AF608054

Guide to the Tuba Repertoire

Indiana Repertoire Guides

Guide to the TUBA *Repertoire*

The New Tuba Source Book

Compiled and Edited by
R. Winston Morris and Daniel Perantoni

Indiana University Press
Bloomington • Indianapolis

This book is a publication of

Indiana University Press
601 North Morton Street
Bloomington, IN 47404-3797 USA

http://iupress.indiana.edu

Telephone orders	800-842-6796
Fax orders	812-855-7931
Orders by e-mail	iuporder@indiana.edu

First edition published 1996 by Indiana
University Press as *The Tuba Source Book,*

The paper used in this publication meets the minimum requirements of American National Standard for Information Sciences—Permanence of Paper for Printed Library Materials, ANSI Z39.48-1984.

Manufactured in the United States of America

Library of Congress Cataloging-in-Publication Data

Tuba source book
Guide to the tuba repertoire : the new tuba source book / compiled and edited by R. Winston Morris and Daniel Perantoni.
p. cm. — (Indiana repertoire guides)
"First edition published 1996 by Indiana University Press as The tuba source book."
Includes bibliographical references and index.
ISBN-13: 978-0-253-34763-3 (cloth : alk. paper)
1. Tuba—Bibliography. 2. Tuba music–Bibliography. 3. Tuba music—Discography. 4. Tubists–Biography. 5. Music—Bio-bibliography. I. Morris, R. Winston. II. Perantoni, Daniel. III. Title. IV. Series.
ML 128.T8T8 2006
788.9'8—dc22
2006005242

1 2 3 4 5 11 10 09 08 07 06

Contributors continued
Gregory Fritze
Craig L. Fuller
Lee Hipp
Donald C. Little
Mark Moore
Shawn Murphy
Daniel T. Perantoni
Harvey Phillips
Gene Pokorny
David Porter
David M. Randolph
James Self
Donald A. Stanley
Kevin J. Stees
William Troiano
Denis Winter

International Consultants
Australia:
Craig Cunningham

Austria:
Edward Hale

Bermuda:
Thomas G. Cremer

Brazil:
Donald Smith

Canada:
Michael Eastep

China:
Xiang-Yu Zhang

Columbia:
Juan Carlos Rodriquez

Denmark:
Jørgen Arnsted

England:
Patrick Harrild

Finland:
Harri Lidsle

France:
Mel Culbertson
Gilles Lutmann

Germany:
Heiko Triebener
Dietrich Unkrodt

Greece:
Nicholas Zervopoulos

Hungary:
Lâszlô Szabô

Ireland:
David J. Murphy

Israel:
Adi Hershko

Italy:
Gregorio Mazzarese

Japan:
Sadayuki Ogura
Kazuhisa Nishida

Korea:
Chong Il Yi
Sung J. Yoo

Lithuania:
Leonardas Ulevicious

Luxembourg:
Patrick Krysatis

Mexico:
Dwight Sullinger

The Netherlands:
Dirk K. Annema

Norway:
Stein Erik Tafjord

Poland:
Jan Pniak

Puerto Rico:
Ricardo Rodriguez

Romania:
Ionel Dumitru

Russia:
Valentin Avvakoumov
Alexander V. Griogoriev

Slovenia:
Igor Krivokapíc

South Africa:
Vurl Bland

Spain:
David Moen

Sultanate of Oman:
Bernard Ebbinghouse

Sweden:
Michael Lind

Switzerland:
David LeClair

Ukraine:
Strelehuk Tury

CONTENTS

FOREWORD (2005)

R. Winston Morris, Senior Editor
Daniel Perantoni, Associate Editor

Before we get beyond the first sentence of this foreword, we want to make sure that credit is given where credit is due and we must acknowledge the incredible work of all the assistant editors on both editions of *The Tuba Source Book*. They are responsible for developing the material that you see in this book. They are listed elsewhere but must be recognized at this point for their commitment, professionalism, and hard work. The assistant editors for this volume are Ronald Davis, David Graves, Timothy Northcut, Philip Sinder, Joseph Skillen, Kenyon Wilson, and Kelly Thomas, our indexer. Editors for the first edition were Ronald Davis, Jeffrey Funderburk, Edward Goldstein, Skip Gray, Charles McAdams, Mark Nelson, and Jerry Young. This publication would not exist without the efforts of these individuals. In addition, we have to recognize the incredible contribution to both issues by the numerous contributors and international consultants. A complete list of all these editors is presented elsewhere and we invite the reader to spend a few minutes absorbing the incredible backgrounds and international recognition represented by these individuals. Please extend your thanks to any of these people you happen to encounter for their dedication and their contributions to these two volumes.

The reader needs to understand exactly what has transpired in relation to the original *The Tuba Source Book* (*TSB*) and the new *Guide to the Tuba Repertoire: The New Tuba Source Book* (*NTSB*). *TSB* was published by Indiana University Press in 1996 (ISBN 0-253-32889-6). The editorial deadline for all information contained in *TSB* was July 1993. This is an important date as it was the final date by which the editors could accept any entries for the *TSB*. The editorial deadline for *NTSB* was January 2005. In other words, almost 12 years transpired between the information gathered for *TSB* and *NTSB*. The *TSB* was an extremely comprehensive publication that basically established the status of the tuba from its inception (Sept. 12, 1835) to 1993. It included the entire repertoire for the instrument along with a complete discography, a bibliography, a biography, and an equipment chapter, and it addressed many other areas of interest. As stated on its front flap, the *TSB* is "a massive research effort by leading professional tubists in 36 countries [which] presents a comprehensive picture of the tuba." For the record, the *TSB* is officially out of print and has been since early 2005. The extremely lucky reader might locate a copy of the 656-page *TSB* still sitting on the shelves of large bookstores or for sale in online auctions. Due to various considerations, primarily length, *NTSB* deals with only the literature and the discography of the tuba because we could best document those areas within the confines of our editorial deadlines. All other chapters of the *TSB* have NOT been updated. That's the bad news. The good news is that **all of the information relative to tuba literature and discography that was contained in** *TSB* is also contained in *NTSB*. The reader does NOT have to have access to *TSB* in order to have a full and complete picture of these two areas of investigation. All of the new entries into these two categories were integrated alphabetically with the original entries from *TSB*. For the most part, the original *TSB* entries have not been altered in any manner. This was not the purpose of *NTSB*. Further, we have not differentiated between the 1993 and the 2005 entries.

We encourage the reader to refer to the introductory/preface/foreword material for *TSB* and for *NTSB*, all of which is included in this edition. All of this material is completely applicable to the present edition and if the reader is to have a true understanding of all the information presented, some time must be spent on this introductory material as well as on the introductory statements to each chapter written by editors of both editions. All of the editors involved have done the very best they could in developing and presenting this information. We make no pretensions that we have accurately presented 100% of every published piece of music for the tuba or every recording that has ever been produced. This would simply be impossible. So we present to you, the reader, our best effort possible and beg your indulgence when necessary.

A couple of areas in particular relative to the annotations are problematic. The price we quote for each publication is the price that appeared on the copy of the publication that we had in our possession. This is almost always stated in dollars and is **always** out of date! The reader should consider prices to be mere guidelines. It is also difficult to ascertain sometimes whether a particular publication is out of print. Please note that our intention is to include everything we can that was ever published (see the preface for further explanation of *published*) regardless of current availability. Anyone who remotely keeps track of the avalanche of tuba-related recordings can attest to the constant explosion of new releases. We are sure that we have missed many pieces that have been recorded, but the careful reader should constantly compare the literature chapters with the discography chapters. If the reader wants a documented evaluation of how much the tuba repertoire is growing, we once again invite you to read the introductory statements all editors have made previous to their chapters.

We also want to draw to the reader's attention that we have not attempted to reconcile the different spellings of composer names (frequently Russian composers). We have presented the spelling for every composer as it appears on the actual publication. Also, we make note of the extremely difficult task of maintaining a current and accurate listing of addresses for publishers, composers and recording companies. The companies go in and out of business, move locations, and are bought up by other companies. The editors present to you the best information we have available to us. We have even listed addresses for some composers we know to be deceased; we present their last known addresses with the hope of providing a way to contact the composers' estates in order to track down pieces of music.

Finally, all the editors who have spent untold hours working on this material want to thank the members of our families for their patience and understanding and we extend a huge "thank you" to everyone at Indiana University Press, one of the finest academic publishers in the world, for their support and expertise.

FOREWORD (1995)

Harvey G. Phillips

Information contained in *The Tuba Source Book* (*TSB*) is thorough and definitive. It will be greeted with grateful enthusiasm by everyone interested in the tuba, most especially by professional performers, teachers, serious students, composers/orchestrators/arrangers, and enthusiasts of every age. The cliché "everything you ever wanted to know about the tuba" applies to this collection of facts about the instrument—its evolution and heritage; those who play it, teach it, study it, and compose for it; and those who just plain love it in all its myriad forms and configurations. Serious researchers and inquisitive laypersons alike will surely find that which they seek about the tuba in this text.

As one whose life has been rapturously and professionally dedicated to music and devoted to the tuba family of instruments, I join countless others of the present and future generations who share deepest gratitude to R. Winston Morris, the mentor of this project. He possessed the vision to conceptualize, structure, implement, and supervise the enormous undertaking of collecting, compiling, editing, and finalizing all materials important to a complete accounting of information about the tuba. As senior editor, he spearheaded the effort to select, assign, supervise, and inspire a staff of outstanding editors, contributors, and consultants for every chapter and topic.

In my many years of association with Winston, my admiration for his strength, professional and personal integrity, patience and understanding, knowledge and wisdom has never diminished. More than any other, he has tenaciously maintained commitment, dignity, and purpose for the cause of the tuba and its rightful place in the art of musical performance. From the beginnings of Tubists Universal Brotherhood Association (TUBA), he was a force in formalizing that organization with a charter, by-laws, and a constitution. He championed the policy that membership is open to everyone interested in the tuba family of instruments. He was founder and first editor of the *TUBA Journal*, the organization's official publication. No one has so consistently and selflessly given of his or her time and expertise to shepherd TUBA to its present preeminence among peer organizations representing brass instruments.

Given that all prejudice is born of ignorance, *The Tuba Source Book* promises to be an important influence in tempering and ultimately eradicating long-suffering prejudice and misunderstanding imposed on the tuba by a heretofore uninformed public audience.

The Tuba Source Book is a monument to the personal and professional expertise of R. Winston Morris and the most recent of his many efforts to benefit his colleagues and the world of music.

PREFACE

The Tuba Source Book (*TSB*) has been one hundred and fifty-eight years in the making. The purpose of the project has been to attempt to define the current status of the tuba and document its growth from its original 1835 conception by Prussian instrument maker Wilhelm Wieprecht (see Clifford Bevan's chapter, "A Brief History of the Tuba") to July 1993, the closing date for the research for the *TSB*. The relative degree of success in this ambitious goal remains for others to decide.

Two important publications that precede the *TSB* and provide a relatively recent basis of comparison primarily in the area of literature available for the tuba are the *Encyclopedia of Literature for the Tuba* by William J. Bell and R. Winston Morris (Colin, 1967) and the *Tuba Music Guide* (*TMG*) by R. Winston Morris (The Instrumentalist Company, 1973). References will be found throughout the *TSB* relating the extraordinary growth in the tuba repertoire in the past twenty years since the publication of the *TMG*.

However, the *TSB* goes much further in documenting the status of the tuba than either one of the earlier publications, which were primarily devoted to literature. A quick glance at the *TSB* Table of Contents is all that is needed to confirm this observation. The heart of this publication is certainly the identification of the literature that has been created for the tuba. Nevertheless, the editors have an equal commitment to documenting other parameters, such as discography, bibliography, biography, history, usage, and equipment.

The procedure utilized in creating the *TSB* indicates the scope of the project and the international involvement in the process. After twenty years of contemplating (since the 1973 *TMG*) and one year of structuring the content of the *TSB*, eight editors were assembled to oversee various aspects of the project. Contributors (twenty-six in all) were identified and solicited who generally would be recognized as having expertise in specific categories. The editors and contributors were given one year (June 1992 to June 1993) to conduct research and prepare chapters on their assigned topic(s). To ensure as much international participation as possible, forty international consultants (mostly professional tuba artists native to the country represented) from thirty-five countries representing most areas of the world were selected. The international consultants supplied as much information as possible from their country on all areas of *TSB* consideration. This information was distributed to the appropriate editor or contributor for incorporation in their final reports.

The international scope and endorsement of the *TSB* is further documented by virtue of official sanctioning by the following professional low brass organizations: Tubists Universal Brotherhood Association (TUBA), Deutsches Tubaforum e. V of Germany, Irish Low Brass Association (ILBA), Japan Euphonium Tuba Association (JETA), and Suomem Pasuuna-ja Tuubaseura ry of Finland.

Information acquired after July 1993 is not included in this edition of the *TSB*. It is also very important that the reader understand that in the areas of literature and discography the major objective was the documentation of materials in these categories that have been created and to one degree or another published. The current availability of these materials was not a primary consideration. Therefore, some of the literature and some of the recordings listed may not be currently available through the normal sources. In such cases, the best possible source of information concerning the acquisition of such materials is given. Some of these items may be currently available through large music and record dealers who have large inventories that contain materials accumulated over the years. Another source for such materials is library systems and private libraries of individuals who might be willing to share information on out-of-print items.

Music included in the *TSB* generally falls into one or the other of the following categories:

1. PUBLISHED—includes all music that is currently available through commercial outlets (this could be anything from the largest established publisher to smaller private publishers).

2. OUT OF PRINT—includes music that was previously published (distributed) but now listed as out of print or not listed at all. If the music could possibly exist in the holdings of a large music retail dealer or even be accessed through libraries (such as the TUBA Resource

Library or other major private, university, or municipal libraries), then it has been included.

3. MANUSCRIPT—includes music in manuscript form that is generally being made available by professional composers/arrangers. If the composer ever copyrighted and distributed music but it is currently unavailable, it would, for *TSB* purposes, be considered "published" but out of print.

For the most part, manuscripts by students and relatively unknown composers/arrangers that have never generally been made available are not included. Also, there was an understanding that only those works specifically designated for tuba would be included. Music published for media other than tuba (vocal music, string bass music, trombone, etc.), while perhaps quite useful and appropriate for study on the tuba, has, nevertheless, not been included in the *TSB*. The astute reader will notice a major omission in the area of literature. An editorial decision was made very early in the planning stages of the *TSB* not to include brass quintet literature. The standard brass quintet utilizing tuba is certainly one of the most important developments in the history of the tuba. It was simply felt that this aspect of the tuba could not be dealt with in the comprehensive manner required. This also applies to the discography section. The only reference to the brass quintet will be found in the section on Brass Chamber Ensembles personnel. Perhaps the *TSB* will serve as an instigating factor in the compilation of a major source work on the modern brass quintet.

To the extent that information was available, the following order and format has been utilized in the presentation of entries for musical literature for the tuba.

1. COMPOSER NAME. (last name first)
2. COMPLETE TITLE. (as it appears on the music)
3. ARRANGER. (arr.)/TRANSCRIBER. (tr.)/EDITOR. (ed.) (first name first)
4. PUBLISHER/SOURCE. (See the Appendix, Addresses of Publishers and Composers, for the complete address for all sources.)
5. INSTRUMENTATION. (for Tuba in Mixed Ensemble and Music for Multiple Tubas)
6. DATE. (copyright date for published works, date of composition for manuscript works, no information when no date is available)
7. PRICE. (publishers' recommended/suggested retail price, generally expressed in dollars, when possible, current July 1993)
8. DURATION. (SOLOS, expressed in minutes as indicated on the printed music or actually timed. COLLECTIONS/COMPILATIONS, etc., expressed in number of pages.)
9. LEVEL.

I—Beginner (up to one year)
II—Intermediate (two to three years)
III—High School
IV—University
V—Professional

combinations: I–II. II–III. III–IV. IV–V.

These are general guidelines and recognized as quite subjective. Level indications describe attributes and requirements of the music more than the expected skills of the player.

LEVEL I—(Beginner) Limited range, approximately one octave: $B\flat_1$–B(d). One year of instruction. Limited rhythmic/technical requirements. No note values shorter than eighth notes, no syncopated rhythms. Music of a tonal nature.

LEVEL II—(Intermediate) Two/Three years of instruction. Range approximately A_1–e (f). Rhythmic/Technical requirements involve simple sixteenth note patterns. Simple, limited syncopated patterns.

LEVEL III—(High School, Secondary School, Pre-college) Range approximately F_1–b (c'). Moderate tessitura. More rhythmic complexity. Extended syncopations, sixteenth note patterns, triplets, etc. Moderate amount of multiple tonguing.

LEVEL IV—(University/College) Range approximately ($B\flat_2$) C1–f' (g'). Higher advanced tessitura. Increased rhythmic complexity/multimetric. Angular melodic lines. Dissonant harmonies/contemporary harmonies. Endurance factors. Introduction to avant-garde techniques (flutter tongue, multiphonics, etc.). Multiple tonguing. Dynamic control and extremes.

LEVEL V—(Professional) Total range: (C_3) D_2–b' (c''+). Extended high tessitura. Rhythmic/Technical complexity of highest order. Angular lines/large skips in melody. Advanced twentieth-century techniques. Extreme dynamic contrasts.

10. RANGE. Every note starting with and including C_1 downward may be referred to as a "pedal tone" (obviously relating to the CC tuba). To the extent that optional pitches (as encountered in *ossia* parts) impact the overall range of a composition, such pitches will be presented in parentheses. (see staff page xv)

11. MOVEMENTS. (specific names and/or numbers)

12. COMMISSION. (name of commissioning party if commissioned)

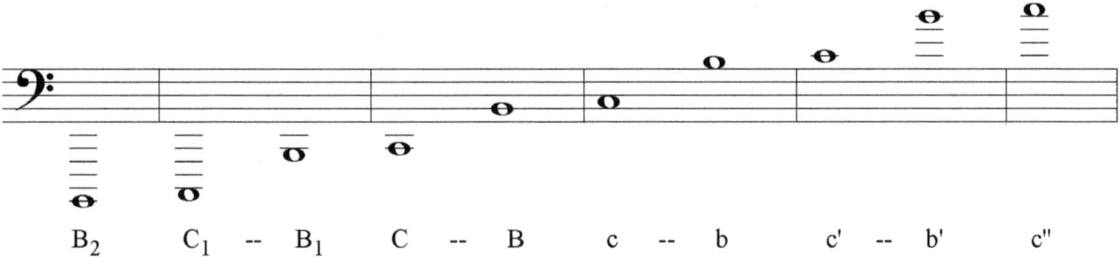

13. DEDICATION. (name of party to whom the composition is dedicated)

14. ANNOTATION. (short, concise, annotative comments concerning the general nature and style of a composition. Any outstanding technical problems or other pertinent information will be noted.)

15. RECORDINGS. (When a particular composition has been recorded, reference will be made to the artist(s) responsible for the recording, and the reader should refer to the main Discography listing, Tuba Recordings by Artist, for complete information.)

16. TAPE ACCOMPANIMENTS. (Reference will be made for those few works that have taped accompaniments.)

17. See: Thompson/Lemke; *French Music for Low Brass Instruments.* Refers the reader to additional information contained in the *French Music for Low Brass Instruments: An Annotated Bibliography* co-authored by J. Mark Thompson and Jeff Lemke and published by Indiana University Press. This publication presents a complete listing and short description of French solo and pedagogical materials generally intended for various low brass instruments but in the case of these references specifically for the French tuba. The French tuba is pitched one octave higher (in C(ut) or B♭(Si♭) than the more commonly encountered contrabass tubas (CC or BB♭). Anyone interested in pursuing this literature should be aware that the solo parts designated for tuba in Si♭ are transposed parts. Tubists accustomed to performing music in concert pitch should always utilize the part designated as "Tuba in ut."

18. See: Bird, Gary, ed.; *Program Notes for the Solo Tuba.* Refers the reader to additional information contained in the *Program Notes for the Solo Tuba* compiled and edited by Gary Bird and published by Indiana University Press. This book contains extensive program notes, mostly written by the composer, for eighty-nine of the more important works that feature the tuba in a solo capacity.

19. A final reference is made when a particular entry is included in more than one chapter of the *TSB.* For example, works for solo tuba and orchestra almost inevitably are also available with piano reduction. Also, some of the works for multiple tubas can be performed by tuba and other low brass instruments; therefore, there will be a cross-reference for those particular entries between Music for Multiple Tubas and Tuba in Mixed Ensemble.

Finally, relative to the entry formatting for musical compositions, it should be noted that when there is no information available in a particular category that "field" will be simply omitted.

For the reader who cannot remember the composer/arranger for a particular composition in the Tuba and Keyboard or Music for Multiple Tubas chapters, listings by title are included.

To the extent that the literature chapters are not primarily concerned with identifying currently available materials but concerned with documenting all literature that has been generated for the tuba, the basic repertoire chapters provide a highly selected listing of recommended literature that should be readily available to the reader. As is the case with every section of the *TSB,* the individuals responsible for identifying the basic recommended repertoire sections are preeminently qualified.

Every section of the *TSB* is without question the most extensive compilation of information ever assembled on that particular tuba subject. The tuba discography presented here is unprecedented in comprehensiveness and scope. The main entry for recordings will be found under Tuba Recordings by Artist (annotated). Very important cross-references are available by consulting the listings "by title" and "by composer."

The biographical sections of the *TSB* present information on as many professional tubists and "tuba composers" possible to identify within the limited time frame of the project. Every attempt was made to contact professional tubists internationally and to acquire information on their activities. Of course, some individuals who have made significant contributions to the advancement of the tuba have been inadvertently excluded because they could not be contacted within the given time frame of the project or they failed to return requests for information. The editors hope that such individuals will receive proper recognition in future editions. The "personnel" sections make an attempt at identifying professional tubists who are (or who have been) active in various types of professional employment. Additional biographical information is available for many of those individuals in the Biographical Sketches section.

The bibliographical entries present a major documentation of past research and publications concerning the tuba. This information represents the "starting point" for all future research efforts on the tuba.

The equipment sections attempt to document currently available materials and services of interest to the tubist.

The large majority of the *TSB* is of a reference nature intended to provide the reader with factual information on the tuba. Some sections are provided to present the reader an historical perspective which will significantly enhance the understanding and relative comprehension of this material. These sections warrant a careful reading and understanding and include chapters by Clifford Bevan on the history of the tuba, Robert E. Eliason on instrument collections, James Self on doubling and freelancing on the tuba, and the chapter compiled by Harvey Phillips representing the thinking on writing for the tuba by twenty-one outstanding composers and arrangers of successful tuba materials. These sections must be required reading for any "student" of the tuba.

Finally, the editors and contributors and consultants for the *TSB* take great pride in presenting this publication which represents the most comprehensive and definitive research effort ever undertaken on a single musical instrument. The tuba is, after all, nothing more or nothing less than an equal partner with all other instruments in the art of making music.

ACKNOWLEDGMENTS

R. Winston Morris (July 1995)

First and foremost, I am immensely grateful to my wife, Barbara, for all the support and help on this project and all the others I have engaged in over the past thirty years. Not only has she provided complete moral support and understanding but she has been the best of all possible English teachers. I only wish I could say that I have learned at least half of everything she has tried to teach me about the English language. She really should be listed as an Editorial Assistant on the *TSB* (Tuba Source Book) as she has expended major amounts of time helping with proofing and editorial considerations. Her "red ink" and support have been crucial.

The two major influences in my professional life have been my teacher, the late William J. Bell, and that indefatigable spirit of tubadom, the great Harvey G. Phillips. I learned from Bill Bell that it is not what you do but how you do it, and I learned from him an immense love and respect for the art of making music. Bill Bell never **played** tuba; he **performed** every time he put the horn on his face. I have written somewhere before that he could make you cry with a C major scale. My relationship with Harvey, a fellow Bell student, began about twenty-five years ago when we first met in Chicago and discussed the continuing formal organization of the Tubists Universal Brotherhood Association. We have been working together on numerous projects since the late 1960s, and his total dedication and enthusiasm have served as a source of inspiration and example for everyone who has had the privilege of knowing him and working with him.

To start naming professional colleagues who over the years have provided encouragement and inspiration to keep on keeping on would be dangerous because inevitably someone very important would be temporarily overlooked, but I must acknowledge the influence of two of my best friends, Daniel T. Perantoni and James Self. Mere words cannot describe the degree of respect and admiration I have for these two long-time colleagues. We have seen many dreams become reality, and this publication documents many of those dreams.

Then there is the "team," the *TSB* team that is. Put this down as a major labor of love for the most dedicated group of individuals I have ever had the honor of being associated with. No, this has not been a profit-making venture. The editors who are contractually committed to the *TSB* will never come anywhere close to being reimbursed for their efforts and expenses. The contributors did just that; they contributed their time and expertise. The consultants made themselves available to everyone else at considerable time and expense. How else to describe such dedication to a profession except as a labor of love? The complete editorial structure for the *TSB* is included elsewhere in this publication; these are the individuals to whom we owe a great debt of gratitude. There are no egos here, no hidden personal agendas, no great individual acclaim, and no funds exchanging hands. Everyone said "yes" and spent one year of his or her life working like crazy to fulfill a personal and professional commitment to the tuba and to future students of the instrument.

It has been a pleasure and honor getting to know and work with Edward R. Goldstein. Ed is one of the finest human beings I know, and he has worked tirelessly and unselfishly on this project. Ed is so nice he became known as the "good cop" on this project. Nevertheless, he was tenacious and unrelenting in pursuing every aspect of the *TSB* to its final conclusion. In the twenty years after the publication of the *Tuba Music Guide* (R. Winston Morris, 1973, The Instrumentalist Company), a number of individuals approached me about future editions and up-dates. I inevitably would explain that I had already been involved in two major publications that documented the literature for tuba (the *TMG* and an earlier publication, *The Encyclopedia of Literature for the Tuba,* William J. Bell and R. Winston Morris, 1965/67, Charles Colin Publishers) and that I really felt that there were other things I needed to be doing, but I certainly wished them well and, to the extent that it was requested, bestowed my blessings on any and all to give it a go themselves. With the exception of Ed, that was the end of that. I believe that everyone else who entertained such ideas quickly realized the work was growing exponentially as each year went by. It had simply grown beyond a one-person project. But Ed was persistent, and periodically we would discuss the possibilities of the project. On the basis of one of our discussions, I started formulating the "team" approach. The feasibility and practicality of this approach made sense. It was doable. Ed and I became much more specific (and ambitious) and structured a tentative table of contents. Then we proceeded to identify those individuals who not only would be the most appropriate editor for a particular section but would be willing to dedicate the time and effort.

Those individuals are designated as assistant editors. All of the editors made a total commitment to the entire project, not just to their individual areas of responsibility. The work of every individual editor, without question, constitutes a major contribution, the magnitude of which would be justified as a separate publication. These six talented individuals—Ronald Davis, Jeffrey L. Funderburk, Skip Gray, Charles A. McAdams, Mark A. Nelson, and Jerry Young—were on-call virtually twenty-four hours a day for over a year. They did their work with a level of competency unparalleled in research on the tuba. My extreme gratitude and profound thanks for the work of these wonderful friends is hereby expressed.

And then there were twenty-six individuals, contributors, who unselfishly made a commitment to research a specific subject for inclusion in the *TSB*. To these dedicated professionals and leaders, listed elsewhere in this publication, go my sincerest gratitude and admiration for a job well done.

And then there were forty individuals from thirty-five different countries around the world, international consultants, who committed to this project to the extent that they could, given their individual circumstances. There were major language problems, there were 3 a.m. facsimile transmissions, there were sometimes large air mail expenses, but yet these world leaders persevered and contributed greatly to the ultimate success of the *TSB*. I am sincerely indebted to these individuals and hope that I can in some small way assist them in the future. The heartfelt responses we received to our solicitations for information from all parts of the world could easily be the subject of another publication.

Our friend Yuri Strelchuk, from Kiev, Ukraine, when asked about the quality of equipment available to the Ukrainian tubist responded, "excuse me please my having held-up of the materials you are waiting from me. I'm not so good in English and I have to ask for translating. The matter is that now we have problems not only with bread and butter but as well with xeroxes, typewriters with Latin keyboards, musics, musical instruments, etc." He goes on to say that in his part of the world there is a total lack of quality instruments and virtually no music available for tuba students. He concludes, "In spite of all this my colleagues and me are looking forward to our co-operation and mutual interest." Yuri requests assistance in acquiring study materials for his students; I have his address.

And what do you suppose of the day-to-day existence of our colleague from Slovenia, Igor Krivokapic, whose first letter promised he would do his best to acquire information for the *TSB* in spite of the fact the it would be difficult "not because of the new born hatred or wartime in the area of the late Yugoslavia, it's just a result of ignorance and lack of knowledge since we lived more or less through separated traditions in the whole history of Yugoslavia"? Igor came through with vital information for the *TSB*.

Then there is the situation for approximately twenty-five percent of all human beings on this planet as authentically reported by our dear friend Xiang-yu Zhang, former tubist with the Shanghai, China, Symphony for twenty years. I quote from the extensive report on the tuba in China from Xiang-yu:

> Before 1966, tubas were only played as bass in military bands. There was certain amount of tuba players at that time, but they did not recognize the characters of tuba enough . . . to ask high-level performing techniques . . . so no one could play solo with tuba at that time in China.
>
> The Great Cultural Revolution from 1966 to 1976 brought a great disaster to the Chinese people in every field, including the tuba. Once, Jiang Qing, the chief leader of "Gang of Four" went to the Central Symphony Orchestra of China. After watching the performance, she pointed to the tuba and said, "What is that big thing? It's useless. Take it away from orchestra." Since then, tuba, which play very important role in orchestras disappeared in China.

Xiang-yu goes on to report,

> Since 1980, the reforming and opening policies have not only brought back great vigour to the economy of China, but also brought a new life to tubas. . . . The important function of tuba in orchestra is gradually recognized by the Chinese people. In recent years, more and more tuba players emerge from the band of factories and farmers. But, the pity is that there is still not one professional tuba teacher in China. . . . That's the reason

> why high level tuba players are still rare in China up to now.
>
> Sometimes, when a orchestra wanted to perform a symphony with tubas, they have to use trombone instead for lacking of tuba players. Of course, the sound effects are very inferior.

Xiang-yu concludes on a positive note,

> Tuba, a musical instrument which plays very important role in symphony orchestra, is being put in an important position in the musical field in China.

And so it goes. If the *TSB* serves the purpose of establishing meaningful communications between our colleagues in troubled parts of the world, surely this represents an accomplishment of a high order. Addresses are available for all of the international consultants and the reader is encouraged to explore the potential for establishing a true universal camaraderie. My eternal gratitude goes to all of the consultants for their unwavering pursuit of artistic ideals and participation in this long-distance project.

I am grateful to Joseph Skillen, a truly outstanding young tubist, who supplied all of the musical examples for the *TSB* through his talents on the computer. I am grateful to Gary Bird and J. Mark Thompson for supplying information on their new publications (see the Preface) so that we could provide valuable references to the work that they have done. I am grateful to my friend, English euphoniumist Steven Mead, for supplying information on music distributors in the U.K. and for helping to establish contact with Clifford Bevan, author of *The Tuba Family*—now, unfortunately, out of print. I am grateful to Dennis Avey of Robert King Music Sales for his cooperation in identifying music publishers and supplying numerous publications for review purposes. I am grateful to Bert Wiley of Bernel Music in Cullowhee, North Carolina, for his assistance in gathering information on recordings and music representative of the British brass band repertoire. I am grateful to Dr. Raoul R. Ronson, President of Seesaw Music Corporation, for his willingness and cooperation in supplying a large number of compositions for review purposes. I am grateful to my good friend Robert Tucci at the Horn and Tuba Center in Munich, who was most cooperative in his help and assistance. I would like to express appreciation to the outstanding German euphoniumist Manfred Heidler for his assistance in helping to identify military musicians in his country. I am also indebted to Markus Hötzel of Wermelskirchen, Germany, for bringing to our attention the existence of the Josef Bühler book *Tuba-Bibliographie* and to Leopold Libal from Austria for sending a copy of his *Die Tuba Literaturliste*. Also, I am appreciative of the cooperation of a number of international music centers; especially the Canadian Music Centre, the Swedish Music Information Centre, and the Scottish Music Information Centre.

I am indebted to and gratefully acknowledge the early support and encouragement we received from everyone involved with Tubists Universal Brotherhood Association. Karen Cotton, David Lewis, and then–TUBA President Marty Erickson were behind this project from the first approach, as were all the other members of the TUBA Executive Committee.

The *TSB* is a product of electronic technology, and to those who assisted in this regard, we owe a debt of gratitude. On my own campus, Tennessee Technological University, I wish to thank Barbara Goodson and Frank Bush of Academic Computing Support for all of their assistance helping to fully utilize the Internet. This publication was essentially written via the network. As senior editor of the project, I was the recipient of massive amounts of computer-generated information from all over the world via modem, disk, or Internet. The final manuscript for the *TSB* was over 2000 pages and accounted for four megabytes of information on disk. This information was handled flawlessly by my trusty Macintosh SE/30 running System 7 with a total of ten megabytes of combined built-in and virtual memory. My eighty-megabyte hard disk drive started getting very pushed toward the end. To the rescue came Jan M. Bodeux, Educational Associate Sales Representative for Microsoft Corporation, who graciously supplied the latest version (5.1a) of Microsoft Word for the Macintosh. The entire manuscript was ultimately prepared in Word for submission to the publishers. Word is unquestionably the state-of-the-art word processing program, and it functioned under tremendous pressure flawlessly. The disks that I was receiving from everyone were produced on every type of computer operating system (Macintosh, MS DOS, Windows, etc.) and with every imaginable word processing program. Thanks are extended to Bonnie L. Orsini of DataViz, Inc. DataViz supplied their MacLinkPlus/Translators™, a program designed for the Macintosh which allows more than seven hundred possible PC to Mac, Mac to PC, and Mac to Mac translations. The tremendous software incompatibilities encountered in this project simply could not have been resolved without this program from DataViz. Finally, as the hard drive was reaching overload status, Fifth Generation Systems, Inc., provided demonstration copies of their AutoDoubler and DiskDoubler programs, which automatically compresses information so that you can literally store twice as much information on floppies or a hard disk. These programs work in tandem, invisibly, and expertly as does all the software from Fifth Generation. I am deeply grateful to these software publishers for their contributions to our project.

I am also grateful to Dr. John E. Taylor, chairperson of the Department of Music and Art at Tennessee Tech during the time of this research, for his strong support and encouragement.

Finally, but certainly not least, as the publication would not exist without their commitment, I would like to express my profound gratitude to everyone at Indiana University Press for their interest in this project. We especially acknowledge the outstanding work of Natalie Wrubel, Editor and Music Sponsor, for her guidance and expertise. It is perhaps almost too logical that Indiana University Press would be the publisher of this document. It was thirty years ago at Indiana University that Bill Bell and I originally conceived and ultimately wrote the *Encyclopedia of Literature for the Tuba*.

ACKNOWLEDGMENTS

Edward R. Goldstein (July 1995)

When I was a student at the Peabody Conservatory back in the 1970s, my teacher David Bragunier suggested that I pick up a copy of the *Tuba Music Guide* [*TMG*] by R. Winston Morris. It quickly became a constant companion. Looking through it was like opening a time capsule. It was then one of the few sources for finding out about the heritage of the literature for the tuba. I started collecting as much of the music as I could find and used it constantly as my primary resource. Unfortunately, I soon became frustrated with the book as nothing past 1972 was included. It was also frustrating looking at outdated information such as the listing for the Bach/Bell arrangement of *Air and Bourree* at a price of seventy-five cents!

In the mid-1970s I wrote to R. Winston Morris and encouraged him to write a sequel to his treatise, updating the book. He wrote back a long and generous note thanking me for my kind words, saying that it was doubtful that he would ever continue the research in a formal way and wished me all of the best in the future.

In the early 1980s I finally met Winston at a United States Army Tuba-Euphonium Conference at Ft. Myer, Virginia. I reminded him of our correspondence and again encouraged him to update the book. Almost ten years had passed and the literature had grown exponentially. He again said, "No way," mentioned that a number of people had been encouraging him to do it, said that he never wanted to look at a file card again, and suggested that I do it myself. Well . . . a seed was planted.

We saw each other again at the International Brass Congress at Indiana University in 1984. I told Winston that I was indeed interested in pursuing the project myself and was enthusiastically told to go for it.

Good intentions notwithstanding, the years passed and the schedule continued to get busier and busier. Winston and I would see each other and would correspond, always with him starting off the conversation with "Well????????????" In 1991 I decided that enough was enough and if I did not just make the time to do it, I would always regret it. I called Winston and declared that the time had come. I think that my timing was just right. He had mellowed a bit about getting involved with another project and suggested a meeting. We got together in January 1992 at the Days Inn across from Ft. Myer the day before the U.S. Army Band Tuba Symposium started. We brainstormed for hours and listed everything that we could possibly imagine, that would be necessary, practical, and impractical to include. We decided that this project should not be an update to the *TMG,* but a new, complete source of information related to the tuba. Everything from recordings to repairmen to music to symposia appeared on our brainstorm list. To this day, nothing has been deleted from that list.

It was already obvious to Winston and he soon convinced me that no one person could do the job with any kind of justice. The sheer amount of information had grown in volume, diversity, and especially in international scope.

A second brainstorming session began with names being attached to the various proposed topics. Ideal marriages were made. Jeff Funderburk, for instance, had already done extensive research on music for unaccompanied tuba; why should someone else start the research from scratch? More names were tossed about, and the excitement continued to grow. Later, virtually everyone that we asked to work on the proposed book said, "Yes."

The talent and creative abilities among the editors were formidable indeed. We met at the International Tuba-Euphonium Symposium in Lexington, Kentucky, in May 1992, and established a timetable for the next year and a half. The editors literally started assembling information that very afternoon. What you have before you on the following pages is the result of that year and a half of efforts.

The editors sincerely hope that an updated *Tuba Source Book* will indeed be available in the future. We owe it to the upcoming generation of performers and composers to document their work on an on-going basis and to make it available to all interested persons. What form that will take remains to be seen. We actively solicit the reader to join us in making future updates possible. Please inform us about new compositions, recordings, festivals, etc. Also it was not possible, given the time frame we were under, to document one hundred percent of the literature for the last one hundred and sixty years. If we could not document materials in an authoritative manner, we chose not to list it in order to maintain the highest degree of accuracy. Mistakes, of course, can and will happen, and we would appreciate your help in correcting future editions.

On a personal note, there are several friends who have made my work smoother and more complete. Thanks are extended to Becky Gutin for key stroking literally thousands of entries; Edith Stark, Blanche Stark, and Sylvia Goldstein for stuffing literally thousands of envelopes; and Maurice the mailman for delivering thousands of pounds of letters and packages. For translation help, I must thank Paul Maillet, Lisa Schultze, and Buddy Wachter. Thanks also go to David Sager and Jim Gregory, two excellent jazz musicians and historians, who really helped to fill in the holes from a first-hand viewpoint. Dr. Michael Marks suggested early on that a history of the tuba should be included. It took a clarinetist to figure that out. Thanks to the hundreds of publishers and composers who responded to our pleas for information, catalogs, and review copies. Of the over 1000 requests sent out, there was only one refusal for help. That is a real tribute to the industry. Without the support of Towson State University, both the music department as well as the computer department, my participation in this project would have been next to impossible. The assistant editors, contributors, and consultants all carried out their appointed tasks with the same degree of confidence and success as Arnold Jacobs buzzing *Pop Goes the Weasel* on his mouthpiece. My sincere thanks for a job well done to each and every one of them. A special expression of gratitude goes to my wife, Ruthie, and to our daughter, Leah, who day after day said, "Can you play with me?" and, when realizing that it was going to be another *Tuba Source Book* day, did not give up. I hope that I can make that lost time up to them.

I would not have even been interested in participating in a project such as this if it had not been for associations over the years with dear friends like Harvey Phillips and John Fletcher. They are among the warmest and most compassionate human beings that I have ever met. Robert Ryker gave me some unbelievably timely words of encouragement after a concert in 1974 that deeply changed the direction of my professional life. I will be grateful to him always and to my teachers, David Bragunier (who took a chance!), Charley Vernon (who showed me how to breathe down to my big toe and told me of the "guy in Chicago"), Arnold Jacobs (the "guy in Chicago"), Ron Friedman (who treated me as a musical peer), Vickie Perkins (who taught me my second and third notes!), and especially Dr. Asher Zlotnick (who gave me my ears and helped validate my professional morals), for giving me the skills to complete this project. You have all been tremendously inspiring to me.

Lastly, this book would not have materialized without the inspiration and past work of R. Winston Morris. Winston is a visionary; nothing is impossible for him. The job will and does get done. He has taught me more about the power of "completing" than perhaps anyone else that I have ever met. Thank you, Winston.

Guide to the Tuba Repertoire

1. Music for Tuba and Keyboard

Joseph Skillen, Assistant Editor, *Guide to the Tuba Repertoire: The New Tuba Source Book*

Edward R. Goldstein, Assistant Editor, *The Tuba Source Book*

Introductory Remarks (July 2005): Joseph Skillen

It is staggering to realize that within the relatively short period between the first *Tuba Source Book* and this edition (roughly eleven years) there has been a considerable expansion in the output and number of composers writing for tuba and piano. This chapter lists over 3,000 works for tuba and piano, while the previous chapter contained 1,900. This degree of output in a little over a decade is astonishing. While I cannot claim that I have included absolutely *every* piece for tuba and piano, I feel that I have given it my best effort.

I approach this introduction with gratitude. Excellent mentors, colleagues, research associates, and family members continue to offer their support throughout my career. To all who made this chapter possible, I offer my sincere thanks.

First and foremost, my thanks go to Winston Morris and Edward Goldstein, the original dreamers and creators of this book. We all owe them a massive debt of gratitude. Mr. Goldstein also compiled the first edition of this chapter and his work is largely unchanged. I have altered his writings only when a particular publisher changed or if a work is now out of print. My compilations and annotations are interspersed with his.

I must also acknowledge the tireless efforts of Bradley Boone and Brian Gallion, my research associates at Louisiana State University. Both of them completed a number of complex tasks with great competence and aplomb. Their efforts allowed me the ability to focus on the content of the chapter rather than every keystroke of data entry. Bradley and Brian assisted me from the very beginning when we contacted publishers, received submissions, re-solicited publishers, and persevered through the final stages of the editing process. I cannot say enough about the support and expertise they brought to this project. Bradley, your dedication was inspirational.

I am most appreciative to the large number of international consultants that kept me ever cognizant of the global growth of tuba literature. All of them, listed in the beginning of this book, were extremely helpful, but David LeClair's assistance with the Swiss publishers gave me a big shot in the arm! Thank you, David. I must also acknowledge the invaluable assistance offered by my fellow associate editors. Remaining in contact with some of the sharpest minds in our business has certainly been a real perk of this project.

I also wish to thank the publishers that so willingly shared their music so that I could annotate the entries that follow. Certainly, the composers who continue to give our musical aspirations a voice deserve great praise. Without them we would be mute.

I wish to acknowledge the continuing support I receive from Louisiana State University to complete such projects. The resources, autonomy, and general direction of excellence I find in my colleagues continue to push me to ever-higher goals.

As with all things, the love and support of family makes our efforts worthwhile. With that thought, I thank my wife Anna-Karin and dedicate my efforts and the words in this chapter to my sons Johan William and Max Gustav Skillen. Their delightful personalities continue to transport me to all of the sunny places on this earth.

Introductory Remarks (July 1995): Edward R. Goldstein

There is, as they say, good news and bad news regarding a tubist performing with a keyboard instrument. The good news is that it adds an infinite palette of colors. It can take a unison sound on the tuba on a harmonic journey that alone could be quite limiting. It is fun to add that extra bit of musical spontaneity, collaborating with another creative mind to create something more than just the sum of both performers' musical contributions. The bad news is that it might not be possible to choose a more unlikely marriage.

The harmonic and acoustical structure of the two instruments is fundamentally different. The tuba is based on the natural overtone system. For the most part, these overtones lie in readiness, waiting for the performer's lips to vibrate sympathetically at the natural acoustical core of each note. To bend them to where they need to be from that core to accommodate the acoustical structure of the keyboard instrument sacrifices a bit of tone quality and demands a flexibility and a degree of musical integrity that is only learned through frequent collaborations with instruments constructed acoustically unlike the tuba.

The temperament of the modern keyboard instrument is an acoustical compromise spreading the natural intonation discrepancies over the total range of the keyboard, thus allowing the instrument to be as in tune as possible, but ultimately placing every note in a different place from the natural acoustics of a perfect harmonic series instrument such as the tuba.

In plain English, the two instruments are not really meant to come together in perfect matrimony. The tubist, being the only one of the pair that can truly alter pitch (modern synthesizers notwithstanding), has to take the role of the supreme musician of the two and must bear the brunt of making the pair sound in tune.

This can, of course, be accomplished by using different valve combinations, adjusting valve slides, or adjusting the aperture, but in the end this needs to be controlled by the ears and the heart, processing the musical stimulus of the collaboration and converting that into a constantly evolving process and anticipating the eventual combination of tones. The more one plays tuba with a keyboard instrument, the more one will have the flexibility of intonation needed for such a collaboration.

That qualification aside, the state of tuba and keyboard is very good indeed. When Bill Bell and Winston Morris compiled the *Encyclopedia of Literature for the Tuba* in 1967, there were 388 or so pieces listed for tuba and keyboard. In 1973 the *Tuba Music Guide* listed 572 pieces. Compare that to the listing in the *Tuba Source Book*. There are almost 1,900 pieces listed for tuba and keyboard with new additions to the list arriving daily. This includes first-class works written by world class composers such as Paul Hindemith, John Williams, Alec Wilder, Ralph Vaughn Williams, and other highly qualified composers. This represents quite an evolution from the time when tubists were limited to arrangements such as *Asleep in the Deep* to program in public performance.

My thanks go out to the hundreds of publishers and composers who responded to requests for information about their offerings. It would be nearly impossible to thank each of them individually. Included are publishers who sent numerous pieces and composers who sent copies of manuscripts for review purposes. Furthermore, all of the editors for the *TSB* consulted with each other almost on a daily basis via electronic mail. This technology provided immediate access to some of the most knowledgeable minds in the brass world today, and their insights and knowledge have made this project an exciting one.

Specific thanks go to all of the international consultants and contacts, particularly Bob Tucci and David LeClair, who provided much information. Thanks are extended to my students and family for their patience and understanding for the past two years. Special thanks go to the hundreds of composers listed on the following pages who have over the years realized the same potential that we as performers recognized when we selected the tuba to express our musical communication. They have given us our lines and our identities in the same way that Shakespeare brought *Hamlet* to life. They have allowed us to have an infinite color palette with which to play.

Works Listed by Composer

Abt, Franz. *Dear Old Songs of Home*. arr. Paul deVille. Carl Fischer Inc. 1906. Out of Print. See: deVille, Paul, *Pleasant Hours,* under Tuba and Keyboard Collections.

Abt, Franz. *Oh, My Home*. arr. Paul deVille. Carl Fischer Inc. 1906. Out of Print. See: deVille, Paul, *Pleasant Hours,* under Tuba and Keyboard Collections.

Adams. *Holy City.* Neil A. Kjos Music Company. 1958. Out of Print. 2:00. II–III. (A_1) D–e♭. No technical problems.

Åkerwall, Martin. *Iceflower.* Amazing Music World. 1995. $18.50. 11:00. V. B♭$_2$–a♭'. Dedicated to Jens Bjørn-Larsen. A very demanding work for both the tubist and pianist. A large range of dynamic control in addition to great facility in the extreme low register is required. Very interesting and appealing sounds with varying textures throughout.

Åkerwall, Martin. *Moments d'été.* ed. Jens Bjørn-Larsen. Amazing Music World. 2001. $21.50. 11:00. IV–V. C–g'. Glow; The Blue Anemone; When The Sun Sets; Naked Trees—for solo tuba; Swan; The Song of May. Dedicated to Pernille Bog. A collection of many small movements that serve as character pieces. Each movement carries its individual challenges, though these are mostly expressive and tuneful. Challenging piano part as well.

Alary, G. *Morceau de Concours.* ed. Himie Voxman. Rubank, Inc. 1972. 4:00. III–IV. B♭$_1$–b♭. Opus 57. "for E♭ Bass." Arpeggios, triplets, technical and lyrical playing with bravura. See: Voxman, Himie,

Concert and Contest Collection, under Tuba and Keyboard Collections.

Albeniz, I. *Mallorca (Barcarola).* arr. J. Amaz. Union Musical Espanola. 1970. 4:00. IV–V. d–b♭' (c''). For "Trombon, Bombardino or Tuba."

Albeniz, I. *Puerta de Tierra (Bolero).* arr. J. Amaz. Union Musical Espanola. 1970. 3:30. IV–V. D–a'. For "Fagot, Bombardino, Trombon or Tuba." High tesitura.

Albéniz, Isaac. *Cantos de España, Op. 232, Nr. 2.* arr. Walter Hilgers. Editions Marc Reift. 1995. $11.80. 3:15. IV. A–d''. Originally for violin and piano from the collection *Cantos de España,* this is a direct adaptation for tuba. The tessitura lies in the upper middle register of the F-tuba. Recorded by Walter Hilgers.

Albéniz, Isaac. *Chant d'amour.* arr. Walter Hilgers. Editions Marc Reift. 1995. $11.80. 3:30. III–IV. B_1–f'. A lyrical transcription of the original work for saxophone. Recorded by Walter Hilgers.

Albéniz, Isaac. *España, Canción Catalan, Op. 165.* arr. Walter Hilgers. Editions Marc Reift. 1995. $16.50. 3:15. IV. A–g'. Originally for violin and piano from the collection *Cantos de España,* this is a direct adaptation for tuba. The tessitura lies in the upper middle register. Recorded by Walter Hilgers.

Albian, Franco. *Alla Siciliana.* Albian Publishing. 2004. III. E_1–b♭. Dedicated to Brian Frederiksen. Composer is completing a piano reduction of the band score. A good theme and variations work suitable for the advanced intermediate player with some multiple tonguing facility. Good test piece or recital work at the intermediate level. See listing under Music for Tuba and Band.

Albinoni. *Sonate en fa majeur.* arr. André Goudenhooft. Gérard Billaudot. III.

Albinoni. *Sonate en re majeur.* arr. André Goudenhooft. Gérard Billaudot.

Albinoni, Tomaso. *Concerto in D Minor, Opus 9, Nr. 2.* arr. Walter Hilgers. Editions Marc Reift. 1995. $16.50. 12:30. IV. D–d'. Allegro e non presto; Adagio; Allegro. Originally for oboe, this is a direct adaptation for tuba. The tessitura lies in the upper middle register. Recorded by Walter Hilgers.

Albinoni, Tomaso. *Konzert B-Dur, Opus 7, Nr. 3.* arr. Branimir Slokar, Urs Flück continuo. Editions Marc Reift. 1998. $17.50. 8:00. III. G–c'. Allegro; Adagio; Allegro. Originally for oboe, this is a direct adaptation for tuba. The limited tessitura makes it very accessible for F or E♭ tuba. Available in bass clef concert pitch or treble clef in B♭.

Alletter, Wilhelm, and Joseph Philip Knight. *Deep Sea Stories.* Carl Fischer Inc. 1938. $3.50. 1:35. II. A♭$_1$–e♭''. E♭ or BB♭ tuba. Easy, accessible solo for the younger player. Uses the tune *Rocked in the Cradle of the Deep.* Would stretch the range of the very beginning BB♭ player.

Ameller, André. *Bamboola.* Gérard Billaudot. 1983.

Ameller, André. *Bassutecy.* Alphonse Leduc. 1983. $5.45. B♭–f'. For French tuba. See review in *TUBA Journal,* Vol. 18, No. 3, Page 17.

Ameller, André. *Batifol.* Éditions M. Combre. 1983. 1:15. II–III. E–e♭'. "pour tuba en ut ou saxhorns en si♭ et piano." For French tuba. Espressivo lyrical section and not too technical playful Allegro section with some syncopations. See: Thompson/Lemke; *French Music for Low Brass Instruments.*

Ameller, André. *Belle Province: Hauterive.* Alphonse Leduc. 1973. $8.60. 2:30. II. E♭–e♭'. Andante espressivo. Cordialement à Jean Arnoult. "pour Tuba en Ut ou Trombone Basse ou Saxhorns si♭ ou mi♭ et Piano." For French tuba. Moderate tempo 3/4 time expressive melody. No rhythms faster than eighth notes. Originally written for saxhorn and would work well played down an octave by an advanced beginner. See: Thompson/Lemke; *French Music for Low Brass Instruments.* Also see review in *TUBA Journal,* Vol. 1, No. 3, Page 6.

Ameller, André. *Dolce Espressivo.* Gérard Billaudot. 1983.

Ameller, André. *Irish-Cante.* Alphonse Leduc. 1977. $11.50. 5:15. IV–V. E♭$_1$–g'. Cordialement à Paul Bernard, Professeur au Conservatoire National Supérieur de Musique. "pour Tuba Ut ou Saxhorn basse Si♭ ou Trombone basse et Piano." For French tuba. Very wide range. See: Thompson/Lemke; *French Music for Low Brass Instruments.* See review in *TUBA Journal,* Vol. 7, No. 2, Page 20.

Ameller, André. *Ive.* Gérard Billaudot. 1981. 1:45. II–III. G–g'. Andante expressivo. "Pour Bugle et pour Baryton-Tuba ténor Si♭–Basse Si♭ et Piano." French tuba tessitura. Lyrical, mostly scale-wise solo.

Ameller, André. *Kryptos.* Hinrichsen Edition. 1958. 5:00. V. G♭$_1$–c'. En Hommage à: Paul Bernard, professeur au Conservatoire National Supérieur de Musique de Paris; Rene Poinsard, professeur au Conservatoire National de Musique Dijon; Maurice Smith, trombone Professor at the Royal College of Music, London. "Etude pour tous les Trombones, ou Tuba, le Saxhorn-basse en si♭ (B♭) et piano." Wide Range. Muted passages. Includes passages in both bass and tenor clefs. Cadenza passages with complex rhythms. See: Thompson/Lemke; *French Music for Low Brass Instruments.*

Ameller, André. *Logos.* Alphonse Leduc. 1982. $18.25. 6:50. V. E_1–a♭'. "pour tuba basse ou tuba en Fa ou Saxhorn basse Si♭ et Piano." Very wide range—has 8vb notes for lower tubas throughout. Strong technique required: double tonguing, wide interval skips, plenty of notes! See: Thompson/Lemke; *French Music for Low Brass Instruments.*

Ameller, André. *Philae.* Gérard Billaudot. 1991. For French tuba.

Ameller, André. *Tuba-Abut.* Éditions Max Eschig. 1975. 5:30. V. ($E\flat_1$) E_1–g'. Cordialement à Paul Bernard, Professeur au Conservatoire National de Musique de Paris. "pour Tuba Ut ou saxhorn si♭ et Piano." Strong technique required: wide interval jumps, wide range, quick tempos. See: Thompson/Lemke; *French Music for Low Brass Instruments.*

Ameller, André. *Tuba-Concert.* Éditions Max Eschig. 1952. 4:40. V. $D\sharp_1$–c''. Cordialement à Paul Bernard, Professeur au Conservatoire National de Musique de Paris. Opus 69. "pour Tuba ut ou Saxhorn basse si♭." Piano reduction. Written for French tuba. Was published for tuba and orchestra. Very wide range—good showcase. See: Thompson/Lemke; *French Music for Low Brass Instruments.*

Amos, K. *Tuba Compositae.* Boosey & Hawkes, Inc. $13.50.

Anderson, Eugene D. *Concert Piece for Tuba and Piano.* Anderson's Arizona Originals. 1971. See: Anderson, Eugene D., *Concert Piece for Tuba and Band,* under Tuba and Band. Also see: Bird, Gary, ed.; *Program Notes for the Solo Tuba.*

Anderson, Eugene D. *Tuba Concerto No. 1 in B Minor.* Anderson's Arizona Originals. 1971. $25.00. See: Anderson, Eugene D., *Tuba Concerto No. 1 in B Minor,* under Tuba and Orchestra. Also see: Bird, Gary, ed.; *Program Notes for the Solo Tuba.*

Anderson, Garland. *Sonata.* Southern Music Company. 1985. $10.00. 12:53 (5:52, 3:26, 3:35). IV–V. A_1–c♯'. Molto Sostenuto/Allegro con brio; Andante Sostenuto; Allegro Amabile. In Memoriam Ralph Allen Anderson. Dedicated to composer's brother. First performed April 25, 1984 at Ball State University by Jeffrey Rideout, tuba, and Garland Anderson, piano. Major work. Good technique required; slurring, sustained playing. Conservative range. Good recital material.

Angerer, Paul. *Tubilustrum.* Available from Spaeth and Schmid. $19.50.

Antoniotti, Giorgio. *Sonata in G Minor, Op. 1 no. 10.* tr. Oscar Zimmerman, ed. and arr. Joseph Skillen. Bernel Music Publications 2000. III–IV. 6:00. Typical four-movement baroque sonata originally for viola da gamba (frequently played on double bass), but requires good interpretation of grace notes. The fast movements require quick breathing and fast finger technique.

Aranyi, Gyorgy. *Kis Humoreszk.* Hungarian publication—available from the Tuba Center.

Aranyi-Aschner, Georg. *Ein kleines Andenken.* Available from Spaeth and Schmid. $19.50.

Arban, J. B. *Carnival of Venice.* arr. Patrick Sheridan. PatrickSheridan.com (Bon Bons Series). $18.00.

Arban, J. B. *Variations on "Carnival of Venice."* arr. Jens-Bjørn Larsen and Ole Hover. SheetMusicNow.com. $14.50.

Arban, J. B. *Variations on "Carnival of Venice."* arr. Øystein Baadsvik. Ovation. $23.01.

Arban, J. B. *Variations on "Carnival of Venice" for Tuba and Symphonic Winds.* arr. and tr. William Schmidt, ed. Sharon Davis. Western International Music, Inc. 1996. $17.00. 8:00. V. C–b♭'. The original Arban solo is complete in this version, but the accompaniment is entirely original "based on the implied harmony of the solo part." Premiered by Daniel Perantoni at the 1988 Mid-West Band and Orchestra Clinic. See listing under Music for Tuba and Band.

Arban, Jean Baptiste. *Arban's Fantasie Brillante.* arr. Carl Weber. J. W. Pepper & Son. 1914. Out of Print. See: Weber, Carl, *Nineteen Solos for E♭ Bass with Piano Accompaniment,* under Tuba and Keyboard Collections.

Arban, Jean Baptiste. *Carnival of Venice, The (Variations).* arr. Herbert Wekselblatt. G. Schirmer Inc. 1972. 1:53. III–IV. $B\flat_1$–f. Flowingly. Theme and (two) Variations. Chorus and two variations based on Arban's variations, but with notes left out for breathing. Good introduction to the heritage of the tune. See: Wekselblatt, Herbert, *First Solos for the Tuba Player, BB♭,* under Tuba and Keyboard Collections.

Arban, Jean Baptiste. *Carnival of Venice in F Major.* arr. Le Clair. Reift. 1993. IV. In preparation.

Arban, Jean Baptiste. *Variations on the "Carnival of Venice."* arr. Richard Domek. Available from the arranger. 1981. For Skip Gray. See: Arban, Jean Baptiste, *Variations on the "Carnival of Venice"* under Tuba and Orchestra and Tuba in Mixed Ensemble.

Arban, Jean Baptiste. *Variations on the "Carnival of Venice."* arr. Schmidt and Davis. Western International Music. In preparation.

Arbel, Chaya. *Roundarounds.* Kibutz Movement League of Composers. Recorded by Adi Herschko.

Arensky, A. *Ballade.* ed. V. Mitegin. Moscow Muzyka. 1969. See: Mitegin, V., *Pieces for Tuba and Piano,* in Tuba and Keyboard Collections.

Armand, Migani. *Tuba Mosaique.*

Arne, Thomas A. *Air from "Comus."* arr. Donald C. Little. CPP/Belwin, Inc. 1978. $4.00. 2:04. II. $B\flat_1$–e♭. Allegro. Stately air in 3/4 time. A few eighth notes, a few slurs, a few accidentals, otherwise, no technical problems. See other listing in this section. See review in *TUBA Journal,* Vol. 7, No. 4, Page 31.

Arne, Thomas A. *Air from "Comus."* arr. Donald C. Little. CPP/Belwin, Inc. 1978. See: Lamb, Jack, *Solo Sounds For Tuba Levels 1–3, Volume 1,* under Tuba and Keyboard Collections. Also see other listing in this section.

Artiga, Angeles Lópes. *Guamiliana.* Publ. D.L., Valencia. 1998. 5:05. IV.

Arutiunian, Alexandre. *Expromt.* arr. A. Lebedev. Military Band Masters Faculty of Moscow Conservatiore. 1971. See: Lebedev, A., Collection of

Pieces for Tuba "Es" and Piano, under Tuba and Keyboard Collections.

Arutunian, Alexander. *Concerto*. Editions BIM. 1993. $22.00. 15:20. IV–V. F_1–g'. Allegro moderato; Andante sostenuto; Allegro ma non troppo. Commissioned by Yamaha Corporation and Editions Bim. Dedicated to Roger Bobo. Piano reduction. For more information see Music for Tuba and Orchestra.

Ascher. *Alice, Where Art Thou?* arr. Carl Weber. J. W. Pepper & Son. 1914. Out of Print. See: Weber, Carl, *Nineteen Solos For E♭ Bass with Piano Accompaniment,* under Tuba and Keyboard Collections.

Assafyev, B. *Scherzo*. ed. S. Melnikov. Military Band Masters Institute–Moscow. 1957. See: Melnikov, S., *Pieces for Tuba and Piano,* under Tuba and Keyboard Collections.

Aubain, Jean Emmanuel. *Thème et Variations*. Amphion. 1975. V. F_1–b♭'. For French tuba. See: Thompson/Lemke; *French Music for Low Brass Instruments.*

Aubert, Jacques. *Air*. arr. Angelo Manzo. Tuba-Euphonium Press. 2001. 3:00. III. E–b. An uptempo baroque tune with some quick technique required in the key of E major.

Aubin, Francine. *Concerto pour Tuba*. Editions Aug. Zurfluh. $33.00.

Autran, Alphonse. *Quadrille En Forme De Ronds D'eau*. Gérard Billaudot. 1990. 3:00. III. E–c'. "pour tuba et piano." For French tuba. Cute tune with no big technical problems. See: Daniel-Lesur, *Collection Panorama,* under Tuba and Keyboard Collections.

Ayma, David. *Rapsodia para Tuba y Piano*. 1989.

Baader-Nobs, Heidi. *Bifurcation*. Éditions BIM. 1991. $22.50. 3:53. V. B_1–a♯'. Morceau imposé du Concours International d'Exécution Musicale–Genève 1991. Modern notation-score needed for performance. Wide range. Contemporary performance requirements: Flutter tongue, glissandos, improvise timing with given pitches. Recorded by Øystein Baadsvik, Jens Bjørn-Larsen.

Bach, C. Ph. *La complaisante*. tr. Lars Holmgaard. SheetMusicNow.com. 2000. $5.00. 3:45. III–IV. D♯–f'. Tuneful work in the early classical style. Mostly lyrical with some fast finger technique at times. Effective piece for learning this style or contrasting material on a recital.

Bach, E. *Spring's Awakening*. Carl Fischer Inc. Out of Print. 3:02. III. (F_1) C–c' (d'). "Fruhlings Erwachen." Written with E♭ tuba in mind. Typical old-style melodic solo.

Bach, Jan. *Tuba Concerto*. Tuba-Euphonium Press. See Music for Tuba and Orchestra.

Bach, J. S. *Arioso*. arr. Øystein Baadsvik. Ovation. $11.43.

Bach, J. S. *Ave Maria*. arr. Charles Gounod, tr. Patrick Sheridan. PatrickSheridan.com (Bon Bons Series). $12.00.

Bach, J. S. *If Thou Be Near*. arr. Richard Thurston. Southern Music Company.

Bach, J. S. *Minuet in G*. arr. Dishinger. Available from Spaeth and Schmid. $7.25.

Bach, J. S. *Planets, Stars, and Airs of Space*. arr. Michael Fischer. Tuba-Euphonium Press. 2001. 1:45. I–II. C–e♭. Easy arrangement of this chorale tune suitable for beginners.

Bach, Johann Sabastian. *Adagio*. Bearbeitung: Walter Hilgers. Editions Marc Reift. 1990. $7.50. 3:18. IV. A_1–d'. "für Tuba und Klavier/Orgel." Good transcription with ornamentation included. Some mordents, trills, etc. Good recital material.

Bach, Johann Sabastian. *Air and Bouree*. arr. William J. Bell. Carl Fischer Inc. 1937. $4.50. 3:25. III–IV. G_1–b♭. One of THE standard solos. Two movements: Air *Komm, Süsser Tod (Come, Sweet Death)*, a very lyrical Chorale and Bourree (from the second violin sonata), scale-wise, very musical transcription. A couple of harmonic seconds will challenge the young ear. Excellent recital material. See: Bach, Johann Sabastian, *Air and Bourree,* under Tuba and Band. Recorded by Rex Conner, Ronald Davis, Harvey Phillips, Peter Popiel. (*Komm Susser Tod* recorded by Karl Megules.)

Bach, Johann Sabastian. *Bouree*. ed. S. Melnikov. Military Band Masters Institute–Moscow. 1957. See: Melnikov, S., *Pieces for Tuba and Piano,* under Tuba and Keyboard Collections.

Bach, Johann Sabastian. *Gavotte*. arr. Ken Swanson. CPP/Belwin, Inc. 1970. $4.00. 1:27. II. A_1–e. Moderato. In cut time. Fastest rhythm is eighth note. All tongued; some accidentals. Good transcription of classic baroque solo. Good advanced beginner recital material.

Bach, Johann Sabastian. *Gavotte*. arr. Ken Swanson. CPP/Belwin, Inc. 1970. See: *CPP/Belwin, Tuba Solos, Level Two,* under Tuba and Keyboard Collections. Also see other listing in this section.

Bach, Johann Sabastian. *Musette*. tr. Ronald C. Dishinger. Medici Music Press. 1982. $3.00. 1:36. II. A_1–c. From *Anna Magdalena Bach Notebook*. Transcription of popular Bach melody. Some syncopation, some sixteenth notes, no big technical problems.

Bach, Johann Sabastian. *O Mensch, bewein' dein' Sünde gross*. Bearbeitung: Walter Hilgers. Editions Marc Reift. 1990. $12.50. 5:33. IV. b♭–g'. BMV 622. For tuba and organ. Transcribed part includes ornamentation: mordents, grace notes, trills. Best on E♭/F tuba due to high tessitura. Some 32nd notes should not be a problem if played at a musical (not too fast) tempo. Recorded by Walter Hilgers.

Bach, Johann Sabastian. *Patron of the Wind from "Phoebus and Pan."* arr. Allen Ostrander. Edition Musicus. 1959. $2.75. 2:20. III. C–g. Allegro giocoso. Good transcription. A few scale-wise eighth notes. No technical problems.

Bach, Johann Sabastian. *Rondo.* tr. Marvin C. Howe. Lawson-Gould. 1965. 1:35. III. (A_1) D–g (a). From Suite in B Minor for flute. Mostly scale-wise motion in this transcription. Some optional 8vb. See: Howe, M., *Three Tuba Solos,* under Tuba and Keyboard Collections.

Bach, Johann Sabastian. *Siciliano.* arr. Quinto Maganini. Edition Musicus. 1950. 3:54. III–IV. D–d♭'. In 6/8 time with eighth note as pulse. Sustained lyrical playing. See: Ostrander, Allen, *Concert Album for Tuba,* under Tuba and Keyboard Collections.

Bach, Johann Sebastian. *Adagio.* arr. Walter Hilgers. Editions Marc Reift. 1998. $6.50. ca. 4:30 (without repeats). II. B_1–f. The tessitura makes this work very performable on a CC or B♭ tuba. Available in violin or bass clef. See listing under Music for Tuba and Organ. Recorded by Walter Hilgers.

Bach, Johann Sebastian. *Badinerie.* arr. John Glenesk Mortimer. Editions Marc Reift. 1998. $6.50. 1:50. III. E♭–c'. An adaptation for tuba and piano of this well-known movement from the *Suite for Orchestra No. 2 in B Minor.* Requires a light and articulate approach. Available in bass clef concert pitch or treble clef in E♭ or B♭.

Bach, Johann Sebastian. *"Ich ruf zu Dir, Herr Jesu Christ," Choral Prelude BMV 639.* arr. Walter Hilgers. Editions Marc Reift. 1988. $6.50. 2:00. II. C–d. Originally for choir and organ; solo part is set so that it could be played along with a church choir with minimal rehearsal time. See listing under Music for Tuba and Organ.

Bach, Johann Sebastian. *Musette.* arr. Herbert Wekselblatt. G. Schirmer Inc. 1972. 1:25. III. $B♭_1$–f. Allegretto. A few wide leaps both articulated and slurred. Fun, musical tune. See: Wekselblatt, Herbert, *First Solos for the Tuba Player, BB♭,* under Tuba and Keyboard Collections.

Bach, Johann Sebastian. *Nun komm' der Heiden Heiland, Choral-Vorspiel BMV 659.* arr. Walter Hilgers. Editions Marc Reift. 1993. $11.80. 6:00. IV. A–g'. This is originally for organ and/or choir. In this arrangement the solo part is in the upper middle to high range. As in the original from Bach the dynamic markings have been kept to an absolute minimum to allow freedom of interpretation. See listing under Music for Tuba and Organ. Recorded by Walter Hilgers.

Bach, Johann Sebastian. *Prelude in D Minor, BWV 539.* arr. Walter Hilgers. Editions Marc Reift. 1998. $6.50. 2:00. II. A_1–g. Originally in D minor, this arrangement has been transposed down a major third to B♭ minor. The tessitura makes this work very performable on a CC or BB♭ tuba. Can be used in combination with other Bach works by the same publisher to form a suite. Available in violin or bass clef. See listing under Music for Tuba and Organ.

Bach, Johann Sebastian. *Prelude XVII from "Das Wohltemperierte Klavier," BWV 862, Teil I.* arr. Walter Hilgers. Editions Marc Reift. 1998. $6.50. 1:45. III. C–c'. Individual melodic lines of the original composition have been set for the tuba solo. Can be used in combination with other Bach works by the same publisher to form a suite. Available in violin or bass clef. See listing under Music for Tuba and Organ.

Bach, Johann Sebastian. *Prelude XX from "Das Wohltemperierte Klavier," BWV 865, Teil I.* arr. Walter Hilgers. Editions Marc Reift. 1998. $6.50. 1:30. II. E_1–f. Individual melodic lines of the original composition have been set for the tuba solo. The tessitura makes this work very performable on a CC or BB♭ tuba. Can be used in combination with other Bach works by the same publisher to form a suite. Available in violin or bass clef. See listing under Music for Tuba and Organ.

Bach, Johann Sebastian. *Prelude XXII from "Das Wohltemperierte Klavier," BWV 867, Teil I.* arr. Walter Hilgers. Editions Marc Reift. 1998. $6.50. 1:30. II. $G♯_1$–e. Individual melodic lines of the original composition have been set for the tuba solo. The tessitura makes this work very performable on a CC or BB♭ tuba. Can be used in combination with other Bach works by the same publisher to form a suite. Available in violin or bass clef. See listing under Music for Tuba and Organ.

Bach, Johann Sebastian. *Sarabande.* arr. Walter Hilgers. Editions Marc Reift. 1998. $14.20. 3:50. III. D–c'. This movement comes from the English Suite No. 2 in A Minor and is a good addition to the growing repertoire of Bach works transcribed for tuba. See listing under Music for Tuba and Organ. Recorded by Walter Hilgers.

Bach, Johann Sebastian. *Second Part from Capriccio.* ed. S. Melnikov. Military Band Masters Institute–Moscow. 1957. See: Melnikov, S., *Pieces for Tuba and Piano,* under Tuba and Keyboard Collections.

Bach, Johann Sebastian. *Siciliano and Chorale.* arr. Daniel Perantoni. Hal Leonard Publishing Corp. 1976. See: Perantoni, Daniel, *Master Solos Intermediate Level,* under Tuba and Keyboard Collections.

Bach, Johann Sebastian. *Siciliano from Sonata No. II.* arr. Harry H. Hall. Brodt Music Company, Inc. 1962. $1.50. 2:49. II–III. C–a. Lovely melody in slow 6/8 time. Requires very lyrical approach. Some flexible slurring involved. Good recital material.

Bach, Johann Sebastian. *Sicilienne d'apres la 1re Sonate en Sol mineur (BMV 1,001) pour Voilin seul.* ed. Philippe Rougeron. Alphonse Leduc. 1983. $3.55. F–f'. For French tuba. See: Thompson/Lemke; *French Music for Low Brass Instruments.*

Bach, Johann Sebastian. *Sonata in Es.* arr. Cooley. Available from Spaeth and Schmid. $22.50.

Bach, Johann Sebastian. *Sonata II.* arr. Hilgers. Editions Marc Reift. 1990. $18.00. 6:00. IV. ($E♭_1$)

D–d♭'. Allegro moderato; Siciliano; Allegro. For tuba and piano or organ. An excellent transcription with some ornamentation and dynamics included.

Bach, Johann Sebastian. *Sonate II for Tuba and Piano.* arr. Wesley Jacobs. Encore Music Publishers. 1992. $10.50. 10:12 (3:40, 2:23, 4:09). IV. D–d'. Three movements: Allegro Moderato; Siciliano; Allegro. Part provided has no expression/dynamic marks. Mostly scale-wise baroque writing. Requires good technique—fun transcription. Last movement requires some breathing planning.

Bach, Johann Sebastian. *Variations on a Theme.* arr. Cordonier. Available from Spaeth and Schmid. $12.00.

Baeyens, H. *Introduction et Cantabile.* Editions Andel Uitgave. 1958. $7.25. 3:00. III. B♭–f'. Upper tessitura; better on F tuba.

Bak, Mikhail Abromovich. *Joke, A.* ed. A. Lebedev. Moscow Muzyka. 1986. Same as Bak, Mikhail Abromovich, *Two Pieces* (second piece) in this section. See: Lebedev, A., *Tuba Tutor Vol. 2,* under Tuba and Keyboard Collections.

Bak, Mikhail Abromovich. *Two Pieces.* 1969. 3:56 (2:02, 1:54). IV. G♭$_1$–c♭'. Melody (Andantino cantabile); Joke (Allegretto scherzando). Melody: Lush, lyrical lullaby in D♭ major. Some slurring; some accidentals; warm vocal approach required. Joke: Requires some flexibility and style. Good recital material.

Baker, Claude. *Omaggi E Fantasie for Tuba and Piano (1981/87).* MMB Music. 1990. 16:00. V. for David Randolph. Playable on C tuba; intended for F tuba. Very modern writing for both instruments: Tuba: complex rhythms, using the instrument and mouthpiece percussively, whispering through horn, muted passages, etc. Piano: striking soundboard, strings, beams, etc. Composer suggests amplifying the piano to enhance the more delicate effects. Score needed for performance. Recorded by David Randolph.

Baksa, Robert. *Tuba Sonata.* Theodore Presser. 1998. $17.00. 13:00. IV. B♭$_1$–e♭'. Lively and flowing; Elegiac, somewhat freely; March. Very good idiomatic writing for the tuba. No major problems technically. An excellent recital selection.

Bales, Kenton. *Fantasy on a Lakota Theme for Tuba and Piano.* Southern Music Company and available from the composer. 1993. $6.50. 4:14. IV–V. F$_1$–b♭ (e♭'). For Craig Fuller. Completed 2/6/92. Some mixed meter. Requires good flexibility, good technique, a good ear, and a strong accompanist.

Ball, Eric. *In the Army.* Salvationist Publishing & Supplies, Ltd. 3:10. III–IV. B♭$_1$–b♭. "Solo for Bombardon in E♭—Advanced Level Test Item." Solo part in treble clef. Traditional showcase solo with a martial flavor: dotted rhythms, octave jumps, theme and variation "feel." Good intermediate solo.

Balthazar, J. L. *Poeme,* op. 10. Editions Andel Uitgave.

Banfield, Pete. *Peaceful Fusion.* Solid Brass Music Company. $7.00. IV. A good solo containing several popular styles including a fine upbeat jazz section.

Barat, J. Edouard. *Introduction and Dance.* arr. Glen Smith. Southern Music Company. 1973. $5.50. 3:54. IV. (C$_2$) E$_1$–g. Baritone part also included. See listing for *Introduction et Danse* in this section. This arrangement is 8vb from original. Also see: Thompson/Lemke; *French Music for Low Brass Instruments.* And see review in *TUBA Journal,* Vol. 1, No. 1, Page 7.

Barat, J. Edouard. *Introduction et Danse.* Alphonse Leduc. $11.50. 3:54. IV–V. C–f'. A mon excellent ami Paul Achard, Administrateur de la Sirène. "pour Saxhorn-Basse Si♭ avec Accompagnement de Piano." See orchestration of *Introduction and Dance,* under Tuba and Band. Also see: Thompson/Lemke; *French Music for Low Brass Instruments.* Recorded by Roger Bobo.

Barat, J. Edouard. *Introduction et Sérénade.* Alphonse Leduc. 1963. $11.50. 4:02. IV–V. F$_1$–f'. "pour tuba ut ou saxhorn basse si♭ ou saxhorn baryton si♭ avec accompagnement de piano." For French tuba. Originally printed 1957. Stately opening section followed by a technical serenade section with scales, arpeggios, and typical French harmonies. See: Thompson/Lemke; *French Music for Low Brass Instruments.*

Barat, J. Edouard. *Morceau de Concours.* Alphonse Leduc. $12.80. 6:10. IV–V. C–a♭'. A l'artiste et Ami J. Balay ex-soliste de la Musique de la Garde et de l'Opéra (de la Garde Républicaine). Lent/Moderato. Contest Piece. "pour Baryton ou Basse si♭ avec Accompagnement de Piano." For French tuba. Requires facility. Good recital material. See: Thompson/Lemke; *French Music for Low Brass Instruments.*

Barat, J. Edouard. *Reminiscences de Navarre.* Alphonse Leduc. 1950. $12.80. 4:00. IV–V. F$_1$–g'. A mon Ami Paul Bernard, Professeur au Conservatoire National de Musique. "pour Tuba en Ut ou Saxhorn basse Si♭ et piano." See: Thompson/ Lemke; *French Music for Low Brass Instruments.*

Baratto, Paolo. *Jumbo-Baby.* Available from the composer. See: Baratto, Paolo, *Jumbo-Baby,* under Tuba and Band. Also written for bassoon or bass trombone with piano.

Baratto, Paolo. *Paprika, Csárdás.* Editions Marc Reift. 2004. $11.80. 2:30. II–III. C–a. Dedicated to Hertha Baratto. A pleasant and relatively simple Czardas. Well suited for a young player getting his feet wet in tempo changes and Hungarian rhythms. Available in bass clef concert pitch or treble clef in E♭ or B♭.

Barber, S. *Adagio and Scherzo from Sonata C Minor.* ed. A. Lebedev. Moscow Muzyka. 1986. 4:02. III–IV. F$_1$–b♭. Some very slow, easy playing combined with Presto quick articulations in

12/8 time. Some three against four in Presto section. See: Lebedev, A., *Tuba Tutor Vol. 2,* under Tuba and Keyboard Collections.

Barboteu, Georges. *Prelude et cadence.* Edition Choudens. 1977. IV–V. E_1–c''. For French tuba. See: Thompson/Lemke; *French Music for Low Brass Instruments.*

Barcos, George. *Preludes.* Editions Marc Reift. In preparation.

Bardwell, William. *Sonata Tuba and Piano.* Robert King Music Co. & Alphonse Leduc. 1974. $5.85. 10:15. V. E_1–e'. Dialogue; Scherzo; Passacaglia. Dedicated to John Fletcher. Written in 1968. Dialogue is a series of cadenza-like speeches between soloist and accompanist (4:45). Scherzo is based on appoggiaturas in 5/8 time with some (unmarked) 2/8. Passacaglia has mixed meter and will take some coordinating with piano part.

Bariller, Robert. *L'Enterrement de Saint-Jean. (The Funeral of St. John.)* Alphonse Leduc. 1960. $8.60. 5:00. II. A_1 (A)–f'. A Paul Bernard, très amicalement. "pour Tuba Ut ou Trombone basse ou Saxhorn basse Si♭ et Piano." Based on A. de Musset's *Fantasio;* Act I, Scene II. Easy rhythms, no technical problems. See: Thompson/Lemke; *French Music for Low Brass Instruments.*

Bariller, Robert. *Hans de Schnokeloch.* Alphonse Leduc. 1961. $11.50. 5:00. II–III. C♯–a'. For French tuba. See: Thompson/Lemke; *French Music for Low Brass Instruments.*

Barnby. *Sweet and Low.* arr. Acton Ostling. CPP/Belwin, Inc. 1969. 0:59. I. D–c. Middle range solo in 6/8 time. Good introduction to 6/8. See: Ostling, Acton, *Tuba (Bass) Soloist, Level One,* under Tuba and Keyboard Collections.

Barnby, Sir Joseph. *Sweet and Low.* arr. John Kinyon. M. Witmark & Sons. 1958. I. See: Kinyon, John, *Breeze-Easy Recital Pieces,* under Tuba and Keyboard Collections.

Barnes, Clifford P. *Arioso and Caprice.* Robbins Music. 1961. $4.00. 2:37. II–III. B♭$_1$–f. Lyrical Andante section followed by an advanced beginner technical Allegretto section. A few sixteenth note scales and a few arpeggios.

Barnes, Clifford P. *Valse Impromptu.* Robbins Music Corporation. 1961. 2:08. III. C–e♭. Allegro. 𝅗𝅥. = 64. Some eighth note scale-wise runs. Depending on tempo, very accessible and challenging to advanced beginner.

Barnes, James, arr. *Sometimes I Feel like a Motherless Child.* CPP/Belwin, Inc. 1980. $4.00. 1:30. I. A_1–A. Published individually as well as included in collections. See other listings in this section. Sad spiritual feel. One-octave range. Ideal for early ability. After piano introduction, eight-measure phrase repeated two times with five-measure tap. Some slurring of eighth notes. Eighth note is fastest rhythm.

Barnes, James, arr. *Sometimes I Feel like a Motherless Child.* CPP/Belwin, Inc. 1980. See: Lamb, Jack, *Classic Festival Solos,* under Tuba and Keyboard Collections. Also see other listing in this section.

Barnes, James, arr. *Sometimes I Feel like a Motherless Child.* CPP/Belwin, Inc. 1980. See: CPP/Belwin, *Tuba Solos, Level Two,* under Tuba and Keyboard Collections. Also see other listing in this section.

Barnes, James. *Concerto for Tuba, Op. 96.* arr. Yukiko Nishimura. Southern Music Company. 1997. $25.00. 19:30. V. C_1–g'. Allegretto giocoso; Lullaby; Rondo. Dedicated to Scott Watson. Very demanding work. It contains virtually every technical "trick in the book": multiple tonguing, large range shifts, quick facility with slurs and fingers. Each movement could stand alone, though the second and third movements are performed attacca. The second movement is written in a ballad style. See listing under Music for Tuba and Orchestra and Music for Tuba and Band.

Barnes, James. *In a Modal Mood.* Belwin Mills Publishing. 1980. 2:07. I–II. A_1–c. Slowly and Sadly. Easy introduction to modes (dorian mode). Mostly quarter and eighth notes at a slow tempo make this solo very accessible to the beginning player. See review in *TUBA Journal,* Vol. 9, No. 4, Page 33.

Barnes, James. *In a Modal Mood.* CPP/Belwin, Inc. 1980. See: CPP/Belwin, *Tuba Solos, Level Two,* under Tuba and Keyboard Collections. Also see other listing in this section.

Barnes, James. *Marching Right Along.* CPP/Belwin, Inc. 1980. $4.00. 1:20. I. B♭$_1$–d. Steady march tempo. Mostly step-wise motion with quarter note as fastest rhythm. Some accents, no technical problems. See other listing in this section.

Barnes, James. *Marching Right Along.* CPP/Belwin, Inc. 1980. See: CPP/Belwin, Inc., *Tuba Solos, Level One,* under Tuba and Keyboard Collections. Also see other listing in this section.

Barnes, James. *Nervous Turkey Rag, The (November Is Here Again).* Medici Music Press. 1982. $3.50. 1:15. II. B♭$_1$–c. Very Comical—Ragtime Feeling. Cute novelty (with a few other tunes thrown in). Tempo chosen will determine difficulty. Solo in cut time; a few eighth notes (optional quarter notes). See review in *TUBA Journal,* Vol. 11, No. 4, Page 22.

Barnes, James. *Whistlin' Tune.* CPP/Belwin, Inc. 1980. $4.00. 0:51. I. B♭–c. Lightly and with humor. Cut time. Short introduction, eight-measure motifs repeated. Limited range. Contains only quarter and half notes. Also has accents, fermatas, ritards, crescendos and makes a nice introduction of these musical devices.

Barnes, James. *Whistlin' Tune.* CPP/Belwin, Inc. See: CPP/Belwin, Inc., *Tuba Solos, Level One,* under Tuba and Keyboard Collections. Also see other listing in this section.

Barnes, James. *Work Song, a "Blues Song" for the Young Tubist.* Belwin Mills, Inc. 1980. Out of Print. 1:35. I–II. B♭$_1$–c. Published separately—see other listings for collection information. Not too fast; very deliberate. Some eighth notes, accents, use of G♭ as a blues note. Blues/rock feel. Good beginner solo.

Barnes, James. *Work Song, a "Blues Song" for the Young Tubist.* CPP/Belwin, Inc. 1980. See: Lamb, Jack, *Classic Festival Solos,* under Tuba and Keyboard Collections. Also see other listing in this section.

Barnes, James. *Work Song, a "Blues Song" for the Young Tubist.* CPP/Belwin, Inc. 1980. See: CPP/Belwin, *Tuba Solos, Level Two,* under Tuba and Keyboard Collections. Also see other listing in this section.

Barnes, W. *Old Time Theme and Variations.* Medici Music Press. 1982. $3.00. 1:49. II. C–e (f). Allegro moderato. Good introduction to theme and variations. Limited Range. Sixteen-measure theme and three variations. Contains some slurring and staccato passages. In 3/4; can be played "in one" for more advanced players.

Barnet, Richard D. *Four Segments.* Fema Music Publications. 1974. $3.75. 4:04 (0:50, 1:47, 0:45, 0:42). IV. F$_1$–c'. Four movements: March (Briskly); Ballad (Tempo rubato); Waltz (Lightly); Dance. To Edward Livingston. Short musical vignettes with plenty of opportunity for expression. Advanced intermediate technique needed; one gliss in first movement.

Barnhouse, Charles Lloyd. *Barbarossa—Air Varie.* arr. Forrest L. Buchtel. C. L. Barnhouse. 1935. $3.50. 5:30. Composed in 1897. Solo for BB♭ tuba or BB♭ bass saxophone. See: Barnhouse, Charles Lloyd, *Barbarossa,* under Tuba and Band.

Barraine, Elsa Jacqueline. *Andante et Allegro.* Editions Salabert. 1958. B♭$_1$–b♭'. For French tuba. See: Thompson/Lemke; *French Music for Low Brass Instruments.*

Barraine, Elsa Jacqueline. *Chiens de Paille. (Straw Dogs.)* Jobert. 1966. V. G$_1$–b♭'. For French tuba. See: Thompson/Lemke; *French Music for Low Brass Instruments.*

Bartles, Alfred. *Scherzo for Tuba and Wind Ensemble.* Sam Fox Publishing. 1970. Out of Print. 4:30. To Harvey G. Phillips. Piano reduction by the composer. See: Bartles, Alfred, *Scherzo for Tuba and Wind Ensemble,* under Tuba and Band.

Bartles, Alfred. *Tubossa—A Concert Bossanova for Solo Tuba and Symphonic Band.* Piano reduction available from composer. See listing under Music for Tuba and Band.

Bartok, Bela. *Adagio.* ed. A. Lebedev. Moscow Muzyka. 1984. 0:50. II. A$_1$–e. Lyrical folk song in A minor and 2/4 time. See: Lebedev, A., *Tuba Tutor Vol. 1,* under Tuba and Keyboard Collections.

Bartok, Bela. *Dance of the Bear.* arr. A. Lebedev. Military Band Masters Faculty of Moscow Conservatiore. 1971. See: Lebedev, A., Collection of Pieces for Tuba "Es" and Piano, under Tuba and Keyboard Collections.

Bartok, Bela. *Dance.* ed. A. Lebedev. Moscow Muzyka. 1984. 0:32. II. F$_1$–d♭. In 2/4 time and with exception of last three notes, three F$_1$'s, range is very limited. See: Lebedev, A., *Tuba Tutor Vol. 1,* under Tuba and Keyboard Collections.

Bartok, Bela. *Dance of the Slovaks.* tr. Ronald C. Dishinger. Studio 224/CPP/Belwin, Inc. 1979. 1:15. II. B♭$_1$–c. Solo in 2/4 time with a variety of articulations: staccatos, tenutos, accents. Modal in nature with limited range. Eighth note is fastest rhythm. Mostly step-wise motion; no technical problems. See: Lamb, Jack, *Classic Festival Solos,* under Tuba and Keyboard Collections.

Bartok, Bela. *Dirge No. 4.* arr. Sharon Davis. Western International Music. 1991. $5.00. 2:37. III–IV. E$_1$ (B$_1$)–b♭. Assai andante. Sustained, lyrical Bartok melody. Some dissonant interval jumps—sevenths, ninths; requires a good ear. Easy rhythmically; a few eighth notes at a very reasonable tempo. Good intermediate twentieth-century writing.

Bartok, Bela. *Hungarian Folk Song.* ed. A. Lebedev. Moscow Muzyka. 1984. 0:55. II–III. B♭$_1$–g♭. Simple rhythms in 2/4 time and in B♭ minor. See: Lebedev, A., *Tuba Tutor Vol. 1,* under Tuba and Keyboard Collections.

Bartok, Bela. *Song, A.* ed. A. Lebedev. Moscow Muzyka. 1984. 1:00. II–III. C–d. In C minor and 4/4 time with all phrases slurred. No technical problems. See: Lebedev, A., *Tuba Tutor Vol. 1,* under Tuba and Keyboard Collections.

Bartsch, Ch. *Adagio et Allegro.* J. Maurer Editions Musicales. 1971. $5.95. 5:20 (1:53, 3:27). IV. F$_1$–c'. Adagio; Allegro moderato. A Norbert Van Ser Jeught. "Pour Bastuba En Ut ou Pour Contrebasse Et Piano." Lyrical Adagio movement followed by a comfortably, musical Allegro section. Good recital material.

Baseler, J. *Happy Thoughts.* Carl Fischer Inc. 1887. Out of Print.

Bashmakov, Leonid. *Mutu.* Tuba-Euphonium Press. 1999. 8:00. IV–V. F$_1$–a'. Commissioned by TUBA See listing under "Music for Tuba in Mixed Ensemble." Piano reduction of work with wind quintet and percussion. Technically demanding with some extreme range considerations. See listing under Music for Tuba in Mixed Ensemble.

Baudrier, Émile. *Relax.* Gérard Billaudot. 1977. 1:57. II–III. F–e'. Moderato. "Pour Trombone Tenor, Trombone Basse, Tuba Ut et Piano." For French tuba. Relaxed tempo, relaxed rhythms, relaxed range. Tenuto and slurred notes throughout—lyrical solo. No technical problems.

Bauer, Guilherme. *Três miniaturas.* Fundação Nacional De Arte. 4:08 (1:30, 1:18, 1:20). IV–V. (D_1) E♯$_1$–d'. Three movements. Mixed meter, modern (tonal) melody, glissando, flutter tongue, technical passages (last movement—quick articulations) make this a worthwhile challenge.

Bayly, T. H. *Long, Long Ago.* arr. Sandy Feldstein. CPP/Belwin, Inc. 1990. I. B♭$_1$–G. See: Feldstein, Sandy, *First Solo Songbook,* under Tuba and Keyboard Collections.

Bayley, Thomas Haynes. *Faith of Our Fathers.* arr. John Kinyon. M. Witmark & Sons. 1958. I. See: Kinyon, John, *Breeze-Easy Recital Pieces,* under Tuba and Keyboard Collections.

Bayley, Thomas Haynes. *Long, Long Ago.* arr. John Kinyon. M. Witmark & Sons. 1958. I. See: Kinyon, John, *Breeze-Easy Recital Pieces,* under Tuba and Keyboard Collections.

Beach, Bennie. *Lamento.* Southern Music Company. 1961. $2.50. Out of Print. 4:20. Reflective lament in 5/4 time. Slow tempo makes this accessible to the player not used to 5/4. Only a few sixteenth notes. Plenty of room for expression. Recorded by Rex Conner, Robert LeBlanc.

Beasley, Rule. *Concerto for Tuba and Band.* Available from the composer. 1968. Commissioned by David Kuehn. See: Beasley, Rule, *Concerto for Tuba and Band,* under Tuba and Band. Also see review in *TUBA Journal,* Vol. 7, No. 3, Page 33. Also see: Bird, Gary, ed.; *Program Notes for the Solo Tuba.*

Beaucamp, Albert. *Cortège.* Alphonse Leduc. 1953. Out of Print. 2:25. II–III. C–g'. A Armand François. Grave. "pour Tuba Ut ou Contrebasse à Cordes ou Saxhorn basse Si♭ ou Trombone basse et Piano." For French tuba. Very melodic (mostly slurred) melody at a slow reflective tempo makes this very accessible to the advanced beginner. See: Thompson/Lemke; *French Music for Low Brass Instruments.*

Beeler, Walter. *Virtuoso, The.* Out of Print. 2:18. II–III. F_1–d. Typical theme and (three) variations solo. First variation has some sixteenth notes, second variation has low tessitura, third variation is based on triplets.

Beethoven, Ludwig von. *Beloved from Afar.* tr. Ronald C. Dishinger. Medici Music Press. 1990. $2.50. 2:52. II–III. B♭$_1$–f. "An die ferne Geliebts, Op. 98, No. 6." A few tempo changes. Some easy slurs, no difficult rhythm or technical problems.

Beethoven, Ludwig von. *Country Dance.* arr. Herbert Wekselblatt. G. Schirmer Inc. 1972. 0:48. III. C–g. Short, quick 2/4 dance with some accidentals and quick sixteenth note articulations. See: Wekselblatt, Herbert, *First Solos for the Tuba Player, BB♭,* under Tuba and Keyboard Collections.

Beethoven, Ludwig von. *Danse villageoise. (Rustic Dance.)* arr. Andre Goudenhooft; Augustin Maillard, piano arr. Gérard Billaudot. 1989. $6.50. 3:00. II–III. C–c'. "Extraite de thèmes variés pour violon." "Adaptation pour le trombone basse et le tuba basse." Wide range for beginning player. Some flexibility needed for slurred arpeggios. See: Thompson/Lemke; *French Music for Low Brass Instruments.*

Beethoven, Ludwig von. *Le Désir.* tr. J. Bilbaut. Editions Salabert. Out of Print.

Beethoven, Ludwig von. *Hymn to Joy.* arr. Wesley Jacobs. Encore Music Publishers. 0:33. I. C–c. Strict time. Short solo with easy rhythms, limited range, some step-wise slurs. See: Jacobs, Wesley, *Solos From The Classics,* under Tuba and Keyboard Collections.

Beethoven, Ludwig von. *May Song.* tr. Ronald C. Dishinger. Medici Music Press. 1990. $2.50. 2:29. II–III. E♭–e♭. *"Mailied, Op. 52, No. 4."* Classical solo in 2/4 time in E♭ major within one octave. Some easy slurring; tenutos, staccatos; no technical problems.

Beethoven, Ludwig von. *Menuet.* arr. Quinto Maganini. Edition Musicus. 1954. 2:00. III. G_1–a♭. Light articulation and flexibility needed. See: Ostrander, Allen, *Concert Album for Tuba,* under Tuba And Keyboard Collections. Recorded by Rex Conner.

Beethoven, Ludwig von. *Nature's Adoration.* arr. Allen Ostrander. Edition Musicus. 1954. 1:36. II. B♭$_1$–f. Maestoso. Well-transcribed advanced beginner solo. Very easy rhythms (one eighth note in entire piece); easy accompaniment. See: Ostrander, Allen, *Concert Album for Tuba,* under Tuba And Keyboard Collections.

Beethoven, Ludwig von. *Ode to Joy.* arr. Bill Boyd, ed. Charles Daellenbach. Hal Leonard Publishing Corp. 1992. 0:45. I. B♭$_1$–B♭. Adapted from Symphony No. 9. A couple of eighth notes; easy rhythms. Comes with practice/performance cassette. See: Daellenbach, Charles, *Book of Beginning Tuba Solos,* under Tuba and Keyboard Collections.

Beethoven, Ludwig von. *Ode to Joy.* arr. Sandy Feldstein. CPP/Belwin, Inc. 1990. I. B♭$_1$–F. See: Feldstein, Sandy, *First Solo Songbook,* under Tuba and Keyboard Collections.

Beethoven, Ludwig von. *Rondo (from Violin Sonata in E♭ Major, Op. 12, No. 3).* arr. Robert Madeson. Tuba-Euphonium Press. 1994. 4:30. III. G_1–b♭. Requires good finger and slurring technique with intermediate range considerations. Available for euphonium and piano also.

Beethoven, Ludwig von. *Sonata in G Major for Tuba and Piano.* tr. Frank Proto. Liben Music Publishers. 1981. $6.00. 9:15 (4:58, 1:00, 3:17). V. G_1–g'. Three movements: Allegro Moderato; Poco Adagio Quasi Andante; Rondo. From the Horn Sonata in F Major, op. 17. Takes a player with great flexibility combined with a French horn "lightness." Mostly upper tessitura and mostly staccato and slurred passages. See review in *TUBA Journal,* Vol. 10, No. 4, Page 36. Recorded by Michael Thornton.

Beethoven, Ludwig von. *Variations on the Theme of "Judas Maccabeus" by G. F. Handel.* tr. William J. Bell. Carl Fischer Inc. 1937. $5.00. 4:45. III–IV. ($F_1$) A_1–b♭. Theme and (four) variations. First variation is piano solo. Second variation is entirely triplets. Third variation introduces sixteenth notes and fourth variation is in cut time with mostly eighth notes. Good intermediate solo. Recorded by William Bell.

Belden, George R. *Black Holes in Space.* ed. Donald C. Little. CPP/Belwin, Inc. 1978. $4.00. 2:17. II. Allegro. A few accidentals and a chance of rushing are the only black holes to avoid. Good beginning solo. See review in *TUBA Journal,* Vol. 8, No. 1, Page 34.

Belden, George R. *Black Holes in Space.* ed. Donald C. Little. CPP/Belwin, Inc. 1978. See: Lamb, Jack, *Solo Sounds for Tuba Levels 1–3,* under Tuba and Keyboard Collections. Also see other listing in this section.

Belden, George R. *Neutron Stars.* arr. Donald C. Little. CPP/Belwin, Inc. 1978. $4.00. 3:45. III. $G♭_1$–g♭. Dramatic/Allegro. Tubist blows air through instrument at two times in this piece for dramatic effect. Some easy 4/4–3/4 meter changes; some syncopation; otherwise good pre-intermediate solo. Plenty of opportunity for dramatic expression (sfp, sfz, etc.). See review in *TUBA Journal,* Vol. 4, No. 3, Page 35.

Bell, J. H. *Sans Pareil.* arr. Carl Weber. J. W. Pepper & Son. 1914. Out of Print. See: Weber, Carl, *Nineteen Solos for E♭ Bass with Piano Accompaniment,* under Tuba and Keyboard Collections. Also see: Bell, J. H., *Sans Pareil,* under Tuba and Band.

Bell, William J. *Chief John.* CPP/Belwin, Inc. 1963. $4.00. 1:13. I. C–e. Dedicated to the late John Kuhn, famous Indian Tuba Player. Solo in cut time and in D minor. Includes great comments by Bill Bell setting the mood for the piece. Quarter note is the fastest rhythm. One upper e, otherwise medium tessitura. A few slurs, a few accents, no technical problems.

Bell, William J. *Chief John.* CPP/Belwin, Inc. 1963. See: CPP/Belwin, *Tuba Solos, Level Two,* under Tuba and Keyboard Collections. Also see other listing in this section.

Bell, William J. *Gavotte.* Carl Fischer Inc. 1935. $2.50. 1:47. I. A_1–c. Tempo di Gavotte. "E♭ or BB♭ tuba." A few eighth notes; no technical problems.

Bell, William J. *Jig Elephantine.* Carl Fischer Inc. 1935. Out of Print. 1:00. II. $b♭_1$–g. At moderate speed. "E♭ or B♭ Tuba." In cut time. A few grace notes, a few arpeggios. Half-valve glissando explained very well by Mr. Bell.

Bell, William J. *Jolly Jumbo.* CPP/Belwin, Inc. 1963. $4.00. 1:01. I–II. ($A♭_1$) D–e♭. Great Descriptive comments by Bill Bell. Elephants dancing with a jolly 6/8 feel. No technical problems.

Bell, William J. *Jolly Jumbo.* CPP/Belwin, Inc. 1963. See: CPP/Belwin, *Tuba Solos, Level Two,* under Tuba and Keyboard Collections. Also see other listing in this section.

Bell, William J. *Low Down Bass.* Carl Fischer Inc. 1935. Out of Print. 1:11. I. $B♭_1$–b♭. With animation and spirit. "E♭ or BB♭ Tuba." Solo in 12/8 for the beginner. Great dynamic range. No technical problems.

Bell, William J. *Melodious Etude.* CPP/Belwin, Inc. 1962. $4.00. 1:32. I. D–c. Moderately. Very limited range, limited rhythms—quarter note is the fastest rhythm. Good beginners' introduction to slurring.

Bell, William J. *Melodious Etude.* CPP/Belwin, Inc. 1963. See: CPP/Belwin, Inc., *Tuba Solos, Level One,* under Tuba and Keyboard Collections. Also see other listing in this section.

Bell, William J. *Nautical John Medley.* Carl Fischer Inc. 1935. $3.25. 3:50. III. ($E♭_1$) $A♭_1$–c'. Based on *Blow the Man Down* and *Rocked in the Cradle of the Deep.* Trills, optional glissando, and a couple of cadenzas. Plenty of opportunity for expression.

Bell, William J. *Sousaphone Polka.* Waterloo Music. 1950. 4:20. III–IV. $B♭_1$–b♭. Written at the request of John Philip Sousa, this was the first composition written by Bill Bell (originally copyrighted in 1924) to show off the first sousaphone. Optional triple tonguing, traditional polka style with two cadenzas.

Bell, William J. *Spartan, The.* CPP/Belwin, Inc. 1963. $4.00. 1:16. I–II. ($B♭_1$) C–f. March tempo. Great descriptive comments by Bill Bell including an encouragement to "sniff breathe." Slightly high range for beginner; otherwise easy rhythms and no technical problems.

Bell, William J. *Spartan, The.* CPP/Belwin, Inc. 1963. See: CPP/Belwin, *Tuba Solos, Level Two,* under Tuba and Keyboard Collections. Also see other listing in this section.

Bell, William J. *Tubaman, The.* (piano arr. L. S.). CPP/Belwin, Inc. 1962. $4.00. 1:05. I. ($B♭_1$) E♭–c. Based on *Blow The Man Down.* Very easy beginning solo. Quarter note is fastest rhythm. No technical problems.

Bell, William J. *Tubaman, The.* CPP/Belwin, Inc. 1962. See: CPP/Belwin, Inc., *Tuba Solos, Level One,* under Tuba and Keyboard Collections. Also see other listing in this section.

Bell, William J. *Tubateer Polka, The.* CPP/Belwin, Inc. 1964. $4.00. 1:24. II–III. ($A♭_1$) C–e♭. Tempo di Polka. (First measure of coda contains incorrect rhythm—never fixed even after all these years!?) Traditional easy polka in A♭ and D♭ major. A few sharps, no technical problems.

Bell, William J., arr. *Folksong Medley.* CPP/Belwin, Inc. 1965. $4.00. 1:39. II. $B♭_1$–f. Three folksongs: Allegro ("Irish Washerwoman"); Meno mosso (Scotch); Allegretto (Russian). Optional notes to leave out for breathing; well-arranged solo.

Bell, William J., arr. *Russian Medley.* CPP/Belwin, Inc. 1964. $4.00. 2:11. I–II. $B♭_1$–d. A majestic

4/4 section (*1812 Overture* and a theme from Tchaikovsky's *4th Symphony*) and a slow 3/4 rhythmic waltz. A few scale-wise eighth note runs in waltz, otherwise no technical problems for slightly advanced beginners.

Bell, William J., arr. *Russian Medley.* CPP/Belwin, Inc. 1964. See: Lamb, Jack, *Solo Sounds For Tuba Levels 1–3, Vol. 1,* under Tuba and Keyboard Collections.

Bella, Domenico della. *Sonata in C Major.* arr. John Glenesk Mortimer. Editions Marc Reift. 1996. $11.80. 5:00. III. G_1–a. Andante; Gigue-Allegro; Largo; Allegro moderato. Transcription in the original key of the Sonata for Cello of this early-eighteenth-century composer. Available in bass clef concert pitch and treble clef in E♭ or B♭. See listing under Music for Tuba and Organ.

Bellini. *Come Brave the Sea.* arr. Paul deVille. Carl Fischer Inc. 1906. Out of Print. See: deVille, Paul, *Pleasant Hours,* under Tuba and Keyboard Collections.

Bencriscutto, Frank. *Concertino for Tuba and Band.* Shawnee Press, Inc. 1971. $7.50. Written for and dedicated to Stanford Freese. See: Bencriscutto, Frank, *Concertino for Tuba and Band,* under Tuba and Band. Some cuts needed in solo (band) part to work with piano (listed in composer's notes). Recorded by Stanford Freese. See review in *TUBA Journal,* Vol. 4, No. 4, Page 25.

Benedict, Julius. *Carnival of Venice.* arr. Bill Boyd. Hal Leonard Publishing Corp. 1992. 0:41. I. B♭$_1$–G. Melody only in 3/4 time; no variations. Quarter note is fastest rhythm. Limited range. Comes with practice/performance cassette. See: Daellenbach, Charles, *Book of Beginning Tuba Solos,* under Tuba and Keyboard Collections.

Benedict, Julius. *Carnival of Venice.* arr. John Kinyon. M. Witmark & Sons. 1958. I. See: Kinyon, John, *Breeze-Easy Recital Pieces,* under Tuba and Keyboard Collections.

Benjamin, Thomas. *Sonata.* Southern Music Company. 1991. $12.00. 12:00. IV–V. G_1–f'. Composed June, 1986, Clearwater Pond, Maine. Three movements. Flutter tongue, cadenza in second movement. Will take some work to prepare, but well worth it. Good recital material. See review in *TUBA Journal,* Vol. 18, No. 4, Page 15.

Benker, Heinz. *Miniaturen-Suite.* Zinneberg Musikverlag. 1986. 10:42 (1:14, 3:16, 1:32, 1:16, 1:50, 1:34.) IV. F_1–e♭'. Leghaft; Nachdenklich; Heiter; Gemütlich; Feierlich; Tänzerisch. für Tuba und Klavier. Very fine modern tonal writing for tuba and piano. Third movement has a few glissandos. Tempos notated are very playable and accessible to strong high school player. Highly recommended.

Bennett, David. *Basses Berserk.* Carl Fischer Inc. 1953. Out of Print. See: Bennett, David, *Basses Berserk,* under Tuba and Band.

Bennett, David. *Voice of the Viking.* Carl Fischer Inc. 1938. $3.25. 4:50. III–IV. F_1–a. Typical solo from the period. Moderate technique required. Slow, fast, loud, soft, slurred, staccato, etc.; it's all included.

Bennett, Malcolm. *Tuba Concerto.* arr. Malcolm Bennett. Tuba-Euphonium Press. 2002. III–IV. B_2–e'. Dedicated to John Elliott. Work in three movements requiring frequent use of a mute. Written in the mid- to low tessitura. See listing under Music for Tuba and Orchestra.

Bennett, Malcolm, arr. *Luzerne Song.* 1988. 0:58. III. (A♭$_1$) E♭–a♭. Leggiero. Part for treble (E♭ bass) included. Traditional tune with a "yodeling feel." See: Bennett, Malcolm, *Five Solos for Tuba,* under Tuba and Keyboard Collections. For a real treat, listen to the recording of John Fletcher playing this tune with the Phillip Jones Brass Ensemble.

Bennett, Malcolm, arr. *McLeods Reel.* 1988. 1:24. III. B♭–c'. Gioviale. Part for treble (E♭ bass) included. Fun reel in cut time. Some octave jumps, some eighth note runs. Pretend that you are a piper! See: Bennett, Malcolm, *Five Solos for Tuba,* under Tuba and Keyboard Collections.

Bennett, Malcolm, arr. *Shenandoah.* 1988. 2:01. II–III. C–a. Semplice. Parts for bass clef and treble (E♭ bass) included. Very lyrical traditional melody repeated with a piano interlude. Great opportunity for making beautiful music! See: Bennett, Malcolm, *Five Solos for Tuba,* under Tuba and Keyboard Collections.

Bennett, Malcolm, arr., Connor, Eddie, selected. *Five Solos For Tuba.* Unlimited Music. 1988. $25.25. II–III. Contains: Connor, Eddie, *McCluskeys Rag;* Molloy, J. L., *Kerry Dance, The;* Traditional, *Luzerne Song;* Traditional, *McLeods Reel;* Traditional, *Shenandoah.*

Benson, Warren. *Arioso.* Hal Leonard Publishing Corp. 1959. $3.95. 1:29. III. D_1–f. To Dirk. Originally published by Piedmont Music. Slowly in 3/2 time. Very lyrical minor tune. Plenty of room for extreme expression. With the exception of last four dotted whole D_1's, not a very difficult piece. Recorded by Peter Popiel.

Benson, Warren. *Helix (Concerto for Solo Tuba and Concert Band).* Carl Fischer Inc. 1976. $7.50. 14:00. for Harvey Phillips. Commissioned by Harvey Phillips; Premiered February 12, 1967, at the 50th Anniversary Eastern Division M.E.N.C. Conference, Boston, Mass., by Harvey Phillips, soloist, and the Ithaca High School Band, Frank L. Battisti, conductor. See: Benson, Warren, *Helix,* under Tuba and Band. Recorded by Harvey Phillips, Jack Robinson, John Turk.

Bentzon, Niels Viggo. *Le chien rouge.* SNYK. 1993.

Bentzon, Niels Viggo. *Concerto.* Available from Spaeth and Schmid. $50.00.

Bentzon, Niels Viggo. *"Fett und Filtz," op. 403d.* Wilhelm Hansen. 1977. This is part four of an *Hommage* to Joseph Beuys in seven parts.

Bentzon, Niels Viggo. *Sonata for Tuba and Piano, op. 277.* Wilhelm Hansen. 1971.

Bentzon, Niels Viggo. *Sonata for Tuba op. 393.* Manuscript. 1976. Work in progress.

Beresford, Arnold. *Smuggler, The.* arr. Elsa Rubin. JTL Publications/G. Scott Music Publishing Co. 1989. $3.50. 3:00. III. D–b♭. Slurred phrases. Spirited 4/4 section and slower 6/8 section. Upper tessitura.

Berg, Thomas. *Bass Solo Polka.* Adlerverlag. 1974. See: Berg, Thomas, *Bass Solo Polka,* under Tuba and Band.

Berlin, A. *Ballade.* ed. G. Voronov. Moscow Muzyka. 1984. See: Voronov, G, *Works for Tuba and Piano by Russian Composers,* under Tuba and Keyboard Collections.

Berlin, Irving. *Puttin' on the Ritz.* arr. James Christensen. Kendor Music, Inc. 2002. $6.00. I–II. 1:45. C–f. Straight-ahead arrangement of this Dixieland-style tune. Good introduction to this style for beginning players.

Berlioz, G. P. *Air Gai.* ed. Himie Voxman. Rubank, Inc. 1972. 3:00. III. ($A♭_1$) C–g. "For E♭ or BB♭ Bass." Solo in 2/4 time with not too many technical problems. See: Voxman, Himie, *Concert and Contest Collection,* under Tuba and Keyboard Collections.

Berlioz, Hector. *Bolero.* arr. Dishinger. Available from Spaeth and Schmid. $8.00.

Berlioz, Hector. *Sanctus.* arr. John Fletcher. Chester Music. 1982. 2:25. II. E♭–f. Adagio. "from *Grande Messe des Morts.*" Slow sustained playing. Listen to *Sanctus* in Berlioz's *Mass* for conception. See: Fletcher, John, *Tuba Solos (Tuba in C), Volume One,* under Tuba and Keyboard Collections.

Bernaud, Alain. *Humoresque.* Éditions Max Eschig. 1964. 9:10. V. F_1–b♭. à Paul Bernard, Professeur au Conservatoire de Paris. "pour Tuba ou Saxhorn-Basse en Si♭ et Piano." For French tuba. Mixed meter; requires great flexibility, full range. See: Thompson/Lemke; *French Music for Low Brass Instruments.*

Bernofsky, Lauren. *Totentanz.* Available from Spaeth and Schmid. $9.75.

Bernstein, Leonard. *Waltz for Mippy.* ed. J. Larin. Moscow Muzyka. 1979. See: Larin, J., Pieces for Tuba and Piano, under Tuba and Keyboard Collections. Also see other listings in this section.

Bernstein, Leonard. *Waltz for Mippy III.* arr. Herbert Wekselblatt. G. Schirmer Inc. 1950. 2:00. III. A_1–g♯. As gracefully as possible under the circumstances. Some passages one octave lower than original making it more accessible to the intermediate player. Some double sharps; leaps of tenths. Muted passage. Feeling of one (3/4) and some mixed meter; trills. Piano uses middle pedal. See: Wekselblatt, H., *Solos for the Tuba Player,* under Tuba and Keyboard Collections. Also see other listing in this section.

Bernstein, Leonard. *Waltz for Mippy III for Tuba and Piano.* Jalni Publications. 1977. $6.00. 2:00. IV. B_1–e'. For my brother Burtie. Was published by G. Schirmer, 1950. "Mippy III was a mongrel belonging to my brother Burtie." Upper tessitura. See other listings in this section.

Beugniot, Jean-Pierre. *Légende.* ed. Fernand Lelong. Gérard Billaudot. 1981. $8.75. 2:15. II. E–f'. "Pour tuba ut ou trombone basse, saxhorn-basse si♭ et piano." For French tuba. No technical problems; only a few sixteenth notes. See: Thompson/Lemke; *French Music for Low Brass Instruments.*

Bevan, Clifford. *G. F. Handel's Third Tuba Concerto.* Piccolo Press. 1990. 5:00 (1:30, 1:50, 1:40). IV. F_1–f'. Courante; Sarabande; Gigue. First performance given by Robert Steadman, soloist, in Wantage Civic Hall, Oxfordshire, on November 28, 1987. Orchestral version available for hire from Piccolo Press. In a baroque style, complete with "Pop Goes the Weasel" interpolated at the end.

Bevan, Clifford. *Händel's Third Tuba Concerto.* Available from Spaeth and Schmid. $8.50.

Beversdorf, Thomas G. *Sonata for Bass Tuba and Piano.* Southern Music Company. 1962. $14.95. 18:00. IV–V. F_1–a. Allegro con moto; Allegretto con grazioso e espress; Allegro con brio. Three movements. Well-written major work for the tuba. Comfortable range; not overwhelming technique needed. Good recital piece. See review in *TUBA Journal,* Vol. 9, No. 1, Page 11. Also see: Bird, Gary, ed.; *Program Notes for the Solo Tuba.* Recorded by Robert LeBlanc.

Bigelow, Albert. *Winter Carousel.* Kendor Music, Inc. 1986. $4.50. 1:35. I. A_1–B♭. Good beginning solo in 3/4 time. Has dotted quarter notes, first and second endings, ritards, fermatas, and some slurring. Limited range.

Bigot, Eugène. *Carillon et Bourdon. (Carillon and Great Bell.)* Alphonse Leduc. 1951. $12.80. 4:00. V. E_1–a♭'. à Monsieur Paul Bernard, Professeur au Conservatoire National de Musique. "pour Tuba en Ut ou Saxhorn basse si♭ et Piano." For French tuba. Some very wide interval jumps, very large range, some quick technical passages. See: Thompson/Lemke; *French Music for Low Brass Instruments.*

Bigot, Pierre. *Cortège. (Procession.)* Éditions M. Combre. 1983. $6.00. 1:23. I–II. F–c'. "pour Tuba en ut (ou Saxhorn basse in si♭ et Piano." Maestoso. Stately beginning solo. Presents no difficult technical challenges for French tuba. Fastest rhythm is eighth note. Good high range practice for BB♭ (CC) tubas. Easy accompaniment. See: Thompson/Lemke; *French Music for Low Brass Instruments.*

Bigot, Pierre. *Tubaria.* Gérard Billaudot. 1991. For French tuba.

Bilbaut, J. *Carnaval de Venise, Le.* Editions Salabert. Out of Print. Theme and variations.

Bilik, Jerry H. *Introduction and Dance.* RBC Publications. 1969. Was published by Samuel French. See: Bilik, Jerry, *Introduction and Dance,* under Tuba and Band.

Billings, William. *Old American Patriotic Song (Chester).* arr. James Barnes. CPP/Belwin, Inc. 1980. $4.00. 1:30. I–II. B♭$_1$–e♭. Very Deliberate. Mostly step-wise motion. Except for a few upper notes (for the beginning player), presents no difficult technical challenges and would be a good confidence builder for the younger student. Fastest rhythm is an eight note. See review in *TUBA Journal,* Vol. 9, No. 2, Page 29.

Billings, William. *Old American Patriotic Song (Chester).* arr. James Barnes. CPP/Belwin, Inc. 1980. See: CPP/Belwin, Inc., *Tuba Solos, Level One,* under Tuba and Keyboard Collections. Also see other listing in this section.

Bitsch, Marcel. *Impromptu.* Alphonse Leduc. 1957. $11.50. 4:15. V. F$_1$–b♭'. à Paul Bernard, Professeur au Conservatoire National de Musique. "pour Saxhorn basse Si♭ ou tuba Ut ou Trombone basse et Piano." Written for French tuba. Requires strong technique. Some tenor clef in part. Cadenza, quick tempos, 5/8 section. See: Thompson/Lemke; *French Music for Low Brass Instruments.*

Bitsch, Marcel. *Intermezzo.* Alphonse Leduc. 1968. $12.80. 5:00. IV. G$_1$–b♭'. A Paul Bernard, professeur au Conservatoire National Supérieur de Musique. "pour Tuba en Ut ou Saxhorn basse Si♭ et Piano." Introductory lyrical section, cadenza, then a technical Allegro moderato section. See: Thompson/Lemke; *French Music for Low Brass Instruments.*

Bitsch, Marcel. *Ritcherkar.* ed. V. Guzii. Moscow Muzyka. 1978. See: Guzii, V., *Pieces for Tuba and Piano,* under Tuba and Keyboard Collections.

Bizet, Georges. *Adagietto from L'Arlésienne.* arr. Quinto Maganini. Edition Musicus. 1949. 1:48. IV. C–f'. Adagio. Some quintuplets; grace notes. Easier on F tuba; playable on lower instrument. All slurred and vocally oriented. See: Ostrander, Allen, *Concert Album for Tuba,* under Tuba and Keyboard Collections.

Bizet, Georges. *Carmen Excerpts.* arr. William J. Bell. CPP/Belwin, Inc. 1965. $4.00. 2:05. III. B♭$_1$–f. Not as faithful as *Toreador's Song,* arr. G. E. Holmes, to the original, but easier rhythms. See other listing in this section.

Bizet, Georges. *Carmen Excerpts.* arr. William J. Bell. CPP/Belwin, Inc. 1965. See: Lamb, Jack, *Solo Sounds for Tuba Levels 3–5, Vol. 1,* under Tuba and Keyboard Collections. See other listing in this section.

Bizet, Georges. *Habanera from "Carmen."* arr. Hiroyuki Yasumoto. Toa Music International Co. 1986. 3:15. III. F–a. Allegretto quasi Andantino. Good transcription for opera aria. See: Yasumoto, Hiroyuki, *Tuba Volume #1,* under Tuba and Keyboard Collections.

Bizet, Georges. *Toreador's Song.* arr. G. E. Holmes and H. Voxman. Rubank, Inc. 1966. 2:07. III. B$_1$♭–f. "Solo Tuba—E♭ or BB♭ tuba." Allegro Moderato. Stately transcription in original keys of F minor/F major of famous Bizet aria. Some syncopation, triplets, grace notes. Good opportunity for musical operatic expression. Wide dynamic range. See: Rubank, *Soloist Folio for Bass (E♭ or BB♭),* under Tuba and Keyboard Collections.

Bizet, Georges. *Toreador's Song from Carmen.* arr. G. E. Holmes. Rubank, Inc. 1939. Published separately. See other listing in this section.

Bjorn, Frank. *Alley Cat.* arr. David Polansky. Kendor Music, Inc. 1961. $5.50. 2:25. I–II. B$_1$♭–c. Dotted rhythms and syncopations throughout. Limited range. Almost all step-wise intervals. Makes for a cute novelty recital piece for an advanced beginning player.

Bland, J. *Carry Me Back to Old Virginny.* arr. Hiroyuki Yasumoto. Toa Music International Co. 1986. 1:08. II. F–f. Moderato. Some syncopations, all slurs, otherwise no technical problems. See: Yasumoto, Hiroyuki, *Tuba Volume #1,* under Tuba and Keyboard Collections.

Blank, Hans. *Variationen uber ein Volkslied.* Musikverlag Siegfried Rundel. See: Blank, Hans, *Variationen uber ein Volkslied,* under Tuba and Band.

Blanquer, Amando. *L'os Hispanic.* Sociedad General de Autores de Espana. 1976. See: Blanquer, Amando, *L'os Hispanic,* under Tuba and Orchestra.

Blazhevich, Vladislav. *Concert Etude.* See: Krotov and Blazhevich, *Concert Etude,* in this section.

Blazhevich, Vladislav. *Concert No. 2 Part 3.* ed. S. Melnikov. Military Band Masters Institute–Moscow. 1957. See: Melnikov, S., *Pieces for Tuba and Piano,* under Tuba and Keyboard Collections.

Blazhevich, Vladislav. *Concert Sketch Nr. 5.* Available from Spaeth and Schmid. $22.00.

Blazhevich, Vladislav. *Miniature No. 7.* ed. S. Melnikov. Military Band Masters Institute–Moscow. 1957. See: Melnikov, S., *Pieces for Tuba and Piano,* under Tuba and Keyboard Collections.

Blazhevich, Vladislav. *Sonatas for Tuba and Piano.* Manuscript. Out of Print. According to A. Lebedev, Vladislav Blazhevich composed fifteen sonatas for tuba and piano. Of these, seven exist in manuscript form and eight have been lost.

Bliss, P. P. *Dare to Be a Daniel.* arr. David E. Smith. David E. Smith Publications. 1985. $2.50. 3:00. I. B$_1$♭–b♭. Alla Den (Adagio). Very easy beginning solo with limited range. Fastest rhythm is quarter note. Modulation with essentially the same musical material.

Blodek, Vilém. *Arie Janeks Aus Der Oper "Im Brunnen."* ed. Václav Hoza. Editio Supraphon,

Praha. 1982. 1:56. IV. E♭–e♭'. Allegretto. Technical aria: scales, triplets alternating with duples, arpeggios. Would lie well on E♭ tuba. See: Hoza, Václav, *Schule Fur Tuba in F und in B,* in Methods and Studies.

Blumenfeld, Aaron. *Sonata for Tuba and Piano.* Trombone Association Publishing. 1989. $14.00. 12:11 (5:28, 4:06, 2:37). V. Three movements. With the exception of a few eighth note rests in the last movement, there are no rests in this piece! This presents endurance challenges. Technical challenges are everywhere: quin-, sex-, septuplets; slurring out of the "Arban's Method"; dissonant interval skips. Unmarked meter changes in lyrical second movement. Third movement has a surprising fun jazz flavor interpolating *Way Down upon the Swanee River* and *Toot Toot Tootsie Good-bye.* Has tricky syncopation. Very challenging piano accompaniment requiring left hand stride playing in last movement.

Boccherini, L. *Menuette.* arr. Hiroyuki Yasumoto. Toa Music International Co. 1986. 3:10. III–IV. $B♭_1$–c'. Tempo di Menuett. Has trills, grace notes, syncopation. Requires lightness and flexibility. See: Yasumoto, Hiroyuki, *Tuba Volume #1,* under Tuba and Keyboard Collections. A different version of this recorded by Zdizislaw Piernik.

Boda, John. *Sonatina.* Robert King Music Co. & Alphonse Leduc. 1968. $4.05. 6:29 (2:56/3:53). IV. G_1–b. Written in 1967. Two movements. First movement: Most complex rhythms are triplets. Moderate tempo. Second movement: Mixed meter and has a recitative-like cadenza. Very playable by strong high school student. Was published by W. D. Stuart Music. Also see: Bird, Gary, ed.; *Program Notes for the Solo Tuba.*

Bogár, István. *Quick Dance.* arr. Peter Wastall. Boosey & Hawkes, Inc. 1979. 0:48. I–II. E♭–f. See: Wastall, Peter, *Learn As You Play Tuba,* under Tuba and Keyboard Collections. Vivace. Hungarian flavor. Some sixteenth notes and one octave-F jump in last measure; otherwise not too demanding.

Bond, Capel. *Concerto No. 6 in B♭.* Editions Marc Reift. 1996. $12.50. 7:30. III. A_1–c' (e♭'). Andante; Adagio; Affetuoso; Allegro. Originally for cello or bassoon, composed by the late-eighteenth-century English composer. The tessitura of this arrangement can be played by all tubas. Requires a light, articulate approach. Available in bass clef concert pitch and treble clef in E♭ or B♭.

Bonheur, Theodore. *Lancer, The.* arr. Harold L. Walters. Rubank, Inc. 1954. $1.50. 2:30. II. $B♭_1$–d. "Solo for E♭ or BB♭ Bass." In 4/4 time with no technical problems.

Bononcini, Giovanni. *Per la Gloria D'Adorarri from "Griselda."* ed. and compiled Harry I. Phillips. Shawnee Press Inc. 1967. 1:32. II. C–e♭. Lyrical, slurred 3/4 transcription. Mostly scale-wise motion. No big technical challenges. See: Phillips, Harry I., *Eight Bel Canto Songs,* under Tuba and Keyboard Collections.

Bordogni, G. M. *No. 4 from 24 Easy Vocalises.* arr. Hiroyuki Yasumoto. Toa Music International Co. 1989. 2:29. III. C–f. All slurred phrases. Same as Rochut/Bordogni #4. See: Yasumoto, Hiroyuki, *Tuba Volume #3,* under Tuba and Keyboard Collections.

Bordogni, G. M. *No. 9 from 24 Easy Vocalises.* arr. Hiroyuki Yasumoto. Toa Music International Co. 1989. 2:05. III. C–a. All slurred phrases. Same as Rochut/Bordogni #9. Some trills, grace notes. See: Yasumoto, Hiroyuki, *Tuba Volume #3,* under Tuba and Keyboard Collections.

Bordogni, G. M. *No. 10 from 24 Easy Vocalises.* arr. Hiroyuki Yasumoto. Toa Music International Co. 1989. 2:33. III. G_1–g. All slurred phrases. Same as Rochut/Bordogni #10. Some grace notes. See: Yasumoto, Hiroyuki, *Tuba Volume #3,* under Tuba and Keyboard Collections.

Bordogni, Marco. *Bordogni Medley.* arr. Richard W. Bowles. CPP/Belwin, Inc. 1973. 2:20. II. C–e (f). Two contrasting melodious etudes, one in 3/4, the other in 2/4 time. Some slurring, syncopation. Good introduction to Bordogni's works. See: Lamb, Jack, *Solo Sounds For Tuba Levels 1–3, Vol. 1,* under Tuba and Keyboard Collections.

Bordogni, Marco. *Bordogni Medley.* arr. Richard W. Bowles. CPP/Belwin, Inc. 1973. See: Lamb, Jack, *Classic Festival Solos,* under Tuba and Keyboard Collections. Also see other listing in this section.

Borg, Kim. *Finnish Rhapsody.* Finnish Music Information Centre. 1980. Three Scetches (sic) for tuba and piano. See: Borg, Kim, *Finnish Rhapsody,* under Tuba and Orchestra.

Borton, Allen L. *Sonata for Tuba and Piano.* Tuba-Euphonium Press. 2001. 7:00. III. E_1–b♭. Dedicated to Bob Piatt. A good sonata in the low tessitura suitable for contrabass tuba.

Bottesini. *Bombardon Polka.* arr. Carl Weber. J. W. Pepper & Son. 1914. Out of Print. See: Weber, Carl, *Nineteen Solos For E♭ Bass with Piano Accompaniment,* under Tuba and Keyboard Collections.

Bottje, Will Gay. *Concerto.* American Composer's Edition. 1973. $21.70. 15:00. See: Bottje, Will Gay, *Concerto for Tuba and Orchestra,* under Tuba and Orchestra. See review in *TUBA Journal,* Vol. 1, No. 2, Page 10 and Vol. 1, No. 2, Page 6.

Bottje, Will Gay. *Prelude and Fugue.* Composers Facsimile Edition. 1959. 5:43 (3:23, 2:20). IV. $b♭_1$–e'. Slowly; Moderato. First movement is lyrical with some more modern intervals; tonal. Second movement has some sixteenth note runs but not overwhelming technical requirements.

Boukhitine, Arnaud. *I Remember Love Supreme.* Robert Martin Editions. 2003. 3:00. III. $A♭_1$–c' (d'). Written in the style of a popular ballad, this is a rhythmically interesting work that will keep an intermediate player interested due to its pop style. Moderate level of technique required.

Boukhitine, Arnaud. *Luxe, calme et volupté.* Robert Martin Editions. 2003. 4:00 III–IV. $B\flat_1$–b. A tonally interesting work that explores lyrical playing with small technical outbursts. A good study piece or short recital piece.

Boukhitine, Arnaud. *Petit Air.* Robert Martin Editions. 2002. 1:30. I. B♭–f. A very brief beginner solo with repetitive rhythmic and scalar patterns.

Boukhitine, Arnaud. *Petite suite en cinq tableaux.* Robert Martin Editions. 2003. 4:30. I. A♭–f. Chanson Chinoise; Waltz for Doriane; Chanson Andalouse; Song for Lydia; Chanson Japonaise. A collection of five very short movements written at the beginner level. Little rhythmic variation and written with predictable linear melodies. Good for teaching different metric emphases for various dance forms.

Bourassa, Richard. *A Time, A Season.* 1982. Commissioned by Rodger Vaughan.

Bourgeois, Derek. *Air and Galumph.* Vanderbeek & Imrie Ltd. 1985. 1:56 (1:00, 0:56). IV. F_1–d♭'. Air; Galumph. "Two Pieces for Tuba and Piano. Opus 53." Treble and bass clef parts included. Air has some slurred arpeggios and lyrical passages. Galumph in 6/8 time. Light accessible tonal modern writing requiring good stylistic sense.

Bourgeois, Derek. *Romance op. 77.* Vanderbeek & Imrie Ltd. 1985. 8:11. IV. $E\flat_1$–f'. Treble and bass clef parts included. Intended for CC or E♭ tuba. Lovely lyrical solo mostly in slow 6/8 time with some mixed meter. Good showcase for moderate flexibility, expressiveness. Good recital material.

Bourgeois, Derek. *Sonata op. 204.* Available from Spaeth and Schmid. $25.00.

Bourgeois, Derek. *Tuba Concerto, Opus 38.* R. Smith & Co. 1972. For John Fletcher. See: Bourgeois, Derek, *Tuba Concerto, Opus 38,* under Tuba and Orchestra.

Bourgéois, Louis, and Thomas Ken. *Doxology.* arr. Bill Boyd, ed. Charles Daellenbach. Hal Leonard Publishing Corp. 1992. 0:32. I. $B\flat_1$–B♭. Chorale style with fermatas. All quarter notes (except last note). Comes with practice/performance cassette. See: Daellenbach, Charles, *Book of Beginning Tuba Solos,* under Tuba and Keyboard Collections.

Boutry, Roger. *Tubacchanale.* Alphonse Leduc. 1956. $14.45. 7:32. V. E_1–b'. A mon ami Paul Bernard, Professeur au Conservatoire National de Musique. "pour tuba en Ut ou Saxhorn basse Si♭ et Piano." Exploits the full range of the tuba; designed for French tuba. Double tonguing, fast tempi, mixed meter, strong technique required! See: Thompson/Lemke; *French Music for Low Brass Instruments.*

Boutry, Roger. *Tubaroque.* Alphonse Leduc. 1955. $11.50. A mon ami Paul Bernard. "Pièce pour tuba Ut ou Saxhorn basse Si♭ ou Trombone basse et Piano." See: Boutry, Roger, *Tubaroque,* under Tuba and Orchestra. Also see: Thompson/Lemke; *French Music for Low Brass Instruments.*

Bowles, Richard W. *Changing Scene.* CPP/Belwin, Inc. 1973. $4.00. 2:55. III. F_1–f. Good solid intermediate solo using mixed meter (3/4, 4/5, 5/4) to give a spacious feeling. Andante rubato quasi-cadenza passages as well as faster allegro passages. Eighth note is fastest rhythm. See other listing in this section.

Bowles, Richard W. *Changing Scene.* CPP/Belwin, Inc. 1973. See: Lamb, Jack, *Solo Sounds For Tuba Levels 3–5, Vol. 1,* under Tuba and Keyboard Collections. See other listing in this section.

Bowles, Richard W. *Deep Rock.* CPP/Belwin, Inc. 1973. $4.00. 2:43. II. $A\flat_1$–e♭. Easy rock tempo; Slow waltz; Tempo 1. Fun light rock feel with not too many technical challenges. Some infrequently used notes for beginning level (c♭, g♭, etc.). Some slurring. See other listing in this section.

Bowles, Richard W. *Deep Rock.* CPP/Belwin, Inc. 1973. See other listing in this section. Also see: Lamb, Jack, *Solo Sounds for Tuba Levels 1–3, Vol. 1,* under Tuba and Keyboard Collections.

Bowles, Richard W. *Venetian Carnival.* CPP/Belwin, Inc. 1973. $4.00. 2:08. II–III. $B_1\flat$–e♭. Intermediate theme and variations based on the classic "Carnival of Venice." Includes a simple cadenza. See other listing in this section. Also see: Bowles, Richard W., *Venetian Carnival,* under Tuba and Band.

Bowles, Richard W. *Venetian Carnival.* CPP/Belwin, Inc. 1973. See: Lamb, Jack, *Solo Sounds for Tuba Levels 1–3, Vol. 1,* under Tuba and Keyboard Collections. Also see other listing in this section.

Boyce, William. *Gavotte from Symphony No. 4.* arr. Anton Vedesky. Medici Music Press. 1982. 2:36. III. C–f. Good transcription of baroque work in cut time. A few eighth note runs, otherwise no technical problems.

Boyd, Bill, arr. *Come, Thou Fount of Every Blessing.* Hal Leonard Publishing Corp. 1992. 1:02. II. $B\flat_1$–c. American folk hymn. See: Daellenbach, Charles, *Book of Easy Tuba Solos,* under Tuba and Keyboard Collections.

Boyd, Bill, arr. *Cruel War Is Raging, The.* ed. Charles Daellenbach. Hal Leonard Publishing Corp. 1992. 0:53. I. C–a. American folksong. Two dotted quarter/eighth note rhythms; otherwise very simple rhythms. Comes with practice/performance cassette. See: Daellenbach, Charles, *Book of Beginning Tuba Solos,* under Tuba and Keyboard Collections.

Boyd, Bill, arr. *Erie Canal, The.* Hal Leonard Publishing Corp. 1992. 0:53. II. D–c. Moderately. American folksong. A few syncopations and dotted rhythms. See: Daellenbach, Charles, *Book of Easy Tuba Solos,* under Tuba and Keyboard Collections.

Boyd, Bill, arr. *Hey, Ho! Nobody Home.* Hal Leonard Publishing Corp. 1992. 0:43. II. C–d. Moderately (not too fast). English folksong. Twice through in F minor, once in G minor. See: Daellenbach, Charles, *Book of Easy Tuba Solos,* under Tuba and Keyboard Collections.

Boyd, Bill, arr. *Loch Lomond.* Hal Leonard Publishing Corp. 1992. 0:48. I. C–d. Moderately. Scottish folksong. See: Daellenbach, Charles, *Book of Easy Tuba Solos,* under Tuba and Keyboard Collections.

Boyd, Bill, arr. *Riddle Song, The.* ed. Charles Daellenbach. Hal Leonard Publishing Corp. 1992. 0:46. I. $B\flat_1$–c. Moderately. English ballad. Quarter note is fastest rhythm. Comes with practice/performance cassette. See: Daellenbach, Charles, *Book of Beginning Tuba Solos,* under Tuba and Keyboard Collections.

Boyd, Bill, arr. *Song of the Volga Boatman.* ed. Charles Daellenbach. Hal Leonard Publishing Corp. 1992. 0:58. I. D–B♭. Russian folksong. Very limited range. A couple of sixteenth notes included. Comes with practice/performance cassette. See: Daellenbach, Charles, *Book of Beginning Tuba Solos,* under Tuba and Keyboard Collections.

Boyd, Bill, arr. *Streets of Laredo.* ed. Charles Daellenbach. Hal Leonard Publishing Corp. 1992. 0:35. I. $B\flat_1$–B♭. American folksong (adapted from old Irish air). In 3/4 time with no technical problems. Comes with practice/performance cassette. See: Daellenbach, Charles, *Book of Beginning Tuba Solos,* under Tuba and Keyboard Collections.

Boyd, Bill, arr. *Wayfaring Stranger, The.* Hal Leonard Publishing Corp. 1992. 0:45. I–II. C–d. Slowly. American folksong See: Daellenbach, Charles, *Book of Easy Tuba Solos,* under Tuba and Keyboard Collections.

Boyd, Bill, arr. *Yankee Doodle.* ed. Charles Daellenbach. Hal Leonard Publishing Corp. 1992. 0:27. I. $B\flat_1$–a. Traditional American. Once through the tune complete with "Shave and a Haircut" at the end. Two dotted eighth/sixteenth patterns; otherwise eighth and quarter notes. Comes with practice/performance cassette. See: Daellenbach, Charles, *Book of Beginning Tuba Solos,* under Tuba and Keyboard Collections.

Boyd, Bill. *Canadian Brass Blues.* ed. Charles Daellenbach. Hal Leonard Publishing Corp. 1992. 0:32. I. E♭–B♭. Very limited range, repetitive blues figure. Some eighth notes. Comes with practice/performance cassette. See: Daellenbach, Charles, *Book of Beginning Tuba Solos,* under Tuba and Keyboard Collections.

Boyle, Rory. *Beelezebub Dances.* Warwick Music Limited. $26.00.

Bozza, Eugène. *Allegro and Finale.* ed. J. Larin. Moscow Muzyka. 1979. See: Larin, J., *Pieces for Tuba and Piano,* under Tuba and Keyboard Collections. Also see other listing in this section.

Bozza, Eugène. *Allegro et Finale.* Alphonse Leduc. 1953. $11.50. 5:35. IV–V. E–a' (b'). "pour Contrebasse à Cordes ou Tuba Ut ou Saxhorn basse Si♭ ou Trombone basse et piano." For French tuba. Neo-baroque writing. Mostly scale-wise writing; a few large interval skips. Good recital material. See: Thompson/Lemke; *French Music for Low Brass Instruments.* And see other listing in this section. Recorded by Gerhard Georgie.

Bozza, Eugène. *Concertino.* Alphonse Leduc. 1967. $19.05. 17:00. Written for Harvey Phillips. "pour Tuba en Ut ou Saxhorn basse en Si♭ et orchestre ou piano." See: Bozza, Eugène, *Concertino for Tuba and Orchestra,* under Tuba and Orchestra. Also see: Thompson/Lemke; *French Music for Low Brass Instruments.* Recorded by Steven Seward.

Bozza, Eugène. *New Orleans.* Alphonse Leduc. 1962. $14.45. 4:30. V. F_1–b♭'. "pour Saxhorn basse Si♭ ou Tuba Ut ou Trombone basse et Piano." Cadenza-like passages. Impressionistic tonal colors throughout combined with pseudo jazz/ragtime syncopation. Wide skips; wide range. See: Thompson/Lemke; *French Music for Low Brass Instruments.*

Bozza, Eugène. *Prelude and Allegro.* ed. J. Larin. Moscow Muzyka. 1979. See: Larin, J., *Pieces for Tuba and Piano,* under Tuba and Keyboard Collections. Also see other listings in this section.

Bozza, Eugène. *Prèlude et Allegro.* Alphonse Leduc. 1953. $11.50. IV. ($A_1$) E–a'. à Monsieur Moulard, Professeur de Contrebasse au Conservatoire National de Valenciennes. "pour contrebasse à Cordes ou Tuba Ut ou saxhorn basse si♭ ou Trombone basse et Piano." For French tuba. One-movement work with several moods including a cadenza in the middle. Primarily conceived as a solo for string bass; still makes a nice addition to the repertoire. See: Thompson/Lemke; *French Music for Low Brass Instruments.* Also see other listings in this section.

Bozza, Eugène. *Prélude et Allegro.* arr. Hiroyuki Yasumoto. Toa Music International Co. 1989. Transposed a major third down from original. See other listings in this section. Also see: Yasumoto, Hiroyuki, *Tuba Volume #3,* under Tuba and Keyboard Collections.

Bozza, Eugène. *Thème Varié.* Alphonse Leduc. 1957. $11.50. 4:00. IV–V. G_1 (f') g. "pour Tuba Ut ou Saxhorn basse Si♭ ou Trombone basse et Piano." Theme and (four) variations with cadenza. Fun piece to play; good recital material. (A variation of the *Elephant* from Saint-Saens, *Carnival of the Animals*) See: Thompson/Lemke; *French Music for Low Brass Instruments.*

Brahms, J. *Lullaby.* arr. Wesley Jacobs. Encore Music Publishers. 0:41. I–II. D–d. Slowly. In D major. With exception of key, level I. Some slurring; some D–d octave jumps. See: Jacobs,

Wesley, *Solos from the Classics,* under Tuba and Keyboard Collections.

Brahms, Johannes. *Cradle Song.* arr. John Kinyon. M. Witmark & Sons. 1958. I. See: Kinyon, John, *Breeze-Easy Recital Pieces,* under Tuba and Keyboard Collections.

Brahms, Johannes. *Der Gang zum Liebchen.* arr. David Green. Encore Music Publishers. 2002. 3:00. II. D–g. Con grazia. A very short piece in a folk style suitable for the beginner to intermediate level.

Brahms, Johannes. *Five Songs.* arr. Donald C. Little. Southern Music Company. $6.50. 8:22 (1:32, 1:28, 1:55, 2:01, 1:26). III–IV. F–b. 1. *Ständchen, Op. 106,* 1889; 2. *O kühler Walk, Op. 72,* 1877; 3. *Minnelied, Op. 71,* 1877; 4. *Sonntag, Op. 47,* 1868; 5. *Vergebliches Ständchen, Op. 84,* 1882. For tuba and piano or bass trombone and piano. Very lyrical transcriptions retaining the wonderful vocal quality of the songs. Good recital material.

Brahms, Johannes. *Gypsy Songs.* arr. Michael Fischer, piano ed. by John Cozza.

Brahms, Johannes. *On the Lake.* arr. Ronald C. Dishinger. Medici Music Press. 1990. $2.50. 3:05. II–III. D–f. "Auf dem See, Op. 59." Limited range. Lyrical solo in 3/4 time with some slurring. No technical problems.

Brahms, Johannes. *Sandman.* arr. Wesley Jacobs. Encore Music Publishers. 0:42. I. C–d. Quietly. Some easy slurring, a couple of dotted quarter notes; no other technical problems. See: Jacobs, Wesley, *Solos from the Classics,* under Tuba and Keyboard Collections.

Brahms, Johannes. *Sunday (Sonntag, Op. 47, 1968).* ed. Don Little. CPP/Belwin, Inc. 1991. See other listing in this section. Also see: Little, Don, *Solo-Pak for Tuba, Part Two,* under Tuba and Keyboard Collections.

Brahms, Johannes. *Sunday.* CPP/Belwin, Inc. Single published piece Out of Print. See other listing in this section. (*Sonntag, Op. 47, 1868*).

Brahms, Johannes. *Trennung.* arr. David Green. Encore Music Publishers. 2002.

Brahms, Johannes. *Two Lieder.* arr. Daniel Perantoni. Hal Leonard Publishing Corp. 1976. See: Perantoni, Daniel, *Master Solos Intermediate Level,* under Tuba and Keyboard Collections.

Brahms, Johannes. *Waltz.* arr. James Graham. TUBA Press. 1991. 2:02. III. G–a. Moderato. Good recital material. See: Graham, James, *Concert Music for Tuba,* under Tuba and Keyboard Collections.

Brahms, Johannes. *Waltz.* arr. Wesley Jacobs. Encore Music Publishers. 1:14. I–II. B_1–d. Slow waltz. Slurring throughout. In 3/4 time and in C major. See: Jacobs, Wesley, *Solos from the Classics,* under Tuba and Keyboard Collections.

Brahms, S (sic). *Waltz.* ed. A. Lebedev. Moscow Muzyka. 1986. 1:15. III. G–b♭. Grazioso. Written by Johannes Brahms. Same as other listing in this section. See: Lebedev, A., *Tuba Tutor Vol. 2,* under Tuba and Keyboard Collections.

Brahmstedt, N. K. *Stupendo.* ed. and compiled Himie Voxman. Rubank, Inc. 1937. $1.50. "Solo Tuba—E♭ or BB♭ tuba." See: Rubank, *Soloist Folio for Bass (E♭ or BB♭),* under Tuba and Keyboard Collections. Also see: Brahmstedt, N. K., *Stupendo,* under Tuba and Band.

Brahmstedt, N. K. *Stupendo.* Rubank, Inc. 1937. Published separately. See other listing in this section.

Brandon, Sy. *American Fantasy.* Tuba-Euphonium Press. 2003. 10:00. III–IV. F_1–c'. Declaration; Introspection; Community. Commissioned by and dedicated to Kenyon Wilson. A three movement work based on American tunes and folk styles.

Brandon, Sy. *Concerto alla Jazz.* Tuba-Euphonium Press. 12:00. IV. (D_1) F_1–e'. Swing; Blues; Latin. Dedicated to Rommel Cordova. Concerto in different jazz styles; no improvisation required.

Brandon, Sy. *Designs and Patters for Tuba and Grand Piano.* TUBA Press. 1973. $7.00. 4:37 (0:51, 0:41, 1:16, 0:57, 1:32). V. C_2–e'. To Barton Cummings. Honorable Mention in 1973 NACWPI Composition Contest. Five movements, fourth mvt. unaccompanied. Very contemporary writing, especially for piano. Pianist must snap strings, rap knuckles on wood, move pedals up and down, roll mallets on strings, etc. Tuba has wide skips, mixed meter, trills, etc. Would take two mature players. Two copies needed for performance. Written Nov. 28, 1973, Boise, Idaho. See review in *TUBA Journal,* Vol. 1, No. 3, Page 6.

Brandon, Sy. *Sonata for Tuba and Piano.* TUBA Press. 1981. $12.00. 15:10 (4:06, 3:20, 7:44). IV–V. F_1–f'. To Harvey Phillips. Three movements. Allegretto; Andante; Allegro Moderato (Rondo-Passacaglia). Contemporary writing with quite a bit of lyricism. Will require a good repetitive tongue, wide range. Has mixed meter, well within the range of an advanced player.

Brandon, Sy. *Sonata Ritmico.* Tuba-Euphonium Press. 2002. 7:00. III–IV. E_1–f'. Allegretto; Adagio; Allegro. Dedicated to John Hardisky. A rhythmic work in three movements with some quick range shifts.

Brandon, Sy. *Three Episodes.* Co-Op Press. 1988. $5.00. 6:40 (2:34, 2:40, 1:26). IV. G_1–b♭. Frolic; Song; March. To Amy. Very lyrical. Each has a slight modal quality and some easy meter changes. Frequent imitation between tuba and piano.

Brass Wind Publications. *Fifteen Introductory Solos.* II. For E♭ Bass/Tuba. Solos by Django Bates; Arthur Butterworth; Nigel Clarke; Douglas Coombes; Robert Ramskill. Treble and bass clef versions available.

Brass Wind Publications. *Up Front Albums Book 1.* I–II. For E♭ bass. Solos by Derek Bourgeois; Arthur

Butterworth; Ian Carr; Gordon Crosse; Edward Gregson; Joseph Horovitz; Raymond Premru; Daryl Runswick; Stan Tracey; Guy Woolfenden. Treble and bass clef versions available.

Brass Wind Publications. *Up Front Albums Book 2.* I–III. For E♭ bass. See: Brass Wind Publications, *Up Front Albums Book 1,* in this section.

Bratton, John W. *Teddy Bears' Picnic, The.* arr. Douglas MacLean. M. Witmark & Sons. 1942. 3:00. II–III. (F_1) B♭$_1$–f (b♭). Complete version of the classic solo associated with the tuba. Makes for a nice recital piece or encore piece as a novelty even for an advanced player.

Braun, Yehezkel. *Three Traditional Tunes for Sabbath (1974).* Israel Music Institute. 1975. III. G–c'. *Adon Olom (Lord Of The Universe)* (Andante); *Yom Ze Meecoubad (This Day Is Honored)* (Larghetto); *Yigdal (Growing)* (Maestoso). Three traditional melodies presented in a simple musical way. No technical problems; easy accompaniment. Upper tessitura—best on F tuba or euphonium.

Braun, Yehezkel. *Three Traditional Tunes for Sabbath Eve (1974).* Israel Music Institute. 1975. III. C–e♭'. *Lecha Dodi (Come My Beloved)* (Andante cantabile); *Sholom Alechem (Peace Unto You)* (Largo e festivo); *Ya Reebom (The Master)* (Andantino). As with the other listing in this section, three traditional melodies presented in a simple musical way. No technical problems; easy accompaniment. Upper tessitura—best on F tuba or euphonium.

Briegel, George F. *Basso Profundo.* Available from the composer. 1952. See: Briegel, George F., *Basso Profundo,* under Tuba and Band.

Briegel, George F. *Mulberry Street Tarantella.* Was available from the composer. 1963. 2:00. II. C–e♭ (g). Good intermediate solo.

Brink, David S. *Three Movements (1988).* Sound Ideas. $16.00. See review in *TUBA Journal,* Vol. 18, No. 3, Page 17.

Britten, Benjamin. *Sentimental Sarabande from the "Simple Symphony" for String Orchestra, The.* ed. A. Lebedev. Moscow Muzyka. 1984. 1:05. III. A♭$_1$–a♭. In 3/2 time. No technical problems. See: Lebedev, A., *Tuba Tutor Vol. 1,* under Tuba and Keyboard Collections.

Broege, Timothy. *Spiritual Bell.* Allaire Music Publications. 2004. D♭–f♯'. Dedicated to Gary Shulze.

Brooks, E. *Message, The.* arr. Forrest L. Buchtel. Neil A. Kjos Music Company. 1952. (renewed 1980). $2.00. 3:19. III. A♭$_1$–f. "Tuba (e♭ or BB♭)." Allegretto; Andante sostenuto; Allegretto. Melodic 3/4 section followed by a 2/4 "polka-like" technical section. Well within intermediate player's grasp.

Brothern, Hartman. *Tuba Sonata in A.* See review in *TUBA Journal,* Vol. 1, No. 2, Page 10.

Broughton, Bruce. *Mosey.* Available from Spaeth and Schmid. $16.50.

Broughton, Bruce. *Sonata (Concerto).* Masters Music Publications. 1976. $7.95. To Tommy Johnson. See: Broughton, Bruce, *Concerto for Tuba Solo and Wind Ensemble,* under Tuba and Band. Also see: Bird, Gary, ed.; *Program Notes for the Solo Tuba.*

Brouquières, Jean. *Au Temps De La Cour. (At the Time of the Heart.)* Éditions Robert Martin. 1982. $4.25. F–b♭. For French tuba. See: Thompson/Lemke; *French Music for Low Brass Instruments.* Also see review in *TUBA Journal,* Vol. 11, No. 4, Page 26.

Brouquières, Jean. *Tubaria.* Éditions Robert Martin. 1983. $4.25. F–f'. For French tuba. See: Thompson/Lemke; *French Music for Low Brass Instruments.*

Brown, Charles. *Récitatif, Lied et Final.* Alphonse Leduc. 1961. Out of Print. 7:00. E_1 (C)–(a') b♭'. A mon ami Paul Bernard, Professeur au Conservatoire National Supérieur de Musique. "pour Saxhorn basse si♭ ou Tuba Ut ou Trombone Basse et Piano." Some passages in tenor clef. See: Thompson/Lemke; *French Music for Low Brass Instruments.*

Brown, Newel Kay. *And Then There Were Six (Variations for Tuba and Piano).* Seesaw Music Corporation. 1978. $14.00. 9:05. V. A♭$_1$–e'. For Gary Bird. Contemporary writing. Will take a soloist with good technique and a good ear. Good rhythmical dialogue between instruments. Strong accompanist required. Completed January 31, 1975, Denton, Tex. See: Bird, Gary, ed.; *Program Notes for the Solo Tuba.*

Brown, Newel Kay. *Prelude and Scherzo.* Seesaw Music Corporation. 1969. $12.00. 5:00. IV–V. B♭–d'. Some large interval skips. See review in *TUBA Journal,* Vol. 7, No. 2, Page 24.

Brown, Rayner. *Diptych.* Western International Music. 1970. $4.00. 5:10 (2:49, 2:21). IV. E_1–e'. Prelude; Fugue. Prelude in 3/2 time has a dialogue going with accompanist, nothing faster than quarter notes at a slow tempo. Fugue in 6/8 with a jump from f to e' and some low articulations. No big technical problems for the suggested level.

Browning, Zack. *For the Funk of It.* Brixton Publications. 1992. $10.00. 5:00. IV–V. E♭$_1$–f'. To Fritz Kaenzig. Multi-styles: Funk and off-beat reggae, contrasted with lyrical passages developed from a twelve-tone set. Need a strong accompanist with a soloist with a strong stylistic and rhythmic sense.

Bruckmann, Ferdinand. *Suite.* Available from Spaeth and Schmid. $19.00.

Bruniau, Aug. *Sur la Montagne (Pastorale).* Gérard Billaudot. 4:25. III–IV. B♭–g (b♭'). Andantino/Allegretto. (Bruniau: Directeur de la Philharmonique et Harmonie de Cognac.) "Baryton Solo ou Basse Si♭ ou Trombone Si♭." For French tuba. Lovely lyrical opening section; moderately technical Allegro section follows.

Buchtel, Forrest Lawrence, arr. *Londonderry Air.* Neil A. Kjos Music Company. 1978. $2.00. 2:29. II–III. A_1–f. Andante. Written for a variety of solo instruments. Traditional melody in D♭ major. Great opportunity for lyricism. Key is the only technical consideration.

Buchtel, Forrest Lawrence, arr. *When the Saints Go Marching In.* Neil A. Kjos Music Company. 1966. Out of Print. 1:25. I. $B\flat_1$–B♭. March Tempo. Familiar solo in cut time. Some eighth notes. No technical problems. Written for a variety of solo instruments.

Buchtel, Forrest Lawrence. *Adonis.* Neil A. Kjos Music Company. 1948. Out of Print. 1:58. I. E♭–(c) e♭. Moderato. Very easy beginning solo in 3/4 time at a reasonable tempo. Quarter note is fastest rhythm.

Buchtel, Forrest Lawrence. *Ajax.* Neil A. Kjos Music Company. 1975. $1.75. 1:44. I. D–d. Andante. Original copyright was 1948. Good beginning solo in 4/4 time. Quarter note is fastest rhythm at reasonable tempo. Mostly step-wise motion.

Buchtel, Forrest Lawrence. *Apollo.* Mills Music. 1945. Out of Print. 3:03. II–III. $B\flat_1$–f. Andante/Allegretto. Advanced beginner-level polka solo. Stately Andante section in 4/4 and 2/4 Allegretto section.

Buchtel, Forrest Lawrence. *Archer, The.* M. M. Cole Publishing Co. 1938. Out of Print. 3:33. II. $B\flat_1$–d (f). #3 Andante and Allegretto. Some repeated sixteenth notes in Allegretto section. See: Buchtel, Forrest Lawrence, *Young Artists First Book of Solos for BB♭ Tuba, The,* under Tuba and Keyboard Collections.

Buchtel, Forrest Lawrence. *At the Ball.* Neil A. Kjos Music Company. 1954. Out of Print. 2:00. I. $B\flat_1$–c. Good beginning solo.

Buchtel, Forrest Lawrence. *Attila.* Neil A. Kjos Music Company. 1948. Out of Print. 1:55. I–II. (D) E♭–e♭. Andante. Mostly step-wise solo in 4/4 time. Faster (Con Moto) section after Andante section.

Buchtel, Forrest Lawrence. *Ballerina, The.* M. M. Cole Publishing Co. 1938. Out of Print. 3:08. II–III. G_1–f. #16 Waltz. In 3/4 time with some eighth note runs. See: Buchtel, Forrest Lawrence, *Young Artists First Book of Solos for BB♭ Tuba, The,* under Tuba and Keyboard Collections.

Buchtel, Forrest Lawrence. *Cavalier, The.* M. M. Cole Publishing Co. 1938. Out of Print. 2:38. II. C–f. #1 Andante and Waltz. A few accidentals; otherwise no technical problems. See: Buchtel, Forrest Lawrence, *Young Artists First Book of Solos for BB♭ Tuba, The,* under Tuba and Keyboard Collections.

Buchtel, Forrest Lawrence. *Courier, The.* M. M. Cole Publishing Co. 1938. Out of Print. 3:05. I–II. $A\flat_1$–d♭. #4 Andante and Waltz. Theme and variation. See: Buchtel, Forrest Lawrence, *Young Artists First Book of Solos for BB♭ Tuba, The,* under Tuba and Keyboard Collections.

Buchtel, Forrest Lawrence. *Flatterer, The.* Mills Music. 1958. Out of Print. 2:00. II. $B\flat_1$–f. No major problems.

Buchtel, Forrest Lawrence. *Gladiator.* Neil A. Kjos Music Company. 1945. Out of Print. 2:00. I. $B\flat_1$–B♭. Very limited range. Good introduction to legato and staccato.

Buchtel, Forrest Lawrence. *Golden Dreams Waltz.* Neil A. Kjos Music Company. 1957. Out of Print. 2:00. I. $B\flat_1$–B♭. Good beginning solo in 3/4 time.

Buchtel, Forrest Lawrence. *Golden Glow.* Mills Music. 1958. 1:00. I. C–B♭. Good beginning solo in 3/4 time.

Buchtel, Forrest Lawrence. *Grenadier, The.* M. M. Cole Publishing Co. 1938. Out of Print. 2:23. II. C–f. #9 Andantino and Allegretto. Andantino section in 6/8. Allegretto section in cut time with syncopation throughout. See: Buchtel, Forrest Lawrence, *Young Artists First Book of Solos for BB♭ Tuba, The,* under Tuba and Keyboard Collections.

Buchtel, Forrest Lawrence. *Harlequin.* Neil A. Kjos Music Company. 1957. Out of Print. 1:55. II. ($A\flat_1$) D–c. Andante/Allegro. "E♭ or BB♭ Tuba." Andante 4/4 section is stately with optional octave choices for ease of range. Difficulty of Allegro 2/2 section depends on choice of tempo.

Buchtel, Forrest Lawrence. *Hercules.* Neil A. Kjos Music Company. 1948. Out of Print. 1:31. I. D–e♭. Con Moto. Mostly step-wise solo in quick 4/4 time. Fastest rhythm is quarter note. Repeated material with eight measures in the middle.

Buchtel, Forrest Lawrence. *Hermes.* Mills Music. 1945. 2:52. III. $B\flat_1$–e♭. Andante/Allegretto. Stately opening andante; polka-style Allegretto section with a cadenza. Minor technical considerations include a couple of interval jumps of sixths, octaves, and—depending on tempo of Allegretto section—articulations.

Buchtel, Forrest Lawrence. *How Can I Leave Thee.* M. M. Cole Publishing Co. 1938. Out of Print. 2:56. II–III. E♭–g. "In different Rhythms." In 4/4, 2/4, and cut time. #12. Short cadenza. Last Allegro section is all syncopated. See: Buchtel, Forrest Lawrence, *Young Artists First Book of Solos for BB♭ Tuba, The,* under Tuba and Keyboard collections.

Buchtel, Forrest Lawrence. *Hussar, The.* M. M. Cole Publishing Co. 1938. Out of Print. 3:29. II. G_1–d♭. Andante/Tempo di Polanaise. #10 Song and Polanaise. Solo in 3/4 time. No technical problems except for three quick articulated lower notes. See: Buchtel, Forrest Lawrence, *Young Artists First Book of Solos for BB♭ Tuba, The,* under Tuba and Keyboard Collections.

Buchtel, Forrest Lawrence. *Introduction and Rondo.* C. L. Barnhouse. 1937. $3.50. 4:30. III. G_1–g. Andantino; Allegretto; Andantino; Presto. Andantino section in 6/8 followed by a cut time Allegretto section with some technical work to master; depending on tempo chosen could be challenging to the early intermediate player.

Buchtel, Forrest Lawrence. *Jolly Sailor.* Mills Music. 1945. 1:13. II. B♭$_1$–f. Allegretto. Cut time allegretto, depending on tempo chosen, could present eighth note articulation challenges. Mostly step-wise motion with a nautical flavor.

Buchtel, Forrest Lawrence. *Juggler, The.* M. M. Cole Publishing Co. 1938. Out of Print. 2:36. II–III. G$_1$–c. Allegretto. #13 Rondo. Cut time or 4/4 time. Repeated and step-wise eighth notes. Short cadenza. See: Buchtel, Forrest Lawrence, *Young Artists First Book of Solos for BB♭ Tuba, The,* under Tuba and Keyboard Collections.

Buchtel, Forrest Lawrence. *King Mydas.* Fillmore. 1935. Out of Print. 4:32. II–III. G$_1$–e♭. Maestoso/Faster. "Solo for BB♭ Bass." Short cadenza, smooth maestoso-like section, and a series of optional cut time polka sections.

Buchtel, Forrest Lawrence. *Mannequin, The.* M. M. Cole Publishing Co. 1938. Out of Print. 2:21. II. C–d. Tempo di Valse. #6 Waltz. Some slurs, some repeated eighth notes. Short cadenza. See: Buchtel, Forrest Lawrence, *Young Artists First Book of Solos for BB♭ Tuba, The,* under Tuba and Keyboard Collections.

Buchtel, Forrest Lawrence. *Mariner, The.* M. M. Cole Publishing Co. 1938. Out of Print. 2:35. II. A♭$_1$–e♭. #7 Andante and Allegretto. Andante section majestic "In a pompous manner." Allegretto section has repeated and step-wise sixteenth notes with a short cadenza. See: Buchtel, Forrest Lawrence, *Young Artists First Book of Solos for BB♭ Tuba, The,* under Tuba and Keyboard Collections.

Buchtel, Forrest Lawrence. *Penseroso e L'Allegro, Il.* Carl Fischer Inc. 1939. $3.25. 3:50. III. (A♭$_1$) B♭$_1$–f. Andante con moto/Allegro. "Solo for Baritone or Tuba." "Tuba E♭–BB♭." Originally published by The Fillmore Bros. Co. Andante section has a lyrical (mostly slurred) vocal quality. Allegro section in 3/4 time has triplets and at tempo given will require some flexibility.

Buchtel, Forrest Lawrence. *Pied Piper.* Neil A. Kjos Music Company. 1957. Out of Print. 2:30. I. B♭$_1$–d. Good beginning solo.

Buchtel, Forrest Lawrence. *Ranger, The.* M. M. Cole Publishing Co. 1938. Out of Print. 3:04. II. D–d (f). #5 Andantino and Allegro. Some repeated eighth notes in cut time Allegro section; otherwise no technical problems. See: Buchtel, Forrest Lawrence, *Young Artists First Book of Solos for BB♭ Tuba, The,* under Tuba and Keyboard Collections.

Buchtel, Forrest Lawrence. *Reluctant Clown, The.* Mills Music. 1945. Out of Print. 1:13. II. D–f. Andantino. Light solo in cut time. A couple of arpeggios, a couple of D octave jumps; otherwise no technical problems for the young player.

Buchtel, Forrest Lawrence. *Salamander, The.* C. L. Barnhouse. 1937. $3.50. 3:44. III. F$_1$–e♭. Andante; Allegro moderato; Tempo di Bolero. Theme and variation form. Some articulation considerations depending on tempo. Some grace note "rips" and a short cadenza.

Buchtel, Forrest Lawrence. *Song of the Sea.* Neil A. Kjos Music Company. 1971. $2.00. 2:10. II–III. B♭$_1$–e♭. Andante; Allegretto. Original copyright date was 1944. Andante section in 12/8. Allegretto in 2/4. Mostly step-wise motion throughout. No technical problems.

Buchtel, Forrest Lawrence. *Song of the Viking.* M. M. Cole Publishing Co. 1938. Out of Print. 1:43. II. G$_1$–d. #8 Moderato; Maestoso. G minor and G major. No technical problems. See: Buchtel, Forrest Lawrence, *Young Artists First Book of Solos for BB♭ Tuba, The,* under Tuba and Keyboard Collections.

Buchtel, Forrest Lawrence. *Spartan, The.* M. M. Cole Publishing Co. 1938. Out of Print. 4:27. III. A♭$_1$–f. #14 Andante and Allegretto. Theme and variations. Last variation in D♭ major. See: Buchtel, Forrest Lawrence, *Young Artists First Book of Solos for BB♭ Tuba, The,* under Tuba and Keyboard Collections.

Buchtel, Forrest Lawrence. *Troubadour, The.* M. M. Cole Publishing Co. 1938. Out of Print. 3:14. III. F$_1$–f. #15 Moderato and Bolero. See: Buchtel, Forrest Lawrence, *Young Artists First Book of Solos for BB♭ Tuba, The,* under Tuba and Keyboard Collections.

Buchtel, Forrest Lawrence. *Volunteer, The.* M. M. Cole Publishing Co. 1938. Out of Print. 4:00. II. B♭$_1$–f. Tempo de Valse. #2 Waltz. Solo in 3/4 time. Some eighth notes; otherwise, no technical problems. See: Buchtel, Forrest Lawrence, *Young Artists First Book of Solos for BB♭ Tuba, The,* under Tuba and Keyboard Collections.

Buchtel, Forrest Lawrence. *Voyageur, The.* M. M. Cole Publishing Co. 1938. Out of Print. 3:25. II–III. A♭$_1$–d♭. #11 Andantino and Waltz. Andantino section in 6/8, Waltz in 3/4. Last section in D♭ major. See: Buchtel, Forrest Lawrence, *Young Artists First Book of Solos for BB♭ Tuba, The,* under Tuba and Keyboard Collections.

Buchtel, Forrest Lawrence. *Wotan.* Neil A. Kjos Music Company. 1975. $1.75. 1:25. I–II. (B♭$_1$) E♭–e♭. Andante; Waltz Tempo. Original copyright was 1948. Stately theme in 4/4 time followed by a Waltz variation in one. No technical problems.

Buchtel, Forrest Lawrence. *Young Artists First Book of Solos for BB♭ Tuba, The.* M. M. Cole Publishing Co. 1938. Out of Print. I–III. Also published for trombone/baritone, cornet/baritone, French horn, E♭ mellophone, alto or bari. sax, oboe, flute. Piano Accompaniment Book available separately. Contains: *The Archer; The Ballerina; The Cavalier; The Courier; The Grenadier; How Can I Leave Thee; The Hussar; The Juggler; The Mannequin; The Mariner; The Ranger; Song of the Viking; The Spartan; The Troubadour; The Volunteer; The Voyageur.*

Bull, E. Hagerup. *Concertino "Giocoso bucolico."* Available from Spaeth and Schmid. $17.00.

Buononcini, Giovanni. *Pupille Nere. (Dark Eyes.)* tr. Mitchell Gershenfeld. Medici Music Press. 1985. 1:50. II. C–d. In 3/4 time; some slurring. See: Gershenfeld, Mitchell, *Medici Masterworks Solos Volume 1,* under Tuba and Keyboard Collections.

Burgstahler, Elton E. *Chansonnoir.* Pro Art Publications. 1974. Out of Print. 4:52. III. G_1–a♭. Andante maestoso/Andante sostenuto. Stately passages combined with lyrical phrases throughout. Cadenza included.

Burgstahler, Elton E. *Tuba Caper.* Pro Art Publications. 1974. Out of Print. 2:31. II. G_1 (C)–f. Easy rhythms, a few octave jumps; good advanced beginner material. Cadenza (with bar lines) included.

Burgstahler, Elton E. *Tubalow.* Pro Art Publications. 1974. Out of Print. 3:04. III. $B♭_1$–g. Theme and variation feel to this piece. Some technical passages, some lyrical ones. Cadenza included (third note from end of cadenza should be E natural).

Burshtin, M. *Legend.* ed. G. Voronov. Moscow Muzyka. 1984. See: Voronov, G., *Works for Tuba and Piano by Russian Composers,* under Tuba and Keyboard Collections.

Butterfield, Don. *Journal of Days.* D. B. Publishing Co. In preparation. For tuba and harpsichord (or piano).

Butterworth, Arthur. *Three Lyric Pieces.* Comus Music. 2003. 8:00. Appassionato, con moto; Valse Lente; Allegro moderato, poco tranquillo. Dedicated to James Gourlay.

Butts, Carrol M. *Suite for Tuba and Piano.* Neil A. Kjos Music Company. 1978. $5.00. 6:21 (3:35, 2:46). IV. C–d'. Andante; Andante meno mosso. Dedicated to Barton Cummings. Middle-upper tessitura. Good opportunity for great lyricism. Not overwhelming technique for level IV player. Recorded by Barton Cummings. See review in *TUBA Journal,* Vol. 8, No. 3, Page 31.

Byrd, William. *Earle of Oxford's Marche, The.* tr. Ronald C. Dishinger. Medici Music Press. 1990. $3.50. 2:20. III. $B♭_1$–f. "From *Fitzwilliam Virginal Book.*" Printed tempo may be a bit fast. A few sixteenth notes; no big technical problems.

Cabus. *Alla Cacia.* Editions Andel Uitgave.

Caccini, Giulia. *Amarilli, Mia Bella.* arr. Don Little. CPP/Belwin, Inc. 1991. 2:50. II. C–d. Lyrical solo in F minor. Good opportunity for musical expression. See: Little, Don, *Solo-Pak for Tuba, Part Two,* under Tuba and Keyboard Collections.

Caccini, Giulio. *Amarilli, Mia Bella.* ed. and compiled Harry I. Phillips. Shawnee Press Inc. 1967. 2:14. II–III. E–e. Moderato affetuoso. Lyrical, slurred 4/4 transcription in a minor key. See: Phillips, Harry I., *Eight Bel Canto Songs,* under Tuba and Keyboard Collections.

Cadee, Jean-Louis. *Ballade pour Tuba.* Available from Spaeth and Schmid. $24.25.

Calabro, Louis. *Sonata-Fantasia for Tuba and Piano.* TUBA Press. 1993. 23:00 (10:57, 3:11, 8:44). V. F_1–a♭'. Slow/Fast/Slow; B Major Paradox; Quasi Rondo. Original copyright 1987 by Louis Calabro. Several melodies heard over an ostinato by the pianist. Some jazz elements. Recorded by Mark Nelson. See review in *TUBA Journal,* Vol. 15, No. 3, Page 39.

Caldara, Antonio. *Sebben, Crudele.* ed. and compiled Harry I. Phillips. Shawnee Press Inc. 1967. 2:07. II. D–e. Allegretto grazioso. Lyrical, slurred 3/4 transcription in a minor key. A couple of grace notes; no difficult technical challenges. See: Phillips, Harry I., *Eight Bel Canto Songs*, under Tuba and Keyboard Collections.

Callahan, Charles. *In the Beginning Biblical Poem for Tuba (Cello) and Organ.* Morning Star Music Publishers. 1993. 4:10. III–IV. In preparation. A–e♭'. Genesis I:1–5. Upper tessitura throughout; easy rhythms. Very lyrical and reflective writing.

Cals. *Piece Preve.* Alphonse Leduc. $18.25.

Capuzzi, Antonio. *Andante and Rondo from Concerto for Double Bass.* arr. Philip Catelinet. Hinrichsen Edition. 1967. $8.95. 8:00. IV–V. ($F_1$) $B♭_1$–g (e♭'). Andante cantabile; Rondo. "for tuba (bass clef), Euphonium/Trombone (treble and bass clef), Bass E♭ and B♭ (treble clef), and Piano." Andante is a lovely lyrical section containing some legato sixteenth note passages. Rondo contains many sixteenth note runs with optional octave ranges. Middle section of Rondo in E♭ minor. Excellent recital material. (A different version of this recorded by James Self.)

Carey, Henry, and Samuel Smith. *America.* arr. Bill Boyd. Hal Leonard Publishing Corp. 1992. 0:37. I. D–c. Once through the melody in 3/4 time. A couple of eighth notes; easy rhythms. Comes with practice/performance cassette. See: Daellenbach, Charles, *Book of Beginning Tuba Solos,* under Tuba and Keyboard Collections.

Carion. *Toccata.* Available from Spaeth and Schmid. $12.75.

Carion, M. *Jumbo.* Editions Andel Uitgave.

Carissimi, Gian Giacomo. *Heart Victorious (Cantata).* arr. Clifford P. Barnes. Jack Spratt Music Co. 1965. $3.00. 1:15. II–III. $B♭_1$–e♭. Allegro con brio. 𝅗𝅥. = 60. Some eighth note runs, depending on tempo, require lightness of articulation. No other technical problems.

Carles, Marc. *Introduction et Toccata.* Alphonse Leduc. 1961. $16.85. 6:25. V. B_1–a'. à Paul Bernard, Professeur au Conservatoire National de Musique. "pour Trombone Basse ou Tuba Ut ou Saxhorn Basse Si♭ et Piano." For French tuba. Wide range, mixed meter, strong technique required. See: Thompson/Lemke; *French Music for Low Brass Instruments.*

Carrier, Loran F. *Tuba Concerto.* Available from the composer. 1969. 12:00. V. $D\flat_1$–f'. Composed and dedicated to Arthur Green. Two movements. Twelve-tone writing with some improvisation. Difficult accompaniment.

Casas, Bartolomé Perez. *Concerto for BB♭ Contrabass Tuba and Piano.* Available from Composer. 10:00. D_1–d'. III. Recorded by Vivente Navarro Más (tuba) and J. M. Garciamontalt (piano). Disciphon LP, C-4502 S.A. (Barcelona).

Casas, Bartolomé Perez. *Concierto Para Tuba Y Piano.* arr. Vicente Navarro Mas. Real Musical. IV–V. D_1–c'. Andante maestoso. Major work by this Spanish composer. Strong articulation and flexible technique required. Recorded by Vicente Navarro Mas.

Casey. *Honeysuckle Polka.* arr. Forrest L. Buchtel. Neil A. Kjos Music Company. 1957. Out of Print. 4:00. III–IV. A_1–g. Traditional polka with cadenzas. Triple tonguing.

Casey. *Remembrance of Liberati.* arr. Forrest L. Buchtel. Neil A. Kjos Music Company. 1957. Out of Print. 4:30. III–IV. $B\flat_1$–a♭. Based on melodies associated with Liberati (cornetist). Triple tonguing throughout.

Castellucci, Louis. *Intermezzo Capriccioso.* Mills Music. 1953. Out of Print. 4:30. IV. F_1–d'. Allegretto grazioso. "Tuba or Bassoon Solo." Polka style requiring flexibility from the tubist.

Castérède, Jacques. *Fantaisie Concertante.* Alphonse Leduc. 1960. $16.85. 7:30. V. B_1–a'. à Paul Bernard, Professeur au Conservatoire National Supérieur de Musique. "pour Trombone bassse ou Tuba Ut ou Saxhorn basse si♭ et Piano." Very wide range and technique required. For French tuba. Mixed meter, crisp articulation, endurance required. See: Thompson/Lemke; *French Music for Low Brass Instruments.*

Castérède, Jacques. *Fantaisie Concertante.* Moscow Muzyka. 1976. See: Guzii, V., *Pieces for Tuba and Piano,* under Tuba and Keyboard Collections. Also see other listing for this piece in this section.

Castérède, Jacques. *Sonatine.* Alphonse Leduc. 1963. $16.85. 7:15. V. E_1–a'. Défilé; Sérénade; Final. à Paul Bernard, Professeur au Conservatoire National Supérieur de Musique. "pour Tuba Ut. ou Saxhorn basse Si♭, et Piano." Wide range, strong technique required. For French tuba. Good recital material. Recorded by Gene Pokorny. See: Thompson/Lemke; *French Music for Low Brass Instruments.*

Catelinet, Philip. *Dith, The.* Obrasso. III.

Catelinet, Philip. *Legend.*

Catelinet, Philip. *Valse Gentile.* Obrasso. III. Written for tuba and brass band. Piano Reduction.

Catozzi, A. *Beelzebub.* arr. Julius S. Seredy. Carl Fischer Inc. 1932. $5.00. 5:30. Dedicated to my friend G. Marquardt, Tuba Soloist. See: Catozzi, A., *Beelzebub,* under Tuba and Band.

Cecconi, Monic. *Tuba—I.* Éditions Rideau Rouge. 1971. $5.50. 4:30. V. F_1–g'. Morceau de Concours du Conservatoire National Supérieur de Musique de Paris 1971. For French tuba. Modern writing: very free playing, glissandos, wide range. See: Thompson/Lemke; *French Music for Low Brass Instruments.*

Censhu, Jiro. *De Profundis: Sonata for Tuba and Piano.* Jiro Censhu. 1985. 8:45. IV–V. C–f'. I; II; III. Available in very neat manuscript from the composer. While not rhythmically complex, the piece contains frequent meter shifts and angular melodic lines and large leaps. Some technical demands, but the main challenges lie in the intervallic content. Good recital material.

Censhu, Jiro. *Hikari-Aru Sora-Wa Shiazukani.* Available from the composer. 1990. IV–V. G_1–e♭. To Shuzo Karakawa. "Bright and Early under the Silent Sky. Prelude for Tuba and Piano." Very free cadenza/recitative playing combined with traditional 6/8 feel. Good recital material.

Censhu, Jiro. *Urban Serenade.* Jiro Censhu. 2004. 5:50. IV. C–f'. Dedicated to Masaya Yamashiro. Available in very neat manuscript. Good ternary form recital piece. The middle section contains the most technical demands—multiple tonguing and writing above the staff. Outer sections are primarily lyrical in the mid- to upper tessitura. Good recital work.

Censhu, Jiro. *Verdurous Aubade for Tuba and Piano.* Toa Music International Co. 1989. 3:39. IV. G_1–f'. For Hiroyuki Yasumoto. Dramatic piece with many quartal intervals. Lyrical and technical sections. Good recital piece. See: Yasumoto, Hiroyuki, *Tuba Volume #3,* under Tuba and Keyboard Collections. Recorded by Hiroyuki Yasumoto.

Chaffin, Lon W. *Formal Persistence.* Tuba-Euphonium Press. 2003. 7:00. III. $B\flat_1$–a. Repetition 18; Imitation 17; Variation 16. Dedicated to Michael Fischer. Each movement pays homage to the forms of a different century. A good recital work.

Challan, Henri. *Intermezzo.* Alphonse Leduc. 1970. $14.95. 6:40. IV–V. A_1–b'. "pour Tuba en Ut ou Saxhorn basse en Si♭ et Piano." For French tuba. Strong lyrical, technical playing equally needed. Cadenza, 15/8, other compound and complex meters included. See: Thompson/Lemke; *French Music for Low Brass Instruments.*

Chambers, W. Paris. *Commodore, The.* arr. Forrest L. Buchtel. Neil A. Kjos Music Company. 1985. $2.50. 3:35. III. A_1–f (g). Original copyright was 1959. Published for a variety of instruments with piano. Cadenza, Andante section, then an Allegretto polka section. Depending on tempo, triple tonguing involved.

Chappot, Edouard. *Concerto.* Editions Marc Reift. $14.50. V. Allegro; Lento; Allegretto. A work that features every aspect of the solo tuba.

Charles, C. *Cortège et Danse.* Éditions Musicales Transatlantiques.

Charpentier, Jacques. *Prélude et Allegro.* Alphonse Leduc. 1959. $12.80. 6:00. V. E_1–b♭' (c''). Prélude-Allegro. "pour Saxhorn basse Si♭ ou Tuba ut ou Contrebasse à Cordes et Piano." Some tenor clef in part with optional 8vb in bass clef. Wide range, strong technique required. For French tuba. See: Thompson/Lemke; *French Music for Low Brass Instruments.*

Chebrou, Michael. *Tubafolia (Concerto).* Editions BIM. 1999. 20:00. IV. $23.00. Piano reduction from the original concerto. For more information see listing under Tuba and Band.

Cheetham, John. *Sonata for Tuba and Piano.* Booneslick Press. 2000. 9:45. IV. $17.50. Moderato, Lamentoso, Giocoso. Commissioned by David Kutz with assistance from the Zeta Chapter of Phi Mu Alpha Sinfonia. A very tuneful work with rhythmic energy and drive throughout (even the slow movement has a fast rhythmic central theme). Good idiomatic writing for both instruments. Excellent recital material and very appropriate for general audiences. Recorded by David Zerkel.

Cherubini, Maria Luigi Sa. *5 Etudes—Trombone (ou Tuba) Basse Seul ou Avec Piano.* arr. Andre Goudenhooft. Editions Billaudot. $21.36. See listing under Methods and Studies.

Childs, Barney. *Mary's Idea.* Seesaw Music Corporation. 1972. 7:20. V. $G♭_1$–e♭'. For Lewis Waldeck. "Deep Springs, September–June 1972." For tuba and harpsichord. "Tuba and piano are hardly this reviewer's vision of the Promised Land. How about tuba and harpsichord?" (Mary Rasmussen in *Brass Quarterly,* Spring 1963, Vol. VI, No. 3 Page 140). "on no account is piano to be substituted." Contemporary writing. Score required for performance; tuba and harpsichord in different meters at times. See: Bird, Gary, ed.; *Program Notes for the Solo Tuba.*

Childs, Barney. *Seaview for Tuba and Piano.* M. M. Cole Publishing Co. 1971. Out of Print. 8:00. IV. E_1–e♭. For Ray Weisling. "Orchestral tuba; upright bell." Contemporary writing. Includes: mixed meter; free playing using given pitches, with performer's own rhythms, dynamics, durations, pauses, etc.; playing fragments in random order; speaking, combined with more structured playing. Pianist must improvise given established pitches. See: Bird, Gary, ed.; *Program Notes for the Solo Tuba.*

Chini, André. *Fleurs artificielles.* SMIC. 1995. Written for F tuba and piano.

Choen, Michael. *Diversita Continua.* Kibutz Movement League of Composers. Recorded by Adi Hershko.

Choi, Hae-Kyung. *Night and Twilight.* Uetz Music Publishers. $14.75. Prize-winning piece of German Musikhochschulen Competition 1995.

Chopin, Frédéric. *Chopin for the Tuba.* Available from Spaeth and Schmid. $9.00.

Chopin, Frederic. *Nocturne Op. 9 no. 2.* tr. Steven Eric Marcus. WindSong Press Limited. 2003. IV–V. 4:50. $E♭_1$–e♭'. A very good transcription of the famous Chopin *Nocturne.* Requires a good bit of both rhythmic and rubato playing. Excellent lyrical facility and dynamic control required. A great recital piece for the mature performer.

Chopin, Frederick. *Etude Op 10 #3.* tr. Ronald C. Dishinger. Medici Music Press. $2.50.

Chopin, Frederick. *Nocturne.* arr. Igor Hudadoff; William Westcott, piano arr. Pro Art Publications. 1967. Out of Print. See: Hudadoff, Igor, *Fifteen Intermediate Tuba Solos,* under Tuba and Keyboard Collections.

Chopin, Frederick. *Op. 28—Preludes No. 3, 2 and 24.* arr. Sharon Davis. Western International Music. 1975. $5.00. 3:49 (1:05, 1:07, 1:36). IV. C–c' (c♯'). Allegro con moto; Lento e legato; Allegro appassionato. Very lyrical transcriptions. Requires a good stylistic sense with good flexibility.

Chopin, Frederick. *Prelude No. 6.* ed. S. Melnikov. Military Band Masters Institute–Moscow. 1957. See: Melnikov, S., *Pieces for Tuba and Piano,* under Tuba and Keyboard Collections.

Chopin, Frederick. *Three Chopin Preludes for Tuba and Piano.* arr. Arthur Frackenpohl. TUBA Press. 1993. $6.00. 3:27 (1:20, 1:03, 1:04). IV. (E_1) G_1–c'. Lento assai (op. 28, no. 6); Molto agitato (op. 28, no. 22); Maestoso (op. 28, no. 9). Very musical transcriptions. Large melodic leaps; flexibility required. Good recital material.

Christensen, James. *Ballad for Tuba.* Kendor Music, Inc. 1963. $4.50. 2:00. III. F–a (c'). Dedicated to Donald Heeren. Upper tessitura with simple rhythms. All slurred phrases. Pretty melody. Comes with flexible recording featuring Barton Cummings, tuba.

Christensen, James. *Bassey Blues.* Kendor Music, Inc. 1994. $5.00. 2:30. I–II. C–a. Good concert introduction to a blues-style piece. No improvisation required, but beginners should have some good facility with accidentals.

Cilensek. *Kontraste.* Available from Spaeth and Schmid. $11.00.

Cioffari, Richard J. *Rhapsody for Tuba and Orchestra.* Trombone Association Publishing. 1975. For Ivan Hammond. See: Cioffari, Richard J., *Rhapsody for Tuba and Orchestra,* under Tuba and Orchestra.

Clais, Tristan. *Tub'88.* Gérard Billaudot. 1990. 2:00. III. c–c'. "pour tuba et piano." For French tuba. Modern notation; three blocks to use with improvised rhythm durations. Composed in 1988. See: Daniel-Lesur, *Collection Panorama,* under Tuba and Keyboard Collections.

Clarke, Herbert L. *The Maid of the Mist.* arr. Wesley Jacobs. Encore Music Publishers. 1995. 4:00.

III–IV. G–e♭'. A mid-range arrangement of this standard cornet solo. Frequent multiple tonguing required.

Clarke, Herbert L. *Stars in the Velvety Sky.* arr. Velvet Brown. Velvet Music Edition.

Clarke, Herbert L. *Twilight Dreams.* arr. Wesley Jacobs. Encore Music Publishers. 1991. $5.00. 2:42. IV. E♭–d♭'. "Waltz Intermezzo For Tuba." Enjoy a dreamy ride through very accessible Herbert L. Clarke transcriptions. Much lyricism and requires strong melodic sense as well as technical strength. Good recital material on any pitch of tuba!

Clarke, Jeremiah. *Trumpet Voluntary.* arr. Clifford Lillya and Merle Lillya. Carl Fischer Inc. 1960. Out of Print. 2:30. II–III. F–g. Allegro moderato. "Formerly attributed to Henry Purcell." As in the trumpet solo, trill from c to d is included. Eight measures on, eight measures off, also per Jeremiah Clarke's conception.

Cleemput, Werner Van. *Caribbean Flush.* J. Maurer Editions Musicales. 1982. $6.35. 5:33. IV. B♭–a'. Tranquillo, volultuoso, un poco mesto. "Voor Bastuba Of: Tuba Bariton Euphonium Trombone En Harmonieorkest Of Piano." Upper tessitura; better on F tuba. In cut time with a Caribbean/Latin flavor. Good recital material.

Clérisse, Robert. *Andante and Allegro.* ed. Himie Voxman. Rubank, Inc. 1972. 3:00. II–III. $B♭_1$–f. "for E♭ or BB♭ Bass." Typical French tuba piece with many fermatas and tempo changes in Andante section. Allegro section in 2/4 time depending on tempo has no big technical problems. See: Voxman, Himie, *Concert and Contest Collection,* under Tuba and Keyboard Collections.

Clérisse, Robert. *Chant d'Amour.* Gérard Billaudot. $5.75. 5:52. IV. D♭–g'. Modéré, sans lenteur. "pour Saxhorn-Baryton ou Basse avec accompagnement de Piano." French tuba tessitura. Lyrical song. Tempo is slow enough to make technical passages accessible. Depending on instrument chosen, tessitura could be a challenge. See: Thompson/Lemke; *French Music for Low Brass Instruments.*

Clérisse, Robert. *Idylle.* Alphonse Leduc. $8.60. 1:56. III. B♭–e♭'. "Basse Si♭." Easy intermediate musical solo starting in 3/4 and ending with a 2/4 section including some sixteenth note scales. For French tuba.

Clérisse, Robert. *Marine.* Éditions M. Combre. 1962. 1:19. III. C–g'. Allargando. "pour Tuba en ut ou Saxhorn Basse Si♭ avec accompagnement de piano." Requires a good ear: intervals of a minor ninth, tenth, tritones, etc. Good recital material. See: Thompson/Lemke; *French Music for Low Brass Instruments.*

Clérisse, Robert. *Pièce Lyrique.* Alphonse Leduc. 1957. $11.50. 6:40. III–IV. B_1 (F)–(f') f♯'. A mon ami D. Candelle Soliste des Concerts Colonne et de la Musique de L'Air. "pour Tuba Ut ou contrebasse à cordes ou Saxhorn basse si♭ ou trombone basse et Piano." For French tuba. See: Thompson/Lemke; *French Music for Low Brass Instruments.*

Clérisse, Robert. *Prélude et divertissement.* Gérard Billaudot. $9.50. III–IV. G♭–g'. "pour Trombone Ut-Basson ou Tuba ou Contrebasse mi♭ ou Baryton si♭ ou Saxophone Ténor si♭ avec accompagnement de Piano." For French tuba. Intermediate flexibility required along with spirit.

Clérisse, Robert. *Romance.* Alphonse Leduc. 1957. $8.60. 2:31. II–III. c–f'. Andante con moto. "Basse Si♭." Stately advanced beginner solo. For French tuba.

Clérisse, Robert. *Soir.* Gérard Billaudot. 1953.

Clérisse, Robert. *Voce Nobile. (Noble Voice.)* Alphonse Leduc. 1953. $7.95. 2:44. III. C–f'. Moderato. "pour Tuba Ut ou contrebasse à Cordes ou Saxhorn basse Si♭ ou Trombone basse et Piano." For French tuba. See: Thompson/Lemke; *French Music for Low Brass Instruments.*

Clews, Eileen. *Quintessence.* Novello & Company.

Clews, Eileen. *Tango.* Novello & Company.

Cliff. *Suite Syncopation (Tuba in Es).* Available from Spaeth and Schmid. $12.25.

Cody, Robert O. *Theater Piece for Tuba and Piano.* See review in *TUBA Journal,* Vol. 1, No. 1, Page 37.

Coeck, L. Jan. *Concertino.* Available from Spaeth and Schmid. $18.25.

Coeck, Louis Jan Alfons Leopold. *Promenade.* de haske muziekuitgave bv. 5:30. IV–V. (C_1) E_1–d'. Good contemporary writing. Combination of textures: glissandos, cadenzas, etc. along with tonal melody.

Cohan, George M. *George M. Cohan Medley.* arr. Igor Hudadoff; William Westcott, piano arr. Pro Art Publications. 1967. Out of Print. See: Hudadoff, Igor, *Fifteen Intermediate Tuba Solos,* under Tuba and Keyboard Collections.

Cohan, George M. *Give My Regards to Broadway.* arr. Bill Boyd, ed. Charles Daellenbach. Hal Leonard Publishing Corp. 1992. 0:38. I. C–B♭. Moderately. In cut time. Quarter note is fastest rhythm. Comes with practice/performance cassette. See: Daellenbach, Charles, *Book of Beginning Tuba Solos,* under Tuba and Keyboard Collections.

Cohen, Sol B. *Romance and Scherzo.* CPP/Belwin, Inc. 1941. $6.50. 4:22. III. G_1–f. Andantino moderato/Scherzo. "BB♭ Bass (Tuba) solo with Piano accompaniment." Lyrical Andantino section in 12/8 followed by a 2/4 Scherzo. No technical problems.

Cohn, James. *Sonata Romantica for Tuba and Piano.* Liben Music Publishers. 1981. $6.00. 10:10 (2:20, 6:30, 1:20). E_1–e'. For Arthur Bialas. Ballade (Allegretto); Theme and Variations (Moderato); Capriccio (Presto). Requires a flexible technique and solid upper range. Good recital material.

Cole, Keith Ramon. *Romance "Homage to Peter Ilyich."* ed. Peter Wastall. Boosey & Hawkes, Inc. 1981. 1:11. I–II. C–e♭. See: Wastall, Peter, *Learn As You Play Tuba,* under Tuba and Keyboard Collections. Lovely lyrical solo in 3/4 time. Some slurred passages; one leap of a major sixth. Good challenging solo for beginning player.

Cole, Keith Ramon. *Solstice.* ed. Peter Wastall. Boosey & Hawkes, Inc. 1980. 1:05. II. F–f. See: Wastall, Peter, *Learn As You Play Tuba,* under Tuba and Keyboard Collections. Misterioso. Easier on E♭ tuba versus BB♭ for younger player.

Comet, T. *Miniature.* Available from Spaeth and Schmid. $8.00.

Compello, Joseph. *Theme and Variations for Tuba.* Joseph Compello Publications. 1987. 3:29 (1:11, 1:24, 1:04). II. F_1–d. Written for Zachary A. Kaminsky. Theme: Ponderous Polka; Lugubrious Landler; Helicon Hyperdrive. "for B♭ tuba or Baritone 8va." Good advanced beginner theme and variations with a cadenza that descends chromatically from $B\flat_1$ to F_1. Otherwise range is very comfortable for the level.

Concone, G. *Etude (Op. 10, No. 11).* arr. Allen Ostrander. Edition Musicus. 1954. 3:14. II–III. G_1–e. Andante Cantabile. Very lyrical etude in 3/4 time. Slurring for four bars at a time. Some grace notes. Good advanced beginner material. See: Ostrander, Allen, *Concert Album for Tuba,* under Tuba And Keyboard Collections.

Concone, Giuseppe. *Allegretto animato.* arr. Stephan Schwotzer. Hofmeister. 1993. 3:01. II–III. $B\flat_1$–e♭. In 3/4 time. Some easy arpeggios. See: Meschke, Dieter, *Zum Uben und Vorspielen/B-Tuba,* under Tuba and Keyboard Collections.

Conley, Lloyd, arr. *Christmas Cameos.* Kendor Music, Inc. 1985. $9.00. II–III. Contains: *The First Noel; Joy to the World; O Come, All Ye Faithful; O Little Town of Bethlehem; Silent Night.*

Conley, Lloyd, arr. *First Noel, The.* Kendor Music, Inc. 1985. 2:20. II. C–e. Melody and some accompaniment by the soloist. Cut for shorter version possible. See: Conley, Lloyd, *Christmas Cameos,* under Tuba and Keyboard Collections.

Conley, Lloyd, arr. *Joy to the World.* Kendor Music, Inc. 1985. 1:13. II–III. C–e. Cut for shorter version possible. See: Conley, Lloyd, *Christmas Cameos,* under Tuba and Keyboard Collections.

Conley, Lloyd, arr. *O Come, All Ye Faithful.* Kendor Music, Inc. 1985. 2:16. II–III. D–e♭. Nice arrangement of the melody and some accompaniment by the soloist. Cut for shorter version possible. See: Conley, Lloyd, *Christmas Cameos,* under Tuba and Keyboard Collections.

Conley, Lloyd, arr. *O Little Town of Bethlehem.* Kendor Music, Inc. 1985. 1:29. II. D–d. Cut for shorter version possible. A few accidentals otherwise, no technical problems. See: Conley, Lloyd, *Christmas Cameos,* under Tuba and Keyboard Collections.

Conley, Lloyd, arr. *Silent Night.* Kendor Music, Inc. 1985. 2:22. II. D–e♭. Cut for shorter version possible. Slurring throughout, and some temporary shifting of key; otherwise no technical problems. See: Conley, Lloyd, *Christmas Cameos,* under Tuba and Keyboard Collections.

Connor. *Five Solos.* Available from Spaeth and Schmid. $19.00.

Connor, Eddie. *McCluskeys Rag.* arr. Malcolm Bennett. 1988. 2:36. III. $B\flat_1$–b♭. Ragtime. Part for treble (E♭ bass) included. Playful ragtime feel complete with syncopations and a few glissandos. Good recital material. See: Bennett, Malcolm, *Five Solos for Tuba,* under Tuba and Keyboard Collections.

Constantinides, Dinos. *Landscape III.* Available from Dinos Constantinides. 2001. 6:15. IV–V. C–f'. Piano reduction of the brass ensemble parts by the composer. A mixture of linear writing interspersed with large leaps and quick angularly melodic rhythmic subdivisions. Good recital piece. Also available for euphonium and piano. See listing under Tuba and Mixed Ensemble.

Constantinides, Dinos. *Mutability Fantasy.* Conners Publications. 1979. $6.00. 4:29. IV–V. D–d' (g'). Lyrical and rhythmical textures. Some very quick articulations required. One octave lower for tuba in spots. "Euphonium or Tuba and Piano." See review in *TUBA Journal,* Vol. 8, No. 4, Page 27. Recorded by Joseph Skillen.

Constantino, Joseph G. *Bill's Tune.* Kendor Music, Inc. 1985. $7.00. 4:25. III–IV. ($C_1$) G_1–c'. Dedicated to Bill Troiano. Lyrical tune in a waltz and rock setting. See review in *TUBA Journal,* Vol. 14, No. 2, Page 40.

Cooman, Carson. *Divertimento for Tuba and Piano.* MMB Music, Inc. 2000. $9.95. 4:00.

Corelli, Arcangelo. *Gigue.* arr. Quinto Maganini. Edition Musicus. 1949. 2:15. III–IV. $B\flat_1$–b♭. Allegro con delicatezza. Gigue in 12/8. One rest in entire transcription. Requires flexibility, endurance, and a good ear. See: Ostrander, Allen, *Concert Album for Tuba,* under Tuba And Keyboard Collections. Recorded by Harvey Phillips.

Corelli, Arcangelo. *Petit piece en fa.* arr. André Goudenhooft. Gérard Billaudot. III.

Corelli, Arcangelo. *Preludio and Allemanda.* arr. Harry H. Hall. Brodt Music Company, Inc. 1962. $2.00. 4:49 (1:29, 3:10). II–III. G_1–e. Preludio; Allemanda. "from *Sonata No. X for Violin.*" Good transcription at conservative tempos with no big technical problems.

Corelli, Arcangelo. *Sarabanda and Gavotta.* ed. Himie Voxman. Rubank, Inc. 1972. 3:00. II–III. D–e♭. "for E♭ or BB♭ Bass." Legato Largo section in 3/4 time followed by an Allegro 4/4 section with mostly step-wise motion. See: Voxman, Himie, *Concert and Contest Collection,* under Tuba and Keyboard Collections.

Corelli, Arcangelo. *Sarabande.* ed. A. Lebedev. Moscow Muzyka. 1986. 1:30. II–III. D–a. Largo. Lyrical transcription utilizing some slurring; no big technical problems other than strong musical demands. See: Lebedev, A., *Tuba Tutor Vol. 2,* under Tuba and Keyboard Collections.

Corelli, Arcangelo. *Sonata No. 9, Opus 5.* arr. James Graham. TUBA Press. 1991. IV. (A_1) B_1–c♯'. Largo; Giga (Allegro—poco moderato); Tempo De Gavotta (Allegro). From violin sonata. Some flexibility required. See: Graham, James, *Concert Music for Tuba,* under Tuba and Keyboard Collections.

Corelli, Arcangelo. *Sonata No. 10, Opus 5.* arr. James Graham. TUBA Press. 1991. IV. G_1–c'. Preludio (Adagio); Allemanda (Allegro moderato); Sarabanda (Largo); Gavotta (Moderato); Giga (Allegro). From violin sonata. See: Graham, James, *Concert Music for Tuba,* under Tuba and Keyboard Collections.

Coriolis, Emmanuel de. *Fantaisie Italienne.* Éditions Musicales Transatlantiques. 1969. 3:12. IV. F–f'. "pour Contrebasse ou Saxhorn Basse avec accompagnement de Piano." "Pseudo" theme and variations in a pseudo-neoclassical feel. High tessitura with growing intensity throughout. Strong technique required: trills; scales with strong, clean articulation; and the flexibility of a contrabass player. Octave basso would be the sounding pitch of a contrabasse and more in the range of a good intermediate tubist.

Corrette, Michel. *Sonata in D Minor.* Editions Marc Reift. 1997. $12.50. 7:00. III. C–c' (d'). Andante; Aria I and II; Allegro staccato. Originally for cello or bassoon, composed by the mid-eighteenth-century French composer; the tessitura of this arrangement makes it playable with all tubas. Requires a light, articulate approach. Available in bass clef concert pitch and treble clef in E♭ or B♭. See listing under Tuba and Organ.

Costa Ciscar, Francisco Javier. *Ambitos.*

Coucounaras, Stelios. *Musik für den Einzelgänger.* Available from Spaeth and Schmid. $14.50.

Couperin, Francois. *Bacchanale.* arr. Dishinger. Available from Spaeth and Schmid. $6.50.

Couperin, Francois. *Le Bavolet Flottant.* tr. Lars Holmgaard. Amazing Music World. Available from SheetMusicNow.com. 2000. 3:45. IV. C–g'. A nice lyrical yet rhythmic concert work in the mid-to-upper tessitura. Most suitable for bass tuba; however, there are no rests for the soloist.

Couperin, Francois. *Concertpièce.* arr. Hiroyuki Yasumoto. Toa Music International Co. 1986. 8:42 (1:38, 2:00, 2:00, 0:55, 2:09). IV. C–e♭'. Prélude; Sicilière; La Tromba; Plainte; Air de Diable. See: Yasumoto, Hiroyuki, *Tuba Volume #1,* under Tuba and Keyboard Collections.

Couperin, Francois. *Marche.* arr. Dishinger. Available from Spaeth and Schmid. $8.00.

Couperin, Francois. *Rondeau.* arr. Dishinger. Available from Spaeth and Schmid. $6.50.

Couperin, Francois. *The Sailor's Song.* arr. Dishinger. Available from Spaeth and Schmid. $8.00.

CPP/Belwin, Inc. *Tuba Solos, Level One.* CPP/Belwin, Inc. 1984. Tuba $4.50 Piano $6.50. I–II. Contains: Barnes, James, *Marching Right Along;* Barnes, James, *Whistlin' Tune;* Bell, William J., *Melodious Etude;* Bell, William J., *Tubaman, The;* Billings, William, *Old American Patriotic Song (Chester);* Gruber, *Silent Night;* Ostling, Acton, *Aurora;* Ostling, Acton, *Deep Cavern;* Ostling, Acton, *King Neptune;* Ostling, Acton, arr., *Blow the Man Down;* Ostling, Acton, arr., *Three Famous Melodies;* Ostling, Acton, arr., *When the Saints Go Marching In;* Popper, David, *Gavotte;* Sousa, John Philip, *Stars and Stripes Forever.*

CPP/Belwin, Inc. *Tuba Solos, Level Two.* CPP/Belwin, Inc. Tuba $4.50 Piano $6.50. II–III. Contains: Bach, Johann Sabastian, *Gavotte;* Barnes, James, *In a Modal Mood;* Barnes, James, *Work Song, a "Blues Song" for the Young Tubist;* Barnes, James, arr., *Sometimes I Feel like a Motherless Child;* Bell, William J., *Chief John;* Bell, William J., *Jolly Jumbo;* Bell, William J., *Spartan, The;* Gounod, Charles, *Valentine Song from "Faust";* Handel, George Frederick, *Bourrée;* Haydn, Franz Joseph, *Haydn Medley (from Symphony No. 94);* Ostling, Acton, arr., *Gallant Captain;* Schubert, Franz, *Moment Musical;* Swanson, Ken, arr., *Blue Bells of Scotland.*

Crockett, Edgar. *Mystique.* TUBA Press. 1989. $8.00. 4:09. IV–V. D–f'. "Intense little ballad" with a Satie flavor, using the upper tessitura of the tubist's range. On F tuba, this piece is a cuddly toy; on CC, it is a lesson in how to relax and sing. "Quick pizzicato jazz bass" part in middle of composition. Requires a strong sensitive accompanist with a relaxed jazz feel. Good recital piece.

Croley, R. *Three Expressioni.* Philharmusica Corp. 1968. $8.50. 2:43 (0:46, 0:33, 1:24). V. D_1–a'. Lento ma non rigido; Adagio molto; Allegro engerico. For Robert Tucci. Composed in 1967. Contemporary writing with strong musical and technical demands. Muted passages.

Cruft, Adrian. *Prelude and Scherzo.* Leeds Music Limited. 1981. 7:00 (5:31, 1:29). III–IV. B♭$_1$–g♯. Prelude (Andante/comodo); Scherzo (Ben ritmico, quasi allegro/comodo). For Eugene Cruft's pupils' pupils. Completed Kent, June 1970. Suggested for tuba (for double bass or other bass clef instrument and pianoforte, op. 65) by Adrian Cruft, who also invites 8vb playing. Sometimes not traditional harmonies; tubist should also adhere to the spirit of the articulation suggested of the bass part (pizzicato and arco). Bassoon/tuba part also included. Prelude has easy meter changes. Scherzo has meter changes and cluster harmonies.

Cui. *Orientale.* arr. Igor Hudadoff; William Westcott, piano arr. Pro Art Publications. 1967. Out of Print. See: Hudadoff, Igor, *Fifteen Intermediate Tuba Solos,* under Tuba and Keyboard Collections.

Cummings, Barton. *Cantilena for Tuba and Piano.* Edition Musicus. 1989. $4.50. 4:00. IV. E_1–e'. One-movement work requiring lyricism, creativity (two cadenza sections) and strong articulation (sixteenth note scale runs in Allegro section). See review in *TUBA Journal,* Vol. 18, No. 2, Page 20.

Cummings, Barton. *Fantasia Breve for Tuba and Piano.* PRB Productions. 1989. $12.00. 11:49 (3:55, 5:22, 2:27). V. E_1–a'. Respectfully dedicated to Mark Nelson. Upper tessitura; best on F tuba. Some quick articulations and flexibility demands. Recorded by Mark Nelson. See review in *TUBA Journal,* Vol. 17, No. 3, Page 25.

Cummings, Barton. *Miniatures for Tuba and Piano.* PRB Productions. 1991. 4:46 (0:43, 0:43, 0:27, 0:24, 0:38, 1:51). IV–V. E–g♯'. Chorale; At Play; Day Dream; Tarentelle; Song Two; Declaration. Short vignettes incorporating upper tessitura, good modern stylistic sense, lyricism, and imagination. Two tacet movements for tuba.

Cummings, Barton. *Remembrance for Tuba and Piano.* TUBA Press. 1991. $7.00. 4:44. IV. D_1–d'. To the Memory of Stuart Snyder. Reflective composition utilizing slow tempos with lyrical phrases, cadenza, and a peppy Allegro section in the middle requiring a light articulation—staccato sixteenth notes at a brisk tempo.

Cummings, Barton. *San Jose Suite.* Solid Brass Music Company. $10.00. V. Written for Tony Clements. *Morning Minute; A Quiet Place; Tarantella, Finale.*

Cummings, Barton. *Soliloquy for Tuba and Piano.* Whaling Music Publishers. 1988. $7.50. 3:36. IV. D♭–c'. Andante. Lovely lyrical ballad interspersed with a cadenza. All legato and slurred playing. Solo lays in the "sweet" upper range of the tuba.

Cummings, Barton. *Suite No. 3.* Tuba-Euphonium Press. 1999. 10:30. IV–V. C_1–f'. Arioso; Variations—Veni Emmanuel; I Sing the Morning; Capriccio—Finale. Commissioned by and dedicated to Mark Nelson. Linear and tonal with many cadenza-like passages.

Cummings, Barton. *Suite No. 4.* Solid Brass Music Company. $15.00. V. Recitative; Dialogue; Drifting; Rollicking. A showpiece for tuba by Barton Cummings.

Cummings, Barton. *Suite No. 5.* Solid Brass Music Company. $15.00. V. Phoenix; Golden Bells; Variations; White Parasol. A flashy tuba solo by Barton Cummings.

Cummings, Barton. *Thu Sau. (Sad Autumn.)* Wimbledon Music Inc. 1983. $4.95. 2:05. III. G–c'. Andante—espressivo rubato. Vietnamese song. A song of strength and pathos; plenty of room for making a strong musical statement. Upper tessitura for CC tuba. Powerful recital piece.

Cunningham, Michael. *Sonata for Tuba, Opus 55.* Seesaw Music Corporation. 1974. $10.00. 9:29 (3:48, 2:40, 3:01). V. F♯$_1$–f♯'. Moderato/Allegro; (Bell Piece) Lento; Allegro. "composed Aug.–Sept. 1972, Bloomington." Contemporary intervals, rhythms (four against three, etc.); wide range and mature approach needed for successful performance. Strong accompanist needed.

Curnow, James. *Concertino.* arr. piano Paul Sainer. TUBA Press. 1988. $12.00. for Barton Cummings. See: Curnow, James, *Concertino for Tuba and Band,* under Tuba and Band. Recorded by Charles McAdams, Daniel Perantoni.

Curnow, James. *Symphonic Variants for Euphonium and Band.* TUBA Press. $20.00. Dedicated to my teacher and friend, Harry Begian, and the University of Illinois Bands. For euphonium, tuba, or trombone and band. Piano reduction. Winner of the 1984 American Bandmasters Association—NABIM Band Composition Award.

Dacre, Harry. *Bicycle Built for Two.* arr. Donald C. Little. CPP/Belwin, Inc. 1977. $4.00. 0:58. I. (B♭$_1$) C–B♭ (c). Moderato. Once through the limited-range tune in 3/4 time. Quarter note is fastest rhythm in this beginning solo. Optional octaves for B♭ and C further reduce (or stretch) range.

Dacre, Harry. *Bicycle Built for Two.* arr. Donald C. Little. CPP/Belwin, Inc. 1977. See: Lamb, Jack, *Solo Sounds for Tuba Levels 1–3, Vol. 1,* under Tuba and Keyboard Collections. Also see other listing in this section.

Dadia, Miguel. *Romanza sin Palabras.* Casa Beethoven. IV.

Daellenbach, Charles, arr. *Book of Beginning Tuba Solos.* Hal Leonard Publishing Corp. 1992. $14.95. I. Contains: Beethoven, L.v., *Ode to Joy;* Benedict, Julius, *Carnival of Venice;* Bourgéois, Louis, and Thomas Ken, *Doxology;* Boyd, Bill, *Canadian Brass Blues;* Boyd, Bill, arr., *Cruel War Is Raging, The;* Boyd, Bill, arr., *Riddle Song, The;* Boyd, Bill, arr., *Song of the Volga Boatman;* Boyd, Bill, arr., *Streets of Laredo;* Boyd, Bill, arr., *Yankee Doodle;* Carey, Henry, and Samuel Smith, *America;* Cohan, George M., *Give My Regards to Broadway;* Foley, Red, *Just a Closer Walk;* Newton, John (lyrics), *Amazing Grace;* Offenbach, Jacques, *Marine's Hymn;* Sibelius, Jean, *Finlandia;* Tilzer, Alber von, and Jack Norworth, *Take Me Out to the Ball Game;* Wauldteufel, Emil, *The Skaters.* Comes with practice/performance cassette. Charles Daellenbach, tuba, and Bill Casey, piano, on A side; piano accompaniments only on B side.

Daellenbach, Charles, arr. *Book of Easy Tuba Solos.* Hal Leonard Publishing Corp. 1992. $14.95. I–II. Contains: Boyd, Bill, arr., *Come, Thou Fount of Every Blessing;* Boyd, Bill, arr., *The Erie Canal;* Boyd, Bill, arr., *Hey, Ho! Nobody Home;* Boyd, Bill, arr., *Loch Lomond;* Boyd, Bill, arr., *The Wayfaring Stranger;* Giordani, Giuseppe, *Love Song (Caro mio ben);* Grieg, Edvard, *The Last Saturday Evening;* Handel, G. F., *Lento;*

Handel, G. F., *Repentance;* Lully, Jean-Baptiste, *The Lonely Forest;* Schwartz, Jean, and William Jerome, *Chinatown, My Chinatown;* Sullivan, Arthur, and W. S. Gilbert, *Miya Sama* from *The Mikado.* Comes with practice/performance cassette. Charles Daellenbach, tuba, and Patrick Hansen, piano, on A side; piano accompaniments only on B side.

Dahlgren, David F. *Folkvisor av Vikingarna. (Folksongs of the Vikings.)* Blis Music Publications. 2003. IV–V. B♭$_2$–e''. Dedicated to the memory of Margit Landberg. This is a very creative theme and variations setting of a number of Scandinavian folk melodies. The piano part is moderately challenging while the solo part requires very good technique, flexibility with large and rapid intervals, and multiphonics. Generally high tessitura.

Damase, Jean-Michel. *Automne.* Gérard Billaudot. 1987. $4.25. 2:00. I. d–d'. "pour saxhorn basse si♭ ou tuba basse et piano." For French tuba. Very lyrical (no slurs) melody in the beginning F tuba/Euphonium range. Good recital material even for advanced player. See: Thompson/Lemke; *French Music for Low Brass Instruments.* See review in *TUBA Journal,* Vol. 18, No. 3, Page 18.

Damase, Jean-Michel. *Bourrée.* Gérard Billaudot. 1987. $8.75. 2:30. II–III. E♭–e♭'. A Fernand LeLong. "pour saxhorn basse si♭ ou tuba basse et piano." For French tuba. Solo in 3/4 time with some slurring, triplets, super triplets, sixteenth notes, tenutos, and hard accents. Good opportunity for stylistic character in playing. See: Thompson/Lemke; *French Music for Low Brass Instruments.* See review in *TUBA Journal,* Vol. 18, No. 4, Page 15.

Damase, Jean-Michel. *Menuet Éclaté.* Gérard Billaudot. 1987. $5.75. 2:20. III. G–d'. Allegretto Moderato. "pour saxhorn basse si♭ ou tuba basse et piano." For French tuba. Some 5/4 time; mostly 3/4. See: Thompson/Lemke; *French Music for Low Brass Instruments.*

Danburg, Russell. *Sonatina.* Wingert-Jones Music, Inc. 1989. $4.00. 5:06 (1:25, 2:01, 1:40). IV. A♭$_1$–c♯'/d♭'. Allegretto Moderato; Lento e Sostenuto (in a relaxed "Blues" style); Allegro Moderato. Mute optional. Very lyrical writing; good audience pleaser. Lyrical playing with a lot of style required. Second movement (blues), eighth notes should be "rolled" with a jazz/blues "triplet" feel.

Dane, Mary. *Las Cañadas.* Editions Marc Reift. 2001. $7.50. 3:30. II. F–d'. A slow, lyric solo. The only difficulty is the relatively high tessitura for young players. This seems to be an arrangement for tuba transcribed from a treble clef instrument or bass trombone.

Daniel-Lesur and Jean-Jacques Werner. *Collection Panorama.* Gérard Billaudot. 1990. $16.00. II–III. D♭–e'. For French tuba. Contains: Autran, Alphonse, *Quadrille En Forme De Ronds D'eau;* Clais, Tristan, *Tub' 88;* Guinot, Georges-Léonce, *Simplex pour tuba et piano;* Huuck, Reinhard, *Ariette;* Renaud, Manuel, *Ton Coeur (Tuba).*

Danks, H. P., and A. E. Harris. *Silver Threads among the Gold and Deep River.* Cundy-Bettoney/Carl Fischer Inc. Out of Print. 3:00 and 2:00. II. B♭$_1$–e♭. Two different beginning solos.

Danmark, Max F. *Scene De Concert.* Ludwig Music Publishing Company. 1979. $4.50. 2:58. III. F$_1$–b♭. "Solo for Trombone or Baritone B.C., Cornet or Baritone T.C., and Tuba." Original copy-right was 1951. Old-style solo requiring moderate technique. Cadenza; some lyrical playing.

Danner, Greg. *Rhapsody.* Tuba-Euphonium Press (Avanti Music). $35.00. 7:00. C$_1$–f'. Commissioned by Scott Tignor. Style is lyrical in a through-composed, non-repetitive form. Some wide leaps.

Danner, Greg. *Tuba Concerto.* Tuba-Euphonium Press. 2002. 13:30. IV. B♭$_1$–f'. Excursion; For Bobbie; Caprice. Dedicated to Winston and Barbara Morris. See listing under Music for Tuba and Orchestra. Technically challenging, with linear and tonal lines. Some large leaps and angular melodic motion in the second and third movements. Recorded by Tim Northcut and the Tennessee Tech Symphony Band for Mark Records.

Daquin, Louis-Claude. *Rigaudon.* arr. Stephan Schwotzer. Hofmeister. 1993. 0:49. II. B♭$_1$–c. In 4/4 time (misprinted time signature) with no technical problems. See: Meschke, Dieter, *Zum Uben und Vorspielen/B-Tuba,* under Tuba and Keyboard Collections.

Dargomijsky, Aleksander S. *Nur Lieben!* tr. Mitchell Gershenfeld. Medici Music Press. 1985. 0:51. II–III. E–e♭. In C minor in 6/8 time. No technical problems. See: Gershenfeld, Mitchell, *Medici Masterworks Solos Volume 1,* under Tuba and Keyboard Collections.

Daucé, Edouard. *Concertino.* Éditions M. Combre. 1961. 4:05. IV. G$_1$–a'. à Monsieur J. Demailly. "pour Tuba en Ut et Piano." For French tuba. Lyrical solo with upper tessitura; very wide range. Aside from range considerations, no technical problems. Good recital material. See: Thompson/Lemke; *French Music for Low Brass Instruments.*

Davidica. *Christ the Lord Is Risen Today.* arr. David McCathren. Solid Brass Music Company. $5.50. III. The favorite Easter hymn, arranged with two intermediate variations.

Davidson, Douglass. *Fantasy on a Theme of Scarlatti.* Douglass Davidson. 1968. See: Davidson, Douglass, *Fantasy on a Theme of Scarlatti,* under Tuba and Band.

Davies, Kenneth. *Excursions for Tuba and Piano.* Kenvad Music, Inc. 1980. $6.00. 5:40. IV. F♯$_1$–b♭. Commissioned by Jay Mueller. Completed October 1980. Starts with rubato lyrical ballad and increases in intensity and tempo throughout to a rock feel. Some fingering patterns to look at, but well within reason at stated tempo. Keep rock eighth notes even; conservative range. Short cadenza. See review in *TUBA Journal,* Vol. 9, No. 1, Page 13.

Davis, William. *Variations on a Theme of Robert Schumann.* Southern Music Company. 1983. $4.95. Also written for B♭ bass clarinet or E♭ baritone saxophone or baritone and piano. See: Davis, William, *Variations on a Theme of Robert Schumann,* under Tuba and Band.

de Grignon, Lamote. *Canco de Maria.* tr. J. Amaz. Union Musical Espanola. 1970. French tuba and piano.

de Grignon, Lamote. *Reverie (Schumanniana).* tr. J. Amaz. Union Musical Espanola. 1970. French tuba and piano.

de Jong, Marinus. *Concert Piece, Op. 50.* Henri Elkan. French tuba and piano.

de Jong, Marinus. *Morceau De Concert-Concertstuk.* Brogneaux. 1953. $7.50. 7:50. IV. B♭$_1$–b♭'. A Mr P. Rouchcinsky, Professeur au Conservatoire Royal d'Anvers. Opus 50. "pour Trombone ou Tuba Ut ou Basson avec accompagnement de piano." Very wide range; upper tessitura. With the exception of a few B♭$_1$'s, better suited for euphonium or trombone than bass tuba. Traditional bravura solo with intermediate technical requirements.

de Ville, Paul, arr. *"Atlas." Grand Air varié.* Carl Fischer Inc. 1919. Out of Print. 7:04. III–IV. (A♭$_1$) B♭$_1$–g. Good intermediate theme and variations within a very conservative range for this genre. Optional cuts for shorter length.

de Ville, Paul, arr. *Happy Be Thy Dreams.* Carl Fischer Inc. 1905. Out of Print. 3:30. II–III. A$_1$–f. Good intermediate solo. No technical problems.

Deason, David. *Two Pieces.* Kiwi Music Press. 1984. $9.00. 2:44 (1:14, 1:30). IV. F♯$_1$–c. Mesto; Allegro. Tricky mixed meter. Strong sense of rhythmic ensemble needed between soloist and accompanist. Short, crisp, fast articulation required in second piece. See review in *TUBA Journal,* Vol. 7, No. 3, Page 30.

Debaar, M. *Legende et Caprice.* Henri Elkan. $3.00. French tuba and piano.

Debaar, Mathieu. *Divertissement.* Available from Spaeth and Schmid. $7.25.

Debaar, Mathieu. *Piece concertante.* Available from Spaeth and Schmid. $10.25.

Debons, Eddy. *A Quia.* Editions Marc Reift. 2002. $15.00. 8:00. III–IV. A♭$_1$ (C$_1$)–d' (g'). Commissioned by Fondation Suisa pour la musique. Dedicated to Maurice Astella. Piano reduction. For more information see Music for Tuba and Band.

Debons, Eddy. *A Bumble Bee's Fantasy.* Editions Marc Reift. 1999. $17.50. 5:30. IV. B♭$_1$–a♭'. Originally for trumpet and piano. As the name implies, this is a work based on the Rimsky-Korsakov "Flight," starting with a cadenza followed by a lyric melody before the chromatic tour de force takes over. Originally for E♭ alto horn, this can be ordered in bass clef concert pitch or treble clef in E♭. Good material for a solo contest.

Debons, Eddy. *Danses païennes. (Pagan Dances.)* Editions Marc Reift. 2001. $15.75. 6:30. IV–V. E♭$_1$–f'. Recitativo; Andante; Recitativo; Allegro barbaro. Dedicated to Claude Romailler. Originally for trumpet and piano. A very dynamic, impressive tour de force. Starting with a cadenza, the 6/8 theme is embellished by the soloist. Another short cadenza follows, leading to a fast dance, "Allegro barbaro," alternating between 12/8 and 4/4. Originally for E♭ alto horn, this can be ordered in bass clef concert pitch or treble clef in E♭. Good material for a solo contest.

Debons, Eddy. *Dinardzade (Rhapsodie orientale).* Editions Marc Reift. 2001. $15.75. 10:00. V. B♭$_1$–g♭' (g'). Dinardzade is Scheherazade's sister. This composition describes her trying to convince Scheherazade not to go to Shahryars' bed, because she will be beheaded in the morning. Following a long introductory cadence, the oriental modal theme is characterized by embellishments. The next section is characterized by a short slow melody in oriental style. The closing section is a very exciting "Allegro vivo" making use of trills, double tonguing, runs, and mordents. Originally for trumpet and piano.

Debons, Eddy. *Divertimento.* Editions Marc Reift. 2001. $15.50. 5:00. IV. E♭–c♭. Originally for trumpet and piano. After the opening cadenza comes a rhythmical Vivace section. The following short Andante is an expressive theme leading to the last Gigue (Allegro). Originally for E♭ alto horn. Suitable for a solo competition at the upper intermediate level.

Debons, Eddy. *Fantasietta.* Editions Marc Reift. 2001. $15.00. 5:30. III. E♭–c♭. Originally for trumpet and piano. The composition begins with a cadenza and is followed by a cantabile theme, after which a short recitative forms a bridge to the Allegro. Although the work is not exceptionally difficult and the range is limited, the keys of B♭ and A♭ minor are a pedagogic challenge for young players.

Debons, Eddy. *Quintus.* Editions Marc Reift. 2004. $11.80. 7:00. III–IV. B♭$_1$–f'. Dedicated to Daniella Vuignier. Originally for trumpet and piano. The composition begins with a cadenza, followed by a slow section with a harmony based on parallel fifths. The Allegro molto is an exciting, very rhythmic dance with changing meters. Good material for a solo contest.

Debussy, Claude. *Golliwogg's Cake-walk.* tr. Arthur Frackenpohl. TUBA Press. 1993. 2:12. IV. (E♭$_1$) G♭$_1$–b♭. Flexibility and good Debussy sense of style required. Good transcription with a bit of Wagner interpolated. Listen to piano original for conception. See: Debussy, Claude, *Two Pieces from "Children's Corner" for Tuba and Piano,* in this section.

Debussy, Claude. *Jimbo's Lullaby.* arr. Sharon Davis. Western International Music. 1984. $6.00. 3:03. III. F_1–g. Moderato. "sweetly and a little clumsy." Good transcription in cut time. Slurring throughout with impressionistic lyricism a must. Eight measures of low-range melody towards end.

Debussy, Claude. *Jimbo's Lullaby.* tr. Arthur Frackenpohl. TUBA Press. 1993. 2:35. IV. ($B\flat_2$) F_1–b♭. Lyrical transcription in 2/2 time. See: Debussy, Claude, *Two Pieces from "Children's Corner" for Tuba and Piano* , in this section.

Debussy, Claude. *Jimbo's Lullaby from "Children's Corner."* arr. Peter Wastall. Boosey & Hawkes, Inc. 1985. 0:52. I–II. $B\flat_1$–e♭. See: Wastall, Peter, *Learn As You Play Tuba,* under Tuba and Keyboard Collections. Impressionistic transcription. Some unaccompanied sections. Use of staccatos and tenutos. Cluster-like piano accompaniment will open younger ears.

Debussy, Claude. *Reverie.* arr. Igor Hudadoff; William Westcott, piano arr. Pro Art Publications. 1967. Out of Print. See: Hudadoff, Igor, *Fifteen Intermediate Tuba Solos,* under Tuba and Keyboard Collections.

Debussy, Claude. *Two Pieces from "Children's Corner" for Tuba and Piano.* tr. Arthur Frackenpohl. TUBA Press. 1993. $8.00. 4:47 (2:35, 2:12). IV. Includes: *Jimbo's Lullaby; Golliwogg's Cakewalk.* See individual listings for annotation.

Dedrick, Art. *Touch of Tuba, A.* Kendor Music, Inc. 1954. $5.50. Dedicated to Harold L. Walters. See: Dedrick, Art, *Touch of Tuba,* A under Tuba and Band. Includes recording with Peter Popiel, tuba.

Defaye, Jean-Michel. *Jogging.* Available from Spaeth and Schmid. $45.00.

Defaye, Jean-Michel. *Morceau De Concours I.* Alphonse Leduc. 1990. $7.95. III. F♯–d'. For French tuba. See: Thompson/Lemke; *French Music for Low Brass Instruments.*

Defaye, Jean-Michel. *Morceau De Concours II.* Alphonse Leduc. 1990. $9.15. IV. C–g'. For French tuba. See: Thompson/Lemke; *French Music for Low Brass Instruments.*

Defaye, Jean-Michel. *Morceau De Concours III.* Alphonse Leduc. 1990. $11.50. V. $E\flat_1$–c'. For French tuba. See: Thompson/Lemke; *French Music for Low Brass Instruments.*

Defaye, Jean-Michel. *Suite Marine.* Alphonse Leduc. 1989. $18.25. E♭–e♭'. For French tuba. L'Otarie; Le Cachalot; Le Requin; L'Elephant; Le Baleineau; Le Dauphin. See: Thompson/Lemke; *French Music for Low Brass Instruments.*

Del Negro, Luca. *Polka Graziosa.* Briegel. 1938. Out of Print. 4:30. III. A_1–f. Typical polka solo with two cadenzas. Conservative range.

Del Negro, Luca. *Sousaphone, The.* Manuscript in the Library of Congress. ca. 1938. 5:40. III–IV. F_1–b♭ (e♭'). Excellent polka-style solo that really showcases the soloist. Two cadenzas that include "advanced player" higher notes as well as optional lower possibilities.

DeLamater, E. *Rocked in the Cradle of the Deep.* ed. Himie Voxman. Rubank, Inc. 1938. $3.00. "Solo Tuba—E♭ or BB♭ tuba." See: *Rocked in the Cradle of the Deep* under Tuba and Band. Also see: Rubank, *Soloist Folio for Bass (E♭ or BB♭),* under Tuba and Keyboard Collections.

DeLamater, E., arr. *Auld Lang Syne (Air and Variations).* Rubank, Inc. 1948. $3.00. "Solo for E♭ or BB♭ Bass." See: DeLamater, E., *Auld Lang Syne,* under Tuba and Band.

DeLamater, E., arr. *Tramp! Tramp! Tramp!* Rubank, Inc. 1948. Out of Print. Also published for baritone or trombone and piano. See: DeLamater, E., *Tramp! Tramp! Tramp!,* under Tuba and Band.

Delbecq, Laurent. *Bassette.* Éditions Robert Martin. 1972. 1:25. I. c–b♭. "pour Basse Si♭ (bass clef) ou Baryton Si♭ (treble clef) et Piano." Beginning solo with limited range. A few eighth notes; otherwise very simple rhythm, no slurs, no technical problems (except for French tuba tessitura).

Delgiudice, Michel. *Abuto.* Alphonse Leduc. 1982. $5.85. 3:30. II. F–d'. "pour Tuba en Ut ou Basse Si♭ avec accompagnement de Piano." For French tuba. Mostly step-wise motion. Some eighth notes; otherwise no technical challenges (except perhaps for one syncopated measure).

Delgiudice, Michel. *Ali-Baba.* Gérard Billaudot. 1977. $4.50. I–II. B♭–d'. Prix de Composition de la Confédération Musicale de France 1977. "pour Saxhorn Si♭ ou Ut et Piano ou Tuba en Ut ou Trombone basse." For French tuba. Stately solo. A few arpeggiated slurs, otherwise no technical problems. See: Thompson/Lemke; *French Music for Low Brass Instruments.* See review in *TUBA Journal,* Vol. 7, No. 2, Page 23.

Delgiudice, Michel. *L'Antre De Polypheme. (The Lair of Polyphemus.)* Éditions Robert Martin. 1981. $11.50. 4:20 (2:20, 2:00). II–III. C–f'. Andante—Les astuces d'Ulysse. See: Thompson/Lemke; *French Music for Low Brass Instruments.* For French tuba. Rhythmically easy; junior high–level solo. See review in *TUBA Journal,* Vol. 11, No. 2, Page 26.

Delgiudice, Michel. *La baleine bleue.* Éditions Robert Martin. 1991. $4.75. For French tuba.

Delgiudice, Michel. *Danse L'Elephant.* Éditions Robert Martin. 1981. $13.50. 2:30. II. E♭–c'. Moderato. In 3/4 time. Some triplets, some syncopation, dotted rhythms; otherwise no rhythmic problems. See review in *TUBA Journal,* Vol. 11, No. 2, Page 26. Also see: Thompson/Lemke; *French Music for Low Brass Instruments.*

Delgiudice, Michel. *Dix Petit Textes. (10 Short Solos.)* Éditions Max Eschig. 1954. 7:27 (0:55, 0:45, 0:52, 0:52, 0:42, 0:31, 0:39, 0:53, 0:48,

0:30). IV–V. G_1–g♯'. Moderato; Andante; Moderato; Andante; Mouvement de Java; Moderato; Moderato; Andante sostenuto; Moderato; Assez vite. à Monsieur P. Bernard, Professeur au Conservatoire de Paris. For French tuba. Short movements with technical demands. Large interval jumps; mixed meter. Good challenging material. See: Thompson/Lemke; *French Music for Low Brass Instruments.*

Delgiudice, Michel. *Gargantua.* Éditions Robert Martin. 1991. $8.50. For French tuba.

Delgiudice, Michel. *Le Petit Baobab.* Éditions Robert Martin. 1981. $12.00. 3:00. II. F–b♭. See: Thompson/Lemke; *French Music for Low Brass Instruments.* "Basse si♭ ou tuba ut (in C) et piano." A few dotted rhythms; otherwise no technical problems. For French tuba. See review in *TUBA Journal,* Vol. 11, No. 2, Page 26.

Delgiudice, Michel. *Le Petit Mamouth.* Éditions Robert Martin. 1981. $13.50. 2:30. II. G–d'. See: Thompson/Lemke; *French Music for Low Brass Instruments.* For French tuba. Solo in 6/8 with some slurring. Mostly step-wise motion with a few arpeggios. See review in *TUBA Journal,* Vol. 11, No. 2, Page 26.

Delgiudice, Michel. *Puissance 4.* Éditions Robert Martin. 1991. $4.75. For French tuba.

Delgiudice, Michel. *Superman.* Éditions Robert Martin. 1991. $4.75. For French tuba.

Delhaye, R. *Dialogue.* Available from Spaeth and Schmid. $11.50.

Delhaye, R. *Rhapsodie.* Available from Spaeth and Schmid. $14.50.

Delhaye, R. *Sonate.* Available from Spaeth and Schmid. $23.75.

Demerssman, J. *Cavatina.* arr. Don Wilson. Gamble Hinged Music Co. 1938. Out of Print. 3:25. III. F_1–f. Opus 47. Traditional solo with Andantino 9/8 section followed by an Allegro Maestoso 4/4 section with some triplets. No technical problems.

Demerssman, J. *Premier Solo de Concert.* tr. Jules Watelle. Editions Salabert. 5:35. V. G–b'. "Transcription pour Saxhorn Basse Si♭." "du Concerto pour Trombone." For French tuba. Technical solo: arpeggios, scales.

Denham, Robert. *Four Ragged Fables.* Tuba-Euphonium Press. 7:30. III–IV. 1999. B_2–e' (f'). Poultry Education ("Learnin' Chickens t' fly"); The Ribbitting (An Nocturnal Hubbub); Sea Slug; Ragbugs. Dedicated to Greg Nickel, Faith Valdez, Chuck Koontz, and Beth Chouinard. Multi-movement work written in a folk style with some rhythmic effects. Suitable variety for recital material.

Denmark, Max F. *Scene de Concert.* Ludwig Music Publishing Company. 1984. $4.50. 2:54. III–IV. F_1–b♭. "Solo for Trombone or Baritone B.C., Cornet or Baritone T.C., and Tuba." Original copyright was 1951. Older-style technical showcase. Needs bravura style and strong intermediate-level technique.

Depelsenaire, Jean-Marie. *Ce que chantait l'aede.* Editions Choudens. 1975. 1:34. II–III. D–e' (f'). á Monsieur Oswald Dehaut. "pour Trombone ou Basse si♭ et piano." For French tuba. Sustained (tenuto and slurred) playing with upper tessitura for French instrument.

Depelsenaire, Jean-Marie. *Funambules. (Tight-Rope Walkers.)* Éditions Musicales Transatlantiques. 1961. $2.50. For French Tuba. See: Thompson/Lemke; *French Music for Low Brass Instruments.*

Depelsenaire, Jean-Marie. *Jeux Chromatiques.* Éditions M. Combre. 1960. 3:43. IV. E–g'. A Monsieur Moulard, Professeur au Conservatoire de Valenciennes. "Chromatic Games." "pour Trombone, Tuba ou Basse in si♭." Much chromatic motion. Full range. For French tuba. See: Thompson/Lemke; *French Music for Low Brass Instruments.*

Depetris. *Eventail.* Available from Spaeth and Schmid. $11.50.

Depetris, C. *Concertino.* J. Maurer Editions Musicales. 1989. $5.50. 6:07 (2:46, 1:31, 1:50). IV–V. (C) E–c". Maestoso (décidé); Andante; Décidé/Allegro. A Dominique Lecomte. Better on euphonium or F tuba. Upper tessitura. Some lyrical and technical playing throughout. Very quick articulations; some triple tonguing.

Depetris, C. *Recitatif Et Allegro.* Editions Andel Uitgave.

Depetris, C. *Roghisness.* Editions Andel Uitgave.

Désenclos, A. *Air.* ed. J. Larin. Moscow Muzyka. 1979. See: Larin, J., *Pieces for Tuba and Piano,* under Tuba and Keyboard Collections.

Désenclos, A. *Suite Brève dans le goôt classique. (Short suite in the Classical Style.)* Alphonse Leduc. 1965. Out of Print. 11:00. V. G_1–c". Prèlude; Fuguette; Aria; Finale. à Monsieur Paul Bernard, Professeur au Conservatoire National Supérieur de Musique. "pour Tuba et Piano." For French tuba. Strong flexibility, range, technique, musicality required. See: Thompson/Lemke; *French Music for Low Brass Instruments.*

Desmond, Walter. *Sea Gong, The.* Belwin, Inc. 1942. Out of Print. 2:55. III. $B♭_1$–b♭. Theme and (four) variations. Fun recital material for beginning intermediate player.

Desportes, Yvonne. *Un Souffle Profond. (A Deep Breath.)* ed. Jean Douay. Gérard Billaudot. 1981. $6.00. 6:00. V. G_1–a♭'. "pour Trombone basse, ou Tuba et Piano." Requires strong technique: triple tonguing, gliss (optional for tuba), quartuplets, trills, endurance (not many rests!). Needs a strong accompanist. Good recital material. See: Thompson/Lemke; *French Music for Low Brass Instruments.*

Desprez, Fernand. *Esquisse Concertante Concertschets.* Editions Andel Uitgave.

Desprez, Fernand. *Fantasie concertante.* Available from Spaeth and Schmid. $14.50.

Deutschmann, Gerhard. *Sonate.* Available from Spaeth and Schmid. $17.00.

deVille, Paul, arr. *Pleasant Hours: A Collection of 20 Standard Melodies.* Carl Fischer Inc. 1906. Out of Print. Written for E♭ bass. Also published for cornet, baritone (b.c. and t.c.), trombone (b.c. and t.c.), E♭ alto saxophone, soprano saxophone, tenor saxophone, alto saxophone, and piano. Contains: Abt, Fr., *Dear Old Songs of Home;* Abt, Franz, *Oh, My Home;* Bellini, *Come Brave the Sea;* Dibdin, *Tom Bowling;* Diehl, Louis, *Water Mill, The;* Fischer, Ludwig, *Down Deep within the Cellar;* Gatty, A. S., *Lights Far Out at Sea;* Glover, S., *Faith;* Glover, S., *Melodies of Many Lands, The;* Handel, G. F., *The Harmonious Blacksmith;* Handel, G. F., *See, the Conquering Hero Comes;* Marzials, *The Fairy Jane;* Mendelssohn, F., *On Wings of Song;* Nelson, *Hour of Prayer, The;* Nelson, S., I; Nicolai, W. F. G., *Minstrel's Song;* Roeckel, J., *Unforgotten Days;* Rubinstein, A., *Romance;* Schubert, Franz, *By the Sea;* Sponholtz, *Peace of Mind.*

Devos, Gérard. *Deux Mouvements Contrastés.* Alphonse Leduc. 1960. Out of Print. 6:50. IV–V. D_1–b♭'. "pour tuba Ut ou Trombone basse ou Saxhorn basse Si♭ et Piano." For French tuba. See: Thompson/Lemke; *French Music for Low Brass Instruments.*

DeWitt, L. O. *Pride of America.* Carl Fischer Inc. 1895. Out of Print. To Mr. Eldon Baker, Premier Tuba Soloist of America. Opus 58. See: DeWitt, L. O., *Pride of America,* under Tuba and Band.

Dibdin. *Tom Bowling.* arr. Paul deVille. Carl Fischer Inc. 1906. Out of Print. See: deVille, Paul, *Pleasant Hours,* under Tuba and Keyboard Collections.

Diehl, Louis. *Water Mill, The.* arr. Paul deVille. Carl Fischer Inc. 1906. Out of Print. See: deVille, Paul, *Pleasant Hours,* under Tuba and Keyboard Collections.

Diercks, John. *Variations on a Theme of Gottschalk.* Theodore Presser Company. 1968. $4.00. 4:30. III–IV. A_1–c'. Theme (Le Bananier). No technical problems.

Dillon, Robert. *Concertpiece for Tuba and Piano.* Available from the composer. 1971. 6:00. IV. F_1–b. Contemporary writing: improvised passages on given pitches, mixed meter. Passage for pulling third valve out to flatten pitch on BB♭ tuba; would have to be compensated for on CC tuba (lip down pitches).

Dobbins, Bill. *Dialogues.* Available from Spaeth and Schmid. $31.00.

Domazlicky, Frantisek. *Concerto for Tuba and Piano op. 53.* Artia Foreign Trade Corporation.

Donahue, Robert. *Bagatelles.* Tempo Music Publications. 1977. 3:24. III. C–f'. "Solo for Trombone, Baritone (B.C.), Bassoon, Cello, Tuba with Piano Accompaniment." Not for contrabass tuba—upper tessitura. Good intermediate piece for F tuba. Theme and (two) variations. Second in a slow 5/8. No technical problems other than tessitura.

Donahue, Robert. *Two Impromptus.* Tempo Music Publications. 1976. 4:17 (2:01, 2:16). II–III. C–e♭. "Solo for Tuba, String Bass, Bassoon, Cello." Very conservative range. Very conservative rhythm patterns. Second impromptu is in an easy 5/4 time; otherwise, no technical problems.

Donati, Guido. *Rondo cantabile.* Available from Spaeth and Schmid. $15.75.

Dondeyne, Désiré. *Cinc (5) Études.* Gérard Billaudot. 1988. $9.25. 19:20 (3:00, 4:30, 2:00, 5:00, 4:30). V. F_1–e'. Written in 1987. "pour tuba ou trombone basse ou saxhorn basse si♭ et piano." Five etudes requiring flexibility and strong technique. Plenty of arpeggios and scales. See: Thompson/Lemke; *French Music for Low Brass Instruments.* See review in *TUBA Journal,* Vol. 18, No. 3, Page 18.

Dondeyne, Désiré. *Cinq (5) Piece Courtes: Pour jeune tubistes.* Gérard Billaudot. 1987. $9.25. 7:15 (2:00, 0:30, 1:00, 1:45, 2:00). II–III. (G_1) C–c'. Andante expressivo; Tempo di Marcia; Modéré; Allegretto; Andante (sans lenteur). à Fernand Lelong, Professeur au C.N.S.M. de Paris. "pour Tuba en ut ou Saxhorn basse si♭ avec accompagnement de Piano." Very melodic little piece requiring some flexibility. See: Thompson/Lemke; *French Music for Low Brass Instruments.*

Dondeyne, Désiré. *Divertimento.* Lino Florenzo. 1978. V. (E_1) F_1–f♯'. "pour Tuba et orchestre." See: Thompson/Lemke; *French Music for Low Brass Instruments.*

Dondeyne, Désiré. *Tubissimo.* ed. Fernand Lelong. Gérard Billaudot. 1983. $7.50. 6:30. IV–V. F_1–e' (g'). à Fernand Lelong. "pour Tuba Basse ou Saxhorn Basse B♭ et Piano." For French tuba. Opens with a cadenza/recitative section, continues with a 4/8 expressivo lyrical section, and ends with a brisk Allegro section. Plenty of opportunity for expression. See: Thompson/Lemke; *French Music for Low Brass Instruments.*

Dondit, Dee Ann, arr. *Still Sweeter Every Day.* David E. Smith Publications. 1990. $3.50. 1:46. III. G_1–f. Theme and variations. Some triplets, dotted rhythms; very accessible to player with advanced beginner/early intermediate technique.

Donovan, Mike. *Sonata for Tuba and Piano.* Solid Brass Music Company. $20.00. IV–V. Bright; Andante; Reflective.

Douliez, Victor. *Andante, Op. 53.* Editions Musicales Brogneaux. $2.40. French tuba and piano.

Dowland, John. *Come Again, Sweet Love Doth Now Invite.* arr. Daniel Perantoni. Hal Leonard Publishing Corp. 1976. See: Perantoni, Daniel, *Master Solos Intermediate Level,* under Tuba and Keyboard Collections.

Dowland, John. *Dear If You Change.* arr. Daniel Perantoni. Hal Leonard Publishing Corp. 1976. See: Perantoni, Daniel, *Master Solos Intermediate Level,* under Tuba and Keyboard Collections.

Dowland, John. *Now, O Now My Needs Must Part.* arr. Daniel Perantoni. Hal Leonard Publishing Corp. 1976. See: Perantoni, Daniel, *Master Solos Intermediate Level,* under Tuba and Keyboard Collections.

Dowland, John. *What If I Never Speed.* arr. Michael Fischer. Tuba-Euphonium Press. 2002. 2:00. I. A_1–B♭. A simple folk melody suitable for beginners.

Dowling, Robert. *His Majesty the Tuba.* CPP/Belwin, Inc. 1940. $4.00. 5:40. III. (B♭$_2$) F_1–c' (f'). Theme and (three) variations. Intermediate technique and flexibility required: scale-wise sixteenths, octave jumps, triple tonguing, optional pedal B♭$_2$ for last note.

Dowling, Robert. *His Majesty the Tuba.* CPP/Belwin, Inc. 1940. See: Lamb, Jack, *Solo Sounds For Tuba Levels 3–5, Vol. 1,* under Tuba and Keyboard Collections. Also see other listing in this section.

Downey, John. *Tabu for Tuba.* Mentor Music. 1965. $4.00. 3:35. C_1–f♯'. To Daniel Neesley. Lyrical. Slow, reflective, lyrical playing throughout a wide range of the horn. Glissandos, trills, wide leaps, dissonant intervals require strong player. Recorded by Harvey Phillips. See: Bird, Gary, ed.; *Program Notes for the Solo Tuba.*

Dragonetti, Domenico. *Kleiner Walzer.* arr. Stephan Schwotzer. Hofmeister. 1993. 0:48. II. F–e♭. Some easy, slow slurring. No big technical problems. See: Meschke, Dieter, *Zum Uben und Vorspielen/B-Tuba,* under Tuba and Keyboard Collections.

Drigo, Richard. *Valse Bluett.* arr. Patrick Sheridan. PatrickSheridan.com (Lollipop Series). $15.00.

Drude, Matthias. *Sonate.* Available from Spaeth and Schmid. $14.00.

Dubois, Pierre Max. *Cornemuse.* Alphonse Leduc. 1961. $14.95. 3:30. III. E–a'. "pour Tuba Ut ou Trombone basse ou Saxhorn basse Si♭ ou Contrebasse à Cordes et Piano." Scales, phrases outlining triads, and a variety of (mostly short) articulations are required. For French tuba. See: Thompson/Lemke; *French Music for Low Brass Instruments.*

Dubois, Pierre Max. *Fantasie.* Editions Choudens. 1965. $12.50. IV–V. F_1–c''. "pour Tuba Ut ou Saxhorn basse Si♭ ou Trombone bass et Piano." For French tuba. See: Thompson/Lemke; *French Music for Low Brass Instruments.*

Dubois, Pierre Max. *Histoires De Tuba Vol. 1: Plantez les gars! (Plant Them Boys!)* Gérard Billaudot. 1984. $4.50. 2:09. II–III. F–(d') f'. "Pour Saxhorn basse en Si♭, Tuba-Tenor en Ut et Tuba-Basse." For French tuba. Good transition solo for F tuba starters. No big technical problems. See: Thompson/Lemke; *French Music for Low Brass Instruments.*

Dubois, Pierre Max. *Histoires De Tuba Vol. 2: Le petit cinéma. (The Little Theater.)* Gérard Billaudot. 1984. $4.50. 2:22. III. A_1–f'. Andantino. "Pour Saxhorn basse en Si♭, Tuba-Tenor en Ut et Tuba-Basse." For French tuba. Wide range required. Some flexibility and light articulations also needed. See: Thompson/Lemke; *French Music for Low Brass Instruments.*

Dubois, Pierre Max. *Histoires De Tuba Vol. 3: Le grand cinéma. (The Big Theater.)* Gérard Billaudot. 1984. $6.25. 4:08. III–IV. G♯$_1$–(f♯') g'. "Pour Saxhorn basse en Si♭, Tuba-Tenor en Ut et Tuba-Basse." For French tuba. Rangewise, more level IV. Flexibility required. See: Thompson/Lemke; *French Music for Low Brass Instruments.*

Dubois, Pierre Max. *Histoires De Tuba Vol. 4: Concert Opéra.* Gérard Billaudot. 1988. $13.00. 9:00 (5:00, 4:00). IV–V. G_1–g♯'. "'V' comme Verdi; 'O' comme Offenbach." "pour tuba basse ou saxhorn basse en si♭ et piano." Composed 1987. For French tuba. Flexibility, lightness required. See: Thompson/Lemke; *French Music for Low Brass Instruments.* See review in *TUBA Journal,* Vol. 17, No. 2, Page 33.

Dubois, Pierre Max. *Piccolo Suite.* Alphonse Leduc. 1957. $14.95. 6:30. V. F_1–a♯'. Prelude; Air; Polka. A Monsieur Paul Bernard, Professeur au Conservatoire. "pour Tuba Ut ou Saxhorn basse Si♭ ou Trombone bass et Piano." For French tuba. Last movement (Polka) has accompaniment available for chamber orchestra (from Leduc). See: Thompson/Lemke; *French Music for Low Brass Instruments.*

Dubrovsky, I. *Song and a Dance,* ed. V. Mitegin. Moscow Muzyka. 1969. See: Mitegin, V., *Pieces for Tuba and Piano,* in Tuba and Keyboard Collections.

Dumitru, Ionel. *Concerto No. 1.* Editions Bim. 1996. $19.80. 20:00. IV–V. C_1–c''. Allegro moderato; Andante dolce; Allegro vivace. Piano reduction. For more information see Music for Tuba and Orchestra.

Dumitru, Ionel. *Fantezie nocturna.* Editions Bim. 1999. $11.80. 7:30. V. C_1–a♭'. A temperamental tonal work which begins and ends with the same cadenza, comprised mainly of triads and chromatic scales. The main section following the cadenza is in ABA form, reminiscent of a fast gypsy dance. Recorded by the composer.

Dumitru, Ionel. *Galop.* Editions Bim. 1999. $7.90. 2:00. IV. B♭–a♭'. Flashy piece in ABA form which lends itself well as an encore. Tonal, high tessitura.

Dumitru, Ionel. *Humoreska.* Available from the composer. 1960. 4:00.

Dumitru, Ionel. *Konzertstück. (Concertpiece.)* Editions Bim. 1996. $16.00. 11:00. IV–V. G_1–g'.

Largo; Allegro molto. Romantic work with traditional harmonies. The high tessitura makes an otherwise relatively simplistic work rather strenuous.

Dumitru, Ionel. *Musical Joke.* Editions Bim. 1996. $9.50. 2:15. IV. C–a'. A lively crowd pleaser, based on conventional harmonies, scale patterns, and arpeggios. The joke is mainly in the piano part, but also in the dialogue between the piano and tuba.

Dumitru, Ionel. *Polka Funurenilor.* Available from the composer. 1961. 3:30.

Dumitru, Ionel. *Preludiu.* Available from the composer. 1947. 7:00.

Dumitru, Ionel. *Rondo International.* Editions Bim. 1996. $9.50. 2:30. IV. C–g'. An incidental piece, based on conventional harmonies, scale patterns, and arpeggios. Not as extreme in range as most of Ionel's works.

Dumitru, Ionel. *Rumanian Dances.* Editions Bim. 1995. $22.00. 18:30. IV. 1. G_1–g'; 2. A_1–a'; 3. E_1–e♭'; 4. E_1–g; 5. D_1–b♭; 6. D–e'. Allegretto—Moderato; Allegro molto—Vivace; Allegro moderato—Moderato largo; Largo—Allegro vivace; Allegro molto—Marcia Polka; Vivace. Interesting crowd pleasers with typical Rumanian gypsy flare. Each individual dance can be used by itself. No. 2 recorded by Roger Bobo, *Tuba Libera,* Crystal Records CD690.

Dumitru, Ionel. *Scherzo Roman for Tuba and Piano.* Uetz Music Publishers. $11.00.

Dumitru, Ionel. *Tuba Diobolica (Polka).* Available from the composer.

Dumitru, Ionel. *Visare. (Dreaming.)* Editions Bim. 1995. $9.50. 2:30. III. D_1–e'. Romantic ballad with conventional harmonies. The tessitura is mainly middle to upper middle range.

Duntriev, G. *Ballada.* ed. A. Lebedev. Moscow Muzyka. 1986. 2:22. IV. F♯$_1$–g (c'). Lyrical tune with meter changes and modern melodic writing. See: Lebedev, A., *Tuba Tutor Vol. 2,* under Tuba and Keyboard Collections.

Dupriez, Christian. *Piccolo Capriccio pour tuba et piano.* Available from the composer. to Mr. Edward R. Goldstein. See: Dupriez, Christian, *Piccolo Capriccio,* under Tuba and Orchestra.

Durand, Eric. *Tournevalse.* Available from Spaeth and Schmid. $11.00.

Durand-Audard, Pierre. *Dialogue.* Alphonse Leduc. 1970. Out of Print. 7:20. V. G♯$_1$–a'. à Monsieur Paul Bernard, Professeur au Conservatoire National Supérieur de Musique. "pour Trombone bass ou Tuba en Ut ou Saxhorn basse Si♭ et Piano." French tuba and piano. Compound meters; wide range and flexibility required. See: Thompson/Lemke; *French Music for Low Brass Instruments.*

Durand-Audard, Pierre. *Tournevalse. (Turning Waltz.)* Gérard Billaudot. 1978. 6:30. IV–V. F_1–(g') b♭'. à Monsieur Paul Bernard, Professeur au Conservatoire. "pour Saxhorn basse (Tuba en ut ou Trombone basse) avec accompagnement de Piano." Flexibility required. See: Thompson/Lemke; *French Music for Low Brass Instruments.*

Durante, Francesco. *Preghiera.* ed. and compiled Harry I. Phillips. Shawnee Press Inc. 1967. 1:35. II–III. C–e♭. Largo. Lyrical, slurred 12/8 transcription in a minor key. A few trills. See: Phillips, Harry I., *Eight Bel Canto Songs*, under Tuba and Keyboard Collections.

Durkó, Zsolt. *Five Pieces for Tuba and Piano.* Editio Musica Budapest. 1979. $9.25. 4:00. V. D_1–g. Szabó Vilmosnak és Schmidt Nórának. Completed in Budapest, 1978 Jánuar 20. Stretching of technique: very low and high playing, mixed meter, complex meters, wide interval jumps, fast articulation, ensemble challenges for accurate performance. Needs an accomplished accompanist versed in modern technique. See review in *TUBA Journal,* Vol. 7, No. 2, Page 20.

Durkó, Zsolt. *Movements.* Editio Musica Budapest (Boosey & Hawkes). 1981. $12.00. 5:00. V. D_1–f♯'. Szabó Vilmosnak és Schmidt Nórának. Completed in Budapest, 1980 Július 22. One movement with different tempi and moods. Modern writing: mixed meters, wide intervals, wide dynamic range, ensemble challenges. Needs two mature performers.

Dutillet, Jacques. *Big Bear Suite.*

Dutillet, Jacques. *Sonata.*

Dutton, Brent. *Rhapsody in Black and Blue.* Available from the composer. 1966. 3:30. IV–V. E♭$_1$–f'. With the exception of high tessitura towards the end of the piece, accessible to the advanced high school player.

Dutton, Brent. *Virtuosity Study No. 1.* Available from the composer. 1967. 4:00. V. F_1–g'. Very technical solo. Very wide range. Works better on F tuba.

Duyck, G. *Dialoog.* Available from Spaeth and Schmid. $8.00.

Dvarionas, B. *Theme and Variations.* ed. S. Melnikov. Military Band Masters Institute–Moscow. 1957. See: Melnikov, S., *Pieces for Tuba and Piano,* under Tuba and Keyboard Collections.

Dvorak, Antonin. *Gypsy Melody.* tr. Mitchell Gershenfeld. Medici Music Press. 1985. 1:12. II–III. A_1–e♭. Poco allegro (Bouncing). Opus 55. A few tempo changes; no technical problems. See: Gershenfeld, Mitchell, *Medici Masterworks Solos Volume 1,* under Tuba and Keyboard Collections.

East, Harold. *Sonatina for Tuba and Piano.* Hal Leonard Corporation. A_1 (E_1)–f'. Three movements. Dedicated to Steven Wassell.

Eccles, H. *First and Second Movements from Violin Sonata.* arr. Hiroyuki Yasumoto. Toa Music International Co. 1986. IV. G_1–d'. Grave; Courente—Allegro con spiritoso. See: Yasumoto, Hiroyuki,

Tuba Volume #1, under Tuba and Keyboard Collections.

Eccles, John. *Minuet.* tr. Ronald C. Dishinger. Studio 224/Belwin, Inc. 1979. 1:30. I. B♭$_1$–F. Very limited range for beginner's level. Solo in 3/4 time; a few slurs, tenuto marks; first and second endings, del segno; no technical problems. See other listing in this section. Published-separately version out of print.

Eccles, John. *Minuet.* tr. Ronald C. Dishinger. Studio 224/CPP/Belwin, Inc. 1979. See: Lamb, Jack, *Classic Festival Solos,* under Tuba and Keyboard Collections. Also see other listing in this section.

Edelson, Edward. *Tango Anyone?* 1986. 1:30. II–III. G$_1$–d. Tempo di Tango. Was originally published as *Tuba Tango* by Pro Art Publications in 1966. Solo in cut time. Has slurs, super triplets, mostly step-wise motion; no technical problems. Keep eighth notes even for tango style. See review in *TUBA Journal,* Vol. 14, No. 4, Page 43.

Edelson, Edward. *Tuba Tango.* Pro Art Publications, Inc. 1966. Out of Print. See: Edelson, Edward, *Tango Anyone?* in this section.

Edmunds, John, arr. *Popular Solos for the Young Bandsman.* Columbia Pictures Publications. 1976. II–III. Written for a variety of instruments; contains twenty-nine popular TV, movie, and rock songs. Some contain tricky syncopations.

Eerola, Lasse. *Amorous Play.* Finnish Music Information Center. 1994. 9:40. V. A$_1$–g'. Dedicated to Harri Miettunen. Rhythmically complex with hocketed rhythms between the solo and piano throughout. Angular melodic lines and continuous fast technical passages make this work an exciting addition to the concert stage.

Eerola, Lasse. *Music for Tuba and Orchestra.* Finnish Music Information Center. 1991. See: Eerola, Lasse, *Music for Tuba and Orchestra,* under Tuba and Orchestra.

Eerola, Lasse. *N-sarja.* Finnish Music Information Centre. 1991. III. F–a. Contains: *Nukkahörtsö* (Bassia hirsuta); *Nurmivihvilä* (Juncus tenuis); *Nittynätkelmä* (Lathyrus pratensis); *Närvanä* (Sibbaldia procumbens); *Nuckkurusokki* (Bidens cernua); *Nukkakärsämö* (Achillea tomentoso); *Nurmitädyke* (Veronica chamaedrys); *Nyylähaarikko* (Sagina nodosa). Eight short stand-alone movements that are suitable for the advanced beginner and intermediate player. Each movement has consistent rhythmic and in-the-staff range demands while each movement introduces a new meter.

Eerola, Lasse. *Rohtokokoelma.* Finnish Music Information Centre. 1991. II–III. F–a. Contains: *Rohtokuirimo* (Cochlearia officinalis); *Rohtopunaluppu* (Sanguisorba officinalis); *Rohtonenätti* (Nasturtium officinale); *Rohtotädyke* (Veronica officinalis); *Rohtopähkämö* (Stachys officinalis); *Rohtoimikkä* (Pulmonaria officinalis). Six short stand-alone movements that are suitable for the advanced beginner and intermediate player. Each movement has consistent rhythmic and in-the-staff range demands while each movement introduces a new meter.

Eerola, Lasse. *Three Pieces for Tuba and Piano.* Finnish Music Information Center. 2002. 11:00. IV–V. D$_1$–f♯'. I; II; III. Sonata-type composition appropriate for an advanced college student or in a professional recital. The movements are mainly rhythmically inspired with ostinato patterns creating a driving energy. Mainly linear melodic content but requires a great deal of tonguing and finger facility.

Ehle, Robert. *Sonatina for Tuba and Piano.* Solid Brass Music Company. $17.00. IV.

Eitel, Butler. *Sting Ray.* Hal Leonard Publishing Corp. 1966. Out of Print. 1:00. I. B♭$_1$–b♭. Mostly an "Ohm-Pah" type of bass line for very beginning player—not a very inspiring melody. From the Hal Leonard Elementary Solo Series.

Eitel, Butler. *Waltzing with a Whirlybird.* Hal Leonard Publishing Corp. 1966. Out of Print. 2:00. I. B♭$_1$–d. Solo in 3/4 time. Fastest rhythm is quarter note. From the Hal Leonard Elementary Solo Series.

Ekkls, H. *Sonata.* ed. S. Melnikov. Military Band Masters Institute–Moscow. 1957. See: Melnikov, S., *Pieces for Tuba and Piano,* under Tuba and Keyboard Collections.

Eklund, Hans. *Concerto per Tuba.* Manuscript available from the Tuba Center. 1982. See: Eklund, Hans, *Concerto per Tuba e Orchestra a Fiato,* under Tuba and Band.

Ekström, Lars. *The Wind and the Bell.* SMI 1997. 15:00. Written for F tuba and piano.

Elgar, Edward. *Chanson de matin.* arr. Michael Fischer, piano ed. John Cozza. Tuba-Euphonium Press. 2000. 3:30. III–IV. A$_1$–e'. Good romantic transcription requiring lyricism interspersed with moments of technique.

Elgar, Edward. *Chanson de nuit.* arr. Michael Fischer, piano ed. John Cozza. Tuba-Euphonium Press. 2000. 2:30. III–IV. G$_1$–e'. Good romantic transcription at the intermediate to advanced level.

Elgar, Edward. *Salut d'amour.* arr. Michael Fischer, piano ed. John Cozza. Tuba-Euphonium Press. 2000. 4:00. II–III. C$_1$–d'. Transcription of a romantic standard work in the middle tessitura.

Elgar, Edward. *Salut d'amour.* arr. Patrick Sheridan and Rich Ridenour. PatrickSheridan.com (Lollipop Series). $15.00.

Elgar, Edward. *Two Songs for Tuba and Piano.* tr. Michael Thornton. Liben Music Publishers. 1981. $5.00. 6:00 (2:37, 3:23). IV. A$_1$–e♭' (g'). *Chanson de Nuit (Op. 15, No. 1)* ; *Chanson de Matin (Op. 15, No. 2).* Well-transcribed songs. Good recital material. Requires strong lyrical sense, flexible technique, and endurance (no rests!). Some mordents, grace notes, and trills included. Recorded by John Fletcher, Michael

Thornton (*Chanson de Matin*). See review in *TUBA Journal,* Vol. 10, No. 4, Page 36.

Elgar, Edward. *Two Songs from Sea Pictures.* arr. Norman Friedman. Southern Music Company. 1983. $3.50. 5:43 (3:29, 2:04). III. E♭–b♭. *Sea Slumber Song; Where Corals Lie.* Upper tessitura—would lay perfectly on E♭ or F tuba although very playable on lower instrument. Requires an expressive melodic approach. No technical problems aside from artistic musical conception considerations.

Ellerby, Martin. *Tuba Concerto.* Maecenas Music, Ltd. Available from Spaeth and Schmid. $25.50.

Enciña, Juan Del. *Triste España Sin Ventura.* tr. Gary A. Buttery. Whaling Music Publishers. 1978. $3.50. 0:50. IV. e–a'. Lament. "Presumably written on the occasion of Queen Isabella's death in the year 1504." Solo for F (or G) tuba or euphonium with harpsichord and optional cello. Solo in cut time with upper tessitura. All slurred and all step-wise motion; requires flexibility.

Endo, Masao. *Sculptured Tradition for Tuba and Piano.* The Japan Federation of Composers. 1983. V. E_1–f♯'. à Hiroyuki Yasumoto. Very free playing; no bar lines. Score needed for performance. Flutter tonguing; extended E_1 section; good ear required.

Engelhardt, Ernst. *Tuba-Sepp'l.* Musikverlag Wilhelm Halter GmbH. 2:20. III. (F_1) C–f. Fun polka-style solo in 2/4 time with some triplet sixteenth notes.

Epstein, Marti. *White Stones.* Encore Music Publishers. 1991. $10.00. V. A_2–g♭'. Written for and dedicated to Sam Pilafian. Modern writing for both instruments. At one point the pianist is instructed to cover bottom strings with "tic-tacs." Mixed meter, extreme dynamics, extreme range.

Everson, Dana F., arr. *Lead on O King Eternal.* David E. Smith Publications. 1992. $3.75. 3:00. II–III. ($F_1$) G_1–f. Strong martial style. March in 6/8 time with staccatos, slurs, and a lot of spirit. Lower 4/4 legato section in middle of piece requires slurring in the lower range.

Everson, Dana F., arr. *My Anchor Holds.* David E. Smith Publications. 1992. $4.00. 2:40. III. G_1–f. Strong march style. March in 4/4 time with a lot of spirit. Middle legato section exploits the lower range.

Ewazen, Eric. *Concerto for Tuba or Bass Trombone.* ed. Eric Ewazen. Southern Music Company. 1998. $20.00. 19:30. IV–V. E_1–f' (a♭'). Andante con moto; Andante Expressivo; Allegro Ritmico. Dedicated to the Julliard School. This piece began as a sonata and a shorter version of this same work may occasionally appear as the *Sonata for Tuba or Bass Trombone* by Eric Ewazen. The outer movements are rhythmically energetic with a challenging accompaniment. The second movement requires a great deal of musical maturity. Angular melodic lines, metric shifts, and some multiple tonguing required. Recorded by Velvet Brown and Joseph Skillen. See listing under Music for Tuba and Orchestra.

Eyser, Eberhard. *Tuba mirum.* SMIC 2003. 17:00. Written for F tuba and piano.

Faillenot, Maurice. *Introduction Et Rigaudon.* Gérard Billaudot. 1985. $5.50. 2:00. II. G–e' (g'). "pour Saxophone tenor en Si♭ ou Saxhorn Baryton en si♭ ou saxhorn basse en si♭ ou tuba en ut et piano." Lyrical playing combined with some easy technical playing. Some syncopation. For French tuba. See: Thompson/Lemke; *French Music for Low Brass Instruments.*

Faillenot, Maurice. *Introduction et ronde.* Robert Martin Editions. 1996. $9.75. 1:20. II–III. F–d'. Written for the beginning saxhorn player, so the tessitura is demanding for the young student though the piece would work well down an octave. As written, it is an intermediate-level piece.

Faillenot, Maurice. *Mardi-Gras.* Robert Martin Editions. 1995. $4.75. 1:45. B–c'. Written for the beginning saxhorn player, so the tessitura is demanding for the young student though the piece would work well down an octave. As written, it is an intermediate-level piece.

Faure, G. *Aprés un Rêve.* arr. Patrick Sheridan. PatrickSheridan. com (Bon Bons Series). $12.00.

Faust, Randall E. *Fantasy for Tuba and Piano.* Manuscript—available from Robert King Music Sales. 1985. 4:24. IV–V. G–e♭'. For Mark Moore. Requires two performers with a strong rhythmical sense. Shifting mixed meter throughout. Well worth the effort! Very tonal and very good recital material.

Fayeulle, Roger. *Bravaccio.* Alphonse Leduc. 1958. $14.95. 5:30. IV–V. A_1–(f') a'. à B. Mari, Tuba solo de l'orchestre du Théatre National de L'Opéra. "pour Tuba Ut ou Saxhorn Basse si♭ ou Trombone Basse et Piano." For French tuba. Some opera quotes included. Requires flexible, dramatic players. See: Thompson/Lemke; *French Music for Low Brass Instruments.*

Featherstone, W. R., and A. J. Gordon. *My Jesus I Love Thee.* arr. David E. Smith. David E. Smith Publications. 1985. $2.50. 2:05. I. C–B♭. Very limited range and rhythm difficulty (fastest rhythm is quarter note). Some slurring, mostly step-wise motion, otherwise no technical problems. Good beginners solo.

Feldman, Enrique C. *Fantasia.* 1994. V. Piece in progress; written for E♭ tuba. Range: 3½ octaves. Extremely difficult; for advanced and professional performers.

Feldstein, Sandy. *Rainy Day Rock.* CPP/Belwin, Inc. 1990. I. $B♭_1$–G. See: Feldstein, Sandy, *First Solo Songbook,* under Tuba and Keyboard Collections.

Feldstein, Sandy, arr. *A-Tisket, A-Tasket.* CPP/Belwin, Inc. 1990. I. $B♭_1$–G. See: Feldstein, Sandy, *First Solo Songbook,* under Tuba and Keyboard Collections.

Feldstein, Sandy, arr. *Aura Lee.* CPP/Belwin, Inc. 1990. I. B♭$_1$–F. See: Feldstein, Sandy, *First Solo Songbook,* under Tuba and Keyboard Collections.

Feldstein, Sandy, arr. *Baa, Baa Black Sheep.* CPP/Belwin, Inc. 1990. I. B♭$_1$–G. See: Feldstein, Sandy, *First Solo Songbook,* under Tuba and Keyboard Collections.

Feldstein, Sandy, arr. *Beautiful Brown Eyes.* CPP/Belwin, Inc. 1990. I. B♭$_1$–E♭. See: Feldstein, Sandy, *First Solo Songbook,* under Tuba and Keyboard Collections.

Feldstein, Sandy, arr. *Caisson Song.* CPP/Belwin, Inc. 1990. I. B♭$_1$–G. See: Feldstein, Sandy, *First Solo Songbook,* under Tuba and Keyboard Collections.

Feldstein, Sandy, arr. *Erie Canal.* CPP/Belwin, Inc. 1990. I. C–G. See: Feldstein, Sandy, *First Solo Songbook,* under Tuba and Keyboard Collections.

Feldstein, Sandy, arr. *First Solo Songbook.* CPP/Belwin, Inc. 1990. Book: $3.95. Book and Cassette: $9.95. I. B♭$_1$–G. "Contains 30 songs using only the first six notes taught in all beginning methods." Bayly, T. H., *Long, Long Ago;* Beethoven, Ludwig von, *Ode to Joy;* Feldstein, Sandy, *Rainy Day Rock;* Feldstein, Sandy, arr., *A-Tisket, A-Tasket;* Feldstein, Sandy, arr., *Aura Lee;* Feldstein, Sandy, arr., *Baa, Baa Black Sheep;* Feldstein, Sandy, arr., *Beautiful Brown Eyes;* Feldstein, Sandy, arr., *Caisson Song;* Feldstein, Sandy, arr., *Erie Canal;* Feldstein, Sandy, arr., *For He's a Jolly Good Fellow;* Feldstein, Sandy, arr., *French Folk Song;* Feldstein, Sandy, arr., *Frère Jacques;* Feldstein, Sandy, arr., *Good King Wenceslas;* Feldstein, Sandy, arr., *Hot Cross Buns;* Feldstein, Sandy, arr., *Jolly Old St. Nicholas;* Feldstein, Sandy, arr., *London Bridge;* Feldstein, Sandy, arr., *Love Somebody;* Feldstein, Sandy, arr., *Lovely Evening;* Feldstein, Sandy, arr., *Old McDonald;* Feldstein, Sandy, arr., *There's a Hole in the Bucket;* Feldstein, Sandy, arr., *This Old Man;* Feldstein, Sandy, arr., *Tom Dooley;* Feldstein, Sandy, arr., *Twinkle, Twinkle Little Star;* Feldstein, Sandy, arr., *The Victors March;* Feldstein, Sandy, arr., *When the Saints Go Marching In;* Foster, Stephen, *Camptown Races;* Hanby, B. R., *Up on the Housetop;* Hart, Lorenz, and Richard Rodgers, *Blue Moon;* Martin, Hugh, and Ralph Blaine, *The Trolley Song;* Pierpont, J., *Jingle Bells.* Optional accompaniment/performance cassette available.

Feldstein, Sandy, arr. *For He's a Jolly Good Fellow.* CPP/Belwin, Inc. 1990. I. B♭$_1$–G. See: Feldstein, Sandy, *First Solo Songbook,* under Tuba and Keyboard Collections.

Feldstein, Sandy, arr. *French Folk Song.* CPP/Belwin, Inc. 1990. I. B♭$_1$–D. *Au Claire de la Lune.* See: Feldstein, Sandy, *First Solo Songbook,* under Tuba and Keyboard Collections.

Feldstein, Sandy, arr. *Frère Jacques.* CPP/Belwin, Inc. 1990. I. B♭$_1$–G. Round. See: Feldstein, Sandy, *First Solo Songbook,* under Tuba and Keyboard Collections.

Feldstein, Sandy, arr. *Good King Wenceslas.* CPP/Belwin, Inc. 1990. I. B♭$_1$–F. See: Feldstein, Sandy, *First Solo Songbook,* under Tuba and Keyboard Collections.

Feldstein, Sandy, arr. *Hot Cross Buns.* CPP/Belwin, Inc. 1990. I. B♭$_1$–D. See: Feldstein, Sandy, *First Solo Songbook,* under Tuba and Keyboard Collections.

Feldstein, Sandy, arr. *Jolly Old St. Nicholas.* CPP/Belwin, Inc. 1990. I. B♭$_1$–G. See: Feldstein, Sandy, *First Solo Songbook,* under Tuba and Keyboard Collections.

Feldstein, Sandy, arr. *London Bridge.* CPP/Belwin, Inc. 1990. I. B♭$_1$–G. See: Feldstein, Sandy, *First Solo Songbook,* under Tuba and Keyboard Collections.

Feldstein, Sandy, arr. *Love Somebody.* CPP/Belwin, Inc. 1990. I. B♭$_1$–F. See: Feldstein, Sandy, *First Solo Songbook,* under Tuba and Keyboard Collections.

Feldstein, Sandy, arr. *Lovely Evening.* CPP/Belwin, Inc. 1990. I. B♭$_1$–G. Round. See: Feldstein, Sandy, *First Solo Songbook,* under Tuba and Keyboard Collections.

Feldstein, Sandy, arr. *Old McDonald.* CPP/Belwin, Inc. 1990. I. B♭$_1$–G. See: Feldstein, Sandy, *First Solo Songbook,* under Tuba and Keyboard Collections.

Feldstein, Sandy, arr. *There's a Hole in the Bucket.* CPP/Belwin, Inc. 1990. I. B♭$_1$–G. See: Feldstein, Sandy, *First Solo Songbook,* under Tuba and Keyboard Collections.

Feldstein, Sandy, arr. *This Old Man.* CPP/Belwin, Inc. 1990. I. B♭$_1$–G. See: Feldstein, Sandy, *First Solo Songbook,* under Tuba and Keyboard Collections.

Feldstein, Sandy, arr. *Tom Dooley.* CPP/Belwin, Inc. 1990. I. B♭$_1$–G. See: Feldstein, Sandy, *First Solo Songbook,* under Tuba and Keyboard Collections.

Feldstein, Sandy, arr. *Twinkle, Twinkle Little Star.* CPP/Belwin, Inc. 1990. I. B♭$_1$–G. See: Feldstein, Sandy, *First Solo Songbook,* under Tuba and Keyboard Collections.

Feldstein, Sandy, arr. *Victors March, The.* CPP/Belwin, Inc. 1990. I. B♭$_1$–G. See: Feldstein, Sandy, *First Solo Songbook,* under Tuba and Keyboard Collections.

Feldstein, Sandy, arr. *When the Saints Go Marching In.* CPP/Belwin, Inc. 1990. I. B♭$_1$–F. See: Feldstein, Sandy, *First Solo Songbook,* under Tuba and Keyboard Collections.

Fernie, Alan. *Caprice.* piano ed. by Roy Newsome. Obrasso-Verlag Ag. 2002. 4:50. IV. C–e♭'. Available with treble clef E♭ part or bass clef tuba part. Technically challenging and exciting concert piece with multiple metric shifts and syncopation. Multiple tonguing and fast finger facility required. Good advanced-level test piece.

Ferriano, Frank. *Sonatina*. Tuba-Euphonium Press. 1998. 8:00. IV. F_1–e♭'. Interplay; Dreamscape; Quasi-Rondo. Commissioned by John Tuinstra. Three-movement work requiring good technique and rhythmic subdivision.

Fesh, D. *Prelude*. arr. A. Lebedev. Military Band Masters Faculty of Moscow Conservatoire. 1971. See. Lebedev, A., *Collection of Pieces for Tuba "Es" and Piano*, under Tuba and Keyboard Collections.

Fiche, Michel. *Monsieur Tuba*. Éditions M. Combre. 1977. 1:38. II. F–d'. "pour Saxhorn Si♭ ou Tuba Ut et Piano." For French tuba. Cute advanced beginner solo that contains a portion of the Bydlo solo! Some slurring and tenuto, easy rhythms (fastest note is eighth note); otherwise no technical problems.

Filas, Juraj. *Sonate*. Editions BIM. 1993. $22.00. 15:00. IV. E_1–f♯'. Moderato; Allegro agitato. Rhythmical, exciting work which makes good use of entire range. In neoclassic style.

Fillmore, Henry. *Deep Bass*. Fillmore Bros. 1927. Out of Print. See: Fillmore, Henry, *Deep Bass*, under Tuba and Band.

Finger, Godfrey. *Sonata in D Minor*. arr. Angelo Manzo. Tuba-Euphonium Press. 2002. 6:00. IV. c–d'. Andante; Allegro; Adagio; Allegretto. Baroque transcription in the mid- to high tessitura.

Fiocco, J. H. *Allegro*. arr. Lars Holmgaard. Amazing Music World. Available from SheetMusicNow.com. 2000. 4:30. IV. B♭$_1$–c'. A good test piece. Continuous baroque-type rhythm throughout with very few rests in the solo part for breathing or rest. Written in the middle tessitura; would work well with either bass or contrabass tuba.

Fischer, Ludwig. *Down Deep within the Cellar*. arr. Paul deVille. Carl Fischer Inc. 1906. Out of Print. See: deVille, Paul, *Pleasant Hours*, under Tuba and Keyboard Collections.

Fischer, Ludwig. *Down in the Deep Deep Cellar*. arr. Herbert Wekselblatt. G. Schirmer Inc. 1972. 1:29. III–IV. B♭$_1$–g. Classic old tuba tune in a theme and variations format. Some wide interval jumps, some arpeggios. Intermediate technique required. See: Wekselblatt, Herbert, *First Solos for the Tuba Player, BB♭*, under Tuba and Keyboard Collections.

Fischer, Ludwig. *Here I Sit in the Deep Cellar*. arr. Lloyd Conley. Kendor Music, Inc. 1981. 4:00. II–III. F_1–f. Novelty theme and (a couple of) variations style with cadenza. Novelty based on playing low F's for effect.

Fleming, Robert. *Concerto for Tuba*. Canadian Music Centre. 1966. Dedicated to Robert Ryker. See: Fleming, Robert, *Concerto for Tuba*, under Tuba and Orchestra.

Fletcher, John, arr. and ed. *Tuba Solos (BB♭ Bass) Volume One*. Chester Music. 1982. $9.95. See: Fletcher, John, *Tuba Solos (Tuba in C), Volume One*, in this section.

Fletcher, John, arr. and ed. *Tuba Solos (E♭ Bass) Volume One*. Chester Music. 1982. $9.95. See: Fletcher, John, *Tuba Solos (Tuba in C), Volume One*, in this section.

Fletcher, John, arr. and ed. *Tuba Solos (Tuba in C) Volume One*. Chester Music. 1982. $9.95. II–III. Contains: Berlioz, Hector, *Sanctus;* Martin, Easthope, *Hey-Ho, Come to the Fair;* Schubert, Franz, *Der lindenbaum;* Sullivan, Arthur, *Oh, Is There Not One Maiden Breast?;* Sullivan, Arthur, *The Policeman's Song;* Sullivan, Arthur, *When Britain Really Ruled the Waves.*

Flowers, Herbie. *Tuba Smarties*. arr. Danzil Stephens. Obrasso. III.

Foley, Red. *Just a Closer Walk*. arr. Bill Boyd, ed. Charles Daellenbach. Hal Leonard Publishing Corp. 1992. 1:03. I. B♭$_1$–c. Arrangement cleverly switches octaves from original to preserve beginning level. Some accidentals, easy syncopation. Comes with practice/performance cassette. See: Daellenbach, Charles, *Book of Beginning Tuba Solos*, under Tuba and Keyboard Collections.

Follas, Ronald W. *Concert Piece for Tuba and Band*. TUBA Press. 1982. $8.00. 11:30. Suggested by Sherman Botts of Des Moines, and David Lewis, Principal Tuba of the North Carolina Symphony. First performed by David Lewis with the East Carolina University Symphonic Wind Ensemble on April 18, 1982, with Herbert L. Carter conducting. Very accessible piano reduction. See: Follas, Ronald W., *Concert Piece for Tuba and Band*, under Tuba and Band. See review in *TUBA Journal*, Vol. 10, No. 4, Page 31.

Foremny, Stephan. *Sonatine für Tuba und Klavier*. manuscript. 1983. 4:57 (2:09, 1:46, 1:02). III. (G_1) B♭$_1$–c'. Gemachlich; Langsam und ausdrucksvoll; Lustig. Completed September 1983. Very musical solo with no major technical problems. Some counting with eighth note as the beat; some leaps of a sixth. Good recital material.

Foremny, Stephan. *Zwei Charakterstuke*. Manuscript. 1992. 2:41 (1:33, 1:08). III. A_1–b. Dolente; Allegretto. Conservative modern melodic language. Some accidentals, syncopation; no technical problems.

Forez, Henri. *Opus Open*. Written for Tuba and harpsichord.

Foster, Stephen. *Camptown Races*. arr. Sandy Feldstein. CPP/Belwin, Inc. 1990. I. B♭$_1$–G. See: Feldstein, Sandy, *First Solo Songbook*, under Tuba and Keyboard Collections.

Foster, Stephen. *Gentle Annie*. arr. Stephen Shoop. Stephen Shoop Music Publications. 2004. I. 3:30. $6.00. D–g. Fine transcription of this well-known early American ballad. Shoop has provided very useful commentary including the text of the ballad and some suggested listening. Excellent for the beginner to develop her or his legato and expressive playing.

Foster, Stephen. *Jeanie with the Light Brown Hair.* arr. Patrick Sheridan and Rich Ridenour. Patrick-Sheridan. com (Bon Bons Series). $12.00.

Foster, Stephen C. *Foster Medley.* arr. Hiroyuki Yasumoto. Toa Music International Co. 1986. 4:06. III. D–g. Andante; Allegretto; Andante. Includes: *Old Black Joe; Nelly Bly; and My Old Kentucky Home.* Very lyrical transcription. No technical problems. See: Yasumoto, Hiroyuki, *Tuba Volume #1,* under Tuba and Keyboard Collections.

Fote, Richard. *Tubadour.* Kendor Music, Inc. 1971. $4.50. 1:13. I. B♭$_1$–B♭. Moderato. A few eighth notes, a few accidentals. Good slightly advanced beginning solo. Comes with song sheet.

Fotek, Jan. *Sonata Romantica per tuba e pianoforte.* Wspolczesna Muzyka Polska. 1985. 20:00. V. E♭$_1$–a♭. Largo Dramatico; Andante Tranquillo; Presto. Zdzislawowi Piernikowi. In three movements. Big piece—endurance required. Wide interval skips, quickness of articulation, wide range.

Frackenpohl, Arthur. *Basso Tomaso.* TUBA Press. 1992. In preparation.

Frackenpohl, Arthur. *Concertino for Tuba and String Orchestra.* Robert King Music Co. & Alphonse Leduc. 1967. $5.85. Written for Abe Torchinsky. See: Frackenpohl, Arthur, *Concertino for Tuba and String Orchestra,* under Tuba and Orchestra.

Frackenpohl, Arthur. *Sonata for Tuba and Piano.* Kendor Music, Inc. 1982. $10.50. 13:20 (4:30, 4:50, 4:00). IV–V. G$_1$♭–c'. Three movements: Fast; Slowly; Lively. For Harvey Phillips. First movement: Some mixed meter, syncopation. Second movement: Legato, lyrical modal/pentatonic feel. Opportunities for great expression. Third Movement: Some mixed meter, syncopation. Good recital piece! See review in *TUBA Journal,* Vol. 11, No. 2, Page 21. Also see: Bird, Gary, ed.; *Program Notes for the Solo Tuba.*

Frackenpohl, Arthur. *Tubarag.* Tuba-Euphonium Press. 1999. 3:00. III. A$_1$–c'. Dedicated to Anne Hardin and Andrew Hyman. Solo in the style of a rag. See listings under Music for Tuba and Band and Music for Tuba and Mixed Ensemble.

Frackenpohl, Arthur. *Variations for Tuba and Piano (The Cobblers Bench).* Shawnee Press. 1973. $6.00. 5:30. For Peter Popiel. See: Frackenpohl, Arthur, *Variations on "The Cobbler's Bench,"* under Tuba and Band. See review in *TUBA Journal,* Vol. 1, No. 2, Page 10, and Vol. 7, No. 4, Page 25. Recorded by Ronald Davis, Peter Popiel.

Françaix, Jean. *Petite Valse Européene.* Schott's Soehne. 1980. $11.95. "pour tuba et double quintette a vents." Piano reduction. Composed in 1979. See: Françaix, Jean, *Petite Valse Européene,* under Tuba and Mixed Ensemble.

Franck, Maurice. *Prélude, arioso et rondo.* Éditions Musicales Transatlantiques. 1969. 6:00. V. A♭$_1$–b♭'. A Paul Bernard, professeur au Conservatoire National Supérieur de Musique. "pour Saxhorn en Si♭, et Trombone Basse ou Tuba et Piano." "Concours du Conservatoire National Supérieur de Musique de Paris (1969)." Requires great flexibility and great range. Mixed meter. For French tuba. See: Thompson/Lemke; *French Music for Low Brass Instruments.*

Franck, Melchior. *Allemande.* arr. Stephan Schwotzer. Hofmeister. 1993. 1:12. II. D–c. In cut time with no technical problems. See: Meschke, Dieter, *Zum Uben und Vorspielen/B-Tuba,* under Tuba and Keyboard Collections.

Franck, Melchior. *Galliarde.* arr. Stephan Schwotzer. Hofmeister. 1993. 1:04. II. C–d. Allegro. In 3/4 time. See: Meschke, Dieter, *Zum Uben und Vorspielen/B-Tuba,* under Tuba and Keyboard Collections.

Frangkiser, Carl. *Cavern Impression, A.* Belwin. 1941. Out of Print. 4:00. III. F$_1$–g. Theme and variations utilizing much step-wise motion.

Frangkiser, Carl. *Melodie Romanza.* Belwin. 1946. Out of Print. 2:55. III. A$_1$–f. Typical theme and variations using turns, triplets, scales.

Frank, Marcel. *Scherzo.* Available from the composer. 1972. 3:30. IV. E♭–d♭'. Light solo that would be accessible to the strong high school player.

Fredrickson, Thomas. *Tubalied for Tuba and Contemporary Wind Ensemble or Piano.* 1975. Commissioned by TUBA and premiered in Carnegie Hall, October 29, 1975, by Daniel Perantoni, tuba. See: Fredrickson, Thomas, *Tubalied for Tuba and Contemporary Wind Ensemble,* under Tuba and Mixed Ensemble. Recorded by Daniel Perantoni.

Frid, G. *Little Birch Tree, A.* ed. A. Lebedev. Moscow Muzyka. 1984. 0:40. II–III. D–d. Mostly unaccompanied entrances. Meter is 3/4, 3/4, 2/4. See: Lebedev, A., *Tuba Tutor Vol. 1,* under Tuba and Keyboard Collections.

Friedman, Norman. *Sonare per Tuba e Piano.* Southern Music Company. 1974. $2.50. 2:55 (0:46, 1:14, 0:55). IV–V. G–e'. Allegro; Andantino; Moderato. Modern melodic writing. Some glissandos, large dissonant leaps. Flexibility required.

Friedrich, Kenneth, D. *Six Airs for Euphonium or Tuba, Vol. 1.* Kenneth Friedrich. 2004. $30.00.

Friedrich, Kenneth, D. *Six Airs for Euphonium or Tuba, Vol. 2.* Kenneth Friedrich. 2004. $30.00.

Frith, John. *Tuba Treat.* Camden Music. 1993. $9.00. G$_1$–d'. Dedicated to Tessa. A good encore piece for the end of a recital. No extreme range demands and idiomatically well written for the tuba.

Fritze, Gregory. *Basso Concertino.* Manuscript. 1987. Synthesizer reduction (or piano). See: Fritze, Gregory, *Basso Concertino,* under Tuba and Mixed Ensemble. Also see: Bird, Gary, ed.; *Program Notes for the Solo Tuba.* Recorded by Gregory Fritze.

Fritze, Gregory. *Sonata for Tuba and Piano.* Manuscript. 1976. 12:43 (3:20, 2:28, 6:55). V. C♯$_1$–b♭'.

To Chester Roberts, for all those train rides to Boston. Three numbered movements. Completed 12/1/76. Very wide glissandos, mixed meter, tricky rhythms, quick dissonant articulation patterns. Requires a mature approach, lyrically and rhythmically. Multiphonics, cadenzas for both players. See: Bird, Gary, ed.; *Program Notes for the Solo Tuba.*

Fucik, Julius. *Der Alte Brummbär.* arr. Norbert Studnitzky. Musikverlag Wilhelm Halter GmbH. 1987. "Polka comique fur Solo-Tuba (od. Bariton) op. 210." Piano reduction. Was published by Molenaar in 1964.

Fux, Johann Joseph. *Allegro.* arr. Gerd Philipp. Hofmeister. 1993. 1:25. II. D–e♭. A little dance in 3/4 time. One F–e♭ leap; no other technical problems. See: Meschke, Dieter, *Zum Uben und Vorspielen/B-Tuba,* under Tuba and Keyboard Collections.

Gabaye, Pierre. *Tubabillage.* Alphonse Leduc. 1959. $12.80. 3:10. III. C–e'. "pour Tuba Ut ou Contrebasse à Cordes ou Saxhorn basse Si♭ ou Trombone basse et Piano." For French tuba. Some duples in 6/8 section; plenty of slurring and staccato; good intermediate solo. See: Thompson/Lemke; *French Music for Low Brass Instruments.*

Gagneux, Renaud. *Sonate.* Available from Spaeth and Schmid. $14.50.

Galán, Carlos. *Tuba Mirum.* Op. 35.

Galliard, Johann Ernst. *Sonata I in A Minor.* arr. John Glenesk Mortimer. Editions Marc Reift. 1999. $11.00 (Complete set of six Sonatas $31.00). 6:00 depending on repeats. III. F_1 (C_1)–a. Cantabile; Moderato spiritoso; Largo; Hornpipe; Vivace. Available individually or as a compilation of all six sonatas. The tessitura lends itself to tubas in all keys, in bass clef concert pitch, or in treble clef in E♭ or B♭. See listing under Tuba and Organ.

Galliard, Johann Ernst. *Sonata II in G Major.* arr. John Glenesk Mortimer. Editions Marc Reift. 1999. $11.00 (Complete set of six Sonatas $31.00). 5:30 depending on repeats. II–III. G_1 (D_1)–g (a). Andante; Vivace; Alla siciliana; Allegro siciliana. Available individually or as a compilation of all six sonatas. The tessitura lends itself to tubas in all keys, in bass clef concert pitch, or in treble clef in E♭ or B♭. See listing under Tuba and Organ.

Galliard, Johann Ernst. *Sonata III in F Major.* arr. John Glenesk Mortimer. Editions Marc Reift. 1999. $11.00 (Complete set of six Sonatas $31.00). 5:30 depending on repeats. III. F_1 (C_1)–g. Largo; Allegro; Quasi recitativo; Allegro spiritoso. Available individually or as a compilation of all six sonatas. The tessitura lends itself to tubas in all keys, in bass clef concert pitch, or in treble clef in E♭ or B♭. See listing under Tuba and Organ.

Galliard, Johann Ernst. *Sonata IV in E Minor.* arr. John Glenesk Mortimer. Editions Marc Reift. 1999. $11.00 (Complete set of six Sonatas $31.00). 7:00 depending on repeats. III. G_1 (E_1)–g. Adagio non troppo; Adagio; Allemanda—Moderato; Corrente—spiritoso; Menuetto. Available individually or as a compilation of all six sonatas. The tessitura lends itself to tubas in all keys, in bass clef concert pitch, or in treble clef in E♭ or B♭. See listing under Tuba and Organ.

Galliard, Johann Ernst. *Sonata V in D Minor.* arr. John Glenesk Mortimer. Editions Marc Reift. 1999. $11.00 (Complete set of six Sonatas $31.00). 6:00 depending on repeats. II–III. A_1–g. Adagio; Allegro spiritoso; Alla siciliana; Allegro assai. Available individually or as a compilation of all six sonatas. The tessitura lends itself to tubas in all keys, in bass clef concert pitch, or in treble clef in E♭ or B♭. See listing under Tuba and Organ.

Galliard, Johann Ernst. *Sonata VI in C Major.* arr. John Glenesk Mortimer. Editions Marc Reift. 1999. $11.00 (Complete set of six Sonatas $31.00). 8:00 depending on repeats. III. G_1 (C_1)–a. Larghetto; Allegro; Sarabanda; Menuet; Menuetto. Available individually or as a compilation of all six sonatas. The tessitura lends itself to tubas in all keys, in bass clef concert pitch, or in treble clef in E♭ or B♭. See listing under Tuba and Organ.

Galliard, John Ernest. *Sonata No. 5.* arr. Wesley Jacobs. Encore Music Publishers. 1991. $15.00. IV. $B♭_1$–e♭'. Adagio; Allegro e spiritoso; Alla Siciliana; Allegro assai. Good transcription of standard brass work. Recorded by Roger Bobo.

Galliard, John Ernest. *Sonata No. 6.* arr. Wesley Jacobs. Encore Music Publishers. 1989. $15.00. III–IV. G_1–g. Larghetto; Alla breve; Sarabanda; Menuett. Good transcription of standard brass work.

Garbarino, Giuseppe. *Sonata per Tuba (Contrabasso) and Piano.*

Gardonyi, Zoltan. *Sonate.* Available from Spaeth and Schmid. $18.25.

Garlick, Antony. *Fantasia.* Seesaw Music Corporation. 1974. $6.00. 7:00. IV. ($E_1$) $G♯_1$–c'. for Carter Leeka. Andante. Completed November 1, 1993. Has two improvised sections using given pitches. Short multi-phonic section. Chromatic glissando. Conservative modern writing.

Garrett, James. *Sonata for Tuba and Piano.* 1970. Manuscript. See review in *TUBA Journal,* Vol. 1, No. 1, Page 7.

Gartenlaub, Odette. *Essai.* Éditions Rideau Rouge. 1970. F_1–g♯'. French tuba and piano. For bass saxhorn, tuba, or bass trombone and piano. See: Thompson/Lemke; *French Music for Low Brass Instruments.*

Garth, J. *Concerto for Tuba.* Henri Elkan. 1960. French tuba and piano.

Gasner, Moshe. *Science Fiction.* Kibutz Movement League of Composers. Recorded by Adi Hershko.

Gatty, A. S. *Lights Far Out at Sea.* arr. Paul deVille. Carl Fischer Inc. 1906. Out of Print. See: deVille, Paul, *Pleasant Hours,* under Tuba and Keyboard Collections.

Gaubert, Philippe. *Madrigal.* arr. Angelo Manzo. Tuba-Euphonium Press. 2001. IV–V. C–f♯'. Transcription of a flute and piano work. Mainly linear lines requiring fast technique.

Gaucet, Charles. *Adagio and Finale from concertino.* ed. Himie Voxman. Rubank, Inc. 1972. 4:30. III–IV. F_1–f. "for BB♭ Bass." Adagio in 12/8 time. Allegro has several technical scale passages. Very expressive transcription of French tuba piece. See: Voxman, Himie, *Concert and Contest Collection,* under Tuba and Keyboard Collections.

Geib, Fred. *Caprice.* Mills Music. 1941. Out of Print. 3:10. III. A_1–a. "In B flat Minor, Op. 4." Dramatic solo in D♭ major/B minor with cadenza. Triplets, scales, dotted rhythms; intermediate-level technique required.

Geib, Fred. *Cavatina.* arr. R. Forst. Mills Music. 1940. Out of Print. 2:30. III. F_1–f. Composed for and Dedicated to The Pennsylvania Forensic and Music League. Andante maestoso. Opus 6. Crisp, light articulation required; some octave jumps; no big technical problems.

Geib, Fred. *Heroic Tale, A.* arr. Frost. Carl Fischer Inc. 1942. $3.25. 3:30. III. G_1–a. Opus 25. "Tuba E♭—C—BB♭." Slow tempo, no outstanding technical problems.

Geib, Fred. *In Solemn Mood.* Stephen Shoop Publications. 2004. 2:00. I–II. G_1–a♭. A low, lyrical piece suitable for beginners.

Geib, Fred. *In the Deep Forest.* Briegel. 1941. Out of Print. 3:00. III. $B♭_1$–a♭. Theme and variations with cadenza. Opus 20.

Geib, Fred. *Introduction and Polka Piquante.* Mills Music. 1946. Out of Print. 5:05. III. B_1–e♭'. Opus 27. A good polka-style solo using mostly stepwise motion. Cadenza uses full range of piece.

Geib, Fred. *The Jolly Sailor.* Stephen Shoop Publications. 2004. 2:30. II. $E♭_1$–a♭. A fine little sea shanty with detached style.

Geib, Fred. *Joyous Dialogue, A.* Mills Music. 1941. Out of Print. "Tuba Solo or Duet." Opus 11. See: Geib, Fred, *Joyous Dialogue, A.,* under Music for Multiple Tubas/Two Parts.

Geib, Fred. *Melody.* arr. Frank Morse. Carl Fischer Inc. 1940. $4.00. 9:00. III–IV. G_1–b♭. Opus 9. Long theme and (five) variations solo. See review in *TUBA Journal,* Vol. 9, No. 3, Page 25.

Geib, Fred. *Nocturne.* arr. R. Forst. Mills Music. 1941. Out of Print. 2:00. II–III. $A♭_1$–g. Opus 7. Some sixteenth notes.

Geib, Fred. *Reverie.* Stephen Shoop Publications. 3:00. II. 2004. F_1–f. A predominantly low and legato slow piece. A good teaching piece for expressive, low playing.

Geib, Fred. *Rustic Polka.* Stephen Shoop Publications. 2004. 3:00. II–III. A–g. A simple tune consisting of a theme and polka section. Includes a cadenza.

Geib, Fred. *Serenade.* arr. R. Forst. Mills Music Inc. 1941. Out of Print. 2:35. II–III. (F_1) A_1–g. Opus 10. Some sixteenth note runs using scales and outlining triads; intermediate technique required.

Geib, Fred. *Song without Words—Air with Variations.* Carl Fischer Inc. 1939. $4.00. 5:00. III–IV. C–b♭ (f'). "Tuba E♭ or BB♭." Theme and (four) variations. High total range for the time period (optional). Intermediate technique required.

Geib, Fred. *Spanish Caprice.* Stephen Shoop Publications. 2004. 3:00. II–III. A♭–a♭. A generally lyrical solo with an opening section requiring considerable technical facility.

Geib, Fred. *Valse.* Stephen Shoop Publications. 2004. 3:30. II–III. B♭–b♭'. Some fairly wide intervallic skips requiring a moderate level of agility and flexibility, but predominantly running eighth note figurations.

Geier, Oskar. *Conzertstuck für Tuba mit Klavierbegleitung.* Musikverlag Barbara Evans. IV.

Gendel, Scott. *Effusion.* Tuba-Euphonium Press. 2003. 6:00. IV–V. E_1–f♯'. Dedicated to James Mitchell. Many meter shifts and angular melodic lines. Rhythmically demanding.

Genzmer, Harald. *Sonate.* Ries & Erler—Distributed by Carl Fischer. 1999. 14:00. IV–V. F_1–g'. Allegro, Lento, Vivace. There are no exceptional technical demands or extreme range considerations. Very idiomatic writing for the tuba with some very challenging moments for the piano. A well-crafted sonata.

George, Thom Ritter. *Concertino for Tuba.* Manuscript available from composer. 1984. See: George, Thom Ritter, *Concertino for Tuba and Wind Ensemble,* under Tuba and Band and under Tuba and Orchestra. Also see: Bird, Gary, ed.; *Program Notes for the Solo Tuba.*

George, Thom Ritter. *Sonata for Tuba and Piano.* Tuba-Euphonium Press. $18.00. 13:57 (2:46, 4:20, 3:18, 3:33). IV–V. $E♭_1$–g'. Vivace e con brio; Vivace assai; Ballad: Mesto (Molto cantabile); Ben ritmato. Major work for tuba and piano. Large tonal jumps and quick articulations will test technique. Well worth the effort! Good recital material. Very lyrical, hypnotic muted second movement. Mixed meter not always notated. Strong accompanist required. See review in *TUBA Journal,* Vol. 9, No. 2, Page 24. Also see: Bird, Gary, ed.; *Program Notes for the Solo Tuba.* Recorded by Daniel Perantoni, David Randolph.

German, Edward. *Romance.* arr. Angelo Manzo. Tuba-Euphonium Press. 2001. 5:00. III–IV. C♯–d'. Good romantic transcription with minor technical passages in the mid- to upper tessitura.

Gerschefski, Edwin. *"America" Variations for Winds.* American Composer's Edition. 1963. $3.15. 1:30. III–IV. $A♭_1$–b♭. Maestoso. Op. 45, no. 1. Solo in 12/8 time; a disjointed, interesting impression of "America."

Gershenfeld, Mitchell, ed. *Medici Masterworks Solos Volume 1.* Medici Music Press. 1985. $10.00. II–III. Contains: Buononcini, Giovanni, *Pupille Nere;* Dargomijsky, Aleksander S., *Nur Lieben!;* Dvorak, Antonin, *Gypsy Melody;* Humperdinck, Engelbert, *Children's Prayer;* Rubenstein, Anton, *Be Not Shy, My Pretty One;* Tchaikovsky, Peter I., *At the Dance.*

Giordani. *My Dearest Love.* arr. Luther Henderson. Solid Brass Music Company. $4.50. II. The popular *Caro mio ben* set in a rock ballad style. Includes cassette.

Giordani, Giuseppe. *Arietta.* arr. Stephan Schwotzer. Hofmeister. 1993. 1:51. II. E♭–e♭. Slow tempo; no technical problems. See: Meschke, Dieter, *Zum Uben und Vorspielen/B-Tuba,* under Tuba and Keyboard Collections.

Giordani, Giuseppe. *Caro mio ben.* arr. Hiroyuki Yasumoto. Toa Music International Co. 1986. 2:15. II. E♭–e♭. Larghetto. All tenuto or slurred. Very vocal approach needed. No technical problems. See: Yasumoto, Hiroyuki, *Tuba Volume #1,* under Tuba and Keyboard Collections.

Giordani, Giuseppe. *Love Song (Caro mio ben).* ed. Charles Daellenbach. Hal Leonard Publishing Corp. 1992. 1:55. II. $B\flat_1$–d. Larghetto. A few eighth/sixteenth dotted rhythms in C major in 4/4 time with a couple of grace notes and accidentals. See: Daellenbach, Charles, *Book of Easy Tuba Solos,* under Tuba and Keyboard Collections.

Giordani, Giuseppe. *My Dearest Love. (Caro mio ben.)* arr. Luther Henderson and ed. Charles Daellenbach. Hal Leonard Publishing Corp. 1989. $14.95. 3:10. III. E♭–g. Rock ballad style. Commercial/popular version of this aria in a rock style. Some syncopation. With performance cassette. See review in *TUBA Journal,* Vol. 18, No. 2, Page 19.

Giovanini, J. *Challenge Concert Polka.* arr. Carl Weber. J. W. Pepper & Son. 1914. Out of Print. See: Weber, Carl, *Nineteen Solos for E♭ Bass with Piano Accompaniment,* under Tuba and Keyboard Collections. Also see: Giovanini, J., *Challenge Concert Polka,* under Tuba and Band.

Gistelinck, E. *Koan II.* Editions Andel Uitgave.

Glass, Jennifer. *Sonatina for Tuba and Piano.* Emerson Edition. 1979. $18.75. 8:00. IV. E_1–f'. To John Fletcher. Allegro non troppo; Lento; Tempo di valse; Presto. Composed in 1963. Wonderful solo that allows for many musical moods—a good tuba showcase. Some mixed meter, glissandos. Strong technique required. See: Bird, Gary, ed.; *Program Notes for the Solo Tuba.* Recorded by John Fletcher.

Glazunov, A. *Chant du Menestrel.* arr. Velvet Brown. Velvet Music Edition.

Gliere, Reinhold. *Intermezzo.* arr. James Graham. TUBA Press. 1991. IV. $B\flat_1$–c'. Andante cantabile. (Horn) Opus 35, No. 11. See: Graham, James, *Concert Music for Tuba,* under Tuba and Keyboard Collections.

Gliere, Reinhold. *Nocturne.* arr. James Graham. TUBA Press. 1991. III–IV. G–d♭'. Andante. (Horn) Opus 35, No. 10. In 9/8 time. See: Graham, James, *Concert Music for Tuba,* under Tuba and Keyboard Collections.

Glinka, M. *Romance.* ed. S. Melnikov. Military Band Masters Institute–Moscow. 1957. See: Melnikov, S., *Pieces for Tuba and Piano,* under Tuba and Keyboard Collections.

Globokar, Vinko. *Juriritubaioka.* Available from Spaeth and Schmid. $45.00.

Glover, S. *Faith.* arr. Paul deVille. Carl Fischer Inc. 1906. Out of Print. See: deVille, Paul, *Pleasant Hours,* under Tuba and Keyboard Collections.

Glover, S. *Melodies of Many Lands, The.* arr. Paul deVille. Carl Fischer Inc. 1906. Out of Print. See: deVille, Paul, *Pleasant Hours,* under Tuba and Keyboard Collections.

Gluck, C. W. *Dance of the Blessed Spirits.* arr. Patrick Sheridan. PatrickSheridan.com (Lollipop Series). $12.00.

Gluck, Chr. *Air.* arr. Quinto Maganini. Edition Musicus. 1954. 2:20. III. E–c'. From Orpheus. In slow 3/4 time. See: Ostrander, Allen, *Concert Album for Tuba,* under Tuba and Keyboard Collections.

Gluck, Christoph W. von. *Melody from "Orpheus and Euridice."* arr. Denis W. Winter. Whaling Music Publishers. $7.00. Originally for flute and strings.

Gluck, K. *Gavotte.* ed. A. Lebedev. Moscow Muzyka. 1984. 1:59. III. E–c'. Written by Christolph Willibald Gluck. In cut time—A major and A minor. No technical problems. See: Lebedev, A., *Tuba Tutor Vol. 1,* under Tuba and Keyboard Collections.

Godel, Didier. *Concerto.* Editions Marc Reift. 1992. $19.80. 14:00. IV. D_1–f'. Allegro non troppo; Modéré; Vivace. Piano reduction. For more information see Music for Tuba and Orchestra.

Godfrey, Fred. *Lucy Long.* arr. Harris, A. E. Cundy-Bettoney/Carl Fischer Inc. 1934. Out of Print. 6:00. III–IV. B_1–c'. Theme and Variations. High tessitura, large leaps.

Goedicke, A. *Dance.* ed. A. Lebedev. Moscow Muzyka. 1984. 0:52. II. D–e♭. In 4/4 time and in D minor. A few eighth notes; no technical problems. See: Lebedev, A., *Tuba Tutor Vol. 1,* under Tuba and Keyboard Collections.

Goedicke, A. *Improvisation.* Mitjagina, V. ed. Muzkya, Moscow. 1969. 1:22. IV. D_1–a♭ (c'). Adagio sostenuto. Melodic writing utilizing middle and lower range. Other than range, no big technical problems. See: Mitjagina, V. ed., *Pieces for Tuba and Piano,* under Tuba and Keyboard Collections.

Goedicke, Alexander. *Concert Etude, Op. 49.* arr. Rudy Emilson. Kendor Music, Inc. 2000.

\$8.00. 3:00. III–IV. A_1–a♭ (d'). Depending on the tempo, this can be a very challenging little piece. It can serve as an encore on a professional recital or a test piece for younger players. A fine arrangement of this familiar trumpet etude. Requires excellent multiple tonguing facility.

Goeller, Dan. *Misty Morning Ride.* Tuba-Euphonium Press. 1996. 6:00. IV. C_1–c'. Dedicated to Dick Cale. Rhythmically challenging work requiring multiphonics and some speaking into the instrument.

Goeyens, A. *All'Antica.* arr. Forrest L. Buchtel. Neil A. Kjos Music Company. 1975. \$5.00. 3:47. III. A_1–g. "Tuba E♭ or BB♭." Baroque style; sixteenth note scale-wise movement, some octave jumps, trills (one mordent); otherwise intermediate technique required. See review in *TUBA Journal,* Vol. 7, No. 1, Page 9.

Goeyvaerts, Karel. *Plikonamu—Micucona.* Available from Spaeth and Schmid. \$10.25.

Gold, Thomas. *5 Terrains 5 Contemporary Pieces.* Available from Spaeth and Schmid. \$29.25.

Goldsmith, James J. *Pastorale.* arr. David R. Werden. Whaling Music Publishers. 1980. \$9.50. 6:07. IV–V. D–e'. For Tucker Jolly. "for Tuba or Euphonium." Upper tesitura—would lie better on E♭/F tuba although possible on lower instrument. Almost a "new age" feel to this lovely piece. Requires endurance, musicality, and flexibility (some sextuplets). Good recital material.

Golland, J. *Scherzo for Tuba.* Hallamshire. Recorded by Stephen Sykes.

Golland, John. *Tuba Concerto.* Available from Spaeth and Schmid. \$23.00.

Goltermann, Georg Edvard. *Concerto No. 4, Opus 65 (Excerpts from).* arr. William J. Bell. Carl Fischer Inc. 1937. \$5.00. 4:40. III–IV. F_1–b♭. Classic tuba transcription of excerpts from cello concerto. Differentiation between triplets and dotted rhythms a consideration. R. Winston Morris suggests putting a dot on the third note of each slurred triplet to separate.

Goode, Jack C. *Tune for Tuba (Sonatina for Tuba and Piano).* Pro Art Publications. 1969. Out of Print. 3:50. III. G_1–b♭. To Bob Danner. Good flowing, lyrical solo with plenty of opportunity for expression. Some slurred and staccato passages. No technical problems.

Goodwin, Gordon. *Alborada.* Southern Music Company. 1976. \$2.50. 3:26. III. C♯–f♯. For Heather Leigh Caffey, 1974. "Spanish-Dawn Song." Lovely little legato, flowing ballad. Requires a flexible tempo combined with bravura and lyricism. Some dissonant intervals, but manageable. Good recital material, even for the advanced player.

Gorb, Adam. *Straightjacket.* Editions BIM. 2002. 11:00. IV–V. Edition in progress.

Gotkovsky, Ida. *Baladins.* Éditions Robert Martin. 1983. \$4.25.

Gotkovsky, Ida. *Suite.* Editions Salabert. 1959. 7:05. V. G_1–b♭'. à Monsieur Paul Bernard, Professeur au Conservatoire National Supérieur de Musique de Paris. Introduction; Andante; Finale. "pour Tuba in ut et Piano." For French tuba. Some septuplets, many arpeggios, much scale-wise motion.

Gottschalk, Arthur. *Sonata for Bass Tuba.* Available from Composer. 2002. 8:00. V. E♭$_1$–e'. Three movements: 1. 5/8; 2. 3/4; 3. 2/4. Written with Abe Torchinsky, Warren Deck, and David Kirk in mind. A challenging work written very idiomatically for the instrument. Each movement has its own character and requires very good rhythmic control in addition to excellent fingering technique in the last movement. A very worthy composition. Best performed on CC tuba.

Gounod, Charles. *Calf of Gold from "Faust."* arr. Allen Ostrander. Edition Musicus. 1965. \$2.75. 2:30. II–III. C–e♭. Allegro Maestoso. For trombone, baritone, or tuba with piano. Stately solo in 6/8 time.

Gounod, Charles. *Funeral March of a Marionette.* arr. Igor Hudadoff; William Westcott, piano arr. Pro Art Publications. 1967. Out of Print. See: Hudadoff, Igor, *Fifteen Intermediate Tuba Solos,* under Tuba and Keyboard Collections.

Gounod, Charles. *March of a Marionette.* arr. Harold L. Walters. Rubank, Inc. 1965. \$2.50. II–III. G_1–a. "Solo E♭ or BB♭ Bass." Very characteristic solo (think Alfred Hitchcock!) in 6/8 time. No technical problems.

Gounod, Charles. *March of a Marionette.* arr. Herbert Wekselblatt. G. Schirmer Inc. 1972. 1:23. III. C–g. Allegretto. Twice through the tune in 6/8 time. See: Wekselblatt, Herbert, *First Solos for the Tuba Player, BB♭,* under Tuba and Keyboard Collections.

Gounod, Charles. *Valentine Song from "Faust."* arr. William J. Bell. CPP/Belwin, Inc. 1970. See: CPP/Belwin, *Tuba Solos, Level Two,* under Tuba and Keyboard Collections. Also see other listing in this section.

Gounod, Charles. *Valentine Song.* arr. William J. Bell. Belwin Mills, Inc. 1970. Out of Print. Separate publication out of print. See other listing in this section.

Gower, Albert. *Sonata.* The Brass Press. 1979. \$4.00. 8:57 (3:00, 2:00, 1:56, 2:01). IV. F_1–f♯'. TUBA Series. Four numbered movements. Was published by Brass Music, Ltd. Conservative modern writing. Some improvising based on given pitches with optional mute in second movement. See review in *TUBA Journal,* Vol. 1, No. 2, Page 10.

Gower, Albert. *Sonata for Tuba and Piano.* Editions Bim. 1979. \$11.80. 6:30. III. F♯$_1$–f♯'. Andante; As fast as possible; Lento; Allegro. Dialogue between tuba and piano in neoclassic style. The piano accompaniment is primarily in octaves. Otherwise the main harmony is the major seventh.

Gower, Albert. *Two Moods for Tuba and Piano.* Theodore Presser. 1995. $9.95. 3:56. G_1–g'. Pensive; Capricious. Dedicated to Tom Stein. Two short movements requiring expressive style and short bursts of high technique in the fast movement.

Gower, William. *Sonata for Tuba and Piano.* See review in *TUBA Journal,* Vol. 7, No. 2, Page 20.

Graap, Lothar. *Suite GWV 209.* Available from Spaeth and Schmid. $22.50.

Graetsch, Hans. *Tuba Kapriolen.* Regina. Piano reduction of tuba and band piece.

Graham, James, arr. *Concert Music for Tuba.* TUBA Press. 1967. $12.00. II–IV. Was published by DePauw University Bands in 1967. Contains: Brahms, J., *Waltz;* Corelli, A., *Sonata No. 10, Opus 5;* Corelli, A., *Sonata No. 9, Opus 5;* Gliere, Reinhold, *Intermezzo;* Gliere, Reinhold, *Nocturne;* Handel, G. F., *Chorus from Judas Maccabaeus;* Mozart, W. A., *Concert Rondo;* Mozart, W. A., *Concerto in D (K. 412);* Mozart, W. A., *Concerto in E flat (K. 417);* Mozart, W. A., *Concerto in E flat (K. 447);* Mozart, W. A., *Concerto in E flat (K. 495);* Saint-Saëns, C., *Romance;* Schumann, R., *Adagio and Allegro;* Scriabine, A., *Romance;* Strauss, R., *Concerto, Opus 11;* Strauss, R., *Second Horn Concerto.*

Granados, E. *Playera.* arr. Igor Hudadoff; William Westcott, piano arr. Pro Art Publications. 1967. Out of Print. See: Hudadoff, Igor, *Fifteen Intermediate Tuba Solos,* under Tuba and Keyboard Collections.

Granados, E. *Spanish Dance No. 2 (Oriental).* tr. J. Amaz. Union Musical Espanola. 1970.

Granados, E. *Spanish Dance No. 5 (Andaluza).* tr. J. Amaz. Union Musical Espanola. 1970.

Grant, Parks. *Concert Duo.* American Composer's Edition. 1954. $8.20. 4:50. V. D_1–e'. "for Tuba and Piano, Op. 48." Conservative contemporary writing. Double tonguing, mixed meter, dissonant intervals, wide range.

Gray, Louis Robert. *Impromptu in G, Op. 7, No. 1.* Boosey & Hawkes, Inc. 1954. Out of Print. 4:45. III. F_1–g. BB♭ bombardon solo. Typical technical solo with cadenza. Conservative intermediate range and technique required. Solo part in treble clef.

Gregor, Frantisek. *Konzertetüde.* ed. Václav Hoza. Editio Supraphon, Praha. 1982. 3:17. IV. G_1–c'. Allegro moderato. Good technical solo. Arpeggios, scales, accents; very playable. See: Hoza, Václav, *Schule Fur Tuba in F und in B,* in Methods and Studies.

Gregson, Edward. *Tuba Concerto.* Novello & Company. 1976. $22.00. For John Fletcher. See: Both listings for Gregson, Edward, *Tuba Concerto,* under Tuba and Band and under Tuba and Orchestra. Also see: Bird, Gary, ed.; *Program Notes for the Solo Tuba.* Recorded by John Fletcher, Michael Lind, Josef Maierhofer, Lennart Nord, Michael Wagner. Refer also to review in *TUBA Journal,* Vol. 6, No. 2, Page 9.

Gregson, Edward, and John Ridgeon. *Nine Miniatures.* Brass Wind Publications. I–II. For E♭ Bass/E♭ tuba. Solos with easy piano accompaniments. Treble and bass clef versions available.

Gretchaninoff, A. *Slumber Song.* arr. Ken Swanson. CPP/Belwin, Inc. 1971. $4.00. 2:20. II–III. $B♭_1$–g. Andantino. Relaxed tempo solo in 4/4 time. A couple of octave jumps from G to g; otherwise no technical problems.

Gretchaninoff, A. *Slumber Song.* arr. Ken Swanson. CPP/Belwin, Inc. 1971. See: Lamb, Jack, *Solo Sounds for Tuba Levels 3–5, Vol. 1,* under Tuba and Keyboard Collections. Also see other listing in this section.

Gretry, Andre. *Air from "Richard Coeur de Lion."* arr. Peter Wastall. Boosey & Hawkes, Inc. 1980. 1:06. I. E♭–e♭. See: Wastall, Peter, *Learn As You Play Tuba,* under Tuba and Keyboard Collections. Stately beginning solo that would be easier on E♭ versus BB♭ for the beginning student. Easy accompaniment.

Grieg, E. *In Spring Time.* ed. A. Lebedev. Moscow Muzyka. 1986. 2:26. IV. C♯–c♯'. Very melodic solo in 6/4 time. See: Lebedev, A., *Tuba Tutor Vol. 2,* under Tuba and Keyboard Collections.

Grieg, Edvard. *In the Hall of the Mountain King.* arr. Fred Weber. CPP/Belwin, Inc. 1973. $4.00. 2:00. II. D–f. Published separately. Good scene-setting instructions from Fred Weber. An accelerando occurs throughout entire piece. Some grace notes, some accidentals. See other listing in this section.

Grieg, Edvard. *In the Hall of the Mountain King.* arr. Fred Weber. CPP/Belwin, Inc. 1973. See: Lamb, Jack, *Solo Sounds for Tuba Levels 3–5, Vol. 1,* under Tuba and Keyboard Collections. See other listing in this section.

Grieg, Edvard. *In the Hall of the Mountain King.* arr. G. E. Holmes. Rubank, Inc. 1939. "Solo Tuba—E♭ or BB♭ tuba." See: In the Hall of the Mountain King under Tuba and Band. Also see: Rubank, *Soloist Folio for Bass (E♭ or BB♭),* under Tuba and Keyboard Collections.

Grieg, Edvard. *In the Hall of the Mountain King (from "Peer Gynt").* arr. Herbert Wekselblatt. G. Schirmer Inc. 1972. 2:13. II–III. D–f♯. Slowly at first then faster. Classic solo with accelerando and some grace notes. See: Wekselblatt, Herbert, *First Solos for the Tuba Player, BB♭,* under Tuba and Keyboard Collections.

Grieg, Edvard. *Last Saturday Evening, The.* ed. Charles Daellenbach. Hal Leonard Publishing Corp. 1992. 1:16. II. (G_1) $B♭_1$–d. Andantino. In 6/8 time and in G minor. Some accidentals. See: Daellenbach, Charles, *Book of Easy Tuba Solos,* under Tuba and Keyboard Collections.

Grieg, Edvard. *My Johann.* arr. Neal Corwell. Kendor Music, Inc. 1988. $5.00. 2:00. II–III. C–g. Allegretto tranquilla e grazioso. Fun transcription for advanced beginner. Liberties with tempos, articulations (including grace notes) will all enhance performance. Good recital material.

Grøndahl, Terje. *Concerto for Tuba and Piano.* Warwick Music Limited. 2003.

Gross, Eric. *Thoughts of Sunraysia.* Manuscript. 1990. 4:00. Opus 172, No. 1.

Gross, Eric. *Tubism.* Manuscript. 1990. 5:15. Opus 172, No. 2.

Gruber. *Silent Night.* arr. Acton Ostling. CPP/Belwin, Inc. 1969. 1:03. I–II. ($A\flat_1$) C–d♭. Adagio cantabile. Melody in A♭ major with a five-bar tag. A few slurs, no technical problems. See: CPP/Belwin, Inc., *Tuba Solos, Level One,* under Tuba and Keyboard Collections.

Gruber. *Silent Night.* arr. Acton Ostling. CPP/Belwin, Inc. 1969. I. See: Ostling, Acton, *Tuba (Bass) Soloist, Level One,* under Tuba and Keyboard Collections. Also see other listing in this section.

Grudzinski, Czeskaw. *Contraste per tuba e pianoforte.* P W. M. Kvakow. 7:12. IV. $G\sharp_1$–e'. Solid, very musical modern writing without many major technical challenges. Conservative tempos. Good introduction to modern melody.

Grundman, Clare. *Tuba Rhapsody.* Boosey & Hawkes, Inc. 1976. $15.50. To Martin D. Erickson, Tuba Soloist, and the U. S. Navy Band. (Optional cut lowers duration to 6:50.) See: Grundman, Clare, *Tuba Rhapsody,* under Tuba and Band. Recorded by Lesley Varner.

Grunelius, Wilhelm von. *Drei lyrische Szenen.* Available from Spaeth and Schmid. $24.25.

Grunelius, Wilhelm von. *Tuba-Triptychon.* Available from Spaeth and Schmid. $20.00.

Gruner, Joachim. *Konzert für Tuba und Orchester.* Bensheimer Verlag. 1977. Recorded by Dietrich Unkrodt.

Gubaidulina, Sofia. *Lamento for Tuba and Piano.* Hal Leonard Corporation. 1991. 6:00 III–IV. F_1–b♭. A work that demands a great deal of musical maturity. Many rubato moments with rhythmic crescendi and decrescendi occurring frequently. Repetitive piano accompaniment. Contrasting slow work for an intermediate recital program.

Gudmen, S. *Dance.* arr. A. Lebedev. Military Band Masters Faculty of Moscow Conservatiore. 1971. See: Lebedev, A., *Collection of Pieces for Tuba "Es" and Piano,* under Tuba and Keyboard Collections.

Guentzel, Gus. *Mastodon.* Mills Music. 1945. 5:00. II–III. $A\flat_1$–f. "for tuba or B♭ Bass Saxophone." Very repetitive polka-style solo for advanced beginner. Conservative range and mostly step-wise motion. Cadenza and lyrical Andante section in addition to running sixteenth note passages in 2/4 time. Good confidence builder.

Guinot, Georges-Léonce. *Simplex pour tuba et piano.* Gérard Billaudot. 1990. 1:25 or 2:00. II. c–c'. "pour tuba et piano." For French tuba. Lyrical playing; no big technical problems. Two durations depending on optional cuts. See: Daniel-Lesur, *Collection Panorama,* under Tuba and Keyboard Collections.

Guion, David M. *Sonata for Tuba.* Available from the composer. 1970–72. 8:00. IV. $A\flat_1$–b. Lento; Misterioso; Allegro. Completed San Diego, Calif., September 14, 1972. Some flutter tonguing. Conservative modern melodic language. Conservative range. Solid writing for tuba and piano.

Gully, Michel. *Recit.* Éditions M. Combre. 1988. 2:15. II. A♭–c'. "pour Tuba ou Saxhorn Basse Si♭ et Piano." For French tuba. Easy rhythms: a few eighth notes at a medium tempo. No technical problems. Good recital material.

Gulya, Robert. *Burlesque.* Editions Bim. 2001. $11.80. 3:40. V. B_2–c". Dedicated to Roland Szentpáli. Extremely high tessitura. Partly written in tenor clef. Wide atonal leaps. interesting harmonies and rhythms. Requires strong pianist.

Gurlitt, Cornelius. *Andante from "First Steps" op. 82.* arr. Peter Wastall. Boosey & Hawkes, Inc. 1980. 0:51. I. D–B♭. See: Wastall, Peter, *Learn As You Play Tuba,* under Tuba and Keyboard Collections. As the title indicates, good melodic, "carefully nurturing," first solo in 3/4 time. Very limited range—fastest rhythm is quarter note. Some step-wise slurring; appropriate to difficulty level.

Guy, Earl. *Carry Me Back to Old Virginny.* arr. G. E. Holmes. Rubank, Inc. 1935. Out of Print. 5:00. III. $G\flat_1$–f. "BB♭ Bass (Sousaphone)." Theme, variation, obligato, two cadenzas, a finale; a "*Carry Me Back to Old Virginny* celebration!" Intermediate technique and planning ahead breath-wise required. Fun solo to play.

Guzii, V., compiled. *Pieces for Tuba and Piano.* Moscow Muzyka. 1976. Contains: Castérède, Jacques, *Fantaisie Concertante;* Ruff, D., *Concert Piece;* Tomasi, Henri, *Etre ou ne pas être.*

Guzii, V., compiled. *Pieces for Tuba and Piano.* Moscow Muzyka. 1978. Contains: Bitch, M., *Ritcherkar;* Hartley, V., *Concertino;* Kikta, V., *Concert for Tuba and Orchestra;* Kling, G., and G. Neuling, *Grand Cadence.*

Haddad, Don. *Scherzino.* Southern Music Company. 1990. $3.50. 1:20. IV. F–c'. Allegro. Would lie well on F tuba; very playable on lower instrument. Needs lightness of articulation with drive at printed tempo. Resembles a quick Irish jig.

Haddad, Don. *Suite for Tuba.* Shawnee Press, Inc. 1966. $10.00. See: Haddad, Don, *Suite for Tuba,* under Tuba and Band. Recorded by Ronald Davis, Rex Conner.

Haddad, Don. *Two Pieces.* Southern Music Company. 1990. $4.00. 2:49 (1:32, 1:17). III. D♭–c'. Andantino; Allegretto. Lyrical and easy rhythmical playing. Good recital material.

Hailstork, Adolphus C. *Duo.* Fema Music Publications. 1981. $5.00. 7:00. V. E_1–c''. For John Turk. Demanding piece from both a technical and musical point of view. Very wide range, mixed meters, quick articulations, flutter tonguing, tricky rhythms. Will take a strong player.

Haines, Edmund. *Modules.* GunMar Music, Incorporated. 1982. $20.00. 10:00. V. $B\flat_1$–f'. Slow; Quite Fast; Very Slow; Dialogue; Fast. For Charles English. Original copyright was 1972 (April 4, 1972, Riverdale), Composers Facsimile Edition. Movements may be played in any order. Very free, unmeasured playing combined with traditional notation. Improvised and random order passages. Flutter tonguing, compound meters, trills; strong technique required. Upper tessitura; best on F tuba.

Halévy, Jacques. *Cardinal's Air from "La Juive," The.* arr. Frank Clark. Edition Musicus. 1965. $2.75. 1:55. III. G_1–e. Andante. For trombone, baritone, or tuba and piano. Slow solo in 2/4. A few eighth note triplets, a short cadenza; no technical problems.

Hall. *Concertante.* Available from Spaeth and Schmid. $5.00.

Hall, Harry H., arr. *Menuet.* Brodt Music Company, Inc. 1962. 1:12. II. D–e♭. "German Folk Song." Simple 24-measure tune in 3/4 time with repeats. A few eighth notes; no technical problems.

Hanby, B. R. *Up on the Housetop.* arr. Sandy Feldstein. CPP/Belwin, Inc. 1990. I. $B\flat_1$–G. See: Feldstein, Sandy, *First Solo Songbook,* under Tuba and Keyboard Collections.

Handel, Georg Friedrich. *As When the Dove.* arr. Velvet Brown. Velvet Music Edition.

Handel, Georg Friedrich. *Concerto Nr. 1 in g-moll.* arr. Walter Hilgers. Editions Marc Reift. 1995. $16.00. 10:30. IV. D–c'. Grave; Allegro; Sarabande—Largo; Allegro. Originally for oboe, Händel Werk Verzeichnis 287, this arrangement is set in the middle register, and requires a solid technical and lyrical approach. Good recital material. Recorded by Walter Hilgers.

Handel, Georg Friedrich. *Dido's Lament.* arr. Velvet Brown. Velvet Music Edition.

Handel, Georg Friedrich. *Prélude et Fugue.* arr. Kurt Sturzenegger. Editions Marc Reift. 1996. $11.80. 5:00. III. F–d'. Because this arrangement was possibly conceived for the bass trombone, the tessitura is set in the middle range and works well on the F tuba. See listing under Tuba and Organ.

Handel, Georg Friedrich. *Tuba Concerto.* ed. Roy Newsome. Obrasso-Verlag Ag. 4:30. III–IV. $E\flat_1$–e♭'. Courante; Sarabande; Gigue. Available with treble clef E♭ part or bass clef tuba part. Piece functions more as a three-movement baroque sonata transcription rather than as a concerto in the classical sense. Melodic writing is typically baroque and the outer movements work well for a intermediate performer. The second movement would work at this level as well if performed down an octave.

Handel, George Frederick. *Adagio and Allegro from Sonata No. 7.* ed. Himie Voxman. Rubank, Inc. 1972. 4:30. III. $B\flat_1$–f. "for E♭ or BB♭ Bass." Adagio in 8 with trills. Attacca Allegro section in 4/4 time with trills, with melody based on inverted triads. See: Voxman, Himie, *Concert and Contest Collection,* under Tuba and Keyboard Collections.

Handel, George Frederick. *Air.* arr. A. Lebedev. Military Band Masters Faculty of Moscow Conservatiore. 1971. See: Lebedev, A., *Collection of Pieces for Tuba "Es" and Piano,* under Tuba and Keyboard Collections.

Handel, George Frederick. *Allegro.* tr. Ronald C. Dishinger. Medici Music Press. 1982. $3.50. 2:26. II. $B\flat_1$–e♭. "from *Concerto Grosso Opus 3, No. 4.*" Distinctions between staccato and tenuto marks as well as dynamics need to be made. Some eighth note scale-like figures, otherwise no technical problems.

Handel, George Frederick. *Allegro from Concerto in F Minor.* arr. Robert M. Barr. Ludwig Music Publishing Company. 1968. $4.00. 2:10. IV. C–b♭. Allegro. Very good transcription. Mostly contains sixteenth note scale-wise runs. Pre-planning breaths will help. Good recital material.

Handel, George Frederick. *Andante.* arr. Allen Ostrander. Edition Musicus. 1954. 3:20. II–III. C–g. Andante Sostenuto. Well-transcribed solo with eighth note as the beat. Good continuo accompaniment. Good recital material (even for an advanced player). See: Ostrander, Allen, *Concert Album for Tuba,* under Tuba And Keyboard Collections.

Handel, George Frederick. *Aria from "Judas Maccabeus."* arr. Harry H. Hall. Brodt Music Company, Inc. 1962. 3:57. II–III. G_1–e♭. Larghetto. Slow sustained lyrical playing. A few slow octave jumps, a few "low" tones, otherwise very accessible to the advanced beginner.

Handel, George Frederick. *Arioso.* arr. Piet de Rooij. Molenaar N. V. 1966. 1:30. III–IV. d–f'. Works well on F tuba. High tessitura for lower instruments. No other technical challenges.

Handel, George Frederick. *Arm, Arm, Ye Brave from "Judas Maccabeus."* arr. Allen Ostrander. Edition Musicus. 1959. $3.00. 3:20. II–III. B_1–e. Andante and Allegro section using a very conservative range. Attention should be paid to articulation: slurred dotted rhythms, staccato notes within slurs. Good transcription.

Handel, George Frederick. *Bouree.* ed. A. Lebedev. Moscow Muzyka. 1984. 1:23. III. D–b. Same as other arrangements of this in this section with a few changed notes. In G major. See: Lebedev, A., *Tuba Tutor Vol. 1,* under Tuba and Keyboard Collections.

Handel, George Frederick. *Bouree.* arr. Quinto Maganini. Edition Musicus. 1954. 1:20. III.

F♯–c'. From the Sixth Flute Sonata. Flexibility required. See: Ostrander, Allen, *Concert Album for Tuba,* under Tuba And Keyboard Collections. Recorded by Rex Conner, Peter Popiel.

Handel, George Frederick. *Bouree.* ed. S. Melnikov. Military Band Masters Institute–Moscow. 1957. See: Melnikov, S., *Pieces for Tuba and Piano,* under Tuba and Keyboard Collections.

Handel, George Frederick. *Bourrée.* arr. Ken Swanson. CPP/Belwin, Inc. 1970. $4.00. 1:36. II. B♭$_1$–f. Moderato. Cut time baroque solo using eighth notes as fastest rhythm. A variety of articulations (staccato, tenuto, slurs) should not be overlooked. See other listings in this section.

Handel, George Frederick. *Bourrée.* arr. Ken Swanson. CPP/Belwin, Inc. 1970. See: Lamb, Jack, *Classic Festival Solos,* under Tuba and Keyboard Collections. Also see other listing in this section.

Handel, George Frederick. *Bourrée.* arr. Ken Swanson. CPP/Belwin, Inc. 1970. See: CPP/Belwin, *Tuba Solos, Level Two,* under Tuba and Keyboard Collections. Also see other listings in this section.

Handel, George Frederick. *Chorus from Judas Maccabaeus.* arr. James Graham. TUBA Press. 1991. II–III. G–g. Maestoso. See: Graham, James, *Concert Music for Tuba,* under Tuba and Keyboard Collections.

Handel, George Frederick. *Concerto No. 3 for Tuba and String Orchestra.* arr. Hiroyuki Yasumoto. Toa Music International Co. 1946. III–IV. D–c'. Grave; Allegro; Largo; Allegro. See: Yasumoto, Hiroyuki arr., *Tuba Volume #2,* under Tuba and Keyboard Collections.

Handel, George Frederick. *Dove Sei from "Rodelinda."* arr. Donald C. Little. See review in *TUBA Journal,* Vol. 7, No. 4, Page 27.

Handel, George Frederick. *Harmonious Blacksmith, The.* arr. Paul deVille. Carl Fischer Inc. 1906. Out of Print. See: deVille, Paul, *Pleasant Hours,* under Tuba and Keyboard Collections.

Handel, George Frederick. *Honor and Arms.* arr. Russell Harvey. G. Schirmer Inc. 1940. $3.00. 4:45. III. (G$_1$) A$_1$–e♭. "from the oratorio 'Samson'." More slurring and tenutos in this arrangement as compared to Bill Bell's arrangement. In comparison this version also has more repeats, and an added section.

Handel, George Frederick. *Honor and Arms.* arr. William J. Bell. CPP/Belwin, Inc. 1965. $4.00. 1:56. II–III. (G$_1$) B♭$_1$–e♭. Plenty of unison with piano for self-confidence in this arrangement. Stately transcription. Some slurring and as in Bill Bell's notes: "played in a very forceful style just as a fine basso would sing it." See other listing in this section.

Handel, George Frederick. *Honor and Arms.* arr. William J. Bell. CPP/Belwin, Inc. 1965. See: Lamb, Jack, *Solo Sounds for Tuba Levels 3–5, Vol. 1,* under Tuba and Keyboard Collections. Also see other listing in this section.

Handel, George Frederick. *Konzert g-Moll.* arr. Mark Evans. Musikverlag Barbara Evans.

Handel, George Frederick. *Larghetto and Allegro.* arr. Donald C. Little. Figured bass realization by Belden, George R. CPP/Belwin, Inc. 1978. $4.00. 4:44. II–III. B♭$_1$–e♭. Larghetto (3/4 time) section followed by an extended Allegro section in 3/8 time. Many sixteenth notes, mostly in step-wise motion. Will require flexibility and facility. Good advanced beginner/early intermediate work. See other listing in this section. Also see review in *TUBA Journal,* Vol. 7, No. 3, Page 35.

Handel, George Frederick. *Larghetto and Allegro.* arr. Donald C. Little. Figured bass realization by George R. Belden. CPP/Belwin, Inc. 1978. See: Lamb, Jack, *Classic Festival Solos,* under Tuba and Keyboard Collections. Also see other listing in this section.

Handel, George Frederick. *Lento.* ed. Charles Daellenbach. Hal Leonard Publishing Corp. 1992. 1:16. II. C♯–c. In 3/2 time. Quarter note is fastest rhythm. A few accidentals. Good introduction to 3/2. See: Daellenbach, Charles, *Book of Easy Tuba Solos,* under Tuba and Keyboard Collections.

Handel, George Frederick. *Love that's true will live forever (Si, Tra I Ceppi, from "Berenice").* arr. James Ord Hume. Boosey & Co. 1906. Out of Print. See: Hume, J. Ord, *Boosey's Bombardon Solo Album,* under Tuba and Keyboard Collections.

Handel, George Frederick. *Menuet from "Alcina."* arr. Harry H. Hall. Brodt Music Company, Inc. 1962. $1.50. 2:30. II. G$_1$–d. Gracefully. Some slurring; eighth note is fastest rhythm; no technical problems.

Handel, George Frederick. *Recitative and Air from "The Messiah."* arr. Charles O'Neill. Waterloo Music Co. 1948. Out of Print. 4:30. III. D♭–b♭. Sustained aria.

Handel, George Frederick. *Repentance.* ed. Charles Daellenbach. Hal Leonard Publishing Corp. 1992. 1:37. II. C–d♭. Adagio. "Chi sprezzando" from *The Passion.* Some large leaps; some accidentals. In 3/4 time with a feeling of six throughout. See: Daellenbach, Charles, *Book of Easy Tuba Solos,* under Tuba and Keyboard Collections.

Handel, George Frederick. *Revenge! Timotheus Cries!* arr. R. Winston Morris. Ludwig Music Publishing Company. 1970. $3.50. 1:35. III. C♯–e. Allegretto. "from *Alexander's Feast.*" Requires lightness of articulation and attention paid to dynamic contrast. Key of D major; conservative range. Good transcription.

Handel, George Frederick. *Sarabande from Concerto in F Minor.* arr. Robert Barr. Ludwig Music Publishing Company. 1968. $4.00. 2:20. II–III. (F$_1$) A♭$_1$–a♭. Largo. Slow 3/4 time solo with a couple of dotted eighth/sixteenth notes.

A few slurs, some optional F_1's. Probably closer to level II, but requires musical intensity.

Handel, George Frederick. *See, the Conquering Hero Comes.* arr. Paul deVille. Carl Fischer Inc. 1906. Out of Print. See: deVille, Paul, *Pleasant Hours,* under Tuba and Keyboard Collections.

Handel, George Frederick. *Sonata No. 6.* tr. R. Winston Morris. Shawnee Press, Inc. 1982. $8.00. 8:30. IV. D–e'. Adagio; Allegro; Largo; Allegro. Composed for violin in E major; transposed to F. Very playable transcription. Adagio in 8, eighth note getting the beat. Some trills included. Requires flexibility and good baroque conception. Four contrasting movements; good opportunity for conceptual variety.

Handel, George Frederick. *Sonate C-Dur für Tuba und Klavier/Orgel.* Bearbeitung: Hilgers, Walter. Editions Marc Reift. 1990. $20.25. 10:54 (2:17, 2:41, 2:24, 1:35, 1:45). IV–V. G–d'. Larghetto; Allegro; Larghetto; Tempo di Gavotte; Allegro. Good transcription from the Sonata for Recorder and Basso Continuo, op. 17. Very full transcription; almost no rests! Challenging musically and technique-wise. Quick articulations, flexibility, and endurance are all factors. Conservative range. Recorded by Walter Hilgers.

Handel, George Frederick. *Sound an Alarm from "Judas Maccabeus."* arr. Clifford P. Barnes. Jack Spratt Music Co. 1965. $3.00. 1:59. III. B♭$_1$–f. Allegro. Sprightly transcription in 6/8 time. Depending on tempo chosen, slurred sixteenth notes could present a challenge; otherwise no big technical problems.

Handel, George Frederick. *Suite in A-flat.* arr. Donald C. Little. See review in *TUBA Journal,* Vol. 7, No. 4, Page 27.

Handel, George Frederick. *Thrice Happy the Monarch from "Alexander Balus."* arr. R. Winston Morris. Ludwig Music Publishing Company. 1970. $5.00. 2:50. III. G_1–f. Allegro. Composed in 1748. Also arranged for trombone, baritone (t.c. and b.c.), or cornet and piano. Transcribed solo in 3/8 time (felt in one). Some sixteenth note runs; some moving in thirds; otherwise flowing solo has no technical problems.

Handel, George Frederick. *Two Short Pieces.* ed. Himie Voxman. Rubank, Inc. 1972. 3:00. II–III. (A_1) B♭$_1$–f. Aria; Bourée. "for E♭ or BB♭ Bass." Aria from Rinaldo in 3/2 time. Bourée in cut time. Both very recognizable. See: Voxman, Himie, *Concert and Contest Collection,* under Tuba and Keyboard Collections.

Handel, George Frederick. *Variations.* arr. A. Lebedev. Military Band Masters Faculty of Moscow Conservatiore. 1971. See: Lebedev, A., *Collection of Pieces for Tuba "Es" and Piano,* under Tuba and Keyboard Collections.

Handel, George Frederick. *Where'er You Walk (from Semele).* arr. Ken Swanson. Belwin Mills, Inc. 1971. Out of Print. 3:35. II. C–d. Moderato. Published separately; see other listings in this section. A few accidentals; a few tonal jumps of a sixth and seventh; mostly scale-wise movement.

Handel, George Frederick. *Where'er You Walk (from Semele).* arr. Ken Swanson. CPP/Belwin, Inc. 1971. See: Lamb, Jack, *Classic Festival Solos,* under Tuba and Keyboard Collections. Also see other listing in this section.

Handel, George Frederick. *Where'er You Walk (from Semele).* arr. Ken Swanson. CPP/Belwin, Inc. 1971. See: Lamb, Jack, *Solo Sounds for Tuba Levels 1–3, Vol. 1,* under Tuba and Keyboard Collections. Also see other listing in this section.

Hanmer, Ronald. *Tuba Tunes.* Emerson Edition. 1979. $10.75. 3:49 (0:50, 1:03, 1:11, 0:45). II. E♭–a♭. Sostenuto (Allegro moderato); Staccato (Allegretto); Cantabile (Andante espressivo); Scherzando (Allegro). Advanced beginner level for E♭ tuba; more difficult for BB♭ due to tessitura. Four contrasting cute vignettes, fun musically and good opportunity for expression. No technical problems. See review in *TUBA Journal,* Vol. 8, No. 4, Page 28.

Hanson, Raymond. *Romance.* Australian Music Centre.

Hanson, Ronald D. *Variations on a Theme for Tuba and Piano.* Edition Musicus. 1980. $6.00. 8:30. V. E♭$_1$–b♭'. Dedicated to Barton Cummings. One-movement work. Extreme range; high tessitura. Glissandos, very wide interval jumps. Complex time signatures. Piece requires a performer with a good ear and strong technique.

Harlow. *Old Home Down on the Farm.* arr. Forrest L. Buchtel. Neil A. Kjos Music Company. 1958. Out of Print. 7:30. III–IV. F_1–g (b♭). Technical theme and variations.

Harmon, John. *Call of the River.* Available from Spaeth and Schmid. $15.25.

Harmon, John. *Silhouette.* Available from Spaeth and Schmid. $13.50.

Harris, Floyd O. *Dancing Silhouettes.* Ludwig Music Publishing Company. 1980. $4.00. 3:49. III. B♭$_1$–f. To my son, Dean A. Harris. For trombone, bassoon, baritone (b.c.), or tuba and piano. Old-style characteristic waltz. Some slurring, some grace notes, cadenza; no technical problems.

Harris, Floyd O. *King's Jester, The.* Ludwig Music Publishing Company. 1950. $3.50. 2:07. II. D–e♭. Allegro. "Solo for E♭, BB♭ Bass." For trombone, baritone (b.c.), or tuba and piano. Solo in 6/8 time with short cadenza. Mostly step-wise motion; no technical problems.

Harris, Floyd O. *Little Caesar.* Ludwig Music Publishing Company. 1982. $3.50. 2:23. II. (E♭$_1$) C–d (e♭). Marcato. Original copyright was 1955. "Solo for E♭, BB♭ Bass, Trombone or Baritone." A 6/8 march using mostly step-wise motion. No technical problems.

Harris, Floyd O. *Little Fiesta.* Ludwig Music Publishing Company. 1950. $3.50. 2:31. II. D–e♭. "E♭, BB♭ Bass." "Polka-Tango, Spanish rhythm." Simple polka-style solo in 2/4 time with a cadenza. Conservative range; no technical problems. Good advanced beginner solo.

Harris, John H. *Tempesta Polka.* Carl Fischer Inc. 1896. $3.25. See: Harris, John H., *Tempesta Polka,* under Tuba and Band. See review in *TUBA Journal,* Vol. 9, No. 3, Page 25.

Hart, Lorenz, and Richard Rodgers. *Blue Moon.* arr. Sandy Feldstein. CPP/Belwin, Inc. 1990. I. $B\flat_1$–G. See: Feldstein, Sandy, *First Solo Songbook,* under Tuba and Keyboard Collections.

Hartley, V. *Concertino.* ed. V. Guzii. Moscow Muzyka. 1978. See: Guzii, V., *Pieces for Tuba and Piano,* under Tuba and Keyboard Collections.

Hartley, Walter S. *Aria for Tuba and Piano.* Elkan-Vogel, Inc. 1968. $3.95. 2:27. III–IV. $b\flat_1$–$b\flat$. Allegretto. "Tuba Part may be played by Bassoon or Euphonium." Composed in 1967. Lyrical modern writing. Part should be harmonically analyzed for greater understanding. Some sixteenth note runs will need work; no other big technical problems.

Hartley, Walter S. *Concertino for Tuba and Wind Ensemble.* Theodore Presser Company. 1969. $21.00. See: Hartley, Walter S., *Concertino for Tuba and Wind Ensemble,* under Tuba and Band. Recorded by John Turk.

Hartley, Walter S. *Fantasia for Tuba and Chamber Orchestra.* Wingert-Jones Music, Inc. 1991. $8.00. Commissioned by Scott Watson with a General Research Grant from the University of Kansas. Composed in 1989. Piano reduction. See: Hartley, Walter S., *Fantasia for Tuba and Chamber Orchestra,* under Tuba and Orchestra.

Hartley, Walter S. *Largo for Tuba and Piano.* Philharmusica Corp. 1974. $7.50. 3:40. IV–V. F_1–f♯'. Dedicated to Michael Lind. Lyrical solo in 6/8 time with a pulse of 6. Wide range; some high and low tessitura with subtle dynamics.

Hartley, Walter S. *Sonata for Tuba and Piano.* Theodore Presser Company. 1967. $9.50. 6:00. IV. G_1–a. Andante; Allegretto grazioso; Adagio sostenuto; Allegro moderato, con anima. Modern melodic writing. Conservative range for the level. Recorded by Robert LeBlanc. See: Bird, Gary, ed.; *Program Notes for the Solo Tuba.*

Hartley, Walter S. *Sonatina.* Fema Music Publications. 1970. $5.00. 6:00. IV. G_1–a. Allegretto; Largo Maestoso; Allegro Moderato. Composed in 1957. Originally published by Tenuto Press in 1958; Interlochen Press in 1961; Fema in 1970. Modern (tonal) writing. Requires flexibility. Recorded by Peter Popiel. See review in *TUBA Journal,* Vol. 1, No. 1, Page 7. Also see: Bird, Gary, ed.; *Program Notes for the Solo Tuba.*

Hartley, Walter S. *Sonatina Giocosa.* 1988.

Hartley, Walter S. *Sonorities for Tuba and Piano.* Philharmusica Corp. 1973. $8.50. C_1–g'. For Rudy Emilson. Adagio. Composed in 1972. Musical textures. Requires solid rhythm control (at a slow speed—some syncopation, quintuplets), wide range, and good modern melodic sense.

Hartley, Walter S. *Tuba Rose (Polka).* Theodore Presser Company. 1977. $2.50. 2:53. IV. $E\flat_1$–b. For Eric Abis. Allegro molto. Several sixteenth note ascending and descending chromatic scales throughout at a quick tempo. Traditional polka feel with a modern harmonic and melodic approach. Good recital piece.

Hartzell, Doug. *Egotistical Elephant, The.* Shawnee Press, Inc. 1967. $5.00. Optional solo instruments: bass clarinet; contra-bass clarinet; baritone saxophone; bassoon; bass trombone. See: Hartzell, Doug, *Egotistical Elephant,* under Tuba and Band.

Harville, Grant. *Concerto for Tuba and Orchestra.* arr. Grant Harville. Tuba-Euphonium Press. 2003. 12:00. IV–V. G_1–g'. Lento—Allegro; Adagio non troppo; Lento—Vivace. See listing under "Music for Tuba and Orchestra." A technically challenging work in three movements.

Hasse-Gower. *Menuet and Bourree.* Rubank, Inc. Out of Print. II.

Hastings, Ross. *Prelude and Faràndola.* TUBA Press. 1987. $8.00. See: Hastings, Ross, *Prelude and Farandola for Tuba and Band,* under Tuba and Band. Accompaniment also available for piano with tambour obligato.

Hatton, J. L. *Simon the Cellarer.* arr. Harry Prendiville. A. Squire. 1888. Out of Print. 1:12. II–III. ($B\flat_1$) C–f. In 6/8 time. "E♭ Bass; or, tuba With Piano or Organ Accompaniment, (ad lib.)." See: Prendiville, Harry, *Six Popular Solos,* under Tuba and Keyboard Collections.

Hatton, J. L. *Simon the Cellarer.* arr. James Ord Hume. Boosey & Co. 1906. Out of Print. See: Hume, J. Ord, *Boosey's Bombardon Solo Album,* under Tuba and Keyboard Collections.

Havens, Daniel. *Cancao.* Available from the composer. IV. Manuscript.

Hayden, Paul. *Chaconne for Tuba and Piano.* Magnolia Music Press. 1999. V. 6:30. C_1–g'. Commissioned and premiered by Joseph Skillen with assistance from the Louisiana Division of the Arts. The opening slow chaconne is based on a progression of six polychords. This opening is followed by eleven short variations. Excellent work with strong technical demands on the soloist and pianist. Written for bass tuba, but requires strong low register. Recorded by Joseph Skillen.

Haydn, Franz Joseph. *Allegro and Minuet.* arr. Igor Hudadoff; William Westcott, piano arr. Pro Art Publications. 1967. Out of Print. See: Hudadoff, Igor, *Fifteen Intermediate Tuba Solos,* under Tuba and Keyboard Collections.

Haydn, Franz Joseph. *Andante.* arr. Scherzer. Musikverlag Johann Kliment KG.

Haydn, Franz Joseph. *Haydn Medley, from Symphony No. 94.* arr. William J. Bell. CPP/Belwin, Inc. 1970. $4.00. 3:00. I. $B\flat_1$–e♭. Three short selections from the *"Surprise Symphony," String Quartets Op. 3,* #5, and *Op. 76,* #5. Suggested tempo is very slow, allowing for beginning level. Some sixteenth notes; at this tempo not a problem.

Haydn, Franz Joseph. *Haydn Medley (from Symphony No. 94).* arr. William J. Bell. CPP/Belwin, Inc. 1970. See: CPP/Belwin, *Tuba Solos, Level Two,* under Tuba and Keyboard Collections. Also see other listing in this section.

Haydn, Franz Joseph. *Papa Haydn's Tune.* arr. John Kinyon. M. Witmark & Sons. 1958. I. See: Kinyon, John, *Breeze-Easy Recital Pieces,* under Tuba and Keyboard Collections.

Haydn, Franz Joseph. *Sonata No. 7.* arr. Richard W. Bowles. CPP/Belwin, Inc. 1973. $4.00. 5:23 (3:50 without repeat in exposition). II–III. $F\sharp_1$–g. Allegro. First movement of Haydn's *Sonata* in sonata form. Good transcription in E♭ major in 4/4 time. Some sixteenth note step-wise runs, some slurs, no big technical problems.

Haydn, Franz Joseph. *Sonata No. 7* (first movement). arr. Richard W. Bowles. CPP/Belwin, Inc. 1973. See: Lamb, Jack, *Solo Sounds for Tuba Levels 3–5, Vol. 1,* under Tuba and Keyboard Collections. Also see other listing in this section.

Haydn, Franz Joseph. *Spacious Firmament on High, The.* arr. Don Little. CPP/Belwin, Inc. 1989. 1:55. I. B♭ C–$B\flat_1$. Limited range, easy rhythms (only a few eighth notes). See: Little, Don, *Solo-Pak for Tuba, Part One,* under Tuba and Keyboard Collections.

Haydn, Franz Joseph. *Trio 48.* tr. Paul Greenstone. PP Music. 1987. $10.00. 9:30 (4:02, 2:06, 3:22). III. $B\flat_1$–b♭. Allegro; Menuet; Finale. Originally for Baryton, Viola, and Cello in D major. Some sixteenth note (mostly step-wise) runs; no other technical problems. Good recital material, even for advanced player.

Haydn, Franz Joseph. *Two Classical Themes.* arr. Daniel Perantoni. Hal Leonard Publishing Corp. 1976. See: Perantoni, Daniel, *Master Solos Intermediate Level,* under Tuba and Keyboard Collections.

Haydn, J. *Hymn.* arr. Wesley Jacobs. Encore Music Publishers. 0:47. I–II. $B\flat_1$–e♭. Singing style. Some slurring and dotted rhythms. Eighth note is fastest rhythm. See: Jacobs, Wesley, *Solos from the Classics,* under Tuba and Keyboard Collections.

Haydn, J. *Spacious Firmament, The.* arr. Wesley Jacobs. Encore Music Publishers. 1:11. I. D–d. With vigor. In G major. A few eighth notes; some slurring; aside from key, no technical problems. See: Jacobs, Wesley, *Solos from the Classics,* under Tuba and Keyboard Collections.

Hayes, Al. *Solo Pomposo.* Carl Fischer Inc. 1911. $3.00. Was published by The Fillmore Bros. See: Hayes, Al, *Solo Pomposo,* under Tuba and Band.

Heiden, Bernard. *Concerto for Tuba and Orchestra.* Peer-Southern Concert Music. 1979. For Harvey Phillips. Composed under a grant from the National Endowment for the Arts. Piano reduction by the composer. Composed in 1976. See: Heiden, Bernard, *Concerto for Tuba and Orchestra,* under Tuba and Orchestra. See review in *TUBA Journal,* Vol. 9, No. 3, Page 23. Also see: Bird, Gary, ed.; *Program Notes for the Solo Tuba.*

Heinick, David. *Three Virtues.* David Heinick. 2003. 5:30. III–IV. $F\sharp_1$–d♭'. Simplicity; Enthusiasm; Serenity. A good recital work with conservative writing for the tuba. Tonally interesting, it would lie well on CC tuba in addition to being a workable piece on bass tuba. Second movement involves many metric shifts.

Heinl, Otto. *Bärentanz.* Musikverlag Wilhelm Halter GmbH. See: Heinl, Otto, *Bärentanz,* under Tuba and Band.

Heins, John. *Sonata for Tuba and Piano.* Available from the composer. Commissioned by Michael Taylor.

Helweg, Kim. *Shlag uns Nöch Liefdo.* SNYK. 23:00. 1994.

Henry, Jean-Claude. *Mouvement.* Alphonse Leduc. 1972. $14.95. 5:45. V. F_1–b'. à Paul Bernard. "pour Tuba, Saxhorn-basse Si♭ ou Trombone-basse et Piano." For French tuba. Very wide range required. Mixed and complex meters; cadenzas. Performer needs strong technique See: Thompson/Lemke; *French Music for Low Brass Instruments.*

Henry, Otto. *Passacaglia and Fugue.* Alphonse Leduc. 1963. 7:30. III–IV. C–f'. Originally written for bass trombone but very workable for tuba. Contains large interval leaps and metric shifts. Rhythmically complex.

Herbert, Victor. *Gypsy Love Song.* arr. Acton Ostling. CPP/Belwin, Inc. 1969. 1:02. I. $B\flat_1$–c. Once through the tune with a big finish. See: Ostling, Acton, *Tuba (Bass) Soloist, Level One,* under Tuba and Keyboard Collections.

Herbert, Victor. *Victor Herbert Medley.* arr. Acton Ostling. CPP/Belwin, Inc. 1969. 1:28. I. $B\flat_1$–d. *Toyland; Because You're You.* Once through each tune. Includes 3/4 and 4/4 time. See: Ostling, Acton, *Tuba (Bass) Soloist, Level One,* under Tuba and Keyboard Collections.

Heuberger, Richard. *Midnight Bells from the "Opera Ball."* arr. Patrick Sheridan. PatrickSheridan.com (Bon Bons Series). $12.00.

Hewitt, Harry. *Prelude No. 1, Opus 376B.* CSI Publication. IV. G_1–a. Part of *Six Preludes.* Available separately.

Hewitt, Harry. *Prelude No. 6, Opus 376C No. 6.* CSI Publication. 1973. 1:45. V. E_1–f♯'. Very low and high playing, 4/4, 5/4, 2/4 sections, modern melody. Composed in 1970. Part of *Twelve Preludes;* available separately.

Hewitt, Harry. *Six Preludes for Tuba and Piano, Op 376B.* CSI Publication. 1950–1970. 14:00. III–IV. G_1–f♯'. Rhythmic solos that can be performed individually or as a suite. Not difficult accompaniment. See review in *TUBA Journal,* Vol. 7, No. 2, Page 21.

Hewitt, Harry. *Sonata No. 1 for Tuba and Piano.* CSI Publication. 1941–1950. 23:30. IV–V. A♭$_1$–b♭. Long one-movement work.

Hewitt, Harry. *Sonata No. 2 for Tuba and Piano.* CSI Publication. 1972. 15:00. IV–V. F$_1$–f'. Four numbered movements. Opus 169, No. 2. Some high- and low-range playing, mostly in middle range. Some 5/8, 5/4 meters involved. Reviewed in *TUBA Journal,* Vol. 7, No. 2, Page 21.

Hewitt, Harry. *Twelve Preludes Tuba and Piano.* TUBA Press. 1973. $13.00. V. D$_1$–a'. Opus 376C. Very wide range required. Differing styles and meters, modern harmony and melody. Requires mature performers.

Hidas, Frigyes. *Allegro Vivace, for Tuba and Four Horns (or Piano)*. Uetz Music Publishers. $18.25. Recorded by Markus Hötzel and the German and American Horn Ensemble.

Hidas, Frigyes. *Scherzo, for Tuba and Four Horns (or Piano).* Available from Spaeth and Schmid. $18.25. For tuba and four horns or piano. See listing under Music for Tuba in Mixed Ensemble.

Hidas, Frigyes. *Tuba Concerto.* Available from Spaeth and Schmid. $32.50.

Higuet, N. *Larghetto e allegretto.* Available from Spaeth and Schmid. $8.00.

Hill, Mildred J. *Happy Birthday.* arr. John Glenesk Mortimer. Editions Marc Reift. 2000. $11.00. 2:00. II. D♭–g. Traditional; March; Valse; Tango. See Music for Tuba in Mixed Ensemble."

Hill, William H. *Conquistadores.* Neil A. Kjos Music Company. 1978. $1.75. 1:32. I. B♭$_1$–c. Moderately. Simple melody with some dotted quarters, some eighths, some slurs, limited range. See review in *TUBA Journal,* Vol. 7, No. 1, Page 8.

Hindemith, Paul. *Sonate. (Sonata for Bass Tuba and Piano.)* European American-Schott. 1955. $14.95. 10:20. IV. G$_1$–c'. Three numbered movements. One of the major pieces written by a master composer. First movement: Main theme uses a major ninth interval (add decay to notes; like a long bell tone). Requires fire and lyricism by both players. Differing meters between piano and tuba require different emphasis to eighths in 6/4 and 9/4 sections. Second movement: Practice with a metronome—especially last line. Work on tightness of ensemble. Third movement: Tempo will ultimately be decided by accompanist's technique. Stress vocal quality of the lines. Cadenza should be analyzed beat by beat initially; then add flexible pace. Listen to recordings for different conceptions of this major work. Familiarize yourself with the piano part as well as your own part. Recorded by Rudiger Augustin, Øystein Baadsvik, Roger Bobo, John Fletcher, Gerhard Georgie, Michael Lind, Daniel Perantoni, Gene Pokorny, Abe Torchinsky, John Turk. See: Bird, Gary, ed.; *Program Notes for the Solo Tuba.*

Hlouschek, Theodor. *Barockes Konzert.* Available from Spaeth and Schmid. $11.50.

Hobbs, Christopher. *Preludes.* Warwick Music Limited. $17.41.

Hobbs, Christopher. *12 Sketches.* Warwick Music. $17.50.

Hogg, Merle E. *Etude 1 for Tuba and Piano.* Music Graphics Press. 1978. $8.50. 7:08. IV–V. (C♯$_1$/D♭$_1$) E$_1$–d'. Composed in 1974. Fine contemporary writing. One-movement work with a lot of seventh and ninth intervals. Two cadenzas offer improvisatory possibilities: Optional multiphonic section; flutter tonguing. Some mixed and compound meters; some quin- and septuplets. Will take work, but worth it. Strong accompanist required. Good recital material. See review in *TUBA Journal,* Vol. 7, No. 3, Page 38.

Hogg, Merle E. *Sonatina for Tuba and Piano.* Lyceum Press. 1967. 8:45. IV–V. F$_1$–d♭'. Allegro; Larghetto; Allegro marcato. Solid piece for tuba and piano. Some possible double tonguing. See: Bird, Gary, ed.; *Program Notes for the Solo Tuba.*

Holliday, Kent. *Sonata for Tuba in F and Piano.* Available from the composer. 1991. 15:04 (5:23, 4:18, 5:59). IV–V. F$_1$–f♯'. Allegro Moderato; Andante Cantabile; Allegro Con Brio. For Skip Gray and Caryl Conger. Major work for tuba and piano. Requires two strong, musical players. Tubist has lyrical playing, dissonant and consonant large jumps. Strong technique and rhythmical sense needed. Good recital material.

Holmboe, Vagn. *Sonate for Tuba and Piano.* Wilhelm Hansen. 1985. Opus 162.

Holmes, G. E. *Carnival of Venice (Fantasia).* Rubank, Inc. 1937. $2.50. 5:00. III. F$_1$–g. "BB♭ Bass (Sousaphone)." Written for cornet or trumpet or tuba and piano. Theme and original technical variations on the classic tune. Good intermediate solo. See review in *TUBA Journal,* Vol. 9, No. 3, Page 25.

Holmes, G. E. *Emmett's Lullaby.* Rubank, Inc. 1933. $2.50. 5:30. III. F$_1$–f. Featured by William Bell, Bass Soloist with Armco Band and Cincinnati Symphony Orchestra. Was published for Tuba and Band. Good theme and variations solo. See review in *TUBA Journal,* Vol. 9, No. 3, Page 25.

Holmes, Paul. *Lento.* Shawnee Press, Inc. 1961. $4.00. IV. E$_1$–d. Composed March 1958. Very lyrical legato composition with two contrasting sections: Lento and Allegro non troppo. Lento section mostly slurred; Allegro section has gentle shifting meters (3/4, 4/4) and easy syncopations. Good recital material. Recorded by Robert LeBlanc, Ronald Davis, Rex Conner.

Holmgaard, Lars. *The Tubagig.* Amazing World Music. Available from SheetMusicNow.com. IV. 6:00. 2000. E♭$_1$–e♭'. While there is no tempo marking, this appears to be a rhythmically driving recital piece. Very few rests provided for the soloist, but an effective melodic design. Suitable for either bass or contrabass tuba.

Holstein, Jean Paul. *Triade.* Editions Choudens. 1973. C–g♯'. For French tuba. See: Thompson/ Lemke; *French Music for Low Brass Instruments.*

Hombsch. *Sonatine.* Available from Spaeth and Schmid. $11.50.

Hopkinson, Michael E. *Concerto for Tuba ("Concerto Euphonique").* Kirklees Music. 1978. 14:14 (5:05, 5:16, 3:53). E♭$_1$–e♭'. IV. Allegro moderato; Adagio; Allegro giocoso. Published for the Alexander Owen Memorial Fund Scholarship 1990. "for B♭ Soloist-B♭ Bass or Euphonium." Solo part in treble clef. Tonal technical and lyrical showcase. Flexibility for arpeggios needed. Optional lip slurs. Mixed meter. Good recital material.

Hopkinson, Michael E. *In Lively Spirits.* Kirklees Music. 1978. 4:30. IV. C–d'. A Re-working of Senaillè's *Andante and Allegro Spiritoso* for E♭ bass. Solo part in treble clef in C minor. A bit updated from the original with different jazzed-up rhythms and melodic twists.

Horovitz, Joseph. *Tuba Concerto.* Manuscript available from the composer. 1989. See: Horovitz, Joseph, *Tuba Concerto,* under Tuba and Band.

Howe, Marvin C., arr. *Three Tuba Solos.* Plymouth Music Co. 1965. $4.00. 6:08. III. G$_1$–g (a). Included: Bach, *Rondo from Suite in B Minor for Flute;* Pergolesi, *Spiritoso;* Purcell, *Next, Winter Comes Slowly.*

Hoza, Václav. *Ländler Für Tuba Und Klavier.* Editio Supraphon, Praha. 1982. 2:42. III. F$_1$–g. Moderato. Ländler style in a broad feeling of one. Fun to play. Eighth note is fastest rhythm. See: Hoza, Václav, *Schule Fur Tuba in F und in B,* in Methods and Studies.

Hoza, Vaclav. *Schule Fur Tuba in F und in B.* Edio Supraphon, Praha. 1983. II–V. Some tuba and piano pieces included in this method book. See *Schule Fur Tuba in F und in B* under Methods and Studies. Includes: Blodek, Vilém, *Arie Janeks Aus Der Oper "Im Brunnen";* Gregor, Frantisek, *Konzertetüde;* Hoza, Václav, *Ländler Für Tuba Und Klavier;* Hoza, Václav, and Hála, Jan, *Mosaik;* Hrdina, Eman, *Slow-Fox-Medium;* Hrdina, Eman, *Walzer;* Hrdina, Eman, *Westernstil;* Kubes, Ladislav, *Alte Bekannte.*

Hoza, Václav, and Jan Hála. *Mosaik.* Editio Supraphon, Praha. 1982. ca. 6:00. V. B♭$_1$–d' (f'). Appasionato. Very modern writing: free rhythms, flutter tonguing, multi-phonics, trills, modern notation with explanations. See: Hoza, Václav, *Schule Fur Tuba in F und in B,* in Methods and Studies.

Hrdina, Eman. *Slow-Fox-Medium.* ed. Václav Hoza. Editio Supraphon, Praha. 1982. 1:14. III. F$_1$–b♭. Slow. Fox trot with syncopation. "Big band" accents. See: Hoza, Václav, *Schule Fur Tuba in F und in B,* in Methods and Studies.

Hrdina, Eman. *Walzer.* ed. Václav Hoza. Editio Supraphon, Praha. 1982. 0:55. II–III. E♭$_1$–B. Tempo di waltz. Low-middle tessitura. Pretty waltz. A couple of very low pitches, otherwise no big technical problems. See: Hoza, Václav, *Schule Fur Tuba in F und in B,* in Methods and Studies.

Hrdina, Eman. *Westernstil.* ed. Václav Hoza. Editio Supraphon, Praha. 1982. 1:35. II–III. F$_1$–g. Foxtrot. Simple foxtrot tune. Some syncopation. Fastest rhythm is eighth note. See: Hoza, Václav, *Schule Fur Tuba in F und in B,* in Methods and Studies.

Huber, Adolf. *Concertino No. IV, Theme from.* arr. J. S. Price. Carl Fischer Inc. 1938. $4.00. 1:35. II. B♭$_1$–d. Moderato. Op. 8. Good interpretive solo for an advanced beginning student. Musically satisfying and obtainable. Eighth note is fastest rhythm. Utilize ritard in last line.

Hubert, P. *Dans les pins.* Thomi-Berg. For French tuba.

Hudadoff, Igor, ed., and Wescott, William, piano acc. *Fifteen Intermediate Tuba Solos.* Pro Art Publications. 1965. Out of Print. II–IV. Published for a variety of instruments with piano. Includes: Chopin, F., *Nocturne;* Cohan, George M., *George M. Cohan Medley;* Cui, *Orientale;* Debussy, *Reverie;* Gounod, *Funeral March of a Marionette;* Granados, *Playera;* Haydn, F. J., *Allegro and Minuet;* Klohr, *Billboard;* Meyerbeer, *Coronation March;* Moussorgsky, M., *Gopak;* Rimsky-Korsakov, N., *Song of India;* Strauss, *Artist's Life;* Tchaikovsky, P. I., *Andante Cantabile;* Tchaikovsky, P. I., *Waltz from Serenade for Strings;* Waldteufel, *Spanish Waltzes.*

Hudadoff, Igor, ed. *Marches, Marches, Marches.* Pro Art Publications. 1974. Out of Print.

Hume, James Ord. *"Te Anau" Fantasia.* Boosey & Hawkes, Inc. 1960. Out of Print. 6:00. III. E$_1$–f. Several cadenzas, several styles and tempos. Plenty of opportunity for many musical colors within a traditional solo style.

Hume, James Ord. *Giralda.* Boosey & Hawkes, Inc. Out of Print. For E♭ bombardon. In bass and treble clef.

Hume, James Ord. *In the Deep, Deep Depths.* Boosey & Hawkes, Inc. 1941. Out of Print. 5:00. III. E$_1$–f. Playing takes place mostly in the lower range of the instrument.

Hume, James Ord. *Qui Tollis.* Boosey & Hawkes, Inc. Out of Print. For B♭ bombardon. In treble clef.

Hume, James Ord. *Romance Espagnuolo.* Boosey & Hawkes, Inc. Out of Print. For E♭ bombardon. In bass and treble clef.

Hume, James Ord. *Soliloquy.* Boosey & Hawkes, Inc. Out of Print. For E♭ bombardon. In bass and treble clef.

Hume, James Ord. *Wakatipu.* Boosey & Hawkes, Inc. Out of Print. Fantasia. For E♭ bombardon. In bass and treble clef.

Hume, James Ord. *Whangaroa.* Boosey & Hawkes, Inc. 1913. Out of Print. 5:07. III. F_1–f. For B♭ bombardon. Traditional style combining lyrical playing with moderate technical work. Three cadenzas!

Hume, James Ord, arr. *Boosey's Bombardon Solo Album.* Boosey & Co. 1906. Solo E♭ bombardon part written in treble clef. Contains: Handel, G. F., *Love That's True Will Live Forever (Si, Tra I Ceppi, From "Berenice");* Hatton, J. L., *Simon the Cellarer;* Knight, J. P., *Rocked in the Cradle of the Deep;* Meyerbeer, *On Heaven's just cause relying and Rataplan Chorus (From "Les Huguenots");* Meyerbeer, *Piff, Paff (Les Huguenots);* Wagner, R., *Heav'n, in pray'r, Thine aid I seek and Good subjects of Brabant, 'tis well! (From Loengrin).*

Hummel, Berthold. *Drei Bagatellen op. 95b.* Available from Spaeth and Schmid. $9.50.

Hummel, Bertold. *Sonatine für Baßtuba und Klavier.* Hofmeister. 1989. 13:35 (4:08, 5:17, 4:10). IV–V. E_1–f'. Allegro; Andante; Rondo vivace. Opus 81a. Utilizes a wide range of the tuba. Lyrical playing throughout; meter changes in last movement. Good recital material.

Humperdinck, Engelbert. *Children's Prayer.* tr. Mitchell Gershenfeld. Medici Music Press. 1985. 1:24. II–III. $B♭_1$–e♭. "from Hansel and Gretel." Lyrical, legato transcription. See: Gershenfeld, Mitchell, *Medici Masterworks Solos Volume 1,* under Tuba and Keyboard Collections.

Hupfield, Herman. *When Tuba Plays the Rumba on the Tuba.* arr. Douglas McLean. Harms. 1946. 2:10. II–III. G_1–e. Tempo de Rumba. Original copyright was 1931. Classic tuba solo in G minor/major. (Different versions of this recorded by William Bell, Harvey Phillips, Joe Tarto, Joe "Country" Washburn.)

Hutchison, Warner. *Deep Calls to Deep.* Seesaw Music Corporation. 1992. $10.00. 8:28 (4:34, 3:54). V. $G♭_1$–f' (a'). For James Shearer. *Deep Calls to Deep—At the Thunder of Your Waterspouts.* Completed: Les Cruces, NM. 4/88. Based on Psalms 42:7. Requires strong technique: rhythm complexity, wide dissonant leaps, wide range, glissandos. Requires tight ensemble with piano.

Huuck, Reinhard. *Ariette.* Gérard Billaudot. 1990. 2:30. III. F–e'. à Jean-Jacques Werner. "pour tuba et piano." For French tuba. Composed in 1989. Impressionistic feel with a French tonality. See: Daniel-Lesur, *Collection Panorama,* under Tuba and Keyboard Collections.

Hyde, Derek. *Promenade.* ed. Peter Wastall. Boosey & Hawkes, Inc. 1980. 0:27. I–II. C–d. Conventional melody with slightly dissonant accompaniment. See: Wastall, Peter, *Learn As You Play Tuba,* under Tuba and Keyboard Collections.

Hyde, Derek. *Tuba-Talk.* ed. Peter Wastall. Boosey & Hawkes, Inc. 1985. 1:13. I–II. C–e♭. Good introductory solo for beginning player, especially on E♭ tuba. Limited range; mostly quarter and eighth notes. Some staccato allows for musical expression. See: Wastall, Peter, *Learn As You Play Tuba,* under Tuba and Keyboard Collections.

Hyman, Dick. *Requiem for Pee Wee Ervin.* manuscript. 1981. 2:46. IV. G–e♭'. Dedicated to Harvey Phillips. Largo (thoughtfully). Very lovely tribute to Pee Wee—very melodic reflective writing. Good recital material. Some meter changes throughout. Requires great lyricism, flexibility. Some left hand stride playing by pianist.

Ideta, Keizo. *Himatsuri.* Kumato Music Junior College.

Ihlenfeld, Dave. *Clouds.* PatrickSheridan.com (Bon Bons Series). $12.00.

Ihlenfeld, Dave. *Clouds.* Tuba-Euphonium Press. 1997. 3:00. IV–V. c–a♭'. A jazz ballad in the high tessitura. Composer provides chord changes in solo part to encourage improvisation on the melody.

Ilvea. *Impromptu.* Manuscript. 1975. 4:20. IV. $F♯_1$–d♭'. Completed 6/19/75. Russian composition in 6/8 time. Very musical and fun to play. Some flexibility required. One-movement sonata-form with very tonal phrases. Good recital material.

Inagaki, Takuzo. *Piece of Tuba.* Academia Music Limited. 1976. 1:52. III–IV. B♭–d'. "for Tuba (or Euphonium) and piano." Opus 6. Cute short solo utilizing some 7/8 meter sections with 3/4 and 4/4 also. Upper tessitura; would lie best on F tuba or euphonium. Some flexibility required.

Innes, F. N. *La Coquette Concert Polka.* arr. Carl Weber. J. W. Pepper & Son. 1914. Out of Print. See: Weber, Carl, *Nineteen Solos for E♭ Bass with Piano Accompaniment,* under Tuba and Keyboard Collections.

Irons, Earl D. *Cedar Vale.* The Fillmore Bros. Co./ Carl Fischer, Inc. 1941. Out of Print. 4:00. II–III. A_1–d (e♭). "Polka. Solo for B♭ Cornet, Trombone, Baritone and BB♭ Bass, with Piano Accompaniment." Typical polka-style solo in an easier level than most in this style.

Irons, Earl D. *Fleur de Lis.* The Fillmore Bros. Co./ Carl Fischer, Inc. 1951. Out of Print. 4:20. III. (G_1) A_1–f. "Solo for Cornet, Trumpet, Baritone, (Bass or Treble Clef) Tuba with Piano Acc." "Bass Solo (E♭—BB♭)." Polka-style solo through a variety of tempos and styles. Short cadenza included.

Isaac, Merle J., arr. *Jolly Dutchman, The.* Carl Fischer Inc. 1939. $2.50. 2:18. I–II. $B♭_1$–e♭. "Adapted from Folk Tunes" by this renowned music educator. Would be level I if not for slightly high tessitura for beginner level. Some slurring, accents, staccato.

Israel, Brian. *Serenade for Tuba and Piano.* Theodore Presser Company. 1980. $4.00. For Jim Martin. March; Waltz; Galop. See review in *TUBA Journal,* Vol. 8, No. 3, Page 32.

Israel, Brian. *Sonata No. 2.* Theodore Presser Company. 1977. $3.00.

Istvàn, Bogar. *Tubaverseny.*

Jackman, Andrew. *Three Tuba Rags.* Novello & Company. 1989. $10.95. 8:35 (3:40, 3:25, 1:30). IV–V. C_1–f♯'. Swing Rag; Music Box Rag; Gravy Train Rag. Both treble and bass clef parts included. Eighth notes are swung in first piece, "straight" (as written) in last two. Muted passages in second rag. Wide range and flexibility required. Glissando and multi-phonics included. Good "showy" recital material. See review in *TUBA Journal,* Vol. 17, No. 1, Page 42.

Jacob, Gordon. *Bagatelles for Tuba.* Emerson Edition. 1980. $11.00. 4:23 (1:13, 0:59, 0:57, 1:13). III. $B\flat_1$–f. To my Godson, Daniel Emerson. *In Tranquil Mood* (Andante); *The Corsair Bold* (Moderato); *A Sprightly Dance* (Allegro Moderato); *After Dinner Speech* (Andante poco pomposo). Both treble and bass clef parts included. Very musical, short, contrasting pieces. Some slurring, dotted rhythms; no big technical problems—just very playable music. Good recital material. See review in *TUBA Journal,* Vol. 9, No. 1, Page 14.

Jacob, Gordon. *Six Little Tuba Pieces.* Emerson Edition. 1978. $13.75. 7:36 (1:11, 1:00, 1:18, 1:01, 1:19, 1:47). III–IV. $B\flat_1$–e♭'. *Restful Prelude* (Andante tranquillo); *Marching Tune* (Alla marcia); *Minuet* (Alla menuetto grazioso); *Hungarian* (Allegro vivace); *In Folk song Style* (Andante moderato); *Scottish* (Vivace). To Emma P. (Parkinson). Very musical suite of intermediate solos with a British (except fourth tune) flavor. A few meters to look out for: 3/2, 5/4, and one mvt. in E♭ minor. A few spots requiring upper range; otherwise no big technical problems. Level III except for range. Good recital material. See review in *TUBA Journal,* Vol. 9, No. 1, Page 14.

Jacob, Gordon. *Tuba Suite.* Boosey & Hawkes, Inc. 1973. $15.00. 17:03 (2:20, 1:39, 3:11, 1:00, 0:48, 1:43, 2:21, 4:06). IV. (D_1) F_1–d' (g'). *Prelude* (Largo); *Hornpipe* (Allegro); *Saraband* (Adagio); *Bourrée* (Allegro giojoso (sic)); *Brief Interlude* (Andante sostenuto); *Mazurka* (Allegro moderato); *Ground* (Jacob's Dream) (Grave); *Galop* (Presto) (with cadenza). To Ian King. Written in 1972. Originally called *Jacob's Suite for Tuba and Strings.* Eight short pieces with a British band feel; eight different moods with great opportunity for musical expression. Includes fast technical playing, slow lyrical playing, etc. Great recital material. Recorded by Eugene Dowling. See review in *TUBA Journal,* Vol. 1, No. 2, Page 10.

Jacobs, Wesley, arr. *Coventry Carole.* Encore Music Publishers. 1:06. I. F♯–d. English carol. Limited range; a few accidentals, some step-wise slurs. Quarter note is fastest rhythm in 3/4 time. See: Jacobs, Wesley, *Solos from the Classics,* under Tuba and Keyboard Collections.

Jacobs, Wesley, arr. *Dona Nobis Pacem.* Encore Music Publishers. 0:50. I–II. C–d. In 3/4 time. Some slurring, a couple of c–C octave jumps. See: Jacobs, Wesley, *Solos from the Classics,* under Tuba and Keyboard Collections.

Jacobs, Wesley, arr. *German Waltz.* Encore Music Publishers. 0:39. I–II. D–e♭. German Folk Song. Waltz in one. Some step-wise slurring; quarter note is fastest rhythm. See: Jacobs, Wesley, *Solos from the Classics,* under Tuba and Keyboard Collections.

Jacobs, Wesley, arr. *Go Down, Moses.* Encore Music Publishers. 1:35. I. D–d. With feeling. Spiritual. Some syncopation. See: Jacobs, Wesley, *Solos from the Classics,* under Tuba and Keyboard Collections.

Jacobs, Wesley, arr. *Greensleeves.* Encore Music Publishers. 0:34. II. A_1–c. Moderato. Old English Air. In 6/8 and D minor. Once through the tune. Some slurring; some accidentals and dotted rhythms. See: Jacobs, Wesley, *Solos from the Classics,* under Tuba and Keyboard Collections.

Jacobs, Wesley, arr. *Harvest Dance.* Encore Music Publishers. 0:27. I. $B\flat_1$–d. Lightly. Czech folk song. Some syncopation. Mostly step-wise motion. In 2/4 time. See: Jacobs, Wesley, *Solos from the Classics,* under Tuba and Keyboard Collections.

Jacobs, Wesley, arr. *In Olden Times.* Encore Music Publishers. 0:47. II. B_1–c. Broadly. German folk song. In G major. Some slurring; some flexibility required. Eighth note is fastest rhythm. See: Jacobs, Wesley, *Solos from the Classics,* under Tuba and Keyboard Collections.

Jacobs, Wesley, arr. *In Springtime.* Encore Music Publishers. 1:02. I–II. C–d. Gaily. German folk song. Some flexibility required for interval jumps. Eighth note is fastest rhythm. See: Jacobs, Wesley, *Solos from the Classics,* under Tuba and Keyboard Collections.

Jacobs, Wesley, arr. *Little Maiden.* Encore Music Publishers. 0:27. I–II. E–d. Lightly. Moravian folk song. Some slurring; easy rhythms. One jump from d–E; otherwise no technical problems. See: Jacobs, Wesley, *Solos from the Classics,* under Tuba and Keyboard Collections.

Jacobs, Wesley, arr. *Mighty Fortress, A.* Encore Music Publishers. 1:02. I. C–c. Broadly. Chorale melody. Typical chorale style; (unwritten) ritards and fermatas. Quarter note is fastest rhythm. See: Jacobs, Wesley, *Solos from the Classics,* under Tuba and Keyboard Collections.

Jacobs, Wesley, arr. *Nightingale.* Encore Music Publishers. 1:17. II. D–c. Moderato. German folk song. In 2/4 with a pulse of 4 (eighth note gets the beat). A couple of written-out turns (32nd notes) and some slurring included. Key of A minor. See: Jacobs, Wesley, *Solos from the Classics,* under Tuba and Keyboard Collections.

Jacobs, Wesley, arr. *Solos from the Classics.* Encore Music Publishers. 1991. $16.50. I–II. Twenty-four classical and folk tunes. Contains: Beethoven, L.v., *Hymn to Joy;* Brahms, J.,

Lullaby; Brahms, J., *Sandman;* Brahms, J, *Waltz;* Haydn, J., *Hymn;* Haydn, J., *The Spacious Firmament;* Jacobs, Wesley, arr., *Coventry Carole;* Jacobs, Wesley, arr., *Dona Nobis Pacem;* Jacobs, Wesley, arr., *German Waltz;* Jacobs, Wesley, arr., *Go Down, Moses;* Jacobs, Wesley, arr., *Greensleeves;* Jacobs, Wesley, arr., *Harvest Dance;* Jacobs, Wesley, arr., *In Olden Times;* Jacobs, Wesley, arr., *In Springtime;* Jacobs, Wesley, arr., *Little Maiden;* Jacobs, Wesley, arr., *A Mighty Fortress;* Jacobs, Wesley, arr., *Nightingale;* Jacobs, Wesley, arr., *Steal Away;* Jacobs, Wesley, arr., *Steeple, The;* Jacobs, Wesley, arr., *Thanksgiving;* Jacobs, Wesley, arr., *Village Dance;* Mendelssohn, F., *Nocturne;* Sibelius, Jean, *Finlandia;* Ward, S. A., *America the Beautiful.*

Jacobs, Wesley, arr. *Steal Away.* Encore Music Publishers. 1:01. II. F–d. Quietly. Spiritual. Some syncopation; limited range. See: Jacobs, Wesley, *Solos from the Classics,* under Tuba and Keyboard Collections.

Jacobs, Wesley, arr. *Steeple, The.* Encore Music Publishers. 1:08. I. C–d. Moderately fast. English folk song. Quarter note is fastest rhythm. A few C–c octave jumps. See: Jacobs, Wesley, *Solos from the Classics,* under Tuba and Keyboard Collections.

Jacobs, Wesley, arr. *Thanksgiving.* Encore Music Publishers. 1:01. I. B♭$_1$–c. Lively. Netherlands air. Solo in 3/4 time. Some slurring, mostly stepwise motion. See: Jacobs, Wesley, *Solos from the Classics,* under Tuba and Keyboard Collections.

Jacobs, Wesley, arr. *Village Dance.* Encore Music Publishers. 0:32. I. E♭–b♭. Playfully. French folk song. Limited range. In 2/4 time with a few eighth notes as fastest rhythm. No technical problems. See: Jacobs, Wesley, *Solos from the Classics,* under Tuba and Keyboard Collections.

Jacobs, Wesley. *Carnival of Venice.* Encore Music Publishers. 1989. $11.00. 5:30. IV–V. C–a♭'. Upper tessitura theme and (three) variations with cadenza. Strong technique required.

Jacobsen, Julius. *Humresque.* Swedish Music Information Center. 1976.

Jacobsen, Julius. *Tuba Buffo.* Swedish Music Information Center. 1977. 7:00. Band accompaniment available. Modest range requirements; also possible on euphonium. Recorded by Michael Lind.

Jacobsen, Julius. *Tuba Buffo: Concerto for Tuba and Wind Band.* Edition Suecia. 2002. 9:30. F$_1$–f♯'. Dedicated to Michael Lind. See listing under Music for Tuba and Band.

Jacobsen, Julius. *Twenty-Four Preludes for Tuba and Piano.* Swedish Music Information Center.

Jaffe, Gerard. *Centone Buffo Concertante.* Southern Music Company. 1973. $5.00. 5:10. III–IV. G$_1$–b♭. Allegro Moderato. Solo in cut time utilizing technical and lyrical playing and two "afterbeat" passages (for those of you who are tired of ohm-pahs). Some quintuplets in cadenza. Fun piece. See review in *TUBA Journal,* Vol. 1, No. 1, Page 7.

Jager, Robert. *Concerto for Bass Tuba.* Hal Leonard Publishing Company. 1978. $7.50. Commissioned by the University of Illinois Band, Harry Begian, director, for Dan Perantoni. See: Jager, Robert, *Concerto for Bass Tuba and Concert Band* under Tuba and Band and under Tuba and Orchestra. Also see: Bird, Gary, ed.; *Program Notes for the Solo Tuba.* Recorded by R. Winston Morris, Daniel Perantoni. See review in *TUBA Journal,* Vol. 9, No. 2, Page 24.

Jager, Robert. *Reflections.* Neil A. Kjos Music Company. 1983. $6.00. 6:15. IV. B♭$_1$–b. Commissioned by Tubists Universal Brotherhood Association. Premiered by R. Winston Morris, tuba, and Barbara Young, piano, May 21, 1980, at the Second National Tuba-Euphonium Symposium-Workshop, University of North Texas, Denton, Tex. Shifting meters throughout. Good recital material.

Jakma Sr., Frits. *Dans der Teddyberen. (Dance of the Teddy Bears.)* Tierolff-Muziekcentrale. 4:38. III. A♭–e♭'. Allegro. "Solo Voor Trombone, Tuba, Bes-Bas of Es-Bas met Begeleiding van Piano." Polka-style solo in cut time with cadenza. Best on F tuba or euphonium.

Jakma Sr., Frits. *Herfstbloemen. (Autumn Flowers.)* Tierolff-Muziekcentrale. 4:00. c–f'. "Intermezzo voor Bugel Piston Trompet Baryton Trombone Tuba Bas in Es—Bes en C met Begeleiding van Piano." Polka-style solo in cut time with short cadenza. Best on F tuba or euphonium.

Jakma, Henk. *Bassenparade. (Parade of the Basses.)* Tierolff-Muziekcentrale. 1965. 3:34. III. B♭–f'. High tessitura; best on F tuba or euphonium. Novelty polka-style work in 4/4 time with cadenza. Intermediate technique required.

James, Ifor. *Song for Michael.* Editions Marc Reift. 1998. $11.00. 3:00. III. C$_1$–d'. Dedicated to Michael Lind. Catchy tune in Beguine style in the middle register; no technical difficulties.

Jeanneau, Francois. *Mini Suite.* Piano four hands and tuba.

Jenkins, Cyril. *Chason Triste.* Boosey & Hawkes. 1922. Out of Print. 3:27. III–IV. C♭–e♭'. "E♭ Bass." Solo part in treble clef. Romantic lyricism throughout. Some triplet arpeggios.

Jenkins, Cyril. *Rondelay.* Boosey & Hawkes. 1922. Out of Print. 1:49. IV. B♭$_1$–f'. "B♭ Bass." Solo part in treble clef. Playful "French sounding" theme in D♭ major that repeats and gets faster and faster throughout the piece until prestissimo. Good showcase and good recital material.

Jenne, Glenn. *Rondo.* Theodore Presser Company. 1968. $2.00. 3:50. IV. F$_1$–b♭. Some mixed meter; quick tempo. Not a technique-buster but a solid challenging piece.

Jennings. *Pomposo Polka.* arr. Carl Weber. J. W. Pepper & Son. 1914. Out of Print. 5:18. III. (F$_1$) B♭$_1$–g. Traditional polka style with no big technical problems. See: Weber, Carl, *Nineteen Solos for E♭ Bass with Piano Accompaniment,* under Tuba and Keyboard Collections.

Jepsen, Irene. *Easy Solos.* Available from Spaeth and Schmid. $24.25. With CD accompaniment or piano accompaniment.

Jepsen, Irene. *Im Spielzeugland.* Available from Spaeth and Schmid. $24.25. With CD accompaniment or piano accompaniment.

Jevtic, Ivan. *Balkan's Ayers Rock.* Editions Bim. 2001. $14.25. 9:00. IV–V. F_1–a♭'. Con rigore; Misterioso; Allegretto. Dedicated to Mel Culbertson. Exciting tour de force. Good recital material. Requires a very proficient pianist. First movement with Balkan flare, second a grandiose description of Balkan's Ayers Rock, the third influenced by Brazilian rhythms.

Jevtic, Ivan. *Concerto for Tuba and Symphony Orchestra.* Éditions BIM. 1992. See: Jevtic, Ivan, *Concerto for Tuba and Symphony Orchestra,* under Tuba and Orchestra.

Johnston, Richard. *Three Pieces for Tuba and Piano.* Canadian Music Centre. 1987. 5:50 (1:35, 2:45, 2:30). III. A_1–g. Conversation; Barcarolle; Quick March. Very well-written suite for intermediate level. Written in a neo-romantic style; lyricism exists throughout. Good recital material.

Jolas, Betsy. *Trois Duos Pour Tuba Et Piano.* Alphonse Leduc. 1985. $12.80. 5:40 (2:30, 1:10, 2:00). IV–V. C_1–g'. pour les quatre-vingts ans de Francis Bott. Composed in 1983. Mixed meter. Wide range. See: Thompson/Lemke; *French Music for Low Brass Instruments.* See reviews in *TUBA Journal,* Vol. 14, No. 4, Page 42, and Vol. 15, No. 1, Page 28.

Jones, Roger. *Andante and Allegro for Tuba and Piano.* Manuscript. 3:14 (1:28, 1:46). IV. F_1–c' (d'). Two numbered movements: Andante; Allegro. At indicated metronome markings, will take great flexibility. Plenty of articulated eighth note triplets and sixteenths to fit into quick cut time tempo. See review in *TUBA Journal,* Vol. 1, No. 3, Page 6.

Jones, Roger. *Dialogs for Tuba and Piano.* Tuba-Euphonium Press. 1997. 9:15. III–IV. A♭–e♭'. Confabulation; Divulgence; Riposté. Dedicated to Jeffrey Funderburk. Three rhythmically diverse movements with mostly conservative range considerations. Mostly linear melodic lines.

Jones, Roger. *Jurassic Tuba! A Mesozoic Menagerie.* Tuba-Euphonium Press. 2000. 12:00. II–III. $E♭_1$–b♭. Dimetrodon; Pterodactyl; Velociraptor; Stegosaurus; Triceratops; T. Rex. Character movements depicting six different dinosaurs. Conservative range demands, but the metric demands are too challenging for an advanced beginner. Some movements alone are appropriate for a beginner.

Jones, Roger. *Manta for Tuba and Piano.* TUBA Press. 1992. $8.00. 5:34. III–IV. F_1–a♭. Completed 6/6/81. One movement work with two tempos: a cut time articulated feel and a 4/4 relaxed lyrical one. Some mixed meter, some syncopation. Good recital material.

Joubert, Claude-Henry. *Ballade Du Moigne Que Nostre Dame Delivera Dou Dyable.* Éditions Robert Martin. 1991. $5.75. 3:00. A_1–d'. Dedicated to Gautier de Coinci. Written as a preparatory solo, it is lyrical with short fast technical outbursts. The range considerations make it more advanced than beginning level.

Joubert, Claude-Henry. *Rudéral.* Gérard Billaudot. 1980. $4.50. 3:30. II–III. B_1–c♯'. "pour Tuba en Ut ou Si♭ et Piano (à une ou deux mains)." Tuba with piano one or two hands. Very easy piano accompaniment. No major technical problems. See: Thompson/Lemke; *French Music for Low Brass Instruments.* See review in *TUBA Journal,* Vol. 9, No. 4, Page 36.

Joubert, Claude-Henry. *Tunuva Tuba.* Éditions M. Combre. 1985. 5:10 (0:45, 0:40, 0:45, 0:20, 0:45, 0:30, 0:20, 0:20, 0:45). III. A_1–d'. Complainte; Marche; Variation 2; Valse; Polanaise; Variation 5; Scherzo; Variations 7 et 8. "pour Tuba (ut ou si♭) et Piano." For French tuba. Theme and (eight) variations. Theme is in 7/8, as is last variation. Others are in 4/4, 3/4, 3/8 time. Theme is step-wise motion making it not too difficult for advanced beginner/intermediate player.

Jous, Christian. *Milonga.* Available from Spaeth and Schmid. $20.75.

Jous, Christian. *Pourquoi.* Available from Spaeth and Schmid. $12.25.

Jude, W. H. *Mighty Deep, The.* arr. Paul de Ville. Carl Fischer Inc. 1898. $2.50. See: Jude, W. H., *The Mighty Deep,* under Tuba and Band.

Jurovsky, V. *March.* arr. A. Lebedev. Military Band Masters Faculty of Moscow Conservatiore. 1971. See: Lebedev, A., *Collection of Pieces for Tuba "Es" and Piano,* under Tuba and Keyboard Collections.

Kabalevsky, D. *Waltz and Galop from Petite Suite.* ed. Himie Voxman. Rubank, Inc. 1972. 2:00. II–III. D–f. Moderato; Allegro. "for E♭ or BB♭ Bass." Moderato in 3/4 time with some slurs. Allegro in 2/4 time with mostly step-wise motion. See: Voxman, Himie, *Concert and Contest Collection,* under Tuba and Keyboard Collections.

Kac, Stefan. *Serenade for Bass Tuba.* Tuba-Euphonium Press. 2003. IV. G_1–f'. Con moto. Rhythmically complex piece with many tempo changes and large intervallic skips.

Kagan, Susan. *Oxford Gavotte.* arr. Herbert Wekselblatt. G. Schirmer Inc. 1972. 1:47. II–III. A_1–f. Tempo di Gavotte. Good introduction to baroque ornamentation: trills and mordent. Solo in cut time. See: Wekselblatt, Herbert, *First Solos for the Tuba Player, BB♭,* under Tuba and Keyboard Collections.

Kaï, Naohiko. *Légende.* Alphonse Leduc. 1962. $16.85. 6:35 (2:20, 4:15). V. $F♯_1$ (B_1)–(a♭'/g♯')

b♭'. A Piacere; Allegro. "pour Tuba Ut ou Trombone basse ou Saxhorn basse Si♭ et Piano." For French tuba. Very wide range. Strong technique and lyricism required. See: Thompson/Lemke; *French Music for Low Brass Instruments.*

Kalinikov, V. *Sad Song, The.* ed. S. Melnikov. Military Band Masters Institute–Moscow. 1957. See: Melnikov, S., *Pieces for Tuba and Piano,* under Tuba and Keyboard Collections.

Kalke, Ernst-Thilo. *Concertino in F for Tuba and Orchestra.* Uetz Music Publishers. $17.25. Virtuosic and entertaining concerto á la *Rhapsody in Blue.* Contest piece for the Markneukirchen International Tuba Competition. Piano reduction available. See listing under Music for Tuba and Orchestra.

Kalke, Ernst-Thilo. *Julep Cup.* Uetz Music Publishers. $13.50.

Kalke, Ernst-Thilo. *Mevagissey Tales, for Tuba and Four Horns (or Piano).* Uetz Music Publishers. $21.00. Recorded by Markus Hötzel and the German and American Horn Ensemble.

Kalke, Ernst-Thilo. *Mevagissey Tales, for Tuba and String Orchestra (or Piano).* Uetz Music Publishers. 1999. $21.00. A concerto in three movements. See listings under Music for Tuba and Orchestra and Music for Tuba and Band.

Kaneda, B. *Long, Long Ago.* arr. A. Lebedev. Military Band Masters Faculty of Moscow Conservatiore. 1971. See: Lebedev, A., *Collection of Pieces for Tuba "Es" and Piano,* under Tuba and Keyboard Collections.

Kappey. *Introduction and Allegretto.* Boosey & Hawkes, Inc. Out of Print. For B♭ bombardon. In treble clef.

Kappey. *O Ruddier than the Cherry.* Boosey & Hawkes, Inc. Out of Print. For E♭ Bbombardon. In bass and treble clef.

Karaev, V. *Dance from Ballet "Seven Beauties."* arr. A. Lebedev. Military Band Masters Faculty of Moscow Conservatiore. 1971. See: Lebedev, A., *Collection of Pieces for Tuba "Es" and Piano,* under Tuba and Keyboard Collections.

Kardos, Istvan. *Poem and Burlesque for Double Bass (Tuba) and Piano.* General Music Publishing Co. 1969. Written for string bass primarily—double stops, extremely high range. Transposed solo part.

Karlsen, Kjell Mork. *Sonata for Tuba and Piano.* Norsk Musikforlag. 1988. 19:38 (6:26, 6:20, 6:52). V. A_1–f' (b♭'). Lamento; Hommage a Sjostakovitsj; Tuba mirum. Op. 74. Major work for tuba and piano. Three very different textures. Lamento is very lyrical; Hommage is very technical; and Tuba mirum is very dynamic, pesante, dissonant, and strong. The entire piece requires endurance, imagination, sharp technique, wide range, and a very strong accompanist. Good recital material.

Kastel, Fabrice. *Concertinetto.* Robert Martin Editions. 1996. $9.75. II–III. (C) G–c'. Written for the beginning saxhorn player, so the tessitura is demanding for the young student though the piece would work well down an octave. Where written, it is an intermediate-level piece.

Katchiturian, A. *Dance from Ballet "Spartak."* arr. A. Lebedev. Military Band Masters Faculty of Moscow Conservatiore. 1971. See: Lebedev, A., *Collection of Pieces for Tuba "Es" and Piano,* under Tuba and Keyboard Collections.

Kazadezins, R. *Spanish Dance.* arr. A. Lebedev. Military Band Masters Faculty of Moscow Conservatiore. 1971. See: Lebedev, A., *Collection of Pieces for Tuba "Es" and Piano,* under Tuba and Keyboard Collections.

Keim, Aaron. *Matins.* Tuba-Euphonium Press. 2002. 5:00. III. F–f'. Commissioned by and dedicated to John Tuinstra. Lyrical and linear piece suitable for recitals.

Kellaway, Roger. *Arcades I.* Manuscript. 1984.

Kellaway, Roger. *Dr. Martin Luther King, In Memoriam (1984).* Editions BIM. Publication in progress.

Kellaway, Roger. *For Harvey.* Manuscript. ca. 1984. For Harvey Phillips. In the collection of Harvey G. Phillips.

Kellaway, Roger. *Morning Song.* Éditions BIM. 1980. $16.00. 7:00. IV–V. F_1–b♭'. For Roger Bobo. Composed in 1978. Almost commercial sounding, this solo is a great crowd pleaser. Formally written for the Roger Kellaway Cello Quartet as a cello solo, *Morning Song* has a "new age/country" feel to it with an extremely lyrical solo part. Strong, flexible technique a must; requires a strong, flexible accompanist. Great recital material. Very wide range. Best on F tuba. Recorded by Jorgen Voight Arnsted, Roger Bobo.

Kellaway, Roger. *Songs of Ascent (Concerto).* Éditions BIM. 1986/89. Piano reduction in preparation (1993). See: Kellaway, Roger, *Songs of Ascent (Concerto),* under Tuba and Orchestra. Also see: Bird, Gary, ed.; *Program Notes for the Solo Tuba.*

Kellaway, Roger. *Westwood Song.* Éditions BIM. 1975, rev. 1982 and 1989. 11:30. IV–V. One of five movements for brass quintet featuring each member. Very lyrical reflective solo. Piano part initially was improvised; this is a realization of that improvisation. Good recital material. Recorded by Roger Bobo.

Kelly, Bryan. *Dordogne Dances.* Emerson Edition. 1995. 6:50. III. G_1–b♭. Impromptu; Pastourelle; Marche; Tarantelle. Four movements each with their own unique rhythmic character. The range and musical demands are suitable for an intermediate player, but the rhythmic subdivisions may be more appropriate for the advanced player.

Kesnar, Maurits. *Prelude.* Carl Fischer Inc. 1954. $3.50. 2:30. III. F_1–g. For Melvin Siener. Was published by: Cundy-Bettoney. Maestoso-regal feel followed by a lyrical section. Some slurred triplets, some low articulations, no major technical problems.

Kiefer, Bruno. *Interrogaçoes.* Fundação Nacional De Arte. 1985. 3:40. IV. A_1–c'. Quick (or triple) tonguing, dissonant phrases, mixed meter, upper tessitura.

Kikta, V. *Concerto for Tuba and Orchestra.* ed. V. Guzii. Moscow Muzyka. 1978. Piano reduction. For tuba and orchestra. See: Guzii, V., *Pieces for Tuba and Piano,* under Tuba and Keyboard Collections.

Kikta, V. *Epic Tale and Procession of the People in Costumes (Festival).* ed. A. Lebedev. Moscow Muzyka. 1986. 4:30 (2:22, 2:08). IV. E_1–e♭'. *Epic Tale (Bilina); Procession of People in Costumes.* Very dramatic modern writing with an old feel. *Epic Tale* is reminiscent of a Gregorian chant. *Procession* has mixed meter combined with a Maestoso dramatic flair. See: Lebedev, A., *Tuba Tutor Vol. 2,* under Tuba and Keyboard Collections.

Killengreen, Christian. *Skjemt.* Norwegian Music Music Center. 1994. 6:00.

Kilon, Moshe. *Sine Nomine.* Kibutz Movement League of Composers. Recorded by Adi Hershko.

King, Karl L. *Octopus and the Mermaid, The.* C. L. Barnhouse Company. 1923. Out of Print. 4:00. III. B♭$_1$–a. Very melodic solo for the intermediate player.

Kinyon, John, arr. *All through the Night.* M. Witmark & Sons. 1958. I. Welsh. See: Kinyon, John, *Breeze-Easy Recital Pieces,* under Tuba and Keyboard Collections.

Kinyon, John, arr. *Ash Grove, The.* M. Witmark & Sons. 1958. I. Welsh. See: Kinyon, John, *Breeze-Easy Recital Pieces,* under Tuba and Keyboard Collections.

Kinyon, John, arr. *Auld Lang Syne.* M. Witmark & Sons. 1958. I. Scottish. See: Kinyon, John, *Breeze-Easy Recital Pieces,* under Tuba and Keyboard Collections.

Kinyon, John, arr. *Bendemeer's Stream.* M. Witmark & Sons. 1958. I. Irish. See: Kinyon, John, *Breeze-Easy Recital Pieces,* under Tuba and Keyboard Collections.

Kinyon, John, arr. *Blue Bells of Scotland, The.* M. Witmark & Sons. 1958. I. Scottish. See: Kinyon, John, *Breeze-Easy Recital Pieces,* under Tuba and Keyboard Collections.

Kinyon, John, arr. *Breeze-Easy Recital Pieces for Tuba.* M. Witmark & Sons. 1958. I–II. Thirty recognizable tunes for tuba and piano. Contains: Barnby, Sir Joseph, *Sweet and Low;* Bayley, Thomas Haynes, *Faith of Our Fathers;* Bayley, Thomas Haynes, *Long, Long Ago;* Benedict, Julius, *Carnival of Venice;* Brahms, J., *Cradle Song;* Haydn, F. J., *Papa Haydn's Tune;* Kinyon, John, arr., *All through the Night;* Kinyon, John, arr., *Ash Grove, The;* Kinyon, John, arr., *Auld Lang Syne;* Kinyon, John, arr., *Bendemeer's Stream;* Kinyon, John, arr., *Blue Bells of Scotland, The;* Kinyon, John arr., *Cockles and Mussels;* Kinyon, John, arr., *Crusaders' Hymn;* Kinyon, John, arr., *Drink to Me Only with Thine Eyes;* Kinyon, John, arr., *The Erie Canal;* Kinyon, John, arr., *German Waltz;* Kinyon, John, arr., *Home on the Range;* Kinyon, John, arr., *John Peel;* Kinyon, John, arr., *Loch Lomond;* Kinyon, John, arr., *Londonderry Air;* Kinyon, John, arr., *Minstrel Boy;* Kinyon, John, arr., *Red River Valley;* Kinyon, John, arr., *Steal Away;* Kinyon, John, arr., *Sweet Betsy from Pike;* Kinyon, John, arr., *When Love Is Kind;* Kinyon, John, arr., *Ye Banks and Braes of Bonny Doon;* Monk, W. H., *Abide with Me;* Spillman, James E., *Flow Gently, Sweet Afton;* Strauss, Johann, *Roses from the South;* Thompson, H. S., *Annie Lisle.*

Kinyon, John, arr. *Cockles and Mussels.* M. Witmark & Sons. 1958. I. Irish. See: Kinyon, John, *Breeze-Easy Recital Pieces,* under Tuba and Keyboard Collections.

Kinyon, John, arr. *Crusaders' Hymn.* M. Witmark & Sons. 1958. I. German. See: Kinyon, John, *Breeze-Easy Recital Pieces,* under Tuba and Keyboard Collections.

Kinyon, John, arr. *Drink to Me Only with Thine Eyes.* M. Witmark & Sons. 1958. I. English folk song. See: Kinyon, John, *Breeze-Easy Recital Pieces,* under Tuba and Keyboard Collections.

Kinyon, John, arr. *Erie Canal, The.* M. Witmark & Sons. 1958. I. American work song. See: Kinyon, John, *Breeze-Easy Recital Pieces,* under Tuba and Keyboard Collections.

Kinyon, John, arr. *German Waltz.* M. Witmark & Sons. 1958. I. See: Kinyon, John, *Breeze-Easy Recital Pieces,* under Tuba and Keyboard Collections.

Kinyon, John, arr. *Home on the Range.* M. Witmark & Sons. 1958. I. American cowboy. See: Kinyon, John, *Breeze-Easy Recital Pieces,* under Tuba and Keyboard Collections.

Kinyon, John, arr. *Instant Band Ensembles (Tuba).* Alfred Music. 1969. Solo book for any solo instrument and band or piano accompaniment. Sixteen popular songs, Christmas songs, etc.

Kinyon, John, arr. *John Peel.* M. Witmark & Sons. 1958. I. English. See: Kinyon, John, *Breeze-Easy Recital Pieces,* under Tuba and Keyboard Collections.

Kinyon, John, arr. *Loch Lomond.* M. Witmark & Sons. 1958. I. Scottish. See: Kinyon, John, *Breeze-Easy Recital Pieces,* under Tuba and Keyboard Collections.

Kinyon, John, arr. *Londonderry Air.* M. Witmark & Sons. 1958. I–II. Irish. See: Kinyon, John, *Breeze-Easy Recital Pieces,* under Tuba and Keyboard Collections.

Kinyon, John, arr. *Minstrel Boy.* M. Witmark & Sons. 1958. I–II. Irish. See: Kinyon, John, *Breeze-Easy Recital Pieces,* under Tuba and Keyboard Collections.

Kinyon, John, arr. *Red River Valley.* M. Witmark & Sons. 1958. I. American cowboy. See: Kinyon, John, *Breeze-Easy Recital Pieces,* under Tuba and Keyboard Collections.

Kinyon, John, arr. *Steal Away.* M. Witmark & Sons. 1958. I. Negro spiritual. See: Kinyon, John, *Breeze-Easy Recital Pieces,* under Tuba and Keyboard Collections.

Kinyon, John, arr. *Sweet Betsy from Pike.* M. Witmark & Sons. 1958. I. English melody. See: Kinyon, John, *Breeze-Easy Recital Pieces,* under Tuba and Keyboard Collections.

Kinyon, John, arr. *When Love Is Kind.* M. Witmark & Sons. 1958. I. Old English melody. See: Kinyon, John, *Breeze-Easy Recital Pieces,* under Tuba and Keyboard Collections.

Kinyon, John, arr. *Ye Banks and Braes of Bonny Doon.* M. Witmark & Sons. 1958. I. Scottish. See: Kinyon, John, *Breeze-Easy Recital Pieces,* under Tuba and Keyboard Collections.

Kistetenyi, Melinda. *Kis Eloeadasi Darab Tubara.* Hungarian Edition—Available from the Tuba Center.

Kitsz, Dennis Bathory. *Sonata for Tuba and Piano.* Westleaf Edition. 1970. IV–V. F♯$_1$–g'. For Stanley Michalowski. (Corrections April 1988.) Contemporary melodic writing. Muted passages, complex time signatures.

Kitts-Turner, John S. *Concertino.* Tuba-Euphonium Press. 1997. 8:00. III–IV. F$_1$–f♭'. See listing under Music for Tuba and Orchestra. A good one-movement concertino in a medium tessitura.

Kladnitzki, W. *Sonate für Tuba und Klavier.* Istazelstwo Musika Moskau. III.

Kling, G., and G. Neuling. *Grand Cadence.* ed. V. Guzii. Moscow Muzyka. 1978. See: Guzii, V., *Pieces for Tuba and Piano,* under Tuba and Keyboard Collections.

Klohr. *Billboard.* arr. Igor Hudadoff; William Westcott, piano arr. Pro Art Publications. 1967. Out of Print. See: Hudadoff, Igor, *Fifteen Intermediate Tuba Solos,* under Tuba and Keyboard Collections.

Klose, Hyacinthe. *Air Varie op. 21.* ed. Fernand Lelong. Gerard Billaudot. Available from Spaeth and Schmid. $12.75.

Knight, J. P. *Rock'd in the Cradle of the Deep.* arr. Harry Prendiville. A. Squire. 1888. Out of Print. 0:50. II–III. (B♭$_1$) F–f. No technical problems. See: Prendiville, Harry, *Six Popular Solos,* under Tuba and Keyboard Collections. "E♭ Bass; or, tuba With Piano or Organ Accompaniment, (ad lib.)."

Knight, J. P. *Rocked in the Cradle of the Deep.* arr. Acton Ostling. CPP/Belwin, Inc. 1969. 1:23. I. (A♭$_1$) D–e♭. Good introduction to slur two-tongue two. Add plenty of spirit to last two measures! See: Ostling, Acton, *Tuba (Bass) Soloist, Level One,* under Tuba and Keyboard Collections.

Knight, J. P. *Rocked in the Cradle of the Deep.* arr. James Ord Hume. Boosey & Co. 1906. Out of Print. See: Hume, J. Ord, *Boosey's Bombardon Solo Album,* under Tuba and Keyboard Collections.

Knight, Morris. *Exchange for Tuba and Piano.* Woodsum Music. 1976. $8.00. 2:40. III–IV. F$_1$–c'. Lyrical solo in 6/8 time in a moderate tempo. Good introduction on an intermediate level to modern melodic writing. See review in *TUBA Journal,* Vol. 4, No. 2, Page 22.

Knight, Morris. *Tuba and Piano Sonata: Three Movements.* Woodsum Music. 1989. $12.00. 12:26 (4:26, 4:00, 4:00). IV. E$_1$–c♯'. Energetically; Lyrically; Burlesquely. For the artistry of John Jones. First movement alternates between 4/4 and 3/4. Second movement is a modern melodic work in 3/4 time. The Burlesquely movement is in 6/8 time utilizing flexibility at a reasonable tempo.

Koch, Erland von. *Concerto for Tuba.* AB Carl Gehrmans Musikforlag. 1979. $20.25. Dedicated to Michael Lind. Completed in 1978. See: Koch, Erland von, *Concerto for Tuba,* under Tuba and Orchestra. See review in *TUBA Journal,* Vol. 10, No. 2, Page 23.

Koch, Erland von. *Tubania for Tuba and Piano.* AB Carl Gehrmans Musikforlag. 1983. Extreme high register for tuba; lies well on euphonium.

Koch, Frederick. *Introduction, Aria and Rondo.* Southern Music Company. 1992. $4.95. 4:33 (0:56, 1:39, 1:58) . IV. F$_1$–f'. *Introduction* (Majestic); *Aria* (Slowly Moving); *Rondo* (Vivace). 1. Melodic regal feel. 2. Lyrical modern lines. 3. Pentatonic-like feel. Upper tessitura. A few trills.

Koch, Johannes H. E. *Sonatine für Tuba (Posaune) und Klavier.* Möseler Verlag. 1988. 6:19 (2:56, 1:46, 1:37). III. E$_1$–f. Breit; Lebhaft; Fugato. "for Tuba (Trombone) and Piano." Some modern, some conventional melodic language. Conservative range; no big technical problems.

Kocher. *For the Beauty of the Earth.* arr. Billy Madison. Solid Brass Music Company. $3.50. I. The old favorite hymn arranged for a beginning tubist.

Koepke, Paul. *Persiflage.* ed. Himie Voxman. Rubank, Inc. 1972. 4:30. III. (A$_1$) B♭$_1$–f. "for E♭ or BB♭ Bass." Lyrical Andante cantabile section followed by a moderately technical Allegro section and a cadenza. See: Voxman, Himie, *Concert and Contest Collection,* under Tuba and Keyboard Collections.

Koerppen, Alfred. *Konzert.* Available from Spaeth and Schmid. $27.50.

Koetsier, Jan. *Concertino.* Éditions BIM. 1990. $17.00. Manfred Hoppert zugeeignet. For tuba and string orchestra, Opus 77. Composed 1978, revised 1982. See: Koetsier, Jan, *Concertino for Tuba and String Orchestra,* under Tuba and Orchestra.

Koetsier, Jan. *Es ist ein Schnitter, der heisst Tod. (There Is a Reaper Named Death.)* Editions Marc Reift. 1997. $16.00. 6:00. III–IV. G$_1$–f'.

Introduktion; Passacaglia; Choral; Variante 1–3. A tonal work with conservative harmonies. Var. 1: tuba obbligato; Var. 2: a dotted eighth and sixteenth embellishment of the melody; Var. 3: fugue. Tessitura is generally in the upper middle register of the F tuba. See listing under Tuba and Organ.

Koetsier, Jan. *Galgenlieder.* Editions Marc Reift. 1997. $16.00. 6:00. III–IV. G_1–f'. Introduktion; Passacaglia; Choral; Variante 1–3. For soprano and tuba! See listing under Tuba and Organ.

Koetsier, Jan. *Sonatina.* Editions Marc Reift. 1970. $14.50. 6:25 (2:45, 1:40, 2:00). IV–V. G_1–e♭'. See: Koetsier, Jan, *Sonatina Tuba e Pianoforte,* in this section.

Koetsier, Jan. *Sonatina Tuba e Pianoforte.* Donemus. 1970. $17.50. 6:25 (2:45, 1:40, 2:00). IV–V. G_1–e♭'. Allegro; Tempo di minuetto; Allegro moderato. op. 57. Solid recital material. Fun to play, fun to listen to. Allegro: Romantic feel. Very tonal, majestic lyrical style. Some jumps of a tenth. Tempo di minuetto: Arpeggios, leaps of a tenth. Allegro moderato: Shifting meter (2/4, 5/8, 3/8). Suited for F tuba; very playable on lower instrument. Completed Unterkagn, February 20, 1970. Recorded by Manfred Hoppert. See review in *TUBA Journal,* Vol. 9, No. 3, Page 24.

Kolodub, L. *Humorous Dance.* ed. G. Voronov. Moscow Muzyka. 1984. See: Voronov, G, *Works for Tuba and Piano by Russian Composers,* under Tuba and Keyboard Collections.

Konagaya, Soichi. *Celebration for Tuba and Piano.* Toa Music International Co. 1989. 9:07. IV. E♭$_1$–f'. For Hiroyuki Yasumoto. September 1979. Big piece with a popular feel. Audience pleaser. See: Yasumoto, Hiroyuki, *Tuba Volume #3,* under Tuba and Keyboard Collections.

Konagaya, Soichi. *Fantasy for Tuba and Piano.* Toa Music International Co. 1979. 7:20. IV–V. C–f'. For Mr. Yasumoto. Was published by TUBA Press. Optional mute. Some contemporary techniques: improvising in cadenza with predetermined pitches; compound meters; double tonguing. See: Yasumoto, Hiroyuki arr., *Tuba Volume #2,* under Tuba and Keyboard Collections. Recorded by Hiroyuki Yasumoto.

Konko, Iwao. *Sonata No. 1 for Tuba and Piano.* Teruo Miyagawa. 1968. 9:00. IV. F_1–b♭'. Three movements. One of the first pieces composed for tuba in Japan. Contemporary writing; pitch bends, etc.

Konko, Iwao. *Sonata No. 2 for Tuba and Piano.* Teruo Miyagawa. 1968.

Köper, Karl-Heinz. *Sonata.* Trombone Association Publishing. 1975. $14.00. 6:57 (3:32, 3:15, 3:10). IV. F_1–f'. Completed September 15, 1975. Some mixed meter, trills, wide range. Good recital material.

Köper, Karl-Heinz. *Tuba-Tabu.* Musikverlag K. H. Köper. 1967. See: Köper, Karl-Heinz, *Tuba-Tabu,* under Tuba and Orchestra. Recorded by Michael Lind.

Kopprasch, C. *Nr. 15, Etüden für Tuba.* arr. Hiroyuki Yasumoto. Toa Music International Co. 1989. 4:02. IV. (D_1) A_1–a. Adagio. Good orchestration of this classic etude for French horn. Solo should have a feeling of relaxed six (sub-divide). Last dynamic on first line should be piano, not forte. Requires great dynamic contrast and strong musical sense. See: Yasumoto, Hiroyuki, arr., *Tuba Volume #2,* under Tuba and Keyboard Collections.

Kopprasch, C. *Nr. 19, Etüden für Tuba.* arr. Hiroyuki Yasumoto. Toa Music International Co. 1989. 4:25. IV. E–a. Feeling of six (sub-dividing) recommended. Extremely lyrical etude-aria quality. Some rhythmic deciphering involved. See: Yasumoto, Hiroyuki, arr., *Tuba Volume #2,* under Tuba and Keyboard Collections.

Kosteck, Gregory. *Enchanted Island, The.* Available from the composer. 1981. See: Kosteck, Gregory, *The Enchanted Island: Symphonic Poem for Tuba and Orchestra,* under Tuba and Orchestra.

Kotshetov, V. *Adagio from the Ballet "Till Eulenspigel."* arr. A. Lebedev. Military Band Masters Faculty of Moscow Conservatiore. 1971. See: Lebedev, A., *Collection of Pieces for Tuba "Es" and Piano,* under Tuba and Keyboard Collections.

Kottaun, Celian. *Billy Blowhard.* Carl Fischer Inc. 1909. Out of Print. See: Kottaun, Celian, *Billy Blowhard,* under Tuba and Band.

Krebs, Johann Ludwig. *Bourrée.* arr. Stephan Schwotzer. Hofmeister. 1993. 2:08. II. C–d♭. In cut time. See: Meschke, Dieter, *Zum Üben und Vorspielen/B-Tuba,* under Tuba and Keyboard Collections.

Kreisler, Alexander von. *Allegretto Grazioso.* Southern Music Company. 1964. $2.50. 2:00. III. B_1–f. In 6/8 time. Some slurring, no big technical problems.

Kreisler, Alexander von. *Rondo.* Southern Music Company. 1965. $1.50. 3:20. II–III. G_1–e. In cut time. Some slurring, no big technical problems.

Kreisler, Fritz. *Liebesfreud.* arr. Hiroyuki Yasumoto. Toa Music International Co. 1989. 2:58. III. B♭$_1$–c'. Player is encouraged to listen to Heifeitz's recording of this for conception. Must have a joyous, flexible, rubato feel in one. Requires strong flexibility as well as musicality. See: Yasumoto, Hiroyuki arr., *Tuba Volume #2,* under Tuba and Keyboard Collections. Recorded by Hiroyuki Yasumoto.

Kreisler, Fritz. *Liebesfreud.* arr. Patrick Sheridan. Available from Spaeth and Schmid. $25.00.

Kreisler, Fritz. *Liebeslied.* arr. Patrick Sheridan. PatrickSheridan. com (Lollipop Series and Bon Bons Series). $18.00.

Kreisler, Fritz. *Schön Rosmarin.* arr. Hiroyuki Yasumoto. Toa Music International Co. 1989. 2:07. IV. B♭$_1$–d'. Violin showpiece. Requires flexibility for arpeggios. Excellent recital encore piece.

See: Yasumoto, Hiroyuki, *Tuba Volume #3,* under Tuba and Keyboard Collections.

Kreisler, Fritz. *Schön Rosmarin.* arr. Patrick Sheridan. PatrickSheridan. com (Lollipop Series). $15.00.

Kremser. *We Gather Together.* arr. David E. Smith. Solid Brass Music Company. $3.50. II. The traditional Dutch hymn arranged for the beginner.

Krivokapic, Igor. *Rhapsody.* Editions Marc Reift. 2003. $17.50. 7:00. IV. F_1–g♭'. Commissioned by Mihael Svagan. One of the only compositions written for cimbasso, this work can also be performed on the tuba, preferably in F, according to the composer, a former tuba player. The first section is a dialogue between tuba and piano; in the second, they walk hand-in-hand to a 5/4 meter. There is a well-written cadence leading to a final Allegro.

Krivokapic, Igor. *Veseli RONDINO.* Sloway Music Editions. 2004.

Kroepsch, F. *Down in the Deep Cellar (Grand Fantasia).* Carl Fischer Inc. 1898. Out of Print. "for B♭ Clarinet, B♭ Cornet, Trombone or Baritone, Bassoon." See: Kroepsch, F., *Down in the Deep Cellar,* under Tuba and Band. See review in *TUBA Journal,* Vol. 9, No. 3, Page 26.

Krol, Bernhard. *Falstaff Concerto op. 119.* Éditions BIM. 1990. $17.00. Commissioned by Editions Bim. See: Krol, Bernhard, *Falstaff Concerto op. 119,* under Tuba and Orchestra.

Krol, Bernhard. *Minuetto Profondo, op. 83, 1.* Hofmeister. 1983. 3:27. IV. F♯$_1$/G♭$_1$–c'. à Mark Evans. Some flexibility and swiftness of articulation, not overwhelming technique, required. Good recital material.

Krol, Bernhard. *Recitativ und Burla op. 83, 2.* Hofmeister. 1987. 4:51 (0:51, 4:00). IV. G_1–c'. Some changing of meters; conservative metronome markings make this accessible with intermediate technique. A few trills and mordents.

Krotov and Blazhevich. *Concert Etude.* arr. Himie Voxman and R. P. Block. Southern Music Company. 1989. $3.75. 3:00. IV. E♭$_1$–e♭'. Technical solo consisting of mainly staccato sixteenth notes and large leaps. Fun and musical way to sharpen technique.

Krotov and Blazhevich. *Concert Etude.* Moscow Muzyka. 1962. See other listing in this section.

Krush, Jay. *Sonata for Tuba and Piano (op. 6).* 1972. 12:18 (4:20, 1:51, 2:45, 3:22). V. E_1–g' (c''). Contemplative; Distraught; Melancholy; Exuberant. For Michael Sanders. Some contemporary techniques: muted passages, half tones, flutter tonguing, improvised passages, bending of pitches. Contemplative movement is very lyrical; Distraught is quick, requiring quick articulations; Melancholy is lyrical and requires some improvisation; Exuberant requires very fast articulation and optional very high tessitura. See review in *TUBA Journal,* Vol. 1, No. 2, Page 10.

Krzywicki, Jan. *Ballade.* Heilman Music. 1984. $6.00. 4:30. III–IV. E–e'. For Paul. First performed by Paul Kryzwicki at the 1983 International Tuba-Euphonium Conference, University of Maryland, College Park. "for Baritone or Tuba and Piano." Would lie best on E♭/F tuba as well as euphonium or advanced player with stamina in upper tessitura. Very accessible musically; simple, nice tune. See review in *TUBA Journal,* Vol. 12, No. 3, Page 22.

Krzywicki, Jan. *Concerto.* Solo Part Only. Tuba-Euphonium Press. 1999. 14:00. V. C_1–g'. De Profundis; In the Woods; Tarantella. Dedicated to Paul Krzywicki. See listing for Tuba and Orchestra. Large range and rhythmic demands. Requires great musical maturity.

Kubes, Ladislav. *Alte Bekannte.* ed. Václav Hoza. Editio Supraphon, Praha. 1982. 1:47. II–III. B♭$_1$–g. Polka. Typical polka style in two parts. See: Hoza, Václav, *Schule Fur Tuba in F und in B,* in Methods and Studies.

Kubicek. *Capriccio.* Available from Spaeth and Schmid. $11.00.

Kühmstedt. *Humoreske.* Available from Spaeth and Schmid. $5.50.

Kulesha, Gary Alan. *Burlesque for Tuba and Piano.* Sonante Publications. 1984. $4.50. 1:51. IV. G♭$_1$–d'. Some changing of meter from 2/4 to 3/8. A few very large leaps and a couple of fast or double-tongued articulations; otherwise no big technical problems. Good recital material. See review in *TUBA Journal,* Vol. 13, No. 1, Page 20.

Kulesha, Gary Alan. *Concerto for Tuba.* Canadian Music Centre. 1979. Piano accompaniment for four hands. See: Kulesha, Gary Alan, *Concerto for Tuba,* under Tuba and Band and under Tuba and Orchestra.

Kulesha, Gary Alan. *Green Apple Two-Step, The.* Sonante Publications. 1993. $5.25. 1:53. III–IV. F_1–b♭ (f'). Written for Scott Irvine. Fast. "for Bass Tuba and Piano." Includes instructions to "blat" on C and F_1 for comedic effect. Polka-style solo with a few large interval jumps. Good novelty recital piece. Played on CBC's Mr. Dressup by Kent Mason.

Kulesha, Gary Alan. *Humoreske in F.* Sonante Publications. 1978. $5.25. 2:20. IV. C_1–c'. Written for Scott Irvine. "for Bass Tuba and Piano." Range is from C up with one pedal C. Cute solo with snappy feel to it; some syncopations and octave jumps. Good recital piece.

Kulesha, Gary Alan. *Sonata for Tuba and Organ.* Canadian Music Centre. 1976. 10:00. IV. C_1–d'. for Scott Irvine. Three numbered movements. Very lyrical addition to this pairing of tuba and organ. Quite a role reversal for the tuba to be playing the "organ pedal point" for a change. Good recital material.

Kulesha, Gary Alan. *Sonatina (1972) for Tuba and Piano.* Canadian Music Centre. 1972. 6:00.

Written for and dedicated to Scott Irvine. Dance; Song; Dance. Sherburne G. McCurdy Festival Series. Dance has mixed meter—5/8, 3/4, 3/8—and is marked "Distinctly bizarre." Song is very lyrical, has an optional muted section and is marked "Passionately brooding." The last Dance is very quick. Marked "Absolutely lunatic," it alternates within 9/8, 4/4, 5/8, 3/4, and 5/4 time and requires flexibility and strong rhythmic sense.

Kulesha, Gary Alan. *Two Little Leprechauns.* Sonante Publications. 1993. $5.25. 1:46. III–IV. $B\flat_1$–g. For J. M. "Moderately Slowly and Very Unsteadily." "for Drunken Tubist and Piano." Shifting mixed meter and slurring (flexibility required). Good novelty recital piece.

Kulesha, Gary Alan. *Visions for Jane.* Canadian Music Centre. 1975. 5:00. IV. G_1–c'. Completed October 30, 1975, 12:05 AM–1:20 AM Very lyrical solo requiring some flexibility; no big technical problems for the level.

Laburda, Jirí. *Sonate.* Gérard Billaudot. 1987. $9.75. 12:40. IV. $F\sharp_1$–f'. Allegro moderato; Larghetto caloroso; Allegro assai. "pour Tuba Et Piano." For French tuba. Range is perhaps the only technical problem in this solo. See: Thompson/Lemke; *French Music for Low Brass Instruments.*

Lackey, Jerry. *Concertpiece for 3 Tubas and Band.* Available from the composer. 1963. See: Lackey, Jerry, *Concertpiece for 3 Tubas and Band,* under Tuba and Band.

Lackey, Jerry. *Jazz Concerto for Tuba and Band.* Available from the composer. 1984. Piano Reduction. Solo tuba and band, drum set, piano, and electric bass. Same as *Jazz Concerto for Tuba and Orchestra.* See: Lackey, Jerry, *Jazz Concerto for Tuba and Band,* under Tuba and Band.

Lackey, Jerry. *Jazz Concerto for Tuba and Orchestra.* Available from the composer. 1984. $35.00. See: Lackey, Jerry, *Jazz Concerto for Tuba and Orchestra,* under Tuba and Orchestra.

Lackey, Jerry. *Short Stuff.* Available from the composer. 1964. $15.00. See: Lackey, Jerry, *Short Stuff,* under Tuba and Band.

Lafont. *Invincible.* Boosey & Hawkes, Inc. Out of Print.

Lamater. *Auld Lang Syne.* Available from Spaeth and Schmid. $7.25.

Lamater. *Rocked in the Cradle of the Deep.* Available from Spaeth and Schmid. $7.25.

Lamb, Jack, ed. *Classic Festival Solos.* CPP/Belwin, Inc. Tuba Part: $4.50 Piano Part: $6:50. I–III. Contains: Barnes, James, *Work Song, a "Blues Song" for the Young Tubist;* Bartok, Bela, *Dance of the Slovaks;* Bordogni, Marco, *Bordogni Medley;* Eccles, John, *Minuet;* Handel, G. F., *Bourrée;* Handel, G. F., *Larghetto and Allegro;* Handel, G. F., *Where'er You Walk (from Semele);* Barnes, James, arr., *Sometimes I Feel like a Motherless Child;* Ostling, Acton, *Aurora;* Ostling, Acton, arr., *Gallant Captain;* Saint-Saëns, C., *Allegro;* Stoutamire, Albert L., *Legend;* Little, Donald, C., arr., *Military March;* Weber, Fred, and Dorothy Garrett, *The Elephant Dance.*

Lamb, Jack, ed. *Solo Sounds for Tuba, Level 1–3, Vol. 1.* CPP/Belwin, Inc. 1987. Tuba: $4.50 Piano $6.50. I–III. Contains: Arne, Thomas A., *Air from "Comus";* Belden, George R., *Black Holes in Space;* Bell, William J., arr., *Russian Medley;* Bordogni, Marco, *Bordogni Medley;* Bowles, Richard W., *Deep Rock;* Bowles, Richard W., *Venetian Carnival;* Dacre, Harry, *Bicycle Built for Two;* Handel, G. F., *Where'er You Walk (from Semele);* Little, Donald C., *Lazy Lullaby;* Little, Donald C., arr., *Military March;* Peter, C., *Jolly Coppersmith, The;* Schumann, Robert, *Sailors' Song;* Weber, Fred, and Dorothy Garrett, *The Elephant Dance.*

Lamb, Jack, ed. *Solo Sounds for Tuba, Level 3–5, Vol. 1.* CPP/Belwin, Inc. 1987. Tuba: $4.50 Piano $6.50. II–III. Contains: Bizet, Georges, *Carmen Excerpts;* Bowles, Richard W., *Changing Scene;* Dowling, Robert, *His Majesty the Tuba;* Gretchaninoff, A., *Slumber Song;* Grieg, Edvard, *In the Hall of the Mountain King;* Handel, G. F., *Honor and Arms;* Haydn, F. J., *Sonata No. 7, First Movement;* Marcello, Benedetto, *Largo and Presto;* Mozart, W. A., *Menuetto;* Vivaldi, Antonio, *Allegro (from Sonata No. 3).*

Lancen, S. *Grave.* Alphonse Leduc. $16.85. For tuba/baritone or saxhorn and piano. For French tuba.

Lange. *Heather Rose Caprice.* arr. Carl Weber. J. W. Pepper & Son. 1914. Out of Print. See: Weber, Carl, *Nineteen Solos for E♭ Bass with Piano Accompaniment,* under Tuba and Keyboard Collections.

Langgaard, Rued. *Dies Irae.* Danish Brass Publishing. 1986. DKR 77,05. 2:17. III. G♯–d. Completed March 18, 1948. Upper tessitura, best on F tuba, playable on lower instrument. Piano part harder than tuba part. Recorded by Jorgen Voight Arnsted.

Lannoy, J. B. de. *Souvenir de Paris.* Schott Frères. Out of Print.

Lantier, Pierre. *Andante et Allegro.* Henri Lemoine & Cie. 1964. $11.00. IV–V. F_1 (A_1)–a'. A Paul Bernard, professeur au Conservatoire National Supérieur de Musique de Paris. "pour Tuba et Piano." For French tuba. See: Thompson/Lemke; *French Music for Low Brass Instruments.*

LaPresti, Ronald. *Sonata for Tuba and Piano.* Manuscript. 1984. 5:00. IV–V. G_1–a'. Written for Daniel Perantoni. Adagio; Allegretto Grazioso; Allegro Con Fuoco. Composed Dec. 1983–Jan. 1984, Tempe, Ariz. Very tonal writing requiring strong technique. In the collection of Daniel Perantoni.

Largent, Edward. *Four Shorts for Tuba and Piano.* Seesaw Music Corporation. 1986. $11.50. 5:30. IV–V. G_1–g♭'. *Rhythms; Spots; Turns; Burlesque.*

Completed July 30, 1984. Flutter tonguing, multi-phonics, glissandos, mixed meter, quintuplets, etc. Requires wide range and strong technique. Recorded by John Turk.

Largent. *Seven Shorts.* Available from Spaeth and Schmid. $46.75.

Larin, J., ed. *Pieces for Tuba and Piano.* Moscow Muzyka. 1979. Contains: Bernstein, Leonard, *Waltz for Mippy;* Bozza, Eugène, *Allegro and Finale;* Bozza, Eugène, *Prelude and Allegro;* Désenclos, A., *Air;* LeClerc, E, *Concertino;* Moro, D., *Piece from Suite "Colours in Movement";* Tchebotarev, S., *Rondo.*

Larsen, Libby. *Concert Piece for Tuba and Piano.* Manuscript. 1993. 3:19. IV–V. G_1–g'. For Mark Nelson. Quick tempo-feeling of one with 2/4 marked. Wide range and some flexibility required. Strong accompanist needed.

Lavalle, Paul, and Joe Tarto. *Big Joe, the Tuba.* arr. F. Henri Klickmann. Stargen Music Corp/Sam Fox Company. 1955. Out of Print. 3:35. III. A♭$_1$–f. March feel in 6/8 time. Key of A♭ and D♭ major. No technical problems.

Lawrance, Peter. *Six Modern Pieces.* Brass Wind Publications. II. For E♭ bass/E♭ tuba. Solos with easy accompaniments. Treble and bass clef versions available.

Lawrence, Lucinda. *Piece for Tuba and Piano.* Hal Leonard Publishing Corp. 1976. F_1–a. In the style of Bartok. Mixed meter. See: Perantoni, Daniel, *Master Solos Intermediate Level,* under Tuba and Keyboard Collections.

Layens, C. G. *Intermede.* Editions Andel Uitgave.

Lebedev, A. *Concerto Allegro.* arr. Glenn P. Smith. University Music Press. 1962. Out of Print. 5:00. IV. (E_1) F_1–c' (e♭'). Neo-romantic feel to this through-composed work. Very lyrical writing; intermediate flexibility and technique required. Good recital material.

Lebedev, A. *Concerto in One Movement.* arr. Allen Ostrander. Edition Musicus. 1960. $6.75. 6:00. IV. (E♭$_1$) E_1–c' (e♭'). Very lyrical, dramatic material. Good recital material. Recorded by Jeffrey Arwood; Manfred Hoppert.

Lebedev, A. *Cradle Song, A.* Moscow Muzyka. 1986. 0:55. III. A_1–a. Tempo di Valse. Andantino. Lullaby. Very musical way of practicing slurs between a sixth and an octave. See: Lebedev, A., *Tuba Tutor Vol. 2,* under Tuba and Keyboard Collections.

Lebedev, A. *Gavotte.* Moscow Muzyka. 1986. 1:21. III. F_1–b♭. Alla Breve. Peasante. Playful little tune that shows the composer's ballet roots. See: Lebedev, A., *Tuba Tutor Vol. 2,* under Tuba and Keyboard Collections.

Lebedev, A. *(Title Unknown).* Manuscript. 1987. $6.75. Third composition for tuba and piano by this Russian master performer and teacher.

Lebedev, A., arr. *Adagio.* Military Band Masters Faculty of Moscow Conservatiore. 1971. Annon. See: Lebedev, A., *Collection of Pieces for Tuba "Es" and Piano,* under Tuba and Keyboard Collections.

Lebedev, A., arr. *Estonian Folk Dance.* Moscow Muzyka. 1974. 0:50. II. E–e. Allegretto. Russian folk song. Pretty tune in 3/4 time with no technical problems. See: Lebedev, A., *Tuba Tutor Vol. 1,* under Tuba and Keyboard Collections.

Lebedev, A., arr. *On the Steep High Mountain.* Moscow Muzyka. 1984. 1:14. III. F–a♭ (b♭). Russian folk song. In 4/4 time in B♭ minor. Some slurring; no technical problems beyond key. See: Lebedev, A., *Tuba Tutor Vol. 1,* under Tuba and Keyboard Collections.

Lebedev, A., arr. *Ring, A.* Moscow Muzyka. 1984. 0:20. II. C–f. Russian folk song. Short lyrical piece in F minor. See: Lebedev, A., *Tuba Tutor Vol. 1,* under Tuba and Keyboard Collections.

Lebedev, A., ed. *Collection of Pieces for Tuba "Es" and Piano.* Military Band Masters Faculty of Moscow Conservatiore. 1971. Contains: Arutiunian, Alexandre, *Expromt;* Bartok, Bela, *Dance of the Bear;* Fesh, D., *Prelude;* Gudmen, S., *Dance;* Handel, G. F., *Air;* Handel, G. F., *Variations;* Jurovsky, V., *March;* Kaneda, B., *Long, Long Ago;* Karaev, V., *Dance from Ballet "Seven Beauties";* Katchiturian, A., *Dance from Ballet "Spartak";* Kazadezins, R., *Spanish Dance;* Kotshetov, V., *Adagio from the Ballet "Till Eulenspigel";* Lebedev, A., arr., *Adagio;* Ledov, A., *Prelude;* Mozart, W. A., *Allegro;* Orthel, L., *Prelude;* Pergolesi, Giovanni Battista, *Air;* Prokofiev, Sergi, *Recitative and Kutuzov's Air from the Opera "War and Peace";* Rachmaninoff, Sergei, *Russian Song;* Rakov, N., *Romance;* Ravel, Maurice, *Pavane;* Rubinstein, A., *A Persian Song;* Schubert, Franz, *Ave Maria;* Scriabine, Alexander, *Etude;* Shostakovitch, Dimitri, *Romance;* Stepovoi, J., *Cantabile;* Stravinsky, Igor, *Russian Song;* Vasilyev, V., *Melody.*

Lebedev, A., ed. *Tuba Tutor Vol. 1.* Moscow Muzyka. 1984. II–III. "School of Playing on Tuba." Contains: Bartok, Bela, *Adagio;* Bartok, Bela, *Dance;* Bartok, Bela, *Hungarian Folk Song;* Bartok, Bela, *A Song;* Britten, Benjamin, *The Sentimental Sarabande from the "Simple Symphony" for String Orchestra;* Frid, G., *A Little Birch Tree;* Gluck, K., *Gavotte;* Goedicke, A., *Dance;* Handel, G. F., *Bouree;* Lebedev, A., arr., *Estonian Folk Dance;* Lebedev, A., arr., *On the Steep High Mountain;* Lebedev, A., arr., *A Ring;* Miaskovskii, N., *Song of the Field;* Monushko, S., *A Fairy Tale;* Pozzoli, E., *Sad Minute, The;* Samonov, A., *Good Night;* Samonov, A., *Grandfather Is Dancing;* Tchaikovsky, Peter I., *Tomsky's Song from the Opera "Queen of Spades";* Zverev, V., *Song.* Also see: Lebedjev, A., *Tuba Tutor, Vol. 1,* under Methods and Studies.

Lebedev, A., ed. *Tuba Tutor Vol. 2.* Moscow Muzyka. 1986. II–IV. "School of Playing on Tuba." Contains: Bak, M., *A Joke;* Barber, S., *Adagio and Scherzo from Sonata C Minor;* Brahms, S. (sic), *Waltz;* Corelli, A., *Sarabanda;* Duntriev, G.,

Ballada; Greig, E., *In Spring Time;* Kikta, V., *Epic Tale and Procession of the People in Costumes (Festival);* Lebedev, A., *A Cradle Song;* Lebedev, A., *Gavotte;* Link, I., *Sonatina Movement IV;* Rakov, N., *Sonatina;* Schedrin, R., *Variations from the Ballet Konick-Gorbunoch;* Smirnova, T., *A Joke;* Sviridov, G., *Iago's Song about King Stephen from the Tragedy "Othello";* Taktakishvili, O., *Aria from the Opera "The Lifes";* Tomasi, G. (sic), *Hamlet's Monologue;* Volkov, K., *A Piece.*

Lebedev, Alexej. *Konzert* (Hofmeister). Available from Spaeth and Schmid. $11.50.

Lebedev, Alexej. *Konzert Nr. 2.* Available from Spaeth and Schmid. $13.25.

Lebedjew, A. *Konzert für Tuba und Klavier.* Hofmeister. 1954. $13.95. ($E\flat_1$) E_1–e♭'. Same as Lebedev, A., *Concerto in One Movement,* in this section.

Lebedjew, Alexej. *Märchen, Wiegenlied und Gavotte.* Available from Spaeth and Schmid. $12.25.

Leclair. *Sonate D-Dur.* Available from Spaeth and Schmid. $14.00.

Leclair, Jean-Marie. *Sarabande.* arr. André Goudenhooft; pno realizations Augustin Maillard. Gérard Billaudot. 1989. $9.50. 2:30. IV. C–f'. "pour le trombone basse et le tuba basse. Extraite de la 3e Sonate pour violon." Packaged with *Courante* by Senaille, Jean Baptiste. See: Thompson/Lemke; *French Music for Low Brass Instruments.*

LeClerc, E. *Concertino.* ed. J. Larin. Moscow Muzyka. 1979. See: Larin, J., *Pieces for Tuba and Piano,* under Tuba and Keyboard Collections.

Ledov, A. *Prelude.* arr. A. Lebedev. Military Band Masters Faculty of Moscow Conservatiore. 1971. See: Lebedev, A., *Collection of Pieces for Tuba "Es" and Piano,* under Tuba and Keyboard Collections.

Leduc. *Andante.* Available from Spaeth and Schmid. $7.25.

Legendre. *Souvenir du Poitou.* arr. Carl Weber. J. W. Pepper & Son. 1914. Out of Print. See: Weber, Carl, *Nineteen Solos for E♭ Bass with Piano Accompaniment,* under Tuba and Keyboard Collections.

Legrady, Thomas. *Tubantella.* Molenaar. 1987. Piano reduction. See: Legrady, Thomas, *Tubantella,* under Tuba and Band.

Lehar, Franz. *Merry Widow Waltz.* arr. Acton Ostling. CPP/Belwin, Inc. 1969. 1:23. I. $B\flat_1$–d. Once through the tune with a tag. No technical problems. See: Ostling, Acton, *Tuba (Bass) Soloist, Level One,* under Tuba and Keyboard Collections.

Lejet, Edith. *Méandres.* Gérard Billaudot. 1985. $7.00. 5:30. V. G_1–g♯'. A Fernand Lelong, professeur au CNSMP. "pour Saxhorn Basse en Si♭ et Piano." Extreme flexibility required. Double tonguing, trills, rhythmic challenges, wide range. See: Thompson/Lemke; *French Music for Low Brass Instruments.*

Lemaire, Jean. *Trois Exercises de Style.* Alphonse Leduc. 1971. Out of Print. 5:45. V. E_1–b♭'. For French tuba. See: Thompson/Lemke; *French Music for Low Brass Instruments.*

Lemaire, Jean. *Variations Sur Un Theme De Purcell.* Editions Rideau Rouge. 1976. 4:45. IV. F_1–g'. "Concours du Conservatoire National Supérieur de Musique de Paris 1976." Wide range. Technical considerations consist mostly of sixteenth note scale-like passages. Requires light articulation and flexibility. "pour Tuba Et Piano." For French tuba.

Lennon, John, and Paul McCartney. *Hey Jude!* arr. Hiroyuki Yasumoto. Toa Music International Co. 1989. 4:10. IV. F_1–f' (g'). Nice transcription of classic Beatles tune. Some syncopation. Wide range. See: Yasumoto, Hiroyuki, *Tuba Volume #3,* under Tuba and Keyboard Collections.

Lennon, John, and Paul McCartney. *Yesterday.* arr. Hiroyuki Yasumoto. Toa Music International Co. 1989. 3:08. III. F_1–g. Good arrangement of the Beatles classic ballad. Strong lyric sense required when tubist plays the melody as well as when accompanying. See: Yasumoto, Hiroyuki, arr., *Tuba Volume #2,* under Tuba and Keyboard Collections. Recorded by Hiroyuki Yasumoto.

Leonov, I. *Etude de concert.* ed. S. Melnikov. Military Band Masters Institute–Moscow. 1957. See: Melnikov, S., *Pieces for Tuba and Piano,* under Tuba and Keyboard Collections.

Lesaffre, Charles. *En Glissant . . . (Upon Sliding.)* ed. Fernand Lelong. Gérard Billaudot. 1984. $4.50. 2:00. II. (B♭) c–d' (e♭'). A mon frère Directeur de l'école de Musique de Dammarie. "Pour saxhorn basse si♭ ou tuba ténor ou trombone en ut et piano." For French tuba. Eighth note is fastest rhythm. Mostly step-wise motion; no technical problems. See: Thompson/Lemke; *French Music for Low Brass Instruments.*

Lesaffre, Charles. *Petite Chansons Pour Marion. (Little Song for Marion.)* Gérard Billaudot. 1988. $5.75. 2:15. II. B♭–e♭' (f'). A ma mère. "pour tuba en ut ou trombone ou baryton ou trompette ou cornet et piano." "Happy is the man who can make a living by his hobby! G. B. Shaw." For French tuba. Pretty tune with a bit of rhythmic variation. A few arpeggios; no big technical problems. See: Thompson/Lemke; *French Music for Low Brass Instruments.*

Levy, Yeuda. *Mediterranean Rondo.* Kibutz Movement League of Composers. Recorded by Adi Hershko.

Lewis, Paul. *Bank Holiday Suite.* Editions Marc Reift. 1998. $19.80. 9:00. IV. E_1–e♭' (a'). Romp; Romance; March. Dedicated to Stephen Wick. Tonal composition spiced with English humor by one of England's most popular television composers. The humorous harmonic twists in the piano part rend a lively tongue-in-cheek character to the work. The highest parts are written optional 8va bassa.

Liadov, Anatol. *Dancing Song.* arr. Dishinger. Available from Spaeth and Schmid. $6.50.

Liagré, Dartagnan. *Souvenir de Calais.* Andrieu Freres/Gérard Billaudot. 1951. $3.50. 4:35. III–IV. B♭$_1$–a'. à mon petit fils Jean-Marie. (Liagre: Soliste a la Musique de la Garde Republicaine). "Baryton en SI♭ ou Basse Si♭." For French tuba. Theme and variations. Mostly scale-wise motion. Good intermediate solo.

Lincke. *Glow Worm, The.* arr. Acton Ostling. CPP/Belwin, Inc. 1969. 1:43. I. E♭–c. Very limited range. A few eighth notes; no technical problems. See: Ostling, Acton, *Tuba (Bass) Soloist, Level One,* under Tuba and Keyboard Collections.

Lincke and Waldteufel. *Waltz Themes.* arr. Acton Ostling. CPP/Belwin, Inc. 1969. 2:03. I. B♭$_1$–B♭. Chimes of Spring; Tres Jolie. In 3/4 time with no technical problems. See: Ostling, Acton, *Tuba (Bass) Soloist, Level One,* under Tuba and Keyboard Collections.

Lincoln. *College March.* arr. Acton Ostling. CPP/Belwin, Inc. 1969. 0:47. I. B♭$_1$–A♭. In 2/4 time. Introduces F♯. See: Ostling, Acton, *Tuba (Bass) Soloist, Level One,* under Tuba and Keyboard Collections.

Link, I. *Sonatina Movement IV.* ed. A. Lebedev. Moscow Muzyka. 1986. 1:11. III–IV. G$_1$–g. In 7/8 time throughout with some flexibility requirements. See: Lebedev, A., *Tuba Tutor Vol. 2,* under Tuba and Keyboard Collections.

Link, Joachim-Dietrich. *Sonatine.* Hofmeister. 1951. Out of Print. 6:00. IV–V. B$_1$–a'. Herrn Kammervirtuos Hans Lachmann. Allegro molto; Adagio improvvisato; Prestissimo. For F tuba. Upper tessitura. Last movement is in 7/8 time.

Linkola, Jukka. *Konzert.* Available from Spaeth and Schmid. $25. 00.

Lischka, Rainer. *Drei Skizzen.* Hofmeister. 1969. 5:55 (1:22, 3:13, 1:20). IV–V. B♭$_1$–f'. "für Baßtuba oder Baßposaune und Klavier." Three movements. Middle to upper tessitura; best on F tuba. Very playable on lower tubas. Rhythmic and lyrical playing throughout. Good recital material.

Little, Don, arr. *Flow Gently, Sweet Afton.* CPP/Belwin, Inc. 1989. I–II. C–d. Traditional. In 3/4 time; some slurring of eighth notes. Mostly step-wise motion with a few jumps, none larger than a sixth. See: Little, Don, *Solo-Pak for Tuba, Part One,* under Tuba and Keyboard Collections.

Little, Donald C. *Lazy Lullaby.* CPP/Belwin, Inc. 1977. $4.00. 2:06. I. C–c. Slowly and expressively. Solo in slow 4/4 time with a few eighth notes. A few slurs covering a third; otherwise no technical problems. Limited range and technique. Recorded by Ronald Davis.

Little, Donald C. *Lazy Lullaby.* CPP/Belwin, Inc. 1977. See: Lamb, Jack, *Solo Sounds for Tuba Levels 1–3, Vol. 1,* under Tuba and Keyboard Collections. Also see other listing in this section.

Little, Donald C., arr. *Military March.* CPP/Belwin, Inc. 1977. $4.00. 1:35. I. (B♭$_1$) C–c. Two American patriotic songs with an eight-measure piano interlude. Solo in cut time with no technical problems. See other listings in this section.

Little, Donald C., arr. *Military March.* CPP/Belwin, Inc. 1977. See: Lamb, Jack, *Classic Festival Solos,* under Tuba and Keyboard Collections. Also see other listings in this section.

Little, Donald C., arr. *Military March.* CPP/Belwin, Inc. 1977. See: Lamb, Jack, *Solo Sounds for Tuba Levels 1–3, Vol. 1,* under Tuba and Keyboard Collections. Also see other listings in this section.

Little, Donald C., arr. *Solo-Pak for Tuba, Part One.* CPP/Belwin, Inc. 1989. $5.00. I. Follows the levels of the Medalist Band Method. Contains: Haydn, Franz Joseph, *The Spacious Firmament on High;* Little, Don, arr., *Flow Gently, Sweet Afton;* Quate, Amy, and Don Little, *Texas Horizons.*

Little, Donald C., arr. *Solo-Pak for Tuba, Part Three.* CPP/Belwin, Inc. 1992. $5.00. II–III. Follows the levels of the Medalist Band Method. Contains: Mozart, W. A., *Aria from La Clemenza di Tito;* Purcell, Henry, *Song from Timon of Athens;* Quate, Amy, *The Feel Good Blues.*

Little, Donald C., arr. *Solo-Pak for Tuba, Part Two.* CPP/Belwin, Inc. 1991. $5.00. I–II. Follows the levels of the Medalist Band Method. Contains: Brahms, Johannes, *Sunday (Sonntag, Op. 47, 1968);* Caccini, Giulia, *Amarilli, Mia Bella;* Quate, Amy, *Los Cocos Locos (Crazy Coconuts).*

Livingston, J., and R. Evans. *To Each His Own.* arr. Hiroyuki Yasumoto. Toa Music International Co. 1989. 4:15. III–IV. F$_1$–e♭. "with Jazz Feeling." A 4/4 ballad with a 12/8 feel. See: Yasumoto, Hiroyuki, *Tuba Volume #3,* under Tuba and Keyboard Collections. Recorded by Hiroyuki Yasumoto.

Lloyd, Gerald. *Three Sketches.* Theodore Presser Company. 1968. $3.00. 4:00 (1:00, 1:10, 1:50). IV. G$_1$–a. Allegro; Recitativo; Allegro. Intermediate technique required.

Lockwood, Harry. *Sonata for Tuba and Piano.* Available from the composer. 1966. IV. For Robert LeBlanc. Four movements.

Lodéon, André. *Campagnarde. (Country Woman.)* Alphonse Leduc. 1964. $9.15. 2:00. II. c–d'. "pour Tuba en Ut ou Saxhorn basse en Si♭ et Piano." For French tuba. Easy rhythms. Can be played as upper tessitura for lower tubas. See: Thompson/Lemke; *French Music for Low Brass Instruments.*

Lodéon, André. *Tuba Show.* Alphonse Leduc. 1968. $12.80. 4:45. IV–V. A$_1$–a' (b♭'). "pour Tuba en Ut ou Saxhorn Basse Si♭ et Piano." For French tuba. Flexibility and strong technique required. Wide range, some mixed meter, cadenza. See: Thompson/Lemke; *French Music for Low Brass Instruments.*

Loeillet, Jean-Baptiste. ***Sonate en do majeur (Sonata in C Major)***. arr. Kurt Sturzenegger. Editions Marc Reift. 1996. \$11.80. 5:30. III. A–d'. Cantabile; Largo; Allegro. Originally for flute and continuo, the arrangement of this baroque composition was obviously conceived for bass trombone. It can also be purchased a major third lower, but in this case it is written in treble clef in B♭. See listing under Tuba and Organ.

Loelliet, Jean-Baptiste. *Vivace, from Sonata in E mi.* arr. Gary Buttery. Whaling Music Publishers. 1978. \$5.00. 3:15. IV. E–d'. "for Blöckflote and Continuo." "Solo Tuba or Euphonium." Continuo part: harpsichord and cello or bassoon. Contains mordents and trills. Brisk cut time. Good recital material.

Löffler. *Der Herr Tubist.* arr. Cosmar. Available from The Tuba Center.

Lohmann, Georg. *Bayrische Polka.* arr. Leeuwen. Available from Spaeth and Schmid. \$8.25.

Lohr, Frederic N. *Out on the Deep.* arr. G. E. Holmes. Rubank, Inc. 1939. 1:10. II. $b\flat_1$–f. "Solo Tuba—E♭ or BB♭." Allegro Moderato. Traditional sea chantey feel in 6/8. A few repeating sixteenth notes; no technical problems. See: Rubank, *Soloist Folio for Bass (E♭ or BB♭)*, under Tuba and Keyboard Collections.

Long, Lela. *Jesus Is the Sweetest Name.* arr. Alan Moss. David E. Smith Publications. 1990. \$3.50. 2:40. II–III. F–g. Lyrical solo with upper tessitura for the level. Much slurring and tenutos.

Lorge, John. *Fantasie.* Tuba-Euphonium Press. 1995. 12:00. V. E_1–g'. I; II; III; IV. See listing for Tuba and Orchestra. A piano reduction by the composer of this very challenging concert piece for tuba and orchestra. Some aleatoric effects, frequent metric shifts, angular rhythms, and extreme dynamics.

Lotzenhiser, G. W. *Hornpipe, A.* Belwin, Inc. 1957. Out of Print. 2:00. II. $B\flat_1$–b♭. To W. J. L. Almost the entire part is in octaves, making the above range deceptive. In cut time with no hard rhythms. Some slurring involved.

Lotzenhiser, G. W. *Solitude.* Belwin, Inc. 1958. Out of Print. 3:00. I–II. (G_1) A_1–B♭. To B. K. Some accidentals; no technical problems.

Louel, Jean. ***Ritmico Ed Arioso.*** Centre Belge de Documentation Musicale. 1980. 4:52. IV–V. $A\flat_1$–e♭'. Muted passages. Complex and compound meters. Contemporary melodic writing. Will take swift articulations (some possible double tonguing) and imaginative lyricism.

Louvier, Alain. *Cromagnon.* Alphonse Leduc. 1973. \$12.20. C♯–c''. For French tuba. See: Thompson/Lemke; *French Music for Low Brass Instruments.*

Lovec, Vladimir. *Requiem for Euphonium or Basstuba and Piano.* ed. W. Boswell and J. Boswell. Philharmusica Corp. 1974. \$3.95. 1:59. IV. E–g'. Lento espressivo. "for Euphonium or Basstuba and Accompaniment." Upper tessitura; better on F tuba or euphonium. Lyrical expressive solo that is mostly slurred. Good opportunity to show off high range and vocal approach.

Lovelock, William. *Concerto for Tuba and Orchestra.* Allans Publishing. ca. 1965. For John Woods. Piano reduction by the composer. See: Lovelock, William, *Concerto for Tuba and Orchestra,* under Tuba and Orchestra.

Lovingood, Kay. *Suite.* Tuba-Euphonium Press. 1997. F_1–f'. 8:00. IV. Variations; Adagio; Fugue. First movement is rhythmically complex with angular melodic lines. The other two movements are more simple in comparison, but the fugue is very rhythmic as well.

Luedeke, Raymond. *Fancies and Interludes I.* American Composer's Edition. 1977. Score: \$17.95, Parts: \$10.30. 14:00. V. B_2–f♯'. Dedicated to Fritz Kaenzig. Commissioned by the University of Northern Iowa. Modern writing with some modern notation (explained). Very strong technique required. Multi-phonics, bending of pitches, improvising, etc. See review in *TUBA Journal,* Vol. 7, No. 1, Page 5.

Lully, Jean-Babtiste. *Gavotte In Rondeau.* tr. S. Post. Medici Music Press. 1981. 2:30. II–III. C–c. In F minor and in 4/4 time. Lyrical solo with a limited range. Good introduction to late Renaissance/early baroque style.

Lully, Jean-Baptiste. *Gavotte.* arr. Herbert Wekselblatt. G. Schirmer Inc. 1972. 1:30. II–III. C–f. Tempo di Gavotte. Stately baroque transcription. See: Wekselblatt, Herbert, *First Solos for the Tuba Player, BB♭,* under Tuba and Keyboard Collections.

Lully, Jean-Baptiste. *Lonely Forest, The. (Bois Épais.)* ed. Charles Daellenbach. Hal Leonard Publishing Corp. 1992. 2:12. II. C–e♭. Largo. A few eighth/sixteenth dotted rhythms; otherwise rhythmically easy. Sustained feel. See: Daellenbach, Charles, *Book of Easy Tuba Solos,* under Tuba and Keyboard Collections.

Lunde, Ivar, Jr. *Designs.* Norsk Musikforlag. 1987. 9:52 (1:41, 2:50, 3:32, 1:49). IV. $F\sharp_1$–d♯'. Interrupted lines; Continuous lines; Expressive lines; Dancing lines. For Jerry and Barbara Young. "Variations for Tuba and Piano Op. 92." Modern melodic writing. Mixed meter, contemporary lyricism. Second movement is entirely muted. End of third movement, tubist is instructed to blow across the open end of a tuba straight mute, producing a BB♭ (optional playing it on tuba). Last movement has a modern ragtime feel with plenty of syncopation and some mixed meter.

Lundin, Dag. *Bourèe burlesque.* SMIC. 2003. Written for F tuba and piano.

Lundquist, Torbjørn Iwan. *Landskap.* 1978. Piano reduction. Recorded by Michael Lind.

Luypaerts, G. Ph. *Suite.* Available from Spaeth and Schmid. \$10.25.

Lysight, Michel. *Thrène.* Available from Spaeth and Schmid. \$10.25.

Lyte, H., and W. Monk. *Abide with Me.* arr. David E. Smith. David E. Smith Publications. 1985. $2.50. 2:06. I. C–B♭. Beginning solo with limited range and easy rhythms—quarter note is fastest rhythm. Some step-wise slurring.

Macbeth, Allan. *Forget Me Not.* arr. G. E. Holmes. Rubank, Inc. 1939. 2:27. II–III. D–f (g). "Solo Tuba—E♭ or BB♭ tuba." Allegretto. Traditional solo in cut time. Some simple arpeggios. Depending on tempo, not too difficult. See: Rubank, *Soloist Folio for Bass (E♭ or BB♭),* under Tuba and Keyboard Collections.

MacDowell, Edward. *Deserted Farm, A.* arr. George Masso. Providence Music Press. 1966. Out of Print. 4:30. III. A_1–a. Woodland Sketches. Opus 15. Also for trombone or baritone (t.c.) and piano. Very lyrical transcription containing all slurred phrases. Good recital material.

Madsen, Trygrave. *Felix, Michael and I: For Tuba and Piano, Op. 102.* Norwegian Music Center.

Madsen, Trygrave. *Michael and I: For Tuba and Piano, Op. 106.* Norwegian Music Center.

Madsen, Trygve. *Introduction and Allegro.* Musikk Husets Forlag. IV. See: Madsen, Trygve, *Introduction and Allegro,* under Tuba and Band.

Madsen, Trygve. *Konzert Op. 35.* Musikk-Huset A/S. 1986. $26.00. See: Madsen, Trygve, *Concerto for Tuba and Orchestra, Opus 35,* under Tuba and Orchestra.

Madsen, Trygve. *Sonata for (F) Tuba and Piano, Op. 34.* Musikk-Huset A/S. 1980. $24.95. IV–V. $B♭_1$–f♯'. To Roger Bobo. Andante sostenuto; Allegro enerfico; Allegro moderato. Flexibility required. As suggested by composer, for F tuba. Recorded by Øystein Baadsvik, Roger Bobo. See review in *TUBA Journal,* Vol. 9, No. 2, Page 25.

Maertens, J. *Cadenza e Allegro Scherzando.* Editions Andel Uitgave.

Maes, J. *Concertstuk (1944).* Editions Musicales Brogneaux. 1953. 5:00. E–c''. "Opgedragen aan de vriend en uitmuntend lerar Mr. P. Roupcinsky." Written for trombone/tuba Ut/bassoon and piano. French tuba and piano.

Maganini, Quinto. *Ancient Greek Melody, An.* Edition Musicus. 1946. 1:37. II–III. C–a♭. Lento. Melody from Aeschylus: *The House of Atreus.* Modal Greek feel; many harmonic second intervals. Easy accompaniment. See: Ostrander, Allen, *Concert Album for Tuba,* under Tuba and Keyboard Collections.

Maganini, Quinto. *L'Apres-Midi d'une Crocodille.* Edition Musicus. 1969. $2. 25. III–IV. E_1–a♭. The afternoon of a lady crocodile. For bassoon and piano (tuba and piano). Interpolated material from: Debussy, Claude, *L'apres-midi d'un faune* and Wagner, Richard, *Liebestod* from *Tristan and Isolde.*

Mahler, Gustav. *Leider Eines Fahrenden Gesellen.* arr. Dan Perantoni and Yutzy. Encore Music Publishers. 1992. $12.50. IV. F♯–f'. Allegro; Gamächlich; Schnell und wild; Alla Marcia. Upper tessitura; best suited for F tuba. Good vocal transcriptions.

Mañas, Adriana Figueroa. *Tango Images.* Tuba-Euphonium Press. 2003. 8:00. IV–V. $B♭_1$–e'. I; II; III; IV. Dedicated to Mark Nelson. Rhythmically interesting and challenging work. Excellent for recitals.

Manas, Franz. *Lustiger Bassist Konzertpolka.* Johann Kliment. 1970. See: Manas, Franz, *Lustiger Bassist Konzertpolka,* under Tuba and Band.

Mancini, Henry. *Pink Panther, The.* arr. Arthur Frackenpohl. Kendor Music, Inc. 1983. $5.00. 2:35. III–IV. C♯–b♭. Groovy misterioso. Contains an "improvise or play as written" section for those who feel comfortable stretching out. Has grace notes, falls, and a commercial feel. Listen to original composition for conception. Good recital piece.

Mancini, Henry. *The Pink Panther.* arr. Scott Richards. Editions Marc Reift. 1964. $7.00. 2:45. II–III. F ($G_1$)–g. Conventional arrangement of the jazz standard. Although available in bass clef concert pitch, or in treble clef in E♭ or B♭, this arrangement lies best on the E♭ or F tuba.

Manen, Christian. *Grave et Scherzo, Op. 107.* Gérard Billaudot. 1978. $9.75. IV–V. F_1–a'. A Paul Bernard, en toute amitié. "pour trombone basse et piano (tuba out saxhorn)." Primarily for bass trombone (or French tuba). Scherzo section has an alternating meter section—7/8, 3/4, 6/8, 7/8, etc.—and cadenza. Very wide range. See: Thompson/Lemke; *French Music for Low Brass Instruments.*

Maniet, Rene. *Piece in C.* Henri Elkan. 1954. French tuba and piano.

Maniet, Rene. *Poco Allegro.* Editions Musicales Brogneaux. 1955. $1.20. French tuba and piano.

Maniet, Rene. *Premier Solo de Concours.* ed. Himie Voxman. Rubank, Inc. 1972. 2:30. II–III. $B♭_1$–e♭. "for E♭ or BB♭ Bass." Very majestic French etude with no big technical problems. See: Voxman, Himie, *Concert and Contest Collection,* under Tuba and Keyboard Collections.

Marcello, Benedetto. *Adagio from Sonata C-Dur.* arr. Gary A. Buttery. Whaling Music Publishers. 1978. $3.50. 4:00. IV. G–c'. Harpsichord and cello or bassoon continuo. For tuba or euphonium. With baroque ornamentation. In eight and in C major. Upper tessitura; mostly crisp dotted rhythms.

Marcello, Benedetto. *Il Mio Bel Foco.* ed. and compiled Harry I. Phillips. Shawnee Press Inc. 1967. 2:30. III. C–g. Recitative/Allegretto affetuoso. Lyrical, slurred transcription in a minor key. In two sections a 4/4 Recitative (felt in eight), and a faster 3/4 Allegretto. See: Phillips, Harry I., *Eight Bel Canto Songs,* under Tuba and Keyboard Collections.

Marcello, Benedetto. *Largo and Allegro.* ed. Himie Voxman. Rubank, Inc. 1972. 3:30. II–III. ($A\flat_1$) $B\flat_1$–f. "for E♭ or BB♭ Bass." Easier transcription of original. Largo in 3/4 time; Allegro in 12/8. See: Voxman, Himie, *Concert and Contest Collection,* under Tuba and Keyboard Collections.

Marcello, Benedetto. *Largo and Allegro.* ed. S. Melnikov. Military Band Masters Institute–Moscow. 1957. See: Melnikov, S., *Pieces for Tuba and Piano,* under Tuba and Keyboard Collections. Also see other listing in this section.

Marcello, Benedetto. *Largo and Presto.* arr. Donald C. Little, figured bass realization by George R. Belden. CPP/Belwin, Inc. 1978. $4.00. 2:45. III. $A\flat_1$–f (g). Well-transcribed arrangement with a melodic 3/4 Largo section followed by a spirited Presto in 2/4 time. Detail should be paid to marked articulations and dynamics. A few trills; intermediate-level technique should be adequate. See other listing in this section.

Marcello, Benedetto. *Largo and Presto.* arr. Donald C. Little, figured bass realization by George R. Belden. CPP/Belwin, Inc. 1978. See: Lamb, Jack, *Solo Sounds for Tuba Levels 3–5, Vol. 1,* under Tuba and Keyboard Collections. Also see other listing in this section.

Marcello, Benedetto. *Sonata.* arr. Joosen. Henri Elkan.

Marcello, Benedetto. *Sonata I, from 6 Solos for a Violoncello.* arr. Hiroyuki Yasumoto. Toa Music International Co. 1989. IV. C–f'. Largo; Allegro; Largo; Allegro. Well-transcribed version of very popular solo. Trills, scales, flexibility, and baroque conception required. See: Yasumoto, Hiroyuki, arr., *Tuba Volume #2,* under Tuba and Keyboard Collections.

Marcello, Benedetto. *Sonata No. 1 in F Major.* arr. Donald C. Little and Richard B. Nelson. Southern Music Company. 1984. $4.95. 9:30 (3.20, 3:16, 0:56, 1:58). IV. A_1–g. Largo; Allegro; Largo; Allegro. Accompaniment: Piano or harpsichord. Many trills included. Light, quick articulation required. Notes in parentheses for optional breaths. Good recital material. (Recorded in different arrangement by: Michael Lind.) See review in *TUBA Journal,* Vol. 12, No. 3, Page 23.

Marcello, Benedetto. *Sonata No. I in F Major.* arr. John Glenesk Mortimer. Editions Marc Reift. 1997. $9.50. (Complete set of six sonatas $23.70.) 6:00. III–IV. A_1 (C_1)–c' (g'). Largo; Allegro; Largo; Allegro. Originally for cello; this transcription is in the original key. The octaves are written so that the player can choose whichever is more comfortable. Available individually or as a compilation of all six sonatas, in bass clef concert pitch, or in treble clef in E♭ or B♭.

Marcello, Benedetto. *Sonata No. 2.* arr. Michael Blostein. Southern Music.

Marcello, Benedetto. *Sonata No. II in E Minor.* arr. John Glenesk Mortimer. Editions Marc Reift. 1997. $9.50 (Complete set of six sonatas $23.70.) 6:00. III–IV. A_1 (E_1)–c'. Adagio; Allegro; Larghetto; Moderato. Originally for cello; this transcription is in the original key. Available individually or as a compilation of all six sonatas, in bass clef concert pitch, or in treble clef in E♭ or B♭.

Marcello, Benedetto. *Sonata No. III in A Minor.* arr. John Glenesk Mortimer. Editions Marc Reift. 1997. $9.50 (Complete set of six sonatas $23.70.) 5:00. III–IV. A_1–d'. Adagio; Allegro; Largo; Allegro. Originally for cello; this transcription is in the original key. Available individually or as a compilation of all six sonatas, in bass clef concert pitch, or in treble clef in E♭ or B♭.

Marcello, Benedetto. *Sonata No. IV in G Minor.* arr. John Glenesk Mortimer. Editions Marc Reift. 1997. $9.50. (Complete set of six sonatas $23.70.) 5:30. III–IV. $E\flat_1$ ($B\flat_1$)–e♭' (g'). Andante; Allegro non troppo; Largo; Allegro. Originally for cello; this transcription is in the original key. Available individually or as a compilation of all six sonatas, in bass clef concert pitch, or in treble clef in E♭ or B♭.

Marcello, Benedetto. *Sonata No. 5 in C Major.* arr. Donald C. Little and Richard B. Nelson. Southern Music Company. 1983. $4.00. 9:53 (3:03, 3:20, 1:05, 2:26). IV. G_1–a. Adagio; Allegro; Largo; Allegro. Accompaniment: Piano or harpsichord. Many trills included. Light, quick articulation required. See review in *TUBA Journal,* Vol. 11, No. 2, Page 23.

Marcello, Benedetto. *Sonata No. V in B♭ Major.* arr. John Glenesk Mortimer. Editions Marc Reift. 1997. $9.50. (Complete set of six sonatas $23.70.) 5:00. III–IV. $B\flat_1$ (G_1)–d' (e♭'). Adagio; Allegro; Largo; Allegro. This transcription is in B♭ instead of the original C major for cello. The octaves are written so that the player can choose whichever is more comfortable. Available individually or as a compilation of all six sonatas, in bass clef concert pitch, or in treble clef in E♭ or B♭.

Marcello, Benedetto. *Sonata No. VI in G Major.* arr. John Glenesk Mortimer. Editions Marc Reift. 1997. $9.50. (Complete set of six sonatas $23.70.) 6:00. III–IV. D (G_1)–d' (e'). Andante; Allegro; Grave; Allegro. Originally for cello; this transcription is in the original key. Available individually or as a compilation of all six sonatas, in bass clef concert pitch, or in treble clef in E♭ or B♭.

Margoni, Alain. *Après une Lecture de Goldoni: Fantaisie dans le style du XVIII siècle. (After a Lecture of Goldoni: Fantasy in the Style of the 18th Century.)* Alphonse Leduc. 1964. $11.50. $G\sharp_1$–f♯'. For French tuba. See: Thompson/Lemke; *French Music for Low Brass Instruments.*

Markl, Max. *Concertino.* Available from the composer. See: Markl, Max, *Concertino,* under Tuba and Orchestra.

Marpurg. *Menuet.* arr. Dishinger. Available from Spaeth and Schmid. $6.50.

Marteau, Marcel. *Morceau Vivant.* arr. Clifford P. Barnes. Jack Spratt Music Co. 1958. $3.50. 3:09. IV. B♭$_1$–b♭. Old-style theme-and-variation-type solo in 4/4 time with some chromatic, slurred sextuplets. Triplet passages, slurred sixteenth note step-wise patterns, crisp staccato passages; fun piece to play. Not overly technically demanding.

Martelli, Henri. *Dialogue.* Éditions Max Eschig. 1966. IV–V. B$_1$–f'. Op. 100. For bass trombone/tuba/saxhorn and piano. For French tuba. See: Thompson/Lemke; *French Music for Low Brass Instruments.*

Martelli, Henri. *Suite pour Tuba.* Éditions Max Eschig. 1954. 7:30. IV–V. G$_1$–a♭'. à Monsieur Paul Bernard, professeur au Conservatoire National de Musique. Op. 83. "Ou saxhorn-basse en Si♭ ou trombone-basse et piano." For French tuba. Very wide range. Extended Lento sections combined with articulated Allegro sections.

Martin, Carroll. *Aeola.* Carl Fischer Inc. 1939. $3.25. 2:48. III. C–f. To John Kuhn. Moderato. "Tuba BB♭–E♭." Melodic solo with slurring, eighth note triplets (in 4/4 time), and parts in A♭ major (still marked F major).

Martin, Carroll. *Pompola.* Carl Fischer Inc. 1939. Out of Print. 2:00. II–III. B♭$_1$–d. Legato and slurred passages throughout in 4/4 time. Some accidentals, a few sixteenth notes. Recorded by Ronald Davis.

Martin, Easthope. *Hey-Ho, Come to the Fair.* arr. John Fletcher. Chester Music. 1982. 1:30. III. (E♭$_1$) D–b♭. Allegro (But Don't Be Silly.) In one (3/4 time) with spirit. See: Fletcher, John, *Tuba Solos (Tuba in C), Volume One,* under Tuba and Keyboard Collections.

Martin, Hugh, and Ralph Blaine. *Trolley Song, The.* arr. Sandy Feldstein. CPP/Belwin, Inc. 1990. I. B♭$_1$–D. See: Feldstein, Sandy, *First Solo Songbook,* under Tuba and Keyboard Collections.

Martin, Vernon. *Concerto for Tuba and Strings.* Composers Autograph Publications. 1956. Out of Print. See: Martin, Vernon, *Concerto for Tuba and Strings,* under Tuba and Orchestra.

Martini, J. P. E. *Piacer d'Aamor.* arr. Hiroyuki Yasumoto. Toa Music International Co. 1986. 2:43. III. C–f. Very vocal approach needed. See: Yasumoto, Hiroyuki, *Tuba Volume #1,* under Tuba and Keyboard Collections. Recorded by Hiroyuki Yasumoto.

Martini, Padre. *Plasir d'Amour.* arr. Quinto Maganini. Edition Musicus. 1954. 2:17. II. C–f (g). Molto Lento. Lyrical (slurred) 6/8 transcription. Good advanced beginner solo. See: Ostrander, Allen, *Concert Album for Tuba,* under Tuba and Keyboard Collections.

Marttinen, Taune. *Elephant and a Mouse, An.* SMOL.

Marzials. *Fairy Jane, The.* arr. Paul deVille. Carl Fischer Inc. 1906. Out of Print. See: deVille, Paul, *Pleasant Hours,* under Tuba and Keyboard Collections.

Masne, D. *Elegia.* ed. S. Melnikov. Military Band Masters Institute–Moscow. 1957. See: Melnikov, S., *Pieces for Tuba and Piano,* under Tuba and Keyboard Collections.

Mason, Roger. *Three Songs for Tuba.* Encore Music Publishers. 1995. 7:30. II–III. F$_1$–c'. Variables; Charlie's Tune; Toccata. Dedicated to Dr. Charles McAdams. A collection of songs where each could stand alone. Range is suitable for the advanced beginner, but the tempos require a very advanced intermediate player with multiple tonguing ability.

Massanet, Jules. *Herod's Air from "Herodiade."* arr. Allen Ostrander. Edition Musicus. 1965. $2.75. 2:30. II–III. B♭$_1$–e♭. In 9/8 time. Plenty of accidentals, some slurring.

Masso, George. *Suite for Louise.* Kendor Music, Inc. 1966. $6.00. See: Masso, George, *Suite for Louise,* under Tuba and Band. Comes with flexible recording featuring Barton Cummings, tuba.

Másson, Askell. *Maes Howe.* Editions Bim. 2000. $19.80. 14:00. V. A$_2$–a'. Dedicated to Harri Lidsle. Piano reduction. For more information see Music for Tuba and Orchestra.

Matchett, Steve. *Walkabout.* RBC Publications. $5.00.

Mattei, Tito. *Mariner, The.* arr. Harold L. Walters. Rubank, Inc. 1954. $1.75. 3:00. II. A$_1$–e♭. "Solo for E♭ or BB♭ Bass." Waltz in 3/4 time with no technical problems.

McCurdy, Gary L. *Four Faces of Tubby.* Tuba Materials Center. 1971. Out of Print. 4:00. IV–V. E♭$_1$–b. In four movements with optional narrator.

McFarland, Michael. *Sketches for Tuba and Piano.* Theodore Presser Company. 1979. $3.50. 7:54. IV. F♭$_1$–b♭. To Fritz Kaenzig. Spirited; Slow and expressive; Marcato. Completed June 1970, Tipp City, Ohio. Conservative modern melodic writing. Mixed meter. Some glissandos on overtone series. Requires crisp articulations. See review in *TUBA Journal,* Vol. 7, No. 2, Page 23.

McHugh, Jim, and Dorothy Fields. *On the Sunny Side of the Street.* arr. Hiroyuki Yasumoto. Toa Music International Co. 1989. 1:57. III. (C$_1$) G$_1$–e. Swing. Soloist plays the melody as well as a "pizzicato" bass line for accompaniment. Player is encouraged to listen to "Fats" Waller's version of this piece for conception. See: Yasumoto, Hiroyuki, arr., *Tuba Volume #2,* under Tuba and Keyboard Collections.

McIntyre, David, L. *Sonata for Tuba and Piano.* Canadian Music Center. 1996. V. 10:00. F$_1$–b'. Moderato; Expressively; Energico. Commissioned by CBC Saskatchewan. Dedicated to John Griffiths and Donna Falconer. A very challenging, but rewarding work that lies best on bass tuba. Contains many metric shifts, large intervallic leaps, multiphonics, and extreme range shifts. Excellent professional recital material. Recorded by John Griffiths.

McKay, George Frederick. *Suite for Bass Clef Instruments.* University Music Press. 1958. Out of Print. 9:00. IV. D_1–b. Sea Spell; Barbaric Dance. Baritone and tuba parts supplied. Prize Composition, 1957–58 National Association of College Wind and Percussion Instructors. Low tessitura work in first movement. Major work for the instrument. Strong accompanist required.

McKimm, Barry. *Andante Tranquillo.* Yarra Yarra Music. 1997. 6:25. IV. G_1–e'. Dedicated to Gene Pokorny, Chicago Symphony Orchestra. Good lyrical piece for advanced college student or professional recital. Slow tempos but complex subdivisions and metric shifts. Mostly linear writing with typical range demands and legato articulations. Challenging piano accompaniment.

McKimm, Barry. *Tuba Concerto.* Yarra Yarra Music Services. 1983. Commissioned by Peter Sykes. See: McKimm, Barry, *Tuba Concerto,* under Tuba and Band.

McLin, Edward, arr. *With Melody for All.* Pro Art Publications. 1963. Out of Print. "20 all-time favorite melodies for band, orchestra, ensemble, unison or solo performance."

McQuaide, George. *Samsonian Polka.* arr. W. E. Barnes. Ludwig Music Publishing Company. 1933. $3.00. 2:30. III. ($B\flat_1$) D♭–g♭. Was published for tuba and band. Polka-style solo in A♭/D♭ major with not many technical challenges other than key. Short cadenza.

Meier, Jost. *Eclipse Finale?* Éditions BIM. 1991. $22.50. "Fantasia uber 'Der Mond ist aufgegangen' 1991." See: Meier, Jost, *Eclipse Finale?,* under Tuba and Orchestra and under Tuba and Band. Recorded by Øystein Baadsvik, Jens Bjørn-Larsen.

Mellilo, Peter. *Solo for Tuba and String Quartet.* D. B. Publishing Co. Out of Print. Piano reduction.

Melnikov, S., ed. *Pieces for Tuba and Piano.* Military Band Masters Institute–Moscow. 1957. Contains: Assafyev, B., *Scherzo;* Bach, J. S., *Bouree;* Bach, J. S., *Second Part from Capriccio;* Blazhevich, Vladislav, *Concert No. 2 Part 3;* Blazhevich, Vladislav, *Miniature No. 7;* Chopin, F., *Prelude No. 6;* Dvarionas, B., *Theme and Variations;* Ekkls, H., *Sonata;* Glinka, M., *Romance;* Handel, G. F., *Bouree;* Kalinikov, V., *The Sad Song;* Leonov, I., *Etude de concert;* Marcello, Benedetto, *Largo and Allegro;* Masne, D., *Elegia;* Moniushko, S., *An Air from the Opera "Halka";* Mozart, W. A., *Concert No. 2 Part One;* Mozart, W. A., *Concert No. 4 Part One;* Mozart, W. A., *Rondo de Concerto;* Rachmaninoff, Sergei, *Elegia;* Rimsky-Korsakov, N., *Song from the Opera "Snow Maiden";* Rubinstein, A., *Romance;* Rubinstein, A., *Song from the Cycle "Persian Songs";* Saint-Saëns, C., *Concert Piece;* Tchaikovsky, Peter I., *The Sad Song;* Vivaldi, A., *Sonata;* Weber, K. M., *Adagio.*

Mendelssohn. *On Wings of Song.* arr. Acton Ostling. CPP/Belwin, Inc. 1969. 1:41. I. $B\flat_1$–c. Andante cantabile. In 3/4 time. Some easy slurring. See: Ostling, Acton, *Tuba (Bass) Soloist, Level One,* under Tuba and Keyboard Collections.

Mendelssohn, F. *Nocturne.* arr. Wesley Jacobs. Encore Music Publishers. 1:27. I–II. D–d. Softly. Repetitive solo in G major. Some slurring, G♯, fermata. No big technical problems other than, in some cases, the key. See: Jacobs, Wesley, *Solos from the Classics,* under Tuba and Keyboard Collections.

Mendelssohn, Felix. *Aria from "Elias."* arr. L. Blaauw. Molenaar N. V. 1959. 2:34. IV. c♯–e♭'. Good F tuba solo; also makes for a good study on lower tubas.

Mendelssohn, Felix. *Auf Flügeln des Gesanges (On Wings of Song).* arr. John Glenesk Mortimer. Editions Marc Reift. 1997. $7.00. 2:00. II. E♭–f. Available in bass clef concert pitch or treble clef in B♭.

Mendelssohn, Felix. *It Is Enough from "Elijah."* arr. Allen Ostrander. Edition Musicus. 1965. $3.00. 4:26. II. $A\flat_1$–e♭. Very musical, expressive solo. Recorded by Peter Popiel.

Mendelssohn, Felix. *On Wings of Song.* arr. Paul deVille. Carl Fischer Inc. 1906. Out of Print. See: deVille, Paul, *Pleasant Hours,* under Tuba and Keyboard Collections.

Mendelssohn, Felix. *Reverie.* arr. Ronald C. Dishinger. Medici Music Press. 1990. $2.50. 2:08. II–III. D–f. Andante espressivo. Op 85, No. 1 (1851). Requires lyrical expressive playing. Limited range.

Mercadante. *Solitude Caprice.* arr. Carl Weber. J. W. Pepper & Son. 1914. Out of Print. See: Weber, Carl, *Nineteen Solos for E♭ Bass with Piano Accompaniment,* under Tuba and Keyboard Collections.

Merle, John. *Demetrius.* Carl Fischer Inc. 1939. Out of Print. 2:00. II. $B\flat_1$–e♭. "Tuba BB♭–E♭." In cut time; quarter note is fastest rhythm. No technical problems.

Merle, John. *Mummers-Danse Grotesque.* Carl Fischer Inc. 1938. Out of Print. See: Merle, John, *Mummers-Danse Grotesque,* under Tuba and Band. Recorded by William Bell.

Merle, John. *Quintero—The Farmer.* Carl Fischer Inc. 1940. Out of Print. 2:22. I–II. D–e♭. "Tuba BB♭—E♭." In cut time; quarter note is fastest rhythm. No technical problems.

Meschke, Dieter. *Musizierbuch für Basstuba.* Pro Musica Verlag Leipzig. II.

Meschke, Dieter, ed. *Zum Uben und Vorspielen/B-Tuba.* arr. Gerd Philipp and Stephan Schwotzer. Hofmeister. 1993. I–III. Contains: Concone, Giuseppe, *Allegretto animato;* Daquin, Louis-Claude, *Rigaudon;* Dragonetti, Domenico,

Kleiner Walzer; Franck, Melchior, *Allemande;* Franck, Melchior, *Galliarde;* Fux, Johann Joseph, *Allegro;* Giordani, Giuseppe, *Arietta;* Krebs, Johann Ludwig, *Bourrée;* Mozart, Leopold, *Bourrée;* Pachelbel, Johann, *Gavotte;* Pergolesi, Giovanni Battista, *Arie;* Pergolesi, Giovanni Battista, *Lied;* Pezel, Johann, *Intrade;* Radolt, Wenzel Ludwig Freiherr von, *Menuett im Kanon;* Saint-Saëns, Camille, *L'Éléphant (Der Elefant);* Schumann, Robert, *Fröhlicher Landmann;* Schwotzer, Stephan, arr., *Altdeutscher Tanz (Narrentanz);* Stanley, John, *Allegretto grazioso;* Witthauer, Johann Georg, *Allegretto und Gavotte.*

Meschke, Dieter, ed. *Zum Uben und Vorspielen/F-Tuba.* arr. Gerd Philipp and Stephan Schwotzer. Hofmeister. 1993. See: Meschke, Dieter, *Zum Uben und Vorspielen/B-Tuba,* in this section.

Meunier, Gérard. *Anapausis. (Repose.)* Gérard Billaudot. 1987. $11.50. 9:45. V. D_1–(g') a♭'. Très lent; Agité; Très lent. A mon cher ami l'incomparable musicien Fernand Lelong, professeur au C.N.S.M. de Paris. "pour tuba et piano." For French tuba. Some mixed meter—7/8, 5/8, 3/4—in second movement. Wide range. See: Thompson/Lemke; *French Music for Low Brass Instruments.* See review in *TUBA Journal,* Vol. 16, No. 3, Page 47.

Meunier, Gérard. *Une nuit d'harmonie.* Thomi-Berg Verlag. For French tuba.

Meunier, Gérard. *Tubabil.* Henri Lemoine & Cie. 1987. $4.75. 2:00. II. F–d'. "pour tuba ou saxhorn (ut ou si bémol) et piano." Mournful little ballad with no technical problems. Easy rhythms. See: Thompson/Lemke; *French Music for Low Brass Instruments.* See review in *TUBA Journal,* Vol. 18, No. 3, Page 19.

Meyerbeer. *Coronation March.* arr. Igor Hudadoff; William Westcott, pno. arr. Pro Art Publications. 1967. Out of Print. See: Hudadoff, Igor, *Fifteen Intermediate Tuba Solos,* under Tuba and Keyboard Collections.

Meyerbeer. *On Heaven's just cause relying and Rataplan Chorus (From "Les Huguenots").* arr. James Ord Hume. Boosey & Co. 1906. Out of Print. See: Hume, J. Ord, *Boosey's Bombardon Solo Album,* under Tuba and Keyboard Collections.

Meyerbeer. *Piff, Paff (Les Huguenots).* arr. James Ord Hume. Boosey & Co. 1906. Out of Print. See: Hume, J. Ord, *Boosey's Bombardon Solo Album,* under Tuba and Keyboard Collections.

Meyerbeer. *Veni Creator.* arr. Allen Ostrander. Edition Musicus. 1954. 1:28. II–III. F–g. In 3/4 time; no big technical problems. See: Ostrander, Allen, *Concert Album for Tuba,* under Tuba and Keyboard Collections.

Meyer-Selb, Horst. *Five Possibilities.* Available from Spaeth and Schmid. $10.25.

Meyer-Selb, Horst. *Fünf Charakterstücke.* Available from Spaeth and Schmid. $10.25.

Miaskovskii, N. *Song of the Field.* ed. A. Lebedev. Moscow Muzyka. 1984. 0:31. II. G_1–g. One-octave range except for last note. All slurred phrases. Lyrical solo in 2/2 time in G minor. See: Lebedev, A., *Tuba Tutor Vol. 1,* under Tuba and Keyboard Collections.

Mignone, Francisco. *Divertimento.* Fundação Nacional De Arte. 1985. 6:31 (1:27, 1:30, 0:45, 1:10, 1:05, 0:34). IV–V. E_1–f'. Moderato; Decidido e amolecado; Moderato/Molto Allegro; Valsa Seresteira; Cançao De Roda; Brejeiro. Six canons. Different feel to each little movement. Requires some flexibility and style. Good recital material.

Mihalovici, M. *Serioso.* Alphonse Leduc. $12.50. Saxhorn Si♭ et Piano. See: Thompson/Lemke; *French Music for Low Brass Instruments.*

Miller, Vernon, Jr. *Four Vignettes for Tuba.* Tuba-Euphonium Press. 1996. 8:00. V. E♭–g♯'. I; II; III; IV. Commissioned and dedicated to Scott Mendoker. Some isolated high range passages and frequent meter shifts and angular melodic lines. Movements are all connected.

Miller, Vernon R. *Tuba Tantrum.* Pro Art Publications. 1962. Out of Print. 2:10. II. $B♭_1$–B♭. Theme and variations. One-octave range with plenty of sixteenth notes.

Miserendino, Joe. *Autumn Moods.* Solid Brass Music Company. $14.00. IV. Summer's Last Hurrah; Serenade for a Soft Fall Night; Witches and Goblins Cavort; Autumn Repose and Dreams of Spring. The first of Joe Miserendino's *Music of the Seasons* suite. Complete suite available for $35.00.

Miserendino, Joe. *Summer Celebration.* Solid Brass Music Company. $14.00. IV. A cheerful celebration of summer. The third of Joe Miserendino's *Music of the Seasons* suite. Complete suite available for $35.00.

Miserendino, Joe. *Winter Song and Spring Dances.* Solid Brass Music Company. $14.00. IV. "The darkness of Winter gives way to lively Spring dances." The second of Joe Miserendino's *Music of the Seasons* suite. Complete suite available for $35.00.

Mitegin, V., ed. *Pieces for Tuba and Piano.* Moscow Muzyka. 1969. Contains: Arensky, A., *Ballade;* Dubrovsky, I., *A Song and a Dance;* Moussorgsky, M., *"Bydlo" from Suite "Pictures of an Exhibition";* Rakov, N., *Air;* Tchaikovsky, Peter I., *Arioso from the Opera "Jolanta."*

Mitjagina, V., ed. *Pieces for Tuba and Piano.* Muzkya, Moscow. 1969. II–IV. Contains: Goedicke, A., *Improvisation;* Moussorgsky, M., *Bydlo from Pictures at an Exhibition;* Mozart, V. (sic), *Liporello's Aria from Don Juan (Don Giovanni);* Saint-Saëns, C., *Cavatina;* Zuerev, V., *Hungarian Melody;* Zuerev, V., *Russian Dance.*

Molloy, J. L. *Kerry Dance, The.* arr. Malcolm Bennett. 1988. 0:54. II–III. F–b♭. Moderato. Parts for bass clef and treble (E♭ bass) included.

Sprightly 6/8 jig with a couple of piano interludes for endurance's sake makes this a good advanced beginner solo. Slurring throughout, a couple of F octave jumps, no technical problems. See: Bennett, Malcolm, *Five Solos for Tuba,* under Tuba and Keyboard Collections.

Moniushko, S. *Air from the Opera "Halka," An.* ed. S. Melnikov. Military Band Masters Institute–Moscow. 1957. See: Melnikov, S., *Pieces for Tuba and Piano,* under Tuba and Keyboard Collections.

Monk. *Abide with Me.* arr. David E. Smith. Solid Brass Music Company. $3.50. I. Good beginning arrangement of an old familiar hymn.

Monk, W. H. *Abide with Me.* arr. John Kinyon. M. Witmark & Sons. 1958. I. See: Kinyon, John, *Breeze-Easy Recital Pieces,* under Tuba and Keyboard Collections.

Monroe, Margrethe. *In the Garden.* arr. Merle J. Isaac. Carl Fischer Inc. 1939. Out of Print. I–II. F–e♭. Tempo di Valse. "Tuba (BB♭–E♭)." Lyrical 3/4 waltz with quarter note as fastest rhythm. Some slurring; a couple of F–d and F–e♭ slurs, otherwise, no technical problems.

Monti, Vittorio. *Csardas.* arr. Marc Reift. Editions Marc Reift. 1997. $13.50. 4:00. IV. G_1–c'. This transcription is written in C minor and is best suited for E♭ tuba. Available in bass clef concert pitch or treble clef in B♭. Recorded by Walter Hilgers.

Monti, Vittorio. *Csardas.* arr. Walter Hilgers. Editions Marc Reift. 1993. $13.50. 5:25. IV. A_1–e' (d"). A one-to-one transcription from the original for violin, except for some of the octave settings. Best suited for F tuba.

Monti, Vittorio. *Czardas.* arr. Øystein Baadsvik. Ovation. $20.98.

Monti, Vittorio. *Czardas.* arr. Patrick Sheridan. PatrickSheridan.com (Lollipop Series). $18.00.

Monushko, S. *Fairy Tail, A.* ed. A. Lebedev. Moscow Muzyka. 1984. 0:41. II–III. C–f. Very imaginative little piece in F minor. See: Lebedev, A., *Tuba Tutor Vol. 1,* under Tuba and Keyboard Collections.

Moquin, Al. *King of the Deep.* The Fillmore Bros. Co. 1948. Out of Print. 3:30. III. A_1–f. "Solo for Tuba (E♭ or BB♭) or Baritone." Introductory section in 12/8, then a 2/4 polka with cadenza.

Moquin, Al. *Sailing the Mighty Deep.* The Fillmore Bros. Co. 1948. Out of Print. 3:00. III. F_1–b♭. "Solo for Tuba (E♭ or BB♭) or Baritone." Polka-style solo utilizing a wide range. Cadenza included.

Moquin, Al. *Sousaphonium.* The Fillmore Bros. Co. 1948. Out of Print. 3:00. III. A♭$_1$–g. "Solo for Tuba (E♭ or BB♭) or Baritone." Polka-style solo with short cadenza. Good intermediate technique required.

Morawetz, Oskar. *Sonata for Tuba.* Aeneas Music. 1984. 12:46 (3:31, 4:25, 4:50). IV–V. E♯$_1$–e'. Allegro; Adagio; Allegro non troppo. Big piece requiring flexibility of technique and strong accompanist.

Moreau, James. *Couleurs en Mouvements. (Moving Colours.)* Alphonse Leduc. 1969. $20.95. 7:10. V. A_1–c". A ma mère, affectueusement. Jaune Cuivre (Copper Yellow); Bleu Azur (Sky Blue); Rouge Flamboyant (Flaming Red). "pour Tuba en Ut ou Saxhorn basse Si♭ et Piano." For French tuba. See: Thompson/Lemke; *French Music for Low Brass Instruments.*

Moreau, James. *Poursuites.* Éditions M. Combre. 1972. 1:54. IV–V. E–a'. "pour basson (ou tuba) et piano." For French tuba. Allegretto section requires flexibility and swift articulations. Lyrical Adagio section in F♯ major.

Moro, D. *Piece from Suite "Colours in Movement."* ed. J. Larin. Moscow Muzyka. 1979. See: Larin, J., *Pieces for Tuba and Piano,* under Tuba and Keyboard Collections.

Morra, Gene. *Nocturnal Serenade.* Carl Fischer Inc. 1964. $2.50. 2:00. II–III. D♭–g♭. Written for a variety of solo instruments with piano. Very lyrical 3/4 solo utilizing slurs and tenutos in D♭ major.

Mortier, W. *Fuguette.* Available from Spaeth and Schmid. $9.75.

Mortimer, John Glenesk. *Happy Birthday.* Available from Spaeth and Schmid. $12.75. With optional keyboard, guitar, drum parts.

Mortimer, John Glenesk. *Tuba Concerto für Tuba und Klavier.* Editions Marc Reift. 1983. $20.25. IV. F_1–g'. Allegro; Adagio non troppo; Tempo di Samba. For David LeClair. See: Mortimer, John Glenesk, *Tuba Concerto für Tuba und Klavier,* under Tuba and Orchestra.

Moss, Alan. *Jesus/Sweetest Name I Know.* David E. Smith Publications. $3.50.

Mountains of Epirus. Available from Dinos Constantinides. 1980. 8:30. IV. F♯$_1$–e'. At the Village; Country Fair. This work is modal and employs characteristic Greek syncopated rhythms and polychordal sonorities. A mixture of linear melodies and rapid rhythmic interjections. See listing under Music for Tuba and Orchestra and Music for Tuba and Band.

Moussorgsky, M. *Bydlo from Pictures at an Exhibition.* arr. V. Mitjagina. Muzkya, Moscow. 1969. 2:17. IV. c♯–g♯'. Mostly straight from the orchestral part. High tessitura. See: Mitjagina, V., ed., *Pieces for Tuba and Piano,* under Tuba and Keyboard Collections.

Moussorgsky, M. *Gopak.* arr. Igor Hudadoff; William Westcott, pno. arr. Pro Art Publications. 1967. Out of Print. See: Hudadoff, Igor, *Fifteen Intermediate Tuba Solos,* under Tuba and Keyboard Collections.

Moussorgsky, M. *Song of the Flea.* arr. Allen Ostrander. Edition Musicus. 1959. $2.75. 2:50. III. C♯–a (b♭). Transcription of aria. Listen to recording of aria for conception. A version of this recorded by John Fletcher.

Mowery, Carl D. *Sonata No. 1 for Tuba and Piano.* See review in *TUBA Journal,* Vol. 1, No. 3, Page 6.

Mowery, Carl D. *Sonata No. 2 for Tuba and Piano.* See review in *TUBA Journal,* Vol. 1, No. 3, Page 6.

Moylan, William. *Solo and Duo for Tuba and Piano.* Seesaw Music Corporation. 1983. $10.00. 11:00. IV–V. A_1–e. Commissioned by the Ball State University Student Chapter of the Tubists Universal Brotherhood Association (TUBA) for OCTUBAFEST IX, August 1982, Muncie, Ind. Designed to be performed as a solo work (six minutes), as a duo (five minutes), or "Solo and Duo" (eleven minutes). Flutter tonguing. Strong technique and strong accompanist required.

Mozart, Leopold. *Bourrée.* arr. Gerd Philipp. Hofmeister. 1993. 2:04. II–III. F–f. In B♭ minor. See: Meschke, Dieter, *Zum Uben und Vorspielen/ B-Tuba,* under Tuba and Keyboard Collections.

Mozart, V. (sic). *Liporello's Aria from Don Juan (Don Giovanni).* arr. V. Mitjagina. Muzkya, Moscow. 1969. 2:23. II–III. (F_1) D–f. Allegro molto. Easy transcription in 4/4 time (B♭ major) with no technical problems. See: Mitjagina, V., ed., *Pieces for Tuba and Piano,* under Tuba and Keyboard Collections.

Mozart, W. A. *Adagio.* arr. Hilgers. Available from Spaeth and Schmid. $6.50.

Mozart, W. A. *Adagio KV 261; Rondo KV 269; Rondo KV 373.* arr. Douay. Available from Spaeth and Schmid. $28.00.

Mozart, W. A. *Ah! Vous dirai-je maman.* arr. Arnaud Boukhitine. Robert Martin Editions. 2002. 1:30. I. B♭–g. Very short piece based on Mozart's "Twinkle Twinkle Little Star."

Mozart, W. A. *All the world is full of lovers.* arr. Arthur Frackenpohl and ed. Charles Daellenbach. Hal Leonard Publishing Corp. 1989. 1:30. III–IV. C–c'. From Act II of *The Magic Flute* . Light vocal approach necessary. See: Mozart, W. A., *Suite No. 1 from The Magic Flute,* under Tuba and Keyboard Collections.

Mozart, W. A. *Allegro.* arr. A. Lebedev. Military Band Masters Faculty of Moscow Conservatiore. 1971. See: Lebedev, A., *Collection of Pieces for Tuba "Es" and Piano,* under Tuba and Keyboard Collections.

Mozart, W. A. *Alleluja, Exultate.* ed. Donald Edward Mathews. Wingert-Jones Music, Inc. 1989. $5.00. 3:40. III. E♭–g (b♭). K. 165. Transcribed famous Mozart melody. Some stepwise sixteenth notes. Light classical approach required.

Mozart, W. A. *Aria from La Clemenza di Tito.* arr. Don Little. CPP/Belwin, Inc. 1992. 1:39. II–III. A_1–d. Allegretto. In 3/4 time, contains some sixteenth notes. See: Little, Don, *Solo-Pak for Tuba, Part Three,* under Tuba and Keyboard Collections.

Mozart, W. A. *Aria "O Isis and Osiris."* arr. Peter Wastall. Boosey & Hawkes, Inc. 1983. 2:28. II–III. B_1♭–f. Often-transcribed aria in the key of B♭ major. See: Wastall, Peter, *Learn As You Play Tuba,* under Tuba and Keyboard Collections.

Mozart, W. A. *Concert No. 2 Part One.* ed. S. Melnikov. Military Band Masters Institute–Moscow. 1957. See: Melnikov, S., *Pieces for Tuba and Piano,* under Tuba and Keyboard Collections.

Mozart, W. A. *Concert No. 4 Part One.* ed. S. Melnikov. Military Band Masters Institute–Moscow. 1957. See: Melnikov, S., *Pieces for Tuba and Piano,* under Tuba and Keyboard Collections.

Mozart, W. A. *Concert Rondo.* arr. James Graham. TUBA Press. 1991. IV. (E♭$_1$) B♭$_1$–b♭. Allegro. K. 371. See: Graham, James, *Concert Music for Tuba,* under Tuba and Keyboard Collections.

Mozart, W. A. *Concerto in D (K. 412).* arr. James Graham. TUBA Press. 1991. III–IV. A–a. Allegro; Rondo (Allegro). From Horn Concerto No. 1. One-octave range. See: Graham, James, *Concert Music for Tuba,* under Tuba and Keyboard Collections.

Mozart, W. A. *Concerto in E flat (K. 417).* arr. James Graham. TUBA Press. 1991. IV. B♭$_1$–c' (e♭'). Allegro maestoso; Andante; Rondo (Allegro). From Horn Concerto No. 2. See: Graham, James, *Concert Music for Tuba,* under Tuba and Keyboard Collections. Recorded by: Zdizislaw Piernik.

Mozart, W. A. *Concerto in E flat (K. 447).* arr. James Graham. TUBA Press. 1991. IV. B♭$_1$–c'. Allegro; Romanze (Larghetto); Rondo (Allegro). From Horn Concerto No. 3. See: Graham, James, *Concert Music for Tuba,* under Tuba and Keyboard Collections.

Mozart, W. A. *Concerto in E flat (K. 495).* arr. James Graham. TUBA Press. 1991. IV. B♭$_1$–e♭'. Allegro moderato; Romanza (Andante); Rondo (Allegro vivace). From Horn Concerto No. 4. See: Graham, James, *Concert Music for Tuba,* under Tuba and Keyboard Collections.

Mozart, W. A. *First Movement from Concerto for Horn.* ed. Himie Voxman. Rubank, Inc. 1972. 4:00. III. F–f. "for E♭ or BB♭ Bass." Trills, slurred and mixed articulation passages. Listen to horn recordings for conception. Only one-octave range! See: Voxman, Himie, *Concert and Contest Collection,* under Tuba and Keyboard Collections.

Mozart, W. A. *Ha! just in the nick of time!* arr. Arthur Frackenpohl and ed. Charles Daellenbach. Hal Leonard Publishing Corp. 1989. 1:44. III–IV. C–c'. From Act I of *The Magic Flute.* See: Mozart, W. A., *Suite No. 2 from The Magic Flute,* under Tuba and Keyboard Collections.

Mozart, W. A. *How strong your tone with magic spell.* arr. Arthur Frackenpohl and ed. Charles Daellenbach. Hal Leonard Publishing Corp. 1989. 2:06. III–IV. C–a♭. From Act I of *The Magic*

Flute. Vocal approach necessary. See: Mozart, W. A., *Suite No. 1 from The Magic Flute,* under Tuba and Keyboard Collections.

Mozart, W. A. *I'd give my finest feather.* arr. Arthur Frackenpohl and ed. Charles Daellenbach. Hal Leonard Publishing Corp. 1989. 1:25. III–IV. D–b♭. From Act II of *The Magic Flute* . See: Mozart, W. A., *Suite No. 2 from The Magic Flute,* under Tuba and Keyboard Collections.

Mozart, W. A. *Marche.* arr. Herbert Wekselblatt. G. Schirmer Inc. 1972. 0:36. III. $B♭_1$–e♭. From *Les Petits Riens.* Suggested tempo is a bit quick; would require much flexibility. In cut time. Some grace notes and one trill. See: Wekselblatt, Herbert, *First Solos for the Tuba Player, BB♭,* under Tuba and Keyboard Collections.

Mozart, W. A. *Menuett.* tr. Lars Holmgaard. Amazing Music World. Available from SheetMusicNow.com. IV. 3:30. 2000. $A♭_1$–f'. A fine transcription of this classic minuet. Would work best on bass tuba since it lies mostly in the mid- to high tessitura. Excellent early work for students transferring to the bass tuba. Very few rests for the soloist.

Mozart, W. A. *Menuetto.* arr. Ken Swanson. CPP/Belwin, Inc. 1971. $4.00. 2:15. II–III. E♭–f. Allegretto. Melodic solo in 3/4 time. Some slurring, mostly step-wise movement. See other listing in this section.

Mozart, W. A. *Menuetto.* arr. Ken Swanson. CPP/Belwin, Inc. 1971. See: Lamb, Jack, *Solo Sounds for Tuba Levels 3–5, Vol. 1,* under Tuba and Keyboard Collections. Also see other listing in this section.

Mozart, W. A. *O Isis and Osiris.* arr. Arthur Frackenpohl and ed. Charles Daellenbach. Hal Leonard Publishing Corp. 1989. 2:25. III–IV. (F_1) G_1–c'. From Act II of *The Magic Flute* . Version in F major. See: Mozart, W. A., *Suite No. 1 from The Magic Flute,* under Tuba and Keyboard Collections.

Mozart, W. A. *O Isis and Osiris.* arr. R. Winston Morris. Editions Bim. 1974. $9.50. 2:25. II. F_1–c'. Well-set arrangement of one of Mozart's most popular arias. Works well on F Tuba.

Mozart, W. A. *O Isis and Osiris (from: The Magic Flute).* arr. Herbert Wekselblatt. G. Schirmer Inc. 1964. 2:23. II–III. B_1♭–f. Adagio. See: Wekselblatt, H., *Solos for the Tuba Player,* under Tuba and Keyboard Collections. Very lyrical accessible solo that even makes for a nice encore for advanced players. Fastest note is eighth note. Version in B♭ major.

Mozart, W. A. *O Isis and Osiris from "The Magic Flute."* ed. R. Winston Morris. Brass Press. 1974. $3.00. 3:00. III–IV. F_1–c'. For Mr. B (William J. Bell). Adagio. Originally published by Manuscripts for Tuba, 1971. This version in F major. Very musical transcription utilizing the "sweet" range of the instrument. Recorded by William Bell, Harvey Phillips.

Mozart, W. A. *Papageno Arie.* arr. Lemarc. Available from Spaeth and Schmid. $12.25.

Mozart, W. A. *Per Questa Bella Mano.* arr. Clifford P. Barnes. Jack Spratt Music Co. 1965. $3.00. 4:00. III. G_1–e♭. K. 612. Several different tempos, good opportunity for musical expression. No big technical problems.

Mozart, W. A. *Presto.* arr. Dishinger. Available from Spaeth and Schmid. $6.50.

Mozart, W. A. *Priester-Aria aus die Zauberflöte. (Aria of the Priests from The Magic Flute.)* arr. Jan Evertse. Tierolff-Muziekcentrale. 1952. 4:30. III. (F) G–d'. Includes *O Isis and Osiris* in F major.

Mozart, W. A. *Romance für F-Tuba.* Uetz Music Publishers. 2003. $8.75. F–c'. See listing under Tuba and Organ.

Mozart, W. A. *Romanze and Rondo (from: Horn Concerto No. 3).* arr. Herbert Wekselblatt. G. Schirmer Inc. 1964. 6:26 (2:37, 3:49). IV. B_1♭–c'. Romanze (Larghetto); Rondo (Allegro). See: Wekselblatt, H., *Solos for the Tuba Player,* under Tuba and Keyboard Collections. Good transcriptions of two movements from Mozart *Horn Concerto #3.*

Mozart, W. A. *Rondo.* arr. Dishinger. Available from Spaeth and Schmid. $8.00.

Mozart, W. A. *Rondo de Concerto.* ed. S. Melnikov. Military Band Masters Institute–Moscow. 1957. See: Melnikov, S., *Pieces for Tuba and Piano,* under Tuba and Keyboard Collections.

Mozart, W. A. *Serenade.* tr. R. Winston Morris. Shawnee Press, Inc. 1982. $7.50. 9:30. IV. D–c'. Allegro; Menuetto; Adagio; Rondo. Composed for alto recorder. Well-transcribed solo requiring a light Mozart approach. Intermediate technique required. Good recital material.

Mozart, W. A. *Serenade from "Don Giovanni."* arr. Allen Ostrander. Edition Musicus. 1965. $2.75. 1:10. II. D–e. In 6/8 time and in D major. No big technical problems.

Mozart, W. A. *Suite No. 1 from The Magic Flute.* arr. Arthur Frackenpohl and ed. Charles Daellenbach. Hal Leonard Publishing Corp. 1989. $14.95. 6:01. III–IV. Contains: *How strong your tone with magic spell; O Isis and Osiris; All the world is full of lovers.* Includes practice/performance cassette by Charles Daellenbach, tuba, and Monica Gaylord, piano. See review in *TUBA Journal,* Vol. 18, No. 2, Page 19.

Mozart, W. A. *Suite No. 2 from The Magic Flute.* arr. Arthur Frackenpohl and ed. Charles Daellenbach. Hal Leonard Publishing Corp. 1989. $14.95. 4:49. III–IV. Contains: *I'd give my finest feather; Within these holy portals; Ha! just in the nick of time!* Includes practice/performance cassette by Charles Daellenbach, tuba, and Monica Gaylord, piano. See review in *TUBA Journal,* Vol. 18, No. 2, Page 20.

Mozart, W. A. *Turkish March.* arr. Amis. Available from Spaeth and Schmid. $17.00.

Mozart, W. A. *Within these holy portals.* arr. Arthur Frackenpohl and ed. Charles Daellenbach. Hal Leonard Publishing Corp. 1989. 1:40. III–IV. (G_1) C–a. From Act II of *The Magic Flute.* See: Mozart, W. A., *Suite No. 2 from The Magic Flute,* under Tuba and Keyboard Collections.

Mozart, Wolfgang. *Suite No. 1 from The Magic Flute.* arr. Arthur Frackenpohl. Solid Brass Music Company. $14.95. III. *How strong your tone with magic spell; O Isis and Osiris; All the world is full of lovers.* Performed by Charles Daellenbach. Includes cassette.

Mueller, Florian. *Concert Music for Bass Tuba.* University Music Press. 1961. Out of Print. To Arnold Jacobs. See: Mueller, Florian, *Concert Music for Bass Tuba,* under Tuba and Orchestra. Recorded by Rex Conner.

Mueller, Frederick A. *Variations on a Theme of Samuel Barber.* Available from the composer. 1972. To Bob Tucci. See: Mueller, Frederick A., *Variations on a Theme of Samuel Barber,* under Tuba and Orchestra.

Mueller, J. I. *Praeludium, Chorale, Variations and Fugue.* arr. Allen Ostrander. Editions Musicus. 1959. $5.50. 7:00. III–IV. F_1–b♭. "From a manuscript dated 1839 for bass (or tenor) trombone and piano (or organ)." Some sixteenth note broken arpeggios that will need to be looked at. Recorded on trombone by Mogens Andressen.

Murgier, Jacques. *Concertstuck.* Éditions Musicales Transatlantiques. 1961. $15.50. 8:30. V. F_1–c♭''. For French tuba. Some mixed meter. Strong flexibility required. See: Thompson/Lemke; *French Music for Low Brass Instruments.*

Murphy, Bower. *Solo Miniature.* ed. Constance Weldon. Charles Colin Publishing. 1969. Out of Print. 4:30. III. $B♭_1$–b♭. Also written for cornet or trumpet. In three sections: Allegro marcato, Andante con moto, Allegro. No big technical problems.

Muscroft, Fred. *Carnival for Bass.* Studio Music Company. 1981. See: Muscroft, Fred, *Carnival for Bass,* under Tuba and Band.

Myers, Theldon. *Daydreams.* Lake State Publications. 1979. $1.25. 1:20. I. D–B♭. Moderato. Beginning solo using a very limited range. Quarter note is fastest rhythm in 4/4 time.

Myers, Theldon. *Just Foolin' Around.* Lake State Publications. 1982. $1.50. 1:10. I. C–B♭. Andante. Beginning solo using a very limited range. Quarter note is fastest rhythm in 4/4 time.

Myers, Theldon. *Lazy Day.* Lake State Publications. 1978. $1.25. 1:15. I. $B♭_1$–B♭. In 3/4 time. Beginning solo using a very limited range. Quarter note is fastest rhythm with a few slurs.

Myers, Theldon. *Waltzing Wind.* Lake State Publications. 1981. $1.50. 1:14. I. $B♭_1$–d♭. Moderate waltz tempo. In A♭ major and 3/4 time. Quarter note is fastest rhythm. Some accidentals.

Naessén, Ray. *Sonata la traviata.* SMIC. 2002. 13:00. Written for F tuba and piano.

Nagel, Paul. *Design for Bass.* D.B. Publishing Co. ca. 1973. For Don Butterfield. Piano reduction. Composed for tuba and band and for tuba and orchestra.

Nash, Gary P. *Deformation IV.* Tuba-Euphonium Press. 1994. 6:30. IV. E_1–d♭'. Rhythmically complex serial composition with frequent tempo changes.

Nelhybel, Vaclav. *Concert Piece.* E. C. Kerby LTD. 1973. $3.50. See: Nelhybel, Vaclav, *Concert Piece,* under Tuba and Band. See review in *TUBA Journal,* Vol. 1, No. 3, Page 6.

Nelhybel, Vaclav. *Suite for Tuba and Piano.* General Music Publishing Co. 1966. $7.95. 6:00. III–IV. F_1–g. Allegro marcato; Quasi improvisando; Allegretto. Some syncopation, mixed meters. Not technically overwhelming.

Nelson. *Hour of Prayer, The.* arr. Paul deVille. Carl Fischer Inc. 1906. Out of Print. See: deVille, Paul, *Pleasant Hours,* under Tuba and Keyboard Collections.

Nelson, S. *Pilot, The.* arr. Harry Prendiville. A. Squire. 1888. Out of Print. 1:38. II. E♭–d♭ (e♭). No technical problems. "E♭ Bass; or, tuba With Piano or Organ Accompaniment, (ad lib.)." See: Prendiville, Harry, *Six Popular Solos,* under Tuba and Keyboard Collections.

Nelson, S. *Pilot, The.* arr. Paul deVille. Carl Fischer Inc. 1906. Out of Print. See: deVille, Paul, *Pleasant Hours,* under Tuba and Keyboard Collections.

Nessler, Victor Ernst. *Der Rattenfänger von Hameln.* arr. Luremann. Available from Spaeth and Schmid. $12.25.

Neuling, Hermann. *Konzert-Cadenz.* Pro Musica Verlag. 1954. $1.50. 2:00. IV. E_1–d. Recitative-like writing; in the form of a cadenza throughout.

Newsome, Roy. *Bass in the Ballroom, The.* Studio Music Company. 1972. $14.00. "Solo for E♭ Bass." See: Newsome, Roy, *Bass in the Ballroom,* under Tuba and Band. Recorded by: Stephen Sykes.

Newsome, Roy. *Basso Brazilio.* Obrasso-Verlag Ag. 5:30. III–IV. 1998. $17.50. 5:30. II. $E♭_1$–d♭'. Available with treble clef E♭ part or bass clef tuba part. Samba-style solo appropriate for the advanced intermediate performer due primarily to range and tessitura. Consistent samba rhythm throughout solo part. Contains cadenza. Typical samba rhythms. No technical problems. Middle- to upper-middle-register tessitura. Bass and treble clef parts are included.

Newsome, Roy. *Swiss Air.* Studio Music Company. See: Newsome, Roy, *Swiss Air,* under Tuba and Band. Recorded by Shaun Crowther.

Newton, John (lyrics). *Amazing Grace.* arr. Bill Boyd, ed. Charles Daellenbach. Hal Leonard Publishing Corp. 1992. 0:47. I. $B♭_1$–B♭. Traditional American melody in 3/4 time. A few eighth notes; no technical problems. Comes with practice/

performance cassette. See: Daellenbach, Charles, *Book of Beginning Tuba Solos,* under Tuba and Keyboard Collections.

Newton, Leonard G. *Modern Lullaby, A.* Boosey & Hawkes, Inc. 1937. Out of Print. 2:30. III. F_1–f. To Henry Cook. "Solo BB♭ Bass." Melodramatic, lyrical writing. Utilizes low range.

Newton, Rodney. *Capriccio.* Rosehill Music. 1990. $14.50. For James Gourlay. See: Newton, Rodney, *Capriccio,* under Tuba and Band.

Nicolai, Otto. *Falstaff's Drinking Song.* arr. Herbert Wekselblatt. G. Schirmer Inc. 1972. 1:28. III. $B♭_1$–b♭. Andante commode. From *The Merry Wives of Windsor.* Some mixed meter with eighth note getting the beat. Will take some interpretive thought. See: Wekselblatt, Herbert, *First Solos for the Tuba Player, BB♭,* under Tuba and Keyboard Collections.

Nicolai, W. F. G. *Minstrel's Song.* arr. Paul deVille. Carl Fischer Inc. 1906. Out of Print. See: deVille, Paul, *Pleasant Hours,* under Tuba and Keyboard Collections.

Nilovic, Janko. *Chain.*

Nilovic, Janko. *Concerto.* Available from Spaeth and Schmid. $35.25.

Nilovic, Janko. *Optimu.* Available from Spaeth and Schmid. $18.25.

Nissim, Mico. *Mirior et L'Eau.*

Niverd, Lucien. *Chant Mélancolique.* Gérard Billaudot/Andrieu Frères. 1939. $2.50. 1:51. II–III. F–d'. Moderato, Cantabile. "for Saxhorn-basse en Si♭ ou Trombone en si♭." See: Niverd, Lucien, *Six Petites Pièces De Style,* under Tuba and Keyboard Collections. F tuba tessitura. Mostly scale-wise motion. A few triplets; no technical problems.

Niverd, Lucien. *Complainte.* Gérard Billaudot/Andrieu Frères. 1939. $2.50. 1:17. II–III. D♯–b. Andantino. "for Saxhorn-basse en Si♭ ou Trombone en si♭." See: Niverd, Lucien, *Six Petites Pièces De Style,* under Tuba and Keyboard Collections. F tuba tessitura. Mostly scale-wise motion in 3/4 time. No technical problems.

Niverd, Lucien. *Historiette Dramatique.* Gérard Billaudot/Andrieu Frères. 1939. $2.00. 1:15. III. D–c' (f'). Modéré, Mélancolique. "for Saxhorn-basse en Si♭ ou Trombone en si♭." See: Niverd, Lucien, *Six Petites Pièces De Style,* under Tuba and Keyboard Collections. F tuba tessitura. Lyrical dramatic melody. Good early intermediate solo.

Niverd, Lucien. *Hymne.* Gérard Billaudot/Andrieu Frères. 1939. $2.00. 1:38. II–III. G–d♭'. Moderato. "for Saxhorn-basse en Si♭ ou Trombone en si♭." See: Niverd, Lucien, *Six Petites Pièces De Style,* under Tuba and Keyboard Collections. F tuba tessitura. A few sixteenth notes; a few triplets, syncopations. Lyrical hymn with a stately flavor. No technical problems.

Niverd, Lucien. *Légende.* Gérard Billaudot/Andrieu Frères. 1939. $9.50. V. E–c''. "pour Trombone ou Basse et Piano." Primarily composed with trombone in mind—"Trombone" on solo part. Tenor clef included.

Niverd, Lucien. *Romance Sentimentale.* Gérard Billaudot/Andrieu Frères. 1939. $1.95. 1:54. II–III. G–c'. Moderato. "for Saxhorn-basse en Si♭ ou Trombone en si♭." See: Niverd, Lucien, *Six Petites Pièces De Style,* under Tuba and Keyboard Collections. F tuba tessitura. Lyrical writing. Some syncopation; some accidentals. No technical problems.

Niverd, Lucien. *Scherzetto.* Gérard Billaudot/Andrieu Frères. 1939. $1.95. 0:45. III. G–d♭'. Vif et léger. "for Saxhorn-basse en Si♭ ou Trombone en si♭." See: Niverd, Lucien, *Six Petites Pièces De Style,* under Tuba and Keyboard Collections. F tuba tessitura. Quick tempo turns an easy piece into a technical challenge. ♩ = 200 in 3/4 time. Mostly scale-wise motion and repeated notes.

Niverd, Lucien. *Six Petites Pièces De Style.* Gérard Billaudot. 1939. $6.25. II–III. "for Saxhorn-basse en Si♭ ou Trombone en si♭." (Also written for horn.) *Hymne; Romance; Sentimentale; Complainte; Historiette Dramatique; Chant Mélancolique; Scherzetto.* See individual listings.

Nodaïra, Ichiro. *Arabesque V.* Henri Lemoine & Cie. 1989. $20.75. V. F_1–a'. à Mel Culbertson. Difficult modern writing. Detailed remarks to both performers in French. Quite a bit of flutter tonguing and glissandos. Very wide interval jumps. Tricky rhythms. Muted passages. Will require two strong players with modern conceptions.

Nordel, Marius. *Toccata.* Manuscript. 1969. 7:00. IV. $G♭_1$–e'. Conservative contemporary writing. Mixed meter.

Norton, Christopher. *Make Mine a Tuba.* ed. Peter Wastall. Boosey & Hawkes, Inc. 1985. 0:38. I–II. E♭–e♭. See: Wastall, Peter, *Learn As You Play Tuba,* under Tuba and Keyboard Collections. Tuba part is doubled in the left hand of the piano for the most part. The right hand has colorful harmonies. The young player will greet the support of the unison accompaniment.

Offenbach, Jacques. *Marine's Hymn.* arr. Bill Boyd, ed. Charles Daellenbach. Hal Leonard Publishing Corp. 1992. 0:40. I. $B♭_1$–B♭. Once through the melody in 2/4 time. No technical problems. Comes with practice/performance cassette. See: Daellenbach, Charles, *Book of Beginning Tuba Solos,* under Tuba and Keyboard Collections.

Olcott. *My Wild Irish Rose.* arr. Acton Ostling. CPP/Belwin, Inc. 1969. 1:43. I. C–c. See: Ostling, Acton, *Tuba (Bass) Soloist, Level One,* under Tuba and Keyboard Collections.

O'Neill, Charles. *Spring Fancy.* Carl Fischer Inc. 1939. Out of Print. 4:40. III. F_1–f. No big technical problems.

Orthel, L. *Prelude.* arr. A. Lebedev. Military Band Masters Faculty of Moscow Conservatiore.

1971. See: Lebedev, A., *Collection of Pieces for Tuba "Es" and Piano,* under Tuba and Keyboard Collections.

Ortiz, Diego. *Recercada on the "Passamezzo Moderno" (1553).* arr. Gordon J. Kinney. Queen City Brass. 1981. $7.50. 1:43. III–IV. F–f'. For Rex Conner. In 3/2 and 6/4 time. Upper tessitura; good F tuba piece. Requires light articulations. Mostly step-wise motion.

Osborne, Chester. *Lowlands.* Pro Art Publications. ca. 1981. Out of Print. II. (E_1) A_1–e♭. Towards the end, soloist has the option of singing through the instrument or playing the portion. See review in *TUBA Journal,* Vol. 8, No. 4, Page 28.

Ostling, Acton. *Aurora.* CPP/Belwin, Inc. 1970. $4.00. 1:35. I. F–c. Moderato. Very limited range for beginners. Quarter note is fastest rhythm in 4/4 time. Mostly step-wise motion. A few simple slurs.

Ostling, Acton. *Aurora.* CPP/Belwin, Inc. 1970. See: CPP/Belwin, Inc., *Tuba Solos, Level One,* under Tuba and Keyboard Collections.

Ostling, Acton. *Aurora.* CPP/Belwin, Inc. 1970. See: Lamb, Jack, *Classic Festival Solos,* under Tuba and Keyboard Collections. Also see other listings in this section.

Ostling, Acton. *Deep Cavern.* CPP/Belwin, Inc. 1970. $4.00. 1:36. I. D–d. Misterioso. Solo in G minor in 4/4 time with a few eighth notes. One-octave range with mostly step-wise motion. No technical problems. Also see other listing in this section.

Ostling, Acton. *Deep Cavern.* CPP/Belwin, Inc. 1970. See: CPP/Belwin, Inc., *Tuba Solos, Level One,* under Tuba and Keyboard Collections. Also see other listing in this section.

Ostling, Acton. *King Neptune.* CPP/Belwin, Inc. 1970. $4.00. 1:35. I. ($B♭_1$) D–c. Pomposo. Limited range in this nautical solo in 3/4 time. Quarter note is fastest rhythm; no technical problems. See other listing in this section.

Ostling, Acton. *King Neptune.* CPP/Belwin, Inc. 1970. See: CPP/Belwin, Inc., *Tuba Solos, Level One,* under Tuba and Keyboard Collections. Also see other listing in this section.

Ostling, Acton, arr. *All through the Night.* CPP/Belwin, Inc. 1969. 1:10. I. $B♭_1$–d. Welsh air. A few dotted rhythms and slurs of a third. See: Ostling, Acton, *Tuba (Bass) Soloist, Level One,* under Tuba and Keyboard Collections.

Ostling, Acton, arr. *Blow the Man Down.* CPP/Belwin, Inc. 1969. 1:40. I–II. C–d. Moderato. Traditional melody in 3/4 time with some light variations on that theme. A few eighth notes; no big technical problems. See: CPP/Belwin, Inc., *Tuba Solos, Level One,* under Tuba and Keyboard Collections.

Ostling, Acton, arr. *Blow the Man Down.* CPP/Belwin, Inc. 1969. I. See other listing in this section. Also see: Ostling, Acton, *Tuba (Bass) Soloist, Level One,* under Tuba and Keyboard Collections.

Ostling, Acton, arr. *Folk Song Melodies.* CPP/Belwin, Inc. 1969. 1:58. I. $B♭_1$–B♭. *Sweet Betsy from Pike; On Top of Old Smoky.* Once through each tune. A few simple step-wise slurs. See: Ostling, Acton, *Tuba (Bass) Soloist, Level One,* under Tuba and Keyboard Collections.

Ostling, Acton, arr. *French Song.* CPP/Belwin, Inc. 1969. 0:38. I. $B♭_1$–G. Very easy familiar French tune. Quarter note is fastest rhythm; limited range. See: Ostling, Acton, *Tuba (Bass) Soloist, Level One,* under Tuba and Keyboard Collections.

Ostling, Acton, arr. *Gallant Captain.* CPP/Belwin, Inc. 1970. $4.00. 1:39. I–II. ($a♭_1$) E♭–c (e♭). Moderato. Sea chantey. "Proud" solo in 4/4 time. Fastest rhythm is eighth note. No technical problems. Published separately; see other listings in this section.

Ostling, Acton, arr. *Gallant Captain.* CPP/Belwin, Inc. 1970. See: Lamb, Jack, *Classic Festival Solos,* under Tuba and Keyboard Collections. Also see other listing in this section.

Ostling, Acton, arr. *Gallant Captain.* CPP/Belwin, Inc. 1970. See: CPP/Belwin, *Tuba Solos, Level Two,* under Tuba and Keyboard Collections.

Ostling, Acton, arr. *Military Marches Melodies.* CPP/Belwin, Inc. 1969. 1:00. I. $B♭_1$–c. Marines; U.S. Army. Once through each tune (with an abbreviated Army tune) in cut time. See: Ostling, Acton, *Tuba (Bass) Soloist, Level One,* under Tuba and Keyboard Collections.

Ostling, Acton, arr. *Three Famous Melodies.* CPP/Belwin, Inc. 1969. 0:56. I. $B♭_1$–A♭. "Yankee Doodle"; "Old MacDonald Had a Farm"; "The Daring Young Man on the Flying Trapeze." Eight measures of first two tunes in 4/4 time, sixteen measures of last tune in 3/4 time with short piano interludes. A few easy slurs. Quarter note is fastest rhythm; no technical problems. See: CPP/Belwin, Inc., *Tuba Solos, Level One,* under Tuba and Keyboard Collections.

Ostling, Acton, arr. *Three Famous Melodies.* CPP/Belwin, Inc. 1969. See: Ostling, Acton, *Tuba (Bass) Soloist, Level One,* under Tuba and Keyboard Collections. Also see other listing in this section.

Ostling, Acton, arr. *When the Saints Go Marching In.* CPP/Belwin, Inc. 1969. 1:09. I–II. E♭–c. Moderate march tempo. Melody and accompaniment section. One slur, some accidentals and accents. Accompaniment part might take some rhythmic clarification for very beginning students; otherwise no technical problems. See: CPP/Belwin, Inc., *Tuba Solos, Level One,* under Tuba and Keyboard Collections.

Ostling, Acton, arr. *When the Saints Go Marching In.* CPP/Belwin, Inc. 1969. See: Ostling, Acton, *Tuba (Bass) Soloist, Level One,* under Tuba and Keyboard Collections. Also see other listing in this section.

Ostling, Acton, and Fred Weber, arr. *Tuba (Bass) Soloist —Book 1.* CPP/Belwin, Inc. 1969. Tuba part: $4.50. Piano part: $6.50. I. Good introduction to basic music concepts: basic slurring, various articulations, different meters. Contains: Herbert, Victor, *Victor Herbert Medley;* Knight, J. P., *Rocked in the Cradle of the Deep;* Lehar, *Merry Widow Waltz;* Lincke, *Glow Worm, The;* Lincke and Waldteufel, *Waltz Themes;* Lincoln, *College March;* Mendelssohn, *On Wings of Song;* Olcott, *My Wild Irish Rose;* Ostling, Acton, arr., *All through the Night;* Ostling, Acton, arr., *Blow the Man Down;* Ostling, Acton, arr., *Folk Song Melodies;* Ostling, Acton, arr., *French Song;* Ostling, Acton, arr., *Military Marches Melodies;* Ostling, Acton, arr., *Three Famous Melodies;* Ostling, Acton, arr., *When the Saints Go Marching In;* Poulton, *Andantino;* Poulton, *Aura Lee;* Sousa, John Philip, *Stars and Stripes Forever;* Waldteufel, *Skater's Waltz;* Weber, *Campus Queen.*

Ostrander, Allen. *Concert Piece in Fugal Style.* Edition Musicus. 1960. $3.75. 4:00. III–IV. ($F_1$) G_1–b♭. No technical problems.

Ostrander, Allen, ed. *Concert Album for Tuba.* Editions Musicus. 1954. $13.00. II–IV. Contains: Bach, J. S., *Siciliano;* Beethoven, L.v., *Menuet;* Beethoven, L. v., *Nature's Adoration;* Bizet, G., *Adagietto from L'Arlésienne;* Concone, G., *Etude (op. 10, no. 11);* Corelli, Arcangelo, *Gigue;* Gluck, Chr., *Air;* Handel, G. F., *Andante;* Handel, G. F., *Bouree;* Maganini, Quinto, *An Ancient Greek Melody;* Martini, Padre, *Plasir d'Amour;* Meyerbeer, *Veni Creator;* Rameau, J. Ph., *Rigaudon;* Rimsky-Korsakov, N., *Song of the East;* Stravinsky, I., *Berceuse.*

Ostransky, Leroy. *Serenade and Scherzo.* ed. Himie Voxman. Rubank, Inc. 1972. 4:30. III–IV. A_1–a♭. "for E♭ or BB♭ Bass." Will require flexibility. See: Voxman, Himie, *Concert and Contest Collection,* under Tuba and Keyboard Collections.

Owen, J. A. *Serenade.* arr. Carl Weber. J. W. Pepper & Son. 1914. Out of Print. See: Weber, Carl, *Nineteen Solos for E♭ Bass with Piano Accompaniment,* under Tuba and Keyboard Collections.

Pachelbel, Johann. *Gavotte.* arr. Stephan Schwotzer. Hofmeister. 1993. 0:29. II. A_1–c. In cut time with a bit of syncopation. See: Meschke, Dieter, *Zum Uben und Vorspielen/B-Tuba,* under Tuba and Keyboard Collections.

Paganini. *Perpetual Motion.* arr. Gary Buttery. Whaling Music Publishers. 1978. $10.00. Piano reduction. See: Paganini, *Perpetual Motion,* under Multiple Tubas. (Other arrangements of this piece recorded.)

Paganini, Niccolo. *Moses Variations: Introduction and Variations on a Theme by Rossini.* arr. Philip Sinder. Encore Music Publishers. 1999. 6:00. IV–V. F_1–f'. Effective romantic theme and variations requiring good phrasing, multiple tonguing, range, and finger facility.

Painparé, H. *Concertpiece.* rev. Himie Voxman. Rubank, Inc. $3.50. 7:00. III. (A♭$_1$) B♭$_1$–a♭. Theme and variations–type solo. Lyrical and technical passages included. Good recital material.

Panetta, Carlo. *Il Dominatore.* Berben Publishers. 2001. 3:45. III. F♯$_1$–b. A short recital work with little melodic and rhythmic variation. Some large intervals, but mostly conservative writing for the intermediate player.

Parfrey, Raymond. *Three Tuba Pieces.* Available from Spaeth and Schmid. $14.00.

Pascal, Claude. *Sonate in 6 minutes 30.* Éditions Durand & Cie. 1958. $29.00. 6:30. IV–V. E_1–b'. à Paul Bernard, Professeur au Conservatoire National Supérieur de Musique de Paris. Anime-Lent et calme. "pour Tuba, ou Trombone-Basse, ou Saxhorn en Si♭ et Piano." For French tuba. Very wide range; quick articulations required. See: Thompson/Lemke; *French Music for Low Brass Instruments.*

Pascuzzi, Gregory. *Andante and Allegretto.* Tuba-Euphonium Press. 1996. 6:00. IV–V. F_1–f♯'. Dedicated to Jay Norris. Good concertpiece with some angular lines and fast technical passages. Piano accompaniment repetitive and challenging.

Pasquet, Luis. *Ten Pieces for Tuba and Piano.* Finnish Music Information Center. 1996. 8:45. II. B♭$_1$–g. Bubbles, Kuplat; Hortuvaisuus, Indecision; Nines, Noonisointuja; A la Manera de Astor Tango, Astorintavalla; Madrigaali, Madrigal; Ystävälle, To a Friend; Muisto Espanjasta, Recuerdo de España; Vahan Romanttinen—Valssi; Tuuba Andeilla, Zamba; Tanssinukke, Pantin. Ten programmatic character pieces for tuba and piano. Published in manuscript that is marginally legible. Another difficulty with this work is that not only is there not a solo part, but the solo part on the piano score is written underneath the piano staff. Thus, this is a work written for an advanced beginner, but the notational aspects makes this work unplayable by such a performer.

Pauer, Jirí. *Tubonetta.* Éditions BIM. 1991. $20.00. 10:00. V. B♭$_2$–b♭'. Intráda; Arie; Rondo. Written in 1976. Quick playing in compound meters—first and third movements. Lyrical cantabile second movement. Very wide range; multiphonics.

Payne, Frank Lynn. *Sonata for Tuba and Piano.* Shawnee Press, Inc. 1979. $5.00. 8:20 (2:00, 3:20, 1:00, 2:00). IV–V. C♯$_1$–f♯'. For Mark Mordue. Some mixed meter. Wide range, good ear, and sharp technique required. See review in *TUBA Journal,* Vol. 7, No. 4, Page 27. Also see: Bird, Gary, ed.; *Program Notes for the Solo Tuba.*

Perantoni, Daniel, ed. *Master Solos Intermediate Level.* Hal Leonard Publishing Corp. 1976. $5.95. Besides a nice selection of solos, has preparation studies and comments for each piece. Contains: Bach, J. S., *Siciliano and Chorale;* Brahms, J., *Two Lieder;* Dowland, John, *Come Again, Sweet Love Doth Now Invite;* Dowland, John, *Dear If You Change;* Dowland, John, *Now, O Now My Needs Must Part;* Haydn, F. J., *Two Classical Themes;* Lawrence, Lucinda, *Piece for Tuba and Piano;* Powell, Morgan, *Introduction and Blues;* Schumann, R., *Romance No. 3.* Includes a performance/practice cassette performed by Daniel Perantoni, tuba, and Eric Dalheim, piano. See review in *TUBA Journal,* Vol. 8, No. 1, Page 35.

Pergolesi, Giovanni Battista. *Air.* arr. A. Lebedev. Military Band Masters Faculty of Moscow Conservatiore. 1971. See: Lebedev, A., *Collection of Pieces for Tuba "Es" and Piano,* under Tuba and Keyboard Collections.

Pergolesi, Giovanni Battista. *Arie.* arr. Stephan Schwotzer. Hofmeister. 1993. 1:43. II. E♭–f. See: Meschke, Dieter, *Zum Uben und Vorspielen/B-Tuba,* under Tuba and Keyboard Collections.

Pergolesi, Giovanni Battista. *Canzona.* arr. Clifford P. Barnes. Jack Spratt Music Co. 1965. $3.00. 3:00. III. G_1–f (a♭). Transcription in 2/4 time. Some repeated slurred patterns; no big technical problems. Good recital material.

Pergolesi, Giovanni Battista. *Lied.* arr. Stephan Schwotzer. Hofmeister. 1993. 1:13. II. F♯–e♭. No technical problems. See: Meschke, Dieter, *Zum Uben und Vorspielen/B-Tuba,* under Tuba and Keyboard Collections.

Pergolesi, Giovanni Battista. *Nina.* ed. and compiled Harry I. Phillips. Shawnee Press Inc. 1967. 1:41. II–III. C♯–d. Andante. Lyrical, slurred transcription in minor key. A few 32nd notes and a few sixteenth note triplets (turns); otherwise not too technically difficult. See: Phillips, Harry I., *Eight Bel Canto Songs,* under Tuba and Keyboard Collections.

Pergolesi, Giovanni Battista. *Spiritoso.* tr. Marvin C. Howe. Lawson-Gould. 1965. 2:39. III. C–g. Fun transcription. Mostly scale-wise baroque writing. Good recital material. See: Howe, M., *Three Tuba Solos,* under Tuba and Keyboard Collections.

Perrie, H. W. *Asleep in the Deep.* arr. Herbert Wekselblatt. G. Schirmer Inc. 1972. 1:48. II–III. $B♭_1$–g. Moderato. Classic solo (verse and chorus) in 12/8. See: Wekselblatt, Herbert, *First Solos for the Tuba Player, BB♭,* under Tuba and Keyboard Collections. Also see: Petrie, H. W. *Asleep in the Deep,* in this section.

Peter, C. *Jolly Coppersmith, The.* arr. William J. Bell. CPP/Belwin, Inc. 1964. $4.00. 1:03. I. D–d. Lively. Solo in 2/4 with a few sixteenth notes. A couple of F–d jumps; otherwise no technical problems. See other listing in this section.

Peter, C. *Jolly Coppersmith, The.* arr. William J. Bell. CPP/Belwin, Inc. 1968. Original copyright was 1964. See: Lamb, Jack, *Solo Sounds for Tuba Levels 1–3, Vol. 1,* under Tuba and Keyboard Collections. Also see other listing in this section.

Peterson, Lawrence. *Sonata for BB♭ Bass and Piano.* Schmidt Publications. 1975. 7:16 (2:34, 1:58, 2:44). III–IV. G_1–g♭ (a). Three numbered movements. 1. Lyrical movement in 7/4. 2. Slow rhythmical writing with quartal intervals. 3. Mixed meter (12/8, 9/8, 6/8). Lyrical writing with shifting tonal center. Good advanced intermediate solo containing (not too) modern compositional material. Copy for judge included—why don't more publishers do that?

Pethel, James. *Brass Talk.* Kendor Music, Inc. 1992. $5.00. 3:25. III. B_1–a. Dedicated to Joe Ray. Slowly and freely. Mostly slurred ballad. Strong flexibility and good ear required. Good recital material.

Pethel, Stan. *Essay for Tuba.* Kendor Music, Inc. 1980. $5.00. 2:42. III. G_1–f. Moderately. Intermediate-level solo in 6/8. No big technical challenges; lyrical writing. See review in *TUBA Journal,* Vol. 8, No. 4, Page 26.

Petit, Alexandre. *Première Étude de Concours.* Gérard Billaudot. $5.25. 4:00. IV. F–d'. à mon ami Gabriel Pares, Chef de musique de la Garde Republicaine. Also written for trumpet or cornet; E♭ clarinet; alto saxophone with piano. Technical etude: dotted rhythms with 32nd notes, cadenza, trill. Requires comfortable technique with creative interpretation.

Petit, Pierre. *Fantaisie.* Alphonse Leduc. 1953. $12.80. 4:00. V. F_1–a'. à mon cher Maître et ami Paul Bernard. "pour Tuba ou Trombone basse en Ut ou Saxhorn basse Si♭ et Piano." For French tuba. Some tenor clef in part. See: Thompson/Lemke; *French Music for Low Brass Instruments.*

Petit, Pierre. *Grave.* Alphonse Leduc. 1952. $8.60. 2:00. IV. $A♭_1$–a'. à Paul Bernard. "pour Tuba Ut ou Trombone basse ou Contrebasse à Cordes ou Saxhorn basse Si♭ et Piano." For French tuba. Some tenor clef in part. See: Thompson/Lemke; *French Music for Low Brass Instruments.*

Petit, Pierre. *Thème Varié.* Alphonse Leduc. 1965. $16.00. 7:30. V. E_1–c''. "pour Saxhorn basse Si♭ ou Tuba Ut et Piano." Theme and (eight) variations. For French tuba. See: Thompson/Lemke; *French Music for Low Brass Instruments.*

Petit, Pierre. *Wagenia.* Alphonse Leduc. 1957. $16.85. 5:30. IV. $A♭_1$–d'. "pour Trombone basse ou Tuba Ut ou Saxhorn basse Si♭ et Piano." See: Thompson/Lemke; *French Music for Low Brass Instruments.*

Petrie, H. W. *Asleep in the Deep.* arr. Forrest L. Buchtel. Neil A. Kjos Music Company. 1958. $2.00. 2:00. I–II. G_1–c. Verse and chorus in 6/8 time in E♭ major. A version of this recorded by William Bell, Barney Mallon. Also see: Perrie, H. W. *Asleep in the Deep,* in this section.

Petrie, H. W. *Asleep in the Deep.* arr. Harold L. Walters. Rubank, Inc. 1954. $2.50. "Solo E♭ or BB♭

Bass." See: Petrie, H. W., *Asleep in the Deep,* under Tuba and Band. A version of this recorded by William Bell, Barney Mallon.

Petrie, H. W. *Asleep in the Deep.* arr. William Teague. Witmark. 1942. 2:00. II. B♭$_1$–g. Verse and chorus in 12/8 time and in B♭ major. A version of this recorded by William Bell, Barney Mallon.

Pezel, Johann. *Intrade.* arr. Gerd Philipp. Hofmeister. 1993. 1:08. II. E♭–e♭. In A♭ major and in 4/4 time. Quarter note is fastest rhythm; no technical problems. See: Meschke, Dieter, *Zum Uben und Vorspielen/B-Tuba,* under Tuba and Keyboard Collections.

Phillips, Harry I., ed. *Eight Bel Canto Songs.* Shawnee Press. 1967. $11.00. II–III. Written for a variety of solo instruments with piano. This collection of Italian songs from the 17th and 18th centuries includes: Bononcini, Giovanni, *Per la Gloria D'Adorarri from "Griselda";* Caccini, Giulio, *Amarilli, Mia Bella;* Caldara, Antonio, *Sebben, Crudele;* Durante, Francesco, *Preghiera;* Marcello, Benedetto, *Il mio bel Foco;* Pergolesi, Giovanni Battista, *Nina;* Scarlatti, Allessandro, *Sento Nel Core;* Stradella, Alessandro, *Pieta, Signore!*

Phillips, L. Z. *Marines' Hymn, The.* arr. G. E. Holmes. Rubank, Inc. 1966. Out of Print. See: Rubank, *Soloist Folio for Bass (E♭ or BB♭),* under Tuba and Keyboard Collections. Also see other listing in this section.

Phillips, L. Z. *Marines' Hymn March, The.* arr. G. E. Holmes. Rubank, Inc. 1939. 1:30. II–III. E♭–e♭. "Solo Tuba—E♭ or BB♭ tuba." "Air Varie." Traditional theme and variations based on the United States Marine Corps Hymn. Mostly sixteenth note scale motion for technical section. Limited range. Single version out of print.

Pichaureau, Claude. *Tubatests, Cycle I.* Alphonse Leduc. 2001. 8:00. III–IV. (A$_1$) F–d'. I; II; III. Written as an accompanied test piece in three movements. The range takes it into the advanced level, but played down an octave it is possible for an intermediate player. Each movement becomes more rhythmically complex with more angular melodies.

Pierpont, J. *Jingle Bells.* arr. Sandy Feldstein. CPP/ Belwin, Inc. 1990. I. B♭$_1$–F. See: Feldstein, Sandy, *First Solo Songbook,* under Tuba and Keyboard Collections.

Pinsuti, Ciro. *Bedouin Love Song.* arr. G. E. Holmes. Rubank, Inc. 1939. 1:56. II. (G$_1$) B♭$_1$–e♭. "Solo Tuba—E♭ or BB♭ tuba." Allegretto moderato. A "middle eastern bolero" feel with some syncopation. Optional lower octaves for BB♭ players. Minor section, slower major section with entire piece repeating. See: Rubank, *Soloist Folio for Bass (E♭ or BB♭),* under Tuba and Keyboard Collections.

Pisciotta, Louis V. *Sonata.* Sound Ideas. 1961. $16.00.

Plagge, Wolfgang. *Musica Sacra, Op. 75: Tuba and Piano.* Norwegian Music Center. 1993. 13:00.

Planel, Robert. *Air et Final.* Alphonse Leduc. 1968. $13.35. 6:45. V. C♭–g'. For French tuba.

Plau, Arild. *Concerto for Tuba and Strings.* Ovation. $45.15. See listing under Music for Tuba and Orchestra. Recorded by Øystein Baadsvik.

Plog, Anthony. *Statements.* Editions Bim. 1995. $11.80. 2:20. III. F$_1$–g. Dedicated to Roger Bobo. Recitative written without bar lines or meter indications; however, an insinuation of tempo should be felt throughout because of the very specific rhythmic writing.

Plog, Anthony. *Three Miniatures.* Éditions BIM. 1991. $16.00. Commissioned by Custom Music Coimpany (sic) and written for Daniel Perantoni. See: Plog, Anthony, *Three Miniatures,* under Tuba and Band. Recorded by Roger Bobo.

Plog, Anthony. *Tuba Concerto.* Editions Bim. 1997. $22.00. 22:00. V. G$_1$–e''. Andante; Slowly; Allegro (theme with four variations). Dedicated to Markus Theinert. For more information see Music for Tuba and Orchestra.

Ponce, M. *Estrellita.* arr. Patrick Sheridan. Patrick-Sheridan. com (Bon Bons Series). $12.00.

Ponlot, M. *Burlesco.* Available from Spaeth and Schmid. $8.00.

Poot, Marcel. *Impromptu.* Éditions Max Eschig. 1933. 4:30. IV–V. G–b'. à E. Dax. "pour Trombone et Piano ou Tuba ou Saxhorn baryton." "Morceau imposé au Concours Du Conservatiore Royal De Bruxelles Année 1931." Part includes passages in tenor clef.

Popper, David. *Gavotte.* arr. William J. Bell. CPP/ Belwin, Inc. 1962. $4.00. 1:33. I. (B♭$_1$) F–e♭. Allegretto. Optional 4/4 or cut time. Optional low notes give the leeway for beginners to chose their level of difficulty. Fastest rhythm is quarter note. Very repetitive eight-measure phrase. A couple of articulated jumps from F to d; otherwise no technical problems.

Popper, David. *Gavotte.* arr. William J. Bell. CPP/ Belwin, Inc. 1962. See: CPP/Belwin, Inc., *Tuba Solos, Level One,* under Tuba and Keyboard Collections. Also see other listing in this section.

Porpora, Nicola Antonio. *Sonata in A♭ Major.* arr. Kurt Sturzenegger. Editions Marc Reift. 1996. $11.00. 4:00. III. C (A♭$_1$)–d♭'. Andante; Adagio; Allegro non presto. Originally for cello by the Italian baroque composer; the tessitura of this arrangement is set in the middle range and is playable on all tubas. See listing under Tuba and Organ.

Porret, Julien. *Fifteenth Solo de Concours.* Molenaar N. V. 1963. 2:30. III. c–e'. Good F tuba solo or high study on lower instrument.

Porret, Julien. *Premier Pièce De Concours.* Gérard Billaudot. 1963. 4:51. IV. G$_1$–d'. "pour Saxhorn Basse en Si♭ et piano." Technical solo. For French tuba. See: Thompson/Lemke; *French Music for Low Brass Instruments.*

Poteenko, Aleksandr. *Tubakonzert.* Available from Spaeth and Schmid. $25.50.

Poullot, F. *L'installation au moulin.*

Poulton. *Andantino.* arr. Acton Ostling. CPP/Belwin, Inc. 1969. 1:00. I. C–d. In cut time. See: Ostling, Acton, *Tuba (Bass) Soloist, Level One,* under Tuba and Keyboard Collections.

Poulton. *Aura Lee.* arr. Acton Ostling. CPP/Belwin, Inc. 1969. 1:17. I. B♭$_1$–A♭. Limited range; no technical problems. See: Ostling, Acton, *Tuba (Bass) Soloist, Level One,* under Tuba and Keyboard Collections.

Poutoire, Patrick. *Petit Air.* Éditions M. Combre. 1983. 2:15. II. G–c'. Majestueux. Regal solo with few technical problems. See: Thompson/Lemke; *French Music for Low Brass Instruments.*

Powell, David. *Sonata for Tuba and Piano.* Tuba-Euphonium Press. 1995. 8:00. V. F$_1$–a♭'. Allegro; Lucentemente; Largamente; Vivace. Dedicated to Sumner Erickson. Published in manuscript. Challenging angular lines, rhythmic demands, metric shifts, and range demands.

Powell, Morgan. *Introduction and Blues.* Hal Leonard Publishing Corp. 1976. See: Perantoni, Daniel, *Master Solos Intermediate Level,* under Tuba and Keyboard Collections.

Pozzoli, E. *Sad Minute, The.* ed. A. Lebedev. Moscow Muzyka. 1984. 1:00. II. B♭–f. Mostly half notes with limited range. A slow, reflective, predominantly lyrical composition. Written for the beginning bass saxhorn so there are the typical tessitura demands, while the musical demands are appropriate for the beginner. See: Lebedev, A., *Tuba Tutor Vol. 1,* under Tuba and Keyboard Collections.

Premru, Raymond. *Concerto for Tuba and Orchestra.* TUBA Press. Dedicated to the memory of John Fletcher. Piano reduction in preparation. See: Premru, Raymond, *Concerto for Tuba and Orchestra,* under Tuba and Orchestra.

Prendiville. *Approach of the Lion, The.* arr. Carl Weber. J. W. Pepper & Son. 1914. Out of Print. See: Weber, Carl, *Nineteen Solos for E♭ Bass with Piano Accompaniment,* under Tuba and Keyboard Collections.

Prendiville, Harry, arr. *Down among the Dead Men.* A. Squire. 1888. Out of Print. 1:20. II. C–e♭. See: Prendiville, Harry, *Six Popular Solos,* under Tuba and Keyboard Collections. "E♭ Bass; or, tuba With Piano or Organ Accompaniment, (ad lib.)."

Prendiville, Harry, arr. *Six Popular Solos.* A. Squire. 1888. Out of Print. II–III. "E♭ Bass; or, Tuba With Piano or Organ Accompaniment, (ad lib.)." Contains: Hatton, J. L., *Simon the Cellarer;* Knight, J. P., *Rock'd in the Cradle of the Deep;* Nelson, S., *The Pilot;* Prendiville, Harry, arr., *Down among the Dead Men;* Russell, H., *The Old Sexton;* Shield, *The Friar of Orders Gray.*

Prescott, John. *Sonata for Tuba and Piano.* TUBA Press. $15.00. 16:16 (5:00, 4:37, 6:29). IV–V. E♭$_1$–a♭'. Commissioned by Scott Watson with a grant from the General Research Fund—University of Kansas. Three numbered movements. Opus 23. Solid writing for tuba and piano. Will take flexibility, wide range, and a strong accompanist. See review in *TUBA Journal,* Vol. 18, No. 2, Page 19.

Presser, William. *Capriccio for Tuba and Band.* Theodore Presser Company. 1969. $7.00. For Rex Conner. See: Presser, William, *Capriccio for Tuba and Band,* under Tuba and Band. Recorded by Michael Astwood. Also see: Bird, Gary, ed.; *Program Notes for the Solo Tuba.*

Presser, William. *Concerto for Tuba and Strings.* Theodore Presser Company. 1970. $8.50. See: Presser, William, *Concerto for Tuba and Strings,* under Tuba and Orchestra. Also see: Bird, Gary, ed.; *Program Notes for the Solo Tuba.*

Presser, William. *Minute Sketches.* Autograph Editions. 1967. $5.95. 5:04 (1:02, 1:02, 1:00, 1:00, 1:00). IV. E$_1$–f♯' (g). Trumgo; Song; Waltz; March; Scherzo. Five contrasting movements of approximately one minute each requiring quick articulations. Modern tonal writing.

Presser, William. *Rondo.* C. L. Barnhouse. 1966. $3.50. 2:13. III. (F$_1$) B♭$_1$–f (b♭). Conservative range; one phrase up to b♭. "Ohm-Pah" section, repeating rhythmical motive.

Presser, William. *Second Sonatina for Tuba and Piano.* Theodore Presser Company. 1974. $8.00. 8:30 (3:52, 2:45, 1:44). IV. E♯$_1$–b♭. Completed June 1973, Green Lake, Michigan. Some lovely lyrical and technical modern melodic lines. See review in *TUBA Journal,* Vol. 1, No. 3, Page 6. Also see: Bird, Gary, ed.; *Program Notes for the Solo Tuba.*

Presser, William. *Sonatina for Tuba and Piano.* Theodore Presser Company. 1973. $4.00. 10:35 (4:38, 3:23, 1:08, 1:26). IV. D$_1$–c'. For William Keck. Allegretto; Allegro; Adagio; Presto. Completed July, 1972, Green Lake, Michigan. Third movement based on Robert Herrick's poem "Another Grace for a Child." Tonal modern writing. Quick articulations, both slurred and tongued. See: Bird, Gary, ed.; *Program Notes for the Solo Tuba.*

Presser, William. *Suite for Tuba.* Lyceum Press (Ensemble Publications). 1967. $4.00. 8:10. For Rex Conner. See: Bird, Gary, ed.; *Program Notes for the Solo Tuba.*

Pro Art (publisher). *Fifty Standard Solos.* Pro Art Publications. 1964. Out of Print. I–IV. Published for a variety of instruments, this series of solo books contains a variety of selections, from easy waltzes and marches to more difficult excerpts from traditional and classical works.

Proctor, Simon. *Tuba Concerto.* Heavy Metal Music. 1995. 10:00. IV. $30.00. F$_1$–f'. Dedicated to and commissioned by Sue Bradley. Available through Windsong Press. Concerto in one movement. Repetitive rhythmic patterns. Linear melodic lines combined with arpeggio and octave leaps. Range demands makes this an advanced-level work. See listing under Music for Tuba and Orchestra.

Proctor, Simon. *Tuber Music.* Available from Spaeth and Schmid. $16.50.

Prokofiev, Sergi. *Recitative and Kutuzov's Air from the Opera "War and Peace."* arr. A. Lebedev. Military Band Masters Faculty of Moscow Conservatiore. 1971. See: Lebedev, A., *Collection of Pieces for Tuba "Es" and Piano,* under Tuba and Keyboard Collections.

Proust, Pascal. *Le Chêne-Chat.* Gérard Billaudot Éditeur. 1993. $8.00. 3:00. III. D–e♭'.

Proust, Pascal. *Élegié.* Gérard Billaudot. 1991. $4.00. 3:00. II–III. D–c'. "pour Tuba en ut (ou saxhorn basse en si♭ ou euphonium) et piano." Very lyrical section and articulated section with some arpeggios. For French tuba.

Proust, Pascal. *Intermezzo.* arr. Unkrodt. Available from Spaeth and Schmid. $19.00.

Proust, Pascal. *Nocturne Et Petite Ronde.* Gérard Billaudot Éditeur. 1997. $6.50. 2:30. G–d'. Written for the bass saxhorn, so there are the typical tessitura demands, while the musical demands are appropriate for the beginner.

Proust, Pascal. *Prélude et Jeu.* Gérard Billaudot Éditeur. 1993. $11.00. 3:40. IV. D–f'. Prélude; Jeu. Written for the advanced beginner on the saxhorn. The upper tessitura makes this an advanced work.

Proust, Pascal. *Premieres Variations.* Available from Spaeth and Schmid. $13.50.

Proust, Pascal. *Tuba Blues.* Available from Spaeth and Schmid. $9.00.

Pryor, Arthur. *Blue Bells of Scotland.* arr. Alan Lourens. Solid Brass Music Company. $12.50. IV. Arrangement available for tuba or euphonium.

Pryor, Arthur. *Exposition Echoes Polka.* arr. Carl Weber. J. W. Pepper & Son. 1914. Out of Print. See: Weber, Carl, *Nineteen Solos for E♭ Bass with Piano Accompaniment,* under Tuba and Keyboard Collections.

Purcell, Henry. *Arise Ye Subterranean Winds.* arr. Allen Ostrander. Edition Musicus. 1959. $2.75. 2:30. III. G_1–f. Some slurred technical passages (sixteenth notes in 4/4 time) included in this fine transcription. Good recital material.

Purcell, Henry. *Gavotte.* arr. Anton Vedeski. Medici Music Press. 1981. 1:42. II–III. B♭$_1$–e♭. From *Harpsichord Suite No. 5.* A variety of marked articulations included. No technical problems. Good recital material.

Purcell, Henry. *Gavotte and Hornpipe.* tr. Ronald C. Dishinger. Medici Music Press.

Purcell, Henry. *March.* arr. Dishinger. Available from Spaeth and Schmid. $8.50.

Purcell, Henry. *Next, Winter Comes Slowly.* tr. Marvin C. Howe. Lawson-Gould. 1965. 1:54. II–III. (G_1) C–g. See: Howe, M., *Three Tuba Solos,* under Tuba and Keyboard Collections.

Purcell, Henry. *Recitative, Song and Chorus.* arr. R. Winston Morris. Southern Music Company. 1972. $2.50. 4:30. III. C–g. From *Dido and Aeneas.* Section in 3/2 time. Very lyrical transcription.

Purcell, Henry. *Song from Timon of Athens.* arr. Don Little. CPP/Belwin, Inc. 1992. 2:16. II–III. (G_1) B♭$_1$–e♭. Solo in 3/4 time at a brisk tempo. Eighth note is fastest rhythm. Some slurring. See: Little, Don, *Solo-Pak for Tuba, Part Three,* under Tuba and Keyboard Collections.

Quate, Amy. *Feel Good Blues, The.* CPP/Belwin, Inc. 1992. 2:30. II–III. C–e. Blues style. "Swung" eighth notes, accidentals, and syncopations throughout. See: Little, Don, *Solo-Pak for Tuba, Part Three,* under Tuba and Keyboard Collections.

Quate, Amy. *Los Cocos Locos. (Crazy Coconuts.)* ed. Don Little. CPP/Belwin, Inc. 1991. 2:02. II. (B♭$_1$) D–e♭. Latin flavor. "After beat" rhythms. Various articulations: tenuto, staccato, accents. See: Little, Don, *Solo-Pak for Tuba, Part Two,* under Tuba and Keyboard Collections.

Quate, Amy, and Don Little. *Texas Horizons.* CPP/Belwin, Inc. 1989. 3:05. I–II. B♭$_1$–d (f). Some slurring of eighth notes at a conservative tempo. No other technical problems. See: Little, Don, *Solo-Pak for Tuba, Part One,* under Tuba and Keyboard Collections.

Quérat, Marcel. *Allegretto Comodo.* Éditions M. Combre. 1971. 2:40. III. G–f'. "pour Saxhorn-Basse et Piano." For French tuba. See: Thompson/Lemke; *French Music for Low Brass Instruments.*

Quérat, Marcel. *Moderation.* Éditions M. Combre. 1991. 2:23. III–IV. A♭$_1$–d'. a Bernard Lienard. "pour Tuba Basse et Piano." Mostly lyrical solo with a French flavor.

Quérat, Marcel. *Relation.* Éditions M. Combre. 1971. 1:47. II. B♭–d'. "pour Basse Si♭ et Piano." No technical problems. For French tuba. See: Thompson/Lemke; *French Music for Low Brass Instruments.*

Rachmaninoff, Sergei. *Elegia.* ed. S. Melnikov. Military Band Masters Institute–Moscow. 1957. See: Melnikov, S., *Pieces for Tuba and Piano,* under Tuba and Keyboard Collections.

Rachmaninoff, Sergei. *Russian Song.* arr. A. Lebedev. Military Band Masters Faculty of Moscow Conservatiore. 1971. See: Lebedev, A., *Collection of Pieces for Tuba "Es" and Piano,* under Tuba and Keyboard Collections.

Rachmaninoff, Sergei. *Vocalise.* arr. Virginia Allen. Ludwig Music Publishing Company. 1992. $5.00. 2:32. III–IV. C–c' (e♭'). Opus 34, no. 14. Transcription of an incredibly lovely melody. Good recital material. A version of this recorded by Robert LeBlanc.

Rachmaninoff, Sergi. *Twilight.* arr. Stephen Shoop. Cimarron Music. 1995. I–II. 3:00. $7.00. B♭$_1$–f♯. A good song-like transcription for the beginner or young intermediate. Good for learning to hear harmonic shifts characteristic of romantic music.

Rachmaninoff, Sergi. *Vocalise.* arr. Patrick Sheridan. PatrickSheridan. com (Bon Bons Series). $15.00.

Radolt, Wenzel Ludwig Freiherr von. *Menuett im Kanon.* arr. Gerd Philipp. Hofmeister. 1993. 1:06. I–II. D–c. No technical problems; in E♭ major and 3/4 time. See: Meschke, Dieter, *Zum Uben und Vorspielen/B-Tuba,* under Tuba and Keyboard Collections.

Rae, Allan. *Serenade for Tuba and Piano.* Canadian Music Centre. 1991. 4:00. IV. A_1–c♯'. Sherburne G. McCurdy Festival Series. Contains metrically free sections and more conventional notation. Nice textural solo. Good recital material. Requires very strong accompanist.

Raich. *Bassistengruß.* Adler Verlag. Piano reduction. See: Raich, *Bassistengruß,* under Tuba and Band.

Rakov, N. *Air.* ed. V. Mitegin. Moscow Muzyka. 1969. See: Mitegin, V., *Pieces for Tuba and Piano,* in Tuba and Keyboard Collections.

Rakov, N. *Romance.* arr. A. Lebedev. Military Band Masters Faculty of Moscow Conservatiore. 1971. See: Lebedev, A., *Collection of Pieces for Tuba "Es" and Piano,* under Tuba and Keyboard Collections.

Rakov, N. *Sonatina.* ed. A. Lebedev. Moscow Muzyka. 1986. 1:51. III. E_1–b♭. Allegro. First seven pitches of this piece based on L E B E D E V. Composed in 1973. Fun piece with a lot of character. Lyrical and pesante playing. See: Lebedev, A., *Tuba Tutor Vol. 2,* under Tuba and Keyboard Collections.

Rakov, N. *Sonatina.* ed. G. Voronov. Moscow Muzyka. 1984. See: Voronov, G, *Works for Tuba and Piano by Russian Composers,* under Tuba and Keyboard Collections. Also see other listing in this section.

Rameau, J. Ph. *Rigaudon.* arr. Quinto Maganini. Edition Musicus. 1954. 1:20. III. E♭–a♭. Alternating slur two, tongue two (eighth note) articulation throughout in cut time. See: Ostrander, Allen, *Concert Album for Tuba,* under Tuba and Keyboard Collections.

Rameau, Jean Philippe. *Rigaudon from Piece de Clavecin.* tr. Ronald C. Dishinger. Medici Music Press.

Rameau, Jean Philippe. *La Villageoise.* arr. Herbert Wekselblatt. G. Schirmer Inc. 1972. 0:48. II. $B♭_1$–e♭. Cute 2/4 dance with no technical problems. See: Wekselblatt, Herbert, *First Solos for the Tuba Player, BB♭,* under Tuba and Keyboard Collections.

Ramskill, Robert. Concerto for Tuba. Warwick Music Limited. $34.90.

Rance, E. (Adjutant). *Rocked in the Cradle of the Deep.* Salvation Army. 3:00. III. $B♭_1$–b♭. "Solo for Bombardon in E♭." Solo part in treble clef.

Rappoldt, Lawrence I. *Concertpiece for Tuba and Piano.* Shawnee Press. 1979. $6.00. 6:20. IV. A_1–d'. Mixed meter. Solid writing for tuba and piano. Will take some rhythmic (meter) inspection. See review in *TUBA Journal,* Vol. 10, No. 2, Page 24.

Raum, Elizabeth. *Concerto del Garda.* Tuba-Euphonium Press. 1998. 15:00. V. F_1–b♭'. I; II; III. Dedicated to John Griffiths. Edition published for F tuba and CC tuba. A very musically and technically demanding work suitable for F tuba. See listing under Music for Tuba and Orchestra, and Music for Tuba and Band.

Raum, Elizabeth. *Faustbuch.* Tuba-Euphonium Press. 2003. 15:00. V. A_1–a♭'. Faust and Mephistopheles; Faust and Gretchen; Walpurgis, Death, and Redemption. Commissioned by and dedicated to Mark Jenkins. A very demanding work with extreme range considerations. The composer notes that it may also may be performed on euphonium. See listing under Music for Tuba and Orchestra.

Raum, Elizabeth. *Legend of Heimdall, The.* Tuba-Euphonium Press. 1998. 12:00. V. G_1–g'. Heimdall's Gjallarhorn; Tale of the Bard; Attack on Asgard. Commissioned by the Canadian Broadcasting Corporation. Dedicated to John Griffiths. A technically and musically challenging work with programmatic content. See listing under Music for Tuba and Orchestra.

Raum, Elizabeth. *Pershing Concerto.* Tuba-Euphonium Press. 2000. 10:00. V. $B♭_1$–f' (a'). Allegro Moderato; II; III. A musically rewarding work with some extreme range considerations. See listing under Music for Tuba and Orchestra.

Raum, Elizabeth. *Romance for Tuba.* Tuba-Euphonium Press. 2001. 5:00. IV–V. $B♭_1$–e♭'. Commissioned by Estelle Gravois-Murr. Dedicated to Ray Murr. A one-movement work with many tempo changes; tonally interesting.

Ravel, Maurice. *Pavane.* arr. A. Lebedev. Military Band Masters Faculty of Moscow Conservatiore. 1971. See: Lebedev, A., *Collection of Pieces for Tuba "Es" and Piano,* under Tuba and Keyboard Collections.

Ravel, Maurice. *Pavane pour une Infante défunte.* ed. and tr. Joseph Skillen. Bernel Music, Ltd. 2000. D–d'. Effective and light transcription of this impressionistic work. Many opportunities for expression, dynamic contrasts, and phrasing considerations. Good recital piece for bass or contrabass tuba.

Ravel, Maurice. *Pièce en forme de Habanera.* arr. Walter Hilgers. Editions Marc Reift. 1991. $11.00. 2:30. III. C–a. Arrangement of the English horn solo in the third movement of Ravel's "Rapsodie espagnole" for symphony orchestra. The difficulty lies in the musical shaping of the rubati lines. Recorded by: Walter Hilgers.

Read, Thomas L. *Enchorial Landscape.* Tuba-Euphonium Press. 2003. 6:00. IV–V. A_1–e♭'.

Dedicated to Mark Nelson. A rhythmically complex work with complex intervals. Good recital piece.

Reed, Alfred. *Fantasia A Due.* Edward B. Marks Music Co. 1979. 5:00. IV–V. G_1–e' (c"). Commissioned by, and dedicated to, TUBA, for the Third International Tuba-Euphonium Symposium-Workshop, 1978. First T.U.B.A.-commissioned work. Solid writing for tuba and piano. Requires strong technique. Good recital material. See review in *TUBA Journal,* Vol. 7, No. 3, Page 31.

Reiche, E. *Adagio from Concerto No. 2.* arr. Hiroyuki Yasumoto. Toa Music International Co. 1989. 3:58. IV. (B_1) D–f'. Would lie better on F tuba although playable on lower instrument. Strong lyrical sense combined with flexibility. Sub-divide in six. See: Yasumoto, Hiroyuki, arr., *Tuba Volume #2,* under Tuba and Keyboard Collections.

Rekhin, Igor. *Sonata for Tuba and Piano.* TUBA Press. $12.00. 9:30 (4:30, 2:00, 3:00). IV–V. D_1–f'. For Scott Watson. Three attacca movements. New-romantic feel. Major work for tuba and piano. Solid writing. Requires flexibility and vocal sense. Good recital material.

Renaud, Manuel. *Ton Coeur (Tuba).* Gérard Billaudot. 1990. 4:00. II–III. D♭–g♭. A Mon père. "pour tuba basse en ut et piano." For French tuba. Extensive use of tritones. Modern melodic writing. Some slurring involved. See: Daniel-Lesur, *Collection Panorama,* under Tuba and Keyboard Collections.

Reynaud, J. *Ah! vous dirai-je maman.* Editions Salabert. Out of Print. Theme and variations.

Reynolds, Verne. *Sonata for Tuba and Piano.* Carl Fischer Inc. 1969. $8.50. 13:00. V. ($A_2$) D_1–a'. Moderately fast; Slow; Variations. For Cherry Beauregard. Difficult work for tuba and piano by this virtuoso French horn teacher and performer, requiring very strong technique as well as strong musicality.

Rich, James, and Randy Randolph. *Yackety Sax.* arr. Hardy Scheiders. Editions Marc Reift. 1963. $9.50. 1:40. III. D–c'. Traditional arrangement of this classic saxophone showpiece, which was used as the theme song on *The Benny Hill Show.*

Richardson, Alan. *In the Lowlands.* Braydeston Press. 1975. $9.95. 5:00 (1:15, 1:15, 1:15, 1:15). III. C–b♭. Alla Marcia—Allegro—In folksong style; Lento moderato; espressivo, ma semplice; Vivace ritmico. For Christine and Henry Erskine-Hill. Four movements with same duration. Very tonal, descriptive musical settings. Lyrical, vocal writing. Technical demands not outstanding. Good recital piece.

Rideout, Alan. *Concertino for Tuba and Strings.* Emerson Edition. 1985. $9.50. See: Rideout, Alan, *Concertino for Tuba and Strings,* under Tuba and Orchestra.

Ridout. *Six Little Tuba Pieces.* Available from Spaeth and Schmid. $11.50.

Ridout, Alan. *Autumn Story.* Emerson Edition. 1996. 3:45. I. D–f. Lost Love; Stacking the Logs; Falling Leaves; Boy Meets Girl; The First Goal of the Season. Good character pieces for the beginning player. No rhythmic complexities, but excellent for training purposes.

Rimsky-Korsakoff, Nikolai. *Hummelflug.* arr. Reift. Available from Spaeth and Schmid. $8.50.

Rimsky-Korsakov, Nicolai. *Flight of the Bumble Bee.* arr. Neal Corwell. Tuba Euphonium Press. 2004. 2:00. III–IV. E_1–b♭. This version of the classical favorite begins and ends in G minor, but features some brief excursions into other related keys. For added punctuation and interest, the arranger has added a coda to bring this encore piece to a rousing and somewhat unexpected close. See listing under Music for Tuba and Electronic Media.

Rimsky-Korsakov, Nicolai. *Flight of the Bumble Bee (in A♭major) (for E♭ tuba).* arr. Patrick Sheridan. PatrickSheridan.com (Lollipop Series). $18.00.

Rimsky-Korsakov, Nicolai. *Flight of the Bumble Bee (in B♭major) (for F tuba).* arr. Patrick Sheridan. PatrickSheridan.com (Lollipop Series). $18.00.

Rimsky-Korsakov, Nikolai. *Andante Cantabile from Concerto.* ed. Himie Voxman. Rubank, Inc. 1972. 3:00. III. C–g♭. "for E♭ or BB♭ Bass. Second movement from trombone concerto including cadenza. As with original, in G♭ major. Very lyrical writing. See: Voxman, Himie, *Concert and Contest Collection,* under Tuba and Keyboard Collections.

Rimsky-Korsakov, Nikolai. *Flight of the Bumble Bee, The.* arr. Marc Reift. Editions Marc Reift. 1997. $7.00. 1:00. IV. A_1–e♭'. This is an arrangement of the original, which can be played by all brass and woodwind instruments. The tessitura is middle to high register. Available in bass clef concert pitch, or in treble clef in E♭ or B♭.

Rimsky-Korsakov, Nikolai. *Song from the Opera "Snow Maiden."* ed. S. Melnikov. Military Band Masters Institute–Moscow. 1957. See: Melnikov, S., *Pieces for Tuba and Piano,* under Tuba and Keyboard Collections.

Rimsky-Korsakov, Nikolai. *Song of India.* arr. Igor Hudadoff; William Westcott, pno. arr. Pro Art Publications. 1967. Out of Print. See: Hudadoff, Igor, *Fifteen Intermediate Tuba Solos,* under Tuba and Keyboard Collections.

Rimsky-Korsakov, Nikolai. *Song of the East.* arr. M. Agounoff. Edition Musicus. 1950. 1:33. II–III. C♯–g. Andante. Quasi cadenza section followed by typical Rimsky-Korsakov recitative-like melody. Some 32nd notes (slow tempo); triplets and dotted rhythms (to differentiate). Middle tessitura throughout. See: Ostrander, Allen, *Concert Album for Tuba,* under Tuba and Keyboard Collections.

Ringleben, J. *Storm King, The.* Carl Fischer Inc. 1897. $3.25. "Grand Fantasia." See: Ringleben, J., *The Storm King—Grand Fantasia,* under Tuba and Band. Also see review in *TUBA Journal,* Vol. 9, No. 3, Page 25.

Rivière, Jean-Pierre. *Ré mineur.* Éditions Max Eschig. 1979. 5:25. IV–V. G_1–g♯'. à Paul Bernard. For French tuba. Great flexibility required. Wide "dissonant" jumps, wide range, glissandos in cadenza.

Roberts, Sue. *Chanson and Divertissement.* 1982. Commissioned by Rodger Vaughan.

Rodgers, Thomas. *Chaconne.* Brass Press. 1974. $3.50. Change of publisher: Editions Bim. $6.50. 3:45. IV. A_1–b. Originally published by Manuscripts for Tuba, 1968. Two legato, lyrical sections separated by a marcato, staccato section. Some sixteenth note triplets; optional mute in last variation. Would take an advanced high school or college player.

Roeckel, J. *Unforgotten Days.* arr. Paul deVille. Carl Fischer Inc. 1906. Out of Print. See: deVille, Paul, *Pleasant Hours,* under Tuba and Keyboard Collections.

Roger, Denise. *Souvenance.* Robert Martin Editions. 1992. $12.50. F–c'. A slow, lyrical piece that stays in the upper tessitura. It is intended to be a beginning piece for the saxhorn player. The upper tessitura makes it more of an advanced beginner piece.

Roikjer, Kjell. *Andante.* Imudico Musikforlaget. $14.00. 3:36. IV–V. F_1–f'. Dedicated to Michael Lind. For Tuba og Klaver, op. 65. Andante sostenuto. Premiered in 1974. Lyrical ballad in 3/2 using the full range of the horn. Depending on tempo, requires flexibility. Good recital material.

Roikjer, Kjell. *Capriccio for Tuba and Orchestra.* Imudico Musikforlaget. 1974. $18.00. Opus 66. See: Roikjer, Kjell, *Capriccio for Tuba and Orchestra, Opus 66,* under Tuba and Orchestra. See review in *TUBA Journal,* Vol. 6, No. 2, Page 10.

Roikjer, Kjell. *Koncert med orkester.* Imudico Musikforlaget. $16.00. Opus 61. See: Roikjer, Kjell, *Concerto for Tuba and Orchestra,* under Tuba and Orchestra.

Roikjer, Kjell. *Sonate for Tuba og Klaver.* Imudico Musikforlaget. 1981. 17:10 (6:30, 6:30, 4:10). IV. A_1–e♭'. Allegro moderato ed energico; Molto lento e pesante; Allegro energico e con agevolezza. Dedicated to Michael Lind. Opus 68. Premiered in 1976. Op. 68. Not too technical. Great on F tuba, playable on lower instruments. Good recital material. See: Bird, Gary, ed.; *Program Notes for the Solo Tuba.*

Roikjer, Kjell. *Tonal Miniature Pieces.* Edition Edtved. 1983. $8.80. 25.00. IV–V. F_1–e'. Dedicated to Michael Lind. Opus 75. Composed Lyngby, November 1981. Fourteen pieces, each in a different major key and the relative minor. Very musical and fun to play. Strong technique required.

Roikjer, Kjell. *Twenty-Four Pieces for Tuba and Piano.* Edition Edtved. 1981. Dedicated to Michael Lind. Twenty-four pieces in all majors and minors.

Roitershteny. *Concertiya Sonatina.* 1986. 4:38. III–IV. F_1–d♭'. Except for some higher tessitura, level III. Cut time throughout. Light, very tonal melody; no hard rhythms. Good introduction to higher range for intermediate student.

Rollé. *Concerto brillant.* Editions Salabert. Out of Print.

Rollin, Robert. *Sonatina for Tuba and Piano.* Seesaw Music Corporation. 1986. $15.00. 6:33 (2:26, 4:07). IV–V. D_1–a♯. Commissioned by John Turk. Modern writing. Strong technique and modern melodic concept and strong accompanist required. Low-range work. Second movement in 3/2 time.

Rollinson, T. H. *Columbia.* arr. Forrest L. Buchtel. Neil A. Kjos Music Company. 1958. Out of Print. III. B_1–g. Theme and variations on *Columbia, Gem of the Ocean.* Much triple tonguing. Traditional polka style.

Rollinson, T. H. *Hear Our Prayer—Paraphrase.* arr. Carl Weber. J. W. Pepper & Son. 1914. Out of Print. See: Weber, Carl, *Nineteen Solos for E♭ Bass with Piano Accompaniment,* under Tuba and Keyboard Collections.

Rollinson, T. H. *Rocked in the Cradle of the Deep.* Cundy-Bettoney/Carl Fischer Inc. 1881. Out of Print. 7:55. III–IV. $B♭_1$–c' (e'). Theme and variations intended for E♭ tuba. Oldest copyright date in this section. Recorded by: Tim Lawhern.

Romberg, Sigmund. *Serenade from "Student Prince."* arr. Patrick Sheridan. PatrickSheridan.com (Lollipop Series). $12.00.

Ronnes, Robert. *Adventure for Tuba and Piano.*

Rønnes, Robert. *Adventure.* Norwegian Music Center. 1980. 3:00.

Roost. *Obsessions.* Available from Spaeth and Schmid. $14.25.

Rose, Phil. S. *Chromatic Concert Polka.* arr. Carl Weber. J. W. Pepper & Son. 1914. Out of Print. See: Weber, Carl, *Nineteen Solos for E♭ Bass with Piano Accompaniment,* under Tuba and Keyboard Collections.

Ross, Walter. *Azure Etudes.* Mark Tezak. 1982. $6.00. 3:56. IV. G_1–d'. With the exception of last note (G_1), all middle to upper tessitura. Melodic, reflective tune. Mostly slurred phrases. Requires vocal approach.

Ross, Walter. *Tuba Concerto.* Boosey & Hawkes, Inc. 1975. $18.50. For R. Winston Morris. Composed in 1973. See: Ross, Walter, *Tuba Concerto,* under Tuba and Band. Also see: Bird, Gary, ed.; *Program Notes for the Solo Tuba.* Recorded by: Harvey Phillips.

Ross, Walter. *Villanella.* TUBA Press. 1992. $8.00. IV. C–b♭. For Mark Nelson. Completed July 17,

1992, Charlottesville, Va. Two contrasting sections: Lento affettuoso, a very lyrical 4/4 introduction; and a 6/8 Allegro burlesco section that requires flexibility and lightness. Conservative range. See review in *TUBA Journal,* Vol. 20, No. 4, Page 16.

Rossini, Gioacchino. *Basilio Aria.* Available from Spaeth and Schmid. $12.75.

Rossini, Gioacchino. *Dance, The.* arr. Lionel Lethbridge. Bernel/R. Smith & Co Ltd. 1991. See: Rossini, Gioacchino, *Two Rossini Pieces,* in this section.

Rossini, Gioacchino. *Introduction, thème et variations sur l'air de Moïse.* Available from Spaeth and Schmid. $12.75.

Rossini, Gioacchino. *L'Italiana in Algeri.* Available from Spaeth and Schmid. $12.25.

Rossini, Gioacchino. *Lord Preserve Me.* arr. Allen Ostrander. Edition Musicus. 1959. $3.00. 2:00. II–III. A_1–e. (*Stabat Mater.*) Dotted eighth/sixteenth note slurred passages must be crisp, especially to contrast with triplets near end.

Rossini, Gioacchino. *Softly, Softly.* arr. Lionel Lethbridge. Bernel/R. Smith & Co Ltd. 1991. See: Rossini, Gioacchino, *Two Rossini Pieces,* in this section.

Rossini, Gioacchino. *Two Rossini Pieces.* arr. Lionel Lethbridge. Bernel/R. Smith & Co Ltd. 1991. $16.75. 4:15 (2:56, 1:19). III. $B\flat_1$–b♭. *Softly, Softly; The Dance. Softly, Softly,* from *The Barber of Seville,* has a light bouncing feel to it in 4/4 time. *The Dance,* from *Soirees Musicales,* is a 6/8, quick, spirited Allegro con brio movement in B♭ major and minor. Good recital material.

Rossini, Gioacchino. *Una Voce M'Ha Colpito.* arr. Lieut. J. Ord Hume. Boosey & Hawkes, Inc. 1913. Out of Print. 5:00. III. $B\flat_1$–f. "L'inganno Fortunato." Andante: sixteenth note triplets and 32nd note figures that need to be treated in a recitativo way. Allegro Vivace: Has cadenza-like, recitativo passages. Triplet passages included.

Rothgarber, Herbert. *Dialogue for Tuba and Piano.* Theodore Presser Company. 1971. $4.00. 7:30. IV–V. F_1–e'. Dedicated to David Winograd. Contemporary "dissonant" melodic language. Mixed meter.

Rottler, Werner. *Konzert für Tuba und Orchestra.* Available from Tuba Center. 1980. For Robert Tucci. See: Rottler, Werner, *Concerto for Tuba and Orchestra,* under Tuba and Orchestra.

Rottler, Werner. *Nachtstück.* Available from the composer. IV. In manuscript.

Rottler, Werner. *Sonatina für Tuba und Klavier.* Hofmeister. 1993. 7:46. IV–V. D_1–f'. Für Robert Tucci. Composed in 1983. Opus 14. Very musical piece requiring some quick articulations, flexibility, wide range, and playfulness. Good recital piece.

Rougeron, Philippe. *Valse Nostalgique.* Gérard Billaudot. 1979. $2.50. 1:48. II. (C) A–c'. "pour Tuba (ou Trombone) Et Piano." For French tuba. Cute waltz with no technical problems. Good recital material. See: Thompson/Lemke; *French Music for Low Brass Instruments.* Also see review in *TUBA Journal,* Vol. 9, No. 1, Page 14.

Rougnon. *Priere.* Alphonse Leduc. $6.75. Saxhorn si♭ et Piano. See: Thompson/Lemke; *French Music for Low Brass Instruments.*

Rougnon. *Sicilienne.* Alphonse Leduc. $5.85. Saxhorn Si♭ et Piano. See: Thompson/Lemke; *French Music for Low Brass Instruments.*

Rougnon. *Valse Lente.* Alphonse Leduc. $7.95. II. C (E)–c'. Instruments En Si♭ et Piano. See: Thompson/Lemke; *French Music for Low Brass Instruments.*

Rubank. *Soloist Folio for Bass (E♭ or BB♭).* Rubank, Inc. 1939. $6.95. II–III. May have been compiled by Himie Voxman. Contains: Bizet, G., *Toreador's Song;* Brahmstedt, N. K., *Stupendo;* DeLamater, E., *Rocked in the Cradle of the Deep;* Grieg, Edvard, *In the Hall of the Mountain King;* Lohr, Frederic N., *Out on the Deep;* Macbeth, Allan, *Forget Me Not;* Phillips, L. Z., *The Marines' Hymn;* Pinsuti, Ciro, *Bedouin Love Song;* Schumann, R., *The Jolly Peasant;* Vander Cook, H. A., *Bombastoso.*

Rubenstein, Anton. *Be Not Shy, My Pretty One.* tr. Mitchell Gershenfeld. Medici Music Press. 1985. 1:42. II–III. E♭–f. Opus 34, no. 11. In A♭ major in 3/4 time. A few sixteenth notes; no technical problems. See: Gershenfeld, Mitchell, *Medici Masterworks Solos Volume 1,* under Tuba and Keyboard Collections.

Rubenstein, Anton. *Melody and Romance.* arr. John Glenesk Mortimer. Editions Marc Reift. 2000. $12.50. 6:00. II. B_1–a♭'. Melody in F, op. 3, no. 1; Romance, op. 44, no. 1. A lyrical arrangement of two popular songs originally for piano. The tessitura lends itself to tubas in all keys.

Rubinstein, A. *Persian Song, A.* arr. A. Lebedev. Military Band Masters Faculty of Moscow Conservatiore. 1971. See: Lebedev, A., *Collection of Pieces for Tuba "Es" and Piano,* under Tuba and Keyboard Collections.

Rubinstein, A. *Romance.* arr. Paul deVille. Carl Fischer Inc. 1906. Out of Print. See: deVille, Paul, *Pleasant Hours,* under Tuba and Keyboard Collections.

Rubinstein, A. *Romance.* ed. S. Melnikov. Military Band Masters Institute–Moscow. 1957. See: Melnikov, S., *Pieces for Tuba and Piano,* under Tuba and Keyboard Collections.

Rubinstein, A. *Song from the Cycle "Persian Songs."* ed. S. Melnikov. Military Band Masters Institute–Moscow. 1957. See: Melnikov, S., *Pieces for Tuba and Piano,* under Tuba and Keyboard Collections.

Ruckauer, H. *Der fidele Bassist.* Rundel. II. Piano reduction. For tuba and band.

Rueff, Jeanine. *Concertstuck.* Alphonse Leduc. 1960. $16.85. 6:45. V. $A\flat_1$–a'. à Paul Bernard,

Professeur au Conservatoire National Supérieur de Musique. "pour Saxhorn basse Si♭ ou Tuba Ut ou Trombone basse et Piano." For French tuba. Some tenor clef in part. See: Thompson/ Lemke; *French Music for Low Brass Instruments.*

Ruelle, F. *Prelude et Danse Guerriere.* Editions Andel Uitgave.

Rufeisen, Arie. *Short Suspense Story, A.* Kibutz Movement League of Composers. Recorded by Adi Hershko.

Ruff, D. *Concert Piece.* Muzyka, Moscow. 1976. See: Guzii, V., *Pieces for Tuba and Piano,* under Tuba and Keyboard Collections.

Russell, Armand. *Suite Concertante.* Accura Music. 1963. $20.50. See: Russell, Armand, *Suite Concertante,* under Tuba in Mixed Ensemble. Also see: Bird, Gary, ed.; *Program Notes for the Solo Tuba.* Recorded by Floyd Cooley.

Russell, H. *Old Sexton, The.* arr. Harry Prendiville. A. Squire. 1888. Out of Print. 1:10. II. D♭–f. Some syncopation and sixteenth/eighth (reverse)–type dotted rhythms. "E♭ Bass; or, tuba With Piano or Organ Accompaniment, (ad lib.)." See: Prendiville, Harry, *Six Popular Solos,* under Tuba and Keyboard Collections.

Sabathil, Ferd. *Divertissement.* arr. Don Wilson. Gamble Hinged Music Co. 1938. Out of Print. 8:45. III. G_1–f. Op. 54; Solo for BB♭ tuba. Long, old-style melodramatic solo. Intermediate technical requirements. Two cadenzas, scales, etc.

Sacco, P. Peter. *Fantasy for Tuba and Piano.* Western International Music. 1972. Out of Print. 4:42. IV–V. G_1–b. Modern melodic language. Meter changes. Possible double tonguing depending on tempo. Muted passages. See review in *TUBA Journal,* Vol. 6, No. 2, Page 9.

Saglietti, Corrado Maria. *Concertissimo.* Editions Bim. 1997. $19.80. 17:00. IV. F_1–f'. Allegro; Adagio; Allegro con spirito. Piano reduction. For more information see Music for Tuba and Band.

Saglietti, Corrado Maria. *Concerto for Tuba and Four Horns.* Éditions BIM. 1985. Publication pending—1993. See: Saglietti, Corrado Maria, *Concerto for Tuba and Four Horns,* under Tuba and Mixed Ensemble.

Sagvik, Stellan. *Svensk Concerto.* Swedish Music Information Center. See: Sagvik, Stellan, *Svensk Concerto,* under Tuba and Orchestra.

Saint-Saëns, Camille. *Allegro.* tr. Ronald C. Dishinger. CPP/Belwin, Inc. 1981. 1:59. I. A_1–B♭. Limited range, just a few eighth notes. Some easy slurring, tenutos. Beginning solo; no technical problems. See: Lamb, Jack, *Classic Festival Solos,* under Tuba and Keyboard Collections.

Saint-Saëns, Camille. *Cavatina.* arr. V. Mitjagina. Muzkya, Moscow. 1969. 4:53. III–IV. E_1–d♭'. Good transcription in D♭ and E major (3/4 time). Wide range but few outstanding technical problems. See: Mitjagina, V., ed., *Pieces for Tuba and Piano,* under Tuba and Keyboard Collections.

Saint-Saëns, Camille. *Concert Piece.* ed. S. Melnikov. Military Band Masters Institute–Moscow. 1957. See: Melnikov, S., *Pieces for Tuba and Piano,* under Tuba and Keyboard Collections.

Saint-Saëns, Camille. *Elephant from "Carnival of Animals."* arr. Hiroyuki Yasumoto. Toa Music International Co. 1986. 0:51. III–IV. E_1–e. Allegretto pomposo. Listen to original bass solo for conception. Needs a light approach; not too heavy of an Elephant. See: Yasumoto, Hiroyuki, *Tuba Volume #1,* under Tuba and Keyboard Collections. Recorded by Hiroyuki Yasumoto. A different arrangement of this recorded by Zdizislaw Piernik.

Saint-Saëns, Camille. *L'Éléphant (Der Elefant).* Hofmeister. 1993. 1:25. III. G_1–e♭. "aus Der Karneval der Tiere." Famous string bass solo in E♭ major and in 3/8 time. See: Meschke, Dieter, *Zum Uben und Vorspielen/B-Tuba,* under Tuba and Keyboard Collections.

Saint-Saëns, Camille. *Romance.* arr. James Graham. TUBA Press. 1991. IV. E–c'. Moderato. (Horn) Opus 36. Very lyrical transcription. See: Graham, James, *Concert Music for Tuba,* under Tuba and Keyboard Collections.

Saint-Saens, Camille. *Romance.* arr. Michael Fischer, piano ed. John Cozza. Tuba-Euphonium Press. 2000. 4:30. III–IV. A–c'. A good romantic transcription in the mid-range. Tessitura suitable for recitals.

Saint-Saens, Camille. *Romance Op. 36.* tr. Jens-Bjørn Larsen. $9.50. Sheetmusicnow.com

Saint-Saens, Camille. *The Swan.* arr. Roger Bobo. Tuba-Euphonium Press. 2003. 3:30. IV. G–f'. Fine arrangement of this standard in the mid- to upper tessitura.

Saint-Saens, Camille. *The Swan from "Carnival of the Animals."* arr. Patrick Sheridan. Patrick Sheridan. com (Lollipop Series). $12.00.

Saint-Saëns, Camilli. *Romance.* arr. John Glenesk Mortimer. Editions Marc Reift. 2002. $7.00. 3:00. III. E–c'. Originally for French horn or cello. This arrangement was probably conceived for bass trombone; therefore the tessitura is relatively high for a young player. This is the only technical difficulty.

Salvation Army Press. *Instrumental Albums Number 14: Solos and Duets for Soprano E♭, Horn E♭, and Bass E♭ with Pianoforte Accompaniment.* Salvation Army Press. 1929. *Nearer My Home* (duet); *O Lovely Peace* (duet); *Swiss Melodies; Whosoever; Sing Glory, Hallelujah; Isle of Beaty; In the Army; Rocked in the Cradle; Shepherd of Israel; Battling for the Lord.*

Salzedo, Leonard. *Sonata.* Chester Music. 1984. $13.95. 11:44 (3:46, 1:31, 2:09, 4:18. IV–V. E_1–g'. Allegro; Lentissimo; Allegretto; Vivace. To John Fletcher. Opus 93. First performed on December 7, 1980, by John Fletcher, tuba, and

Robert Noble, piano, in "Music at the Green," at Southgate Music Club. Modern melodic language. Wide range. Large work requiring flexibility, strong technique, and musicality. A bit of tenor clef in part.

Samonov, A. *Good Night.* ed. A. Lebedev. Moscow Muzyka. 1984. 0:57. II. F–f. Lyrical lullaby in 2/4 time. A few eighth notes, mostly half notes. See: Lebedev, A., *Tuba Tutor Vol. 1,* under Tuba and Keyboard Collections.

Samonov, A. *Grandfather Is Dancing.* ed. A. Lebedev. Moscow Muzyka. 1984. 0:33. II–III. ($A\flat_1$) E♭–a♭. Some accidentals and "dissonant" melody. See: Lebedev, A., *Tuba Tutor Vol. 1,* under Tuba and Keyboard Collections.

Sarasate, Pablo de. *Zigeunerweisen (Gypsy Airs).* arr. Timofei Dokshitser. Editions Marc Reift. 2001. $11.80. 5:30. IV–V. C–f' (a♭'). Originally for violin and orchestra, this is a transcription of T. Dokshitser's well-known arrangement for trumpet and piano. The brilliant introductory cadence is followed by a short slow melody in typical Hungarian style. The closing Allegro molto vivace is a flashy tour de force pulling all the registers of double tonguing.

Sassetti, Bernardo. *Sonata.* Lusitanius Editions, Portugal. Comissioned by and dedicated to Sérgio Carolino. To be premiered in 2005. A very jazzy piece. Requires some improvisation.

Saul, Walter. *Cetacea.* Tuba-Euphonium Press. 1997. 3:30. III–IV. D_1–c'. Commissioned by Daniel Cole-McCullough. Dedicated to Arthur Kelly. Lyrical work in the extreme low register.

Saul III., Walter B. *De Profundis.* TUBA Press. 1983. $5.00. 5:00. IV. F_1–a. Largo misterioso. December 1983, Misenheimer, North Carolina. From Psalm 130:1–4. Dark textural piece requiring some quick articulations. Conservative modern melodic language. Good recital piece.

Sauter, Eddie. *Conjectures.* Mentor Music. 1968. $6.00. Written for Harvey Phillips. Piano accompaniment with optional percussion. Originally titled *Harvey Phillips—Tuba.* See: Sauter, Eddie, *Conjectures,* under Tuba and Band. Recorded by: Harvey Phillips.

Scarlatti, Alessandro. *Aria.* arr. Clifford P. Barnes. Jack Spratt Music Co. 1965. $3.00. 2:30. II–III. $B\flat_1$–f. "From the Opera *Tigraine.*" No technical problems. Some slurring; vocal approach necessary.

Scarlatti, Allessandro. *Sento Nel Core.* ed. and compiled Harry I. Phillips. Shawnee Press Inc. 1967. 4:17. II. C♯–d. Adagio. Lyrical, slurred transcription in 3/4 time. Good recital material. See: Phillips, Harry I., *Eight Bel Canto Songs,* under Tuba and Keyboard Collections.

Scarmolin, A. Louis. *Introduction and Dance.* Ludwig Music Publishing Company. 1960. $4.50. 3:00. III. $B\flat_1$–f. "for Tuba, Cello, String Bass and Piano." Good opportunity to show off advanced beginner technique.

Scarmolin, A. Louis. *Polka Giocoso.* C. L. Barnhouse. 1953. $3.50. 3:30. III. C–f. Polka-style solo with a somewhat tricky "road map" of D.S. al coda, etc. Mostly step-wise motion.

Scarmolin, A. Louis. *Pomp and Dignity.* Pro Art Publications. 1941. Out of Print. 4:25. II–III. G_1–e. Maestoso. Some triplets in step-wise motion.

Schaefer, August H. *Gay Caballero.* The Fillmore Bros. Co. 1941. Out of Print. 5:00. $F\sharp_1$–f. "Solo for Tuba, Baritone (Bass or Treble), and B♭ Saxophones." Good opportunity to show off advanced beginner/intermediate technique.

Schedrin, R. *Variations from the Ballet Konick-Gorbunoch.* ed. A. Lebedev. Moscow Muzyka. 1986. 1:37. IV. ($E\flat_1$) G_1–b♭. Requires flexibility and strong musical sense. See: Lebedev, A., *Tuba Tutor Vol. 2,* under Tuba and Keyboard Collections.

Schlemüller, Hugo. *Cradle Song.* arr. J. S. Price. Carl Fischer Inc. 1937. Out of Print. 2:00. I. $B\flat_1$–B♭. In 6/8 time with no technical problems.

Schlemüller, Hugo. *Prayer, A.* arr. J. S. Price. Carl Fischer Inc. 1937. $2.50. 2:00. I. A_1–B♭. All half and whole notes. No technical problems. Ideal for beginner.

Schlenker, Manfred. *Rondo Variato.* Available from Spaeth and Schmid. $11.00.

Schlesinger, Scott. *Two Duets for Tuba and Piano.* Tuba-Euphonium Press. 2002. 4:30. IV–V. A_1–e'. Duet No. 1; Duet No. 2. The "duet" refers to the tuba and piano combination and not a work for two tubas and piano. Technically and metrically demanding.

Schmid, Heinrich Kaspar. *"Im tiefsten Walde." (In the Deep Forest.)* arr. Thomas Bacon. Southern Music Company.

Schmidt, A. *Divertissement.* Editions Andel Uitgave. 1974.

Schmidt, A. *Ostinato.* Editions Andel Uitgave.

Schmidt, Ole. *Concerto for Tuba and Orchestra.* Chester Music. 1976. $26.95. See: Schmidt, Ole, *Concerto for Tuba and Orchestra,* under Tuba and Orchestra. Also see: Bird, Gary, ed.; *Program Notes for the Solo Tuba.* Recorded by Michael Lind. See review in *TUBA Journal,* Vol. 7, No. 4, Page 26.

Schmidt, Ole. *Sonata for Tuba and Piano.* MS Publications.

Schmidt, William. *Phantasy on an American Spiritual for Tuba and Piano.* Western International Music, Inc. 1997. $10.00. G_1–c'.

Schmidt, William. *Serenade.* Western International Music. 1962. $7.00. 9:00. IV. F_1–c'. Romanza; Waltz; Dirge; March. For Tommy Johnson. Composed in 1958. Solid contemporary writing for tuba. See: Bird, Gary, ed.; *Program Notes for the Solo Tuba.* Recorded by Rex Conner, John Thomas (Tommy) Johnson.

Schmidt, William. *Sonata.* Western International Music. 1984. $13.00. 17:19 (6:14, 5:15, 5:50).

IV–V. F_1–g'. for Mel Culbertson. World premiere on May 24, 1982, by Mel Culbertson, tuba, and Chantal de Buchy, piano, at the Paris Conservatory of Music. American premiere: Ron Davis, tuba, and Barbara Worsley, piano, March 17, 1984, at Univ. of Southern California. Would rest best on F tuba. Meter changes, muted passages, glissandos. Flexibility and modern lyrical approach necessary. See review in *TUBA Journal,* Vol. 13, No. 2, Page 27. Also see: Bird, Gary, ed.; *Program Notes for the Solo Tuba.*

Schmutz, Albert D. *Chorale Prelude.* Available from the composer. 1971. For tuba and organ.

Schneebiegl, Rolf. *Der kellermeister.* Bosworth & Co. 1979. See: Schneebiegl, Rolf, *Der kellermeister,* under Tuba and Band.

Schnyder, Daniel. *Sonata for Bass Trombone (Tuba) and Piano.* Editions Marc Reift. 1996. $19.80. 11:00. IV. D_1–g'. Blues; An American Ballad; Below Surface. Dedicated to David Taylor. Very dynamic work with a contemporary jazz flare; first prize in the 1996 International Trumpet Guild Composition Contest.

Scholtes, Walter. *My Tuba Solo.* Waterloo Music Company. 1950. 6:10. III. (A_1) $B♭_1$–a♭. Traditional solo.

Scholtes, Walter, arr. *Rocked in the Cradle of the Deep.* Waterloo Music Company. 1950. Out of Print. 5:00. II–III. ($A♭_1$) C–f. Theme and variations.

Schooley, John. *Serenata.* Heilman Music. 1976. $6.00. 6:36 (1:11, 2:03, 0:35, 1:39, 1:08). IV. (D_1) F_1–c♭'. Intrada (Allegro con spirito); Air (Andante e rubato); Cabaletta (Allegro); Recitative (Andante maestoso); Paspy (Allegretto e leggiero). Dedicated to the Goals of TUBA. First Performed by Paul Kryzwicki at the 1970 Aspen Music Festival. Conservative contemporary melodic language. Lyrical and rhythmical playing. Some 5/8, 7/8 meters. See review in *TUBA Journal,* Vol. 3, No. 3, Page 7.

Schoonenbeek, Kees. *Suite Concertante.* de haske muziekuitgave bv. 1990. 11:44. IV. $B♭_1$–b♭. Four attacca movements: Allegretto; Allegro Giocoso; Valse lente; Allegro. Very lyrical, tonal, modern writing. Some meter changes. Last movement entirely in 5/8 time. Requires quick articulations in spots. Good recital material.

Schostakowitsch, Dimitri. *Introduction and Dance.* arr. Musser. Available from Spaeth and Schmid. $9.00.

Schrijver, Karel de. *Concertino.* Tierolff-Muziekcentrale. 1968. 8:40 (3:29, 2:19, 2:52). IV–V. F–b♭'. Deel I; Deel II; Deel III. "voor Bariton-Trombone-Tuba si♭ (Trombone-Euphonium Ut) met Piano Begeleiding." NOT for contrabass tuba! Very lyrical and technical solo for higher instrument. Strong technique and lyricism required.

Schrijver, Karel de. *Six Petits Morceaux.* Scherzando Editions Musicales.

Schroen, B. *Fantasie.* arr. John Spencer. Cundy-Bettoney/Carl Fischer Inc. 1938. $4.00. 5:00. III. F_1–g. "Solo BB♭ Tuba." Several tempos and styles.

Schubert, Franz. *After Work.* arr. David Green. Encore Music Publishers. 2001. 2:30. II–III. $B♭_1$–f. A short piece in folk style.

Schubert, Franz. *Ave Maria.* arr. A. Lebedev. Military Band Masters Faculty of Moscow Conservatiore. 1971. See: Lebedev, A., *Collection of Pieces for Tuba "Es" and Piano,* under Tuba and Keyboard Collections.

Schubert, Franz. *Ave Maria.* arr. Øystein Baadsvik. Ovation. $11.43.

Schubert, Franz. *By the Sea.* arr. Paul deVille. Carl Fischer Inc. 1906. Out of Print. See: deVille, Paul, *Pleasant Hours,* under Tuba and Keyboard Collections.

Schubert, Franz. *Der lindenbaum. (The Linden Tree.)* arr. John Fletcher. Chester Music. 1982. 3:10. II–III. D–g. Andante con moto. Expressive song in 3/4 time. Requires vocal approach. No technical problems. See: Fletcher, John, *Tuba Solos (Tuba in C), Volume One,* under Tuba and Keyboard Collections.

Schubert, Franz. *Die böse Farbe.* tr. Enrique C. Feldman. Arizona University Music Press. 1987. 1:50. IV. B–e♭'. Ziemlich geschwind (Allegro assai). Upper tessitura. Some flexibility required. See: Schubert, Franz, *Songs from Die Schöene Müellerin,* in this section.

Schubert, Franz. *Die liebe Farbe.* tr. Enrique C. Feldman. Arizona University Music Press. 1987. 1:55. III. d–d'. Etwas langsam (Poco Lento). Upper tessitura. No other technical problems. See: Schubert, Franz, *Songs from Die Schöene Müellerin,* in this section.

Schubert, Franz. *Entr'acte from "Rosamunde."* arr. George Masso. Kendor Music, Inc. 1967. $5.50. 4:10. II. E♭–f. In 2/4 time. Some triplets, some slurring; no big technical problems. Good recital material.

Schubert, Franz. *Fruhlingsglaube. (Faith in Spring.)* arr. Michael Fischer, piano ed. John Cozza. Tuba-Euphonium Press. 2000. 4:00. III–IV. F–g. Good arrangement of Schubert art song. Conservative range, but challenging rhythmic subdivision for the intermediate player.

Schubert, Franz. *Mein!* tr. Enrique C. Feldman. Arizona University Music Press. 1987. 4:58. IV. C–e'. Massig geschwind (Allegro moderato). Upper tessitura. Best on F tuba; endurance could be a factor with lower instrument. Some flexibility required. See: Schubert, Franz, *Songs from Die Schöene Müellerin,* in this section.

Schubert, Franz. *Moment Musical.* arr. Ken Swanson. CPP/Belwin, Inc. 1970. See: CPP/Belwin, *Tuba Solos, Level Two,* under Tuba and Keyboard Collections.

Schubert, Franz. *My Sweetheart's Eyes.* tr. Ronald C. Dishinger. Medici Music Press. 1990. $2.50.

1:53. II. C–e. "Geheimes, Op. 14, No. 2, 1824." In 2/4 time and in F major with no technical problems.

Schubert, Franz. *Serenade.* arr. Roger Bobo. Encore Music Publishers. 4:30. IV–V. d–g'. Fine arrangement of this standard serenade in a very high tessitura.

Schubert, Franz. *Serenade D957 No. 4.* arr. John Glenesk Mortimer. Editions Marc Reift. 1997. $7.00. 4:00. II. D–g. Conventional arrangement of the original song "Ständchen" by Schubert. Available in bass clef concert pitch, or in treble clef in E♭ or B♭.

Schubert, Franz. *Songs from Die Schöene Müellerin.* tr. Enrique C. Feldman. Arizona University Music Press. 1987. 10:33. III–IV. B–e'. Dedicated to James Andrews. Best on F tuba or euphonium. Contains *Die böse Farbe, Die liebe Farbe, Mein!* and *Wohin?*

Schubert, Franz. *Ständchen.* arr. Hiroyuki Yasumoto. Toa Music International Co. 1989. 3:10. IV. D–g'. Lovely transcription. High tessitura; best on F tuba. See: Yasumoto, Hiroyuki, *Tuba Volume #3,* under Tuba and Keyboard Collections. Different arrangements of this recorded by Roger Bobo, The Contraband, Zdizislaw Piernik.

Schubert, Franz. *Swan Song.* arr. Allen Ostrander. Edition Musicus. 1959. $3.00. 2:25. II. G_1–e♭. "My Last Abode." Several octave jumps throughout and slurring; no other big technical problems.

Schubert, Franz. *Wohin?* tr. Enrique C. Feldman. Arizona University Music Press. 1987. 1:50. IV. B–e'. Maasig (Moderato). Upper tesitura. Some flexibility required. See: Schubert, Franz, *Songs from Die Schöene Müellerin,* in this section.

Schuller, Gunther. *Capriccio for Tuba and Small Orchestra.* Mentor Music. 1969. See: Schuller, Gunther, *Capriccio for Tuba and Small Orchestra,* under Tuba and Orchestra. Also see: Bird, Gary, ed.; *Program Notes for the Solo Tuba.* Recorded by: Harvey Phillips.

Schumann, Robert. *Adagio and Allegro.* arr. Cooley. Available from Spaeth and Schmid. $22.50.

Schumann, Robert. *Adagio and Allegro.* arr. James Graham. TUBA Press. 1991. IV. $B♭_1$–e♭'. Slow with expression; Quick, with animation. (Horn) Opus 70. See: Graham, James, *Concert Music for Tuba,* under Tuba and Keyboard Collections. Recorded by Eugene Dowling.

Schumann, Robert. *Fantasiestücke.* arr. Cooley. Available from Spaeth and Schmid. $22.50.

Schumann, Robert. *Fantasiestucke, Op. 73.* Solo part only. arr. Henry Howey. Tuba-Euphonium Press. 1996. 14:00. IV. G_1–d'. Zart und mit ausdruck; Lebhaft, leicht; Rasch und mit Feuer. The performer must use the piano part from the original work or from another transcription in the original key. Musically demanding transcription of this romantic masterpiece. Contains arrangement for euphonium solo as well.

Schumann, Robert. *Fröhlicher Landmann.* arr. Stephan Schwotzer. Hofmeister. 1993. 0:54. II–III. A_1–d. Frisch und munter. "von der Arbeit zurückkehrend aus Album für die Jugent, op. 68." Familiar tune in D major. See: Meschke, Dieter, *Zum Uben und Vorspielen/B-Tuba,* under Tuba and Keyboard Collections.

Schumann, Robert. *Happy Farmer, The (Variations from "Album for the Young").* arr. Herbert Wekselblatt. G. Schirmer Inc. 1972. 1:30. III. C–f. Brisk and lively. Fun set of theme and (two) variations. Double tonguing possible, depending on tempo chosen. Otherwise some crisply articulated sixteenth note repeated notes as well as step-wise passages. Good early intermediate material. See: Wekselblatt, Herbert, *First Solos for the Tuba Player, BB♭,* under Tuba and Keyboard Collections.

Schumann, Robert. *Jolly Farmer Goes to Town, The.* arr. William J. Bell. Carl Fischer Inc. 1938. $3.50. 2:30. III–IV. G_1–a. Theme and variations. (Optional) triple tonguing passages. Listen to Bill Bell's recording! Recorded by William Bell.

Schumann, Robert. *Jolly Peasant, The.* arr. G. E. Holmes. Rubank, Inc. 1939. 1:32. II–III. C–f. "Solo Tuba-E♭ or BB♭." Moderato. Short theme and variations. Mostly scale-wise motion for sixteenth note technical section. Very accessible to advanced beginner. See: Rubank, *Soloist Folio for Bass (E♭ or BB♭),* under Tuba and Keyboard Collections.

Schumann, Robert. *Jolly Peasant, The.* arr. G. E. Holmes. Rubank, Inc. 1966. $2.00. Published separately. See other listing in this section.

Schumann, Robert. *Märchenbilder.* arr. Cooley. Available from Spaeth and Schmid. $25.00.

Schumann, Robert. *Merry Peasant, The, from "Album for the Young."* arr. Peter Wastall. Boosey & Hawkes, Inc. 1985. 0:43. I–II. C–f. See: Wastall, Peter, *Learn As You Play Tuba,* under Tuba and Keyboard Collections. Nice arrangement of this classic tune. Good introduction to staccato and tenutos. Easy accompaniment.

Schumann, Robert. *Romance No. 2.* arr. David R. Werden. Whaling Music Publishers. 1993. $8.00. 4:49. IV–V. C♯–c♯'. Arranged for euphonium, trombone, or tuba with piano. Lovely lyrical transcription. Mostly slurred; some skips of a tenth. Easy rhythms, some upper tessitura if played on lower tubas.

Schumann, Robert. *Romance No. 3.* arr. Daniel Perantoni. Hal Leonard Publishing Corp. 1976. See: Perantoni, Daniel, *Master Solos Intermediate Level,* under Tuba and Keyboard Collections.

Schumann, Robert. *Sailors' Song.* arr. Donald C. Little. CPP/Belwin, Inc. 1978. $4.00. 2:29. II. ($G_1$) A_1–e♭. Moderato. From the *Album for the Young.* In 4/4 time and in G minor. Some eighth notes and some slurs. Variety of articulations: staccato, tenuto, accents. Lyrical approach very necessary. See review in *TUBA Journal,* Vol. 8, No. 1, Page 34.

Schumann, Robert. *Sailors' Song.* arr. Donald C. Little. CPP/Belwin, Inc. 1978. See: Lamb, Jack, *Solo Sounds for Tuba Levels 1–3, Vol. 1,* under Tuba and Keyboard Collections. Also see other listing in this section.

Schumann, Robert. *Scenes from Childhood, Op. 15.* arr. James Self. Bassett Hound Music. $15.00. 11:20 (1:35, 1:09, 0:55, 2:38, 1:03, 1:37, 2:23). IV–V. C$\sharp_1$–g'. *About Strange Lands and People; Curious Story; Important Event; The Poet Speaks; At the Fireside; Frightening; Reverie.* Composed in 1938. Very lyrical set of transcriptions utilizing a wide range. Recorded by James Self.

Schumann, Robert. *Three Romances.* arr. Cooley. Available from Spaeth and Schmid. $22.50.

Schumann, Robert. *Träumeri.* arr. Hiroyuki Yasumoto. Toa Music International Co. 1989. 1:44. III. F–e$\flat$'. Beautiful lyrical transcription. Lies best on F tuba; playable on lower instrument. See: Yasumoto, Hiroyuki, arr., *Tuba Volume #2,* under Tuba and Keyboard Collections. A different version recorded by Melton Tuba-Quartett, Zdizislaw Piernik.

Schumann, Robert. *Wild Horseman, The.* arr. Herbert Wekselblatt. G. Schirmer Inc. 1972. 0:32. III. D–g. Fast. From *Album for the Young.* Short (even shorter depending on tempo chosen) romp in 6/8 time. Requires some flexibility. See: Wekselblatt, Herbert, *First Solos for the Tuba Player, BB$\flat$,* under Tuba and Keyboard Collections.

Schumann, Robert. *Your Ring on My Finger.* tr. Ronald C. Dishinger. Medici Music Press. 1990. $2.50. 2:01. II–III. C–f. Innig (Passionate). "Frauenliebe und Leben, Op. 42, No. 4." Well-transcribed solo with some slurring, some accidentals.

Schürch, Cyrill. *Hors-d'Oeuvre.* Editions Marc Reift. 1995. $12.50. 3:30. III. B$\flat_1$–f'. Dedicated to Marc Unternährer. An upbeat work with rhythmical ostinato figures trading off between tuba and piano.

Schürch, Cyrill. *Sonate.* Editions Marc Reift. 1997. $19.00. 15:00. III–IV. G$\flat_1$–f'. A tonal composition in three movements, only the third of which has a tempo indication: Allegro. The first movement is based on an ostinato; the second is a very lyric, flowing melody; the third movement requires a good double tongue. A fun work which does not require a great amount of rehearsal time.

Schwartz, Elliot. *Three Inventions.* Tuba-Euphonium Press. 2002. 7:30. IV. E$\flat_1$–c$\flat$'. I; II; III. Dedicated to Scott Vaillancourt. Requires a mute. Aleatoric passages and rhythmically demanding piano accompaniment.

Schwartz, Elliott. *Flame.* American Composer's Edition. 1988. 10:00. V. E$\flat_1$–g$\sharp$'. Commissioned by Scott Watson, with the support of a University of Kansas research grant. Completed June 1988, Brunswick, Maine. Modern writing and notation. Pitches based on the letters F L A M E, C H A R, and S E A R. Spatial/proportional notation; each section fifteen seconds. Sung and spoken material for tubist. Piano also has contemporary techniques.

Schwartz, Jean, and William Jerome. *Chinatown, My Chinatown.* arr. Bill Boyd. Hal Leonard Publishing Corp. 1992. 0:34. I–II. B$\flat_1$–D. Old jazz standard in cut time. Once through the melody in B$\flat$ major. See: Daellenbach, Charles, *Book of Easy Tuba Solos,* under Tuba and Keyboard Collections.

Schwotzer, Stephan, arr. *Altdeutscher Tanz (Narrentanz).* Hofmeister. 1993. 1:08. I–II. C–d. "Anoymus (um 1590)." No technical problems; quarter note is fastest rhythm. See: Meschke, Dieter, *Zum Uben und Vorspielen/B-Tuba,* under Tuba and Keyboard Collections.

Scott, Kathleen. *Andante and Allegro.* Queen City Brass Publications/PP Music. 1984. $7.50. 5:13. IV. F$_1$–d'. Commissioned by Rodger Vaughan for his Fiftieth Birthday Tuba Recital. Composed 1981. Lyrical Andante section followed by moderately technical Allegro section. A few octave jumps; no big technical problems. Conventional tonal writing.

Scriabine, Alexander. *Etude.* arr. A. Lebedev. Military Band Masters Faculty of Moscow Conservatiore. 1971. See: Lebedev, A., *Collection of Pieces for Tuba "Es" and Piano,* under Tuba and Keyboard Collections.

Scriabine, Alexander. *Romance.* arr. James Graham. TUBA Press. 1991. III. E–a. (Horn). See: Graham, James, *Concert Music for Tuba,* under Tuba and Keyboard Collections.

Sear, Walter. *Sonatina for Tuba and Piano.* Cor Publishing Co. 1974. $5.00. 7:00. II–III. A$_1$–f. Three numbered movements. Original copyright date was 1969. Major work for advanced beginner. Recorded by: Ronald Davis; Karl Megules.

Séguin, Pierre. *Cortège. (Procession.)* Alphonse Leduc. 1984. $5.45. D–f'. For French tuba. See: Thompson/Lemke; *French Music for Low Brass Instruments.*

Séguin, Pierre. *Rupture.* Alphonse Leduc. 1987. 2:00. III–IV. F–f'. Elementary work for bass saxhorn. Range makes this piece an advanced work, but it would be suitable for an intermediate player to read the piece down an octave. Linear melodies and some minor rhythmic subdivision.

Séguin, Pierre. *Tubavardage. (Tuba Chatter.)* Alphonse Leduc. 1987. $5.45. C–e$\flat$'. For French Tuba. See: Thompson/Lemke; *French Music for Low Brass Instruments.*

Semler-Collery, Jules. *Barcarolle et Chanson Bachique. (Barcarolle and Drinking Song.)* Alphonse Leduc. 1953. $12.80. IV. B$\flat_1$–g$\flat$'. à Paul

Bernard. "pour Tuba Ut ou Contrebasse à Cordes ou Saxhorn basse Si♭ ou Trombone basse et Piano." For French tuba. See: Thompson/Lemke; *French Music for Low Brass Instruments.*

Semler-Collery, Jules. *Cantabile et divertissement pour tuba et orchestre.* Éditions Max Eschig. 1963. V. B♭$_1$–f♯'. Reduction pour tuba (ou saxhorn basse) et piano. See: Thompson/Lemke; *French Music for Low Brass Instruments.*

Semler-Collery, Jules. *Deux Pièces brèves.* Éditions Max Eschig. 1973. IV. F$_1$–f♯'. For French tuba (ou saxhorn basse). See: Thompson/Lemke; *French Music for Low Brass Instruments.*

Semler-Collery, Jules. *Saxhornia.* Alphonse Leduc. 1959. $14.45. V. F$_1$–a♭'. Cantus Recitativo-Tarentella. "pour Saxhorn-basse Si♭ ou Tuba Ut ou Trombone basse et Piano." For French tuba. See: Thompson/Lemke; *French Music for Low Brass Instruments.*

Semler-Collery, Jules. *Tubanova.* Éditions Max Eschig. 1967. 6:15. V. A♭$_1$ (E♭)–g'. Andantino espressivo; Allegretto spiritoso. à Paul Bernard, Professeur au Conservatoire National Supérieur de Musique de Paris en toute amitié. "pour Tuba ou Saxhorn-basse Si♭ ou Trombone-basse ou Contrebasse Si♭ ou Contrebasse a Cordes et Piano." "Solo De Concours." For French tuba. See: Thompson/Lemke; *French Music for Low Brass Instruments.*

Senaillè, Jean Baptiste. *Allegro Spiritoso.* arr. Richard E. Thurston. Southern Music Company. 1992. $4.50. 2:18. IV. C–a (a'). Third movement of a Sonata in D minor. This arrangement in C minor. Some ornamentation included. Very quick indicated tempo (120) requiring quick articulations. See other listings in this section.

Senaillè, Jean Baptiste. *Allegro Spiritoso.* arr. Wesley Jacobs. Encore Music Publishers. 1990. $5.50. 2:49. IV. G$_1$–c'. trés vif. Similar to Catelinet arrangement but in a minor key. Some octave changes and a few notes left out to facilitate tuba performance. No ornamentation included. See other listing in this section.

Senaillè, Jean Baptiste. *Courante.* arr. André Goudenhooft; pno realizations by Augustin Maillard. Gérard Billaudot. 1989. $9.50. 2:30. IV. G$_1$–b. "pour le trombone basse et le tuba basse. Extraite de la 8e Sonate, pour violon." Packaged with *Sarabande* by Jean-Marie Leclair. Flexibility and quick articulations. See: Thompson/Lemke; *French Music for Low Brass Instruments.*

Senaillè, Jean Baptiste. *In Lively Spirits.* Hopkinson, Michael E. Kirklees Music. 1978. A Re-Working of J. B. Senaille's *Andante and Allegro Spiritoso* for E♭ bass. See: Hopkinson, Michael E., *In Lively Spirits,* in this section.

Senaillè, Jean Baptiste. *Introduction and Allegro Spiritoso.* arr. Philip Catelinet. Hinrichsen Edition. 1964. $8.40. 2:49 (1:03, 1:46). IV. B♭$_1$–d♭'. Two attacca sections: Andante; Allegro Spiritoso. "For Tuba (B.C.), Euphonium/Trombone (T.C. and B.C.), Bass E♭ (T.C.) and Piano." Andante: Very lyrical writing with several e♭ to f trills. All slurred phrases. Allegro spiritoso in B♭ minor. Metronome marking (132) quicker than other arrangements in this section, requiring strong technique, both articulation and flexibility. Good recital material.

Senaillé, Jean-Baptiste. *Andante and Allegro Spiritoso.* Editions Marc Reift. 1997. $14.25. 3:00. III. B♭$_1$–c'. Originally for violin and continuo, this arrangement is an adaptation for tuba from a collection of fifty violin sonatas composed by this baroque composer and violinist. Good recital material beginning with a short lyric introduction and followed by a C minor Allegro based on scale patterns. Available in bass clef concert pitch, or in treble clef in E♭ or B♭.

Senaillé, Jean-Baptiste. *Andante and Allegro Spiritoso* (B♭ bass). arr. Mortimer. Available from Spaeth and Schmid. $16.50.

Senon, G. *Elemntarite.*

Senon, Gilles. *Tuba or Not Tuba.* Available from Spaeth and Schmid. $18.25.

Shaughnessy, Robert. *Concertino for Tuba and String Orchestra.* Peer-Southern Organization. 1969. $10.00. See: Shaughnessy, Robert, *Concertino for Tuba and String Orchestra,* under Tuba and Orchestra.

Shekov, Ivan. *Prelude und Scherzo für Tuba und Klavier.* Blasmusikverlag Fritz Schultz GmbH. 1986. 4:33 (2:48, 1:45). III. G$_1$–f. Prelude (Andante); Scherzo (Allegro). Treble and bass clef parts included. Some accidentals; otherwise no technical problems. Prelude is mostly lyrical with modern tonal writing. Scherzo is playful with mostly articulated passages.

Sheridan, Patrick, arr. *Danny Boy.* PatrickSheridan.com (Lollipop Series). $12.00.

Sheridan, Patrick, arr. *Jenny Wren.* PatrickSheridan.com (Bon Bons Series). $15.00.

Shield. *Friar of Orders Gray, The.* arr. Harry Prendiville. A. Squire. 1888. Out of Print. 1:25. II–III. (B♭$_1$) C–f. In 6/8 time. Spirited solo with a nautical feel. One trill. "E♭ Bass; or, tuba With Piano or Organ Accompaniment, (ad lib.)." See: Prendiville, Harry, *Six Popular Solos,* under Tuba and Keyboard Collections.

Shoop, Stephen. *Five Whistling Tunes.* piano ed. Robert Brazier. Stephen Shoop Music Publications. 2004. 6:00. $9.00. I–II. B♭$_1$–f. Happy!; Reflective and Lyrical; Jazzy; Close Intervals; March. Five short movements to be performed as if whistling. These are very good solos for the young beginner to explore musical expression in varying styles. Excellent for early solo and ensemble work.

Shoop, Stephen. *Highland Melody.* piano ed. Robert Brazier. Stephen Shoop Music Publications. 2004. 2:45. $7.00. I. B♭$_1$–c'. While a bit repetitive, this is another excellent tune for the beginner.

Very good for a contrasting piece on an early recital or solo and ensemble contest.

Shostakovitch, Dimitri. *Adagio for Tuba and Piano.* Recorded by Roger Bobo.

Shostakovitch, Dimitri. *Polka from: The Age of Gold.* arr. Herbert Wekselblatt. G. Schirmer Inc. 1964. 2:17. IV–V. G_1–f. Allegretto. Fun transcription! Wide range combined with "Shostakovitch intervals" (tritone, sevenths, ninths, etc.) make for some technical challenges. Good encore piece. See: Wekselblatt, H., *Solos for the Tuba Player,* under Tuba and Keyboard Collections.

Shostakovitch, Dimitri. *Romance.* arr. A. Lebedev. Military Band Masters Faculty of Moscow Conservatiore. 1971. See: Lebedev, A., *Collection of Pieces for Tuba "Es" and Piano,* under Tuba and Keyboard Collections.

Sibbing, Robert. *Sonata for Tuba and Piano.* Theodore Presser Company. 1973. $12.00. 10:30 (4:00, 3:50, 2:40). IV. F_1–c'. Allegro Moderato; Larghetto; Allegro Giocoso. For Kent Campbell. Written in Quincy, Illinois, November 1963. Very playable recital material. Good combination of lyricism and rhythm. Uses all ranges of the bass tuba. See: Bird, Gary, ed.; *Program Notes for the Solo Tuba.* Recorded by Daniel Perantoni.

Sibelius, Jean. *Finlandia.* arr. Bill Boyd, ed. Charles Daellenbach. Hal Leonard Publishing Corp. 1992. 1:06. I. E♭–c. In E♭ major. Only one eighth note; easy rhythms. Comes with practice/performance cassette. See: Daellenbach, Charles, *Book of Beginning Tuba Solos,* under Tuba and Keyboard Collections.

Sibelius, Jean. *Finlandia.* arr. Wesley Jacobs. Encore Music Publishers. 1:00. I–II. D–B. With dignity. In D major. With exception of key, level I. Limited range, some slurring. The main "tune" from Finlandia. See: Jacobs, Wesley, *Solos from the Classics,* under Tuba and Keyboard Collections.

Siebert, Edrich. *Bombastic Bombardon.* Molenaar. 1952. III. Piano reduction. See: Siebert, Edrich, Bombastic Bombardon, under Tuba and Band.

Siebert, Edrich. *Dear to My Heart.* Studio Music Company. 1972. $14.00. See: Siebert, Edrich, *Dear to My Heart,* under Tuba and Band.

Siekmann, Frank H. *Parable for Tuba and Piano.* Manuscript. 1993. 3:51. III. B_1♭–g. Stately; not too demanding; limited range; intermediate solo. Good introduction to cadenzas, trill from A to B♭, brief passage in D♭ major.

Siekmann, Frank. *Once upon a Funicula.* Available from Spaeth and Schmid. $15.75.

Siennicki, Edmund J. *Happy Song.* Ludwig Music Publishing Company. 1990. $3.50. 1:52. I. B♭$_1$–B♭. Written for a variety of solo instruments. Easy piano accompaniment. Simple tune in B♭ major (4/4 time) with no technical problems. Quarter note is fastest rhythm.

Siennicki, Edmund J. *Harvest Waltz.* Ludwig Music Publishing Company. 1987. $2.95. 1:40. I. C–A. Written for a variety of solo instruments. Limited range. Waltz in C major in 3/4 time. Some dotted rhythms; some slurs. No other technical problems. Easy piano accompaniment. See review in *TUBA Journal,* Vol. 18, No. 4, Page 15.

Siennicki, Edmund J. *Memphis Ridge.* See review in *TUBA Journal,* Vol. 9, No. 4, Page 33.

Siennicki, Edmund J. *Rooster, The.* Ludwig Music Publishing Company. 1990. $3.50. 2:07. I. B♭$_1$–B♭. Written for a variety of solo instruments. Beginning solo in 4/4 time with quarter note as fastest rhythm. A few slurs, a few tenutos; no technical problems.

Siennicki, Edmund J. *Swan, The.* Ludwig Music Publishing Company. 1990. $3.50. 1:56. I. C–B♭. Limited-range solo in 3/4 time. Some slurring; a few dotted quarter/eighth note rhythms; no technical problems. Written for a variety of solo instruments.

Sikora, Elzbieta. *Il Viaggio 1 per tuba solo con pianoforte.* Recorded by Zdizislaw Piernik.

Simon, Frank. *Zillertal.* Rubank, Inc. 1974. Out of Print. 4:13. III–IV. B♭$_1$–g (b♭). To Harold Walters. Old-style technical solo involving several different meters and technical challenges including triple tonguing.

Simpson, Michael M. *Reveries.* Tuba-Euphonium Press. 2003. 5:00. III–IV. G♯$_1$–e'. Alternates between lyrical and technical passages. Technical passages with frequent accidentals.

Sivelöv, Niklas. *Sonata Op. 5.* SMIC 1992. 10:00. Written for F tuba and piano. Recorded by Øystein Baadsvik.

Sivic, Pavel. *Piece de concert.* Sloway Music Editions. 2004.

Skolnik, Walter. *Sonata.* Theodore Presser Company. 1985. $8.50. 10:00. IV. F♯$_1$–c'. Pesante; Sostenuto; Allegretto. Conservative modern writing. Good introduction to contemporary tonal melody. Some meter changes.

Skolnik, Walter. *Valse Caprice.* Theodore Presser Company. 1973. $2.50. 2:32. III–IV. F_1–g. For tuba or string bass and piano. Completed August 1973, New York. Both solo parts included. One-movement work in 3/4 time. Fun tonal writing. Some flexibility needed; no big technical problems. See review in *TUBA Journal,* Vol. 1, No. 2, Page 10.

Smedvig, Egil. *Toga Virilis.* Saga Music Press. 1984. $5.50. 4:00. III. (B♭$_1$) C–g. To Samuel Pilafian. Written for tuba or bassoon and piano. Cut solo with optional cadenza. A few quartel moves in cadenza; no big technical problems.

Smirnova, T. *Joke, A.* ed. A. Lebedev. Moscow Muzyka. 1986. 1:47. III–IV. G_1–c'. Opus 18, no. 4. Alternating 2/4 and 3/4 time with some "joking" lines. See: Lebedev, A., *Tuba Tutor Vol. 2,* under Tuba and Keyboard Collections.

Smironova, T. *Sonata.* ed. G. Voronov. Moscow Muzyka. 1984. See: Voronov, G, *Works for Tuba and Piano by Russian Composers,* under Tuba and Keyboard Collections.

Smironova, T. *Tale, A.* ed. G. Voronov. Moscow Muzyka. 1984. See: Voronov, G, *Works for Tuba and Piano by Russian Composers,* under Tuba and Keyboard Collections.

Smith, Claude T. *Abide with Me.* Available from Spaeth and Schmid. $5.00.

Smith, Claude T. *Ballad and Presto Dance.* Wingert-Jones Music, Inc. 1988. $6.00. See: Smith, Claude T., *Ballad and Presto Dance,* under Tuba and Band. Recorded by Robert Daniel.

Smith, Claude T. *Dare to Be a Daniel.* Available from Spaeth and Schmid. $5.00.

Smith, Claude T. *Jesus Loves Me.* Available from Spaeth and Schmid. $5.50.

Smith, Claude T. *My Jesus I Love Thee.* Available from Spaeth and Schmid. $5.50.

Smith, David E., arr. *Away in a Manger.* David E. Smith Publications. 1985. $2.50. 2:27. II. $B\flat_1$–e♭ (f). Simple solo in 3/4 time with some slurring; no other technical problems.

Smith, David E., arr. *Cross of Jesus, The.* David E. Smith Publications. 1987. $4.50. 3:59. III. $A\flat_1$–b♭. Several different keys, meters, and textures within this solo. A few flashy 32nd note scales and possible triple tonguing near end depending on tempo. Good showcase solo for intermediate player.

Smith, David E., arr. *Hallelujah! What a Saviour!* David E. Smith Publications. 1988. $2.50. 1:46. II. D–d. Theme and variations style. Some slurring; no big technical problems.

Smith, David E., arr. *Praise Him, All Ye Little Children.* David E. Smith Publications. 1985. $2.50. 1:25. I. $B\flat_1$–B♭. Anonymous. Solo in B♭ major (4/4 time) with no technical problems. Quarter note is fastest rhythm.

Smith, David E., arr. *Stand Up, Stand Up for Jesus.* David E. Smith Publications. 1985. $3.50. 3:24. II–III. (C) E♭–f (g). Optional octave changes ease difficulty. Some technical articulations.

Smith, David E., arr. *Tis So Sweet to Trust in Jesus.* David E. Smith Publications. 1988. $2.50. 2:09. I–II. $B\flat_1$–c (e). Easy rhythms; one dotted rhythm. Some slurring. Modulates between F and E♭ and back to F major.

Smith, David E., arr. *We Gather Together.* David E. Smith Publications. 1984. $2.50. 1:58. I–II. A_1–d. Netherlands folk song. Simple rhythms in 3/4 time. Some slurring. No technical problems.

Smith, David E., arr. *Young Tuba Soloist.* David E. Smith Publications. All selections available separately. Contains: *Abide with Me; Away in a Manger; Dare to be a Daniel; Hallelujah What a Survivor!; My Jesus I Love Thee; Praise Him Little Children; Tis So Sweet to Trust in Jesus; We Gather Together.*

Smith, Douglas, arr. *I Wonder As I Wander.* David E. Smith Publications. 1989. $3.50. 3:06. II. $B\flat_1$–f. Solo in 3/4 time and B♭ and D♭ major. Some slurring; no big technical problems.

Smith, Glenn. *Salicastrum.* Seesaw Music Corporation. 1992. $11.00. 8:23. V. $B\flat_2$–a'. For John Turk. Completed Bloomington, Ind., Nov. 1971. Modern writing. Very strong technique required. Multi-phonics, muted passage, very quick articulations, optional circular breathing, rhythmic challenges. Difficult piano part.

Smith, Kile. *Sonata for Tuba and Piano.* Manuscript. 1986. 12:15 (4:25, 2:48, 5:02). IV–V. F_1–f'. For Brian Brown. Tonal modern melodic language. Strong technique required. Low slurred articulations as well as high melodic writing. Flexibility needed. Some meter shifting throughout. Good recital material.

Smolanoff, Michael. *Set of Three.* Southern Music Company. 1973. $2.50. 6:46 (3:27, 2:09, 1:10). IV. $F\sharp_1$–c'. Opus 17. Three numbered movements. 1. Slow tempo with eighth note as beat. Modern melody and harmony. 2. Slow tempo again with lyrical modern writing. 3. A bit quicker with syncopation and some easy meter changes. See review in *TUBA Journal,* Vol. 1, No. 1, Page 7.

Snyder, Randall. *Soundpiece.* Available from the composer. 1970. 3:00. V. C_1–f'. Contemporary writing with intricate rhythms and dissonant intervals. Slow tempo.

Solomon, Edward S. *One Tough Tuba.* Southern Music Company. 1991. $2.50. 2:07. II–III. $B\flat_1$–e. Easy jazz. Eighth notes should be "swung" like triplets. Some syncopations; some accidentals. No big technical problems.

Solomon, Edward S. *Tuba Solos for the Young Player.* Available from Spaeth and Schmid. $28.00.

Soule, Edmund F. *Suite for Tuba and Piano.* TUBA Press. 1980. $12.00. 12:32 (4:19, 4:35, 3:38). IV–V. $E\flat_1$–g'. Molto moderato; Adagio; Marcia moderato, ma vigoroso. Written for David Grosvenor. Completed Eugene, Ore., 1980. Modern writing. Technical challenges include wide range, meter changes, tricky rhythms. Written for E♭ tuba.

Sousa, John Philip. *Stars and Stripes Forever.* arr. Acton Ostling. CPP/Belwin, Inc. 1969. 0:35. I–II. $B\flat_1$–b♭. March tempo. In cut time, fastest rhythm is quarter note. Melody of last stain of march only (Trio section) with melody altered a bit to fit into conservative range. A few slurs, a few accidentals. No technical problems. See: CPP/Belwin, Inc., *Tuba Solos, Level One,* under Tuba and Keyboard Collections.

Sousa, John Philip. *Stars and Stripes Forever.* arr. Acton Ostling. CPP/Belwin, Inc. 1969. I. March tempo. See: Ostling, Acton, *Tuba (Bass) Soloist, Level One,* under Tuba and Keyboard Collections. Also see other listing in this section.

Southwell, George. *My Tuba Solo.* arr. Aldo Di Ianni. Volkwein Bros. 1954. See: Southwell, George, *My Tuba Solo,* under Tuba and Band.

Sowerby, Leo. *Chaconne.* Carl Fischer Inc. 1938. $3.25. 4:47. III. $B\flat_1$–b♭. Continually metamorphosing set of variations. Lyrical playing combined with technical demands include slurring and some scale-like passages with quick articulations. Good intermediate solo. Recorded by Ron Davis.

Spaniola, Joseph. *Letters from a Friend.* TUBA Press. 1992. $8.00. 12:00 (3:37, 5:53, 2:40). IV. A_1–c♯'. Sleepless Nights; The Journey; The Hope of Tomorrow. For euphonium or tuba and piano. Modern impressionistic writing. Meter changes, flexibility, and modern melodic appreciation required.

Spillman, James E. *Flow Gently, Sweet Afton.* arr. John Kinyon. M. Witmark & Sons. 1958. I. See: Kinyon, John, *Breeze-Easy Recital Pieces,* under Tuba and Keyboard Collections.

Spillman, Robert. *Concerto.* Edition Musicus. 1962. $14.00. 8:00. IV. E_1–f'. High tessitura. Solid tonal contemporary writing. Requires strong technique.

Spillman, Robert. *Two Songs.* Edition Musicus. 1963. $8.50. 5:00. IV. $G\flat_1$–e'. For Roger Bobo. Two numbered movements. Another solid piece by this composer. Moderate range—only one section up to e'. Second song in 3/2 time. Good recital material. Recorded by Roger Bobo.

Spohr, Ludwig. *Adagio.* arr. Mark Evans. Musikverlag Barbara Evans.

Sponholtz. *Peace of Mind.* arr. Paul deVille. Carl Fischer Inc. 1906. Out of Print. See: deVille, Paul, *Pleasant Hours,* under Tuba and Keyboard Collections.

St. Clair, Floyd P. *Golden Days (Serenade).* J. E. Agnew. 1931. Out of Print. 1:25. II. $B\flat_1$–f. "Solo Tuba E♭ or BB♭." Sounds like an old school song. Simple rhythms, in 6/8 time.

Stabile, James. *Sonata for Tuba and Piano.* Western International Music. 1970. Out of Print. III–IV. (C_1) G_1–d♭'. Allegro vivace; Moderato; Piu mosso. Solid tonal writing for tuba and piano. Second and third movements attacca. Some quick articulations in first movement. Second and third much less demanding.

Stamitz, Karl. *Rondo Alla Scherzo (from: Clarinet Concerto in E♭).* arr. Herbert Wekselblatt. G. Schirmer Inc. 1964. 4:34. IV. D–b♭. Allegro Moderato. Generally higher tessitura—would be ideal on E♭ (F) tuba, although very playable on lower instrument. Would develop steady mid-high range on BB♭ (CC) tuba. Some sixteenth note runs, depending on tempo, could be challenging. Some grace notes. 6/8 time throughout. See: Wekselblatt, H., *Solos for the Tuba Player,* under Tuba and Keyboard Collections.

Standford, Patric. *Invocation for Tuba and Piano.* Redcliffe. 1984. 5:19. IV. D_1–g♭'. Also published for tuba and strings. Very melodic writing. Aside from full range, no major technical problems for the level.

Stanley, John. *Allegretto grazioso.* arr. Stephan Schwotzer. Hofmeister. 1993. 1:35. II–III. C–d. In cut time and in F major. See: Meschke, Dieter, *Zum Uben und Vorspielen/B-Tuba,* under Tuba and Keyboard Collections.

Staples, James. *Suite for Tuba and Piano.* Manuscript. 1989. 1:17, 3:16, 2:09, 3:06, 1:21. IV–V. E_1–g'. Allegro scherzando; Adagio mesto; Moderato con moto; Adagio espressivo; Allegro vivace. Commissioned by and dedicated to Gary Bird. Major work for tuba and piano requiring strong technique and endurance. Better on F tuba; high tessitura. Quick articulations throughout. One short muted passage. See: Bird, Gary, ed.; *Program Notes for the Solo Tuba.*

Steckar, Franck. *Au Coeur de la Nuit.*

Steinquest, Eugene W. *Variations on a Theme of Roy Harris.* See review in *TUBA Journal,* Vol. 1, No. 3, Page 6.

Stekl, Konrad. *Sonate für Basstuba und Klavier (oder Baßposaune).* Adler Verlag. 1976. 11:01 (4:08, 3:26, 3:27). IV–V. (B_1) C–e♭' (g'). Three numbered movements. Op. 113a. Contemporary technical and lyrical writing. Conventional melodic second movement. Upper tessitura; best on F tuba. See review in *TUBA Journal,* Vol. 8, No. 1, Page 28.

Stephens. *Albertie* (Tuba in Es). Available from Spaeth and Schmid. $6.50.

Stephens. *The Imp* (Tuba in Es). Available from Spaeth and Schmid. $6.50.

Stephens. *Rondo Rotundo* (Tuba in Es). Available from Spaeth and Schmid. $6.50.

Stephens, Denzil. *Dancing Tuba, The.* Obrasso. III. Piano reduction of tuba and brass band piece. See: Stephens, Denzil, *Dancing Tuba, The,* under Tuba and Band.

Stepovoi, J. *Cantabile.* arr. A. Lebedev. Military Band Masters Faculty of Moscow Conservatiore. 1971. See: Lebedev, A., *Collection of Pieces for Tuba "Es" and Piano,* under Tuba and Keyboard Collections.

Steptoe, Roger. *Concerto for Tuba and Strings.* Stainer & Bell. 1983. $17.50. For James Gourlay. See: Steptoe, Roger, *Concerto for Tuba and Strings,* under Tuba and Orchestra. See review in *TUBA Journal,* Vol. 18, No. 3, Page 19.

Stevens, Halsey. *Sonatina for Tuba and Piano.* Peer-Southern. 1968. $6.50. 9:00. IV. G_1–f'. For Don Waldrop. Original copyright date was 1960. Originally *Sonatina for Bass Tuba and Piano.* Mixed meter. "New Age" feel; lyrical solo with many colors. Opportunity for great expression. Part for trombone included. Upper tessitura; best on F tuba. Requires strong accompanist. See: Bird, Gary, ed.; *Program Notes for the Solo Tuba.* Recorded by Donald Knaub, Daniel Perantoni, David Randolph, James Self.

Stevens, John. *Journey.* Editions Bim. 2001. $22.00. 28:00. V. A_2–g'. Morning in the Yard; Midnight in the Mountains; Highballing through Town. Piano reduction. For more information see Music for Tuba and Orchestra.

Stevens, John. *Liberation of Sisyphus.* Editions Bim. 1999. 10:50. V. $16. 60. Piano reduction of the original. For more information see Music for Multiple Tubas.

Stevens, Thomas. *Variations in Olden Style (d'apres J. S. Bach).* Éditions BIM. 1990. For Bozo the Great. Written in 1989 for Roger Bobo. See: Stevens, Thomas, *Variations in Olden Style (after Bach),* under Tuba and Orchestra. Recorded by Roger Bobo.

Stewart, Joseph. *Tuba.* Kendor Music, Inc. 1977. $6.50. Dedicated to Andy Peruzzini and the Maryvale High School Chorale. See: Stewart, Joseph, *Tuba,* under Tuba and Band. Comes with a flexible recording featuring A. Peruzzini, tubist.

Stewart, Robert. *Quiet Piece, A.* 1982. Commissioned by Rodger Vaughan.

Storm, Charles W. *Bold and Brave.* Lavell Publishing Co. 1961. Out of Print. See: Storm, Charles W., *Bold and Brave,* under Tuba and Band.

Storm, Charles W. *Bouquet for Basses.* Volkwein Bros. 1954. Out of Print. See: Storm, Charles W., *Bouquet for Basses,* under Tuba and Band.

Stoutamire, Albert L. *Legend.* Pro Art Publications/CPP/Belwin, Inc. 1970. 3:20. II–III. (G_1) A_1–f. Rather slow but with motion. In a minor and 4/4 time. Some triplets/duplets to be concise about. Some slurring, some optional low range. See: Lamb, Jack, *Classic Festival Solos,* under Tuba and Keyboard Collections.

Stoutamire, Albert L. *Legend.* Pro Art Publications. 1970. Out of Print. Was published separately. See other listing in this section.

Stoutamire, Albert L. *Praeludium and Fughetta.* Ludwig Music Publishing Company. 1976. $4.00. 4:16. IV. ($F_1$) $B\flat_1$–c'. Stately solo with lyrical Prelude section "Pensively" in 4/4 time, and Fugue "Jocularly" in cut time. No technical problems. See review in *TUBA Journal,* Vol. 1, No. 3, Page 3, and Vol. 7, No. 1, Page 9.

Stradella, Alessandro. *Pieta, Signore!* ed. and compiled Harry I. Phillips. Shawnee Press Inc. 1967. 4:38. II–III. (C) D–f. Andantino. Lyrical slurred transcription in 3/4 time. Minor key. A couple of trills; grace notes. See: Phillips, Harry I., *Eight Bel Canto Songs,* under Tuba and Keyboard Collections. Recorded by: Karl Megules.

Stradella, Alessandro. *Pieta, Signore!* tr. Clyde Felix. Edition Musicus. 1960. $3.00. 4:00. III. F_1–g. No technical problems.

Stratton, Don. *In F.* Trombone Association Publishing. 1979. $7.00. 6:00. IV. F_1–d♭'. For tuba and harpsichord. Completed Dec. 31, 1979, Bangor, Me. Chance music. Six improvised sections lasting one minute each. Performers are requested not to rehearse or discuss the piece with anyone including each other prior to performance. Muted passages. Harpsichordist must also improvise.

Strauss. *Artist's Life.* arr. Igor Hudadoff; William Westcott, pno. arr. Pro Art Publications. 1967. Out of Print. See: Hudadoff, Igor, *Fifteen Intermediate Tuba Solos,* under Tuba and Keyboard Collections.

Strauss, Franz. *Nocture, Op. 7.* arr. Michael Fischer, piano ed. John Cozza. Tuba-Euphonium Press. 2000. 4:30. IV. $C\flat_1$ ($D\flat_1$)–d♭. Good transcription from the original for solo horn. Works very well on tuba with reasonable advanced range demands.

Strauss, Franz. *Nocturno, Op. 7.* arr. Rudy Emilson. Kendor Music, Inc. 2001. $7.00. 6:00. IV. $D\flat_1$–d♭'. Good transcription from the original for solo horn. Works very well on bass tuba or contrabass tuba. Musical style is one of the big issues in performing this work.

Strauss, Johann. *Roses from the South.* arr. John Kinyon. M. Witmark & Sons. 1958. I. See: Kinyon, John, *Breeze-Easy Recital Pieces,* under Tuba and Keyboard Collections.

Strauss, Richard. *Concerto, Opus 11.* arr. James Graham. TUBA Press. 1991. IV. $B\flat_1$–e♭'. Allegro; Andante; Allegro. (Horn). See: Graham, James, *Concert Music for Tuba,* under Tuba and Keyboard Collections.

Strauss, Richard. *Horn Concerto Nr. 1 (Solostimme).* arr. Anderson. Available from Spaeth and Schmid. $11.00.

Strauss, Richard. *Second Horn Concerto.* arr. James Graham. TUBA Press. 1991. IV. $A\flat_1$–d♭'. Andante con Moto. Second movement only. See: Graham, James, *Concert Music for Tuba,* under Tuba and Keyboard Collections.

Stravinsky, Igor. *Berceuse.* arr. Quinto Maganini. Edition Musicus. 1948. 2:30. III. E–a. From *The Firebird.* Legato (slurred) solo. See: Ostrander, Allen, *Concert Album for Tuba,* under Tuba And Keyboard Collections.

Stravinsky, Igor. *Russian Song.* arr. A. Lebedev. Military Band Masters Faculty of Moscow Conservatiore. 1971. See: Lebedev, A., *Collection of Pieces for Tuba "Es" and Piano,* under Tuba and Keyboard Collections.

Strebel, Neal. *Sonata for Bass Horn and Piano.* Available from the composer. 1962. 9:50. V. E_1–e'. Complex rhythms; large dissonant intervals.

Strukov, V. *Lento Elegiaco.* ed. G. Voronov. Moscow Muzyka. 1984. See: Voronov, G., *Works for Tuba and Piano by Russian Composers,* under Tuba and Keyboard Collections.

Strukow, Valery. *Concerto for Tuba and Orchestra.* Éditions BIM. 1991. $19.00. Written in 1980. See: Strukow, Valery, *Concerto for Tuba and Orchestra,* under Tuba and Orchestra. Recorded by Jens Bjørn-Larsen.

Strukow, Valery. *Elegie*. Editions Bim. 1991. $9.50. 3:00. III. d♭–f'. Very lyric, tonal work in a style reminiscent of Franz Schubert. Only difficulty is the high tessitura.

Sullivan, Arthur. *Oh, Is There Not One Maiden Breast?* arr. John Fletcher. Chester Music. 1982. 1:35. II–III. G–a♭. Andante. From *Pirates of Penzance*. Some accidentals at a slow tempo; otherwise no technical problems. See: Fletcher, John, *Tuba Solos (Tuba in C), Volume One*, under Tuba and Keyboard Collections.

Sullivan, Arthur. *Policeman's Song, The*. arr. John Fletcher. Chester Music. 1982. 1:00. II. ($B♭_1$) F–f. Allegro non troppo. From *Pirates of Penzance*. Mostly eighth notes with a quick tempo. Listen to aria in operetta for conception. See: Fletcher, John, *Tuba Solos (Tuba in C), Volume One*, under Tuba and Keyboard Collections.

Sullivan, Arthur. *When Britain Really Ruled the Waves*. arr. John Fletcher. Chester Music. 1982. 1:00. II–III. G–a. Maestoso. From *Iolanthe*. Listen to aria for conception. Song in 3/4 with dotted rhythms and plenty of spirit. See: Fletcher, John, *Tuba Solos (Tuba in C), Volume One*, under Tuba and Keyboard Collections.

Sullivan, Arthur, and W. S. Gilbert. *Miya Sama from The Mikado*. ed. Charles Daellenbach. Hal Leonard Publishing Corp. 1992. 1:03. I. D–c. Allegro moderato. A few slurs, mostly quarter notes in 4/4 time with a Japanese flavor. See: Daellenbach, Charles, *Book of Easy Tuba Solos*, under Tuba and Keyboard Collections.

Sviridov, G. *Iago's Song about King Stephen from the Tragedy Othello*. ed. A. Lebedev. Moscow Muzyka. 1986. 1:06. IV. G_1–c'. Some quick articulations—possible double tonguing. See: Lebedev, A., *Tuba Tutor Vol. 2*, under Tuba and Keyboard Collections.

Swann, Donald. *Two Moods for Tuba*. Chamber Music Library. 1961. $3.50. 5:00. IV. $G♭_1$–f'. Dedicated to Gerard Hoffnung. Elegy (Affettuoso); Scherzo (Scherzando). Two attacca movements. Muted passages. Upper tessitura. Best on F tuba. Good recital material. See: Bird, Gary, ed.; *Program Notes for the Solo Tuba*. Recorded by: Harvey Phillips.

Swanson, Ken, arr. *Blue Bells of Scotland*. CPP/Belwin, Inc. 1970. $4.00. 1:58. II. $B♭_1$–f. Moderato. Theme and (one) variation of this traditional tune in 4/4 time. Eighth notes in variation; one scale and one arpeggio up to f; otherwise very comfortable tessitura. No technical problems. See review in *TUBA Journal*, Vol. 9, No. 2, Page 29.

Swanson, Ken, arr. *Blue Bells of Scotland*. CPP/Belwin, Inc. 1970. See: CPP/Belwin, *Tuba Solos, Level Two*, under Tuba and Keyboard Collections.

Swiergiel, Waldemar. *Concerto for Tuba*. Available from Spaeth and Schmid. $22.50.

Swinnen, Hans. *Grave en Allegro*. J. Maurer Editions Musicales. 1984. $2.10. 2:15. IV. G–g'. "Voor Solo instrument En Piano: Viola Violoncello Fagotto Corno Sax-Tenore Flicorno (Saxhorn) Tuba Bariton." Fun solo best suited for F tuba. Upper tessitura. Lyrical Grave section followed by a baroque-like Allegro section in a comfortable cut time.

Szentpáli, Roland. *Ballade*. Editions Bim. 2002. $31.70. 11:00. IV–V. E_1–g'. Dedicated to Meister Anton Meinl for his eightieth birthday. Piano reduction. For more information see Music for Tuba and Mixed Ensemble (String Quartet).

Szentpáli, Roland. *Concerto*. Editions Bim. 2002. $22.00. 17:00. V. D_1–a'. Moderato; Andante; Moderato. Commissioned by Concours international de Guebwiller (Alsace, France) with the support of the SUISA Music Foundation. Piano reduction. For more information see Music for Tuba and Orchestra.

Szkutko, John. *King Arthur Variations*. John Szkutko SZK Music. 1995. 7:30. V. $B♭_2$–g. A challenging theme-and-variations solo with large leaps and excellent diatonic finger facility required. Some fast technique in the low register also required. Challenging piano part with a catchy theme.

Szkutko, John. *Phantasi*. John Szkutko SZK Music. 1995. 7:00. V. $B♭_2$–b♭'. A very challenging work with extreme range demands. Challenging piano part as well, but worth the effort. Very virtuosic writing, suitable for a recital show piece.

Szkutko, John. *Trojan*. John Szkutko SZK Music. 1996. 4:45. III. $B♭_2$–g. A good intermediate solo that features predominantly low playing. Some moderate technique required, but very playable by a younger player.

Szkutko, John. *Tuba Miniatures*. John Szkutko SZK Music. 1995. 6:45. III–IV. $B♭_2$–a♭'. *A Dance; Bull Frog; Teddy Bear; T-Rex; Metropolis; Birds of a Feather*. A very good collection of short character pieces suitable as etudes or for a concert suite. Generally the technical demands are intermediate, though there are some sudden range and technique demands that make some movements more appropriate for an advanced player. Some challenging piano moments as well.

Tacuchian, Ricardo. *Os Mestres Cantores Da Lapa*. Fundação Nacional De Arte. 1985. 5:06. IV. $D♭_1$–d♭'. Moderato section has nationalistic rhythmical feel. Allegro section has repetitive patterns and requires intermediate technique. Some trills.

Takács, Jeno. *Sonata Capricciosa*. Ludwig Doblinger. 1967. $21.00. 9:00. IV. A_1–d'. To Eva. Op. 81. Conservative contemporary writing. Strong technique required: double and triple tonguing, flutter tongue, half valve pitches, etc. Recorded by David Randolph. See review in *TUBA Journal*, Vol. 9, No. 3, Page 24.

Takalo, Arttu. *"Kaipaus."* Finnish Music Information Center. 2002. 4:45. III–IV. B_1–g'. Published in virtually unreadable manuscript. Mostly lyrical work in the mid- to high tessitura. There is no separate solo tuba part; one must perform from the piano score.

Taktakishvili, O. *Aria from the Opera "Three Lives."* ed. A. Lebedev. Moscow Muzyka. 1986. 1:28. III. E♭–b♭. No technical problems. See: Lebedev, A., *Tuba Tutor Vol. 2,* under Tuba and Keyboard Collections.

Takumi, Hedetoshi. *Impromptu No. 1.* Tuba-Euphonium Press. 1999. 8:00. IV–V. B_2–f'. Technically challenging and rhythmically complex. Frequent extreme tempo fluctuations and very challenging accompaniment.

Tal, Joseph. *Movement for Tuba and Piano (1980).* Israel Music Institute. 1981. 8:00. V. C–g'. To Michael Margulies. Modern feel—no barlines. Muted passages. High tessitura; best on F tuba. Strong technique required.

Tchaikovsky, Peter I. *Andante Cantabile.* arr. Igor Hudadoff; William Westcott, pno. arr. Pro Art Publications. 1967. Out of Print. See: Hudadoff, Igor, *Fifteen Intermediate Tuba Solos,* under Tuba and Keyboard Collections.

Tchaikovsky, Peter I. *Aria of the King Rene.* Encore Music Publishers. 1997. 3:50. II. F_1–e♭. A good lyrical study piece or short recital piece for the contrabass tuba. Challenges lie in creating expressive lines while making the low playing lyrical.

Tchaikovsky, Peter I. *Arioso from the Opera "Jolanta."* ed. V. Mitegin. Moscow Muzyka. 1969. See: Mitegin, V., *Pieces for Tuba and Piano,* in Tuba and Keyboard Collections.

Tchaikovsky, Peter I. *At the Dance.* tr. Mitchell Gershenfeld. Medici Music Press. 1985. 1:58. III. A_1–f. Moderato. Opus 39. In 3/8 time and in D minor. See: Gershenfeld, Mitchell, *Medici Masterworks Solos Volume 1,* under Tuba and Keyboard Collections.

Tchaikovsky, Peter I. *Canzonetta from Violin Concerto, Op. 35.* arr. Kenneth Drobnak. Tuba-Euphonium Press. 2000. 5:30. IV. G_1–e♭' (b♭'). Good romantic transcription suitable for recital. Requires musical maturity. Contains optional high register notes up to b♭'; otherwise, range is in the medium to high tessitura.

Tchaikovsky, Peter I. *None But the Lonely Heart, Op. 6.* arr. Herbert Wekselblatt. G. Schirmer Inc. 1964. 2:22. II–III. D–g. Andante non tanto. Expressive lyrical solo. Some jumps of a sixth; otherwise not too technically challenging. See: Wekselblatt, H., *Solos for the Tuba Player,* under Tuba and Keyboard Collections.

Tchaikovsky, Peter I. *Sad Song, The.* ed. S. Melnikov. Military Band Masters Institute–Moscow. 1957. See: Melnikov, S., *Pieces for Tuba and Piano,* under Tuba and Keyboard Collections.

Tchaikovsky, Peter I. *Tomsky's Song from the Opera "Queen of Spades."* ed. A. Lebedev. Moscow Muzyka. 1984. 0:55. II. D–f. Little aria in 2/4 with no technical problems. See: Lebedev, A., *Tuba Tutor Vol. 1,* under Tuba and Keyboard Collections.

Tchaikovsky, Peter I. *Waltz from Serenade for Strings.* arr. Igor Hudadoff; William Westcott, pno. arr. Pro Art Publications. 1967. Out of Print. See: Hudadoff, Igor, *Fifteen Intermediate Tuba Solos,* under Tuba and Keyboard Collections.

Tchebotarev, S. *Rondo.* ed. J. Larin. Moscow Muzyka. 1979. See: Larin, J., *Pieces for Tuba and Piano,* under Tuba and Keyboard Collections.

Tchérépnine, Alexandre. *Andante.* M. P. Belaieff. 1950. $8.00. 5:00. III–IV. $A♭_1$–d'. à la memoire de mon chere père. "pour Tuba ou Trombone et Piano." Alternative trombone part also included. Theme and variations. Solid melodic writing. One passage in G♭ major. Recorded by Manfred Hoppert.

Telemann, Georg P. *Sonata.* tr. and ed. Kenneth Drobnak. Tuba-Euphonium Press. 2002. 6:00. III–IV. D_1–d'. Triste; Allegro; Andante; Vivace. A transcription of the popular sonata in F minor moved to the key of c minor. Contains an optional part for cello continuo.

Telemann, Georg P. *Sonata in C Major.* tr. and ed. Kenneth Drobnak; piano ed. Wilhelm Weismann. Tuba-Euphonium Press. 1999. 6:00. IV. $A♭_1$–b♭. Cantabile; Allegro; Grave; Vivace. Technically demanding transcription from the original work in C major, though this arrangement is in E♭ major. The transcriber offers ornamentation options and figured bass options for the pianist.

Telemann, Georg Philipp. *Adagio and Allegro.* arr. Norman Friedman F. Southern Music Company. 1977. $3.00. 3:40 (2:02, 1:38). IV. $B♭_1$–c'. Adagio; Allegro. From the Trumpet Concerto in D major. Adagio in 8; Allegro in 4/4 time. Typical baroque transcription. Good recital material. See review in *TUBA Journal,* Vol. 5, No. 3, Page 22.

Telemann, Georg Philipp. *Andante and Allegro.* arr. L. W. Chidester. Southern Music Company. 1973. $3.50. 2:13 (1:01, 1:12). III. G_1–g♭. Andante; Allegro. Andante in 3/2 time in D♭ major. Allegro in 2/4 time. No major technical problems.

Telemann, Georg Philipp. *Prelude and Allegretto.* arr. L. W. Chidester. Southern Music Company. 1966. $2.95. II–III. $A♭_1$–f. Prelude (Adagio); Allegretto (Tempo di minuetto). Prelude from Sonata in G minor and Allegretto from Sonata in B♭ major. Solid baroque transcriptions. Adagio has eighth note pulse in 4/4 time (8/8). Allegretto is in a brisk 3/8 time.

Telemann, Georg Philipp. *Sonata in F Major.* tr. Kenneth Drobnak. TUBA Press. 9:19 (2:22,

2:35, 2:07, 2:15). IV. D–d'. Andante; Vivace; Grave; Allegro. Harmonization by Frans Brüggen. In preparation. Well-transcribed baroque solo with four contrasting movements. Andante has a pulse of eight; Vivace is in 3/4 time with some syncopations; Grave is in 3/2 time; and Allegro has baroque arpeggios and scales. Flexibility, good stylistic sense required. Good recital material.

Telemann, Georg Philipp. *Sonata in F Minor.* arr. John Glenesk Mortimer. Editions Marc Reift. 1996. $15.00. 10:00. III. C–d♭'. Andante; Allegro; Andante; Vivace. Originally for bassoon, this arrangement is a very playable and is good recital material without being too strenuous. Available in bass clef concert pitch or in treble clef in E♭ and B♭.

Telemann, Georg Philipp. *Suite in A Minor for Flute and Strings.* arr. Ronald Davis. Manuscript available from the arranger. 1982. 15:00. V. G–g'. Air Ala Italien; La Plasir; Allegro/Overture; Rejouissance. Very high tessitura. Very agile flute transcription. Suggested ornamentation included. Solo part only.

Thompson, H. S. *Annie Lisle.* arr. John Kinyon. M. Witmark & Sons. 1958. I. See: Kinyon, John, *Breeze-Easy Recital Pieces,* under Tuba and Keyboard Collections.

Thomson, Virgil. *Jay Rozen Portrait and Fugue.* Heilman Music. 1984, 1985. $4.00. 1:52 (1:42, 1:10). IV. $G♭_1$–f'. Commissioned by the Yale University Music Library by means of gifts from American and Canadian tubists. First performed by Jay Rozen and Newel Kay Brown at the National Conference of the American Society of University Composers, March 2, 1985, University of Missouri at Columbia. *Portrait* completed New York, April 1984. *Fugue* completed New York, February 1985. Requires full range and good ear. Tonal contemporary writing. Good recital material.

Tihomirov, A. *Concert Piece for Tuba and Piano.* (Russian publisher.) 4:26. IV. $E♭_1$–f'. One-movement work with meter changes throughout. Melodic and technical challenges throughout. Good ear, good rhythmic sense, and quick articulations required.

Tilzer, Alber von, and Jack Norworth. *Take Me Out to the Ball Game.* arr. Bill Boyd, ed. Charles Daellenbach. Hal Leonard Publishing Corp. 1992. 0:39. I. $B♭_1$–c. Once through the melody in 3/4 time. Quarter note is the fastest rhythm. Comes with practice/performance cassette. See: Daellenbach, Charles, *Book of Beginning Tuba Solos,* under Tuba and Keyboard Collections.

Toldra, Eduardo. *Ave Maria from "6 Sonnets."* tr. J. Amaz. Union Musical Espanola. 1970. 4:10. IV. G–g'. Good smaller tuba piece in E major.

Toldra, Eduardo. *Dels Quatre Vents from "6 Sonnets."* tr. J. Amaz. Union Musical Espanola. 1970. 2:00. III–IV. G♯–c♯'. Molto Lento. Easy intermediate solo in B major. Easy accompaniment.

Toldra, Eduardo. *Oracio al Main from "6 Sonnets."* tr. J. Amaz. Union Musical Espanola. 1970.

Toldra, Eduardo. *Serenada d'Hivern from "6 Sonnets."* tr. J. Amaz. Union Musical Espanola. 1970.

Tomasi, G. (sic). *Hamlet's Monologue.* ed. A. Lebedev. Moscow Muzyka. 1986. 4:23. IV. B_1–d'. Composed by Henri Tomasi. Recitative style with modern melodic lines. Imagination and dynamic contrast required. See: Lebedev, A., *Tuba Tutor Vol. 2,* under Tuba and Keyboard Collections.

Tomasi, Henri. *Danse Sacrée. (Ritual Dance.)* Alphonse Leduc. 1960. $10.75. 3:00. "No. 3 des Cinq profanes et sacreés." "pour Tuba Ut ou Trombone ou Saxhorn basse Si♭ et Piano ou accompagnement d'Orchestre de Chambre." See: Tomasi, Henri, *Danse Sacrée no. 3 des "Cinq profanes et sacreés,"* under Tuba and Orchestra. Also see: Thompson/Lemke; *French Music for Low Brass Instruments.*

Tomasi, Henri. *Etre ou ne pas être.* Alphonse Leduc. 1963. $7.95. See: Tomasi, Henri, *Etre ou ne pas être,* under Tuba and Mixed Ensemble. Also see: Thompson/Lemke; *French Music for Low Brass Instruments.* And see other listing in this section. Recorded by Arnold Jacobs and Toby Hanks; a trombone quartet version recorded by the Leningrad Trombone Quartet.

Tomasi, Henri. *Etre ou ne pas être.* Moscow Muzyka. 1976. See: Guzii, V., *Pieces for Tuba and Piano,* under Tuba and Keyboard Collections. Also see other listing in this section. Recorded by Arnold Jacobs and Toby Hanks.

Toulon, Jacques. *Trois caricatures.* Éditions Robert Martin. 1989. $4.00. G_1–b♭'. For French tuba. See: Thompson/Lemke; *French Music for Low Brass Instruments.*

Tournier, Franz. *Récit et Rondo.* Éditions Rideau Rouge. 1969. IV. F_1–b♭'. Concours du Conservatoire National Supèrieur de Musique de Paris 1969. Récit; Rondo. "pour Tuba ou Saxhorn Basse Si♭ et Piano." For French tuba. Great flexibility and wide range required. See: Thompson/Lemke; *French Music for Low Brass Instruments.*

Traditional. *Away in a Manger.* arr. David E. Smith. Solid Brass Music Company. $3.50. II.

Traditional. *Hallejulah! What A Saviour.* arr. David E. Smith. Solid Brass Music Company. $3.50. II.

Traditional. *I Wonder As I Wander.* arr. David E. Smith. Solid Brass Music Company. $4.50. II.

Traditional. *The Old Rugged Cross.* arr. Dana Everson. Solid Brass Music Company. $4.50. II.

Traditional. *Stand Up, Stand Up for Jesus.* arr. David E. Smith. Solid Brass Music Company. $4.50. II–III.

Troje-Miller, N. *Sonatina Classica.* CPP/Belwin, Inc. 1941. $4.00. 6:00. III. $B♭_1$–a (b♭). Andante con moto; Andante grazioso; Allegro moderato. Challenging but approachable, solid work for intermediate level. No big technical problems.

Truillard, R. *Divertissement classique.* Truillard-Arpeges. For French Tuba.

Tuba-Euphonium Press. 2001. 8:00. II–III. D–g. Allegro agitato; Allegro molto; Allegretto; Vivace grazioso; Allegro giocoso; Vivace giocoso; Andantino grazioso; Allegro. A collection of several very short movements suitable for recitals or etude study at the intermediate level.

Tuthill, Burnet. *Fantasia for Tuba or Bass Trombone with Band or Piano Accompaniment Op. 57.* Lyceum Press. 1970. $5.00. For Rex Conner. Composed in 1968. See: Tuthill, Burnet, *Fantasia for Tuba, Op. 57,* under Tuba and Band. See review in *TUBA Journal,* Vol. 1, No. 3, Page 6.

Uber, David. *Autumn Afternoon.* Kendor Music, Inc. 1992. $5.00. 2:35. III. G♯$_1$–f. Andante, molto espressivo. For solo trombone, baritone horn, or tuba with piano accompaniment. Lyrical piece with mostly slurred phrases. No technical problems. Good recital material.

Uber, David. *Ballad of Enob Mort, The.* Southern Music Company. 1979. $5.00. 5:46 (2:29, 3:17). IV. G$_1$–c'. Allegretto, agitato; Allegro. The title is, of course, "trombone" spelled backwards in two words. Allegretto section is extremely lyrical and reflective. Allegro section requires flexibility. Good recital material.

Uber, David. *Bayou Legend for Solo Tuba and Piano.* Manuscript. 1992. 3:20. III. A♭$_1$–f. Op. 297. Melodic ballad section in 4/4 time and Più Mosso section in 2/4. No big technical problems.

Uber, David. *Danza Espanola.* Virgo Music Publishers. 1987. $6.95. In memory of Gordon Pulis. Allegro con fuoco. Written for trombone (euphonium, tuba) and piano. Opening tempo should be ca. 100.

Uber, David. *Delaware Rhapsody, A.* Kendor Music, Inc. 1981. $6.50. 5:45. III–IV. C–a♭ (d♭'). For solo trombone, baritone horn, or tuba with piano accompaniment. In 5/4 (3+2) time. Lyrical and moderately technical passages. See review in *TUBA Journal,* Vol. 10, No. 2, Page 26.

Uber, David. *Evensong.* Kendor Music, Inc. 1980. $7.00. 5:20. III–IV. C–b♭. Respectfully Dedicated To The Memory Of Art Dedrick. Op. 64. Written for tuba or bass trombone. Conceived as a series of invocations with alternate responses by the piano. Reflective lyrical first half with occasional quintuplets. Middle section contains syncopated figures. Last section returns to the feeling of the beginning. Limited range; could be played by strong high school player. See review in *TUBA Journal,* Vol. 8, No. 4, Page 26.

Uber, David. *A Jazz Rhapsody.* Tuba-Euphonium Press. 2002. 4:00. III. G$_1$–f (f'). One-movement solo in a jazz style with conservative range demands. Good for an intermediate performer's first entry into jazz sonorities.

Uber, David. *Legend of Lake St. Catherine.* Kendor Music, Inc. 1996. $7.00. III. 3:40. G$_1$–c'. Lyrical work exploring the mid- to low register. Suitable recital material for contrabass tuba.

Uber, David. *Legend of Purple Hills, The.* Southern Music Company. 1980. $5.00. 7:10. IV. A$_1$–f'. For Scott Mendoker. Op. 137. Very lyrical ballad; mostly slurred phrases. Wide range; technical facility a must. See review in *TUBA Journal,* Vol. 7, No. 3, Page 31.

Uber, David. *Legend of the Sleeping Bear.* Kendor Music, Inc. 1986. $7.00. 6:10. IV. A$_1$–c'. Dedicated to Don Butterfield. Originally titled *Sound Sketches.* Flexibility required. Lyrical writing. See review in *TUBA Journal,* Vol. 14, No. 4, Page 42.

Uber, David. *"Mr. Tuba" on Broadway.* Kendor Music, Inc. 1987. $7.50. 6:00. IV. E$_1$–b♭ (f'). Dedicated to my good friend, Harvey Phillips. Originally called *Caricatura* (1970). Flexibility required. See review in *TUBA Journal,* Vol. 16, No. 3, Page 48. Also see: Uber, David, *Caricatura,* under Tuba and Mixed Ensemble.

Uber, David. *Pantomime.* Charles Colin Publishing. 1967. $4.95. 6:00. III–IV. B♭$_1$–a♭ (b♭). Advanced intermediate technique sufficient. Some "jazz rhythms" involved.

Uber, David. *Pantomime.* Encore Music Publishers. 2001. 4:30. III–IV. B♭$_1$–a♭(g'). A technically challenging work in the middle register.

Uber, David. *Rhapsody in C Minor.* Kendor Music, Inc. 1998. $7.00. 4:15. III–IV. G$_1$–g. Fine work in the middle tessitura (suitable for contrabass tuba) that explores changing articulations and the tonal colors available in C minor. Suitable as either an etude or concert piece.

Uber, David. *Rock Bottom.* Tuba-Euphonium Press. 2002. 4:00. F$_1$–f.

Uber, David. *Romance.* Kendor Music, Inc. 1986. $6.00. 6:00. III. A♭$_1$–f (g). Very lyrical solo requiring some flexibility. See review in *TUBA Journal,* Vol. 14, No. 4, Page 43.

Uber, David. *Skylines.* Hidalgo Music. 1992. $10.00. Composed for and dedicated to Douglas Yeo. Manhattan; Chicago; Boston. See: Uber, David, *Skylines,* under Tuba and Mixed Ensemble.

Uber, David. *Sonata Di Bravura.* TUBA Press. 1992. 9:45 (3:30, 2:30, 3:45). IV. F$_1$–d'. Commissioned by Scott Mendoker, 1992. Allegro ma non troppo; Andantino espress; Allegro assai. Publication pending. Opus 298. Lovely lyrical writing combined with some technical demands consisting mainly of flexibility and some quick articulations. Good recital material.

Uber, David. *Sonata for Bass Tuba and Piano.* Edition Musicus. 1978. $9.50. 9:42 (5:15, 2:57, 1:40). IV. C–b♭ (d♭'). Commissioned by Frank H. Meredith. Allegro Moderato; Andante, Poco Agitato; Allegro. Also known as *Sonata for Euphonium or Bass Tuba and Piano.* Major work; lyrical and technical playing required. Technique involves mostly quick articulations and flexibility. Third movement in D♭ major.

Uber, David. *Sonata in One Movement.* Encore Music Publishers. 2001. III–IV. G_1–b♭. Commissioned by and composed for Ross Tolbert. Range suitable for intermediate level though technical demands are more appropriate for advanced player.

Uber, David. *Sonatina.* Southern Music Company. 1985. $5.00. 6:45 (2:40, 1:47, 2:18). III–IV. A♭$_1$–a♭ (c'). Allegro moderato; Lento; Allegro moderato. Also for trombone, euphonium, or horn in F and piano. Involves technical, flexible playing. Optional octave placement eases difficulty.

Uber, David. *Sonatine No. 1.* TUBA Press. 9:43 (3:39, 3:27, 2:37). IV. (G_1) A_1–c' (f'). Publication pending. Solid writing. Requires flexible technique and quick fingers. Fun to play.

Uber, David. *Sonatine No. 2.* TUBA Press. 4:39. IV. A_1–b♭. Publication pending. One-movement work requiring swift articulations, flexibility, and lyrical playing.

Uber, David. *Sonatuba.* TUBA Press. 1991. 7:45 (3:40, 1:40, 2:25). Completed Summer 1991, Tinmouth, Vt. See: Uber, David, *Sonatuba,* under Tuba and Mixed Ensemble.

Uber, David. *Summer Nocturne.* Southern Music Company. 1983. $6.00. 8:10. III–IV. A_1–b♭ (c'). Also for trombone or horn and piano. One-movement lyrical ballad requiring intermediate-level flexibility.

Uber, David. *Theater Piece.* Encore Music Publishers. 1992. $9.00. 3:35. IV. C–c'. In preparation. For euphonium or tuba and piano. Cute solo utilizing syncopation and technical and lyrical playing. Good recital material.

Uber, David, arr. *Deep River.* Kendor Music, Inc. 1996. $6.00. 3:35. C–g. Dedicated to Mary Ann Craig.

Uga, Pierre. *Promenade.* ed. Jean Douay. Gérard Billaudot. 1978. $9.50. 2:36. III. C–e'. Andantino/Allegretto. "pour Trombone Ténor, Trombone Basse, Tuba ut ou Saxhorn si♭." French tuba tessitura. Mostly scale-wise motion. Some triplets; some sixteenth notes. Depending on instrument chosen, no technical problems. See: Thompson/Lemke; *French Music for Low Brass Instruments.*

Usher, Julia. *Venezia.* Primarera. 1982. 9:45 (1:39, 1:30, 1:40, 3:02, 0:33, 1:21). IV. (F_1) (A_1)–d'. Orient Express; Campanile; Piazza; San Marco; Emilio Panfido; Regatta Storica. "Six Sketches For Tuba and Piano of Sights and Sounds of Venice." Musical portraits; conservative modern tonality. Some quick articulations.

Van Der Roost, J. *Obsessions.* Editions Andel Uitgave.

Vander Cook, H. A. *Arbutus.* arr. Forrest L. Buchtel. Neil A. Kjos Music Company. 1954. Out of Print. 2:55. III. A_1–g. Typical polka style.

Vander Cook, H. A. *Behemoth.* Rubank, Inc. 1941. $2.00. 4:00. III. F_1–f. "Solo for BB♭ Bass." Polka-style solo with cadenza.

Vander Cook, H. A. *Bombastoso.* ed. and compiled by Himie Voxman. Rubank, Inc. 1941. 3:01. II. B♭$_1$–f. "Solo Tuba—E♭ or BB♭ tuba." Caprice. Traditional theme and variations split up with solo piano interludes. Mostly sixteenth note scale-wise motion in technical section. Good advanced beginner solo. Limited range. See: Rubank, *Soloist Folio for Bass (E♭ or BB♭),* under Tuba and Keyboard Collections.

Vander Cook, H. A. *Bombastoso.* ed. and compiled by Himie Voxman. Rubank, Inc. 1941. Out of Print. Separately published version. See other listing.

Vander Cook, H. A. *Chrysanthemum.* arr. Forrest L. Buchtel. Neil A. Kjos Music Company. 1960. Out of Print. 3:00. III. B♭$_1$–f. "Basses (E♭ or BB♭)." Traditional solo in two parts: Tempo di Bolero and Allegretto. Technical playing in a bolero and polka format. Triple tonguing or optional single notes. Cadenza.

Vander Cook, H. A. *Colossus.* Rubank, Inc. 1941. $3.50. 4:00. II–III. B♭$_1$–e♭. "Air and Variations." Theme and (three) variations.

Vander Cook, H. A. *Columbine.* arr. Forrest L. Buchtel. Neil A. Kjos Music Company. 1955. Out of Print. 2:05. II. A_1–f. Easy advanced beginner solo. A few sixteenth notes.

Vander Cook, H. A. *Daisies.* arr. Forrest L. Buchtel. Neil A. Kjos Music Company. 1957. Out of Print. 3:05. II–III. B♭$_1$–f. Typical polka style.

Vander Cook, H. A. *Dewdrops.* arr. Forrest L. Buchtel. Neil A. Kjos Music Company. 1957. Out of Print. 2:55. II–III. B♭$_1$–f. Typical polka style with a little triple tonguing.

Vander Cook, H. A. *Hyacinthe.* arr. Forrest L. Buchtel. Neil A. Kjos Music Company. 1952. Out of Print. 3:04. II–III. B♭$_1$–f. Typical polka style. See review in *TUBA Journal,* Vol. 8, No. 4, Page 28.

Vander Cook, H. A. *Ivy.* arr. Forrest L. Buchtel. Neil A. Kjos Music Company. 1963. Out of Print. 4:00. III. A_1–f♯. Lyrical 6/8 section, followed by a polka-style section.

Vander Cook, H. A. *Lily.* arr. Forrest L. Buchtel. Neil A. Kjos Music Company. 1952. Out of Print. 3:00. II–III. A_1–f. "Tuba E♭ or BB♭." Lyrical section in 4/4 followed by a polka section.

Vander Cook, H. A. *Magnolia.* arr. Forrest L. Buchtel. Neil A. Kjos Music Company. 1980. $2.50. 4:00. III. G_1–a♭. Original copyright was 1952. Moderately technical/lyrical section in 4/4 time followed by a polka. Tessitura a bit higher than others by Vander Cook.

Vander Cook, H. A. *Marigold.* arr. Forrest L. Buchtel. Neil A. Kjos Music Company. 1952. Out of Print. 3:55. II. G_1–e♭. Typical polka style.

Vander Cook, H. A. *Morning Glory.* arr. Forrest L. Buchtel. Neil A. Kjos Music Company. 1952. Out of Print. 4:00. II–III. G_1–e♭. "Tuba (E♭ or BB♭)." Andante section in 4/4 time followed by a polka.

Vander Cook, H. A. *Moss Rose.* arr. Forrest L. Buchtel. Neil A. Kjos Music Company. 1957. Out of Print. 3:20. III–IV. $G\sharp_1$–f. Typical polka style with triple tonguing.

Vander Cook, H. A. *Pansies.* arr. Forrest L. Buchtel. Neil A. Kjos Music Company. 1957. Out of Print. 3:20. II–III. $B\flat_1$–f. Typical polka style.

Vander Cook, H. A. *Peony.* arr. Forrest L. Buchtel. Neil A. Kjos Music Company. 1952. Out of Print. 3:20. II–III. G_1–f. Typical polka style.

Vander Cook, H. A. *Rosebuds.* arr. Forrest L. Buchtel. Neil A. Kjos Music Company. 1954. $2.50. 4:00. II. ($A_1$) C–f. "Tuba (E♭ and BB♭)." Andante section in 4/4, cadenza, polka. More limited in range than other Vander Cook pieces.

Vander Cook, H. A. *Tulip.* arr. Forrest L. Buchtel. Neil A. Kjos Music Company. 1980. $2.00. 3:00. II. $B\flat_1$–e♭. "Tuba (E♭ or BB♭)." Original copyright date was 1952. Andante cantabile section followed by an Allegretto polka. Easier than other Vander Cook solos.

Vander Cook, H. A. *Wild Rose.* arr. Forrest L. Buchtel. Neil A. Kjos Music Company. 1952. Out of Print. 3:45. III. A_1–g. Typical polka style.

Vanheel, L. *Tecnica In Aba.* Editions Andel Uitgave. 1981.

Vanherenthals, J. *Ballade.* Available from Spaeth and Schmid. $11.50.

Vansteenkiste, M. *Legende.* Editions Andel Uitgave.

Vasconi, Eugene. *Shades of Tuba.* Southern Music Company. 1993. $3.95.

Vasilyev, V. *Melody.* arr. A. Lebedev. Military Band Masters Faculty of Moscow Conservatiore. 1971. See: Lebedev, A., *Collection of Pieces for Tuba "Es" and Piano,* under Tuba and Keyboard Collections.

Vaughan, Rodger. *Concertpiece No. 1.* Fema Music Publications. 1970. $6.00. 5:00. IV. $F\sharp_1$–c'. Composed in 1959. Previously published by Interlochen Press in 1961. Conservative contemporary writing. Solid piece for tuba and piano. Recorded by: Rex Conner; Ronald Davis.

Vaughan, Rodger. *Concertpiece No. 2.* Fema Music Publications. 1981. $6.00. 6:00. IV. f_1–c'. For Heidi Werth. Fine contemporary melodic writing. A few meter changes.

Vaughan, Rodger. *Elegy.* Available from the composer. 1986–87. See: Vaughan, Rodger, *Elegy,* under Tuba and Band.

Vaughan, Rodger. *Manchester Parade (a British Slow-March).* TUBA Press. 1981. $5.00. 2:05. III–IV. G_1–b♭. For Marianne Forster. Composed on a theme by H. K. Werth, December 1981. "A British Slow-March for Tuba and Piano." In cut time. Requires moderate flexibility. No big technical problems. Fun to play.

Vaughan Williams, Ralph. *Concerto for Bass Tuba.* Oxford University Press. 1955. $18.95. See: Vaughan Williams, Ralph, *Concerto for Bass Tuba,* under Tuba and Orchestra and under Tuba and Band. Also see: Bird, Gary, ed.; *Program Notes for the Solo Tuba.* Also see: Villiams, V. R., *Concerto for Bass Tuba,* in this section. Recorded by Jeffrey Arwood, Philip Catelinet, Floyd Cooley, Eugene Dowling, John Fletcher, Patrick Harrild, Manfred Hoppert, Arnold Jacobs, Ian King, Michael Lind, Richard Nahatzki, Daniel Perantoni, Harvey Phillips, Donald Strand.

Vaughan Williams, Ralph. *Six Studies in English Folk-Song.* tr. Michael Wagner. Galaxy Music Corp/ECS Publishing/Stainer & Bell. 1927. $8.95. 8:36 (1:37, 1:25, 1:32, 1:51, 1:27, 0:44). IV. G_1–d. Adagio; Andante Sostenuto; Larghetto; Lento; Andante tranquillo; Allegro vivace. To May Mukle. For violoncello and pianoforte with alternate versions for violin, viola, clarinet, English horn, alto saxophone, bassoon, or tuba (and transposed versions by Paul Droste for euphonium, baritone, tenor saxophone, or bass clarinet). Very lyrical writing. With exception of last movement, mostly slurred phrases. Excellent recital material. Recorded by Eugene Dowling, Gene Pokorny.

Verdi, Giuseppe. *Aria from "Don Carlos."* arr. Allen Ostrander. Edition Musicus. 1959. $2.75. 3:00. III. G_1–e. Listen to aria for conception. Vocal interpretation a must. Some sextuplets included.

Verdi, Giuseppe. *Aria from Falstaff.* arr. Carl Weber. J. W. Pepper & Son. 1914. Out of Print. See: Weber, Carl, *Nineteen Solos for E♭ Bass with Piano Accompaniment,* under Tuba and Keyboard Collections.

Verdi, Giuseppe. *Grand Air from "The Masked Ball."* arr. Allen Ostrander. Edition Musicus. 1965. $2.75. 2:50. III. A_1–g. Some dotted rhythms; very accessible, easy intermediate solo.

Vergauwen, A. *Ballade.* Editions Andel Uitgave.

Villette, Pierre. *Fantaisie Contante.* Alphonse Leduc. 1962. $12.80. Au Maître Paul Bernard, Professeur au Conservatoire National Supérieur de Musique. See: Villette, Pierre, *Fantaisie Contante,* under Tuba and Orchestra. Also see: Thompson/Lemke; *French Music for Low Brass Instruments.*

Villiams, V. R. (Vaughan Williams, Ralph.) *Concerto for Tuba and Orchestra.* Moscow Muzyka. 1955. See: Vaughan Williams, Ralph, *Concerto for Bass Tuba,* under Tuba and Orchestra and under Tuba and Band. Also see other listing in this section.

Viola, Anselm. *Concerto.* arr. John Glenesk Mortimer. Editions Marc Reift. 1997. $15.00. 16:00. III–IV. F_1–d'. Molto moderato; Andante; Allegro. An arrangement of this late-eighteenth-century composer's work. It is a very active composition, based on scale patterns and arpeggios and requiring clean articulation. Available in bass clef concert pitch or in treble clef in E♭ and B♭.

Vivaldi, Antonio. *Allegro (from Sonata No. 3)*. arr. Ken Swanson. CPP/Belwin, Inc. 1971. $4.00. 2:18. III. ($G_1$) C–f. Allegro. Crisp, light articulation is the biggest consideration in this quick 2/4 baroque transcription. Syncopations throughout. Practice with metronome. See other listing in this section.

Vivaldi, Antonio. *Allegro (from Sonata No. 3)*. arr. Ken Swanson. CPP/Belwin, Inc. 1971. See: Lamb, Jack, *Solo Sounds for Tuba Levels 3–5, Vol. 1,* under Tuba and Keyboard Collections. Also see other listing in this section.

Vivaldi, Antonio. *Concerto in A Minor.* arr. Allen Ostrander. Edition Musicus. 1958. $11.00. 9:00. IV. B_1–d' (d♯'). Allegro molto; Andante molto; Allegro. Breathing can be tricky—plan ahead. Requires flexibility. Good transcription. Upper tessitura.

Vivaldi, Antonio. *Praeludium in C Minor.* arr. Quinto Maganini. Edition Musicus. 1965. $2.75. 3:00. III. G_1–a♭. Alternative baritone and trombone parts also included. In 3/2 time. Some flexibility required.

Vivaldi, Antonio. *Sonata*. ed. S. Melnikov. Military Band Masters Institute–Moscow. 1957. See: Melnikov, S., *Pieces for Tuba and Piano,* under Tuba and Keyboard Collections.

Vivaldi, Antonio. *Sonata in A Minor.* arr. Kenneth Drobnak, piano ed. Gian Francesco Malipiero. Tuba-Euphonium Press. 1996. 6:00. III. G_1–e'. Largo; Allegro; Largo; Allegro. Transcriber provides two solo parts, one with performance practice suggestions and the other without. Also provided are figured bass parts and a continuo part for cello. Same composition as the Winston Morris transcription.

Vivaldi, Antonio. *Sonata No. I in B♭ Major.* arr. John Glenesk Mortimer. Editions Marc Reift. 1997. $11.00 (Complete set of six sonatas $31.00). 6:00–10:00 depending on repeats. III. B♭$_1$ (F_1)–e♭'. Largo; Allegro; Andante; Allegro. Originally for violin; this transcription is in the original key. Available individually or as a compilation of all six sonatas, in bass clef concert pitch, or in treble clef in E♭ or B♭. The octave settings vary depending on which instrument is used.

Vivaldi, Antonio. *Sonata No. 2 from "Pastor Fido."* arr. Cooley. Available from Spaeth and Schmid. $18.25.

Vivaldi, Antonio. *Sonata No. II in F Major.* arr. John Glenesk Mortimer. Editions Marc Reift. 1998. $11.00 (Complete set of six sonatas $31.00). 6:30–13:00 depending on repeats. III. F_1–c'. Andante; Allegro; Largo; Allegro. Originally for violin; this transcription is in the original key. Available individually or as a compilation of all six sonatas, in bass clef concert pitch, or in treble clef in E♭ or B♭.

Vivaldi, Antonio. *Sonata No. 3 a-moll.* arr. Morris. Available from Spaeth and Schmid. $15.25.

Vivaldi, Antonio. *Sonata No. III in A Minor.* arr. John Glenesk Mortimer. Editions Marc Reift. 1998. $11.00 (Complete set of six sonatas $31.00). 8:00–16:00 depending on repeats. III. G_1 (C_1)–c'. Largo; Allegro; Largo; Allegro. Originally for violin; this transcription is in the original key. Available individually or as a compilation of all six sonatas, in bass clef concert pitch, or in treble clef in E♭ or B♭. Works well on CC tuba.

Vivaldi, Antonio. *Sonata No. 3 in A Minor.* arr. R. Winston Morris. Shawnee Press, Inc. 1982. $7.00. 17:45 (6:00, 4:15, 4:25, 3:05). IV. G_1–c'. Largo; Allegro; Largo; Allegro. Large work—duration could be shortened if preferred by eliminating repeats. Combination of slow sustained playing and fast flexible passages. Good recital material.

Vivaldi, Antonio. *Sonata No. IV in B♭ Major.* arr. John Glenesk Mortimer. Editions Marc Reift. 1998. $11.00 (Complete set of six sonatas $31.00). 6:00–10:00 depending on repeats. III. F_1 (D_1)–b♭e♭'. Largo; Allegro; Largo; Allegro. Originally for violin; this transcription is in the original key. Available individually or as a compilation of all six sonatas, in bass clef concert pitch, or in treble clef in E♭ or B♭. The octave settings vary depending on which instrument is used.

Vivaldi, Antonio. *Sonata No. V in E Minor.* arr. John Glenesk Mortimer. Editions Marc Reift. 1998. $11.00 (Complete set of six Sonatas $31.00). 6:00–10:00 depending on repeats. III. G_1 (D_1)–c'. Largo; Allegro; Largo; Allegro. Originally for violin; this transcription is in the original key. Available individually or as a compilation of all six sonatas, in bass clef concert pitch, or in treble clef in E♭ or B♭. The octave settings vary depending on which instrument is used.

Vivaldi, Antonio. *Sonata No. VI in B♭ Major.* arr. John Glenesk Mortimer. Editions Marc Reift. 1998. $11.00 (Complete set of six sonatas $31.00). 6:00–10:00 depending on repeats. III. F_1 (E♭$_1$)–b♭. Largo; Allegro; Largo; Allegro. Originally for violin; this transcription is in the original key. Available individually or as a compilation of all six sonatas, in bass clef concert pitch, or in treble clef in E♭ or B♭. The octave settings vary depending on which instrument is used. See listing under Tuba and Organ.

Vogel, Roger C. *Temporal Landscape No. 1.* Shawnee Press, Inc. 1978. $3.00. 5:00. IV–V. Lowest note possible: e♭'. for David Randolph. Modern writing. Contemporary techniques for both players. For tubist: tapping instrument with fingers, clicking valves, glissando, huge dissonant interval jumps, etc. Pianist: Stopping strings vibrating with hand, rubbing strings, plucking strings, etc. Muted passages. See review in *TUBA Journal,* Vol. 8, No. 1, Page 28.

Vogel, Roger C. *Temporal Landscape No. 4.* Theodore Presser Company. 1980. $3.50. 4:00. IV–V. E_1–e♭'. For David Randolph. Muted passages. Relatively more conventional than *Temporal Landscape No. 1.* Multi-phonics, wide dissonant jumps. Will take a strong ear as well as a strong accompanist. See review in *TUBA Journal,* Vol. 8, No. 3, Page 27.

Volkmann, Rudy. *Suite Babu, (Are You My).* William Grant Still Music. 1982. 3:30. III–IV. B♭$_1$–b♭. For Vicky Burke. Opus 6. Theme and variations style. Some cantabile playing as well as technical playing required. Some triple tonguing possible. Fun piece to play. Not overwhelming technical demands. See review in *TUBA Journal,* Vol. 10, No. 4, Page 37.

Volkov, K. *Piece, A.* ed. A. Lebedev. Moscow Muzyka. 1986. 3:14. IV. E_1–c'. Beautiful lyrical modern dissonant and consonant lines all presented in a very musical way. See: Lebedev, A., *Tuba Tutor Vol. 2,* under Tuba and Keyboard Collections.

Volle, Bjarne. *Canarie nr. 2: Tuba ag Piano.* Norwegian Music Center. 1996.

Vollrath, Carl. *Epode for Tuba and Piano.* Trombone Association Publishing. 1988. $9.00. 7:54. IV–V. B♭$_2$–f'. Very wide range only in a few passages. Modern tonal writing. Not overwhelming technique for the suggested level.

Vollrath, Carl. *Recital Piece No. 1.* Tuba-Euphonium Press. 1999. 6:00. IV. F_1–e♭'. Incorporates bouncy style into this single-movement work with large jumps and syncopated rhythms.

Voronov, G., ed. *Works for Tuba and Piano by Russian Composers.* Moscow Muzyka. 1984. Contains: Berlin, A., *Ballade;* Burshtin, M., *Legend;* Kolodub, L., *Humorous Dance;* Rakov, N., *Sonatina;* Smironova, T., *Sonata;* Smironova, T., *A Tale;* Strukov, V., *Lento Elegiaco;* Zverev, V., *Concertino;* and for tuba solo: Burshtin, M., *Suite;* Ekimovsky, V., *Romance and Capriccio.*

Vosk, Jay. *Showdown!* Tuba-Euphonium Press. 2001. 3:30. III–IV. A_1–d'. Bright, up-tempo showpiece suitable for recitals.

Voxman, H. *Soloist Folio.* Available from Spaeth and Schmid. $13.25.

Voxman, Himie, compiled and ed. *Concert and Contest Collection.* Rubank, Inc. 1972. $10.45. II–IV. "for E♭ or BB♭ Bass (Tuba-Sousaphone)." Piano accompaniment available separately. Contains: Alary, G., *Morceau de Concours;* Berlioz, G. P., *Air Gai;* Clérisse, Robert, *Andante and Allegro;* Corelli, Arcangelo, *Sarabanda and Gavotta;* Gaucet, Charles, *Adagio and Finale from Concertino;* Handel, G. F., *Adagio and Allegro from Sonata No. 7;* Handel, G. F., *Two Short Pieces;* Kabalevsky, D., *Waltz and Galop from Petite Suite;* Koepke, Paul, *Persiflage;* Maniet, Rene, *Premier Solo de Concours;* Marcello, Benedetto, *Largo and Allegro;* Mozart, W. A., *First Movement from Concerto for Horn;* Ostransky, Leroy, *Serenade and Scherzo;* Rimsky-Korsakov, N., *Andante Cantabile from Concerto.*

Vuori, Harri. *Digderidoo.* Available from Spaeth and Schmid. $22.50.

Wadowick, James L., arr., and Donald E. McCathren, ed. *Christ the Lord Is Risen Today.* David E. Smith Publications. 1987. $4.50. 3:12. II–III. A_1–f. Theme and variations on traditional hymn melody. Last variation in D♭ major. A few sixteenth notes; otherwise no technical problems.

Wadowick, James L., arr., and Donald E. McCathren, ed. *Dona Nobis Pacem.* David E. Smith Publications. 1986. $4.00. 2:47. III. B♭$_1$–f. Theme and (five) variations.

Wadowick, James L., arr., and Donald E. McCathren, ed. *O Mighty God.* David E. Smith Publications. 1987. $3.50. 2:20. II–III. C–f. Some slurring; no big technical problems.

Wagner, Richard. *Die Meistersinger von Nürnberg.* arr. Hiroyuki Yasumoto. Toa Music International Co. 1986. 2:40. IV. A_1–e'. Piano and tuba transcription of the most famous of tuba orchestral excerpts. Listen to orchestral version for conception. See: Yasumoto, Hiroyuki, *Tuba Volume #1,* under Tuba and Keyboard Collections.

Wagner, Richard. *Die Meistersinger Von Nurnberg (from the Prelude, Act One).* arr. Herbert Wekselblatt. G. Schirmer Inc. 1964. 2:56. IV–V. A_1–e'. See: Wekselblatt, H., *Solos for the Tuba Player,* under Tuba and Keyboard Collections. Tuba and piano transcription of perhaps the #1 tuba orchestral excerpt.

Wagner, Richard. *Die Walkure (from Act III).* arr. Herbert Wekselblatt. G. Schirmer Inc. 1964. 1:57. IV–V. E_1–c♯. See: Wekselblatt, H., *Solos for the Tuba Player,* under Tuba and Keyboard Collections. Two excerpts from Act III. Great opportunity to work on standard orchestral tuba excerpts with piano accompaniment.

Wagner, Richard. *Heav'n, in pray'r, Thine aid I seek and Good subjects of Brabant, 'tis well! (From Loengrin).* arr. James Ord Hume. Boosey & Co. 1906. Out of Print. See: Hume, J. Ord, *Boosey's Bombardon Solo Album,* under Tuba and Keyboard Collections.

Wagner, Richard. *O du mein holcler Abendstern, from "Tanhöuser."* arr. Hiroyuki Yasumoto. Toa Music International Co. 1986. 1:11. III. D–g. Andante mosso. Very lyrical transcription. All slurred. See: Yasumoto, Hiroyuki, *Tuba Volume #1,* under Tuba and Keyboard Collections. A different version of this recorded by John Fletcher.

Wagner, Richard. *Ride of the Valkyries (from Die Walkure).* arr. David Uber. Kendor Music, Inc. 2002. $7.00. III. 2:35. F♯$_1$–a. Concert version of the prelude to Act Three of *Die Walkure.* The piano reduction provides some of the excitement of the orchestral original. The tuba plays much more than the expected excerpt. A good, accompanied way for intermediate players to learn this difficult excerpt.

Wagner, Richard. *Siegfried (from Act II, Prelude and First Scene)* . arr. Herbert Wekselblatt. G. Schirmer Inc. 1964. 4:34. IV–V. F_1–a. See: Wekselblatt, H., *Solos for the Tuba Player,* under Tuba and Keyboard Collections. Low, sustained, legato transcription. Good introduction to this excerpt as well as to Wagner's low tessitura writing for the tuba.

Wagner, Richard. *Walther's Prize Song.* arr. George Masso. Kendor Music, Inc. 1966. 3:00. II. E–a. From *Der Meistersingers.* All slurred phrases. Upper tessitura for younger BB♭ player. Good, usable transcription.

Waignein, A. *First Contest.* Editions Andel Uitgave.

Waignein, A. *Galejade.* Editions Andel Uitgave.

Waignein, André. *Apopol.* Available from Spaeth and Schmid. $8.00.

Waignein, André. *Concertino.* Available from Spaeth and Schmid. $9.75.

Waignein, André. *Structures.* Available from Spaeth and Schmid. $9.75.

Waldteufel. *Skater's Waltz.* arr. Acton Ostling. CPP/Belwin, Inc. 1969. 1:09. I. $B♭_1$–c. Simple version of the tune. Some slurring from F–B♭. See: Ostling, Acton, *Tuba (Bass) Soloist, Level One,* under Tuba and Keyboard Collections.

Waldteufel. *Spanish Waltzes.* arr. Igor Hudadoff; William Westcott, pno. arr. Pro Art Publications. 1967. Out of Print. See: Hudadoff, Igor, *Fifteen Intermediate Tuba Solos,* under Tuba and Keyboard Collections.

Walker, Gwyneth. *Chanties and Ballads: Songs of the Sea for Tuba and Orchestra.* MMB Music, Inc. 1995. $19.95. 15:00. See listing under Music for Tuba and Orchestra and Music for Tuba and Band.

Wallace. *Let Me like a Soldier Fall.* arr. Carl Weber. J. W. Pepper & Son. 1914. Out of Print. 0:46. II–III. E–g. From "Maritana." No technical problems. See: Weber, Carl, *Nineteen Solos for E♭ Bass with Piano Accompaniment,* under Tuba and Keyboard Collections.

Walters, Harold L. *Concertante.* Rubank, Inc. 1960. $2.50. See: Walters, Harold L., *Concertante,* under Tuba and Band.

Walters, Harold L. *Concertante.* Tierolff-Muziekcentrale. See other listing in this section.

Walters, Harold L. *Forty Fathoms.* Rubank, Inc. 1952. $3.50. "Solo for E♭ or BB♭ Bass." See: Walters, Harold L., *Forty Fathoms,* under Tuba and Band.

Walters, Harold L. *Leprechauns Patrol.* Rubank, Inc. 1954. Out of Print. 2:30. II. G_1–d. "Solo for E♭ or BB♭ Bass." In 6/8 time. No technical problems.

Walters, Harold L. *Scherzo Pomposo.* Rubank, Inc. 1958. $3.00. See: Walters, Harold L., *Scherzo Pomposo,* under Tuba and Band.

Walters, Harold L. *Tarantelle.* Ludwig Music Publishing Company. 1946. $5.00. See: Walters, Harold L., *Tarantelle,* under Tuba and Band.

Walters, Harold L., arr. *Blow the Man Down.* Rubank, Inc. 1954. $2.50. 4:00. II–III. $A♭_1$–e♭. "Solo for E♭ or BB♭ Bass." "Chantey and Variations." Theme and variations with cadenza.

Walters, Harold L., arr. *Christmas Nocturne.* Rubank, Inc. 1954. Out of Print. 1:55. I. E♭–c. Beginning solo. Includes: *Lullaby, Thou Little Tiny Child* and *My Sheep Were Grazing.*

Walters, Harold L., arr. *Down in the Valley.* Rubank, Inc. 1960. $2.95. 3:00. I. ($F_1$) C–c. "Fantasy On A Folk Song. Solo for E♭ or BB♭ and Piano." Nice solo for beginning student in 3/4 time. Easy rhythms. With the exception of last note (an optional F_1) this piece is within one octave.

Ward, Norman. *Happy Hippo, The.* Kendor Music, Inc. 1967. $5.00. See: Ward, Norman, *The Happy Hippo,* under Tuba and Band. Comes with flexible recording featuring Barton Cummings, tubist.

Ward, S. A. *America the Beautiful.* arr. Wesley Jacobs. Encore Music Publishers. 0:38. I. C–d. Moderato. Once through the tune. Some slurring, accidentals, one jump from F to d. See: Jacobs, Wesley, *Solos from the Classics,* under Tuba and Keyboard Collections.

Warner and Bradbury. *Jesus Loves Me.* arr. David E. Smith. David E. Smith Publications. 1984. $3.00. 1:30. II. $B♭_1$–f. Some slurring; no technical problems.

Warner. *Jesus Loves Me.* arr. David E. Smith. Solid Brass Music Company. $4.00. II.

Warrack, Guy. *Pieces for Tuba (Grades 3 and 4).* The Associated Board of the Royal Schools of Music. 2000. 5:00. I–II. $B♭_1$–f. The Sandman; Gavotte. Two test pieces written at the beginner level and transposed into various keys to teach transposition and new fingerings to the same tune. One tune is lyrical while the other is a bit more technical. Parts available in treble and bass clef.

Warren, David. *Mantis Dance.* Ludwig Music Publishing Company. 1987. $3.50. 2:00. II. $B♭_1$–e♭. Original copyright date was 1959. Lyrical playing and articulated sections with no technical problems.

Warren, Frank E. *Music for Tuba and Piano.* ed. Chester Roberts. Frank E. Warren Music Service. 1991. $5.00. 8:30. IV. ($D_1$) F_1–d♭'. Op. 28a. Conservative modern tonal writing. No major technical problems.

Warren, Frank E. *Sonata for Tuba and Piano.* Frank E. Warren Music Service. 1975. $12.00. 11:00. IV–V. C_1–f'. for Rob Welle and Lucille Gaita. Three numbered movements. Op. 1. Completed 12/75. First performance: 4/22/76, Boston, Mass., Rob Weller, tuba, Lucille Gaita, piano. Some multi-phonics for tubist. Currently being revised.

Warren, Frank E. *Song for Tuba and Piano.* Frank E. Warren Music Service. 1989. $6.00. 8:30. IV. $B\flat_1$–b♭. for Robert A. Orr. Op. 25. The first performance was given by Robert A. Orr and Hyeran Kim at Boston Conservatory of Music on April 21, 1990. Lyrical pentatonic main theme. Some quick articulations required as well as lyrical playing.

Wastall, Peter, ed. *Learn As You Play Tuba.* Boosey & Hawkes, Inc. 1985. Tuba part: $6.75; Piano part: $7.50. I–III. Contains: Bogár, István, *Quick Dance;* Cole, Keith Ramon, *Romance Homage to Peter Ilyich;* Cole, Keith Ramon, *Solstice;* Debussy, Claude, *Jimbo's Lullaby from Children's Corner;* Gretry, Andre, *Air from Richard Coeur de Lion;* Gurlitt, Cornelius, *Andante from First Steps, op. 82;* Hyde, Derek, *Promenade;* Hyde, Derek, *Tuba-Talk;* Mozart, W. A., *Aria O Isis and Osiris;* Norton, Christopher, *Make Mine a Tuba;* Schumann, R., *The Merry Peasant from Album for the Young.*

Watelle, J. *Grand solo de concert.* Editions Salabert.

Watz, Franz. *Concertino for Tuba and Klavier.* Rundel O. J.

Wauldteufel, Emil. *Skaters, The.* arr. Bill Boyd, ed. Charles Daellenbach. Hal Leonard Publishing Corp. 1992. 0:25. I. $B\flat_1$–c. Traditional skating tune in 3/4 time. Easy rhythms. Comes with practice/performance cassette. See: Daellenbach, Charles, *Book of Beginning Tuba Solos,* under Tuba and Keyboard Collections.

Weber. *Campus Queen.* arr. Acton Ostling. CPP/Belwin, Inc. 1969. 2:05. I. C–c. A lot of music in a small solo! Lyrical, Cantabile verse in B♭. Chorus (Allegro) has great opportunity for style. A couple of natural signs; no technical problems. See: Ostling, Acton, *Tuba (Bass) Soloist, Level One,* under Tuba and Keyboard Collections.

Weber, Alain. *Soliloque.* Alphonse Leduc. 1969. $16.00. 6:45. V. G_1–a♯'. A Monsieur Paul Bernard, Professeur au Conservatoire National Supérieur de Musique. "pour Trombone Basse, ou Tuba en Ut, ou Saxhorn en Si♭ et Piano." For French tuba. Strong technique required. See: Thompson/Lemke; *French Music for Low Brass Instruments.*

Weber, Carl Maria von. *Un Adagio.* arr. André Goudenhooft, pno realizations by Augustin Maillard. Gérard Billaudot. 1986. $5.25. 2:00. III. G_1–e. "pour trombone basse (ou tuba) et piano." Classical transcription with a few slurred sixteenth notes with no major technical problems. See: Thompson/Lemke; *French Music for Low Brass Instruments.*

Weber, Carl, arr. *First Solo Album (Bass Clef).* Theodore Presser Company. $1.00. I–II. Easy beginning solos—55 recognizable tunes.

Weber, Carl, arr. *Nineteen Solos for E♭ Bass with Piano Accompaniment.* J. W. Pepper & Son. 1914. Out of Print. Contains: Arban, Jean Baptiste, *Arban's Fantasie Brillante;* Ascher, *Alice, Where Art Thou?;* Bell, J. H., *Sans Pareil;* Bottesini, *Bombardon Polka;* Giovanini, J., *Challenge Concert Polka;* Innes, F. N., *La Coquette Concert Polka;* Jennings, *Pomposo Polka;* Lange, *Heather Rose Caprice;* Legendre, *Souvenir du Poitou;* Mercadante, *Solitude Caprice;* Owen, J. A., *Serenade;* Prendiville, *The Approach of the Lion;* Pryor, Arthur, *Exposition Echoes Polka;* Rollinson, T. H., *Hear Our Prayer-Paraphrase;* Rose, Phil. S., *Chromatic Concert Polka;* Verdi, Giuseppe, *Aria from Falstaff;* Wallace, *Let Me like a Soldier Fall from "Maritana";* Weber, Carl, arr., *The Old Sexton;* Weber, Carl, arr., *Pretty as a Butterfly.*

Weber, Carl, arr. *Old Sexton, The.* J. W. Pepper & Son. 1914. Out of Print. 0:47. II–III. D♭–f. Old English. A few reverse dotted rhythms and syncopations. See: Weber, Carl, *Nineteen Solos for E♭ Bass with Piano Accompaniment,* under Tuba and Keyboard Collections.

Weber, Carl, arr. *Pretty as a Butterfly.* J. W. Pepper & Son. 1914. Out of Print. 2:05. III. E♭–b♭ (d♭'). Dotted rhythms and triplets. See: Weber, Carl, *Nineteen Solos for E♭ Bass with Piano Accompaniment,* under Tuba and Keyboard Collections.

Weber, Fred. *Big Boy.* Belwin. 1945. Out of Print. See: Weber, Fred, *Big Boy,* under Tuba and Band.

Weber, Fred, arr. *Three Favorites.* Belwin, Inc. 1947. Out of Print. 2:00. I. $B\flat_1$–b♭. Includes: "Massa's in the Cold, Cold Ground"; "Grandfathers Clock"; "Marine's Hymn." Beginning solo.

Weber, Fred, and Dorothy Garrett. *Elephant Dance, The.* Belwin Mills, Inc. 1953. Out of Print. 1:11. I–II. D–e♭. Solo in G minor and in 6/8 time. Mostly step-wise motion with a couple of d–D jumps and a few accidentals. Separately published solo by Belwin is Out of Print. See other listings in this section.

Weber, Fred, and Dorothy Garrett. *Elephant Dance, The.* CPP/Belwin, Inc. 1953. See: Lamb, Jack, *Classic Festival Solos,* under Tuba and Keyboard Collections. Also see other listings in this section (Dorothy Garrett not listed in music).

Weber, Fred, and Dorothy Garrett. *Elephant Dance, The.* CPP/Belwin, Inc. 1953. See: Lamb, Jack, *Solo Sounds for Tuba Levels 1–3, Vol. 1,* under Tuba and Keyboard Collections. Also see other listings in this section. Dorothy Garrett not listed in music.

Weber, K. M. *Adagio.* ed. S. Melnikov. Military Band Masters Institute–Moscow. 1957. See: Melnikov, S., *Pieces for Tuba and Piano,* under Tuba and Keyboard Collections.

Weeks, Clifford M. *Triptych for Tuba and Piano.* Robert King Music Co. & Alphonse Leduc. 1964. $3.55. 6:00. C–d1. Three movements: Adagio/Allegro; Lento; Allegro. Substitute parts for baritone/trombone included. Good dialogue between piano and tuba. Not demanding range, not demanding accompaniment. Recorded by Karl Megules.

Weiner, Lawrence. *Serenade.* Southern Music Company. 1989. $5.50. 6:22. IV. G_1–c♯'. Written for William Mayson. Conservative contemporary writing. Some lovely lyrical lines. Slow tempo makes any technical work very approachable. Some "dissonant" intervals requires sharp ear. Good recital material.

Weiner, Lawrence. *Sonata.* Available from Spaeth and Schmid. $26.25.

Weiss, W. H. *Village Blacksmith, The.* arr. Harry Prendiville. Carl Fischer Inc. 1898. Out of Print. 3:35. II. B♭$_1$–d. Easy advanced beginning solo.

Wekselblatt, Herbert. *First Solos for the Tuba Player.* Available from Spaeth and Schmid. $22.00.

Wekselblatt, Herbert. *Solos for the Tuba Player.* Available from Spaeth and Schmid. $23.00.

Wekselblatt, Herbert, arr. *Civil War Medley.* G. Schirmer Inc. 1972. 1:41. II. D–d. Uses "Battle Hymn of the Republic" and "When Johnny Comes Marching Home." Piece consists of just playing through each tune. Battle Hymn is in a slow 4/4 with dotted rhythms. Johnny is in 6/8. See: Wekselblatt, Herbert, *First Solos for the Tuba Player, BB♭,* under Tuba and Keyboard Collections.

Wekselblatt, Herbert, arr. *Hornpipe.* G. Schirmer Inc. 1972. 1:52. III. B♭$_1$–g. Allegro. American folk dance. Show stopper—sounds harder than it really is! Many sixteenth notes that will take some practice, but well worth it. Good recital material, even for advanced players. See: Wekselblatt, Herbert, *First Solos for the Tuba Player, BB♭,* under Tuba and Keyboard Collections.

Wekselblatt, Herbert, arr. *Military Suite.* G. Schirmer Inc. 1972. 1:59. II. E♭–g. March tempo. Cut time medley includes *The Marine's Hymn; The Caisson Song; Anchors Aweigh.* Melody of all three songs separated by an eight-measure piano interlude. Slightly upper range for this level on BB♭ tuba. See: Wekselblatt, Herbert, *First Solos for the Tuba Player, BB♭,* under Tuba and Keyboard Collections.

Wekselblatt, Herbert, arr., and Susan Kagan, pno realizations. *First Solos for the Tuba Player.* G. Schirmer Inc. 1972. $9.95. II–IV. Contains: American Folk Dance, *Hornpipe;* Arban, J. B., *Carnival of Venice, The (Variations);* Bach, J. S., *Musette;* Beethoven, L. v., *Country Dance;* Fischer, Ludwig, *Down in the Deep Deep Cellar;* Gounod, Charles, *March of a Marionette;* Grieg, Edvard, *In the Hall of the Mountain King (from Peer Gynt);* Kagan, Susan, *Oxford Gavotte;* Lully, Jean-Baptiste, *Gavotte;* Mozart, W. A., *Marche (from Les Petits Riens);* Nicolai, Otto, *Falstaff's Drinking Song (from The Merry Wives of Windsor);* Perrie, H. W., *Asleep in the Deep;* Rameau, Jean Philippe, *La Villageoise;* Schumann, Robert, *Happy Farmer, The (Variations from "Album for the Young");* Schumann, Robert, *Wild Horseman, The (from "Album for the Young");* Various Composers, *Seven Duets;* Wekselblatt, Herbert, arr., *Civil War Medley;* Wekselblatt, Herbert, arr., *Military Suite.* See review in *TUBA Journal,* Vol. 12, No. 2, Page 16.

Wekselblatt, Herbert, ed. *Solos for the Tuba Player.* G. Schirmer Inc. 1972. $13.95. II–V. Contains: Bernstein, Leonard, *Waltz for Mippy III;* Mozart, W. A., *O Isis and Osiris (from: The Magic Flute);* Mozart, W. A., *Romanze And Rondo (from: Horn Concerto No. 3);* Shostakovitch, Dimitri, *Polka from: The Age of Gold;* Stamitz, Karl, *Rondo Alla Scherzo (from: Clarinet Concerto in E♭);* Tchaikovsky, Peter I., *None but the Lonely Heart, op. 6;* Wagner, Richard, *Die Meistersinger Von Nurnberg (from the Prelude, Act One);* Wagner, Richard, *Die Walkure (from Act III);* Wagner, Richard, *Siegfried (from Act II, Prelude and First Scene).* See review in *TUBA Journal,* Vol. 12, No. 2, Page 16.

Wells, John. *Tuba Suite.* Available from Spaeth and Schmid. $62.25.

Wenström-Lekare, Lennart. *Sonata for Tuba and Piano.* Available from the composer. 1991.

Wenstrom-Lekare, Lennart. *Three Pieces for Tuba and Piano.* Svens Musik.

Werle, Floyd E. *Concertino for Three Brass and Band.* Bourne Co. 1970. See: Werle, Floyd E., *Concertino for Three Brass and Band,* under Tuba and Band. Recorded by Ken Angerstein.

Werner, Jean-Jacques. *Concerto.* Gérard Billaudot Éditeur. 1996. $27.95. V. 19:00. G_1–g♯'. Souvenirs; Fulgurances; Ténèbres Solaires. Dedicated to Pierre Wissmer. Extremely demanding work for the professional tubist. Many difficult intervals, extreme range demands, complex rhythms, metric shifts, and many musical decisions for optimal performance. Excellent professional recital material. See listing under Music for Tuba and Orchestra and Music for Tuba and Band.

Werner, Jean-Jacques. *Libre-episode. (Free Episode.)* Éditions Musicales Transatlantiques. 1979. $6.75. F_1–a♭'. For French tuba. See: Thompson/Lemke; *French Music for Low Brass Instruments.* See review in *TUBA Journal,* Vol. 8, No. 3, Page 28.

Wessman, Harri. *Sonata for Tuba and Piano.* Finnish Music Information Center. 12:30. 1995. 12:30. IV. (B♭$_1$) F_1–e'. I; II; III. Three solid movements showcasing rhythmic motives. Reasonable range demands with clear melodic writing. Good conservative college-level piece.

Whatley, G. Larry. *Sonata for Tuba and Piano.* TUBA Press. 1991. $8.00. 12:56 (5:12, 3:44, 4:00). IV. B♭$_1$–c'. Three numbered movements. Contemporary melodic language. Some very lyrical playing in second movement. First and third movement has mixed meter throughout.

White, David Ashley. *Dance and Aria.* Shawnee Press, Inc. 1978. $10.00. 6:24. IV–V. A♭$_1$–e♭'. To William Rose. "for Tuba, Tenor Trombone

(Euphonium) or Bass Trombone and Piano." One-movement work including lyrical passages and utilizing mixed meter. Some quick articulations and tempos; a few glissandos. See review in *TUBA Journal,* Vol. 7, No. 4, Page 23.

White, Donald H. *Sonata for Tuba.* Ludwig Music Publishing Company. 1979. $16.00. 15:08 (5:25, 5:53, 4:00). V. F_1–a♭'. Commissioned by Custom Music Company, sole distributors of Hirsbrunner, Rudolf Meinl, and Sanders Tubas, in cooperation with Tubists Universal Brotherhood Association. Premiered by Steven Bryant, tuba, and Jean Barr, piano; May 19, 1980, at the Second National Tuba-Euphonium Symposium-Workshop; University of North Texas, Denton, Tex. Major work for tuba and piano. First movement: Syncopation and beat displacements. Double tonguing and large interval jumps. Second movement: Lyrical writing. Third movement: Very fast tempo marking. Mixed meter: 7/8 and 2/4 time. Very quick articulations. Requires strong technique and strong accompanist. Recorded by: Fritz Kaenzig.

White, John. *Sonata no. 3 "Basingstoke."* Warwick Music Limited. $17.

Widmer, Ernst. *Torre Aludu.* Fundação Nacional De Arte. 1985. 4:30. IV. E_1–d'. Conservative tempos. No major technical problems. Optional glissandos. Conservative contemporary melodic language.

Wiegand, George. *Levithan, The.* J. R. Lafleur & Son & Harry Coleman. 1894. Out of Print. 5:00. IV. B♭$_1$–e♭'. "Fantasia for E♭ Tuba." Old traditional-style solo with cadenza. See: Wiegand, George, *Levithan, The,* under Tuba and Band.

Wiggins, Bram. *Preludes for Pachyderms.* Available from Spaeth and Schmid. $14.00.

Wiggins, Bram. *The Tuba Player's Debut.* Available from Spaeth and Schmid. $11.00.

Wigy, Fr. *Legende.* Available from Spaeth and Schmid. $8.00.

Wilder, Alec. *Concerto for Tuba and Concert Band.* tr. Robert George Waddell. Margun Music, Incorporated. 1965. $15.00. For Harvey Phillips. See: Wilder, Alec, *Concerto for Tuba and Concert Band,* under Tuba and Band. Also see review in *TUBA Journal,* Vol. 10, No. 3, Page 22.

Wilder, Alec. *Elegy for the Whale.* Margun Music, Incorporated. 1982. $6.00. See: Wilder, Alec, *Elegy for the Whale,* under Tuba and Orchestra. Also see review in *TUBA Journal,* Vol. 10, No. 3, Page 23.

Wilder, Alec. *Encore Piece for Tuba and Piano.* ed. Gunther Schuller. Margun Music, Incorporated. 1981. $5.00. 0:55. V. A_1–a♭'. A one-minute showcase of flexibility and technique. Arpeggios, fast articulations, trills, glissando, extreme range. Recorded by Roger Bobo.

Wilder, Alec. *Small Suite for Bass (Tuba) and Piano.* ed. Gunther Schuller. Margun Music, Incorporated. 1981. $9.00. 10:27 (2:31, 2:52, 2:18, 2:26). IV–V. F♯$_1$–f♯' (a'). Smoothly; Romantically; Flowingly; Quasi Jazz. for Gary Karr. Original copyright date was 1963. Written with the breathing requirements of a string bass in mind—not many rests. Some sustained upper tessitura in second movement. Very playable, lyrical solo; no major technical problems other than wide range.

Wilder, Alec. *Sonata for Tuba and Piano.* Mentor Music. 1963. $9.00. 10:31 (3:12, 2:11, 3:23, 1:45). IV. F_1–d'. For Harvey Phillips. Lovely solo. Lyrical playing combined with some technical demands: flexibility and strong stylistic sense. Switching between a fast technical section and a swing section in second movement. Good recital material. See: Wilder, Alec, *Sonata for Tuba and Piano,* under Tuba and Orchestra. Also see: Bird, Gary, ed.; *Program Notes for the Solo Tuba.* Recorded by: Harvey Phillips.

Wilder, Alec. *Sonata No. 2 for Tuba and Piano.* Margun Music, Incorporated. 1976. $15.00. 17:27 (3:53, 2:37, 5:23, 3:14, 2:20). IV–V. G_1–a♭'. Espressivo; Jazz Style; Slowly; Air; Energetically. For Lottie Phillips. Dedicated to Harvey Phillips's mother. Completed 1975. Big piece utilizing strong technique combined with mature, sensitive, lyrical playing.

Wilder, Alec. *Song for Carol.* Margun Music, Incorporated. 1981. $2.00. 2:15. IV. A_1–f'. Tenderly. Upper tessitura. All tenuto and slurred. Lovely lyrical tune dedicated to Carol Phillips. Recorded by Harvey Phillips.

Wilder, Alec. *Suite No. 1 for Tuba and Piano ("Effie Suite").* Margun Music, Incorporated. 1968. $11.00. 11:00. IV. F_1–e'. Effie Chases a Monkey; Effie Falls in Love; Effie Takes a Dancing Lesson; Effie Joins the Carnival; Effie Goes Folk Dancing; Effie Sings a Lullaby. One of the most popular tuba and piano solos, for good musical reasons. Requires the entire spectrum from the tuba: Very vocal, lyrical playing; quick articulated playing; slurred flexibility; and most importantly, an imaginative, lyrical approach. Great crowd pleaser—excellent recital material. Also see: Wilder, Alec, *Suite No. 1 for Tuba and Orchestra "Effie,"* under Tuba and Orchestra. Also see: Wilder, Alec, *Effie Joins the Carnival from Suite No. 1,* and Wilder, Alec, *Suite No. 1 "Effie" for Tuba and Woodwind Quintet,* under Tuba and Mixed Ensemble. Also see: Bird, Gary, ed.; *Program Notes for the Solo Tuba.* Recorded by Roger Bobo, Walter Hilgers, Michael Lind, Harvey Phillips.

Wilder, Alec. *Suite No. 2 for Tuba and Piano (Jesse Suite).* Margun Music. 1964. 4:25 (0:50, 1:18, 0:42, 1:35). IV. C–e'. Four numbered movements. Written on the occasion of the birth of Jesse Emmett Phillips, Feb. 14, 1964. In preparation—Available Fall 1993. Was published by Sam Fox Publishing. Playful solo requiring lyrical playing and quick articulations. Although titled "Suite No. 2," this is actually the third suite for tuba and piano composed by Alec Wilder. Recorded by Harvey Phillips.

Wilder, Alec. *Suite No. 3 for Tuba and Piano "Suite for Little Harvey."* Margun Music, Incorporated. 1980. $6.50. 4:53 (1:32, 0:57, 1:34, 0:50). IV–V. C–a♭'. Four numbered movements: Andantino; II; Moderato; IV. Written on the occasion of the birth of Harvey Gene Phillips, Jr., Sept. 16, 1966. Original copyright date was 1966. Some quick articulations and lyrical playing. Upper tessitura. Last movement in 5/4 time with flutter tonguing on g♭'. Although titled "Suite No. 3," this is actually the fourth suite for tuba and piano composed by Alec Wilder. Recorded by Harvey Phillips.

Wilder, Alec. *Suite No. 4 for Tuba and Piano "Thomas Suite."* Margun Music, Incorporated. 1982. $6.50. 2:20 (0:41, 1:10, 0:33, 0:26). IV. D_1–e'. Four numbered movements. Written on the occasion of the birth of Thomas Alexander Phillips, Sept. 23, 1968. Upper tessitura (only one really low pitch—D_1). Very lyrical playing required in this short Suite. Although titled "Suite No. 4," this is actually the fifth suite for tuba and piano composed by Alec Wilder. Recorded by Harvey Phillips.

Wilder, Alec. *Suite No. 5 for Tuba and Piano (Ethan Ayer).* Margun Music, Incorporated. 1964. $10.00. 5:00. IV–V. $A♭_1$–e♭'. Dedicated to a loyal friend. Written during a New York Brass Quintet tour in 1963. Ethan Ayer was a big arts philanthropist. Although titled "Suite No. 5," this is actually the second suite for tuba and piano composed by Alec Wilder. Recorded by Harvey Phillips.

Wiley, Frank. *Caverns.* Ludwig Music Publishing Company. $7.95.

Wilhelm, Rolf. *Concertino for Tuba and Winds.* Available from Tuba Center. 1983. Written for Robert Tucci. See: Wilhelm, Rolf, *Concertino for Tuba and Winds,* under Tuba and Band. Also see: Bird, Gary, ed.; *Program Notes for the Solo Tuba.* Recorded by Michael Bunn, Jens Bjørn-Larsen.

Wilkenschildt, Georg. *Arie and Humuresque.* MS Publications.

Williams, Ernest. *Concerto No. 2.* Charles Colin Publishing. 1937. $5.95. IV. ($E♭_1$) A_1–c'. Allegro moderato; Adagio; Rondo. Transposed version of Ernest Williams's second trumpet concerto. Technical challenges throughout. See: Williams, Ernest, *Concerto No. 2,* under Tuba and Band.

Williams, John. *Concerto for Tuba and Orchestra.* Hal Leonard Corporation. 1988. $19.95. 18:35. F_1–g'. Allegro Moderato; Andante; Allegro Molto. Dedicated to Chester Schmitz. See listing under Music for Tuba and Orchestra.

Winteregg, Steven. *Concerto for Tuba.* Tuba-Euphonium Press. 1998. 14:00. V. $B♭_2$–f'. Heroic; Lyric; Dramatic. Dedicated to Samuel Gnagey, Samuel Green, and Robert Leblanc. Dramatic work requiring great agility and dynamic control. Technically demanding with angular melodic lines. See listing under Music for Tuba and Orchestra.

Winteregg, Steven. *Three Movements for Tuba and Piano.* Pastiche Music. 1977. 6:02 (1:47, 2:46, 1:29). IV. F_1–e'. Three numbered movements. Meter changes. Quick articulations in last movement. Good recital material.

Witthauer, Johann Georg. *Allegretto und Gavotte.* arr. Gerd Philipp. Hofmeister. 1993. 1:53 (1:00, 0:53). II. D♭–f. Allegretto; Gavotte. In D♭ major and B♭ minor respectively. See: Meschke, Dieter, *Zum Uben und Vorspielen/ B-Tuba,* under Tuba and Keyboard Collections.

Woestyne, David Van de. *Muziek (1976).* Centre Belge de Documentation Musicale. 1977. 6:30. IV. A_1–g♭'. "voor tuba-saxhorn (c) en piano." Composed in 1976. Better on F tuba—upper tessitura throughout.

Wolf, Hugo. *Der Genesene an die Hoffnung.* arr. Walter Hilgers. Editions Marc Reift. 1998. $9.50. 4:30. III. G–f'. A direct transcription of the original song from the Mörike-Lieder. Mörike's text has been included under the tuba part as a guideline for phrasing. Recorded by Walter Hilgers.

Woodward, James. *Tuba Concerto.* Tuba-Euphonium Press. 2000. 20:00. V. E_1–a'. Joyously; Freely; Slowly, Freely; Brilliantly. Dedicated to Alan Baer. Very demanding work for tuba and orchestra. The piano reduction by the composer is quite workable. Extreme range demands and great technical facility required. See listing under Music for Tuba and Orchestra.

Woolf, Gregory. *Per Tuba ad Astram.* Previously available from the composer. For Daniel Perantoni. See: Woolf, Gregory, *Per Tuba ad Astram,* under Tuba and Orchestra.

Worth, George E. *Serpent of the Brass.* Rubank, Inc. 1942. $2.00. 2:00. II–III. D–f. "Solo for E♭ or BB♭ Bass." Was copyright 1941 by George E. Worth. Some optional triple tonguing. Not very technically demanding.

Wunder, Richard. *Song after Battle for Tuba and Piano.* Manuscript available from the composer. ca. 1983. A_1–e'. Written for Gene Pokorny. Battle-Song. See review in *TUBA Journal,* Vol. 10, No. 4, Page 34.

Wurmser, Lucien. *Solo de Concourts.* Gérard Billaudot/ Andrieu Freres. 1955. $3.50. 2:56. III. G–f'. à Mr Fernamd Anne, President Fon Stes Mles de Normandie. Largement Quasi récitativo/Allegro. "Basse ou Baryton ou Saxo ténor, Basson ou Tuba ou Trombones." French tuba tessitura. Recitative-like passages combined with lyrical lines. Good recital material. Busy accompaniment part.

Wurmser, Lucien. *Tendres Mélodies.* Gérard Billaudot. 1956. $3.50. 1:48 (1:01, 0:47). III. F–f'. Two movements. Lent; Andante. en hommage à Mr Adrien Maltête President de la Féderation des societés musicales du Sud-Ouest. "Petites Pièces De Concours." "Pour Basse si♭ ou Baryton ou saxo si♭ ou trombone, basson ou tuba." French tuba tessitura. Two lyrical songs. Depending on instrument chosen, only technical problem is that of tessitura.

Wyss. *The Thomas Wyss Tuba Collection (Tuba in Es).* Available from Spaeth and Schmid. $15.75.

Yarrow, Peter, and Leonard Lipton. *Puff (The Magic Dragon).* arr. Richard Maltby. Warner Bros. 1967. See: Yarrow, Peter, and Leonard Lipton, *Puff (The Magic Dragon),* under Tuba and Band.

Yasumoto, Hiroyuki, arr. *Barcarolle for Tuba.* Toa Music International Co. 1986. 1:27. III. C–c'. Cantabile. Very lyrical solo requiring flexibility. See: Yasumoto, Hiroyuki, *Tuba Volume #1,* under Tuba and Keyboard Collections.

Yasumoto, Hiroyuki, arr. *Londonderry Air.* Toa Music International Co. 1986. 2:14. II–III. C–g. Andante sostenuto. "Irish Tune." Very legato with a strong vocal sense. No technical problems. See: Yasumoto, Hiroyuki, *Tuba Volume #1,* under Tuba and Keyboard Collections.

Yasumoto, Hiroyuki, arr. *Nobody Knows the Trouble I've Seen.* Toa Music International Co. 1986. 1:50. II. F–f. Religioso. "Negro Spirituals." All slurred with some syncopation. No technical problems. See: Yasumoto, Hiroyuki, *Tuba Volume #1,* under Tuba and Keyboard Collections.

Yasumoto, Hiroyuki, arr. *Tuba Volume #1.* Toa Music International Co. 1986. II–IV. Contains: Bizet, G., *Habanera from Carmen;* Bland, J., *Carry Me Back to Old Virginny;* Boccherini, L., *Menuette;* Couperin, F., *Concertpièce;* Eccles, H., *First and Second Movements from Violin Sonata;* Foster, Stephen C., *Foster Medley;* Giordani, Giuseppe, *Caro mio ben;* Martini, J. P. E., *Piacer d'Aamor;* Saint-Saëns, C., *Elephant from Carnival of Animals;* Wagner, Richard, *Die Meistersinger von Nürnberg;* Wagner, Richard, *O du mein holcler Abendstern, from "Tanhöuser";* Yasumoto, Hiroyuki, arr., *Barcarolle for Tuba;* Yasumoto, Hiroyuki, arr., *Londonderry Air;* Yasumoto, Hiroyuki, arr., *Nobody Knows the Trouble I've Seen.*

Yasumoto, Hiroyuki, arr. *Tuba Volume #2.* Toa Music International Co. 1989. III–IV. Contains: Tanimunei, Kocho, *Fantasy for Tuba and Piano;* Handel, G. F., *Concerto No. 3 for Tuba and String Orchestra;* Kopprasch, C., *Nr. 15, Etüden für Tuba;* Kopprasch, C., *Nr. 19, Etüden für Tuba;* Kreisler, F., *Libesfreud;* Lennon, John, and Paul McCartney, *Yesterday;* Marcello, B., *Sonata I, from 6 Solos for a Violoncello;* McHugh, Jim, and Dorothy Fields, *On the Sunny Side of the Street;* Reiche, E., *Adagio from Concerto No. 2;* Schumann, Robert, *Träumeri.*

Yasumoto, Hiroyuki, arr. *Tuba Volume #3.* Toa Music International Co. 1989. III–IV. Contains: Bach, J. S., *Sarabande (from BWV 1013 Solo Tuba);* Bordogni, G. M., *No. 10 from 24 Easy Vocalises;* Bordogni, G. M., *No. 4 from 24 Easy Vocalises;* Bordogni, G. M., *No. 9 from 24 Easy Vocalises;* Bozza, Eugène, *Prélude et Allegro;* Censhu, Jiro, *Verdurous Aubade for Tuba and Piano;* Konagaya, Soichi, *Celebration for Tuba and Piano;* Kreisler, Fritz, *Schön Rosmarin;* Lennon, John, and Paul McCartney, *Hey Jude!;* Livingston, J., and R. Evans, *To Each His Own;* Schubert, F., *Ständchen.*

Yoffe, Shlomo. *Andante and Rondo.* Kibutz Movement League of Composers. Recorded by Adi Hershko.

York, Barbara. *Arioso Gloria.* Tuba-Euphonium Press. 2003. 4:30. III. $B\flat_1$–c'. Dedicated to Michael Fischer. One-movement work in compound meter.

York, Barbara. *Sea Dreams; Three Pieces for Tuba and Piano.* Tuba-Euphonium Press. 2002. 7:00. III–IV. F_1–b♭. Down Under; Whales; Dolphins. Dedicated to Michael Fischer. Three programmatic movements requiring some technical facility. Written in the middle to low tessitura.

Yuhas, D. *Three Miniatures for Tuba and Piano.* Manuscript. 2:38 (0:49, 1:17, 0:32). IV. $B\flat_1$–a. Three numbered movements. Conservative contemporary melodic language. Some mixed meters.

Zajaczek, Roman. *Tema Cantabile con Piernicazioni per tuba universale e pianoforte.* Recorded by Zdizislaw Piernik.

Zámencník. *Concertino.* Editions Bim. 1999. $31.70. 13:00. III–IV. $F\sharp_1$–b♭'. Preludio; Canzona I; Quasi danza; Canzona II; Finale. Composed for the International Competition, "Mährischer Herbst," Brno 2000. First movement is a neoclassic, rhythmical prelude interspersed with short cadenzas; second movement is a lyrical song in a tonal setting; third movement a scherzando dance with rhythms that often land on the wrong foot; fourth movement is a song built on fourths harmonically; Finale is a quick dialogue with the piano.

Zaninelli, Luigi. *Peg Leg Pete.* Boosey & Hawkes, Inc. 1963. $7.00. "Burla for Tuba and Piano." See: Zaninelli, Luigi, *Peg Leg Pete,* under Tuba and Band.

Zaninelli. Luigi. *Mamminga Rag.* Theodore Presser. 1991. $10.95. 3:00. C_1–a. Dedicated to Kevin and Sara. Part available for euphonium and trombone in this edition. A good concert selection in the ragtime vein. Very good low-register technique required for the tuba version. A good closing piece for a recital.

Zbar. *Jeu 3.* Alphonse Leduc. $12.80.

Zeman, Thomas. *Sonata.* Available from the composer. 1967. 12:00. IV–V. C_1–e'. Andante; Vivace; Allegro. For Winston Morris. Major piece; contemporary writing. Requires mute and strong accompanist.

Zettler, Richard. *Alt und New für Zwei.* Thomi-Berg.

Zettler, Richard. *Concerto classico.* Available from Spaeth and Schmid. $22.00.

Zhurbin, Lev. *Sonata for Tuba and Piano.* Tuba-Euphonium Press. 2000. 5:30. IV. $G\flat_1$–f'. Commissioned by and dedicated to Benjamin Massin. Jazz-influenced work with some free improvisation in the piano part. Large leaps and dynamic contrasts.

Ziev. *Divertimento.* Available from Spaeth and Schmid. $20.25.

Zinos, Fredrick. *Elegy for Tuba and Piano.* Neil A. Kjos Music Company. 1968. $1.50. 6:35. III–IV. A_1–b (c♭'). Respectfully Dedicated to Barton Cummings. One-movement work requiring flexibility and lyrical approach. Conservative contemporary melodic writing. Conservative range. Recorded by Barton Cummings.

Zoccatelli, V. *Ossur.* Available from Spaeth and Schmid. $8.50.

Zuerev, V. *Hungarian Melody.* ed. V. Mitjagina. Muzkya, Moscow. 1969. 1:23. III–IV. G_1–a. Mournful, lyrical tune with some syncopation. See: Mitjagina, V., ed., *Pieces for Tuba and Piano,* under Tuba and Keyboard Collections.

Zuerev, V. *Russian Dance.* ed. V. Mitjagina. Muzkya, Moscow. 1969. 2:19. II–III. G_1–g. Simple tune with easy melody and rhythms. See: Mitjagina, V., ed., *Pieces for Tuba and Piano,* under Tuba and Keyboard Collections.

Zverev, V. *Concertino.* ed. G. Voronov. Moscow Muzyka. 1984. See: Voronov, G, *Works for Tuba and Piano by Russian Composers,* under Tuba and Keyboard Collections.

Zverev, V. *Song.* ed. A. Lebedev. Moscow Muzyka. 1984. 0:52. III. $B\flat_1$–g. A song of strength. In C minor and 3/4 time. See: Lebedev, A., *Tuba Tutor Vol. 1,* under Tuba and Keyboard Collections.

Works Listed by Title

For annotations, see Works Listed by Composer, Tuba and Keyboard Collections, and Tuba and Keyboard Other than Piano. Titles beginning with an English article are alphabetized according to the first substantive word.

A

A Quia, Debons, Eddy.
Abide with Me, Lyte, H., and Monk, W.
Abide with Me, Monk (arr. David E. Smith).
Abide with Me, Monk, W. H.
Abide with Me, Smith, Claude T.
Abuto, Delgiudice, Michel.
Acrobatics, David Uber.
Adagietto from L'Arlésienne, Bizet, Georges.
Adagio, Bach, J. S. (Walter Hilgers).
Adagio, Bach, Johann Sabastian.
Adagio, Bach, Johann Sebastian (arr. Walter Hilgers).
Adagio, Bartok, Bela.
Adagio, Lebedev, A. (arr.).
Adagio, Mozart, W. A. (arr. Hilgers).
Adagio, Spohr, Ludwig.
Adagio, Weber, K. M.
Adagio and Allegretto, Gluck (arr. Willard Musser).
Adagio and Allegro, Schumann, Robert.
Adagio and Allegro, Schumann, Robert (arr. Cooley).
Adagio and Allegro, Telemann, Georg Philipp.
Adagio and Allegro from Sonata No. 7, Handel, George Frederick.
Adagio and Finale from Concertino, Gaucet, Charles.
Adagio and Scherzo from Sonata C Minor, Barber, S.
Adagio et Allegro, Bartsch, Ch.
Adagio for Tuba and Piano, Shostakovitch, Dimitri.
Adagio from Concerto No. 2, Reiche, E.
Adagio from Sonata C-Dur, Marcello, Benedetto.
Adagio from the Ballet "Till Eulenspigel," Kotshetov, V.
Adagio KV 261; Rondo KV 269; Rondo KV 373, Mozart, W. A. (arr. Douay).
Adagio KV 580a, Mozart, W. A. (arr. Walter Hilgers).
Adonis, Buchtel, Forrest Lawrence.
Adventure, Rønnes, Robert.
Adventure for Tuba and Piano, Ronnes, Robert.
Aeola, Martin, Carroll.
After Work, Schubert, Franz (arr. David Green).
Ah! Vous dirai-je maman, Mozart, W. A. (arr. Arnaud Boukhitine).
Ah! vous dirai-je maman, Reynaud, J.
Air, Aubert, Jacques.
Air, Bach (ed. Marlatt, David).
Air, Désenclos, A.
Air, Gluck, Chr.
Air, Handel.
Air, Pergolesi, Giovanni Battista.
Air, Rakov, N.
Air and Bouree, Bach, Johann Sabastian.
Air and Galumph, Bourgeois, Derek.
Air de Don José (extrait de Carmen), Bizet, G. (arr. Patrice Sciortino).
Air de Papageno (extrait de la flûte enchantée), Mozart, W. A. (arr. Patrice Sciortino).
Air du Toreador (extrait de Carmen), Bizet, G. (arr. Patrice Sciortino).
Air et Final, Planel, Robert.
Air from "Comus," Arne, Thomas A.
Air from "Richard Coeur de Lion," Gretry, Andre.
Air from the Opera "Halka," An, Moniushko, S.
Air Gai, Berlioz, G. P.

Air Varie, Op. 21, Klose, Hyacinthe.
Ajax, Buchtel, Forrest Lawrence.
Albertie (Tu in Es), Stephens.
Alborada, Goodwin, Gordon.
Ali-Baba, Delgiudice, Michel.
Alice, Where Art Thou? Ascher.
All 'Antica, Goeyens, A.
All People That on Earth Do Dwell, Borton, Allen (arr.).
All the world is full of lovers, Mozart, Wolfgang Amadeus.
All through the Night, Kinyon, John (arr.).
All through the Night, Ostling, Acton (arr.).
Alla Cacia, Cabus.
Alla Siciliana, Albian, Franco.
Allegretto animato, Concone, Giuseppe.
Allegretto Comodo, Quérat, Marcel.
Allegretto Grazioso, Kreisler, Alexander von.
Allegretto grazioso, Stanley, John.
Allegretto und Gavotte, Witthauer, Johann Georg.
Allegro, Fiocco, J. H.
Allegro, Fux, Johann Joseph.
Allegro, Handel, George Frederick.
Allegro, Mozart, Wolfgang Amadeus.
Allegro, Saint-Saëns, Camille.
Allegro, Vivaldi (ed. Marlatt, David).
Allegro and Finale, Bozza, Eugène.
Allegro and Minuet, Haydn, Franz Joseph.
Allegro et Finale, Bozza, Eugène.
Allegro from Concerto in F Minor, Handel, George Frederick.
Allegro (from Sonata No. 3), Vivaldi, Antonio.
Allegro non Troppo, Seitz (arr. Willard Musser).
Allegro Spiritoso, Senaillè, Jean Baptiste.
Allegro Vivace, for Tuba and Four Horns (or Piano), Hidas, Frigyes.
Alleluja, Exultate, Mozart, Wolfgang Amadeus.
Allemande, Franck, Melchior.
Allemande, Gervaise, Claude (arr. Patrice Sciortino).
Alley Cat, Bjorn, Frank.
Almighty, The, Borton, Allen (arr.).
Alt und New für Zwei, Zettler, Richard.
Altdeutscher Tanz (Narrentanz), Schwotzer, Stephan (arr.).
Alte Bekannte, Kubes, Ladislav.
Amarilli, Mia Bella, Caccini, Giulia.
Amarilli, Mia Bella, Caccini, Giulio.
Amazing Grace, Borton, Allen (arr.).
Amazing Grace, Newton, John.
Ambitos, Costa Ciscar, Francisco Javier.
America, Carey, Henry, and Smith, Samuel.
America the Beautiful, Ward, S. A.
"America" Variations for Winds, Gerschefski, Edwin.
American Fantasy, Brandon, Sy.
Amorous Play, Eerola, Lasse.
Anapausis, Meunier, Gérard.
Ancient Greek Melody, An, Maganini, Quinto.
And Then There Were Six, Brown, Newel Kay.
Andante, Handel, George Frederick.
Andante, Haydn, Franz Joseph.
Andante, Leduc.
Andante, Roikjer, Kjell.
Andante, Tchérépnine, Alexandre.
Andante, Op. 53, Douliez, Victor.
Andante and Allegretto, Pascuzzi, Gregory.
Andante and Allegro, Clérisse, Robert.
Andante and Allegro, Scott, Kathleen.
Andante and Allegro, Telemann, Georg Philipp.
Andante and Allegro for Tuba and Piano, Jones, Roger.
Andante and Allegro Spiritoso, Senaillé, Jean-Baptiste.
Andante and Allegro Spiritoso (B♭ Bass), Senaillé, Jean-Baptiste (arr. Mortimer).
Andante and Rondo, Yoffe, Shlomo.
Andante and Rondo from Concerto for Double Bass, Capuzzi, Antonio.
Andante Cantabile, Tchaikovsky, Peter I.
Andante Cantabile from Concerto, Rimsky-Korsakov, N.
Andante et Allegro, Barraine, Elsa Jacqueline.
Andante et Allegro, Lantier, Pierre.
Andante from "First Steps" Op. 82, Gurlitt, Cornelius.
Andante Tranquillo, McKimm, Barry.
Andantino, Poulton.
Anitra's Dance, Grieg (ed. Marlatt, David).
Annie Lisle, Thompson, H. S.
Antre De Polypheme, L', Delgiudice, Michel.
Apollo, Buchtel, Forrest Lawrence.
Apopol, Waignein, André.
Approach of the Lion, The, Prendiville.
Aprés un Rêve, Faure, G. (arr. Patrick Sheridan).
Après une Lecture de Goldoni: Fantaisie dans le style du XVIII siècle, Margoni, Alain.
Apres-Midi d'une Crocodille, L', Maganini, Quinto.
Aquarium, Proust, Pascal (Robert Martin Editions).
Arabesque V, Nodaïra, Ichiro.
Arban's Fantasie Brillante, Arban, Jean Baptiste.
Arbutus, Vander Cook, H. A.
Arcades I, Kellaway, Roger.
Archer, The, Buchtel, Forrest Lawrence.
Aria, Bach, J. S. (arr. Patrice Sciortino).
Aria, Scarlatti, Alessandro.
Aria for Tuba and Piano, Hartley, Walter S.
Aria from "Don Carlos," Verdi, Giuseppe.
Aria from "Elias," Mendelssohn, Felix.
Aria from Falstaff, Verdi, Giuseppe.
Aria from "Judas Maccabeus," Handel, George Frederick.
Aria from La Clemenza di Tito, Mozart, W. A.
Aria from La Clemenza di Tito, Mozart, Wolfgang Amadeus.
Aria from the Opera "Three Lives," Taktakishvili, O.
Aria "O Isis and Osiris," Mozart, Wolfgang Amadeus.
Aria of the King Rene, Tchaikovsky, Peter I.
Arie, Pergolesi, Giovanni Battista.
Arie and Humuresque, Wilkenschildt, Georg.

Arie Janeks Aus Der Oper "Im Brunnen," Blodek, Vilém.
Arietta, Giordani, Giuseppe.
Ariette, Huuck, Reinhard.
Arioso, Bach, J. S. (arr. Øystein Baadsvik).
Arioso, Benson, Warren.
Arioso, Handel, George Frederick.
Arioso and Caprice, Barnes, Clifford P.
Arioso from the Opera "Jolanta," Tchaikovsky, Peter I.
Arioso Gloria, York, Barbara.
Arise Ye Subterranean Winds, Purcell, Henry.
Arm, Arm, Ye Brave from "Judas Maccabeus," Handel, George Frederick.
Artist's Life, Strauss.
As When the Dove, Handel, G. F. (arr. Velvet Brown).
Ash Grove, The, Kinyon, John (arr.).
Asleep in the Deep, Petrie, H. W.
At the Ball, Buchtel, Forrest Lawrence.
At the Dance, Tchaikovsky, Peter I.
A-Tisket, A-Tasket, Feldstein, Sandy (arr.).
"Atlas" Grand Air varié, de Ville, Paul (arr.).
Attila, Buchtel, Forrest Lawrence.
Au Coeur de la Nuit, Steckar, Franck.
. . . Au fond des bois, Naulais, Jerôme (Robert Martin Editions).
Au Temps De La Cour, Brouquières, Jean.
Auf Flügeln des Gesanges (On Wings of Song), Mendelssohn, Felix (arr. John Glenesk Mortimer).
Auld Lang Syne, DeLamater, E. (arr.).
Auld Lang Syne, Kinyon, John (arr.).
Auld Lang Syne, Lamater.
Aura Lee, Feldstein, Sandy (arr.).
Aura Lee, Poulton.
Aurora, Ostling, Acton.
Automne, Damase, Jean-Michel.
Autumn Afternoon, Uber, David.
Autumn Moods, Miserendino, Joe.
Autumn Story, Ridout, Alan.
Ave Maria, Bach, J. S. (arr. Charles Gounod, tran. Patrick Sheridan).
Ave Maria, Gounod, Charles (J. S. Bach) (arr. Patrice Sciortino).
Ave Maria, Schubert, Franz.
Ave Maria, Schubert, Franz (arr. Kalke).
Ave Maria, Schubert, Franz (arr. Øystein Baadsvik).
Ave Maria from "6 Sonnets," Toldra, Eduardo.
Ave Verum, Mozart, W. A. (arr. Patrice Sciortino).
Away in a Manger, Borton, Allen (arr.).
Away in a Manger, Smith, David E. (arr.).
Away in a Manger, Traditional (arr. David E. Smith).
Azure Etudes, Ross, Walter.

B

Baa, Baa Black Sheep, Feldstein, Sandy (arr.).
Bacchanale, Couperin, Francois (arr. Dishinger).
Badinerie, Bach, J. S. (arr. John Glenesk Mortimer).
Bagatelles, Donahue, Robert.
Bagatelles for Tuba, Jacob, Gordon.
Baladins, Gotkovsky, Ida.
Baleine bleue, La, Delgiudice, Michel.
Balkan's Ayers Rock, Jevtic, Ivan.
Ballad and Presto Dance, Smith, Claude T.
Ballad for Tuba, Christensen, James.
Ballad of Enob Mort, The, Uber, David.
Ballada, Duntriev, G.
Ballade, Arensky, A.
Ballade, Berlin, A.
Ballade, Krzywicki, Jan.
Ballade, Szentpáli, Roland.
Ballade, Vanherenthals, J.
Ballade, Vergauwen, A.
Ballade Du Moigne Que Nostre Dame Delivera Dou Dyable, Joubert, Claude-Henry.
Ballade pour Tuba, Cadee, Jean-Louis.
Ballerina, The, Buchtel, Forrest Lawrence.
Bamboola, Ameller, André.
Bank Holiday Suite, Lewis, Paul.
Barbarossa-Air Varie, Barnhouse, Charles Lloyd.
Barcarolle et Chanson Bachique, Semler-Collery, Jules.
Barcarolle for Tuba, Yasumoto, Hiroyuki (arr.).
Bärentanz, Heinl, Otto.
Barockes Konzert, Hlouschek, Theodor.
Basilio Aria, Rossini, Gioacchino.
Bass in the Ballroom, The, Newsome, Roy.
Bass Solo Polka, Berg, Thomas.
Bassenparade, Jakma, Henk.
Basses Berserk, Bennett, David.
Bassette, Delbecq, Laurent.
Bassey Blues, Christensen, James.
Bassistengruß, Raich.
Basso Brazilio, Newsome, Roy.
Basso Concertino, Fritze, Gregory.
Basso Profundo, Briegel, George F.
Basso Tomaso, Frackenpohl, Arthur.
Bassutecy, Ameller, André.
Batifol, Ameller, André.
Bayou Legend for Solo Tuba and Piano, Uber, David.
Bayrische Polka, Lohmann, Georg.
Be Not Shy, My Pretty One, Rubenstein, Anton.
Beatles, The, Lennon, John, and McCartney, Paul (arr. John Glenesk Mortimer).
Beautiful Brown Eyes, Feldstein, Sandy (arr.).
Bedouin Love Song, Pinsuti, Ciro.
Beelzebub, Catozzi, A.
Beelezebub Dances, Boyle, Rory.
Behemoth, Vander Cook, H. A.
Belle Province: Hauterive, Ameller, André.
Beloved from Afar, Beethoven, Ludwig von.
Bendemeer's Stream, Kinyon, John (arr.).
Beneath the Cross of Jesus, Borton, Allen (arr.).
Berceuse, Stravinsky, Igor.
Bicycle Built for Two, Dacre, Harry.
Bifurcation, Baader-Nobs, Heidi.
Big Bear Suite, Dutillet, Jacques.
Big Boy, Weber, Fred.
Big Joe, the Tuba, Lavalle, Paul, and Tarto, Joe.

Billboard, Klohr.
Bill's Tune, Constantino, Joseph G.
Billy and His Sweetheart, Copland, Aaron (arr. Quincy Hilliard).
Billy Blowhard, Kottaun, Celian.
Black Holes in Space, Belden, George R.
Blessed Assurance, Borton, Allen (arr.).
Blow the Man Down, Ostling, Acton (arr.).
Blow the Man Down, Walters, Harold L. (arr.).
Blue Bells of Scotland, Pryor, Arthur (arr. Alan Lourens).
Blue Bells of Scotland, Swanson, Ken (arr.).
Blue Bells of Scotland, The, Kinyon, John (arr.).
Blue Moon, Hart, Lorenz, and Rodgers, Richard.
Blues, Goddard, Mark.
Bold and Brave, Storm, Charles W.
Bolero, Berlioz, Hector (arr. Dishinger).
Bombardon Polka, Bottesini.
Bombastic Bombardon, Siebert, Edrich.
Bombastoso, Vander Cook, H. A.
Boogie, Goddard, Mark.
Book of Beginning Tuba Solos, Daellenbach, Charles (arr.).
Book of Easy Tuba Solos, Daellenbach, Charles (arr.).
Boosey's Bombardon Solo Album, Hume, James Ord (arr.).
Bordogni Medley, Bordogni, Marco.
Bouquet for Basses, Storm, Charles W.
Bouree, Bach, Johann Sabastian.
Bourrée, Damase, Jean-Michel.
Bourrée, Handel, George Frederick.
Bourrée, Krebs, Johann Ludwig.
Bourrée, Mozart, Leopold.
Bourèe burlesque, Lundin, Dag.
Brass: Series One, First and Second Grades, Australian Music Examinations Board.
Brass: Series One, Third and Fourth Grades, Australian Music Examinations Board.
Brass Talk, Pethel, James.
Bravaccio, Fayeulle, Roger.
Break Thou the Bread of Life, Borton, Allen (arr.).
Breeze-Easy Recital Pieces for Tuba, Kinyon, John (arr.).
A Bumble Bee's Fantasy, Debons, Eddy.
Burlesco, Ponlot, M.
Burlesque, Gulya, Robert.
Burlesque for Tuba and Piano, Kulesha, Gary Alan.
By the Sea, Schubert, Fr. (tr. Wesley Jacobs and P. Laville).
By the Sea, Schubert, Franz.
Bydlo (extrait des Tableaux d'une exposition no. 4), Moussorgsky, M. (arr. Patrice Sciortino).
Bydlo from Pictures at an Exibition, Moussorgsky, M.

C

Cadenza e Allegro Scherzando, Maertens, J.
Caisson Song, Feldstein, Sandy (arr.).
Calf of Gold from "Faust," Gounod, Charles.
Call of the River, Harmon, John.
Campagnarde, Lodéon, André.
Camptown Races, Foster, Stephen.
Campus Queen, Weber.
Canadian Brass Blues, Boyd, Bill.
Canadian Brass Book of Beginning Tuba Solos (Finlandia; Carnival of Venice; Volga Boatman, etc.), Daellenbach, Charles (ed.).
Canadian Brass Book of Easy Tuba Solos (Erie Canal; Loch Lomond; Come Thou Fount of Every Blessing; etc.), Daellenbach, Charles (ed.).
Canadian Brass Book of Intermediate Tuba Solos (To Music (Schubert); *Where E'er You Walk* (Handel); *Solace* (Joplin); etc.), Daellenbach, Charles (ed.).
Canadian Brass Christmas Solos (First Noel; Angels We Have Heard on High; Silent Night; etc.), Daellenbach, Charles (ed.).
Canarie nr. 2: Tuba ag Piano, Volle, Bjarne.
Cancao, Havens, Daniel.
Canco de Maria, de Grignon, Lamote.
Cantabile, Stepovoi, J.
Cantabile et divertissement pour tuba et orchestre, Semler-Collery, Jules.
Cantate BWV 26 Ach Wie Flüchtig, Ach Wie Nichtig (extrait: Aria pour voix de basse), Bach, J. S. (arr. François Poullot).
Cantilena for Tuba and Piano, Cummings, Barton.
Cantos de España, Op. 232, Nr. 2, Albéniz, Isaac.
Canzona, Pergolesi, G. B.
Canzonetta from Violin Concerto, Op. 35, Tchaikovsky, Peter I. (arr. Kenneth Drobnak).
Capriccio, Kubicek.
Capriccio, Newton, Rodney.
Capriccio for Tuba and Band, Presser, William.
Capriccio for Tuba and Orchestra, Roikjer, Kjell.
Capriccio for Tuba and Small Orchestra, Schuller, Gunther.
Caprice, Fernie, Alan (arr. Roy Newsome).
Caprice, Geib, Fred.
Cardinal's Air from "La Juive," The, Halévy, Jacques.
Caribbean Flush, Cleemput, Werner Van.
Carillon et Bourdon, Bigot, Eugène.
Carmen (extrait: Acte II: Vivat! Vivat le torero!), Bizet, G. (arr. François Poullot).
Carmen Excerpts, Bizet, Georges.
Carnaval de Venise, Le, Bilbaut, J.
Carnaval Time, Brizzi, Aldo.
Carnival for Bass, Muscroft, Fred.
Carnival of Venice, Arban, J. B. (arr. Patrick Sheridan).
Carnival of Venice, Benedict, Julius.
Carnival of Venice, Jacobs, Wesley.
Carnival of Venice (Fantasia), Holmes, G. E.
Carnival of Venice in F Major, Arban, Jean Baptiste.
Carnival of Venice, The (Variations), Arban, Jean Baptiste.
Caro mio ben, Giordani, Giuseppe.
Carry Me back to Old Virginny, Bland, J.
Carry Me Back to Old Virginny, Guy, Earl.

Cavalier, The, Buchtel, Forrest Lawrence.
Cavatina, Demerssman, J.
Cavatina, Geib, Fred.
Cavatina, Saint-Saëns, Camille.
Cavern Impression, A, Frangkiser, Carl.
Caverns, Wiley, Frank.
Ce que chantait l'aede, Depelsenaire, Jean-Marie.
Cedar Vale, Irons, Earl D.
Celebration for Tuba and Piano, Konagaya, Soichi.
Celestial Keys, Walker, Gwyneth.
Centone Buffo Concertante, Jaffe, Gerard.
Cetacea, Saul, Walter.
Chaconne, Purcell, Henry (arr. Morris).
Chaconne, Rodgers, Thomas.
Chaconne, Sowerby, Leo.
Chaconne for Tuba and Piano, Hayden, Paul.
Chain, Nilovic, Janko.
Challenge Concert Polka, Giovanini, J.
Changing Scene, Bowles, Richard W.
Chanson de matin, Elgar, Edward (arr. Michael Fischer, piano ed. John Cozza).
Chanson de nuit, Elgar, Edward (arr. Michael Fischer, piano ed. John Cozza).
Chanson de Solvejg, Grieg, E. (arr. Patrice Sciortino).
Chansonnoir, Burgstahler, Elton E.
Chant d'amour, Albéniz, Isaac.
Chant d'Amour, Clérisse, Robert.
Chant du Menestrel, Glazunov, A.
Chant Mélancolique, Niverd, Lucien.
Chanties and Ballads: Songs of the Sea for Tuba and Orchestra, Walker, Gwyneth.
Charlbury Charleston, Goddard, Mark.
Chason and Divertissement, Roberts, Sue.
Chason Triste, Jenkins, Cyril.
Chief John, Bell, William J.
Chiens de Paille, Barraine, Elsa Jacqueline.
Children of the Heavenly Father, Borton, Allen (arr.).
Children's Prayer, Humperdinck, Engelbert.
Chinatown, My Chinatown, Schwartz, Jean, and Jerome, William.
Ching-a-Ring Chaw, Copland, Aaron (arr. Quincy Hilliard).
Chopin for the Tuba, Chopin, Frédéric.
Choral Fantasy, Opus 93, Koetsier, Jan.
Chorale Prelude, Schmutz, Albert D.
Chorus from Judas Maccabaeus, Handel, George Frederick.
Christ the Lord Is Risen Today, Borton, Allen (arr.).
Christ the Lord Is Risen Today, Davidica (arr. David McCathren).
Christ the Lord Is Risen Today, Wadowick, James L. (arr.), and McCathren, Donald E. (ed.).
Christmas Cameos, Conley, Lloyd (arr.).
Christmas Nocturne, Walters, Harold L. (arr.).
Chromatic Concert Polka, Rose, Phil. S.
Chrysanthemum, Vander Cook, H. A.
Church's One Foundation, The, Borton, Allen (arr.).
5 Etudes—Trombone (ou Tuba) Basse Seul ou Avec Piano, Cherbubini, Maria Luigi Sa.
Cinc (5) Études, Dondeyne, Désiré.
Cinq (5) Piece Courtes: Pour jeune tubistes, Dondeyne, Désiré.
Civil War Medley, Wekselblatt, Herbert (arr.).
Classic Festival Solos, Lamb, Jack (ed.).
Classic Festival Solos, Vol. 2, Lamb, Jack (ed.).
Classical Jazz Suite, Copeland, R.
Clouds, Ihlenfeld, Dave.
Cockles and Mussels, Kinyon, John (arr.).
Collection of Pieces for Tuba "Es" and Piano, Lebedev, A. (ed.).
Collection Panorama, Daniel-Lesur and Werner, Jean-Jacques.
College March, Lincoln.
Colossus, Vander Cook, H. A.
Columbia, Rollinson, T. H.
Columbine, Vander Cook, H. A.
Come Again, Sweet Love Doth Now Invite, Dowland, John.
Come Brave the Sea, Bellini.
Come Brave the Sea, Bellini (tr. Wesley Jacobs and P. Laville).
Come, Christians, Join to Sing, Borton, Allen (arr.).
Come, Thou Fount of Every Blessing, Boyd, Bill (arr.).
Come, Ye Thankful People, Come, Borton, Allen (arr.).
Commodore, The, Chambers, W. Paris.
Complainte, Niverd, Lucien.
Concert Album for Tuba, Ostrander, Allen (ed.).
Concert and Contest Collection, Voxman, Himie (compiled and ed.).
Concert Duo, Grant, Parks.
Concert Etude, Krotov and Blazhevich.
Concert Etude, Op. 49, Goedicke, Alexander.
Concert Music for Bass Tuba, Mueller, Florian.
Concert Music for Tuba, Graham, James (arr.).
Concert No. 2 Part One, Mozart, Wolfgang Amadeus.
Concert No. 2 Part 3, Blazhevich, Vladislav.
Concert No. 4 Part One, Mozart, Wolfgang Amadeus.
Concert Piece, Nelhybel, Vaclav.
Concert Piece, Ruff, D.
Concert Piece, Saint-Saëns, Camille.
Concert Piece for Tuba and Band, Follas, Ronald W.
Concert Piece for Tuba and Piano, Anderson, Eugene D.
Concert Piece for Tuba and Piano, Larsen, Libby.
Concert Piece for Tuba and Piano, Tihomirov, A.
Concert Piece in Fugal Style, Ostrander, Allen.
Concert Piece, Op. 50, De Jong, M.
Concert Rondo, Mozart, Wolfgang Amadeus.
Concert Sketch Nr. 5, Blazhevich, Vladislav.
Concertante, Hall.
Concertante, Walters, Harold L.
Concertinetto, Kastel, Fabrice.
Concertino, Bozza, Eugène.
Concertino, Coeck, L. Jan.
Concertino, Curnow, James.
Concertino, Daucé, Edouard.

Concertino, Depetris, C.
Concertino, Hartley, V.
Concertino, Kitts-Turner, John S.
Concertino, Koetsier, Jan.
Concertino, LeClerc, E.
Concertino, Markl, Max.
Concertino, Schrijver, Karel de.
Concertino, Waignein, André.
Concertino, Zámencnik.
Concertino, Zverev, V.
Concertino for Euphonium or Tuba and Wind Orchestra: Mountains of Epirus, Constantinides, Dinos.
Concertino for Three Brass and Band, Werle, Floyd E.
Concertino for Tuba, George, Thom Ritter.
Concertino for Tuba and Band, Bencriscutto, Frank.
Concertino for Tuba and Klavier, Watz, Franz.
Concertino for Tuba and String Orchestra, Frackenpohl, Arthur.
Concertino for Tuba and String Orchestra, Shaughnessy, Robert.
Concertino for Tuba and Strings, Rideout, Alan.
Concertino for Tuba and Wind Ensemble, Hartley, Walter S.
Concertino for Tuba and Winds, Wilhelm, Rolf.
Concertino "Giocoso bucolico," Bull, Hagerup E.
Concertino in F for Tuba and Orchestra, Kalke, Ernst-Thilo.
Concertino No. IV, Theme from, Huber, Adolf.
Concertissimo, Saglietti, Corrado Maria.
Concertiya Sonatina, Roitershteny.
Concerto, Bentzon, Niels Viggo.
Concerto, Bottje, Will Gay.
Concerto, Chappot, Edouard.
Concerto, Godel, Didier.
Concerto, Krzywicki, Jan.
Concerto, Mortimer, John Glenesk.
Concerto, Nilovic, Janko.
Concerto, Spillman, Robert.
Concerto, Szentpáli, Roland.
Concerto, Viola, Anselm.
Concerto, Werner, Jean-Jacques.
Concerto, Opus 11, Strauss, Richard.
Concerto alla Jazz, Brandon, Sy.
Concerto Allegro, Lebedev, A.
Concerto brillant, Rollé.
Concerto classico, Zettler, Richard.
Concerto del Garda, Raum, Elizabeth.
Concerto for Bass Tuba, Jager, Robert.
Concerto for Bass Tuba, Vaughan Williams, Ralph.
Concerto for Tuba, Fleming, Robert.
Concerto for Tuba, Garth, J.
Concerto for Tuba, Koch, Erland von.
Concerto for Tuba, Kulesha, Gary Alan.
Concerto for Tuba, Ramskill, Robert.
Concerto for Tuba, Swiergiel, Waldemar.
Concerto for Tuba, Winteregg, Steven.
Concerto for Tuba ("Concerto Euphonique"), Hopkinson, Michael E.
Concerto for Tuba, Op. 96, Barnes, James (arr. Yukiko Nishimura).
Concerto for Tuba and Band, Beasley, Rule.
Concerto for Tuba and Concert Band, Wilder, Alec.
Concerto for Tuba and Four Horns, Saglietti, Corrado Maria.
Concerto for Tuba and Orchestra, Arutiunian, Alexandre.
Concerto for Tuba and Orchestra, Harville, Grant.
Concerto for Tuba and Orchestra, Heiden, Bernard.
Concerto for Tuba and Orchestra, Kikta, V.
Concerto for Tuba and Orchestra, Lovelock, William.
Concerto for Tuba and Orchestra, Premru, Raymond.
Concerto for Tuba and Orchestra, Schmidt, Ole.
Concerto for Tuba and Orchestra, Strukow, Valery.
Concerto for Tuba and Orchestra, Villiams, V. R. (Vaughan Williams, Ralph).
Concerto for Tuba and Orchestra, Williams, John.
Concerto for Tuba and Piano, Dumitru, Ionel.
Concerto for Tuba and Piano, Grøndahl, Terje.
Concerto for Tuba and Piano, Op. 53, Domazlicky, Frantisek.
Concerto for Tuba and Strings, Martin, Vernon.
Concerto for Tuba and Strings, Plau, Arild.
Concerto for Tuba and Strings, Presser, William.
Concerto for Tuba and Strings, Steptoe, Roger.
Concerto for Tuba and Symphony Orchestra, Jevtic, Ivan.
Concerto for Tuba or Bass Trombone, Ewazen, Eric.
Concerto in A Minor, Vivaldi, Antonio.
Concerto in D (K.412), Mozart, Wolfgang Amadeus.
Concerto in D Minor, Opus 9, Nr. 2, Albinoni, Tomaso.
Concerto in E flat (K.417), Mozart, Wolfgang Amadeus.
Concerto in E flat (K.447), Mozart, Wolfgang Amadeus.
Concerto in E flat (K.495), Mozart, Wolfgang Amadeus.
Concerto in One Movement, Lebedev, A.
Concerto No. 1, Dumitru, Ionel.
Concerto No. 2, Williams, Ernest.
Concerto No. 3 for Tuba and String Orchestra, Handel, George Frederick.
Concerto No. 4, Opus 65 (Excerpts from), Goltermann, Georg Edvard.
Concerto No. 6 in B♭, Bond, Capel.
Concerto Nr. 1 in g-moll, Handel, G. F. (arr. Walter Hilgers).
Concerto per Tuba, Eklund, Hans.
Concerto pour Tuba, Aubin, Francine.
Concertpièce, Couperin, F.
Concertpiece, Painparé, H.
Concertpiece for 3 Tubas and Band, Lackey, Jerry.
Concertpiece for Tuba and Piano, Dillon, Robert.
Concertpiece for Tuba and Piano, Rappoldt, Lawrence I.

Concertpiece No. 1, Vaughan, Rodger.
Concertpiece No. 2, Vaughan, Rodger.
Concertstuck, Murgier, Jacques.
Concertstuck, Rueff, Jeanine.
Concertstuk (1944), Maes, J.
Concierto Para Tuba Y Piano, Casas, Bartolomé Perez.
Concone Suite, A, Concone, Giuseppe (arr. Barton Cummings).
Conjectures, Sauter, Eddie.
Conquistadores, Hill, William H.
Contraste per tuba e pianoforte, Grudzinski, Czeskaw.
Conzertstuck für Tuba mit Klavierbegleitung, Geier, Oskar.
Coquette, La Concert Polka, Innes, F. N.
Cornemuse, Dubois, Pierre Max.
Coronation March, Meyerbeer.
Cortège, Beaucamp, Albert.
Cortège, Bigot, Pierre.
Cortège, Séguin, Pierre.
Cortège et Danse, Charles, C.
Couleurs en Mouvements, Moreau, James.
Country Dance, Beethoven, Ludwig von.
Courante, Senaillè, Jean Baptiste.
Courier, The, Buchtel, Forrest Lawrence.
Coventry Carole, Jacobs, Wesley (arr.).
Cradle Song, A, Lebedev, A.
Cradle Song, Brahms, Johannes.
Cradle Song, Schlemüller, Hugo.
Cromagnon, Louvier, Alain.
Cross of Jesus, The, Smith, David E. (arr.).
Crown Him with Many Crowns, Borton, Allen (arr.).
Cruel War Is Raging, The, Boyd, Bill (arr.).
Crusaders' Hymn, Kinyon, John (arr.).
Csardas, Monti, Vittorio (arr. Marc Reift).
Csardas, Monti, Vittorio (arr. Walter Hilgers).
Czardas, Monti, Vittorio (arr. Øystein Baadsvik).
Czardas, Monti, Vittorio (arr. Patrick Sheridan).

D

Daisies, Vander Cook, H. A.
Dance, Bartok, Bela.
Dance, Goedicke, A.
Dance, Gudmen, S.
Dance, The, Rossini, Gioacchino.
Dance and Aria, White, David Ashley.
Dance from Ballet "Seven Beauties," Karaev, V.
Dance from Ballet "Spartak," Katchiturian, A.
Dance of the Bear, Bartok, Bela.
Dance of the Blessed Spirits, Gluck, C. W.
Dance of the Slovaks, Bartok, Bela.
Dancing Silhouettes, Harris, Floyd O.
Dancing Song, Liadov, Anatol.
Dancing Tuba, The, Stephens, Denzil.
Danny Boy, Sheridan, Patrick (arr.).
Dans der Teddyberen, Jakma Sr., Frits.
Dans les pins, Hubert, P.
Danse de L'Éléphant, Delguidice, Michel.
Danse L'Elephant, Delgiudice, Michel.
Danse Sacrée, Tomasi, Henri.
Danse villageoise, Beethoven, Ludwig von.
Danses païennes (Pagan Dances), Debons, Eddy.
Danza Espanola, Uber, David.
Dare to Be a Daniel, Bliss, P. P.
Dare to Be a Daniel, Smith, Claude T.
Daydreams, Goddard, Mark.
Daydreams, Myers, Theldon.
De Profundis, Saul III, Walter B.
De Profundis: Sonata for Tuba and Piano, Censhu, Jiro.
Dear If You Change, Dowland, John.
Dear Lord and Father of Mankind, Borton, Allen (arr.).
Dear Old Songs of Home, Abt, Fr.
Dear Old Songs of Home, Abt, Franz (tr. Wesley Jacobs and P. Laville).
Dear to My Heart, Siebert, Edrich.
Deux Mouvements Contrastés, Devos, Gérard.
Deep Bass, Fillmore, Henry.
Deep Calls to Deep, Hutchison, Warner.
Deep Cavern, Ostling, Acton.
Deep River, Uber, David (arr.).
Deep Rock, Bowles, Richard W.
Deep Sea Stories, Alletter, Wilhelm, and Knight, Joseph Philip.
Deformation IV, Nash, Gary P.
Delaware Rhapsody, A, Uber, David.
Dels Quatre Vents from "6 Sonnets," Toldra, Eduardo.
Demetrius, Merle, John.
Der Alte Brummbär, Fucik, Julius.
Der fidele Bassist, Ruckauer, H.
Der Gang zum Liebchen, Brahms, Johannes (arr. David Green).
Der Genesene an die Hoffnung, Wolf, Hugo (arr. Walter Hilgers).
Der Herr Tubist, Löffler.
Der kellermeister, Schneebiegl, Rolf.
Der lindenbaum, Schubert, Franz.
Der Rattenfänger von Hameln, Nessler, Victor Ernst.
Des hortensias sous la pluie, Tanaka, Kumiko (Robert Martin Editions).
Deserted Farm, A, MacDowell, Edward.
Design for Bass, Nagel, Paul.
Designs, Lunde Jr., Ivar.
Designs and Patters for Tuba and Grand Piano, Brandon, Sy.
Désir, Le, Beethoven, Ludwig von.
Deux Pièces brèves, Semler-Collery, Jules.
Dewdrops, Vander Cook, H. A.
Dialogue, Durand-Audard, Pierre.
Dialogue, Martelli, Henri.
Dialogue for Tuba and Piano, Rothgarber, Herbert.
Dialogues, Dobbins, Bill.
Dialoog, Duyck, G.
Dido's Lament, Handel, G. F. (arr. Velvet Brown).
Die liebe Farbe, Schubert, Franz.

Die Meistersinger von Nürnberg, Wagner, Richard.
Die Walkure (from Act III), Wagner, Richard.
Dies Irae, Langgaard, Rued.
Digderidoo, Vuori, Harri.
Dinardzade (Rhapsodie orientale), Debons, Eddy.
Diptych, Brown, Rayner.
Dirge in Woods, Copland, Aaron (arr. Quincy Hilliard).
Dirge No. 4, Bartok, Bela.
Dith, The, Catelinet, Philip.
Diversita Continua, Choen, Michael.
Divertimento, Debons, Eddy.
Divertimento, Dondeyne, Désiré.
Divertimento, Mignone, Francisco.
Divertimento, Ziev.
Divertimento for Tuba and Piano, Cooman, Carson.
Divertissement, Debaar, Mathieu.
Divertissement, Sabathil, Ferd.
Divertissement, Schmidt, A.
Divertissement classique, Truillard, R.
Dix Petit Textes, Delgiudice, Michel.
Dolce Espressivo, Ameller, André.
Dona Nobis Pacem, Jacobs, Wesley (arr.).
Dona Nobis Pacem, Wadowick, James L. (arr.), and McCathren, Donald E. (ed.).
Dordogne Dances, Kelly, Bryan.
Dove Sei from "Rodelinda," Handel, George Frederick.
Down among the Dead Men, Prendiville, Harry (arr.).
Down Deep within the Cellar, Fischer (tr. Wesley Jacobs and P. Laville).
Down Deep within the Cellar, Fischer, Ludwig.
Down in the Deep Cellar, Kroepsch, F.
Down in the Deep Deep Cellar, Fischer, Ludwig.
Down in the Valley, Walters, Harold L. (arr.).
Doxology, Bourgéois, Louis, and Ken, Thomas.
Dr. Martin Luther King, In Memoriam (1984), Kellaway, Roger.
Dragons and Deeps, Pinkham, Daniel.
Drei Bagatellen, Op. 95b, Hummel, Berthold.
Drei lyrische Szenen, Grunelius, Wilhelm von.
Drei Skizzen, Lischka, Rainer.
3 Stücke, Ehmann, Wilhelm.
Drink to Me Only with Thine Eyes, Kinyon, John (arr.).
Duo, Hailstork, Adolphus C.
Duo, Op. 69, Näther, Gisbert.

E

Earle of Oxford's Marche, The, Byrd, William.
Easy Solos, Jepsen, Irene.
Eclipse Finale? Meier, Jost.
Effusion, Gendel, Scott.
Egotistical Elephant, The, Hartzell, Doug.
Eight Bel Canto Songs, Phillips, Harry I. (ed.).
Ein kleines Andenken, Aranyi-Aschner, Georg.
Eleanor Rigby, Lennon, John, and McCartney, Paul (arr. John Glenesk Mortimer).
Elegia, Masne, D.
Elegia, Rachmaninoff, Sergei.
Élegié, Proust, Pascal.
Elegie, Strukow, Valery.
Elegy, Vaughan, Rodger.
Elegy for the Whale, Wilder, Alec.
Elegy for Tuba and Piano, Zinos, Fredrick.
Elemntarite, Senon, G.
Éléphant (Der Elefant), L', Saint-Saëns, Camille.
Elephant and a Mouse, An, Marttinen, Taune.
Elephant Dance, The, Weber, Fred, and Dorothy Garrett.
Elephant from "Carnival of Animals," Saint-Saëns, Camille.
Emmett's Lullaby, Holmes, G. E.
En Glissant . . . , Lesaffre, Charles.
Enchanted Island, The, Kosteck, Gregory.
Enchorial Landscape, Read, Thomas L.
Encore Piece for Tuba and Piano, Wilder, Alec.
Enterrement de Saint-Jean, L', Bariller, Robert.
Entr'acte from "Rosamunde," Schubert, Franz.
Entrevous for 2 Tubas and Piano, Jous, Christian.
Epic Tale and Procession of the People in Costumes (Festival), Kikta, V.
Epode for Tuba and Piano, Vollrath, Carl.
Erie Canal, Feldstein, Sandy (arr.).
Erie Canal, The, Boyd, Bill (arr.).
Erie Canal, The, Kinyon, John (arr.).
Es ist ein Schnitter, der heisst Tod (There Is a Reaper Named Death), Koetsier, Jan.
España, Canción Catalan, Op. 165, Albéniz, Isaac.
Esquisse Concertante Concertschets, Desprez, F.
Essai, Gartenlaub, Odette.
Essay for Tuba, Pethel, Stan.
Estonian Folk Dance, Lebedev, A. (arr.).
Estrellita, Ponce, M.
Etre ou ne pas être, Tomasi, Henri.
Etude, Scriabine, Alexander.
Etude (op. 10, no. 11), Concone, G.
Etude de concert, Leonov, I.
Etude 1 for Tuba and Piano, Hogg, Merle E.
Etude, Op. 10 #3, Chopin, Frederick.
Eusebius, Schumann, R. (arr. Patrice Sciortino).
Evensong, Uber, David.
Eventail, Depetris.
Exchange for Tuba and Piano, Knight, Morris.
Excursions for Tuba and Piano, Davies, Kenneth.
Exposition Echoes Polka, Pryor, Arthur.
Expromt, Arutiunian, Alexandre.

F

Fairest Lord Jesus, Borton, Allen (arr.).
Fairy Jane, The, Marzials.
Fairy Jane, The, Marzials (tr. Wesley Jacobs and P. Laville).
Fairy Tail, A, Monushko, S.
Faith, Glover, S.
Faith, Glover, S. (tr. Wesley Jacobs and P. Laville).
Faith of Our Fathers, Bayley, Thomas Haynes.
Falstaff Concerto, Op. 119, Krol, Bernhard.

Falstaff's Drinking Song, Nicolai, Otto.
Famous Themes—Symphonic Works, Volume 1, Marlatt, David.
Fancies and Interludes I, Luedeke, Raymond.
Fanfare for the Common Man, Copland, Aaron (arr. Quincy Hilliard).
Fantaisie, Petit, Pierre.
Fantaisie Concertante, Castérède, Jacques.
Fantaisie Contante, Villette, Pierre.
Fantaisie Italienne, Coriolis, Emmanuel de.
Fantasia, Feldman, Enrique C.
Fantasia, Garlick, Antony.
Fantasia A Due, Reed, Alfred.
Fantasia Breve for Tuba and Piano, Cummings, Barton.
Fantasia for Tuba and Chamber Orchestra, Hartley, Walter S.
Fantasia for Tuba or Bass Trombone with Band or Piano Accompaniment, Op. 57, Tuthill, Burnet.
Fantasie, Dubois, Pierre Max.
Fantasie, Lorge, John.
Fantasie, Schroen, B.
Fantasie concertante, Desprez, Fernand.
Fantasiestücke, Schumann, Robert (arr. Cooley).
Fantasiestucke, Op. 73, Schumann, Robert (arr. Henry Howey).
Fantasietta, Debons, Eddy.
Fantasy for Tuba and Piano, Faust, Randall E.
Fantasy for Tuba and Piano, Konagaya, Soichi.
Fantasy for Tuba and Piano, Sacco, P. Peter.
Fantasy on a Lakota Theme for Tuba and Piano, Bales, Kenton.
Fantasy on a Theme of Scarlatti, Davidson, Douglass.
Fantezie nocturna, Dumitru, Ionel.
Faust (extrait: Acte IV, 2nd Tableau: Mephistophélès), Gounod, C. (arr. François Poullot).
Faustbuch, Raum, Elizabeth.
Feel Good Blues, The, Quate, Amy.
Felix, Michael and I: For Tuba and Piano, Op. 102, Madsen, Trygrave.
"Fett und Filtz," Op. 403d, Bentzon, Niels Viggo.
Fifteen Intermediate Tuba Solos, Hudadoff, Igor (ed.), and Wescott, William (pno. acc.).
Fifteen Introductory Solos, Brass Wind Publications.
Fifteenth Solo de Concours, Porret, Julien.
Fifty Standard Solos, Pro Art (publisher).
Finlandia, Sibelius, Jean.
Finnish Rhapsody, Borg, Kim.
First and Second Movements from Violin Sonata, Eccles, H.
First Contest, Waignein, A.
First Movement from Concerto for Horn, Mozart, Wolfgang Amadeus.
First Noel, The, Conley, Lloyd (arr.).
First Solo Album, Weber, Carl (arr.).
First Solo Songbook, Feldstein, Sandy (arr.).
First Solos for the Tuba Player, Wekselblatt, Herbert.
Five Pieces for Tuba and Piano, Durkó, Zsolt.
Five Possibilities, Meyer-Selb, Horst.
Five Solos, Connor.
Five Solos for Tuba, Bennett, Malcolm (arr.), Connor, Eddie (selected).
Five Songs, Brahms, Johannes.
5 Terrains 5 Contemporary Pieces, Gold, Thomas.
Five Whistling Tunes, Shoop, Stephen.
Flame, Schwartz, Elliott.
Flatterer, The, Buchtel, Forrest Lawrence.
Fleur de Lis, Irons, Earl D.
Fleurs artificielles, Chini, Andrè.
Flight of the Bumble Bee, Rimsky-Korsakov, Nicolai (arr. Neal Corwell).
Flight of the Bumble Bee (in A♭ major) (for E♭ Tuba), Rimsky-Korsakov, Nicolai (arr. Patrick Sheridan).
Flight of the Bumble Bee (in B♭ major) (for F♭ Tuba), Rimsky-Korsakov, Nicolai (arr. Patrick Sheridan).
Flight of the Bumble Bee, The, Rimsky-Korsakov, Nikolai (arr. Marc Reift).
Flow Gently, Sweet Afton, Little (arr.).
Flow Gently, Sweet Afton, Spillman, James E.
Folk Song Melodies, Ostling and Weber (arr.).
Folksong Medley, Bell, William J. (arr.).
Folkvisor av Vikingarna (Folksongs of the Vikings), Dahlgren, David F.
For All the Saints, Borton, Allen (arr.).
For Harvey, Kellaway, Roger.
For He's a Jolly Good Fellow, Feldstein, Sandy (arr.).
For the Beauty of the Earth, Borton, Allen (arr.).
For the Beauty of the Earth, Kocher.
For the Funk of It, Browning, Zack.
Forget Me Not, Macbeth, Allan.
Formal Persistence, Chaffin, Lon W.
Forty Fathoms, Walters, Harold L.
Foster Medley, Foster, Stephen C.
Four Classics for Young Brass Players, Musser, Willard.
Four Faces of Tubby, McCurdy, Gary L.
Four Ragged Fables, Denham, Robert.
Four Segments, Barnet, Richard D.
Four Shorts for Tuba and Piano, Largent, Edward.
Four Vignettes for Tuba, Miller, Vernon, Jr.
French Dance, Gluck (arr. Willard Musser).
French Folk Song, Feldstein, Sandy (arr.).
French Song, Ostling, Acton (arr.).
Frère Jacques, Feldstein, Sandy (arr.).
Frère Jacques, Sciortino, Patrice (arr.).
Friar of Orders Gray, The, Shield.
Fröhlicher Landmann, Schumann, Robert.
Fruhlingsglaube (Faith in Spring), Schubert, Franz (arr. Michael Fischer, piano ed. John Cozza).
Fuguette, Mortier, W.
Funambules, Depelsenaire, Jean-Marie.
Funeral March of a Marionette, Gounod, Charles.
Fünf Charakterstücke, Meyer-Selb, Horst.

G

G. F. Handel's Third Tuba Concerto, Bevan, Clifford.

Galantine, Joubert, Claude-Henry.
Galejade, Waignein, A.
Galgenlieder, Koetsier, Jan.
Gallant Captain, Ostling, Acton (arr.).
Galliarde, Franck, Melchior.
Galop, Dumitru, Ionel.
Gargantua, Delgiudice, Michel.
Gavotte, Bach, Johann Sabastian.
Gavotte, Bell, William J.
Gavotte, Gluck, K.
Gavotte, Lebedev, A.
Gavotte, Lully, Jean-Baptiste.
Gavotte, Pachelbel, Johann.
Gavotte, Popper, David.
Gavotte, Purcell, Henry.
Gavotte and Hornpipe, Purcell, Henry.
Gavotte from Symphony No. 4, Boyce, William.
Gavotte in Rondeau, Lully, Jean-Babtiste.
Gay Caballero, Schaefer, August H.
Gentle Annie, Foster, Stephen (arr. Stephen Shoop).
George M. Cohan Medley, Cohan, George M.
German Waltz, Jacobs, Wesley (arr.).
German Waltz, Kinyon, John (arr.).
Gigue, Corelli, Arcangelo.
Giralda, Hume, James Ord.
Give My Regards to Broadway, Cohan, George M.
Gladiator, Buchtel, Forrest Lawrence.
Glow Worm, The, Lincke.
Go Down, Moses, Jacobs, Wesley (arr.).
God of our Fathers, Borton, Allen (arr.).
Going to Heaven, Copland, Aaron (arr. Quincy Hilliard).
Golden Days (Serenade), St. Clair, Floyd P.
Golden Dreams Waltz, Buchtel, Forrest Lawrence.
Golden Glow, Buchtel, Forrest Lawrence.
Golliwogg's Cake-walk, Debussy, Claude.
Good King Wenceslas, Feldstein, Sandy (arr.).
Good Night, Samonov, A.
Gopak, Moussorgsky, M.
Grand Air from "The Masked Ball," Verdi, Giuseppe.
Grand Cadence, Kling, G., and Neuling, G.
Grand solo de concert, Watelle, J.
Grandfather Is Dancing, Samonov, A.
Grave, Lancen, S.
Grave, Petit, Pierre.
Grave en Allegro, Swinnen, Hans.
Grave et Scherzo, Op. 107, Manen, Christian.
Great Is Thy Faithfulness, Borton, Allen (arr.).
Green Apple Two-Step, The, Kulesha, Gary Alan.
Greensleeves, Jacobs, Wesley (arr.).
Greensleeves, Sauvignet, Marie-Angès (arr.) (Robert Martin Editions).
Grenadier, The, Buchtel, Forrest Lawrence.
Grieg Collection (Anitra's Dance; A Dream; Norwegian Dance No. 1.), Baadsvik, Øystein (arr.).
Gypsy Love Song, Herbert, Victor.
Gypsy Melody, Dvorak, Antonin.
Gypsy Songs, Brahms, Johannes (arr. Michael Fischer, piano ed. by John Cozza).

H

Ha! just in the nick of time! Mozart, Wolfgang Amadeus.
Habanera (extrait de Carmen), Bizet, G. (arr. Patrice Sciortino).
Habanera from "Carmen," Bizet, Georges.
Habanera nocturne, Pelegri, Stéphane (Robert Martin Editions).
Hallejulah! What a Saviour, Traditional (arr. David E. Smith).
Hamlet's Monologue, Tomasi, G. (sic).
Händel's Third Tuba Concerto, Bevan, Clifford.
Hans de Schnokeloch, Bariller, Robert.
Happy Be Thy Dreams, de Ville, Paul (arr.).
Happy Birthday, Hill, Mildred J. (arr. John Glenesk Mortimer).
Happy Birthday, Mortimer, John Glenesk.
Happy Farmer, The, Schumann, Robert.
Happy Hippo, The, Ward, Norman.
Happy Song, Siennicki, Edmund J.
Happy Thoughts, Baseler, J.
Harlequin, Buchtel, Forrest Lawrence.
Harmonious Blacksmith, The, Handel, George Frederick.
Harmonious Blacksmith, The, Handel (tr. Wesley Jacobs and P. Laville).
Harvest Dance, Jacobs, Wesley (arr.).
Harvest Waltz, Siennicki, Edmund J.
Haydn Medley, from Symphony No. 94, Haydn, Franz Joseph.
Hear Our Prayer—Paraphrase, Rollinson, T. H.
Heart Victorious (Cantata), Carissimi, Gian Giacomo.
Heather Rose Caprice, Lange.
Heav'n, in pray'r, Thine aid I seek and Good subjects of Brabant, 'tis well! (From Loengrin), Wagner, Richard.
Helix (Concerto for Solo Tuba and Concert Band), Benson, Warren.
Hercules, Buchtel, Forrest Lawrence.
Here I Sit in the Deep Cellar, Fischer, Ludwig.
Herfstbloemen, Jakma Sr., Frits.
Hermes, Buchtel, Forrest Lawrence.
Herod's Air from "Herodiade," Massanet, Jules.
Heroic Tale, A, Geib, Fred.
Hey, Ho! Nobody Home, Boyd, Bill (arr.).
Hey-Ho, Come to the Fair, Martin, Easthope.
Hey Jude! Lennon, John, and McCartney, Paul.
Hey Jude, Lennon, John, and McCartney, Paul (arr. John Glenesk Mortimer).
Highland Melody, Shoop, Stephen.
Hikari-Aru Sora-Wa Shiazukani, Censhu, Jiro.
Himatsuri, Ideta, Keizo.
His Majesty the Tuba, Dowling, Robert.
Histoires De Tuba Vol. 1: Plantez les gars! Dubois, Pierre Max.
Histoires De Tuba Vol. 2: Le petit cinéma, Dubois, Pierre Max.
Histoires De Tuba Vol. 3: Le grand cinéma, Dubois, Pierre Max.

Histoires De Tuba Vol. 4: Concert Opéra, Dubois, Pierre Max.
Historiette Dramatique, Niverd, Lucien.
Holy City, Adams.
Holy, Holy, Holy, Borton, Allen (arr.).
Home on the Range, Kinyon, John (arr.).
Honeysuckle Polka, Casey.
Honor and Arms, Handel, George Frederick.
Horn Concerto Nr. 1 (Solostimme), Strauss, Richard (arr. Anderson).
Hornpipe, A, Lotzenhiser, G. W.
Hornpipe, Goddard, Mark.
Hornpipe, Wekselblatt, Herbert (arr.).
Hors-d'Oeuvre, Schürch, Cyrill.
Hot Cross Buns, Feldstein, Sandy (arr.).
Hour of Prayer, The, Nelson (tr. Wesley Jacobs and P. Laville).
How Can I Leave Thee, Buchtel, Forrest Lawrence.
How strong your tone with magic spell, Mozart, Wolfgang Amadeus.
Hummelflug, Rimsky-Korsakoff, Nikolai (arr. Reift).
Humoreska, Dumitru, Ionel.
Humoreske, Kühmstedt.
Humoreske in F, Kulesha, Gary Alan.
Humoresque, Bernaud, Alain.
Humorous Dance, Kolodub, L.
Humresque, Jacobsen, Julius.
Hungarian Folk Song, Bartok, Bela.
Hungarian Melody, Zuerev, V.
Hussar, The, Buchtel, Forrest Lawrence.
Hyacinthe, Vander Cook, H. A.
Hymn to Joy, Beethoven, Ludwig von.
Hymn, Haydn, J.
Hymne, Niverd, Lucien.
Hymne a la Nuit, Rameau, J. P. (arr. Patrice Sciortino).

I

I Bought Me a Cat, Copland, Aaron (arr. Quincy Hilliard).
I Love to Tell the Story, Borton, Allen (arr.).
I Need Thee Every Hour, Borton, Allen (arr.).
I Remember Love Supreme, Boukhitine, Arnaud.
I Wanna Hold Your Hand, Lennon, John, and McCartney, Paul (arr. John Glenesk Mortimer).
I Wonder As I Wander, Smith, Douglas (arr.).
I Wonder As I Wander, Traditional (arr. David E. Smith).
Iago's Song about King Stephen from the Tragedy Othello, Sviridov, G.
Iceflower, Åkerwall, Martin.
"Ich ruf zu Dir, Herr Jesu Christ," Choral Prelude BMV 639, Bach, J. S. (arr. Walter Hilgers).
I'd give my finest feather, Mozart, Wolfgang Amadeus.
Idylle, Clérisse, Robert.
If Thou Be Near, Bach, J. S. (arr. Richard Thurston).
Il Dominatore, Panetta, Carlo.
Il Mio Bel Foco, Marcello, Benedetto.
Il Viaggio 1 per tuba solo con pianoforte, Sikora, Elzbieta.
Im Spielzeugland, Jepsen, Irene.
Im tiefsten Walde (In the Deep Forest), Schmid, Heinrich Kaspar.
Imp, The (Tuba in Es), Stephens.
Impromptu, Bitsch, Marcel.
Impromptu, Ilvea.
Impromptu, Poot, Marcel.
Impromptu in G, Op. 7, No. 1, Gray, Louis Robert.
Impromptu No. 1, Takumi, Hedetoshi.
Improvisation, Goedicke, A.
In a Modal Mood, Barnes, James.
In F, Stratton, Don.
In Lively Spirits, Hopkinson, Michael E.
In Lively Spirits, Senaillè, Jean Baptiste.
In Olden Times, Jacobs, Wesley (arr.).
In Spring Time, Grieg, E.
In Springtime, Jacobs, Wesley (arr.).
In the Army, Ball, Eric.
In the Beginning Biblical Poem for Tuba (Cello) and Organ, Callahan, Charles.
In the Deep Forest, Geib, Fred.
In the Deep, Deep Depths, Hume, James Ord.
In the Garden, Monroe, Margrethe.
In the Hall of the Mountain King, Grieg, Edvard.
In the Lowlands, Richardson, Alan.
Installation au moulin, L', Poullot, F.
Instant Band Ensembles (Tuba), Kinyon, John (arr.).
Instrumental Albums Number 14: Solos and Duets for Soprano E♭, Horn E♭, and Bass E♭ with Pianoforte Accompaniment, Salvation Army Press.
Intermede, Layens, C. G.
Intermezzo, Bitsch, Marcel.
Intermezzo, Challan, Henri.
Intermezzo, Gliere, Reinhold.
Intermezzo, Provost, Pascal.
Intermezzo Capriccioso, Castellucci, Louis.
Interrogaçoes, Kiefer, Bruno.
Intrade, Pezel, Johann.
Introduction and Allegretto, Kappey.
Introduction and Allegro, Madsen, Trygve.
Introduction and Allegro Spiritoso, Senaillè, Jean Baptiste.
Introduction and Andante, Op. 54, Douliez, Victor.
Introduction and Blues, Powell, Morgan.
Introduction and Dance, Barat, J. Edouard.
Introduction and Dance, Bilik, Jerry H.
Introduction and Dance, Scarmolin, A. Louis.
Introduction and Dance, Schostakowitsch, Dimitri (arr. Musser).
Introduction and Polka Piquante, Geib, Fred.
Introduction and Rondo, Buchtel, Forrest Lawrence.
Introduction, Aria and Rondo, Koch, Frederick.
Introduction Et Cantabile, Baeyens, H.
Introduction et Danse, Barat, J. Edouard.
Introduction Et Rigaudon, Faillenot, Maurice.
Introduction et ronde, Faillenot, Maurice.
Introduction et Sérénade, Barat, J. Edouard.

Introduction et Toccata, Carles, Marc.
Introduction, thème et variations sur l'air de Moïse, Rossini, Gioacchino.
Invincible, Lafont.
Invocation for Tuba and Piano, Standford, Patric.
Irish-Cante, Ameller, André.
It Is Enough from "Elijah," Mendelssohn, Felix.
It Is Well with My Soul, Borton, Allen (arr.).
Ive, Ameller, André.
I've Heard an Organ Talk, Copland, Aaron (arr. Quincy Hilliard).
Ivy, Vander Cook, H. A.

J

Jay Rozen Portrait and Fugue, Thomson, Virgil.
Jazz Concerto for Tuba and Band, Lackey, Jerry.
Jazz Concerto for Tuba and Orchestra, Lackey, Jerry.
A Jazz Rhapsody, Uber, David.
Jeanie with the Light Brown Hair, Foster, Stephen (arr. Patrick Sheridan and Rich Ridenour).
Jenny Wren, Sheridan, Patrick (arr.).
Jesus Is the Sweetest Name, Long, Lela.
Jesus Loves Me, Borton, Allen (arr.).
Jesus Loves Me, Smith, Claude T.
Jesus Loves Me, Warner (arr. David E. Smith).
Jesus Loves Me, Warner and Bradbury.
Jesus Shall Reign, Borton, Allen (arr.).
Jesus/Sweetest Name I Know, Moss, Alan.
Jeu 3, Zbar.
Jeux Chromatiques, Depelsenaire, Jean-Marie.
Jig Elephantine, Bell, William J.
Jimbo's Lullaby, Debussy, Claude.
Jingle Bells, Pierpont, J.
Jogging, Defaye, Jean-Michel.
John Peel, Kinyon, John (arr.).
Joke, A, Bak, Mikhail Abromovich.
Joke, A, Smirnova, T.
Jolly Coppersmith, The, Peter, C.
Jolly Dutchman, The, Issac, Merle J. (arr.).
Jolly Farmer Goes to Town, The, Schumann, Robert.
Jolly Jumbo, Bell, William J.
Jolly Old St. Nicholas, Feldstein, Sandy (arr.).
Jolly Peasant, The, Schumann, Robert.
Jolly Sailor, Buchtel, Forrest Lawrence.
Journal of Days, Butterfield, Don.
Journey, Stevens, John.
Joy to the World, Borton, Allen (arr.).
Joy to the World, Conley, Lloyd (arr.).
Joyous Dialogue, A, Geib, Fred.
Juggler, The, Buchtel, Forrest Lawrence.
Julep Cup, Kalke, Ernst-Thilo.
Jumbo, Carion, M.
Jumbo-Baby, Baratto, Paolo.
Jurassic Tuba! A Mesozoic Menagerie, Jones, Roger.
Juriritubaioka, Globokar, Vinko.
Just a Closer Walk, Foley, Red.
Just As I Am, Borton, Allen (arr.).
Just Foolin' Around, Myers, Theldon.

K

"Kaipaus," Takalo, Arttu.
Kerry Dance, The, Molloy, J. L.
King Arthur Variations, Szkutko, John.
King Mydas, Buchtel, Forrest Lawrence.
King Neptune, Ostling, Acton.
King of the Deep, Moquin, Al.
King's Jester, The, Harris, Floyd O.
Kis Eloeadasi Darab Tubara, Kistetenyi, Melinda.
Kis Humoreszk, Aranyi, Gyorgy.
Kleiner Walzer, Dragonetti, Domenico.
Koan II, Gistelinck, E.
Koncert med orkester, Roikjer, Kjell.
Kontraste, Cilensek.
Konzert, Koerppen, Alfred.
Konzert, Linkola, Jukka.
Konzert (hofmeister), Lebedev, Alexej.
Konzert B-Dur, Opus 7, Nr. 3, Albinoni, Tomaso.
Konzert für Tuba und Klavier, Lebedjew, A.
Konzert für Tuba und Orchester, Gruner, Joachim.
Konzert für Tuba und Orchestra, Rottler, Werner.
Konzert g-Moll, Handel, George Frederick.
Konzert Nr. 2, Lebedev, Alexej.
Konzert, Op. 35, Madsen, Trygve.
Konzert-Cadenz, Neuling, Hermann.
Konzertetüde, Gregor, Frantisek.
Konzertstück (Concertpiece), Dumitru, Ionel.
Kryptos, Ameller, André.

L

L'Antre de Polypheme, Delguidice, Michel.
L'Italiana in Algeri, Rossini, Gioacchino.
La Baliene Bleue, Delguidice, Michel.
La complaisante, Bach, C. Ph.
La Flûte Enchantée (extrait: O Isis und Osiris), Mozart, W. A. (arr. François Poullot).
La Truite, Schubert, F. (arr. Patrice Sciortino).
Lamento, Beach, Bennie.
Lamento for Tuba and Piano, Gubaidulina, Sofia.
Lancer, The, Bonheur, Theodore.
Ländler Für Tuba Und Klavier, Hoza, Václav.
Landscape III, Constantinides, Dinos.
Landskap, Lundquist, Torbjørn Iwan.
Larghetto and Allegro, Handel, George Frederick.
Larghetto e allegretto, Higuet, N.
Largo, Dvorak (ed. David Marlatt).
Largo, Handel (ed. David Marlatt).
Largo, Vivaldi (ed. David Marlatt).
Largo and Allegro, Marcello, Benedetto.
Largo and Presto, Marcello, Benedetto.
Largo for Tuba and Piano, Hartley, Walter S.
Las Cañadas, Dane, Mary.
Last Saturday Evening, The, Grieg, Edvard.
Laurie's Song, Copland, Aaron (arr. Quincy Hilliard).
Lazy Day, Myers, Theldon.
Lazy Lullaby, Little, Donald C.
Le Bavolet Flottant, Couperin, Francois (tr. Lars Holmgaard).
Le Chêne-Chat, Proust, Pascal.

Le chien rouge, Bentzon, Niels Viggo.
Le diamant bleu, Basteau, Jean-François (Robert Martin Editions).
Le jardin sur la lagune, Naulais, Jerôme (Robert Martin Editions).
Le Petit Baobab, Delguidice, Michel.
Le Petit Mammouth, Delguidice, Michel.
Le Tuba Classique, Recueil 1, Poullot, François (arr.).
Le Voyage d'Hadrien, Crepin, Alain (Robert Martin Editions).
Lead on O King Eternal, Everson, Dana F. (arr.).
Learn As You Play Tuba, Wastall, Peter (ed.).
Legend, Burshtin, M.
Legend, Catelinet, Philip.
Legend, Stoutamire, Albert L.
Legend of Heimdall, The, Raum, Elizabeth.
Legend of Lake St. Catherine, Uber, David.
Legend of Purple Hills, The, Uber, David.
Legend of the Sleeping Bear, Uber, David.
Legende et Caprice, Debaar, M.
Légende, Beugniot, Jean-Pierre.
Légende, Kaï, Naohiko.
Légende, Niverd, Lucien.
Legende, Vansteenkiste, M.
Legende, Wigy, Fr.
Leider Eines Fahrenden Gesellen, Mahler, Gustav.
Lento, Handel, George Frederick.
Lento, Holmes, Paul.
Lento Elegiaco, Strukov, V.
Leprechauns Patrol, Walters, Harold L.
Let Me like a Soldier Fall, Wallace.
Letters from a Friend, Spaniola, Joseph.
Levithan, The, Wiegand, George.
Liberation of Sisyphus, Stevens, John.
Libre-episode, Werner, Jean-Jacques.
Liebesfreud, Kreisler, Fritz.
Liebesfreud, Kreisler, Fritz (arr. Sheridan).
Liebeslied, Kreisler, Fritz.
Lied, Pergolesi, Giovanni Battista.
Lift High the Cross, Borton, Allen (arr.).
Lights Far Out at Sea, Gatty, A. S. (tr. Wesley Jacobs and P. Laville).
Lily, Vander Cook, H. A.
Liporello's Aria from Don Juan (Don Giovanni), Mozart, V. (sic).
Little Birch Tree, A, Frid, G.
Little Caesar, Harris, Floyd O.
Little Fiesta, Harris, Floyd O.
Little Horses, The, Copland, Aaron (arr. Quincy Hilliard).
Little Maiden, Jacobs, Wesley (arr.).
Loch Lomond, Boyd, Bill (arr.).
Loch Lomond, Kinyon, John (arr.).
Logos, Ameller, André.
London Bridge, Feldstein, Sandy (arr.).
Londonderry Air, Buchtel, Forrest Lawrence (arr.).
Londonderry Air, Kinyon, John (arr.).
Londonderry Air, Yasumoto, Hiroyuki (arr.).
Lonely Forest, The, Lully, Jean-Baptiste.
Long, Long Ago, Bayley, Thomas Haynes.
Long, Long Ago, Kaneda, B.
Longing for Spring, Mozart (arr. Willard Musser).
Lord Preserve Me, Rossini, Gioacchino.
Los Cocos Locos, Quate, Amy.
L'os Hispanic, Blanquer, Amando.
Love Somebody, Feldstein, Sandy (arr.).
Love Song (Caro mio ben), Giordani, Giuseppe.
Love that's true will live forever (Si, Tra I Ceppi, from "Berenice"), Handel, George Frederick.
Lovely Evening, Feldstein, Sandy (arr.).
Low Down Bass, Bell, William J.
Lowlands, Osborne, Chester.
Lucy Long, Godfrey, Fred.
Lullaby, Brahms, J.
Lustiger Bassist Konzertpolka, Manas, Franz.
Luxe, calme et volupté, Boukhitine, Arnaud.
Luzerne Song, Bennett, Malcolm (arr.).

M

Madrigal, Gaubert, Philippe.
Maes Howe, Másson, Askell.
Magnolia, Vander Cook, H. A.
Maid of the Mist, The, Clarke, Herbert L. (arr. Wesley Jacobs).
Make Mine a Tuba, Norton, Christopher.
Mallorca (Barcarola), Albeniz, I.
Mamminga Rag, Zaninelli, Luigi.
Manchester Parade (A British Slow-March), Vaughan, Rodger.
Mannequin, The, Buchtel, Forrest Lawrence.
Manta for Tuba and Piano, Jones, Roger.
Mantis Dance, Warren, David.
March, Jurovsky, V.
March, Purcell, Henry (arr. Dishinger).
March of a Marionette, Gounod, Charles.
Marche, Couperin, Francois (arr. Dishinger).
Marche, Mozart, Wolfgang Amadeus.
Marche Funèbre (extrait de la Sonate op. 35), Chopin, F. (arr. Patrice Sciortino).
Märchen, Wiegenlied und Gavotte, Lebedjew, Alexej.
Märchenbilder, Schumann, Robert (arr. Cooley).
Marches, Marches, Marches, Hudadoff, Igor (ed.).
Marching Right Along, Barnes, James.
Mardi-Gras, Faillenot, Maurice.
Marigold, Vander Cook, H. A.
Marine, Clérisse, Robert.
Mariner, The, Buchtel, Forrest Lawrence.
Mariner, The, Mattei, Tito.
Marines' Hymn March, The, Phillips, L. Z.
Marine's Hymn, Offenbach, Jacques.
Mary's Idea, Childs, Barney.
Mass from Stone, for Tuba and Organ, Weinhart, Christoph.
Master Solos Intermediate Level, Perantoni, Daniel (ed.).
Mastodon, Guentzel, Gus.
Matins, Keim, Aaron.
May Jesus Christ Be Praised, Borton, Allen (arr.).
May Song, Beethoven, Ludwig von.

McCluskeys Rag, Connor, Eddie.
McLeods Reel, Bennett, Malcolm (arr.).
Méandres, Lejet, Edith.
Medici Masterworks Solos Volume 1, Gershenfeld, Mitchell (ed.).
Meditation, Åkerwall, Martin.
Mediterranean Rondo, Levy, Yeuda.
Mein! Schubert, Franz.
Melodie Romanza, Frangkiser, Carl.
Melodies of Many Lands, The, Glover, S. (tr. Wesley Jacobs and P. Laville).
Melodious Etude, Bell, William J.
Melody, Geib, Fred.
Melody, Vasilyev, V.
Melody and Romance, Rubenstein, Anton.
Melody from "Orpheus and Euridice," Gluck, Christoph W. von.
Méloman, Gastinelle, Gerard.
Memphis Ridge, Siennicki, Edmund J.
Menuet, Beethoven, Ludwig von.
Menuet, Exaudet, A. (arr. Patrice Sciortino).
Menuet, Hall, Harry H. (arr.).
Menuet, Marpurg.
Menuet (extrait du Petit livre d'Anna Magdalena Bach), Bach, J. S. (arr. Patrice Sciortino).
Menuet and Bourree, Hasse-Gower.
Menuet Éclaté, Damase, Jean-Michel.
Menuet from "Alcina," Handel, George Frederick.
Menuett im Kanon, Radolt, Wenzel Ludwig Freiherr von.
Menuett, Mozart, W. A. (tr. Lars Holmgaard).
Menuette, Boccherini, L.
Menuetto, Mozart, Wolfgang Amadeus.
Menuetto (extrait de la sonate no. X), Mozart, W. A. (arr. Patrice Sciortino).
Merry Peasant, The, from "Album for the Young," Schumann, Robert.
Merry Widow Waltz, Lehar, Franz.
Message, The, Brooks, E.
Messe Solennelle (extrait: Quoniam pour voix de basse), Rossini, G. (arr. Poullot, François).
Michael and I: For Tuba and Piano, Op. 106, Madsen, Trygrave.
Michele, Lennon, John, and McCartney, Paul (arr. John Glenesk Mortimer).
Midnight Bells from the "Opera Ball," Heuberger, Richard.
Mighty Deep, The, Jude, W. H.
Mighty Fortress, A, Jacobs, Wesley (arr.).
A Mighty Fortress Is Our God, Borton, Allen (arr.).
Military March, Little, Donald C. (arr.).
Military Marches Melodies, Ostling, Acton (arr.).
Military Suite, Wekselblatt, Herbert (arr.).
Milonga, Jous, Christian.
Mini Suite, Jeanneau, Francois.
Miniature, Comet, T.
Miniature No. 7, Blazhevich, Vladislav.
Miniaturen-Suite, Benker, Heinz.
Miniatures for Tuba and Piano, Cummings, Barton.
Minstrel Boy, Kinyon, John (arr.).
Minstrel's Song, Nicolai, W. F. G. (tr. Wesley Jacobs and P. Laville).
Minuet, Eccles, John.
Minuet in G, Bach, J. S. (arr. Dishinger).
Minuetto Profondo, Op. 83, 1, Krol, Bernhard.
Minute Sketches, Presser, William.
Mirior et L'Eau, Nissim, Mico.
Misty Morning Ride, Goeller, Dan.
Miya Sama from The Mikado, Sullivan, Arthur and Gilbert, W. S.
Moderation, Quérat, Marcel.
Modern Lullaby, A, Newton, Leonard G.
Modules, Haines, Edmund.
Moment Musical, Schubert, Franz.
Moments d'été, Åkerwall, Martin.
Monsieur Tuba, Fiche, Michel.
Morceau De Concert-Concertstuk, de Jong, Marinus.
Morceau de Concours, Alary, G.
Morceau de Concours, Barat, J. Edouard.
Morceau De Concours I, Defaye, Jean-Michel.
Morceau De Concours II, Defaye, Jean-Michel.
Morceau De Concours III, Defaye, Jean-Michel.
Morceau Vivant, Marteau, Marcel.
More Classics for Young Brass Players, Musser, Willard.
Morning Glory, Vander Cook, H. A.
Morning Song, Kellaway, Roger.
Mosaik, Hoza, Václav, and Hála, Jan.
Moses Variations: Introduction and Variations on a Theme by Rossini, Paganini, Niccolo (arr. Philip Sinder).
Mosey, Broughton, Bruce.
Moss Rose, Vander Cook, H. A.
Mouvement, Henry, Jean-Claude.
Movement for Tuba and Piano (1980), Tal, Joseph.
Movements, Durkó, Zsolt.
"Mr. Tuba" on Broadway, Uber, David.
Mulberry Street Tarantella, Briegel, George F.
Mummers-Danse Grotesque, Merle, John.
Musette, Bach, Johann Sabastian.
Music for Tuba and Orchestra, Eerola, Lasse.
Music for Tuba and Piano, Warren, Frank E.
Music of the Seasons, Miserendino, Joe.
Musica Sacra, Op. 75: Tuba and Piano, Plagge, Wolfgang.
Musical Joke, Dumitru, Ionel.
Musik für den Einzelgänger, Coucounaras, Stelios.
Musizierbuch für Basstuba, Meschke, Dieter.
Mutability Fantasy, Constantinides, Dinos.
Mutu, Bashmakov, Leonid.
Muziek (1976), Woestyne, David Van de.
My Anchor Holds, Everson, Dana F. (arr.).
My Dearest Love (Caro mio ben), Giordani, Giuseppe.
My Faith Looks Up to Thee, Borton, Allen (arr.).
My Jesus I Love Thee, Featherstone, W. R. and Gordon, A. J.
My Jesus I Love Thee, Smith, Claude T.
My Johann, Grieg, Edvard.
My Sweetheart's Eyes, Schubert, Franz.

My Tuba Solo, Scholtes, Walter.
My Tuba Solo, Southwell, George.
My Wild Irish Rose, Olcott.
Mystique, Crockett, Edgar.

N

Nabucco (extrait: Première Partie: Léviti), Verdi, G. (arr. François Poullot).
Nachtstück, Rottler, Werner.
Nature's Adoration, Beethoven, Ludwig von.
Nautical John Medley, Bell, William J.
Nearer, My God, to Thee, Borton, Allen (arr.).
Nervous Turkey Rag, The (November Is Here Again), Barnes, James.
Neutron Stars, Belden, George R.
New Orleans, Bozza, Eugène.
Next, Winter Comes Slowly, Purcell, Henry.
Night and Twilight, Choi, Hae-Kyung.
Nightingale, Jacobs, Wesley (arr.).
Nina, Pergolesi, Giovanni Battista.
Nine Miniatures, Gregson, Edward, and Ridgeon, John.
Nineteen Solos for E♭ Bass with Piano Accompaniment, Weber, Carl (arr.).
No. 4 from 24 Easy Vocalises, Bordogni, G. M.
No. 9 from 24 Easy Vocalises, Bordogni, G. M.
No. 10 from 24 Easy Vocalises, Bordogni, G. M.
Nobody Knows the Trouble I've Seen, Yasumoto, Hiroyuki (arr.).
Nobody Knows the Trouble I've Seen, Heinrich, Claus-Erhard (arr.).
Nocturnal Serenade, Morra, Gene.
Nocturne, Chopin, Frederick.
Nocturne, Geib, Fred.
Nocturne, Gliere, Reinhold.
Nocturne, Mendelssohn, F.
Nocturne (extrait de l'op. 15 no. 3), Chopin, F. (arr. Patrice Sciortino).
Nocturne Et Petite Ronde, Proust, Pascal.
Nocture, Op. 7, Strauss, Franz (arr. Michael Fischer, piano ed. John Cozza).
Nocturne, Op. 9, No. 2, Chopin, Frederic (tr. Steven Eric Marcus).
Nocturno, Op. 7, Strauss, Franz (arr. Rudy Emilson).
None but the Lonely Heart, Op. 6, Tchaikovsky, Peter I.
Now, O Now My Needs Must Part, Dowland, John.
Nr. 15, Etüden für Tuba, Kopprasch, C.
Nr. 19, Etüden für Tuba, Kopprasch, C.
N-sarja, Eerola, Lasse.
Nun komm' der Heiden Heiland, Choral-Vorspiel BMV 659, Bach, J. S. (arr. Walter Hilgers).
Nur Lieben! Dargomijsky, Aleksander S.

O

O Come, All Ye Faithful, Borton, Allen (arr.).
O Come, All Ye Faithful, Conley, Lloyd (arr.).
O du mein holcler Abendstern, from "Tanhöuser," Wagner, Richard.
O God Our Help in Ages Past, Borton, Allen (arr.).
O Isis and Osiris, Mozart, W. A. (arr. R. Winston Morris).
O Isis and Osiris, Mozart, Wolfgang Amadeus.
O Isis and Osiris from "The Magic Flute," Mozart, Wolfgang Amadeus.
O Little Town of Bethlehem, Conley, Lloyd (arr.).
O Mensch, bewein' dein' Sünde gross, Bach, Johann Sabastian.
O Mighty God, Wadowick, James L. (arr.), and McCathren, Donald E. (ed.).
O Ruddier than the Cherry, Kappey.
Ob-la-di, Ob-la-da, Lennon, John, and McCartney, Paul (arr. John Glenesk Mortimer).
Obsessions, Van Der Roost, J.
Octopus and the Mermaid, The, King, Karl L.
Ode to Joy, Beethoven, Ludwig von.
Oh, Is There Not One Maiden Breast? Sullivan, Arthur.
Oh, My Home, Abt, Franz (tr. Wesley Jacobs and P. Laville).
Old American Patriotic Song (Chester), Billings, William.
Old and New Folksongs, Hegenhauser, Marc (Robert Martin Editions).
Old Home Down on the Farm, Harlow.
Old McDonald, Feldstein, Sandy (arr.).
Old Poem, Copland, Aaron (arr. Quincy Hilliard).
Old Rugged Cross, The, Borton, Allen (arr.).
Old Rugged Cross, The, Traditional (arr. Dana Everson).
Old Sexton, The, Russell, H.
Old Sexton, The, Weber, Carl (arr.).
Old Time Theme and Variations, Barnes, W.
Omaggi E Fantasie for Tuba and Piano (1981/87), Baker, Claude.
On Heaven's just cause relying and Rataplan Chorus (From "Les Huguenots"), Meyerbeer.
On the Lake, Brahms, Johannes.
On the Steep High Mountain, Lebedev, A. (arr.).
On the Sunny Side of the Street, McHugh, Jim, and Fields, Dorothy.
On Wings of Song, Mendelssohn (arr. Ostling and Weber).
On Wings of Song, Mendelssohn (tr. Wesley Jacobs and P. Laville).
Once upon A Funicula, Siekmann, Frank.
One Tough Tuba, Solomon, Edward S.
Op. 28—Preludes No. 3, 2 and 24, Chopin, Frederick.
Optima, Nilovic, Janko.
Opus Open, Forez, Henri.
Oracio al Main from "6 Sonnets," Toldra, Eduardo.
Orientale, Cui.
Os Mestres Cantores Da Lapa, Tacuchian, Ricardo.
Ossur, Zoccatelli, V.
Ostinato, Schmidt, A.
Out on the Deep, Lohr, Frederic N.
Oxford Gavotte, Kagan, Susan.

P

Pallas, Dondeyne, Dèsirè (Robert Martin Editions).
Pansies, Vander Cook, H. A.
Pantomime, Uber, David.
Papa Haydn's Tune, Haydn, Franz Joseph.
Papageno Arie, Mozart, W. A. (arr. Lemarc).
Paprika, Csárdás, Baratto, Paolo.
Parable for Tuba and Piano, Siekmann, Frank H.
Passacaglia and Fugue, Henry, Otto.
Pastorale, Goldsmith, James J.
Patron of the Wind from "Phoebus and Pan," Bach, Johann Sabastian.
Pavane, Ravel, Maurice.
Pavane pour une Infante défunte, Ravel, Maurice (ed. and tr. Joseph Skillen).
Peace of Mind, Sponholtz (tr. Wesley Jacobs and P. Laville).
Peaceful Fusion, Banfield, Pete.
Peg Leg Pete, Zaninelli, Luigi.
Penny Lane, Lennon, John, and McCartney, Paul (arr. John Glenesk Mortimer).
Penseroso e L'Allegro, Il, Buchtel, Forrest Lawrence.
Peony, Vander Cook, H. A.
Per la Gloria D'Adorarri from "Griselda," Bononcini, Giovanni.
Per Questa Bella Mano, Mozart, Wolfgang Amadeus.
Per Tuba ad Astram, Woolf, Gregory.
Perpetual Motion, Paganini.
Pershing Concerto, Raum, Elizabeth.
Persian Song, A, Rubinstein, A.
Persiflage, Koepke, Paul.
Petit Air, Boukhitine, Arnaud.
Petit Air, Poutoire, Patrick.
Petit Baobab, Le, Delgiudice, Michel.
Petit Mamouth, Le, Delgiudice, Michel.
Petit piece en fa, Corelli, Arcangelo.
Petite Chansons Pour Marion, Lesaffre, Charles.
Petite suite en cinq tableaux, Boukhitine, Arnaud.
Petite Valse Européene, Françaix, Jean.
Phantasi, Szkutko, John.
Phantasy on an American Spiritual for Tuba and Piano, Schmidt, William.
Philae, Ameller, André.
Piacer d'Aamor, Martini, J. P. E.
Piccolo Capriccio pour tuba et piano, Dupriez, Christian.
Piccolo Suite, Dubois, Pierre Max.
Picture of Dorian Blue, Solid Brass Music Company.
Piece concertante, Debaar, Mathieu.
Piece de concert, Sivic, Pavel.
Piece, A, Volkov, K.
Pièce en forme de Habanera, Ravel, Maurice (arr. Walter Hilgers).
Piece for Tuba and Piano, Lawrence, Lucinda.
Piece from Suite "Colours in Movement," Moro, D.
Piece in C, Maniet, Rene.
Pièce Lyrique, Clérisse, Robert.
Piece of Tuba, Inagaki, Takuzo.
Piece Preve, Cals.
Pièces Classiques, Volume 1, Sciortino, Patrice (arr.).
Pièces Classiques, Volume 2, Sciortino, Patrice (arr.).
Pièces Classiques, Volume 3, Sciortino, Patrice (arr.).
Pièces Classiques, Volume 4, Sciortino, Patrice (arr.).
Pièces Classiques, Volume 5, Sciortino, Patrice (arr.).
Pieces for Tuba (Grades 3 and 4), Warrack, Guy.
Pieces for Tuba and Piano, Guzii, V. (compiled).
Pieces for Tuba and Piano, Larin, J. (ed.).
Pieces for Tuba and Piano, Melnikov, S. (ed.).
Pieces for Tuba and Piano, Mitegin, V. (ed.).
Pieces for Tuba and Piano, Mitjagina, V. (ed.).
Pied Piper, Buchtel, Forrest Lawrence.
Pieta, Signore! Stradella, Alessandro.
Piff, Paff (Les Huguenots), Meyerbeer.
Pilot, The, Nelson, S. (tr. Wesley Jacobs and P. Laville).
Pink Panther, The, Mancini, Henry (arr. Scott Richards).
Planets, Stars, and Airs of Space, Bach, J. S. (arr. Michael Fischer).
Plasir d'Amour, Martini, Padre.
Playera, Granados, E.
Pleasant Hours: A Collection of 20 Standard Melodies, deVille, Paul (arr.).
Plikonumu—Micucona, Goeyvaerts, Karel.
Poco Allegro, Maniet, Rene.
Poem and Burlesque for Double Bass (Tuba) and Piano, Kardos, Istvan.
Poeme, Op. 10, Balthazar, J. L.
Policeman's Song, The, Sullivan, Arthur.
Polka from: The Age of Gold, Shostakovitch, Dimitri.
Polka Funurenilor, Dumitru, Ionel.
Polka Giocoso, Scarmolin, A. Louis.
Polka Graziosa, Del Negro, Luca.
Pomp and Dignity, Scarmolin, A. Louis.
Pompola, Martin, Carroll.
Pomposo Polka, Jennings.
Pop Duets, Story, Michael (arr.).
Popular Solos For The Young Bandsman, Edmunds, John (arr.).
Pourquoi??? Jous, Christian.
Poursuites . . . , Moreau, James.
Praeludium and Fughetta, Stoutamire, Albert L.
Praeludium, Chorale, Variations and Fugue, Mueller, J. I.
Praeludium in C Minor, Vivaldi, Antonio.
Praise Him, All Ye Little Children, Smith, David E. (arr.).
Praise to the Lord, Borton, Allen (arr.).
Prayer, A, Schlemüller, Hugo.
Preghiera, Durante, Francesco.
Prelude, Fesh, D.
Prelude, Kesnar, Maurits.
Prelude, Ledov, A.
Prelude, Orthel, L.
Prélude, Op. 28, No. 4, Chopin, F. (arr. Patrice Sciortino).
Prélude, Op. 28, No. 7 et No. 15, Chopin, F. (arr. Patrice Sciortino).

Prelude and Allegretto, Telemann, Georg Philipp.
Prelude and Allegro, Bozza, Eugène.
Prelude and Faràndola, Hastings, Ross.
Prelude and Fugue, Bottje, Will Gay.
Prelude and Scherzo, Brown, Newel Kay.
Prelude and Scherzo, Cruft, Adrian.
Prélude, arioso et rondo, Franck, Maurice.
Prèlude et Allegro, Bozza, Eugène.
Prélude et Allegro, Charpentier, Jacques.
Prelude et cadence, Barboteu, Georges.
Prelude et Danse Guerriere, Ruelle, F.
Prélude et divertissement, Clérisse, Robert.
Prélude et Fugue, Handel, Georg Friedrich (arr. Kurt Sturzenegger).
Prélude et Jeu, Proust, Pascal.
Prelude in D Minor, BWV 539, Bach, J. S. (arr. Walter Hilgers).
Prelude No. 1, Opus 376B, Hewitt, Harry.
Prelude No. 6, Chopin, Frederick.
Prelude No. 6, Opus 376C, No. 6, Hewitt, Harry.
Prelude XVII from "Das Wohltemperierte Klavier," BWV 862, Teil I, Bach, J. S. (arr. Walter Hilgers).
Prelude XX from "Das Wohltemperierte Klavier," BWV 865, Teil I, Bach, J. S. (arr. Walter Hilgers).
Prelude XXII from "Das Wohltemperierte Klavier," BWV 867, Teil I, Bach, J. S. (arr. Walter Hilgers).
Prelude und Scherzo für Tuba und Klavier, Shekov, Ivan.
Preludes, Barcos, George.
Preludes, Hobbs, Christopher.
Preludes for Pachyderms, Wiggins, Bram.
Preludio and Allemanda, Corelli, Arcangelo.
Preludiu, Dumitru, Ionel.
Premier Pièce De Concours, Porret, Julien.
Premier Solo de Concert, Demerssman, J.
Premier Solo de Concours, Maniet, Rene.
Première Étude de Concours, Petit, Alexandre.
Premieres Variations, Proust, Pascal.
Presto, Mozart, W. A. (arr. Dishinger).
Pretty as a Butterfly, Weber, Carl (arr.).
Pride of America, DeWitt, L. O.
Priere, Rougnon.
Prière D'Elisabeth, Wagner, Richard (arr. Patrice Sciortino).
Priester-Aria aus die Zauberflöte, Mozart, Wolfgang Amadeus.
Prince and the Princess, The, Rimsky-Korsakov (ed. Marlatt, David).
Printemps, Schubert, F. (arr. Patrice Sciortino).
Promenade, Coeck, Louis Jan Alfons Leopold.
Promenade, Hyde, Derek.
Promenade, Joubert, Claude-Henry.
Promenade, Uga, Pierre.
Puerta de Tierra (Bolero), Albeniz, I.
Puff (The Magic Dragon), Yarrow, Peter, and Leonard Lipton.
Puissance 4, Delguidice, Michel.
Pupille Nere, Buononcini, Giovanni.
Puttin' On The Ritz, Berlin, Irving (arr. James Christensen).

Q

Quadrille En Forme De Ronds D'eau, Autran, Alphonse.
Qui Tollis, Hume, James Ord.
Quick Dance, Bogár, István.
Quiet Piece, A, Stewart, Robert.
Quintero—The Farmer, Merle, John.
Quintessence, Clews, Eileen.
Quintus, Debons, Eddy.

R

Ragamuffin, Goddard, Mark.
Rainy Day Rock, Feldstein, Sandy.
Ranger, The, Buchtel, Forrest Lawrence.
Rapsodia para Tuba y Piano, Ayma, David.
Ré mineur, Rivière, Jean-Pierre.
Recercada On The "Passamezzo Moderno" (1553), Ortiz, Diego.
Recit, Gully, Michel.
Récit et Rondo, Tournier, Franz.
Récit et Theme Variations Op. 37, Büsser, P. Henri.
Recital Piece No. 1, Vollrath, Carl.
Recitatif Et Allegro, Depetris, C.
Récitatif, Lied et Final, Brown, Charles.
Recitativ und Burla, Op. 83, 2, Krol, Bernhard.
Recitative and Air from "The Messiah," Handel, George Frederick.
Recitative and Kutuzov's Air from the Opera "War and Peace," Prokofiev, Sergi.
Recitative, Song and Chorus, Purcell, Henry.
Red River Valley, Kinyon, John (arr.).
Reflections, Jager, Robert.
Rejoice, Ye Pure in Heart, Borton, Allen (arr.).
Relation, Quérat, Marcel.
Relax, Baudrier, Émile.
Reluctant Clown, The, Buchtel, Forrest Lawrence.
Remembrance for Tuba and Piano, Cummings, Barton.
Remembrance of Liberati, Casey.
Reminiscences de Navarre, Barat, J. Edouard.
Repentance, Handel, George Frederick.
Requiem for Euphonium or Basstuba and Piano, Lovec, Vladimir.
Requiem for Pee Wee Ervin, Hyman, Dick.
Rêve de choux . . . , Joubert, Claude-Henry.
Revenge! Timotheus Cries! Handel, George Frederick.
Reverie, Debussy, Claude.
Reverie, Mendelssohn, Felix.
Reverie (Schumanniana), de Grignon, Lamote.
Reveries, Simpson, Michael M.
Rhapsodie, Delhaye, R.
Rhapsody, Krivokapic, Igor.
Rhapsody for Tuba and Orchestra, Cioffari, Richard J.

Rhapsody in Black and Blue, Dutton, Brent.
Rhapsody in C Minor, Uber, David.
Riddle Song, The, Boyd, Bill (arr.).
Ride of the Valkyries (from "Die Walkure"), Wagner, Richard (arr. David Uber).
Riff Rock, Sarvello.
Rigaudon, Daquin, Louis-Claude.
Rigaudon, Rameau, J. Ph.
Rigaudon from Piece de Clavecin, Rameau, Jean Philippe.
Ring, A, Lebedev, A. (arr.).
Ritcherkar, Bitch, M.
Ritmico Ed Arioso, Louel, Jean.
Rock Bottom, Uber, David.
Rock'd in the Cradle of the Deep, Knight, J. P.
Rocked in the Cradle of the Deep, DeLamater, E.
Rocked in the Cradle of the Deep, Knight (arr. Ostling and Weber).
Rocked in the Cradle of the Deep, Rance, E. (Adjutant).
Rocked in the Cradle of the Deep, Rollinson, T. H.
Rocked in the Cradle of the Deep, Scholtes, Walter (arr.).
Roghisness, Depetris, C.
Rohtokokoelma, Eerola, Lasse.
Romance, Clérisse, Robert.
Romance, German, Edward.
Romance, Glinka, M.
Romance, Hanson, Raymond.
Romance, Rakov, N.
Romance, Rubinstein, A. (tr. Wesley Jacobs and P. Laville).
Romance, Saint-Saëns, Camille.
Romance, Saint-Saens, Camille (arr. Michael Fischer, piano ed. John Cozza).
Romance, Saint-Saëns, Camilli (arr. John Glenesk Mortimer).
Romance, Scriabine, Alexander.
Romance, Shostakovitch, Dimitri.
Romance, Uber, David.
Romance and Scherzo, Cohen, Sol B.
Romance Espagnuolo, Hume, James Ord.
Romance for Tuba, Raum, Elizabeth.
Romance für F-Tuba, Mozart, W. A.
Romance "Homage to Peter Ilyich," Cole, Keith Ramon.
Romance No. 2, Schumann, Robert.
Romance No. 3, Schumann, Robert.
Romance, Op. 36, Saint-Saens, Camille (tr. Jens-Bjørn Larsen).
Romance, Op. 77, Bourgeois, Derek.
Romance Sentimentale, Niverd, Lucien.
Romanze, Reger, Max (arr. Wisskirchen).
Romanze and Rondo (from: Horn Concerto No. 3), Mozart, Wolfgang Amadeus.
Rondeau, Couperin, Francois (arr. Dishinger).
Rondelay, Jenkins, Cyril.
Rondo, Bach, Johann Sabastian.
Rondo, Jenne, Glenn.
Rondo, Kreisler, Alexander von.
Rondo, Mozart, W. A. (arr. Dishinger).
Rondo, Presser, William.
Rondo, Tchebotarev, S.
Rondo (from Violin Sonata in E♭ Major, op. 12, no. 3), Beethoven, Ludwig von.
Rondo Alla Scherzo (from: Clarinet Concerto in E♭), Stamitz, Karl.
Rondo cantabile, Donati, Guido.
Rondo de Concerto, Mozart, Wolfgang Amadeus.
Rondo International, Dumitru, Ionel.
Rondo Rotundo (Tu in Es), Stephens.
Rondo Variato, Schlenker, Manfred.
Rooster, The, Siennicki, Edmund J.
Rosebuds, Vander Cook, H. A.
Roses from the South, Strauss, Johann.
Roundarounds, Arbel, Chaya.
Rudéral, Joubert, Claude-Henry.
Rumanian Dance No.2, Dumitru, Ionel.
Rumanian Dances, Dumitru, Ionel.
Rupture, Séguin, Pierre.
Russian Dance, Zuerev, V.
Russian Medley, Bell, William J. (arr.).
Russian Song, Rachmaninoff, Sergei.
Russian Song, Stravinsky, Igor.

S

Sad Minute, The, Pozzoli, E.
Sad Song, The, Kalinikov, V.
Sad Song, The, Tchaikovsky, Peter I.
Sailing the Mighty Deep, Moquin, Al.
Sailors' Song, Schumann, Robert.
Sailor's Song, The, Couperin, Francois (arr. Dishinger).
Salamander, The, Buchtel, Forrest Lawrence.
Salicastrum, Smith, Glenn.
Salut d'amour, Elgar, Edward (arr. Michael Fischer, piano ed. John Cozza).
Salut d'amour, Elgar, Edward (arr. Patrick Sheridan and Rich Ridenour).
Samsonian Polka, McQuaide, George.
San Jose Suite, Cummings, Barton.
Sanctus, Berlioz, Hector.
Sandman, Brahms, J.
Sans Pareil, Bell, J. H.
Sarabanda and Gavotta, Corelli, Arcangelo.
Sarabande, Bach, J. S. (arr. Walter Hilgers).
Sarabande, Bach, Johann Sebastian (arr. Walter Hilgers).
Sarabande, Corelli, Arcangelo.
Sarabande, Leclair, Jean-Marie.
Sarabande from Concerto in F Minor, Handel, George Frederick.
Saxhornia, Semler-Collery, Jules.
Scene De Concert, Danmark, Max F.
Scènes du Far West, Proust, Pascal (Robert Martin Editions).
Scenes from Childhood, Op. 15, Schumann, Robert.
Scherzetto, Niverd, Lucien.
Scherzino, Haddad, Don.
Scherzo, Assafyev, B.
Scherzo, Dumitru, Ionel.

Scherzo, Frank, Marcel.
Scherzo, Dumitru, Ionel.
Scherzo for Tuba, Golland, J.
Scherzo, for Tuba and four Horns (or piano), Hidas, Frigyes.
Scherzo for Tuba and Wind Ensemble, Bartles, Alfred.
Scherzo Pomposo, Walters, Harold L.
Scherzo Roman for Tuba and Piano, Ionel, Dumitrul.
Schön Rosmarin, Kreisler, Fritz.
Schule Fur Tuba in F und in B, Hoza, Vaclav.
Science Fiction, Gasner, Moshe.
Sculptured Tradition for Tuba and Piano, Endo, Masao.
Sea Dreams; Three Pieces for Tuba and Piano, York, Barbara.
Sea Gong, The, Desmond, Walter.
Seaview for Tuba and Piano, Childs, Barney.
Sebben, Crudele, Caldara, Antonio.
Second Horn Concerto, Strauss, Richard.
Second Part from Capriccio, Bach, Johann Sebastian.
Second Sonatina for Tuba and Piano, Presser, William.
See, the Conquering Hero Comes, Handel (tr. Wesley Jacobs and P. Laville).
See, the Conquering Hero Comes, Handel, George Frederick.
Sentimental Sarabande from the "Simple Symphony" for String Orchestra, The, Britten, Benjamin.
Sento Nel Core, Scarlatti, Allessandro.
Serenada d'Hivern from "6 Sonnets," Toldra, Eduardo.
Serenade, Geib, Fred.
Serenade, Mozart, Wolfgang Amadeus.
Serenade, Owen, J. A.
Serenade, Schmidt, William.
Sérénade, Schubert, F. (arr. Patrice Sciortino).
Serenade, Schubert, Franz (arr. Roger Bobo).
Serenade, Weiner, Lawrence.
Serenade and Scherzo, Ostransky, Leroy.
Serenade D957 No. 4, Schubert, Franz (arr. John Glenesk Mortimer).
Serenade for Bass Tuba, Kac, Stefan.
Serenade for Tuba and Piano, Israel, Brian.
Serenade for Tuba and Piano, Rae, Allan.
Serenade from "Don Giovanni," Mozart, Wolfgang Amadeus.
Serenade from "Student Prince," Romberg, Sigmund.
Serenata, Schooley, John.
Serial Stomp, Gale.
Serioso, Mihalovici, M.
Serpent of the Brass, Worth, George E.
Set of Three, Smolanoff, Michael.
Seven Shorts, Largent.
Shades of Tuba, Vasconi, Eugene.
Shenandoah, Bennett, Malcolm (arr.).
Shlag uns Nöch Liefdo, Helweg, Kim.
Short Stuff, Lackey, Jerry.
Short Suspense Story, A, Rufeisen, Arie.
Showdown! Vosk, Jay.
Siciliano, Bach, Johann Sabastian.
Siciliano and Chorale, Bach, Johann Sebastian.
Siciliano from Sonata No. II, Bach, Johann Sabastian.
Sicilienne, Rougnon.
Sicilienne d'apres la 1re Sonate en Sol mineur (BMV 1,001) pour Voilin seul, Bach, Johann Sabastian.
Siegfried (from Act II, Prelude and First Scene), Wagner, Richard.
Silent Night, Borton, Allen (arr.).
Silent Night, Conley, Lloyd (arr.).
Silent Night, Gruber.
Silhouette, Harmon, John.
Silver Threads among the Gold and Deep River, Danks, H. P. and Harris, A. E.
Simon the Cellarer, Hatton, J. L.
Simple Gifts, Copland, Aaron (arr. Quincy Hilliard).
Simplex pour tuba et piano, Guinot, Georges-Léonce.
Sine Nomine, Kilon, Moshe.
Six Airs for Euphonium or Tuba, Vol. 1, Friedrich, Kenneth, D.
Six Airs for Euphonium or Tuba, Vol. 2, Friedrich, Kenneth, D.
Six Little Tuba Pieces, Jacob, Gordon.
Six Little Tuba Pieces, Ridout, Alan.
Six Modern Pieces, Lawrance, Peter.
Six Petites Pièces De Style, Niverd, Lucien.
Six Petits Morceaux, Schrijver, Karel de.
Six Popular Solos, Prendiville, Harry (arr.).
Six Preludes for Tuba and Piano, Op 376B, Hewitt, Harry.
Six Studies in English Folk-Song, Vaughan Williams, Ralph.
Skaters, The, Wauldteufel, Emil.
Skater's Waltz, Waldteufel.
Sketches for Tuba and Piano, McFarland, Michael.
Skjemt, Killengreen, Christian.
Skylines, Uber, David.
Slow-Fox-Medium, Hrdina, Eman.
Slumber Song, Gretchaninoff, A.
Small Suite for Bass (Tuba) and Piano, Wilder, Alec.
Smuggler, The, Beresford, Arnold.
Softly, Softly, Rossini, Gioacchino.
Soir, Clérisse, Robert.
Soliloque, Weber, Alain.
Solioquy, Hume, James Ord.
Soliloquy for Tuba and Piano, Cummings, Barton.
Solitude, Lotzenhiser, G. W.
Solitude Caprice, Mercadante.
Solo and Duo for Tuba and Piano, Moylan, William.
Solo de Concourts, Wurmser, Lucien.
Solo for Tuba and String Quartet, Mellilo, Peter.
Solo Miniature, Murphy, Bower.
Solo Pomposo, Hayes, Al.

Solo Sounds for Tuba, Level 1–3, Vol 1, Lamb, Jack (ed.).
Solo Sounds for Tuba, Level 3–5, Vol 1, Lamb, Jack (ed.).
Soloist Folio, Voxman, H.
Soloist Folio for Bass (E♭ or BB♭), Rubank.
Solo-Pak for Tuba, Part One, Little, Donald C. (arr.).
Solo-Pak for Tuba, Part Three, Little, Donald C. (arr.).
Solo-Pak for Tuba, Part Two, Little, Donald C. (arr.).
Solos for the Tuba Player, Wekselblatt, Herbert.
Solos for the Tuba Player, Wekselblatt, Herbert (ed.).
Solos from the Classics, Jacobs, Wesley (arr.).
Solstice, Cole, Keith Ramon.
Sometimes I Feel like a Motherless Child, Barnes, James (arr.).
Sonare per Tuba e Piano, Friedman, Norman.
Sonata, Anderson, Garland.
Sonata, Benjamin, Thomas.
Sonata, Dutillet, Jacques.
Sonata, Ekkls, H.
Sonata, Gower, Albert.
Sonata, Köper, Karl-Heinz.
Sonata, Marcello, Benedetto.
Sonata, Pisciotta, Louis V.
Sonata, Salzedo, Leonard.
Sonata, Schmidt, William.
Sonata, Skolnik, Walter.
Sonata, Smironova, T.
Sonata, Telemann, Georg P. (tr. and ed. Kenneth Drobnak).
Sonata, Vivaldi, Antonio.
Sonata, Weiner, Lawrence.
Sonata, Zeman, Thomas.
Sonata I, from 6 Solos for a Violoncello, Marcello, Benedetto.
Sonata I in A Minor, Galliard, Johann Ernst (arr. John Glenesk Mortimer).
Sonata II, Bach, Johann Sabastian.
Sonata II in G Major, Galliard, Johann Ernst (arr. John Glenesk Mortimer).
Sonata III in F Major, Galliard, Johann Ernst (arr. John Glenesk Mortimer).
Sonata IV in E Minor, Galliard, Johann Ernst (arr. John Glenesk Mortimer).
Sonata V in D Minor, Galliard, Johann Ernst (arr. John Glenesk Mortimer).
Sonata VI in C Major, Galliard, Johann Ernst (arr. John Glenesk Mortimer).
Sonata Capricciosa, Takács, Jeno.
Sonata (Concerto), Broughton, Bruce.
Sonata Da Chiesa, Corelli, Archangelo (arr. Morris).
Sonata Di Bravura, Uber, David.
Sonata for Bass Horn and Piano, Strebel, Neal.
Sonata for Bass Trombone (Tuba) and Piano, Schnyder, Daniel.
Sonata for Bass Tuba, Gottschalk, Arthur.
Sonata for Bass Tuba and Piano, Beversdorf, Thomas G.
Sonata for Bass Tuba and Piano, Uber, David.
Sonata for BB♭ Bass and Piano, Peterson, Lawrence.
Sonata for (F) Tuba and Piano, Op.34, Madsen, Trygve.
Sonata for Tuba, Guion, David M.
Sonata for Tuba, Morawetz, Oskar.
Sonata for Tuba, White, Donald H.
Sonata for Tuba and Organ, Kulesha, Gary Alan.
Sonata for Tuba and Piano, Blumenfeld, Aaron.
Sonata for Tuba and Piano, Borton, Allen L.
Sonata for Tuba and Piano, Brandon, Sy.
Sonata for Tuba and Piano, Donovan, Mike.
Sonata for Tuba and Piano, Frackenpohl, Arthur.
Sonata for Tuba and Piano, Fritze, Gregory.
Sonata for Tuba and Piano, Garrett, James.
Sonata for Tuba and Piano, George, Thom Ritter.
Sonata for Tuba and Piano, Gower, Albert.
Sonata for Tuba and Piano, Hartley, Walter S.
Sonata for Tuba and Piano, Karlsen, Kjell Mork.
Sonata for Tuba and Piano, Kitsz, Dennis Bathory.
Sonata for Tuba and Piano, LaPresti, Ronald.
Sonata for Tuba and Piano, Lockwood, Harry.
Sonata for Tuba and Piano, McIntyre, David, L.
Sonata for Tuba and Piano, Payne, Frank Lynn.
Sonata for Tuba and Piano, Powell, David.
Sonata for Tuba and Piano, Prescott, John.
Sonata for Tuba and Piano, Rekhin, Igor.
Sonata for Tuba and Piano, Reynolds, Verne.
Sonata for Tuba and Piano, Schmidt, Ole.
Sonata for Tuba and Piano, Sibbing, Robert.
Sonata for Tuba and Piano, Sivelov, Niklas.
Sonata for Tuba and Piano, Smith, Kile.
Sonata for Tuba and Piano, Stabile, James.
Sonata for Tuba and Piano, Warren, Frank E.
Sonata for Tuba and Piano, Wenström-Lekare, Lennart.
Sonata for Tuba and Piano, Wessman, Harri.
Sonata for Tuba and Piano, Whatley, G. Larry.
Sonata for Tuba and Piano, Wilder, Alec.
Sonata for Tuba and Piano, Zhurbin, Lev.
Sonata for Tuba and Piano (Op. 6), Krush, Jay.
Sonata for Tuba and Piano, Op. 162, Homboe, Vagn.
Sonata for Tuba and Piano, Op. 277, Bentzon, Niels Viggo.
Sonata for Tuba and Piano, Op. 393, Bentzon, Niels Viggo.
Sonata for Tuba in F and Piano, Holliday, Kent.
Sonata for Tuba, Opus 55, Cunningham, Michael.
Sonata for Tuba, Op. 393, Bentzon, Niels Viggo.
Sonata in A Minor, Vivaldi, Antonio (arr. Kenneth Drobnak, piano ed. Gian Francesco Malipiero).
Sonata in A♭ Major, Porpora, Nicola Antonio (arr. Kurt Sturzenegger).
Sonata in C Major, Bella, Domenico della (arr. John Glenesk Mortimer).

Sonata in C Major, Telemann, Georg P. (tr. and ed. Kenneth Drobnak, piano ed. Wilhelm Weismann).
Sonata in D Minor, Corrette, Michel.
Sonata in D Minor, Finger, Godfrey.
Sonata in Es, Bach, J. S. (arr. Cooley).
Sonata in F Major, Telemann, Georg Philipp.
Sonata in F Minor, Telemann, Georg Philipp (arr. John Glenesk Mortimer).
Sonata in G Major for Tuba and Piano, Beethoven, Ludwig von.
Sonata in G Minor, Op. 1, No. 10, Antoniotti, Giorgio.
Sonata in One Movement, Uber, David.
Sonata in 6 Min. 30 Seconds, Pascal.
Sonata la traviata, Naessén, Ray.
Sonata No. 1 for Tuba and Piano, Hewitt, Harry.
Sonata No. 1 for Tuba and Piano, Konko, Iwao.
Sonata No. 1 for Tuba and Piano, Mowery, Carl D.
Sonata No. I in B♭ Major, Vivaldi, Antonio (arr. John Glenesk Mortimer).
Sonata No. 1 in F Major, Marcello, Benedetto.
Sonata No. I in F Major, Marcello, Benedetto (arr. John Glenesk Mortimer).
Sonata No. 2, Israel, Brian.
Sonata No. 2, Marcello, Benedetto (arr. Michael Blostein).
Sonata No. 2 for Tuba and Piano, Hewitt, Harry.
Sonata No. 2 for Tuba and Piano, Konko, Iwao.
Sonata No. 2 for Tuba and Piano, Mowery, Carl D.
Sonata No. 2 for Tuba and Piano, Wilder, Alec.
Sonata No. 2 from "Pastor Fido," Vivaldi, Antonio (arr. Cooley).
Sonata No. II in E Minor, Marcello, Benedetto (arr. John Glenesk Mortimer).
Sonata No. II in F Major, Vivaldi, Antonio (arr. John Glenesk Mortimer).
Sonata No. 3 "Basingstoke," White, John.
Sonata No. 3 a-moll, Vivaldi, Antonio (arr. Morris).
Sonata No. III in A Minor, Marcello, Benedetto (arr. John Glenesk Mortimer).
Sonata No. 3 in A Minor, Vivaldi, Antonio.
Sonata No. III in A Minor, Vivaldi, Antonio (arr. John Glenesk Mortimer).
Sonata No. IV in B♭ Major, Vivaldi, Antonio (arr. John Glenesk Mortimer).
Sonata No. IV in G Minor, Marcello, Benedetto (arr. John Glenesk Mortimer).
Sonata No. 5, Galliard, John Ernest.
Sonata No. V in B♭ Major, Marcello, Benedetto (arr. John Glenesk Mortimer).
Sonata No. 5 in C Major, Marcello, Benedetto.
Sonata No. V in E Minor, Vivaldi, Antonio (arr. John Glenesk Mortimer).
Sonata No. 6, Galliard, John Ernest.
Sonata No. 6, Handel, George Frederick.
Sonata No. VI in B♭ Major, Vivaldi, Antonio (arr. John Glenesk Mortimer).
Sonata No. VI in G Major, Marcello, Benedetto (arr. John Glenesk Mortimer).
Sonata No. 7, Haydn, Franz Joseph.
Sonata No. 7, First Movement, Haydn, Franz Joseph.
Sonata No. 9, Opus 5, Corelli, Arcangelo.
Sonata No. 10, Opus 5, Corelli, Arcangelo.
Sonata, Op. 5, Sivelöv, Niklas.
Sonata, Op. 204, Bourgeois, Derek.
Sonata per Tuba (Contrabasso) and Piano, Garbarino, Giuseppe.
Sonata Ritmico, Brandon, Sy.
Sonata Romantica for Tuba and Piano, Cohn, James.
Sonata Romantica per tuba e pianoforte, Fotek, Jan.
Sonata Tuba and Piano, Bardwell, William.
Sonata-Fantasia for Tuba and Piano, Calabro, Louis.
Sonatas for Tuba and Piano, Blazhevich, Vladislav.
Sonatas I–VI, Galliard, Johann Ernst (arr. John Glenesk Mortimer).
Sonatas I–VI, Marcello, Benedetto (arr. John Glenesk Mortimer).
Sonatas I–VI, Vivaldi, Antonio (arr. John Glenesk Mortimer).
Sonate, Delhaye, R.
Sonate, Deutschmann, Gerhard.
Sonate, Drude, Matthias.
Sonate, Filas, Juraj.
Sonate, Gagneux, Renaud.
Sonate, Gardonyi, Zoltan.
Sonate, Genzmer, Harald.
Sonate, Hindemith, Paul.
Sonate, Laburda, Jirí.
Sonate, Schürch, Cyrill.
Sonate II for Tuba and Piano, Bach, Johann Sabastian.
Sonate XVII, Mozart, W. A. (arr. Patrice Sciortino).
Sonate C-Dur für Tuba und Klavier/Orgel, Handel, George Frederick.
Sonate D-Dur, Leclair.
Sonate en do majeur (Sonata in C Major), Loeillet, Jean-Baptiste.
Sonate en do majeur (Sonata in C Major), Loeillet, Jean-Baptiste (arr. Kurt Sturzenegger).
Sonate en fa majeur, Albinoni.
Sonate en re majeur, Albinoni.
Sonate for Tuba and Piano, Holmboe, Vagn.
Sonate for Tuba og Klaver, Roikjer, Kjell.
Sonate für Basstuba und Klavier, Stekl, Konrad.
Sonate für Tuba und Klavier, Kladnitzki, W.
Sonate in 6 Minutes 30, Pascal, Claude.
Sonatina, Boda, John.
Sonatina, Danburg, Russell.
Sonatina, Ferriano, Frank.
Sonatina, Hartley, Walter S.
Sonatina, Koetsier, Jan.
Sonatina, Rakov, N.
Sonatina, Uber, David.
Sonatina (1972) for Tuba and Piano, Kulesha, Gary Alan.
Sonatina Classica, Troje-Miller, N.
Sonatina for Tuba and Piano, East, Harold.
Sonatina for Tuba and Piano, Ehle, Robert.

Sonatina for Tuba and Piano, Glass, Jennifer.
Sonatina for Tuba and Piano, Hogg, Merle E.
Sonatina for Tuba and Piano, Presser, William.
Sonatina for Tuba and Piano, Rollin, Robert.
Sonatina for Tuba and Piano, Sear, Walter.
Sonatina for Tuba and Piano, Stevens, Halsey.
Sonatina für Tuba und Klavier, Rottler, Werner.
Sonatina Giocosa, Hartley, Walter S.
Sonatina Movement IV, Link, I.
Sonatina Tuba e Pianoforte, Koetsier, Jan.
Sonatine, Castérède, Jacques.
Sonatine, Hombsch.
Sonatine, Link, Joachim-Dietrich.
Sonatine für Baßtuba und Klavier, Hummel, Bertold.
Sonatine für Tuba (Posaune) und Klavier, Koch, Johannes H. E.
Sonatine für Tuba und Klavier, Foremny, Stephan.
Sonatine No. 1, Uber, David.
Sonatine No. 2, Uber, David.
Sonatuba, Uber, David.
Song, Zverev, V.
Song, A, Bartok, Bela.
Song after Battle for Tuba and Piano, Wunder, Richard.
Song and a Dance, A, Dubrovsky, I.
Song for Carol, Wilder, Alec.
Song for Michael, James, Ifor.
Song for Tuba and Piano, Warren, Frank E.
Song from the Cycle "Persian Songs," Rubinstein, A.
Song from the Opera "Snow Maiden," Rimsky-Korsakov, N.
Song from Timon of Athens, Purcell (arr. Little).
Song of India, Rimsky-Korsakov, N.
Song of the Bethrothed, Schumann (arr. Willard Musser, Willard).
Song of the East, Rimsky-Korsakov, N.
Song of the Field, Miaskovskii, N.
Song of the Flea, Moussorgsky, M.
Song of the Sea, Buchtel, Forrest Lawrence.
Song of the Viking, Buchtel, Forrest Lawrence.
Song of the Volga Boatman, Boyd, Bill (arr.).
Song without Words—Air with Variations, Geib, Fred.
Songs from Die Schöene Müellerin, Schubert, Franz.
Songs of Ascent (Concerto), Kellaway, Roger.
Sonorities for Tuba and Piano, Hartley, Walter S.
Sound an Alarm from "Judas Maccabeus," Handel, George Frederick.
Soundpiece, Snyder, Randall.
Sousaphone, The, Del Negro, Luca.
Sousaphone Polka, Bell, William J.
Sousaphonium, Moquin, Al.
Souvenance, Roger, Denise.
Souvenir de Calais, Liagré, Dartagnan.
Souvenir de Paris, Lannoy, J. B. de.
Souvenir du Poitou, Legendre.
Spacious Firmament, The, Haydn, J.
Spacious Firmament on High, The, Haydn, Franz Joseph.
Spanish Dance, Kazadezins, R.
Spanish Dance No. 2 (Oriental), Granados, E.
Spanish Dance No. 5 (Andaluza), Granados, E.
Spanish Waltzes, Waldteufel.
Spartan, The, Bell, William J.
Spartan, The, Buchtel, Forrest Lawrence.
Spiritoso, Pergolesi.
Spiritual Bell, Broege, Timothy.
Spring Fancy, O'Neill, Charles.
Spring's Awakening, Bach, E.
Stand Up, Stand Up for Jesus, Traditional (arr. David E. Smith).
Ständchen, Schubert, Franz.
Stars and Stripes Forever, Sousa, John Philip.
Stars in the Velvety Sky, Clarke, Herbert L. (arr. Velvet Brown).
Statements, Plog, Anthony.
Steal Away, Jacobs, Wesley (arr.).
Steal Away, Kinyon, John (arr.).
Steeple, The, Jacobs, Wesley (arr.).
Still Sweeter Every Day, Dondit, Dee Ann (arr.).
Sting Ray, Eitel, Butler.
Stocking Stuffers, Cummings, Barton.
Storm King, The, Ringleben, J.
Straitjacket, Gorb, Adam.
Streets of Laredo, Boyd, Bill (arr.).
Structures, Waignein, André.
Stupendo, Brahmstedt, N. K.
Suite, Bruckmann, Ferdinand.
Suite, Gotkovsky, Ida.
Suite, Lovingood, Kay.
Suite, Luypaerts, G. Ph.
Suite Babu, (Are You My), Volkmann, Rudy.
Suite Brève dans le goût classique, Désenclos, A.
Suite Concertante, Russell, Armand.
Suite Concertante, Schoonenbeek, Kees.
Suite for Bass Clef Instruments, McKay, George Frederick.
Suite for Brass, Skeen.
Suite for Louise, Masso, George.
Suite for Tuba, Haddad, Don.
Suite for Tuba, Presser, William.
Suite for Tuba and Piano, Butts, Carrol M.
Suite for Tuba and Piano, Nelhybel, Vaclav.
Suite for Tuba and Piano, Soule, Edmund F.
Suite for Tuba and Piano, Staples, James.
Suite GWV 209, Graap, Lothar.
Suite in A Minor for Flute and Strings, Telemann, Georg Philipp.
Suite in A-flat, Handel, George Frederick.
Suite Marine, Defaye, Jean-Michel.
Suite No. 1 for Tuba and Piano ("Effie Suite"), Wilder, Alec.
Suite No. 1 from The Magic Flute, Mozart, W. A. (arr. Arthur Frackenpohl).
Suite No. 1 from The Magic Flute, Mozart, Wolfgang Amadeus.
Suite No. 2 for Tuba and Piano (Jesse Suite), Wilder, Alec.
Suite No. 2 from The Magic Flute, Mozart, Wolfgang Amadeus.
Suite No. 3, Cummings, Barton.

Suite No. 3 for Tuba and Piano "Suite for Little Harvey," Wilder, Alec.
Suite No. 4, Cummings, Barton.
Suite No. 4 for Tuba and Piano "Thomas Suite," Wilder, Alec.
Suite No. 5, Cummings, Barton.
Suite No. 5 for Tuba and Piano (Ethan Ayer), Wilder, Alec.
Suite pour Tuba, Martelli, Henri.
Suite Syncopation (Tu in Es), Cliff.
Suleika, Mendelssohn (arr. Willard Musser).
Summer Celebration, Miserendino, Joe.
Summer Nocturne, Uber, David.
Sunday, Brahms, Johannes.
Sunday, Brahms (arr. Little).
Sunday, Brahms (arr. Willard Musser).
Sunday (Sonntag, Op. 47, 1968), Brahms, Johannes.
Superman, Delguidice, Michel.
Sur la Montagne (Pastorale), Bruniau, Aug.
Svensk Concerto, Sagvik, Stellan.
Swan, The, Saint-Saens, Camille (arr. Roger Bobo).
Swan, The, Siennicki, Edmund J.
Swan from "Carnival of the Animals," The, Saint-Saens, Camille (arr. Patrick Sheridan).
Swan Song, Schubert, Franz.
Sweet and Low, Barnby, Sir Joseph.
Sweet Betsy from Pike, Kinyon, John (arr.).
Sweets for Brass, Solid Brass Music Company.
Swing for brass, Muller, Thierry (Robert Martin Editions).
Swingin', Goddard, Mark.
Swiss Air, Newsome, Roy.
Symphonic Variants for Euphonium and Band, Curnow, James.
Symphonie No. 7 (extrait), Beethoven, L.v. (arr. Patrice Sciortino).
Symphonie No. IX (extrait), Dvorak, A. (arr. Patrice Sciortino).

T

Tabu for Tuba, Downey, John.
Take Me Out to the Ball Game, Tilzer, Alber von, and Norworth, Jack.
Tale, A, Smironova, T.
Tambourin, Rameau, J. P. (arr. Patrice Sciortino).
Tango, Clews, Eileen.
Tango Anyone? Edelson, Edward.
Tango Images, Mañas, Adriana Figueroa.
Tannhäuser (extrait: Acte II, Scéne III: Air du Landgrave), Wagner, R. (arr. François Poullot).
Tannhäuser (extrait: Acte II, Scéne IV: Autre air du Landgrave), Wagner, R. (arr. François Poullot).
Tarantelle, Walters, Harold L.
"Te Anau" Fantasia, Hume, James Ord.
Tecnica In Aba, Vanheel, L.
Teddy Bears' Picnic, The, Bratton, John W.
Tema Cantabile con Piernicazioni per tuba universale e pianoforte, Zajaczek, Roman.
Tempesta Polka, Harris, John H.
Temporal Landscape No. 1, Vogel, Roger C.
Temporal Landscape No. 4, Vogel, Roger C.
Ten Pieces for Tuba and Piano, Pasquet, Luis.
Tendres Mélodies, Wurmser, Lucien.
Texas Horizons, Quate and Little.
Texas Horizons, Quate, Amy, and Little, Don.
Thanksgiving, Jacobs, Wesley (arr.).
Theater Piece, Uber, David.
Theater Piece for Tuba and Piano, Cody, Robert O.
Theme and Variations, Dvarionas, B.
Theme and Variations for Tuba, Compello, Joseph.
Thème et Variations, Aubain, Jean Emmanuel.
Thème Varié, Bozza, Eugène.
Thème Varié, Petit, Pierre.
There's a Hole in the Bucket, Feldstein, Sandy (arr.).
Thine Is the Glory, Borton, Allen (arr.).
This Old Man, Feldstein, Sandy (arr.).
Thomas Wyss Tuba Collection (Tu in Es), The, Wyss.
Thoughts of Sunraysia, Gross, Eric.
Three Chopin Preludes for Tuba and Piano, Chopin, Frederick.
Three Episodes, Brandon, Sy.
Three Expressioni, Croley, R.
Three Famous Melodies, Ostling, Acton (arr.).
Three Favorites, Weber, Fred (arr.).
Three Inventions, Schwartz, Elliot.
Three Lyric Pieces, Butterworth, Arthur.
Three Miniatures, Plog, Anthony.
Three Miniatures for Tuba and Piano, Yuhas, D.
Three Movements (1988), Brink, David S.
Three Movements for Tuba and Piano, Winteregg, Steven.
Three Pieces for Tuba and Piano, Eerola, Lasse.
Three Pieces for Tuba and Piano, Johnston, Richard.
Three Pieces for Tuba and Piano, Wenstrom-Lekare, Lennart.
Three Romances, Schumann, Robert (arr. Cooley).
Three Sketches, Lloyd, Gerald.
Three Songs for Tuba, Mason, Roger.
Three Traditional Tunes for Sabbath (1974), Braun, Yehezkel.
Three Traditional Tunes for Sabbath Eve (1974), Braun, Yehezkel.
Three Tuba Pieces, Parfrey, Raymond.
Three Tuba Rags, Jackman, Andrew.
Three Tuba Solos, Howe, Marvin C. (arr.).
Three Virtues, Heinick, David.
Thrène, Lysight, Michel.
Thrice Happy the Monarch from "Alexander Balus," Handel, George Frederick.
Thu Sau, Cummings, Barton.
Time, A Season, A, Bourassa, Richard.
Tis So Sweet to Trust in Jesus, Smith, David E. (arr.).
To Each His Own, Livingston, J., and Evans, R.
Toccata, Carion.
Toccata, Nordel, Marius.
Toga Virilis, Smedvig, Egil.
Tom Bowling, Dibdin, Tom Bowling (tr. Wesley Jacobs and P. Laville).
Tom Dooley, Feldstein, Sandy (arr.).
Tomsky's Song from the Opera "Queen of Spades," Tchaikovsky, Peter I.

Ton Coeur (Tuba), Renaud, Manuel.
Tonal Miniature Pieces, Roikjer, Kjell.
Toreador's Song, Bizet, Georges.
Torre Alada, Widmer, Ernst.
Totentanz, Bernofsky, Lauren.
Touch of Tuba, A, Dedrick, Art.
Tournevalse, Durand, Eric.
Tournevalse, Durand-Audard, Pierre.
Tramp! Tramp! Tramp! DeLamater, E. (arr.).
Träumeri, Schumann, Robert.
Trennung, Brahms, Johannes (arr. David Green).
Três miniaturas, Bauer, Guilherme.
Triade, Holstein, Jean Paul.
Trio 48, Haydn, Franz Joseph.
Trio No. 3, Beethoven, L.v. (arr. Patrice Sciortino).
Triptych for Tuba and Piano, Weeks, Clifford M.
Triste España Sin Ventura, Enciña, Juan Del.
Trois caricatures, Toulon, Jacques.
Trois Duos Pour Tuba Et Piano, Jolas, Betsy.
Trois Exercises de Style, Lemaire, Jean.
Trojan, Szkutko, John.
Trolley Song, The, Martin, Hugh, and Blaine, Ralph.
Troubadour, The, Buchtel, Forrest Lawrence.
Trumpet Voluntary, Clarke, Jeremiah.
Tub' 88, Clais, Tristan.
Tuba, Stewart, Joseph.
Tuba and Piano Sonata: Three Movements, Knight, Morris.
Tuba (Bass) Soloist-Book 1, Ostling, Acton, and Weber, Fred (arr.).
Tuba Blues, Proust, Pascal.
Tuba Buffo, Jacobsen, Julius.
Tuba Buffo: Concerto for Tuba and Wind Band, Jacobsen, Julius.
Tuba Caper, Burgstahler, Elton E.
Tuba Compositae, Amos, K.
Tuba Concerto, Bach, Jan.
Tuba Concerto, Bennett, Malcolm.
Tuba Concerto, Carrier, Loran F.
Tuba Concerto, Ellerby, Martin.
Tuba Concerto, Godel, Didier.
Tuba Concerto, Golland, John.
Tuba Concerto, Gregson, Edward.
Tuba Concerto, Handel, G. F. (ed. Roy Newsome).
(Tuba) Concerto, Handel, G. F. (piano ed. Roy Newsome).
Tuba Concerto, Hidas, Frigyes.
Tuba Concerto, Horovitz, Joseph.
Tuba Concerto, McKimm, Barry.
Tuba Concerto, Plog, Anthony.
Tuba Concerto, Proctor, Simon.
Tuba Concerto, Ross, Walter.
Tuba Concerto, Woodward, James.
Tuba Concerto für Tuba und Klavier, Mortimer, John Glenesk.
Tuba Concerto No. 1 in B Minor, Anderson, Eugene D.
Tuba Concerto, Opus 38, Bourgeois, Derek.
Tuba d'Amore, Robert Martin Editions.
Tuba Diobolica (Polka), Dumitru, Ionel.
Tuba Kapriolen, Graetsch, Hans.
Tuba Miniatures, Szkutko, John.
Tuba mirum, Eyser, Eberhard.
Tuba Mirum, Op. 35, Galán, Carlos.
Tuba Mosaique, Armand, Migani.
Tuba or Not Tuba, Senon, Gilles.
Tuba Player's Debut, The, Wiggins, Bram.
Tuba Rhapsody, Grundman, Clare.
Tuba Rose (Polka), Hartley, Walter S.
Tuba Show, Lodéon, André.
Tuba Smarties, Flowers, Herbie.
Tuba Solos (BB♭ Bass) Volume One, Fletcher, John (arr.).
Tuba Solos (E♭ Bass) Volume One, Fletcher, John (arr.).
Tuba Solos (Tuba in C) Volume One, Fletcher, John (arr.).
Tuba Solos for the Young Player, Solomon, Edward S.
Tuba Solos, Level One, CPP/Belwin, Inc.
Tuba Solos, Level Two, CPP/Belwin, Inc.
Tuba Sonata, Baksa, Robert.
Tuba Sonata in A, Brothern, Hartman.
Tuba Suite, Jacob, Gordon.
Tuba Suite, Wells, John.
Tuba Tango, Edelson, Edward.
Tuba Tantrum, Miller, Vernon R.
Tuba Treat, Frith, John.
Tuba Tunes, Hanmer, Ronald.
Tuba Tutor Vol. 1, Lebedev, A (ed.).
Tuba Tutor Vol. 2, Lebedev, A (ed.).
Tuba Volume #1, Yasumoto, Hiroyuki (arr.).
Tuba Volume #2, Yasumoto, Hiroyuki (arr.).
Tuba Volume #3, Yasumoto, Hiroyuki (arr.).
Tuba-Abut, Ameller, André.
Tubabil, Meunier, Gérard.
Tubabillage, Gabaye, Pierre.
Tubacchanale, Boutry, Roger.
Tuba-Concert, Ameller, André.
Tubadour, Fote, Richard.
Tubafolia (Concerto), Chebrou, Michael.
Tubagig, The, Holmgaard, Lars.
Tuba-I, Cecconi, Monic.
Tubakonzert, Poteenko, Aleksandr.
Tubalied for Tuba and Contemporary Wind Ensemble or Piano, Fredrickson, Thomas.
Tubalow, Burgstahler, Elton E.
Tubaman, The, Bell, William J.
Tubania for Tuba and Piano, Koch, Erland von.
Tubanova, Semler-Collery, Jules.
Tubantella, Legrady, Thomas.
Tubarag, Frackenpohl, Arthur.
Tubaria, Bigot, Pierre.
Tubaria, Brouquières, Jean.
Tubaroque, Boutry, Roger.
Tuba-Sepp'l, Engelhardt, Ernst.
Tuba-Tabu, Köper, Karl-Heinz.
Tuba-Talk, Hyde, Derek.
Tubateer Polka, The, Bell (arr.).
Tubatests, Cycle I, Pichaureau, Claude.
Tuba-Triptychon, Grunelius, Wilhelm von.
Tubavardage, Séguin, Pierre.

Tubaverseny, Istvàn, Bogar.
Tuber Music, Proctor, Simon.
Tubilustrum, Angerer, Paul.
Tubism, Gross, Eric.
Tubissimo, Dondeyne, Désiré.
Tubonetta, Pauer, Jirí.
Tubossa—A Concert Bossanova for Solo Tuba and Symphonic Band, Bartles, Alfred.
Tulip, Vander Cook, H. A.
Tune for Tuba (Sonatina for Tuba and Piano), Goode, Jack C.
Tunuva Tuba, Joubert, Claude-Henry.
Turkish March, Mozart, W. A. (arr. Amis).
Twelve Preludes Tuba and Piano, Hewitt, Harry.
12 Sketches, Hobbs, Christopher.
Twenty-Four Pieces for Tuba and Piano, Roikjer, Kjell.
Twenty-Four Preludes for Tuba and Piano, Jacobsen, Julius.
Twenty-Four Preludes for Tuba and Piano, Roikjer, Kjell.
Twilight, Rachmaninoff, Sergi (arr. Stephen Shoop).
Twilight Dreams, Clarke, Herbert L.
Twinkle, Twinkle Little Star, Feldstein, Sandy (arr.).
Two Classical Themes, Haydn, Franz Joseph.
Two Duets for Tuba and Piano, Schlesinger, Scott.
Two Impromptus, Donahue, Robert.
Two Lieder, Brahms, Johannes.
Two Little Leprechauns, Kulesha, Gary Alan.
Two Moods for Tuba, Swann, Donald.
Two Moods for Tuba and Piano, Gower, Albert.
Two Pieces, Bak, Mikhail Abromovich.
Two Pieces, Deason, David.
Two Pieces, Haddad, Don.
Two Pieces from "Children's Corner" for Tuba and Piano, Debussy, Claude.
Two Rossini Pieces, Rossini, Gioacchino.
Two Short Pieces, Handel, George Frederick.
Two Songs, Spillman, Robert.
Two Songs for Tuba and Piano, Elgar, Edward.
Two Songs from Sea Pictures, Elgar, Edward.

U

Un Adagio, Weber, Carl Maria von.
Un Souffle Profond, Desportes, Yvonne.
Una Voce M'Ha Colpito, Rossini, Gioacchino.
Unforgotten Days, Roeckel, J. (tr. Wesley Jacobs and P. Laville).
Up Front Albums Book 1, Brass Wind Publications.
Up Front Albums Book 2, Brass Wind Publications.
Up on the Housetop, Hanby, B. R.
Urban Serenade, Censhu, Jiro.

V

Valentine Song, Gounod, Charles.
Valentine Song from "Faust," Gounod, Charles.
Valse, Brahms, J. (arr. Patrice Sciortino).
Valse, Op. 69, No. 1, Chopin, F. (arr. Patrice Sciortino).
Valse, Op. 69, No. 2, Chopin, F. (arr. Patrice Sciortino).
Valse Bluett, Drigo, Richard (arr. Patrick Sheridan).
Valse Caprice, Skolnik, Walter.
Valse Gentile, Catelinet, Philip.
Valse Impromptu, Barnes, Clifford P.
Valse Lente, Rougnon.
Valse Nostalgique, Rougeron, Philippe.
Variationen uber ein Volkslied, Blank, Hans.
Variations, Handel, George Frederick.
Variations for Tuba and Piano (The Cobblers Bench), Frackenpohl, Arthur.
Variations from the Ballet Konick-Gorbunoch, Schedrin, R.
Variations in Olden Style (d'apres J. S. Bach), Stevens, Thomas.
Variations on a Theme, Bach, J. S. (arr. Cordonier).
Variations on a Theme for Tuba and Piano, Hanson, Ronald D.
Variations on a Theme of Gottschalk, Diercks, John.
Variations on a Theme of Robert Schumann, Davis, William.
Variations on a Theme of Roy Harris, Steinquest, Eugene W.
Variations on a Theme of Samuel Barber, Mueller, Frederick A.
Variations on "Carnival of Venice," Arban, J. B. (arr. Jens-Bjørn Larsen and Ole Hover).
Variations on "Carnival of Venice," Arban, J. B. (arr. Øystein Baadsvik).
Variations on "Carnival of Venice" for Tuba and Symphonic Winds, Arban, J. B. (arr. and tr. William Schmidt, ed. Sharon Davis).
Variations on the "Carnival of Venice," Arban, Jean Baptiste.
Variations on the Theme of "Judas Maccabeus" by G. F. Handel, Beethoven, Ludwig von.
Variations Sur Un Theme De Purcell, Lemaire, Jean.
Venetian Carnival, Bowles, Richard W.
Venezia, Usher, Julia.
Veni Creator, Meyerbeer.
Verdurous Aubade for Tuba and Piano, Censhu, Jiro.
Verrat—Lied, Brahms, J. (arr. François Poullot).
Version lente de Swing for brass, Muller, Thierry (Robert Martin Editions).
Veseli RONDINO, Krivokapic, Igor.
Victor Herbert Medley, Herbert, Victor.
Victors March, The, Feldstein, Sandy (arr.).
Village Blacksmith, The, Weiss, W. H.
Village Dance, Jacobs, Wesley (arr.).
Villageoise, La, Rameau, Jean Philippe.
Villanella, Ross, Walter.
Virtuosity Study No. 1, Dutton, Brent.
Virtuoso, The, Beeler, Walter.
Visare (Dreaming), Dumitru, Ionel.
Visions for Jane, Kulesha, Gary Alan.
Vivace, from Sonata in E mi, Loelliet, Jean-Baptiste.

Vocalise, Rachmaninoff, Sergei.
Vocalise, Rachmaninoff, Sergi (arr. Patrick Sheridan).
Voce Nobile, Clérisse, Robert.
Voice of the Viking, Bennett, David.
Volunteer, The, Buchtel, Forrest Lawrence.
Voyageur, The, Buchtel, Forrest Lawrence.

W

Wachet Auf, Ruft Uns Die Stimme, Bach, J. S. (arr. Patrice Sciortino).
Wagenia, Petit, Pierre.
Wakatipu, Hume, James Ord.
Walkabout, Matchett, Steve.
Walther's Prize Song, Wagner, Richard.
Waltz, Brahms, J.
Waltz, Brahms, S (sic).
Waltz and Galop from Petite Suite, Kabalevsky, D.
Waltz for Mippy III for Tuba and Piano, Bernstein, Leonard.
Waltz from Serenade for Strings, Tchaikovsky, Peter I.
Waltz Themes, Lincke and Waldteufel.
Waltzing Wind, Myers, Theldon.
Waltzing with a Whirlybird, Eitel, Butler.
Walzer, Hrdina, Eman.
Water Mill, The, Diehl, Louis (tr. Wesley Jacobs and P. Laville).
Wayfaring Stranger, The, Boyd, Bill (arr.).
We Gather Together, Borton, Allen (arr.).
We Gather Together, Kremser (arr. David E. Smith).
Westernstil, Hrdina, Eman.
Westwood Song, Kellaway, Roger.
Whangaroa, Hume, James Ord.
What a Friend We Have in Jesus, Borton, Allen (arr.).
What If I Never Speed, Dowland, John (arr. Michael Fischer).
When Britain Really Ruled the Waves, Sullivan, Arthur.
When Love Is Kind, Kinyon, John (arr.).
When the Saints Go Marching In, Buchtel, Forrest Lawrence (arr.).
When the Saints Go Marching In, Feldstein, Sandy (arr.).
When the Saints Go Marching In, Ostling, Acton (arr.).
When Yuba Plays the Rumba on the Tuba, Hupfield, Herman.
Where'er You Walk (from Semele), Handel, George Frederick.
Whistlin' Tune, Barnes, James.
White Stones, Epstein, Marti.
Wild Horseman, The, Schumann, Robert.
Wild Rose, Vander Cook, H. A.
Wind and the Bell, The, Ekström, Lars.
Winter Carousel, Bigelow, Albert.
Winter Song and Spring Dances, Miserendino, Joe.
Winterballade, Thiel, Wolfgang.
With Melody for All, McLin, Edward (arr.).
Within these holy portals, Mozart, Wolfgang Amadeus.
Wohin? Schubert, Franz.
Work Song, a "Blues Song" for the Young Tubist, Barnes, James.
Works for Tuba and Piano by Russian Composers, Voronov, G. (ed.).
Wotan, Buchtel, Forrest Lawrence.

XYZ

Yackety Sax, Rich, James, and Randolph, Randy.
Yankee Doodle, Boyd, Bill (arr.).
Ye Banks and Braes of Bonny Doon, Kinyon, John (arr.).
Yellow Submarine, Lennon, John, and McCartney, Paul (arr. John Glenesk Mortimer).
Yesterday, Lennon, John, and McCartney, Paul.
Yesterday, Lennon, John, and McCartney, Paul (arr. John Glenesk Mortimer).
Young Artists First Book of Solos for BBb Tuba, The, Buchtel, Forrest Lawrence.
Young Tuba Soloist, Smith, David E. (arr.).
Your Ring on My Finger, Schumann, Robert.
Zébulon le faisan, Joubert, Claude-Henry.
Zénobie la Perdrix: Scène champêtre en six tableautins, Joubert, Claude-Henry.
Zigeunerweisen (Gypsy Airs), Sarasate, Pablo de (arr. Timofei Dokshitser).
Zillertal, Simon, Frank.
Zion's Walls, Copland, Aaron (arr. Quincy Hilliard).
Zoé la Pintade, Joubert, Claude-Henry.
Zoltan le canard sauvage, Joubert, Claude-Henry.
Zum Uben und Vorspielen/B-Tuba, Meschke, Dieter (ed.).
Zum Uben und Vorspielen/F-Tuba, Meschke, Dieter (ed.).
Zwei Charakterstuke, Foremny, Stephan.

Tuba and Keyboard Collections

Many of the selections included in these collections have been and are still published separately. Acquiring these collections is a great way to build up a large library of tuba solos on a budget.

Australian Music Examinations Board. *Brass: Series One, First and Second Grades.* ed. Gary McPherson, Janice Stockigt, and Ian Burk. Allans Publishing. 1998. $22.56. 24 pp. I. A primer for the widely-used Australian music examinations, in accordance with the AMEB Band Syllabus. Included are basic studies in articulation, as well as a variety of brief solos w/piano accompaniment. A separate accompaniment part is included, and the method, though suitable for individual study, is designed for use in groups of like-keyed instruments. Published versions include treble clef E♭ and B♭, as well as bass clef C (non-transposing). There is also a version specifically for CC tuba. See also Methods and Studies.

Australian Music Examinations Board. *Brass: Series One, Third and Fourth Grades.* ed. Gary McPherson, Janice Stockigt, and Ian Burk. Allans Publishing. 1998. $22.56. 28 pp. II–III. Similar in format to volume one of the same series, but more challenging technically.

Baadsvik, Øystein, arr. *Grieg Collection.* Ovation. $31.84. Contains: *Anitra's Dance; A Dream; Norwegian Dance No. 1.*

Bennett, Malcolm, arr., Connor, Eddie (selected). *Five Solos for Tuba.* Unlimited Music. 1988. $25.25. II–III. Contains: Connor, Eddie, *McCluskeys Rag;* Molloy, J. L., *Kerry Dance, The;* Traditional, *Luzerne Song;* Traditional, *McLeods Reel;* Traditional, *Shenandoah.*

Borton, Allen, arr. *Tuba Hymns.* Tuba-Euphonium Press. 2001. F–c'. II. Commissioned by David Miles. Dedicated to John Robert Van Nice. Contains: *A Mighty Fortress Is Our God; All People That on Earth Do Dwell; Amazing Grace; Away in a Manger; Beneath the Cross of Jesus; Blessed Assurance; Break Thou the Bread of Life; Children of the Heavenly Father; Christ the Lord Is Risen Today; Come, Christians, Join to Sing; Come, Ye Thankful People, Come; Crown Him with Many Crowns; Dear Lord and Father of Mankind; Fairest Lord Jesus; For All the Saints; For the Beauty of the Earth; God of Our Fathers; Great Is Thy Faithfulness; Holy, Holy, Holy; I Love to Tell the Story; I Need Thee Every Hour; It Is Well with My Soul; Jesus Loves Me; Jesus Shall Reign; Joy to the World; Just As I Am; Lift High the Cross; May Jesus Christ Be Praised; My Faith Looks Up to Thee; Nearer, My God, to Thee; O Come, All Ye Faithful; O God Our Help in Ages Past; Praise to the Lord; The Almighty; Rejoice, Ye Pure in Heart; Silent Night; The Church's One Foundation; The Old Rugged Cross; Thine Is the Glory; We Gather Together; What a Friend We Have in Jesus.*

Brass Wind Publications. *Fifteen Introductory Solos.* II. For E♭ Bass/Tuba. Solos by Django Bates; Arthur Butterworth; Nigel Clarke; Douglas Coombes; Robert Ramskill. Treble and bass clef versions available.

Brass Wind Publications. *Up Front Albums Book 1.* I–II. For E♭ bass. Solos by Derek Bourgeois; Arthur Butterworth; Ian Carr; Gordon Crosse; Edward Gregson; Joseph Horovitz; Raymond Premru; Daryl Runswick; Stan Tracey; Guy Woolfenden. Treble and bass clef versions available.

Brass Wind Publications. *Up Front Albums Book 2.* I–III. For E♭ bass. See: Brass Wind Publications, *Up Front Albums Book 1* in this section.

Buchtel, Forrest Lawrence. *Young Artists First Book of Solos for BB♭ Tuba, The.* M. M. Cole Publishing Co. 1938. Out of Print. I–III. Also published for Trombone/baritone, cornet/baritone, French horn, E♭ mellophone, alto or bari. sax, oboe, flute. Piano Accompaniment Book available separately. Contains: *The Archer; The Ballerina; The Cavalier; The Courier; The Grenadier; How Can I Leave Thee; The Hussar; The Juggler; The Mannequin; The Mariner; The Ranger; Song of the Viking; The Spartan; The Troubadour; The Volunteer; The Voyageur.*

Concone, Giuseppe. *A Concone Suite.* arr. Barton Cummings. Solid Brass Music Company. $18.00. III–IV. A collection of eight vocalises by nineteenth-century composer Giuseppe Concone.

Conley, Lloyd, arr. *Christmas Cameos.* Kendor Music, Inc. 1985. $9.00. II–III. Contains: *The First Noel; Joy to the World; O Come, All Ye Faithful; O Little Town of Bethlehem; Silent Night.*

Copland, Aaron. *Copland for Tuba.* Arranged by Quincy Hilliard. Solid Brass Music Company. $24.90. III. A collection of twelve songs by Aaron Copland, arranged by Quincy Hilliard. *Simple Gifts; I've Heard an Organ Talk; Old Poem; I Bought Me a Cat; Laurie's Song; Billy and His Sweetheart; Dirge in Woods; Zion's Walls; Ching-a-Ring Chaw; The Little Horses; Going to Heaven; Fanfare for the Common Man.*

CPP/Belwin, Inc. *Tuba Solos, Level One.* CPP/Belwin, Inc. 1984. Tuba: $4.50. Piano: $6.50. I–II. Contains: Barnes, James, *Marching Right Along;* Barnes, James, *Whistlin' Tune;* Bell, William J., *Melodious Etude;* Bell, William J., *Tubaman, The;* Billings, William, *Old American Patriotic Song (Chester);* Gruber, *Silent Night;* Ostling, Acton, *Aurora;* Ostling, Acton, *Deep Cavern;* Ostling, Acton, *King Neptune;* Ostling, Acton, arr., *Blow the Man Down;* Ostling, Acton, arr., *Three Famous Melodies;* Ostling, Acton, arr., *When the Saints Go Marching In;* Popper, David, *Gavotte;* Sousa, John Philip, *Stars and Stripes Forever.*

CPP/Belwin, Inc. *Tuba Solos, Level Two.* CPP/Belwin, Inc. Tuba: $4.50. Piano: $6.50. II–III. Contains: Bach, J. S., *Gavotte;* Barnes, James, *In a Modal Mood;* Barnes, James, *Work Song, a "Blues Song" for the Young Tubist;* Barnes, James, arr., *Sometimes I Feel like a Motherless Child;* Bell, William J., *Chief John;* Bell, William J., *Jolly Jumbo;* Bell, William J., *Spartan, The;* Gounod, Charles, *Valentine Song from "Faust";* Handel, G. F., *Bourrée;* Haydn, F. J., *Haydn Medley (from Symphony No. 94);* Ostling, Acton, arr., *Gallant Captain;* Schubert, Franz, *Moment Musical;* Swanson, Ken, arr., *Blue Bells of Scotland.*

Cummings, Barton. *Stocking Stuffers.* $8.00. II. A collection of ten familiar Christmas carols, arranged by Barton Cummings for the beginning tubist.

Daellenbach, Charles, arr. *Book of Beginning Tuba Solos.* Hal Leonard Publishing Corp. 1992. $14.95. I. Contains: Beethoven, L.v., *Ode to Joy;* Benedict, Julius, *Carnival of Venice;* Bourgéois, Louis, and Ken, Thomas, *Doxology;* Boyd, Bill, *Canadian Brass Blues;* Boyd, Bill, arr., *Cruel War Is Raging, The;* Boyd, Bill, arr., *Riddle Song, The;* Boyd, Bill, arr., *Song of the Volga Boatman;* Boyd, Bill, arr., *Streets of Laredo;* Boyd, Bill, arr., *Yankee Doodle;* Carey, Henry, and Smith, Samuel, *America;* Cohan, George M., *Give My Regards to Broadway;* Foley, Red, *Just a Closer Walk;* Newton, John, *Amazing Grace;* Offenbach, Jacques, *Marine's Hymn;* Sibelius, Jean, *Finlandia;* Tilzer, Alber von, and Norworth, Jack, *Take Me Out to the Ball Game;* Wauldteufel, Emil, *The Skaters.* Comes with practice/performance cassette. Charles Daellenbach, tuba, and Bill Casey, piano, on A side; piano accompaniments only on B side.

Daellenbach, Charles, arr. *Book of Easy Tuba Solos.* Hal Leonard Publishing Corp. 1992. $14.95. I–II. Contains: Boyd, Bill, arr., *Come, Thou Fount of Every Blessing;* Boyd, Bill, arr., *The Erie Canal;* Boyd, Bill, arr., *Hey, Ho! Nobody Home;* Boyd, Bill, arr., *Loch Lomond;* Boyd, Bill, arr., *The Wayfaring Stranger;* Giordani, Giuseppe, *Love Song (Caro mio ben);* Grieg, Edvard, *The Last Saturday Evening;* Handel, G. F., *Lento;* Handel, G. F., *Repentance;* Lully, Jean-Baptiste, *The Lonely Forest;* Schwartz, Jean, and Jerome, William, *Chinatown, My Chinatown;* Sullivan, Arthur, and Gilbert, W. S., *Miya Sama* from *The Mikado.* Comes with practice/performance cassette. Charles Daellenbach, tuba, and Patrick Hansen, piano, on A side; piano accompaniments only on B side.

Daellenbach, Charles, ed. *Canadian Brass Book of Beginning Tuba Solos.* Solid Brass Music Company. $16.95. I. Seventeen beginning solos, including *Finlandia; Carnival of Venice; Volga Boatman,* etc. Edited by Charles Daellenbach of the Canadian Brass. Includes CD.

Daellenbach, Charles, ed. *Canadian Brass Book of Easy Tuba Solos.* Solid Brass Music Company. $16.95. II. Twelve easy solos, including *Erie Canal; Loch Lomond; Come Thou Fount of Every Blessing,* etc. Edited by Charles Daellenbach of the Canadian Brass. Includes CD.

Daellenbach, Charles, ed. *Canadian Brass Book of Intermediate Tuba Solos.* Solid Brass Music Company. $16.95. III. Twelve intermediate solos, including *To Music* (Schubert); *Where E'er You Walk* (Handel); *Solace* (Joplin), etc. Edited by Charles Daellenbach of the Canadian Brass. Includes cassette.

Daellenbach, Charles, ed. *Canadian Brass Christmas Solos.* Solid Brass Music Company. $16.95. III. Ten intermediate carols, including *First Noel; Angels We Have Heard on High; Silent Night,* etc. Edited by Charles Daellenbach of the Canadian Brass. Includes CD.

Daniel-Lesur and Werner, Jean-Jacques. *Collection Panorama.* Gérard Billaudot. 1990. $16.00. II–III. D♭–e'. For French tuba. Contains: Autran, Alphonse, *Quadrille En Forme De Ronds D'eau;* Clais, Tristan, *Tub' 88;* Guinot, Georges-Léonce, *Simplex pour tuba et piano;* Huuck, Reinhard, *Ariette;* Renaud, Manuel, *Ton Coeur (Tuba).*

Delguidice, Michel. *Collection pour la Jeunesse.* Robert Martin Editions. Contains: *Le Petit Baobab; Danse de L'Éléphant; Puissance 4; Le Petit Mammouth; Superman; L'Antre de Polypheme; La Baliene Bleue; Gargantua.*

deVille, Paul, arr. *Pleasant Hours: A Collection of 20 Standard Melodies.* Carl Fischer Inc. 1906. Out of Print. Written for E♭ Bass. Also published for cornet, baritone (b.c. and t.c.), trombone (b.c. and t.c.), E♭ alto saxophone, soprano saxophone, tenor saxophone, alto saxophone, and piano. Contains: Abt, Fr., *Dear Old Songs of Home;* Abt, Franz, *Oh, My Home;* Bellini, *Come Brave the Sea;* Dibdin, *Tom Bowling;* Diehl, Louis, *Water Mill, The;* Fischer, Ludwig, *Down Deep within the Cellar;* Gatty, A. S., *Lights Far Out at Sea;* Glover, S., *Faith;* Glover, S., *Melodies of Many Lands, The;* Handel, G. F., *The Harmonious Blacksmith;* Handel, G. F., *See, The Conquering Hero Comes;* Marzials, *The Fairy Jane;* Mendelssohn, Felix, *On Wings of Song;* Nelson, *Hour of Prayer, The;* Nelson, S., *I;* Nicolai, W. F. G., *Minstrel's Song;* Roeckel, J., *Unforgotten Days;* Rubinstein, A., *Romance;* Schubert, Franz, *By the Sea;* Sponholtz, *Peace of Mind.*

Edmunds, John, arr. *Popular Solos for the Young Bandsman.* Columbia Pictures Publications. 1976. II–III. Written for a variety of instruments; contains 29 popular TV, movie, and rock songs. Some contain tricky syncopations.

Eerola, Lasse. *N-sarja.* Finnish Music Information Centre. 1991. III. F–a. Contains: *Nukkahörtsö* (Bassia hirsuta); *Nurmivihvilä* (Juncus tenuis); *Nittynätkelmä* (Lathyrus pratensis); *Närvanä* (Sibbaldia procumbens); *Nuckkurusokki* (Bidens cernua); *Nukkakärsämö* (Achillea tomentoso); *Nurmitädyke* (Veronica chamaedrys); *Nyylähaarikko* (Sagina nodosa).

Eerola, Lasse. *Rohtokokoelma.* Finnish Music Information Centre. 1991. II–III. F–a. Contains: *Rohtokuirimo* (Cochlearia officinalis); *Rohtopunaluppu* (Sanguisorba officinalis); *Rohtonenätti* (Nasturtium officinale); *Rohtotädyke* (Veronica officinalis); *Rohtopähkämö* (Stachys officinalis); *Rohtoimikkä* (Pulmonaria officinalis).

Encore Music Publishers. *19th Century Melodies.* tr. Wesley Jacobs and P. Laville. Encore Music Publishers. 1999. I–II. B♭$_1$–f. Contains: Gatty, A. S., *Lights Far Out at Sea;* Fischer, *Down Deep within the Cellar;* Diehl, Louis, *The Water Mill;* Roeckel, J., *Unforgotten Days;* Schubert, Fr., *By the Sea;* Rubinstein, A., *Romance;* Nelson, S., *The Pilot;* Dibdin, *Tom Bowling;* Nicolai, W. F. G., *Minstrel's Song;* Bellini, *Come Brave the Sea;* Abt, Franz, *Oh, My Home* and *Dear Old Songs of Home;* Glover, S., *The Melodies of Many Lands* and *Faith;* Marzials, *The Fairy Jane;* Händel, *The Harmonious Blacksmith* and *See, the Conquering Hero Comes;* Nelson, *The Hour of Prayer;* Sponholtz, *Peace of Mind;* Mendelssohn, *On Wings of Song.*

Feldstein, Sandy, arr. *First Solo Songbook*. CPP/Belwin, Inc. 1990. Book: $3.95. Book and Cassette: $9.95. I. B♭$_1$–G. "Contains 30 songs using only the first six notes taught in all beginning methods." Bayly, T. H., *Long, Long Ago;* Beethoven, L.v., *Ode to Joy; Rainy Day Rock; A-Tisket, A-Tasket; Aura Lee; Baa, Baa Black Sheep; Beautiful Brown Eyes; Caisson Song; Erie Canal; For He's a Jolly Good Fellow; French Folk Song; Frère Jacques; Good King Wenceslas; Hot Cross Buns; Jolly Old St. Nicholas; London Bridge; Love Somebody; Lovely Evening; Old McDonald; There's a Hole in the Bucket; This Old Man; Tom Dooley; Twinkle, Twinkle Little Star; The Victors March; When the Saints Go Marching In;* Foster, Stephen, *Camptown Races;* Hanby, B. R., *Up on the Housetop;* Hart, Lorenz, and Rodgers, Richard, *Blue Moon;* Martin, Hugh, and Blaine, Ralph, *The Trolley Song;* Pierpont, J., *Jingle Bells.* Optional accompaniment/performance cassette available.

Fletcher, John, arr. and ed. *Tuba Solos (BB♭ Bass) Volume One*. Chester Music. 1982. $9.95. See: Fletcher, John, *Tuba Solos (Tuba in C), Volume One,* in this section.

Fletcher, John, arr. and ed. *Tuba Solos (E♭ Bass) Volume One*. Chester Music. 1982. $9.95. See: Fletcher, John, *Tuba Solos (Tuba in C), Volume One,* in this section.

Fletcher, John, arr. and ed. *Tuba Solos (Tuba in C) Volume One*. Chester Music. 1982. $9.95. II–III. Contains: Berlioz, Hector, *Sanctus;* Martin, Easthope, *Hey-Ho, Come to the Fair;* Schubert, Franz, *Der lindenbaum;* Sullivan, Arthur, *Oh, Is There Not One Maiden Breast?;* Sullivan, Arthur, *The Policeman's Song;* Sullivan, Arthur, *When Britain Really Ruled The Waves.*

Galliard, Johann Ernst. *Sonatas I–VI*. arr. John Glenesk Mortimer. Editions Marc Reift. 1999. $31.00. Available individually or as a compilation of all six sonatas, in bass clef concert pitch, or in treble clef in E♭ or B♭. The tessitura lends itself to tubas in all keys. See listings under Music for Tuba and Keyboard/Works Listed by Composer and Tuba and Organ.

Gershenfeld, Mitchell, ed. *Medici Masterworks Solos Volume 1*. Medici Music Press. 1985. $10.00. II–III. Contains: Buononcini, Giovanni, *Pupille Nere;* Dargomijsky, Aleksander S., *Nur Lieben!;* Dvorak, A., *Gypsy Melody;* Humperdinck, E., *Children's Prayer;* Rubenstein, A., *Be Not Shy, My Pretty One;* Tchaikovsky, Peter I., *At the Dance.*

Goddard, Mark. *Party Pieces*. Spartan Press. 2001. $14.95. I–II. E♭–b♭. Contains: *Swingin'; Blues; Hornpipe; Daydreams; Boogie; Charlbury Charleston; Ragamuffin.* Collection of simple tunes for the beginning bass tuba player. One drawback is that it is published only with the e♭ treble clef part. Good opportunities to explore different musical styles.

Graham, James, arr. *Concert Music for Tuba*. TUBA Press. 1967. $12.00. II–IV. Was published by DePauw University Bands in 1967. Contains: Brahms, J., *Waltz;* Corelli, A., *Sonata No. 10, Opus 5;* Corelli, A., *Sonata No. 9, Opus 5;* Gliere, Reinhold, *Intermezzo;* Gliere, Reinhold, *Nocturne;* Handel, G. F., *Chorus from Judas Maccabaeus;* Mozart, W. A., *Concert Rondo;* Mozart, W. A., *Concerto in D (K. 412);* Mozart, W. A., *Concerto in E flat (K. 417);* Mozart, W. A., *Concerto in E flat (K. 447);* Mozart, W. A., *Concerto in E flat (K. 495);* Saint-Saëns, C., *Romance;* Schumann, R., *Adagio and Allegro;* Scriabine, Alexander, *Romance;* Strauss, R., *Concerto, Opus 11;* Strauss, R., *Second Horn Concerto.*

Gregson, Edward, and Ridgeon, John. *Nine Miniatures*. Brass Wind Publications. I–II. For E♭ bass/E♭ tuba. Solos with easy piano accompaniments. Treble and bass clef versions available.

Guzii, V., compiled. *Pieces for Tuba and Piano*. Moscow Muzyka. 1976. Contains: Castérède, Jacques, *Fantaisie Concertante;* Ruff, D., *Concert Piece;* Tomasi, Henri, *Etre ou ne pas être.*

Guzii, V., compiled. *Pieces for Tuba and Piano*. Moscow Muzyka. 1978. Contains: Bitch, M., *Ritcherkar;* Hartley, V., *Concertino;* Kikta, V., *Concert for Tuba and Orchestra;* Kling, G., and Neuling, G., *Grand Cadence.*

He's Not Heavy, He's My Tuba. Solid Brass Music Company. $29.98. III–IV. "Thirteen pieces featuring the New York Brass Quintet and YOU"—*Lazy Blues, Boogie Brasses, Mambo for 5, Brass Bop* (Lebow), *Three Salutations* (End), *Brass Quintet* (Wilder), *Little Brown Jug, Impressions of a Parade,* five others. Includes CD.

Howe, Marvin C., arr. *Three Tuba Solos*. Plymouth Music Co. 1965. $4.00. 6:08. III. G$_1$–g (a). Included: Bach, *Rondo from Suite in B Minor for Flute;* Pergolesi, *Spiritoso;* Purcell, *Next, Winter Comes Slowly.*

Hoza, Vaclav. *Schule Fur Tuba in F und in B*. Edio Supraphon Praha. 1983. II–V. See *Schule Fur Tuba in F und in B* under Methods and Studies. Includes: Blodek, Vilém, *Arie Janeks Aus Der Oper "Im Brunnen";* Gregor, Frantisek, *Konzertetüde;* Hoza, Václav, *Ländler Für Tuba Und Klavier;* Hoza, Václav, and Hála, Jan, *Mosaik;* Hrdina, Eman, *Slow-Fox-Medium;* Hrdina, Eman, *Walzer;* Hrdina, Eman, *Westernstil;* Kubes, Ladislav, *Alte Bekannte.*

Hudadoff, Igor, ed., and Wescott, William, pno. acc. *Fifteen Intermediate Tuba Solos*. Pro Art Publications. 1965. Out of Print. II–IV. Published for a variety of instruments with piano. Includes: Chopin, F., *Nocturne;* Cohan, George M., *George M. Cohan Medley;* Cui, *Orientale;* Debussy, C., *Reverie;* Gounod, C., *Funeral March of a Marionette;* Granados, *Playera;* Haydn, F. J., *Allegro and Minuet;* Klohr, *Billboard;* Meyerbeer, *Coronation March;* Moussorgsky, M., *Gopak;* Rimsky-Korsakov, N., *Song of India;*

Strauss, *Artist's Life;* Tchaikovsky, Peter I., *Andante Cantabile;* Tchaikovsky, Peter I., *Waltz from Serenade for Strings;* Waldteufel, *Spanish Waltzes.*

Hume, James Ord, arr. *Boosey's Bombardon Solo Album.* Boosey & Co. 1906. Solo E♭ Bombardon part written in treble clef. Contains: Handel, G. F., *Love That's True Will Live Forever (Si, Tra I Ceppi, From "Berenice");* Hatton, J. L., *Simon the Cellarer;* Knight, J. P., *Rocked in the Cradle of the Deep;* Meyerbeer, *On Heaven's just cause relying and Rataplan Chorus (from "Les Huguenots");* Meyerbeer, *Piff, Paff (Les Huguenots);* Wagner, R., *Heav'n, in pray'r, Thine aid I seek and Good subjects of Brabant, 'tis well! (From Loengrin).*

Jacobs, Wesley, arr. *Solos from the Classics.* Encore Music Publishers. 1991. $16.50. I–II. Twenty-four classical and folk tunes. Contains: Beethoven, L.v., *Hymn to Joy;* Brahms, J., *Lullaby;* Brahms, J., *Sandman;* Brahms, J, *Waltz;* Haydn, J., *Hymn;* Haydn, J., *The Spacious Firmament;* Jacobs, Wesley, arr., *Coventry Carole;* Jacobs, Wesley, arr., *Dona Nobis Pacem;* Jacobs, Wesley, arr., *German Waltz;* Jacobs, Wesley, arr., *Go Down, Moses;* Jacobs, Wesley, arr., *Greensleeves;* Jacobs, Wesley, arr., *Harvest Dance;* Jacobs, Wesley, arr., *In Olden Times;* Jacobs, Wesley, arr., *In Springtime;* Jacobs, Wesley, arr., *Little Maiden;* Jacobs, Wesley, arr., *A Mighty Fortress;* Jacobs, Wesley, arr., *Nightingale;* Jacobs, Wesley, arr., *Steal Away;* Jacobs, Wesley, arr., *Steeple, The;* Jacobs, Wesley, arr., *Thanksgiving;* Jacobs, Wesley, arr., *Village Dance;* Mendelssohn, F., *Nocturne;* Sibelius, Jean, *Finlandia;* Ward, S. A., *America the Beautiful.*

Joubert, Claude-Henry. *Zénobie la Perdrix: Scène champêtre en six tableautins.* Robert Martin Editions. 1997. $13.25. 5:00. I–II. G–d'. Contains: *Promenade; Rêve de choux. . . ; Galantine; Zoltan le canard sauvage; Zébulon le faisan; Zoé la Pintade.* Dedicated to Nicolas Biget. Elementary-level collection of short solos. Suitable for bass tuba.

Kinyon, John, arr. *Breeze-Easy Recital Pieces for Tuba.* M. Witmark & Sons. 1958. I–II. Thirty recognizable tunes for tuba and piano. Contains: Barnby, Sir Joseph, *Sweet and Low;* Bayley, Thomas Haynes, *Faith of Our Fathers;* Bayley, Thomas Haynes, *Long, Long Ago;* Benedict, Julius, *Carnival of Venice;* Brahms, J., *Cradle Song;* Haydn, F. J., *Papa Haydn's Tune;* Kinyon, John, arr., *All through the Night;* Kinyon, John, arr., *Ash Grove, The;* Kinyon, John, arr., *Auld Lang Syne;* Kinyon, John, arr., *Bendemeer's Stream;* Kinyon, John, arr., *Blue Bells of Scotland, The;* Kinyon, John, arr., *Cockles and Mussels;* Kinyon, John, arr., *Crusaders' Hymn;* Kinyon, John, arr., *Drink to Me Only with Thine Eyes;* Kinyon, John, arr., *The Erie Canal;* Kinyon, John, arr., *German Waltz;* Kinyon, John, arr., *Home on the Range;* Kinyon, John, arr., *John Peel;* Kinyon, John, arr., *Loch Lomond;* Kinyon, John, arr., *Londonderry Air;* Kinyon, John, arr., *Minstrel Boy;* Kinyon, John, arr., *Red River Valley;* Kinyon, John, arr., *Steal Away;* Kinyon, John, arr., *Sweet Betsy from Pike;* Kinyon, John, arr., *When Love Is Kind;* Kinyon, John, arr., *Ye Banks and Braes of Bonny Doon;* Monk, W. H., *Abide with Me;* Spillman, James E., *Flow Gently, Sweet Afton;* Strauss, Johann, *Roses from the South;* Thompson, H. S., *Annie Lisle.*

Kinyon, John, arr. *Instant Band Ensembles (Tuba).* Alfred Music. 1969. Solo book for any solo instrument and band or piano accompaniment. Sixteen popular songs, Christmas songs, etc.

Lamb, Jack, ed. *Classic Festival Solos, Vol. 1.* CPP/Belwin, Inc. Tuba Part: $4.50. Piano Part: $6.50. I–III. Contains: Barnes, James, *Work Song, a "Blues Song" for the Young Tubist;* Bartok, Bela, *Dance of the Slovaks;* Bordogni, Marco, *Bordogni Medley;* Eccles, John, *Minuet;* Handel, G. F., *Bourrée;* Handel, G. F., *Larghetto and Allegro;* Handel, G. F., *Where'er You Walk (from Semele);* Barnes, James, arr., *Sometimes I Feel like a Motherless Child;* Ostling, Acton, *Aurora;* Ostling, Acton, arr., *Gallant Captain;* Saint-Saëns, C., *Allegro;* Stoutamire, Albert L., *Legend; Little,* Donald, C. arr., *Military March;* Weber, Fred, and Dorothy Garrett, *The Elephant Dance.*

Lamb, Jack, ed. *Classic Festival Solos, Vol 2.* CPP/Belwin, Inc. Contains: Mozart, W. A., arr. Little, *Aria from La Clemenza di Tito;* Weber, *Campus Queen;* arr. Little, *Flow Gently, Sweet Afton;* arr. Ostling and Weber, *Folk Song Melodies;* Belden, ed. Little, *Neutron Stars;* Mendelssohn, arr. Ostling and Weber, *On Wings of Song;* Knight, arr. Ostling and Weber, *Rocked in the Cradle of the Deep;* Cohen, *Romance and Scherzo;* Purcell, arr. Little, *Song from Timon of Athens;* Brahms, arr. Little, *Sunday;* Quate and Little, *Texas Horizons;* arr. Bell, *The Tubateer Polka.*

Lamb, Jack, ed. *Solo Sounds for Tuba, Level 1–3,* Vol. 1. CPP/Belwin, Inc. 1987. Tuba: $4.50. Piano: $6.50. I–III. Contains: Arne, Thomas A., *Air from "Comus";* Belden, George R., *Black Holes in Space;* Bell, William J., arr., *Russian Medley;* Bordogni, Marco, *Bordogni Medley;* Bowles, Richard W., *Deep Rock;* Bowles, Richard W., *Venetian Carnival;* Dacre, Harry, *Bicycle Built for Two;* Handel, G. F., *Where'er You Walk (from Semele);* Little, Donald C., *Lazy Lullaby;* Little, Donald C., arr., *Military March;* Peter, C., *Jolly Coppersmith, The;* Schumann, R., *Sailors' Song;* Weber, Fred, and Dorothy Garrett, *The Elephant Dance.*

Lamb, Jack, ed. *Solo Sounds for Tuba, Level 3–5, Vol. 1.* CPP/Belwin, Inc. 1987. Tuba: $4.50. Piano: $6.50. II–III. Contains: Bizet, G., *Carmen Excerpts;* Bowles, Richard W., *Changing Scene;* Dowling, Robert, *His Majesty the Tuba;* Gretchaninoff, A., *Slumber Song;* Grieg, Edvard, *In the Hall of the Mountain King;* Handel, G. F.,

Honor and Arms; Haydn, F. J., *Sonata No. 7, First Movement;* Marcello, Benedetto, *Largo and Presto;* Mozart, W. A., *Menuetto;* Vivaldi, A., *Allegro (from Sonata No. 3).*

Larin, J., ed. *Pieces for Tuba and Piano.* Moscow Muzyka. 1979. Contains: Bernstein, Leonard, *Waltz for Mippy;* Bozza, Eugène, *Allegro and Finale;* Bozza, Eugène, *Prelude and Allegro;* Désenclos, A., *Air;* LeClerc, E., *Concertino;* Moro, D., *Piece from Suite "Colours in Movement";* Tchebotarev, S., *Rondo.*

Lawrance, Peter. *Six Modern Pieces.* Brass Wind Publications. II. For E♭ bass/E♭ tuba. Solos with easy accompaniments. Treble and bass clef versions available.

Lebedev, A., ed. *Collection of Pieces for Tuba "Es" and Piano.* Military Band Masters Faculty of Moscow Conservatiore. 1971. Contains: Arutiunian, Alexandre, *Expromt;* Bartok, Bela, *Dance of the Bear;* Fesh, D., *Prelude;* Gudmen, S., *Dance;* Handel, G. F., *Air;* Handel, G. F., *Variations;* Jurovsky, V., *March;* Kaneda, B., *Long, Long Ago;* Karaev, V., *Dance from Ballet "Seven Beauties";* Katchiturian, A., *Dance from Ballet "Spartak";* Kazadezins, R., *Spanish Dance;* Kotshetov, V., *Adagio from the Ballet "Till Eulenspigel";* Lebedev, A., arr., *Adagio;* Ledov, A., *Prelude;* Mozart, W. A., *Allegro;* Orthel, L., *Prelude;* Pergolesi, Giovanni Battista, *Air;* Prokofiev, Sergi, *Recitative and Kutuzov's Air from the Opera "War and Peace";* Rachmaninoff, Sergei, *Russian Song;* Rakov, N., *Romance;* Ravel, M., *Pavane;* Rubinstein, A., *A Persian Song;* Schubert, F., *Ave Maria;* Scriabine, Alexander, *Etude;* Shostakovitch, D., *Romance;* Stepovoi, J., *Cantabile;* Stravinsky, I., *Russian Song;* Vasilyev, V., *Melody.*

Lebedev, A., ed. *Tuba Tutor Vol. 1.* Moscow Muzyka. 1984. II–III. "School Of Playing On Tuba." Contains: Bartok, Bela, *Adagio;* Bartok, Bela, *Dance;* Bartok, Bela, *Hungarian Folk Song;* Bartok, Bela, *A Song;* Britten, Benjamin, *The Sentimental Sarabande from the "Simple Symphony" for String Orchestra;* Frid, G., *A Little Birch Tree;* Gluck, K., *Gavotte;* Goedicke, A., *Dance;* Handel, G. F., *Bouree;* Lebedev, A., arr., *Estonian Folk Dance;* Lebedev, A., arr., *On the Steep High Mountain;* Lebedev, A., arr., *A Ring;* Miaskovskii, N., *Song of the Field;* Monushko, S., *A Fairy Tail;* Pozzoli, E., *Sad Minute, The;* Samonov, A., *Good Night;* Samonov, A., *Grandfather Is Dancing;* Tchaikovsky, Peter I., *Tomsky's Song from the Opera "Queen Of Spades";* Zverev, V., *Song.* Also see: Lebedjev, A., *Tuba Tutor, Vol. 1,* under Methods and Studies.

Lebedev, A., ed. *Tuba Tutor Vol. 2.* Moscow Muzyka. 1986. II–IV. "School Of Playing On Tuba." Contains: Bak. M., *A Joke;* Barber, S., *Adagio and Scherzo from Sonata C Minor;* Brahms, S. (sic), *Waltz;* Corelli, A., *Sarabanda;* Duntriev, G., *Ballada;* Greig, E., *In Spring Time;* Kikta, V., *Epic Tale and Procession of the People in Costumes (Festival);* Lebedev, A., *A Cradle Song;* Lebedev, A., *Gavotte;* Link, I., *Sonatina Movement IV;* Rakov, N., *Sonatina;* Schedrin, R., *Variations from the Ballet Konick-Gorbunoch;* Smirnova, T., *A Joke;* Sviridov, G., *Iago's Song about King Stephen from the Tragedy Othello;* Taktakishvili, O., *Aria from the Opera "The Lifes";* Tomasi, G. (sic), *Hamlet's Monologue;* Volkov, K, *A Piece.*

Lennon, John, and McCartney, Paul. *The Beatles.* arr. John Glenesk Mortimer. Editions Marc Reift. $19.80. 15:00. II. $B\flat_1$–$d\flat'$. Collection of eight popular Beatles tunes: *I Wanna Hold Your Hand; Yesterday; Michele; Yellow Submarine; Eleanor Rigby; Penny Lane; Hey Jude; Ob-la-di, Ob-la-da.* Short, well-written arrangements for the aspiring young player.

Little, Donald C., arr. *Solo-Pak for Tuba, Part One.* CPP/Belwin, Inc. 1989. $5.00. I. Follows the levels of the Medalist Band Method. Contains: Haydn, F. J., *The Spacious Firmament on High;* Little, Don, arr., *Flow Gently, Sweet Afton;* Quate, Amy, and Little, Don, *Texas Horizons.*

Little, Donald C., arr. *Solo-Pak for Tuba, Part Two.* CPP/Belwin, Inc. 1991. $5.00. I–II. Follows the levels of the Medalist Band Method. Contains: Brahms, J., *Sunday (Sonntag, Op. 47, 1968);* Caccini, Giulia, *Amarilli, Mia Bella;* Quate, Amy, *Los Cocos Locos (Crazy Coconuts).*

Little, Donald C., arr. *Solo-Pak for Tuba, Part Three.* CPP/Belwin, Inc. 1992. $5.00. II–III. Follows the levels of the Medalist Band Method. Contains: Mozart, W. A., *Aria from La Clemenza di Tito;* Purcell, Henry, *Song from Timon of Athens;* Quate, Amy, *The Feel Good Blues.*

Marcello, Benedetto. *Sonatas I–VI.* arr. John Glenesk Mortimer. Editions Marc Reift. 1997. Complete set of six sonatas $23.70. Originally for cello; this transcription is in the original key. Available individually or as a compilation of all six sonatas, in bass clef concert pitch, or in treble clef in E♭ or B♭. See listing under Works Listed by Composer.

Marlatt, David. *Famous Themes—Symphonic Works, Volume 1.* Solid Brass Music Company. $25.00. III. Dvorak, *Largo;* Grieg, *Anitra's Dance;* Vivaldi, *Largo;* Rimsky-Korsakov, *The Prince and the Princess;* Bach, *Air;* Vivaldi, *Allegro;* Handel, *Largo.*

McLin, Edward, arr. *With Melody for All.* Pro Art Publications. 1963. Out of Print. "20 all-time favorite melodies for band, orchestra, ensemble, unison or solo performance."

Melnikov, S., ed. *Pieces for Tuba and Piano.* Military Band Masters Institute–Moscow. 1957. Contains: Assafyev, B., *Scherzo;* Bach, J. S., *Bouree;* Bach, J. S., *Second Part from Capriccio;* Blazhevich, Vladislav, *Concert No. 2 Part 3;* Blazhevich, Vladislav, *Miniature No. 7;* Chopin, F., *Prelude No. 6;* Dvarionas, B., *Theme and Variations;* Ekkls, H, *Sonata;* Glinka, M., *Romance;*

Handel, G. F., *Bouree;* Kalinikov, V., *The Sad Song;* Leonov, I., *Etude de concert;* Marcello, Benedetto, *Largo and Allegro;* Masne, D., *Elegia;* Moniushko, S., *An Air from the Opera "Halka";* Mozart, W. A., *Concert No. 2 Part One;* Mozart, W. A., *Concert No. 4 Part One;* Mozart, W. A., *Rondo de Concerto;* Rachmaninoff, S., *Elegia;* Rimsky-Korsakov, N., *Song from the Opera "Snow Maiden";* Rubinstein, A., *Romance;* Rubinstein, A., *Song from the Cycle "Persian Songs";* Saint-Saëns, C., *Concert Piece;* Tchaikovsky, Peter I.., *The Sad Song;* Vivaldi, A., *Sonata;* Weber, K. M., *Adagio.*

Meschke, Dieter, ed. *Zum Uben und Vorspielen/ B-Tuba.* arr. Gerd Philipp and Stephan Schwotzer. Hofmeister. 1993. I–III. Contains: Concone, Giuseppe, *Allegretto animato;* Daquin, Louis-Claude, *Rigaudon;* Dragonetti, Domenico, *Kleiner Walzer;* Franck, Melchior, *Allemande;* Franck, Melchior, *Galliarde;* Fux, Johann Joseph, *Allegro;* Giordani, Giuseppe, *Arietta;* Krebs, Johann Ludwig, *Bourrée;* Mozart, Leopold, *Bourrée;* Pachelbel, Johann, *Gavotte;* Pergolesi, Giovanni Battista, *Arie;* Pergolesi, Giovanni Battista, *Lied;* Pezel, Johann, *Intrade;* Radolt, Wenzel Ludwig Freiherr von, *Menuett im Kanon;* Saint-Saëns, Camille, *L'Éléphant (Der Elefant);* Schumann, Robert, *Fröhlicher Landmann;* Schwotzer, Stephan, arr., *Altdeutscher Tanz (Narrentanz);* Stanley, John, *Allegretto grazioso;* Witthauer, Johann Georg, *Allegretto und Gavotte.*

Meschke, Dieter, ed. *Zum Uben und Vorspielen/ F-Tuba.* arr. Gerd Philipp and Stephan Schwotzer. Hofmeister. 1993. See: Meschke, Dieter, *Zum Uben und Vorspielen/B-Tuba,* in this section.

Miserendino, Joe. *Music of the Seasons.* Solid Brass Music Company. $35.00. IV. The complete suite by Joe Miserendino—*Autumn Moods, Winter Song and Spring Dances, Summer Celebration.*

Mitegin, V., ed. *Pieces for Tuba and Piano.* Moscow Muzyka. 1969. Contains: Arensky, A., *Ballade;* Dubrovsky, I., *A Song and a Dance;* Moussorgsky, M., *"Bydlo" from Suite "Pictures at an Exhibition";* Rakov, N., *Air;* Tchaikovsky, Peter I., *Arioso from the Opera "Jolanta."*

Mitjagina, V., ed. *Pieces for Tuba and Piano.* Muzkya, Moscow. 1969. II–IV. Contains: Goedicke, A., *Improvisation;* Moussorgsky, M., *Bydlo from Pictures At an Exhibition;* Mozart, V. (sic), *Liporello's Aria from Don Juan (Don Giovanni);* Saint-Saëns, Camille, *Cavatina;* Zuerev, V., *Hungarian Melody;* Zuerev, V., *Russian Dance.*

Mozart, Wolfgang Amadeus. *Suite No. 1 from The Magic Flute.* arr. Arthur Frackenpohl, ed. Charles Daellenbach. Hal Leonard Publishing Corp. 1989. $14.95. 6:01. III–IV. Contains: *How strong your tone with magic spell; O Isis and Osiris; All the world is full of lovers.* Includes practice/performance cassette by Charles Daellenbach, tuba, and Monica Gaylord, piano. See review in *T. U. B. A. Journal,* Vol. 18, No. 2, Page 19.

Mozart, Wolfgang Amadeus. *Suite No. 2 from The Magic Flute.* arr. Arthur Frackenpohl, ed. Charles Daellenbach. Hal Leonard Publishing Corp. 1989. $14.95. 4:49. III–IV. Contains: *I'd give my finest feather; Within these holy portals; Ha! just in the nick of time!* Includes practice/ performance cassette by Charles Daellenbach, tuba, and Monica Gaylord, piano. See review in *TUBA Journal,* Vol. 18, No. 2, Page 20.

Musser, Willard. *Four Classics for Young Brass Players.* Solid Brass Music Company. $8.00. II. Mozart, *Longing for Spring;* Brahms, *Sunday;* Mendelssohn, *Suleika;* Schumann, *Song of the Bethrothed.* Arranged by Willard Musser. Solo parts for trumpet, horn, trombone, and tuba.

Musser, Willard. *More Classics for Young Brass Players.* Solid Brass Music Company. $8.00. II. Gluck, *French Dance; Adagio and Allegretto;* Seitz, *Allegro non Troppo.* Arranged by Willard Musser. Solo parts for trumpet, horn, trombone, and tuba.

Niverd, Lucien. *Six Petites Pièces De Style.* Gérard Billaudot. 1939. $6.25. II–III. "For Saxhorn-basse en Si♭ ou Trombone en si♭." Also written for horn. *Hymne; Romance Sentimentale; Complainte; Historiette Dramatique; Chant Mélancolique; Scherzetto.*

Ostling, Acton, and Weber, Fred, arr. *Tuba (Bass) Soloist —Book 1.* CPP/Belwin, Inc. 1969. Tuba part: $4.50. Piano part: $6.50. I. Contains: *Song;* Herbert, Victor, *Victor Herbert Medley;* Knight, J. P., *Rocked in the Cradle of the Deep;* Lehar, *Merry Widow Waltz;* Lincke, *Glow Worm, The;* Lincke and Waldteufel, *Waltz Themes;* Lincoln, *College March;* Mendelssohn, *On Wings of Song;* Olcott, *My Wild Irish Rose;* Ostling, Acton, arr., *All through the Night;* Ostling, Acton, arr., *Blow the Man Down;* Ostling, Acton, arr., *Folk Song Melodies;* Ostling, Acton, arr., *French Song;* Ostling, Acton, arr., *Military Marches Melodies;* Ostling, Acton, arr., *Three Famous Melodies;* Ostling, Acton, arr., *When the Saints Go Marching In;* Poulton, *Andantino;* Poulton, *Aura Lee;* Sousa, John Philip, *Stars and Stripes Forever;* Waldteufel, *Skater's Waltz;* Weber, *Campus Queen.*

Ostrander, Allen, ed. *Concert Album for Tuba.* Editions Musicus. 1954. $13.00. II–IV. Contains: Bach, J. S., *Siciliano;* Beethoven, L. v., *Menuet;* Beethoven, L. v., *Nature's Adoration;* Bizet, G., *Adagietto from L'Arlésienne;* Concone, G., *Etude (Op. 10, No. 11);* Corelli, Arcangelo, *Gigue;* Gluck, Chr., *Air;* Handel, G. F., *Andante;* Handel, G. F., *Bouree;* Maganini, Quinto, *An Ancient Greek Melody;* Martini, Padre, *Plasir d'Amour;* Meyerbeer, *Veni Creator;* Rameau, J. Ph., *Rigaudon;* Rimsky-Korsakov, N., *Song of the East;* Stravinsky, Igor, *Berceuse.*

Perantoni, Daniel, ed. *Master Solos Intermediate Level.* Hal Leonard Publishing Corp. 1976.

$5.95. Contains: Bach, J. S., *Siciliano and Chorale;* Brahms, J., *Two Lieder;* Dowland, John, *Come Again, Sweet Love Doth Now Invite;* Dowland, John, *Dear If You Change;* Dowland, John, *Now, O Now My Needs Must Part;* Haydn, F. J., *Two Classical Themes;* Lawrence, Lucinda, *Piece for Tuba and Piano;* Powell, Morgan, *Introduction and Blues;* Schumann, R., *Romance No. 3.* Includes a performance/practice cassette performed by Daniel Perantoni, tuba, and Eric Dalheim, piano. See review in *TUBA Journal,* Vol. 8, No. 1, Page 35.

Poullot, François, arr. *Le Tuba Classique, Recueil 1.* Editions M. Combre. 1999. $27.95. I–II. E♭–d'. Contains: Mozart, W. A., *La Flûte Enchantée (extrait: O Isis und Osiris);* Wagner, R., *Tannhäuser (extrait: Acte II, Scéne III: Air du Landgrave);* Verdi, G., *Nabucco (extrait: Première Partie: Léviti);* Brahms, J., *Verrat—Lied;* Wagner, R., *Tannhäuser (extrait: Acte II, Scéne IV: Autre air du Landgrave);* Gounod, C., *Faust (extrait: Acte IV, 2nd Tableau: Mephistophélès);* Mozart, W. A., *La Flûte Enchantée (extrait: Air du Papageno);* Bizet, G., *Carmen (extrait: Acte II: Vivat! Vivat le torero!);* Bach, J. S., *Cantate BWV 26 Ach Wie Flüchtig, Ach Wie Nichtig (extrait: Aria pour voix de basse);* Rossini, G., *Messe Solennelle (extrait: Quoniam pour voix de basse).* Collection containing melodic orchestral and operatic excerpts written for beginning bass tuba players.

Prendiville, Harry, arr. *Six Popular Solos.* A. Squire. 1888. Out of Print. II–III. "E♭ Bass; or, Tuba With Piano or Organ Accompaniment, (ad lib.)." Contains: Hatton, J. L., *Simon the Cellarer;* Knight, J. P., *Rock'd in the Cradle of the Deep;* Nelson, S., *The Pilot;* Prendiville, Harry arr., *Down among the Dead Men;* Russell, H., *The Old Sexton;* Shield, *The Friar of Orders Gray.*

Pro Art, publisher. *Fifty Standard Solos.* Pro Art Publications. 1964. Out of Print. I–IV. Published for a variety of instruments, this series of solo books contains a variety of selections, from easy waltzes and marches to more difficult excerpts from traditional and classical works.

Robert Martin Editions. *Tuba d'Amore.* Robert Martin Editions. 2002. 12:00. II. G–g' (a'). Contains: Basteau, Jean-François, *Le diamant bleu;* Tanaka, Kumiko, *Des hortensias sous la pluie;* Crepin, Alain, *Le Voyage d'Hadrien;* Sauvignet, Marie-Angès, arr., *Greensleeves;* Naulais, Jerôme, . . . *Au fond des bois* and *Le jardin sur la lagune;* Proust, Pascal, *Aquarium* and *Scènes du Far West;* Hegenhauser, Marc, *Old and New Folksongs;* Dondeyne, Dèsirè, *Pallas;* Pelegri, Stéphane, *Habanera nocturne;* Muller, Thierry, *Swing for Brass* and *Version lente de Swing for brass.* Collection of twelve character pieces for bass saxhorn or euphonium. Would be most appropriate for the beginner student capable of reading the music down one octave.

Roikjer, Kjell. *Tonal Miniature Pieces.* Edition Edtved. 1983. $8.80. 25:00. IV–V. F_1–e'. Dedicated to Michael Lind. Opus 75. Fourteen pieces, each in a different major key and the relative minor.

Rubank. *Soloist Folio for Bass (E♭ or BB♭).* Rubank, Inc. 1939. $6.95. II–III. May have been compiled by Himie Voxman. Contains: Bizet, G., *Toreador's Song;* Brahmstedt, N. K., *Stupendo;* DeLamater, E., *Rocked in the Cradle of the Deep;* Grieg, Edvard, *In the Hall of the Mountain King;* Lohr, Frederic N., *Out on the Deep;* Macbeth, Allan, *Forget Me Not;* Phillips, L. Z., *The Marines' Hymn;* Pinsuti, Ciro, *Bedouin Love Song;* Schumann, Robert, *The Jolly Peasant;* Vander Cook, H. A., *Bombastoso.*

Salvation Army Press. *Instrumental Albums Number 14: Solos and Duets for Soprano E♭, Horn E♭, and Bass E♭ with Pianoforte Accompaniment.* Salvation Army Press. 1929. *Nearer My Home* (duet); *O Lovely Peace* (duet); *Swiss Melodies; Whosoever; Sing Glory, Hallelujah; Isle of Beaty; In the Army; Rocked in the Cradle; Shepherd of Israel; Battling for the Lord.*

Schubert, Franz. *Songs From Die Schöene Müellerin.* tr. Enrique C. Feldman. Arizona University Music Press. 1987. 10:33. III–IV. B–e'. Contains: *Die böse Farbe; Die liebe Farbe; Mein!; Wohin?*

Sciortino, Patrice, arr. *Pièces Classiques, Volume 1.* Gérard Billaudot Éditeur. 1993. $12.95. I. (See comments below.) 11:20. F–e♭'. Contains: Anonymous, *Frère Jacques;* Schubert, F., *Printemps;* Gounod, Charles—Bach, J. S., *Ave Maria;* Gervaise, Claude, *Allemande;* Rameau, J. P., *Hymne a la Nuit;* Schubert, F., *La Truite;* Exaudet, A., *Menuet;* Mozart, W. A., *Ave Verum.* Collection of elementary classical solos for the bass saxhorn. While it may be elementary for that instrument, the basstuba performer will find the range demands to be less than elementary.

Sciortino, Patrice, arr. *Pièces Classiques, Volume 2.* Gérard Billaudot Éditeur. 1993. $11.95. I–II. 13:20. F–d' (e♭'). Contains: Mozart, W. A., *Air de Papageno (extrait de la flûte enchantée);* Bach, J. S., *Menuet (extrait du Petit livre de Magdalena Bach);* Chopin, F., *Nocturne (extrait de l'op. 15 no. 3);* Beethoven, L. v., *Trio No. 3;* Mozart, W. A., *Menuetto (extrait de la sonate no. X);* Chopin, F., *Marche Funèbre (extrait de la Sonate op. 35);* Grieg, E., *Chanson de Solvejg;* Dvorak, A., *Symphonie No. IX (extrait).* Collection of elementary classical solos for the bass saxhorn. While it may be elementary for that instrument, the basstuba performer will find the range demands to be less than elementary.

Sciortino, Patrice, arr. *Pièces Classiques, Volume 3.* Gérard Billaudot Éditeur. 1993. $14.50. II–III. 10:50. F–e♭'. Contains: Moussorgsky, M., *Bydlo (extrait des Tableaux d'une exposition no. 4);* Bach, J. S., *Menuet (extrait du Petit livre d'Anna*

Magdalena Bach); Chopin, F., *Prélude, op. 28 no. 7 et no. 15;* Beethoven, L. v., *Symphonie No. 7 (extrait);* Bizet, G., *Air du Toreador (extrait de Carmen);* Mozart, W. A., *Sonate XVII.* Collection of moderate classical solos for the bass saxhorn. While it may be moderate for that instrument, the basstuba performer will find the range demands to be less than elementary.

Sciortino, Patrice, arr. *Pièces Classiques, Volume 4.* Gérard Billaudot Éditeur. 1993. $14.50. III. 11:30. F–g'. Contains: Schumann, R., *Eusebius;* Chopin, F., *Valse, op. 69 no. 1;* Bizet, G., *Habanera (extrait de Carmen);* Schubert, F., *Sérénade;* Chopin, F., *Prélude, op. 28 no. 4;* Rameau, J. P., *Tambourin.* Collection intermediate classical solos for the bass saxhorn. While it may be intermediate for that instrument, the basstuba performer will find the range demands to be less than elementary.

Sciortino, Patrice, arr. *Pièces Classiques, Volume 5.* Gérard Billaudot Éditeur. 1993. $13.95. III–IV. 17:30. F–g'. Contains: Chopin, F., *Valse, op. 69 no. 2;* Bach, J. S., *Wachet Auf, Ruft Uns Die Stimme;* Wagner, Richard, *Prière D'Elisabeth;* Bach, J. S., *Aria;* Brahms, J., *Valse;* Bizet, G., *Air de Don José (extrait de Carmen).* Collection of moderate to advanced classical solos for the bass saxhorn. While it may be moderate for that instrument, the basstuba performer will find the range demands to be a challenge.

Smith, David E., arr. *Young Tuba Soloist.* David E. Smith Publications. All selections available separately. Contains: *Abide with Me; Away in a Manger; Dare to Be a Daniel; Hallelujah What a Survivor!; My Jesus I Love Thee; Praise Him Little Children; Tis So Sweet to Trust in Jesus; We Gather Together.*

Solid Brass Music Company. *Sweets for Brass.* Solid Brass Music Company. $29.98. III–IV. "15 contemporary works featuring the Contemporary Brass Quintet and YOU." Contains: *Picture of Dorian Blue;* Gale, *Serial Stomp;* Skeen, *Suite for Brass;* Sarvello, *Riff Rock;* R. Copeland, *Classical Jazz Suite;* ten others. Includes CD.

Vivaldi, Antonio. *Sonatas I–VI.* arr. John Glenesk Mortimer. Editions Marc Reift. 1997. Complete set of six sonatas $31.00. Originally for violin; this transcription is in the original key. Available individually or as a compilation of all six sonatas, in bass clef concert pitch, or in treble clef in E♭ or B♭. The octave settings vary depending on which instrument is used. See listing under Works Listed by Composer.

Voronov, G., ed. *Works for Tuba and Piano by Russian Composers.* Moscow Muzyka. 1984. Contains: Berlin, A., *Ballade;* Burshtin, M., *Legend;* Kolodub, L., *Humorous Dance;* Rakov, N., *Sonatina;* Smironova, T., *Sonata;* Smironova, T., *A Tale;* Strukov, V., *Lento Elegiaco;* Zverev, V., *Concertino;* and for tuba solo: Burshtin, M., *Suite;* Ekimovsky, V., *Romance and Capriccio.*

Voxman, Himie, compiled and edited. *Concert and Contest Collection.* Rubank, Inc. 1972. $10.45. II–IV. "For E♭ or BB♭ Bass (Tuba-Sousaphone)." Piano accompaniment available separately. Contains: Alary, G., *Morceau de Concours;* Berlioz, G. P., *Air Gai;* Clérisse, Robert, *Andante and Allegro;* Corelli, Arcangelo, *Sarabanda and Gavotta;* Gaucet, Charles, *Adagio and Finale from Concertino;* Handel, G. F., *Adagio and Allegro from Sonata No. 7;* Handel, G. F., *Two Short Pieces;* Kabalevsky, D., *Waltz and Galop from Petite Suite;* Koepke, Paul, *Persiflage;* Maniet, Rene, *Premier Solo de Concours;* Marcello, Benedetto, *Largo and Allegro;* Mozart, W. A., *First Movement from Concerto for Horn;* Ostransky, Leroy, *Serenade and Scherzo;* Rimsky-Korsakov, N., *Andante Cantabile from Concerto.*

Wastall, Peter, ed. *Learn As You Play Tuba.* Boosey & Hawkes, Inc. 1985. Tuba part: $6.75. Piano part: $7.50. I–III. Contains: Bogár, István, *Quick Dance;* Cole, Keith Ramon, *Romance Homage to Peter Ilyich;* Cole, Keith Ramon, *Solstice;* Debussy, C., *Jimbo's Lullaby from "Children's Corner";* Gretry, Andre, *Air from Richard Coeur de Lion;* Gurlitt, Cornelius, *Andante from First Steps, Op. 82;* Hyde, Derek, *Promenade;* Hyde, Derek, *Tuba-Talk;* Mozart, W. A., *Aria O Isis and Osiris;* Norton, Christopher, *Make Mine a Tuba;* Schumann, R., *The Merry Peasant from Album for the Young.*

Weber, Carl, arr. *First Solo Album (Bass Clef).* Theodore Presser Company. $1.00. I–II. Easy beginning solos—55 recognizable tunes.

Weber, Carl, arr. *Nineteen Solos for E♭ Bass with Piano Accompaniment.* J. W. Pepper & Son. 1914. Out of Print. Contains: Arban, Jean Baptiste, *Arban's Fantasie Brillante;* Ascher, *Alice, Where Art Thou?;* Bell, J. H., *Sans Pareil;* Bottesini, *Bombardon Polka;* Giovanini, J., *Challenge Concert Polka;* Innes, F. N., *La Coquette Concert Polka;* Jennings, *Pomposo Polka;* Lange, *Heather Rose Caprice;* Legendre, *Souvenir du Poitou;* Mercadante, *Solitude Caprice;* Owen, J. A., *Serenade;* Prendiville, *The Approach of the Lion;* Pryor, Arthur, *Exposition Echoes Polka;* Rollinson, T. H., *Hear Our Prayer—Paraphrase;* Rose, Phil. S., *Chromatic Concert Polka;* Verdi, Giuseppe, *Aria from Falstaff;* Wallace, *Let Me like a Soldier Fall from "Maritana";* Weber, Carl, arr., *The Old Sexton;* Weber, Carl, arr., *Pretty as a Butterfly.*

Wekselblatt, Herbert, arr., and Kagan, Susan, piano realizations. *First Solos for the Tuba Player.* G. Schirmer Inc. 1972. $9.95. II–IV. Contains: American Folk Dance, *Hornpipe;* Arban, J. B., *Carnival of Venice, The (Variations);* Bach, J. S., *Musette;* Beethoven, L. v., *Country Dance;* Fischer, Ludwig, *Down in the Deep Deep Cellar;* Gounod, Charles, *March of a Marionette;* Grieg, Edvard, *In the Hall of the Mountain King (from Peer Gynt);* Kagan, Susan, *Oxford Gavotte;* Lully,

Jean-Baptiste, *Gavotte;* Mozart, W. A., *Marche (from Les Petits Riens:);* Nicolai, Otto, *Falstaff's Drinking Song (from The Merry Wives of Windsor);* Perrie, H. W., *Asleep in the Deep;* Rameau, Jean Philippe, *La Villageoise;* Schumann, R., *Happy Farmer, The (Variations from "Album for the Young");* Schumann, R., *Wild Horseman, The (from Album for the Young);* Various Composers, *Seven Duets;* Wekselblatt, Herbert, arr., *Civil War Medley;* Wekselblatt, Herbert, arr., *Military Suite.* See review in *TUBA Journal,* Vol. 12, No. 2, Page 16.

Wekselblatt, Herbert, ed. *Solos for the Tuba Player.* G. Schirmer Inc. 1972. $13.95. II–V. Contains: Bernstein, Leonard, *Waltz for Mippy III;* Mozart, W. A., *O Isis And Osiris (from: The Magic Flute);* Mozart, W. A., *Romanze and Rondo (from: Horn Concerto No. 3);* Shostakovitch, D., *Polka from: The Age of Gold;* Stamitz, Karl, *Rondo Alla Scherzo (from: Clarinet Concerto in E♭);* Tchaikovsky, Peter I., *None But the Lonely Heart, Op. 6;* Wagner, Richard, *Die Meistersinger Von Nurnberg (from the Prelude, Act One);* Wagner, Richard, *Die Walkure (from Act III);* Wagner, Richard, *Siegfried (from Act II, Prelude and First Scene).* See review in *TUBA Journal,* Vol. 12, No. 2, Page 16.

Yasumoto, Hiroyuki, arr. *Tuba Volume #1.* Toa Music International Co. 1986. II–IV. Contains: Bizet, G., *Habanera from Carmen;* Bland, J., *Carry Me Back to Old Virginny;* Boccherini, L., *Menuette;* Couperin, F., *Concertpièce;* Eccles, H., *First and Second Movements from Violin Sonata;* Foster, Stephen C., *Foster Medley;* Giordani, Giuseppe, *Caro mio ben;* Martini, J. P. E., *Piacer d'Aamor;* Saint-Saëns, C., *Elephant from Carnival of Animals;* Wagner, Richard, *Die Meistersinger von Nürnberg;* Wagner, Richard, *O du mein holcler Abendstern, from "Tanhöuser";* Yasumoto, Hiroyuki, arr., *Barcarolle for Tuba;* Yasumoto, Hiroyuki, arr., *Londonderry Air;* Yasumoto, Hiroyuki, arr., *Nobody Know the Trouble I've Seen.*

Yasumoto, Hiroyuki, arr. *Tuba Volume #2.* Toa Music International Co. 1989. III–IV. Contains: Tanimunei, Kocho, *Fantasy for Tuba and Piano;* Handel, G. F., *Concerto No. 3 for Tuba and String Orchestra;* Kopprasch, C., *Nr. 15, Etüden für Tuba;* Kopprasch, C., *Nr. 19, Etüden für Tuba;* Kreisler, F., *Libesfreud;* Lennon, John, and McCartney, Paul, *Yesterday;* Marcello, B., *Sonata I, from 6 Solos for a Violoncello;* McHugh, Jim, and Fields, Dorothy, *On the Sunny Side of the Street;* Reiche, E., *Adagio from Concerto No. 2;* Schumann, Robert, *Träumeri.*

Yasumoto, Hiroyuki, arr. *Tuba Volume #3.* Toa Music International Co. 1989. III–IV. Contains: Bach, J. S., *Sarabande (from BWV 1013 Solo Tuba);* Bordogni, G. M., *No. 10 from 24 Easy Vocalises;* Bordogni, G. M., *No. 4 from 24 Easy Vocalises;* Bordogni, G. M., *No. 9 from 24 Easy Vocalises;* Bozza, Eugène, *Prélude et Allegro;* Censhu, Jiro, *Verdurous Aubade for Tuba and Piano;* Konagaya, Soichi, *Celebration for Tuba and Piano;* Kreisler, Fritz, *Schön Rosmarin;* Lennon, John, and McCartney, Paul, *Hey Jude!* Livingston, J., and Evans, R, *To Each His Own;* Schubert, Franz, *Ständchen.*

Tuba and Keyboard Other than Piano

The following list is offered for the performer interested in a recital featuring tuba with organ, harpsichord, or synthesizer. Most pieces listed can also be performed with piano. Some, as in the case of *Mary's Idea,* are expressly requested not to be played with piano. Refer to the Tuba and Keyboard/Works Listed by Composer section for specific information.

Tuba and Organ

Åkerwall, Martin. *Meditation.* ed. Jens-Bjørn Larsen. SheetMusicNow.com.

Bach, Johann Sabastian. *O Mensch, bewein' dein' Sünde gross.* Bearbeitung: Hilgers, Walter. Editions Marc Reift.

Bach, Johann Sabastian. *Sonata II.* arr. Walter Hilgers. Editions Marc Reift.

Bach, Johann Sebastian. *"Ich ruf zu Dir, Herr Jesu Christ," Choral Prelude BMV 639.* arr. Walter Hilgers. Editions Marc Reift. 1988. 2:00. $6.50. II. C–d. Originally for choir and organ; solo part is set so that it could be played along with a church choir with minimal rehearsal time. See listing under Music for Tuba and Keyboard/ Works Listed by Composer.

Bach, Johann Sebastian. *Adagio.* arr. Walter Hilgers. Editions Marc Reift. 1998. $6.50. ca. 4:30 (without repeats). II. B_1–f. The tessitura makes this work very performable on a CC or B♭ tuba. Available in violin or bass clef. See listing under Music for Tuba and Keyboard/Works Listed by Composer. Recorded by Walter Hilgers.

Bach, Johann Sebastian. *Nun komm' der Heiden Heiland, Choral-Vorspiel BMV 659.* arr. Walter Hilgers. Editions Marc Reift. 1993. $11.80. 6:00. IV. A–g'. This is originally for organ and/ or choir. In this arrangement the solo part is in the upper middle to high range. As in the original from Bach, the dynamic markings have been kept to an absolute minimum to allow freedom of interpretation. See listing under Music for Tuba and Keyboard/Works Listed by Composer. Recorded Walter Hilgers.

Bach, Johann Sebastian. *Prelude in D Minor, BWV 539.* arr. Walter Hilgers. Editions Marc Reift. 1998. $6.50. 2:00. II. A_1–g. Originally in D minor; this arrangement has been transposed down a major third to B♭ minor. The tessitura makes this work very performable on a CC or

BB♭ tuba. Can be used in combination with other Bach works by the same publisher to form a suite. Available in violin or bass clef. See listing under Music for Tuba and Keyboard/Works Listed by Composer.

Bach, Johann Sebastian. *Prelude XVII from "Das Wohltemperierte Klavier," BWV 862, Teil I.* arr. Walter Hilgers. Editions Marc Reift. 1998. $6.50. 1:45. III. C–c'. Individual melodic lines of the original composition have been set for the tuba solo. Can be used in combination with other Bach works by the same publisher to form a suite. Available in violin or bass clef. See listing under Music for Tuba and Keyboard/Works Listed by Composer.

Bach, Johann Sebastian. *Prelude XX from "Das Wohltemperierte Klavier," BWV 865, Teil I.* arr. Walter Hilgers. Editions Marc Reift. 1998. $6.50. 1:30. II. E_1–f. Individual melodic lines of the original composition have been set for the tuba solo. The tessitura makes this work very performable on a CC or BB♭ tuba. Can be used in combination with other Bach works by the same publisher to form a suite. Available in violin or bass clef. See listing under Music for Tuba and Keyboard/Works Listed by Composer.

Bach, Johann Sebastian. *Prelude XXII from "Das Wohltemperierte Klavier," BWV 867, Teil I.* arr. Walter Hilgers. Editions Marc Reift. 1998. $6.50. 1:30. II. $G\sharp_1$–e. Individual melodic lines of the original composition have been set for the tuba solo. The tessitura makes this work very performable on a CC or BB♭ tuba. Can be used in combination with other Bach works by the same publisher to form a suite. Available in violin or bass clef. See listing under Music for Tuba and Keyboard: Works Listed by Composer.

Bach, Johann Sebastian. *Sarabande.* arr. Walter Hilgers. Editions Marc Reift. 1998. $14.20. 3:50. III. D–c'. This movement comes from the *English Suite Nr. 2 in A Minor* and is a good addition to the growing repertoire of Bach works transcribed for tuba. See listing under Music for Tuba and Keyboard/Works Listed by Composer. Recorded by Walter Hilgers.

Bella, Domenico della. *Sonata in C Major.* arr. John Glenesk Mortimer. Editions Marc Reift. 1996. $11.80. 5:00. III. G_1–a. Andante; Gigue-Allegro; Largo; Allegro moderato. Transcription in the original key of the *Sonata for Cello* of this early-eighteenth-century composer. Available in bass clef concert pitch and treble clef in E♭ or B♭. See listing under Music for Tuba and Keyboard/Works Listed by Composer.

Callahan, Charles. *In the Beginning: Biblical Poem for Tuba (Cello) and Organ.* Morning Star Music Publishers.

Corrette, Michel. *Sonata in D Minor.* Editions Marc Reift. 1997. $12.50. 7:00. III. C–c' (d'). Andante; Aria; Allegro staccato. While this piece by the mid-eighteenth-century French composer was originally for cello or bassoon, the tessitura of this arrangement makes it playable with all tubas. Requires a light, articulate approach. Available in bass clef concert pitch and treble clef in E♭ or B♭. See listing under Music for Tuba and Keyboard/Works Listed by Composer.

Drude, Matthias. *Sonate.* Available from Spaeth and Schmid. $15.75.

Ehmann, Wilhelm. *3 Stücke.* Available from Spaeth and Schmid. $9.75.

Galliard, Johann Ernst. *Sonata I in A Minor.* arr. John Glenesk Mortimer. Editions Marc Reift. 1999. $11.00 (Complete set of six sonatas $31.00). 6:00 depending on repeats. III. F_1 (C_1)–a. Cantabile; Moderato spiritoso; Largo; Hornpipe; Vivace. Available individually or as a compilation of all six sonatas, in bass clef concert pitch, or in treble clef in E♭ or B♭. The tessitura lends itself to tubas in all keys. See listing under Music for Tuba and Keyboard/Works Listed by Composer.

Galliard, Johann Ernst. *Sonata II in G Major.* arr. John Glenesk Mortimer. Editions Marc Reift. 1999. $11.00 (Complete set of six sonatas $31.00). 5:30 depending on repeats. II–III. G_1 (D_1)–g (a). Andante; Vivace; Alla siciliana; Allegro siciliana. Available individually or as a compilation of all six sonatas, in bass clef concert pitch, or in treble clef in E♭ or B♭. The tessitura lends itself to tubas in all keys. See listing under Music for Tuba and Keyboard/Works Listed by Composer.

Galliard, Johann Ernst. *Sonata III in F Major.* arr. John Glenesk Mortimer. Editions Marc Reift. 1999. $11.00 (Complete set of six sonatas $31.00). 5:30 depending on repeats. III. F_1 (C_1)–g. Largo; Allegro; Quasi recitativo; Allegro spiritoso. Available individually or as a compilation of all six sonatas, in bass clef concert pitch, or in treble clef in E♭ or B♭. The tessitura lends itself to tubas in all keys. See listing under Music for Tuba and Keyboard/Works Listed by Composer.

Galliard, Johann Ernst. *Sonata IV in E Minor.* arr. John Glenesk Mortimer. Editions Marc Reift. 1999. $11.00 (Complete set of six sonatas $31.00). 7:00 depending on repeats. III. G_1 (E_1)–g. Adagio non troppo; Adagio; Allemanda—Moderato; Corrente—spiritoso; Menuetto. Available individually or as a compilation of all six sonatas, in bass clef concert pitch, or in treble clef in E♭ or B♭. The tessitura lends itself to tubas in all keys. See listing under Music for Tuba and Keyboard/Works Listed by Composer.

Galliard, Johann Ernst. *Sonata V in D Minor.* arr. John Glenesk Mortimer. Editions Marc Reift. 1999. $11.00 (Complete set of six sonatas $31.00). 6:00 depending on repeats. II–III. A_1–g. Adagio; Allegro spiritoso; Alla siciliana; Allegro assai. Available individually or as a compilation of all six sonatas, in bass clef concert pitch, or in treble clef in E♭ or B♭. The tessitura lends itself to tubas in all keys. See listing under

Music for Tuba and Keyboard/Works Listed by Composer.

Galliard, Johann Ernst. *Sonata VI in C Major.* arr. John Glenesk Mortimer. Editions Marc Reift. 1999. $11.00 (Complete set of six sonatas $31.00). 8:00 depending on repeats. III. G_1 (C_1)–a. Larghetto; Allegro; Sarabanda; Menuet; Menuetto. Available individually or as a compilation of all six sonatas, in bass clef concert pitch, or in treble clef in E♭ or B♭. The tessitura lends itself to tubas in all keys. See listing under Music for Tuba and Keyboard/Works Listed by Composer.

Handel, Georg Friedrich. *Prélude et Fugue.* arr. Kurt Sturzenegger. Editions Marc Reift. 1996. $11.80. 5:00. III. F–d'. Because this arrangement was possibly conceived for the bass trombone, the tessitura is set in the middle range and works well on the F tuba. See listing under Music for Tuba and Keyboard/Works Listed by Composer.

Hatton, J. L. *Simon the Cellarer.* arr. Harry Prendiville. A. Squire.

Heinrich, Claus-Erhard, arr. *Nobody Knows the Trouble I've Seen.* Uetz Music Publishers. 2003. $10.00. F–f'. Also for trombone and tenorhorn.

Hlouschek, Theodor. *Barockes Konzert.* Available from Spaeth and Schmid. $15.50.

Knight, J. P. *Rock'd in the Cradle of the Deep.* arr. Harry Prendiville. A. Squire.

Koetsier, Jan. *Choral Fantasy, Opus 93.* Solid Brass Music Company. $15.50. IV. Lyrical concert work for tuba and organ.

Koetsier, Jan. *Es ist ein Schnitter, der heisst Tod. (There is a Reaper named Death.)* Editions Marc Reift. 1997. $16.00. 6:00. III–IV. G_1–f'. Introduktion; Passacaglia; Choral; Variante 1–3. A tonal work with conservative harmonies. Var. 1: tuba obbligato; Var. 2: a dotted eighth and sixteenth embellishment of the melody; Var. 3: fugue. Tessitura is generally in the upper middle register of the F tuba. See listing under Music for Tuba and Keyboard/Works Listed by Composer.

Koetsier, Jan. *Galgenlieder.* Editions Marc Reift. 1997. $16.00. 6:00. III–IV. G_1–f'. Introduktion; Passacaglia; Choral; Variante 1–3. For soprano and tuba! See listing under Music for Tuba and Keyboard/Works Listed by Composer.

Kulesha, Gary Alan. *Sonata for Tuba and Organ.* Canadian Music Centre.

Loeillet, Jean-Baptiste. *Sonate en do majeur. (Sonata in C Major.)* arr. Kurt Sturzenegger. Editions Marc Reift. 1996. $11.80. 5:30. III. A–d'. Cantabile; Largo; Allegro. Originally for flute and continuo, the arrangement of this baroque composition was obviously conceived for bass trombone. It can also be purchased a major third lower, but in this case it is written in treble clef in B♭. See listing under Music for Tuba and Keyboard/Works Listed by Composer.

Mozart, W. A. *Adagio KV 580a.* arr. Walter Hilgers. Available from Spaeth and Schmid. $7.25.

Mozart, W. A. *Romance für F-Tuba.* Uetz Music Publishers. 2003. $8.50. F–c'. See listing under Music for Tuba and Keyboard/Works Listed by Composer.

Mueller, J. I. *Praeludium, Chorale, Variations and Fugue.* arr. Allen Ostrander. Editions Musicus.

Näther, Gisbert. *Duo, Op. 69.* Available from Spaeth and Schmid. $9.50.

Nelson, S. *Pilot, The.* arr. Harry Prendiville. A. Squire.

Pinkham, Daniel. *Dragons and Deeps.* Ione Press. 2001. 5:00. IV. For Randal Montgomery. Written for bass tuba in F. Based on a biblical text from Psalm 148, the work depicts praise in many small sections. A good balance of lyrical, linear playing juxtaposed against faster staccato passages with large leaps. Relatively simple accompaniment.

Porpora, Nicola Antonio. *Sonata in A♭ Major.* arr. Kurt Sturzenegger. Editions Marc Reift. 1996. $11.00. 4:00. III. C ($A♭_1$)–d♭'. Andante; Adagio; Allegro non presto. Originally for cello by the Italian baroque composer; the tessitura of this arrangement is set in the middle range and is playable on all tubas. See listing under Music for Tuba and Keyboard/Works Listed by Composer.

Prendiville, Harry arr. *Down among the Dead Men.* A. Squire.

Prendiville, Harry arr. *Six Popular Solos.* A. Squire.

Reger, Max. *Romanze.* arr. Wisskirchen. Available from Spaeth and Schmid. $8.75.

Russell, H. *Old Sexton, The.* arr. Harry Prendiville. A. Squire.

Schmutz, Albert D. *Chorale Prelude.* Available from the composer.

Schubert, Franz. *Ave Maria.* arr. Kalke. Available from Spaeth and Schmid. $8.50.

Shield. *Friar of Orders Gray, The.* arr. Harry Prendiville. A. Squire.

Thiel, Wolfgang. *Winterballade.* Available from Spaeth and Schmid. $12.25.

Vivaldi, Antonio. *Sonata No. VI in B♭ Major.* arr. John Glenesk Mortimer. Editions Marc Reift. 1998. $11.00 (Complete set of six sonatas $31.00). 6:00–10:00 depending on repeats. III. F_1 ($E♭_1$)–b♭. Largo; Allegro; Largo; Allegro. Originally for violin; this transcription is in the original key. Available individually or as a compilation of all six sonatas, in bass clef concert pitch, or in treble clef in E♭ or B♭. The octave settings vary depending on which instrument is used. See listing under Music for Tuba and Keyboard/Works Listed by Composer.

Walker, Gwyneth. *Celestial Keys.* MMB Music, Inc. 2004. $28.95. 14:00.

Weinhart, Christoph. *Mass from Stone, for Tuba and Organ.* Uetz Music Publishers. $17.00.

Tuba and Harpsichord

Butterfield, Don. *Journal of Days.* D. B. Publishing Co.

Childs, Barney. *Mary's Idea*. Seesaw Music Corporation.

Enciña, Juan Del. *Triste España Sin Ventura*. tr. Gary A. Buttery. Whaling Music Publishers.

Forez, Henri. *Opus Open*.

Loelliet, Jean-Baptiste. *Vivace, from Sonata in E mi.* arr. Gary Buttery. Whaling Music Publishers.

Marcello, Benedetto. *Adagio from Sonata C-Dur.* arr. Gary Buttery. Whaling Music Publishers.

Marcello, Benedetto. *Sonata No. 1 in F Major.* arr. Donald C. Little and Richard B. Nelson. Southern Music Company.

Marcello, Benedetto. *Sonata No. 5 in C Major.* arr. Donald C. Little and Richard B. Nelson. Southern Music Company.

Purcell, Henry. *Gavotte*. arr. Anton Vedeski. Medici Music Press.

Stratton, Don. *In F.* Trombone Association Publishing.

Tuba and Synthesizer

Fritze, Gregory. *Basso Concertino*. Manuscript.

Tuba and Lute

Garcia: cuerdas, vientos, y voces. Kallisti Music Press. 2003.

2. Music for Tuba and Band

Timothy J. Northcut, Assistant Editor, *Guide to the Tuba Repertoire: The New Tuba Source Book*

Julia Piorkowski and Bobbie Zajkowski, Editorial Assistants

Skip Gray, Assistant Editor, *The Tuba Source Book*

Introductory Remarks (July, 2005): Timothy J. Northcut

The primary goal of this chapter is to provide an updated list of compositions written for tuba and band. Not having been involved with the research for the first edition of *The Tuba Source Book,* I would like to congratulate Skip Gray for the exceptional job he did. When my mentor, Winston Morris, contacted me about joining the team for this publication as an assistant editor, I immediately responded "yes," recognizing the importance of updating such information. I also knew that "no" was not an acceptable answer. Almost thirteen years have passed since the closing date for research for the first edition of *The Tuba Source Book* (July 1993), and the repertoire for tuba and band has experienced significant growth. In the present survey of these materials, it is apparent that as the quantity of the repertoire has increased, so has the quality.

The corresponding chapter in the first edition of *The Tuba Source Book* included 234 entries for tuba and band. For this publication, I have added 67 new entries and updated 5 entries from the first edition. Regrettably, I was compelled to withhold a number of compositions due to lack of information and as a result, there will be compositions that have been omitted. My responsibility as editor is to maintain the excellence in research that was established in *The Tuba Source Book,* and it is my hope that this was accomplished and you find this material to be extremely helpful.

This chapter is the culmination of the work of many volunteers and was truly a labor of love. It is with profound gratitude that I thank those who assisted:

• Julia Piorkowski and Bobbie Zajkowski. I express my extreme gratitude for the work of these wonderful friends who served as my editorial assistants. They each were totally committed to the completion of this project. I cannot thank you enough!

• Winston Morris, for his trust in my abilities to conduct research and for his words of encouragement and support in all of my musical endeavors.

• David Adams, Chair of the Performance Studies Division in the University of Cincinnati College-Conservatory of Music, for monetary support for the initial mailing to hundreds of publishers and composers.

• To the publishers and composers who responded to requests for information, catalogs, and review copies, especially David Miles (Tuba-Euphonium Press).

• To the International Consultants, especially Jørgen Voigt Arnsted, Øystein Baadsvik, Sergio Carolino, John Elliott, Alessandro Fossi, James Gourlay, John Griffiths, Chitate Kagawa, David LeClair, Gilles Lutmann, and Steve Rosse.

• Jennifer Northcut. I am immensely grateful to my wife for her patience and tolerance beyond reason.

• Nicholas and Claire Northcut. A special expression of gratitude goes to my children, who day to day patiently waited for dad to come out and play.

Introductory Remarks (July, 1995): Skip Gray

The tuba's true beginnings as a featured solo instrument can best be traced back to the last decades of the nineteenth century, when the growth of professional and town bands was at its zenith. The earliest known original solo works for the tuba include such works as *The Thunderer* (1891) by J. S. Cox, *Tuba Polka* (1886) by J. J. Davis, *The Beauty Polka* (1887) by D. L. Ferrazzi, and *Dream of Peace* (1888) by W. C. Ripley. Composer George Southwell is credited with at least five works for solo tuba with band between the years 1881 and 1902. Most of these early solo pieces are formal relatives to the cornet solos by composers such as Herbert L. Clarke which are well known and are still played often. The standard structure of these works consists of an introduction, a brief cadenza, a polka, and a trio. Although most of these early pieces for solo tuba and band are out of print or have become lost, several publishing companies are beginning to make some available again, and as they reappear, it becomes evident that these works offered significant technical and musical challenges to tubists of more than one hundred years ago.

In the early to middle twentieth century, the public school music education movement created a need and new market for music of wide ability levels. There were more concerts and new contests for not only bands, but ensembles and soloists on every instrument. Beginners through advanced students needed solo material fit to their level of proficiency, and band directors wanted to spotlight their young "artists" in front of the group in concerts. Publishers began making available series of "graded" solo literature for every instrument, and the tubist received a great deal of literature from composers such as H. A. VanderCook, Forrest Buchtel, and Fred Weber.

The 1960s and '70s produced a conscious movement to make the tuba an equal of all other instruments, to gain respect for it as a "musical" instrument in its own right, and to attain opportunities for artists of the instrument. The great players of this period, paired with the uninhibited experimental spirit of composers, led to a large body of works in a wide variety of styles. In this time period, many colleges and universities added tuba professors to faculty rosters and many works for solo tuba and band were commissioned to help promote these new artists in residence as well as to attract students for them to teach. In addition to college bands and the professional military bands who sought new works featuring tuba soloists, professional tubists needed works to play with high school groups and at the ever-growing number of music conventions and conferences.

Compositions featuring the solo tubist with band have evolved beyond the "polka and trio" into the complete spectrum of styles, from modern, experimental works with avant-garde techniques required of both soloist and band members, to works which could function well as sound-tracks for the latest Hollywood cinema production.

A scholarly study which has been most helpful in preparing this listing of compositions for solo tuba and band, especially for the very early works, is "An Annotated Bibliography of Tuba Solos with Band Accompaniment" by L. Richmond Sparks, available from University Microfilms in Ann Arbor, Michigan. Special thanks also to Bert Wiley at Bernel Music for his assistance with works for tuba and brass band.

Åkerwall, Martin. *The Answered Question.* Available from the composer. Tuba and Brass Band. 1998. 10:00. V. F_1–g'. Extremely soft dynamics with exposed tuba writing. This piece is a humble tribute to Charles Ives and is similar in form to his *Unanswered Question.* Available for Tuba and Organ.

Akiyoshi, Toshiko. *I Ain't Gonna Ask No More.* Kendor Music, Inc. Solo Tuba (or Bass Trombone) and Jazz Ensemble. 1974. 5:30. III. F_1–f. Single movement. A good bluesy solo with great back-up licks. Also contains an open ad lib solo with simple changes. Recorded by Toshiko Akiyoshi/Lew Tabackin Big Band.

Albian, Franco. *Alla Siciliana (Aria and Variations).* Available from the composer. Solo Tuba and Band. 1993. 6:30. III. F_1–b♭. This work is comprised of a theme and five variations, with two solo cadenzas. Musically, the piece is very conservative, typical of solo works written in the late eighteen hundreds, centering in B♭ major and closely related keys. A strong Italian flavor permeates this piece, which is fun for both the player and the audience.

Anderson, Eugene D. *Concert Piece for Tuba and Band.* Anderson's Arizona Originals. Solo Tuba and Concert Band. $30.00. 6:00. III–IV. F_1–f'. Single movement in four sections. Dedicated to the Mesa City Band. Tuba solo part is primarily diatonic with several chordal passages. The work is centered in B♭ major with departures to the parallel minor and a Largo section in C major. Band accompaniment is playable by most high school and community bands. See: Bird, Gary, ed.; *Program Notes for the Solo Tuba.*

Andrieu, Fernand. *L'Angelus du soir—Melodie.* Editions Musicales. Solo Tuba (or Saxophone, Baritone, Horn, Trombone) and Band. 3:30. III. G–c'. See: Sparks, L. Richmond; "An Annotated Bibliography of Tuba Solos with Band Accompaniment."

Angst, Adolf. *Die swingende Tuba—Solo for Tuba in E-flat or B-flat.* Eigentum u. Verlag. Solo Tuba and Band. 4:30. III–IV. F_1–d♭'. A German march written in swing style. See: Sparks, L. Richmond; "An Annotated Bibliography of Tuba Solos with Band Accompaniment."

Arban, Jean Baptiste. *Variations on the Carnival of Venice.* arr. Frank Berry. Carl Fischer, Inc. Solo Tuba (in F) and Band (also for Tuba and Orchestra). 1988. Score and parts are rental from the publisher. 8:00. V. C–b♭'. For Roger Bobo. This version in the key of B♭ major sits well for the F tuba and has accompanimental sections scored so that the soloist will not be over-balanced. Recorded by Roger Bobo.

Arban, Jean Baptiste. *Variations on the Carnival of Venice.* arr. William Schmidt. Western International Music, Inc. Solo Tuba (in F) and Symphonic Wind Ensemble. 1993. Score and parts are rental. 8:00. V. C–b♭'. For Ron Davis. This version in the key of B♭ major sits well for the F tuba and has accompanimental sections scored so that the soloist will not be over-balanced.

Arend, A. Den. *Concerto—Voor Tuba, Basse Solo, Baryton or Tenorhorn—Harmonie Fanfare.* Molenaar N.V. Solo Tuba and Band. 1963. 9:30. IV. F_1–a. Continuous movement with an introduction, theme, and variations. See: Sparks, L. Richmond; "An Annotated Bibliography of Tuba Solos with Band Accompaniment."

Arutiunian, Alexandre. *Concerto for Tuba and Orchestra.* arr. Johann de Meij. Editions BIM. Solo Tuba and Band. 1993 (1992). 15:20. IV–V. F_1–g'. Three movements: Allegro moderato; Andante sostenuto; Allegro ma non troppo. Commissioned by Yamaha Corporation and Editions BIM. Dedicated to Roger Bobo. Tonal work with contemporary colors; generally high tessitura. Available for Tuba and Piano, Tuba and Orchestra. Reviewed in the Spring 1998 and Summer 1998 issues of the *TUBA Journal* (Vol. 25, Nos. 3 and 4).

Baadsvik, Øystein. *Déjà vu.* Ovation. Solo Tuba and Brass Band. 1994. 3:00. III. $41.97. The name of this piece comes from the fact that the theme was never composed tone by tone. Baadsvik wrote, "When the theme came to me it felt like I had heard it several times before. I checked with some friends to find out if this actually was an existing piece of music. It turned out to be new! My first experience simply was a 'Déjà vu.'" Available for Solo Tuba and Wind Band.

Baadsvik, Øystein. *Did You Do?* Ovation. Solo Tuba and Brass Band. 2003. 3:00. II. $65.12. The name of the piece is a joke upon the word *Didgeridoo.* It was commissioned by the Trondheim Military Band to be performed in a series of children's concerts. The idea behind the piece was to show the origin of brass instruments and the use of lip vibration to produce sound. A big challenge was to deal with the fact that the didgeridoo only has one single note (a d♭) that is present during the whole piece. It starts as a call from far away presented by a duet between the didgeridoo and the flugelhorn. The euphoniums and the marimba continue with a beautiful legato line that carries the four-bar chord progression that the whole piece is built upon. One by one the instrument groups join in on an optimistic little fanfare until everything is suddenly interrupted by a heavy rock groove (!) on the didgeridoo. The trombone kicks off a groovy solo followed by a fugue in the cornets before the beat is calmed down by the euphonium and marimba legato line at the end. Available for Solo Tuba and Wind Band.

Baadsvik, Øystein. *Fnugg Blue.* arr. Svein H. Giske. Ovation. Solo Tuba and Brass Band. 2003. $94.07. 8:00. IV. D♭–d♭. This version of *Fnugg Blue* was made for the gala concert of the European Brass Band Championship in Bergen in May 2003. It was premiered by Øystein Baadsvik and Stavanger Brass Band. The score includes a relatively easy part for synthesizer. The player is also controlling the start and stop of two electronic rhythm loops played either from a CD player or from a sampler, drum machine, or a keyboard with this option built in. The loops are included on an audio CD. It is highly recommended that the soloist and the synthesizer are amplified through a speaker system for the performance. Available for Solo Tuba and Wind Band.

Bach, Jan. *Tuba Concerto.* Tuba-Euphonium Press. See Tuba and Orchestra.

Bach, Johann Sebastian. *Air and Bouree.* arr. William Bell/Jerry Lackey. Carl Fischer, Inc. Solo tuba and Band. Rental. 5:00. III. An easy-moderate band arrangement of the William Bell classic arrangement for tuba and piano.

Barat, J., ed. *Introduction and Dance.* arr. Daniel Phillips. TUBA Press. Solo Tuba and Band (Piano accompaniment available). $30.00. 4:00. IV. C–g♭'. An easy band arrangement of the standard tuba solo. See listing under Tuba and Keyboard.

Baratto, Paolo. *Jumbo-Baby.* Available from the composer. Solo Tuba (or Bass Trombone, Bassoon) with Wind Band or Brass Band (Piano reduction available). 2:30. II. C–g. A simple and cute little work with an easy accompaniment.

Barnes, James. *Concerto for Tuba, Op. 96.* Southern Music Company. Rental only. arr. R. Mark Rogers. Solo Tuba and Band. 1997. 19:30. V. C_1–g'. Three movements: Allegretto giocoso; Lullaby; Rondo. Written for and premiered by Scott Watson. Very demanding work. It contains virtually every technical "trick in the book": multiple tonguing, large range shifts, quick facility with slur and fingers. Each movement could stand alone, though the second and third movements are performed attacca. The second movement is written in ballad style. Written with CC tuba in mind. Recorded by Patrick Sheridan. Available for Tuba and Piano, Tuba and Symphony Orchestra. Reviewed in the Winter 1998 issue of the *TUBA Journal* (Vol. 25, No. 2).

Barnhouse, Charles L. *Barbarossa—Air Varie.* C.L. Barnhouse. Solo Tuba and Band (Piano accompaniment available). 1897. Out of Print. 5:30. III. $E\flat_1$–e♭'. A true classic in the turn-of-the-century repertoire.

Barry, Darrol. *Impromptu for Tuba.* Studio Music. Solo Tuba and Brass Band. 1981. 5:22. III–IV. $B\flat_1$ (F_1)–f'. Written for Ian Duckworth. A tuneful work with most material for the soloist diatonic and a nice cadenza. Recorded by Kenneth Ferguson and the Desford Colliery Caterpillar Band.

Bartles, Alfred. *Scherzo for Tuba and Wind Ensemble.* Sam Fox Publishing. Tuba and Wind Ensemble (Piano reduction out of print). 1970. Rental through Theodore Presser Co. 4:30. III–IV. F_1–d♯'. Single movement. To Harvey Phillips. An enjoyable, tuneful piece with jazz influences in both tuba solo part and accompaniment.

Bartles, Alfred. *Tubossa—A Concert Bossanova for Solo Tuba and Symphonic Band.* Available from the composer. Solo Tuba and Symphonic Band. 2004. 5:30. IV. $B♭_1$–f'. Dedicated to R. Winston Morris. Premiered by Timothy Northcut with the Tennessee Tech Symphony Band. The piece was conceived as a kind of concert bossa nova that explores the lyric possibilities of the tuba while backing up the solo with a harmonically rich and challenging accompaniment. Available for Tuba and Piano. Recorded by Timothy Northcut.

Bavicchi, John. *Concerto for Tuba and Concert Band.* BKJ Publications. 1994. 12:00. IV. $D♭_1$–b♭'. Five sections in one continuous movement. Written for Greg Fritze. Based on a previous work, *Concertino for Tuba and Brass Quartet,* also written for Greg Fritze. Premiered at the University of Delaware with the MIT Concert Band. The solo part as well as the band parts would be accessible to most college-level players. The band orchestration is nicely scored so the soloist will be easily heard.

Beasley, Rule. *Concerto for Tuba and Band.* Available from the composer. Solo Tuba and Band (Piano reduction available). 1969. 13:30. III–IV. F_1–f'. Three movements: Allegro moderato; Adagio; Allegro. Commissioned by David Kuehn. The music sounds modern yet conventional. See: Bird, Gary, ed.; *Program Notes for the Solo Tuba.*

Bell, J. H. *Sans Pareil.* J. W. Pepper and Son. Solo Tuba and Band. 1901. Out of Print. 3:45. III–IV. $A♭_1$–f'. See: Sparks, L. Richmond; "An Annotated Bibliography of Tuba Solos with Band Accompaniment."

Bell, William J. *Tubaman, The.* arr. Fred Weber. Belwin Mills Publishing Corporation. Solo Tuba and Band (Piano accompaniment available). 1962. Out of Print. 2:00. I. $B♭_1$–c. A very easy solo and band accompaniment from Fred Weber's "First Division Band Course."

Bencriscutto, Frank. *Concertino for Tuba and Band.* Shawnee Press. Tuba and band (Piano reduction available). 1969. $50.00. 10:00. III. $E♭_1$–c'. Single movement work. For Stanford Freese. A diatonic work centered in the tuba's middle register with two extensive solo cadenzas. Band accompaniment is easy. Recorded by Stanford Freese.

Bennet, David. *Basses Berserk.* Carl Fischer, Inc. Tuba Section (or Tuba Solo) and Band. 1953. Out of Print. 2:30. II. B♭–f. A simple, entertaining work performable by high school or good junior high players.

Bennett, Malcolm. *Concerto No. 2.* Available from the composer. Solo Tuba and Brass Band. 1988. 18:45. IV. D_1–b'. Three movements: Allegro; Adagio; Allegro. Available for Tuba and Piano.

Benson, Warren. *Helix.* Carl Fischer. Solo Tuba and Concert Band (piano reduction available). 1967. $6.00 (score), parts on rental. 14:00. III–IV. F_1–e'. Two movements: Dancing-rollicking; Singing-pensive. Commissioned by and dedicated to Harvey Phillips. Tuba part not extremely demanding. Band accompaniment difficult and requiring extensive percussion. Recorded by Harvey Phillips, Jack Robinson, and John Turk.

Berg, Thomas. *Bass-Solo—Polka.* Adlerverlag. Solo Tuba and Band. 1974. 2:50. III. C–b♭. See: Sparks, L. Richmond; "An Annotated Bibliography of Tuba Solos with Band Accompaniment."

Bewley, Norlan. *Santa Wants a Tuba for Christmas.* Bewley Music. Solo Tuba and Band. 1992. 4:00. IV. B♭–f'. Written for Harvey Phillips. An exceptionally cute tune, especially when used with the vocal solo. A good swing feel is necessary for all players. Fun to play and delightful for audiences. Recorded by Harvey Phillips. Originally for Solo Tuba and Tuba Ensemble; also available for Solo Tuba and Orchestra.

Bilik, Jerry. *Introduction and Dance.* RBC Publications. Solo Tuba and Band. 1969. $50.00. 4:30. II–III. G_1–b. Continuous work in three sections: Andante; Allegro ma non troppo; Allegro ma non troppo. A musically simple yet solid composition. This music could be handled by a good junior high school–level soloist and band.

Blank, Allan. *Divertimento for Tuba and Band.* American Composers Alliance. 1979. 28:00.

Blank, Hans. *Variationen uber ein Volkslied (Ein Mannlein steht im Walde).* Musikverlag Siegfried Rundel. Solo Tuba (or Baritone, Bassoon) and Band. 4:00. III. $E♭_1$–e♭. See: Sparks, L. Richmond; "An Annotated Bibliography of Tuba Solos with Band Accompaniment."

Blemant, L. *Le Triomphe—Fantasie pour Tuba.* Editions Robert Martin. Solo Tuba (or Trombone, Baritone) and Band. 7:00. III–IV. D–c'. Continuous work in four sections with solo cadenza. See: Sparks, L. Richmond; "An Annotated Bibliography of Tuba Solos with Band Accompaniment."

Bourgeois, Derek. *Rondo Grottesco.* William Allen Music, Inc. Solo Tuba and Band. $70.00.

Bowles, Richard. *Venetian Carnival.* Belwin Mills Publishing Inc. Solo Tuba and Band. 1973. 2:30. II. B♭–e♭. An easy solo with brief cadenza based on the melody "The Carnival of Venice."

Brahmstedt, N. K. *Stupendo—Concert Polka.* Rubank, Inc. Solo Tuba and Band (Piano accompaniment available). 1937. 3:30. II–III. A_1–a♭. An easy, mostly diatonic work.

Brand, Michael. *Four Temperaments (Variations for Tuba)*. G&M Brand Music. Solo Tuba and Band. One movement in four sections. Reviewed in the Winter 1999 issue of the *TUBA Journal* (Vol. 27, No. 2).

Brand, Michael. *Tuba Tapestry.* R. Smith & Co. Ltd. Solo Tuba with Brass Band. 1978. $34.00. 4:45. IV. D–g'. Single movement. Written for John Fletcher and the Fodens' Band. A pretty, tuneful piece with a fairly extensive cadenza for the solo tubist. Recorded by Hans Anderson, John Fletcher, Sibley Graham, and Tim Norris.

Brandon, Sy. *Concerto alla Jazz.* Tuba-Euphonium Press. Solo Tuba and Band. 2001. 10:30. IV. D_1–e'. Three movements: Swing; Blues; Latin. Concerto in different jazz styles; no improvisation is required. Limited technical demands. Band accompaniment could be played by advanced high school band. To Rommel Cordova.

Briccetti, Thomas. *Ecologue No. 4 for Solo Tuba and Concert Band.* Available from the composer. Solo Tuba and Band. 1962. 9:00. III. E_1–b♭. Two movements: Lento; Allegro. Composed for the Pinellas County (Florida) School System under a grant from the Contemporary Music Project, funded by the Ford Foundation and administered by Music Educators National Conference. A good solo tuba and symphonic band work with a melodic, rhythmic, and coloristic interest. The solo part contains little technically difficult material. The second movement has some meter changes which will be challenging to high school groups.

Briegel, George F. *Basso Profundo.* Available from the composer. Solo Tuba and Band (Piano accompaniment available). 1952. 3:30. B♭–f. An easy "polka" for solo tuba.

Broughton, Bruce. *Concerto for Tuba Solo and Wind Ensemble.* Edwin F. Kalmus & Co. Solo Tuba and Wind Ensemble (Piano accompaniment available as *Sonata for Tuba and Piano*). 1976 (1985). $60.00. 7:30. IV. C_1–e'. Three movements: Allegro moderato; Aria; Allegro Leggero. For Tommy Johnson. The composer's arrangement of his *Sonata for Tuba and Piano* works very well, and the very coloristic scoring includes harp. See: Bird, Gary, ed.; *Program Notes for the Solo Tuba.*

Brubaker, Jerry. *Song and Dance.* Horizon Press. Tuba (or Euphonium) Solo and Band. $85.00.

Bruniau, A. *Sur la montagne.* Editions Billaudot. Tuba and Band (also Tuba and Brass Band).

Brusick, William R. *Concerto for Tuba and Wind Orchestra.* Available from the composer. Tuba and Band. 2003. 26:30. V. A_2–g'. Three movements: Lento Espressivo—Vivace; Romanza; Allegro Energico. Commissioned by and dedicated to Timothy Northcut. Premiered by Paul Ebbers with the Florida State University Wind Orchestra, James Croft, conductor. Encompassing an introduction and three movements, which are played without pause, the concerto is held together by the use of a single motive, a chant-like melody, which is played by the solo tuba at the outset of the work. The Lento introduction serves as a commentary by the orchestra on the soloist's long opening statement by developing the melodic elements in the chant motive and by exploiting some of the rich harmonies inherent in the motive. The second movement begins softly with a harmonized whole-tone scale. A slow but continuous crescendo culminates in the cadenza, which is based in part on the chant motive. The last movement is set in sonata-rondo form with two main themes: an agitated theme accompanied by heavy punctuations from the orchestra, and a contrasting legato theme. The climax of this movement and of the whole concerto occurs when the chant is presented in a three-voice canon by the full brass section. Available for Tuba and Piano. Recorded by Timothy Northcut.

Bugby, Colin. *Mr. C. Takes a Stroll.* Available from composer. Solo Tuba and Brass Band. 2002. 3:17. III. A_2 (optional A)–f. Good for a young soloist. Fun to play and delightful for audiences. For John Coleman. Available for Tuba and Wind Band, Tuba and Piano.

Camphouse, Mark. *Poème for Solo Tuba and Symphonic Band.* Manuscript available from the composer. Solo Tuba and Symphonic Band. 1986. 12:00. IV–V. E–a'. Single movement. For Jeffrey Arwood and the United States Army Band. A slow, brooding work with many wide leaps in the solo tuba part. There are long sections in which the soloist does not play as well as interludes in which the tubist plays unaccompanied or with just one other instrument. The emotional work is difficult but is not perceived as "virtuosic." Recorded by Jeffrey Arwood.

Cardillo, S. *Catari, Catari.* Molenaar Music N.V. Solo Tuba (or Euphonium) and Band. 1912. 2:30. IV. C–g'. See: Sparks, L. Richmond; "An Annotated Bibliography of Tuba Solos with Band Accompaniment."

Carroll, Gregory. *Studies in American Folk Idiom.* Bernel Music LTD. Solo Tuba and Band. Available for Solo Tuba and Orchestra, Tuba and Piano.

Catelinet, Philip. *Three Sketches for Tuba.* Solo Tuba and Brass Band. Available from Bernel Music LTD. $53.00.

Catozzi, A. *Beelzebub.* arr. Julius S. Seredy. Carl Fischer, Inc. Tuba and Band (Piano reduction available). 1932. $30.00. 5:30. III. A_1–c' (e♭'). Theme and four variations. Dedicated to G. Marquardt, Tuba Soloist. A classic air and variation solo portraying several characters. A good technical showpiece with short cadenza. See listing under Tuba and Keyboard.

Chappot, Edward. *Concerto pour Tuba, Percussion et Brass Band.* Editions Marc Reift. Tuba, Percussion, and Brass Band. 1999. 11:00. IV. F_1–g♯'. Three movements: Allegro moderato; Lento sostenuto espress. Funèbre; Rondo, Allegro Giocoso. Dedicated to Pierre Pilloud. A traditionally written double concerto. The first movement is a dialogue between tuba and xylophone or marimba, interspersed with glockenspiel. There is a short cadenza for the tuba at the end of the movement. In the second movement, a funeral march, the percussionist plays tamtam and tubular bells in addition to xylophone. The third movement is lively with the solo instruments trading off arpeggio- and scale-like patterns. The ensemble writing for brass band is well orchestrated.

Chebrou, Michel. *Tubafolia.* Editions Bim. Tuba and Wind Band. 2000 (1999). 20:00. IV. G_1–g' (optional a'). Three movements: Allegretto; Andante Molto Moderato; Rondo. Dedicated to Bernard Liénard. High tessitura. Tonal composition with some triple tonguing. Effective work with lyrical and rhythmic appeal. Available for Tuba and Piano.

Childs, Barney. *Concert Piece for Tuba and Band.* Manuscript available from the composer. Solo Tuba and Band. 1973. 9:00. III–IV. D_1–d' (f' or B♭'). Six connected sections: Introduction; Lively; Dialogue; Surprises, . . . ; . . . Cadenza . . . ; . . . and Coda. Commissioned by and dedicated to Rex Conner, Ivan Hammond, David Kuehn, R. Winston Morris, Dan Perantoni, Harvey Phillips, Jack C. Robinson, James Self. An interesting, modern work with moderately easy band accompaniment. Tuba solo part contains little of difficulty other than some hemiola and five- against four-beat passages. This work could serve as a good introduction to modern sounds for a younger group.

Clark, Maurice. *Tyrolean Tubas.* Molenaar Music N.V. Solo Tuba(s) and Brass Band. 1963. $22.00. 3:30. III–IV. G_1–f'. See: Sparks, L. Richmond; "An Annotated Bibliography of Tuba Solos with Band Accompaniment." Recorded by Mary Stern.

Clarke, Herbert L. *Cousins.* arr. John Glenesk Mortimer. Editions Marc Reift. Tuba and Brass Band. 1993. 4:30. III. Part I: $B♭_1$–e♭'; Part II: G_1 (optional $E♭_1$)–f". A brass band arrangement for any two instruments. The parts can be ordered in E♭ or B♭.

Condon, Leslie. *Celestial Morn.* Salvationist Publishing and Supplies, Ltd. Solo Tuba and Brass Band. 1962. 9:00. IV. $E♭_1$–e♭'. A beautiful, neoromantic solo work for tuba and brass band. Recorded by Albert Hornsberger.

Condon, Leslie. *Radiant Pathway.* Salvationist Publishing and Supplies, Ltd. Tuba Duet (or Euphonium-Tuba Duet, Solo Tuba) and Brass Band. 1975. 7:00. IV. Tuba I: $B♭_1$ ($E♭_1$)–f' (b♭'); Tuba II: $E♭_1$ ($G♭_1$)–d♭'. Continuous work in three sections: Allegro moderato; Largo con espressivo; Allegro ritmico. A nicely written work intended as a duet for E♭ and B♭ tubas with brass band. A devotional showpiece with lots of finger technique required. Recorded by Graham Patterson, David Stokes.

Constantinides, Dinos. *Concertino for Euphonium or Tuba and Wind Orchestra: Mountains of Epirus.* Available from the composer. 1980. 8:30. IV. $F♯_1$–e'. This work is modal and employs characteristic Greek syncopated rhythms and polychordal sonorities. A mixture of linear melodies and rapid rhythmic interjections. Available for Tuba and Orchestra, Tuba and Piano.

Corwell, Neal. *Catoctin, Opus 34.* Nicolai Music. Solo Tuba with Symphonic Wind Ensemble. 1999. 10:00. IV. F_1–g♭'. Single-movement work in two sections: Beginnings; Echoes. Commissioned by Steve Dillon. Premiered by Kelly O'Bryant and the United States Army Band. The piece is inspired by the Catoctin Mountains of Northwest Maryland which have borne witness to ecological onslaught, the American Civil war, and clashes between Native Americans and early white settlers. Demanding work for both soloist and ensemble. Reviewed in the Summer 2000 issue of the *TUBA Journal* (Vol. 27, No. 4).

Cox, J. S. *The Thunderer—Solo for Bombardon.* Jean White. Solo Tuba and Band. 1891. Out of Print. 2:45. III. B♭–e♭'. See: Sparks, L. Richmond; "An Annotated Bibliography of Tuba Solos with Band Accompaniment."

Cummings, Barton. *Concerto for Tuba.* Solid Brass Music Company. Solo Tuba and Wind Ensemble. 2001. V. C_1–g'. Commissioned by Robert Daniel, Mark Nelson, Raúl I. Rodríguez, James Self, James Shearer, Kenyon Wilson, Micky Wrobleski, and Jerry Young. Four movements: Almost Invisible; Things You Cannot See; Of Dreams Remembered; In Amber Salute. The intention of this piece was to create a composition that would be a virtuoso piece allowing the entire spectrum of the tuba and wind ensemble to be explored without restrictions or time constraints. Each movement has a unique sound environment to accompany the solo tuba. The first movement is scored for solo tuba, brass, keyboards, and percussion, while movement two utilizes the solo tuba, woodwinds minus saxophones, keyboards, and percussion. Movement three features the solo tuba, saxophones, double bass, keyboards, and percussion with the fourth movement combining the solo tuba and what would be called the traditional concert band. "Almost Invisible" is a dance-like movement that explores the ability of the tuba to be graceful and highlights the tuba's ability to negotiate rapid technical passages in a light and flexible fashion. "Things You Cannot See" presents the tuba in a slow, introspective, and moody atmosphere. The dark quality of the music changes to one of brilliance in a virtuoso display of pyrotechnics from the tuba. "Of Dreams Remembered" has a haunting and reflective atmosphere that explores the expressive singing quality of the tuba. "In Amber Salute" is the finale and begins softly and slowly. This leads into a rollicking hornpipe style that continually develops and eventually returns to the opening ideas followed by a brief cadenza and a final blazing outburst of sound in the hornpipe tempo. Available for Tuba and Piano. Reviewed in the Winter 2004 issue of the *ITEA Journal* (Vol. 31, No. 2).

Cummings, Barton. *Remembrance.* Solid Brass Music Company. Solo Tuba and Brass Band. 2003. 4:45. III–IV. D_1–d'. Three sections. The first section is in a lyrical, singing style. The second section is fast and technical and leads to a brief cadenza. The third section takes the piece back to the opening motives and finishes in a very quiet fashion. Brass band parts are accessible by intermediate-level performers. In memory of Stuart Snyder.

Curnow, Jim. *Concertino for Tuba and Band.* TUBA Press. Tuba and Band. 1980. $27.00. 6:30. III–IV. F_1 ($A\flat_2$)–c♭'. Single movement in three sections. For Barton Cummings. A tuneful piece with traditional harmonic orientation. Heavy scoring creates balance problems with large accompanying ensembles. Recorded by Charles McAdams, Daniel Perantoni.

Curnow, Jim. *Fantasia for Tuba and Band.* TUBA Press. Solo Tuba and Band. 1987. $50.00. 8:00. IV. D_1–f'. Continuous movement with six sections. Commissioned by the Roanoke Rapids Band Boosters. Dedicated to the Roanoke Rapids High School Band, Roanoke Rapids, North Carolina, David L. Hanks, Director. A dramatic work with much quartal and diatonic writing in the solo tuba part typical of Curnow's style. Band accompaniment is easily playable by most high school bands and does not impede the tuba soloist being heard.

Daniels, George F. *Orpheus.* J. G. Richards & Co. Solo Tuba and Band. 1891. Out of Print. 2:30. II–III. D♭–f. See: Sparks, L. Richmond; "An Annotated Bibliography of Tuba Solos with Band Accompaniment."

Danner, Greg. *Concerto for Tuba and Band.* Tuba-Euphonium Press. Solo Tuba and Band. $80.00. 19:30. IV–V. $B\flat_1$–g'. Three Movements: Excursion; For Bobbie; Caprice. Dedicated to R. Winston and Barbara Morris. Premiered by Timothy Northcut with the Tennessee Tech Symphony Band. Throughout the work, the emphasis is on melody, supported by clearly defined forms and harmonic structure. The first movement is in an arch design, with a declamatory opening section giving way to a lyrical theme. The second movement is a musical poem beginning with tuba alone stating a lyrical melody. The music grows out of this material, developing melodically and harmonically, with rather transparent scoring throughout. The last movement begins with a playful melody tossed back and forth between soloist and ensemble. Animated rhythms and frequently changing meters characterize this rondo tune. Available for Tuba and Piano. Recorded by Timothy Northcut.

Davis, J. J. *Tuba Polka—The Eureka.* Publisher not listed. Solo Tuba and Band. 1886. Out of Print. 3:00. III. $B\flat_1$–a♭. Original copy in United States Library of Congress. See: Sparks, L. Richmond; "An Annotated Bibliography of Tuba Solos with Band Accompaniment."

Davis, William. *Variations on a Theme of Robert Schumann—"The Happy Farmer."* Southern Music Company. Solo Tuba (or bass other instruments in the band) and Band (Piano accompaniment available). 1983. $40.00. 4:15. IV. $B\flat_1$–c'. A great deal of technique and flexibility required of the soloist throughout the four variations and in the cadenza.

Debons, Eddy. *A Quia.* Editions Marc Reift. Tuba and Brass Band. 2002. 8:00. III–IV. $A\flat_1$–d' (optional C_1–g'). Commissioned by Fondation Suisa pour la musique. Dedicated to Maurice Astella. A dramatic work with an oriental flare. Conservative tessitura, well set in the middle range of an F or E♭ tuba. The first section is a Burlesque, followed by a Funèbre, after which a cadenza bridges to the final Danse. The Danse is very rhythmical with changing meters. Available for Tuba and Piano.

DeCosta, Harry, and the Original Dixieland Band. *Tuba Tiger Rag.* arr. Luther Henderson, adapted for band by David Marshall. Hal Leonard Publishing Corporation. Solo Tuba and Band. 1991. $55.00. 5:00. III. F_1 ($B\flat_2$)–b♭ (c'). A fun solo tuba feature of the old Dixieland favorite. Band accompaniment is fairly easy. Recorded by the Canadian Brass.

Dedrick, Art. *A Touch of Tuba.* Kendor Music Inc. Tuba and Concert Band (Piano reduction available). 1959. $32.00. 4:00. II. F_1–b♭ (e♭'). One movement with two sections: Moderato; Fast. Dedicated to Harold L. Walters. A good solo work for a young high school or junior high school student. A cadenza links the two large sections of the piece. Recorded by Peter Popiel. Recorded accompaniment available: *Vivace: A Complete Practice System.*

DeLamater, E. *Auld Lang Syne.* Rubank, Inc. Solo Tuba and Band (Piano accompaniment available). 1948. 4:00. II. C–f. A traditional solo in format of Introduction, Theme, and two variations. The material is mostly diatonic with the closing variation in triplets containing the most technical difficulty. Recorded accompaniment available.

DeLamater, E. *Rocked in the Cradle of the Deep.* Rubank, Inc. Solo Tuba and Band (Piano accompaniment available). 1937. 3:00. II. B♭$_1$–f. Theme with two variations. Active yet mostly diatonic writing for the soloist, lying mostly in the staff. The second variation is in triplets.

DeLamater, E. *Tramp! Tramp! Tramp!* Rubank, Inc. Solo Tuba and Band (Piano accompaniment available). 1948. 3:30. II. B♭$_1$–e♭. Theme with two variations. Mostly diatonic writing with greatest technical demand in the second variation comprised of running triplets. Contains several short cadenzas.

Delbecq, Alfred. *Air Varie.* Molenaar Music N.V. Solo Tuba and Band. 1968. 4:00. III–IV. E♭–e♭'. See: Sparks, L. Richmond; "An Annotated Bibliography of Tuba Solos with Band Accompaniment."

Dersen. *Im Winzerkeller.* Huhn/Nobile Verlag. arr. Kothera. Tuba and Band (Piano accompaniment available).

DeWitt, L. O. *Pride of America—Polka.* Carl Fischer, Inc. Solo Tuba and Band. 1895. Out of Print. 5:00. III–IV. B♭–e♭'. Dedicated to Eldon Baker. See: Sparks, L. Richmond; "An Annotated Bibliography of Tuba Solos with Band Accompaniment."

Dumitru, Ionel. *Romanian Dance.* In preparation by Editions Bim. Solo Tuba and Band. 1993.

Duncan, Andrew. *Rhapsody for Tuba and Piano and Band.* Lewis Music Press. C$_1$–a♭'. Written for Gavin Woods, tuba, and Stewart Death, piano. Single movement in three distinct sections. This is an extremely virtuosic piece.

Dutton, Brent. *Divertissment.* Solo Tuba and Brass Band. Brassquake Press. 2003. V. F$_1$–d". Three movements: C'est Possible?; Ouvre ton Coeur; Ouvre Ton Chemise. Commissioned by Tubamania for the 1999 Tubamania Conference. Premiered by the composer. Solo part very demanding. Accompanying parts are not difficult and do not cause any balance problems for the soloist.

Dutton, Brent. *Tuba Concerto No. 3.* Brassquake Press. Solo Tuba and Brass Band. Premiered at TubaMania Conference in 1999 by the composer.

Eklund, Hans. *Concerto per Tuba e Orchestra a Fiati.* Manuscript available from the Tuba Center. Solo Tuba and Band. 1982. 8:00. IV. F♯$_1$–f'. See: Sparks, L. Richmond; "An Annotated Bibliography of Tuba Solos with Band Accompaniment."

Ellerby, Martin. *Tuba Concerto.* Maecenas Music. Solo Tuba and Concert Band. 1988. 13:00. G$_1$–g' (*ossia*). Continuous work in two sections: Andante ma non troppo; Allegro con brio. Dedicated to Stephen Sykes. Recorded by James Gourlay, Patrick Harrild, Patrick Sheridan, and Stephen Sykes. Available for Solo Tuba and Brass Band, Solo Tuba and Orchestra, Tuba and Piano. Reviewed in the Winter 1995 issue of the *TUBA Journal* (Vol. 22, No. 2).

Ely, Robert. *Concerto for Tuba.* Bandleader Publications, distributed by Mother Lode Music. 1993. 10:00. IV. F$_1$–e♭'. Three movements. Available for Tuba and Piano. Reviewed in the Summer 1999 issue of the *TUBA Journal* (Vol. 26, No. 4).

Engelhardt, Ernst. *Tuba—Sepp'l.* Musikverlag Wilhelm Halter GmbH. Solo Tuba and Band (Piano accompaniment available). 2:30. III. F$_1$–b♭. A concert polka featuring the solo tuba. See: Sparks, L. Richmond; "An Annotated Bibliography of Tuba Solos with Band Accompaniment."

Ewazen, Eric. *Concerto for Tuba or Bass Trombone.* arr. Virginia Allen. Southern Music Company. Solo Tuba and Band. 19:30. IV–V. E$_1$–a♭'. Three movements: Andante con moto; Andante Expressivo; Allegro Ritmico. This piece began as the *Sonata for Tuba or Bass Trombone and Piano;* the tuba version is written for and dedicated to Karl Kramer. Premiered by Karl Kramer in 1996. The outer movements are rhythmically energetic. The second movement requires musical maturity. Angular melodic lines, metric shifts, and multiple tonguing required. Available for Solo Tuba and Orchestra, Tuba and Piano. Reviewed in the Summer 2000 issue of the *TUBA Journal* (Vol. 27, No. 4).

Ferrazzi, D. L. *"The Beauty" Polka.* Originally published by Carl Fischer, republished and available from Piston, Reed, Stick, and Bow. Solo Tuba and Band. 1887. $15.00. 3:15. III. B♭–b♭. A typical turn-of-the-century solo with Introduction (Cadenza)—Polka—Trio form.

Fillmore, Henry. *Deep Bass.* Carl Fischer, Inc. Solo Tuba and Band (Piano accompaniment available). 1927. 1:00. I–II. F$_1$–e. A very easy solo with a short cadenza.

Flowers, Herbie. *Tuba Smarties.* arr. Denzil Stephens. Sarnia Music. Solo Tuba and Brass Band (Wind Band arrangement also available). 1982. 2:20. III. B♭$_1$–b♭. A clever novelty solo for the tuba. Recorded by Herbie Flowers.

Follas, Ronald W. *Concertpiece for Tuba and Band.* TUBA Press. Tuba and Concert Band (Piano reduction available). 1982. $45.00. 11:30. IV. F♯2–f♯'. One single continuous movement. The very easy band parts and "Hollywood" sound makes this an appealing work. The solo part is both tuneful and flashy. An extensive cadenza towards the end of the piece explores the tuba's wide range.

Forte, Aldo Rafael. *Dance Rhapsody for Tuba and Band.* Tuba-Euphonium Press. 2003. 12:00. IV. G$_1$–f'. Three movements: Airs; Grooves; Animations. Composed for, premiered, and recorded by Andrew Rummel, Principal Tubist with the United States Air Force Heritage of America Band, Major Larry H. Lang, Commander/Conductor. The three contrasting movements are played without pause. Each movement is faster in tempo than the preceding movement. Most of the thematic material for the work is derived from major and minor thirds. The work exploits the wide pitch range of the tuba as well as the expressive and technical possibilities.

Foster, Stephen. *Gentle Tuba (Old Black Joe)*. arr. Conley and Lloyd. Studio PR Publications. Solo Tuba and Band. 1980. $36.00. 3:00. II. E♭–e♭. An easy arrangement with updated harmonies.

Frackenpohl, Arthur. *Song and Dance for Euphonium, Tuba, and Band.* Horizon Press. Solo Euphonium, Solo Tuba, and Band. 1991. Commissioned by the Lake Braddock Secondary School Band, Roy C. Holder, Director, Burke, Virginia. Recorded by David Porter.

Frackenpohl, Arthur. *Tubarag*. Tuba-Euphonium Press. Solo Tuba with Band. 1999. 3:00. II–III. $B♭_1$–c'. For Anne Hardin, Director of Bands, E. L. Wright Middle School, Columbia, S.C., and Andrew Hyman, First Chair Tuba, 1996 S.C. Jr. All-State Band. Good for a young soloist on a popular concert. Available for Tuba and Piano, Solo Tuba and Brass Quintet.

Frackenpohl, Arthur. *Variations on "The Cobbler's Bench."* Shawnee Press, Inc. Tuba and Concert Band (Piano reduction available). 1973. $25.00. 5:30. III–IV. G_1–c' (c♭'). Theme and four variations with cadenza. For Peter Popiel. A nicely scored work which allows the soloist to be heard easily. Recorded by Ronald Davis, Peter Popiel. Recorded accompaniment available: *Vivace: A Complete Practice System.* For further information, see listing under Recorded Accompaniments.

François, Claude, and Revaus, Jacques. *My Way.* arr. Hardy Schneiders. Editions Marc Reift. Tuba and Brass Band. 1993. 4:00. II. $B♭_1$–g'. A good, light arrangement of the popular chanson. Good for a young soloist.

Fritze, Gregory. *Concertino for Tuba and Band.* Music Nova USA. Solo Tuba and Band. 2003. 14:00. IV. $F♯_1$–g'. Commissioned by Gary Bird and Mary Ann Craig. Adopted from an earlier composition, *Concertino for Euphonium and Band,* published in 1995 by TubaPress. Differences from the original include cadenzas, orchestrations, and key changes. A one-movement composition with a fast-slow-fast form. The solo part as well as the band parts would be accessible to most college-level players. The band orchestration is nicely scored so the soloist will be easily heard. Available for Tuba and Orchestra. Tuba and Piano reduction in progress.

Fucik, Julius. *Der Alte Brummbär (Basse Solo).* arr. John Maston. Musikverlag Wilhelm Halter GmbH. Solo Tuba (or Bassoon, Saxophone, Baritone) and Band (Piano accompaniment available). 1964. 3:45. III. C–b. Traditional concert polka with the solo part staying in the upper tessitura. See: Sparks, L. Richmond; "An Annotated Bibliography of Tuba Solos with Band Accompaniment."

George, Thom Ritter. *Concertino for Tuba and Wind Ensemble.* Manuscript available from the composer. Solo Tuba and Wind Ensemble (also for Solo Tuba with String Orchestra and Solo Tuba and Piano). 1984. 7:30. IV. B♭–e♭'. Three movements: Allegro ma non troppo; Cantabile e simplice; Vivace. Traditional melodic writing with modern harmonies. See: Bird, Gary, ed.; *Program Notes for the Solo Tuba.*

Giovanini, J. *Challenge Concert Polka.* J. W. Pepper. Solo Tuba and Band. 1901. Out of Print. 4:00. II–III. D♭–a♭. See: Sparks, L. Richmond; "An Annotated Bibliography of Tuba Solos with Band Accompaniment."

Giroux, George. *Solo Blues.* Southern Music Company. Solo Tuba (or Clarinet, Saxophone, Trumpet, Trombone, Baritone). 1974. $20.00. 1:30. I. C–d♭. A very easy work with a pop-music sound.

Gliere, Reinhold. *"Andante" from Concerto for Coloratura Soprano and Orchestra.* arr. Timothy Northcut. Available from Arranger. Solo Tuba and Band. 2003. 7:53. IV. C–d♭'. Written in 1942–43 when Gliere was in his late sixties, the *Concerto* has two movements—a lyrical *Andante* and a brilliant *Allegro.* A mournful, unharmonized tune introduces the *Andante* movement before the soloist enters. The solo drives the movement from climax to climax by providing great spans of melody thrown against a backdrop of rich orchestral texture. Available for Tuba and Piano. Recorded by Timothy Northcut.

Gourlay, James. *Alpine Tuba.* Editions Marc Reift. Tuba and Brass Band. 1999. 4:30. III. $E♭_1$–e♭' (optional g'). Dedicated to Shaun Crowther. A humorous work requiring a shade of theatrics. After an introduction depicting the Alps, the tuba enters, playing bits of a melody which are echoed first in the soprano cornet and then in the cow bells. The melody develops into a Laendler and is then followed by virtuosic variations. In the polka section, a second soloist can play along as a duet (optional).

Graetsch, Hans. *Chiemgauer—Bass—Sololander.* arr. Karl Jugel-Janson. Wilhelm Halter GmbH. Solo Tuba and Band (Piano accompaniment available). 4:00. II. $A♭_1$–e♭. A waltz in three sections. See: Sparks, L. Richmond; "An Annotated Bibliography of Tuba Solos with Band Accompaniment."

Graetsch, Hans. *Tuba Kapriolen.* Regina. Tuba and Band (Piano accompaniment available).

Gregson, Edward. *Tuba Concerto.* Novello & Co., Ltd. Solo Tuba and Brass Band (Solo Tuba and Concert Band, Solo Tuba and Orchestra, and Piano reduction available). 1976. 15:00. IV. D_1–e'. Three movements: Allegro deciso; Lento e mesto; Allegro giocoso. Commissioned by the Besses O 'Th'Barn Band with funds from the Arts Council of Great Britain. For John Fletcher. See: Bird, Gary, ed.; *Program Notes for the Solo*

Tuba. Recorded by John Fletcher, Michael Lind, Michael Wagner.

Gregson, Edward. *Tuba Concerto*. Novello & Co., Ltd. Solo Tuba and Concert Band (Solo Tuba and Brass Band, Solo Tuba and Orchestra, and Piano reduction available). 1976. $75.00. 15:00. IV. D_1–e'. Three movements: Allegro deciso; Lento e mesto; Allegro giocoso. Commissioned by the Besses O 'Th'Barn Band with funds from the Arts Council of Great Britain. For John Fletcher. An excellent accompaniment lets the soloist shine in this finely crafted work. Nice melodies and cadenzas provide a perfect solo vehicle for the tubist. See: Bird, Gary, ed.; *Program Notes for the Solo Tuba*. Recorded with wind band by Josef Maierhofer, Lennart Nord.

Grieg, Edvard. *In the Hall of the Mountain King*. arr. G. E. Holmes. Rubank, Inc. Solo Tuba and Band (Piano accompaniment available). 1939. 2:00. II. C–e. A popular melody from the classics which works well for the young tubist. Mostly diatonic writing with some chromatic alterations and accidentals carrying through the bar which will demand the attention of a novice player.

Grundman, Claire. *Tuba Rhapsody*. Boosey and Hawkes. Tuba and Concert Band (Piano reduction available). 1976. $65.00. 9:30. III. G_1–b♭. One continuous movement. To Martin D. Erickson, Tuba Soloist, and the U.S. Navy Band. Simple tunes and light scoring in solo passages allow the tubist to be heard. Band parts are moderate in difficulty, playable by most high school groups. Recorded by Lesley Varner.

Haddad, Don. *Suite for Tuba*. arr. Robert E. Clemons. Shawnee Press. Tuba and concert band (Piano accompaniment available). 1978. $50.00. 9:00. III. $B♭_1$–c'. Three movements: Allegro Maestoso; Andante Espressivo; Allegro con Brio. Nice melodies and sensible scoring make this an effective work for tuba soloists, whether they be accomplished students or professionals. The band parts are playable by a good high school band. Tuba and Piano version recorded by Rex Conner, Ronald Davis. Recorded accompaniment available: *Vivace: A Complete Practice System*. For further information, see listing under Recorded Accompaniments.

Hall, George. *Concertante for E-flat Tuba and Brass Band*. Piccolo Press. Solo Tuba and Brass Band. 5:00. III–IV. $E♭_1$–g. Available for Tuba and Piano. Reviewed in the Winter 1999 issue of the *TUBA Journal* (Vol. 26, No. 2).

Harris, John H. *Tempesta Polka*. Carl Fischer, Inc. Solo Tuba and Band (Piano accompaniment available). 1896. Out of Print. 5:00. III–IV. B♭–e♭'. See: Sparks, L. Richmond; "An Annotated Bibliography of Tuba Solos with Band Accompaniment."

Hartley, Walter. *Concertino for Tuba and Wind Ensemble*. Theodore Presser Co. Tuba and Wind Ensemble (Piano reduction available). 1968–69. $21.00. 9:00. IV. F_1–e♭'. Two movements: Lento; Allegro non troppo. For Rex Conner. Requires sensitive playing by the soloist as well as the ability to execute a triple forte which takes place at the work's main climax just prior to the cadenza in the second movement. Recorded by John Turk.

Hartzell, Doug. *Ballad for Young Cats*. Shawnee Press. Solo Tuba and Band. $18.00. II.

Hartzell, Doug. *Egotistical Elephant, The*. Shawnee Press. Tuba and Concert Band (Piano reduction available). 1967. $18.00. 3:30. II. C–d♭. Single movement. A simple, melodic work appropriate for a first- or second-year student. Band accompaniment is very easy.

Hastings, Ross. *Prelude and Faràndola for Tuba and Band*. TUBA Press. Solo Tuba and Band (Piano reduction available). 1987. $30.00. 6:30. III–IV. F_1–e♭'. Two movements. The Prelude is melodic and quite expressive. The Faràndola is a driving dance with some changing meters and several tricky rhythmic passages. Throughout, the tuba solo contains few wide intervallic leaps. Other than the occasionally changing meters, the band parts contain little of difficulty.

Hayes, Al. *Solo Pomposo*. Carl Fischer Inc. Tuba and Band (Piano reduction available). 1911. $35.00. 4:00. II–III. $B♭_1$–b♭. An old, traditional tuba solo in the Introduction-Cadenza-Polka-Trio format. The solo part is mostly diatonic in the key of B♭ and E♭ and in the lower half of the bass clef staff.

Heinl, Otto. *Barentanz*. Musikverlag Wilhelm Halter GmbH. Solo Tuba and Band (Piano accompaniment available). 3:00. III. B♭–f'. See: Sparks, L. Richmond; "An Annotated Bibliography of Tuba Solos with Band Accompaniment."

Heinl, Otto. *Der verliebte Teddybär*. Musikverlag Wilhelm Halter GmbH. Solo Tuba and Band. 3:00. III. A_1 (C_1)–f'. Simple diatonic and chordal melodies in this cute, novelty solo. The tuba solo part is mostly in the upper tessitura and, although technically simple, might be suited best for the F or E♭ tuba.

Holmes, G. E. *Emmett's Lullaby*. Rubank, Inc. Solo Tuba and Band (Piano accompaniment available). 1933. 5:30. III. F_1–f. An old favorite theme and variations solo. See listing under Tuba and Keyboard.

Hopkinson, Michael E. *Concerto for Tuba*. Solo Tuba and Brass Band. Kirklees Music. $18.90.

Hopkinson, Michael E. *In Lively Spirits*. Solo Tuba and Brass Band (Piano accompaniment available). Kirklees Music. 1992. $9.50. 4:30. III–IV. G_1–e♭'. A quasi jazz-style arrangement of *Andante and Allegro Spiritoso* by J. B. Senaille. The main challenge to the soloist is playing with a swing feeling; there are no substantial technical demands.

Horovitz, Joseph. *Tuba Concerto*. Manuscript available from the composer. Solo Tuba and Brass

Band (Concerto Band accompaniment in preparation, piano reduction available). 1989. 21:00. IV–V. F_1–f♯'. Three movements: Allegro; Andante; Con moto. Commissioned by the Besses O 'Th' Barn Band, for James Gourlay, with funds from the Musicians' Union. A substantial concerto consisting of modern harmonies and traditional style. A good deal of interplay between soloist and accompanying ensemble creates a texture allowing the tubist to be heard. An extensive cadenza is placed following the dramatic climax towards the end of the third movement. Recorded by James Gourlay.

Hoshina, Hiroshi. *Concertino for Tuba and Winds.* Japan Tuba Center. 1998. G_1–f'. Commissioned by Chitate Kagawa. Dedicated to Harvey G. Phillips. A single-movement work with sections that are clearly outlined beginning with Grave; L'istesso tempo con gusto; Meno mosso; Allegro con brio and returning to the original Grave. Throughout the work, lyricism is emphasized over technical facility, which results in beautiful dialogues between the solo tuba and wind ensemble. Available for Tuba and Piano. Recorded by Takashi Abo. Reviewed in the Spring 1999 issue of the *TUBA Journal* (Vol. 26, No. 3) and Summer 2002 issue of the *ITEA Journal* (Vol. 29, No. 4).

Hubert, Roger. *Elegie.* Editions Robert Martin. Solo Tuba (or Saxophone, Horn, Trombone, Baritone) and Band. 1961. 2:30. I–II. F–b. A very simple work, probably intended primarily for horn solo. See: Sparks, L. Richmond; "An Annotated Bibliography of Tuba Solos with Band Accompaniment."

Huffine, G. *Them Basses.* Carl Fischer Inc. Tuba/Low-Brass Soli with Band. $30.00. III. A traditional march in 6/8 featuring the low brass section.

Hupfield, Herman. *When Yuba Plays the Rumba on the Tuba.* arr. Bob Foster. Warner Bros. Publications Inc. Solo Tuba (or Tubas) with Marching Band. 1982. 2:00. II. B♭$_1$–f. Single movement. A fun and easy arrangement of the popular, classic tuba solo. Recorded by William Bell, Harvey Phillips, Joe Tarto, Joe "Country" Washburn.

Hyldgaard, Soren. *Bagatelle.* De Haske/Hal Leonard. Solo Tuba (or Euphonium) and Wind Orchestra. 2001. 4:10. IV. A–g'. Dedicated to Jens Bjørn-Larsen. Written as an encore. A simple, haunting piece that allows the tuba to sing in upper tessitura. Accompanying parts are not difficult and do not cause any balance problems for the soloist. Recorded by Jens Bjørn-Larsen.

Jacobsen, Julius. *Tuba buffo (Concerto for Tuba and Wind Orchestra).* Swedish Music Information Center. Solo Tuba and Wind Ensemble. 1977. 9:30. IV–V. A truly humorous and tuneful work. Recorded by Michael Lind.

Jager, Robert. *Concerto for Bass Tuba and Concert Band.* Belwin-Mills, Inc. Solo Tuba and Concert Band (Piano reduction available). 1978. Score and parts available on rental. 13:20. IV–V. D_1–a♭'. One continuous movement with five sections. Commissioned by the University of Illinois Band for Daniel Perantoni. A beautiful concerto in the romantic style reminiscent of Rachmaninoff or Brahms. See: Bird, Gary, ed.; *Program Notes for the Solo Tuba.* Recorded by R. Winston Morris, Daniel Perantoni.

Jansson, Leif A. *Lassie.* Lema Musikförlag, Sweden. Solo Tuba and Band. 1990. 7:00. IV.

Jude, W. H. *The Mighty Deep.* arr. Paul de Ville. Originally published by Carl Fisher, Inc.; republished and available from Piston Reed Stick and Bow. Solo Tuba and Band. 1898. $15.00. 3:30. II–III. B♭$_1$–a. An easy tuneful solo.

Kabec, Vlad. *Der Wurzelseppl'—Polka for Tuba.* Musikverlag Wilhelm Halter GmbH. Solo Tuba and Band. 1986. 2:45. II. B♭–f. Published in tandem with a horn solo piece entitled *Harlem—Lullaby* by Jean Treves.

Kalke, Ernst-Thilo. *Mevagissey Tales.* Musikverlag Bruno Uetz. Solo Tuba and Wind Band. 2001. 16:00. V. C_1–d''. Three movements: Cornish Dawn; King's Arms; The Smuggler's Wife. First movement originally for horn quartet with solo tuba. Expanded to three movements for wind band by suggestion of Skip Gray. The three movements provide impressions of an English coastal village. Cornwall is distinguished by soaring cliffs that precipitate steeply into the sea, interrupted only by inlets of estuaries emerging from creeks and brooks. In such an inlet lies concealed the place called Mevagissey. In the first movement, the scene is set in the early morning hours when the fog rises from the sea and crawls up the cliffs. One is not only transported back to the mythical world of King Arthur and Merlin, but the stories of pirates and buccaneers also come to life. The second movement is named for an actual pub in Mevagissey. It is filled with armor and pictures of warriors that at one time fought in the area. The third movement is entitled "The Smuggler's Wife." Mevagissey was the base for an extensive smuggling business with France. The punishment for smuggling was very severe. Once, when a smuggler had been imprisoned by the coast guard, his captors became so enchanted by his young and beautiful wife that they let her husband, the smuggler, go free. Available for Tuba in Mixed Ensemble, Tuba and Orchestra, Tuba and Piano.

Kellaway, Roger. *Morning Song.* Editions BIM. Tuba and Brass Band. 1979. 7:00. IV–V. F_1–b♭'. For Roger Bobo. Originally written for the Roger Kellaway Cello Quartet, then arranged for Tuba and Piano.

Kenny, Terry. *Sullivan at Sea.* Bandleader Publications, distributed by Mother Lode Music. Solo Tuba and Band or Brass Band. 1993. IV. F_1–b♭. A potpourri of five songs that involve men and the action of the ocean. They are strung together in a clever and engaging way. Available for Solo Tuba and Piano. Reviewed in the Summer 1999 issue of the *TUBA Journal* (Vol. 26, No. 4).

Kessler, James. *Solo Overture for Tuba and Band.* Available from the composer. Solo Tuba and Band. 1977. 11:00. III–IV. F_1–d♯'. Written for Jeff Arwood. A work characterized as dark and brooding with a great deal of shifting meters and repetitive melodic fragments.

King, Karl L. *The Devil and the Deep Blue Sea–Humoreske.* Originally published by C. L. Barnhouse; republished and available from Piston Reed Stick and Bow. Solo Tuba and Band. $15.00. 3:30. II–III. C–g. A novelty solo from the early twentieth century.

Kleinsinger, George. *Tubby the Tuba.* arr. George Roach. G. Schirmer. Tuba and Band (Also available for Tuba and Orchestra). 1945. $75.00. 12:00. III. $E♭_1$–e♭'. Single movement. The classic work featuring the tuba in a story setting with narrator and ensemble. The beautiful tuba melody and nice story make this a good "pops" or children's concert piece. Numerous recordings and videos are available.

Kolditz, Hans. *Die Kellerasseln.* Musikverlag Wilhelm Halter GmbH. Tuba and Band.

Kolditz, Hans. *Rondo for Tuba and Large Wind Orchestra.* Musikverlag Wilhelm Halter GmbH. Solo Tuba and Band. 1988. 3:45. II–III. $B♭_1$–e♭. Continuous work in three sections: Allegro; Andante cantabile; Allegro. An easy, tuneful work in A-B-A form. Band parts are not difficult.

Kothera, Georg. *Mit Lust und Liebe.* Georg Bauer Musikverlag. Solo Tuba and Band. 1977. 3:20. II. $B♭_1$–g. See: Sparks, L. Richmond; "An Annotated Bibliography of Tuba Solos with Band Accompaniment."

Kottaun, Celian. *Billy Blowhard—Concert Polka.* Carl Fischer, Inc. Solo Tuba and Band (Piano accompaniment available). 1909. 4:00. II–III. $B♭_1$–b♭. An "old standard" in the tuba solo with band repertoire.

Koumans, R. *Concerto for Basstuba and Band.* Molenaar Music N.V. Solo Tuba and Band. In preparation.

Kroepsch, F. *Down in the Deep Cellar—Grand Fantasia.* arr. L. P. Laurendeau. Carl Fischer, Inc. Solo Tuba (or Clarinet, Cornet, Trombone, Baritone) and Band (Solo Tuba with Brass Quintet and Solo Tuba and Piano also available). 1908. Out of Print. 6:45. IV. $E♭_1$–g'. A traditional yet technically demanding work for the solo tubist.

Kulesha, Gary. *Concerto for Tuba.* Canadian Music Centre. Solo Tuba and Band (Orchestra Accompaniment and Piano Accompaniment Four Hands also available). 1979. Rental from the publisher. 18:00. IV. C_1–d'. Three movements: Prelude and Fugue; Scherzo; Finale. Commissioned by the Scarborough Concert Band of Ontario, Canada.

Kumstedt, Paul. *Humoreske for Tuba and Wind Orchestra.* Georg Bauer Musikverlag. Solo Tuba and Band. 1985. 3:30. III. F_1–d'. A well-scored piece with pop music influences. See: Sparks, L. Richmond; "An Annotated Bibliography of Tuba Solos with Band Accompaniment."

Lackey, Jerry. *Concertpiece for 3 Tubas and Band.* Available from the composer. 3 Solo Tubas (1 small, 2 large) and Band (Piano reduction available). 1963. Score and parts rental (Tubas and piano $25.00). 8:00. IV. Part I: A_1–f♯'; Part II: $G♭_1$–d'; Part III: E_1 (D_1)–d'. One movement with multiple sections.

Lackey, Jerry. *Jazz Concerto for Tuba and Band.* Available from the composer. Solo Tuba and Band, Drum Set, Piano, and Electric Bass (Also versions for Tuba and Orchestra, Tuba and Piano). 1984. Rental from composer. 12:00. IV. G_2–b♭'. Three movements: Fast Swing, Rock, Simple Waltz, Fast Swing; Slow, Tranquillo; Fast, with Energy. This arrangement by the composer of his work originally for solo tuba and orchestra is great solo tuba showpiece, especially for "pops" concerts.

Lackey, Jerry. *Short Stuff.* Available from the composer. Solo Tuba and Band. 1964. Tuba and band rental from composer (Piano reduction $15.00). 1:00. IV. G_1–c'. Written for William Bell. A quick, humorous encore piece.

Lange, Willy. *Launische Tuba—Heitere Polka für Tuba.* Musikverlag Wilhelm Halter GmbH. Solo Tuba and Band. 2:30. II. $A♭_1$–f. See: Sparks, L. Richmond; "An Annotated Bibliography of Tuba Solos with Band Accompaniment."

Lange, Willy. *Tubistenfreud, Op. 176.* Musikverlag Wilhelm Halter GmbH. Solo Tuba and Band (Piano accompaniment available). 3:00. II–III. $E♭_1$–e♭. See: Sparks, L. Richmond; "An Annotated Bibliography of Tuba Solos with Band Accompaniment."

Lange, Willy. *Tubistenlaune.* Musikverlag Wilhelm Halter GmbH. Solo Tuba and Band. 1:30. II–III. F–a (b♭). An easy polka with no substantial technical demands.

Lange, Willy. *Tubistenscherz, Ein.* Musikverlag Wilhelm Halter GmbH. Solo Tuba and Band. 1:45. III. F_1–f'. A technical polka-style solo which lies mostly in and above the bass clef staff. There are several arpeggios which demand dexterity and rapid passages which require double tonguing as well as a cadenza requiring some triple tonguing.

Lange, Willy. *Tubistenschreck, Op. 77.* Musikverlag Wilhelm Halter GmbH. Solo Tuba and Band. 1983. 3:30. IV. C_1 (F_1)–a' (a). See: Sparks, L. Richmond; "An Annotated Bibliography of Tuba Solos with Band Accompaniment."

Lange, Willy. *Tubistentraum, Op. 216.* Musikverlag Wilhelm Halter GmbH. Solo Tuba and Band. 1983. 2:00. III–IV. F (F_1)–b♭' (b♭). See: Sparks, L. Richmond; "An Annotated Bibliography of Tuba Solos with Band Accompaniment."

Laurendeau, L. P. *Elephantine Polka.* Originally published by Carl Fischer, Inc., republished and available from Piston Reed Stick and Bow. Solo Tuba and Band. 1903. $15.00. 1:30. III. D♭–d♭'. A good solo in Polka and Trio form with two short cadenzas.

Legrady, Thomas. *Tubantella.* Molenaar Music N.V. Solo Tuba and Band. 1987. 2:40. II. F_1–b♭. A simple tarantella with no substantial technical demands on the soloist.

Loder, E. J. *The Diver—Tuba Solo.* arr. Paul de Ville. Carl Fischer, Inc. Solo Tuba and Band. 1893. Out of Print. 3:30. II. A_1–g. See: Sparks, L. Richmond; "An Annotated Bibliography of Tuba Solos with Band Accompaniment."

Loeffler. *Der Herr Tubist.* arr. Cosmar. Musikverlag Rundel GmbH. Tuba and Band (Piano accompaniment available).

Losch, Margot. *Auf Freierstuber—Polka.* arr. H. Ruckauer. Margot Losch Musikverlag. Solo Tuba and Band. 1978. 2:30. II. G_1–f. A concert polka featuring the soloist in the bread and butter register.

Madsen, Trygve. *Introduction and Allegro.* Norwegian Music Information Center. Tuba and Band. 10:00. IV V. For Michael Lind.

Manas, Franz. *Lustiger Bassist Konzertpolka.* Johann Kliment. Solo Tuba and Band. 1970. 2:30. II. A_1–f. See: Sparks, L. Richmond; "An Annotated Bibliography of Tuba Solos with Band Accompaniment."

Marais, Marin. *Le Basque.* tr. Dan Phillips. Thompson Edition. Tuba and Band. 1987. $35.00. 1:00. IV. C–c'. Single movement. A short, light, flashy work which serves as a nice encore. Easy band accompaniment.

Marques, Carlos. *Concerto for Tuba.* Editions BIM, in progress. Solo Tuba and Symphonic Wind Band. In progress. 15:00. V. Commissioned by the Oporto National Orchestra. Dedicated to Sergio Carolino. Available for Solo Tuba and Symphony Orchestra.

Martin, W., arr. *Rocked in the Cradle.* Wright & Round, Ltd. Solo Tuba with Brass Band. 1985. $23.00. 1:30. II. A♭–E♭. A very simple arrangement in a paired edition which also contains a solo tenor horn version of *Annie Laurie Variations.*

Masso, George. *Suite for Louise.* arr. Robert Rÿker. Kendor Music, Inc. Solo Tuba and Concert Band (Piano accompaniment available). 1966. 5:40. II. A_1–f. Three movements: Bourée; Pavane; Gigue. Three simple movements of contrasting character make this a nice solo for a young tubist. Band accompaniment is easy.

Matteson, Rich. *Be-Bop Minor.* Available from the composer. Solo Tuba and Jazz Ensemble. 1978. 3–5 minutes. V. B_1–g'. Commissioned by and composed for Michael Lind. A hot and difficult chart with several openings for ad lib solos. Several written solos are provided with the arrangement.

Matteson, Rich. *Just the Two of Us.* Available from the composer. Solo Tuba and Jazz Ensemble. 1978. 4:00. IV–V. C–a'. Commissioned by and composed for Michael Lind. A pretty ballad with completely notated solo part which stays in the upper tessitura.

McBeth, Francis. *Daniel in the Lion's Den.* Southern Music Company. Solo Tuba and Concert Band. 1992. Rental from the publisher. 3:10. V. G_1–b'. Composed for and dedicated to Daniel Perantoni. A technical tour de force, nearly always lying at the top of and above the bass clef staff, intended as an encore piece for tuba soloist with band. Very high tessitura and some difficult sixteenth note passages. Premiered by Dan Perantoni with the United States Air Force Band at the 1992 International Tuba-Euphonium Conference in Lexington, Kentucky.

McKimm, Barry. *Tuba Concerto.* Yarra Yarra Music Services. Tuba and Concert Band (Piano reduction available). 1983. 18:00. III. G–c♯'. Three movements: Andante sostenuto—Allegro; Adagio; Allegro vigoroso. Commissioned by Peter Sykes. An introspective, lyrical work intended for the contrabass tuba. The original version of this concerto, for tuba and piano, has been abbreviated considerably in overall duration. The concert band parts are somewhat difficult, probably requiring college-level players. An edition for solo tuba with brass band is in preparation by the composer.

Medberg, Gunnar. *Divertimento.* Swedish Music Information Center. Solo Tuba and Wind Ensemble. 1988. Four movements: Allegro con brio; Andante; Allegretto; Allegro vivace.

Meier, Jost. *Eclipse finale?* Editions Bim. Solo Tuba with Brass Band (also available for Tuba and Chamber Orchestra, Tuba and Piano). 1991. Rental from the publisher. 19:30. V. D_1–a♭'. Commissioned for the 1991 Geneva Competition by the Christiane and Jean Henneberger-Mercier Foundation. Variations on the German folksong "Der Mond is aufgegangen" (The moon has risen). The tuba solo plays a dramatic role portraying humanity's increasing concern at the destruction of nature and the environment. A dramatic and difficult modern work with wide, irregular intervals, complex rhythms and ensemble cuings, and other avant-garde effects. Recorded by Øystein Baadsvik and the Bienne Brass Band. Reviewed in the Summer 1997 issue of the *TUBA Journal* (Vol. 24, No. 4).

Menoche, Charles Paul. *Chamber Concerto.* Available from composer. Solo Tuba and Thirteen Players (Flute, Oboe, Clarinet, Alto Saxophone, 2 Trumpets, Horn Trombone, 2 Percussion, 2 Synthesizers). 2002. 17:00. IV–V. C_1–g♭'. Dedicated to Tracey Rudnick. This piece pays homage to the composer's roots as a tubist. It draws inspiration from American poet Charles Olson's 1950 essay *Projective Verse.* A rhythmically aggressive and energetic work that is challenging for both tubist and ensemble. Despite the small ensemble, a conductor is necessary. Extensive work-out throughout the concerto. See listing under Tuba in Mixed Ensemble.

Merle, John. *Mummers—Danse Grotesque.* Carl Fischer, Inc. Solo Tuba and Band (Piano accompaniment available). 1938. Out of Print. 2:00. I–II. G_1–c. An easy little solo in 6/8 time. Recorded by William Bell.

Methehen. *Ramses.* Tuba Center. Tuba and Band.

Michel, Jean-François. *Sambatuba.* Woodbrass Music SA. Tuba and Brass Band. 2004. 3:00. III. F_1–e' (optional B♭$_2$–b♭'). Dedicated to Ernst, Martha, and Manfred Obrecht. A rhythmical work that is fun to play and delightful for the audience. A good addition to the popular literature.

Monti, Victorio. *Czardas.* arr. Sergio Carolino. Lusitanus Editions, Portugal. Solo Tuba and Symphonic Wind Band. 1995. 6:00. V. C_1–f". An arrangement of the standard violin virtuoso piece. Multiphonics, double and triple tonguing are used in the cadenza. A fantastic show piece for the tuba.

Monti, Vittorio. *Csárdás.* arr. Øystein Baadsvik. Ovation. Solo Tuba and Wind Band. 1992. $50.65. 5:00. IV. G_1–a♭'. Originally written for the violin, this display piece has tempted numerous performers. In this arrangement the tuba is the star of the show. Fun to play and delightful for audiences. The solo part can be played on different instruments and the set is delivered with solo part in treble clef in E♭ and bass clef. Recorded by Øystein Baadsvik. Available for Solo Tuba and Piano, Solo Tuba and String Orchestra, Solo Tuba and Brass Band, Solo Tuba and Wind Quintet.

Moore, David Arthur. *Winter Concerto.* Available from the composer. Solo Tuba and Wind Orchestra. 1986. $50.00. 20:00. V. A_2–f'. Nine movements that follow continuously without pause: Introit: Frost Music; Passacaglia I: Winter Dream Variations; Cadenza I; Fantasia: Storm Music I; Passacaglia II: Nifleheim Variations; Toccata and Fugue: Storm Music II; Cadenza II; Passacaglia III: Muspelheim Variations; Abschied. The piece is based on a three note motive, A, E♭, A♭, which in turn generates a nine-tone chromatic infinity series and a twelve-tone row based on four tri-chords. Each passacaglia has nine variations. Dedicated to the memory of Arthur K. Smart. Available for Solo Tuba and Piano.

Morricone, Enrico. *Gabriel's Oboe.* arr. Øystein Baadsvik. Ovation. Solo Tuba (or Euphonium) and Brass Band. 2001. $56.44. 7:00. IV. B♭–g'. Available for Solo Tuba and Symphony Orchestra, Solo Tuba and Wind Band.

Mozart, W. A. *Concert Rondo.* arr. Andy Clark. C. L. Barnhouse Co. Solo Tuba (Baritone, or Horn) and Band. $55.00.

Mozart, W. A. *Horn Concerto No. 1.* tr. Otto Zurmuhle. Molenaar Music N.V. Solo Tuba (or Tenorhorn, Baritone) and Band. 1959. 9:00. III. F–g♭. A good band arrangement of this classic standard.

Mueller, Florian. *Concert Music for Bass Tuba and Concert Band.* arr. Richard Schwartz. Warwick Music Ltd. 2003. $52.41. 5:00. III–IV. E_1–e'. Completed in 1946, Florian Mueller's *Concert Music for Bass Tuba and Orchestra* was composed for and first performed by Arnold Jacobs and the Chicago Symphony Orchestra. Its date of composition places it as one of the earliest original works for solo tuba and orchestra. Dr. Richard Schwartz, Professor of Music at Virginia State University, created this faithful band transcription of the work using Mueller's handwritten manuscript. Band parts are not difficult and do not cause any balance problems for the soloist.

Mueller, Frederick. *Variations on a Theme of Samuel Barber.* Manuscript available from the composer. Solo Tuba and Band (also Solo Tuba and Strings, Solo Tuba and Piano). See listing under Tuba and Orchestra.

Muscroft, Fred. *Carnival for Bass.* Studio Music Co. Solo Tuba with Brass Band (Piano accompaniment available). 1981. $22.75. 5:00. III–IV. B♭$_1$–e♭'. A theme and variation solo based upon the Carnival of Venice complete with opening cadenza, theme, and three variation sections. Recorded by Fred Baker.

Nelhybel, Vaclav. *Concert Piece.* E. C. Kerby, Ltd. Tuba (or Alto Saxophone, Tenor Saxophone, Baritone Saxophone, Trumpet, Trombone, or Baritone) and Band (Piano accompaniment available). 1973. $27.00. 4:00. III. C–f. Three continuous sections: Allegro marcato; Piu vivo; Molto vivo. A dramatic dialogue between the solo tuba and band.

Nelhybel, Vaclav. *Concerto for Tuba (or Horn).* Great Works Publishing, Inc. Solo Tuba (or Horn), 2 Flutes, Oboe, English Horn, 2 Clarinets, Bassoon, Harp, Double Bass, 2 Trumpets, Trombone, 3 Percussion (Vibraphone, Bells, Xylophone). 1993. 14:00. IV. Three movements: Allegro; Adagio; Moderato—Allegro. An effectively written work which, although employing many of the composer's familiar idioms, sounds especially fresh because of the orchestration.

Nelhybel, Vaclav. *Concerto Grosso for Tubas and Band.* Hope Publishing Co. Tuba(s) and band. 1980. $28.00. 10:00. III. G_1–d♭. Three movements: Con brio; Sostenuto; Allegro. Commissioned by the Dauphin County Music Educators Association, Harrisburg, Pennsylvania. Music typical of the composer's well-known style and sound. For good balance, at least four tubists are recommended to perform this work with a typical "symphonic" band.

Nelson, S. *Bonnie Mary of Argyle*. arr. A. Kriek. Molenaar Music N.V. Solo Tuba and Band. 1960. 2:30. II. C–g. An easy folksong arrangement.

Newsome, Roy. *Bass in the Ballroom, The*. Studio Music Company. Solo Tuba and Brass Band (Piano accompaniment available). 1971. $14.00. 4:45. III–IV. A_1–e♭'. A good "pops concert" arrangement which takes the solo tuba through two dance styles: tango and waltz. Recorded by Stephen Sykes and Gavin Woods.

Newsome, Roy. *Swiss Air*. Studio Music Company. Solo Tuba and Brass Band (Piano accompaniment available). $14.00. Recorded by Shaun Crowther.

Newton, Rodney. *Capriccio*. Rosehill Music Publishing Company. Solo Tuba and Brass Band (Piano accompaniment available). 1991. $35.50. 8:30. IV. E_1–e'. Single movement. For James Gourlay. An interesting work which presents two contrasting themes, the first somewhat dance-like, the second lyrical and romantic. A very nice display piece for the solo tubist which includes one short and two fairly extensive cadenzas. Recorded by Stephen Sykes and James Gourlay.

Newton, Rodney. *Millennium Concerto*. Studio Music Company. Solo Tuba and Wind Orchestra. 2000. Composed for James Gourlay. This work was commissioned by the tuba virtuoso James Gourlay, with funding from the British Association of Symphonic Wind Band and Ensembles, in celebration of the new millennium and may be regarded as a musical journey from darkness to light. There are four sections played without a break: Into the Unknown (Lento)—two dark chords are answered by a rising phrase from the soloist. Material is passed from the band to the soloist and back, rising and falling in emotional intensity. The atmosphere of this opening section is questioning and uneasy and, after a powerful central climax, subsides and leads directly to the second section, Hazards (Allegro agitato). The music is fast and edgy with the use of odd meters, giving the music a frantic, awkward feel. Eventually, after two short cadenzas for the soloist, the atmosphere becomes calmer and the third section, Reflections (Adagio ma con moto), is reached. This passage is of a lyrical nature and the harmonic landscape more consonant. A warm climax brings a sense of relief and from here onwards the mood lightens until we reach the final section, Into the Light (Allegro con brio). The soloist plays a broad, Lydian mode melody surrounded by swirling figures in the accompaniment. This gives way to a central fugal section of a slightly capricious nature before the main theme reappears. The fugal material is reprised and the work ends with the primary material stated in a triumphant blaze of sound. Available for Solo Tuba and Brass Band and Tuba and Piano. Recorded by James Gourlay.

Newton, Rodney. *The Kraken*. Studio Music Company. Solo Tuba and Wind Band. 2002. 12:30. C_2–f'. *The Kraken* is a concerto in all but name. Commissioned by James Gourlay with funding from the Royal Northern College of Music, the work received its premiere performance by James Gourlay with the Royal Northern College of Music Junior Wind Orchestra under the direction of Roger Bobo on 15th September 2003. It is scored for a large ensemble (with contrabass clarinet and contra bassoon) together with parts for harp and organ (the latter optional). Subtitled "an aquerelle" (with tongue in cheek!), it was inspired by lines from Lord Tennyson's poem *The Kraken*. When listening to this piece, one may imagine a gigantic creature lying at the bottom of an ocean trench for countless millennia until, roused by the trumpets of the Last Judgment, it rises, only to perish on the surface. This one movement work uses the full range of the tuba and the full resources of the wind orchestra together with the organ to give an impression of vastness and immense power. The death of the titanic creature is graphically described in the solo writing toward the end of the work. Available for Solo Tuba and Orchestra.

Norbury, Kevin. *Badinage*. The Salvation Army USA Eastern Territory. Solo Tuba and Brass Band. 2001. 5:00. Norbury features a handful of motifs from Leslie Condon's *Celestial Morn* as the basis for this solo. It was specifically written for the New York Staff Band and tuba soloist Patrick Sheridan. A brisk but lyrical piece that concludes with technical challenges and fun rhythms. Recorded by Patrick Sheridan.

Novello, Ivor. *Shine through My Dreams*. Molenaar Music N.V. Solo Tuba (or Tenorhorn, Trombone, Baritone, Euphonium) and Band. 1935. 2:30. I–II. D♭–f. See: Sparks, L. Richmond; "An Annotated Bibliography of Tuba Solos with Band Accompaniment."

Payer. *Tuba Capriolen*. arr. Gottlöber. Simton Musikproduktion und Verlag. Solo Tuba and Band.

Petrie, H. W. *Asleep in the Deep*. arr. Harold L. Walters. Rubank, Inc. Solo Tuba and Band (Piano accompaniment available). 1954. 3:00. II. C (F_1)–d. A popular, old theme and variations solo. Recorded by William Bell, Barney Mallon.

Pettee, W. E. M. *Tuba Solo—Osceola*. J. G. Richards & Co. Solo Tuba and Band. 1889. Out of Print. 3:30. I–II. B♭–a♭. See: Sparks, L. Richmond; "An Annotated Bibliography of Tuba Solos with Band Accompaniment."

Plog, Anthony. *Three Miniatures*. Editions Bim. Tuba and Wind Ensemble (Originally for Tuba and Piano, also available from the publisher). 1992. CHF 35.00 (score), parts rental. 5:30. V. D–e'. Three movements: Allegro; Freely-Slowly; Allegro vivace. For Daniel Perantoni. Version for Solo Tuba and Wind Ensemble premiered by Dan Perantoni with the United States Air Force Band at the 1992 International Tuba-Euphonium Conference in Lexington, Kentucky. See also listing under Tuba and Keyboard. Recorded in tuba-piano edition by Roger Bobo and Daniel Perantoni.

Ployhar, James D. *Tubas on the Run.* CPP/Belwin Inc. Tuba and/or Baritone Section Soli with Band. 1992. $32.00. 2:00. II.

Precker, Jean. *Air et Divertissement.* Molenaar Music N.V. Solo Tuba and Band. 1971. $45.00. 5:40. III. D♭$_1$–a♭. Two movements. A tuneful work with no substantial technical difficulties.

Presser, William. *Capriccio for Tuba and Band.* Tenuto Publications. Tuba and band (Piano reduction available). 1969. $22.00. 5:26. III–IV. E$_1$–cc. One continuous movement. For Rex Conner. A quick showpiece without too many technical difficulties. Two extended cadenzas allow the soloist to also display some expressive quality. Band scoring does not cover the soloist. See: Bird, Gary, ed.; *Program Notes for the Solo Tuba.* Recorded by Michael Astwood.

Puccini, Giacomo. *"E Lucevan le Stella" from Tosca.* arr. William Brusick. Available from arranger. Solo Tuba and Band. 2003. 3:45. IV. G–f'. Commissioned by and dedicated to Timothy Northcut. A beautiful, dramatic melody providing the soloist with opportunity to emote and show musicality. Accompanying parts are not difficult.

Puccini, Giacomo. *"Nessun Dorma" from Turandot.* arr. William Brusick. Available from arranger. Solo Tuba and Band. 2003. 2:57. IV. c–f'. Commissioned by and dedicated to Timothy Northcut. Sung at the beginning of the third act by Calaf, the most heroic of all Puccini's tenor roles. The rescoring of the orchestral parts is masterfully done with sonorities that allows the tuba to sing and soar in the tenor soloist's role. Recorded by Timothy Northcut.

Putnam, C. S. *The Elephant's Dance (A Jungle Episode).* Fillmore Bros. Co. Solo Tuba and Band. 1940. Out of Print. 6:00. III. F$_1$–c'. A melodic work written in traditional form of band solo works in the early twentieth century. This time, an elephant dances a polka.

Raich. *Bassistengruss.* Adler Musikverlag. Solo Tuba and Band (Piano accompaniment available).

Ramsdell, E. C. *Polka di Basso—Tuba Solo.* E. C. Ramsdell. Solo Tuba and Band. 1896. Out of Print. 3:00. III. B♭$_1$–a♭. See: Sparks, L. Richmond; "An Annotated Bibliography of Tuba Solos with Band Accompaniment."

Raum, Elizabeth. *Pershing Concerto.* Tuba-Euphonium Press. Solo Euphonium or Tuba and Band (originally written as *Concerto for Euphonium and Piano*). 2000. 10:00. $60.00. V. F$_1$ (*ossia*)–b♭' (*ossia*). Commissioned by Richard Raum and John Griffiths. Dedicated to John Griffiths. Three movements: Allegro Moderato; Andante; Allegro non troppo. The outer movements reflect the courage of leaders such as General "Black Jack" Pershing and men like him. The middle movement is waltz-like and more lyrical, portraying the sadness of losing loved ones as Pershing did. Brass calls and percussion cadences echoing the music of the military permeate the entire work. A musically rewarding work with some extreme range considerations. Available for Solo Tuba and Orchestra, Tuba and Piano. Reviewed in the Fall 2001 issue of the *ITEA Journal* (Vol. 29, No. 1).

Raum, Elizabeth. *T for Tuba.* Virgo Music House. Solo Tuba and Young Student Band. 1991. 5:00. Commissioned by Regina Junior Lions Band. Premiered by John Griffiths at the 45th Annual MidWest International Band and Orchestra Clinic. Two versions of the solo part: difficult and easy. Available for Tuba and Piano.

Read, L. C. *"Thunderer" Polka.* W. H. Cundy Publishers. Solo Tuba and Band. 1881. Out of Print. 3:30. III–IV. A♭$_1$–e♭'. See: Sparks, L. Richmond; "An Annotated Bibliography of Tuba Solos with Band Accompaniment."

Rehfeld, Kurt. *Elefanten-Ballet.* Georg Bauer Musikverlag. Solo Tuba and Band. 1978. 3:15. II. G$_1$–g. A very easy, tuneful work for young tubist and band. See: Sparks, L. Richmond; "An Annotated Bibliography of Tuba Solos with Band Accompaniment."

Rehfeld, Kurt. *Launische Tuba.* Georg Bauer Musikverlag. Solo Tuba and Band. 1978. 3:30. III–IV. F$_1$–f'. A technically demanding work for the soloist reminiscent of the "Can-can" music hall dance. See: Sparks, L. Richmond; "An Annotated Bibliography of Tuba Solos with Band Accompaniment."

Reinhart, Wolfgang. *Bombardon—Polka fur Bass-Solo.* Georg Bauer Musikverlag. Solo Tuba and Band. 1985. 3:15. III. F–c'. See: Sparks, L. Richmond; "An Annotated Bibliography of Tuba Solos with Band Accompaniment."

Relton, William. *"The trouble with the Tuba is . . . "* Kirklees Music. Solo Tuba and Brass Band. 1991. $27.00. 4:30. III. B♭–b. Single movement in four sections: Maestoso, Allegro, Andante, Allegro. For Colin Aspinall. A humorous work with few technical demands.

Rimmer, William. *Variations on Jenny Jones.* arr. Thomas Wyss. Kirklees Music. Solo Tuba and Brass Band. 1989. $25.50. 5:00. IV. A$_1$–f'. Continuous work with introduction, cadenza, theme, and three variations. A nice arrangement of the traditional British song providing ample display of the solo tubist's technique.

Rimsky-Korsakov, Nikolai. *Flight of the Bumble Bee.* arr. Thomas Wyss. Kirklees Music. Solo Tuba and Brass Band. 1989. $21.00. 1:30. IV. A$_1$–e'. The traditional virtuoso display piece arranged nicely for solo tuba and brass band.

Ringleben, J. *The Storm King—Grand Fantasia.* Originally published by Carl Fischer, Inc., republished and available from Piston Reed Stick and Bow. Solo Tuba and Band (Piano accompaniment available). 1896. $15.00. 6:00. III–IV. $B\flat_1$–c' (f'). A challenging, traditional theme and variations solo.

Ripley, W. C. *The Close of Day.* George Southwell Publishers. Solo Tuba and Band. 1891. Out of Print. 3:30. II. $B\flat_1$–e♭. See: Sparks, L. Richmond; "An Annotated Bibliography of Tuba Solos with Band Accompaniment."

Ripley, W. C. *Dream of Peace.* J. G. Richards & Co. Solo Tuba and Band. 1888. Out of Print. 3:00. II–III. $B\flat_1$–g♭. See: Sparks, L. Richmond; "An Annotated Bibliography of Tuba Solos with Band Accompaniment."

Ripley, W. C. *Tuba Obligato—Majenta.* J. C. Richards & Co. Tuba Section Soli with Band. 1885. 3:30. II–III. $B\flat_1$–e♭. See: Sparks, L. Richmond; "An Annotated Bibliography of Tuba Solos with Band Accompaniment."

Robertson, Dave. *Tuba-riff-ic.* Laissez-Faire Music. Solo Tuba (or Tuba Section) and Band. 1981. Out of Print. 2:00. II. F_1–g. A cute, pop-oriented piece which is usable as a solo or featuring the entire tuba section.

Rollinson, T. H. *Bombastes Polka.* W. H. Cundy Publishers. Solo Tuba and Band. 1886. Out of Print. 3:30. III. $B\flat_1$–c'. This work would have been considered a true virtuoso tuba solo piece in the late nineteenth century with high tessitura and a fair amount of technique required. See: Sparks, L. Richmond; "An Annotated Bibliography of Tuba Solos with Band Accompaniment."

Rooy, J. de. *Watching the Wheat.* Molenaar Music N.V. Solo Tuba (or Baritone) and Band. 1961. 2:40. II. E♭–a. A nice arrangement of the Dutch folksong.

Rooy, Jan de. *Twelve Rovers, The (Les douze Brigands).* Molenaar Music N.V. Solo Tuba (or Euphonium) and Band. 1961. 2:00. I–II. C–c. See: Sparks, L. Richmond; "An Annotated Bibliography of Tuba Solos with Band Accompaniment."

Ross, Walter. *Tuba Concerto.* Boosey and Hawkes. Tuba and Band (Piano reduction available). 1973. $36.00. 11:30. IV. $F\sharp_1$–e♭'. Three movements: Overture; Berceuse; Toccata. For R. Winston Morris. A well-scored work for full symphonic band craftily written so that the soloist is not obscured. An interesting accompaniment easily playable by a good high school band. Very good use of solo tuba with percussion. See: Bird, Gary, ed.; *Program Notes for the Solo Tuba.* Recorded by Harvey Phillips.

Rossini, Gioacchino. *Largo al Factotum.* arr. Stephen Roberts. Obrasso Verlag AG. Solo Tuba and Brass Band. 1992. $72.50. 4:30. III. $B\flat_1$–e♭'. The famous operatic solo arranged well for tuba with brass band. Recorded by Shaun Crowther, James Gourlay.

Round, H. *The Men of Harlech—Air Varie.* arr. Red Fences. Molenaar Music N.V. Solo Tuba (or Trombone, Euphonium) and Band. 1966. 6:45. II–III. E♭–g. Theme and five interesting contrasted variations.

Rückauer, H. *Der fidele Bassist.* Musikverlag Rundel GmbH. Solo Tuba and Band (Piano accompaniment available).

Saglietti, Corrado Maria. *Concertissimo.* Editions Bim. Tuba and Wind Band. 1997. 17:00. IV. F_1–f'. Premiered at the 1997 ITEC. Three movements: Allegro; Adagio; Allegro con spirito. Well-set tonal work for F tuba, reminiscent of Richard Strauss. Available for Tuba and Piano.

Saint Saens, Camille. *Chumbo the Elephant from "Carnival of the Animals."* arr. D. W. Stauffer. Stauffer Press. Solo tuba and concert band. $10.00. 1:20. II. $A\flat_1$–e.

Sauter, Eddie. *Conjectures.* Mentor Music, Inc. Solo Tuba Band (Piano accompaniment with optional percussion available). 1968. Band accompaniment rental from the publisher. 9:00. IV–V. $F\sharp_1$–e'. Two connected movements. Written for and first performed by Harvey Phillips, the work contains a great deal of rubato and expression as one might infer from the title. Prevalent tempo changes, unstable tonality, dramatic scoring, and extensive use of percussion make this a difficult yet interesting work. Recorded by Harvey Phillips.

Schmidt, William. *Tuba Mirum—Variations on a Gregorian Chant.* Western International Music, Inc. Solo Tuba and Winds, Percussion, with Harp and Piano. 1984. $80.00. 18:22. IV. A_1–f'. One continuous movement. For Michael Lind. This interesting and significant work in the wind ensemble literature could constitute a focal point on a group's program. It contains imaginative variations and colorful orchestration sensitive to the soloist. See: Bird, Gary, ed.; *Program Notes for the Solo Tuba.*

Schmidt, William. *Tunes.* Western International Music, Inc. Solo Tuba, Winds, and Percussion. 1990. 12:22. V. F_1–b'. Three movements: A Little Off; A Little Under; A Little Out. Commissioned by the Sapporo International Music Festival '90 and dedicated to Tubists Universal Brotherhood Association. A demanding work for soloist and accompanying ensemble. In the first movement, which has a Latin feel, the tubist is required to use alternate fingerings for intonation shadings. A cup mute is specified for the second movement which is blues-oriented. The third movement contrasts "straight" and jazz musical styles. See: Bird, Gary, ed.; *Program Notes for the Solo Tuba.*

Schneebiegl, Rolf. *Der Kellermeister—Konzertpolka.* Bosworth & Co. Solo Tuba and Band. 1979. 2:40. III. F_1–b♭. A cute, novelty solo containing little difficult technical material except for some melodic leaps.

Schneiders, Hardy. *Tubanera.* Editions Marc Reift. Tuba and Wind Band. 2000. 2.30. II. A cute solo in the form of Habañera. Good for a young soloist in a popular concert. Recorded by Karel Malimánek.

Senaille, J. B. *In Lively Spirits.* See: Hopkinson, Michael E., in this section.

Shahin, Ray. *Mr. Bass.* Southern Music Company. Solo Tuba (or Baritone) and Band. 1962. $25.00. 2:30. II. B♭–e♭. A very easy work for both solo tuba and band.

Shire, David. *Marlows Theme.* arr. Staffan Lundén Velden. Ovation. Solo Tuba and Wind Band. 1988. $51.37. 3:00. III. F–g'. Available for Tuba and Brass Quintet.

Siebert, Edrich. *Bombastic Bombardon, The.* Molenaar Music N.V. Solo Tuba and Band. 1952. 4:15. II–III. A_1–f. A traditional concerto polka featuring the tuba.

Siebert, Edrich. *Dear to My Heart—Air Varie.* Studio Music Company. Solo Tuba and Brass Band (Piano accompaniment available). 1972. $21.00. 3:45. II–III. D ($A♭_1$)–b♭ (e♭'). A traditional waltz-like theme with three variations and brief cadenza before the closing coda.

Smith, Claude T. *Ballade and Presto Dance.* arr. Gary Lewis. In preparation by Wingert-Jones. Solo Tuba and Band (Piano accompaniment available). 1988. 7:30. IV. F–a'. Written for Steve Seward. See listing under Tuba and Keyboard. Recorded by Robert Daniel.

Sorbon, Kurt. *"Die Poltergeist . . . Polka."* Musikverlag Wilhelm Halter GmbH. Solo Tuba and Concert Band. 1990. 1:40. A–c'. A traditional German polka in basic arrangement for solo tuba.

Southwell, George. *Monte Cristo.* George Southwell Publisher. Solo Tuba and Band. 1895. Out of Print. 4:00. III–IV. D–f' (a♭). A late-nineteenth-century virtuoso work. See: Sparks, L. Richmond; "An Annotated Bibliography of Tuba Solos with Band Accompaniment."

Southwell, George. *My Tuba Solo.* Volkwein Bros., Inc. Solo Tuba and Band (Piano accompaniment available). 1954. Out of Print. 4:30. III. C–a♭ (c'). A typical concert polka for solo tuba. The work originally was published in 1887.

Southwell, George. *Natoma.* George Southwell Publications. Solo Tuba and Band. 1902. 2:15. II. C–f. A very easy concert polka. See: Sparks, L. Richmond; "An Annotated Bibliography of Tuba Solos with Band Accompaniment."

Southwell, George. *Quickstep (Fun for the Basses).* Southwell & Streeter Publishers. Tuba Section Soli and Band. 1881. Out of Print. 1:50. II–III. C–a♭. An easy novelty march with mostly diatonic writing for the tubas. See: Sparks, L. Richmond; "An Annotated Bibliography of Tuba Solos with Band Accompaniment."

Southwell, George. *Sounds from the Tuba.* George Southwell Publisher. Solo Tuba and Band. 1886. Out of Print. 3:45. III. $B♭_1$–a♭. See: Sparks, L. Richmond; "An Annotated Bibliography of Tuba Solos with Band Accompaniment."

Sparke, Philip. *Concertino for Tuba and Brass Band.* Studio Music. Solo Tuba and Brass Band. 1988. 13:00. IV–V. C_1–g'. Two large connected sections: Lento; Vivo. An extensive, technically difficult solo work for tuba. The opening Lento is highly melismatic—with the tuba playing many notes per beat, similar to the middle section of the Romanza from Vaughan Williams Concerto—and has two moderate solo cadenzas. The Vivo contains non-stop tonal pyrotechnics for the solo tuba and an extensive written and ad-lib cadenza. This work is a major virtuoso showpiece for tuba and brass band.

Steadman-Allen, Ray. *Dashing Away with the Smoothing Iron.* Rosehill Music Publishing Company. Solo Tuba and Brass Band. 1991. $27.50. 3:00. III–IV. A♭–e♭'. Continuous movement in three sections: Allegro giocoso; Andante; Allegro vivace. A good arrangement of the traditional British tune with some humorous moments.

Steckar, Marc. *Tubaobab: Concerto in Four Movements for Tuba and Big Wind Band.* Ed. Feeling Musique. 1994. 8:59. Recorded by Philippe Legris.

Stephens, Denzil. *Dancing Tuba, The.* Sarnia Music. Solo Tuba and Band. 1985. 3:30. III–IV. C–e♭'. A waltz featuring the solo tuba.

Stephens, Denzil S. *Albertie.* Wright & Round, Ltd. Solo Tuba and Brass Band. 1984. $23.00. 3:30. III. A_1–c' (d'). A novelty solo with no significant technical or musical demands.

Stephens, Denzil S. *Imp, The.* Wright & Round, Ltd. Solo Tuba and Brass Band. $23.00. 3:00. III. $B♭_1$ (G_1)–d'. A little rondo with cute tunes and nice contrasting sections.

Stewart, Joseph. *Tuba.* Kendor Music, Inc. Tuba and Band with optional SATB choral parts (Piano accompaniment available). 1977. $42.00. 3:00. III. $B♭_1$–b♭. Two connected sections: Presto; Jazz Waltz. Dedicated to Andy Peruzzini and the Maryvale High School Chorale. Some stylistic and technical challenges for the soloist. Band accompaniment is fairly easy.

Storm, Charles W. *Bouquet for Basses.* Volkwein Bros., Inc. Solo Tuba and Brass Band (Piano accompaniment available). 1954. Out of Print. 5:00. II. $B♭_1$–e♭. A traditional polka for tuba solo.

Strauss, Richard. *Concerto No. 1 for Horn and Symphonic Band.* Band transcription by John Boyd. Tuba solo part transcribed by John Anderson. Thompson Edition, Inc. Tuba and Band. 1987. Purchase price $120.00; also available from the publisher on rental. 18:00. IV. G_1–e♭'. Three connected movements: Allegro; Andante; Allegro. Band arrangement is dedicated "For Louis Stout." A good arrangement of the great romantic horn concerto which works very well for tuba. Recorded by Arnold Jacobs.

Sullivan, Arthur. *Lost Chord, The.* arr. A. C. van Leeuwen. Molenaar Music N.V. Solo Tuba (or Trombone) and Band. 1950. 3:30. I. C–c. A very easy melodic solo for tuba and band.

Sutton, E. *Cavalier, The.* Molenaar N.V. Solo Tuba (or Tenorhorn, Baritone) and Band. 4:15. II–III. G_1–a♭. An old-style theme and polka. See: Sparks, L. Richmond; "An Annotated Bibliography of Tuba Solos with Band Accompaniment."

Szkutko, John. *King Arthur Variations.* SZK Music. Solo Tuba and Concert Band. 1995. V. $B\flat_2$–b♭'. A simple melody followed by virtuosic variations. Band parts are not difficult.

Thingnæs, Frode. *Song for Michael—To Be or Not Tuba.* Frost Music A/S. Solo Tuba (or Baritone) and Concert Band. $60.00. 4:00. IV. A♭–g'. For Michael Lind. A pretty, lyrical work displaying the tuba's upper register.

Traditional. *Amazing Grace.* arr. Øystein Baadsvik. Ovation. Solo Tuba and Wind Band. 1995. 4:00 II. F–f'.

Tuthill, Burnett. *Fantasia for Tuba, Op. 57.* Lyceum Press. Solo Tuba (or Bass Trombone) and Band (Piano accompaniment available). 1968. 8:00. III–IV. G_1–g' (e'). For Rex Conner. Brief Andante introduction is followed by an Allegro. Relatively traditional tonal writing with some larger, irregular intervals for the soloist in and above the staff.

Vadala, Chris. *Lonely Road.* Whaling Music. Solo Tuba (or Euphonium) and Jazz Band (or Concert Band and Rhythm Section). 1978. $30.00. 5:00. III–IV. D–d'. A slow jazz ballad. Contains choice of written-out or improvised solos.

Vaughan, Rodger. *Elegy.* Available from the composer. Solo Tuba and Wind Ensemble (Piano accompaniment also available). 1986–87. 3:45. III–IV. A_1–c'. Single movement. For Roger Bobo. A slow, gentle, expressive work. Band accompaniment is very easy.

Vaughan Williams, Ralph. *Concerto for Bass Tuba.* arr. Robert Hare. Oxford University Press. Tuba and Band (Also Tuba and Orchestra, Tuba and Piano). 1976. Score and parts rental from the publisher. Arranged for Daniel Perantoni. This arrangement is as difficult and heavily scored as the original orchestral version and takes a great deal of preparation and care to ensure a successful performance. See listing under Tuba and Orchestra and Tuba and Keyboard. See: Bird, Gary, ed.; *Program Notes for the Solo Tuba.* Recorded by Jeffrey Arwood, Daniel Perantoni. Recorded accompaniment available: *Vivace: A Complete Practice System.* For further information, see listing under Recorded Accompaniments.

Vivaldi, Antonio. *Concerto in A Minor (First movement).* arr. Richard R. Trevarthen. Bernel Music LTD. Solo Tuba and Brass Band. 1993. $35.00. 3:45. III. A_1–d♯'. A good arrangement of this standard tuba solo (See: Tuba and Keyboard: Vivaldi/Ostrander). There are some fairly wide intervallic leaps and rapid scale passages, but mostly in the middle register.

Wagner, Richard. *Lied Aan de Avondster.* arr. F. Diepenbeek. Molenaar Music N.V. Solo Tuba (or Baritone) and Band. 1949. 2:45. III. B–e♭'. An arrangement of an aria from the third act of *Tannhauser.*

Walters, Harold L. *Concertante.* Rubank, Inc. Solo Tuba and Band (Piano accompaniment available). 1960. $19.50. 4:45. III–IV. $E\flat_1$–d'. Continuous work in three sections.

Walters, Harold L. *Forty Fathoms.* Rubank, Inc. Solo Tuba and Band (Piano accompaniment available). 1952. 3:00. III. $A\flat_1$–e♭. An easy work with a nautical flavor.

Walters, Harold L. *Scherzo Pomposo.* Rubank, Inc. Solo Tuba and Band (Piano accompaniment available). 1958. 4:00. II–III. $B\flat_1$–f (b♭ or e♭'). This melodic work contains trills, hemiola, and optional quintuplets and triplet scale passages which can be added to increase the difficulty of the piece. There are several descending chromatic sequences which will challenge the younger player.

Walters, Harold L. *Tarantelle.* Ludwig. Tuba and Band (Piano accompaniment available). 1946. $42.50. 3:30. II. B_1–f. Continuous work in two sections: Andante; Allegro. Opening Andante section is majestic and primarily diatonic. Allegro is a rollicking 6/8 in F minor.

Wantier, Firmin. *Air et Variations.* Editions Musicales Brogneaux. Solo Tuba (or Saxophone, Trombone, Baritone) and Band. 1957. Out of Print. 6:30. IV. $A\flat_1$–g'. A substantial and characteristically French work with a theme and three variations. See: Sparks, L. Richmond; "An Annotated Bibliography of Tuba Solos with Band Accompaniment."

Ward, Norman. *Happy Hippo, The.* Kendor Music, Inc. Solo Tuba and Band (Piano accompaniment available). 1967. Out of Print. 3:00. II. $B\flat_1$–f. A very easy work for the soloist; band parts are slightly more difficult.

Watz, Franz. *Concertino in drei Saetzen.* Musikverlag Rundel GmbH. Solo Tuba and Band (Piano accompaniment available).

Watz, Franz. *Fröiche Tubist, Der.* Ewoton Musikverlag. Solo Tuba and Band (Piano accompaniment available).

Weber, Fred. *Big Boy.* arr. Howard Kilbert. Belwin Mill Corporation. Solo Tuba and Band (Piano accompaniment available). 1953. Out of Print. 1:30. I. E♭–d♭. A very easy arrangement for solo tuba and band.

Werle, Floyd E. *Concertino for Three Brass and Band.* Bourne Co. Solo Trumpet, Trombone, Tuba and Band (Piano reduction available). 1970. $30.00. 6:30. III. B_1–c'. Three movements: Vintage Foxtrot; Lullaby; Greek Dance. A well-scored work with a "pop" feel showcasing three solo brass. The first movement is in a fast two, the second is a slow interplay between the three solo instruments, and the final "Greek Dance" is a driving movement in a 7/8 meter. Recorded by Fred Angerstein.

White, Winton. *Allegro Sardonicus.* Available from the composer. Solo Tuba and Band. 2004. 6:30. IV. F_1–f'. Premiered by Chuck Koontz, tubist, and the Biola Symphonic Winds on May 21, 2004. Through the use of syncopation, piercing timbres, dissonant sonorities, and sometimes wildly disjunct lines for the solo tuba, the qualities of comic sarcasm and barbed irony are created. The composer's intentions for this piece is to add to the solo tuba repertoire a unique style that is technically challenging yet playable by college-level performers.

Wiegand, George. *The Leviathan—Fantasia.* Harry Coleman Publisher. Solo Tuba and Band (Piano accompaniment available). 1894. Out of Print. 6:45. III–IV. $B\flat_1$–e♭'. A substantial and demanding work for the solo tubist. See: Sparks, L. Richmond; "An Annotated Bibliography of Tuba Solos with Band Accompaniment."

Wilder, Alec. *Concerto for Tuba and Concert Band.* Margun Music, Inc. Solo Tuba and Concert Band (Piano reduction available). 1965. Score and parts rental from the publisher. 12:00. IV. $F\sharp_1$–g'. Four movements: Lively; Andante; Jauntily; Allegro. For Harvey Phillips. A work containing lyrical and technical demands typical of most of Wilder's tuba music. Some wide, irregular intervals.

Wilhelm, Rolf. *Concertino for Tuba.* Tuba Center. Solo Tuba and Band (Piano reduction available). 1983. 11:45. IV–V. F_1–f'. Three movements: Moderato, deciso; Andante lirico; Allegro comodo. Written for Robert Tucci. A delightful work which excellently displays both the virtuosity and the musicianship of the soloist. See: Bird, Gary, ed.; *Program Notes for the Solo Tuba.* Recorded by Michael Bunn, Jens Bjørn-Larsen.

Williams, Ernest. *Concerto No. 2.* Charles Colin. Solo Tuba (or Trumpet) and Band (Piano accompaniment available). 1937. 17:00. III–IV. $E\flat_1$–b♭. Three movements: Allegro Moderato; Adagio; Allegro. See listing under Tuba and Keyboard.

Wilson, Curtis. *Rainbows.* Available from the composer. Solo Tuba and Wind Ensemble. 2003. IV. G_1–f'. Premiered by Markus Theinert. Written as a meditative, lyrical elegy in remembrance of Chris Baker, a tuba student at Texas Christian University who was killed in a plane crash. The piece contains a quotation from the well-known tune of *Somewhere over the Rainbow* and ends with the solo tuba playing a passacaglia theme along with the tuba section of the band.

Woods, J. H. *Carter's March.* Thompson & Odell Publishers. Solo Tuba and Band. 1887. Out of Print. 3:30. II. $B\flat_1$–e♭. Dedicated to T. M. Carter, Esquire. See: Sparks, L. Richmond; "An Annotated Bibliography of Tuba Solos with Band Accompaniment."

Woods, J. H. *Castle in Spain, A, Op. 48.* Thompson & Odell Publishers. Solo Tuba and Band. 1887. Out of Print. 4:20. II–III. F_1–e♭. See: Sparks, L. Richmond; "An Annotated Bibliography of Tuba Solos with Band Accompaniment."

Woods, J. H. *Helicon Schottische, Opus 46.* Thompson & Odell Publishers. Solo Tuba and Band. 1887. Out of Print. 2:30. III. $B\flat_1$–c'. See: Sparks, L. Richmond; "An Annotated Bibliography of Tuba Solos with Band Accompaniment."

Woodward, James. *Tuba Concerto.* Tuba-Euphonium Press. Solo Tuba and Band. 2000. IV. E_1–c". Four movements: Joyously, light; Freely-Quirky; Slowly, Freely; Brilliantly. Written for Alan Baer and premiered at the 2000 ITEC with Mr. Baer as the soloist. The work is characterized by lively outer movements that are driven by rhythmic motifs in the solo voice. While not a minimalist piece, some of its harmonic language is reminiscent of the music of John Adams. The inner movements are more complex and feature substantial cadenzas for the soloist. High tessitura required of the soloist. The concerto is written in a totally accessible harmonic language and is enjoyable for both the audience and the performer. Available for Tuba and Orchestra. Recorded by David Zerkel.

Wuorinen, Charles. *Chamber Concerto for Tuba with 12 Winds and 12 Drums.* C. F. Peters Corporation. Solo Tuba, 4 Flutes (Doubling Piccolo and Alto Flute), 2 Oboes (Doubling English Horn), 2 Bassoons (Doubling Contrabassoon), 4 Horns, Percussion (Single Player Requiring 12 Equidistant Drums). 1970. Available on rental from the publisher. 17:00. IV–V. C_1–f♯'. A very demanding contemporary work with difficult parts for all players. Recorded by David Brainard, Don Butterfield.

Yarrow, Peter, and Lipton, Leonard. *Puff (The Magic Dragon).* arr. Richard Maltby. Warner Bros. Solo Tuba (or Tuba Section) and Band (Piano accompaniment available). 1967. Out of Print. 3:00. II–III. $A\flat_1$–a'. A nice arrangement in variations of the sixties pop tune.

Youmans, Vincent. *The Carioca.* arr. Lon Norman. Manuscript. Solo Tuba and Band. 1972. Out of Print. 3:15. IV. $E\flat_1$–e♭'. Arranged for Harvey Phillips and the U.S. Army Band. A classic rumba which works as a great popular feature for the solo tuba. Recorded by Jeffrey Arwood, Harvey Phillips, Sam Pilafian.

Zaninelli, Luigi. *Peg Leg Pete.* Boosey & Hawkes. Solo Tuba (or Bass Clarinet) and Band (Piano accompaniment available). 1963. Out of Print. 2:30. II. $B\flat_1$ ($A\flat_1$)–f. A tuneful novelty solo with a cadenza and the added demand on the soloist to produce several half-valve glissandos.

Zinke, Gerhard. *Der Basskarle—Polka.* Wilhelm Halter GmbH. Solo Tuba and Band. 2:30. II–III.

C–a. See: Sparks, L. Richmond; "An Annotated Bibliography of Tuba Solos with Band Accompaniment."

Zinke, Gerhard. *Der Klettermaxe Polka.* Musikverlag Wilhelm Halter GmbH. Solo Tuba (or Tenorhorn, Baritone, Trombone, or Bassoon) and Concert Band. 3:00. III. G_1–d♭. A good novelty solo to play with the "town band."

Zonn, Paul Martin. *Exchanges.* Available from the composer. Solo Tuba and Symphonic Wind Ensemble. 1980. 8:00. IV–V. E_1–g'. For the Depaul University Wind Ensemble and Don DeRoche, Conductor. To the memory of Thomas Harris. A difficult, contemporary work for solo tuba and wind ensemble with gestural writing including wide, irregular intervallic leaps and difficult poly-rhythms. Interesting ensemble colors.

3. Music for Tuba and Orchestra

Timothy J. Northcut, Assistant Editor, *Guide to the Tuba Repertoire: The New Tuba Source Book*

Julia Piorkowski and Bobbie Zajkowski, Editorial Assistants

Skip Gray, Assistant Editor, *The Tuba Source Book*

Introductory Remarks (July 2005): Timothy J. Northcut

The primary goal of this chapter is to provide an updated list of compositions written for tuba and orchestra. Not having been involved with the research for the first edition of *The Tuba Source Book,* I would like to congratulate Skip Gray for the exceptional job he did. When my mentor, Winston Morris, contacted me about joining the team for this publication as an assistant editor, I immediately responded "yes," recognizing the importance of updating such information. I also knew that "no" was not an acceptable answer. Almost thirteen years have passed since the closing date for research for the first edition of *The Tuba Source Book* (July 1993), and the repertoire for tuba and orchestra has experienced significant growth. In the present survey of these materials, it is apparent that as the quantity of the repertoire has increased, so has the quality.

The corresponding chapter in the first edition of *The Tuba Source Book* included 106 entries for tuba and orchestra. For this publication, I have added 69 new entries and updated 16 entries from the first edition. Regrettably, I was compelled to withhold a number of compositions due to lack of information and as a result, there will be compositions that have been omitted. My responsibility as editor is to maintain the excellence in research that was established in *The Tuba Source Book,* and it is my hope that this was accomplished and you find this material to be extremely helpful.

This chapter is the culmination of the work of many volunteers and was truly a labor of love. It is with profound gratitude that I thank those who assisted:

• Julia Piorkowski and Bobbie Zajkowski. I express my extreme gratitude for the work of these wonderful friends who served as my editorial assistants. They each were totally committed to the completion of this project. I cannot thank you enough!

• Winston Morris, for his trust in my abilities to conduct research and for his words of encouragement and support in all of my musical endeavors.

• David Adams, Chair of the Performance Studies Division in the University of Cincinnati College-Conservatory of Music, for monetary support for the initial mailing to hundreds of publishers and composers.

• To the publishers and composers who responded to requests for information, catalogs, and review copies, especially David Miles (Tuba-Euphonium Press).

• To the International Consultants, especially Jørgen Voigt Arnsted, Øystein Baadsvik, Sergio Carolino, John Elliott, Alessandro Fossi, James Gourlay, John Griffiths, Chitate Kagawa, David LeClair, Gilles Lutmann, and Steve Rosse.

• Jennifer Northcut. I am immensely grateful to my wife for her patience and tolerance beyond reason.

• Nicholas and Claire Northcut. A special expression of gratitude goes to my children, who day to day patiently waited for dad to come out and play.

Introductory Remarks (July 1995): Skip Gray

It has not been many years since the time when tubists had very little choice in works they could perform as a solo with orchestral accompaniment. The venerable Ralph Vaughan Williams' *Concerto for Bass Tuba* was the usual selection, not necessarily because it was regarded as a great piece of music, but, more often than not, because it was the only piece by a "major composer" available to the instrument. In the first comprehensive guide to tuba repertoire, the *Encyclopedia of Literature for the Tuba* by William J. Bell and R. Winston Morris published in 1967, only six original works for solo tuba and orchestra are identified. By 1973 and the publication of Morris' *Tuba Music Guide,* twenty-six works are listed in this genre. Today, well over one hundred works exist featuring the solo tuba with strings spanning the wide palette from pops to experimental, and from works in traditional forms to those which are almost completely improvisatory.

For a composer, the creation of a major work for solo tuba and orchestra is a true labor of love. Some of the pieces have been commissioned with a fairly substantial fee or grant, but many of these compositions have been written by a composer for a tubist-friend, a musician whom the composer honestly respects, even admires. This is evidenced in Joachim Grunner's *Concerto for Tuba and Orchestra,* written for Dietrich Unkrodt as well as John Williams' *Tuba Concerto,* dedicated to Chester Schmitz. There are also compositions of significant duration, some as long and intricate as symphonies. These works show great care and devotion to the instrument as the composer must realize, down-deep, that the great investment of thought, time, and creative turmoil will probably not be rewarded in a manner similar to compositional output for more traditional musical media. Tuba concerti are simply not performed as regularly (or usually as critically regarded) as symphonies, tone poems, or even solo works for the more "popular" orchestral instruments. Yet composers are writing works of sizable duration, complexity, and intellect for tuba and orchestra, for example Derek Bourgeois' *Tuba Concerto, Opus 38* (duration 43 minutes), Eugene Anderson's *Tuba Concerto No. 1 in B Minor* (36 minutes), and Frank Proto's *Sinfonia Concertante for Solo Tuba, Percussion, Flutes, and Strings* (33 minutes), to name a few.

In addition to formal concerti for tuba and orchestra, there are now works putting the solo tubist in new solo roles with the orchestra. William Kraft's *Concerto for Tuba with 3 Chamber Groups and Orchestra* actually has the soloist moving to various locations onstage depending on the tubist's accompaniment in various sections of the work. A new work by Canadian composer Elizabeth Raum entitled *The Legend of Heimdall for Solo Tuba and Orchestra* is a sort of music drama with the solo tuba cast in the leading role. In the more popular vein, the solo tubist has works like Jerry Lackey's *Jazz Concerto for Tuba and Orchestra.*

The works briefly highlighted here are just the tip of the iceberg in portraying the diversity of fine literature available for solo tuba and orchestra. Today, tubists can make a true choice from a wide range of music featuring them with orchestra and can select from various roles in which they desire to be portrayed. This variety of literature should not only open doors for more tubists to be heard and appreciated but hopefully offer greater opportunities for tuba players to receive critical respect and acclaim.

Aagaard-Nilsen, Torstein. *Concerto for Tuba and Orchestra.* Music Information Centre Norway. 1997. 15:00.

Ahmas, Harri. *Concerto for Tuba, Strings and Percussion.* Finnish Music Information Center. 1995. V. B_2–g♭'. Reviewed in the Spring 2000 issue of the *TUBA Journal* (Vol. 27, No. 3).

Albam, Manny. *Concertino for Tuba and Chamber Orchestra.* Manuscript available from the composer. Solo Tuba, Strings, and Harp. Three movements. For Michael Lind.

Almila, Atso. *Concerto for Tuba and String Orchestra.* Finnish Music Information Center. Solo Tuba and String Orchestra. 1986. Rental from the publisher. 16:00. IV. F_1–d'. Three movements: Moderato; Tranquillo; Presto. To Michael Lind. Good, colorful string scoring with many opportunities for expressive interpretation by the soloist, whose part is fairly straightforward. There is an extensive cadenza in the first movement and mute is required in the second.

Anderson, Eugene D. *Tuba Concerto No. 1 in B-Minor.* Anderson's Arizona Originals. Solo Tuba and Symphony Orchestra (Piano reduction available). 1970. Score and parts $90.00 (also available on rental). Original version 35:50. Revised version 27:00. IV. C_1–g♯'. Three movements: Legato expressivo—Allegro; Largo; Allegro. To Arnold Jacobs. With its lush harmonies and melodic lines, this concerto could be considered neo-romantic. Although the main body of the solo tuba part is in or below the staff, the work's very long duration with little rest makes it physically demanding. Orchestral scoring is sometimes very heavy and attention needs to be directed to maintaining correct balance for the soloist. Reviewed in *TUBA Journal,* Winter 1991. See: Bird, Gary, ed.; *Program Notes for the Solo Tuba.* Recorded by Samuel Pilafian.

Andriessen, Jurriaan. *Concertino.* Donemus Publishing House. Solo Tuba and Orchestra (part indicates "solo sousaphone in e-flat"). 1967. $32.50. 12:00. IV. C–c". A work mostly in the very upper tessitura.

Arban, Jean Baptiste. *Carnival of Venice.* Ovation. arr. Anna Baadsvik. Solo Tuba and String Orchestra. 2002. 8:00. V. $A♭_1$–a♭'. $50.65. An extremely technically demanding variation piece based on an easy folk melody. Recorded by Øystein Baadsvik.

Arban, Jean Baptiste. *Variations on the "Carnival of Venice."* arr. Frank Berry. Carl Fischer, Inc. Solo Tuba and Orchestra. Rental. 8 minutes. V.

G_1–a. For Roger Bobo. This arrangement is in the key of B-flat, so it will lie well for the F tuba. Recorded by Roger Bobo.

Arban, Jean Baptiste. *Variations on the "Carnival of Venice."* arr. Jerry Lackey. Carl Fischer. Solo Tuba and Orchestra. Rental. 8:00. V. G_1–a. This arrangement is in the key of F, so it will lie well for the C tuba.

Arban, Jean Baptiste. *Variations on the "Carnival of Venice."* arr. Richard Domek. Available from Richard Domek. Solo Tuba and Orchestra (this arrangement also available for Tuba and Piano, Tuba and Woodwind Quintet). 1983. Rental. 8:00. V. C–d' (B♭)'. For Skip Gray. This arrangement is in the key of B-flat and is well suited to the F tuba. Contains interesting new material in the accompanying episodes between solo sections.

Arutiunian, Alexandre. *Concerto for Tuba and Orchestra.* Editions BIM. Solo Tuba and Orchestra. 1993 (1992). 15:20. IV–V. F_1–g'. Three movements: I. Allegro moderato; II. Andante sostenuto; III. Allegro ma non troppo. Commissioned by Yamaha Corporation and Editions BIM. Dedicated to Roger Bobo. Premiered and recorded by Harri Lidsle. Tonal work with contemporary colors; generally high tessitura. Available for Tuba and Piano, Tuba and Band. Reviewed in the Spring 1998 and Summer 1998 issues of the *TUBA Journal* (Vol. 25, No. 3 and No. 4). Recorded by Harri Lidsle.

Aubin, Francine. *Concerto pour Tuba.* Editions Auguste Zurfluh. Solo Tuba and Orchestra. 2003. 17:15. IV–V. F_1–a'. Three movements: Maestoso; Allegretto; Tempo di Marcia. Composed for Stéphane Labeyrie. Available for Tuba and Piano.

Bach, Jan. *Tuba Concerto.* Tuba-Euphonium Press. Tuba and Orchestra. 2003. 18:00. C_1–a'. Three movements: March; Lament; Variations. Commissioned by The Florida West Coast Symphony Orchestra, Leif Bjaland, Artistic Director. Dedicated to "His Lowness Jay Hunsberger." The March is fast and virtuosic and demands agile playing in all ranges of the tuba, especially the low range. Orchestration features active percussion writing (including "marching machine") and quotes of "Turkey in the Straw." The Lament begins with the most "serious" writing of the work: sinewy, lyrical lines in the tuba against lush orchestration. The movement suddenly gives way to a rock/funk/samba section (based on earlier material). There is a short return to the first material from this movement before a segue into the final movement, Variations. The theme is an old folk song, "Sweet and Low," first played by the oboe and violins. The tuba follows with five variations plus a cadenza. The piece ends with a musical "tribute" to a performance by Louis Armstrong that Bach witnessed as a young man. Band and keyboard versions are in preparation.

Baker, David N. *Concerto.* MMB Music, Inc. Solo Tuba and Orchestra. 2004. 17:07. E_1–g'. Three movements: B's; Berceuse; Blues. The three movements reflect the composer's fondness for alliteration, and each is intended to be descriptive as well as euphonious. Movement I plays homage to three of his favorite composers: Brahms, Bartok, and Berg. This is done through the use of quotes, gestures, and harmonies. Movement II is very much a contemporary cradle song or lullaby. The principal melodies consist of sweeping romantic lines, with the strings and winds providing lush cushions of sound and melodic reinforcement. Movement III utilizes the blues form, gestures, and scales. Commissioned by and written for Daniel Perantoni. Recorded by Daniel Perantoni.

Bakke, Ruth. *Tubazzo: Concerto for Tuba and Orchestra.* Music Information Centre Norway. Solo Tuba and Orchestra. 1998. 20:00.

Bales, Kenton. *The Rocks.* Available from the composer. Solo Tuba and Orchestra. 1997. 17:00. V. A♭$_1$–a'. Four movements: Big Black Rocks; Slick Rocks; Smooth Rocks; Rough Red Rocks. Composed for and premiered by Craig Fuller and the Omaha Symphony Orchestra.

Barnes, James. *Concerto for Tuba.* Southern Music Company. Rental only. Solo Tuba and Orchestra. 1997. 19:30. V. C_1–g'. Three movements: Allegretto giocoso; Lullaby; Rondo. Composed for and premiered by Scott Watson. Very demanding work. It contains virtually every technical "trick in the book": multiple tonguing, large range shifts, and quick facility with slurs and fingers. Each movement could stand alone, though the second and third movements are performed attacca. The second movement is written in ballad style. Written with the CC tuba in mind. Available for Tuba and Piano, Tuba and Band. Reviewed in the Winter 1998 issue of the *TUBA Journal* (Vol. 15, No. 2).

Bennett, Malcolm. *Tuba Concerto.* Available from the composer. Solo Tuba and Orchestra. 1980. 13:00. III–IV. B♭$_2$–e'. Three movements: Allegro; Slowly and Simply; Brisk. Dedicated to John Elliott. Available for Tuba and Piano. Reviewed in the Spring 1998 issue of the *TUBA Journal* (Vol. 25, No. 3).

Bentzon, Niels Viggo. *Capriccio, Opus 396.* Edition Wilhelm Hansen. Solo Tuba, Trumpet, Percussion, Piano, Strings. 1977. Rental from the publisher. 7:00.

Bentzon, Niels Viggo. *Concerto for Tuba, Opus 373.* Edition Wilhelm Hansen. Solo Tuba and Orchestra. 1975. Rental from the publisher. 20:00.

Bewley, Norlan. *Santa Wants a Tuba for Christmas.* Bewley Music. Solo Tuba and Orchestra. 1992. 4:00. IV. B♭–f'. Written for Harvey Phillips. An exceptionally cute tune, especially when used with the vocal solo. A good swing feel is necessary for all players. Fun to play and delightful for audiences. Originally for Solo Tuba and Tuba Ensemble. Available for Solo Tuba and Band. Recorded by Harvey Phillips.

Birtwistle, Harrison. *Cry of Anubis.* Tuba and Orchestra. Boosey & Hawkes, Inc. 1995.

Blank, Alan. *Divertimento for Tuba and String Orchestra.* American Composers Alliance. 1979. 28:00.

Blanquer, Amando. *L'os hispànic.* Sociedad General de Autores de España. Solo Tuba with Orchestra (Piano reduction available). 1976. 6:00. Four movements: De gaubança; La Passió; L'espera; La tombearella. Original contrabass version dedicated to Jaime Antonio Robles. A work originally for contrabass and piano arranged by the composer for tuba, later tuba and orchestra.

Borg, Kim. *Finnish Rhapsody, Opus 32B.* Finnish Music Information Centre. Solo Tuba, Flute, Oboe, Clarinet, Bassoon, Horn, Trumpet, and Strings (Piano accompaniment available). 1985. 6:30. III–IV. A_1–d'. Three movements: On the Road; Summer Night; Wedding. A light, tuneful work nicely scored so that the solo tubist will be easily heard. Reviewed in the Summer 1999 issue of the *TUBA Journal* (Vol. 26, No. 4).

Bottje, Will Gay. *Concerto for Tuba and Orchestra.* American Composers Alliance. Solo Tuba and Orchestra (Piano accompaniment available). 1973. 16:00. III–IV. E_1–c'. Three movements: Very Quietly; Dance Variations; Dramatic. A work with few difficult range or intervallic demands. The second movement contains continually shifting polymeters.

Bourgeois, Derek. *Tuba Concerto, Opus 38.* R. Smith & Company. Solo Tuba and Orchestra (Piano reduction available). 1972. Rental from the publisher. 43:00. IV–V. F_1($G\sharp_2$ in cadenza)–f'. Four movements: Allegro moderato; Rondo (Grave); Scherzo (Allegro Scherzando); Finale (Maestoso—Allegro vivace). For John Fletcher. A major, extended work blending jazz and popular elements into a classical setting. Rhythmic writing in some places quite difficult. Scored for large orchestra. Recorded by John Fletcher.

Boutry, Roger. *Tubaroque.* Alphonse Leduc. Solo Tuba with Orchestra (Piano accompaniment available). 1955. Rental from the publisher. 4:30. IV. A_1–g' (a♭'). For Paul Bernard. See listing under Tuba and Keyboard. Also see: Thompson/Lemke; *French Music for Low Brass Instruments.*

Bozza, Eugene. *Concertino for Tuba and Orchestra.* Alphonse Leduc. Solo Tuba and Orchestra (Piano reduction also available). 1967. Rental from the publisher. 13:00. V. $F\sharp_1$–a♭'. Three movements: Allegro vivo; Andante ma non troppo; Allegro vivo. A true technical and musical showpiece with important cadenzas in each movement. Although the work was originally intended for the small French tuba, it is regularly performed on both the bass and sometimes contrabass tubas. The work is full of interesting, tuneful melodies, rapid chromatic passages, and wide leaps. Orchestral scoring is light and presents no balance problems for the soloist. See: Thompson/Lemke; *French Music for Low Brass Instruments.* Tuba and Piano version recorded by Steven Seward.

Brehm, Alvin. *Concerto for Tuba.* G. Schirmer. Solo Tuba and Orchestra. 1982. Rental from the publisher. 22:00.

Broadstock, Brenton. *Tuba Concerto.* G. Schirmer (Australia). Tuba and Orchestra. 1985. Score and parts rental from the publisher. 17:00. V. $F\sharp_1$–b' (also a notation to "very high note"). Two movements: Pensoso sempre sostenuto; Drammatico. A lyrical work in a modern style with tone clusters, string harmonics, mutings, stopped effects, and quarter tone trills. A major work of great difficulty both to the soloist and accompanying ensemble. There are four extensive solo cadenzas which also contain support/interaction from the orchestra. This work is actually Broadstock's second major concerto for the tuba. The first is much more conservative in musical nature and difficulty and, at this time, not available for performance.

Broughton, Bruce. *Concerto for Tuba Solo and Orchestra.* Edwin F. Kalmus & Co. Solo Tuba and Orchestra. Piano accompaniment available as *Sonata for Tuba and Piano.* 7:30. IV. C_1–e'. Three movements: Allegro moderato; Aria; Allegro Leggero. For Tommy Johnson. The composer's arrangement of his *Sonata for Tuba and Piano* works very well and the coloristic scoring includes harp. Available for Tuba and Wind Ensemble. See: Bird, Gary, ed.; *Program Notes for the Solo Tuba.*

Brown, Jonathan Bruce. *Lyric Variations for Tuba and String Orchestra.* Seesaw Music Corporation. Tuba and Strings. 1975. $13.50 (score). 5:15. III–IV. $A\flat_1$–e♭'. A work of mainly diatonic, melodic nature for the soloist with a theme and seven variations.

Bull, Edvard Hagerup. *Giocoso Bucolico: La Muse Legère: Concertino for Tuba and Chamber Orchestra.* Norwegian Music Information Center. Solo Tuba, Flute, Oboe, Horn, Piano, Strings. 1992. 12:00. IV–V. $C\sharp_1$–c''. Three movements: Allegretto; Adagio; Allegro Energico. In memoriam Darius Milhaud. The score specifies "Tuba (à 6 Pistons en Ut)" signifying the "French Tuba." The solo part lies in an extremely high tessitura (35 c''s, and many instances of b' and b♭') throughout, which is truly the primary difficulty presented in this overall nice, conservative, French-influenced work.

Carrapatoso, Eurico. *Concertino for Tuba.* Editions BIM. Tuba Solo and Chamber Orchestra with Percussion. 2005. 12:00. Commissioned by and dedicated to Sérgio Carolino. Premiered with the Lisbon Sinfonietta Chamber Orchestra.

A very nice piece based on traditional Portuguese music.

Carroll, Gregory. *Studies in American Folk Idiom.* Bernel Music LTD. Solo Tuba and Orchestra. Available for Solo Tuba and Band, Tuba and Piano.

Cioffari, Richard J. *Rhapsody for Tuba and Orchestra.* Trombone Association Publishing. Solo Tuba and Orchestra (Piano reduction available). 1975. $75.00. 7:30. III–IV. G_1–b. For Ivan Hammond. The soloist plays continuously with few rests. The part lies mostly in the staff with the main difficulty, other than endurance, being a few wide intervallic leaps.

Colding-Jorgensen, Henrik. *Ballade.* Samfundet. Solo Tuba and Chamber Orchestra. 1979. 15:00. V. E♭–g'. Two movements with several sections that contain a mixture of traditional writing and a non-metered (with pitches given) improvisatory style of writing. A difficult and complex work for both soloist and orchestra. Adequate rehearsal time is needed. Dedicated to Jørgen Arnsted.

Constantinides, Dinos. *Concertino for Euphonium or Tuba and Wind Orchestra: Mountains of Epirus.* Available from the composer. 8:30. IV. F♯$_1$–e'. This work is modal and employs characteristic Greek syncopated rhythms and polychordal sonorities. A mixture of linear melodies and rapid rhythmic interjections. Available for Tuba and Wind Orchestra, Tuba and Piano.

Dahlgren, David. *Folkvisor av Vikingarna.* Blis Music Publications. Tuba and String Orchestra. 12:00. 2003. This piece is a setting of three Swedish folk tunes: *Flowers of Joy, Swerege* (the Swedish national anthem), and *Who Can Sail?* Written for and premiered by John Griffiths at the Prairie New Music Festival. Available for Tuba and Piano. Recorded by John Griffiths (tuba and piano version).

Daniel-Lesur. *Mélodrame.* Gérard Billaudot. Tuba and Orchestra. Available for Tuba and Piano.

Dennison, Sam. *Lyric Piece and Rondo for Tuba and Strings.* Kalmus. Tuba and Strings. 1982. $32.00. Lyric Piece 5:00. Rondo 3:20. IV. F_1–g'. Two movements. A tuneful work which presents no major difficulties and goes together very easily with the accompanying string ensemble.

Domazlicky, Frantisek. *Concerto, Opus 53.* Artia Foreign Trade Corporation of Czechoslovakia. Solo Tuba and String Orchestra. 1983. IV.

Dupriez, Christian. *Piccolo Capriccio.* Available from the composer. Tuba and Orchestra (Piano accompaniment also available). 2:30. IV. A_1–g'. Dedicated to Mr. Edward R. Goldstein. A melodic little work in four sections.

Easton, Ian. *Airloom.* Solo Tuba and Chamber Orchestra. Available from the composer. Premiered by Steve Rosse at TubaMania Conference 1995. Available for Tuba and CD, Tuba and Piano.

Ecclès, Henry. *Sonata.* Gérard Billaudot. Solo Bass Tuba and Orchestra. Available for Bass Tuba and Piano.

Eerola, Lasse. *Music for Tuba and Orchestra.* Finnish Music Information Center. Solo Tuba, 2 Flutes, 2 Clarinets, Bassoon, 2 Horns in F, Piano, 2 Percussion, Strings (Piano reduction available). 1991. 11:00. IV–V. F_1–a♭'. Two movements: Adagio; Scherzo. Extensive solo cadenzas precede each movement (and actually link the two together) and foreshadow material to come. A difficult work for both soloist and orchestra.

Ellerby, Martin. *Tuba Concerto.* Maecenas Music. Solo Tuba and Orchestra. 1988. 13:00. G_1–g' (*ossia*). Continuous work in two sections: Andante ma non troppo; Allegro con brio. Dedicated to Stephen Sykes. Recorded by Pat Sheridan. Available for Tuba and Brass Band, Tuba and Concert Band, Tuba and Piano. Reviewed in the Winter 1995 issue of the *TUBA Journal* (Vol. 22, No. 2).

Ewazen, Eric. *Concerto for Tuba or Bass Trombone.* Southern Music Company. Solo Tuba and Orchestra. 1998. 19:30. V. E_1–a♭'. Three movements: Andante con moto; Andante Expressivo; Allegro Ritmico. This piece began as a *Sonata for Tuba or Bass Trombone and Piano.* The tuba version is written for and dedicated to Karl Kramer. Premiered by Karl Kramer in 1996. The outer movements are rhythmically energetic. The second movement requires musical maturity. Angular melodies, metric shifts, and multiple tonguing are required. Available for Solo Tuba and Band, Tuba and Piano. Reviewed in the Summer 2000 issue of the *TUBA Journal* (Vol. 27, No. 4).

Faillenot, Maurice. *Tuba Concerto.* Editions Robert Martin. Solo Tuba and Orchestra. 1999. 12:30. IV–V. E♭$_1$–g♯'. Three movements: Allegro; Lento; Final. Written for Stephane Labeyrie.

Fleming, Robert. *Concerto for Tuba.* Canadian Music Centre. Solo Tuba and Orchestra (2 flutes, Oboe, 2 Clarinets, Bassoon, 2 Horns, Timpani, Strings) (Piano reduction available). 1966. Orchestral part rental. 13:00. III–IV. E♭$_1$–f♯'. Three movements: Allegro con Moto; Andantino e Grazioso; Allegro Vivace. Dedicated to Robert Ryker. A good, conservatively written work.

Frackenpohl, Arthur. *Concertino for Tuba and String Orchestra.* Robert King Music. Tuba and Strings (Piano reduction available). 1962. $17.25. 8:45. III. G_1–c'. Three movements: Moderato; Lento; Allegro. Written for Abe Torchinsky. A tuneful, approachable work easily put together. Recorded by Benjamin Irmer.

Gagneux, Renaud. *Concerto.* Editions Durand et Cie. Solo Tuba and Orchestra. 1984. Rental from the publisher.

Gagneux, Renaud. *La Chasse des carillons crie dans les gorges pour tuba, cor, et orchestra.* Editions Durand et Cie. Tuba, Horn, and Orchestra.

1991. Rental from the publisher. Premiered by Hervé Brisse.

George, Thom Ritter. *Concertino for Tuba and String Orchestra.* Available from the composer. Solo Tuba and Strings (Also versions for Solo Tuba and Wind Ensemble, Solo Tuba and Piano). 1984. Three movements: Allegro ma non troppo; Cantabile e simplice; Vivace. See: Bird, Gary, ed.; *Program Notes for the Solo Tuba.*

Godel, Didier. *Concerto for Tuba and Orchestra.* Editions Marc Reift, Switzerland. Tuba and Orchestra. 1992. 14:00. III–IV. D_1–f'. Three movements: I. Allegro non troppo; II. Modéré; III. Vivace. A well-written composition in neoclassic style. Good recital material. Available for Tuba and Piano. Reviewed in the Fall 1996 issue of the *TUBA Journal* (Vol. 24, No. 1).

Grant, James. *Three Furies for Tuba and Orchestra.* Grantwood Music Press. 1995. 11:00. C_1–g'. Rental from the publisher. Three movements: Decidedly Jocular; Very Clean—Gently Inebriated; Relentless. Reviewed in the Fall 1995 issue of the *TUBA Journal* (Vol. 23, No. 1).

Gregson, Edward. *Concerto for Tuba.* Novello and Co., LTD. Solo Tuba and Orchestra (Solo Tuba and Concert Band, Solo Tuba and Brass Band, and Piano reduction available). 1976. Rental from the publisher. See listing under Tuba and Band. See: Bird, Gary, ed.; *Program Notes for the Solo Tuba.*

Grieg, Edvard. *Anitra's Dance.* arr. Øystein Baadsvik. Ovation. Solo Tuba and String Orchestra. 2002. 4:00. IV. E–b'. $57.89. Recorded by Øystein Baadsvik. Available for Tuba and Piano.

Grieg, Edvard. *Norwegian Dance No. 1.* arr. Øystein Baadsvik. Ovation. Solo Tuba and String Orchestra. 2002. 5:00. V. D–e'. $76.00.Grieg's starting point was Ludwig M. Lindeman's important collection of folk melodies—and for the *Norwegian Dance No. 1* he chose melody No. 302, although he treated the original with considerable freedom. Even though he composed the dances for piano four hands, the music seems to be crying out for orchestral sonority. Grieg himself tried to orchestrate the dances, but ultimately abandoned the attempt. Many others have since tried their luck, with varying degrees of success. This is Øystein Baadsvik's transformation of the dance for tuba and strings. Recorded by Øystein Baadsvik. Available for Tuba and Piano.

Grunner, Joachim. *Double Concerto for Contrabass Clarinet and Tuba.* Available from the composer. Solo Contrabass Clarinet, Solo Tuba, and Orchestra. 1991. 22:00. Four movements: Parallel; Trionfante; Etude; Passacaglia.

Grunner, Joachim. *Konzert fur Tuba und Orchester.* Verlag Neue Musik Berlin. Solo Tuba and Orchestra. 1977. Score $29.95. Parts rental from the publisher. 22:00. V. E_1–a'. Three movements: Recitative; Aria; Scenes. For Dietrich Unkrodt. A dramatic, energetic work requiring a great deal of control of the instrument from the soloist, who, in addition to playing notated pitches, must sing and play during three poignant sections of the "Aria," ad lib, and make some very quick mute changes. Recorded by Dietrich Unkrodt.

Grunner, Joachim. *Triple Concerto for Trumpet, Trombone, Tuba and Large Orchestra.* Verlag Neue Musik Berlin. Solo Trumpet, Solo Trombone, Solo Tuba, and Orchestra. 1983–84. Rental from the publisher. 21:00. Four movements.

Hahn, Gunnar. *Per Svinagerde: Ballad.* Swedish Music Information Center. Solo Tuba and String Orchestra. 1982.

Hartley, Walter S. *Fantasia for Tuba and Chamber Orchestra.* Wingert-Jones Music, Inc. Solo Tuba, 2 Flutes, Oboe, Bassoon, 2 Clarinets, 2 Trumpets, 2 Horns, 2 Trombones, and Strings (Piano reduction available). 1991. $35.00. 8:30. IV–V. $E\flat_1$–a'. Continuous work in four sections: Andante; Allegro molto; Adagio; Presto. Commissioned by Scott Watson with a General Research Grant from the University of Kansas. A solid musical work, conservative in compositional style yet approachable by a wide body of listeners.

Harville, Grant. *Concerto for Tuba and Orchestra.* Tuba-Euphonium Press. 2003. 12:00. IV–V. G_1–g'. Three movements: Lento—Allegro; Adagio non troppo; Lento—Vivace. A technically challenging work. Available for Tuba and Piano.

Heiden, Bernard. *Concerto for Tuba and Orchestra.* Southern Music Publishing Company (dist. by Theodore Presser). Piano reduction available. 1976. Rental from the publisher. 17:00. IV. D_1–f♯'. Three movements: Allegro risoluto; Andante; Vivace. Composed under a grant from the National Endowment for the Arts. For Harvey Phillips. A waltz-like first movement quickly takes the tubist through nearly the entire range required in the composition in the opening, dancing solo phrase. The Andante has the tuba playing lyrical variations mostly over a fifteen-note ground. The final Vivace combines a diatonic, march-like melody with a chromatically varied sixteenth note line played in varied forms later by the soloist. A traditionally written work with few excessive demands on the soloist. See: Bird, Gary, ed.; *Program Notes for the Solo Tuba.*

Holmboe, Vagn. *Concerto for Tuba, Opus 127.* G. Schirmer, Inc. Solo Tuba and Orchestra. 17:00. V. Recorded by Jens Bjørn-Larsen.

Holmboe, Vagn. *Intermezzo Concertante.* G. Schirmer, Inc. Solo Tuba and Orchestra. 8:00. Recorded by Jens Bjørn-Larsen.

Ionel, Dumitru. *Concerto No. 1.* Editions BIM. Tuba and Orchestra (Score and parts in preparation). 1996 (1958). 20:00. IV–V. C_1–c''. Three movements: Allegro moderato; Andante dolce; Allegro vivace. Tonal work with very classical harmonies, based on scales and arpeggios. The generally high tessitura is the only technical challenge. Available for Tuba and Piano.

Ionel, Dumitru. *Konzertstuck*. Editions BIM. Tuba and String Orchestra. 1960. 11:00. IV. In preparation.

Jager, Robert. *Concerto for Bass Tuba and Symphony Orchestra*. Belwin-Mills Music Corporation. Solo Tuba and Orchestra (Also Tuba and Band, Tuba and Piano). 1981. Rental from the publisher. 13:00. See listing under Tuba and Band. See: Bird, Gary, ed.; *Program Notes for the Solo Tuba*.

Jevtic, Ivan. *Concerto for Tuba and Symphony Orchestra*. Editions BIM. Solo Tuba and Orchestra (Piano reduction available). 1992. Rental from the publisher. 22:00. IV–V. F_1–a♭'. Four movements: Maestoso; Scherzo diabolico; Adagio; Allegro giusto. A powerful, major work for solo tuba and orchestra. Melodically oriented writing with no avant-garde techniques required. Reviewed in the Summer 1997 issue of the *TUBA Journal* (Vol. 24, No. 4).

Kalke, Ernst-Thilo. *Concertino in F*. Musikverlag Bruno Uetz. Tuba and Orchestra. 1997. 11:25. III–IV. C_1–g'. Straightforward piece of music that is not technically demanding for soloist or orchestra. Available for Tuba and Piano.

Kalke, Ernst-Thilo. *Mevagissey Tales*. Musikverlag Bruno Uetz. Solo Tuba and String Orchestra. 1999. 16:00. V. C_1–d''. Three movements: Cornish Dawn; King's Arms; The Smuggler's Wife. First movement originally for horn quartet with tuba. Expanded to three movements for wind band by suggestion of Skip Gray. Descriptive of an English village along the south coast of Cornwall. Available for Tuba in Mixed Ensemble, Tuba and Band, Tuba and Piano.

Karkoff, Maurice. *Concertino for Tuba and String Orchestra*. Swedish Music Information Center. Solo Tuba and Strings. 1991. 12:00. Three movements: Moderato; Adagio; Finale.

Karlsen, Kjell Mørk. *Concerto Furvus, Op. 97*. Music Information Centre Norway. Tuba and Orchestra. 1990. 17:00.

Kayser, Leif. *Concerto for Tuba and String Orchestra*. Leif Kayser. Solo Tuba and String Orchestra. 1979.

Kellaway, Roger. *Songs of Ascent (Concerto)*. Editions BIM. Tuba and Orchestra (Piano reduction in preparation). 1988/89. Rental from the publisher. V. Extremely high tessitura for the soloist throughout. See: Bird, Gary, ed.; *Program Notes for the Solo Tuba*. Reviewed in the Summer 1997 issue of the *TUBA Journal* (Vol. 24, No. 4).

Kenny, Michael. *Concerto for Tuba and Orchestra*. Kelly Sebastian Music Publishers. 1981. For Peter Whish-Wilson. Three movements: Movement 1; Serenade; Gigue. Available for Tuba and Piano. Reviewed in the Summer 1992 issue of the *ITEA Journal* (Vol. 19, No. 4).

Kitts-Turner, John S. *Concertino*. Tuba-Euphonium Press. Solo Tuba and Orchestra. 1997. 8:00. III–IV. F_1–f♭'. A good one-movement composition in a medium tessitura. Available for Tuba and Piano.

Kleinsinger, George. *Further Adventures of Tubby the Tuba, The*. Music Theatre International. Solo Tuba and Orchestra. Rental from the publisher. Of the "Tubby" pieces, contains the most involved playing for the tubist, including much lyrical playing and extensive technical material toward the end of the work. Recorded by Tommy Johnson.

Kleinsinger, George. *Tubby Joins the Circus*. Music Theatre International. Solo Tuba and Orchestra. Rental from the publisher. Less playing than the other "Tubby" works for the tubist. Recorded by Tommy Johnson.

Kleinsinger, George. *Tubby Meets the Jazz Band*. Music Theatre International. Solo Tuba, Clarinet, Trumpet, Trombone, Drums, Piano, and Orchestra. Rental from the publisher. Recorded by Tommy Johnson.

Kleinsinger, George. *Tubby the Tuba*. Music Theatre International. Solo Tuba and Orchestra (Tuba and Band arrangement available). 1945. Rental from the publisher. 12:00. III. E♭$_1$–e♭'. Narration by Paul Tripp. The classic story of the tuba wanting to play a melody. Beautiful tunes and a nice story. Many recordings available.

Koch, Erland von. *Concerto for Tuba*. AB Carl Gehrmans Musikforlag. Tuba and Strings (Piano reduction available). 1978. Score $19.50, Parts rental from the publisher. 14:00. IV–V. E_1 (F♯$_1$)–g' (a♭'). Three movements: Allegro moderato; Siciliano; Presto. Dedicated to Michael Lind. A conservative melodic work somewhat romantic in character.

Koetsier, Jan. *Concertino for Tuba and String Orchestra, Opus 77*. Editions Bim. Tuba and String Orchestra (Piano reduction available). 1978, revised 1982. Parts rental from the publisher. 15:00. V. F_1–g♭'. Three movements: Allegro con brio; Romanza e Scherzino; Rondo Bavarese. Dedicated to Manfred Hoppert. A tonal, melodic work with virtuosic and humorous moments. Tessitura and agility required would suggest appropriateness of an F or E-flat tuba in the performance of this work. Recorded by Manfred Hoppert, Velvet Brown, and Thomas Walsh.

Köper, Karl-Heinz. *Tuba-Tabu*. Musikverlag K. H. Köper. Tuba and Orchestra (Tuba and piano version also published). 10:00. IV. F_1–f'. One continuous movement with four large sections. A pleasant, tuneful work with few outstanding technical demands. Recorded by Michael Lind.

Koppel, Anders. *Concerto for Tuba and Orchestra*. Edition Wilhelm Hansen. 2003. 20:00. IV–V.

C_1–a♭'. Three movements: Moderato; Andante Misterioso; Lento-Allegro Assai. Commissioned by Mattias Johansson and supported by The Danish State Art Foundation. For Ulla. Premiered by Mattias Johansson. This three-movement composition is challenging for the soloist. Very rhythmically complex throughout with technical difficulty. Frequent metric shifts and tempo changes. Angular lines. Accompanying parts are not difficult and do not cause balance problems for the soloist.

Kosteck, Gregory. *The Enchanted Island: Symphonic Poem for Tuba and Orchestra.* Manuscript previously available from the composer. Solo Tuba and Symphony Orchestra (Piano reduction available). 1981. Out of Print. 11:00. IV. C_1–e'. Continuous work in four large sections plus a coda (Tranquillo; Scherzando; Arioso; Finale; Adagio). Commissioned by, composed for, and dedicated to Sande and Paula MacMorran. An extensive, coloristic, modern tone poem for orchestra with a great deal of soloistic tuba writing. Although the piece is not a "virtuoso" solo work, the solo tubist serves as a principal melodic component. Because of the tessitura of the part and weight of orchestration, a contrabass tuba would probably work best in performance of this piece.

Kraft, William. *Tuba Concerto.* New Music West. Solo Tuba with Three Chamber Groups and Orchestra. 1979. Rental from the publisher. 18:00. V. F♯$_2$–a♯'. Commissioned by Zubin Mehta for Roger Bobo and the Los Angeles Philharmonic with partial assistance of a grant from the National Endowment for the Arts. An extensive contemporary work, revised and rescored by the composer from his 1977 work *Andirivieni.* The work contains material very reminiscent of the composer's *Encounters II for Solo Tuba,* including rapid, non-tonal passages, very wide intervallic leaps, the complete spectrum of dynamics, and various avant-garde effects including singing into the instrument, double stops, glisses, etc. A demanding piece for both the performers and audience. See: Bird, Gary, ed.; *Program Notes for the Solo Tuba.*

Krol, Bernhard. *Falstaff Concerto, Op. 119.* Editions Bim. Solo Tuba and String Orchestra (Piano reduction available). 1990. Rental from the publisher. 15:00. IV–V. G_1–f♯'. Three movements. Commissioned by Editions Bim. A neoclassical work in regard to both melodic style and form. The second movement contains some beautiful, lyrical writing while the greatest technical demands for the tubist come forth in the driving and humorous third movement, entitled "Homage to Guisseppe Verdi."

Krzywicki, Jan. *Concerto.* Tuba-Euphonium Press. Solo Tuba and Orchestra. 1999. 25:00. IV. C_1–g'. Three movements: De Profundis; In the Woods; Tarantella. Dedicated to Paul Krzywicki. Neo-romantic with emotion ranging from driving intensity to sensitive lyricism. Large range and rhythmic demands. Requires great musical maturity. Available for Tuba and Piano. Reviewed in the Winter 1998 issue of the *TUBA Journal* (Vol. 25, No. 2).

Krzywicki, Jan. *Fantasy for Tuba and Strings.* Available from the composer. Solo Tuba and String Orchestra. 1964. 8:00. III. E_1–b. Two movements: Andante; Allegro. For Abe Torchinsky. A melodic work with the tuba part written in and below the bass clef staff.

Kulesha, Gary. *Concerto for Tuba and Orchestra.* Canadian Music Centre. Solo Tuba and Orchestra (Band accompaniment and piano accompaniment (four hands) also available). 1979. Rental from the publisher. 18:00. IV. C_1–d'. Three movements: Prelude and Fugue; Scherzo; Finale. Commissioned by the Scarborough Concert Band of Ontario, Canada. Written for Scott Irvine. See annotation under Music for Tuba and Band.

Kupferman, Meyer. *Concerto for Tuba.* Soundspells Productions. 1982, revised 2002. V. Two movements. The first movement is designed as a dramatic aria. The tuba melody repeats over and over while gradually assuming new colors and variations. Its line always begins in the darkest bass before projecting into high lyrical episodes of considerable fire. The second movement resembles a scherzo. Short "kindergarten" tunes shape the dance-like character. The tuba finally returns to the opening mood of the concerto. The deep melodic aria slowly emerges once more but this time rising to a powerful climax—only to descend into the darkest regions of its world. Recorded by Edwin Diefes and the Czech National Symphony Orchestra.

Lachenmann, Helmut. *Harmonica—Music for Full Orchestra with Tuba-Solo.* Breitkopf & Härtel. Large Orchestra with Tuba Solo. 1981–83. 31:00. V. A_2–c'' (highest note possible). For Richard Nahatzki. A difficult and complex work for both solo tubist and orchestra. Extensive range and leaps, very challenging rhythms and polymeters, and other avant-garde effects throughout. Recorded by Richard Nahatzki.

Lackey, Jerry. *Jazz Concerto for Tuba and Orchestra.* Available from the composer. Solo Tuba and Orchestra, Drum Set, Piano, and Electric Bass (also versions for Tuba and Band, Tuba and Piano). 1984. Rental from composer. 12 minutes. V. G_2–b♭'. Three movements: Fast Swing, Rock, Simple Waltz, Fast Swing; Slow, Tranquillo; Fast, with Energy. A very good, challenging pops-style feature work for tuba and orchestra.

Larsson, Mats. *Homage to the Neon Sign of las Palaz Bingo: Concerto for Tuba and String Orchestra.* Swedish Music Information Center. Solo Tuba and Strings. 1991. 14:00–15:00. For Gene Pokorny.

Leichtling, Alan. *Concerto for Tuba, Strings, and Two Harps, Opus 83.* Seesaw Music Corporation. Solo Tuba, 2 Harps, and Strings. 1980–81. 21:00. IV–V. F_1–g'. Two movements: Aria with fantasy variations; Finale: allegro con brio. Dedicated to Robert Starer. Primarily diatonic writing in the solo part with some difficult polymeters and rhythmic interaction between solo part and ensemble. An extensive cadenza precedes the brief transition between the last variation in the first movement and the Finale.

Levy, Frank. *Dialogue.* Seesaw Music Corporation. Tuba, Harp, Timpani, and Strings. 1962. $13.00 (score). 10:00. IV. F_1–f'. The work is in two connected large sections: Adagio e molto mesto; Allegro marcato. Open scoring and effective use of dissonance make this an interesting work although by no means virtuosic. "Contrabass" tuba is specified in the score but an F or E-flat tuba would also be effective within the instrumentation, especially in sections juxtaposing the tuba with harp.

Linkola, Jukka. *Concerto for Tuba and Orchestra.* Finnish Music Information Center. Solo Tuba and Orchestra. 1992. 24:00. V. F_1–b♭'. Three movements: Introduction; Choral; Shades of Rhythm. Commissioned by NOMUS. Dedicated to Michael Lind. An extensive, virtuosic work employing less exploratory melodic and harmonic styles yet still possessing interesting, coloristic writing in both the solo and the accompanying ensemble. Reviewed in the Summer 1999 issue of the *TUBA Journal* (Vol. 26, No. 4).

Lorge, John S. *Fantasia for Tuba and Orchestra.* Available from the composer. Solo Tuba and Orchestra. 1992. 15:00. IV. E_1–g'. Four movements: Andante, Allegro non Troppo molto pesante; Andante; Senza Misura, Poco Allegretto, Senza Misura Ancora; Allegro. For Matthew Garbutt. A substantial, modern work in which the soloist is often playing dialogues with various orchestral combinations. Wide, irregular intervallic leaps throughout. There are no avant-garde effects except some improvised half-valve passages in the third movement.

Lovelock, William. *Concerto for Tuba and Orchestra.* Allans Publishing Pty. Ltd. Solo Tuba and Orchestra (Piano reduction by the composer). ca. 1965. Out of Print. 11:30. IV–V. F_1–f'. Continuous work in three large sections: Allegro; Adagio; Tempo primo. For John Woods. A tonal, neo-romantic work written in Australia with some very demanding technical passages. Works best on the F or E-flat tuba.

Lundquist, Torbjørn Iwan. *Landskap for Tuba and Orchestra.* Swedish Music Information Center. Tuba and Strings. 1978. 16:00. IV–V. F_1–a♭'. Continuous work in three large sections. For Michael Lind. A beautiful work possessing nice melodies with quartal and chromatic melodic and harmonic influences. The opening section with allegro moderato feeling proceeds into an expressive Largamente, followed by a substantial cadenza which provides the transition to the final Presto. Recorded by Michael Lind.

Luther, Michael. *Concerto for Tuba and Orchestra.* JML Publications. 1998. 21:15. D_1–a'. Processional; Ballade; Native American Song. For Norm Pearson, tubist of the Los Angeles Philharmonic. Written in a traditional three-movement fast-slow-fast pattern. An excellent addition to the repertory. Available for Tuba and Piano. Wonderful review in the Summer 2000 issue of the *TUBA Journal* (Vol. 27, No. 4).

Madsen, Trige. *Concerto for Tuba and Orchestra, Opus 35.* Musikk-Huset Forlag, Norway. Solo Tuba and Orchestra (Piano reduction available). 1986. IV.

Manas, Adriana I. Figueroa. *Fantasia.* Available from composer. Solo Tuba and Orchestra. 1999. In two sections. Available for Tuba and Piano. Reviewed in the Summer 2002 issue of the *ITEA Journal* (Vol. 29, No. 4).

Marcellino, Rafaelle. *The Art of Resonance.* Australian Music Centre. Solo Tuba and Symphony Orchestra. 1997. 20:00. Commissioned by Steve Rosse and Symphony Australia. Premiered by Steve Rosse and the Sydney Symphony in February, 1998.

Markl, Max. *Concertino for Tuba and Orchestra.* Tuba Center. Tuba and Orchestra.

Marques, Carlos. *Concerto for Tuba.* Editions BIM, in progress. Solo Tuba and Symphony Orchestra. 15:00. V. Commissioned by the Oporto National Orchestra. Dedicated to Sergio Carolino. Available for Tuba and Symphonic Wind Band.

Marthinsen, Niels. *Concerto for Tuba.* Edition Wilhelm Hansen. Solo Tuba and Orchestra. 1994. 22:00. V. E_1–b♭'. Three movements. Commissioned by the Danish Radio Symphony Orchestra. Dedicated to Jens Bjørn-Larsen. Movement I contains syncopated angular lines with a demanding range. Movement II requires musical maturity due to frequent metric shifts, a high tessitura, and fragmented passages. Movement III is technically difficult. A major work of great difficulty for the soloist. Accompanying parts are not as difficult.

Martin, Vernon. *Concerto for Tuba and Strings.* Composers Autograph Publications. Tuba and Strings (Piano reduction available). 1956. Out of Print. 14:00. III–IV. G_1–e♭'. Three movements. Conservative writing for the tuba and orchestra.

Másson, Askell. *Maes Howe Concerto.* Editions BIM. Tuba and Chamber Orchestra. 2000 (1999). Rental parts. 14:00. V. A_2–a'. Commissioned by Harri Lidsle with funds from NOMUS and the Kulturverein Island-Finland for the 2001 ITEC in Lahti, Finland. Dedicated to Harri Lidsle. Based on an Icelandic folk melody; Maes Howe was a burial mound in the Orkney Islands some 5000 years ago. The work employs extensive use of alternate fingerings on rapid repeated notes. Available for Tuba and Piano.

Meier, Jost. *Eclipse finale?* Editions Bim. Solo Tuba and Chamber Orchestra (also available for Tuba and Brass Band, Tuba and Piano). 1991. Rental from the publisher. 19:30. V. See listing under Tuba and Band. Reviewed in the Summer 1997 issue of the *TUBA Journal* (Vol. 25, No. 4).

Miserendino, Joseph. *Autumn Moods.* Available from the composer. Solo Tuba and Strings. 2003. 7:31. Four sections: Summer's Last Hurrah; Song of a Soft Fall Night; Witches and Goblins Cavort; Autumn Repose and Dreams of Spring. Available for Tuba and Piano, Tuba and Organ.

Miserendino, Joseph. *Canzona della notte scura.* Available from the composer. Solo Tuba and Strings. 2003. 3:27. IV. F–g♭'. Available for Tuba and Piano, Tuba and Organ.

Miserendino, Joseph. *Canzona di una notte tranquillo.* Available from the composer. Solo Tuba and Strings. 2003. 4:26. IV. B–g'.

Miserendino, Joseph. *Summer Celebration.* Available from the composer. Solo Tuba and Strings. 2003. 4:27. IV. F–f'. High tessitura and technical throughout. Available for Tuba and Piano.

Miserendino, Joseph. *Winter Song and Spring Dances.* Available from the composer. Solo Tuba and Strings. 2002. 6:16. IV. F_1–f'. Available for Tuba and Piano, Tuba and Organ, Tuba and Woodwind Choir.

Monti, Vittorio. *Csárdás.* arr. Øystein Baadsvik. Ovation. Solo Tuba and String Orchestra. 1992. 5:00. IV. G_1–a♭'. $50.65. Originally written for the violin, this display piece has tempted numerous performers. In this arrangement the tuba is the star of the show. Fun to play and delightful for audiences. The solo part can be played on different instruments and the set is delivered with solo part in treble clef in E♭ and bass clef. Recorded by Øystein Baadsvik. Available for Solo Tuba and Piano, Solo Tuba and Wind Band, Solo Tuba and Brass Band, Solo Tuba and Wind Quintet.

Morricone, Enrico. *Gabriel's Oboe.* arr. Øystein Baadsvik. Ovation. Solo Tuba and Symphony Orchestra. 2001. 7:00. IV. B♭–g'. $94.07. Available for Solo Tuba and Wind Band, Solo Tuba and Brass Band.

Mortimer, John Glenesk. *Tuba Concerto.* Editions Marc Reift. Tuba and String Orchestra. 1983. For David LeClair. 9:30. IV. F_1–g'. Three movements: Allegro; Adagio non troppo; Tempo di Samba. A tonal composition demanding a lyrical approach and rhythmical accuracy. Solid ensemble writing in the accompaniment. Available for Tuba and Piano. Reviewed in the Fall 1991 issue of the *TUBA Journal* (Vol. 19, No. 1).

Mueller, Florian. *Concert Music for Tuba.* University Publications. Tuba and Orchestra (2 Flutes doubling Piccolo, 2 Oboes, 2 Clarinets, 2 Bassoons, 2 Horns, Strings) (Piano reduction available). 1961. Out of Print. 5:00. III–IV. E_1–e'. For Arnold Jacobs. See listing under Tuba and Keyboard. Tuba and Piano version recorded by Rex Conner.

Mueller, Frederick. *Variations on a Theme of Samuel Barber.* Manuscript available from the composer. Solo Tuba and Strings (also Solo Tuba and Band, Solo Tuba and Piano). 1972. 9:00. III–IV. C♯–d' (g'). Commissioned by and dedicated to Robert Tucci. A mostly lyrical work in seven variations with a cadenza.

Muradian, Vazgen. *Concerto for Tuba and Orchestra, Opus 85.* Rental from the composer. Solo Tuba and String Orchestra (Piano reduction available). 1984. 15:30. IV. C_1–g'. Three movements: Allegro grazioso; Romanza; Presto. A melodic, neo-romantic work which takes the soloist through much of their range in a mostly diatonic fashion. The music contains passion reminiscent of the composer's Armenian homeland. Vazgen Muradian has written a very large body of music including concerti for every orchestral instrument. His *Concerto for Contrabassoon and String Orchestra* also works quite well for the tuba and is in the same style.

Newton, Rodney. *The Kraken.* Studio Music Company. Solo Tuba and Symphony Orchestra. 2002. 12:30. C_2–F'. *The Kraken* is a concerto in all but name. Commissioned by James Gourlay with funding from the Royal Northern College of Music, the work received its premiere performance by James Gourlay with the Royal Northern College of Music Junior Wind Orchestra under the direction of Roger Bobo on 15th September 2003. It is scored for a large ensemble (with contrabass clarinet and contra bassoon) together with parts for harp and organ (the latter optional). Subtitled "an aquerelle" (with tongue in cheek!), it was inspired by lines from Lord Tennyson's poem *The Kraken.* When listening to this piece, one may imagine a gigantic creature lying at the bottom of an ocean trench for countless millennia until, roused by the trumpets of the Last Judgment, it rises, only to perish on the surface. This one-movement work uses the full range of the tuba and the full resources of the wind orchestra together with the organ to give an impression of vastness and immense power. The death of the titanic creature is graphically described in the solo writing toward the end of the work. Available for Solo Tuba and Wind Orchestra.

Osmon, Leroy. *Elegy for Tuba and Small Orchestra.* RBC Publications. Solo Tuba, Flute, Trumpet, Trombone, Piano and String Orchestra (or String Quartet). 1999. 6:00. IV. $F♯_1$–d'. Single movement. Commissioned by Andrew S. Kesten in memory of his grandfather, David Kesten. This piece is a reflective work using the tuba in a lyrical, singing style. The middle section is an extended duet with the first violin.

Pape, Andy. *Concerto Grosso in Maggiore e in minore.* Edition Wilhelm Hansen. Recorder Solo, Cello Solo, Tuba Solo, and Symphony Orchestra. 1996. 24:00. V. A_2–a'. Three movements. Commissioned by the Danish Radio Symphony Orchestra. Inspired by and dedicated to Michala Petri, Morten Zeuthen and Jens Bjørn Larsen. Written in a traditional three-movement fast-slow-fast pattern. The recorder, cello, and tuba solo parts require virtuoso performers. The tuba solo part is very demanding in regard to technique, range, and balancing the other two soloists. A well-written composition that challenges the most experienced performers.

Plau, Arild. *Concerto for Tuba and Strings.* Music Information Centre Norway. 1990. 18:00. IV–V. A_1–g'. Three movements: Prologue; Canzone; Finale. The grief-ridden middle movement of this piece was composed in memory of the composer's wife, who had just passed away. Premiered by Øystein Baadsvik in 2001 with the Wratislavia (Poland) Chamber Orchestra. Recorded by Øystein Baadsvik.

Plog, Anthony. *Nocturne for Tuba and Strings.* Editions BIM, in preparation. Solo Tuba and String Orchestra. 2004. 9:30. IV. C–e♭'. For Kent Eshelman. A lyrical piece that allows the instrument to sing. Alternates quiet reflective passages with animated allegro writing.

Plog, Anthony. *Tuba Concerto.* Editions BIM. Tuba and Symphony Orchestra. 1997 (1992). Rental parts. 22:00. V. G_1–e". Three movements: Andante; Slowly; Allegro (theme with four variations). Dedicated to Markus Theinert. Chromatically based first and third movements. The second movement starts with a cadenza for the tuba followed by an expressive duet with clarinet and pizzicato string accompaniment. A worthwhile work making good use of dissonance and rhythmic interplay. Available for Tuba and Piano.

Premru, Raymond. *Concerto for Tuba and Orchestra.* Publication pending. Solo Tuba and Orchestra (Piano accompaniment available). 1992. 15:00. IV. F_1–f'. Three movements: Adagio—Allegro ma non troppo; Molto Allegro; Adagio. Commissioned by Tubists Universal Brotherhood Association and premiered at the 1992 International Tuba-Euphonium Conference in Lexington, Kentucky. Dedicated to the memory of John Fletcher. A highly melodic work in which the composer depicts the personality and memories of his friend and colleague John Fletcher. The hauntingly beautiful third movement, a soliloquy for solo tuba with strings, is about seven minutes in duration and can very effectively stand by itself in performance.

Presser, William. *Concerto for Tuba and Strings.* Theodore Presser Company. Solo Tuba and String Orchestra (Piano reduction available). 1970. Rental from the publisher. 16:30. IV. C_1–e'. Three movements. See: Bird, Gary, ed.; *Program Notes for the Solo Tuba.*

Proctor, Simon. *Tuba Concerto.* Heavy Metal Music. Tuba and Orchestra. 1995. $60.00. 15:00–20:00. V. F_1–f'. Commissioned by and dedicated to Sue Bradley. Advised by Harvey Phillips. Single movement in three distinct sections. The opening *Presto scherzando* provides opportunities for virtuosity and musicianship. The cadenza at the end of this movement is unique, requiring the orchestral (*tutti*) tuba and solo tuba to play the cadenza as a duet. This is followed by the remaining two sections, one of which includes jazz fragments. The end of the concerto includes the most technically challenging passages, marked "Arbanistic." Available for Tuba and Piano, Piano accompaniment tape. Reviewed in the Fall 1999 issue of the *TUBA Journal* (Vol. 27, No. 1).

Proto, Frank. *The Four Seasons.* Liben Music Publishers. Tuba, Percussion, Strings, and Tape. 1980. Score and parts rental from the publisher. 30:00. IV–V. A_2–a'. Five movements: Introduction; Spring; Summer; Autumn; Winter. Commissioned by the Cincinnati Symphony Orchestra. A fulfilling work, from both performers' and audience perspectives, which combines popular and modern musical idioms. A work which is truly a duo concertante for tuba and percussion with orchestra and tape. Recorded by Michael Thornton.

Proto, Frank. *The New Seasons—Sinfonia Concertante for Tuba, Percussion, Flutes and Strings.* Liben Music Publishers. Solo Tuba, 2 Solo Percussion, 4 Flutes (with Piccolos and Alto Flutes), 2 Tutti Percussion, and Strings. 1991. Rental from the publisher. 32:30. IV–V. $E♭_1$–g♭'. Three movements. An extensive, modern work with a demanding tuba solo part and very demanding percussion solo parts. Although probably not a work that would fit on a "pops" concert, there are jazz and popular influences apparent in the composition. Both solo percussion parts require improvisation within a jazz style.

Raum, Elizabeth. *Concerto del Garda.* Tuba-Euphonium Press. Solo Tuba and Orchestra (originally composed as *Sonata for Tuba and Piano*). 1998. $75.00. 15:00. V. G_1–b♭'. Three movements: Moderato grandioso; Lento; Allegretto con anima. Dedicated to John Griffiths. This piece recalls a more classical approach of clarity and balance. The solo part in the outer movements uses extensive range and alternates between expansive melodic passages and scalar and arpeggiated sequences. The middle movement is full of expressive melodic sequences and remains in the high F tuba register for most of the movement. A very musically and technically demanding work suitable for F tuba. Piano version premiered by John Griffiths at the 1997 ITEC. Orchestral version premiered by Roger Bobo at the 1998 ITEC. Recorded by John Griffiths. Reviewed in the Winter 1999 issue of the *TUBA Journal* (Vol. 27, No. 2) and the Fall 2001 issue of the *ITEA Journal* (Vol. 29, No. 1).

Raum, Elizabeth. *The Legend of Heimdall for Solo Tuba and Orchestra*. Available from the composer. Solo Tuba and Orchestra. 1991. 19:00. IV–V. G_1–g'. Three movements: Heimdall's Gjallarhorn; The Song of the Bard; The Battle of Asgard. Commissioned by the Canadian Broadcasting Corporation and dedicated to John Griffiths. Lyrical program music in a neo-romantic style based upon themes from Norse myths. The composer specifies CC tuba for the outer movements and F on the middle movement. Recorded by John Griffiths.

Raum, Elizabeth. *Pershing Concerto*. Tuba-Euphonium Press. Solo Euphonium or Tuba and Orchestra (originally composed as *Sonata for Euphonium and Piano*). 2000. 14:00. $70.00. V. F_1 (*ossia*)–b♭' (*ossia*). Three movements: Allegro Moderato; Andante; Allegro non troppo. For John Griffiths. Commissioned by Richard Raum and John Griffiths. The outer movements reflect the courage of leaders such as General "Black Jack" Pershing and men like him. The middle movement is waltz-like and more lyrical, portraying the sadness of losing loved ones as Pershing did. Brass calls and percussion cadences, echoing the music of the military, permeate the entire work. A musically rewarding work with some extreme range considerations. Recorded by John Griffiths. Available for Tuba and Band, Tuba and Piano. Reviewed in the Fall 2001 issue of the *ITEA Journal* (Vol. 29, No. 1).

Ridout, Alan. *Concertino for Tuba and Strings*. Emerson Edition. Solo Tuba and Strings or String Quartet (Piano reduction available). 1985. 4:45. IV. F_1–e'. Three movements: Allegro; Lento; Vivace. Tuneful, conservative music. Meter in third movement shifts irregularly between three and two beats per bar.

Roikjer, Kjell. *Capriccio for Tuba and Orchestra, Opus 66*. Musikforlaget IMUDICO. Solo Tuba and Orchestra (Piano reduction available). 1974. 7:30. IV–V. F_1–g'. Continuous work in three large sections. For Michael Lind. A flashy work for the solo tuba with mostly diatonic and chordal writing.

Roikjer, Kjell. *Concerto for Tuba and Orchestra*. Musikforlaget IMUDICO. Solo Tuba and Orchestra (Piano reduction available).

Rottler, Werner. *Concerto for Tuba and Orchestra*. Available from the composer. Solo Tuba and Orchestra (Piano accompaniment available). 1980. IV. Three movements: Allegro moderato; Adagio quieto e religioso; Allegretto vivace. For Robert Tucci.

Saglietti, Corrado Maria. *Piazze di Torino*. Animando Edizioni Musicali Sas, Italy. Solo Tuba and String Orchestra. 2004. 16:00. IV–V. G_1–f'. Three Sections: Piazza San Carlo—Allegro; Piazzetta Maria Teresa—Andante fantastico; Porta Palazzo—Allegro. Premiered by Alessandro Fossi at the 2004 ITEC. A very approachable, melodic work.

Sagvik, Stellan. *Svensk Concertino, Opus 114j*. Swedish Music Information Center. Solo Tuba and String Orchestra. 1983. 10:00. IV.

Sampson, David. *Three Portraits for Tuba and Chamber Orchestra*. Available from the composer. Solo Tuba and Chamber Orchestra. 1990. 18:00. V. $D♭_1$–B♭'. Commissioned by Scott Mendoker. Three movements; each portrait depicts different aspects of Sampson's relationship with Mendoker. First impressions are the subject of Portrait One. The music is light and engaging. Portrait Two shows a deeper side, more intimate and sensitive. The music is quieter, richer, and more delicate. Portrait Three shows the individual in crisis: angry, hurt, and confused. The music is angular and complex. When this burst of emotion is spent, the music becomes introverted and a peaceful stillness gradually replaces the pain. The movement ends meditatively. A worthwhile piece with emotion ranging from intense to lyrical. Recorded by Scott Mendoker. Reviewed in the Spring 1995 issue of the *TUBA Journal* (Vol. 22, No. 3).

Schilling, Hans Ludwig. *Tuba & Co.—Concerto for Baßtuba und Streichorchester*. Available from the composer. Solo Tuba and String Orchestra.

Schmidt, Ole. *Concerto for Tuba and Orchestra*. Edition Wilhelm Hansen. Tuba and Orchestra (Piano reduction available). 1976. 14:20. V. Three movements: Allegro moderato; Lento; Allegro giusto. See: Bird, Gary, ed.; *Program Notes for the Solo Tuba*. Recorded by Michael Lind.

Schmidt, William. *Concerto for Tuba and Chamber Orchestra*. Available from the composer. Solo Tuba and Chamber Orchestra (Flute, Oboe, Clarinet, Bassoon, Trumpet, 2 Horns, Bass Trombone, Percussion, and Strings). 1993. Rental. 15:30. IV. A_1–g♯'. Three movements. A great deal of interplay between soloist and accompanying ensemble and some very coloristic instrumental doublings make this an interesting yet not overly difficult work. The third movement contains extensive shifting meters.

Schuller, Gunther. *Capriccio for Tuba and Orchestra*. Mentor Music, Inc. Solo Tuba and Small Orchestra (Piano reduction available). 1969. Rental from the publisher. 10:00. IV. $E♭_1$–e'. For Harvey Phillips. Substantial technical demands made on the soloist including extensive lip trills. See: Bird, Gary, ed.; *Program Notes for the Solo Tuba*. Recorded by Harvey Phillips.

Segerstam, Leif. *Orchestral Diary Sheet No. 11i*. Finnish Music Information Center. Solo Tuba (or Trombone) in Orchestra. 1981. V. An unmetered orchestral sound-piece with solo obligato instrumental solo, originally cello and later rewritten by the composer for various solo instruments.

Shaughnessy, Robert. *Concertino for Tuba and String Orchestra.* Peer International Corp. Tuba and String Orchestra (Piano reduction available). 1969. Score and parts on rental from the publisher. 12:00. III–IV. A_1–b. Three movements: I; II. Lento; III. Allegro non troppo. A work without significant difficulty, unusual in that all three movements are in a compound meter—the first movement in 6/4, the second in 9/8, and the third in 12/8.

Sorensen, Erling Ingemann. *Sensonner, Opus 10.* Danish Music Information Center. Solo Tuba and String Orchestra. 1981. 10:00. IV.

Steptoe, Roger. *Concerto for Tuba and Strings.* Stainer & Bell. Solo Tuba and Strings (Piano reduction available). 1983. Rental from the publisher. 15:00. V. F_1–g'. Three movements: Con poco moto—Allegro; Giocoso; Molto calmo. For James Gourlay. The openings of the first movement and the third movement are quite melodic. Very difficult technical material which, depending on the tempo, will require double tonguing.

Stevens, John. *Journey.* Editions BIM. Contrabass Tuba and Orchestra. 2001 (1998). Parts on rental. 28:00. V. A_2–g'. Three movements: Morning in the Yard; Midnight in the Mountains; Highballing through Town. Commissioned by the Edward F. Schmidt Family Commissioning Fund. Composed for and premiered by Gene Pokorny and the Chicago Symphony Orchestra. Rhythmically complex work; effective and picturesque writing; Each movement can be played alone, or movements I and II, or II and III, may be played together. Although written for contrabass tuba, this work can also be played on the bass tuba in F or E♭. Available for Tuba and Piano.

Stevens, Thomas. *Variations in Olden Style (after Bach).* Editions Bim. Solo Tuba, Strings, Continuo (Piano accompaniment available). 1989. Parts on rental from the publisher. 4:45. IV. F–f'. Theme and five variations. For Roger Bobo. Good, traditional theme and variations based on the Sarabande from J. S. Bach's *Sixth Cello Suite.* The tuba part is all in or slightly above the staff and lies very well for the F tuba. Recorded in tuba-piano version by Roger Bobo.

Stokes, Eric. *A Center Harbor Holiday.* Manuscript. Tuba and Orchestra. 1963; revised 1972. 14:00. IV. E_1–g'. For Roger Bobo. A concerto in one movement with patriotic American flavor.

Strukow, Valerie. *Concerto for Tuba and Orchestra.* Editions Bim. Solo Tuba and Orchestra (Piano reduction available). 1980. Rental from the publisher. 13:45. V. C_1–a' (with suggested *ossia* sections down an octave). Three movements: Allegro moderato; Lento elegiaco; Vivo scherzando. A technically demanding modern work in a style interesting and accessible to broad audiences. The first movement contains many hybrid scale passages, which quickly take the player through much of the tuba's range, and ends with an extensive solo cadenza. The second movement is lyrical and expressive and is followed by the finale, which resembles a wild tarantella. Recorded by Jens Bjørn-Larsen.

Szentpáli Roland. *Concerto.* Editions BIM. Tuba and Orchestra. 2002. Scores for purchase, parts on rental. 17:00. V. D_1–a'. Three movements: Moderato; Andante; Moderato. Commissioned by Concours International de Guebwiller (Alsace, France) with the support of the SUISA Music Foundation. Written in a style reminiscent of Bartok. The tessitura is very high, requiring enormous endurance. Good mixture of lyric and technical passages. Available for Tuba and Piano. Reviewed in the Spring 2003 issue of the *ITEA Journal* (Vol. 30, No. 3).

Tischhauser, Franz. *Eve's Meditation on Love.* Amadeus. Soprano, Solo Tuba, and Orchestra. 1992 (1970/71). Score available for purchase, parts on rental. 24:00. III–IV. D_1–f'. Seven movements: I. Hypothesis; II. Test for Cheerfulness; III. Test for Tenderness; IV. Test for Industry; V. Test for Teachability; VI. Test for Patience; VII. Conclusion. Humorous work based on texts from Mark Twain and adapted by the composer. A soprano sings the role of Eve, and Adam is the tuba. There are no particular technical difficulties for the tuba. The work is written in a quasi-revue style. Solo instruments in the orchestra portray the different animals used to underline the different personal qualities of Adam: first violin is the lark, second violin the cat, viola the bee, cello the dog, and contrabass the sheep.

Tomasi, Henri. *Danse Sacrée: No. 3 from "Cinc danses profanes et sacrées."* Alphonse Leduc. Solo Tuba and Chamber Orchestra (Piano reduction available). 1960. 5:00. III. G_1–a♭'. See: Thompson/Lemke; *French Music for Low Brass Instruments.*

Vaughan Williams, Ralph. *Concerto for Bass Tuba.* Oxford University Press. Solo Tuba and Orchestra (Solo Tuba and Band, Piano reduction also available). 1954. Rental from the publisher. 13:00. IV. $E♭_1$–f' (a♭'). Three movements: Prelude (Allegro moderato); Romanza; Finale—Rondo all Tedesca. Dedicated to the London Symphony Orchestra. Although written in 1954, this is a truly conservative work, firmly within the bounds of traditional harmony, tonality, and notation. Despite the fact that there are now over one hundred works for solo tuba and orchestra, the Vaughan Williams is still regarded by many musicians and conductors as the primary work in the tubist's solo repertoire and is a required selection for many auditions and competitions. The first movement takes the soloist through much of the instrument's range, from pedal e-flat to optional high a-flats in the cadenza. The Romanza is a beautifully expressive, melodic scene providing the soloist with a very nice vehicle to emote and exhibit musicality. The Finale contains some opportunity for pyrotechnic display, although it winds to a halt with the final cadenza and ends with an unsatisfying fizzle. See: Bird, Gary, ed.; *Program Notes for the Solo Tuba.* Recorded by Philip Catelinet, Eugene Dowling, John Fletcher, Patrick Harrild, Manfred Hoppert, Arnold Jacobs, Ian King, Michael Lind, Richard Nahatzki, Harvey Phillips, Donald Strand, Floyd Cooley. Recorded accompaniment available: *Vivace: A Complete Practice System.* For further information, see listing under Recorded Accompaniments.

Vea, Ketil. *Concerto for Tuba and Orchestra.* Music Information Centre Norway. 1990. 21:00.

Velden, Staffan Lunden. *Kesh Jig Concerto.* Ovation. Tuba Solo and String Orchestra. 2002. 4:00. G_1–f'. Recorded by Øystein Baadsvik.

Villette, Pierre. *Fantaisie concertante.* Alphonse Leduc. Solo Tuba and Chamber Orchestra (Piano reduction available). 1962. Rental from the publisher. IV–V. G_1–a♭'. See: Thompson/Lemke; *French Music for Low Brass Instruments.*

Vivaldi, Antonio. *The Winter.* arr. Øystein Baadsvik. Ovation. Solo Tuba and String Orchestra. 2002. 9:00. V. G_1–g'. $65.12. Recorded by Øystein Baadsvik.

Walker, Gwyneth. *Chanties and Ballads: Songs of the Sea for Tuba and Orchestra.* MMB Music, Inc. 1995. 15:00. D_1–g'. Three movements: Coming Up for Air; Far from Home; Bonny Tuba. The first movement features a jaunty melody for the tuba with ascending scale-runs and glissandi suggestive of rising up to the surface. The second movement is a ballad—perhaps a lament sung by a homesick sailor. Sounds of the ship's rigging may be heard in the percussion. The final movement is a set of variations on a well-known melody. There is the customarily somber (perhaps sunken) variation in the minor mode followed by a virtuosic triplet arpeggiation variation. Premiered by Mark Nelson and the Millikin-Decatur Symphony Orchestra.

Werner, Jean-Jacques. *Concerto for Tuba and Orchestra.* G. Billaudot Editions. Available solely from Theodore Presser. 1996. 19:00. V. Three movements: Souvenirs; Fulgurances; Tenebres Solaires. Available for Tuba and Piano. Reviewed in the Spring 1998 issue of the *TUBA Journal* (Vol. 25, No. 3).

Werner, Sven Erik. *Windfall.* Samfundet. Solo Tuba and Orchestra. 1993. 17:30. V. G–b♭'. One movement with sections. Numerous mixed meters. The title has two meanings: *Wind* represents "fruit that has blown down from the trees" and *fall* represents "a plum on one's lap." The association with autumn weather, ripening, decay, and death can be traced in the music. The music changes to grim, humorous excitement in an attempt to throw light on the paradox of the title. Commissioned by Jørgen Voigt Arnsted.

White, Joseph Pollard. *Concerto for Tuba and Orchestra.* Available from the composer. Solo Tuba and Orchestra. 1990. IV. D_1–d'. Three movements: Allegro molto vivace; Andante tranquillo; Allegro assai. Intended to be a fun piece and to show off the sound of the tuba in various contexts. A mute is required in the third movement. The solo part as well as the orchestra parts would be accessible to most college-level players. Premiered by Robert Shuster and the Rainier Symphony.

Wilder, Alec. *Elegy for the Whale.* Margun Music Inc. Solo Tuba and Orchestra (Piano accompaniment also available). Rental from the publisher. 1981. 3:20. IV. F_1–g'. Written for Harvey Phillips. A somber, brooding piece. The tuba part is mostly in the upper register and contains many intricate, irregular tonal shifts. Although melodic in nature, this work lacks the "popular feel" inherent in much of Wilder's music and is a truly difficult piece for performer and audience alike.

Wilder, Alec. *Sonata for Tuba and Orchestra.* Wilder Music Inc. Tuba and Orchestra (Tuba and Piano available). Out of Print. An arrangement for orchestral accompaniment of the composer's *Sonata for Tuba and Piano.*

Wilder, Alec. *Suite No. 1 for Tuba and Orchestra "Effie."* Margun Music Inc. Tuba and Orchestra. Rental from the publisher. The popular solo tuba work arranged nicely for orchestral accompaniment. See listings also under Tuba and Keyboard and Tuba in Mixed Ensemble.

Williams, John. *Concerto for Tuba.* Withdrawn by the composer from performance. Solo Tuba and Orchestra (Piano reduction available). 1985. 16:30. V. F_1–g'. Three movements: Allegro moderato; Andante; Allegro molto. To Chester Schmitz. An incredible, virtuosic work with John Williams's familiar melodic and harmonic style. Some of the technical demands in the solo part arise because of the string-like nature of the writing, with rapid, smooth arpeggiations and double tongue sections perhaps more idiomatic to bowed instruments. See: Bird, Gary, ed.; *Program Notes for the Solo Tuba.*

Winteregg, Steven. *Concerto for Tuba.* Available from the composer. Tuba and Orchestra (Flute, Clarinet, Bassoon, Horn, Trumpet, Trombone, 2 Percussion, Strings). 1992. Rental from the composer. 16:30. IV. G_1–e'. Three movements. Written with the CC tuba in mind, although the piece would certainly work very well on one of the smaller tubas. A modern, dramatic work very well scored for the soloist to be easily heard.

Woodward, James. *Tuba Concerto*. Tuba-Euphonium Press. Solo Tuba and Orchestra. 2000. IV. E_1–c''. Four movements: Joyously, light; Freely—Quirky; Slowly, Freely; Brilliantly. Written for Alan Baer and premiered at the 2000 ITEC with Mr. Baer as the soloist. The work, in four movements, is characterized by lively outer movements that are driven by rhythmic motifs in the solo voice. While not a minimalist piece by any stretch of the imagination, some of the harmonic language is reminiscent of the music of John Adams. The inner movements are more complex and feature substantial cadenzas for the soloist. What one will notice most quickly about this concerto is the high tessitura required of the soloist. The work hovers at or above the staff for much of the duration of the piece. The most notable foray into the stratosphere occurs within the last four measures of the piece, after twenty minutes of playing; the solo part rips up to the C above middle C, uncharted territory for a concerto for bass tuba (possibly with the exception of Kellaway's *Song of Ascent*). The concerto is written in a totally accessible harmonic language and is enjoyable for both the audience and the performer. Recorded by David Zerkel. Available for Tuba and Band.

Woolf, Gregory. *Per Tuba Ad Astram (A Concertino for Tuba in Stilo Antico)*. Previously available from the composer. Solo Tuba and Orchestra (Piano reduction by the composer). Out of Print. 12:00. IV. F_1–g'. Three movements: Allegro; Adagio; Molto Allegro. For Daniel Perantoni. An expressive work filled with haunting, quirky melodies which truly demonstrate the performer's ability to "sing" with their instrument.

4. Music for Tuba in Mixed Ensemble

Timothy J. Northcut, Assistant Editor, *Guide to the Tuba Repertoire: The New Tuba Source Book*

Julia Piorkowski and Bobbie Zajkowski, Editorial Assistants

Skip Gray, Assistant Editor, *The Tuba Source Book*

Introductory Remarks (July 2005): Timothy J. Northcut

The primary goal of this chapter is to provide an updated list of compositions written for tuba and mixed ensemble. Not having been involved with the research for the first edition of *The Tuba Source Book,* I would like to congratulate Skip Gray for the exceptional job he did. When my mentor, Winston Morris, contacted me about joining the team for this publication as an assistant editor, I immediately responded "yes," recognizing the importance of updating such information. I also knew that "no" was not an acceptable answer. Almost thirteen years have passed since the closing date for research for the first edition of *The Tuba Source Book* (July 1993), and the repertoire for tuba and mixed ensemble has experienced significant growth. In the present survey of these materials, it is apparent that as the quantity of the repertoire has increased, so has the quality.

The corresponding chapter in the first edition of *The Tuba Source Book* included 389 entries for tuba in mixed ensemble. For this publication, I have added 142 new entries and updated 17 entries from the first edition. Regrettably, I was compelled to withhold a number of compositions due to the lack of information and as a result, there will be compositions that have been omitted. My responsibility as editor is to maintain the excellence in research that was established in *The Tuba Source Book,* and it is my hope that this was accomplished and you find this material to be extremely helpful.

This chapter is the culmination of the work of many volunteers and was truly a labor of love. It is with profound gratitude that I thank those who assisted:

• Julia Piorkowski and Bobbie Zajkowski. I express my extreme gratitude for the work of these wonderful friends who served as my editorial assistants. They each were totally committed to the completion of this project. I cannot thank you enough!

• Winston Morris, for his trust in my abilities to conduct research and for his words of encouragement and support in all of my musical endeavors.

• David Adams, Chair of the Performance Studies Division in the University of Cincinnati College-Conservatory of Music, for monetary support for the initial mailing to hundreds of publishers and composers.

• To the publishers and composers who responded to requests for information, catalogs, and review copies, especially David Miles (Tuba-Euphonium Press).

• To the International Consultants, especially Jørgen Voigt Arnsted, Øystein Baadsvik, Sergio Carolino, John Elliott, Alessandro Fossi, James Gourlay, John Griffiths, Chitate Kagawa, David LeClair, Gilles Lutmann, and Steve Rosse.

• Jennifer Northcut. I am immensely grateful to my wife for her patience and tolerance beyond reason.

• Nicholas and Claire Northcut. A special expression of gratitude goes to my children, who day to day patiently waited for dad to come out and play.

Introductory Remarks (July 1995): Skip Gray

Over the past twenty-five years, there has been tremendous growth in the number of works for tuba in various chamber music ensemble settings. The desire is always present among both composers and performers to experiment and discover new sounds and innovative media for expression. Works for tuba in mixed ensemble often exemplify this creative spirit. Another primary motivation for tubists seeking works with different musical combinations is to reach audiences who might not have been exposed to the tuba's capabilities or those who simply reject the pairing of tuba with piano. Certainly, if a tuba player can convince a string quartet to perform a work which also includes the tuba on one of their concerts, the tubist will undoubtedly be cast in front of a new group of listeners. By performing with a fine vocalist, flutist, or other musician, there is the solid opportunity to draw an expanded audience, persons who may not have previously been interested in attending a tuba recital.

Several works with chamber ensemble have established themselves as standard tuba solo repertoire; the Armand Russell *Suite Concertante for Tuba and Woodwind Quintet* and the *Suite No. 1 for French Horn, Tuba, and Piano* by Alec Wilder come immediately to mind. But as can be seen in the following pages, works exist for many diverse combinations featuring or at least employing the tuba as an equal partner. For example, compositions for tuba with established chamber ensembles such as string quartet, horn quartet, rhythm section, and percussion ensemble, in addition to a multitude of experimental combinations, appear on programs and recitals.

The works listed in this chapter include pieces which feature the tuba in chamber settings as well as those in which the tuba is an equal partner in the ensemble. The established brass quintet repertoire has been omitted here, with the exception of works specifically emphasizing the tuba.

Adderley, Mark. *Bass Substances: For Tuba and Double Bass.* Music Information Centre Norway. 1999.

Adomavicis, T. *Ballade Aria.* Valentin Avvakoumov. Trombone and Tuba. 1985. 2:30. III. Trombone: c♯–a♭'; Tuba: A_1–a♭. A nicely written little rondo in conventional tonality featuring the trombone as the melodic voice.

Åkerwall, Martin. *Leaves of Blue Frost: Buddhi for kor og tuba.* Available from the composer. Tuba and Mixed Choir. 2002. 11:00. V. E♭$_1$–g♭'. The term "Buddhi" in the title is the name of an especially powerful kind of healing technique developed in Denmark. The composer was asked by the man who created this technique to compose some music he could use for meditation and "Buddhi." The overall mood of the piece is very peaceful and serene. The composer instructs the tubist to perform "with incredible tenderness and warmth." There are no great technical difficulties for the tuba other than execution of the extreme soft dynamics and sustaining of notes at a very slow tempo. Interesting vocal writing adds great coloristic effect. Sensitive playing is a requisite so that the choir is not overshadowed. An excellent addition to the repertoire.

Åkerwall, Martin. *Manden med Tubaen.* Available from the composer. Tuba, Harp and Cello.

Åkerwall, Martin. *Meditation for Tuba and Organ.* Available from the composer. Tuba and Organ. 2001. 3:00. V. E♭–g'. Very exposed writing in the upper tessitura of the tuba. Controlled soft playing is required.

Åkerwall, Martin. *Trimendious.* Available from the composer. Trio for Tuba, Trombone, and Piano. 2001. 15:30. V. B♭$_2$–g'. Three movements: Joyfully Dancing; In a Misty Mood; To Jens. Commissioned by Statens Kunstfond. Lots of mixed meters; rhythmically challenging. An interactive dialogue composition that is very rhythmical with changing meters between the soloists and pianist. A great chamber music work that will require adequate rehearsal time. This work will challenge the most experienced performers.

Åkerwall, Martin. *What Darwin Didn't Know.* Available from the composer. Tuba and Flute. 2004. IV–V. B♭$_2$–e♭'. Dedicated to Anna Dina and Jens Bjørn-Larsen. A great deal of musical interplay between the two instruments. Adequate rehearsal time is needed due to frequent metric shifts.

Albam, Manny. *Quintet for Tuba and Stings.* Manuscript available from the composer. Solo Tuba and String Quartet. For Harvey Phillips.

Albam, Manny. *Sextet for Tuba and Winds.* Manuscript available from the composer. Solo Tuba and Woodwind Quintet. For Harvey Phillips.

Alexander, Josef. *Three Miniatures from Two Extremes.* Margun Music. Piccolo and Tuba (F). 1987. $20.00. 10:45. IV–V. F♯$_1$–f'. Three movements: Downstream; Midstream; Upstream. Mixed meters and wide, non-melodic intervallic leaps add difficulty to this unusual yet interesting work.

Amato, Bruno. *Two Together.* Seesaw Music Corporation. Soprano and Tuba. 1971. $20.00. 8:00. V. F♯$_1$–e'. In six sections. To Les Varner. Text by Walt Whitman. A very demanding "new music" work for both soprano and tubist with difficult rhythms and wide melodic leaps. For the tubist, there are extensive sing and play sections as well as moments of simultaneously playing and tapping on the tuba. Recorded by John Turk.

Ameller, Andre. *Epigraphe.* Alphonse Leduc. 3 Trombones and Tuba. $16.00.

Amis, Kenneth. *Suite for Bass Tuba.* Seesaw Music Corporation. Tuba, Violin, Viola, Violoncello, 3 Flutes, Piano, 3 Percussion. 1987. $26.00. 7:00. IV. B♭$_2$–f'. Five movements: Pastorale; Anima; Agitato; Impromptu; Allegro. Each of the five movements consists of a different instrumental combination (1. tuba and piano; 2. tuba and percussion; 3.tuba and flutes; 4. tuba and strings; 5. tuba and full ensemble) accompanying the tuba in traditional tonal idioms. Except for the wide range of the brief cadenza at the end of the fifth movement, the tuba part lies very comfortably below and in the staff and is mostly diatonic.

Anderson, Eugene. *Baroque 'n Brass.* Cimarron Music and Productions. Trumpet and Tuba. 5:00. Commissioned by and dedicated to David L. Aubuchon. A delightful duet that displays both lyric and technical gestures. Requires virtuoso performers. Recorded by Timothy Morrison and Samuel Pilafian.

Anderson, Eugene. *Baroque 'n Jazz Trio.* Cimarron Music and Productions. Tuba, Clarinet, and Drums. 2004. 4:30. IV. D_1–f'. Single movement. Dedicated to Samuel Pilafian. Dixieland style.

Anderson, Eugene. *The Bass'n Blues.* Cimarron Music and Productions. Tuba, Clarinet, Tenor Saxophone, String Bass, and Drums. 2004. 3:20. IV. C_1–g'. Single movement. Dedicated to Samuel Pilafian. Jazz.

Anderson, Eugene. *Fugue for Low Brass Trio.* Anderson's Arizona Originals. Horn, Trombone, Tuba. 1988. $6.00. 4:30. III. G_1–b♭'. Lack of rests could present endurance problems for less developed players. A good opportunity for three players to work on matching style.

Anderson, Eugene. *Quintuple Overlays.* Anderson's Arizona Originals. 2 Trumpets, 2 Euphoniums, 2 Tubas, 3 Percussion (Snare Drum; Cymbals; Timpani). 1988. $9.00. 2:30. III–IV. Tuba I: D♯–c♯'; Tuba II: D_1–g. An interesting instrumental combination, literally an extended tuba-euphonium ensemble with percussion. Tonal and melodic aspects are very conventional. Tuba II part requires good technique below the staff, going down to pedal D.

Applebaum, Allyson Brown. *Premises.* MMB Music, Inc. Solo Tuba, 2 Trumpets, 2 Horns, 2 Trombones, Narrator or pre-recorded narration. 1984. Rental from the publisher. 10:00. IV–V. D_1–g'. Three movements: Emergence; Point of Departure; Elements. A well-written modern piece, melodic in overall character. Although unlike a renaissance canzona, the first movement has a contrapuntal flavor. The second movement is a tuba cadenza accompanying the reading of a poem (by live or pre-recorded speaker). The final movement is comprised of melodic fragments and gestures. There are several avant-garde techniques required of the tubist, including limited double stops and "pitch boxes" in which notes are given for the player to play with varied rhythms and articulations.

Arban, Jean Baptiste. *Variations on the "Carnival of Venice."* arr. Richard Domek. Available from Richard Domek. Solo Tuba and Woodwind Quintet (this arrangement also available for Solo Tuba and Piano, Solo Tuba and Chamber Orchestra). 1982. 8:00. V. C–d' (B♭)'. For Skip Gray. This arrangement is in the key of B♭ and is well suited to the F tuba. Contains interesting new material in the accompanying episodes between solo sections. Well scored for the accompanying woodwind quintet.

Arban, Jean-Baptiste. *Carnival of Venice.* arr. Staffan Lundén Velden. Ovation. Tuba and Brass Quintet. 2002. 8:00. V. $A♭_1$–a♭'. $41.97. An extremely technically demanding variation piece based on an easy folk melody.

Arban, Jean-Baptiste. *Der Carneval von Venedig (Carnival of Venice).* arr. John Challis. Musikverlag Bruno Uetz. Solo Tuba in Brass Quintet. 1994. 8:00. V. C–d'. This arrangement is in the key of B♭ and is well suited for the F or E♭ tuba. Scored well for the accompanying brass.

Arensky, Anton. *Serenade No. 3 for 3 Trombones and Tuba, Opus 39.* ed. Keith Brown. International Music Company. 3 Trombones and Tuba. $5.50.

Aronson, Lee. *Suite for Tuba and Electric Guitar.* Tuba-Euphonium Press. 2000. $12.00. 9:30. III. $B♭_1$–f. Four movements: Allemande; Courante; Sarabande; Gigue. Dedicated to Rodger Vaughan. A collection of four dances in baroque style with traditional harmonies. Demonstrates effective use of two-part contrapuntal writing. Unusual instrument combination.

Arrigo, G. *Petit Requiem.* Aldo Bruzzichelli. Horn, Trombone, Tuba, Violin, Cello, Bass, Piano, Percussion. Score $10.00.

Asheim, Nils Henrik. *Scream Soft.* Music Information Centre Norway. Tuba and Percussion. 15:00.

Baadsvik, Øystein. *Déjà vu.* Ovation. Solo Tuba and Big Band. $36.90. The name of this piece comes from the fact that the theme was not composed tone by tone. Baadsvik wrote, "When the theme came to me it felt like I had heard it several times before. I checked with some friends to find out if this actually was an existing piece of music. It turned out to be new! My first experience simply was a 'Déjà vu.'" Available for Solo Tuba and Wind Band, Solo Tuba and Brass Band.

Baadsvik, Øystein. *FNUGG.* Ovation. Tuba, String Quartet, Jazz Piano. $12.88. Originally for unaccompanied tuba. An improvisational work with elements from the Australian Aboriginal didgeridoo and Norwegian folk music. The techniques involved are multiphonics and Baadsvik's own invention, "lip beat" (percussive tuba). *Fnugg* is a Norwegian work describing something very small and weightless. Available for Tuba and Brass Band. Recorded by Øystein Baadsvik.

Bach, J. S. *Bach Duets for B-flat and Bass Clef Instruments.* arr. Branch. Accentuate Music. Trumpet and Tuba (or Trombone). $4.95.

Bach, J. S. *Bandinerie.* arr. Jan Koetsier. Donemus. Tuba, 2 Trumpets, Horn, Trombone. IV.

Bach, J. S. *Contrapunctus I from "Art of Fugue."* arr. Lewis Waldeck. Cor Publishing Company. Trumpet, Horn, Trombone, Tuba. $4.00.

Bach, J. S. *Goldberg Suite from "Aria with Thirty Variations."* arr. Arthur Frackenpohl. TUBA

Press. Horn and Tuba. 1989. $7.00. 8:50. III–IV. F_1–e♭'. Four movements: Overture; Canon; Gigue; Finale. For Phil Myers and Warren Deck. Good music which works well for the combination of horn and tuba. A musical challenge for seasoned professionals as well as students.

Bach, J. S. *Motet, BWV 118.* Nichols Music Company. 2 Trumpets, 2 Horns, Trombone, Tuba and Voices. $10.00.

Bach, J. S. *Prelude et Fugue, BWV 549.* arr. Fabrice Chollet. Editions Fertile Plaine, France. Solo Tuba; Choir 1: 2 Trumpets and 2 Trombones; Choir 2: 2 Trumpets, Horn, Trombone. 2004. IV. C–c'. A nice arrangement that is very playable by a college student. Accompanying parts are not difficult and do not cause any balance problems for the soloist.

Bach, J. S. *Two Choruses from the Motet "Jesu, meine Freude."* arr. Lowell E. Shaw. The Hornists Nest. Four Horns and Tuba (or Five Horns). 1970. $4.00. 4:45. III. B_1–a. Two movements: Andante; Allegro non tanto—Andante. An effective arrangement for five horns (the tuba is a substitute part for Horn 4).

Bach, Jan. *Quintet for Solo Tuba and Strings.* TUBA Press. Solo Tuba and String Quartet. 1978. $30.00. 23:00. IV–V. E_1–b'. Four movements: Introit; Scherzo in moto perpetuo; Chaconne; Ripresa e fandango. To Harvey Phillips. A notey work with little gratification for the soloist. Interesting string writing adds great coloristic effect. A demanding work for all members of the quintet. See: Bird, Gary, ed.; *Program Notes for the Solo Tuba.*

Bach, P. D. Q. (Peter Schickele). *"Dutch" Suite in G Major.* Theodore Presser Company. Bassoon and Tuba. 1980. $5.50. 10:00. III–IV. C_1–e'. Four movements: Mr. Minuit's Minuet; Panther Dance; Dance of the Grand Dams; The Lowland Fling. For Ellen Brinkman and Jon Jackson. A work laden with the typical compositional humor of Peter Schickele. A challenge for the tubist to balance artistically with the bassoon. Recorded by Ronald Bishop.

Bach, P. D. Q. (Peter Schickele). *The Only Piece Written for Violin and Tuba.* Theodore Presser Company. Tuba and Violin. 2003. $9.95. 7:30. IV–V. Four movements: Andante Alighieri; Shake Allegro; Lento nice 'n' easyo; Allegro, but not too mucho. Reviewed in the Fall 2003 issue of the *ITEA Journal* (Vol. 31, No. 1).

Bach, P. D. Q. (Peter Schickele). *Trio Sonata.* Theodore Presser Company. 2 Flutes, Tambourine, and Tuba. $7.95.

Baer, Howard J., arr. *Amazing Grace.* Sonante Publications. 2 Trumpets, Trombone, Tuba. 1989. $5.50. 2:45. II–III. B♭–a. An easy, conventional brass quartet arrangement with two tasteful variation sections.

Baker, David. *Sonata for Tuba and String Quartet.* MMB Music, Inc. Tuba and String Quartet. 1982. $24.95. 18:30. IV. C_1–f♯'. Four movements: Slow-Moderato; Easy Swing "Blues"; Very Slow; Fast. To Harvey Phillips. An extensive solo work for the tubist. Although individual string parts are not extremely difficult, extended harmonies and shifting meters make adequate rehearsal time a requisite. See: Bird, Gary, ed.; *Program Notes for the Solo Tuba.* Recorded by Harvey Phillips.

Bakke, Ruth. *Rock Bottom.* Norwegian Music Information Center. Tuba and Timpani. 1988. 12:00. IV–V. Absence of bar lines makes this a very free piece in terms of rhythm.

Baldwin, David. *Divertimento for Flute and Tuba.* Cleveland Chamber Music Publishers. Flute and Tuba. 1973. 9:00. IV. A_2–e'. Three movements: Largo-mysterioso, Allegro; Andante espressivo; Quasi pomposo, Allegro vivo. For Kenneth and Elizabeth Singleton. Modern music for flute and tuba with wide irregular leaps and rhythms, nonmetered aleatoric passages, and avant-garde effects including long rips, screaming through the tuba, pitch bends, flutter tonguing, and feet stomps.

Baldwin, David. *Last Days, The.* Philharmusica Corporation. Horn and Tuba. 1974. $10.00. 8:00. IV. C_1–b♭'. A modern, interactive dialogue work with some difficult cross-rhythms between the parts and a limited number of effects including glissandi, flutter tonguing, pitch bending, and kicking over music stands.

Banco, Gerhart. *Trio in 4 Styles.* Edition Helbling. Trumpet, Tenor Horn (or Trombone), and Tuba. $18.00. Four movements: A la invention; Adagio espressivo; Sehr lebhaft; Mäßig rasch, musikantisch. The four movements are each written in the style of a specific composer: J. S. Bach, Beethoven, and Bruckner.

Baratto, Paolo. *Hoch und Tief.* Editions BIM. Piccolo Flute, Tuba, and Piano. 1993 (1975). 4:00. I–II. B♭$_1$–e♭. Simple fantasy variations on a well-known Swiss folksong. Appropriate for a junior high school recital. Parts in bass clef concert pitch, or in treble clef in E♭ or B♭.

Barber, Clarence. *Theme and Variations for Tuba and Percussion.* Music for Percussion, Inc. Tuba and Percussion (Single player requiring 4 Timpani, 3 Glass Bowls, Ice Bell, Bongo, Small Tamtam, Bucket of Water, Wind Gong). 1987. $4.00. 6:20. IV. G_1–f'. Theme and four variations (Lightly; Freely; Serenely; Barbaric, driving). To Mark Carson and Gilbert Corella. A well-written work which uses the instruments idiomatically. A limited amount of poly-rhythms. The tubist is required to perform several avant-garde effects including some easy double stops and flutter tonguing. Mute is required.

Barber, Clarence. *Uriel: A Flourish of Joy.* Great Works Publishing, Inc. Euphonium, Tuba, and Percussion (Vibraphone, Snare Drum, 4 Tom-toms, Bass Drum). 1993. 5:30. III–IV.

Euphonium: F–c''; Tuba: F♯$_1$–g. The high tessitura of the euphonium part and constantly shifting meters make this nicely written, tuneful piece deceivingly difficult. The percussion part is playable by a single performer.

Barboteu, Georges. *Divertissement for Tuba and Brass Quartet.* Editions Choudens. Solo Tuba, 2 Trumpets, Horn, and Trombone. 1973. $27.75. 2:30. V. Dedicated to E. Raynaud. Recorded by Walter Hilgers.

Bartles, Alfred. *Beersheba Neo-Baroque Suite.* Brass Press. Tuba and Cello (or Euphonium, Trombone). 1975. $5.00. 7:30. III–IV. D$_1$–e'. Four movements: Prelude; Gavotte; Sarabande; Gigue-Postlude. To R. Winston Morris. A well-written duet in baroque style idiomatically suited for any of the instrumental combinations. See also listing under Music for Multiple Tubas.

Bashmakov, Leonid. *Mutu.* Tuba-Euphonium Press. Solo Tuba, Woodwind Quintet, and Percussion. 1999. $30.00. 8:00. IV. F$_1$–a'. Nine short sections are played continuously. Commissioned by the Tubists Universal Brotherhood Association (TUBA) in 1997. Premiered by Harri Miettunen and the Tampere Philharmonic Orchestra in 2000. The range and technical demands are challenging for all players involved. The extreme high register playing is well written and approached in a scalar fashion. Trills and quintuplet and sextuplet passages are used frequently. An excellent addition to the repertoire. Available for Solo Tuba and Piano. Reviewed in the Fall 2001 issue of the *ITEA Journal* (Vol. 29, No. 1).

Bassett, Leslie. *Nonet.* C. F. Peters Corporation. Flute, Oboe, Clarinet, Bassoon, Trumpet, Horn, Trombone, Tuba, and Piano. $17.05.

Baxley, W. S. *Chorale in E Major.* Clark-Baxley Publications. Horn, Trombone, Euphonium, and Tuba. $7.25.

Beach, Bennie. *Dance Suite for Tuba and Triangle.* Neil A. Kjos Music Co. Tuba and Triangle. 1978. $5.00. 6:00. III–IV. A$_1$–d'. Three movements: Cracovienne; Roundance; Jazz. Dedicated to Barton Cummings. Wide intervallic leaps and shifting tonal centers produce primary difficulties in this work comprised of three movements of well-contrasted character. Recorded by Barton Cummings.

Becker, Günther. *Un poco giocoso—Konzertante Szenen für Baßtuba und Kammerensemble.* Breitkopf & Härtel. Solo Tuba and Chamber Ensemble (Flute, Oboe, Clarinet, Bassoon, Horn, Trumpet, Trombone, Percussion, Harp, Piano, Violin, Viola, Cello, Bass). 1983. Rental from the publisher. 20:00. V. B♭$_2$–f'. Continuous multisection work. Dedicated to Dr. Wilfried Brennecke. Premiered by Melvyn Poore and the Düsseldorf Chamber Ensemble. A difficult and powerful work for both tubist and ensemble members. In addition to standard notation of music, the soloist is asked to ad lib, flutter tongue, produce wide glissandos, sing and play, mutter vocal sounds, and play the tuba with a saxophone mouthpiece and bassoon reed.

Beethoven, Ludwig van. *Excerpt from the "Appassionata Sonata."* arr. J. Strautman. Valentin Avvakoumov. Solo Tuba and 4 Trombones. 1986. 0:45. II–III. G$_1$(E♭$_1$)–c. A nice little arrangement featuring the tuba in the "bread and butter" register.

Beethoven, Ludwig van. *Joyful, Joyful.* arr. Howard J. Baer. Sonante Publications. 2 Trumpets, Trombone, Tuba (or Bass Trombone). 1982. $5.50. 2:00. II. F$_1$–g. An easy arrangement of the "Song of Joy" from Beethoven's ninth symphony.

Belden, George. *They All Have Flown Away.* Manuscript available from the composer. Tuba, Horn, and Percussion (Single player requiring Marimba, 4 Tom-toms, Suspended Cymbals, Maracas, Triangle, and Tambourine). 1978. 8:10. III–IV. F$_1$–d'. Commissioned by and dedicated to Sue Hudson and Mark Wolfe. The work in three large connected sections is traditionally notated and contains idiomatically written parts for all three players. A good chamber music work.

Bennet, Roy, and Sid Tepper. *Nuttin' for Christmas.* arr. Paul Frederick. Chappell & Co. Solo Tuba in Brass Quintet. 1996. 1:30. III. A$_1$–g. A nice, light arrangement for a holiday concert. Accompanying parts are not difficult.

Bennett, Malcolm. *Tuba Concerto No. 2.* Available from the composer. Solo Tuba and Brass Band. 18:45. IV. D$_1$–b'. Three movements: Allegro; Adagio; Allegro. A very nice, listenable piece with a lot of repetition. The solo part is playable by most college-level players. Available for Tuba and Piano.

Benson, Warren. *Canon.* Carl Fischer. Tuba and Hand Drum. 1971. $10.00. 3:15. IV. Approximate pitch notation used with all notes being in or slightly above the staff. Single movement. Commissioned by Harvey Phillips in memory of William Bell. The tubist creates only percussive effects throughout including half-valve pitches, pitches sung into the horn, fingernail on the bell, horn slaps, etc., in this canonic duet with hand drum.

Bentzon, Niels Viggo. *Micro-Trio, Opus 573.* Edition Wilhelm Hansen. Percussion, Cello, and Tuba. 1993. 10:00. IV. F$_1$–g♯'. Dedicated to the Slaatto Brothers. Single movement in several sections.

Berg, Fred Jonny. *Beyond Mystic Forest, Op. 12.* Music Information Centre Norway. Trumpet, Tuba and Piano. 1992. 3:00.

Bergsma, W. *Suite.* Carl Fischer. 2 Trumpets, Trombone, and Tuba. $6.50.

Bernstein, Leonard. *Fanfare for Bima.* Boosey & Hawkes. Trumpet, Horn, Trombone, and Tuba. $8.50. 1:00. III–IV.

Blahnik, J. *Die Weinhnacht—Christmas.* GIA Publications, Inc. 2 Trumpets, Trombone, and Tuba. $7.00.

Blank, Allan. *American Medley.* Associated Music Publishers. Flute, 2 Trumpets, Horn, Trombone, Tuba, and Percussion. $22.50.

Bliss, P. P. *Wonderful Words.* arr. Howard J. Baer. Sonante Publications. 2 Trumpets, Trombone, Tuba. 1989. $5.50. 1:45. II. E♭ (E♭$_1$)–g. A good, simple church arrangement.

Blum, Thomas. *Confutatis.* Swedish Music Information Center. Soprano, Tuba, and Piano. 1992. 5:00. For Kerstin Pettersson, Mattias Johansson, and Mattias Gummesson.

Blumenfeld, A. *Trio Sonata.* T.A.P. Music Sales. Flute, Tuba, and Piano. $22.00.

Bogar, I. *Three Movements.* Editio Musica Budapest. 2 Trumpets, Trombone, and Tuba. $12.50.

Bortnyansky, Dmitry. *Sacred Concerto No. 15.* arr. V. Pachkayev. Parow'sche Musikalien. Three Trombones and Tuba. 4:56. Recorded by the Russian National Symphony Orchestra Low Brass Section.

Börtz, Daniel. *Winter Pieces 1.* Swedish Music Information Center. Tuba, Piano, and Percussion. 1981–82. 8:00.

Bradbury, William B. *Just As I Am.* arr. Gordon A. Adnams. Sonante Publications. Cornet, Flugelhorn, Euphonium, and Tuba. 1982. $5.50. 1:20. I–II. B♭ (E♭$_1$)–e♭. A very easy devotional piece arranged for all conical instruments but playable by alternative instrumentation (trumpets, trombone).

Brahms, Johannes. *Three Songs from Opus 62.* arr. Howland. Touch of Brass Publications. Trumpet, Horn, Trombone, and Tuba. $9.00.

Brandon, Sy. *Serenade for Oboe and Tuba.* Co-op Press. Oboe and Tuba. 1979. $4.00. 3:00. III–IV. F$_1$–e♭'. One continuous movement with three sections. To Harry and Betty Hewitt. Some interesting music; very poor quality of manuscript produces greatest performance difficulty.

Brandon, Sy. *Summer Suite for Oboe and Tuba.* Co-op Press. Oboe and Tuba. 1987. $6.00. 8:45. IV. F$_1$–f'. Four movements: Rain Dance; Garden Serenade; Harvest Dance; Celebration Dance. For Anita. "An exploration of the use of the twelve tones around a changing tonal center."

Brandon, Sy. *Three Amusement Park Pieces.* Co-op Press. Tuba and Percussionist. 1988. $4.00. 4:15. III–IV. G$_1$–e'. Three movements: Shooting Gallery; Carousel; Rollercoaster. Three light, contrasting pieces. Several wide intervallic leaps for the tubist, but mostly diatonic writing in dialogue with the percussionist.

Breit, Stan, and Ward, Norman. *The Boy Who Wanted a Tuba—A Christmas Story.* Byron-Douglas Publications. Flute, Clarinet, Trumpet, Tuba, and Narrator. 1971. 3:00. I–II. F–D'. A simple yet cute story with small ensemble geared towards young children.

Briegel, George F., arr. *Im Tiefen Keller.* George F. Briegel. Solo Tuba (or Trombone) and 3 Trumpets. 1937. Out of Print. 3:00. III. F–f'. A traditional tuba solo with trumpet accompaniment. Trumpet parts are not difficult and contain nice fanfare introduction and interlude.

Broege, Timothy. *Benedictus.* Allaire Music Publications. Mezzo-soprano or Contralto Voice, Tuba, and Piano. 1971. 4:30. IV–V. D$_1$–f'. One continuous movement. Composed for Gary and Barbara Shulze. "In memory of my Father." Except for three very difficult measures in the tuba part consisting of wide intervallic leaps, the tuba part is not extremely difficult. Sensitive playing is a requisite so that the voice and transparent piano are not overshadowed.

Brott, A. *World Sophisticate.* Berandol Music. 2 Trumpets, Horn, Trombone, Tuba, Soprano, and Percussion. $12.50.

Broughton, Bruce. *Bipartition for Tuba and Cello.* Available from the composer. Tuba and Amplified Cello. 1980. 7:00. V. G♭$_1$–a'. Two movements, basically a "theme" and seven variations. The tubist and cellist are presented with a variety of challenges including rhythmic diversity, wide intervals, extended range, and dynamic contrasts. For Keith and Tommy Johnson. The composer suggests the use of F tuba for the work. Reviewed in the Spring 1992 issue of the *TUBA Journal* (Vol. 19, No. 3).

Brown, Jonathan Bruce. *Strata: Five Pieces for Percussion Quintet and Tuba.* Seesaw Music Corporation. 5 Percussionists (Playing: 5 Timpani, Vibraphone, Orchestra Chimes, Suspended Cymbals, Mixing Bowls, Claves, Wood Blocks, Bongos, Piccolo Snare Drum, Bass Drum, Marimba) and Tuba. 1974. $19.00. 10:45. III–IV. E♭$_1$–d'. Five movements: Andante; Moderately Slow, Reflective; Allegro con fuoco; Lento Espressivo; Allegro Moderato, Maestoso. An extensive percussion ensemble work with a non-strenuous tuba obligato which serves as an effective coloristic addition. Tuba part is not technically demanding.

Brown, Newel Kay. *Silhouettes.* Seesaw Music Corporation. Trumpet and Tuba. 1978. 6:30. IV. A$_1$–f♯'. Continuous work in seven sections. To Robert Levy and Robert Yeats. Each of the work's sections are in a contrasting character, from the chant-like opening to non-specific, chance music dialogues.

Brown, Newell Kay. *Dialogue and Dance.* Seesaw Music Corporation. Trombone and Tuba. $11.00.

Brown, Newell Kay. *Windart 1.* Seesaw. Tuba, Soprano, Piano. 1978. $17.00. 9:00. IV–V. E♭$_1$–a♭'. Continuous work in seven sections. For Cherry Beauregard. Text based on the poem "Leben" by G. Meurer. Difficult yet expressive chamber music in a non-tonal setting.

Brown, Raynor. *6 Fugues.* Western International Music. Horn, Trombone, and Tuba. 1969. $9.00. 13:00. III–IV. E_1–d'. There are few technical problems presented in this music, which contains no tempo markings and very few expressive indications. The trombone has the most difficult part with a range of $B\flat_1$–c''. Endurance could also be a problem as there are very few rests.

Brown, Raynor. *Variations.* Western International Music. 2 Trumpets, Horn, Trombone, Tuba, and Piano. 1973. $15.00. 18:40. III–IV. G_1–b. Theme and ten variations. For Sharon Davis. The piano part, while not incredibly difficult, is the most demanding writing of this interesting, modern chamber music work.

Brün, Herbert. *'twice upon three times . . .'* Smith Publications. Bass Clarinet and Tuba. 1988. 4:30. V. B_2–a'. Three movements. Interesting timbral effects resultant from orchestration and harmonic intervals between bass clarinet and tuba parts. Difficulties imposed upon the tubist include wide, non-tonal leaps and balancing the volume level of the bass clarinet to attain the composer's desired sonorities.

Bury, Peter, arranger. *Deep Down in the Cellar—Demonstration Piece for Tuba.* Camara Music Publishers. Solo Tuba in Brass Quintet. 1966. $7.50. 3:00. III. $B\flat_2$–g. A good, light arrangement of the traditional tuba solo. Accompanying parts are not difficult and do not cause any balance problems for the soloist.

Buss, H. J. *Sonic Fables.* Brixton Publications. 2 Trumpets, Horn, Trombone, Tuba, and Percussion. $27.50.

Buss, H. J. *Trigon.* Brixton Publications. Trumpet, Trombone, and Tuba. $17.00.

Cahn, William L. *Quiet Music.* HoneyRock. Tuba, Timpani and Percussion. 1977. $20.00. 12:30. IV. E_1–f'. Dedicated to Cherry Beauregard. The piece is centered around an interplay of timbres between the tuba and timpani, contrasted against the high pitched sounds of metallic percussion (chimes, crotales, tam tam, tuned gongs, sleighbells, and suspended glockenspiel). The music tends to the contemplative rather than the bombastic possibilities of the ensemble.

Capuzzi, Antonio. *Concerto for Double Bass.* arr. Jim Self. Basset Hound Music. Solo Tuba, 2 Trumpets, Horn, Tenor Trombone, Bass Trombone (or Euphonium). 1993. 14:45. IV. F_1–g'. Three movements: Allegro moderato; Andante cantabile; Rondo Allegro. The complete concerto, of which only the Andante and Rondo (second and third movements) are usually performed, is nicely arranged for solo tuba with brass quintet. The key is changed from the standard version to B♭, which, because of the higher tessitura, lies much better on the F or E♭ tuba. Third movement recorded by Jim Self.

Carion, M. *Toccata Sax.* J. Maurer Editions Musicales. Saxophone and Tuba. $7.95.

Carolino, Sergio. *Lili's Funk.* arr. Adelino Mota. Lusitanus Editions, Portugal. Solo Tuba and Big Band. 2004. 7:00. V. C_1–f''. A funk-style piece with a strong bass line. Requires improvisation. A very energetic and rhythmic piece. Recorded by Sergio Carolino.

Carpenter, Bud. *Basso Bossa.* Swing Lane Publications. Tuba (or Bass Trombone, Bassoon), Guitar, Bass, Piano (Vibes, Accordion, and/or Electric Guitar), Drums. 1963. 2:15. II–III. C–g. A good little piece for tuba and rhythm section.

Casterede, Jacques. *Prelude et Danse.* Alphonse Leduc. 3 Trombones, Tuba, Piano, Percussion. $37.00.

Chamberlin, Robert. *Daysong.* Available from the composer. Tuba, Marimba, and Tape. 1985. 9:30. IV. $D\flat_1$–g'. Single-movement work. For Scott and Mary Watson. Most of this work, which can be described as a "sound piece," is in non-metered, time-delineated sections. In addition to normal pitch material, the tuba is required to perform several effects, including producing wind sounds, singing, double stops, and playing sub-tones. This piece could serve as a good introduction to contemporary performance styles for a younger student as there are no great technical difficulties except for a few isolated high note entrances. See: Bird, Gary, ed.; *Program Notes for the Solo Tuba.*

Chihara, P. *Willow, Willow.* C. F. Peters Corporation. Tuba, Amplified Bass Flute, 3 Percussion. 1968. $14.50. 8:00. IV. C–f'. Four movements. To Sheridan Stokes. The amplified bass flute is featured in this sound piece whose largest demand on the tubist is putting together their part within the ensemble.

Childs, Barney. *Mary's Idea.* Seesaw Music Corporation. Tuba and Harpsichord. $10.00. See: Bird, Gary, ed.; *Program Notes for the Solo Tuba.* Also see listing under Tuba and Keyboard.

Childs, Barney. *A Question of Summer for Tuba and Harp.* Composers Facsimile Edition. Tuba and Harp. 1976. 9:20. IV–V. C_1–b'. One continuous movement. Commissioned by Ivan Hammond. Although both parts are precisely notated, there is a great deal of truly independent activity taking place between the tuba and harp. This is chamber music in which the performers need to not listen to each other much of the time. Contains jazz influences and some avant-garde effects. See: Bird, Gary, ed.; *Program Notes for the Solo Tuba.* Recorded by Ivan Hammond.

Christensen, James. *Ballad for Tuba.* Whaling Music. Solo Tuba and Brass Ensemble. $12.00. 2:30. IV.

Coles, G. *Chorale Variations on Oh Sacred Head Sore and Wounded.* Berandol Music. 2 Trumpets, Trombone, and Tuba. $12.50.

Corwell, Neal. *Denali.* Tuba-Euphonium Press. Euphonium, Tuba, String Quartet, and Piano. 1998. $35.00. 12:00. IV. D_1–d♭'. Commissioned by the Garrett Lakes Arts Festival, Erick Friedman, music director. Also known as Mount McKinley, the highest peak in North America was called by the Alaska Natives "Denali," which means "the high one." The music attempts to express the sense of awe one may feel while contemplating the strength, beauty, and majesty of the peak.

Corwell, Neal. *Drum Taps.* Tuba-Euphonium Press. Solo Tuba with Horn, Euphonium, and Drums. 2002. $15.00. 11:45. IV. F_1–g'. Written for Velvet M. Brown and Julianne Fish. Inspired by "Drum Taps," a collection of poems penned by Walt Whitman and based upon his experiences during the American Civil War.

Corwell, Neal. *Zeke and Zebedee.* Tuba-Euphonium Press. Solo Tuba (or Euphonium) and Narrator. 1995. $10.00. 6:30. III. C_1–b♭. A fun "little ditty" about a serious subject. The narration tells the story of two men, Zeke and Zebedee. Zeke is a farmer and Zebedee is a musician. There is a great deal of interaction between the two parts as the tuba (or euphonium) paints much of what the narrator is reciting. The piece includes a number of musical quotes from Bach to rock. Corwell includes several theatrical instructions. Strong technical skills are required. Reviewed in the Spring 2002 issue of the *ITEA Journal* (Vol. 29, No. 3).

Couperin, F. *Les Ondes.* arr. Krzywicki. Theodore Presser Company. Trombone (or Baritone) and Tuba. $7.50.

Cummings, Barton. *Song of the Trouveres.* Tuba and Self-Played Percussion. See listing under Unaccompanied Tuba.

Curnow, Jim. *Variations on an Aboriginal Melody.* TUBA Press. Tuba and Woodwind Quintet. 1982. $20.00. 10:00. IV–V. E_1–g'. Four movements: Allegro con Spirito; Andante moderato con espressivo; Allegro Giocoso; Allegro con Energetico. For Skip Gray. A melodic tour de force for solo tuba within the accompanying woodwind quintet.

D'Almeida, António Victorino. *O número do Trapézio.* Lusitanus Editions, Portugal. Tuba and Piccolo. 1991. 2:30. V. G–g'. This is a very nice piece written as a circus number. Wide intervals. Good agility and flexibility are required from the tubist.

Danielsson, Christer. *Little Suite for Four Brass.* Throre Ehrling Musik AB.Trombone, Trombone (or Horn), Trombone (or Baritone), and Tuba (or Bass Trombone). 1972. $22.50. 8:00. III–IV. Part I: d–c"; Part II: d♭–a'; Part III: A♭–d'; Part IV: A_1–e♭. Three movements: Moderato; Lento; Scherzo. Tuneful work with a great deal of pop-jazz influences. Because of the general high tessitura of all parts, this piece also works well played by tuba-euphonium ensemble.

Danielsson, Crister. *Capriccio da Camera.* Nordiska Musikförlag. Solo Tuba, 2 Trumpets, Horn, 2 Trombones. 1976. 6:45. IV. A_1–f'. One continuous movement in three sections. Dedicated to Michael Lind and the Stockholm Philharmonic Brass ensemble. A tuneful, brief showpiece for the solo tuba. Recorded by Michael Lind, Walter Hilgers, and Finn Schumacker.

Danielsson, Crister. *Suite Concertante.* Gehrmans Musikförlag. Tuba and four horns (alternate parts also for other brass instrument combinations). 1977. 12:30. IV. F♯$_1$–e'. Four movements: Largo—Allegro Vivo; Moderato misterioso; Andante con Sentimento; Alla Marcia. Composed for Michael Lind and the First Swedish Tuba Workshop. Nice, melodic music, scored very effectively, showcasing both the solo tubist and horns. Recorded by Michael Lind, Walter Hilgers, and Markus Hötzel.

Davidson, John. *Sonata.* T.A.P. Music Sales. Trombone, Tuba, and Piano. $18.00.

Deason, David. *Sy-Anita Suite for Tuba and Oboe.* TUBA Press. Oboe and Tuba. $5.00. 4:00. B_1–e♭'. Three movements: Andante; Lento; Allegretto. Contains shifting meters and some wide intervallic leaps.

DeCosta, Harry, and the Original Dixieland Band. *Tuba Tiger Rag.* arr. Luther Henderson. Brassworks Music (G. Schirmer). Tuba in Brass Quintet. $34.00. 5:00. III. F_1 (B♭$_2$)–b♭ (c'). Recorded by the Canadian Brass.

Degtyaryov, Stepan. *Christmas Concerto.* arr. A. Skobelev. Parow'sche Musikalien. Three Trombones and Tuba. 4:27. Recorded by the Russian National Symphony Orchestra Low Brass Section.

Diemente, E. *Forms of Flight.* Smith Publications. 2 Trumpets, Horn, Trombone, Tuba, Soprano. $35.50.

Diercks, John. *Figures on China.* Theodore Presser Company. Horn, Trombone, and Tuba. $4.00.

Doane, William H. *To God Be the Glory.* arr. Howard J. Baer. Sonante Publications. 2 Trumpets, Trombone, Tuba (or Bass Trombone). 1978. $5.50. 2:15. II–III. A_1–b♭.

Dorsey, A. *Brass Music II.* MS Publications. 2 Trumpets, Trombone, and Tuba. $6.00.

Dresser, Mark. *Althaus.* DelDresser. Tuba, Clarinet, Cello, Alto Saxophone, String Bass. 2000. $25.00. 18:00. V. D_1–b♭'. Commissioned by and dedicated to David LeClair. Mark Dresser: "*Althaus* aims to explore various expressive areas of the instrument, i.e. the sonic potentials of tuba as timbre generator, focused improvised transitions within thematic writing, a virtuoso cadenza over an odd meter groove and lastly the lyric potential of the tuba over a harmonic progression." Improvisation and an entire palette of contemporary techniques are required.

Dresser, Mark. *Loss of the Innocents.* DelDresser. Clarinet, Cello, Tuba. 1997. $15.00. 9:00. V. C_1–highest note possible. In memory of the innocent victims of TWA flight 800. Mark Dresser: "I worked closely with the tubist, Marcus Rojas, clarinetist Chris Speed, and cellist Erik Friedlander in the composition. The clarinet part is written with a melismatic style and microtonal ornamentation inspired by the great Balkan clarinet tradition. The tuba integrates some dramatic extremes of the instrument."

Druckman, Jacob. *Dark upon the Harp.* Theodore Presser. 2 Trumpets, Horn, Trombone, Tuba, Soprano, and Percussion. Rental from the publisher (Score $4.00). V. A difficult, non-tonal work. The soprano must have perfect pitch.

Dubenski, Arcady. *Concerto Grosso.* Ricordi. 3 Trombones, Tuba, Orchestra. 1950. Orchestral accompaniment rental from the publisher. 6:30. III–IV. A_1–c♯'. Three movements (if played without orchestral accompaniment): Prelude; Toccata; Fugue. Five movements (if played with orchestral accompaniment): Introduction (Tacet for Solo Instruments); Prelude; Toccata; Interlude (Tacet for Solo Instruments); Fugue. A good neoclassical work which may be performed with or without the orchestral accompaniment. Written in the truly orchestral keys of A and E major.

Dubois, Rob. *Espaces a Remplir.* Donemus. 2 Clarinets, Saxophone, Trumpet, Trombone, Tuba, Bass, Piano, Vibraphone, Percussion. $30.00.

Dubois, Rob. *Trio Agitato.* Donemus. Horn, Trombone, and Tuba. 1969. $29.75. Indeterminate length. IV. G_1–f♯'. For Kees Blokker. A non-metered work with only pitch group successions given. Contemporary techniques required also include "approximate pitch notation" and flutter tonguing. There are a great number of wide leaps and mute is required.

Dutton, Brent. *Brass Trio.* Seesaw Music Corporation. Trumpet, Trombone, Tuba. 1968–71. $13.50. 4:30. IV. $E♭_1$–c'. Three movements: 7th. Yellow Song; Squelch; March for an Invalid. Conventional writing in the first and third movements. The second movement contains modern effects including flutter tonguing, gestures played "as fast as possible," wide glisses over the harmonic series, and simultaneous singing and playing.

Dutton, Brent. *Evidently, Occasional Music.* Seesaw Music. Cello, Double Bass, Tuba. 1973. $16.00. 8:45. IV. C–d'. Three movements: Muzerwug's Skither; Folktune; Ending. Written for Mark Jamison and Guy Fouquet. This work presents the tubist with various challenges, including rapidly shifting meters and balancing to a cellist and double bassist, as well as a brief improvisatory passage.

Dutton, Brent. *Tuba Concerto No. 1.* Seesaw Music Corporation. Tuba, 3 Trumpets, 3 Trombones, Percussion (single player on timpani and vibes), Piano. 1968. $50.00. 9:00. IV–V. C_1–g'. Three movements: Andante—Allegro; Andante; Allegro. A very challenging work which lies outside the bounds of common tonality. The tuba soloist encounters wide, irregular intervallic leaps as well as many changes in tempo and meter.

Dutton, Brent. *Tuba Concerto No. 2.* BrassQuake Press. Solo Tuba and Brass Ensemble. 1998. 15:00. IV–V. $E♭_1$–c''. Three movements. Composed for and premiered by Steve Rossé at ITEC 1998. The solo part (except for a couple of passages) as well as the brass ensemble parts are accessible to most college-level players. Nicely scored so that the soloist will be easily heard.

Dutton, Brent. *Tuesday Overture.* Seesaw Music Corporation. Tuba and Percussion. 1975. $15.00. 4:00. IV. D_1–d'. An interactive piece for percussionist and tuba with extensive avant-garde requirements for the tubist, including hissing sounds, simultaneous singing and playing, and improvised sections. Very little conventional pitch notation other than eight bars in D major and several other brief passages.

Edgerton, Michael E. *Ai.* Tuba-Euphonium Press. Trumpet in C, Trombone, Tuba. 1998. $15.00. 10:10. IV–V. $F♯_1$–a♭'. Dedicated to Jeffery Jarvis. Features the F tuba as a prominent melodic member alongside the trumpet and trombone. This piece was premiered by Phil Sinder (tuba), Curtis Olsen (trombone), and Kim Walker (trumpet) at Michigan State University in 1987. The work is in three broad sections in which two slower outer sections, featuring the high melodic F tuba intertwined in a three-part counterpoint of high lyricism, frame a central fast inner section. The piece is somewhat reminiscent of the American tradition of brass playing and writing.

Ellerby, Martin. *Epitaph V: Winter Music (Leningrad).* Studio Music Company, London. Solo Tuba, 2 Percussion, 2 Piano. 2002. 9:00. IV. $E♭_1$–g♭'. Written for James Gourlay. Recorded by James Gourlay.

Elvey, George J. *Crown Him with Many Crowns.* arr. Howard J. Baer. Sonante Publications. 2 Trumpets, Trombone, Tuba, or Bass Trombone. 1982. $5.50. 1:45. III. $G♭_1$–e♭'.

Erb, Donald. *Three Pieces.* Merion Music, Inc. 2 Trumpets, Horn, Trombone, Tuba, and Piano. 1973. 6:15. III–IV. B_1–a. Three movements. A contemporary work requiring effects including tapping on bell, muttering, hissing into instrument, kissing sounds, etc.

Faure, Gabriel. *Lydia.* Nichols Music Company. 2 Trumpets, Horn, and Tuba. $4.00.

Fauré, Gabriel. *Pavane.* arr. Walter Hilgers. Editions Marc Reift. Flute, Cello, Tuba, and Piano. 1995. 6:00. IV. G♯–f♯'. Originally for orchestra and choir, this is a chamber music arrangement, which treats all four instruments equally. Requires very light playing in the high tessitura. There are no technical difficulties.

Favre, Pascal. *Celebration.* Editions BIM. Flute, Clarinet, Alto Saxophone, 2 Trumpets, Trombone, Tuba, Timpani, and Percussion. 2000. 4:30.

II–III. B♭$_1$–c♭. Olivier Cuendet, Directuer du Conservatoire de musique de Lausanne. Composed for the 10th anniversary of the new building, the 40th anniversary of the department of dramatic arts, and the 140th anniversary of the foundation of the Conservatory in Lausanne, Switzerland. Well-written fanfare. Tuba is not featured.

Feldman, Enrique Cañez. *Sueños Negros.* Available from the composer. Tuba, Piano, Percussion (4 Tom-toms and Suspended Cymbal). 1991. 6:30. IV. B$_2$–g♭'. A dramatic, generally melodic work which, as the composer states in his preface, "is a musical depiction of the human mind during its dream state." Its high tessitura make performance on the F tuba advisable.

Feldman, Morton. *Durations III for Violin, Tuba, and Piano.* C. F. Peters Corporation. Violin, Tuba, and Piano. 1961. $15.00. 10:00. IV. F♯$_1$–g'. An example of "chance music." Tuba is muted throughout. Pitches are notated but rhythms are free. Recorded by Don Butterfield.

Fernandez, C. *Musical Confrontations.* Margun Music. Woodwind Quintet and Brass Quintet. $40.00.

Ferriano, Frank. *Nocturne.* Really Good Music, LLC. Tuba and String Quartet. 1998. $30.00. This combination of instruments results in surprisingly mellow music. Great for a break from an expanded version of the composer's *Nocturne for Tuba and Piano.* See listing under Tuba and Piano.

Filippi, Amedeo di. *Divertimento for Brass Duo.* Robert King Music Company. Baritone (or Horn) and Tuba. 1968. $5.85. 9:00. III. G$_1$–c'. Five movements: March; Intermezzo I; Tempo de Valse; Intermezzo II; Rondino. A straight-ahead little suite of tonal music.

Finko, David. *The Klezmers (One Act Opera).* Dako Publishers. Bass-baritone, Mezzo-soprano, 2 Violins, Double Bass, Clarinet, Cornet, Tuba, Percussion. 1989. 20:00. IV. F$_1$–d'. Dedicated to Dr. Lawrence Bernstein. An interesting little opera resplendent with glimpses of Jewish culture. As a member of the klezmer band, the tubist actually performs onstage and the part contains some difficult passages, especially those interplaying with the cornet.

Fischer, Ludwig. *Here I Sit in the Deep, Dark Cellar.* arr. John Beyrent. BVD Press. Brass Quintet featuring Tuba Solo. 2002. 3:00. IV. F$_1$–f'. Theme and variations. A good, light arrangement. Accompanying parts are not difficult. Nice recital material for a young artist.

Forbes, Michael. *Lullaby.* Tuba-Euphonium Press. Tuba and Euphonium Duet with Brass Tenet. 2001. $12.00. 5:30. IV. B♭–f'. This is a light yet effective piece that has several expressive lyrical themes effectively dispersed amongst the soloists and the ensemble. It is most appropriate for college students and professionals due to the range and endurance of the tuba solo, which remains in the high register for long periods of time. The tuba part is longer and more challenging than the euphonium part. The technical demands of both parts are not a problem due to the suggested tempo of the work (quarter note equals 68), the keys (E♭ and F major), and the smooth lines. Reviewed in the Fall 2003 issue of the *ITEA Journal* (Vol. 31, No. 1).

Fote, R. *12 Christmas Carols.* Kendor Publications, Inc. Trumpet, Horn (or Trombone), and Tuba (or Trombone). $19.50.

Frackenpohl, Arthur. *Air and Dance.* Tuba-Euphonium Press. Violin and Tuba. 1995. $8.00. 5:00. IV. G$_1$–d♭'. Commissioned by Eugene Dowdy and Christopher Radanovic. Written in memory of Catherine Radanovic. A tonal piece with a great deal of dialogue activity between the two parts.

Frackenpohl, Arthur. *Brass Duo.* Robert King Music Company. Horn (or Baritone) and Tuba. 1972. $5.55. 6:45. III. F$_1$–b♭. Four movements: Prelude; Ballad; Scherzo; Variations. Traditional writing with few difficulties except an occasional irregular rhythm and shifting meters. Reviewed in the Spring 1992 issue of the *TUBA Journal* (Vol. 20, No. 3).

Frackenpohl, Arthur. *Pop Suite No. 2.* Horizon Press. Trombone (or Euphonium) and Tuba. 1991.

Frackenpohl, Arthur. *Sonata for Trumpet, Tuba and Piano.* PP Music. Trumpet, Tuba, and Piano. 1977. For Ivan Hammond.

Frackenpohl, Arthur. *Song and Dance.* Horizon Publications. Tuba, Euphonium, and Piano. $10.00. See listing under Tuba and Band.

Frackenpohl, Arthur. *Three Dances for Horn and Tuba.* Tenuto Publications. Horn and Tuba. 1989. $7.00. 8:00. IV. G$_1$–c'. Three movements: Rag; Waltz; Bossa. For Phil Myers and Warren Deck. Light music with enough difficulty to make interesting recital material.

Frackenpohl, Arthur. *Tubarag.* Tuba-Euphonium Press. For Solo Tuba and Brass Quintet. 1999. $12.00. 3:00. For Anne Hardin and Andrew Hyman. Good for a young soloist on a recital. See listing under Tuba and Band.

Françaix, Jean. *Petite Valse Européenne.* B. Schott's Söhne. Tuba and Double Wind Quintet (Piano reduction available). 1979. Parts are rental from the publisher. 8:00. IV–V. G$_1$–a♭'. One continuous movement. "For my little son Eric." High tessitura and wide leaps permeate this brief, entertaining work. Certainly intended for the F tuba. Recorded by Christoph Schneider.

Franck, César. *Arioso from "L'Organist, Vol. 1."* tr. Howard J. Baer. Sonante Publications. 2 Trumpets, Trombone, Tuba (or Bass Trombone). 1982. $5.50. 1:45. II. E–e.

Frederickson, Thomas. *Tubalied.* Available from the composer. Solo Tuba and chamber ensemble (Piano reduction also available). V. D$_1$–f♯'. For

Daniel Perantoni. A very difficult, "new music" piece for solo tuba and chamber ensemble. Piano reduction is very difficult. Recorded by Dan Perantoni.

Friedman, Stanley. *Parodie III.* Seesaw Music Corporation. $40.00. Solo Tuba, Solo Trumpet, and Brass Quintet. V.

Friedman, Stanley. *Parodie VI.* Seewaw Music Corporation. $85.00. Solo Tuba, 2 Horns, 2 Trumpets, 2 Trombones, Percussion. V.

Fritze, Gregory. *Basso Concertino.* Available from the composer. Solo Tuba (or Bass Trombone), 2 Trumpets, Horn, Trombone (Version for Solo Tuba and Synthesizer available). 1984. 7:00. IV–V. C_1–a'. A serial work which serves as a very nice, lyrical display for the solo tuba in the traditional brass quintet instrumentation. Recorded by Gregory Fritze and the Cambridge Symphonic Brass Ensemble.

Gaathaug, Morten. *Sonata Concertante for Tuba and Brass Quintet, Opus 41.* Norwegian Music Information Centre. Solo Tuba 2 Trumpets, Horn, Trombone, and Tuba. 1991–92. 18:00. IV–V. E_1–a♭' (c"). Three connected movements: Allegro; Andante molto moderato; Molto allegro. To Øystein Baadsvik. A tuneful, pyrotechnic display piece for the tubist; the very high tessitura would make performance on the F tuba a wise choice. Fun music for performers and listeners alike. Recorded by Øystein Baadsvik.

Gabrieli, Andrea. *3 Ricercare.* arr. Lewis Waldeck. Cor Publishing Company. 2 Trumpets, Trombone, Tuba. $5.00.

García, Orlando Jacinto. *cuerdas, vientos, y voces (strings, winds, and voices).* Kallisti Music Press. Mandolin and Tuba. 1998. $24.00. 11:30. V. $A\sharp_2$–c".

Gates, Crawford. *Suite for Tuba with Percussion, Celesta, Harp, and Piano, Opus 53.* Pacific Publications. Tuba, Percussion, Celesta, Harp, and Piano. 1978. 14:30. IV–V. D_1–g'. Six movements: Intrada; Allemande; Courante; Sarabande; Gavotte; Gigue. Commissioned by Cherry Beauregard. Unique, well-crafted orchestration and good writing for the solo tuba.

Geier, Oskar. *Conzert-Fantasie.* Musikverlag Barbara Evans. Trumpet, Tuba, and Piano.

Geminiani, F. *Concerto Grosso.* Shawnee Press, Inc. 2 Trombones (or Euphoniums) and Tuba. $12.50. See listing under Music for Multiple Tubas.

Gerhard, R. *Hymnody.* Oxford University Press. Flute, Oboe, Clarinets, Trumpet, Horn, Trombone, Tuba, 2 Pianos, Percussion. Rental from the publisher (Score $7.35).

Ghiselin, Johannes. *La Alfonsina.* ed. the Empire Brass Quintet. G. Schirmer. Horn, Trombone, and Tuba (or Baritone). 1979. $3.95. 1:20. III–IV. G–d'. A renaissance contrapuntal work which works well for low brass trio.

Gillingham, David R. *Divertimento.* Tuba-Euphonium Press. Horn, Tuba, and Piano. 1994. $30.00. IV–V. A_1–g'. Five movements: Fanfare; March; Nocturne; Scherzo; Prelude and Ritual Dance. Commissioned by Philip Sinder, Professor of Tuba, and Janine Gaboury-Sly, Professor of Horn, Michigan State University. Reviewed in the Fall 1996 issue of the *TUBA Journal* (Vol. 24, No. 1). Recorded by Philip Sinder.

Gillis, L. *10 Duets.* Virgo Music Publishers. Bass Trombone and Tuba. $7.95.

Gillis, L. *10 More Duets.* Virgo Music Publishers. Bass Trombone and Tuba (or 2 Bass Trombones). $9.00.

Glandien, Lutz. *"4:1." for Four Trombones and Tuba.* Verlag Neue Musik Berlin. 4 Trombones and Tuba. 1985. 9:00. IV. D_1–f'. Four movements. Good, modern chamber music for four trombones and tuba.

Goedicke, Alexander. *Concert Suite.* Philharmusica Corporation. Trombone (or Euphonium) and Tuba. $5.95

Gottschalk, Arthur. *Fanfare.* Seesaw Music Corporation. Trumpet, Horn, Trombone, and Tuba. $9.00.

Gould, Morton. *Tuba Suite.* G. Schirmer. Solo Tuba and Three Horns. 1971. $12.00. 9:30. IV. F_1–E♭'. Five movements: Prelude; Chorale; Waltz; Elegy; Quickstep. For Bill Bell in memoriam. The solo tuba part is substantially more difficult than the horn accompaniment parts. See: Bird, Gary, ed.; *Program Notes for the Solo Tuba.* Recorded by Harvey Phillips and Markus Hötzel.

Grape, John T. *Jesus Paid It All.* arr. Howard J. Baer. Sonante Publications. Cornet/Flugelhorn, Flugelhorn, Trombone, Tuba. 1989. $5.50. 3:15. III. F_1–a.

Gryc, Stephen. *Music for Tuba and Timpani.* Robert King Music Company. Tuba and Timpani. 1990. $6.75. 7:15. III. G_1–a♭. Three movements: Deciso; Lirico; Energico. Commissioned by Rosemary Small. Dedicated to Alexander Lepak. Very few difficulties for the tubist other than staying together with the timpanist. The timpani part is substantially more demanding than the tuba part.

Guy, Noa. *The Forbidden Fruit.* Available from the composer. Tuba and Female Choir. 1992. 20:00. IV. $G\sharp_1$–g'. Three movements: The Garden of Eden; The Seduction; The Realization. Dedicated to Roger Bobo. An extensive, modern tuba solo work which interacts in dialogues with the female choir. The choir is required to perform standard vocalization, sprechstimme, clapping, finger snapping, and hand rubbing sounds. Text is by the composer.

Hackbarth, Glenn. *Duo.* Smith Publications. Tuba and Percussion (Xylophone, Vibraphone, 4 Tom-toms, 3 Cymbals). 1976. $13.00. 4:45. V. D_1–a'. Single movement. For Dan Perantoni. A typical experimental work from the seventies comprised of gestures passed between tubist and percussionist, poly-rhythms, "free" sections, and other effects.

Hallnäs, Eyvind. *Myggan och elefanten.* Swedish Music Information Center. Piccolo and Tuba. 1983. 3:30.

Handel, G. F. *The Trumpet Shall Sound.* Editions Musicus. Trombone and Tuba (with optional Piano accompaniment). $4.50.

Hartley, Walter. *Concerto for Tuba and Percussion Orchestra.* Accura Music, Inc. Tuba and Six Percussionists. 1974. $60.00. 15:00. IV–V. B_2–g♯'. Four movements: Adagio—Allegro; Molto vivace; Largo; Allegro molto. Dedicated to C. Rudolph Emilson (tubist) and Theodore C. Frazeur (percussionist). A work full of interesting colors and worth the work of preparation for performance. Recorded by Jeffrey Jarvis.

Hartley, Walter. *Double Concerto for Saxophone, Tuba, and Wind Octet.* Theodore Presser. Saxophone, Tuba, Flute, Oboe, Bassoon, 2 Trumpets, Horn, and Trombone. 1969. $18.00. 5:00. III–IV. F_1–c♭'. Three movements: Allegro con brio; Andante; Presto. An interesting instrumental combination and an overall good chamber work. Recorded by Martin Erickson.

Hartley, Walter. *Duet for Flute and Tuba.* Theodore Presser. Flute and Tuba. 1963. $6.00. 3:00. III. G_1–b. Three movements: Allegretto; Andante; Vivace. Pleasant music which goes together easily. Recorded by Harvey Phillips.

Hartley, Walter. *Quartet for Low Brass and Piano.* Tuba-Euphonium Press. Trombone, Euphonium, Tuba, and Piano. 2003. $24.00. III/IV. G_1–d1'. Four Movements: Allegro Moderato; Scherzando; Adagio; Vivace. Good chamber music with a lot of interplay between the instruments.

Hartley, Walter. *Three Inventions for Trumpet and Tuba.* Nichols Music Company. 1996. $6.00. F_1–f'. Three movements: Allegro; Andante; March. Reviewed in the Fall 2000 issue of the *TUBA Journal* (Vol. 28, No. 1).

Harvey, Paul. *Six for Six in Six Inns.* Manuscript available from the composer. Tuba and Woodwind Quintet. 1981. 12:00. IV. F_1–d'. Six movements: The Royal Oak; The Golden Ball; The Lord Nelson; Pope's Grotto; The Lemon Tree; The Coach and Horses. To Skip Gray. Delightful chamber music picturing six pubs in London, England, frequented by musicians.

Heiden, Bernhard. *Divertimento for Tuba and 8 Solo Instruments.* MMB Music, Inc. Flute, Clarinet, Viola, Cello, Double Bass, Alto Saxophone, Marimba, Harp and Solo Tuba. 1992. 17:00. IV–V. F_1–f'. Six Movements: Chorale; Ostinato; Perpetuum Mobile; Dialogue; Fancy; Conclusion. Commissioned by Camerata for Harvey Phillips.

Heiden, Bernhard. *Four Fancies.* MMB Music, Inc. Alto Saxophone, Marimba and Tuba. 1992. 7:00. IV. G_1–e'. Four movements: Ostinato; Perpetuum Mobile; Dialogue; Fancy.

Heiden, Bernhard. *Variations for Solo Tuba and Nine Horns.* Associated Music Publishers. Solo Tuba and Nine Horns. 1974. $12.00. 12:00. IV–V. D_1–f'. Single movement with nine sections. Written for Harvey Phillips and dedicated to the memory of John Barrows. See: Bird, Gary, ed.; *Program Notes for the Solo Tuba.* Recorded by Harvey Phillips and Markus Hötzel.

Heilmann, Harald. *Trauerode für 4 Wagner-Tuben und Kontrabaßtuba.* Heinrichshofen Verlag (C. F. Peters Corporation). 4 Wagner Tubas and Contrabass Tuba.

Heinichen, Johannes David. *Sonata in C Minor.* tr. Skip Gray. Available from Skip Gray. Horn and Tuba. $4.00. 6:00. III–IV. G_1–B♭. Four movements: Grave; Allegro; Larghetto e cantabile; Allegro. A baroque duo originally for oboe and bassoon.

Heiss, J. *Inventions, Contours, and Colors.* Boosey & Hawkes. Flute, Clarinet, Bassoon, Tuba, Violin, Viola, Cello, Bass. Rental from the publisher (Score $7.50).

Hellvin, Roy. *Sinfonia Concer-Onkel for Horn, Tuba, Piano and Violin.* Music Information Centre Norway. 1992. 9:00.

Helperin, Salomon. *Capris 41.* Swedish Music Information Center. Tuba, Clarinet, and Electroaccoustic instruments. 1986.

Hendze, Jesper. *Spin-Off.* Edition Samfundet. Tuba, Clarinet, Cello, and Percussion. 2004. 8:45. V. E_1–g♯'. Commissioned by tubist Janus Mogensen for his debut with The Royal Danish Academy of Music, Copenhagen, on November 7, 2001, and written with support from the Danish Arts Foundation and "Gurli og Paul Madsens Fond." This one-movement work will challenge the most experienced performers. Rhythmically complex, frequent tempo changes and metric shifts. Well-crafted orchestration.

Heussenstamm, George. *Dialogue.* Dorn Publications Inc. Tuba and Sax. $15.00.

Hewitt, Harry. *Discourse for Tuba and Guitar (Opus 452, No. 3).* Harry Hewitt. Tuba and Guitar. 1983. 3:30. IV. F♯$_1$–g♭'. Single movement.

Hewitt, Harry. *Leaf in the Stream (Opus 456, No. 2).* Harry Hewitt. Oboe and Tuba. 1979. 4:00. III–IV. D♭–f'. Single movement. The piece is comprised of a series of rubato gestures with rather free interplay between oboe and tuba parts.

Hewitt, Harry. *Six Preludes for Flute and Tuba (Opus 452, No. 1).* TUBA Press. Flute and Tuba. 1977. $5.00. 12:15. IV. E♭$_1$–a'. Six movements. Reviewed in the Winter 1996 issue of the *TUBA Journal* (Vol. 24, No. 2).

Hidas, Frigyes. *Quartettino.* Editio Musica Budapest. 2 Trumpets, Trombone, and Tuba. $11.75.

Hidas, Frigyes. *Scherzo.* Musikverlag Bruno Uetz. Tuba and Four Horns. 2004. 2:30. IV. B♭$_1$–e'. Available for Tuba and Piano.

Hidas, Frigyes. *Trio for Horn, Trombone, and Tuba.* Editio Musica Budapest. Horn, Trombone, and Tuba. 1981. $12.00. 4:15. III–IV. A_1–d♭'. Single movement with four sections. Some engaging harmonies and shifting meters.

Hill, Mildred J. *Happy Birthday.* arr. John Glenesk Mortimer. Editions Marc Reift. Tuba, Piano or Keyboard or Guitar, Drums optional. 2000. II. D♭–g. Four movements: I. Traditional; II. March; III. Valse; IV. Tango. Theme and three variations. Good for a young student who would like to serenade his or her parents on their birthdays.

Hoag, Charles. *TUBAPLAY.* Manuscript available from the composer. Solo Tuba and Self-Played Percussion. 1985. 6:00. IV. D_1–a'. Eight movements: Prelude; Gong with the Wind; Interlude; Tango; Interlude; Soft-Shoe Dance; Interlude; Final Bounce. Commissioned by Scott Watson, Skip Gray, and Jerry Young. The performer is required to play the tuba and, simultaneously in various movements, gong, pedal bass drum, and suspended cymbal. An effective work both for its music as well as theatrical appeal. See also listing under Unaccompanied Tuba.

Hogg, Merle E. *Seven for Four.* Music Graphics Press. Trumpet, Horn, Trombone, and Tuba. $105.75.

Hollingworth, W. *Dear Is My Little Vale.* Molenaar Music N.V. 2 Trumpets, Horn, and Tuba. $8.00.

Holmes, Brian. *Roger Bobo Plays the Tuba.* Roger Dean Publishing Company. Treble Chorus (SSA), Tuba, and Piano. 2002. $2.25. III. F_1–g. Commissioned by the Cantabile Children's Chorus of Los Altos, California, directed by Signe Boyer. The text is a poem by John Updike that plays humorously with the words "tuba" and "Bobo." The chorus part is suitable for either a children or women's chorus. Reviewed in the Fall 2003 issue of the *ITEA Journal* (Vol. 31, No. 1).

Horovitz, Joseph. *Brass Polka.* Chester Music. Trumpet, Horn, Trombone, and Tuba. $14.95.

Horwood, M. S. *Residue.* Theodore Presser. Tuba and Vibraphone. 1981. $4.00. V.

Hovhaness, Alan. *Tower Music.* Broude Brothers. Woodwind Quintet and Brass Quintet. Rental from the publisher.

Hoyt, George M. *Introduction and Allegro for Brass Trio.* Hoyt Editions. Horn in F, Trombone, and Tuba. 1983. $12/00. 5:30. III–IV. B_1–e♭'. Single continuous movement. For Bill and Jack. Reviewed in the Winter 1999 issue of the *TUBA Journal* (Vol. 26, No. 2).

Hoyt, George M. *Suite for Horn and Tuba.* Hoyt Editions. Horn and Tuba. $14.00. 12:00. III–IV. F_1–d'. Five movements: Chorale; Canonic Invention; Poem; Elegy; Dance. Reviewed in the Winter 1999 issue of the *TUBA Journal* (Vol. 26, No. 2).

Iannacone, Anthony. *Sonatina for Trumpet and Tuba.* Theodore Presser. Trumpet and Tuba. 1976. $4.50. 10:15. III–IV. F_1–d'. For Carter Eggers and J. R. Smith. A modern work with hybrid scales, shifting meters, and irregular rhythms. A work very playable by college students with the major difficulty being endurance problems which may arise from the absence of rest periods for both parts. Recorded by J. R. Smith.

Irish Traditional. *Be Thou My Vision.* arr. Howard J. Baer. Sonante Publications. 2 Trumpets, Trombone, Tuba. 1989. $5.50. 3:15. II–III. A♭$_1$–a♭. A nice arrangement whose main difficulty is the 5/4 middle section which also goes into the key of E major. A good piece for church services.

Isaac, Heinrich. *Four Pieces.* tr. Kenneth Singleton. Peer International Corporation. Horn, Trombone (or Baritone), Tuba (or Bass Trombone). 1976. $8.00. 3:45. II–III. F–g. Four renaissance contrapuntal pieces with little technical difficulty other than occasional imitative entrances on "odd" parts of the beat.

Jacobsen, Julius. *Tuba Ballet.* Swedish Music Information Center. Tuba and Woodwind Quintet. 1978. 7:45. IV. F_1–e'. Four movements: Arabesque—Battement; Pas de Deux; Gr. Battement; Polka—Can Can. Commissioned by Rikskonserter for Michael Lind. Delightful music inspired by the ballet. Recorded by Michael Lind.

Jager, Robert. *Fantasy Variations.* TUBA Press. Flute (doubling Piccolo), Tuba, and Piano. 1982. $10.00. 7:30. IV. A_1–e♭'. Continuous work with theme and five variations. Interesting yet conservative chamber music for an unusual instrumental combination.

Johansen, Bertil Palmar. *Partita for Tuba and Percussion.* Music Information Centre Norway. 1998. 11:00.

Johnson, Geir. *Body Theory: For Brass Quartet and Percussion.* Music Information Centre Norway. Trumpet, Horn, Trombone, Tuba. 2000.

Johnston, Ben. *Pursuit.* Smith Publications. Bassoon and Tuba. 1996. V. B_2–c'. For Johnny Reinhard.

Josquin Des Prez. *De Tous Biens Playne.* Southern Music Company. Trumpet, Horn, Trombone, and Tuba. $3.00.

Josquin Des Prez. *Se je perdu mon ami.* arr. George M. Hoyt. Hoyt Editions. Horn, Trombone, and Tuba. $10.00.

Kalke, Ernst-Thilo. *Mevagissey Tales.* Musikverlag Bruno Uetz. Tuba and Four Horns. 1996. 5:50. V. C_1–d". Single movement, later named Cornish Dawn. Descriptive of an English village along the south coast of Cornwall. Also available for solo tuba with two trumpets, horn and trombone. See additional listings for expanded versions under: Tuba and Orchestra; Tuba and Band; Tuba and Keyboard. Recorded by Markus Hötzel (tuba and four horn version).

Kalke, Ernst-Thilo. *More Short Encores.* Musikverlag Bruno Uetz. Trumpet, Tuba, and Piano. 2001. 7:00. IV. F_1–f'. Three movements: Vivace, Lento espressivo; Jazz Waltz.

Kalke, Ernst-Thilo. *Three Short Encores.* Musikverlag Bruno Uetz. Trumpet, Tuba, and Piano. 2001. 7:10. IV. C_1–e'. Three movements: Bright; Slowly; Swing.

Kalke, Ernst-Thilo. *Tubism.* Musikverlag Bruno Uetz. Tuba, Four Trumpets, Horn, Four Trombones, and Percussion. 2003. 2:30. IV. $B\flat_1$–f'. Single movement. A Latin rock groove that is fun to play and delightful for the audience. Accompanying parts are not difficult.

Kapr, J. *Omaggio alla Tromba.* Artia Foreign Trade Corporation. 2 Trumpets, 3 Horns, Trombone, Tuba, Piccolo, Flute, Clarinet, Bass Clarinet, Contrabassoon, Piano, and Timpani. $8.00.

Karlsen, Kjell Mørk. *Concerto Grosso, Opus 98 No. 2.* Music Information Centre Norway. Cornet, Horn, Euphonium, Tuba, and Piano. 2000. 15:00.

Karlsen, Kjell Mørk. *Three Pieces for Violin and Tuba.* Music Information Centre Norway.

Kayser, Leif. *In dulci jubilo.* Leif Kayser. Trumpet, Horn, Trombone, and Tuba. 1955.

Kayser, Leif. *Notturno saccro.* Leif Kayser. Trumpet, Horn, Trombone, and Tuba. 1958.

Kayser, Leif. *Variationer over Lovet være du Jesu Christ.* Leif Kayser. Trumpet, Horn, Trombone, and Tuba. 1957.

Kellaway, Roger. *Dance of the Ocean Breeze.* Edition BIM. Horn, Tuba, and Piano. 1979. 3:45. III–IV. F_1–c'. Single movement. For Froydis Vekre and Roger Bobo. A delightful, light piece. Recorded by Roger Bobo.

Kellaway, Roger. *Sonoro.* Edition BIM. Tuba, Horn, and Piano. 1979. 10:00. IV. C_1–d'. Single, multisection movement. For Froydis Vekre and Roger Bobo. Very lyrical writing and a tricky bridge section in 5/16. Recorded by Roger Bobo.

Kershner, Brian. *Duo Fantasia.* Tuba-Euphonium Press. Tuba and Percussion. 2002. $15.00. IV–V. C_1–g♭'. For Scott Mendoker and Hsin-Yi Wu. Duet will challenge the most experienced performers. Angular lines for tubists and multiple percussion equipment for percussionist. A great chamber music piece.

Kirby, Ben. *All We Do.* Tuba-Euphonium Press. Tuba and Acoustic Guitar. 1997. $10.00. IV. B_1–g'. A single-movement work consisting of several sections and tempo changes that provide contrast. Classical and folk idioms are employed. The piece begins with a slow introduction by the guitar and the tuba enters with a lyrical melody. The character of the piece begins to change with the addition of triplet and sixteenth note patterns. A more technical passage marked "Bebop!" is followed by a cadenza and a passage requiring double tonguing from the tubist. The piece ends slowly and quietly the way it began. Reviewed in the Winter 1999 issue of the *TUBA Journal* (Vol. 26, No. 2).

Kirby, Ben. *Folk Music.* Tuba-Euphonium Press. Tuba and Acoustic Guitar. 1998. $8.00. IV. F♯–e'. A work very playable by college students. Requires controlled soft playing in upper tessitura for the tubist.

Knox, Charles. *Solo for Tuba with Brass Trio.* Tenuto Publications. Solo Tuba, Trumpet, Horn, and Trombone. 1968. $4.50. 8:45. III–IV. F_1–c'. Three movements. A good work with modern harmonies, easily put together.

Kodaly, Zoltan. *Lament.* arr. Skip Gray. Shawnee Press, Inc. Trombone (or Euphonium) and 2 Tubas. $5.00. See listing under Music for Multiple Tubas.

Koetsier, Jan. *Falstaffiade, Opus 134b.* Editions Marc Reift. Tuba and Four Horns. 1996. 5:00. IV. F_1–a♭' (optional b♭'). Introduktion—Adagio maestoso; Thema—Allegretto commodo; Var. I—Allegro; Var. II—Tempo di Valse; Var. III—Marcia funebre; Var. IV—Allegramente. Introduction, theme, and four variations based on Falstaff's drinking song in Otto Nicolai's opera "The Merry Wives of Windsor." Conventional writing.

Koetsier, Jan. *Galgenlieder.* Editions Marc Reift. Tuba and soprano/tenor. 1993 (1992). 14:00. III–IV. D_1–f'. Eight movements: I. Das Geburtslied; II. Das Hemmed; III. Die zwei Wurzeln; IV. Die Luft; V. Fisches Nachtgesang; VI. Igel and Agel; VII. Die beiden Esel; VIII. Das Gebet. A tonal composition based on texts from Christian Morgenstern. The main difficulty in performing these songs is balancing and blending with the singer. Except for the fifth movement, a tuba solo connoting the blubbering of a fish at night, both parts are equally soloistic.

Kont, P. *Quartet #2.* Ludwig Doblinger. Trumpet, Horn, Trombone, and Tuba. $20.50.

Koppel, Anders. *Scherzo.* Edition Wilhelm Hansen. Marimba, Violin, Viola, Violoncello, and Tuba. 2001. 8:30. IV. $E\flat_1$–d♭'. An interesting combination of instruments. A good chamber music composition.

Kraft, William. *Double Trio for Piano, Prepared Piano, and Small Ensemble.* New Music West. Trio I: Piano, Tuba, Percussion; Trio II: Prepared Piano, Electric Guitar, Percussion. 1966. Rental from the publisher. 24:13. V. A_2 (or lowest possible note)–g' (highest note possible). Five movements: Prelude: Presto Energico; Tempo Rubato e Andante; Presto Delicato; Cadenze: Adagio; Allegro Molto. Difficult and complex contemporary chamber music with various avant-garde effects. Recorded with Roger Bobo (Cambria CD 1071).

Kraft, William. *Nonet for Brass and Percussion.* New Music West. 2 Trumpets, Horn, Trombone, Tuba, 4 Percussion. 1958. $25.00. 25:00. III–IV. E_1–b♭. Six movements: Presto; Andante;

Interlude 1—Scherzo a Tre; Allegretto; Interlude 2: Scherzo a Quatro; Maestoso e Rubato. Chamber music for brass quintet and percussion. The percussion parts are extensive.

Krol, Bernard. *Cathedrale in Three Naves, Op. 85.* Bote & Bock K.G. Horn (or Alto Trombone), Trombone, and Tuba (or Bass Trombone). 1982. $15.50. 7:45. III. G_1–a♭. Three movements: Natus est nobis hodie; Victimae paschali laudes; Veni, Creator Spiritus. Music influenced by chant and ecclesiastical modes. Parts are melodically inspired and sound like medieval music in new clothing. Very little of technical difficulty.

Kröpsch, Fritz. *Im tiefen Keller (Down in the Deep Cellar)—Große Fantasie.* arr. Mark Evans. Musikverlag Barbara Evans. Solo Tuba in Brass Quintet (Piano accompaniment also available). 1989. 6:45. IV. $E♭_1$–g'. A good transcription for brass quartet accompaniment of the classical, old "Grand Fantasia" for solo tuba published in 1908.

Krush, Jay. *Two Madrigals.* Plymouth Music Company. Horn, Trombone (or Euphonium), and Tuba. $5.95.

Kulesha, Gary. *Three Complacencies.* Sonante Publications. Bass Clarinet and Tuba. 1978. $4.00. 3:00. III–IV. G_1–d'. Three movements. Humorous little contrasting pieces written in conventional tonality. A few difficult leaps in the tuba part.

Kupferman, Meyer. *Saturnalis.* Soundspells Productions. Tuba and Amplified Cello. 1974. 14:00. V. D♭–a♯'. Difficult to read due to very poor manuscript. Requires virtuoso performers. Recorded by Roger Bobo.

Langer, K. *Cortege for Tuba.* Encore Music Publishers. Tuba and Three Percussion (Marimba and Gong, 2 Timpanists). 1986. $13.00. 4:00. III. F_1–g♯. Continuous work in cantabile style. Some effective writing, especially in section requiring glissandi by the tubist in counterpoint with timpani.

Langley, James W. *Suite.* Hinrichsen Editions Ltd. 3 Trombones and Tuba (or 4 Trombones). 1961. 7:00. III. Part I: c–b♭'; Part II: A–g'; Part III: G♭–e♭'; Tuba Part: D–d'. Five movements: Intrada; Chorale; Scherzetto; Canon; Moto Perpetuo. Upper two parts are in tenor clef. A nice demonstration piece for the orchestral trombone section or contest piece for high school students. Also usable by tuba-euphonium quartet or ensemble.

Lanza, A. *Eidesis II.* Boosey & Hawkes. 2 Horns, 2 Trombones, Tuba, 3 Cellos, 2 Basses, 3 Percussion. $3.00.

Lassus, Orlandus. *2 Pieces.* tr. Randall Block. Philharmusica Corporation. Flute (or Oboe) and Tuba. 1975. $4.50. 3:00. II–III. F–b♭. Two movements. The tuba part stays in the staff throughout and moves at moderate pace in mostly diatonic motion. There is no rest, so endurance could be a problem for a younger player.

Lemay, Robert. *Maniwaki.* Canadian Music Centre. Tuba and Percussion. 1997. 10:00. C_2–g', mostly E♭–d. Premiered by tubist Brent Longstoff and percussionist Darrell Bueckert. A virtuosic piece which includes playing backstage, mute tapping, playing with the mute, and walking to several positions on the stage. This composer is well known for his timbre exploration and unconventional use of the concert hall space. Reviewed in the Winter 1999 issue of the *TUBA Journal* (Vol. 27, No. 2).

Lendvay, Kamilló. *Five Movements in Quotation-Marks.* Editio Musica Budapest. Horn, Trombone, and Tuba. 1980. $13.00. 7:15. IV. $G♭_1$–e'. Five movements: "Hommage à Stravinsky"; "Hommage à Count Basie"; "Hommage à Johann Strauß"; "Hommage à Robert Stolz"; "Hommage à Moi. . . ." For Horst Küblböck and his ensemble.

Leontyev, A. *Folk Song for 3 Trombones and Tuba.* ed. Keith Brown. International Music Company. 3 Trombones and Tuba. $5.50.

Lerstad, Terje Bjørn. *Doell for Trombone and Tuba, Op. 154.* Music Information Centre Norway. 1983. 9:00.

Lerstad, Terje Bjørn. *Straumkvædet, Op. 91.* Music Information Centre Norway. Clarinet, Tuba, and Piano. 1980. 7:30.

Lerstad, Terje Bjørn. *Wachet auf, Op. 143: Chorale Variation on M. Praetorius and J. S. Bach.* Music Information Centre Norway. Tuba, Trombone, Horn. 1981. 6:00.

Levinas, M. *Clov et Hamm.* Éditions Salabert. Trombone, Tuba, Percussion, and Tape. 1974. 8:00. III. $D♭_1$–b. For Marcel Galiegue and Fernand Lelong. A work reliant nearly completely on the tape. Tuba and trombone parts not difficult. Some non-metered sections.

Levine, Bruce. *A Day.* The Franklin Edition. Soprano and Tuba. 1971. $6.00. 3:30. III–IV. A_1–g. Single movement. An atmospheric work with text written by Howard Moss specifically for this piece. Difficulties imposed upon the tubist include balancing and blending with the soprano.

Lézé, Jean-François. *Canções Lunares* (Songs from the Moon). Rivera Editores, Valencia, Spain. Tuba, Horn, and Piano. 2004. 6:00. IV. D_1–c'. Four small movements: Grave e inquieto; Andante; Adagio; Allegro Moderato. Dedicated to Sérgio Carolino, tuba, and José Bernardo Silva, horn. Premiered at the 36th International Horn Symposium 2004 in Valencia, Spain.

Lézé, Jean-François. *O Sapo Vermelho* (The Red Frog). Rivera Editores, Valencia, Spain. Tuba and Vibraphone. 2002. 5:00. IV–V. A_2–g'. Dedicated to Sérgio Carolino. This piece requires some improvisation.

Lézé, Jean-François. *Tango e Passo Doble.* Rivera Editores, Valencia, Spain. Tuba, Horn, and Piano.

2004. 3:00. IV. E_1–f. Dedicated to Sérgio Carolino, tuba, and José Bernardo Silva, horn. Premiered at the 36th International Horn Symposium 2004 in Valencia, Spain. This piece is written in the Argentine traditional music style of "tango" with tributes to the Spanish music "passo doble." A very nice piece for both players and audience.

Lillebjerka, Sigmund. *Lamentoso.* Music Information Centre Norway. Horn, Bass Trombone, Tuba, and Piano.

Lindberg, Nils. *Movements for Tuba and Wind Quintet.* Swedish Music Information Center. Tuba, Alto Flute, English Horn, Bass Clarinet, Horn, and Bassoon. 1979.

Locke, Matthew. *One Dozen Duets.* MS Publications. Trombone and Tuba (or 2 Trombones). $5.00.

Locke, Matthew. *Suite No. 2.* arr. Lewis Waldeck. Cor Publishing Company. Trumpet, Horn, Trombone, Tuba. $4.00.

Loeb, D. *Aubade and Villanelle.* Accentuate Music. Tuba, Violin, and Percussion. $20.00 (score).

Loeb, D. *3 Invocations.* Accentuate Music. Horn and Tuba. $4.50.

Lovreglio, E. *Évocation.* Editions Musicales Transatlantiques. 3 Trombones, Tuba, Timpani. 1972. $26.00. 10:00. IV. $F\sharp_1$–f♯'. An episodic work with many tempo changes. Good post-romantic chamber music in which all instrumental parts are fairly equal.

Luedeke, Raymond. *Krishna.* Seesaw Music Corporation. Tuba, Seven Percussion, and Piano. 1975. $52.00. 8:30. V. C_1–e♭'. Single movement with five sections. For Don Harry. A dramatic work incorporating the tuba into the percussion ensemble. The piece employs no avant-garde effects other than singing and playing.

Luedeke, Raymond. *New Hampshire—His Majesty the Tuba.* Seesaw Music Corporation. Tuba, Tenor, and Piano. 1968. 2:50. III–IV. E_1–f♯'. Two brief, whimsical songs. Some wide leaps in the tuba part, which serves as a true equal to the tenor.

Lund, Erik. *Music for Tuba and Mallet Instruments.* TUBA Press. Tuba and Percussion (single performer playing Crotale, Vibraphone, Marimba with low a). 1983. $12.00. 8:00. V. $D\sharp_1$–c'' (continuing as high as possible). A difficult work for both tubist and percussionist, consisting mainly of dialogues and gestures passed between the two performers.

Lunde, Ivar, Jr. *Embellishments, Opus 60, No. 1.* Norsk Musikforlag. Piccolo Trumpet and Tuba. 1976. 2:30. IV. G_1–d'. Single movement in two sections: Moderately Fast, Majestic; Very Fast and Light. To Gary Albrecht and Steve Allen. Difficult rhythms and mixed meters throughout.

Lunde, Ivar, Jr. *Pulsations, Opus 89.* Music Information Centre Norway. Four Trombones and Tuba. 1985. 10:00.

Macero, Teo. *One-Three Quarters.* C. F. Peters Corporation. 2 Pianos, Piccolo/Flute, Violin, Cello, Trombone, and Tuba. 1970. $7.50. 8:00. An colorful exploratory piece with dramatic gestures. One piano is required to be tuned down a quarter tone with quarter tone pitch variances in other parts.

Madsen, Trygve. *Divertimento, Opus 43.* Musikk-Huset Forlag, Norway. Horn and Tuba. 8:00. V.

Madsen, Trygve. *Trombones, Michael and I, Op. 127.* Music Information Centre Norway. Three Trombones, Bass Trombone, and Tuba.

Maganini, Quinto. *The Boa-Constrictor and the Bobolink (Humorous Sketch).* Editions Musicus. Piccolo and Tuba. $2.50. 1:30. III. C–b♭. Single movement in waltz tempo.

Maneri, J. *Ephphatha.* Margun Music. Clarinet, Trombone, Tuba, and Piano. $35.00.

Mantia, Simone. *Believe Me If All Those Endearing Young Charms.* arr. David R. Werden. Whaling Music Publishers. Tuba Solo in Brass Quintet. 1983. $9.50. 6:00. V. F_1–g' (a'). The great barnburner solo nicely arranged with brass quartet accompaniment.

Marcello, Benedetto. *Adagio from Sonata in C Major.* arr. Gary Buttery. Whaling Music. Tuba, Harp, Cello, Bassoon. $3.50.

Marks, Günther. *Hymnus für 4 Wagner-Tuben und Kontrabass-Tuba.* Edition Kunzelmann. 4 Wagner Tubas and Contrabass Tuba. Published 1985. 4:40. II. G_1–a♭. Single movement in three parts. A work inspired by the Adagio from Bruckner's seventh symphony.

Maros, Miklós. *Concertino for Tuba (or Contrabass) and Winds.* Swedish Music Information Center. Solo Tuba (or Bass), Flute, Clarinet, Bari. Sax, Trumpet, Horn, Percussion. 1971. 9:00.

Martinson, Rolf. *Monogram, Op. 30 for basstuba och blaskvintett.* Swedish Music Information Center. Tuba and Woodwind Quintet. 1991.

Más, Vicente Navarro. *Dualismo.* Available from the composer. Tuba and Flute. 6:00. IV. Three movements: Andante; Larghetto; Allegro. Recorded by Vivente Navarro Más, tuba, and A. Pich Santasusana, flute.

Matthus, Siegfried. *Sonate for Brass, Piano and Timpani.* VEB Deutscher Verlag für Musik. Trumpet in B♭, Horn, Trombone, Tuba, Piano, and Timpani. 1983. Rental from publisher. 4:30. III–IV. $F\sharp_1$–f. Continuous work in seven sections. A "sound" piece with few technical demands other than some difficult rhythmic interplay and two sections in which all players' parts are in completely different meters.

McCarthy, Daniel. *Blithe Spirit.* Tuba-Euphonium Press. Solo Tuba, Clarinet, Horn, Bassoon, and Cello. Optional Bass Clarinet. Composer has withdrawn publication.

Meister, Scott R. *Arabic Dances.* HoneyRock. Tuba and Percussion. 2001. $22.95. IV–V. D_1–g♯'. Three movements: Saba; Bayati; Hijaz. Scored for tuba and one multi-percussionist, this is a challenging and unique work inspired by elements of music of the Middle East. The tubist is required to use extended techniques such as multiphonics, singing through the horn, use of wide vibrato, and playing as fast as possible with proportional rhythm. A great selection for either brass or percussion recitals.

Mendelssohn, Felix. *Scherzo.* arr. A. E. Goldstein. Cor Publishing Company. Trumpet, Horn, Trombone, and Tuba. $5.00.

Menoche, Charles Paul. *Chamber Concerto.* Available from composer. Solo Tuba and Thirteen Players (Flute, Oboe, Clarinet, Alto Saxophone, 2 Trumpets, Horn Trombone, 2 Percussion, 2 Synthesizers). 2002. 17:00. IV–V. C_1–g♭'. Dedicated to Tracey Rudnick. This piece pays homage to the composer's roots as a tubist. It draws inspiration from American poet Charles Olson's 1950 essay, *Projective Verse.* A rhythmically aggressive and energetic work that is challenging for both the tubist and the ensemble. Despite the small ensemble, a conductor is necessary. Extensive workout throughout the concerto. See listing under Tuba and Band.

Miller Ragne, Philip. *Interlacements.* Swedish Music Information Center. Flute, Oboe, Clarinet, Trumpet, Horn, and Tuba. 1989.

Mitchell, W. Roy. *Jazz Suite for Tuba and Jazz Trio.* TUBA Press. Solo Tuba, Piano, Bass, and Drums. 1988. $16.00. 19:00. IV–V. $B♭_2$–b♭'. Three movements: Samba; Ballad; Fusion-Rock. Written especially for Gary Bird. Although F tuba is specified for the Samba and Fusion-Rock, and CC tuba for the Ballad, it is completely playable on either instrument. The Fusion-Rock movement requires a great deal of agility and contains optional "open" ad-lib solo sections.

Moland, Eirik. *Et fjellsavn.* Music Information Centre Norway. Clarinet, Horn, Tuba, Triangle, 2 Jew's Harps, and Synthesizer. 1990. 8:00.

Molineux, Allen. *Dichotomic Diversion for Tuba and Percussionists.* TUBA Press. Tuba and 3 Percussionists (playing multiple set-ups). $15.00. 8:00. IV. E_1–c'. Nice percussion writing and muted tuba passages create timbral variety. No significant ensemble problems.

Monti, Vittorio. *Csárdás.* arr. Øystein Baadsvik. Ovation. Solo Tuba and Wind Quintet. 1992. 5:00. IV. G_1–a♭'. $50.65. Originally written for the violin, this display piece has tempted numerous performers. In this arrangement the tuba is the star of the show. Fun to play and delightful for audiences. The solo part can be played on different instruments, and the set is delivered with solo part in treble clef in E♭ and bass clef. Recorded by Øystein Baadsvik. Available for Solo Tuba and Piano, Solo Tuba and Wind Band, Solo Tuba and Brass Band, Solo Tuba and Orchestra.

Moreira, Pedro. *Tuba Jazz Quintet.* Editions BIM. Tuba Solo and Saxophone Quartet. 9:00. Commissioned by and dedicated to Sérgio Carolino and the *Saxofinia* Saxophone Quartet. A jazzy piece that requires some improvisation.

Mozart, W. A. *Aria No. 14 "Queen of the Night" from The Magic Flute.* arr. David Kosmyna. BVD Press. Brass Quintet with Tuba as the featured soloist. 2003. 2:30. IV. $A♭_1$–e♭'. A nice arrangement for contrast on a brass quintet performance. Arrangement in the key of C minor.

Mozart, W. A. *Aria of the Queen of the Night from Die Zauberflöte.* arr. André Becker. Musikverlag Bruno Uetz. Solo Tuba and Brass Ensemble (Four Trumpets, Horn, Three Trombones and Euphonium). 1999. 2:30. IV. F–f'. A nice arrangement in the key of D minor that requires a light approach.

Mozart, W. A. *Fugue, K. 401.* Robert King Music Sales. Flexible Brass Quartet with Tuba. $3.40.

Mozart, W. A. *O Isis and Osiris from "The Magic Flute."* tr. Arthur Frackenpohl. Brassworks Music. Solo Tuba in Brass Quintet (Trumpets playing Fluegelhorns). 1985. $15.00. 2:30. III. F_1–c'. A good version of the standard tuba solo transcription, mostly in the staff. A nice opportunity for the tubist to be featured playing a beautiful melody.

Mozart, W. A. *Two Themes.* Robert King Music Sales. Flexible Brass Quartet with Tuba. $3.40.

Murray, Greg. *". . . a whale for the killing."* Music for Percussion, Inc. Tuba and 2 Percussionists. 1983. 8:30. V. $D♭_1$–g♭'. Single movement with eleven episodes. Written for Daniel Perantoni and the Rosewood Percussion Duo. An effective, introspective work with many demands placed upon the tubist, including various non-traditional techniques (wind sounds, singing/playing, rips, etc.).

Nagel, Robert. *Suite.* Mentor Music. Trumpet, Horn, Trombone, Tuba, and Piano. $6.50.

Nash, Richard. *Trio Number 1 for Tuba, Horn, and Piano.* TUBA Press. Tuba, Horn, and Piano. 1992. $8.00. 7:30. IV. $B♭_2$–e'. Three movements: Marche; Adagio; Allegro. Music which looks like that of Alec Wilder but lacking the melodic character. Reviewed in the Spring 1993 issue of the *TUBA Journal* (Vol. 21, No. 3).

Nash, Richard T. *Variations for Tuba.* Available from the composer. Solo Tuba in Brass Quintet. 6:30. IV. A_2–e'. Three movements. Dedicated to Tommy Johnson. Three contrasting movements with a strong post-romantic flavor. The tuba part is lyrical with few technical difficulties and contains a solo cadenza in the third movement.

Naulais, Jerôme. *Choral.* Alphonse Leduc & Cie. 3 Trombones and Tuba. 1986. $9.50. 2:45. II–III. $B♭_1$–f♯.

Nelhybel, Vaclav. *Concerto for Tuba (or Horn).* Great Works Publishing, Inc. Solo Tuba (or Horn), 2 Flutes, Oboe, English Horn, 2 Clarinets, Bassoon, Harp, Double Bass, 2 Trumpets, Trombone, 3 Percussion (Vibraphone, Bells, Xylophone). See listing under Tuba and Band.

Nelhybel, Vaclav. *Octet*. Jerona Music Corporation. Tuba, Bass Guitar, Strings, Percussion. $44.00.

Nelson, Steve, and Jack Rollins. *Frosty the Snowman*. arr. Sandy Smith. Wright and Round Limited. Available from Solid Brass Music Company. E♭ or F Tuba and Brass Choir. 5:30. IV. F_1–g'. An accessible arrangement of a holiday favorite that is nicely scored so that the soloist is easily heard.

Newman, Ron. *Duo for Bass Trombone and Tuba*. Available from he composer. Bass Trombone and Tuba. 1991. 10:45. IV–V. Bass Trombone: $G♭_1$–g♭'; Tuba: E_1–f'. Three movements: That Old Refrain; Jobim; Ritual Fire Fugue. Written for Curtis Olson and Philip Sinder. Constantly shifting polymeters permeate the first movement (14/16—2/4—12/16—13/16 for the first four measures!) and require a great deal of diligent preparation. In the second movement, the tuba spins out a liquid melody high above the bossa nova rhythms in the bass trombone. The Ritual Fire Fugue is a study of metric modulation with a modern jazz feel. This work is not a duet which can be quickly "thrown together," but can be rewarding for a bass trombonist and tubist who desire to spend the time to realize a fine performance of this good piece of music.

Nicotra, Alfredo. *Mitt hjerte er med deg, Opus 28, No. 2*. Music Information Centre Norway. 2 Trumpets, Tuba, Percussion and Piano. 1999. 6:00.

Nilsson, Bo. *Bass*. Edition Reimers. Tuba, Percussion (6 Buckelgongs, Tamtam) and Electric Sound Reinforcement. 1977. $6.75. 10:30. IV–V. E_1–g♯'. Continuous work in nine sections. For Michael Lind. A new-music electro-acoustical composition requiring amplification and filtered sound processing of the tuba and percussion. Although the part is notated in strict meters, the music is comprised of gestures and melodic passages. Recorded by Michael Lind.

Nono, Luigi. *Guai ai gelidi Mostri*. Ricordi. 2 Altos, Flute, Clarinet, Tuba, Viola, Cello, Bass, Live Electronics. 1987.

Nono, Luigi. *Hommage to Gyorgy Kurtag*. Ricordi. Alto, Flute, Clarinet, Tuba. 1986.

Nono, Luigi. *Risonanze Erranti*. Ricordi. Alto, Flute, Tuba, Percussion, Live Electronics. 1987.

Nordhagen, Stig. *Equilibrium for Tuba and Two Percussionists*. Norwegian Music Information Centre. Tuba, 2 Percussion (each playing multiple set-ups). 1991. 12:10. IV–V. G_1–g♯'. Continuous work in three sections. Written for Sten Cranner, Tomas Nilsson, and Rolf Lennart Stenso. A modern work a great deal of difficult rhythmic interaction between the tubist and percussionists.

Nordstrøm, Hans-Henrik. *Afsked med Orion*. Edition A. Tuba and String Quartet. 1993. 16:00. V. E_1–a♭'. Dedicated to and premiered by Jørgen Arnsted and The Kontra Quartet. *Farewell to Orion* was composed during the months of February and March when the constellation Orion begins to disappear from the night sky. The disappearance of Orion signals the end of Winter and the coming of Spring.

Nordstrøm, Hans-Henrik. *Dialog*. Samfundet. Tuba and Percussion. 1991. 12:00. V. B_2–a♭'. Four movements. Commissioned and premiered by Jørgen Arnsted. This piece is a dialogue between the deep, lyrical, expressive, dramatic, calm, grotesque, and giddy tuba and different types of percussion including the vibraphone which sings, plays, and teases.

Nunes, Emmanuel. *Machina-Mundi*. Bühnen- und Musikverlag G. Ricordi & Co. Mixed Chorus, Symphony Orchestra, Tape and 4 Soloists: Tuba, Flute, Clarinet, and Percussion. 1992. 62:05. V. Commissioned by the Commission Nationale pour les Commémorations des découvertes Portugaises. Recorded by the Gulbenkian Orchestra and Chorus (Lisbon) conducted by Fabrice Bollon with Gerard Buquet, tuba.

Nytch, Jeffrey. *Three Songs of War*. Tuba-Euphonium Press. Tuba and Countertenor. 1992. IV–V. D_1–e'. Three movements: Dulce et Decorum Est; Asleep (Part 1); Asleep (Part 2). Text by English poet Wilfred Owen, a pacifist who was killed during WWI. Commissioned by Jim Court. According to the program notes, "the poems graphically depict the hell of the western front, the destruction of innocence, and the poet's despair over the death of a friend . . . the widely differing timbres of the dark, brooding tuba and the ghostly, other-worldly countertenor provide a dramatic tension reflective of the dehumanizing struggles—physical, psychological, and spiritual—of waging war." The tuba part includes multiphonics and at one point the composer indicates to "play as low as possible." Reviewed in the Fall 2002 issue of the *ITEA Journal* (Vol. 30, No. 1).

Orowan, T. *Trio No. 1*. Editions Musicus. Trombone, Euphonium, and Tuba. 1965. $6.00. 10:00. IV. $E♭_1$–e♭. A technical work with the tuba part mostly in the low register.

Orrego-Salas, Juan. *De Profundis*. MMB Music, Inc. Tuba and Four Cellos. 1979. D_1–e'. Commissioned by Harvey Phillips.

Orrego-Salas, Juan. *Midsummer Diversions*. MMB Music, Inc. Cello and Tuba. 1987. 10:10. V. D_1–e'. Four movements: Milonga; Ragtime; Modinha; Zingaresca. Commissioned by the Eva Janzer Cello Center. Dedicated to Janos Starker and Harvey Phillips.

Osmon, Leroy. *The Kesten Suite for Flute and Tuba*. RBC Publications. Flute and Tuba. 2004. 10.00. IV. $G♭_1$–d'. Dedicated to R. Winston Morris, Dave Kirk, and Andrew S. Kesten. Five Movements: Slowly; Moderately Fast; Gently and Rubato; Moderate March Tempo; Expressivo, Allegro. The movements are of contrasting style and the work could serve as a good change of pace on a recital. This piece is second in a projected series of duets for flute and various other instruments (the first is *The Kole Suite* for flute and violin). Each movement of *The Kesten Suite* is a portrait or caricature of the person named in the title. The original titles are listed at random in the program notes and not placed at the heading of the movements. Unlike *The Kole Suite,* the composer wanted the performer, as well as the listener, to decide which title goes with which movement. The titles are taken from events in the life of Andrew Kesten.

Paasch, Antony. *Baroque Suite.* Tuba-Euphonium Press. Bassoon and Tuba. 2002. $10.00. IV. E_1–b. Prelude; Gavotte; Courante; Sarabande; Minuet; Gigue. Dedicated to Judy and Gary Buttery. Good music which works well for the combination of bassoon and tuba.

Pachelbel, Johann. *Fugue on "Ein Feste Burg."* tr. J. Kent Mason. Sonante Publications. 2 Trumpets, Trombone, Tuba (or Bass Trombone). 1978. $5.50. 1:30. II–III. D–a.

Pachelbel, Johann. *2 Magnificats.* Robert King Music Sales. Flexible Brass Quartet with Tuba. $3.40.

Palestrina, G. P. *Adoramus.* arr. Lewis Waldeck. Cor Publishing Company. Trumpet, Horn, Trombone, Tuba. $3.00.

Palestrina, G. P. *Ricercare del Primo Tono.* Robert King Music Sales. Flexible Brass Quartet with Tuba. $4.20.

Palestrina, G. P. *Three Hymns.* Robert King Music Sales. Flexible Brass Quartet with Tuba. $3.40.

Parker, J. *Music for Two—Six Duets.* Patterson's Publications. Trombone and Tuba (or Euphonium). $8.95.

Payne, Frank Lynn. *Canzona de Sonare.* Manuscript available from the composer. Tuba and Woodwind Quintet. 1982. 10:00. IV. E_1–f'. Single movement with three sections. To Skip Gray. An energetic chamber music work exploring renaissance counterpoint ideas within modern tonal and harmonic practice. See: Bird, Gary, ed.; *Program Notes for the Solo Tuba.*

Pearsall, Ed. *Duet for Tuba and Piccolo.* TUBA Press. Tuba and Piccolo. 1991. $10.00. 12:00. III. F_1–c'. Two movements: Lightly; Slowly. Simple, characteristic writing for the piccolo and tuba.

Peaslee, Richard. *The Devil's Herald.* Margun Music. Tuba, 4 Horns, Percussion. 1975. $15.00. 8:45. V. E♭$_1$–a♭'. One continuous movement. For Harvey Phillips. An interesting and powerful work with varied colors yielded from both orchestration and effects including wind sounds and fluttertongue sections. See: Bird, Gary, ed.; *Program Notes for the Solo Tuba.*

Penn, William. *Capriccio for Tuba and Marimba.* Keyboard Percussion Publications. Tuba and Marimba. 1992. 9:10. III–IV. F_1–e' (gliss from nondescript low note to highest note possible). Continuous work in rondo form. Written for John Turk and Rosemary Small. A tuneful, entertaining work reminiscent of movie soundtrack music. Well-written parts for both tuba and marimba. Recorded by Jeffrey Jarvis and Gene Pokorny.

Persichetti, Vincent. *Serenade No. 1 for Ten Wind Instruments, Opus 1.* Elkan-Vogel Inc. Flute, Oboe, Clarinet, Bassoon, 2 Trumpets, 2 Horns, Trombone, Tuba. 1929. $20.00. 6:30. III. F♯$_1$–g♭. Five movements: Prelude; Episode; Song; Interlude; Dance. Pleasant chamber music foreshadowing the *Serenade No. 12* for solo tuba, which is much more demanding. Recorded by the United States Coast Guard Band.

Peterson, T. *Allegro.* arr. J. Strautman. Valentin Avvakoumov. 4 Trombones and Tuba. 1978. 1:30. III–IV. G_1–b♭. A energetic, melodic work employing romantic harmonies. A good opener or encore piece for a concert or recital.

Petit, Philip. *Les 4 Vents.* Alphonse Leduc. Trumpet, 2 Horns, and Tuba. $42.00.

Pimentel, Tomás. *Tema Baixo (Low Theme).* Lusitanus Editions, Portugal. Two Tubas, Accordion and Drums. 2003. 10:00. V. Tuba 1: D_1–g♭'. Tuba 2: G_1–a♭'. Commissioned by and dedicated to Sérgio Carolino. This jazz piece requires improvisation on both tubas. Premiered at the ITEC 2004 by Sérgio Carolino and Janos Mazura.

Plagge, Wolfgang. *Trio for Trombone, Tuba and Piano, Opus 95.* Music Information Centre Norway. 1997. 10:00.

Plog, Anthony. *Dialogue.* Editions BIM. Horn in F, Tuba, Piano. 1992. 5:00. III. C–e'. As the name depicts, a conversational composition, the melodic lines generally trading off between the two solo instruments. The piano functions mainly as accompaniment. No exceptional difficulties.

Pluister, S. *Divertimento.* Donemus. 2 Flutes, Oboe, Clarinet, Bassoon, Trumpet, Horn, Tuba, Bass, Percussion. $15.50.

Polin, Claire. *The Death of Procris (Studies after a Painting by Piero de Cosimo).* Seesaw Music Corporation. Flute and Tuba. 1972–73. $11.00. 5:30. IV–V. D_1–e'. Two movements: Background; Foreground. Commissioned by Kenneth and Elizabeth Singleton. A difficult, "modern" work requiring much rhythmically free interplay between flute and tuba. Contains some nontraditional performance requirements including humming, slap-clicks, and extensive multiphonics in the flute part.

Powell, Morgan. *Transitions for Solo Tuba and Chamber Ensemble.* TUBA Press. Solo Tuba, Flute, Clarinet, Oboe, Tenor Saxophone, Trumpet, Trombone, Violin, Bass, 2 Percussion, Piano. 1991. $30.00. 10:20. V. E♭$_1$–b♭' (also "highest note possible" indicated). For Daniel Perantoni and Edwin London. A very difficult work featuring the solo tuba, requiring performers to play strict rhythms in some sections while in others making free gestures. The work is recorded and was performed live preceded by Morgan Powell's unaccompanied tuba solo *Midnight Realities.* Recorded by Daniel Perantoni.

Presser, William. *5 Duets for Trombone and Tuba.* Theodore Presser Company. Trombone and Tuba. $7.00.

Presser, William. *5 Duets for Trumpet and Tuba.* Theodore Presser Company. Trumpet and Tuba. 1985. $6.00. 6:19. III–IV. G_1–a (Trumpet part goes to high c). Five movements: Adagio; Allegretto; Allegretto; Allegro; Adagio. The movements are of contrasting style and the work could serve as a good change of pace on a recital. There is little rest, so endurance could be a problem for the trumpet whose part lies mainly in the top and above the staff.

Presser, William. *Five Duets for Tuba and Timpani.* Theodore Presser Company. Tuba and Timpani. 1981. $4.00. 6:30. III. G_1–c'. Five movements: Adagio; Andante; Tempo de valce; Andante; Finale. A simple work with lots of interplay between the tuba and timpani.

Presser, William. *Quintet for Horns and Tuba.* Tenuto Publications. 4 Horns and Tuba. 1988. $12.00. 5:15. III. F_1–b♭. Four movements: Allegretto; Adagio; Poco allegro; Allegro moderato. Tuba part is somewhat simple yet soloistic.

Presser, William. *Seven Duets for Horn and Tuba.* Seesaw Music Corporation. Horn and Tuba. 1972. $9.00. 7:00. III–IV. E_1 (D_1)–d'. Seven movements: Andante; Allegro; Allegro; Allegro molto; Adagio-Allegro; Vivace; Allegro. These duets, reminiscent of Bach two-part inventions employing more modern tonal boundaries, are music which can be used for casual playing encounters or possibly in recital.

Presser, William. *7 Duets for Tuba and Violin.* Theodore Presser. Tuba and Violin. $4.50.

Prokofiev, Sergey. *"March" from A Love for Three Oranges.* arr. G. Strautman. Parow'sche Musikalien. 3 Trombones and Tuba. 1:46. Recorded by the Russian National Symphony Orchestra Low Brass Section.

Pryor, Arthur. *The Whistler and His Dog—A Caprice.* arr. John Hoesly. Piston Reed Stick and Bow Publisher. Solo Tuba in Brass Quintet. 1985. $11.00. 2:45. II–III. $B♭_1$–g. An easy arrangement of an old classic tune.

Purcell, Henry. *Allegro and Air from "King Arthur."* Robert King Music Sales. Flexible Brass Quartet with Tuba. $3.40.

Purcell, Henry. *Canon on a Ground Bass.* arr. Skip Gray. Shawnee Press, Inc. Trombone (or Euphonium) and 2 Tubas. $4.00. See listing under Music for Multiple Tubas.

Purcell, Henry. *Fantasia #1.* arr. Irving Rosenthal. Western International Music. Horn, Trombone, and Tuba. 1968. $5.00. 2:00. III–IV. G_1–d♭'. A good arrangement for low brass trio. The tuba part is mostly in the upper tessitura.

Purcell, Henry. *Music for Queen Mary II .* Robert King Music Sales. Flexible Brass Quartet with Tuba. $3.40.

Purcell, Henry. *Two Trumpet Tunes and Air.* Robert King Music Sales. Flexible Brass Quartet with Tuba. $5.55.

Rasmussen, Mary, arr. *Christmas Music (40 Carols).* Robert King Music Sales. Flexible Brass Quartet with Tuba. $26.45.

Raum, Elizabeth. *Aegean Perspective.* Canadian Music Centre. 1999. Flute, Clarinet, Saxophone, Tuba, Percussion, and Narrator. 14:00. Seven movements: Pluto and Persephone; Arachne and Minerva; The Graces; The Fates; Sisyphus; Ariadne and Theseus; Atlas. Commissioned by saxophonist Shelley Jagow and Wright State University. Premiered at ITEC 2000 with tubist Jason Smith. *Aegean Perspective* is a Mycenaean Greek mythology with a modern slant. The musicians themselves narrate as well as play, and the stories, although taken from original Greek legend, will have their own particular contemporary flavor. The unusual combination of saxophone, flute, clarinet, tuba, and percussion is especially effective for creating the wide palette of musical colors needed for this piece.

Read, Thomas. *Brillenbass.* ACA Music Publishers. Solo Tuba and Celeste (also playing 2 Suspended Cymbals). 1993. $18.00. 11:00. IV. C_1–f'. Single movement with contrasting sections. For Mark Nelson. A powerful work with melodic material reminiscent of chant or folk songs. Controlled soft playing in the pedal register is required as well as long forte sections above the staff.

Reed, Alfred. *Double Wind Quintet.* Marks Music Corporation. Flute, Oboe, Clarinet, Bassoon, 2 Trumpets, 2 Horns, Trombone, Tuba. 1973. $25.00. 16:00. IV. G_1–b♭. Three movements: Intrada (Fanfares, Entrances and Marches); Pavane (Elegy); Toccata (Rock). This enjoyable chamber music is of a generally popular nature. Although the tuba part is not soloistic, the player has plenty of material with which to keep themselves occupied and will definitely be noticed!

Reiche, Gottfried. *Sonatas No. 1, 15, 18, 19, 24, 7, 21 and 22.* Robert King Music Sales. Flexible Brass Quartet with Tuba. $3.40 each.

Revueltas, Sylvestre. *3 Sonetos.* Southern Music Publishing Company (dist. by Theodore Presser). 2 Clarinets, Bass Clarinet, Bassoon, 2 Trumpets, Horn, Tuba, Piano, Percussion. $12.00.

Reynolds, R. *Blind Men.* C. F. Peters Corporation. 3 Trumpets, 3 Trombones, Tuba, Percussion, and Piano. $10.00.

Reynolds, R. *Wedge.* C. F. Peters Corporation. 2 Trumpets, 2 Trombones, Tuba, 2 Flutes, Bass, Piano, Percussion, and Celeste. Rental from the publisher.

Reynolds, Verne. *Signals for Trumpet, Tuba, and Brass Ensemble.* Available from the composer. Solo Trumpet, Solo Tuba, and Brass Ensemble. 1976. 10:50. IV–V. D_1–a♭'. Continuous work in three large sections. Commissioned by Thomas Stevens and Roger Bobo. There are several sections in which the soloists are required to play somewhat freely over ostinato figures in the brass ensemble. Many wide, irregular leaps, and interactive dovetailing between solo parts. Recorded by Roger Bobo.

Reynolds, Verne. *Trio for Horn, Trombone, and Tuba.* Margun Music. Horn, Trombone, and Tuba. 1978. $16.00.

Rice, Thomas. *Bass Quartet.* Seesaw Music Corporation. Tuba, String Bass, Contrabassoon, Timpani. $18.00.

Rice, Thomas. *Music for Brass Duo, Opus 53F.* Seesaw Music Corporation. Trumpet and Tuba. $9.00.

Rice, Thomas. *Music for Brass Quartet, Opus 53A.* Seesaw Music Corporation. Trumpet, Horn, Trombone, and Tuba. $30.00.

Rice, Thomas. *Thing for Tuba and Timpani, Opus 52.* Seesaw Music Corporation. Tuba and Timpani. 1982. $15.00 6:10. III. G_1–b♭. Single movement with four sections. No substantial demands in this work in which neither instrument is used particularly melodically but most often pass timpani-like figures between one another.

Riddle, Peter. *Concertino.* Seesaw Music Corporation. Tuba, Flute, 6 Percussion. V.

Ridout, Alan. *Concertino for Tuba and Strings.* Emerson Edition LTD. Solo Tuba and Strings or String Quartet (Piano reduction available). See listing under Tuba and Orchestra.

Rimsky-Korsakov, Nicolai. *Flight of the Tuba Bee.* arr. Howard Cable. Canadian Brass Publications (G. Schirmer). Solo Tuba, 2 Trumpets, Horn, Trombone. 1979. $16.00. 1:30. V. E_1–e'. The classic virtuoso encore arranged excellently for solo tuba in brass quintet. Recorded by the Canadian Brass.

Roikjer, Kjell. *Variations and Fugue.* Wilhelm Hansen Musikforlag. 2 Trumpets, Trombone, and Tuba. $9.25.

Rollin, Robert. *Chamber Concerto.* Seesaw Music Corporation. Solo Tuba, Piccolo, Oboe, Clarinet, Saxophone, Trumpet, Trombone, and Percussion. 1993.

Rollin, Robert. *Concertino No. 2.* Seesaw Music Corporation. Flute, Tuba, Percussion Ensemble. $30.00.

Rollin, Robert. *The Raven and the First Men.* Seesaw Music Corporation. Horn, Tuba, Piano, Tape. $40.00.

Rollin, Robert. *Trio for Trumpet, Trombone, and Tuba.* Seesaw Music Corporation. Trumpet, Trombone, and Tuba. 1993.

Rønnes, Robert. *Scherzetto.* Music Information Centre Norway. Tuba and Percussion. 1981. 2:00.

Rossini, Gioacchino. *Overture to the Opera William Tell.* arr. Kenneth P. Drobnak. Tuba-Euphonium Press. Brass Quintet featuring Solo Tuba. 1997. $16.00. 5:00. V. C–c''. Dedicated to Mrs. Kenneth Ledford. A challenging arrangement of this well-known work featuring the tuba. Tubist must have strong technique and proficient double-tonguing. Nicely scored so that the tubist will be easily heard.

Rubenstein, Arthur B. *Bruegel-Dance Visions.* Editions BIM. Solo Tuba, Viola, Cello, Bass, Harp, Percussion, and Synthesizer. 1991. 14:45. IV. F♯$_1$–g♭'. Four movements: Aubade (The Misanthrope); Estampie (Children's Games); Pavanne (Land of Cockaigne); Rondeau (Struggle Between Carnival and Lent). Commissioned by Jim Self. Four movements based on paintings by the sixteenth-century Flemish painter Pieter Bruegel. Some difficult rhythmic writing. Reviewed in the Summer 1997 issue of the *TUBA Journal* (Vol. 24, No. 4). Recorded by Jim Self.

Russell, Armand. *Suite Concertante.* Accura Music. Tuba and Woodwind Quintet (Piano reduction available). 1961. $36.00. 11:15. IV. G_1–f♯'. Four movements: Capriccio; Ballade; Scherzo; Burlesca. Good chamber music employing traditional musical idioms. See: Bird, Gary, ed.; *Program Notes for the Solo Tuba.* Recorded by Floyd Cooley.

Rybrant, Stig. *Deep Brass Joke: Scherzo.* H. Busch. (Swedish Music Information Center). 4 Trombones and Tuba. 1954. 3:30.

Ryker, Robert. *Petite Marche, Op.11.* Ryker Associates, Inc. Bass Trombone (or Euphonium), Bass Tuba, and Pianoforte. 1983. A march in three short sections based on a melodic motive repeatedly imitated between the two brass instruments.

Sabatini, G. *Ecstasy.* Camara Music Publishers. Solo Tuba, 2 Trumpets, Horn, Trombone, Violin, and Harp. $9.00.

Saglietti, Corrado Maria. *Concerto for Tuba and Four Horns.* Edition BIM. Tuba and Four Horns (Piano accompaniment also available). 1985. 8:45. III–IV. G♭$_1$–e'. Three movements: Allegro; Adagio; Allegro con Spirito. Very approachable, melodic work with difficult horn parts. Reviewed in the Fall 1999 issue of the *TUBA Journal* (Vol. 27, No. 1). Recored by Markus Hötzel.

Salotti, Harry. *Music.* Tuba-Euphonium Press. Tuba and Woodwind Quintet. 2001. $20.00. 6:00. IV. F_1–e'. Good chamber music with accompanying parts not causing any balance problems for the soloist.

Sandström, Sven-David. *Ratio.* Swedish Music Information Center. Tuba and Bass Drum. 1974. 6:00.

Sassetti, Bernardo. *Suite á Procura de um nome.* Available from the composer. Tuba, Marimba, and Piano. 2002. 10:00. IV. C_2–f'. Four movements: Preludio; Vontade; O Fado e o Tempo; Construção. Commissioned by the Caldas da Rainha Music Festival and dedicated to the Caldas da Rainha Music Conservatory. Premiered in the Caldas da Rainha Music Festival in 2002 with the composer Bernardo Sassetti on piano,

Sérgio Carolino, tuba, and Jean-François Lézé, marimba. Some improvisation required.

Schelle, Michael. *Blue Plate Special.* American Composers Edition, Inc. Solo Tuba and Percussion. 1983. $6.35. 18:00.

Schickele, Peter. *Little Suite for Winter.* Theodore Presser Company. Clarinet and Tuba. 1981. $18.00. 11:00. III–IV. E♭$_1$–c♯'. Five movements: Fantasia; Blues Bounce; Lullaby; Rondo; Traveling Music. Commissioned by Rodger Vaughan for the occasion of his 50th birthday tuba recital. Nice, effervescent chamber music for clarinet and tuba.

Schilling, Hans Ludwig. *Meeting.* Hans Ludwig Schilling. Tuba and Contrabassoon.

Schilling, Hans Ludwig. *Sonate en Trio.* J. P. Tonger Verlag, Köln. Trumpet, Tuba, and Piano.

Schmidt, F. *Tullnerbacher Blasmusik.* Ludwig Doblinger K.G. 2 Trumpets, 3 Horns, Tuba, and 2 Oboes. $15.15.

Schmidt, William. *Concertino.* Western International Music, Inc. Piano, 2 Trumpets, Horn, Trombone, and Tuba (or Bass Trombone). 1969. IV. Three movements: Allegro con brio; Largo; Allegro con spirito. A true mini-concerto with extended albeit conservative harmonies and influences of American musical idioms.

Schmidt, William. *Concertino for Tuba (or Bass Trombone) and Woodwind Quintet.* Western International Music, Inc. Tuba (or Bass Trombone) and Woodwind Quintet. 1980. $15.00. 12:00. III. A♭$_1$–c♯'. Three movements. For Terry Cravens. Good chamber music featuring the tuba which goes together without difficulty. Tuba mute is required in the second movement. See: Bird, Gary, ed.; *Program Notes for the Solo Tuba.*

Schmidt, William. *Latin Rhythms.* Western International Music, Inc. Tuba and Percussion. 1989. $18.00. 9:00. IV. E$_1$–g'. Four movements: Introduction; Tangoletto; Bossalina Nova; Chat Chat Chat. To Gary Brittin. Fairly complex rhythms pervade this work which, much of the time, scores the tuba like an extension of the percussion instruments. A true chamber duet. Bucket and cup mutes required of the tubist.

Schmidt, William. *Music for Scrimshaws.* Western International Music, Inc. 2 Trumpets, Horn, Trombone, Tuba, and Harp. $15.00.

Schmidt, William. *Sonatina.* Western International Music, Inc. Horn, Trombone, and Tuba. $7.00.

Schmidt, William. *Tony and The Elephant or Jim and The Road Runner.* Western International Music Inc. Trumpet and Tuba. 1984. $8.00. 8:30. IV–V. G$_1$–e'. Five movements: Stomp'n'; Waltz'n'; Blues'n'; Swing'n'; Trip'n'. For Tony Plog and Jim Self. Cup, bucket, and straight mutes requested. Contrasting movements present a stylistic challenge. See: Bird, Gary, ed.; *Program Notes for the Solo Tuba.*

Schmitt, F. *Quatuor.* Editions Billaudot. 3 Trombones and Tuba. $29.00.

Schmitt, M. *Trio.* Bote & Bock K.G. Trumpet, Trombone, and Tuba. $26.40.

Schooley, John H. *Partita for Brass Quartet.* Kendor Music, Inc. 2 Trumpets, Trombone, Tuba. 1969. 6:20. II–III. F$_1$–a. Six movements: Chorale; Invention for Two Trumpets; Pastorale; Invention for Trombone and Tuba; Fugato; Finale. A good contest or recital work for a high school group.

Schuback, Peter. *Lignes paralleles.* Swedish Music Information Center. Flute, Alto, and Tuba. 1975.

Schubert, Franz. *Ave Maria.* arr. Ernst-Thilo Kalke. Musikverlag Bruno Uetz. Tuba and Brass Ensemble (4 Trumpets, Horn, 4 Trombones). 2003. 2:30. IV. A♭$_1$–e♭'. Nice opportunity for the tubist to be featured playing a beautiful melody. Because of the high tessitura, this arrangement is suitable for E♭ or F tuba. Orchestration is colorful, but light so that the soloist can be easily heard.

Schuller, Gunther. *Little Brass Music.* Mentor Music. Trumpet, Horn, Trombone, and Tuba. 1963. $5.00. 4:00. IV–V. F$_1$–d♭'. A difficult modern chamber music work.

Schuller, Gunther. *Perpetuum Mobile.* Margun Music Inc. 4 Horns and Tuba (or Bassoon). $10.00. Horns are muted throughout in this light work reminiscent of twentieth-century French chamber music.

Schust, Alfred. *Duo for Tuba and Flute.* Musikverlag Barbara Evans. Tuba and Flute. 1989. 7:45. IV. G$_1$–g'. Four movements: I; II. Presto agitato; III. Adagio; IV. Presto. Good post-romantic chamber music. The tubist is required to change registers and roles (from accompanying to lead) quite rapidly. Some difficult, irregular chromatic alterations in some passages, especially in the fourth movement.

Schust, Alfred. *Trio for Flute (doubling Piccolo), Alto Sax, and Tuba.* Musikverlag Barbara Evans. Flute, Alto Sax, and Tuba. 1984. 7:15. III–IV. E♯$_1$ (D$_1$)–e'. Three movements. Nice neo-romantic chamber music in three well-balanced, contrasting movements—an opening Allegro moderato, Waltz "à la mode," and a concluding march-like movement. Although the flute is truly the lead voice, the saxophone and tuba parts are challenging and rewarding to play.

Schwartz, Elliott. *Spectrum.* Tuba-Euphonium Press. For Horn, Cello, and Tuba. 2002. $12.00. 8:00. IV–V. F♯$_1$–d'. Composed for Richard Francis and Scott Vallaincourt. Conceived as a set of seven very brief variations. A difficult and complex work that will require careful rehearsal and attention to detail. Performers are called upon to speak very rapidly into their instruments real phrases and sentences that are punctuated by abrupt pauses. The words that are spoken are taken from the mnemonic that was used to teach children the colors of the spectrum: ROY G BIV, commonly known as red, orange, yellow, green, blue, indigo, and violet. Requires virtuoso performers. Reviewed in the Summer 2001 issue of the *TUBA Journal* (Vol. 28, No. 4).

Sear, Walter. *Quartet.* Cor Publishing. 2 Trumpets, Trombone, and Tuba. $14.00.

Self, Jim. *Contra-Dictions.* Basset Hound Music. Two Solo Tubas, Two Antiphonal Brass Sextets, Percussion. 1998. 10:30. Premiered by Daniel Perantoni and Robert Tucci.

Self, Jim. *Courante.* Basset Hound Music. Tuba, Trombone, Alto Saxophone. 1991. 6:30. IV–V. Tuba: D_1–a' (Trombone: A_1–e♭"!). The work is based on the French baroque dance form, in triple meter with rhythmic variations. Includes an improvisatory section for the tubist. The trombone part may be considered more difficult than the tuba part with its high tessitura, wide intervallic leaps, and lack of rests which could present an endurance challenge. Recorded by Jim Self.

Self, Jim. *Tail Spins.* Basset Hound Music. Flute, Violin, Viola, Tuba. 2001. 5:00. One movement.

Self, Jim. *Winks 'n Jinks.* Basset Hound Music. Solo Tuba and Four Trombones. 1995. 8:00. One movement. Written for Norm Pearson and LA Philharmonic Trombones.

Seráns, X. Carlos. *Four pezas para tuba solista e trombones.* Published by the composer. Solo Tuba and Trombone Quartet. 2000. IV–V. Four movements: Alborada; Balada; Vals; Pasarruás.

Sermila, Jarmo. *Quasi come Quasimodo.* Edition Wilhelm Hansen. Tuba and Percussion. 1997. 10:00. IV. F_1–f'. A long, single-movement piece with many different sections and styles. This piece is full of wide, dissonant intervals and extreme dynamic changes. Reviewed in the Summer 1999 issue of the *TUBA Journal* (Vol. 26, No. 4).

Shire, David. *Marlows Theme.* arr. Staffan Lundén Velden. Ovation. Tuba and Brass Quintet. 1988. $34.01. 3:00. III. F–g'. Written for Trombone, but adapted for Tuba in this arrangement for Brass Quintet and Solo Tuba. The solo part can be played on other instruments and the set is delivered with solo parts in B♭, C, E♭, G, and bass clef. Arrangement also available for Solo Tuba and Brass Sextet.

Sigurbjörsson, Thorkell. *Donkey Dance.* Iceland Music Information Centre. Tuba, Double Bass, and Piano. 4:00. V. E_1–f♯'. A work which attempts to imitate the polymetric freedom of ethnic folk music.

Silverman, Faye-Ellen. *Dialogue.* Seesaw Music Corporation. Horn and Tuba. 1975–76. $10.00. 4:30. III. F_1–d'. Continuous work in two sections. The opening section consists of steady eighth notes and long, sustained trill passages handed between horn and tuba. The second section is contrapuntal, featuring frequent dissonance, several half-valve glisses, and one short phrase requiring simultaneous singing and playing by the tubist.

Singleton, Ken, tr. and ed. *Ars Nova Duets.* PP Music. F Horn and Tuba. 1984. $9.00. 22 pages. III. b♭–d'. Fifteen individual works included in the volume. Very little music from the fourteenth century is available transcribed for tubists, and this collection is a good introduction. These duets, lying in and slightly above the staff, will also extend a younger player's range and security in the upper register.

Skjelbred, Bjørn Bolstad. *Heavy Metal: En Rip-Off for Bass Tuba and Slagverk.* Music Information Centre Norway. Tuba and Percussion. 1995. 7:30.

Smit, Leo, arr. *Taps.* Theodore Presser Company. Five Trombones and Tuba. 1980. $6.00. 0:35. II. E_1 (optional octave higher)–G_1. Composed for the 1980 Brevard Music Center Trombone Choir. A simple harmonization of the old standard bugle call featuring the first trombone on the melody.

Smith, Glenn. *Beyond the Dream and to the Sun.* Seesaw Music Corporation. Solo Tuba, Flute, Oboe, Bass Clarinet, Bassoon, Piano. $26.50.

Smith, Glenn. *Forowen.* Seesaw Music Corporation. Alto Flute and Tuba. 1972. $7.00. 3:45. IV. B♭$_2$–highest note possible (highest notated pitch is e'). Dedicated to John and Sally Turk. Interestingly orchestrated music requiring both players to simultaneously sing and play in several sections. The three *Forowen* pieces work very well performed as a set on a recital program.

Smith, Glenn. *Forowen 2.* Seesaw Music Corporation. Flute and Tuba. 1979. $7.00. 3:00. IV. C_1–g'. A brief, reflective work with a haunting melody and unresolved dissonance which can truly leave the conservative listener unnerved. The composer uses a wide range in both parts to attain coloristic variety. A brief section with some difficult sixteenth note interplay with wide intervallic leaps.

Smith, Glenn. *Forowen 3.* Seesaw Music Corporation. Piccolo and Tuba. 1979. $7.00. 2:30. IV. F_1–g'. For John and Laurie Turk. An interesting, two-part invention with some difficult non-tonal sixteenth note passages and simultaneous sing-play sections. *Forowen 3* contains fewer traditional dissonances than its two predecessors but is much more energetic and technically demanding. Recorded by John Turk.

Smith, Glenn. *Music for Horns, Tuba, and Violas.* Seesaw Music Corporation. 2 Horns, Tuba, 2 Violas. $28.00.

Sønstevold, Gunnar. *Duet for Harp and Tuba.* Music Information Centre Norway.

St. Saens, Camille. *Adagio from the "Third Symphony."* arr. J. Strautman. Valentin Avvakoumov. 4 Trombones and Tuba. 1978. 4:00. III. A♭$_1$–g. A nice low brass arrangement of the famous chorale from the "Organ Symphony."

St. Saens, Camille, and Mussorgsky, Modest. *Two Tuba Solos: The Elephant and Bydlo.* arr. David Camesi. Western International Music, Inc. Solo Tuba in Brass Quintet. 1974. $7.00. 2:00. III. E_1–e'. Two separate movements which can be played by themselves. A good arrangement, mostly in the bread and butter range, of two works often associated with the tuba. Bydlo is a major third lower than the Ravel orchestral key and thus much more easily playable.

Stallings, Lee. *Rhapsody for Tuba.* Les Stallings Music Group. 1999. 11:25. IV. F_1–f'. Three movements: Emergence; Kathy's Song; Free Flight. Commissioned by the Denver Brass for tuba soloist Kathleen Aylsworth-Brantigan and the Aries Brass Quintet. Premiered June 1997. This is a three-movement work for solo tuba within a brass quintet setting. This is a difficult piece, technically demanding for both soloist and ensemble.

Stepanyan, A. *Nocturne for 3 Trombones and Tuba.* ed. Keith Brown. International Music Company. 3 Trombones and Tuba. $5.50.

Stephens, Denzil. *Rondo Rotundo.* Sarnia Music. Solo Tuba with Brass Ensemble or Brass Band. 1989. $23.00. 3:00. IV. G_1–f'. A brisk tuba showpiece with contrasting technical and lyric sections.

Stevens, John. *City Suite.* Available from the composer. Tuba, Flute, Flugelhorn, Trombone, Vibes, Guitar, Piano, Bass, and Drums. 1978. 20:00. IV. $B♭_1$–f'. Three movements: Home Again; Central Park Down; Crush Hour. Composed for Toby Hanks. A jazz work featuring the tuba and requiring improvisation.

Stevens, John. *Country Suite.* Available from the composer. Tuba, Flute, Flugelhorn, Vibes, Guitar, Piano, Bass, and Drums. 1977. 20:00. IV. C–d'. Three movements: Amazing Place "How Sweet the Sound"; Lazy Day Song; Saturday Night Stompin'. Composed for Toby Hanks. A companion jazz suite, featuring the tuba, to *City Suite.* Improvisation by the tubist is required.

Stevens, John. *Dialogues for Horn and Tuba.* Manuscript from the composer. Horn and Tuba. 1987. 12:00. IV–V. C_1–e'. Five movements: Prologue and Dance; March; Scherzo; Lament; Dance and Epilogue. Style of movements contrasting with pop and jazz influences throughout. The tuba part is quite rhythmically demanding.

Stevens, John. *Dialogues for Trombone and Tuba.* Southern Music Publishing Company (in N.Y.; See: Theodore Presser). Trombone and Tuba. 1987. $8.50. 10:00. IV–V. E_1–f♯'. Four movements: Fanfare; Aria; Scherzo; Finale. A great deal of melodic and rhythmic interaction between the two instruments. The "fast" tempos are extremely quick and the tuba part is rhythmically demanding.

Stevens, John. *Dialogues for Trumpet and Tuba.* Manuscript available from the composer. Trumpet and Tuba. 1988. 10:00. IV–V. $E♭_1$–g'. Four movements: Fanfare; Scherzo; Chant; Finale. More exploratory than typical of Mr. Stevens's work, with greater use of dissonance and free sections, multiphonics, and mute required of the tubist.

Stevens, John. *Triangles.* Gordon V. Thompson Music. Horn, Trombone, and Tuba. 1978. $18.00. 11:00. IV–V. G_1–f'. A one-movement work with four sections each connected by a solo cadenza. Good chamber music employing jazz rhythms and style throughout. Recorded by John Stevens.

Stewart, Joseph. *TUBA.* Kendor Music, Inc. Solo Tuba, SATB Chorus, String Bass (Versions for Solo Tuba and Band, Solo Tuba and Piano available). 1973. 3:00. III. $B♭_1$–b♭. Two connected sections: Presto; Jazz Waltz. Dedicated to Andy Peruzzini and the Maryvale High School Chorale. Some stylistic and technical challenges for the soloist. The choral accompaniment is more difficult than the band accompaniment and may require the piano accompaniment also be played.

Stewart, Robert. *Heart Attack.* American Composers Alliance. Tuba and 2 Percussionists (I: Xylophone, Vibes, Orchestra Bells; II: Conga, Timbales, Brake Drum, Triangle, Maracas). 1973. 9:00. $D♭_1$–a♭'. For Barton Cummings. A difficult contemporary work with wide intervals, disjunct note groupings, and several effects including glissandi and slapping the instrument

Strautman, J. *Ragtime.* Valentin Avvakoumov. 4 Trombones and Tuba. 1991. 5:30. III. $B♭_1$–a. A well-crafted little rag with a tricky six-bar tuba solo in the middle.

Strautman, J. *Serenade.* Valentin Avvakoumov. 4 Trombones and Tuba. 1990. 3:00. III–IV. G–b♭. An expressive, melodic work which features the tuba.

Strautman, J. *Waltz in "5 X 5."* Valentin Avvakoumov. 4 Trombones and Tuba. 1992. 4:00. III–IV. $A♭_1$–d♭'. A traditional waltz-style work in quintuple meter. Although the tuba does not have the principal part throughout, it is the featured part.

Sundstrups, Leif. *Azira Phal's.* TubaMania International. Solo Tuba and Brass Choir (4 Trumpets, 4 Horns, 4 Trombones, Tuba, Timpani, and 1 Percussionist). 1996. 3:00. Written for Steve Rossé and the Sydney Symphony Brass. A short composition in the style of a fanfare and prayer.

Szentpáli, Roland. *Ballade.* Editions BIM. Tuba and String Quartet (or String Orchestra). 2002. 11:00. IV–V. E_1–g'. Dedicated to Meister Anton Meinl for his eightieth birthday. A lyrical composition in a tonal setting. No exceptional technical difficulties except for a few wide tonal leaps in the third movement. The tessitura is not as high as in most of this composer's writings. The string quartet plays mainly the role of accompanist, intertwining with the tuba part, which is always soloistic.

Szentpáli, Roland. *Earth Voices.* Editions BIM. Solo Tuba, 4 Euphoniums, 4 Tubas, and Narrator. Text by Levente Kovesdi. 2000. 9:00. V. $42.50.

Szentpáli, Roland. *Jazz Quintet.* Editions BIM. Solo Tuba and Saxophone Quartet. 1995/96. 9:00. IV–V. Also available as Brass Quintet.

Szkutko, John. *5 Episodes for Brass.* SZK Music. 2 Cornets, Tenor Horn, and Tuba. IV–V. E♭$_1$–f'. Five sections: March; Hymn; I Say, I Say, I Say; 30 Second Waltz; Finale. Good chamber music that will challenge the performers, with the major difficulty being endurance problems due to the absence of rests.

Szkutko, John. *4 Frogs and a Fly.* SZK Music. Cornet, Horn in E♭, Euphonium, and Tuba. IV–V. B♭$_2$–g'. A character piece that employs traditional musical idioms.

Tackett, Fred. *Yellow Bird.* Hoceanna Music. Solo Tuba, Guitar, Piano, Bass, Drums. 1971–72. 15:45. V. C–b♭'. Three sections: Fast; Not So Fast; Real Fast. Commissioned by and written for Roger Bobo. One of the first pop-jazz works featuring the tuba. Contains ad lib solo section. Recorded by Roger Bobo. See: Bird, Gary, ed.; *Program Notes for the Solo Tuba.*

Talvitie, Riika. *Sulatto for Tuba, Piano, and Percussion.* The Finnish Music Information Centre. 1998. 7:00. V. B$_2$–e'. Premiered by Harri Lidsle, Tarmo Jarvilento, and Olli-Pekka Martikainen in 1997. A virtuosic work of contemporary nature. Rhythmic complexity with contrapuntal activity, frequent metric shifts, and tempo changes. Contains extended technique such as multiphonics and flutter tonguing. Requires rehearsal and mature musicians with impeccable rhythmic activity. Reviewed in the Winter 1999 issue of the *TUBA Journal* (Vol. 27, No. 2).

Tartini, Giusseppe. *Andante Cantabile.* arr. A. Reisman. Camara Music Publishers. Solo Tuba, 2 Trumpets, Horn, Trombone, Violin. $6.00.

Tautenhahn, G. *Trio No. 2.* Seesaw Music Corporation. Tuba, English Horn, Glockenspiel. $16.00.

Tchesnokov, Pavel. *Let My Prayer Come True.* arr. A. Skobelev. Parow'sche Musikalien. Three Trombones and Tuba. 4:48. Recorded by the Russian National Symphony Orchestra Low Brass Section.

Telemann, G. P. *Three Chorale Preludes.* arr. Arthur Frackenpohl. Horizon Press. Trombone (or Euphonium) and Tuba. 1991.

Telemann, G. P. *Three Dances in A Minor.* arr. Walter Hartley. Ensemble Publications, Inc. Flute and Tuba. 1972. $4.00. 5:00. III–IV. A$_1$–c'. Three movements: Moderato; Allegro; Vivace. Chamber music which works very well for flute and tuba.

Tenney, J. *3 Indigenous Songs.* Smith Publications. Tuba or Bassoon, 2 Piccolos, Alto Flute, 2 Percussion. $75.00.

Teuber, Fred W. *Duet Set for Horn and Tuba.* Broad River Press, Inc. Horn and Tuba. 1975. $4.00. 6:15. IV. A♭$_1$–c♯'. Five movements: Starter; Song-Like; Near March; Rock-a-bye; Bog-Hunt Chase. Fun music to play when getting together with a hornist friend.

Thomas, T. Donley. *Bicinia.* Medici Music. Trombone (or Euphonium) and Tuba. $10.00. See listing under Music for Multiple Tubas.

Thommessen, Olav Anton. *MiniaTEXture for Tuba and Percussion.* Music Information Centre Norway. 1985. 6:00.

Tomasi, Henri. *Être ou ne pas être.* Alphonse Leduc. Solo Tuba (or Bass Trombone) and 3 Trombones (Piano accompaniment also available). 1963. $12.20. 6:10. IV. B♭$_1$–d'. Single movement. For the Trombone Quartet of the National Orchestra of the French Radio Theater. A dramatic musical setting of the famous monologue from Shakespeare's Hamlet. Recorded by Arnold Jacobs and Toby Hanks.

Tómasson, Jónas. *Sonata XVII.* Iceland Music Information Centre. Horn, Tuba, and Piano. 1986. 12:00. III–IV. F$_1$–f'. Six movements: Preludia; Intermezzo I; Danza; Canto; Intermezzo II; Finale. Interesting chamber music with some difficult rhythmic interplay in the Danza and Finale movements.

Traditional. *Nobody Knows.* arr. Gordon A. Adnams. Sonante Publications. 2 Trumpets, Trombone, Tuba (or Bass Trombone). 1982. $5.50. 1:45. II. C–c. An easy arrangement in slow swing of the old favorite.

Tull, Fisher. *Concerto da Camera.* Southern Music Company. Alto Sax, 2 Trumpets, Horn, Trombone, and Tuba. $29.95.

Tull, Fisher. *Lament, Opus 32.* Manuscript available from the composer. Four Horns and Tuba. 5:30. III. B$_1$–a. Single movement. Good chamber music featuring the first horn.

Uber, David. *Caricatura, Opus 89.* Available from the composer. Solo Tuba and Brass Ensemble. 1970. 5:20. III. B♭$_1$–c'. Single movement. Commissioned by Harvey Phillips. A tuneful piece with mostly diatonic writing for the soloist. The brass ensemble parts are not difficult and this is an easy work to put together.

Uber, David. *Double Portraits—The City—Concert Sketches for Trombone and Tuba.* Brodt Music Company. Trombone and Tuba. 1967. $4.00. 7:30. III–IV. A♭$_1$–b♭'. Three movements: Times Square; Twilight; The City Awakens. Light music with "pop" sound. Recorded by Michael Lind.

Uber, David. *Giraffe and the Bear, The: A Concert Duo for Flute and Tuba.* Medici Music. Flute and Tuba. 1981. $13.00. 6:40. IV. A♭$_1$–e♭' (f'). Three movements: Allegro vivo; Andante tranquillo; Allegro con fuoco. A tonal piece with a great deal of dialogue activity between the two parts. Third movement has a great deal of shifting polymeters (5/8—4/8—7/8, etc.).

Uber, David. *Rhythmic Contours (Opus 135)*. Available from the composer. Solo Tuba and Percussion (4 players) (Piano reduction available from the composer). $15.00. 10:30. IV–V. A_1–b♭'. One continuous work in five sections. Composed for Barton Cummings. A driving work with little rest for the tubist. Good, active percussion writing keeps the composition moving forward.

Uber, David. *Skylines (Opus 296)*. Hidalgo Music. Solo Tuba (Bass Trombone) and Brass Ensemble. 1992. $30.00. 7:15. IV–V. G_1–a'. Three movements: Manhattan; Chicago; Boston. Composed for and dedicated to Douglas Yeo. Movements have highly individual characters. High tessitura of the solo part make performance on an E♭ or F tuba logical.

Uber, David. *Sonatuba for Solo Tuba, Brass and Percussion (Opus 291)*. TUBA Press. Solo Tuba, Brass, and Percussion (Piano reduction available). 1991. $30.00. 8:00. IV. A♭$_1$–f' (a♭'). Three movements: Allegro moderato; Valse, poco lento; Allegro. For Harvey Phillips. A tuneful work nicely scored so that the tuba is not over-balanced.

Uber, David. *Three Cameos*. Tuba-Euphonium Press. Solo Tuba and Saxophone Quartet. 1993. A♭$_1$–f'. For Harvey Phillips. Three movements. Tuba serves as both soloist and accompanist. Reviewed in the Winter 1997 issue of the *TUBA Journal* (Vol. 25, No. 2).

Van der Velden, Renier. *Concertino*. Centre Belge de Documentation. 2 Pianos, 2 Trumpets, Horn, Trombone, and Tuba. 1965. 12:00.

Van Vactor, David. *Song and Dance (Economy Band No. 2 for Horn, Tuba, and Percussion)*. Roger Rhodes Music, Ltd. Horn, Tuba, and Percussion (Playable by a single performer requiring Bells, Chimes, Marimba, Bass Drum, Snare Drum, Timpani, Cymbal). 1969. Out of Print. 7:00. III–IV. E_1–c'. Two connected sections: Lento—(Meno mosso, con licenza)—Allegretto. A good, conventional work. The inclusion of few rests in the horn part could present endurance problems.

Vasconi, Eugene. *Images*. Southern Music Company, Inc. 2 Trumpets, Trombone, Tuba. $10.00.

Vasconi, Eugene. *Promenade*. Southern Music Company, Inc. 2 Trumpets, Trombone (or Euphonium), Tuba. $5.00. See listing under Music for Multiple Tubas.

Vaughan, Rodger. *Five Carols*. Tuba-Euphonium Press. Tuba and Bassoon. 1999. $8.00. III. E♭$_1$–g. For Marc Dickey. Five Christmas Carols: Good King, Old Wensc; We Three Kings; Silent Night; Jingle Duo; We Wish You. A simple arrangement with a lot of interplay between the two instruments.

Vaughan, Rodger. *Have You Ever?* Tuba-Euphonium Press. Six Songs for Soprano and Tuba. 2002. $8.00. III. E_1–g. Six songs using poems by students from Ms. Major's third grade class, Palmer Lake Elementary School, Colorado. A cute composition with a lot of interplay between the soprano and tuba. Very similar to Anthony Plog's *Animal Ditties* for Narrator, Trumpet, and Piano.

Vaughan, Rodger. *Quattro Bicinie for Clarinet and Tuba*. Philharmusica Corporation. Tuba and B♭ Clarinet. 1967. $7.95. 5:00. III–IV. F_1–d'. Four movements: Intrada; Gavotte; Sarabande; Gigue. To Donal Michalsky. Light music requiring tasteful playing by the tubist.

Vaughan, Rodger. *Quinte Bicinie for Viola and Tuba*. Rodger Vaughan. Viola and Tuba. 1972. 8:00. III–IV. G_1–c'. Five movements: Preludio; Basse Danse; Pavane; Passamezzo; Saltarello. Commissioned by Pamela Goldsmith. For Pam Goldsmith. Effective chamber music with some nice lines and colors, including a small amount of sing/play sections in the tuba part.

Vaughan, Rodger. *Ronda's First Suite*. Tuba-Euphonium Press. Duet for Horn and Tuba. 1994. III. $8.00. A_1–b♭. Four movements: March; Song; Minuet; Galop. For Ronda Ellis. Fun, original composition appropriate for younger performers. The melody is predominantly in the horn part. Also scored for Euphonium and Tuba.

Vaughan, Rodger. *Three Miniatures*. TUBA Press. Tuba and Cello. 1982. $4.00. 5:20. III. C–b♭. Three movements: Allegretto; Canon at the Inversion; Greeley Jazz. For Mattie Robinson on her twelfth birthday. Simple yet interesting works for a change of pace on a recital or a brief fling with a cellist.

Vaughan, Rodger. *3 Songs for Soprano and Tuba—Poems by John Updike*. Trigram Music. Soprano and Tuba. 1968. $7.95. 5:15. IV. E♭$_1$–e♭'. Three movements: The Clan; Lament, for Cocoa; Headline in the Times. For Marjorie Tall. Settings for soprano and tuba of poems by John Updike.

Vazzana, Anthony. *Cambi for Tuba and Percussion*. Available from the composer. Tuba (in F) and Percussionist. 1976. 9:00. V. D_1–b♭'. Three movements: Toccata; Canzona; Giga. For James Self. A difficult work in both technical and ensemble aspects. Some very interesting colors and musical interplay between tubist and percussionist. Piece uses micro tones, singing through instrument, and multiphonics. See: Bird, Gary, ed.; *Program Notes for the Solo Tuba*.

Vesala, Edward. *Taksenta*. Finnish Music Information Centre. Tuba and Percussion. 1998. D♭$_1$–d♭$_2$. Exploration of possibilities in pitch, rhythm, and color with twentieth-century effects including glissandi, flutter tonguing, vocal singing, multiphonics, striking the mouthpiece, and hitting the tuba. Reviewed in the Summer 2000 issue of the *TUBA Journal* (Vol. 27, No. 4).

Vitali, T. *Ciaccona*. arr. G. Sabatini. Camara Music Publishers. Solo Tuba, 2 Trumpets, Horn, Trombone, Violin. $22.00.

Vizzutti, Allen. *Fantasia for Solo Tuba, Brass and Percussion.* Allen Vizzutti. Solo Tuba, Brass Ensemble, and Percussion (Piano reduction available). 1990. 8:00. V. C–g' (c"). Single movement with three sections. Commissioned by and written for Skip Gray. A showpiece for solo tuba with both rapid, technical and lyrical, expressive sections.

Volle, Bjarne. *Canariduett No. 1.* Music Information Centre Norway. Piccolo trumpet and tuba. 1994. IV. An extended one-movement work that contains complex time signatures and extreme note values. Reviewed in the Spring 1998 issue of the *TUBA Journal* (Vol. 25, No. 3).

Vosk, Jay. *Fantasy Duo.* Tuba-Euphonium Press. Horn in F and Tuba. 2003. $12.00. IV. B♭?–b♭. Three movements: Lyrical, Evocative; Energetic; Come Prima. For Victor Valenzuela and Mark Nelson.

Wallach, Joelle. *Cantares de los Peredis.* American Composers Alliance. Mezzo Soprano, Baritone, Tenor or Soprano, Tuba, Timpani, Crotales. 1987. 11:00.

Warren, Frank E. *Music for Tuba with Violoncello and Vibraharp.* Frank E. Warren Music Service. Tuba, Violoncello, and Vibraharp. 1989. 10:30. IV. F_1–f'. Single movement. For Richard Armandi. Chamber music for tuba, cello, and vibes. Requires tuba mute.

Warren, Frank E. *7 Duets for Tuba and Bassoon.* Frank E. Warren Music Service. Bassoon and Tuba. 1983. $5.00. 11:00. IV. C–f'. Seven movements. Commissioned by Gary and Judy Buttery. Dedicated to Gary and Judy Buttery. A good, interactive composition for bassoon and tuba. The movements are in contrasting styles, and balance between the instruments is usually not a major problem.

Washburn, Robert. *Concertino for Wind and Brass Quintets.* Oxford University Press. Flute, Oboe, Clarinet, Bassoon, 2 Trumpets, 2 Horns, Trombone, Tuba. 1971. $15.00. 8:00. III–IV. G_1–a. Two movements: Adagio—Allegro vivo; Theme and Variants. Allegro vivo section of first movement contains many meter changes with 3, 4, 5, 6, 7, 8, or 9 eighth notes to the bar. Tuba part in Theme and Variants contains a rapid sixteenth note passage.

White, Ian. *Undertones (in memoriam Tony Hancock).* Available from composer. Solo Tuba and String Quartet. 1997. 15:00. V. B_2–a'. Three movements, the first being an optional tuba cadenza. This work won the Clements Prize for Chamber Music. Tony Hancock was a very popular radio comedian in Britain in the 1950s, later moving into television. His theme tune was a jaunty tuba solo (written by Angela Morley), which summed up his pompous character perfectly. The cadenza and the first movement convey the pathos of his stage persona, while the second movement, subtitled "Epilogue," reflects more on Hancock's real-life loneliness and insecurity resulting in his alcoholism and suicide. This piece is of extreme technical difficulty for all players involved, and needs a conductor to keep the performance together. The tuba part uses several modern techniques including multiphonics, and a mute is required. The string parts also require knowledge of modern music techniques. A challenging but worthwhile composition.

Wilder, Alec. *Effie Joins the Carnival from "Suite No. 1."* arr. Ronald Bishop. Margun Music. Tuba in Brass Quintet. $7.00. III.

Wilder, Alec. *Elegy.* Margun Music Inc. Solo Tuba and Brass Ensemble (3 Trumpets, 3 Horns, 3 Trombones). 1971. 4:00. III–IV. A_1–f♯'. Written in tribute to and in memory of William Bell. A beautiful, lyrical work. Accompanying brass ensemble parts are very easy.

Wilder, Alec. *Movement III. Tuba Showpiece from "Brass Quintet No. 1."* Margun Music, Inc. Tuba in Brass Quintet. 1959. $12.00 (complete work). 2:45. IV. F_1–b♭'. Written for the New York Brass Quintet. This single movement featuring the tuba is part of a six-movement work which showcases each member of the brass quintet. The movements may be performed as a suite or separately. Recorded by Harvey Phillips.

Wilder, Alec. *Nonet for Brass.* Margun Music. 8 Horns, Tuba. $28.00. IV. Four movements. Jazz style throughout. Recorded by Markus Hötzel.

Wilder, Alec. *Suite for Brass Quintet and Strings.* Margun Music Inc. 2 Trumpets, Horn, Trombone, Tuba, Strings, Percussion (one player). 1979. 11:45. III–IV. G_1–e♭'. Four movements. Music typical of Alec Wilder, with no substantial difficulties in any parts. The fourth movement is in a jazz style and is the only movement in which the percussion plays, simply providing time.

Wilder, Alec. *Suite for Trumpet and Tuba.* Margun Music, Inc. Trumpet and Tuba. Published in 1980. $15.00. 7:00. IV. G_1–f'. Six movements. Nicely written music which sounds good for the difficult combination of trumpet and tuba.

Wilder, Alec. *Suite No. 1 "Effie" for Tuba and Woodwind Quintet.* arr. William Stanton. Margun Music, Inc. Tuba and Woodwind Quintet. 1991. 11:15. III–IV. F_1–e'. Six movements: Effie Chases a Monkey; Effie Falls in Love; Effie Takes a Dancing Lesson; Effie Joins the Carnival; Effie Goes Folk Dancing; Effie Sings a Lullabye.

Wilder, Alec. *Suite No. 1 for Horn, Tuba, and Piano.* Margun Music, Inc. Horn, Tuba, and Piano. 1971. $15.00. 14:00. IV–V. $A♭_1$–g'. Five movements: Maestoso; Pesante; In a Jazz Manner; Berceuse (for Carol); Alla cacia. For John Barrows and Harvey Phillips. Challenging chamber music. See: Bird, Gary, ed.; *Program Notes for the Solo Tuba.* Recorded by Harvey Phillips.

Wilder, Alec. *Suite No. 1 for Tuba "Effie the Elephant."* arr. Walter Hilgers. Available from the arranger. Solo Tuba and Brass Quintet. 1988. 12:30. See listing under Tuba and Keyboard. Recorded by Walter Hilgers.

Wilder, Alec. *Suite No. 1 for Tuba, Double Bass, and Piano.* Margun Music. Tuba, Double Bass, Piano. 1962. $12.00. 10:00. IV. F_1–g'. Written for bassist Gary Karr and tubist Harvey Phillips.

Wilder, Alec. *Suite No. 2 ("Jesse").* arr. Kenyon D. Wilson. Margun Music. Tuba and Woodwind Quintet. 1998. 4:25. IV. C–e'. Written on the occasion of the birth of Jesse Emmett Phillips, February14, 1964. Four numbered movements. Originally with piano accompaniment.

Wilder, Alec. *Suite No. 2 for Horn, Tuba, and Piano.* Margun Music. Horn, Tuba, and Piano. 1971. 10:00. IV–V. F_1–f'. Five movements. Written for John Barrows and Harvey Phillips. Recorded by Harvey Phillips.

Wilder, Alec. *Twelve Duets for Horn and Tuba.* Margun Music, Inc. (In preparation 1992.) Horn and Tuba. 1968.

Wilson, Ted. *Hopkinton Road.* Tuba-Euphonium Press. Tuba (or tubas) and Rhythm Section (Piano, Bass, Guitar, Drums). 1993. $10.00. 6:00. IV. E♭–c'. A good jazz chart that requires some improvisation. This piece is a good change of pace for a recital program.

Wreede, Katrina. *Tuba Beguine for Solo Tuba and Brass Ensemble.* MMB Music. Solo Tuba, 1 Piccolo Trumpet or B♭ Trumpet, 3 B♭ Trumpets, 4 Horns, Euphonium, Tenor Trombone, Bass Trombone, Optional Percussion. 1998. 6:00. C–b. For Barbara Day Turner and the San Jose Chamber Orchestra. A light, tuneful composition that is nicely scored.

Wright, Rayburn. *Undercurrents.* Seesaw Music Corporation. Flute, 7 Tubas, 2 Percussion. See listing under Music for Multiple Tubas.

Wyatt, Scott. *Lifepoints.* Available from the composer. Solo Tuba, Percussion, Electronic Tape. 1990. See listing under Tuba and Electronic Media.

Wyre, John. *Maruba for Tuba and Marimba.* Malarkey Music. Tuba and Marimba (with low A). 1987. 12:30. III. C–d'. Single movement with three sections. Commissioned by Ex Tenebris with assistance of the Ontario Arts Council. Written for and dedicated to Beverly Johnson and J. Scott Irvine. A work containing interesting colors, somewhat "New Age" in character.

Xenakis, Iannis. *Linaia-Agon.* Éditions Salabert. Horn, Trombone, and Tuba. 1972. At least 13:30. V. G_1–a'. Dedicated to Lina Lalandi. This atonal work is a true musical game or play depicting a fight between the classical gods Linos and Apollo, each player assuming the role of one of the adversaries. In addition to the conventionally notated prelude, entr'acte music, and closing music, the four internal episodes which represent combat between the gods is chance music chosen by the players in interactive response to what other players have chosen to play and determined with a scoring matrix.

Yen Lu. *Quartet.* Seesaw Music Corporation. Clarinet, Tuba, 2 Percussionists (playing multiple set-ups). 1970. $14.00. 6:30. IV–V. B♭$_2$–f'. Continuous work in four sections (Adagio; Allegro; Andante; Adagio). Many interactive, free gestures with notated pitches, air sound, and simultaneous singing and playing. Music duration is notated in approximate time spans rather than meters.

Yoran, Victor. *Duo for Violin and Tuba.* Tuba-Euphonium Press. 1995. $24.00. 26:00. V. A_2–f♯'. Four movements: Allegro Giocoso; Andante; Impetuoso; Lento. A virtuosic composition for both performers written in traditional notation. Technically demanding. Good agility and flexibility required for the tubist due to wide intervallic leaps and difficult rhythms. Manuscript is hand-printed and difficult to read.

Zaninelli, Luigi. *Berlin Suite.* Shawnee Press. Trumpet, Trombone, and Tuba. $10.00.

Ziffrin, Marilyn. *Trio.* Available from the composer. Xylophone, Soprano, and Tuba. 8:30. IV. D_1–g'. Continuous work. For Barton Cummings. An atonal, non-metered work. All three parts are quite active. The soprano is required to produce nineteen different vocal sounds, all notated on specific pitches. Recorded by Barton Cummings.

Zonn, Paul Martin. *Divertimento #1.* Available from the composer. Tuba, Double Bass, 2 Percussion (I: Marimba and Xylophone; II: Vibraphone and Xylophone). 1965. 10:00. IV–V. B♭$_2$–f'. Three movements: Moderato; Poco Lento; Allegro. For Robert Whaley. A contemporary, virtuoso piece for all members of the ensemble, written in traditional notation. The tuba part contains some half-valve glisses, flutter tongue, and muted passages. Wide, irregular intervals throughout. Recorded by Daniel Perantoni.

Zonn, Paul Martin. *Varia V.* Available from the composer. Clarinet, Trumpet, Trombone, Tuba, and Piano. 1979. 5:00. IV–V. C_1–g'. Interesting contemporary chamber music with wide intervallic leaps and difficult rhythms. The work is comprised of five sections which could be construed as four variations and a concluding theme (*Livery Stable Blues* in "Dixieland" style).

Zonn, Paul Martin. *Winter Paths.* Available from the composer. Tuba and Woodwind Quintet. 1982. 10:30. V. A_1–g♯'. Single movement. For Skip Gray. An interesting and demanding chamber music work containing traditional, unmetered, and aleatoric notation. There are wide, irregular intervallic leaps and difficult rhythmic relationships.

5. Music for Unaccompanied Tuba

Philip Sinder, Assistant Editor, *Guide to the Tuba Repertoire: The New Tuba Source Book*
Jeffrey L. Funderburk, Assistant Editor, *The Tuba Source Book*

Introductory Remarks (July 2005): Philip Sinder

Countless times during my research of unaccompanied works for the *Guide to the Tuba Repertoire: The New Tuba Source Book,* I would uncover what I expected to be a work that could be added to the new listings, only to discover that Jeff Funderburk, editor for this chapter in the initial edition, had already located the piece and had written a concise, accurate, and helpful entry! Bravo to Jeff for his first edition efforts. I hope that the new works and updates cited here are as complete and useful.

The first edition of *The Tuba Source Book* included 257 unaccompanied works for tuba, and many of these works had annotated listings. In the *Guide to the Tuba Repertoire: The New Tuba Source Book,* I have added 98 new listings, and have updated the annotations and recording information for an additional 22 works. This marks an impressive gain for the instrument in a span of less than ten years from the time *The Tuba Source Book* was first published. Additional pieces beyond this total were also identified, but sparseness of information about publication, availability, or the work itself caused me to withhold it from the printing of this edition. And, several very recent compositions by known composers were listed, even though actual publication details were uncertain at this time.

Several collections titled "concert etudes" appear both in this chapter and in the chapter Methods and Studies. In many cases, a short suite of a work of this sort could be an effective recital or competition option.

I want to recognize all of the people who provided assistance in identifying, locating, and commenting on these pieces. While I had direct contact with many publishers and composers, I also want to thank David LeClair, Jeff Parker, David Graves, Sergio Carolino, James Gourlay, and Heiko Triebener for their assistance.

As editor, I have sought to maintain the standards of evaluation that were utilized in *The Tuba Source Book* regarding levels of difficulty, general musical style, and the annotation detail. I sincerely hope that you find the information useful and accurate.

Introductory Remarks (July 1995): Jeffrey L. Funderburk

The unaccompanied medium presents a great diversity of musical styles and experiences. The unique limitations and inherent freedom of this medium have encouraged experimentation by composers. Due to the limited number of sounds produced by an unaccompanied instrument, many new techniques have evolved with this medium and are often incorporated into the texture of the work. This is not to say, however, that all of this literature relies on extended technique. While many works represent a high degree of experimentation and exploration of the instrument's possibilities, other works represent very traditional musical experiences.

Besides the presentation of new and nontraditional performance techniques, there are other important merits of examining the unaccompanied literature. The performer benefits from the unaccompanied solo by becoming, more than ever before, fully aware of all aspects of playing. Without accompaniment to help furnish melodic, rhythmic, and dynamic contrasts, the tubist is totally in charge of the musical product, thus having total control of interpretation. For a performer, this is a valuable expansion of musical experience. Keyboard musicians have long been faced with total control of the musical performance, which forces them to take absolute responsibility for the product. With the unaccompanied medium, the tubist can also have the experience of total control of the music and hopefully grow musically from the increased responsibilities.

It is believed that with proper selection, unaccompanied literature need not be reserved for only the more advanced students and professionals but may be used by all tuba performers in order to enrich the performance experience. Careful selection of works can serve to bolster etude experiences by emphasizing similar techniques in a purely musical context.

A few explanations should help clarify terminology used in the following annotations. Because of the great diversity of compositional and notational styles within the medium, this author has chosen to categorize works in order to give the reader a clearer sense of the work being discussed. Three categories of composition were identified: traditional, contemporary, and avant-garde.

Traditional: These works rely on traditional technique and range. The musical language is based on traditional harmony and is represented in standard notation.

Contemporary: These works often represent a more modern use of the instrument in terms of technical demands. The range is generally expanded and some extended techniques may be used. The basic material lies within the realm of traditional performance practice but represent a limited departure from the norm for performer and audience. Notation is primarily standard though some use of newer techniques may appear.

Avant-garde: These works make extensive use of expanded range and extended techniques. Use of non-traditional notation and theatrical techniques may be in evidence. These works are the most challenging for the general audience and least familiar to the average performer.

The notational systems were identified as belonging to one of four categories: traditional, proportional, frame, or graphic. *Traditional* is that notation used in the "common practice" period of music history. *Proportional* refers to notation in which durational values are given proportionally, often by extending the ligatures of the notes. *Frame notation* employs a frame or enclosure which contains the events to be performed in a specified amount of time. *Graphic notation* employs pictures or drawings which are to be interpreted by the performer.

Special thanks are extended to W. Ryan Thomas for his hours of assistance in helping to make this project possible.

Adler, Samuel. *Canto VII.* Boosey & Hawkes, Inc. 1974. \$6.50. 9:00. IV–V. D_1–f'. Four movements: Quite Fast; Light, Fluffy and Quick; Slowly and with Great Expression; Fast and Triumphant. For Harvey Phillips. This piece, composed in 1972, is interesting and very approachable. The general range requirements are moderate with most playing in the middle register while utilizing the entire range of the instrument. The general compositional style is contemporary with traditional notation, sometimes modified to represent the non-pitched sounds. Perhaps the most interesting movement is the second, which combines percussive effects with played sounds sometimes altered with flutter-tonguing. This movement effectively converts the tuba to a percussion instrument. The other three movements rely on traditional performance techniques. Wide intervals are the greatest technical demand. Brief explanations of the symbols used are provided. Extended techniques are used, including breath sounds, fingernails on the bell, valve clicks, flutter-tonguing, glissandi, white noise. See: Bird, Gary, ed.; *Program Notes for the Solo Tuba.* Recorded by Cherry Beauregard.

Agrell, Jeffrey. *Eccentric Dances.* Editions BIM. Composed 1997, published 1999. 8:00. III. F_1–e♭'. Six movements: Ponderoso/Impudent; Insouciant; Spooky; Con Ritmo Latino; Bluesy; Slowly-Declamatory/Fast. For Remo Capra. Interesting work with somewhat modest range demands; will work well on any size tuba. Quite unusual to find so many special effects in a piece at this level: flutter tongue, foot stomps, singing, groaning, wind sounds, toe taps, and others are all used to help create an effective and engaging musical composition (movements III and IV are the only ones which use special effects). The composer provides helpful comments for each movement. A suite of just a few of the movements is also feasible.

Albert, Thomas. *Latticework.* 1973. 4:00. IV. E♭–d'. One movement. For Daniel Perantoni. This is an avant-garde work which relies entirely on proportional and frame notation. There is a good explanation of the notation included. Multiphonics and general interpretation are the primary challenges.

Anderson, Eugene. *Lyri-Tech I.* Anderson's Arizona Originals. 1991. 6:00. III–IV. D_1–e'. One movement. Commissioned by and dedicated to David Aubuchon. This work is rhythmically simple and theatrically based. There are no particular technical challenges, but the work will require attention in order to achieve an interesting musical presentation. Recorded by Sam Pilafian.

Anonymous. *Chansons et Rondes Enfantines.* arr. Fernand Lelong. Editions Billaudot. 1992. 14:20. I–III. c–g'. A collection of 33 French children's songs and rounds, ranging from ten seconds to one minute in duration. Only six keys are used: C, G, F, and B♭ major, and A and E minor. Many of the melodies are easily recognizable, and employ simple rhythms with largely scalar and arpeggiated tunes. The disparity in the difficulty rating is due to the range employed: clearly a bass tuba or even euphonium would be appropriate. This collection could serve as a fine early training book for upper register on F or E♭ tuba, and could also be used effectively down an octave on all tubas.

Anonymous. *Hijazker Longa.* Gary Buttery. Whaling Music Publishers. 1978. $2.50. 5:00. III. C–e♭'. One movement. This is an interesting and entertaining transcription of a traditional Syrian Oud concert piece. This dance-like work is tuneful and within the normal technical demands of the instrument.

Antoniou, Theodor. *Six Likes for Solo Tuba.* Bärenreiter-Verlag, Kassel. 1968. $18.00. 12:00. V. A♭$_2$–b♭'. Six movements: Like a Duet; Like a Study; Like a March; Like a Cackling; Like a Song; Like a Murmuring. Composed in 1967, this is an avant-garde composition which relies on both traditional and proportional notation. The general tessitura is quite high, with considerable demands made upon the upper middle and extreme high register. Perhaps its most effective utilization is as a study piece in extended techniques. Each movement is a depiction of its title. This is a very difficult work with great demands on multiphonics and coordination of finger taps in the "March." Very wide interval glissandi are required in "Like a Cackling." A clear explanation of symbols is included. Extended techniques used include bends, breath sounds, valve clicks, finger taps, flutter-tonguing, glissandi, indefinite rhythm, multiphonics, quarter tone bends, trills, vocal sounds (singing). See: Bird, Gary, ed.; *Program Notes for the Solo Tuba.*

Arakaki, Renee. *Trinity.* Media Press. 1999. 8:00. In three movements: Mind; Spirit; Body.

Aranda, Pablo. *PerTUBAdo.* Manuscript. 1995. III–IV. E$_1$–d'. A Chilean work in one movement written for unaccompanied tuba using an ambient piano for resonance. Extremes in dynamic employed. Uses three- and four-note pitch sets, and places considerable importance on tone color. Straightforward rhythmic work, with no special effects (outside of the ambient piano). A good contemporary work for a less experienced college tubist.

Arnold, Malcolm. *Fantasy for Tuba.* Faber Music Inc. 1969. $6.95. 5:00. III–IV. F$_1$–c'. One movement. The range requirements of this work are modest, with most playing in the middle and lower middle register. The compositional style and notational systems are traditional. The work is a traditional fantasy with a recurring melodic theme contrasted by various sections, in an almost rondo-like fashion. With the exception of a few measures in the Allegro section at letter C, it is a very easy work for the performer. The rapid arpeggiated passages at that point are difficult. This is a light work with few demands on performer or audience. Recorded by John Fletcher, James Gourlay, Tim Norris.

Baadsvik, Øystein. *Fnugg.* Ovation Music, see www.baadsvik.com. 2002. 4:00. IV. E♭$_1$–B♭ (played), B♭–d♭' (sung). One-movement specialty piece written by the Norwegian tubist/composer. Baadsvik writes, "It's originally an improvisation with elements from the Australian Aboriginal instrument didgeridoo and Norwegian folk music. 'Fnugg' is a Norwegian word describing something very small and weightless." Pitch range is very narrow, to incorporate the extensive multiphonics. Simple and repetitive melodic material cast in a slow introduction followed by a "very steady rock groove." There are specific instructions for vowel sounds on the multiphonics, which is an effective technique. Also requires a percussive "lip beat," achieved by stopping the air with the tongue in a "smack-like" manner. Will require excellent balance and intonation on the multiphonics. Effective and fun study piece; could be well used in an encore setting. Recorded by Øystein Baadsvik.

Bach, Johann Sebastion. *Allemande from Partita II in D Minor.* arr. Paul Hartin. 3:30. III–IV. G♯–d'. One movement. This work is a well-conceived transcription. The primary difficulty will be one of phrasing and breathing without disrupting the musical flow.

Bach, Johann Sebastian. *Dance Movements.* arr. Abe Torchinsky. G. Schirmer. 1974. $2.50. IV. D–G'. These are selected dances from the unaccompanied cello suite. Similar to other collections.

Bach, Johann Sebastian. *Partita in A Minor.* arr. Floyd Cooley. Tuba Classics. 1994. 13:30. IV–V. D–a'. Four movements: Allemande; Corrente; Sarabande; Bourree Anglaise. Well-known work that has been dropped two octaves from the flute original and lies extremely well on F tuba and a bit less so on E♭ tuba. Range is somewhat misleading, as there is only one a' in the entire work, and all other pitches are at e' or below. The Allemande and Corrente are considerably more challenging than the final two movements, requiring musical maturity, thoughtful interpretation/breathing, and embouchure strength. This edition contains suggestions for dynamics, articulations, and breath marks. The performer should use these as a starting point and adapt interpretation further to suit individual taste. Recorded by Gene Pokorny.

Bach, Johann Sebastian. *Partita in A Minor for Flute Alone.* arr. Russell Tinkham. Tuba-Euphonium Press. 1997. 13:30. IV–V. D–a'. (Please see notes above for Cooley arrangement of this same work.) This version, by design, lacks any dynamics, articulations, or breath marks. The performer should study and listen to several flute versions in order to make an informed interpretation. Recorded by Gene Pokorny.

Bach, Johann Sebastian. *Partitas et Sonates.* arr. André Goudenhooft. Editions Billaudot. 1996. 1:37:30 (!) (with all repeats taken). IV. G$_1$–e'.

Twenty-two movements adapted from six different Bach works for solo violin, spanning twenty-nine pages of music. While the cover indicates that these arrangements are designed for bass trombone, the title page lists bass trombone and bass tuba. A number of these movements are more rapid in nature and seem to lie best on tuba. A limited number of ornaments are included, and only a modest number of dynamic suggestions. There are regular suggestions for breath spots, including possible note omissions on more active passage work. This is fantastic music—all of it a significant challenge for the tubist regarding endurance and interpretation. Excellent for study purposes, as well as in a grouping of movements or an entire Sonata or Partita as a recital vehicle.

Bach, Johann Sebastian. *Sarabande and Preludio.* arr. Neal Corwell. Nicolai Music. 2004. 7:15. IV. A_1–f'. Two movements adapted from the solo string music of J. S. Bach. The Sarabande is from the *Suite No. 6* for solo cello, and the Preludio from the *Partita No. 3* for solo violin. Nicely accommodates breath spots for the tuba while retaining the intended musical line. Both movements are in F major, making the considerable technique and flexibility needed for the second movement to work ideally on the F tuba.

Bach, Johann Sebastian. *Six Short Solo Suites.* arr. Robert King. Robert King Music Company. 1990. $4.80. III. E_1–a. 22 movements. This collection of selected movements from each of J. S. Bach's six suites for unaccompanied cello is well suited to the tuba and is not technically demanding. Selections should serve as great study and recital material, and prove to be musically satisfying to the performer.

Bach, Johann Sebastian. *Suite #1 (cello).* Cazes Cuivres.

Bach, Johann Sebastian. *Suite per basso.* Hofmeister.

Bach, Johann Sebastian. *Unaccompanied Suites, BWV 1007–1012.* arr. Ralph Sauer. Cherry Classics Music. 2004. ca. 1 hour 30 minutes. III–IV. G_1–d'. This new version of the well-known cello suites of J. S. Bach will prove to be an attractive alternative for the advanced tubist. Each Suite has been transposed down a perfect fourth from the original cello key, putting this great music more in the heart of the tuba's comfort zone. Indeed, these would lie well on either bass or contrabass tuba. Phrase and slur markings are included, but dynamic level choices are left to the individual performer. There are also many wise breath indications by the editor (a trombonist). The publisher is distributing these suites only in electronic media formats, allowing performers to customize the printed versions to their own tastes.

Badian, Maya. *Mosaiques Sonores.* Lucian Badian Editions, available from the Canadian Music Centre. Composed 1990, published 1996. ca. 10:00. V. $B\flat_2$–g'. In three movements: Ironicamente; Deciso; Burlesco. An avant-garde work which employs virtually every extended technique possible on tuba. Two pages at the outset describe, in both French and English, the notation and desired effect for each element. The work includes examples of traditional, proportional, frame, and graphic notation. There are several improvisatory moments using a prescribed set of pitches. Considerable flutter tongue employed. Several muted passages indicated. This piece could make an interesting "theatrical"-style unaccompanied tuba offering, but it will take a great deal of effort to master all of the challenges.

Baker, Claude. *Canzonet.* Southern Music Company. 1973. $1.00. IV. F_1–e'. One movement. For Alan Estes. This work is rhythmically complex and has an improvisational character. It relies entirely on traditional technique and notation. Rhythmic interpretation and wide intervals should prove the primary technical challenges.

Ballif, Claude. *Solfeggietto VII.*

Bamert, Matthias. *Icon-sequenza.* G. Schirmer Inc. 1973. $1.50. 4:30. V. E_1–f♯'. One movement. To Ronald Bishop. This is an avant-garde composition which makes considerable use of proportional and graphic notation. This work relies heavily on extended technique and extramusical sounds. Many techniques are required, including singing in the horn, playing tam-tam and tambourine, and mouthpiece popping.

Bashmakov, Leonid. *Cassazione.* Edition Fazer, Helsinki. 1976. $5.50. 5:00. IV–V. E_1–d'. One movement. Commissioned by 1976 Brass Congress. The general range requirements are moderate with an emphasis on performance below and just in the staff. This work is particularly idiomatic for the large tuba. It exploits the instrument without resorting to extreme registers or non-traditional techniques. The compositional style and notational system are traditional. This is a multisection work with numerous tempo and style changes. A brief introduction presents much of the basic material for the composition. A motive involving slurred harmonics from the second to the tenth recurs three times through the composition and serves as a unifying element. Technically, many extended passages of rapid notes, both slurred and articulated, are the primary challenge. Tremolos are the only extended technique used.

Bates, Jeremiah. *Variations on a Theme of Villa-Lobos.* Musical Evergreen. 1977. $6.50. 2:30. III–IV. F_1–a♭'. One movement. The general tessitura of this work is moderate to somewhat high with most of the requirements in the staff. The range is much less an issue on the smaller tuba. The compositional style and notational system employed are traditional. The work is marked by frequent tempo shifts. Formally, it is a set of variations in which sections are clearly marked with fermatas between each section. Technical demands beyond range requirements are quite modest, though some instances of wide interval work are demanding. Trills are the only extended technique employed.

Baxley, Wayne S. *Tuba McDifficult Unaccompanied Multi-phonic Solo.* Clark-Baxley Publications. 1989. $5.50. 1:30. IV. G_1–e'. One movement. The general range requirements are moderate, with most of the playing within the staff. Generally, the work should provide no particular problems provided the performer is capable of multiphonics. The general compositional style and notational system are traditional. Musically, the work is loosely organized in an ABA' form. A short melody in eighth notes marked by wide intervals serves as the primary musical theme. As the subtitle suggests, multiphonics are a dominant idea in the work and basically serve as the purpose of the work.

Baxton, Anthony. *Golden Gate Scenes.*

Beach, Bennie. *Divertissement for Tuba.* Tenuto Publications. 1975. $2.00. 6:00. IV. $B\flat_1$–$d\flat'$. Three movements: Statement; Waltz; Chant. For Kent Campbell. This composition relies on solid control of the middle register and should present no special endurance concerns. This is a simple piece, most interesting for the younger or less advanced performer. It should be a successful recital piece. The general style of this work is traditional, tending toward the contemporary and using traditional notation. There are no great technical demands. The first movement is organized around a rhythmic/thematic motive of two sixteenths and an eighth. The second movement is a fast waltz in one. The final movement is based on an opening chant-like motive. Following the initial slow tempo, the work moves to a middle section, which is quicker and uses many compound/complex meters with much of the same thematic material as before, and then returns to the opening style and tempo. See: Bird, Gary, ed.; *Program Notes for the Solo Tuba.*

Beck, Jeremy. *Tempus Fugit.* Tuba-Euphonium Press. Composed 1998, published 2001. 3:00. IV. $G\sharp_1$–e'. One movement. For Jeffrey Funderburk. Alternates brief lyrical and technical motives in a focused contemporary manner. Needs precise rhythmic skills. The title translates to "time flies." Designed as a potential encore piece. Good choice for a college-level player on F or E♭ tuba, but also very viable on a larger instrument. Recorded by Jeffrey Funderburk.

Bernaud. *Humoresque.* Associated Music Publishers.

Beveridge, Thomas. *Etude in piano e forte.* TUBA Gem, Vol. 12, No. 1. (1981). 3:00. III–IV. D♭–f'. One movement.

Bingham, Judith. *Der Spuk.* Maecenas Music. 2001. 7:00. IV. $E\flat_1$–f'. For James Gourlay. The music serves to tell the story of a Bavarian folk tale in which a giant ghost is finally scared away by villagers blowing alphorns. An interesting variety of demands for the tubist, but nothing too extreme, and the music is well suited to the instrument. A few brief multiphonics are found. This solo would work well on either bass or contrabass tuba.

Bittinger, James. *Four Island Phantasies.* Pocono Mountain Music Publishing. 1994. 8:45. II–III. $A\flat_1$–g. Four movements: Cairns Island Phantasy; Burns Island Phantasy; Kipp Island Phantasy; Epply Island Phantasy. Three composers listed for each "phantasy": James Bittinger, Willard Musser, and Donald Whittekind. Generic pieces with settings of these available for all brass, woodwind, and mallet percussion. As such, they lack much of a tuba identity, but are still well conceived in terms of range, key choices, and difficulty level. Movements alternate slow-fast.

Blank, Allan. *Three for Barton.* Associated Music Publishers. 1974. $3.50. 6:00. IV–V. D_1–$g\flat'$. Three movements: A Short Fantasy; Burlesque; Scene. For Barton Cummings. The general tessitura of this work is moderate with a well-dispersed use of the middle register. There is significant use of the upper middle register throughout, but always balanced with lower playing. The piece was written in 1973, and its compositional style would best be described as contemporary. Most of the notation is traditional, though often unmetered, but there are instances of proportional notation as well. The first movement is comprised of contrasting sections, one dominated by repeated notes while the other is slower, more legato and marked by multiphonics. The second movement is roughly in the form of an ABA'B'(C)A". The third movement utilizes a single prominent theme set off by short episodes. Repeated note figures hark back to the first movement. The work is technically challenging, but not unattainable for most strong players. Most technical demands lie in the areas of range, wide intervals, and control of extended techniques. Extended techniques employed include breath sounds, foot stamps, high/low sounds/noises, flutter-tonguing, glissandi, indefinite pitch, multiphonics, quarter tone bends, one half air/one half tone.

Blatter, Alfred. *Cameos.* Media Press.

Bliss, Marilyn. *Aria.* 1:00. IV. $D\sharp_1$–e'. One movement. This brief work written in 1982 explores the lyric qualities of the tuba. Wide intervals, often slurred, are the primary technical challenge other than range. The work should prove interesting for study and be very functional in many performance settings due to its brevity.

Bliss, Marilyn. *Evocations.* New York Women Composers, Inc. 5:30. IV–V. $E\flat_1$–f'. Four movements: Praeludium; Burlesque; Arioso; Largo-Finale. To Albert Plugasch. Written in 1982, this work seeks, in the composer's words, to "explore the broad range of sound, timbre, register, and emotion obtainable" with the tuba. This mildly contemporary piece relies entirely on traditional notation. Technically the primary challenges involve range and extended rapid passages as well as heavy reliance on multiphonics in the final movement. This is an interesting work worthy of study and performance.

Borkowski, M. *Vox per uno strumento at ottone.* Polskie Wydawnictwo Muzyczne. 5:40.

Borwick, Doug. *Tuba Sonata.* Three movements: Recitative and Aria; Theme and Variations; Rondo. See: Bird, Gary, ed.; *Program Notes for the Solo Tuba.*

Bourgeois, Derek. *Fantasy Pieces.* Brass Wind Publications. 1996. 19:00. III–IV. D_1–f'. Nine movements: Allegro moderato; Adagio cantabile; Moderato con moto; Commodo; Allegro moderato e pesante; Allegro moderato; Adagio—Allegro vivace; Moderato pesante; Allegro vivace. An interesting set of pieces all in a traditional tonal style, written to be used as test pieces for the National Youth Orchestra of Great Britain. Performance suggestions provided for each piece. These works would be ideal as supplementary study material for the advanced high school or college-level performer. Several of them could be grouped effectively as recital, examination, or competition material. Upper tessitura use is limited. Many of the pieces require strong finger/tongue coordination, and more advanced flexibility. The metronome markings seem aggressive, but the composer notes that these "need not be strictly observed." Viable on any key of tuba. An enjoyable set of varied pieces that really suit the instrument well.

Braun, Yehezkel. *Tubae Cantus Ante Lucem.* Israeli Music Institute. 1975. 3:30. III–IV. G–f'. Four movements. This is a melodic work of interest because of its rhythmic diversity. Often dance-like, this work should prove entertaining for performer and audience.

Brings, Allen. *Berceuse for Solo Tuba.* Seesaw Music Corporation. 1992. 2:20. III–IV. F_1–f'. One-movement work all written in a lyrical and expressive contemporary style. Tempo and metric activity stays relaxed throughout. The composer makes a special note regarding the seven levels of dynamic intensity as found in the score. Appearing easy on first glance, this work contains challenging intervallic structure and will need excellent control throughout the indicated range.

Brings, Allen. *Scherzetto.* Seesaw Music Corp. 1975. $3.00. 1:20. IV. F_1–f'. One movement. This composition places moderate demands on range but utilizes the complete range. The compositional style is contemporary, mainly due to its non-tonal organization. It relies entirely on traditional notation. It is a very melodic work in general format. The material is based on elements of the serial technique. Without fully utilizing a single row, there are extended passages of non-repeated pitches. It is a very short work which is rich in potential study material, particularly from a compositional standpoint. Technically, extended rapid passages of a non-scalar nature combine with wide intervallic work and a very wide range to make this a rather difficult work.

Brizzi, Aldo. *De La Tramutazione Dei Metalli II.*

Brown, Anthony. *Interim Structures.* Seesaw Music Corp. 1977. $10.00. 9:00. IV. C–b♭. One movement. Range requirements in the traditional sense are not applicable here. The limited traditional playing is in a very modest register. Slides were not provided with the score and must be sought from another source. This is an avant-garde composition. The primary notational system is graphic with some instances of unmetered traditional notation. The soloist enters, lights candles, and begins with the slides. There are three musical/sound events set off between four slide sections. The primary challenge of the work is interpreting the symbols. There is a good explanation of all symbols used, which is helpful. Very little of the piece requires actual playing and only one of these short played passages is at all difficult. Extended techniques employed include breath sounds, fingernails on bell, half-valve, indefinite pitch, mouthpiece buzzing (with sung pitch), theatrics, vocal sounds (mumbling through horn), white noise.

Brown, Francis James. *Small Suite for Tuba Solo.* American Composer's Edition. $6.98. 6:00.

Bujanovsky, Vitali. *Improvisation.* 4:00. IV. F_1–c'. One movement. The compositional style and notational systems are traditional. Many brief sections of contrasting styles and tempi are connected by a recurrent thematic motive. There are no particular technical demands other than occasional wide intervals. The work should prove interesting for study and performance.

Bujanovsky, Vitali. *Monodie.* 2:00. III. F_1–d♭'. One movement. This brief work in a traditional style is essentially a short monologue for tuba. There are no particular technical demands. The melodic basis of the work should be interesting particularly for younger players.

Burghardt, Daryl. *Hieronymus.* Manuscript. 1999. 7:30. III. $B♭_2$–e♭'. Three movements: Hell; Paradise; Garden of Earthly Delights. Written for the Leonard Falcone International Euphonium and Tuba Festival. Extensive notes to the performer regarding musical interpretation, and a brief description of the inspiration for this work—artist Hieronymus Bosch and his bizarre and fascinating inner panels for the triptych "Garden of Earthly Delights." All low register pitches below $E♭_1$ offer an upper-octave option. A well-written and attractive solo with three distinct movements. Will require musical maturity, yet the technical demands are not overwhelming.

An advanced high school player or interested undergraduate tubist would find this work attractive.

Buss, Howard J. *A Day in the City: 7 Vignettes for Unaccompanied Tuba or Bass Trombone.* Brixton Publications. 1986. $4.75. 9:30. III. G♭₁–a. Seven movements: Another Sunrise; Off to a Busy Day; Lost Key Episode; The Waitin' in Line Blues; Romantic Interlude; Sudden Storm; Out on the Town. Range requirements throughout are quite modest with demands limited to middle-register playing. The compositional style and notation are traditional. The work is mildly programmatic, as each vignette is titled with a descriptive heading. Traditional tonal techniques are the primary harmonic language. Movements are in varying styles and show some jazz influences. The second movement has an awkward rhythmic repeated-note passage and several rapid passages. The fourth movement is marked by a series of wide intervals which consistently return to a constant lower pitch. Technically, there are no great demands.

Buttery, Gary. *Suite for Unaccompanied Broque Tuba (and Tubaist).* Whaling Music Publishers. 1975. $3.00. 4:00. III. F₁–f'. Three movements: Allemande; Sarabande; Gigue. This work tends to linger in the upper middle register and above. Written in 1973, this is an excellent work for study of the baroque dance forms, but it is also very entertaining for performer and audience and should be an effective recital piece. The compositional style and notation of this work are traditional. It is a suite in the baroque tradition. Though contemporary music, the form remains true to the baroque suite in style and selection of dance movements. The extended passages of rapid sixteenths are the primary technical challenge other than the general tessitura.

Cáceres, Eduardo. *Tubular I.* Manuscript. 1989.

Campbell, D. E. *Sonata for Unaccompanied Tuba.* TUBA Gem, Vol. 12, No. 2.

Castells, Adrés Valero. *Impromptu AV 17.* Publ. D.L., Valencia. 1999. 5:45. V.

Chamberlain, Robert. *Elegy.* MMB Music Inc. $2.95. 5:00. IV. One movement. For Jerry Young. This work is contemporary in style and uses some non-traditional notation. The work is intended to be played into the lid of a grand piano with the damper pedal held down. The work was written in 1981 in response to the assassination of Anwar Sadat and the resulting strong feelings experienced by the composer. Extended techniques utilized include multiphonics, glissandi, speaking into the instrument, half-valve notes, and the use of a mute. This is a very effective work in performance. See: Bird, Gary, ed.; *Program Notes for the Solo Tuba.*

Choi, Hae-Kyung. *Nacht und Dämmerung.* Musikverlag Bruno Uetz. Composed in 1995, published in 2001. 7:30. IV–V. E₁–g♭'. Three movements: Abenddämmerung, Nacht, Morgendämmerung. An avant-garde composition which was the first prize winner of the 1995 German Musikhochschulen Composition Competition. The work features over a dozen extended techniques, and it will take considerable effort to have command over each effect. Once the effects and notation are mastered, this solo offers both performer and listener an engaging musical platform. Appears best suited to the bass tuba.

Christiansen, Henning. *Kirkeby and Munch.*

Christiansen, Henning. *Kredslobsforstyrrelse.*

Cionek. *Lamentations for Manfred (Tuba and Narrator).* Tuba-Euphonium Music Pub.

Císcar, Javier Costa. *Ambitos: 4 piezas para tuba.* Publ. D.L., Valencia. 1993. IV.

Clark, William. *Jeremy.* RBC Publications. 1989. $3.50. 2:00. I. C–e♭. One movement. This work is an excellent introduction to the unaccompanied literature and a fine teaching piece. There is an extended middle section intended for bell tree and triangle which may be performed by a non-skilled percussionist. No rhythms are present which are more complicated than the dotted eighth and sixteenth note pattern.

Clark, William. *Timothy.* RBC Publications. 1989. $3.50. 2:30. II. E♭–g. One movement. This simple work should be interesting study material for the young tubist. The middle section, which is written for brake drum and twenty-penny nail, is a nice break. The only technical concern may be the reliance on performance in the staff.

Clark, William. *The Water Valley Flash.* RBC Publications. 1989. $3.50. 1:30. I. B♭–d. One movement. For Jim Shearer. This simple piece is intended for the beginner player. The jazz style should be entertaining. A middle section for suspended cymbal gives a break and musical contrast. There are no rhythms more complicated than dotted eighth and sixteenth note patterns.

Colding-Jørgensen, Henrik. *Boast.* Dansk Musik. 1984. 3:00. V. D₁–g'. One movement. For Michael Lind. This composition relies heavily on the extreme high register. The work was composed in 1980. As the name suggests, perhaps the greatest value of the work is to boast of one's technical prowess. Nevertheless, if performed convincingly, it should prove an audience thriller. The general compositional style is traditional as is the notational system, though unmetered. The work is basically from the tradition of the fantasia, and is in many regards an extended, stand-alone cadenza. The single movement is marked in sections by many tempo and style changes. The work relies heavily on advanced traditional technique, particularly in its use of extended rapid passages often in the extreme high register. Very wide intervallic leaps and phrases of extreme range are commonplace. Glissandi are the only extended technique. Recorded by József Basinka.

Colding-Jorgensen, Henrik. *Sourires.* 1997. 6:00.

Constantinides, Dinos. *Piece for Solo Tuba.* T.A.P. 1979. $2.00. 4:00. IV–V. F♯$_1$–f'. One movement. This work in a contemporary style is rhythmically rather complex. There is significant use of proportional notation. Technical challenges include rapid arpeggiated slurs as well as wide leaps.

Coolidge, Richard. *Three Monologues.* Tuba-Euphonium Press. Composed 1994, published 1997. 8:30. IV. F$_1$–a♭'. Three untitled movements. For J. Mark Thompson. Indicates that the work is for either tuba or bass trombone. Includes a number of octave displacements when the musical line heads above f'. A contemporary work, but includes no special effects. Generally lyrical and dramatic writing.

Cooman, Carson. *Dream Etudes, Book III.* MMB Music, Inc. 2002. 7:00. III. C♯$_1$–e♭'. In three movements: Interrupting; Folding; Prancing. For Mark Nelson. The composer indicates that this work is his opus 355, and that it follows his other sets of *Dream Etudes* which are written for solo clarinet and solo piano. Intervallically challenging in spots, the music is stylistically very cohesive while providing excellent variety. Range demands are modest, and a contrabass tuba should be the ideal choice. Excellent preparatory notes.

Cooper, Steve. *7 Modal Tunes for Tuba.* TUBA Gem, Vol. 11, No. 2. (1978). 3:00. III. A–b♭'. Seven movements: Dorian; Aeolian; Lydian; Phrygian; Ionian; Locrian; Mixolydian. Extended passages of rapid notes and occasional wide leaps dominate these short studies.

Cope, David. *BTRB.* Brass Music Ltd. 1974. $7.00. IV. One movement. For Tom Everett. This work is theatrical in nature and relies almost entirely on extramusical sounds. Various special effects are achieved by using bassoon reeds, foot stomps, and the like. The work was originally written for bass trombone but may be adapted for any brass instrument.

Cresswell, Lyell. *Drones IV.* ALM. 1977. 6:00. IV–V. G$_1$–f♯'. One movement. For Melvyn Poore. This is an avant-garde composition that primarily is a sound painting. This work calls for the inclusion of any high pitched drone. Notation is entirely proportional and graphic. Events are measured in seconds. There is considerable use of vocalization.

Creuze, Roland. *Eria.* Editions Gérard Billaudot. 1985. $6.50. 6:30. V. G♭$_1$–a'. One movement. For Fernand Lelong. This composition was written in 1980 and relies on high register playing. An explanation of the symbols would be helpful as there are several non-traditional symbols used. The general compositional style of this work is contemporary and relies on unmetered traditional notation with some instances of proportional notation. There is considerable use of flutter-tongued passages and repeated note patterns in proportional notation which accelerate or slow. Technically, extended flutter-tongued passages of often rapidly changing pitches are difficult. Changes between normal tonguing and flutter-tonguing occur regularly within a line. Awkward intervals and a rather disjunct style are additional difficulties encountered. Extended techniques utilized include bends and flutter-tonguing. Recorded by Fernand LeLong, Phillippe Legris. See: Thompson/Lemke; *French Music for Low Brass Instruments.*

Croley, Randel. *Variazioni.* Avant Music. 1968. $4.95. 7:00. III–IV. E$_1$–b. One movement. Range requirements of this work are moderate, requiring control throughout the middle register. The majority of the writing is in the staff. The single greatest challenge is to make the composition musically interesting, as it has a tendency to ramble. The general compositional style is contemporary and relies on traditional notation that is unmetered but uses bar lines. The single movement is highly sectionalized with many tempo and style changes. There are two primary sections which serve as thematic material for the variation. No special demands on technique exist, though control of the middle register and accurate rhythmic interpretation are essential.

Cummings, Barton. *Brief Moments.* PRB Productions. 1989. $6.00. 4:30. III. F$_1$–e'. Four movements: Sprightly Dance; Melancholia; Crisply Walzing; Marching. The simple melodic character and reliance on basic technique should make this an excellent first unaccompanied work. Technical demands are limited to sixteenth note passages which are not extensive except in the third movement.

Cummings, Barton. *Musings.* Kiwi Music Press. 1985. $1.50. 2:00. IV. E$_1$–e'. Three movements: Reflections; Currents; Reflections Two. The general range use is moderate with a tendency to emphasize the upper middle and high registers, with most writing in the staff. The compositional style is contemporary, and the notation system is primarily traditional though often unmetered and uses a single incident of proportional notation. The outer movements are lyric in general character and, though unmetered, are primarily dominated by a quarter note pulse. The second movement begins with a brief quasi cadenza, moves to a rapid section of frequently shifting meter emphasizing the compound subdivisions, returns to the quasi-cadenza style and finally finishes with a brief allegro. Technically, the demands are quite modest, with wide slurred intervals and control of range the major concerns.

Cummings, Barton. *Three Moods.* Musical Evergreen. 1976. $3.95. 3:00. III. C$_1$–f'. Three movements: Lightly; Lento-Rubato; Lightly-Staccato. The general range requirements of this work are moderate. The compositional style and notation system used are traditional. Very wide dynamic shifts occur throughout the work. Technically, demands are moderate. Low register passages in the second movement and rapid rearticulated pitches in the third movement are the primary technical requirements.

Cummings, Barton, arr. *Song of the Trouveres.* Edition Musicus. 1980. $2.50. 5:00. II–III. E–a. Seven movements: En ma dame; Ja nuns hon pris; C'est la fin; Douce dame; E, dame jolie; Vos n'aler; Pour mon cuer. These are simple tunes from the Renaissance and middle ages with suggested (optional) percussion parts. The works provide no particular technical challenges but may prove an interesting experience in an often neglected musical style.

Dalbavie, Marc-André. *Petit Interlude.* Editions Billaudot. 1992. 3:50. IV. C–g'. One-movement French work designated for bass saxhorn or bass tuba, with the expected higher tuba tessitura. This piece is designed to be performed with a steady slow pulse, yet it is unmetered. Interest comes from a wide spectrum of juxtaposed rhythmic subdivisions with consistent intervallic structure, and from the execution of highly specific dynamic markings. Would serve as an interesting contemporary solo or study piece.

Danburg, Russell. *Five Extemporizations.* Kendor Music Company Inc. 1985. $5.00. 9:00. IV. F_1–d'. Five movements: Lento e doloroso; Andante maestoso (tempo di polacca) with fervor but not fast; Adagio con espressivo; Allegretto (tempo di valse); Adantino giocoso (tempo di boogie) in a rollicking style, but not fast. For Harvey Phillips. This work relies on middle and upper middle register playing, making the general range demands moderate with most requirements in the staff. This work should prove very approachable for most good performers and all audiences. The general compositional style and notation are traditional. The four movements are in a slow, fast, slow, fast arrangement with slow movements being song-like while fast movements are dance-like. Solid control of lyric playing, particularly in sometimes wide intervals, is required throughout. Technical demands are modest, though control of sixteenth triplets in the second movement and accurate dotted eighths and sixteenths in contrast to eighth triplets in the fifth movement are essential.

Danburg, Russell. *Sonatina.* Wing. $4.00.

Degl'Antonij, G. B. *Ricercata Quarta.* arr. by Gordon J. Kinney. Queen City Brass Publications. 1981. $6.50. 4:00. IV. $B\flat_1$–g'. Originally a work for cello, this is an interesting study in baroque style. Technical requirements are limited to range and extended rapid passages. It is well edited and should prove an interesting work for study and performance.

Denham, Robert. *Three Predicaments.* Tuba-Euphonium Press. Composed in 1999, published 2003. 7:00. IV. C_1–f'. Three movements: The Sound of Fury; Solitary Confinement; What If the Hypotenuse Is Missing? An equal division of labor throughout the indicated pitch range, but F or E♭ tuba would be the preferred choice. Each movement has a number of unexpected 8vb markings. Movement I is more aggressive in nature and features a considerable number of trills in all registers. Movement II, the longest of the three, is rhapsodic and lyrical. Movement III, a scherzo, will require good upper register pitch accuracy and excellent rapid slurred scalar technique. A diverse and difficult solo for the advanced college student.

Dobrowolski, Andrzej. *Muzyka na tube.* Polskie Wydawnictwo Muzyczne. 12:05. V–V. Three movements. Written in 1973, this is an avant-garde work which is unusual for its use of "prepared" tuba in the second movement. Besides great demands on traditional technique, a large portion of the work relies on extended techniques. Primarily this is an exploration of the sound possibilities of the tuba.

Donatoni, Franco. *Che: For Tuba.* Ricordi. 1997. For Luigi Pestalozza. In two unmetered movements.

Dondeyne, Desire. *5 Pieces Courtes.* Editions Billaudot.

Dragonetti, D. *Concert Etude.* arr. Randall Block. Musical Evergreen. $3.95. 2:30. III–IV. E–g'. One movement. The primary technical demands of this work are extended passages of sixteenths and the somewhat high tessitura. It is an entertaining work that works particularly well on the F tuba.

Dubrovay, László. *Solo No. 3.* Editio Musica Budapest. 1986. 8:40. V. B_2–d♭''. Three movements. This work relies almost entirely on graphic notation. The notation is fully explained, though in German. Musically it is an exploration of sounds and colors with considerable latitude for performer interpretation. Recorded by József Basinka.

Dutton, Brent. *Four Expansions.* Seesaw Music Corp. 1976. $5.00. 3:00. V. $B\flat_2$–b♭'. Four movements: Moderato; Slow; Dance; Moderato. For Ron Bishop. While this work generally lies in the middle register, there are frequent occurrences of both extremes. It demands complete control of the instrument's entire range. The general compositional style is contemporary and relies on traditional notation. An additional challenge of this work is the cluttered appearance of the manuscript. Glissandi are the only extended technique.

Dutton, Brent. *Polis for Unaided Tuba.* Seesaw Music Corp. 1977. $6.00. 3:00. V. $B\flat_2$–e♭''. One movement. The general range requirements of this work are quite extensive and relatively evenly divided between the extreme high and low registers. This is an avant-garde composition, written in 1970, which utilizes proportional, frame, and traditional notation. A glissando effect intended to simulate a motorcycle serves as a unifying element by its occurrence at the beginning and end as well as once more in the body of the work. Another more traditional line serves as a second unifying motive and occurs twice. There are many contrasts which are exploited in this work, such as the juxtaposition of great range extremes, muted versus natural sounds, and breath sounds versus played pitches. Once the substantial technical demands of range and coordination of mute insertion and withdrawal while performing are surmounted, there remains the great challenge to make musical sense of the work. The extensive notes are helpful in interpretation, but their occasional inclusion between lines adds to the untidy appearance of the score. Extended techniques used include breath sounds, glissandi, multiphonics; a mute is required.

Dutton, Brent. *Thème Varié*. Seesaw Music Corp. 1980. $4.00. 5:30. V. B_2–a'. One movement. Though most of the work is in the middle register, there are extended passages during the opening which place great demands on the high register. The general compositional style is contemporary and utilizes primarily traditional notation with significant use of proportional notation as well. The work is a very free set of variations. Sections are generally marked by a fermata at the end of the previous section and often a tempo change for the new section. The work culminates in a final three-to-five-second section of "totally chaotic playing" which is entirely without notation except to give the final pitch. Extensive use of multiphonics with independence of each line is a particular technical demand of the work. The work also makes great technical demands in extended sections of rapid arpeggiated passages, which are sometimes played and sometimes sung in a multiphonic. Extended techniques employed include multiphonics and random pitch selection.

Emmerson, Simon. *Variations for Tuba*. Arts Lab Music Publishing. 1977. $7.00. 3:00. V. $E\flat_2$–e♭''. One movement. The general range requirements of this work are extensive in each direction, with an equal emphasis on the high and low registers. The piece was written in 1976, and its general compositional style is contemporary and utilizes proportional notation almost entirely, with some minor instances of graphic notation depicting general contour of glissando lines. This work has an improvisatory character. The opening is dominated by sustained pitches with increased activity between each occurrence as the pace increases. The body of the work is dominated by a series of pitches performed as fast as possible. The wide range and long passages of rapid pitches with irregular accents are the primary technical difficulties of the work. Extended techniques employed include bends, glissandi, indefinite pitch, microtonal pitch (in sung parts only), multiphonics, mouthpiece buzzing, timbre trills, trills.

Etzel, Bernhard. *Divertimento bassobavarese*. Recorded by Thomas Walsh.

Etzel, Bernhard. *Five Miniatures for Solo Tuba*. Recorded by Thomas Walsh.

Feiler, Christian. *Fünf Schritte*. E_1–c♯'. Five movements. See Unkrodt, Dietrich, *Reige Vortragsliteratur, Tuba 1 und Tuba 2*.

Fennelly, Brian. *Tesserae V*. American Composer's Edition. 1980. 7:00. V. C_1–g♯'. Three movements: Introduction—Pilafony I—Sombre Sounds (A); Pilafony II—Sombre Sounds (B)—Solemn Song; Coda: Toccata. This is a rhythmically and technically complex work. Absolute technical control will be required to achieve an effective musical performance. There are a few extended techniques required, including multiphonics and tonguing noises as well as mild theatrical instructions.

Flory, Neal. *Suite for Unaccompanied Solo Tuba*. Tuba-Euphonium Press. Composed in 1999, published in 2003. 7:30. IV. E_1–e'. Four movements: Nocturne; Dance; Rhapsody; Finale. For Yutaka Kono. Movements alternate between lyrical and technical styles. While the composer notes that he would prefer the use of F tuba on this work, the range and technical demands would allow success on a variety of keyed tubas. Each of the fast movements includes brief use of flutter tongue, and the final movement will require a solid triple tongue as well. Contemporary work that offers considerable variety.

Fodi, John. *Four Bagatelles*. Canadian Music Centre. 1979. 4:00. IV. E_1–f♯'. Four movements: ♩ = 72; ♩ = 64; ♩ = 84; ♩ = 72. Rhythmic complexities with a great deal of syncopation and wide intervals will prove to be challenging technical aspects of this work. Without careful interpretation, these movements take on a rambling character.

Frackenpohl, Arthur. *Five Sketches for Solo Tuba*. Tuba-Euphonium Press. Composed in 1997, published in 1998. 9:20. III–IV. E_1 (optional $B\flat_2$)–c'. Also titled *Divertimento for Solo Tuba*. Five movements: Intrada; Air; Scherzo; Blues; Rondo. For Ron D. and Andrew H. Traditional tonal work in the typical lighter styles favored by the composer. Required range quite conservative, but technical demands and rhythmic challenges make the work more involved. Effective recital material. A fun work which will develop flexibility.

Frackenpohl, Arthur. *Music for a Tuba Guy*. Manuscript. 2004. 8:30. III. F_1 (optional C_1)–f'. In three movements: Fast; Slowly; Lively. For

Charles Guy. Although this work contains serial elements and has a fair amount of chromaticism, it is tonal and demonstrates many of the rhythmic and melodic elements that are typical of this composer. The tessitura is largely in the staff, and the work could be handled by either bass or contrabass tuba. Excellent contrast of technical and lyrical elements. Enjoyable for both performer and listener.

Frackenpohl, Arthur. *Sonata for Solo Tuba*. TUBA Press. 1993. 8:35. IV. C_1–d'. Four movements: Slowly; Very Fast; Freely; Fast. With the exception of the third movement, which is unmetered and has proportional notation, this work is essentially traditional in style. It requires absolute technical control of the instrument, with many extended passages of rapid notes and disjunct intervals.

Frackenpohl, Arthur. *Studies on Christmas Carol*. Kendor Music Company Inc. 1981. $6.50. II–III. G_1–b♭. Twelve songs: *O Come, All Ye Faithful; We Wish You a Merry Christmas; Away in a Manger; Go, Tell It on the Mountain; Angels We Have Heard on High; The Friendly Beasts; Jolly Old St. Nicholas; Hark! The Herald Angels Sing; What Child Is This?; Jingle Bells; Fum! Fum! Fum!; Deck the Halls*. Each of these traditional carols is dealt with in a simple theme and variation form. They should prove interesting for younger players and very functional for seasonal performances by any performer.

Frackenpohl, Arthur. *Tubatunes*. Almitra Music/ Kendor Music. 1981. $6.00. 15:00 (10:30 w/ cuts). III. C_1–e♭' (F_1–c♯'). Four movements: Rag; Waltz Ballad; Latin Jazz; Blues. For Daniel Perantoni. Range requirements throughout are moderate, with all demands within the middle register. The compositional style and notational system of this work are traditional. Musically, the work is very light with considerable jazz influence. The movements are very simple, with optional cuts and *ossia* parts provided to make this work accessible to the younger player who would most enjoy it. There are optional improvisation sections in the third and fourth movements, with chord symbols provided. Technically, the most difficult aspect is coordinating playing and percussive effects within a single integrated line. Otherwise, technical demands are quite modest and confined to rapid articulations in sixteenths and smooth, lyric performance in the staff. Extended techniques employed include bends, foot stamps, glissandi, timbre trill (articulation with valves).

Frank, Marcel G. *Andante and Allegro*. 3:00. III. $B♭_1$–e♭'. Two movements: Moderately Slow; Lively. Written in 1973, this work is traditional in notation and style. There are no unusual technical demands.

Frank, Marcel G. *Sonata*. 7:30. III–IV. $D♭_1$–e'. Five movements: Brightly; Moderately; Slowly; Gaily; Moderately Fast. To Winston Morris. This work is written entirely in traditional notation and in a traditional style. The music is thematically and melodically based. There are no particular technical challenges.

Freedman, Harry. *Caper*. Canadian Music Centre. 1978. 5:00. IV. A_1–f'. One movement. Commissioned by Dennis Miller with the assistance of the Canada Council. This is an interesting work of a mildly theatrical nature. Foot stomps, valve clicks, multiphonics, and vocalization permeate the work. There is a great element of humor in this composition. When the technical aspects of the work are fully controlled, this should prove a very successful and entertaining work.

Friedman, Stan. *Ossia*. Seesaw Music Corp. 1984. $6.00. 8:00. IV–V. $C♯_1$–f♯'. One movement. North Carolina State Music Teachers Association. The general range requirements of this work are moderate with generally well-balanced use of the entire middle register with some emphasis on the upper middle and upper register. Composed in 1980 (revised 1983), the work is in contemporary compositional style and relies entirely on proportional notation. Tempo is estimated by the statement that each system is approximately 10 seconds in duration. Interpreting all symbols and presenting all accents and nuances are critical to the success of the work. There are very few explanations; even so, the work is generally easy to interpret. Technically, control of wide slurs, often into the high register, rapid slurred passages, and control of multiphonics are the primary challenges. Extended techniques employed include glissandi, multiphonics, trills.

Fritze, Gregory. *Yevrah Yad Thrib Bypah*. $5.00. 7:00. IV. C_1–f'. Four movements: Slow and Dramatic; Lento Rubato; Dancelike; Allegro non troppo. To Harvey Phillips. This work relies primarily on traditional notation, though there are instances of approximate pitch notation. The compositional style is essentially traditional, with the addition of extended techniques including multiphonics, mouthpiece pops, and taps to extend the sound palate. Wide intervals should prove the primary technical challenge. See: Bird, Gary, ed.; *Program Notes for the Solo Tuba*.

Fulkerson, James. *Patterns III*. Media Press. 1969. 4:00. IV. $B♭_2$–g'. One movement. This work relies heavily on extended techniques but uses the full range of the instrument, including extremes in both directions, during traditional performance sections. This is a very difficult work in every regard. It is an avant-garde composition which utilizes frame and graphic notation as well as traditional notation. There is an adequate explanation of symbols included, which is helpful in interpreting the score. The work is an exploration of sound possibilities. Some sections are pointillistic, as isolated notes occur in varied registers. The work may be best described as a "sound-scape," a painting with sounds. Technically, besides the great range requirements, there are intricate alternations between singing, playing, and vocal clicks/clucks within a continuous line. Also, the work calls for the removal of the mute while maintaining a multiphonic. Many extended techniques are used, including breath sounds, Doppler effect, mouthpiece pops, flutter-tonguing, multiphonics, timbre trill, trills, vocal sounds, whistle tone, white noise, mute.

Gabrieli, Domenico. *Ricercar.* arr. R. Winston Morris. Shawnee Press Inc. 1974. $1.75. 3:30. III–IV. G_1–c'. One movement. This work was originally for unaccompanied cello. It is an excellent study or recital piece in the baroque style. Technical demands are limited to extended passages of sixteenth notes. Careful attention to interpretation is required for the success of the work. Recorded by Ronald Davis.

Gallagher, Jack. *Sonata Breve.* The Brass Press. 1983. $4.00. 4:30. III. G_1–c' (G_1–e♭'). Four movements: With Conviction; Introspectively; Swaggeringly; With Energy. For Tucker Jolly. This work relies heavily on the middle register, thereby making limited demands on endurance or general range. It is interesting for its use of a traditional classical structure in an unaccompanied work and therefore is good as a study and teaching piece. The first movement is in sonata-allegro form. The second movement is song-like. The third movement is a dance in compound time, and the fourth movement is a short rondo-like movement.

Galloway, Scott. *Essay for Tuba.*

Geissler, Siegfried. *Studie V für Tuba.* 3:30. F_1–g'. One movement. See Unkrodt, Dietrich, *Reige Vortragsliteratur, Tuba 1 und Tuba 2.*

Germanavicius, Vytautas. *Eos: For Tuba Solo.* Lithuaniun Music Information and Publishing Centre. 1995. 9:00.

Ghezzo, Dinu. *Sound Shapes II.* Seesaw Music Corp.

Gilbert, Anthony. *Kauri, for Tuba Solo.* University of York Music Press. 2002. 10:30. IV–V. $D\sharp_1$–a'. For James Gourlay. This work serves to celebrate the Kauri tree, a New Zealand tree species which has enjoyed a resurgence in recent years. The work is primarily lyric in nature, and will demand excellent intervallic sense, along with a full spectrum of dynamics and control. Several brief phrases employ multiphonics. Despite the wide range (and even brief use of treble clef), the upper register demands are not too taxing. Still, best suited for an F or E♭ tuba.

Glaser, Verner Wolf. *Two Tuba Tunes.* Swedish Music Information Center.

Glass, Jennifer. *Prelude, Waltz, and Finale.* Griffiths Edition. Composed 1984, published 1996. 5:30. IV–V. $E\flat_1$–a'. Three-movement work dedicated to John Fletcher. Contemporary in nature, yet no extended techniques. A considerable amount of upper tessitura work makes this best suited to F or E♭ tuba. The opening Prelude is unmetered throughout, cadenza-like with wide intervallic leaps. Flexibility, technique, and a strong intervallic sense are tested to a greater degree in the final two movements, which are both metered. A challenging and effective work at the advanced level.

Globokar, Vinko. *Echanges für einen Blechbläser.* Henry Litolff's Verlag/C. F. Peters. 1975. $44.35. 8:00. IV. One movement. Written in 1973, the work employs an avant-garde compositional style, and its notational system is entirely graphic. This composition is intended for any brass instrument. A tone row is given and may be used in interpreting the symbols. A microphone and loudspeakers are also used, with the microphone placed near specific slide/valve openings and the loudspeakers behind the audience. The work is basically an exploration of sounds and sound possibilities. The primary difficulty is in interpreting the symbols. An explanation is given in German without translation. A great deal of time and effort is required to prepare this work. Extended techniques utilized include bends, flutter-tonguing, glissandi, trills, mute, varied mouthpieces and reeds.

Globokar, Vinko. *Introspection d'un Tubist.*

Globokar, Vinko. *Res/As/Ex/Ins-pirer.*

Golightly, D. F. *Serenade for Solo Tuba, Op. 4.* Modrana. 1979. $2.45. 4:30. IV. D_1–a♯'. Three movements: March; Elegy; Galop. For James Anderson. Range requirements in this work are quite significant, with frequent use of extreme registers in both directions requiring complete control of the instrument. The compositional style and notation system are traditional. The title of each movement is an accurate portrayal of the material which follows. Technically, the primary demands are related to the very wide range and the use of wide intervals. In addition, the March uses extended passages of articulated sixteenth notes and the Galop contains some rather complicated rhythmic subdivisions of the beat.

Golob, Jani. *TubaBlues.*

Gordon, David. *Three Etudes for Solo Tuba.* Tuba-Euphonium Press. Composed 2000, published 2001. 6:15. III–IV. D_1–f♯'. Three movements: Lyrical; Aggressive/Relaxed; Driving. Each movement is quite distinct in style, yet all employ traditional techniques save one note that is flutter tongued. Movement I employs legato arpeggiations and includes a fair amount of upper tessitura work. Movement II is more technical and has increased metric interest. Movement III is a study in rhythm, with several metric modulations, tempo changes, and varied meters. The pitch content is much easier on this final movement. The piece is well suited to either bass or contrabass tuba. Also listed in the chapter Methods and Studies.

Grant, James. *Stuff.* Tuba-Euphonium Press (or http://www.jamesgrantmusic.com). 2001. 5:45. III–IV. F_1 (C_1)–b. A theme with seven variations for solo tuba. Dedicated to the 76 members of the 2001 Solstice/Equinox Commissioning Consortium for Tubists. Best suited to the contrabass tuba. Pitch range is modest, with the C_1 option indicated for the final note of the piece only. The main challenge in this work is to handle the seven distinct moods in each of the variations, which showcase significant tempo and stylistic variety in a traditional setting. Also, some of the phrasing and transitional details will need careful consideration. Score is extremely well marked. Variation VII requires a command of swing-style eighths. Excellent study or recital material for a strong high school player or younger college tubist.

Grant, James. *Three Furies.* Grantwood Music Press. 1993. $9.50 (+$1.50 shipping). 10:15. V. $C\flat_1$–g'. Three movements: Fury I; Fury II; Fury III. For Mark Nelson. This work in a contemporary style relies entirely on traditional notation. Rhythmically, the work is very complex. Technically, extended rapid passages, very wide leaps, and passages encompassing extremes of range make this a tremendously difficult work. The only extended technique involves half-valve effects. Motivically based, this is a very interesting work. Recorded by Mark Nelson.

Gregson, Edward. *Alarum.* Intrada Music Publishing. Composed in 1993, published in 1995. 8:00. IV–V. $E\flat_1$–g'. A one-movement work in three larger sections. For James Gourlay. Contemporary work that includes a few instances of flutter tongue and some proportional notation. Opening four-note motive (A-E-E♭-G) is a musical play on the dedicatee's name. A good deal of this work exploits upper and lower pitch extremes of the tuba. A strong player with wide dynamic abilities is a necessity. The title means a "call to arms," and there are many aggressive, fanfare-like moments. A dance-influenced mixed-meter third section eventually culminates in a brief restatement of the opening motive. A major work for the instrument. Recorded by James Gourlay, Hans Nickel.

Grunelius, Wilhelm von. *emBRASSing Ovid, No. 2, "Jupiter and Europa."* Editions Marc Reift. 1996. 5:00. IV–V. $D\sharp_1$ (optional G_2)–g'. For Walter Hilgers. A work depicting Jupiter disguising himself as a young bull and seducing the beautiful princess Europa.

Gruner, Joachim. *Solo für Tuba.* 5:00. C_1–a'. One movement. See Unkrodt, Dietrich, *Reige Vortragsliteratur, Tuba 1 und Tuba 2.*

Ha, Jae Eun. *Three Abstracts for Tuba.* Neil A. Kjos Music Company. 1978. $6.00. 8:00. IV–V. C_1–a♭' ($E\flat_1$–a♭'). Three movements: With much freedom in improvisational style; Molto tranquillo; Freely and fantastically. To Barton Cummings. Generally, the range requirements of this work are quite demanding, from extreme low to extreme high. Complete flexibility within and between registers is required. This is a very difficult work which is very effective in performance. This is an avant-garde composition which utilizes proportional, frame, and graphic notation as well as unmetered traditional notation. Generally, motives tend to grow from a basic germ of an idea to a larger form by extension. Technically this work is tremendously demanding, involving extreme range, very rapid passages, and very wide intervallic work. Extended techniques employed include breath sounds, flutter-tonguing, glissandi, key clicks, quarter tone bends, tremolos, and use of a mute. Recorded by Barton Cummings.

Haddad, Don. *Short Suite.* Seesaw Music Corp. 1975. $5.50. 4:00. III. G_1–e♭'. Four movements: Freely; 𝅗𝅥. = ca. 60; Freely; ♩ = ca. 138. The range demands of this work are moderate with an emphasis on work in the staff. A good introductory work for those unfamiliar with the unaccompanied genre. The compositional style and notation are traditional. Each movement is short, simple, and tuneful, more in the style of well-crafted etudes. Technical demands are modest in every regard. There is consistent passage work in sixteenth notes with frequent accidentals, but most lines are scalar with all notes true to a given key.

Hahn, Gunnar. *4 Winds.*

Hanks, Paul. *Solo No.1; Three Short Pieces.* Tomorrow Brass Series. 4:00. IV. $C\sharp_1$–f'. Three movements: ♩ = 90; ♩ = 50; ♩ = 90. For Tom Hancock. This work in a contemporary style takes the character of a series of monologues. Two of the three movements are unmetered and there are many instances of proportional notation. A great deal of flutter tonguing is required as well as use of a mute. Rhythmically, the work is complex.

Hanson, Ronald D. *Escapement.* To Mark Nelson. 7:00. V. F_1–e♭'. One movement. This work relies entirely on traditional notation with a very complex rhythmic palette. Because of the constant rhythmic flow, this is a tremendously difficult work.

Harmon, R. C. *Suite for Solo Tuba.* 8:30. IV. G_1–f'. Six movements: Praeludium; Marcia; Sarabande; Bourre; Minuetto; Finale. This work is traditional in style and primarily based on thematic and motivic development. Notation is traditional. Wide leaps and passages which span a very wide range are the primary technical challenge.

Harris, Roger. *Suite for Solo Tuba.* Seesaw Music Corp. 1976. $7.50. 4:45. III. F_1–c'. Four movements: Fanfare; Badinage; Laure; March. The general range requirements of this work are modest, with emphasis on the middle register and an avoidance of extreme registers. The work was composed in 1970, and its compositional style and notational system are traditional. This work is dominated throughout by melodic/thematic material.

Hartley, Walter S. *Music for Tuba Solo.* Philharmusica Corp. 1974. $7.50. 5:00. IV. E♭$_1$–g'. Four movements: I. Andante; II. Allegro; III. Largo; IV. Presto. For Harvey Phillips. The general range requirements of this work are moderate, relying primarily on a well-distributed use of the middle register. The compositional style is contemporary and relies entirely on traditional notation. The first movement is dominated by wide intervals, usually in the context of long phrases. The second movement is in 5/8 time with shifting subdivision of the bar. The third movement is a Largo with very wide intervals reached by glissando, rapid passages of 32nd notes and very wide intervals within sixteenth note passages. This is technically the most demanding movement. The fourth movement is in cut time, utilizing a repeated-note motive in eighth notes contrasted with passages of moving eighth notes. Extended techniques employed include flutter-tonguing, glissandi, trills.

Hartley, Walter S. *Suite for Unaccompanied Tuba.* Elkan-Vogel. 1964. $2.00. 5:00. IV. G$_1$–b. Four movements: Intrada; Valse; Air; Galop. Range demands of the work are moderate with emphasis on upper middle register playing. Written in 1962, this work is widely used as an introductory piece to the unaccompanied literature for tuba. The compositional style is mildly contemporary and utilizes traditional notation. This is a loose interpretation of the dance suite, not relying on actual dance forms, but making movements dance-like. The primary difficulty lies in the disjunct nature of the melodic/harmonic contour, which makes use of many awkward intervals. Pitch accuracy and interpretive skills are the major challenges technically and musically for the performer. See: Bird, Gary, ed.; *Program Notes for the Solo Tuba.* Recorded by Peter Popiel, John Fletcher, and Rex Conner.

Hartzell, Eugene. *Monologue 17: Toying for Tuba.* Ludwig Doblinger KG. 1987. $11.10. 6:00. IV. C$_1$–c'. One movement. The general range requirements of this work, written in 1983, are moderate with an emphasis on the lower middle register. This is a solid composition worthy of attention. The general compositional style is contemporary with a reliance on traditional notation. There is considerable rhythmic diversity throughout the work, which utilizes duple subdivisions as small as the 32nd note as well as triplets, sextuplets, and septuplets. Instances of excellent melodic use of the extreme low register present challenges. Several tempo shifts mark sections of the work. The only extended techniques required are trills and the use of a mute.

Harville, Grant. *Suite in B♭ Minor.* Tuba-Euphonium Press. 2003. 12:30. IV. B♭$_2$–g♭'. Six movements: Comodo; Andante Rubato; Allegretto grazioso; Adagio non troppo; Allegro non troppo; Vivo. Varied dance-like movements seemingly designed after Bach cello suites. The composer, an accomplished tubist himself, has created an accessible and engaging work at an advanced level. Use of more extreme registers is kept to a minimum, on both ends of the spectrum. Use of an F or E♭ tuba appears to be a logical choice. There exists a considerable amount of harmonic interest. An effective and engaging work for both performer and listener.

Hendze, Jesper. *Stunt.* Available from the composer (ashendze@danishcomposers.dk). 1999. 4:00

Hermanson, Christer. *Waves.* MIC.

Hewitt, Harry. *Twelve Preludes, Opus 376, A.* 1973. 17:00. IV. D$_1$–a♭'. Twelve Preludes. This work is intended for performances with or without tape accompaniment prepared by the performer. The work could also be performed as a duet with two tubas. In any event, the work seems to be lacking without both parts. Range is the only technical problem.

Hilprecht, Uwe. *Vier Haltungen zu einem alten Thema.* A♭$_2$–a♭''. Five movements: Thema; Der Melancholiker; Der Sanguiniker; Der Phlegmatiker; Der Choleriker. See Unkrodt, Dietrich, *Reige Vortragsliteratur, Tuba 1 und Tuba 2.*

Hlouschek, Theodore. *Variazioni classici per tuba solo.* Hofmeister.

Hoag, Charles. *Tubaplay.* 6:00. V. B♭$_2$–a'. Eight movements: Prelude; Gong with the Wind; Interlude; Tango; Interlude; Soft-shoe Dance; Interlude; Final Bounce. Commissioned by Scott Watson, Skip Gray, and Jerry Young. In addition to playing tuba, the performer in this work is required to play gong, bass drum, and suspended cymbal. Probably the greatest challenge of the work is the coordination required between the percussion and tuba playing as the parts are thoroughly integrated. The piece is very effective in performances, but will require extensive preparation.

Homs, Joaquin. *2 Monologs per a tuba.* Manuscript. 1979. 7:00. V.

Israel, Brian. *Suite for Unaccompanied Tuba.* Tritone Press. 1982. $2.50. 5:30. III–IV. F$_1$–d'. Four movements: Allemande; Courante; Gavotte; Gigue. For Randal Foil. This work was written in 1980, and its general range requirements are moderate with some significant upper middle register passages. Every effort should be made to understand and portray the traditional dance form of each movement in order to allow the contrast of the more modern extended tonality to work. The compositional style is essentially traditional and utilizes traditional notation. The work applies the broad architecture of the baroque dance suite to a more modern tonal palette. The tonal twists of the melodies make the work challenging in initial stages of study. Extended passages of rapid notes both scalar and arpeggiated, often with numerous accidentals, are the primary technical demand.

Jager, Robert. *Diverse Moments #1*. Wingert-Jones Music Inc. 1978. $4.00. 5:30. III. B_1–c'. Five movements: March; Elegy; Waltz; Ballad; Scherzo. For R. Winston Morris. This work relies primarily on middle and lower middle register playing. The compositional style and notational system are traditional. Technical and musical demands are kept to a minimum throughout the work. Technically, the moving eighth note passages in the Waltz (in one) and the alteration between cut time and 3/4 meter in the Scherzo are challenging.

Jalbert, Pierre. *Two Character Pieces*. Bernel Music. Composed in 2000, published in 2002. 6:00. IV–V. F♯$_1$–f♯'. Two movements: Lament; Perpetuum. For Mark Nelson. Contemporary solo with two very distinct movements. Overall range is somewhat less taxing than that of other difficult unaccompanied works, but challenges in musicality and technique more than compensate. Movement I requires excellent control at softer dynamics, and leaps from low to high motives often. The "sigh-like" descending semitone and overall nature will need excellent musical ability. Movement II contains strings of rapid mid-register slurred scalar material, and a metric structure that will force careful study and assimilation. The player will have to budget air well to maintain the momentum. An excellent work, by an award-winning young composer, that pushes the tuba in new directions.

Johnson, Tom. *Monologue for Tuba*. Two-Eighteen Press. 1976. A theatrical work for tuba, talking and playing, which is a fun piece for performer and audience alike.

Johnson, Tom. *Tilework*. Editions 75. 2003. 8:30. IV. F_1–f♯. Subtitle indicates "Three movements in one tempo." The composer provides extensive notes on the relationship of the title "Tilework" to this musical context, which is minimalist in nature. Recurring pitch groups and metric patterns come and go in a four-repetition loop. The work is clearly cast in three larger sections. One of the few works for tuba in this style. There appear to be four omissions/concerns: 1) no dynamics are marked at any point; 2) some of the busier patterns are really a stretch in one breath on tuba; 3) the second and third sections include notation of overlaid patterns in a score-like manner, which is awkward to read; and 4) a statement confirming that accidentals hold through each new system is missing.

Jones, Roger. *Design No. 1*. Laissez-Faire Music/TUBA Press. 1983. 4:00. IV. E_1–e'. Two movements: ♩ = ca. 60; 𝅗𝅥 = ca. 72. For Constance Weldon. The general range requirements of this work are moderate, with a well-balanced use of the entire middle register and some emphasis on the upper register. The compositional style and notation are traditional. The general style of the work is simple. There are numerous technical demands throughout, including wide intervals and rather complicated rhythmic activity. Perhaps the greatest challenge, however, is to arrive at an interesting interpretation of the music.

Joubert, Claude-Henry. *Petite Suite*. Editions M. Combre. 1982. $6.00. 6:30. III. A_1–e'. Four movements: Prélude et Fugue; Sarabande; Menuet; Gigue. For Jean-Pierre Besançon. The general requirements are moderate, with an emphasis on the upper middle register. This is an excellent study and recital piece, particularly effective for use in the study of traditional dance forms. It is entertaining for audience and performer alike. This work is light in style and is essentially a reinterpretation of the unaccompanied suite. It is designated as an elementary piece on the score and with some minor octave transposition would work quite well on euphonium as an elementary piece. This is a very lyrical work that makes solid demands on technique. Wide intervals are not uncommon and the general style concerns of each dance are important to proper interpretation.

Kagel, Mauricio. *Mirum*. Universal Edition A.G. 1974. $4.00. IV. D♭$_1$–g'. One movement. The general tessitura of this work is quite high. Composed in 1965, this work is particularly worthy of performance and study due to the international stature of the composer and the rather unusual quality of the work. This is an avant-garde composition which relies heavily on theatrics. The pitch/rhythmic notation is traditional, but short staves are used without meter to notate individual events, each set off from the next by text. The work is essentially a series of events often using words or other theatrical elements between performed passages. Technically, there are several isolated passages which are quite difficult and require special attention in order to master. In general, individual passages are relatively less difficult than pacing and continuity considerations of the work as a whole. Extended techniques employed include flutter-tonguing and glissandi.

Karkoff, Maurice. *Two Pieces for Solo Tuba*. DaCapo Press.

Kasai, Kiyoshiro. *Music for Tuba*. 1985. 4:00. IV–V. G_2–c''. One movement. For Takashi Abo. This work is very free in style and contemporary in its musical language. There are passages of graphic notation as well as note stems without pitch designation. The extreme range will prove the greatest challenge of the work.

Katzenbeier, Hubert. *Drei Speilstücke für Tuba Solo*. 7:25. D_1–f'. Three movements: Speilstücke I; Speilstücke II; Speilstücke III. See Unkrodt,

Dietrich, *Reige Vortragsliteratur, Tuba 1 und Tuba 2.* Recorded by Phillippe Legris.

Kaufman, Christopher. *Effulgence.* Chiron Publications.

Kavanaugh, Patrick. *Debussy Variations: No. 14 for Solo Tuba.* Pembroke Music Co. 1977. $5.00. 5:00. IV–V. One movement. For Lynn Robinson. The score is rather cluttered in general appearance and will take considerable time to interpret. Coordination of slide removal and the like is at least as much of a challenge as performance technique. The compositional style is avant-garde and relies considerably on proportional and graphic notation. This is an extensive exploration of non-traditional sounds on the tuba. The single greatest challenge is interpreting the score. Valve slides must be almost constantly manipulated, often removed quickly to produce a "pop." Often, several staves are intended to be interpreted simultaneously. Even though extensive explanations are given, some notation is not completely clear. In general character, the work relies on gestures and rapid flourishes to create a sound environment. Many extended techniques are employed, including breath sounds, mouthpiece pops, flutter-tonguing, half-valve, lip trills, lip buzzing, multiphonics, removal of slides quickly, finger-stopping slides, vocal sounds.

Kayser, Leif. *Monolog for Solo Tuba.*

Kessler, Jim. *Etude.* 0:30. III. D_1–c'. One movement. This very short work is useful a study in 7/8 meter. There are no unusual technical challenges.

Khoudoyan, Adam. *Elégie.* Editions BIM. Composed in 1990, published in 1991. 4:00. III. G_1–d'. One-movement work, all at a marking of "Adagio con dolore." The composer (b. 1921), a native of Armenia, has created a traditional work which attempts to express, with a simple lyrical style, the suffering of the Armenian people. While the tessitura would allow this work to be played on any key of tuba, it would be best suited for the BB♭ or CC tuba. Challenges include frequent accidentals, longer phrases, and a wide span of expressive dynamics. Excellent study and recital material.

Kibbe, Michael. *Three Lyric Pieces.* Seesaw Music Corp. 1975. $5.50. 2:30. III. F_1–c'. Three movements: Andante; Allegro; Moderato. Composed in 1968. The general demands on range are quite modest. This work is useful as study material for younger students. The compositional style and notational system are traditional, and the harmonic language is tonal. Three very short movements are more like study etudes than concert material. These make minimal demands on technique and will prove sight-reading material for many good players. The primary demand is control of legato playing.

Kinney, Gordon J. *Improvisation for Solo Tuba.* TUBA Gem. 1976. 1:30. III–IV. A♭–f'. One movement. For Rex Conner. This work is traditional in style and notation. There are no particular technical challenges other than a somewhat high tessitura and a couple of rapid passages.

Kinney, Gordon J. *Little Suite for Tuba.* Studio P/R. 1973. $2.50. 7:00. III. G_1–e♭'. Four movements: Prelude; Caprice; Air tendre; Bourrée. For Rex Conner. The general range requirements of this work are moderate with an emphasis on the upper middle register. The compositional style and notational system of this work are traditional. This is a suite by virtue of its general form of a collection of dances and dance-like movements. The work as a whole is simple and tuneful. Technically, the work requires solid control of the middle and upper middle register. Wide interval slurs are often required and are probably the single most demanding technical aspect.

Kinney, Gordon J. *Ricercar for Tuba.* Studio P/R. 1973. $2.00. 2:00. III. B_1–d'. One movement. Range requirements are moderate with no extreme demands in either direction. The bulk of the composition lies in the staff. The compositional style and notation of this work are traditional. This is a very simple work in ABA' form with each section labeled in the score. It is very short and makes no significant technical demands other than control of lyric playing in the upper middle register.

Kjär, Vildfred. *3 Plays the Tuba.*

Klauss. *Sonata for Solo Tuba.* Composers Autograph Pub.

Klucevsek, Guy. *Elegy for Solo Tuba.* 2:30. III–IV. G♯$_1$–g♯'. One movement. In memory of Dr. Martin Luther King, Jr. Written in 1970, this work relies on traditional notation. The general character of the work is improvisatory. The often high tessitura is the primary technical challenge of the work. This is an interesting and evocative work.

Knudsen, Per Egil. *Tre Miniatyrer.*

Koch, Erland von. *Monolog nr 9.* Carl Gehrmans Musikförlag. 1977. $8.00. 5:00. III–IV. F_1–b♭' (F_1–e'). Two movements: Andante; Allegro vivace. Range requirements are moderate if the lower *ossia* parts are performed. Most of the work is in the staff with extended use of upper middle register playing. Without *ossia* parts, there are significant high register demands. Composed in 1975, this is an entertaining work which is equally pleasurable for performer and audience. The compositional style and notation are traditional. Each movement begins with the statement of a theme which forms the basis for the movement. The work is very melodic and simple in form. The compositional style is direct, musically light, and very pleasing. The primary technical demand is range, which in most cases is simplified in an *ossia* part. See: Bird, Gary, ed.; *Program Notes for the Solo Tuba.* Recorded by Michael Lind.

Kochan, Günter. *Monolog.* $G\flat_1$–g'. One movement. See Unkrodt, Dietrich, *Reige Vortragsliteratur, Tuba 1 und Tuba 2.*

Kohlenberg, Oliver. *Le torre di Bologna/The Towers of Bologna.* Jasemusiikki. 1991. IV. $E\flat_1$–f'. Seven movements and coda: A. Maestoso e lugubre; B. Poco agitato; C. Piu agitato; D. Cantabile; E. Lugubre e sombre; F. Poco scherzando; G. Lamentoso, con dolore; Coda. The composer suggests that the performer should always begin with movement A and end with movement G and Coda, but may play other movements in any order or leave them out. Each movement is marked with a repeat which is also to be considered optional. The composer also suggests that pauses of any length may occur between movements or other program selections may take place during pauses. The work uses traditional notation throughout but utilizes syncopations to break the normal feel of the meter. Melodic lines are angular and contemporary in style.

Kraft, William. *Encounters II.* MCA Music/Editions BIM. 1970/1991. 6:00. V. C_2–b♭'. One movement. For Roger Bobo. This work exploits the complete range of the tuba, with particular emphasis on the upper middle register and high register. Composed in 1966, this is one of the most performed works in the tuba's repertoire. The general compositional style of this work is contemporary and relies on traditional notation. It is, according to the composer, a set of variations, though not obviously such. Each section is marked by a double bar and a change of tempo and/or style. The extended multiphonic section demands pitch accuracy for effective performance and the technical demands of the final page are very substantial. The overall technical demands are enormous, but the greater challenge is to surmount the technical obstacles and move toward a purely musical interpretation and performance. Extended techniques employed include glissandi, multiphonics, timbre trills, trills. See: Bird, Gary, ed.; *Program Notes for the Solo Tuba.* Recorded by Roger Bobo, József Basinka, Heo Jae Young.

Krush, Jay. *I Will Speak Briefly On. . . .* 9:00. IV. C_1–c'. One movement. This is a theatre piece which has a very long text with brief musical passages interspersed. These are passages of proportional notation and passages which are based on vocalizations through the instrument. This work was written in 1973 and is rather unusual within the tuba repertoire.

Krzanowski, Andrzej. *Sonata.* Polskie Wydawnictwo Muzyczne. 1985. 14:00. IV. $C\sharp_1$–a♭'. One movement. For Zdzislawowi Piernikowi. Primarily, the range requirements of this work are modest with a few extended passages in the high register. The greatest endurance factor is the extended duration without a significant break. Written in 1978, this is an important piece in the genre because of its minimalist tendencies. It is not a piece appropriate for every audience and will not prove fulfilling for many performers, but it is unique within the literature and worthy of study. The general style of this work is contemporary and, though there is some use of proportional notation, it primarily employs a modified traditional notation without use of meter. This is a minimalist piece which relies on a basic motivic idea repeated endlessly with slight variation. Distinct sections are marked by tempo changes and fermatas. As an element of contrast, there are slow, lyric passages at much lower dynamic levels, but the original cell always dominates. If the range is within grasp, the only technical difficulty is endurance. The only extended technique employed is indefinite pitch. Recorded by Zdzislaw Piernik.

Kuehn, Mikel. *Jigsaw.* Available from the composer. 9:15. V. B_1–g'. Three movements. Written for Mark Cox, dedicated to David Kuehn. As the composer states, "each movement possesses a separate structural design and emphasizes a different model of time—movement I is non-linear, movement II linear, and movement III combines both non-linear and linear elements." The work relies primarily on very advanced traditional notation. Rhythmically the work is very advanced and uses complex subdivisions of the beat. Non-traditional notation is clearly explained in performance notes. Wide intervals and very complex rhythmic patterns are the primary technical demands. Extended techniques include flutter tonguing, multiphonics, glissandi, tone alteration, and circular breathing.

Kuhn, Charles. *Improvisation for Unaccompanied Tuba.* Tomorrow Brass Series. 1972. 3:00. IV. D–e♭'. One movement. This work is traditional in general style and relies on traditional notation. Other than a few wide leaps and rapid passages, this work should present no special challenges.

Kühnl, Claus. *Homage à Schubert.* Breitkopf & Härtel. 1986. 5:00. F_1–e''. One movement. For Malte Burba and Klaus Burger. This work is intended for alphorn or any brass instrument. It is a theatrical piece which relies heavily on the performer's acting ability in the portrayal of frame characters. Extended techniques employed include breath sounds, multiphonics, and knocking on the instrument. There are extensive explanatory notes covering notation and performance suggestions.

Kurylewicz, A. *Tubesque for Solo Tuba.* TUBA Press. $7.00. 9:00. V. C_1–a'. Four movements: Allegro; Canzona; Tango-Grotesque; Presto. This work employs graphic and frame notation as well as traditional notation. All movements are without meter designation. Technically, this is a very difficult work requiring wide intervals, often with glissando, extreme range, and extended rapid passages. There is no explanation of notation included and the copy of the manuscript is sometimes missing notes. Movements are based on motives, which should make the work more easily understood by performer and audience.

Laiosa, Mark. *Traun.* 2:00. III–IV. A_1–f'. One movement. This short lyric piece presents no special problems. The work relies on traditional style and traditional notation and is melodic in nature.

Lang. *Are You Experienced.*

Láng, István. *Aria di Coloratura.* Editio Musica Budapest. 1984. $7.00. 5:00. V. C_1–g'. One movement. For László Ujfalusi. This work uses a wide and well-distributed range. Most work is within the middle register, but there is definite emphasis on both extremes. The compositional style of this work is contemporary and utilizes unmetered traditional notation as well as some proportional notation. The single movement is divided into sections by tempo changes. The extended opening in a slow tempo with many fermatas gradually reveals an eleven-note row through a process of gradual addition of notes. Throughout, the work maintains an improvisatory character. Technically, the most demanding aspects are rapid note passages often encompassing a very wide range, sometimes as much as 2½ octaves. Extended techniques employed include flutter-tonguing, multiphonics, trills, tremolos with tongue, tongue clicking, vocal sounds. Recorded by József Basinka.

Langgård, Rued. *Dies Irae.* RDB.

Lawes, William. *5 Pieces.* arr. Gordon J. Kinney. Queen City Brass Publications. 1981. $6.50. 3:00. III. G_1–d'. Five movements. For Rex Conner. These simple baroque dance tunes are entertaining. They should prove excellent for study material with limited technical demands.

Lebedev, I. *Three Pieces.* Musical Evergreen. 1975. $5.50. 4:00. III–IV. E_1–g. Three movements: Allegro moderato; Moderato; Grave. The range requirements of this work are modest with most writing below the staff. The compositional style and notation are traditional. The work presents no particular special problems for the performer. The material is melodic in nature. Technical demands are very modest with the main challenges being some rather low articulated eighth note passages in the second movement and octave leaps in the middle register in the third movement.

Leichtling, Alan. *Fantasy Piece VII.* Seesaw Music Corp. 1983. $6.00. 8:00. IV. F_1–f♯'. One movement. For Barton Cummings. Composed in 1982, this work uses a rather wide well-distributed range, with some emphasis on the upper middle and high register. The general compositional style is contemporary and uses traditional notation. Rhythmically, this work is very complex, utilizing many meter changes and a great variety of subdivisions of the individual beat and multiple beats. Most of the work is marked at an eighth note pulse, which makes rhythm more manageable. Considerable time may be spent in interpretation of the rather complex use of traditional notation.

Leitermeyer, F. *Tubissimo.* 1990. $7.95. 5:00. IV. C_1–g'. This work is traditional in its use of thematic material and unmetered traditional notation. The primary technical challenge is its use of very wide intervals, often slurred and exceeding two octaves. Sections of contrasting styles combine to make a very interesting work.

Lendvay, Kamillo. *Five Movements in Quotation Marks.* Manuscript.

Lennon/McCartney. *Blackbird.* arr. Lars Holmgaard. 3:00. IV. B♭$_1$–e♭'. One movement. The primary technical challenge of this work is the extensive use of multiphonics. Besides solid technical control, an accurate stylistic approach is essential for effective performance.

Lerstad, Terje. *Piece for Solo Tuba.*

Lerstad, Terje. *2 Pieces for Solo Tuba.*

Lewis, Robert Hall. *Monophony IX.* Ludwig Doblinger KG. 1977. $5.00. 9:00. IV–V. F♯$_1$–f'. Five movements: Liveramente; Adagio; Moderato; Quasi Cadenza; Moderato. For Harvey Phillips. This composition relies on upper middle register playing, which is taxing. Though CC tuba would clearly work, the F tuba allows for greater comfort and control in prolonged playing through this somewhat high work. The general compositional style of this work is contemporary and relies on traditional notation. The work has a tendency to ramble, much in the style of a literary monologue. There are five clearly marked sections. Extended techniques employed include breath sounds, flutter-tonguing, glissandi, multiphonics, trills, tremolos, and use of a mute.

Lézé, Jean-Francois. *Mirages Contraires.* Lusitanus Editions, Portugal. 2003. 7:00. V. C_1–c'. For Sérgio Carolino. This work utilizes wide intervals, and requires multiphonics and multiple tonguing. Good synchronization will also be needed for the self-played percussion instruments, which include crotales and bass drum.

Lipp, Charles. *Tuba Magritte.* TUBA Press. 1991. $5.00. 4:30. IV. G_1–f♯'. Three movements: The Fair Captive; Threatening Weather; Ladder of Fire. Wide intervals and accurate rhythmic execution should prove to be the primary technical challenge of this work. The second movement employs a mute throughout and requires flutter-tonguing and multiphonics. Overall, this is a challenging work which should be musically satisfying.

Lippe, Cort. *Solo Tuba Music.* Borik Press. 1993. 7:00. For Mel Culbertson. Recorded by József Basinka.

List, Garret. *Le Maire de Courbevoie.*

Lubet, Alex. *Lament.* Alex Lubet. 1979. $5.00. 1:30. IV. E_1–e♭'. One movement. Range demands of this work are moderate and well distributed throughout the middle register. The general compositional style of this work is contemporary and uses traditional notation. Rhythmic complexity is the primary technical challenge of this very short etude-like work. It is interesting for its use of serial technique, specifically for its use of a tone row. The only extended techniques employed are eighth-tone bends.

Lys, Marc. *Tubastone.* Editions Robert Martin. 1988. $7.50. 3:00. IV–V. F_1–a♭'. One movement. Though there are instances of extreme high requirements, these are well balanced with lower middle register performance making the general endurance demands moderate. *Ossia* parts simplify some extreme high demands, but much remains. The general compositional style is contemporary, with use of traditional notation. Tenor clef is used briefly in the ninth variation. The work is a set of variations based on elements of the opening theme. Following the statement of the theme, there are ten variations, each clearly marked. Technical demands abound in the work. Rhythmically, this work is very complex and is dominated by extended rapid passages, sometimes with very wide intervals as well.

Macauley, Janice. *Tuba Contra Mundum.* TUBA Press. 1991. $4.00. 3:00. IV. G_2–c''. One movement. This work, other than range, makes no unusual demands on technique. Phrases alternate moods with instructions such as "jokingly" and "wistful." This should prove a very effective and interesting work for study and performance.

MacBride, David. *Tuba Mirum.* American Composer's Edition. $2.98. 6:00.

Macy, Carleton. *Music for Tuba Alone.* 7:00. IV. A_1–b''. Five movements: I. Allegro Moderato; Prelude; II. Andante Sostenuto; Prelude; III. Fugue. For Carla Rutschman. This contemporary composition relies on a combination of traditional, proportional, and graphic notation. Extended rapid passages and wide leaps are the primary technical challenges.

Mannino, Franco. *Tre Impressioni Serial.* Edizioni Curci. 1990. 11:00. IV. C♯$_1$–g♭'. Three movements: L'infinito; Marcetta; Canto D'amore. Movements one and three are unmetered, but otherwise these works are traditionally notated. Each is essentially based on a theme or motive. Range is the primary technical challenge.

Maros, Miklos. *Etudes for Tuba (Etyder för Tuba).* Nordiska Musikforlag. 6:30.

Marques, Carlos. *Arabesque V: 4 Temperaments of a Esquisafrenic, for Solo Tuba.* Lusitanus Editions, Portugal. 2003. 9:00. V. C_1–d''. For Sérgio Carolino. Many wide intervals and several contemporary effects, including wind effect, slap tongue, multiphonics, and glissandi. A strong musical theatre work.

Martelli. *Suite, Opus 83.* Associated Music Publishers.

Martin, Robert. *Aldebaran.* Merion Music. Composed 1994, published 1999. 5:45. IV. F_1–f'. A one-movement, four-section work with ten changes of tempo and mood. Difficulties include rhythmic structure, exacting dynamic schemes, challenging intervals in a predominantly atonal context, and navigation of the musical transitions. The pitch range tends to be more conservative, with only a small number of passages above c', yet the player must save energy for a commanding ascent to a fortissimo sustained f' in the closing measures. This is a musically effective and compelling work.

Martínez, Jorge. *Migraciones.* Manuscript. 1994. III–IV. D_1–e'. In three movements. The outer movements are considerably easier than the middle one, which includes a number of avant-garde techniques. Movements one and three make use of motivic material taken from Chilean folk tunes. The middle movement contains boxed notation and includes snippets of other works as well as folk tunes. The performer must create, through note sequences and dramatic delivery, a clear connection to the audience. Contains some multiphonics and moments of improvisation.

Martinsson, Rolf. *Monodi, Op. 31.* Swedish Music Information Center. 9:00. For Sven-Olof Juvas.

Masson, Askell. *Aeolus.* Editions BIM, and Summer 2003 ITEA Journal "Gem Series." 2003. 3:00. IV. E_1–g'. One-movement work cast in three sections. One brief passage above the staff, otherwise quite tame in pitch range used. Several special effects, including an awkward rapid half-valved effect. The fast slurred technique in the middle section will take some work to master. Appropriate on either a bass or contrabass tuba.

Masson, Askell. *Boreas.* Editions BIM. Composed 1999, published 2000. 6:00. IV. A_2–f'. In one movement. Boreas stands for the North Wind of Greek mythology, and this composition is based upon a melody from Icelandic folklore. Though metered, the tempo can be somewhat free throughout. Several "wind sound" effects are used, plus one flutter-tongued note and a few measures with easier multiphonics. Makes extensive use of alternate fingerings on rapid repeated notes. Limited number of indicated dynamics. Would work on any key of tuba. Good audience piece.

Mattern, Daniell. *Five Sequential Studies for Solo Tuba.* 8:00. IV. E_1–b♭. Four movements: Fast; Slow; Fast; Slow, Rubato. Written in 1969, this work is traditional in style and notation. Movements are based on motivic development. There are no particular technical challenges. This work is useful as a study piece due to its use of middle register without required high register work.

McCarty, Frank. *Color-Etudes.* Media Press. 1970. 6:50. III. E♭$_1$–e'. Three movements: Black; Green; Red. For Rodger Vaughan. The playing requirements of this work are well distributed through the general range with limited use of either extreme. This is a very playable and entertaining work to study and perform. The compositional style of this work is contemporary, but it uses traditional notation. Motivically, repeated notes are important in all movements. The first movement is marked by a "swell" motive, so called for its crescendo and decrescendo repeated on a sustained pitch. In the second movement, the repetition of a pitch three times at the beginning of a line is particularly important. The third movement utilizes a constant motion in eighth notes with few interruptions, and the repeated note continues to be an important device. The third movement will take work for the rapid execution and the constant motion, but other requirements are minimal.

McIntosh, Ian. *Inner Voices.*

Menoche, Charles. *Perceptions for Solo Tuba.*

Miles, Ben. *Perspectives.* Manuscript (contact the composer at milestba@hotmail.com). 2004. 3:45. III. E_1–d♭'. This solo was designed to be at an appropriate level for an advanced high school tubist, and would also work well for many undergraduate students. The range and overall technique are best suited to the contrabass tuba. Written in one movement with six connected sections, the piece alternates slow/lyrical playing with more animated passage work. A good test of dynamic and tonal control with significant intervallic challenges.

Mitsuoka, I. *Whales.* Musical Evergreen. 1976. $5.50. 5:00. IV. Indeterminate range. One movement. This is an avant-garde composition which relies entirely on graphic notation. Pitch is approximated by horizontal lines and lines of different shapes on a staff. Time is denoted by numbers over the staff which represent seconds. Lengths of individual occurrences as well as the total length of the work is flexible according to the interpretation of the performer, but it is marked to proceed slowly. The work is presumed to mimic whale song. Pitch level and direction of musical line is represented by straight, jagged, and curved lines. There are no explanatory notes, but the score is easily interpreted. Technically, the challenge is obtaining an effective glissando sound which can work throughout the registers of the tuba and controlling this in order to bring out marked accents within the line, as well as accurately representing the contour of each line.

Morecki, Krzysztof. *Quasars.* Musical Evergreen. 1976. $3.89. 2:00. IV. G_1–b'. One movement. The majority of the pitches in this work are in the extreme high register. This is an avant-garde composition which makes use of a varied form of proportional notation. In this work, a time line is drawn above the staff on which 2 cm. is approximately equal to a metronome marking of 52 beats per minute. There are no notes of explanation or performance suggestions other than the indication regarding the time line. Pitches are placed on a staff with no indication of rhythm. Density of the occurrences are determined by the approximate placement of the pitches on the staff in relation to the time line. The work is essentially pointillistic, with individual pitches treated as occurrences. The density of occurrences varies, however, and with the exception of two flourishes, the texture is quite sparse. Extreme intervals are often juxtaposed. The primary technical demands other than the generally high tessitura are the wide intervals and pitch accuracy, as high pitches regularly occur following extended rests.

Morgenstern, Tobias. *1–2–3 für Tuba.* C–e'. Three Movements: Mäßig Schreitend; II; Schnelle Viertel. See Unkrodt, Dietrich, *Reige Vortragsliteratur, Tuba 1 und Tuba 2.*

Morrison, John. *String of Pearls for Solo Tuba.* Manuscript (available from the composer at http://www.johnmorrison.org). 1994. 5:30. III–IV. F_1–f'. For Benedict Kirby. Seven short and diverse movements, with some challenging rhythmic figures (and rests)! The composer suggests the use of CC tuba, and the general tessitura supports this plan. Considerable control needed to capture the essence of each movement. No special effects required. The title refers to the name scientists gave the collision pattern found by the comet Schumaker-Levy 9, as it relates to the organization of the movements. An effective undergraduate-level solo.

Moylan, William. *Solo and Duo.* See same in Tuba and Keyboard.

Mozart. *Alleluja, Exultate.* arr. Matthews. WING. $5.00.

Muczynski, Robert. *Impromptus.* G. Schirmer. 1973. $2.00. 4:30. III. D_1–e♭'. Five movements: Allegro con moto; Andante; Allegro Moderato; Moderato; Allegro giocoso. This composition relies on middle-register playing with few demands in either extreme, making very modest demands on endurance. This work is entertaining for performer and audience alike. It should be easily playable by anyone who can manage the range requirements. This work relies on a traditional compositional style and notation system. It is a very entertaining work. Syncopations and accents are important elements of the first, third, and fifth movements, which are each dance-like in general character. The second movement is a lyric, song-like movement which uses the upper middle register and demands control of legato style in a soft dynamic setting. The fourth movement is again song-like, but in a 5/8 meter and lower tessitura than the second movement. Another technical concern may be the fifth movement's alternations between 6/8 and 3/4 meter.

Müller, Achim. *Vier Kapitel für Tuba Solo.* arr. by Weinberg. 10:30. E_1–f'. Four movements:

Evolution; Stagnation; Depression; Revolution. See Unkrodt, Dietrich, *Reige Vortragsliteratur, Tuba 1 und Tuba 2.*

Nelson, Gary. *Verdigris.* TUBA Press. 1991. $4.00. 5:30. IV. E_1–e♭'. Rhythmically, this work is simple, though it uses no metric marking. Careful interpretation of the many dynamic markings is essential for accurate interpretation. A poem is spoken in fragments throughout the piece, which adds an interesting wrinkle to the composition.

Newman, Ron. *Three Pieces for Tuba.* Tuba-Euphonium Press. Composed 1997, published 1999. 9:15. IV–V. D♭$_1$–g♭' (optional d♭"). Three movements: Soliloquy; Pavane; Rich Matteson. For the Leonard Falcone International Euphonium and Tuba Festival. A challenging contemporary work with distinct stylistic demands in each of the movements. The composer provides extensive notes in the preface regarding interpretation, including a lengthy set of hints for the proper jazz articulation style in movement III. Uses the full range of the tuba, but no extended techniques. The first movement is quite free, but there are several important metric modulations. Movement II attempts to mirror the style of a Bach cello suite, and will need considerable soft control in the upper register. Movement III pays tribute to tuba/euphonium jazz great Rich Matteson, with a set of four choruses and coda based on "rhythm changes." Please note that the 1999 version contains an abbreviated third movement as compared to the original setting.

Nielsen, John. *Landlig Suite for Solo Tuba.*

Olson, C. G. Sparre. *Canto II.* Norsk Musikforlag. 1981. 1:30. II–III. G_1–f♯. One movement. This is a lively work in an ABA form with a short lyric section as the B section. The general folk dance character of the outer sections combined with the simple eighth note dominant rhythmic patterns should provide a fun work for younger tubists.

Osmon, Leroy. *Concert Etudes for Solo Tuba, Volume I and II.* Southern Music Company. 1991. Volume I: 11:45. Volume II: 10:00. III–IV. Volume I: C_1–e♭'. Volume II: D_1–f'. Five movements in each volume. Volume I: From F. M.; To J. W. P.; For the Children of Hiroshima; Obsédant (for Cay); Comme Une Ombre Mouvante. Volume II: F. B. W.; P. W.; P. B.; M. H.; A. M. For Frank Woodruff (volume I) and David Kirk (volume II). Varied musical settings in a traditional tonal style. Seem best suited to contrabass tuba. A good test of control and musicianship. Upper register lip trills required in spots. Only a few passages venture above the staff. Excellent study or recital material. Recorded by David Kirk. Also listed in the chapter Methods and Studies.

Paasch, Antony. *Suite for Solo Tuba Alone by Itself without Accompaniment.* Tuba-Euphonium Press. 2003. 13:30. III. E_1–e♭'. Six movements: Not too fast!; Andante; Allegro; Adagio; Moderato; Presto. Each movement is in binary form with a repeat marked, and the overall timing reflects taking all of the repeats. The composer utilizes a variety of unusual time signatures, yet the writing is conventional in other ways, with many scalar and arpeggiated lines, and a limited number of accidentals. Only larger-scale dynamics are given. The third movement is considerably more challenging than the other five, with greater range and flexibility needed in this 11/16 meter. Good study material.

Paganini. *Theme and Variations.* arr. Holmgaard. Sheet Music Now.

Paganini, Niccolo. *4 Caprices.* arr. David Werden. Whaling Music Publishers. $12.50.

Para, D. J. *Variations.* TUBA Gem. 1975. 1:30. IV. F–b'. One movement. This very short avant-garde composition is based on a series of pitches derived from the name of tubist Robert Whaley. The notation is a mixture of traditional, frame, proportional notation.

Parker, Charlie. *Charlie Parker Omnibook.* Atlantic Music Supply Corporation. 1978. $11.95. IV. E♭–a♭'. This collection of sixty solos transcribed from recordings of Charlie Parker is intended for use by any bass clef instrument. Also included is a scale syllabus which explains chord symbols, lists scales which can be used with each symbol and spells various types of scales. Each solo provides the head and solo as well as the appropriate chord changes. Technique is quite demanding at the marked tempi and considering the range. These are excellent and entertaining study material. Many may be used down an octave.

Paxton, Steve. *Tubachants.* Manuscript.

Pearsall, Ed. *2 Motets.* TUBA Press. $5.00. 4:30. IV–V. A_1–g'. Two movements: Intrada; Aire. This is an interesting but very difficult work. Absolute control of multiphonics is required and a majority of the composition relies on this technique. An added twist is the use of finger taps in the first movement. The work should prove both interesting and challenging for the performer and will work well as a recital piece.

Pehrson, Joseph. *Tuba Miracle.* Seesaw Music Corp. Composed in 2000, published 2001. 9:45. III–IV. E♭$_1$–d♭'. In two movements. Written for Michael Thurlow. Both movements are completely unmetered, yet traditional metric figures and markings abound. Several tonal centers predominate; however, the music has considerable accidentals and intervallic challenges. This work appears best suited to a BB♭ or CC tuba, as there are frequent forays below the staff, and a rather limited upper tessitura. Alternates musical material between lyrical demands and hefty low register orchestral-like passagework.

Pellay, Paul. *Capriccio for Tuba, Op. 41a.* 1989. 5:30. IV–V. E♭$_1$–f'. One movement. This work is improvisatory in style and relies entirely on traditional technique.

Penderecki, Krzysztof. *Capriccio.* B. Schott's Sohne Mainz. 1987. $8.95. 5:00. V. E♭$_1$–g'. One movement. The general tessitura tends to be moderately high with an emphasis on performance in and above the staff. Composed in 1980, this is an excellent work deserving the attention of every serious tubist. The general compositional style is contemporary and uses unmetered traditional notation with but two exceptions. There is notation depicting highest and lowest possible pitch and note flags representing rhythm without note heads, but rather a curved line denoting the general musical contour. The majority of the work remains in a quick tempo, with a brief middle section in a waltz style and slightly slower. There is an opening theme which supplies most of the motivic material for the work and returns following the waltz section. The primary technical demands beyond those of range are wide intervals and extended passages of rapid sixteenths. The notation and sparse markings leave a great deal of freedom for interpretation, requiring special attention on the part of the performer to arrive at a satisfactory musical solution. Extended techniques employed include flutter-tonguing, glissandi, indefinite pitch, trills. Recorded by Roger Bobo, Zdzislaw Piernik, József Basinka, Jeffrey Funderburk, Heo Jae Young, Stephane Labeyrie, Phillippe Legris, Dan Perantoni, Gavin Woods, James Gourlay.

Penderecki, Krzysztof. *Piernikiana.* Polskie Wydawnictwo Muzyczne.

Penn, William. *Three Essays.* Seesaw Music Corp. 1975. $9.00. 10:55. V. A$_2$–c'. Three movements: Prelude; Interlude; Postlude. For Gene Pokorny. Dedicated to Barney Childs. The primary demands on traditional techniques are in the upper middle register with use of extremes in each direction. Composed in 1973, this is a very interesting work, particularly for study, and certainly worthy of performance. This is an avant-garde composition which utilizes proportional and frame notation as well as traditional notation. There is a very good explanation of the symbols used, which greatly aids in the interpretation of the score. The first movement emphasizes repeated patterns. The second movement uses an indefinite time notation with notes and effects spaced on the staff to reflect relative time. The third movement is lyric and uses many very wide slurs in succession. The opening two thirds of the movement are traditionally notated and performed; then the third slide is withdrawn, and the final section is a mixture of natural and altered sounds produced by playing and singing through the unsealed third valve. Extended techniques employed include glissandi, indefinite pitch, tremolos (with voice), vocal sounds, removal of slides. Recorded by Eugene Pokorny, John Turk.

Persichetti, Vincent. *Parable XXII.* Elkan-Vogel. 1983. $4.00. 13:30. V. D$_1$–g'. One movement. For Harvey Phillips. This work requires a very wide range with full use of both extremes. Control of both upper and lower registers is required, and due to the length, endurance is a concern. A very significant commitment of time will be required of any player in order to give an effective rendering of this work. Though limited in its use of extended techniques, it requires complete control of all traditional techniques at a professional performance level. The compositional style is contemporary, but the work relies entirely on traditional notation. Though it is a single continuous movement, there are sections marked by tempo changes. Very rapid tongued passages coupled with wide, sometimes awkward intervals are particularly demanding. Musically the work demands considerable attention in order to arrive at an adequate interpretation. Extended techniques employed include glissandi, trills. See: Bird, Gary, ed.; *Program Notes for the Solo Tuba.* Recorded by Mark Nelson, József Basinka.

Persichetti, Vincent. *Serenade No. 12.* Elkan-Vogel. 1963. $3.00. 7:00. IV. D$_1$–e'. Six movements: Intrada; Arietta; Mascherata; Capriccio; Intermezzo; Marcia. For Harvey Phillips. Generally the range requirements are moderate to high with extremes utilized in both directions. Though this work is normally performed on CC, it does work well on F tuba. This work is a mainstay of the genre and deserves the attention and study of every serious tubist. The compositional style and notation in this work are traditional. It is essentially a set of dance-like movements. Though no extended techniques are required, the work relies on a very advanced level of traditional technique. The first and sixth movements require control of wide interval slurs and sudden dynamic changes which must not be allowed to interfere with the flow of the melody. The second and fifth movements explore the lyric qualities of the instrument in long phrases. The third movement is the most awkward musically and generally requires the greatest interpretive efforts. The fourth movement is technically difficult due to its speed and the awkward slurs within the triplet line. See: Bird, Gary, ed.; *Program Notes for the Solo Tuba.* Recorded by Harvey Phillips, Phillippe Legris, David Zerkel.

Pinkham, Daniel. *Tucket IV.* E. C. Schirmer Company Inc. 1981. 1:30. IV. G$_1$–e♭'. One movement. This is a very short work in a contemporary style which is chromatic in nature. Wide intervals and changing meter are the primary technical challenges. The work is an exciting short piece, excellent as a possible encore piece.

Poore, Melvyn. *Variations.*

Poore, Melvyn. *Vox Superius.* Arts Lab Music Publishing. 1977. $8.00. 8:00. IV–V. B♭$_1$–f'. One movement. This work was composed in 1976, and the general compositional style is best described as contemporary bordering on the avant-garde. The general tessitura is moderate with most playing in the staff. This work is perhaps a bit long. The dominant notational system is proportional, with some use of rather advanced traditional notation of rhythm. There is an adequate explanation of symbols and the score is very clean and clear, making interpretation less difficult. This is a study in timbres and effects which are possible with the tuba and an exploration of the instrument's "other" potentials. An interesting effect is the use in a multiphonic section of pronounced syllables and even words with the sung line. Some patterns do emerge, such as a motif of wide repeated intervals alternating rather rapidly. Wide leaps, frequent use of multiphonics, and rapid passages containing extreme dynamic shifts are among the more demanding technical aspects of this work. Extended techniques employed include flutter-tonguing, multiphonics, trills (valve trill while singing), tremolos, vocal sounds, and use of a mute.

Poulheim, Bert. *Groteske Miniaturen.* Recorded by Phillippe Legris.

Powell, Morgan. *Midnight Realities.* Brass Music, Lt. 1974. $3.50. 5:00. V. C_1–a'. One movement. For Daniel Perantoni. Composed in 1972, this is a tremendously difficult work. It is an avant-garde composition which uses proportional and frame notation as well as traditional notation. Events are sometimes given time designation in seconds. The work is a sound painting more than a traditional form. The music is based on timbres sometimes produced by effects such as multiphonics and percussive sounds. These are used to create a descriptive atmosphere. Though most of the piece relies on non-traditional technique and sounds, that which is traditional tends to be quite high. Many difficulties are encountered, including a multiphonic section in which each part is fully independent and passages of very rapid articulated notes which encompass a very wide range. Extended techniques employed include breath sounds, valve clicks, glissandi, indefinite pitch, multiphonics, and use of a mute. See: Bird, Gary, ed.; *Program Notes for the Solo Tuba.* Recorded by Daniel Perantoni.

Presser, William. *Eight Episodes.* Tenuto Publications. 1999. 8:45. III. F_1–c'. Eight short movements: Allegretto; Andante; Andante; Allegro; Allegro; Allegretto; Vivo; Allegretto. These brief settings are written in a traditional tonal style, featuring considerable rapid technical activity that is largely scalar. Six of the movements include one or more changes in tempo, and a few feature unexpected metric groupings. They appear to be ideal for the contrabass tuba. Best as study material, or perhaps a grouping of the episodes as recital material.

Presser, William. *Suite.* Ensemble Publications/Lyceum Music Press. 1967. $4.00. 8:10. III–IV. E_1–e♭'. Three movements: Allegretto; Adagio; Adagio. For Rex Conner. Range demands are very modest with most playing below the staff or just in the staff. This piece is one of few pieces in the unaccompanied literature which relies on lower middle register playing almost exclusively, so that range should be no problem for any performer. The general compositional style and notation system are traditional. The three movements contain no great technical demands. The second and third movements each have a short opening in a slow tempo before moving to the dominant moderately rapid pace of the total composition.

Ptaszynska, Marta. *Two Poems.* Polskie Wydawnictwo Muzyczne (Marks Music). 1979. $5.00. 8:00. V. $F\sharp_1$–f♯'. Two movements: Cantabile, con-espressione; Scherzando, con bravura. The range of the tuba is thoroughly exploited throughout the work with special emphasis on the high register. Endurance is an important consideration. Composed in 1975, the work uses a generally contemporary compositional style tending toward the avant-garde. There is use of proportional notation, though most of the notation is traditional or modified so that it includes bar lines with a number appearing over each bar line when there is a change in the pulse from the previous measure. The number represents the number of quarters or eighths contained within the measure. A brief explanation of the symbols used is provided. The first movement is slow and expressive with a rearticulated pitch "motif" serving as a main unifying element. Multiphonics occur throughout, often with both parts moving in rhythmic unison as intervals continuously change. Another difficulty of the multiphonics section involves sung pitches below the played line. The second movement, a scherzo-like movement, involves some very rapid runs sometimes coupled with very wide intervallic leaps. Interesting is the use of vocal syllables to alter timbre of the played sound. Very rapid triple-tonguing is also required. Extended techniques employed include flutter-tonguing, glissandi, multiphonics, quarter tone bends, vocal sounds.

Raum, Elizabeth. *Sweet Dances.* Tuba-Euphonium Press. 2002. 9:00. IV–V. F_1 (D_1 optional)–a' (d♭" optional). Four movements: Blew Tango; Dot Polka; Waltzin' Matuba; A Hard Knight's Day. For John Griffiths. Four varied dance settings in a tonal style. Multiphonics required in the final movement; otherwise all traditional playing and notation. As a whole, not quite as stratospheric in range as some of this composer's other offerings. The primary challenge is to capture the proper dance style for each movement while navigating some busy technical passages. John

Griffiths has provided quite a few suggested octave alterations for the final movement, which is written in a rock style.

Raum, Elizabeth. *Will There Be a Time.* Tuba-Euphonium Press. Composed 1996, published 1998. 10:00. V. F_2–d♭''. Four linked movements: Moderato; The Neighbors; Fighting Zone; Will There Ever Be a Time. For John Griffiths. An avant-garde dramatic piece which serves as a commentary on the horror of violence throughout the world. There are a number of moments with spoken text, plus flutter tongue, multiphonics, and a variety of other special effects. The composer requests "solo tuba in F." Many awkward wide leaps, and a significant amount of demanding upper register work, including several treble clef notated pitches. An unusual and riveting work. Recorded by John Griffiths.

Reck, David. *Five Studies.* Edition Peters. 1968. $9.25. 10:00. V. B_2–f'. Five movements: Tempo Rubato; As Fast as Possible, with Clarity; Like a Song; Make like a Wallenda, Man!; Blues. The total range of the tuba is fully exploited in this work, but generally demands are well paced for endurance considerations. This work is an excellent study piece, particularly for study of alternative notational systems. The explanations and symbols are clear enough for the work to be used as a first study piece in this genre provided the player is technically very strong. This is an avant-garde work which employs proportional and frame notation as well as unmetered traditional notation. The five studies or movements explore a wide range of styles. Notation is perhaps the most interesting feature, as it makes extensive use of frame notation for both sound and silence. Technically, the work is quite difficult, requiring control of rapidly articulated, non-scalar passages, wide leaps in rapid succession with changing accent patterns, multiphonics, and a very wide range. Extended techniques employed include breath sounds, flutter-tonguing, glissandi, multiphonics, lip trills. See: Bird, Gary, ed.; *Program Notes for the Solo Tuba.* Recorded by Toby Hanks.

Reed, Marlyce P. *Two Autumn Moods.*

Reményi, Attila. *Solo for Tuba.* Editio Musica Budapest.

Remson, Michael. *Fanfare and Air.* Tuba-Euphonium Press. Composed in 1996, published in 1997. 6:20. III–IV. G♯$_1$–d'. In one movement. The publisher distributes this work in one bound set containing versions for euphonium, bass trombone, and tuba (pp. 9–12). The cover only lists the work as a euphonium solo, which may indeed be the original intent. For tuba the range is quite modest, and it would be a good work to perform on contrabass tuba. The solo alternates between energetic and lyric styles, but there are more moments that would constitute an "Air." A few half-valved glissandi are the only non-traditional requests. Considerable tempo variation and transitions throughout.

Renn, Donald S. *Rhapsody.* Tuba-Euphonium Press. 1998. 4:00. III–IV. C_1–e♭'. One-movement work in six short sections. Fairly traditional writing in a tonal setting, lacking any extended techniques. Nice variety of styles present. More difficult passages are fairly "tuba-friendly." Well suited to any key of tuba.

Roger, Denise. *Jeux De Cuivre.* Editions Robert Martin. 1992. 4:45. IV–V. A♯$_2$–a♭'. Two movements: Parlando-Anime; Expressif-Rythmique. Each movement offers a range of lyrical and technical playing, at a high level of difficulty. The writing is bombastic at one moment, and light and playful soon after. The composer uses a large pitch range, with considerable upper tessitura demands. With frequent awkward intervals and a regular stream of accidentals, this music will take considerable effort to master. Still, it offers a great deal of variety, seems well suited to the bass tuba, and appears to have considerable audience appeal.

Roikjer, Kjell. *Five Unaccompanied Pieces, Op. 88.* Engstrom and Sodring.

Roikjer, Kjell. *Study for Tuba Solo.* 1:30. IV. C–f'. One movement. This short work, written in 1979, is traditional in style and notation. The improvisatory character and flowing lines are very entertaining. Rapid slurred passages across a wide range are the primary technical challenges.

Rosolino, Richard. *Variations on Amazing Grace.* Hidalgo Music. 1994. 3:25. III. G_2–d'. Introduction, theme, and four variations on this well-known melody, cast in the key of G major. Well suited to the contrabass tuba. Quite a few ornamental notes are included, and several scooped notes are indicated in the gospel style variation. G_2 found only on the final note of the piece; otherwise G_1 is the bottom pitch.

Ross, Walter. *Escher's Sketches.* Mark Tezak. 1986. 8:00. IV. G♭$_1$–f'. Five movements: Comodo; Estravagante; Agitato; Ballo Lento; Fantastico. This contemporary work uses very traditional musical language. All movements are without meter; however, rhythm and pulse are simple throughout. Each movement is based on a lithograph by M. C. Escher and uses musical devices to depict that picture. This is an interesting work worthy of study, and a solid recital piece. Recorded by Mark Nelson.

Rozen, Jay. *In the 90% (Sturgeon's Law).* Tuba-Euphonium Press. 1998. 3:15. IV. G_1–g' (or possibly higher using F tuba on harmonic series–based lyrical section). One-movement work written by tubist/composer. A tonal and fun romp for the tuba, with no pretensions of being a serious piece of art music. The title makes reference to author Theodore Sturgeon, who once remarked while speaking of literature that "90 percent of everything is crap." Challenges in this work include brief multiphonics, maintaining the tempo through alternating two and three note groupings that are rapidly tongued, handling a fair amount of upper register work, and making the breaths work out properly on some long phrases. Seems designed for a CC tuba, but many will prefer E♭ or F tuba.

Russell, Gilmour. *Mud.* American Music Center.

Sacco, Peter. *Tuba Mirum.* Western International Music. 1969. $2.00. 10:00. IV. $E\flat_1$–$e\flat'$. Five movements: Tuba Mirum; Lacrymosa; Libera Me; Sanctus Benedictus; Allegro con Brio. This work presents moderate range requirements, with most playing well distributed in the middle register. An effective approach to performance of this work employs a narrator to read the text prior to each movement. The general compositional style is traditional though unique in this medium for its coupling of a religious text with the music. Notation is traditional throughout. Though five movements are labeled, due to the lack of pause from movement four to five and the da capo which returns to the beginning of the fourth movement, there are in practical terms only four movements. Each of the four movements is titled with a label from the Catholic liturgy and a text precedes it which is in keeping with the religious title. Musically, the movements reflect the sentiments of the preceding text. For example, the mention of the trumpet call in the text of the first movement is reflected in the double dotted rhythm reminiscent of trumpet fanfares in that movement. The second movement is marked by a sob motive. Technically the work presents no unusual demands.

Samkopf. *Solo Piece for Tuba.*

Sandgren, Joachim. *Rave.* Swedish Music Information Center.

Sandgren, Joachim. *Resonance.* Swedish Music Information Center.

Sarcich, Paul. *Chaconne.* American Music Center. 6:00.

Saul, Walter. *De Profundis.* TUBA Press.

Sauter, Ed. *Eight Random Thoughts.* 11:00. IV. F_1–$a\flat'$. Eight movements: ♩ = 88; ♩ = 112; ♩ = 104; ♩ = 48; ♩ = 66; ♩ = 48; ♩ = 60; ♩ = 66. To Kurt Vonnegut, Jr. This is an interesting work which takes traditional technique to the limits. Wide intervals of as much as two octaves are common and a smooth legato style is required throughout.

Scelsi, Giac. *Maknongan.* Salabert. 1956.

Schilling, Hans Ludwig. *Tuba Prima.* Möseler Verlag. 1981. 6:00. V. $B\flat_1$–$b\flat''$. Two movements: Recitando; Valse musette. This is an extremely difficult work in a contemporary style. While notation is entirely traditional, rhythmic notation is quite complex in the first movement. Considerable use of multiphonics, very rapid passages covering a wide range, and a non-stop rapid rhythmic flow in the waltz are the primary technical challenges.

Schlünz, Annette. *Ach, es . . . Musik für Tuba Solo.* Bote & Bock. 1993. 7:00. V. C_1–$e\flat'$. One movement. For Michael Vogt. Written in 1991, this is a tremendously difficult work in a contemporary style. Notation is a mix of traditional and proportional notation, with many notational markings which signify extended techniques. All symbols are clearly explained. The rhythmic notation is complex. Musically, the work is a collage of sound colors and flourishes. A short poem by the composer and a quote from René Char suggest the general emotional character of the work. Though very demanding, this work has great potential in performance. Recorded by Michael Vogt.

Schneider, John. *TBA.*

Schudel, Thomas. *Line Drawings.* Canadian Music Centre. 1985. 3:30. IV. G_1–$g\flat'$. Two movements: Adagio; Allegro con brio. For Michael Moran. This work is melodic and essentially traditional in its general character. The primary technical demand is range, while all other aspects of this work are well within normal technical demands. This is a solid composition of value both as a study piece and a recital work.

Sciortino, Patrice. *15 Etudes de Concours.* Editions Billaudot. 1999. ca.40:00. IV–V. F_1–$a\flat'$. This collection of studies is the culminating work in an eight-volume set of bass tuba material composed by Anthony Girard and Patrice Sciortino, from easy levels through very advanced. These fifteen cadenza-like etudes work to challenge every facet of tuba playing: technique, flexibility, varied articulations, range and strength, large intervals, etc. Plus, they present a significant musical challenge. Oddly, this book includes scant dynamic markings, and only general tempo indications. Excellent study material for the F or E♭ tuba. A single etude or short grouping of them could be an effective recital vehicle. Also listed in the chapter Methods and Studies.

Sczerba, Michael. *Three Meditations.* Frank E. Warren Music. 1999. 14:00.

Sear, Walter E. *Sonata.* Western International Music. 1966. $3.00. 8:00. III. F_1–d'. Four movements: Andante; Presto; Andantino; Giocoso. Range requirements throughout are moderate, with much of the work in the lower middle register. This composition should work well as study material to supplement basic etudes. The compositional style and notation are traditional. No special technical demands are made of the performer. The work is melodic in character. The first movement is smooth with extended slurred passages across intervals which are generally a perfect fifth or less. The second movement is marked by a double-dotted eighth note and 32nd note figure in a very fast tempo. The third movement is similar in tempo and style to the first movement.

Selmer-Collery. *Tuba Nova.* Associated Music Publishers.

Sera, Carlo. *Lyric Suite.* Musical Evergreen. 1977. \$3.89. 3:30. III–IV. E_1–f♯'. Four movements: Allegro molto; Adagio; Allegretto; Allegro. Range requirements of this work are generally moderate, with most playing in the staff. Composed in 1976, this work should prove excellent study material to supplement basic etudes and is a worthy recital piece, though rather short. The compositional style and notation system are traditional. The first movement is dominated by very wide leaps and a very sparse texture with a sporadic, rhythmic flow. The second movement is more lyric, again dominated by wide intervals often slurred. The third movement returns to a thin texture reminiscent of movement one, though in a 3/8 meter and a somewhat higher general tessitura. The final movement is marked by frequent meter changes, wide intervals, and a sometimes sporadic rhythmic flow, here created by a reliance on syncopations and irregularly placed accents. Technical demands are moderate. Pitch accuracy is critical, particularly in the first movement where high register notes regularly occur after rests.

Sharman, Rodney. *Boa Constrictor.* Canadian Music Centre. 2000. 2:00. II–III. F♯$_1$–e. For David Gordon Duke. A work supported as part of the BC (British Columbia) Millennium Series and designed for the developing tubist. While the required range is quite modest, the lengthy phrases and chromatic nature of this work will pose a challenge to the younger player. A solid effort dynamically and lyrically will be essential in capturing the essence of this piece.

Silverman, Faye-Ellen. *Zigzags.* Seesaw Music Corp. 1988. \$7.00. 8:30. IV–V. C♯$_1$–b♭'. One movement. This work tends to emphasize the high register. Few if any breaks make this a very taxing work. This is a very difficult work and will require a significant time commitment. The general compositional style is contemporary but relies on traditional notation. Though a single movement, there are many tempo changes which mark style and section changes. Tempo markings are numbered up to VII (i.e., Tempo I, Tempo II, etc.) and are recurrent throughout. Each successive tempo marking is referenced to a previous tempo; for instance, Tempo VI is three times the speed of Tempo I. While perhaps seemingly complicated at first, these references do aid in matching style with previous sections and assist in rapidly understanding the relationship between sections. Technically, wide leaps and rapid passages across a very wide range abound. These coupled with the endurance factor and the extended techniques make this a very demanding composition. Extended techniques employed include flutter-tonguing, glissandi, multiphonics. Recorded by Velvet Brown.

Slavicky, Milan. *Echoes.* Editions BIM. Composed in 1981, published in 2000. 10:45. IV–V. F♯$_1$–f♯'. Three movements: Echo 1; Danza; Echo 2. Rhythmic and generally aggressive contemporary work by this Czech Republic composer. Appears best suited for F or E♭ tuba. Requires flutter tongue, multiphonics, and several longer freely pitched trills. Effective and exciting composition, requiring power and control.

Smith, Glenn. *Magniloquentia.* 4:00. V. C–d'. Two movements. Extended passages of rapid notes and complex rhythmic figures dominate this work. The second movement makes extensive use of multiphonics. While notationally the work is traditional, the general musical effect is that of a contemporary work and a technical exploration of the instrument.

Smith, Glenn. *The Survival.* 7:00. V. E♭$_2$–c''. Two movements: Future Schock; Discorporation. For John Turk. Written in 1972, this contemporary composition uses passages of proportional and graphic notation as well as traditional notation. Multiphonics, extended passages of multiple tonguing, and vocalizations are used. This is a very difficult and long work.

Songer, Lewis. *Tuballet.* KoKo Enterprises. 1983. \$3.50. 5:00. III–IV. G_1–e♭'. Four movements: Stately-Mysterious; Moderato, dolce e simplice; Easy 1; Spirited. This work involves modest range requirements, as most playing is well distributed in the middle register. This is an excellent study piece for the advancing student and is good sight-reading material for the more advanced. The compositional style and notation used are traditional. Each movement is motivically oriented with a basic theme or motive dominating each. Technical demands are modest. The first movement utilizes rapid passages of sixteenth notes as well as eighth and sixteenth triplets and presents rhythmically the most diverse palate.

Spillman, Robert A. *Four Greek Preludes.* Edition Musicus. 1969. \$3.75. 13:00. IV. E_1–f'. Four movements: Lento, molto liberamente; Andante moderato e cantabile; Recitativo: largamente; Allegro giocoso. For Rex Conner. This work relies on middle register playing, making the general demands moderate for endurance though extremes of range are used. These preludes are very approachable and enjoyable for any advanced player. They are worthy of programming, but should probably not be performed as a full set due to length and similarity of the movements. The general compositional style is traditional and uses traditional notation which is unmetered in the first and third movements. The work maintains a modal character throughout, which gives it a unique flavor. Movements I, II, and III are highly melodic in character with very singable themes. The third movement is dominated by a fanfare motive and remains somewhat tentative in its progress, never developing into a full theme. Technically, these are moderately challenging with rapid scalar passages the dominant technical feature. The greatest musical challenge is to maintain the character of each movement despite the technical demands.

Stanley, Helen. *Excursions for Solo Tuba.* TUBA Press. 1986. $4.00. 4:00. III. F_1–d'. Three movements: Allegro dramatico; Andantino romantico; Allegretto burlando. This interesting work should prove a useful introductory work to the unaccompanied medium. All movements are thematically based. Occasional wide intervals should prove the only technical challenge, while the musical context should maintain the interest of performer and audience.

Steadman, Robert. *Sonata in One Movement.* MGP. 1983. $1.00. 8.25. IV–V. A_2–f'. One movement. This work is dominated by changing meters, with sections marked by tempo changes. The drive of the work is primarily rhythmic with some motivic use.

Stein, Leon. *Solo Sonata for Tuba.* Composers Facsimile Edition. 10:00. IV. F♯$_1$–c'. Two movements: Variations; Recitative. This very long work is traditional in style and notation. There are many style and time changes through each movement. Extended passages of rapidly articulated notes are the primary technical challenge.

Stein, Leon. *Two Pieces.* Dorn Publications Inc. 1981. 6:30. III–IV. F♯$_1$–c'. Two movements: Transformations (twelve mini-etudes in variation form); Duplex. The general range demands of this work are moderate, with most playing in the staff. Composed in 1969, the work employs traditional compositional style and notation. The first movement is a set of variations that place great demands on the performer's facility through numerous rapid passages which are primarily scalar. The second movement utilizes two themes which serve as the basic thematic material in a sectionalized movement. The primary technical demands are extended passages of sixteenth notes which seem to proceed endlessly.

Stephens. *Slow Melody Solos.*

Stern, Jacob. *Adventure for Solo Tuba, Opus 43.* Manuscript. 2001. 8:00. III–IV. F_1–d♯'. For Mark Nelson. A single-movement work, all played at a consistent slow tempo, featuring twelve phrases which provide melodic and rhythmic variations on the opening motives. Would be equally suited to bass or contrabass tuba. The lack of notated dynamics and the generally "dry" nature of this work serve to make it an effective study piece, but one that has rather limited audience appeal.

Stevens, John. *Remembrance.* Editions BIM. Composed in 1995, published in 2000. 7:20. IV. E_1–a♭'. A one-movement work in six larger sections. For John Tuinstra, who commissioned the work in memory of Jerry Bramblett. The composer writes: "The music is meant to reflect aspects of Jerry Bramblett's personality as well as the emotions he felt as he battled the cancer that prematurely ended his life." The solo balances longer sections of flowing melodic lines with several more aggressive moments. The indicated range is a bit deceptive, as the music contains only one high a♭'—well prepared—and otherwise only ascends to e'. One note requires flutter tongue. The closing section includes extended multiphonics in a chorale-like setting which will need excellent balance, control, and intonation. An effective contemporary work consistent with other offerings from this composer.

Stevens, John. *Salve Venere, Salve Marte.* Editions BIM. 1995. 9:00. V. G♭$_1$–g♭'. One-movement composition in four larger sections. For Roger Bobo. The title—Hail to Venus, Hail to Mars—results in an expressive and rhythmic musical dialogue between the Roman goddess of love and beauty, and the god of war. Notation is generally conventional. Dynamic contrast is paramount. Considerable diversity also achieved through melodic motives, articulations, and rhythmic schemes. It contains a large number of rapid wide leaps, and a considerable amount of upper tessitura playing. Best on F or E♭ tuba. Another effective and demanding work from this composer/tubist. Recorded by Velvet Brown.

Stevens, John. *Suite #1.* Philharmusica Corp. Manduca Music Publications. 1977. 6:00. IV–V. E_1–f'. Five movements: Slow and Rubato; Ponderous; Slow and Freely; March; Slow and Sombre. This work is primarily melodic in nature with traditional demands on technique. With limited use of the high register, it should prove a valuable piece for study and performance. See: Bird, Gary, ed.; *Program Notes for the Solo Tuba.* Recorded by John Stevens.

Stevens, John. *Triumph of the Demon Gods.* Queen City Brass Publications. 1981. $5.00. 3:30. IV. E♭$_1$–e'. One movement. The range requirements are well balanced, with somewhat more emphasis on the middle and low register. The compositional style is essentially traditional though not particularly tonal, and the notational system employed is traditional. The music depicts a struggle between the forces of good and evil. Sections contrast a relatively low tessitura line with a marked style utilizing accents and short/long rhythm and a higher, more legato melodic section. There are frequent tempo shifts and meter shifts, but always in a quarter note pulse. Technically, requirements are moderate, with rapid sixteenth note passages and regular style shifts the primary demands. See: Bird, Gary, ed.; *Program Notes for the Solo Tuba.* Recorded by John Stevens.

Stevens, Thomas. *Encore: Boz.* Wimbledon Music Inc. 1977. $4.00. 3:00. IV. C–c''. One movement.

For Roger Bobo. This work calls for use of the performer's complete range. Though much of the playing is in the upper and upper middle register, the short duration should prevent endurance problems. Composed in 1976, the work employs a generally contemporary compositional style and relies primarily on traditional notation with some examples of proportional notation. This is a "mirror piece" in that the material is presented and then played in retrograde, making the end and the beginning identical. At the center of the composition, between the presentation and the retrograde, is a "Little Concert" to be improvised. Instructions for the "Little Concert" call for a gradual crescendo from pianissimo to fortissimo and a return to the pianissimo to maintain the mirror idea. It is also suggested in the score that rather than the improvised section, the opening and closing of the work may be used as a general entrance and exit for another work or group of works and this is in fact as the work is recorded. Technically the greatest demands are the very wide intervals required. Thematically the piece is a decreasing interval beginning from highest possible to lowest possible pitch and arriving at a unison. Also challenging is the use of flutter-tonguing on individual notes within a rapid line. Extended techniques employed include foot stamps, flutter-tonguing, indefinite pitch. Recorded by Roger Bobo.

Stewart, Michael. *Five Bagatelles.* Tuba-Euphonium Press. Composed in 1997, published in 1998. 5:40. III. F_1–e♭'. Five movements: Fanfare; Broadly, with Strength; Scherzo; Reflective; Dance. Generally well written for tuba in a traditional style and enjoyable for the performer. Upper register (c' and higher) used sparingly. No extended techniques required. Movement III becomes quite active towards the end, with rapid articulations/technique in the low register. The final movement is of perpetual motion and will require smart budgeting of air and a clean style. Good study or recital selection.

Stöckigt, Michael. *Monogramm.* F_1–f'. One movement. See Unkrodt, Dietrich, *Reige Vortragsliteratur, Tuba 1 und Tuba 2.*

Stratton, Don. *Won't He Get Lonely?* PP Music. 1986. $5.00. 3:30. III. F_1–d'. One movement. For George Shaffer. This work uses a well-distributed range primarily in the middle register. Of modest difficulty, this work should prove to be good study material for a younger tubist. The compositional style and notation are traditional. Though a single movement, the work contains many sections marked by tempo and style changes. Many instances of arpeggiation and arpeggiated sequences are perhaps the most demanding technical elements. Numerous meter changes and extensive use of compound meters give a rhythmic vitality to the composition.

Stroud, Richard. *A Variation of East African Calls.* One movement. For R. Winston Morris. See: Bird, Gary, ed.; *Program Notes for the Solo Tuba.*

Sturzenegger, Kurt. *Tuba mirum spargens sonum.* Editions Marc Reift. 1997. 4:00. III–IV. E♭$_1$ (optional C_1)–f♭'. For Pierre Pilloud. One-movement contemporary setting by Swiss composer/trombonist which alternates soft and lyrical low register lines with several aggressive and technical sections. One brief phrase employing multiphonics. Incorporates the famous "Dies Irae" motive. Effective on either bass or contrabass tuba.

Szalonek, W. *Piernikiana.* Polskie Wydawnictwo Muzyczne. 12:05. Recorded by Zdzislaw Piernik.

Szentpali, Roland. *Caprice No. 1.* Editions BIM. Composed in 1993, published in 2001. 4:20. V. F♯$_1$–c''. No specific tempo indication. For Roger Bobo. An energetic piece written in a highly difficult technical manner. Best suited to bass tuba.

Szentpali, Roland. *Caprice No. 2.* Editions BIM. Composed in 1997, published in 2001. 3:30. V. A_2–a♭'. For John Stevens. Tempo is Allegro. Focus tends to be more on legato playing than is the case with the other two works in this series. Still, considerable range and skill necessary.

Szentpali, Roland. *Caprice No. 3.* Editions BIM, and the Spring 2003 *ITEA Journal,* page 34. 2003. 2:30. IV–V. A_2–b♭'. Short one-movement work in two sections. Written to commemorate the International Tuba-Euphonium Association's thirtieth anniversary. Part of the ITEA Gem Series, but also published by Editions BIM. No special effects, but plenty of technical skills required for success on this work. Rather orchestral in nature. A few brief forays to the extreme upper register make this work suited to the bass tuba. Good for study or recital–it would be a perfect encore piece!

Szentpali, Roland. *Variations on a Hungarian Children Song.* Composed in 1999, published in 2002. 6:50. V. C_1–c''. Theme along with five very technical variations. Calls for double tongue as well as multiphonics. This is a tonal work which includes significant arpeggiated action. F tuba is the ideal choice. Recorded by Roland Szentpali.

Szeto, Caroline. *Study No. 1.*

Szeto, Caroline. *Study No. 2.*

Szkutko, John. *Buffus.* SZK Music. 1995. 3:30. IV–V. B♭$_2$–b♭' (multiphonics: d–a'). A one-movement work with five larger sections, designed to be a tuba showpiece. In addition to the large pitch range, it incorporates multiple tongue, rapid technique, and several extended sections utilizing multiphonics. Very tonal and largely anchored in B♭ major. A straightforward and fun romp for the tuba, but will require advanced skills.

Takahashi, Tohru. *Canzon.* 4:00. IV–V. D_1–f'. One movement. To Tsutomu Morimoto. Written in

1982, this is an avant-garde composition which utilizes proportional, graphic, and traditional notation. There are extended passages of indefinite pitch and much use of vocalization.

Terzakis, D. *Stixis III for Tuba Solo.* Breitkopf & Härtel. 1974. 3:00. III. A_1–d'. One movement. The primary challenge of this work is musical interpretation. Notation includes some nontraditional markings which are not explained and may not be familiar to some. Compositionally, the work relies on short patterns which are repeated, generally with an increase in speed before beginning the next pattern.

Thommesen, Olav Anton. *2 Pieces.*

Thow, John. *Living Room Music.* 2:30. III–IV. A_1–e♭'. One movement. To Michael A. McClain. Written in 1967, this work is traditional in style and notation. Regular meter changes and tempo changes mark several sections. This work is probably best used as a study piece.

Tisné, Antoine. *Monodie III.* Editions Billandot. 1990. $7.00. 9:30. V. B_2–f'. One movement. For Fernand Lelong. This very difficult work relies almost entirely on proportional notation. Those sections in traditional notation use complex time signatures. Rapid articulated passages which are rhythmically complex couple with very wide intervals to make a technically challenging work. Recorded by Phillippe Legris.

Toulon, Jacques. *Trois Caricatures.* Editions Robert Martin. 1989. $4.00. 2:10. III. G_1–b♭'. Three movements: Dinosaurus; Valse; Presto. The general tessitura is high and is generally more appropriate to the euphonium. This is a very pleasant work which would be very appropriate for a lower-level euphonium student, but of very limited value to the tubist. The general compositional style and notation are traditional. Musically, the three movements are organized around traditional melodic and thematic ideas. The work is listed as an elementary work, but due to the range this is not appropriate technically for the tuba; musically, however, this is a very accurate characterization. The general high tessitura and the passages of extended sixteenth notes in the third movement constitute the only technical challenges.

Triebman, Karl Ottomar. *Ballade.* Hofmeister.

Tuominen, Seppo. *Tubaniana.* FMI Finnish Music Information Centre. 3:00. III. D_1–d♭'. One movement. This work is simple in concept and should present no problems other than range for the average high school student. There are few extended passages of sixteenth runs.

Tuthill, Burnet. *Ten Tiny Tunes for Tuba.* Tenuto Publications. 1974. $2.00. 10:33. IV. F_1–f' (D_1–e♭). Ten movements: Slow; Allegro; Andante; Vivace; Allegretto; Moderato, cantabile; Snappy; Allegro; Slowly; Fast. For R. Winston Morris. All movements are characterized by moderate middle register demands, well within the general range of the instrument. Endurance should be no problem, particularly with the many chances to pause between movements. As study pieces, these are quite effective due to their brevity and the option to choose appropriate movements. If performance is desired, all or a selection may be used. The general compositional style is traditional with reliance on traditional notation. The ten movements are very short; half are a minute or less in length. Technical demands are minimal for the most part, though movements VIII, IX, and X present more challenge due to rapid passages, sometimes in arpeggiation and sometimes as florid embellishment to the line.

Uber, David. *Solo Etudes for Tuba.* Tuba-Euphonium Press. III. A collection of twelve etudes, each of which is suitable for concert performance. A variety of meters and musical styles. Multimetricism, a 2½ octave range, and extensive use of accidentals make this a challenging yet suitable work for high school tuba players. Also listed in the chapter Methods and Studies.

Unkrodt, Dietrich. *Reige Vortragsliteratur, Tuba 1 und Tuba 2.* Verlag Neue Musik, Berlin. 1989. V. This two-volume collection contains a total of eleven works for solo tuba. These works represent a wide variety of styles tending toward the contemporary and avant-garde. Most rely to some extent on extended techniques. The general tessitura tends to be rather high.

Vadala, C. *Lonely Road.* Whaling Music Publishers. $5.00.

Van der Slice, John. *Solo for Tuba.* Tuba-Euphonium Press. Composed in 1990, published in 1993. 5:15. IV. A_2–g'. Music is laid out on three portrait view sheets, and is easy to read despite being in manuscript. Outside of the concluding upper tessitura flourish, there are very few moments above a c'. The work appears to be ideal for the CC tuba. There are a few special effects in this contemporary work, and the composer provides a helpful glossary. Flutter tongue, various popping sounds, and an unusual ascending multiphonic glissando near the conclusion are all utilized. The general tempo is slow. Barring of measures is a bit haphazard, and there are some unusual yet significant metric challenges.

Van Hoy, Marjorie. *Seven Melodic Etudes.* Tuba-Euphonium Press. 1994. 12:00. III. E_1–e♭'. Seven varied tonal studies: Con Brio; Lullaby; Con espressione; Con grazia; Trills; Maestoso; Leggiero. A variety of keys are employed, and this music looks best suited to contrabass tuba. The writing is very consistent within each etude. Most of the etudes are just under two minutes in duration. A set of three or four as a grouping could be an effective contest or recital vehicle. Also listed in the chapter Methods and Studies.

Van Nostrand, Burr. *Tuba-Tuba.* American Composer's Edition. $2.45. 5:00.

Vaughan, Rodger. *Suite for Tuba.* Joseph Boonin. 1976. 7:00. III–IV. F_1–c'. Four movements: ♩ = 112; ♩ = 112–116; ♩ = 72–76; 𝅗𝅥 = 96. For Benton Minor. The general tessitura is moderate with no extended high register demands. Composed in 1971, the work is traditional both in compositional style and notation. This work is very approachable technically and musically by any good player. Placement of accents in the first movement, accurate handling of the meter in the second movement, and accurate rendering of triplets versus dotted eighths and sixteenths in the third movement should prove the major technical demands.

Vazzana, Anthony. *Self Portraits for Solo Tuba.* Tuba-Euphonium Press. 1994. 15:30. IV–V. D♯$_1$–c''. Seven Movements: Large Strides; Ascent and Descent; Melos; Leapfrog; Melancolia; Play; On a Fast Track. For James Self. Excellent composer-supplied notes regarding each of the seven settings. A nice variety of material, most of it fairly difficult. Will require an F or E♭ tuba. Interesting rhythms, large leaps, clearly specified dynamics. All movements except the third explore the upper limits of the instrument. The composer suggests that a shorter grouping of movements, if contrasting, would also be effective in performance. Very consistent compositional style and excellent musical interest.

Waagemans, Peter-Jan. *Nuage Gris.*

Wanamaker, Greg. *TubaSuite.* Manuscript (see http://home.twcny.rr.com/gregorywanamaker). 2003. 10:30. V. E♭$_1$–b♭'. Five movements: To Begin with; Recitative; Bloozba; Arietta; Full Circle (. . . repeat and fade). For Charles Guy. This work requires professional-caliber range, technique, and control. It pushes the tubist with musical styles and patterns in a manner that is outside the normal realm of the unaccompanied solo. Will need significant musical interpretation as well as strong mechanics. Upper register is utilized extensively. No extended techniques are required. Interesting preface from the composer, which includes the following: "Rather than emphasizing the oompah cliché, I focused on other ideas from baroque continuo lines to the popular undulating techno-bass. I did not completely throw lyric melody to the curb, however. I gave some to the tuba." An impressive and rewarding unaccompanied work.

Warren, Frank E. *Leeann.* Seesaw Music Corp. 1975. $5.00. 5:00. V. G_2–e♭'. One movement. For Rob Weller and Leeann. The range use in this work is well distributed throughout the middle register, with considerable low register demands as well. Composed in 1974, this work utilizes a contemporary general compositional style and traditional notation. There is a brief key to the notation for extended techniques, which is helpful. The dominant tempo throughout is slow and the general character is lyric. Control of multiphonics is necessary for an effective performance as there are somewhat extended passages of melodic work in the voice part. Also problematic is the half-valve melodic section. Extended techniques employed include glissandi, half-valve, multiphonics, trills.

Warren, Frank E. *Tuba Music, Opus 13.* Frank E. Warren Music Service. 1980. $4.50. 5:00. IV–V. F_2–e'. One movement. The general range demands of this work are moderate, with well-distributed requirements primarily in the middle register. The compositional style and notation are traditional. Several tempo changes mark sections within the movement. The prevalent tempo is quick with many rapid-note passages. Many of the more extended rapid passages have *ossia* parts to simplify demands. Some extreme low passages may be problematic. One interesting section involves bringing out a two-part counterpoint within the context of a constantly moving sixteenth note line.

Watz, Franz. *Fantasie.*

Wefelmeyer, Bernd. *Sieben durch Acht.* C–f♯. One movement. See Unkrodt, Dietrich, *Reige Vortragsliteratur, Tuba 1 und Tuba 2.* Recorded by Phillippe Legris.

Werner, Sven Erik. *Tale for Tuba.*

Wiggins, Christopher D. *Soliloquy X.* Studio Music Company. 1997. 4:30. IV–V. F_1–f'. A single-movement contemporary work with Allegro opening and closing sections, and a more lyrical middle section. Many challenging wider intervallic leaps. No extended techniques present. This solo would be best suited for an F or E♭ tuba. Score is well marked and features significant challenges in dynamic contrast. Exciting writing that would serve as an excellent recital or competition offering.

Wilby, Philip. *Four Winds.* Warwick Music.

Wilder, Alec. *Convalescence Suite.* Margun Music Inc. 1982. $9.50. 20:00. IV. E♭$_1$–g'. Eighteen movements (in three parts): Dolce; ♩ = 120; 𝅗𝅥. = 50; Gently and Otherwise; Forcefully; ♩ = 144; Expressive e rubato; Muscularly; Giocoso; Dolce; As Fast as 16ths Will Permit; Gently and Romantically; Fast; ♪ = 160; Andante; Flowingly Rubato; Up Tempo Jazz Style; Epilogue. For Harvey Phillips. The range over the course of this very lengthy work tends to favor the upper and upper middle registers. Endurance considerations will depend entirely on selection of movements for performance. This is an exceptionally long work in three parts, not appropriate for performance as a single unit. It is an excellent source of study material with many possible combinations of movements for performance. The compositional style and notational system of this work are traditional. Much of this work displays definite jazz influence. A primary technical demand of the composition is control of smooth, lyric playing, sometimes in more rapid tempos. Melodic lines tend to cover a wide range in the course of a phrase, with direction of motion changing often. Though harmony is traditional, many resolutions require careful attention to establish firmly in the ear. Performance demands are traditional, but tax all aspects of technique to the fullest extent. Extended techniques employed include flutter-tonguing, glissandi, trills.

Wiley, Frank. *Caverns.* Ludwig Music.

Wilhelm, Rolf. *Five Etudes for Solo Tuba.* Also listed in the chapter Methods and Studies.

Wilson, Richard. *Civilization and Its Discontents, for Solo Tuba.* Peer Music. Composed in 1992, published in 1995. 5:45. III–IV. F♯$_1$–e♭'. Five movements: Overcoming the Forces of Nature; Soap as a Measure of Civilization; Love, Necessity, and the Death Instinct; The Aggressive Impulse Thwarted; Bad Conscience and the Superego. A humorous link to the Sigmund Freud essay of 1930 has resulted in this unaccompanied tuba work. The style is contemporary, but most of the writing is conventional. Extended flutter tongue while muted can be found in the fourth movement. Despite the relatively modest range requirements, the composer has provided a number of alternate octave displacements to further enable performance on any size tuba. These five short varied movements are interesting and stylistically unified. Recorded by Stephen Johns.

Wilson, Richard. *Transfigured Goat.* Recorded by Stephen Johns.

Winsor, P. *Asleep in the Deep.* Carl Fischer Inc. $45.00.

Winteregg, Steven. *A Time for. . . .* Pasticcio Music. 1991. 3:30. IV. A$_1$–e♭'. Two movements: Searching; Living. To Robert LeBlanc. The compositional style of this work is contemporary with a reliance on traditional notation and technique. Rhythmic complexity may prove the primary technical challenge. The driving second movement is exciting and enjoyable.

Wolff, Christian. *Tuba Song.* C. F. Peters Corp. 1992.

Woodson, Thomas. *Canticle for Solo Tuba.* Manuscript.

Wrobleski, Micky. *Night Music for Solo Tuba.* Chicken Scratch Press. 2002. 6:00. IV–V. B$_2$–a♭'. For Jerome Stover. A one-movement setting with three sections: Adagio—Allegretto et molto marcato e pesante—Adagio. Challenging due to large pitch range, technique, and required special effects. An effective solo that generally lies well on the tuba, especially a smaller instrument in F or E♭. There are a variety of extended techniques included, and they have good musical purpose. Unfortunately, the composer does not provide a complete glossary of the notated effects, leaving the performer to guess at the desired sound in a few places. The extended techniques include multiphonics, clicks/whispers, large glissandi, and other spoken syllables.

Wrobleski, Micky. *Reflected Projections.* Chicken Scratch Press. Composed 1999, published 2002. 7:30. IV. B$_2$–g'. For Gene. One continuous movement at a mostly slower tempo. Calls for considerable control of dynamics along with a high level of agility. Equal division of labor between upper and lower registers makes this work well suited to a CC tuba, but certainly possible on any instrument. Quite a few trills and ornamental notes, but no extended techniques. Lengthy phrases in places. Good work for study or recital.

Yost, Michael. *Variations on a Theme for Tuba.* 3:00. III–IV. G$_1$–d'. One movement. This contemporary work notates pitch but no rhythm. The success of this work is entirely dependent on the performer's interpretive abilities.

Zerbe, Hannes. *Gamma.* G$_1$–e'. One movement. See Unkrodt, Dietrich, *Reige Vortragsliteratur, Tuba 1 und Tuba 2.*

Ziffrin, Marilyn J. *Four Pieces for Tuba.* Music Graphics Press. 1982. $4.95. 10:00. IV. E$_2$–g' (B♭$_2$–g'). Four movements: ♩ = 68; ♩ = 100; Largo; Fast, but Very Rhythmical. For Barton Cummings. This work utilizes the complete range of the instrument, including extremes in both directions, with a general tendency to be somewhat high. The general compositional style is contemporary and the work uses traditional notation. The first movement is characterized by an opening fanfare motive which recurs near the end of the movement in inversion. The second movement is based on a rapidly repeated note pattern. The third movement is slow and melodic in character, with repeated note passages which hearken back to the previous movement. The fourth movement is quick and rhythmically challenging. Extended techniques employed include flutter-tonguing and glissandi. Recorded by Barton Cummings.

Zonn, Paul. *Red Wiggler.* TUBA Gem. 1:30. IV. F$_1$–f'. One movement. This short work utilizes proportional and graphic as well as traditional notation. Wide intervals and multiphonics are the primary technical demands. This work is a brief exploration of the tuba's extramusical possibilities in a contemporary musical setting.

6. Music for Tuba and Electronic Media

Philip Sinder, Assistant Editor, *Guide to the Tuba Repertoire: The New Tuba Source Book*
Jeffrey L. Funderburk, Assistant Editor, *The Tuba Source Book*

Introductory Remarks (July 2005): Philip Sinder

In his comments preceding the Tuba and Tape chapter from the first edition of *The Tuba Source Book,* editor Jeffrey Funderburk suggested that this chapter might be more accurately labeled (in future years) in such a way as to represent a wider range of playback formats (tape, compact disc, digital audio tape, etc.) as well as to incorporate the small number of works found employing electronics which are controlled and manipulated in a live manner during performance. So, the chapter has been officially renamed.

The Tuba Source Book listed 53 works in this medium. I have uncovered an additional 28 compositions, plus provided complete annotations for 3 works that were cited in the first edition. As with many unaccompanied works, compositions for tuba and electronic media tend to be more difficult in nature—targeted for advanced undergraduate and graduate students, as well as professionals.

The portability of these works, as well as the infinite array of colors and musical materials available to the composer working in this medium, stand to provide the tubist with considerable options for a recital vehicle. The performer must strive to maintain the musical integrity and interest of each work.

I am grateful to all who provided assistance in the update to this chapter, especially Neal Corwell, Sergio Carolino, Steve Rosse, and James Gourlay.

Introductory Remarks (July 1995): Jeffrey L. Funderburk

The medium described as tuba and tape is actually expanding to include tuba and electronic media of greater variety. With the increasing capabilities of the current generation of synthesizers and developments in electronic music, it is expected that there will be a significant increase in composition within this medium in coming years. This is particularly welcomed by many tubists who have never been totally satisfied with the acoustic combination of tuba and piano. This medium combines the independence of the unaccompanied medium with a much broader tonal palate provided by the tape or electronic accompaniment.

Unfortunately, it would appear that these works have not been as successful as works in other mediums in securing publication. For this reason, most of these works are available from very small publishers or directly from the composer. It is hoped that with greater attention by performers and an increase in compositions, these works will become more available in coming years. This medium offers a truly unlimited potential for the tubist and can be one of the most interesting and exciting areas of performance and programming available to the soloist.

I would like to thank Barton Cummings, who was particularly helpful in identifying works in this area and provided information on several of the works included here.

Ayers, Jesse. *The Dancing King.* TUBA Press. 1991. $15.00. 6:00. IV–V. F_1–g'. One movement. For Frank Banton. This work utilizes a tape-recorded synthesized accompaniment. This is a rhythmically very driving work in an almost popular style. The tape provided contains several versions, including an accompaniment track for performance, a performance track which has a synthesized tuba sound performing the solo part, and a slow practice track. The technical challenges in the work are substantial primarily due to extended passages of rapid sixteenth notes. A weakness of the piece is the lack of a score which represents the tape part. Complex meters and a severe lack of rests make this an even more difficult work.

Bales, Kenton. *Collage 3 for Solo Tuba and Electronics.* Manuscript, available from the composer. The electronic component on this work consists of processed live sounds.

Bark, Jan. *Malumna (Music-Theatre for Tuba and Tape).* Swedish Music Information Center.

Báthory-Kitsz, Dennis. *Llama Butter.* Westleaf Editions. 1993. 23:00. IV–V. $D\flat_1$–$c\flat'$. One movement. Commissioned by Mark Nelson. In addition to the tuba and tape, this piece has two recommended stage settings, and the score suggests that dancers should be used as well. Careful instructions are provided for staging and costuming. The tape primarily provides environmental sounds—a combination of breathing sounds, viols, vocalizations, and animal sounds. The tuba part is synchronized by timings and the tuba score does not attempt to give a graphic rendering of the tape. Most of the tuba part is traditionally notated, though there are passages of graphic notation and the entire work is without meter. There are also extended multiphonic sections with both parts moving in unison rhythm.

Beck, Jeremy. *HoUsE miX.* Tuba-Euphonium Press. Composed 1995, published 1997. 4:30. IV. G_1–g'. One-movement work written for Jeffrey Funderburk. Piece is designated for tuba and synthesizer, with the synthesizer portion of the work designed specifically for the Korg 01/W. Distributed by the publisher with a DAT (Digital Audio Tape) of the synthesized sounds. The composer includes detailed notes on how to begin the work in both formats. A fun and energetic work with materials and gestures borrowed from the language of techno dance music. Not particularly difficult in range of technical demands, but requires considerable metric security. Well-designed cue line with only a few awkward page turns. No special effects. Recorded by Jeffrey Funderburk.

Berling, David. *Colloquy.* 6:00. IV. $E\flat$–f'. One movement. Written in 1992. This work is unusual in that it calls for the tape to be turned on and off at various points, allowing for very free passages of solo tuba. The score offers no graphic representation of the tape, but does provide timings.

Biggs, John. *Invention for Tuba and Tape.* Consort Press. 1985. 7:15. III. C_1–a. For Scott Watson. An excellent introductory work in this medium. Limited range and modest technical demands in a work best suited to contrabass tuba. Well-notated score and cue line. The "tape" part is now distributed on compact disc, and consists exclusively of sounds from inside the piano, with strings being strummed, hammered, and muted in different ways. The tubist must negotiate a fair amount of mixed-meter writing, but all at a moderate or slow tempo.

Bottje, Will Gay. *Triangles.* Composers Facsimile Edition. 1972. 7:00. One movement. Written for tuba, trumpet, and tape, this is an aleatoric work in which each performer has three different parts for the piece. Each part consists of five sections from which to chose. At the performance, each player selects five sections from the three available sets.

Burns, Kristine. *Atanos II.* Tuba-Euphonium Press. Composed 1994, published 1999. 8:59. IV–V. $E\flat_1$–$a\flat'$. The pre-recorded CD contains well-engineered and interesting electronic sounds, which begin in a dream-like manner and gradually grow more agitated. The tuba part also follows this plan with increasing activity and difficulty. However, it will take considerable study and practice to align the tuba part with the CD. The cue line is difficult to follow, and the indicated timings on the score do not link up with the CD. There is a large amount of lower tessitura writing for tuba in this piece.

Byers, David. *St. Columbus and the Crane.*

Cisternino, Nic. *Morgana . . . il segreto del quarto tempo.*

Cope, David. *Spirals.* Seesaw. 6:30. IV. E_1–$g\sharp'$. One movement. For Barton Cummings. This work utilizes a tape prepared by the performer. The tape part is traditionally notated and involves four tracks of music. Full instructions are included.

Corwell, Neal. *Aboriginal Voices.* Nicolai Music. Composed 1994, published 1995. 7:37. IV. G_1–$e\flat'$. For Mark Nelson. Musical content inspired by Australian native Aborigines; the recorded CD includes a digitally sampled didgeridoo, as well as vocal and percussive effects. The tubist encounters a modest range, yet significant technical challenges. The work contains a few fairly lengthy phrases, but is well written for the tuba overall. The composer also sanctions performances with bass trombone or euphonium as the solo instrument, with octave changes as necessary. Fun to play and exciting for the listener. Multiphonics required. Recorded by Mark Nelson and Neal Corwell.

Corwell, Neal. *The Dream.* Tuba-Euphonium Press. 1995. 6:45. III–IV. $E\flat_1$–c' (tuba). For Velvet Brown. This work is scored for tuba, euphonium, and pre-recorded sounds. It consists of an opening slow section that grows more animated and leads to a concluding march-like section. For tuba, this work is not quite as technically demanding as some of this composer's other pieces. The performance score consists of the two instrumental lines with minimal cues for the electronics, but it does not appear too awkward to stay on track. Recorded by Neal Corwell and Velvet Brown.

Corwell, Neal. *House of the Rising Sun.* Nicolai Music. 2001. 4:38. III–IV. D_1–e'. A setting of this popular folk/blues/rock tune for solo tuba with CD accompaniment. With guitar as the pre-recorded voice, the arranger offers a variety of background styles and tempos. Corwell also provides comments which indicate that the performer should use great freedom with this setting, from octave choices to rubato to extended improvised phrases if desired. Recorded by Neal Corwell.

Corwell, Neal. *Hungarian Hallucination.* Nicolai Music. 2000. 5:05. IV. A♭$_1$–e♭' (tuba range). A whimsical setting for euphonium and tuba with CD accompaniment (or solo euphonium with CD) based on themes from Franz Liszt's Hungarian Rhapsody No. 2. Also includes brief forays into several other highly recognizable melodies from opera and elsewhere. The arranger states, "this piece has no serious intentions. The composer/arranger's only objective was to create a piece which would be fun for all involved, both audiences and performers." The pitch range for tuba is modest, but the piece will require excellent rapid finger and tongue technique.

Corwell, Neal. *New England Reveries.* Nicolai Music. $21.00 (+$2.00 shipping). 8:45. IV. D$_1$–b♭'. One movement. For Mark Nelson. Despite the medium, this is essentially a very traditional work which is very melodic in character with definite pop music influences. The score is very clear and easily followed as it is entirely notated in traditional notation. The tape is a synthesized voicing of the accompaniment. The work should prove very pleasant and entertaining in performance. Other than extended passages of sextuplets, the tuba part should present no special technical problems.

Corwell, Neal. *Quiet Mountain, Opus 37.* Nicolai Music. 2000. 8:00. III–IV. F$_1$–d' (tuba). Scored for trombone, tuba, and pre-recorded sounds. Inspired by a view of Mt. Eniaa, in Hokkaido, Japan, on a foggy morning. Opens with a duo cadenza, and has several varied musical sections requiring a wide dynamic range and excellent coordination with the trombonist. Modest technical demands. Recorded by Neal Corwell.

Corwell, Neal. *Ritual.* Nicolai Music. 1997. 9:35. IV–V. F$_1$–f' (tuba). This work is scored for euphonium and tuba with CD accompaniment, and is a "musical evocation of the meditative, celebratory, and sacrificial elements of one culture's ceremony." There is a considerable amount of rapid slurred and tongued passage work, and an excellent triple tongue ability will be needed. The tuba part rarely heads above the staff. The performance score is well marked and fairly easy to follow. Recorded by Neal Corwell and Velvet Brown.

Corwell, Neal. *2 a.m., Opus 32.* Nicolai Music. 1998. 6:00. IV. G–b♭'. Dedicated to the memory of Otis Wilson, and premiered with the composer as soloist. Originally a euphonium solo piece, but sanctioned by the composer for performance on trombone or tuba as well. If performed on tuba, the composer suggests octave alterations as needed, and also to avoid using a mute. The work is all in a slow tempo, and with a lyrical solo line cast over an improvisatory guitar background. Recorded by Neal Corwell.

Corwell, Neal. *Venetian Carnival Animals.* Nicolai Music. 1998. 7:10. IV–V. F$_1$–g'. A set of variations based on the Arban *Carnival of Venice* solo, and also uses the "Elephant Song" from Saint Saens' *Carnival of the Animals* as source material. Pitched in B♭ so as to lie best on the F tuba. A humorous accompaniment includes synthesized bellowing animal sounds in strategic locations. Will require top-notch finger and tongue technique to keep up with the pre-recorded accompaniment. A fun new treatment of this time-tested solo. Recorded by Neal Corwell.

Cresswell, Lyell. *Drones IV.* See same work under Music for Unaccompanied Tuba.

Davis, D. Edward. *Accidots, for Tuba-Euphonium Quartet and CD.* Manuscript, available from the composer at eddie@warmsilence.org. 2002. ca. 6:00. IV. The pre-recorded CD fades in several minutes into the work, and provides background textures that do not require direct alignment with the quartet. But, the writing for the tuba-euphonium quartet is quite challenging metrically and will be difficult to perform unless the parts have substantial cues or perhaps the players perform from the score. The end of the work is chorale-like, echoing in a loose manner the material on the CD. A few spoken phrases and mouthpiece slaps for the players.

Davis, D. Edward. *Let There Be Funk.* Manuscript, available from the composer at eddie@warmsilence.org. 2001. 8:51. IV. E♭$_1$–e'. For Rex Martin. A one-movement work for live tuba and pre-recorded CD which includes elements of funk, hip-hop, salsa, R&B, and soul. A real workout for the tubist due to the constantly driving bass lines and melodic fragments, with only a few extended rests where pages can be moved along. And the frequent interjections of tempo and style variants, along with some mixed meter passages, make portions of this work a significant challenge to keep in the intended groove. This would be a really fun piece for both tubist and audience! Best on the CC tuba.

Davis, D. Edward. *Scadicot, for Tuba-Euphonium Quartet and CD.* Manuscript, available from the composer at eddie@warmsilence.org. 2000. 6:15. IV. Begins with a four-part tuba-euphonium chorale-like setting which is interrupted by a funk tuba bass line. Gradually the other three players join in the fun, and then the CD rhythm track comes on board as well. Extended work with mouthpiece slaps for all four players, and some spoken moments for the euphoniums. Euphonium I has a brief improvised solo near the conclusion. A fun and totally different style of writing for tuba-euphonium quartet.

Dunn, David. *Interjacence.* 20:00. Written for Barton Cummings. Written in 1977, the final realization has no live performers. The work includes non-traditional notation utilizing frame notation of indeterminate length. There is a pre-recorded tape part, which is used with live instruments including tuba, clarinet, and tam-tam to make a final tape that is presented in the final performance.

Dutton, Brent. *Subterrestrial Sounds.* Seesaw Music. 1978. $34.00. 7:00. IV. C_1–f'. Four movements: Prologue; II; III; Epilogue. This work is intended for use with a tape made by the performer. The score includes five staves, four of which should be recorded. Alternative performance is possible with five tubists. The compositional style is contemporary. Occasional non-traditional notation is used, but performance notes make these markings clear. Range and general timing of the solo with the tape will be primary concerns. It is suggested that a technician run the tape in performance to assist with timings as the tape needs to be stopped and restarted several times. Essentially the work is based on sections dominated by color while other sections are canonic.

Easton, Ian. *Airloom for Tuba and Synthesizer.* Manuscript, available from the composer. This work exists in three formats, including tuba with prerecorded CD, tuba with chamber orchestra, and tuba with piano (Country Dance movement only).

Ernst, David. *Coludes for Tuba and Tape.* 10:00. V. One movement. Written for Barton Cummings. A very colorful work using "musique-concrete" for the tape. An extremely difficult work that will require significant rehearsal time with tape and a stop watch.

Escobar, Aylton. *Poética IV.* Editora Novas Metas. 1980. V. This very interesting work requires the performer to prepare a rather elaborate tape, which will require a studio to produce. Two scores are provided, one for performance and one for preparation of the tape. The tape is primarily tuba performance on multiple tracks with various electronic manipulations. The performer personalizes the tape at the end by including his or her name in the final text. This work requires a significant commitment of time, but should result in a very effective performance.

Felciano. *"And from the Abyss" for Tuba and Tape.* Recorded by Floyd Cooley.

Furukawa, Kiyoshi. *Music for Tuba and Tonband.*

Giuliano, Giuseppe. *Aleph Infinito.*

Hamlin, Peter. *Clones.* Tuba-Euphonium Press. Composed 1998, published 2000. 11:15. IV–V. D_1–c''. For Jeffrey Funderburk. A difficult yet engaging work requiring a wide pitch range, strong technique, excellent tonal control, and a keen metric sense. The composer attempts to clone and mutate the tuba sound through rapidly repeating short motives. The eight larger sections of this work contain varied lyrical and technical moments. It will take considerable effort to be in sync with the CD accompaniment. Final section includes a lyrical line in the extreme upper register marked "harmonics"—and is notated to work best on the F tuba harmonic series. Recorded by Jeffrey Funderburk.

Hanson, Stan. *Play Power 6.* Medi.

Hatzis, Christos. *Pavilliones en l'air.*

Hewitt, Harry. *12 Preludes for Solo Tuba.* See same work under Music for Unaccompanied Tuba.

Hiller, Lejaren. *Malta.* Theodore Presser Co. 1971. $15.00. 20:16. IV–V. B_1–b♯''. Four movements: Geographical; Historical; Carnival; Personal. To Barton Cummings. This is a very difficult work primarily due to its extensive range and length. The tape is a mixture of sounds on two separate channels, primarily acoustic sounds ranging from a narrator to church bells to a village band. The score graphically represents events on the tape and also gives clock timings in order that synchronization may be simplified. The tuba part is often in treble clef and is dominated by very wide intervals, a reliance on the extreme high register, and many extended passages of rapid notes. Recorded by Barton Cummings.

Jacobs, Kenneth. *Children of the Hermit and Their Mountain Handywork.* Seesaw. 1987. $42.00. 15:00. IV–V. $B♭_1$–g♭'. This composition relies on traditional performance technique from the tubist and uses unmetered traditional notation. The score provides a rather sketchy depiction of the tape events.

Kärkkäinen, Tommi. *Music for Trombone and/or Tuba and Tape.* Warner/Chappell, via the Finnish Music Information Centre (FIMIC # 15098). 2000. For Harri Lidsle.

Krieger, Arthur. *Double Knot for Tuba and Electronic Sounds.* Manuscript.

Kulesha, Gary. *Demons.*

Larson, Forrest. *Syncronic for Tuba and Tape.* 8:00. IV. G_1–d♯'. One movement. For Phil Vanouse. Composed in 1993. Performance requires use of a stopwatch, as the score offers no graphic representation of the tape. A brief work with minimal endurance requirements, as the tuba plays only about half the time.

Lazarof, Henri. *Cadence VI.* Bote & Bock. 1974. $12.25. 6:25. V. G_2–a♭'. One movement. Commissioned by and dedicated to Roger Bobo. This work utilizes a tape prepared by the performer. The score presents both parts. Except for three clusters of four notes near the end, this is essentially a duet. Compositionally, the piece is a set of variations based on a six-note tone row. This work utilizes proportional notation and a little graphic notation in addition to unmetered traditional notation. Multiphonics and use of a mute expand the sound palate. Recorded by Roger Bobo.

McLean, Priscilla. *Beneath the Horizon III.* MLC. 1978. 12:30. IV–V. C_1–a'. One movement. This is a very interesting work as it combines a tape of recorded whale sounds (sometimes electronically manipulated) with live performance on tuba that is dominated by extended techniques resulting in non-traditional sounds. The score uses graphic representations of events on the tape as well as a time line which gives the placement, in number of minutes and seconds, of large events on the tape. The composer suggests using a stopwatch in the learning process to aid the synchronization of the work. Many extended techniques are required, including fingernail tapping, glissandi, whistling with the mouthpiece, flutter-tonguing, and vocalizations. Thorough explanatory notes are included to aid interpretation of the score. Recorded by Melvyn Poore.

Melby, John. *Passages.* Presser (Merion Music). A work for tuba and computer.

Montague, Stephen. *Paramell IV.*

Nono, Luigi. *Post-prae-ludium per Donau.* Ricordi. 1987. To Giancarlo Schiaffini.

Olson, Curtis. *Incurzion for Tuba and Synthesizer.* Tuba-Euphonium Press. 1995. 16:30. IV. G_1–e'. For Philip Sinder. A three-movement work that is part of a series of pieces by this trombonist/composer for solo brass with electronic pre-recorded accompaniment. An incursion is a military invasion, and the composer has used this concept with a slightly altered spelling for each of the works in this series. The outer movements are quite fast and will require considerable technique in numerous passages. All movements are a good test of dynamic control and endurance. The cue line is active and well marked, and the pages go by quickly. A riveting and relentless synthesized line creates strong audience appeal.

Ostrander, Linda. *Time Out for Tuba and Tape Recorder.* V. For Barton Cummings. Written in 1979, this work calls for a tape made by the performer which will require multi-track recording equipment, a stop watch, and a lot of patience.

Ott, Joseph. *Bart's Piece.* Claude Benny Press. $9.00. 9:30. III–IV. A_1–a. One movement. For Barton Cummings. The score of this work graphically represents the tape and also gives event timings in seconds for the tuba part. Primarily there is only a loose synchronization to the piece and there are sections of improvisation. Notation and performance techniques are primarily traditional, though there are notations for highest and lowest possible notes. Recorded by Barton Cummings.

Ott, Joseph. *Concerto with Tape.* Claude Benny Press. 1974. $14.00. 18:00. IV. D_1–d♭'. One movement. Performance of this work will require a technician, as the tape must be stopped and restarted several times on cue. The score gives a reasonably clear representation of the tape. The tuba part makes no unusual demands on the performer. Notation of the tuba part is primarily traditional, though sometimes unmetered, with a few instances of proportional notation.

Ott, Joseph. *Music for Tuba and Two Channel Tape.* Benny Press. 1972. 8:00–10:00. IV. C_1–c♯'. One movement. Composed at the request of Barton Cummings. This work calls for the performer to make the tape. The tape part in the score consists of eight staves (four per channel) and a tape overlay at certain points. The tape part is composed primarily of clusters and sequenced statements and will require considerable time to be adequately realized. The tuba part uses several extended techniques including double tonguing, glissandi, and key clicks. There are instances of proportional notation and sections of free improvisation. The overall effect is that of a very large tuba ensemble.

Penn, William. *Capriccio.* Keyboard Percussion Publications. 1992. 9:10. IV. F_1–e' (also includes several glisses to highest note possible). Two versions of this work exist, including the original setting for tuba and marimba and a setting done by the composer with a synthesized marimba part. Contact the composer at Aurec@Aurec.com for further information on the synthesized version, which was employed by Gene Pokorny on his recording of the work. The synthesized marimba version obviously provides a fine practice vehicle for the tubist, but also gives the work an expanded palette of sound that is quite attractive. Well written for the tuba, and equally suited to a bass or contrabass tuba. See also listing under Tuba and Mixed Ensemble. Recorded by Gene Pokorny (synthesized version) and Jeffery Jarvis (marimba version).

Poore, Melvyn. *And Finally . . . for tuba and Live Electronics.*

Poore, Melvyn. *One, Two, Three for Tuba and Delay System.*

Poore, Melvyn. *Playback I for Tuba and Recording/Playback System.*

Poore, Melvyn. *Tubassoon for Tuba and 4-Channel Amplification System.*

Raum, Elizabeth. *Nation: Theme and Variations for Tuba and CD.* Tuba-Euphonium Press. 1998. 10:45. IV–V. E_1–a'. For John Griffiths. Theme and five variations which depict various aspects of Canada. The variations are labeled: I. Coast; II. City; III. Frozen North; IV. Trains across the Prairies; V. Majesty of the Mountains. Very diverse musical moments, from chorale-like settings to aggressive programmatic material in a chromatic style. Includes several multiphonics. A considerable upper tessitura workout.

Raum, Elizabeth. *Secret: A Melodrama for Tuba and CD.* Tuba-Euphonium Press. 1998. ca. 12:00. V. A_1–a'. For John Griffiths. A highly personalized work involving both text and music which chronicles the life and career of tubist John Griffiths. Includes the tubist's choice of several humorous introductory statements. A large amount of upper tessitura playing, with frequent changes in style and tempo. Frequent interjections of text provided by the tubist during the performance. A challenge for tubists other than the dedicatee to deliver a convincing rendition of this work. Distributed in a two-work set which also includes Raum's *Nation.*

Riley, James. *Tubagogic.* This work requires significant studio taping and is very difficult.

Rimsky-Korsakov, Nicolai. *Flight of the Bumble Bee.* arr. Neal Corwell. Tuba-Euphonium Press. 1994/2002/2004. 2:00. IV–V. E_1–a♭. Distributed in a bundle with the euphonium, trumpet, and tuba solo parts. All are in the concert key of G minor, and most all of the playing is in the middle register. On the latest version (2004) of the accompanying CD, the arranger provides seven different grades of tempo from which to choose for practice and performance. These range from a slow practice speed all the way up to m.m. = 178. Corwell also re-mixed the accompaniment slightly in the 2004 version. Several intelligent rests are included in this arrangement, and linking with the CD accompaniment ensures the steady delivery of the solo part.

Rollin, Robert. *The Raven and the First Men.* Seesaw Music. 1983. 7:30. III–IV. E_1–a (tuba range). Written for tubist John Turk and hornist William Slocum. An unusual instrumentation of horn, tuba, and piano along with pre-recorded electronics. The work is based upon the creation myth of the Haida Indians of British Columbia. Each instrument represents various aspects of the myth. The performance score which all players use clearly indicates the material found on the pre-recorded tape. This work would be most effective on a contrabass tuba. Recorded by John Turk.

Ross, Walter. *Midnight Variations.* Dorn. 1971. 7:00. IV. $F\sharp_1$–c'. One movement. For Barton Cummings. This is an effective if somewhat dated composition for tuba and tape. The score very clearly depicts events on the tape with graphic notation. The tape is primarily electronically produced sounds. Most of the tuba part relies on extended techniques including vocalizations, half-valve performance, and glissandi. See: Bird, Gary, ed.; *Program Notes for the Solo Tuba.* Recorded by Barton Cummings.

Ross, Walter. *Piltdown Fragments.* Walter Ross. 1975. 9:15. IV–V. F_1–e'. One movement. For Barton Cummings. This is a very interesting work of many colors. The tape is primarily electronically generated with some vocalization as well. The texture tends to be thin throughout. The score uses a very clear graphic depiction of events on the tape and provides a time line with slashes representing a pulse to help place events in a time frame. The tuba part is primarily notated in a traditional fashion, though it occasionally uses vocalizations and half-valved effects which are depicted graphically. This is an excellent work worthy of attention. Recorded by Barton Cummings.

Ruggiero, Charles. *Fractured Mambos.* $45.00. 10:00. V. $E\flat_1$–e'. One movement. For Philip Sinder. The tape combines recorded acoustic sounds as well as synthesized sounds in a dance/jazz setting. The rehearsal tape that is provided has an excellent tuba performance, which is very helpful in learning the work. The piece is more an ensemble feature than a technical display and should prove very popular in performance. See: Bird, Gary, ed., *Program Notes for the Solo Tuba.* Recorded by Philip Sinder.

Schiaffini, Giancarlo. *Canzon "La volupiense."* Edipan. 1986.

Scott, Andy. *Going Down.* Astute Music (also http://www.andyscott.org.uk). 2003. 9:45. IV–V. C_1–a'. For James Gourlay. An exciting and spirited work which uses the full range of the instrument. Solo cadenzas begin and end the piece, but the main body of the work is an up-tempo jazz/funk-style setting for tuba and CD. The CD consists solely of tuba-originated sounds, from breathing to key clicks and other percussive effects, as well as multi-tuba layering. The work ends as the title suggests, gradually exploring greater register depths, which generally have been avoided to this point. Appears best suited to F or E♭ tuba.

Sezudo, Ricardo. *Work for Tuba and Live Electronics.* Manuscript, available from tubist Sergio Carolino (sergiofbc@hotmail.com). 2002. ca.10:00. V. A contemporary work written for Sergio Carolino, and commissioned by "Jornadas Nova Música" (Aveiro University Contemporary Music Festival).

Smith, Glenn. *Space Tuba for Tuba and Electronic Sounds.* Manuscript. 1992. 5:25.

Souster, Tim. *Heavy Reductions.*

Stevens, John D. *Soliloquy—Peace in Our Time with Tape.* 9:00. One movement. This composition relies entirely on improvisation. The tape is a prerecorded improvisation by the composer and is entirely piano. There is no written music for the tuba. See: Bird, Gary, ed.; *Program Notes for the Solo Tuba.*

Stockhausen, Karlheinz. *Solo for Tuba and Tape.* Universal Edition. V. Written for tuba and tape prepared by the performer.

Sundstrup, Leif. *Azira Phal'e.* TubaMania Press. An Australian work available in two formats: tuba solo with brass and percussion ensemble accompaniment, or tuba solo with prerecorded CD accompaniment.

Winsor, Phillip. *Asleep in the Deep-A Fantasy.*

Wintle, James. *Tuba Mirum.* Manuscript. Work is scored for tuba, piano, and electronics.

Witkin, Beatrice. *Breath and Sounds.* Belwin-Mills. 1975. $15.00. 9:00. IV. C_1–g♯'. Four movements. The tape comes with both a performance track and a recorded performance of the work by Toby Hanks. The depiction of the tape in the score is sketchy but adequate. In addition to the graphic portrayal of the tape, every second on the work is marked by a dotted line and the number of seconds, thus essentially setting a pulse. Much of the tuba part is freely interpreted. The third movement involves only vocalizations and non-traditional sounds.

Wraggett, Wes. *Cetecea.*

Wyatt, Scott A. *Lifepoints for Tuba with Percussion and Tape.* Scott Wyatt. 1990. 9:00. V. A♭$_1$–a'. Three movements. Commisioned for and dedicated to Skip Gray. This work is tremendously difficult from an ensemble standpoint. A high degree of proficiency is required of both musicians. The tape is a combination of electronically generated sounds and recorded acoustic sounds. The score combines both performers' parts and the tape part on three staves in traditional notation. The tuba part is extremely demanding technically. Compositionally, this is a contemporary work with instances of minimalist influence.

Wyatt, Scott A. *Three for One.* TUBA Press. $18.00. 10:30. IV–V. C$_1$–a'. Three movements. This is a very entertaining and challenging work. Though in three movements, the tape runs continuously. The score clearly depicts events on the tape in a modified traditional notation. The tape consists of electronically generated sounds as well as recorded acoustic sounds. Of particular interest is the second movement's use of prerecorded tuba sounds which combine with the live performance to create echo effects. This is a tremendously effective work, worthy of study and performance. Recorded by Daniel Perantoni.

7. Music for Multiple Tubas

Kenyon Wilson, Assistant Editor, *Guide to the Tuba Repertoire: The New Tuba Source Book*

Charles A. McAdams, Assistant Editor, *The Tuba Source Book*

Introductory Remarks (July 2005): Kenyon Wilson

The published repertoire for multiple tubas has grown enormously over the past decade, and it may well be the fastest-growing genre of tuba-related literature. From fewer than 200 works listed in the *Tuba Music Guide* (Morris 1973), to just over 1,100 works in the *Tuba Source Book* (Morris and Goldstein 1996), this chapter contains almost 2,000 entries.

Although many of these compositions for multiple tubas are available from established publishers, there has been a recent increase in the number of smaller publishers specializing in literature for low brass. The increasing popularity of the Internet has spawned numerous sites where composers and arrangers can offer their works directly, with some even sending the files to your computer for printing. As a result, purchasing music from across the globe can be as easy as using a local music store.

"Multiple tubas" is defined as two or more tubas or any combination of euphoniums and tubas. However, for a composition to be listed here at least one of the parts has to be marked "tuba." Compositions for four euphoniums are not included, but compositions for three euphoniums and one tuba are. Music for multiple euphoniums is listed in the *Euphonium Music Guide*. Although there are many compositions for multiple trombones, bassoons, celli, or string basses that are easily adapted for tuba and euphonium ensembles, the present listing is limited to those works composed or arranged specifically for tubas.

Publishers and composers, in addition to our international consultants, provided materials and information to examine for this project. If part of an entry for a work is missing (e.g., price, copyright date, range), it is because that information was not provided or could not be verified. Compositions whose entries are incomplete may also be more difficult to obtain.

The duration and grade levels listed for each piece are meant to be guides, not absolutes. A composition for four tubas may be extremely challenging because of the range and technical demands of the first and second parts. However, with euphoniums performing the first two parts, the composition may be as much as a grade level easier and more approachable. The annotations indicate whether a euphonium may be substituted for a tuba part, or vice versa. The instrumentation given in the listing is exactly what appears on the printed score or part. Performers are encouraged to consult the ranges listed and should feel free to use whatever instrumentation best fits their needs.

The research for this chapter was an enormous undertaking, and I need to thank those who made this possible. First of all, Charles McAdams did a thorough job preparing the corresponding chapter in the *Tuba Source Book,* and this chapter incorporates his research and builds upon the excellent relationships he established with publishers. My counterpart for the *Euphonium Source Book,* Seth Fletcher, also provided a great deal of assistance, as several pieces are listed in both books. Several composers and publishers went out of their way to provide help, including Mike Forbes, Kenneth Friedrich, Ray Grim, Paul Luhring, David Miles, Winston Morris, Mark Nelson, Paul Schmidt, Stephen Shoop, and David Werden. Finally, the scope and breadth of this chapter would be greatly limited without the international consultants representing the musical achievements of their countries. I am indebted to the following musicians for their essential contribution: Jørgen Arnsted, Sérgio Carolino, Alessandro Fossi, John Griffiths, David LeClair, Harri Lidsle, Giles Lutmann, Kazuhisa Nishida, Heiko Triebener, and Paul Walton.

Introductory Remarks (July 1995): Charles A. McAdams

The published repertoire for multiple tubas has grown enormously in the last twenty years. The growth has occurred not only in arrangements and transcriptions but also in original compositions. The 1,058 compositions listed in this chapter indicate this recent growth. As a matter of fact, *The Tuba Source Book* contains more two-part listings than all multiple tuba entries in the *Tuba Music Guide* (Morris 1973). Fortunately, as the quantity of literature has increased, so has the quality. Composers continue to discover the potential for expression with an ensemble consisting of tubas or euphoniums and tubas.

Many of these compositions for multiple tubas are available from more established publishers (i.e., Kendor, Shawnee Press, Theodore Presser, etc.); however, the bulk of this literature is being produced by smaller publishers who often devote a majority of their catalogs to publications for the tuba.

Multiple tubas is defined as two or more tubas or any combination of euphoniums and tubas. However, for a composition to be included in this listing at least one of the parts had to be marked *tuba*. For instance, compositions for four euphoniums are not included, but compositions for three euphoniums and one tuba are listed. While there are numerous compositions for multiple trombones, bassoons, celli, or string basses that may be easily adapted for ensembles of multiple tubas and euphoniums, the listing here is limited to those works actually composed or published for tubas.

Publishers and composers, in addition to the *TSB* international consultants, provided materials and information to examine for this project. If part of an entry for a composition is missing (i.e., price, copyright date, ranges, etc.), it is because that information was not provided or could not be verified. Compositions whose entries are incomplete may also be more difficult to obtain.

The duration and grade level listed for each piece are meant to be a guide, not an absolute. A composition for four tubas may be extremely challenging due to the range and technical demands of the first and second parts. However, with euphoniums playing the first or second parts, the composition may be as much as a grade level easier and more approachable.

If a euphonium may be substituted for a tuba part or vice versa, this will be indicated in the annotation. There are, of course, tuba duets, trios, quartets, etc., where the composer had in mind only tubas, not tubas and euphoniums. The instruments listed in the instrumentation entry indicate exactly what is printed on the score or part. Tubists have been "transcribing" music for years. Certainly Scott Joplin did not envision ragtime melodies played by euphonium and tubas, yet there are twenty of Joplin's "rags" published for two euphoniums and two tubas. Generally, performers should feel free to use whatever instrumentation fits their needs best.

Purchasing music from publishers and composers encourages publishers to continue to publish music for multiple tubas. Unfortunately, there are several works listed as "out of print" and no longer available. Supporting the publishers of this music can prevent further loss of literature.

The research for a chapter of this magnitude was an enormous undertaking. I would like to take this opportunity to thank those individuals who helped with this task. First, I would like to thank those publishers and composers who provided examination copies. Second, I would like to thank Michael Bersin, Central Missouri State University, for his assistance in developing a database program to store and manage the information on all the compositions; Wesley True, Central Missouri State University, for his assistance with translations of many international publications; and Kazuhisa Nishida, Osaka University of Arts, for his invaluable assistance in obtaining and translating numerous Japanese publications. Others who provided invaluable information and materials include Jim Self, freelance artist, Los Angeles; David Miles, editor of TUBA Press; Jan Bodeux and the Microsoft Corporation; and the staff at Wingert-Jones Music, Kansas City, Missouri. I would also like to thank my fellow assistant editors, Ron Davis, Jeff Funderburk, Skip Gray, Mark Nelson, and Jerry Young, for their assistance and encouragement. A special thanks is in order to Ed Goldstein for pushing for many years to get this project moving. I would also like to thank Winston Morris for asking me to write this section of *The Tuba Source Book* and for being an invaluable resource.

And finally to my wife, Carol, and my children, James and Kathryn, I would like to express my gratitude for their support and patience. A project of this nature and scope is truly a labor of love. While the work has at times been frustrating, tedious, and time-consuming, I have enjoyed the opportunity to be a part of this project.

Two Parts

Albam, Manny. *Odd Couple, The.* Manncy Music. Two tubas.

Albert, Thomas. *Five for Two Tubas.* Brass Music Limited (The Brass Press). Two tubas. 1971. \$3.50. 5:00. IV. Part I: A_1–a; Part II: F_1–a. Five movements: Prelude; Rondo; Meditation; Scherzo; Postlude. To Daniel Perantoni. This piece uses very contemporary harmonies and rhythms. The first two movements are in mixed meter, and the third movement requires a mute for both parts. Some sections are technically challenging.

Anderson, Eugene. *Baroque'n Brass.* Anderson's Arizona Originals. One trumpet or euphonium and one tuba. 1991. \$6.00. 5:00. IV. Part I: G♯–d''; Part II: D_1–d'. Commissioned by and dedicated to David L. Aubuchon, U.S. Army Band, Ft. Dix, New Jersey. A moderate tempo fugue. Technically challenging for both players, and the tessitura of the first part is high.

Anderson, Eugene. *Teuphm'isms I.* Anderson's Arizona Originals. One euphonium and one tuba. 1990. \$5.00. 5:00. IV. Part I: G–c''; Part II: F_1–f'. Dedicated to Brian Bowman and Harvey Phillips. Technically challenging for both parts. The tessitura of the first part is high. There are many syncopated rhythms in both parts.

Anderson, Eugene. *Teuphm'isms II.* Anderson's Arizona Originals. One euphonium and one tuba. 1992. \$5.00. 5:00. IV. Part I: G–c♯''; Part II: E_1–f'. Dedicated to Brian Bowman and Harvey Phillips. Fanfare-like in character. Switches back and forth from 6/8 to 2/4. Both parts are challenging technically and have large range demands.

Anderson, Eugene. *Three Contrasts for Two Tubas.* Anderson's Arizona Originals. Two tubas. 1988. \$5.00. 4:30. IV. Part I: G_1–d'; Part II: E_1–b♭. Three movements: Allegretto; Rubato Espressivo; Forcefully. The first movement is in a canon-like style. The last movement has a few meter changes with many syncopated rhythms.

Aronson, Lee. *Suite for Tuba and Euphonium.* Tuba-Euphonium Press. One euphonium and one tuba. 2001. \$12.00. 10:00. II–III. Part I: A–e'; Part II: A_1–e. Four movements: Allemande; Courante; Sarabande; Gigue. A collection of four dances in baroque style with traditional harmonies. Demonstrates effective use of two-part contrapuntal writing. Individual movements can stand alone on a concert.

Bach, Johann Sebastian. *Aria–Duet from Cantata No. 78.* arr. David Werden. Cimarron Music and Productions. One euphonium and one tuba with piano. 1995. \$10.00. II–III. Part I: d–b♭'; Part II: A–e♭'. Effective arrangement of this highly imitative work in ternary form. Ranges and style are appropriate for young and intermediate-level performers. Second part may also be performed on euphonium. Euphonium parts also available in treble clef.

Bach, Johann Sebastian. *Bach for Two Tubas.* arr. Scott MacMorran. Tuba/Euphonium Music Publications. Two tubas. Out of Print. III–IV. Part I: D–d; Part II: G_1–f♯. A collection of twelve minuets, marches, and one bourrée. Each lasts approximately two minutes. Select movements may be combined into a suite for concert use.

Bach, Johann Sebastian. *Duets and Trios.* arr. Daniel S. Augustine. Southern Music Company. Two or three tubas. 1972. \$7.95. 17 pp. III–IV. Part I: F–f'; Part II: F_1–b♭; Part III: F_1–f. This is a collection of short minuets, marches, and other dances. Ten of the sixteen arrangements are from the Clavier Book of Anna Magdalena Bach, the composer's second wife. There are thirteen duets and three trios. The first part works equally well on euphonium. Individual movements may be played alone or combined into a suite.

Bach, Johann Sebastian. *Minuet I from Partita No. 1.* arr. Jeffrey Lazar. Lyric Brass Publishing. One euphonium and one tuba. 1998. \$2.50.

Bach, Johann Sebastian. *Suite in D Minor, Cello Suite No. 2.* arr. Arthur Frackenpohl. Tuba-Euphonium Press. One euphonium and one tuba. 1997. \$12.00. III. Part I: F–g'; Part II: F_1–c' (d'). Six movements. A good teaching piece for understanding of baroque contrapuntal style. Both parts have been given ample amounts of melodic work and harmonic support. Euphonium part also available in treble clef. Also reviewed in the Summer 1999 issue of the *TUBA Journal* (Vol. 26, No. 4).

Bach, Johann Sebastian. *Tuba Duo Nine.* arr. James Self. Basset Hound Music. Two tubas. 1988. \$5.00. 4:00. IV–V. Part I: G_1–d'; Part II: G_1–d'. This transcription is from the second movement or Largo of Bach's concerto for two violins. A beautiful melody that is lyrical and technically challenging. Works very well.

Bach, Johann Sebastian. *Twelve Duets.* arr. Ronald Dishinger. Medici Music Press. Two tubas. 1993. \$9.50.

Bach, Johann Sebastian. *Twelve Two Part Inventions.* arr. David McNaughtan Miller. Two tubas.

Bach, Johann Sebastian. *Two Part Inventions.* arr. Allen Ostrander. Kendor Music, Incorporated. Two tubas. 1976. \$6.50. 5:20. IV–V. Part I: C–e♭'; Part II: (F_1) G_1–d'. Four movements: 1; 3; 12; 15. To Bill Bell. Bach wrote 15 two-part inventions and 15 three-part inventions for the clavier. Ostrander selected the first, third, twelfth, and fifteenth movements of the two-part inventions and transposed them down a major sixth for the tuba. The movements may be played alone or in any combination. The movements contrast in meter and tempo and are very challenging to play at the tempos marked.

Bach, Johann Sebastian. *Two-Part Inventions.* arr. Andrew B. Spang and Jeffrey Lazar. Lyric Brass Publishing. One euphonium and one tuba. 2000. $17.50. III. Part I: F–c"; Part II: C_1–c'. Fifteen movements. This is a straightforward transcription with the original ornaments. The euphonium part is scored in tenor clef in three of the movements. Also reviewed in the Winter 2001 issue of the *TUBA Journal* (Vol. 28, No. 2).

Bach, Johann Sebastian. *Vivace from Concerto No. 3 in D Minor.* arr. James Self. Wimbledon Music, Incorporated. Two tubas. 1979. $7.00. 5:00. IV. Part I: A_1–d'; Part II: G_1–d'. This concerto was originally written for two violins. Written in a fugal style, this composition requires good technique and a strong sense of rhythm. Effective as a finale in a recital.

Bach, W. F. *Tuba Duo Five.* arr. James Self. Basset Hound Music. Two tubas. 1984. $5.00. 4:45. IV. Part I: $B\flat_1$–e♭'; Part II: $E\flat_1$–e♭'. The texture is very polyphonic. There are many large skips and the work will require light and agile playing. Many technically challenging sections.

Bach, W. F. *Tuba Duo Six.* arr. James Self. Basset Hound Music. Two tubas. 1985. $5.00. 4:00. IV. Part I: C–d'; Part II: A_1–d'. Both parts are technically challenging. The texture is very polyphonic and the parts are quite interesting. Will require strong players.

Badarak, Mary Lynn. *Bass Lied and Valse to Bass. TUBA Journal.* One euphonium and one tuba. 1976. $7.50. 2:30. IV. Part I: A–d'; Part II: F_1–a. Two movements: Bass Lied; Valse to Bass. The first movement is slow and lyrical with contemporary harmonies. The valse is multimetric, alternating between 5/8, 4/8, and 6/8. Written as part of the TUBA Gem series and distributed in the *TUBA Journal,* Vol. 3, No. 3. It is available by purchasing this issue of the *TUBA Journal.*

Bartles, Alfred H. *Beersheba Neo-Baroque Suite.* Brass Music Limited (The Brass Press). Tuba and cello (or euphonium). 1975. $5.00. 5:30. IV. Part I: G–g; Part II: F_1–e'. Four movements: Prelude; Gavotte; Sarabande; Gigue-Postlude. For Winston Morris. The first part may be played on cello, euphonium, or trombone. See same work under Tuba and Mixed Ensemble.

Bartles, Alfred H. *T.U.B.A. Canon. TUBA Journal.* Two tubas. 1975. $7.50. 2:30. IV. Part I: D_1–c♯'; Part II: D_1–c♯'. For Winston Morris. The first section is a canon two measures apart. The second section is a canon one measure apart with a 6/4 time signature. Written as part of the TUBA Gem Series and distributed in the *TUBA Journal,* Vol. 2, No. 3. It is available by purchasing this back issue of the *TUBA Journal.*

Beasley, R. *Four Miniatures for Trombone and Tuba.* One trombone and one tuba.

Beck, Jeremy. *Prelude, Dance, and Fanfare.* Tuba-Euphonium Press. One euphonium and one tuba. 2001. $10.00. 7:00. III. Part I: c♯–f♯'; Part II: G♭–d'. Three movements: Prelude; Dance; Fanfare. A complex original composition that will also work for two tubas. Each part has large intervals in a pointillistic style. Also reviewed in the Winter 2002 issue of the *ITEA Journal* (Vol. 29, No. 2).

Belden, George R. *Ginnungigap. TUBA Journal.* One euphonium and one tuba. 1977. $7.50. 2:30. IV. Part I: F♯–b♭'; Part II: $F\sharp_1$–f'. This is a programmatic description of the creation of the world as told in Scandinavian mythology. Both parts are difficult and have extreme range demands. Very contemporary harmonies. Written as part of the TUBA Gem series and distributed in the *TUBA Journal,* Vol. 5, No. 1. It is available by purchasing this issue of the *TUBA Journal.*

Belden, George R. *Ragnarok.* Tenuto Publications. One euphonium and one tuba. 1983. $3.50. 2:20. IV. Part I: c–b♭'; Part II: E_1–b♭. This work was originally written in 1978 and is a programmatic description of the final destruction of the world. This is a companion piece to Ginnungigap. Contains many syncopated rhythms.

Bell, William, arr. *Artistic Solos and Duets.* Charles Colin. One euphonium and one tuba. 1975. $5.95. 15 pp. IV. Part I: B–a'; Part II: F–f'. A collection of thirteen duets arranged for two low brass instruments. These are from the *Complete Tuba Method* by William Bell. While the duets are not technically difficult, the tessitura of the second part is high. Several of the passages may be played down an octave. See also Methods and Studies.

Benson, Warren. *Serpentine Shadows. TUBA Journal.* Two tubas. 1973. $7.50. 4:15. III–IV. Part I: C_1–e♭'; Part II: C_1–e♭'. Four movements: Song; Dance; Hymn; Riff. Written as part of the TUBA Gem Series and distributed in the *TUBA Journal,* Vol. 1, No. 2. It is available by purchasing this back issue of the *TUBA Journal.*

Blazhevich, Vladislav. *Two Concert Duets.* arr. Herbert Wekselblatt. G. Schirmer Incorporated. Two tubas. 1964. $13.95. 2:30. III–IV. Part I: G_1–c'; Part II: F_1–g. Two movements: Andante; Allegro Vivo. The first movement is very slow and lyrical. The second movement is in a bright 6/8 meter in a polyphonic style. This is one of two duets published in a collection of tuba solos. See Wekselblatt, Herbert, ed., *Solos for the Tuba Player* in Tuba and Keyboard Collections.

Boccherini, Luigi. *Tuba Duo Eleven, Op. 5.* arr. James Self. Basset Hound Music. Two tubas. 1990. $5.00. 5:30. IV–V. Part I: $B\flat_1$–e♭'; Part II: G_1–e♭'. A nice melody that is technically challenging and frequently passed between the two parts. There are many large skips in the second part. Works very well. Will require strong players.

Bourgeois, Derek. *March and Fugue for Two Tubas, Op. 40 and 55.* Vanderbeek and Imirie Limited. Two Tubas. 1985. 5:30. IV. Part I: $B\flat_1$–e'; Part

II: E♭$_1$–g. Two movements: March; Fugue. The top part is written for an E♭ or F tuba. Most of the work is in the first part. There are some meter changes and the harmonies in the first movement are dissonant. The last two measures of the first movement require multiphonics in both parts. Originally published by Tuba/Euphonium Ensemble Publications, a project of the local chapter of TUBA at Ball State University.

Bowder, Jerry. *Canons and Hockets.* Manduca Music Publications. One euphonium and one tuba. 1995. $10.00. 5:45. III–IV. Part I: D–c"; Part II: (F$_1$) B♭$_1$–e♭' (g♭'). A tour-de-force duet suitable for advanced players and based on a 1930s jazz motif. Both parts are imitative and highly contrapuntal, including several passages written in parallel ninths or sevenths. Each part is in score form to assist with the ensemble.

Brandon, Sy. *Recital Duets for Two Tubas.* Tuba-Euphonium Press. Two tubas. 1981. $7.00. 9:00. III–IV. Part I: A$_1$–a; Part II: G♭$_1$–a. Seven movements: Fanfare; Waltz; Chorale; March; Bel Canto; Canons; Gigue. Utilizes traditional harmonies. The fifth movement contains several recitatives and rubato sections. Players will need to listen and count carefully. Playable by good high school players.

Brown, Newel Kay. *Dialogue and Dance.* Seesaw Music Corporation. One trombone (euphonium) and one tuba. 1978. $12.00. 6:00. IV–V. Part I: G$_1$–b♭'; Part II: A♭$_1$–e'. Two movements: Resolutely; Gay. Dedicated to David Kuehn and G. B. Lane. Very contemporary harmonies and technical challenges for both parts. Sections of the first part are printed in tenor clef. Both players read off a single score. This will require strong players.

Butterfield, Don. *Seven Duets for Tubas.* DB Publishing Company. Two tubas. 1960. 15:00. III–IV. Part I: C–c; Part II: E♭$_1$–g. Seven movements: To the Spartans; Archaic Portrait; Swingsville; Toccata; Abstraction; Sound Imagery; Construction in Keys. Dedicated to William J. Bell. A collection of duets in varying styles. Technical difficulty ranges from moderate to very difficult. The first part may also be played on euphonium. The duets may be performed individually or arranged together into a suite.

Buttery, Gary. *Wallowed Out.* Whaling Music Publishers. Two tubas. 1975. $5.00. 4:30. IV. Part I: F♯–g'; Part II: G$_1$–b. Three movements: June 17, 1972; Periodicity of Infinity; "Pardon Me" March. The first movement alternates between 3/4 and 4/4 with the 3/4 section played in one. The third movement is marked "very rapid" in 6/8. Buttery wrote this for a composition recital, and the work was premiered on June 18, 1975. The composition is programmatic and is a satire of the Watergate affair. The first part may be played on euphonium.

Carnardy, J. *Thirty Progressive Duos.* Two tubas.

Catelinet, Philip. *The Alpha Suite.* Philip Catelinet. One euphonium and one tuba. Out of Print. 7:30. IV. Part I: B♭–a♯'; Part II: A$_1$–a♭. Three movements: Aerimony; Amiability; Affinity. All three movements are very polyphonic. No significant technical problems, but players will need to count carefully. Fairly traditional in its harmonic structure.

Catelinet, Philip. *Suite in Miniature.* Hinrichsen Edition Limited (C. F. Peters). Two tubas. 1952. $4.20. 5:30. III–IV. Part I: E♭–d'; Part II: C–a. Three movements: Minuet; Invocata; Ecossaise. Three movements in contrasting styles published for trombones, euphoniums, or tubas. The first part may be performed on either euphonium or tuba. First and third movements are recorded by Karl Megules, Recorded Publications, Company, Z434471.

Chedeville, Philippe. *Three Rococo Dances.* arr. Randall Block. The Musical Evergreen. Two tubas. 1975. $3.50. 4:30. III–IV. Part I: F–c'; Part II: F–b♭. Three movements: Rondeau; Contredance; Gigue. Dances are very polyphonic and typical of the style invoked by the title.

Conley, Lloyd, arr. *Christmas for Two.* Kendor Music, Incorporated. One euphonium and one tuba. 1981. $9.50. 21 pp. III. Part I: A–f'; Part II: A♭$_1$–f. Easy arrangements of ten familiar Christmas carols: *O Come All Ye Faithful; We Three Kings; Deck the Halls; O Little Town; The First Noel; Hark, the Herald; It Came upon a Midnight Clear; Jingle Bells; Silent Night;* and *Joy to the World.* Traditional harmonies are used in an often contrapuntal style. Arrangements are very appropriate for high school concerts or church. The last three are more technically challenging.

Constantinides, Dinos. *Dedications for Baritone and Tuba.* Available from the composer. One euphonium and one tuba. 1989. $5.00. 6:20. IV–V. Part I: G–a'; Part II: G$_1$–f'. Three movements: Pandiatonic; Polytonal; Quartal. Good technique is required of both players at the tempo marked. Harmonies are representative of the names of the movements. The third movement is multimetric and the second movement has some tenor clef lines in the first part. This was originally written in 1970.

Corelli, Arcangelo. *Sonata Da Chiesa.* arr. R. Winston Morris. Ludwig Music Publishing Company. Two tubas and piano. 1970. $7.00. 8:00. IV. Part I: D–d'; Part II: C–d'. Five movements: Grave; Allegro Moderato; Allegretto; Adagio; Allegro Vivace. Very nice baroque melodies. The music is polyphonic, but not overly demanding technically. A harpsichord could be substituted for the piano. Fun to play.

Cummings, Barton. *Vignettes for Euphonium, Tuba and Piano.* Solid Brass Music Company. One euphonium, one tuba, and piano. 1996. $18.00. 12:30. III–IV. Part I: E–c"; Part II: G$_1$–g'. Five movements: In Olden Style; Morning Reveries;

Lazy Day; Cantilena; Random Flight. Very challenging work with large intervals and fast technical passages in both parts. Middle three movements are slow and lyrical, whereas the outer movements are fast and technical. Third movement contains jazz elements. Parts are of equal difficulty.

Danburg, Russell. *Prelude and Tarantella.* Wingert-Jones Music, Incorporated. Two tubas. 1982. $5.00. 4:00. IV. Part I: F_1–c'; Part II: A♭$_1$–c'. Two movements: Prelude; Tarantella. The first movement is slow and lyrical and provides some very interesting harmonies as it weaves in and out of major and minor modes. The second movement is a frolicking dance. Both parts have similar range demands and responsibilities.

De Filippi, Amedeo. *Divertimento.* Robert King Music Company. One euphonium and one tuba. 1968. $5.55. 9:00. III. Part I: c–g'; Part II: G_1–b♭. Five movements: March; Intermezzo I; Tempo Di Valse; Intermezzo II; Rondino. Ranges and technical difficulty make this very appropriate for high school use.

De Jong, Conrad. *Music for Two Tubas.* Elkan-Vogel Company. Two tubas. 1964. $1.95. 5:00. III. Part I: D–c'; Part II: G_1–e♭. Three movements: Fanfare; Canon; Finale. Dedicated to Dick and Don. Three contrasting movements. The canon is in a lyrical style. These work particularly well for high school students. The first part may be played by a euphonium. Enjoyable to play.

Defaye, Jean-Michel. *Six Etude.* Alphonse Leduc Editions. Two tubas.

Devienne, Francois. *Duet in F.* arr. Kenneth Singleton. Peer International Corporation. Two tubas. 1976. Out of Print. $3.50. 8:00. IV. Part I: E–e'; Part II: E–e'. Two movements: Allegro; Grazioso con Variatione. This was originally part of *Six Duets, Op. 18* for flutes. The second movement is a theme and variations, the final variation is quite technical with the melody constantly switching between the two parts.

Devienne, Francois. *Four Duets, Op. 82.* arr. Mitchell Gershenfeld. Medici Music Press. Two tubas. 1984. $9.50. 9:00. III–IV. Part I: C–b♭; Part II: G_1–g. Four movements. The movements contrast in key and meter, but they all begin with a moderate-tempo section, followed by a Rondo/Trio. No significant technical problems. Works well.

Dutton, Brent. *One Slow, One Fast.* Seesaw Music Corporation. Two tubas. 1978. $12.00. 5:30. IV. Part I: F_1–f'; Part II: F_1–e♭'. Two movements: I; II. Rondo. For Stevie. The first movement is slow and fairly conservative. The second movement is multimetric and more challenging technically. Some dissonant harmonies.

Dutton, Brent. *Pretty Forms.* Seesaw Music Corporation. Two tubas. 1977. $12.00. 4:00. V. Part I: A_1–e'; Part II: B♭$_2$–g'. Four movements: Liturgical Circles; Spots; Fugue; A Very Peasant Dance. Extreme technical and range demands required of both parts. The second movement contains mostly multiphonics. Very contemporary in character.

Dutton, Brent. *Some Loose Canons.* Seesaw Music Corporation. Two tubas. 1977. $12.00. 6:00. IV–V. Part I: D♭$_1$–e'; Part II: B♭$_2$–e'. Six movements. Dedicated to Ronald Bishop. A few mixed meters with many triplets, quintuplet, and septuplets. Numerous octave, eleventh, and thirteenth skips in the melody. Originally written in 1971, very challenging to play.

Dutton, Brent. *Then and Now.* Seesaw Music Corporation. One euphonium and one tuba. 1978. $12.00. 5:00. IV–V. Part I: G♭–b♭'; Part II: G♭$_1$–d'. Two movements: Then; Now. Written for Ken Henning and Mark Edwards. The second movement contains many twentieth-century techniques including singing and yelling through the horn, slapping the bell, and foot stomps. The first movement is in a more traditional style. Very difficult.

Ferstl, Herbert, arr. *Twenty Six Tuba Duette.* Georg Bauer. Two tubas. 1987. $12.00. 24 pp. III. Part I: E–b♭; Part II: F_1–f. A collection of 26 melodies by German and French composers. There are no significant range or technical problems. Each duet is short and excellent for study, or the duets may be grouped together as a suite for performance.

Forbes, Michael. *Six Roundabouts.* Editions BIM. Two tubas. 2003. CHF 20.00. 7:00. IV. Part I: G♭$_1$–g♭'; Part II: G♭$_1$–g♭'. Six movements: Allegro ma non troppo; Adagio espressivo; Allegro con spirito; Allegro moderato; Lento; Allegro spiritoso. Commissioned by Brian Kiser, Tuba/Euphonium Instructor, Indiana State University. Canonic duets with contemporary harmonies and rhythms, which intertwine and result in fascinating combinations. Although the work is written for bass tuba, the general tessitura is high and would also work for euphonium or trombone.

Frackenpohl, Arthur. *Brass Duo.* Robert King Music Company. One horn (euphonium) and one tuba. 1972. $5.55. 7:00. IV. Part I: B♭–b'(c"); Part II: F_1–b♭. Four movements: Prelude; Ballad; Scherzo; Variations. Fine traditional writing. May be performed with F Horn and tuba or euphonium and tuba. The tessitura of the first part is high. See same work under Tuba and Mixed Ensemble.

Frackenpohl, Arthur. *Pop Suite No. 2.* Horizon Press. One euphonium and one tuba. 1991. $5.00. 9:30. IV. Part I: c–c"; Part II: F_1–b♭. Three movements: Tango; Waltz; March. The tango and march are very syncopated and will require very careful counting. All three movements are tuneful and fun to play, but challenging.

Frackenpohl, Arthur. *Song and Dance.* Horizon Press. One euphonium, one tuba, and piano.

1991. $10.00. 8:00. IV–V. Part I: B♭–c'; Part II: G_1–c♭'. Two movements: Slowly; Moderately. A challenging piece for both parts. Each part has an opportunity to play the melody. *Ossia* sections provide alternatives to some of the rhythmic and range demands.

Frackenpohl, Arthur, arr. *Five Bach Duos for Euphonium and Tuba.* Williams Music Publishing Company. One euphonium and one tuba. 1993. $10.00. 8:45. IV. Part I: B♭–c"; Part II: F_1–b♭. Five movements: Two-part Invention #4; Sarabande; Aria; Minuett; Chorale Prelude. Traditional arrangement of these famous Bach melodies. The first part is printed in tenor clef.

Fritze, Gregory. *Fifteen Spectrum Duets for Tubas.* Available from the composer. Two tubas. 1990. $10.00. 30 pp. IV–V. Part I: C_1–f'; Part II: C_1–c'. Fifteen movements: Serenade; Gallop; Waltz; Dance; Rock and Jazz; Dance; Pastoral; Song; Nine; Invention; Light Swing; Double/Half Tempo; Song; Gallop; Fanfare. These contrasting fifteen movements are all in a traditional style except one that is very contemporary in design. Both parts have melodic responsibility and have many technical challenges. The duets may be played individually or in small groups as a suite.

Fux, Johann Joseph. *Sonata Pastorale (K. 397).* arr. Paul F. Hartin. Cellar Press. Two tubas and piano. 1974. 3:00. III–IV. Part I: D–d'; Part II: E–a. Two movements: Adagio; Un poco allegro. Two contrasting movements in a classical style. Not technically difficult, playable by high school students.

Garrett, James A. *Duet for Tubas.* The Brass Press. Two tubas. 1974. Out of Print. 5:00. III–IV. Part I: A$♭_1$–c'; Part II: G$♭_1$–c'. A one-movement work in 3/8 with both marcato and lyrical sections. Not rhythmically difficult, but there are some large skips in the melody.

Garrett, James A. *Fantasia for Tuba Duo.* The Brass Press. Two tubas. 1974. $3.50. 5:00. IV. Part I: A_1–e♭'; Part II: A$♭_1$–c'. Three movements: Adagio Sonoro; Agitato; Andante Sonoro. Very interesting writing in these three movements of contrasting sections. Numerous meter and style changes. Both parts are of equal difficulty.

Gearhart, Livingston, arr. *Bass Clef Sessions.* Shawnee Press, Incorporated. 1954. $7.50. 50 pp. III–IV. Part I: c–b♭'; Part II: F–g'. A collection of 62 two-, three-, and four-part arrangements for euphonium and tuba. Styles of the collection range from Renaissance to Jazz. See also Music for Multiple Tubas, Four Parts.

Geer, Karen. *Suite for Two Tubas.* Ludwig Music Publishing Company. Two tubas. 1984. $4.50. 5:00. III–IV. Part I: C–e♭'; Part II: E_1–c'. Three movements: March; Canon; Waltz. The march contains many instances of major seventh and ninth intervals. The last movement is very tonal and simple harmonically. The texture of the outer two movements is homophonic.

Geib, Fred. *A Joyous Dialogue, Op. 11.* Mills Music. Two tubas. 1941. Out of Print. 3:00. III. Part I: C–g; Part II: E–b♭. Primarily for tuba and piano with an optional second tuba part making the work possible as a tuba duet. Contains a traditional theme, cadenza, and variation section.

Gibbons, Orlando. *Fantasia.* The Musical Evergreen. Two tubas. 1971. $2.50. 2:00. IV. Part I: D♭–c'; Part II: D♭–c'. Typical Renaissance polyphonic fantasia. A lot of syncopation and rhythmic challenges associated with this type of close canon-like writing.

Gillam, Russell C. *Tuba Duet No. 1.* Two tubas and piano. 1967. 3:00. III. Part I: C–f; Part II: G_1–e. Very usable by high school players as the piano accompaniment strongly supports the melody. No real technical problems.

Gillingham, David. *Diverse Elements.* Tuba-Euphonium Press. One euphonium, one tuba, and piano. 1996. $30.00. 11:15. IV. Part I: G♯–c"; Part II: F_1–g♭'. Five movements: Intrada; Jazz Walk; Euphony; Caccia; Fanfare-March. Commissioned by Sande MacMorran, Professor of Tuba and Euphonium, University of Tennessee, Knoxville, Tennessee. Challenging original work in five contrasting movements. Style includes large intervals, syncopated rhythms, and technically challenging passages. Both parts are of equal difficulty.

Gillis, Lew. *Ten Duets.* Virgo Music Publishers. One trombone (euphonium) and one tuba. 1986. $7.95. 13 pp. IV. Part I: D$♭_1$–f'; Part II: G–a'. Movements vary in difficulty, depending on their ranges, as well as in style, key, and tempo. Several combinations of movements will work on a program.

Gillis, Lew. *Ten More Duets, Book 2.* Virgo Music Publishers.

Giuliani, Mauro. *Tuba Duets.* tr. Mark Mordue. Tuba-Euphonium Press. Two tubas. 1998. $10.00. 9 pp. II–III. Part I: G_1–f'; Part II: E$♭_1$–g. Four duets. Excerpted from Mauro's *Guitar Etudes, Op. 1 and Op. 14.* Originally scored for one guitar, but with clear melody and harmony lines, the duets work best as a pairing of a bass tuba and a contrabass tuba. Melodic material is primarily in the first part, though both parts require technical dexterity. Individual movements can stand alone in a concert.

Goble, Joseph. *Five Graded Intermediate Duets.* Tuba-Euphonium Press. One euphonium and one tuba. 1996. $15.00. 22 pp. II–III. Part I: B♭–b♭'; Part II: F_1–a♭. Five movements: Bombardon Dance; Zéllaphon; Champ; Abrélatas; Phanfare and Presto. Progressively arranged collection of duets specifically composed for intermediate-level performers. Fourth movement calls for optional percussion, including cabasa, claves, castanets, timbales, agogo bell, cowbell, vibra slap, and congas. Euphonium parts also available in treble clef. Individual movements can stand alone on a concert.

Goedicke, Alexander. *Concert Suite*. Philharmusica Corporation. One euphonium and one tuba. 1974. $6.00. 7:30. IV. Part I: B♭–a♭'; Part II: $B♭_1$–e♭'. Six movements. Very polyphonic, but not technically difficult. The tessitura of both parts is high.

Goldman, Richard Franko. *Duo for Tubas*. Mercury Music Corporation. Two tubas. 1950. Out of Print. 3:00. IV. Part I: G_1–c'; Part II: F_1–b. Three movements: Allegro commodo; Andante pessimistico; Vigoroso. For Frederick W. Prausnitz. Written in twelve-tone technique. Movement two is based on an inversion of the theme; movement three is based on the retrograde. The work is not rhythmically challenging.

Handel, George Frederic. *Nine Duets*. arr. Ronald Dishinger. Medici Music Press. Two tubas. 1993. $10.50.

Handel, George Frederic. *Va Tácito from Giulio Césare*. arr. Todd Cranson. Cimarron Music and Productions. One euphonium, one tuba, and piano. $11.50. 4:15. III. Part I: F–f'; Part II: c–d'. Effective arrangement of Handel's popular *Huntsman's Aria* originally scored for voice, horn, and orchestra. Euphonium parts also available in treble clef.

Hartin, Paul F. *Two Midaeval Carols*. Cellar Press. Two tubas. 1974. IV. Part I: c–d'; Part II: C–f. Two movements: Parit Virgo Filium; Cantilena: Princeps Serenissine. Typical Renaissance syncopated rhythms. Euphonium may be used on the first part.

Hartley, Walter. *Bivalve Suite*. Autograph Editions. One euphonium and one tuba. 1971. $8.50. 3:00. IV. Part I: F–a'; Part II: $E♭_1$–d♭'. Three movements: Allegro moderato; Lento; Presto. For Edward Bahr and C. Rudolph Emilson. Fun to play but there are several challenging ensemble problems for the players. Recorded by Robert LeBlanc and Paul Droste, *Euphonium Favorites for Recital and Contest*, Coronet, LPS 3203.

Hartman. *Choix D'Airs*. arr. Abe Torchinsky. Tuba-Euphonium Press. Two tubas. 1994. $11.00. 14 pp. II–III. Part I: E_1–f'; Part II: A_1–d'. Thirteen duets. Excerpted from *Extraits Des Meilleurs Compositeur*, published early in the nineteenth century, these brief duets are accessible by young players though almost every key signature is covered, up to seven sharps and seven flats. Individual movements can stand alone in a concert.

Hartman. *Six Duets*. arr. Abe Torchinsky. Tuba-Euphonium Press. Two tubas. 1994. $17.00. 16 pp. II–III. Part I: $B♭_1$–f'; Part II: $G♯_1$–b♭. Six duets. Originally published for two ophicleides early in the nineteenth century, these duets have been transposed down to a comfortable tuba range. The melodic material is predominantly in the first part, which is more suited for a bass tuba. Individual movements can stand alone in a concert.

Hartzell, Doug. *Ten Jazz Duos and Solos*. Shawnee Press, Incorporated. One euphonium and one tuba. 1974. $6.00. 7:30. IV–V. Part I: B♭–a♭'; Part II: F–a♭'. Six movements: Funky Monkeys; Split-Level; Swingin' in Seven; Tri-Level; Rock Pile; Short Ballad for Short Chicks. This is from a collection of ten jazz melodies: four solos, five duets, and one trio. These are written for any two bass clef instruments but would work best with one euphonium and one tuba. Technically challenging for both parts. Chord symbols are included so piano, bass, and drums may be easily added for concert use.

Haugland, A. Oscar. *Suite No. 16 for Two Tubas*. HOA Music Publishers Two tubas. 1993. $4.00. 4:20. IV. Part I: F♯–c'; Part II: F♯–d♭. Four movements: Allegro con brio; Allegretto; Tempo giusto; Andantino. Traditional harmonic structure. No significant technical demands, with the exception of the third movement which is multimetric. This suite works pretty well.

Haugland, A. Oscar. *Suite No. 17 for Two Tubas*. HOA Music Publishers. Two tubas. 1993. $4.00. 4:20. IV. Part I: G–b; Part II: E_1–c. Four movements: Allegro; Moderato; Lento; Allegretto. The technical demands and harmonies are more complex than in Suite No. 16. No range problems. Good reading material.

Haugland, A. Oscar. *Suite No. 18 for Two Tubas*. HOA Music Publishers. Two tubas. 1993. $5.00. 6:00. IV. Part I: E–b; Part II: E_1–e. Five movements: Allegro non troppo; Lento; Allegretto amabile; Allegretto; Scherzo. These movements are more complicated regarding key and technique. The movements contrast in style, meter, and key. Interesting writing.

Haugland, A. Oscar. *Suite No. 19 for Two Tubas*. HOA Music Publishers. Two tubas. 1993. $5.00. 4:30. IV. Part I: A–c♯'; Part II: A_1–g♯. Five movements: Andantino; Andante; Andante; Adagio; Risoluto. Both parts have equal responsibility for the melody. Melodies are frequently passed back and forth between parts. Movements contrast in key and style.

Haugland, A. Oscar. *Suite No. 20 for Two Tubas*. HOA Music Publishers. Two tubas. 1993. $5.00. 6:00. IV. Part I: G–e'; Part II: G_1–d. Five movements: Allegro giocoso; Allegro moderato; Allegro; Moderato; Allegro non troppo. More challenging technically than the other suites by Haugland. Rhythms are more complex and syncopated; the third movement is multimetric and complicated. Will require strong players.

Hawkins, Alan, arr. *Twenty Duets from Symphonic Masterworks*. Shawnee Press, Incorporated. One euphonium and one tuba. 1985. $4.95. 32 pp. IV. Part I: G–c''; Part II: $B♭_1$–f. A collection of twenty famous classical melodies arranged for euphonium and tuba. These melodies are select movements from symphonies of Haydn, Mozart, Beethoven, Schubert, Brahms, etc. The first part is responsible for the melody most of the time. Because of the familiarity of the melodies, these are enjoyable to play.

Haydn, F. J. *Tuba Duo Ten, Op. 99.* arr. James Self. Basset Hound Music. Two tubas. 1989. $5.00. 4:45. IV–V. Part I: A_1–e♭'; Part II: A_1–d'. A very nice melody. This is technically challenging. There are several skips ranging in length from one to two octaves. Both parts are of equal difficulty. Fun to play.

Henry, Eric. *Three Jazz Duets.* Tuba-Euphonium Press. Two tubas. 1995. $10.00. 5:00. II–III. Part I: C–g'; Part II: G_1–g. Three movements: Tuba for Two; Latin; Rock Swing. Study piece in jazz with frequent passages in octaves. Use of multiphonics is required in the second part. Individual movements can stand alone in a concert. Also reviewed in the Fall 1998 issue of the *TUBA Journal* (Vol. 26, No. 1).

Hewitt, Harry. *Six Preludes for Euphonium and Tuba, Op. 246C.* TUBA Press. One euphonium and one tuba. 1991. Out of Print. 14:00. IV. Part I: A♭–g♭'; Part II: $B♭_1$–f♭'. Six challenging movements in a contemporary harmonic setting. There are technical and rhythmic challenges, especially in the fourth movement. Several movements have ad-lib sections requiring players to watch the score and listen carefully. Will require strong players. Originally written in 1983 and titled *Six Preludes for Baritone and Tuba.*

Hewitt, Harry. *Suite for Harp and Two Tubas.* Available from the composer. Two tubas and harp. 1977. 8:00. IV. Part I: E–f♯'; Part II: F_1–f♯. Four movements. The harp part may be played by celeste or vibes. Tuba parts are not very interesting or challenging except for the range demands of the first part. The tubas are primarily providing accompaniment for the harp.

Hewitt, Harry. *Suite for Tuba Duo, Op. 376.* Available from the composer. Two tubas. 1972. 9:30. IV. Part I: $A♭_1$–e'(a♭'); Part II: F_1–e♭. Five movements. Contemporary tonal style with each movement differing in key and tempo. In some movements the first part may be played by a euphonium.

Hoesly, John, arr. *Christmas Collection—Duets for Brass.* Piston Reed Stick and Bow Publisher. Two tubas. 1990. $17.00. 19 pp. III–IV. Part I: $B♭_1$–b♭; Part II: G_1–g. Fourteen movements: Jingle Bells; Good King Wenceslas; We Three Kings; Deck the Halls; God Rest Ye Merry Gentlemen; Angels We Have Heard on High; O Come All Ye Faithful; O, Christmas Tree; It Came upon a Midnight Clear; Joy to the World; We Wish You a Merry Christmas; Hark, the Herald Angels Sing; The First Noel; Silent Night. Both parts have only moderate technical challenges and no range problems. Ideal for good high school players or anyone looking for fun arrangements of Christmas music. There is another version available for one euphonium and one tuba. The parts and score are all sold separately.

Hudadoff, Igor, arr. *Concert and Ensemble Folio (Bandsembles).* Pro Art. Two tubas. 1961. Out of Print. 24 pp. II–III. A collection of 22 popular tunes usable as easy duets for junior high or high school.

Israel, Brian. *Sonata No. One.* Tritone Press. Two tubas. 1979. $4.00. 6:05. IV. Part I: F_1–d♭; Part II: F_1–c'. Three movements. To Rick and Al Balestra. Moderate technical challenges. Both parts have equal responsibility for the melody. Interesting two-part writing.

Israel, Brian. *Sonata No. Two.* Tritone Press. Two tubas. 1977. $3.00 4:30. III–IV. Part I: $B♭_1$–c♯'; Part II: A_1–b. Three movements: Allegro non troppo; Andante; Vivace. Question and answer style in the first movement. Part one may be played by a euphonium in the first two movements.

Jesus, Nelson. *Duos for Two Tubas.* Lusitanus Editions, Portugal. Two tubas. 2003. 10:00. IV. $A♯_2$–b'. Four movements: Caminhada; Jogos; Pequena Dança; Confusão. Commissioned by and dedicated to Pedro Santos and Pedro Henriques.

Jones, Roger. *Airs and Dances.* Tuba-Euphonium Press. One euphonium and one tuba. 2000. $10.00. 18 pp. III. Part I: (F) G–a'; Part II: (F_1) $B♭_1$–c♭'. Seven movements: Tarentella; Air No. 1; Waltz; Air No. 2; Scherzo; Air No. 3; Ritual Dance. Collection of seven contrasting duets. The three Airs are slow and lyrical, while the other movements are lively and dance-like with syncopation and occasional meter changes. Individual movements can stand alone on a concert.

Jones, Roger. *Four Duets.* Tuba-Euphonium Press. One euphonium and one tuba. 1999. $8.00. 7:00. III. Part I: $B♭_1$–g'; Part II: (G_1) A_1–b♭. Four movements. Dedicated to my good friend Doug Baer. This collection of four contrasting duets is written in a modern, contrapuntal style. Melodic material is divided between both voices. Individual movements can stand alone on a concert.

Jones, Roger. *Three Tubas Two.* Tuba-Euphonium Press. Two or three tubas. 2000. $8.00. 5:00. II. Part I: ($A♭_1$) $B♭_1$–g (c'); Part II: ($A♭_1$) $B♭_1$–f'; Part III: $A♭_1$–c. Described by the composer as a duet with optional third part, this piece is in rondo form with contrasting tempos. The optional third part fills in harmonies and adds texture, but the duet is effective without it.

Jones, Roger. *21 Distinctive Duets for Tuba.* University of Miami Press. Two tubas. 1973. Out of Print. 32 pp. III–IV. Part I: G_1–d'; Part II: F_1–a. A collection of 21 duets, each in a different style and tempo. Many of these will work well for good high school players. May be played individually or arranged in small suites. Some of the movements are quite tuneful. Duet No. 12

recorded by the University of Miami Tuba Ensemble, Miami United Tuba Society, 14568.

Jones, Roger. *Two Tuba Suites, Book 1.* Available from the composer. Two tubas. 1981. $10.00. 24 pp. IV. Part I: G_1–g; Part II: F_1–f. Six suites. Suites 1, 2, 3, and 5 contain three movements, Suites 4 and 6 and have four movements. Both parts are interesting and share melodic responsibilities. The movements in each suite contrast in meter and key. These work well.

Jones, Roger. *Two Tuba Suites, Book 2.* Available from the composer. Two tubas. 1988. $15.00. 42 pp. IV. Part I: F_1–c'; Part II: F_1–g. Four suites: 7; 8; 9; 10. Each suite contains four movements. The movements contrast in meter and tempo. The melodies are often syncopated and at times technically challenging.

Joplin, Scott. *Euphonic Sounds.* arr. Arthur Frackenpohl. Tuba-Euphonium Press. One euphonium and one tuba. 1997. $8.00. 3:45. III. Part I: G–a♭' (b♭'); Part II: $G♭_1$–c'. For Mary Ann Craig. Effective arrangement of one of Joplin's more popular syncopated two-steps. Both parts are challenging, with frequent arpeggiated passages and syncopated rhythms. Includes alternative passages for more advanced performers.

Joubert, Claude-Henry. *Ten Duos Concertants.*

Jous, Christian. *Entrevue.* Editions du Petit Page. Two tubas and piano. €19.00.

Kelly, Michael S. *Sonata.* One euphonium and one tuba. 1979.

Knight, Steve. *Conversations.* Cimarron Music and Productions. One euphonium and one tuba. $6.50.

Krush, Jay. *Largo and Allegro.* The Brass Press. Two tubas. 1974. $3.50. 3:00. III–IV. Part I: G–a; Part II: C_1–a. One-movement work that alternates in tempo between largo and allegro. Works well with high school students but also interesting for university level.

Lasso, Orlando di. *Fantasias.* arr. Richard E. Powell. Southern Music Company. One euphonium and one tuba. 1970. Out of Print. 4:00. IV.

Lasso, Orlando di. *Two Renaissance Duets.* arr. Andrew Spang. Lyric Brass Publishing. One euphonium and one tuba. $2.50. From *O Magnum Musicum.*

Leavitt, Daniel Joe. *Sub-Voce Entropy.* West Wind Music Company. Two tubas. 1986. $3:00. 3:30. IV. Part I: E–e♭'; Part II: E–e♭'. This is an aleatoric composition. Both players read from a chart consisting of forty measures. Each player starts on a measure of his choice and plays the measures in any order he chooses as long as he plays all the measures only once. Technical demands depend on the speed of the performance. Good introduction to aleatoric music.

Luedeke, Raymond. *Eight Bagatelles.* Tenuto Publications. Two tubas. 1970. $7.00. 9:00. IV. Part I: E_1–e♭'; Part II: $B♭_2$–c'. For Lee Richardson. These may be performed as a total work or as selections chosen for a suite. The second part has several pedal B's and C♯'s above pedal C. Several technically challenging sections, two-octave leaps, etc. Movements VI and VII are in mixed meter.

Luedeke, Raymond. *Wonderland Duets.* Tenuto Publications. Two tubas and narrator. 1971. $6.00. 5:00. IV. Part I: D_1–d♭'; Part II: D_1–d♭'. Based on Lewis Carroll's *Alice in Wonderland.* The tuba parts are very challenging. The narrator should be able to read text in rhythm. Good recital material, a real audience pleaser.

Manzo, Angelo. *Three Short Duets.* Tuba-Euphonium Press. One euphonium and one tuba. 2001. $10.00. 3:00. II–III. Part I: G–f'; Part II: C_1–c'. Three movements: Gigue; Romance; Fugue. These duets, each shorter than a minute, are all in the key of C minor. The outer movements are fast while the contrasting inner movement is slow. Also reviewed in the Spring 2003 issue of the *ITEA Journal* (Vol. 30, No. 3).

Matchett, Steve D., arr. *Sixteen Christmas Duets.* Gulf Wind Music Press. Two tubas. 1998. $8.50. 16 pp. III. Sixteen movements: Deck the Halls; O Christmas Tree; Silent Night; Away in a Manger; Up on the Housetop; God Rest Ye Merry Gentlemen; O Come, All Ye Faithful; We Wish You a Merry Christmas; Jingle Bells; Joy to the World; Hark the Herald Angels Sing; It Came upon a Midnight Clear; We Three Kings of Orient Are; The First Noel; O Little Town of Bethlehem; Good King Wenceslas. The collection of duets may be performed as is, or with the collections scored for other wind instruments.

McCurdy, Gary L. *Chorale and Gigue.* TMC Music. One euphonium and one tuba. Out of Print.

McCurdy, Gary L. *The Coloring Book.* TMC Music. Two tubas. 1975. Out of Print. 4:00. II–III. Part I: C–d; Part II: $B♭_1$–c. Four movements: Blue; Green; Yellow; Red. Four programmatic movements representing four major colors. Range and technical demands make this playable by young tubists.

McCurdy, Gary L. *Prelude and Fugue.* TMC Music. Two tubas. 1971. Out of Print. 3:00. III. Part I: C–c'; Part II: A_1–g. Fugue is a typical baroque-style fugue, very polyphonic. Technical demands, however, allow this to be performed by high school players.

McCurdy, Gary L. *Twelve Duets for Tubas.* TMC Music. Two tubas. 1971. Out of Print. 9 pp. III–IV. Part I: $B♭_1$–c'; Part II: F_1–e. Twelve short duets, each of twelve measures in length in twelve different keys. The challenges of these movements are the different keys and some slight technical demands.

McCurdy, Gary L. *Two Impressions.* TMC Music. Two tubas. 1971. Out of Print. 2:00. III. Part I: B♭–f; Part II: E_1–d♭.

McCurdy, Gary L. *Waltz of the Walrus.* TMC Music. Two tubas. 1972. Out of Print. 2:00. III–IV.

Part I: F–f; Part II: B♭$_1$–e♭. May be performed with two tubas or tuba with piano accompaniment or band accompaniment.

Morley, Thomas. *Tuba Duets.* arr. Leigh Anne Hunsaker. Harold Gore Publishing Company. Two tubas. 1991. $10.00. 41 pp. III. Part I: G$_1$–g; Part II: F$_1$–g. A collection of 21 songs by Thomas Morley transcribed for two tubas. There are very few technical demands and the ranges are well within a high school player's ability.

Mozart, Wolfgang Amadeus. *Duets for Tuba.* arr. Wesley Jacobs. Encore Music Publishers. Two tubas. 1989. $16.00. 23 pp. IV. Part I: D–d'; Part II: F♯$_1$–a♭. Twelve movements. Each movement varies in technical and range demands, key, meter, and style. Several of the movements are very tuneful and enjoyable to play.

Mozart, Wolfgang Amadeus. *Eleven Mozart Duets for Bass Clef Instruments.* arr. Richard E. Powell. Shawnee Press, Incorporated. Two bass clef instruments. 1972. $7.00. 15 pp. IV. Part I: d–c''; Part II: c$_1$–f'. A collection of eleven duets of varying style and tempo that were originally written for two horns. The first part should be played on euphonium and the second part on tuba. Younger tubists may wish to play some of the passages down an octave.

Mozart, Wolfgang Amadeus. *Five Duets.* arr. Paul F. Hartin. Cellar Press. Two tubas. 1974. 6:00. IV. Part I: F–f'; Part II: F$_1$–g♭. Five movements: Allegro; Menuetto; Polonaise; Larghetto; Allegro. Five contrasting movements of familiar Mozart melodies. First part is very playable by a euphonium. Arrangements work very well.

Mozart, Wolfgang Amadeus. *Seven Menuets KV65A.* arr. Ronald C. Dishinger. Medici Music Press. Two tubas. 1990. $7.50. 8 pp. III–IV. Part I: C$_1$–c'; Part II: F$_1$–f. Seven movements. All seven movements are in standard minuet-trio-minuet form and were originally written by Mozart when he was 13 years old. All are in the key of B♭ except for the first movement, which is in A♭. Movements may be performed individually or grouped together in any number. A couple of these work really well.

Mozart, Wolfgang Amadeus. *Sonata for Two Tubas, K.V. 292.* arr. Rex Conner. PP Music. Two tubas. 1993. $6.50. 13:00. IV. Part I: C–d'; Part II: B♭$_1$–c'. Three movements: Moderato; Andante; Rondo-Allegro. This was originally written for bassoon and cello and has been transposed a fifth lower than the original. Both parts are tuneful and technically challenging. Would also work well for one euphonium and one tuba. Will require strong players.

Mozart, Wolfgang Amadeus. *Tuba Duo Eight.* arr. James Self. Basset Hound Music. Two tubas. 1987. $5.00. 4:45. IV–V. Part I: G$_1$–f'; Part II: F$_1$–d'. A very lyrical but challenging melody. Both parts have the opportunity to play the melody. Good writing.

Mozart, Wolfgang Amadeus. *Tuba Duo Four, K. 380.* arr. James Self. Basset Hound Music. Two tubas. 1983. $5.00. 5:30. IV–V. Part I: G$_1$–f'; Part II: F$_1$–d'. A transcription of the first movement of the *Sonata for Klavier and Violin in E♭,* 1781. Both parts have equal responsibility for the melody and are very demanding regarding range and technique. Interesting writing.

Mozart, Wolfgang Amadeus. *Tuba Duo One, K. 378.* arr. James Self. Basset Hound Music. Two tubas. 1976. $5.00. 7:30. IV–V. Part I: G$_1$–d'; Part II: F$_1$–d'. This is from the first movement of a *Sonata for Klavier and Violin,* 1779. A very melodic but challenging duet. Both parts are of equal difficulty and have the opportunity to play the melody. This duet works very well.

Mozart, Wolfgang Amadeus. *Tuba Duo Seven, K. 380.* arr. James Self. Basset Hound Music. Two tubas. 1986. $5.00. 6:00. IV–V. Part I: F$_1$–f'; Part II: E$_1$–c'. This is third movement, Rondo, of the *Sonata for Klavier and Violin,* 1781. In a moderate 6/8 meter, the parts are very challenging but also quite interesting. A lot of work, but well worth the effort.

Mozart, Wolfgang Amadeus. *Tuba Duo Three, K. 454.* arr. James Self. Basset Hound Music. Two tubas. 1981. $5.00. 5:00. IV–V. Part I: G$_1$–e'; Part II: (C$_1$)E$_1$–e'. This is the first movement of the *Sonata for Klavier and Violin,* 1784. The melody is very lyrical and is played by both parts. There are many range and technical challenges for both parts. Works well.

Mozart, Wolfgang Amadeus. *Tuba Duo Two (Rondo alla Tubas) K. 564.* arr. James Self. Basset Hound Music. Two tubas. 1979. $5.00. 5:00. IV–V. Part I: F$_1$–f'; Part II: F$_1$–d'. This is the Rondo from *Trio for Klavier, Violin, and Cello,* 1788. Both parts are interesting and technically very challenging. Excellent writing.

Mozart, Wolfgang Amadeus. *Twelve Duets, K.V. 487.* arr. Ronald Dishinger. Medici Music Press. Two tubas. 1993. $9.50. 12 pp. III–IV. Part I: C–d'; Part II: F$_1$–f. Each duet varies in style, tempo, and meter. Most are very tuneful and not technically difficult. A couple of these could be played by good high school students.

Mozart, Wolfgang Amadeus. *Twelve Duets for Horn (Tubas).* arr. Edward McKee. Tuba-Euphonium Press. Two tubas. 1994. $10.00. 11 pp. II–III. Part I: F–f'; Part II: B♭$_2$–b♭. Twelve duets. This arrangement of these popular horn duets is a good resource for study and sight-reading. The key choice fits the instruments well and there is little voice-crossing. As such, the top part would be more appropriate for a smaller tuba or a more advanced player, while the bottom part is accessible to intermediate-level performers. Individual movements can stand alone in a concert. Also reviewed in the Winter 1995 issue of the *TUBA Journal* (Vol. 22, No. 2).

Mozart, Wolfgang Amadeus. *Twelve Duos for Two Tubas.* arr. Rex A. Conner. Queen City Brass Publications. Two tubas. 1981. $8.00. 15 pp. IV. Part I: E♭–e♭'; Part II: E♭$_1$–g♭. A collection of minuets, andantes, and polonaises. The first part may easily be played on euphonium or F tuba. Movements may be used individually or a small number may be selected as a suite for concert use.

Mozart, Wolfgang Amadeus. *Twelve Easy Duets for Winds.* arr. Henry Charles Smith. G. Schirmer. One euphonium and one tuba. 1972. Out of Print.

Mozart, Wolfgang Amadeus. *Two Wind Duets (K.487).* arr. Randall Block. The Musical Evergreen. One euphonium and one tuba. 1975. $3.50. 3:00. III–IV. Part I: B♭–c'; Part II: B♭$_1$–g. Two movements: Allegro; Andante. Two contrasting movements in a classical style. Parts are of equal difficulty.

Mueller, Frederick. *Duet.* Available from the composer. One euphonium and one tuba. $6.00.

Nakagawa, Ryohei, arr. *My Melody Book.* Sohgaku-Sha. Two tubas. 1990. $42.00. 160 pp. III–IV. Part I: B♭$_1$–b♭; Part II: F$_1$–f. Dedicated to K. Yamashita. A collection of 109 familiar melodies. There are European folk songs, American folk songs, popular and Christmas songs, jazz, and a few Japanese folk songs. The technical challenges range from moderate to moderately difficult. Many of these work quite well and would be appropriate for study, concert use, or just for fun. This book contains an incredible amount of music.

Nelhybel, Vaclav. *Counterpoint No. 6.* Barta Music Company. Two tubas. 1979. $6.50. 9 pp. IV. Part I: A♭$_1$–g; Part II: G$_1$–a♭. Eight movements. A collection of original polyphonic duets. Movements are of varying difficulty depending on their rhythmic complexity. Ranges are not a problem and the first three movements are very playable by high school students.

Nelhybel, Vaclav. *Eleven Duets for Tuba.* General Music Publishing Company. Two tubas. 1966. $4.95. 8 pp. II–IV. Part I: A$_1$–e; Part II: A$_1$–e. Rhythmically quite interesting. Select movements may be chosen as suites for concerts. Rhythms are moderately challenging. Tempos may be varied for high school players.

Paasch, Antony. *Seven Miniatures (Based on Native American Themes).* Tuba-Euphonium Press. One euphonium and one tuba. 2002. $8.00. 7:00. III. Part I: B–f'; Part II: B♭$_2$–g. Seven movements: Freely; With War-Like Intensity; Lively; Delicately; Chanted; Driving; Smoothly. Challenging work with shifting meter and mixed meter. Each movement is in a new key, and there is effective use of dissonance and modern harmonies. Also reviewed in the Spring 2004 issue of the *ITEA Journal* (Vol. 31, No. 3).

Patterson, Merlin E. *Two-Part Inventions.* One euphonium and one tuba. 1974. 5:50. IV. Part I: A♭–b♭'; Part II: G♯$_1$–c'. Four movements: Fughetta; Ostinato; Gigue; Allemande. Euphonium part is printed in tenor clef. Movements are in mixed meter and rhythmically very challenging.

Pederson, Tommy. *Ten Duets for Bass Trombone.* Kendor Music, Incorporated. Two bass trombones (tubas). 1976. $9.50. 20 pp. IV. Part I: G$_1$–d'; Part II: F$_1$–e♭'. Ten movements: Empty Boxes; The Whether Man; Hippo in the Cabbage Patch; Rumble on 6th Street; Riot of the Red Ants; Fibulee, Tibula; Melissa; The Walrus Ordered Waffles; Tigger Talk; Adrift on a Waterbed. Very tuneful and humorous duets. Movements vary in technical and range demands, but all require strong players. Fun to play.

Perfeito, Paulo. *BTT.* Lusitanus Editions, Portugal. Two tubas and drums. 2004. 8:00. V. Part I: F$_1$–c"; Part II: C$_1$–a'. Commissioned by and dedicated to Sérgio Carolino. A very nice piece in a jazzy style. Some improvisation required in the first part. Second part requires multiphonics and a strong bass line.

Pires, Isabel. *Para Duas Tubas.* Lusitanus Editions, Portugal. Two tubas. 1999. 7:00. V. Part I: F$_1$–f'; Part II: F$_1$–f'. Dedicated to Nuno Carvalho. Premiered in the Lisbon Superior Music School. Contemporary music notation.

Porret, Julien. *Twelve Divertissements en Duos, Op. 670.* Editions Robert Martin. Two tubas. 1980. $16.00. 23 pp. IV. Part I: B–e'; Part II: G–e'. Twelve movements. Twelve original duets that may be performed individually or in any order. Both parts are of equal technical difficulty. Predominantly polyphonic in character, but not technically challenging. The tessitura is a little high for both parts. The first part could be played by a euphonium or tuba.

Powell, Morgan. *Short Piece for Tuba and Euphonium. TUBA Journal.* One euphonium and one tuba. 1974. $7.50. 1:30. IV. Part I: B♭–b♭"; Part II: G–d'. Short duet with mixed meters and numerous tempo changes. Challenging rhythmically to put together. Uses some flutter tonguing, and the last note is muted. This was written as part of the TUBA Gem series and is distributed with the *TUBA Journal,* Vol. 1, No. 3. It is available by purchasing this issue of the *TUBA Journal.*

Presser, William. *Five Hag Pieces.* Theodore Presser. One euphonium and one tuba. 1987. $5.50. 4:20. IV. Part I: E–b♭'; Part II: E$_1$–b♭. Five movements: Gee, Dad Gaffed a Faded Hag; H.H.A. Beach Egged a Caged Hag; Abe Bach Bagged a Bead-Headed Hag; Each Fagged Hag Had a Bad Headache; A Chafed Hag Fed a Chef Chaff. Using German spellings (B = B♭ and H = B), the themes spell out the titles of each movement. Both parts have equal responsibility for the melody. Some technical challenges in both parts. Interesting writing and fun to play. This composition is a sequel to *Two Hag*

Pieces, published by the *TUBA Journal,* Winter, 1984.

Presser, William. *Seven Tuba Duets.* Tenuto Publications. Two tubas. 1970. $6.00. 9:00. IV. Part I: F_1–b♭; Part II: E_1–b♭. Seven movements: Prologue; Invention I; Passacaglia; Invention II; Fugue; Invention III; Epilogue. The movements contrast in style, meter, and key. They are short and may be performed alone or in a variety of combinations. Some movements are technically challenging, especially at the tempos indicated.

Presser, William. *Two Hag Pieces for Euphonium and Tuba. TUBA Journal.* One euphonium and one tuba. 1984. $7.50. 2:50. IV. Part I: G–b♭'; Part II: G_1–a. Two movements: A Deaf, Aged, Bad Hag; A Gagged Hag Abed, Dead, Hee-Hee, Ha-Ha. Using German spellings (B = B♭ and H = B), the themes from each movement spell out the title. The first movement begins like a canon and remains polyphonic throughout. The second movement is in 6/8 and has traditional harmonies. Written as part of the TUBA Gem series and is distributed in the *TUBA Journal,* Vol. 11, No. 3. It is available by purchasing this issue of the *TUBA Journal.*

Purcell, Henry. *Chaconne.* arr. R. Winston Morris. Shawnee Press, Incorporated. Two tubas with optional piano or harpsichord. 1982. $7.00. 2:20. III–IV. Part I: G–d'; Part II: G–d'. Effective arrangement of this famous "Chaconne." The addition of the harpsichord can add a baroque flavor and a tone color not often heard with two tubas. The arrangement works very well.

Purvis, Stanley H. *Appalachian Echos.* Kendor Music, Incorporated. Two tubas. 1991. $5.00. 2:50. III–IV. Part I: E♭–b♭(c'); Part II: E♭$_1$–f. The melody is like a folk song that is presented in a question and answer format. There are several tempo changes within the basic ABA (slow-fast-slow) form. Very tuneful and enjoyable to play.

Quantz, Johann. *Twelve Duets, Op. 2 and Op. 5.* arr. Paul Schmidt. Heavy Metal Music. Two tubas. $15.00. Twelve movements. Both parts may also be performed on euphonium. Euphonium parts also available in treble clef. Individual movements can stand alone on a concert.

Raum, Elizabeth. *Requiem for Wounded Knee.* Available from the composer. Two tubas, narrator, and piano. 20:00.

Rener, Hermann. *Spielheft 1.* Philipp Grosch Musikverlag. One euphonium and one tuba. $10.00. 10:00. IV. Part I: c–f'; Part II: F–d'. Ten movements. Written for two trombones or any two bass clef instruments, this can work well with one euphonium and one tuba. Both parts have equal responsibility for the melody. A lot of imitation, though not technically difficult.

Roikjer, Kjell. *Ten Inventions for Two Tubas, Op. 55.* Wilhelm Hansen Musikverlag. Two tubas. 1969. $16.00. 17 pp. IV. Part I: B_1–e'; Part II: F_1–a. These inventions are excellent study material. Quite challenging rhythmically and in terms of key.

Rønnes, Robert. *Three Pieces for Toby the Tuba.* Norway Music Information Centre. Two tubas. 3:00. Three movements.

Ryker, Robert. *Petite Marche.* One euphonium and one tuba and piano. 1983. 4:00. IV. Part I: C♭–b♭'; Part II: C–d♭'. A lot of imitation between the piano accompaniment and the tuba and euphonium parts. Both parts are of equal difficulty.

Ryker, Robert. *Sonata for Two Bass Tubas.* Robert King Music Company. Two tubas. 1959. Out of Print. 4:00. IV. Part I: D_1–d'; Part II: D_1–d'. Both parts are of equal difficulty. Texture is mostly homophonic with three sections of varying tempo. First performed on March 23, 1959. A good recital piece.

Ryker, Robert. *Sonata for Two Bass Tubas.* Tuba-Euphonium Press. Two tubas. 1995. $10.00. 5:00. II–III. Part I: D_1–d'; Part II: D_1–d'. For Phi Mu Alpha Sinfonia at Indiana University. This single-movement work is the middle movement of an unfinished composition. The texture is predominantly contrapuntal, and the form is ternary. The melodic material is divided between both parts.

Saari, Jarmo. *Suo-duo.* Finnish Music Information Centre. Two tubas. 1998. *Suo-duo* is a zingy, rhythmic work in a distinct style. It demands much of the performers and makes use of the lowest register. Both parts call for multiphonics and tapping rhythms on the instrument. The first part may also be performed on euphonium.

Sainte-Jacome. *Duet.* arr. Herbert G. Wekselblatt. Schirmer, Incorporated. Two tubas. 1964. $13.95. 3:20. III–IV. Part I: F_1–g; Part II: F_1–g. Very polyphonic and technically challenging in a few sections. Players will need to count carefully. Originally written for two trumpets. This is one of two duets published in a collection of tuba solos. See Wekselblatt, Herbert, ed., *Solos for the Tuba Player,* under Tuba and Keyboard Collections.

Samuel, Gerhard. *Pezzo Serioso.* MMB Music. Two tubas and one percussion. 1978. $5.95. 6:00.

Scarmolin, A. Louis. *Duet Time.* arr. Michael Boo. Ludwig Music Publishing Company. One euphonium and one tuba. 1982. $5.50. 15 pp. IV. Part I: F–f'; Part II: F–e♭'. Twelve movements: Dialogue; Rondolette; Jumpin' Bean; Andantino; Fiesta; Drawing Room; Here and There; Swans; Spring Dance; Bambolina; Follow Me; Fughetta. The melodies are very traditional in style and harmonic structure. The parts are of equal difficulty. There are no significant technical problems. May be performed individually or a small number may be grouped together for a suite. Fun to play. Originally copyrighted in 1966.

Scherzer, Edward. *Twenty-Four Duette, Op. 73.* Two tubas.

Schlesinger, Scott. *Six Tuba Duets.* Tuba-Euphonium Press. Two tubas. 2002. $12.00. 16 pp. III. Part I: A_1–f'; Part II: (F_1) G_1–e'. Six duets. Collection of original duets in contrasting styles, including rock, baroque invention, and jazz. First part may also be performed on euphonium. Individual movements can stand alone in a concert. Also reviewed in the Spring 2004 issue of the *ITEA Journal* (Vol. 31, No. 3).

Schmidt, Paul, ed. *Leviathan Love.* Heavy Metal Music. Two tubas. $20.00. 40 pp. III. Part I: F_1–a; Part II: D_1–a♭. Thirty movements. Commissioned and published by members of the Heavy Metal Society Tuba Quartet. The first eight movements are from a book of duets for bass viols, published in 1638 by Michael East. The next five are by Gerard Turnhout and date from the mid-sixteenth century. Next are eleven works by Thomas Morley, including two canzonettas and nine fantasies. The final six pieces are from the Anna Magdalena Notebook. The style of the duets is generally contrapuntal and imitative. The range of the parts is more appropriate for contrabass tuba than bass tuba. Individual movements can stand alone in a concert.

Schmidt, William. *Variations on a Theme of Prokofieff.* Western International Music, Incorporated. One euphonium and one tuba. 1990. $5.00. 5:00. IV. Part I: B–g'; Part II: D♯–e'. Scored for either two euphoniums or one euphonium and one tuba. The range demands on the second part are not great, but the tessitura is high. Technically challenging in only a couple of spots, but the harmonies are quite dissonant and very contemporary in nature.

Sear, Walter. *Advanced Duets for Tuba, Volume I.* Cor Publishing Company. Two tubas. 1969. $6.00. 24 pp. III–IV. Part I: F_1–d'; Part II: F_1–d'. A collection of 21 original duets in contrasting tempo and style. Difficulty of the movements ranges from moderate to difficult. Many of these are very tuneful and are enjoyable to play and listen to. The duets may be performed individually or in small groups as a suite.

Sear, Walter. *Advanced Duets for Tuba, Volume II.* Cor Publishing Company. Two tubas. 1974. $6.00. 24 pp. IV. Part I: F♯$_1$–d'; Part II: E_1–c'. Ten different movements mostly in the style of strict canons and inventions. Movements vary in range and technical demands but are generally more difficult and less tuneful than the duets in Volume I by Sear. These may also be played individually or in small numbers as a suite.

Self, Jim, arr. *Concert Duets, Vol I.* Tuba-Euphonium Press. Two tubas. 1997. $15.00. 23 pp. III–IV. Part I: F_1–f'; Part II: E♭$_1$–d'. Six duets. Includes four works by Mozart and two by W. F. Bach. These challenging duets were arranged over a fifteen-year period and taken primarily from eighteenth-century trio sonatas. Both parts require technical dexterity and musicality. Also reviewed in the Spring 1998 issue of the *TUBA Journal* (Vol. 25, No. 3).

Self, Jim, arr. *Concert Duets, Vol II.* Tuba-Euphonium Press. Two tubas. 1997. $15.00. 21 pp. III–IV. Part I: (E_1) F_1–g♭'; Part II: E_1–e♭'. Six duets. Includes arrangements of Mozart, J. S. Bach, Haydn, and Boccherini, plus an original composition by Jim Self. These challenging duets were arranged over a fifteen-year period and taken primarily from eighteenth-century trio sonatas. Both parts require technical dexterity and musicality. Also reviewed in the Spring 1998 issue of the *TUBA Journal* (Vol. 25, No. 3).

Self, Jim. *Duh Suite.* Basset Hound Music. Two tubas and drum set. 1998. $30.00. IV. Part I: C_1–c"; Part II: B♭$_2$–b♭'. Six movements: Duh Intro; Duh Odds; Duh Fool Professors; Duh Blooze; Duh Yaz; Duh KoDa. For Dennis Askew and Kelly O'Bryant. A tour-de-force duet with challenging technical passages, large intervals, and register extremes. Several movements have a jazz texture, and the second movement contains frequent meter changes. Percussion parts require a drum set and "tingly" things. Recorded by Dennis Askew and Kelly O'Bryant on the compact disc *Carolina Morning,* KoDa Records.

Sibbing, Robert. *Canon and Scherzo.* Tuba-Euphonium Press. Two tubas and piano. 1999. $12.00. 7:00. II–III. Part I: G_1–d'; Part II: E♭$_1$–a♭. Two movements. This original work for two tubas and piano is predominantly homophonic in texture, with several passages in octaves or parallel intervals between the tubas. Both parts are of equal difficulty.

Siekmann, Frank H., arr. *Beautiful Savior (Crusader's Hymn).* Brelmat Music. One euphonium, one tuba, and piano. 2001. $10.00. 4:45. III. Part I: G–g' (b♭'); Part II: B♭–d'. This arrangement of the traditional hymn is scored for euphonium, tuba, and piano and works well in both church and recital settings. Parts are of equal difficulty.

Singleton, Kenneth, arr. *Three Renaissance Duets.* Peer International Corporation. Two tubas. 1976. $8.00. 5:00. IV. Part I: D–d'; Part II: D–c'. Three movements: Fantasia; Canon; Duo. These duets represent the imitative polyphony typical of the 15th and 16th centuries. Fantasia was originally written for two bass viols. The Canon is originally by Obrecht and served as a Credo for the Missa Salve Dive Parens. Technically not very difficult, but counting correctly can be a challenge.

Singleton, Kenneth, arr. *Twenty-Five Baroque and Classical Duets, Book I.* Peer International Corporation. Two tubas. 1981. $8.00. 24 pp. IV. Part I: B♭$_1$–d'; Part II: B♭$_1$–c'. Book one contains the first 13 of the 25 different melodies. All were originally composed for two flutes and recorders.

Most of the pieces are individual movements from larger compositions, but a few are entire suites. The movements vary in technical and range demands. Most are very tuneful and work exceptionally well for two tubas.

Singleton, Kenneth, arr. *Twenty-Five Baroque and Classical Duets, Book II.* Peer International Corporation. Two tubas. 1981. $8.00. 24 pp. IV. Part I: D–d'; Part II: C–d'. This volume contains the last 12 movements of the set of 25. Each piece is a different movement from a larger composition written for two flutes. Each movement presents different range and technical demands. These duets are fun to play and work quite well for two tubas.

Sparke, Philip, arr. *Sweet 'n' Low, Book 1.* Studio Music Company. One euphonium and one tuba. 1989. $8.00. 8 pp. III. Part I: d–f'; Part II: $B\flat_1$–$e\flat$. Eight duets: Barbara Allen; Loch Lomond; Silver Threads among the Gold; The Ash Grove; Drink to Me Only; When the Saints; Swing Low, Sweet Chariot; Early One Morning. All five books of these duets follow the same format. Each duet appears in the book twice, once in bass clef, once in treble clef. These same duets are also available for treble clef instruments in *Mix 'n' Match* by the same arranger and publisher. Consequently the tuba may be combined with any other bass or treble clef instrument to play these same melodies. These are not technically challenging and very appropriate for high school students.

Sparke, Philip, arr. *Sweet 'n' Low, Book 2.* Studio Music Company. One euphonium and one tuba. 1989. $8.00. 8 pp. III. Part I: $E\flat$–f'; Part II: $B\flat$–$e\flat$. Eight duets: The Blue Bells of Scotland; Marching through Georgia; All through the Night; Cockles and Mussels; Santa Lucia; Muss I Denn?; Ye Banks and Braes; The Camptown Races. The duets in this series may be played individually or grouped together as a suite. No technical problems.

Sparke, Philip, arr. *Sweet 'n' Low, Book 3: A First Christmas Selection.* Studio Music Company. One euphonium and one tuba. 1989. $8.00. 8 pp. III. Part I: d–f. Part II: $B\flat$–$e\flat$. Eight duets: Away in a Manger; Ding Dong, Merrily on High; The First Noel; God Rest Ye Merry, Gentlemen; Good King Wenceslas; Hark, the Herald Angels Sing; The Holly and the Ivy; Jingle Bells. Both parts have the opportunity to play the melody. Not technically difficult. Each movement lasts approximately one minute.

Sparke, Philip, arr. *Sweet 'n' Low, Book 4: A Second Christmas Selection.* Studio Music Company. One euphonium and one tuba. 1989. $8.00. 8 pp. II III. Part I: c–f'; Part II: $B\flat_1$–$e\flat$. Eight duets: Infant Holy; O Come, All Ye Faithful; Silent Night; O Little Town of Bethlehem; One in Royal David's City; We Three Kings of Orient Are; While Shepherds Watched; We Wish You a Merry Christmas. Both parts are of equal difficulty. The movements are short and are fun for young players.

Sparke, Philip, arr. *Sweet 'n' Low, Book 5: Caribbean Cocktail.* Studio Music Company. One euphonium and one tuba. 1989. $8.00. 8 pp. III. Part I: d–f'; Part II: $B\flat_1$–$e\flat$. Eight duets: Banana Boat Song; Mary Ann; The Mocking Bird; Mango Walk; Sloop John B; Sly Mongoose; Matilda; Jamaican Farewell. Both parts have opportunities to play the melody. No significant technical problems. These melodies are very fun to play and appropriate for young players.

Stamitz, Karl. *Duet for Tubas.* arr. Newell H. Long. The Brass Press. Two tubas. 1974. Out of Print. 2:00. III. Part I: G–c'; Part II: $B\flat_1$–$e\flat$. Works very well for high school students. The first part may be played on euphonium; treble and bass clef parts are provided for the first part.

Stevens, John. *Splinters. TUBA Journal.* Two tubas. 1982. $7.50. 1:00. IV. Part I: ($B\flat_1$)F–f'; Part II: F_1–f. A short rock duet with challenging rhythmic figures. The first part will need a strong tuba player because of the range. The score indicates that a euphonium may also be used for the first part. Rhythmically and dynamically fun but challenging to play. Written as part of the TUBA Gem Series and distributed in the *TUBA Journal,* Vol. 9, No. 4. It is available by purchasing this issue of the *TUBA Journal.* Recorded by John Stevens, "Power Classical," Mark Records, MRS 20699.

Stevens, John. *Suite for Two.* Brassworks Music, Gordon V. Thompson Music. Two tubas. 1985. $20.00. 6:00. IV. Part I: A_1–d'; Part II: F_1–c'. Four movements: Prelude; Scherzo; Song; Coda. The Scherzo and Coda are in a jazz style. Both parts have equal responsibility for the melody. Good writing for two tubas. Recorded by John Stevens, "Power Classical," Mark Records, MRS 20699.

Stoker, Richard. *Four Dialogues.* Hinrichsen Edition Limited. One euphonium and one tuba. 1966. Out of Print. 5:00. IV. Part I: A–d'; Part II: C–g. Four movements: Interview; Debate; Interrogation; Argument. The duet is playable with two tubas or a euphonium and tuba. The third movement is in 5/8 but is not very difficult technically.

Stouffer, Paul, arr. *Easy Classics for Two.* Kendor Music, Incorporated. Two tubas. 1993. $5.50. 5:30. II. Part I: G_1–d; Part II: G_1–d. Six movements: Andante (Mozart); Bouree (Telemann); Dance (Haydn); Andantino (Schubert); Minuet (Purcell); Imitation (Baton). No technical or range problems. Both parts have an opportunity to play the melody. Ideal for young players.

Stoutamire, Albert, and Kenneth Henderson, arr. *Duets for All.* CPP Belwin, Incorporated. Two tubas. 1973. $5.00. 24 pp. III–IV. Part I: D–c'; Part II: $A\flat_1$–c'. A collection of eighteen different melodies from famous composers ranging from baroque to contemporary styles. These same duets are arranged for a variety of instruments (i.e., two flutes, two trumpets, etc.) so you can have a tuba play the first part, and a trumpet or clarinet play the second part. Excellent material to challenge or reward those intermediate to advanced high school players. The higher parts are all written with 8vb for younger players.

Stroud, Richard. *Tubantiphon*. Seesaw Music Corporation. Two tubas. 1976. $12.00. 5:30. IV. Part I: G_1–b♭'; Part II: G_1–b♭. This is very complex rhythmically. There are multimetric sections, several sixteenth note runs, syncopations, and trills. Will require strong players.

Sweelinck, Jan P. *Polyphonic Rhyme No. 4*. arr. Randall Block. The Musical Evergreen. Two tubas. 1974. $2.50. 2:30. III. Part I: F–a♭; Part II: $B♭_1$–c. Duet is marked "Alla Breve" but there are no bar lines. Not technically difficult, but varying the tempo can make this playable by high school students or more challenging for college students.

Sweelinck, Jan P. *Lo Mi Son Giovinetta*. arr. Paul F. Hartin. Cellar Press. Two tubas. 1974. 3:30. III–IV. Part I: G–c'; Part II: C–f. The first part is easily performed on euphonium, making this very playable by high school students. Not rhythmically complex.

Sweelinck, Jan P. *Vioci du Gai Printemps*. arr. Paul F. Hartin. Cellar Press. Two tubas. 1974. 2:30. III–IV. Part I: B♭–c'; Part II: $B♭_1$–f. Two movements: Allegro; March-like. A lively duet featuring contrasting lyrical and technical sections. The first part may be performed on euphonium.

Szkutko, John. *Teddy Bears*. SZK Music. One euphonium and one tuba with piano. 1996. $20.00 (Australian). 5:00. III–IV. Part I: E♭–e♭''; Part II: $E♭_1$–f'. Challenging, yet lighthearted original composition which includes "Teddy Bear's Picnic" as its final theme. Includes complicated technical passages, large intervals, trills, and flutter tonguing.

Telemann, Georg Philipp. *Largo and Allegro from Sonata No. 4*. arr. Kenneth P. Drobnak. Tuba-Euphonium Press. Two tubas. 1997. $8.00. 5:00. II–III. Part I: C–d'; Part II: C–c'. Two movements: Largo; Allegro. For Deanna Swoboda. Straightforward arrangement in a contrapuntal texture. Both parts require technical dexterity.

Telemann, Georg Philipp. *Six Canonic Sonatas*. tr. Mike Forbes. Tuba-Euphonium Press. Two bass tubas. 1998. $20.00. 26 pp. III. Part I: F–f'; Part II: F–f'. Six sonatas of three movements each. Large collection of six of Telemann's three-movement sonatas in a contrapuntal texture. Both parts are challenging and are scored for bass tubas. This entire collection is also available transposed down a fourth for contrabass tubas. Individual movements can stand alone on a concert.

Telemann, Georg Philipp. *Six Canonic Sonatas*. tr. Mike Forbes. Tuba-Euphonium Press. Two contrabass tubas. 1998. $20.00. 26 pp. III. Part I: C–c'; Part II: C–c'. Six sonatas of three movements each. Large collection of six of Telemann's three-movement sonatas in a contrapuntal texture. Both parts are challenging and are scored for contrabass tubas. This entire collection is also available transposed up a fourth for bass tubas. Individual movements can stand alone on a concert.

Telemann, Georg Philipp. *Six Duets*. tr. Kenneth P. Drobnak. Tuba-Euphonium Press. Two tubas. 1997. $24.00. 50 pp. II–III. Part I: $B♭_1$–d'; Part II: $B♭_1$–d'. Six duets of four movements each. For Tucker Jolly. Large collection of six of Telemann's four-movement duets in a contrapuntal texture. Both parts are interesting and challenging. Individual movements can stand alone in a concert.

Telemann, Georg Philipp. *Six Sonatas for Two Tubas*. arr. Paul Erion. Lyric Brass Publishing. Two tubas. 2000. $25.00.

Telemann, George Phillip. *Canonic Sonata*. arr. Paul F. Hartin. Cellar Press. Two tubas. 1974. 5:00. IV. Part I: D–d'; Part II: D–d'. Three movements: Spirituoso; Larghetto; Allegro assai. Each movement is a pure canon. The first player begins and the second player, reading off the same music, starts at the beginning when the first player reaches the second measure. There is a fermata at the end of each movement for the two players to catch up to each other. Rhythmically very challenging.

Telemann, George Phillip. *Sonata, Op. 5, No. 4*. arr. Brent Dutton. Available from the arranger. Two tubas. 1973. $5.00. 6:00. IV. Part I: F–f'; Part II: F–f'. Three movements: Vivace; Piacevole; Presto. Typical baroque style. Both parts are technically difficult in some section, and the tessitura of both parts is high. Other instrumentation possibilities include one euphonium and one tuba, or two F tubas.

Telemann, George Phillip. *Three Chorale Preludes*. arr. Arthur Frackenpohl. Horizon Press. One euphonium and one tuba. 1991. $5.00. 6:30. IV. Part I: G–b♭'; Part II: G_1–a'. Three movements: Allein gott In Der Hoh Sei Ehr (All Glory Be to God on High); Vater Unser Im Himmelreich (Our Father in Heaven); Christ Lag In Todesbanden (Christ Lay in Death's Bonds). Both parts take turns playing the slow chorale theme then the faster accompaniment. No significant technical problems. Works well.

Thomas, T. Donley. *Bicinia, Op. 5*. Medici Music Press. One trombone (euphonium) and one tuba. 1986. $11.00. 10:00. IV. Part I: G♭–b'; Part II: A_1–a. Five movements: Pomposo, Quasi Marcia; Allegro con Fuoco; Andante Cantabile; Scherzo; Maestoso. Both parts are interesting and challenging. The movements are multimetric and rhythmically very interesting. The third movement is in a theme and variations form.

Thornton, Michael. *Two English Madrigals.* PP Music. Two tubas.

Tignor, Scott. *Boats and Ships.* Cimarron Music and Productions. One euphonium and one tuba with piano. 1997. $18.50. 10:00. III. Part I: C–g'; Part II: B♭$_1$–c'. Three movements: Tug Boat; Sail Boat; Battleship. Written for Kelly Diamond. Lively, original duet with piano accompaniment. The outer movements are upbeat and employ mixed meter while the inner movement features more lyrical passages. Each part is of equal difficulty. Euphonium part is also available in treble clef. First part may also be performed on tuba.

Torchinsky, Abe, arr. *Duets for Tuba.* Tuba-Euphonium Press. Two tubas. 1994. $15.00. 14 pp. II–III. Part I: C–f'; Part II: A♭$_1$–e♭'. Ten duets. Excerpted from *Ten Duos for Ophicleides* by Hartman and *The New Method for Bass Ophicleide* by F. Vobaron, published in the nineteenth century. These duets have been transposed down to modern tuba range. Individual movements can stand alone in a concert.

Torchinsky, Abe, arr. *Ten Duets.* Encore Music Publishers. Two tubas. 1988. $16.00. 29 pp. IV–V. Part I: D–f'; Part II: A$_1$–g'. Ten movements. These are transcriptions of ten duets for ophicleides by Hartman and F. Vobaron. The difficulty ranges from moderate to very difficult because of the varying technical and range demands.

Uber, David. *Acrobatics.* Tuba-Euphonium Press. Two euphoniums or two tubas and piano. 1994. $10.00. 3:30. II–III. Part I: D–a; Part II: G$_1$–f. For Thomas Juzwiak and Robert Kenny. May be performed with any combination of euphoniums and tubas. The form is ternary with compound meter in the outer sections and simple meter in the middle. Both parts are challenging and interesting.

Uber, David. *Double Portraits.* Brodt Music Company. One euphonium and one tuba. 1967. $4.00. 7:30. III–IV. Part I: B♭–g'; Part II: A♭$_1$–b'. Four movements: The City; Times Square; Twilight; The City Awakes. A programmatic description of life in a big city. Originally written for trombone and tuba, it is often performed with euphonium and tuba. Excellent recital piece. See same work under Tuba in Mixed Ensemble. Recorded by Michael Lind and Christer Torge, Trombone & Bass Tuba, BIS LP95.

Uber, David. *Duo Concertante for Two Tubas, Op. 97.* Almitra Music Company/Kendor Music, Incorporated. Two tubas. 1978. $6.00. 5:40. III–IV. Part I: C♭–c; Part II: G$_1$–g. Three movements: Poco Allegretto; Andante, Poco Agitato; Allegro Moderato. Works well for good high school or college players. The first movement is very rhythmic, the second movement is lyrical, and the third movement is a bouncy 6/8. Moderate technical demands on both players. Other instrumentation possibilities include euphonium and tuba, and bass trombone and tuba.

Uber, David. *Silent Streets for Euphonium and Tuba.* REBU Music Publications. One euphonium and one tuba. 1993. $5.00. 2:20.

Vaughan, Rodger, arr. *Five Carols.* Tuba-Euphonium Press. One euphonium and one tuba. 1997. $8.00. 7:00. III. Part I: D–g'; Part II: E♭$_1$–g. Five movements: Good King Wenceslas; Silent Night; The Three of Us; Jingle, Jingle; We Wish You a Merry Christmas. Humorous setting of five Christmas carols with unusual modulations, atypical cadences, and jazz elements. Tuba part calls briefly for multiphonics. Also reviewed in the Fall 2000 issue of the *TUBA Journal* (Vol. 28, No. 1).

Vaughan, Rodger. *Ronda's First Suite (Duet for Two Tubas).* Tuba-Euphonium Press. Two tubas. 1994. $8.00. 7:00. II. Part I: A$_1$–b♭'; Part II: A$_1$–c. Four movements: March; Song; Minuet; Galop. For Ronda Ellis. Fun original composition appropriate for younger performers. The melody is predominantly in the first part. Also reviewed in the Fall 2001 issue of the *ITEA Journal* (Vol. 29, No. 1).

Vaughan, Rodger. *Sonatina for Two Tubas.* Available from the composer. Two tubas. 1975. $5.00. 7:30. IV. Part I: G$_1$–g'; Part II: D$_1$–b♭. Three movements. For James Self. The first part would work well on F tuba because of the range. Very interesting writing and dynamic contrasts, especially in the last movement. A few meter changes in the last movement.

Wadowick, James L. *Two for the Tuba.* Concert Music Publishing Company. Two tubas and piano. 1969. 4:00. III. Part I: D♭–b♭; Part II: A♭$_1$–e♭. A very usable duet for high school players with piano accompaniment. In a traditional tonal style.

Warren, Christopher. *Four Etudes for Two Tubas.* Tuba-Euphonium Press. Two tubas. 1992. $10.00. 6:30. IV. Part I: E$_1$–d'; Part II: E♭$_1$–c'. Four movements: Bouncy; Moderate; Mysterious; Marcia. This composition is included at the end of the book *Twenty Etudes.* The movements reflect a very contemporary style. Both parts are technically challenging in some sections.

White, William. *Fantasia.* arr. David Baldwin. The Musical Evergreen. Two tubas. 1975. $2.50. 2:00. III–IV. Part I: C$_1$–a; Part II: A$_1$–a. Polyphonic texture with some syncopation. Playable by high school students at a slightly slower tempo. There are a few 32nd note patterns in the first part.

White, William. *Fantasia.* arr. Paul F. Hartin. Cellar Press. Two tubas. 1975. 2:00. Part I: F–d'; Part II: D–d'. This fantasia by White is transposed from the original in C to the key of F. Playable by high school or college students.

Wienhorst, R. *Two Mean Old Tubas (Intrada No. 6).* ECS Publishing. Two tubas. 1:00. II–III.

Part I: A–c'; Part II: C♯–c. Brief, original composition in 6/8 time with frequent use of the tritone interval. First part may also be performed on euphonium.

Wilder, Alec. *Suite for Two Tubas.* Margun Music Incorporated. Two tubas. 1971. $8.00. 14:00. IV. Part I: D_1–f♯; Part II: F_1–e♭'. Written at the request of Harvey Phillips. A collection of ten original duets with classic Wilder melodic and harmonic writing. These can be organized into small suites for performance. Large interval skips make this a challenging work.

Wilhelm, Rolf. *Ragtime. TUBA Journal.* Two tubas. 1986. $7.50. 1:45. IV. Part I: A–f'; Part II: $A♭_1$–a♭. A nice rag that features both parts equally. The first part has a high tessitura and may be played on an F tuba. Written as part of the TUBA Gem Series and distributed in the *TUBA Journal,* Vol. 13, No. 3. It is available by purchasing this issue of the *TUBA Journal.*

Wilson, David. *Duet for Two Tubas and Understanding Audience.* Cleveland Chamber Music Publishers (Philharmusica Corporation). Two tubas. 1973. 2:30. IV. Part I: F–d'; Part II: F_1–a. Four movements: Arrive; Volta; Song; Humoresque. Not difficult except for the second movement. Could be used by high school students with a euphonium on the first part. Traditional harmonies.

Wilson, Kenyon D. *Tubaku.* Available from the composer. Two tubas. 2002. 3:30. III. Part I: C_1–d'; Part II: C_1–g. To Ali Hajiev, Professor of Tuba, Baku Music Academy, Azerbaijan. Original composition with melodic material divided among both parts. Includes a large middle section in 11/8 meter, and the final, driving section is influenced by Azerbaijani scales and rhythms.

Wolfe, Gordon. *Canon in the Lydian Mode. TUBA Journal.* One euphonium and one tuba. 1983. $7.50. 1:30. III–IV. Part I: F♯–e♭'; Part II: B_1–a♭. The canon is written in treble clef. The tuba plays it as an E♭ instrument (read the notation as if it were in bass clef and add three flats) while the euphonium plays the canon as a B♭ transposing instrument. Not technically difficult. Written as part of the TUBA Gem series and distributed in the *TUBA Journal,* Vol. 10, No. 4. It is available by purchasing this issue of the *TUBA Journal.*

Zemp, Daniel. *Twenty Petits Duos.* Editions Billaudot. Two tubas. 1985. $14.50. 6:00. IV. Part I: A–f'; Part II: D–e'. Twenty movements. The tessitura of the second part is high. This could also be played by two F tubas. Not technically demanding until the last movement. The movements can be grouped together in any number or order. Both parts have equal responsibility for the melody.

Zettler, Richard. *Alt und Neu fur Zwei (Old and New for Two).* Elisabeth Thomi-Berg. One euphonium and one tuba. $8.50. 12:30. IV. Part I: (E♭)A–a'; Part II: F–f'. Six movements: I-Andante; Menuett; Allegretto Commodo; II-Tango Sentimental; Valse Vienneoise; Tarantella. Both parts have equal responsibility for the melody. No significant technical problems. The tessitura of the second part is high, but there are some *ossia* sections.

Zychowicz, James L. *Six Baroque Pieces for Two Tubas.* Shawnee Press, Incorporated. Two tubas. 1981. Out of Print. 8:00. III–IV. Part I: F–b♭; Part II: E_1–G. A transcription of six different baroque songs by six different composers. Range is not demanding and a few of the movements are playable by high school students. A couple of the movements are quite tuneful and work very well. They may be performed individually or grouped together in small suites.

Three Parts

Anderson, Eugene. *Fugue for Low Brass Trio.* Cimarron Music and Productions. Two euphoniums and one tuba. 1996. $7.00. 4:00. II–III. Part I: c–c''; Part II: G–g'; Part III: G_1–b♭. This fugue in traditional style is originally for horn, trombone, and tuba. Alternate euphonium parts in both treble and bass clef are available for the top two parts.

Anderson, Eugene. *Sea Chanty for Three.* Anderson's Arizona Originals. Three tubas. 1990. $5.00. 2:20. III–IV. Part I: D–g; Part II: $B♭_1$–e♭; Part III: G_1–B♭. Most of the melody is in the top part. There are moderate technical demands and traditional harmonies. Parts may be doubled for a large ensemble.

Bach, Johann Sebastian. *Air on a G String.* arr. Chris Hendricks. Hidalgo Music. Three tubas. 1994. $6.00. 4:00. III. Part I: C♯–d'; Part II: B_1–c'; Part III: C–d'. Closely scored arrangement of this well-known work. Each part performs the melody and the bass line at some point.

Bach, Johann Sebastian. *Come, Sweet Death.* arr. Eddie Sauter. *TUBA Journal.* One euphonium and two tubas. 1973. 1:30. III–IV. Part I: c–g'; Part II: G–c'; Part III: G_1–c'. To the memory of William J. Bell. Arranged May 26, 1973, at the conclusion of the first International Tuba Symposium Workshop. Some of the third part may be played down one octave to make it playable by high school students. Works great for large ensembles. A traditional closer for many Octubafest concerts and TUBA Conferences. Distributed in the first TUBA Newsletter, Fall, 1973. There is a misprint in the original score: the third line, third measure, second beat of the first tuba part should be a d♭, not d♮. This arrangement was given to TUBA by Eddie Sauter and may be freely duplicated by tubists everywhere and performed in the memory of William J. Bell. Recorded by the Tennessee Technological University

Tuba Ensemble, Golden Crest Records, CRS 4139; Garden State Tuba Ensemble, "Karl Megules," Recorded Publications Company, Z434471; and Harvey Phillips/TubaChristmas, Harvey Phillips Foundation, HPF NR1111.

Bach, Johann Sebastian. *Fugue a 3.* arr. Paul Schmidt. Heavy Metal Music. Two euphoniums and one tuba. 1994. $7.00. 3:15. II–III. Part I: B♭–g'; Part II: c–a♭'; Part III: D–b♭. This three-voice fugue is an effective teaching piece for contrapuntal technique. Ranges are appropriate for intermediate-level performers. Parts may be doubled for a large ensemble. Score is not provided.

Bach, Johann Sebastian. *Fugue in C Minor for Low Brass.* arr. R. Winston Morris. Ludwig Music Publishing Company. One euphonium and two tubas. 1992. 1:40. III–IV. Part I: d–b♭'; Part II: C–c'; Part III: G_1–d. Arranged for the Tennessee Technological University Tuba Ensemble. A transcription of a well-known Bach fugue. The style is meant to be smooth and lyrical. The first part is printed in bass and treble clef. The tessitura of the first part is high. Parts may be doubled for a large ensemble.

Bach, Johann Sebastian. *Fugue in F Major.* arr. Paul Schmidt. Heavy Metal Music. Two euphoniums and one tuba. 1991. $7.00. 2:20. IV. Part I: G–f'; Part II: D–f'; Part III: (F_1) C–f. Will require very clean playing in the low register of all parts. Works well for this instrumentation. No score available. Parts may be doubled for a large ensemble.

Bassano, Giovanni. *Fantasie a tre voci, Volume I.* arr. Michael Fischer. Tuba-Euphonium Press. One euphonium and two tubas or two euphoniums and one tuba. 2001. $20.00. 20 pp. II. Part I: A–g'; Part II: C–c'; Part III: F_1–f. Ten fantasias. Nice collection of ten pieces in a contrapuntal style, with most of them canonic in nature. Each piece is one to two minutes in duration and is appropriate for intermediate-level performers. Individual movements can stand alone on a concert. Parts may be doubled for a large ensemble. Also reviewed in the Spring 2002 issue of the *ITEA Journal* (Vol. 29, No. 3).

Bassano, Giovanni. *Fantasie a tre voci, Volume II.* arr. Michael Fischer. Tuba-Euphonium Press. One euphonium and two tubas or two euphoniums and one tuba. 2001. $20.00. 20 pp. II. Part I: A–g'; Part II: C–d'; Part III: G_1–g. Ten fantasias. Nice collection of ten pieces in a contrapuntal style, with most of them canonic in nature. Each piece is one to two minutes in duration and is appropriate for intermediate-level performers. Individual movements can stand alone on a concert. Parts may be doubled for a large ensemble. Also reviewed in the Spring 2002 issue of the *ITEA Journal* (Vol. 29, No. 3).

Bergenfeld, Nathan. *Chaconne.* Tempo Music Publications. Two euphoniums and one tuba. 1975. Out of Print. 4:00. III. Part I: f–f'; Part II: d–d♭'; Part III: G–a♭. A fairly easy composition with simple rhythms. Very appropriate for high school concerts or contests.

Bewley, Norlan. *Pinata.* Bewley Music Incorporated. Two euphoniums and one tuba. 1991. $10.00. 1:20. III–IV. Part I: d–f'; Part II: A–b♭; Part III: G_1–d. Could also be played with one euphonium and two tubas. A lot of syncopation, but not technically difficult. All three parts have an opportunity to play the melody. Parts may be doubled for a large ensemble.

Blair, Dean. *Serious Suite for Three Tubas, The.* T.A.P. Music. Three tubas. 1986. $6.00. 4:20. IV. Part I: c–d''; Part II: E_1–a; Part III: F_1–c'. Four movements: Moderato; March; Chant; Finale. Technically not very demanding, but the tessitura of the first part is high. The third part is higher and more challenging than the second part. There is no score available. Originally written and copyrighted by Blair in 1970.

Bruckner, Anton. *Aequale.* arr. Paul Schmidt. Heavy Metal Music. One euphonium and two tubas. $3.00. 1:20. III. Part I: f♯–f'; Part II: G–c'; Part III: G_1–g. A very slow chorale. The second part may be played by a euphonium or tuba. Players read from a score. Parts may be doubled for a large ensemble.

Butterfield, Don, arr. *Them Baces.* DB Publishing Company. One euphonium and two tubas. 1973. 4:00. IV. Part I: F–f'; Part II: F_1–b♭; Part III: F_1–g. Dedicated to the memory of William J. Bell. A cute arrangement that paraphrases "Them Basses," "Under the Double Eagle," "Bombasto," "When Yuba Plays the Rhumba," and "Tubby the Tuba." This was written to be performed at the first Annual New York Brass Conference for Scholarships, held February 3 and 4, 1973.

Byrd, William. *In Crystal Towers from Psalms, Songs, and Sonnets.* arr. Paul F. Hartin. Cellar Press. Three tubas. 1974. 3:00. III. Part I: G–c'; Part II: A–c'; Part III: G_1–d. Will work best for high school ensembles with a euphonium on the first part. Rhythms are not difficult and harmonic structure is consistent with baroque writings. Parts may be doubled for a large ensemble.

Carmody, Bill. *Disco Tuba. TUBA Journal.* One euphonium and two tubas. 1978. $7.50. 3:00. IV. Part I: B–a'; Part II: C_1–d'; Part III: A_1–e. Bass line is in a funk-like style. A few challenging rhythmic figures for all parts. There is a four-measure section that may be repeated for improvisation. Parts may be doubled for a large ensemble. Very fun to play. Written as part of the TUBA Gem Series and distributed in the *TUBA Journal,* Vol. 6, No. 1. It is available by purchasing this issue of the *TUBA Journal.*

Censhu, Jiro. *Doguu Sansai (Three Clay Puppets).* Available from the composer. Three tubas. 1986. $10.00. 4:00. IV. Part I: d–f'; Part II: G–e'; Part III: F_1–a. Three movements: Con moto;

Con grazia; Con spirito. For R. Winston Morris. The first and second parts could easily be played on euphonium. The last movement is very lively and interesting to play. Revised in 1988.

Corelli, Arcangelo. *Sonata Da Chiesa A Tre.* arr. Brent Dutton. Available from the arranger. Three tubas. 1970. $5.00. 5:30. IV. Part I: D–d'; Part II: D–d'; Part III: D–f. Four movements: Grave; Presto; Adagio; Allegro. The top two parts are the solo parts and the third part is the continuo. Requires light playing, works well.

Corelli, Arcangelo. *Sonata da Chiesa in E Minor, Op. 3, No. 7.* arr. Larry Pitts. The Brass Press. Three tubas. 1974. Out of Print. 5:30. III–IV. Part I: E–d'; Part II: E–d'; Part III: E_1–e. Four movements: Grave; Allegro; Adagio; Allegro. In the style of a typical baroque sonata. Excellent for teaching baroque style. Very playable by high school players, especially if the second movement is taken at a moderate tempo.

Corelli, Arcangelo. *Trio Sonata, Op. 1, No. 5.* arr. Paul Schmidt. Heavy Metal Music. Two euphoniums and one tuba. 1990. $7.00. 6:30. IV. Part I: c–g'; Part II: A–g'; Part III: C–g (c'). Four movements: Grave; Allegro; Adagio; Allegro. Parts one and two are the melody and part three is primarily the continuo part. The third movement alternates every few measures between 3/2 and 4/4 and a slow and fast tempo. No score available.

Corelli, Arcangelo. *Trio Sonata, Op. 1, No. 10.* arr. Paul Schmidt. Heavy Metal Music. Two euphoniums and one tuba. 1990. $7.00. 6:45. IV. Part I: E–a'; Part II: A–f'; Part III: A–a. Four movements: Grave; Allegro; Adagio; Allegro. The top two parts are more challenging than in the other Corelli sonatas arranged by Schmidt. The third part (continuo) is also more challenging, but very interesting to play. No score available.

Corelli, Arcangelo. *Trio Sonata, Op. 3, No. 2.* arr. Paul Schmidt. Heavy Metal Music. Two euphoniums and one tuba. 1990. $7.00. 7:00. IV. Part I: F–f'; Part II: G–d'; Part III: F_1–g. Four movements: Grave; Allegro; Adagio; Allegro. The first two parts have the polyphonic melody. There are moderate technical demands on all parts. No score available.

Corelli, Arcangelo. *Trio Sonata, Op. 3 No. 2.* arr. Todd Cranson. Cimarron Music and Productions. Two euphoniums and one tuba. 1997. $7.00. III. Part I: A–b♭'; Part II: A–b♭'; Part III: ($B♭_2$) F_1–d (a♭). Four movements: Grave; Allegro; Adagio; Allegro. Straightforward arrangement of this baroque work originally for two violins and continuo. The two top parts present the melodic material polyphonically, while the third performs the steady continuo. Also reviewed in the Winter 1999 issue of the *TUBA Journal* (Vol. 26, No. 2).

Corelli, Arcangelo. *Trio Sonata, Op. 3, No. 7.* arr. Paul Schmidt. Heavy Metal Music. Two euphoniums and one tuba. 1990. $7.00. 6:30. IV. Part I: B♭–f'; Part II: G–f'; Part III: G_1–g. Four movements: Grave; Allegro; Adagio; Allegro. The top two parts are polyphonic and very syncopated, but not technically challenging. The third part plays the continuo part. These arrangements work well for this instrumentation. No score available.

Couperin, Francois. *Les Ondes Rondeau.* arr. Jan Krzywicki. Theodore Presser Company. Two euphoniums and one tuba. 1984. $7.50. 2:30. IV. Part I: A–e'; Part II: F–f'; Part III: F_1–f. For Paul, Pete, and Hal. Originally written for harpsichord in 1713. This is a slow, flowing, lyrical melody in 6/8. No significant technical or range problems. This can also be performed by three tubas or one euphonium and two tubas.

Danburg, Russell. *Nocturne and Dance for Three Tubas.* Wingert-Jones Music, Incorporated. Three tubas. 1983. $6.00. 3:20. IV. Part I: G–c'; Part II: C_1–b♭; Part III: F_1–b♭. Two movements: Nocturne; Dance. All three parts have equal responsibility for the melody. The Dance is especially rhythmic and exciting. There is a brief cadenza in the Dance for the first part. Range of the parts is not high but the technical challenges will require three strong players.

Daughtry, Russ. *Pains of Esdraelon, The.* Tuba-Euphonium Ensemble Publications. One euphonium and two tubas. Out of Print. 3:30. IV. Part I: B–d'; Part II: G_1–a♭; Part III: G_1–d. Each part is featured as a soloist at different times during this mixed meter trio. Technically challenging, especially for the first and second parts.

Dutton, Brent. *Choral and Folksong.* Available from the composer. Two trombones (euphoniums), one tuba, and piano. 1968. $10.00. 6:00. IV–V. Part I: E–b'; Part II: F–g♯'; Part III: $B♭_2$–g♭'. Two movements: Choral; Folksong. Very contemporary in harmony and notation. Most of the second movement uses spatial notation for all parts. The piano part is very difficult. There are extreme range demands for the third part.

Dutton, Brent. *Troisieme Suite.* Seesaw Music Corporation. Three tubas. 1977. $17.00. 4:00. IV. Part I: A_1–e'; Part II: F_1–d'; Part III: $D♭_1$–f'. The third part has the largest range of the three, although all three are equal in technical difficulty. Some special techniques are required of all players, including multiphonics and improvisation, and all parts will require a mute. Challenging to play.

Elliott, John. *I Do, I Undo, I Redo.* Tuba-Euphonium Press. Three tubas and percussion. 2002. $20.00. III–IV. Part I: $B♭_1$–g'; Part II: A_1–e'; Part III: C_1–b. The title comes from an abstract steel sculpture by Louise Bourgeois, and the form of the piece is a series of contrasting sections connected by promenades. Modern techniques are employed, including multiphonics, flutter tonguing, and muted tubas. It is scored for two bass tubas and one contrabass tuba, though the first part may work on euphonium. The one percussion part includes tam-tam, suspended symbol, snare drum, mart tree, hand bongos, and temple bowls. Also reviewed in the Summer 2004 issue of the *ITEA Journal* (Vol. 31, No. 4).

Garbáge, Pierre. *Chaser #1.* James Garrett. Two euphoniums and one tuba. 1972. $10.00. 1:20. IV. Part I: a–f'; Part II: d–d'; Part III: B_1–c (b). Written for R. Winston Morris and the Tennessee Technological University Tuba Ensemble. A highly syncopated melody at a "hoedown" tempo. This could also be performed with one euphonium and two tubas. Fun to play. Pierre Garbáge says of this composition, "Heavy in every way but one." Parts may be doubled for a large ensemble.

Garrett, James, arr. *Red River Valley.* James Garrett. One euphonium and two tubas. 1971. $5.00. 1:00. I–II. Part I: B♭–c'; Part II: G–e♭; Part III: $B♭_1$–c. A simple arrangement of this American folk song. The third part has the melody for half of the song. No technical or range problems. Ideal for very young players. Parts may be doubled for a large ensemble.

Garrett, James A., arr. *Clementine.* James Garrett. One euphonium and two tubas. 1971. $5.00. 1:00. II–III. Part I: B♭–c'; Part II: F–e♭; Part III: $B♭_1$–B♭. A very usable arrangement for junior high school students. The second part could be played on euphonium or tuba. Parts may be doubled for a large ensemble.

Garrett, James A., arr. *Im Wald und duf der Heide.* James Garrett. Two euphoniums and one tuba. 1974. $5.00. 1:00. III. Part I: d–f'; Part II: B♭–d; Part III: $B♭_1$–f. Very traditional harmonies. Easily playable by young students. Could also be performed with one euphonium and two tubas. Parts may be doubled for a large ensemble.

Garrett, James A., arr. *I've Been Working on the Railroad.* James Garrett. One euphonium and two tubas. 1971. $5.00. 1:00. II–III. Part I: B♭–a♭; Part II: G–g; Part III: $B♭_1$–B♭. Could also be played with two euphoniums and one tuba or by three tubas. No technical or range problems. Parts may be doubled for a large ensemble.

Geminiani, Francesco. *Concerto Grosso.* arr. R. Winston Morris. Shawnee Press, Incorporated. Two euphoniums and one tuba. 1974. $12.50. 6:30. III–IV. Part I: c–a'; Part II: A–a'; Part III: G_1–e (g). Three movements: Moderato; Adagio; Allegro. Written for the Tennessee Technological University Tuba Ensemble. Both euphonium parts are printed in bass and treble clef. Easily playable by high school students if the euphonium players have a good high a (a'). The arrangement is not muddy at all and works very well. Parts may be doubled for a large ensemble.

Gershenfeld, Mitchell, arr. *Two English Madrigals.* Medici Music Press. Three tubas. 1983. $5.00. 4:30. III–IV. Part I: F♯–a; Part II: E–a; Part III: G_1–c. Two movements: Weep, Oh Mine Eyes; In the Merry Month of May. Two short madrigals originally by John Wilbye and Henry Youll, respectively. The texture is very polyphonic, but not technically challenging. Works well. Parts may be doubled for a large ensemble.

Gessner, John M. *Two Pieces for Three Tubas.* Three tubas. 1969. 5:00. IV. Part I: F♯–f♯; Part II: E–b; Part III: $F♯_1$–f♯. Two movements: Slowly, Very fast. First part has a high tessitura and may require an F tuba. Many complex rhythms; will require three strong players.

Gilfish, Trident (Gigger). *Crawfish Crawl.* arr. James Garrett. Cimarron Music and Productions. Two euphoniums and one tuba. 1996. $9.00. 5:00. III. Part I: F♯–b♭'; Part II: A♭–e♭'; Part III: $B♭_1$–f. Lighthearted original composition by James Garrett written under one of his pseudonyms. The piece is in an easy ragtime feel, and the melodic material is divided among all three voices. The frequent use of accidentals may challenge young performers. Euphonium parts also available in treble clef.

Gillam, Russell C. *Innocuous Incident.* Three tubas. 1971. 4:00. III. Part I: G–d'; Part II: C–b♭; Part III: G_1–a. The first part can be performed by a euphonium and thus easily performed by high school ensembles.

Hancock, Thomas M., arr. *Tuba Carols.* Ludwig Music Publishing Company. One euphonium and two tubas. 1987. $5.00. 14 pp. III–IV. Part I: B♭–c'; Part II: F–b; Part III: F_1–c. A collection of twelve familiar Christmas carols. Music is printed as a score with no separate parts. Because of the ranges other possible instrumentations are three tubas, or two euphoniums and one tuba. The first and second parts are printed in treble clef at the end of the book. Some of these work really well. Parts may be doubled for a large ensemble.

Handel, George Frederic. *Sonata No. 4.* arr. George R. Belden and Donald C. Little. Great Works Publishing, Incorporated. Two euphoniums and one tuba. 1992. $8.00. 6:00. IV. Part I: c–b♭'; Part II: c–c''; Part III: F_1–c'. Four movements: Adagio; Allegro; Largo; Allegro. In a trio sonata format with the top two parts playing the solo parts and the tuba playing the continuo. The tessitura of both euphonium parts is high. Technically challenging for all parts.

Hartin, Paul F., arr. *A Suite of Elizabethan Madrigals.* Cellar Press. 1974. 4:30. III. Part I: B♭–c'; Part II: B♭–c'; Part III: A_1–c. Four movements: O Sleep, Fond Fancy; Ha Ha, This World Doth Pass; Come Sirrah Jack, Ho!; The Nightingale. The first and second parts can both be played on euphonium, making this very playable by a high school ensemble. Parts may be doubled for a large ensemble.

Hastings, Ross. *Little Madrigal for Big Horns.* Southern Music Company. One euphonium and two tubas. 1972. Out of Print. 2:30. III–IV. Part I: c–g'; Part II: G–c'; Part III: F_1–d♭. Nice melodic madrigal; not very polyphonic. Frequent meter changes, but the quarter note remains constant. Very tuneful: a lot of music in this short composition. Parts may be doubled for a large ensemble. Recorded by the University of Miami Tuba Ensemble, Miami United Tuba Ensemble Society, 14568.

Heger, Owe, arr. *Leichte Ragtime-Trios (Easy Ragtime Trios).* Noetzel Edition (C. F. Peters). Two euphoniums and one tuba. 1988. $15.95. 18:00. IV. Part I: F–g'; Part II: F–g'; Part III: F–d'. Five movements: The Easy Winners; The Entertainer; Dickie's Rag; The Strenuous Life; The Sycamore. Dedicated to Wilhelm Ebeling. A collection of one original and four Joplin rags. A lot of syncopation, with some technical challenges in all three parts. The movements are complete rags and may be played alone or grouped together in small numbers. Fun to play.

Heger, Owe, arr. *Leichte Volkslieder-Trios 6 (Easy Folksong Trios).* Noetzel Edition (C. F. Peters). Three tubas. 1988. $14.50. 8:30. IV. Part I: F–d'; Part II: F–d'; Part III: F–d'. Six movements: Guten Abend, Gute Nacht; Bruder Jaiob; Weißt du, Wieviel Sternlein Stehen; Guter Mond, du Stehst so Stille; Dat du min Leevsten büst; Es Warren Zwei Königskinder. Dedicated to Volker Kähler and Gerke Swyter. These are arranged for any three bass clef instruments. The movements are short and are not technically challenging. The same melodies are arranged for three trumpets or three horns, thus allowing combinations of any three brass instruments.

Henderson, Kenneth, and Albert Stoutamire, arr. *Trios for All.* CPP Belwin, Incorporated. Two euphoniums and one tuba. 1974. $5.00. 21 pp. II–III. Part I: B♭–g'; Part II: A–e♭'; Part III: F_1–e. A collection of seventeen different compositions including works by Purcell, Mozart, Shostakovich, Grieg, and thirteen other notable composers. Some of these work very well for junior high as well as high school players. Parts may be doubled for a large ensemble.

Hewitt, Harry. *Three Preludes for Three Tubas, Op. 376C.* Available from the composer. Three tubas. 1968. $4.00. 7:00. IV. Part I: F_1–d'; Part II: D_1–b; Part III: F_1–d. Three movements. Technical challenges are primarily in the first and second parts. Very dissonant harmonies at times. Performers play from a score.

Hilton, John. *Ten Ayres or FaLa's for 3.* arr. Daniel Helman, ed. Paul Schmidt. Heavy Metal Music. Two euphoniums and one tuba. 1995. $7.00. Part I: A–g'; Part II: A–g'; Part III: C–a. Ten movements, including Now Is the Summer Springing; Love Laid His Yoke upon Me; Your Lovers That Have Loved Astray; My Mistress Frowns When She Should Play. Based on *Ballets,* first published in 1627. All are in ternary form, and the first two performers are asked to swap parts on the repeat of the first section. Also reviewed in the Fall 1998 issue of the *TUBA Journal* (Vol. 26, No. 1).

Hounsell, Clare. *A Low-Down Trio.* PEL Music Publications. $8.50.

Isbell, Thomas, arr. *Dona Nobis Pacem.* The Brass Press. One euphonium and two tubas. 1969. $3.50. 3:00. II–III. Part I: c–d'; Part II: C–d; Part III: C–d. Written for R. Winston Morris and the Tennessee Technological University Tuba Ensemble. The first part may be played by a tuba or euphonium. The second and third parts are relatively easy, with no technical or range problems. Excellent piece for young students, or any players wanting to work on lyrical playing. Parts may be doubled for a large ensemble.

Israel, Brian. *Tower Music.* Tritone Press. Two euphoniums and one tuba. 1983. $3.50. 4:17. III–IV. Part I: G–d'; Part II: F♯–b; Part III: G_1–g♭. Three movements: Praeludium; Fugua; Carol. To Jack Gallagher. The second part is not that high and could be performed on tuba. The Fugua and Carol are lively and playable by good high school players. Parts may be doubled for a large ensemble.

Jacobson, I. D. *Three Temperaments for Tubas.* Israel Composers League. Three tubas. 1963. Out of Print. 3:30. III–IV. Part I: G–f'; Part II: G_1–a. Part III: C–d'. Three movements. The tessitura of the top part is high and could be played on euphonium or F tuba. No technical demands; very traditional harmonies. Parts may be doubled for a large ensemble.

Jager, Robert. *Variations on a Motive by Wagner.* Elkan-Vogel, Incorporated. One euphonium and two tubas. 1976. $15.00. 5:00. IV. Part I: G–b♭'; Part II: D♯–d'; Part III: $D\sharp_1$–f. Composed for Harvey Phillips, Earle Louder, and R. Winston Morris. A single movement with contrasting sections. The last section is particularly challenging technically, but worth the effort.

Jones, Roger. *Suite for Three Tubas.* Available from the composer. Three tubas. 1992. $15.00. 5.00. IV. Part I: F♯–d'; Part II: $B\flat_1$–g; Part III: F_1–e. Three movements: Moderately Fast and with a Steady Pulse; Very Slow; Fast. All three parts are challenging and have responsibility for the melody. The melodies are often syncopated but are tuneful and work very well.

Jones, Roger. *Switched-Down Bach.* Available from the composer. One euphonium and two tubas. 1992. $5.00. 2:00. IV. Part I: A♭–f; Part II: $A\flat_1$–a; Part III: $A\flat_1$–d♭. Written in a jazz style. All three parts play the melody at different times. The melody is syncopated and will require a good jazz feel of all players. The top part may also be played by a tuba. Parts may be doubled for a large ensemble.

Jones, Roger. *Three Tubas Two.* Available from the composer. Three tubas. 1971. $6.00. 3:30. III–IV.

Part I: C–f (c'); Part II: $A\flat_1$–f; Part III: $A\flat_1$–c. The melody is primarily in the first and second parts. The melody has some syncopations but contains very traditional harmonies. The top part may be played on euphonium, making this very playable by high school students.

Jones, Roger. *Toe Tapping Tuba Tune.* Available from the composer. Three tubas. 1993. $5.00. 2:30. IV. Part I: $A\flat_1$–a♭; Part II: $B\flat_1$–f; Part III: F_1–d. The melody is very syncopated and multimetric. No significant technical problems. Parts may be doubled for a large ensemble.

Jones, Roger. *Trio for Tubas.* Available from the composer. One euphonium and two tubas. 1970. $10.00. 4:20. IV. Part I: G–a'; Part II: F–d'; Part III: C–c'. Two movements: Slow but Moving; Lively. The second movement is multimetric and rhythmically challenging. All three parts are interesting to play.

Joyful Euphonium Tuba Ensemble, Book 1. Kyodo Music. Two euphoniums and one tuba. ¥2100. 63 pp. III. Part I: A–a♭'; Part II: F–f'; Part III: C♯–a. Twenty-eight movements: Eine Kleine Nacht Musick, Second and Third Movement by Mozart; Ases Tod from *Peer Gynt* by Grieg; In the Hall of the Mountain King by Grieg; Gavotte by Gossec; Theme and Variations from *Ah, Vous dirais-je, maman* by Mozart; Csikos Post by Necke; March from *Nutcracker* by Tchaikovsky; Serenade for Strings, First Movement by Tchaikovsky; Scene from *Swan Lake* by Tchaikovsky; Serenade by Schubert; Unfinished Symphony by Schubert; Overture from the *Barber of Seville* by Rossini; Brindisi from *La Traviata* by Verdi; Cantata No. 147 by J. S. Bach; Etude No. 77 by Beyer; Etude No. 78 by Beyer; Farandole from *L'Arlesienne* by Bizet; Humoreske by Dvorak; Pomp and Circumstance No. 1 by Elgar; Scheherazade, Third Movement by Rimsky-Korsakov; Emperor Waltz by Strauss; Symphony No. 9, Fourth Movement by Dvorák; Stars and Stripes Forever by Sousa; Great Gate of Kiev from *Pictures at an Exhibition* by Mussorgsky; An der Schonen Blauen Donau by Strauss; Beautiful Dreamer by Foster; Theme from Judas Maccabeus by Handel. Large collection of popular arrangements. The majority are scored for trio, though eleven are scored for duet.

Joyful Euphonium Tuba Ensemble, Book 2. Kyodo Music. Two euphoniums and one tuba. ¥2100. 63 pp. III. Part I: A–a'; Part II: G–a'; Part III: E♭–b. Seventeen movements: Pavane for a Dead Infant by Ravel; Jupiter from *The Planets* by Holst; Prelude to Die Meistersinger by Wagner; Symphony No. 40, First and Third Movements by Mozart; Symphony No. 5, Four Movements by Beethoven; March Lorraine by Ganne; Night on Bald Mountain by Mussorgsky; The Fairest of the Fair March by Sousa; Overture to La Forza del Destino by Verdi; Danza dell'ore from *La Gioconda* by Ponchielli; Bolero by Ravel; Overture to Die fledermaus by Strauss; Aragonaise from *Carmen* by Bizet. Large collection of popular arrangements.

Joyful Euphonium Tuba Ensemble, Book 3. Kyodo Music. Two euphoniums and one tuba. ¥2100. 62 pp. III. Part I: G–a'; Part II: D–f'; Part III: B_1–a. Nineteen movements: Lullaby by Mozart; Berceuse from *Jocelyn* by Godard; Blue Bells of Scotland; Song of Sorveig by Grieg; Toreador Song from *Carmen* by Bizet; Slavic Dance No. 10 by Dvorak; Turkish March by Beethoven; Carry Me Back to Old Virginny by Brand; La Paloma by Yradier; Washington Post March by Sousa; Symphony No. 6, All Four Movements by Tchaikovsky; Ich Liebe Dich by Grieg; Panis Angelicus by Frank; Sentimental Waltz by Tchaikovsky; Overture to the Light Calvary; Last Rose of Summer. Large collection of popular arrangements. The majority are scored for trio, though one is scored for duet.

Joyful Euphonium Tuba Ensemble, Book 4. Kyodo Music. Two euphoniums and one tuba. ¥2100. 63 pp. III. Part I: F–a'; Part II: D–a'; Part III: C–a. Twenty-two movements: Salut d'Amour by Elgar; The Entertainer by Joplin; Andante Cantabile by Tchaikovsky; Pavane by Faure; Emperor String Quartet, Second Movement by Haydn; Waltz from *Coppelia* by Delibes; Overture from *Nutcracker* by Tchaikovsky; Clair de Lune by Debussy; Slavic March by Tchaikovsky; Minute from *L'Arlesienne* by Bizet; Hungarian Dance No. 5 by Brahms; Symphony No. 3, Third Movement by Brahms; Trumpet Voluntary by Clarke; Gymnopedie No. 1 by Satie; Als die Alle Mutter by Dvorak; Polonase from *Orchestral Suite No. 2* by J. S. Bach; Minuet from *Orchestral Suite No. 2* by J. S. Bach; Canon by Pachebel; Concerto for flute and Harp, Second Movement by Mozart; Piano Concerto No. 21 by Mozart; Etude No. 3 in E Major by Chopin. Large collection of popular arrangements. The majority are scored for trio, though six are scored for duet.

Joyful Euphonium Tuba Ensemble, Book 5. Kyodo Music. Two euphoniums and one tuba. ¥2100. 63 pp. III. Part I: G–a'; Part II: G–g'; Part III: C–e'. Eighteen movements: Adagio by Albinoni; Overture from *Tanhauser* by Wagner; Hallelujah Chorus by Handel; Egmont Overture by Beethoven; Prelude No. 15 by Chopin; Symphony No. 101, Second Movement by Haydn; Spring from *The Four Seasons;* Summer from *The Four Seasons;* Autumn from *The Four Seasons;* Winter from *The Four Seasons;* Aufforderung zum Tanz by Weber; Concerto for Two Violins, First Movement by J. S. Bach; Romance in F Major by Beethoven; The Moldau by Smetana; Nocturne from *String Quartet No. 2* by Borodin; Waltz from *Serenade for Strings* by Tchaikovsky; Waltz of the Flowers from *Nutcracker* by Tchaikovsky; Hungarian Rhapsody No. 2 by

Liszt. Large collection of popular arrangements. The majority are scored for trio, though four are scored for duet.

Joyful Euphonium Tuba Ensemble, Book 6. Kyodo Music. Two euphoniums and one tuba. ¥2100. 30 pp. III. Part I: A–a♭'; Part II: F♯–g'; Part III: C–a. Six movements: Schafe konnen Sicher Weiden from *Cantata,* BWV 208 by J. S. Bach; Dance of the Sugar Plum Fairy from *Nutcracker* by Tchaikovsky; Amaryllis, a French Folksong; Finale from *Carmen Suite No. 1* by Bizet; Waltz from *Swan Lake* by Tchaikovsky; Lacrimosa from *Requiem* by Mozart. Large collection of popular arrangements.

Kerll, J. C. *Canzone.* arr. Newell H. Long. The Brass Press. One euphonium and two tubas. 1974. $3.50. 2:00. III. Part I: A–e'; Part II: A_1–f; Part III: A_1–f. Imitative counterpoint that works very well for euphoniums and tubas. No real technical problems, but players will need to count carefully. Parts may be doubled.

Kinyon, John, arr. *Fun for Band.* Alfred Publishing Company. 1972. Out of Print. 16 pp. I–II. Part I: A♭–f; Part II: A♭–f; Part III: A♭–f. A collection of easy duets and trios. Works great for tubists who have only been playing one or two years.

Kodály, Zoltan. *Lament.* arr. Skip Gray. Shawnee Press, Incorporated. One euphonium and two tubas. 1980. $6.95. 2:30. III–IV. Part I: c♭–c"; Part II: C–f; Part III: F_1–B♭. The first part is written in tenor clef in the score although the part is in bass clef. Parts are technically easy but the range of the first part makes this difficult for the euphonium. This arrangement works very well. Parts may be doubled for a large ensemble.

Larrick, Geary. *Trio for Tubas.* Available from the composer. Three Tubas. 1992. $12.00. 4:00. III. Part I: C–f♯; Part II: C–e; Part III: $B♭_1$–f♯. Three movements: Recitative; Song; March. No range or technical problems. The texture is very thin; it is rare for even two parts to play at the same time.

Lasso, Orlando Di. *Motet "Cantate Domino."* arr. William Schmidt. Western International Music, Inc. Two euphoniums and one tuba. 1995. $5.00. 2:00. II. Part I: B–d'; Part II: D–f; Part III: G_1–A. This arrangement of the Renaissance motet is scored in A minor. Second part may also be performed on tuba. Independence of parts is the most challenging element.

Lindenfeld, Harris. *Inflation.* Tritone Press. Three tubas. 1975. $6.00. 8:30. IV. Part I: A_1–d'; Part II: $A♭_1$–c♯'; Part III: G_1–g. Three movements: Moderately and smoothly; Very slowly; Fast and light. The technical demands are moderate but there are many ensemble challenges, especially in the multimetric third movement. The piece is atonal and thus quite dissonant.

Lupo, Thomas. *Fantasia.* arr. David Baldwin. The Musical Evergreen. Three tubas. 1974. $3.50. 2:00. IV. Part I: C–a; Part II: B–b; Part III: A_1–a. Very contrapuntal and syncopated in nature. While range is not a problem for high school players, the piece is rhythmically and technically challenging.

Lupo, Thomas. *Fantasia.* arr. Paul F. Hartin. Cellar Press. Three tubas. 1975. 2:00. IV. Part I: F–d'; Part II: E–e'; Part III: D_1–d. Same as the Baldwin arrangement, just transposed up a fourth to the key of C.

Marcellus, John, arr. *Trios for Brass, Volume I, Advanced.* CPP Belwin, Incorporated. Two euphoniums and one tuba. 1986. $6.50. 15 pp. III–IV. Part I: F–b♭'; Part II: A–g'; Part III: $A♭_1$–f. A collection of five melodies from the baroque and classical style periods. As with the other books in this series, a treble clef book is available, allowing any combination of brass instruments to play these trios. The tessitura of the top part is much higher than in the other books in this series, and there are more technical challenges. Parts may be doubled for a large ensemble.

Marcellus, John, arr. *Trios for Brass, Volume I, Easy-Intermediate.* CPP Belwin, Incorporated. Two euphoniums and one tuba. 1986. $6.50. 15 pp. II–III. Part I: B♭–g'; Part II: B♭–f'; Part III: G_1–f. A collection of eight melodies from the Renaissance, baroque, and classical periods. Very appropriate for young players. There is a treble clef book available, so any combination of brass instruments is possible. Parts may be doubled for a large ensemble.

Marcellus, John, arr. *Trios for Brass, Volume I, Intermediate.* CPP Belwin, Incorporated. Two euphoniums and one tuba. 1986. $6.50. 15 pp. III. Part I: F–a'; Part II: F–e'; Part III: A_1–f. A collection of eight melodies from the baroque and classical periods. These melodies are more polyphonic and slightly more challenging than the Easy-Intermediate arrangements. Parts may be doubled for a large ensemble.

McAdams, Charles A., arr. *Swing Low, Sweet Chariot.* Encore Music Publishers. One euphonium and two tubas. 1991. $8.50. 3:00. III–IV. Part I: f–g'; Part II: B♭–b♭'; Part III: $B♭_1$–c. The tubas begin this familiar melody in a slow lyrical fashion. The middle section is an up tempo swing treatment of the melody with the slow lyrical section returning at the end. Drum set may be added. Works well and is a good introduction to teaching swing style. Parts may be doubled for a large ensemble.

McCurdy, Gary. *Chorale.* TMC Publications. Two euphoniums and one tuba. 1973. Out of Print. 2:00. III. Part I: B♭–d'; Part II: A–c'; Part III: C–d. The top part could also be played by a tuba. The chorale is in a very traditional style with the melody primarily in the top part. Parts may be doubled for a large ensemble.

McCurdy, Gary. *Demon Dance.* TMC Publications. Three tubas. 1971. Out of Print. 2:00. III. Part I: B♭–d'; Part II: D–a; Part III: F_1–A.

McCurdy, Gary. *Five Hundred Pound Polka.* TMC Publications. Three tubas with piano. 1971. Out of Print. 2:00. II–III. Part I: A–g; Part II: E–d; Part III: C–d.

McCurdy, Gary. *Three Dances for Three Tubas.* TMC Publications. Three tubas. 1971. Out of Print. 4:00. IV. Part I: G♭–d'; Part II: E–b♭; Part III: F_1–d. Three movements: Minuet; Two-Step; Tango.

Milford, Gene, arr. *Mountain Songs.* Great Works Publishing, Inc. Two euphoniums and one tuba. 1995. $7.00. 2:30. I–II. Part I: B♭–e♭'; Part II: B♭–e♭'; Part III: $A♭_1$–c. Two movements: Little Mohee; Billy Boy. An arrangement of two folk songs intended for beginning to intermediate players. Top two parts are also available in treble clef. Parts may be doubled for a large ensemble.

Morita, Kazuhiro, arr. *Euphonium and Tuba: Ensemble Works for the First Time.* Yamaha Kyohan Company Limited. Two euphoniums and one tuba. 1983. $8.00. 20 pp. III–IV. Part I: B♭–g'; Part II: A–f'; Part III: G_1–d. A collection of seven duets (two euphoniums) and seven trios (two euphoniums and one tuba). Three of the duets have an optional third part (tuba), so these also are notated as three-part compositions. All but one of the compositions are by Western composers including Grieg, Mussorgsky, Brahms, Bach, and Beethoven. The arrangements are short and are of moderate technical difficulty.

Mozart, Wolfgang Amadeus. *Allegro.* arr. Stephen Shoop. Stephen Shoop Music Publications. One euphonium and two tubas. 1997. $5.50. 1:15. II. Part I: A–b♭; Part II: D–e♭; Part III: $A♭_1$–c. Originally for piano, this trio consists predominantly of eighth notes performed in a detached style. Parts may be doubled for a large ensemble. The top voice may be also performed on tuba.

Mozart, Wolfgang Amadeus. *Divertimento No. 1, K. 229.* arr. Paul Schmidt. Heavy Metal Music. Two euphoniums and one tuba. 1992. $5.00. 4:30. IV. Part I: c–f'; Part II: F–e'; Part III: $B♭_1$–f. This is the Allegro movement from this Divertimento. A workout for all three parts, but fun to play. No score available.

Mueller, Frederick A. *Tuba Trio.* Available from the composer. One euphonium and two tubas. 1973. $12.00. 8:30. IV. Part I: E–a♭'; Part II: A_1–e♭'; Part III: E_1–d♭'. Five movements: Adagio; Presto-staccato; Lament; Cadenca; Perpetuum mobile. To Earle, David, and Winston, in memory of William J. Bell. Very interesting trio. Parts are challenging to put together, with a few twentieth-century techniques and very modern harmonies.

Murzin, V. *Impromptu.* The Musical Evergreen. Two trombones (euphoniums) and one tuba. 1975. $7.50. 1:20. III–IV. Part I: g–a'; Part II: f–e; Part III: A–f. The first two parts may be played on euphonium as well as trombone. The top two parts are written in tenor clef. The melody is primarily in the third part.

Nelhybel, Vaclav. *Ludus for Three Tubas.* E. C. Kerby Limited (Hal Leonard). Three tubas. 1975. $10.00. 9:00. V. Part I: G_1–g'; Part II: G_1–g'; Part III: $F♯_1$–g'. Three movements. Commissioned by Rudolf Meinl Tubas and dedicated to the First International Tuba Symposium, 1973. First performed by Daniel Perantoni, Robert Tucci, and J. Lesley Varner. Extensive technical and range demands on all parts. There are frequent and extreme dynamic contrasts, complex rhythms, large skips, and a contemporary harmonic structure. This work is very demanding but is also an exciting piece of music.

Olsen, Ole. *Fanitul.* arr. L. A. Rauchut. KIWI Music Publishing. Two euphoniums and one tuba. Out of Print. 2:00. IV. Part I: c–a'; Part II: G♯–e'; Part III: A_1–c'. The technical demands are greatest on the two euphonium parts. Brief high sections of the tuba part may be played an octave lower if necessary.

O'Reilly, J., and J. Kinyon, arr. *Yamaha Band Ensembles, Tuba/Book 1.* Alfred Publishing Company Incorporated. Three tubas with optional piano. 1990. $4.50. 23 pp. I–II. Part I: $B♭_1$–c; Part II: A_1–A♭; Part III: A_1–A♭. A collection of seventeen different American folk and Christmas songs. These correlate with the Yamaha Band Student Method Book Series. Other arrangements of these same melodies for several different groups of instruments may be purchased separately. The top line is always the melody, the second line the harmony, and the third line an accompaniment. Very appropriate for beginning and young players.

O'Reilly, J., and J. Kinyon, arr. *Yamaha Band Ensembles, Tuba/Book 2.* Alfred Music Publishing Company Incorporated. Three tubas with optional piano. 1990. $4.50. 23 pp. II. Part I: $B♭_1$–e♭; Part II: $A♭_1$–B♭; Part III: G_1–c. A collection of fourteen different melodies arranged for three tubas and correlating with Book 2 of the Yamaha Band Student. No range or technical problems.

O'Reilly, J., and J. Kinyon, arr. *Yamaha Band Ensembles, Tuba/Book 3.* Alfred Publishing Company Incorporated. Three tubas with optional piano. 1990. $4.50. 23 pp. II–III. Part I: A_1–e♭; Part II: A_1–c; Part III: A_1–c. A collection of thirteen different melodies arranged to correlate with the Yamaha Band Student Method Book. Though they can get muddy at times, these are great for giving young tuba players a chance to play melodies and harmonies.

Potter, David. *Aria and Rondo.* Southern Music Company. Two euphoniums and one tuba. 1983. $5.95. 4:30. IV. Part I: c♯–b'; Part II: c♯–g'; Part III: G_1–e♭'. Two movements: Aria; Rondo. For Susan Smith, Dan Satterwhite, and a friend. The Rondo is in mixed meter with alternating technical and lyrical sections. Brief sections of the tuba part may be played an octave lower if necessary as the tessitura of the tuba part is a bit high.

Presser, William. *Suite for Three Tubas.* Tenuto Publications. Three tubas. 1968. $6.00. 8:00. III–IV. Part I: A_1–a; Part II: A_1–a♭; Part III: E_1–d. Three movements: Allegretto; Andante; Allegro. Although individual parts are not difficult, there are some complicated rhythmic figures in the first movement that can cause ensemble problems. Good program material.

Purcell, Henry. *Canon on a Ground Bass.* arr. Skip Gray. Shawnee Press, Incorporated. One euphonium and two tubas. 1980. $7.50. 2:20. III–IV. Part I: e–a'; Part II: E–b; Part III: A_1–e. This is from an instrumental interlude from Purcell's Opera *Dioclessian.* The third part plays the ground bass while the top two parts play the melody in canon. Very tuneful and enjoyable to play and listen to. Good for high school ensemble, although the second part may get a little high for some high school players. Parts may be doubled for a large ensemble.

Purcell, Henry. *Chaconne.* arr. Paul F. Hartin. Cellar Press. Three tubas. 1975. 2:30. III. Part I: G_1–$a\flat^1$; Part II: G_1–e♭'; Part III: G_1–b♭. Arrangement of the same Purcell *Canon* that Gray arranged. First part should be played on the euphonium or F tuba. Parts may be doubled for a large ensemble.

Racussen, David. *Canonic Etudes.* Shawnee Press, Incorporated. Three tubas. 1971. Out of Print. 37 pp. III–IV. A collection of canons for one to four players. The books were printed for all wind instruments.

Reicha, Anton. *Six Trios for Three Horns.* tr. Barton Cummings. Solid Brass Music Company. Three tubas. 2003. $15.00. 17:00. II–III. Part I: G–d♭'; Part II: B♭–c'; Part III: $E\flat_1$–g. Originally a collection of trios for horn. First part maintains a high tessitura–could be performed on euphonium. Each part is interesting with a few technical challenges. Individual movements could be performed separately.

Rodgers, Thomas. *Three Pieces For Low Brass Trio.* The Brass Press. Two euphoniums and one tuba. 1974. Out of Print. 7:00. IV. Part I: c♭–g'; Part II: G–f; Part III: G_1–b♭. Three movements: Fanfare; Contrapunctus; Scherzo. Written for R. Winston Morris and the Tennessee Technological University Tuba Ensemble. While range is not a problem for any of the parts, there are several sections that challenge the ensemble. A good concert piece.

Roikjer, Kjell. *Ten Inventions for Three Tubas.* Engstrøm and Sodring. Three tubas. 1990. 8 pp. IV–V. Part I: c–e'; Part II: c♯–e'; Part III: A_1–c. A collection of ten contrasting movements. Excellent writing for this genre. Movements are musically and technically challenging for the advanced player. Movements may be performed individually or selected in small numbers to perform as a suite.

Ross, Walter. *Fancy Dances.* Dorn Publications Incorporated. Three tubas. 1972. 6:00. IV. Part I: B_1–e♭'; Part II: $A\flat_1$–^{c}; Part III: $F\sharp_1$–f. Three movements: Galop; Saraband; Saltarello. All parts are of equal difficulty. The third movement is especially rhythmically challenging. Recorded by the New York Tuba Quartet, "Tubby's Revenge," Crystal Records, S221.

Rossini, Giacchino. *Who Am I, or Dost Thou Mock Me.* arr. Andrew Hoefle. Tuba-Euphonium Press. One euphonium and two tubas. 1997. $8.00. 4:45. I–III. Part I: B–b'; Part II: D–f♯'; Part III: G_1–g. Excerpted from the *Barber of Seville, Act I, No. 7.* All parts have challenging sixteenth note passages, and the melodic material is divided among the voices. Parts may be doubled for a large ensemble.

Sarcich, Paul. *Dance Suite for Three Tubas.* Warwick Music. Three Tubas. £14.95.

Scheidt, Samuel. *Selections from Symphonien auff Conzerten-Manier.* arr. Paul F. Hartin. Cellar Press. Three tubas. 1974. 5:00. IV. Part I: c♯–b'; Part II: A–f'; Part III: $F\sharp_1$–e. Four movements. The first part should be played on euphonium and the second part may require an F tuba. While the third movement is very challenging technically, the others do not present much of a problem.

Schein, Johann Hermann. *Six Trios.* arr. Paul Schmidt and Daniel Heiman. Heavy Metal Music. Two euphoniums and one tuba. 1997. $7.00. Part I: c–g'; Part II: B♭–f'; Part III: G_1–b♭. Six movements. These six short trios are transcribed from secular vocal works for two sopranos and bass from *Musica boscareccia.* Each trio contains dance-like rhythmic syncopations, and three of the movements contain a meter shift from duple to triple. An optional fourth part doubles the third part an octave lower. Individual movements can stand alone on a concert. Also reviewed in the Fall 2000 issue of the *TUBA Journal* (Vol. 28, No. 1).

Schmidt, Paul, arr. *Five Trios of King Henry VIII.* Heavy Metal Music. Two euphoniums and one tuba. 1992. $5.00. 5:00. III–IV. Part I: F–f'; Part II: F–e♭'; Part III: $B\flat_1$–f. Five movements: Pastime with Good Company; If Love Now Reigned; O My Hart; Fantasy; With Owt Dyscorde. Nice arrangement of these famous English melodies. Younger players will need a conductor due to the many fermatas and tempo changes. No score available; parts may be doubled for a large ensemble.

Schubert, Franz. *Four Choruses.* arr. Kenneth Singleton. Peer International Corporation. Three tubas. 1977. $8.50. 5:00. IV. Part I: F–d'; Part II: F–d'; Part III: D–f'. Four movements: Dessen Fahne Donnesturme Wallte (The Colors

Churn within the Thunderstorm); Die Zwei Tugendwege (The Two Ways of Virtue); Totengraberlied (Grave Digger's Song); Tronend auf Erhabnem Sitz (In Majesty upon the Sublime Throne). All three parts are of equal difficulty and have the same range. The tessitura of the first part is higher and would be appropriate on euphonium or F tuba. The movements are tuneful and are in a traditional harmonic setting.

Schumann, Clara. *Fugue No. 1.* arr. Angelo Manzo. Tuba-Euphonium Press. One euphonium and two tubas. 2001. $12.00. 2:00. II–III. Part I: B♭–g'; Part II: E–e♭'; Part III: E♭$_1$–f. Brief three-voice fugue in a traditional contrapuntal style. Parts may be doubled for a large ensemble. Also reviewed in the Spring 2003 issue of the *ITEA Journal* (Vol. 30, No. 3).

Schumann, Robert. *Two Canons.* arr. Kenneth Singleton. Peer International Corporation. Three tubas. 1977. Out of Print. 1:45. IV. Part I: F–e♭'; Part II: F–d'; Part III: F–d'. Two movements: Gebt Mir Zu Trinken! (Let Me Drink!); Lásst Lautenspiel und Becherklang Nicht Rasten (Let the Lute Playing and the Clinking of Goblets not Cease). Two contrasting canons, the first very aggressive and fast, the second a little slower-paced. Range and technical demands of all parts are equal. F tubas or euphoniums could easily be used on any of the parts.

Singleton, Kenneth, arr. *Two English Madrigals.* Peer International Corporation. Three tubas. 1977. Out of Print. 2:30. IV. Part I: E♭–d'; Part II: D–d'; Part III: D–d'. Two movements: Come, Merry Lads, Let Us Away; Lady Those Eyes. All three parts are of equal difficulty regarding range. The first madrigal is polyphonic; the second is in a canon-like style. Will require three strong players.

Stewart, Frank G. *Heavyweights.* Seesaw Music Corporation. Three tubas. 1974. $18.00. 5:00. IV. Part I: D–e'; Part II: D–b♭; Part III: F♯$_1$–a. Several contrasting sections within one movement. There are mixed meters (3/8, 6/8, 7/8, etc.) in the fast section. The first part may be played on euphonium.

Telemann, G. P. *Three Chorale Preludes.* arr. William Schmidt. Western International Music. One euphoniums and two tubas. 1985. $7.00. 5:30. IV. Part I: d–f'; Part II: D–c'; Part III: G$_1$–f. Three movements: Komm, Heiliger Geist, Herr Gott; Vater unser im Himmelreich; Herr Jesu Christ, Dich zu uns Wend. The chorale melodies are in the top part. Interesting writing in the second and third parts. There are no articulation marking, so tubists will need to exercise sensitivity in phrasing. Parts may be doubled for a large ensemble.

Thornton, Michael, arr. *Three Diverse Drinking Songs.* Queen City Brass Publications. Three tubas. 1991. $8.00. 2:00. IV. Part I: C–e♭'; Part II: C–c'; Part III: C–b♭. Three movements: Would You Have a Young Virgin?; He That Will an Alehouse Keepe; Trinklied im Winter. A lively collection of three different songs. A euphonium may be used for the first part. Parts may be doubled for a large ensemble. Originally copyrighted in 1980.

Thornton, Michael, arr. *Three Pieces from King Henry VIII.* Queen City Brass Publications. Three tubas. 1980. $5.00. 2:30. IV. Part I: F–e'; Part II: F–e♭'; Part III: G$_1$–d'. Three movements: O My Hart; Blow Thy Horne Hunter; With Owt Dyscorde. A transcription of three Renaissance songs. Not technically difficult but the range requirements make this more suited for college players.

Uber, David. *Signals for Tuba Trio.* Tuba-Euphonium Press. Three tubas. 1992. $10.00. 3:00. IV. Part I: F–b♭; Part II: B♭–g; Part III: G$_1$–e♭. Three movements. Technically challenging, but no range problems. All parts have equal melodic and technical responsibilities. Will require three strong players. Interesting writing and fun to play.

Vivaldi, Antonio. *Vivaldi Trio Sonata.* ed. Paul Schmidt. Heavy Metal Music. Two euphoniums and one tuba. 1997. $7.00. Part I: c–g'; Part II: E♭–c'; Part III: B♭$_1$–a♭. Based on *Diverse Concerto in G Minor,* this transcription is transposed to C minor. The second part may be performed on tuba. Also reviewed in the Summer 1998 issue of the *TUBA Journal* (Vol. 25, No. 4).

Weelkes, Thomas. *Three Madrigals.* arr. Paul Schmidt. Heavy Metal Music. Two euphoniums and one tuba. 1990. $7.00. 4:00. IV. Part I: e♭–f'; Part II: B♭–e♭'; Part III: E♭–f. Three movements: Come, Sirrah Jack, Ho!; Since Robin Hood; Strike It Up, Tabor. Three very spirited madrigals. The third is the most polyphonic, though none of the movements are difficult technically. No score available, parts may be doubled.

Westby, Oivind. *3 Miniatures.* Nordic Sounds. Three tubas and percussion. 2001. 7:00.

Wilder, Alec. *Ten Trios for Tubas.* Margun Music, Incorporated. Three tubas. 1980. $8.00. 7 pp. IV. Part I: G$_1$–g'; Part II: G$_1$–g♭'; Part III: F$_1$–d'. A collection of ten movements in contrasting styles including jazz. The first part may be played on euphonium or F tuba because of the high tessitura. The technical and range demands will require advanced players.

Wilder, Alec. *Tuba Trio Number 1.* Margun Music, Incorporated. Three tubas. 1983. $4.50. 1:45. IV. Part I: G♭–f'; Part II: D–f'; Part III: C–d'. Very polyphonic in nature; canon-like in the middle section. Harmonies are rich and typical of Wilder's music, and consequently angular melodies and skips are common.

Willaert, Adrian. *Ricerdar a Tre Voci.* arr. Paul F. Hartin. Cellar Press. Three tubas. 1974. 2:00. III–IV. Part I: A–d'; Part II: E–g; Part III: G$_1$–B♭. Has a limited range for all parts. Very usable with a high school ensemble with a euphonium on the first part. Parts may be doubled for a large ensemble.

Zindars, Earl. *Tuba Trio. TUBA Journal.* Three tubas. 1981. $7.50. 1:00. III–IV. Part I: d–e'; Part II: A–d'; Part III: G_1–a. Top two parts are much more suited to euphoniums or F tubas. No real technical difficulties; may be performed by high schools players if euphoniums are playing the first two parts. Parts may be doubled for a large ensemble. Written as part of the TUBA Gem Series and distributed in the *TUBA Journal,* Vol. 9, No. 2. It is available by purchasing this issue of the *TUBA Journal.*

Four Parts

Aagaard-Nilsen, Torstein. *Efflorescent.* Nordic Sounds Limited. Tuba quartet. 1998.

Abt, Franz. *Postlude on "Willingham."* arr. Gregory Bright. Tuba/Euphonium Music Publications. Two euphoniums and two tubas. Out of Print. 4:00. III.

Adson, John. *Two Airs.* arr. John Stevens. Encore Music Publishers. Two euphoniums and two tubas. 1988. $12.50. 2:20. III–IV. Part I: d–g'; Part II: d–e'; Part III: A–a; Part IV: A_1–d. Two movements: Allegro; Allegretto. Most of the melody is in the first euphonium part. The second movement has primarily tutti rhythms in a very traditional harmonic setting. An arrangement very playable by high school or college ensembles. Parts may be doubled for a large ensemble.

Ahrendt, Karl. *Three Movements for Four Tubas.* T.A.P. Music. Four tubas. 1989. $15.00. 12:00. IV. Part I: B♭–b♭'; Part II: F–f'; Part III: C–d'; Part IV: C_1–g. Three movements: Intrada; Aria; Canzona. The top two parts indicate a tuba in F, though a euphonium could also be used. Some sections are technically difficult; strong players will be required to put this together. A score is available for an extra four dollars.

Albeniz, I. M. F. *Tango Espana.* arr. Paul Schmidt. Heavy Metal Music. Two euphoniums and two tubas. 1991. $7.00. 1:30. IV. Part I: G–f'; Part II: G–b♭; Part III: G–d♭'(e♭'); Part IV: G_1–a♭. Rhythmically complex for the top three parts. Several large skips in the first part. Fun to play. No score available. Parts may be doubled for a large ensemble.

Albert, Thomas. *TubaCanon. TUBA Journal.* Four tubas. 1975. $7.50. Indeterminate. IV–V. Part I: G–g; Part II: G–g; Part III: G–g; Part IV: G–g. Based on a larger indeterminate (aleatoric) work titled *A Maze with Grace.* All players read from the score. The players begin one at a time, each starting in the upper left hand corner, then proceeding to the other notes in any order they choose. The length and structure players will use should be decided prior to the performance. This was written as part of the TUBA Gem series and distributed with the *TUBA Journal,* Vol. 2, No. 2. It is available by purchasing this issue of the *TUBA Journal.*

Albinoni, Tomaso. *Adagio.* arr. Hirokazu Hiraishi. Sonic Arts, Incorporated. Four euphoniums. 1992. $11.00. 6:00. III–IV. Part I: G–a'; Part II: F–e'; Part III: F–d♭'; Part IV: C–c'. May also be played with two euphoniums and two tubas or three euphoniums and one tuba. A slow lyrical melody with most of the melodic responsibility in the top two parts. No significant technical problems. Parts may be doubled for a large ensemble.

Alexander, Joseph. *Dyad for Four Tubas.* Margun Music, Incorporated. Four tubas. 1989. $30.00. 8:30. IV–V. Part I: C♯–g'; Part II: D–f'; Part III: A_1–g'; Part IV: F♯$_1$–f'. Two movements. The range demands are extensive for all four parts. This could be performed by two euphoniums and two tubas. Technically very challenging, both movements are multimetric. Harmonies are contemporary and very dissonant.

Alexander, Lois, arr. *Prelude on Theme of Chesnokov.* Cimarron Music and Productions. Two euphoniums and two tubas with chimes. $10.00. Euphonium parts also available in treble clef.

Alexander, Lois, arr. *Swing Low, Sweet Chariot.* Southern Music Company. Two euphoniums and two tubas. 1990. $5.00. 3:00. IV. Part I: c–c"; Part II: A–b♭'; Part III: B♭$_1$–b♭; Part IV: E♭$_1$–f. Tessitura of the first two parts is quite high. The middle section is pointillistic in character. Parts may be doubled for a large ensemble.

Alford, Kenneth. *Colonel Bogey March.* arr. Norlan Bewley. Bewley Music, Incorporated. Two euphoniums and two tubas. 1995. $12.00. 3:30. II. Part I: d♭–g♭'; Part II: B♭–f'; Part III: F–b♭; Part IV: F_1–d♭. This well-known march was made popular by its use in the movie *The Bridge on the River Kwai.* Part of the Octubafest Music collection, this arrangement is appropriate for intermediate-level ensembles, though key signatures of five and six flats may prove challenging. Melodic material is divided among all four voices. Parts may be doubled for a large ensemble. Euphonium parts also available in treble clef.

Alford, Kenneth. *Colonel Bogey March.* arr. Robert Wilkinson. Cimarron Music and Productions. Two euphoniums and two tubas. 1997. $11.00. 3:30. This well-known march was made popular by its use in the movie *The Bridge on the River Kwai.* Euphonium parts also available in treble clef.

Alford, Kenneth. *Colonel Bogey March (Bridge over the River Kwai).* arr. Paul Schmidt. Heavy Metal Music. Two euphoniums and two tubas. 1991. $7.00. 3:20. IV. Part I: A–a'; Part II: F–c'; Part III: F–c'; Part IV: F_1–c. Good arrangement of the march used in the motion picture *The Bridge on the River Kwai.* Most of the melody is in the first part. No score available. Parts may be doubled for a large ensemble.

Alfred. *Army of the Nile*. arr. Robert Wilkinson. Cimarron Music and Productions. Two euphoniums and two tubas. $13.00. Euphonium parts also available in treble clef.

Alpert, Herb. *El Solo Toro—Mariachi*. arr. James Self. Available from the composer. Two euphoniums and two tubas. Out of Print. 2:30. III. Part I: c–f'; Part II: G–b♭; Part III: (F_1) $B♭_1$–f; Part IV: F_1–c. No technical problems. The piece has a Mexican flavor and is designed for young players.

Ameller, André. *Adagio, Choral et Scherzetto*. André Ameller. Four tubas. 1981.

Ameller, André. *Concertstuck*. André Ameller. Four tubas. 1982.

Ameller, André. *Lento Espressivo*. *TUBA Journal*. Four tubas. 1980. $7.50. 2:00. IV. Part I: g–g♭'; Part II: C–c'; Part III: F–d♭'; Part IV: F_1–d. The tessitura of the first part is high and may require an F tuba. A very lyrical chorale, this was written as part of the TUBA Gem Series and distributed with the *TUBA Journal*, Vol. 8, No. 1. It is available by purchasing this issue of the *TUBA Journal*.

Anderson, Eugene. *Celebration*. Anderson's Arizona Originals. Three euphoniums and one tuba. 1988. $5.00. 1:45. III–IV. Part I: g–a'; Part II: g–e♭'; Part III: G–b; Part IV: (C_1) G_1–e♭. A fanfare with all parts having equal melodic responsibility and technical demands. Good for a concert opener. Parts may be doubled for a large ensemble.

Anderson, Eugene. *Chorale Quartet*. Anderson's Arizona Originals. Two euphoniums and two tubas. 1989. $5.00. 2:30. III. Part I: A–a'; Part II: E–c♯'; Part III: F–c♯; Part IV: (D_1) E–d. A very lyrical chorale. No technical problems; very appropriate for younger players. Parts may be doubled for a large ensemble.

Anderson, Eugene. *Fanfare for Tubafour*. Anderson's Arizona Originals. Two euphoniums and two tubas. 1988. $5.00. 1:45. IV. Part I: d–b♭'; Part II: d–e'; Part III: G–b; Part IV: $G♭_1$–d. This fanfare is slow and mysterious in character. The melody is based on dotted eighth note and triplet figures. Parts may be doubled for a large ensemble.

Anderson, Eugene. *Great Chromatic Fugue in G*. Anderson's Arizona Originals. Three euphoniums and one tuba. 1988. $6.00. 3:00. IV. Part I: d–c''; Part II: G–g'; Part III: D–a; Part IV: G_1–b♭. The technical challenges are moderate. The tessitura of the first part is high. Players will need to count carefully.

Anderson, Eugene. *Heavy Metal*. Anderson's Arizona Originals. Two euphoniums, two tubas, and drum set. 1989. $5.00. 2:30. IV. Part I: B♭–b♭'; Part II: A–f'; Part III: f–d'; Part IV: $A♭_1$–d♭. A rock-style composition with most of the melody in the first part. The tubas have an interesting bass line. The drum set helps establish a rock feel. The tessitura of the first part is high. Parts may be doubled for a large ensemble.

Anderson, Eugene. *Outback Brass*. Anderson's Arizona Originals. Two euphoniums and two tubas. 1989. $5.00. 1:30. IV. Part I: e–b♭'; Part II: F–d'; Part III: E–b♭; Part IV: G_1–f. Based on an Aboriginal melody dating from 1788. There are many driving rhythmic figures and large skips. Interesting writing. Parts may be doubled for a large ensemble.

Anderson, Eugene. *Quintuple Overlays*. Cimarron Music and Productions. Two euphoniums and two tubas with two trumpets and percussion. 1997. $14.00. 3:00. III–IV. Part I: G–a♭'; Part II: G–a♭'; Part III: D♯–c♯'; Part IV: D_1–g. This original work for brass choir features a tuba/euphonium quartet with two trumpets and three percussion parts: snare drum, cymbal, and timpani. Syncopation, chromatic lines, and large intervals are challenging elements of each part. First two parts also available in treble clef. Works well as a concert opener.

Anderson, Eugene. *Theme and Six Derivations*. Anderson's Arizona Originals. Two euphoniums and two tubas. 1988. $8.00. 11:00. IV. Part I: G–c''; Part II: G–a♭'; Part III: $B♭_1$–f'; Part IV: D_1–g. A single movement with seven different sections. The derivations contrast in key, tempo, and style. Only moderate technical demands, but the tessitura for the first part is high. Mutes are required.

Anderson, Eugene, arr. *Beautiful Savior*. Anderson's Arizona Originals. Two euphoniums and two tubas. 1988. $5.00. 2:20. IV. Part I: f♯–g'; Part II: d–d'; Part III: G–d'; Part IV: G_1–a. Arrangement in a lyrical and chorale style of the hymn "Fairest Lord Jesus." No significant technical problems. Parts may be doubled for a large ensemble.

Anderson, Eugene, arr. *Beer Barrel Polka*. Anderson's Arizona Originals. Two euphoniums and two tubas. 1990. $5.00. 1:45. IV. Part I: B♭–b♭'; Part II: F–f'; Part III: F–f'; Part IV: F_1–f. The first part has primary melodic responsibility throughout the piece. The tessitura of the first and third part is high. Perfect for those Octubafest parties! Parts may be doubled for a large ensemble.

Anderson, Eugene, arr. *Bells-a-Plenty*. Cimarron Music and Productions. Two euphoniums and two tubas. 1995. $6.50. 4:00. III. Part I: e♭–b♭'; Part II: E–f'; Part III: D–d'; Part IV: $E♭_1$–g. Medley of three Christmas carols: "Carol of the Bells," "I Heard the Bells on Christmas Day," and "Children's Bell Carol." First two parts also available in treble clef. Third part may be performed on euphonium.

Anderson, Eugene, arr. *The Caroling Quartet*. Anderson's Arizona Originals. Two euphoniums and two tubas. 1988. $5.00. 2:00. IV. Part I: e♭–b♭'; Part II: B♭–a'; Part III: A–d'; Part IV: F_1–b♭. A Christmas medley featuring brief excerpts of "Do You Hear What I Hear?" "Santa Claus Comes Tonight," "Jingle Bells," and "Rudolph the

Red-Nosed Reindeer." Most of the melody is in the first part and the tessitura of the first part is high. Parts may be doubled for a large ensemble.

Anderson, Eugene, arr. *Chiapanecas (Advanced).* Anderson's Arizona Originals. Three euphoniums and one tuba. 1988. $5.00. 2:30. IV–V. Part I: g–b♭'; Part II: F–g'; Part III: F–g♭'; Part IV: F_1–e♭'. A fun arrangement of the "Mexican Hat Dance." The tessitura of the first and fourth parts is high. A few technical challenges. Parts may be doubled for a large ensemble.

Anderson, Eugene, arr. *Chiapanecas (Easy).* Anderson's Arizona Originals. Two euphoniums and two tubas. 1988. $5.00. 2:30. III–IV. Part I: g–b♭'; Part II: d–g'; Part III: B♭–c (d'); Part IV: F_1–c. An easier arrangement of the same Mexican melody. The tessitura of the top part is still a little high, but the fourth part is much more suited to younger players. Parts may be doubled for a large ensemble.

Anderson, Eugene, arr. *Christmas Bells A-Plenty.* Anderson's Arizona Originals. Two euphoniums and two tubas. 1988. $5.00. 3:00. IV. Part I: d–b♭'; Part II: E–f'; Part III: D–e♭'; Part IV: E♭$_1$–c'. An arrangement of three Christmas melodies, all with the word "Bell" in the title: "Ring Christmas Bells"; "I Heard the Bells on Christmas Day"; and "Children's Bell Choir." The melody is primarily in the first part. Parts may be doubled for a large ensemble.

Anderson, Eugene, arr. *Coventry Carol.* Cimarron Music and Productions. Two euphoniums and two tubas. 1995. $6.50. 2:00. II–III. Part I: B–f'; Part II: G♯–a; Part III: A–e'; Part IV: G♯$_1$–f. Predominantly homophonic arrangement of this Christmas carol with traditional harmonies. Melody is present in both the first and fourth parts. First tuba part is scored frequently above the second euphonium. First two parts also available in treble clef. Parts may be doubled for a large ensemble.

Anderson, Eugene, arr. *Deutschland Über Alles.* Anderson's Arizona Originals. Two euphoniums and two tubas. 1988. $5.00. 2:00. III–IV. Part I: c–g'; Part II: A–e'; Part III: A–c'; Part IV: G_1–g. A chorale-like arrangement of the German national anthem. Most of the melodic responsibility is in the first part. Parts may be doubled for a large ensemble.

Anderson, Eugene, arr. *The Echo Carol.* Anderson's Arizona Originals. Two euphoniums and two tubas. 1990. $5.00. 2:30. IV. Part I: c♯–a'; Part II: A–f'; Part III: F–c'; Part IV: F_1–f'. Good arrangement of this traditional melody. No significant technical demands. Parts may be doubled for a large ensemble.

Anderson, Eugene, arr. *Joseph, Dearest—Joseph, Mine.* Cimarron Music and Productions. Two euphoniums and two tubas. 1995. $7.50. 1:30. II. Part I: d–b♭'; Part II: B–e♭'; Part III: E♭–e♭'; Part IV: A♭'–d. Nice arrangement of this Christmas carol in D and E♭ major. Texture is predominantly homophonic. First two parts also available in treble clef. Parts may be doubled for a large ensemble.

Anderson, Eugene, arr. *Kimiga-Yo.* Anderson's Arizona Originals. Two euphoniums and two tubas. 1989. $5.00. 2:00. III–IV. Part I: c–a'; Part II: b–e'; Part III: D–a; Part IV: D_1–d. A traditional setting of this Japanese melody. The melody is primarily in the first part. Parts may be doubled for a large ensemble.

Anderson, Eugene, arr. *Minuet.* Anderson's Arizona Originals. Two euphoniums and two tubas. 1988. $5.00. 2:00. IV. Part I: A–g'; Part II: f–e'; Part III: F–f'; Part IV: F_1–f. The tessitura of the third part is high and may be played by a euphonium. Uses very traditional harmonies, and works very well. Parts may be doubled for a large ensemble.

Anderson, Eugene, arr. *Sixteen Tons.* Anderson's Arizona Originals. Solo tuba and three euphoniums. 1988. $5.00. 1:45. III–IV. Part I: A♭$_1$–b♭; Part II: A♭–b; Part III: A–f; Part IV: (B♭$_1$) E–d'. A light jazzy arrangement of this Tennessee Ernie Ford classic. This features a tuba solo with three euphoniums accompanying. Swing feel is necessary. Could be used to highlight a high school tuba player with trombones or euphoniums playing the other parts. A tuba III part is included that combines parts II and III for use in a trio. Parts may be doubled for a large ensemble.

Anderson, Eugene, arr. *Variations on Jingle Bells.* Cimarron Music and Productions. Two euphoniums and two tubas. 1995. $7.50. 1:15. II–III. Part I: B♭–b♭'; Part II: B♭–a♭'; Part III: A–d'; Part IV: A♭$_1$–f. Brief theme and variations based on motives from "Jingle Bells." All parts are interesting, and melodic material is divided equally among all four voices. Euphonium parts also available in treble clef. Parts may be doubled for a large ensemble.

Anderson, Leroy. *Sleigh Ride.* arr. Peter Rauch. Ohio Valley Tuba Quartet Press. Two euphoniums and two tubas. $13.00. 3:45. IV. Part I: d–a'; Part II: c–g'; Part III: C–b; Part IV: C_1–A. A fun arrangement of this Anderson wintery classic. The melody is primarily in the first and third parts. The tessitura of the first part is high. Sleigh bells and slap stick may be added for effect. Parts may be doubled for a large ensemble.

Aoshima, Hiroshi. *Gnome.* Tokyo Bari-Tuba Ensemble. Two euphoniums and two tubas.

Arcadelt, Jacob. *Ave Maria.* arr. James Self. Wimbledon Music Incorporated. Four tubas. 1979. $7.00. 2:30. III–IV. Part I: d♭–d♭'; Part II: c–b♭; Part III: A♭–f; Part IV: D♭–d. While the published title suggests four tubas, the first two parts are listed as "tenor tuba" on the music. This can be played with four tubas, but it is very playable by high school students with euphoniums on the first and second parts. A very nice setting of this slow chorale. Recorded by the Melton Tuba-Quartett, *Premiere,* Diavolo Records, DR-D-93-C-001.

Arlen. *Stormy Weather.* arr. Stephens, Denzil. Sarnia Music. Two euphoniums and two tubas.

Auberg, Jamie. *Navigating the Noland Trail.* Tuba-Euphonium Press. Two euphoniums and two tubas. 1999. $18.00. 12:00. III. Part I: F–a' (b'); Part II: F–f'; Part III: C–d'; Part IV: $E\flat_1$–g. Five movements: At the Beginning; Observation 1: The Lake; The Wildlife; The Thicket of Thin Trees; The Home Stretch. Programmatic original composition based on the five-mile scenic trail in Eastern Virginia. The style of the slow movements is generally lyrical with traditional harmonies, and the fast movements are rhythmically driven. Double-tonguing may be required in the final movement. Parts may be doubled for a large ensemble.

Ayers, Jesse. *Into the Magical Rain Forest for Tuba/Euphonium Ensemble and Tape.* Tuba-Euphonium Press. Two euphoniums, two tubas, and tape. 1993. $15.00. 5:30. IV. Part I: f–g'; Part II: A–f'; Part III: E–a♭; Part IV: E_1–d. Commissioned by R. Winston Morris and the Tennessee Technological University Tuba Ensemble. The tape has many melodic and percussive sounds and is often the primary focal point of the composition. The composition is tonal but with some very interesting harmonies. No significant technical problems. Enjoyable for both performers and audience. Parts may be doubled for a large ensemble. Also available in a six-part version.

Baadsvik, Øystein, arr. *Allt Under Himlens Fäste (Everything under the Sky).* Baadsvik Music Shop. Two euphoniums and two tubas. €17.80.

Bach, C. P. E. *Solfeggietto.* arr. F. Chester Roberts. Southern Music Company. Two euphoniums and two tubas. 1986. $3.00. 1:30. IV. Part I: G–a'; Part II: E♭–c'; Part III: $A\flat_1$–a♭; Part IV: G_1–g. Dedicated to the U.S. Coast Guard Tuba-Euphonium Quartet. A very usable arrangement of C. P. E. Bach's most famous keyboard composition. Constant sixteenth note runs traded between the parts; technically very challenging. Players must count carefully to make the phrases seamless as the technical melody is passed from one part to the next.

Bach, C. P. E. *Solfegietto.* arr. Michael Howard. BTQ Publications. Two euphoniums and two tubas. 1993. $8.00.

Bach, Erik. *Fregat Galop, Op. 52.* Available from the composer. Two euphoniums and two tubas. 1993. 4:00.

Bach, Johann Sebastian. *Air from Suite in D.* arr. Wood. Available from Tubalaté. Two euphoniums and two tubas. 3:30. Recorded by Tubalaté on the compact disc, *Episodes.*

Bach, Johann Sebastian. *Air from Suite No. 3 in D.* arr. David Werden. Whaling Music Publishers. Two euphoniums and two tubas. 1978. $5.00. 3:10. IV. Part I: c–b♭'; Part II: B♭–a'; Part III: A–f'; Part IV: G_1–d'. The tessitura of the third part is high and may be played on an F tuba or euphonium. The first part is printed only in treble clef. This arrangement is in the key of C, transposed up from the original in G. This beautiful simple melody requires a great deal of finesse to play as an ensemble. Parts may be doubled for a large ensemble. Recorded by the Atlantic Tuba Quartet, Golden Crest Records, CRS 4173; the British Tuba Quartet, *Euphonic Sounds,* Polyphonic Reproductions Limited, QPRZ 009D.

Bach, Johann Sebastian. *Air from Suite No. 3 in D Major.* arr. Øystein Baadsvik. Baadsvik Music Shop. Two euphoniums and two tubas. €17.80. 3:30. II–III. All parts available in both bass and treble clef.

Bach, Johann Sebastian. *Air on the G String.* arr. Joseph D. Goble. Tuba-Euphonium Press. Two euphoniums and two tubas. 1994. $6.00. 3:30. II. Part I: f–a♭'; Part II: A–f'; Part III: F–b; Part IV: A_1–c'. The arrangement retains the melody exclusively in the first euphonium part. The counter melody and harmonic movement are the role of the inner voices, while the second tuba provides the well-known pizzicato bass line. The work is accessible to younger ensembles provided the stronger players are performing the outer parts. Parts may be doubled for a large ensemble. Also reviewed in the Spring 1995 issue of the *TUBA Journal* (Vol. 22, No. 3).

Bach, Johann Sebastian. *Anna Magdalena Suite.* arr. John Stevens. Available from the arranger. Two euphoniums and two tubas. 1981. 7:00. III–IV. Part I: G–a♭'; Part II: F–A'; Part III: $B\flat_1$–c'; Part IV: F_1–e♭. Four movements: Menuet; Musette; Bist Du Bei Mir; Marche. A straightforward transcription of this group of well-known piano pieces.

Bach, Johann Sebastian. *Arioso from Cantata 156.* arr. Frank H. Siekmann. Brelmat Music. Two euphoniums and two tubas. 2002. $10.00. 3:00. II–III. Part I: B–b'; Part II: d–a'; Part III: A_1–c'; Part IV: G_1–b. This straightforward arrangement of Bach's famous cantata allows each of the parts to perform the melody at some point, accompanied by the other three parts. Each part has a challenging range when performing the melody and a simple rhythmic accompaniment otherwise. More appropriate for a quartet than for a large ensemble.

Bach, Johann Sebastian. *Bist Du Bei Mir.* arr. David Werden. Whaling Music Publishers. Two euphoniums and two tubas. 1978. $5.00. 2:30. III–IV. Part I: d–a♭'; Part II: B♭–e♭; Part III: F–f'; Part IV: G_1–d. An excellent arrangement of one of Bach's most famous secular songs, written as a love song for his first wife, Anna Magdalena. The two euphonium parts are in tenor clef in the score and the first euphonium part is printed in treble clef only. Not difficult rhythmically;

the challenge here is playing together as an ensemble. The first tuba part may be too high for high school tuba players, and a euphonium may be substituted for this part. Recorded by the Atlantic Tuba Quartet, Golden Crest Records, CRS 4173; the Melton Tuba-Quartett, *Premiere,* Diavolo Records, DR-D-93-C-001; U.S. Armed Forces Tuba/Euphonium Ensemble and Massed Ensemble, U.S. Army Records.

Bach, Johann Sebastian. *Bist Du bei mir.* arr. Stefan Winternheimer. Musikverlag Bruno Uetz. Two euphoniums and two tubas. 2000. €10.00. 2:30. Parts may be doubled for a large ensemble. Recorded by the Melton Tuba-Quartett on the compact disc *Premiere.*

Bach, Johann Sebastian. *Choral No. 3 (Blessed Jesus, We Are Here).* tr. Gérard Buquet. Editions Combre. Two euphoniums and two tubas. 1991. 2:30. II–III. Part I: f♯–b♭'; Part II: B♭–b♭; Part III: G–g; Part IV: F_1–d. The melody is predominantly in the first part in this arrangement. The other parts are accessible by intermediate-level performers. Parts may be doubled for a large ensemble.

Bach, Johann Sebastian. *Chorale Prelude from Cantata No. 140.* arr. Barton Cummings. Solid Brass Music Co. Two euphoniums and two tubas. $8.00. 5:45. II–III. Part I: B♭–g'; Part II: A♭–f'; Part III: E♭–a; Part IV: D_1–c. Arrangement of Bach's "Wachet auf, ruft uns die Stimme." Melody is passed around the top three parts while the fourth part maintains a low tessitura. Ornaments provide the greatest challenge and most of them are written out. More appropriate for a quartet than for a large ensemble.

Bach, Johann Sebastian. *Come Sweet Death.* arr. Eugene Anderson. Anderson's Arizona Originals. Two euphoniums and two tubas. 1988. $5.00. 1:30. III–IV. Part I: c–g'; Part II: G–c'; Part III: C–b♭; Part IV: (C_1) F_1–c. A four-part version and slightly easier arrangement of the same Bach melody that Sauter arranged for one euphonium and two tubas. The euphonium parts are not high and the first tuba part is not overly challenging. Parts may be doubled for a large ensemble.

Bach, Johann Sebastian. *Come, Thou Long Expected Jesus.* arr. Chris Warren. Cimarron Music and Productions. Two euphoniums and two tubas. $10.50. Euphonium parts also available in treble clef.

Bach, Johann Sebastian. *Contrapunctus III from Art of Fugue.* arr. Mark Nelson. Whaling Music Publishers. Two euphoniums and two tubas. 1991. $15.00. 3:20. IV. Part I: c♯–b♭'; Part II: G–f'; Part III: $B♭_1$–g; Part IV: (D_1) F_1–d. Very polyphonic and challenging technically at times. Players will need to count carefully. There are no significant range demands.

Bach, Johann Sebastian. *Contrapunctus IX.* arr. Larry Pitts. The Brass Press. Two euphoniums and two tubas. Out of Print. 4:45. IV. Part I: c–a'; Part II: G♯–e'; Part III: D–c'; Part IV: $G♯_1$–d. Written for R. Winston Morris and the Tennessee Technological University Tuba Ensemble. Good arrangement of this very contrapuntal composition. This is in a key which does not pose great range demands on any of the parts. All parts are technically demanding and need to be played very light and clean. Parts may be carefully doubled for a large ensemble.

Bach, Johann Sebastian. *Contrapunctus IX.* arr. Mike Forbes. Tuba-Euphonium Press. Two euphoniums and two tubas. 1999. $10.00. 3:00. II–III. Part I: d–b♭'; Part II: A–f'; Part III: E–e'; Part IV: (E_1) G_1–b♭. Nice arrangement of this well-known four-voice fugue. The arranger has clearly indicated in all parts which part should be prominent during particular passages. For this reason, this work serves well as a study piece for young ensembles and a concert piece for intermediate-level ensembles. Parts may be doubled for a large ensemble. Recorded by Tubalaté on the compact disc *Hall of Mirrors.*

Bach, Johann Sebastian. *Contrapunctus IX.* arr. Paul Schmidt. Heavy Metal Music. Two euphoniums and two tubas. 1991. $7.00. 4:45. IV. Part I: G–d'; Part II: F–d'; Part III: C♯–a; Part IV: F_1–g. All parts have the opportunity to play the theme. Technically challenging at times; all players will need to count carefully. No score available. Parts may be doubled for a large ensemble.

Bach, Johann Sebastian. *Contrapunctus IX.* arr. Peter Rauch. Ohio Valley Tuba Quartet Press. Two euphoniums and two tubas. 1988. $10.00. 4:45. IV–V. Part I: d–c''; Part II: G♯–b♭'; Part III: C–a; Part IV: D_1–d. This fugue is very challenging for all four parts. The tessitura of the first part is high, but there are some *ossia* 8vb sections included. Written in four, this fugue should be felt in two when performed. Will require four strong players.

Bach, Johann Sebastian. *Fantasia in C.* arr. David Sabourin. Touch of Brass Music Corporation. Two euphoniums and two tubas. 1981. 1:20. IV. Part I: c–c''; Part II: c♯–a'; Part III: F–a; Part IV: A_1–f'. While this work is technically not extremely difficult, putting the parts together can be challenging because of its polyphonic nature. The tessitura of the top two parts is quite high. The score indicates a copyright date of 1981; the parts show a date of 1982.

Bach, Johann Sebastian. *Five Selections from Anna Magdalena's Notebook.* arr. Stephen Shoop. Cimarron Music and Productions. Two euphoniums and two tubas. 1995. $12.00. 6:15. II. Part I: G–b♭'; Part II: A–b♭'; Part III: A_1–c'; Part IV: (F_1) G_1–c. Excellent teaching arrangement for younger ensembles. All parts are interesting, but the ranges and rhythms are accessible for younger performers, and the movements are brief. Individual movements can stand alone in a concert. Euphonium parts also available in treble clef. Parts may be doubled for a large ensemble.

Bach, Johann Sebastian. *Four Bach Chorales.* arr. Keith Mehlan. Horizon Press. Two euphoniums and two tubas. 1991. $12.00. 6:30. IV. Part I: d–b♭'; Part II: A–a♭'; Part III: B♭–f'; Part IV: D_1–e♭. Four movements: Haupt Voll Blunt und Wunden; Ein Feste Burg ist unser Gott; Christ Lag in Todesbanden; In Dulci Jubilo. Four widely contrasting movements. All parts have an opportunity to play the melody. The tessitura of the top three parts is high. This arrangement could also work well with three euphoniums and one tuba.

Bach, Johann Sebastian. *Fuga No. 7 from Organ Works IX.* tr. Yutaka Kono. Tuba-Euphonium Press. Two euphoniums and two tubas. 1999. $10.00. 3:30. III. Part I: G–b'; Part II: F♯–d'; Part III: A_1–a; Part IV: D_1–g. Straightforward arrangement of this fugue from one of Bach's standard collections. Long technical passages make this more appropriate for advanced performers, though it is accessible by intermediate-level performers. All parts are interesting and challenging. Parts may be doubled for a large ensemble.

Bach, Johann Sebastian. *Fuga No. 7 from the Well Tempered Clavier, Book II.* arr. Andrew Spang. Lyric Brass Publishing. Two euphoniums and two tubas. 1994. $9.00. 3:00. Arranged for TUBA+, the tuba-euphonium ensemble at the Eastman School of Music. First part is in tenor clef. Parts may be doubled for a large ensemble.

Bach, Johann Sebastian. *Fuga VII from WTC.* arr. James Self. Available from the arranger. Two euphoniums and two tubas. 1972. Out of Print. 2:00. IV. Part I: e♭–c"; Part II: B♭–g'; Part III: D–b♭; Part IV: F♭$_1$–e♭. Very polyphonic; players must count carefully.

Bach, Johann Sebastian. *Fugue in G Minor (Little).* arr. Albert Peoples. Southern Music Company. Two euphoniums and two tubas. 1990. $8.00. 4:00. IV. Part I: A–c"; Part II: F–a♭'; Part III: F♯$_1$–b♭; Part IV: D_1–c. The tessitura of the first part is high. Technically demanding, especially on the first and third parts. Will require strong players. Parts may be carefully doubled for a large ensemble.

Bach, Johann Sebastian. *Fugue in G Minor (Little).* arr. Dean A. Somerville. Tuba-Euphonium Press. Two euphoniums and two tubas. 1998. $6.00. 3:00. III. Part I: A–b♭'; Part II: E♭–e♭'; Part III: E♭$_1$–b♭; Part IV: F_1–e♭. Nice arrangement of this well-known four-voice fugue. Long technical passages make this more appropriate for advanced performers, though it is accessible by intermediate-level performers. All parts are interesting and challenging. Parts may be doubled for a large ensemble.

Bach, Johann Sebastian. *Fugue in G Minor (Little).* arr. Skip Gray. Shawnee Press, Incorporated. Two euphoniums and two tubas. 1984. $9.00. 3:15. IV. Part I: A–c'; Part II: F–a♭'; Part III: B♭$_1$–b♭; Part IV: G_1–d. While the greatest technical demands are on the two euphonium parts, all four parts have the subject and countersubject in exposed places. The first euphonium part is printed in tenor clef. Requires very light and clean playing by all parts. A first-rate arrangement of Bach's best-known fugue. Parts may be doubled for a large ensemble. Recorded by the British Tuba Quartet *In at the Deep End,* Heavyweight Records, Limited, HR008/D.

Bach, Johann Sebastian. *Fugue in G Minor from Fantasia and Fugue, BWV 542.* arr. Peter Smalley. Studio Music Company. Two euphoniums and two tubas. 1996. Part I: F♯–c"; Part II: F3–c"; Part III: C_1–c'; Part IV: C_1–c'. Challenging fugue in the traditional style. Each part contains an optional muted section. Euphonium parts also available in treble clef, first tuba parts also available in E♭ treble clef, and second tuba parts also available in both E♭ and B♭ treble clef. Also reviewed in the Spring 1997 issue of the *TUBA Journal* (Vol. 24, No. 3). Recorded by the British Tuba Quartet on their compact disc *March to the Scaffold,* Polyphonic Records, and by Tubalaté on the compact disc *Move.*

Bach, Johann Sebastian. *Fugue No. 16 for Four Low Brass Instruments.* arr. Ray Grim. Prima Musica. Two euphoniums and two tubas. 1988. 2:00. IV. Part I: c♯–b♭'; Part II: E–f'; Part III: C–f; Part IV: D_1–d. This has been transcribed from *The Well-Tempered Clavier,* Book I. Technically this is not very demanding but the first part will require a strong player due to the range demands. The fourth part will need very clean articulation in the low register.

Bach, Johann Sebastian. *Italian Concerto, BWV 971, Movement I.* arr. Todd Cranson. Cimarron Music and Productions. Two euphoniums and two tubas. $11.50. 4:15. III. Part I: c–c"; Part II: G–c"; Part III: E_1–d'; Part IV: F_1–c'. A challenging arrangement of one of Bach's more famous piano works. All parts require technical dexterity to maintain the style and tempo. Euphonium parts also available in treble clef. Also reviewed in the Spring 1999 issue of the *TUBA Journal* (Vol. 26, No. 3).

Bach, Johann Sebastian. *Jesu, Joy of Man's Desiring.* arr. David Werden. Whaling Music Publishers. Two euphoniums and two tubas. 1978. $5.00. 2:10. IV. Part I: c–g'; Part II: B♭–f'; Part III: E–b♭; Part IV: F_1–B♭. Nice arrangement of this famous melody. No real technical problems, but a lyrical triplet feel must be maintained throughout. The top part is printed in tenor clef and parts one and two are in tenor clef in the score. Parts may be doubled for a large ensemble. Recorded by the British Tuba Quartet, *In at the Deep End,* Heavyweight Records Limited, HR008/D.

Bach, Johann Sebastian. *Jesu, Joy of Man's Desiring.* arr. H. Hiraishi. Sonic Arts, Incorporated. Two euphoniums and two tubas. 1986. $11.00. 2:10. III–IV. Part I: E–f'; Part II: E–c'; Part III: D–g; Part IV: G_1–e. The tessitura of the top two parts is low. The melody is in the euphonium parts exclusively. No technical difficulties. Parts may be doubled for a large ensemble.

Bach, Johann Sebastian. *Jesu, Joy of Man's Desiring.* arr. Richard E. Thurston. Southern Music Co. Two euphoniums and two tubas. 1993. $10.00. 3:00. III. Part I: G–b♭'; Part II: G–g'; Part III: F–c'; Part IV: F_1–b♭. Effective arrangement of one of Bach's more popular works. The flowing melodic line is divided among the upper three voices. Parts may be doubled for a large ensemble.

Bach, Johann Sebastian. *Minuet.* arr. Paul Schmidt. Heavy Metal Music. Two euphoniums and two tubas. 1991. $3.00. 1:20. III. Part I: d–d'; Part II: c♯–g'; Part III: F–g; Part IV: C♯–d. An interesting minuet with a highly polyphonic middle section. The second part has a higher tessitura and is more challenging than the first part. No score available. Parts may be doubled for a large ensemble.

Bach, Johann Sebastian. *Musette.* tr. Paul Luhring. PEL Music Publications. Four tubas. 1999. $8.50. 2:00. I–II. Part I: A–f; Part II: F–d; Part III: C–B♭; Part IV: F_1–F. For the Peshtigo High School Tuba Quartet. Straightforward transcription appropriate for young performers. Melodic material is predominately in the first part. Parts may be doubled for a large ensemble.

Bach, Johann Sebastian. *Prelude and Fugue.* arr. Maurice Bale. Godiva Music. Two euphoniums and two tubas. £6.00. From *Eight Short Preludes and Fugues.*

Bach, Johann Sebastian. *Prelude and Fugue in C Minor.* arr. Skip Gray. Shawnee Press, Incorporated. Two euphoniums and two tubas. 1984. $9.00. 3:00. IV. Part I: A♭–b♭'; Part II: A♭–f'; Part III: E♭$_1$–a; Part IV: D_1–f. This was originally written for keyboard instruments and published in Book I of *The Well-Tempered Clavier* (1722). Typical of this style, there is a flowing sixteenth note melodic line passed between parts one and three and parts two and four. Most of the first euphonium part is notated in tenor clef. Parts may be doubled for a large ensemble, but the two measures of cadenza-like material should be played as a solo.

Bach, Johann Sebastian. *Prelude and Fugue in G.* arr. David Sabourin. Touch of Brass Music Corporation. Two euphoniums and two tubas. $10.00. 3:00. IV. Part I: B♭–a'; Part II: B♭–a'; Part III: D–c'; Part IV: F_1–d. No significant technical challenges but the fugue section should not be played too quickly. Parts may be carefully doubled for a large ensemble.

Bach, Johann Sebastian. *Prelude and Fugue in G Minor.* arr. James Barnes. Two euphoniums and two tubas. 2002. $10.00. 3:45. III. Part I: c♯–c''; Part II: A–g'; Part III: C–c' (d'); Part IV: (E_1) F_1–e♭. Two movements: Prelude; Fugue. Arrangement of Fugue No. XVI from Book I of *The Well-Tempered Clavier,* and an excellent study piece of contrapuntal style. Euphonium parts also available in treble clef. Parts may be doubled for a large ensemble.

Bach, Johann Sebastian. *Prelude and Fugue in G Minor.* arr. David Sabourin. Touch of Brass Music Corporation. Two euphoniums and two tubas.

Bach, Johann Sebastian. *Prelude and Fugue in G Minor, BWV 558.* arr. Kenyon D. Wilson. Tuba-Euphonium Press. Two euphoniums and two tubas. 1997. $8.00. 3:15. II. Part I: d–g' (a'); Part II: A–d'; Part III: F–c'; Part IV: (F_1) G_1–d. Effective arrangement of this well-known prelude and four-voice fugue in the traditional style. Range and style are appropriate for intermediate-level performers, though all parts are interesting and have the melody at some point. Parts may be doubled for a large ensemble.

Bach, Johann Sebastian. *Prelude and Fugue No. 16.* arr. Paul Schmidt. Heavy Metal Music. Two euphoniums and two tubas. 1992. $5.00. 3:30. IV. Part I: G♯–g'; Part II: A–f'; Part III: B♭$_1$–c'; Part IV: G_1–a'. Two movements: Prelude; Fugue. Challenging for all four parts. The fugue is from Book I of *The Well Tempered Clavier.* No score available. Parts may be doubled for a large ensemble.

Bach, Johann Sebastian. *Prelude and Fugue No. 22.* arr. David Schanke. Music Arts Publishing Company. Two euphoniums and two tubas. 1993. $14.00. 3:45. II–III. Part I: B–g'; Part II: A♭–d♭'; Part III: E–a♭ (b♭); Part IV: G_1–d♭. Two movements: Prelude; Fugue. Nice arrangement of this prelude and fugue from Book I of *The Well-Tempered Clavier.* Limited range makes this appropriate for intermediate-level performers, though the independence of parts in the fugue may be challenging. Euphonium parts also available in treble clef. Parts may be doubled for a large ensemble.

Bach, Johann Sebastian. *Sarabande.* arr. Michael Howard. BTQ Publications. Two euphoniums and two tubas. 1993. $9.00.

Bach, Johann Sebastian. *Sarabande.* arr. Michael Howard. Studio Music Company. Two euphoniums and two tubas. 1996. £6.00. 3:00. III. Part I: E–b'; Part II: C♯–a'; Part III: B–e; Part IV: G_1–g. Arranged for the British Tuba Quartet. From Bach's *French Suite No. 1 in D Minor.* Third part may also be performed on euphonium. Euphonium parts also available in treble clef, first tuba parts also available in E♭ treble clef, and second tuba parts also available in B♭ treble clef. More appropriate for a quartet than for a large ensemble. Also reviewed in the Summer 1997 issue of the *TUBA Journal* (Vol. 24, No. 4).

Bach, Johann Sebastian. *Sarabande and Bouree.* arr. Akira Yodo. Tuba-Euphonium Press. Two euphoniums and two tubas. 1991. $6.00. 7:00. IV.

Part I: A♭–b♭'; Part II: G–g'; Part III: F–b♭; Part IV: G_1–f. Two movements: Sarabande; Bourree. No real range or technical difficulties. The Bouree is more polyphonic and consequently more difficult to play together. Though in a different key, this is the same violin partita that Bill Bell transcribed for tuba and piano in *Air and Bourree*. Parts may be doubled for a large ensemble.

Bach, Johann Sebastian. *Sarabande, Gavottes, and Gigue from Cello Suite VI*. arr. Arthur Frackenpohl. Tuba-Euphonium Press. Two euphoniums and two tubas. 1993. $15.00. 8:45. III. Part I: G–c"; Part II: G–a'; Part III: G_1–d'; Part IV: G_1–a. Four movements: Sarabande; Gavotte I; Gavotte II; Gigue. For the U.S. Navy Band Tuba Quartet. Effective arrangement of four dances from this Bach cello suite. The sarabande is in a slow triple meter, while the gavottes and gigue are in a fast duple meter. All parts are interesting and have melodic material at some point. Euphonium parts are scored entirely in tenor clef. Parts may be doubled for a large ensemble. Individual movements can stand alone on a concert.

Bach, Johann Sebastian. *Sheep May Safely Graze*. arr. Gail Robertson. Tuba-Euphonium Press. Two euphoniums and two tubas. 1998. $12.00. 4:00. III. Part I: c–c"; Part II: B♭–a♭'; Part III: A♭–c' (e♭'); Part IV: (C_2) F_1–f. Nice arrangement of this well-known chorale that combines a lyrical, flowing melody with a sustained hymn passage. Melodic material is divided between the top three voices, and all parts are interesting. Euphonium parts also available in treble clef. Parts may be doubled for a large ensemble.

Bach, Johann Sebastian. *Sonate en Trio Vivace*. arr. Alain Cazes. Cazes-Cuivres. Four tubas. 1986. 2:00. IV. Part I: G–c"; Part II: B♭–b♭'; Part III: C–c; Part IV: D_1–e♭. The tessitura of the top two parts is quite high. Both of these parts are printed in tenor clef. Technical demands are greatest on the first part.

Bach, Johann Sebastian. *Toccata and Fugue in D Minor*. arr. Allyn Lindsey. Cimarron Music and Productions. Two euphoniums and two tubas. $16.00. Euphonium parts also available in treble clef.

Bach, Johann Sebastian. *Toccata and Fugue in D Minor*. arr. Todd Fiegel. Celluloid Tubas. Two euphoniums and two tubas. 2000. $25.00. IV. Part I: D–b♭'; Part II: D–a'; Part III: A_1–f'; Part IV: G_1–f'. With best wishes to Junction. Challenging arrangement of this famous piece by Bach. Requires four strong players, as the quartet texture allows for little rest. More appropriate for a quartet than for an ensemble.

Bach, Johann Sebastian. *Two Bach Chorales*. arr. Stephen Shoop. Stephen Shoop Music Publications. Two euphoniums and two tubas. 1997. $7.50. 2:15. I–II. Part I: B♭–g'; Part II: A–d'; Part III: A_1–a; Part IV: (F_1) G_1–c (d). Two movements. Both movements are homophonic with traditional harmonies and serve well as warm-up pieces for young ensembles. Euphonium parts also available in treble clef. Parts may be doubled for a large ensemble. Individual movements can stand alone on a concert.

Bach, Johann Sebastian. *Two Chorales*. arr. Velvet Brown. Velvet Music Edition. Two euphoniums and two tubas.

Bach, Johann Sebastian. *Wachet Auf*. arr. Gary A. Buttery. Whaling Music Publishers. Two euphoniums and two tubas. 1978. $9.00. 3:20. IV. Part I: G–a♭'; Part II: G–a'; Part III: G_1–e♭'; Part IV: F_1–c'. Nice arrangement of this beautiful melody from Bach's Cantata No. 104. The melody is passed around through all four parts. Very lyrical in style at a moderate tempo. Both tuba parts have a high tessitura. Parts may be doubled for a large ensemble.

Bagley, E. E. *National Emblem March*. arr. Robert Wilkinson. Cimarron Music and Productions. Two euphoniums and two tubas. 1997. $13.00. 3:00. Euphonium parts also available in treble clef.

Baker, John, arr. *Lute Dances for Four Part Tuba Ensemble*. The Brass Press. Two euphoniums and two tubas. 1975. $4.00. 1:40. II–III. Part I: e–c'; Part II: d–d'; Part III: B–f♯; Part IV: (A_1) B_1–A. Two movements: Der Prinzentanz; Proportz. Written for R. Winston Morris and the Tennessee Technological University Tuba Ensemble. The limited range and simple rhythms allow this to work well for high school or college ensembles. The difficulty of the performance is determined by the tempo at which the second movement is taken. The Proportz is written in 3/4 but should be felt in one. The first and second parts are printed in both treble and bass clefs. Parts may be doubled for a large ensemble. Recorded by the British Tuba Quartet, *In at the Deep End*, Heavyweight Records Limited, HR008/D.

Bale, Maurice. *Tubalation Rag*. Godiva Music. Two euphoniums and two tubas. £6.00.

Bale, Maurice, arr. *David of the White Rock*. Godiva Music. Two euphoniums and two tubas. £6.00. Welsh air.

Bale, Maurice, arr. *Four English Madrigals*. Godiva Music. Two euphoniums and two tubas. 1994. £5.00. 3:30. II–III. Part I: e–g'; Part II: c–c'; Part III: C_1–g; Part IV: F_1–e. Four movements: Now Is the Month of Maying; The Silver Swan; Awake, Sweet Love; My Bonny Lass She Smileth.

Bale, Maurice, arr. *Oh Dear, What Can the Matter Be?* Godiva Music. Four tubas. 1994. £6.00. 2:00. III. Part I: B♭$_1$–b♭'; Part II: B♭$_1$–g; Part III: B♭$_1$–f; Part IV: (B♭$_2$) F_1–e♭.

Bale, Maurice, arr. *Two Russian Pieces*. Godiva Music. Four tubas. 1994. £5.00. 3:30. II–III. Part I: G–e♭'; Part II: F–g; Part III: C–e♭; Part IV: (C_1) F_1–c.

Ball, Eric. *Friendly Giants.* R. Smith and Company Limited. Four tubas. 1961. $5.00. 5:45. IV. Part I: $B\flat_1$–e♭'; Part II: $B\flat_1$–b♭; Part III: A–e♭'; Part IV: E–d. Two movements. All four parts are printed in treble clef. Parts one and two are for E♭ tubas and parts three and four are for B♭ tubas. Very traditional harmonies. The second movement is technically challenging and contains exposed sections for all parts.

Ball, Eric. *Quartet for Tubas.* R. Smith and Company Limited. Two E♭ tubas and two BB♭ tubas. 1950. $10.00. 5:30. IV. Part I: A–d'; Part II: B♭–b♭; Part III: A–d'; Part IV: F–d'. Two movements: Moderato; Largo. A very traditional-style work. No real technical challenges. The score and parts are both printed in treble clef and must be transposed.

Barber, Samuel. *Adagio for Strings.* arr. Allyn Lindsey. Cimarron Music and Productions. Two euphoniums and two tubas. 2001. $11.50. 4:45. Euphonium parts also available in treble clef. More appropriate for a large ensemble.

Barber, Samuel. *Adagio for Strings.* arr. Kenyon D. Wilson. Tuba-Euphonium Press. Two euphoniums and two tubas. 1999. $12.00. 4:45. III. Part I: c–c♭"; Part II: B♭–g♭'; Part III: E♭–d♭'; Part IV: A_1–g♭. Challenging arrangement in the original key based on Barber's initial four-part *Adagio,* which was the slow movement of one of his early string quartets. There are two possible endings: one with the final phrase performed as *divisi* tubas, and the other which includes euphoniums if there is only one on a part. More appropriate for a large ensemble. Also reviewed in the Summer 2001 issue of the *TUBA Journal* (Vol. 28, No. 4).

Barbera, Giuseppe. *Waphan Touba.* Animado Music Publisher, Sondrio. Two euphoniums and two tubas. 2001. 4:00. III. Part I: c–c"; Part II: E–b'; Part III: $E\flat_1$–e'; Part IV: C_1–e'. Individual parts are challenging, though the scoring is not difficult to rehearse. The strong, syncopated bass line helps the mixed-meter passages. Both euphonium parts have passages in tenor clef.

Barroso, Ari. *Brazil.* arr. Hans Weichselbaumer. Musikverlag Bruno Uetz. One euphonium and three tubas. 1995. €12.00. 1:45. Recorded by the Melton Tuba-Quartett on the compact disc *Lazy Elephants,* Diavolo Records.

Bartles, Alfred H. *When Tubas Waltz.* Kendor Music, Incorporated. Two euphoniums and two tubas. 1976. $11.00. 4:20. IV. Part I: d–b♭'; Part II: B♭–g'; Part III: $B\flat_1$–b; Part IV: $B\flat_1$–b♭. Dedicated to R. Winston Morris and the Tennessee Technological University Tuba Ensemble. A classic early composition for tuba/euphonium ensemble. A jazz waltz in a scherzo-trio-scherzo form. Players must have a good jazz feel. Not easy to play, but works very well. Trap set with brushes can be used to support the feel of a jazz waltz. Parts may be doubled for a large ensemble. Recorded by the Tennessee Technological University Tuba Ensemble, Golden Crest Records, CRS 4139; the Tubadours, *Ya Ve Iss Da Mighty Tubadours,* Crystal Records, S421; David LeClair, *Swingin' Low,* Marcophon.

Bavicchi, John. *Cavatina.* BKJ Publications. Two euphoniums and two tubas. 1999. 1:15. III. Part I: B♭–g♭'; Part II: G–g'; Part III: F–c'; Part IV: $A\flat_1$–a♯. Written for the Colonial Tuba Quartet. Original composition employing modern harmonies including quartal and quintal textures. Frequent use of accidentals and large intervals are the more challenging aspects. Parts may be doubled for a large ensemble.

Bayliss, Colin. *Ale and Arty.* Da Capo Music. One euphonium and two tubas with narrator. £10.00. Narrator performs poems and tales about beer drinking. Recorded by Tubalaté on the compact disc *Earth and Moon.*

Bayliss, Colin. *The Lyke Wake Dirge.* Da Capo Music. Two euphoniums and two tubas. £10.00.

Bayliss, Colin. *Tubalaté Tango.* Da Capo Music. Two euphoniums and two tubas. £8.00.

Beadell, Robert. *Three Sketches.* Brass Music Limited/The Brass Press. Two euphoniums and two tubas. 1974. Out of Print. 6:00. IV. Part I: A♭–c♭" (d♭"); Part II: G♯–g'; Part III: $B\flat_1$–c'; Part IV: $B\flat_1$–c'. Three movements. Commissioned by R. Winston Morris and the Tennessee Technological University Tuba Ensemble. There are many syncopated and jazz-influenced rhythms. The texture can get very thick at times. The third movement is especially technically challenging. Originally published in 1970 by Manuscripts for Tuba.

Beethoven, Ludwig van. *Conga from Symphony No. 7.* arr. Maurice Bale. Godiva Music. Two euphoniums and two tubas. £5.00. A slight revision of the slow movement.

Beethoven, Ludwig van. *Egmont Overture.* arr. Maurice Bale. Godiva Music. Two euphoniums and two tubas. £8.00.

Beethoven, Ludwig van. *Rule Britannia.* arr. David Werden. Cimarron Music and Productions. Two euphoniums and two tubas. 2003. $10.50. 4:15. III. Part I: A–b♭'; Part II: F–a'; Part III: $B\flat_1$–b♭; Part IV: $E\flat_1$–a. Theme and four variations. Quartet showpiece based on the famous theme by Thomas Arne. All parts are technically demanding with large arpeggios and fast lines that are passed between performers. Works great as a concert closer or encore. Euphonium parts also available in treble clef. More appropriate for a quartet than for an ensemble.

Beethoven, Ludwig van. *Sonata "Pathetique."* arr. David R. Werden. Whaling Music Publishers. Two euphoniums and two tubas. 1993. $9.00. IV. Part I: c–d"; Part II: c–b♭'; Part III: C–f♭'; Part IV: $E\flat_1$–d♭'. This is the second movement of the *Piano Sonata in C Minor, Op. 13* (1798). Slow and very melodic, but challenging to play.

The tessitura of the first part is high. The first part is printed in bass and treble clefs. Parts may be doubled for a large ensemble.

Bennet, John. *Weep, O Mine Eyes.* Sarnia Music. Two euphoniums and two tubas. £9.99.

Benzi, Franco. *Fly Down.* Animado Music Publisher, Sondrio. Tuba Quartet. 2003. 11:00. III. Part I: D–e♭'; Part II: C–d'; Part III: G$_1$–g♭; Part IV: G$_1$–f. Dedicated to Renate. Described as a concertino for tuba quartet, the piece is multi-sectional. Each part has exposed melodic lines, though the texture is mostly homophonic. Calls for flutter tonguing in all parts.

Berlin, Irving. *Alexander's Ragtime Band.* arr. John Hoesly. Piston Reed Stick and Bow Publisher. Two euphoniums and two tubas. 1991. $7.00. 2:20. IV. Part I: d–b♭'; Part II: F♯–f'; Part III: C–c♭'; Part IV: F$_1$–g. A good jazz style is required for this swinging arrangement. Some technical challenges in all parts. Drums may be added for stylistic effect. There is no score available. Parts may be doubled for a large ensemble.

Berlin, Irving. *Alexander's Ragtime Band.* arr. Paul Schmidt. Heavy Metal Music. Two euphoniums and two tubas. 1990. $5.00. 1:45. III–IV. Part I: B♭–f'; Part II: A–e♭'; Part III: E♭–e♭; Part IV: F$_1$–A♭. Good arrangement of this famous melody. Most of the melody is in the first part. No score available. Parts may be doubled for a large ensemble.

Berlin, Irving. *Puttin' on the Ritz.* arr. Lennie Niehaus. Kendor Music, Incorporated. Two euphoniums and two tubas. 2002. $11.00. 3:10. III–IV. Part I: f–g'; Part II: B♭–f'; Part III: E♭–g; Part IV: B♭$_1$–d♭. Swing arrangement at a fast tempo. Interesting parts for all performers as each part has the melody at some point. Many tutti rhythms. There is a section with chord symbols in the first part for an improvised solo, or the performer may elect to play the optional solo written in the part. Parts may be doubled for a large ensemble. Also reviewed in the Spring 2003 issue of the *ITEA Journal* (Vol. 30, No. 3).

Berlioz, Hector. *Hungarian March from The Damnation of Faust.* arr. David R. Werden. Whaling Music Publishers. Two euphoniums and two tubas. 1979. $9.00. 2:30. IV. Part I: G–c''; Part II: c–a'; Part III: G–e'; Part IV: G$_1$–a. Technically challenging for the first and second parts. The tessitura of the first and third parts is high. This will require mature players. The first part is printed in treble and tenor clef.

Bernie, Ben, Maceo Pinkard, and Kenneth Casey. *Sweet Georgia Brown.* arr. Jack Fragomeni. Manduca Music Publications. Two euphoniums and two tubas. 1996. $12.00. 4:00. III. Part I: A♭–c''; Part II: c–a'; Part III: G–d'; Part IV: C–g. Fun, light arrangement of this popular work that includes non-jazz and jazz sections. All parts are interesting, with written-out jazz lines and optional improvisation. The fourth part serves as the walking bass line under the written-out improvisation passage. Parts may be doubled for a large ensemble.

Bewley, Norlan. *Cinnamon Downs.* Bewley Music Incorporated. Two euphoniums, two tubas, and three harps. 1992. $25.00. 5:00. IV. Part I: c–a'; Part II: c–a'; Part III: G$_1$–c'; Part IV: G$_1$–d. With the exception of a few solo sections, the primary role of the euphoniums and tubas is to accompany the three harps. All parts are very syncopated and rhythmical in character. Will require precise rhythmic execution between the harps and tubas. The parts are demanding of the harpists.

Bewley, Norlan. *The Instrumentalist March.* Bewley Music, Incorporated. Two euphoniums and two tubas. 1994. $15.00. 4:45. II. Part I: d–b♭'; Part II: F–f'; Part III: C–c'; Part IV: E♭$_1$–g. Part of the Octubafest Music collection, this original composition is appropriate for intermediate-level ensembles. Melodic material is divided among all four voices. Parts may be doubled for a large ensemble. Euphonium parts also available in treble clef.

Bewley, Norlan. *Just Do It.* Bewley Music, Incorporated. Two euphoniums and two tubas. $15.00. 4:45. III. Part I: e♭–c''; Part II: c–b♭'; Part III: A♭–f'; Part IV: E♭$_1$–g. Part of the Octubafest Music collection, this original composition is in a driving, rock style. All parts have the melody at some point. Parts may be doubled for a large ensemble. Euphonium parts also available in treble clef.

Bewley, Norlan. *Octubafest Song, The.* Bewley Music Incorporated. Two euphoniums, two tubas, and vocal solo. 1992. $20.00. 2:30. IV. Part I: B♭–a♭'; Part II: B♭–a♭'; Part III: E♭–e♭'; Part IV: E♭$_1$–g. The text and vocal melody are fairly simple. However, the middle instrumental interlude is challenging, especially for the euphoniums. The tessitura of the third part is high. Parts may be doubled for a large ensemble.

Bewley, Norlan. *The Polka March.* Bewley Music, Incorporated. Two euphoniums and two tubas. 1995. $15.00. 3:15. II. Part I: F–a'; Part II: F–d'; Part III: D–c'; Part IV: F$_1$–d. Part of the Octubafest Music collection, this composition is appropriate for intermediate-level ensembles. Melodic material is divided among all four voices. Parts may be doubled for a large ensemble. Euphonium parts also available in treble clef.

Bewley, Norlan. *Runabout.* Bewley Music Incorporated. Two euphoniums and two tubas. 1993. $15.00. 4:30. IV. Part I: f–b♭'; Part II: c–f'; Part III: F–f'; Part IV: F–g. A good jazz feel is necessary with all the syncopation and swing eighth notes. All parts have the opportunity to play the melody. Drums may be added for effect. Parts may be doubled for a large ensemble.

Bewley, Norlan. *Santa Wants a Tuba for Christmas.* Bewley Music Incorporated. Two euphoniums, two tubas, optional vocal and rhythm. 1992. $20.00. 4:00. IV. Part I: B♭–a'; Part II: B♭–e♭'; Part III: B♭$_1$–f'; Part IV: F$_1$–c. An exceptionally cute tune, especially when used with the vocal solo and rhythm. The first tuba part has two challenging sections, but otherwise, the parts are not difficult. A good swing feel is necessary for all players. The second part has extended *divisi* sections. Fun to play and delightful for audiences. Parts may be doubled for a large ensemble. Recorded by Harvey Phillips and his TubaSantas and Merry TubaChristmas, HPF #1000–1.

Bewley, Norlan, arr. *Barbara and Helena Polka*. Bewley Music, Incorporated. Two euphoniums and two tubas. $10.00. 3:00. II. Part I: B–a'; Part II: B–d'; Part III: G–a; Part IV: F$_1$–c. Part of the Octubafest Music collection, this medley of these two polkas is appropriate for intermediate-level ensembles. Melodic material is predominantly in the top two voices. Parts may be doubled for a large ensemble. Euphonium parts also available in treble clef.

Bewley, Norlan, arr. *The Clarinet Polka*. Bewley Music, Incorporated. Two euphoniums and two tubas. 1995. $10.00. 1:30. II–III. Part I: d–b♭'; Part II: d–a♭'; Part III: B♭$_1$–d'; Part IV: B♭$_1$–a. Part of the Octubafest Music collection. Originally a feature piece for clarinet; this arrangement divides the solo part between all four voices. Parts may be doubled for a large ensemble. Euphonium parts also available in treble clef.

Bewley, Norlan, arr. *Ein Prosit!* Bewley Music, Incorporated. Two euphoniums and two tubas. 1995. $5.00. 0:30. II. Part I: d–b♭'; Part II: d–d'; Part III: F–g; Part IV: F$_1$–d. This brief arrangement of this beer-hall favorite is part of the Octubafest Music collection. Parts may be doubled for a large ensemble. Euphonium parts also available in treble clef.

Bewley, Norlan, arr. *El Tuba*. Bewley Music, Incorporated. Two euphoniums and two tubas. $12.00. 2:45. II. Part I: f–a'; Part II: c–f'; Part III: F–b♭; Part IV: G$_1$–A♭. Part of the Octubafest Music collection, this arrangement is in a Spanish/Mexican style. Parts may be doubled for a large ensemble. Euphonium parts also available in treble clef.

Bewley, Norlan, arr. *Famous Waltzes of the Opera and Ballet*. Bewley Music, Incorporated. Two euphoniums and two tubas. 1995. $15.00. 2:30. II. Part I: B♭–b♭'; Part II: F♯–f♯'; Part III: B♭$_1$–c'; Part IV: F$_1$–f. This medley of several popular waltzes is part of the Octubafest Music collection. Each part performs the melody at some point. Parts may be doubled for a large ensemble. Euphonium parts also available in treble clef.

Bewley, Norlan, arr. *Heel and Toe and Jenny Lind Polkas*. Bewley Music, Incorporated. Two euphoniums and two tubas. $10.00. 2:00. II. Part I: A–e'; Part II: A♭–e'; Part III: G–c'; Part IV: G$_1$–G. Part of the Octubafest Music collection, this medley of these two polkas is appropriate for intermediate-level ensembles. Melodic material is divided among the top three voices. Parts may be doubled for a large ensemble. Euphonium parts also available in treble clef.

Bewley, Norlan, arr. *In Ein Hofbrau Haus/Augustin/Du, Du, Liegst Mir Im Herzen*. Bewley Music, Incorporated. Two euphoniums and two tubas. 1995. $10.00. 1:30. II. Part I: B♭–a♭'; Part II: B♭–f'; Part III: B♭$_1$–c'; Part IV: E♭$_1$–e♭. Part of the Octubafest Music collection, this medley of three popular waltzes is appropriate for intermediate-level ensembles. Melodic material is divided among all four voices. Parts may be doubled for a large ensemble. Euphonium parts also available in treble clef.

Bewley, Norlan, arr. *In Heaven There Is No Beer*. Bewley Music, Incorporated. Two euphoniums and two tubas. 1995. $10.00. 2:00. II. Part I: d♭–a♭'; Part II: E♭–g'; Part III: E♭–d♭'; Part IV: E♭$_1$–d♭. Part of the Octubafest Music collection, the arrangement of this beer-hall favorite is appropriate for intermediate-level ensembles. Lyrics not included. Parts may be doubled for a large ensemble. Euphonium parts also available in treble clef.

Bewley, Norlan, arr. *La Cucaracha*. Bewley Music, Incorporated. Two euphoniums and two tubas. $8.00. 1:45. II. Part I: F–f'; Part II: F–d'; Part III: C–g; Part IV: F$_1$–d. This fun arrangement of a well-known Mexican tune is part of the Octubafest Music collection and is appropriate for intermediate-level performers. Parts may be doubled for a large ensemble. Euphonium parts also available in treble clef.

Bewley, Norlan, arr. *Mexican Hat Dance*. Bewley Music, Incorporated. Two euphoniums and two tubas. $10.00. 3:00. II. Part I: F–b♭'; Part II: F–g'; Part III: B♭$_1$–f; Part IV: F$_1$–d. This fun arrangement of a well-known Mexican tune is part of the Octubafest Music collection and is appropriate for intermediate-level performers. Parts may be doubled for a large ensemble. Euphonium parts also available in treble clef.

Bewley, Norlan, arr. *Peanuts Polka*. Bewley Music, Incorporated. Two euphoniums and two tubas. $12.00. 2:15. II. Part I: e♭–f'; Part II: d–e♭'; Part III: A♭–a♭; Part IV: A♭$_1$–a♭. Part of the Octubafest Music collection, this arrangement is appropriate for intermediate-level ensembles. Melodic material is predominantly in the top two voices. Parts may be doubled for a large ensemble. Euphonium parts also available in treble clef.

Bewley, Norlan, arr. *Red Raven Polka*. Bewley Music, Incorporated. Two euphoniums and two tubas. $10.00. 2:30. II. Part I: c–a'; Part II: c–c'; Part III: D–c'; Part IV: B♭$_1$–f. Part of the Octubafest Music collection, this arrangement is appropriate for intermediate-level ensembles. Melodic material is divided among all four voices.

Parts may be doubled for a large ensemble. Euphonium parts also available in treble clef.

Bewley, Norlan, arr. *Red Wing Polka.* Bewley Music, Incorporated. Two euphoniums and two tubas. 1995. $10.00. 1:00. II. Part I: F–f'; Part II: F–f'; Part III: F–c'; Part IV: F_1–c. Part of the Octubafest Music collection, this arrangement is appropriate for intermediate-level ensembles. Melodic material is divided among the top three voices. Parts may be doubled for a large ensemble. Euphonium parts also available in treble clef.

Bewley, Norlan, arr. *There Is a Tavern in the Town.* Bewley Music, Incorporated. Two euphoniums and two tubas. 1995. $10.00. 3:15. II–III. Part I: c–b♭'; Part II: c–g'; Part III: C–d'; Part IV: F_1–d. Part of the Octubafest Music collection, this arrangement is appropriate for intermediate-level ensembles. Melodic material is divided among all four voices, though the tubas are featured. Parts may be doubled for a large ensemble. Euphonium parts also available in treble clef.

Bewley, Norlan, arr. *The Tinker Polka.* Bewley Music, Incorporated. Two euphoniums and two tubas. 1995. $10.00. 2:30. II–III. Part I: e♭–b♭'; Part II: A♭–g'; Part III: E♭–b♭; Part IV: $E\flat_1$–B♭. Part of the Octubafest Music collection, this arrangement is one of the more challenging in the collection, as all parts have brief sixteenth note runs and arpeggios. Parts may be doubled for a large ensemble. Euphonium parts also available in treble clef.

Billings, William. *Canon.* arr. Paul Schmidt. Heavy Metal Music. Two euphoniums and two tubas. 1991. $5.00. 2:30. III. Part I: c–f'; Part II: A–d'; Part III: C–a; Part IV: F_1–c. The melody and technical demands are most appropriate for high school students. All parts have the opportunity to play the melody. No score available. Parts may be doubled for a large ensemble.

Bizet, George. *Overture from Carmen.* arr. Bruno Seitz. Musikverlag Martin Scherbacher. Two euphoniums and two tubas. 1993. $15.00. 5.00. IV. Part I: B♭–b♭'; Part II: F–g'; Part III: C–b♭; Part IV: F_1–g. Fun arrangement of this famous overture. Technically challenging for the top three parts. The top part is printed in bass and treble clef. Parts may be doubled for a large ensemble.

Bizet, Georges. *Habanera.* arr. Frank J. Halferty. Kendor Music, Incorporated. Two euphoniums and two tubas. 2003. $9.00. 3:00. Part I: A–g'; Part II: G–d'; Part III: D–f♯; Part IV: A_1–e. Melody is evenly distributed among the parts in this well-known work from the opera *Carmen.* Also reviewed in the Spring 2004 issue of the *ITEA Journal* (Vol. 31, No. 3).

Bizet, Georges. *Toreador Song from Carmen.* arr. Byron Gray. Cimarron Music and Productions. Two euphoniums and two tubas. 1998. $13.00. 2:45. Euphonium parts also available in treble clef.

Bizet, Georges. *Toreador Song from Carmen.* arr. Maurice Bale. Godiva Music. Four tubas. 1994. £6.00. 4:00. III. Part I: F–f'; Part II: F–b♭; Part III: $B\flat_1$–f; Part IV: $E\flat_1$–c.

Blahnik, F., and E. Gratz. *The Last Polka.* arr. Paul Schmidt. Heavy Metal Music. Two euphoniums and two tubas. 1992. $7.00. 3:00. IV. Part I: G♭–e♭'; Part II: G♭–f'; Part III: $A\flat_1$–b♭; Part IV: G_1–d♭ (e♭). While the melody is primarily in the first part, the second part is technically more challenging. A good arrangement for those Octubafests and other social events. No score available. Parts may be doubled for a large ensemble.

Blank, Allan. *Music for Tubas.* T.A.P. Music. Four tubas. 1977. $12.00. 9:30. IV–V. Part I: C–b'; Part II: C–b'; Part III: A_1–a'; Part IV: E_1–c'. Three movements. There are extreme range and technical demands for all parts. Euphoniums could be used on any of the first three parts. Will require four strong players. Score not available.

Blatter, Alfred. *Images for Tuba Quartet.* Available from the composer. Four tubas. 1974. 5:20. IV–V. Part I: B♭–f'; Part II: $D\flat_1$–f♯; Part III: C–f♯; Part IV: $E\flat_1$–e♭. Dedicated to the great musicians in TUBA. An early avant-garde work for tuba quartet. This uses mutes and several twentieth-century techniques including flutter tonguing, multiphonics, and some improvisation. Each measure lasts approximately five seconds. Will require four strong players.

Bock, Jerry. *Sunrise Sunset.* arr. Eugene Anderson. Anderson's Arizona Originals. Three euphoniums and one tuba. 1988. $5.00. 2:10. III–IV. Part I: A–g'; Part II: A–g'; Part III: G–g'; Part IV: G_1–g. Probably the most famous selection from *Fiddler on the Roof.* No real technical challenges; the melody is primarily in the top two parts. Parts may be doubled for a large ensemble.

Borodin, Alexander. *Scherzo from Symphony No. 2.* arr. Maurice Bale. Godiva Music. Two euphoniums and two tubas. 1996. £8.00. 4:00. III. Part I: A–c''; Part II: A_1–b♭; Part III: F–b♭; Part IV: D_1–f.

Bottje, Will Gay. *Incognitos.* The Brass Press. Two euphoniums and two tubas. 1974. Out of Print. 7:00. IV. Part I: G–b'; Part II: F♯–g'; Part III: G–e♭'; Part IV: $F\sharp_1$–c'. Two movements. Commissioned by R. Winston Morris and the Tennessee Technological University Tuba Ensemble. Very contemporary-sounding harmonies with many dissonances. The second movement is multimetric and more challenging to play. Will require four strong players.

Bousted, Donald. *Tears.* Available from Tubalaté. Two euphoniums and two tubas. Recorded by Tubalaté on the compact disc *Earth and Moon.*

Bowman, Euday. *Twelfth Street Rag.* arr. David Schanke. Music Arts Publishing Company. Two euphoniums and two tubas. 2001. $14.00. 1:45. II. Part I: B♭–d'; Part II: B♭–b♭; Part III: B♭–g; Part IV: ($B\flat_1$) F–d (f). A straightforward arrangement appropriate for intermediate-level performers. Third part may also be performed on euphonium. Parts may be doubled for a large ensemble.

Boyce, William. *Alleluia.* arr. F. H. Laws. Ohio Valley Tuba Quartet Press. Two euphoniums and two tubas. 1988. $9.00. 1:45. III–IV. Part I: c–f'; Part II: c–e'; Part III: C–d; Part IV: G_1–d. This features an eight-measure theme that is repeated by each part. The texture is very polyphonic, but fits together quite well. Parts may be doubled for a large ensemble.

Boyce, William. *Alleluia from "William Tell Overture."* arr. F. H. Laws. Cimarron Music and Productions. Two euphoniums and two tubas. 1998. $10.50. 3:00. III. Part I: c–f'; Part II: c–e'; Part III: C–g; Part IV: G_1–c. Arrangement of the chorale section in ternary form. The outer parts are homophonic while the middle section contains a four-part fugal texture. Euphonium parts also available in treble clef. Parts may be doubled for a large ensemble.

Brahms, Johaness. *Marienlieder, Op. 22* arr. John Stevens. Available from the arranger. Two euphoniums and two tubas. 1987. 8:30. IV. Part I: f–b♭'; Part II: d♭–g'; Part III: B♭–d'; Part IV: $B\flat_1$–g♭. Seven movements: Con Moto; Andante con Moto; Con Moto; Allegro; Poco Adagio–Legato; Poco Lento; Allegro. Seven characteristic Brahms vocal works transcribed for euphoniums and tubas.

Brahms, Johannes. *Dem dunkeln Schoss der heilgen Erde.* arr. Angelo Manzo. Tuba-Euphonium Press. Two euphoniums and two tubas. 2002. $8.00. 2:15. I–II. Part I: f–b♭'; Part II: c–d'; Part III: F–b♭; Part IV: A_1–d. Originally scored for mixed a cappella chorus and based on a text by Schiller. The texture is predominantly homophonic with the melody in the top voice. Parts may be doubled for a large ensemble. Also reviewed in the Spring 2004 issue of the *ITEA Journal* (Vol. 31, No. 3).

Brahms, Johannes. *Es ist ein Ros' enstprungen.* arr. Stephen Shoop. Cimarron Music and Productions. Two euphoniums and two tubas. 1995. $7.50. 2:30. II. Part I: e–b♭'; Part II: c–e♭'; Part III: E♭–b♭; Part IV: $B\flat_1$–e♭. Also known as "Lo, How a Rose E'er Blooming," this simple chorale is set with traditional harmonies. Range and style are appropriate for young ensembles. Euphonium parts also available in treble clef. Parts may be doubled for a large ensemble.

Brahms, Johannes. *Four Brahms Folk Songs.* tr. Frank Ferriano. Tuba-Euphonium Press. Two euphoniums and two tubas. 2000. $8.00. 5:30. I–II. Part I: e♭–a'; Part II: d–e♭'; Part III: G–c'; Part IV: ($A\flat_1$) $B\flat_1$–f. Four movements: In Stiller Nacht; Erlaube mir; Abschiedslied; Da untem im tale. Effective collection of arrangements by Brahms appropriate for young ensembles. Each work is predominantly homophonic in texture with the melody in the first part. Serves well as study pieces for ensemble intonation and legato playing. Parts may be doubled for a large ensemble. Individual movements can stand alone on a concert.

Brahms, Johannes. *Hungarian Dance No. 5.* arr. Bruno Seitz. Musikverlag Martin Scherbacher. Four tubas. 1993. $15.00. 3:30. IV. Part I: c–a♭'; Part II: B♭–d'; Part III: F–f; Part IV: F_1–c. The tessitura of the first part is high. Euphoniums may be used on the top two parts to make this playable by most college and some high school students. The melody is primarily in the top part. Parts may be doubled for a large ensemble.

Brahms, Johannes. *Hungarian Dance No. 5.* arr. David Woodcock. Green Bay Music. Two euphoniums and two tubas. 1992. $22.00. 2:20. IV. Part I: d–b♭'; Part II: c♯–f'; Part III: F♯–b♭; Part IV: C–f. The euphonium parts are the most challenging, as they have primary melodic responsibility. There are several tempo changes. Players will need to play in a clean and light style. All four parts are printed in bass and treble clef.

Brahms, Johannes. *Hungarian Dance No. 5.* arr. Frank J. Halferty. Kendor Music, Inc. Two euphoniums and two tubas. 2002. $9.00. 2:15. IV. Part I: A–a'; Part II: A–f'; Part III: A_1–f; Part IV: G_1–f. Challenging arrangement of this popular piece in the key of D. Each part has the melody at some point. Two-octave arpeggios in the first part and technical passages in the first and second parts provide the greatest challenge. Parts may be doubled for a large ensemble. Also reviewed in the Spring 2003 issue of the *ITEA Journal* (Vol. 30, No. 3).

Brahms, Johannes. *Six German Folk Songs.* arr. Stephen Shoop. Cimarron Music and Productions. Two euphoniums and two tubas. 1995. $9.00. 4:00. I–II. Part I: d–a'; Part II: G–e♭'; Part III: D–c'; Part IV: (G_1) $B\flat_1$–e♭. Six movements: I'd Enter Your Garden; The Fiddler; How Sad Flow the Streams; At Night; Awake, Awake!; A House Stands 'Neath the Willows' Shade. Originally for vocal ensemble, the songs in this collection are based on folk songs collected by Brahms. The songs are relatively easy and offer a variety of styles. Euphonium parts also available in treble clef. Parts may be doubled for a large ensemble. Individual movements can stand alone on a concert.

Brahms, Johannes. *Three Pieces from Brahms.* tr. William R. Lee. Tuba-Euphonium Press. Two euphoniums and two tubas. 1997. $12.00. 5:45. II–III. Part I: e♭–b♭'; Part II: d–g'; Part III: B♭–c' (e♭'); Part IV: C–c'. Three movements: Geleit; Freiwilliger her!; Marschieren. Apart from the range considerations, this set of transcriptions is accessible by intermediate-level performers. The outer march movements are contrasted slightly by the upbeat middle movement in three. Individual movements can stand alone in a concert.

Divisi passages make the work more appropriate for a large ensemble. Also reviewed in the Summer 1998 issue of the *TUBA Journal* (Vol. 25, No. 4).

Brahms, Johannes. *Waldesnacht, clu Wunder Kühle (Wondrous Cool, Thou Woodland Quiet).* arr. Mark Nelson. Whaling Music Publishers. Two euphoniums and two tubas. 1988. $5.50. 1:45. III–IV. Part I: f♯–a'; Part II: d–e'; Part III: G–a; Part IV: G_1–d. Nice chorale-like arrangement of this tranquil melody. No significant technical or range problems. Parts may be doubled for a large ensemble.

Brahms, Johannes. *Wonderous Cool, Thou Woodland Quiet.* arr. Mark Nelson. Cimarron Music and Productions. Two euphoniums and two tubas. $11.00. Parts I–II: d–a'; Parts III–IV: G_1–a. A lyrical and expressive work with Brahms' typical light dissonance and chromaticism. Melodic material is primarily in the first part. Euphonium parts also available in treble clef. Parts may be doubled for a large ensemble. Also reviewed in the Winter 1996 issue of the *TUBA Journal* (Vol. 23, No. 2).

Brandon, Sy. *In Rememberance, September 11, 2001.* Tuba-Euphonium Press. Three euphoniums and one tuba. 2002. $20.00. 12:30. III. Part I: e–c''; Part II: A–g'; Part III: E–e♭'; Part IV: E_1–a. Four movements: Fanfare to Fallen Heroes; Elegy for the Innocent; Justice; Prayer for Peace. To the Euphouria Quartet. Challenging large-scale work in response to the events of September 11, 2001. The opening movement is a maestoso fanfare, the second movement is an andante elegy, the third movement faster with "battle motives," and the final movement is a slow chaconne in mixed meter. Parts may be doubled for a large ensemble. Also reviewed in the Spring 2004 issue of the *ITEA Journal* (Vol. 31, No. 3).

Brandon, Sy. *Quartet for Tubas.* Co-op Press. Two euphoniums and two tubas. 1988. 4:20. IV. Part I: f–c''; Part II: c–g'; Part III: F–b♭; Part IV: F_1–c. No real technical problems, but there are several high b♭'s in the first part. Some interesting melodic passages and tasteful contemporary harmonies. Good writing. Parts may be doubled for a large ensemble.

Brandon, Sy, arr. *Music for International Tuba Day, Book I.* Tuba-Euphonium Press. Two euphoniums and two tubas. 1991. $12.00. 21 pp. II. Part I: G–g' (a'); Part II: G–e♭'; Part III: G_1–g; Part IV: F_1–e♭. Thirteen pieces: Polly Wolly Doodle; All through the Night; Sailor's Hornpipe; Israeli Medley; Du, Du, liegst mir im Herzen; Camptown Races; Waltzing Matilda; Cielito Lindo; My Old Kentucky Home; Oh Suzanna; International Tuba Day March; Yankee Doodle; America, the Beautiful. Collection of straightforward arrangements compiled for use in International Tuba Day celebrations, which fall on the first Friday of May. All performers read off the flip-folder-sized score, and the parts are accessible by young to intermediate-level performers. Parts may be doubled for a large ensemble. Individual movements can stand alone on a concert.

Brandon, Sy, arr. *Music for International Tuba Day, Book II.* Tuba-Euphonium Press. Two euphoniums and two tubas. 1991. $12.00. 20 pp. II. Part I: G–a' (c''); Part II: G–f'; Part III: G_1–g; Part IV: F_1–f. Twelve pieces: Blue Tail Fly; Santa Lucia; Home on the Range; The Girl I Left behind Me; Steal Away/Swing Low; Railroad Medley; Sakura; Blow the Man Down; Red River Valley; Alouette; Sidewalks of New York; Evening Prayer. Collection of straightforward arrangements compiled for use in International Tuba Day celebrations, which fall on the first Friday of May. All performers read off the flip-folder-sized score, and the parts are accessible by young to intermediate-level performers. Parts may be doubled for a large ensemble. Individual movements can stand alone on a concert.

Bratton. *The Teddy Bears' Picnic.* arr. Maurice Bale. Godiva Music. Two euphoniums and two tubas. £7.00.

Bright Euphonium Tuba Ensemble, Book 1. Kyodo Music. Two euphoniums and two tubas. ¥2266. 70 pp. III. Part I: F–b♭' (c''); Part II: F♯–g' (b♭'); Part III: $B♭_1$–b; Part IV: A_1–a. Twelve movements: Air on a G String by J. S. Bach; Minuet in G by Beethoven; Traumerei by Schumann; Eine Kleine Nacht Musick, First Movement by Mozart; Moments Musicaux No. 3 by Schubert; Humoreske by Dvorák; Minuet by Boccherini; Andante Cantabile by Tchaikovsky; Hungarian Dance No. 5 by Brahms; Gavotte by Gossee; Salut d'amour by Elgar; Symphony No. 1, Third Movement by Mahler. Large collection of popular arrangements. The majority are scored for quartet, though four are for trio, two are for duet, and one is for a quintet.

Britain, Radie. *The World Does Not Wish for Beauty.* T.A.P. Music. Four tubas. 1980. $5.00. 4:20. IV. Part I: E♭–f'; Part II: C–c'; Part III: B_1–g♭; Part IV: E_1–b♭. The tessitura of the first part is high. No significant technical problems. Parts may be doubled for a large ensemble. Score is not available.

Broeniman, Ernest, arr. *Wooden Heart "Muss I Denn."* ed. Paul Luhring. PEL Music Publications. Two euphoniums and two tubas. 1996. $9.25. 1:45. II–III. Part I: e♭–a♭'; Part II: B♭–f'; Part III: E♭–a♭; Part IV: G_1–f. Effective arrangement in a light march style. All parts are interesting, and melodic material is divided among all four voices. Range and style are appropriate for intermediate-level performers. Parts may be doubled for a large ensemble.

Brown, Lew, Wladimie Timm, and Jaromin Vejouda. *Beer Barrel Polka* arr. Ray Grim. Cimarron Music and Productions. Two euphoniums and two tubas. 1996. $10.00. 2:15. II. Part I: B♭–e♭'; Part II: B♭–c'; Part III: $B♭_1$–f; Part IV: (F_1) G_1–f.

Straightforward arrangement of this beer-hall standard–part of the TubaMeisters Collection. Melodic material is divided among all four parts. Parts may be doubled for a large ensemble. Euphonium parts also available in treble clef.

Brown, Nacio Herb. *Singing in the Rain*. arr. Denzil Stephens. Sarnia Music. Two euphoniums and two tubas.

Brown, Velvet. *Two Chorales*. Velvet Music Edition. Two euphoniums and two tubas.

Bruckner, Anton. *Ave Maria*. arr. David Sabourin. Touch of Brass Music Corporation. Two euphoniums and two tubas. $6.50.

Bruckner, Anton. *Graduale: Locus Iste*. Musikverlag Bruno Uetz. One euphonium and three tubas. €10.00. Second part may be also performed on euphonium. Recorded by the Melton Tuba-Quartett on the compact disc *Lazy Elephants,* and by the Dutch Tuba Quartet on the compact disc *Escape from Oom-Pah Land,* World Wind Music.

Bruckner, Anton. *Locus Iste*. arr. David Sabourin. Touch of Brass Music Corporation. Two euphoniums and two tubas. $6.50.

Bruckner, Anton. *Three Bruckner Motets*. arr. John Stevens. Tuba-Euphonium Press. Two euphoniums and two tubas. 1995. $10.00. 6:00. II. Part I: d–b♭'; Part II: B♭–d'; Part III: E♭–c'; Part IV: $A\flat_1$–e♭. Three movements: Vexilla Regis; Locus Iste; Pangue Langua. Collection of three motets in a late-romantic style. Each motet is predominantly homophonic in texture and is appropriate for intermediate-level performers. Individual movements can stand alone on a concert. Parts may be doubled for a large ensemble.

Bruckner, Anton. *Three Motets*. arr. John Stevens. Available from the arranger. Two euphoniums and two tubas. 1986. 6:00. IV. Part I: d–b♭'; Part II: B♭–d'; Part III: E♭–c'; Part IV: G_1–f. Three movements: Vexilla Reqis; Locus Iste; Pange Linqua. Three very sonorous vocal motets. Very polyphonic.

Bull, John. *The King's Hunt*. arr. Michael Howard. BTQ Publications. Two euphoniums and two tubas. 1993. $9.00. 2:30. Recorded by the British Tuba Quartet *Elite Syncopations,* Polyphonic Reproductions Limited, QPRZ 012D.

Bull, John. *The King's Hunt*. arr. Michael Howard. Studio Music Company. Two euphoniums and two tubas. 1996. Part I: F–a'; Part II: F–a'; Part III: F_1–d'; Part IV: F_1–d'. Challenging arrangement that works well as a show piece. All parts are technically challenging and require double-tonguing. Euphonium parts also available in treble clef, first tuba parts also available in E♭ treble clef, and second tuba parts also available in both E♭ and B♭ treble clef. Also reviewed in the Spring 1997 issue of the *TUBA Journal* (Vol. 24, No. 3). Recorded by the British Tuba Quartet on the compact disc *Elite Syncopations,* Polyphonic Records.

Bulla, Stephen. *Celestial Suite*. Rosehill Music Publishing Company. Two euphoniums and two tubas. 1989. $14.95. 8:00. IV. Part I: c–c"; Part II: F–g♭'; Part III: C–c'; Part IV: E_1–f. Three movements: Eclipse; Canzone Lunaire; Solar Plexus. A very tuneful virtuosic work for tuba/euphonium quartet. The tessitura of the first part is high. All four parts are challenging technically. The third part has a brief improvised cadenza, and the player has to blow into his instrument to imitate the sound of wind. All four parts are printed in treble and bass clef. Recorded by the British Tuba Quartet, *Euphonic Sounds,* Polyphonic Reproductions Limited, QPRZ 009D.

Bulla, Stephen. *Quartet for Low Brass*. Kendor Music, Incorporated. Two euphoniums and two tubas. 1978. Out of Print. 4:00. IV. Part I: A–e'; Part II: G–c'; Part III: C–f; Part IV: G_1–d. A single-movement work in three sections: a bright fanfare, a lyrical middle section, and a march-like finale. Range is not demanding. A couple of technical sections can be tricky, but the piece generally fits together quite nicely. The composition works very well and is a good audience pleaser. Parts may be doubled for a large ensemble. Recorded by the British Tuba Quartet, *In at the Deep End,* Heavyweight Records, HR008/D; The U.S. Navy Tuba Quartet, The U.S. Navy Band.

Bulla, Stephen, arr. *Quartets for Low Brass, Volume I: Traditional Favorites*. Tuba-Euphonium Press. Two euphoniums and two tubas. 1992. $25.00. 16 pp. III–IV. Part I: A♭–c"; Part II: G–g'; Part III: $A\flat_1$–a♭; Part IV: F_1–e♭. Ten movements: The Blue Bells of Scotland; Blow the Man Down; Auld Lang Syne; Polly Wolly Doodle; Listen to the Mockingbird; Sourwood Mountain; Oh, Susanna; The Last Rose of Summer; He's a Jolly Good Fellow; Good Night Ladies. The range demands vary greatly from one movement to another. Since there are very few technical challenges, many of these are very playable by high school ensembles. The arrangements are very short and are most appropriate for recreational use, not a formal concert. The settings of the movements are very traditional. The top two parts are printed in bass and treble clef. Parts may be doubled for a large ensemble.

Bulla, Stephen, arr. *Quartets for Low Brass, Volume II: Spirituals*. Tuba-Euphonium Press. Two euphoniums and two tubas. 1992. $25.00. 11 pp. IV. Part I: F–c" (d"); Part II: F–g'; Part III: C–b♭; Part IV: F_1–e. Ten movements: Little David Play; Down by the Riverside; Go Down Moses; Deep River; Swing Low, Sweet Chariot; Every Time I Feel the Spirit; Amazing Grace; Joshua; Precious Lord Take My Hand; Hand Me Down My Silver Tuba. These arrangements are of moderate technical difficulty, but the tessitura of the first part is high. Each movement is a different spiritual and is relatively short–just one verse of each song. These are designed for school or recreational use, not necessarily a formal concert. The top two parts are printed in both treble and bass clef. Parts may be doubled for a large ensemble.

Bulla, Stephen, arr. *Quartets for Low Brass, Volume III: Fanfares and Anthems.* Tuba-Euphonium Press. Two euphoniums and two tubas. 1992. $25.00. 13 pp. III–IV. Part I: B♭–b♭'; Part II: B♭–e♭; Part III: B♭$_1$–b♭; Part IV: F$_1$–d. Twelve movements: Hail to the Chief; Star Spangled Banner; America the Beautiful; God Save the Queen (My Country 'Tis of Thee); O Canada; Rule Britannia; La Marseillaise; Fanfare of Tribute; Fanfare D'Sousa; Canonic Fanfare; Quartre Fanfares Generique; Choral Anthem ("Now the Day Is Over"). Short traditional arrangements of twelve familiar fanfares and national anthems. No significant technical problems. Designed as study material or for use on specific occasions. Parts may be doubled for a large ensemble.

Bullet, William. *Greensleeves.* arr. Gary A. Buttery. Whaling Music Publishers. Two euphoniums and two tubas. 1978. $5.00. 2:00. III–IV. Part I: B♭–f'; Part II: A–e'; Part III: D–a; Part IV: D$_1$–B♭. A very lush arrangement of this traditional melody. The melody is all in the euphonium parts, but the tessitura is not high. The first tuba part has several measures of flowing sixteenth notes. Parts may be doubled for a large ensemble. Recorded by the Atlantic Tuba Quartet, *Euphonic Sounds,* Golden Crest Records, CRS 4173; the British Tuba Quartet, *Euphonic Sounds,* Polyphonic Records, QPRZ009D.

Burn, Chris. *Hall of Mirrors.* Available from Tubalaté. Two euphoniums and two tubas. Recorded by Tubalaté on the compact disc *Hall of Mirrors.*

Buttery, Gary. *An English Folk Christmas.* Whaling Music Publishers. Four tubas. 1978. $7.50. 3:30. IV–V. Part I: B♭–b♭^{1}; Part II: G–g'; Part III: E♭–e; Part IV: F♯$_1$–e. A nice medley in a single movement of five English folk/Christmas songs: Gloucestershire Wassail, God Rest Ye Merry Gentlemen, All You That Are to Mirth Inclined, King Herod and the Cock, and Here We Come A-Wassailing. Each part has the opportunity to play one of the melodies. The tessitura of the first part is high. Euphoniums may be used for the first and second parts. Parts may be doubled for a large ensemble. Recorded by the U.S. Coast Guard Tuba/Euphonium Quartet, U.S. Coast Guard Recordings.

Buttery, Gary. *Musica De Lupus: Scenarios for the Continued Existence of a Misunderstood Friend–The Wolf.* Whaling Music Publishers. Four tubas. 1978. $12.00. 12:30. IV–V. Part I: F–g♯'; Part II: D–f'; Part III: (D$_1$) E$_1$–f'; Part IV: B$_2$–d♯. A very contemporary programmatic work. The single movement contains four sections: Vocalise for the Survivors, The Hunted, Orphans of the Wind, and A Right to Life. The music portrays the struggle faced by the wolf in the never-ending encroachment upon its wilderness home. The work is technically very challenging and places great range demands on all four parts. Twentieth-century techniques required include glissandos, blowing wind through the tuba, half-valve notes, quarter tones, and a free rhythmic section. This composition requires mutes for all four parts. Won Honorable Mention in the 1978 Mirafone Tuba Quartet Composition Competition.

Buttery, Gary, arr. *An English Christmas Country Dance.* Cimarron Music and Productions. Two euphoniums and two tubas. $14.00.

Buttery, Gary, arr. *Fantasia of Eastern Europe Village Dances.* Cimarron Music and Productions. Two euphoniums and two tubas. $18.00. 10:45. Euphonium parts also available in treble clef. Recorded by the Alchemy Tuba Quartet on the compact disc *Village Dances,* Alchemy.

Buttery, Gary, arr. *Sponger Money.* Whaling Music Publishers. Two euphoniums, two tubas, and percussion. 1983. $7.50. 2:50. IV. Part I: A–d"; Part II: A–c"; Part III: C–f'; Part IV: F$_1$–f. Good arrangement of this familiar Latin melody with a calypso beat. The percussion parts are written in the euphonium and tuba parts and are to be played by those players. There is a section with chord symbols for both tuba parts to improvise solos. The top part requires a mute and the bottom three parts are asked to sing. The tessitura is high for the top three parts. Fun for performers and audience.

Butts, Carol M. *March and Chorale.* Pro Art Publications, Incorporated. Two trombones (euphoniums) and two tubas. 1971. Out of Print. 3:00. III–IV. Part I: e♭–g♭'; Part II: B♭–f'; Part III: B♭$_1$–f; Part IV: B♭$_1$–e♭. Published originally for trombones and tubas, this works just as well with euphoniums on the first and second parts. Very basic rhythms in the 6/8 section, and the chorale section is in cut time. Traditional harmonies. Parts may be doubled for a large ensemble.

Buxtehude, Dietrich. *Alles, was Ihr Tut (All You Do in Life).* arr. William D. Pardus. Creation Station. Two euphoniums and two tubas. 2001. $12.00. 2:00. II–III. Part I: e–f'; Part II: B♭–d'; Part III: D–a; Part IV: G$_1$–d. Originally scored for SATB chorus, strings, and continuo. Parts may be doubled for a larger ensemble. Euphonium parts also available in treble clef. Also reviewed in the Spring 2003 issue of the *ITEA Journal* (Vol. 30, No. 3).

Buxtehude, Dietrich. *Canzona in d.* arr. Angelo Manzo. Tuba-Euphonium Press. Two euphoniums and two tubas. 2002. $8.00. 3:15. II–III. Part I: d–a'; Part II: A–d'; Part III: C–b♭; Part IV: G♯$_1$–d. Highly imitative contrapuntal work in ternary form, with the outer sections marked at a moderate tempo in quadruple meter and the middle section much faster and in triple meter. Parts are of equal difficulty, and the melodic material is divided among all four voices. Parts may be doubled for a large ensemble.

Byrd, William. *Ave Verum.* arr. Patrick Schulz. Tuba-Euphonium Press. Two euphoniums and two tubas. 1998. $8.00. 3:30. II. Part I: b–a'; Part II: c–c'; Part III: c–c'; Part IV: C–f. This work is typical of music from this era, with many points of imitation and open harmonies. All parts are equally difficult and accessible by intermediate-level performers. Parts may be doubled for a large ensemble. Also reviewed in the Fall 2001 issue of the *ITEA Journal* (Vol. 29, No. 1).

Byrd, William. *Ave Verum Corpus.* arr. Michael Howard. BTQ Publications. Two euphoniums and two tubas. 1993. $8.00.

Byrd, William. *Ave Verum Corpus.* arr. Paul Schmidt. Heavy Metal Music. Two euphoniums and two tubas. 1991. $5.00. 4:00. III. Part I: e–e'; Part II: G–a; Part III: G–g; Part IV: A_1–c. All parts have a chance to play the theme. This is very polyphonic, but fits together very nicely. No score available. Parts may be doubled for a large ensemble.

Byrd, William. *Earle of Oxford March.* arr. Allyn Lindsey. Cimarron Music and Productions. Two euphoniums and two tubas. $16.00. Euphonium parts also available in treble clef.

Byrd, William. *Earle of Oxford Marche.* arr. Kenyon D. Wilson. Tuba-Euphonium Press. Two euphoniums and two tubas. 1998. $10.00. 1:15. III. Part I: d–a'; Part II: G–e'; Part III: C–a; Part IV: G_1–g. This stately march is in ternary form, with a metric modulation to double time in the middle section. Melodic material is divided among the four voices, and all parts have challenging technical passages. Euphonium parts also available in treble clef. Parts may be doubled for a large ensemble. Also reviewed in the Spring 2002 issue of the *ITEA Journal* (Vol. 29, No. 3).

Byrd, William. *Jhon Come Kisse Me Now.* arr. Denis Winter. Whaling Music Publisher. Two euphoniums and two tubas. 1978. $7.00. 2:00. IV. Part I: F–g'; Part II: F–g'; Part III: C–e'; Part IV: F_1–c'. A nice lyrical melody. The high tessitura of the third and fourth parts will require mature players. Good rhythmic accuracy is required. The first and second parts are printed in treble clef. Recorded by the Atlantic Tuba Quartet, *Euphonic Sounds,* Golden Crest Records, CRS 4173; the British Tuba Quartet, *Euphonic Sounds,* Polyphonic Reproductions Limited, QPRZ009D.

Byrd, William. *Stately Procession.* arr. Gregory Bright. Tuba/Euphonium Music Publications. Two euphoniums and two tubas. Out of Print. 4:00. III. Permanently out of print.

Byrd, William. *Wolsey's Wilde.* arr. Gordon Jacob and Gail Robertson. Tuba-Euphonium Press. Two euphoniums and two tubas. 1998. $12.00. 1:00. III. Part I: d–b♭'; Part II: B♭–f'; Part III: E♭–b♭; Part IV: (F_1) G_1–B♭. This arrangement is based on a movement from the *William Byrd Suite,* arranged for concert band by Gordon Jacob. It is in the form of a light gigue, and the melodic material is divided among the four voices. Euphonium parts also available in treble clef. Parts may be doubled for a large ensemble, and there are *divisi* passages in the second euphonium part. Also reviewed in the Spring 2002 issue of the *ITEA Journal* (Vol. 29, No. 3).

Camphouse, Mark. *Ceremonial Sketch.* Available from the arranger. Two euphoniums and two tubas. 1988. $6.00. 4:30. IV–V. Part I: G–d♭"; Part II: G♭–c"; Part III: G_1–f'; Part IV: D♯$_1$–c'. Written for R. Winston Morris and the Tennessee Technological University Tuba Ensemble. A major work. Many sections of all parts are *divisi,* making it necessary to double the players on each part. Range demands are extreme and will require strong players on all four parts. Recorded by the Tennessee Technological University Tuba Ensemble, Mark Custom Recording Service, MENC88-1-4; the U.S. Armed Forces Tuba/Euphonium Ensemble and Massed Ensemble, U.S. Army Band.

Cannon, Hughie. *Rev Bill Bailey.* arr. Rodger Vaughan. Available from the arranger. Two euphoniums and two tubas. 1986. $5.00. 1:20. IV. Part I: f–b♭', Part II: e♭–f', Part III: F♯–b♭, Part IV: C-d. For Bert Harclerode's birthday. A medium-tempo version of Bill Bailey. No significant technical problems. The melody is primarily in the first part. Drums may be added for stylistic effect. There is no score available. Parts may be doubled for a large ensemble.

Canter, James A. *Appalachian Carol (Quartet No. 2).* Tuba-Euphonium Press. Two euphoniums and two tubas. 1992. $10.00. 5:20. IV. Part I: A–a♭'; Part II: A–d'; Part III: B♭$_1$–e♭; Part IV: A_1–d. Written for R. Winston Morris and the Tennessee Technological University Tuba Ensemble. An exceptional and tuneful composition based on the hymn "What Wondrous Love Is This?" The composition is in a slow-fast-slow-fast form. Some brief technical challenges. Fun to play and enjoyable for audiences. Parts may be doubled for a large ensemble. Originally copyrighted in 1980 and published by Kendor Music, Incorporated. Recorded by the U.S. Armed Forces Tuba/Euphonium Ensemble and Massed Ensemble, U.S. Army Band Records.

Canter, James A. *Paraklesis.* Tuba-Euphonium Press. Two euphoniums, two tubas, and tambourine. 1993. $15.00. 5:00. V. Part I: A_1–g'; Part II: A_1–e'; Part III: G_1–a; Part IV: F_1–c♯. Commissioned by and written for R. Winston Morris and the Tennessee Technological University Tuba Ensemble. A very contemporary and complex composition. There are numerous twentieth-century techniques required, including blowing through the instrument, bending pitches, quarter tones, playing pitches and rhythms in a random order, and frequent odd meter changes. Will require very strong players. Originally written and first performed in 1981. Parts may be doubled for a large ensemble.

Canter, James A. *Siamang Suite.* Tuba-Euphonium Press. Two euphoniums and two tubas. 1992. $10.00. 6:00. IV. Part I: c–d♭''; Part II: c–a'; Part III: $B♭_1$–c'; Part IV: G_1–a. Three movements: Introduction; Song; Dance. To the Tennessee Technological University Tuba Ensemble, R. Winston Morris, Director. A classic work for tuba/euphonium ensemble. All four parts require a mute in the eerie-sounding second movement. The third movement is a fast-paced, vibrant multimetric dance. Technically the composition is moderately demanding, but a challenge to put together without a conductor. Parts may be doubled for a large ensemble. Originally published by Kendor Music, Incorporated, and copyrighted in 1978.

Canter, James A., arr. *12 Days of Housetops!* Kendor Music, Incorporated. Two euphoniums and two tubas. 1985. $9.50. 3:15. III–IV. Part I: B♭–g'; Part II: A–$e♭_1$; Part III: $A♭_1$–g♭; Part IV: F_1–B. Commissioned by the Franklin (Tenn.) Junior H.S. Tuba Ensemble, Bill Marley and Bob Horne, directors. A cute arrangement combining "The Twelve Days of Christmas" and "Up on the Housetop." Players are asked to speak through their instruments and some parts are required to play half-valve glissandos. Many tempo and style changes. Very entertaining for both performers and audience. Parts may be doubled for a large ensemble.

Carmichael, Hoagy. *Georgia on My Mind.* arr. David LeClair. Editions Marc Reift. Two euphoniums and two tubas. 1992. CHF 20.00. 4:00. IV. Part I: g♭–b'; Part II: c♯–g'; Part III: E♭–e♭'; Part IV: C_1–c♯'. In addition to bass clef parts, euphonium parts are also available in treble, first tuba parts also available in E♭ treble, and second tuba also available in E♭ and B♭ treble clef. Parts may be doubled for a large ensemble. Recorded by Contraband on the compact disc *Singin' Low,* Marcophon Records.

Carmody, Bill. *Fifteen Easy Pieces for Bass Clef Instruments.* Whaling Music Publishers. Two euphoniums and two tubas. $15.00. 18 pp. III–IV. Part I: (B♭) c–e♭'; Part II: B♭–c'; Part III: E♭–c'; Part IV: $A♭_1$–d. A collection of fifteen short compositions contrasting in key, style, and tempo. Of the fifteen pieces there are two duets, two trios, one euphonium solo with trio accompaniment, and ten quartets. Most are not technically demanding and would be suitable for a good high school ensemble. Parts are printed in a booklet with parts one and two in one booklet and parts three and four in the other. Parts may be doubled for a large ensemble. Fun to play.

Carmody, Bill, and Mike Francis. *Hard Way.* Whaling Music Publishers. Four tubas. $5.00. 4:00. IV. Part I: d–c''; Part II: F–f'; Part III: F_1–f'; Part IV: F_1–e♭. A hard rock bass line passed between the third and fourth parts becomes the foundation of this piece. There is a section with chord symbols in all four parts for improvised solos and bass lines. The tessitura of the first two parts is high, and they may be played by euphonium. Drums may be added for stylistic effect. Parts may be doubled for a large ensemble.

Carolino, Sérgio. *Lili's Funk.* Lusitanus Editions, Portugal. Four tubas and rhythm section. 2000. 6:00. V. Dedicated to the Tubophonia Jazz Ensemble. Funky groove style. Some improvisation required. Rhythm section includes electric bass, electric guitar, and drums.

Carolino, Sérgio. *TGV.* Lusitanus Editions, Portugal. Four tubas and rhythm section. 2004. 5:00. V. Dedicated to the Tubophonia Jazz Ensemble. New Orleans street-parade groove-music style. Very high tessitura for the first and second parts–may also be performed on euphoniums. Rhythm section includes electric bass, electric guitar, and drums.

Carolino, Sérgio. *TUrBulênciA Sonora.* Lusitanus Editions, Portugal. Four tubas and optional vibraphone. 2004. 6:00. V. Dedicated to the Portugal Tuba Ensemble "Tubophonia." A very rhythmical and energetic piece! Improvisation is required on the first tuba and vibraphone. A very strong bass line on the fourth tuba part.

Censhu, Jiro. *No No Hate Yori (From beyond the Field).* Available from the composer. Two euphoniums and two tubas. 1992. $10.00. 9:30. IV. Part I: e♭–c''; Part II: B♭–a'; Part III: G_1–f'; Part IV: G_1–g. Commissioned by and dedicated to the Sendai Tuba/Euphonium Ensemble. A slow introduction in 3/4 followed by a very fast animated section in 4/4. The melody is primarily in the euphoniums but all parts are interesting. The tessitura of the first part is very high. There is a challenging cadenza for the third part. Works well. Parts may be doubled for a large ensemble.

Censhu, Jiro. *Sai Kai (The Reunion).* Available from the composer. Two euphoniums and two tubas. 1992. $10.00. 5:00. IV. Part I: c–a'; Part II: F–f'; Part III: E♭–b♭; Part IV: A_1–b♭. Commissioned by and dedicated to the Sendai Tuba/Euphonium Ensemble. The melody is in a moderate 6/8 tempo with very traditional harmonies. No significant range or technical problems. Parts may be doubled for a large ensemble.

Censhu, Jiro. *Shinju (May Tree).* Available from the composer. Two euphoniums and two tubas. 1991. $10.00. 8:30. IV. Part I: c–b♭'; Part II: G–b♭'; Part III: C–c'; Part IV: F_1–b♭. Two movements. Commissioned by and dedicated to the Sendai Tuba/Euphonium Ensemble. The first movement is in a slow 4/4 and the second movement is in a spirited 6/8. All four parts are interesting and challenging. The tessitura of the first part is high. Parts may be doubled for a large ensemble.

Charpentier, Marc-Antoine. *Prelude from "Te Deum."* arr. Paul Schmidt. Heavy Metal Music. Two euphoniums and two tubas. 1997. $7.00. 3:00. Part I: F–g'; Part II: G–g'; Part III: D–c'; Part IV: F_1–c. This baroque-style arrangement is accessible for intermediate-level performers and is appropriate as a fanfare or concert opener. The melody alternates between the first two parts, providing each player with adequate rest. Also reviewed in the Winter 1999 issue of the *TUBA Journal* (Vol. 26, No. 2).

Cheetham, John. *Consortium for Euphoniums and Tubas.* Shawnee Press, Incorporated. Two euphoniums and two tubas. 1980. $18.00. 5:30. IV. Part I: F–$b\flat_1$; Part II: F♯–g'; Part III: C–c'; Part IV: F_1–g. Commissioned by R. Winston Morris for the Tennessee Technological University Tuba Ensemble. While the piece comprises four parts, there are numerous *divisi* sections in all parts requiring a minimum of four euphonium and four tuba players to play all the written notes. The first section contains a lyrical melody and the second section contains a technical aggressive treatment of the same melody. A first-rate work appropriate for any program. Will require tuba players who can articulate cleanly in the low register. Euphonium parts are also printed in treble clef. This composition is designed to be performed by a large ensemble. Recorded by the Tennessee Technological University Tuba Ensemble, KM Records, KM 4631; the U.S. Armed Forces Tuba/Euphonium Ensemble, Mark Records, MW89MCD-8; and the British Tuba Quartet, *In at the Deep End,* Heavyweight Records Limited, HR008/D.

Cheyette, Irving, and Charles Roberts, arr. *Fourtone Folio, Volume I.* Carl Fischer. Three euphoniums and one tuba. 1931. Out of Print. 16 pp. I–II. Part I: c–g'; Part II: d–g'; Part III: B♭–e'; Part IV: $B\flat_1$–a. A collection of thirteen arrangements of classical and folk tunes. Actually published for any four bass clef instruments but works best with euphoniums on the first three parts. Good for junior high school students. The melody is always in the top part. Parts may be doubled for a large ensemble.

Cheyette, Irving, and Charles Roberts, arr. *Fourtone Folio, Volume II (More 4-Tones).* Carl Fischer. Three euphoniums and one tuba. 1933. Out of Print. 15 pp. II. Part I: c–a'; Part II: c–f'; Part III: B♭–e♭'; Part IV: $A\flat_1$–e♭. Eleven short arrangements of popular baroque, classical, and romantic melodies. The top part always has the melody. These are slightly more challenging than those in Volume I, but still very playable by young students.

Childs, Barney. *Quartet Fantasy.* Available from the composer. Four tubas. 1978. 15:00. IV–V. Part I: $B\flat_2$–f' (a♭'); Part II: D_1–c♯'; Part III: E_1–d'; Part IV: E_1–c♯'. Two movements. To Gene Pokorny, Ivan Hammond, Daniel Perantoni, and Bart Cummings. All parts are technically challenging and have many exposed places. The harmonies are contemporary and the meter is constantly changing. There are a couple of twentieth-century techniques required, but most of the work involves traditional performance techniques. Will require four strong players.

Chopin, Frederic. *Four Preludes Op. 28, Nos. 4, 7, 22, 28.* arr. Peter Rauch. Ohio Valley Tuba Quartet Press. Two euphoniums and two tubas. 1988. $12.00. 4:00. IV. Part I: B–c"; Part II: G–a♯'; Part III: E♭–c'; Part IV: E_1–c. Four movements. Four well-known piano preludes transcribed for tuba/euphonium quartet. Careful dynamic control is necessary to maintain proper balance.

Chopin, Frederic. *Mazurka No. 48, Op. 68 No. 2 "The Hoffnung Quartet."* arr. Eugene Anderson. Cimarron Music and Productions. Four tubas. 1995. $7.50. 2:30. II–III. Part I: E♭–c'; Part II: $B\flat_1$–a♭; Part III: $B\flat_1$–f; Part IV: F_1–f. This Chopin Mazurka is scored for four tubas in the key of B♭ minor. Each part is interesting and challenging. Written trills lie well for most tubas. All parts have optional muted passages. Parts may be doubled for a large ensemble.

Chopin, Frederic. *Military Polonaise* arr. Maurice Bale. Godiva Music. Two euphonium and two tubas. 1994. £6.00. 4:00. III. Part I: E♭–e♭'; Part II: E♭–g; Part III: $B\flat_1$–e♭; Part IV: $E\flat_1$ ($A\flat_1$)–b.

Chopin, Frederic. *"Minute" Waltz.* arr. Benjamin Roundtree. Roundtree Music. Two euphoniums and two tubas. 2002. $12.00. 2:00. III. Part I: G–c"; Part II: d♭–g'; Part III: A♭–e♭'; Part IV: $A\flat_1$–e♭. Straightforward arrangement of this well-known work. Melodic material is divided among all four voices, though the technically challenging passages are contained entirely in the euphonium parts. Parts may be doubled for a large ensemble.

Chopin, Frederic. *Minute Waltz.* arr. David R. Werden. Whaling Music Publishers. Two euphoniums and two tubas. 1979. $5.50. 1:20. IV–V. Part I: A–d"; Part II: B♭–b♭'; Part III: c–f'; Part IV: $B\flat_1$–f. Arranged for a solo euphonium with an accompaniment of one euphonium and two tubas. The solo part is virtuosic in its technical demands and its tessitura is very high. The accompanying parts are not difficult.

Chopin, Frederic. *Minute Waltz.* arr. Steven Mead. BTQ Publications. Two euphoniums and two tubas. 1993. 1:45. Recorded by the British Tuba Quartet, *Elite Syncopations,* Polyphonic Reproductions Limited, QPRZ 012D.

Chopin, Frederic. *Prelude #4 for Tuba Quartet.* arr. Chris Hendricks. Hidalgo Music. Four tubas. 1992. $4.00. 2:00. IV. Part I: F–f'; Part II: (A_1) D♯–a; Part III: e–b; Part IV: E–f. Nice arrangement of this Chopin prelude. Other than a single high note in the first part (f') the parts are all playable by high school students. Parts may be doubled for a large ensemble.

Chopin, Frederic. *Three Short Preludes.* arr. Maurice Bale. Godiva Music. Four tubas. 1994. £6.00. 5:00. III. Part I: A–e♭'; Part II: G–b; Part III: C–g; Part IV: (C_1) F_1–B♭.

Chopin, Frederic. *Tuba Quartet-Chopin Mazurka, Op. 68, No. 48.* arr. Eugene Anderson. Anderson's Arizona Originals. Four tubas. 1988. $5.00. 2:30. III–IV. Part I: F–c'; Part II: $B\flat_1$–a♭; Part III: $B\flat_1$–f; Part IV: F_1–c'. Dedicated to Professor Raymond F. Dvorak. The melody is primarily in the first part. The score indicates a euphonium may be used for the first part. The fourth part requires a high c (c'), so a stronger tuba player will be needed for that part than for the second or third parts. Anderson includes an additional part that is a combination of the second and third part, allowing this to be played as a trio if desired. Parts may be doubled for a large ensemble.

Clarke, Herbert. *Trumpet Voluntary.* arr. Maurice Bale. Godiva Music. Two euphoniums and two tubas. 1996. £5.00. 5:00. III. Part I: g–a'; Part II: e–c'; Part III: G–a; Part IV: G_1–d. Revision of the 1994 arrangement, transposed to C rather than A♭.

Clews, Eileen. *Partita for Tuba Quartet.* Broadbent and Dunn Ltd. Four tubas. 1995. $16.50. III. Three movements. The first two parts may also be performed on euphonium. The piece is tonal with fast, technical outer movements and a slow, lyrical second movement. Also reviewed in the Winter 1999 issue of the *TUBA Journal* (Vol. 26, No. 2).

Collins, Judy. *Since You've Asked.* arr. Gary Buttery. Whaling Music Publishers. Two euphoniums and two tubas. 1967. $7.50. 2:20. IV. Part I: F–g'; Part II: f–g'; Part III: D–c'; Part IV: C–a. A very lyrical flowing melody, primarily in the first two parts. Parts may be doubled for a large ensemble. Recorded by the Atlantic Tuba Quartet, *Euphonic Sounds,* Golden Crest, CRS 4173.

Collins-Rice, Hugh. *Earth and Moon.* Available from Tubalaté. Two euphoniums and two tubas. Recorded by Tubalaté on the compact disc *Earth and Moon.*

Confrey, Zez. *Charleston Chuckles.* arr. Rodger Vaughan. Available from the arranger. Two euphoniums and two tubas. 1988. $5.00. 1:20. IV. Part I: f–b♭'; Part II: f–e♭'; Part III: B♭–a; Part IV: $B\flat_1$–d♭. A toe-tapping syncopated melody. The melody is primarily in the top two parts. Drums may be added for stylistic enhancement. Parts may be doubled for a large ensemble.

Confrey, Zez. *Dizzy Fingers.* arr. Rodger Vaughan. Available from the arranger. Two euphoniums and two tubas. 1989. $5.00. 3:30. IV. Part I: d–b♭'; Part II: B♭–e'; Part III: B♭–b♭; Part IV: $B\flat_1$–f. Arranged for the Tubadours. An up-tempo arrangement of this jazz-like melody. Technically challenging for the top two parts. Fun to play and for audiences.

Confrey, Zez. *High Hattin' from African Suite.* arr. Rodger Vaughan. Available from the arranger. Two euphoniums and two tubas. 1988. $5.00. 2:10. IV. Part I: c♯–b♭'; Part II: f–e♭'; Part III: B♭–a♭; Part IV: $B\flat_1$–d. For the Tubadours. A jazz melody from the 1920s. Most of the melody is in the first part. Drums may be added to enhance the jazz style. Fun to play. Parts may be doubled for a large ensemble.

Constantinides, Dinos. *Eight Miniatures for Four Tubas.* T.A.P. Music. Four tubas. 1978. $10.00. 12:00. IV–V. Part I: E♭–a'; Part II: C–f♯'; Part III: F_1–d♯'; Part IV: D_1–b♭. Eight movements. A virtuoso-level quartet. Extreme range and technical demands in all parts. Could also be performed with one euphonium and three tubas. Odd meters and complicated rhythms are common. Contains many contemporary-sounding harmonies. Winner of Honorable Mention in the Tuba Quartet Composition Contest sponsored by the Mirafone Corporation and the Los Angeles Tuba Quartet.

Constantinides, Dinos. *I Never Saw a Moor for Four Tubas.* T.A.P. Music. Four tubas. 1980. $4.00. 3:00. III–IV. Part I: B–e'; Part II: G♯–e'; Part III: D–g; Part IV: (F_1) G_1–e. For Lennax. The tessitura of the top two parts is high; top parts could be played on euphonium. No real technical demands. No parts available, so players must read off score. Parts may be doubled for a large ensemble.

Cook, Kenneth. *Introduction and Rondino.* Hinrichsen Edition Limited. Four tubas. 1951. Out of Print. 4:45. IV. Part I: D–c'; Part II: F♭–b♭; Part III: $A\flat_1$–e♭; Part IV: $F\flat_1$–B♭. This is composed in the British Brass Band tradition and is one of the first tuba quartet compositions ever published. All four parts are in treble clef. The first and second parts are in E♭ and the third and fourth parts are for B♭ tubas. There is a slow chorale-like section followed by a more aggressive and lively second half.

Cooman, Carson. *Midsummer Songs.* MMB Music. Two euphoniums and two tubas. 2001. $34.95. 8:00. Three movements. Commissioned and dedicated to Tubalaté. Movements are based on and proceeded by epigraphs from William Shakespeare's famous play *A Midsummer Night's Dream.*

Corelli. *Sonata No. 10, Op. 5.* arr. Robert Madeson. Cimarron Music and Productions. Two euphoniums and two tubas. $16.00. Euphonium parts also available in treble clef.

Cornelius, Peter. *Aetherische Geisterstimmen.* arr. Angelo Manzo. Tuba-Euphonium Press. Two euphoniums and two tubas. 2002. $8.00. 2:30. II. Part I: e♭–g'; Part II: B♭–e♭'; Part III: D–b♭; Part IV: F_1–d. The title might translate as *Ethereal Spirit Voices.* Tonal work in the style of Brahms and with the feel of a processional. Parts may be doubled for a large ensemble. Also reviewed in the Spring 2004 issue of the *ITEA Journal* (Vol. 31, No. 3).

Corwell, Neal. *Threnody.* Tuba-Euphonium Press. Solo flute with two euphoniums and two tubas. 2002. $15.00. 6:00. IV. Part I: A–b♭'; Part II: A–a♭'; Part III: C–a; Part IV: $E♭_1$–c. For the voices silenced on September 11, 2001. A "threnody" is a song of lamentation, and this work was written to mourn the tragic loss of life brought about by the terrorist attacks in the United States on September 11, 2001. The quartet serves both as equal partner to the flute and in an accompanimental role, and the composer makes effective use of modern harmonies and dissonance. All parts call for trilling and flutter tonguing. Parts may be doubled for a large ensemble.

Coucounarás, Stelios. *Elegy for Four Tubas.* Editions Marc Reift. Two euphoniums and two tubas. 2001. CHF 23.00. 8:00. II. Part I: C♯–f'; Part II: G_1–e♭'; Part III: G_1–d♭'; Part IV: F_1–e♭. Three movements: Melodie gegen 12-ton; Rondo; Elegy in Major. Dedicated to Walter Hilgers. A tonal composition with folklore elements. Effective and easy to put together.

Couperin, François. *Les Baricades Mistérieuses.* arr. Kenyon D. Wilson. Tuba-Euphonium Press. Two euphoniums and two tubas. 1997. $8.00. 4:00. II. Part I: f–g'; Part II: e♭–e♭'; Part III: G–b♭; Part IV: G_1–f. Originally for harpsichord, this work employs traditional harmonies and is in rondo form. The individual parts are simple and repetitive, forming an aggregate rhythm of straight eighth notes. Nice study piece for ensemble playing. Parts may be doubled for a large ensemble.

Crist, Tim. *Lyric.* Cimarron Music and Productions. Two euphoniums and two tubas. $16.00.

Cruger, Johann. *Nun Danket Alle Gott.* arr. Roger Mason. Tuba-Euphonium Press. Two euphoniums and two tubas. 1996. $13.00. 4:45. II. Part I: e–a♭'; Part II: c–d'; Part III: C–g; Part IV: F_1–d. Effective arrangement of the standard hymn tune *Now Thank We All Our God.* Serves well as an intonation/balance study piece for younger ensembles. Parts may be doubled for a large ensemble. Also reviewed in the Summer 1998 issue of the *TUBA Journal* (Vol. 25, No. 4).

Crump, Peter. *The March of the Hare.* Available from Tubalaté. Two euphoniums and two tubas. Recorded by Tubalaté on the compact disc *Earth and Moon.*

Cummings, Barton. *Five Fragments.* Cimarron Music and Productions. Two euphoniums and two tubas. 1995. $10.50. III. Five movements. A virtuoso piece consisting of five contrasting movements and intended for college-level performers. Mutes are required for all parts. Euphonium parts also available in treble clef. Individual movements can stand alone in a concert. Also reviewed in the Summer 1995 issue of the *TUBA Journal* (Vol. 22, No. 4).

Cummings, Barton. *From Darkness . . . Emerging.* Tuba-Euphonium Press. Two euphoniums and two tubas. 1992. $10.00. 6:30. IV. Part I: E–c''; Part II: A–b♭'; Part III: E_1–b♭; Part IV: E_1–b♭. Three movements. This is technically challenging, and the tessitura of the first part is high. Dissonant harmonies reflect the title of the composition. The first and third parts have cadenzas in the last movement.

Cummings, Barton. *In Darkness . . . Dreaming.* Heavy Metal Music. Two euphoniums and two tubas. 1991. $10.00. 6:50. IV–V. Part I: F–b♭'; Part II: E♭–a'; Part III: F_1–f'; Part IV: D_1–f'. Three movements: The Last Dying Rays; Flight; To Wake. Dedicated to the Colonial Tuba Quartet. A programmatic work whose dissonant harmonies and technical challenges reflect the titles of the movements. There are extreme range demands in all parts. Very interesting writing. The first, third, and fourth parts all have cadenzas in the last movement.

Cummings, Barton. *Ohlone Suite.* Solid Brass Music Company. Two euphoniums and two tubas. 2003. $15.00. 8:00. II–III. Part I: d–a♭'; Part II: B♭–e♭'; Part III: E♭–c'; Part IV: F_1–e♭. Four movements: March; Waltz; Serenade; Galop. For the Ohlone College Euphonium-Tuba Ensemble, Tony Clements, Conductor. Nice composition aimed at college-level ensembles but accessible for intermediate-level performers. There are a few challenging technical passages, but the ensemble is easy to rehearse. The title of each movement indicates its style and form. Parts may be doubled for a large ensemble.

Cummings, Barton, arr. *Three Renaissance Quartets.* Edition Musicus. Two euphoniums and two tubas. 1980. $5.00. 8:00. IV. Part I: c–g'; Part II: E–d'; Part III: D–a; Part IV: F_1–c. Three movements: Canzona; Canzona; Song. The first movement was composed by Florentio Maschera, and the second and third movements were composed by Heinrich Issac. Range is not challenging, but the highly polyphonic canzonas can be challenging to put together. The top two parts could be played by F tubas for use in a tuba quartet. Parts may be doubled for a large ensemble.

Cunningham, Michael G. *Chaconne, Op. 148.* Seesaw Music Corporation. Two euphoniums and two tubas. 1991. $12.00. 4:00. IV. Part I: D♭–b♭'; Part II: A–f'; Part III: d–e♭'; Part IV: G_1–g. Technically challenging, especially for the euphoniums. Very contemporary harmonies. All players read from a five-page score.

Danburg, Russell. *Chorale and Gigue for a Quartet of Tubas.* Wingert-Jones Music, Incorporated. Four tubas. 1990. $7.00. 4:20. IV. Part I: A–c'; Part II: F–c'; Part III: A_1–a♭; Part IV: G_1–c♯. Two movements: Chorale; Gigue. Dedicated to my grandson, Jarrid. The Chorale is quite lyrical and traditional in its harmony. The Gigue is more rhythmically complex but contains mostly tutti rhythms. The top two parts are often pitted melodically against the bottom two parts. Parts may be doubled for a large ensemble.

Davidson, Matthew. *Coraggio.* Available from Tubalaté. Two euphoniums and two tubas. Recorded by Tubalaté on the compact disc *Hall of Mirrors.*

Davidson, Matthew. *Move.* Available from Tubalaté. Two euphoniums and two tubas. Recorded by Tubalaté on the compact disc *Move.*

Davison, Peter. *Tuba Quartet.* Available from the composer. Four tubas. 1977. V. Part I: c–c"; Part II: A–c"; Part III: D–g♯'; Part IV: $E\sharp_1$–f♯'. A very challenging work. The tessitura is extremely high for all four parts (numerous double c's [c"]). Skips of an octave or greater are frequent.

Day, Joel, arr. *International Tuba Day Music Books, Numbers 1 and 2.* Available from the arranger. Two euphoniums and two tubas. $5.00.

De Filippi, Amedeo. *Cassation for Four Tubas.* General Music Publications Company, Incorporated. Four tubas. 1975. $8.50. 8:00. IV. Part I: e♭–a♭'; Part II: G♭–f'; Part III: $G\flat_1$–e♭'; Part IV: $F\sharp_1$–d♯'. Three movements: Cortége; Nocturne; Rondo Alla Caccia. Fun to play but very challenging. The top two parts may be played by euphoniums or F tubas; otherwise the range is very demanding. The third movement is marked Allegro Giocoso and is in 6/8. Mutes are needed by all four parts in the second movement. Parts may be doubled for a large ensemble.

De Jong, Conrad. *Grab Bag.* Brass Music Limited (The Brass Press). Four tubas. 1974. $6.00. 3:30. IV. Part I: a–a'; Part II: A♭–d♭'; Part III: A–g; Part IV: $F\sharp_1$–G♭. Three movements: Warm-Up; Sear and Yellow Leaf (MacBeth); Fanfare Variations. Commissioned by R. Winston Morris and the Tennessee Technological University Tuba Ensemble, R. Winston Morris, Director. The first tuba part should be played on euphonium or F tuba. The first movement contains fragments from nineteen different tuba solo, ensemble, and orchestral literature. Players perform at least eight to ten of the fragments in random order. Fragments may be segmented, or repeated in any fashion as one would in a practice session. The third movement contains sections where only the rhythms are notated and the players are free to choose their own pitches. This last movement is based on the first movement of De Jong's tuba duet. For more information on that composition, see Music for Multiple Tubas, Two Parts.

De Vento, Ivo. *Die Brinlein die Fliessen.* arr. Paul Schmidt. Heavy Metal Music. Two euphoniums and two tubas. 1990. $5.00. 1:00. III–IV. Part I: c–c'; Part II: f–g'; Part III: D–d; Part IV: F_1–B♭. The second part has a much higher tessitura than the first part. No significant technical problems. No score available. Parts may be doubled for a large ensemble.

De Vittoria, Tomas Luis. *O Magnum Misterium.* arr. Barton Cummings. Solid Brass Music Company. Two euphoniums and two tubas. 1998. $9.00. 4:00. II. Part I: e–e'; Part II: G–b; Part III: E–f; Part IV: G_1–B. Nice arrangement of this Renaissance motet. Limited ranges and repetitive elements make this piece accessible for intermediate- or beginner-level performers. Parts may be doubled for a large ensemble.

Deak, Csaba. *Quartet for Tubas.* Swedish Music Information Center. One euphonium and three tubas. 1990. $11.00. 10:00. IV–V. Part I: D♭–c"; Part II: F♯$_1$–f'; Part III: F_1–e♭'; Part IV: $E\flat_1$–b. A demanding work regarding both technique and range. The composition has very contemporary harmonies and uses pitch bending, flutter tonguing, blowing air through the instrument, and mutes.

Debussy, Claude. *Golliwogg's Cakewalk.* arr. Bryan V. Doughty. Cimarron Music and Productions. Two euphoniums and two tubas. 1998. $11.50. 2:15. Euphonium parts also available in treble clef. Recorded by the Dutch Tuba Quartet on the compact disc *Wolkenschatten.*

Debussy, Claude. *Golliwogg's Cakewalk.* arr. Paul Schmidt. Heavy Metal Music. Two euphoniums and two tubas. 1991. $7.00. 2:10. IV. Part I: ($B\flat_1$) G♭–g'; Part II: F–g'; Part III: B♭–d' (e♭'); Part IV: $E\flat_1$–a♭. All parts have an opportunity to play the melody. No significant technical problems, but requires light and lyrical playing. No score available. Parts may be doubled for a large ensemble.

Debussy, Claude. *The Little Negro.* arr. Hirokazu Hiraishi. Sonic Arts, Incorporated. Two euphoniums and two tubas. 1986. $11.00. 2:00. IV. Part I: E–g'; Part II: G–d'; Part III: C–f; Part IV: E_1–c♯. The melody begins syncopated and ends very lyrical. All parts have an opportunity to play the melody. Parts may be doubled for a large ensemble.

Debussy, Claude. *Trois Chansons.* tr. Jeremy Lane. Tuba-Euphonium Press. Two euphoniums, two tubas, and contralto vocalist. 2002. $18.00. 4:30. II–III. Part I: c♯–f♯'; Part II: A–e'; Part III: E–c'; Part IV: E_1–d♯. Three movements: Dieu! Qu'il la fait bon regarder!; Quant j'ai ouy le tabourin; Yver, vous n'ests qu'un villain. Originally for voice, this is a nice collection of songs in the French style. Parts may be doubled for a large ensemble. Vocal part may also be performed on euphonium or tuba. Also reviewed in the Spring 2004 issue of the *ITEA Journal* (Vol. 31, No. 3).

Dempsey, Ray. *Now Hear This!* Tuba-Euphonium Press. Two euphoniums and two tubas. 1998. $10.00. 3:00. III. Part I: e♭–b♭'; Part II: c–a♭'; Part III: G–c'; Part IV: G_1–g♭. Rhythmically driven original composition that works well as a concert opener. Opens with a fanfare, and contains technically challenging passages in all four parts. Parts may be doubled for a large ensemble. Recorded by the British Tuba Quartet on the compact disc *Fireworks,* Polyphonic Records, and by the Monarch Tuba-Euphonium Quartet on the compact disc *Metamorphosis,* Campro Productions.

Dempsey, Raymond. *Quatre Chansons Pour Tuba Quatuor (French Suite for Tuba Quartet).* Horizon Press. Two euphoniums and two tubas. 1991. $16.00. 9:00. IV. Part I: A–b'; Part II: g–e'; Part III: E–e'; Part IV: E_1–e'. Four movements: Ma Normandie; Vila L'bon Vent; Le Temps des Cerises; Aupres de ma blonde. The second movement is very challenging; all four parts have an extended cadenza. The French text and English translation are provided for each chanson. Parts may be doubled for a large ensemble. The first, third, and fourth movements are recorded by the British Tuba Quartet, *Elite Syncopations,* Polyphonic Reproductions Ltd., QPRZ012D; and the Monarch Tuba/Euphonium Quartet.

Desmond, Paul. *Take Five.* arr. Ingo Luis. Musikverlag Bruno Uetz. One euphonium and three tubas. 1995. €17.00. 4:15. Second part may also be performed on euphonium. Recorded by the Melton Tuba-Quartett on the compact disc *Lazy Elephants,* Diavolo Records.

Desprez, Josquin. *Absalon, Fili Mi.* arr. Stephen Shoop. Cimarron Music and Productions. Two euphoniums and two tubas. 1995. $7.00. 3:30. II–III. Part I: f–a♭'; Part II: A♭–c'; Part III: F–b♭; Part IV: $B♭_1$–e♭. Nice arrangement of this slow, canonical work. All parts are interesting. The independence of parts provides the greatest challenge, but the conservative ranges make the piece accessible to intermediate-level performers. Euphonium parts also available in treble clef. Parts may be doubled for a large ensemble.

Desprez, Josquin. *Ave Maria.* arr. Andrew Spang. Lyric Brass Publishing. Two euphoniums and two tubas. 2001. $9.00. 2:45. Arranged for TUBA+, the tuba-euphonium ensemble at the Eastman School of Music. First part is in tenor clef. Parts may be doubled for a large ensemble.

Diero, Pietro. *March: Il Ritorno.* arr. Ken Ferguson. Studio Music Company. Two euphoniums and two tubas. 2:50. Recorded by the British Tuba Quartet, *Euphonic Sounds,* Polyphonic Reproductions Limited, QPRZ 009D.

DiGiovanni, Rocco. *Tubas at Play.* Available from the composer. Four tubas. 1978. $18.00. 3:30. IV–V. Part I: C–f'; Part II: A_1–d♯'; Part III: G_1–a; Part IV: F_1–g. The tessitura of the first part is high. This piece is very melodically driven, with most of the melody in the top two parts. Very rich harmonies; nice lyrical writing. Formerly called *Shining Star.* A euphonium may be used for the first and second parts. Parts may be doubled for a large ensemble.

Dowland. *Come Again, Sweet Love.* arr. David Werden. Cimarron Music and Productions. Two euphoniums and two tubas. 1992. $5.50. 1:00. I–II. Part I: e♭–f'; Part II: c–c'; Part III: A♭–f; Part IV: $A♭_1$–A♭. Brief chorale with a homophonic texture and traditional harmonies. Serves well as a study piece for ensemble intonation. Euphonium parts also available in treble clef. Parts may be doubled for a large ensemble.

Dowland, John. *Two Madrigals.* arr. Mark Nelson. Whaling Music Publishers. Two euphoniums and two tubas. 1988. $5.50. 3:30. III. Part I: d–e'; Part II: G–b♭; Part III: F♯–g; Part IV: $F♯_1$–G. Two movements: What If I Never Speed?; Now, O Now I Needs Must Part. Good arrangement of two simple madrigals. Very appropriate for high school students. The texture is homophonic much of the time. Parts may be doubled for a large ensemble.

Dressler. *Four Quartets.* Two euphoniums and two tubas.

Dressler. *Scherziapriori II.* Two euphoniums and two tubas.

Drobnak, Ken, arr. *Renaissance Choral Music, Vol. I.* Tuba-Euphonium Press. Two euphoniums and two tubas. 2001. $15.00. 16 pp. II. Part I: B♭–f'; Part II: G–f'; Part III: D–c'; Part IV: G_1–d. Six movements: Come from Thy Home by Eustache DuCaurroy; Lord, Now Lettest Thou Thy Servant Depart by Melchior Frank; On Thy True Word, O God by Johann Walther; Help, Lord, My God, in This My Need by Nikolaus Selneccer; Upon the Mount of Olives by Giovanni Croce; On This Most Joyful Easter Day by Johann Eccard. Nice collection of six pieces from the Renaissance period. Each piece is about three minutes in duration and is appropriate for intermediate-level performers. Individual movements can stand alone on a concert. Parts may be doubled for a large ensemble. Also reviewed in the Summer 2002 issue of the *ITEA Journal* (Vol. 29, No. 4).

Drobnak, Ken, arr. *Renaissance Choral Music, Vol. II.* Tuba-Euphonium Press. Two euphoniums and two tubas. 2001. $15.00. 15 pp. II. Part I: c–f'; Part II: A♭–e♭'; Part III: E♭–d♭'; Part IV: $G♭_1$–f. Six movements: O Most Blessed Sacrament by Giovanni Croce; When Buried Was Our Lord by Jakob Handl; Praise Be Thine by Orlandus Lassus; O Thou Glorious King by Luca Marenzio; Lift High the Banner of the Lord by Giovanni Battista Pergolesi; Behold in What Manner the Just One Dies by Tomas L. da Vittoria. Nice collection of six pieces from the Renaissance period. Each piece is about three minutes in duration and is appropriate for intermediate-level performers. Individual movements can stand alone on a concert. Parts may be doubled for a large ensemble. Also reviewed in the Summer 2002 issue of the *ITEA Journal* (Vol. 29, No. 4).

Durufle, Maurice. *Ubi Caritas*. tr. R. Winston Morris. Cimarron Music and Productions. Two euphoniums and two tubas. 1997. $11.00. 1:45. II–III. Part I: f–b♭'; Part II: B♭–f'; Part III: A–d'; Part IV: B♭$_1$–g. Effective arrangement of this chorale. Euphonium parts also available in treble clef. More appropriate for a large ensemble, as both tuba parts contain *divisi* passages. Recorded by Symphonia on the compact disc *Symphonia Two: La Morte dell Oom*, Mark Records.

Dutton, Brent. *Resonances*. Seesaw Music Corporation. Two euphoniums and two tubas. 1991. $17.00. 4:45. IV. Part I: e♭–b♭'; Part II: B♭–g'; Part III: F$_1$–a; Part IV: E♭$_1$–f. Not difficult technically. A very approachable and playable dissonant, contemporary quartet. Parts may be doubled for a large ensemble.

Dutton, Brent. *Song and Dance No. 3*. Seesaw Music Corporation. Four tubas. 1979. $17.00. 3:30. IV–V. Part I: G♭$_1$–f'; Part II: E♭$_1$–c'; Part III: E♭$_1$–e♭'; Part IV: D♭$_1$–e♭'. A fast-paced work with very contemporary harmonies, changing meters, and large range requirements for all parts. Technically challenging for all four parts. Mutes needed for third and fourth parts.

Dvorák, Anton. *Humoresk, Op. 101, No. 7*. arr. Paul Schmidt. Heavy Metal Music. Two euphoniums and two tubas. 1992. $7.00. 2:20. IV. Part I: B♭–a'; Part II: G–g♭'; Part III: A♭$_1$–c'; Part IV: F$_1$–g♭. A cute arrangement of this famous work in which the tubas frequently have the melody. No score available; parts may be doubled for a large ensemble.

Elgar, Edward. *Salut d'Amour*. arr. Gail Robertson. Tuba-Euphonium Press. Two euphoniums and two tubas. 1998. $14.00. 3:30. III. Part I: B♭–a♭'; Part II: B♭–a♭'; Part III: B♭$_1$–e♭'; Part IV: E♭$_1$–e♭. For the Interservice Tuba/Euphonium Quartet. This moderate-tempo song is driven by a syncopated accompaniment. Melodic material is divided evenly between the four voices and the harmonies are traditional. Euphonium parts also available in treble clef. Parts may be doubled for a large ensemble.

Ellin, Ben. *Quartet 4*. Available from the composer. Four tubas. 2004. 8:00. III–IV. Ensemble range: B♭$_2$–e♭'. Commissioned by the London Tuba Quartet. Rhythmically driven original composition for tuba quartet. Parts may be doubled for a large ensemble.

Ellington, Duke. *Mean Thing Swing*. arr. Rodger Vaughan. Available from the arranger. Two euphoniums and two tubas. 1990. $5.00. 2:20. IV–V. Part I: g♭–g'; Part II: c–f'; Part III: F–b♭; Part IV: G$_1$–f. For the Tubadours. A fun arrangement of the jazz classic "It Don't Mean a Thing If It Ain't Got That Swing." Technically challenging for all parts at the tempo indicated. Performers will need a good jazz feel.

Ellington, Duke. *Mood Indigo*. arr. Rodger Vaughan. Available from the arranger. Two euphoniums and two tubas. 1976. $5.00. 3:00. III–IV. Part I: g♯–f'; Part II: c–d'; Part III: B–b♭; Part IV: F$_1$–e. Nice arrangement of this classic jazz ballad. Drums may be added to support the jazz style. Most of the melody is in the first part. Parts may be doubled for a large ensemble. Recorded by the Tubadours, *Ve Iss Da Mighty Tubadours Ya?* Crystal Records, S421.

Ellington, Duke. *Satin Doll*. arr. Denzil Stephens. Sarnia Music. Two euphoniums and two tubas.

Ellington, Duke. *Satin Doll*. arr. Rodger Vaughan. Available from the arranger. Two euphoniums and two tubas. 1978. $5.00. 1:30. IV. Part I: f–g'; Part II: g–e'; Part III: c–b♭; Part IV: F$_1$–f. A famous moderate swing melody. This arrangement works well for this instrumentation. Drums may be added for effect. No score available. Parts may be doubled for a large ensemble. Recorded by the Tubadours, *Ve Iss Da Mighty Tubadours Ya?* Crystal Records, S421.

Ellmenreich, Albert. *Spinning Song*. arr. Peter Rauch. Ohio Valley Tuba Quartet Press. Two euphoniums and two tubas. 1990. $9.00. 1:20. IV. Part I: g–a'; Part II: A–f'; Part III: F–f; Part IV: F$_1$–d. A fairly aggressive syncopated melody. Most of the melodic responsibility is in the top two parts. Some interesting harmonies in the accompaniment. Parts may be doubled for a large ensemble.

Emberson, Steven, arr. *Five Foot Two–Eyes of Blue*. Available from the arranger. Two euphoniums and two tubas.

Emberson, Steven, arr. *From a Distance*. Available from the arranger. Two euphoniums and two tubas.

Emberson, Steven, arr. *Happy Birthday with Fanfare*. Available from the arranger. Two euphoniums and two tubas.

Emberson, Steven, arr. *Longer*. Available from the arranger. Two euphoniums and two tubas. 3:00. IV. Part I: A♭–a♭'; Part II: A♭–g'; Part III: A♭$_1$–a♭; Part IV: A♭$_1$–g♭. This is an arrangement of the folk/rock melody made famous by Dan Fogelberg. The melody is primarily in the top two parts. No significant technical problems. Parts may be doubled for a large ensemble.

Emberson, Steven, arr. *New York, New York*. Available from the arranger. Two euphoniums and two tubas.

Emberson, Steven, arr. *You Light Up My Life*. Available from the arranger. Two euphoniums and two tubas.

Ernst-Thilo, Kalke. *Jumbos Holiday*. Musikverlag Bruno Uetz. One euphonium and three tubas. 1995. €12.00. 2:00. Second part may also be performed on euphonium. Recorded by the Melton Tuba-Quartett on the compact disc *Lazy Elephants*.

Ernst-Thilo, Kalke. *Requiem for a Dead Little Cat.* Musikverlag Bruno Uetz. One euphonium and three tubas. 1995. €12.00. 2:00. Second part may also be performed on euphonium and parts may be doubled for a large ensemble. Recorded by the Melton Tuba-Quartett on the compact disc *Lazy Elephants.*

Evans, G. *In the Good Old Summertime.* arr. Arthur Frackenpohl. T.A.P. Music. Two euphoniums and two tubas. 1990. $16.00. 1:30. IV. Part I: B♭–b♭'; Part II: A–f'; Part III: A_1–b♭; Part IV: G_1–b♭. For Harvey Phillips and Friends. Fun arrangement of this familiar melody. Technical challenges depend on the performance tempo. Parts may be doubled for a large ensemble.

Ewazen, Eric. *Devil Septet.* Seesaw Music Corporation. Four tubas, piano, and percussion. 1976. $33.00. 7:00. IV–V. Part I: F♯$_1$–f'; Part II: A_1–f'; Part III: A♭$_1$–e'; Part IV: F_1–e'. Very contemporary and dissonant. Techniques used include singing, talking, hissing, and roaring through the mouthpiece. There are two different improvisation sections for all four parts and a spot for the house and stage lights to dim. This can be a very effective piece. Will require four strong players.

Farmer, John. *Fair Phyliss.* arr. Robert Wilkinson. Cimarron Music and Productions. Two euphoniums and two tubas. $11.00. Euphonium parts also available in treble clef.

Farmer, John. *Fair Phyllis I Saw.* Sarnia Music. Two euphoniums and two tubas. £9.99.

Fasce, Albert. *Quatour.* Editions du Petit Page. Four tubas. €19.00.

Fauré, Gabriel. *Canticle of Jean Racine.* arr. Kenneth Drobnak. Tuba-Euphonium Press. Two euphoniums and two tubas. 1994. $8.00. 3:45. II. Part I: e♭–a♭'; Part II: c–d♭'; Part III: F–b♭; Part IV: G_1–c. Composed in late-romantic style, this work consists of several sections built in layers starting with the lowest voice and progressing upward. As such, all parts are interesting and contain melodic material. The slow tempo and chorale texture makes this work appropriate for young ensembles. Parts may be doubled for a large ensemble.

Fauré, Gabriel. *Pavane.* arr. Maurice Bale. Godiva Music. Two euphoniums and two tubas. £6.00.

Fauré, Gabriel. *Pavane, Op. 50.* arr. Kenyon D. Wilson. Tuba-Euphonium Press. Two euphoniums and two tubas. 1998. $10.00. 5:00. III. Part I: A–a♭'; Part II: F–d♭'; Part III: C♯–a♭; Part IV: G–d. Effective arrangement of this work originally for orchestra and chorus. Melodic material is distributed among the four voices and the harmonies are traditional. Euphonium parts also available in treble clef. Parts may be doubled for a large ensemble. Recorded by the Tennessee Tech Tuba Ensemble on their compact disc *Carnegie VI,* Mark Records.

Fauré, Gabriel. *Pie Jesu.* arr. Paul Walton. Breakthrough Music. Two euphoniums and two tubas. Part I: c–f'; Part II: c–f'; Part III: A_1–b; Part IV: B♭$_1$–d'. Effective arrangement suitable for young ensemble.

Fentress, Stephen S. *Song of Memory. TUBA Journal.* Three euphoniums and one tuba. 1980. $7.50. 1:00. III–IV. Part I: g–e♭"; Part II: d–g♭'; Part III: G–d♭'; Part IV: B♭$_1$–a♭. A slow, lyrical song in a minor key. Meter constantly shifts between 2/4, 3/4, and 4/4. The first part is written in treble clef though in concert pitch, unlike the normal transposition. Players read from the score. Parts may be doubled for a large ensemble. Written as part of the TUBA Gem Series and distributed in the *TUBA Journal,* Vol. 8, No. 4. It is available by purchasing this issue of the *TUBA Journal.*

Ferguson, Edmund. *Total Tubosity.* Heavy Metal Music. Two euphoniums and two tubas. 1991. $5.00. 2:45. IV. Part I: c–a♭'; Part II: c–g'; Part III: F–b♭; Part IV: A♭$_1$–g. For the Heavy Metal Society Tuba Quartet. The second tuba part plays a rock bass line with a euphonium melody above. A tutti rhythmic shout chorus is in the middle. Fun to play. Drums may be added for style enhance ment. No score available. Parts may be doubled for a large ensemble.

Ferguson, Ken, arr. *Fascinatin' Gershwin.* BTQ Publications. Two euphoniums and two tubas. 1993. $15.00. 8:45. A medley of "Swanee," "Fascinatin' Rhythm," "It Ain't Necessarily So," "A Foggy Day," and "Strike Up the Band." Recorded by the British Tuba Quartet, *Elite Syncopations,* Polyphonic Reproductions Limited, QPRZ 012D.

Ferriano, Frank. *Four Folk Songs.* Tap Music Sales. Tuba/euphonium quartet. $8.00.

Ferriano, Frank. *Rag.* Tuba-Euphonium Press. Two euphoniums and two tubas. 2001. $10.00. 1:30. II–III. Part I: F–f'; Part II: c–f'; Part III: F–b♭; Part IV: F_1–d (f). Brief original composition based on rhythms from the ragtime era with a modern chordal vocabulary. Parts may be doubled for a large ensemble. Also reviewed in the Fall 2001 issue of the *ITEA Journal* (Vol. 29, No. 1).

Ferriano, Frank. *Scherzo.* Tuba-Euphonium Press. Two euphoniums and two tubas. 2001. $10.00. 2:15. II–III. Part I: A–a'; Part II: A–f'; Part III: A–b♭; Part IV: A_1–a. Lively original composition with modern harmonies and effective use of dissonance. Rhythmically challenging with borrowed rhythms and hemiolas. Calls for one euphonium mute. Parts may be doubled for a large ensemble.

Ferriano, Frank. *Two Jazz Moods.* Tuba-Euphonium Press. Two euphoniums and two tubas. 2002. $12.00. 4:30. III. Part I: d♭–c"; Part II: c–a'; Part III: A♭–e♭'; Part IV: A♭$_1$–a♭. Two movements: Blues; Swing Riffs. The first mood consists of three blues choruses with a brief snippet from *In the Hall of the Mountain King* added for humor. The second mood, Swing Riffs, is scored with a bitonal texture, with the euphoniums and tubas in different keys. *Divisi* passages make this piece more appropriate for a large ensemble than for a quartet. First euphonium part is in tenor clef only. Also reviewed in the Summer 2004 issue of the *ITEA Journal* (Vol. 31, No. 4).

Finnissy, Michael. *Violet, Slingsby, Guy and Lionel.* Available from Tubalaté. Two euphoniums and two tubas. Three movements. Recorded by Tubalaté on the compact disc *Hall of Mirrors.*

Fischer, Fred. *Come Josephine (In My Flying Machine).* arr. Paul Schmidt. Heavy Metal Music. Two euphoniums and two tubas. 1990. $3.00. 2:00. III. Part I: e–e'; Part II: G–c'; Part III: E–f; Part IV: G$_1$–B. A moderate waltz with the melody in the first part. Very playable by high school students. No score available. Parts may be doubled for a large ensemble.

Fodi, John. *Quartet, Op. 73.* Canadian Music Centre. Two euphoniums and two tubas. 1984. 5 pp.

Forbes, Michael. *Auburn Is the Colour. . . .* Editions BIM. Two euphoniums and two tubas. 2003. CHF 25.00. 5:45. Part I: e–b'; Part II: d–a'; Part III: F–f'; Part IV: G–d'. For Sotto Voce. Quasi rock ballad written, according to the composer, with the intent of representing a visual color with an aural art form. Recorded by Sotto Voce on the compact disc *Consequences,* Summit Records.

Forbes, Michael. *Consequences.* Editions BIM. Two euphoniums and two tubas. 2003. CHF 25.00. 6:00. III–IV. Part I: B♭–c''; Part II: G–b♭'; Part III: C–f'; Part IV: C$_1$–c'. For Sotto Voce. Rhythmical work in rock style. All parts are rhythmically challenging and interesting to play. Well-written ensemble sections. Melody is mainly in the first euphonium part. Recorded by Sotto Voce on the compact disc *Consequences,* Summit Records.

Forbes, Michael. *Cosmic Voyage.* Editions BIM. Two euphoniums and two tubas. 2003. CHF 25.00. 5:45. III–IV. Part I: c–a' (c''); Part II: B–g'; Part III: G$_1$–c'; Part IV: (D$_1$) E$_1$–d♭. Commissioned through a grant from the Valdosta State University Faculty Research Fund. Written for the Valdosta State University Tuba/Euphonium Ensemble, Dr. Kenyon Wilson, director. Well-written, effective tonal work. The first section is forceful and based on stacked fifths, followed by a cadenza for each instrument. The voyage is a lively 5/8 melody which moves in and out of 2/4, 3/4, 6/8, and 7/8. An exciting addition to the growing tuba quartet repertoire. Recorded by Sotto Voce on the compact disc *Consequences,* Summit Records.

Forbes, Michael. *Four Miniatures.* Editions BIM. Two euphoniums and two tubas. 2003. €23.00. 10:00. III–IV. Part I: B♭–c''; Part II: D–a'; Part III: C–f'; Part IV: E♭$_1$–d♭'. Four movements: Salutation; Toccata; Lament; Jubilation. To Roland Szentpali and Janos Mazura. Written for the Budapest ITEC 2004 Quartet Competition. Calls for mutes and multiple tonguing in all parts. The first movement is loosely based on the bugle call *Taps,* and the second movement is in the style of the second movement of Anthony Plog's *Four Sketches.* The third movement features the tubas, and the final movement is rhythmically driven with frequent meter changes. Parts may be doubled for a large ensemble.

Forbes, Michael, arr. *Loch Lomond. ITEA Journal* (Vol. 31, No. 2), Winter 2004. Two euphoniums and two tubas. 2004. 2:30. II. Part I: c–f'; Part II: B♭–d'; Part III: c–d'; Part IV: (F$_1$) F–a. For the Sotto Voce Quartet. Included in the *ITEA Journal* as part of the Gem Series, this arrangement is accessible for intermediate-level performers. This arrangement treats the folk tune in a traditional choral style. The first and third verses are performed, and the middle verse is intended to be sung. Parts may be doubled for a large ensemble. Recorded by Tubalaté on the compact disc *Hall of Mirrors.*

Forte, Aldo. *Adagio and Rondo.* Tuba-Euphonium Press. Two euphoniums and two tubas. 1992. $10.00. 4:00. IV. Part I: C–c''; Part II: B–a'; Part III: E–d'; Part IV: G♯$_1$–a. Written for R. Winston Morris and the Tennessee Technological University Tuba Ensemble. The tessitura of the first part is high. The rondo section is challenging technically, very fast-paced, and multimetric. Contains some contemporary-sounding harmonies; a very exciting composition. Parts may be doubled for a large ensemble. Originally copyrighted by the composer in 1973.

Foster. *Swanee River.* arr. Chris Warren. Cimarron Music and Productions. Two euphoniums and two tubas. $12.50. Euphonium parts also available in treble clef.

Frackenpohl, Arthur. *A Little Four Tuba Music.* T.A.P. Music. Four tubas. 1990. $10.00. 12:30. IV. Part I: E$_1$–d'; Part II: E$_1$–d♭'; Part III: E$_1$–d♭'; Part IV: E$_1$–b♭. Five movements: Prelude; Waltz; Air; Dance; Intro and March. All four parts require good range and technical facility. Some of the movements are tuneful and have fairly traditional harmonies. A conductor may be helpful in the fourth and fifth movements because of the complicated meter changes.

Frackenpohl, Arthur. *Pop Suite.* Kendor Music, Incorporated. Two euphoniums and two tubas. 1974. $10.50. 7:00. IV. Part I: B♭–b♭'; Part II: B♭–g'; Part III: B♭$_1$–a♭; Part IV: G$_1$–a♭. Three movements: Rock; Refrain; Rag. Written for R. Winston Morris and the Tennessee Technological University Tuba Ensemble. This is exactly like the brass quintet composition with the same name. The first movement is slightly stilted for rock enthusiasts, but the Refrain is a beautiful melody and the Rag works quite well. All parts have written-out solos to play. While the range is not demanding, rhythmically there are enough challenges to make this primarily a college-level piece. Parts may be doubled for a large ensemble. Recorded by the University of Miami Tuba Ensemble, Miami United Tuba Society, 14568; Karl Megules, *Garden State Tuba Ensemble*, Recorded Publications, Company, Z43471; the British Tuba Quartet, *In at the Deep End*, Heavyweight Records Limited, HR008/D.

Frackenpohl, Arthur. *St. Nicholas Ground*. Tuba-Euphonium Press. Two euphoniums and two tubas. 1993. $10.00. 2:30. II. Part I: B♭–b♭'; Part II: B♭–a'; Part III: $B♭_1$–a; Part IV: $B♭_1$–g. Written for Harvey Phillips, founder of TubaChristmas. Based on the tune "Jolly Old St. Nicholas," Frackenpohl employs the tune as a ground bass with five variations. Parts may be doubled for a large ensemble. Also reviewed in the Fall 1995 issue of the *TUBA Journal* (Vol. 23, No. 1) and the Fall 1996 issue of the *TUBA Journal* (Vol. 24, No. 1).

Frackenpohl, Arthur. *Suite for Tuba Quartet*. Horizon Press. Two euphoniums and two tubas. 1991. $16.00. 6:50. IV. Part I: B–b♭'; Part II: B–a♭'; Part III: $B♭_1$–c'; Part IV: $A♭_1$–e♭. Three movements: Fanfare; Air; March. Commissioned by the Colonial Tuba Quartet. Nice writing for tuba/euphonium quartet. The last movement is multimetric and more technically challenging, but also very aggressive and exciting. The top two parts are printed in treble clef. Parts may be doubled for a large ensemble.

Frackenpohl, Arthur. *Suite No. 2 for Tuba Quartet*. Tuba-Euphonium Press. Two euphoniums and two tubas. 1999. $20.00. 10:00. III. Part I: G–b♭'; Part II: G–b♭'; Part III: G_1–c' (c♯'); Part IV: $G♭_1$–g. Three movements: March; Hymn; Jig. Written for the U.S. Navy Tuba-Euphonium Quartet. Effective original composition accessible by intermediate-level performers. Melodic material is divided among the four voices. The march movement contains several meter changes, including a passage in triple meter. The hymn movement gives each voice a solo passage in a homophonic texture, and the final gig is lively and rhythmically driven. Parts may be doubled for a large ensemble.

Frank, Melchior. *Vier Deutscher Tänzen*. PEL Music Publications. Two euphoniums and two tubas. 2003. $9.50. 5:15. II–III. Part I: f–b♭'; Part II: c–f'; Part III: G–d'; Part IV: G_1–e♭. Four movements. Collection of four German dances in traditional style. Parts may be doubled for a large ensemble. Individual movements can stand alone on a concert.

Franz, Robert. *Ave Maria*. arr. Angelo Manzo. Tuba-Euphonium Press. Two euphoniums and two tubas. 2002. $8.00. 2:30. II. Part I: d–g'; Part II: c♯–d'; Part III: F♯–b; Part IV: $F♯_1$–d. This brief arrangement distributes melodic material equally among all four voices. Although each part is not technically challenging, endurance is a factor with younger ensembles as all parts perform essentially without a break. Parts may be doubled for a large ensemble. Also reviewed in the Summer 2004 issue of the *ITEA Journal* (Vol. 31, No. 4).

Frescobaldi, Girolamo. *Canzona a Quarti Toni*. arr. Paul Schmidt. Heavy Metal Music. Two euphoniums and two tubas. 1997. $7.00. II–III. Part I: c♯–f'; Part II: F♯–a; Part III: D–e; Part IV: $G♯_1$–c. This brief work in ternary form is an effective piece for teaching contrapuntal technique and independence of parts. Parts may be doubled for a large ensemble. Also reviewed in the Fall 2000 issue of the *TUBA Journal* (Vol. 28, No. 1).

Frescobaldi, Girolamo. *Canzona Sesta a 4*. arr. Paul Schmidt. Heavy Metal Music. Two euphoniums and two tubas. 1997. $7.00. 2:00. II–III. Part I: d–f'; Part II: G–a; Part III: C–f; Part IV: F_1–c. This brief work in ternary form is an effective teaching piece for contrapuntal technique and independence of parts. All parts are highly imitative. Ranges are appropriate for intermediate-level performers. Parts may be doubled for a large ensemble.

Friederich, G. W. E. *Lilly Bell Quick Step*. arr. Paul Schmidt. Heavy Metal Music. Two euphoniums and two tubas. 1991. $7.00. 2:00. IV. Part I: e♭–a♭'; Part II: A♭–d♭'; Part III: $A♭_1$–a♭; Part IV: $A♭_1$–A♭. A lively march with the melody shared among the top three parts. There are some technical challenges depending on performance tempos. No score available. Parts may be doubled for a large ensemble.

Friederich, G. W. E. *Ocean Tide March with Hail Columbia*. arr. Paul Schmidt. Heavy Metal Music. Two euphoniums and two tubas. 1990. $7.00. 3:30. IV. Part I: B♭–g'; Part II: F–f'; Part III: D–e♭'; Part IV: F_1–f. "Hail Columbia" serves as a 29-measure introduction to this march. The melody is passed between the upper three parts. There are some range and technical demands on the top three parts. No score available. Parts may be doubled for a large ensemble.

Friederich, G. W. E. *Prima Dona Waltz*. arr. Paul Schmidt. Heavy Metal Music. Two euphoniums and two tubas. 1991. $7.00. 2:20. III–IV. Part I: c–g'; Part II: G–a'; Part III: $A♭_1$–f; Part IV: ($E♭_1$) F_1–g. All parts have an opportunity to play the melody in this waltz. No significant technical problems. No score available. Parts may be doubled for a large ensemble.

Friedrich, Kenneth D. *Legend of Camino Real*. Available from the composer. Two euphoniums and two tubas. 2003. $10.00. 6:00. III–IV. Part I: E–b'; Part II: G–a'; Part III: D_1–a; Part IV: E_1–a. Challenging programmatic work based on a road that stretches through the deserts and mountains between Mexico City and Santa Fe. Each part is interesting with exposed solo passages at some time. Extended ranges and large intervals make this work accessible for advanced quartets only.

Friedrich, Kenneth D. *Pathos.* Cimarron Music and Productions. Three euphoniums and one tuba. $12.00. 4:00. III. Part I: E–b♭'; Part II: A♭–b♭'; Part III: F–f'; Part IV: C–g. Following a brief introductory lyrical passage, this work contains driving lines over a repeating eighth note *ostinato.* Works well as a concert opener. Also scored for trombone quartet. Euphonium parts also available in treble clef. Parts may be doubled for a large ensemble.

Friedrich, Kenneth D. *Suite for Tuba Quartet.* Available from the composer. Two euphoniums and two tubas. 2003. $15.00. 17:30. III–IV. Part I: B♭–b♭'; Part II: F–b♭'; Part III: G_1–c'; Part IV: $E\flat_1$–b♭. Challenging original composition for tuba/euphonium quartet. Each part has an extended range and fast technical passages. More appropriate for a quartet than for an ensemble.

Friedrich, Kenneth D. *Suite No. 2 for Tuba Quartet.* Available from the composer. Two euphoniums and two tubas. 2003. $15.00. 15:45. III. Part I: c–b♭'; Part II: E♭–a♭'; Part III: C–d'; Part IV: F_1–a♭. Four movements. Challenging original composition for tuba/euphonium quartet. Each part has an extended range and fast technical passages. All parts are interesting. More appropriate for a quartet than for an ensemble.

Friedrich, Kenneth D. *Tubuus.* Available from the composer. One euphonium and three tubas. 2004. $12.50. 5:00. II–III. Part I: B♭–a'; Part II: F♭–a♭'; Part III: $A\flat_1$–g; Part IV: $E\flat_1$–e♭. Straightforward original composition in rondo form. Parts may be doubled for a larger ensemble.

Fritze, Gregory. *Pacman Gets Caught.* Available from the composer. Two euphoniums and two tubas. 1982. $10.00. 4:00. IV. Part I: B♭–b♭'; Part II: B♭–g♭'; Part III: $B\flat_1$–c'; Part IV: $A\flat_1$–g♭. For the Boston Tuba-Four. One melody is "chased" by the rest of the parts and is finally caught. (Programmatic of the popular late-1970s video game.) All parts are interesting and challenging. Parts may be doubled for a large ensemble.

Fritze, Gregory. *Prelude and Dance.* Tuba-Euphonium Press. Two euphoniums and two tubas. 1990. $18.00. 9:00. IV. Part I: G–b♭'; Part II: F–b♭'; Part III: B♭–f♭'; Part IV: $F\sharp_1$–a♭. Commissioned by and composed for the Colonial Tuba Quartet. The Prelude is very lyrical; the Dance is in a "rock" style. The tessitura is a little high for the first tuba part. Great writing for mature players. The first performance of this piece was at the International TUBA Conference in Sapporo, Japan, August, 1990.

Fucik, Julius. *Entry of the Gladiators.* arr. Bruno Seitz. Musikverlag Martin Scherbacher. Two euphoniums and two tubas. 1993. $15.00. 4:00. IV. Part I: e♭–b♭'; Part II: A♭–e♭'; Part III: E♭–d'; Part IV: G_1–d♭. Good arrangement of this famous fanfare. All four parts are interesting and challenging. Parts may be doubled for a large ensemble.

Fucik, Julius. *Entry of the Gladiators (Thunder and Blazes).* arr. J. Kelly Diamond. Tuba-Euphonium Press. Two euphoniums and two tubas. 1996. $8.00. 3:00. III. Part I: A–b♭'; Part II: (A♭) d♭–g♭'; Part III: E♭–d♭'; Part IV: G_1–f. Effective arrangement of this well-known march. All parts are technically challenging and interesting. Parts may be doubled for a large ensemble. Also reviewed in the Winter 2002 issue of the *ITEA Journal* (Vol. 29, No. 2).

Fucik, Julius. *Florentiner Marsch.* arr. Franz Watz. Musikverlag Bruno Uetz. One euphonium and three tubas. 1995. €14.00. 4:30. Second part may also be performed on euphonium. Recorded by the Melton Tuba-Quartett on the compact disc *Lazy Elephants,* Diavolo Records.

Fucik, Julius. *Thunder and Blazes.* arr. Skip Gray. Dedicated to the Tokyo Bari-Tuba Ensemble.

Gabrieli, A. *Canzona.* arr. J. Lesley Varner. Tuba/Euphonium Music Publications. Two euphoniums and two tubas. Out of Print.

Gabrieli, Andrea. *Ricercar Del Duodecimo Tuono.* arr. Paul Schmidt. Heavy Metal Music. Two euphoniums and two tubas. 1990. $7.00. 2:30. III. Part I: A♭–e♭'; Part II: G–a♭; Part III: D♭–f; Part IV: $A\flat_1$–B♭. A typical late Renaissance instrumental canzona with the middle section in triple meter. Very polyphonic, but not technically difficult. Ideal for high school students. No score available. Parts may be doubled for a large ensemble.

Gabrieli, Andrea. *Ricercar Del Duodecimo Tuono.* arr. Richard Barth. Music Arts Company. Two euphoniums and two tubas. 1979. $10.00. 3:20. III–IV. Part I: B♭–g'; Part II: A–c'; Part III: E♭–g; Part IV: $B\flat_1$–c. An instrumental canzona, very polyphonic, but not technically demanding. Top two parts are printed in bass and treble clef. Fun to play; works very well. Parts may be doubled for a large ensemble.

Gabrieli, Andrea. *Ricercare del Duodècimo Tono.* tr. Ronald Davis. Tuba-Euphonium Press. Two euphoniums and two tubas. 2002. $8.00. 2:15. II. Part I: B♭–g'; Part II: A–c'; Part III: E♭–g; Part IV: $B\flat_1$–c. This work is in the form of a canzona–a work divided into distinct sections, each with its own theme developed through imitation–and is one of Gabrieli's best-known compositions. Euphonium parts also available in treble clef. Parts may be doubled for a large ensemble. Also reviewed in the Winter 2004 issue of the *ITEA Journal* (Vol. 31, No. 2).

Gabrieli, Antonio. *Ricercar.* arr. Maurice Bale. Godiva Music. Two euphoniums and two tubas. £5.00. Melodic material is divided among all four voices.

Gabrieli, Giovanni. *Canzona, "La Spiritata."* arr. Peter Rauch. Ohio Valley Tuba Quartet Press. Two euphoniums and two tubas. 1988. $9.00.

1988. III–IV. Part I: d–a'; Part II: B♭–d'; Part III: B♭$_1$–b♭; Part IV: G$_1$–e♭. Typical polyphonic instrumental canzona. All parts have the opportunity to play the theme. Players must count carefully and play cleanly. Recorded by the British Tuba Quartet, *Elite Syncopations,* Polyphonic Reproductions Limited.

Gabrieli, Giovanni. *Canzona per Sonare II.* arr. Paul Schmidt. Heavy Metal Music. Two euphoniums and two tubas. 1992. $7.00. 3:00. IV. Part I: e♭–g'; Part II: A–c'; Part III: E–g; Part IV: F$_1$–c. An instrumental canzona well known in the brass quintet repertoire. All parts have an opportunity to play the melody. Technical difficulty depends on performance tempo. No score available.

Gabrieli, Giovanni. *Canzona per Sonare No. 1.* arr. Allyn Lindsey. Cimarron Music and Productions. Two euphoniums and two tubas. $12.00. Euphonium parts also available in treble clef.

Gabrieli, Giovanni. *Canzona per Sonare No. 1 "La Spiritata."* arr. Barton Cummings. Solid Brass Music Company. Two euphoniums and two tubas. 1996. $10.00. 2:30. II. Part I: c–g'; Part II: A♭–c'; Part III: E–a♭; Part IV: F$_1$–f. Nice arrangement of this Renaissance motet. All parts are interesting. Limited ranges make this piece accessible for intermediate-level performers. Parts may be doubled for a large ensemble.

Gabrieli, Giovanni. *Canzona per sonare No. 2.* arr. Benjamin Roundtree. Roundtree Music. Two euphoniums and two tubas. 2002. $12.00. 2:15. III. Part I: e–g'; Part II: B♭–g'; Part III: F–c'; Part IV: F$_1$–c. Nice arrangement of this highly imitative contrapuntal work in traditional Renaissance style. All parts are interesting and equally challenging. Parts may be doubled for a large ensemble.

Gabrieli, Giovanni. *Canzona per sonare No. 4.* arr. Benjamin Roundtree. Roundtree Music. Two euphoniums and two tubas. 2002. $12.00. 2:00. III. Part I: e–g'; Part II: d–g'; Part III: E♭–b♭; Part IV: F$_1$–c. Nice arrangement of this highly imitative contrapuntal work in traditional Renaissance style. All parts are interesting and equally challenging. Parts may be doubled for a large ensemble.

Gabrieli, Giovanni. *Canzona per sonare No. 4.* arr. Skip Gray. Musikverlag Bruno Uetz. One euphonium and three tubas. 1995. €10.00. 2:30. Second part may also be performed on euphonium. Parts may be doubled for a large ensemble. Recorded by the Melton Tuba-Quartett on the compact disc *Lazy Elephants,* Diavolo Records, and by Gerhard Meinl's Tuba Quartet on the compact disc *Tuba! A Six-Tuba Musical Romp,* Angel Music.

Gabrieli, Giovanni. *Sonata.* arr. Paul Schmidt. Heavy Metal Music. Two euphoniums and two tubas. 1991. $7.00. 4:00. IV. Part I: B♭–e♭'; Part II: F–e♭'; Part III: F–c'; Part IV: B♭$_1$–a♭. A polyphonic instrumental work that shifts back and forth from duple to triple meter. Not technically difficult. No score available. Parts may be doubled for a large ensemble.

Garbáge, Pierre. *Chaser #3.* James Garrett. Two euphoniums and two tubas. 1974. $10.00. 2:00. IV. Part I: (B♭$_1$) d–f' (c"); Part II: (B♭$_1$) B♭–d'; Part III: (C$_1$) G$_1$–b; Part IV: (C$_1$) G$_1$–d. Written for R. Winston Morris and the Tennessee Technological University Tuba Ensemble. The melody is primarily in the fourth part. Although written in cut time, this should be performed in a moderate four. This work has lyrics for group sing-along activities and is also known as "I'm Walkin' the Dog." A very catchy melody. Parts may be doubled for a large ensemble. As Pierre says, "Real heavy, nearly."

Garbáge, Pierre. *Songs in the Fight against Rum (Songs of Might to Cheer the Fight in the Blight of Liquordom).* James Garrett. Two euphoniums, two tubas, tenor solo, barbershop quartet, mixed chorus, female speaker, male speaker, country band, chimes, collection takers, and three clarinets. 1975. $75.00. 25:00. IV–V. Part I: E–b♭'; Part II: G–e♭'; Part III: F♯$_1$–c'; Part IV: B♭$_2$–f♯. A monumental work requiring strong performers on all parts. This opera-like production has vocal solos, chorus selections, instrumental interludes, and speaking parts. The tongue-in-cheek melodies and text must be performed genuinely yet in the spirit of pure fun. Very enjoyable for performers and audience. All parts require mutes. Parts may be doubled for a large ensemble. Pierre says, "A burning plea for Bromo-Seltzer."

Garner, Erroll. *Misty.* arr. Denzil Stephens. Sarnia Music. Two euphoniums and two tubas.

Garrett, James. *Ho-Ho-Hoedown.* Cimarron Music and Productions. Two euphoniums and two tubas. 1996. $9.50. 1:30. II. Part I: e♭–b♭'; Part II: d♭–f'; Part III: B♭$_1$–g; Part IV: B♭$_1$–g. Fearlessly edited, annotated, updated, and relentlessly criticized by Dr. Pierre X. Garbage. Fun original composition in a hoedown style. Includes humorous transitions and other lighthearted elements. Euphonium parts also available in treble clef. Parts may be doubled for a large ensemble.

Garrett, James. *Tubalee Jubalee.* Cimarron Music and Productions. Two euphoniums and two tubas. 1995. $13.50. 4:45. III. Part I: B♭–b♭'; Part II: A–g'; Part III: F$_1$–b♭; Part IV: F$_1$–f. Dedicated with deep appreciation to R. Winston Morris and all past and present members of the great Tennessee Tech Tuba Ensemble. Medley of eight Dixie favorites, including *South, Darktown Strutter's Ball, Muskrat Ramble, St. James Infirmary, Basin Street Blues, That's a Plenty, South Rampart Street Parade,* and *Tiger Rag.* Requires a cowbell and drums. Recorded by the Tennessee Tech Tuba Ensemble on the album *The Tennessee Technological University Tuba Ensemble,* KM Educational Library, and by the United States Armed Forces Tuba-Euphonium

Ensemble on the compact disc *Forty-third Annual Mid-West International Band and Orchestra Clinic,* Mark Records.

Garrett, James A. *Miniature Jazz Suite.* James Garrett. Two euphoniums and two tubas, piano, bass, and drums. 1977. $35.00. 6:50. IV. Part I: a♭–b'; Part II: D–b'; Part III: C–c♯'; Part IV: G_1–c♭. Written for R. Winston Morris and the Tennessee Technological University Tuba Ensemble. This single-movement suite contains sections in moderate swing, slow swing, and rock. There are written-out solos and sections for improvised solos. Many tutti lines in the accompaniment. Technically challenging in some spots. Parts may be doubled for a large ensemble. Recorded by the Tennessee Technological University Tuba Ensemble, *Heavy Metal,* Mark Records, MES-20759.

Garrett, James A. *Mystical Music.* The Brass Press. Two euphoniums and two tubas. 1974. Out of Print. 7:30. IV. Part I: e♭–b♭'; Part II: G♯–a'; Part III: $G\sharp_1$–c♭'; Part IV: F_1–g♯. A single movement with several contrasting sections. The tessitura of the first part is high. Technically challenging at times for the first two parts. Most effective with all four parts doubled.

Garrett, James, arr. *Bill Bailey.* James Garrett. Two euphoniums and two tubas with optional keyboard and drums. 1984. $15.00. 4:00. IV. Part I: B♭–f♯'; Part II: B♭–e♭'; Part III: $B\flat_1$–a♭; Part IV: $B\flat_1$–e♭. Commissioned by and dedicated to Allen Jaffee. A fun but technically difficult arrangement of this popular tune. The melody and accompaniment are very syncopated. There is a 32-measure section that may be repeated for improvised solos. Will require strong players. Parts may be doubled for a large ensemble. Recorded by the Tennessee Technological University Tuba Ensemble, *All That Jazz,* Mark Records, MES-20608.

Garrett, James, arr. *Chimes Blues.* James Garrett. Two euphoniums and two tubas with optional keyboard and drums. 1984. $10.00. 4:50. IV. Part I: f–f'; Part II: B♭–b♭; Part III: B♭–g; Part IV: G_1–f. Commissioned by and dedicated to Allen Jaffee. Nice arrangement of this Dixieland standard. Twelve-bar blues in B♭. No significant range or technical challenges. Tubas have major responsibility for the melody. Parts I and II are available in treble and bass clefs. The top two parts have *divisi* sections. Parts may be doubled for a large ensemble. Recorded by the Tennessee Technological University Tuba Ensemble, *All That Jazz,* Mark Records, MES-20608.

Garrett, James, arr. *Down on the Farm.* James Garrett. Two euphoniums and two tubas. 1984. $10.00. 2:30. IV. Part I: B–f'; Part II: B–f'; Part III: $B\flat_1$–a♭; Part IV: $B\flat_1$–f. Good Dixieland-style arrangement. There is a section open in the middle for improvised solos (sixteen measures in B♭). This is followed by a unison shout chorus. Some technical challenges, but fun to play. Parts may be doubled for a large ensemble.

Garrett, James, arr. *Flow Gently Sweet Afton.* Cimarron Music and Productions. Two euphoniums and two tubas. 1995. $8.00. 2:00. II. Part I: f–g' (b♭'); Part II: d–e'; Part III: F–a; Part IV: $B\flat_1$–d. Dedicated to the memory of Allen Jaffe, Great Tubist, and Great Friend. Straightforward arrangement of this well-known chorale appropriate for young ensembles. The repeated melody is presented in four different settings, and the melodic material is divided among all four voices. Parts may be doubled for a large ensemble.

Garrett, James, arr. *Hanukkah Song.* Cimarron Music and Productions. Two euphoniums and two tubas. 1995. $6.50. 2:00. II. Part I: d–f'; Part II: d–d'; Part III: D–g; Part IV: D–d. Straightforward arrangement suitable for intermediate performers. Parts may be doubled for a large ensemble. Euphonium parts also available in treble clef.

Garrett, James, arr. *Joe Avery.* James Garrett. Two euphoniums and two tubas. 1984. $10.00. 2:00. IV. Part I: B♭–f'; Part II: B♭–d'; Part III: $B\flat_1$–a♭; Part IV: $B\flat_1$–e♭. Twelve-bar blues in B♭. The middle section may be repeated for improvised solos. The addition of drums is suggested. Parts may be doubled for a large ensemble.

Garrett, James, arr. *Just a Closer Walk with Thee.* James Garrett. Two euphoniums and two tubas with optional keyboard and drums. 1984. $10.00. 3:00. IV. Part I: e–e'; Part II: c–c'; Part III: C–g; Part IV: C–c. Commissioned by and dedicated to Allen Jaffee. This arrangement begins slow and solemn and ends with a fast swing feel. A lot of syncopated, jazz rhythms. Works very well. Parts may be doubled for a large ensemble. Recorded by the Tennessee Technological University Tuba Ensemble, *All That Jazz,* Mark Records, MES-20608.

Garrett, James, arr. *Loch Lomond.* Cimarron Music and Productions. Two euphoniums and two tubas. 1996. $9.50. 1:45. II. Part I: f–b♭'; Part II: c–c'; Part III: F–b♭; Part IV: $B\flat_1$–g. Rich harmonic setting of this traditional Scottish song. Melodic material is divided evenly among all four voices. Parts may be doubled for a large ensemble. Euphonium parts also available in treble clef.

Garrett, James, arr. *Mardi Gras Collection.* Cimarron Music and Productions. Two euphoniums and two tubas. $40.00. Seven movements: When the Saints Go Marching In; Chimes Blues; Joe Avery; Bill Bailey; Closer Walk with Thee; Rip 'Em Up, Joe; Down on the Farm. Dedicated to and commissioned by the late, great Allen Jaffe, founder and tubist of the Preservation Hall in New Orleans. Excellent collection of standard New Orleans favorites. Pieces may be performed as written or with optional ad-lib improvisational passages. Euphonium parts also available in treble clef. Ad-lib solos included. Individual movements can stand alone in a concert. Also reviewed in the Summer 1998 issue of the *TUBA Journal* (Vol. 25, No. 4).

Garrett, James, arr. *Rip 'Em Up, Joe.* James Garrett. Two euphoniums and two tubas with optional keyboard and drums. 1984. $10.00. 2:20. IV. Part I: f–g'; Part II: e–f'; Part III: G♯–g; Part IV: A_1–d. Commissioned by and dedicated to Allen Jaffee. Sixteen-bar blues in F at a moderate tempo. Sections may be repeated with chord symbols for improvised solos. Parts may be doubled for a large ensemble.

Garrett, James, arr. *Scotch-Irish Medley.* Cimarron Music and Productions. Two euphoniums and two tubas. 1996. $10.00. 2:00. II. Part I: c–b♭'; Part II: A♭–d'; Part III: C–a♭; Part IV: A_1–d. Fun, light arrangement appropriate for intermediate-level performers. Medley includes *Haggis Wha Hae* and *Wearin' of the Green.* Melodic material is divided among all four voices. Parts may be doubled for a large ensemble. Euphonium parts also available in treble clef.

Garrett, James, arr. *Wabash Canon Ball for Tuba-Euphonium Ensemble.* Ludwig Music Publishing Company. Two euphoniums and two tubas. 1987. $15.50. 1:45. III–IV. Part I: A♭–g'; Part II: A♭–f'; Part III: B♭$_1$–g; Part IV: A♭$_1$–f. Written for R. Winston Morris and the Tennessee Technological University Tuba Ensemble. Excellent arrangement of this classic country/folk song. The melody is in both euphonium and tuba parts. The work can be a challenge to keep together at fast tempos. This could be played by a tuba quartet with F tubas on the first two parts. The top two parts are printed in both bass and treble clefs. Parts may be doubled for a large ensemble. Recorded by the British Tuba Quartet, *In at the Deep End,* Heavyweight Records Limited, HR008/D.

Garrett, James, arr. *When the Saints Come Marchin' In.* James Garrett. Two euphoniums and two tubas. 1984. $10.00. 2:00. IV. Part I: B–f'; Part II: B–f'; Part III: B_1–a; Part IV: B_1–f. A fast-paced arrangement that includes a repeated section for improvised solos. There is a sixteen-measure "shout chorus" that follows the improvised solos. This is technically challenging, especially at the tempos indicated. Parts may be doubled for a large ensemble.

Gates, Crawford. *Tuba Quartet, Op. 59.* Intrada Music Group. Two euphoniums and two tubas. 1991. $15.00. 14:05. IV–V. Part I: B–c''; Part II: E–a♭'; Part III: G_1–f'; Part IV: G_2–e♭'. Three movements: Preludium; Chorale; Finale. Commissioned by Mitch Gershenfeld. The second part is marked E♭ tuba or second euphonium, although a euphonium is typically used on this part as the tessitura of the part is high. This is a wonderful work for tuba/euphonium ensemble, but there are great range and technical demands for all parts. The second movement is very lyrical with lush harmonies. The outer two movements are very technical and full of energy. This will require four very strong players. Parts may be doubled for a large ensemble. Recorded by the Tennessee Technological University Tuba Ensemble, Mark Records, MES 20759.

Gautier, Leonard. *Le Secret.* arr. David R. Werden. Whaling Music Publishers. Three euphoniums and one tuba. 1979. $6.00. 2:10. IV. Part I: B♭–g'; Part II: G–b♭'; Part III: B♭–g'; Part IV: E♭$_1$–b♭. Arrangement for solo euphonium and accompaniment of two euphoniums and one tuba. Excellent for showing off a strong euphonium player. The other three parts are not technically demanding. Parts may be doubled for a large ensemble.

Gearhart, Livingston, Don Cassel, and Wallace Hornibrook. *Bass Clef Sessions.* Shawnee Press, Incorporated. Two euphoniums and two tubas. 1954. $7.50. 50 pp. III–IV. Part I: c–b♭'; Part II: F–g'; Part III: G–d'; Part IV: F_1–g. A collection of 62 two-, three-, and four-part arrangements for euphonium and tuba. Styles of the collection range from Palestrina to jazz. Technical challenges vary from easy to moderately difficult. Parts may be doubled for a large ensemble.

George, Thom Ritter. *Tubamobile.* Tuba-Euphonium Press. Two euphoniums and two tubas. 1995. $15.00. 3:30. III–IV. Part I: c–b♭'; Part II: c–a♭'; Part III: G_1–c'; Part IV: F_1–b. For R. Winston Morris. Rhythmically driven original composition. Melodic material is divided among all four voices. First part also available in tenor clef. Parts may be doubled for a large ensemble. Recorded by Symphonia on the compact disc *Symphonia—Super Sonic Ensemble in the Alternate Clef,* Mark Records.

George, Thom Ritter. *Tubasonatina.* Available from the composer. Two euphoniums and two tubas. 1977. $13.00. 8:20. IV. Part I: B♭–b♭'; Part II: G–b♭'; Part III: B_1–d'; Part IV: F_1–b. Three movements: Sea Chanty; Meditation; Dance. Commissioned by and dedicated to R. Winston Morris and the Tennessee Technological University Tuba Ensemble. A real classic in the tuba ensemble repertoire. A very tuneful composition in which all four parts have an opportunity to play a melodic role. The second movement requires mutes for all parts. The last movement is fast-paced and challenging to play with all the mixed meters. Enjoyable for performers and for audiences. Parts may be doubled for a large ensemble. Recorded by the Tennessee Technological University Tuba Ensemble, KM Records, KM 6431.

Gershenfeld, Mitchell, arr. *Three Chorales.* Medici Music Press. Four tubas. 1983. $5.00. 3:00. III–IV. Part I: c–d'; Part II: G–a; Part III: D–e♭; Part IV: F_1–B. Three movements: Christ Lag In Todes Banden; Wer Nur Den Lieben Gott Lásst Walten; Lobt Gott, Unsern Herren In

Seinem Heiligtum. A very nice setting of three chorales originally composed by J. S. Bach, G. Neumark, and M. Praetorius, respectively. No real technical difficulties. Easily playable by high school students if euphoniums are used for the top two parts. Parts may be doubled for a large ensemble.

Gershwin, George. *I Got Rhythm.* arr. Denzil Stephens. Sarnia Music. Two euphoniums and two tubas. £15.00.

Gershwin, George. *Impromptu in Two Keys.* arr. David LeClair. Editions Marc Reift. Two euphoniums and two tubas with drums. 2001. €14.00. 2:15. III. Part I: e♭–b♭'; Part II: B♭–g'; Part III: G–e♭'; Part IV: $B♭_1$–e'. Straightforward arrangement of this brief work for piano. Melody is predominantly in the first tuba part. In addition to bass clef parts, euphonium parts are also available in treble, first tuba parts also available in E♭ treble, and second tuba also available in E♭ and B♭ treble clef. Parts may be doubled for a large ensemble. Recorded by Contraband on the compact disc *The Dragon's Dance,* Marcophon Records.

Gershwin, George. *Prelude I.* arr. Willibald Kresin. Editions Marc Reift. Two euphoniums and two tubas with drums. 2001. €14.00. 1:45. III–IV. Part I: F–c''; Part II: F–a'; Part III: F–e♭'; Part IV: F_1–b♭. First in a series of three preludes originally for piano. Melody is predominantly in the first part, though each part is challenging and interesting. In addition to bass clef parts, euphonium parts are also available in treble, first tuba parts also available in E♭ treble, and second tuba also available in E♭ and B♭ treble clef. Recorded by Contraband on the compact disc *The Dragon's Dance,* Marcophon Records.

Gershwin, George. *Prelude II.* arr. Willibald Kresin. Editions Marc Reift. Two euphoniums and two tubas with drums. 2001. €14.00. 3:15. III. Part I: c–b♭'; Part II: c–a'; Part III: F–b; Part IV: F_1–g. Second, and probably the best known, in a series of three preludes originally for piano. It is in a slow blues style and the melody is predominantly in the first euphonium and first tuba part. In addition to bass clef parts, euphonium parts are also available in treble, first tuba parts also available in E♭ treble, and second tuba also available in E♭ and B♭ treble clef. Recorded by Contraband on the compact disc *The Dragon's Dance,* Marcophon Records.

Gershwin, George. *Prelude III.* arr. Willibald Kresin. Editions Marc Reift. Two euphoniums and two tubas with drums. 2001. €14.00. 1:30. III. Part I: c♭–b'; Part II: G–a♭'; Part III: F–d'; Part IV: F_1–a♭. Third in a series of three preludes originally for piano—a challenging but effective work. In addition to bass clef parts, euphonium parts are also available in treble, first tuba parts also available in E♭ treble, and second tuba also available in E♭ and B♭ treble clef. Recorded by Contraband on the compact disc *The Dragon's Dance,* Marcophon Records.

Gershwin, George. *Strike Up the Band.* arr. Maurice Bale. Godiva Music. Two euphoniums and two tubas. 1996. £6.00. 2:00. III. Part I: d–g'; Part II: A–c'; Part III: F–g (e♭); Part IV: ($E♭_1$) $A♭_1$–c.

Gershwin, George. *Summertime.* arr. Denzil Stephens. Sarnia Music. Two euphoniums and two tubas. £15.00.

Gervaise, Claude. *Dance Suite.* arr. David R. Werden. Whaling Music Publishers. Two euphoniums and two tubas. 1979. $8.50. 5:00. III–IV. Part I: c–b♭'; Part II: d–f'; Part III: B♭–a♭; Part IV: $A♭_1$–e♭. Three movements: Bransle de Bourgone; Bransle Gai; Allemande. Three French Renaissance dances. Technically very playable by high school ensembles. The first part is printed in treble clef. Parts may be doubled for a large ensemble.

Gesualdo. *Moro Lasso.* Two euphoniums and two tubas.

Gibbons. *Fantasia in Foure Parts.* arr. Bryan V. Doughty. Cimarron Music and Productions. Two euphoniums and two tubas. 1998. $14.00. 3:30. II–III. Part I: B–a'; Part II: A–a'; Part III: F_1–c'; Part IV: F_1–g. Tonal composition in a canonical style. Individual parts are accessible for younger performers, though the independence of parts may prove challenging for younger ensembles. Euphonium parts also available in treble clef. Parts may be doubled for a large ensemble.

Gibbons, Orlando. *Prelude and Voluntary for Four Tubas.* arr. James Self. Wimbledon Music Incorporated. Four tubas. 1979. $7.00. 2:50. IV. Part I: e–a'; Part II: G–d'; Part III: D–b♭; Part IV: C_1–f. Two movements: Prelude; Voluntary. The tessitura of the first part is high and will require a very strong player on F tuba or euphonium. Rhythms in the Voluntary are not difficult but players must count carefully due to the close counterpoint. There is a *divisi* on the last measure in the top three parts. Parts may be doubled for a large ensemble.

Gilfish, Trident (Gigger). *Bullfrog Rag.* arr. James Garrett. Cimarron Music and Productions. Two euphoniums and two tubas. 1995. $8.50. 3:00. III. Part I: A–b♭'; Part II: A–e♭'; Part III: A_1–a♭ (b♭); Part IV: (C_1) G_1–g. Lighthearted original composition by James Garrett, written under one of his pseudonyms. The piece is in an easy ragtime feel, and the melodic material is divided among all four voices. The melodic scoops, rips, and frequent use of accidentals may challenge young performers. Requires a good low voice range for the vocalized "Ribbet!" Euphonium parts also available in treble clef. Parts may be doubled for a large ensemble. Recorded by the Tennessee Tech Alumni Tuba Ensemble on the compact disc *Pierre Garbáge Festival,* Mark Records.

Gillis, Lew. *Four Kuehn ("Keen") Guys*. Virgo Music Publishers. Four tubas. 1986. $8.95. 3:00. IV. Part I: C_1–f'; Part II: A♭–f'; Part III: G–d'; Part IV: $B♭_1$–f'. Range demands will require four strong players; in fact the fourth part is higher than the third part. Sections of the music alternate between 6/8, 9/8, and 4/4. Written for David Kuehn when he was Dean of the School of Music at the University of North Texas.

Gliere, Reinhold. *Russian Sailor's Dance*. arr. J. Kelly Diamond. Tuba-Euphonium Press. Two euphoniums and two tubas. 2000. $12.00. 4:00. III. Part I: A–b♭'; Part II: E–a'; Part III: A_1–c'; Part IV: E_1–a. Written for and dedicated to the United States Navy Band Tuba-Euphonium Quartet. Good arrangement of this well-known work. All parts are interesting with challenging, technical passages being passed from player to player. More appropriate for a quartet than for an ensemble. Also reviewed in the Summer 2001 issue of the *TUBA Journal* (Vol. 28, No. 4).

Glinka, Michael. *Overture from Russlan and Ludmila*. arr. Ken Ferguson. BTQ Publications. Two euphoniums and two tubas. 1993. $12.00. 5:20. Recorded by the British Tuba Quartet, *Elite Syncopations,* Polyphonic Reproductions Limited, QPRZ 012D.

Glover, Jim, arr. *Amazing Grace*. Available from the arranger. Two euphoniums and two tubas. 1982. $12.00.

Glover, Jim, arr. *Frosty the Snowman*. Available from the arranger. Two euphoniums and two tubas. 1992. $8.00.

Glover, Jim, arr. *God Save the Queen*. Available from the arranger. Two euphoniums and two tubas. 1991. $3.50.

Glover, Jim, arr. *In Heaven There Is No Beer*. Available from the arranger. Two euphoniums and two tubas. 1992. $12.00.

Glover, Jim, arr. *Moon River*. Available from the arranger. Two euphoniums and two tubas. 1992. $12.00.

Glover, Jim, arr. *O Canada*. Available from the arranger. Two euphoniums and two tubas. 1991. $3.50.

Glover, Jim, arr. *Old Comrades (Alte Kamaraden)*. Available from the arranger. Two euphoniums and two tubas. 1992. $12.00.

Glover, Jim, arr. *Paloma Blanca*. Available from the arranger. Two euphoniums and two tubas. 1991. $10.00.

Glover, Jim, arr. *Sleigh Ride*. Available from the arranger. Two euphoniums and two tubas. 1993. $10.00.

Glover, Jim, arr. *Star Spangled Banner*. Available from the arranger. Two euphoniums and two tubas. 1991. $3.50.

Glover, Jim, arr. *Those Lazy, Hazy, Crazy Days of Summer*. Available from the arranger. Two euphoniums and two tubas. 1991. $12.00. 2:00. III–IV. Part I: d–g'; Part II: c–g'; Part III: C–g; Part IV: C–e. Moderately difficult; could be played by high school ensembles depending on the performance tempo. All four parts have the opportunity to play the melody. Parts may be doubled for a large ensemble.

Glover, Jim, arr. *Too Fat Polka*. Available from the arranger. Two euphoniums and two tubas. 1991. $12.00.

Goble, Joseph. *Highway 336*. Tuba-Euphonium Press. Two euphoniums and two tubas. 2003. $12.00. 2:15. III. Part I: f–b♭'; Part II: B♭–f'; Part III: F–a♭; Part IV: F_1–B♭. Rhythmically driven original composition with a rock influence. Range and style are appropriate for intermediate-level performers. Euphonium parts also available in treble clef. Parts may be doubled for a large ensemble.

Goble, Joseph. *Sault Suite*. Tuba-Euphonium Press. Two euphoniums and two tubas. 2002. $24.00. 9:30. III. Part I: B♭–b♭'; Part II: F–g'; Part III: $B♭_1$–d♭'; Part IV: F_1–f. Five movements: In the St. Mary's Channel at Rotary Park; Locking through the Poe; Mariner's Hymn; Bay Mills; Big Waters (Superior). For the Well-Tempered Tuba/Euphonium Quartet at Northwestern University. Programmatic work based on the composer's memories of Sault Saint Marie, Michigan. Technical passages and key signatures up to five flats may prove challenging to intermediate-level performers. Euphonium parts also available in treble clef. Parts may be doubled for a large ensemble. Also reviewed in the Spring 2003 issue of the *ITEA Journal* (Vol. 30, No. 3).

Goble, Joseph. *Toad Patrol*. Tuba-Euphonium Press. Two euphoniums and two tubas. 1997. $6.00. 3:00. II. Part I: c–b♭'; Part II: B♭–a♭'; Part III: C–c'; Part IV: G_1–d. This original march-like composition is accessible by intermediate-level performers. Melodic material is divided evenly between the four voices. Euphonium parts also available in treble clef. Parts may be doubled for a large ensemble.

Goble, Joseph D. *Leviathans*. Tuba-Euphonium Press. Two euphoniums and two tubas. 1993. $5.00. 1:20. IV. Part I: B♭–a♭'; Part II: B♭–e♭'; Part III: B_1–a♭; Part IV: G_1–g. For the T.O.P. Quartet: Andy, Phil, Kary, and Matt. Fanfare-like in character in a brisk 6/8 meter. All parts are interesting and moderately challenging. Parts may be doubled for a large ensemble.

Goeller, Dan. *The Cheesy Tuba Quartet*. Tuba-Euphonium Press. Two euphoniums and two tubas. 1996. $10.00. 4:30. II–III. Part I: B♭–g'; Part II: G–b♭'; Part III: F_1–a; Part IV: F_1–b♭. Three movements. Aptly named quartet complete with singing and probably the worst collection of tuba-related jokes available. It is set in a Vaudeville style and will function as a break from the serious literature. More appropriate as a quartet than as a large ensemble piece. Also reviewed in the Summer 2002 issue of the *ITEA Journal* (Vol. 29, No. 4).

Gorb, Adam. *Tubaccata*. Breakthrough Music. Two euphoniums and two tubas. Part I: B♭–e♭''; Part II: E♭–c''; Part III: $E♭_1$–f♯'; Part IV: B_2–f'. Written especially for Tubalaté's 2003 U.S. tour, *Tubaccata* showcases the tuba-euphonium medium. Its time changes and span of the ranges only serve to heighten the excitement.

Gossec. *Tambourin*. arr. Maurice Bale. Godiva Music. Two euphoniums and two tubas. £5.00.

Gottschalk, Arthur. *Tubas at Christmas*. Available from the composer. One euphonium and three tubas. 1974. 2:45. IV. Part I: c–g'; Part II: C–c'; Part III: C–a; Part IV: C_1–c. Three movements: Deck the Halls; Silent Night; Jolly Old St. Nicholas. A traditional arrangement of these three Christmas melodies. All parts have an opportunity to play the melody. No significant technical problems. Parts may be doubled for a large ensemble.

Gottschalk, L. *Galop*. arr. Velvet Brown. Velvet Music Edition. Two euphoniums and two tubas. $16.00.

Gounod, Charles François. *Finale from the Foust Ballet Music*. arr. Maurice Bale. Godiva Music. Two euphoniums and two tubas. £7.00.

Gounod, Charles François. *Funeral March of a Marionette*. arr. Arthur Frackenpohl. Almitra Music Company, Incorporated (Kendor Music, Incorporated). Two euphoniums and two tubas. 1992. $11.00. 4:00. IV. Part I: A–g'; Part II: G–g'; Part III: G_1–c'; Part IV: G_1–a♭. A fun arrangement of the melody used as the theme to the Alfred Hitchcock television series. Technically not a problem once the 6/8 feel is established. Parts may be doubled for a large ensemble.

Gounod, Charles François. *Funeral March of a Marionette*. arr. Paul Schmidt. Heavy Metal Music. Two euphoniums and two tubas. 1990. $7.00. 4:20. III–IV. Part I: c–f'; Part II: F–d'; Part III: D–d'; Part IV: C–d. The range and technical demands of the euphonium parts are well within the abilities of good high school students. The first tuba part is high in some sections but does have 8vb *ossia* parts written. No score available. Parts may be doubled for a large ensemble.

Gourlay, James. *Scènes de Paris*. Editions Marc Reift. Two euphoniums and two tubas. 2001. CHF 35.00. 6:00. IV. Part I: B–e''; Part II: C–e''; Part III: $D♭_1$–f'; Part IV: C_1–d'. Written for Fernand Lelong. Inspired by a trip to Paris, this is a theme with variations paying homage to various composers. A tonal work with a charming flair. In addition to bass clef parts, euphonium parts are also available in treble and second tuba is available in E♭ treble clef.

Grafulla. *Washington Grays*. arr. Robert Wilkinson. Cimarron Music and Productions. Two euphoniums and two tubas. $13.00. Euphonium parts also available in treble clef.

Gray, Byron, arr. *Patapan*. Cimarron Music and Productions. Two euphoniums and two tubas. $11.00. Euphonium parts also available in treble clef.

Gray, Byron, arr. *Rings*. Cimarron Music and Productions. Two euphoniums and two tubas. $11.00. Euphonium parts also available in treble clef.

Gray, Byron, arr. *Yuba Play the Tuba*. Cimarron Music and Productions. Two euphoniums and two tubas. $11.00. Euphonium parts also available in treble clef.

Gray, Robert. *Contrasts for Brass*. Available from the composer. Two euphoniums and two tubas. 1992. $10.00. 3:00. II. Part I: c–e'; Part II: c–e'; Part III: A_1–f; Part IV: A_1–f. Written in ternary form, the slow middle section is contrasted with the outer allegro moderato material. The piece is rooted in the keys of E♭ and D♭ major, so the key may prove challenging to younger players. Parts may be doubled for a large ensemble. Also reviewed in the Summer 1995 issue of the *TUBA Journal* (Vol. 22, No. 4).

Gray, Skip, arr. *Concert and Contest Collection for Tuba-Euphonium Quartet (Grade III–IV)*. Tuba-Euphonium Press. Two euphoniums and two tubas. 2003. $24.00. 23 pp. II. Part I: c–a♭'; Part II: A♭–f'; Part III: C–g; Part IV: F_1–d. Eight pieces: Chorale: Aus tiefer Not by Johann Walter; Lied der Braut by Robert Schumann; Two Dances from Terpsichore by Michael Praetorius; Bist du bei mir by Johann Sebastian Bach; Der Wegweiser from Winterreise by Franz Schubert; Two Pieces by Henry Purcell; March for the Prince of Wales by Franz Joseph Haydn; Howndawg Stomp by Skip Gray. Nice collection of works appropriate for younger ensembles. Includes Dr. Gray's article entitled "Keys to Establishing a Successful Tuba-Euphonium Quartet." Euphonium parts also available in treble clef. Parts may be doubled for a large ensemble. Individual movements can stand alone in a concert. Also reviewed in the Spring 2004 issue of the *ITEA Journal* (Vol. 31, No. 3).

Grieg, Edvard. *Gavotte and Musette*. arr. Maurice Bale. Godiva Music. Four tubas. 1999. £6.00. 5:00. III. Part I: D–e♭'; Part II: $B♭_1$–A♭; Part III: $B♭_1$–F; Part IV: $B♭_2$–B♭. An arrangement for the standard brass band tuba quartet, consisting of two E♭ bass tubas and two BB♭ contrabass tubas. The score and parts are in bass clef.

Grieg, Edvard. *In the Hall of the Mountain King*. arr. Frank J. Halferty. Kendor Music, Incorporated. Two euphoniums and two tubas. 2001. $10.00. 3:00. III–IV. Part I: f–b♭'; Part II: G–g'; Part III: D–a; Part IV: G_1–g♭. Range provides the greatest challenge in this arrangement. The fourth part has a two-octave leap, and parts will often cross. Each of the top three parts has the melody at some point. Double-tonguing may be necessary depending upon the accelerando to the end. Parts may be doubled for a large ensemble. Also reviewed in the Winter 2002 issue of the *ITEA Journal* (Vol. 29, No. 2).

Grieg, Edvard. *In the Hall of the Mountain King*. arr. Robert Wilkinson. Cimarron Music and Productions. Two euphoniums and two tubas. 1996. $11.00. 3:00. III. Part I: A–a'; Part II: A–g'; Part III: G_1–a; Part IV: A_1–e. This arrangement of this popular movement from the Peer Gynt Suite divides the melodic material among all four parts. The difficulty is determined primarily by the speed of the accelerando to the end. Euphonium parts also available in treble clef. Parts may be doubled for a large ensemble.

Grieg, Edward. *Arietta and Waltz*. arr. Hirokazu Hiraishi. Sonic Arts, Incorporated. Two euphoniums and two tubas. 1987. $11.00. 2:45. IV. Part I: d–g'; Part II: F–c♭'; Part III: E♭–g; Part IV: $A♭_1$–d. Two movements: Arietta; Waltz. A fairly simple melody in a very traditional setting. No significant technical problems. Parts may be doubled for a large ensemble.

Grieg, Edward. *Four Pieces*. arr. Peter Rauch. Ohio Valley Tuba Quartet Press. Two euphoniums and two tubas. 1988. $12.00. 5:00. IV. Part I: c–a♭'; Part II: G♯–a♭'; Part III: c–b♭; Part IV: C_1–d. Four movements: National Song; At Home; Sailors Song; Waltz. Most of the melody is in the top two parts. Contains mostly tutti rhythms and traditional harmonies in the accompaniment. Parts may be doubled for a large ensemble.

Grieg, Edward. *In the Hall of the Mountain King*. arr. David R. Werden. Whaling Music Publishers. Two euphoniums and two tubas. 1992. $9.00. 3:00. IV. Part I: F–$b♭_1$; Part II: E–b♭'; Part III: $B♭_1$–d♭'; Part IV: $B♭_1$–a♭. A quartet arrangement of this fun melody known to tuba players as one of the melodies played by William Bell on his solo album. All parts have the opportunity to play the melody. The tessitura of the first part is high. Parts may be doubled for a large ensemble.

Grieg, Edward. *Wachterleid (Watchman's Song), Op. 12*. arr. Paul Schmidt. Heavy Metal Music. Two euphoniums and two tubas. 1991. $5.00. 2:00. III. Part I: c–g♭'; Part II: A–d'; Part III: A_1–b♭; Part IV: F_1–d. Nice arrangement of this familiar song. Very appropriate for high school students. No score available. Parts may be doubled for a large ensemble.

Grim, Ray. *TubaMeister Polka*. Cimarron Music and Productions. Two euphoniums and two tubas. 1999. $11.50. 2:45. II. Part I: d–b♭'; Part II: c–g'; Part III: D–b♭; Part IV: $B♭_1$–c. Part of the TubaMeisters Collection, this original polka is accessible for intermediate-level performers. All parts are interesting and may be doubled for a large ensemble. Euphonium parts also available in treble clef.

Grim, Ray, arr. *Barbara Polka*. Cimarron Music and Productions. Two euphoniums and two tubas. 1996. $8.00. 1:15. II. Part I: d–g'; Part II: d–e♭'; Part III: A♭–g; Part IV: $B♭_1$–c. Part of the TubaMeisters Collection, this brief arrangement of this standard polka is accessible by intermediate-level performers. Parts may be doubled for a large ensemble. Euphonium parts also available in treble clef.

Grim, Ray, arr. *Clarinet Polka*. Cimarron Music and Productions. Two euphoniums and two tubas. 1996. $8.50. 1:45. II–III. Part I: B♭–c"; Part II: B♭–a'; Part III: $B♭_1$–c'; Part IV: $A♭_1$–F. Part of the TubaMeisters Collection. This work was originally a show piece for clarinet, and this arrangement features the first euphonium with arpeggiated passages that can be challenging depending upon the tempo. The remaining three voices serve an accompanimental role and are appropriate for intermediate-level performers. Parts may be doubled for a large ensemble. Euphonium parts also available in treble clef.

Grim, Ray, arr. *Jenny Lind Polka*. Cimarron Music and Productions. Two euphoniums and two tubas. 1996. $10.00. 0:45. II. Part I: e♭–g'; Part II: d–g'; Part III: E♭–a♭; Part IV: $A♭_1$–g. Part of the TubaMeisters Collection, this brief arrangement divides the melodic material equally among all four voices. Parts may be doubled for a large ensemble. Euphonium parts also available in treble clef.

Grim, Ray, arr. *St. Paul Waltz*. Cimarron Music and Productions. Two euphoniums and two tubas. 1996. $9.50. 3:00. II. Part I: d–c"; Part II: c–c'; Part III: F–e♭; Part IV: F_1–B♭. Part of the TubaMeisters Collection, this light waltz is effectively arranged for intermediate-level performers. Melodic material is predominantly in the first part. Parts may be doubled for a large ensemble. Euphonium parts also available in treble clef.

Grim, Ray, arr. *Susie Polka*. Cimarron Music and Productions. Two euphoniums and two tubas. 1996. $10.00. 2:15. II–III. Part I: e♭–b♭'; Part II: c–e♭'; Part III: A–c'; Part IV: F_1–e♭. Nice arrangement of this upbeat polka—part of the TubaMeisters Collection. All parts are interesting, and melodic material is divided among all four voices. First part contains several trills. Parts may be doubled for a large ensemble. Euphonium parts also available in treble clef.

Grim, Ray, arr. *Tulak Polka*. Cimarron Music and Productions. Two euphoniums and two tubas. 1996. $9.00. 1:15. II. Part I: d–b♭'; Part II: d–g'; Part III: F–b♭; Part IV: G_1–c. Part of the TubaMeisters Collection, this moderate-tempo polka is accessible for intermediate-level performers. Melodic material is predominantly in the first part. Parts may be doubled for a large ensemble. Euphonium parts also available in treble clef.

Grim, Ray, arr. *Woodland Polka*. Cimarron Music and Productions. Two euphoniums and two tubas. 1996. $10.00. 3:00. II–III. Part I: d–a♭'; Part II: B♭–f'; Part III: $A♭_1$–b♭; Part IV: $A♭_1$–f. Part of the

TubaMeisters Collection, this polka is accessible by intermediate-level performers. All parts are interesting and technically challenging. Melodic material is divided equally among all four voices. Parts may be doubled for a large ensemble. Euphonium parts also available in treble clef.

Grim, Ray, arr. *Zepperl Polka.* Cimarron Music and Productions. Two euphoniums and two tubas. 1996. $8.00. 1:30. II. Part I: f–g'; Part II: d–e♭'; Part III: F–a♭; Part IV: B♭$_1$–B♭. Part of the TubaMeisters Collection, this moderately slow polka arrangement is based on an Austrian folk dance. Melodic material is predominantly in the first part. Parts may be doubled for a large ensemble. Euphonium parts also available in treble clef.

Gruber, Franz. *Silent Night.* arr. Rodger Vaughan. Cimarron Music and Productions. Two euphoniums and two tubas. 2002. $9.00. 1:15. Euphonium parts also available in treble clef.

Gussago. *La Nicolina.* arr. Paul Schmidt. Heavy Metal Music. Two euphoniums and two tubas. 1992. $7.00. 3:40. III–IV. Part I: d–g'; Part II: A♭–b♭; Part III: E♭–a♭; Part IV: A♭$_1$–d. A canon without any real technical problems. Players will need to count carefully. No score is available, and parts may be doubled for a large ensemble.

Habegger, Christa, arr. *Alas, and Did My Savior Bleed.* Cimarron Music and Productions. Two euphoniums and two tubas. $7.00.

Habegger, Christa, arr. *Children of the Heavenly Father.* Cimarron Music and Productions. Two euphoniums and two tubas. $7.50.

Habegger, Christa, arr. *Jesus Saves.* Cimarron Music and Productions. Two euphoniums and two tubas. $8.50.

Habegger, Christa, arr. *My Faith Looks Up to Thee.* Cimarron Music and Productions. Two euphoniums and two tubas. $7.00.

Haddad, Don. *Quartet for Tubas.* Available from the composer. Four tubas. 1974. 3:00. IV. Part I: F–f'; Part II: B♭–c'; Part III: E♭–f; Part IV: B♭$_1$–c. The first part has primary responsibility for the melody and is the most challenging technically. The other three parts are not very difficult. The tessitura of the first part is high and may be played by a euphonium.

Hall, Percy. *Chorale and Clog Dance.* Great Works Publishing, Incorporated. Two euphoniums and two tubas. 1999. $14.00. 2:30. I. Part I: d–e♭'; Part II: B♭–c'; Part III: E♭–e♭; Part IV: G$_1$–B♭. Two movements: Chorale; Clog Dance. Dedicated to Gary Tirey, Band Director, Otterbein College, Westerville, Ohio. An excellent work for young players. The slow chorale and moderate dance movements provide contrast to keep young players interested. Third part may be performed on tuba or euphonium. Top three parts are also available in treble clef, and the top part may also be performed on French horn. Parts may be doubled for a large ensemble.

Hall, Percy. *Dirge and Slow Dance.* Great Works Publishing, Incorporated. Three euphoniums and one tuba. 1999. $10.00. 3:00. I. Part I: f–f'; Part II: c–d♭'; Part III: B♭–c'; Part IV: B♭$_1$–d♭. Two movements: Dirge; Slow Dance. Dedicated to Mike Schwall, Band Director, Ontario Schools, Ohio. An excellent work for young players. Top three parts are also available in treble clef, and the top part may also be performed on French horn. Parts may be doubled for a large ensemble.

Hall, Percy. *Waltz and March.* Great Works Publishing, Incorporated. Three euphoniums and one tuba. 1999. $10.00. 2:30. I. Part I: c–c'; Part II: c–c'; Part III: A–b♭; Part IV: A♭$_1$–e♭. Two movements: Vintage Waltz; Two-Step March. Dedicated to Dale Schubert, Band Director, Napoleon, Ohio. An excellent work for young players. The slow waltz and moderate march movements provide contrast to keep young players interested. Top three parts are also available in treble clef, and the top part may also be performed on French horn. Parts may be doubled for a large ensemble.

Handel, George Frederic. *Air from Water Music.* arr. David Minchin. Available from Tubalaté. Two euphoniums and two tubas. 2:15. Recorded by Tubalaté on the compact disc *Light Metal.*

Handel, George Frederic. *All We like Sheep.* arr. Benjamin Roundtree. Roundtree Music. Two euphoniums and two tubas. 2002. $12.00. 3:00. III. Part I: c–b♭'; Part II: A–b♭'; Part III: A$_1$–b♭ (e♭'); Part IV: F$_1$–f. Effective arrangement from Handel's *Messiah.* Texture is both contrapuntal and homophonic. Parts may be doubled for a large ensemble.

Handel, George Frederic. *Allegro, from Water Music.* arr. Peter Rauch. Ohio Valley Tuba Quartet Press. Two euphoniums and two tubas. 1988. $11.00. 3:00. IV. Part I: d–b♭'; Part II: A–a'; Part III: F–b♭; Part IV: D$_1$–d. Nice arrangement of this famous movement of Handel's *Water Music.* Most challenging for the top two parts. Parts must be played cleanly and lightly.

Handel, George Frederic. *Allegro Maestoso from Water Music.* arr. Allyn Lindsey. Cimarron Music and Productions. Two euphoniums and two tubas. $14.50. Euphonium parts also available in treble clef.

Handel, George Frederic. *Almirena's Aria "Lascia ch'io pianga."* arr. William Schmidt. Western International Music, Inc. Two euphoniums and two tubas. 1998. $8.00. 3:00. II. Part I: f–g'; Part II: c–f'; Part III: D–a; Part IV: (E$_1$) G$_1$–d. Nice chorale with traditional harmonies. Rhythm is predominantly homophonic. Limited range and rhythms make this piece appropriate for intermediate-level performers. Parts may be doubled for a large ensemble.

Handel, George Frederic. *Halleluja Chorus.* arr. Robert Wilkinson. Cimarron Music and Productions. Two euphoniums and two tubas. 1995. $11.00. 5:15. Euphonium parts also available in treble clef.

Handel, George Frederic. *The Hallelujah Chorus.* arr. David Sabourin. Touch of Brass Music Corporation. Two euphoniums and two tubas. 1981. $10.00. 3:00. IV. Part I: B♭–b♭'; Part II: A–b♭'; Part III: F–a; Part IV: F_1–f. A good arrangement of this classic baroque choral work. Will require euphonium players with a strong high b♭' and clean and light articulation in the low tuba register. The arrangement works well. Parts may be doubled for a large ensemble.

Handel, George Frederic. *Hallelujah Chorus.* arr. John Stevens. Available from the arranger. Two euphoniums and two tubas. 1986. 2:00. III–IV. Part I: c–g'; Part II: F–E'; Part III: C–g; Part IV: F_1–c.

Handel, George Frederic. *Hallelujah! from "Messiah."* arr. Daniel Heiman. Heavy Metal Music. Two euphoniums and two tubas. 1991. $7.00. 8:00. III–IV. Part I: c–a♭'; Part II: F–d'; Part III: C–g; Part IV: F_1–d. Three movements: Hallelujah Chorus; Pifa; And with His Stripes We Are Healed. Most of the melodic responsibility is in the top two parts. No score available. Parts may be doubled for a large ensemble.

Handel, George Frederic. *Largo from Xerxes.* tr. Joseph Skillen. Tuba-Euphonium Press. Two euphoniums and two tubas. 2001. $8.00. 4:00. II. Part I: c–f'; Part II: A–f'; Part III: C–a; Part IV: (C_1) F_1–f. Effective transcription of this well-known work. Individual parts are not difficult and will serve as an excellent study piece in legato playing and ensemble intonation. More appropriate for a large ensemble, as the top three parts contain *divisi* passages. Also reviewed in the Winter 2002 issue of the *ITEA Journal* (Vol. 29, No. 2).

Handel, George Frederic. *Let the Bright Seraphim.* arr. Robert Madeson. Cimarron Music and Productions. Two euphoniums and two tubas. $10.00. Euphonium parts also available in treble clef.

Handel, George Frederic. *Menuets.* arr. Frank J. Halferty. Kendor Music, Incorporated. Two euphoniums and two tubas. $10.00. 2:30. II–III. Excerpted from Handel's famous *Music for the Royal Fireworks.*

Handel, George Frederic. *Messiah Suite.* arr. Daniel F. Heiman and Paul Schmidt. Heavy Metal Music. Two euphoniums and two tubas. 1992. $10.00. 14:30. III. Part I: c–a♭' (b'); Part II: F–d♭'; Part III: $B♭_1$–g; Part IV: F_1–e♭. Five movements: Hallelujah!; Pifa; And with His Stripes We Are Healed; He Trusted in God; Amen! Collection of five works by Handel. Includes the well-known "Hallelujah" chorus, a four-voice fugue, and two lyrical choral works. Parts may be doubled for a large ensemble. Individual movements can stand alone on a concert.

Handel, George Frederic. *Nations So Furiously Rage.* arr. Robert Wilkinson. Cimarron Music and Productions. Two euphoniums and two tubas. $13.00. Euphonium parts also available in treble clef.

Handel, George Frederic. *Sarabande and Variations.* arr. Richard Barth. Music Arts Company. Two euphoniums and two tubas. 1978. $10.00. 5:00. III. Part I: B–e♭'; Part II: A–c'; Part III: B_1–g; Part IV: (C_1) G_1–c. Very moderate technical demands. Good for young players. The top two parts are printed in both bass and treble clef. Parts may be doubled for a large ensemble.

Handel, George Frederic. *The Trumpet Shall Sound.* arr. Robert Wilkinson. Cimarron Music and Productions. Two euphoniums and two tubas. $13.00. Euphonium parts also available in treble clef.

Handel, George Frederic. *Two Baroque Dances.* arr. Grady Greene. Music Arts Company. Two euphoniums and two tubas. 1987. $15.00. 2:30. III–IV. Part I: e–a♭'; Part II: B♭–f'; Part III: A–g; Part IV: $A♭_1$–d♭. Two movements: Gavotte; Gigue. Works well for high school or college ensembles as there are no significant technical problems. The top two parts are printed in both bass and treble clef. Parts may be doubled for a large ensemble.

Handel, George Frederic. *Water and Fireworks Music.* arr. Daniel Heiman. Heavy Metal Music. Two euphoniums and two tubas. 1991. $5.00. 3:20. IV. Part I: G–g'; Part II: G–e♭'; Part III: A_1–a; Part IV: F_1–g. Three movements: Hornpipe; Coro; Bourree. The melody is primarily in the first part. Performers will need to play lightly and cleanly to avoid making the melody muddy in the low register of the euphonium. No score available. Parts may be doubled for a large ensemble.

Handy, W. C. *St. Louis Blues.* arr. Bill Holcombe. Musicians Publications. Two euphoniums and two tubas. 1992. $12.00. 5:00. IV. Part I: d♯–g'; Part II: G–e'; Part III: D–b; Part IV: G_1–e. Fun arrangement of this classic blues melody. All four parts have interesting lines and the harmonization is typical of this style. Drums may be added for effect. Parts may be doubled for a large ensemble. Recorded by the Melton Tuba-Quartett, *Premiere,* Diavolo Records, DR-D-93–C 001.

Hardt, Victor H. *Lullaby and Dance.* Tempo Music Publications, Incorporated. Two euphoniums and two tubas. 1968. Out of Print. 2:30. III–IV. Part I: e–f♯'; Part II: d♭–f'; Part III: A♭–d'; Part IV: F–d'. Two movements: Lullaby; Dance. Not very difficult, but there are some very musical sections in both movements. The Dance has some rhythmic challenges, so high school ensembles may need to perform at a more conservative tempo. There are two measures that high school tuba players may wish to play down an octave; all other range requirements are appropriate. Parts may be doubled for a large ensemble.

Harrison, Wayne. *Beneath the Surface.* Laissez-Faire Music Publishing Company. Two euphoniums, two tubas, piano, guitar, bass, and drums. 1981. Out of Print. 4:30. IV. Part I: d–b♭; Part II: d–f'; Part III: B♭$_1$–d'; Part IV: F$_1$–f. Dedicated to R. Winston Morris and the Tennessee Technological University Tuba Ensemble. This composition starts in a swing style and then has sections in bossa nova and funk. Not too difficult rhythmically, but challenging stylistically. The tessitura of the first euphonium part is high and will require a strong player; all players will need a good jazz feel. Parts may be doubled for a large ensemble. Recorded by the Tennessee Technological University Tuba Ensemble, *All That Jazz,* Mark Records, MES 20608.

Harrold, Robert. *The Night (It Has a Thousand Faces).* Tuba-Euphonium Press. Two euphoniums and two tubas. 1991. $10.00. 4:00. IV. Part I: c–b♭'; Part II: c–f; Part III: F$_1$–b♭; Part IV: F$_1$–b♭. For Laura. The first section features a slow lyrical melody accompanied by sustained block chords. The second section begins with a rhythmic bass line passed between the third and fourth parts underneath a syncopated melody. No great technical demands, but a strong sense of rhythm and a good upper register for the euphoniums are required. Top two parts are printed in both bass and treble clef. Parts may be doubled for a large ensemble.

Harrold, Robert. *Three Traveling Shorts.* Tuba-Euphonium Press. Two euphoniums and two tubas. 1991. $10.00. 6:00. IV. Part I: A–c' (a"); Part II: G–g' (a'); Part III: C$_1$–g; Part IV: F$_1$–e♭. Three movements. The first movement is fast and multimetric, constantly repeating 3/8, 2/8, and 4/4. The second movement is slower-paced and uses traditional harmonies in a chorale-like style. The third movement is very fast and more technically demanding for the first euphonium player. The last twelve measures of the third movement get significantly slower, perhaps signifying the end of the "trip," and thus the composition. The top two parts are printed in both treble and bass clef. Parts may be doubled for a large ensemble.

Hartin, Paul F., arr. *An Old German Folk Song.* Cellar Press. Two euphoniums and two tubas. 1975. 2:00. II–III. Part I: g–e'; Part II: e♭–c'; Part III: c–a♭; Part IV: A♭$_1$–f. A nice chorale setting of the German folk song "Ich Schwing mein Horn in Jammersthal." The melodic characteristics, range, and technical demands make this excellent for high school students. Parts may be doubled for a large ensemble.

Hartley, Walter. *Miniatures for Four Valve Instruments.* Galaxy Music Corporation. Two euphoniums and two tubas. 1984. $11.25. 5:20. IV. Part I: F–b♭'; Part II: F–g♭'; Part III: B–e♭'; Part IV: E♭$_1$–c'. Four movements: Marche Manquee; Shizo; Pavane; Four Valve Rag. The first movement is a short multimetric march; the last movement is the most challenging of the piece. The euphoniums are placed under greater technical and range demands than the tubas. Written in 1976, published in 1984. Recorded by the Atlantic Tuba Quartet, Golden Crest Records, CRS 4173.

Hartley, Walter S., arr. *Shape-Note Songs.* Stephen Shoop Music Publications. Two euphoniums and two tubas. 1997. $8.50. 3:30. II. Part I: B♭–g'; Part II: B♭–g'; Part III: F–g; Part IV: (F$_1$) G$_1$–d. Four movements: Holy Manna by William Moore; Sweet Prospect by William Walker; Idumea by A. Davisson; Burk by B. F. White. Originally for a cappella choir, these songs are excerpted from *The Sacred Harp* (1844) and older folk collections. Melodic material is divided between the four voices and clearly marked. Euphonium parts also available in treble clef. Parts may be doubled for a large ensemble. Individual movements can stand alone on a concert.

Hassler, Hans Leo. *Two Motets.* arr. Paul Schmidt. Heavy Metal Music. Two euphoniums and two tubas. 1991. $5.00. 3:00. III–IV. Part I: d–e'; Part II: A–b♭; Part III: A–a; Part IV: C–e. Two movements. The first movement is homophonic with mostly tutti rhythms. The second movement is polyphonic. No significant technical problems. No score available. Parts may be doubled for a large ensemble.

Hawker, John. *Romance for Bass Tuba. TUBA Journal.* Solo tuba, two euphoniums, and one tuba. 1977. $7.50. 3:30. IV. Part I: e–g'; Part II: B$_1$–c'; Part III: F$_1$–b; Solo/Part IV: E♭$_1$–e'. Challenging tuba solo with an accompaniment of two euphoniums and one tuba. Contrasting sections of a fast 3/8, slow 3/4, and fast 2/4. Written as part of the TUBA GEM Series and distributed in the *TUBA Journal,* Vol. 5, No. 2. It is available by purchasing this issue of the *TUBA Journal.*

Hawkins, Erskine. *Tuxedo Junction.* arr. Paul Schmidt. Heavy Metal Music. Two euphoniums and two tubas. 1991. $7.00. 4:30. IV. Part I: F–g'; Part II: B♭–b♭'; Part III: D–b♭; Part IV: A$_1$–d♭. Fun arrangement of this big band classic. The top three parts require mutes to produce closed and open effects (players are instructed to use the lid of a plastic bucket). Opportunities exist for improvisation. Drums may be added to enhance swing style. No score available. Parts may be doubled for a large ensemble.

Hawkins, Johnson, and Dash. *Tuxedo Junction.* arr. Ingo Luis. Musikverlag Bruno Uetz. One euphonium and three tubas. 1995. €17.00. 4:00. Second part may also be performed on euphonium. Recorded by the Melton Tuba-Quartett on the compact disc *Lazy Elephants,* Diavolo Records.

Haydn, Franz J. *Menuett, from Quartet Op. 75, No. 13.* arr. Karl Humble. T.A.P. Music. Two euphoniums and two tubas. 1989. $5.00. 4:00. IV. Part I: F♯–b♭'; Part II: G–f'; Part III: D–b♭; Part IV: E_1–e. A nice transcription of the third movement of this Haydn string quartet, often referred to as the "Kaiser Quartet." No extreme range or technical demands. Parts may be carefully doubled for a large ensemble. There is a misprint on the parts: this is quartet op. 76, no. 3, not no. 13.

Haydn, Franz Joseph. *Achieved Is the Glorious Work.* arr. Mike Forbes. Tuba-Euphonium Press. Two euphoniums and two tubas. 1999. $8.00. 2:45. II–III. Part I: A♭–g♭'; Part II: A♭–f'; Part III: A♭–d♭'; Part IV: ($E\flat_1$) F_1–d♭. For the U.S. Army Tuba/Euphonium Quartet. Effective arrangement of this work. Works well as a concert opener with its opening fanfare and contrapuntal treatment of the themes. Parts may be doubled for a large ensemble. Recorded by Sotto Voce on the compact disc *Consequences,* Summit Records.

Heiman, Daniel. *La Guercia.* Heavy Metal Music. Two euphoniums and two tubas. 1991. $5.00. 1:45. III–IV. Part I: d–f'; Part II: (C) G–b♭; Part III: E♭–c'; Part IV: $B\flat_1$–f. All parts are syncopated and the texture is polyphonic. No significant technical demands. No score available. Parts may be doubled for a large ensemble.

Heiman, Daniel, arr. *Three Barbershop Songs.* Heavy Metal Music. Two euphoniums and two tubas. 1991. $7.00. 4:00. III. Part I: g♭–f'; Part II: B–c'; Part III: G–a; Part IV: D♭–f. Three movements: I Had a Dream Dear; My Old Kentucky Home; Aura Lee. A very traditional arrangement of these three barbershop favorites. Most of the melody is in the top two parts. Not difficult, but fun to play. No score available. Parts may be doubled for a large ensemble.

Heiman, Daniel, arr. *Three Motets.* Heavy Metal Music. Two euphoniums and two tubas. 1991. $7.00. 4:00. IV. Part I: d–f'; Part II: c–c'; Part III: C♯–b♭; Part IV: (D_1) F_1–e♭. Three movements: Sanctus; Motet for Four Voices; Cantate Domino. Three very polyphonic motets written by Byrd, Crose, and Hassler, respectively. There are many meter changes, though the work is not technically difficult. No score available. Parts may be doubled for a large ensemble.

Henderson, Ray. *Five Foot Two, Eyes of Blue (Has Anybody Seen My Kim?).* arr. Steve Emberson. Available from the arranger. Two euphoniums and two tubas. 2:00. IV. Part I: b♭–b♭'; Part II: a–g'; Part III: B♭–d'; Part IV: F_1–g. Cute arrangement of this peppy classic melody. It is written in four but should be played in cut time. Technical difficulty is determined by the speed of performance. Parts may be doubled for a large ensemble.

Henry, Eric, arr. *Infant Holy, Infant Lowly.* Tuba-Euphonium Press. Two euphoniums and two tubas. 1994. $10.00. 2:30. II. Part I: f♯–a'; Part II: c–a'; Part III: F–b; Part IV: A_1–g. Also reviewed in the Summer 2002 issue of the *ITEA Journal* (Vol. 29, No. 4).

Hensel-Mendelssohn, Fanny. *Schweigt der Menschen laute Lust.* arr. Angelo Manzo. Tuba-Euphonium Press. Two euphoniums and two tubas. 2002. $8.00. 1:45. I–II. Part I: e♭–g'; Part II: c–d♭'; Part III: E♭–g♭; Part IV: $A\flat_1$–d♭. Brief tonal work appropriate for young performers. The texture is homophonic, and the melody is predominantly in the first part. Parts may be doubled for a large ensemble. Also reviewed in the Spring 2004 issue of the *ITEA Journal* (Vol. 31, No. 3).

Heussenstamm, George. *Tuba Quartet, Op. 65, No. 3.* Available from the composer. Four tubas. 1977. $22.00. 9:00. IV. Part I: F_1–f♯'; Part II: D_1–a♭'; Part III: $D\sharp_1$–e'; Part IV: E_1–d. Written for four F tubas. A contemporary composition with many complicated rhythms and mixed meters. There are some spoken parts and mouthpiece buzzing. The score indicates a specific staging for the performance.

Heussenstamm, George. *Tubacussion, Op. 62.* Seesaw Music Corporation. Four tubas and percussion. 1977. $31.00. 10:00. IV–V. Part I: c–e♭'; Part II: $A\sharp_1$–b; Part III: E_1–e♭'; Part IV: $E\flat_1$–a♭. An avant-garde work with many twentieth-century techniques, including tapping the instrument, floor stomps, humming, rattling of keys, indeterminate sections, and random selection of pitches. A very difficult work.

Heussenstamm, George. *TubaFour, Op. 30.* Seesaw Music Corporation. One euphonium and three tubas. 1976. $24.00. 8:30. IV. Part I: $D\flat_1$–b'; Part II: B_1–d'; Part III: G_1–b; Part IV: D_1–b. In a contemporary style. The pitches are determined in some sections based on the position of dots on the page. Very challenging due to technical demands and the complex harmonic structure. The composer indicates a conductor will be necessary. Recorded by the New York Tuba Quartet, *Tubby's Revenge,* Crystal Records, S221.

Hewitt, Harry. *Bird in the Forest, Op. 376F.* Available from the composer. Four tubas with a high solo and optional echo part. 1972. $15.00. 3:00. IV. Part I: D♭–f♯'; Part II: D♭–b; Part III: D♭–b; Part IV: D♭–b. To R. Winston Morris and the Tennessee Technological University Tuba Ensemble. This involves a high solo instrument (flute or clarinet) and four tubas. There is a second optional high part that echoes the solo part. The solo and echo parts often play in a manner that is totally unrelated to the tuba ensemble. There are numerous dynamic contrasts and tempo changes. With a few adjustments, the top part could be played by a euphonium.

Hewitt, Harry. *Four Preludes for Four Tubas.* Available from the composer. Four tubas. 1973. $9.00. 13:00. IV. Part I: B♭–f'; Part II: $B\flat_1$–c'; Part

III: G♭$_1$–c'; Part IV: E$_1$–c'. Four movements. Four movements contrasting in tempo and character with contemporary harmonies. Very interesting interplay between the parts. No extreme technical demands, but the parts are still challenging. Originally composed and copyrighted in 1971.

Hewitt, Harry. *In the Shadows, Op. 376B.* Available from the composer. Four tubas and celeste. 1971. $8.00. 4:00. IV. Part I: A♭–f'; Part II: B♭$_1$–c'; Part III: F$_1$–c; Part IV: E$_1$–A. The fourth part is an optional part that only plays for 22 measures. The first part is high and may be played on an F tuba or euphonium. While the piece is technically only moderately challenging, there are numerous tempo and meter changes. A conductor will be necessary.

Hidas, Frigyes. *Tubaquartett.* Musikverlag Bruno Uetz. One euphonium and three tubas. 1995. €17.00. 3:00. Second part may also be performed on euphonium. Recorded by the Melton Tuba-Quartett on the compact disc *Lazy Elephants,* Diavolo Records.

Hill, William H. *Fantasia on "Dies Irae" for Tuba Ensemble.* Neil A. Kjos Music Company. Two euphoniums and two tubas. 1980. $7.00. 5:00. IV. Part I: G–b'; Part II: F–b$_1$; Part III: G$_1$–c'; Part IV: F$_1$–b. Commissioned by the Tubists Universal Brotherhood Association for the 1980 Second National Tuba/Euphonium Workshop. Based on the Gregorian chant "Dies Irae." The first section is a plainsong line introduction, and it is followed by a very dissonant contrasting Allegro molto section. The first and second tuba parts have *divisi* sections; all parts use mutes. Good writing for tuba/euphonium ensemble. Parts may be doubled for a large ensemble.

Hindemith, Paul. *Six Chansons.* tr. Jeremy S. Lane. Tuba-Euphonium Press. Two euphoniums and two tubas. 2002. $15.00. 6:15. II. Part I: c–a♭'; Part II: B♭–d'; Part III: C–g♭; Part IV: E♭$_1$–c♯. Six movements: The Doe; The Swan; Since All Is Passing; Spring Time; In Winter; Orchard. Originally composed for mixed chorus and based on a text by German poet Rainer Maria Rilke. The texture is homophonic and the melody is primarily in the first euphonium. Parts may be doubled for a large ensemble. Also reviewed in the Summer 2004 issue of the *ITEA Journal* (Vol. 31, No. 4).

Hoesly, John. *Quadrant.* Piston Reed Stick and Bow Publisher. Two euphoniums and two tubas. 1992. $15.00. 20:00. IV–V. Part I: F–b'; Part II: A♭–a'; Part III: A♭$_1$–c'; Part IV: F$_1$–b♭. Four movements: Amorphous; Bemorphous; Seamorphous; Fourmorphous. A contemporary tonal composition. There are numerous meter changes, a multiphonic section, and glissandos, and players are asked to blow air through their instruments at different pitch levels. All four parts are technically challenging. Very interesting writing. The score is available for an extra four dollars.

Hoesly, John, arr. *Ballin' the Jack.* Piston Reed Stick and Bow Publisher. Two euphoniums and two tubas. 1990. $7.00. 2:00. IV. Part I: c–a♭'; Part II: F♯–e'; Part III: C–g♭; Part IV: (D$_1$) G$_1$–e. This begins with a slow introduction followed by a moderate jazz section. The first and second parts are the most technically challenging. The score is available for an additional two dollars. Parts may be doubled for a large ensemble.

Hoesly, John, arr. *Just a Closer Walk with Thee.* Piston Reed Stick and Bow Publisher. Two euphoniums and two tubas. 1990. $7.00. 3:00. IV. Part I: B♭–b♭'; Part II: A–e♭$_1$; Part III: B♭$_1$–a♭; Part IV: B♭$_1$–d (b♭). Begins with a slow chorale, then moves to swing and then Dixieland, and ends slowly. Most challenging for the top two parts. Drums may be added for stylistic support. The score is available for an additional two dollars. Parts may be doubled for a large ensemble.

Hoesly, John, arr. *St. Louis Blues.* Piston Reed Stick and Bow Publisher. Two euphoniums and two tubas. 1990. $7.00. 4:30. IV. Part I: e–g'; Part II: B♭–f'; Part III: B♭$_1$–f; Part IV: G$_1$–e♭. Good arrangement of this famous blues melody. Most of the melodic responsibility is in the first part. Many syncopated rhythms in the melody and accompaniment. Fun to play. A score is available for an additional two dollars.

Hoesly, John, arr. *That's a Plenty.* Piston Reed Stick and Bow Publisher. Two euphoniums and two tubas. 1990. $7.00. 3:00. IV. Part I: B♭–g'; Part II: B♭–f'; Part III: D–a; Part IV: A$_1$–f. The melody is primarily in the first and second parts. A middle section with chord symbols may be repeated for improvised solos. A rhythm section is recommended for stylistic effect. A score is available for an additional two dollars. Parts may be doubled for a large ensemble.

Holborne, Anthony. *Ten Pieces for Tuba Ensemble.* arr. John Stevens. Tuba-Euphonium Press. Two euphoniums and two tubas. 1992. $10.00. 14:00. IV. Part I: d–g'; Part II: G–g'; Part III: F–c'; Part IV: F$_1$–d. Ten movements: Muy Linda; Honie-Suckle; Pavan; The Marie-Golde; The Choice; Patiencia; The New Yeres Gift; Night Watch; Last Will and Testament; Galliard. A conglomeration of Renaissance-style songs in a variety of keys, meters, and styles. While technically not difficult, there are many polyphonic sections. Some movements could be played by high school ensembles. Parts may be doubled for a large ensemble. The music is sold as parts only; there is no score available.

Holmes, Paul. *Quartet for Tubas.* TRN Music Publishers. Two euphoniums and two tubas. 1980. $20.00. 10:00. IV. Part I: B–g'; Part II: B–e'; Part III: D–b; Part IV: G$_1$–a. Four movements: Adagio; Andante and Allegro; Lento; Allegro Moderato in a Jazz Style. Commissioned by

R. Winston Morris and the Tennessee Technological University Tuba Ensemble. Very melodic and rhythmically interesting composition. Second and fourth movements have a lot of syncopated rhythms, hemiolas, etc. Fun to play and satisfying for audiences. Parts may be doubled for a large ensemble. Recorded by the University of Michigan Tuba and Euphonium Ensemble, University of Michigan Records, SM0011; the British Tuba Quartet, *In at the Deep End,* Heavyweight Records Limited, HR008/D.

Holst, Gustav. *Intermezzo and March from Suite in E♭ Major.* arr. Scott Schlesinger. Tuba-Euphonium Press. Two euphoniums and two tubas. 2002. $24.00. 5:30. III. Part I: F–c''; Part II: G–f'; Part III: F_1–g'; Part IV: F_1–f'. Two movements: Intermezzo; March. Challenging arrangement that is true to the original. The passages transcribed from woodwind parts present the greatest challenge, though the arrangement is effective. Parts may be doubled for a large ensemble. Also reviewed in the Spring 2004 issue of the *ITEA Journal* (Vol. 31, No. 3).

Holst, Gustav. *Jupiter (Chorale) from "The Planets."* arr. Joseph Goble. Tuba-Euphonium Press. Two euphoniums and two tubas. $8.00. 2:15. II. Part I: c–g'; Part II: G–d'; Part III: G_1–b♭; Part IV: G_1–f. Brief setting of the chorale from the "Jupiter" movement of *The Planets.* Melodic material is divided evenly among the four voices, and the arrangement is appropriate for younger ensembles. Parts may be doubled for a large ensemble.

Holst, Gustav. *March from Second Suite in F for Military Band.* arr. David Werden. Cimarron Music and Productions. Two euphoniums and two tubas. 1997. $13.00. 4:30. III. Part I: A♭–c''; Part II: c–b♭'; Part III: C–b♭; Part IV: C_1–f. Excellent arrangement of this popular work for wind band. All parts are challenging, and the melodic material is divided among the top three voices. Euphonium parts also available in treble clef. Parts may be doubled for a large ensemble. Also available in a six-part version from the same arranger and publisher.

Hook, James. *Rondo.* arr. James A. Garrett. James Garrett. Two euphoniums and two tubas. 1973. $15.00. 2:00. IV. Part I: f–g'; Part II: c–d'; Part III: F–b♭; Part IV: A_1–f. Written for R. Winston Morris and the Tennessee Technological University Tuba Ensemble. A very energetic melody equally demanding for all instruments. This transcription works very well for tubas and euphoniums. The top two parts are available in bass and treble clef. Parts may be doubled for a large ensemble. Recorded by the British Tuba Quartet, *In at the Deep End,* Heavyweight Records Limited, HR008/D.

Howard, Ronald. *Chorale.* Available from the composer. Two euphoniums and two tubas. 1979. 1:10. III–IV. Part I: d♭–e'; Part II: F–f; Part III: F–a; Part IV: B_1–d. A very slow chorale, alternating between 3/4, 5/4, and 6/4. Uses contemporary harmonies. Players read from a score. No significant technical problems. Parts may be doubled for a large ensemble.

Huffine, G. F. *Them Basses.* arr. Joseph Goble. Tuba-Euphonium Press. Two euphoniums and two tubas. 2001. $8.00. 3:00. II–III. Part I: c–b♭'; Part II: B♭–f'; Part III: $B♭_1$–f; Part IV: F_1–f. For the Amazing Tuba/Euphonium Quartet. Like the original march, this arrangement is scored with the melody in the lowest part with the other parts serving an accompanimental role. Euphonium parts also available in treble clef. Parts may be doubled for a large ensemble. Also reviewed in the Spring 2003 issue of the *ITEA Journal* (Vol. 30, No. 3).

Hughey, J., and P. Jernigan, arr. *Gay 90's Medley.* University of Tennessee Series. Two euphoniums and two tubas. 1971. Out of Print. 4:00. IV. Part I: d–d♭'; Part II: F–a♭; Part III: F–f; Part IV: $B♭_1$–d.

Humperdink, Engelbert. *Gebet aus Hänsel und Gretel.* arr. Bruno Seitz. Musikverlag Martin Scherbacher. Two euphoniums and two tubas. 1991. $13.50. 3:30. IV. Part I: B♭–b♭'; Part II: A–g; Part III: $B♭_1$–d'; Part IV: E_1–g. A slow and very lyrical melody. The melody is primarily in the first part. No significant technical problems. Parts may be doubled for a large ensemble.

Hurt, Eddie. *Melissma.* Queen City Brass Publications. Four tubas. 1981. $6.50. 2:00. IV. Part I: B♭–b♭'; Part II: A♭–c'; Part III: C–f; Part IV: $B♭_1$–e♭. For Rex Conner. The major demand of this piece is range, not technique. This would be considered a grade V if tubas were to play all four parts. If performed with two euphoniums and two tubas, this piece is playable by a good high school ensemble. Parts may be doubled for a large ensemble.

Hutchinson, Terry. *Tuba Juba Duba.* The Brass Press. Two euphoniums and two tubas. 1974. $5.00. 3:10. III. Part I: c♯–g' (b'); Part II: c♯–c'; Part III: D–e; Part IV: B–d. The simple catchy melody makes this a thoroughly fun piece to perform and to listen to. There are simple mixed meters along with a slow lyrical middle section. Also includes a finger snaps or woodblock part and a foot stomp at the end. Very entertaining! Parts may be doubled for a large ensemble. Recorded by the Tennessee Technological University Tuba Ensemble, Golden Crest Records, CRS 4139; the Melton Tuba-Quartett, *Premiere,* Diavolo Records, DR-D-93-C-001.

Iannaccone, Anthony. *Hades.* Seesaw Music Corporation. Two euphoniums and two tubas. 1975. $12.00. 5:30. IV–V. Part I: c–b♭'; Part II: A–a'; Part III: D–d'; Part IV: D_1–b. Very contemporary in harmony and style. Special techniques required include blowing through the instrument while clicking valves, as well as quarter tones, glissandos, and multiphonics. All four parts will require mutes. There are many difficult rhythmic figures; this will require four strong players. Recorded by the University of Michigan Tuba/Euphonium Ensemble, Golden Crest Records, CRS-4145.

Iannaccone, Anthony. *Three Mythical Sketches.* Tenuto Publications. Two euphoniums and two tubas. 1973. $4.00. 6:30. IV. Part I: A–a'; Part II: A–g♭'; Part III: C♯–e♭'; Part IV: G_1–c♯'. Three movements: Pluto; Persephone; Poseidon. All parts are technically and rhythmically challenging. Harmonically very dissonant at times, and all parts need mutes. Will require four strong players. Recorded by the University of Michigan Tuba/Euphonium Ensemble, Golden Crest Records, CRS-4145.

Ionel, Dumitru. *Quartet.* Editions BIM. Four tubas. 1996. CHF 15.00. 2:30. II. Part I: F♯–f'; Part II: F–e♭'; Part III: B♭$_1$–a♭; Part IV: F_1–g. Conservative writing with simple harmonies and rhythms—easy to interpret. First and second parts may also be performed on euphonium. Appropriate for young ensembles.

Israel, Brian. *Canzona and Hornpipe.* Tritone Press. Four tubas. 1982. $5.00. 5:20. IV. Part I: A_1–d'; Part II: A_1–d'; Part III: A_1–d'; Part IV: E_1–d'. Two movements: Canzone; Hornpipe. The Canzone is very contrapuntal; the Hornpipe is also very imitative and rhythmically more challenging than the Canzone. All parts are similar in their range demands (all four tubas have a high d'). This will require four strong players.

Ivanovici, J. *Waves of the Danube.* arr. Soichi Konagaya. Sonic Arts, Incorporated. Two euphoniums and two tubas. 1986. $12.00. 3:45. IV. Part I: c–a♭'; Part II: B♭–a♭'; Part III: D–a♭; Part IV: (E♭$_1$) F_1–d. A medley of three different moderate waltzes. There is a brief cadenza for the first part near the beginning of the piece. All parts play portions of the melody. Parts may be doubled for a large ensemble.

Jacob, Gordon. *Four Pieces for Tuba Quartet.* Whaling Music Publishers. Two euphoniums and two tubas. 1981. $15.00. 6:00. IV. Part I: d–c"; Part II: G–b♭'; Part III: E♭–d'; Part IV: E♭$_1$–b♭. Four movements. Dedicated to the Denis Winter Quartet. The movements are in a variety of meters with the melody often written in a folk style. While only the first euphonium part is printed in treble clef, both parts are notated in treble clef in the score. A high tessitura will require strong euphonium players. Parts may be doubled for a large ensemble.

Jager, Robert. *Mixtures and Mutations.* Tuba-Euphonium Press. Two euphoniums and two tubas. 1992. $10.00. 6:30. IV. Part I: c–c"; Part II: G♭–g♭'; Part III: G_1–b; Part IV: F_1–g♭. Four movements: Slowly; Aggressively; Moderately; Boldly. To R. Winston Morris and the Tennessee Technological University Tuba Ensemble. Contemporary harmonies; rhythmically intricate in some of the movements. The fourth movement is multimetric and the tessitura of the first part is high. Mutes are required of all parts. This was originally published by Laissez-Faire Music Publishing Company and copyrighted in 1981.

Jessel, Leon. *Parade of the Wooden Tubas.* arr. D. L. Shirer. Available from the arranger. One baritone, one euphonium, and two tubas. 2003. 3:15. II. Part I: f–a♭'; Part II: c–f'; Part III: F–b♭; Part IV: (F_1) G_1–e♭. Light arrangement based on *Parade of the Wooden Soldiers.* Each part has the melody at some time. Parts may be doubled for a large ensemble.

Johnson, Charles Leslie. *Dill Pickles Rag.* arr. Mark Nelson. Tuba-Euphonium Press. Two euphoniums and two tubas. 1994. $8.00. 3:30. II–III. Part I: B–a' (c"); Part II: d–f♯'; Part III: D–a; Part IV: (C_1) G_1–d. For the Hokkaido Euphonium/Tuba Camp. Traditional ragtime two-step arranged with melodic material in all four voices. The syncopated rhythms and range are challenging, but still accessible to intermediate-level performers. Parts may be doubled for a large ensemble.

Jones, Roger. *Allegro for Tuba Quartet.* Available from the composer. Four tubas. 1969. $12.00. 5:00. IV. Part I: G–e'; Part II: B♭$_1$–b♭; Part III: G_1–g; Part IV: F_1–d. The melody and accompaniment are very syncopated. The first and third parts are the most technically challenging. Works well.

Jones, Roger. *Canticles.* Available from the composer. Four tubas. 1978. $50.00. 15:00. IV. Part I: A–a'; Part II: C–e'; Part III: E_1–d'; Part IV: D_1–g. Three movements. A major work for tuba/euphonium quartet. The music is multimetric and complex harmonically, and there are cadenzas in many of the parts. All parts require mutes and are technically challenging.

Jones, Roger. *Cantilena.* Available from the composer. Two euphoniums and two tubas. 1975. $5.00. 1:45. III–IV. Part I: c–f'; Part II: c–c'; Part III: C–a♭; Part IV: F_1–e. A nice lyrical melody in a slow 3/4. No technical problems. Very appropriate for high school students. Parts may be doubled for a large ensemble.

Jones, Roger. *Chant and Fantasie.* Available from the composer. Four tubas. 1969. $20.00. 5:00. IV. Part I: C–e♭'; Part II: C–b♭; Part III: G_1–f; Part IV: F_1–d. Two movements: Chant; Fantasie. The first movement is slow and somber. The second movement shifts frequently between 2/4 and 3/4. All parts play portions of the melody. No significant technical difficulties, but players will need to count carefully.

Jones, Roger. *Quartet for Tubas.* Available from the composer. Four tubas. 1972. $10.00. 4:50. IV. Part I: C–e'; Part II: C–b♭; Part III: C–g; Part IV: F_1–c. Three movements: Intrada; Air; Ballabile. Very good writing for tuba quartet. The third movement is rhythmically more interesting and challenging. All parts require mutes.

Jones, Roger. *Tubafugalfanfare*. Available from the composer. Four tubas. 1992. $6.00. 1:20. IV. Part I: F–a; Part II: $G\flat_1$–d; Part III: F–f; Part IV: F_1–d. A short but dramatic fanfare based on one main fugal subject. All parts have equal responsibility for the melody. Works very well. Parts may be doubled for a large ensemble.

Joplin, Scott. *The Easy Winners*. arr. David R. Werden. Whaling Music Publishers. Two euphoniums and two tubas. 1980. $6.00. 2:45. IV. Part I: G–b♭'; Part II: G–a'; Part III: G–d'; Part IV: F_1–a. The tessitura is high for the top two parts of this Joplin rag. A few tricky rhythms; will require strong players. The first euphonium part is printed in treble clef. Parts may be doubled for a large ensemble.

Joplin, Scott. *Easy Winners*. arr. Denzil Stephens. Sarnia Music. Two euphoniums and two tubas.

Joplin, Scott. *The Easy Winners*. arr. Hirokazu Hiraishi. Sonic Arts, Incorporated. Two euphoniums and two tubas. 1986. $12.00. 2:45. IV. Part I: G–a'; Part II: F–a'; Part III: F–c'; Part IV: F_1–e♭. All parts have the opportunity to play this syncopated melody. Technically challenging in several sections. Fun to play.

Joplin, Scott. *The Easy Winners*. arr. Paul Schmidt. Heavy Metal Music. Two euphoniums and two tubas. 1991. $7.00. 2:45. IV. Part I: f–a♭'; Part II: E♭–g'; Part III: $B\flat_1$–c'; Part IV: $E\flat_1$–a. Highly syncopated melody. Technically challenging for all parts, but fun to play. There is no score available.

Joplin, Scott. *Elite Syncopations*. arr. William Picher. PP Music. Two euphoniums and two tubas. 1986. $8.00. 3:30. IV. Part I: B♭–c'; Part II: B♭–g'; Part III: D–d'; Part IV: $A\flat_1$–g. Not many technical difficulties, but counting can be tricky and the primary challenge of most of these Joplin rags. The tubas get a brief opportunity to play the melody, but most of the work is in the euphoniums. The first part is printed in treble clef in the score and the part. Parts may be doubled for a large ensemble. Recorded by the British Tuba Quartet, *Elite Syncopations*, Polyphonic Reproductions Ltd., QPRZ012D.

Joplin, Scott. *The Entertainer*. arr. Byron Gray. Cimarron Music and Productions. Two euphoniums and two tubas. 1998. $13.00. 1:25. Euphonium parts also available in treble clef.

Joplin, Scott. *The Entertainer*. arr. David Schanke. Music Arts Publishing Company. Two euphoniums and two tubas. 1996. $16.00. 4:15. II–III. Part I: A–g'; Part II: c–e♭'; Part III: C–f; Part IV: $B\flat_1$–d. Nice arrangement of this popular rag. It is challenging, but still accessible by intermediate-level performers. Euphonium parts also available in treble clef. Parts may be doubled for a large ensemble.

Joplin, Scott. *The Entertainer*. arr. Denzil Stephens. Sarnia Music. Two euphoniums and two tubas.

Joplin, Scott. *The Entertainer*. arr. Hirokazu Hiraishi. Sonic Arts, Incorporated. Three euphoniums and one tuba. 1987. $12.00. 3:30. IV. Part I: d–a'; Part II: A–g'; Part III: G–e'; Part IV: F_1–d. The third part could be played by a tuba, as the tessitura is not high. The melody is primarily in the top three parts. Fun to play. Parts may be doubled for a large ensemble.

Joplin, Scott. *Euphonic Sounds*. arr. David R. Werden. Whaling Music Publishers. Two euphoniums and two tubas. 1978. $8.00. 2:50. IV. Part I: c–d''; Part II: c–a'; Part III: c♯–c'; Part IV: F_1–f. A medium-tempo rag with a very syncopated melody and accompaniment. Most of the melodic work is in the first and second parts. Both of these parts are printed in treble clef. Generally these Joplin arrangements are challenging to play, but, played correctly, are enjoyable for both performers and audience. Recorded by the Atlantic Tuba Quartet, *Euphonic Sounds*, Golden Crest, CRS 4173; the British Tuba Quartet, *Euphonic Sounds*, Polyphonic Reproductions Limited, QPRZ009D.

Joplin, Scott. *Euphonic Sounds*. arr. Hirokazu Hiraishi. Sonic Arts, Incorporated. Two euphoniums and two tubas. 1986. $12.00. 2:50. IV. Part I: G–b♭'; Part II: F♯–e♭'; Part III: D♭–f; Part IV: $G\flat_1$–d. A very syncopated melody shared by all parts. Will require light and clean playing. Technically challenging in some sections. Parts may be doubled for a large ensemble.

Joplin, Scott. *The Favorite Rag*. arr. David Sabourin. Touch of Brass Music Corporation. Two euphoniums and two tubas. 1981. $10.00. 2:20. IV. Part I: c–g'; Part II: c–d'; Part III: G–b; Part IV: A_1–e. Technically quite challenging for the euphoniums. Tubas have primarily an accompaniment function. Parts may be doubled for a large ensemble.

Joplin, Scott. *The Great Crush Collision*. arr. Paul Schmidt. Heavy Metal Music. Two euphoniums and two tubas. 1991. $7.00. 2:30. IV. Part I: A–f'; Part II: E–f'; Part III: $G\sharp_1$–b♭; Part IV: F_1–c. Originally written by Joplin to describe a staged steam locomotive crash in 1896. The parts are challenging, but fun to play. There is no score available.

Joplin, Scott. *Maple Leaf Rag*. arr. Karl Humble. T.A.P. Music. Two euphoniums and two tubas. 1989. $6.00. 3:20. IV. Part I: c–c''; Part II: A♭–c''; Part III: D♭–b♭; Part IV: $E\flat_1$–f♭. Technically challenging for the top three parts. The tessitura of the first part is high. Players will need to count carefully. Fun to play.

Joplin, Scott. *Peacherine Rag*. arr. Hirokazu Hiraishi. Sonic Arts, Incorporated. Two euphoniums and two tubas. 1992. $11.00. 4:00. III–IV. Part I: d–a♭; Part II: G–e♭; Part III: F–c'; Part IV: F_1–d. A moderate-tempo rag. No significant technical problems, but many of the rhythmic patterns are very syncopated. Parts may be doubled for a large ensemble.

Joplin, Scott. *Pineapple Rag.* arr. Hirokazu Hiraishi. Sonic Arts, Incorporated. Two euphoniums and two tubas. 1986. $12.00. 4:00. IV. Part I: B♭–g'; Part II: F–e♭'; Part III: E–g; Part IV: G_1–c. A moderate-tempo rag. The melody is primarily in the top two parts. There is a lot of syncopation, which will require accurate counting and playing. Parts may be doubled for a large ensemble.

Joplin, Scott. *Pleasant Moments Rag.* arr. Paul Schmidt. Heavy Metal Music. Two euphoniums and two tubas. 1990. $7.00. 2:30. IV. Part I: F–f'; Part II: F–d'; Part III: F_1–b♭; Part IV: F_1–f. A rag in 3/4 time. A lot of syncopation in the top three parts. Challenging, but fun to play. No score available.

Joplin, Scott. *Rag-Time Dance.* arr. David R. Werden. Whaling Music Publishers. Two euphoniums and two tubas. 1979. $7.00. 2:45. IV–V. Part I: A♭–b♭' (d"); Part II: A♭–b♭'; Part III: A♭$_1$–e♭'; Part IV: A♭$_1$–e♭'. Medium-tempo rag. While most of the work is in the first part, both tuba parts have opportunities to play the melody. Technically challenging, and the tessitura of all four parts is high. Recorded by the U.S. Navy Tuba Quartet, U.S. Navy Band recordings.

Joplin, Scott. *Rag-Time Dance.* arr. Paul Schmidt. Heavy Metal Music. Two euphoniums and two tubas. 1991. $7.00. 3:30. IV. Part I: F–g'; Part II: C–f'; Part III: E–b; Part IV: F_1–c. The top two parts have the most technical demands. A very interesting rag. No score available.

Joplin, Scott. *The Strenuous Life.* arr. Hirokazu Hiraishi. Sonic Arts, Incorporated. Two euphoniums and two tubas. 1986. $12.00. 4:00. IV. Part I: A–g'; Part II: A–e'; Part III: C–g; Part IV: G_1–d. All parts have the opportunity to play this syncopated melody. No range problems. Parts may be doubled for a large ensemble.

Joplin, Scott. *The Strenuous Life: A Ragtime Two-Step.* arr. Walter Lex. PP Music. Two euphoniums and two tubas. 1986. $8.00. 4:00. IV–V. Part I: d–c"; Part II: F–b♭'; Part III: C–d'; Part IV: E♭$_1$–f. To Roger Behrend. A challenging Joplin rag. The tessitura of both euphonium parts is quite high. There are several technical demands that will require strong players in order to produce a flowing ragtime feel. All four parts have responsibility for the melody.

Joplin, Scott. *Swipesy.* arr. David R. Werden. Whaling Music Publishers. Two euphoniums and two tubas. 1981. $7.00. 3:00. IV. Part I: c–c♭"; Part II: d♭–b♭'; Part III: A♭–d♭'; Part IV: A♭$_1$–f. Rhythmically challenging, and the euphoniums have a high tessitura. The first euphonium part is printed in treble clef. This arrangement works very well. Parts may be doubled for a large ensemble.

Joplin, Scott. *Two Rags, Volume 1.* arr. David Sabourin. Touch of Brass Music Corporation. Two euphoniums and two tubas. $10.00. Two movements: The Cascades; The Favorite Rag. The Cascades is recorded by the British Tuba Quartet, *In at the Deep End,* Heavyweight Records, Limited, HR008/D.

Joplin, Scott. *Two Rags, Volume 2.* arr. David Sabourin. Touch of Brass Music Corporation. Two euphoniums and two tubas. $10.00. Two movements: Pleasant Moments; Heliotrope Bouquet.

Jous, Christian. *Fine Ale.* Editions du Petit Page. Two euphoniums and two tubas. €19.00.

Jous, Christian. *L'Emir aphone.* Editions du Petit Page. Two euphoniums and two tubas. €19.00.

Joyful Euphonium Tuba Ensemble, Book 7. Kyodo Music. Two euphoniums and two tubas. ¥2100. 31 pp. III. Part I: A–a♭'; Part II: G–e'; Part III: D–c'; Part IV: G_1–b♭. Seven movements: Grand March from Aida by Verdi; Enterrrement de la Poupée by Tchaikovsky; Ave Verum Corpus by Mozart; Petite Nigro by Debussy; Suite No. 3 by Respighi; William Tell Overture by Rossini; Slavic Dance No. 3 by Dvorák. Large collection of popular arrangements.

Kassler, David. *Chorale Prelude and Fugue on Puer Nobis.* Tuba-Euphonium Press. Two euphoniums and two tubas. 2003. $15.00. 6:30. III. Part I: G–c"; Part II: D–f♯'; Part III: G_1–b♭; Part IV: D_1–a. Original composition in D major in the style of a traditional chorale prelude and fugue for organ. More appropriate for an ensemble than a quartet, as the first and third parts contain *divisi* passages and the fourth part is best achieved with two performers stagger-breathing on the sustained low organ "pedal notes."

Kauffman, Steve, and Andrew Spang, arr. *Nanourissma.* Lyric Brass Publishing. Two euphoniums and two tubas. 1994. $9.00. 2:30. Both euphonium parts contain passages in tenor clef. Parts may be doubled for a large ensemble.

Keating, Geoff. *Et Tu Bop.* Breakthrough Music. Two euphoniums and two tubas. £14.95. Part I: c–d♯"; Part II: c–b'; Part III: B_1–e'; Part IV: G_1–c♯'. A fun lively work.

Keating, Geoff. *Shall We Dance?* Breakthrough Music. Two euphoniums and two tubas. £11.95. Four movements: Tango; Foxtrot; Waltz; Charleston. A fun, light piece popular with audiences of all ages.

Keating, Geoff. *Such Sweet Sorrow.* Breakthrough Music. Two euphoniums and two tubas. £11.95. Part I: e♭–b'; Part II: d♯–b'; Part III: B♭$_1$–c♯'; Part IV: E_1–b. This is a slow, sentimental ballad showing the sweet side of the instruments.

Kern, Jerome. *They Didn't Believe Me.* arr. Bill Holcombe. Musicians Publications. Two euphoniums and two tubas. 1991. $12.00. 2:45. IV. Part I: e♭–e'; Part II: c–d'; Part III: B♭–g; Part IV: F_1–e. A nice lyrical melody with lush jazz harmonies. The second section is in a faster swing style. This arrangement works quite well. Drums may be added for effect. Parts may be doubled for a large ensemble. Recorded by the British Tuba Quartet, *Euphonic Sounds,* Polyphonic Reproductions Limited, QPRZ 009D.

Kerwin, Simon. *Bass Camp*. Breakthrough Music. Two euphoniums and two tubas. £14.95. Part I: B♭–e♭"; Part II: A♭–b♭'; Part III: F$_1$–c♭'; Part IV: E♭$_1$–f'. A work that examines and dispels popular theories about the tuba. The work cleverly includes references to *Tubby the Tuba, Ugly Duckling, The Thunderer, The Stars and Stripes,* and *Carnival of Venice*, and also a film music quotation from *Close Encounters of the Third Kind.* The piece requires a duck call and a whistle.

Kerwin, Simon. *Illustrations.* Kirklees Music. Two euphoniums and two tubas. £10.50. 7:45. Three movements. Core repertoire work in a traditional fast, slow, fast form. Recorded by Tubalaté on the compact disc *Episodes.*

Kerwin, Simon. *March—FroT.* Breakthrough Music. Two euphoniums and two tubas. £11.95. Part I: A–d♭"; Part II: A–d♭'; Part III: B♭$_1$–c'; Part IV: F$_1$–d♭. This technically demanding work was commissioned by Tubalaté by way of a thank you to their FROTs (Friends of Tubalaté) for their continued support. The march is written as a traditional brass band contest march. Recorded by Tubalaté on the compact disc *Move.*

Ketchum, Leo K. *Elegy and Presto.* Tuba-Euphonium Press. Two euphoniums and two tubas. 1997. $12.00. 4:00. III. Part I: B♭–c"; Part II: (F) G–g♭'; Part III: C–b♭; Part IV: B♭$_2$–f. Original composition consisting of two contrasting sections. The first is slow with little rhythmic activity at the beginning and end, whereas the middle section is livelier. The second section is more upbeat, with technical passages and trills in the upper three voices. Euphonium parts also available in treble clef. Parts may be doubled for a large ensemble.

Key, Francis Scott. *The Star Spangled Banner.* arr. Eugene Anderson. Anderson's Arizona Originals. Three euphoniums and one tuba. 1988. $5.00. 1:10. IV. Part I: B♭–b♭'; Part II: B♭–d'; Part III: G–f'; Part IV: F$_1$–f. Technically not very difficult, but will require a strong player on the first part due to the five high b♭'s. Parts may be doubled for a large ensemble.

Key, Francis Scott, and John Stafford Smith. *The Star Spangled Banner.* arr. Gail Robertson. Tuba-Euphonium Press. Two euphoniums and two tubas. 1998. $10.00. 1:15. II. Part I: B♭–f'; Part II: B♭–d'; Part III: F–b♭; Part IV: F$_1$–d. Straightforward arrangement of the United States national anthem. Melody is entirely in the first part. Euphonium parts also available in treble clef. Parts may be doubled for a large ensemble. Parts are formatted to fit into a flip-folder. Also reviewed in the Fall 2001 issue of the *ITEA Journal* (Vol. 29, No. 1).

Key, Francis Scott, and John Stafford Smith. *The Star Spangled Banner.* arr. Steve D. Matchett. Gulf Wind Music Press. Two euphoniums and two tubas. 2002. $12.00. 1:15. II–III. Third part may also be performed on euphonium. Euphonium parts also available in treble clef. Parts may be doubled for a large ensemble.

Khatchaturian, Aram. *Sabeltanz.* arr. Bruno Seitz. Musikverlag Martin Scherbacher. Two euphoniums and two tubas. 1991. $13.50. 2:00. IV. Part I: B–g'; Part II: F–d'; Part III: F–b♭; Part IV: F$_1$–f. This is Khatchaturian's well-known fast-paced melody, often played as a solo. While most of the melodic work is in the first part, there are numerous tutti figures that make this technically challenging for all parts. Performers will need to play cleanly and lightly. The first part is printed in treble clef. Parts may be doubled for a large ensemble.

King, Karl. *The Melody Shop.* arr. David R. Werden. Whaling Music Publishers. Two euphoniums and two tubas. 1987. $8.00. 2:30. IV–V. Part I: B♭–c"; Part II: B♭–a♭'; Part III: B♭–e♭'; Part IV: A♭$_1$–e♭. Good arrangement of this famous march. Technically most demanding for the top two parts. The tessitura of the first part is especially high. The top two parts are printed in bass and treble clef. Challenging, but worth the effort. Recorded by the U.S. Armed Forces Tuba/Euphonium Ensemble, Mark Records, MW89MCD-8.

King, Karl L. *Barnum and Bailey's Favorite.* arr. J. Kelly Diamond. Tuba-Euphonium Press. Two euphoniums and two tubas. 1996. $8.00. 1:30. III. Part I: e♭–a♭' (d"); Part II: d♭–f'; Part III: F–d♭'; Part IV: A♭$_1$–a♭. Challenging arrangement of this standard march, especially at a circus march tempo. Melodic material is divided among all four voices, and all parts are interesting and challenging. Parts may be doubled for a large ensemble. Also reviewed in the Winter 2003 issue of the *ITEA Journal* (Vol. 30, No. 2).

King, Karl L. *Kentucky Sunrise March.* arr. David Butler. Tuba-Euphonium Press. Two euphoniums and two tubas. 2002. $12.00. 2:15. III. Part I: f–b♭'; Part II: F–e♭'; Part III: G–b♭; Part IV: G$_1$–g. Nice arrangement of this march in a ragtime feel. The melody is evenly distributed between all parts, and all parts are interesting. Euphonium parts also available in treble clef. Parts may be doubled for a large ensemble. Also reviewed in the Spring 2004 issue of the *ITEA Journal* (Vol. 31, No. 3).

Knoener, Ronald C., arr. *Evergreen Polka.* Tuba-Euphonium Press. Two euphoniums and two tubas. 1997. $8.00. 2:30. II. Part I: c–b♭'; Part II: B♭–e♭'; Part III: E♭–g; Part IV: A♭$_1$–B♭. Straightforward arrangement of this standard polka. Range is appropriate for intermediate-level performers. Parts may be doubled for a large ensemble, and there are *divisi* notes in the second euphonium part.

Knoener, Ronald C., arr. *Helena Polka.* Tuba-Euphonium Press. Two euphoniums and two tubas. 1997. $8.00. 2:00. II–III. Part I: f–a♭'; Part II: c–f'; Part III: $B\flat_1$–a; Part IV: A_1–c. Straightforward arrangement of this standard polka. Range is appropriate for intermediate-level performers. Parts may be doubled for a large ensemble, and there are *divisi* notes in the first part.

Knoener, Ronald C., arr. *Rosamünde.* PEL Music Publications. Two euphoniums and two tubas. 1996. $9.95. 4:45. II–III. Part I: e♭–a♭'; Part II: B♭–f'; Part III: $A\flat_1$–f; Part IV: $A\flat_1$–f. Melody is scored predominantly in the euphoniums in this arrangement of this beer-hall standard. Also known as the *Beer Barrel Polka.* More appropriate for a large ensemble, as there are *divisi* notes in the second part. Parts may be doubled for a large ensemble. Also reviewed in the Summer 1997 issue of the *TUBA Journal* (Vol. 24, No. 4).

Knoener, Ronald C., arr. *Springtime Polka.* Tuba-Euphonium Press. Two euphoniums and two tubas. 1997. $8.00. 2:30. II–III. Part I: G–a'; Part II: G–e♭'; Part III: C–g; Part IV: F_1–c. Straightforward arrangement of this standard polka. Range is appropriate for intermediate-level performers. Parts may be doubled for a large ensemble, and there are *divisi* notes in the first part.

Knoener, Ronald C., arr. *The "Tuba-Nette" Polka.* Tuba-Euphonium Press. Two euphoniums and two tubas. 1997. $8.00. 3:00. III. Part I: G–b♭'; Part II: E–a'; Part III: E_1–a; Part IV: $B\flat_2$–a. Originally titled the *Clarinet Polka,* this arrangement features virtuosic, arpeggiated passages in all four voices. Parts may be doubled for a large ensemble, and there are *divisi* notes in the first part.

Kochan, Gunter. *Sieben Miniaturen Fur Vier Tuben (Seven Miniatures for Four Tubas).* Verlan Neve Musik Berlin. Four tubas. 1978. $11.00. 13:00. V. Part I: $G\flat_1$–a♭'; Part II: F_1–g♭'; Part III: G_1–f♯'; Part IV: F_1–e♭'. Seven movements: Moderato; Lento; Allegretto; Largo-Agitato; Allegro Molto; Adagio; Prestissimo. For Dietrich Unkrodt. A virtuosic piece. Extremely challenging rhythmically and in terms of range. All four parts were written with an F tuba in mind. This has some elements of "third stream music" and contains many twentieth-century techniques. These include multiphonics, flutter tonguing, and glissandos. Winner of first prize in the 1978 tuba quartet composition contest sponsored by The Los Angeles Tuba Quartet and the Mirafone Corporation. Recorded by Jim Self on his album *Changing Colors,* Summit Records, DCD 132.

Koetsier, Jan. *Wolkenschatten, Op. 136.* Editions Marc Reift. One euphonium and three tubas. 1994. CHF 22.00. 6:30. III. Part I: B♭–c''; Part II: E–f'; Part III: A_1–d'; Part IV: E_1–a. Three movements: Tranquillo; Presto; Allegro giocoso. An effective tonal composition and aural representation of the title, which translates to "Cloud Shadows." Recorded by the Alchemy Tuba Quartet on the compact disc *Village Dances,* Alchemy, and by the Dutch Tuba Quartet on the compact disc *Wolkenschatten.*

Koltz, Michael. *Tuba Quartet: Study in Motion, Hymn, and Finale.* Tuba-Euphonium Press. Two euphoniums and two tubas. 1992. $12.00. 3:20. IV. Part I: F♯–e''; Part II: D–f♯'; Part III: d–f♯'; Part IV: F_1–c'. Three movements: Motion; Hymn; Finale. The first movement is fast, multimetric, and technically challenging. The tessitura of the first part is high. Portions of the first part are printed in tenor clef. Very interesting writing.

Kosteck, Gregory. *Serene Voices: Music for Tuba Quartet.* Rochester Music Company, Incorporated. Four tubas. 1978. 5:15. V. Part I: D–f'; Part II: $A\sharp_1$–e'; Part III: G_1–d♭'; Part IV: C_1–d'. Three movements: Motivic Theme; Fantasie; Canons. Composed especially for and dedicated to Sande MacMorran. Extreme ranges and technical demands in all four parts. Very interesting writing. This will require four superb players.

Kotscher, Edmund, and Rudi Lindt. *Liechtensteiner Polka.* arr. Gail Robertson. Tuba-Euphonium Press. Two euphoniums and two tubas. 1999. $14.00. 2:30. II. Part I: c–f'; Part II: c–e'; Part III: (F_1) E_1–b♭; Part IV: (E_1) $B\flat_1$–d (f). For the First Annual Octubafest at Florida Community College at Jacksonville. Effective arrangement of this standard polka. Melodic material is divided among all the parts, and the first euphonium even has a few passages to be sung. Ranges are accessible to intermediate-level performers. Euphonium parts also available in treble clef. Parts may be doubled for a large ensemble, and there the second part includes *divisi* notes.

Kotscher, Edmund, and Rudi Lindt. *Liechtensteiner Polka.* arr. Ray Grim. Cimarron Music and Productions. Two euphoniums and two tubas. 1996. $10.00. 1:45. II–III. Part I: e♭–a♭'; Part II: d♭–f'; Part III: E♭–a; Part IV: $A\flat_1$–A♭. Part of the TubaMeisters Collection, this polka is accessible to intermediate-level performers. Melodic material is divided among all four voices. Parts may be doubled for a large ensemble. Euphonium parts also available in treble clef.

Krebs, Johann Ludwig. *Fugue on B.A.C.H.* arr. Rayner Brown. Western International Music. Two euphoniums and two tubas. 1986. $7.00. 4:30. IV. Part I: D–g'; Part II: c–e♭'; Part III: E♭–d'; Part IV: G_1–b♭. Nice arrangement of this fugue. At times the brief low tessitura of the first part can make this arrangement sound a bit muddy. Parts may be doubled with care.

Kreisler, Fritz. *Liebeslied.* arr. David Woodcock. Green Bay Music. Two euphoniums and two tubas. 1992. $22.00. 3:20. IV. Part I: c–b♭'; Part II: d–g'; Part III: G–b♭; Part IV: G_1–d. A moderate-tempo waltz with the melody in the first and second parts. No significant technical problems. Parts may be doubled for a large ensemble.

Kresin, Willibald. *Movin'—Groovin'*. Editions Marc Reift. Two euphoniums and two tubas with drums. 2001. €17.50. 3:45. III. Part I: c–d"; Part II: E–c"; Part III: E♭–f'; Part IV: C–d'. Piece has two sections: the first contains a rhythmically syncopated jazz feel, and the second is in a Latin style. All parts are interesting and challenging. In addition to bass clef parts, euphonium parts are also available in treble, first tuba parts also available in E♭ treble, and second tuba also available in E♭ and B♭ treble clef. Parts may be doubled for a large ensemble. Recorded by Contraband on the compact disc *The Dragon's Dance,* Marcophon Records.

Kresin, Willibald. *On a Rocky Road.* Editions Marc Reift. Two euphoniums and two tubas with drums. 2001. €17.50. 2:30. III. Part I: B♭–c"; Part II: c–a♭'; Part III: ($B♭_1$) F–g'; Part IV: F_1–a♭. Interesting original composition in a jazz/rock style. All parts are rhythmically challenging with extensive syncopation. In addition to bass clef parts, euphonium parts are also available in treble, first tuba parts also available in E♭ treble, and second tuba also available in E♭ and B♭ treble clef. Parts may be doubled for a large ensemble. Recorded by Contraband on the compact disc *The Dragon's Dance,* Marcophon Records.

Kresin, Willibald. *Tango.* Editions Marc Reift. Two euphoniums and two tubas with drums. 2001. €17.50. 4:00. III. Part I: A–c"; Part II: A–c"; Part III: A_1–d'; Part IV: F_1–g♯. This tango features the euphoniums with the tubas performing the appropriate habanera bass line. All parts are interesting yet accessible by intermediate-level performers. In addition to bass clef parts, euphonium parts are also available in treble, first tuba parts also available in E♭ treble, and second tuba also available in E♭ and B♭ treble clef. Parts may be doubled for a large ensemble. Recorded by Contraband on the compact disc *The Dragon's Dance,* Marcophon Records.

Kresin, Willibald. *Tuba Rodeo.* Editions Marc Reift. Two euphoniums and two tubas with drums. 2001. €17.50. 3:00. III. Part I: B♭–b♭'; Part II: B♭–b♭'; Part III: E♭–b♭; Part IV: $B♭_1$–b♭. Fun original composition in a fast tempo. All parts are accessible by intermediate-level performers. In addition to bass clef parts, euphonium parts are also available in treble, first tuba parts also available in E♭ treble, and second tuba also available in E♭ and B♭ treble clef. Parts may be doubled for a large ensemble. Recorded by Contraband on the compact disc *The Dragon's Dance,* Marcophon Records.

Kresin, Willibald. *Mr. Bach Goes to Town (Prelude and Fugue in Swing).* Editions Marc Reift. Two euphoniums and two tubas with drums. 2001. €17.50. 3:15. III. Part I: G–c"; Part II: A♭–a'; Part III: C–d'; Part IV: F_1–f. Two movements: Prelude; Fugue. An original composition that intermixes contrapuntal sections in the style of Bach with jazz and swing sections based on similar motives. The second movement is a jazz fugue. In addition to bass clef parts, euphonium parts are also available in treble, first tuba parts also available in E♭ treble, and second tuba also available in E♭ and B♭ treble clef. Parts may be doubled for a large ensemble. Recorded by Contraband on the compact disc *The Dragon's Dance,* Marcophon Records.

Kupferman, Meyer. *Kierkegaard for Four Tubas.* General Music Publishing Company, Incorporated. Four tubas. 1982. $8.00. 3:20. IV–V. Part I: C♯–e'; Part II: E–e♭'; Part III: C–d'; Part IV: $E♭_1$–g♭. For Roger Bobo. A slow but very rhythmically challenging composition. Scoring is very thick. The first two parts could be played on euphonium. A conductor might be helpful for some quartets.

Langer. *Sea Songs.* Nichols Music. Two euphoniums and two tubas. $10.00. Setting of three traditional sea chanties.

Langer. *Solemn Promise.* Nichols Music. Two euphoniums and two tubas. $12.00.

Lasso, Orlando di. *I Know a Younge Maiden.* arr. Barton Cummings. Solid Brass Music Company. Two euphoniums and two tubas. 1996. $9.00. 1:30. II. Part I: f–g♭'; Part II: d♭–b♭; Part III: G–f; Part IV: $B♭_1$–B♭. Nice arrangement of this Renaissance motet. Limited ranges and repetitive elements make this piece accessible for intermediate- or beginner-level performers. Parts may be doubled for a large ensemble.

Lasso, Orlando di. *Mon Coeur se Recommende á Vous: Madrigal for Tuba Quartet.* arr. Jack Robinson. Whaling Music Publishers. Four tubas. 1979. $5.00. 2:00. III. Part I: e–f'; Part II: c–b♭; Part III: F–f; Part IV: F_1–b♭. Playable by high school students if the first two parts are played by euphoniums. The madrigal has both chorale and imitative sections. While technically very easy, there are some beautiful melodic sections. A very nice short concert piece. Parts may be doubled for a large ensemble. Recorded by the British Tuba Quartet, *Euphonic Sounds,* Polyphonic Reproductions Limited, QPRZ009D.

Lasso, Orlando di. *Two Madrigals.* arr. Frank Ferriano. Tuba-Euphonium Press. Two euphoniums and two tubas. 2001. $10.00. 3:00. II. Part I: g–a♭'; Part II: d–d'; Part III: B♭–b♭; Part IV: $B♭_1$–e♭. Two movements: O Eyes of My Beloved; I Know a Young Maiden Wondrous Fair. Effective way to introduce madrigal style to younger ensembles. Parts may be doubled for a large ensemble. Also reviewed in the Spring 2004 issue of the *ITEA Journal* (Vol. 31, No. 3).

LeClair, David. *Der Unvollendeten Vollendung (The Finishing of the Unfinished).* Editions Marc Reift. Two euphoniums and two tubas with drums. 2001. €17.50. 8:15. III. Part I: c–b♭'; Part II: F–b♭'; Part III: C–c'; Part IV: D_1–b. Fun original composition, based on Schubert's *Unfinished*

Symphony, set in a light jazz setting with frequent meter changes, time changes, and mixed meter. The composer also includes brief excerpts from other well-known works, including Schubert's *Trout Quartet,* Wagner's *Die Meistersinger,* and Strauss' *Die Fleidermous.* In addition to bass clef parts, euphonium parts are also available in treble, first tuba parts also available in E♭ treble, and second tuba also available in E♭ and B♭ treble clef. Recorded by Contraband on the compact disc *The Dragon's Dance,* Marcophon Records.

LeClair, David. *The Dragon's Dance.* Editions Marc Reift. Two euphoniums and two tubas with drums and four marimbas. 2001. €19.60. 5:15. III. Part I: c♯–b♭'; Part II: B♭–b♭'; Part III: D♭–d♭'; Part IV: C_1–c'. Interesting work featuring the marimba quartet as equal partners with the brass quartet. Piece is rhythmically driving and challenging. All parts are interesting and have the melody at some point. In addition to bass clef parts, euphonium parts are also available in treble, first tuba parts also available in E♭ treble, and second tuba also available in E♭ and B♭ treble clef. Recorded by Contraband on the compact disc *The Dragon's Dance,* Marcophon Records.

LeClair, David. *Elegy.* Editions Marc Reift. Two euphoniums and two tubas with four marimbas. 2001. €14.00. 3:30. II–III. Part I: c–b♭'; Part II: f–g'; Part III: D–c♭'; Part IV: F_1–g. Slow work with the melody primarily in the first euphonium. The marimbas serve an accompanimental role for the majority of the piece. In addition to bass clef parts, euphonium parts are also available in treble, first tuba parts also available in E♭ treble, and second tuba also available in E♭ and B♭ treble clef. Recorded by Contraband on the compact disc *The Dragon's Dance,* Marcophon Records.

LeClair, David. *For Heaven's Sake.* Editions Marc Reift. Two euphoniums and two tubas with optional drums. 2001. CHF 20.00. 2:30. V. Part I: d–d"; Part II: A–a'; Part III: C–e♭'; Part IV: F_1–b♭. Original composition in big-band style. The various transitions between swing and jazz waltz are rhythmically challenging to put together. In addition to bass clef parts, euphonium parts are also available in treble, first tuba parts also available in E♭ treble, and second tuba also available in E♭ and B♭ treble clef. Recorded by Contraband on the compact disc *The Dragon's Dance,* Marcophon.

LeClair, David. *Forever and a Day.* Editions Marc Reift. Two euphoniums and two tubas with drums. 2001. €14.00. 3:15. III. Part I: e–c"; Part II: e–g'; Part III: G–c♯'; Part IV: G_1–b♭. Nice jazz ballad with a bossa nova feel. In addition to bass clef parts, euphonium parts are also available in treble, first tuba parts also available in E♭ treble, and second tuba also available in E♭ and B♭ treble clef. Parts may be doubled for a large ensemble. Recorded by Contraband on the compact disc *The Dragon's Dance,* Marcophon Records.

LeClair, David. *Formidable.* Editions Marc Reift. Two euphoniums and two tubas with optional drums. 2001. CHF 25.00. 2:30. IV. Part I: d–d♭"; Part II: d–a'; Part III: B♭–d'; Part IV: G_1–c. Euphonium solo over a walking bass line. The refrain is in a big-band style. In addition to bass clef parts, euphonium parts are also available in treble, first tuba parts also available in E♭ treble, and second tuba also available in E♭ and B♭ treble clef.

LeClair, David. *Forte!* Editions Marc Reift. Two euphoniums and two tubas with drums. 2001. €17.50. 5:45. III–IV. Part I: c–d♭"; Part II: c–a'; Part III: C–e'; Part IV: E_1–c'. A challenging original composition with a jazz influence. Meter changes, mixed meters, and range provide the greatest challenges. Serves well as a concert opener. In addition to bass clef parts, euphonium parts are also available in treble, first tuba parts also available in E♭ treble, and second tuba also available in E♭ and B♭ treble clef. Parts may be doubled for a large ensemble. Recorded by Contraband on the compact disc *The Dragon's Dance,* Marcophon Records.

Lee, Christopher. *Prelude and Groove.* Tuba-Euphonium Press. Two euphoniums and two tubas. 2000. $15.00. 9:30. III–IV. Part I: c–c"; Part II: B♭–g'; Part III: $B♭_1$–d'; Part IV: E_1–a♭. For Gary Buttery and Alchemy. Original composition with jazz influences. The Prelude section is slow and features each voice with exposed passages. The Groove section is rhythmically driven with frequent changes of meter and mixed meter. More appropriate for an advanced ensemble.

Lee, Lester, and Zeke Manners. *Pennsylvania Polka.* arr. Gail Robertson. Tuba-Euphonium Press. Two euphoniums and two tubas. 1999. $14.00. 2:00. II. Part I: c–f' (b♭'); Part II: F–e♭'; Part III: (C) F–b♭; Part IV: F_1–d (g). Fun arrangement that is appropriate for intermediate-level ensembles. Melody is predominantly in the first part. Euphonium parts also available in treble clef. Parts may be doubled for a large ensemble, and there are *divisi* notes in the second part.

Lee, Lester, and Zeke Manners. *Pennsylvania Polka.* arr. Ray Grim. Cimarron Music and Productions. Two euphoniums and two tubas. $10.00. 2:00. II. Part I: c–a'; Part II: A–g'; Part III: $B♭_1$–e♭'; Part IV: F_1–d. Nice arrangement of this standard polka, accessible by intermediate-level performers. Melodic material is divided among the top three voices. Euphonium parts also available in treble clef. Parts may be doubled for a large ensemble.

LeJeune, Claude. *Revecy venir du printans.* arr. Benjamin Roundtree. Roundtree Music. Two euphoniums and two tubas. 2002. $12.00. 2:30. II–III. Part I: c–g'; Part II: A–d'; Part III: C–c'; Part IV: F_1–d. This arrangement of "Here

Again Comes the Spring" is homophonic and employs traditional harmonies. Range and style are accessible by intermediate-level performers. Parts may be doubled for a large ensemble.

LeJune, Claude. *Quand La Terre Au Printemps.* Available from the composer. Four tubas. 1974. 1:30. III–IV. Part I: F–b♭; Part II: E♭–g; Part III: E♭–e♭; Part IV: B♭–c.

Lemeland. *Partita, Op. 109.* Four tubas.

Lennon, John, and Paul McCartney. *Michelle.* arr. Rodger Vaughan. Available from the arranger. Two euphoniums and two tubas. 1990. $5.00. 2:10. III–IV. Part I: e–f'; Part II: c–d♭'; Part III: A–a; Part IV: A_1–f. For the Tubadours. A lyrical chorale-like arrangement of this Beatles ballad. Most of the melody is in the top part. Playable by good high school players. Parts may be doubled for a large ensemble.

Lennon, John, and Paul McCartney. *Yesterday.* arr. Akira Miyagawa. Yamaha Music Foundation. Two euphoniums and two tubas. 1990. $21.00. 3:00. IV. Part I: d–a'; Part II: c♯–f'; Part III: A–a'; Part IV: A_1–f. A very interesting arrangement of this famous Beatles melody. The first part has primary responsibility for the melody. This works quite well. Parts may be doubled for a large ensemble.

Leontovich, M. *Ukrainian Carol (Ring Christmas Bells).* arr. Peter Rauch. Ohio Valley Tuba Quartet Press. Two euphoniums and two tubas. 1990. $6.00. 1:10. IV. Part I: f–b♭'; Part II: f–d'; Part III: B♭–b♭; Part IV: B♭$_1$–B♭. Also known as "Carol of the Bells." This melody seems natural for a tuba/euphonium ensemble. The melody is primarily in the first part. Enjoyable to play. Parts may be doubled for a large ensemble.

Liszt, Franz. *Ave Maria.* arr. Angelo Manzo. Tuba-Euphonium Press. Two euphoniums and two tubas. 2001. $12.00. 3:15. I–II. Part I: f–g'; Part II: d♭–e♭'; Part III: F♯–c'; Part IV: G_1–g. Originally for piano; this arrangement divides the melodic material among all four voices and is appropriate for young performers. Parts may be doubled for a large ensemble. Also reviewed in the Winter 2003 issue of the *ITEA Journal* (Vol. 30, No. 2).

Liszt, Franz. *Hungarian Rhapsodie No. 2.* arr. Bruno Seitz. Musikverlag Martin Scherbacher. Two euphoniums and two tubas. 1990. $13.50. 2:30. IV. Part I: B–b♭'; Part II: F–f'; Part III: B_1–d'; Part IV: F_1–f. A fun arrangement of this famous Hungarian melody. No significant technical problems. Parts may be doubled for a large ensemble.

Liszt, Franz. *Pater Noster.* arr. Angelo Manzo. Tuba-Euphonium Press. Two euphoniums and two tubas. 2002. $8.00. 2:00. II. Part I: e–f'; Part II: e–e'; Part III: A–c♯'; Part IV: A_1–g. This chorale-like work is appropriate for young ensembles. Parts may be doubled for a large ensemble. Also reviewed in the Spring 2004 issue of the *ITEA Journal* (Vol. 31, No. 3).

Livingston and Evans. *Buttons and Bows.* arr. Paul Schmidt. Heavy Metal Music. Two euphoniums and two tubas. 1990. $7.00. 1:30. IV. Part I: F–g'; Part II: G–e♭'; Part III: A♭–e♭'; Part IV: B♭$_1$–d. Most of this familiar melody is in the first part. Some range challenges for the third part. Fun to play. No score available. Parts may be doubled for a large ensemble.

London, Edwin. *Love in the Afternoon: A Tone Poem.* Henmar Press Incorporated. Four tubas. 1979. $17.50. 4:00. IV–V. Part I: C_1–d'; Part II: C_1–e'; Part III: D_1–e'; Part IV: B_2–e♭'. A programmatic work designed to depict the physical act of love. The tessitura of all four parts is quite low. The work involves many twentieth-century techniques, including flutter tonguing, double/triple tonguing, extra wide vibrato, and a free non-metered section. This humorous piece will require four strong players.

Lowry, Robert. *Three Hymns by Robert Lowry.* arr. Stephen Shoop. Stephen Shoop Music Publications. Two euphoniums and two tubas. 1997. $7.50. 4:00. I–II. Part I: f–f'; Part II: d–c'; Part III: G–g; Part IV: A_1–A♭. Three movements: Something for Jesus; I Need Thee Every Hour; Beautiful River. Straightforward arrangement of these three American Sunday-school songs. The texture is homophonic and the melody is predominantly in the first part. Euphonium parts also available in treble clef. Parts may be doubled for a large ensemble. Individual movements can stand alone on a concert.

Luhring, Paul, arr. *Irish Tubas.* PEL Music Publications. Two euphoniums and two tubas. 2000. $11.95. 4:15. II–III. Part I: d–c''; Part II: A♭–f'; Part III: B♭$_1$–e♭'; Part IV: F_1–c. This fun arrangement is a medley of *When Irish Eyes Are Smiling, Irish Washerwoman, That's an Irish Lullaby,* and *Oh, Danny Boy.* Melodic material is divided among the four voices, though it is predominantly in the first part. Range and style are appropriate for intermediate-level performers. Parts may be doubled for a large ensemble.

Luis, Ingo. *Lazy Elephant Blues.* Musikverlag Bruno Uetz. One euphonium and three tubas. 1995. €15.00. 3:30. Second part may be performed on euphonium as well. Recorded by the Melton Tuba-Quartett on the compact disc *Lazy Elephants,* Diavolo Records.

Luis, Ingo. *Little Lullaby.* Musikverlag Bruno Uetz. One euphonium and three tubas. 2000. €12.00. 2:00. Second part may be performed on euphonium as well. Recorded by the Melton Tuba-Quartett on the compact disc *Power.*

Lully, Jean-Baptiste. *Air from Amadis.* arr. Paul E. Hartin. Cellar Press. Four tubas. 1975. 2:00. III. Part I: d–f; Part II: A–c'; Part III: F–a; Part IV: C–e. Works especially well for high schools if euphoniums are used on the first two parts.

A college quartet should use four tubas. Good writing in this genre. Parts may be doubled for a large ensemble.

Lundquist, Torbjørn. *Triplet for Four Tubas.* Swedish Music Information Center. Four tubas. 1977. $12.00. 5:00. IV. Part I: d–a♭'; Part II: G♯–d'; Part III: E♭–c♯; Part IV: E_1–e♭. Three movements. The tessitura of the first part is high and may require an F tuba or euphonium. The first and third movements are slow with contemporary harmonies. The second movement is fast, more rhythmically challenging, and multimetric.

Lupo, Thomas. *Fantasia for Basses.* arr. Paul Schmidt. Heavy Metal Music. Two euphoniums and two tubas. 1992. $5.00. 4:00. IV. Part I: A♭–g'; Part II: A♭–g'; Part III: F–c'; Part IV: F_1–f. A slow tempo, but very polyphonic. Players will need to count carefully. Parts are included to allow this to be played as a trio with just three euphoniums. No score available, but parts may be doubled for a large ensemble.

Lyon, Max J. *Suite for Four Bass Instruments.* Shawnee Press, Incorporated. Two euphoniums and two tubas. 1975. $10.00. 5:00. IV. Part I: c♯–a'; Part II: B♭–e♭'; Part III: C♯–b; Part IV: $A\flat_1$–g♯. Three movements: Chorale; Rhyme; Motion. Could also be performed with one euphonium and three tubas. The second movement is in a moderate 3/8 and the last movement alternates between 3/8, 5/8, and 7/8 in a lively tempo. The piece does fit together well. Parts may be doubled for a large ensemble. Recorded by the Atlantic Tuba Quartet, Golden Crest Records, CRS 4173.

Maccolini, Emilio. *Iracunde.* Animado Music Publisher, Sondrio. Two euphoniums and two tubas. 2001. 4:00. II–III. Part I: d–b♭'; Part II: B♭–g♭'; Part III: D–b♭; Part IV: G_1–e. Composition is ternary, with driving outer sections and a slow ballad in the middle. Texture is predominantly homophonic, which makes this piece accessible to intermediate-level players. Parts may be doubled for a large ensemble.

MacDowell, Edward. *To a Wild Rose.* arr. Gail Robertson. Tuba-Euphonium Press. Two euphoniums and two tubas. 1999. $10.00. 1:45. II. Part I: d–a'; Part II: A–f♯'; Part III: G♯–c♯'; Part IV: A_1–d♯. Simple ballad scored with the melody predominantly in the first part, though the inner voices have brief melodic passages. Parts are appropriate for young players. Euphonium parts also available in treble clef. Parts may be doubled for a large ensemble.

MacDowell, Edward. *To a Wild Rose.* arr. Peter Rauch. Ohio Valley Tuba Quartet Press. Two euphoniums and two tubas. 1990. $8.00. 1:45. IV. Part I: d–b♭'; Part II: D–b♭'; Part III: $B\flat_1$–b♭; Part IV: F_1–b♭. All parts have the opportunity to play this very lyrical melody. Very traditional harmonies. Parts may be doubled for a large ensemble.

Mack, Cecil. *Charleston.* arr. Clifford Bevan and Paul Schmidt. Heavy Metal Music. Two euphoniums and two tubas. 1991. $7.00. 2:00. IV. Part I: B–f'; Part II: F–e♭'; Part III: $B\flat_1$–b♭; Part IV: F_1–g♭. A fun arrangement of this melody associated with the "roaring '20s." Most of the melody is in the first part. Very syncopated, but no significant technical problems. No score available. Parts may be doubled for a large ensemble.

Makela, Steven. *Folk Fantasy.* Tuba-Euphonium Press. Two euphoniums and two tubas. 1997. $10.00. 3:30. III. Part I: c–b♭'; Part II: c–d♭'; Part III: F–f; Part IV: F_1–c. This single-movement work starts with a slow, introductory section and ends with a lively, upbeat section. The motives and themes give the impression that this work is based on folk songs, though no program notes are provided. Parts may be doubled for a large ensemble.

Mancini, Henry. *Baby Elephant Walk.* arr. Eugene Anderson. Anderson's Arizona Originals. Two euphoniums and two tubas. 1988. $5.00. 2:45. IV. Part I: G♯–a'; Part II: F–a'; Part III: F–d'; Part IV: F_1–a. Fun arrangement of this familiar Mancini melody. The melody is primarily in the fourth part, alternating some with the first part. The first and second parts will need a secure high a'. Parts may be doubled for a large ensemble.

Mancini, Henry. *Baby Elephant Walk.* arr. Ingo Luis. Musikverlag Bruno Uetz. One euphonium and three tubas. €15.00. 2:15. Second part may be performed on euphonium as well. Recorded by the Melton Tuba Quartett on the compact disc *Premiere,* Diavolo Records.

Mancini, Henry. *Baby Elephant Walk.* arr. Lennie Niehaus. Kendor Music, Inc. Two euphoniums and two tubas. $9.00. 2:30. This arrangement is based on the version used in the Paramount Picture *Harari.* Parts may be doubled for a large ensemble.

Mancini, Henry. *The Pink Panther.* arr. Jay Krush. Northride Music, Incorporated/Kendor Music, Incorporated. Two euphoniums and two tubas. 1982. $8.50. 3:45. III–IV. Part I: d–b♭'; Part II: G–d♯'; Part III: C–b♭; Part IV: E_1–e. A cute jazzy arrangement of this familiar tune. While not very fast, this is rhythmically challenging in a couple of sections. Fun to play and to listen to. Parts may be doubled for a large ensemble. Recorded by the British Tuba Quartet, *Euphonic Sounds,* Polyphonic Reproductions Limited, QPRZ009D; the Melton Tuba Quartett, *Premiere,* Diavolo Records, DR-D-93-C-001; and the Northern Tuba Lights.

Marcellus, John, arr. *Quartets for Brass, Volume I; Advanced.* CPP Belwin, Incorporated. Three euphoniums and one tuba. 1986. $6.50. 15 pp. III–IV. Part I: c–c"; Part II: c–f'; Part III: F–d'; Part IV: A_1–e. A collection of seven melodies from the baroque, classical, and romantic style periods. The first parts in two of the arrangements are printed in tenor clef. Treble clef books are available, allowing these to be performed by any combination of brass instruments. Parts may be doubled for a large ensemble.

Marcellus, John, arr. *Quartets for Brass, Volume I; Easy-Intermediate.* CPP Belwin, Incorporated. Three euphoniums and one tuba. 1986. $6.50. 15 pp. II–III. Part I: d–a'; Part II: B♭–f'; Part III: A–d'; Part IV: $B\flat_1$–f♯. A collection of nine melodies from the baroque and classical style periods. The parts are technically very easy. The third part may be played by an advanced tuba player, but it is designed for a euphonium. The quartets start out very easy but get increasingly difficult. Treble clef books are available, allowing these quartets to be played by almost any combination of brass instruments. Parts may be doubled for a large ensemble.

Marcellus, John, arr. *Quartets for Brass, Volume I; Intermediate.* CPP Belwin, Incorporated. Three euphoniums and one tuba. 1986. $6.50. 15 pp. III. Part I: e♭–b♭'; Part II: c–g♭'; Part III: A–f'; Part IV: F–e♭. A collection of eight melodies from the baroque, classical, and romantic style periods. The tessitura of the first part is high and that part has most of the technical challenges as well. Treble clef books are available, allowing these arrangements to be played by almost any combination of brass instruments. Parts may be doubled for a large ensemble.

Marks, Johnny. *Rudolph the Red-Nosed Reindeer.* arr. Keith Mehlan. PP Music. Two euphoniums and two tubas. 1987. $10.00. 2:20. IV. Part I: c'–c"; Part II: c–g'; Part III: c–c'; Part IV: $B\flat_1$–d. Technically fairly easy, but the tessitura of the first part is quite high. The melody is featured in both euphonium and tuba parts. Parts may be doubled for a large ensemble.

Martino, Ralph. *Fantasy for Tuba/Euphonium Quartet.* PP Music. Two euphoniums and two tubas. 1992. $11.00. 5:00. IV. Part I: c♯–b'; Part II: c♯–b♭'; Part III: B_1–c♭'; Part IV: F_1–a. Written for the U.S. Navy Band Tuba/Euphonium Quartet. A very driving and exciting composition. It is technically challenging and is often multimetric as it progresses through different styles. Works very well. Recorded by the British Tuba Quartet, *Elite Syncopations,* Polyphonic Reproductions Limited, QPRZ 012D; and the Monarch Tuba/Euphonium Quartet.

Maschwitz, Eric. *A Nightingale Sang in Berkeley Square.* arr. Peter Smalley. Studio Music Company. Two euphoniums and two tubas. 1996. £7.50. 5:00. III. Part I: B♭–b♭'; Part II: G_1–g'; Part III: G–e♭'; Part IV: $E\flat_1$–g. A slow jazz standard, arranged for the British Tuba Quartet. Euphonium parts also available in treble clef, first tuba parts also available in E♭ treble, and second tuba parts also available in both E♭ and B♭ treble clef. Parts may be doubled for a large ensemble. Also reviewed in the Winter 1997 issue of the *TUBA Journal* (Vol. 24, No. 2). Recorded by the British Tuba Quartet on the compact disc *Elite Syncopations,* Polyphonic Records.

Mason, Lowell. *Three Hymns by Lowell Mason.* arr. Stephen Shoop. Stephen Shoop Music Publications. Two euphoniums and two tubas. 1997. $7.50. 2:00. II. Part I: B♭–f'; Part II: d–b♭; Part III: E♭–g; Part IV: (F_1) $B\flat_1$–B♭. Three movements: Work, for the Night Is Coming; There Is a Fountain; Nearer, My God, to Thee. These arrangements of three nineteenth-century church hymns are appropriate for young ensembles and can serve either as warm-up pieces or as concert works. The texture is homophonic and the melody is predominantly in the first part. Euphonium parts also available in treble clef. Parts may be doubled for a large ensemble. Individual movements can stand alone on a concert.

Mason, Roger. *A Christmas Gathering.* Tuba-Euphonium Press. Two euphoniums and two tubas. 1997. $15.00. 5:00. II–III. Part I: c–b♭'; Part II: B–g'; Part III: C–a; Part IV: G_1–g. Humorous collage of short excerpts from traditional Christmas songs. All parts are interesting and have melodic material. Parts may be doubled for a large ensemble.

Massenet, J. E. F. *Aragonaise from "Le Cid."* arr. M. S. Erickson. PP Music. Two euphoniums and two tubas. 1986. $6.00. 1:45. IV. Part I: e♭–c"; Part II: c–f'; Part III: E♭–a♭; Part IV: $A\flat_1$–d♭. The "Aragonaise" is taken from Massenet's opera *Le Cid,* written in 1885. This march-like composition is in 6/8 and is technically challenging for all four parts. Good writing. Recorded by the U.S. Navy Tuba Quartet, U.S. Navy Band Records; and the Monarch Tuba/Euphonium Quartet.

Masson, Iain. *On Platform 2.* Four tubas. 2004. Commissioned by the London Tuba Quartet.

Masuda, Kouzou. *Suite for Four Tubas.* Tokyo Bari-Tuba Ensemble. Four tubas.

Matchett, Steve. *Medieval Night.* Gulf Wind Music Press. Two euphoniums and two tubas. 2001. $11.00. 3:15. Original composition consisting of two contrasting sections. The first section, titled "Monks Assembled," is slow and chant-like, and the second section, titled "Peasant Revelers," is a dance section in compound meter. Second euphonium part also available in treble clef. Parts may be doubled for a large ensemble.

Matchett, Steve. *Sounding for Tuba/Euphonium Quartet.* RBC Publications. Two euphoniums and two tubas. 1991. $8.00. 7:20. IV. Part I: B♭–a♭'; Part II: G–g♭'; Part III: $B\flat_1$–c♭'; Part IV: F_1–f. Two movements. Dedicated to Joe Gannon, Robert Muñoz, Glenn Pistoll, and Larry Porter. The first movement is chorale-like in character. The second movement is very aggressive rhythmically with several meter changes. All parts play portions of the melody and are technically challenging at times. The first and second parts are printed in treble and bass clefs. Parts may be doubled for a large ensemble.

Matchett, Steve. *Township Suite.* Gulf Wind Music Press. Two euphoniums and two tubas. 2001. $11.00. 4:00. Three movements: Mayor's March; Glee Club; Fairgrounds. Humorous work for intermediate-level quartet. The first movement is marked "Pompously" and includes intentionally wrong-sounding notes. The second movement has a barbershop texture, and the last movement is a march in a carnival style. Third part may also be performed on euphonium. Euphonium parts also available in treble clef. Parts may be doubled for a large ensemble.

McAdams, Charles A., arr. *The Saints.* Encore Music Publishers. Two euphoniums and two tubas. 1991. $8.50. 1:30. III–IV. Part I: b♭–b♭'; Part II: f–d'; Part III: B♭–b♭; Part IV: $B♭_1$–e♭. A swing arrangement of this traditional Dixieland tune. A slower middle section features the first tuba part. Ranges are easy except for the b', the last note of the first part. Parts may be doubled for a large ensemble.

McCurdy, Gary. *Bentonsport 1895.* TMC Publications. Four tubas. 1981. Out of Print. 1:45. III–IV. Part I: B♭–f'; Part II: B♭–d; Part III: B♭–f; Part IV: $B♭_1$–b♭. A fast, old-fashioned-sounding waltz. Can work well for high schools if the first and second parts are played on euphonium. Not difficult rhythmically. Parts may be doubled for a large ensemble.

McCurdy, Gary. *Blues for Bill.* TMC Publications. Four tubas. 1980. Out of Print. 2:45. III–IV. Part I: B♭–e♭'; Part II: B♭–d'; Part III: $B♭_1$–d; Part IV: $A♭_1$–d♭. Dedicated to the late William J. Bell. Basic twelve-bar blues in B♭. The middle sections may be used for improvised solos. A rhythm section may be added, though it is not called for in the score. Top two parts will need to be played by euphoniums for the piece to be performed by high school students. Parts may be doubled for a large ensemble.

McCurdy, Gary. *Recitative for Four Tubas and Cantor.* TMC Publications. Four tubas and male vocalist. 1971. Out of Print. 2:00. III. Part I: c–f; Part II: E–A; Part III: $F♯_1$–E; Part IV: C_1–C. A short humorous piece for tuba quartet and male vocalist.

McCurdy, Gary. *Things Are Tough All Over, Tubby.* TMC Publications. Four tubas and male vocalist. 1971. Out of Print. 2:00. III–IV. Part I: A–g; Part II: G–d; Part III: E–A; Part IV: C–E. A humorous piece for tuba quartet and male vocalist.

McCurdy, Gary. *Two Folk Songs.* TMC Publications. Two euphoniums and two tubas. 1973. Out of Print. 2:00. III. Part I: c–g'; Part II: B♭–e♭'; Part III: $B♭_1$–f; Part IV: A_1–c. Melody and harmony in a very traditional style. No technical problems. Parts may be doubled for a large ensemble.

McCurdy, Gary, arr. *Saints.* TMC Publications. Four tubas. 1979. Out of Print. 1:30. II–III. Part I: B♭–f'; Part II: B♭–c'; Part III: B♭–g; Part IV: $B♭_1$–e♭. Easily playable by high school students if the first two parts are played by euphoniums. Not technically difficult; melody stays in the top two parts and the moving bass line is doubled in the third and fourth parts. Parts may be doubled for a large ensemble.

McCurdy, Gary, arr. *Two Patriotic Songs.* TMC Publications. Four tubas. 1976. Out of Print. 1:45. II–III. Part I: A–e♭'; Part II: A–e♭'; Part III: A_1–d; Part IV: A_1–B♭. Two movements: My Country Tis of Thee; Yankee Doodle. Very playable by junior or senior high school students if the first and second parts are played by euphoniums. No real technical difficulties. Fun for students to play. Parts may be doubled for a large ensemble.

McGarr, Peter. *Memory Trace.* Breakthrough Music. Two euphoniums, two tubas, and media. £25.00. Part I: G–a♭'; Part II: G–a♭'; Part III: G–c'; Part IV: G–c'. Written at the request of Tubalaté. The work uses a CD partway through, the first and fourth parts play harmonicas (in B♭ and A♭), and the second part has an option to play trumpet/bass trumpet. A bell tree is required. A video is also available for multimedia performance. Recorded by Tubalaté on the compact disc *Hall of Mirrors.*

McGarr, Peter. *Night Time.* Breakthrough Music. Two euphoniums and two tubas with recorded accompaniment. Part I: e♭–c"; Part II: e♭–c"; Part III: e♭–f'; Part IV: e♭–f'. This work, a follow on to *Memory Trace,* uses a CD throughout. The tessitura is quite high and dynamics are very soft; mute options are given. A short but very effective work.

McLean, Stuart. *Describe the Evening.* Breakthrough Music. Two euphoniums and two tubas. Part I: E–d♭"; Part II: F–d"; Part III: D_1–e♭'; Part IV: E_1–e♭'. Written for Tubalaté, after a visit to the Liverpool Institute for the Performing Arts. The work contains solo and duet passages.

McQueen, Ian. *Heights of Halifax.* Available from Tubalaté. Two euphoniums and two tubas. Recorded by Tubalaté on the compact disc *Earth and Moon.*

Meacham, F. W. *American Tuba Patrol.* arr. Soichi Konagaya. Sonic Arts, Incorporated. Two euphoniums and two tubas. 1986. $12.00. 3:20. III–IV. Part I: B♭–g'; Part II: F–e♭'; Part III: $B♭_1$–g; Part IV: ($E♭_1$) F_1–e♭. An arrangement of the "American Patrol March." The melody is in both the tuba and the euphonium parts. No real technical or range problems. Fun to play. Parts may be doubled for a large ensemble.

Medek, Ivo. *Reflections.* T.A.P. Music. Four tubas. 1985. $6.00. 8:00. IV–V. Part I: A–a'; Part II: E♭–a'; Part III: F–d'; Part IV: F_1–a. Three movements. Extreme technical and range demands in all four parts. This could be performed with two euphoniums and two tubas. Some contemporary harmonies.

Mehlan, Keith. *Bottoms Up Rag*. Horizon Press. Two euphoniums and two tubas. 1991. $8.00. 2:45. IV. Part I: e–c"; Part II: e♭–a'; Part III: f–b♭; Part IV: F_1–f. Each part has the opportunity to play this ragtime melody. The top two parts always have the melody together. Works very well. Parts may be doubled for a large ensemble. Recorded by the Monarch Tuba/Euphonium Quartet.

Mehlan, Keith. *Tubalation Rag*. PP Music. Two euphoniums and two tubas. 1987. $8.00. 3:00. IV. Part I: d–a'; Part II: c–f'; Part III: $B\flat_1$–b♭; Part IV: A_1–g. An original composition in the ragtime style of Scott Joplin. All four parts have an opportunity to play the solo. Fun to play. Parts may be doubled for a large ensemble.

Mehlan, Keith, arr. *Londonderry Air*. Horizon Press. Two euphoniums and two tubas. 1991. $7.00. 2:20. IV. Part I: c♯–a'; Part II: d–f'; Part III: G–d'; Part IV: F_1–d. Begins with a solo euphonium, and then the melody is traded between all four parts. The phrases are clearly marked and should be followed exactly. Works well for this genre. Parts may be doubled for a large ensemble. Recorded by the Monarch Tuba/Euphonium Quartet.

Mendelssohn, Felix. *Nocturne from Midsummer-night's Dream*. arr. Maurice Bale. Godiva Music. Two euphoniums and two tubas. £5.00.

Mendelssohn, Felix. *Tarantella from Songs without Words, Op. 182, No. 3*. arr. Norihisa Yamamoto. KIWI Music Press. Two euphoniums and two tubas. 1987. $3.95. 1:20. IV. Part I: e♭–b♭'; Part II: B♭–d'; Part III: F♯–g; Part IV: $A\flat_1$–e♭. Most of the melodic work is in the top three parts with numerous triplets at a fast rate of speed. The first part is printed in tenor clef and requires a mute. Parts may be doubled for a large ensemble.

Mercer, Johnny, and Harold Allen. *That Old Black Magic*. Kendor Music, Inc. Two euphoniums and two tubas. $10.00. 2:30. III. Part I: c–a'; Part II: c–f'; Part III: D–b♭; Part IV: F_1–g. Challenging up-tempo swing chart, especially at the indicated tempo of 208 beats per minute. Not appropriate for ensembles unfamiliar with the jazz idiom. Parts may be doubled for a large ensemble. Also reviewed in the Summer 2004 issue of the *ITEA Journal* (Vol. 31, No. 4).

Michel, Jean-François, arr. *Quartett Album*. Editions Marc Reift. Two euphoniums and two tubas. 1995. CHF 30.00. Eight pieces: Marche by Lully; Ave Verum by Mozart; Allemande by Phalèse; Intrada by Franck; O vos Omnes by Victoria; Ave Maria by Schubert; Trumpet Voluntary by Clarke; Trumpet Tune and March by Clarke. A collection of short and simple quartet arrangements of well-known classical compositions. In addition to bass clef parts, euphonium parts are also available in treble, first tuba parts also available in E♭ treble, and second tuba also available in E♭ and B♭ treble clef.

Milford, Gene, arr. *Three American Folk Songs*. Great Works Publishing, Incorporated. Two euphoniums and two tubas. 1993. $8.00. 2:30. I. Part I: B♭–b♭; Part II: B♭–a♭; Part III: $B\flat_1$–c; Part IV: G_1–A♭. Three movements: Aura Lee; Skip to My Lou; Hush Little Baby. Dedicated to L. Timothy DeStefano. An arrangement of three popular folk songs intended as teaching pieces for young players. Top two parts are also available in treble clef. Parts may be doubled for a large ensemble.

Minerd, Doug, arr. *Ding Dong Merrily (on Low)*. Cimarron Music and Productions. Two euphoniums and two tubas. 2002. $14.00. 3:30. III. Part I: G–c"; Part II: G–c"; Part III: D_1–c'; Part IV: C_1–c'. Highly embellished arrangement of this standard Christmas song. All parts are interesting, and range is the most difficult aspect. Euphonium parts also available in treble clef. Parts may be doubled for a large ensemble.

Minerd, Doug, arr. *Sea Tubas*. Whaling Music Publishers. Two euphoniums and two tubas. 1982. $12.50. 5:10. IV. Part I: F–g'; Part II: F–e'; Part III: A_1–c'; Part IV: F_1–g'. A very cute medley of "What Do You Do with a Drunken Sailor," "Blow the Man Down," "Asleep in the Deep," "Barnacle Bill the Sailor," and "Shenandoah." Technically challenging for all parts, with the potential for some ensemble problems. Well received by audiences. The first part is printed in treble clef. Parts may be doubled for a large ensemble. Recorded by the Northern Tuba Lights.

Miserendino, Joe. *Grecian Gambol*. Available from the composer. Three euphoniums and one tuba. 2004. $12.00. 3:00. II–III. Part I: F♯–b'; Part II: E–a'; Part III: D–a'; Part IV: $B\flat_1$–f♯. Light character piece that is fun and accessible to intermediate-level players. The form is ternary with fast, driving outer sections and a slow middle section. Frequent tempo changes are challenging for the ensemble. Parts may be doubled for a large ensemble.

Miserendino, Joe. *Lighthearted and Lowpitched*. Available from the composer. Three euphoniums and one tuba. 2003. $12.00. 4:00. I–II. Part I: B♭–g'; Part II: E♭–a'; Part III: $B\flat_1$–g'; Part IV: A_1–a. Light character piece that is fun and accessible to younger players. Texture is predominantly homophonic and the rhythms are simple, though each part is interesting. Parts may be doubled for a large ensemble.

Mitchell-Davidson, Paul. *Tubafication*. Breakthrough Music. Two euphoniums and two tubas. £11.95. 4:30. Part I: c–a'; Part II: A♭–g♭'; Part III: E–e'; Part IV: F_1–a♭. Commissioned by Tubalaté, *Tubafication* is a bebop-style piece. The work involves a small amount of improvisation (help is offered by the composer!). *Tubafication* was selected as a piece for the ITEC 2002 Quartet Competition. Recorded by Tubalaté on the compact disc *Episodes*.

Miura, Mari. *Composition.* Tuba-Euphonium Press. Two euphoniums and two tubas. 1997. $15.00. 7:30. III–IV. Part I: E–a♭' (c"); Part II: D–g'; Part III: F_1–c'; Part IV: $E\flat_1$–b. Five movements: Introduction; Episode; Confusion; Dream; Movement. Original composition with modern harmonies, poly-rhythms, and mixed meter. More appropriate for advanced performers. Calls for one euphonium and one tuba mute. Both euphonium parts contain passages in tenor clef. Parts may be doubled for a large ensemble.

Monaco, Keith. *You Made Me Love You.* arr. Bill Holcombe. Musicians Publications. Two euphoniums and two tubas. 1991. $12.00. 3:20. IV. Part I: d–a'; Part II: B–e'; Part III: D–c'; Part IV: $F\sharp_1$–d♭. Good arrangement of this old popular song. It begins in a slow ballad style then ends with an up-tempo swing section. A good swing feel is necessary in all players. Drums may be added for effect. Recorded by the British Tuba Quartet, *Euphonic Sounds,* Polyphonic Reproductions, Limited, QPRZ 009D.

Monteverdi, Claudio. *Toccata for L'Orfeo.* arr. Donald C. Little. KIWI Music Press. Two euphoniums and two tubas. 1987. $2.75. 1:30. III. Part I: b♭–g'; Part II: B♭–b♭; Part III: F–d; Part IV: $B\flat_1$–$B\flat_1$ (e'). The fourth part has the same pitch for the entire piece. But there are optional *divisi* chords in the fourth part for up to four different pitches. Other possible instrumentations include one euphonium and three tubas or four tubas. No real technical problems. All players read from a single score. Parts may be doubled for a large ensemble.

Monti, Vittorio. *Czardas.* arr. David LeClair. Editions Marc Reift. Two euphoniums and two tubas with optional drums. 2001. €17.50. 4:15. III–IV. Part I: f–b♭'; Part II: c♯–a'; Part III: $C\sharp_1$–a'; Part IV: G_1–b♭. Arrangement features the first tubist with other parts serving as accompaniment. Solo part is virtuosic, with double-tonguing and a wide tessitura. Optional drum parts include snare, bass, tambourine, and glockenspiel and may be performed by one player. In addition to bass clef parts, euphonium parts are also available in treble, first tuba parts also available in E♭ treble, and second tuba also available in E♭ and B♭ treble clef. More appropriate for a quartet than for an ensemble. Recorded by Contraband on the compact disc *The Dragon's Dance,* Marcophon Records.

Monti, Vittorio. *Czardas.* arr. J. Kelly Diamond. Tuba-Euphonium Press. Two euphoniums and two tubas. 2000. $10.00. 3:00. III–IV. Part I: F–b♭' (f"); Part II: B♭–e♭'; Part III: $B\flat_1$–e♭'; Part IV: ($B\flat_2$) F_1–e♭. Written for and dedicated to the United States Navy Band Tuba-Euphonium Quartet. Arrangement features all four members of the quartet rather than one player, as the virtuosic lines are passed between the parts. More appropriate for advanced players. More effective as a quartet than as an ensemble.

Moore, Timothy. *Three Piece Suite.* Breakthrough Music. Two euphoniums and two tubas. £11.95. 6:15. Part I: F–b♭'; Part II: F–a♭'; Part III: F–d'; Part IV: F_1–b. Three movements: Rag; Blues; Stomp. Popular original composition commissioned by the quartet Tubalaté. Recorded by Tubalaté on the compact disc *Light Metal.*

Moore, Timothy, arr. *Three Spirituals.* Breakthrough Music. Two euphoniums and two tubas. £11.95. Part I: B♭–e♭"; Part II: B♭–c♭"; Part III: $E\flat_1$–e♭'; Part IV: $E\flat_1$–e♭'. Three movements: Elijah Rock; Sometimes I Feel like a Motherless Child; Nobody Knows. Parts may be doubled for a large ensemble. Recorded by Tubalaté on the compact disc *Move.*

Morel, Jean-Marie. *Sept Péchés Capitauz (Seven Major Sins).* Editions Robert Martin. Four tubas. 1989. $35.00. 9:45. IV–V. Part I: B♭–b♭'; Part II: G–a♭'; Part III: $G\sharp_1$–g♭'; Part IV: D_1–g♭'. Seven movements: L'ORGUEIL est une estime exagéreé de soi-même (PRIDE is an inordinate self-esteem); L'AVARICE nous fait user de nos richesses avec une excessive parcimonie (AVARICE make us dispose of our wealth with parsimony); LA LUXURE est un abandon immodéré aux plaisirs de la chair (LUST means unrestrained addition to the pleasures of the flesh); L'ENVIE consiste à s'attrister du bien et à se réjouir du mal qui arrive au prochain (ENVY makes us sad about the good fortune of others and delights us about their misfortune); LA GOURMANDISE est l'amour déréglé du manger et du boire (GREEDINESS means an immoderate love for food and drink); LA COLÈRE est un mouvement déréglé de l'âme, qui fait que l'on s'emporte contre ce qui déplait (ANGER is a disordered state of mind which makes us lose our temper when something displeases us); LA PARESSE est un amour excessif du repos (LAZINESS means an immoderate love for rest). A programmatic work describing in detail the seven major sins. The tessitura of all four parts is quite high. The top two parts will require F tubas or euphoniums. There are a few technical problems; players will need to count carefully. Directions from the composer are to "loudly give notice of the subtitles before each number."

Morley, Thomas. *April Is in My Mistress' Face.* arr. Mark Nelson. Whaling Music Publishers. Two euphoniums and two tubas. 1991. $8.00. 1:30. III–IV. Part I: g–f'; Part II: d–c'; Part III: G–f; Part IV: G_1–B♭. Good arrangement of this famous Renaissance madrigal. Easily playable by good high school students. Parts may be doubled for a large ensemble.

Morley, Thomas. *April Is in My Mistress Face.* arr. Michael Howard. BTQ Publications. Two euphoniums and two tubas. 1993. $8.00.

Morley, Thomas. *April Is in My Mistress' Face.* Sarnia Music. Two euphoniums and two tubas. £9.99.

Morley, Thomas. *It Was a Lover and His Lass.* arr. Maurice Bale. Godiva Music. Two euphoniums and two tubas. 1994. £5.00. 1:30. II–III. Part I: d–e♭'; Part II: B♭–c'; Part III: F–g; Part IV: F_1–e♭.

Mortaro, Antonia. *L'Albergona.* arr. Daniel Heiman. Heavy Metal Music. Two euphoniums and two tubas. 1991. $5.00. 1:45. IV. Part I: d–f'; Part II: F–c'; Part III: E♭–g; Part IV: $A\flat_1$–c. Not technically difficult, but very polyphonic. Players will need to count carefully. No score available. Parts may be doubled for a large ensemble.

Mouret, Jean Joseph. *Fanfare and Rondeau from "Premiere Suite."* arr. Paul Schmidt. Heavy Metal Music. Two euphoniums and two tubas. 1991. $7.00. 2:45. IV. Part I: G–f'; Part II: G–f'; Part III: E–f'; Part IV: G_1–g. Two movements: Fanfare; Rondeau. The tessitura of the third part is high and may be played on euphonium. The Rondeau and the Fanfare work well together. No score available. Parts may be doubled for a large ensemble.

Mouret, Jean-Joseph. *Rondeau.* arr. Benjamin Roundtree. Roundtree Music. Two euphoniums and two tubas. 2002. $12.00. 1:45. II–III. Part I: c–b♭'; Part II: c–g'; Part III: E–c'; Part IV: F_1–c. Effective arrangement of this well-known piece, also known as the theme from *Masterpiece Theatre.* All parts are interesting, though the euphonium parts are more technically challenging than the tuba parts. Parts may be doubled for a large ensemble.

Mouret, Jean Joseph. *Rondeau.* arr. John Stevens. Encore Music Publishers. Two euphoniums and two tubas. 1988. $13.00. 1:30. IV. Part I: c–b♭'; Part II: c–g'; Part III: E–c'; Part IV: G_1–e♭. A very playable arrangement of this famous *Masterpiece Theatre* theme. No significant technical or range problems. Parts may be doubled but care should be taken to keep the character light and articulations clean.

Mozart, Wolfgang Amadeus. *Adoramus Te, Christe.* arr. Mark Nelson. Whaling Music Publishers. Two euphoniums and two tubas. 1991. $8.00. 1:30. III. Part I: d–f'; Part II: A–b♭; Part III: G–g; Part IV: G_1–B♭. Nice slow chorale. Very playable by high school students, but with enough musical material for mature ensembles. Parts may be doubled for a large ensemble.

Mozart, Wolfgang Amadeus. *Allegro from Eine Kleine Nachtmusik, K. 525.* arr. Albert Peoples. Southern Music Company. Two euphoniums and two tubas. 1990. $12.50. 5:00. IV. Part I: D–e'; Part II: B–e'; Part III: A_1–d'; Part IV: G_1–e. Good arrangement of this familiar melody. Most of the melodic work is in the first part. Parts may be doubled for a large ensemble.

Mozart, Wolfgang Amadeus. *Ave Verum.* arr. David Sabourin. Touch of Brass Music Corporation. Two euphoniums and two tubas. $6.50.

Mozart, Wolfgang Amadeus. *Ave Verum Corpus.* arr. Bruno Seitz. Musikverlag Martin Scherbacher. Two euphoniums and two tubas. 1993. $13.00. 2:30. III–IV. Part I: f–g'; Part II: d–c'; Part III: B♭–g; Part IV: B–d. Nice chorale with traditional harmonies. Ranges lie well for high school players. The euphonium parts are printed in bass and treble clefs. Parts may be doubled for a large ensemble.

Mozart, Wolfgang Amadeus. *Ave Verum Corpus (K. 618).* arr. Rudy Emilson. Kendor Music, Inc. Two euphoniums and two tubas. 2000. $7.00. 2:35. II. Part I: f–g♭'; Part II: c–c'; Part III: G–g; Part IV: B_1–d. Nice chorale with traditional harmonies. Range is appropriate for intermediate-level performers. Parts may be doubled for a large ensemble. Also reviewed in the Spring 2001 issue of the *TUBA Journal* (Vol. 28, No. 3).

Mozart, Wolfgang Amadeus. *Das Butterbrot.* arr. Hans Dorner. Four tubas.

Mozart, Wolfgang Amadeus. *Eine Kleine Nachtmusik.* arr. Bruno Seitz. Musikverlag Martin Scherbacher. Two euphoniums and two tubas. 1989. $15.00. 5:00. IV. Part I: B♭–g'; Part II: F–d'; Part III: $B\flat_1$–g; Part IV: E_1–f. Arranged in the key of B♭, the tessitura of the first part is approachable by many high school students. The melody remains primarily in the euphoniums. Parts may be doubled for a large ensemble.

Mozart, Wolfgang Amadeus. *Eine Kleine Nachtmusik for Tuba Quartet.* arr. James Self. Basset Hound Music. Four tubas. 1976. $10.00. 5:00. IV. Part I: B♭–a'; Part II: G–g'; Part III: G_1–a; Part IV: F_1–a. The tessitura of the top two parts is high and could be played by euphoniums. Technically challenging in some sections depending on the performance tempo. This transcription is in the key of C and works very well for two euphoniums and two tubas. Parts may be doubled for a large ensemble. Recorded by the Tubadours, *Ve Iss Da Mighty Tubadours Ya?* Crystal Records, S421.

Mozart, Wolfgang Amadeus. *Eine Kleine Nachtmusik, K. 525.* arr. Grady Greene. Music Arts Company. Two euphoniums and two tubas. 1987. $15.00. 5:00. IV. Part I: c–g'; Part II: G–d'; Part III: B–g; Part IV: G_1–d. Moderate technical challenges and no real range problems. This arrangement works better for less experienced performers. The top two parts are printed in bass and treble clef. Parts may be doubled for a large ensemble.

Mozart, Wolfgang Amadeus. *Eine Kleine Nachtmusik K. 525.* arr. Paul Schmidt. Heavy Metal Music. Two euphoniums and two tubas. 1991. $20.00. 22:30. IV–V. Part I: ($B\flat_1$) E–g'; Part II: C–f'; Part III: $B\flat_1$–d'; Part IV: $E\flat_1$–g. Four movements: Allegro; Romance; Menuetto; Rondo. This is the complete serenade. The melody is primarily in the euphoniums and most challenging for them. This arrangements works well for this genre. No score available. Parts may be doubled for a large ensemble.

Mozart, Wolfgang Amadeus. *Eine Kleine Nachtmusik, Mvt. I.* arr. Aaron Booz. Tuba-Euphonium Press. Two euphoniums and two tubas. 2000. $10.00. 6:00. III. Part I: c–a' (c"); Part II: G–f'; Part III: B_1–d'; Part IV: G_1–e. Effective arrangement of this well-known work. Inner voices may require double-tonguing, and the top part has several trills. Parts may be doubled for a large ensemble.

Mozart, Wolfgang Amadeus. *Fugue K. 401.* arr. Paul Schmidt. Heavy Metal Music. Two euphoniums and two tubas. 1990. $7.00. 4:00. IV. Part I: d–g'; Part II: A–c'; Part III: C♯–b; Part IV: G_1–d. All parts are challenging. Players will need to count carefully and play cleanly and lightly. No score available.

Mozart, Wolfgang Amadeus. *Kyrie from Requiem.* arr. Tiffani McGainey. Tuba-Euphonium Press. Two euphoniums and two tubas. 2001. $10.00. 2:00. III. Part I: c–b♭'; Part II: G–d'; Part III: C–g; Part IV: G_1–c. Straightforward arrangement with added dynamic markings for clarity. Melodic material is divided among all four parts. More appropriate for a quartet than for a large ensemble. Euphonium parts also available in treble clef. Also reviewed in the Winter 2003 issue of the *ITEA Journal* (Vol. 30, No. 2).

Mozart, Wolfgang Amadeus. *The Magic Flute (Die Zauberflote).* arr. Bryan V. Doughty. Cimarron Music and Productions. Two euphoniums and two tubas. 1998. $12.00. 8:30. III. Part I: G–b♭'; Part II: F–a♭'; Part III: $A\flat_1$–b♭; Part IV: F_1–a♭. This challenging arrangement of this popular overture divides the melodic material between all four parts. Requires clear, technical playing from all performers. Euphonium parts also available in treble clef. More appropriate for a quartet than for an ensemble.

Mozart, Wolfgang Amadeus. *The Magic Flute Overture.* arr. Maurice Bale. Godiva Music. Two euphoniums and two tubas. 1995. £8.00. 5:30. III. Part I: e–c"; Part II: G–g'; Part III: E♭–d♭'; Part IV: ($E\flat_1$) G_1–a♭.

Mozart, Wolfgang Amadeus. *March of the Priests from "The Magic Flute."* arr. Donald Sherman. Horizon Press. Two euphoniums and two tubas. 1991. $6.00. 3:00. III. Part I: c–f'; Part II: A–d'; Part III: A–f; Part IV: $B\flat_1$–d. The melody is primarily in the top two parts. Not technically challenging, and very appropriate for high school students. Parts may be doubled for a large ensemble.

Mozart, Wolfgang Amadeus. *Marriage of Figaro.* arr. Al Fabrizio. Tuba-Euphonium Press. Two euphoniums and two tubas. 1994. $12.00. 3:45. II–III. Part I: c–b♭' (d"); Part II: G–b♭'; Part III: $B\flat_1$–f'; Part IV: F_1–f. Dedicated to the U.S. Navy Tuba Ensemble. Challenging arrangement that is faithful to the original overture. Melodic material is divided among all voices. Parts may be doubled for a large ensemble. Also reviewed in the Spring 1996 issue of the *TUBA Journal* (Vol. 23, No. 3). Recorded by the Monarch Tuba-Euphonium Quartet on the compact disc *Metamorphosis,* Campro Productions.

Mozart, Wolfgang Amadeus. *Overture from the Marriage of Figaro.* arr. Ken Ferguson. BTQ Publications. Two euphoniums and two tubas. $15.00. Recorded by the British Tuba Quartet, *In at the Deep End,* Heavyweight Records Limited, HR008/D.

Mozart, Wolfgang Amadeus. *Overture to The Magic Flute.* arr. Jay Rozen. KIWI Music Press. Two euphoniums and two tubas. 1987. $10.00. 6:30. IV. Part I: B♭–b♭'; Part II: B♭–g'; Part III: B♭–f'; Part IV: G–d♭'. Dedicated to the Little Big Horns. This is a transcription of an arrangement for four male voices (TTBB) done by an anonymous arranger in the 1830s. There are only moderate technical demands, but the tessitura of the third and fourth parts is high. However, the higher sections do have optional 8vb sections for younger players.

Mozart, Wolfgang Amadeus. *Serenade Eine Kleine Tuba Musik for Four Tubas, K. 525.* arr. John Fletcher. Emerson Edition. Four tubas. 1984. $21.50. 5:00. IV. Part I: G–a; Part II: E–e'; Part III: A_1–g; Part IV: G_1–e. Fine arrangement of this classic composition. The tessitura of the top two parts is high. According to the score, "the top part can be played on a euphonium, but a bass (F) tuba is preferable." There are several turns and trills in the top two parts. Parts may be doubled for a large ensemble. Recorded by the Melton Tuba Quartett, *Premiere,* Diavolo Records, DR-D-93-C-001; John Fletcher and the Philip Hones Brass Ensemble, Argo Records, ZRG895.

Mozart, Wolfgang Amadeus. *Sonata No. 1.* arr. Robert Wilkinson. Cimarron Music and Productions. Two euphoniums and two tubas. $19.00. Three movements. Euphonium parts also available in treble clef.

Mozart, Wolfgang Amadeus. *Turkish March K. 331.* arr. Keith Mehlan. PP Music. Two euphoniums and two tubas. 1986. $8.00. 3:30. IV. Part I: B♭–c"; Part II: B♭–a'; Part III: $B\flat_1$–d'; Part IV: $B\flat_1$–b♭. Nice arrangement of this march. Tessitura is high for all four parts. Technically challenging if played at the tempo indicated. Recorded by the Monarch Tuba/Euphonium Quartet.

Mozart, Wolfgang Amadeus. *Twinkle, Twinkle. . . .* arr. Bryan V. Doughty. Cimarron Music and Productions. Two euphoniums and two tubas. 1999. $16.00. 17 pp. III. Theme and twelve variations. Part I: G–c"; Part II: G–c"; Part III: C_1–e'; Part IV: C_1–c'. Quartet showpiece based on *Twinkle, Twinkle Little Star.* All parts are technically demanding with large arpeggios and fast lines that are passed between performers. Works well as a concert closer or encore. Euphonium parts also available in treble clef. More appropriate for a quartet than for an ensemble.

Mozart, Wolfgang Amadeus. *Twinkle, Twinkle Little Star.* arr. David Werden. Cimarron Music and Productions. Two euphoniums and two tubas. 1994. $13.00. Theme and nine variations. This arrangement is based on variations on Mozart's *Ah! Vous Dirais-Je, Maman.* All parts are technically demanding. Melodic material is divided among the parts, and there is frequent voice-crossing. Works well as a concert closer or encore. Euphonium parts also available in treble clef. More appropriate for a quartet than for a large ensemble.

Mozart, Wolfgang Amadeus. *Two Waltzes, K. 600, #1 and 4.* arr. Paul Schmidt. Heavy Metal Music. Two euphoniums and two tubas. 1990. $5.00. 2:50. III–IV. Part I: B♭–f'; Part II: F–e♭'; Part III: $B♭_1$–b♭; Part IV: A_1–e♭. Two movements. All parts have an opportunity to play the melody. Technically not difficult, but the tessitura of the second part is low. No score available. Parts may be doubled for a large ensemble.

Muller, Francisco J. *The Death of Beowulf.* Francisco Muller. Four tubas. 1969. 5:50. IV. Part I: f–f'; Part II: G♯–d♭; Part III: E–b; Part IV: E_1–d. Could also be performed with one euphonium and three tubas. While the tempo is slow, there are many meter changes and challenging rhythmic figures.

Munsonins, H., and H. Ackermann. *Wenzel Polka.* arr. Ray Grim. Cimarron Music and Productions. Two euphoniums and two tubas. 1996. $10.00. 2:00. II. Part I: f–f'; Part II: c–d'; Part III: F–a; Part IV: F_1–d. Part of the TubaMeisters Collection, this fun polka arrangement is appropriate for intermediate-level performers. All parts are interesting, and parts may be doubled for a large ensemble. Euphonium parts also available in treble clef.

Mussorgsky, Modeste. *Miniatures at an Exhibition.* arr. Simon Proctor. Heavy Metal Music. Two euphoniums and two tubas. 1995. $10.00. 10:00. III–IV. Part I: c–g'; Part II: B–f'; Part III: B_1–c'; Part IV: F_1–f. This arrangement is a re-composed work based on the original piano score of *Pictures at an Exhibition,* reduced to make the piece playable and interesting to hear in the quartet texture. Also reviewed in the Summer 1998 issue of the *TUBA Journal* (Vol. 25, No. 4).

Mussorgsky, Modeste. *Pictures at an Exhibition.* arr. Scott Schlesinger. Tuba-Euphonium Press. Two euphoniums and two tubas. 2003. $35.00. 8:00. II–III. Part I: G–b♭'; Part II: G–g♯'; Part III: D_1–c'; Part IV: $E♭_1$–g. Seven movements: Promenade; Bydlo; Ballet of Unhatched Chickens; Sepulcrum Romanum; Catacombs; Hut of the Baba-Yaga; Great Gate of Kiev. Originally for piano, this work is best known as the orchestra arrangement by Ravel. According to the arranger, this collection contains the seven movements that work best for tuba quartet, and some of the movements have been abridged for similar reasons. More appropriate for a large ensemble than for a quartet.

Mussorgsky, Modeste. *Promenade from "Pictures at an Exhibition."* arr. Lisa Golas. Tuba-Euphonium Press. Two euphoniums and two tubas. 1995. $10.00. 1:30. II. Part I: f–c''; Part II: c–f'; Part III: F–b♭; Part IV: F_1–d. An arrangement of the first *Promenade* from this popular work. More effective with a large ensemble, as the piece begins with an exchange between a solo player and the tutti ensemble. Euphonium parts also available in treble clef. Several other movements from this work are available separately from the same arranger.

Naftel, Frederick. *I Saw a Snake. . . .* Breakthrough Music. Two euphoniums and two tubas. £19.95. Part I: B♭–c''; Part II: A♭–a'; Part III: E_1–c'; Part IV: F_1–f♯'. Naftel's own version of the *Carnival of the Animals,* including snakes, preying mantis, dogs, the fly, and, of course, the elephant! Two movements are for solo instruments.

Naftel, Frederick. *Pascal's Victim.* Da Capo Music. Two euphoniums and two tubas. £12.00. Three movements. Written for the quartet Tubalaté and selected for ITEC 2002 Quartet competition. The movements are in the traditional fast, slow, fast form, with tricky time changes in the third movement. Recorded by Tubalaté on the compact disc *Move.*

Nash, Richard. *Tublue.* Whaling Music Publishers. Four tubas, piano, bass, and drums. 1979. $14.00. 5:30. IV. Part I: d–c'' (d''); Part II: E–f' (g'); Part III: B–c' (d'); Part IV: (C_1) E_1–c'. Written for the Los Angeles Tuba Quartet: Roger Bobo, Tommy Johnson, Jim Self, and Don Waldrop. An original composition for tuba quartet in a jazz idiom. All players will need good jazz phrasing and style. The tessitura of the first two parts is high. Other possible instrumentations include one euphonium and three tubas, or two euphoniums and two tubas. The first part is printed in treble clef.

Necke, Hermann. *Csikos Post.* arr. Paul Schmidt. Heavy Metal Music. Two euphoniums and two tubas. 1990. $5.00. 1:45. IV. Part I: G–a♭; Part II: F♯–g'; Part III: E♭–e♭'; Part IV: F_1–e♭. Cute arrangement of the "Daffy Duck Song," associated with Disney cartoons. Fast-paced and technically challenging in some spots. No score available. Parts may be doubled for a large ensemble.

Necke, Hermann. *Csikos Post.* arr. Soichi Konagaya. Sonic Arts, Incorporated. Two euphoniums and two tubas. 1986. $12.00. 2:20. IV. Part I: B–b'; Part II: B–b; Part III: C–a; Part IV: E_1–f♯. Fun melody that is passed back and forth between the euphoniums and tubas. A lot of sudden dynamic changes. No significant technical problems. Parts may be doubled for a large ensemble.

Newsome. *Dead Man's Cove.* Two euphoniums and two tubas.

Newsome, Roy. *The Basics.* Breakthrough Music. Two euphoniums and two tubas. £11.95. Part I: c–c"; Part II: F–b♭'; Part III: D♭–d'; Part IV: F_1–b♭. Three movements. *The Basics,* as its title suggests, calls on the performers to draw on the basics of performance: scales, chords, and rhythms. *The Basics* was selected for the ITEC 2002 Quartet competition. Recorded by Tubalaté on the compact disc *Move.*

Newsome, Roy. *Jubilate (for Tubalaté).* Breakthrough Music. Two euphoniums and two tubas. £11.95. Part I: c–c"; Part II: E♭–b♭'; Part III: $B\flat_1$–e♭'; Part IV: F_1–g. Based on the Salvationist tune "O Be Joyful in the Lord."

Nicotra, Alfredo. *Fra hele Buenos Aires.* Norway Music Information Centre. Two euphoniums and two tubas. 7:30.

Niehaus, Lennie. *All Too Soon.* Kendor Music, Incorporated. Two euphoniums and two tubas. 1986. $9.00. 2:45. IV. Part I: c♭–g'; Part II: B–e♭'; Part III: E♭–f; Part IV: A_1–d. A moderate jazz waltz with traditional eight-measure phrases. Melodies are tossed between all four parts. Ranges of the Niehaus arrangements are generally not a problem. Drums may be added for additional jazz feel. Parts may be doubled for a large ensemble.

Niehaus, Lennie. *Brass Tacks.* Kendor Music, Incorporated. Two euphoniums and two tubas. 1983. $9.00. 2:40. IV. Part I: e♭–a'; Part II: c–f'; Part III: F–g; Part IV: A_1–f. Swing-style composition at a moderate tempo. While the euphoniums carry much of the responsibility, the two tuba parts do have some written solos. Drum set may be added to enhance the swing feel. This arrangement works very well. Parts may be doubled for a large ensemble. Recorded by the Northern Tuba Lights.

Niehaus, Lennie. *Grand Slam.* Kendor Music, Incorporated. Two euphoniums and two tubas. 1986. $9.50. 3:00. IV. Part I: d–g'; Part II: c–c'; Part III: C–f; Part IV: A_1–c. An original bright swing composition. Range is not demanding on the first euphonium and there are many tutti jazz rhythms between parts. All four parts share melodic responsibility. Parts may be doubled for a large ensemble. Recorded by the British Tuba Quartet, *Elite Syncopations,* Polyphonic Reproductions Limited, QPRZ012D.

Niehaus, Lennie. *Keystone Chops.* Kendor Music, Incorporated. Two euphoniums and two tubas. 1986. $9.00. 3:10. IV. Part I: B♭–f'; Part II: B♭–c'; Part III: C–g♭; Part IV: G_1–c. A swing tune that works at a moderate or bright tempo, depending on the abilities of the ensemble. Range is not demanding, but players must be able to swing to make the composition work. This is one of the better examples of this genre. Parts may be doubled for a large ensemble.

Niehaus, Lennie. *Miniature Jazz Suite #1.* Kendor Music, Incorporated. Two euphoniums and two tubas. 1987. $12.00. 9:45. IV. Part I: B♭–g'; Part II: B♭–c'; Part III: B♭–f♯; Part IV: (F_1) $A\flat_1$–e♭. Four movements: Tubalues; Bebop and Ballad; Change of Heart; Barimetricks. Each movement in the suite represents a contrast in jazz styles: swing, ballad, jazz waltz, and swing. The fourth movement has a section where players may improvise. This is technically more challenging than the other Niehaus compositions. A good swing feel is necessary for an appropriate performance of this piece. Parts may be doubled for a large ensemble. Recorded by the Melton Tuba Quartett, *Premiere,* Diavolo Records, DR-D-93-C-001.

Niehaus, Lennie. *Pachyderms in Paradise.* Kendor Music, Incorporated. Two euphoniums and two tubas. 1989. $9.50. 3:00. IV. Part I: c–f'; Part II: B♭–d'; Part III: $B\flat_1$–f; Part IV: $A\sharp_1$–e♭. Range and technical demands make this possible for a good high school quartet. A good swing feel is necessary. All parts have written solos as well as tutti rhythmic accompaniments. The first third of the piece changes meter frequently, but the quarter note remains constant. There is an eight-measure section with chord symbols in the third part for an improvised solo, though the player may play what is written in the part. Parts may be doubled for a large ensemble.

Niehaus, Lennie. *Sleeping Giants.* Kendor Music, Incorporated. Two euphoniums and two tubas. 1986. $9.50. 3:15. IV. Part I: c♯–f'; Part II: c–d'; Part III: E♭–g♭; Part IV: G_1–e♭. An original swing tune, with no real range demands, but players must have a good swing feel to make the piece work. Drum set may be added to help with tempo and style. Many tutti swing rhythms. Parts may be doubled for a large ensemble. Recorded by David LeClair, *Swingin' Low,* Marcophon.

Niehaus, Lennie. *Stephen Foster Jazz Suite.* Kendor Music, Incorporated. Two euphoniums and two tubas. 1989. $11.00. 8:30. IV. Part I: B–g'; Part II: c–c'; Part III: E–g; Part IV: (F_1) $A\flat_1$–c. Four movements: Beautiful Dreamer; My Old Kentucky Home; Oh! Susanna; Camptown Races. The first and last movements are in a fast swing style. The second movement is a ballad and the third movement is a jazz waltz. Range is not hard, but a good swing feel is necessary. The fourth movement contains a section with chord symbols in the first part for an improvised solo, or the player may elect to play the solo written in the part. Any of the movements could stand alone in a concert. Parts may be doubled for a large ensemble.

Niehaus, Lennie. *Tuba Turf.* Cojarro Music, Incorporated (Kendor Music, Incorporated). Two euphoniums and two tubas. 1992. $10.00. 2:50. III–IV. Part I: e–f'; Part II: c–c'; Part III: D–f; Part IV: (F_1) $B\flat_1$–d. A jazz waltz at a moderate tempo. Many tutti passages and sections where two parts pass the melody back and forth. The addition of a drum set would be beneficial. Parts may be doubled for a large ensemble.

Niehaus, Lennie. *Tubalation.* Kendor Music, Incorporated. Two euphoniums and two tubas. 1987. $9.50. 3:35. IV. Part I: f–g'; Part II: d–d'; Part III: E♭–f; Part IV: B♭$_1$–c. A moderate swing-style composition. The melody is often passed back and forth between the euphoniums and tubas. Each part has the opportunity to play the melody as a brief solo. No great technical or range demands. Parts may be doubled for a large ensemble.

Niehaus, Lennie. *Tubarometer.* Kendor Music, Incorporated. Two euphoniums and two tubas. 1991. $9.50. 2:55. IV. Part I: B♭–f'; Part II: B♭–c'; Part III: B♭$_1$–f; Part IV: B♭$_1$–d♭. As the "barometer" rises, so does the key. This moderate swing tune modulates from B♭ to B and then finally to the key of C. There are a few meter changes, but no real technical challenges. A good swing feel is essential. Parts may be doubled for a large ensemble.

Niehaus, Lennie. *A Whale's Tale.* Kendor Music, Incorporated. Two euphoniums and two tubas. 1984. $9.00. 2:20. IV. Part I: f–g'; Part II: d–c'; Part III: F–a; Part IV: A$_1$–e♭. A jazz waltz at a moderate tempo. Individual parts are more exposed than in other Niehaus compositions as the melody shifts from part to part. Not difficult technically, but challenging to count in three. Parts may be doubled for a large ensemble.

Niehaus, Lennie, arr. *Christmas Jazz Favorites No. 1.* Kendor Music, Incorporated. Two euphoniums and two tubas. 1994. $17.00. 8:00. III–IV. Part I: f–g'; Part II: A–d'; Part III: D–g♭; Part IV: B♭$_1$–f. Four movements: O Come, All Ye Faithful; The First Noel; It Came upon the Midnight Clear; God Rest Ye Merry Gentlemen. The first and fourth movements are in a fast swing style. The second movement is a ballad, and the third movement is a jazz waltz. Range is not hard, but a good swing feel is necessary. Any of the movements can stand alone in a concert. Parts may be doubled for a larger ensemble.

Niehaus, Lennie, arr. *Christmas Jazz Favorites No. 2.* Kendor Music, Incorporated. Two euphoniums and two tubas. 1996. $14.00. 7:40. III–IV. Part I: f–g'; Part II: B♭–c'; Part III: F–f; Part IV: (F$_1$) B♭$_1$–c. Three movements: The Boar's Head Carol; Cantique de Noel; Jolly Old St. Nicholas. The first and third movements are in a fast swing style. The second movement is a ballad. Range is not hard, but a good swing feel is necessary. Third movement modulates up to five flats. Any of the movements can stand alone in a concert. Parts may be doubled for a larger ensemble.

Niehaus, Lennie, arr. *Christmas Jazz Favorites No. 3.* Kendor Music, Incorporated. Two euphoniums and two tubas. 1997. $17.00. 8:25. III–IV. Part I: d–g' (b♭'); Part II: c–e' (f'); Part III: E♭–g; Part IV: A$_1$–e♭. Four movements: O Little Town of Bethlehem; The Twelve Days of Christmas; Rise Up, Shepherd and Follow; Jingle Bells. The first and fourth movements are in a fast swing style. The third movement is a jazz waltz. Range is not hard, but a good swing feel is necessary. The first and fourth movements contain sections with chord symbols in the second part for an improvised solo, though the player may elect to play the optional solo written in the part. Any of the movements can stand alone in a concert. Parts may be doubled for a larger ensemble. Also reviewed in the Spring 1998 issue of the *TUBA Journal* (Vol. 25, No. 3).

Niehaus, Lennie, arr. *A Christmas Jazz Medley.* Kendor Music, Incorporated. Two euphoniums and two tubas. 1984. $9.00. 3:30. IV. Part I: f–g'; Part II: c–e♭; Part III: F–g; Part IV: B♭$_1$–e♭. A fun and light medley of "It Came upon the Midnight Clear," "Hark the Herald Angels Sing," and "Jingle Bells." All of Niehaus's compositions have very playable ranges for all the parts. Not technically difficult, but challenging to make clean and stylistically correct at the tempos indicated: moderate swing, ballad, and bright swing. Fun for both performer and audience. Parts may be doubled for a large ensemble.

Niehaus, Lennie, arr. *Gay 90's Jazz Suite.* Kendor Music, Incorporated. Two euphoniums and two tubas. 1993. $14.00. 8:45. III–IV. Part I: d–g'; Part II: c–f'; Part III: C–g♭; Part IV: A♭$_1$–e♭. Four movements: The Man on the Flying Trapeze; After the Ball; The Sidewalks of New York; While Strolling through the Park One Day. The first and last movements are in a fast swing style. The second movement is a ballad, and the third movement is a jazz waltz. Range is not hard, but a good jazz swing feel is necessary. Any of the movements can stand alone in a concert. Parts may be doubled for a large ensemble.

Niehaus, Lennie, arr. *I Heard the Bells on Christmas Day.* Kendor Music, Incorporated. Two euphoniums and two tubas. 2002. $7.00. 2:40. II–III. Part I: e♭–f'; Part II: B♭–e'; Part III: D–f; Part IV: B♭$_1$–B♭. Jazz-ballad arrangement of this carol. Range is appropriate for intermediate-level performers. Parts may be doubled for a large ensemble.

Niehaus, Lennie, arr. *Lo, How a Rose E'er Blooming.* Kendor Music, Incorporated. Two euphoniums and two tubas. 2001. $7.00. 3:00. II. Part I: e♭–f'; Part II: c–d♭'; Part III: G–f; Part IV: A♭$_1$–d♭. Jazz-ballad arrangement of this carol. Range is appropriate for intermediate-level performers. Parts may be doubled for a large ensemble. Also reviewed in the Winter 2002 issue of the *ITEA Journal* (Vol. 29, No. 2).

Niehaus, Lennie, arr. *Londonderry Air.* Kendor Music, Incorporated. Two euphoniums and two tubas. 1997. $12.00. 2:40. III–IV. Part I: c–g';

Part II: c–d'; Part III: E♭–g; Part IV: $B♭_1$–e♭. Fast-swing arrangement. Range is not difficult, but a good swing feel is necessary. Many tutti swing rhythms. Parts may be doubled for a large ensemble. Also reviewed in the Fall 1997 issue of the *TUBA Journal* (Vol. 25, No. 1).

Niehaus, Lennie, arr. *Old King Cole.* Kendor Music, Incorporated. Two euphoniums and two tubas. 2002. $10.00. 2:40. III–IV. Part I: e–f'; Part II: e♭–e♭'; Part III: F♯–g; Part IV: $A♭_1$–c. A fast swing arrangement. Many tutti rhythms and passages where two parts pass the melody back and forth. Parts may be doubled for a large ensemble.

Niehaus, Lennie, arr. *Spiritual Jazz Suite.* Kendor Music, Incorporated. Two euphoniums and two tubas. 1990. $17.00. 8:50. IV. Part I: F–g'; Part II: F–d'; Part III: C–f; Part IV: F_1–d. Four movements: Joshua Fought the Battle of Jerico; Deep River; Nobody Knows the Trouble I've Seen; Swing Low, Sweet Chariot. These four well-known spirituals are set in contrasting styles: swing, ballad, jazz waltz, and swing. Range is not a problem, but a good swing feel is necessary. This arrangement works very well. Parts may be doubled for a large ensemble. Recorded by the British Tuba Quartet, *Euphonic Sounds,* Polyphonic Reproductions Limited, QPRA009D.

Niehaus, Lennie, arr. *Swingin' Ukrainian Christmas.* Kendor Music, Incorporated. Two euphoniums and two tubas. 2003. $8.00. 2:35. III. Part I: c–f'; Part II: B♭–a♭; Part III: C–f; Part IV: $A♭_1$–B♭. Arrangement of "Carol of the Bells" in a jazz-waltz style; includes a section in 4/4. Many repeated rhythms and tutti sections. Parts may be doubled for a large ensemble.

Niehaus, Lennie, arr. *Yuletide Jazz Suite #1.* Kendor Music, Incorporated. Two euphoniums and two tubas. 1990. $11.00. 7:30. IV. Part I: d–g'; Part II: c–d'; Part III: F–f; Part IV: (F_1) $A♭_1$–f. Four movements: Joy to the World; Angels We Have Heard on High; We Three Kings; O Little Town of Bethlehem. The first movement has a medium swing feel, second movement is a ballad, third movement a jazz waltz, and the last movement a bright swing. Good swing feel required to make this work. The movements could be performed separately. Parts may be doubled for a large ensemble.

Niehaus, Lennie, arr. *Yuletide Jazz Suite #2.* Kendor Music, Incorporated. Two euphoniums and two tubas. 1993. $16.00. 7:45. IV. Part I: c♯–g'; Part II: c–e♭'; Part III: D–f; Part IV: G_1–d. Three movements: Deck the Halls; What Child Is This?; The Wassail Song. The three movements are in a moderate swing, a jazz waltz, and a bright swing respectively. A good swing feel is necessary for all players. Drums may be added for effect. All parts have the opportunity to play the melody. Parts may be doubled for a large ensemble.

Nilovic, Janko. *Variations aux Quatre Vents.* Symphony Land. Four tubas. 1980. 6:30. III–IV. Part I: c–a'; Part II: G♯–f♯'; Part III: F♯–c♯'; Part IV: $F♯_1$–g. The first two parts could be played on the euphonium to make the quartet accessible to high school students. There are no technical demands, but the harmony is very dissonant.

Nordhagen, Stig. *Music for Tuba Quartet.* Norway Music Information Centre. Tuba quartet. 14:00. Four movements: Giocoso; Nocturne; Tema med variasioner; Finale.

Olsen, Ole. *Gammel Jegermarsj (Old Hunter March).* arr. Øystein Baadsvik. Baadsvik Music Shop. Two euphoniums and two tubas. €19.00. Famous Norwegian march arranged for quartet. All parts are available in both bass and treble clef.

Orzechowski, H. *Grey Horse Polka.* arr. Paul Schmidt. Heavy Metal Music. Two euphoniums and two tubas. 1990. $7.00. 1:30. IV. Part I: B♭–e♭'; Part II: B♭–e♭'; Part III: D♭–a♭; Part IV: G_1–e'. A medium difficult polka. The tessitura of part two is higher than that of part one. No score available. Parts may be doubled for a large ensemble.

Ostermann, W. *Einmal Am Rhein.* arr. Ray Grim. Cimarron Music and Productions. Two euphoniums and two tubas. 1996. $10.00. 2:00. II. Part I: g–b♭'; Part II: e♭–f'; Part III: B♭–a; Part IV: G_1–B♭. Part of the TubaMeisters Collection, this waltz arrangement is appropriate for intermediate-level performers. Melody is predominantly in the first part. Parts may be doubled for a large ensemble. Euphonium parts also available in treble clef.

Ott, Joseph. *7 22 73 for Tuba Quartet.* Claude Benny Press. Two euphoniums, two tubas, and tape. 1973. $10.00. 9:30. IV. Part I: d–a'; Part II: B–g'; Part III: A–b'; Part IV: F_1–g. Three movements. Commissioned by R. Winston Morris. Title reflects the date the composition was completed. A taped accompaniment is used in movements I and III. Very contemporary (half-valve notes, hissing through the instrument, etc.) and very dissonant. More appropriate for a large ensemble than for a quartet.

Owen, Blythe. *Saraband and Gigue for Tuba Quartet Op. 43.* Hall-Orion Music Press. Four tubas. 1973. $6.00. 4:00. III–IV. Part I: c–f'; Part II: E♭–e♭'; Part III: B_1–a; Part IV: E_1–c. The first and second parts may be played on euphonium by high school students, F tuba by college students. The tessitura of the fourth part remains quite low and will require very clean playing. A nice light work for tuba quartet. Parts may be doubled for a large ensemble.

Paasch, Antony. *Native American Suite.* Cimarron Music and Productions. Two euphoniums and two tubas. $12.00.

Paasch, Antony. *Prairie Suite.* Tuba-Euphonium Press. Two euphoniums and two tubas. 2001. $15.00. 8:30. II–III. Part I: f–c''; Part II: A–g';

Part III: C–d'; Part IV: F_1–a. Four movements: Dawn; Hoedown; The Solitary Cowboy; Roundup. Dedicated to Gary Buttery. Programmatic work based on Paasch's poem *Tis a Noble Thing*. All parts are interesting and have melodic material at some point. Individual movements can stand alone in a concert. Parts may be doubled for a large ensemble. Also reviewed in the Spring 2003 issue of the *ITEA Journal* (Vol. 30, No. 3).

Palestrina, Giovanni de. *Alla Rivea del Tebro.* tr. Gary Nelson. Tuba-Euphonium Press. Four tubas. 1995. $10.00. 1:45. II. Part I: d–g'; Part II: B♭–c'; Part III: F–a; Part IV: B♭$_1$–d. Highly imitative work in the Renaissance style. Individual parts are not difficult and are appropriate for intermediate-level performers. Parts may be doubled for a large ensemble.

Palestrina, Giovanni de. *In Festo Transfigurationis Domini.* tr. Doug Bristol. Tuba-Euphonium Press. Two euphoniums and two tubas. 2000. $10.00. 4:15. II. Part I: e♭–e♭'; Part II: G–b♭; Part III: E♭–g; Part IV: C–e♭. For the Alabama Tuba Quartet. Highly imitative work and an excellent study in early counterpoint. Appropriate for intermediate-level performers. Parts may be doubled for a large ensemble.

Palestrina, Giovanni de. *Magnificat.* tr. Doug Bristol. Tuba-Euphonium Press. Two euphoniums and two tubas. 2000. $12.00. 7:00. II. Part I: G–g'; Part II: G–f'; Part III: F–c'; Part IV: C–a. For the Alabama Tuba Quartet. Highly imitative piece in the Renaissance style. Range is appropriate for intermediate-level performers. Parts may be doubled for a large ensemble.

Palestrina, Giovanni Pierluigi. *Motet "Christe, Lux Vera."* arr. Randall Block. The Musical Evergreen (Philharmusica). Four tubas. 1976. $8.50. 1:45. III. Part I: A♭–a♭; Part II: E♭–c; Part III: B♭$_1$–e♭; Part IV: B♭$_1$–A♭. A polyphonic work, but not difficult technically. Ranges are limited and the piece is very appropriate for high school students. Players must count carefully. Parts may be doubled for a large ensemble.

Palestrina, Giovanni Pierluigi. *Ricercar del Primo Tuono.* arr. Paul Schmidt. Heavy Metal Music. Two euphoniums and two tubas. 1992. $5.00. 2:00. III–IV. Part I: f–f'; Part II: G–c'; Part III: F–a; Part IV: G_1–d. Very polyphonic; all parts are of equal difficulty. A limited range, very appropriate for high school ensembles. No score available. Parts may be doubled for a large ensemble.

Pardus, William D. *Loconic Overture.* Creation Station. Two euphoniums and two tubas. $20.00. 4:15. Typical piece in ternary form with melodic material in each of the four voices. Euphonium parts also available in treble clef. Also reviewed in the Summer 2001 issue of the *TUBA Journal* (Vol. 28, No. 4).

Pardus, William D., arr. *Three Madrigals.* Creation Station. Two euphoniums and two tubas. $20.00. 4:15. II–III. Part I: d–a'; Part II: B–d'; Part III: F–g; Part IV: B♭$_1$–g. Three movements: If Loveliest of Spirits by Philippe de Monte; April Is in My Mistress' Face by Thomas Morley; Thyrsis, Sleepest Thou? by John Bennet. Three madrigals in the Franco-Flemish and English traditions of the late sixteenth century. Euphonium parts also available in treble clef. Also reviewed in the Summer 2001 issue of the *TUBA Journal* (Vol. 28, No. 4).

Parfrey, Raymond. *Male Voice for Brass.* Available from Tubalaté. Two euphoniums and two tubas. Three movements: Song for a Star; Southern Memories; Oriental Barber's Shop. Recorded by Tubalaté on the compact disc *Earth and Moon.*

Parfrey, Raymond. *Tributes to Tunesmiths.* Available from Tubalaté. Two euphoniums and two tubas. Three movements: Movie Tune; Folk-like Tune; Waltz Tune. Recorded by Tubalaté on the compact disc *Earth and Moon.*

Parker. *Deep Harmony.* arr. Paul Walton. Breakthrough Music. Two euphoniums and two tubas. 2:00. Part I: e♭–g♭'; Part II: c–g'; Part III: E♭$_1$–c'; Part IV: E♭$_1$–c'. Beautiful hymn tune featuring the first euphonium on the first verse and the first tuba on the second verse. Recorded by Tubalaté on the compact disc *Episodes.*

Parry. *Jerusalem.* arr. Maurice Bale. Godiva Music. Two euphoniums and two tubas. £5.00.

Passereau, Pierre. *Il est bel et bon.* arr. Lisa Scoggin. Tuba-Euphonium Press. Two euphoniums and two tubas. 1997. $8.00. 1:15. I–II. Part I: g–a'; Part II: d–e'; Part III: A–b; Part IV: A_1–e. Highly imitative piece in the Renaissance style. Range is appropriate for young and intermediate-level performers. Parts may be doubled for a large ensemble.

Payne, Frank Lynn. *Quartet for Tubas.* Shawnee Press, Incorporated. Four tubas. 1971. $18.00. 11:00. IV. Part I: G–e'; Part II: F–d'; Part III: B_1–d'; Part IV: D_1–a. Three movements: Allegro; Andante; Vivo. The first part has a high tessitura. No real technical problems, but the work will require four strong players. Good challenging writing for tuba quartet. Awarded first place in the 1969 International Tuba Ensemble Composition Contest sponsored by the University of Miami School of Music. Recorded by the University of Michigan Tuba and Euphonium Ensemble, University of Michigan Records, SM0011; the University of Miami Tuba Ensemble, Miami United Tuba Ensemble Society, 14568; and the Melton Tuba Quartett, *Premiere,* Diavolo Records, DR-D-93-C-001.

Payne, Frank Lynn. *Tubaphonic Suite.* T.A.P. Music. Four tubas. 1989. $7.00. 15:00. IV. Part I: D–f'; Part II: A–f'; Part III: E_1–d'; Part IV: D_1–a. Six movements: Concept; Divergence; Exploration; Postulate; Retreat Canon; Synthesis. A massive work. The first and last movements change meter frequently and are very contemporary in nature.

Texture is very thick at times. Range and technical demands will require four strong players. A score is available for four dollars extra.

Payne, Roger. *Suite in Blue.* Fortune Music Publications. Four tubas. 1976. $10.00. 7:30. IV. Part I: C–b♭; Part II: D–f♯; Part III: F_1–f; Part IV: G_1–d. Three movements: March Two-Step; Meander; Danse Triste. Commissioned by the William Davis Construction Group Band. Dedicated to Charlie Longridge and Phil Porter. The score and parts are printed in treble clef, as the first two parts are for E♭ tubas and the third and fourth parts for B♭ tubas. Some technical problems, especially in the third movement. Fairly traditional harmonies. Players must count carefully.

Pelecis, Georgs. *Almost a Fugue.* Available from Tubalaté. Two euphoniums and two tubas. Recorded by Tubalaté on the compact disc *Hall of Mirrors.*

Peterson, Oscar. *Noreen's Nocturne.* arr. Keating. Breakthrough Music. Two euphoniums and two tubas. Part I: d♯–d"; Part II: B♭–b♭'; Part III: C–f'; Part IV: A_1–d'. Arranged specially for the quartet Tubalaté, this arrangement includes quotes from several other standards. Recorded by Tubalaté on the compact disc *Hall of Mirrors.*

Petrie. *Asleep in the Deep.* arr. Paul Schmidt. Heavy Metal Music. Two euphoniums and two tubas. 1990. $5.00. 1:20. III–IV. Part I: (F_1) F–d'; Part II: G–c'; Part III: G–b♭; Part IV: F_1–f. Written for euphonium or ophicleide solo with accompaniment. No significant technical problems; very playable by high school students. No score available. Parts may be doubled for a large ensemble.

Pezel, John. *Sonata No. 2.* arr. John Stevens. Encore Music Publishers. Two euphoniums and two tubas. 1988. $10.00. 2:00. III–IV. Part I: e–f'; Part II: G–c'; Part III: C–g; Part IV: F_1–g. This is a single movement typical of Renaissance instrumental music. The first section is in 4/4 and then proceeds to 3/2. Very playable by high school or university ensembles. Parts may be doubled for a large ensemble.

Pezold. *Menuet from Anna Magdalena's Notebook.* arr. Stephen Shoop. Cimarron Music and Productions. Two euphoniums and two tubas. 1995. $9.00. 1:45. I–II. Part I: B–f'; Part II: A–d'; Part III: G_1–d; Part IV: G_1–c. Straightforward arrangement of this well-known work with traditional harmonies. This is an excellent piece for young ensembles, as melodic material is divided among all four voices. Euphonium parts also available in treble clef. Parts may be doubled for a large ensemble.

Pierpont, James. *Jingle Bells.* arr. James A. Garrett. James Garrett. Two euphoniums and tubas. 1990. $10.00. 1:00. III–IV. Part I: B♭–b♭'; Part II: B♭–e♭'; Part III: B♭$_1$–b♭; Part IV: B♭$_1$–g. A fun arrangement of this popular Christmas song. No significant technical challenges. Other than a couple of high b♭'s, range is not a problem.

Pierpont, James. *Jingle Bells.* arr. Rodger Vaughan. Available from the arranger. Two euphoniums and two tubas. 1990. $5.00. 1:10. III–IV. Part I: a–b♭'; Part II: f–f'; Part III: F–b♭; Part IV: B♭$_1$–g. For the Tubadours. The melody is divided between the first and fourth parts. The arrangement works quite well. No score available. Parts may be doubled for a large ensemble.

Pierpont, James. *Jingle Bells.* arr. Timothy Olt. Tuba-Euphonium Press. Two euphoniums and two tubas. 2003. $10.00. 1:30. II. Part I: f–b♭'; Part II: G–d'; Part III: G–g; Part IV: B♭$_2$–g. Fun arrangement of this standard Christmas song. The tune is presented as a march, as a multimetric waltz, and in other humorous settings. Parts may be doubled for a large ensemble.

Pilkington. *All in a Cave.* Sarnia Music. Two euphoniums and two tubas. £9.99.

Pilkington. *Amyntas with His Phyllis Fair.* Sarnia Music. Two euphoniums and two tubas. £9.99.

Pilkington. *Have I Found Her?* Sarnia Music. Two euphoniums and two tubas. £9.99.

Pilkington. *Love Is a Secret Feeding Fire.* Sarnia Music. Two euphoniums and two tubas. £9.99.

Pilkington. *The Messenger of Spring.* Sarnia Music. Two euphoniums and two tubas. £9.99.

Pilkington. *What Though Her Frowns.* Sarnia Music. Two euphoniums and two tubas. £9.99.

Pilkington. *Why Do I Fret?* Sarnia Music. Two euphoniums and two tubas. £9.99.

Pilkington. *Why Should I Grieve?* Sarnia Music. Two euphoniums and two tubas. £9.99.

Pitoni, Giuseppe. *Cantate Domini and What Child Is This?* arr. Paul Schmidt. Heavy Metal Music. Two euphoniums and two tubas. 1991. $3.00. 1:45. III. Part I: c–e♭'; Part II: B♭–c'; Part III: F–f; Part IV: G_1–d. An arrangement of two famous Christmas season melodies. Very appropriate for high school students. No score available. Parts may be doubled for a large ensemble.

Pleshak, Sergei. *Searching for the Truth.* Breakthrough Music. Two euphoniums and two tubas. Part I: d–c♭"; Part II: B♭–g'; Part III: C♭–c♭'; Part IV: F_1–a. This original composition was awarded runner-up prize in the British Council Composition Competition (in association with Tubalaté and Besson). A good solid repertoire work. Recorded by Tubalaté on the compact disc *Hall of Mirrors.*

Porter, Cole. *From This Moment On.* arr. Denzil Stephens. Sarnia Music. Two euphoniums and two tubas. £15.00.

Powell, Baden. *Bocoxe.* arr. Gary Buttery. Whaling Music Publishers. Two euphoniums and two tubas. 1978. $5.00. 1:45. IV. Part I: c–g' (c"); Part II: A–e♭'; Part III: F–c'; Part IV: F_1–f. A lively melody with the feel switching from 6/8 to 2/4 to 3/4. All parts have the opportunity to play the melody. Parts may be doubled for a large ensemble. Recorded by the Atlantic Tuba Quartet, *Euphonic Sounds,* Golden Crest, CRS

4173; and the British Tuba Quartet, *Euphonic Sounds,* Polyphonic Reproductions Limited, QPRZ009D.

Praetorius, Michael. *Lo, How a Rose E'er Blooming.* arr. Andrew Spang. Lyric Brass Publishing. Two euphoniums and two tubas. 1994. $9.00. Parts may be doubled for a large ensemble. Also available in a six-part arrangement by the same arranger and publisher.

Praetorius, Michael. *Partita in Four Parts.* arr. John Bina. PEL Music Publications. Two euphoniums and two tubas. 2003. $9.50. 3:45. II–III. Part I: f–a♭'; Part II: d♭–e♭'; Part III: A♭–b♭; Part IV: $A♭_1$–e♭. Four movements: Bransle Simple; Bransle Gay; Bransle Gentil; Courante. Collection of four dances in a late Renaissance/early baroque style. Two movements are in duple meter, and two are in triple meter. Style and range are appropriate for intermediate-level performers, though the key signatures of four and five flats may prove challenging. Parts may be doubled for a large ensemble. Individual movements can stand alone on a concert.

Praetorius, Michael. *Three Bourees from "Terpsichore."* arr. Paul F. Hartin. Cellar Press. Four tubas. 1975. 4:00. IV. Part I: d–e'; Part II: B–a; Part III: F♯–f; Part IV: G_1–G. Three movements. The three pieces are in the same style. Harmony is very traditional. A little muddy at times.

Presser, William. *Serenade for Four Tubas.* Tenuto Publications. Four tubas. 1972. $6.00. 6:00. IV. Part I: E–c'; Part II: $B♭_1$–b♭; Part III: F_1–f; Part IV: d_1–e♭. Three movements: Allegretto; Adagio (Canon); Allegro. No outstanding range or technical problems; however, the fourth part gets quite low (D_1). Good writing for tuba quartet. This composition received third place in the 1969 University of Miami International Tuba Ensemble Composition Contest. The Allegro (third movement) was recorded by the University of Michigan Tuba and Euphonium Ensemble, Golden Crest Records, CRS-4145.

Proctor, Simon. *Light Metal.* Heavy Metal Music. Two euphoniums and two tubas. 1992. $10.00. 11:30. IV. Part I: c–g'; Part II: A–f'; Part III: C–b; Part IV: F–f. Four movements: Talatasco; Schmaltz Waltz; Chorale; Jazz Fugue. For the Heavy Metal Society Tuba Quartet and published in the memory of our friend Christopher Monk. A challenging composition encompassing a wide variety of styles. A good jazz style is necessary of all players. All parts have solos. Parts may be doubled for a large ensemble.

Prokofiev, Sergei. *Troika from "Lt. Kjie Suite."* arr. David Butler. Tuba-Euphonium Press. Two euphoniums and two tubas with optional percussion. 2003. $15.00. 2:45. III. Part I: c♯–a♭'; Part II: c♯–f♯'; Part III: C–g; Part IV: F_1–g♭. Excerpted from the film score of *Lt. Kije,* this arrangement depicts a ride in a traditional three-horse sleigh, complete with bells on the harnesses. Optional percussion includes sleigh bells, triangle, and tambourine. Calls for mutes for two euphoniums and one tuba. Parts may be doubled for a large ensemble. Euphonium parts also available in treble clef. Recorded by the Tennessee Tech Tuba Ensemble on the compact disc *Carnegie VI,* Mark Records.

Puccini, Giacomo. *March from "La Boheme."* arr. David Butler. Tuba-Euphonium Press. Two euphoniums and two tubas. 1998. $12.00. 2:15. II. Part I: B♭–g'; Part II: B♭–e♭'; Part III: $A♭_1$–b♭; Part IV: F_1–f. Effective arrangement that is appropriate for younger ensembles. Melodic material is divided among the top three parts. Parts may be doubled for a large ensemble.

Puccini, Giacomo. *Nessun Dorma.* arr. Paul Walton. Breakthrough Music. Two euphoniums and two tubas. £8.00. Part I: c–a'; Part II: c–f'; Part III: c–g; Part IV: C–e. Effective arrangement. Suitable for younger ensemble.

Puccini, Giocomo. *Turandot; Two Choruses.* arr. Donald Sherman. Horizon Press. Two euphoniums and two tubas. 1991. $7.00. 2:00. III. Part I: c–g'; Part II: A♭–c'; Part III: D♭–f; Part IV: F_1–f. A single movement containing two different Puccini melodies. All parts have the opportunity to play the melody. No significant technical problems. Parts may be doubled for a large ensemble.

Pullig, Ken. *Dances; Four Tubas: A Short Piece for Tuba Quartet.* Tuba-Euphonium Press. Two euphoniums and two tubas. 1993. $15.00. 5:30. IV. Part I: d–b♭"; Part II: F–a'; Part III: F–c'; Part IV: (G_1) $B♭_1$–e♭. Good writing for tuba/euphonium quartet. Several tempo and meter changes and some technical challenges. All four parts are interesting, though the tessitura of the first part is high. Parts may be doubled for a large ensemble.

Purcell, H., and J. Clarke. *Two Trumpet Tunes and Trumpet Voluntary.* arr. Peter Rauch. Ohio Valley Tuba Quartet Press. Two euphoniums and two tubas. 1988. $12.00. 6:20. IV. Part I: A–b'; Part II: B♭–b'; Part III: $B♭_1$–a (d'); Part IV: (C_1) G_1–A. Three movements: Trumpet Tune A; Trumpet Tune B; Trumpet Voluntary. Very usable arrangement of these three familiar baroque trumpet melodies. Most of the melodic responsibility is in the first two parts. Precision in the dotted eighth and sixteenth note figures and in execution of trills is vital. Parts may be carefully doubled for a large ensemble.

Purcell, Henry. *Fanfare.* arr. Allyn Lindsey. Cimarron Music and Productions. Two euphoniums and two tubas. 2001. $9.00. 0:45. Euphonium parts also available in treble clef.

Purcell, Henry. *Two Trumpet Tunes and Ayre.* arr. Karl Humble. T.A.P. Music. Two euphoniums and two tubas. 1989. $5.00. 3:20. III–IV. Part I: B♭–g'; Part II: A–e♭'; Part III: $B♭_1$–f; Part IV: A_1–e♭. Three movements: Tune I; Ayre; Tune II.

The first tune is the famous "Trumpet Voluntary" that we now know was actually written by Jeremiah Clarke (?–1707). There are no significant technical or range problems. The movements may be played in any order or by themselves. Parts may be doubled for a large ensemble.

Puw, Guto Pryderi. *Visages*. Available from Tubalaté. Two euphoniums and two tubas. Recorded by Tubalaté on the compact disc *Earth and Moon*.

Pygott, Richard. *Quid Petis O Fili*. arr. Michael Thornton. Queen City Brass Publications. Four tubas. 1980. $6.50. 3:10. III–IV. Part I: f–d'; Part II: A–c'; Part III: D–f; Part IV: B♭–d. The first and second parts could be played by euphonium to be playable by high school ensembles. A lot of imitation typical of Renaissance instrumental music. Parts may be doubled for a large ensemble.

Ramsoe, Wilhelm. *Quartet for Brass*. arr. Gary Buttery. Whaling Music Publishers. Two euphoniums and two tubas. 1978. $12.00. 9:00. IV–V. Part I: A–a'; Part II: G–g'; Part III: E–g'; Part IV: G_1–e♭'. Three movements: Scherzo; Andante quasi Allegretto; Allegro Molto. Three contrasting movements based on the works of the French composer Ramsoe. Tessitura of all four parts is high. All parts are rhythmically and musically challenging, especially at the suggested tempos. Recorded by the Atlantic Tuba Quartet, *Euphonic Sounds,* Golden Crest, CRS 4173; the British Tuba Quartet, *Euphonic Sounds,* Polyphonic Reproductions Limited, #QPRZ009D; the Melton Tuba Quartett, *Premiere,* Diavolo Records, DR-D-93-C-01; U.S. Coast Guard Tuba/Euphonium Quartet, *Soloists and Chamber Players,* U.S.C.G., 122678–A; U.S. Navy Tuba/Euphonium Quartet, U.S. Navy Band Records.

Randalls, Jeremy. *Tuba Quartet*. Scottish Music Information Centre. Four tubas. 1986. $8.00. 7:15. IV. Part I: E♭–f'; Part II: C♯–e'; Part III: G_1–e'; Part IV: D_1–d♭'. To Willie Young. The Allegro section is multimetric and can be challenging. All parts have an opportunity to play the melody. The tessitura of the top two parts is high and would be most appropriate on F tubas or perhaps euphoniums.

Raposo, Joe. *Sesame Street*. arr. Rodger Vaughan. Available from the arranger. Two euphoniums and two tubas. 1988. $5.00. 2:30. IV. Part I: f–a♭'; Part II: B♭–e'; Part III: B♭–c'; Part IV: F_1–f. This is the theme from the popular children's television show. The syncopated melody is bounced between the first and third parts. Fun to play. No score available. Parts may be doubled for a large ensemble.

Raton, Rodente (Mousey). *Mouse Trap Blues*. arr. James Garrett. Cimarron Music and Productions. Two euphoniums and two tubas. 1996. $9.50. 2:45. III. Part I: c♯–g'; Part II: c♯–d'; Part III: $B\flat_1$–g; Part IV: $B\flat_1$–e♭. Lighthearted, original composition in a blues texture written by James Garrett under one of his pseudonyms. Calls for slapstick to simulate the mousetrap sounds. Requires a good falsetto voice for shouting "eek!" Euphonium parts also available in treble clef. Parts may be doubled for a large ensemble.

Rauch, Peter. *Folksong Medley*. Ohio Valley Tuba Quartet Press. Two euphoniums and two tubas. 1991. $12.00. 4:00. IV. Part I: B♭–b♭'; Part II: B♭–a'; Part III: C–b♭; Part IV: $E\flat_1$–f. A medley of Camptown Races, Oh Suzanna, My Old Kentucky Home, Shennandoah, and Dixie. All parts have an opportunity to play the melody. Some mixed meters. Parts may be doubled for a large ensemble.

Rauch, Peter. *TubaFunk*. Cimarron Music and Productions. Two euphoniums and two tubas. 1998. $12.00. 3:45. III. Part I: c–b♭' (c''); Part II: G–g'; Part III: F–b; Part IV: (F_1) G_1–d. Fun original composition in a rock, funk style. The texture is predominantly a layering of different rhythmic motives. A repeating solo section is labeled with chord changes for the first euphonium to improvise. Euphonium parts also available in treble clef. Parts may be doubled for a large ensemble.

Rauch, Peter, arr. *Greensleeves*. Ohio Valley Tuba Quartet Press. Two euphoniums and two tubas. 1990. $10.00. 2:00. IV. Part I: B–c''; Part II: B–b♭'; Part III: E–g; Part IV: D_1–f. All four parts have an opportunity to play the melody. Not technically difficult, but the tessitura of the first and second parts is high. Parts may be doubled for a large ensemble.

Rauch, Peter, arr. *With a Little Bit of Flash*. Ohio Valley Tuba Quartet Press. Two euphoniums and two tubas. 1992. $12.00. 3:45. IV–V. Part I: c–b♭'; Part II: B♭–b♭'; Part III: F_1–a♭; Part IV: E_1–a. A fanfare with many driving eighth and sixteenth note patterns. The accompaniment is very syncopated, and the meter changes frequently. Most demanding technically of the first part. An exciting piece that will require four strong players.

Read, Thomas. *Meet These People*. American Composers Alliance. Two euphoniums and two tubas. 1987. $20.00. 7:00. V. Part I: $B\flat_1$–a♭'; Part II: $F\sharp_1$–f♯'; Part III: c–g'; Part IV: C_1–g'. Written for the University of Vermont Tuba/Euphonium Ensemble. A very technically challenging piece with extensive range demands for all parts. This contains very contemporary harmonies. Players are directed to sit very far apart on the stage to surround the audience with sound.

Reeman, John. *Episodes*. Studio Music Company. Two euphoniums and two tubas. 10:45. Five movements. Written specially for Tubalaté, this published version is pitched a third lower than the original. The movements alternate between slow and fast. Recorded by Tubalaté on the compact disc *Episodes*.

Regan, Michael. *Quartet*. Breakthrough Music. Two euphoniums and two tubas. £14.95. Part I: B♭–b♭';

Part II: F–b♭'; Part III: G_1–e♭'; Part IV: G_1–g♯. Written for the quartet Tubalaté, this is a work which will help form the core repertoire of any tuba-euphonium quartet. Recorded by Tubalaté on the compact disc *Earth and Moon.*

Reger, Max. *Abschied.* arr. William Schmidt. Western International Music, Inc. Two euphoniums and two tubas. 1996. $6.00. 2:00. II–III. Part I: c–f♭'; Part II: A–b; Part III: E–a♭; Part IV: $B\flat_1$–e♭. Nice arrangement with traditional harmonies in a compound meter. Range and style are appropriate for intermediate-level performers. Parts may be doubled for a large ensemble.

Reicha, Anton. *Four Quartets.* arr. David R. Werden. Whaling Music Publishers. Two euphoniums and two tubas. 1983. $9.50. 8:20. IV. Part I: B♭–b♭'; Part II: F–b♭'; Part III: F–g♭'; Part IV: $B\flat_1$–g. Four movements: Theme and Variations; Minuetto; Andante; Allegro. All parts are technically challenging, though most of the melodic responsibility is in the first part. The last movement features a driving syncopated melody. The first part is printed in treble clef. Parts may be doubled for a large ensemble.

Reiche, Gottfried. *Sonata #15.* arr. Paul Schmidt. Heavy Metal Music. Two euphoniums and two tubas. 1991. $5.00. 3:10. III. Part I: d–f'; Part II: A–g; Part III: $B\flat_1$–d; Part IV: F_1–d♭. Two movements: Tenuto; Allegro. The first movement is in a chorale style. The second movement is very polyphonic, but not technically challenging. No score available. Parts may be doubled for a large ensemble.

Reiche, Gottfried. *Sonata #18.* arr. Paul Schmidt. Heavy Metal Music. Two euphoniums and two tubas. 1991. $5.00. 3:30. III–IV. Part I: B♭–g'; Part II: F–a; Part III: $B\flat_1$–f; Part IV: F_1–d. The texture is much less polyphonic than what is typical for this style period. Not technically difficult; very appropriate for high school ensembles. No score available. Parts may be doubled for a large ensemble.

Reinhardt, Django. *Nuages.* John Wessner. Two euphoniums and two tubas. 1993. $5.00. 2:00. IV. Part I: d–e♭"; Part II: B–c"; Part III: G_1–d' (a'); Part IV: G_1–b. The tessitura of the top two parts is high. The fourth part contains a section for an improvised jazz solo. Rhythm parts are included.

Renwick, Wilke. *Dance.* arr. Kenyon D. Wilson. Tromba Music Publishers. Two euphoniums and two tubas. 1994. 1:00. III. Part I: f–d"; Part II: d–b♭'; Part III: A–c'; Part IV: $B\flat_1$–f. Effective arrangement of this standard work for brass quintet. Depending upon tempo, double-tonguing may be required in the euphonium parts. Parts may be doubled for a large ensemble. Recorded by Symphonia on the compact disc *Symphonia Two: La Morte dell Oom,* Mark Records.

Richardson, Sharon. *Three Statements for Four Tubas.* Southern Music Company. Four tubas. 1971. Out of Print. 5:00. IV. Part I: A–f'; Part II: C–e'; Part III: C–d'; Part IV: F_1–g. Three movements. Could also be performed with a euphonium on the first or first and second parts. The second movement requires the second and third players to sing the syllable "doo" through their instrument. The last movement is the most challenging technically.

Rimmer. *The Mery Men.* Two euphoniums and two tubas.

Rimsky-Korsakov, Nicholai. *Procession of the Nobles.* arr. David Butler. Tuba-Euphonium Press. Two euphoniums and two tubas. 1993. $15.00. 3:30. IV. Part I: G–b♭'; Part II: A♭–e♭'; Part III: A♭–c'; Part IV: $A\flat_1$–a♭. Written for R. Winston Morris and the Tennessee Technological University Tuba Ensemble. Excellent arrangement of this familiar melody. Technically challenging for all parts. Will require a minimum of eight players (two on a part) as all parts have numerous *divisi* sections.

Rimsky-Korsakov, Nicolai. *Dance of the Tumblers.* arr. Al Fabrizio. Tuba-Euphonium Press. Two euphoniums and two tubas. 2000. $12.00. 3:30. III. Part I: (B♭) d♭–b♭'; Part II: c–b♭'; Part III: F–b♭; Part IV: F_1–e♭. To my friend Roger Behrend and the Navy Band Quartet. Challenging arrangement of this popular work. At the indicated tempo of quarter note equals 132–138, the nearly constant sixteenth note patterns will require technical dexterity. More appropriate for a quartet than for an ensemble.

Rimsky-Korsakov, Nicolai. *Flight of the Bumble Bee.* arr. Franz Watz. Musikverlag Bruno Uetz. One euphonium and three tubas. 1995. €14.00. 2:30. Second part may be performed on euphonium as well. More appropriate for a quartet than for an ensemble. Recorded by the Melton Tuba Quartett on the compact disc *Lazy Elephants,* Diavolo Records.

Rimsky-Korsakov, Nicolai. *Flight of the Bumble Bee.* arr. Maurice Bale. Godiva Music. Two euphoniums and two tubas. 1997. £6.00. 1:15. IV. Part I: G–d"; Part II: G–c"; Part III: F♯–d; Part IV: G_1–g. For Steven Mead.

Ripley, Hosea. *Fireman's Polka.* arr. Paul Schmidt. Heavy Metal Music. Two euphoniums and two tubas. $7.00. Part I: A–f'; Part II: F–a; Part III: E–c'; Part IV: $B\flat_1$–d. Interesting light polka, complete with fire bell, shouting, and singing. Parts may be doubled for a large ensemble.

Roark, Larry. *Intonation I. TUBA Journal.* Two euphoniums and two tubas. 1978. $7.50. 1:45. III. Part I: b♭–g'; Part II: e♭–c'; Part III: G–f; Part IV: C–d. Very playable for high school ensembles. Very pleasant quartal harmonies. Not technically demanding. Parts may be doubled for a large ensemble. Written as part of the TUBA Gem Series and distributed in the *TUBA Journal,* Vol. 7, No. 1. Available by purchasing this issue of the *TUBA Journal.*

Roark, Larry. *Intonation II.* Available from the composer. Two euphoniums and two tubas. 1:00. IV. Part I: f–b♭^{1}; Part II: c–e♭'; Part III: F♯–a♭'; Part IV: $G♭_1$–d♭. A nice chorale-like composition. Similar in style to *Intonation I,* but the range is slightly more demanding. Parts may be doubled for a large ensemble.

Robertson, Donna N. *Lullaby.* TMC Publications. Four tubas. Out of Print. 2:00. III–IV. Part I: d–f'; Part II: c–a; Part III: D–f; Part IV: A_1–d. This arrangement is based on a thirteenth-century noel. While written for four tubas, this would be easily playable by high school students if the first or first and second parts were played on euphonium. Very simple rhythmically. Parts may be doubled for a large ensemble.

Robertson, Gail, arr. *All Things Bright and Beautiful.* Tuba-Euphonium Press. Two euphoniums and two tubas. 1998. $12.00. 3:00. III–IV. Part I: G_1–c"; Part II: c–c"; Part III: G_1–c♭'; Part IV: F_1–a. Written for Laura Lineberger, euphonium soloist, U.S. Army Brass Band. Challenging set of theme and three variations. All parts contain virtuosic passages accompanied by the remaining three members. Serves well as an encore piece. Euphonium parts also available in treble clef. Also reviewed in the Summer 1999 issue of the *TUBA Journal* (Vol. 26, No. 4).

Robertson, Gail, arr. *Amazing Grace.* Tuba-Euphonium Press. Two euphoniums and two tubas. 1998. $10.00. 2:00. II. Part I: f♯–g'; Part II: c–d'; Part III: A_1–g; Part IV: (C_1) G_1–d. Dedicated to "Mamom." Effective arrangement of this traditional hymn. The verse is presented four times, with a different member of the ensemble performing the melody each time. Euphonium parts also available in treble clef. Parts may be doubled for a large ensemble.

Robertson, Gail, arr. *Jingle Bells.* Tuba-Euphonium Press. Two euphoniums and two tubas. 1997. $12.00. 1:30. II. Part I: c–a'; Part II: f–f'; Part III: F–b♭; Part IV: F_1–f. Straightforward arrangement of this Christmas song with the melodic material divided among all voices. Parts are formatted so they may be reduced to fit in a flip-folder. Parts may be doubled for a large ensemble.

Robertson, Gail, arr. *We Wish You a Merry Christmas.* Tuba-Euphonium Press. Two euphoniums and two tubas. 1998. $10.00. 2:00. II. Part I: G–g' (c"); Part II: G–g'; Part III: C–b♭; Part IV: C_1–e. This seasonal arrangement is in ternary form. The first section treats the tune in a traditional manner, the second shifts the meter from 3/4 to 4/4, and the final returns to the original meter with an ornamented flourish. It is accessible by intermediate-level performers. Parts may be doubled for a large ensemble. Also reviewed in the Summer 1999 issue of the *TUBA Journal* (Vol. 26, No. 4).

Roblee, Richard. *4-Tuba-Blues.* Musikverlag Bruno Uetz. One euphonium and three tubas. €17.00. Second part may be performed on euphonium as well. Recorded by the Melton Tuba Quartett on the compact disc *Power.*

Rodgers, Thomas. *Air for Tuba Ensemble.* Tuba-Euphonium Press. Two euphoniums and two tubas. 1993. $6.00. 4:00. IV. Part I: d–b♭'; Part II: d–f'; Part III: D–c'; Part IV: G_1–g. Written for R. Winston Morris and the Tennessee Technological University Tuba Ensemble. There are no real technical problems; the challenges are with range and playing lyrically. Musically very rewarding for both performers and audience. Written for and works best with a large ensemble. Originally copyrighted in 1981 and published by Laissez-Faire Music Publishing Company.

Rodgers, Thomas. *Preludio.* Two euphoniums and two tubas. 2:00. III–IV. Part I: d♭–e'; Part II: B♭–b♭; Part III: G–a; Part IV: F_1–d. Written for R. Winston Morris and the Tennessee Technological University Tuba Ensemble. Chorale-like in style with at least one part moving by itself on each beat of the measure. Many dynamic contrasts. Appropriate for high school students, especially to teach intonation and phrasing. Parts may be doubled for a large ensemble.

Rodgers, Thomas. *Thematic Permutations.* Tuba-Euphonium Press. Two euphoniums and two tubas. 1993. $10.00. 6:40. IV. Part I: A♭–b♭'; Part II: F–g♭'; Part III: A_1–c'; Part IV: F_1–a. Written for R. Winston Morris and the Tennessee Technological University Tuba Ensemble. A single movement with contrasting sections based on one main theme with several polyphonic sections. Several sections of the first part are notated in tenor clef. Good writing for tuba quartet. Originally published by Laissez-Faire Music Publishing Company and copyrighted in 1981. Parts may be doubled for a large ensemble.

Rodrigues, G. Matos. *La Cumparsita.* arr. David Schanke. Music Arts Publishing Company. Two euphoniums and two tubas with optional percussion. 1998. $16.00. 3:00. II. Part I: B♭–g'; Part II: B♭–f'; Part III: ($B♭_1$) F–f(g); Part IV: $B♭_1$–f. Fun arrangement based on this Argentine tango and appropriate for intermediate-level ensembles. First two parts are also available in treble clef, and the third part may also be performed on euphonium. Optional percussion includes snare and bass drums. Parts may be doubled for a large ensemble.

Roikjer, Kjell. *Ten Inventions for Four Tubaer Op. 64.* Engstrom and Sodring. Four tubas. 1990. 9 pp. IV. Part I: B–g♭'; Part II: E–d♭'; Part III: C–c'; Part IV: E_1–d'. The first part should be played on an F tuba or perhaps a euphonium. The movements contrast in tempo, meter, and key. They may be selected to form a suite or performed individually. Will require skilled performances by all four players.

Rollin, Robert. *Quodlibitus Bibendum (The Drinking Quodlibet) for Tuba Quartet.* Seesaw Music Corporation. Four tubas. 1983. $24.00. 3:00. IV. Part I: B♭–g♯'; Part II: F♯–b; Part III: $B\flat_1$–f♯'; Part IV: G_1–b. For John Turk, Ronald Bishop, Tucker Jolly, and Sumner Erickson. A euphonium may be used on the first part. The piece contains small quotations of Irish, French, English, German, and Scottish drinking songs. Not difficult technically, but the tessitura of the first part is high. Parts may be doubled for a large ensemble.

Rollin, Robert. *The Raven and the First Man.* Two euphoniums and two tubas.

Roper, Antony. *String of Tones.* Available from Tubalaté. Two euphoniums and two tubas. Recorded by Tubalaté on the compact disc *Earth and Moon.*

Rosenberger, W. *The Lyric Tuba Waltz.* Musikverlag Martin Scherbacher. Two euphoniums and two tubas. 1993. $15.00. 2:20. IV. Part I: A–b♭'; Part II: A–g'; Part III: D♯–b; Part IV: B_2–g. All parts have an opportunity to play portions of the melody. No significant technical problems. The top part is printed in bass and treble clef. Parts may be doubled for a large ensemble.

Ross, John. *Hymn.* Cimarron Music and Productions. Two euphoniums and two tubas. $14.50.

Ross, John. *Study on a Theme from Peter Grimes.* Cimarron Music and Productions. Two euphoniums and two tubas. $14.50.

Ross, Walter. *Shapes in Bronze.* Tuba-Euphonium Press. Two euphoniums and two tubas. 1992. $15.00. 11:00. IV. Part I: B♭–g'; Part II: F–f'; Part III: G_1–b♭; Part IV: F_1–g. Four movements. For R. Winston Morris and the Tennessee Technological University Tuba Ensemble. Four contrasting movements with the last movement the most technically demanding of the four. The tubas frequently have the melody throughout the work. Works very well, especially with the parts doubled.

Rossini, Giacchino. *Barber of Seville.* arr. Bryan V. Doughty. Cimarron Music and Productions. Two euphoniums and two tubas. 1997. $16.00. 7:00. III. Part I: A–a'; Part II: G–g'; Part III: A_1–b; Part IV: $F\sharp_1$–b. Abridged arrangement of this popular overture. The melodic material is shared among all members of the quartet. Euphonium parts also available in treble clef.

Rossini, Giacchino. *Dueling Barbers (of Seville).* arr. Robert Wilkinson. Cimarron Music and Productions. Two euphoniums and two tubas. 1995. $13.50. 4:15. III. Part I: B♭–b♭'; Part II: B♭–f'; Part III: F_1–g; Part IV: $B\flat_1$–f. Entertaining arrangement of the *Barber of Seville Overture* that features the first euphonium and first tuba in somewhat competitive roles, trading melodic material. Euphonium parts also available in treble clef. More appropriate for a quartet than for an ensemble.

Rossini, Giacchino. *La Danza.* arr. Peter Smalley. Studio Music Company. Two euphoniums and two tubas. 1996. Part I: G–b♭'; Part II: D–g'; Part III: C–e♭'; Part IV: G_1–g. Straightforward arrangement of a Neapolitan *Tarantella.* Euphonium parts also available in treble clef, first tuba parts also available in E♭ treble clef, and second tuba parts also available in B♭ treble clef. More appropriate for a quartet than for a large ensemble. Also reviewed in the Summer 1997 issue of the *TUBA Journal* (Vol. 24, No. 4). Recorded by the British Tuba Quartet on the compact disc *Elite Syncopations,* Polyphonic Records.

Rossini, Giacchino. *Tancredi Overture.* arr. Maurice Bale. Godiva Music. Two euphoniums and two tubas. £8.00.

Rossini, Giacchino. *William Tell Overture.* arr. Corey Dawson. Tuba-Euphonium Press. Two euphoniums and two tubas. 2001. $12.00. 1:30. III. Part I: c–c"; Part II: c–c"; Part III: C–c'; Part IV: F_1–a. This arrangement is excerpted from the final and best-known section of the overture. Depending upon the tempo, double-tonguing may be required in all parts. Melodic material is divided among the parts. Parts may be doubled for a large ensemble. Also reviewed in the Spring 2002 issue of the *ITEA Journal* (Vol. 29, No. 3).

Rossini, Giacchino. *William Tell Overture.* arr. David Schanke. Music Arts Publishing Company. Two euphoniums and two tubas. 2001. $16.00. 2:15. III. Part I: B♭–g' (b♭'); Part II: B♭–c'; Part III: ($B\flat_1$) G–g (b♭); Part IV: $B\flat_1$–e♭. This arrangement is excerpted from the final and best-known section of the overture. Depending upon the tempo, double-tonguing may be required in all parts. The first two parts are also available in treble clef, and the third part may also be performed on euphonium. Parts may be doubled for a large ensemble.

Rossini, Giacchino. *William Tell Overture.* arr. Peter Smalley. Studio Music Company. Two euphoniums and two tubas. £10.50. III–IV. Part I: G–e♭"; Part II: G–c"; Part III: $B\flat_1$–f'; Part IV: $E\flat_1$–b♭. Challenging arrangement of this well-known work. Every member of the quartet needs to be proficient in double-tonguing. More appropriate for a quartet than for a large ensemble. Euphonium parts also available in treble clef. Also reviewed in the Summer 2001 issue of the *TUBA Journal* (Vol. 28, No. 4). Recorded by the British Tuba Quartet on the compact disc *Euphonic Sounds,* Polyphonic Records.

Rossini, Gioacchino. *Allegro from William Tell Overture.* arr. Peter Rauch. Ohio Valley Tuba Quartet Press. Two euphoniums and two tubas. 1992. $10.00. 7:30. IV. Part I: A–b♭'; Part II: G–e♭'; Part III: $B\flat_1$–c'; Part IV: $E\flat_1$–e♭. Most of the melodic responsibility is in the top two parts, but the technical challenges are greatest on the top part. All players need accurate multiple tonguing skills. Will require four strong players.

Rossini, Gioacchino. *Overture to Wilhelm Tell.* arr. Bruno Seitz. Musikverlag Martin Scherbacher. Two euphoniums and two tubas. 1990. $13.50. 1:45. IV. Part I: B♭–c''; Part II: A–e♭'; Part III: D–c'; Part IV: E♭$_1$–e♭. The first part is the most challenging technically and has a high tessitura. All parts need to be played lightly and cleanly. Parts may be doubled for a large ensemble.

Rossini, Gioacchino. *Petit Caprice: In the Style of Offenbach.* arr. Ron Davis. Tuba-Euphonium Press. Two euphoniums and two tubas. 1993. $5.00. 3:20. IV. Part I: B♭–c''; Part II: E♭–g'; Part III: B♭$_1$–c'; Part IV: E♭$_1$–f♯. A very lively piece, challenging for all parts. The tessitura of the first part is high and the fourth part is quite low. Works well. Parts may be doubled for a large ensemble.

Rossini, Gioacchino. *William Tell Overture (abridged).* arr. Paul Schmidt. Heavy Metal Music. Two euphoniums and two tubas. 1991. $7.00. 1:30. IV. Part I: F–g'; Part II: F–f'; Part III: F–c♯'; Part IV: F$_1$–f. A shortened version of this famous overture. The melody is passed between the first, second, and third parts. Works very well for this genre and is fun to play. No score available. Parts may be doubled for a large ensemble.

Roundtree, Benjamin, arr. *Two Advent Chorals.* Roundtree Music. Two euphoniums and two tubas. 2003. $8.00. 2:00. II. Part I: d–b♭'; Part II: d–g'; Part III: c–c'; Part IV: F$_1$–f. Two movements: Lo! How a Rose E'er Blooming by Michael Praetorius; Break Forth, O Beauteous Heavenly Light by Johann Sebastian Bach. These arrangements, appropriate for intermediate-level performers, serve well as study pieces for warm-up and ensemble playing. The texture is homophonic and the harmonies are traditional. Parts may be doubled for a large ensemble.

Rozen, Jay. *Melody (x3).* Available from the composer. Two euphoniums and two tubas. 1994. A challenging one-movement piece in a driving, rhythmic style. Range considerations make the piece more appropriate for advanced players. Also reviewed in the Spring 1995 issue of the *TUBA Journal* (Vol. 22, No. 3).

Russell, Armand. *Transforming Realms.* Available from the composer. Two euphoniums and two tubas. 1983. $15.00. 9:00. IV. Part I: F–b♭'; Part II: F♯–g'; Part III: G$_1$–c'; Part IV: F♯$_1$–a♭. Technically challenging with several meter changes. Very contemporary harmonies, and many polychords and dissonant intervals.

Russell, Henry. *Ship on Fire.* arr. William R. Lee. Tuba-Euphonium Press. Two euphoniums, two tubas, and voice. 2003. $12.00. 3:30. II–III. Part I: A♭–g'; Part II: G–d'; Part III: B♭$_1$–g; Part IV: F♯$_1$–e♭. Combining voice with tuba/euphonium quartet, this piece is based on lyrics by Charles MacKay. The quartet serves an accompanimental role, and the parts are accessible by intermediate-level performers. Parts may be doubled for a large ensemble.

Ryder, Keith, and Paul Schmidt, arr. *Four German Pieces for Tuba Quartet.* Heavy Metal Music. Two euphoniums and two tubas. $7.00. Four movements: Lauterbach; Wintergrun; Eisenkeinest; Alte Kath. Written for the Heavy Metal Tuba Society Tuba Quartet. Fun work in the Bavarian style, designed for lighter performance settings. The first part contains most of the melodic material, though each part is interesting. Also reviewed in the Winter 1999 issue of the *TUBA Journal* (Vol. 26, No. 2).

Saint-Saëns, Camille. *Adagio from Symphony #3.* arr. Steve Hanson. KIWI Music Press. Two euphoniums and two tubas. $5.00. 3:00. III–IV. Part I: d–g'; Part II: c–f'; Part III: C–d'; Part IV: B♭$_1$–d♭. Nice arrangement of this familiar melody. No real technical or range problems. Parts may be doubled for a large ensemble.

Saint-Saëns, Camille. *Bacchanale from Samson and Delilah.* arr. Kenyon D. Wilson. Tuba-Euphonium Press. Two euphoniums, two tubas, and optional percussion. 1994. $15.00. 6:15. III. Part I: A–b♭' (c''); Part II: A–g'; Part III: F–c'; Part IV: G$_1$–e. Challenging arrangement of this popular piece known for its final dance section. Melodic material is divided among all voices, and there is an opening cadenza in the first euphonium part. The optional percussion includes timpani and castanets. Double-tonguing may be required at the indicated tempo. More appropriate for a large ensemble, as all parts have *divisi* passages. Also reviewed in the Spring 2002 issue of the *ITEA Journal* (Vol. 29, No. 3).

Saint-Saëns, Camille. *Two Movements from Carnival of the Animals.* arr. David Minchin. Breakthrough Music. Two euphoniums and two tubas. £8.00. 4:15. Part I: G–b♭'; Part II: G–b♭'; Part III: E♭$_1$–e♭'; Part IV: E♭$_1$–e♭'. Two movements: The Swan; The Elephant. The first movement features the euphoniums, while the second movement features the tubas. Recorded by Tubalaté on the compact disc *Light Metal.*

Salotti, Harry. *The Quest.* Tuba-Euphonium Press. Two euphoniums and two tubas. 1996. $12.00. 6:45. III. Part I: E–b♭'; Part II: A–b♭'; Part III: D♭–e'; Part IV: E$_1$–b♭. Multisectional original composition with modern harmonies. Melodic material is divided among all four voices, and there is a brief cadenza in the first part. Parts may be doubled for a large ensemble.

Sample, Steve, arr. *Cole Porter Medley.* T.A.P. Music. Two euphoniums, two tubas, piano/guitar, bass, and drums. 1978. $22.00. 3:45. IV–V. Part I: f–c''; Part II: G–a♭'; Part III: E♭–f'; Part IV: C–a. Written for R. Winston Morris and the Tennessee Technological University Tuba Ensemble. An excellent arrangement of "Easy to Love," "So in Love," and "You'd Be So Nice to Come Home to." The arrangement features both swing and bossa nova styles. All parts have interesting soli sections. Players will need a good swing feel. The top three parts have several *divisi* sections requiring seven players total to play all the parts. Will require strong players because of the high tessitura of the top three parts. Very enjoyable for performers and audience. Parts may be further doubled for a large ensemble. Recorded by the Tennessee Technological University Tuba Ensemble, KM Records, KM 4631.

Sample, Steve, arr. *Ellington Medley.* SOS Music Services. Two euphoniums, two tubas, piano/guitar, bass, and drums. 1974. Out of Print. 12:00. IV. Part I: d–c''; Part II: B♭–f♯'; Part III: B♭$_1$–c'; Part IV: A$_1$–a. Written for R. Winston Morris and the Tennessee Technological University Tuba Ensemble. One of the first jazz medleys for multiple tubas. This arrangement includes the selections "Satin Doll," "Mood Indigo," "Don't Get Around Much Anymore," "Sophisticated Lady," and "Take the A Train." There are several tempo and key changes. The tessitura of the top part is quite high and will require a strong player. All parts have some *divisi,* so two on a part are required to play all the written notes. Recorded by the Tennessee Technological University Tuba Ensemble, Golden Crest Records, CRS 4139.

Sample, Steve, arr. *Gershwin Medley.* T.A.P. Music. Two euphoniums, two tubas, piano/guitar, bass, and drums. 1979. $15.00. 3:20. IV–V. Part I: f–c''; Part II: e–a'; Part III: G–e♭'; Part IV: A$_1$–b♭. Written for R. Winston Morris and the Tennessee Technological University Tuba Ensemble. A swing medley of "They Can't Take That Away from Me," "Soon," and "A Foggy Day." Both euphoniums have a high tessitura and will require a good swing feel to work stylistically. Both tuba parts are featured melodically in different sections. This arrangement works quite well and is a real audience pleaser. All parts (except the fourth) require two players because of the extensive *divisi* sections. Parts may be further doubled for a large ensemble. Recorded by the Tennessee Technological University Tuba Ensemble, *Live!* KM Records, KM 5661; and the U.S. Armed Forces Tuba/Euphonium Ensemble, Mark Records, MW89MCD-8.

Sample, Steve, arr. *Harold Arlen Medley.* SOS Music Services. Two euphoniums, two tubas, piano/guitar, bass, and drums. 1982. $50.00. 5:20. IV. Part I: f–c''; Part II: B♭–g'; Part III: C–d♭'; Part IV: B♭$_1$–a. Written for R. Winston Morris and the Tennessee Technological University Tuba Ensemble. A medley of "Somewhere over the Rainbow," "My Shining Hour," "That Old Black Magic," and "Out of This World." Players will need a good jazz feel. The tessitura of the first part is high. The top three parts have numerous *divisi* sections, requiring a minimum of seven players for this arrangement. Parts may be further doubled for a large ensemble.

Sample, Steve, arr. *Nostalgia Medley.* SOS Music Services. Two euphoniums, two tubas, piano/guitar, bass, and drums. 1975. Out of Print. IV. Dedication: Written for R. Winston Morris and the Tennessee Technological University Tuba Ensemble.

Sample, Steve, arr. *Stella by Starlight.* SOS Music Services. Two euphoniums, two tubas, piano/guitar, bass, and drums. 1986. $50.00. 4:30. IV. Part I: g–c''; Part II: e–g'; Part III: C–c'; Part IV: A$_1$–g. The top two parts require a minimum of two players each. There is a section open for improvised solos. Chord changes are on all parts. The tessitura of the first part is high. A swing feel is necessary in all players. Parts may be further doubled for a large ensemble.

Sample, Steve, arr. *Tennessee Waltz.* SOS Music Services. Two euphoniums, two tubas, piano/guitar, bass, and drums. 1986. Out of Print. 4:30. IV. Part I: e♭–b♭'; Part II: c–f'; Part III: G–b♭; Part IV: B♭$_1$–g. Written for R. Winston Morris and the Tennessee Technological University Tuba Ensemble. The waltz has sections in 3/4, 2/4, 2/2, 4/4, and 5/4. There is a section with chord symbols in all parts for improvised solos. Rhythm parts are essential to the performance. Parts may be doubled for a large ensemble.

Sample, Steve, arr. *Two Tunes by Nacio Herb Brown.* SOS Music Services. Two euphoniums, two tubas, piano/guitar, bass, and drums. 1983. $50.00. 5:00. IV–V. Part I: g–d''; Part II: c–f'; Part III: G–d'; Part IV: G$_1$–g. Written for R. Winston Morris and the Tennessee Technological University Tuba Ensemble. A medley of "You Stepped out of a Dream" and "Temptation." The tessitura of the first part is very high. The first section is in a mambo style and bongos, tambourines, and other rhythm instruments should be used. The second section is a fast swing. Requires a good rhythmic feel in all players. Parts I, II, and IV require a minimum of two players each. Parts may be further doubled for a large ensemble. Recorded by the Tennessee Technological University Tuba Ensemble, *All That Jazz,* Mark Records, MES-20608.

Sample, Steve, arr. *Waltzing with Irving.* SOS Music Services. Two euphoniums, two tubas, piano/guitar, bass, and drums. 1984. $50.00. 3:30. IV. Part I: f–b♭'; Part II: d–a'; Part III: F–d'; Part IV: B♭$_1$–b♭. Written for R. Winston Morris and the Tennessee Technological University Tuba Ensemble. A medley of "What'll I Do?" "Always," and "Remember." The tessitura of the top part is high. The top three parts have many *divisi* sections and will require two players each. Rhythm parts are essential to maintain a good jazz waltz feel. Works well. Parts may be further doubled for a large ensemble.

Sanson, Dacide. *Scherzo.* Animado Music Publisher, Sondrio. Two euphoniums and two tubas. 2000.

4:30. III. Part I: F–a'; Part II: f–a'; Part III: C–c'; Part IV: F_1–a♭. This scherzo is a lively multimetric work with large passages in 7/8. All parts are interesting, and the syncopation and overlapping of lines provide the greatest challenges to the ensemble. Works well as a concert opener. Parts may be doubled for a large ensemble.

Satie, Erik. *First Gymnopedie.* arr. Peter Rauch. Ohio Valley Tuba Quartet Press. Two euphoniums and two tubas. 1988. $8.00. 2:10. IV. Part I: e–a'; Part II: d–a'; Part III: A_1–b; Part IV: (D_1) A_1–a. A very lyrical melody passed primarily between the top three parts. No significant technical problems. Parts may be doubled for a large ensemble.

Satie, Eric. *Gymnopedia No. 1 from Three Gymnopedies.* arr. Peter Rauch. Cimarron Music and Productions. Two euphoniums and two tubas. 1998. $10.00. 3:00. II–III. Part I: f♯–a'; Part II: d–a'; Part III: A_1–b; Part IV: (D_1) A_1–a. Originally for piano. This arrangement divides the melodic material evenly among the four parts. The texture is homophonic with the traditional *gymnopedia* accompaniment emphasizing the first and second beats. Euphonium parts also available in treble clef. Parts may be doubled for a larger ensemble.

Satie, Erik. *Le Piccadilly.* arr. Hirokazu Hiraishi. Sonic Arts, Incorporated. Two euphoniums and two tubas. 1986. $11.00. 2:00. IV. Part I: F–a'; Part II: F–d'; Part III: C–f; Part IV: F_1–d. A cute syncopated melody passed around to each part. No significant technical problems. Parts may be doubled for a large ensemble.

Scarlatti, Alessandro. *Sonata.* arr. Paul Schmidt. Heavy Metal Music. Two euphoniums and two tubas. $7.00. III. Part I: G–e'; Part II: F–d'; Part III: A–e'; Part IV: A_1–f♯. Three movements. Straightforward arrangement of this baroque work likely written for flute, two violins, and continuo. The upper three voices perform in a contrapuntal, imitative fashion, while the fourth part performs the basso continuo. Third part may also be performed on euphonium.

Schanke, David, arr. *American Song Suite.* Music Arts Publishing Company. Two euphoniums and two tubas. 2000. $16.00. 5:30. II. Part I: B♭–a♭'; Part II: B♭–e♭'; Part III: ($B\flat_1$) F–a♭; Part IV: $B\flat_1$–f. Three movements: Shenandoah; Sweet Betsy from Pike; Listen to the Mocking Bird. American folk songs in a nice arrangement appropriate for intermediate-level performers. Each part has the melody at some point. The first two parts are also available in treble clef, and the third part may also be performed on euphonium. Parts may be doubled for a large ensemble. Any of the move ments can stand alone in a concert.

Schanke, David, arr. *Mexican Song Medley, Set No. 1.* Music Arts Publishing Company. Two euphoniums and two tubas. 1997. $16.00. 3:45. II. Part I: c–a♭'; Part II: c–d♭'; Part III: C–g; Part IV: ($A\flat_1$) $B\flat_1$–d. Single-movement medley includes "Cielito Lindo," "Las Gaviotas," "La Cucaracha," and "Jarabe Tapatio." Each part has the melody at some point, and the piece is appropriate for intermediate-level performers. Euphonium parts also available in treble clef. Parts may be doubled for a large ensemble.

Schanke, David, arr. *Mexican Song Medley, Set No. 2.* Music Arts Publishing Company. Two euphoniums and two tubas. 2003. $16.00. 4:30. II. Part I: e♭–g'; Part II: d–g'; Part III: (E♭) G–f; Part IV: $B\flat_1$–e♭. Single-movement medley includes "Chiapanecas," "Carmela," "Ay, Ay, Ay," and "Zacatecas." Each part has the melody at some point, and the piece is appropriate for intermediate-level performers. The first two parts are also available in treble clef, and the third part may also be performed on euphonium. Parts may be doubled for a large ensemble.

Scheidt, Samuel. *Galliard Battaglia.* arr. Allyn Lindsey. Cimarron Music and Productions. Two euphoniums and two tubas. $16.00. Euphonium parts also available in treble clef.

Schein, Johann H. *Pavan a 4.* arr. Paul Schmidt. Heavy Metal Music. Two euphoniums and two tubas. 1991. $5.00. 1:45. IV. Part I: d–d'; Part II: B–g; Part III: G–g; Part IV: $B\flat_1$–B♭. Very polyphonic; technically the most challenging for the first part. No score available. Parts may be doubled for a large ensemble.

Schlesinger, Scott. *Song without Words.* Tuba-Euphonium Press. Two euphoniums and two tubas. 2002. $12.00. 3:30. III. Part I: d–a'; Part II: d–e♭'; Part III: $B\flat_1$–d♯'; Part IV: $F\sharp_1$–g. Effective original composition with rock and swing elements. All parts are rhythmically driven with syncopated patterns and frequent meter changes. Parts may be doubled for a large ensemble.

Schlesinger, Scott, arr. *Four Polkas.* Tuba-Euphonium Press. One euphonium and three tubas. 2003. $12.00. 5 pp. II. Part I: c–a'; Part II: c–f'; Part III: D–c'; Part IV: F_1–d. Four movements: Das Wandern ist des Mullers Lust; Die Wacht am Rhein; Um die Ecke rum; Wenzel Polka. This collection of four polkas contains two traditionally scored ones and two that lack the characteristic bass line. Parts may be doubled for a large ensemble. Individual movements can stand alone on a concert.

Schmelzer, J. H. *Three Pieces for Horseballet.* arr. Paul Schmidt. Heavy Metal Music. Two euphoniums and two tubas. 1990. $3.00. 2:45. III. Part I: e♭–f'; Part II: c–f'; Part III: E♭–a♭; Part IV: $A\flat_1$–E♭. Three movements: Courante for His Majesty the King and All His Calvary; Follia to Begin More of the Jumping and Other Horse Exercises; Sarabande for Concluding the Ballet. A traditional homophonic texture with the melody primarily in the first part. No significant technical problems. No score available. Parts may be doubled for a large ensemble.

Schmidt, Dankwart, arr. *Bayerische Polka*. Editions Marc Reift. Two euphoniums and two tubas. 1994. CHF 22.00. 2:30. III. Part I: E♭$_1$–a♭'; Part II: E♭$_1$–e♭'; Part III: E♭$_1$–c'; Part IV: E♭$_1$–a♭. Fun and well-set arrangement of this popular Bavarian folk song. Recorded by Contraband on the compact disc *Swingin' Low,* Marcophon.

Schmidt, Dankwart, arr. *Tuba Muckl*. Editions Marc Reift. Two euphoniums and two tubas. 1994. CHF 19.00. 1:15. IV. Part I: B♭$_1$–b♭'; Part II: B♭$_1$–b♭'; Part III: F–b♭; Part IV: F$_1$–f. A popular Bavarian tune, originally for clarinet; the virtuosic solo part is in the first euphonium. Recorded by Contraband on the compact disc *Swingin' Low,* Marcophon.

Schmidt, Nicklas. *The Day We Buried Vanya*. Available from Tubalaté. Two euphoniums and two tubas. Recorded by Tubalaté on the compact disc *Hall of Mirrors.*

Schmidt, Paul, arr. *Christmas Bell Songs*. Heavy Metal Music. Two euphoniums and two tubas. 1991. $5.00. 2:30. III–IV. Part I: c–f'; Part II: B♭–a♭; Part III: F–e♭; Part IV: F$_1$–B♭. Two movements: Carol of the Bells; Jingle Bells. Very playable arrangement of these two familiar melodies. The melody is in the first part. No score available. Parts may be doubled for a large ensemble.

Schmidt, Paul, arr. *Civil War Suite No. 1.* Heavy Metal Music. Two euphoniums and two tubas. 1994. $7.00. 5:00. II–III. Part I: d–g'; Part II: G–e♭'; Part III: E♭–e♭'; Part IV: G$_1$–e♭. Three movements: Gary Owen; Stonewall Jackson's Way; Just before the Battle by George Root. A collection of pieces dating from the American Civil War. The first movement is the famous Irish jig usually associated with leprechauns. The second and third movements are a chorale and a ballad, respectively. Individual movements can stand alone in a concert. Parts may be doubled for a large ensemble. Also reviewed in the Spring 1995 issue of the *TUBA Journal* (Vol. 22, No. 3).

Schmidt, Paul, arr. *Civil War Suite No. 2.* Heavy Metal Music. Two euphoniums and two tubas. 1994. $7.00. 5:15. II–III. Part I: B♭–f'; Part II: F–d♭'; Part III: C–c'; Part IV: (F$_1$) A♭$_1$–d. Three movements: The Battle Cry of Freedom; Shenandoah; When Johnny Comes Marching Home. A collection of pieces dating from the American Civil War. The first and third movements are marches, and the second is a folk song. All parts are interesting and may be doubled for a large ensemble. Individual movements can stand alone in a concert.

Schmidt, Paul, arr. *Civil War Suite No. 3.* Heavy Metal Music. Two euphoniums and two tubas. 1993. $7.00. 2:30. II–III. Part I: B♭–f'; Part II: A–f'; Part III: B♭$_1$–d'; Part IV: F$_1$–c. Two movements: Battle Hymn of the Republic; Dixie. A collection of pieces dating from the American Civil War. The first movement is a march and the second movement is an upbeat song. Parts may be doubled for a large ensemble. Individual movements can stand alone in a concert.

Schmidt, Paul, arr. *The Cuckoo.* Heavy Metal Music. Two euphoniums, two tubas, with optional flute, recorder, or whistle. 1990. $5.00. 1:20. IV. Part I: B♭–g'; Part II: c–f'; Part III: F–b♭; Part IV: C–e♭. Cute arrangement of this humorous traditional Swiss melody. The Cuckoo notes are written in the fourth part. No score available. Parts may be doubled for a large ensemble.

Schmidt, Paul, arr. *Emilia Polka*. Heavy Metal Music. Two euphoniums and two tubas. 1991. $7.00. 3:30. IV. Part I: B♭–e♭'; Part II: A♭–d'; Part III: C–c'; Part IV: G$_1$–d♭. A traditional polka with most of the melody in the top part. No range problems. No score available. Parts may be doubled for a large ensemble.

Schmidt, Paul, arr. *Evergreen Polka*. Heavy Metal Music. Two euphoniums and two tubas. 1990. $7.00. 3:30. IV. Part I: c–f'; Part II: A–g'; Part III: C–b♭; Part IV: F$_1$–B♭. Most of the melodic responsibility lies in the top two parts. Drums can be added for stylistic enhancement. Very traditional harmonies. No score available. Parts may be doubled for a large ensemble.

Schmidt, Paul, arr. *Helena Polka*. Heavy Metal Music. Two euphoniums and two tubas. 1991. $7.00. 3:30. IV. Part I: e♭–f'; Part II: c–a♭'; Part III: E♭–e♭'; Part IV: F$_1$–e♭. Good arrangement of this traditional polka. Most of the melody is in the top part. No significant technical challenges. No score available. Parts may be doubled for a large ensemble.

Schmidt, Paul, arr. *Three Christmas Carols*. Heavy Metal Music. Two euphoniums and two tubas. 1991. $5.00. 2:45. III. Part I: c–f'; Part II: G–c'; Part III: D–g; Part IV: F$_1$–A. Three movements: O Holy Night; O How Joyfully; O Come, Little Children. A fairly easy arrangement of these three familiar melodies. The melody is primarily in the top part. No score available. Parts may be doubled for a large ensemble.

Schmidt, Paul, arr. *Three Christmas Carols I.* Heavy Metal Music. Two euphoniums and two tubas. 1991. $5.00. 2:30. III–IV. Part I: d–g'; Part II: B♭–e♭'; Part III: D–g; Part IV: F$_1$–c. Three movements: Vom Himmel Hoch; In the Bleak Midwinter; O Tannenbaum. Three short and contrasting Christmas melodies in a traditional setting. Very appropriate for high school students. No score available. Parts may be doubled for a large ensemble.

Schmidt, Paul, arr. *Three Christmas Carols II.* Heavy Metal Music. Two euphoniums and two tubas. 1991. $7.00. 3:00. III. Part I: B♭–f'; Part II: A–d♭'; Part III: F–a♭; Part IV: G$_1$–f. Three movements: Macht auf die Tor; Make We Joy; Übers Gebirg Maria Geht. A very traditional arrangement of three familiar Christmas melodies. The third movement has a polyphonic texture, but is not difficult technically. Very appropriate for high school players. No score available. Parts may be doubled for a large ensemble.

Schmidt, Paul, arr. *Three German Songs*. Heavy Metal Music. Two euphoniums and two tubas. 1990. $7.00. 4:30. III–IV. Part I: B–f'; Part II: G–e♭'; Part III: $B\flat^1$–e♭'; Part IV: F_1–a (b♭). Three movements: Deutschland Uber Alles; Tomorrow Belongs to Me; Edelweiss. Nice arrangement of these traditional German and Austrian melodies. With just a couple of exceptions, the melody is in the first part. Good programming for those fall German festivals. No score available. Parts may be doubled for a large ensemble.

Schmidt, Paul, arr. *Tinker Polka*. Heavy Metal Music. Two euphoniums two tubas. 1990. $7.00. 3:30. III–IV. Part I: d–g'; Part II: G–b♭; Part III: F–b♭; Part IV: $B\flat_1$–f. Not technically difficult. The melody is primarily in the top part. No score available. Parts may be doubled for a large ensemble.

Schmidt, Paul, arr. *Two Christmas Carols*. Heavy Metal Music. Two euphoniums and two tubas. 1991. $5.00. 2:00. III–IV. Part I: B♭–g♭'; Part II: A f'; Part III: $B\flat_1$–b♭; Part IV: F_1–e♭. Two movements: Masters in This Hall; Once in Royal David's City. Each part has an opportunity to play the melody. No significant technical problems. No score available. Parts may be doubled for a large ensemble.

Schmidt, Paul, arr. *Two Madrigals*. Heavy Metal Music. Two euphoniums and two tubas. 1990. $7.00. 3:00. III–IV. Part I: d–e'; Part II: A–d'; Part III: E–f; Part IV: F_1–c. Two movements: Weep, O Mine Eyes; Fair Phyllis I Saw. The first movement is slow and somber, while the second is fast and has a humorous character. Both movements are very polyphonic, though not technically difficult. No score available. Parts may be doubled for a large ensemble.

Schmidt, Paul, arr. *Two Old Songs*. Heavy Metal Music. Two euphoniums and two tubas. 1990. $5.00. 2:10. IV. Part I: B–g'; Part II: F–f'; Part III: $A\flat_1$–g; Part IV: G_1–d. Two movements: K-K-K-Katy; Toot, Toot Tootsie Goodbye. Fun arrangement of two melodies from the 1920s. No significant technical problems. Drums may be added for effect. No score available. Parts may be doubled for a large ensemble.

Schmidt, Paul, arr. *Two Sackbut Quartets*. Heavy Metal Music. Two euphoniums and two tubas. 1992. $7.00. 3:00. IV. Part I: c–g'; Part II: B♭–b♭; Part III: $B\flat_1$–b♭; Part IV: F_1–f. Two movements: In Te Domini, Speravi; In Nomine. For Ascanio Sforza. These two works are by Josquin des Prez and Orlando Gibbons respectively. They are very polyphonic, with primary melodic responsibility in the top three parts. No score available. Parts may be doubled for a large ensemble.

Schoendorff, Matthew. *Adagio*. Tuba-Euphonium Press. Two euphoniums and two tubas. 2002. $10.00. 4:45. II. Part I: d–a♭'; Part II: B♭–a♭' (b'); Part III: F–b♭; Part IV: C–f. Transcription by the composer of his *Adagio* for four euphoniums. It is a tonal work in ternary form with flowing melodies and sonorous harmonies. All parts require mutes, and parts may be doubled for a large ensemble. Also reviewed in the Spring 2004 issue of the *ITEA Journal* (Vol. 31, No. 3).

Schoendorff, Matthew. *The Bridge*. Tuba-Euphonium Press. Two euphoniums and two tubas. 2002. $10.00. 5:00. III. Part I: c–a'; Part II: A♭–g'; Part III: $G\flat_1$–g; Part IV: E_1–c. Nice original composition with dissonance and harmonic tension throughout. Parts may be doubled for a large ensemble. Optional mutes are indicated in both euphonium parts. Parts may be doubled for a large ensemble. Also reviewed in the Spring 2004 issue of the *ITEA Journal* (Vol. 31, No. 3).

Schooley, John. *Cherokee for Tuba Quartet*. Heilman Music. Two euphoniums and two tubas. 1984. $15.00. 5:00. IV. Part I: G–a'; Part II: G–e'; Part III: D–b♭; Part IV: D_1–g. Dedicated to Melodie. Schooley refers to this as a tone poem for tuba ensemble. The piece does progress through different styles, tempos, and tonalities. One section shifts frequently between 3/4, 5/8, and 7/8. The two euphonium parts are printed in both bass and treble clef. Offers a change of pace in a recital program. Parts may be doubled for a large ensemble. Recorded by Northern Tuba Lights.

Schooley, John. *Toccata for Euphonium/Tuba Quartet*. Heilman Music. Two euphoniums and two tubas. 1984. $15.00. 5:00. IV. Part I: B–b♭'; Part II: F–a♭'; Part III: C–b♭; Part IV: (C_1) $E\flat_1$–f. Dedicated to Jonathan. A tuneful original composition, very contrapuntal in style. Technically not too difficult; most of the melodic activity is in the top two euphonium parts and both parts are printed in bass and treble clef. Parts may be doubled for a large ensemble.

Schroeder, John. *Aria*. arr. Jan Krzywicki. Tuba-Euphonium Press. Two euphoniums and two tubas. 2000. $8.00. 1:45. I. Part I: c–g'; Part II: A♭–d'; Part III: A♭–a♭; Part IV: F_1–c. For Pete and friends. This brief ballad with traditional harmonies is appropriate for young ensembles. All players read from the score, which helps this piece serve as an intonation study. Parts may be doubled for a large ensemble. Euphonium parts available only in treble clef.

Schubert, Franz. *Ballet Music from Rosamunde*. arr. Maurice Bale. Godiva Music. Two euphoniums and two tubas. £6.00.

Schubert, Franz. *Chor der Engel*. arr. Angelo Manzo. Tuba-Euphonium Press. Two euphoniums and two tubas. 2002. $10.00. 2:30. I. Part I: f–g'; Part II: c♯–c'; Part III: D–g; Part IV: A_1–e♭. Four-part chorale with traditional harmonies. This arrangement is an excellent piece for younger performers and can serve effectively as an intonation study for more advanced ensembles. Also reviewed in the Summer 2004 issue of the *ITEA Journal* (Vol. 31, No. 4).

Schubert, Franz. *Die Forelle (The Trout)*. arr. David LeClair. Editions Marc Reift. Two euphoniums and two tubas with drums. 2001. €17.50. 7:15. III. Part I: f–c"; Part II: c♯–g'; Part III: C–d♭'; Part IV: D_1–a. Theme and five variations based on Schubert's *Trout Quintet*. The opening section is a direct arrangement of Schubert's work, but the subsequent variations are composed by LeClair with a jazz influence. In addition to bass clef parts, euphonium parts are also available in treble, first tuba parts also available in E♭ treble, and second tuba also available in E♭ and B♭ treble clef. Parts may be doubled for a large ensemble. Recorded by Contraband on the compact disc *The Dragon's Dance,* Marcophon Records.

Schubert, Franz. *Minuet and Trio from Symphony No. 5.* arr. Maurice Bale. Godiva Music. Two euphoniums and two tubas. £6.00.

Schubert, Franz. *Serenade.* arr. Gail Robertson. Tuba-Euphonium Press. Two euphoniums and two tubas. 1999. $10.00. 2:45. II–III. Part I: d–a'; Part II: c–g'; Part III: G–b; Part IV: (D_1) F_1–g. Slow, lyrical ballad arranged with melodic material divided among the top three parts. Individual parts are not difficult. Euphonium parts also available in treble clef. Parts may be doubled for a large ensemble.

Schuller, Gunther. *Five Moods for Tuba Quartet.* Associated Music Publishers. Four tubas. 1976. Out of Print. 6:45. V. Part I: $F\sharp_1$–b'; Part II: E_1–$f\sharp^1$; Part III: E_1–d'; Part IV: $E\flat_1$–d'. Five movements: Lament; Allegro moderato; Adagio misterioso; Molto lento, Broodingly; Allegro Volando. Commissioned by Harvey Phillips. Dedicated to the memory of William Bell. According to the composer, this composition "tries to capture in vignette portraits the different characteristic traits of this remarkable man." Extreme ranges, technical demands, and wide skips make this a most complex and challenging work. An F tuba would be needed on the first and probably the second parts. Many contemporary techniques including multiphonics and tapping the mouthpiece and horn. Mutes are required for all four parts. Written for the First International Tuba Symposium-Workshop. Recorded by the New York Tuba Quartet, *Tubby's Revenge,* Crystal Records, S221.

Schulz, Patrick. *Tuba Quartet No. 1.* Tuba-Euphonium Press. Two euphoniums and two tubas. 1999. $25.00. 12:00. III–IV. Part I: F♯–b♭'; Part II: E–a♭'; Part III: B_1–d'; Part IV: $B\flat_2$–b♭. Five movements. To the Sotto Voce Tuba Quartet. Challenging original composition consisting of five contrasting movements with modern harmonies, frequent meter changes, and cross-voicing. The slow movements feature each part with exposed lyrical passages, while the fast movements are rhythmically driving. Parts may be doubled for a large ensemble.

Schumann, Clara. *Fugue No. 2.* arr. Angelo Manzo. Tuba-Euphonium Press. Two euphoniums and two tubas. 2001. $12.00. 2:00. II. Part I: d–a'; Part II: A–d'; Part III: C–g; Part IV: G_1–d. Brief four-voice fugue in a traditional contrapuntal style. Parts may be doubled for a large ensemble. Also reviewed in the Spring 2003 issue of the *ITEA Journal* (Vol. 30, No. 3).

Schumann, Clara. *Prelude and Fugue No. 3.* tr. Angelo Manzo. Tuba-Euphonium Press. Two euphoniums and two tubas. 2002. $12.00. 4:00. II. Part I: c♯–b♭'; Part II: G–e'; Part III: D–b♭; Part IV: F_1–e♭. Straightforward arrangement of this four-voice fugue in a traditional style. All parts are interesting yet rhythmically simple, which makes this work appropriate to younger ensembles. Parts may be doubled for a large ensemble. Also reviewed in the Spring 2004 issue of the *ITEA Journal* (Vol. 31, No. 3).

Schumann, Robert. *Classics for Low Brass Quartet, Set No. 1.* arr. David Schanke. Music Arts Company. Two euphoniums and two tubas. 1991. $12.50. 2:00. III. Part I: B♭–e♭'; Part II: B♭–c'; Part III: A–f; Part IV: $A\flat_1$–e♭. Two movements: The Merry Farmer, op. 68, no. 10; Soldier's March, op. 68, no. 2. Easy arrangement of two songs by Schumann. Excellent for young players. The top two parts are printed in bass and treble clef. Parts may be doubled for a large ensemble.

Schumann, Robert. *Classics for Low Brass Quartet, Set No. 2.* arr. David Schanke. Music Arts Company. Two euphoniums and two tubas. 1991. $12.50. 2:20. III–IV. Part I: B♭–e♭'; Part II: B♭–c'; Part III: A♭–g; Part IV: $A\flat_1$–d♭. Two movements: Andante con Expresione, op. 68, no. 26; The Wild Horseman, op. 68, no. 8. The two songs contrast in style and meter. No significant range or technical problems. The top two parts are printed in both bass and treble clef. Parts may be doubled for a large ensemble.

Schumann, Robert. *The Horseman.* arr. Robert Wilkinson. Cimarron Music and Productions. Two euphoniums and two tubas. $11.00. Euphonium parts also available in treble clef.

Schumann, Robert. *Norse Song.* arr. Robert Wilkinson. Cimarron Music and Productions. Two euphoniums and two tubas. $10.00. Euphonium parts also available in treble clef.

Schumann, Robert. *Piece in Folk Style.* arr. David R. Werden. Whaling Music Publishers. Three euphoniums and one tubas. 1981. $5.00. 2:20. IV. Part I: F–b♭'; Part II: B♭–a♭'; Part III: G♭–e♭'; Part IV: $G\flat_1$–a♭. This is an arrangement for euphonium/tuba quartet of the second movement from *Five Pieces in a Folk Style,* which Paul Droste transcribed for euphonium and piano. No real technical difficulties. The first euphonium part is printed in treble clef. Parts may be doubled for a large ensemble.

Schumann, Robert. *Suite from Album for the Young.* arr. David R. Werden. Whaling Music Publishers. Two euphoniums and two tubas. 1980. $9.50. 5:00. IV. Part I: B–c"; Part II: G–g'; Part III: G_1–f'; Part IV: G_1–g. Four movements: Wilder Reiter (Wild Rider); Armes Waisenkind (Poor Orphan); Frohlicher Landman (Happy Farmer); Kriegslied (War Song). Good arrangement of four contrasting Schumann songs. The tessitura of the first part is high. The top two parts are printed in treble clef. No significant technical challenges. Parts may be doubled for a large ensemble.

Schumann, Robert. *Suite from Album for the Young.* arr. Stephen Shoop. Southern Music Company. Two euphoniums and two tubas. 1993. $7.95. 4:45. III–IV. Part I: B♭–e♭'; Part II: A–d'; Part III: A♭$_1$–f; Part IV: F_1–e♭. Five movements: Chorale; The Happy Farmer; Melody; The Wild Rider; Soldier's March. All four parts have an opportunity to play the melody. No significant range or technical problems. Very appropriate for good high school players. Parts may be doubled for a large ensemble.

Schumann, Robert. *Suite No. 2 from Album for the Young.* arr. Stephen Shoop. Cimarron Music and Productions. Two euphoniums and two tubas. 1995. $11.00. 6:45. II. Part I: G–b♭'; Part II: F–g'; Part III: C–b♭; Part IV: F_1–d. Five movements: Rustic Song; Folk Song; Sailors' Song; Little Romance; Harvest Song. All four parts have an opportunity to perform the melody in this arrangement for young ensembles. Euphonium parts also available in treble clef. Parts may be doubled for a large ensemble.

Schumann, Robert. *Three Hunting Songs.* arr. Rudy Emilson. Kendor Music, Incorporated. Two euphoniums and two tubas. 2001. $10.00. 6:20. III. Part I: B–g'; Part II: B♭–f'; Part III: G–d'; Part IV: G_1–c'. Three movements: Wake Up! The Hunt Is Glorious; Be Intent!; Drinking Song. Arrangement of three songs from Schumann's *Five Hunting Songs,* op. 137. Large leaps and ranges in the third and fourth parts may be challenging for intermediate-level performers. Traditional harmonies with frequent tutti rhythms. Parts may be doubled for a large ensemble.

Schumann, Robert. *Traumerei.* arr. Bruno Seitz. Musikverlag Martin Scherbacher. Two euphoniums and two tubas. 1991. $13.50. 2:50. III–IV. Part I: A♭–g♭'; Part II: G♭–c'; Part III: D♭–f; Part IV: F_1–B♭. Very lyrical with the melody predominantly in the first part. This may also be played with one euphonium and three tubas. The first part is printed in bass and treble clef. Parts may be doubled for a large ensemble. Recorded by the Melton Tuba Quartett, *Premiere,* Diavolo Records, DR-D-93–C001.

Schutz, Heinrich. *Chorale (Psalm 97).* arr. Daniel Heiman. Heavy Metal Music. Two euphoniums and two tubas. 1992. $5.00. 1:00. III–IV. Part I: d–f'; Part II: A–a; Part III: D–f; Part IV: G_1–A. A slow, lyrical chorale. The meter is constantly shifting. No range problems. Players read from a single score. Parts may be doubled for a large ensemble.

Schutz, Heinrich. *Ego Sum Tui Plaga Doloris.* arr. Mark Nelson. Whaling Music Publishers. Two euphoniums and two tubas. 1991. $10.00. 2:20. III–IV. Part I: f–g'; Part II: B♭–c'; Part III: E♭–g; Part IV: B♭$_1$–e♭. Very playable by high school students. The texture is polyphonic but it is not difficult technically. Parts may be doubled for a large ensemble.

Sciortino, Patrice. *Figures.* Editions Billaudot. Four tubas. €50.25.

Scott, James. *Frog Legs Rag.* arr. Stephen Shoop. Cimarron Music and Productions. Two euphoniums and two tubas. 1995. $10.50. 4:45. II. Part I: G–a'; Part II: F–f'; Part III: A_1–a; Part IV: A_1–g. Originally for piano, this rag is one of the composer's more popular ones and is in the same style as Scott Joplin's rags. The parts are rhythmically challenging, and each voice has melodic material at some point. Euphonium parts also available in treble clef. Parts may be doubled for a large ensemble.

Scott, Stuart. *Fellscape.* Breakthrough Music. Two euphoniums and two tubas. £11.95. Part I: B–a♯'; Part II: A–g'; Part III: G_1–e♭'; Part IV: G_1–g. Written especially for the quartet Tubalaté and inspired by the composer's visits, observations, and feelings about the northern fells. Fellscape was selected for the ITEC 2002 Quartet competition. Recorded by Tubalaté on the compact disc *Earth and Moon.*

Seitz, Bruno. *Four Tuben im 3/4 Takt-Volksweise.* Musikverlag Martin Scherbacher. Four tubas. 1988. $13.50. 1:45. III–IV. Part I: B♭–e♭'; Part II: G–d'; Part III: G–g; Part IV: G_1–d. A nice lyrical melody with no technical problems. Easily playable by high school students if a euphonium is used on the first and second parts. The parts may be doubled for a large ensemble.

Seitz, Bruno. *Tuba Muckl Polka.* Musikverlag Martin Scherbacher. Two euphoniums and two tubas. 1988. $13.50. 2:20. IV. Part I: G–f'; Part II: E♭–d'; Part III: E♭–b♭; Part IV: F_1–d. Could also be played with one euphonium and three tubas or four tubas. A short, fun polka with most of the melody and technical challenges in the first part. The parts may be doubled for a large ensemble.

Seitz, Lockhart. *The World Is Waiting for the Sunrise.* arr. David Butler. Tuba-Euphonium Press. Two euphoniums and two tubas. 1996. $10.00. 2:45. III. Part I: d–b♭' (e♭"); Part II: d–a♭'; Part III: A–c'; Part IV: (E♭$_1$) F_1–e♭. For the Tennessee Tech Tuba Ensemble. This march has long been a favorite of brass players, especially for the familiar euphonium obbligato, which has been left intact in this arrangement. The lower three parts are accessible to intermediate-level performers, though the top part requires strong players. Euphonium parts also available in treble clef. More appropriate for a large ensemble, as all parts contain *divisi* passages. Recorded by the Tennessee Tech Tuba Ensemble on the compact disc *Unleash the Beast!*, Mark Records.

Seivewright, Andrew. *Gowbarrow Gavotte*. Available from Tubalaté. Two euphoniums and two tubas. Recorded by Tubalaté on the compact disc *Earth and Moon*.

Self, James. *Poker Chips*. Basset Hound Music. Four tubas and vibraphone. 1993. IV–V. A multi-movement work with the name of each movement representing a different term in poker and a musical aspect (i.e., Five-Card Stud will be in 5/4). Interesting timbres with the vibraphone. A fun piece for audiences. Work in progress.

Self, James, arr. *Carolina*. James Self. Two euphoniums and two tubas. 1969. Out of Print. 1:30. III–IV. Part I: c–c' (a'); Part II: A–a♭ (f'); Part III: F–g (c'); Part IV: C–f. Barbershop style harmonies of this familiar folk song. No significant technical problems.

Senfl, Ludwig. *Kanon*. arr. William D. Pardus. Creation Station. Two euphoniums and two tubas. $12.00. 2:30. Part I: d–g'; Part II: d–g'; Part III: $B\flat_1$–f; Part IV: $B\flat_1$–f. This brief Renaissance arrangement is unusual in that the primary melodic responsibility falls to the second and fourth parts. Euphonium parts also available in treble clef. Also reviewed in the Summer 2001 issue of the *TUBA Journal* (Vol. 28, No. 4).

Shoop, Stephen. *A Little Hymn*. Stephen Shoop Music Publications. Two euphoniums and two tubas. 1997. $6.00. 1:45. I–II. Part I: c–c'; Part II: c–b♭; Part III: F–e (f); Part IV: C–c. Written in the style of Robert Schumann, this original composition is appropriate for young ensembles. Euphonium parts also available in treble clef. Parts may be doubled for a large ensemble.

Shoop, Stephen, arr. *Bendemeer's Stream*. Cimarron Music and Productions. Two euphoniums and two tubas. 1995. $9.00. 1:45. I–II. Part I: B♭–b♭; Part II: A–d'; Part III: $B\flat_1$–e♭; Part IV: $B\flat_1$–B♭. This brief, tonal piece is arranged for young ensembles. The texture is homophonic and the melody is predominantly in the first euphonium. Euphonium parts also available in treble clef. Parts may be doubled for a large ensemble.

Shoop, Stephen, arr. *Sakura, Sakura*. Stephen Shoop Music Publications. Two euphoniums and two tubas. 1997. $4.50. 1:00. I–II. Part I: g♭–g♭'; Part II: e♭–b♭; Part III: B♭–f; Part IV: $B\flat_1$–F. Originally written for the koto, a thirteen-stringed instrument, this piece is based on the Japanese folk song *Song of the Blooming Cherry Tree*. The piece is based on a pentatonic scale and serves well as a study piece for young ensembles. Euphonium parts also available in treble clef. Parts may be doubled for a large ensemble.

Shoop, Stephen, arr. *Three Southern Hymns*. Stephen Shoop Music Publications. Two euphoniums and two tubas. 1997. $7.50. 2:15. I–II. Part I: c♯–g'; Part II: A–d'; Part III: E♭–f; Part IV: A_1–c. Three movements: Boundless Mercy; Salvation; Resignation. In memorium: Opal Linville Shoop. These hymns are from two well-known early tuba hymn books, *Southern Harmony* and *Kentucky Harmony*. The texture is homophonic, with the melody predominantly in the first part. Serves well as a study piece for young ensembles. Euphonium parts also available in treble clef. Parts may be doubled for a large ensemble. Individual movements can stand alone on a concert.

Shostakovich, Dimitri. *Four Preludes, Op. 34, Nos. 4, 7, 14, 16*. arr. Peter Rauch. Ohio Valley Tuba Quartet Press. Two euphoniums and two tubas. 1992. $12.00. 7:30. IV. Part I: B–c"; Part II: A–a♭'; Part III: B–a♭; Part IV: C_1–d. Four movements. Each movement contrasts in key, meter, and style. The tessitura of the first part is high, but there are no significant technical problems. Parts may be doubled for a large ensemble.

Siecznski, Rudolph. *Wein, DuStadt Meiner Traume*. arr. Ray Grim. Cimarron Music and Productions. Two euphoniums and two tubas. 1995. $10.00. 3:00. II. Part I: d–g'; Part II: c–e♭'; Part III: A♭–c'; Part IV: $A\flat_1$–e♭. Part of the TubaMeisters Collection. Traditional slow waltz with the melody primarily in the first euphonium part. Arrangement is accessible for intermediate-level performers. Euphonium parts also available in treble clef. Parts may be doubled for a large ensemble.

Siekmann, Frank H., arr. *Were You There?* Brelmat Music. Two euphoniums and two tubas. 1995. $12.00. 5:00. III. Part I: d–b♭'; Part II: c–g'; Part III: E–d'; Part IV: $B\flat_1$–g. This arrangement of the traditional spiritual includes excerpts from the "Goin' Home" theme of Dvorák's New World Symphony. Rhythms and harmonies are not hard, but ranges add to the difficulty. Parts may be doubled for a large ensemble. Also available in a double-quartet version from the same publisher.

Silcher, Von Fr. *Die Lorelei*. arr. Bruno Seitz. Musikverlag Martin Scherbacher. Four tubas. 1993. $15.00. 3:00. IV. Part I: e♭–g'; Part II: B♭–c'; Part III: E♭–e♭; Part IV: F_1–B♭. A standard arrangement of this famous German waltz. The tessitura of the top part is high and may be played on euphonium. No technical problems. Playable by high school students if euphoniums are used on the top two parts. Parts may be doubled for a large ensemble.

Singleton, Kenneth, arr. *Three 16th Century Flemish Pieces*. Queen City Brass Publications. Two euphoniums and two tubas. 1984. $7.50. 3:00.

III. Part I: f–g'; Part II: c–d'; Part III: B♭–b♭; Part IV: $B♭_1$–e♭. Three movements: Holla hoi per lanerta hoi; Sauff aus ünd machsnit lang; Hilf glüch mit freuden. Fairly easy arrangements of melodies typical of the Renaissance polyphonic style. Measure 15 in the first part of the first movement is missing a half rest. Parts may be doubled for a large ensemble. Recorded by the Monarch Tuba/Euphonium Quartet.

Skempton, Howard. *Rest and Recreation.* Oxford University Press. Two euphoniums and two tubas. Two movements. Written for Tubalaté. Minimalist in style with a lyrical first movement and rhythmic second movement. Recorded by Tubalaté on the compact disc *Move.*

Sloan, Gerald, arr. *Tuba Sunday for Tuba Choir.* Available from the arranger. Two euphoniums and two tubas. 1983. $5.00. 2:10. III. Part I: d–f'; Part II: d♭–e'; Part III: F–g; Part IV: $B♭_1$–d. Two movements: How Firm a Foundation; Amazing Grace. For Dr. Jerry Young and his students at Interlochen. Nice arrangement of two traditional protestant hymns. All parts have an opportunity to play the melody. Very playable by high school students. Parts may be doubled for a large ensemble.

Smaller and Adler. *That Lovin' Rag.* arr. Rodger Vaughan. Available from the arranger. Two euphoniums and two tubas. 1988. $5.00. 2:00. IV. Part I: f–a'; Part II: e–e'; Part III: F–a'; Part IV: F_1–d. An up-tempo very syncopated rag. Technical challenges depend on the performance tempo.

Smalley, Peter. *A Cool Suite for Tuba/Euphonium Quartet.* Studio Music Company. Two euphoniums and two tubas with optional percussion. £16.50. Four movements: Strollin'; Lazin'; Hangin' Out; Cruisin'. Nice collection of light swing pieces. Euphonium parts are also available in treble clef, and tuba parts are available in E♭ and B♭ treble clef. Parts may be doubled for a large ensemble. Also reviewed in the Spring 1999 issue of the *TUBA Journal* (Vol. 26, No. 3). Recorded by the British Tuba Quartet on the compact disc *Fireworks,* Polyphonic Records.

Smalley, Peter. *Quartet No. 1, "Glyder Landscape."* Studio Music Company. Two euphoniums and two tubas with optional percussion. 1996. Four movements: Twll Du; Cantilever; Cwm Idwall; Castell y Gwynt. Written for the British Tuba Quartet. Challenging programmatic work with movements named after the physical features of mountains in Snowdonia, North Wales. All parts call for double-tonguing. Also reviewed in the Summer 1997 issue of the *TUBA Journal* (Vol. 24, No. 4). Recorded by the British Tuba Quartet on the compact disc *March to the Scaffold,* Polyphonic Records.

Smalley, Peter. *Tuba Sauce.* Studio Music Company. Two euphoniums and two tubas. £16.50. II–III. Part I: G–a'; Part II: F–f'; Part III: G_1–c'; Part IV: $E♭_1$–a. Four movements: Ketchup; Gravy; Caramel; Custard. A light piece with several jazz elements. Each part is afforded the opportunity to be featured soloing over a driving bass line. Euphonium parts also available in treble clef, first tuba part also available in E♭ treble, and the second tuba part also available in both E♭ and B♭ treble. Parts may be doubled for a large ensemble. Also reviewed in the Summer 2001 issue of the *TUBA Journal* (Vol. 28, No. 4).

Snow, David. *Elephants Exotiques.* Available from the composer. Four tubas. 1978. 9:30. IV–V. Part I: E–b♭'; Part II: E–e♭'; Part III: E–e♭'; Part IV: $E♭_1$–e♭'. Four movements: Preludio Pachydermus; Looking for Peanuts (in the Jungle); Elephant Love Song; Mating Season. The piece is fun to listen to but because of the very contemporary harmonies it is also difficult to play. At the end of the third movement the fourth tuba player stands and recites two paragraphs of text printed in French. The fourth movement is multimetric and involves glissandos and slapping the hand against the mouthpiece. The tessitura of the top two parts is very high and may be played by euphoniums. All players read from a score. Winner of second place in the Los Angeles Tuba Quartet/Mirafone Composition Contest.

Solomons, David. *Pieces of Eight.* Da Capo Music. Two euphoniums and two tubas. £16.00. Four movements: Catch that Bee; Rag; Relax a Bit; Henry's Tune. Recorded by Tubalaté on the compact disc *Earth and Moon.*

Solomons, David. *Prayer before the Close of Day.* Da Capo Music. Two euphoniums and two tubas. £10.00. 6:30. Based on original plainchant. Recorded by Tubalaté on the compact disc *Move.*

Sousa, John Philip. *Belle of Chicago March.* arr. Skip Gray. Shawnee Press, Incorporated. Two euphoniums and two tubas. 1984. $8.00. 2:20. III–IV. Part I: d♭–f'; Part II: B♭–e♭'; Part III: E♭–g; Part IV: $A♭_1$–c. This arrangement poses the fewest technical demands of any of the Sousa marches published for tuba/euphonium quartet. Range requirements also make this a good high school or college recital piece. The melody is primarily in the euphoniums. Parts may be doubled for a large ensemble.

Sousa, John Philip. *El Capitan.* arr. R. Winston Morris. The Brass Press. Two euphoniums and two tuba. 1974. $5.00. 2:20. III–IV. Part I: B♭–g'; Part II: c–f'; Part III: G–a♭; Part IV: A_1–e♭. Written for the Tennessee Technological University Tuba Ensemble. This transcription is in the same key as the original, with most of the melody in the top two parts. This arrangement works well and is effective at concerts. Parts may be doubled for a large ensemble. Recorded by the British Tuba Quartet, *In at the Deep End,* Heavyweight Records Limited, HR008/D; and the Monarch Tuba/Euphonium Quartet.

Sousa, John Philip. *The Gladiator March.* arr. David Butler. Tuba-Euphonium Press. Two euphoniums and two tubas. 1998. $12.00. 3:00. II–III. Part I: c–g'; Part II: E–f'; Part III: C–g; Part IV: E_1–f. This arrangement of this march provides interesting lines for each performer, giving a significant part of the melodic material to each of the top three parts. The octave grace notes and arpeggios in the first part may be challenging, but otherwise the piece is accessible for young ensembles. Euphonium parts also available in treble clef. Parts may be doubled for a large ensemble. Also reviewed in the Summer 1999 issue of the *TUBA Journal* (Vol. 26, No. 4).

Sousa, John Philip. *Hands across the Sea.* arr. David R. Werden. Whaling Music Publishers. Two euphoniums and two tubas. 1983. $8.00. 3:30. IV. Part I: d–d"; Part II: c–b♭'; Part III: C–e♭'; Part IV: F_1–f. Dedicated to the Tokyo Bari-Tuba Ensemble. Tessitura of both euphonium parts is high. The first euphonium part is printed in treble clef. The arrangement works well. Parts may be doubled for a large ensemble. Recorded by the Northern Tuba Lights.

Sousa, John Philip. *The Liberty Bell.* arr. Gail Robertson. Tuba-Euphonium Press. Two euphoniums and two tubas. 1999. $12.00. 3:30. II. Part I: c–a' (b♭'); Part II: G–f'; Part III: C–c'; Part IV: G_1–a. Written for Andrew "Trout" Couse. Straightforward arrangement of one of Sousa's more popular marches. Melodic material is divided among all four parts. Parts are formatted so they may be reduced to fit in a flip-folder. Euphonium parts also available in treble clef. Parts may be doubled for a large ensemble.

Sousa, John Philip. *New York Hippodrome.* arr. Ronald Knoener. Tuba-Euphonium Press. Two euphoniums and two tubas. 1999. $12.00. 3:45. II–III. Part I: A–g' (b♭'); Part II: A–g' (b♭'); Part III: B♭$_1$–a; Part IV: A♭$_1$–e♭. Straightforward arrangement of this march in 6/8 time. Melodic material is primarily in top two parts. The piece is appropriate for intermediate-level performers. More appropriate for a large ensemble, as there are *divisi* sections in both euphonium parts.

Sousa, John Philip. *Semper Fidelis.* arr. David Sabourin. Touch of Brass Music Corporation. Two euphoniums and two tubas. 1982. $7.50. 2:30. IV. Part I: G–b♭'; Part II: G–e♭'; Part III: B♭$_1$–b♭; Part IV: A♭$_1$–e♭. Good arrangement of this classic march. Tessitura of the first part is high. Most of the work is in the top two parts. Transposed up a fourth from the original key. Parts may be doubled for a large ensemble.

Sousa, John Philip. *Semper Fidelis.* arr. Maurice Bale. Godiva Music. Two euphoniums and two tubas. £6.00.

Sousa, John Philip. *Semper Fidelis.* arr. R. Winston Morris. Ludwig Music Publishing Company. Two euphoniums and two tubas. 1988. $15.50. 2:30. III–IV. Part I: B–g'; Part II: B♭–f'; Part III: C–g; Part IV: G_1–f. Written for the Tennessee Technological University Tuba Ensemble. Excellent arrangement of this traditional Sousa march. Technically not overly challenging, but the moving lines must be played cleanly by all parts. Both euphonium parts are printed in bass and treble clef. Arrangement works very well. Parts may be doubled for a large ensemble. Recorded by the British Tuba Quartet, *In at the Deep End,* Heavyweight Records, HR008/D.

Sousa, John Philip. *The Stars and Stripes Forever.* arr. David R. Werden. Whaling Music Publishers. Two euphoniums and two tubas. 1992. $8.00. 2:00. IV. Part I: B♭–b♭'; Part II: A–b♭'; Part III: F–f'; Part IV: A_1–c'. Tessitura of the first three parts is high; an F tuba or a euphonium may be used on the third part. The first and second parts are printed in treble clef and the third and fourth parts are printed in both treble and bass clef for E♭ tubas. Good arrangement. Originally copyrighted in 1979. Parts may be doubled for a large ensemble. Recorded by the Atlantic Tuba Quartet, Golden Crest Records, CRS 4173; and the Northern Tuba Lights.

Sousa, John Philip. *The Stars and Stripes Forever.* arr. Lennie Niehaus. Kendor Music, Inc. Two euphoniums and two tubas. 2002. $10.00. 2:35. III–IV. Part I: c–f'; Part II: B♭–c'; Part III: C–g; Part IV: B♭$_1$–d. Jazz arrangement based on themes from Sousa's march. Many tutti rhythms with interesting elements in each part. Range is not difficult, but a good swing feel is necessary. Parts may be doubled for a large ensemble.

Sousa, John Philip. *The Stars and Stripes Forever.* arr. Paul Schmidt. Heavy Metal Music. Two euphoniums and two tubas. 1990. $7.00. 2:00. III–IV. Part I: B♭–f'; Part II: B♭–f'; Part III: C♭–g (e♭'); Part IV: F_1–e♭. The range and technical demands are very appropriate for good high school players. Drums may be added for effect. No score available. Parts may be added for a large ensemble.

Sousa, John Philip. *The Thunderer.* arr. David R. Werden. Whaling Music Publishers. Two euphoniums and two tubas. 1989. $8.00. 2:30. IV. Part I: c–b♭'; Part II: c–a'; Part III: C–c'; Part IV: F_1–c'. Most of the melody is in the first part while the other three parts have a tutti rhythmic accompaniment. Parts may be doubled for a large ensemble.

Sousa, John Philip. *The Thunderer.* arr. Peter Smalley. Studio Music Company. Two euphoniums and two tubas. 1996. III. Part I: F–e♭"; Part II: c–c"; Part III: C–f'; Part IV: A_1–f. Euphonium parts also available in treble clef and tuba parts also available in E♭ treble clef. Also reviewed in the Summer 1997 issue of the *TUBA Journal* (Vol. 24, No. 4). Recorded by the British Tuba Quartet on the compact disc *March to the Scaffold,* Polyphonic Records.

Sousa, John Philip. *Washington Post.* arr. David R. Werden. Whaling Music Publishers. Two euphoniums and two tubas. 1983. $8.50. 2:30. IV. Part I: F–b♭'; Part II: A–g'; Part III: F–f'; Part IV: $B♭_1$–e♭'. Nice arrangement of this famous Sousa march. The tessitura of the third part is high; an F tuba is recommended. The first part is printed in tenor clef. Parts may be doubled for a large ensemble. Recorded by David LeClair, *Swingin' Low,* Marcophon.

Sousa, John Philip. *Washington Post.* arr. David Sabourin. Touch of Brass Music Corporation. Two euphoniums and two tubas. 1981. $8.50. 2:30. IV. Part I: B♭–f'; Part II: F–e♭'; Part III: F–b♭; Part IV: F_1–c. Excellent arrangement of this traditional march. No real range or technical difficulties for this level. Parts may be doubled for a large ensemble. Recorded by the British Tuba Quartet, *In at the Deep End,* Heavyweight Records, HR008/D; the Melton Tuba Quartett, *Premiere,* Diavolo Records, DR-D-93-C-001.

Spears, Jared. *Divertimento.* Available from the composer. Two euphoniums and two tubas. 1980. $50.00. 10:45. IV–V. Part I: B♭–c''; Part II: F–g'; Part III: F–e'; Part IV: $F♯_1$–b. Five movements: Invention; Melodrama; Dance; Chorale; Toccata. Written for R. Winston Morris and the Tennessee Technological University Tuba Ensemble. There are considerable range and technical demands on all parts. All four parts have numerous *divisi* sections and each will require at least two players. Movements I, III, and V are high-spirited and full of energy. Mutes are required for the top three parts. An exceptional piece for an advanced ensemble. Parts may be doubled for a large ensemble. Recorded by the Tennessee Technological University Tuba Ensemble, *Composer Festival,* KM Records, KM 6549.

Speer, Daniel. *Sonata.* arr. Paul Schmidt. Heavy Metal Music. Two euphoniums and two tubas. 1991. $5.00. 3:00. III–IV. Part I: e–e♭; Part II: B♭–c'; Part III: A–b♭; Part IV: $B♭_1$–f. All parts have the same rhythmical technical demands. No range problems. The texture is polyphonic in some sections. No score available. Parts may be doubled for a large ensemble.

Stechlik. *Whoop It Up Polka.* arr. Ray Grim. Cimarron Music and Productions. Two euphoniums and two tubas. 1996. $10.00. 2:15. II. Part I: d–g'; Part II: c–b♭; Part III: $B♭_1$–e♭; Part IV: $B♭_1$–g. Part of the TubaMeisters Collection, this upbeat polka arrangement is appropriate for intermediate-level performers. Melodic material is divided among the first, second, and fourth parts. Parts may be doubled for a large ensemble. Euphonium parts also available in treble clef.

Steffe, W. *Battle Hymn.* arr. Thomas Isbell. The Brass Press. Two euphoniums and two tubas. 1974. $4.00. 2:00. III. Part I: D–f'; Part II: B♭–f'; Part III: E♭–f; Part IV: G_1–b♭. Written for R. Winston Morris and the Tennessee Technological University Tuba Ensemble. The first part has an extended solo in the first section in a free expressive style. The second section is a march-like version of this traditional patriotic melody. Very usable with high school students. Parts may be doubled for a large ensemble.

Steinke, Greg. *Suspended in Frozen Velocity: Image Music IX from "Songs of the Fire Circles."* Tuba-Euphonium Press. Two euphoniums and two tubas. 1992. $12.00. 6:00. IV–V. Ranges for all parts: lowest note possible to highest note possible. Dedicated to those dying for freedom as this is played. This is another in a series of pieces of "Image Music" which explore Native American culture based on the "Songs of the Fire Circles." There are numerous twentieth-century techniques called for: various "free" pitch and meter sections, randomly chosen rhythms, and glissandos. There are extreme technical and range challenges for all four parts. All parts require mutes.

Steinke, Greg A. *Native American Notes II: The Bitter Roots of Peace for Tuba-Euphonium Quartet.* Tierra del Mar Music. Two euphoniums and two tubas with narrator. $50.00. 17:00. III–IV. Part I: D–a♯'; Part II: E♭–b♭'; Part III: C–f'; Part IV: C_1–d♯'. Arrangement dedicated to Don Harry. This is an arrangement by the composer of a programmatic work, originally for string quartet, attempting to compare and contrast historical events in Eastern Europe and North America. Modern playing techniques required include half-valve glissandos, rhythmic tapping on the instrument, use of mutes, and improvisation/aleatoric passages. Parts may be doubled for a large ensemble. Also reviewed in the Winter 1998 issue of the *TUBA Journal* (Vol. 25, No. 2).

Stephens, David. *The String Band Polka* arr. Ray Grim. Cimarron Music and Productions. Two euphoniums and two tubas. 1996. $10.00. 1:30. II. Part I: f–g'; Part II: c–g'; Part III: $B♭_1$–b♭; Part IV: G_1–e♭. Part of the TubaMeisters Collection, this polka is effectively arranged for intermediate-level performers. Melody is predominantly in the first part. Parts may be doubled for a large ensemble. Euphonium parts also available in treble clef.

Stevens, John. *Ballade.* Available from the composer. Two euphoniums and two tubas. 1990. 2:00. III. Part I: F–e♭'; Part II: d–a; Part III: D–f; Part IV: $B♭_1$–d. A short jazz ballad. Very sonorous, and legato in style throughout. Written especially for high school players.

Stevens, John. *Benediction.* Tuba-Euphonium Press. Two euphoniums and two tubas. 2003. $10.00. 3:15. II. Part I: g–b♭'; Part II: e–f'; Part III: G–c'; Part IV: G_1–a♭. For the Sotto Voce Quartet. Brief, original composition in a lyrical hymn setting with rich sonorities. Melody is primarily in the first euphonium and first tuba parts. Parts may be doubled for a large ensemble. Recorded by Sotto Voce on the compact disc *The Complete Quartets of John Stevens,* Summit Records.

Stevens, John. *Dances.* Peer International Corporation. Solo tuba and three tubas. 1978. $12.00. 7:30. IV–V. Part I: c–f'; Part II: C–c'; Part III: B♭$_1$–g; Part IV: B♭$_1$–c. This one-movement composition is in three sections: moderate 2/2, slow 3/4, and fast 6/8. Rhythmically challenging for the soloist as well as the other three parts. A solo cadenza separates each section. The solo part may be played on euphonium. A very exciting aggressive-sounding composition. See: Bird, Gary, ed.; *Program Notes for the Solo Tuba.* Recorded by Toby Hanks, *Sampler,* Crystal Records, S395; the Melton Tuba Quartett, *Premiere,* Diavolo Records, DR-D-93–C-001; the Northern Tuba Lights; and by the Sotto Voce Tuba Quartet, *Viva Voci!*

Stevens, John. *Diversions.* Editions BIM. Four tubas. 1978. 14:00. IV. Part I: C–a♭'; Part II: E–A♭'; Part III: C–d'; Part IV: G$_1$–b♭. Five movements: Prologue; Latin Feel; Free—Very Down Home; Fast; Epilogue. A jazz composition requiring improvisation by the second and third parts. The Prologue and Epilogue are short and in a jazz ballad style. The second movement is a funk/rock tune featuring the fourth part in an intricate bass line and the third movement is a fast jazz waltz. The top two parts may be played on euphonium.

Stevens, John. *Diversions.* Encore Music. Four tubas. Out of Print.

Stevens, John. *Jammin'.* Available from the composer. Two euphoniums and two tubas. 1990. 2:30. III. Part I: c–e♭'; Part II: c–e♭'; Part III: C–G♭; Part IV: A♭$_1$–d♭. A short piece in a rock style. Rock rhythms, syncopations, and unison ensemble figures are stressed.

Stevens, John. *Manhattan Suite.* Southern Music Publishing Company Incorporated. Four tubas. 1979. $12.00. 15:20. IV. Part I: B♭–b♭'; Part II: B♭$_1$–g'; Part III: F$_1$–e♭; Part IV: E♭$_1$–f. Four movements: Rock; Slow Swing; Jazz Waltz; Slow and Free. While the score indicates four tubas, the parts suggest that the first part may be played by a euphonium and the second part played by a euphonium or F tuba. The top three parts have a section for improvised solos. As an alternative to improvisation, players may use solos written by the composer. This is a very lively piece with four contrasting movements. There are a few ensemble challenges, and the piece will require four strong players. Recorded by the University of Michigan Tuba and Euphonium Ensemble, University of Michigan Records, SM0011.

Stevens, John. *Moondance.* Editions BIM. Four tubas. 1991. 7:00. V. Part I: C–g♭'; Part II: C–e♭'; Part III: E♭$_1$–d♭'; Part IV: E♭$_1$–e♭'. Commissioned by and dedicated to the Summit Tuba Quartet. A slow and legato opening section is followed by a solo cadenza that leads to a very rapid, rhythmically energetic section. The opening material returns at the end. The piece is tonal and has a jazz flavor. Very challenging. Recorded by the Summit Tuba Quartet, *Summit Brass-American Tribute,* Summit Records, DCD 127.

Stevens, John. *Music 4 Tubas.* Peer International Corporation. Four tubas. 1978. $12.00. 8:00. IV. Part I: C–f'; Part II: B♭$_1$–g'; Part III: G$_1$–d♭'; Part IV: G$_1$–d'. Three movements: Lively; Largo; Rock. A very interesting work. The tessitura is rather high for the first two parts, and even the fourth part goes up to a high d'. A challenge to play but worth the effort. Recorded by the New York Tuba Quartet, *Tubby's Revenge,* Crystal Records, S221.

Stevens, John. *Power for Four Tubas.* Peer International Corporation. Four tubas. 1978. $12.00. 2:10. IV. Part I: G–e♭'; Part II: c–e♭'; Part III: C–f; Part IV: G$_1$–c. This is a driving jazz-like composition which alternates between 2/2 and 7/4. It is very challenging, especially at the tempo marked. May also be performed with two euphoniums and two tubas. This exciting piece makes a terrific opener. Recorded by John Stevens, *Power,* Mark Records, MRS-20699; and the Northern Tuba Lights.

Stevens, John. *Viva Voce!* Tuba-Euphonium Press. Two euphoniums and two tubas. 2003. $12.00. 2:30. III. Part I: B♭–c''; Part II: B♭–a'; Part III: B♭$_1$–f'; Part IV: B♭$_1$–e'. For the Sotto Voce Quartet. Challenging original composition with rock and swing influences. Range considerations and technical complexities make this more appropriate for an advanced ensemble. More appropriate for a quartet than for an ensemble. Recorded by Sotto Voce on the compact disc *The Complete Quartets of John Stevens,* Summit Records.

Stevens, John, arr. *Twenty-Four Christmas Carols.* Available from the arranger. Two euphoniums and two tubas. 1982. 24 pp. IV. Part I: F–b♭'; Part II: F–g'; Part III: G$_1$–c'; Part IV: F$_1$–a♭. Twenty-four traditional carols arranged in a variety of traditional classical styles. Use of modulations, trills, ornaments, and counter melodies predominates.

Stolc, C. *Forge in the Forest Polka.* arr. Paul Schmidt. Heavy Metal Music. Two euphoniums and two tubas. 1990. $7.00. 3:00. IV. Part I: A–e♭'; Part II: F–e♭'; Part III: E♭–b♭; Part IV: F$_1$–f. There are many technical challenges for the top two parts, especially if played at a fast tempo. Perfect for Octubafest concerts. No score available. Parts may be doubled for a large ensemble.

Stoll, David. *Octave Variations.* Breakthrough Music. Two euphoniums and two tubas. £16.00. Part I: G–b♭'; Part II: G–a'; Part III: B♭$_1$–e♭'; Part IV: E♭$_1$–c'. This piece opens with a fanfare section and then develops the theme through a waltz, ragtime, and fugue. Melodic material is divided among the four voices.

Stolzel, Gottfried Heinrich. *Bist Du bei mir.* arr. Stephen Shoop. Cimarron Music and Productions. Two euphoniums and two tubas. 1995. $8.50. 3:45. II–III. Part I: f–a♭'; Part II: A–e♭'; Part III: D–g; Part IV: A_1–B♭. Translated to "When Thou Art Near," this tonal work is arranged for young to intermediate-level performers. The melody is predominantly in the first part. Euphonium parts also available in treble clef. Parts may be doubled for a large ensemble.

Stoutamire, Albert, and Kenneth Henderson. *Quartets for All.* CPP Belwin, Incorporated. Three euphoniums and one tuba. 1975. $5.00. 23 pp. III. Part I: B♭–g'; Part II: B♭–f'; Part III: A♭–f'; Part IV: B♭$_1$–f. A collection of twelve songs from a variety of composers and styles. No significant technical problems, and the melody is almost exclusively in the first part. Works very well for junior high and high school students. Parts may be doubled for a large ensemble.

Strauss, Johann. *An der Schöen Blauen Donau (Blue Danube Waltz).* arr. Bruno Seitz. Musikverlag Martin Scherbacher. Two euphoniums and two tubas. 1989. $15.00. 4:30. IV. Part I: A♭–c''; Part II: G♭–e♭'; Part III: C–d♭'; Part IV: E♭$_1$–e♭. Good arrangement of this famous waltz. The first part has the melody the majority of the time and is the most difficult technically. Fun to play, but also challenging. Parts may be doubled for a large ensemble.

Strauss, Johann. *Egyptian March.* arr. Paul Schmidt. Heavy Metal Music. Two euphoniums and two tubas. 1994. $7.00. II–III. Part I: c–a♭'; Part II: F–a♭'; Part III: C–e♭'; Part IV: E_1–e♭. Commissioned by the Heavy Metal Society Tuba Quartet. Light, encore-style arrangement that employs special effects such as singing through the instruments and timpani effects simulated by the tubas. Optional *divisi* sections are included for use by large ensemble. Also reviewed in the Winter 1995 issue of the *TUBA Journal* (Vol. 22, No. 2).

Strauss, Johann. *Pizzacato Polka.* arr. Maurice Bale. Godiva Music. Two euphoniums and two tubas. £6.00.

Strauss, Johann. *The Pizzacato Polka.* arr. Norlan Bewley. Bewley Music, Incorporated. Two euphoniums and two tubas. 1995. $10.00. 2:00. II. Part I: e–b♭'; Part II: c–e♭'; Part III: G–b♭; Part IV: G_1–c. Straightforward arrangement of this polka originally for strings—part of the Octubafest Collection. The melodic material is predominantly in the first part, which requires more advanced technical skills than the other three. Parts may be doubled for a large ensemble. Euphonium parts also available in treble clef.

Strauss, Johann. *Pizzacato Polka.* arr. Ray Grim. Cimarron Music and Productions. Two euphoniums and two tubas. 1996. $9.00. 1:15. II–III. Part I: e–b♭'; Part II: c–f'; Part III: G–g; Part IV: G_1–e♭. Nice arrangement of this polka originally for strings—part of the TubaMeisters Collection. The melodic material is predominantly in the first part, which requires more advanced technical skills than the other three. Parts may be doubled for a large ensemble. Euphonium parts also available in treble clef.

Strauss, Johann. *Radetzky March.* arr. Ray Grim. Cimarron Music and Productions. Two euphoniums and two tubas. $8.50. Part of the TubaMeisters Collection. Euphonium parts also available in treble clef.

Strauss, Johann. *Radetzky March.* arr. Ronald Knoener. Tuba-Euphonium Press. Two euphoniums and two tubas. 1998. $12.00. 2:00. II–III. Part I: d–b♭'; Part II: B♭–b♭'; Part III: E–g; Part IV: F_1–f. Typical Strauss march with the melody primarily in the first part and the other three serving an accompanimental role. Parts may be doubled for a large ensemble. Also reviewed in the Fall 1999 issue of the *TUBA Journal* (Vol. 27, No. 1).

Strauss, Johann. *Strauss Waltzes.* arr. Norlan Bewley. Bewley Music, Incorporated. Two euphoniums and two tubas. 1995. $15.00. 3:00. II–III. Part I: B♭–c''; Part II: A–g'; Part III: F–e♭'; Part IV: F_1–e♭. Part of the Octubafest Music collection, this medley of waltzes is appropriate for intermediate-level ensembles. Melodic material is divided among all four voices. Parts may be doubled for a large ensemble. Euphonium parts also available in treble clef.

Strauss, Johann. *Tritsch-Tratsch Polka.* arr. Bruno Seitz. Musikverlag Martin Scherbacher. Two euphoniums and two tubas. 1988. $13.50. 2:20. IV. Part I: c–b♭'; Part II: G–f'; Part III: D♭–a♭; Part IV: F_1–A♭. A high-spirited polka, technically challenging for the top three parts. Many subito dynamic contrasts for stylistic effect. Fun to play. Parts may be doubled for a large ensemble.

Strauss, Johann. *The Tritsch Tratsch Polka.* arr. Norlan Bewley. Bewley Music, Incorporated. Two euphoniums and two tubas. 1995. $10.00. 2:00. II. Part I: B–g'; Part II: B–e'; Part III: G–b; Part IV: G_1–d. Part of the Octubafest Music collection, this arrangement is appropriate for intermediate-level ensembles. Melodic material is predominantly in the first part. Parts may be doubled for a large ensemble. Euphonium parts also available in treble clef.

Strauss, Johann. *Valse from Die Fledermaus.* arr. David Schanke. Music Arts Company. Two euphoniums and two tubas. 1992. $10.00. 1:45. III–IV. Part I: e♭–g'; Part II: F♯–c'; Part III: E♭–a♭; Part IV: G_1–e♭. A fun arrangement of this classic Strauss waltz. Most of the work is in the first euphonium part, though all four parts get a chance to play the melody occasionally. The top two parts are printed in both bass and treble clef. Parts may be doubled for a large ensemble.

Strauss, Johann. *Waltzes from "Die Fledermaus" and the "Gypsy Baron."* arr. George Whetmore, ed. Paul Luhring. PEL Music Publications. Four tubas. 1998. $8.50. 2:45. II. Part I: F–c'; Part II: G–a♭; Part III: E♭–e♭; Part IV: F_1–F. For the Pulaski High School Tuba Quartet. This single-movement arrangement is a medley of two well-known Strauss waltzes. Range and style are appropriate for intermediate-level performers. Parts may be doubled for a large ensemble.

Streisand, Barbra. *Evergreen.* arr. Denzil Stephens. Sarnia Music. Two euphoniums and two tubas. £15.00.

Stroud, Richard. *Night Train for Tubas.* Available from the composer. Two euphoniums and two tubas. $12.00. 2:30. IV. Part I: d♭–a♭'; Part II: c–g'; Part III: B♭–c'; Part IV: $B♭_1$–f. Twelve-bar blues in B♭. There is a written-out walking bass line in the fourth part. The melody is primarily in the first and second parts. There is a section that may be repeated for improvised solos. Parts may be doubled for a large ensemble. See: Bird, Gary, ed.; *Program Notes for the Solo Tuba.*

Stroud, Richard. *Treatments for Tuba.* Seesaw Music Corporation. Two euphoniums and two tubas. 1976. $33.00. 8:00. IV–V. Part I: A♭–a'; Part II: A♭–d'; Part III: G_1–b♭; Part IV: G_1–a♭. Three movements. Rhythmically complex and very dissonant. There is a brief aleatoric section in the second movement. Very interesting writing, and challenging to play.

Stroud, Richard, arr. *Silver Bells.* Available from the arranger. Two euphoniums and two tubas. $10.00. 1:20. IV. Part I: d–g'; Part II: d–e♭'; Part III: $B♭_1$–g; Part IV: D–d. This arrangement is of "Carol of the Bells," not the popular secular Christmas song "Silver Bells." Much of the melodic work is in the top two parts, though there are some tutti rhythmic passages in all four parts. No real range or technical demands. The tempo really determines the difficulty of this composition. Parts may be doubled for a large ensemble.

Strukow, Valery. *Tuba Quartet.* Editions BIM. Four tubas. 1992. $22.50.

Stuart, Hugh M. *Soft Shoo for Two Euphoniums and Two Tubas.* Shawnee Press, Incorporated. Two euphoniums and two tubas. 1987. $11.00. 2:00. IV. Part I: e–b♭'; Part II: e–a'; Part III: $B♭_1$–a; Part IV: $B♭_1$–g. A single soft-shoe-style melody is passed around to each part. Technically this is fairly easy, but the range demands require an advanced player on the first part.

Sturzenegger, Kurt. *Tubarium.* Editions Marc Reift. Two euphoniums and two tubas. 1995. CHF 26.00. 7:00. III. Part I: c–b♭'; Part II: G–e♭'; Part III: C–b♭; Part IV: ($E♭_1$) F_1–d. Three movements: Marche; Tango; Finale (Pot-pourri). A characteristic, tonal work with no specific technical difficulties. The Fafner motive from Wagner's *Siegfried* appears in a short section of the Finale between two rhythmical 5/8 sections. In addition to bass clef parts, euphonium parts are also available in treble, first tuba parts also available in E♭ treble, and second tuba parts also available B♭ treble clef.

Sullivan, Arthur. *The Long Day Closes.* arr. Angelo Manzo. Tuba-Euphonium Press. Four tubas. 2001. $10.00. 2:30. II. Part I: c–e♭'; Part II: A♭–c'; Part III: C–g♭; Part IV: G_1–d♭. Brief hymn in a homophonic texture with traditional harmonies. The melody is predominantly in the first part. Parts may be doubled for a large ensemble.

Susato, Tielman. *Ronde and Saltarelle.* arr. Denis Winter. Whaling Music Publishers. Two euphoniums and two tubas. 1978. $7.00. 2:00. IV. Part I: d–a♭'; Part II: d–a♭'; Part III: B♭–g; Part IV: $B♭_1$–d. A nice melody in a fast-slow-fast form. No significant technical problems. The top two parts are written in tenor clef. Parts may be doubled for a large ensemble. Recorded by the Atlantic Tuba Quartet, *Euphonic Sounds,* Golden Crest, CRS 4173.

Susato, Tilman. *Suite No. 1 from the Danserye.* arr. Paul Schmidt. Heavy Metal Music. Two euphoniums and two tubas. 1993. $7.00. II. Part I: c–f'; Part II: F–b♭; Part III: F–f; Part IV: G_1–B♭. Five movements: Mohrentanz; Die Schlact; Schafertanz; Nachtanz; Warum. This collection of five short Renaissance dances is intended to be performed without pause. All the dances are in typical binary form. Conservative ranges and simple keys make this piece accessible to younger ensembles. Also reviewed in the Spring 1995 issue of the *TUBA Journal* (Vol. 22, No. 3).

Susato, Tilman. *Three Dances.* arr. Barton Cummings. Solid Brass Music Company. Two euphoniums and two tubas. 1996. $9.00. 5:00. II. Part I: c–d'; Part II: G–f; Part III: D–d; Part IV: D_1–b♭. Three movements: Rondo; Pavane; Salterelle. Great arrangement for young ensembles. Predominantly homophonic with traditional harmonies. Parts may be doubled for a large ensemble. Also reviewed in the Summer 1997 issue of the *TUBA Journal* (Vol. 24, No. 4).

Sydeman, William. *Music for Low Brass.* Seesaw Music Corporation. Two trombones (euphoniums) and two tubas. 1967. $19.00. 6:30. IV. Part I: E–b♭'; Part II: $B♭_1$–a; Part III: C–f'; Part IV: E_1–b♭. Two movements. Originally written for three trombones and one tuba, and euphoniums could be used on the top two or three parts. Only moderately difficult, but the harmonies are quite dissonant. Some of the top two parts are written in tenor clef. The top three parts require mutes.

Szkutko, John. *Big Fat Polka.* SZK Music. Four tubas. 1994. $25.00 (Australian). 2:15. III. Part I: $B♭_2$–f'; Part II: $B♭_2$–e♭'; Part III: $B♭_2$–e♭'; Part IV: $B♭_2$–b♭. German-style polka with *big* and *fat* melodies thrown in the middle section, including *We Shall Not Be Moved, The Elephant,* and *In Cellar Cool.* At the indicated tempo, the first and third parts may require triple-tonguing. Parts may be doubled for a large ensemble.

Szkutko, John. *Dragon Land.* SZK Music. Four tubas. 1996. $25.00 (Australian). 2:30. III. Part I: F–b♭; Part II: F–g; Part III: F_1–d♭; Part IV: $B♭_2$–d♭. A mysterious, and at times dark, programmatic dragon-themed work in the key of B♭ minor. All parts are interesting, and the fourth part requires technical agility in the low register. Parts may be doubled for a large ensemble.

Szkutko, John. *Dune Buggy.* SZK Music. Two euphoniums and two tubas. 1992. 2:00. A technically challenging upbeat work in mixed meter. The melodic material is divided evenly between the four parts.

Szkutko, John. *Hippo Trot.* SZK Music. Four tubas. 1990. 3:00. Overall range: $B♭_1$–e♭'. A slow, programmatic hippo-themed work.

Szkutko, John. *Jones & Co.* SZK Music. One euphonium and three tubas. 1994. 3:00. A quartet with sections of varied character, including a tarantella, waltz, and ballad.

Szkutko, John. *March.* SZK Music. Two euphoniums and two tubas. 1992. 2:00. Composed primarily in the style of a brass band march; the trio section is replaced by a fugue.

Szkutko, John. *Mountains.* SZK Music. Two euphoniums and two tubas. 1992. 6:30. Original composition with a Scottish sound.

Szkutko, John. *Walking Giants.* SZK Music. Four tubas. 1992. $25.00 (Australian). 3:45. III. Part I: A–g'; Part II: D–d'; Part III: D–c'; Part IV: D_1–A. Original composition with traditional harmonies. All parts are interesting and the melodic material is divided among the four voices. The fourth part requires technical agility in the low register, and the first part contains several trills. Parts may be doubled for a large ensemble.

Szpakowski, Michael. *Dancing Music.* Breakthrough Music. Two euphoniums and two tubas. £11.95. Part I: G–g'; Part II: c–g'; Part III: D_1–d; Part IV: C–g. Written for the quartet Tubalaté, the piece uses African harmonies. Parts may be doubled for a large ensemble. Recorded by Tubalaté on the compact disc *Hall of Mirrors.*

Szpakowski, Michael. *Variations on a Yiddish Folksong.* Breakthrough Music. Two euphoniums and two tubas. £11.95. A set of fun variations based on an old Yiddish folk song. The piece offers an option for the first euphonium to sing the melody!

Tamura, Toru. *Quartet for Tubas.* Tokyo Bari-Tuba Ensemble. Four tubas.

Tautenhahn, Gunther. *Alte Kameraden.* Two euphoniums and two tubas.

Tautenhahn, Gunther. *In-Phase-Out.* Seesaw Music Corporation. Four tubas. 1978. $19.00. 9:00. IV–V. Part I: C–e'; Part II: A_1–e'; Part III: G_1–e'; Part IV: $G♭_1$–e♭'. This is designed to alternate phases of sound with silence. There are very contemporary harmonies and all four parts have large range demands. There are several contrasting sections within this single movement.

Taylor, Jeff. *Fanfare No. 1.* Horizon Press. Two euphoniums and two tubas. 1991. $6.00. 2:30. IV. Part I: c–c♯"; Part II: c–g'; Part III: $A♭_1$–g; Part IV: F_1–f. A technically challenging fanfare for all four parts. The tessitura of the first part is high. An exciting fanfare.

Tchaikovsky, Peter. *Andante Cantabile from String Quartet No. 1.* arr. Ken Drobnak. Tuba-Euphonium Press. Two euphoniums and two tubas. 2002. $10.00. 2:45. II–III. Part I: d♭–g'; Part II: B♭–g'; Part III: $B♭_1$–c'; Part IV: A_1–e♭. This work, originally for strings, is an excellent study in lyrical playing and ensemble legato. Melodic material is divided among the parts. Parts may be doubled for a large ensemble. Also reviewed in the Spring 2004 issue of the *ITEA Journal* (Vol. 31, No. 3).

Tchaikovsky, Peter. *Dance of the Little ~~Swans~~ Tubas.* arr. Paul Schmidt. Heavy Metal Music. Two euphoniums and two tubas. 1994. $7.00. 1:30. II–III. Part I: A–g'; Part II: A–a; Part III: F–a; Part IV: A_1–g. Short, light arrangement of *Dance of the Little Swans.* The melody is predominantly in the first part. Works well as a concert opener. Parts may be doubled for a large ensemble.

Tchaikovsky, Peter. *Dance of the Little Tubas (Swans).* arr. Joseph Goble. Tuba-Euphonium Press. Two euphoniums and two tubas. 1993. $8.00. 1:30. II–III. Part I: e♭–g'; Part II: B♭–g'; Part III: G–b♭; Part IV: F_1–d. To Jayme. This short, light arrangement of *Dance of the Little Swans* gives each part equal opportunity with the melodic material. Works well as an opener, closer, or encore piece. Euphonium parts also available in treble clef. Also reviewed in the Spring 1995 issue of the *TUBA Journal* (Vol. 22, No. 3).

Tchaikovsky, Peter. *Finale from Symphony No. 4.* arr. David Butler. Tuba-Euphonium Press. Two euphoniums and two tubas. 1998. $18.00. 8:00. III–IV. Part I: G–a'; Part II: F–g'; Part III: G_1–c'; Part IV: F_1–b. For the Tennessee Tech Tuba Ensemble. Effective arrangement of the fourth movement. All parts require advanced technical dexterity, and the melodic material is divided among the parts. Euphonium parts also available in treble clef. More appropriate for a large ensemble, as there are *divisi* sections in each part.

Tchaikovsky, Peter. *Little Russian March from Symphony No. 2 in C Minor.* arr. Joseph Goble. Tuba-Euphonium Press. Two euphoniums and two tubas. 1998. $8.00. 4:00. II–III. Part I: e♭–g'; Part II: A–e♭'; Part III: $B♭_1$–b♭'; Part IV: G_1–f. Originally scored for orchestra, this dark march is accessible for intermediate-level performers. Melodic material is divided among the voices. Parts may be doubled for a large ensemble.

Tchaikovsky, Peter. *March of the Toy Soldiers from the "Nutcracker."* arr. David Woodcock. Green Bay Music. Two euphoniums and two tubas. 1993.

$22.00. 1:45. IV. Part I: c–b♭'; Part II: B♭–b♭'; Part III: D–b; Part IV: G$_1$–g. Technically challenging for the first and second parts. All parts need to be played lightly and cleanly. Parts may be doubled for a large ensemble.

Tchaikovsky, Peter. *Sleeping Tuba Waltz.* arr. John Fletcher. Emerson Edition. Four tubas. 1983. $24.50. 3:20. IV–V. Part I: B♭$_1$–b♭'; Part II: B♭$_1$–f'; Part III: B♭$_2$–b♭; Part IV: B♭$_2$–d. Originally written by Tchaikovsky for the ballet *Sleeping Beauty* and also used in the cartoon version made by Walt Disney. Though quite high, parts one and two were originally conceived for an F or E♭ tuba but may be played on euphonium. Fun to play but challenging to perform at the tempo marked. Recorded by John Fletcher and The Philip Jones Brass Ensemble, *Brass Splendour,* London 411 9552 and on *Divertimento,* Argo, ARG 851.

Teike, C. *Old Comrades.* arr. Norlan Bewley. Bewley Music, Incorporated. Two euphoniums and two tubas. 1995. $12.00. 3:30. II. Part I: A–b♭'; Part II: A–g'; Part III: D–d♭'; Part IV: A♭$_1$–f. Part of the Octubafest Music collection, this arrangement is appropriate for intermediate-level ensembles. Melodic material is divided among all four voices. Parts may be doubled for a large ensemble. Euphonium parts also available in treble clef.

Teike, Carl. *Alte Kameraden March.* arr. Paul Schmidt. Heavy Metal Music. Two euphoniums and two tubas. 1992. $7.00. 2:20. IV. Part I: A–g'; Part II: A♭–d'; Part III: A–f; Part IV: G$_1$–f. With just a couple of exceptions, the first euphonium has primary responsibility for the melody. No significant technical challenges. No score available; Parts may be doubled for a large ensemble.

Texidor, Jamie. *Amparito Roco.* arr. Robert Wilkinson. Cimarron Music and Productions. Two euphoniums and two tubas. 1998. 2:45. $14.00. III. Part I: B♭–a'; Part II: B♭–g'; Part III: B♭$_1$–c'; Part IV: B♭$_1$–g. This arrangement of the popular Spanish march allows each part to perform the melody at some point. Euphonium parts also available in treble clef. Parts may be doubled for a large ensemble.

Texidor, Jamie. *Amparito Roca.* arr. Steven Emberson. Available from the arranger. Two or three euphoniums and two or three tubas. 1993. 3:00. II–III. Part I: B–a♭'; Part II: c–g'; Part III: G–d'; Part IV: E♭–f'; Part V: G–a♭; Part VI: E♭$_1$–g. Commissioned by Tubalation. Second and third parts are optional. Straightforward arrangement of this popular Spanish march accessible for intermediate-level performers. All parts are interesting and perform the melody at some point. Parts may be doubled for a large ensemble.

Thielmans, Jean ("Boots"). *Bluesette.* arr. Rodger Vaughan. Available from the arranger. Two euphoniums and two tubas. 1991. $5.00. 3:30. IV. Part I: c–a'; Part II: d♭–d'; Part III: G–a; Part IV: B♭$_1$–f. For the Tubadours. A jazz waltz. The melody is primarily in the top three parts. Drums may be added to enhance the jazz feel. Parts may be doubled for a large ensemble.

Thompson, Bruce G. *Three Miniatures for Tuba Quartet.* Available from the composer. Four tubas. 5:00. III–IV. Part I: F–c' (d'); Part II: F♯$_1$–c'; Part III: G$_1$–a; Part IV: F$_1$–g. Three movements: Prelude; Song; Introduction and March. A euphonium could be used on the first part to make this playable by high school students. No significant technical problems. Parts may be doubled for a large ensemble.

Thompson, Randall. *Alleluia.* arr. Robert Wilkinson. Cimarron Music and Productions. Two euphoniums and two tubas. 1997. $14.50. 4:00. Euphonium parts also available in treble clef.

Thornton, Michael, arr. *Two English Madrigals.* PP Music. Four tubas. 1992. $6.50. 2:10. IV. Part I: E–d'; Part II: A$_1$–d'; Part III: G$_1$–f'; Part IV: B♭$_1$–f'. Two movements: Tosse Not My Soule; Thus Saith My Cloris Bright. An arrangement of two madrigals by John Dowland and John Wilbye, respectively. Range demands are greater for the third and fourth parts than for the first and second. This will require four strong players. Originally published by Queen City Brass Publications and copyrighted in 1980.

Tignor, Scott. *Irish Landscape.* Cimarron Music and Productions. Two euphoniums and two tubas. 1997. $11.50. 8:00. III. Part I: B♭–c"; Part II: G–f'; Part III: A$_1$–d'; Part IV: F$_1$–d. Written for the Tennessee Tech Tuba Ensemble, Winston Morris, director. Multisectional work with traditional harmonies. All parts are interesting. Euphonium parts also available in treble clef. Parts may be doubled for a large ensemble.

Tignor, Scott. *Three Little London Variations.* Cimarron Music and Productions. Two euphoniums and two tubas. 1997. $18.00. 5:45. III. Part I: B♭–c"; Part II: F–a'; Part III: F$_1$–b♭; Part IV: F$_1$–e♭. Three movements: Off to Jail; Dense Fog; Tumbling Down. Set of three light variations based upon *London Bridge Is Falling Down.* Euphonium parts also available in treble clef. Parts may be doubled for a large ensemble.

Toda, Akira. *Euphonium Tuba Quartet.* Yamaha Kyohan Company Limited. Two euphoniums and two tubas. 1989. $17.50. 30 pp. III–IV. Part I: B♭–g'; Part II: A–d'; Part III: C–g; Part IV: A–e♭. A collection of 29 American folk songs and Christmas songs. There are no significant technical or range challenges. These are short arrangements and are very playable by high school students, yet interesting enough for university students. Parts may be doubled for a large ensemble.

Tomkins, Thomas. *Oyez! Has Any Found a Lad?* arr. Paul Schmidt. Heavy Metal Music. Two euphoniums and two tubas. 1991. $7.00. 2:00.

IV. Part I: d–g'; Part II: c–d'; Part III: A_1–g; Part IV: A_1–f. An aggressive melody primarily in the upper three parts in a traditional harmonic style. No significant technical problems, but players will need to count carefully. No score available. Parts may be doubled for a large ensemble.

Torme, Mel. *The Christmas Song.* arr. Rodger Vaughan. Available from the arranger. Two euphoniums and two tubas. 1987. $5.00. 2:00. IV. Part I: F–g'; Part II: e–e'; Part III: D–b; Part IV: G_1–g. For the Tubadours. Probably the most popular secular Christmas holiday song written in the last century. The top three parts take turns playing the melody. Works very well. No score available. Parts may be doubled for a large ensemble.

Uber, David. *Chronicles.* Tuba-Euphonium Press. Two euphoniums and two tubas. 1996. $10.00. 4:30. III. Part I: B♭–c" (d"); Part II: G–e'; Part III: C–g; Part IV: F_1–f. For Karl Megules and the Garden State Tuba Ensemble. Upbeat original composition with melodic material in all parts. Parts may be doubled for a large ensemble. Euphonium parts also available in treble clef.

Uber, David. *Deep River.* Manduca Music Publica tions. Two euphoniums and two tubas. $8.00. 3:30. II–III. Part I: d–a'; Part II: A–f♯'; Part III: G–a; Part IV: G_1–e. Expressive original ballad with close-voiced harmonies and a lot of motion in the inner voices. All parts are interesting and require a good legato articulation. Parts may be doubled for a large ensemble.

Uber, David. *Divertimento.* Tuba-Euphonium Press. Two euphoniums and two tubas. 1992. $12.00. 6:00. IV. Part I: d–d♭"; Part II: c–f'; Part III: D–b; Part IV: G_1–g. Three movements: Scherzo; Legend; Marchette. The first movement is very fast and should be felt in one, not three. The second movement is very lyrical and the third movement is a slow march. The tessitura of the first part is high. There are no range demands placed on the tubas. The third movement has a fugue-like section and is the most technically challenging in the piece. Originally published by Almitra Music Company, Incorporated (Kendor Music, Incorporated) and copyrighted in 1981. Parts may be doubled for a large ensemble.

Uber, David. *Divertimento, No. 2, Op. 130.* Encore Music Publishers. Two euphoniums and two tubas. 1990. $24.50. 9:00. IV–V. Part I: d♭–c"; Part II: B♭–g'; Part III: B♭$_1$–b♭; Part IV: F_1–g. Five movements: Prologue; Dance; Diversion; Fete; Celebration. A very interesting and complex work for tuba/euphonium quartet. The tessitura and technical demands are greatest on the first part. Several sections are multimetric. This will require four strong players.

Uber, David. *Music for the Stage, Op. 283.* Rebu Music Publications. Two euphoniums and two tubas. 1993. $12.00. 7:50. IV. Part I: d–b♭'; Part II: c–e'; Part III: D♭–a; Part IV: G_1–f. Three movements: I. Opening Curtain–Act I; II. Entr'Acte; III. Finale—Act II, Closing Curtain. Designed as a show piece; each part has numerous solo sections. All four parts are challenging but interesting. Close adherence to written dynamics is essential. Parts may be doubled for a large ensemble.

Uber, David. *Shadow-Graph.* Tuba-Euphonium Press. Three euphoniums and one tuba. 2002. $12.00. 6:00. III. Part I: B♭–c"; Part II: B♭$_1$–g'; Part III: A–e♭'; Part IV: A_1–b. For Shinya Suzuki and Ikuko Miura. This one-movement composition is divided into five contrasting sections. The textures range from quartal harmonies to traditional sonorities to added-note modern chords. The melodic ideas are well distributed among all four voices. Parts may be doubled for a large ensemble. May also be performed by four euphoniums. Also reviewed in the Summer 2004 issue of the *ITEA Journal* (Vol. 31, No. 4).

Uber, David. *Suite for Four Bass Tubas, Op. 67.* Almitra Music Company (Kendor Music, Incorporated). Four tubas. 1976. $11.00. 5:30. III–IV. Part I: F_1–b♭; Part II: A♭$_1$–a♭; Part III: B♭$_1$–g; Part IV: F_1–e♭. Four movements: Allegretto Misterioso; Allegro; Andante; Scherzo Allegro Molto. A classic work for tuba quartet. Technically it is not very challenging, but players must count carefully. Works well for good high school players or college students. Fun to play and to listen to.

Uber, David. *Three Bagatelles for Euphonium/Tuba Quartet, Op. 286.* Hidalgo Music. Two euphoniums and two tubas. 1992. $9.50. 5:15. IV. Part I: d♭–a♭'; Part II: c–f'; Part III: C–b♭; Part IV: G_1–e. Three movements. Three short, fairly easy movements that contrast in key, meter, and style. The final movement is a bit more challenging than the first two. Parts may be doubled for a large ensemble.

Uber, David. *Vaudeville.* Touch of Brass Music Corporation. Two euphoniums and two tubas. 1982. $12.00. 8:00. IV. Part I: c–c"; Part II: c–b♭; Part III: B♭$_1$–b♭; Part IV: F_1–b♭. Four movements: Moderato; Very Rhythmic; Tempo di Blues; Allegro. Four contrasting movements in styles representative of their titles. The top two parts have a high tessitura and all four parts are challenging technically. Fun to play.

Uber, David. *A Vermont Gathering.* Tuba-Euphonium Press. Two euphoniums and two tuba. 2001. $10.00. 2:15. II. Part I: f♯–g'; Part II: c♯–f'; Part III: B–f'; Part IV: E♭–a♭. This brief original composition consists of four contrasting sections. The texture is predominantly lyrical with the melodic material divided between all parts. Parts may be doubled for a large ensemble. May also be performed by four euphoniums.

Uber, David, arr. *Amazing Grace.* Tuba-Euphonium Press. Two euphoniums and two tubas. 1999.

$10.00. 2:15. II. Part I: A♭–a♭'; Part II: B♭–f'; Part III: D♭–a♭; Part IV: G_1–d♭. Popular hymn arranged in three settings with traditional harmonies. Settings are connected with brief introductions. Parts may be doubled for a large ensemble.

Uber, David, arr. *Eternal Hymns.* Kendor Music, Incorporated. Two euphoniums and two tubas. 2000. $10.00. 6:00. II–III. Part I: f–g'; Part II: A–e♭'; Part III: C–B♭; Part IV: F_1–c. Six movements: Rock of Ages (Hastings, Thomas); Nearer, My God to Thee (Mason, Lowell); Day Is Dying in the West (Sherwin, William F.); What a Friend We Have in Jesus (Converse, Charles C.); Beneath the Cross of Jesus (Maker, Fredrick C.); Eternal Father, Strong to Save (Dykes, John B.). Set of chorales with traditional harmonies. Range is appropriate for intermediate-level performers, though third part may be more difficult. Any of the movements can stand alone in a concert. Parts may be doubled for a large ensemble. Also reviewed in the Spring 2001 issue of the *TUBA Journal* (Vol. 28, No. 3).

Uber, David, arr. *Give Me That Old Time Religion.* Wehr's Music House. Two euphoniums and two tubas. 2003. $10.50. 3:15. II. Part I: c–a'; Part II: B♭–e'; Part III: C–a♭; Part IV: F_1–f. For Ovella Linton Ebron. Fun arrangement of this upbeat folk song that includes hand clapping. Melodic material is divided among the four voices. Includes nine statements of the chorus with the theme treated differently each time. Euphonium parts also available in treble clef.

Uber, David, arr. *Hymns for Many Occasions.* Tuba-Euphonium Press. Two euphoniums and two tubas. 2000. $12.00. 11 pp. II. Part I: e♭–b♭'; Part II: B♭–f'; Part III: E♭–b♭; Part IV: F_1–f. Seven movements: Bringing in the Sheaves; In the Garden; What a Friend We Have in Jesus; May Jesus Christ Be Praised; I Love to Tell the Story; God of our Fathers; Day Is Dying in the West. Useful collection of traditional hymns set in a four-part choral texture. Each hymn is preceded by a brief introduction, and the melody is primarily in the first part. Range is appropriate for intermediate-level performers. Parts may be doubled for a large ensemble. Individual movements can stand alone on a concert.

Uber, David, arr. *National Songs of America.* Kendor Music, Incorporated. Two euphoniums and two tubas. 2001. $10.00. 5:30 without repeats. II–III. Part I: B♭–f'; Part II: B♭–f'; Part III: G_1–f; Part IV: F_1–e♭. Five movements: America; America, the Beautiful; Yankee Doodle; Battle Hymn of the Republic; The Star Spangled Banner. Set of arrangements with traditional harmonies. Range is appropriate for intermediate-level performers, though there is occasional voice-crossing. Any of the movements can stand alone in a concert. Parts may be doubled for a large ensemble. Also reviewed in the Summer 2001 issue of the *TUBA Journal* (Vol. 28, No. 4).

Van Hoy, Marjorie A. *Four Contrapuntal Pieces.* Tuba-Euphonium Press. Two euphoniums and two tubas. 1994. $15.00. 4:00. I–II. Part I: d–b'; Part II: G–a'; Part III: C–c♯'; Part IV: G_1–f. Four movements: Kyrie Eleison; Christe Eleison; Kyrie Eleison; Gloria. Original composition in traditional contrapuntal style. Individual parts are not difficult, though the independence of parts may be challenging to younger players. The third movement is scored for three euphoniums and two tubas. Individual movements can stand alone on a concert. Parts may be doubled for a large ensemble.

Van Vactor, David. *Quartetto for Four Tubas.* Southern Music Company. Two euphoniums and two tubas. 1974. Out of Print. 13:00. IV. Part I: G–b♭' (c"); Part II: G–f'; Part III: C–c'; Part IV: ($B♭_2$) F_1–f♯. Four movements: Chorales; Allegro Scherzando; Intermezzo; Allegretto Giusto. The movements contrast greatly in style, meter, and key. The second and fourth movements are technically challenging at times. Good writing; fun to play.

Vasconi, Eugene. *Promenade.* Southern Music Company. Two euphoniums and two tubas. 1989. $5.00. 2:30. IV. Part I: d–f'; Part II: G–d'; Part III: G–a; Part IV: $B♭_1$–f. Technically not very challenging, and the melody and harmonies are very traditional. The melody is often fugue-like in character. Works quite well for large ensembles. Parts may be doubled for a large ensemble.

Vaughan, Rodger. *Fanfares.* Available from the composer. Two euphoniums and two tubas. 1988. $5.00. 2:00. IV. Part I: d–b♭'; Part II: c–f'; Part III: c–b♭; Part IV: A_1–f. Commissioned by Skip Gray and written for the University of Kentucky Tuba Ensemble. A moderate-tempo fanfare with the first and second parts often playing in an echo manner with the third and fourth parts. Some *divisi* sections in the top three parts. Very effective. Parts may be doubled for a large ensemble.

Vaughan, Rodger. *Marce's Blues.* Available from the composer. Two euphoniums and two tubas. 1993. $5.00. 2:45. IV. Part I: f–a'; Part II: e–a'; Part III: F–a; Part IV: F_1–e♭. For the nineteenth birthday of Cecilia Nocum. A traditional blues progression and format. Most of the melody is in the top two parts. Drums may be added. Parts may be doubled for a large ensemble.

Vaughan, Rodger. *Petite and Powerful: A Rag for Tuba/Euphonium Quartet.* Available from the composer. Two euphoniums and two tubas. 1991. $5.00. 2:45. IV. Part I: c–b♭'; Part II: c–e♭'; Part III: C–c♭; Part IV: $D♭_1$–g. Composed for the 21st birthday of Roxane Requio. A medium-tempo rag. The melody is very syncopated, especially in the top two parts. Parts may be doubled for a large ensemble.

Vaughan, Rodger. *Riverwest Rag.* Available from the composer. Two euphoniums and two tubas. 1989. $5.00. 2:30. IV. Part I: b♭–g'; Part II: B♭–e♭'; Part III: B♭–b♭; Part IV: E♭$_1$–e♭. Composed for the 21st birthday of Minako Kawanishi. An up-tempo rag. The lively melody is primarily in the top two parts. Fun for both performers and audiences. No score available. Parts may be doubled for a large ensemble.

Vaughan, Rodger. *Two (More) Birthday Rags.* Tuba-Euphonium Press. Two euphoniums and two tubas. 2001. $10.00. 6:00. II. Part I: f–a♭'; Part II: c–d'; Part III: F–a; Part IV: F$_1$–f♯. Two movements: Skis and Skates; Marce's Snowshoes. For Jane C. Kim and Cecilia Nocum. Like his original *Two Birthday Rags,* both movements are in the style of ragtime jazz. Each composition is completely notated, so no improvisation is required. Parts may be doubled for a large ensemble. No score is provided. Also reviewed in the Summer 2004 issue of the *ITEA Journal* (Vol. 31, No. 4).

Vaughan, Rodger. *Two Birthday Rags.* Tuba-Euphonium Press. Two euphoniums and two tubas. 1999. $10.00. 6:00. II. Part I: f–a'; Part II: c–f'; Part III: F–b; Part IV: F$_1$–f. Two movements: Colorado Cool; Kansas Kindling. For Melanie S. Chan and LeeLee Truong. Both movements are in the style of ragtime jazz. Each composition is completely notated, so no improvisation is required. Parts may be doubled for a large ensemble. No score is provided. Also reviewed in the Summer 2001 issue of the *TUBA Journal* (Vol. 28, No. 4).

Vaughan, Rodger. *Wiggleworm Squirm: The Neighbor Note Nocturne, The Semitone Serenade, A Rag.* Available from the composer. Two euphoniums and two tubas. 1989. $5.00. 6:00. IV. Part I: g–b♭'; Part II: B♭–d'; Part III: E♭–a♭; Part IV: D$_1$–e. Written for the Tubadours and dedicated to Minako Kawanishi. A very fun rag to play. No significant technical difficulties, though the melody is quite syncopated. Drums may be added for effect. No score available. Parts may be doubled for a large ensemble.

Vaughan, Rodger, arr. *Amazing Grace.* Available from the arranger. Two euphoniums, two tubas, and garden hose. $5.00.

Vaughan, Rodger, arr. *American Favorites: Tuba Euphonium Quartets.* Tuba-Euphonium Press. Two euphoniums and two tubas. 1992. $15.00. 14 pp. III–IV. Part I: B♭–a♭'; Part II: B♭–f'; Part III: B♭$_1$–b♭; Part IV: E♭$_1$–f. A delightful set of light arrangements of traditional American folk melodies. All parts are featured with the melody at one time or another. No significant technical problems. The euphonium parts are printed in bass and treble clef. Originally published in 1977 by the Mirafone Corporation. Parts may be doubled for a large ensemble.

Vaughan, Rodger, arr. *Away in a Manger.* Available from the arranger. Two euphoniums and two tubas. 1984. $5.00.

Vaughan, Rodger, arr. *Down by the Old Mill Stream.* Available from the arranger. Two euphoniums and two tubas. 1990. $5.00. 1:30. III–IV. Part I: c–f'; Part II: c–d'; Part III: c–a; Part IV: C–e. For the Tubadours. Cute arrangement of this familiar melody. Very appropriate for high school or college students. No score available. Parts may be doubled for a large ensemble. Recorded by the Tubadours, *Ve Iss Da Mighty Tubadours Ya?* Crystal Records, S421.

Vaughan, Rodger, arr. *Dream.* Available from the arranger. Two euphoniums and two tubas. 1988. $5.00. 1:30. IV. Part I: e♭–g'; Part II: e♭–e♭'; Part III: E♭–a♭; Part IV: E♭$_1$–e♭. For Abe Torchinsky and the Aspentubas. Nice arrangement of this classic "Big Band"–era ballad. The lyrical melody is primarily in the euphoniums. No score available. Parts may be doubled for a large ensemble.

Vaughan, Rodger, arr. *Eight Days of Christmas.* Available from the arranger. Two euphoniums and two tubas. 1982. $5.00.

Vaughan, Rodger, arr. *God Rest Ye, Merry Gentlemen.* Available from the arranger. Two euphoniums and two tubas. $5.00. 2:00. IV. Part I: f–b♭'; Part II: d–e♭'; Part III: G–b♭; Part IV: B♭$_1$–g. For the Tubadours. Good arrangement of this traditional Christmas carol. No significant technical problems. Parts may be doubled for a large ensemble. Recorded by the Tubadours, *Merry Christmas Album,* Crystal Records, S422.

Vaughan, Rodger, arr. *Good Christian Men Rejoice.* Available from the arranger. Two euphoniums and two tubas. 1984. $5.00.

Vaughan, Rodger, arr. *Greensleeves.* Available from the arranger. Two euphoniums and two tubas. 1976. $5.00.

Vaughan, Rodger, arr. *In Dulci Jubilo/Jingle Bells.* Cimarron Music and Productions. Two euphoniums and two tubas. 1982. $9.00. 1:45. II. Part I: f–a♭'; Part II: d–f'; Part III: A♭–c'; Part IV: G$_1$–f. For the Tubadours. Straightforward medley of two popular Christmas carols. Melody is predominantly in the first and third parts. Parts may be doubled for a large ensemble. Euphonium parts also available in treble clef.

Vaughan, Rodger, arr. *Infant Holy.* Available from the arranger. Two euphoniums and two tubas. 1982. $5.00.

Vaughan, Rodger, arr. *Java.* Available from the arranger. Two euphoniums and two tubas. 1990. $5.00. 3:00. IV. Part I: d♭–a♭'; Part II: d♭–a♭'; Part III: A♭–c'; Part IV: A♭$_1$–f. For the Tubadours. Interesting arrangement of this jazz standard. The melody is primarily in the first and second euphonium parts. Several meter changes in the middle section. No score available. Parts may be doubled for a large ensemble.

Vaughan, Rodger, arr. *Jingle Bells Waltz.* Available from the arranger. Two euphoniums and two tubas. $5.00. 2:00. IV. Part I: e♭–b♭'; Part II: A♭–f'; Part III: A♭–d♭'; Part IV: D♭–g♭. For the Tubadours. A very interesting and fast-paced waltz version of "Jingle Bells." The meter repeats the pattern 3+3+3+2. Drums may be added for effect. Fun to play. No score available. Parts may be doubled for a large ensemble.

Vaughan, Rodger, arr. *Lo How a Rose.* Available from the arranger. Two euphoniums and two tubas. 1984. $5.00.

Vaughan, Rodger, arr. *Mack, the Knight.* Available from the arranger. Two euphoniums and two tubas. 1988. $5.00. 2:00. IV. Part I: g–g'; Part II: f–d'; Part III: A–b♭; Part IV: $B♭_1$–g. For the Tubadours. A humorous combination of "Mack, the Knife" and the music from a McDonald's restaurant commercial featuring "Mac Tonight." Most of the melody is in the upper two parts and the fourth part. Fun to play. Parts may be doubled for a large ensemble. No score available. Premiered at the Octubafest at the University of Kansas, 1988.

Vaughan, Rodger, arr. *March of The Toys.* Available from the arranger. Two euphoniums and two tubas. 1975. $5.00.

Vaughan, Rodger, arr. *Moonglow.* Available from the arranger. Two euphoniums and two tubas. 1991. $5.00. 2:10. III–IV. Part I: g♯–g'; Part II: d–d'; Part III: F–b♭; Part IV: $B♭_1$–f. For the Tubadours. A nice slow swing melody with most of the work in the euphonium. Not difficult technically. No score available. Parts may be doubled for a large ensemble.

Vaughan, Rodger, arr. *Only Eight Days of Christmas.* Cimarron Music and Productions. Two euphoniums and two tubas. 1995. $9.00. 2:45. III. Part I: d♭–a♭'; Part II: B♭–f'; Part III: E♭–c'; Part IV: F_1–f. For the Tubadours. Light, abbreviated arrangement of *The Twelve Days of Christmas.* Melodic material is divided among all four voices. Parts may be doubled for a large ensemble. Euphonium parts also available in treble clef.

Vaughan, Rodger, arr. *Santa Claus Is Coming to Town.* Available from the arranger. Two euphoniums and two tubas. 1984. $5.00. 1:30. IV. Part I: f–a'; Part II: d–f'; Part III: F–b♭; Part IV: F_1–e. For the Tubadours. Cute arrangement of this fun Christmas melody. There are many tempo and style changes. Parts may be doubled for a large ensemble. Recorded by the Tubadours, *Merry Christmas Album,* Crystal Records, S422.

Vaughan, Rodger, arr. *Santa's Favorites.* Cimarron Music and Productions. Two euphoniums and two tubas. 1995. $40.00. Part I: d–b♭'; Part II: B♭–g'; Part III: D–d'; Part IV: F_1–a♭. Fifteen movements: Coventry Carol; God Rest Ye Merry Gentlemen; Hail to the Lord's Anointed; 'Neath Bethlehem Starlit Night; Jingle Bells—Traditional; Lo How a Rose E'er Blooming; O Little Town of Bethlehem; Good Christian Men Rejoice; Jingle Bells—Jazz Waltz; Santa Claus Is Comin' to Town; Greensleeves; March of the Wooden Soldiers; Away in the Manger; Bells of St. Mary's; March of the Toys. Nice collection of Christmas songs with each part having the melody at some point. Accessible for a variety of players, depending upon the movement. Individual movements can stand alone in a concert. Euphonium parts also available in treble clef. Parts may be doubled for a large ensemble. Also reviewed in the Winter 1996 issue of the *TUBA Journal* (Vol. 23, No. 2).

Vaughan, Rodger, arr. *Sentimental Journey.* Available from the arranger. Two euphoniums and two tubas. 1977. $5.00. 1:45. IV. Part I: g♯–f'; Part II: d–d'; Part III: G♭–b♭; Part IV: $B♭_1$–c. For the Tubadours. A moderate swing tune with most of the melody primarily in the top two parts. No significant technical problems. Drums may be added. Parts may be doubled for a large ensemble.

Vaughan, Rodger, arr. *Silent Night.* Available from the arranger. Two euphoniums and two tubas. 1984. $5.00.

Vaughan, Rodger, arr. *Speak Low.* Available from the arranger. Two euphoniums and two tubas. 1990. $5.00.

Vaughan, Rodger, arr. *Take Me Out to the Ballgame.* Available from the arranger. Two euphoniums and two tubas. 1988. $5.00.

Vaughan, Rodger, arr. *Undecided.* Available from the arranger. Two euphoniums and two tubas. 1988. $5.00. 3:20. IV. Part I: f–a♭'; Part II: f–e♭'; Part III: F–g; Part IV: F_1–d. For the Tubadours. A famous dance melody from the "Big Band" era. Contains an extended tuba solo. Drums may be added for style enhancement. No score available. Parts may be doubled for a large ensemble.

Vaughan, Rodger, arr. *Veni Emmanuel.* Available from the arranger. Two euphoniums and two tubas. 1983. $5.00. 3:00. IV. Part I: f–f'; Part II: c–g'; Part III: G–a; Part IV: G_1–e. A very lyrical and traditional arrangement. Works well. Parts may be doubled for a large ensemble.

Vaughan Williams, Ralph. *Flourish.* arr. David Butler. Tuba-Euphonium Press. Two euphoniums and two tubas. 2002. $10.00. 2:00. II. Part I: d–g'; Part II: c–e♭'; Part III: F–b♭; Part IV: F_1–c. Originally for wind band, this piece is a stately fanfare in ternary form using contrasting dynamics and articulations to define the sections. Melody is predominantly in the first part, though there is some exchange between the tubas and euphoniums. Euphonium parts also available in treble clef. Parts may be doubled for a large ensemble. Also reviewed in the Spring 2004 issue of the *ITEA Journal* (Vol. 31, No. 3).

Vaughan Williams, Ralph. *Seventeen Come Sunday.* arr. David Butler. Tuba-Euphonium Press. Two euphoniums and two tubas. 1998. $15.00. 3:30. II. Part I: c–b♭'; Part II: c–a♭'; Part III: E♭–b♭; Part IV: F_1–d♭. An excellent arrangement of the first movement of Vaughan Williams' *Folk Song Suite.* It is in ternary form with the light British march style in the outer sections being contrasted with the legato melody of the middle section. Each part is interesting and performs a substantial melodic role at some point. Euphonium parts also available in treble clef. Parts may be doubled for a large ensemble. Also reviewed in the Fall 1999 issue of the *TUBA Journal* (Vol. 27, No. 1).

Vazzana, Anthony. *Montaggi for Four Tubas.* Tuba-Euphonium Press. Four tubas. 1993. $40.00. 12:00. V. Part I: A_1–a'; Part II: A_1–g'; Part III: A_1–e'; Part IV: $C\sharp_1$–c'. A contemporary work that is very technically demanding of all four parts. Twentieth-century techniques required include multiphonics, quarter tones, hand clapping, shouting, singing, and chanting in the instrument. Each player reads from the score. All parts require mutes and players are asked in one section to play from their lowest possible note to their highest possible note. A very dissonant and complex work. Originally written in 1978; won Honorable Mention in the Tuba Quartet Composition Contest sponsored by the Los Angeles Tuba Quartet and the Mirafone Corporation.

Verdi, Giuseppe. *Choro di Schiavi Ebrei (Chor der Gefangenen aus der Opera "Nabucco").* arr. Mark Evans. Musikverlag Barbara Evans. Two euphoniums and two tubas. 1992. $15.00. 3:30. IV. Part I: F–g'; Part II: B–f'; Part III: F_1–d'; Part IV: F_1–f. All parts have an opportunity to play the lyrical melody. Numerous repeating patterns of triplets and sextuplets accompany the melody. The tempo is quite slow and the rhythm patterns can be a challenge to fit together. Parts may be doubled for a large ensemble.

Verdi, Giuseppe. *La donna é mobile.* arr. Benjamin Roundtree. Roundtree Music. Two euphoniums and two tubas. 2002. $12.00. 2:00. II–III. Part I: f–g' (b♭'); Part II: d–e♭'; Part III: F–b♭; Part IV: F_1–B♭. Nice arrangement of this popular aria. Melodic material is divided between the first euphonium and first tuba parts. The remaining parts are accessible for intermediate-level performers. Parts may be doubled for a large ensemble.

Verdi, Guiseppe. *La Donna e Mobile.* arr. Gail Robertson. Tuba-Euphonium Press. Two euphoniums and two tubas. 1999. $10.00. 2:30. II. Part I: f–b♭'; Part II: f–b♭'; Part III: F–d'; Part IV: ($E\flat_1$) $B\flat_1$–f. For Carmen Russo. Straightforward arrangement of this standard aria. Melodic material is divided among the top three parts. Parts are formatted to be reduced for use in a flip folder. Euphonium parts also available in treble clef. Parts may be doubled for a large ensemble.

Verdi, Guiseppe. *Nabucco Overture.* arr. Maurice Bale. Godiva Music. Two euphoniums and two tubas. £8.00.

Verdi, Guiseppe. *Questa o Quella.* arr. Robert Wilkinson. Cimarron Music and Productions. Two euphoniums and two tubas. $12.50. Euphonium parts also available in treble clef.

Victoria, Thomas Luis de. *O Regem Coeli for Tuba Quartet.* arr. Joseph Schwartz. The Unicorn Music Company, Incorporated. Four tubas. 1990. 4:30. IV. Part I: c–f'; Part II: e♭–e♭'; Part III: E♭–b♭'; Part IV: E♭–b♭'. Two movements: Part I; Part II. A very nice arrangement of this Renaissance madrigal. The tessitura of the first part is high. Playable by high school students if the first and second parts are played on euphonium. Part II is faster and more polyphonic than Part I. No real technical challenges. Parts may be doubled for a large ensemble.

Victoria, Thomas Luis de. *O Vos Omnes (Motet).* arr. James Self. Wimbledon Music Incorporated. Four tubas. 1979. $7.00. 2:30. II–III. Part I: f–e♭'; Part II: d–e♭'; Part III: A♭–g♭; Part IV: ($E\flat_1$) $A\flat_1$–e♭. This motet is marked lento with the main theme primarily in the first two parts. The arranger suggests the ideal instrumentation would be for euphoniums to play the first and second parts and tubas to play the third and fourth parts. The motet is not rhythmically challenging and with the euphoniums playing the top two parts this is easily playable by high school students. Parts may be doubled for a large ensemble.

Vittoria, Thomas Luis de. *Ave Maria.* arr. John Tuinstra. Tuba-Euphonium Press. Two euphoniums and two tubas. 1993. $8.00. 1:45. I–II. Part I: f–f'; Part II: d–e♭'; Part III: B♭–a; Part IV: $B\flat_1$–e♭. Brief arrangement of a work by the great Spanish contemporary of Palestrina. Appropriate for young ensembles. Parts may be doubled for a large ensemble. Also reviewed in the Summer 1995 issue of the *TUBA Journal* (Vol. 22, No. 4).

Vivaldi, Antonio. *Concerto.* arr. Karl Humble. T.A.P. Music. Two euphoniums and two tubas. 1990. $10.00. 6:00. IV–V. Part I: f–c''; Part II: c–b♭'; Part III: $B\flat_1$–d'; Part IV: F_1–b♭. Three movements: Allegro; Largo; Allegro. Originally written for two trumpets and orchestra in the key of C. The tessitura of the first two parts is quite high. Technically challenging in some spots depending on the tempos used. Parts may be doubled for a large ensemble. No score available.

Von Suppe, Franz. *Morning, Noon, and Night in Vienna Overture.* arr. David Butler. Tuba-Euphonium Press. Two euphoniums and two tubas. 2002. $20.00. 6:00. III. Part I: E–b♭'; Part II: G–f'; Part III: $B\flat_1$–c'; Part IV: ($E\flat_1$) F_1–c'. Challenging arrangement that works well as a concert opener. All parts require technical dexterity and the melodic material is divided among all four voices. Euphonium parts also available in treble clef. More appropriate for a large ensemble than for a quartet, as all parts have *divisi* passages. Also reviewed in the Spring 2004 issue of the *ITEA Journal* (Vol. 31, No. 3).

Wagner, J. F. *Under the Double Eagle*. arr. Norlan Bewley. Bewley Music, Incorporated. Two euphoniums and two tubas. 1995. $12.00. 1:15. II. Part I: c–b♭'; Part II: c–b♭'; Part III: G–e♭'; Part IV: A♭$_1$–f. Part of the Octubafest Music collection, this arrangement is appropriate for intermediate-level ensembles. Melodic material is divided among all four voices. Parts may be doubled for a large ensemble. Euphonium parts also available in treble clef.

Wagner, J. F. *Under the Double Eagle*. arr. Paul Schmidt. Heavy Metal Music. Two euphoniums and two tubas. 1990. $7.00. 2:45. IV. Part I: B♭–g'; Part II: G–g'; Part III: D–c'; Part IV: F$_1$–e (a). All four parts have an opportunity to play the melody. No significant technical challenges. No score available. Parts may be doubled for a large ensemble.

Wagner, Richard. *Bridal Chorus from Lohengrin*. arr. Dan Oliver. Cimarron Music and Productions. Two euphoniums and two tubas. $10.50. 2:15. III. Part I: d–g'; Part II: d–d'; Part III: G–a; Part IV: B♭$_1$–B♭. Straightforward arrangement of this popular wedding song. The texture is homophonic, and the melody is predominantly in the first part. Euphonium parts also available in treble clef. Parts may be doubled for a large ensemble.

Wagner, Richard. *Bridal Chorus from Lohengrin*. arr. Dan Oliver. Ohio Valley Tuba Quartet Press. Two euphoniums and two tubas. 1988. $9.00. 2:30. III–IV. Part I: d–g'; Part II: d–d'; Part III: G–a; Part IV: B♭$_1$–B♭. Very usable arrangement of this famous wedding introit. The melody is primarily in the first part, so the piece is really not demanding for any of the players. Parts may be doubled for a large ensemble.

Wagner, Richard. *Elsa's Procession to the Cathedral*. arr. Gail Robertson. Tuba-Euphonium Press. Two euphoniums and two tubas. 1998. $14.00. 4:00. III. Part I: B–b♭'; Part II: B♭–b♭'; Part III: B♭$_1$–c'; Part IV: (E♭$_1$) G$_1$–c♯'. For Scott and Sarah Battunis' wedding. Nice arrangement of this lyrical work. Though not technically difficult, this piece requires endurance and musicality from each performer. Modulates to four sharps. Euphonium parts also available in treble clef. Parts may be doubled for a large ensemble.

Wagner, Richard. *Pilgerchor aus Tannhäuser*. arr. Bruno Seitz. Musikverlag Martin Scherbacher. Four tubas. 1988. $15.00. 3:00. IV. Part I: A♭$_1$–f'; Part II: A♭$_1$–c'; Part III: F–a♯; Part IV: F$_1$–e♭. Nice arrangement of this famous melody from Tannhauser. No significant technical problems. The first and second parts are written for tubas in F. A euphonium could be used on the first part. Works quite well. Parts may be doubled for a large ensemble.

Wagner, Richard. *Pilgrim's Chorus from Tannhäuser*. arr. Paul Schmidt. Heavy Metal Music. Two euphoniums and two tubas. 1991. $7.00. 3:20. IV. Part I: A♭–f'; Part II: A♭–d'; Part III: F–c'; Part IV: G♭$_1$–g♭. Nice arrangement of this famous melody. No technical or range problems. A conductor will help the ensemble performance. Parts may be doubled for a large ensemble.

Wagner, Richard. *Ride of the Valkyries*. arr. David Uber. Kendor Music, Incorporated. Two euphoniums and two tubas. 2002. $9.00. 2:35. IV–V. Part I: B–b'; Part II: A♯–f♯'; Part III: A♯$_1$–a♯; Part IV: F♯$_1$–f♯. Challenging arrangement including large leaps in each part, 32nd notes in the lower parts, and trilling in the first part. Modulates into five sharps. Parts may be doubled for a large ensemble. Also reviewed in the Spring 2003 issue of the *ITEA Journal* (Vol. 30, No. 3).

Waldteufel, E. *The Skaters' Waltzes*. arr. Soichi Konagaya. Sonic Arts, Incorporated. Two euphoniums and two tubas. 1986. $12.00. 5:30. IV. Part I: e♭–a♭'; Part II: B♭–e♭'; Part III: C–a♭; Part IV: G$_1$–e♭. A medley of three popular waltzes. The melody is primarily in the first part. No range or technical problems. Parts may be doubled for a large ensemble.

Walton, Nicky. *Vite!* Breakthrough Music. Two euphoniums and two tubas. Part I: d–c''; Part II: d–f'; Part III: A♭$_1$–c'; Part IV: A♭$_1$–c'. Written by the wife of a founding member of the quartet Tubalaté, this piece is influenced by minimalism. Works really well with large ensemble. Recorded by Tubalaté on the compact disc *Hall of Mirrors*.

Walton, Paul, arr. *Danny Boy*. Breakthrough Music. Two euphoniums and two tubas. Part I: B♭–g'; Part II: c–f'; Part III: B♭–g; Part IV: B♭$_1$–b♭. Effective arrangement. One verse only. Works well with large ensemble.

Warren, Charles, arr. *Down in the River to Pray*. Cimarron Music and Productions. Two euphoniums and two tubas. $12.50. Euphonium parts also available in treble clef.

Warren, Charles, arr. *Short'in Bread*. Cimarron Music and Productions. Four tubas. $9.50.

Warren, Charles, arr. *Wore a Yellow Ribbon*. Cimarron Music and Productions. Two euphoniums and two tubas. $11.00. Euphonium parts also available in treble clef.

Warren, Chris, arr. *O' Come Emmanuel*. Cimarron Music and Productions. Two euphoniums and two tubas. $7.50. Euphonium parts also available in treble clef.

Warren, Harry. *The Kiss Polka*. arr. Ray Grim. Cimarron Music and Productions. Two euphoniums and two tubas. 1996. $10.00. 1:45. II. Part I: d–b♭'; Part II: B♭–f'; Part III: C–b♭; Part IV: A♭$_1$–g. Part of the TubaMeisters Collection, this arrangement is appropriate for intermediate-level performers. Melodic material is predominantly in the first part, though all parts are interesting. Parts may be doubled for a large ensemble. Euphonium parts also available in treble clef.

Warren, Harry. *Selections from 42nd Street.* arr. Doug Minerd. PP Music. Two euphoniums and two tubas. 1989. $20.00. 6:00. IV. Part I: B–a'; Part II: B–a'; Part III: G_1–e'; Part IV: G_1–f'. The medley includes "We're in the Money," "Lullaby of Broadway," "Forty-Second Street," and "Shuffle Off to Buffalo." The range of all four parts is quite high. A good swing feel is necessary. The addition of a drum set would benefit the ensemble. Works very well. Parts may be doubled for a large ensemble. Recorded by the British Tuba Quartet, *Elite Syncopations,* Polyphonic Reproductions Limited, QPRZ 012D; and the Monarch Tuba/Euphonium Quartet.

Watts, Charles. *Suite in D♭ for Tubas and Euphoniums.* Available from the composer. Two euphoniums and two tubas. 1992. $5.00. 6:30. IV. Part I: c–b♭'; Part II: c–g♭'; Part III: $A\flat_1$–b♭; Part IV: $A\flat_1$–a♭. Three movements: Alla Marcia; Moderato; Chaconne. Rhythmically not very difficult, and the melody and harmonies are very traditional. The three movements contrast in key, meter, and style. Parts may be doubled for a large ensemble.

Weber, Carl Maria von. *Hunter's Chorus from Der Freischutz.* arr. F. H. Laws. Cimarron Music and Productions. Two euphoniums and two tubas. 1998. $11.50. 1:00. Euphonium parts also available in treble clef.

Weber, Carl Maria von. *Hunter's Chorus from "Der Freischütz."* arr. F. H. Laws. Ohio Valley Tuba Quartet Press. Two euphoniums and two tubas. 1988. $9.00. 1:20. III–IV. Part I: f–a'; Part II: d–d'; Part III: c–b♭; Part IV: E♭–f. Very traditional in its harmonic and rhythmic treatment of this melody. No significant technical problems. Parts may be doubled for a large ensemble.

Weber, Carl Maria von. *Hunter's Chorus from "Der Freischütz."* arr. Paul Schmidt. Heavy Metal Music. Two euphoniums and two tubas. 1991. $7.00. 1:20. III–IV. Part I: c–e'; Part II: A–a; Part III: G–f; Part IV: $B\flat_1$–f. The melody is primarily in the top two parts. No significant technical problems. No score available. Parts may be doubled for a large ensemble.

Weber, Carl Maria von. *Huntsmen's Choruses.* arr. Rudy Emilson. Kendor Music, Incorporated. Two euphoniums and two tubas. 2000. $10.00. 3:00. IV. Part I: f–b♭'; Part II: d–f'; Part III: E♭–b♭; Part IV: $B\flat_1$–f. Two movements: From the Opera "Der Freischutz"; From the Opera "Euryanthe." Challenging arrangement of two of Weber's hunting choruses. All parts may require double-tonguing if performed at the indicated tempos. Either of the movements can stand alone in a concert. Parts may be doubled for a large ensemble. Also reviewed in the Spring 2002 issue of the *ITEA Journal* (Vol. 29, No. 3).

Wedner, Henry Lewis. *O Little Town of Bethlehem.* arr. Rodger Vaughan. Available from the arranger. Two euphoniums and two tubas. 1984. $5.00. 2:25. III–IV. Part I: d–a'; Part II: d–d'; Part III: D–a; Part IV: F_1–d. For the Tubadours. A traditional very arrangement. The melody is primarily in the top two parts. Works well. Parts may be doubled for a large ensemble. Recorded by the Tubadours, *Merry Christmas Album,* Crystal Records, S422.

Weelkes, Thomas. *Lo, Country Sports.* arr. Paul F. Hartin. Cellar Press. Four tubas. 1974. 2:00. III–IV. Part I: B♭–c'; Part II: B♭–c; Part III: $B\flat_1$–f; Part IV: A_1–c. Playable by high school students if the first and second parts are played on euphonium. A typical contrapuntal madrigal. Not difficult technic ally. Parts may be doubled for a large ensemble.

Welcher, Dan. *Hauntings for Tuba Ensemble.* Available from the composer. Two euphoniums and two tubas. 1986. $25.00. 7:30. IV. Part I: G–c"; Part II: $A\sharp_1$–b'; Part III: $F\sharp_1$–d♯'; Part IV: D_1–c♯'. Four movements: In the Twilight; Kaspar; Poltergeist; Il Commendatore (without pause). Commissioned by Tubists Universal Brotherhood Association. Contemporary tonal harmonies, along with basic twentieth-century techniques. The tessitura of the first two parts is high and will require strong players. All parts will require mutes. Parts may be doubled for a large ensemble. First performed by the College All-Star Tuba/Euphonium Ensemble at the 1986 International Tuba-Euphonium Conference.

Werden, David, arr. *Good Cheer Collection.* Cimarron Music and Productions. Two euphoniums and two tubas. $45.00. II–III. Sixteen movements: Joy to the World; Bring a Torch Jeanette Isabella; On the Day Earth Shall Ring; Lo, How a Rose E'er Blooming; Oh Come All Ye Faithful; The First Noel; Good Christian Men Rejoice; Deck the Halls; In the Bleak Mid Winter; Go Tell It on the Mountain; Good King Wenceslas, Jingle Bells; Silent Night; Hark the Herald Angels Sing; I Heard the Bells; Jolly Old Saint Nicholas. This collection of popular Christmas songs is available in full-sized and march-sized parts. Euphonium parts also available in treble clef. Parts may be doubled for a large ensemble. Also reviewed in the Summer 1995 issue of the *TUBA Journal* (Vol. 22, No. 4) and in the Spring 1996 issue of the *TUBA Journal* (Vol. 23, No. 3).

Werden, David, arr. *Lo, How a Rose E'er Blooming.* Cimarron Music and Productions. Two euphoniums and two tubas. $10.00. 1:45. I–II. Part I: d–e'; Part II: B–d'; Part III: G–a; Part IV: A_1–e. Straightforward arrangement of this popular Christmas chorale. Parts are formatted to fit into flip folders. Euphonium parts also available in treble clef. Parts may be doubled for a large ensemble.

Werden, David, arr. *On This Day.* Cimarron Music and Productions. Two euphoniums and two tubas. 2003. $11.00. 3:00. II. Part I: d–g'; Part II: B–f''; Part III: E–c'; Part IV: B♭$_1$–f. Straightforward arrangement of this SATB chorale. The melody is in the first euphonium in the outer sections, and the second tuba has the melody in the contrasting middle section. Euphonium parts also available in treble clef. Parts may be doubled for a large ensemble.

Werden, David, arr. *Songs of the British Isles.* Whaling Music Publishers. Two euphoniums and two tubas. 1986. $9.50. 6:30. III–IV. Part I: B♭$_1$–g'; Part II: G–f' (g'); Part III: (C) E♭–c'; Part IV: (E♭$_1$) B♭$_1$–g. Four movements: The Minstrel Boy; Molly Malone; Danny Boy; English Country Garden. A collection of four short familiar British folk songs. Technically not challenging and consequently very appropriate for good high school ensembles. The first part is printed in treble clef. Parts may be doubled for a large ensemble.

Werner-Kersten, Max. *Bummel-Petrus (Lazy Pete).* arr. Ronald C. Knoener. Tuba-Euphonium Press. Two euphoniums and two tubas. 1997. $8.00. 1:30. II–III. Part I: c–g'; Part II: B♭–e♭'; Part III: C–g; Part IV: B♭$_1$–A♭ (B♭). Straightforward arrangement of this popular polka. Melodic material is divided primarily between the first euphonium and first tuba. Parts may be doubled for a large ensemble, and there are *divisi* passages in the second part.

Wilbye, John. *Adieu, Sweet Amaryllis.* Sarnia Music. Two euphoniums and two tubas. £9.99.

Wilbye, John. *Lady, When I Behold.* Sarnia Music. Two euphoniums and two tubas. £9.99.

Wilder, Alec, arr. *Carols for a MERRY TUBACHRISTMAS.* Harvey Phillips Foundation. Two euphoniums and two tubas. 1977. $5.00. 20 pp. III–IV. Part I: e–a♭'; Part II: A–e; Part III: C–c'; Part IV: E♭$_1$–d. Commissioned by Harvey Phillips. Dedicated to William J. Bell. This is the book of Christmas carols arranged for use in the TubaChristmas concerts held each year all over the world. There are nineteen familiar carols plus the Eddie Sauter arrangement of Come, Sweet Death (three-part). While the technical and range demands are not great, these carols should not be considered easy. These carols will require four moderately strong players as the melody shifts between all four parts. With Wilder, even the accompaniment parts are interesting, but challenging to play. These are designed to have, and actually work much better with, multiple players on a part. A treble clef book is available for the first and second parts. Available from the Harvey Phillips Foundation or at any TubaChristmas concert. Recorded by Harvey Phillips/TubaChristmas, Harvey Phillips Foundation, HPF NR-1111; and Harvey Phillips and his TUBASANTAS, Harvey Phillips Foundation, HPF 1000–1.

Wilder, Alec, and Norlan Bewley, arr. *Carols for a MERRY TUBACHRISTMAS, Volume II.* Harvey Phillips Foundation. Two euphoniums and two tubas. 1992. $6.00. 66 pp. III–IV. Part I: e–a♭'; Part II: A–e; Part III: C–c'; Part IV: E♭$_1$–d. Commissioned by Harvey Phillips. Dedicated to William J. Bell and Alec Wilder. This contains all the carols from Volume I plus 13 new carols arranged by Norlan Bewley for a total of 32 Christmas carols. All arrangements, except for three, are in score form. Technical demands are moderate. A treble clef book is also available. These are designed for a quartet or mass ensemble. Recorded by Harvey Phillips and his TUBASANTAS, Harvey Phillips Foundation, HPF 1000–1.

Wilhelm, Rolf. *Bavarian Stew.* Musikverlag Bruno Uetz. One euphonium and three tubas. €13.00. Second part may be performed on euphonium as well.

Wilkinson, Robert. *El Tubadore.* Cimarron Music and Productions. Two euphoniums and two tubas. $12.50. Euphonium parts also available in treble clef.

Wilkinson, Robert. *Strange Man.* Cimarron Music and Productions. Tuba/euphonium quartet. $11.00.

Wilkinson, Robert. *TuBach.* Cimarron Music and Productions. Two euphoniums and two tubas. $9.00. Euphonium parts also available in treble clef.

Wilkinson, Robert. *Tubasity.* Cimarron Music and Productions. Two euphoniums and two tubas. $11.00. Euphonium parts also available in treble clef.

Wilkinson, Robert. *Waltzing MaTubas.* Cimarron Music and Productions. Two euphoniums and two tubas. 1997. $11.50. 2:15. Euphonium parts also available in treble clef.

Wilkinson, Robert, arr. *Auld Lang Syne.* Cimarron Music and Productions. Two euphoniums and two tubas. $8.50. Euphonium parts also available in treble clef.

Wilkinson, Robert, arr. *Chanukah Medley.* Cimarron Music and Productions. Two euphoniums and two tubas. $11.00. Euphonium parts also available in treble clef.

Wilkinson, Robert, arr. *Dona Nobis Tubas.* Cimarron Music and Productions. Two euphoniums and two tubas. 1996. $9.00. 2:45. Euphonium parts also available in treble clef.

Wilkinson, Robert, arr. *A Folk Song.* Cimarron Music and Productions. Two euphoniums and two tubas. $8.50. Euphonium parts also available in treble clef.

Wilkinson, Robert, arr. *Freilach Ora.* Cimarron Music and Productions. Two euphoniums and two tubas. $10.00. Euphonium parts also available in treble clef.

Wilkinson, Robert, arr. *Halleluya*. Cimarron Music and Productions. Two euphoniums and two tubas. $9.50. Euphonium parts also available in treble clef.

Wilkinson, Robert, arr. *The Happy Soul*. Cimarron Music and Productions. Two euphoniums and two tubas. $12.00. Euphonium parts also available in treble clef.

Wilkinson, Robert, arr. *Hava Nigila*. Cimarron Music and Productions. Two euphoniums and two tubas. $10.00. Euphonium parts also available in treble clef.

Wilkinson, Robert, arr. *Klezmer Collection "To Life."* Cimarron Music and Productions. Two euphoniums and two tubas. $70.00. Euphonium parts also available in treble clef.

Wilkinson, Robert, arr. *Lo, How a Rose E'er Blooming*. Cimarron Music and Productions. Two euphoniums and two tubas. $8.50. Euphonium parts also available in treble clef.

Wilkinson, Robert, arr. *My Father's Nigun Song*. Cimarron Music and Productions. Two euphoniums and two tubas. $8.50. Euphonium parts also available in treble clef.

Wilkinson, Robert, arr. *On Sabbath Day*. Cimarron Music and Productions. Two euphoniums and two tubas. $10.00. Euphonium parts also available in treble clef.

Wilkinson, Robert, arr. *Sammy's Freilach*. Cimarron Music and Productions. Two euphoniums and two tubas. $7.00. Euphonium parts also available in treble clef.

Wilkinson, Robert, arr. *Sherelle*. Cimarron Music and Productions. Two euphoniums and two tubas. $10.00. Euphonium parts also available in treble clef.

Wilkinson, Robert, arr. *Tish Nigon (Table Song)*. Cimarron Music and Productions. Two euphoniums and two tubas. $10.00. Euphonium parts also available in treble clef.

Wilkinson, Robert, arr. *Zacatecas March*. Cimarron Music and Productions. Two euphoniums and two tubas. $11.50. Euphonium parts also available in treble clef.

Williams, William N. *Little Suite for Tuba Quartet*. T.A.P. Music. Four tubas. 1990. $12.00. 10:00. IV. Part I: C–a♭'; Part II: B♭$_1$–g'; Part III: C–g'; Part IV: G$_1$–e♭'. Three movements: Barcarole; Scherzo; March. Range is very demanding in all four parts. Other instrumentation possibilities include two euphoniums and two tubas or three euphoniums and one tuba. The third player is asked to rhythmically tap the rim of his bell with a metal mallet. Parts may be doubled for a large ensemble.

Willis, Richard. *Prelude and Rondino*. Tuba-Euphonium Press. Two euphoniums and two tubas. 1998. $10.00. 3:15. II. Part I: A♭–g'; Part II: A♭–c♯'; Part III: B♭$_1$–a; Part IV: A$_1$–g♭. Two movements: Prelude; Rondino. Original composition appropriate for younger performers. The first movement is homophonic and based on traditional harmonies, which contrasts with the fast-paced second movement. Each part has melodic material at some point. Parts may be doubled for a large ensemble.

Wilson, Kenyon D. *Dance No. 1*. Tuba-Euphonium Press. Two euphoniums and two tubas. 1993. $5.00. 2:00. IV. Part I: f–c''; Part II: B♭–f'; Part III: F–b♭; Part IV: F$_1$–B♭. A very lively melody that is multimetric and primarily in the euphoniums. All parts are interesting and have some technical challenges, depending on the performance tempo. Works well for a concert opener. Parts may be doubled for a large ensemble. Recorded by the Tennessee Tech Alumni Tuba Ensemble on the compact disc *For the Kings of Brass*, Mark Records.

Wilson, Kenyon D. *Shades of Gray*. Available from the composer. Two euphoniums and two tubas. 1996. 6:00. I–II. Part I: A–f'; Part II: A–e♭'; Part III: A$_1$–d; Part IV: A$_1$–B♭. Three movements: Fanfare; Round; March. Original composition specifically designed for younger ensembles. The outer movements are homophonic in texture at a moderato tempo, while the middle movement is a four-part round in D minor. All parts are interesting and may be doubled for a large ensemble.

Wilson, Kenyon D. *Tuba Quartet No. 1 in C Minor*. Tuba-Euphonium Press. Two euphoniums and two tubas. 1994. $24.00. 6:30. III. Part I: G–a♭'; Part II: A–f'; Part III: D–b♭; Part IV: G$_1$–d. Three movements: Fugue; Lament; Dance. To my brother Kevin and his wife Stephanie on their wedding day. Third Place Winner in the 1994 Harvey Phillips Tuba-Euphonium Quartet Composition Contest. This three-movement original composition starts with a four-voice fugue in the traditional style. The second movement features the first euphonium and first tuba and starts in D minor before modulating to D major. The final movement is a fast-paced rondo with frequent meter changes. All parts are challenging and interesting. Parts may be doubled for a large ensemble. Recorded by the Tennessee Tech Tuba Ensemble on the compact disc *Unleash the Beast!* Mark Records.

Winteregg, Steven L. *Time Structures*. Available from the composer. Four tubas. 1979. 11:00. IV–V. Part I: B♭–g'; Part II: G–e♭'; Part III: C–a; Part IV: C$_1$–g. Four movements: Gothic Cathedral; Brunelleschi's Dome; Bayreuth Festspielhaus; Art Deco Skyscraper. The four contrasting movements vary in tempo and style. All are multimetric and are complex rhythmically. The top two parts could be played by euphonium but are intended to be performed by tubas. A very interesting work, though complex. Will require four strong players.

Wolking, Henry. *Tuba Blues Medley*. Touch of Brass Music Corporation. Two euphoniums, two tubas, and drums. 1984. $10.00. 5:30. IV. Part I: c–b'; Part II: B♭–g'; Part III: G_1–a♭; Part IV: E_1–c♯'. A cute basic twelve-bar blues in the key of C. This composition features written-out solos for the first tuba part in the slow blues section, then a section opened up for anyone to improvise in the faster swing section. The feel switches back and forth between half time and double time. Drums really help to make the tempo and style changes work. Parts may be doubled for a large ensemble. Recorded by the British Tuba Quartet, *Elite Syncopations,* Polyphonic Reproductions Limited, QPRZ012D; and the Northern Tuba Lights.

Wood, Derek. *Tubafusion.* Available from Tubalaté. Two euphoniums and two tubas. Recorded by Tubalaté on the compact disc *Earth and Moon.*

Woodcock, David. *Tiny Tuba Tunes.* Green Bay Music. Two euphoniums and two tubas. 1993. $22.00. 3:34. III. Part I: c–c'; Part II: G–a; Part III: D–e; Part IV: A_1–c. Five movements: Austrian Folk Song; Oh, Susanna; Old MacDonald Had a Farm; When the Saints Go Marching In; Greensleeves. Very easy and playable melodies. The melody is passed around between all parts. Ideal for younger players. All four parts are printed in bass and treble clef. Parts may be doubled for a large ensemble.

Woodcock, David, arr. *How Much Is That Doggy in the Window?* Green Bay Music. Two euphoniums and two tubas. 1993. $22.00. 1:30. IV. Part I: A–b♭'; Part II: c–g'; Part III: C–b; Part IV: F_1–e♭. Cute arrangement of this classic children's melody. The tubas have much of the melodic responsibility. No range and technical problems. Parts may be doubled for a large ensemble.

Woods. *Paddlin' Madelin Home.* arr. Goble. Tuba-Euphonium Press. Two euphoniums and two tubas. 1999. $8.00. 1:30. II. Part I: e♭–g'; Part II: d–g'; Part III: A♭$_1$–g; Part IV: B♭$_1$–e♭. This light arrangement divides the melodic material equally between all four voices. The simple rhythms and limited range make this an excellent piece for younger ensembles. Parts may be doubled for a large ensemble.

Five Parts

Alford, Harry. *The Purple Carnival.* arr. Ron Knoener. PEL Music Publications. Three euphoniums and two tubas. 1997. $9.95. 3:30. II–III. Part I: e♭–b♭'; Part II: G♭–f'; Part III: F–f'; Part IV: D♭–a; Part V: A♭$_1$–a♭. Technically challenging arrangement of this march in 6/8 meter. Melodic material is divided among the five voices, and all parts are interesting. Flutter tonguing is required in the first part, and the key signatures of four and five flats may prove challenging. Parts may be doubled for a large ensemble.

Anderson, Eugene. *Hawaiian Quintet '88.* Anderson's Arizona Originals. Three euphoniums and two tubas. 1988. $5.00. 2:00. IV. Part I: f–g'; Part II: c–d'; Part III: d–a♭'; Part IV: B♭–d♭'; Part V: F_1–b♭. A fanfare-like melody in 6/8. Some syncopation, and the tubas have an interesting bass line. The two euphoniums parts were originally written for two conch shells.

Anderson, Eugene, arr. *Take Me Out to the Ballgame.* Anderson's Arizona Originals. Three euphoniums and two tubas. 1988. $5.00. 1:10. III–IV. Part I: g–a'; Part II: c–f'; Part III: G–c'; Part IV: A–d'; Part V: G_1–d. Fairly easy arrangement of this familiar melody. The first tuba part is too high for most high school players; a euphonium may be used for this part or the tuba player may take some of the passages down an octave. There is a part printed that combines the second and third parts so the arrangement can be played as a quartet. Parts may be doubled for a large ensemble.

Bach, Johann Sebastian. *Contrapunctas I.* arr. R. Winston Morris. The Brass Press. Two euphoniums and three tubas. 1974. $5.00. 4:00. IV. Part I: G–a♭'; Part II: G–g'; Part III: F–a♭; Part IV: A_1–f; Part V: (C_1) F_1–d. Good arrangement of this popular Bach fugue. No real technical or range demands; the challenge is counting correctly to avoid incorrect entrances. Other possible instrumentations include three euphoniums and two tubas or two euphoniums, one F tuba, and two CC tubas. Parts may be doubled with care. Recorded by Tennessee Technological University Tuba Ensemble, *The Golden Sound of Euphoniums,* Mirafone Corporation promotional recording.

Bach, Johann Sebastian. *Contrapunctus I.* arr. Barton Cummings. Solid Brass Music Co. Two euphoniums and three tubas. 1996. $10.00. 3:30. II. Part I: c–b♭'; Part II: A–a'; Part III: G–b♭; Part IV: B_1–g; Part V: (D_1) G_1–e. A straightforward arrangement of this popular fugue. Appropriate for intermediate-level performers. Parts may be doubled for a large ensemble. Also reviewed in the Fall 1996 issue of the *TUBA Journal* (Vol. 24, No. 1).

Bach, Johann Sebastian. *Passacaglia and Fugue in C Minor.* arr. James A. Garrett. James Garrett. Two euphoniums and three tubas. 1987. $50.00. 14:00. IV–V. Part I: c–c"; Part II: A–c"; Part III: C_1–e♭'; Part IV: C_1–c'; Part V: C_1–a♭. The tessitura of the first two parts is high. Technical demands are extensive on all five parts. Fine writing. Will require five strong players.

Bach, Johann Sebastian. *Prelude in C.* arr. Stephen Shoop. Cimarron Music and Productions. Three euphoniums and two tubas. 1995. $4.00. 2:45. II. Part I: B–b'; Part II: A–f'; Part III: F♯–e'; Part IV: A_1–a; Part V: F♯$_1$–e. Originally for organ, this piece is in a highly imitative contrapuntal style. Each part is interesting and the melodic material is divided among the voices. Euphonium parts also available in treble clef. Third part may also be performed on tuba. Parts may be doubled for a large ensemble.

Bach, Johann Sebastian. *Thus Do You Fare, My Jesus.* arr. John Martin. Tuba-Euphonium Press. Two euphoniums and three tubas. 1999. $8.00. 3:45. II. Part I: d–b♭'; Part II: B♭–a♭'; Part III: E♭–d'; Part IV: F–b; Part V: F_1–d. The work begins with a simple chorale with traditional harmonies, which then is repeated with an added, moving countermelody that is passed among the top four voices. It is accessible for intermediate-level performers. Parts may be doubled for a large ensemble.

Bagley, E. E. *National Emblem March.* arr. John Martin. Tuba-Euphonium Press. Two euphoniums and three tubas. 1998. $10.00. 3:15. II. Part I: B♭–a'; Part II: B♭–g'; Part III: E♭–b♭; Part IV: A♭$_1$–g; Part V: A♭$_1$–e♭. Straightforward arrangement of this popular march. All parts are interesting and accessible for intermediate-level performers. Both euphonium parts include a written trill. Parts may be doubled for a large ensemble.

Baker, David N. *Piece for Solo Tuba and Tuba Quartet.* MMB Music. Solo tuba with two euphoniums and two tubas. 1990. $19.95. 12:00. Composed for Harvey Phillips.

Baskin, Bernard. *Four Excursions for Five Tubas.* Available from the composer. Five tubas. 1971. 8:00. IV. Part I: F_1–f; Part II: F_1–f; Part III: F_1–g; Part IV: F_1–a; Part V: F_1–a. Four movements. Technically not very difficult. The harmonies are quite dissonant with numerous seconds, ninths, and augmented fourths. There are many meter changes, but all with the quarter note remaining constant. A conductor for the piece is strongly recommended.

Báthory-Kitsz, Dennis. *Quintet.* Frog Peak Music. One euphonium and four tubas. 1974. $25.00. 12:00. IV–V. Part I: A♭$_1$–d♭"; Part II: F–b♭'; Part III: A♭$_1$–g'; Part IV: E♭$_1$–e♭'; Part V: C_1–b♭. Three movements. Written for the Trenton Tuba Ensemble. Challenging original composition with frequent meter changes, asymmetrical meters, and large melodic leaps. All parts require strong performers, as each part includes extreme ranges, long trilled sections, and flutter-tongued passages. Euphonium part also available in treble clef.

Carolino, Sérgio. *Shoes.* Lusitanus Editions, Portugal. Five tubas and rhythm section. 2000. 7:00. V. Dedicated to the Tubophonia Jazz Ensemble. Funky rock groove–style music. Improvisation required. Very high tessitura for the first and second parts—may also be performed on euphoniums. Rhythm section includes electric bass, electric guitar, and drums.

Corwell, Neal. *The Waste Land.* Tuba-Euphonium Press. Solo tuba with two euphoniums and two tubas. 2000. $15.00. 7:30. IV. Part I: D_1–e♭'; Part II: B♭–b♭'; Part III: F–g♭'; Part IV: E–b♭; Part V: F_1–e. Written for, and dedicated to, Stacy Baker and the Morehead State University Ensemble. Dark, programmatic work based on the T. S. Eliot poem of the same name. The ensemble parts are conservatively written, with the most challenging passages in the solo part. Harmonies are understandably dissonant, though the piece ends with a lighter texture. Accompanimental parts may be doubled for a large ensemble. Also reviewed in the Summer 2001 issue of the *TUBA Journal* (Vol. 28, No. 4). Recorded by Symphonia on the compact disc *Symphonia Three: Symphonia Fantastique,* Mark Custom Recording Service.

Cottrell, Jeff. *Rosa Mystica.* Tuba-Euphonium Press. Three euphoniums and two tubas. 2002. $12.00. 5:30. II–III. Part I: d–c"; Part II: c–a'; Part III: F–e♭'; Part IV: G_1–f; Part V: G_1–f. This lyrical ballad features each of the five voices with exposed solo passages. The harmonies are traditional. Rhythm and texture are appropriate for intermediate-level performers, though the ranges of the first euphonium may prove challenging. Parts may be doubled for a large ensemble.

Cottrell, Jeff. *Wexford Carol.* Cimarron Music and Productions. Five-part tuba/euphonium ensemble. $14.00. Euphonium parts also available in treble clef.

Cummings, Barton. *Toward the Millennium.* Wehr's Music House. Solo tuba with two euphoniums and two tubas. 2000. $14.00. 6:00. III–IV. Part I: G_1–g'; Part II: d–b♭'; Part III: G–e'; Part IV: D–c'; Part V: D_1–d. For Kelly O'Bryant and the University of North Carolina Tuba Ensemble, Dr. Dennis AsKew, Conductor. An excellent feature piece for solo tuba and four-part accompaniment. The solo part is rhythmically challenging with several large intervals and a relatively high tessitura. Accompanimental parts are less challenging but require strong ensemble playing, as there are several passages where all four parts are scored in technically challenging parallel lines. Euphonium parts also available in treble clef. Accompanimental parts may be doubled for a large ensemble.

Cummings, Barton, arr. *Sonata from "Die Bankelsangerlieder."* Solid Brass Music Company. Two euphoniums and three tubas. 1996. $9.00. 2:45. II. Part I: g–a'; Part II: e–f'; Part III: C–a; Part IV: E–a; Part V: E_1–c. Straightforward arrangement in A minor of this standard brass quintet work. All parts are interesting.

Debussy, Claude. *Golliwog's Cake Walk.* arr. Norihisa Yamamoto. KIWI Music Press. Two euphoniums and three tubas. 1988. $4.95. 2:10. IV. Part I: d–b♭'; Part II: B♭–a♭'; Part III: E♭–f'; Part IV: E♭$_1$–c'; Part V: E♭$_1$–a♭. Good arrangement of this famous melody. No significant technical problems. Fun to play. The first part is printed in tenor clef. There is no score available. Parts may be doubled for a large ensemble.

Dorff, Daniel. *Taps for Tubas.* Tenuto Publications. Two euphoniums and three tubas. 2004. 2:30. II–III. Part I: f–b♭' (f"); Part II: f♯–e♭'; Part III: B♭–d'; Part IV: G–d'; Part V: G_1–a♭. An interesting piece based on the bugle-call of taps, but set in a habañera dance style with the characteristic bass line. The outer parts are challenging, but the inner voices are appropriate for intermediate-level performers. Parts may be doubled for a large ensemble.

Dörsam, Franz-Jörgen. *Intermezzo.* Lusitanus Editions, Portugal. Five tubas. 1999. 8:00. V. Commissioned by and dedicated to Sérgio Carolino and the Portugal tuba ensemble Tubophonia. A very nice and funny piece.

Dutton, Brent. *Sub-Terrestrial Sounds.* Seesaw Music Corporation. Five tubas. 1978. $36.00. IV–V. Solo tuba: C_1–f'; Part II: $G\flat_1$–a♭; Part III: $G\flat_1$–a♭; Part IV: E_1–d♭'; Part V: C_1–a'. For solo tuba with four tubas accompanying or solo tuba and tape. Very contemporary and containing enormous range demands, multiphonics, and improvisation. See same work under Tuba and Electronic Media.

Dvorák, Antonin. *Serenade for String Orchestra (Fifth Movement—Allegro Vivace).* arr. Sy Brandon. Tuba-Euphonium Press. Three euphoniums and two tubas. 1996. $18.00. 6:00. III–IV. Part I: A–c" (e♭"); Part II: E–b♭'; Part III: F–f'; Part IV: F_1–a♭; Part V: $E\flat_1$–f. Energetic final movement from Dvorák's famous *Serenade.* Contains technically challenging passages in all five voices. Parts may be doubled for a large ensemble. Arrangements of the four other movements are available separately from the publisher.

Dvorák, Antonin. *Serenade for String Orchestra (First Movement—Moderato).* arr. Sy Brandon. Tuba-Euphonium Press. Three euphoniums and two tubas. 1996. $8.00. 3:45. III. Part I: B♭–b♭'; Part II: G–g'; Part III: F–f'; Part IV: $B\flat_1$–a♭; Part V: D_1–e♭. Serene introductory movement from Dvorák's famous *Serenade.* Parts may be doubled for a large ensemble. Arrangements of the four other movements are available separately from the publisher.

Dvorák, Antonin. *Serenade for String Orchestra (Fourth Movement—Larghetto).* arr. Sy Brandon. Tuba-Euphonium Press. Three euphoniums and two tubas. 1996. $8.00. 5:00. III. Part I: B♭–c"; Part II: G♭–a♭'; Part III: F–d♭'; Part IV: F_1–b♭; Part V: $D\flat_1$–c. Slow, lyrical fourth movement from Dvorák's famous *Serenade.* Contains frequent voice crossings. Parts may be doubled for a large ensemble. Arrangements of the four other movements are available separately from the publisher.

Dvorák, Antonin. *Serenade for String Orchestra (Second Movement—Tempo di Valse).* arr. Sy Brandon. Tuba-Euphonium Press. Three euphoniums and two tubas. 1996. $10.00. 6:00. II–III. Part I: G♯–c"; Part II: E–g'; Part III: E♭–g'; Part IV: $G\sharp_1$–f♯; Part V: $E\flat_1$–c. Light waltz movement in one from Dvorák's famous *Serenade.* Melodic material is divided among the voices. Parts may be doubled for a large ensemble. Arrangements of the four other movements are available separately from the publisher.

Dvorák, Antonin. *Serenade for String Orchestra (Third Movement—Vivace).* arr. Sy Brandon. Tuba-Euphonium Press. Three euphoniums and two tubas. 1996. $16.00. 5:30. III–IV. Part I: B♭–b'; Part II: E–a'; Part III: E–e♭'; Part IV: A_1–c; Part V: E_1–a♭. Driving third movement from Dvorák's famous *Serenade.* The style is similar to that of Tchaikovsky's *String Serenade,* composed following this work. Contains technically challenging passages in all five voices. Parts may be doubled for a large ensemble. Arrangements of the four other movements are available separately from the publisher.

Dvorák, Antonin. *Slavonic Dances, Op. 46, No. 1.* arr. David Butler. Tuba-Euphonium Press. Two euphoniums and three tubas. 2003. $24.00. 5:30. III. Part I: B♭–b♭'; Part II: B♭–g'; Part III: E♭–b; Part IV: A_1–b♭; Part V: ($E\flat_1$) G–f. Originally scored for two pianos and arranged for orchestra by the composer, this popular work is a setting of a Furiant, which is a Bohemian dance of great energy and fire. It is marked *presto,* and alternates between a duple and triple pulse while written in triple meter throughout. Euphonium parts also available in treble clef. Parts may be doubled for a large ensemble.

Eberlin, Johann Ernest. *Toccata and Fugue.* arr. Ronald C. Knoener. Tuba-Euphonium Press. Three euphoniums and two tubas. 1997. $20.00. 5:30. III. Part I: c–b♭'; Part II: G–g'; Part III: F–e♭'; Part IV: A_1–a♭; Part V: G_1–d. Two movements. For Dr. Jerry Young and Basically Brass. Arrangement of a toccata and four-voice fugue in a traditional, contrapuntal style. All parts are interesting and contain melodic material. More appropriate for a large ensemble, as most parts contain *divisi* passages.

Fabrizio, Al. *Theme and Variations.* Tuba-Euphonium Press. Solo tuba with two euphoniums and two tubas. 2002. $10.00. 3:30. III–IV. Part I: $B\flat_2$–b♭'; Part II: A–d'; Part III: A–b♭; Part IV: $B\flat_1$–f; Part V: F_1–B♭. Penfield Commission Project. Scored for solo tuba and with quartet accompaniment, this work is in the form of a theme and two variations. The accompanimental parts are not difficult, though the solo part contains technically challenging passages and an unwritten ad-lib cadenza. Accompanimental parts may be doubled for a large ensemble.

Fiegel, Todd, arr. *Medley of the Third Kind.* UNI-TUBA Press. Three euphoniums and two tubas. 1978. Out of Print. 7:00. IV. Part I: G–a'; Part II: B♭–b'; Part III: F–f'; Part IV: $E\flat_1$–b♭; Part

V: A♭$_1$–f. To the Unitubas. A humorous medley of a theme from *Close Encounters of the Third Kind,* the William Tell Overture, and a theme from *Star Wars.* Parts may be doubled for a large ensemble.

Forte, Aldo. *Tubas Latinas (Overture for Tuba Ensemble).* Tuba-Euphonium Press. Two euphoniums, three tubas, and two optional percussion. 1992. $10.00. 7:00. IV–V. Part I: c–b♭'; Part II: c–a'; Part III: F–e♭'; Part IV: G$_1$–b; Part V: F$_1$–b. Commissioned by Ernie Walls for the Tennessee Technological University Tuba Ensemble, R. Winston Morris, Director. Consists of four sections in a slow-fast-slow-fast format with styles of Spanish, Latin American, and jazz rhythms. The tessitura of the first part is very high and all parts are technically demanding. The second and third parts have several *divisi* sections. Will require strong players. Parts may be doubled for a large ensemble. The composition was premiered at the 1992 National MENC Convention in New Orleans.

Frank, Marcel G. *Ballad for Five Tubas.* Available from the composer. Two euphoniums and three tubas. 1972. 4:30. IV. Part I: f–b♭'; Part II: c♯–f♯'; Part III: F♯–b♭; Part IV: E–f; Part V: A$_1$–d. A very slow lyrical composition. Responsibility for the melody lies primarily in the first part. The tessitura of the first part is high, but the other parts are not very challenging. Will require players with mature sounds.

Frank, Marcel G. *Lyric Poem for Five Tubas.* University of Miami Press. Two euphoniums and three tubas. 1971. Out of Print. $6.00. 4:30. IV. Part I: e♭–b♭'; Part II: F♯–g'; Part III: F♯–b♭; Part IV: E–f; Part V: A$_1$–d. To Connie Weldon. Recommended instrumentation is two euphoniums, one F tuba, and two CC tubas. A melodically rich composition with most of the difficulty in the first part. The first part has a very high tessitura, but the two tuba parts are not demanding. Parts may be doubled for a large ensemble. Recorded by the University of Miami Tuba Ensemble, Miami United Tuba Society, 14568; U.S. Armed Forces Tuba/Euphonium Ensemble and Massed Ensemble, U.S. Army Band Recordings.

Frederick, Donald R., arr. *Fourteen Familiar Hymns, Carols, and Spirituals.* Accura Music. Three euphoniums and two tubas. 1991. 8 pp. III–IV. Part I: e♭–a'; Part II: c–f'; Part III: A–c'; Part IV: C–a♭; F$_1$–A♭. A collection of Christmas Carols, church hymns, and spirituals. As the fifth part doubles the fourth part at the octave, these could be played as quartets. Very useful for those occasions when sacred music is appropriate. Parts may be doubled for a large ensemble.

Friedrich, Kenneth D. *Miniatures.* Cimarron Music and Productions. Three euphoniums and two tubas. $14.00. 24 pp. III. Part I: G–a'; Part II: F–b'; Part III: F–f♯'; Part IV: B♭$_1$–b; Part V: F$_1$–a♭. Six movements. Collection of six contrasting pieces employing a variety of styles. Two of the movements contain frequent meter changes and mixed meter. Euphonium parts also available in treble clef. Parts may be doubled for a large ensemble. Individual movements can stand alone on a concert.

Fritze, Gregory. *Octubafest Polka for Tuba Ensemble.* Available from the composer. Two euphoniums and three tubas. 1976. $10.00. 4:00. IV. Part I: A♭–a♭'; Part II: A♭–f'; Part III: E♭–d♭'; Part IV: A♭$_1$–f; Part V: A♭$_1$–c. Commissioned by Harvey Phillips in celebration of the annual Octubafest. A very cute melody with the beginning and end utilizing a brief excerpt from Wagner's "Ride of the Valkyrie." Not difficult and fun to play. Parts may be doubled for a large ensemble.

Fritze, Gregory. *Salutation Fanfare.* Available from the composer. Three euphoniums and two tubas. 1985. $10.00. 2:00. III–IV. Part I: B♭–a♭'; Part II: B♭–f♯'; Part III: B♭–e'; Part IV: B♭$_1$–b♭; Part V: A$_1$–f. Commissioned by and written for the 1985 New York Brass Conference. A very syncopated fanfare melody and accompaniment. The melody is not technically challenging and most moving lines are played by two or more parts at once. Parts may be doubled for a large ensemble.

Fritze, Gregory, arr. *Simple Gifts.* Available from the arranger. Solo tuba, two euphoniums, and two tubas. 1990. $10.00. 4:00. IV. Solo tuba: C–c'; Part II: d–g'; Part III: A–e'; Part IV: F–g; Part V: F$_1$–c. This famous folk melody is played by a solo tuba with a simple and very lyrical accompaniment. This is also available for solo tuba and three-part accompaniment. Parts may be doubled for a large ensemble.

Fucik, Julius. *Florentiner.* arr. John Martin. Tuba-Euphonium Press. Two euphoniums and three tubas. 1999. $12.00. 2:30. II–III. Part I: d–b♭'; Part II: c–g'; Part III: C–b♭; Part IV: G$_1$–c'; Part V: G$_1$–d. Effective arrangement of this well-known march. Melodic material is divided among the five parts. Range and style are accessible for intermediate-level performers. Parts may be doubled for a large ensemble.

Garrett, James A., arr. *Londonderry Air.* Ludwig Music Publishing Company. Three euphoniums and two tubas. 1987. $15.50. 2:20. III–IV. Part I: G–a'; Part II: d–g'; Part III: c–e'; Part IV: F–c'; Part V: F$_1$–d. This is for solo euphonium and four-part tuba/euphonium accompaniment. The arrangement is very lyrical and contains some very lush harmonies. Both euphonium parts are available in treble and bass clefs. This would be an excellent selection to use to feature a guest soloist or outstanding student euphoniumist. Parts may be doubled for a large ensemble. Recorded by the U.S. Armed Forces Tuba/Euphonium Ensemble, Mark Records, MW89MCD-8.

Gates, Crawford. *Psalm.* Intrada Music Group. Three trombones, one euphonium, and one tuba. 1984. \$7.50. 3:00. IV. Part I: e–c"; Part II: B–g'; Part III: G–e'; Part IV: G–f'; Part V: E–b. Commissioned by M. Dee Stewart and first performed at the 1984 International Brass Congress. First three parts may be played on euphonium. Nice chorale writing, very melodic. The tessitura of the first part is quite high and will require a very mature player. Mutes are required for all players. Parts may be doubled for a large ensemble. See same work under Tuba in Mixed Ensemble.

Gesualdo, Carlo. *Moro Lasso.* arr. Eugene Anderson. Anderson's Arizona Originals. Three euphoniums and two tubas. 1988. \$5.00. 3:00. III–IV. Part I: f–g'; Part II: B♭–e'; Part III: B–c'; Part IV: E–g; Part V: A_1–c. A highly polyphonic madrigal. All parts have the opportunity to play the theme. No significant technical problems. Parts may be doubled for a large ensemble.

Gesualdo, Carlo. *Moro Lasso from Madrigal, Book VI.* arr. Eugene Anderson. Cimarron Music and Productions. Three euphoniums and two tubas. 1995. \$8.00. 4:00. II–III. Part I: f–g'; Part II: B♭–e'; Part III: A–c'; Part IV: E–g; Part V: A_1–c. Effective arrangement of a Renaissance work appropriate for intermediate-level performers. First and second euphonium parts also available in treble clef. Fourth part may also be performed on euphonium. Parts may be doubled for a large ensemble.

Gesualdo, P. *Madrigale.* arr. John McClernan. Tuba/Euphonium Music Publications. Two euphoniums and three tubas. 1971. Out of Print. 5:00. III–IV.

Goble, Joseph. *Totally Tuba March.* Tuba-Euphonium Press. Three euphoniums and two tubas. 1996. \$10.00. 2:00. II–III. Part I: B♭–a♭'; Part II: B♭–g'; Part III: G–e♭'; Part IV: A♭$_1$–a♭; Part V: A♭$_1$–f. Lighthearted, original composition in the traditional 6/8 march style. Melodic material is divided among the five voices. Euphonium parts also available in treble clef. Parts may be doubled for a large ensemble. Also reviewed in the Spring 2002 issue of the *ITEA Journal* (Vol. 29, No. 3).

Henderson, Ray. *Five Foot Two, Eyes of Blue (Has Anybody Seen My Girl?).* arr. Mark Nelson. Whaling Music Publishers. Two euphoniums and three tubas. 1988. \$7.50. 2:00. IV. Part I: b♭–b♭'; Part II: a–g'; Part III: F–d'; Part IV: C–a; Part V: B♭$_2$–A. Could also be played by three euphoniums and two tubas. A lot of syncopation. The top part has most of the melodic responsibility. Parts may be doubled for a large ensemble.

Hilgers, Walter. *Präludium.* Editions Marc Reift. One euphonium and four tubas. 1999. €8.40. Recorded by Gerhard Meinl's Tuba Quartet on the compact disc *Tuba! A Six-Tuba Musical Romp,* Angel Music.

Holborne, Antony. *Pavan: The Funerals.* arr. Paul F. Hartin. Cellar Press. Five tubas. 1975. 2:30. III–IV. Part I: f–f'; Part II: B♭–c'; Part III: F–a♭; Part IV: F–b♭; Part V: F_1–d. The tessitura of the first part is high and may be played on an F tuba or euphonium. Not very difficult technically. Parts may be doubled for a large ensemble.

Hounsell, Clare. *Heritage Hill Suite.* arr. Paul Luhring. PEL Music Publications. Three euphoniums and two tubas. 1995. \$15.95. 6:00. II–III. Part I: f–d♭"; Part II: c–c"; Part III: F–f'; Part IV: F–c'; Part V: F_1–c. Three movements: Parade Ground—Fort Howard; A Waltz at Astor House; "Auntie" Cotton's Polka. Programmatic work depicting the places and people in the early days of the city of Green Bay, Wisconsin. The first movement is a concert march, the second is a moderate-tempo waltz, and the final movement is a polka in folk style. Parts may be doubled for a large ensemble. Individual movements can stand alone on a concert.

Howard, Bart. *Fly Me to the Moon.* arr. Robert Hughes. Hampshire House Publishing Corporation (Mark Tezak). Four trombones (euphoniums) and one tuba. 1986. 4:00. IV. Part I: g–c♯"; Part II: f–a"; Part III: e–d"; Part IV: A–g'; Part V: F_1–d'. Originally written for four trombones and tuba. The top four parts may be played by euphoniums. This is a popular jazz tune arranged in a bossa nova style moving to swing style and then back to bossa nova. Drums may be added for style enhancement.

Humperdinck, Engelbert. *Evening Prayer.* arr. Angelo Manzo. Tuba-Euphonium Press. Two euphoniums and three tubas. 2001. \$10.00. 1:30. II–III. Part I: B♭–g'; Part II: B♭–e♭'; Part III: F–b♭; Part IV: F_1–a; Part V: B♭$_1$–B♭. This brief arrangement is taken from the opera *Hansel and Gretel* and is a good study piece for ensembles wishing to work on their legato playing. Also reviewed in the Spring 2003 issue of the *ITEA Journal* (Vol. 30, No. 3).

Jager, Robert. *Three Ludes for Tuba.* Masters Music Publications, Incorporated. Solo tuba with two euphoniums and two tubas. 1998. \$14.95. 8:15. III. Part I: A♭$_1$–d'; Part II: c–a♭'; Part III: A–e♭'; Part IV: C–b♭; Part V: A♭$_1$–e♭. Three movements: Prelude; Interlude; Postlude. Commissioned by students and alumni of R. Winston Morris in celebration of his thirtieth anniversary, 1996–97, as the tuba professor at Tennessee Technological University. Fun, original composition scored for solo tuba with quartet accompaniment, though the soloist is tacet for the middle movement. The solo part is challenging, but the accompaniment is accessible to intermediate-level performers. *Prelude* is a fanfare-like movement that features a dialogue between soloist and quartet. The coda includes a brief reference to the Tennessee Tech Hymn. The second movement is a slow passacaglia with seven variations. *Postlude* is an upbeat movement in ternary form with the middle section containing frequent meter changes and mixed meter which may be challenging to young ensembles. Accompanimental parts may be doubled for a large ensemble. Also featured in an article in the Winter 2003 issue of the *ITEA Journal* (Vol. 30, No. 2). Recorded by Symphonia on the compact disc *Symphonia Two: La Morte dell Oom,* Mark Records.

Jobim, António Carlos. *Wave.* arr. Sérgio Carolino. Lusitanus Editions, Portugal. Solo euphonium with four tubas and rhythm section. 2000. 7:00. V. Dedicated to the Portugal tuba ensemble Tubophonia. A Brazilian-style bossa nova standard. Improvisation is required. Solo part may also be performed on tuba. Rhythm section includes bass, guitar, Brazilian guitar (cavaquinho), and drums.

Jones, Roger. *Yankee Tunes for Tubas.* Available from the composer. Two euphoniums and three tubas. 1993. $12.00. 4:00. IV. Part I: B♭–g'; Part II: B♭–f'; Part III: C–d'; Part IV: A♭–a'; Part V: F_1–c. A medley of "Chester," "Yankee Men of War," and "Drunken Sailor." Very tuneful with traditional harmonies. No significant technical problems. Parts may be doubled for a large ensemble.

Joplin, Scott. *Great Crush Collision March.* arr. L. A. Rauchut. KIWI Music Press. Three euphoniums and two tubas. 1985. $7.95. 2:10. IV. Part I: d–b♭'; Part II: (c♯) e–f'; Part III: A–c'; Part IV: C–c'; Part V: F_1–g. While the euphoniums have primary responsibility for the melody, the tubas do have the melody for 32 measures. The fifth part has 16 measures of *divisi,* but these can be easily covered in the other parts. Parts may be doubled for a large ensemble.

King, Karl L. *Broadway One-Step.* arr. Ronald C. Knoener. Tuba-Euphonium Press. Three euphoniums and two tubas. 2002. $12.00. 3:30. II–III. Part I: d–b♭'; Part II: d–a♭'; Part III: G–f'; Part IV: D–f; Part V: A♭$_1$–d♭. For Dawn Holte. Effective arrangement accessible for young to intermediate-level performers. It is more dance-like than King's typical marches and not as technically challenging. Parts may be doubled for a large ensemble. Also reviewed in the Summer 2004 issue of the *ITEA Journal* (Vol. 31, No. 4).

King, Karl L. *Kentucky Sunrise March.* arr. Ronald C. Knoener. PEL Music Publications. Three euphoniums and two tubas. $9.95. 3:00. II–III. Part I: f–b♭'; Part II: A–d'; Part III: A–d'; Part IV: C–g; Part V: B♭$_1$–f. This arrangement is written for the composer's daughter, Lori Knoener, tubist. Although the score calls for five players, the third part alternates doubling the second and fourth parts. Thus the piece can be performed as a quartet, or parts may be doubled for a large ensemble. Also reviewed in the Summer 1998 issue of the *TUBA Journal* (Vol. 25, No. 4).

Klohr, John. *The Billboard March.* arr. John T. Martin. Tuba-Euphonium Press. Two euphoniums and three tubas. 1999. $8.00. 2:15. II–III. Part I: c–a♭'; Part II: c–e♭'; Part III: F–b♭; Part IV: F–a♭; Part V: A♭$_1$–e♭. Straightforward arrangement of this standard march. Appropriate for intermediate-level performers. Melodic material is divided among the top four voices. Parts may be doubled for a large ensemble.

Knoener, Ron, arr. *Tinker Polka.* PEL Music Publications. Three euphoniums and two tubas. 1996. $8.50. 3:00. II. Part I: e♭–a♭'; Part II: e♭–g'; Part III: B♭–e♭'; Part IV: A♭$_1$–g; Part V: A♭$_1$–e♭. Straightforward arrangement of this traditional polka appropriate for intermediate-level performers. The bass line is divided between the two tuba parts, and the melodic material is shared among the top four voices. Parts may be doubled for a large ensemble.

Konagaya, Soichi. *Illusion.* Tuba-Euphonium Press. Two euphoniums, three tubas, and percussion. 1979. 9:00. IV–V. Part I: e♭–b♭'; Part II: A–g♭'; Part III: A–c'; Part IV: F–c'; Part V: F_1–e♭. Dedicated to R. Winston Morris and the Tennessee Technological University Tuba Ensemble. Percussion parts include suspended cymbals, timpani, gong, vibraphone, and chimes; all can be played by one player. While tonal, this piece does contain some contemporary harmonies, oriental sounds, and many unique timbral effects not always associated with a tuba/euphonium ensemble. Effects include blowing air through the instrument without the mouthpiece and playing a roll on a suspended cymbal that is upside down on the timpani, and the most interesting sound is the Bala-euphonium. Recorded by the Tennessee Technological University Tuba Ensemble, *LIVE!* KM Records, KM 5661.

Krive, Rick. *Lil Short'nin Funk. TUBA Journal.* Five tubas. 1976. $7.50. 1:30. IV. Part I: b♭$_1$–g♭'; Part II: B♭$_1$–d♭'; Part III: B♭$_1$–a♭; Part IV: B♭$_1$–e; Part V: G_1–c. A jazz-rock feel that is rhythmically exciting and challenging to play. There is a brief multimetric section and one measure where all four parts are asked to sing through their instruments. Will require five strong players. This was written as part of the TUBA Gem series and is distributed with the *TUBA Journal,* Vol. 4, No. 1. It is available by purchasing this issue of the *Journal.*

Krol, Bernhard. *Feiertagsmusik (Festive Music).* Editions BIM. Three euphoniums and two tubas. 1989. $22.50. 7:30. IV–V. Part I: c–a'; Part II: G–f'; Part III: A–d♭'; Part IV: E–a; Part V: D♭$_1$–e. Commissioned by R. Winston Morris for the Tennessee Technological University Tuba Ensemble's April 2, 1990, performance at Weil Recital Hall, Carnegie Hall, New York City. Excellent writing, though not technically challenging. Tessitura of the first part is high. The work is slow, lyrical, and musically challenging. Parts may be doubled for a large ensemble.

Martin, Glenn. *Bluesin' Tubas.* Tuba-Euphonium Press. Three euphoniums, two tubas, piano, bass, drums, guitar. 1984. $10.00. 4:10. IV. Part I: B–c"; Part II: d–a'; Part III: c–e'; Part IV: B♭–c'; Part V: B♭–e♭. Dedicated to R. Winston Morris and the Tennessee Technological University Tuba Ensemble. An original jazz tune with a medium swing feel. Sections can be opened up for improvised solos. Originally published by Laissez-Faire Music Publishing Company. Recorded by the Tennessee Technological University Tuba Ensemble, *Heavy Metal,* Mark Records, MES 20759.

Martin, Glenn. *Chops!* Tuba-Euphonium Press. Three euphoniums, two tubas, and rhythm. 1984. $10.00. 2:40. IV. Part I: d–c"; Part II: d–e'; Part III: d–e'; Part IV: C–a; Part V: A–e♭'. Dedicated to R. Winston Morris and the Tennessee Technological University Tuba Ensemble. This is in a fast swing style with sections for improvised solos. As the title implies, strong players are needed as the piece makes range and technical demands in addition to requiring a good swing style of all players. Parts may be doubled for a large ensemble. Originally published by Laissez-Faire Music Publishing Company. Recorded by the Tennessee Technological University Tuba Ensemble, *All That Jazz,* Mark Records, MES 20608.

Mauer, Ludwig. *Four Pieces.* arr. John Stevens. Tuba-Euphonium Press. Two euphoniums and three tubas. 1998. $15.00. 6:45. II–III. Part I: c–a'; Part II: c–f'; Part III: A_1–c'; Part IV: A_1–a; Part V: G_1–g. Four movements. Effective arrangement of this standard brass quintet work. The ranges and style are appropriate for intermediate-level performers. Parts may be doubled for a large ensemble.

Meacham, F. W. *American Patrol.* arr. William R. Lee. Cimarron Music and Productions. Three euphoniums and two tubas. 2002. $14.50. 4:00. III. Part I: A–a♭'; Part II: A–g'; Part III: G–g'; Part IV: A♭$_1$–a♭; Part V: G_1–f. This fun arrangement includes excerpts from E. E. Bagley's *National Emblem March* and Claude J. Rouget's *Marseillaise.* Melodic material is divided among the five voices. Parts may be doubled for a large ensemble.

Mendelssohn-Bartholdy, Felix. *Andante Tranquillo from Organ Sonata in A, Op. 65 No. 3.* tr. Mark Prater. Wehr's Music House. Three euphoniums and two tubas. 2001. $6.00. 1:45. II. Part I: c–b♭'; Part II: G–g'; Part III: A–d'; Part IV: E♭–g; Part V: (E♭$_1$) F_1–B♭. In memoriam Douglas C. Lemmon. Slow movement from this work originally for organ. The texture is predominantly homophonic and the harmonies are traditional. Requires good legato articulation from all performers. Range and style are appropriate for young ensembles. First euphonium part available only in tenor or treble clef. Parts may be doubled for a large ensemble.

Monteverdi, Claudio. *Ecco Mormorar L'onde.* arr. Gary Lee Nelson. Tuba-Euphonium Press. Two euphoniums and three tubas. 1991. $8.00. 3:00. IV. Part I: f–b♭'; Part II: f–g'; Part III: B♭–b♭; Part IV: F–b♭; Part V: B♭$_1$–e♭. This is very polyphonic, though there are no significant technical problems. Players will need to count carefully. Parts may be doubled for a large ensemble.

Monteverdi, Claudio. *Two Pieces from "Orfeo."* arr. Daniel Heiman. Heavy Metal Music. Three euphoniums and two tubas. 1991. $5.00. 1:30. IV. Part I: f–g'; Part II: d–d'; Part III: B♭–a; Part IV: E♭–g; Part V: F_1–c. Two movements: Sinfonia; Ballo. The first movement is in a chorale style. The second movement is polyphonic and more challenging. The third part may be played by a euphonium or tuba. No score available. Parts may be doubled for a large ensemble.

Morley, Thomas. *Two Morley Madrigals.* arr. Frank Ferriano. Tuba-Euphonium Press. Two euphoniums and three tubas. 2002. $12.00. 4:45. II. Part I: c–g'; Part II: d–g'; Part III: G–d'; Part IV: (B♭$_1$) C–a; Part V: C–d. Two movements: April Is in My Mistress' Face; Now Is the Month of Maying. The first madrigal is scored for a standard quartet, and the second is scored for five parts. Arrangement is appropriate for intermediate-level performers. Parts may be doubled for a large ensemble. Individual movements can stand alone on a concert.

Moulu, Pierre. *A Lament for Anne of Brittany.* arr. Richard Jacoby. Ludwig Music Publishing Company. Three euphoniums and two tubas. 1986. $9.95. 4:00. III–IV. Part I: g–f'; Part II: d–d'; Part III: G_1–c'; Part IV: F–f; Part V: A_1–c. This is based on a cantus firmus that Josquin Du Prez used in his lament on the death of Ockeghem. No significant technical or range problems. A translation of the text and performance suggestions are included. Parts may be doubled for a large ensemble.

Mouret, Jean Joseph. *Rondeau.* arr. Barton Cummings. Solid Brass Music Company. Two euphoniums and three tubas. 1996. $9.00. 2:00. II. Part I: f–b♭'; Part II: c–f'; Part III: A–g; Part IV: E–e♭; Part V: F_1–c. Popularly known as the theme from *Masterpiece Theater.* Euphonium parts are more challenging than tuba parts. Appropriate for intermediate-level performers. Parts may be doubled for a large ensemble.

Mozart, Wolfgang Amadeus. *The Impresario Overture.* arr. Ronald C. Knoener. Tuba-Euphonium Press. Three euphoniums and two tubas. 2002. $20.00. 6:00. III. Part I: B♭–a'; Part II: A–g'; Part III: G–g'; Part IV: B♭$_1$–g; Part V: F_1–f. Arranged for Basically Brass. Straightforward arrangement that works well as a concert opener. All parts are interesting. *Divisi* passages make the piece more appropriate for a large ensemble than for a quintet. Also reviewed in the Winter 2004 issue of the *ITEA Journal* (Vol. 31, No. 2).

Mozart, Wolfgang Amadeus. *Marriage of Figaro Overture.* arr. Charles Warren. Cimarron Music and Productions. Two euphoniums and three tubas. $14.50.

Mozart, Wolfgang Amadeus. *Minuet from Symphony No. 40.* tr. Frank Ferriano. Tuba-Euphonium Press. Three euphoniums and two tubas. 2001. $12.00. 5:45. II–III. Part I: d–c' (e♭"); Part II: c–a' (d"); Part III: B♭–g'; Part IV: C–c' (e'); Part V: G_1–a. Straightforward transcription of the third movement from this well-known symphony. First euphonium is scored entirely in tenor clef, and the second euphonium has a large section in tenor clef. Parts may be doubled for a large ensemble. Also reviewed in the Spring 2002 issue of the *ITEA Journal* (Vol. 29, No. 3).

Mozart, Wolfgang Amadeus. *Overture to the "Marriage of Figaro."* arr. Arthur Gottschalk. Shawnee Press, Incorporated. Three euphoniums and two tubas. 1981. $14.00. 3:45. IV–V. Part I: A–d"; Part II: A–a'; Part III: G–f♯'; Part IV: D–e'; Part V: D–c'. Technically challenging for all parts, but fun to play. The tessitura of the tuba parts is high. The three euphonium parts are printed in tenor clef. Will require strong players. Parts may be doubled for a large ensemble. Recorded by the University of Michigan Tuba Ensemble; and the U.S. Armed Forces Tuba/Euphonium Massed Ensemble, U.S. Army Records.

Nicolai, O. *Merry Wives of Windsor Overture.* arr. John T. Martin. Tuba-Euphonium Press. Two euphoniums and three tubas. 1998. $20.00. 4:00. III. Part I: B♭–b♭'; Part II: B♭–b♭'; Part III: $B♭_1$–e♭'; Part IV: F_1–c'; Part V: F_1–b♭. This transcription from orchestra to quintet produces challenging passages excerpted from the runs in the strings and woodwinds. All parts are interesting and the melodic material is divided among all voices. Serves as a nice concert opener. Parts may be doubled for a large ensemble.

Pachelbel, Johann. *Two Contrasting Pachelbel Fugues.* arr. Frank Ferriano. Tuba-Euphonium Press. Three euphoniums and two tubas. 2002. $12.00. 4:00. II. Part I: B♭–b♭'; Part II: G–a♭'; Part III: B–d'; Part IV: $B♭_1$–a; Part V: E_1–a. Two movements: Chromatic in D Minor; Magnificat Fugue. This collection of two fugues serves as a nice programming contrast to the large volume of contrapuntal works by J. S. Bach. Individual parts are not difficult. Third part may also be performed on tuba. First euphonium is scored entirely in tenor clef, and the second euphonium is scored entirely in tenor clef for the first fugue. Also reviewed in the Spring 2004 issue of the *ITEA Journal* (Vol. 31, No. 3).

Palestrina, Giovanni de. *Litaniae de Beata Virgine Mary.* arr. Doug Bristol. Tuba-Euphonium Press. Three euphoniums and two tubas. 2000. $10.00. 5:30. II. Part I: f–g'; Part II: c–c'; Part III: F–a♭; Part IV: F–g; Part V: $B♭_1$–d♭. Highly imitative piece in the Renaissance style. Range is appropriate for intermediate-level performers and serves well as a study piece for college ensembles. Parts may be doubled for a large ensemble. Also reviewed in the Summer 2002 issue of the *ITEA Journal* (Vol. 29, No. 4).

Pezel, Johann. *Sonata No. 2.* arr. Barton Cummings. Solid Brass Music Company. Two euphoniums and three tubas. 1996. $9.00. 8:00. II. Part I: e–f'; Part II: B♭–d'; Part III: F–a; Part IV: C–g; Part V: F_1–c. Nice arrangement of this chorale with simple rhythms traditional harmonies. Predominately homophonic and appropriate for intermediate-level performers. Parts may be doubled for a large ensemble.

Pezel, Johann. *Sonata No. 3.* arr. Barton Cummings. Solid Brass Music Company. Three euphoniums and two tubas. 1996. $9.00. 2:45. II. Part I: f–f'; Part II: B♭–d'; Part III: c–e♭'; Part IV: B♭–d'; Part V: $B♭_1$–e♭. First tuba part has a high tessitura with the same range as the second euphonium part; a bass tuba or euphonium would thus be more appropriate than a contrabass tuba. Uses traditional harmonies and works well for intermediate-level performers. Parts may be doubled for a large ensemble.

Pezel, Johann. *Sonata No. 22.* arr. Barton Cummings. Solid Brass Music Company. Three euphoniums and two tubas. 1996. $9.00. 2:45. II. Part I: c–g'; Part II: c–e♭'; Part III: g–f'; Part IV: e♭–d♭'; Part V: F_1–f. Brief technical passages in the first two parts provide moderate challenge. Otherwise, the arrangement works well for intermediate-level performers. Parts may be doubled for a large ensemble.

Pezel, Johann. *Three German Dances.* arr. Daniel Heiman. Heavy Metal Music. Two euphoniums and three tubas. 1991. $7.00. 3:30. IV. Part I: f–b♭'; Part II: c–a'; Part III: F–g; Part IV: C–d; Part V: F_1–G. Three movements: Intrade 10; Intrade 16; Allemande 17. Very close polyphony in the upper four parts. Players will need to count very carefully. No score available.

Pezel, Johann. *Three Pieces.* arr. Barton Cummings. Solid Brass Music Co. Two euphoniums and three tubas. 1996. $9.00. 4:15. II. Part I: d–g'; Part II: A–f'; Part III: E♭–a; Part IV: C–g; Part V: F_1–g. Three movements: Intrada; Sarabande; Bal. First movement is contrapuntal with frequent part-crossing. Second and third movements are predominantly homophonic and easier. Excellent work for younger performers with a good range. Parts may be doubled for a large ensemble.

Prenner, Georgivs. *Qvem uidistis pastores.* tr. Angelo Manzo. Tuba-Euphonium Press. Solo euphonium with two euphoniums and two tubas. 2001. $15.00. 2:45. II. Part I: d–g'; Part II: d–g'; Part III: G–c; Part IV: G–a; Part V: C–f.

Scored for solo euphonium and quartet, this Renaissance motet is accessible for young to intermediate-level performers. The solo part has the fewest moving notes and acts more as a descant above the more active quartet. Parts may be doubled for a large ensemble.

Presser, William. *Divertimento*. Tenuto Publications. Two euphoniums and three tubas. 1976. $7.00. 6:30. IV. Part I: G–b♭'; Part II: F–g'; Part III: C–f♯'; Part IV: G_1–a; Part V: E♭$_1$–f♯. Three movements. A challenging piece in terms of both technique and range. Technical demands are greatest in the third movement. Good solid writing. Parts may be doubled for a large ensemble.

Robinson, Keith J. *Father, Forgive Them*. Tuba-Euphonium Press. Two euphoniums and three tubas. 2002. $10.00. 4:00. II. Part I: B♭–b♭; Part II: A♭–b♭; Part III: B♭$_1$–b♭; Part IV: B♭$_1$–b♭; Part V: F_1–d♭. Original composition in B♭ minor based on Luke 23:34. It opens with a lyrical, mournful passage that evolves into a canon based on the theme. Parts may be doubled for a large ensemble.

Rossini, Gioacchino. *The Barber of Seville Overture*. arr. Jeff Kile. Masters Music Publications, Inc. Two euphoniums and three tubas. 1999. $17.50. 3:00. III. Part I: G–c"; Part II: G–c"; Part III: B♭$_1$–e'; Part IV: G_1–d'; Part V: C_1–c'. Nice arrangement of this popular work. Each part is technically challenging and the ranges are difficult. Parts may be doubled for a large ensemble, and there are *divisi* passages in the first tuba part.

Scheidt, Samuel. *Canzona XXX*. arr. Skip Gray. Shawnee Press, Incorporated. Two euphoniums and three tubas. 1980. $14.00. 5:30. IV. Part I: c–a'; Part II: B–e'; Part III: F–a; Part IV: C–g; Part V: (C_1) G_1–d. Nice arrangement of this canzona that has been a staple of brass quintet literature for years. Lightness and clarity of the moving lines are a necessity, as the piece is very polyphonic and technically demanding of all parts. The two euphonium parts are printed in tenor clef in the score, but the parts are printed in bass clef. The arrangement remains true to the original metric form of duple-triple-duple. Parts may be cautiously doubled for a large ensemble.

Schelokov, V. *Movement for Five Tubas*. The Musical Evergreen. Five tubas. 1976. $11.50. 2:20. IV. Part I: G♭–b♭; Part II: E♭–g; Part III: D♭–e♭; Part IV: D♭–d; Part V: B♭$_1$–B♭. Not very demanding technically for any of the parts. The first and fourth parts do have challenging triplet figures in the fast middle section. Some dissonances in the harmonies. This can sound muddy at times if the players are not careful.

Schulz, Patrick. *Dark Forest*. Tuba-Euphonium Press. Three euphoniums and two tubas. 1995. $25.00. 8:00. III. Part I: B♭–c"; Part II: B♭–a♭'; Part III: B♭–f'; Part IV: F_1–b♭; Part V: (E♭$_1$) G♭$_1$–B♭. This multi-sectioned original composition features rich sonorities and lyrical passages. Melodic material is divided among all five parts, and there is a written cadenza in the first tuba part. Mutes are required in all three euphonium parts. Parts may be doubled for a large ensemble.

Shiner, Marty. *Mexican Carnival*. Kendor Music, Incorporated. Four trombones (euphoniums) and one tuba. 1972. $8.00. 2:00. IV. Part I: e♭–d"; Part II: e♭–g'; Part III: A♭–e♭'; Part IV: A♭–d'; Part V: A♭$_1$–e♭. Other possible instrumentations include three euphoniums and two tubas. A fun piece with a Mexican flavor. It is not difficult technically, but the tessitura of the first part is quite high. Parts may be doubled for a large ensemble.

Sousa, John Philip. *The Liberty Bell March*. arr. L. A. Rauchut. KIWI Music Press. Three euphoniums and two tubas. $6.95. 3:30. IV. Part I: c–b♭'; Part II: c–f'; Part III: B♭–f'; Part IV: E–d♭'; Part V: F♯$_1$–f. Good arrangement of this famous Sousa march. Most of the melody is in the first euphonium part. There are several *divisi* sections in the fourth part. Parts may be doubled for a large ensemble.

Sousa, John Philip. *Washington Post*. arr. James Self. Basset Hound Music. Two euphoniums and three tubas. 1993. $7.00. 3:00. IV. Part I: A–g'; Part II: A–f'; Part III: A_1–b♭; Part IV: A_1–f; Part V: F_1–f. A good arrangement of this march with some humorous sections. Fun to play. Parts may be doubled for a large ensemble.

Stevens, John. *Fanfare for a Friend*. Tuba-Euphonium Press. Five tubas. 1991. $5.00. 1:30. IV. Part I: B–g'; Part II: B–f'; Part III: B_1–b♭; Part IV: G_1–g; Part V: G_1–d. For Dietrich Unkrodt and the Berlin Tubists. A very driving and energetic fanfare. The rhythms are complex and syncopated, but most of the time there are two to five parts playing the same rhythm. The tessitura of the first part is very high and may be played by a euphonium.

Stevens, John, arr. *Suite of English Madrigals*. Encore Music Publishers. Two euphoniums and three tubas. 1988. $19.00. 6:00. IV. Part I: f–b♭'; Part II: c–a'; Part III: B♭–d'; Part IV: F–b♭; Part V: B♭$_1$–g. Four movements: Down the Hills; Cruel, Wilt Thou Per Server; To the Shady Woods; Now Is the Month of Maying. A collection of four different English madrigals. No significant technical problems. Good arrangement. Parts may be doubled for a large ensemble.

Telemann, George Phillip. *Alleluia*. arr. Daniel Heiman. Heavy Metal Music. Two euphoniums and three tubas. 1991. $5.00. 1:20. III–IV. Part I: f–g'; Part II: d–e♭'; Part III: G–b♭; Part IV: B♭–f; Part V: F_1–d. This piece is based on the last movement of a cantata by Telemann. The only text is the word "alleluia," repeated over and over. No significant range or technical problems. Parts may be doubled for a large ensemble.

Tschesnokoff, Pavel. *Salvation Is Created.* arr. Ronald Knoener. PEL Music Publications. Three euphoniums and two tubas. 1996. $9.95. 2:30. II. Part I: f–f'; Part II: c–d'; Part III: c–a; Part IV: F–f; Part V: F_1–e♭. Straightforward arrangement of this chorale, suitable for younger ensembles. More appropriate for a large ensemble as there are frequent *divisi* passages in the second part. Also reviewed in the Summer 1997 issue of the *TUBA Journal* (Vol. 24, No. 4).

Uber, David. *Exhibitions, Op. 98.* Kendor Music, Incorporated. Four euphoniums and one tuba. 1977. Out of Print. 3:30. IV. Part I: e♭–b'; Part II: f–g'; Part III: e♭–e♭'; Part IV: B♭–e♭'; Part V: (B♭$_1$) F–b. The solo euphonium has a high tessitura and is difficult technically. This work can be performed by all euphoniums or by as many as three tubas, depending on the strengths of the players. All parts are challenging as the piece moves through several different styles. Very enjoyable for performers and audience.

Uber, David. *Explorations for Tuba Quintet, Op. 85.* Tuba-Euphonium Press. Five tubas. 1992. $12.00. 8:00. IV. Part I: D–c'; Part II: G_1–g; Part III: F_1–g; Part IV: F_1–f; Part V: F_1–c♭. All parts have equal technical demands and are interesting to play. No range problems, but the group will need a conductor as there are many challenging rhythmic figures and entrances.

Vaughan, Rodger. *Offering: A Sketch for Euphonium Solo and Tuba/Euphonium Quartet.* Available from the composer. Three euphoniums and two tubas. 1992. $5.00. 1:20. III–IV. Solo euphonium: f–g♭'; Part II: e–e'; Part III: c–c♯'; Part IV: E♭–f♯; Part V: A♭$_1$–d. A very lyrical and tranquil euphonium solo with a fairly simple accompaniment. None of the parts are technically demanding. Parts may be doubled for a large ensemble.

Vaughan, Rodger, arr. *Swing Low, Sweet Chariot.* Tuba-Euphonium Press. Three euphoniums and two tubas. 1999. $8.00. 2:45. II. Part I: e♭–a♭'; Part II: c–g'; Part III: A♭–e♭'; Part IV: D♭–a♭; Part V: A♭$_1$–e♭. For the Astoria Tuba-Euphonium Quartet plus one. Straightforward arrangement of this traditional hymn in F major and A♭ major. The melody is predominantly in the second part. Parts may be doubled for a large ensemble. No score is provided.

Von Suppe, Franz. *Poet and Peasant Overture.* arr. Gregory Bright. Tuba/Euphonium Music Publications. Two euphoniums and three tubas. Out of Print. 8:00. IV.

Wagner, Richard. *Intro. to Act III, Die Meistersinger.* arr. John Martin. Tuba-Euphonium Press. Two euphoniums and three tubas. 1999. $10.00. 3:15. II–III. Part I: G–a'; Part II: F–f♯'; Part III: G–b; Part IV: D–b♭; Part V: G_1–d. Lyrical playing is highlighted in this five-part arrangement from one of Wagner's operas. The range and rhythms are accessible to younger performers, but the musical phrasing and dynamic changes require a more experienced ensemble. Parts may be doubled for a large ensemble.

Wagner, Richard. *Rienzi Overture.* arr. Gregory Bright. Tuba/Euphonium Music Publications. Two euphoniums and three tubas. Out of Print.

Wagner, Richard. *Siegfreid's Funeral March.* arr. Gregory Bright. Tuba/Euphonium Music Publications. Two euphoniums and three tubas. Out of Print. 6:00. IV.

Werden, David, arr. *Joy to the World.* Cimarron Music and Productions. Solo tuba with four-part tuba/euphonium ensemble. 2001. $6.00.

Wesley, Samuel. *O Sing unto My Roundelay.* arr. Angelo Manzo. Tuba-Euphonium Press. Two euphoniums and three tubas. 2002. $12.00. 4:30. II. Part I: c–g'; Part II: c♯–g'; Part III: F–b; Part IV: C–a; Part V: G_1–c. Nice "vocal" arrangement appropriate for younger performers. The piece begins in D minor and modulates to D major halfway through. Parts may be doubled for a large ensemble. Also reviewed in the Summer 2004 issue of the *ITEA Journal* (Vol. 31, No. 4).

White, Ian. *Quintet.* John D. Elliott. Three euphoniums and two tubas. 8:00. IV–V. Part I: c–b"; Part II: B–b♭'; Part III: G–d'; Part IV: c♯–a; Part V: D♯$_1$–g. Three movements. An exciting and challenging work. The tessitura of the first part is high. The movements are all multimetric and technically challenging. Parts may be doubled for a large ensemble.

Wilson, Ted. *Wot Shigona Dew?* Tuba-Euphonium Press. Three euphoniums, two tubas, and rhythm. 1983. $10.00. 4:00. IV. Part I: e♭–c"; Part II: c–b♭'; Part III: c–a♭'; Part IV: B♭$_1$–b♭; Part V: B♭$_1$–f. A very catchy blues tune with some very nice harmonies. There is a section with just chord symbols for any instrumentalist to play an improvised solo. Technically not very difficult, but a good swing feel is crucial. Works well at a variety of tempos. Originally published by Laissez-Faire Music Publishing Company. Parts may be doubled for a large ensemble. Recorded by the Tennessee Technological University Tuba Ensemble, *Heavy Metal,* Mark Records, MES 20759.

Six Parts

Arlen, Harold. *Somewhere over the Rainbow.* arr. Rich Matteson. Tuba-Euphonium Press. Three euphoniums, three tubas, and rhythm. 1993. Written for the Matteson-Phillips Tubajazz Consort.

Ayers, Jesse. *The Magical, Mystical Rain Forest.* Tuba-Euphonium Press. Three euphoniums and three tubas and recorded accompaniment. 1999. $20.00. 5:30. II. Part I: f–b♭'; Part II: d♭–g'; Part III: B♭–f' (g'); Part IV: E♭–d♭; Part V: E♭–g; Part VI: (E_1) A♭$_1$–d♭. Commissioned by the Tennessee

Tech Tuba-Euphonium Ensemble, R. Winston Morris, founder and conductor. This is a revision of the 1991 version of *Into the Magical Rain Forest* by this same composer. This revision expands the piece from four parts to six parts to simplify the individual parts and allow shorter phrases. The recorded accompaniment is now available in compact disc rather than tape. This version is more appropriate for use with younger ensembles. Parts may be doubled for a large ensemble.

Barber, Samuel. *Adagio for Strings.* arr. David Spies. Tuba-Euphonium Press. Three euphoniums and three tubas. 2000. $14.00. 4:45. III. Part I: d–b♭'; Part II: G–f'; Part III: G–c'; Part IV: B_1–e'; Part V: E–c'; Part VI: E_1–e. Challenging arrangement based on Barber's orchestral version of *Adagio.* A minimum of twelve performers is required, and the arranger recommends nineteen. Also reviewed in the Summer 2001 issue of the *TUBA Journal* (Vol. 28, No. 4).

Bartles, Alfred H. *The New When Tubas Waltz.* Tuba-Euphonium Press. Three euphoniums and three tubas. 2001. $12.00. 5:00. III. Part I: B–b♭' (c"); Part II: B–b♭'; Part III: F–a'; Part IV: F–d'; Part V: F–c♭'; Part VI: B♭$_1$–b♭. For Winston, to Bobbie. New original composition in the light, jazzy style of the original *When Tubas Waltz* by the same composer. All parts are interesting. Parts may be doubled for a large ensemble. Also reviewed in the Winter 2002 issue of the *ITEA Journal* (Vol. 29, No. 2). Recorded by Symphonia on the compact disc *Symphonia Three: Symphonia Fantastique,* Mark Records.

Baylock, Alan. *A Lift of the Foot.* Tuba-Euphonium Press. Three euphoniums and three tubas with piano, acoustic bass, and drums. 1996. $25.00. 5:00. IV. Part I: B♭–e♭"; Part II: B–d♭"; Part III: B–a♭'; Part IV: C–f'; Part V: B_1–d♭'; Part VI: D♭$_1$–b♭'. Commissioned by the University of North Texas Tuba/Euphonium Ensemble, John Rider and Marc Dickman, directors; Don Little, faculty advisor. Original composition in a "funk shuffle, swing" style. Instrumentation is patterned after the Matteson-Phillips TubaJazz Consort. First euphonium part contains chord changes for an unwritten, improvised solo passage. More appropriate for a large ensemble, as four of the parts contain *divisi* passages.

Beethoven, Ludwig van. *Funeral March on the Death of a Hero, Op. 26.* arr. Arthur Frackenpohl. Tuba-Euphonium Press. Three euphoniums and three tubas with tympani. 1994. $10.00. 5:00. III. Part I: G–c" (d"); Part II: G–a'; Part III: G–f♯'; Part IV: G–c' (d'); Part V: G_1–a; Part VI: F_1–f♯. For Winston Morris and "Symphonia." Effective arrangement of this well-known work. Individual parts are not rhythmically or stylistically difficult, though their ranges may prove challenging. First and second euphonium parts also available in tenor clef. Fourth part may also be performed on euphonium. Parts may be doubled for a large ensemble.

Bewley, Norlan. *Rich Tradition: A Tribute to Rich Matteson.* Bewley Music Incorporated. Three euphoniums, three tubas, and rhythm. 1992. $30.00. 5:45. IV–V. Solo euphonium: d♭–b♭' (f"); Part II: f–b♭'; Part III: B♭–f'; Part IV: C–c♯'; Part V: C–c♯'; Part VI: B♭$_2$–e♭. Three movements: Chorale; The Call; Jubilee. The first part is for solo euphonium and the fourth part for solo tuba. The second movement is for the solo euphonium a cappella. The last movement alternates between a Dixieland and a swing style. While the two solo parts are the most demanding, there are many tutti sections requiring a good swing feel of all players. A very exciting work.

Blostein, Michael D. *Nebulous.* Tuba-Euphonium Press. Three euphoniums and three tubas. 2001. $18.00. 4:00. III. Part I: c–a♭'; Part II: e♭–a♭'; Part III: G–d'; Part IV: B♭$_1$–d'; Part V: B♭$_1$–a; Part VI: C_1–A♭. Original composition set in a minimalistic texture with a layering of the individual lines. More appropriate for a large ensemble, as there are *divisi* passages in all parts.

Boone, Dan. *Three Moods.* The Brass Press. Four euphoniums and two tubas. 1971. $5.00. 4:00. III. Part I: c–g'; Part II: e♭–a♭; Part III: c–f'; Part IV: G–f'; Part V: C–f; Part VI: F_1–f. Three movements: Allegro; Larghetto; Allegro. Written for R. Winston Morris and the Tennessee Technological University Tuba Ensemble. A delightful work playable by high school ensembles. The three contrasting movements provide a wide musical variety. The second movement is very lyrical and the third movement is multimetric and fits together very well. The first four parts are printed in both treble and bass clefs. Very enjoyable to play. Parts may be doubled for a large ensemble. Recorded by the University of Miami Tuba Ensemble, Miami United Tuba Society, 14568.

Brahms, Johannes. *Es ist eine Rose Entsprungen.* arr. Fumio Gotoh. Tuba-Euphonium Press. Three euphoniums and three tubas. 1992. $6.00. 1:20. III–IV. Part I: c–g'; Part II: c–d'; Part III: e♭–a♭'; Part IV: F–b♭; Part V: E♭–a♭; Part VI: G_1–d♭. Parts one and two are marked "euphonium" and part three is marked "tenor tuba" and has a higher range and tessitura than the first two parts. A very nice arrangement of this beautiful melody. No technical problems. Almost all the parts have some *divisi* sections, so parts will need to be doubled as this was transcribed for a large ensemble.

Brahms, Johannes. *Rhapsody in G Minor, Op. 79, No. 2.* arr. Frank H. Siekmann. Brelmat Music. Four euphoniums and two tubas. 1995. $30.00. 6:00. III–IV. Part I: A–b♭'; Part II: F♯–b♭' (c"); Part III: F♯–a'; Part IV: G–b'; Part V: G_1–b♭; Part VI: E_1–b♭. Instrumentation not specified in this six-part arrangement, though range considerations suggest four euphonium and two tuba parts.

This is a challenging work with cross-rhythms (triplets vs. dotted eighth or sixteenth note patterns), wide ranges, and large intervals in inner voices. All parts are of equal difficulty, and parts may be doubled for a large ensemble.

Carmichael, Hoagy. *Georgia on My Mind.* arr. Rich Matteson. Tuba-Euphonium Press. Three euphoniums, three tubas, and rhythm. 1993. 4:40. Written for the Matteson-Phillips Tubajazz Consort. Recorded by the Matteson-Phillips Tubajazz Consort, *Super Horn,* Mark Records, MJS 57591.

Childs, Barney. *Music for Tubas . . . Six of 'Em.* Facsimile Editions (Carl Fischer). Six tubas. 1969. $18.00. 10:00. IV. Part I: B♭$_1$–f♯; Part II: G–d; Part III: A♯$_1$–d♭'; Part IV: A♯$_1$–e♯'; Part V: G$_1$–c♯'; Part VI: F$_1$–e♭'. Four movements. For Barton Cummings. This piece has many complicated rhythms and is challenging to put together. There are many twentieth-century techniques required, including flutter tonguing, lip trills, and glissandos. Multiple tonguing and mutes are also required of all players. May need to use a conductor to help keep the ensemble together.

Cottrell, Jeff. *Tuba Loca.* Tuba-Euphonium Press. Three euphoniums and three tubas. 2001. $15.00. 3:45. III–IV. Part I: c–d"; Part II: G–b♭'; Part III: G–d"; Part IV: B♭$_1$–c'; Part V: F$_1$–a; Part VI: F$_1$–a. Original composition in a light, Latin style. All parts are interesting and challenging. The third part contains a written-out solo, and chord changes are provided should the performer wish to improvise. More appropriate for a sextet than for a large ensemble. Also reviewed in the Spring 2003 issue of the *ITEA Journal* (Vol. 30, No. 3).

Cummings, Barton. *Fanfare and Chant.* Kendor Music, Incorporated. Four euphoniums and two tubas. 1978. Out of Print. 2:30. IV. Part I: e–c"; Part II: e–c"; Part III: A–f♯'; Part IV: A–f♯; Part V: E–b; Part VI: A$_1$–c. Two movements: Fanfare; Chant. The tessitura of the first part is very high. There are many tutti rhythms in the chant. Parts may be doubled for a large ensemble.

Després, Josquin. *In nominee Iesu omne genuflectatur.* tr. Angelo Manzo. Tuba-Euphonium Press. Two euphoniums and four tubas. 2001. $12.00. 2:45. II. Part I: d–f'; Part II: c–e'; Part III: G–b; Part IV: G–a; Part V: A$_1$–d; Part VI: E$_1$–A. Highly imitative composition set in a medieval or Renaissance style. Individual parts are not difficult, though the staggered entrances and independent lines may prove challenging for younger performers. Parts may be doubled for a large ensemble.

DiGiovanni, Rocco. *Tuba Magic for Tuba Ensemble.* Shawnee Press, Incorporated. Two euphoniums and four tubas. 1981. $25.00. 6:30. IV–V. Part I: F♯–b♭'; Part II: G–a'; Part III: B♭$_1$–e'; Part IV: B♭$_1$–e♭'; Part V: F$_1$–d♭'; Part VI: F$_1$–a. Written for R. Winston Morris and the Tennessee Technological University Tuba Ensemble. A majestic-sounding piece with very lush harmonies. There is a cadenza for the first euphonium in the middle section. The lyrical qualities of the euphonium and tuba are explored. The ranges of all parts are high and will require strong players on all parts. The top two parts are printed in both bass and treble clef. Very enjoyable for performers and audience. Parts may be doubled for a large ensemble. Recorded by the Tennessee Technological University Tuba Ensemble, *LIVE!* KM Records, KM 5661; and the U.S. Armed Forces Tuba/Euphonium Ensemble and Massed Ensemble, U.S. Army Band Records.

DiGiovanni, Rocco. *Tubarhumba.* Available from the composer. Two euphoniums, four tubas, guitar, bass, drums, claves, and maracas. 1984. $20.00. 4:00. IV. Part I: e–b♭'; Part II: e–b♭'; Part III: D–f'; Part IV: D–f'; Part V: A♭$_1$–e♭'; Part VI: F$_1$–c'. Written for R. Winston Morris and the Tennessee Technological University Tuba Ensemble. A fun melody in a bright rumba and swing style. The first euphonium part is very demanding. A good feel for these two styles is necessary. The rhythm section is a key ingredient to this piece. The tessitura of the first tuba part is high. Parts may be doubled for a large ensemble.

Dutton, Brent. *Warring.* Seesaw Music Corporation. Three euphoniums and three tubas. 1980. $17.00. 7:30. IV. Part I: B–b♭'; Part II: G–b♭'; Part III: F–b♭'; Part IV: G$_1$–b; Part V: E♭$_1$–f; Part VI: E♭$_1$–f. Dedicated to the Central Michigan University Tuba Ensemble. This is designed for a large ensemble with each part doubled, ideally 12 to 24 players. The euphoniums should be physically situated as far from the tubas as possible (i.e., one group on the stage the other group in a balcony). Technically challenging at times; the players are also required to sing through their instruments, ad-lib sections for each part, and produce contemporary harmonies.

Elgar, Edward. *Nimrod from "Enigma Variations."* arr. Mike Forbes, Mike. Tuba-Euphonium Press. Three euphoniums and three tubas. 2000. $8.00. 2:30. II–III. Part I: c–c"; Part II: A–f'; Part III: E–f'; Part IV: A–e'; Part V: D–f; Part VI: (C$_1$) D$_1$–c. Excerpted from Elgar's *Enigma Variations,* this slow movement features a lyrical texture. Melodic material is divided among the voices. Rhythm and texture are appropriate for intermediate-level performers, though the ranges may prove difficult. Parts may be doubled for a large ensemble.

Ellington, Duke. *In a Mello Tone.* arr. Rich Matteson. Tuba-Euphonium Press. Three euphoniums, three tubas, and rhythm. 1990. Written for the Matteson-Phillips Tubajazz Consort.

Ellington, Mercer. *Things Ain't What They Used to Be.* arr. Rich Matteson. Tuba-Euphonium Press. Three euphoniums, three tubas, and rhythm. 1993. 7:30. Written for the Matteson-Phillips

Tubajazz Consort. Recorded by the Matteson-Phillips Tubajazz Consort, *Super Horn,* Mark Records, MJS 57591

Endo, M. *Meiso No Inga.* Tokyo Bari-Tuba Ensemble. Five euphoniums and one tuba.

Erdmann, Richard. *The Third Day.* Tuba-Euphonium Press. Four euphoniums and two tubas. 1996. $12.00. 6:00. III. Part I: c–b'; Part II: c–g♯'; Part III: A–f'; Part IV: A_1–e'; Part V: G–d'; Part VI: A_1–d. Originally titled *On the Third Day He Rose from the Dead,* this programmatic work contains frequent meter changes and traditional harmonies. One euphonium mute is required. Parts may be doubled for a large ensemble. Also reviewed in the Spring 1999 issue of the *TUBA Journal* (Vol. 26, No. 3).

Fiegel, E. Todd. *Celluloid Tubas: A Score for Barney Oldfield's Race for a Life (1913).* Celluloid Tubas. Three euphoniums, three tubas, motion picture equipment. 1992. Rental. 15:00. IV–V. Part I: G–d♭'; Part II: B♭–a'; Part III: G–f♯'; Part IV: $B♭_1$–a; Part V: $B♭_2$–a; Part VI: A_2–d. For Fritz Kaenzig with profound admiration. The performance is designed to accompany a select portion of the film *Barney Oldfield's Race for a Life.* Challenging for all parts due to tempo and meter changes and the need to stay with the film. A low tessitura required for the fifth and sixth parts. Very enjoyable for performers and audience. Contact the composer for exact rental and performance information.

Frescobaldi, Girolamo. *Toccata.* arr. Joseph Skillen. Tuba-Euphonium Press. Three euphoniums and three tubas. 1992. $10.00. 2:20. IV. Part I: c–c''; Part II: G–a'; Part III: G–f'; Part IV: E–c'; Part V: G_1–a; Part VI: (C_1) E_1–g. Written for R. Winston Morris and the Tennessee Technological University Tuba Ensemble. Most of the melody and the technical challenges are in the top three parts. The tessitura of the first part is high. Works well. Parts may be doubled for a large ensemble.

Friedrich, Kenneth D. *El Toro Loco.* Available from the composer. Four euphoniums and two tubas. 2003. $12.50. 3:30. III. Part I: c–c''; Part II: G–a♭'; Part III: B♭–b♭'; Part IV: G–g; Part V: $A♭_1$–a; Part VI: F_1–g. Light, programmatic work in a Spanish style. All parts have challenging lines, but parts are typically paired rhythmically, so the piece is easy to rehearse and accessible to intermediate-level performers.

Friedrich, Kenneth D. *Winds of Spring.* Cimarron Music and Productions. Four euphoniums and two tubas. $11.00. 3:30. II–III. Part I: B♭–b'; Part II: B♭–g'; Part III: B♭–f'; Part IV: F–b♭; Part V: D–g; Part VI: F_1–B♭. Flowing, lyrical work with traditional harmonies. Euphonium parts also available in treble clef. Parts may be doubled for a large ensemble.

Friedrich, Kenneth D. *W.O.L. (With Out Lyrics).* Cimarron Music and Productions. Four euphoniums and two tubas. $21.00. 4:15. II–III. Part I: g–b'; Part II: A♭–g'; Part III: e♭–e♭'; Part IV: d♭–e♭'; Part V: F–e; Part VI: G_1–d. Lyrical, original composition with traditional harmonies and several tempo changes. Melodic material is primarily in the first two parts. Parts may be doubled for a large ensemble.

Fritze, Gregory. *Kilimanjaro.* Available from the composer. Three trombones (euphoniums), one euphonium, and two tubas. 1991. $10.00. 9:00. V. Part I: F–d♭''; Part II: A♭–d♭''; Part III: F_1–f♯'; Part IV: E_1–d♭''; Part V: E_1–a♭'; Part VI: E_1–a♭'. Composed for Gary Bird and the Indiana University Low Brass Faculty. The top three parts may be played on trombones or euphoniums. This is a very challenging work with extensive range demands. There are several smears and glissandos for all parts and numerous meter changes. Will require very strong players.

Fritze, Gregory. *Tubafest Shuffle.* Available from the composer. Three euphoniums, three tubas, and rhythm. 1988. $10.00. 3:30. IV. Part I: f–g'; Part II: d–e♭'; Part III: F–e♭'; Part IV: F–f; Part V: A_1–e♭; Part VI: G_1–e♭. Composed for the Berklee Heavy Metal. A driving funk-rock-style composition. A basic funk rhythm is repeated throughout the piece. There is a twelve-measure section that can be repeated for improvised solos. Some technical challenges. There is also a version available that includes two French horns. Parts may be doubled for a large ensemble.

Fritze, Gregory. *Tu-Bop.* Available from the composer. Three euphoniums, three tubas, and rhythm. 1981. $10.00. 10:00. IV. Part I: f–d''; Part II: c–b♭'; Part III: B♭–f♯'; Part IV: A_1–e'; Part V: B_1–c'; Part VI: F_1–a. Composed for the Berklee Heavy Metal. An up-tempo swing composition with improvised solos for the first, second, and fourth parts. Very syncopated; a good swing feel is necessary in all players. Parts may be doubled for a large ensemble.

Garbáge, Pierre. *Sousa Surrenders.* James Garrett. Three euphoniums, three tubas, and optional timpani. 1974. $35.00. 10:30. IV–V. Part I: c♭–b♭'; Part II: A♭–g♭'; Part III: E♭–f'; Part IV: D–c'; Part V: $B♭_1$–c'; Part VI: D_1–c'. Written for R. Winston Morris and the Tennessee Technological University Tuba Ensemble. A humorous arrangement of several Sousa marches. The third part could be played by a euphonium or tuba. Technically challenging for all parts. All parts require mutes. Expect the unexpected from this arrangement. A lot of fun for performers and audience. Dr. Garbáge writes, "Sousa Surrenders and Pierre graciously accepts his sword." Recorded by the U.S. Armed Forces Tuba/Euphonium Ensemble and Massed Ensemble, U.S. Army Band Records.

Garrett, James A. *Expose for Tubas.* James Garrett. Four euphoniums and two tubas. 1976. $20.00. 2:20. IV. Part I: g–c''; Part II: g–g'; Part III: c–e';

Part IV: E♭–d♭'; Part V: A♭$_1$–f; Part VI: C$_1$–c. Written for R. Winston Morris and the Tennessee Technological University Tuba Ensemble. A single movement that progresses through several different moods in a short period of time. The tessitura of the first part is high. Most of the technical work is for the top two parts. Very dissonant harmonies at times. The top two euphonium parts require mutes. There are several *divisi* sections in all parts. Parts may be doubled for a large ensemble.

Garrett, James A. *Fanfare.* The Brass Press. Three euphoniums and three tubas. 1966. $3.50. 1:00. III–IV. Part I: g–a♭'; Part II: c–f'; Part III: d–d'; Part IV: c–b♭; Part V: F–f; Part VI: G$_1$–f. Designed as a fun opener to a concert. Not technically difficult. Parts may be doubled for a large ensemble.

Garrett, James A., arr. *Espana Cami.* James Garrett. Three euphoniums and three tubas. 1970. $20.00. 3:00. IV. Part I: f–b♭'; Part II: d♭–f'; Part III: B♭–f'; Part IV: G–f'; Part V: G–b♭; Part VI: B♭$_1$–b♭. A fun arrangement of this classic Mexican melody. Several syncopated and triplet rhythms, though most rhythm patterns are played by two or more parts. Drums and other percussion instruments may be added for stylistic enhancement. Parts may be doubled for a large ensemble.

Glivar, David B. *A Cry Out.* Ohio University ITEA Chapter Composition Series. Three euphoniums and three tubas. 2004. 5:30. III. Part I: A♭–c''; Part II: A♭–c'; Part III: B–c'; Part IV: D–b; Part V: B$_1$–a; Part VI: F$_1$–c. Two movements. Rhythmically driven work in a minimalist style. Parts may be doubled for a large ensemble.

Glover, Jim, arr. *Florentiner March.* Available from the arranger. Three euphoniums and three tubas. 1992. $15.00.

Glover, Jim, arr. *Here Comes Santa Claus.* Available from the arranger. Four euphoniums and two tubas. 1992. $8.00.

Glover, Jim, arr. *Jingle Bell Rock.* Available from the arranger. Four euphoniums and two tubas. 1992. $8.00.

Glover, Jim, arr. *Let It Snow.* Available from the arranger. Four euphoniums and two tubas. 1992. $8.00.

Glover, Jim, arr. *Santa Claus Is Comin' to Town.* Available from the arranger. Four euphoniums and two tubas. 1992. $8.00.

Glover, Jim, arr. *Silver Bells.* Available from the arranger. Four euphoniums and two tubas. 1992. $8.00.

Goodman, Benny, Chick Webb, and Edgar Sampson. *Stompin' at the Savoy.* arr. Rich Matteson. Tuba-Euphonium Press. Three euphoniums, three tubas, and rhythm. 1976. 6:50. Written for the Matteson-Phillips Tubajazz Consort. Recorded by the Matteson-Phillips Tubajazz Consort, *Super Horn,* Mark Records, MJS 57591.

Handel, George Frederic. *Allegro from "Water Music."* arr. James Self. Basset Hound Music. Two euphoniums and four tubas. 1972. $10.00. 3:00. IV. Part I: B♭–b♭'; Part II: B♭–b♭'; Part III: B♭$_1$–b♭; Part IV: F$_1$–b♭; Part V: F$_1$–b♭; Part VI: F$_1$–b♭. Good arrangement of this baroque melody. There are some technical challenges especially in the top four parts. Will require good lyrical and detached playing. Some syncopated rhythms.

Hayakawa, M. *Divertimento.* Tokyo Bari-Tuba Ensemble. Three euphoniums and three tubas.

Hill, William H. *Fantasia on "Dies Irae."* Neil A. Kjos Music Company. Two euphoniums and four tubas. 1988. $7.00. 5:30. IV. Part I: G–b♭'; Part II: G–b♭'; Part III: F$_1$–b; Part IV: F$_1$–b; Part V: F$_1$–b; Part VI: F$_1$–b. Commissioned by TUBA. The two euphonium parts call for two players each, requiring a minimum of eight players for this piece. There are two contrasting sections: a slow chant-like introduction followed by a dissonant allegro section. All parts are interesting and have sections that are technically challenging.

Holst, Gustav. *March from Second Suite in F for Military Band* arr. David Werden. Cimarron Music and Productions. Three euphoniums and three tubas. 1997. $18.00. 4:30. III. Part I: A♭–c''; Part II: c–b♭'; Part III: B♭–b♭'; Part IV: B♭$_1$–f'; Part V: E♭–b♭; Part VI: C$_1$–d. Excellent arrangement of this popular work for wind band. All parts are challenging and the melodic material is divided among the top five voices. Euphonium parts also available in treble clef. Parts may be doubled for a large ensemble. Also available in a four-part version from the same arranger and publisher. Recorded by Symphonia on the compact disc *Symphonia Two: La Morte dell Oom,* Mark Records.

Holst, Gustav. *Mars, The Bringer of War, from "The Planets."* arr. David Butler. Tuba-Euphonium Press. Three euphoniums and three tubas. 1993. $15.00. 7:00. IV. Part I: B–c''; Part II: B–g'; Part III: B–g'; Part IV: C–d♭'; Part V: c–b♭; Part VI: F$_1$–d'. Written for R. Winston Morris and the Tennessee Technological University Tuba Ensemble. A solid arrangement: the piece almost seems best suited for euphoniums and tubas. Technically challenging for all parts. Players need to count carefully and play cleanly. There are several *divisi* sections; this is intended for a large ensemble. Fun to play.

Jarrett, Keith. *Lucky Southern.* arr. Rich Matteson. Tuba-Euphonium Press. Three euphoniums, three tubas, and rhythm. 1976. 4:30. Written for the Matteson-Phillips Tubajazz Consort. Recorded by the Matteson-Phillips Tubajazz Consort, Mark Records, MJS 57587.

Knight, Morris. *Colossi.* Woodsum Music, Limited. Six Tubas. 1990. $25.00. 14:00. IV. Part I: D♯–e'; Part II: A$_1$–b; Part III: F$_1$–c♯'; Part IV: A$_1$–b; Part V: A$_1$–b; Part VI: F$_1$–d♭. Seven movements:

Elephants; Hippopotamus; Moose; Giraffe; Rhinoceros; Ostrich; Whales. Dedicated to Harvey and Toby and Les and J. S. and John and Sande and Phil and so many other colossal tubists I've always looked "down" to for great performances. The movements contrast in style, meter, and key. There are some technical challenges, especially in the bottom two parts. The score and parts are very difficult to read because of the awkward manner in which the ledger lines are printed.

Lamb, Marvin. *Heavy Metal.* Carl Fischer, Incorporated. Two euphoniums and four tubas. 1985. Rental. 5:12. IV–V. Part I: B♭–b♭'; Part II: A♭–b♭'; Part III: C–e'; Part IV: (F_1) G_1–b; Part V: E_1–d'; Part VI: $F\sharp_1$–b♭. Written for R. Winston Morris and the Tennessee Technological University Tuba Ensemble and dedicated to the memory of John Dunstable and the Pointer Sisters. This piece stretches the timbres normally associated with the tuba/euphonium ensemble. After a muted, eerie-sounding introduction, a funk feel evolving into a swing section follows. In addition to playing their instruments, performers are asked to sing swing nonsense syllables and perform hand jives (clapping the legs, chest, and hands to a written rhythm). Several sixteenth note and triplet runs make this technically challenging and exciting to play. Parts may be doubled for a large ensemble. Recorded by the Tennessee Technological University Tuba Ensemble, *Heavy Metal,* Mark Records, MES 20759.

Lawn, Rick. *Hippochondriac.* UNITUBA Press. Four euphoniums and two tubas. Out of Print. 4:00. IV. Part I: a–c"; Part II: d–b♭'; Part III: g–f'; Part IV: E–c'; Part V: E–c'; Part VI: C–a. Other instrumentation possibilities include three euphoniums and three tubas. A good jazz feel is necessary to perform this work. No significant technical demands, but the tessitura of the top two parts is high. The use of a drum set is strongly recommended. Parts may be doubled for a large ensemble.

Matteson, Rich. *Little Ole Softy.* Tuba-Euphonium Press. Three euphoniums, three tubas, and rhythm. 1980. 5:30. Written for the Matteson-Phillips Tubajazz Consort. Recorded by the Matteson-Phillips Tubajazz Consort, *Super Horn,* Mark Records, MJS 57591.

Matteson, Rich. *Spoofy.* Tuba-Euphonium Press. Three euphoniums, three tubas, and rhythm. 1976. 11:45. Written for the Matteson-Phillips Tubajazz Consort. Recorded by the Matteson-Phillips Tubajazz Consort, Mark Records, MJS 57587.

Mendelssohn, Felix. *Nocturne from "Midsummer Night's Dream."* arr. Dean A. Sommerville. Tuba-Euphonium Press. Four euphoniums and two tubas. 1998. $8.00. 1:30. II. Part I: f–f'; Part II: c–d'; Part III: A–c'; Part IV: F–g; Part V: E♭–e♭; Part VI: $B\flat_1$–g. Brief arrangement in a homophonic texture. Range is appropriate for intermediate-level performers. Melody is primarily in the first part. Parts may be doubled for a large ensemble.

Morris, Mike. *Tubology.* Laissez-Faire Music Publishing Company. Three euphoniums, three tubas, and rhythm. Out of Print.

Mozart, Wolfgang Amadeus. *O Isis und Osiris.* arr. Andrew Spang. Lyric Brass Publishing. Two euphoniums and four tubas. 1993. $10.00. 3:00. Arrangement is for solo tuba with quintet accompaniment. First euphonium part is in tenor clef.

Mussorgsky, Modeste. *Bydlo from "Pictures at an Exhibition."* arr. Lisa Golas. Tuba-Euphonium Press. Three euphoniums and three tubas. 1995. $10.00. 2:30. III. Part I: d♯–g♯'; Part II: A♯–c♯'; Part III: A–g♯'; Part IV: C♯–g♯; Part V: $G\sharp_1$–d♯'; Part VI: E_1–A. Originally for piano, this work is best known as an arrangement for orchestra by Ravel. The well-known solo, originally scored for French tuba, is contained in the third euphonium part. The key of five sharps may present a challenge for intermediate-level performers, but the tempo is slow. Parts may be doubled for a large ensemble. Euphonium parts also available in treble clef. Several other movements from this work are available separately from the same arranger.

Mussorgsky, Modeste. *The Old Castle from "Pictures at an Exhibition."* arr. Lisa Golas. Tuba-Euphonium Press. Three euphoniums and three tubas. 1995. $24.00. 4:00. II–III. Part I: d♯–a'; Part II: G♯–f♯'; Part III: G♯–d'; Part IV: $G\sharp_1$–a; Part V: $G\sharp_1$–e'; Part VI: $G\sharp_1$–f♯. Originally for piano, this work is best known as an arrangement for orchestra by Ravel. Melodic material is distributed among the voices, and the key signature of five sharps may provide the greatest challenge to intermediate-level performers. Euphonium parts also available in treble clef. Several other movements from this work are available separately from the same arranger.

Ott, Joseph. *Suite for Six Tubas.* Claude Benny Press. Six tubas. 1968. $9.00. 7:00. IV. Part I: G_1–b; Part II: $B\flat_1$–a; Part III: G_1–a; Part IV: G_1–g; Part V: $B\flat_1$–b; Part VI: G_1–g. Three movements. No major technical problems, but putting the ensemble together can be challenging. The writing has some close harmonies and tone clusters. Very dissonant at times—can get muddy if not careful. Interesting writing.

Paganini, N. *Perpetual Motion.* arr. Gary Buttery. Whaling Music Publishers. Two to seven players with piano. 1978. $10.00. 4:20. V. All parts: C_1–d' (e'). For two to seven tubas with piano accompaniment. Eighty percent of the composition is in unison. Technically very challenging. Players must have excellent technique and a good sense of rhythm.

Palestrina, Giovanni de. *Agnus Dei.* arr. Bryan V. Doughty. Cimarron Music and Productions. Three euphoniums and three tubas. $16.00.

Praetorius, Michael. *Lo, How a Rose E'er Blooming.* arr. Andrew Spang. Lyric Brass Publishing. Two euphoniums and four tubas. 1993. $12.00. Arranged for TUBA+, the tuba-euphonium ensemble at the Eastman School of Music. Part I: d–b'; Part II: c♯–g'; Part III: A–a; Part IV: G–g; Part V: C–g; Part VI: (C_1) D_1–g. Straightforward arrangement of this popular Christmas song. Melody is predominantly in the first part. Parts may be doubled for a large ensemble. Also available in a four-part arrangement by the same arranger and publisher.

Presser, William. *Suite for Six Tubas.* Tenuto Publications. Six tubas. 1967. $6.00. 7:00. IV. Part I: B_1–e♭'; Part II: B♭$_1$–b; Part III: G♭$_1$–b♭; Part IV: A♭$_1$–d'; Part V: A♭$_1$–b; Part VI: E♭$_1$–b. Three movements: March; Echo; Song and Scherzo. Dedication: For Rex Conner. All parts are of equal difficulty. Several melodic and rhythmic tutti sections. The melody frequently alternates between the top three and bottom three parts.

Raum, Elizabeth. *Jason and the Golden Fleece.* Tuba-Euphonium Press. Two euphoniums and four tubas with percussion. 2001. $30.00. 12:30. III–IV. Part I: c–b♭'; Part II: G♭–a'; Part III: C–d'; Part IV: E–d'; Part V: G_1–a♯'; Part VI: F–e♭. Five movements: Jason and the Argonauts; The Symplegades (Clashing Islands); Medea; Sowing the Dragon's Teeth; The Golden Fleece. Commissioned by Winston Morris and the tuba ensemble Symphonia, with assistance from the Saskatchewan Arts Board. This programmatic original work is a challenge for all performers. The percussion includes timpani, wind chimes, flexatone, suspended cymbal, snare drum, and castanets. Third and fourth tuba parts also double on percussion. Parts may be doubled for a large ensemble. Premiered at ITEC 2000. Recorded by Symphonia on the compact disc *Symphonia Three: Symphonia Fantastique,* Mark Records.

Rollins, Sonny. *Oleo.* arr. Rich Matteson. Tuba-Euphonium Press. Three euphoniums, three tubas, and rhythm. 1993. 4:30. Written for the Matteson-Phillips Tubajazz Consort. Recorded by the Matteson-Phillips Tubajazz Consort, Mark Records, MJS 57587.

Sandstrom, Sven-David. *Fanfare for Six Tubas.* Swedish Music Information Center. Six Tubas. 1979. 6:30.

Schmidt, Dankwart. *Bayrische Polka.* Available from the composer. Two euphoniums and four tubas. 2:35. Recorded by Gerhard Meinl's Tuba Sextet, *A Six-Tuba Musical Romp,* Angel, 54729; and David LeClair, *Swingin' Low,* Marcophon.

Schmidt, Dankwart. *Bayrische Zell.* Available from the composer. Two euphoniums and four tubas. 2:50. Recorded by Gerhard Meinl's Tuba Sextet, *A Six-Tuba Musical Romp,* Angel, 54729.

Self, James, arr. *Basic Psych-Rock.* James Self. Two euphoniums and four tubas. Out of Print. 5:00. IV. Part I: c–b♭'; Part II: e♭–f'; Part III: e–b♭; Part IV: E–g; Part V: G_1–f; Part VI: G_1–f. A hard rock style with rhythm section. Parts may be doubled for a large ensemble.

Shinihara, Keisuke. *Japanese Songs.* Tokyo Bari-Tuba Ensemble. Four euphoniums and two tubas.

Sibelius, Jean. *Finlandia.* arr. James Self. Basset Hound Music. Two euphoniums and four tubas. 1993. $12.00. 8:00. IV. Part I: c–a'; Part II: A–e♭'; Part III: C–b♭; Part IV: C–g; Part V: F_1–f; Part VI: F_1–d. A very good chorale-like arrangement of this nice melody. Parts may be doubled for a large ensemble.

Silver, Horace. *Gregory Is Here.* arr. Rich Matteson. Tuba-Euphonium Press. Three euphoniums, three tubas, and rhythm. 1993. 7:50. Written for the Matteson-Phillips Tubajazz Consort. Recorded by the Matteson-Phillips Tubajazz Consort, Mark Records, MJS 57587.

Strauss, Richard. *Allerseelen. (All Souls' Day.)* arr. Fumio Gotoh. Tuba-Euphonium Press. Three euphoniums and three tubas. 1991. $6.00. 2:45. IV. Part I: c–a♭'; Part II: A♭–a♭'; Part III: G–b♭'; Part IV: F–e♭'; Part V: G_1–a♭; Part VI: E♭$_1$–d. Part three is marked "tenor tuba" and has a higher range and tessitura than the first and second parts. No real technical demands other than range. All parts have *divisi* sections, so twelve players will be required to perform the arrangement as written (though the bottom two parts have only two or three notes marked *divisi*). The bottom tuba part requires several precise low E♭$_1$'s.

Sullivan, Arthur. *The Lost Chord.* arr. Barton Cummings. Tuba-Euphonium Press. Three euphoniums and three tubas. 1991. $5.00. 3:30. IV. Part I: c–c''; Part II: c–g'; Part III: B♭–c'; Part IV: C–g; Part V: C–d; Part VI: F_1–A. Other than a single high c in the first part, the arrangement is not difficult. Attention should be paid to the lyricism and dynamics. Parts may be doubled for a large ensemble.

Svarda, William E. *Piece for Six Tubas.* Available from the composer. Six tubas. 1969. 6:00. III–IV. Part I: D–c'; Part II: B♭$_1$–b; Part III: D♭–g; Part IV: A♭$_1$–g; Part V: E_1–c; Part VI: F_1–d♭. Four movements: Moderato; Moderato; Andante; Presto. Traditional harmonies and rhythms. Frequent unison and octave playing; no significant technical or range problems. Parts may be doubled for a large ensemble.

Tchaikovsky, Peter. *1812 Overture.* Wehr's Music House. tr. Chris Sharp. Three euphoniums and three tubas. 1995. $27.00. 8:00. III. Part I: G–e♭''; Part II: G–b♭'; Part III: B♭–g'; Part IV: G_1–e♭'; Part V: G_1–b♭; Part VI: B♭$_2$–a♭. For Gail Robertson and the 1994 Central Florida Octubafest Tuba Choir. This arrangement encompasses the final eight minutes of the original composition. Though not technically difficult, the extreme range of the first parts provides the greatest challenge. Euphonium parts also available in treble clef. Parts may be doubled for a large ensemble.

Also reviewed in the Fall 1995 issue of the *TUBA Journal* (Vol. 23, No. 1).

Tchaikovsky, Peter. *Finale from Symphony No. 4 in F Minor.* arr. Jim Self. Basset Hound Music. Two euphoniums and four tubas with percussion. 1995. $30.00. IV. Part I: F–d♭"; Part II: E–c"; Part III: C–g'; Part IV: C–f'; Part V: F_1–c'; Part VI: B_2–a. For Los Tubas. Effective arrangement of the final movement of this popular symphony. All parts are challenging and require technical agility. Percussion parts require cymbals, bass drum, and triangle. Parts may be doubled for a large ensemble. Recorded by Los Tubas on the compact disc *The Big Stretch,* Basset Hound Music.

Toyama, Yuzo. *Essay.* Yuzo Toyama. Three euphoniums and three tubas. 1993. $15.00. 4:00. V. Part I: B–c'; Part II: A–b♭'; Part III: G–b♭'; Part IV: G_1–d'; Part V: $G\flat_1$–c'; Part VI: F_1–c'. Commissioned by TUBA. Very complex rhythmically and technically challenging to play. The tessitura of the first two parts is high. This piece was premiered by the International All-Star College Ensemble, R. Winston Morris, Director, August 12, 1990, at the International Tuba/ Euphonium Conference, Sapporo, Japan.

Tschesnokoff, Pavel. *Salvation Is Created.* arr. William R. Lee. Cimarron Music and Productions. Three euphoniums and three tubas. $11.00. 2:30. II–III. Part I: d–c"; Part II: d–f'; Part III: A–c'; Part IV: A–f♯; Part V: C–d; Part VI: D_1–d. Straightforward arrangement of this chorale suitable for intermediate-level performers. The texture is homophonic and the melodic material is predominantly in the first part. Euphonium parts also available in treble clef. Parts may be doubled for a large ensemble.

Uber, David. *Declarations.* Tuba-Euphonium Press. Three euphoniums and three tubas. 2001. $15.00. 4:00. III. Part I: f–b♭'; Part II: c–g'; Part III: c–g'; Part IV: F–e♭'; Part V: $A\flat_1$–a♭; Part VI: G_1–g. For BASSically Brass. This single-movement work is divided into five contrasting sections. Each part has featured solos, and all parts require technically strong performers. Parts may be doubled for a large ensemble. Also reviewed in the Summer 2004 issue of the *ITEA Journal* (Vol. 31, No. 4).

Uber, David. *Intrada, Romanze, and Scherzo.* T.A.P. Music. Four euphoniums and two tubas. 1989. $20.00. 8:00. IV. Part I: d–c"; Part II: d–g'; Part III: d♭–f'; Part IV: F–g'; Part V: $A\flat_1$–g; Part VI: F_1–g. Three movements: Intrada; Romanza; Scherzo. The tessitura of the top two parts is high. Some technical challenges in all parts. Good writing.

Uber, David. *Puppetry.* Tuba-Euphonium Press. Four euphoniums and two tubas. 2002. $15.00. 3:00. II–III. Part I: A♭–b♭'; Part II: e♭–g'; Part III: c–f'; Part IV: F–e♭'; Part V: G_1–a'; Part VI: F_1–f. For Jerry Young and the U.W.E.C. Low Brass Ensemble. Light character work with modern harmonies. Rhythmically challenging with simple and compound division of the beat. Parts may be doubled for a large ensemble.

Vaughan, Rodger. *Five Canons for Tuba/ Euphonium Sextet.* Available from the composer. 1977. $8.00.

Vaughan, Rodger, arr. *Tubagirls I.* Available from the arranger. Two euphoniums and four tubas. 1977. $5.00. 6:30. IV. Part I: f–b♭'; Part II: c–a♭'; Part III: E♭–c'; Part IV: G_1–b; Part V: F_1–c'; Part VI: $E\flat_1$–c. This is a medley of "Sweet Sue," "Laura," "Sweet Georgia Brown," "Nancy," and "Liza." All parts except the first part have numerous *divisi* sections requiring two on a part.

Vaughan, Rodger, arr. *Tubagirls II.* Available from the arranger. Two euphoniums and four tubas. 1978. $5.00. 6:00. IV. Part I: B♭–c"; Part II: B♭–g'; Part III: E♭–d'; Part IV: F_1–c'; Part V: G_1–b♭; Part VI: $E\flat_1$–b♭. A medley of "Sioux City Sue," "Georgia on My Mind," "Jean," "Amy," and "Tootsie." All parts have an opportunity to play the melody. The tessitura of the first part is high. Drums may be added for effect. No score available. Parts may be doubled for a large ensemble.

Vaughan Williams, Ralph. *Folk Song Suite.* arr. Michael Forbes. Tuba-Euphonium Press. Three euphoniums and three tubas with optional percussion. 2001. $40.00. 15:00. III. Part I: A♭–c"; Part II: B♭–b♭'; Part III: F–g'; Part IV: E♭–f' (g'); Part V: $B\flat_1$–c'; Part VI: ($B\flat_2$) $E\flat_1$–e♭. Four movements: March—"Seventeen Come Sunday"; Scherzo—"Sea Songs"; Intermezzo—"My Bonnie Boy"; March—"Folk Songs from Somerset." This work was originally published as a three-movement work for military band in 1923, but this arrangement restores the original second movement that had been removed and released separately by the publisher. Melodic material is divided among all the parts, and all parts are challenging and interesting. Optional percussion parts include snare drum, bass drum, cymbal, and triangle. Parts may be doubled for a large ensemble. Also reviewed in the Winter 2003 issue of the *ITEA Journal* (Vol. 30, No. 2).

Verdi, Guiseppe. *Dies Irae from Requiem.* arr. Jason Cole. Tuba-Euphonium Press. Two euphoniums and four tubas. 2001. $15.00. 1:45. III–IV. Part I: G–c"; Part II: G–g'; Part III: G_1–b; Part IV: G_1–g; Part V: G_1–g; Part VI: $E\flat_1$–B♭. Challenging arrangement of the explosive *Dies Irae* from Verdi's *Requiem.* The famous bass drum passage is rescored for low contrabass tubas. Trills and fast technical passages make this more appropriate for an advanced ensemble. Parts may be doubled for a large ensemble.

Von Suppe, Franz. *Poet and Peasant Overture.* arr. Mike Forbes. Tuba-Euphonium Press. Three euphoniums, three tubas, and optional percussion. 1999. $24.00. 10:00. III. Part I: B♭–d"; Part

II: G♯–b♭' (d"); Part III: G♯–g'; Part IV: D–g'; Part V: F_1–b♭'; Part VI: D_1–a. Dedicated to John Stevens and the University of Wisconsin–Madison Tuba/Euphonium Ensemble. The arrangement of this popular overture works well as a concert opener. All parts are technically challenging, with trills, written-out tremolos, and fast passages being passed between the voices. Optional percussion includes snare drum, bass drum, and cymbals (two players). Limiting performers to no more than two per part is recommended.

Weisling, Raymond. *Tuba Club.* Raymond Weisling. Six tubas. 1969. Out of Print. 7:00. IV. Part I–VI: All parts range from their lowest note possible to their highest note possible. This composition is intended as an exploration into the "total sound resources" of six tubas. Contemporary notation and techniques required, including flutter tonguing, glissandos, lip trills, and whistling. The piece is very challenging. A conductor is necessary.

Werden, David, arr. *Joy to the World.* Cimarron Music and Productions. Solo tuba with two euphoniums and three tubas. $6.00. 1:15. III. Part I: B♭–f'; Part II: B♭–e♭'; Part III: G–e♭'; Part IV: E♭–b♭; Part V: E♭–g; Part VI: E♭$_1$–e♭. "To: Harvey Phillips—From: Santa." Fun arrangement of this standard Christmas work, scored for solo tuba and five-part ensemble. Ensemble parts are interesting but not difficult, and the challenging solo part includes both straightforward melodic material and contrapuntal descant material. Euphonium parts also available in treble clef. Accompaniment parts may be doubled for a large ensemble.

Werle, Floyd E. *Variations on an Old Hymn Tune.* Available from the composer. Two euphoniums and four tubas. 1988. 5:50. IV. Part I: g–a'; Part II: e–f'; Part III: A♯–c'; Part IV: C–g; Part V: G_1–g♭; Part VI: F_1–A. For R. Winston Morris, Ernie Walls, and the Tennessee Technological University Tuba Ensemble. After the statement of the hymn tune there are five variations, all in different tempos. The sections in the fast tempos are more technically challenging. No significant range demands. Good six-part writing. Parts may be doubled for a large ensemble. Recorded by the Tennessee Technological University Tuba Ensemble, Mark Custom Recording Service, MENC88-1-4; and the U.S. Armed Forces Tuba/Euphonium Massed Ensemble, U.S. Army Records.

Seven or More Parts

Bach, Johann Sebastian. *Jesu, Joy of Man's Desiring.* arr. N. Yamamoto. Tuba-Euphonium Press. Six euphoniums and two tubas. 1985. $6.00. 2:00. IV. Part I: B♭–b♭'; Part II: B♭–f'; Part III: A–f'; Part IV: F_1–b♭; Part V: f–e♭'; Part VI: e–c'; Part VII: F–g; Part VIII: F_1–a. Dedicated to Peggy Heinkel and to the Tokyo Bari-Tuba Ensemble. Beautiful arrangement of this famous Bach melody. Technically it is not very difficult, but rhythmic accuracy is necessary to keep the texture from sounding muddy. A tuba may be used on at least one of the other euphonium parts. Four of the euphonium parts are printed in tenor clef. Parts may be doubled for a large ensemble.

Bach, Johann Sebastian. *Prelude and Fugue in D Minor (BWV 554).* arr. James Barnes. Southern Music Co. Four euphoniums and four tubas. 1999. $15.00. 5:15. III. Part I: d–b♭'; Part II: d–b♭'; Part III: A–a'; Part IV: A–f'; Part V: C–b♭; Part VI: C–b♭; Part VII: F_1–d; Part VIII: (D_1) F_1–d. To commemorate the twentieth anniversary of the appointment of Scott Watson, Professor of Tuba at the University of Kansas, to his position of studio teaching. Nice arrangement of this prelude and fugue originally for organ. Appropriate for college-level performers. Parts may be doubled for a large ensemble. Also reviewed in the Winter 1999 issue of the *TUBA Journal* (Vol. 27, No. 2). Recorded by Symphonia on the compact disc *Symphonia Three: Symphonia Fantastique,* Mark Custom Recording Service.

Barnes, James. *Tangents: An Overture for Tuba Ensemble.* Southern Music Company. Four euphoniums and four tubas. 2001. $25.00. 5:45. III–IV. Part I: e–c"; Part II: e–c"; Part III: d–a'; Part IV: c♯–a'; Part V: E♭–d'; Part VI: B♭$_1$–c♯'; Part VII: F♭$_1$–f; Part VIII: E_1–d. For the Wild Bunch. Challenging original composition that works well as a concert opener. Top two euphonium and tuba parts maintain a high tessitura, and the composer recommends E♭ or F tubas for the top tuba parts. All parts have several solo passages to allow the rest of the section to rest. Three euphonium mutes required, and all euphonium parts also available in treble clef. More appropriate for a large ensemble. Also reviewed in the Winter 2002 issue of the *ITEA Journal* (Vol. 29, No. 2). Recorded by Symphonia on the compact disc *Symphonia Three: Symphonia Fantastique,* Mark Records.

Barnes, James. *Yorkshire Ballad.* Southern Music Company. Four euphoniums and three tubas. 1996. $12.50. 3:00. III. Part I: f–c" (e♭"); Part II: c–a'; Part III: c–g'; Part IV: B♭–b♭'; Part V: A–f'; Part VI: F–f'; Part VII: (B♭$_2$) F_1–f. Scored for trombone choir or tuba/euphonium ensemble. Most parts maintain a high tessitura. First part contains tenor clef and offers an *ossia* option during the highest passage. Good ensemble performing is essential. More appropriate for a large ensemble, as two parts contain *divisi* passages. Recorded by Symphonia on the compact disc *Symphonia Two: La Morte dell Oom,* Mark Records.

Beale, David. *Reflections on a Park Bench.* David Beale. Six euphoniums and six tubas. 1973. Out of Print. 24:00. IV–V. Part I: E–c''; Part II: E–c''; Part III: E–c''; Part IV: E–b♭'; Part V: E–b♭'; Part VI: E–b♭'; Part VII: E_1–a; Part VIII: E_1–a; Part IX: E_1–b♭; Part X: E_1–c'; Part XI: E_1–c'; Part XII: E_1–c'. Written for R. Winston Morris and the Tennessee Technological University Tuba Ensemble. This is a mammoth work written for three tuba/euphonium quartets. A very complex, challenging, and programmatic work based on an inscription found on the back of a park bench, "To those who shall sit here rejoicing, to those who shall sit here mourning, sympathy and greeting: So have we done in our time, 1892 A.D.W.-H.M.W." This work is extremely difficult and will require twelve strong players. Recorded by the Tennessee Technological University Tuba Ensemble, *Carnegie Hall*, Golden Crest Records, CRSQ-4152.

Beethoven, Ludwig van. *Finale from Symphony No. 5*. arr. Maurice Bale. Godiva Music. Six euphoniums and five tubas. £20.00. Intended to be a play-in at tuba conferences—has an additional four parts specifically written for inexperienced performers.

Beethoven, Ludwig van. *Symphony No. 1 (First Movement)*. arr. Charles Warren. Cimarron Music and Productions. Eight-part tuba/euphonium ensemble. $28.00.

Berlioz, Hector. *Dream of the Witches' Sabbath from Symphonie Fantastique*. tr. Todd Fiegel. Celluloid Tubas. Four euphoniums and four tubas with percussion. 2000. $30.00. 9:30. IV. Part I: E♭–f''; Part II: G–c''; Part III: $B♭_1$–b♭'; Part IV: $B♭_1$–c''; Part V: G_1–b♭'; Part VI: C–f'; Part VII: C_1–c'; Part VIII: C_1–g. To Winston Morris and Symphonia. An excellent tour-de-force arrangement of the final movement of *Symphonie Fantastique*. All parts are challenging, with extreme registers and fast, technical passages. Percussion parts call for timpani, bass drum, tubular bells, and suspended cymbal. Calls for one euphonium mute. Recorded by Symphonia on the compact disc *Symphonia Three: Symphonia Fantastique*, Mark Records.

Berlioz, Hector. *March to the Scaffold from Symphonie Fantastique*. arr. William Granger. Shawnee Press, Incorporated. Four euphoniums and six tubas. 1986. $30.00. 4:30. IV. Part I: G–d''; Part II: G–b'; Part III: E♭–b♭'; Part IV: E♭–b♭'; Part V: G_1–c♭'; Part VI: $B♭_1$–e♭'; Part VII: G_1–b♭; Part VIII: G_1–a♭; Part IX: G_1–g; Part X: G_1–g. Dedicated to the University of Georgia Tuba-Euphonium Ensemble. Good arrangement of this famous orchestral excerpt. This will require four strong euphonium players because of the high tessituras of these parts. Technically not very difficult, but it is challenging to fit all the parts together cleanly. Parts may be doubled for a large ensemble.

Bizet, Georges. *The Soldiers' Chorus from Faust*. arr. Maurice Bale. Godiva Music. Six euphoniums and five tubas. £20.00. Intended to be a play-in at tuba conferences—has an additional four parts specifically written for inexperienced performers.

Bonelli. *Toccata*. arr. Charles Warren. Cimarron Music and Productions. Eight-part tuba/euphonium ensemble. $18.00.

Borton, Allen L. *The Glory of Low Brass*. Tuba-Euphonium Press. Three euphoniums and five tubas. 2001. $12.00. 1:45. III. Part I: F–b♭'; Part II: F–g'; Part III: E♭–e♭'; Part IV: G–f'; Part V: E♭–f'; Part VI: C–c'; Part VII: F_1–f; Part VIII: C_1–g. To the University of Michigan Euphonium/Tuba Ensemble, Fritz Kaenzig, director. Original composition in ternary form with traditional harmonies. The first section is a brief and stately fanfare, followed by a rhythmically driven middle section in mixed meter. The final section contains several meter changes before ending in duple. Parts may be doubled for a large ensemble.

Brahms, Johannes. *Ballad in D Minor, Op. 10, No. 1*. arr. Frank H. Siekmann, Frank H. Brelmat Music. Five euphoniums and two tubas. 1994. $35.00. 6:00. III–IV. Part I: A–c''; Part II: A–g'; Part III: E–g'; Part IV: E–f♯'; Part V: D–f♯'; Part VI: A_1–d'; Part VII: A_1 (F_1)–f♯. Premiered by the Armed Forces Tuba/Euphonium Ensemble, Fort Myer, Va., February 1995, John Stevens, conducting. Instrumentation not specified in this seven-part arrangement, though range considerations imply that only two parts will be performed on tuba. The rhythms are not difficult and are largely homophonic. Three parts have *divisi* passages. More appropriate for a large ensemble.

Brahms, Johannes. *Festive and Commorative*. arr. Charles Warren. Cimarron Music and Productions. Eight-part tuba/euphonium ensemble. $24.00.

Broughton, Bruce. *Suite from "Silverado."* arr. Todd Fiegel. Celluloid Tubas. Four euphoniums, four tubas, two percussion, and film. 2002. Rental only. III–IV. Part I: F♯–c♯''; Part II: E–c♯''; Part III: C–b'; Part IV: C–b♭'; Part V: $A♭_1$–f♯'; Part VI: D–d'; Part VII: F_1–d'; Part VIII: E_1–a. Four movements: Escape; Wagon Train; Ambush; We'll Be Back. Challenging adaptation of the original film score. Two euphonium mutes are required.

Bruckner, Anton. *Os Justi*. arr. David Sabourin. Touch of Brass Music Corporation. Four euphoniums and four tubas. $8.50.

Canter, James, A. *Circle VIII: Bowge IV*. Tuba-Euphonium Press. Four euphoniums and four tubas. 1993. $15.00. 8:30. IV. Part I: A♭–g'; Part II: A♭–g'; Part III: A♭–f♯'; Part IV: A♭–f♯'; Part V: $B♭_1$–a♭; Part VI: $A♭_1$–e♭; Part VII: A_1–e; Part VIII: G_1–A♭. Written for R. Winston Morris and the Tennessee Technological University Tuba Ensemble. A very contemporary piece, with numerous half and whole step intervals in the tuba parts. Some basic twentieth-century techniques required. Tubas are muted. No significant range or technical demands on any part.

Censhu, Jiro. *Chi Ni Hikari Arite (Lux in Terra).* Available from the composer. Four euphoniums and four tubas. 1987. \$15.00. 10:00. IV. Part I: F–b♭'; Part II: F–b♭'; Part III: G–b♭'; Part IV: F–a'; Part V: D–e'; Part VI: F_1–c'; Part VII: F_1–e♭'; Part VIII: F_1–a. Three movements. Commissioned by the Osaka Bari-Tuba Ensemble. Players are arranged into two tuba/euphonium quartets. The third movement features a brief cadenza for the first part in each quartet. The tessitura of the euphonium parts is high. Technically challenging in some spots. Good writing.

Chopin, Frederic. *Revolutionary Étude* arr. Maurice Bale. Godiva Music. Four euphoniums and three tubas. £10.00. Difficult arrangement with extensive ranges.

Clinard, Fred L. *Diversion for Seven Bass Clef Instruments.* Shawnee Press, Incorporated. Four euphoniums and three tubas. 1979. \$16.00. 5:00. IV. Part I: e–c"; Part II: e–c"; Part III: c♯–g'; Part IV: c♯–g'; Part V: C–a; Part VI: C–a; Part VII: D_1–e. Written for R. Winston Morris and the Tennessee Technological University Tuba Ensemble. A one-movement work in a fast-slow-fast form. The fast section contains a driving multimetric section. The slow section features a hauntingly beautiful melody for a solo euphonium with ensemble accompaniment. The tessitura of the first two parts is very high and will require strong players. Very enjoyable for audiences and performers. Parts may be doubled for a large ensemble.

Corwell, Neal. *The Furies.* Tuba-Euphonium Press. Four euphoniums and four tubas. 1995. \$20.00. 6:30. III–IV. Part I: G–d"; Part II: G–d"; Part III: F–b♭'; Part IV: F–a♭'; Part V: C–e♭'; Part VI: B♭$_1$–b; Part VII: D_1–a; Part VIII: D_1–a. Premiered on April 1, 1995, at the Arizona Low Brass Symposium II in Tucson by the Symphonia tuba/euphonium ensemble, R. Winston Morris, director. This original composition is a programmatic work depicting the Furies, which are mythical characters employed in many of the classical Greek tragedies to seek revenge for those who have been murdered. This is a challenging work with rhythmic complexities and effective use of dissonance. Modern techniques, such as mouthpiece slaps, glissandos, trills, hand claps, and chanting through the horn, are employed. Parts may be doubled for a large ensemble. Recorded by Symphonia on the compact disc *Symphonia—Super Sonic Ensemble in the Alternate Clef,* Mark Records, and by Neal Corwell and Velvet Brown on the compact disc *Heart of a Wolf,* Nicolai Music.

Cummings, Barton. *A Miniature Suite.* Tuba-Euphonium Press. Five euphoniums, five tubas, percussion, piano, and bass. 2000. \$50.00. 11:00. IV–V. Part I: E–c"; Part II: E–b'; Part III: E–a'; Part IV: E–a'; Part V: E–a'; Part VI: E_1–f'; Part VII: E_1–d'; Part VIII: E_1–c'; Part IX: C_1–b♭'; Part X: C_1–c. Five movements: Fanfare; The Clouds of Autumn; Scherzo; Chorale; Remembering Rich. For Winston Morris and Symphonia. Challenging collection of five contrasting movements. The piece opens with a rhythmically driven fanfare, followed by a slow descriptive movement. The scherzo movement is a fast-paced rondo, while the chorale is slow and homophonic with modern added-note chords. The final movement is a tribute to Rich Matteson, set in an easy swing style. Percussion parts include timpani, marimba, tambourine, triangle, and drum set and require a minimum of two performers. Individual movements can stand alone on a concert. Parts may be doubled for a large ensemble.

Danner, Greg. *Beast!* Tuba-Euphonium Press. Four euphoniums and four tubas. 1996. \$24.00. 4:00. III. Part I: G♯–b'; Part II: E–b'; Part III: E–f'; Part IV: F♯–f'; Part V: F_1–e♭'; Part VI: E_1–b♭; Part VII: E_1–e; Part VIII: D_1–f. For Winston Morris and the Tennessee Technological Tuba Ensemble. Driving, original composition based on the octatonic scale. Melodic material is divided among all eight parts. Includes glissandos, clapping, taping the instrument with a coin, and chanting. Parts may be doubled for a large ensemble. Also reviewed in the Summer 2002 issue of the *ITEA Journal* (Vol. 29, No. 4). Recorded by the Tennessee Tech Tuba Ensemble on the compact disc *Unleash the Beast!* Mark Records.

DiGiovanni, Rocco. *Tuba Musicale.* Available from the composer. Five euphoniums and five tubas. 1990. \$20.00. 6:00. IV–V. Part I: d–a'; Part II: d–a'; Part III: G–f'; Part IV: G–f'; Part V: D–c'; Part VI: D–c'; Part VII: F_1–d'; Part VIII: F_1–d'; Part IX: E♭$_1$–b♭; Part X: E♭$_1$–f. Written for R. Winston Morris and the Tennessee Technological University Tuba Ensemble. A beautiful melody with a slow 3/4 feel. All parts have an opportunity to play the melody, but most of the melodic responsibility is in the top four parts. Will require strong players.

Dukas. *The Sorcerer's Apprentice.* arr. Maurice Bale. Godiva Music. Six euphoniums and five tubas with percussion. £30.00. Difficult arrangement with extreme ranges.

Dutton, Brent. *Suite for Seven Tubas.* Seesaw Music Corporation. Seven tubas. 1978. \$26.00. 10:00. IV–V. Part I: B♭$_1$–f'; Part II: G_1–a; Part III: E♭$_1$–e♭'; Part IV: G_1–e'; Part V: D_1–b♭; Part VI: C_1–g; Part VII: B♭$_2$–B♭. Seven movements. Each movement is written for the same number of players as the number of the movement. So the first movement is for one tuba, the second movement for two, etc. The last movement is very challenging. The tessitura of the bottom three parts is very low.

Dvorák, Antonin. *Variations on the New World Symphony.* arr. James Woodward. Tuba-Euphonium Press. Four euphoniums and three tubas. 1994. \$12.00. 3:15. III. Part I: B♭–b♭'; Part II: d–g';

Part III: B♭–e♭'; Part IV: B♭–c'; Part V: E♭–g; Part VI: $A\flat_1$–c; Part VII: $E\flat_1$–B♭. Scored for solo euphonium with sextet accompaniment, the arrangement is adapted from the choral arrangement by William Arms Fisher. It is a set of theme and three variations based on the famous "Going Home" melody. The accompaniment parts are accessible to young performers, though the solo part contains more advanced passages. Accompanimental parts may be doubled for a large ensemble.

Fiegel, E. Todd. *Pachydermus Pinkus Lowus-Blowus; Adapted from the Score for Dumbo* (1941). Celluloid Tubas. Four euphoniums, four tubas, auxiliary percussion, and film equipment. 1992. Rental. 8:00. V. Part I: f–d"; Part II: F–d"; Part III: c–d"; Part IV: F–a'; Part V: $B\flat_1$–e♭'; Part VI: D–e♭'; Part VII: E_1–c'; Part VIII: E_1–d. For "Mr. Tuba" and the University of Michigan Euphonium/Tuba Ensemble. A tuba ensemble adaptation of a segment of the soundtrack from the Disney cartoon classic *Dumbo.* Technically challenging at times, and the range demands are extensive for the top euphoniums and the bottom parts. All parts require mutes. This is fun to play and VERY entertaining for audiences.

Fiegel, Todd. *The Three Little Pigs (Twisted Tuba Tales No. 1).* Celluloid Tubas. Four euphoniums and four tubas with narrator. 2000. $20.00. III. Part I: $A\flat_1$–b'; Part II: $A\flat_1$–g♭'; Part III: $A\flat_1$–f♯'; Part IV: $A\flat_1$–d'; Part V: $C\sharp_1$–c♯'; Part VI: $F\sharp_1$–e♭'; Part VII: $E\flat_1$–c'; Part VIII: $E\flat_1$–b♭. To Susie, with love. A modern and tuba-euphoniumistically slanted retelling of this classic fable starring Euphie, Bari, Used-to-be-a (whose middle name is Cornet), and the villain, DesiRay. This arrangement is accessible for college-level ensembles and popular with the audiences. Parts may be doubled for a large ensemble.

Florinza, Lino. *Typic Rhythm.* Florent Lemirre. Four euphoniums and four tubas. 1987. $55.00. 7:20. IV. Part I: B♭–a'; Part II: B♭–a♭'; Part III: G–a♭'; Part IV: F–e♭'; Part V: E♭–g'; Part VI: E♭–e♭'; Part VII: $B\flat_1$–a♭; Part VIII: $E\flat_1$–g. Four movements: Mambo Calypso; Bolero; Bossa Nova; Samba. Dedicated to Hervé Brisse in total friendship. Each movement rhythmically represents its title. Some technical challenges in all parts. The use of drums is strongly recommended. Lino Florenzo is a pseudonym for the French composer Florent Lemirre.

Forbes, Michael. *Textures.* Tuba-Euphonium Press. Six euphoniums and six tubas. 2001. $40.00. 20:00. IV. Part I: c–c"; Part II: A–c♭"; Part III: A♭–b'; Part IV: A♭–a'; Part V: G–a'; Part VI: G–g'; Part VII: $B\flat_1$–f'; Part VIII: $B\flat_1$–e'; Part IX: F_1–a; Part X: F_1–g; Part XI: C_1–f; Part XII: $A\flat_2$–f. Three movements: Transparent; Translucent; Opaque. Commissioned by Marty Erickson and the Penn State Tuba/Euphonium Ensemble. Challenging original composition for advanced ensemble. The piece is intended to explore the different levels of thickness in a tuba/euphonium ensemble. The first movement explores pentatonic harmonies, the second movement explores traditional diatonic textures, and the final movement employs chords containing as many as twelve different pitches. Six euphonium mutes and four tuba mutes are required. Parts may be doubled for a large ensemble. Individual movements can stand alone on a concert. Also reviewed in the Winter 2003 issue of the *ITEA Journal* (Vol. 30, No. 2).

Forte, Aldo Rafael. *Seguidillas: Repetitions and Ostinatos for Tuba Ensemble.* Masters Music Publications, Inc. Four euphoniums, four tubas, and two optional percussion. 1996. $30.00. 4:00. III. Part I: d–c" (f"); Part II: d–b♭'; Part III: G–b♭'; Part IV: c–g'; Part V: C–d'; Part VI: G_1–d'; Part VII: G_1–a; Part VIII: (F_2) F_1–c. Commissioned by Stephen E. Panoff for R. Winston Morris and Symphonia. "Seguidillas" literally means something that is repeated seemingly without end. The composition is therefore unified through the consistent use of several repetitive motives in a Spanish style. All euphonium parts are also available in treble clef. The two optional percussion parts include tambourine, timbales, maracas, and mounted castanets. Parts may be doubled for a large ensemble, and there are *divisi* passages in the second part. Recorded by Symphonia on the compact disc *Symphonia—Super Sonic Ensemble in the Alternate Clef,* Mark Records.

Frackenpohl, Arthur. *Eine Kleine Octubamusic.* T.A.P. Music. Eight tubas. 1990. $25.00. 10:00. IV. Part I: $F\sharp_1$–c'; Part II: $F\sharp_1$–b♭; Part III: $F\sharp_1$–b♭; Part IV: E_1–b♭; Part V: E_1–b; Part VI: $F\sharp_1$–b♭; Part VII: F_1–b♭; Part VIII: E_1–b♭. Five movements: Unison Prelude; Round Dance; Sad Waltz; Pair Dance; Intro and March. Each part has an opportunity to play the melody. Often a single part has a portion of the melody without any accompaniment. The pair dance features two parts at a time passing the melody back and forth.

Frank, Melchior, and Giovanni Gabrieli. *Antiphonal Suite.* arr. Michael Forbes and Demondrae Thurman. Tuba-Euphonium Press. Four euphoniums and four tubas. 2001. $32.00. 8:00. II–III. Part I: e–b♭'; Part II: c–a'; Part III: g–b♭'; Part IV: A–a'; Part V: A♭–d'; Part VI: G_1–a♭; Part VII: G–b♭; Part VIII: (D_1) F_1–e. Three movements: Intrada; Canzon duedecimi toni; Canzon septimi toni No. 2. Scored for two quartets, this piece works best when the quartets are spaced apart for a truly antiphonal effect. Individual movements can stand alone in a concert. Parts may be doubled for a large ensemble. Also reviewed in the Spring 2003 issue of the *ITEA Journal* (Vol. 30, No. 3).

Fredrickson, Thomas. *Antiphonies.* Available from the composer. Four euphoniums and four tubas. 1983. $15.00. 6:00. IV. Part I: F♯–b';

Part II: F♯–a♭'; Part III: F♯$_1$–d'; Part IV: F♯$_1$–b♭; Part V: F♯–a'; Part VI: F♯–g'; Part VII: F♯$_1$–c'; Part VIII: E$_1$–c'. Commissioned by Tubists Universal Brotherhood Association for the 1983 International Tuba/Euphonium Conference. A very contemporary piece written for two tuba/euphonium quartets. Technically and metrically very complex. A very interesting contemporary composition.

Friedrich, Kenneth D. *Entrada.* Available from the composer. Four euphoniums and four tubas. 2003. $15.00. 4:30. II–III. Part I: E♭–b♭'; Part II: B♭–g'; Part III: B♭–g'; Part IV: F–e♭'; Part V: A♭$_1$–b♭; Part VI: A♭$_1$–g; Part VII: F$_1$–g; Part VIII: F$_1$–g. As the name implies, this eight-part piece works well as a concert opener, opening with a fanfare flourish. The parts are generally paired, and the rhythms and ranges make this piece accessible for intermediate-level players. Parts may be doubled for a large ensemble.

Friedrich, Kenneth D. *March of the Times.* Cimarron Music and Productions. Two baritones, two euphoniums, and four tubas. $14.00. 2:00. III. Part I: c–b♭'; Part II: c–g'; Part III: B♭–a; Part IV: F–f♯; Part V: D–c'; Part VI: F$_1$–f♯; Part VII: F$_1$–d; Part VIII: F$_1$–B♭. Original composition in a traditional quick march form. Range and style are appropriate for intermediate-level performers, though the initial key signature of D♭ major may challenge younger performers. Baritone parts may also be performed on euphonium. Parts may be doubled for a large ensemble.

Friedrich, Kenneth D. *New Frontiers.* Cimarron Music and Productions. Four euphoniums and four tubas. $21.00. 17 pp. III. Part I: A♭–b'; Part II: G♭–f'; Part III: B♭–f'; Part IV: A♭–e'; Part V: D♭$_1$–a; Part VI: B♭$_1$–g♭; Part VII: A♭$_1$–e; Part VIII: A♭$_1$–d♭. Multi-sectional work with slow, lyrical sections alternating with rhythmically active fast sections. Employs predominantly traditional harmonies. Key signatures up to six flats may prove challenging to younger performers. All parts are interesting, and the first euphonium has a written cadenza. Parts may be doubled for a large ensemble.

Friedrich, Kenneth D. *Sequences.* Cimarron Music and Productions. Four euphoniums and three tubas. $14.00. 7:00. III. Part I: A–c''; Part II: F–b♭'; Part III: A♭–g'; Part IV: F–e♭'; Part V: C–d♭'; Part VI: B♭$_1$–g; Part VII: F$_1$–d. Original composition based on repeating, rhythmic motives. Each part contains at least one exposed solo passage. Parts may be doubled for a large ensemble.

Friedrich, Kenneth D. *Southwestern Brass.* Cimarron Music and Productions. Four euphoniums and four tubas. $24.00. III. Part I: A–c''; Part II: A♭–a'; Part III: d–a'; Part IV: c–f'; Part V: E♭$_1$–a; Part VI: E♭$_1$–g; Part VII: F$_1$–g; Part VIII: F$_1$–g. Three movements: A Bit O' Southwestern Flavor; Dance of the Senoritas; A Night on the Town. This light suite is based on southwestern themes and is appropriate for intermediate-level performers. The outer movements have an upbeat lyrical texture, and the second movement is a tango. Parts may be doubled for a large ensemble.

Friedrich, Kenneth D. *Tubamania!* Cimarron Music and Productions. Four euphoniums and four tubas. $21.00. 2:00. III. Part I: E♭–c''; Part II: e♭–a♭'; Part III: A♭–b♭'; Part IV: A♭–f'; Part V: A♭$_1$–c'; Part VI: D♭–g; Part VII: E♭–g; Part VIII: A♭$_1$–E♭. Fun original composition in a rock style. The first part contains an improvisation passage with an optional written-out solo. Parts may be doubled for a large ensemble.

Gabrieli, Giovanni. *Antiphony No. 2 for Double Tuba/Euphonium Choir.* arr. Art Conner. Tuba/Euphonium Music Publications. Four euphoniums and four tubas. Out of Print. 4:00. III–IV.

Gabrieli, Giovanni. *Canzon a 12 in Echo.* tr. Todd Fiegel. Celluloid Tubas. Six euphoniums and six tubas. 2002. $20.00. 3:00. II. Part I: d–a♭'; Part II: c–e♭'; Part III: c–g'; Part IV: c–d'; Part V: d–a♭'; Part VI: c–d'; Part VII: F–a; Part VIII: A$_1$–e♭; Part IX: F–g; Part X: F$_1$–d; Part XI: F–a; Part XII: G$_1$–d. To Kirt and Dixie. Arrangement is scored for triple quartet and is accessible to intermediate-level performers. Most effective when the quartets are spaced antiphonally. Parts may be doubled for a large ensemble.

Gabrieli, Giovanni. *Canzon noni toni from Sacrae Symphoniae.* arr. Andrew Spang. Lyric Brass Publishing. Four euphoniums and four tubas. 1993. $9.00. 3:30. Arranged for TUBA+, the tuba-euphonium ensemble at the Eastman School of Music. Arrangement for double quartet. Parts may be doubled for a large ensemble.

Gabrieli, Giovanni. *Sonata No. 13 for Double Tuba/Euphonium Choir.* arr. J. Lesley Varner. Tuba/Euphonium Music Publications. Four euphoniums and four tubas. Out of Print. 4:30. IV.

Gabrieli, Giovanni. *Sonata Pian e Forte.* arr. Charles Warren. Cimarron Music and Productions. Eight-part tuba/euphonium ensemble. $24.50.

George, Thom Ritter. *Two Interplays.* Thom Ritter George. Three tenor trombones, one bass trombone, two euphoniums, and two tubas. 1985. $7.50. 7:30. IV. Part I: e–b'; Part II: A♭–g'; Part III: E–a'; Part IV: E–g♭; Part V: E–a'; Part VI: E–e♭'; Part VII: E$_1$–f♯; Part VIII: E♭$_1$–c. Two movements: Andante Sempre; Vivo. Commissioned by the Morehead State University Chapters of the ITA and TUBA. Other possible instrumentations include five euphoniums and three tubas. The composition focuses on the interplay between two quartets. There are some technical challenges in the second movement. Solid writing. See same work under Tuba in Mixed Ensemble.

Gliere, Reinhold. *Russian Sailors' Dance from the Red Poppy.* arr. Michael Weaver. Athens Music

Publishing. Four euphoniums and three tubas. 2000. $30.00. 4:00. III. Part I: E–b'; Part II: E–a'; Part III: E–b♭'; Part IV: A–a'; Part V: E–d'; Part VI: A_1–a; Part VII: E_1–a. More appropriate for a large ensemble than for a septet. Also reviewed in the Winter 2001 issue of the *TUBA Journal* (Vol. 28, No. 2).

Gottschalk, Arthur. *Substructures I.* Seesaw Music Corporation. Two euphoniums and eight tubas. 1975. $31.00. 6:00. IV–V. Part I: D–e'; Part II: F♯$_1$–d♭'; Part III: F♯$_1$–a; Part IV: F♯$_1$–a; Part V: e–b♭'; Part VI: e–b♭'; Part VII: B–c; Part VIII: G_1–b♭; Part IX: E_1–b; Part X: E_1–c. Parts five and six are for euphoniums. The players are divided into three different groups on the stage. Not very difficult technically, but a challenge to put together. The tessitura of the bottom two parts is very low. Harmonically very dissonant. Recorded by the University of Michigan Tuba/Euphonium Ensemble, Golden Crest Records, CRS 4145.

Gounod, Charles François. *The Funeral March of a Marionette.* arr. Maurice Bale. Godiva Music. Four euphoniums and four tubas. £10.00.

Grainger, Percy Aldridge. *The "Duke of Marlborough" Fanfare.* arr. Todd Fiegel. Celluloid Tubas. Four euphoniums and four tubas with percussion. 2002. $15.00. 1:45. III. Part I: g–b'; Part II: d–g♯'; Part III: G–f'; Part IV: G♭–b'; Part V: A–b; Part VI: D♭–g♯; Part VII: G_1–f; Part VIII: G_1–d♭. This brief fanfare includes passages for offstage euphonium which can be performed by the fourth euphoniumist. Includes brief passages in mixed meter. Percussion includes suspended cymbal.

Haddad, Don. *Knoxville, 1974.* Seesaw Music Corporation. Two euphoniums and six tubas. 1975. $12.00. 5:20. IV. Part I: g–d"; Part II: c♯–a'; Part III: G–d'; Part IV: C–d'; Part V: g–d"; Part VI: A–g'; Part VII: C–e♭'; Part VIII: F_1–c♯. Written for two choirs of one euphonium and three tubas each. The tessitura of the first and second parts of each choir is very high. The second part of each choir may be played by a euphonium. No significant technical problems. No score available.

Hartley, Walter. *Triple Quartet.* Masters Music Publications, Inc. Eight euphoniums and four tubas. 1997. $20.00. 6:40. III–IV. Part I: d♭–c"; Part II: F♯–a♭'; Part III: F–a♭'; Part IV: D–c'; Part V: F–c"; Part VI: D♯–g'; Part VII: E–e'; Part VIII: E–g'; Part IX: G_1–e'; Part X: G♯$_1$–a; Part XI: A♭$_1$–a; Part XII: C_1–g♭. Three movements: Allegro con brio; Lento; Allegro vivace. This is a challenging work with thick textures. It is a triple-quartet piece scored for trombone quartet (parts I–IV), euphonium quartet (parts V–VIII), and tuba quartet (parts IX–XII). All the trombone parts and the first tuba part are labeled as optional euphonium, though it is most effective when performed with the original scoring. The top six parts contain passages in tenor clef.

Hoshina, Hiroshi. *Dialogue.* Tokyo Bari-Tuba Ensemble. Four euphoniums and six tubas.

Ishii, Maki. *Yama No Hibiki.* Tokyo Bari-Tuba Ensemble. Six euphoniums and six tubas.

Ito, Yasuhide. *Cadenzas for 8 Players.* Tokyo Bari-Tuba Ensemble. Four euphoniums and four tubas.

Knox, Charles. *Scherzando for Tubular Octet.* Available from the composer. Four euphoniums and four tubas. 1979. $25.00. 5:45. IV. Part I: B–c"; Part II: B♭–a'; Part III: B♭–a'; Part IV: A–a'; Part V: A_1–c'; Part VI: A_1–c'; Part VII: A_1–a; Part VIII: F♯$_1$–a. Dedicated to R. Winston Morris and the Tennessee Technological University Tuba Ensemble. Excellent writing for eight-part tuba ensemble. Technically not that difficult, but it is challenging to fit together and will require a conductor. Recorded by the Tennessee Technological University Tuba Ensemble, *LIVE!* KM Records, KM 5661.

Konagaya, Soichi. *Celebration.* Tokyo Bari-Tuba Ensemble. Solo tuba, three euphoniums, and three tubas. Written for Harvey Phillips.

Konagaya, Soichi. *Prophecy.* Tokyo Bari-Tuba Ensemble. Solo euphonium, four euphoniums, and four tubas.

Lasso, Orlando di. *Echo Fantasy for Double Tuba/Euphonium Ensemble.* arr. James Derby. Tuba/Euphonium Music Publications. Four euphoniums and six tubas. Out of Print. 3:00. IV.

Lecuona, Ernesto. *Malaguena.* arr. Tom Senff. Tuba-Euphonium Press. Four euphoniums and four tubas. 2002. $20.00. 5:00. III–IV. Part I: A♭–e♭"; Part II: c–d♭"; Part III: G–a♭'; Part IV: c–a♭'; Part V: C–c' (g'); Part VI: C–c' (g'); Part VII: G_1–g; Part VIII: G_1–g. Straightforward arrangement of this well-known piece. Melodic material is primarily divided between the first two parts, which are in tenor clef. Parts may be doubled for a large ensemble.

Lemirre, Florent. *Circus Life.* Available from the composer. Four euphoniums and four tubas. 1987. $55.00. 7:30. IV–V. Part I: d–b♭'; Part II: A–g'; Part III: A♭–e♭'; Part IV: G–e♭'; Part V: F–f'; Part VI: E♭–e♭'; Part VII: D♭–e♭'; Part VIII: E♭$_1$–a♭. Four movements: La Parade (the Parade); Clown et Funambules (Clowns and Tightrope Walkers); Trapèze Volant (Flying Trapeze); Fauves et Dompteur (Beasts and Animal Tamers). Dedicated to Hervé Brisse in total friendship. Four programmatic character pieces. Technical and range demands are great on all parts. This is also the most complex harmonically of Lemirre's compositions. Will require eight strong players.

Lemirre, Florent. *Esquisse Villageoise (Country Sketches).* Available from the composer. Four euphoniums and four tubas. 1987. $55.00. 5:50. IV. Part I: d–a♭'; Part II: G–a♭'; Part III: A♭–g'; Part IV: B♭$_1$–f'; Part V: E♭–f'; Part VI: E♭–d'; Part VII: B♭$_1$–c'; Part VIII: A♭$_1$–a♭. Four movements: Cloche Dans Le Matin (Morning Bells); Calme et Serein (Calm and Serene); Rone Enfantine (Children's Round Dance); Farandole De Fête (Festival Farandole). Dedicated to Hervé Brisse in total friendship. Tessitura of the first two tuba parts is high. The harmonies are very traditional but there are several technically demanding sections.

Lemirre, Florent. *Tuba Séduction (Ballade)*. Available from the composer. Four euphoniums and four tubas. 1987. $30.00. 4:30. IV. Part I: f–a♭'; Part II: d–f'; Part III: c–f'; Part IV: G–f'; Part V: B♭–a'; Part VI: F–e'; Part VII: $B♭_1$–c'; Part VIII: G_1–f. Dedicated to Hervé Brisse in total friendship. The tessitura of the first tuba part is quite high, in fact higher than the first euphonium part. This may be performed with six euphoniums and two tubas. The melody is primarily in the top two parts. No significant technical problems. The composer's last name is spelled with only one "r" on some parts and some compositions.

Liszt, Franz. *Hungarian Rhapsody No. 2*. arr. Todd Fiegel. Celluloid Tubas. Four euphoniums and four tubas. 2002. $25.00. III–IV. Part I: E–c" (d"); Part II: C–c" (d"); Part III: $B♭_1$–c"; Part IV: $B♭_1$–g'; Part V: A_1–a'; Part VI: A_1–f'; Part VII: $B♭_2$–c'; Part VIII: $B♭_2$–d. Arranged for the ITEC 2002 World Honors Euphonium-Tuba Ensemble and dedicated with love to Kirt and Dixie. Challenging arrangement of this famous rhapsody. More appropriate for a large ensemble than for an octet, as four parts have *divisi* passages.

McCarthy, Daniel. *Two Pieces for Tuba/Euphonium Ensemble*. Tuba-Euphonium Press. Six euphoniums and two tubas. 1993. $20.00. 7:30. IV. Part I: c♯–b♭'; Part II: B♭–g'; Part III: G–f♯'; Part IV: B_1–a; Part V: C–b♭'; Part VI: B♭–f♯'; Part VII: G–f'; Part VIII: E_1–a. Two movements: Dark Towers; Wind and Wuthering. Dedicated to Elliot Chasanov. Written for two tuba/euphonium quartets. All parts are challenging in part because of the constantly changing meters and dissonant harmonies. The composition is very programmatic, depicting the names of the movements. Winner of the 1992 Connie Weldon Tuba/ Euphonium Ensemble Contest, sponsored by TUBA and the University of Miami.

McGuire, Michael. *A Brief History of a Star*. Tuba-Euphonium Press. Four euphoniums and four tubas with three percussion. 1998. $30.00. 5:30. III. Part I: f–b♭'; Part II: e–g'; Part III: d–g'; Part IV: c–g'; Part V: $E♭_1$–c'; Part VI: D_1–f; Part VII: E♭–a; Part VIII: A_1–f. With special thanks to Mr. James Barnes, Mr. Scott Watson, and the K.U. Tuba and Euphonium Ensemble. Programmatic work attempting to describe the life of a star from Big Bang to black hole. Theatrical requirements include dry ice, white and red spotlights, stand lights, colored flashlights, disco ball, slide projectors, and screens. Piece may also be performed in a concert setting without the theatrical elements. Parts may be doubled for a large ensemble.

McKimm, Barry. *Serenade for Tubas*. Available from the composer. Four euphoniums and four tubas. 1982. 7:30. IV. Part I: B♭–d♭"; Part II: B♭–c♭"; Part III: G♭–b♭'; Part IV: G♭–g'; Part V: $B♭_1$–c'; Part VI: $B♭_1$–c'; Part VII: $G♭_1$–d♭; Part VIII: ($E♭_1$) $G♭_1$–A. A large single-movement work with several different sections. The tessitura of the top part is high. Some syncopated and complex rhythms in a traditional harmonic style.

McKimm, Barry, arr. *Irish Tune from County Derry*. Available from the arranger. Four euphoniums and four tubas. 1983. 2:20. IV. Part I: A–c"; Part II: A–a'; Part III: A–a'; Part IV: A–b♭'; Part V: E♭–d'; Part VI: D–d'; Part VII: $A♭_1$–e♭; Part VIII: $E♭_1$–d♭. Arranged for the Solitaire Tuba/ Euphonium Ensemble. The tessitura of the first part is high. Scoring is a little thick at times. The style is very lyrical.

McLean, Stuart. *Mollusca*. Breakthrough Music. Four euphoniums and four tubas. Part I: F–c♯"; Part II: G–d"; Part III: c–c"; Part IV: A–c"; Part V: F_1–e'; Part VI: B♭–c'; Part VII: E_1–e'; Part VIII: E_1–c'. An octet, premiered by Tubalaté and Sotto Voce. All parts are challenging.

Mendelssohn-Bartholdy, Felix. *Heilig*. arr. David Butler. Tuba-Euphonium Press. Four euphoniums and four tubas. 2003. $15.00. 3:00. II. Part I: g–a♭'; Part II: g–a♭'; Part III: e♭–e♭'; Part IV: d–d'; Part V: B♭–a; Part VI: B♭–c'; Part VII: $B♭_1$–g; Part VIII: $E♭_1$–a♭. Originally written for two SATB choirs, this arrangement is scored for double quartets and may be performed antiphonally. Appropriate for young or intermediate-level performers. Euphonium parts also available in treble clef. Parts may be doubled for a large ensemble.

Mobberley, James C. *On Thin Ice*. Cautious Music. Four euphoniums and five tubas. 1990. $50.00. 5:15. V. Part I: G–d♭"; Part II: F♯–b♭'; Part III: F–b♭'; Part IV: $B♭_1$–a'; Part V: E_1–e♭'; Part VI: $F♯_1$–d♯'; Part VII: F_1–d♭'; Part VIII: E_1–c'; Part IX: $E♭_1$–g♭. Commissioned by Ernie Walls and dedicated to R. Winston Morris and the Tennessee Technological University Tuba Ensemble. A very well-written and difficult composition. Range demands are extensive for the euphoniums. There are several odd meter changes as well as isolated sixteenth notes in the parts that can be difficult to place. Performance techniques required include glissandos, flutter tonguing, and mutes. Parts may be doubled, but the lowest parts should be doubled first. Originally titled "Bull in a China Shop." This received its international premiere at the International Tuba/ Euphonium Conference by the All-Star University Tuba/Euphonium Ensemble, in August 1990, Sapporo, Japan.

Mussorgsky, Modeste. *Baba Yaga from "Pictures at an Exhibition."* arr. Lisa Golas. Tuba-Euphonium

Press. Four euphoniums and four tubas. 1995. $24.00. 3:30. III–IV. Part I: G–c"; Part II: D–a'; Part III: D–g'; Part IV: D–g'; Part V: G_1–e♭'; Part VI: D_1–a♭'; Part VII: D_1–a♭; Part VIII: D_1–a♭. Originally for piano, this work is best known as an arrangement for orchestra by Ravel. This movement contains several large intervals in each part. Calls for four euphonium and two tuba mutes. Parts may be doubled for a large ensemble. Euphonium parts also available in treble clef. Several other movements from this work are available separately from the same arranger.

Mussorgsky, Modeste. *Great Gate at Kiev from "Pictures at an Exhibition."* arr. Lisa Golas. Tuba-Euphonium Press. Four euphoniums and four tubas. 1995. $24.00. 5:30. III. Part I: B♭–b♭'; Part II: D–b♭'; Part III: D–g'; Part IV: D–g'; Part V: $A♭_1$–f'; Part VI: C_1–e♭'; Part VII: C_1–b♭; Part VIII: C_1–g♭. Originally for piano, this work is best known as an arrangement for orchestra by Ravel. This arrangement of the final movement requires strong ensemble playing to depict the Great Gate. Parts may be doubled for a large ensemble. Euphonium parts also available in treble clef. Several other movements from this work are available separately from the same arranger.

Mussorgsky, Modeste. *Night on Bald Mountain.* arr. Maurice Bale. Godiva Music. Six euphoniums and six tubas with percussion. £30.00. Difficult arrangement with extreme ranges.

Mussorgsky, Modeste. *Night on Bald Mountain.* arr. Reginald Curtis. Tuba-Euphonium Press. Five euphoniums and four tubas with optional percussion. 2003. $45.00. 7:15. III–IV. Part I: c♯–d♭"; Part II: c–d♭"; Part III: A–a'; Part IV: A–a'; Part V: E–a"; Part VI: C–f'; Part VII: B_1–e'; Part VIII: F_1–a♭; Part IX: ($B♯_2$) E_1–g. Effective arrangement of this original work for orchestra. The trills and quick, technical passages make this appropriate for advanced ensembles. Optional percussion includes cymbal, bass drum, tam tam, and tubular bells. Parts may be doubled for a large ensemble.

Nelhybel, Vaclav. *Canzona.* Great Works Publishing, Incorporated. Four euphoniums and four tubas. 1997. $24.00. 3:45. II–III. Part I: c♯–b♭'; Part II: c♯–g'; Part III: A–d'; Part IV: G–d'; Part V: C–a; Part VI: C♯–f; Part VII: A_1–d; Part VIII: F_1–B♭. Composed for and dedicated to the St. Olaf College Tuba-Euphonium Ensemble, Paul Niemisto, conductor. Effective original work for eight-part ensemble. It contains both rhythmic and harmonic challenges—employing both traditional and contemporary chord structure. The range and voicing are accessible to intermediate-level players. Parts may be doubled for a large ensemble.

Nørgård, Per. *Nu dækker sne den hele jord.* Edition Wilhelm Hansen. Four euphoniums and four tubas. 1976. 18:00. Premiered in Montreux (International Brass Congress) in 1976. This piece brings together and mixes two 1976 works: *Nu dækker sne den hele jord* for eight tubas and the choral part from *Vinterkantate/Winter Hymn.*

Osmon, Leroy. *Frescos de Bonampak (Octet No. 2).* RBC Music. Four euphoniums and four tubas. 2004. 9:15. III–IV. Part I: c♯–c"; Part II: B♭–g'; Part III: B–g'; Part IV: G–a'; Part V: $D♭_1$–c'; Part VI: $E♭_1$–f♯'; Part VII: C_1–c; Part VIII: $D♭_1$–c. Commissioned by Mark Morette. Dedicated to my wife and Yucatecan friends. Programmatic work based on the violent paintings of the *frescos* with effective use of dissonance, mixed meter, and changing meter. Optional mutes are indicated for third and fourth euphonium parts. Parts may be doubled for a large ensemble. Recorded by the Tennessee Tech Tuba Ensemble on the compact disc *Carnegie VI,* Mark Records.

Pearsal, Robert. *Lay a Garland.* arr. Angelo Manzo. Tuba-Euphonium Press. Four euphoniums and four tubas. 2001. $12.00. 1:45. II. Part I: e♭–g'; Part II: d–f'; Part III: B♭–b♭; Part IV: B♭–b♭; Part V: E♭–g; Part VI: C–e♭; Part VII: $B♭_1$–c; Part VIII: G_1–B♭. Effective arrangement of this Renaissance work. The individual parts are not difficult, but the layering of voices and imitative entrances make this an excellent study piece for college or younger ensembles. Parts may be doubled for a large ensemble. Also reviewed in the Summer 2003 issue of the *ITEA Journal* (Vol. 30, No. 4).

Pegram, Wayne. *Howdy!* Ludwig Music Publishing Company. Three euphoniums, four tubas, and drums. 1992. $17.50. 2:40. IV. Part I: c–a'; Part II: c–f'; Part III: B♭–b♭; Part IV: G_1–d'; Part V: G_1–b♭; Part VI: G_1–b♭; Part VII: G_1–b♭. Written for R. Winston Morris and the Tennessee Technological University Tuba Ensemble. A high-energy, fast-paced opening fanfare that is exciting for both performers and audience. A few technical challenges. Parts may be doubled for a large ensemble, and many often are. Recorded by the Tennessee Technological University Tuba Ensemble, *Heavy Metal,* Mark Records, MES 20759, and the U.S. Armed Forces Tuba/Euphonium Ensemble, Mark Records, MW89MCD-8.

Piltzecker, Ted. *Cacology.* Tuba-Euphonium Press. Three euphoniums and five tubas. 1992. $10.00. 2:20. IV. Part I: B♭–b♭'; Part II: d–g♭'; Part III: B–d♭'; Part IV: C–c'; Part V: D–b♭; Part VI: F_1–b♭; Part VII: $B♭_1$–b♭; Part VIII: F_1–g♭. Commissioned by John Stevens and the University of Wisconsin Tuba/Euphonium Ensemble. A challenging work for all eight parts. Very interesting writing, very appropriate for recital material. Premiered by the College All-Star Ensemble at the 1992 International Tuba/Euphonium Conference.

Raum, Elizabeth. *A Little Monster Music.* Tuba-Euphonium Press. Four euphoniums and twelve tubas. 2001. $40.00. 12:00. IV. Part I: A♭–b';

Part II: A♭–b'; Part III: A♭–b'; Part IV: A♭–b'; Part V: C–g'; Part VI: C–g'; Part VII: C–f'; Part VIII: C–f'; Part IX: G_1–e'; Part X: C_1–e'; Part XI: G_1–d'; Part XII: G_1–d'; Part XIII: E_1–d'; Part XIV: E_1–d'; Part XV: C_1–b♭; Part XVI: C_1–b♭. Four movements: Hydra; Nessie; Fafner; St. George and the Dragon. Commissioned by tubist Roger Bobo for his tuba ensemble, Stuba. Premiered at ITEC 2000, in Regina, Saskatchewan. Programmatic work depicting four noted monsters. The first movement depicts Hydra, the nine-headed beast from Greek mythology, with a fast, rhythmically driven movement. The second movement depicts the gentler Nessie, Scotland's *Loch Ness* monster. Through the use of Wagner quotes, the third movement depicts Fafner from the opera *Sigfried,* while the final movement describes the battle between St. George and his dragon. Individual movements can stand alone on a concert. Also reviewed in the Spring 2003 issue of the *ITEA Journal* (Vol. 30, No. 3).

Respighi, Ottorino. *Pines of the Appian Way from "The Pines of Rome."* arr. Michael Forbes. Tuba-Euphonium Press. Five euphoniums, four tubas, and percussion. 2001. $18.00. 4:45. III–IV. Part I: f–e♭"; Part II: B♭–b♭'; Part III: $B\flat_1$–g♭'; Part IV: f–d"; Part V: B♭–a'; Part VI: B♭–f'; Part VII: $B\flat_1$–e♭'; Part VIII: (F_1) $B\flat_1$–a; Part IX: $B\flat_2$–e♭. Premiered by the 2001 Armed Forces Tuba/ Euphonium Ensemble (AFTEE). Effective yet challenging arrangement of this popular work. Originally arranged with three trombone parts, three euphonium parts, and three tuba parts, though the arranger indicates that the scoring for five euphoniums and four tubas is an acceptable alternative. More appropriate for a large ensemble, as all parts contain *divisi* passages. Mutes are required for all but the two lowest parts, and all of the euphonium parts contain passages in tenor clef. Also reviewed in the Summer 2002 issue of the *ITEA Journal* (Vol. 29, No. 4).

Rimsky-Korsakov, Nicolas. *Flight of the Bumblebones.* arr. Wally Gladwin. T.A.P. Music. Six euphoniums and two tubas. 1986. $15.00. 3:45. IV–V. Part I: B_1–a'; Part II: B_1–g'; Part III: $B\flat_1$–f'; Part IV: $B\flat_1$–d♭'; Part V: A_1–f'; Part VI: A_1–f'; Part VII: A_1–a'; Part VIII: A_1–e'. The ranges are extreme and the tessituras of all parts are very high. This can be performed with a variety of instrumentations, especially if some sections are played an octave lower. Technically challenging in several sections.

Ross, Walter. *Concerto Basso.* Dorn Publications, Incorporated. Four euphoniums and four tubas. 1974. 11:00. IV. Part I: c–g♯'; Part II: B♭–g'; Part III: B♭–f; Part IV: $F\sharp_1$–B♭; Part V: d♭–g'; Part VI: B–g'; Part VII: F–f; Part VIII: $F\sharp_1$–e. Three movements. Written for two euphonium/ tuba quartets. Parts one through four represent one quartet; parts five through eight, the second quartet. The third movement is multimetric and is more technically challenging. The top four parts require mutes. Recorded by the Tennessee Technological University Tuba Ensemble, Golden Crest Records, QCRS 4139.

Schaphorst. *When the Moon Jumps.* Nichols Music. Four euphoniums and four tubas. $10.00.

Schlesinger, Scott. *Que Pasa.* Tuba-Euphonium Press. One euphonium and six tubas. 2002. $12.00. 4:15. III. Part I: G–g'; Part II: G–f'; Part III: G–f'; Part IV: $A\flat_1$–e♭'; Part V: $A\flat_1$–e♭'; Part VI: E_1–b♭; Part VII: E_1–b♭. Rhythmically driven original composition with jazz and rock influences. There are several tutti passages in octaves that will require a strong ensemble to execute cleanly. Chord changes are provided in the first two parts for improvised solos. Parts may be doubled for a large ensemble.

Schubert. *Trauermarcshe, Op. 55.* arr. Charles Warren. Cimarron Music and Productions. Eight-part tuba/euphonium ensemble. $22.00.

Schudel, Thomas. *Richter 7.8 for 12 Low Brass Instruments.* T.A.P. Music. Three euphoniums and nine tubas. 1981. $25.00. 6:00. IV. Part I: c–g'; Part II: c♯–g'; Part III: c–f♯'; Part IV: G♯–d'; Part V: G–d♭'; Part VI: G♯–c♯'; Part VII: C–b♭; Part VIII: C♯–a; Part IX: C–b♭; Part X: G_1–e; Part XI: $F\sharp_1$–f; Part XII: F_1–e. Dedicated to John Griffiths. The ensemble is divided into three groups of four players, with one euphonium and three tubas in each group. The texture is very thick and the harmonies very dissonant. It is what one would expect from a piece with a title named after a device used to measure the force of earthquakes. A very interesting piece.

Schutz, Heinrich. *Antiphony No. 1 for Double Tuba/ Euphonium Choir.* arr. Tom Hancock. Tuba/ Euphonium Music Publications. Four euphoniums and six tubas. Out of Print. 4:00. III–IV.

Self, Jim. *La Morte dell' Oom (No Pah Intended).* Basset Hound Music. Six euphoniums, six tubas, and two percussionists. 1997. $40.00. 6:15. IV. Part I: B♭–d"; Part II: B♭–d"; Part III: G–d♭"; Part IV: G–b'; Part V: G–b'; Part VI: G–b'; Part VII: C–g'; Part VIII: C–f♯'; Part IX: C–e'; Part X: G_1–e♭'; Part XI: C_1–e♭'; Part XII: C_1–e♭'. For Winston Morris and Symphonia. Challenging original work for large ensemble and percussion. Includes brief quotes from standard tuba excerpts, including *Symphony Fantastique, Lohengrin Prelude to Act III,* the "Bear" solo from *Petruchka,* and "Bydlo" from *Pictures at an Exhibition.* Percussion parts require cymbals, snare drum, bass drum, bongos, toms, shaker, and cow bell. Parts may be doubled for a large ensemble. Recorded by Symphonia on the compact disc *Symphonia Two: La Morte dell Oom,* Mark Records.

Siekmann, Frank H., arr. *Were You There?* Brelmat Music. Six euphoniums and two tubas. 1995. $19.00. 5:00. III. Part I: A♭–b♭' (d♭"); Part II: A♭–b♭'; Part III: F–f'; Part IV: D♭–e♭'; Part V: f–b♭';

Part VI: B♭–a♭'; Part VII: G♭–d♭'; Part VIII: C♯–c'. This arrangement of the traditional spiritual is scored for double tuba-euphonium quartet and includes excerpts from the "Goin' Home" theme of Dvorák's New World Symphony. The instrumentation is not specified, but the ranges suggest the top three parts in both choirs should be performed on euphonium. Parts may be doubled for a large ensemble. Also available in a quartet version by the same publisher.

Stalling, Carl, and Milt Franklyn. *Eine Kleine Tubamusik für Roadrunner und Coyote.* arr. Todd Fiegel. Celluloid Tubas. Four euphoniums, four tubas, two percussion, and film. 1995. Rental only. 7:00. III–IV. Part I: E–c"; Part II: E–c"; Part III: E–g'; Part IV: E–g'; Part V: G_1–d♯' (b'); Part VI: C–c'; Part VII: C_1–f'; Part VIII: C_1–f. "For Fritz 'Beep-beep' Kaenzig, who is the reason I do this." Crowd-pleasing arrangement of the original score for a cartoon. Calls for two euphonium plunger mutes. Percussion includes drum set, xylophone, and tympani.

Stevens, John. *Adagio.* Editions BIM. Four euphoniums and four tubas. 1991. 9:00. IV. Part I: g–b♭'; Part II: g–a'; Part III: d–d'; Part IV: c–d'; Part V: E–c'; Part VI: C–c'; Part VII: G_1–f; Part VIII: F_1–e. Commissioned by the Tubists Universal Brotherhood Association for the 1992 International Tuba/Euphonium Conference, Lexington, Ky. A slow, single-movement work in a Romantic style. Lush harmonies and sonorous qualities of the instruments are emphasized.

Stevens, John. *Higashi-Nishi (East-West).* Editions BIM. Four euphoniums and four tubas. 1984. 12:00. V. Part I: F–c"; Part II: D♭–c"; Part III: D♭–g♭'; Part IV: D♭–g♭'; Part V: F_1–c'; Part VI: F_1–c'; Part VII: F_1–g; Part VIII: $D♭_1$–f. Written for the Tokyo Bari-Tuba Ensemble. Although a one-movement work, this composition is in four distinct sections: Slow, Fast, Slow, Fast. The harmonies and melodies have a distinct oriental influence combined with more "American" rhythms.

Stevens, John. *The Liberation of Sisyphus.* Editions BIM. Solo tuba, four euphoniums, and four tubas. 1990. $43.50. 6:00. IV–V. Solo tuba: A_1–c"; Part II: G–b♭'; Part III: F–a♭'; Part IV: G–f'; Part V: F–d'; Part VI: F_1–c'; Part VII: F_1–b; Part VIII: F_1–f; Part IX: F_1–f. For Roger Bobo. The solo part is written for virtuosic skills. The part spans a huge range and is very demanding technically. The ensemble parts are also very challenging. This is a very exciting and demanding composition. See: Bird, Gary, ed.; *Program Notes for the Solo Tuba.* Recorded by Roger Bobo, *The Liberation of Sisyphus,* Crystal Records.

Susato, Tylman. *Five Dances.* arr. John Stevens. Encore Music Publishers. Four euphoniums and four tubas. 1988. $23.00. 8:30. IV. Part I: f–a'; Part II: d–g'; Part III: c–f'; Part IV: F–c'; Part V: G–c'; Part VI: D–c'; Part VII: C–a♭; Part VIII: C_1–c. Five movements: La Mourisque; Bransle Quatre Bransles; Ronde; Ronde Mon Amy; Pavane Battaille. Five movements contrasting in style, meter, and key. No significant technical problems. Works well for a large ensemble. No score available.

Szentpáli, Roland, and Levente Kövesdi. *Earth Voices.* Editions BIM. Solo tuba with four euphoniums, four tubas, and narrator. 2001. CHF 55.00. 9:00. IV–V. Four movements: Daybreak; Desertion; Desolation; Epilogue. For Roger Bobo and the Stuba Ensemble. Very high tessitura. The solo part is also feasible on euphonium. The different sections describe the text, which the narrator reads while the music provides the background. Between text sections, the music evolves descriptively on the text themes.

Tchaikovsky, Peter. *Andante Cantabile from Symphony No. 5.* arr. Mike Forbes. Tuba-Euphonium Press. Four euphoniums and four tubas. 1999. $10.00. 5:00. III. Part I: G♭–d"; Part II: F–b♭'; Part III: F–b♭'; Part IV: F–g♭'; Part V: C–d'; Part VI: C–b♭'; Part VII: $G♭_1$–b♭; Part VIII: $D♭_1$–f. Originally scored for orchestra featuring horn, this arrangement features solo euphonium. Individual parts are not difficult, but the piece demands a high level of musicality. More appropriate for a large ensemble, as there are *divisi* passages in each part.

Tchaikovsky, Peter. *Overture Solennelle (1812).* arr. Charles Warren. Cimarron Music and Productions. Eight-part tuba/euphonium ensemble. $28.00.

Tchaikovsky, Peter. *Overture Solennelle (1812).* arr. Clifford Bevan. Piccolo Press. Nine-part tuba/euphonium ensemble. 1995. £11.95. Scored for two antiphonal tuba/euphonium quartets and a massed tuba ensemble, this abridged arrangement omits the parts better suited for woodwinds while retaining the character of the piece. Best suited for a large number of players in the massed ensemble. Also reviewed in the Spring 1996 issue of the *TUBA Journal* (Vol. 23, No. 3).

Tchesnokov, Pavel. *Salvation Is Created.* arr. Lisa Golas. Tuba-Euphonium Press. Four euphoniums and four tubas. 1998. $8.00. 2:00. I–II. Part I: g–f'; Part II: c–f'; Part III: D–d'; Part IV: D–b♭; Part V: D–c'; Part VI: E♭–g; Part VII: G_1–e♭; Part VIII: ($B♭_2$) F_1–G. Originally a Russian Orthodox chorale, this arrangement is scored for two choirs, euphoniums versus tubas, which alternate statements until joining for the finale. Parts may be doubled for a large ensemble. Also reviewed in the Summer 2002 issue of the *ITEA Journal* (Vol. 29, No. 4).

Tinoco, Luis. *Untitled Work.* Available from composer. Solo tuba with six tubas. 2005. V. Commissioned by Sérgio Carolino and dedicated to the Portugal tuba ensemble Tubophonia. Very contemporary harmonies.

Torqvet, Daniel. *Cantatibus organis, Caecilia virgo.* arr. Angelo Manzo. Tuba-Euphonium Press. Four euphoniums and four tubas. 2001. $15.00. 3:15. I. Part I: f–f'; Part II: f–f'; Part III: F–g; Part IV: G–a; Part V: C–f; Part VI: D–f; Part VII: G_1–A; Part VIII: G_1–A. Renaissance-style transcription accessible by young performers. Most entrances are as trios or quartets. Parts may be doubled for a large ensemble.

Torre, Javier De La. *Preludio and Fuga a 8 for Tuba and Euphonium Octet.* Available from the composer. Four euphoniums and four tubas. 1987. 10:00. V. Part I: E–a♯'; Part II: F–g♭'; Part III: E–g'; Part IV: E–g♯'; Part V: F_1–d'; Part VI: F_1–d♯'; Part VII: F_1–e'; Part VIII: F_1–f'. Very contemporary piece with many twentieth-century compositional techniques, including flutter tonguing, circular breathing, glissandos, murmuring in the instrument, complex notation, and complex meters. The bottom two tuba parts have higher range requirements than the first two tuba parts. This will require very strong players on each part.

Tull, Fisher. *Tubular Octad.* Boosey and Hawkes, Incorporated. Four euphoniums and four tubas. 1980. $19.00. 8:00. IV–V. Part I: F–c''; Part II: G–b♭'; Part III: F–a'; Part IV: F–a'; Part V: G_1–d♭'; Part VI: G_1–b♭; Part VII: G_1–b♭; Part VIII: G_1–a♭. Commissioned by the Tubists Universal Brotherhood Association. The work is in a single movement but has several distinct sections, including a canonic passage and a scherzo, within an overall arch form. There are two double cadenzas featuring one euphonium and one tuba. Range and technical demands will require eight very strong players. Premiered May 22, 1980, by the National Collegiate All-Star Tuba-Euphonium Ensemble at the Second National Tuba/Euphonium Symposium/Workshop.

Vaughan, Rodger. *Winds: Five Descriptive Pieces for Tuba/Euphonium Octet.* Tuba-Euphonium Press. Four euphoniums and four tubas. 1992. $20.00. 10:30. IV. Part I: B♭–c♭'; Part II: B♭–a♭'; Part III: B♭–f♯'; Part IV: B♭–f'; Part V: C–b♭; Part VI: C–a; Part VII: C_1–a; Part VIII: C_1–f. Five movements: Khamsin; Zephyrs; Bora; Doldrums; Sirocco. For Jerry Young and his low-down musicians at the University of Wisconsin, Eau Claire. Not technically difficult, but a challenge due to the numerous meter changes. Rhythmically very interesting and exciting at times. Enjoyable to play.

Williams, John. *The March from "1941."* arr. Todd Fiegel. Celluloid Tubas. Four euphoniums and four tubas with percussion. 1995. $25.00. 4:00. III–IV. Part I: G–d♭''; Part II: G–c''; Part III: B♭–b♭'; Part IV: F–a'; Part V: G_1–f'; Part VI: G_1–e'; Part VII: G_1–c'; Part VIII: F_1–b. Arrangement dedicated "with great respect and appreciation to Jerry Young, who turned the propeller and got it airborne again." Popular arrangement of this march from the movie *1941.* Percussion parts include snare and bass drums, cymbals, and orchestral bells. Recorded by Symphonia on the compact disc *Symphonia Two: La Morte dell Oom,* Mark Records.

Wright, Rayburn. *Undercurrents.* Seesaw Music Corporation. One flute, seven tubas, and two percussion. 1980. $99.00. 18:00. IV–V. Part I: E♭–e♭'; Part II: E♭–e♭'; Part III: $B♭_1$–b♭; Part IV: $G♭_1$–c♯'; Part V: $G♭_1$–a; Part VI: $G♭_1$–c♯'; Part VII: $F♯_1$–g. A large and complex work with numerous tempo and meter changes. Technically challenging and containing very dissonant harmonies. All parts require mutes. Will require strong players and a conductor. See same work under Tuba in Mixed Ensemble.

Yoshizawa, Kentaro. *Tuba Chan Chaka Chan.* Tokyo Bari-Tuba Ensemble. Four euphoniums and four tubas.

Ensemble Master List by Title

Note: Titles beginning with an English article are alphabetized according to the first substantive word.

A

Absalon, Fili Mi. Desprez/Shoop. Two euphoniums and two tubas.

Abschied. Reger/Schmidt. Two euphoniums and two tubas.

Achieved Is the Glorious Work. Haydn/Forbes. Two euphoniums and two tubas.

Acrobatics. Uber. Two euphoniums or two tubas and piano.

Adagio. Albinoni/Hiraishi. Four euphoniums.

Adagio. Schoendorff. Two euphoniums and two tubas.

Adagio. Stevens. Four euphoniums and four tubas.

Adagio and Rondo. Forte. Two euphoniums and two tubas.

Adagio, Choral et Scherzetto. Ameller. Four tubas.

Adagio for Strings. Barber/Lindsey. Two euphoniums and two tubas.

Adagio for Strings. Barber/Spies. Three euphoniums and three tubas.

Adagio for Strings. Barber/Wilson. Two euphoniums and two tubas.

Adagio from Symphony #3. Saint-Saens/Hanson. Two euphoniums and two tubas.

Adieu, Sweet Amaryllis. Wilbye. Two euphoniums and two tubas.

Adoramus Te, Christe. Mozart/Nelson. Two euphoniums and two tubas.

Advanced Duets for Tuba. Volume I. Sear. Two tubas.

Advanced Duets for Tuba. Volume II. Sear. Two tubas.

Aequale. Bruckner/Schmidt. One euphonium and two tubas.

Aetherische Geisterstimmen. Cornelius/Manzo. Two euphoniums and two tubas.
Agnus Dei. Palestrina/Doughty. Three euphoniums and three tubas.
Air for Tuba Ensemble. Rodgers. Two euphoniums and two tubas.
Air from Amadis. Lully/Hartin. Four tubas.
Air from Suite in D. Bach/Wood. Two euphoniums and two tubas.
Air from Suite No. 3 in D. Bach/Werden. Two euphoniums and two tubas.
Air from Suite No. 3 in D Major. Bach/Baadsvik. Two euphoniums and two tubas.
Air from Water Music. Handel/Minchin. Two euphoniums and two tubas.
Air on a G String. Bach/Hendricks. Three tubas.
Air on the G String. Bach/Goble. Two euphoniums and two tubas.
Airs and Dances. Jones. One euphonium and one tuba.
Alas, and Did My Savior Bleed. Habegger. Two euphoniums and two tubas.
Ale and Arty. Bayliss. One euphonium and two tubas with narrator.
Alexander's Ragtime Band. Berlin/Hoesly. Two euphoniums and two tubas.
Alexander's Ragtime Band. Berlin/Schmidt. Two euphoniums and two tubas.
All in a Cave. Pilkington. Two euphoniums and two tubas.
All Things Bright and Beautiful. Robertson. Two euphoniums and two tubas.
All Too Soon. Niehaus. Two euphoniums and two tubas.
All We like Sheep. Handel/Roundtree. Two euphoniums and two tubas.
Alla Rivea del Tebro. Palestrina/Nelson. Four tubas.
Allegro. Mozart/Shoop. One euphonium and two tubas.
Allegro for Tuba Quartet. Jones. Four tubas.
Allegro from Eine Kleine Nachtmusik. Mozart/Peoples. Two euphoniums and two tubas.
Allegro from Water Music. Handel/Rauch. Two euphoniums and two tubas.
Allegro from "Water Music." Handel/Self. Two euphoniums and four tubas.
Allegro from William Tell Overture. Rossini/Rauch. Two euphoniums and two tubas.
Allegro Maestoso from Water Music. Handel/Lindsey. Two euphoniums and two tubas.
Alleluia. Boyce/Laws. Two euphoniums and two tubas.
Alleluia. Telemann/Heiman. Two euphoniums and three tubas.
Alleluia. Thompson/Wilkinson. Two euphoniums and two tubas.
Alleluia from "William Tell Overture." Boyce/Laws. Two euphoniums and two tubas.
Allerseelen (All Souls' Day). Strauss/Gotoh. Three euphoniums and three tubas.
Alles, was Ihr Tut (All You Do in Life). Buxtehude/Pardus. Two euphoniums and two tubas.
Allt Under Himlens Fäste (Everything under the Sky). Baadsvik. Two euphoniums and two tubas.
Almirena's Aria "Lascia ch'io pianga." Handel/Schmidt. Two euphoniums and two tubas.
Almost a Fugue. Pelecis. Two euphoniums and two tubas.
Alpha Suite, The. Catelinet. One euphonium and one tuba.
Alt und Neu fur Zwei (Old and New for Two). Zettler. One euphonium and one tuba.
Alte Kameraden. Tautenhahn. Two euphoniums and two tubas.
Alte Kameraden March. Teike/Schmidt. Two euphoniums and two tubas.
Amazing Grace. Glover. Two euphoniums and two tubas.
Amazing Grace. Robertson. Two euphoniums and two tubas.
Amazing Grace. Uber. Two euphoniums and two tubas.
Amazing Grace. Vaughan. Two euphoniums, two tubas, and garden hose.
American Favorites: Tuba Euphonium Quartets. Vaughan. Two euphoniums and two tubas.
American Patrol. Meacham/Lee. Three euphoniums and two tubas.
American Song Suite. Schanke. Two euphoniums and two tubas.
American Tuba Patrol. Meacham/Konagaya. Two euphoniums and two tubas.
Amparito Roca. Texidor/Emberson. Two euphoniums and two tubas.
Amparito Roco. Texidor/Wilkinson. Two euphoniums and two tubas.
Amyntas with His Phyllis Fair. Pilkington. Two euphoniums and two tubas.
An der Schoen Blauen Donau (Blue Danube Waltz). Strauss/Seitz. Two euphoniums and two tubas.
Andante Cantabile from String Quartet No. 1. Tchaikovsky/Drobnak. Two euphoniums and two tubas.
Andante Cantabile from Symphony No. 5. Tchaikovsky/Forbes. Four euphoniums and four tubas.
Andante Tranquillo from Organ Sonata in A, Op. 65 No. 3. Mendelssohn-Bartholdy/Prater. Three euphoniums and two tubas.
Anna Magdalena Suite. Bach/Stevens. Two euphoniums and two tubas.
Antiphonal Suite. Frank and Gabrieli/Forbes and Thurman. Four euphoniums and four tubas.
Antiphonies. Fredrickson. Four euphoniums and four tubas.
Antiphony No. 1 for Double T/E Choir. Schutz/Hancock. Four euphoniums and six tubas.
Antiphony No. 2 for Double T/E Choir. Gabrieli/Conner. Four euphoniums and four tubas.
Appalachian Carol (Quartet No. 2). Canter. Two euphoniums and two tubas.

Appalachian Echos. Purvis. Two tubas.

April Is in My Mistress' Face. Morley. Two euphoniums and two tubas.

April Is in My Mistress' Face. Morley/Howard. Two euphoniums and two tubas.

April Is in My Mistress' Face. Morley/Nelson. Two euphoniums and two tubas.

Aragonaise from "Le Cid." Massenet/Erickson. Two euphoniums and two tubas.

Aria. Schroeder/Krzywicki. Two euphoniums and two tubas.

Aria and Rondo. Potter. Two euphoniums and one tuba.

Aria—Duet from Cantata No. 78. Bach/Werden. One euphonium and one tuba with piano.

Arietta and Waltz. Grieg/Hiraishi. Two euphoniums and two tubas.

Arioso from Contata 156. Bach/Siekmann. Two euphoniums and two tubas.

Army of the Nile. Alfred/Wilkinson. Two euphoniums and two tubas.

Artistic Solos and Duets. Bell. One euphonium and one tuba.

Asleep in the Deep. Petrie/Schmidt. Two euphoniums and two tubas.

Auburn Is the Colour. . . . Forbes. Two euphoniums and two tubas.

Auld Lang Syne. Wilkinson. Two euphoniums and two tubas.

Ave Maria. Arcadelt/Self. Four tubas.

Ave Maria. Bruckner/Sabourin. Two euphoniums and two tubas.

Ave Maria. Desprez/Spang. Two euphoniums and two tubas.

Ave Maria. Franz/Manzo. Two euphoniums and two tubas.

Ave Maria. Liszt/Manzo. Two euphoniums and two tubas.

Ave Maria. Vittoria/Tuinstra. Two euphoniums and two tubas.

Ave Verum. Byrd/Schulz. Two euphoniums and two tubas.

Ave Verum. Mozart/Sabourin. Two euphoniums and two tubas.

Ave Verum Corpus. Byrd/Howard. Two euphoniums and two tubas.

Ave Verum Corpus. Byrd/Schmidt. Two euphoniums and two tubas.

Ave Verum Corpus. Mozart/Seitz. Two euphoniums and two tubas.

Ave Verum Corpus (K. 618). Mozart/Emilson. Two euphoniums and two tubas.

Away in a Manger. Vaughan. Two euphoniums and two tubas.

B

Baba Yaga from "Pictures at an Exhibition." Mussorgsky/Golas. Four euphoniums and four tubas.

Baby Elephant Walk. Mancini/Anderson. Two euphoniums and two tubas.

Baby Elephant Walk. Mancini/Luis. One euphonium and three tubas.

Baby Elephant Walk. Mancini/Niehaus. Two euphoniums and two tubas.

Bacchanale from Samson and Delilah. Saint-Saëns/Wilson. Two euphoniums, two tubas, and optional percussion.

Bach for Two Tubas. Bach/MacMorran. Two tubas.

Ballad for Five Tubas. Frank. Two euphoniums and three tubas.

Ballad in D Minor, Op. 10, No. 1. Brahms/Siekmann. Five euphoniums and two tubas.

Ballade. Stevens. Two euphoniums and two tubas.

Ballet Music from Rosamunde. Schubert/Bale. Two euphoniums and two tubas.

Ballin' The Jack. Hoesly. Two euphoniums and two tubas.

Barbara and Helena Polka. Bewley. Two euphoniums and two tubas.

Barbara Polka. Grim. Two euphoniums and two tubas.

Barber of Seville. Rossini/Doughty. Two euphoniums and two tubas.

Barber of Seville Overture, The. Rossini/Kile. Two euphoniums and three tubas.

Barnum and Bailey's Favorite. King/Diamond. Two euphoniums and two tubas.

Baroque'n Brass. Anderson. One trumpet or euphonium and one tuba.

Basic Psych-Rock. Self. Two euphoniums and four tubas.

Basics, The. Newsome. Two euphoniums and two tubas.

Bass Camp. Kerwin. Two euphoniums and two tubas.

Bass Clef Sessions. Gearhart/Cassel/Hornibrook. Two euphoniums and two tubas.

Bass Lied and Valse to Bass. Badarak. One euphonium and one tuba.

Battle Hymn. Steffe/Isbell. Two euphoniums and two tubas.

Bavarian Stew. Wilhelm. One euphonium and three tubas.

Bayerische Polka. Schmidt. Two euphoniums and two tubas.

Bayrische Polka. Schmidt. Two euphoniums and four tubas.

Bayrische Zell. Schmidt. Two euphoniums and four tubas.

Beast! Danner. Four euphoniums and four tubas.

Beautiful Savior. Anderson. Two euphoniums and two tubas.

Beautiful Savior (Crusader's Hymn). Siekmann. One euphonium, one tuba, and piano.

Beer Barrel Polka. Anderson. Two euphoniums and two tubas.

Beer Barrel Polka. Brown, Timm, and Vejouda/Grim. Two euphoniums and two tubas.

Beersheba Neo-Baroque Suite. Bartles. Tuba and cello (or euphonium).
Belle of Chicago March. Sousa/Ray. Two euphoniums and two tubas.
Bells-a-Plenty. Anderson. Two euphoniums and two tubas.
Bendemeer's Stream. Shoop. Two euphoniums and two tubas.
Beneath the Surface. Harrison. Two euphoniums, two tubas, piano, guitar, bass, and drums.
Benediction. Stevens. Two euphoniums and two tubas.
Bentonsport 1895. McCurdy. Four tubas.
Bicinia, Op. 5. Thomas. One trombone (euphonium) and one tuba.
Big Fat Polka. Szkutko. Four tubas.
Bill Bailey. Garrett. Two euphoniums and two tubas with optional keyboard and drums.
Billboard March, The. Klohr/Martin. Two euphoniums and three tubas.
Bird in the Forest, Op. 376F. Hewitt. Four tubas with a high solo and optional echo part.
Bist Du Bei Mir. Bach/Werden. Two euphoniums and two tubas.
Bist Du bei mir. Bach/Winternheimer. Two euphoniums and two tubas.
Bist Du bei mir. Stolzel/Shoop. Two euphoniums and two tubas.
Bivalve Suite. Hartley. One euphonium and one tuba.
Blues for Bill. McCurdy. Four tubas.
Bluesette. Thielmans/Vaughan. Two euphoniums and two tubas.
Bluesin' Tubas. Martin. Three euphoniums, two tubas, piano, bass, drums, and guitar.
Boats and Ships. Tignor. One euphonium and one tuba with piano.
Bocoxe. Powell/Buttery. Two euphoniums and two tubas.
Bottoms Up Rag. Mehlan. Two euphoniums and two tubas.
Brass Duo. Frackenpohl. One horn (euphonium) and one tuba.
Brass Tacks. Niehaus. Two euphoniums and two tubas.
Brazil. Barroso/Weichselbaumer. One euphonium and three tubas.
Bridal Chorus from Lohengrin. Wagner/Oliver. Two euphoniums and two tubas.
Bridal Chorus from Lohengrin. Wagner/Oliver. Two euphoniums and two tubas.
Bridge, The. Schoendorff. Two euphoniums and two tubas.
Brief History of a Star, A. McGuire. Four euphoniums and four tubas with three percussion.
Bright Euphonium Tuba Ensemble, Book 1. Two euphoniums and two tubas.
Brinlein die Fliessen, Die. De Vento/Schmidt. Two euphoniums and two tubas.
Broadway One-Step. King/Knoener. Three euphoniums and two tubas.
BTT. Perfeito. Two tubas and drums.
Bullfrog Rag. Gilfish/Garrett. Two euphoniums and two tubas.
Bummel-Petrus (Lazy Pete). Werner-Kersten/Knoener. Two euphoniums and two tubas.
Buttons and Bows. Livingston and Schmidt. Two euphoniums and two tubas.
Bydlo from "Pictures at an Exhibition." Mussorgsky/Golas. Three euphoniums and three tubas.

C

Cacology. Piltzecker. Three euphoniums and five tubas.
Cadenzas for 8 Players. Ito. Four euphoniums and four tubas.
Canon. Billings/Schmidt. Two euphoniums and two tubas.
Canon and Scherzo. Sibbing. Two tubas and piano.
Canon in the Lydian Mode. Wolfe. One euphonium and one tuba.
Canon on a Ground Bass. Purcell/Gray. One euphonium and two tubas.
Canonic Etudes. Racussen. Three tubas.
Canonic Sonata. Telemann/Hartin. Two tubas.
Canons and Hockets. Bowder. One euphonium and one tuba.
Cantate Domini and What Child Is This? Pitoni/Schmidt. Two euphoniums and two tubas.
Cantatibus organis, Caecilia virgo. Torqvet/Manzo. Four euphoniums and four tubas.
Canticle of Jean Racine. Fauré/Drobnak. Two euphoniums and two tubas.
Canticles. Jones. Four tubas.
Cantilena. Jones. Two euphoniums and two tubas.
Canzon a 12 in Echo. Gabrieli/Fiegel. Six euphoniums and six tubas.
Canzon noni toni from Sacrae Symphoniae. Gabrieli/Spang. Four euphoniums and four tubas.
Canzona. Gabrieli/Varner. Two euphoniums and two tubas.
Canzona. Nelhybel. Four euphoniums and four tubas.
Canzone. Kerll/Long. One euphonium and two tubas.
Canzona a Quarti Toni. Frescobaldi/Schmidt. Two euphoniums and two tubas.
Canzona and Hornpipe. Israel. Four tubas.
Canzona in d. Buxtehude/Manzo. Two euphoniums and two tubas.
Canzona, "La Spiritata." Gabrieli/Rauch. Two euphoniums and two tubas.
Canzona per Sonare II. Gabrieli/Schmidt. Two euphoniums and two tubas.
Canzona per Sonare No. 1. Gabrieli/Lindsey. Two euphoniums and two tubas.
Canzona per Sonare No. 1 "La Spiritata." Gabrieli/Cummings. Two euphoniums and two tubas.
Canzona per sonare No. 2. Gabrieli/Roundtree. Two euphoniums and two tubas.

Canzona per sonare No. 4. Gabrieli/Gray. One euphonium and three tubas.
Canzona per sonare No. 4. Gabrieli/Roundtree. Two euphoniums and two tubas.
Canzona Sesta a 4. Frescobaldi/Schmidt. Two euphoniums and two tubas.
Canzona XXX. Scheidt/Gray. Two euphoniums and three tubas.
Carolina. Self. Two euphoniums and two tubas.
Caroling Quartet, The. Anderson. Two euphoniums and two tubas.
Carols for a Merry TubaChristmas. Wilder. Two euphoniums and two tubas.
Carols for a Merry TubaChristmas, Vol. II. Wilder. Two euphoniums and two tubas.
Cassation for Four Tubas. De Filippi. Four tubas.
Cavatina. Bavicchi. Two euphoniums and two tubas.
Celebration. Anderson. Three euphoniums and one tuba.
Celebration. Konagaya. Solo tuba. Three euphoniums, and three tubas.
Celestial Suite. Bulla. Two euphoniums and two tubas.
Celluloid Tubas: A Score for Barney Oldfield's Race for a Life (1913). Fiegel. Three euphoniums, three tubas, and motion picture equipment.
Ceremonial Sketch. Camphouse. Two euphoniums and two tubas.
Chaconne. Bergenfeld. Two euphoniums and one tuba.
Chaconne. Purcell/Hartin. Three tubas.
Chaconne. Purcell/Morris. Two tubas with optional piano or harpsichord.
Chaconne, Op. 148. Cunningham. Two euphoniums and two tubas.
Chant and Fantasie. Jones. Four tubas.
Chanukah Medley. Wilkinson. Two euphoniums and two tubas.
Charleston. Mack/Bevan and Schmidt. Two euphoniums and two tubas.
Charleston Chuckles. Confrey/Vaughan. Two euphoniums and two tubas.
Chaser #1. Garbáge. Two euphoniums and one tuba.
Chaser #3. Garbáge. Two euphoniums and two tubas.
Cheesy Tuba Quartet, The. Goeller. Two euphoniums and two tubas.
Cherokee for Tuba Quartet. Schooley. Two euphoniums and two tubas.
Chi Ni Hikari Arite (Lux in Terra). Censhu. Four euphoniums and four tubas.
Chiapanecas (Easy). Anderson. Two euphoniums and two tubas.
Chiapanecas (Advanced). Anderson. Three euphoniums and one tuba.
Children of the Heavenly Father. Habegger. Two euphoniums and two tubas.
Chimes Blues. Garrett. Two euphoniums and two tubas with optional keyboard and drums.
Choix D'Airs. Hartman/Torchinsky. Two tubas.
Chops! Martin. Three euphoniums, two tubas, and rhythm.
Chor der Engel. Schubert/Manzo. Two euphoniums and two tubas.
Choral and Folksong. Dutton. Two trombones (euphoniums), one tuba, and piano.
Choral No. 3 (Blessed Jesus, We Are Here). Bach/Buquet. Two euphoniums and two tubas.
Chorale. Howard. Two euphoniums and two tubas.
Chorale. McCurdy. Two euphoniums and one tuba.
Chorale and Clog Dance. Hall. Two euphoniums and two tubas.
Chorale and Gigue. McCurdy. One euphonium and one tuba.
Chorale and Gigue for A Quartet of Tubas. Danburg. Four tubas.
Chorale Prelude and Fugue on Puer Nobis. Kassler. Two euphoniums and two tubas.
Chorale Prelude from Contata No. 140. Bach/Cummings. Two euphoniums and two tubas.
Chorale (Psalm 97). Schutz/Heiman. Two euphoniums and two tubas.
Chorale Quartet. Anderson. Two euphoniums and two tubas.
Choro di Schiavi Ebrei (from "Nabucco"). Verdi/Evans. Two euphoniums and two tubas.
Christmas Bell Songs. Schmidt. Two euphoniums and two tubas.
Christmas Bells A-Plenty. Anderson. Two euphoniums and two tubas.
Christmas Collection—Duets for Brass. Hoesly. Two tubas.
Christmas for Two. Conley. One euphonium and one tuba.
Christmas Gathering, A. Mason. Two euphoniums and two tubas.
Christmas Jazz Favorites No. 1. Niehaus. Two euphoniums and two tubas.
Christmas Jazz Favorites No. 2. Niehaus. Two euphoniums and two tubas.
Christmas Jazz Favorites No. 3. Niehaus. Two euphoniums and two tubas.
A Christmas Jazz Medley. Niehaus. Two euphoniums and two tubas.
Christmas Song, The. Torme/Vaughan. Two euphoniums and two tubas.
Chronicles. Uber. Two euphoniums and two tubas.
Cinnamon Downs. Bewley. Two euphoniums, two tubas, and three harps.
Circle VIII: Bowge IV. Canter. Four euphoniums and four tubas.
Circus Life. Lemirre. Four euphoniums and four tubas.
Civil War Suite No. 1. Schmidt. Two euphoniums and two tubas.
Civil War Suite No. 2. Schmidt. Two euphoniums and two tubas.

Civil War Suite No. 3. Schmidt. Two euphoniums and two tubas.

Clarinet Polka, The. Bewley. Two euphoniums and two tubas.

Clarinet Polka. Grim. Two euphoniums and two tubas.

Classics for Low Brass Quartet, Set No. 1. Schumann/Schanke. Two euphoniums and two tubas.

Classics for Low Brass Quartet, Set No. 2. Schumann/Schanke. Two euphoniums and two tubas.

Clementine. Garrett. One euphonium and two tubas.

Cole Porter Medley. Sample. Two euphoniums, two tubas, piano/guitar, bass, and drums.

Colonel Bogey March. Alford/Bewley. Two euphoniums and two tubas.

Colonel Bogey March. Alford/Schmidt. Two euphoniums and two tubas.

Colonel Bogey March. Alford/Wilkinson. Two euphoniums and two tubas.

Coloring Book, The. McCurdy. Two tubas.

Colossi. Knight. Six tubas.

Come Again, Sweet Love. Dowland/Werden. Two euphoniums and two tubas.

Come Josephine (In My Flying Machine). Fischer/Schmidt. Two euphoniums and two tubas.

Come Sweet Death. Bach/Anderson. Two euphoniums and two tubas.

Come Sweet Death. Bach/Sauter. One euphonium and two tubas.

Come, Thou Long Expected Jesus. Bach/Warren. Two euphoniums and two tubas.

Composition. Miura. Two euphoniums and two tubas.

Concert and Contest Collection for Tuba-Euphonium Quartet (Grade III-IV). Gray. Two euphoniums and two tubas.

Concert and Ensemble Folio (Bandsembles). Hudadoff. Two tubas.

Concert Duets, Vol I. Self. Two tubas.

Concert Duets, Vol II. Self. Two tubas.

Concert Suite. Goedicke. One euphonium and one tuba.

Concerto. Vivaldi/Humble. Two euphoniums and two tubas.

Concerto Basso. Ross. Four euphoniums and four tubas.

Concerto Grosso. Geminiani/Morris. Two euphoniums and one tuba.

Concertstuck. Ameller. Four tubas.

Conga from Symphony No. 7. Beethoven/Bale. Two euphoniums and two tubas.

Consequences. Forbes. Two euphoniums and two tubas.

Consortium for Euphoniums and Tubas. Cheetham. Two euphoniums and two tubas.

Contrapunctas I. Bach/Morris. Two euphoniums and three tubas.

Contrapunctus I. Bach/Cummings. Two euphoniums and three tubas.

Contrapunctus III from Art of Fugue. Bach/Nelson. Two euphoniums and two tubas.

Contrapunctus IX. Bach/Forbes. Two euphoniums and two tubas.

Contrapunctus IX. Bach/Pitts. Two euphoniums and two tubas.

Contrapunctus IX. Bach/Rauch. Two euphoniums and two tubas.

Contrapunctus IX. Bach/Schmidt. Two euphoniums and two tubas.

Contrasts for Brass. Gray. Two euphoniums and two tubas.

Conversations. Knight. One euphonium and one tuba.

Cool Suite for Tuba/Euphonium Quartet, A. Smalley. Two euphoniums and two tubas with optional percussion.

Coraggio. Davidson. Two euphoniums and two tubas.

Cosmic Voyage. Forbes. Two euphoniums and two tubas.

Counterpoint No. 6. Nelhybel. Two tubas.

Coventry Carol. Anderson. Two euphoniums and two tubas.

Crawfish Crawl. Gilfish/Garrett. Two euphoniums and one tuba.

Cry Out, A. Glivar. Three euphoniums and three tubas.

Csikos Post. Necke/Konagaya. Two euphoniums and two tubas.

Csikos Post. Necke/Schmidt. Two euphoniums and two tubas.

Cuckoo, The. Schmidt. Two euphoniums and two tubas, with optional flute, recorder, or whistle.

Czardas. Monti/Diamond. Two euphoniums and two tubas.

Czardas. Monti/LeClair. Two euphoniums and two tubas with optional drums.

D

Dance. Renwick/Wilson. Two euphoniums and two tubas.

Dance No. 1. Wilson. Two euphoniums and two tubas.

Dance of the Little ~~(Swans)~~ Tubas. Tchaikovsky/Schmidt. Two euphoniums and two tubas.

Dance of the Little Tubas (Swans). Tchaikovsky/Goble. Two euphoniums and two tubas.

Dance of the Tumblers. Rimsky-Korsakov/Fabrizio. Two euphoniums and two tubas.

Dance Suite. Gervaise/Werden. Two euphoniums and two tubas.

Dance Suite for Three Tubas. Sarcich. Three tubas.

Dances. Stevens. Solo tuba and three tubas.

Dances; Four Tubas: A Short Piece for Tuba Quartet. Pullig. Two euphoniums and two tubas.

Dancing Music. Szpakowski. Two euphoniums and two tubas.

Danny Boy. Walton. Two euphoniums and two tubas.
Dark Forest. Schulz. Three euphoniums and two tubas.
Das Butterbrot. Mozart/Dorner. Four tubas.
David of the White Rock. Bale. Two euphoniums and two tubas.
Day We Buried Vanya, The. Schmidt. Two euphoniums and two tubas.
Dead Man's Cove. Newsome. Two euphoniums and two tubas.
Death of Beowulf, The. Muller. Four tubas.
Declarations. Uber. Three euphoniums and three tubas.
Dedications for Baritone and Tuba. Constantinides. One euphonium and one tuba.
Deep Harmony. Parker/Walton. Two euphoniums and two tubas.
Deep River. Uber. Two euphoniums and two tubas.
Dem dunkeln Schoss der heilgen Erde. Brahms/Manzo. Two euphoniums and two tubas.
Demon Dance. McCurdy. Three tubas.
Der Unvollendeten Vollendung (The Finishing of the Unfinished). LeClair. Two euphoniums and two tubas with drums.
Describe the Evening. McLean. Two euphoniums and two tubas.
Deutschland Uber Alles. Anderson. Two euphoniums and two tubas.
Devil Septet. Ewazen. Four tubas, piano, and percussion.
Dialog for Tubas. Atherton. Four tubas.
Dialogue. Hoshina. Four euphoniums and six tubas.
Dialogue and Dance. Brown. One trombone (euphonium) and one tuba.
Die Forelle (The Trout). Schubert/LeClair. Two euphoniums and two tubas with drums.
Die Lorelei. Silcher/Seitz. Four tubas.
Dies Irae from Requiem. Verdi/Cole. Two euphoniums and four tubas.
Dill Pickles Rag. Johnson/Nelson. Two euphoniums and two tubas.
Ding Dong Merrily (on Low). Minerd. Two euphoniums and two tubas.
Dirge and Slow Dance. Hall. Three euphoniums and one tuba.
Disco Tuba. Carmody. One euphonium and two tubas.
Diverse Elements. Gillingham. One euphonium, one tuba, and piano.
Diversion for Seven Bass Clef Instruments. Clinard. Four euphoniums and three tubas.
Diversions. Stevens. Four tubas.
Diversions. Stevens. Four tubas.
Divertimento. De Filippi. One euphonium and one tuba.
Divertimento. Hayakawa. Three euphoniums and three tubas.
Divertimento. Presser. Two euphoniums and three tubas.
Divertimento. Spears. Two euphoniums and two tubas.
Divertimento. Uber. Two euphoniums and two tubas.
Divertimento No. 1, K. 229. Mozart/Schmidt. Two euphoniums and one tuba.
Divertimento, No. 2, Op. 130. Uber. Two euphoniums and two tubas.
Dizzy Fingers. Confrey/Vaughan. Two euphoniums and two tubas.
Doguu Sansai (Three Clay Puppets). Censhu. Three tubas.
Dona Nobis Pacem. Isbell. One euphonium and two tubas.
Dona Nobis Tubas. Wilkinson. Two euphoniums and two tubas.
Double Portraits. Uber. One euphonium and one tuba.
Down by the Old Mill Stream. Vaughan. Two euphoniums and two tubas.
Down in the River to Pray. Warren. Two euphoniums and two tubas.
Down on the Farm. Garrett. Two euphoniums and two tubas.
Dragon Land. Szkutko. Four tubas.
Dragon's Dance, The. LeClair. Two euphoniums and two tubas with drums and four marimbas.
Dream. Vaughan. Two euphoniums and two tubas.
Dream of the Witches' Sabbath from Symphonie Fantastique. Berlioz/Fiegel. Four euphoniums and four tubas with percussion.
Dueling Barbers (of Seville). Rossini/Wilkinson. Two euphoniums and two tubas.
Duet. Mueller. One euphonium and one tuba.
Duet. Sainte-Jacome/Wekselblatt. Two tubas.
Duet for Tubas. Garrett. Two tubas.
Duet for Tubas. Stamitz/Long. Two tubas.
Duet for Two Tubas and Understanding Audience. Wilson. Two tubas.
Duet in F. Devienne/Singleton. Two tubas.
Duet Time. Scarmolin/Boo. One euphonium and one tuba.
Duets and Trios. Bach/Augustine. Two or three tubas.
Duets for All. Stoutamire and Albert. Two tubas.
Duets for Tuba. Mozart/Jacobs. Two tubas.
Duets for Tuba. Torchinsky. Two tubas.
Duh Suite. Self. Two tubas and drum set.
Duke of Marlborough Fanfare, The. Grainger/Fiegel. Four euphoniums and four tubas with percussion.
Dune Buggy. Szkutko. Two euphoniums and two tubas.
Duo Concertante for Two Tubas, Op. 97. Uber. Two tubas.
Duo for Tubas. Goldman. Two tubas.
Duos for Two Tubas. Jesus. Two tubas.
Dyad for Four Tubas. Alexander. Four tubas.

E

Earle of Oxford March. Byrd/Lindsey. Two euphoniums and two tubas.
Earle of Oxford Marche. Byrd/Wilson. Two euphoniums and two tubas.
Earth and Moon. Collins-Rice. Two euphoniums and two tubas.
Earth Voices. Szentpáli and Kövesdi. Solo tuba with four euphoniums, four tubas, and narrator.
Easy Classics for Two. Stouffer. Two tubas.
Easy Winners. Joplin/Stephens. Two euphoniums and two tubas.
Easy Winners, The. Joplin/Hiraishi. Two euphoniums and two tubas.
Easy Winners, The. Joplin/Schmidt. Two euphoniums and two tubas.
Easy Winners, The. Joplin/Werden. Two euphoniums and two tubas.
Ecco Mormorar L'onde. Monteverdi/Nelson. Two euphoniums and three tubas.
Echo Carol, The. Anderson. Two euphoniums and two tubas.
Echo Fantasy for Double T/E Ensemble. Lasso/Derby. Four euphoniums and six tubas.
Efflorescent. Aagaard-Nilsen. Tuba quartet.
Egmont Overture. Beethoven/Bale. Two euphoniums and two tubas.
Ego Sum Tui Plaga Doloris. Schutz/Nelson. Two euphoniums and two tubas.
Egyptian March. Strauss/Schmidt. Two euphoniums and two tubas.
Eight Bagatelles. Luedeke. Two tubas.
Eight Days of Christmas. Vaughan. Two euphoniums and two tubas.
Eight Miniatures for Four Tubas. Constantinides. Four tubas.
1812 Overture. Tchaikovsky/Sharp. Three euphoniums and three tubas.
Ein Prosit! Bewley. Two euphoniums and two tubas.
Eine Kleine Nachtmusik. Mozart/Seitz. Two euphoniums and two tubas.
Eine Kleine Nachtmusik for Tuba Quartet. Mozart/Self. Four tubas.
Eine Kleine Nachtmusik, K. 525. Mozart/Greene. Two euphoniums and two tubas.
Eine Kleine Nachtmusik, K. 525. Mozart/Schmidt. Two euphoniums and two tubas.
Eine Kleine Nachtmusik, Mvt. I. Mozart/Booz. Two euphoniums and two tubas.
Eine Kleine Octubamusic. Frackenpohl. Eight tubas.
Eine Kleine Tubamusik für Roadrunner und Coyote. Stalling and Franklyn/Fiegel. Four euphoniums, four tubas, two percussion, and film.
Einmal Am Rhein. Ostermann/Grim. Two euphoniums and two tubas.
El Capitan. Sousa/Morris. Two euphoniums and two tuba.
El Solo Toro—Marriachi. Alpert/Self. Two euphoniums and two tubas.
El Toro Loco. Friedrich. Four euphoniums and two tubas.
El Tuba. Bewley. Two euphoniums and two tubas.
El Tubadore. Wilkinson. Two euphoniums and two tubas.
Elegy. LeClair. Two euphoniums and two tubas with four marimbas.
Elegy and Presto. Ketchum. Two euphoniums and two tubas.
Elegy for Four Tubas. Coucounaras. Four tubas.
Elephants Exotiques. Snow. Four tubas.
Eleven Duets for Tuba. Nelhybel. Two tubas.
Eleven Mozart Duets for Bass Clef Instruments. Mozart/Powell. Two bass clef instruments.
Elite Syncopations. Joplin/Picher. Two euphoniums and two tubas.
Ellington Medley. Sample. Two euphoniums, two tubas, piano/guitar, bass, and drums.
Elsa's Procession to the Cathedral. Wagner/Robertson. Two euphoniums and two tubas.
Emilia Polka. Schmidt. Two euphoniums and two tubas.
English Christmas Country Dance, An. Buttery. Two euphoniums and two tubas.
An English Folk Christmas. Buttery. Four tubas.
Entertainer, The. Joplin/Gray. Two euphoniums and two tubas.
Entertainer, The. Joplin/Hiraishi. Three euphoniums and one tuba.
Entertainer, The. Joplin/Schanke. Two euphoniums and two tubas.
Entertainer, The. Joplin/Stephens. Two euphoniums and two tubas.
Entrada. Friedrich. Four euphoniums and four tubas.
Entrevue. Jous. Two tubas and piano.
Entry of the Gladiators. Fucik/Seitz. Two euphoniums and two tubas.
Entry of the Gladiators (Thunder and Blazes). Fucik/Diamond. Two euphoniums and two tubas.
Episodes. Reeman. Two euphoniums and two tubas.
Es ist ein Ros' enstprungen. Brahms/Shoop. Two euphoniums and two tubas.
Es ist eine Rose Entsprungen. Brahms/Gotoh. Three euphoniums and three tubas.
Espana Cami. Garrett. Three euphoniums and three tubas.
Esquisse Villageoise (Country Sketches). Lemirre. Four euphoniums and four tubas.
Essay. Toyama. Three euphoniums and three tubas.
Et Tu Bop. Keating. Two euphoniums and two tubas.
Eternal Hymns. Uber. Two euphoniums and two tubas.
Euphonic Sounds. Joplin/Frackenpohl. One euphonium and one tuba.
Euphonic Sounds. Joplin/Hiraishi. Two euphoniums and two tubas.
Euphonic Sounds. Joplin/Werden. Two euphoniums and two tubas.

Euphonium and Tuba: Ens. Works for the First Time. Morita. Two euphoniums and one tuba.
Euphonium Tuba Quartet. Toda. Two euphoniums and two tubas.
Evening Prayer. Humperdinck/Manzo. Two euphoniums and three tubas.
Evergreen. Streisand/Stephens. Two euphoniums and two tubas.
Evergreen Polka. Knoener. Two euphoniums and two tubas.
Evergreen Polka. Schmidt. Two euphoniums and two tubas.
Exhibitions, Op. 98. Uber. Four euphoniums and one tuba.
Explorations for Tuba Quintet, Op. 85. Uber. Five tubas.
Expose for Tubas. Garrett. Four euphoniums and two tubas.

F

Fair Phyliss. Farmer/Wilkinson. Two euphoniums and two tubas.
Fair Phyllis I Saw. Farmer. Two euphoniums and two tubas.
Famous Waltzes of the Opera and Ballet. Bewley. Two euphoniums and two tubas.
Fancy Dances. Ross. Three tubas.
Fanfare. Garrett. Three euphoniums and three tubas.
Fanfare. Purcell/Lindsey. Two euphoniums and two tubas.
Fanfare and Chant. Cummings. Four euphoniums and two tubas.
Fanfare and Rondeau. Mouret/Schmidt. Two euphoniums and two tubas.
Fanfare for a Friend. Stevens. Five tubas.
Fanfare for Six Tubas. Sandstrom. Six tubas.
Fanfare for Tubafour. Anderson. Two euphoniums and two tubas.
Fanfare No. 1. Taylor. Two euphoniums and two tubas.
Fanfares. Vaughan. Two euphoniums and two tubas.
Fanitul. Olsen/Rauchut. Two euphoniums and one tuba.
Fantasia. Gibbons. Two tubas.
Fantasia. Lupo/Baldwin. Three tubas.
Fantasia. Lupo/Hartin. Three tubas.
Fantasia. White/Baldwin. Two tubas.
Fantasia. White/Hartin. Two tubas.
Fantasia for Basses. Lupo/Schmidt. Two euphoniums and two tubas.
Fantasia for Tuba Duo. Garrett. Two tubas.
Fantasia in C. Bach/Sabourin. Two euphoniums and two tubas.
Fantasia in Foure Parts. Gibbons/Doughty. Two euphoniums and two tubas.
Fantasia of Eastern Europe Village Dances. Buttery. Two euphoniums and two tubas.
Fantasia on "Dies Irae." Hill. Two euphoniums and four tubas.
Fantasias. Lasso/Powell. One euphonium and one tuba.
Fantasie a tre voci, Volume I. Bassano/Fischer. One euphonium and two tubas.
Fantasie a tre voci, Volume II. Bassano/Fischer. One euphonium and two tubas.
Fantasy for Tuba/Euphonium Quartet. Martino. Two euphoniums and two tubas.
Fascinatin' Gershwin. Ferguson. Two euphoniums and two tubas.
Father, Forgive Them. Robinson. Two euphoniums and three tubas.
Favorite Rag, The. Joplin/Sabourin. Two euphoniums and two tubas.
Feiertagsmusik (Festive Music). Krol. Three euphoniums and two tubas.
Fellscape. Scott. Two euphoniums and two tubas.
Festive and Commorative. Brahms/Warren. Eight-part tuba/euphonium ensemble.
Fifteen Easy Pieces for Bass Clef Instruments. Carmody. Two euphoniums and two tubas.
Fifteen Spectrum Duets for Tubas. Fritze. Two tubas.
Figures. Sciortino. Four tubas.
Finale from Symphony No. 4. Tchaikovsky/Butler. Two euphoniums and two tubas.
Finale from Symphony No. 4 in F Minor. Tchaikovsky/Self. Two euphoniums and four tubas with percussion.
Finale from Symphony No. 5. Beethoven/Bale. Six euphoniums and five tubas.
Finale from the Foust Ballet Music. Gounod/Bale. Two euphoniums and two tubas.
Fine Ale. Jous. Two euphoniums and two tubas.
Finlandia. Sibelius/Self. Two euphoniums and four tubas.
Fireman's Polka. Ripley/Schmidt. Two euphoniums and two tubas.
First Gymnopedie. Satie/Rauch. Two euphoniums and two tubas.
Five Bach Duos for Euphonium and Tuba. Frackenpohl. One euphonium and one tuba.
Five Canons for Tuba/Euphonium Sextet. Vaughan.
Five Carols. Vaughan. One euphonium and one tuba.
Five Dances. Susato/Stevens. Four euphoniums and four tubas.
Five Duets. Mozart/Hartin. Two tubas.
Five Foot Two—Eyes of Blue. Emberson. Two euphoniums and two tubas.
Five Foot Two, Eyes of Blue. Henderson/Emberson. Two euphoniums and two tubas.
Five Foot Two, Eyes of Blue. Henderson/Nelson. Two euphoniums and three tubas.
Five for Two Tubas. Albert. Two tubas.
Five Fragments. Cummings. Two euphoniums and two tubas.
Five Graded Intermediate Duets. Goble. One euphonium and one tuba.

Five Hag Pieces. Presser. One euphonium and one tuba.
Five Hundred Pound Polka. McCurdy. Three tubas with piano.
Five Moods for Tuba Quartet. Schuller. Four tubas.
Five Selections from Anna Magdalena's Notebook. Bach/Shoop. Two euphoniums and two tubas.
Five Trios of King Henry VIII. Schmidt. Two euphoniums and one tuba.
Flight of the Bumble Bee. Rimsky-Korsakov/Bale. Two euphoniums and two tubas.
Flight of the Bumble Bee. Rimsky-Korsakov/Watz. One euphonium and three tubas.
Flight of the Bumblebones. Rimsky-Korsakov/Gladwin. Six euphoniums and two tubas.
Florentiner. Fucik/Martin. Two euphoniums and three tubas.
Florentiner March. Glover. Three euphoniums and three tubas.
Florentiner Marsch. Fucik/Watz. One euphonium and three tubas.
Flourish. Vaughan Williams/Butler. Two euphoniums and two tubas.
Flow Gently Sweet Afton. Garrett. Two euphoniums and two tubas.
Fly Down. Benzi. Tuba Quartet.
Fly Me to the Moon. Howard/Hughes. Four trombones (euphoniums) and one tuba.
Folk Fantasy. Makela. Two euphoniums and two tubas.
Folk Song, A. Wilkinson. Two euphoniums and two tubas.
Folk Song Suite. Vaughan Williams/Forbes. Three euphoniums and three tubas with optional percussion.
Folksong Medley. Rauch. Two euphoniums and two tubas.
For Heaven's Sake. LeClair. Two euphoniums and two tubas with optional drums.
Forever and a Day. LeClair. Two euphoniums and two tubas with drums.
Forge in the Forest Polka. Stolc/Schmidt. Two euphoniums and two tubas.
Formidable. LeClair. Two euphoniums and two tubas with optional drums.
Forte! LeClair. Two euphoniums and two tubas with drums.
Four Bach Chorales. Bach/Mehlan. Two euphoniums and two tubas.
Four Brahms Folk Songs. Brahms/Ferriano. Two euphoniums and two tubas.
Four Choruses. Schubert/Singleton. Three tubas.
Four Contrapuntal Pieces. Van Hoy. Two euphoniums and two tubas.
Four Dialogues. Stoker. One euphonium and one tuba.
Four Duets. Jones. One euphonium and one tuba.
Four Duets, Op. 82. Devienne/Gershenfeld. Two tubas.
Four English Madrigals. Bale. Two euphoniums and two tubas.
Four Etudes for Two Tubas. Warren. Two tubas.
Four Excursions for Five Tubas. Baskin. Five tubas.
Four Folk Songs. Ferriano. Tuba/euphonium quartet.
Four German Pieces for Tuba Quartet. Ryder, Keith, and Schmidt. Two euphoniums and two tubas.
Four Kuehn ("Keen") Guys. Gillis. Four tubas.
Four Miniatures. Forbes. Two euphoniums and two tubas.
Four Miniatures for Trombone and Tuba. Beasley. One trombone and one tuba.
Four Pieces. Grieg/Rauch. Two euphoniums and two tubas.
Four Pieces. Mauer/Stevens. Two euphoniums and three tubas.
Four Pieces for Tuba Quartet. Jacob. Two euphoniums and two tubas.
Four Polkas. Schlesinger. One euphonium and three tubas.
Four Preludes for Four Tubas. Hewitt. Four tubas.
Four Preludes, Op. 28, Nos. 4, 7, 22, 28. Chopin/Rauch. Two euphoniums and two tubas.
Four Preludes, Op. 34. Shostakovich/Rauch. Two euphoniums and two tubas.
Four Quartets. Dressler. Two euphoniums and two tubas.
Four Quartets. Reicha/Werden. Two euphoniums and two tubas.
4-Tuba-Blues. Roblee. One euphonium and three tubas.
Four Tuben im 3/4 Takt-Volksweise. Seitz. Four tubas.
Fourteen Familiar Hymns, Carols, and Spirituals. Frederick. Three euphoniums and two tubas.
Fourtone Folio, Volume I. Cheyette. Three euphoniums and one tuba.
Fourtone Folio Volume II. Cheyette. Three euphoniums and one tuba.
Fra hele Buenos Aires. Nicotra. Two euphoniums and two tubas.
Fregat Galop, Op. 52. Bach, E. Two euphoniums and two tubas.
Freilach Ora. Wilkinson. Two euphoniums and two tubas.
Frescos de Bonampak (Octet No. 2). Osmon. Four euphoniums and four tubas.
Friendly Giants. Ball. Four tubas.
Frog Legs Rag. Scott/Shoop. Two euphoniums and two tubas.
From a Distance. Emberson. Two euphoniums and two tubas.
From Darkness . . . Emerging. Cummings. Two euphoniums and two tubas.
From This Moment On. Porter/Stephens. Two euphoniums and two tubas.
Frosty the Snowman. Glover. Two euphoniums and two tubas.
Fuga No. 7 from Organ Works IX. Bach/Kono. Two euphoniums and two tubas.
Fuga No. 7 from the Well Tempered Clavier, Book II. Bach/Spang. Two euphoniums and two tubas.
Fuga VII from WTC. Bach/Self. Two euphoniums and two tubas.

Fugue a 3. Bach/Schmidt. Two euphoniums and one tuba.
Fugue for Low Brass Trio. Anderson. Two euphoniums and one tuba.
Fugue in C Minor for Low Brass. Bach/Morris. One euphonium and two tubas.
Fugue in F Major. Bach/Schmidt. Two euphoniums and one tuba.
Fugue in G Minor from Fantasia and Fugue, BWV 542. Bach/Smalley. Two euphoniums and two tubas.
Fugue in G Minor (Little). Bach/Gray. Two euphoniums and two tubas.
Fugue in G Minor (Little). Bach/Peoples. Two euphoniums and two tubas.
Fugue in G Minor (Little). Bach/Somerville. Two euphoniums and two tubas.
Fugue K. 401. Mozart/Schmidt. Two euphoniums and two tubas.
Fugue No. 1. Schumann, C./Manzo One euphonium and two tubas.
Fugue No. 2. Schumann, C./Manzo Two euphoniums and two tubas.
Fugue No. 16 for Four Low Brass Instruments. Bach/Grim. Two euphoniums and two tubas.
Fugue on B.A.C.H. Krebs/Brown. Two euphoniums and two tubas.
Fun for Band. Kinyon.
Funeral March of a Marionette. Gounod/Frackenpohl. Two euphoniums and two tubas.
Funeral March of a Marionette. Gounod/Schmidt. Two euphoniums and two tubas.
Funeral March of a Marionette, The. Gounod/Bale. Four euphoniums and four tubas.
Funeral March on the Death of a Hero, Op. 26. Beethoven/Frackenpohl. Three euphoniums and three tubas with tympani.
Furies, The. Corwell. Four euphoniums and four tubas.

G

Galliard Battaglia. Scheidt/Lindsey. Two euphoniums and two tubas.
Galop. Gottschalk/Brown. Two euphoniums and two tubas.
Gammel Jegermarsj (Old Hunter March). Olsen/Baadsvik. Two euphoniums and two tubas.
Gavotte and Musette. Grieg/Bale. Four tubas.
Gay 90's Jazz Suite. Niehaus. Two euphoniums and two tubas.
Gay 90's Medley. Hughey. Two euphoniums and two tubas.
Gebet aus "Hansel und Gretel." Humperdink/Seitz. Two euphoniums and two tubas.
Georgia on My Mind. Carmichael/LeClair. Two euphoniums and two tubas.
Georgia on My Mind. Carmichael/Matteson. Three euphoniums, three tubas, and rhythm.
Gershwin Medley. Sample. Two euphoniums, two tubas, piano/guitar, bass, and drums.
Ginnungigap. Belden. One euphonium and one tuba.
Give Me That Old Time Religion. Uber. Two euphoniums and two tubas.
Gladiator March, The. Sousa/Butler. Two euphoniums and two tubas.
Glory of Low Brass, The. Borton. Three euphoniums and five tubas.
Gnome. Aoshima. Two euphoniums and two tubas.
God Rest Ye, Merry Gentlemen. Vaughan. Two euphoniums and two tubas.
God Save the Queen. Glover. Two euphoniums and two tubas.
Golliwogg's Cakewalk. Debussy/Doughty. Two euphoniums and two tubas.
Golliwogg's Cakewalk. Debussy/Schmidt. Two euphoniums and two tubas.
Golliwog's Cake Walk. Debussy/Yamamoto. Two euphoniums and three tubas.
Good Cheer Collection. Werden. Two euphoniums and two tubas.
Good Christian Men Rejoice. Vaughan. Two euphoniums and two tubas.
Gowbarrow Gavotte. Seivewright. Two euphoniums and two tubas.
Grab Bag. De Jong. Four tubas.
Graduale: Locus Iste. Bruckner. One euphonium and three tubas.
Grand Slam. Niehaus. Two euphoniums and two tubas.
Great Chromatic Fugue in G. Anderson. Three euphoniums and one tuba.
Great Crush Collision, The. Joplin/Schmidt. Two euphoniums and two tubas.
Great Crush Collision March. Joplin/Rauchut. Three euphoniums and two tubas.
Great Gate at Kiev from "Pictures at an Exhibition." Mussorgsky/Golas. Four euphoniums and four tubas.
Grecian Gambol. Miserendino. Three euphoniums and one tuba.
Greensleeves. Bullet/Buttery. Two euphoniums and two tubas.
Greensleeves. Rauch. Two euphoniums and two tubas.
Greensleeves. Vaughan. Two euphoniums and two tubas.
Gregory Is Here. Silver/Matteson. Three euphoniums, three tubas, and rhythm.
Grey Horse Polka. Orzechowski/Schmidt. Two euphoniums and two tubas.
Gymnopedia No. 1 from Three Gymnopedies. Satie/Rauch. Two euphoniums and two tubas.

H

Habanera. Bizet/Halferty. Two euphoniums and two tubas.
Hades. Iannaccone. Two euphoniums and two tubas.
Hall of Mirrors. Burn. Two euphoniums and two tubas.

Halleluja Chorus. Handel/Wilkinson. Two euphoniums and two tubas.
Hallelujah Chorus, The. Handel/Sabourin. Two euphoniums and two tubas.
Hallelujah Chorus, The. Handel/Stevens. Two euphoniums and two tubas.
Hallelujah! from "Messiah." Handel/Heiman. Two euphoniums and two tubas.
Halleluya. Wilkinson. Two euphoniums and two tubas.
Hands across the Sea. Sousa/Werden. Two euphoniums and two tubas.
Hanukkah Song. Garrett. Two euphoniums and two tubas.
Happy Birthday with Fanfare. Emberson. Two euphoniums and two tubas.
Happy Soul, The. Wilkinson. Two euphoniums and two tubas.
Hard Way. Carmody. Four tubas.
Harold Arlen Medley. Sample. Two euphoniums, two tubas, piano/guitar, bass, and drums.
Hauntings for Tuba Ensemble. Welcher. Two euphoniums and two tubas.
Hava Nigila. Wilkinson. Two euphoniums and two tubas.
Have I Found Her? Pilkington. Two euphoniums and two tubas.
Hawaiian Quintet '88. Anderson. Three euphoniums and two tubas.
Heavy Metal. Anderson. Two euphoniums, two tubas, and drum set.
Heavy Metal. Lamb. Two euphoniums and four tubas.
Heavyweights. Stewart. Three tubas.
Heel and Toe and Jenny Lind Polkas. Bewley. Two euphoniums and two tubas.
Heights of Halifax. McQueen. Two euphoniums and two tubas.
Heilig. Mendelssohn-Bartholdy/Butler. Four euphoniums and four tubas.
Helena Polka. Knoener. Two euphoniums and two tubas.
Helena Polka. Schmidt. Two euphoniums and two tubas.
Here Comes Santa Claus. Glover. Four euphoniums and two tubas.
Heritage Hill Suite. Hounsell/Luhring. Three euphoniums and two tubas.
Higashi-Nishi (East-West). Stevens. Four euphoniums and four tubas.
High Hattin' from "African Suite." Confrey/Vaughan. Two euphoniums and two tubas.
Highway 336. Goble. Two euphoniums and two tubas.
Hippo Trot. Szkutko. Four tubas.
Hippochondriac. Lawn. Four euphoniums and two tubas.
Hoffnung Festival. Hoffnung. Two euphoniums and two tubas.
Ho-Ho-Hoedown. Garrett. Two euphoniums and two tubas.
Horseman, The. Schumann/Wilkinson. Two euphoniums and two tubas.
How Much Is That Doggy in the Window? Woodcock. Two euphoniums and two tubas.
Howdy! Pegram. Three euphoniums, four tubas, and drums.
Humoresk, Op. 101, No. 7. Dvorák/Schmidt. Two euphoniums and two tubas.
Hungarian Dance No. 5. Brahms/Halferty. Two euphoniums and two tubas.
Hungarian Dance No. 5. Brahms/Seitz. Four tubas.
Hungarian Dance No. 5. Brahms/Woodcock. Two euphoniums and two tubas.
Hungarian March from "Faust." Berlioz/Werden. Two euphoniums and two tubas.
Hungarian Rhapsodie No. 2. Liszt/Seitz. Two euphoniums and two tubas.
Hungarian Rhapsody No. 2. Liszt/Fiegel. Four euphoniums and four tubas.
Hunter's Chorus from "Der Freischut." Weber/Schmidt. Two euphoniums and two tubas.
Hunter's Chorus from "Der Freischutz." Weber/Laws. Two euphoniums and two tubas.
Hunter's Chorus from Der Freischutz. Weber/Laws. Two euphoniums and two tubas.
Huntsmen's Choruses. Weber/Emilson. Two euphoniums and two tubas.
Hymn. Ross. Two euphoniums and two tubas.
Hymns for Many Occasions. Uber. Two euphoniums and two tubas.

I

I Do, I Undo, I Redo. Elliott. Three tubas and percussion.
I Got Rhythm. Gershwin/Stephens. Two euphoniums and two tubas.
I Heard the Bells on Christmas Day. Niehaus. Two euphoniums and two tubas.
I Know a Younge Maiden. Di Lasso/Cummings. Two euphoniums and two tubas.
I Never Saw a Moor for Four Tubas. Constantinides. Four tubas.
I Saw a Snake. . . . Naftel. Two euphoniums and two tubas.
Il est bel et bon. Passereau/Scoggin. Two euphoniums and two tubas.
Illusion. Konagaya. Two euphoniums, three tubas, and percussion.
Illustrations. Kerwin. Two euphoniums and two tubas.
Im Wald und duf der Heide. Garrett. Two euphoniums and one tuba.
Images for Tuba Quartet. Blatter. Four tubas.
Impresario Overture, The. Mozart/Knoener. Three euphoniums and two tubas.
Impromptu. Murzin. Two trombones (euphoniums) and one tuba.
Impromptu in Two Keys. Gershwin/LeClair. Two euphoniums and two tubas with drums.

In a Mello Tone. Ellington/Matteson. Three euphoniums, three tubas, and rhythm.

In Crystal Towers from Psalms, Songs, and Sonnets. Byrd/Hartin. Three tubas.

In Darkness . . . Dreaming. Cummings. Two euphoniums and two tubas.

In Dulci Jubilo/Jingle Bells. Vaughan. Two euphoniums and two tubas.

In Ein Hofbrau Haus/Augustin/Du, Du, Liegst Mir Im Herzen. Bewley. Two euphoniums and two tubas.

In Festo Transfigurationis Domini. Palestrina/Bristol. Tuba-Euphonium Press.

In Heaven There Is No Beer. Bewley. Two euphoniums and two tubas.

In Heaven There Is No Beer. Glover. Two euphoniums and two tubas.

In nominee Iesu omne genuflectatur. Després/Manzo. Two euphoniums and four tubas.

In Rememberance, September 11, 2001. Brandon. Three euphoniums and one tuba.

In the Good Old Summertime. Evans/Frackenpohl. Two euphoniums and two tubas.

In the Hall of the Mountain King. Grieg/Halferty. Two euphoniums and two tubas.

In the Hall of the Mountain King. Grieg/Werden. Two euphoniums and two tubas.

In the Hall of the Mountain King. Grieg/Wilkinson. Two euphoniums and two tubas.

In the Shadows, Op. 376B. Hewitt. Four tubas and celeste.

Incognitos. Bottje. Two euphoniums and two tubas.

Infant Holy. Vaughan. Two euphoniums and two tubas.

Infant Holy, Infant Lowly. Henry. Two euphoniums and two tubas.

Inflation. Lindenfeld. Three tubas.

Innocuous Incident. Gillam. Three tubas.

In-Phase-Out. Tautenhahn. Four tubas.

Instrumentalist March, The. Bewley. Two euphoniums and two tubas.

Intermezzo. Dörsam. Five tubas.

Intermezzo and March from Suite in E-flat Major. Holst/Schlesinger. Two euphoniums and two tubas.

International Tuba Day Music Books, Numbers 1 and 2. Day. Two euphoniums and two tubas.

Into the Magical Rain Forest for T/E Ens. and Tape. Ayers. Two euphoniums, two tubas, and tape.

Intonation I. Roark. Two euphoniums and two tubas.

Intonation II. Roark. Two euphoniums and two tubas.

Intrada, Romanze, and Scherzo. Uber. Four euphoniums and two tubas.

Intro. to Act III, Die Meistersinger. Wagner/Martin. Two euphoniums and three tubas.

Introduction and Rondino. Cook. Four tubas.

Iracunde. Maccolini. Two euphoniums and two tubas.

Irish Landscape. Tignor. Two euphoniums and two tubas.

Irish Tubas. Luhring. Two euphoniums and two tubas.

Irish Tune from County Derry. McKimm. Four euphoniums and four tubas.

It Was a Lover and His Lass. Morley/Bale. Two euphoniums and two tubas.

Italian Concerto, BWV 971, Movement I. Bach/Cranson. Two euphoniums and two tubas.

I've Been Working on the Railroad. Garrett. One euphonium and two tubas.

J

Jammin'. Stevens. Two euphoniums and two tubas.

Japanese Songs. Shinihara. Four euphoniums and two tubas.

Jason and the Golden Fleece. Raum. Two euphoniums and four tubas with percussion.

Java. Vaughan. Two euphoniums and two tubas.

Jenny Lind Polka. Grim. Two euphoniums and two tubas.

Jerusalem. Parry/Bale. Two euphoniums and two tubas.

Jesu, Joy of Man's Desiring. Bach/Hiraishi. Two euphoniums and two tubas.

Jesu, Joy of Man's Desiring. Bach/Thurston. Tuba quartet.

Jesu, Joy of Man's Desiring. Bach/Werden. Two euphoniums and two tubas.

Jesu, Joy of Man's Desiring. Bach/Yamamoto. Six euphoniums and two tubas.

Jesus Saves. Habegger. Two euphoniums and two tubas.

Jhon Come Kisse Me Now. Byrd/Winter. Two euphonium and two tubas.

Jingle Bell Rock. Glover. Four euphoniums and two tubas.

Jingle Bells. Pierpont/Garrett. Two euphoniums and tubas.

Jingle Bells. Pierpont/Vaughan. Two euphoniums and two tubas.

Jingle Bells. Pierpont/Olt. Two euphoniums and two tubas.

Jingle Bells. Robertson. Two euphoniums and two tubas.

Jingle Bells Waltz. Vaughan. Two euphoniums and two tubas.

Joe Avery. Garrett. Two euphoniums and two tubas.

Jones & Co. Szkutko. One euphonium and three tubas.

Joseph, Dearest—Joseph, Mine. Anderson. Two euphoniums and two tubas.

Joy to the World. Werden. Solo tuba with four-part tuba/euphonium ensemble.

Joy to the World. Werden. Solo tuba with two euphoniums and three tubas.

Joyful Euphonium Tuba Ensemble, Book 1. Two euphoniums and one tuba.

Joyful Euphonium Tuba Ensemble, Book 2. Two euphoniums and one tuba.

Joyful Euphonium Tuba Ensemble, Book 3. Two euphoniums and one tuba.

Joyful Euphonium Tuba Ensemble, Book 4. Two euphoniums and one tuba.

Joyful Euphonium Tuba Ensemble, Book 5. Two euphoniums and one tuba.

Joyful Euphonium Tuba Ensemble, Book 6. Two euphoniums and one tuba.

Joyful Euphonium Tuba Ensemble, Book 7. Two euphoniums and two tubas.

A Joyous Dialogue, Op. 11. Geib. Two tubas.

Jubilate (for Tubalaté). Newsome. Two euphoniums and two tubas.

Jumbos Holiday. Ernst-Thilo. One euphonium and three tubas.

Jupiter (Chorale) from "The Planets." Holst/Goble. Two euphoniums and two tubas.

Just a Closer Walk with Thee. Garrett. Two euphoniums and two tubas with optional keyboard and drums.

Just a Closer Walk with Thee. Hoesly. Two euphoniums and two tubas.

Just Do It. Bewley. Two euphoniums and two tubas.

K

Kanon. Senfl/Pardus. Two euphoniums and two tubas.

Kentucky Sunrise March. King/Butler. Two euphoniums and two tubas.

Kentucky Sunrise March. King/Knoener. Three euphoniums and two tubas.

Keystone Chops. Niehaus. Two euphoniums and two tubas.

Kierkegaard for Four Tubas. Kupferman. Four tubas.

Kilimanjaro. Fritze. Three trombones (euphoniums), one euphonium, and two tubas.

Kimiga-Yo. Anderson. Two euphoniums and two tubas.

King's Hunt, The. Bull/Howard. Two euphoniums and two tubas.

King's Hunt, The. Bull/Howard. Two euphoniums and two tubas.

Kiss Polka, The. Warren/Grim. Two euphoniums and two tubas.

Klezmer Collection "To Life." Wilkinson. Two euphoniums and two tubas.

Knoxville, 1974. Haddad. Two euphoniums and six tubas.

Kyrie from Requiem. Mozart/McGainey. Two euphoniums and two tubas.

L

La Cucaracha. Bewley. Two euphoniums and two tubas.

La Cumparsita. Rodrigues/Schanke. Two euphoniums and two tubas with optional percussion.

La Danza. Rossini/Smalley. Two euphoniums and two tubas.

La Donna e Mobile. Verdi/Robertson. Two euphoniums and two tubas.

La donna é mobile. Verdi/Roundtree. Two euphoniums and two tubas.

La Guercia. Heiman. Two euphoniums and two tubas.

La Morte dell' Oom (No Pah Intended). Self. Six euphoniums, six tubas, and two percussionists.

La Nicolina. Gussago/Schmidt. Two euphoniums and two tubas.

Lady, When I Behold. Wilbye. Two euphoniums and two tubas.

L'Albergona. Mortaro/Heiman. Two euphoniums and two tubas.

Lament. Kodaly/Gray. One euphonium and two tubas.

A Lament for Anne of Brittany. Moulu/Jacoby. Three euphoniums and two tubas.

Largo and Allegro. Krush. Two tubas.

Largo and Allegro from Sonata No. 4. Telemann/Drobnak. Two tubas.

Largo from Xerxes. Handel/Skillen. Two euphoniums and two tubas.

Last Polka, The. Blahnik and Schmidt. Two euphoniums and two tubas.

Lay a Garland. Pearsal/Manzo. Four euphoniums and four tubas.

Lazy Elephant Blues. Luis. One euphonium and three tubas.

Le Piccadilly. Satie/Hiraishi. Two euphoniums and two tubas.

Le Secret. Gautier/Werden. Three euphoniums and one tuba.

Legend of Camino Real. Friedrich. Two euphoniums and two tubas.

Leichte Ragtime-Trios (Easy Ragtime Trios). Heger. Two euphoniums and one tuba.

Leichte Volkslieder-Trios 6 (Easy Folksong Trios). Heger. Three tubas.

L'Emir aphone. Jous. Two euphoniums and two tubas.

Lento Espressivo. Ameller. Four tubas.

Les Baricades Mistérieuses. Couperin/Wilson. Two euphoniums and two tubas.

Les Ondes Rondeau. Couperin/Krzywicki. Two euphoniums and one tuba.

Let It Snow. Glover. Four euphoniums and two tubas.

Let the Bright Seraphim. Handel/Madeson. Two euphoniums and two tubas.

Leviathan Love. Schmidt. Two tubas.

Leviathans. Goble. Two euphoniums and two tubas.

Liberation of Sisyphus, The. Stevens. Solo tuba, four euphoniums, and four tubas.

Liberty Bell, The. Sousa/Robertson. Two euphoniums and two tubas.

Liberty Bell March, The. Sousa/Rauchut. Three euphoniums and two tubas.

Liebeslied. Kreisler/Woodcock. Two euphoniums and two tubas.
Liechtensteiner Polka. Kotscher and Lindt/Grim. Two euphoniums and two tubas.
Liechtensteiner Polka. Kotscher and Lindt/Robertson. Two euphoniums and two tubas.
Lift of the Foot, A. Baylock. Three euphoniums and three tubas with piano, acoustic bass, and drums.
Light Metal. Proctor. Two euphoniums and two tubas.
Lighthearted and Lowpitched. Miserendino. Three euphoniums and one tuba.
Lil Short'nin Funk. Krive. Five tubas.
Lili's Funk. Carolino. Four tubas and rhythm section.
Lilly Bell Quick Step. Friederich/Schmidt. Two euphoniums and two tubas.
Litaniae de Beata Virgine Mary. Palestrina/Bristol. Three euphoniums and two tubas.
A Little Four Tuba Music. Frackenpohl. Four tubas.
Little Hymn, A. Shoop. Two euphoniums and two tubas.
Little Lullaby. Luis. One euphonium and three tubas.
Little Madrigal for Big Horns. Hastings. One euphonium and two tubas.
Little Monster Music, A. Raum. Four euphoniums and twelve tubas.
Little Negro, The. Debussy/Hiraishi. Two euphoniums and two tubas.
Little Ole Softy. Matteson. Three euphoniums, three tubas, and rhythm.
Little Russian March from Symphony No. 2 in C Minor. Tchaikovsky/Goble. Two euphoniums and two tubas.
Little Suite for Tuba Quartet. Williams. Four tubas.
Lo, Country Sports. Weelkes/Hartin. Four tubas.
Lo, How a Rose. Vaughan. Two euphoniums and two tubas.
Lo, How a Rose E'er Blooming. Niehaus. Two euphoniums and two tubas.
Lo, How a Rose E'er Blooming. Praetorius/Spang. Two euphoniums and four tubas.
Lo, How a Rose E'er Blooming. Praetorius/Spang. Two euphoniums and two tubas.
Lo, How a Rose E'er Blooming. Werden. Two euphoniums and two tubas.
Lo, How a Rose E'er Blooming. Wilkinson. Two euphoniums and two tubas.
Lo Mi Son Giovinetta. Sweelinck/Hartin. Two tubas.
Loch Lomond. Forbes. Two euphoniums and two tubas.
Loch Lomond. Garrett. Two euphoniums and two tubas.
Loconic Overture. Pardus. Two euphoniums and two tubas.
Locus Iste. Bruckner/Sabourin. Two euphoniums and two tubas.
Londonderry Air. Garrett. Three euphoniums and two tubas.
Londonderry Air. Mehlan. Two euphoniums and two tubas.
Londonderry Air. Niehaus. Two euphoniums and two tubas.
Long Day Closes, The. Sullivan/Manzo. Four tubas.
Longer. Emberson. Two euphoniums and two tubas.
Lost Chord, The. Sullivan/Cummings. Three euphoniums and three tubas.
Love in the Afternoon: A Tone Poem. London. Four tubas.
Love Is a Secret Feeding Fire. Pilkington. Two euphoniums and two tubas.
Low-Down Trio, A. Hounsell. Tuba/euphonium trio.
Lucky Southern. Jarrett/Matteson. Three euphoniums, three tubas, and rhythm.
Ludus for Three Tubas. Nelhybel. Three tubas.
Lullaby. Robertson. Four tubas.
Lullaby and Dance. Hardt. Two euphoniums and two tubas.
Lute Dances. Baker. Two euphoniums and two tubas.
Lyke Wake Dirge, The. Bayliss. Two euphoniums and two tubas.
Lyric. Crist. Two euphoniums and two tubas.
Lyric Poem for Five Tubas. Frank. Two euphoniums and three tubas.
Lyric Tuba Waltz, The. Rosenberger. Two euphoniums and two tubas.

M

Mack, the Knight. Vaughan. Two euphoniums and two tubas.
Madrigale. Gesualdo/McClernan. Two euphoniums and three tubas.
Magic Flute (Die Zauberflote). Mozart/Doughty. Two euphoniums and two tubas.
Magic Flute Overture, The. Mozart/Bale. Two euphoniums and two tubas.
Magical, Mystical Rain Forest, The. Ayers. Three euphoniums and three tubas and recorded accompaniment.
Magnificat. Palestrina/Bristol. Two euphoniums and two tubas.
Malaguena. Lecuona/Senff. Four euphoniums and four tubas.
Male Voice for Brass. Parfrey. Two euphoniums and two tubas.
Manhattan Suite. Stevens. Four tubas.
Maple Leaf Rag. Joplin/Humble. Two euphoniums and two tubas.
Marce's Blues. Vaughan. Two euphoniums and two tubas.
March. Szkutko. Two euphoniums and two tubas.
March and Chorale. Butts. Two trombones (euphoniums) and two tubas.

March and Fugue for Two Tubas, Op. 40 and 55. Bourgeois. Two tubas.
March from "La Boheme." Puccini/Butler. Two euphoniums and two tubas.
March from "1941," The. Williams/Fiegel. Four euphoniums and four tubas with percussion.
March from Second Suite in F for Military Band. Holst/Werden. Three euphoniums and three tubas.
March from Second Suite in F for Military Band. Holst/Werden. Two euphoniums and two tubas.
March—FroT. Kerwin. Two euphoniums and two tubas.
March: Il Ritorno. Diero/Ferguson. Two euphoniums and two tubas.
March of Hare, The. Crump. Two euphoniums and two tubas.
March of the Priests from "The Magic Flute." Mozart/Sherman. Two euphoniums and two tubas.
March of the Times. Friedrich. Four euphoniums and four tubas.
March of the Toy Soldiers from the "Nutcracker." Tchaikovsky/Woodcock. Two euphoniums and two tubas.
March of the Toys. Vaughan. Two euphoniums and two tubas.
March to the Scaffold from Symphonie Fantastique. Berlioz/Granger. Four euphoniums and six tubas.
Mardi Gras Collection. Garrett. Two euphoniums and two tubas.
Marienlieder, Op. 22. Brahms/Stevens. Two euphoniums and two tubas.
Marriage of Figaro. Mozart/Fabrizio. Two euphoniums and two tubas.
Marriage of Figaro Overture. Mozart/Warren. Two euphoniums and three tubas.
Mars, The Bringer of War, from "The Planets." Holst/Butler. Three euphoniums and three tubas.
Mazurka No. 48, Op. 68 No. 2 "The Hoffnung Quartet." Chopin/Anderson. Four tubas.
Mean Thing Swing. Ellington/Vaughan. Two euphoniums and two tubas.
Medieval Night. Matchett. Two euphoniums and two tubas.
Medley of the Third Kind. Fiegel. Three euphoniums and two tubas.
Meet These People. Read. Two euphoniums and two tubas.
Meiso No Inga. Endo. Five euphoniums and one tuba.
Melissma. Hurt. Four tubas.
Melody (x3). Rozen. Two euphoniums and two tubas.
Melody Shop, The. King/Werden. Two euphoniums and two tubas.
Memory Trace. McGarr. Two euphoniums, two tubas, and media.
Menuet from Anna Magdalena's Notebook. Pezold/Shoop. Two euphoniums and two tubas.
Menuets. Handel/Halferty. Two euphoniums and two tubas.
Menuett, from Quartet, Op. 75. No. 13. Haydn/Humble. Two euphoniums and two tubas.
Merry Wives of Windsor Overture. Nicolai/Martin. Two euphoniums and three tubas.
Mery Men, The. Rimmer. Two euphoniums and two tubas.
Messenger of Spring, The. Pilkington. Two euphoniums and two tubas.
Messiah Suite. Handel/Heiman and Schmidt. Two euphoniums and two tubas.
Mexican Carnival. Shiner. Four trombones (euphoniums) and one tuba.
Mexican Hat Dance. Bewley. Two euphoniums and two tubas.
Mexican Song Medley, Set No. 1. Schanke. Two euphoniums and two tubas.
Mexican Song Medley, Set No. 2. Schanke. Two euphoniums and two tubas.
Michelle. Lennon and McCartney/Vaughan. Two euphoniums and two tubas.
Midsummer Songs. Cooman. Two euphoniums and two tubas.
Military Polonaise. Chopin/Bale. Two euphonium and two tubas.
Miniature Jazz Suite. Garrett. Two euphoniums and two tubas, piano, bass, and drums.
Miniature Jazz Suite #1. Niehaus. Two euphoniums and two tubas.
Miniature Suite, A. Cummings. Five euphoniums, five tubas, percussion, piano, and bass.
Miniatures. Friedrich. Three euphoniums and two tubas.
Miniatures at an Exhibition. Mussorgsky/Proctor. Two euphoniums and two tubas.
Miniatures for Four Valve Instruments. Hartley. Two euphoniums and two tubas.
Minuet. Anderson. Two euphoniums and two tubas.
Minuet. Bach/Schmidt. Two euphoniums and two tubas.
Minuet and Trio from Symphony No. 5. Schubert/Bale. Two euphoniums and two tubas.
Minuet from Symphony No. 40. Mozart/Ferriano. Three euphoniums and two tubas.
Minuet I from Partita No. 1. Bach/Lazar. One euphonium and one tuba.
Minute Waltz. Chopin/Mead. Two euphoniums and two tubas.
Minute Waltz. Chopin/Roundtree. Two euphoniums and two tubas.
Minute Waltz. Chopin/Werden. Two euphoniums and two tubas.
Misty. Garner/Stephens. Two euphoniums and two tubas.
Mixtures and Mutations. Jager. Two euphoniums and two tubas.

Mollusca. McLean. Four euphoniums and four tubas.
Mon Coeur se Recommende a Vous: Madrigal. Lasso/Robinson. Four tubas.
Montaggi for Four Tubas. Vazzana. Four tubas.
Mood Indigo. Ellington/Vaughan. Two euphoniums and two tubas.
Moon River. Glover. Two euphoniums and two tubas.
Moondance. Stevens. Four tubas.
Moonglow. Vaughan. Two euphoniums and two tubas.
Morning, Noon, and Night in Vienna Overture. Von Suppe/Butler. Two euphoniums and two tubas.
Moro Lasso. Gesualdo. Two euphoniums and two tubas.
Moro Lasso. Gesualdo/Anderson. Three euphoniums and two tubas.
Moro Lasso from Madrigal, Book VI. Gesualdo/Anderson. Three euphoniums and two tubas.
Motet "Cantate Domino." Di Lasso/Schmidt. Two euphoniums and one tuba.
Motet "Christe, Lux Vera." Palestrina/Block. Four tubas.
Mountain Songs. Milford. Two euphoniums and one tuba.
Mountains. Szkutko. Two euphoniums and two tubas.
Mouse Trap Blues. Raton/Garrett. Two euphoniums and two tubas.
Move. Davidson. Two euphoniums and two tubas.
Movement for Five Tubas. Schelokov. Five tubas.
Movin'—Groovin'. Kresin. Two euphoniums and two tubas with drums.
Mr. Bach Goes to Town (Prelude and Fugue in Swing). Kresin. Two euphoniums and two tubas with drums.
Musette. Bach/Luhring. Four tubas.
Music for International Tuba Day, Book I. Brandon. Two euphoniums and two tubas.
Music for International Tuba Day, Book II. Brandon. Two euphoniums and two tubas.
Music for Low Brass. Sydeman. Two trombones (euphoniums) and two tubas.
Music for the Stage, Op. 283. Uber. Two euphoniums and two tubas.
Music for Tuba Quartet. Nordhagen. Tuba quartet.
Music for Tubas. Blank. Four tubas.
Music for Tubas . . . Six of 'Em. Childs. Six tubas.
Music for Two Tubas. De Jong. Two tubas.
Music 4 Tubas. Stevens. Four tubas.
Musica De Lupus: Scenarios for the Continued Existence of a Misunderstood Friend—The Wolf. Buttery. Four tubas.
My Faith Looks Up to Thee. Habegger. Two euphoniums and two tubas.
My Father's Nigun Song. Wilkinson. Two euphoniums and two tubas.
My Melody Book. Nakagawa. Two tubas.
Mystical Music. Garrett. Two euphoniums and two tubas.

N

Nabucco Overture. Verdi/Bale. Two euphoniums and two tubas.
Nanourissma. Kauffman and Spang. Two euphoniums and two tubas.
National Emblem March. Bagley/Martin. Two euphoniums and three tubas.
National Emblem March. Bagley/Wilkinson. Two euphoniums and two tubas.
National Songs of America. Uber. Two euphoniums and two tubas.
Nations So Furiously Rage. Handel/Wilkinson. Two euphoniums and two tubas.
Native American Notes II: The Bitter Roots of Peace for Tuba-Euphonium Quartet. Steinke. Two euphoniums and two tubas with narrator.
Native American Suite. Paasch. Two euphoniums and two tubas.
Navigating the Noland Trail. Auberg. Two euphoniums and two tubas.
Nebulous. Blostein. Three euphoniums and three tubas.
Nessun Dorma. Puccini/Walton. Two euphoniums and two tubas.
New Frontiers. Friedrich. Four euphoniums and four tubas.
New When Tubas Waltz, The. Bartles. Three euphoniums and three tubas.
New York Hippodrome. Sousa/Knoener. Two euphoniums and two tubas.
New York, New York. Emberson. Two euphoniums and two tubas.
Night, The (It Has a Thousand Faces). Harrold. Two euphoniums and two tubas.
Night on Bald Mountain. Mussorgsky/Bale. Six euphoniums and six tubas with percussion.
Night on Bald Mountain. Mussorgsky/Curtis. Five euphoniums and four tubas with optional percussion.
Night Time. McGarr. Two euphoniums and two tubas with recorded accompaniment.
Night Train for Tubas. Stroud. Two euphoniums and two tubas.
Nightingale Sang in Berkeley Square, A. Maschwitz/Smalley. Two euphoniums and two tubas.
Nimrod from "Enigma Variations." Elgar/Forbes. Three euphoniums and three tubas.
Nine Duets. Handel/Dishinger. Two tubas.
No No Hate Yori (From beyond the Field). Censhu. Two euphoniums and two tubas.
Nocturne and Dance for Three Tubas. Danburg. Three tubas.
Nocturne from "Midsummer Night's Dream." Mendelssohn/Sommerville. Four euphoniums and two tubas.
Nocturne from Midsummernight's Dream. Mendelssohn/Bale. Two euphoniums and two tubas.

Noreen's Nocturne. Peterson/Keating. Two euphoniums and two tubas.
Norse Song. Schumann/Wilkinson. Two euphoniums and two tubas.
Nostalgia Medley. Sample. Two euphoniums, two tubas, piano/guitar, bass, and drums.
Now Hear This! Dempsey. Two euphoniums and two tubas.
Nu dækker sne den hele jord. Nørgård. Four euphoniums and four tubas.
Nuages. Reinhardt. Two euphoniums and two tubas.
Nun Danket Alle Gott. Cruger/Mason. Two euphoniums and two tubas.

O

O Canada. Glover. Two euphoniums and two tubas.
O' Come Emmanuel. Warren. Two euphoniums and two tubas.
O Isis und Osiris. Mozart/Spang. Two euphoniums and four tubas.
O Little Town of Bethlehem. Wedner/Vaughan. Two euphoniums and two tubas.
O Magnum Misterium. De Vittoria/Cummings. Two euphoniums and two tubas.
O Regem Coeli for Tuba Quartet. Victoria/Schwartz. Four tubas.
O Sing unto My Roundelay. Wesley/Manzo. Two euphoniums and three tubas.
O Vos Omnes (Motet). Victoria/Self. Four tubas.
Ocean Tide March with Hail Columbia. Friederich/Schmidt. Two euphoniums and two tubas.
Octave Variations. Stoll. Two euphoniums and two tubas.
Octubafest Polka for Tuba Ensemble. Fritze. Two euphoniums and three tubas.
Octubafest Song, The. Bewley. Two euphoniums, two tubas, and vocal solo.
Odd Couple, The. Albam. Two tubas.
Offering: A Sketch for Euphonium Solo and Tuba/Euphonium Quartet. Vaughan. Three euphoniums and two tubas.
Oh Dear, What Can the Matter Be? Bale. Four tubas.
Ohlone Suite. Cummings. Two euphoniums and two tubas.
Old Castle from "Pictures at an Exhibition," The. Mussorgsky/Golas. Three euphoniums and three tubas.
Old Comrades. Teike/Bewley. Two euphoniums and two tubas.
Old Comrades (Alte Kamaraden). Glover. Two euphoniums and two tubas.
Old German Folk Song, An. Hartin. Two euphoniums and two tubas.
Old King Cole. Niehaus. Two euphoniums and two tubas.
Oleo. Rollins/Matteson. Three euphoniums, three tubas, and rhythm.
On a Rocky Road. Kresin. Two euphoniums and two tubas with drums.
On Platform 2. Masson. Four tubas.
On Sabbath Day. Wilkinson. Two euphoniums and two tubas.
On Thin Ice. Mobberley. Four euphoniums and five tubas.
On This Day. Werden. Two euphoniums and two tubas.
One Slow. One Fast. Dutton. Two tubas.
Only Eight Days of Christmas. Vaughan. Two euphoniums and two tubas.
Os Justi. Bruckner/Sabourin. Four euphoniums and four tubas.
Outback Brass. Anderson. Two euphoniums and two tubas.
Overture from Carmen. Bizet/Seitz. Two euphoniums and two tubas.
Overture from Russlan and Ludmila. Glinka/Ferguson. Two euphoniums and two tubas.
Overture from the Marriage of Figaro. Mozart/Ferguson. Two euphoniums and two tubas.
Overture Solennelle (1812). Tchaikovsky/Bevan. Nine-part tuba/euphonium ensemble.
Overture Solennelle (1812). Tchaikovsky/Warren. Eight-part tuba/euphonium ensemble.
Overture to "The Magic Flute." Mozart/Rozen. Two euphoniums and two tubas.
Overture to the "Marriage of Figaro." Mozart/Gottschalk. Three euphoniums and two tubas.
Overture to Wilhelm Tell. Rossini/Seitz. Two euphoniums and two tubas.
Oyez! Has Any Found a Lad? Tomkins/Schmidt. Two euphoniums and two tubas.

P

Pachyderms in Paradise. Niehaus. Two euphoniums and two tubas.
Pachydermus Pinkus Lowus-Blowus; Adapted from the Score for Dumbo (1941). Fiegel. Four euphoniums, four tubas, auxiliary percussion, and film equipment.
Pacman Gets Caught. Fritze. Two euphoniums and two tubas.
Paddlin' Madelin Home. Woods/Goble. Two euphoniums and two tubas.
Pains of Esdraelon, The. Daughtry. One euphonium and two tubas.
Paloma Blanca. Glover. Two euphoniums and two tubas.
Para Duas Tubas. Pires. Two tubas.
Parade of the Wooden Tubas. Jessel/Shirer. One baritone, one euphonium, and two tubas.
Paraklesis. Canter. Two euphoniums, two tubas, and tambourine.
Partita for Tuba Quartet. Clews. Four tubas.
Partita in Four Parts. Praetorius/Bina. Two euphoniums and two tubas.

Partita, Op. 109. Lemeland. Four tubas.
Pascal's Victim. Naftel. Two euphoniums and two tubas.
Passacaglia and Fugue in C Minor. Bach/Garrett. Two euphoniums and three tubas.
Patapan. Gray. Two euphoniums and two tubas.
Pater Noster. Liszt/Manzo. Two euphoniums and two tubas.
Pathos. Friedrich. Three euphoniums and one tuba.
Pavan a 4. Schein/Schmidt. Two euphoniums and two tubas.
Pavan: The Funerals. Holborne/Hartin. Five tubas.
Pavane. Fauré/Bale. Two euphoniums and two tubas.
Pavane, Op. 50. Fauré/Wilson. Two euphoniums and two tubas.
Peacherine Rag. Joplin/Hiraishi. Two euphoniums and two tubas.
Peanuts Polka. Bewley. Two euphoniums and two tubas.
Pennsylvania Polka. Lee and Manners/Grim. Two euphoniums and two tubas.
Pennsylvania Polka. Lee and Manners/Robertson. Two euphoniums and two tubas.
Perpetual Motion. Paganini/Buttery. Two to seven players with piano.
Petit Caprice: In the Style of Offenbach. Rossini/Davis. Two euphoniums and two tubas.
Petite and Powerful: A Rag for T/E Quartet. Vaughan. Two euphoniums and two tubas.
Petite Marche. Ryker. One euphonium and one tuba and piano.
Pezzo Serioso. Samuel. Two tubas and one percussion.
Pictures at an Exhibition. Mussorgsky/Schlesinger. Two euphoniums and two tubas.
Pie Jesu. Fauré/Walton. Two euphoniums and two tubas.
Piece for Six Tubas. Svarda. Six tubas.
Piece for Solo Tuba and Tuba Quartet. Baker. Solo tuba with two euphoniums and two tubas.
Piece in Folk Style. Schumann/Werden. Three euphoniums and one tuba.
Pieces of Eight. Solomons. Two euphoniums and two tubas.
Pilgerchor aus Tannhäuser. Wagner/Seitz. Four tubas.
Pilgrim's Chorus from Tannhäuser. Wagner/Schmidt. Two euphoniums and two tubas.
Pinata. Bewley. Two euphoniums and one tuba.
Pineapple Rag. Joplin/Hiraishi. Two euphoniums and two tubas.
Pines of the Appian Way from "The Pines of Rome." Respighi/Forbes. Five euphoniums, four tubas, and percussion.
Pink Panther, The. Mancini/Krush. Two euphoniums and two tubas.
Pizzacato Polka. Strauss/Bale. Two euphoniums and two tubas.
Pizzacato Polka. Strauss/Bewley. Two euphoniums and two tubas.
Pizzacato Polka. Strauss/Grim. Two euphoniums and two tubas.
Pleasant Moments Rag. Joplin/Schmidt. Two euphoniums and two tubas.
Poet and Peasant Overture. Von Suppe/Bright. Two euphoniums and three tubas.
Poet and Peasant Overture. Von Suppe/Forbes. Three euphoniums, three tubas, and optional percussion.
Poker Chips. Self. Four tubas and vibraphone.
Polka March, The. Bewley. Two euphoniums and two tubas.
Polyphonic Rhyme No. 4. Sweelinck/Block. Two tubas.
Pop Suite. Frackenpohl. Two euphoniums and two tubas.
Pop Suite No. 2. Frackenpohl. One euphonium and one tuba.
Postlude on "Willingham." Abt/Bright. Two euphoniums and two tubas.
Power for Four Tubas. Stevens. Four tubas.
Prairie Suite. Paasch. Two euphoniums and two tubas.
Präludium. Hilgers. One euphonium and four tubas.
Prayer before the Close of Day. Solomons. Two euphoniums and two tubas.
Prelude I. Gershwin/Kresin. Two euphoniums and two tubas with drums.
Prelude II. Gershwin/Kresin. Two euphoniums and two tubas with drums.
Prelude III. Gershwin/Kresin. Two euphoniums and two tubas with drums.
Prelude and Dance. Fritze. Two euphoniums and two tubas.
Prelude and Fugue. Bach/Bale. Two euphoniums and two tubas.
Prelude and Fugue. McCurdy. Two tubas.
Prelude and Fugue in C Minor. Bach/Gray. Two euphoniums and two tubas.
Prelude and Fugue in D Minor (BWV 554). Bach/Barnes. Four euphoniums and four tubas.
Prelude and Fugue in G. Bach/Sabourin. Two euphoniums and two tubas.
Prelude and Fugue in G Minor. Bach/Barnes. Tuba-euphonium quartet.
Prelude and Fugue in G Minor. Bach/Sabourin. Two euphoniums and two tubas.
Prelude and Fugue in G Minor, BWV 558. Bach/Wilson. Two euphoniums and two tubas.
Prelude and Fugue No. 3. Schumann, C./Manzo. Two euphoniums and two tubas.
Prelude and Fugue No. 16. Bach/Schmidt. Two euphoniums and two tubas.
Prelude and Fugue No. 22. Bach/Schanke. Two euphoniums and two tubas.
Prelude and Groove. Lee. Two euphoniums and two tubas.

Prelude and Rondino. Willis. Two euphoniums and two tubas.
Prelude and Tarantella. Danburg. Two tubas.
Prelude and Voluntary for Four Tubas. Gibbons/Self. Four tubas.
Prelude, Dance, and Fanfare. Beck. One euphonium and one tuba.
Prelude from "Te Deum." Charpentier/Schmidt. Two euphoniums and two tubas.
Prelude in C. Bach/Shoop. Three euphoniums and two tubas.
Prelude #4 for Tuba Quartet. Chopin/Hendricks. Four tubas.
Prelude on Theme of Chesnokov. Alexander. Two euphoniums and two tubas with chimes.
Preludio. Rodgers. Two euphoniums and two tubas.
Preludio and Fuga a 8 for Tuba and Euphonium Octet. Torre. Four euphoniums and four tubas.
Pretty Forms. Dutton. Two tubas.
Prima Dona Waltz. Friederich/Schmidt. Two euphoniums and two tubas.
Procession of the Nobles. Rimsky-Korsakov/Butler. Two euphoniums and two tubas.
Promenade. Vasconi. Two euphoniums and two tubas.
Promenade from "Pictures at an Exhibition." Mussorgsky/Golas. Two euphoniums and two tubas.
Prophecy. Konagaya. Solo euphonium, four euphoniums, and four tubas.
Psalm. Gates. Three trombones, one euphonium, and one tuba.
Puppetry. Uber. Four euphoniums and two tubas.
Purple Carnival, The. Alford/Knoener. Three euphoniums and two tubas.
Puttin' on the Ritz. Berlin/Niehaus. Two euphoniums and two tubas.

Q

Quadrant. Hoesly. Two euphoniums and two tubas.
Quand La Terre Au Printemps. LeJune. Four tubas.
Quartet. Ionel. Four tubas.
Quartet. Regan. Two euphoniums and two tubas.
Quartet Fantasy. Childs. Four tubas.
Quartet for Brass. Ramsoe/Buttery. Two euphoniums and two tubas.
Quartet for Low Brass. Bulla. Two euphoniums and two tubas.
Quartet for Tubas. Ball. Two E♭ tubas and two BB♭ tubas.
Quartet for Tubas. Brandon. Two euphoniums and two tubas.
Quartet for Tubas. Deak. One euphonium and three tubas.
Quartet for Tubas. Haddad. Four tubas.
Quartet for Tubas. Holmes. Two euphoniums and two tubas.
Quartet for Tubas. Jones. Four tubas.
Quartet for Tubas. Payne. Four tubas.
Quartet for Tubas. Tamura. Four tubas.
Quartet 4. Ellin. Four tubas.
Quartet No. 1, "Glyder Landscape." Smalley. Two euphoniums and two tubas with optional percussion.
Quartet, Op. 73. Fodi. Two euphoniums and two tubas.
Quartets for All. Stoutamire. Three euphoniums and one tuba.
Quartets for Brass, Volume I; Advanced. Marcellus. Three euphoniums and one tuba.
Quartets for Brass, Volume I; Easy-Intermediate. Marcellus. Three euphoniums and one tuba.
Quartets for Brass, Volume I; Intermediate. Marcellus. Three euphoniums and one tuba.
Quartets for Low Brass, Volume I: Traditional Favorites. Bulla. Two euphoniums and two tubas.
Quartets for Low Brass, Volume II: Spirituals. Bulla. Two euphoniums and two tubas.
Quartets for Low Brass, Volume III: Fanfares and Anthems. Bulla. Two euphoniums and two tubas.
Quartett Album. Michel. Two euphoniums and two tubas.
Quartetto for Four Tubas. Van Vactor. Two euphoniums and two tubas.
Quartour pour Tubas. Fasce. Four tubas.
Quatour. Fasce. Four tubas.
Quatre Chansons Pour Tuba Quatuor (French Suite for Tuba Quartet). Dempsey. Two euphoniums and two tubas.
Que Pasa. Schlesinger. One euphonium and six tubas.
Quest, The. Salotti. Two euphoniums and two tubas.
Questa o Quella. Verdi/Wilkinson. Two euphoniums and two tubas.
Quid Petis O Fili. Pygott/Thornton. Four tubas.
Quintet. Báthory-Kitsz. One euphonium and four tubas.
Quintet. White. Three euphoniums and two tubas.
Quintuple Overlays. Anderson. Two euphoniums and two tubas with two trumpets and percussion.
Quodlibitus Bibendum (The Drinking Quodlibet) for Tuba Quartet. Rollin. Four tubas.
Qvem uidistis pastores. Prenner/Manzo. Solo euphonium with two euphoniums and two tubas.

R

Radetzky March. Strauss/Grim. Two euphoniums and two tubas.
Radetzky March. Strauss/Knoener. Two euphoniums and two tubas.
Rag. Ferriano. Two euphoniums and two tubas.
Ragnarok. Belden. One euphonium and one tuba.
Rag-time Dance. Joplin/Schmidt. Two euphoniums and two tubas.
Rag-Time Dance. Joplin/Werden. Two euphoniums and two tubas.

Ragtime. Wilhelm. Two tubas.
Raven and the First Man, The. Rollin. Two euphoniums and two tubas.
Recital Duets for Two Tubas. Brandon. Two tubas.
Recitative for Four Tubas and Cantor. McCurdy. Four tubas and male vocalist.
Red Raven Polka. Bewley. Two euphoniums and two tubas.
Red River Valley. Garrett. One euphonium and two tubas.
Red Wing Polka. Bewley. Two euphoniums and two tubas.
Reflections. Medek. Four tubas.
Reflections on a Park Bench. Beale. Six euphoniums and six tubas.
Renaissance Choral Music, Vol. I. Drobnak. Two euphoniums and two tubas.
Renaissance Choral Music, Vol. II. Drobnak. Two euphoniums and two tubas.
Requiem for a Dead Little Cat. Ernst-Thilo. One euphonium and three tubas.
Requiem for Wounded Knee. Raum. Two tubas, narrator, and piano.
Resonances. Dutton. Two euphoniums and two tubas.
Rest and Recreation. Skempton. Two euphoniums and two tubas.
Rev Bill Bailey. Cannon/Vaughan. Two euphoniums and two tubas.
Revecy venir du printans. LeJeune/Roundtree. Two euphoniums and two tubas.
Revolutionary Étude. Chopin/Bale. Four euphoniums and three tubas.
Rhapsody in G Minor, Op. 79, No. 2. Brahms/Siekmann. Four euphoniums and two tubas.
Ricercar. Gabrieli/Bale. Two euphoniums and two tubas.
Ricercar Del Duodecimo Tuono. Gabrieli/Barth. Two euphoniums and two tubas.
Ricercar Del Duodecimo Tuono. Gabrieli/Schmidt. Two euphoniums and two tubas.
Ricercar del Primo Tuono. Palestrina/Schmidt. Two euphoniums and two tubas.
Ricercare del Duodècimo Tono. Gabrieli/Davis. Two euphoniums and two tubas.
Ricerdar a Tre Voci. Willaert/Hartin. Three tubas.
Rich Tradition: A Tribute to Rich Matteson. Bewley. Three euphoniums, three tubas, and rhythm.
Richter 7.8 for 12 Low Brass Instruments. Schudel. Three euphoniums and nine tubas.
Ride of the Valkyries. Wagner/Uber. Two euphoniums and two tubas.
Rienzi Overture. Wagner/Bright. Two euphoniums and three tubas.
Rings. Gray. Two euphoniums and two tubas.
Rip 'Em Up, Joe. Garrett. Two euphoniums and two tubas with optional keyboard and drums.
Riverwest Rag. Vaughan. Two euphoniums and two tubas.
Romance for Bass Tuba. Hawker. Solo tuba, two euphoniums, and one tuba.
Ronda's First Suite (Duet for Two Tubas). Vaughan. Two tubas.
Ronde and Saltarelle. Susato/Winter. Two euphoniums and two tubas.
Rondeau. Mouret/Cummings. Two euphoniums and three tubas.
Rondeau. Mouret/Roundtree. Two euphoniums and two tubas.
Rondeau. Mouret/Stevens. Two euphoniums and two tubas.
Rondo. Hook/Garrett. Two euphoniums and two tubas.
Rosa Mystica. Cottrell. Three euphoniums and two tubas.
Rosamünde. Knoener. Two euphoniums and two tubas.
Rudolph the Red-Nosed Reindeer. Marks/Mehlan. Two euphoniums and two tubas.
Rule Brittania. Beethoven/Werden. Two euphoniums and two tubas.
Runabout. Bewley. Two euphoniums and two tubas.
Russian Sailor's Dance. Gliere/Diamond. Two euphoniums and two tubas.
Russian Sailors' Dance from the Red Poppy. Gliere/Weaver. Four euphoniums and three tubas.

S

Sabeltanz. Khatchaturian/Seitz. Two euphoniums and two tubas.
Sai Kai (The Reunion). Censhu. Two euphoniums and two tubas.
Saints. McCurdy. Four tubas.
Saints, The. McAdams. Two euphoniums and two tubas.
Sakura, Sakura. Shoop. Two euphoniums and two tubas.
Salut d'Amour. Elgar/Robertson. Two euphoniums and two tubas.
Salutation Fanfare. Fritze. Three euphoniums and two tubas.
Salvation Is Created. Tchesnokov/Golas. Four euphoniums and four tubas.
Salvation Is Created. Tschesnokoff/Knoener. Three euphoniums and two tubas.
Salvation Is Created. Tschesnokoff/Lee. Three euphoniums and three tubas.
Sammy's Freilach. Wilkinson. Two euphoniums and two tubas.
Santa Claus Is Comin' to Town. Glover. Four euphoniums and two tubas.
Santa Claus Is Coming to Town. Vaughan. Two euphoniums and two tubas.
Santa Wants a Tuba for Christmas. Bewley. Two euphoniums, two tubas, opt. vocal, and rhythm.
Santa's Favorites. Vaughan. Two euphoniums and two tubas.
Saraband and Gigue for Tuba Quartet, Op. 43. Owen. Four tubas.

Sarabande. Bach/Howard. Two euphoniums and two tubas.
Sarabande. Bach/Howard. Two euphoniums and two tubas.
Sarabande and Bouree. Bach/Yodo. Two euphoniums and two tubas.
Sarabande and Variations. Handel/Barth. Two euphoniums and two tubas.
Sarabande, Gavottes, and Gigue from Cello Suite VI. Bach/Frackenpohl. Two euphoniums and two tubas.
Satin Doll. Ellington/Stephens. Two euphoniums and two tubas.
Satin Doll. Ellington/Vaughan. Two euphoniums and two tubas.
Sault Suite. Goble. Two euphoniums and two tubas.
Scènes de Paris. Gourlay. Two euphoniums and two tubas.
Scherzando for Tubular Octet. Knox. Four euphoniums and four tubas.
Scherziapriori II. Dressler. Two euphoniums and two tubas.
Scherzo. Ferriano. Two euphoniums and two tubas.
Scherzo. Sanson. Two euphoniums and two tubas.
Scherzo from Symphony No. 2. Borodin/Bale. Two euphoniums and two tubas.
Schweigt der Menschen laute Lust. Hensel-Mendelssohn/Manzo. Two euphoniums and two tubas.
Scotch-Irish Medley. Garrett. Two euphoniums and two tubas.
Sea Chanty for Three. Anderson. Three tubas.
Sea Songs. Langer. Two euphoniums and two tubas.
Sea Tubas. Minerd. Two euphoniums and two tubas.
Searching for the Truth. Pleshak. Two euphoniums and two tubas.
Seguidillas: Repetitions and Ostinatos for Tuba Ensemble. Forte. Four euphoniums, four tubas, and two optional percussion.
Selections from 42nd Street. Warren/Minerd. Two euphoniums and two tubas.
Selections from Symphonien auff Conzerten-Manier. Scheidt/Hartin. Three tubas.
Semper Fidelis. Sousa/Bale. Two euphoniums and two tubas.
Semper Fidelis. Sousa/Morris. Two euphoniums and two tubas.
Semper Fidelis. Sousa/Sabourin. Two euphoniums and two tubas.
Sentimental Journey. Vaughan. Two euphoniums and two tubas.
Sept Peches Capitauz (Seven Major Sins). Morel. Four tubas.
Sequences. Friedrich. Four euphoniums and four tubas.
Serenade. Schubert/Robertson. Two euphoniums and two tubas.
Serenade Eine Kleine Tuba Musik for Four Tubas. K. 525. Mozart/Fletcher. Four tubas.
Serenade for Four Tubas. Presser. Four tubas.
Serenade for String Orchestra (Fifth Movement—Allegro Vivace). Dvorák/Brandon. Three euphoniums and two tubas.
Serenade for String Orchestra (First Movement—Moderato). Dvorák/Brandon. Three euphoniums and two tubas.
Serenade for String Orchestra (Fourth Movement—Larghetto). Dvorák/Brandon. Three euphoniums and two tubas.
Serenade for String Orchestra (Second Movement—Tempo di Valse). Dvorák/Brandon. Three euphoniums and two tubas.
Serenade for String Orchestra (Third Movement—Vivace). Dvorák/Brandon. Three euphoniums and two tubas.
Serenade for Tubas. McKimm. Four euphoniums and four tubas.
Serene Voices: Music for Tuba Quartet. Kosteck. Four tubas.
Serious Suite for Three Tubas, The. Blair. Three tubas.
Serpentine Shadows. Benson. Two tubas.
Sesame Street. Raposo. Vaughan. Two euphoniums and two tubas.
Seven Duets for Tubas. Butterfield. Two tubas.
Seven Menuets KV65A. Mozart/Dishinger. Two tubas.
Seven Miniatures (Based on Native American Themes). Paasch. One euphonium and one tuba.
Seven Tuba Duets. Presser. Two tubas.
7 22 73 for Tuba Quartet. Ott. Two euphoniums, two tubas, and tape.
Seventeen Come Sunday. Vaughan Williams/Butler. Two euphoniums and two tubas.
Shades of Gray. Wilson. Two euphoniums and two tubas.
Shadow-Graph. Uber. Three euphoniums and one tuba.
Shall We Dance? Keating. Two euphoniums and two tubas.
Shape-Note Songs. Hartley. Two euphoniums and two tubas.
Shapes ïn Bronze. Ross. Two euphoniums and two tubas.
Sheep May Safely Graze. Bach/Robertson. Two euphoniums and two tubas.
Sherelle. Wilkinson. Two euphoniums and two tubas.
Shinju (May Tree). Censhu. Two euphoniums and two tubas.
Ship on Fire. Russell/Lee. Two euphoniums, two tubas, and voice.
Shoes. Carolino. Five tubas and rhythm section.
Short Piece for Tuba and Euphonium. Powell. One euphonium and one tuba.
Short'in Bread. Warren. Four tubas.
Siamang Suite. Canter. Two euphoniums and two tubas.
Sieben Miniaturen Fur Vier Tuben (Seven Miniatures for Four Tubas). Kochan. Four tubas.

Siegfried's Funeral March. Wagner/Bright. Two euphoniums and three tubas.
Signals for Tuba Trio. Uber. Three tubas.
Silent Night. Gruber/Vaughan. Two euphoniums and two tubas.
Silent Night. Vaughan. Two euphoniums and two tubas.
Silent Streets for Euphonium and Tuba. Uber. One euphonium and one tuba.
Silver Bells. Glover. Four euphoniums and two tubas.
Silver Bells. Stroud. Two euphoniums and two tubas.
Simple Gifts. Fritze. Solo tuba. two euphoniums, and two tubas.
Since You've Asked. Collins/Buttery. Two euphoniums and two tubas.
Singing in the Rain. Brown/Stephens. Two euphoniums and two tubas.
Six Baroque Pieces for Two Tubas. Zychowicz. Two tubas.
Six Canonic Sonatas. Telemann/Forbes. Two bass tubas.
Six Canonic Sonatas. Telemann/Forbes. Two contrabass tubas.
Six Chansons. Hindemith/Lane. Two euphoniums and two tubas.
Six Duets. Hartman/Torchinsky. Two tubas.
Six Duets. Telemann/Drobnak. Two tubas.
Six Etude. Defaye. Two tubas.
Six German Folk Songs. Brahms/Shoop. Two euphoniums and two tubas.
Six Preludes for Euphonium and Tuba, Op. 246C. Hewitt. One euphonium and one tuba.
Six Roundabouts. Forbes. Two tubas.
Six Sonatas for Two Tubas. Telemann/Erion. Two tubas.
Six Trios. Schein/Schmidt and Heiman. Two euphoniums and one tuba.
Six Tuba Duets. Schlesinger. Two tubas.
Sixteen Christmas Duets. Matchett. Two tubas.
Sixteen Tons. Anderson. Solo tuba and three euphoniums.
Skaters' Waltzes, The. Waldteufel/Konagaya. Two euphoniums and two tubas.
Slavonic Dances, Op. 46, No. 1. Dvorák/Butler. Two euphoniums and three tubas.
Sleeping Giants. Niehaus. Two euphoniums and two tubas.
Sleeping Tuba Waltz. Tchaikovsky/Fletcher. Four tubas.
Sleigh Ride. Anderson/Glover. Two euphoniums and two tubas.
Sleigh Ride. Anderson/Rauch. Two euphoniums and two tubas.
Soft Shoo for Two Euphoniums and Two Tubas. Stuart. Two euphoniums and two tubas.
Soldiers' Chorus from Faust, The. Bizet/Bale. Six euphoniums and five tubas.
Solemn Promise. Langer. Two euphoniums and two tubas.
Solfeggietto. Bach, C. P. E./Roberts. Two euphoniums and two tubas.
Solfegietto. Bach, C. P. E./Howard. Two euphoniums and two tubas.
Some Loose Canons. Dutton. Two tubas.
Somewhere over the Rainbow. Arlen/Matteson. Three euphoniums, three tubas, and rhythm.
Sonata. Gabrieli/Schmidt. Two euphoniums and two tubas.
Sonata. Kelly. One euphonium and one tuba.
Sonata. Scarlatti/Schmidt. Two euphoniums and two tubas.
Sonata. Speer/Schmidt. Two euphoniums and two tubas.
Sonata Da Chiesa. Corelli/Morris. Two tubas and piano.
Sonata Da Chiesa A Tre. Corelli/Dutton. Three tubas.
Sonata da Chiesa in E Minor, Op. 3. No. 7. Corelli/Pitts. Three tubas.
Sonata for Two Bass Tubas. Ryker. Two tubas.
Sonata for Two Bass Tubas. Rÿker. Two tubas.
Sonata for Two Tubas. K.V. 292. Mozart/Conner. Two tubas.
Sonata from "Die Bankelsangerlieder." Cummings. Two euphoniums and three tubas.
Sonata No. 1. Mozart/Wilkinson. Two euphoniums and two tubas.
Sonata No. One. Israel. Two tubas.
Sonata No. 2. Pezel/Cummings. Two euphoniums and three tubas.
Sonata No. 2. Pezel/Stevens. Two euphoniums and two tubas.
Sonata No. Two. Israel. Two tubas.
Sonata No. 3. Pezel/Cummings. Three euphoniums and two tubas.
Sonata No. 4. Handel/Little. Two euphoniums and one tuba.
Sonata No. 10, Op. 5. Corelli/Madeson. Two euphoniums and two tubas.
Sonata No. 13 for Double T/E Choir. Gabrieli/Varner. Four euphoniums and four tubas.
Sonata #15. Reiche/Schmidt. Two euphoniums and two tubas.
Sonata #18. Reiche/Schmidt. Two euphoniums and two tubas.
Sonata No. 22. Pezel/Cummings. Three euphoniums and two tubas.
Sonata, Op. 5. No. 4. Telemann/Dutton. Two tubas.
Sonata Pastorale (K. 397). Fux/Hartin. Two tubas and piano.
Sonata "Pathetique." Beethoven/Werden. Two euphoniums and two tubas.
Sonata Pian e Forte. Gabrieli/Warren. Eight-part tuba/euphonium ensemble.
Sonate en Trio Vivace. Bach/Cazes. Four tubas.
Sonatina for Two Tubas. Vaughan. Two tubas.
Song and Dance. Frackenpohl. One euphonium, one tuba, and piano.
Song and Dance No. 3. Dutton. Four tubas.

Song of Memory. Fentress. Three euphoniums and one tuba.
Song without Words. Schlesinger. Two euphoniums and two tubas.
Songs in the Fight against Rum (Songs of Might to Cheer the Fight in the Blight of Liquordom). Garbáge. Two euphoniums, two tubas, tenor solo, barbershop quartet, and mixed chorus.
Songs of the British Isles. Werden. Two euphoniums and two tubas.
Sorcerer's Apprentice, The. Dukas/Bale. Six euphoniums and five tubas with percussion.
Sounding for Tuba/Euphonium Quartet. Matchett. Two euphoniums and two tubas.
Sousa Surrenders. Garbáge. Three euphoniums, three tubas, and optional timpani.
Southwestern Brass. Friedrich. Four euphoniums and four tubas.
Speak Low. Vaughan. Two euphoniums and two tubas.
Spielheft 1. Rener. One euphonium and one tuba.
Spinning Song. Ellmenreich/Rauch. Two euphoniums and two tubas.
Spiritual Jazz Suite. Niehaus. Two euphoniums and two tubas.
Splinters. Stevens. Two tubas.
Sponger Money. Buttery. Two euphoniums, two tubas, and percussion.
Spoofy. Matteson. Three euphoniums, three tubas, and rhythm.
Springtime Polka. Knoener. Two euphoniums and two tubas.
St. Louis Blues. Handy/Holcombe. Two euphoniums and two tubas.
St. Louis Blues. Hoesly. Two euphoniums and two tubas.
St. Nicholas Ground. Frackenpohl. Two euphoniums and two tubas.
St. Paul Waltz. Grim. Two euphoniums and two tubas.
Star Spangled Banner. Glover. Two euphoniums and two tubas.
Star Spangled Banner, The. Key and Smith/Matchett. Two euphoniums and two tubas.
Star Spangled Banner, The. Key and Smith/Robertson. Two euphoniums and two tubas.
Star Spangled Banner, The. Key/Anderson. Three euphoniums and one tuba.
Stars and Stripes Forever, The. Sousa/Niehaus. Two euphoniums and two tubas.
Stars and Stripes Forever, The. Sousa/Schmidt. Two euphoniums and two tubas.
Stars and Stripes Forever, The. Sousa/Werden. Two euphoniums and two tubas.
Stately Procession. Byrd/Bright. Two euphoniums and two tubas.
Stella by Starlight. Sample. Two euphoniums, two tubas, piano/guitar, bass, and drums.
Stephen Foster Jazz Suite. Niehaus. Two euphoniums and two tubas.
Stompin' at the Savoy. Goodman/Matteson. Three euphoniums, three tubas, and rhythm.
Stormy Weather. Arlen/Stephens. Two euphoniums and two tubas.
Strange Man. Wilkinson. Tuba/euphonium quartet.
Strauss Waltzes. Strauss/Bewley. Two euphoniums and two tubas.
Strenuous Life, The. Joplin/Hiraishi. Two euphoniums and two tubas.
Strenuous Life, The: A Ragtime Two-Step. Joplin/Lex. Two euphoniums and two tubas.
Strike Up the Band. Gershwin/Bale. Two euphoniums and two tubas.
String Band Polka, The. Stephens/Grim. Two euphoniums and two tubas.
String of Tones. Roper. Two euphoniums and two tubas.
Study on a Theme from Peter Grimes. Ross. Two euphoniums and two tubas.
Substructures I. Gottschalk. Two euphoniums and eight tubas.
Sub-Terrestrial Sounds. Dutton. Five tubas.
Sub-Voce Entropy. Leavitt. Two tubas.
Such Sweet Sorrow. Keating. Two euphoniums and two tubas.
Suite for Four Bass Instruments. Lyon. Two euphoniums and two tubas.
Suite for Four Bass Tubas, Op. 67. Uber. Four tubas.
Suite for Four Tubas. Masuda. Four tubas.
Suite for Harp and Two Tubas. Hewitt. Two tubas and harp.
Suite for Seven Tubas. Dutton. Seven tubas.
Suite for Six Tubas. Ott. Six tubas.
Suite for Six Tubas. Presser. Six tubas.
Suite for Three Tubas. Jones. Three tubas.
Suite for Three Tubas. Presser. Three tubas.
Suite for Tuba and Euphonium. Lee. One euphonium and one tuba.
Suite for Tuba Duo, Op. 376. Hewitt. Two tubas.
Suite for Tuba Quartet. Frackenpohl. Two euphoniums and two tubas.
Suite for Tuba Quartet. Friedrich. Two euphoniums and two tubas.
Suite for Two. Stevens. Two tubas.
Suite for Two Tubas. Geer. Two tubas.
Suite for Two Tubas. Wilder. Two tubas.
Suite from Album for the Young. Schumann/Shoop. Two euphoniums and two tubas.
Suite from Album for the Young. Schumann/Werden. Two euphoniums and two tubas.
Suite from "Silverado." Broughton/Fiegel. Four euphoniums, four tubas, two percussion, and film.
Suite in Blue. Payne. Four tubas.
Suite in D♭ for Tubas and Euphoniums. Watts. Two euphoniums and two tubas.
Suite in D Minor, Cello Suite No. 2. Bach/Frackenpohl. One euphonium and one tuba.
Suite in Miniature. Catelinet. Two tubas.
Suite No. 1 from the Danserye. Susato/Schmidt. Two euphoniums and two tubas.

Suite No. 2 for Tuba Quartet. Frackenpohl. Two euphoniums and two tubas.
Suite No. 2 for Tuba Quartet. Friedrich. Two euphoniums and two tubas.
Suite No. 2 from Album for the Young. Schumann/Shoop. Two euphoniums and two tubas.
Suite No. 16 for Two Tubas. Haugland. Two tubas.
Suite No. 17 for Two Tubas. Haugland. Two tubas.
Suite No. 18 for Two Tubas. Haugland. Two tubas.
Suite No. 19 for Two Tubas. Haugland. Two tubas.
Suite No. 20 for Two Tubas. Haugland. Two tubas.
A Suite of Elizabethan Madrigals. Hartin.
Suite of English Madrigals. Stevens. Two euphoniums and three tubas.
Summertime. Gershwin/Stephens. Two euphoniums and two tubas.
Sunrise Sunset. Bock/Anderson. Three euphoniums and one tuba.
Suo-duo. Saari. Two tubas.
Susie Polka. Grim. Two euphoniums and two tubas.
Suspended in Frozen Velocity: Image Music IX from "Songs of the Fire Circles." Steinke. Two euphoniums and two tubas.
Swanee River. Foster/Warren. Two euphoniums and two tubas.
Sweet Georgia Brown. Bernie, Pinkard, and Casey/Fragomeni. Two euphoniums and two tubas.
Sweet 'n' Low, Book 1. Sparke. One euphonium and one tuba.
Sweet 'n' Low, Book 2. Sparke. One euphonium and one tuba.
Sweet 'n' Low, Book 3: A First Christmas Selection. Sparke. One euphonium and one tuba.
Sweet 'n' Low, Book 4: A Second Christmas Selection. Sparke. One euphonium and one tuba.
Sweet 'n' Low, Book 5: Caribbean Cocktail. Sparke. One euphonium and one tuba.
Swing Low, Sweet Chariot. Alexander. Two euphoniums and two tubas.
Swing Low, Sweet Chariot. McAdams. One euphonium and two tubas.
Swing Low, Sweet Chariot. Vaughan. Three euphoniums and two tubas.
Swingin' Ukrainian Christmas. Niehaus. Two euphoniums and two tubas.
Swipesy. Joplin/Werden. Two euphoniums and two tubas.
Switched-Down Bach. Jones. One euphonium and two tubas.
Symphony No. 1 (First Movement). Beethoven/Warren. Eight-part tuba/euphonium ensemble.

T

Take Five. Desmond/Luis. One euphonium and three tubas.
Take Me Out to the Ballgame. Anderson. Three euphoniums and two tubas.
Take Me Out to the Ballgame. Vaughan. Two euphoniums and two tubas.
Tambourin. Gossec/Bale. Two euphoniums and two tubas.
Tancredi Overture. Rossini/Bale. Two euphoniums and two tubas.
Tangents: An Overture for Tuba Ensemble. Barnes. Four euphoniums and four tubas.
Tango. Kresin. Two euphoniums and two tubas with drums.
Tango Espana. Albeniz/Schmidt. Two euphoniums and two tubas.
Taps for Tubas. Dorff. Two euphoniums and three tubas.
Tarantella from Songs without Words, Op. 182, No. 3. Mendelssohn/Yamamoto. Two euphoniums and two tubas.
Tears. Bousted. Two euphoniums and two tubas.
Teddy Bears. Szkutko. One euphonium and one tuba with piano.
Teddy Bears' Picnic, The. Bratton/Bale. Two euphoniums and two tubas.
Ten Ayres or FaLa's for 3. Hilton/Helman. Two euphoniums and one tuba.
Ten Duets. Gillis. One trombone (euphonium) and one tuba.
Ten Duets. Torchinsky. Two tubas.
Ten Duets for Bass Trombone. Pederson. Two bass trombones (tubas).
Ten Duos Concertants. Joubert.
Ten Inventions for Four Tubaer, Op. 64. Roikjer. Four tubas.
Ten Inventions for Three Tubas. Roikjer. Three tubas.
Ten Inventions for Two Tubas, Op. 55. Roikjer. Two tubas.
Ten Jazz Duos and Solos. Hartzell. One euphonium and one tuba.
Ten More Duets, Book 2. Gillis.
Ten Pieces for Tuba Ensemble. Holborne/Stevens. Two euphoniums and two tubas.
Ten Trios for Tubas. Wilder. Three tubas.
Tennessee Waltz. Sample. Two euphoniums, two tubas, piano/guitar, bass, and drums.
Teuphm'isms I. Anderson. One euphonium and one tuba.
Teuphm'isms II. Anderson. One euphonium and one tuba.
Textures. Forbes. Six euphoniums and six tubas.
TGV. Carolino. Four tubas and rhythm section.
That Lovin' Rag. Smaller and Adler/Vaughan. Two euphoniums and two tubas.
That Old Black Magic. Mercer and Allen. Two euphoniums and two tubas.
That's a Plenty. Hoesly. Two euphoniums and two tubas.
Them Baces. Butterfield. One euphonium and two tubas.
Them Basses. Huffine/Goble. Two euphoniums and two tubas.
Thematic Permutations. Rodgers. Two euphoniums and two tubas.

Theme and Six Derivations. Anderson. Two euphoniums and two tubas.
Theme and Variations. Fabrizio. Solo tuba with two euphoniums and two tubas.
Then and Now. Dutton. One euphonium and one tuba.
There Is a Tavern in the Town. Bewley. Two euphoniums and two tubas.
They Didn't Believe Me. Kern/Holcombe. Two euphoniums and two tubas.
Thing's Ain't What They Used to Be. Ellington/Matteson. Three euphoniums, three tubas, and rhythm.
Things Are Tough All Over, Tubby. McCurdy. Four tubas and male vocalist.
Third Day, The. Erdmann. Four euphoniums and two tubas.
Thirty Progressive Duos. Carnardy. Two tubas.
Those Lazy, Hazy, Crazy Days of Summer. Glover. Two euphoniums and two tubas.
Three American Folk Songs. Milford. Two euphoniums and two tubas.
Three Bagatelles for Euphonium/Tuba Quartet. Uber. Two euphoniums and two tubas.
Three Barbershop Songs. Heiman. Two euphoniums and two tubas.
Three Bourees from "Terpsichore." Praetorius/Hartin. Four tubas.
Three Bruckner Motets. Bruckner/Stevens. Two euphoniums and two tubas.
Three Chorale Preludes. Telemann/Frackenpohl. One euphonium and one tuba.
Three Chorale Preludes. Telemann/Schmidt. One euphonium and two tubas.
Three Chorales. Gershenfeld. Four tubas.
Three Christmas Carols. Schmidt. Two euphoniums and two tubas.
Three Christmas Carols I. Schmidt. Two euphoniums and two tubas.
Three Christmas Carols II. Schmidt. Two euphoniums and two tubas.
Three Contrasts for Two Tubas. Anderson. Two tubas.
Three Dances. Susato/Cummings. Two euphoniums and two tubas.
Three Dances for Three Tubas. McCurdy. Three tubas.
Three Diverse Drinking Songs. Thornton. Three tubas.
Three German Dances. Pezel/Heiman. Two euphoniums and three tubas.
Three German Songs. Schmidt. Two euphoniums and two tubas.
Three Hunting Songs. Schumann/Emilson. Two euphoniums and two tubas.
Three Hymns by Lowell Mason. Mason/Shoop. Two euphoniums and two tubas.
Three Hymns by Robert Lowry. Lowry/Shoop. Two euphoniums and two tubas.
Three Jazz Duets. Henry. Two tubas.
Three Little London Variations. Tignor. Two euphoniums and two tubas.
Three Little Pigs, The (Twisted Tuba Tales No. 1). Fiegel. Four euphoniums and four tubas with narrator.
Three Ludes for Tuba. Jager. Solo tuba with two euphoniums and two tubas.
Three Madrigals. Pardus. Two euphoniums and two tubas.
Three Madrigals. Weelkes/Schmidt. Two euphoniums and one tuba.
3 Miniatures. Westby. Three tubas and percussion.
Three Miniatures for Tuba Quartet. Thompson. Four tubas.
Three Moods. Boone. Four euphoniums and two tubas.
Three Motets. Bruckner/Stevens. Two euphoniums and two tubas.
Three Motets. Heiman. Two euphoniums and two tubas.
Three Movements for Four Tubas. Ahrendt. Four tubas.
Three Mythical Sketches. Iannaccone. Two euphoniums and two tubas.
Three Piece Suite. Moore. Two euphoniums and two tubas.
Three Pieces. Pezel/Cummings. Two euphoniums and three tubas.
Three Pieces for Horseballet. Schmelzer/Schmidt. Two euphoniums and two tubas.
Three Pieces for Low Brass Trio. Rodgers. Two euphoniums and one tuba.
Three Pieces for Toby the Tuba. Rønnes. Two tubas.
Three Pieces from Brahms. Brahms/Lee. Two euphoniums and two tubas.
Three Pieces from King Henry VIII. Thornton. Three tubas.
Three Preludes for Three Tubas, Op. 376C. Hewitt. Three tubas.
Three Renaissance Duets. Singleton. Two tubas.
Three Renaissance Quartets. Cummings. Two euphoniums and two tubas.
Three Rococo Dances. Chedeville/Block. Two tubas.
Three Short Duets. Manzo. One euphonium and one tuba.
Three Short Preludes. Chopin/Bale. Four tubas.
Three 16th Century Flemish Pieces. Singleton. Two euphoniums and two tubas.
Three Sketches. Beadell. Two euphoniums and two tubas.
Three Southern Hymns. Shoop. Two euphoniums and two tubas.
Three Spirituals. Moore. Two euphoniums and two tubas.
Three Statements for Four Tubas. Richardson. Four tubas.
Three Temperaments for Tubas. Jacobson. Three tubas.
Three Traveling Shorts. Harrold. Two euphoniums and two tubas.
Three Tubas Two. Jones. Three tubas.

Three Tubas Two. Jones. Two or three tubas.
Threnody. Corwell. Two euphoniums, two tubas, and flute.
Thunder and Blazes. Fucik/Gray.
Thunderer, The. Sousa/Smalley. Two euphoniums and two tubas.
Thunderer, The. Sousa/Werden. Two euphoniums and two tubas.
Thus Do You Fare, My Jesus. Bach/Martin. Two euphoniums and three tubas.
Time Structures. Winteregg. Four tubas.
Tinker Polka. Bewley. Two euphoniums and two tubas.
Tinker Polka. Knoener. Three euphoniums and two tubas.
Tinker Polka. Schmidt. Two euphoniums and two tubas.
Tiny Tuba Tunes. Woodcock. Two euphoniums and two tubas.
Tish Nigon (Table Song). Wilkinson. Two euphoniums and two tubas.
To a Wild Rose. MacDowell/Rauch. Two euphoniums and two tubas.
To a Wild Rose. MacDowell/Robertson. Two euphoniums and two tubas.
Toad Patrol. Goble. Two euphoniums and two tubas.
Toccata. Bonelli/Warren. Eight-part tuba/euphonium ensemble.
Toccata. Frescobaldi/Skillen. Three euphoniums and three tubas.
Toccata and Fugue. Eberlin/Knoener. Three euphoniums and two tubas.
Toccata and Fugue in D Minor. Bach/Fiegel. Two euphoniums and two tubas.
Toccata and Fugue in D Minor. Bach/Lindsey. Two euphoniums and two tubas.
Toccata for Euphonium/Tuba Quartet. Schooley. Two euphoniums and two tubas.
Toccata for L'Orfeo. Monteverdi/Little. Two euphoniums and two tubas.
Toe Tapping Tuba Tune. Jones. Three tubas.
Too Fat Polka. Glover. Two euphoniums and two tubas.
Toreador Song from Carmen. Bizet/Bale. Four tubas.
Toreador Song from Carmen. Bizet/Gray. Two euphoniums and two tubas.
Total Tubosity. Ferguson. Two euphoniums and two tubas.
Totally Tuba March. Goble. Three euphoniums and two tubas.
Toward the Millennium. Cummings. Solo tuba with two euphoniums and two tubas.
Tower Music. Israel. Two euphoniums and one tuba.
Township Suite. Matchett. Two euphoniums and two tubas.
Transforming Realms. Russell. Two euphoniums and two tubas.
Trauermarcshe, Op. 55. Schubert/Warren. Eight-part tuba/euphonium ensemble.
Traumerei. Schumann/Seitz. Two euphoniums and two tubas.
Treatments for Tuba. Stroud. Two euphoniums and two tubas.
Tributes to Tunesmiths. Parfrey. Two euphoniums and two tubas.
Trio for Three Tubas. Keays. Three tubas.
Trio for Tubas. Jones. One euphonium and two tubas.
Trio for Tubas. Larrick. Three tubas.
Trio Sonata, Op. 1, No. 5. Corelli/Schmidt. Two euphoniums and one tuba.
Trio Sonata, Op. 1, No. 10. Corelli/Schmidt. Two euphoniums and one tuba.
Trio Sonata, Op. 3, No. 2. Corelli/Cranson. Two euphoniums and one tuba.
Trio Sonata, Op. 3, No. 2. Corelli/Schmidt. Two euphoniums and one tuba.
Trio Sonata, Op. 3, No. 7. Corelli/Schmidt. Two euphoniums and one tuba.
Trios for All. Henderson. Two euphoniums and one tuba.
Trios for Brass, Volume I, Advanced. Marcellus. Two euphoniums and one tuba.
Trios for Brass, Volume I, Easy-Intermediate. Marcellus. Two euphoniums and one tuba.
Trios for Brass, Volume I, Intermediate. Marcellus. Two euphoniums and one tuba.
Triple Quartet. Hartley. Eight euphoniums and four tubas.
Triplet for Four Tubas. Lundquist. Four tubas.
Tritsch-Tratsch Polka. Strauss/Seitz. Two euphoniums and two tubas.
Tritsch Tratsch Polka, The. Strauss/Bewley. Two euphoniums and two tubas.
Troika from "Lt. Kjie Suite." Prokofiev/Butler. Two euphoniums and two tubas with optional percussion.
Trois Chansons. Debussy/Lane. Two euphoniums, two tubas, and contralto vocalist.
Troisieme Suite. Dutton. Three tubas.
Trumpet Shall Sound, The. Handel/Wilkinson. Two euphoniums and two tubas.
Trumpet Voluntary. Clarke/Bale. Two euphoniums and two tubas.
Tuba Blues Medley. Wolking. Two euphoniums, two tubas, and drums.
T.U.B.A. Canon. Bartles. Two tubas.
Tuba Carols. Hancock. One euphonium and two tubas.
Tuba Chan Chaka Chan. Yoshizawa. Four euphoniums and four tubas.
Tuba Club. Weisling. Six tubas.
Tuba Duet No. 1. Gillam. Two tubas and piano.
Tuba Duets. Giuliani/Mordue. Two tubas.
Tuba Duets. Morley/Hunsaker. Two tubas.
Tuba Duo Eight. Mozart/Self. Two tubas.
Tuba Duo Eleven, Op. 5. Boccherini/Self. Two tubas.
Tuba Duo Five. Bach/Self. Two tubas.
Tuba Duo Four, K. 380. Mozart/Self. Two tubas.
Tuba Duo Nine. Bach/Self. Two tubas.

Tuba Duo One, K. 378. Mozart/Self. Two tubas.
Tuba Duo Seven, K. 380. Mozart/Self. Two tubas.
Tuba Duo Six. Bach/Self. Two tubas.
Tuba Duo Ten, Op. 99. Haydn/Self. Two tubas.
Tuba Duo Three, K. 454. Mozart/Self. Two tubas.
Tuba Duo Two (Rondo alla Tubas) K. 564. Mozart/Self. Two tubas.
Tuba Juba Duba. Hutchinson. Two euphoniums and two tubas.
Tuba Loca. Cottrell. Three euphoniums and three tubas.
Tuba Magic for Tuba Ensemble. DiGiovanni. Two euphoniums and four tubas.
Tuba Muckl. Schmidt. Two euphoniums and two tubas.
Tuba Muckl Polka. Seitz. Two euphoniums and two tubas.
Tuba Musicale. DiGiovanni. Five euphoniums and five tubas.
Tuba Quartet. Davison. Four tubas.
Tuba Quartet. Randalls. Four tubas.
Tuba Quartet. Strukow. Four tubas.
Tuba Quartet—Chopin Mazurka, Op. 68, No. 48. Chopin/Anderson. Four tubas.
Tuba Quartet No. 1. Schulz. Two euphoniums and two tubas.
Tuba Quartet No. 1 in C Minor. Wilson. Two euphoniums and two tubas.
Tuba Quartet, Op. 59. Gates. Two euphoniums and two tubas.
Tuba Quartet, Op. 65, No. 3. Heussenstamm. Four tubas.
Tuba Quartet: Study in Motion, Hymn, and Finale. Koltz. Two euphoniums and two tubas.
Tuba Rodeo. Kresin. Two euphoniums and two tubas with drums.
Tuba Sauce. Smalley. Two euphoniums and two tubas.
Tuba Seduction (Ballade). Lemirre. Four euphoniums and four tubas.
Tuba Sunday for Tuba Choir. Sloan. Two euphoniums and two tubas.
Tuba Trio. Mueller. One euphonium and two tubas.
Tuba Trio. Zindars. Three tubas.
Tuba Trio Number 1. Wilder. Three tubas.
Tuba Turf. Niehaus. Two euphoniums and two tubas.
TubaCanon. Albert. Four tubas.
Tubaccata. Gorb. Two euphoniums and two tubas.
TuBach. Wilkinson. Two euphoniums and two tubas.
Tubacussion, Op. 62. Heussenstamm. Four tubas and percussion.
Tubafest Shuffle. Fritze. Three euphoniums, three tubas, and rhythm.
Tubafication. Mitchell-Davidson. Two euphoniums and two tubas.
TubaFour, Op. 30. Heussenstamm. One euphonium and three tubas.
Tubafugalfanfare. Jones. Four tubas.
TubaFunk. Rauch. Two euphoniums and two tubas.
Tubafusion. Wood. Two euphoniums and two tubas.
Tubagirls I. Vaughan. Two euphoniums and four tubas.
Tubagirls II. Vaughan. Two euphoniums and four tubas.
Tubaku. Wilson. Two tubas.
Tubalaté Tango. Bayliss. Two euphoniums and two tubas.
Tubalation. Niehaus. Two euphoniums and two tubas.
Tubalation Rag. Bale. Two euphoniums and two tubas.
Tubalation Rag. Mehlan. Two euphoniums and two tubas.
Tubalee Jubalee. Garrett. Two euphoniums and two tubas.
Tubamania! Friedrich. Four euphoniums and four tubas.
TubaMeister Polka. Grim. Two euphoniums and two tubas.
Tubamobile. George. Two euphoniums and two tubas.
Tuba-Nette Polka, The. Knoener. Two euphoniums and two tubas.
Tubantiphon. Stroud. Two tubas.
Tubaphonic Suite. Payne. Four tubas.
Tubaquartett. Hidas. One euphonium and three tubas.
Tubarhumba. DiGiovanni. Two euphoniums, four tubas, and rhythm.
Tubarium. Sturzenegger. Two euphoniums and two tubas.
Tubarometer. Niehaus. Two euphoniums and two tubas.
Tubas at Christmas. Gottschalk. One euphonium and three tubas.
Tubas at Play. DiGiovanni. Four tubas.
Tubas Latinas (Overture for Tuba Ensemble). Forte. Two euphoniums, three tubas, and two optional percussion.
Tubasity. Wilkinson. Two euphoniums and two tubas.
Tubasonatina. George. Two euphoniums and two tubas.
Tublue. Nash. Four tubas, piano, bass, and drums.
Tubology. Morris. Three euphoniums, three tubas, and rhythm.
Tu-Bop. Fritze. Three euphoniums, three tubas, and rhythm.
Tubular Octad. Tull. Four euphoniums and four tubas.
Tubuus. Friedrich. One euphonium and three tubas.
Tulak Polka. Grim. Two euphoniums and two tubas.
Turandot; Two Choruses. Puccini/Sherman. Two euphoniums and two tubas.

TUrBulênciA Sonora. Carolino. Four tubas and optional vibraphone.
Turkish March K. 331. Mozart/Mehlan. Two euphoniums and two tubas.
Tuxedo Junction. Hawkins, Johnson, and Dash/Luis. One euphonium and three tubas.
Tuxedo Junction. Hawkins/Schmidt. Two euphoniums and two tubas.
Twelfth Street Rag. Bowman/Schanke. Two euphoniums and two tubas.
12 Days of Housetops! Canter. Two euphoniums and two tubas.
Twelve Divertissements en Duos, Op. 670. Porret. Two tubas.
Twelve Duets. Bach/Dishinger. Two tubas.
Twelve Duets for Horn (Tubas). Mozart/McKee. Two tubas.
Twelve Duets for Tubas. McCurdy. Two tubas.
Twelve Duets. K.V. 487. Mozart/Dishinger. Two tubas.
Twelve Duets, Op. 2 and Op. 5. Quantz/Schmidt. Two tubas.
Twelve Duos for Two Tubas. Mozart/Conner. Two tubas.
Twelve Easy Duets for Winds. Mozart/Smith. One euphonium and one tuba.
Twelve Two Part Inventions. Bach/Miller. Two tubas.
Twenty Duets from Symphonic Masterworks. Hawkins. One euphonium and one tuba.
Twenty Petits Duos. Zemp. Two tubas.
Twenty-Five Baroque and Classical Duets, Book 1. Singleton. Two tubas.
Twenty-Five Baroque and Classical Duets, Book II. Singleton. Two tubas.
Twenty-Four Christmas Carols. Stevens. Two euphoniums and two tubas.
Twenty-Four Duette, Op. 73. Scherzer. Two tubas.
21 Distinctive Duets for Tuba. Jones. Two tubas.
Twenty Six Tuba Duette. Ferstl. Two tubas.
Twinkle, Twinkle. . . . Mozart/Doughty. Two euphoniums and two tubas.
Twinkle, Twinkle Little Star. Mozart/Werden. Two euphoniums and two tubas.
Two Advent Chorals. Roundtree. Two euphoniums and two tubas.
Two Airs. Adson/Stevens. Two euphoniums and two tubas.
Two Bach Chorales. Bach/Shoop. Two euphoniums and two tubas.
Two Baroque Dances. Handel/Greene. Two euphoniums and two tubas.
Two Birthday Rags. Vaughan. Two euphoniums and two tubas.
Two Canons. Schumann/Singleton. Three tubas.
Two Chorales. Bach/Brown. Two euphoniums and two tubas.
Two Chorales. Brown. Two euphoniums and two tubas.
Two Christmas Carols. Schmidt. Two euphoniums and two tubas.
Two Concert Duets. Blazhevich/Wekselblatt. Two tubas.
Two Contrasting Pachelbel Fugues. Pachelbel/Ferriano. Three euphoniums and two tubas.
Two English Madrigals. Gershenfeld. Three tubas.
Two English Madrigals. Singleton. Three tubas.
Two English Madrigals. Thornton. Four tubas.
Two English Madrigals. Thornton. Two tubas.
Two Folk Songs. McCurdy. Two euphoniums and two tubas.
Two for the Tuba. Wadowick. Two tubas and piano.
Two Hag Pieces for Euphonium and Tuba. Presser. One euphonium and one tuba.
Two Impressions. McCurdy. Two tubas.
Two Interplays. George. Three tenor trombones, one bass trombone, two euphoniums, and tuba.
Two Jazz Moods. Ferriano. Two euphoniums and two tubas.
Two Madrigals. Di Lasso/Ferriano. Two euphoniums and two tubas.
Two Madrigals. Dowland/Nelson. Two euphoniums and two tubas.
Two Madrigals. Schmidt. Two euphoniums and two tubas.
Two Mean Old Tubas (Intrada) No. 6. Wienhorst. Two tubas.
Two Midaeval Carols. Hartin. Two tubas.
Two (More) Birthday Rags. Vaughan. Two euphoniums and two tubas.
Two Morley Madrigals. Morley/Ferriano. Two euphoniums and three tubas.
Two Motets. Hassler/Schmidt. Two euphoniums and two tubas.
Two Movements from Carnival of the Animals. Saint-Saëns/Minchin. Two euphoniums and two tubas.
Two Old Songs. Schmidt. Two euphoniums and two tubas.
Two Part Inventions. Bach/Ostrander. Two tubas.
Two-Part Inventions. Bach/Spang and Lazar. One euphonium and one tuba.
Two-Part Inventions. Patterson. One euphonium and one tuba.
Two Patriotic Songs. McCurdy. Four tubas.
Two Pieces for Three Tubas. Gessner. Three tubas.
Two Pieces for Tuba/Euphonium Ensemble. McCarthy. Six euphoniums and two tubas.
Two Pieces from "Orfeo." Monteverdi/Heiman. Three euphoniums and two tubas.
Two Rags, Volume 1. Joplin/Sabourin. Two euphoniums and two tubas.
Two Rags, Volume 2. Joplin/Sabourin. Two euphoniums and two tubas.
Two Renaissance Duets. Di Lassus/Spang. One euphonium and one tuba.
Two Russian Pieces. Bale. Four tubas.
Two Sackbut Quartets. Schmidt. Two euphoniums and two tubas.
Two Trumpet Tunes and Ayre. Purcell/Humble. Two euphoniums and two tubas.

Two Trumpet Tunes and Trumpet Voluntary. Purcell/Rauch. Two euphoniums and two tubas.
Two Tuba Suites, Book 1. Jones. Two tubas.
Two Tuba Suites, Book 2. Jones. Two tubas.
Two Tunes by Herb Brown. Sample. Two euphoniums, two tubas, piano/guitar, bass, and drums.
Two Waltzes, K. 600, #1 and 4. Mozart/Schmidt. Two euphoniums and two tubas.
Two Wind Duets (K.487). Mozart/Block. One euphonium and one tuba.
Typic Rhythm. Florinza. Four euphoniums and four tubas.

U

Ubi Caritas. Durufle/Morris. Two euphoniums and two tubas.
Ukrainian Carol (Ring Christmas Bells). Leontovich/Rauch. Two euphoniums and two tubas.
Undecided. Vaughan. Two euphoniums and two tubas.
Under the Double Eagle. Wagner, J. F./Bewley. Two euphoniums and two tubas.
Under the Double Eagle. Wagner/Schmidt. Two euphoniums and two tubas.
Undercurrents. Wright. One flute, seven tubas, and two percussion.
Untitled Work. Tinoco. Solo tuba with six tubas.

V

Va Tacito. Handel/Cranson. One euphonium, one tuba, and piano.
Valse from Die Fledermaus. Strauss/Schanke. Two euphoniums and two tubas.
Variations aux Quatre Vents. Nilovic. Four tubas.
Variations on a Motive by Wagner. Jager. One euphonium and two tubas.
Variations on a Theme of Prokofieff. Schmidt. One euphonium and one tuba.
Variations on a Yiddish Folksong. Szpakowski. Two euphoniums and two tubas.
Variations on an Old Hymn Tune. Werle. Two euphoniums and four tubas.
Variations on Jingle Bells. Anderson. Two euphoniums and two tubas.
Variations on the New World Symphony. Dvorák/Woodward. Four euphoniums and three tubas.
Vaudeville. Uber. Two euphoniums and two tubas.
Veni Emmanuel. Vaughan. Two euphoniums and two tubas.
Vermont Gathering, A. Uber. Two euphoniums and two tuba.
Vier Deutscher Tánzen. Frank. Two euphoniums and two tubas.
Vignettes for Euphonium, Tuba and Piano. Cummings. One euphonium, one tuba, and piano.
Vioci du Gai Printemps. Sweelinck/Hartin. Two tubas.
Violet, Slingsby, Guy and Lionel. Finnissy. Two euphoniums and two tubas.
Visages. Puw. Two euphoniums and two tubas.
Vite! Walton. Two euphoniums and two tubas.
Viva Voce! Stevens. Two euphoniums and two tubas.
Vivace from Concerto No. 3 in D minor. Bach/Self. Two tubas.
Vivaldi Trio Sonata. Vivaldi/Schmidt. Two euphoniums and one tuba.

W

Wabash Canon Ball for Tuba-Euphonium Ensemble. Garrett. Two euphoniums and two tubas.
Wachet Auf. Bach/Buttery. Two euphoniums and two tubas.
Wachterleid (Watchman's Song), Op. 12. Grieg/Schmidt. Two euphoniums and two tubas.
Waldesnacht, clu Wunder Kuhle (Wondrous Cool. . . .). Brahms/Nelson. Two euphoniums and two tubas.
Walking Giants. Szkutko. Four tubas.
Wallowed Out. Buttery. Two tubas.
Waltz and March. Hall. Three euphoniums and one tuba.
Waltz of the Walrus. McCurdy. Two tubas.
Waltzes from "Die Fledermaus" and the "Gypsy Baron." Strauss/Whetmore. Four tubas.
Waltzing MaTubas. Wilkinson. Two euphoniums and two tubas.
Waltzing with Irving. Sample. Two euphoniums, two tubas, piano/guitar, bass, and drums.
Waphan Touba. Barbera. Two euphoniums and two tubas.
Warring. Dutton. Three euphoniums and three tubas.
Washington Grays. Grafulla/Wilkinson. Two euphoniums and two tubas.
Washington Post. Sousa/Sabourin. Two euphoniums and two tubas.
Washington Post. Sousa/Self. Two euphoniums and three tubas.
Washington Post. Sousa/Werden. Two euphoniums and two tubas.
Waste Land, The. Corwell. Solo tuba with two euphoniums and two tubas.
Water and Fireworks Music. Handel/Heiman. Two euphoniums and two tubas.
Wave. Jobim/Carolino. Solo euphonium with four tubas and rhythm section.
Waves of the Danube. Ivanovici/Konagaya. Two euphoniums and two tubas.
We Run Them In. Offenbach. Three tubas.
We Wish You a Merry Christmas. Robertson. Two euphoniums and two tubas.
Wedding March. Mendelssohn/Emberson. Two euphoniums and two tubas.
Weep, O Mine Eyes. Bennet. Two euphoniums and two tubas.

Wein, DuStadt Meiner Traume. Siecznski/Grim. Two euphoniums and two tubas.

Wenzel Polka. Munsonins and Ackermann/Grim. Two euphoniums and two tubas.

Were You There? Siekmann. Six euphoniums and two tubas.

Were You There? Siekmann. Two euphoniums and two tubas.

Wexford Carol. Cottrell. Five-part tuba/euphonium ensemble.

A Whale's Tale. Niehaus. Two euphoniums and two tubas.

What Though Her Frowns. Pilkington. Two euphoniums and two tubas.

When the Moon Jumps. Schaphorst. Four euphoniums and four tubas.

When the Saints Come Marchin' In. Garrett. Two euphoniums and two tubas.

When Tubas Waltz. Bartles. Two euphoniums and two tubas.

Who Am I, or Dost Thou Mock Me. Rossini/Hoefle. One euphonium and two tubas.

Whoop It Up Polka. Stechlik/Grim. Two euphoniums and two tubas.

Why Do I Fret? Pilkington. Two euphoniums and two tubas.

Why Should I Grieve? Pilkington. Two euphoniums and two tubas.

Wiggleworm Squirm. Vaughan. Two euphoniums and two tubas.

William Tell Overture. Rossini/Dawson. Two euphoniums and two tubas.

William Tell Overture. Rossini/Schanke. Two euphoniums and two tubas.

William Tell Overture. Rossini/Smalley. Two euphoniums and two tubas.

William Tell Overture (abridged). Rossini/Schmidt. Two euphoniums and two tubas.

Winds: Five Descriptive Pieces for T/E Octet. Vaughan. Four euphoniums and four tubas.

Winds of Spring. Friedrich. Four euphoniums and two tubas.

With a Little Bit of Flash. Rauch. Two euphoniums and two tubas.

W.O.L. (With Out Lyrics). Friedrich. Four euphoniums and two tubas.

Wolkenschatten, Op. 136. Koetsier. One euphonium and three tubas.

Wolsey's Wilde. Byrd/Jacob and Robertson. Two euphoniums and two tubas.

Wonderland Duets. Luedeke. Two tubas and narrator.

Wonderous Cool, Thou Woodland Quiet. Brahms/Nelson. Two euphoniums and two tubas.

Wooden Heart "Muss I Denn." Broeniman. Two euphoniums and two tubas.

Woodland Polka. Grim. Two euphoniums and two tubas.

Wore a Yellow Ribbon. Warren. Two euphoniums and two tubas.

World Does Not Wish for Beauty, The. Britain. Four tubas.

World Is Waiting for Sunrise, The. Seitz/Butler. Two euphoniums and two tubas.

Wot Shigona Dew? Wilson. Three euphoniums, two tubas, and rhythm.

Y

Yama No Hibiki. Ishii. Six euphoniums and six tubas.

Yamaha Band Ensembles, Tuba/Book 1. O'Reilly. Three tubas with optional piano.

Yamaha Band Ensembles, Tuba/Book 2. O'Reilly. Three tubas with optional piano.

Yamaha Band Ensembles, Tuba/Book 3. O'Reilly. Three tubas with optional piano.

Yankee Tunes for Tubas. Jones. Two euphoniums and three tubas.

Yesterday. Lennon and McCartney/Miyagawa. Two euphoniums and two tubas.

Yorkshire Ballad. Barnes. Four euphoniums and three tubas.

You Light up My Life. Emberson. Two euphoniums and two tubas.

You Made Me Love You. Monaco/Holcombe. Two euphoniums and two tubas.

Yuba Play the Tuba. Gray. Two euphoniums and two tubas.

Yuletide Jazz Suite #1. Niehaus. Two euphoniums and two tubas.

Yuletide Jazz Suite #2. Niehaus. Two euphoniums and two tubas.

Z

Zacatecas March. Wilkinson. Two euphoniums and two tubas.

Zepperl Polka. Grim. Two euphoniums and two tubas.

8. Methods and Studies

David D. Graves, Assistant Editor, *Guide to the Tuba Repertoire: The New Tuba Source Book*

Jerry A. Young, Assistant Editor, and David D. Graves, Editorial Assistant, *The Tuba Source Book*

Introductory Remarks (July 2005): David D. Graves

As in the first edition, the primary goal of this chapter is the annotation of any method or study book composed specifically for the tuba. The only stipulation is that the work must be published, or at the very least, available for purchase from the composer. In the case of out of print material, the work must still be in circulation. Due to the scope of such an undertaking, it is understood that works may have been unintentionally omitted, though every effort has been made to avoid such omission. The stated price reflects the most up-to-date information at the time of this chapter's preparation. Finally, due to the limited availability of review materials, bibliographical information for some works may be missing or incomplete.

Thanks are extended to the following, for their invaluable assistance in the completion of this chapter:

- Jerry Young—an extraordinary scholar, musician, and mentor—for his guidance in the first edition and his trust in my abilities regarding the second edition
- Linda Stewart—administrative assistant in the Baylor University School of Music—for addressing and mailing approximately four hundred letters, resulting in the availability of review materials for this chapter
- Colin Campbell—an outstanding young tubist and overall nice guy—for spending several hours on the phone, thereby ensuring the accuracy of much of the information contained in this chapter
- David LeClair and Heiko Triebener—international consultants for this edition—for going above and beyond the call by annotating several of the international methods and studies included in this chapter
- The many composers and publishers who provided review materials for this chapter
- Winston Morris—editorial genius and grandfather of tubadom—for his infinite patience and flexible deadlines
- Denise, Andrea, Evan, and Jeremy Graves—my family—for their love, support, and understanding, particularly while I have been confined to the *Tuba Source Book* room (formerly known as the laundry room) of our house. Perhaps now we can locate the missing laundry.

Introductory Remarks (July 1995): Jerry A. Young and David D. Graves

Pedagogical literature for the tuba dates from the nineteenth century. Early tubists likely borrowed study materials from brass methods for trumpet, horn, and trombone and studies from the vocal literature, as well as studies for the serpent and/or ophicleide, with material specific to the tuba emerging in the last half of the nineteenth century. In this study and survey of these materials, it is apparent that pedagogical practice has changed drastically over the years with common practice becoming slightly more standardized over the past ten to fifteen years.

Publishing house catalogs, computer databases, and numerous other sources provided information for this portion of *The Tuba Source Book*. Almost all currently available materials and a very large portion of materials that have been in print in the past are included here. This is the most comprehensive and accurate annotated source of tuba study materials assembled to date, and it should prove to be of significant value to the music teaching profession.

Thanks are extended to those in the music publishing industry who furnished review copies of pedagogical materials, as well as to the music retailers who allowed access to their inventory, particularly Groth Music of Minneapolis,

Minnesota, and Alan Hager of that firm. Thanks also to the numerous *TSB* international consultants who furnished copies of works available in their countries and to low brass colleagues across the United States who provided materials from their libraries. Finally, special thanks go to the University of Wisconsin–Eau Claire School of Graduate Study and Research, Dr. Ronald Satz, Dean; and the Department of Music, Dr. David Baker, Chair. Through their generous support, Mr. David Graves (tubist, scholar, teacher, and master's degree candidate) was able to assist with the research for and preparation of this portion of *The Tuba Source Book*. Without Mr. Graves' diligent assistance and thoughtful input, the completion of this portion of the book likely would not have been possible.

General comments regarding this annotated bibliography:

1) The goal for this chapter was to determine the availability of published methods and studies for the tuba. When it was determined that a given work was out of print, this was indicated in the bibliographic information presented. However, lack of an "out of print" notation does not guarantee that the given item is indeed available.

2) The prices given indicate the most recent price for each piece. In the case of out of print material or where no other source was available, the cover price is listed with the assumption that this information might be of interest. Since every publisher did not furnish a current catalog with current price information, there is no guarantee that all prices were accurate as of the publication deadline.

3) Entries that appear in the following listing without annotation and/or with incomplete bibliographic information were not made available to the editor for examination. The editorial staff of *The Tuba Source Book* felt that it was important that all items be documented in this project, regardless of current availability. Some items were not furnished for review by the publisher while others (appearing in old catalogs or bibliographies) have presumably long since been out of print and lost.

Adler, Samuel. *Tubetudes.* Southern Music Company. 1978. $3.50. 7 pp. II–III. These etudes range from very playable by an intermediate student to challenging for a good high school student. All sixteen etudes are written to be musical studies, as well as to challenge some technical aspect of musicianship, and would be appropriate for recital presentation. A particularly good choice for the pedagogical library of the junior and senior high school teacher.

Amis, K. *Pre-Audition Warm-up for Tuba.* Seesaw Music Corporation. $29.00.

Anderson, Eugene, and Harvey Phillips. *Musically Mastering the Low Range of the Tuba and Euphonium: A College Method Book.* Anderson's Arizona Originals. 1992. 75 pp. III–IV. Although designed for the college-level student, these etudes will work well for the very advanced high school student. The etudes are organized in sets of three with each set working one half step lower than the previous one. Each set includes etudes in baroque, romantic, and contemporary styles, and a variety of performance techniques are employed. Also includes pedagogical hints sections and fingering charts.

Appelghem und Zemp. *Methode pour Tuba I et II.* Lille. 1982.

Arban, J. B. *Arban-Bell Interpretations.* ed. William Bell. Charles Colin. 1975. $25.00. 126 pp. III–V. This volume presents significant portions of the original Arban *Complete Method for Trumpet* in bass clef for the tubist or euphoniumist (all exercises are presented in octaves). Some of the sections included here: studies in dotted eighths and sixteenths, lip slurs, the simple grace note, the triple tongue, the double tongue, etc. All sections are accompanied by instructive comments from the legendary William Bell.

Arban, J. B. *Arban Scales.* ed. Wesley Jacobs. Encore Music Publishers. $20.00. 98 pp. II–V. Arban scale patterns are presented in all keys complete with articulation and rhythmic variations. This represents a good resource for developing thorough acquaintance with scales from the intermediate years forward.

Arban, J. B. *Exercises in Double Crotchets.* tr./ed. Wesley Jacobs. Encore Music Publishers. 1988. $20.00. 99 pp. IV–V. The original Arban double crotchet studies transposed into all keys, complete with listing of all Arban articulation variations plus additional articulation variations from the editor. This is a fine route to better time and articulation while improving reading in all keys.

Arban, Jean Baptiste. *Arban Characteristic Studies for Tuba.* tr. and ed. Wesley Jacobs. Tuba-Euphonium Press. 1994. $19.00. 31 pp. IV–V. Arban's fourteen virtuosic etudes, conservatively edited to make them more suitable for performance on the tuba. Transcribed in such a manner as to preserve Arban's intended fingering patterns when the CC tuba is used.

Arban, Jean Baptiste. *Arban Complete Method for the Tuba.* tr. and ed. Jerry Young and Wesley Jacobs. Encore Music Publishers. 2000. $56.95. 334 pp. I–V. Dedicated to Barbara G. Young, James B. and Artie L. Young, Harvey G. Phillips, Gerald Sloan, William N. Shaver III, Ronald Garner, Bliss Alexander, and most especially, Daniel Perantoni. A complete tuba method in every sense. Includes not only Arban's full array of technical and musical exercises designed to develop every aspect of brass performance, but also updated pedagogical commentary. Transcribed in such a manner as to preserve Arban's intended fingering patterns when the CC tuba is used.

Arban, Jean Baptiste. *My First Arban for the Developing Student.* ed. Robert Foster. Carl Fischer. 2001. $6.95. 32 pp. I–II. A synopsis of Arban's complete method, compiled and edited especially for first- and second-year tuba players. Includes exercises from the following sections of the original Arban method: first studies, scale studies, chromatic scales, intervals, major/minor arpeggios, the art of phrasing, and duets. Also includes an abridged version of "The Carnival of Venice."

Arban, Joseph Jean Baptiste Laurent. *The Arban-Bell Tuba Method.* ed. William J. Bell. Charles Colin. 1968. Out of Print. 196 pp. III–IV. Although this volume is out of print, it can be found in the *Bell Complete Method for Tuba* from the same publisher.

Arban-Prescott. *Arban-Prescott First and Second Year.* Carl Fischer, Incorporated. 1937. $8.50. 51 pp. I–III. An abbreviated version of the complete Arban method designed especially for use in heterogeneous brass instrument class settings. This book emphasizes the most fundamental aspects of proper brass playing.

Associated Board of the Royal Schools of Music, The. *Scales and Arpeggios for Tuba (Grades 1–8).* ed. John Wallace and Ian Denley. ABRSM. 1995. $9.06. 43 pp. I–III. Intended to assist with the thorough mastery of scales and arpeggios, this method includes a comprehensive fingering chart and table of harmonics for BB♭, CC, E♭, and F tubas, as well as a suggested practice regimen for passing each grade level of the ABRSM exam. Includes helpful pedagogical commentary.

Associated Board of the Royal Schools of Music, The. *Specimen Sight-Reading Tests for Baritone, Euphonium and Tuba (Grades 1–5).* ABRSM. 1995. $5.95. 32 pp. I–II. Short melodic exercises intended to prepare candidates for the Associated Board examinations. Also useful to anyone wanting sight-reading practice. The exercises explore different keys, styles, and tempi, and they are organized by ABRSM grade level.

Associated Board of the Royal Schools of Music, The. *Specimen Sight-Reading Tests for Baritone, Euphonium and Tuba (Grades 6–8).* ABRSM. 1998. $7.23. 24 pp. II–III. Short melodic exercises intended to prepare candidates for the Associated Board examinations. Also useful to anyone wanting sight-reading practice. The exercises explore different keys, styles, and tempi, and they are organized by ABRSM grade level.

Associated Board (United Kingdom). *Studies for Tuba, Grades III–VIII.* Associated Board of the Royal Schools of Music.

Augustine, Daniel S. *Seventeen Etudes for Tuba.* Daniel Augustine. 1975. 12 pp. IV–V. Only the most advanced student or professional player would benefit from these etudes. Very wide leaps to both extreme registers combined with difficult and odd technical and rhythmic figures make these very difficult and challenging studies. This is excellent material for the athletic tubist who needs to "stretch."

Australian Music Examinations Board. *Brass: Series One, First and Second Grades.* ed. Gary McPherson, Janice Stockigt, and Ian Burk. Allans Publishing. 1998. $22.56. 24 pp. I. A primer for the Australian music examinations, in accordance with the AMEB Band Syllabus. Included are basic studies in articulation, as well as a variety of brief solos with piano accompaniment. A separate accompaniment part is included, and the method, though suitable for individual study, is designed for use in groups of like-keyed instruments. Published versions include treble clef E♭ and B♭, as well as bass clef C (non-transposing). See Music for Tuba and Keyboard.

Australian Music Examinations Board. *Brass: Series One, Third and Fourth Grades.* ed. Gary McPherson, Janice Stockigt, and Ian Burk. Allans Publishing. 1998. $22.56. 28 pp. II–III. Similar in format to volume I (first and second grades) of the same series, but more challenging technically. See Music for Tuba and Keyboard.

Australian Music Examinations Board. *Orchestral Brass: Tuba Series One, Grades One and Two.* ed. David Agg, John Weretka, and John Woods. Allans Publishing. 2004. $22.56. 48 pp. I–II. Similar in format to the *Brass* series by the same publisher, but incorporates melodic material by more mainstream composers and is only published in the bass clef. Includes a separate piano part, as well as historical information and performance suggestions for each selection. Very useful as both melodic study material for beginning students and sight-reading material for slightly more advanced students. See Music for Tuba and Keyboard.

Australian Music Examinations Board. *Orchestral Brass: Tuba Series One, Grades Three and Four.* ed. David Agg, John Weretka, and John Woods. Allans Publishing. 2004. $22.56. 62 pp. II–III. Similar in format to volume I (grades one and two) of the same series, but more challenging technically. See Music for Tuba and Keyboard.

Australian Music Examinations Board. *Trombone, Tuba and Euphonium Technical Work Book.* Allans Publishing. 2004. $22.56.

Bach, J. S. *Bach for the Tuba, Volume I.* arr./tr. Douglas Bixby/Roger Bobo. Western International Music. 1971. $8.00. 34 pp. IV–V. Study of the music of Bach with emphasis on phrasing, low register, style, and ornamentation. This volume is intended to function as preparatory exercises for a second volume (see following entry). Some selections are appropriate for solo performance.

Bach, J. S. *Bach for the Tuba, Volume II.* arr./tr. Douglas Bixby/Roger Bobo. Western International Music. 1972. $8.00. 36 pp. IV–V. Continued study of the music of Bach with emphasis on phrasing, low register, style, and ornamentation. This volume consists largely of arrangements of works suitable for recital use, as well as study.

Badía, Miguel. *Flexibilidade, Volumes 1 e 2.* Casa Beethoven. 1977. IV.

Balent, Andrew. *Sounds Spectacular Band Course (Tuba), Books I and II.* Carl Fischer, Incorporated. 1991. $4.95. 32 pp. I–II. This is an attractively covered band method which includes instruction in theory (with an emphasis on terminology) and ensemble playing. Included are theory puzzles and full band arrangements.

Balent, Andrew, and Quincy Hilliard. *Sounds Spectacular Skill Builders: Warmups and Technical Studies for the Developing Performer (Tuba), Book I.* Carl Fischer, Incorporated. 1992. $3.95. 16 pp. I–II. Intended as a supplement to the Sounds Spectacular Band Course, this work is divided into separate units, with exercises specifically designed for the proper development of embouchure, breathing, counting, and articulation, in addition to ensemble balance.

Bauer, G. *Elementarschule für Bläser in B, Es, C im violin/Baßschlüssel.* Georg Bauer Musikverlag. 1980.

Bauer, G. *Technisch-rythmische Studien für Bläser (Baßschlüssel).* Georg Bauer Musikverlag. 1965.

Becker, G. *Method for the B♭ Tuba.* In three volumes. Remick.

Beeler, Walter. *Method for BB flat Tuba—Book I.* Warner Brothers Music. 1946. $7.95. 72 pp. I–II. A "first book" for private instruction. It includes many familiar tunes and logically introduces new notes, keys, and concepts. An outstanding feature is the inclusion of duets for teacher and student to perform together.

Beeler, Walter. *Method for BB flat Tuba—Book II.* Remick. 1962. $7.95. 48 pp. II–III. Intended for the advanced intermediate to advanced high school student, this book continues with familiar traditional and classical melodies and concludes with a good set of characteristic etudes. This work includes fine material for use in high school–level auditions.

Beeler, Walter. *Play Away! for BB♭ and E♭ Tubas (Sousaphone).* G. Schirmer, Incorporated. 1960. $1.00. 32 pp. I. Typical of the fine pedagogical thought of Walter Beeler, this book provides a decelerated approach for the very young beginner. It proceeds at a very slow pace and provides plenty of review as new ideas and concepts are introduced.

Behm. *Sharps and Flats (Tuba).* Belwin-Mills.

Bell, William. *Artistic Solos and Duets for Tuba, Trombone and Baritone.* Charles Colin Publications. 1975. $12.50. 58 pp. II–IV. A collection of solos and duets for the development of melodic interpretation and phrasing skills. Solo material includes works from Arban's *Complete Method (Art of Phrasing)*, transcriptions of sonatas by both Marcello and Bach, and two original works, "Gus the Hippo" and "Tuba Man." The solo transcriptions and duet material are either on or above the bass clef staff and therefore might prove to be additionally challenging for most high school tuba players. This work is included in its entirety in the William Bell *Complete Tuba Method.*

Bell, William. *William Bell Daily Routine for Tuba.* ed. Abe Torchinsky. Encore Music Publishers. 1989. $17.50. 28 pp. III–IV. Here is the daily routine recommended by the great William Bell, edited, clarified, and explained by his student and tuba legend Abe Torchinsky, retired tubist from the Philadelphia Orchestra and the University of Michigan. Exercises in breathing, flexibility, tonguing, etc. are all included with specific directions with regard to how Bell intended them to be played.

Bell, William J. *Blazhevich Tuba Interpretations.* Charles Colin. 1975. $7.95. 79 pp. III–IV. These studies, edited by the famous William Bell, are presented with very instructive comments by the master pedagogue. Characteristic of Blazhevich, these studies present a variety of unusual meters, as well as a variety of keys. Whether used for concentrated study or as a resource for challenging sight-reading material, this is an excellent text. (Also included in the *Bell Complete Method.*)

Bell, William J. *Complete Method for Tuba.* Charles Colin. 1975. $45.00. 260 pp. I–IV. Here William Bell presents a comprehensive text for tuba study. Included is an abridged and edited version of the Arban *Complete Method for Trumpet* (including some of *The Art of Phrasing* and duets from that text), as well as the Bell *Blazhevich Interpretations* (also available from the publisher in separate editions). The section "Artistic Solos and Duets" include classics such as "The Carnival of Venice."

Bell, William J. *Daily Routine and Blazhevich Interpretations, Volume 1 and 2.* ed. Charles Colin. New Sounds in Modern Music. 1954. Out of Print. $1.95. 31 pp. III–IV. This method includes a brief introduction to Mr. Bell's pedagogical approach plus the solo parts to two solos: "Tuba Man" and "Gus the Hippo." This is one of the most historically significant methods in the repertoire.

Bell, William J. *Foundation to Tuba and Sousaphone Playing.* Carl Fischer, Incorporated. 1931. $12.00. 106 pp. I–III Written by one of the greatest legends in tuba performance and teaching, this work covers fundamentals of tuba playing with pedagogical comments directed to the teacher. A variety of progressive etudes and some simple solo works are included.

Bell, William J. *Tuba Warm-Ups and Daily Routine.* Charles Colin. 1975. Out of Print. $3.50. 39 pp. III–IV. This text includes William Bell's prescribed warm-up procedure, covering long tones, flexibilities, tonguing, scales and arpeggios, interval studies, etc. (This material is included in its entirety in the Bell *Complete Method* from the same publisher.)

Belloli, Agostino. *8 ausgewählte Etüden.* Friedrich Hofmeister Leipzig. $12.88.

Bencriscutto, Frank, and Hal Freese. *Total Musicianship (Tuba).* Neil A. Kjos Music Company. 1983. $4.50. 48 pp. III–IV. Designed for the intermediate to advanced musician, this method is appropriate for individual or group study. The primary objectives of the method are establishing a solid warm-up routine, developing technique, and learning to improvise in the jazz idiom. Especially helpful are the simplicity of the improvisation section and the scope of the fingering chart (for BB♭, CC, E♭, and F tubas).

Bergeim, Joseph. *Instrumental Course for E flat and BB flat Tubas.* Joseph E. Skornicka. Boosey & Hawkes, Incorporated. 1946. 48 pp. I.

Bernard, Paul. *12 Pieces Melodiques.* Alphonse Leduc Editions Musicales. 1947. $14.25. 16 pp. III–IV. (See Thompson/Lemke: *French Music for Low Brass Instruments.*)

Bernard, Paul. *Etudes et Exercises pour Tuba et Saxhorn Basse.* ed. J. Forestier. Alphonse Leduc Editions Musicales. 1948. $14.20. 17 pp. III–IV. Good studies in a variety of keys. They will work best on F tuba or even tenor tuba, although they present reasonable range challenges for the contrabass tubist. Only the most advanced high school student would be interested in these studies. These are very reasonable studies for the second-year (or higher) college student. (See Thompson/Lemke: *French Music for Low Brass Instruments.*)

Bernard, Paul. *Forty Etudes D'Apres Forestier.* Alphonse Leduc Editions Musicales. 1948. $14.20. 17 pp. III–IV. (See Thompson/Lemke: *French Music for Low Brass Instruments.*)

Bernard, Paul. *Methode Complete pour Trombone Basse, Tuba, Saxhorns Basses et Contrebasse.* Alphonse Leduc Editions Musicales. 1960. $36.50. 136 pp. I–IV. This work, although directed toward the broader low brass family, is best suited to the tenor tuba. Because of the high tessitura of the exercises, it is likely intended for the French C tuba, an instrument that is actually smaller than the euphonium in physical dimensions. (See Thompson/Lemke: *French Music for Low Brass Instruments.*)

Berninger, H. *Bläserübungen, Tonleitern und tägliche Studien für Baß-Tuba oder Helikon.* Friedrich Hofmeister.

Bianchini. *Popular Method.* Editions Salabert.

Bing, W. *The Bing Book.* Whipple Music. $21.00.

Bitsch, M. *14 Etudes de Rythme (Greiner).* Alphonse Leduc Editions Musicales. 1988. 29 pp. IV–V. (See Thompson/Lemke: *French Music for Low Brass Instruments*).

Blazewitsch, Vladislav. *Advanced Daily Drills for Trombone and Tuba.* ed. Alan Ostrander. Editions Musicus. 1961. $5.60. 18 pp. III–IV. These studies can be used as either warm-up or study material. Focus is on development of tone, articulation, and flexibility through intensive scale study. The author's pedagogical approach is presented briefly in English translation at the beginning of the text.

Blazhevich, V. *26 Melodic Studies in Sequences.* ed. Joel Zimmerman. Shawnee Press. 1988. $10.00. 53 pp. IV. Challenging etudes that cover a variety of rhythmic and phrasing problems. A broad range of meters and keys are represented. These are excellent studies for the advanced college student who needs to refine reading skills and improve general musicality.

Blazhevich, V. M. *Textbook for Tuba in B♭.* Encore Music Publishers. 1939/1990. $32.00. 62 pp. II–V. The first Russian etude book specifically for tuba. These etudes are totally different from those transcribed from the trombone etudes in the King and Knaub Blazhevich editions. This is a complete method for tuba in the spirit of Arban.

Blazhevich, Vladislav. *70 Studies for BB flat Tuba, Vol. I and II.* Robert King Music Company. 1965. $3.40. 52 pp. III–IV. Excellent studies in all keys for low range, odd meters. These studies (transcribed from the original trombone etudes) have become a "standard" of tuba pedagogical repertoire. (See also: Knaub, D., *Progressive Techniques for Tuba.*)

Blazhewitsch, V. *Schule für Baß-Tuba in B* (Hochschule der Künste Berlin). SSV. 1925.

Bleger, M. *10 Caprices.* Alphonse Leduc Editions Musicales.

Bleger, M. *31 Etudes Brillantes.* Alphonse Leduc Editions Musicales.

Bleger, M. *Methode Complete de Saxhorn-Basse.* ed. M. Job. Alphonse Leduc Editions Musicales. 1932. 83 pp. IV.

Bleger, M. *Methode Elementaire.*

Bleger, M. *Nouvelle Méthode Complète.* Alphonse Leduc Editions Musicales. 1932.

Blume, O. *36 Übungen, Band 1–3.* ed. Emil Teuchert. C. F. Schmidt. 1972.

Bobo, Roger. *Mastering the Tuba (in Three Volumes).* Editions BIM. 1993. Soon to become available from Swiss publisher BIM and master artist/teacher Roger Bobo, the first volume of this set will cover fundamental exercises and warm-ups, the second volume (anticipated release in 1994) will include special etudes by contemporary composers with special instructional material for each etude, and the third volume (anticipated release 1995) will be on "how to be your own teacher."

Böhme, Oskar. *24 Melodic Studies.* Editions Marc Reift. 2003. $12.16. IV–V. A new edition of Böhme's *24 Etudes.* The etudes are melodic and cover just about all facets of brass playing: articulation, slurs, rhythm, tempo, dynamics, cantabile playing, syncopation, scales, trills, arpeggios, and multiple tonguing—all in a variety of keys. Available in treble clef.

Boosey and Hawkes. *The Complete Boosey and Hawkes Tuba Scale Book.* Boosey and Hawkes. 1995. $8.00. 49 pp. III–IV. Useful not only as a primer for graded examinations but also as a tool for improving technique through the incorporation of advanced scale patterns. Incorporates all major, minor (harmonic and melodic), chromatic, and whole tone scales, with arpeggios and intervallic exercises as well.

Bordogni, Marco. *43 Bel Canto Studies for Tuba.* ed. Chester Roberts. Robert King Music Company. 1972. 52 pp. III–IV. These studies, transcribed from Bordogni vocalises, focus on phrasing and lyricism. Roberts has transposed many of the etudes from their original keys. This is a standard college/university text in the United States.

Bordogni, Marco. *Legato Etudes for Tuba, Volume I.* trans. Wesley Jacobs. Encore Music Publishers. 1990. $10.00. 16 pp. III–V. Here are fifteen etudes from the vocalises of Bordogni emphasizing lyric style and phrasing. This edition has recorded accompaniments, available from the publisher.

Bordogni, Marco. *Legato Etudes for Tuba, Volume 2.* tr. Wesley Jacobs. Encore Music Publishers. 1995. $15.00. 28 pp. III–IV. Contains twenty-one of Bordogni's vocalises as presented in Rochut's *Melodious Etudes for Trombone* (etudes 16–36), but presented here an octave lower. Several exercises in this particular volume contain complex rhythms and require familiarity with the keys of D♭, E, and A major.

Bordogni, Marco. *Legato Etudes for Tuba, Volume 3.* tr. Wesley Jacobs. Encore Music Publishers. 1995. $15.00. 35 pp. III–IV. Contains twenty-four of Bordogni's vocalises as presented in Rochut's *Melodious Etudes for Trombone* (etudes 37–60), but presented here an octave lower. Due to the presence of frequent intervallic leaps, there is a greater need for flexibility than in previous volumes of this series.

Bordogni, Marco. *Low Legato Etudes for Tuba, Volume I.* tr. Wesley Jacobs. Encore Music Publishers. 1990. $11.00. 17 pp. IV–V. These five etudes are from the vocalises of Bordogni. Each is presented an octave lower than in other editions and in three different (progressively lower) keys (for an actual total of fifteen etudes). This is an excellent approach to low register study.

Bordogni, Marco. *Low Legato Etudes for Tuba, Volume 2.* tr. Wesley Jacobs. Encore Music Publishers. 1995. $15.00. 32 pp. III–IV. Contains twenty-two of Bordogni's vocalises as presented in Rochut's *Melodious Etudes for Trombone* (etudes 16–37), but presented here almost entirely below the bass clef staff, to aid in the development of low register playing. Several exercises in this particular volume contain complex rhythms and require familiarity with the keys of both E and A major.

Bordogni, Marco. *Low Legato Etudes for Tuba, Volume 3.* tr. Wesley Jacobs. Encore Music Publishers. 1995. $15.00. 30 pp. III–IV. Contains nineteen of Bordogni's vocalises as presented in Rochut's *Melodious Etudes for Trombone* (etudes 38–56), but presented here almost entirely below the bass clef staff, to aid in the development of low register playing. Due to the presence of frequent intervallic leaps, there is a greater need for flexibility than in previous volumes of this series.

Bousquet, N. *Thirty-Six Celebrated Studies for the Tuba.* tr. and ed. Peter Popiel and Matthew Wilson. Carl Fischer. 1998. $11.95. 79 pp. IV–V. A collection of advanced technical exercises incorporating wide intervallic leaps, arpeggios, and challenging rhythmic figures. Conservatively edited from the original trumpet version to make the exercises suitable for performance on the tuba.

Bower-Colin. *Advanced Rhythms.*

Bower-Colin. *Rhythms, Volumes I and II.*

Brandon, Sy. *Holiday Etudes for Tuba.* Tuba-Euphonium Press. 1996. $10.00. 29 pp. I–II. Winner of the 1996 ITEA Composition Contest for tuba etudes at the elementary level. Twenty-eight etudes suitable for study by first- and second-year tuba players. Each etude is named after a particular holiday and, in spite of limited range, the book incorporates a wide variety of meters, dynamics, and articulations.

Brightmore, Victor. *Forty-Three Easy Melodic Studies for Beginners on Brass Instruments (Bass Clef Edition).* Chappell & Company, Limited. II.

Brightmore, Victor. *25 Melodic Studies for Brass (Bass Clef Version).* Chappell & Company, Limited. 1964. 12 pp. III–IV.

Bruggen, P. van. *Etudes.*

Buck, Lawrence. *Elementary Method for Tuba (E♭ or BB♭).* Neil A. Kjos Music Company. 1954. Out of Print. $1.25. 40 pp. I. Although it is billed as a method for like-instrument or private instruction, this text is most suitable for the private setting. A new idea or concept is introduced every one to two pages, and considerable individual attention/explanation from the teacher would be desirable, as there is no explanatory text in the body of the book.

Buehlman, Barbara, and Ken Whitcomb. *Sessions in Sound, Books I and II (Tuba/Sousaphone).* Heritage Music Press. 1976. $4.50. 32 pp. I–II. This is a beginning band method which introduces new ideas at the top of each page and contains a brief glossary at the end of the book.

Burba, Malte. *Omnibus.* Editions Marc Reift. 2003. $24.33. III. A German-only text, of which the first half is dedicated to a detailed description of the physiological aspects of brass playing. The second half includes musical exercises intended to develop articulation, pitch accuracy, and familiarity with a variety of contemporary styles, including jazz.

Burden, James H. *Head Start Band Method, Book 1 (Tuba).* Columbia Lady Music. 1977. $5.50. 24 pp. I–II. This is a beginning band method which highlights new ideas and concepts with textual coloration and cartoon drawings.

Butterfield, Don. *Advanced Solo-Studies for Bass Clef Instruments.* D. B. Publishing Company.

Carbone, E. *Methodo teorico-practico: Posaune, Tuba, Bombardon.* Carisch Edizioni Musicali.

Carnaud, Jeune. *Complete Method, Volumes I and II.*

Carnaud, Jeune. *25 Etudes pour Tuba.*

Carnaud, Jeune. *25 Exercises pour Saxhorn basse.*

Caruso, Carmine, Hal Graham, and Shelton Booth. *Caruso Band Method (Tuba)—Book I.* Samuel French. 1969. $2.00. 30 pp. I. A beginning method for group instruction, this approach is based in the pedagogical ideas of prominent brass teacher Carmine Caruso. The tuba book has very good pedagogical comments, but little material of melodic interest for the young student.

Catelinet, Philip. *The Essential Tubaist.* Cinque Port Music Publishers. 1985. 30 pp. III–IV. This book is offered as a guide to daily practice which covers tone flexibility, precision and pitch, scales, and arpeggios. Presented in a format that takes the student from Monday through Saturday (resting on Sunday), all keys are covered. Pedagogical suggestions are offered at the beginning of the book.

Caton. *Progressive E♭ Tuba Instruction for Public School Classes.* Volkwein.

Charlier, Théo. *Trente-deux études de perfectionnement pour trombone in si bénik á 4 pistons ou tuba.* Henri Lemoine and Cie. 1946. 55 pp. III–IV. (See Thompson/Lemke: *French Music for Low Brass Instruments.*)

Cherubini, Maria Luigi Sa. *5 Etudes—Trombone (ou Tuba) Basse Seul ou Avec Piano.* arr. Andre Goudenhooft. Editions Billaudot. $21.36.

Cherubini, Maria Luigi Sa. *Etudes Diverses—Trombone Basse ou Tuba Basse.* arr. Andre Goudenhooft. Editions Billaudot. $19.95.

Childs, Robert and Nicholas. *Warm-ups and Studies.* Obrasso—Verlag AG. 1988. 11 pp. II–IV. Comprising six warm-up studies and two etudes, this book is intended for all brass instruments. Long tones, flexibilities, articulation, and technique are represented. As the work is aimed principally at a brass band audience, notation is presented in treble clef only. Text is presented in English and German.

Christensen, Kerstein. *Tuba Skole.* Wilhelm Hansen Musikforlag. 1949. $4.00. 67 pp. I–III. Aimed principally at the beginning tubist who is using the F tuba, this small book is not dissimilar to the abbreviated versions of the Arban *Method,* covering all basic fundamentals of performance. At the end of the book are a few good, intermediate–early advanced etudes. Text is printed in Scandinavian.

Cimera, Jaroslav. *73 Advanced Tuba Studies.* Belwin-Mills. 1955. $5.50. 31 pp. IV. These etudes emphasize technical and rhythmic development. A variety of keys and meters are represented. The style of the etudes compares favorably with Tyrell or Kopprasch studies.

Clark, Andy. *Five Minutes a Day (Tuba).* C. L. Barnhouse Company. 1992. $3.95. 12 pp. II–III. This method for band contains twelve individual lessons, including chorales, technical studies, and tuning exercises.

Clarke, Harry F. *Elementary Method for Tuba.* Belwin-Mills. I.

Clodomir. *Methode Complete pour tous les Saxhorns.* Alphonse Leduc Editions Musicales. 1948. 112 pp. IV.

Clodomir. *Methodes Elementaires pour tous les Saxhorns.* Alphonse Leduc Editions Musicales.

Clodomir, Pierre F. *70 kleine Etüden.* Friedrich Hofmeister Leipzig.

Colin, C. *100 Original Warm-Ups.*

Concone and Marchesi. *60 Musical Studies for Tuba (Book I).* tr. David L. Kuehn. Southern Music Company. 1969. $7.50. 21 pp. II–III. Studies in legato style from the vocalises of Concone and Marchesi, with special attention to phrasing and reading problems. On the whole, these studies are less challenging than traditional Rochut-style studies, but are very worthwhile for the late intermediate/early advanced student.

Concone, G. *Advanced Concone Studies.* ed. Reinhardt. Theodore Presser Company. $5.50.

Concone, Giuseppe. *The Complete Solfeggi: Legato Etudes for Tuba.* tr. and ed. Wesley Jacobs. Encore Music Publishers. 2000. $20.00. 144 pp. II–IV. A comprehensive method for developing mature legato style. Includes a wide range of material, from short scalar exercises intended for daily use to full-length vocalises suitable for performance. Includes brief pedagogical commentary by both the composer and the editor.

Cooman, Carson. *Dream Etudes, Book III.* MMB Music. See Music for Unaccompanied Tuba.

Cugnot, Alexandre. *15 ausgewählte Etüden.* Friedrich Hofmeister Leipzig. $11.66.

Culbertson, Melvin. *Muscle Up, Volumes I and II.*

Cummings, Barton. *Seventeen Virtuoso Studies after Maxime-Alphonse for Tuba, Bass Trombone, Bass and Contrebass Saxhorn.* Alphonse Leduc Editions Musicales. $16.25. (See Thompson/

Lemke: *French Music for Low Brass Instruments*).

Cummings, Barton. *Thirty Studies for Tuba, Bass Trombone, Bass and Contrabass Saxhorn after Maxime-Alphonse.* Alphonse Leduc Editions Musicales. 1978. $11.40. 12 pp. III–IV. These etudes are especially fine for work on articulation and technique. They would work especially well for the advanced high school or beginning college student. Per Mr. Cummings's reputation as a fine composer as well as gifted tuba artist, the etudes are very musical in character. (See Thompson/Lemke: *French Music for Low Brass Instruments*).

de Ville, Paul. *The Eclipse Self Instructor for BB♭ Bass.* Carl Fischer, Incorporated. 1905. Out of Print. 64 pp. II–III. Although the title indication is for contrabass tuba, the tessitura of all exercises appears to be principally for euphoniumor trombone. A thorough introduction to rudiments of music is included together with a few early exercises and "seventy-three standard national and sacred melodies." Pedagogical comments of interest to the scholar of pedagogical history are included at the beginning of the method.

Defaye. *Six Etudes—Two Tubas.* Alphonse Leduc Editions Musicales. $25.30.

Defaye. *Six Etudes Tuba.* Alphonse Leduc Editions Musicales. $11.40. (See Thompson/Lemke: *French Music for Low Brass Instruments*).

Delgiudice, Michel. *Douze Etudes Rythmiques et Melodiques.* Eschig. 1954. 25 pp. IV. (See Thompson/Lemke: *French Music for Low Brass Instruments*).

Delgiudice, Michel. *10 Kleine Text.*

D'Erasmo. *Method (Tuba).* Editions Salabert.

Dijoux, Marc. *Dechiffrage du debutant.*

Dodson, Thomas. *Music Creativity (Tuba).* Neil A. Kjos Music Company. 1991. $4.95. 32 pp. I. The uniqueness of this method is found in its emphasis on developing the creative process. Typical etudes are presented in alternation with incomplete etudes. The student is given guidelines within which to complete the incomplete etude, after which it is to be performed.

Dondeyne, D. *5 Etudes.*

Dondeyne, D. *12 Dechiffrages.* (See Thompson/Lemke: *French Music for Low Brass Instruments*).

Dondeyne, D. *9 Dechiffrages.*

Dondeyne, D. *13 Dechiffrages.*

Dondeyne, Desire. *12 Dechiffrages Superieur, Volume B.* Editions Billaudot. $6.28.

Dondeyne, Desire. *12 Dechiffrages Superieur, Volume C.* Editions Billaudot. $6.28

Dondeyne, Desire. *13 Dechiffrages Moyen, Volume B.* Editions Billaudot. $6.82.

Dondeyne, Desire. *13 Dechiffrages Moyen, Volume C.* Editions Billaudot. $6.82.

Dondeyne, Desire. *9 Dechiffrages Preparatoire, Volume B.* Editions Billaudot. $5.20.

Dondeyne, Desire. *9 Dechiffrages Preparatoire, Volume C.* Editions Billaudot. $5.20.

Douglas, Wayne, and Fred Weber. *Belwin Band Builder for Bass (Tuba) in 3 Volumes.* Belwin-Mills. 1953/57. $5.50. 27 pp. I–II. This classic band method quickly introduces the tuba as both a soloistic and accompanimental instrument. This is accomplished through the early presentation of several harmonized tunes, each of which includes both the melody and a bass part. Volumes II and III give additional attention to the development of technique through progressive scale studies.

Downey and Meehan. *Ensemble Techniques in Two Volumes (Tuba).* Hal Leonard Publishing Corporation. $2.95.

Dubois, Pierre Max. *12 Soli en form D'Etudes.* Alphonse Leduc Editions Musicales. 1961. $14.25. 16 pp. IV. (See Thompson/Lemke: *French Music for Low Brass Instruments*).

Dufresne, Gaston. *Sight Reading Studies for Bass Trombone/Tuba.* ed. Don Schaeffer. Charles Colin. 1964. 25 pp. IV.

Dutton, Brent. *Twelve Etudes for Solo Tuba or Bass Trombone.* Brass Quake Press. 2003. $15.00. 14 pp. III–V. Dedicated to Ron Bishop. A collection of advanced etudes, most of which incorporate extensive low register, wide intervallic leaps, frequent chromaticism, and/or multiple meter shifts.

Eby, Walter M. *Eby's Scientific Method for BB flat Bass, Sousaphone, E flat Tuba and CC Bass Part 1.* Walter Jacobs (Big Three). 1930. Out of Print. 60 pp. I–II. One of the early methods emphasizing the contrabass tuba, this method was intended for private instruction, covering all fundamental areas of performance and providing detailed explanation of pedagogical practice.

Eby, Walter M. *Eby's Scientific Method for BB flat Bass, Sousaphone, E flat Tuba and CC Bass Part 2.* Walter Jacobs (Big Three). 1930. Out of Print. 175 pp. III. A continuation of the Eby *Method, Part I.* This section of the work is aimed toward the more advanced player, developing and building on ideas presented in part I.

Eerola, Lasse. *Thirty Etydia Tuuballe.* Finnish Music Information Centre. 1992. 30 pp. II. This is a particularly fine book of etudes for the serious young student. Virtually all basic rhythm problems are addressed, and the etudes really focus on developing the middle register of the instrument, an important focus for any young student. Various studies focus on intervals, flexibility, articulation, etc.

Eidson, Alonzo B. *Belwin Brass Bass Method, Book I and II.* ed. Nilo W. Hovey. Belwin-Mills. 1947. $1.25. 32 pp. I–II. This basic, beginning method includes several piano accompaniments for exercises within the book and a fingering chart which extends up to f'.

Elledge, Robert, and Donald Haddad. *Band Technique–Step by Step (Tuba).* Neil A. Kjos Music Company. 1992. $4.95. 36 pp. II. An intermediate-level method which progresses through most major and minor keys, this work features enrichment through "Advanced Rhythms" pages and through an extensive fingering chart which both extends to BBB♭ and includes fingerings for F, E♭, CC, and BB♭ tubas.

Ellis, James L. *Back to Basics for Tuba.* L. S. Publications. 2002. $10.00. 57 pp. II–III. Intended as a "private lesson book for first-year students and a permanent resource warm-up guide for more advanced students." Addresses basic principles of both theory and performance, including music notation, tone production, practice technique, lip slurs, basic scales, and range development.

Endresen, R. M. *BB♭ Tuba Method (Two Books).* M. M. Cole Publishing Company. 1937. Out of Print. $1.00. 63 pp. I–II. Intended for private instruction, this classic method introduces basic music fundamentals at an accelerated pace. In addition to etudes emphasizing all aspects of development, a number of recognizable melodies and duets for student and teacher are included.

Endresen, R. M. *E♭ Tuba Method (Two Books).* M. M. Cole Publishing Company. 1937. Out of Print. $1.00. 63 pp. I–II. This text is essentially identical to the previously described Endresen *BB♭ Tuba Method.* A few different photographs are included and the foreword is different; however, all instructional material is the same.

Endressen, R. M. *Supplementary Studies for E flat or BB flat Bass.* Rubank, Incorporated. 1936. $3.95. 24 pp. II–III. Containing progressively arranged, brief etudes in various styles emphasizing various aspects of melodic and technical playing, this is a good review/sight-reading book for junior or senior high.

Erickson, Frank. *Belwin Comprehensive Band Method (BB♭ Tuba), Volumes I, II, and III.* Belwin-Mills. 1988/88/89. $5.00. 40 pp. I–II. Designed for either individual or group instruction, this method contains three volumes, each of which are subsequently divided into two sections: one for individual instruction and another for group study. Features of each section include harmonized etudes, progressively introduced rhythmic patterns, and (volume III only) alternating etudes/program works.

Erickson, Frank. *Technique through Melody for Band (Tuba).* Belwin-Mills. 1983. $5.50. 24 pp. II–III. With an emphasis on lyrical playing, this method includes both modal and tonal etudes, some of which are designed for aural development through the repetition of specific intervallic relationships.

Erickson, Frank, Eric Osterling, and James D. Ployhar. *Band Today, Part I.* Belwin-Mills. 1977. $5.50. 32 pp. I. This is a traditional band method designed for group or individual instruction. Covers fundamentals of music reading and playing.

Feldstein, Sandy. *Alfred's New Band Method, Book I.* Alfred Music Company. $4.95. I.

Feldstein, Sandy, and John O'Reilly. *Alfred's Basic Band Method, I, II, III (Tuba).* Alfred Music Company. 1977. $5.50. 32 pp. I–II. Each section/chapter within this method begins with the new material for that section and continues with reinforcing etudes, occasionally including a duet for two tubas.

Feldstein, Sandy, and John O'Reilly. *Yamaha Band Student, Books I and II (Tuba).* Alfred Music Company. 1988. $5.50. 31 pp. I. Containing a variety of repertoire, this is a widely used band method with increased visual appeal. Newly introduced fundamentals are presented in highlighted areas.

Feldstein, Sandy, and Joseph Scianni. *The Sound of Rock (Tuba).* Alfred Music Company. 1971. $1.95. 32 pp. II–III. This is a method designed to introduce elements of rock/jazz to the student through group instruction. Emphasis is on rhythm patterns and articulation styles typically found in rock music. The tuba part emphasizes bass-like playing, but with opportunities to play solos.

Fink, Reginald H., ed. and compiler. *Studies in Legato.* Carl Fischer, Incorporated. 1967. $9.00. 43 pp. III–IV. Legato studies for tuba or bass trombone "Based on the works of Concone, Marchesi and Panofka." Includes suggestions for efficient study of each etude. These studies would be well suited to the advanced high school or beginning college student.

Fischer, Carl. *Carl Fischer's New and Revised Edition of Celebrated Tutors: BB♭ Bass.* Carl Fischer, Incorporated. 1908. Out of Print. 77 pp. II–III. This method is virtually identical to the later method attributed to Otto Langey and published by Carl Fischer, apparently printed from the same plates. (See *Langey–Carl Fischer Tutors for BB♭ Bass.*)

Fitchhorn, E. *Practical Procedures for Sight Reading for Band (Tuba).* ed. O. W. Margrave. Henri Elkan Music Publisher.

Franz, A. *Schule für Tuba oder Helikon in F mit 4 Ventilen.* Bellmann & Thymer O.J.

Franz, Oskar. *10 Grosse Concert-Etüden.* Friedrich Hofmeister Leipzig. $9.56.

Freese, Hal. *Advanced Band Method (Tuba).* Belwin-Mills. 1972. $5.50. 39 pp. II. The third in a series of three volumes, this book is a logical continuation of the second (Intermediate) volume.

Freese, Hal. *Elementary Band Method (Tuba).* Belwin Mills. 1967. $5.50. 33 pp. I. The first in a series of three volumes, this volume is progressively organized and addresses the fundamental concepts of first-year tuba playing.

Freese, Hal. *Intermediate Band Method (Tuba).* Belwin-Mills. 1968. $5.50. 40 pp. I–II. The second in a series of three volumes, this volume is a logical continuation of the first (Elementary) volume.

Fritze, Gregory. *Twenty Characteristic Etudes for Tuba.* TUBA Press. 1991. $12.00. 40 pp. III–IV. Winner of the 1992 TUBA Etude Contest, this book is directed toward preparation for orchestral, chamber, and solo literature and principally toward the advanced collegiate or professional performer. The composer notes that there are several direct quotations from the repertoire to help direct learning. All keys are represented, and the etudes are intended for tubas in all keys.

Froseth, James O. *The Comprehensive Music Instructor for Band, Books I, II, III (Tuba).* Gia Publications, Incorporated. $4.95.

Froseth, James O. *Do It! Play Tuba, Book One.* GIA Publications. 1997. $6.95. 48 pp. I. Though intended as a beginning method for mixed and like-instrument instruction, this is also suitable as a method for individual instruction. Includes a fingering chart for BB♭ and E♭ tubas, illustrations, and separate glossaries for musical symbols, basic terminology, and rhythmic patterns. Also includes an audio CD with both accompaniment and demonstration tracks for each exercise. Demonstration tracks feature tubist Fritz Kaenzig. See Discography: Kaenzig, Fritz.

Froseth, James O. *The Individualized Instructor, Books I, II, III (Tuba).* Gia Publications, Incorporated. 1970/72/73. $4.95. 31 pp. I–III. This series is designed for use as a self-guided, individual course. Characteristics of this series include rhythm exercises, technical studies, and ensembles.

Froseth, James O. *The Individualized Instructor, Preliminary Book (Tuba).* Gia Publications, Incorporated. $5.95.

Froseth, James. *Listen, Move, Sing and Play for Band (Tuba), Book 1.* Gia Publications, Incorporated. 1984. $3.50. 33 pp. I. This highly comprehensive band method emphasizes the firm establishment of fundamental performance skills through a variety of exercises and etudes, including rounds, duets, and rhythmic drills.

Froseth, James. *Listen, Move, Sing and Play for Band (Tuba), Book 2.* Gia Publications, Incorporated. 1984. $3.95. 31 pp. I–II. The second in a series of two books, this is a logical continuation of the first book.

Gallay, J. F. *30 Etudes for Tuba, Op.13.* ed. Robert King. Robert King Music Company. 1978. $3.95. 31 pp. IV. Originally for valveless horn, these difficult etudes present exceptional challenges in flexibility and overall technique for either an advanced college student or a professional player who is seeking to "stretch."

Gallay, Jacques. *12 Etudes.* ed. Estevan Dax. Editions Billaudot. $9.50. 15 pp. IV.

Gallay, Jacques. *15 Style Studies.* ed. Gerard Billaudot. Editions Billaudot. 1974. $9.25. 14 pp. IV–V. Played in the written octave, this method provides excellent melodic material for the F tuba, and the longer studies may be used as performance works.

Gallay, Jacques F. *12 Grandes Etudes Brillantes, Op.43.* Friedrich Hofmeister Leipzig. $13.26.

Gallay, Jacques F. *Forty Preludes for F Tuba, Op.27.* ed. Robert King. Alphonse Leduc. 1993. $9.15. 28 pp. IV–V. Originally composed for the horn, this collection is comprised of both measured and non-measured etudes, most of which place high technical demands on the performer. Lip flexibility and breath control are prerequisites to mastering most of the etudes in this method. Intended for use with the bass tuba but also suitable for middle and high register development on the contrabass tuba.

Geib, Fred. *The Geib Method for Tuba.* Carl Fischer, Incorporated. 1941. $12.00. 117 pp. I–III. Written by one of the early great figures in tuba pedagogy, this text is similar to the Arban method for trumpet, but at an overall simpler level. The work does not have melodies, but does incorporate a few orchestral excerpts at its conclusion. (See orchestra studies section for a listing of excerpts.)

Geib, Fred. *Tuba Studies and Solos.* Tuba-Euphonium Press. 1994. $13.00. 30 pp. III–IV. A compilation of exercises and solos with emphasis upon contrasting articulations. Prominent use of broken chords, chromaticism, and melodic sequencing.

Getchell, Robert W. *Practical Studies (Book I and II).* ed. Nilo Hovey. Belwin-Mills. 1955. $6.50. 32 pp. II–III. These books serve as an introduction to the study of technique and, particularly, rhythm. Basic rhythmic figures receive concentrated treatment in brief, interesting etudes.

Giovannoli, S. *Method for E♭ and B♭ Bass for Beginners, Part I: Rudiments and Easy Exercises.* New York: Middle Village. 1959. $1.50. 31 pp. I–II. Intended as a beginning method for private instruction, this simple text introduces basic rudiments of playing, together with very easy exercises for the beginning and early intermediate student. There are no pedagogical comments in the book; however, the simple etudes would work well as supplementary material for the young person.

Girard, Anthony. *50 Etudes Faciles et Progressives, Volume 1.* Editions Billaudot. $9.76.

Girard, Anthony. *50 Etudes Faciles et Progressives, Volume 2.* Editions Billaudot. $9.76.

Girard, Anthony. *24 Etudes De Flexibilite—Tuba Basse.* Editions Billaudot. $10.12.

Girard, Anthony. *24 Etudes De Rythme et De Detache—Tuba Basse.* Editions Billaudot. $21.36.

Girard, Anthony. *24 Etudes D'Intonation et De Respiration—Tuba Basse.* Editions Billaudot. $13.43.

Giuffre, Jimmy. *Jazz Phrasing and Interpretation (Bass Instruments)*. Associated Music Publishers. 1969. 61 pp. III–IV.

Gland, H., and A. Franz. *Schule für Tuba oder Helikon in B mit 4 Ventilen*. Bellman & Thymer, O.J.

Goldman, Edwin Franko. *Daily Embouchure Studies*. Carl Fischer, Incorporated. 1909. Out of Print. 9 pp. III–IV.

Gordon, David. *Three Etudes for Solo Tuba*. Tuba-Euphonium Press. 2001. $8.00. III–IV. Intended for performance and comprising three movements: Lyrical; Aggressive/Relaxed; Driving. Each movement is quite distinct in style, yet all employ traditional techniques, save one note that is flutter-tongued. Movement I employs legato arpeggiations and includes a fair amount of upper tessitura work. Movement II is more technical and has increased metric interest. Movement III is a study in rhythm, with several metric modulations, tempo changes, and varied meters. Pitch content is much easier on this movement. Overall, the piece is well suited to either bass or contrabass tuba. See Music for Unaccompanied Tuba.

Gornston, David. *Fun with Scales in Bass Clef.* MCA.

Gornston, David. *The Very First BB♭ or E♭ Bass method*. Edward Schuberth & Co. 1953. 60¢. 32 pp. I.

Gornston, David, and W. Musser. *Tuba Dailies*. Neil A. Kjos Music Company. 1960. $1.00. 17 pp. I–V. This is a book (principally) of lip slurs, with various rhythms and articulations. It is intended as a guide to establishing a daily routine, drilling fundamentals of good playing.

Goudenhooft, Andre. *15 Etudes complementaires*. Editions Billadout. (See Thompson/Lemke: *French Music for Low Brass Instruments*).

Goudenhooft, Andre. *15 Etudes Complementaires D'Apres Differents Auteurs Anciens*. Editions Billaudot. $15.10.

Goudenhooft, Andre. *32 Etudes—Trombone Basse ou Tuba Basse*. Editions Billaudot. $17.31.

Goudenhooft, Andre. *Twenty-Four Etudes pour le Trombone Basse et le Tuba Basse*. ed. Gerard Billaudot. Editions Billaudot. 1985. $19.50. 30 pp. V. Use of wide range, various keys, contrasting articulations, and tenor clef make this a challenging method for the most advanced performers. (See Thompson/Lemke: *French Music for Low Brass Instruments*).

Gouse, Charles F. *Learn to Play the Tuba! (Books I and II)*. Alfred Music Company. 1970. 48 pp. I. This is part of a method series intended for group brass instruction or for use as a private tutor. It covers basics of music reading and playing fundamentals.

Gower, William, and Himie Voxman. *Rubank Advanced Method for E flat or BB flat Bass, Vol. I*. Rubank, Incorporated. 1951. $6.95. 72 pp. III. This method provides excellent challenges for the serious young high school student. Short etudes cover scales, arpeggios, flexibility, and other aspects of development of good, fundamental playing skills.

Gower, William, and Himie Voxman. *Rubank Advanced Method for E flat or BB flat Bass, Vol. II*. Rubank, Incorporated. 1959. $6.95. 95 pp. III–IV. These etudes emphasize articulation, flexibility, ornamentation, and scales. The book also includes several full-length solos.

Green, Barry, and Timothy Gallwey. *The Inner Game of Music: Workbook for Band (Tuba/String Bass)*. Gia Publications, Incorporated. 1991. $4.50. 21 pp. II–III. Designed as a supplement to the text *The Inner Game of Music*, this method reinforces positive performance concepts with musical examples from the classical music repertoire.

Gregson, E. *New Horizons for the Young Brass Player (Tuba)*.

Gregson, E. *Twenty Supplementary Tunes*.

Grigoriev, Boris. *50 Etudes for Tuba, Volume 1*. ed. Keating Johnson. Encore Music Publishers. 1986. $15.00. 27 pp. III–IV. Etudes in all keys are represented in this book with particular emphasis on low register. These etudes are best suited to students who have established good fundamentals, as well as to professional players.

Grigoriev, Boris. *50 Etudes for Tuba, Volume 2*. ed. Keating Johnson. Encore Music Publishers. 1986. $15.00. 29 pp. III–V. The second in a series of two books, this volume is a logical continuation of volume I.

Grigoriev, Boris. *78 Studies for Tuba*. Robert King Music Company. 1983. $5.20. 72 pp. III–IV. These etudes cover all keys (major and relative minor), moving through sharps and flats progressively. Although some technical problems are presented, the emphasis of the book is on lyric playing and low register, very comparable in some ways to the Blazhevich studies published by Robert King.

Grunow, Richard F., and Edwin E. Gordon. *Jump Right In! Book I (Tuba)*. Gia Publications, Incorporated. $4.95.

Gugel, Heinrich. *12 Etüden*. Friedrich Hofmeister Leipzig. $9.58.

Guthrie, James. *Twenty-Nine Etudes for Tuba*. TUBA Press. 1992. $12.00. 35 pp. IV–V. Not for the faint of heart, these etudes are recommended for the very advanced and serious student or the professional. Very good, challenging rhythmic problems are presented, in terms of both meters and basic time, and range and technical demands really push the performer to the limit. An excellent choice for the performer who needs to be totally prepared in any reading situation.

Haddad, Don. *20 Short Etudes*. Southern Music Company. 1990. $7.95. 15 pp. II–III. Very nice etudes for the intermediate to early advanced player. Melodic and rhythmic problems are presented in a musically attractive way. These etudes appropriately test the range of the young player to middle C.

Haines, Harry, and J. R. McEntyre. *Division of Beat (Tuba/Bass), Books Ia, Ib, and II.* Southern Music Company. 1981/81/89. $4.50. I–II. This band method places emphasis on the development of correct rhythmic skills through the use of a breath impulse. It is recommended that the method be used in conjunction with matching rhythm slides, also available from Southern Music Company.

Hawkes and Sons. *Simplicity Tutor.*

Hejda. *Etudes for BB flat Tuba.* Artia, Foreign Trade Corporation. 1958.

Herfurth, C. Paul, and Hugh M. Stuart. *Our Band Class Book for Basses (Levels I and II for BB flat and E flat Tubas).* Carl Fischer, Incorporated. 1967. $3.95. 34 pp. I.

Herfurth, C. Paul, and Hugh M. Stuart. *Sounds of the Winds (Tuba), Book I and II.* Carl Fischer, Incorporated.

Herfurth, C. Paul, and Vernon R. Miller. *A Tune a Day for Tuba or Sousaphone.* Boston Music Company. 1954. $6.95. 48 pp. I. This book includes a review of musical and playing fundamentals, but the main content focuses on essentially American folk and hymn tunes presented in a simple format.

Hilgers, Walter. *Daily Exercises.* Editions Marc Reift. 1993. $20.79. III–IV. A wide array of etudes, from simple long tone exercises to articulation drills containing a variety of rhythmic patterns. Arpeggios and scales are introduced in all registers, with a variety of articulations.

Hindsley, Mark H. *Carl Fischer Basic Method for BB♭ Tuba.* Carl Fischer, Incorporated. 1938. Out of Print. $1.00. 48 pp. I–II. This is a rapidly moving yet well-organized method covering various rhythms, keys, and interpretive skills.

Hofmeister, ed. *Tonleitern und tägliche Studien: Baß-Tuba und Helikon.* Friedrich Hofmeister. 1933/53.

Hoppert, Manfred. *B-Tuba/Kontrabasstuba Grifftabellen.* Wilhelm Zimmerman.

Hornung, A., and O. Heinl. *Schule für Blasorchester: Tuba.* Halter O.J. 1968.

Hovey, Howard. *Universal's Fundamental Method for the Tuba and Sousaphone.* Universal Music Publishers. 1942. Out of Print. $1.75. 48 pp. I–II. A basic elementary method for private instruction that includes an introduction to basic musicianship skills and a variety of short solos and familiar tunes.

Hovey, Nilo W. *Advanced Techniques for E♭ and BB♭ Basses.* M. M. Cole Publishing Company.

Hovey, Nilo W. *Basic Technique for E♭ or BB♭ Bass.* M. M. Cole Publishing Company.

Hovey, Nilo W. *Rubank Elementary Method—E flat or BB flat Bass.* Rubank, Incorporated. 1934. $4.95. 48 pp. I–II. This book rapidly introduces basic musical concepts and most major keys. It works particularly well as an initial text for private study.

Hovey, Nilo W. *Supplementary Drill Book for E♭ and BB♭ Basses.* M. M. Cole Publishing Company.

Hovey, Nilo W. *T-I-P-P-S for Bands (Bass/Tuba).* Belwin-Mills. 1959. $4.50. 23 pp. II–III. With studies in most "band keys," this is an ensemble method which emphasizes fundamentals such as tone, intonation, phrasing, precision, and style through the use of scalar, arpeggiated, and chorale-type studies.

Hoza, Vaclav, ed. *One Hundred Etudes for Tuba.* Editio Supraphon veb Deutscher Verlag für Musik Leipzig.

Hoza, Vaclav. *Schule für Tuba in F und in B.* Editio Supraphon veb Deutscher Verlag für Musik Leipzig. 1983. 135 pp. I–IV. Vaclav Hoza is a legendary performer and teacher in Czechoslovakia. This comprehensive method includes a history of the tuba and a complete introduction to musicianship skills and brass playing skills. Similar in format to the Arban *Method,* it presents one of the most sensible progressive approaches to playing in existence for tuba players. All text is printed in Czech and German.

Hubbell, Fred. *Rounds Plus.* Heritage Music Press. 1991. $3.95. 24 pp. I–II. This method is comprised of scales and short melodies which may be played as rounds, and it is organized by key.

Hudadoff, Igor. *A Rhythm a Day.* Pro Art Publications. 1963. 24 pp. II–III.

Hudadoff, Igor, and Norman Ward. *Sight Reader for Young Bands (Tuba)—Book I.* Shawnee Press. 1968. 16 pp. I.

Hudadoff, Igor, and Norman Ward. *Sight Reader for Young Bands (Tuba)—Book II.* Shawnee Press. 1969. 16 pp. I–II.

Huston, J. August. *Twenty-Two Etudes for Tuba.* ed. Wesley Jacobs. Tuba-Euphonium Press. 2000. $9.00. 12 pp. II–III. A collection of short etudes progressing in difficulty from middle school to college level. Includes a variety of tempi, styles, and articulations. Probably composed originally for E♭ tuba.

Jacobs, Wesley. *Daily Routine and Warm Up Studies for Tuba.* Encore Music Publishers. 1990. $12.00. 16 pp. I–V. A complete warm-up routine covering flexibility, articulation, intervals, scales, and tone production. Each section is preceded by practice suggestions.

Jacobs, Wesley. *Flexibility Studies for Tuba.* Encore Music Publishers. 1989. $11.00. 23 pp. III–V. Flexibility etudes are each presented in a variety of keys, covering a variety of interval problems. The book opens with detailed practice hints and suggestions.

Jacobs, Wesley. *Low Register Studies for Tuba.* Encore Music Publishers. $22.00. 121 pp. II–V. A progressive book for study of low register that includes fingering charts and a guide to practice.

Each chapter has exercises followed by musical etudes.

Jacobs, Wesley. *Restructured Etudes for Tuba, Volume I.* ed. Wesley Jacobs. Encore Music Publishers. 1989. $12.00. 22 pp. IV–V. Five etudes are in this volume with each presented three times, each time in a different key. Each presents interesting technical and musical challenges, and suggestions for effective study from the editor are included. The editor recommends these etudes for tubas in all keys.

Jacobs, Wesley. *Restructured Etudes for Tuba, Volume II.* ed. Wesley Jacobs. Encore Music Publishers. 1986. $15.00. 45 pp. IV–V. Each etude in this volume is presented three times, each time in a different key, and one of the three times in a different meter. As in volume I, the etudes are musically interesting and present challenges in all areas of technique. The editor recommends these etudes for tubas in all keys.

Jacobs, Wesley. *Restructured Etudes for Tuba, Volume III.* ed. Wesley Jacobs. Encore Music Publishers. 1986. $13.50. 37 pp. IV–V. As in the previous two volumes, each etude in this volume is presented three times, each time in a different key, and, as in volume II, one of the three times in a different meter. The editor recommends these etudes for tubas in all keys.

Jacobs, Wesley. *Restructured Etudes for Tuba, Volume IV.* ed. Wesley Jacobs. Encore Music Publishers. 1986. $12.00. 33 pp. IV–V. The format for this volume is identical to that of the previous volumes in the same series.

Jacobs, Wesley. *Restructured Etudes for Tuba, Volume V.* ed. Wesley Jacobs. Encore Music Publishers. 1991. $17.00. 27 pp. IV–V. The format for this volume is identical to that of the previous volumes in the same series.

Jacobs, Wesley. *Technical Studies for Tuba.* Encore Music Publishers. 1990. $15.00. 40 pp. IV–V. A series of etudes (presented in all keys) that present a variety of pattern and interval studies together with a variety of suggested rhythm and articulation patterns. Excellent study repertoire for the serious student or the professional who wants material to maintain or sharpen skills.

Jenson, Art. *Learning Unlimited—Audio Visual/Cassette Series (BB♭ Bass), Levels I and II.* Hal Leonard Publishing Corporation. 1971. $9.95. 48 pp. I–II. Designed primarily for individual instruction, this is a combination book/cassette method which is usable both by groups of like instruments and as supplementary material for any band method. The material is progressively organized according to complexity of each concept, beginning (in level I) with buzzing the mouthpiece and concluding (in level II) with playing in compound meter.

Jenson, Art. *Learning Unlimited—Class Series (BB♭ Bass), Level I.* Hal Leonard Publishing Corporation. 1973. $4.95. 64 pp. I. This is a beginning band method whose primary features include reference charts (listing each exercise by primary concept emphasized and as unison, duet, or full band), illustrations, and textual coloration.

Jenson, Art. *Learning Unlimited—Class Series (BB♭ Bass), Level II.* Hal Leonard Publishing Corporation. 1974. $4.95. 48 pp. II. The second in a series of two books, this is a logical continuation of the first book and includes the expansion of harmonic, formal, and expressive skills.

Job., M., ed. *Ecole de Chant et de Style—Trente Airs Classiques.* Alphonse Leduc Editions Musicales. 1949. 11 pp. IV. (See Thompson/Lemke: *French Music for Low Brass Instruments*).

Johnson, Harold M. *Aeolian Method for E♭ or BB♭ Bass.* H. T. Fitzsimmons. 1945. Out of Print. $1.00. 48 pp. I–II. Although billed as a method for group or private instruction, this method is definitely best suited to the individual lesson format, as little supplemental or explanatory material is included, and the pace is brisk. The selection of melodies included is excellent and the brief etudes are well written.

Johnson, Keith. *Progressive Studies for the High Register.* Harold Gore Publishing. 1991. $10.00. 35 pp. III–V. These progressive studies in range development are intended for use as part of the player's daily routine. A good guide to study is provided at the beginning of the book.

Johnson, Stuart. *New Horizons Tuneful Tuba.*

Johnson, Tommy, Mark McDunn, and Harold Rusch. *The Tommy Johnson Tuba Methods, Book 1.* Neil A. Kjos Music Company. 1975. $1.75. 32 pp. I. Tommy Johnson is best known in the tuba world as a leading studio musician. For many years he has also been a successful teacher of young students. Here are his ideas for teaching the young tubist. The method includes familiar melodies and good preliminary comments on playing fundamentals.

Kietzer, R. *Schule für Tuba in F, Es (Helikon) d.e.r.* Zimmermann-Frankfurt. $12.24.

Kietzer, Robert. *Schule für Tuba in B♭ or C, Helikon, bombardon, Sousaphon, Op. 85. (complete or in two parts).* Wilhelm Zimmerman. 112 pp. II–III. Here is an early German tuba tutor. In the beginning of the text a review of basic fundamentals of music reading and instrument address are presented. The volume consists principally of short etudes in all keys suitable for the intermediate to advanced high school student. All fundamental areas of brass study are covered thoroughly. Text is presented in German, English, and Russian.

Kietzer, Robert. *Schule für Tuba in F und E♭ oder Helikon, Op. 84.* Wilhelm Zimmerman. $13.25. 87 pp. I–IV.

Kinyon, John. *Basic Training Course for Tuba, Book 1.* Alfred Music Company. 1970. $5.50. 32 pp. I. Book I of a two-book series, this method is progressively organized and contains many short melodies. Although it is indicated as being intended for private instruction, like-instrument classes, mixed ensembles, or beginning bands, its most appropriate use is probably as part of a beginning band course.

Kinyon, John. *Basic Training Course for Tuba, Book 2.* Alfred Music Company. 1971. $5.50. 32 pp. I–II. The second in a two-book series, this method is a logical continuation of the first book.

Kinyon, John. *Breeze-Easy Method for BB flat Tuba, Book I.* Witmark. 1954. $5.95. 32 pp. I. A true classic, this text is designed for use individually or with other brass instruments. It introduces principles of musicianship and basic musical skills, as well as performance fundamentals, in a thorough, logical manner.

Kinyon, John. *Breeze-Easy Method for BB flat Tuba, Book II.* Witmark. 1960. $5.95. 32 pp. I–II. This is a logical continuation of the first book of this series described above.

Kinyon, John. *Daily Half Dozens for Young Bands (tuba).* Alfred Music Company. 1968. $1.00. 15 pp. I–II. Intended for group instruction, this book includes seven six-exercise pre-rehearsal routines for full band. Each set includes a warm-up, a scale study, a rhythm exercise, a round, and a technique drill. The last page of the book has a good narrative regarding suggestions for home practice.

Kinyon, John. *The MPH John Kinyon Band Method (Tuba).* Warner Brothers Music.

Kinyon, John. *Stepping Stones to Band Performance (Tuba).* Alfred Music Company. 1970. $1.00. 17 pp. I–II. This simple book is for group instruction and intended to move the ensemble from playing unison melodies to playing independent lines in a full band composition. Except for two full-length compositions at the end of the book, exercises are two to three lines long.

Kitchner, O. *Schule für Tuba* (Stadt Bibliotheken, München). Domkowsky O.J. ca. 1910.

Kleefoot, Michael. *Einfach fit.* Friedrich Hofmeister Leipzig. $22.72.

Kliment. *Anfänger-Schule für B-Tuba.*

Kliment. *Anfänger-Schule für F-Tuba oder Baß Posaune.*

Kliment. *B-Baß-Schule für Fortgeschrittene.*

Kliment. *Grifftabelle and Anfangsbrunde.*

Kling, H. *Leicht faßliche praktische Schule.* Louis Oertle. 1898. Out of Print.

Kling, Henri. *32 Technical and Musical Studies for Tuba or Bass Trombone.* tr. Peter Popiel. Accura Music. $15.95. III–IV.

Kling, Henry. *30 Etüden.* Friedrich Hofmeister Leipzig. $11.67.

Kling, Henry. *10 Etüden.* Friedrich Hofmeister Leipzig. $8.60.

Klose-Vanasek. *270 Tone and Technique Exercises.*

Knaub, Donald. *Progressive Techniques for Tuba.* Hal Leonard Publishing Corporation. 1970. $14.95. 128 pp. III–IV. This method contains the seventy studies by Blazhevich with the addition of warm-up studies, scale studies, and editorial comments. The warm-up routine based on the famous Emory Remington warm-up studies, together with Professor Knaub's pedagogical comments, make this a particularly valuable work for the tubist's library.

Kohlman, Charles. *Thirty-One Etudes for Bass Trombone or F/E♭ Tuba.* Tuba-Euphonium Press. 1999. $15.00. 32 pp. IV–V. Though originally composed for bass trombone, these etudes are well suited for advanced study on either the F or the E♭ tuba. Extensive range and wide intervallic leaps make this a challenging method, even for the most advanced college tubist.

Komischke, Uwe. *Daily Drills.* Editions Marc Reift. 1996. $20.27. III–IV. Written in treble clef, these exercises emphasize the development of embouchure strength through articulation and interval training. Preface includes helpful insights regarding practice strategy.

Komischke, Uwe. *24 Studies.* Editions Marc Reift. 1996. $16.22. III–IV. Well-structured etudes, each focusing on a specific meter, rhythm, or articulation. Written in treble clef, the studies incorporate a conservative range, rarely extending beyond the staff in either direction.

Komischke, Uwe. *Virtuosity Drills.* Editions Marc Reift. 1996. $16.22. IV–V. Drills designed to develop technical proficiency through the use of tonally irregular sequences. Though varying articulations is suggested, the exercises are written without articulation or tempo indications in order to give the performer complete control in determining his/her own rate of progress. Written in treble clef.

Komischke, Uwe. *Warm-Ups.* Editions Marc Reift. 1996. $16.22. IV–V. A wide array of difficult exercises in a variety of registers, including lip slurs, scale patterns, and articulation drills. Originally for trumpet, the exercises are published in treble clef.

Kopprasch, C. *Sechzig usgewahlte Etuden (60 Etudes)—Two volumes.* ed. Franz Seyffarth (Hofmeister). Freidrich Hofmeister. 27 pp. III–IV. This book (originally from the horn repertoire) represents one of the basic resources for study of brass technique, with a wealth of interval and articulation studies. Also published for trumpet and trombone, this work should be in every player's library. (NOTE: Now also available from Hofmeister in a single volume.)

Kopprasch, C. *Sixty Studies for Tuba.* Robert King Music Company. $4.80. 52 pp. III–IV. (See previous entry.)

Krzystek, W. *Studia na puzon i tube.* Polish Music Edition (P.W.M.) Krakow.

Kuhn, John M., and Jaroslav Cimera. *Kuhn-Cimera Method for Tuba (BB flat and E flat).* Belwin-Mills. 1941. $5.50. 48 pp. I–II. This book is intended as an introductory method for private study and was written by two of the "giants" of low brass pedagogy early in this century. In addition to coverage of basic fundamentals, familiar tunes from classical and folk repertoire are included.

Laas, Bill, and Fred Weber. *Advanced Fun with Fundamentals (Tuba)*. Belwin-Mills. $5.50. II–III.

Laas, Bill, and Fred Weber. *Fun with Fundamentals (Tuba)*. Belwin-Mills. 1963. $5.50. 28 pp. I–II. This is a supplemental method which emphasizes technical development through elementary scales, etudes, and duets.

Laas, Bill, and Fred Weber. *Studies and Melodious Etudes for Tuba (Bass), Level I*. Belwin-Mills. 1969. $5.50. 32 pp. I–II. The first in a series of three books, this book (like books II and III—see Swanson, Kenneth) was designed to be used as a supplementary technique book with the Tuba (Bass) Student Instrumental Course and addresses the development of musicianship through scales and technical/melodic etudes.

Labole, P. *Methode Complete I et II*. (See Thompson/Lemke: *French Music for Low Brass Instruments*.)

Lachmann, Hans. *25 Etuden nach Josef Hrabe*. Friedrich Hofmeister. 1956. IV–V.

Lachmann, Hans. *26 Etudes for Tuba*. Friedrich Hofmeister. 1956. 15 pp. III. These are fine etudes for the average high school student or good intermediate student, although they also present good fundamental review possibilities for the beginning college student. They are principally studies in technique, time, and articulation, similar to the Robert Getchell studies.

Lange, W. *Etüden und Vortragstücke: Tuba I (F–Es)*. Schulz. 1980.

Lange, W. *Etüden und Vortragstücke: Tuba II (C)*. Schulz. 1980.

Langey, Otto. *The Bass*.

Langey, Otto. *Langey–Carl Fischer Tutors for BB♭ Bass*. Carl Fischer, Incorporated. 1944. Out of Print. $1.50. 80 pp. II–III. Although an introduction to the rudiments of music is included at the outset of the text, this method is likely not intended for a beginner, as it moves at an accelerated pace through all fundamental aspects of playing. Studies are arranged according to key. This method is not dissimilar to the Arban or Rubank methods in approach to introduction of new material and exercises.

Langey, Otto. *Practical Tutor for B♭ Bass*. Boosey & Hawkes, Incorporated.

Langey, Otto. *Practical Tutor for E♭ Bass*. Boosey & Hawkes, Incorporated.

Lautzenheiser, Tim, et al. *Essential Elements 2000, Book One*. Hal Leonard Corporation. 1999. $6.95. 48 pp. I. Also composed by John Higgins, Charles Menghini, Paul Lavender, Tom C. Rhodes, and Don Bierschenk. A comprehensive beginning method which includes not only duets and trios but also separate rhythm and scale/arpeggio exercises. The accompanying CD features not only demonstration performances but also accompaniment tracks.

Lebedjev, A. *Tuba Tutor, Vol. 1*. Moscow Muzyka. 1984. 70 pp. II–III. This method by the most famous of the Russian tuba pedagogues has written text in Russian only. It includes warm-up etudes in various keys and progressive technical and melodic etudes and solos. Piano accompaniment material is included for most etudes and solos. The material presented would be well suited to the average high school student.

Lebedjew, Alexej. *Etüden*. Friedrich Hofmeister Leipzig. $13.27.

Lee, William F., and James Progris. *I Wanna Play the Tuba*. Charles Hanson II Music and Books of California, Inc. 1979. $2.95. 33 pp. I. Here is a very basic beginning method for private instruction. It introduces music reading and fundamentals using simple but (generally) well-known melodies.

Lehman, Cliff, and Susan Taylor. *Sound Method for Band in Four Volumes (Tuba)*. Belwin-Mills. $5.50.

Leidig, Vernon. *Visual Band Method, Books I and II (Tuba—E♭ and BB♭)*. ed. Lennie Niehaus. Highland Music Company. 1965. $1.00. 35 pp. I–II. Here is a method intended for full beginning band instruction. The presentation of material is very typical of such methods with regard to presentation of basic material and very short etudes and melodies. Fingerings for new notes are supplemented with photographs of a valve section with fingers depressing appropriate valves.

Leidig, Vernon, and Lennie Niehaus. *Visual Intermediate Band Method (Tuba—E♭ and BB♭)*. Highland Music Company. 1968. $1.25. 27 pp. II. A continuation of the beginning method described above, the intermediate method includes eight lessons covering eight major and two minor keys with scales and thirds and varied articulations, rhythms, and meters. Several parts for works for full band are included at the end of the book.

Lelong, F. *Special Exercises for Flexibility and Scales for B♭ Euphonium and Tenor and Bass Tuba in Two Books*. Alphonse Leduc Editions Musicales. 1981. $15.00. 20 pp. I–IV. The first book in this series by Paris Conservatoire Professor Lelong deals with flexibility exercises, and the second with development of technique through scales. The exercises can be adapted to virtually any level of student and provide good material for any daily routine.

Lelong, F. *Tuba Method, Books I, II, III*. Editions Billaudot. $13.25.

LeLong, Fernand. *L'ABC du Jeune Tubiste, Volume 1*. Editions Billaudot. $18.12.

LeLong, Fernand. *L'ABC du Jeune Tubiste, Volume 2*. Editions Billaudot. $26.90.

LeLong, Fernand. *L'ABC du Jeune Tubiste, Volume 3.* Editions Billaudot. $16.22.

Lesaffre, C., and Lelong. *Petite Chanson pour Marion.* Editions Billaudot. $5.75.

Liebmann, Hans. *Elementar-Technik, Vol. 1.* Editions Marc Reift. 1994. $28.37. IV–V. Contrary to the title, this is a collection of exercises, which progress according to key, intended for the development of advanced technique in all keys and all registers. Includes studies in articulation, dynamics, and rhythm. Written in treble clef.

Liebmann, Hans. *Elementar-Technik, Vol. 2.* Editions Marc Reift. 1994. $20.27. IV–V. A continuation of volume I. Includes studies on diatonic, chromatic, and twelve-tone scales; chords and sequences; intervals; multiple tonguing; velocity; and endurance. Includes a transcription of Mozart's *Sonata for Piano, KV 331.* Written in treble clef.

Linderman. *Melodious Fundamentals.*

Lindkvist, Janne. *Tore Tuba's Første Spelbok; Nybørjarskola För Tuba.* Mo Brass Musikförlag, Sweden. 1988. 46 pp. I. A book intended for private instruction at the beginning level, this volume is filled with entertaining caricatures and simple songs (with Scandinavian text), duets, and tunes with piano harmonization. The prologue states that the work is intended primarily for beginning E♭ tubists, but that it is also suitable for the BB♭ tuba.

Linke, E., ed. *Tonstudien und Orchesterauszüge berühmter Meister für F und Es-Tuba* (Hochschule der Künste, Berlin). Verlag Militärmusik-Zeitung.

Little, Donald C., with James D. Ployhar. *Practical Hints on Playing the Tuba.* Belwin-Mills. 1984. $5.50. 41 pp. II–III. A concise method-text with several explanatory pages devoted to proper instrument/mouthpiece selection, playing position, tone production, instrument maintenance, and other aspects of playing. The work includes photos.

Little, Lowell. *Embouchure Builder for BB♭ Bass (Tuba).* Pro Art Publications. 1954. $4.50. 16 pp. II–III. Designed as a supplementary method, this book stresses long tone and flexibility practice and is intended for use during the warm-up period.

Maddy, J. E., and Thadeus P. Giddings. *Universal Teacher for Orchestra and Band (E♭ and BB♭ tuba).* Willis Music Company. 1923. Out of Print. $3.00. 34 pp. II–III. This is the historic first method written for group band instruction. (Maddy and Giddings were also the founders of the Interlochen National Music Camp.) A rapidly moving, progressive method, the book includes band parts to works arranged by Maddy as well as developmental etudes.

Maenz, Otto. *20 Studien für Tuba.* Friedrich Hofmeister Leipzig. $11.67.

Maenz, Otto. *Zwölf Spezialastudien für Tuba.* Freidrich Hofmeister. $12.25. 16 pp. IV.

Magnell, Elmer P. *68 Pares Studies for E♭ or BB♭ Tuba.* Belwin-Mills. 1957. II–III.

Magnell, Elmer P. *29 Schantl Studies for Tuba.* Belwin-Mills. 1959. III.

Makela, Steven. *Thirteen Etudes for Tuba.* TUBA Press. 1992. $8.00. 25 pp. III–V. These etudes are intended primarily for the college or professional player, although a few of the etudes would be useful for the serious high school student. While the studies are very musical in nature, the technical emphasis is on development of even tone across the full range of the tuba, with most etudes covering a three-octave range.

Marchesi and Panofka. *28 Advanced Studies for Tuba.* tr. David L. Kuehn. Southern Music Company. 1972. $15.00. 55 pp. IV–V. These are advanced etudes in legato style and technique and would be suitable for the advanced, serious high school student, as well as good, interesting practice material for the college or professional player. A variety of keys and meters are covered.

Marchesi, Mathilde. *24 Vokalisen.* Friedrich Hofmeister Leipzig. $12.89.

Mariani, A. *Popular Method for Tuba.* Editions Salabert.

Mariani, Giuseppe. *Metodo Popolare per Flicorno Contrabasso Si♭.* G. Ricordi & Company. 1957.

Maros, M. *Etydes for Tuba.* AB Nordiska Musikforlaget. 1943.

Maxwell, Roger. *Fourteen Weeks to a Better Band (Tuba), Vol. I.* C. L. Barnhouse Company. $4.00. I–II. Designed for grades 7–9, this is a group method intended to improve sight-reading through the study of basic rhythmic figures and their use across musical styles.

Maxwell, Roger. *Fourteen Weeks to a Better Band (Tuba), Vol. II.* C. L. Barnhouse Company. $4.50. II–III. Designed for grades 9–12, this is an advanced version of the first volume in this series. The rhythmic figures are virtually the same as in the first book, but more challenging exercises are presented for the high school–level student.

Maxwell, Roger. *Fourteen Weeks to an Improved Band (Tuba).* Roger Maxwell Publications. 1985. $3.50. 31 pp. I–II. Though designed for students in grades 5–7, this is a rapidly progressive method which quickly addresses dotted eighth/sixteenth note rhythms, syncopation, and other intermediate skills.

McLeod, James, and Norman Staska. *Rhythm Etudes (Tuba).* Belwin-Mills. 1966. $5.00. 31 pp. II. This is a progressively organized method with emphasis on a variety of keys and meters.

McLeod, James, and Norman Staska. *Scale Etudes (Tuba, String Bass).* Belwin-Mills. 1963. $5.50. 33 pp. I–II. This method contains scale-based etudes, each written in octaves.

Meschke, D. *Tuba Fibel.*

Meschke, Dieter. *60 Etüden für Kontrabaßtuba.* Freidrich Hofmeister.

Mestdagh, P. *Methoden voor Trombone, Tuba.* Metropolis.

Michalek, J. *Method.*

Michel, J. Fr. *Blattlese-Schule.* Editions Marc Reift.

Michel, J. Fr. *Schule für B und Es Bass.* Editions Marc Reift.

Mityagin. *37 Selected Etudes for Tuba.* MCA.

Moeck, Walter. *Tuba Warm-Ups.* C. L. Barnhouse Company. 1976. $1.50. 5 pp. II–III. This booklet includes a warm-up routine with lip slurs in various meters and up to c'. A good "taking-off place" in establishing a solid daily routine.

Moore, E. C. *Elements of Band Technic (Tuba).* Summy-Birchard Publishing Company. 1958. 16 pp. III.

Moore, E. C. *The Moore Band Course (BB♭ Bass).* Carl Fischer, Incorporated. 1930. Out of Print. 39 pp. I–II. Intended for group instruction, this early band method includes rudiments of musicianship and numerous exercises in solo and duet form based on familiar tunes. It is notable that each exercise throughout the book has pedagogical comments on the facing page describing the exercise's intent and suggestions for accomplishment.

Moore, E. C. *The Moore Band Course (E♭ Bass).* Carl Fischer, Incorporated. 1930. Out of Print. 39 pp. I–II. This method book is identical to the Moore book for BB♭ tuba with appropriate adjustments for range, etc., applicable to the E♭ tuba.

Moore, E. C., and A. O. Sieg. *Preparatory Instructor for Basses (BB♭ and E♭).* Carl Fischer, Incorporated. 1937/67. 75¢. 32 pp. I–II. An elementary tutor intended for private instruction, this book gives a rudimentary introduction to addressing the instrument, breath, and articulation. Although the exercises presented are somewhat pedantic, they are pedagogically well thought out, and, supplemented with melodic material, they would be quite useful.

Moser, Karl. *Ubungen zum Zusammenspiel, Heft 4.* Siegfried Rundel Musikverlag. 60 pp. I. An "old school" group method which contains an unusually large number of musical exercises versus a combination of musical exercises and pedagogical commentary. This particular volume is published for all low brass instruments and includes many melodies and duets from the classical repertoire. Includes a brief musical glossary and an index of tunes used for the exercises. All text is in German.

Mühlbacher, F. *Schule für Bass-Tuba in B oder C, F und Es-Tuba/Helikon.* Solistenverlag.

Müller. *Technische Studien für Baßposaune und Tuba.*

Murphy, Bower. *Advanced Tuba Etudes.* ed. Constance Weldon. Charles Colin. 1969. 63 pp. III–IV. These etudes, authored by a noted American brass pedagogue, are in all major and minor keys and cover both lyric and technical styles. Very good for use with serious high school students, and excellent, challenging reading material for the college student.

Muzzi, Pietro. *Raccolta di pezzi di autori classici per Flicorni Bassi Gravi e Contrabassi (Tube).* Musicali Ortipe.

Newell, David. *Bach and Before for Band.* Neil A. Kjos Music Company. 2002. $5.95. 40 pp. I. A collection of nineteen four-part chorales from the sixteenth, seventeenth, and eighteenth centuries. All four parts to each chorale are included, creating the possibility for a variety of small ensembles. The piano accompaniment to each chorale is also included, along with a fingering chart for BB♭, CC, E♭, and F tubas.

O'Reilly, John, and John Kinyon. *Yamaha Band Student, Book III (Tuba).* Alfred Music Company. 1989. $5.50. 31 pp. II. A continuation of the first two volumes (see Feldstein, Sandy), this work is directed more towards skill improvement for intermediate players. Compound meters and more major and minor keys are explored.

Osman, Leroy. *Concert Etudes for Solo Tuba.* Southern Music Company. 1991. $3.50. 7 pp. IV–V. Intended for concert performance, these etudes are somewhat programmatic and definitely challenging for the most serious performer. High range, technique, and flexibility are all thoroughly tested.

Osmon, Leroy. *Concert Etudes for Solo Tuba, Volume 2.* Southern Music Company. 1991. $5.00. 11 pp. IV–V. Dedicated to David Kirk. The second of a two-volume series, this volume contains etudes 6–10, all of which are suitable for concert performance. Difficult for even the most seasoned professional, due to the complex rhythmic nature of the etudes. Compound meter, multimetricism, and unmeasured writing are all incorporated. Recorded by David Kirk. See Discography: Kirk, David; See also Music for Unaccompanied Tuba.

Ostling, Acton, and Fred Weber. *Tunes for Tuba (Bass) Technic, Levels I and II.* Belwin-Mills. 1969/70. $5.50. 32 pp. I–II. Like the Studies and Melodious Etudes for Tuba (Bass) series (see under Laas, Bill), this series is a member of the Belwin Student Instrumental Course and is designed as a supplement to the primary series, The Tuba (Bass) Student. Whereas the Studies and Melodious Etudes series is primarily of a technical nature, the Tunes for Tuba series is purely melodic and thus emphasizes the development of musicality.

Ostling Hovey. *Section Studies for Low Range Basses.* Belwin-Mills.

Ostrander, Allen. *Low Tone Studies.* Charles Colin. $4.95.

Ostrander, Allen. *Shifting Meter Studies for Bass Trombone or Tuba.* Robert King Music Company. 1965. $2.00. 20 pp. III–IV. Primarily intended for study of use of the double-valved bass trombone, these studies provide excellent material for the student who needs to improve his/her sense of time and sight-reading. The studies do not provide undue technical challenges, allowing the student to focus on the principal objective of the etudes.

Ostrander, Allen. *20-Minute Warmup.* Charles Colin.

Pares, G. *Daily Exercises and Scales for BB flat Bass.* revised E. Claus. Carl Fischer, Incorporated. 1912. $6.00. 32 pp. II–III. This is the classic text for scale study for band students. Emphasis is on flat major and minor keys with short sections on chromatic scales and arpeggios. Scales are presented in a variety of rhythmic and articulation patterns.

Pares, G. *Méthode de Contrebasse (ou Saxhorn-Contrebasse).* Chez Henry Lemoine. 47 pp.

Pares, G. *Methode Elementaire de Tuba.*

Pares, G. *Pares Scales for BB♭ Bass.* revised/ed. by Harvey S. Whistler. Rubank, Incorporated. 1946. $4.95. 48 pp. II–III. This method contains all major and minor scales in a variety of rhythmic patterns. An excellent review or introductory text for scale study.

Pares, G. *Pares Scales for E flat Tuba.* revised/ed. by Harvey S. Whistler. Rubank, Incorporated. 1946. $4.95. 48 pp. II–III. This text is identical to the above listed book for BB flat tuba with appropriate adjustments made for the E flat instrument.

Paudert, Ernst. *Etudes for Tuba.* Encore Music Publishers. $9.00. 12 pp. IV–V. Emphasis in these studies is on technique for the advanced player. They are well suited for F tuba, as well as euphonium, and cover all major keys.

Paulson, Joseph. *Get in Rhythm (Basses and String Bass).* Pro Art Publications. 1948. 31 pp. I–II.

Paulson, Joseph. *Play Right Away.* Pro Art Publications. 1953. Out of Print. 36 pp. I. This is a march-size publication for beginning instruction.

Pearson, Bruce. *Best in Class, Books I and II (Tuba).* ed. Gerald Anderson and Charles Forque. Neil A. Kjos Music Company. 1982/83. $4.95. 32 pp. I. This is a standard band method which is correlated with a series of compositions for full band and is published for both E♭ and BB♭ tubas, in both treble and bass clefs.

Pearson, Bruce. *Encore (Tuba)!* ed. Gerald Anderson and Charles Forque. Neil A. Kjos Music Company. 1985. $3.95. 32 pp. I. Intended for use as a supplement to the Best in Class series of method books, this book provides solos, duets, trios, rounds, and full band arrangements (tuba part) as a reinforcement for basic performance skills.

Pearson, Bruce. *Standard of Excellence, Book 1.* Neil A. Kjos Music Company. 1993. $6.45. 48 pp. I. A standard band method which includes practice and progress charts, rhythm and scale exercises, and a glossary with page references. Also includes many colorful diagrams, ensemble arrangements, and solos with keyboard accompaniment. Published for both E♭ and BB♭ tuba, in both treble and bass clef. Recorded accompaniment available from the publisher.

Pearson, Bruce. *Standard of Excellence, Book 2.* Neil A. Kjos Music Company. 1993. $6.45. 48 pp. I–II. See volume I. Recorded accompaniment available from the publisher.

Pearson, Bruce. *Standard of Excellence, Book 3.* Neil A. Kjos Music Company. 1996. $6.45. 48 pp. II. See volume I. Recorded accompaniment available from the publisher.

Pearson, Bruce, and Chuck Elledge. *A Best in Class Christmas (Tuba).* Neil A. Kjos Music Company. 1988. $3.45. 24 pp. I. A supplement to the Best in Class series of method books, this book includes several familiar carols, all of which include the melody, the bass part, and a harmony part.

Pearson, Bruce, and Chuck Elledge. *A Best in Class Showcase (Tuba).* Neil A. Kjos Music Company. 1989. $3.95. 24 pp. I. This book differs from *A Best in Class Christmas* in its presentation of popular march, folk, or classical melodies rather than Christmas carols.

Pease, Donald J. *Pro Art E flat or BB flat Bass (Tuba and Sousaphone) Method.* Pro Art Publications. 1964. $5.00. 48 pp. I–II. This is a rapidly progressive method which places special emphasis on exposure to a variety of keys.

Pease, Donald J. *Starting the Band—Basses.* Pro Art Publications. 1951. 36 pp. I. This is a march-sized publication intended for beginning instruction.

Pepper, J. W. *J. W. Pepper's New and Popular Self Instructor for the B♭ Bass.* J. W. Pepper. 1886. Out of Print. 64 pp. I–III. This very early American method for the tuba or euphonium includes rudiments of musicianship and a wealth of melodies that were from important contemporary European and American composers and in many cases remain important today. Also included are beginning etudes introducing various concepts important to the development of basic skills.

Peters, Charles S. *Master Method for Band, Book I (Basses).* ed. Paul Yoder. Neil A. Kjos Music Company. 1958. $3.45. 32 pp. I. The first in a series of three books, this book rapidly progresses through the first year of instrumental instruction with an emphasis on rhythmic, harmonic, and pedagogical development through "count-time" exercises, duets, and instructional ideas within each lesson.

Peters, Charles S. *Master Method for Band, Book II (Basses).* ed. Paul Yoder. Neil A. Kjos Music Company. 1959. $3.45. 32 pp. I–II. The second in a series of three books, this book is a logical yet rapidly progressive continuation of book I, with the addition of "artist variation" exercises—exercises which are technically oriented variations of previously introduced etudes.

Peters, Charles S. *Master Method for Band, Book III (Basses)*. ed. Paul Yoder. Neil A. Kjos Music Company. 1964. $3.45. 31 pp. II–III. The third in a series of three books, this book emphasizes the development of articulation, phrasing, and ensemble skills. Also, this book continues the "artist variation" concept of book II, with the addition of concert-length full band accompaniments to the variations.

Peters, Charles S. *Total Range (Tuba)*. Neil A. Kjos Music Company. 1976. $2.45. 36 pp. II–V. This text presents a progressive, cumulative approach to range development from low to high. Lessons are presented in a format of weekly goals and exercises, always building on and including material studied previously.

Peters, Charles, and Matt Betton. *Take One (Basses)*. Neil A. Kjos Music Company. 1972. $1.95. 32 pp. I. This is a beginning method which is both traditional in its introduction of fundamental theory and basic playing skills and non-traditional in its inclusion of several contest-length solos (including piano accompaniment), band-related photographs, and jazz pedagogy.

Peters, Charles S., and Paul Yoder. *Master Drills: Scales and Skills (Basses)*. Neil A. Kjos Music Company. 1962. 17 pp. I–II.

Pethel, Stan. *Twenty Etudes for Tuba*. TUBA Press. 1992. $10.00. 41 pp. IV. These are advanced etudes that cover a broad range of styles (song, waltz, blues, etc.) and keys. Most focus on the middle range of the instrument and avoid the extreme outside ranges. Recommended for the serious college student.

Phillips, Harry I. *Silver Burdett Instrumental Series (E♭ and BB♭ Tubas), Volumes I and II*. Hal Leonard Publishing Corporation. 1969. $3.95. 74 pp. I–III. This is a simple yet thorough method by one of the most respected music textbook publishers. The method includes duets and trios in addition to technical and lyrical studies.

Phillips, Harvey G., and William Winkle. *The Art of Tuba and Euphonium*. Summy-Birchard Publishing Company. 1992. $14.95. 98 pp. I–V. Principally a text covering all aspects of tuba performance and pedagogy, this work includes a chapter on developing and maintaining performance skills which includes a suggested warm-up routine and short exercises emphasizing aspects of proper fundamental development.

Pilant, F. *Bass Tuba School*.

Pilant, F. *Pro Art Method*.

Ployhar, James D. *Band Today, Part I and II (Tuba)*. Belwin-Mills. 1977. $5.50. 32 pp. I–II. The first two in a series of three books, this is a standard band method designed for individual or group instruction.

Ployhar, James D. *Band Today, Part III*. Belwin-Mills. 1978. $5.50. 32 pp. II. The third in a series of three books, this book contains a small amount of work in G♭ major and a section which teaches rudimental ornamentation.

Ployhar, James D. *I Recommend*. Belwin-Mills. 1972. $5.50. 32 pp. II–III. Intended as a supplemental warm-up book, this volume covers scales and arpeggios as well as articulation, intervals, dynamics, and rhythm. A review of musical rudiments is included at the book's conclusion.

Ployhar, James D. *Medalist Band Method (Tuba) in Three Volumes*. Belwin-Mills. $5.00. I–II.

Ployhar, James D. *Technic Today (Tuba) in Three Volumes*. Belwin-Mills. 1977/78/79. $5.50. 24 pp. I–III. This is a supplemental series which is organized according to key.

Ployhar, James, and George Zepp. *3-D Band Book (Bass/Tuba)*. Belwin-Mills. 1983. $5.50. 40 pp. II–III. Designed as a supplemental method for full band, this work emphasizes the development of tuning, counting, and scale skills.

Ployhar, James D., and George Zepp. *Tone and Technic through Chorales and Etudes (Tuba)*. Belwin-Mills. $5.50. II. This book includes exercises in four-part harmony, duets, and technical studies for individual instruments. All are intended to be used in the ensemble setting, although the technical studies may be used in individual practice as well.

Pniak, Jan. *Mala Szdola na Tube*. Polish Music Edition (P.W.M.) Krakow. 1986.

Pniak, Jan. *Szkola na tube BB, CC, Es, F.* Polish Music Edition (P.W.M.) Krakow. In progress.

Popiel, Peter. *Thirty Vocalises for Tuba*. Accura Music. 1992. 64 pp. IV. These etudes are taken from works of composers of the baroque, classical, and romantic periods and emphasize low-register legato style. The etudes are organized from least to most difficult, progressively. Each etude is well thought out and presents an excellent challenge for the college student.

Porret, J. *Mecanisme (A)*.

Porret, J. *Methode Progressive*.

Porret, J. *24 Etudes Melodiques*.

Poullot, Francois. *A Propos du Tuba*. Editions Billaudot. $10.12.

Poullot, Francois. *Preambule (Preamble), Book 1. Saxhorn Basse/Contrebasse Sib., Tuba in ut (six valves)*. Alphonse Leduc Editions Musicales. 1982. $37.95. 55 pp. I–II. This is an elementary text for the tuba, introducing very basic aspects of playing (tone production, rhythm reading, basic scales, etc.). It also includes a basic history of the tuba and euphonium. The mode of presentation in this book is not far removed from that of the classic Arban method.

Poullot, Francois. *Preambule (Preamble), Book 2. Saxhorn Basse/Contrebasse Sib., Tuba in ut (six valves)*. Alphonse Leduc Editions Musicales.

1982. $37.95. 58 pp. III–IV. Systematically organized according to meter, this book includes scalar, intervallic, and arpeggiated exercises in the keys of C major, A minor, F major, D minor, G major, and E minor. This is a book for only the very serious intermediate to early advanced player. There are considerable upper register demands. Pedagogical comments are included.

Poullot, Francois. *Preambule (Preamble), Book 3. Saxhorn Basse/Contrebasse Sib., Tuba in ut (six valves).* Alphonse Leduc Editions Musicales. 1986. $44.35. 74 pp. III–IV. Essentially developed along the same lines as volume II, this continuation of the series is a more involved study of range and meter.

Poullot, Francois. *Traite des Gammes D'Apres Balay Volume 1 Tuba/Saxhorns Basses.* Alphonse Leduc Editions Musicales. $25.30.

Poullot, Francois. *Traite des Gammes D'Apres Balay Volume 2 Tuba/Saxhorns Basses.* Alphonse Leduc Editions Musicales. $25.30.

Prescott, Gerald R. *The Prescott Technic System, Parts I and II.* Carl Fischer, Incorporated. 1935/63. $1.40. 10 pp. This is a set of lesson plans designed for use as a guide to teaching from the *Arban Complete Method.* Part I includes first and second sets of preparatory exercises and plans for the first through fourth years of studies. Part II includes fifth- through twelfth-year lesson plans.

Prevet, H. *Methode pour Saxhorn Basse.*

Pröpper, Klemens. *Before You Begin.* Zimmermann-Frankfurt. 1998. $13.07. 24 pp. III–IV. A compilation of pedagogical commentary and special exercises for the proper development and maintenance of the embouchure muscles. Though most of the exercises appear to have been written with the F tuba in mind, the material is suitable for use on any tuba. Very useful pedagogical information.

Pröpper, Klemens. *Progressive Technique and Blowing Procedure for Low Brass Instruments.* Zimmermann-Frankfurt. 1995. $22.49. 76 pp. III–IV. With text in both German and English, this method is very informative pedagogically and addresses many physiological aspects of brass playing, including embouchure formation, breathing function, and articulation. Musical exercises appear to have been conceived with the F tuba in mind. Though the material is applicable to all levels, the manner in which it is presented is most appropriate for advanced high school players and beyond.

Pucci, Salvatore. *Studi per Bassi Gravi e Contrabassi Si♭.* Musicali Florio.

Ranieri, V. *30 Instruktive und Melodisce Übungsstücke für Tuba oder Fagott (in Three Volumes).* Louis Oertel & Co. Out of Print. 11 pp. III–IV. Each volume of this set contains ten tonal etudes in progressively more difficult keys.

Ranieri, Vincenz. *60 Etüden für Kontrabaßtuba.* Friedrich Hofmeister Leipzig. $13.27.

Rascusen, David. *Canonic Etudes.* See same work under Music for Multiple Tubas/Three Parts.

Reger, Wayne M. *The Talking Tuba.* Charles Colin. 1967. $4.95. 24 pp. I–III. A basic method designed to supplement other texts and emphasize very basic fundamentals. This work features cartoon illustrations with a humorous flavor.

Reift, Marc. *Einspielübung.* Editions Marc Reift.

Reift, Marc. *Rhythmus-Schule.* Editions Marc Reift.

Rhodes, Tom, and Donald Bierschenk. *Symphonic Band Technique (Tuba).* Southern Music Company. 1986. $4.50. 32 pp. III–IV. Designed for the high school or college-level band, this is a supplemental warm-up method which places emphasis not only on the development of tone and phrasing, but also on the development of technique through major and minor scale study in various meters, with various articulations.

Rhodes, Tom C., Donald Bierscheule, and Tim Lautzenheiser. *Essential Elements: A Comprehensive Band Method, Books I and II (Tuba).* Neil A. Kjos Music Company. 1991. $5.50. 32 pp. I–II. This is a beginning method book intended for classroom use. It includes instrument-specific comments and utilizes popular, folk, and classical repertoire.

Ridgeon, John. *Brass for Beginners: Studies for Brass Instruments in Bass Clef.* Boosey & Hawkes, Incorporated.

Ridgeon, John. *Eight Graded Lip Flexibility Studies.* Belwin-Mills. 1981. I.

Rieunier, Françoise. *22 Rhythmic Instrumental Sightreading Exercises (for All Instruments).* Alphonse Leduc Editions Musicales. 1972. 15 pp. IV–V. These challenging and interesting etudes provide the ultimate in sight-reading practice for the advanced student or professional. None of the etudes have clefs or keys, so those factors may be adjusted for each instrument appropriately. In addition to standard meters, beat groupings of 5½, 3½, etc. are found. (See Thompson/Lemke: *French Music for Low Brass Instruments.*)

Rinderspacher. *Neue Schule für Tuba in F oder Es.*

Rinderspacher. *Schule für Tuba in B oder C.*

Robinson, Jack. *Advanced Conditioning Studies.* Whaling Music Publishers. $12.50. 72 pp. III–V. This is a comprehensive text on warm-up and daily routine as related to building strength and endurance. Extensive text explaining the author's position and pedagogical philosophy is included together with exercises for implementation. Of particular note/interest is the fact that the author was influenced in his writing by experts in Nautilus training as well as tuba pedagogues William Bell and Don Harry.

Robinson, Jack. *Musical Tuba Playing.* Tuba-Euphonium Press. $32.00. 116 pp. III–V. A comprehensive pedagogical method which addresses many fundamental aspects of tuba performance, including tone production, intonation, articulation, and flexibility. Thorough commentary is included with each section of the method, and there are separate chapters and musical exercises for the BB♭, CC, and F tubas. Due to the extreme range of some of the exercises, the material is best suited to college- and professional-level tuba players.

Robinson, Keith. *Rain Forest Etudes: Twenty-Five Musical Studies for the Young Tubist.* Tuba-Euphonium Press. 1997. $10.00. 22 pp. I–II. A collection of programmatic etudes written to provide young tuba players with material that is both "fun and musically rewarding." The etudes are relatively short, yet each is presented as a musical work rather than just an etude. Limited range and technical requirements make this text suitable for first-year tuba players. Helpful introductory comments and a glossary of musical terms are included. See Discography: Swoboda, Deanna.

Rollinson, T. H. *Modern School.*

Ronka, Ilmari. *Modern Daily Warm-ups and Drills.* Carl Fischer, Incorporated.

Rossari/Muzzi. *Studi di Perfezionamento per Tuba (Flicorno Basso Grave e Contrabasso) in 2 Volumes.* Musicali Ortipe.

Rusch. *24 Arban-Klose-Concone Studies.* Belwin-Mills. 1956. $5.50. 29 pp. II–III. This set of studies is designed for private lesson or class/full band instruction. Specific etudes have been chosen from the more complete methods listed in the title to provide focus for specific performance problems, generally based in rhythm. Each of the 24 studies consists of a unison etude and an accompaniment part to be played by other class members when used in a band setting.

Rusch, Harold W. *18 Barrett and Jancourt Studies for Tuba.* Belwin-Mills.

Rusch, Harold W. *Hal Leonard Advanced Band Method for Basses.* Hal Leonard Publishing Corporation. 1963. 64 pp. III–IV. This work includes nineteen pages of exercises and etudes composed and/or compiled by Arnold Jacobs with brief commentary by this legendary master teacher. The remainder of the book is a class method for band.

Rusch, Harold W. *Hal Leonard Elementary Band Method (Tuba).* Hal Leonard Publishing Corporation. $3.50.

Rusch, Harold W. *Hal Leonard Intermediate Band Method (Tuba).* Hal Leonard Publishing Corporation. 1961. $3.50. 44 pp. I–II. This method places an emphasis on rhythmic development through the use of rhythm charts.

Rusch, Harold W. *25 Lazarus-Concone Studies for Tuba.* Belwin-Mills. 1956. $5.50. 28 pp. II–III. Intended as a follow-up text to the *24 Arban-Klose-Concone Studies* by Rusch (above), this book is set up in a similar fashion but with emphasis on articulation, phrasing, and dynamics rather than rhythm. Each of the 25 etudes has a direct and obvious emphasis on correct performance of a particular fundamental area.

Rusch, Harold W., and Alfred F. Barto. *Breath Control and Tuning and Intonation Studies for Wind Instrument Players.* Fillmore Music House. 1949. Out of Print. $1.25. 32 pp. III. This text begins with detailed pedagogical suggestions for breath control and tuning that apply to all instruments, followed by specific intonation correction solutions for each of the traditional bass clef band instruments. Sixteen lessons follow, each with specific objectives and pedagogical comments regarding improvement of breath and intonation. Although much of the information is outdated, much remains valuable.

Rys. *50 Etudes de Perfectionnement Tuba Contrebasse Ut, Tuba B, Tenor Ut.* Alphonse Leduc Editions Musicales. $16.40. (See Thompson/Lemke: *French Music for Low Brass Instruments.*)

Rys. *50 Etudes Faciles Tuba Contrebasse Ut, Tuba Basse Fa, Tuba Tenor Ut.* Alphonse Leduc Editions Musicales. $22.40. (See Thompson/Lemke: *French Music for Low Brass Instruments.*)

Rys. *50 Etudes Progressives.* Robert Martin Editions Musicales. $12.50. (See Thompson/Lemke: *French Music for Low Brass Instruments.*)

Salotti, Harry. *Etudes with Style: Music for the Tuba.* Tuba-Euphonium Press. 2004. II–III. Winner of the 2003 ITEA Composition Contest for tuba etudes at the intermediate level. A collection of twenty-five etudes in a wide variety of musical styles. The etudes are organized by four headings: Music over the Ages, Dance Music around the World, American Music, and Movie Music. Included is an extensive forward by Harvey Phillips and an audio CD which features both accompaniment and demonstration tracks for each etude, with Patrick Sheridan playing the demonstration tracks. Also includes an appendix which identifies specific composers, works, performers, and recordings that represent each of the musical styles represented by the etudes. See Discography: Sheridan, Patrick.

Salvo, Victor. *Fun Workbook for Tuba.* Pro Art Publications. 1973. $1.50. 37 pp. I–II. This is a book of theory worksheets at the beginning level applied to the tuba range. Includes fingering charts. This is a possible supplement to any method book.

Salvo, Victor V. *241 Double and Triple Tonguing Exercises for Trombone-Baritone-Tuba.* Belwin-Mills. 1973. $5.50. 36 pp. III–IV. A progressive method for study of multiple tonguing, this work includes suggestions for practice procedures and measuring progress, as well as suggestions for additional sources of material.

Sargent, W. A. Barrington. *Lip Builders or Daily Stimulants.* Cundy-Bettoney. 1911. Out of Print. 75¢. 8 pp. I–III. These are very simple-to-play warm-up and flexibility studies designed to improve tone quality, endurance, and articulation.

Pedagogical suggestions are included at the beginning of the book, as well as between the four series of studies.

Sawhill, Clarence, and Frank Erickson. *Bourne Guide to the Band (Tuba), Book I.* Bourne Company. 1955. 31 pp. I. Intended only for group instruction, this method integrates unison melodies and exercises with short pieces in parts, requiring independence on the part of each section.

Sawhill, Clarence, and Frank Erickson. *Bourne Guide to the Band (Tuba), Book II.* Bourne Company. 1956. 28 pp. I–II. This is a logical continuation of the first book in this series, moving the student to material suitable for an early intermediate player.

Sciortino, Patrice. *15 Etudes de Concours Tuba Basse.* Editions Billaudot. 1999. $18.11. IV–V. This collection of studies is the culminating work of an eight-volume set of bass tuba material composed by Anthony Girard and Patrice Sciortino, ranging in difficulty from easy to advanced. These fifteen cadenza-like etudes serve to challenge every facet of tuba playing: technique, flexibility, articulation, range, and so forth. With sparse dynamic and tempo indications, the exercises also present a significant musical challenge. Excellent study and performance material for the F or E♭ tuba. See Music for Unaccompanied Tuba.

Sciortino, Patrice. *15 Etudes De Phrase et De Velocite Tuba Basse.* Editions Billaudot. $13.43.

Sciortino, Patrice. *28 Etudes De Virtuosite.* Editions Billaudot. $38.08.

Sciortino, Patrice. *24 Etudes: Flexibilite.* Editions Billaudot. $9.77.

Sciortino, Patrice. *24 Etudes: Intonation et Respiration.* Editions Billaudot. $9.77.

Sciortino, Patrice. *24 Etudes: Rythme et Detache.* Editions Billaudot. $12.00.

Sciortino, Patrice. *24 Etudes: Tessiture et Technique.* Editions Billaudot. $16.21.

Sear, Walter. *Etudes for Tuba.* Cor Publishing Company. 1969. $6.00. 32 pp. IV. Forty-five challenging etudes for the advanced tubist that present balanced study of upper and lower registers. Excerpted arrangements from three of the Bach cello suites are at the end of the book.

Sebesky, Gerald. *Fundamentals for Beginning Bands (Tuba).* C. L. Barnhouse Company. $2.25. I. This book, intended to be used as supplementary material for group methods, is essentially an activity book to enhance study of music fundamentals for the young students.

Senon, G. *Preludes Faciles Pour Tuba Tenor (Vol. 1).* Robert Martin Editions Musicales. 1983. $12.75. 32 pp. III–IV. Though the first several pages of this method are playable by an advanced junior high student, the work is generally suited to the high school and college levels, due to the overall high tessitura and abundant changing meter studies.

Senon, G., and Ferdinand Lelong. *Kaleidoscope (in Three Volumes).* Editions Billaudot. 1983. $13.50. 23 pp. III–IV. Although designated as elementary etudes, these etudes would be challenging melodically and rhythmically to the advanced intermediate student, and range-wise to the advanced student. A very good choice for the developing F or E♭ tuba player. (See Thompson/Lemke: *French Music for Low Brass Instruments.*)

Shoemaker, John. *Legato Etudes for Tuba Based on the Vocalises of Giuseppe Concone.* Carl Fischer, Incorporated. 1969. $8.00. 30 pp. III–IV. These etudes, similar to the Concone etudes edited by David Kuehn, focus on the development of good interpretation of legato phrasing. Very good pedagogical comments on legato style and how to perform that style properly are included in the foreword.

Sieber, Ferdinand. *60 Musical Studies for Tuba (Book II).* tr. David L. Kuehn. Southern Music Company. 1969. $7.50. 21 pp. III–IV. Studies in legato style from the vocalises of Concone and Marchesi, with special attention to phrasing and reading problems. Very nice studies for the high school student or a good beginning lyrical study book for the college student.

Siekmann, Frank. *Tuba Etudes at the Elementary Level.* Tuba-Euphonium Press. 1997. $8.00. 24 pp. II. Twenty-six elementary etudes progressively arranged, from long tone studies to chromatic exercises having both meter and key changes. Equal treatment of major and minor keys, with many different musical styles.

Singer, Larry. *Etudes for Tuba, Volume I.* ed. Wesley Jacobs. Encore Music Publishers. 1986. $15.00. 43 pp. III–V. Etudes very appropriate for bass or contrabass tubas. Some etudes are built on familiar melodies. Some excellent challenges are presented in the areas of interval study and unusual rhythmic figures. Also, all etudes are presented three times, each time in a different key.

Singer, Larry. *Etudes for Tuba, Volume II.* ed. Wesley Jacobs. Encore Music Publishers. 1986. $15.00. 45 pp. III–V. The second in a series of two books, this is a logical continuation of volume I.

Skornicka, J. E., and E. G. Boltz. *Rubank Intermediate Method for E flat and BB flat Bass.* Rubank, Incorporated. 1934. $4.95. 48 pp. II–III. A continuation of the Hovey *Rubank Elementary Method,* this work progresses through various keys and uses pleasing, familiar melodies. This is a perennial good choice for the interested, young student who needs listenable tunes to help in attending to solving fundamental problems.

Skornicka, J. E., and Joseph Bergheim. *The Boosey and Hawkes Band Method (Tuba).* Boosey & Hawkes, Incorporated. 1947. Out of Print. 75¢. 32 pp. I–II. Intended as a method for group band study, this text introduces basic rudiments of musicianship using familiar tunes. Pedagogical comments given at the beginning of the book are spare.

Slama, Anton. *66 Etudes in All Major and Minor Keys for Trombone, Tuba, Bassoon, String Bass.* Carl Fischer, Incorporated. 1922. $7.00. 45 pp. III–V. These etudes provide the advanced student with fine material for all aspects of study of articulation and technique. The material is particularly well-suited to the F tuba; however, it would also be very beneficial to the contrabass tubist who needs to improve upper register facility, or it could be read down one octave for solid work on technique and articulation.

Slokar, B. *Tägliche Ubungen.* Editions Marc Reift.

Slokar, B. *Tonleitern/Gammes/Scales, Vol. I und II.* ed. Marc Reift. Editions Marc Reift.

Slokar, Branimir, and Marc Reift. *Flexibility.* Editions Marc Reift. 1993. $20.27. III–V. Originally for trombone, these etudes are presented in treble clef and include progressively challenging lip slurs, up to a range of two octaves. The use of strategically placed accents, syncopation, and alternating duple/triple rhythmic patterns provides additional challenge.

Smith, Claude, Paul Yoder, and Harold Bachman. *Smith-Yoder-Bachman Ensemble Band Method (Basses).* Neil A. Kjos Music Company. 1939. $1.00. 32 pp. I. This method is principally intended as a group method with emphasis on developing player independence through use of two-, three-, and four-part exercises, as well as full band arrangements. A series of theory lessons is included, as well as familiar melodies.

Smith, Claude B. *All-State Band Method.* Pro Art Publications. 1961. 24 pp. I.

Smith, Claude T. *Symphonic Rhythms and Scales (Tuba).* Hal Leonard Publishing Corporation. 1984. $3.95. 24 pp. II–III. This is a supplementary method with emphasis on rhythmic development through the use of syncopation, ties, and accentuation.

Smith, Claude T. *Symphonic Techniques for Band (Tuba).* Hal Leonard Publishing Corporation. 1987. $3.95. 32 pp. III–IV. This method consists primarily of technical studies and chorales for full band.

Smith, Claude T. *Symphonic Warm-Ups for Band (Tuba).* Hal Leonard Publishing Corporation. 1982. $4.95. 24 pp. II–IV. This supplementary method emphasizes the development of tone, technique, and style through scales, etudes, and chorales.

Smith, Leonard B. *A Treasury of Scales for Band and Orchestra (Tuba).* Belwin-Mills. 1952. $4.00. 8 pp. I–II. This is a collection of all major and minor scales.

Snedecor, Phil. *Low Etudes for Tuba.* PAS Music. 1991. $8.95. 34 pp. III–V. Containing etudes in various keys and styles, this is a collection of etudes for the development of the tuba's low register. Designed with both the professional and advanced student tubist in mind, the book contains mostly original material, with the addition of two excerpt-based etudes at the end of the book.

Sparke, Philip. *Scales and Arpeggios, Grades 1–8 in Grade Order.*

Steckeler. *Tuba-Schule für Anfänger (für Tuba in B, F, Es aus: Neue Trossinger Instrumentalmethoden).*

Stegmann. *Elementarschule.* Richard Stegmann. $15.60.

Street, A. *Scales and Arpeggios for the Tuba.* Boosey & Hawkes, Incorporated. 1977. $6.00. 16 pp. III–IV. This book was designed for the student preparing for the Royal Schools of Music board exams and presents a detailed practice regimen for preparation of scales and arpeggios for all major and minor scales, as well as chromatic and whole tone scales. The student's attention is directed to variance of phrasing and articulation patterns and the need to practice intonation as well as technique.

Stuart-Herfurth. *Sounds of the Winds.*

Sueta, Ed. *Band Method, Volumes I, II, III (Tuba).* Macie Publishing Co. 1974. $5.50. 40 pp. I–II. This is an unusual band method which places emphasis on rhythmic reading and perception through use of familiar repertoire. Pedagogical comments peculiar to the tuba are included in the tuba book.

Swan. *Practice Routine.* Trombacor Music. $10.00.

Swanson, Kenneth, and James Ployhar. *Tunes for Tuba (Bass) Technic, Level III.* Belwin-Mills. 1971. $5.50. 32 pp. II–III. The third in a series of three books/levels (see Ostling, Acton for levels I and II), this book is a logical continuation of book II and emphasizes the development of musicality through the presentation of advanced-intermediate-level melodies.

Swanson, Kenneth, Herman Vincent, and James Ployhar. *Studies and Melodious Etudes for Tuba (Bass), Levels II and III.* Belwin-Mills. 1970/71. $5.50. 32 pp. II–III. The second and third books in a series of three (see Laas, Bill for first book information), these books are a logical continuation of the first book, with the additional coverage of advanced meters and keys.

Swanson, Kenneth, Herman Vincent, and James Ployhar. *Tuba (Bass) Student, Level III.* Belwin-Mills. 1971. $5.50. 40 pp. II–III. The third in a series of three books/levels (see Weber, Fred for books I and II), this book is a logical continuation of book II and includes technical etudes in a variety of meters and keys.

Swearingen, James. *Go for Technique (Tuba), Books I, II, and III.* Belwin-Mills. 1990. $5.00. 24 pp. I–II. Each book of this method is divided into individual units, and each unit contains "technique builders," rhythmic studies, scale studies, and melodious etudes.

Swearingen, James. *Unison Plus (Tuba)*. Heritage Music Press. 1988. $2.50. 15 pp. I. This book contains eight popular folk tunes, each including both the basic melody and the tuba part to a full band arrangement.

Swearingen, James, and Barbara Buehlman. *Band Encounters, Book 1 (Tuba)*. Heritage Music Press. 1984. $4.50. 32 pp. I. The first in a series of two books, this band method uses a combined theoretical and cartoon approach to introduce the fundamentals of first-year performance.

Swearingen, James, and Barbara Buehlman. *Band Encounters, Book 2 (Tuba)*. Heritage Music Press. 1984. $4.50. 32 pp. I–II. A continuation of book I, this book introduces sixteenth notes, expressive terminology, and other basic concepts of musical performance.

Swearingen, James, and Barbara Buehlman. *Band Plus, Book 1 (Tuba)*. Heritage Music Press. 1989. $4.95. 48 pp. I. The first in a series of two books, this band method contains the Band Encounters series plus a number of theory puzzles (find-a-word, word scramble, matching, etc.).

Swearingen, James, and Barbara Buehlman. *Band Plus, Book 2 (Tuba)*. Heritage Music Press. 1989. $4.95. 48 pp. I–II. A continuation of book I, this book introduces sixteenth notes, expressive terminology, and other basic concepts of musical performance.

Swearingen, James, and Barbara Buehlman. *Technique Encounters, Books 1 and 2 (Tuba)*. Heritage Music Press. 1984. $1.95. 15 pp. I–II. Ideal as a supplement to any beginning method book, book I places emphasis on rhythmic development at the beginning level while book II introduces more complex rhythms in a progressive manner.

Tarto, Joe. *Basic Rhythms and the Art of Jazz Improvisation*. Charles Colin. 1976. $7.50. 102 pp. III–V. Written by one of the original tuba artist/teacher virtuosi, this book serves as a thorough introduction to jazz playing for the bass line player. It includes pattern drills and a good representation of standard tunes from the early to middle years of the development of the jazz art form. The blues, boogie-woogie, and Latin styles are among those introduced along with basic techniques such as "walking bass."

Tarto, Joe. *Bass Noodles: Modulation Breaks and Hot Choruses for Tuba, Trombone, Mellophone, String Bass, and Bari Sax.* Alfred and Company. 1929. $1.00. 33 pp. III–IV. This text by jazz virtuoso Joe Tarto includes a variety of examples of modulation breaks in a variety of keys in addition to several solos and choruses as performed by Tarto himself. This is a valuable work for the aspiring young bass player, regardless of the particular bass instrument chosen.

Taube, L. H. *Leichte Übungen für Bläser–Heft I: Baritone/Tuba*. ed. Otto Ebner. Pro Musica Verlag.

Taylor, Maurice. *Easy Steps to the Band (Tuba)*. Belwin-Mills. 1939. $3.95. 32 pp. I–II. This is a rapidly progressing method which is divided into 25 individual lessons, including scale studies, duets, and full band arrangements (tuba part).

Taylor, Maurice D. *Band Fundamentals in Easy Steps (Basses)—Books One, Two, Three.* Belwin-Mills. 1960/63/66. 32 pp. I–II. This method is principally intended for group band instruction. It includes a good introduction to basic musicianship fundamentals and one- to two-line exercises and melodies, as well as band-type parts.

Taylor, Maurice D. *Easy Steps to Band (Basses)*. Belwin-Mills. 1967. 32 pp. I.

Taylor, Maurice D. *Intermediate Steps to Band (Basses)*. Belwin-Mills. 1947. 32 pp. II. A method intended primarily for class use with early intermediate students, this book includes thirty lessons, each with a clearly stated objective dealing with a specific area such as rhythm, phrasing, articulation, etc. Exercises are typically only one or two lines in length.

Teuchert, Emil. *Große Praktische Tubaschule*. Carl Fischer, Incorporated.

Teuchert, Emil. *Lehrgang*.

Teuchert, Emil. *Schule für B oder C-Tuba, Teil I.* Freidrich Hofmeister.

Teuchert, Emil. *Schule für die Basstuba in F oder E♭ und für Kontrabass-tuba in CC or BB♭*. ed. Franz Seyffarth. Freidrich Hofmeister. 63 pp. II–III. This method offers a good approach to private instruction for the late intermediate student. Scale and interval studies are presented together with short and interesting etudes in virtually all keys. A review of music fundamentals is presented in the introductory section. All text is in German.

Teuchert, Emil. *Tägliche Übungen für Tuba mit einem Anhang der Schwierigsten Orchesterstellen und Soli aus Blas und Streichmusik*. Seeling/Erdmann. 1936/64.

Teuchert, Emil, und Bruno Uetz. *26 Studien in allen Dur- und moll-Tonarten und (Uetz) Technische Studien.* Freidrich Hofmeister.

Todorov, G. *School.*

Tyrrell, H. W. *Advanced Studies for BB♭ Bass.* Boosey & Hawkes, Incorporated. 1948. $9.00. 40 pp. III–IV. A standard method for the serious high school student, with particular focus on rhythmic and melodic patterns. An excellent resource for private study and for audition material for honors bands, etc.

Tyrrell, H. W. *Advanced Studies for E♭ Bass.* Boosey & Hawkes, Incorporated. 1948. 40 pp. III–IV. The etudes in this work are identical to those in the BB♭ book, but with appropriate editing for range, etc., to facilitate development of skills appropriate to the E♭ tuba.

Uber, David. *Concert Etudes for Tuba (or Bass Trombone)*. Robert King Music Company. 1985. $3.50. 32 pp. IV. These etudes will challenge the advanced performer both musically and technically. The composer explores a variety of keys and both extremes of range for the tuba, as well as interesting rhythmic challenges, in studies that represent better than usual the musical satisfaction to be found in worthwhile etudes.

Uber, David. *David Uber Warm Up Procedure for Tuba.* Charles Colin. 1980. $5.95. 20 pp. II–IV. This text presents a well-thought-out routine which may be used as a whole or in parts. All basic, fundamental aspects of performance are covered, including long tones, scales, flexibilities, etc. Pedagogically sound instructions are included at the beginning of the text, as well as accompanying each emphasis area.

Uber, David. *15 Progressive Etudes for Tuba (or Bass Trombone).* Touch of Brass. $7.95.

Uber, David. *Fifty Short Beginning Studies for the Tuba Player.* Wehr's Music House. 2002. $9.00. 18 pp. I–II. A collection of fifty short etudes, most of which are set in rudimentary meters and keys. Includes limited exposure to chromaticism, syncopation, and sixteenth notes. Especially suitable as a method for first-year students who are transitioning into their second year of study.

Uber, David. *First Studies for BB♭ Tuba.* Kendor Music Company. 1988. $9.00. 25 pp. II–III. These etudes will work well with the intermediate or early advanced player. The composer has made a special effort to accommodate the problems encountered by the young student with orthodontic braces.

Uber, David. *Solo Etudes for Tuba.* Tuba-Euphonium Press. 2002. $10.00. 12 pp. III. A collection of twelve etudes, each of which is suitable for concert performance. A variety of meters and musical styles. Multimetricism, a 2½ octave range, and extensive use of accidentals make this a challenging yet suitable work for high school tuba players. See Music for Unaccompanied Tuba.

Uber, David. *Thirty Studies for the Bass Tuba.* Southern Music Company. 1977. $3.75. 28 pp. III–IV. These are excellent, musical etudes for the advanced student. Challenges are represented for all areas of musical skills. Only the most advanced high school students should tackle these studies, as they are most appropriate to the student in the midst of college study.

Uber, David. *Thirty-five Conservatory Etudes.* Touch of Brass. $9.95.

Uber, David. *Thirty-Five Elementary Etudes for BB♭ Tuba.* Tuba-Euphonium Press. 2002. $12.00. 22 pp. II–III. A collection of thirty-five short etudes, with emphasis upon rhythmic acuity. Frequent use of compound meter and, in the second half of the text, frequent meter changes within each etude make this a suitable method for developing a good sense of rhythm, especially for the advanced middle school student.

Uber, David. *Tuba Method (in Three Books).* Peer-Southern Organization.

Uber, David. *Twenty-five Early Studies for Tuba.* Southern Music Company. 1980. $7.50. 28 pp. II–III. Appropriate etudes for the second- or third-year tuba student. These are fine musical studies that emphasize tonguing, legato, rhythm, breath control, and phrasing. Tonally, principally flat keys are represented.

Uetz. *Elementarschule für Tuba in B.*

Uetz. *Technische Studien mit Toneleiterstudein nach Arban (I und II).*

Ujfalusi, Laszlo, Andras Pehl, and Jozsef Perlaki. *Tubaiskola (Tubaschule).* Editio Musica Budapest. 1962. 133 pp. I–IV. Including parallel Hungarian and German text, this is a comprehensive method, intended for use with the F tuba, which includes rudimentary studies, exercises in all keys, and several solos including piano accompaniment.

U.S. Department of the Army. *Soldier's Manual: Tuba Player, Levels I, II, and III.* Washington Department of Defense, Department of the Army. 1978. 109 pp.

Uth, Lothar. *Schule für Tuba.* Uth O.J.

Van Beekum, Jan. *Fondamento.*

Van Hoy, Marjorie A. *Seven Melodic Etudes for Tuba.* Tuba-Euphonium Press. 1994. $7.00. 8 pp. IV. Dedicated to Andras Szentkiralyi. A short collection of technically challenging etudes, each of which is suitable for concert performance. Wide intervallic leaps, extensive broken chord patterns, and frequent tempo changes make this a challenging work for even the most astute college-level tuba player. See Music for Unaccompanied Tuba.

Van Uffelen, P. C. *Voordrachtstukken en Etudes.* Molenaar N.V. 1963. 18 pp. IV.

Vander Cook, H. A. *Vander Cook Etudes for E flat or BB flat Bass (Tuba).* Rubank, Incorporated. 1941. $3.50. 26 pp. II–III. From one of the great legends of instrumental pedagogy, here are principally short etudes representing a variety of styles and covering the broad range of fundamental areas from legato tonguing to technical development. The volume concludes with two of Vander Cook's classic solos, "Bombastoso" and "Colossus."

Vasiliev, S. *24 Melodious Etudes for Tuba.* Robert King Music Company. $3.40. 39 pp. III–IV. These are good studies for phrasing, interpretation, and flexibility in mostly lyric settings. These etudes are a nice alternative to Bordogni and are, in some instances, more challenging in terms of range and technique.

Vaughan, Rodger. *Randolph Etudes for Tuba and Bass Trombone, Book 1 (Introductory).* 1991. 24 pp. II. At press time these etudes have been submitted for publication. Contact the composer at the California State University–Fullerton for publication information. Designed with the very young player in mind, these are mainly interesting half note/quarter note studies in which modal, as well as major and minor, keys are explored. All studies are lyrical in nature.

Vaughan, Rodger. *Randolph Etudes for Tuba and Bass Trombone, Book 2 (Intermediate)*. 1991. 25 pp. II–III. At press time these etudes have been submitted for publication. Contact the composer at the California State University–Fullerton for publication information. These studies, exploring modal and major/minor keys, would be suitable for the advanced junior high or early senior high student. More rhythmic challenges are presented than in volume I of this series.

Vaughan, Rodger. *Randolph Etudes for Tuba and Bass Trombone, Book 3 (Advanced)*. 1991. 26 pp. III. At press time these etudes have been submitted for publication. Contact the composer at the California State University–Fullerton for publication information. A logical continuation of volumes I and II, this set of etudes presents an excellent set of challenges for the high school tubist and tunes the ear to work well in keys outside the standard major and minor fare.

Vazzana, Anthony. *A Book of Studies for Tuba*. Tuba-Euphonium Press. 1997. $12.00. 27 pp. III. Twenty-six etudes designed to introduce the young tubist to a wide array of musical styles and technical challenges. A wide variety of meters, extreme dynamic contrasts, and challenging rhythms provide the performer with material that is stimulating yet accessible.

Victor. *Victor Method (Tuba)*. Belwin-Mills.

Vieulou. *Etudes Caracteristiques*. Editions Gras. $44.75. (See Thompson/Lemke: *French Music for Low Brass Instruments*).

Vieulou. *Etudes Caracteristiques Saxhorn Basse, 4/5/6 Pistons*. Alphonse Leduc Editions Musicales. $22.40.

Ward, N. *Elementary School Beginner for E♭ Tuba*. Consolidated. 1956.

Warren, Christopher. *Twenty Etudes for Tuba*. TUBA Press. 1992. $10.00. 48 pp. III–IV. This is a very helpful text that includes a comprehensive section on scales, a warm-up routine, and etudes in a variety of styles with pedagogical suggestions included to help guide the student who might not have a professional tuba teacher accessible. A very good selection for the library of any serious high school student or early college student, the book concludes with four nice duets for two tubas.

Wastall, Peter. *Learn As You Play Tuba*. Boosey & Hawkes, Incorporated. $11.50.

Wastall, Peter. *Scales and Arpeggios for Tuba*. Boosey & Hawkes, Incorporated. 1990. $6.50. 19 pp. II–III. This text includes the scale and arpeggio exercises required for the five levels of the Associated Board of the Royal Schools of Music in England for E♭ and BB♭ tubas. All scales and arpeggios for each grade are included, together with a practice planner and an area for comments from the teacher. This would be a good resource for any student who needs extra work on scales.

Watelle, Jules. *Grande Méthode de Basse et Tuba*. Editions Salabert. 1912. Out of Print. 196 pp. III–V. This French method is aimed particularly at the French tuba in C, although much of the material would be useful to the student studying the F tuba in development of upper register facility. The etudes are, for the most part, very advanced and cover every aspect of technical development. A few melodic studies and solos are included.

Weast. *Valuable Repetitions*. McGinnis & Marx Music Publications. $10.00.

Weber, Fred. *Belwin Elementary Band Method for Bass (Tuba)*. ed. Nilo W. Hovey. Belwin-Mills. 1945. $1.00. 39 pp. I. This is a beginning method for full band instruction. Some simple melodies are included along with ensemble works for the full band. As the book progresses, less emphasis is placed on the melodic aspect of the tuba, and more emphasis is placed on the tuba as an accompaniment/background instrument.

Weber, Fred. *Belwin Intermediate Band Method for Bass (Tuba)*. ed. Nilo W. Hovey. Belwin-Mills. 1947. $5.50. 31 pp. II. A continuation of the Belwin Elementary Method, this method places more emphasis upon the development of individual technique.

Weber, Fred. *Belwin Progressive Band Studies for Bass (Tuba)*. Belwin-Mills. 1949. II–III.

Weber, Fred. *First Division Band Method for Tuba, Parts I, II, III, and IV*. Belwin-Mills. 1962/63/64/65. $5.50. I–III. This is a classic, progressive group method for band that has enjoyed immense popularity in the United States over the past thirty years. Presentation of fundamentals is combined with singable melodies and brief ensemble works.

Weber, Fred. *Rehearsal Fundamentals for Bass (Tuba)*. Belwin-Mills. 1956. II–III.

Weber, Fred. *Tuba Note Speller*. Belwin-Mills. 1951. $5.50. 32 pp. I. Here is a workbook designed to assist the young student with note reading, fingerings, and rhythmic reading.

Weber, Fred, and Kenneth Swanson. *Tuba (Bass) Student, Levels I and II*. Belwin-Mills. 1969/70. $5.50. 40 pp. I–II. This three-volume method (volume III is listed under Swanson, Kenneth) is designed for use in private instruction from the elementary through the advanced-intermediate levels. It includes the introduction and review of fundamentals throughout.

White, William C., ed. and compiler. *Unisonal Scales, Chords and Rhythmic Studies for Bands–Tuba*. Carl Fischer, Incorporated. 1921. Out of Print. 30 pp. II–III.

Wilhelm, Rolf. *Five Etudes for Solo Tuba*. See Music for Unaccompanied Tuba.

Williams, Richard, and Jeff King. *Foundations for Superior Performance.* Neil A Kjos Music Company. 1998. $5.95. 48 pp. II–III. A collection of warm-ups and technical exercises intended for group instruction but also suitable for individual study. Of special interest to the individual are the full-range (two-octave) scales and arpeggios at the back of the book.

Wltschek. *Lippenbindungen für Tuba in F und B.*

Woodruff. *24 Artistic Studies for Tuba.* Southern Music Company. 1986. $7.50. 32 pp. III. This is a collection of studies from the etudes of Bordogni, Blazhevich, Vasiliev, and Kopprasch freely edited by Mr. Woodruff. His purpose in re-working the etudes is to make them better suited for competition or other uses. Stylistic, tempo, and other expressive indications have been added to give the performer more ideas for musical interpretation of the etudes.

Wouda. *Voordrachstukken Etudes Ten Behoeve van de Muziekexamens.* Uitgave Molenaar, N. V.

Wright D., and H. Round. *Complete Method.* Wright.

Yaus, Grover C. *40 Rhythmical Studies for Basses (E♭ and BB♭).* Belwin-Mills. 1958. $2.95. 23 pp. II–III. These studies are designed for unison band; however, they will work very well for private instruction, particularly for intermediate or early advanced students who need help with rhythm. Rhythms presented are common figures, not "tricks" presented for difficulty's sake.

Yaus, Grover C. *47 Foundation Studies for E♭ or BB♭ Tuba.* Belwin-Mills. II.

Yaus, Grover C. *Harmonized Rest Patterns (Tuba).* Belwin-Mills.

Yaus, Grover C. *101 Rhythmic Rest Patterns (for Basses).* Belwin-Mills. 1953. $5.50. 21 pp. I–II. This method, published for unison band, focuses on the development of rhythmic reading skills.

Yaus, Grover C. *127 Original Exercises for Bass Clef Instruments.* Belwin-Mills. 1956. III.

Yaus, Grover C. *32 All in One Studies for Basses.* Belwin-Mills.

Yaus, Grover C. *20 Rhythmical Studies for Basses (E♭ or BB♭).* Belwin-Mills. 1952. $3.95. 21 pp. II–III. This method places an emphasis upon rhythmic development through the inclusion of various meters and the strategic placement of accentuation.

Yaus, Grover C., ed. and compiler. *Division of Measure for E♭ and BB♭.* Belwin-Mills. II–III.

Yaus, Grover C., and Roy C. Miller. *150 Original Exercises for Bass Clef Instruments.* Belwin-Mills. 1944.

Zechmeister, Gerhard. *Concert Tuba.* Doblinger. 110 pp. I–IV. Dedicated to Professor Leopold Kolar. Intended as a comprehensive method for the Viennese F tuba, this text addresses breathing, embouchure, tone, range, and articulation with an extensive amount of pedagogical commentary and a wide range of musical exercises. The commentary is provided in both German and English, and the exercises span the entire range of musical development, from long tones to four-octave lip slurs. Photos, diagrams, and an exhaustive set of fingering charts are included.

Zepp, George. *Notes for Today (Bass), Parts I and II.* Belwin-Mills. 1977/78. $5.00 each. 24 pp. each. I–II. This is a book of word games intended as a supplement to any band method for the reinforcement of basic music theory skills.

9. Orchestral Excerpts

David D. Graves, Assistant Editor, *Guide to the Tuba Repertoire: The New Tuba Source Book*

Jerry A. Young, Assistant Editor, and David D. Graves, Editorial Assistant, *The Tuba Source Book*

Introductory Remarks (July 2005): David D. Graves

As in the first edition, the primary goal of this chapter is the annotation of any excerpt collection compiled specifically for the tuba. The only stipulations are that the collection must be *legal* and available for purchase or, in the case of out of print works, still in circulation. Due to the scope of such an undertaking, it is understood that works may have been unintentionally omitted, though every effort has been made to avoid such omission. The stated price reflects the most up-to-date information at the time of this chapter's preparation. Due to the limited availability of review materials, bibliographical information for some collections may be missing or incomplete. Furthermore, with the current rate of technological development, particularly with regard to printed media, it is worth noting that many of the more comprehensive excerpt collections are now in electronic format. Also, many of the once-obscure orchestral LPs have now been re-released as compact discs. Subsequently, the personal computer and CD player have earned a place alongside the metronome and tuner as valuable tools in the thorough study of orchestral repertoire.

Thanks are extended to the following, for their invaluable assistance in the completion of this chapter:

- Jerry Young—an extraordinary scholar, musician and mentor—for his guidance in the first edition and his trust in my abilities with the second edition
- Linda Stewart—administrative assistant in the Baylor University School of Music—for addressing and mailing approximately four hundred letters, resulting in the availability of review materials for this chapter
- Colin Campbell—an outstanding young tubist and overall nice guy—for spending many hours on the phone, thereby ensuring the accuracy of much of the information contained in this chapter
- The many composers and publishers who provided review materials for this chapter
- Winston Morris—editorial genius and grandfather of tubadom—for his infinite patience and flexible deadlines
- Denise, Andrea, Evan, and Jeremy Graves—my family—for their love, support, and understanding, particularly while I have been confined to the *Tuba Source Book* room (formerly known as the laundry room) of our house. Perhaps now we can locate the missing laundry.

Introductory Remarks (July 1995): Jerry A. Young and David D. Graves

The study of orchestral repertoire consumes a considerable portion of the serious tubist's practice time. In addition to the *Albums of Orchestra Parts* published by Kalmus, numerous publishers have created publications that furnish either entire parts or important passages for the tubist. Many contain specific pedagogical and interpretational information and suggestions. Although the bulk of the literature for tuba in this area has been produced since the late 1940s, such materials for tuba have existed since the latter part of the nineteenth century.

Special thanks are extended to Eugene Pokorny of the Chicago Symphony Orchestra, Ronald Bishop of the Cleveland Orchestra, and Douglas Yeo of the Boston Symphony Orchestra for their assistance in obtaining some of the more difficult-to-locate orchestral study texts. Thanks are also due to several *TSB* international consultants for providing information about publications from their respective parts of the world. In addition, special thanks go to the University of Wisconsin–Eau Claire School of Graduate Study and Research, Dr. Ronald Satz, Dean; and the

Department of Music, Dr. David Baker, Chair. Because of their generous support, Mr. David Graves was able to assist with the research for and preparation of this portion of *The Tuba Source Book.*

General comments regarding this annotated bibliography:

1) The goal for this chapter was to determine the availability of published orchestral excerpts for the tuba. When it was determined that a given work was out of print, this was indicated in the bibliographic information presented. However, lack of an "out of print" notation does not guarantee that the given item is indeed available.

2) The prices given indicate the most recent price for each piece. In the case of out of print material or where no other source was available, the cover price is listed with the assumption that this information might be of interest. Since every publisher did not furnish a current catalog with current price information, there is no guarantee that all prices were accurate as of the publication deadline.

3) Entries that appear in the following listing without annotation and/or with incomplete bibliographic information were not made available to the editor for examination. The editorial staff of *The Tuba Source Book* felt that it was important that all items be documented in this project, regardless of current availability. Some items were not furnished for review by the publisher while others (appearing in old catalogs or bibliographies) have presumably long since been out of print and lost.

4) Where entries are published for both trombone and tuba, all contents of the text are listed. Every work listed does not necessarily include a tuba part.

5) Spelling of names of composers and works appear here in identical form to the way they appear in the table of contents of the individual publication. No attempt has been made to be consistent with spellings in this publication. It should be noted, likewise, that rules of capitalization, etc., vary from language to language and, again, all entries here appear as seen in tables of contents.

Bartok, Bela. *Albums of Orchestra Parts, # 8610.* Edwin F. Kalmus. $9.00. This is a set of complete parts to *2 Portraits op. 5; 2 Pictures op. 10; 1st Suite.*

Beethoven, Ludwig von, et al. *The Orchestra Musician's CD-ROM Library, Volume 1 (Beethoven, Schubert and More)—Low Brass.* Hal Leonard. $19.98. The first of five volumes; includes (in portable display format [.pdf]) the complete low brass parts to ninety orchestral works by Auber, Beethoven, Berlioz, Cherubini, Donizetti, Mendelssohn, Rossini, Schubert, and Weber. A complete listing of contents is available at www.orchmusiclibrary.com. Published for Violin I and II, Viola, Cello, Bass, Flute and Piccolo, Clarinet, Oboe and English Horn, Horn, Bassoon, Contrabassoon, Trumpet and Cornet, Low Brass (which includes Trombone, Euphonium, and Tuba), and Timpani/Percussion.

Belwin-Mills. *Tuba Excerpts from Standard Orchestral Repertoire, Book One.* Belwin-Mills. $6.50. 57 pp. Contains excerpts from D'Albert: *Der Rubin; Gernot.* Bantock: *Der Zeitgeist; Helena.* Berger: *Symphonie B dur.* Berlioz: *Symphony Fantastique; Romeo and Juliet; Trojan Marsch; Requiem; Damnation of Faust; Benvenuto Cellini.* Chabrier: *Gwendoline.* Donizetti: *Lucia di Lammermoor.* Dräseke: *Herat.* Glazounow: *Symphony.* Halevy: *Die Jüdin.* Kretzschmer: *Die Folkunger.* Liszt: *Ce qu'on entend sur la montagne, Symphonische Dichtung Nr. 1; Tasso, Symphonische Dichtung Nr. 2; Die Ideale, Symphonische Dichtung Nr. 12.* Mascagni: *Cavalleria Rusticana.* Mendelssohn: *Midsummer Night's Dream.* Nicode: *Das Meer.* Novak: *von ewiger Sehnsucht; Tondichtung.* Saint-Saëns: *Samson and Delilah.* Sibelius: *Symphony Nr. 1; Symphony Nr. 2.* Strauss: *Til Eulenspiegel; Also Sprach Zarathustra.* Thomas: *Hamlet.* Tinel: *Franziskus; Drei Symphonische Tongemälde; Overture, Godoleva.* Tchaikowsky: *Symphony Nr. 4.* Verdi: *Rigoletto.* Volbach: *Es waren zwei Königskinder.* Wagner: *Lohengrin; Tristan and Isolde; Eine Faust Overture.* Weingartner: *Symphony Nr.2.* Zoellner: *Der Überfall; Die versunkene Glocke.*

Belwin-Mills. *Tuba Excerpts from Standard Orchestral Repertoire, Book Three.* Belwin-Mills. $4.00. 25 pp. Contains excerpts from Wagner's *Die Meistersinger, Das Rheingold, Die Walküre, Siegfried, Götterdämmerung, Parsifal, Eine Faust-Ouvertüre, Huldigungs-Marsch.*

Belwin-Mills. *Tuba Excerpts from Standard Orchestral Repertoire, Book Two.* Belwin-Mills. $4.00. 25 pp. Contains excerpts from Wagner: *Rienzi, Der Fliegende Holländer, Tannhäuser, Lohengrin, Tristan und Isolde.*

Berlioz, Hector. *Albums of Orchestra Parts, #8616.* Edwin F. Kalmus. $9.00. This is a set of complete parts to overtures: *King Lear, Judges of the Secret Court, Der Corsair, Benvenuto Cellini.*

Berlioz, Hector. *Albums of Orchestra Parts, #8617.* Edwin F. Kalmus. $9.00. This is a set of complete parts to *Romeo and Juliet, Fantastic Symphony, Harold in Italy.*

Berlioz, Hector. *Orchester Studien Tuba: Berlioz.* ed. Manfred Hoppert. Zimmermann-Frankfurt. 1995. $26.68. 91 pp. Contains excerpts from the following works by Berlioz: *Symphonie*

Fantastique, Harold in Italy, Grand Death-Mass (Requiem), Romeo and Juliet, Triumphal and Funeral Symphony, The Damnation of Faust, Te Deum, and *The Trojans;* and overtures to *The Judges of the Secret Court, King Lear, The Corsair,* and *Benvenuto Cellini.* Each excerpt is presented with an indication of other instruments within the orchestra that share the same part and/or the trombone parts in score format, so the performer can see how the tuba part fits into the entire low brass timbral spectrum. Also includes a glossary of abbreviations with translation into English, as well as a listing of passages that are likely to show up on an audition. Text is in English, French, and German.

Bernard, Paul. *Traits Difficiles: Tuba.* Alphonse Leduc Editions Musicales. 4 pp. This collection contains excerpts for tuba from the following works: Delvincourt: *Radio Serenade;* Wagner: *La Walkyrie, Eine Faust;* Roussel: *Fourth Symphony;* Stravinsky: *Petrouchka;* Tchaikowsky: *Fourth Symphony;* Liszt: *Les Ideals di Schiller;* Halevy: *La Juive;* Berlioz: *Requiem;* Saint-Saens: *Le Deluge;* Thomas: *Hamlet.*

Bernard, Paul. *Traits Difficiles, Volume 1.* Alphonse Leduc. 1948. 8 pp. Parts one and two of a four-part series. Part One is the same as the above-listed work and contains tuba passages from Delvincourt: *Radio Serenade;* Wagner: *La Walkyrie* and *Une Ouverture pour Faust;* Roussel: *Symphony No. 4;* Stravinsky: *Petrouchka;* Tchaikovsky: *Symphony No. 4;* Liszt: *Les Ideals de Schiller;* Halévy: *La Juive;* Berlioz: *Requiem;* Saint-Saëns: *Le Déluge;* and Thomas: *Hamlet.* Part Two contains tuba passages from Delvincourt: *Bal Vénitien;* D'Indy: *Le Camp de Wallenstein;* Berlioz: *La Damnation de Faust, Benvenuto Cellini* and *Symphonie Fantastique;* Liszt: *Le Tasse;* Saint-Saëns: *Samson et Dalila;* Chabrier: *Gwendoline;* Masiagni: *Cavalleria Rusticana;* Wagner: *Lohengrin;* Verdi: *Rigoletto;* Schmitt: *La Tragédie de Salomé;* and Glazounow: *Symphony No. 2.*

Bernard, Paul. *Traits Difficiles, Volume 2.* Alphonse Leduc. 1951. 8 pp. Parts three and four of a four-part series. Part Three contains bass trombone passages from Delvincourt: *Le Toit du Monde* and Respighi: *Les Pins de Rome;* a tenor tuba passage from R. Strauss: *Don Quichotte;* and bass/contrabass tuba passages from Delvincourt: *Le Toit du Monde,* Liszt: *Ce Que L'On Entend Sur la Montagne,* R. Strauss: *Till Eulenspiegels [Merry Pranks],* Wagner: *Tristan et Isolde,* and Donizetti: *Lucie de Lammermoor.* Part Four contains bass trombone passages from Moussorgsky: *Tableaux D'Une Exposition* and Liszt: *Piano Concerto No. 4.* Also included in Part Four are tuba passages from Bachelet: *Scémo,* Verdi: *Force du Destin,* Moussorgsky: *Tableaux D'Une Exposition,* and Wagner: *L'Or du Rhin.*

Berthold, Otto. *Orchesterstudien: Strauss (Symphonic Werken).*

Beversdorf, Thomas. *Orchestral Literature for Trombone and Tuba.* $15.00.

Borodin, Alexander, and Reinhold Gliere. *Albums of Orchestra Parts, #8608.* Edwin F. Kalmus. $9.00. This is a set of complete parts to Borodin: *Symphony No. 2, Prince Igor Overture, Polovetsian Dances;* and Gliere: *Russian Sailors' Dance.*

Brahms, Johannes, and Max Bruch. *Albums of Orchestra Parts, #8609.* Edwin F. Kalmus. $9.00. This is a set of complete parts to Brahms: Academic Festival Overture, Tragic Overture, Symphony No. 2; and Bruch: *Scottish Fantasie op. 46.*

Brahms, Johannes, et al. *The Orchestra Musician's CD-ROM Library, Volume 3 (Brahms, Schumann and More)—Low Brass.* Hal Leonard. $19.98. The third of five volumes. Includes (in .pdf format) the complete low brass parts to 74 orchestral works by Brahms, Chabrier, Chausson, Chopin, Franck, Lalo, Liszt, Offenbach, Sarasate, Schumann, and von Suppe. A complete listing of contents is available at www.orchmusiclibrary.com. Published for Violin I and II, Viola, Cello, Bass, Flute and Piccolo, Clarinet, Oboe and English Horn, Horn, Bassoon, Contrabassoon, Trumpet and Cornet, Low Brass (which includes Trombone, Euphonium, and Tuba), and Timpani/Percussion.

Brahms, Johannes. *Orchestral Literature für Trombone und Tuba: Die 4 Sinfonien + 2 Ouvertüren.*

Brahms, Johannes. *Orchester Studien Posaune/Tuba: Brahms.* ed. Martin Göss. Zimmermann-Frankfurt. 1993. $22.49. 52 pp. Contains trombone and tuba excerpts from the following works by Brahms: *Symphonies No. 1–4, Academic Festival Overture, Tragic Overture, A German Requiem, Song of Destiny, Nänie,* and *Song of the Fates.* Excerpts are presented in score format, and many cues for other instruments within the orchestra are indicated, to facilitate a greater sense of ensemble. Text is in English, French, and German.

Brown, Keith, ed. *Orchestral Excerpts from the Symphonic Repertoire for Trombone, Vol. I.* International Music Company. 1964. $9.00. 63 pp. This collection of orchestral studies includes trombone and tuba (when applicable) excerpts from the following works: Berlioz: *Hungarian March from "The Damnation of Faust," Overture to the Roman Carnival;* Borodin: *Symphony No. 2;* Brahms: *Symphony No. 2, Tragic Overture;* Dvorak: *Symphony Nos. 8 and 9;* Elgar: *Enigma Variations;* Hindemith: *Konzertmusik for Strings and Brass;* d'Indy: *Symphony on a French Mountain Air;* Liszt: *Les Preludes;* Prokofiev: *Symphony No. 5;* Rimsky-Korsakow: *Russian Easter Overture;* Rossini: *Overture la Gaza Ladra;* Schumann: *Symphony No. 4;* Sibelius: *Symphony No. 2;* Stravinsky: *Firebird Suite;* Tchaikovsky: *Symphony No. 4, 1812 Overture;* Vaughan Williams: *A London Symphony;* Verdi: *Othello;* Weber: *Overture "Der Freischutz."*

Brown, Keith, ed. *Orchestral Excerpts from the Symphonic Repertoire for Trombone, Vol. II.* International Music Company. 1965. $9.00. 62 pp. This collection of orchestral studies contains trombone and tuba (when applicable) excerpts from the following works: Berlioz: *Symphony Fantastique;* Brahms: *Academic Festival Overture;* Chausson: *Symphony in B♭;* Delibes: *Coppelia;* Prokofiev: *Lt. Kije;* Rachmaninoff: *Isle of the Dead;* Saint-Saens: *Symphony No. 3 in C;* Schumann: *Symphonies Nos. 2 and 3;* Shostakovich: *Symphony No. 1;* Sibelius: *Finalandia;* Smetana: *Overture to "The Bartered Bride";* Strauss: *Ein Heldenleben, Don Juan, Salome's Dance, Till Eulenspiegel;* Stravinsky: *Fireworks, Petrouchka;* Tchaikowsky: *Francesca da Rimini;* Verdi: *Aida.*

Brown, Keith, ed. *Orchestral Excerpts from the Symphonic Repertoire for Trombone, Vol. III.* International Music Company. 1965. $9.00. 62 pp. This collection of orchestral studies contains trombone and tuba (where applicable) excerpts from the following works: Berlioz: *Overture to "Beatrice and Benedict";* Bizet: *L'Arlesienne Suite No. 2;* Borodin: *Polovetsian Dances;* Brahms: *Requiem, Symphonies Nos. 1 and 2;* Bruckner: *Symphony No. 4;* Debussy: *Nocturnes;* Dukas: *The Sorcerer's Apprentice;* Franck: *Symphony in D Minor;* Humperdinck: *Hansel and Gretel;* d'Indy: *Istar;* Kabalevsky: *Overture to Colas Breugnon;* Lalo: *Overture to Le Roi d'Ya;* Mahler: *Symphony No. 1;* Mussorgsky: *Night on the Bare Mountain;* Rimsky Korsakov: *Symphony No. 2, Suite Coq d'Or;* Shostakovich: *Symphony No. 5;* Stravinsky: *L'Histoire du Soldat, Le Sacre du Printeps;* Tchaikowsky: *Symphony No. 6;* Verdi: *Overture la Forza del Destino, Requiem;* Weber: *Overture Euryanthe.*

Brown, Keith, ed. *Orchestral Excerpts from the Symphonic Repertoire for Trombone, Vol. IV.* International Music Company. 1965. $9.00. 62 pp. This collection of orchestral studies contains trombone and tuba (where applicable) excerpts from the following works: Berlioz: *Harold in Italy, Overture to "Judges of the Secret Court";* Brahms: *Symphony No. 4;* Chabrier: *Espana;* Dvorak: *Cello Concerto;* Hindemith: *Symphonic Metamorphosis;* Liszt: *Piano Concerto No. 2;* Milhaud: *The Creation of the World;* Orff: *Carmina Burana;* Prokofiev: *Romeo and Juliet Suites 1 and 2, Scythia Suite;* Rachmaninoff: *Symphony No. 2;* Ravel: *Alborada del Gracioso;* Sibelius: *Symphony No. 1;* Strauss: *Don Quixote;* Stravinsky: *Song of the Nightingale;* Tchaikowsky: *Suite No. 3.*

Brown, Keith, ed. *Orchestral Excerpts from the Symphonic Repertoire for Trombone, Vol. V.* International Music Company. 1966. $9.00. 62 pp. This collection of orchestral studies contains trombone and tuba (where applicable) excerpts from the following works: Berg: *Violin Concerto;* Berlioz: *Funeral Oration from "Symphonic Funebre et Triomphale";* Bruckner: *Symphony No. 5;* Chabrier: *Overture "Gwendoline";* Hindemith: *Sinfonietta;* Kodaly: *Hary Janos Suite;* Mahler: *Symphony No. 5;* Mendelssohn: *Symphony No. 5, Wedding March;* Prokofiev: *Symphony No. 6;* Sibelius: *Symphony No. 5;* Strauss: *Also Sprach Zarathustra;* Stravinsky: *Symphony in C;* Tchaikovsky: *Symphony No. 5.*

Brown, Keith, ed. *Orchestral Excerpts from the Symphonic Repertoire for Trombone, Vol. VI.* International Music Company. 1967. $9.00. 62 pp. This collection of orchestral studies contains trombone and tuba (where applicable) excerpts from the following works: Berg: *Kammerkonzert;* Bruckner: *Symphony No. 7;* Dvorak: *Scherzo Cappricioso;* Gliere: *Symphony No. 3;* Hindemith: *Harmonie der Welt;* Mahler: *Symphony No. 7;* Poulenc: *Suite Francaise;* Ravel: *L'Heure Espagnole, Piano Concerto for the Left Hand, L'Infant les Sortileges;* Rimsky-Korsakow: *Scheherazade;* Schoenberg: *Variations;* Tchaikovsky: *Nutcracker Suite;* Verdi: *Don Carlo.*

Brown, Keith, ed. *Orchestral Excerpts from the Symphonic Repertoire for Trombone, Vol. VII.* International Music Company. 1967. $9.00. 62 pp. This collection of orchestral studies contains trombone and tuba (where applicable) excerpts from the following works: Berg: *Wozzeck;* Berlioz: *Romeo and Juliet;* Bruckner: *Symphony No. 6;* Glazunov: *Symphony No. 4;* Hindemith: *Nobilissima Vissione;* Mahler: *Symphonies Nos. 5 and 8;* Shostakovich: *Symphony No. 9;* Tchaikowsky: *Swan Lake;* Webern: *Six Pieces.*

Brown, Keith, ed. *Orchestral Excerpts from the Symphonic Repertoire for Trombone, Vol. VIII.* International Music Company. 1968. $9.00. 62 pp. This collection of orchestral studies contains trombone and tuba (where applicable) excerpts from the following works: Berlioz: *Requiem;* Blacher: *Variations on a Theme by Paganini;* Bruckner: *Symphony No. 1;* Debussy: *Le Martyre de St. Sebastian;* Dukas: *Fanfare La Peri;* Hindemith: *Mathis der Maler;* Ibert: *Divertissement;* Janacek: *Sinfonietta;* Mahler: *Symphony No. 3;* Poulenc: *Suite Francaise;* Ravel: *Daphnis et Chloe Suites I and II, La Valse;* Roussel: *Symphony No. 4;* Sibelius: *Symphony No. 3;* Strauss: *Le Bourgeois Gentilhomme, Tod und Verklärung;* Stravinsky: *Symphony in Three Movements;* Tchaikowsky: *Manfred Symphony, The Sleeping Beauty;* Verdi: *Nabucco.*

Brown, Keith, ed. *Orchestral Excerpts from the Symphonic Repertoire for Trombone, Vol. IX.* International Music Company. 1969. $9.00. 62 pp. This collection of orchestral studies contains trombone and tuba (where applicable) excerpts from the following works: Berg: *Lulu;* Berlioz: *The Damnation of Faust;* Bruckner: *Symphony No. 8;* Hindemith: *Cello Concerto;* Liszt: *Hungarian Rhapsody No. 2;* Mahler: *Symphonies Nos. 6 and 9;* Ravel: *Bolero;* Sibelius: *Symphony No. 7;*

Smetana: *From Bohemia's Fields and Meadows;* Strauss: *Salome;* Tchaikowsky: *Symphony No. 2.*

Brown, Keith, ed. *Orchestral Excerpts from the Symphonic Repertoire for Trombone, Vol. X.* International Music Company. 1970. $9.00. 62 pp. This collection of orchestral studies contains trombone and tuba (where applicable) excerpts from the following works: Berlioz: *The Royal Hunt and Storm;* Bruckner: *Symphonies Nos. 3 and 9;* Debussy: *Iberia;* Dvorak: *Symphony No. 7;* Franck: *Le Chasseur Mardit;* Ibert: *Escales;* Mussorgsky: *Boris Godunov;* Puccini: *La Boheme, Tosca.* Ravel: *Rhapsodie Espagnole;* Rimsky-Korsakow: *Capriccio Espagnole;* Rosinni: *Overture William Tell;* Roussel: *Symphony No. 3;* Strauss: *McBeth;* Stravinsky: *Jeu de Cartes;* Tchaikowsky: *Hamlet Overture-Fantasy, Romeo and Juliet;* Vaughan Williams: *Symphony No. 4;* Verdi: *Falstaff, La Forza del Destino, Rigoletto.*

Brown, Keith, ed. *Orchestral Excerpts from the Symphonic Repertoire for Trombone–Strauss.* International Music Company. 1969. $9.00. 28 pp. This collection of orchestral studies from the works of Strauss contains trombone and tuba (where applicable) excerpts from the following works: *Don Juan, Til Eulenspiegel, Tod und Verklärung, Salome's Dance, Also Sprach Zarathustra, Le Bourgeois Gentilhomme, Ein Heldenleben, Don Quixote, Symphonica Domestica.*

Brown, T. Conway. *Tuba Passages (Bass Clef), Band Edition.* Boosey & Hawkes, Incorporated. 1940. Out of Print. $1.00. 48 pp. This book contains excerpts from the following band works/transcriptions: Bach: *Air* (from celebrated movement, *3rd Suite*). *Fugue A La Gigue;* Beethoven: *In the Steppes of Central Asia;* Coleridge-Taylor: *The Bamboula (Rhapsodic Dance), Petite Suite De Concert, Christmas Overture;* Curzon: *La Gitana (Czardas), Robin Hood (Suite), Zingaresca (Gipsy Caprice);* Debussy: *The Children's Corner (Suite);* Dukas: *L'Apprenti Sorcier (Scherzo);* Dvorak: *Largo and Scherzo* (from *"New World" Symphony*); Enesco: *Roumanian Rhapsody #1;* Friedemann: *Slavonic Rhapsody #1, Slavonic Rhapsody #2;* Glinka: *Russlan and Ludmilla* (Overture); Liszt: *Hungarian Rhapsody #2;* Mancini, S.: *Symphonic March;* Mozart: *The Marriage of Figaro* (Overture); Nicolai: *Merry Wives of Windsor* (Overture); Rachmaninoff: *Prelude in G Minor (op. 23, #5), Prelude;* Rimsky-Korsakov: *Scherazade, Capriccio Espagnol, Dance of the Tumblers* (from *The Snow Maiden*), *The Flight of the Bumble Bee, Polonaise* (from *Christmas Night*); Saint-Saens: *Marche Heroique;* Sibelius: *Valse Lyrique, Valse Triste, Finlandia;* Tschaikowsky: *Two Movements from the Fifth Symphony, Valse Des Fleurs* (from *The Nutcracker*), *Two Excerpts from the Pathetique Symphony;* Wagner: *Lohengrin* (*Introduction to Act III* and *Bridal Chorus*); Wallace: *Maritana* (Overture); Woodforde-Finden: *Four Indian Love Lyrics;* Wood: *Frescoes (Suite).*

Bruckner, Anton. *Albums of Orchestra Parts, #8611.* Edwin F. Kalmus. $9.00. This is a set of complete parts to symphonies nos. 4, 7, 8, 9.

Bruckner-Seyffarth. *Orchesterstudien, Volume One.*

Bruckner-Seyffarth. *Orchesterstudien, Volume Two.*

Chabrier, Emmanuel, and Ernest Chausson. *Albums of Orchestra Parts, #8612.* Edwin F. Kalmus. $9.00. This is a set of complete parts to Chabrier: *Marche Joyeuse, Espana;* and Chausson: *Symphony in B♭.*

Cherry, Gordon. *The Complete Low Brass Excerpt Collection.* Cherry Classics Music. $89.00. A comprehensive collection of complete low brass parts on CD-ROM (.pdf format). Includes over 280 works on over 8,000 pages. Periodic updates are made available at no extra charge. A complete and up-to-date listing of contents may be found at www.cherry-classics.com/catalogue.pdf.

de Ville, Paul. *The Tuba Player's Studio.* Carl Fischer, Incorporated. Out of Print. This collection includes excerpts for tuba from the following works: Tchaikowsky: *1812 Overture, Capriccio Italien;* Moses-Tobani: *Auld Lang Syne, Unfinished Symphony* (Schubert), *Fantasia* from *Fidelio* (Beethoven), *Grand War March and Battle Hymn* from *Rienzi* (Wagner), *Souvenir de Meyerbeer,* Andante from *Fifth Symphony* (Beethoven), *Selections from Martha* (Flowtow), *Souvenir de Meyerbeer (Fantasia), Fantasia* from *Götterdamerung* (Wagner), *Attila* (selection from Verdi's opera), *The Bohemian Girl* (selection from Balfe's opera), *Creme de la Creme, A Trip to Coney Island, Grand Fantasia* from *Siegfried* (Wagner), *Vorspiel* to *Der Meistersinger von Nurnburg* (Wagner); Johnson: *The Death of Custer* (from *The Battle of Little Big Horn*); Suppe: *Isabella Overture, Pique Dame* (Overture); Laurendeau: *Selections from Samson and Delilah* (Saint-Saens); Godfrey: *Reminiscences of Scotland (Grand Selection of Scotch Melodies), Reminiscences of Verdi (Grand Selection);* Kucken: *The Warriors Return (Descriptive Fantasia);* Mendelssohn-Bartholdy: *Ruy Blas Overture;* Moszkowski: *From Foreign Lands;* Lassen: *Fest Overture (Festival);* Thomas: *Mignon Overture;* Luscombe: *A Trip to the Country (Descriptive Fantasia);* Baetens: *Albion (Grand Fantasia on Scotch, Irish and English Airs);* Ackermann: *Arie Concertante;* Rossini: *Semiriamide Overture;* Wagner: *Tannhauser (March), Rienzi Overture;* Auber: *Zanetta Overture, Le Lac des Fees;* Bishop: *Guy Mannering Overture;* Mercadante: Overture from *Stabat Mater* (Rossini); Flowtow: *Martha Overture;* Suppe: *Poet and Peasant Overture;* Litolff: *Maximillian Robespierre Overture;* Beethoven: *Overture Leonore (Fidelio);* Herman: *Columbus (Grand Descriptive Fantasia);* Meyrelles: Andante from *Surprise Symphony* (Haydn), *Selection from Tanhauser* (Wagner), *Bouquet of Melodies (Potpourri);* Luigini: *Ballet Egyptien;* Massenet: *Scenes Pittoresques;* Langey: *Sounds from England;* Gomez: *Il Guarany;* Bizet: *L'Arlesienne (Suite de Concert);* Keler-Bela: *Roumanian Festival Overture.*

Debussy, Claude, and Leo Delibes. *Albums of Orchestra Parts, #8613.* Edwin F. Kalmus. $9.00. This is a set of complete parts to Debussy: *La Mer* and *Nocturnes;* and Delibes: *Prelude and Mazurka, Ballade and Theme, Entr' Acte,* and *Waltz* from *Coppelia Ballet.*

Debussy, Claude et al. *The Orchestra Musician's CD-ROM Library, Volume 2 (Debussy, Mahler and More)–Low Brass.* Hal Leonard. $19.98. The second of five volumes, includes (in .pdf format) the complete low brass parts to 61 orchestral works by Bizet, Bruch, Bruckner, Busoni, Debussy, Fauré, Grieg, Mahler, Reger, and Saint-Saëns. A complete listing of contents is available at www.orchmusiclibrary.com. Published for Violin I and II, Viola, Cello, Bass, Flute and Piccolo, Clarinet, Oboe and English Horn, Horn, Bassoon, Contrabassoon, Trumpet and Cornet, Low Brass (which includes Trombone, Euphonium, and Tuba), and Timpani/Percussion.

Dreyer, Franz. *Orchestral Studies from Operas for the Trombone, Volume 6.* C. F. Schmidt. (See annotation for volume 1.) This volume contains excerpts from Meyerbeer: *Hugenotten;* Bizet: *Djamileh;* Bittner: *Der Bergsee;* Cornelius: *Gunlod;* Goldmark: *Merlin;* Lortzing: *Zar und Zimmermann;* Nessler: *Trompeter von Sackingen;* Herold: *Zampa;* and Offenbach: *Hoffmann's Erzahlungen.*

Dreyer, Franz. *Orchestral Studies from Operas for the Trombone, Volume 1.* C. F. Schmidt. This entire series of excerpts contains portions of the tuba parts (when applicable) to the following: Wagner: *Rienzi, Fliegende Hollander,* and *Tannhauser;* Weber: *Freischutz;* Verdi: *Rigoletto;* Tschaikowsky: *Iolanthe;* Spohr: *Jessonda;* Smetana: *Der Kuss;* Oberleithner: *Aphrodite;* Mozart: *Don Juan* and *Zauberflote;* Mascagni: *Rantzau;* Lortzing: *Undine;* Donizetti: *Don Pasquale;* and Flotow: *Martha.*

Dreyer, Franz. *Orchestral Studies from Operas for the Trombone, Volume 2.* C. F. Schmidt. $4.00. 61 pp. (See annotation for volume 1.) This volume contains excerpts from Wagner: *Parsifal, Tristan und Isolde,* and *Lohengrin;* Waltershausen: *Oberst Chabert;* Verdi: *Othello;* Tschaikowsky: *Eugen Onegin;* Smareglia: *Der Vasall von Szigeth;* Schillings: *Moloch;* and Meyerbeer: *Nordstern.*

Dreyer, Franz. *Orchestral Studies from Operas for the Trombone, Volume 3.* C. F. Schmidt. (See annotation for volume 1.) This volume contains excerpts from Wagner: *Rheingold, Walkure,* and *Meistersinger;* Weber: *Euryanthe;* Verdi: *Falstaff;* Saint-Saens: *Samson and Dalila;* Rossini: *Diebische Elster;* Puccini: *Manon Lescaut;* Mascagni: *Freund Fritz;* Gounod: *Faust (Margarethe);* Kienzl: *Evangelimann;* Herold and Halevy: *Ludovic;* Wallace: *Maritana;* and Thomas: *Hamlet.*

Dreyer, Franz. *Orchestral Studies from Operas for the Trombone, Volume 4.* C. F. Schmidt. (See annotation for volume 1.) This volume contains excerpts from Wagner: *Siegfried* and *Gotterdammerung;* Nicolai: *Die lustigen Weiber;* Verdi: *Troubadour* and *Maskenball;* Puccini: *Boheme;* Meyerbeer: *Robert der Teufel;* Goldmark: *Heimchen am Herd* and *Gotz von Berlichingen;* and Schumann: *Genoveva.*

Dreyer, Franz. *Orchestral Studies from Operas for the Trombone, Volume 5.* C. F. Schmidt. (See annotation for volume 1.) This volume contains excerpts from Auber: *Stumme von Portici;* d'Albert: *Tiefland;* Berlioz: *Benvenuto Cellini;* Bittner: *Der Musikant;* Cornelius: *Barbier von Bagdad;* Donizetti: *Regimentstochter;* Goldmark: *Konigin von Saba;* Lortzing: *Der Wildschutz;* Halevy: *Der Blitz;* Istel: *Tribunals Gebot;* and Gorter: *Das susse Gift.*

Dreyer, Franz. *Orchestral Studies from Operas for the Trombone, Volume 7.* C. F. Schmidt. (See annotation for volume 1.) This volume contains excerpts from Meyerbeer: *Der Prophet;* Massenet: *Werther;* Mendelssohn: *Loreley;* Smetana: *Dalibor and Die verkaufte Braut;* Thomas: *Mignon;* Rossini: *Wilhelm Tell;* Gluck: *Orpheus;* Boito: *Mephistofeles;* and Dohnanyi: *Der Schleier der Pierrette.*

Dreyer, Franz. *Orchestral Studies from Operas for the Trombone, Volume 8.* C. F. Schmidt. (See annotation for volume 1.) This volume contains excerpts from Auber: *Fra Diavolo;* d'Albert: *Kain;* Berlioz: *Die Trojaner;* Beethoven: *Fidelio* and *Leonoren Ouverture Nr. 2;* Bizet: *Carmen;* Delibes: *Lakme;* Flotow: *Stradella;* Kaskel: *Der Gefangene der Zarin;* Kreutzer: *Nachtlager;* Marschner: *Vampyr;* Massenet: *Der Gaukler unserer l. Frau;* Cherubini: *Wassertrager;* and Brull: *Prince Gringoire.*

Dreyer, Franz. *Orchestral Studies from Operas for the Trombone, Volume 9.* C. F. Schmidt. (See annotation for volume 1.) This volume contains excerpts from Verdi: *Aida;* Puccini: *Tosca;* Meyerbeer: *Afrikanerin;* Marschner: *Hans Heiling;* Marenco: *Excelsior;* Goldmark: *Die Kriegsgefangene;* Gluck: *Jphigenie auf Tauris* and *Alceste;* Giordano: *Fedora;* Mascagni: *Cavalleria Rusticana;* and Bittner: *Die rote Gred.*

Dreyer, Franz. *Orchestral Studies from Operas for the Trombone, Volume 10.* C. F. Schmidt. (See annotation for volume 1.) This volume contains excerpts from Verdi: *Ernani;* Tschaikowsky: *Pique Dame;* Reznicek: *Donna Diana;* Puccini: *Madame Butterfly;* Nougues: *Quo vadis?;* Marschner: *Templer & Judin;* Maillart: *Glockchen des Eremiten;* Goldmark: *Wintermarchen;* and Goldberger: *Mondweibchen.*

Dvorak, Antonin. *Albums of Orchestra Parts, #8614.* Edwin F. Kalmus. $9.00. This is a complete set of parts to *Carnival Overture, Scherzo Capriccioso op. 66, Cello Concerto.*

Dvorak, Antonin. *Albums of Orchestra Parts, #8615.* Edwin F. Kalmus. $9.00. This is a set of complete parts to symphonies nos. 1, 4, 5.

Dvorak, Antonin, et al. *The Orchestra Musician's CD-ROM Library, Volume 5 (Dvorak, Rimsky-Korsakov and More)—Low Brass.* Hal Leonard. $19.98. The fifth of five volumes, includes (in .pdf format) the complete low brass parts to 64 orchestral works by Borodin, Dvorak, Rimsky-Korsakov, Scriabin, and Smetana. A complete listing of contents is available at www.orchmusiclibrary.com. Published for Violin I and II, Viola, Cello, Bass, Flute and Piccolo, Clarinet, Oboe and English Horn, Horn, Bassoon, Contrabassoon, Trumpet and Cornet, Low Brass (which includes Trombone, Euphonium, and Tuba), and Timpani/Percussion.

Elgar, Edward. *Albums of Orchestra Parts, #8618.* Edwin F. Kalmus. $9.00. This is a set of complete parts to *Enigma Variations, Cockaigne Overture, Pomp and Circumstance No. 1.*

Evans, Mark, and Klemens Pröpper. *Orchester Probespiel (Test Pieces for Orchestral Auditions).* Edition Peters. 1993. $43.36. 63 pp. Excerpts from the operatic and concert repertoire, including Bartok: *Concerto for Orchestra;* Berg: *Wozzeck;* Berlioz: *Symphonie Fantastique, Romeo and Juliet, Damnation of Faust,* and *Grand Death-Mass (Requiem);* Bruckner: *Symphonies No. 4, 7* and *8;* Delibes: *Coppelia;* Hindemith: *Symphonic Metamorphosis* and *Mathis der Mahler;* Leoncavallo: *Der Bajazzo;* Mahler: *Symphony No. 1;* Mascagni: *Cavalleria Rusticana;* Mendelssohn: *A Midsummer Night's Dream;* Mussorgsky/Ravel: *Pictures at an Exhibition* (*Bydlo* only); Prokofiev: *Cinderella, Romeo and Juliet,* and *Symphony No. 5;* R. Strauss: *Death and Transfiguration, Till Eulenspiegel's Merry Pranks, Also Sprach Zarathustra, Ein Heldenleben, Don Quixote, Salome, Elektra,* and *Der Rosenkavalier;* Stravinsky: *Petrouchka;* Tchaikovsky: *Symphonies No. 4* and *6;* Verdi: *Aida, Falstaff,* and *Rigoletto;* and Wagner: *Eine Faust (Overture), The Flying Dutchman, Tannhäuser, Lohengrin, Die Meistersinger von Nürnberg, Tristan and Isolde, Das Rheingold, Die Walküre, Siegfried,* and *Götterdämmerung.*

Ferrari, Bruno. *Passi Difficili e "A Solo" per trombone e basso tuba, Vol. I.* G. Ricordi & Company. 1970. $18.00. 43 pp. This collection contains trombone and tuba (where applicable) excerpts from the following Italian operatic works: Rossini: *La Gazza Ladra;* Verdi: *Nabucco, Macbeth, Aida;* Catalani: *Loreley;* Puccini: *Manon Lescaut, La Boheme;* Macagni: *Iris.*

Ferrari, Bruno. *Passi Difficili e "A Solo" per trombone e basso tuba, Vol. II.* G. Ricordi & Company. 1970. $10.50. 39 pp. This collection contains trombone and tuba (where applicable) excerpts from the following Italian operatic works: Rossini: *Guglielmo Tell;* Verdi: *Ernani, La Forza del Destino, Falstaff;* Catalani: *La Wally;* Puccini: *Madama Butterfly;* Mascagni: *Cavalleria Rusticana;* Giordano: *Fedora.*

Ferrari, Bruno. *Passi Difficili e "A Solo" per Trombone e Basso Tuba, Vol. III.* G. Ricordi & Company. 1970. $10.50. 39 pp. This collection contains trombone and tuba (where applicable) excerpts from the following Italian operatic works: Donizetti: *Lucia di Lammermoor;* Verdi: *Il trovatore, Messa di Requiem, Simon Boccanegra, Don Carlo;* Leoncavallo: *I Pagliacci;* Puccini: *Tosca* and *la Faniciulla del West.*

Ferrari, Bruno. *Passi Difficili e "A Solo" per Trombone e Basso Tuba, Vol. IV.* G. Ricordi & Company. 1970. $10.50. 49 pp. This collection contains trombone and tuba (where applicable) excerpts from the following Italian operatic works: Donizetti: *La Favorita;* Verdi: *La Battaglia di Legnano, Rigoletto, I Vespri Siciliani, Otello;* Boito: *Mefistofele;* Puccini: *Turandot;* Mascagni: *L'amico Fritz.*

Franck, Cesar, and Leo Delibes. *Albums of Orchestra Parts, #8619.* Edwin F. Kalmus. $9.00. This is a set of complete parts to Franck: *Symphony in D Minor* and *Le Chasseur Maudit;* Delibes: *Sylvia Ballet Suite.*

Geib, Fred. *The Geib Method for Tuba.* Carl Fischer, Incorporated. 1941. $12.00. 117 pp. Basically an etude/method book, this work contains excerpts from the following works: Meyerbeer: *Fackeltanz;* Gounod: *Queen of Sheba;* Strauss: *Death and Transfiguration* and *Till Eulenspiegel;* Mascagni: *Cavalleria Rusticana;* Franck: *Symphony in D Minor;* Berlioz: *Symphony Fantastique;* Delibes: *Sylvia;* Bach: *Fugue a la Gigue;* Berlioz: *Benvenuto Cellini.*

Grieg, Edvard. *Albums of Orchestra Parts, #8620.* Edwin F. Kalmus. $9.00. This is a set of complete parts to *Peer Gynt Suites Nos. 1 and 2, Norwegian Dance op. 35, Lyric Suite, Symphonic Dances.*

Heber, P., and Müller, H. *Orchesterstudien für Tuba Symphonien von Bruckner und Bach.* Friedrich Hofmeister. 1974.

Hoppert, Manfred. *Orchester Studien für Tuba: Wagner I.* Zimmermann-Frankfurt. 51 pp. This collection contains tuba excerpts from the following works of Richard Wagner: *The Flying Dutchman, Tannhäuser, Lohengrin, Tristan und Isolde, Die Meistersinger von Nürnberg, Parsifal, Eine Faust Ouverture.*

Hoppert, Manfred. *Orchester Studien für Tuba: Wagner: Der Ring des Nibelungen.* Zimmermann-Frankfurt. 47 pp. This collection contains tuba excerpts from the Ring operas, including *Das Rheingold, Die Walküre, Siegfried,* and *Götterdämmerung.*

Kabalevsky, Dmitri, and Aram Khachaturian. *Albums of Orchestra Parts, #8621.* Edwin F. Kalmus. $9.00. This is a set of complete parts to Kabalevsky: *Colas Breugnon Overture*and *The Comedians;* Khachaturian: *Masquerade Suite.*

Kalmus, Edwin. *Tuba Excerpts from Standard Orchestral Repertoire, Book One*. Edwin F. Kalmus.

Kalmus, Edwin. *Tuba Excerpts from Standard Orchestral Repertoire, Book Two*. Edwin F. Kalmus.

Kalmus, Edwin. *Tuba Excerpts from Standard Orchestral Repertoire, Book Three*. Edwin F. Kalmus.

Kalmus, Edwin. *Tuba Excerpts from Standard Orchestral Repertoire, Book Four.* Edwin F. Kalmus. $5.50. 24 pp. Contains excerpts from: Auber: *Die Stumme von Portici;* Bendel: *Rotkäppchen;* Reger: *Variationen und Fugue;* Wallace: *Maritana;* Büttner-Tartier: *Die Heilblume;* Hartmann: *Eine nordische Heerfahrt;* Lortzing: *Undine;* Smetana: *Richard III;* Verdi: *La Traviata;* Volbach: *Sinfonie H-moll;* Leoncavallo: *Der Bajazzo;* Scheinpffug: *Frühling;* Verdi: *Falstaff.*

Kalmus, Edwin. *Tuba Excerpts from Standard Orchestral Repertoire, Book Five*. Edwin F. Kalmus. $5.50. 22 pp. Contains excerpts from Hausmann: *Fortuna;* Huber: *Sinfonie No. 3;* Kalafati: *Ouverture-Fantasie;* Pierson: *Musik zu "Faust";* Berlioz: *Marsch für die Überreichung der Fahnen* (from *Te Deum*); Schmidt: *Sinfonie in E-dur;* Smetana: *Aus Böhmens Hain und Flur;* Verdi: *Aida;* Wolf: *Penthesilea;* Berlioz: *Trauermarsch* (from *Hamlet*), *Heroide funebre*, and *Die Vehmrichter;* Dohnanyi: *Der Schleier der Pierrette;* Lange: *Komisches Sextett.*

Kalmus, Edwin. *Tuba Excerpts from Standard Orchestral Repertoire, Book Six.* Edwin F. Kalmus. $4.00. 36 pp. Contains excerpts from Berlioz: *Damnation of Faust, Symphonie Fantastique, Corsair Overture, Harold in Italy, King Lear Overture;* Mendelssohn: *Elijah, St. Paul, Midsummer Night's Dream;* Meyerbeer: *The African, The Huguenots, The Prophet, Roberto Diavolo, Fackeltanz No. 1.*

Liszt, Franz. *Albums of Orchestra Parts, #8622.* Edwin F. Kalmus. $9.00. This is a set of complete parts to *Faust Symphony, Tasso, Totendance, Mephisto Waltz, Mazeppa.*

Mahler, Gustav. *Albums of Orchestra Parts, #8623.* Edwin F. Kalmus. $9.00. This is a set of complete parts to symphonies nos. 1, 2, 5.

Mahler, Gustav. *Sinfonie Nr. 1–6 (für Posaune und Tuba).* ed. Göss.

Mahler, Gustav. *Sinfonie Nr. 7–10 und Das Lied von der Erde (für Posaune und Tuba).* ed. Göss.

Massenet, Jules, and Giacomo Meyerbeer. *Albums or Orchestra Parts, #8624.* Edwin F. Kalmus. $9.00. This is a set of complete parts to Massenet: *Phedre Overture* and *Le Cid Ballet;* and Meyerbeer: *Coronation March from the "Prophet."*

Meschke, Dieter, ed. *Orchestral Studies: Tuba.* VEB Deutscher Verlag für Musik Leipzig. 1989. 127 pp. This collection of orchestral studies contains excerpts from the following works: Meyerbeer: *Fackeltanz–Torch Dance;* Lortzing: *Undine;* Adam: *Giselle;* Berlioz: *Symphonie Fantastique, The Corsair, Benvenuto Cellini, The Damnation of Faust;* Mendelssohn: *Calm Sea and Prosperous Voyage, A Midsummer Night's Dream, St. Paul, Elijah;* Liszt: *Les Preludes;* Wallace: *Maritana;* von Flotow: *Martha;* Wagner: *Eine Faust Overture, Rienzi, The Flying Dutchman, Tannhäuser, Lohengrin, Das Rheingold, Die Walküre, Siegfried, Götterdämmerung, Tristan und Isolde, Die Meistersinger, Parsifal;* Verdi: *Nabucco, Macbeth, Luisa Miller, Rigoletto, Il Trovatore, La Traviata, Simone Boccanegra, La forza del destino, Don Carlos, Aida, Othello, Falstaff, Requiem;* Moniuszko: *Halka;* Franck: *Symphony in D Minor, Psyche;* Smetana: *Richard III, Wallenstein's Camp, Hakon Jarl, Ma Vlast, Vysehrad, Die Moldau, Sarka, From the Fields and Groves of Bohemia, Tabor, Blanik;* Bruckner: *Symphonies Nos. 4–9, Te Deum;* Brahms: *Symphony No. 2, Academic Festival Overture, Overture in C Minor, Ein Deutsches Requiem;* Borodin: *Symphony No. 2, Prince Igor.*

Morris, R. Winston. *An Introduction to Orchestral Excerpts for Tuba.* Shawnee Press. 1974. $8.00. 39 pp. Excellent for the introduction of orchestral playing, this anthology includes excerpts from Prokofiev: *Kije's Wedding* (from *Lieutenant Kije*); Moussorgsky: *Night on Bald Mountain;* Rimsky-Korsakoff: *Russian Easter Overture;* Mahler: *Symphony No. 1* (mvt. III); Saint-Saens: *Symphony No. 3* (mvt. II); Shostakovich: *Polka and Dance* (from *The Age of Gold*), *Symphony No. 5* (mvts. I and IV), *Symphony No. 9* (*Finale*), and *Festival Overture;* Liszt: *Les Preludes;* Sibelius: *Finlandia;* Brahms: *Academic Festival Overture;* Tchaikowsky: *Symphony No. 6* (mvts. I, II, and III), *Romeo et Juliette, Symphony No. 4* (mvt. IV), and *Overture 1812;* Franck: *Symphony in D Minor* (mvts. I and III); Wagner: *Ride of the Valkyries, Die Meistersinger* (Prelude to Act I), and *Lohengrin* (Prelude to Act III); Berlioz: *The Damnation of Faust (Hungarian March)* and *Symphonie Fantastique* (mvts. IV and V).

Müller, Heinz. *Intonation Studies for Trombone.* VEB Friedrich Hofmeister—Leipzig. 56 pp. Though written for trombone, this book includes portions of the following tuba parts: Bruckner: *Symphony No. 4* (mvt. IV), *Symphony No. 5* (mvt. IV), *Symphony No. 6* (mvts. II and IV), and *Symphony No. 9* (mvts. I and III); Brahms: *Symphony No. 2* (mvts. I and II); Tschaikowski: *Symphony No. 4* (mvt. I), *Symphony No. 6* (mvts. I and IV), and *Schwanensee;* Dvorak: *Symphony No. 9* ("New World," mvt. II); Verdi: *Don Carlos, Nabucco,* and *Othello;* Wagner: *The Flying Dutchman, Tannhauser,* and *Lohengrin.*

Müller, R., und Teuchert, E. *Orchesterstudien für Tuba: Strauss.* ed. F. Seyffarth. Friedrich Hofmeister.

Nielsen, Carl. *Orchestral Studies for Trombone and Tuba, Volume One.* Edition Wilhelm Hansen. 1984. 29 pp. This volume includes excerpts from Nielsen: *Symphony No. 1 in G Minor; Aladdin* (No. 6: *Dance of the Prisoners*); *Symphony No. 2*

(The Four Temperaments); Concerto for Flute and Orchestra; Rhapsodic Overture; and *Masquerade (Overture* and *Cock's Dance).*

Nielsen, Carl. *Orchestral Studies for Trombone and Tuba, Volume Two.* Edition Wilhelm Hansen. 1984. 35 pp. This volume contains excerpts from Nielsen: *Symphony No. 3 (Sinfonia Expansive)* and *Symphony No. 4 (The Inextinguishable).*

Nielsen, Carl. *Orchestral Studies for Trombone and Tuba, Volume Three.* Edition Wilhelm Hansen. 1984. 19 pp. This volume contains excerpts from Nielsen: *Symphony No. 5, Concerto for Violin and Orchestra, Symphony No. 6 (Sinfonia Semplice),* and *Saul and David* (Prelude to the 2nd Act).

Pniak, Jan. *Studia orkiestrowe na tube.* In preparation.

Prokofieff, Serge. *Albums of Orchestra Parts, #8625.* Edwin F. Kalmus. $9.00. This is a set of complete parts to symphonies nos. 5, 6, 7.

Prokofieff, Serge. *Albums of Orchestra Parts, #8626.* Edwin F. Kalmus. $9.00. This is a set of complete parts to *Suite from the Love for 3 Oranges op. 33 bis, Lt. Kije Suite op. 60, Cinderella Suite No. 3.*

Prokofieff, Serge. *Albums of Orchestra Parts, #8627.* Edwin F. Kalmus. $9.00. This is a set of complete parts to *Romeo and Juliet Suites Nos. 1, 2, 3.*

Prokofieff, Serge. *Albums of Orchestra Parts, #8628.* Edwin F. Kalmus. $9. This is a set of complete parts to *Piano Concertos Nos. 1* and *5,* and *Violin Concerto No. 1.*

Rachmaninoff, Serge. *Albums of Orchestra Parts, #8629.* Edwin F. Kalmus. $9.00. This is a set of complete parts to *Piano Concertos Nos. 2* and *3,* and *Isle of the Dead.*

Rimsky-Korsakoff, Nicholas. *Albums of Orchestra Parts, #8630.* Edwin F. Kalmus. $9.00. This is a set of complete parts to *Capriccio Espagnol, Sheherazade, Russian Easter Overture.*

Rimsky-Korsakoff, Nicholas. *Albums of Orchestra Parts, #8631.* Edwin F. Kalmus. $9.00. This is a set of complete parts to *Le Coq d'Or Introduction, Le Coq d'Or Suite, Mlada Suite, Polonaise from Christmas Eve.*

Saint-Saens, Camille. *Albums of Orchestra Parts, #8632.* Edwin F. Kalmus. $9.00. This is a set of complete parts to *Bacchanale* from *Samson, Symphony No. 3 op. 78, Suite Algerienne op. 60.*

Sear, Walter, and Lewis Waldeck. *Tuba Excerpts, Volume I.* Cor Publishing Company. 1966. $6.00. 32 pp. Contains excerpts from Berlioz: *Damnation of Faust, Symphonie Fantastique, Corsaire Overture, Harold in Italy, Benvenuto Cellini, Romeo and Juliet, Trojan March, Requiem, King Lear, Funeral March* from *Hamlet, Heroide Funebre;* Brahms: *Academic Festival Overture, Symphony No. 2, Tragic Overture;* Bach: *Passacaglia and Fugue in C Minor;* Borodin: *Symphony No. 2;* Bruckner: *Symphony No. 4, Symphony No. 5, Symphony No. 6, Symphony No. 7, Symphony No. 8, Symphony No. 9, Te Deum;* Donizetti: *Lucia di Lammermoor;* Debussy: *Iberia, La Mer;* Delibes: *Coppelia;* Elgar: *Cockaigne Overture.*

Sear, Walter, and Lewis Waldeck. *Tuba Excerpts, Volume II.* Cor Publishing Company. 1966. $6.00. 32 pp. Contains excerpts from: Elgar: *Enigma Variations;* Franck: *Symphony in D Minor;* Ibert: *Escales;* Leoncavallo: *I Pagliacci;* Liszt: *Les Preludes;* Mahler: *Das Lied von der Erde, Symphonies 1, 2, 9, 10;* Mascagni: *Cavalleria Rusticana;* Mendelssohn: *Midsummer Night's Dream;* Meyerbeer: *Fackeltanz;* Mussorgsky: *Night on Bald Mountain;* Prokofiev: *Lt. Kije, Piano Concerto No. 1, Symphony No. 5, Romeo and Juliet No. 2, Scythian Suite;* Respighi: *Pines of Rome, Feste Romane, Fountains of Rome;* Shostakovich: *Symphony No. 1, Symphony No. 5, Symphony No. 6, Symphony No. 7, Symphony No. 9, Golden Age;* Sibelius: *Finlandia, Symphonies 1, 2;* Smetana: *Die Moldau, From Bohemia's Fields and Forest;* Strauss: *Don Quixote, Ein Heldenleben, Death and Transfiguration, Don Juan, Macbeth, Also Sprach Zarathustra, Til Eulenspiegel's Lustige Streiche;* Tchaikowsky: *Symphonies 4, 5, 6, Sleeping Beauty, Romeo and Juliet, 1812 Overture;* Rossini: *Thieving Magpie;* Rimsky-Korsakov: *Capriccio Espagnol, Russian Easter Overture, Coq D'or, Sheherazade.*

Sear, Walter, and Lewis Waldeck. *Tuba Excerpts, Volume III.* Cor Publishing Company. 1969. $6.00. 32 pp. Contains excerpts from Wagner's *Der Fliegende Hollander, Tannhauser, Lohengrin, Die Meistersinger, Das Rheingold, Die Walkure, Siegfried, Eine Faust Overture, Gotterdammerung, Parsifal.*

Seyffarth, F. *Orchesterstudien (Complete), Volume One.*

Seyffarth, F. *Orchesterstudien (Complete), Volume Two.*

Shifrin, Ken, and Danny Longstaff. *British Orchestral Excerpts for Trombone and Tuba, Volume I.* Virgo Music Publishers. 1986. 58 pp. This collection of orchestral studies contains trombone and tuba (where applicable) excerpts from the following works: Arnold: *Tam O'Shanter Overture;* Britten: *Peter Grimes—Four Sea Interludes from the Opera, War Requiem, The Young Person's Guide to the Orchestra;* Elgar: *The Dream of Gerontius;* Holst: *The Perfect Fool Ballet;* Walton: *Concerto for Viola and Orchestra.*

Shifrin, Ken, and Danny Longstaff. *British Orchestral Excerpts for Trombone and Tuba, Volume II.* Virgo Music Publishers. In preparation. This collection of orchestral studies contains trombone and tuba (where applicable) excerpts from the following works: Britten: Sinfonia da Requiem; Elgar: Symphony No.2; Holst: The Planets; Tippett: Child of Our Time; Vaughan Williams: Sea Symphony; Walton: Symphony No. 1.

Shifrin, Ken, and Danny Longstaff. *British Orchestral Excerpts for Trombone and Tuba, Volume III.*

Virgo Music Publishers. In preparation. This collection of orchestral studies contains trombone and tuba (where applicable) excerpts from the following works: Britten: *Spring Symphony;* Delius: *Brigg Fair;* Elgar: *Symphony No. 1;* Vaughan Williams: *Symphony No. 5;* Walton: *Belshazzar's Feast;* Wood: *Sea Songs.*

Shifrin, Ken, and Danny Longstaff. *British Orchestral Excerpts for Trombone and Tuba, Volume IV.* Virgo Music Publishers. In preparation. This collection of orchestral studies contains trombone and tuba (where applicable) excerpts from the following works: Bax: *Tentagel;* Britten: *Passacaglia from "Peter Grimes";* Elgar: *Cockaigne Overture, Music Makers, Pomp and Circumstance No. 1;* Tippett: *Symphony No. 4;* Vaughan Williams: *Symphony No. 6;* Walton: *Henry V, Portsmouth Point.*

Shostakovich, Dmitri. *Albums of Orchestra Parts, #8633.* Edwin F. Kalmus. $9.00. This is a set of complete parts to *Symphonies Nos. 5, 9, 10.*

Shostakovich, Dmitri. *Albums of Orchestra Parts, #8634.* Edwin F. Kalmus. $9.00. This is a set of complete parts to *Hamlet, Festive Overture, Golden Age Ballet Suite.*

Sibelius, Jean. *Albums of Orchestra Parts, #8635.* Edwin F. Kalmus. $9.00. This is a set of complete parts to *Symphonies Nos. 1* and *2, Finlandia, Karelia Suite.*

Smetana, Frederick. *Albums of Orchestra Parts, #8636.* Edwin F. Kalmus. $9.00. This is a set of complete parts to *Moldau, Sarka, Blanik, From Bohemia's Meadows and Forests.*

Stoneberg, Alfred. *Moderne Orchesterstudien fur Posaune und Basstuba, Volume 1.* Musikverlage Hans Gerig Koln. 1953. $17.50. 35 pp. This collection of orchestral studies includes trombone and tuba (when applicable) excerpts from "the most technically difficult passages in operatic and concert music." Included in the first volume are excerpts from Mozart: *Tuba mirum aus dem Requiem;* Berlioz: *Faust's Verdammung op. 24;* Schumann: *Symphonie Nr. 2 in C-Dur* and *Symphonie Nr. 3 in Es-Dur;* Rimsky-Korsakow: *Scheherazade;* D'Albert: *Tiefland;* Brahms: *Symphonie Nr. 1 in C-Moll op. 68* and *Symphonie Nr. 2 in D-Dur op. 73;* Ravel: *Bolero;* Strawinsky: *Pulcinella, Petruschka,* and *Psalmen Symphonie;* Hindemith: *Sinfonische Metamorphosen;* and Barber: *Medea.*

Stoneberg, Alfred. *Moderne Orchesterstudien fur Posaune und Basstuba, Volume 2.* Musikverlage Hans Gerig Koln. 1953. $17.50. 34 pp. (See annotation for volume 1.) This volume contains excerpts from Berlioz: *Roman Carnival Ouverture;* Tschaikowsky: *Klavier-Konzert Nr. 1, Francesca da Rimini,* and *1812 Ouverture Solenelle;* Borodine: *Die Polewetzer Tanze a.d. Oper "Furst Igor";* Reger: *Requiem;* Wolf-Ferrari: *Der Schmuck der Madonna;* Ravel: *La Valse* and *Daphnis et Cloe;* Strawinsky: *Der Feuervogel* and *Symphonie en Ut;* and Hindemith: *Konzertmusik fur Streicher und Blechblaser.*

Stoneberg, Alfred. *Moderne Orchesterstudien fur Posaune und Basstuba, Volume 3.* Musikverlage Hans Gerig Koln. 1953. $17.50. 39 pp. (See annotation for volume 1.) This volume contains excerpts from Schumann: *Symphonie Nr. 4 in D-moll;* Verdi: *Die Macht des Schicksals (Ouverture);* Cornelius: *Der Barbier von Bagdad;* Bruckner: *Symphonie Nr. 3 in D-moll (2. Fassung v. 1878), Symphonie Nr. 4 in Es-Dur (Originalfassung),* and *Symphonie Nr. 5 in B-Dur (Originalfassung);* Mussorgsky: *Tableaux d'une exposition (Bilder einer Ausstellung);* Bartok: *Konzert fur Orchester* and *Violin-Konzert;* Weinberger: *Schwanda der Dudelsackpfeifer;* and Prokofieff: *Peter and the Wolf (Opus 67).*

Stoneberg, Alfred. *Moderne Orchesterstudien fur Posaune und Basstuba, Volume 4.* Musikverlage Hans Gerig Koln. 1953. $17.50. 49 pp. (See annotation for volume 1.) This volume contains excerpts from Bruckner: *Symphonie Nr. 7 E-Dur (Originalfassung)* and *Symphonie Nr. 8 C-Moll (Originalfassung);* Brahms: *Tragische Ouverture;* Dvorak: *Symphonie Nr. 5 (Aus der neuen Welt);* Rimsky-Korsakoff: *Russiche Ostern (Ouverture);* Martin: *Konzert fur sieben Blaser und Orchester;* Bartok: *Tanz-Suite;* Blacher: *Orchestervariationen uber ein Thema von Paganini;* Tschaikowsky: *Symphonie Nr. 4 F-Moll* and *Symphonie Nr. 6 H-Moll (Pathetique);* Berg: *Violin-Konzert;* Mahler: *Symphonie Nr. 3;* and Liszt: *Les Preludes* and *Zweite Ungarische Rhapsodie.*

Stoneberg, Alfred. *Moderne Orchesterstudien fur Posaune und Basstuba, Volume 5.* Musikverlage Hans Gerig Koln. 1953. $17.50. 47 pp. (See annotation for volume 1.) This volume contains excerpts from Bach: *Christ lag in Todesbanden (Kantate am Osterfeste);* Rietz: *Ouverture A-Dur;* Smetana: *Die verkaufte Braut (Ouverture);* Strauss: *Eine Alpensinfonie* and *Der Burger als Edelmann;* Pfitzner: *Palestrina* and *Von Deutscher Seele;* and Mohaupt: *Die Gaunerstreiche der Courasche.*

Stoneberg, Alfred. *Moderne Orchesterstudien fur Posaune und Basstuba, Volume 6.* Musikverlage Hans Gerig Koln. 1953. $17.50. 44 pp. (See annotation for volume 1.) This volume contains excerpts from Beethoven: *Symphonie Nr. 5 op. 67, Fidelio op. 72, Missa Solemnis op. 123,* and *Symphonie Nr. 9 op. 125;* Maillart: *Das Glockchen des Eremiten;* Berlioz: *Phantastische Symphonie;* Pfitzner: *Konzert fur Violine h-moll;* and Orff: *Carmina Burana.*

Stoneberg, Alfred. *Moderne Orchesterstudien fur Posaune und Basstuba, Volume 7.* Musikverlage Hans Gerig Koln. 1953. $17.50. 42 pp. (See annotation for volume 1.) This volume contains excerpts from Bruckner: *Symphonie Nr. 1 in c-moll (Linzer Fassung), Symphonie Nr. 2 in c-moll*

(Originalfassung), Symphonie Nr. 4 in A-dur (Originalfassung), and *Symphonie Nr. 9 in d-moll (Originalfassung);* and Hindemith: *Mathis der Maler (Oper in sieben Bildern).*

Stoneberg, Alfred. *Moderne Orchesterstudien fur Posaune und Basstuba, Volume 8.* Musikverlage Hans Gerig Koln. 1953. $17.50. 46 pp. (See annotation for volume 1.) This volume contains excerpts from Mozart: *Die Zauberflote* and *Don Juan (Don Giovanni);* Humperdinck: *Hanselund Gretel;* and Berg: *Wozzeck.*

Stöneberg, Alfred. *Verdi Orchesterstudien, Vol. I.* Musikverlage Hans Gerig Koln. $19.50. This collection contains trombone and tuba (where applicable) excerpts from the following Verdi operas: *Troubadour, Macbeth.*

Stöneberg, Alfred. *Verdi Orchesterstudien, Vol. II.* Musikverlage Hans Gerig Koln. $13.50. This collection contains trombone and tuba (where applicable) excerpts from the following Verdi operas: *Aida, Sizilianische Vesper.*

Stöneberg, Alfred. *Verdi Orchesterstudien, Vol. III.* Musikverlage Hans Gerig Koln. $13.50. This collection contains trombone and tuba (where applicable) excerpts from the following Verdi operas: *Othello, Nabucco.*

Stöneberg, Alfred. *Verdi Orchesterstudien, Vol. IV.* Musikverlage Hans Gerig Koln. $13.50. This collection contains trombone and tuba (where applicable) excerpts from the following Verdi operas: *Don Carlos, Rigoletto.*

Stöneberg, Alfred. *Verdi Orchesterstudien, Vol. V.* Musikverlage Hans Gerig Koln. $13.50. This collection contains trombone and tuba (where applicable) excerpts from the following Verdi operas: *Macht des Schicksals, Simone Boccanegra, La Traviata.*

Stöneberg, Alfred. *Verdi Orchesterstudien, Vol. VI.* Musikverlage Hans Gerig Koln. $13.50. This collection contains trombone and tuba (where applicable) excerpts from the following Verdi operas: *Maskenball, Falstaff.*

Strauss, Johann. *Albums of Orchestra Parts, #8641.* Edwin F. Kalmus. $9.00. This is a set of complete parts to *Tales from the Vienna Woods, Blue Danube Waltz, Artists Life, Thunder and Lightning.*

Strauss, Richard. *Albums of Orchestra Parts, #8639.* Edwin F. Kalmus. $9.00. This is a set of complete parts to *Death and Transfiguration, Till Eulenspiegel, Don Juan.*

Strauss, Richard. *Albums of Orchestra Parts, #8640.* Edwin F. Kalmus. $9.00. This is a set of complete parts to *Also Sprach Zarathustra, Don Quixote, Ein Heldenleben.*

Strauss, Richard. *Don Juan.* ed. Edwin Anderson. Manduca Music Publications. 1997. 10 pp. Includes complete trombone and tuba parts to Strauss's *Don Juan,* in score format, as well as a glossary of terms.

Strauss-Berthold. *Orchestra Studies.*

Stravinsky, Igor. *Albums of Orchestra Parts, #8637.* Edwin F. Kalmus. $9.00. This is a set of complete parts to *Petroushka, Firebird (1919), Fireworks.*

Stravinsky, Igor. *Albums of Orchestra Parts, #8638.* Edwin F. Kalmus. $9.00. This is a set of complete parts to *The Rites of Spring, Symphony No. 1.*

Stravinsky, Igor. *Orchester Studien Posaune/Basstrompete/Tuba: Stravinsky.* ed. Hans Hombsch. Zimmermann-Frankfurt. 1999. $36.90. 179 pp. Contains trombone, bass trumpet, and tuba excerpts from the following works by Stravinsky: *Faun et Bergère op. 2, Feu d'artifice op. 4, L'Oiseaux de Feu—(3ème) Suitede ballet, Petrouchka, Le Sacre du Printemps, Le Rossignol, Chant du Rossignol, Quatre ètudes pour Orchestre, Histoire du Soldat, Pulcinella (Suite), Symphonies d'instruments à vent, Mavra, Octuor pour instruments à vent, Concerto for Piano and Wind Instruments, Œdipus Rex, Le Baiser de la Fee—Ballet, Symphonie de Psaumes, Concerto en Ré pour violon et orchestre, Persèphone, Jeu de cartes, Symphonie in C, Tango, Pas-de-deux, Circus Polka, Four Norwegian Moods, Babel, Scherzo à la russe, Scènes de Ballet, Symphonie in three movements, Orpheus, Mass, In Memoriam Dylan Thomas, Canticum Sacrum, Choral-Variationen, Agon, Threni, The Flood—"A Musical Play," Abraham and Isaac,* and *Requiem canticles.* Excerpts are presented in score format. Also includes a list of abbreviations, a legend explaining the symbols used, and an exhaustive table of contents which includes dates of composition, instrumentation, and approximate duration of each selection. Text is in English, French, and German.

Tchaikovsky, Peter, et al. *The Orchestra Musician's CD-ROM Library, Volume 4 (Tchaikovsky and More)–Low Brass.* Hal Leonard. $19.98. The fourth of five volumes, includes (in.pdf format) the complete low brass parts to 42 orchestral works by Glinka, Mussorgsky, and Tchaikovsky. A complete listing of contents is available at www.orchmusiclibrary.com. Published for Violin I and II, Viola, Cello, Bass, Flute and Piccolo, Clarinet, Oboe and English Horn, Horn, Bassoon, Contrabassoon, Trumpet and Cornet, Low Brass (which includes Trombone, Euphonium, and Tuba), and Timpani/Percussion.

Teuchert, E. T. *Orchesterstudien für Baßtuba.* Breitkopf & Haertel, Leipzig. 57 pp. This collection contains tuba excerpts from the following works: d'Albert: *Der Rubin, Gernot;* Bantock: *Der Zeitgeist, Helena;* Berger, *Symphonie B dur;* Berlioz: *Phantastische Symphonie, Trojanischer Marsch, Requiem, Fausts Verdammung, Benvenuto Cellini;* Chabrier: *Gwendoline;* Donizetti: *Lucia di Lammermoor;* Dräske: *Herrat;* Glazounow: *Symphonie;* Halevy: *Die Jüdin;* Kretzschmer: *Die Folkunger;* Liszt: *Ce qu'on entend sur la montage, Tasso, Die Ideale;* Mascagni: *Cavalleria Rusticana;* Mendelssohn: *Musik zu Shakespeares Sommernachtstraum;* Nicode: *Das Meer;* Novak: *Von ewiger Sehnsucht;* Saint-Saens: *Samson und Dalila;* Sibelius: *Symphonie Nrs. 1 und 2;* Strauss: *Till Eulenspiegels lustige Streiche, Also sprach Zarathustra;* Thomas: *Hamlet;* Tinel: *Franziskus, Drei symphonische Tongemälde, Godoleva;* Tschaikowsky: *Symphonie Nr. 4;* Verdi: *Rigoletto;* Volbach: *Es waren zwei Königskinder;* Wagner: *Lohengrin, Tristan und Isolde, Eine Faust-Ouvertüre;* Weingartner: *Symphonie Nr. 2;* Zoellner: *Der Überfall, Die versunkene Glocke.*

Teuchert, Emil. *Tägliche Übungen fur Tuba, mit Anhang d. Schwierigsten Orchesterstellen.* Seeling/ Erdmann. 1936/64.

Torchinsky, Abe. *The Tuba Player's Orchestral Repertoire, Volume One.* European American Music Corporation. 1975. Out of Print. $14.95. 68 pp. This volume contains complete parts from Mendelssohn: *A Midsummer Night's Dream, Elijah;* and Berlioz: *King Lear, Waverly, The Judges of the Secret Court (tubas I and II), Grand Death-Mass (orchestras I and II), Fantastic Symphony (tubas I and II), Harold in Italy, Romeo and Juliet, The Corsair, Te Deum (tubas I and II), Benvenuto Cellini, The Damnation of Faust, Trojan March, Symphonie Descriptive: Chasse et Orange, Lelio, Funeral and Triumphal Symphony (tubas I and II).*

Torchinsky, Abe. *The Tuba Player's Orchestral Repertoire, Volume Two.* European American Music Corporation. 1976. Out of Print. $10.00. 26 pp. Currently out of print, this volume contains complete parts from Wagner: *A Faust Overture; Overture to Rienzi; Overture to The Flying Dutchman; Tannhauser* (*Overture, Overture and Scene One [Venusberg],* and *Chorus ["Arrival of the Guests at Wartburg"]*); *Lohengrin* (*Prelude to the Opera* and *Introduction to Act III*); *The Mastersingers of Nuremberg* (*Prelude to the Opera, Prelude to Act III, Dance of the Apprentices, Procession of the Mastersingers,* and *Greeting to Hans Sachs*); *Prelude* and *Isolde's Love Death* from *Tristan and Isolde; Entrance of the Gods into Valhalla* from *The Rhinegold; The Valkyrie* (*The Ride of the Valkyries, Wotan's Farewell,* and *Magic Fire Music*); *The Twilight of the Gods* (*Siegfried's Rhine Journey* and *Siegfried's Narrative/Death with Funeral March*); and *Parsifal* (*End of the Third Act* and *Good Friday Spell*).

Torchinsky, Abe. *The Tuba Player's Orchestral Repertoire, Volume Three.* Encore Music Publishers. 1989. $24.00. 58 pp. Previously published by Joseph Boonin, Incorporated, this volume contains complete parts from Brahms: *A German Requiem, Symphony No. 2, Academic Festival Overture, Tragic Overture,* and *Song of the Fates;* and Dvorak: *Symphony in E♭ Major (No. 3), Symphony in D Major (No. 6, old No. 3), Scherzo Capriccioso, Husitska, Symphony in G Major (No. 8, old No. 4), Requiem Mass, Carnival, In Nature's Realm, Othello, Symphony in E Minor (No. 9, old No. 5), Suite in A Major, Concerto for Violoncello and Orchestra, The Noon Witch,* and *The Golden Spinning Wheel.*

Torchinsky, Abe. *The Tuba Player's Orchestral Repertoire, Volume Four.* Encore Music Publishers. $27.00. 63 pp. Previously published by Joseph Boonin, Incorporated, this volume contains complete parts from Strauss: *Serenade in E♭ Major, Don Juan, Macbeth, Tod und Verklarung, Till Eulens-piegels Lustige Streiche, Also Sprach Zarathustra* (tubas I and II), *Don Quixote* (tenor tuba in B♭, tenor tuba in C, and bass tuba parts), *Ein Heldenleben* (tenor tuba in B♭, tenor tuba in C, and bass tuba parts), *Symphonia Domestica, Eine Alpensinfonie* (tubas I and II), and *Salomes Tanz.*

Torchinsky, Abe. *The Tuba Player's Orchestral Repertoire, Volume Five.* Jerona Music Corporation. 1980. $11.95. 35 pp. This volume contains complete parts from Tchaikovsky: *Symphony No. 1, Symphony No. 2, Symphony No. 3, Symphony No. 4, Symphony No. 5,* and *Symphony No. 6.*

Torchinsky, Abe. *The Tuba Player's Orchestral Repertoire, Volume Six.* Jerona Music Corporation. 1980. $10.95. 35 pp. This volume contains complete parts from Tchaikovsky: *The Tempest, Swan Lake Suite, Marche Slave, Francesca da Rimini, Capriccio Italien, 1812 Overture, Suite No. 2,* and *Suite No. 3.*

Torchinsky, Abe. *The Tuba Player's Orchestral Repertoire, Volume Seven.* Jerona Music Corporation. 1980. $7.95. 28 pp. This volume contains complete parts from Tchaikovsky: *Manfred Symphony, Sleeping Beauty Suite, Hamlet, The Nutcracker Suite, Concerto No. 3 for Piano and Orchestra, Overture to "L'Orage," Fatum, Le Voyvode, Marche Solennelle,* and *Romeo and Juliet.*

Torchinsky, Abe. *The Tuba Player's Orchestral Repertoire, Volume Eight.* Jerona Music Corporation. 1981. $14.95. 78 pp. This volume contains complete parts from Prokofiev: *Symphony No. 2, Symphony No. 3, Symphony No. 4, Symphony No. 5, Symphony No. 6,* and *Symphony No. 7.*

Torchinsky, Abe. *The Tuba Player's Orchestral Repertoire, Volume Nine.* Jerona Music Corporation. 1981. $16.95. 87 pp. This volume contains complete parts from Prokofiev: *Piano Concerto No. 1, Piano Concerto No. 2, Violin Concerto No. 1, Symphonic Suite from "The Love of Three Oranges," Piano Concerto No. 5, Lieutenant Kije Suite, Romeo and Juliet (Suites No. 1, 2 and 3), Alexander Nevsky, Cinderella (Suites No. 1 and 3),* and *Summer Night Suite.*

Torchinsky, Abe. *The Tuba Player's Orchestral Repertoire, Volume Ten.* Jerona Music Corporation. 1982. $11.95. 50 pp. This volume contains complete parts from Stravinsky: *The Rite of Spring* (tubas I and II), *Firebird Suite* (1919 edition), and *Petrouchka.*

Torchinsky, Abe. *The Tuba Player's Orchestral Repertoire, Volume Eleven.* Jerona Music Corporation.

1983. $13.95. 53 pp. This volume contains complete parts from Mahler: *Symphony No. 1, Symphony No. 2, Symphony No. 3, Symphony No. 5,* and *Symphony No. 6.*

Torchinsky, Abe. *The Tuba Player's Orchestral Repertoire, Volume Twelve.* Jerona Music Corporation. 1985. $7.95. 23 pp. This volume contains complete parts from Franck: *Symphony in D Minor;* Saint-Saens: *Third Symphony;* Chausson: *Symphony in B♭ Major;* and Debussy: *Nocturnes, La Mer.*

Torchinsky, Abe. *The Tuba Player's Orchestral Repertoire, Volume Thirteen.* Jerona Music Corporation. 1985. $17.95. 56 pp. This volume contains complete parts from Bruckner (Nowak edition): *Symphony No. 4, Symphony No. 5, Symphony No. 6, Symphony No. 7, Symphony No. 8,* and *Symphony No. 9.*

Torchinsky, Abe. *The Tuba Player's Orchestral Repertoire, Volume 14.* Encore Music Publishers. 1995. 64 pp. Contains complete parts to Shostakovich *Symphonies Number 1–7,* along with editorial corrections and expert performance commentary by the author. Currently out of print.

Torchinsky, Abe. *The Tuba Player's Orchestral Repertoire, Volume 15.* Encore Music Publishers. 1995. 63 pp. Contains complete parts to Shostakovich *Symphonies Number 8–12,* along with editorial corrections and expert performance commentary by the author. Currently out of print.

Torchinsky, Abe. *The Tuba Player's Orchestral Repertoire, Volume 16.* Encore Music Publishers. 1996. $22.50. 54 pp. Contains complete parts to Mahler *Symphonies Number 7–9,* including the tenor tuba part to *Symphony Number 7.* Also includes editorial corrections and expert performance commentary by the author.

Torchinsky, Abe. *The Tuba Player's Orchestral Repertoire, Volume 17.* Encore Music Publishers. 2002. $25.00. 51 pp. Contains complete parts to the following works by Elgar: *Cockaigne Overture, Pomp and Circumstance, Enigma Variations, Symphonies 1* and *2,* and *Violin Concerto.* Also includes editorial corrections and expert performance commentary by the author.

Torchinsky, Abe. *Twentieth Century Orchestra Studies for Tuba.* G. Schirmer, Incorporated. 1969. $13.75. 79 pp. Contains excerpts from: Barber: *Medea's Meditation, Second Essay;* Bernstein: *On the Waterfront;* Bloch: *Schelomo;* Carter: *Variations;* Creston: *Invocation and Dance;* Diamond: *Fourth Symphony;* Einem: *Concerto for Orchestra;* Harris: *Third Symphony;* Hartmann: *Sixth Symphony;* Hindemith: *Konzertmusik, Mathis der Maler, Nobilissima Visione, Symphonic Metamorphosis;* Holst: *The Planets;* Mahler: *Tenth Symphony;* Orff: *Carmina Burana;* Piston: *The Incredible Flutist;* Prokofiev: *Cinderella Suite No. 1, Lieutenant Kije Suite, Romeo and Juliet No. 1, Romeo and Juliet No. 2, Scythian Suite, Fifth Symphony, Sixth Symphony, Seventh Symphony, Violin Concerto No. 1;* Revueltas: *Sensemaya;* Riegger: *Third Symphony;* Schoenberg: *Theme and Variations;* Schuman: *Circus Overture, Third Symphony, Sixth Symphony;* Sessions: *Second Symphony;* Shostakovitch: *The Golden Age, First Symphony, Fifth Symphony, Seventh Symphony, Ninth Symphony;* Stravinsky: *Circus Polka, Scenes de Ballet, Symphony in Three Movements;* Thomson: *Louisiana Story, The Seine at Night, A Solemn Music;* Villa-Lobos: *Choros No. 8;* Weinberger: *Fugue from "Shvanda."*

Tschaikowsky, Peter Ilich. *Albums of Orchestra Parts, #8643.* Edwin F. Kalmus. $9.00. This is a set of complete parts to symphonies nos. 1, 2, 3.

Tschaikowsky, Peter Ilich. *Albums of Orchestra Parts, #8644.* Edwin F. Kalmus. $9.00. This is a set of complete parts to symphonies nos. 4, 5, 6.

Tschaikowsky, Peter Ilich. *Albums of Orchestra Parts, #8645.* Edwin F. Kalmus. $9.00. This is a set of complete parts to *Marche Slave, Fransesca da Rimini, 1812 Overture, Romeo and Juliet Overture.*

Tschaikowsky, Peter Ilich. *Albums of Orchestra Parts, #8646.* Edwin F. Kalmus. $9.00. This is a set of complete parts to *Swan Lake Suite, Sleeping Beauty Suite, Nutcracker Suite No. 1.*

Tschaikowsky, Peter Ilich. *Albums of Orchestra Parts, #8647.* Edwin F. Kalmus. $9.00. This is a set of complete parts to *Suite No. 3, Nutcracker Suite No. 2, Capriccio Italien.*

Verdi, Giuseppe. *Albums of Orchestra Parts, #8642.* Edwin F. Kalmus. $9.00. This is a set of complete parts to *I Vespri Siciliani Overture, Forza del Destino Overture, Nabucco Overture.*

Wagner, Richard. *Albums of Orchestra Parts, #8648.* Edwin F. Kalmus. $9.00. This is a set of complete parts to Overtures: *Flying Dutchman, Tannhauser; Prelude* and *Love Death* from *Tristan; Meistersinger, Rienzi.*

Wagner, Richard. *Albums of Orchestra Parts, #8649.* Edwin F. Kalmus. $9.00. This is a set of complete parts to *The Ride of the Valkyries, Entry of the Gods into Valhalla, Siegfried's Rhine Journey, Wotan's Farewell* and *Magic Fire Music.*

Wagner, Richard. *Albums of Orchestra Parts, #8650.* Edwin F. Kalmus. $9.00. This is a set of complete parts to *Siegfried's Death and Funeral Music, Arrival of the Guests at Wartburg, Faust Overture, Venusberg Music.*

Wagner, Richard. *Wagner Orchester-Studien.* ed. F. Seyffarth. DV.

Wagner, Richard. *Werke Orchesterstudien aus seinen Bühnen und Konzertwerken: Tuba.* ed. Emil Teuchert. Breitkopf & Haertel. ca. 1910.

Wekselblat, Herbert. *Solos for the Tuba Player.* G. Schirmer, Incorporated. 1964. $13.95. 38 pp. Principally a collection of solos, this book also contains several orchestral studies. Works represented include Berlioz: *Hungarian March, Symphonie*

Fantastique; Verdi: *Rigolletto, Ernani, Otello, Falstaff;* Wagner: *Lohenghrin, Eine Faust Overture, Siegfried, Das Rheingold;* Strauss: *Salome, Also Sprach Zarathustra.*

Yeo, Douglas. *Orchestral Excerpts for Trombone and Tuba, Vol. I: Shostakovich.* Virgo Music Publishers. 1989. $12.50. 24 pp. This volume contains excerpts from the Shostakovich third and fourth symphonies. This edition is distinguished by the fact that it contains comments in the excerpted portions of score describing texture and other information critical to proper performance. Additionally, historical notes about each work and a suggested discography are included.

10. Discography

Ronald Davis, Assistant Editor, *Guide to the Tuba Repertoire: The New Tuba Source Book*

Ronald Davis, Assistant Editor, *The Tuba Source Book*

Introductory Remarks (July 2005): Ronald Davis

I am a survivor, the only original *Tuba Source Book* assistant editor to sign up for a return engagement.

The first time around was a great experience. The original *Tuba Source Book* staff (Jerry Young, Mark Nelson, Charlie McAdams, Skip Gray, Jeff Funderburk, and myself, along with Winston Morris and Ed Goldstein) was a team. In the beginning we all met together in one room to get things started. We knew it was a technology-driven project, so I had to master skills with word processing, databases, and e-mail. That last one was not convenient back then. I had to leave my office in our music building and walk over to the basement of the Humanities Building to the College Technology Center. There I had to take out my list of computer commands, long strings of codes that only a hacker could love, and attempt to send and receive messages. Sometimes I got so frustrated that I just went back to the office and made a telephone call instead. The majority of the information that appeared in the *Tuba Source Book* discography was taken directly from hard copies, either the actual albums or from photocopies. I had great confidence in the accuracy of that information.

The *Guide to the Tuba Repertoire: The New Tuba Source Book* has been a completely different experience, due mostly to the incredible changes in technology over the last decade. During this whole process I have never seen another editor face to face, and the number of telephone calls I have made can be counted on one hand. Almost all communication has been handled by e-mail. Instead of trips to the Computer Center or to the library, now I simply use the computer on the desk in my studio. The most revolutionary change of the last decade is the influence of the World Wide Web and our ability to instantly access massive amounts of information: record catalogues, library files, inventory lists, and personal websites. The blessing is also a curse. The number of recordings has increased exponentially and the goal was to track them all down. Every time I thought we had exhausted one source I would be instantly linked in new directions. If the book is ever to be published you have to stop some time, even though you know there is just a little bit more you could do. It feels similar to what George Lucas said about film-making: "Movies are never finished; they are abandoned."

I made several judgment calls while compiling this version of the discography. With so many players in the larger ensembles the cross-references became unwieldy, so not every ensemble member is listed separately. Another challenge has been trying to verify the current address information for each record label. There are over 350 different label names, many of which are independent desktop publishers with limited distribution. The final editing process revealed the infinite number of inconsistencies existing in the original source material. *Wabash Blues* is one well-known standard tune, but the three artists who recorded it had the composer information listed three different ways ("Meinken and Ringle," "Ringle and Meinken," and "Fred Reinken"). In this and other cases I selected one designation as a main composer entry and cross-referenced the other entries to it. In instances where slightly differing titles refer to the same composition (e.g., Stravinsky: *Petroushka (excerpt)* and Stravinsky: *Bear Solo from "Petroushka"*), the entries are kept separate.

I am proud to have participated in both editions of the *Tuba Source Book,* but when the inevitable third edition comes I will be joining my five original colleagues in the "Assistant Editors Emeritus Club."

I would like to thank Eric Paull, my doppelgänger over at the *Euphonium Source Book,* for his regular assistance over the last year. And special thanks also to Steven Shoop for invaluable contributions in the entries of William Bell and Harvey Phillips.

Introductory Remarks (July 1995): Ronald Davis

In 1978 the *Tuba Music Guide* discography identified 33 record albums. While compiling for the *Tuba Source Book* discography, information on over 400 recordings was received, and considering the enormity of the subject, it was certain that some information would be overlooked. The main section of this chapter includes albums that feature the tuba as a prominent solo instrument. Solo tuba, tuba and piano, tuba and orchestra or band, tuba and brass ensembles, tuba/euphonium ensembles, and jazz recordings are all included. Several categories were not included: orchestral recordings with the tuba as a section instrument, brass quintets, and with one or two careful exceptions, promotional recordings from publishers. All recording formats were included: long playing records, cassette tapes, and compact discs.

The first and main approach to this research was to consult every issue of the *TUBA Journal* for recording information and to enter it into a database. The next step was to survey all available sources and to fill in the missing information. For a complete entry, the following information was included: the name of the tuba artist, the album title, other personnel performing, the record label, the year of recording or release, the format (long playing record "LP," cassette tape "CS," compact disc "CD"), the catalogue number(s), and the selections on the album that feature the tuba listed by composer, arranger, and title. Compositions are generally listed in the order in which they appear on the album. Originally it was attempted to determine the price and availability of each album, but by publishing time, this information was so inconsistent that it was eliminated from the final draft. Be advised that the main purpose of this discography is to identify those recordings that have been produced. Many albums listed may no longer be available. Every attempt was made to secure copies of each recording for accurate, first-hand information. Record catalogues, record stores, distributors, and music libraries were consulted. Other discographies, most notably the Schwann catalogues and the *Trombone/Euphonium Discography* by Edward Bahr, were referenced. Often, incomplete secondary information would be added to the database in the hopes of ultimately finding the album or that more information could be verified by the publishing deadline. In many instances references were so thin that many, reluctantly, were dropped from the final chapter.

The main section of this chapter documents recordings by artist, and all information available is included here. Recordings by title and recordings by composer list minimum information for cross-reference purposes. For the section on conference recordings, the directors of each conference were asked about the availability of recordings from that conference. In cases where tapes were available the information is listed.

In the address section, every attempt was made to secure the most recent address for each company with the Schwann catalogue serving as the major reference source. Many of these companies have moved, merged, or gone out of business. In such instances the best reference is provided.

Several individuals need to be sincerely thanked for their assistance with this chapter: First, Dr. Reginald Bain of the University of South Carolina School of Music for all of his computer expertise, for his cheerful good humor, and his readiness to help at all times; and Barton Cummings for his careful reading, his input, and his encouragement with this project. Mr. Cummings has written extensive record articles and reviews for the *TUBA Journal,* and his advice was invaluable. Also, Bert Wiley with Bernel Music contributed in the area of British brass bands. Thanks are also extended to Ted Meyer for an outstanding job of proofreading. And finally, a loving thank you to my wife, Phyllis, for enduring this entire project.

Tuba Recordings by Artist

Acuff, Bill; see Tennessee Tech Tuba-Euphonium Quintet; *The Golden Sound of Euphoniums*

Albertasaurus Tuba Quartet
- Album Title: *Albertasaurus*
- Personnel: Scott Whethem, Michael Eastep, tubas; John McPherson, David Reid, euphoniums
- Label: Arktos, 2000, CD: TUAL02
- Massenet, J. E. F.: *Aragonaise*
- Bach, Johann Sebastian: *Vivace from Trio Sonata in C for Organ, BWV 526*
- Beethoven, Ludwig van/McPherson: *Piano Sonata No. 8 "Pathetique"*
- Mozart, Wolfgang Amadeus: *Turkish March (from Piano Sonata in A, K331)*
- Mozart, Wolfgang Amadeus: *Andante Cantabile (from Piano Sonata in C, K330)*
- McPherson, John: *Hugo Hugo*
- Chopin, Frédéric/Werden: *Minute Waltz*
- Verdi, Giuseppi/Eastep-Whetham: *Two Selections from "La Traviata"*
- Ketelby, Albert/McPherson: *A Night in a Persian Caravan*

Shearing, George/Reid: *Lullaby of Birdland*
Joplin, Scott/Lex: *The Strenuous Life*
Turpin, Tom/Sabourin: *Harlem Rag*

Alchemy (previously the Atlantic Tuba Quartet)
Album Title: *Village Dances*
Personnel: Gary Buttery, Joanna Hersey, tubas; Danny Vinson, James Jackson, euphoniums
Label: Alchemy, 1997, CD: TUAL20
Buttery, Gary: *Fanfare for the Millennium*
Buttery, Gary: *Fantasia of Eastern European Village Dances*
Buttery, Gary: *Xmas Tuba of the British Isles*
Aquino, Baden Powell de/Buttery: *Bocoxe*
Gibbons, Orlando/Campbell: *Tuba Voluntary*
Gautier, L./Werden: *Le Secret*
Koetsier, Jan: *Wolkenschatten, Op. 136*
Susato, Tielman/Buttery: *Shepherd's Dance*
Villa-Lobos, Heitor: *Danza Martelo from Bachianas Brasilieras #5*
Vinson, Danny: *Memoirs of the American Civil War*
Hart, Bill/Buttery: *Brass Cuckoo*
Mozart, Wolfgang Amadeus/Werden: *Ah!, Vous Dirai-Je Maman, K.26*
Traditional/Buttery: *Sponger Money*
Traditional/Buttery: *While Soft Winds Shake the Barley*

Amberst, Nigel; see Hoffnung, Gerard; *Hoffnung Music Festival Concert*

Andersen, Hans
Album Title: *Betrayal, Opus 144*
Personnel: Laura Helasvuo Simonsen, violin; Lise Errboe, vibraphone
Label: Borgen Records, 1982, LP: 5202-8
Christiansen, Henning: *Betrayal for Tuba, Violin and Vibraphone, Op. 144*

Anderson, Hans
Album Title: *Brass Ability* (see full reference under Holmgaard, Lars)
Handel, George Friderik/Andersen: *Music for the Royal Fireworks*
Schidlt, M./Andersen: *Gleichwie das Feuer*
Bach, Johann Sebastian: *Fugue in G minor*
Grieg, Edvard/Andersen: *Hyldingsmarch*
Laumann, H.: *Song for Oliver*
Laumann, H.: *Live and Let Live*

Anderson, Hans
Album Title: *Kirkeby and Edvard Munch*
Personnel:
Label: Borgen Records/Weltmelodie 1983, LP: WM-LP-4718
Christiansen, Henning: *Kirkeby and Edvard Munch (in twelve movements)*

Anderson, Hans
Album Title:
Personnel:
Label: Rondo Grammofon, LP: RLP 8317
Brand, Michael: *Tuba Tapestry for Tuba and Brass Band*

Anderson, Hans
Album Title:
Personnel:
Label: Borgen Records, LP: ISBN 87-418-7146-4
Christiansen, Henning: *Maskemåned for Trumpet and Tuba, Op. 148*

Angerer, Ali; see Heavy Tuba

Angerstein, Fred
Album Title: *University of Houston Wind Ensemble, Vol. VI*
Personnel: James Matthews, conductor
Label: Century Records, 1970, LP: Houston Music Series Vol. 4
Werle, Floyd: *Concertino for Three Brass and Band*

ANON
Album Title: *Diadem of Gold*
Personnel: Brighouse & Rastick Band
Label: Polyphonic, CS: CPRL 017
Brand, Michael: *Tuba Tapestry*

ANON
Album Title: *Masterpieces for Brass, Vol. 1*
Personnel:
Label: Rondo Grammofon, CD: RCD 8322 (Also RLP 8315 and RMC 8315 under title *Music from the Old Tivoli Bandstand*)
Nielsen, Hans Peter: *The Satyr*

ANON
Album Title: *Mid-West National Band and Orchestra Clinic 1981*
Personnel: Northshore Concert Band; John Painter, conductor
Label: Silver Crest, 1981, LP: MID-81-15C
Nelhybel, Vaclav: *Concerto Grosso for Tubas and Band*

ANON
Album Title: *Tubby the Tuba*
Personnel: Johnny Andrews, narrator
Label: Peter Pan, LP: S8044
Kleinsinger, George, and Paul Tripp: *Tubby the Tuba*

ANON
Album Title: *Tell Me a Story*
Personnel: MGM Orchestra; José Ferrer, narrator
Label: MGM, LP: PX 106
Kleinsinger, George, and Paul Tripp: *Tubby the Tuba*

ANON
Album Title: *Tubby the Tuba*
Personnel:
Label: Simon Says, LP: 19
Kleinsinger, George, and Paul Tripp: *Tubby the Tuba*

ANON
Album Title: *Tubby the Tuba*
Personnel:
Label: Wonderland, LP: 8
Kleinsinger, George, and Paul Tripp: *Tubby the Tuba*

ANON
Album Title: *Tubby the Tuba*
Personnel: Peter Pan Players and Orchestra
Label: Peter Pan Records, 45 RPM: PP1020/8044
Kleinsinger, George, and Paul Tripp: *Tubby the Tuba*

ANON
Album Title: *Tubby the Tuba*
Personnel: Stuttgart Symphony Orchestra; Carl Bamberger, conductor; Paul Tripp, narrator
Label: Golden Records, LP: GLP 8
Kleinsinger, George, and Paul Tripp: *Tubby the Tuba*

ANON
Album Title: *Tubby the Tuba (Peter and the Wolf, The Story of Celeste)*
Personnel: Not Listed
Label: MGM Children's Series, LP: CHS 505
Kleinsinger, George, and Paul Tripp: *Tubby the Tuba*

ANON
Album Title:
Personnel:
Label: Mark Educational Recordings, LP: 1244
Vaughan Williams, Ralph: *Concerto for Bass Tuba and Orchestra*

Antens, Ron; see Dutch Tuba Quartet

Aranda, Pablo
Album Title: *PerTUBAdo*
Personnel:
Label: Nueve Composiciones de Camara, 2003, CD

Arnsted, Jørgen Voight
Album Title: *Masterpieces for Brass, Vol. 2*
Personnel:
Label: Rondo Grammofon, CD: RCD 8333

Arnsted, Jørgen Voight
Album Title: *Old Danish Masterpieces for Brass, Vol. 1*
Personnel:
Label: Rondo Grammofon, LP: RLP 8314; CS: RMC 8314
Langgaard, Rued: *Dies Irae for Tuba and Piano*

Arnsted, Jørgen Voight
Album Title: *Scandinavian Trombone*
Personnel:
Label: Rondo Grammofon, LP: RLP 8307; CS: RMC 8307
Holmboe, Vagn: *Notater for Three Trombones and Tuba*

Arwood, Jeffrey
Album Title: *The Army Ground Forces Band in Concert—Texas Bandmasters Association*
Personnel: The Army Ground Forces Band (Atlanta, Georgia); Major Michael Pyatt, conductor, Forces Command, Ft. McPherson
Label: The Army Ground Forces Band, 1990, CS: Public Service/Not for Sale
Camphouse, Mark: *Poeme*

Arwood, Jeffrey
Album Title: *ASBDA Convention, June 1985, Charlotte, NC*
Personnel: The United States Army Band "Pershing's Own"; Colonel Eugene W. Allen, conductor
Label: New Age Sight and Sound, 1985, CS:
Vaughan Williams, Ralph/Hare: *Concerto for Bass Tuba and Band*

Arwood, Jeffrey
Album Title: *Augustiana College 32nd Annual Concert Band Festival*
Personnel: Augustiana College Concert Band; Dr. Bruce T. Amman, conductor
Label: Westmark Tapes, 1989, CS:
Taylor, Mark: *Latin Fantasy*
Abreu, Zequinha/A. Smith: *Tico-Tico*

Arwood, Jeffrey
Album Title: *Pennsylvania Inter-Collegiate Band Festival Concert—1989*
Personnel: Pennsylvania Inter-Collegiate; Dr. Stanley F. Michalski, Jr., conductor
Label: Al Teare Digital Recordings, 1989, CS:
Lebedev, Alexi/A. Cohen: *Concerto in One Movement*
Abreu, Zequinha/A. Smith: *Tico-Tico*

Arwood, Jeffrey
Album Title: *South Dakota State University Symphonic Band—1975*
Personnel: South Dakota State University Symphonic Band; Dr. Darwin Walker, conductor
Label: Mark Records, 1975, LP: MC6106
Youmans, Vincent/Norman: *Carioca*
Rogers, Walter: *The Volunteer*
Brennard, George/Arwood: *The Old Rugged Cross*

Arwood, Jeffrey
Album Title: *27th Annual South Dakota All-State Band*
Personnel: South Dakota All-State Band; Major Allen C. Crowell, conductor
Label: Mark Records, 1977, LP: MC 6107
Galliard, Johann Ernst/R. Clemons: *Allegro from Sonata No. 3 in F major*
Van Heusen, Jimmy and Phil Silvers/A. Smith: *Nancy with the Laughing Face*
Abreu, Zequinha/A. Smith: *Tico-Tico*

Arwood, Jeffrey
Album Title: *The United States Army Band featuring Overture "1812"*
Personnel: The United States Army Band "Pershing's Own"; Colonel Samuel R. Loboda, conductor
Label: United States Army Band, 1974, LP: S 19741 Public Service/Not for Sale
Abreu, Zequinha/A. Smith: *Tico-Tico*

Arwood, Jeffrey
Album Title: *The United States Army Band in Residence—Wilber M. Brucker Hall*
Personnel: The United States Army Band "Pershing's Own"; Colonel Eugene W. Allen, conductor
Label: United States Army Band, 1979, LP: S 19791 Public Service/Not for Sale
Taylor, Mark: *Latin Fantasy*

AsKew, Dennis; see O'Bryant, Kelly; *Carolina Morning*

Astwood, Michael
Album Title: *1974 Mid-West Band and Orchestra Clinic*
Personnel: Coronado High School Symphonic Band
Label: Crest, 1974, LP: MID-74-13
Presser, William: *Capriccio for Tuba and Band*

Atlantic Tuba Quartet
Album Title: *Euphonic Sounds*
Personnel: David Werden, Dennis Winter, euphoniums; Gary Buttery, David Chaput, tubas
Label: Golden Crest, 1978, LP: CRS 4173
Susato, Tielman/Winter: *Ronde and Saltarelle "Pour Quoy"*
Bach, Johann Sebastian/Myers: *Allegro from Toccata in D minor for Klavier, BWV 913*
Bach, Johann Sebastian/Werden: *Bist du bei mir, BWV 508*
Lyon, Max J.: *Suite for Four Bass Instruments*
Anonymous/Buttery: *Greensleeves*
Joplin, Scott/Werden: *Euphonic Sounds*
Sousa, John Philip/Werden: *Stars and Stripes Forever*
Bach, Johann Sebastian/Werden: *"Air" from Suite No. 3 in D major for Orchestra, BWV 1068*
Ramsöe, Emilio Wilhelm/Buttery: *Allegro molto from Quartet No. 4*
Byrd, William/Winter: *Jhon Come Kisse Me Now*
Hartley, Walter: *Miniatures for Four Four-Valve Instruments*
Collins, Judy/Buttery: *Since You've Asked*
Aquino, Baden Powell de/Buttery: *Bocoxe*
Best, Denzil Decosta/Buttery: *Move*

Audenaert, Guy
Album Title: *Hindemith: Complete Brass Sonatas*
Personnel: Alain de Rudder, Geert Callaert, et al.
Label: Rene Gailly, 2000, CD #92024
Hindemith, Paul: *Sonata for Bass Tuba and Piano*

Augustin, Rudiger
Album Title: *Hindemith Chamber Works, Vol. II*
Personnel: Richard Laugs, piano
Label: Musical Heritage Society Orpheus, LP: OR H-290
Hindemith, Paul: *Sonata for Bass Tuba and Piano*

Baadsvik, Øystein
Album Title: *International Competition for Musical Performers Geneva 1991*
Personnel: Bienne Brass Band; Martin Aakerwall, piano; Orchester de la Orchester de la Suisse-Romande
Label: Musica Helvetica, 1992, CD: MH CD 77.2
Meier, Jost: *Eclipse Finale? For Tuba and Brass Band*
[see cross reference under Bjørn-Larsen, Jens]

Baadsvik, Øystein
Album Title: *Tuba Carnival*
Personnel: Musica Vitae; Bjørn Sagstad, conductor
Label: BIS, 2003, CD: 1285
Baadsvik, Øystein: *Fnugg*
Vivaldi, Antonio: *L'Inverno (Winter) from The Four Seasons*
Grieg, Edvard: *Anitra's Dance*
Plau, Arild: *Concerto for Tuba and Strings*
Grieg, Edvard/Baadsvik: *Norwegian Dance No. 1*
Traditional/Lunden-Welden: *Kesh Jig*
Stevens, Thomas: *Variations in Olden Style*
Arban, Jean-Baptiste/Baadsvik: *Variations on the Carnival of Venice*
Monti, Vittorio/Baadsvik: *Csárdás*

Baadsvik, Øystein
Album Title: *Tuba Works by Øystein Baadsvik*
Personnel: Niklas Sivelöv, piano; Swedish Brass Quintet
Label: Pro Musica, 1993, CD: PSC 1101
Kraft, William: *Encounters II for Solo Tuba*
Hindemith, Paul: *Sonata for Bass Tuba and Piano*
Madsen, Trygve: *Sonata for Tuba and Piano*
Sivelov, Niklas: *Sonata for Tuba and Piano*
Gaathaug, Morten: *Sonata Concertante for Solo Tuba and Brass Quintet*

Baev, Bayo
Album Title: *Music of Irwin Bazelon*
Personnel: Rousse Philharmonic, Harold Farberman, conductor
Label: Troy Records, 2000, CD: TROY363
Bazelon, Irwin: *For Tuba . . . With Strings Attached*

Baker, Fred
Album Title: *Brass Ablaze*
Personnel: Hammonds Sause Works Band
Label: Polyphonic, CS: CPRL 005
Muscroft, Fred: *Carnival for Bass*

Banker, John; see United States Coast Tuba-Ephonium Quartet; *The Musical Sounds of the Seasons*

Barber, John William (Bill)
Album Title: *Miles Davis, Birth of the Cool*
Personnel: Miles Davis Groups, 1948—50
Label: Capital, LP: DT1974

Best, Denzil Decosta: *Move*
Wallington, George: *Godchild*
Henry, Cleo: *Boplicity*
Barber, John William (Bill)
Album Title: *Miles Davis—Porgy and Bess*
Personnel: Miles Davis
Label: Columbia, 1958, LP: 8085
Gershwin, George/Evans: *The Buzzard Song*
Barber, John William (Bill)
Album Title: *Rugolomania*
Personnel: Pete Rugolo and his Orchestra with the Rugolettes
Label: Philips, LP: BBL 7069
Adamson/B. Lane: *Everything I Have Is Yours*
Bargeron, Dave
Album Title: *Blood, Sweat and Tears—Live and Improvised*
Personnel: Blood, Sweat and Tears
Label: Columbia Legacy/Sony Music Entertainment 2CDs: C2K4618/2CS: C2T46918
Traditional/Hooker, John Lee/Clayton-Thomas: *One Room Country Shack*
Bargeron, Dave
Album Title: *Blood, Sweat and Tears Featuring David Clayton-Thomas/New City*
Personnel: Blood, Sweat and Tears
Label: Columbia, 1975, LP: 33484
Traditional/Hooker, John Lee/Clayton-Thomas: *One Room Country Shack*
Bargeron, Dave
Album Title: *Dance of Passion*
Personnel: Johnny Griffin Quartet Plus 3
Label: Antilles/Polygram, 1993, CD: 314512604-2
Griffin, Johnny: *Dance of Passion*
Griffin, Johnny: *You've Never Been There*
Bargeron, Dave
Album Title: *TubaTuba*
Personnel: Michel Godard, tuba; Joe "Sunny" Barbato, accompaniment; Kenwood Dennard, drums
Label: ENJA, 2001, CD: 9133-2
Bargeron, Dave: *To Be Tuba*
Bargeron, Dave: *Soji*
Godard, Michel: *Puligny Montrachet*
Bargeron, Dave: *Valencia*
Coltrane, John: *Giant Steps*
Godard, Michel: *Bass Bees*
Bargeron, Dave: *Joanda*
Godard, Michel: *The Night Is Still Young*
Davis, Miles: *Donna Lee*
Bargeron, Dave: *TubaTuba*
Bargeron, Dave: *What I See in Your Eyes*
Bargeron, Dave
Album Title: *TubaTuba Tu*
Personnel: Michel Godard, tuba; Joe "Sunny" Barbato, accompaniment; Kenwood Dennard, drums
Label: ENJA
Oww
Passmezzo
Sweet Georgia Brown
Choro Loco
Clara C
Pultany Bridge
Murmure
Old Town
Chiacona
Bargeron, Dave; see Johnson, Howard; *Howard Johnson & Gravity!!!; Right Now!*
Barsotti, Mario
Album Title: *Hindemith: Sonatas for Wind and Piano, Vol. 2*
Personnel: Massimiliano Damerini, piano
Label: Arts Music, 1997, CD: #47123-2
Hindemith, Paul: *Sonata for Bass Tuba and Piano*
Bazsinka, József
Album Title: *Contemporary Hungarian Wind Music*
Personnel: Budapest Symphonic Band; Laszlo Marosi, conductor
Label: Hungaroton Classics, HCD 31612
Bogar, Istvan: *Concerto for Tuba*
Bazsinka, József
Album Title: *French Connection*
Personnel: Irina Ivanitskaia, piano; Ferenc Kócziás, Peter Bálint, Sándor Balogh, trombones; Zoltán Varga, Gabor Kérdö, percussion
Label: Hungaroton, 2001, CD: 31953
Barat, Joseph Eduoard: *Introduction and Dance*
Bozza, Eugène: *Concertino for Tuba and Piano*
Desenclos, Alfred: *Suite Brève*
Charpentier, Jacques: *Prélude and Allegro*
Bozza, Eugène: *New Orleans*
Emler, Andy: *Tuba Stone*
Tomasi, Henri: *Être Ou Ne Pas Être! (monolog D'Hamlet)* with three trombones
Schmitt, Florent: *Quatuor, Op. 109*
Castérède, Jacques: *Prélude et Dance*
Bazsinka, József
Album Title: *Waves*
Personnel: Andras Fejer, Ferenc Kócziás, Peter Bálint, Sándor Balogh, euphoniums; Laszlo Szabo, Zsolt Szekely, Roland Szentpáli, Tamas Kelemen, tubas
Label: Hungaroton, 1996, CD: HCD 31642
Hilprecht, Uwe: *Haltungen (4) zu einem alten Thema, for tuba*
Dubrovay, Laszlo: *Solo No. 3 for Tuba*
Persichetti, Vincent: *Parable for Solo Tuba, Op. 147*
Penderecki, Krzysztof: *Capriccio for Solo Tuba*
Lang, Istvan: *Aria di coloratura*
Colding-Jargensen, Henrik: *Boast*
Kraft, William: *Encounters II for Solo Tuba*
Lippe, Cort: *Solo Tuba Music*

Stevens, John: *The Liberation of Sisyphus* (solo tuba with euphonium/tuba ensemble)
Beauregard, Cherry
Album Title: *Music of Samuel Adler*
Personnel:
Label: Mark Educational Recordings, LP: MM 1117
Adler, Samuel: *Canto VII for Solo Tuba*
Bell, William
Album Title: *The Best of Crest*
Personnel:
Label: Golden Crest, 7 inch 33⅓ record: CRS 7
Merle, John: *Mummers (Dance Grotesque)*
Bell, William
Album Title: *The Best of Crest*
Personnel:
Label: Golden Crest, 33⅓ record: CRS 12
Petrie, H. W.: *Asleep in the Deep*
Bell, William
Album Title: *Bill Bell and His Tuba*
Personnel:
Label: Golden Crest, LP: CR 4027; CS: CRS4211
Hupfeld, Herman: *When Yuba Plays the Rhumba on the Tuba Down in Cuba*
Petrie, H. W.: *Asleep in the Deep*
Grieg, Edvard: *In the Hall of the Mountain King*
Carr, S./Bell: *Tuba Man*
Landes, B.: *The Elephant's Tango*
Merle, John: *Mummers (Dance Grotesque)*
Arban, Jean-Baptiste/Bell: *Carnival of Venice*
Mozart, Wolfgang Amadeus: *O Isis and Osiris*
Beethoven, Ludwig van/Bell: *Variations on a Theme from "Judas Maccabeus"*
Schumann, Robert/Bell: *The Jolly Farmer Goes to Town*
Bell, William
Album Title: *A Children's Introduction to the Orchestra*
Personnel: The Golden Symphony Orchestra and Sandpiper Chorus; Mitch Miller, conductor
Label: Golden Records, LP: GLP 1
Wilder, Alec: *Poobah the Tuba*
Bell, William
Album Title: *Decca Presents the Symphony Orchestra, Vol. 3: The Brass Family*
Personnel: Decca Little Symphony Orchestra; David Mendoza, conductor
Label: Decca Personality Series, 78 rpm record: Album No. 92
Schumann, Robert/Bell: *The Jolly Farmer Goes to Town*
Bell, William
Album Title: *The Directors Band*
Personnel: Directors Band, Morehead State University; Robert Hawkins, conductor
Label: Audicom Corporation, 7 inch record: KM2038 R634 (First released by Morehead State University Book Store)
Landes, B.: *The Elephant's Tango*
Paganini, Niccolò: *Moto Perpetuo* (with Arnold Jacobs and Harvey Phillips)
Bell, William
Album Title: *The Neighbors Band*
Personnel: Robert McClellend, trumpet; Joseph Songer, horn; Lawrence Alpeter, trombone
Label: Young People's 78 rpm: 726-A
Bell, William
Album Title: *The Revelli Years*
Personnel: University of Michigan Symphonic Band
Label: Golden Crest, 1981, LP:
Paganini, Niccolò/Bell: *Moto Perpetuo*
Bell, William
Album Title: *Tubby the Tuba*
Personnel: Mitch Miller and Orchestra; The Sandpiper Chorus; Paul Tripp
Label: Golden Records, 5 inch 33⅓ rpm record: R257
Kleinsinger, George, and Paul Tripp: *Tubby the Tuba*
Kleinsinger, George, and Paul Tripp: *Tubby the Tuba* (solo and instrumental)
Bell, William
Album Title: *Tubby the Tuba*
Personnel: Victor Young Orchestra; Danny Kaye, narrator
Label: MCA, LP: 148
Kleinsinger, George, and Paul Tripp: *Tubby the Tuba*
Bird, Gary; see Colonial Tuba Quartet
Birnie, Stuart; see "British Tuba Quartet"
Bishop, Ronald
Album Title: *P. D. Q. Bach: Music for an Awful Lot of Winds and Percussion*
Personnel: David McGill, bassoon
Label: Telarc, 1992, CD/CS: #80307
Bach, P. D. Q. [Schikele, Peter]: *"Dutch" Suite (S. -16) for Bassoon and Tuba*
Bjørn-Larsen, Jens
Album Title: *Concert Band Music*
Personnel: Danish Concert Band
Label: Rondo Grammofon, CD: RCD 8331
Wilhelm, Rolf: *Concertino for Tuba and Concert Band*
Bjørn-Larsen, Jens
Album Title: *Contemporary Concert Band Music*
Personnel: Danish Concert Band; Jorgen Jensen, conductor
Label: Rondo Grammofon, 1995, CD: #8340
Plog, Anthony: *Three Miniatures for Tuba and Piano*
Bjørn-Larsen, Jens
Album Title: *International Competition for Musical Performers Geneva 1991*

Baader-Nobs, Heidi: *Bifurcation for Tuba and Piano*
Strukov, Valery: *Concerto for Tuba and Orchestra*
[see full reference under Baadsvik, Øystein]

Bjørn-Larsen, Jens
Album Title: *Vagn Holmboe: Brass Concertos*
Personnel: Aalborg Symphony Orchestra; Owain Arwel Hughes, conductor
Label: Grammafon-BIS, 1996, CD: BIS-CD-802
Holmboe, Vagn: *Concerto for Tuba and Orchestra, Op. 52*
Holmboe, Vagn: *Intermezzo Concertante for Tuba and Orchestra, Op. 171*

Bobo, Roger
Album Title: *Bobissimo! The Best of Roger Bobo*
Personnel: Ralph Grierson, piano
Label: Crystal, 1991, CD: CD125
Galliard, Johann Ernst: *Sonata No. 5 in D minor*
Barat, Joseph Eduoard: *Introduction and Dance*
Hindemith, Paul: *Sonata for Bass Tuba and Piano*
Wilder, Alec: *Suite No. 1 for Tuba and Piano (Effie the Elephant)*
Kraft, William: *Encounters II for Solo Tuba*
Spillman, Robert: *Two Songs*
Lazarof, Henri: *Cadence VI for Tuba and Tape*
Wilder, Alec: *Encore Piece (A Tubist's Showcase)*

Bobo, Roger
Album Title: *BOTUBA*
Personnel: Thomas Stevens, trumpet; Ralph Grierson, piano
Label: Crystal, 1978, LP: S392; CS: C392
Stevens, Thomas: *Encore Boz*
Spillman, Robert: *Two Songs*
Kraft, William: *Encounters II for Solo Tuba*
Wilder, Alec: *Encore Piece (A Tubist's Showcase)*
Lazarof, Henri: *Cadence VI for Tuba and Tape*
Reynolds, Verne: *Signals for Trumpet, Tuba, and Brass Choir*
samohT, snevetS: *zoB erocnE*

Bobo, Roger
Album Title: *Gravity Is Light Today*
Personnel: Emily Harris, synthesizer; Roger Kellaway, piano; Fred Tackett, guitar; Ralph Grierson, piano; Skip Mosher, bass; Ray Rich, drums; Frøydis Ree Wekre, horn; Roger Bobo, bass horn
Label: Crystal, 1979, LP: S396 CD396
Kellaway, Roger: *The Morning Song*
Kellaway, Roger: *The Westwood Song*
Tackett, Fred: *The Yellow Bird*
Kellaway, Roger: *Sonoro* (on CD release only)
Kellaway, Roger: *Dance of the Ocean Breeze* (on CD release only)

Bobo, Roger
Album Title: *Music of Henry Lazarof*
Personnel:
Label: Avant, 1974, LP: AV 1019
Lazarof, Henri: *Cadence VI for Tuba and Tape*

Bobo, Roger
Album Title: *Prunes*
Personnel: Frøydis Ree Werke, horn; Zita Carno, piano; Roger Kellaway, piano
Label: Crystal, 1980, LP: S126
Bach, Johann Sebastian: *Air for the G String*
Sinigaglia, Leone: *Song & Humoreske*
Schubert, Franz Peter: *Serenade*
Cui, Cesar: *Perpetual Motion*
Kellaway, Roger: *Sonoro for Horn, Bass Horn and Piano*
Kellaway, Roger: *Dance of the Ocean Breeze for Horn, Bass Horn and Piano*

Bobo, Roger
Album Title: *Roger Bobo and Tuba*
Personnel: Ralph Grierson, piano
Label: Crystal, 1969, LP: S125
Galliard, Johann Ernst: *Sonata No. 5 in D minor*
Hindemith, Paul: *Sonata for Bass Tuba and Piano*
Barat, Joseph Eduoard: *Introduction and Dance*
Kraft, William: *Encounters II for Solo Tuba*
Wilder, Alec: *Suite No. 1 for Tuba and Piano (Effie the Elephant)*

Bobo, Roger
Album Title: *Roger Bobo, Tuba Libera*
Personnel: European Tuba Octet; Marie Condamin, piano.
Label: Crystal, 1994, CD: 690
Bach, Johann Sebastian: *Bourree I and II from Suite for Solo Cello*
Stevens, Thomas: *Variations in Olden Style*
Penderecki, Krzysztof: *Capriccio for Solo Tuba*
Madsen, Trygve: *Sonata for Tuba and Piano*
Plog, Anthony: *Three Miniatures for Tuba and Piano*
Arban, Jean-Baptiste/Berry: *Fantaisie and Variations on the "Carnival of Venice"*
Dumitru, Ionel: *Romanian Dance No. 2*
Shostakovich, Dmitri: *Adagio*
Stevens, John: *The Liberation of Sisyphus* (solo tuba with euphonium/tuba ensemble)

Bobo, Roger
Album Title: *Solo Brass: New Perspectives*
Personnel: Fred Tackett, guitar; Ralph Grierson, piano; Skip Moser, bass; Ray Rich, drums
Label: Avant, LP: AV 1009
Tackett, Fred: *The Yellow Bird*

Bobo, Roger
Album Title: *Thomas Stevens, trumpet*
Label: Crystal, CD: CD667
Reynolds, Verne: *Signals for Trumpet, Tuba, and Brass Choir*

Bobo, Roger
Album Title: *Tuba Nova*
Personnel: Dan Rothmuller, cello; Ralph Grierson, piano
Label: Crystal, 1981, LP: S398
Kupferman, Meyer: *Saturnalis* (tuba and amplified cello)
Subatnik, Morton: *First Dream of Light* (tuba, piano, electronic ghost score)

Bobo, Roger; see Summit Tubas; *American Tribute-Summit Brass;* see Szentpáli, Roland; *I Killed My Lips;* see United States Army Band "Pershing's Own"; *United States Army Band Tuba-Euphonium Workshop Grand Concert*

Braynard, David
Album Title: *Wuorinen: Two Part Symphony/ Chamber Concerto for Tuba*
Personnel: Columbia University Group for Contemporary Music; Charles Wuorinen, conductor
Label: Composers Recordings, 1997, CD: #744 / LP: SD491
Wuorinen, Charles: *Chamber Concerto for Tuba with 12 Winds and 12 Drums*

Breen, Ryan; see Tubalaté

Brewer, Robert
Album Title: *An Die Musik*
Personnel:
Label: None, CD: #00
Stevens, Halsey: *Sonatina for Tuba and Piano*
Schumann, Robert: *Adagio and Allegro in A♭, Op. 70*
Brahms, Johannes: *Vier ernste Gesänge*
George, Thom Ritter: *Sonata*
Schubert, Franz Peter: *An die Musik, Op. 88, No. 4*

British Tuba Quartet
Album Title: *Boosey and Hawkes National Brass Band Championship of Great Britain 1991*
Personnel: Steven Mead, Michael Howard, euphoniums; Ken Ferguson, Stuart Birnie, tubas
Label: Polyphonic, 1991, CD: QDRL 049D
Frackenpohl, Arthur: *Pop Suite (last movement)*

British Tuba Quartet
Album Title: *Elite Syncopations*
Personnel: Steven Mead, Michael Howard, euphoniums; Ken Ferguson, Stuart Birnie, tubas
Label: Polyphonic, 1993, CD: QPRZ 012D
Glinka, Michael/Smalley: *Overture to Russlan and Ludmila*
Rossini, Gioacchino/Smalley: *La Danza*
Chopin, Frédéric/Mead: *Minute Waltz*
Martino, Ralph: *Fantasy*
Bull, John/Howard: *The King's Hunt*
Gabrieli, Giovanni/Rauch: *Canzona, La Spiritata*
Tchaikovsky, Peter Ilyitch/Smalley: *Trepek*
Strauss, Johann Jr./Smalley: *Chit Chat Polka*
Gershwin, George/Ferguson: *Fascinatin' Gershwin*
Sherwin, Manning/Smalley: *A Nightingale Sang in Berkley Square*
Dubin and Warren/Minard: *42nd Street Selections*
Schoenberg, C. M./Mead: *On My Own from "Les Miserables"*
Joplin, Scott/Picher: *Elite Syncopations*
Horovitz, Joseph: *Rumpole of the Bailey*
Berlin, Irving/Gout: *Puttin' on the Ritz*
arr. Dempsey: *Three Movements from "Quatre Chansons"*
Niehaus, Lennie: *Grand Slam*
Wolking, Henry: *Tuba Blues*

British Tuba Quartet
Album Title: *Euphonic Sounds*
Personnel: Steven Mead, Michael Howard, euphoniums; Ken Ferguson, Stuart Birnie, tubas
Label: Polyphonic, 1992, CD: QPRZ 009D
Bulla, Stephen: *Celestial Suite*
Diero/Ferguson: *Il Ritorno*
Kern, Jerome/Holcombe: *They Didn't Believe Me*
Ramsöe, Emilio Wilhelm/Buttery: *Quartet for Brass*
Di Lasso, Orlando/Robinson: *Mon Coeur se Recommende a Vous*
Byrd, William/Winter: *Jhon Come Kisse Me Now*
Aquino, Baden Powell de/Buttery: *Bocoxe*
Joplin, Scott/Powell: *The Favorite Rag*
arr. Niehaus: *Spiritual Jazz Suite*
arr. Buttery: *Greensleeves*
Lerner, Alan Jay/Belsha: *Get Me to the Church on Time*
Bach, Johann Sebastian/Werden: *Air from Suite No. 3*
Mancini, Henry/Krush: *The Pink Panther*
Joplin, Scott/Werden: *Euphonic Sounds*
Monaco/Holcombe: *You Made Me Love You*
Rossini, Gioacchino/Smalley: *William Tell Overture*

British Tuba Quartet
Album Title: *Fireworks*
Personnel: Steven Mead, Michael Howard, euphoniums; Ken Ferguson, Stuart Birnie, tubas
Label: Polyphonic, 1997, CD: 20
Taylor, Jeffrey: *Fanfare No. 1*
Nicolai, Otto/Smith: *Merry Wives of Windsor Overture*
Delibes, F./Mead: *Flower Duet from "Lakmé"*
Dempsey, Raymond: *Now Hear This*
Purcell, Henry/Smalley: *Distressed Innocence Overture*
Amos, Keith: *Flander's Cauldron*
Verdi, Giuseppi/Smalley: *Force of Destiny Overture*

Ridout, Alan: *Pigs*
Forsyth, Kieran: *Westminster Intrada*
Kupferman, Meyer: *Kierkegaard, for Tuba Quartet*
Frith, John: *Fireworks*
Rossini, Gioacchino/Davis: *Petit Caprice in the Style of Offenbach*
Prokofiev, Sergey/Smalley: *Montagues and Capulets*
Strauss, Johann/Smalley: *Perpetuum Mobile*
Smalley, Peter: *A Cool Suite*
Traditional/Schmidt: *Bavarian Polka*

British Tuba Quartet
Album Title: *In at the Deep End*
Personnel: Steven Mead, Michael Howard, euphoniums; Ken Ferguson, Stuart Birnie, tubas
Label: Heavyweight Records LTD, 1991, CD: HR008/D
Bulla, Stephen: *Quartet for Low Brass*
Sousa, John Philip/Morris: *Semper Fidelis*
Frackenpohl, Arthur: *Pop Suite*
Saint-Saëns, Camille/Murley: *Adagio from Symphony No. 3*
Bach, Johann Sebastian/Werden: *Jesu, Joy of Man's Desiring*
Mozart, Wolfgang Amadeus/Ferguson: *Overture from the "Marriage of Figaro"*
Rimsky-Korsakov, Nicholas: *Notturno*
Heusen, Van/Barton: *Here's That Rainy Day*
Bach, Johann Sebastian/Gray: *Fugue in G minor*
Sousa, John Philip/Morris: *El Capitan*
Cheetham, John: *Consortium*
Joplin, Scott/Sabourin: *The Cascades*
Anonymous/Baker: *Lute Dances*
Holmes, Paul: *Quartet for Tubas*
Hook, J./Garrett: *Rondo*
Bach, Johann Sebastian/Howard: *Rondo*
Traditional/Garrett: *Wabash Cannonball*
Traditional/Trippet/Howard: *Steal Away*
Sousa, John Philip/Sabourin: *Washington Post March*

British Tuba Quartet
Album Title: *March to the Scaffold*
Personnel: Steven Mead, Michael Howard, euphoniums; Ken Ferguson, Stuart Birnie, tubas
Label: Polyphonic, 1997, CD: #013
Sousa, John Philip/Smalley: *The Thunderer*
Traditional/Woodfield: *Havah Nagilah*
Tchaikovsky, Peter Ilyitch/Smalley: *Dance of the Sugar Plum Fairy*
McHugh, J., and D. Fields: *On the Sunny Side of the Street*
Smalley, Peter: *The Glyder Landscape*
Lefebure-Wely/Howard: *Sortie in E♭*
Lundquist, Torbjørn Iwan: *Triplet for 4 Tubas*
Bach, Johann Sebastian/Smalley: *Fugue from Fantasia and Fugue in G*
Jewell, Fred/Smalley: *Battle Royal*
Purcell, Henry/Smalley: *Dido's Lament from "Dido and Aeneas"*
Hartley, Walter: *Miniatures for Four Four-Valve Instruments*
Mozart, Wolfgang Amadeus/Mehlan: *Rondo alla Turca*
Premru, Ray: *In Memoriam*
Morley/Howard: *April Is in My Mistress' Face*
Reeman, John: *Sonatina for Tuba Quartet*
Berlioz, Hector/Granger: *March to the Scaffold*

Brown, Velvet
Album Title: *The Composer's Voice: New Music from Bowling Green*
Personnel: Bowling Green Philharmonia; Emily Freeman Brown, conductor
Label: Albany Records, 2004, CD: TROY 633
Williams, John: Concerto for Tuba

Brown, Velvet
Album Title: *Heart of a Wolf*
Personnel: Neal Corwell, euphonium
Label: Nicolai Music, 2000, CD: NC6400
Corwell, Neal: *Ritual* (tuba/euphonium duo with CD acc.)
Corwell, Neal: *Aboriginal Voices* (solo tuba)
Corwell, Neal: *The Furies* (eight-part tuba-euphonium ensemble work)

Brown, Velvet
Album Title: *Music for Velvet*
Personnel: Roberto Arosio, piano; Neal Corwell, euphonium
Label: Crystal Records, 2003, CD: CD693
Ewazen, Eric: *Sonata*
Reynolds, Verne: *Sonata*
Corwell, Neal: *2 AM*
Brown, Velvet: *Te Dago Mi* (Tuba/Euphonium/Piano)
Silverman, Faye-Ellen: *Zigzags* (unacc.)
Gomez, Alice: *Bonampak*
Tomasi, Henri: *Danse Sacrée*

Brown, Velvet
Album Title: *Velvet Brown, Tuba*
Personnel: Roberto Arosio, piano; Trombones: David Garcia, Massimo Oldani, Emily Harris, Fabio Costa
Label: Crystal Records, 1999, CD: CD 692
Castérède, Jacques: *Sonatina for Tuba and Piano*
Stevens, John: *Salve Venere, Salve Marte*
Handel, George Friderik: *"As When the Dove" from "Acis and Galatea"*
Koetsier, Jan: *Concertino for Tuba and String Orchestra, Op. 77*
Broughton, Bruce: *Sonata [Concerto] for Tuba and Piano*
Clarke, Herbert L.: *Stars in a Velvety Sky*
Brown, Velvet: *Negro Spirituals (Deep River, The Gospel Train, Sometimes I Feel like a Motherless Child, Joshua Fought the Battle of Jericho)*

Bruno, Jerry
Album Title: *Tubby the Tuba*
Personnel: The Playmates and Orchestra; Maury Laws, conductor
Label: Cricket Records, 45 rpm: C-46A
Kleinsinger, George, and Paul Tripp: *Tubby the Tuba*
Bunn, Michael; see United States Army Band "Pershing's Own"; *United States Army Band Tuba-Euphonium Workshop Grand Concert*

Butterfield, Don
Album Title: *Music of Morton Feldman and Earle Brown*
Personnel: Don Hammond, alto flute; David Tudor, piano; Philip Kraus, vibraphone; Matthew Raimondi, violin; David Soyer, cello
Label: Time Records, LP: 58007
Feldman, Morton: *Durations 3 for Violin, Tuba and Piano*

Buttery, Gary
Album Title: *A Different Village*
Personnel: David Schoenfeld, Deborah Szajnbeng, Premjit Talwar, Bruce Batts, Tony Morris, Sue Lowenkron Morris
Label: 1992, CD: CS:
Traditional/Buttery: *Tsiganochka* (solo tuba, guitar, mandocello, accordion, and bazuki)

Buttery, Gary; see Atlantic Tuba Quartet; *Euphonic Sounds*

Callender, George Sylvester "Red"
Album Title: *Basin Street Brass*
Personnel: Al Aarons, trumpet; Grover Mitchell, trombone; Buddy Collette, reeds; Harold Jones, Walter Sage, drums; Al Viola, guitar/banjo; Leroy Vinnegar, bass; Patrick Boyle,tambourine
Label: Legend Record Company, 1973, LP: 1003
Williams, Spencer/Mitchell: *Basin Street Blues*
arr. Boyle: *Primrose Lane*
arr. Boyle: *When the Saints Go Marchin' In*
arr. Boyle: *Just a Closer Walk with Thee*
Ellington, Edward Kennedy "Duke"/ Callender: *Sophisticated Lady*
arr. Callender: *Dedicated to the Blues*
arr. Mitchell: *I Want a Little Girl*
arr. Mitchell: *Magna*
arr. Mitchell: *Fat Cat*
arr. Callender: *Lush Life*

Callender, George Sylvester "Red"
Album Title: *The Lowest*
Personnel: Buddy Collete, flute; Gerald Wilson, trumpet; Gerald Wiggins, piano; Billy Bean, guitar; Bill Douglass, drums; Red Mitchell, bass; Hymic Gunklcr, alto saxophone; Martin Berman, baritone saxophone; John "Stream" Ewing, trombone; Eddie Beal, piano; Bill Pitman, guitar
Label: 2002, LP
Autumn in New York
Pickin', Pluckin', Whistlin' and Walkin'
The Lowest
Of Thee I Sing
Dedicated to the Blues
They Can't Take That Away from Me
Five-Four Blues
Tea for Two
Another Blues
Volume, Too
I'll Be Around

Callender, George Sylvester "Red"
Album Title: *Moon Mist Blues*
Personnel:
Label: Hemisphere Records, LP: 1002
Callender, Red: *Moon Mist Blues*

Callender, George Sylvester "Red"
Album Title: *Red Callender Speaks Low*
Personnel: Vince DeRosa, horn; Bob Bain, guitar; Bill Douglas, drums; Buddy Collette, reeds; Irving Rosenthal, horn; Red Mitchell, bass
Label: Crown Records, 1957, LP: CLP 5012
Weill, Kurt/Nash: *Speak Low*
Collette, Buddy: *Nice Day*
Ellington, Edward Kennedy "Duke": *In a Sentimental Mood*
Gershwin, George: *Foggy Day*
Callender, Red: *Cris*
De-Lange/Van Heusen: *Darn That Dream*
Wrubel/Magidson: *Gone with the Wind*

Carolino, Sérgio
Album Title: *TGB TUBAGUITARRA& BATERIA*
Personnel: Márlo Delagado, guitar, dobro; Alexandre Frazão, drums, melodica
Label: Clean-feed Records, 2004, CD: CFO23CD
Frazão, Alexandre: *Pipa Baquigrafo*
Barretto, C.: *3.4.7*
Frazão, Alexandre: *Inercia*
Delgado, Márlo: *Pascoal Joins the Dark Force*
Carolino, Sérgio: *Lilli's Funk—Intro*
Carolino, Sérgio: *Lilli's Funk (to Lillana)—Theme*
Monk, Thelonius: *Brilliant Corners*
Palma, J.: *Só*
Powell, B.: *Un Poco Loco*
Page/Plant/Jones: *Black Dog*

Catelinet, Philip
Album Title: *British Composers*
Personnel: London Symphony Orchestra; Sir John Barbirolli, conductor
Label: EMI Records, 1998, CD:
Vaughan Williams, Ralph: *Concerto for Bass Tuba and Orchestra*

Catelinet, Philip
Album Title:
Personnel: London Symphony Orchestra; Sir John Barbirolli, conductor

Label: Barbirolli Society, 1955, LP: SJB102
Vaughan Williams, Ralph: *Concerto for Bass Tuba and Orchestra*
Chaput, David; see Atlantic Tuba Quartet; *Euphonic Sounds*
Clark, Willie; see Tuba 4's
Colonial Tuba Quartet
Album Title: *Spectraphonics*
Personnel: Mary Ann Craig, Jay Hildebrandt, euphoniums; Gary Bird, Gregory Fritze, tubas
Label: Mark, 1995, CD: 1909
Stamp, Jack: *Colonial Express*
Frackenpohl, Arthur: *Suite for Tuba Quartet*
Bernie, Pinkard, and Casey: *Sweet Georgia Brown*
Fritze, Gregory: *Prelude and Dance*
Traditional: *Simple Gifts/Yankee Doodle/When Jesus Wept/Chester/Edelweiss*
Melillo, Stephen: *Erich*
Cummings, Barton: *In Darkness Dreaming*
Mozart, Wolfgang Amadeus: *Allegro from Eine kleine Nachtmusik*
Picchi, Ermanno: *Fantasie Original*
Arlen, Harold: *Somewhere over the Rainbow*
Pullig, Ken: *Dances*
Banchieri, Adriano: *2 Fantasias*
Sousa, John Philip: *Washington Post March*
Conner, Rex
Album Title: *1969 Midwest National Band and Orchestra Clinic*
Personnel: Waukegan Grade School Band; Bernard Stiner, director
Label: Golden Crest, 1969, LP: MID 69-6
Boccalari, E./Akers: *Fantasia di Concerto*
Conner, Rex
Album Title: *Rex Conner National Contest List Tuba Solos*
Personnel: Patricia Lasswell, piano
Label: Coronet, LP: LPS 1259
Handel, George Friderik: *Air and Bourree*
Beethoven, Ludwig van: *Minuet*
Schmidt, William: *Serenade for Tuba and Piano*
Vaughan, Rodger: *Concertpiece No. 1*
Bach, Johann Sebastian/Bell: *Air and Bourree*
Beach, Bennie: *Lamento*
Haddad, Don: *Suite for Tuba*
Mueller, Florian: *Concert Music for Bass Tuba*
Holmes, Paul: *Lento*
Hartley, Walter: *Suite for Unaccompanied Tuba*
Contraband (The)
Album Title: *Swingin' Low*
Personnel: Martin Kym, Martin Meier, euphoniums; Ernest May, David LeClair, tubas; Andy Lüscher, drums; Thomas Thüring, piano
Label: Marcophon, 1993, CD: CD 940-2
LeClair, David: *Heidentüblein*
Spiritual/Kresin: *Swing Low, Sweet Chariot*
Schubert, Franz Peter/LeClair: *Ständchen*
Carmichael, Hoagy/LeClair: *Georgia on My Mind*
Bartles, Alfred: *When Tubas Waltz*
Niehaus, Lennie: *Sleeping Giants*
arr. Dankwart Schmidt: *Tuba Muckl*
Lohmann, Georg/Schmidt: *Bayerische Polka*
LeClair, David: *Carnival of Venice*
Schubert, Franz Peter/LeClair: *Militärmarsch*
Kresin, Willibald: *Chin Up!*
Sousa, John Philip/Werden: *Washington Post March*
LeClair, David: *Growing Up Together* (euphonium and tuba)
Joplin, Scott/LeClair: *The Easy Winners*
Clarke, Herbert L./LeClair: *Cousins*
Contraband Tuba Quartet
Album Title: *The Dragon's Dance*
Personnel: Martin Kym, Martin Meier, euphoniums; Ernest May, David LeClair, tubas; Andy Lüscher, drums; Thomas Thüring, piano
Label: Marcophon, CD: 7031
LeClair, David: *Forte/Formidable/Fortune/The Dragon's Dance*
Schubert, Franz Peter/LeClair: *Die Forelle (Trout) Theme & Variations 1—5*
Kresin, Willibald: *Movin Groovin/Tuba Rodeo/Tango*
Templeton, Alec/Kresin: *Mr. Bach Goes to Town*
Templeton, Alec: *On a Rocky Road*
Gershwin, George/LeClair: *Impromptu in 2 Keys*
Gershwin, George/Kresin: *Three Preludes*
Monti, Vittorio/LeClair: *Csárdás*
Cooley, Floyd
Album Title: *"and from the abyss"*
Personnel:
Label: Opus One, LP: 29
Felciano, Richard: *"and from the abyss" for tuba and tape*
Cooley, Floyd
Album Title: *DePaul University Wind Ensemble, Vol. 3*
Personnel: DePaul University Wind Ensemble; Donald DeRoche, conductor
Label: Troy Records, 2001, CD: Troy 501
Vaughan Williams, Ralph: *Concerto for Bass Tuba and Orchestra*
Gregson, Edward: *Tuba Concerto*
Strauss, Richard: *Concerto No. 1 for Horn, Op. 11*
Cooley, Floyd
Album Title: *Friends in Low Places*
Personnel: DePaul University Wind Ensemble; Donald DeRoche, conductor
Label: Albany Records, 2002, CD: 501
Vaughan Williams, Ralph: *Concerto for Bass Tuba and Orchestra*
Gregson, Edward: *Tuba Concerto*

Strauss, Richard: *Concerto No. 1 for Horn, Op. 11*
Cooley, Floyd
Album Title: *The Romantic Tuba*
Personnel: Naomi Cooley, harpsichord and piano
Label: Crystal, 1983, LP: S120 (A rerelease of Avant Records 1020)
Bach, Johann Sebastian: *Sonata in E♭ major*
Brahms, Johannes: *Vier Ernste Gesange*
Zindars, Earl: *Trigon*
Russell, Armand: *Suite Concertante*
Cooley, Floyd
Album Title: *School Broadcast "Music Makers"—BRASS*
Personnel:
Label: SoCal, 1975, CS: M-51
Vaughan Williams, Ralph: *Concerto for Bass Tuba and Orchestra*
Wagner, Richard: *Siegfried (excerpts)*
Brahms, Johannes: *Vier Ernste Gesange (excerpts)*
Cooley, Floyd
Album Title: *A Schumann Fantasy*
Personnel: Robin Southerland, piano
Label: Summit Records, 1993, CD: DCD 156
Schumann, Robert: *Fantasiestücke, Op. 73*
Schumann, Robert: *Drei Romanzen, Op. 94*
Schumann, Robert: *Märchenbilder (Pictures of Fairyland), Op. 113*
Schumann, Robert: *Adagio and Allegro, Op. 70*
Corella, Gil
Album Title: *Unnatural Ax—The Bear*
Personnel: Stephen DiBonaventura, banjo; Ken Hall, guitar; Randy Jennings, drums
Label: Sterling Productions, 1998, CD:
Beethoven, Ludwig van: *Beethoven's 5½*
Bonfa, Luis: *Samba de Orfeu*
Bassman, George: *I'm Getting Sentimental*
Jacobs, Jacob: *The Bear*
Reinhardt, Django: *Minor Swing*
Rossini, Gioacchino: *William Fell over the Chair*
Schertzinger, Victor: *Tangerine*
Rimsky-Korsakov, Nicholas: *Fright of the Fumblebee*
Hanley and McDonald: *Indiana*
Raye, Don: *I'll Remember April*
Evans, Ray: *Mona Lisa*
DeCosta and LaRocca: *Tiger Rag*
Cohan: *Banjos and Tubas Forever*
Crowther, Shaun
Album Title: *Let's Go*
Personnel: Williams Fairey Engineering
Label: Abrasso, CD: 832
Rossini, Gioacchino/Roberts: *Largo al factotum from "The Barber of Seville"*
Crowther, Shaun
Album Title: *Master Brass, Vol. 1*
Personnel: Williams Fairey Engineering Band; Major Peter Parks, director
Label: Polyphonic, 1990, CD: QDRL 046D
Butler/Gay: *The Sun Has Got His Hat On*
Crowther, Shaun
Album Title:
Personnel: Williams Fairey Engineering
Label: Grasmere, CD: GRCD 35
Butler/Gay, Sparke: *The Sun Has Got His Hat On*
Relton, William: *The Trouble with the Tuba Is*
Newsome, Roy: *Swiss Air*
Cummings, Barton
Album Title: *Barton Cummings, Music for Tuba*
Personnel: Sharon Dudley, piano; Pat Pfiffner, percussion
Label: Coronet, LP: LPS 3065
Butts, Carrol: *Suite for Tuba and Piano*
Ott, Joseph: *Bart's Piece for Tuba and Electronic Tape*
Rasbach, Oscar: *Trees*
Beach, Bennie: *Dance Suite for Tuba and Triangle*
Williams, Howard: *Concertino for Tuba, Percussion and Piano*
Cummings, Barton
Album Title: *Hilles*
Personnel:
Label: Capra, 1979, LP: 1206
Hilles, Lejaren: *Malta for Tuba and Tape*
Cummings, Barton
Album Title: *On Tuba: Barton Cummings*
Personnel: Mary Jane Moore, piano
Label: Crystal, LP: S391
Ross, Walter: *Piltdown Fragments* (tuba and tape)
Ziffrin, Marilyn J.: *Four Pieces for Tuba*
Zinos, Frederick: *Elegy*
Ha, Jae Eu: *Three Pieces*
Cummings, Barton
Album Title: *Paths*
Personnel: Dean Anderson, xylophone; Neva Pilgrim, soprano
Label: Capra, 1981, LP: CRS 1210
Ross, Walter: *Midnight Variations for Tuba and Tape*
Ziffrin, Marilyn J.: *Trio for Xylophone, Soprano and Tuba*
Cummings, Barton
Album Title: *A Retrospective*
Personnel:
Label: C&CC, 1999, CD: C&CCD 101
Grundman, Clare: *Tuba Rhapsody*
Ostrander, Linda: *Time Out for Tuba (movement I—Cycles)*
Uber, David: *Rhythmic Contours (movement I)*
Schubert, Franz Peter: *Serenade*
Saint-Saëns, Camille: *The Swan from "Carnival of the Animals"*
Beversdorf, Thomas: *Sonata (movement I)*
Williams, Danny: *Blues for Bart*
Hollomon, Samuel: *Music for Tuba*

Christensen, James: *Ballad for Tuba*
Ross, Walter: *Midnight Variations for tuba and tape*
Ha, Jae Eu: *Three Pieces*
Curnow, James: *Concertino*

Daellenbach, Charles
Album Title: *Canadian Brass Beginning Solos*
Personnel: Bill Casey, piano
Label: Hal Leonard, 1992, solo collection with CD/CS: HL63000590
Traditional American: *Amazing Grace*
Carey, Henry: *America*
Boyd, Bill: *Canadian Brass Blues*
Benedict, Julius: *Carnival of Venice*
American Folksong: *The Cruel War Is Raging*
Bourgeois, Louis: *Doxology*
Sibelius, Jean: *Finlandia*
Cohan, George M.: *Give My Regards to Broadway*
Foley, Red: *Just a Closer Walk with Thee*
Offenbach, Jacques: *Marine's Hymn*
Beethoven, Ludwig van: *Ode to Joy*
English Ballad: *Riddle Song*
Wauldteufel, Emil: *Skater's Waltz*
Russian Folksong: *Song of the Volga Boatman*
American Folksong: *Streets of Laredo*
Tilzer, Albert von: *Take Me Out to the Ball Game*
Traditional American: *Yankee Doodle*

Daellenbach, Charles
Album Title: *Canadian Brass Easy Solos*
Personnel: Patrick Hansen, piano
Label: Hal Leonard, 1992, solo collection with CD/CS: HL63000586
Schwartz, Jean: *Chinatown, My Chinatown*
American Folk Hymn: *Come, Thou Fount of Every Blessing*
American Folksong: *Erie Canal*
English Folksong: *Hey, Ho! Nobody Home*
Handel, George Friderik: *Lento*
Scottish Folksong: *Loch Lomond*
Lully, Jean Baptiste: *Lonely Forest*
Giordani, Giuseppi: *Love Song (Caro mio ben)*
Sullivan, Arthur: *Miya Sama from "The Mikado"*
Handel, George Friderik: *Repentance (Chi sprezzando)*
American Folksong: *Wayfaring Stranger*

Daellenbach, Charles
Album Title: *Canadian Brass Intermediate Solos*
Personnel: Patrick Hansen, piano
Label: Hal Leonard, 1992, solo collection with CD/CS:
Schubert, Franz Peter: *An die Musik, Op. 88, No. 4*
Bononcini, Giovanni: *Arietta (Non posso disperar)*
Puccini, Giacomo: *Colline's Aria*
Donizetti, Gaetano: *Drinking Song from "Lucrezia Borgia"*
Herbert, Victor: *Italian Street Song*
Sullivan, Arthur: *Pale Young Curate*
Verdi, Giuseppi: *Prayer (Il lascerato spirito)*
Fauré, Gabriel: *The Secret*
Joplin, Scott: *Solace*
Brahms, Johannes: *Sunday*
Handel, George Friderik: *Where E'er You Walk*
Schubert, Franz Peter: *Who Is Sylvia?*

Daley, Joe
Album Title: *Crystals*
Personnel: Sam Rivers
Label: Impulse, LP:
Daley, Joe; see Johnson, Howard; *Howard Johnson & Gravity!!!; Right Now!; Second Childhood; Taj Mahal: The Real Thing*

Daniel, Robert
Album Title: *Archival Series, Volume 1: Solo Flight*
Personnel: United States Air Force Band
Label: U.S. Air Force, 1990, CS: BOL-8908T Public Service/Not for Sale
Smith, Claude T.: *Ballade and Presto Dance*

Daniel, Robert; see United States Army Band "Pershing's Own"; *United States Army Band Tuba-Euphonium Workshop Grand Concert*

Davis, Ronald
Album Title: *American Opus: Music for Ballroom Dancing Volume 1*
Personnel: Doug Graham, clarinet; Dick Goodwin, trumpet, keyboards; Ron Davis, banjo; Jim Hall, drums
Label: Dance Opus, LLC, 1998
Traditional/Goodwin: *Clarinet Polka*

Davis, Ronald
Album Title: *The Magic Place*
Personnel: Robbie Clement, guitar; John Berquist, button accordion
Label: Tomorrow River Music, 1985, CS: E1232
Marxsen, Dale: *Waltzing with Bears*

Davis, Ronald
Album Title: *SoloPro: Contest Music for Tuba*
Personnel: Theodor Lichtmann, Piano
Label: Summit Records, 1990, CS: DCD 106
Haddad, Don: *Suite for Tuba*
Holmes, Paul: *Lento*
Gabrieli, Dominico/R. W. Morris: *Ricercar*
Frackenpohl, Arthur: *Variations for Tuba and Winds (Cobbler's Bench)*
Vaughan, Rodger: *Concertpiece No. 1*
Bach, Johann Sebastian/Bell: *Air and Bourree*
Sowerby, Leo: *Chaconne*
Sear, Walter: *Sonatina*
Martin, Carroll: *Pompola*
Little, Donald: *Lazy Lullaby*

Deck, Warren
Album Title: *New York Legends, Joseph Alessi, Trombone*

Personnel: Jonathan Feldman, Virginia Perry Lamb, John McNeely, pianos
Label: Cala Records, 1997, CD: CACD0508
Bernstein, Leonard: *Waltz for Mippy III*

Deck, Warren; see Gerhard Meinl's Tuba Sextet; *Tubas! A Six-Tuba Musical Romp*

Dites-Le-Moi Tuba
Album title: *Pleasant Moments*
Personnel: Guy Michel, Bernard Trinchan, tenor tubas; Nicolas Papaux, José Niquille, tubas; Itsvan Barga, drums, washboard
Label: Artlab, CD: 93745
Niehaus, Lennie: *Tubalation*
Gale, Jack: *Jazz Suite*
Joplin, Scott: *Pleasant Moments*
Gershwin, George: *A Portrait*
Williams, Cootie, and Thelonius Monk/Hampton: *'Round Midnight*
Niehaus, Lennie: *Spiritual Jazz Suite*
Bartles, Alfred: *When Tubas Waltz*
Collins, Judy: *Since You've Asked*
Ruga, Claudio: *Swing Castle*
Frackenpohl, Arthur: *Pop Suite*
Carmichael, Hoagy/Luis: *Georgia on My Mind*
Joplin, Scott: *The Cascades*
Gale, Jack: *Mellon Dance*

Dixie Power Trio
Album Title: *Ain't My Fault*
Personnel: Andy Kochenour, tuba; Zack Smith, cornet; Bert Carlson, banjo; Byron McWilliams, drums
Label: DPT, 2000, CD: DPT-004
Byrd, Roy: *Mardi Gras in New Orleans*
Braham-Furber: *Limehouse Blues*
Smith, Zachary: *The Woman Is Right*
Dural, Stanley: *Zydeco Boogaloo*
Burwell, C.: *Sweet Lorraine*
Swanstone, McCarron, and Morgan: *The Blues My Naughty Sweetie Gives to Me*
Smith, Zachary: *Baby, You Keep Me Up All Night*
The Old Rugged Cross
Smith, Zachary: *Can't Let Go That Zydeco*
Johnson, Joseph: *Ain't My Fault*
Smith, Zachary: *Regardez La Femme Charmante*

Dixie Power Trio
Album Title: *Greetings from Gumboville*
Personnel: Andy Kochenour, tuba; Zack Smith, cornet; Bert Carlson, banjo; Byron McWilliams, drums
Label: DPT, 1995, CD: DPT-002
Hoover, J.: *The Rhythm King*
Berry, C.: *Too Much Monkey Business*
Smith, Zachary: *Wicked Jerk Chicken*
Morton, F. "Jelly Roll": *Buddy Bolden's Blues*
Carlson, B.: *Quittin' Time*
Stitzel, Mel: *The Chant*
Smith, Zachary: *Can't Let Go That Zydeco*
Barbarin, P.: *Second Line*
Justman, S.: *Centerfold*
Primrose, Joe: *St. James Infirmary*
Smith, Zachary: *She Loves Me Anyway*
Smith, Zachary: *The Good, the Bad, and the Banjo*
Smith, Zachary: *DPT Second Line*
Byrne, Eno: *Once in a Lifetime*
Muse, C.: *Sleepytime Down South*

Dixie Power Trio
Album Title: *Out of Control*
Personnel: Andy Kochenour, tuba; Zack Smith, cornet; Bert Carlson, banjo; Byron McWilliams, drums
Label: DPT, 1993, CD: DPT-001
Gaines and Quezerque: *Big Chief*
Montrell: *That Mellow Sousaphone*
Ellington, Edward Kennedy "Duke": *Just Squeeze Me*
Raye and Slack: *The House of Blue Lights*
Welsch, Elliot, and Adams: *Mardi Gras Mambo*
Webster and Harris: *Spiderman*
Smith, Zachary: *Baby Got Banjo*
Lauper and Hyman: *Time after Time*
Plant and Page: *Stairway to Heaven*
Berry, Chuck: *School Day*
Dural, Stanley: *Zydeco Boogaloo*
Lennon, John, and Paul McCartney: *I Saw Her Standing There*
Byrd, Roeland: *Baby Let Me Hold Your Hand*
Original Dixieland Jazz Band: *Fidgety Feet*
Skill: *That's What I Like about You*

Dowling, Eugene
Album Title: *The English Tuba*
Personnel: London Symphony; Edward Norman, conductor
Label: Fanfare, 1992, CD: CD D595
Vaughan Williams, Ralph: *Concerto for Bass Tuba and Orchestra*
Vaughan Williams, Ralph: *Six Studies in English Folksong*
Handel, George Friderik: *Air con Variazioni from Suite No. 5 in E major*
Elgar, Edward: *Romance*
Jacob, Gordon: *Tuba Suite*

Dowling, Eugene
Album Title: *Music Featuring the Tuba*
Personnel: London Symphony Orchestra; Paul Freeman, conductor
Label: Digitally Encoded Cassette Classics, CS: EC-6033
Vaughan Williams, Ralph: *Concerto for Bass Tuba and Orchestra*
Vaughan Williams, Ralph: *Six Studies in English Folksong*
Bach, Johann Sebastian/Dowling/Norman: *Sonata No. 4 in C*
Ravel, Maurice: *Pièce en form de Habanera*
Schumann, Robert: *Adagio and Allegro in A♭, Op. 70*

Draper, Ray
Album Title: *Award Winning Drummer—Max Roach*
Personnel: Max Roach, drums; Booker Little, trumpet; Arthur Davis, bass; George Coleman, tenor saxophone
Label: Time Jazz Series, 1980, CD: BCD1042
Tuba de Nod
Milano
Variations on the Scene
Pies of Quincy
Old Folks
Sadiga
Gandolfo's Bounce

Draper, Ray
Album Title: *Jackie McLean and Company*
Personnel: Jackie McLean, alto saxophone; Bill Hardman, trumpet; Mal Waldron, piano; Doug Watkins, bass; Arthur Taylor, drums
Label: Prestige, 1992 (recorded in 1957), LP/CD: OJCCD-074-2
Waldron, Mal: *Flickers*
Draper, Ray: *Minor Dream*

Draper, Ray
Album Title: *John Coltrane/Ray Draper Quintet*
Personnel: John Coltrane, tenor sax; Gil Coggins, piano; Spanky De Brest, bass; Larry Ritchie, drums
Label: Prestige, 1980, LP: MPP 2507
Draper, Ray: *Clifford's Kappa*
Draper, Ray: *Filidia*
Draper, Ray: *Two Sons*
Draper, Ray: *Paul's Pal*
Draper, Ray: *Under Paris Skies*
Draper, Ray: *I Hadn't Anyone Till You*

Draper, Ray
Album Title: *Red Beans and Rice*
Personnel: Phil Wood, trumpet; Richard Aplan, reeds; David Dahlsten, trombone; Bob Hogans, organ; Tommy Trujillo, guitar; Ron Johnson, bass; Paul Lagos, drums; Rodney Gooden, bass clarinet
Label: Epic, 1969, LP: BN 26461
Draper, Ray: *Happiness*
Draper, Ray: *Empty Streets*
Wood, Philip D.: *Trilogy*
Wood, Philip D.: *Gentle Old Sea*
Draper, Ray, and Richard Aplan: *Let My People Go*
Draper, Ray: *Mess Around*
Wood, Philip D.: *Home*
Trujillo, Tommy: *If You Ever Wanna*

Draper, Ray
Album Title: *A Tuba Jazz*
Personnel: John Coltrane, tenor sax; John Maher, piano; Spanky De Brest, bass; Larry Ritchie, drums
Label: Fresh Sound Records, 1958, LP/1989, CD: FSR-CD 20
Draper, Ray: *Essii's Dance*
Rollins, Sonny: *Doxy*
Lerner, Alan Jay: *I Talk to the Trees*
Harbach, Otto, and Jerome Kern: *Yesterday's*
Rollins, Sonny: *Oleo*
Dennis, Matt, and Earl Brent: *Angel Eyes*

Drums and Tuba
Album Title: *Box Fetish*
Personnel: Brian Wolff, tuba; Tony Nozero, drums
Label: My Pal God, 1999, CD: MPG036
Drums and Tuba: *Does It Suck to Be You*
Drums and Tuba: *The Inspector*
Drums and Tuba: *Adventures of Poo-Poo and Pee-Pee*
Drums and Tuba: *Carrots*
Drums and Tuba: *Loteria*
Drums and Tuba: *Open Case*
Drums and Tuba: *Kuc to Luc*
Drums and Tuba: *Gimpel the Fool*
Drums and Tuba: *5.24.94*
Drums and Tuba: *In Case*
Drums and Tuba: *Meat*
Drums and Tuba: *The Butcher*
Drums and Tuba: *Tuba Song*
Drums and Tuba: *No Good with Words*
Drums and Tuba: *Close Case*
Drums and Tuba: *Curtains*
Drums and Tuba: *Brief Case*
Drums and Tuba: *Out of Case*
Drums and Tuba: *Pete's Dance*

Drums and Tuba
Album Title: *The Flying Ballerina*
Personnel: Brian Wolff, tuba; Tony Nozero, drums
Label: My Pal God, 1998, CD: MPG037
Drums and Tuba: *Fits of Spaghetti*
Drums and Tuba: *Kermit*
Drums and Tuba: *Chummus, A Challa, and a Whole Lot of Chutzpah*
Drums and Tuba: *The Inspector Returns*
Drums and Tuba: *Lots of Luc*
Drums and Tuba: *Blazevitch*
Drums and Tuba: *The Flying Ballerina*
Baron, Joey: *Scottie Pippen*
Mingus, Charles: *Boogie Stop Shuffle*
Drums and Tuba: *Neal Hamburger*
The Minuteman: *God Bows to Math*
Drums and Tuba: *Pig Ears for Lily*
Drums and Tuba: *Meter Maid*
Drums and Tuba: *Bertone*
Drums and Tuba: *There Is a Monster*

Drums and Tuba
Album Title: *Vinyl Killer*
Personnel: Brian Wolff, tuba; Tony Nozero, drums
Label: Righteous Babe, 2001, CD: RBR023-D
Drums and Tuba: *The Diagram*

Drums and Tuba: *The Donkey and the Walrus*
Drums and Tuba: *Royronus*
Drums and Tuba: *The 10 Attacks of Dagger*
Drums and Tuba: *Territory*
Drums and Tuba: *Topolino*
Drums and Tuba: *The Sauce Maker*
Drums and Tuba: *Eli*
Drums and Tuba: *The Horse and the Tree*
Drums and Tuba: *Chapeau Russia*
Drums and Tuba: *Prince Meets the Phantom*
Drums and Tuba: *No Accommodation for Buffalo*
Drums and Tuba: *Carlos the Cat*

Dumitru, Ionel
Album Title: *Tuba Recital*
Personnel: Irina Botez, piano
Label: Electrecord 7 inch, $33^1/_3$: ECC 839
Paganini, Niccolò: *Theme and Variations*
Wieniawski: *Mazurcă*
Dumitru, Ionel: *Fantezie Pentru Tuba si Pian*

Dutch Tuba Quartet
Album Title: *Escape from Oom-Pah Land*
Personnel: Ron Antens, Jan van de Sanden, tubas; Hugo Verweij, Arjen Bos, euphoniums
Label: World Wind Music, 1998, CD: 500042
Wilkinson, Robert: *Happy Soul*
Hawkins, Erskin/Johnson/Johnson: *Tuxedo Junction*
Hidas, Frigyes: *Tuphonium*
Sousa, John Philip/Smalley: *The Thunderer*
Payne, Frank Lynn: *Quartet for Tubas (The Condor)*
Bruckner, Anton/Sabourin: *Locus Iste*
Stevens, John: *Dances*
Joplin, Scott/Sabourin: *Pleasant Moments*
DeCosta and LaRocca/Gale: *Tiger Rag*
Uber, David: *Music for the Stage*
Gabrieli, Giovanni/Gray: *Canzona per Sonare No. 4*
Spiritual/Alexander: *Swing Low, Sweet Chariot*
Mancini, Henry/Krush: *Pink Panther*

Dutch Tuba Quartet
Album Title: *Four Keen Guys*
Personnel: Ron Antens, Jan van de Sanden, tubas; Hugo Verweij, Arjen Bos, euphoniums
Label: World Wind, CD: WWM 500023
Beal, Keith: *Three Movements for Four Tubas*
Berlioz, Hector/Werden: *Hungarian March*
Frackenpohl, Arthur: *Pop Suite*
Gillis, Lew: *Four Keen Guys*
Handy, W. C./Holcombe: *St. Louis Blues*
Jacob, Gordon: *Four Pieces for Tuba Quartet*
Joplin, Scott/Werden: *The Easy Winners*
Mertens, Hardy: *Scyths*
Stevens, John: *Manhattan Suite*

Dutch Tuba Quartet
Album Title: *Wolkenschatten*
Personnel: Ron Antens, Jan van de Sanden, tubas; Hugo Verweij, Arjen Bos, euphoniums
Label: BES, CD: 0240
Joule, James: *The Eagle Thunders*
Nordhagen, Stig: *Nocturne*
Debussy, Claude/Doughty: *Golliwogg's Cakewalk*
Koetsier, Jan: *Wolkenschatten für Tubaquartet, Op. 136 (movement I—Tranquillo)*
Stevens, John: *Moondance*
Williams, John/Damson: *March from 1941*
Traditional/Verweij: *Freylekhs fun der Khupe*
Traditional/Verweij: *Der Khusid geyt Tantsn*
Brown, Clifford/Wilkenson: *Daahoud*
Schaars, Peter Kleine: *Wolf the Cat*

Easener, Marc
Album Title: *20th Century Concerti*
Personnel: Foundation Philharmonic; David Snell, conductor
Label: ASV Living Era, 2002, CD: CD DCA 1126
Williams, John: *Concerto for Tuba*

Eastep, Michael; see Albertasaurus Tuba Quartet

Erickson, Martin
Album Title: *Dale Underwood, Saxophone Soloist*
Personnel:
Label: Golden Crest, LP: 4136
Hartley, Walter: *Double Concerto for Saxophone, Tuba and Winds*
Whitney: *Introduction and Samba*

Erickson, Martin
Album Title: *Millennium Brass*
Personnel: Vince DiMartino, Rich Illman, trumpets; Lisa Bontrager, horn; Scott Hartman, trombone
Label: Walking Frog Records, 2000, CD: WFR601
Monti, Vittorio/Duncan: *Csárdás*

Erickson, Martin
Album Title: *Music from America's Golden Age*
Personnel: George Foreman, conductor
Label: Walking Frog, 2002, CD: #111
Kling, Henri: *The Elephant and the Fly, Op. 520,* for piccolo, tuba, and band

Erickson, Martin
Album Title: *My Very Good Friend*
Personnel: John Sheridan, piano
Label: Bear Productions, 1997, CD:
Parker, Charlie: *Yardbird Suite*
Ellington, Edward Kennedy "Duke"/Gaines: *Just Squeeze Me*
Wolf/Melling: *My One and Only Love*
Burke/Spina: *My Very Good Friend, The Milkman*
Rodgers, Richard, and Hart, Lorenz: *You Took Advantage of Me*
Taylor, Billy: *One for the Whoofer*

Zindars, Earl: *How My Heart Sings*
Traditional: *Just a Closer Walk with Thee*
Perkins: *Grooveyard*
Sheridan, John: *All Alone Blues*
Berlin, Irving: *Always*
Parker, Charlie: *My Little Suede Shoes*
Waller, Thomas "Fats": *Honeysuckle Rose*
Ellington, Edward Kennedy "Duke": *I Let the Song Go Out of My Heart*
Youmans/Ceasar: *Tea for Two*

Erickson, Martin
Album Title: *Smile—The Music of Marty Erickson*
Personnel: Marvin Stamm, trumpet; Frank Mantooth, piano; Steve Houghton, drums; Ron Newman, piano
Label: Willson/DEG Music, 2002, CD:
Tchaikovsky, Peter Ilyitch/Newman: *Boss-Swan-Nova*
Rollins, Sonny/Erickson: *Doxy*
Newman, Ron/Newman: *This Won't Hurt a Bit*
Noble, Ray/Newman: *Cherokee*
Jones, Thad/Erickson: *A Child Is Born*
Bulla, Stephen: *Bluzenfunky*
Bulla, Stephen: *Clearfield Driving*
Herbert, Victor/Newman: *Indian Summer*
Brubeck, Dave/Taylor: *It's a Raggy Waltz*
Chaplin, Charlie/Newman: *Smile*

Erickson, Martin
Album Title: *The Teddy Bears' Picnic*
Personnel: New Columbian Brass Band; George Foreman, conductor
Label: Dorian Recordings, 2000, CD: #93201
Laurendeau, L. P.: *Elephantine Polka*

Erickson, Martin; see Monarch Tuba-Euphonium Quartet; see Symphonia; see United States Navy Band Tuba-Euphonium Quartet

Eskelin, Ellory
Album Title: *Figure of Speech*
Personnel:
Label: Soul Note, 1993, CD: 121232-2
Eskelin, Ellery: *#107*
Eskelin, Ellery: *Short Story*
Eskelin, Ellery: *Figure of Speech*
Eskelin, Ellery: *Whispered*
Eskelin, Ellery: *It Doesn't Wait*

European Tuba Quartet
Album Title: *Heavy Metal—Light Industry*
Personnel: Larry Fishkind, Benoit Veridaz, Pinguin Moschner, Melvyn Poore, tubas
Label: FMP, 1987, CD: 1200
Five Short Pieces
Jerkle Cirque
Brass Tax
Golden Gate
Blue Wail
Running Around
Silver Shadows
On Chor

European Tuba Quartet
Album Title: *Low and Behold*
Personnel: Larry Fishkind, Carl Ludwig Hübsch, Pinguin Moschner, Melvyn Poore, tubas
Label: JazzHausMusik, 2000, CD: JHM 110
Hübsch, Carl Ludwig: *Bird*
Wauschke: *Desert Song*
Moschner, Pinguin/Fishkind: *Round the Block*
Moschner, Pinguin: *Duett Duell*
Hübsch, Carl Ludwig: *Red Thread*
Robinson, Perry: *Angels*
Fishkind, Larry: *Four Miniatures*
Fishkind, Larry: *Reed Hornets*
Hübsch, Carl Ludwig: *Material Girls*
Fishkind, Larry: *Trash Dance*
Moschner, Pinguin: *Moonlight Elephants*
Moschner, Pinguin: *Moving Clusters*

Feldman, Enrique "Hank" C.
Album Title: *Tubesia*
Personnel: Marie A. Sierra, piano; Willie Hill, Jr., tenor sax; Rene Camacho, bass; Jeff Haskell, jazz piano; Robin Horn, drums; Guillermo "Bubba" Fass, Arturo Rodriguez, Latin percussion; Darin J. Wadle, classical percussion
Label: Mark, 2001, CD: MCD 2275
Rachmaninoff, Sergei: *Floods of Spring*
Feldman, Hank C.: *Suenos Negros*
Rachmaninoff, Sergei: *Vocalise, Op. 34, No. 14*
Feldman, Hank C.: *Images*
Curtis, Eduardo de: *Torna a Surriento*
Henderson, Joe/Hill: *Recordame*
Gillespie, Dizzy/Feldman: *Birks Werks*
Gillespie, Dizzy/Hill: *Night in Tunisia*
Traditional/Feldman: *Yisrael V'oraita*
Monk, Thelonius/Hill: *Straight, No Chaser*
Ellington, Edward Kennedy "Duke"/ Feldman: *In a Sentimental Mood*
Romberg, Sigmund, and Hammerstein, O./ Hill: *Softly, as a Morning Sunrise*

Feldman, Enrique "Hank" C.; see Symphonia

Felt, Brad
Album Title: *Exordium*
Personnel: Gary Schunk, piano; Jaribu Shahid, bass; Gerald Cleaver, drums
Label: D Flat Records, 1995, CD:
Felt, Brad: *Don't Hold On*
Felt, Brad: *Portrait of Teresa*
Felt, Brad: *Blues to Nasir*
Golson, Benny: *Whisper Not*
Antonio, Luis: *Minina Moca (Young Lady)*
Felt, Brad: *Carol's Theme*
Burke and Van Heusen: *It Could Happen to You*
Felt, Brad: *"P.J. Lids"*

Ferguson, Kenneth
Album Title: *Desford Live in Canada*
Personnel: Desford Colliery Catapillar Band

Label: Hermitage, 1990, CD: HMCD 001 (Same recording released as *Making Tracks,* Polyphonic, QPRL 045D)
Barry, Darrol: *Impromptu for Tuba*
Ferguson, Kenneth; see British Tuba Quartet
Fishkind, Larry
Album Title: *Calistrophy*
Personnel: Klez-thetics; Akos Laki, clarinet; Roberto Haliffi, drums; Burton Greene, piano
Label: BV Haast, 2003, CD: CD 0802
Fishkind, Larry
Album Title: *Jew-azzic Park*
Personnel: Michael Moore, clarinet; Roberto Haliffi, drums; Burton Greene, piano; Patricia Beysens, vocals and flugelhorn; Perry Robinson, clarinet; Hans Mekel, clarinet and sax
Label: BVHaast, 1995, CD: CD 9506
Fishkind, Larry
Album Title: *KlezMokum*
Personnel: KlezMokum; Michael Moore, clarinet; Roberto Haliffi, drums; Burton Greene, piano
Label: BVHaast, 1992, CD: CD 9209
Fishkind, Larry
Album Title: *Le Dor Va Dor*
Personnel: Sovali (Sofie van Lier), vocals; Michael Moore, clarinet; Roberto Haliffi, drums; Burton Greene, piano; Patricia Beysens, vocals and flugelhorn; Perry Robinson, clarinet; Hans Mekel, clarinet and sax
Label: BV Haast, 2000, CD: 0700
Fishkind, Larry
Album Title: *ReJew-venation*
Personnel: Michael Moore, clarinet; Roberto Haliffi, drums; Burton Greene, piano; Patricia Beysens, vocals and flugelhorn; Perry Robinson, clarinet; Hans Mekel, clarinet and sax
Label: BV Haast, 1998, CD: CD 9809
Fishkind, Larry; see European Tuba Quartet
Fletcher, John
Album Title: *Baroque Brass: The Philip Jones Ensemble*
Personnel: The Philip Jones Brass Ensemble
Label: Argo, LP: ZRG 898
Bach, Johann Sebastian: *Suite No. 1 in G major for Solo Cello* (Minuet, Courante)
Fletcher, John
Album Title: *The Best of Fletch*
Personnel: Besses o' th' Barn Band; Roy Newsome, conductor/London Symphony Orchestra; Andre Previn, conductor
Label: John Fletcher Trust Fund, 1988, CS:
Mozart, Wolfgang Amadeus/Fletcher: *Tuba Serenade (Eine Kleine Nachtmusik)*
Gregson, Edward: *Tuba Concerto*
Ramsöe, Emilio Wilhelm: *Allegro Vivace from Quartet No. 5, Op. 38*
Howarth, Elgar: *Carnival of Venice*
Rimsky-Korsakov, Nicholas/Fletcher: *Flight of the Bumblebee*
Arnold, Malcolm: *Fantasy for Solo Tuba*
arr. Howarth: *The Cuckoo, Lucerne Song*
Bach, Johann Sebastian: *Suite No. 1 in G major for Solo Cello (Minuet, Courante)*
Vaughan Williams, Ralph: *Concerto for Bass Tuba and Orchestra*
Tchaikovsky, Peter Ilyitch/Fletcher: *Waltz from "Sleeping Beauty"*
Fletcher, John
Album Title: *Brass Splendour*
Personnel: The Philip Jones Brass Ensemble
Label: London, 1984, CD: 411 955-2 LH
Tchaikovsky, Peter Ilyitch/Fletcher: *Waltz from "Sleeping Beauty"*
Fletcher, John
Album Title: *Composers: Edward Gregson, Gordon Langford*
Personnel: Besses o' th' Barn Band; Roy Newsome, conductor
Label: Chandos, 1994, CD #4526
Edward, Gregson: *Tuba Concerto*
Fletcher, John
Album Title: *Divertimento*
Personnel: The Philip Jones Brass Ensemble
Label: Argo, LP: ZRG 851
Tchaikovsky, Peter Ilyitch/Fletcher: *Waltz from "Sleeping Beauty"*
Fletcher, John
Album Title: *Easy Winners*
Personnel: The Philip Jones Brass Ensemble
Label: Argo, 1978, LP: ZRG 895; CS: KZRC 895
Mozart, Wolfgang Amadeus/Fletcher: *Eine Kleine Nachtmusik*
Fletcher, John
Album Title: *Oliver Cromwell*
Personnel: Stanshawe Band (Bristol); Walter Hargreaves, conductor
Label: Twoten, LP: TT 001
Brand, Michael: *Tuba Tapestry*
Arnold, Malcolm: *Fantasy for Solo Tuba*
Fletcher, John
Album Title: *Le Tuba Enchantee*
Personnel: Michael Reeves, piano
Label: Seven Seas Records 1980, LP: K28C-65
Tchaikovsky, Peter Ilyitch: *Overture Miniature from "Nutcracker"*
Elgar, Edward: *Chanson de Matin, Op. 15, No. 2*
Wagner, Richard: *O Du Mein Holder Abendstern from "Tannhauser"*
Mussorgsky, Modest: *Song of the Flea*
Mozart, Wolfgang Amadeus: *Non Pui Andrai from "Le Nozze di Figaro"*
Hartley, Walter: *Suite for Unaccompanied Tuba*

Hindemith, Paul: *Sonata for Bass Tuba and Piano*
Glass, Jennifer: *Sonatine for Basstuba and Piano*
Fletcher, John
Album Title: *Twentieth Century Soloists*
Personnel: Besses o' th' Barn Band; Roy Newsome, conductor
Label: Chandos, 1982, LP: BBR 1013
Gregson, Edward: *Tuba Concerto*
Fletcher, John
Album Title: *Vaughan Williams: Pastoral Symphony/Tuba Concerto*
Personnel: London Symphony Orchestra; Andre Previn, conductor
Label: RCA Red Seal, 1972, LP: LSC-3281; CD: 60586-2-RG; CS: AGK1-5872
Vaughan Williams, Ralph: *Concerto for Bass Tuba and Orchestra*
Flowers, Herbie
Album Title: *Sky 2*
Personnel:
Label: Ariola, LP: 204510
Traditional: *Tuba Smarties*
Flowers, Herbie
Album Title: *Sky 3*
Personnel:
Label: Ariola, LP: 203413-320
Traditional: *Dance of the Big Fairries*
Forman, Steven
Album Title: *Nine Stellar Pieces*
Personnel:
Label: Furious Artisans, 2000, CD: 6803
Martin, Robert: *Aldebaran,* for solo tuba
Frazier, Philip; see New Orleans Jazz Bands; *Down Yonder*
Frazier, Richard
Album Title: *The Brass and the Band*
Personnel: Dallas Symphonic Wind Ensemble
Label: Crystal, 1987, CD: 431
Clarke, Herbert L.: *Bride of the Waves*
Freese, Stanford
Album Title: *25th Anniversary Midwest National Band and Orchestra Clinic*
Personnel: Thomas Jefferson Senior High School Band-Earl Benson, director
Label: Golden Crest, 1971, LP: MID-71-7
Bencriscutto, Frank: *Concertino for Tuba and Band*
Frey, Michael
Album title: *3 Voices Et a Tuba—Live at Moods*
Personnel: Marianne Racine, Peggy Chew, vocals; Samira Mall-Darby, vocals and percussion
Label: Jecklin Red Note, CD: JC 108-2
Jones, Sam: *Unit Seven*
Lennon, John, and Paul McCartney: *Come Together*
List, G./Racine, Marianne: *Prélude*
Mahal, Taj: *Cakewalk into Town*
Monk, Thelonius/Mall-Darby, Samira: *Epistrophy*
Ronell, Ann: *Willow Weep for Me*
Mall-Darby, Samira: *Whose Reality Is This Anyway?*
Urbaniak, Michael: *New York Polka*
Chinese traditional: *The Alisan Girl*
Mall, Philippe: *The Hymn*
Davis, Miles: *Blue in Green*
Mingus, Charles: *Better Git It in Your Soul*
Mahal, Taj: *Encore: Cakewalk into Town*
Fritsch, Philippe; see Steckar Elephant Tuba Horde
Fritze, Gregory
Album Title: *Cambridge Symphonic Brass Ensemble*
Personnel: Russell De Vuyst, Ken Pullis, trumpets; Richard Hudson, horn; Kevin Henry, trombone
Label: Crystal, 1986, LP: S552
Fritze, Gregory: *Basso Continuo*
Holmes, Brian: *Tales of the Cultural Revolution*
Fritze, Gregory; see Colonial Tuba Quartet
Funderburk, Jeff
Album Title: *Journeys*
Personnel: Abbie Conant, trombone; Iva Návratová, piano; Uli Kieckbusch, piano
Label: Mark, CD: 3176-MCD
Thompson, Troy: *Allegro from Sonatina for Tuba*
Bloch, Ernst: *The Jewish Life*
Penderecki, Krzysztof: *Capriccio for Solo Tuba*
Hindemith, Paul: *Sonata for Bass Tuba and Piano*
Beck, Jeremy: *Variationen/Tempus Fugit/ HoUsE miX* (with synthesizer)
Dumitru, Ionel: *Romanian Dance No. 2*
Hamlin, Peter: *Clones* (with tape)
Impre a tre
Funderburk, Jeff
Album Title: *Passages*
Personnel: Robin Guy, Oksana Skidan, piano
Label: Mark, 1996, CD: 2199-MCD
Lebedev, Alexei: *Concert Allegro*
Lebedev, Alexei: *Concerto in One Movement*
Koetsier, Jan: *Sonatina*
Capuzzi, Antonio: *Andante and Rondo from Concerto for Double Bass*
Vaughan, Rodger: *Concertpiece No. 1*
Jones, Robert: *Dialogs*
Mozart, Wolfgang Amadeus/Morris: *O Isis and Osiris*
Broughton, Bruce: *Sonata [Concerto] for Tuba and Piano*
Funderburk, Jeff
Album Title: *Requiem*
Personnel: Northern Iowa Wind Symphony; Ronald Johnson, conductor
Label: Mark Custom Recording, 1997, CD: 2332-MCD

Bukvich, Daniel: *Meditations on the Writings of Vasily Kandinsky*
Funderburk, Jeff
Album Title: *Romantic Connections*
Personnel: Iva Návratová, piano
Label: Mark Custom Recording, 2001, CD: 3748-MCD
Ecclés, Henry: *Sonate*
Castérède, Jacques: *Sonatine*
Ewazen, Eric: *Sonata (Concerto)*
Fauré, Gabriel: *Après un Rêve*
Fauré, Gabriel: *Sicilienne*
Bruch, Max: *Kol Nidrei*
Schumann, Robert: *Adagio and Allegro in A♭, Op. 70*
Kellaway, Roger: *The Morning Song*
Funderburk, Jeff; see Symphonia
Gallet, Philippe; see Miraphone Tuba Quartet
Galmant, Olivier; see Miraphone Tuba Quartet
Gannett, Dave
Album Title: *Christmas Cookies*
Personnel: Randy Morris, piano and frets; Charles Bertini, trumpet and flugelhorn; Renee Dover, strings; Ed Metz, drums
Label: Arbor Jazz Records, 1993, CD: CS:
Gannett, Dave
Album Title: *Out-of-Season*
Personnel: Randy Morris, piano and frets; Charles Bertini, trumpet and flugelhorn; Renee Dover, strings; Ed Metz, drums
Label: AppleJazz, 2000, CD: AJCD0595
Ellington, Edward Kennedy "Duke": *In a Mellow Tone*
Jenkins: *This Is All I Ask*
Brown and Ayer: *Oh, You Beautiful Doll*
Carmichael, Hoagy: *Skylark*
Burke and Van Heusen: *Here's That Rainy Day*
Brown: *The Blues Walk*
McCarthy and Monaco: *You Made Me Love You*
Porter, Cole: *You'd Be So Nice to Come Home to*
Jobim, Antonio Carlos: *Quiet Nights of Quiet Stars*
Ernesto and Battista: *Come Back to Sorrento*
Wood and Hines: *Rosetta*
Ellington, Edward Kennedy "Duke": *Do Nothing' Til You Hear from Me*
Ellington, Edward Kennedy "Duke": *Mood Indigo*
Rodgers, Richard, and Oscar Hammerstein: *It Might As Well Be Spring*
Steiner: *Dudley Do-Right of the Mounties*
Steiner: *Dudley Do-Wrong!*
Gannett, Dave
Album Title: *Tubas from Hell*
Personnel: Tom Hook, keyboards, trombone, frets, percussion; Ed Metz, drums; Renee Dover, strings; Randy Morris, piano, marimba, mandolin; Anthony Dixon, banjo
Label: Summit Records, 1993, CD: DCD 155
Hirsch/Rose:' *Deed I Do*
Waller, Thomas "Fats": *Keepin' Out of Mischief Now*
Fields and McHugh: *On the Sunny Side of the Street*
Anonymous (c. 1927): *Tubas in the Moonlight*
Mercer, Johnny: *Tangerine*
Pinkard, Young, and Meyer: *Sugar*
Williams, Mason: *Samba Beach*
Loesser, Frank: *On a Slow Boat to China*
Carmichael, Hoagy: *Ol' Rockin' Chair's Got Me*
Burke and Johnston: *Pennies from Heaven*
Joplin, Scott: *Solace*
Randolph, Boots: *Yakkety Tuba*
Gay, Les
Album Title: *Music of BL Lacerta*
Personnel: Robert Price, winds; Maurice Hood, viola and violin; David Anderson, flute, percussion, and electronics
Label: IRIDA, 1981, LP: IR-0009
BL Lacerta: *High Energy*
BL Lacerta: *Starts Same but Beautiful*
BL Lacerta: *Flutes and Tuba*
BL Lacerta: *Powerful*
BL Lacerta: *Estampie*
BL Lacerta: *My Mother Is Here*
BL Lacerta: *Stravinsky*
BL Lacerta: *Third*
BL Lacerta: *Monkey Chant*
Georgie, Gerhard
Album Title:
Personnel: Maria Bergman, piano
Label: Tontraeger, LP: 0123506 SWF
Bozza, Eugène: *Allegro et Finale*
Georgie, Gerhard
Album Title:
Personnel: Maria Bergman, piano
Label: Tontraeger, LP: 0123505 SWF
Hindemith, Paul: *Sonata for Bass Tuba and Piano*
Gerhard Meinl's Tuba Sextet
Album Title: *Tuba! A Six-Tuba Musical Romp*
Personnel: Enrique Crespo, Warren Deck, Walter Hilgers, Samuel Pilafian, Jonathon Sass, Dankwart Schmidt
Label: Angel, 1992, CD: CDC 7 54729 2 (USA: CDC 54729)
Mozart, Wolfgang Amadeus/Crespo, Hilgers, Pilafian: *Divertimento No. 2 in B♭*
Bach, Johann Sebastian/D. Schmidt: *Fugue in G minor*
Couperin, F./Pilafian: *Les Baricades Misterieuses*
Di Lasso, Orlando/Pilafian: *Ola, O che bon eccho*
Gabrieli, Giovanni/Gray: *Canzona per Sonare No. 4*
Rosler, J. J./D. Schmidt: *Partita—Polacca*
Hilgers, Walter: *Praeludium*
Crespo, Enrique: *Bruckner Etude*

Crespo, Enrique: *Three Milongas*
Denson, Frank: *Three Folksongs for Four Brass*
Sass, Jonathon: *Meltdown*
Watz, Franz: *Melton Marsch*
Traditional/D. Schmidt: *Bayerische Zell*
Lohmann, Georg/D. Schmidt: *Bayerische Polka*

Glynn, Patrick; see Tuba 4's

Godard, Michel; see Bargeron, Dave; *TubaTuba;* see Steckar Tubapack

Gourlay, James
Album Title: *CWS Glasgow Band Meet the Sovereign Soloists*
Personnel: CWS Glasgow Band; John Hudson, conductor
Label: Doyen, 1991, CD: DOY CD 012; CS: DOY MC 012
Rossini, Gioacchino/Roberts: *Largo al factotum from "The Barber of Seville"*
Rimsky-Korsakov, Nicholas/Gourlay: *Flight of the Bumblebee*

Gourlay, James
Album Title: *East Meets West*
Personnel: John Wilson, Jonathan Scott, piano; Grimethorpe Colliery Band; Gary Cutt, conductor
Label: Doyen, CD
Hindemith, Paul: *Sonata for Bass Tuba and Piano*
Ellerby, Martin: *Epitaph V*
Lebedev, Alexi: *Concerto in One Movement*
Vaughan Williams, Ralph/Littlemore: *Concerto for Bass Tuba and Brass Band*
Carpenter, Gary: *Fantasia on China Song*

Gourlay, James
Album Title: *Gourlay Plays Tuba*
Personnel: Britannia Building Society Band, Howard Snell, conductor
Label: Doyen Records, 1997, CD: DOY CD 028
Gregson, Edward: *Tuba Concerto*
Arnold, Malcolm: *Fantasy for Solo Tuba*
Newton, Rodney: *Capriccio in E♭ major*
Gregson, Edward: *Alarum for solo tuba*
Horovitz, Joseph: *Concerto for Tuba and Brass Band*

Gourlay, James
Album Title: *Joseph Horovitz: Music for Brass*
Personnel: CWS (Glasgow) Band; Joseph Horovitz, conductor
Label: Serendipity, 1995, CD: SERCD1900
Horovitz, Joseph: *Concerto for Tuba and Brass Band*

Gourlay, James
Album Title: *Tristan Encounters*
Personnel: Williams Fairey Band; Brian Grant, conductor
Label: Polyphonic, CD: QPRL 210D
Ellerby, Martin: *Tuba Concerto*

Green, Carlton; see Johnson, Howard; *Second Childhood*

Greene, Fred; see Self, James; *The Big Stretch*

Griffiths, John
Album Title: *Canadian Chops*
Personnel: David McIntyre, piano; Jim Gallagher, piano
Label: CBC (unnumbered)
McIntyre, David: *Sonata for Tuba and Piano*
Raum, Elizabeth: *Concerto del Garda*
Raum, Elizabeth: *The Legend of Heimdall*
Raum, Elizabeth: *Will There Be a Time?*
Raum, Elizabeth: *"T" for Tuba*

Griffiths, John
Album Title: *The Legend of Heimdall*
Personnel: Orchestra of the Cappella of St. Petersburg; Richard Raum, conductor
Label: Saskatchewan Arts Board, 2001, CD: LOH 14342
Raum, Elizabeth: *The Legend of Heimdall*
Raum, Elizabeth: *Concerto del Garda*
Raum, Elizabeth: *Pershing Concerto*

Griffiths, John
Album Title: *The National Youth Band of Canada*
Personnel: National Youth Band of Canada; Lt. Col. R. A. Herriot, conductor
Label:
Hidas, Frigyes: *Tuba Concerto*
Mantia, Simone/Howly: *Believe Me If All Those Endearing Young Charms*

Gutternigg, H. G.; see Heavy Tubas; *Sagenhaft*

Haas, Uli; see Melton Tuba-Quartett

Hackl, Helmut; see Heavy Tuba

Hammond, Ivan
Album Title:
Personnel: Ruth Inglefield, harp
Label: Composer's Recording, Inc., CD: CRI SD-556
Childs, Barney: *A Question of Summer for Harp and Tuba*

Hanks, Thompson (Toby)
Album Title: *He's Not Heavy, He's My Tuba*
Personnel: New York Brass Quintet; Robert Nagel, Allan Dean, trumpets; Paul Ingraham, French horn; John Swallow, trombone
Label: Music Minus One, CD: 4701 (Play-along CD has full performance and accompaniment-only tracks—includes sheet music)
Lebow, Leonard: *Popular Suite*
End, Jack: *Three Salutations*
Wilder, Alec: *Brass Quintet No. 2*
arr. Rosenthal: *Little Brown Jug*
Nagel, Robert: *This Old Man*
Uber, David: *A Day at the Camptown Races*
Uber, David: *Beachcombers Dance*
Baron, Samuel: *Impressions of a Parade*

Hanks, Thompson (Toby)
Album Title: *Music of Beatrice Witkin*
Personnel:
Label: Opus One, LP: 12

Witkin, Beatrice: *Breath and Sounds for Tuba and Tape*

Hanks, Thompson (Toby)
Album Title: *Sampler*
Personnel: Gary Kirkpatrick, piano; New York Tuba Quartet; NY City Ballet Orchestra Trombones; Frederic Hand, guitar
Label: Crystal, LP: S395; rereleased 2000, CD: CD395
Telemann, Georg Philipp: *Fantasy in C minor*
Hindemith, Paul: *Three Easy Pieces*
Stevens, John: *Dances*
Tomasi, Henri: *Être Ou Ne Pas Être! (monolog D'Hamlet)* with three trombones
Reck, David: *Five Studies for Tuba Alone*
Clarke, Herbert L.: *From the Shores of the Mighty Pacific*
Wilder, Alec: *Elegy for the Whale* (on CD release only)
Fay, Tom: *Some Music* (on CD release only)
Hand, Frederic: *Toby and Lynn* (on CD release only)

Hanks, Toby
Album Title: *Sonata*
Personnel: David Pearl, piano
Label: Plainsong, 1996, CD: PS101
Castérède, Jacques: *Sonatine*
Schmidt, William: *Sonata for Tuba and Piano*
Wilder, Alec: *Elegy for the Whale*
Koetsier, Jan: *Sonatina*
Schumann, Robert: *Adagio and Allegro in A♭, Op. 70*
Pisciotta, Louis V: *Sonata*

Hanks, Thompson (Toby); see Megules, Karl; *Karl I. Megules, Tuba;* see New York Tuba Quartet; *Tubby's Revenge*

Harclerode, Albert; see Mighty Tubadours

Harrild, Patrick
Album Title: *Kent Youth Wind Orchestra—Music by British Composers*
Personnel: Kent Youth Wind Orchestra, Alan Hutt, conductor
Label: Euphonia, 1993, CD EUPCD012
Ellerby, Martin: *Tuba Concerto*

Harrild, Patrick
Album Title: *Vaughan Williams*
Personnel: London Symphony Orchestra; Bryden Thomson, conductor
Label: Chandos, 1989, LP: ABTD 1379; CD: CHAN-8740
Vaughan Williams, Ralph: *Concerto for Bass Tuba and Orchestra*

Havet, Didier; see Steckar Elephant Tuba Horde/ Steckar Tubapack

Heasley, Tom
Album Title: *On the Sensations of Tone*
Personnel:
Label: Innove Records, 2001, CD: 566
Prelude
Thonis

Heasley, Tom
Album Title: *Where the Earth Meets the Sky*
Personnel:
Label: Hypnos Recordings, 2001, CD
Ground Zero
Western Sky
Monterey Bay
Where the Earth Meets the Sky

Heavy Tuba
Album Title: *Faces—Live*
Personnel: Jonathon Sass, Ali Angerer, Helmut Hackl, Reinhold Schmid, W. Krempl, tubas; Robert Bachner, Anton Miesenberger, Herbert Hubinger, Thomas Aitzetmüller, Petra Krumphuber, Helmut Hörtenhuber, Stefan Pernegger, tenor tubas; Kurt Erlmoser, guitar; Helmar Hill, piano; Wener Lederbauer, bass; Markus Mitterhumer, drums; Herwig Stieger, percussion; Heimo Schmid, leader
Label: ATS, 1994, CD: CD-0450-0894
Hendrix, Jimi: *Voodoo Chile*
Pethel, Stan: *Monday Night*
Sass, Jonathon: *148 Street Blues*
Tautenhahn, G.: *In—Phase—Out*
Thomas, D. C.: *Spinning Wheel*
Sass, Jonathon: *Meltdown*
Bach, Johann Sebastian: *Prelude*
McDonald, Barry: *Las Zorras Pocas*
McDonald, Barry: *Pork Fat and Black-Eyed Peas*
Pecha, Antonin: *Hvezdonicka*
Patorius, Jaco: *Fanny Mae*
Sass, Jonathon: *Going Uptown*

Heavy Tuba
Album Title: *Sagenhaft*
Personnel: Jonathon Sass, Ali Angerer, H. G. Gutternigg, tubas; Robert Bachner, Anton Miesenberger, Petra Krumphuber, Bernard Ortner, tenor tubas; Kurt Erlmoser, guitar; Helmar Hill, piano; Wener Lederbauer, bass; Ewald Zach, drums; Herwig Stieger, percussion; Heimo Schmid, leader
Label: ATS, 1997, CD: CD-0490
Strauss, Richard: *Zarathustra's Reincarnation*
Chase, Bill: *Get It On*
Cech, Christoph: *Sagenhaft*
Sass, Jonathon: *Blue Lights*
Chase, Bill: *Handbags and Gladrags*
Lennon, John, and Paul McCartney: *Helter Skelter*
Chase, Bill: *Livin In Heat*
Sass, Jonathon: *Ripsey's Rumble*
Hill, Helmar: *Ballade*

Hershko, Shmuel "Adi"
Album Title: *And Two-ba Too*
Personnel: Yaron Shavit, piano
Label: ACUM, CD: TO11
Arbel, Chaya: *Roundarounds*
Yoffe, Shlomo: *Andante and Rondo*
Choen, Michael: *Diversita Continua*

Rufeisen, Arie: *A Short Suspense Story*
Gasner, Moshe: *Science Fiction*
Kilon, Moshe: *Sine Nomine*
Levy, Yeuda: *Mediterranean Rondo*

Hershko, Shmuel "Adi"; see Mighty Tubadours; *Ve Iss Da Mighty Tubadours, Ya?*

Hilgers, Walter
Album Title: *Around the World 2*
Personnel: German Brass
Label: German Brass Productions, CD: 27.304 LC 2194

Hilgers, Walter
Album Title: *Bach 2000*
Personnel: German Brass
Label: German Brass Productions, CD: 27.305 LC 2194

Hilgers, Walter
Album Title: *Hindemith: Complete Sonatas Vol. 7*
Personnel: Kalle Randalu, piano
Label: MD&G Records, 1997, CD: #3040697
Hindemith, Paul: *Sonata for Bass Tuba and Piano*

Hilgers, Walter
Album Title: *On Tour*
Personnel: Juergen Wirth, Heiko Triebener, tubas
Label: Kreuz Verlag, CD: LC 06190

Hilgers, Walter
Album Title: *Tuba Tubissima*
Personnel: The Hamburg Brass Soloists; Herbert Drees, organ
Label: Audite Schallplatten, 1988, CD: 97.403
Bach, Johann Sebastian/Hilgers: *Adagio from Toccata, Adagio and Fugue in C major*
Handel, George Friderik/Hilgers: *Sonata in C major, Op. 1, No. 7 for Tuba and Organ*
Bach, Johann Sebastian/Hilgers: *"O Mensch bewein' dein Sünde gross,"* *BWV 622*
Danielssohn, Christer: *Capriccio Da Camera for Solo Tuba and Brass Quintet*
Wilder, Alec/Hilgers: *Suite No. 1 for Tuba and Brass Quintet (Effie the Elephant)*
Barboteu, Georges: *Divertissement for Tuba and Brass Quartet*

Hilgers, Walter
Album Title: *Tubadour*
Personnel: Sebastian Knauer, piano and cembalo
Label: Marcophon, 1993, CD: CD939-2
Bach, Johann Sebastian: *Nun komm'der Heiden Heiland, BWV 659*
Bach, Johann Sebastian: *Sonata II for Tuba and Cembalo*
Wolf, Hugo: *Der Genesene an die Hoffnung*
Crespo, Enrique: *Escenas Latinas*
Monti, Vittorio: *Csárdás*
Danielssohn, Christer: *Concertante Suite for Tuba and Four Horns*

Hilgers, Walter
Album Title: *Tubaroque*
Personnel: Sebastian Knauer, piano; Leonie Brockmann, flute; Christoph Groth, cello
Label: Marcophon, 1994, CD: 949-2
Handel, George Friderik: *Concerto #1 in G*
Bach, Johann Sebastian: *Sarabande from English Suite #2 in A*
Albinoni, Tomaso: *Concerto, Op. 9, No. 2 in D*
Albeniz, Isaac: *aus "España," Op. 165*
Albeniz, Isaac: *aus Cantros de España, Op. 232, No. 2, "Chant d'Amour"*
Fauré, Gabriel: *Pavane, Op. 50*
Ravel, Maurice: *Pièce en form de Habanera*

Hilgers, Walter; see Gerhard Meinl's Tuba Sextet; *Tubas! A Six-Tuba Musical Romp*

Hoffnung, Gerard
Album Title: *Hoffnung Music Festival Concert*
Personnel: Hoffnung Tuba Quartet; Niegel Amberst, Gerard Hoffnung, Jim Powell, John L. Wilson
Label: Angel, 1956, LP: 35500
Chopin, Frédéric/Abrams: *Mazurka No. 49*

Hohmann, Hubert
Album Title: *Bajazzo*
Personnel: Unterbiberger Hofmusik, Claudio Roditi
Label: Himpsl Records, CD: No. 9501

Hohmann, Hubert
Album Title: *Vivamus*
Personnel: Unterbiberger Hofmusik
Label: Himpsl Records, CD: No. 9701

Holmgaard, Lars
Album Title: *Brass Ability* (see also under Andersen, Hans)
Personnel: Royal Danish Brass
Label: Rondo Grammofon, 1993, CD: RCD 8334
Lennon, John, and Paul McCartney/ Holmgaard: *Blackbird*

Hoppert, Manfred
Album Title:
Personnel:
Label: Colosseum Records/Bayerischen Rundfunkes, LP: SM 631
Hindemith, Paul: *Sonata for Bass Tuba and Piano*
Koetsier, Jan: *Concertino for Tuba and String Orchestra*
Koetsier, Jan: *Sonatina for Tuba and Piano*
Lebedev, Alexi: *Concerto in One Movement*
Tscherepnin, Alexander: *Andante for Tuba and Piano*
Vaughan Williams, Ralph: *Concerto for Bass Tuba and Orchestra*

Hornsberger, Albert
Album Title:
Personnel: New York Staff Band—Salvation Army

Label:
Condon, Leslie: *Celestial Morn*

Hötzel, Markus
Album Title: *Variations*
Personnel: American and German Horn Ensemble; Robert Ross, conductor
Label: Saarlandischer Rundfunk (no specific number)
Koetsier, Jan: *Hymne*
Saglietti, Corrado Maria: *Concerto*
Schlenker, Manfred: *Rondo Variato*
Danielssohn, Christer: *Concertante Suite for Tuba and Four Horns*
Hidas, Frigyes: *Allegro Vivace*
Heiden, Bernhard: *Variations for Tuba and Nine Horns*
Gould, Morton: *Tuba Suite for Tuba and Three Horns*
Kalke, Ernst-Thilo: *Mevagissey Tales*
Wilder, Alec: *Nonet*

Hübsch, Carl Ludwig
Album Title: *119 Ways to Begin* (unacc.)
Personnel:
Label: Nurnichtnur, CD: 1021018
45 minutes live aufgenommen im Feedbackstudio Koln

Hübsch, Carl Ludwig
Album Title: *Post No Bills*
Personnel:
Label: Nurnichtnur, 2002, CD: 1030825

Hübsch, Carl Ludwig; see European Tuba Quartet

Irmer, Benjamin
Album Title: *Deutsches Musikschulorchester*
Personnel: Deutsches Musiksculorchester; Hoerg-Peter Weigle, conductor
Label: Aru Musici, AM 1189-2
Frackenpohl, Arthur: *Concertino for Tuba and Strings*

Jacobs, Arnold
Album Title: *Concert Works and Orchestral Excerpts from Wagner, Berlioz, Mahler and More!*
Personnel: Chicago Symphony Orchestra Trombone and Tuba Section
Label: Educational Brass Recordings, 1971, LP: Stereo ERB 1000; reissued 2002, CD
Berlioz, Hector: *Rakoczy (Hungarian) March from "Damnation of Faust" (excerpt)*
Brahms, Johannes/Fote: *Chorale Prelude, Op. 122, No. 8, "Es ist ein Ros' entsprungen"*
Bruckner, Anton: *Symphony No. 4 (first movement excerpt)*
Bruckner, Anton: *Symphony No. 8 (fourth movement excerpt)*
Holst, Gustav: *Mars from "The Planets" (excerpts with tenor tuba)*
Kreines: *Chorale Variations, "Jesu meine Fruede"*
Mahler, Gustav: *Symphony No. 2 (fifth movement excerpt)*
Mahler, Gustav: *Symphony No. 3 (first movement excerpts)*
Tchaikovsky, Peter Ilyitch: *1812 Overture (excerpt)*
Tchaikovsky, Peter Ilyitch: *Symphony No. 6 (fourth movement)*
Tomasi, Henri: *Être Ou Ne Pas Être! (monolog D'Hamlet)* with three trombones
Verdi, Giuseppi: *Nabucco Overture (excerpt)*
Wagner, Richard: *Valkyrie (Magic Fire Music, Ride of the Valkyries)*
Wagner, Richard: *Lohengrin (Introduction to Act III)*
Wagner, Richard: *Tannhauser Overture*

Jacobs, Arnold
Album Title: *Concerto for Tuba*
Personnel: Chicago Symphony Orchestra
Label: Deutsche Grammophone, LP: 2530 906
Vaughan Williams, Ralph: *Concerto for Bass Tuba and Orchestra*

Jacobs, Arnold
Album Title: *Portrait of an Artist*
Personnel: Adolph Herseth, Vincent Cichowicz, William Scarlett, Charles Geyer, trumpets; Dale Clevenger, Richard Oldberg, horns; Jay Friedman, Frank Crisafulli, trombones; Gunnison Music Camp Directors' Band, Robert Hawkins, conductor; Chicago Symphony Orchestra, Carlo Maria Giulini, Fritz Reiner, James Levine, Jean Martinon, Daniel Barenboim, conductors
Label: Summit Records, 2000, CD: SMT 267
Buxtehude, Dietrich: *Fanfare*
Strauss, Richard: *Concerto No. 1 for Horn, Op. 11*
Rimsky-Korsakov, Nicholas: *Scheherezade*
Monti, Vittorio: *Csárdás*
Clarke, Herbert L.: *Carnival of Venice*
Vaughan Williams, Ralph: *Concerto for Bass Tuba and Orchestra (movement I)*
Gugel/Pottag: *Etude No. 24*
Gabrieli, Giovanni: *Canzon per Sonare No. 2*
Wagner, Richard: *Lohengrin (Introduction to Act III)*
Berlioz, Hector: *Dies Irae from "Symphonie Fantastique"*
Bozza, Eugène: *Sonatine*
Berlioz, Hector: *Romeo and Juliet excerpt*
Bartók, Béla: *Concerto for Orchestra excerpt*
Stravinsky, Igor: *Bear Solo from "Petrouchka"*
Neilsen, Carl: *Symphony No. 4 excerpt*
Bruckner, Anton: *Symphony No. 4*
Mussorgsky, Modest/Ravel: *Great Gate of Kiev from "Pictures at an Exhibition"*

Jacobs, Arnold
Album Title:
Personnel: Directors Band, Gunnison Music Camp; Robert Hawkins, conductor
Label: Century Recordings, LP: V15357

Strauss, Richard: *Concerto No. 1 for Horn, Op. 11*
Jacobs, Arnold; see Bell, William; *The Directors Band*
Jae Young, Heo
Album Title: *Tuba Recital—Live*
Personnel: Kyung Hee Lee, piano; Soung Jong Kim, piano; Kyung Won Brass Ensemble
Label: SEM Gramophone, 1995, CD DE 0025
Wilder, Alec: *Sonata No. 1 for Tuba and Piano*
Leopold, Louis J.: *Promendade*
Uber, David: *Ballad of Enob Mort*
Danielssohn, Christer: *Capriccio Da Camera for Solo Tuba and Brass Quintet*
Gregson, Edward: *Tuba Concerto*
Smith, Claude T.: *Ballade and Presto Dance*
Monti, Vittorio: *Csárdás*
Grieg, Edvard: *Solvejg's Lied*
Rimsky-Korsakov, Nicholas: *Flight of the Bumblebee*
Jae Young, Heo
Album Title: *Tuba Recital 2*
Personnel: Jee-Won Lee, piano
Label: TMK Köln, 1996, CD: 9773
Telemann, Georg Philipp: *Sonata in F minor for Bassoon*
Schubert, Franz Peter: *Arpeggione Sonata*
Uber, David: *Sonata for Bass Tuba and Piano*
Kraft, William: *Encounters II for Solo Tuba*
Uber, David: *Romance*
Arban, Jean-Baptiste: *Variations on the "Carnival of Venice"*
Rachmaninoff, Sergei: *Vocalise, Op. 34, No. 14*
Jae Young, Heo
Album Title: *Tuba Recital 3*
Personnel: Young Kyung Hyun, piano
Label: Woong-Jin Records, 1999, CD:
Capuzzi, Antonio/Catelinet: *Andante and Rondo*
Barat, Joseph Eduoard: *Introduction and Dance*
Catozzi, A.: *Beelzebub*
Bach, Johann Sebastian: *Sonata in E♭Major*
Penderecki, Krzysztof: *Capriccio for Solo Tuba*
Cummings, Barton: *Fantasia Breve*
Arban, Jean-Baptiste: *Fantaisie and Variations on the "Carnival of Venice"*
Jarvis, Jeffrey
Album Title: *Athletic Conveyances—Music for Tuba and Percussion*
Personnel: Mark Ford, percussion; East Carolina University Percussion Ensemble
Label: AR University, 1999, CD: AUR CD 3061
Penn, William: *Capriccio for Tuba and Marimba*
Taggart, Mark: *Athletic Conveyance*
Wyre, John: *Maruba*
Hartley, Walter: *Concerto for Tuba and Percussion Orchestra*
Jenkel, Herbert
Album Title: *Tubby the Tuba*
Personnel: All-American Orchestra; Leon Barzin, conductor; Victor Jory, narrator
Label: Columbia Records, 1945, LP: CL 671
Kleinsinger, George, and Paul Tripp: *Tubby the Tuba*
Jenkins, James; see Stevens, John; *Power*
Johns, Steven
Album Title: *Affirmations: Four Works by Richard Wilson*
Personnel:
Label: Albany Records, 2000, CD: #389
Wilson, Richard Edward: *Civilization and Its Discontents,* for solo tuba
Wilson, Richard Edward: *Transfigured Goat,* for solo tuba
Johns, Steven; see New York Tuba Quartet; *Tubby's Revenge*
Johnson, Howard
Album Title: *Album, Album*
Personnel: Jack De Johnette's Special Edition
Label: ECM, LP: 1280 823 467-1 (LC 2516)
Johnson, Howard: *Album, Album*
Johnson, Howard
Album Title: *But Not for Me: A Chet Baker Studio Discovery*
Personnel: Chet Baker, trumpet; James Newton, flute; Kenny Barron, piano; Charlie Haden, bass; Ben Riley, drums
Label: Stash Records, 1994, CD: ST-CD-584
Lament
Davis, Miles: *Four*
Mulligan, Gerry: *Line for Lyons*
Haden, Charlie: *Ellen David*
Gershwin, George and Ira: *But Not for Me*
Luxion, Dennis: *Prayer for the Newborn*
Johnson, Howard
Album Title: *Composers Workshop Ensemble*
Personnel: Composers Workshop Ensemble
Label: Strata-East Records, 1972, LP: SES 1972-3
Taylor, Coleridge: *Substructure*
Smith, Warren: *Lament*
Smith, Warren: *Blues for E. L. C.*
Monk, Thelonius: *Blues by Monk*
Smith, Warren: *Hello Julius*
Smith, Warren: *Introduction to the Blues*
Johnson, Howard
Album Title: *Dreamer*
Personnel: Erica Lindsay, tenor saxophone; Francesca Tanksley, piano; Anthony Cox, bass; Newman Baker, drums; Robin Eubanks, trombone
Label: Candid, 1989, CD: 79040
Lindsay, Erica: *First Movement*
Ellington, Edward Kennedy "Duke": *Day Dream*

Lindsay, Erica: *Walking Together*
Lindsay, Erica: *Dreamer*
Lindsay, Erica: *At the Last Moment*
Lindsay, Erica: *Gratitude*

Johnson, Howard
Album Title: *Gunther Schuller—Jumpin' in the Future*
Personnel: George Garzone, tenor saxophone; Kenny Wenzel, Rick Stepton, trombones; Bevan Manson, piano; Matt Darrieu, alto saxophone; George Schuller, drums
Label: GM Recordings, 1998, CD: GM3010CD
Kern, Jerome/Schuller: *Yesterdays*

Johnson, Howard
Album Title: *Howard Johnson & Gravity!!!*
Personnel: Dave Bargeron, Joe Daley, Nedra Johnson, Carl Kleinsteuber, Tom Malone, Earl McIntyre, Marcus Rojas, Bob Stewart, tubas; Paul Shaffer, keyboards
Label: Verve, 1996, CD: 314 531 021-2
Pullen, Don: *Big Alice*
Nelson, Oliver: *Stolen Moments*
Perkinson, Coleridge: *Way 'Cross Georgia*
Kelly, Wynton: *Kelly Blue*
Johnson, Howard: *Be No Evil*
Kern, Jerome/Harbach: *Yesterdays*
Johnson, Howard: *Here Comes Sonny Man*
McLean, Jackie: *Appointment in Ghana*
Monk, Thelonius: *'Round Midnight*
Blue, Kelly: *And Then Again. . .*

Johnson, Howard
Album Title: *Mitschnitte vom Jazz Fest Berlin 1984*
Personnel:
Label: Bayerischen Rundfunk

Johnson, Howard
Album Title: *The Rest of Gil Evans Live at Royal Festival Hall, London*
Personnel:
Label: Mole Records, 1978, LP:
Where Flamingos Fly

Johnson, Howard
Album Title: *Right Now!*
Personnel: Dave Bargeron, Joe Daley, Carl Kleinsteuber, Earl McIntyre, Bob Stewart, tubas; Ray Chew, piano; James Cammack, bass; Kenwood Dennard, drums; Taj Mahal, vocals
Label: Verve, 1997, CD: 314 537 801-2
Tolliver, Charles: *Right Now*
Barron, Ronnie: *It's Getter Harder to Survive*
Hancock, Herbie: *Tell Me a Bedtime Story*
Hampton, Slide: *Frame for the Blues*
Greene, Joe: *Don't Let the Sun Catch You Cryin'*
Semanya, Caiphus: *Ma-Ma*
Evans, Gil: *Svengali's Summer/Waltz*
John, Little Willie:*Fever*
Johnson, Howard:*O Raggedy Man*

Johnson, Howard
Album Title: *Roadway*
Personnel: Gary Wittner, guitar; Bruce Ditmas, drums; Dominic Richards, bass
Label: Invisible Music, 1999, CD:
Monk, Thelonius: *Thelonius*
Wittner, Gary: *Chompers*
Miller, Yount, Williams: *Release Me*
Wittner, Gary: *Squeaky*
Monk, Thelonius: *Criss-Cross*
Monk, Thelonius: *Crespuscule with Nellie*
Wittner, Gary: *Roadway*
Traditional: *John Brown's Body*
Wittner, Gary: *Another Moment in the Past*
Wittner, Gary: *Big Forehead*
Williams, Hank: *I'm So Lonesome I Could Cry*
Wittner, Gary: *Year's End*

Johnson, Howard
Album Title: *Second Childhood*
Personnel: Phoebe Snow; Howard Johnson, John Stevens, Carleton Green, Joseph Daley
Label: Columbia, 1976, LP: 33952
Snow, Phoebe: *Sweet Disposition* (tubas arranged by Howard Johnson)

Johnson, Howard
Album Title: *Taj Mahal: The Real Thing*
Personnel: Bob Stewart, Howard Johnson, Joseph Daley, Earl McIntyre, tubas
Label: Columbia Records, 1971, LP: CG 30619
Thomas, Henry/Mahal: *Fishin' Blues*
Mahal, Taj: *Ain't Gwine to Whistle Dixie Any Mo'*
Mahal, Taj: *Sweet Mama Janisse*
Mahal, Taj: *Going Up to the Country and Paint My Mailbox Blue*
Mahal, Taj: *Big Kneed Gal*
Johnson, Blind Willie/Mahal: *You're Going to Need Somebody on Your Bond*
Mahal, Taj: *Tom and Sally Drake*
Estes, Sleepy John/Mahal: *Diving Duck Blues*
Mahal, Taj: John, *Ain't It Hard?*
Mahal, Taj: *You Ain't No Streetwalker, Mama Honey, But I Do Love the Way You Strutt Your Stuff*

Johnson, Howard
Album Title:
Personnel:
Label: East Coasting, LP: JW001311
Johnson, Howard: *Music Written for Monterey*

Johnson, Howard
Album Title:
Personnel: Dicky Wells
Label: Prestige, LP: PRT 7593

Johnson, John Thomas (Tommy)
Album Title: *Beetlejuice [motion picture soundtrack]*
Personnel: Music by Danny Elfman
Label: Geffin Records, 1988, CD: 24202-2; CS: M5G-24202

Johnson, John Thomas (Tommy)
Album Title: *Brass Tacks*
Personnel: Sharon Davis, piano
Label: Western International Music, LP: WIMR-14
Schmidt, William: *Serenade for Tuba and Piano*

Johnson, John Thomas (Tommy)
Album Title: *Capricorn One [motion picture soundtrack]*
Personnel: Music by Jerry Goldsmith
Label: Warner Brothers

Johnson, John Thomas (Tommy)
Album Title: *Crimson Tide [motion picture soundtrack]*
Personnel: Music by Hans Zimmer
Label:

Johnson, John Thomas (Tommy)
Album Title: *Jaws [motion picture soundtrack]*
Personnel: Music by John Williams
Label: Twentieth Century Fox/MCA, 1974

Johnson, John Thomas (Tommy)
Album Title: *Kermit the Frog Presents the Muppet Musicians of Bremen [TV soundtrack]*
Personnel: Guido Basso, trumpet; Ed Bickert, banjo; Rob McConnell, trombone; Moe Koffman, clarinet; lyrics by Jerry Juhl; music by Jack Elliott
Label: Children's Records of America, 1972, LP: CTW 22073

Johnson, John Thomas (Tommy)
Album Title: *The Manhattan Transfer Meets Tubby the Tuba*
Personnel: Naples Philharmonic (Florida); Tim Russell, conductor
Label: Summit Records, 1993, CD: DCD152
Kleinsinger, George, and Paul Tripp: *Tubby the Tuba*
Kleinsinger, George, and Paul Tripp: *Tubby the Tuba Joins the Circus*
Kleinsinger, George, and Paul Tripp: *Tubby the Tuba Joins the Jazz Band*
Kleinsinger, George, and Paul Tripp: *The Further Adventures of Tubby the Tuba*

Johnson, John Thomas (Tommy)
Album Title: *Music from the TV Series—The Mancini Generation*
Personnel: Henry Mancini and his Orchestra
Label: RCA Victor, 1972, LP: LSP-4689
Mancini, Henry: *Amazing Grace*

Johnson, John Thomas (Tommy)
Album Title: *Pearl Harbor [motion picture soundtrack]*
Personnel: Music by Hans Zimmer
Label:

Johnson, John Thomas (Tommy)
Album Title: *Planet of the Apes [motion picture soundtrack]*
Personnel: Music by Danny Elfman
Label:

Johnson, John Thomas (Tommy)
Album Title: *Rampal Plays Scott Joplin*
Personnel: Jean-Pierre Rampal, flute; John Steele Ritter, piano and harpsichord; Shelly Manne, drums
Label: Columbia Records, 1983, LP: M 37818
Joplin, Scott: *Maple Leaf Rag*
Joplin, Scott: *Elite Syncopations*
Joplin, Scott: *Combination March*
Joplin, Scott: *The Entertainer*
Joplin, Scott: *The Cascades*
Joplin, Scott: *Cleopha*
Joplin, Scott: *The Ragtime Dance*
Joplin, Scott: *The Chrysanthemum*
Joplin, Scott: *The Favorite*
Joplin, Scott: *Original Rags*
Joplin, Scott: *Harmony Club Waltz*
Joplin, Scott: *Great Crush Collision*

Johnson, John Thomas (Tommy)
Album Title: *Spiderman [motion picture soundtrack]*
Personnel: Music by Danny Elfman
Label:

Johnson, John Thomas (Tommy)
Album Title: *Spiderman 2 [motion picture soundtrack]*
Personnel: Music by Danny Elfman
Label:

Johnson, John Thomas (Tommy)
Album Title: *Star Trek—The Motion Picture [motion picture soundtrack]*
Personnel: Music by Jerry Goldsmith
Label: Columbia, 1979, CD: CK-3633; CS: PST-36334

Johnson, John Thomas (Tommy)
Album Title: *The Tigger Movie [motion picture soundtrack]*
Personnel: Music by Harry Gregson-Williams
Label: Disney

Johnson, John Thomas (Tommy)
Album Title: *Tubby the Tuba*
Personnel: Annette Funicello, narrator
Label: Disneyland 1963, LP: 1287
Kleinsinger, George, and Paul Tripp: *Tubby the Tuba*

Johnson, John Thomas (Tommy); see Pearson, Norm; *Edward Scissorhands;* see Self, James; *The Big Stretch*

Johnson, Nedra; see Johnson, Howard; *Howard Johnson & Gravity!!!*

Joseph, Kirk
Album Title: *Mardi Gras in Montreaux*
Personnel: Dirty Dozen Brass Band
Label: Rounder Records, 1985, CD: 2052

Joseph, Kirk
Album Title: *My Feet Can't Fail Me Now*
Personnel: Dirty Dozen Brass Band

Label: Concord Jazz, 1984, GW-3005
Joseph, Kirk
Album Title: *Voodoo*
Personnel: Dirty Dozen Brass Band
Label: Columbia Records, 1987, FC 45042
Joseph, Kirk
Album Title: *Whatcha Gonna Do for the Rest of Your Life*
Personnel: The Dirty Dozen Brass Band
Label: Columbia, 1991, CD: 47383
Joseph, Kirk; see New Orleans Jazz Bands; *Down Yonder*
Jun, Obana; see Rustic Bari-Tuba Ensemble
Kaenzig, Fritz
Album Title: *Do It! Play Tuba*
Personnel:
Label: GIA Publications, method book and CD: MLR-481
Kaenzig, Fritz
Album Title: *Hindemith: Sonatas for Brass*
Personnel: Siglind Bruhn, piano
Label: Equilibrium Records, 1999, CD: 10
Hindemith, Paul: *Sonata for Bass Tuba and Piano*
Kaenzig, Fritz
Album Title: *Mixed Doubles*
Michael Tunnell, trumpet; Meme Tunnell, piano
Label: Coronet, LP: LPS 3210; reissued 1995, CD COR-401-2
White, Donald: Sonata for Tuba and Piano
Liptak, David: *Mixed Doubles* for trumpet, tuba, violin, and contrabass
McFarland, Michael: *Sketches* (CD only)
Kaenzig, Fritz; see Symphonia
Karella, Clarence
Album Title: *Danny Kaye's Hans Christian Andersen*
Personnel: Danny Kaye, narrator; Victor Young Orchestra
Label: Decca, LP: DL 8479
Kleinsinger, George, and Paul Tripp: *Tubby the Tuba*
Kleinsinger, George, and Paul Tripp: *Tubby the Tuba at the Circus*
King, Ian
Album Title: *Golden Sounds*
Personnel:
Label:
Falla, Manuel de
Corelli, Archangelo
Rimsky-Korsakov, Nicholas
Debussy, Claude
Ravel, Maurice
Gershwin, George
King, Ian
Album Title: *Tuba Magnifique*
Personnel: Margaret Schofield, Dean Sky-Lucas, pianos
Label: Move Records, 2001, CD: MD3236
Albeniz, Isaac: *Malagueña*
Granados, Enrique: *Spanish Dance, Op. 37, Nos. 2 and 5/Intermezzo from "Goyescas"*
Bach, Johann Sebastian: *Two Bourrees from Suite No. 3 for Solo Cello*
Bach, Johann Sebastian: *Two Menuets and Gigue from Suite No. 1 for Solo Cello*
Kreisler, Fritz: *Sch'n Rosmarin/Liebeslied/ Liebesfreud/Caprice Viennois*
Saint-Saëns, Camille: *The Swan from "Carnival of the Animals"*
Fauré, Gabriel: *Sicilienne*
Fauré, Gabriel: *Après un Rêve*
Traditional: *Deep River/Swing Low Sweet Chariot*
Cassado: *Requiebros,*
Monti, Vittorio: *Csárdás*
King, Ian
Album Title: *Tuba Recital*
Personnel: Paul Hamberger, Margaret Schofield, pianos
Label: Move Records, 2000 (recorded 1970), CD: MD3226
Bach, Johann Sebastian: *Viola da Gamba Sonata #1*
Bach, Johann Sebastian: *Viola da Gamba Sonata in G*
Vivaldi, Antonio: *Cello Sonata #5 in E*
Beethoven, Ludwig van: *Horn Sonata in F, Op. 17*
Hindemith, Paul: *Sonata for Bass Tuba and Piano*
King, Ian
Album Title:
Personnel: SWF Orchester
Label: SWF, 1962, LP: 11652
Vaughan Williams, Ralph: *Concerto for Bass Tuba and Orchestra*
Kirk, David
Album Title: *Music of Leroy Osmon*
Personnel:
Label: Mark, 1996, CD: MCD 1975
Osmon, Leroy: *Concert Etudes for Solo Tuba*
Kleinsteuber, Carl; see Johnson, Howard; *Howard Johnson & Gravity!!!; Right Now!*
Kochenour, Andy; see Dixie Power Trio
Korevaar, David
Album Title: *Hindemith: The 5 Sonatas for Brass and Piano*
Personnel: Joseph Anderer, piano
Label: Kleos, 2002, CD: #5118
Hindemith, Paul: *Sonata for Bass Tuba and Piano*
Krempl, W; see Heavy Tuba
Krzywicki, Paul
Album Title: *The Philadelphia Lower Brass Section*
Personnel: M. Dee Stewart, Glenn Dodson, Joseph Alessi, Charles Vernon
Label: Excerpt Recording Company, LP:
Labeyrie, Stéphane
Album Title: *Rencontre*

Personnel: Gaëlle Thouvenin, harp; Thierry Thibault, tuba; Jean-Philippe Chavey, horn; Philippe Monferan and Sylvaine Vallespir, piano
Label: Edition BIM, CD:
Madsen, Trygve: *Sonate pour tuba et piano*
Bizet, Georges: *Extrait des pêcheurs de perles*
Schubert, Franz Peter: *Lieder, Op. 135, D921*
Boismortier, Joseph Bodin: *Deuxième sonate, Op. XIV*
Kellaway, Roger: *Sonoro* pour tuba, cor, et piano
Kellaway, Roger: *Dance of the Ocean Breeze* pour tuba, cor, et piano
Penderecki, Krzysztof: *Capriccio for Solo Tuba*
Emler, Andy: *Tubastone*

Lacen, Anthony "Tuba Fats"
Album Title: *Anthony "Tuba Fats" Lacen*
Personnel: Rue Conti Jazz Band; Orange Kellin; Dan Pawson
Label: GHB Records, 1995, CD: BCD-344
My Memphis Baby
Oh How I Miss You Tonight
Ting a Ling
Muskrat Ramble
In the Sweet Bye and Bye
Yearning
Shake It and Break It
Big Leg Woman
In the Gloryland

Lacen, Anthony "Tuba Fats"; see New Orleans Jazz Bands; *Down Yonder*

Landréat, Daniel; see Steckar Elephant Tuba Horde/Steckar Tubapack

Lawhern, Tim
Album Title: *Mr. Jack Daniel's Original Silver Cornet Band on Tour across America*
Personnel: Mr. Jack Daniel's Original Silver Cornet Band
Label: Silver Cornet Productions CD
Rollinson, T. H.: *Rocked in the Cradle of the Deep*

LeBlanc, Robert
Album Title: *Euphonium Favorites for Recital and Contest*
Personnel: Paul Droste, euphonium
Label: Coronet, 1986, LP: LPS 3203
Hartley, Walter: *Bivalve Suite for Euphonium and Tuba*

LeBlanc, Robert
Album Title: *Robert LeBlanc Tuba Solos*
Personnel: Myra Baker, piano
Label: Coronet, LP: 1721
Holmes, Paul: *Lento*
Beach, Bennie: *Lamento*
Hartley, Walter: *Sonata*
Rachmaninoff, Sergei: *Vocalise Op. 34, No. 14*
Beversdorf, Thomas: *Sonata for Bass Tuba and Piano*

LeClair, David
Album Title: *Galina Ustvolskaya Nr. 2*
Personnel: Marianne Schroeder, piano; Felix Renggli, piccolo
Label: Hat Art, 1993, CD: CD 6130
Ustvolskaya, Galina: *Dona Nobis Pacem for Piccolo, Tuba and Piano*

LeClair, David; see Contraband (The)

Legris, Philippe
Album Title: *Musical Feeling (Feeling des Grands Solistes)*
Personnel: Orchestre D'Harmonie de la Police Nationale (French National Police Force Band); Benoit Girault, conductor
Label: Pierre Verany, 1994, CD: PV 794115
Steckar, Marc: *"Tubaobab"—Concerto in Four Movements for Tuba and Big Wind Band*

Legris, Philippe
Album Title: *Tuba "Solo"*
Personnel:
Label: 1995, CD: 020 DDD
Bach, Johann Sebastian: *Prelude*
Creuze, Roland: *Eria*
Katzenbeier, Hubert: *Drei Spielstucke*
Penderecki, Krzysztof: *Capriccio for Solo Tuba*
Persichetti, Vincent: *Serenade No. 12*
Poulheim, Bert: *Groteske Miniaturen*
Steckar, Marc: *Tu bats le fer etc . . .*
Tisne, Antoine: *Monodie III*
Wefelmeyer, Bernd: *Sieben Durch Acht*

Legris, Philippe; see Steckar Elephant Tuba Horde/Steckar Tubapack

Lehr, David "Red"
Album Title: *The Jazz Incredibles . . . an Incredible Trio*
Personnel: John Becker, banjo; Jean Kitrell, piano
Label: Red Lehr, LP: JI-84; CS: MCRP-85
Williams, Spencer: *Basin Street Blues*
Lockhart and Seitz: *The World Is Waiting for the Sunrise*
Muir and Edgar: *Ragtime Rosie*
Steele and Melrose: *High Society*
Joplin, Scott: *Original Rags*
Robin and Shavers: *Undecided Now*
Fields and McHugh: *I Can't Give You Anything but Love*
Cumana
Hanley, James F.: *Zing Went the Strings of My Heart*
Pollack, Lew: *That's A-Plenty*

Lehr, David "Red"
Album Title: *The Old St. Louis Levee Band Live at the Rockville Opry House*
Personnel: The Old St. Louis Levee Band
Label: LP: OSLLB-85-104; CS:
Hanley and McDonald: *Indiana*
Oh, Daddy
Henderson, Ray: *Alabamy Bound*
Ringle and Meinken: *Wabash Blues*
Traditional: *Wabash Cannonball*

Morton, F. "Jelly Roll": *Wolverine Blues*
Traditional: *Just a Closer Walk with Thee*
DeCosta and LaRocca: *Tiger Rag*
Howe, Julia Ward: *Battle Hymn of the Republic*

Lehr, David "Red"
Album Title: *The Old St. Louis Levee Band Plays the Blues*
Personnel: The Old St. Louis Levee Band
Label: Red Lehr, LP: OSLLB-1091; CS:
Handy, W. C.: *St. Louis Blues*
Williams, Spencer: *Basin Street Blues*
Swanstone, McCarron, and Morgan: *The Blues My Naughty Sweetie Gives to Me*
Trombone Man Blues
Williams, Clarence, and Williams, Spencer: *Royal Garden Blues*
Handy, W. C.: *Beale Street Blues*
Schoebel, Maras, and Rapollo: *Farewell Blues*

Lidsle, Harri
Album Title: *Concertos for Tuba, French Horn and Trombone*
Personnel: Oulu Symphony Orchestra (Finland); Atso Almila, conductor
Label: MILS, 1996, CD: MILS 9651
Arutiunian, Alexander: *Concerto for Tuba and Orchestra*

Lienard, Bernard
Album Title: *D'un Souffle de Lumiere*
Personnel: Nicolas Dessenne, piano; Valerie Hartmann-Claverie, ondes martenot
Label: NVA Production, 1995, CD: PT 1995.11.010
Arban, Jean-Baptiste: *Fantaisie Brillante*
Castérède, Jacques: *Fantaisie Concertante*
Creuze, Roland: *D'un Souffle de Lumiere*
Ecclés, Henry: *Sonate*

Lienard, Bernard; see Steckar Elephant Tuba Horde

Lind, Michael
Album Title: *Christer Torgé, Trombone, and Michael Lind, Tuba*
Personnel: Steven Harlos, piano
Label: Grammofonfirma BIS, 1978, LP: BIS LP 95 (Reissued 1996, BIS CD 95)
Marcello, Benedetto: *Sonata in F major for Tuba and Piano*
Hindemith, Paul: *Sonata for Bass Tuba and Piano*
Uber, David: *Double Portraits for Trombone and Tuba*

Lind, Michael
Album Title: *Michael Lind—Tuba*
Personnel: Swedish Radio Symphony Orchestra; Stig Westerberg, conductor; Andreas Roehn, Violin Solo; Stockholm Philharmonic Brass Ensemble; Dlaes Stroemblad and Gunnar Schmidt, trumpets; John Petersen/Rune Bodin, trombone; Ib Lanzky-Otto, French Horn; Bjoern Liljequist, percussion; Malmoe Symphony Orchestra; Gunnar Stern, conductor; Royal Stockholm Philharmonic Orchestra; Leif Segerstam, conductor
Label: Caprice Records, 1979, LP: CAP 1143; CD: CAP 21493
Lundquist, Torbjørn Iwan: *Landscape for Tuba and Strings*
Vaughan Williams, Ralph: *Concerto for Bass Tuba and Orchestra*
Jacobsen, Julius: *Tuba Buffo*
Nilsson, Bo: *Bass, for Solo Tuba and Percussion*

Lind, Michael
Album Title: *Michael Lind Plays Tuba*
Personnel: Steve Harlos, piano; Stockholm Philharmonic Winds and Brass
Label: Four Leaf Records, 1980, LP: FLC 5045; CD: FLC CD 102
Arban, Jean-Baptiste: *Fantaisie and Variations on the "Carnival of Venice"*
Koch, Erland von: *Monolog No. 9 for Unaccompanied Tuba*
Jacobsen, Julius: *Tuba Ballet for Tuba and Woodwind Quintet*
Wilder, Alec: *Suite No. 1 for Tuba and Piano (Effie the Elephant)*
Danielssohn, Christer: *Concertante Suite for Tuba and Four Horns*
Gregson, Edward: *Tuba Concerto* (on CD only)

Lind, Michael
Album Title: *National Brass Band Festival 1979*
Personnel: Besses o' th' Barn Brass Band; Roy Newsome, conductor
Label: Chandos, 1979, LP: BBR 103
Arban, Jean-Baptiste: *Fantaisie and Variations on the "Carnival of Venice"*

Lind, Michael
Album Title: *Ole Schmidt Plays Ole Schmidt: Concertos for Brass Instruments*
Personnel: Aarhus Symphony Orchestra; Ole Schmidt, conductor
Label: Edition Wilhelm Hansen, LP: LPWH 111
Schmidt, Ole: *Concerto for Tuba and Orchestra*

Lind, Michael
Album Title: *Paul Hindemith: Chamber Music*
Personnel: Steven Harlos, piano
Label: BIS, 1994, CD: #159
Hindemith, Paul: *Sonata for Bass Tuba and Piano*

Lind, Michael
Album Title: *Virtuoso Tuba*
Personnel: Malmo Symphony Orchestra; Gunnar Stern, conductor; Royal Stockholm Philharmonic Orchestra; Leif Segerstam, conductor
Label: Caprice, 1995, CD: CAP 21493
Lundquist, Torbjørn Iwan: *Landscape for Tuba and Strings*

Danielssohn, Christer: *Capriccio Da Camera for Solo Tuba and Brass Quintet*
Nilsson, Bo: *Bass, for Solo Tuba and Percussion*
Jacobsen, Julius: *Tuba Buffo*
Vaughan Williams, Ralph: *Concerto for Bass Tuba and Orchestra*

Lind, Michael
Album Title:
Personnel: Stockholm Philharmonic Brass Ensemble
Label: Swedish Society Discofil, LP: SLT-33254
Danielssohn, Christer: *Capriccio Da Camera for Solo Tuba and Brass Quintet*

Lind, Michael; see Scandinavian Tuba Jazz

Lusher, David; see Mighty Tubadours

M'N'M Trio
Album Title: *Halfway to Heaven*
Personnel: Eli Newberger, tuba; Jimmy Mazzy, banjo and vocals; Joe Muranyi, clarinet and vocals
Label: Stomp Off, 1996, CD: CD-1319
Eaton and Shand: *I Double Dare You*
You'll Long for Me
Salama and Grebenka: *Dark Eyes*
Young, Schuster, and Little: *In a Shanty in Old Town Sweet Girl*
Morton, F. "Jelly Roll": *Good Old New York*
Jolson and Brown: *Sonny Boy*
Barbarin and Armstrong: *Don't Forget to Mess Around*
De Rose and Hill: *So Little Time*
Straight and Kahn: *Santa Claus Blues*
Theard, Sam: *You Rascal You*
Brooks, George: *Send Me to the 'Lectric Chair*
Brooks and Chaplin: *You Wonderful You*
Rose and Richman: *Muddy Water*
Venable and Armstrong: *Irish Black Bottom*
Grainger and Robbins: *Tain't Nobody's Bizness If I Do*
Dubin and Russell: *Half-Way to Heaven*
Brooks, Shelton: *Jazzbo Jenkins*

Maierhofer, Josef
Album Title: *Secunda Volta vom Pannonischen Blasorchester*
Personnel: Pannonischen Blasorchester; Peter Forcher, conductor
Label: Sica-Sound-Music, 1992, CD: CD 020145-2; CS: MC 020-145-4
Gregson, Edward: *Tuba Concerto*

Mallon, Barney
Album Title: *Circus Time with the Dukes of Dixieland*
Personnel: Frank Assunto, trumpet; Fred Assunto, trombone; Jack Mahev, clarinet; Stanley Mendelson, piano; Tommy Rundell, drums
Label: Audio Fidelity, LP: AFLP 1863
Petrie, H. W./Lamb: *Asleep in the Deep*

Malone, Tom; see Johnson, Howard; *Howard Johnson & Gravity!!!*

Marshall, Oren
Album Title: *Clowning Around: London Brass Entertains*
Personnel: London Brass
Label: Teldec, 1990, CD: 2292-46069-2
Bach, Johann Sebastian: *Badinerie*

Martin, Rex; see Symphonia

Martinez, Jorge
Album Title: *Migraciones*
Personnel:
Label: Música de Arte, 1999, CD

Mas, Vicente Navarro
Album Title:
Personnel: Fermin Ruiz Escovez, flute
Label: Discophon
Casas, Bartolomé Perez/Mas: *Concerto for Tuba*
Escovez, Fermin Ruiz: *Dualismo for Tuba and Flute*

Matteson, Rich
Album Title: *Best of Dixieland*
Personnel: Bob Scobey's Frisco Jazz Band; Rich Matteson, helicon
Label: RCA Victor, 1964, LP: LSP-2982(e)
Barris and Cavanaugh: *Mississippi Mud*

Matteson, Rich
Album Title: *18th and 19th on Chestnut Street*
Personnel: Bob Scobey's Frisco Jazz Band; Rich Matteson, helicon
Label: RCA Victor, 1959, LP:

Matteson, Rich
Album Title: *Louie and the Dukes of Dixieland*
Personnel: Frank Assunto, trumpet; Fred Assunto, trombone; Jerry Fuller, clarinet; Jack Assunto, banjo; Stanley Mendelson, piano; Owen Mahoney, drums
Label: Audio Fidelity, 1960, LP: AFSD 5924 (Reissued as CD: S522; CS: S524, Leisure Audio, 1988)
Charles, Moten, and Hayes: *South*
Robbins, Allen, and Sheafe: *Washington and Lee Swing*
Rose, Jolson, and DeSylva: *Avalon*
Bernie, Pinkard, and Casey: *Sweet Georgia Brown*
Furber and Braham: *Limehouse Blues*

Matteson, Rich
Album Title: *The Riverboat Five on a Swinging Date*
Personnel: Rich Matteson, helicon; Rick Nelson, trombone; Baird Jones, piano; Ed Reed, clarinet; Nappy Lamare, banjo; Ray Baudue, drums
Label: Mercury, 1959, LP: MG 20509
Palmer and Williams: *I Found a New Baby*
Bernie, Pinkard, and Casey: *Sweet Georgia Brown*

Matteson, Rich
Album Title: *Rompin' and Stompin'*
Personnel: Bob Scobey's Frisco Jazz Band; Rich Matteson, helicon

Label: RCA Victor, 1958, LP: LSP 2086
The Chant
Original Dixieland Jazz Band: *Fidgety Feet*
Matteson, Rich
Album Title: *Something's Always Happening on the River*
Personnel: Bob Scobey's Frisco Jazz Band; Rich Matteson, helicon and bass trumpet
Label: RCA Victor, 1958, LP: LPM-1889
Barris and Cavanaugh: *Mississippi Mud Riverboat Shuffle*
Foster, Stephen: *Swannee River*
Matteson, Rich
Album Title: *Sound of the Wasp*
Personnel: Rich Matteson, tuba; Phil Wilson, trombone; Jack Peterson, guitar; Lyle Mays, piano; Ed Soph, drums; Kirby Stewart, bass
Label: ASI Records, 1975, LP: 203
Wilson, Phil: *The Sound of the Wasp*
Wilson, Phil: *What's Her Name?*
Matteson, Rich
Album Title: *Tuba-Euphonium Legacy Project, Volume 1*
Personnel: Louis Armstrong, Riverboat Five, Dukes of Dixieland, Phil Wilson, Pete Barbutti
Palmer and Williams: *I Found a New Baby*
Rose, Jolson, and DeSylva: *Avalon*
Bernie, Pinkard, and Casey: *Sweet Georgia Brown*
The Prisoner's Song
Wilson, Phil: *I'll Never Forget Old What's Her Name*
Wilson, Phil: *The Sound of the Wasp*
Matteson-Phillips TubaJazz Consort
Album Title: *Matteson-Phillips TubaJazz Consort*
Personnel: Rich Matteson, Ashley Alexander, Buddy Baker, euphoniums; Harvey Phillips, Dan Perantoni, Winston Morris, tubas; Jack Petersen, guitar; Tommy Ferguson, Dan Haerle, piano; Rufus Reid, bass; Ed Soph, drums
Label: A & R Records, 1976, LP:
Silver, Horace/Matteson: *Gregory Is Here*
Jarrett, Keith/Matteson: *Lucky Southern*
Gershwin, George/Matteson: *Summertime*
Rollins, Sonny/Matteson: *Oleo*
Matteson, Rich: *Spoofy*
Matteson-Phillips TubaJazz Consort
Album Title: *Superhorn*
Personnel: Rich Matteson, Ashley Alexander, Buddy Baker, euphoniums; Harvey Phillips, Dan Perantoni, Winston Morris, tubas; Jack Petersen, guitar; Tommy Ferguson, Dan Haerle, piano; Kelli Sills, Rufus Reid, bass; Ed Soph, Steve Houghton, drums
Label: Mark Recordings, CD: MJS 57626CD
Matteson-Phillips TubaJazz Consort and *Superhorns* LPs combined on one CD.
Matteson-Phillips TubaJazz Consort
Album Title: *Superhorns*
Personnel: Rich Matteson, Ashley Alexander, Buddy Baker, euphoniums; Harvey Phillips, Dan Perantoni, Winston Morris, tubas; Jack Petersen, guitar; Tommy Ferguson, piano; Kelli Sills, bass; Steve Houghton, drums
Label: Mark Recordings, 1982, LP: MJS 57591
Razaf/Goodman/Webb/Sampson: *Stompin' at the Savoy*
Matteson, Rich: *Little Ole Softy*
Peterson, Oscar/J. Petersen: *Noreen's Nocturn*
Ellington, Edward Kennedy "Duke"/ Matteson: *Things Ain't What They Used to Be*
Carmichael, Hoagy/Matteson: *Georgia on My Mind*
arr. Matteson: *Waltzing Matilda*
Matteson-Phillips TubaJazz Consort
Album Title: *TubaJazz Superhorns*
Personnel:
Label: HPF-Tubajazz-CD 3
Matteson, Rich: *Spoofy*
Jarrett, Keith/Matteson: *Lucky Southern*
Rollins, Sonny/Matteson: *Oleo*
Matteson, Rich: *Little Ole Softy*
Sampson/Racaf/Good/Mattesonman/ Webb: *Stompin' at the Savoy*
Silver, Horace/Matteson: *Gregory Is Here*
Gershwin, George/Matteson: *Summertime*
Peterson, Oscar/Peterson: *Noreen's Nocturne*
Carmichael, Hoagy/Matteson: *Georgia on My Mind*
Ellington, Edward Kennedy "Duke"/ Matteson: *Things Ain't What They Used to Be*
arr. Matteson: *Waltzing Matilda*
Matteson-Phillips TubaJazz Consort
Album Title: *TubaJazz Superhorns Live!!!*
Personnel:
Label: HPF-TJ-CD 4
Ellington, Edward Kennedy "Duke"/ Matteson: *In a Mellow Tone*
Silver, Horace/Matteson: *Señor Blues*
Low/Gray/Bennett/Ha/Matteson: *Bye Bye Blues*
Terry, Clark/Matteson: *C. T.'s Blues (Finger Filibuster)*
Matteson, Rich: *Introduction to Shuckin' and Jivin'*
Matteson, Rich: *Shuckin' and Jivin'*
Rollins, Sonny/Matteson: *Oleo*
Sheldon, Jack/Wilson: *Your Mama Ain't Got No Draws*
May, Ernest; see Contraband (The)
Mazura, János
Album Title: *I Let the Song . . .*
Personnel: György Vukán; The Creative Arts Trio

Label: Periferic, 1998, CD: BGCD 030
Parker, Charlie: *Au Privave*
Rollins, Sonny: *Doxy*
Pederson, Tommy: *Elephant in the Livingroom*
Charles, Dick: *Mad about Him, Sad without Him, How Can I Be Glad without Him Blues*
Ellington, Edward Kennedy "Duke": *I Let the Song Go Out of My Heart*
Szalóky, Béla: *Truesome Whosome*
Parker, Charlie: *Scrapple from an Apple*
Ellington, Edward Kennedy "Duke": *Satin Doll*
Parker, Charlie: *Billie's Bounce*
Fritz, József Róbert: *Blues for Louie*
Parker, Charlie: *My Little Suede Shoes*
Hubbel, Raymond: *Poor Butterfly*
Henderson, Ray: *Bye Bye Blackbird*

McAdams, Charles
Album Title: *The Forty-First Annual Mid-West International Band and Orchestra Clinic—1987*
Personnel: North Side Junior High Band; Jackson, Tennessee; Janet Warren, conductor
Label: Mark Records, 1988, CS: MW87-MC-13
Curnow, James: *Concertino for Tuba and Band*

McIntosh, Nat
Album Title: *Youngblood Brass Band—Center: level:roar*
Personnel: David Henzie-Skogen, drums; Tom Reschke, bass drum and cymbal; Alex Wilkins, tenor Saxophone; Joe Goltz, trombone; Charles Wagner, trumpet; Jeff Madden, trumpet; Mike Boman, trumpet
Label: Ozone Music, 2002, CD:
To Come Together
Round One
Culture:envy:war
Brooklyn
Diaspora
Human Nature Part 2
Thursday
The Moment
Avalanche
Nat McIntosh Handbills for No Man
Camouflage
Is an Elegy
Under Your Influence
V. I. P.
And Leave Alone

McIntosh, Nat
Album Title: *Youngblood Brass Band—Unlearn*
Personnel: David Henzie-Skogen, drums; Tom Reschke, bass drum and cymbal; Alex Wilkins, tenor saxophone; Joe Goltz, trombone; Charles Wagner, trumpet; Jeff Madden, trumpet; Mike Boman, trumpet
Label:
Bloodshot
Acousticon Theme
Human Nature
Da Bomba
The Warrior Comes Out to Play
Pastime Paradise
Peace
The Trilogy vs. Dr. Skooly
From Now On
Ya'll Stay Up
It's All Over
Chinatown

McIntosh, Nat: see Sotto Voce

McIntyre, Earl
Album Title: *Carla Bley: Dinner Music*
Personnel:
Label: Watt Works, 1976, LP: 6
Social Studies

McIntyre, Earl
Album Title: *Taj Mahal: Happy Just to Be like I Am*
Personnel:
Label: Columbia Records, LP:

McIntyre, Earl; see Johnson, Howard; *Howard Johnson & Gravity!!!; Right Now!; Taj Mahal: The Real Thing*

Megules, Karl
Album Title: *Karl I. Megules, Tuba*
Personnel: Bernie Leighton, piano; Garden State Tuba Ensemble; Toby Hanks, guest artist
Label: Recorded Publications Company, 1976, LP: Z 434471
Weeks, Clifford: *Triptych*
Ferreira and Einhorn/Megules: *Batida Diferente*
Stradella, Alessandro: *Pieta, Signora*
Bach, Johann Sebastian/Sauter: *Komm Süsser Tod*
Frackenpohl, Arthur: *Pop Suite*
Sear, Walter: *Sonatina*
Croft: *Duet for Tenor Tuba and Bass Tuba*
Tarlow, Lawrence: *Quintet for Tubas*
Ecclés, Henry/Megules: *Adagio*
Catelinet, Philip: *Suite in Miniature (first and third movements)*
Butts, Carrol: *Ode to Low Brass*

Mehlan, Keith; see Monarch Tuba-Euphonium Quartet; see United States Navy Band Tuba-Euphonium Quartet

Melton Tuba-Quartett
Album Title: *Lazy Elephants*
Personnel: Uli Haas, Heiko Triebener, Henrik Tietz, Hartmut Müller
Label: Diavolo Records, CD: DR-D-95-C-003 LC 5351
Bach, Johann Sebastian/Hermann: *Badinerie*
Gabrieli, Giovanni/Gray: *Canzona per Sonare No. 4*
Victoria, Thomas Luis de/Self: *O Vos Omnes*

Mozart, Wolfgang Amadeus/Doerner: *Das Butterbrot*
Liszt, Franz/Seitz: *Hungarian Rhapsody #2*
Hidas, Frigyes: *Tuba Quartett*
Strauss, Johann/Seitz: *Tritsch-Tratsch Polka*
Rimsky-Korsakov, Nicholas/Watz: *Flight of the Bumblebee*
Khatchaturian, Aram/Seitz: *Sabre Dance*
Kalke, Ernst-Thilo: *Requiem to a Dead Little Cat*
Kalke, Ernst-Thilo: *Jumbo's Holiday*
Schooley, John: *Cherokee*
Barroso, Ary/Weichselbaumer: *Brazil*
Hawkins, Erskine/Luis: *Tuxedo Junction*
Desmond, Paul/Luis: *Take Five*
Luis, Ingo: *Lazy Elephant Blues*

Melton Tuba-Quartett
Album Title: *Melton Tuba-Quartett "Premiere"*
Personnel: Uli Haas, Heiko Triebener, Henrik Tietz, Hartmut Müller
Label: Diavolo Records, 1993, CD: DR-D-93-C-001 LC 5351
Sousa, John Philip/Sabourin: *Washington Post March*
Frackenpohl, Arthur: *Ragtime*
Handy, W. C./Holcombe: *St. Louis Blues*
Mozart, Wolfgang Amadeus/Fletcher: *Eine Kleine Nachtmusik*
Ramsöe, Emilio Wilhelm/Buttery: *Andante Quasi Allegretto*
Payne, Frank Lynn: *Quartet for Tubas (The Condor)*
Arcadelt, Jacob/Self: *Ave Maria*
Niehaus, Lennie: *Miniature Jazz Suite*
Mancini, Henry/Luis: *Baby Elephant Walk*
Stevens, John: *Dances*
Bach, Johann Sebastian/Werden: *Bist du bei mir, BWV 508*
Schumann, Robert/Seitz: *Traumerei*
Mancini, Henry/Krush: *The Pink Panther*
Hutchison, Terry: *Tuba Juba Duba*

Melton Tuba-Quartett
Album Title: *Power*
Personnel: Uli Haas, Heiko Triebener, Henrik Tietz, Hartmut Müller
Label: Diavolo Records, CD: MT299 LC 5351
Stevens, John: *Power*
Stevens, John: *Moondance*
Traditional: *The Londonderry Air*
Traditional: *Greensleeves*
Traditional: *Old Star*
Dempsey, Raymond: *Quatre Chansons*
Luis, Ingo: *Little Lullaby*
Wolking, Henry: *Tuba Blues Medley*
Aquino, Baden Powell de: *Bocoxe*
Roblee, Richard: *Four Tuba Blues*
Wilhelm, Rolf: *Bavarian Stew*
Watz, Franz: *Melton Marsch*

Mendoker, Scott
Album Title: *Monument: The Music of David Sampson*
Personnel: Czech Philharmonic Chamber Orchestra; Alan Balter, conductor
Label: Summit Records, 1999, CD: DCD 237
Sampson, David: *Three Portraits for Tuba and Chamber Orchestra*

Mendoker, Scott
Album Title: *The Symphonic Wind Music of David R. Holsinger, Vol. 6*
Personnel: Rutgers Wind Ensemble, William Berz, conductor
Label: Mark, CD: 2824-MCD
Holsinger, David: *Kansas City Dances*

Michel, Guy
Album title: *Recital*
Personnel: Dominique Schweizer, piano
Label: Artlab, CD: 93743
Bach, Johann Sebastian: *Sonata in G Dur, BWV 1027*
Lantier, Pierre: *Andante et Allegro*
Hopkinson: *Concerto for Tuba "Concerto Euphonique"*
Hindemith, Paul: *Sonata for Bass Tuba and Piano*

Mighty Tubadours
Album Title: *The Mighty Tubadours Merry Christmas Album*
Personnel: Albert Harclerode, Norm Pearson, tubas; Loren Marstellar, Gil Zimmerman,euphoniums
Label: Crystal, 1984, LP: S422
Herbert, Victor/Vaughan: *March of the Toy Soldiers*
Redner/Vaughan: *Oh Little Town of Bethlehem*
arr. Vaughan: *Hail the Lord's Annointed*
arr. Harclerode: *March of the Three Kings*
Mueller/Vaughan: *Away in a Manger*
Hopkins/Lycan: *We Three Kings*
Bach, Johann Sebastian/Falconer: *Von Himmel Hoch*
arr. Harclerode: *Glousteshire Wassail Song*
arr. Vaughan: *O Come, O Come Emmanuel*
Tchaikovsky, Peter Ilyitch/Self: *Dance of the Reedpipes*
Tchaikovsky, Peter Ilyitch/Charlton: *March-Overture from "Nutcracker"*
arr. Vaughan: *Coventry Carol*
arr. Harclerode: *O Tannenbaum*
Kingsbury/Harclerode: *Infant Holy*
Schop/Vaughan: *Break Forth O Beauteous Light*
Willis/Harclerode: *It Came upon a Midnight Clear*
arr. Charlton: *First Noel*
Berlin, Irving/Vaughan: *White Christmas*
arr. Harclerode: *O Sanctissumus*
Gillespie/Vaughan: *Santa Claus Is Coming to Town*

arr. Harclerode: *Good King Wenceslas; Il Est Ne*
arr. Vaughan: *God Rest Ye Merry, Gentlemen*
Schulz/Harclerode: *O Come Little Children*

Mighty Tubadours
Album Title: *Ve Iss Da Mighty Tubadours, Ya?*
Personnel: Frank Berry, Loren Marstellar, Gil Zimmerman, euphoniums; Albert Harclerode, Adi Hershko, David Lusher, Norman Pearson, Timothy Reilly, tubas
Label: Crystal, 1991, CD: CD420 (combines *Ya, Ve Iss Da Mighty Tubadours* and *Tubadour Merry Christmas* albums)
Vaughan, Rodger: *Jingle Bell Waltz*

Mighty Tubadours
Album Title: *Ya, Ve Iss Da Mighty Tubadours*
Personnel: Frank Berry, euphonium; Albert Harclerode, Adi Hershko, David Lusher, Timothy Reilly, tubas
Label: Crystal, 1978, LP: S42
Herbert, Victor/Vaughan: *March of the Toy Soldiers*
Strauss, Johann Jr./Berry: *Waltz from "Die Fledermaus"*
King, Karl L./Berry: *Barnum and Bailey's Favorite*
Bartles, Alfred: *When Tubas Waltz*
Mouret, Jean Joseph/Self: *Rondo*
Taylor, Tell/Vaughan: *Down by the Old Mill Stream*
Tchaikovsky, Peter Ilyitch/Self: *Dance of the Reedpipes*
Gounod, Charles/Berry: *Funeral March for a Marionette*
Bach, Johann Sebastian/Berry: *Fugue in G minor*
Anonymous/Lusher: *Come Dearest, the Daylight Is Gone*
Richardson, Arthur/McLean/Whitcomb: *Too Fat Polka*
Kabalevski, Dmitri/Berry: *Comedian's Galop*
Ellington, Edward Kennedy "Duke"/ Vaughan: *Mood Indigo/Satin Doll*
Mozart, Wolfgang Amadeus/Self: *Allegro from Eine Kleine Nachtmusik*

Miraphone Tuba Quartet
Album Title: *International Marschparade*
Personnel: Patrick Couttet, Philippe Wendling, euphoniums; Philippe Gallet, Olivier Galmant, tubas
Label: Koch International, 1998, CD: 324 199 PC08 LC 5680
Fucik, Julius: *Einzug Der Gladiatoren*
Fucik, Julius: *Unter Der Admiralsflagge*
Sousa, John Philip: *Washington Post*
Beethoven, Ludwig van: *Yorkscher Marsch*
Teike, Carl: *Graf Zeppelin Marsch*
Fucik, Julius: *Florentiner Marsch*
Sprick, Geert: *Mens Sana in Corpore Sano*
Novacek, Rudolf: *Castaldo Marsch*
Teike, Carl: *Alte Kameraden*
Volksweise: *Petersburger Marsch*
Strauss, Johann: *Radetzky Marsch*
Piefke, Gottfried: *Preussens Gloria*
Sousa, John Philip: *Stars and Stripes Forever*

Miraphone Tuba Quartet
Album Title: *Miraphone Tuba Quartet*
Personnel: Patrick Couttet, Philippe Wendling, euphoniums; Philippe Gallet, Olivier Galmant, tubas
Label: Koch International, CD: 323 759 G1 LC 5680
Mozart, Wolfgang Amadeus/Rozen: *Overture from the "Magic Flute"*
Martino, Ralph: *Fantasy*
Stevens, John: *Manhattan Suite*
Frackenpohl, Arthur: *Refrain from "Pop Suite"*
Glinka, Michael/Ferguson: *Overture to "Russlan and Ludmila"*
Traditional/Buttery: *Greensleeves*
Niehaus, Lennie: *Tubalation*
Joplin, Scott/Walter: *The Strenuous Life*
Agrell, Jeffrey: *Gospel Time*
Shaw, Lowell: *Frippery*
Lennon, John, and Paul McCartney/Luis: *Hey Jude*
Steckar, Marc: *Bassacat*

Miraphone Tuba Quartet
Album Title: *Pictural*
Personnel: Patrick Couttet, Philippe Wendling, euphoniums; Philippe Gallet, Olivier Galmant, tubas
Label: Koch, CD: 324653
La Danza
The Casbah of Tetouan
Pictural
Entrevue/ Tribal
Schoenberg, Claude-Michel: *On My Own from "Les Miserables"*
Stevens, John: *Power*
Under the Sea
King, Karl L.: *The Melody Shop*
Lohmann, Georg: *Bayerische Polka*

Modern Jazz Tuba Project
Album Title: *Live at the Bottom Line*
Personnel: Bill Huber, Barry Green, Marc Dickman, euphoniums; Joe Murphy, Richard Perry, R. Winston Morris, tubas; Paul Carrol Binkley, electric/acoustic guitars; Steven Willets, piano/keyboards; Jim Ferguson, acoustic bass; Bob Mater, drums/percussion
Label: Heartdance Music, 2003, CD: HDM-1090
Noble, Ray/Matteson: *Cherokee*
Martin, Glenn: *Valvin' on a Riff*
Carmichael, Hoagy/Matteson: *Skylark*
Toledo, Rene Luis/Murphy: *Rene's Song*
Silver, Horace/Perry: *Cookin' at the Continental*
Brown, Clifford/Perry: *Sandu*
LeGrand, Michel/Williamson: *Summer Knows*

Brubeck, Dave/Elseck and Murphy: *Blue Rondo a la Turk*
Esleck, David L.: *I-95*
Rollins, Sonny/Matteson: *Oleo*
Modern Jazz Tuba Project
Album Title: *My Favorite Things*
Personnel: Bill Huber, Barry Green, Marc Dickman, euphoniums; Joe Murphy, Richard Perry, R. Winston Morris, tubas; Paul Carrol Binkley, electric/acoustic guitars; Steven Willets, piano/keyboards; Jim Ferguson, acoustic bass; Bob Mater, drums/percussion
Label: Heartdance Music, 2003, CD: HDM-1120
Rodgers, Richard, and Oscar Hammerstein: *My Favorite Things*
Theme for Malcolm
Strange Thing
Hey Man!
Silver, Horace/Matteson: *Gregory Is Here*
Pearl Casters
This Masquerade
Carmichael, Hoagy: *Georgia on My Mind*
Pick Up the Pieces
Kool Kube
Sing, Sing, Sing
Monarch Tuba-Euphonium Quartet
Album Title: *Metamorphosis*
Personnel: Roger Behrend, David Miles, euphoniums; Martin Erickson, Keith Mehlan, tubas
Label: Campro Productions, 1993, CD:
arr. Singleton, Kenneth: *Three Sixteenth Century Flemish Pieces*
Rossini, Gioacchino/Davis: *Petit Caprice in the Style of Offenbach*
Mehlan, Keith: *Eine Kleine Schrecken Musik (A Little Fright Music)*
Sousa, John Philip/Morris: *El Capitan*
Martino, Ralph: *Fantasy*
arr. Dempsey: *Quatro Chansons*
Dempsey, Raymond: *Now Hear This*
Mozart, Wolfgang Amadeus/Fabrizio: *Overture from the "Marriage of Figaro"*
Taylor, Jeffrey: *Fanfare No. 1*
LeClair, David: *Carnival of Venice*
Sherwin, Manning/Mehlan: *A Nightingale Sang in Berkley Square*
arr. Mehlan: *The Londonderry Air*
Mozart, Wolfgang Amadeus/Mehlan: *Turkish Rondo*
Massenet, Jules/Margaret Erickson: *Argonaise from "Le Cid"*
Mehlan, Keith: *Bottoms Up Rag*
Morgan, Kevin
Album Title: *Virtuoso Tuba*
Personnel: Paul Bateman, piano; Gareth Bimson, John Young, trumpets; John Thurgood, horn; Lindsay Shilling, trombone
Label: White Line, 1996, CD: WHL 2098
Giampieri/Rimmer: *Carnival of Venice*
Saint-Saëns, Camille/Stephens: *The Swan from "Carnival of the Animals"*
Schoenberg, Claude-Michel/Barry: *On My Own from "Les Miserables"*
Kander, John Harold: *Cabaret*
Rimsky-Korsakov, Nicholas/Lewington: *Flight of the Bumblebee*
Mozart, Wolfgang Amadeus: *Horn Concerto No. 4 in E♭major, K. 495* (Rondo)
Rimmer, William: *Jenny Jones,* for tuba solo
Loewe, Frederick: *I Could Have Danced All Night*
Verdi, Giuseppi: *"Fairest daughter of the graces" from Rigoletto*
Kronk: *Mr. Bumble*
Work, Henry Clay/Doughty: *Variations on "Grandfather's Clock"*
Vaughan Williams, Ralph: *Concerto for Bass Tuba and Orchestra*
Waller, Thomas "Fats": *Ain't Misbehavin'*
Hartmann, John/Mortimer: *Facilita*
Bratton, John/Nash: *Teddy Bears' Picnic*
Garner, Erroll: *Misty*
Gilkyson, Terry: *The Bare Necessities*
Rossini, Gioacchino/Roberts: *Largo al factotum from "The Barber of Seville"*
Carmichael, Hoagy: *Stardust*
Denza, Luigi/Shilling: *Funiculì Funiculà*
Morris, Jim
Album Title: *Sweets for Brass*
Personnel:
Label: Music Minus One, CD w/book-4702
For Bass Trombone or Tuba Players (Play-along CD with accompaniment-only tracks—includes sheet music)
Gale, Jack: *A Picture of Dorian Blue*
Skeen, Lewis: *Suite for Brass*
Foust, Alan: *1 x 1 x 5*
Sarvello, Frank: *Riff Rock*
Copeland, Ray: *Classical Jazz Suite*
O' Reilly, John: *Metropolitan 5tet*
Rood, Hale: *Simplis Sonor*
Danser, Jahn: *Suite*
Albam, Manny: *Morrisania Motion*
Morris, Jim: *Jaroque Waltz/Mood*
Morris, R. Winston
Album Title: *Music of Robert Jager*
Personnel: Tokyo Kosei Wind Orchestra; Robert Jager, conductor
Label: Kosei Publishing Company, 1986, LP: KOR8104; CD: KOCD-3504
Jager, Robert: *Concerto for Bass Tuba and Band*
Morris, R. Winston; see Matteson-Phillips TubaJazz Consort; see Modern Jazz Tuba Project; see Self, James; *The Big Stretch;* see Tennessee Tech Alumni Ensemble; see Tennessee Tech Tuba-Euphonium Ensemble; see Symphonia.

Moschner, Pinguin
Album Title: *Hannes Zerbe Blech Band*
Personnel: Hannes Zerbe Blech Band
Label: Plaene, LP: 88416 (LC 0972)
Moschner, Pinguin
Album Title: *If 69 Were 96—The Music of Jimi Hendrix*
Personnel: Joe Sachse, guitar
Label: AHO, 1994, CD: AHO CD 1016
Hendrix, Jimi: *Highway Child*
Moschner and Sachse: *Aus Allen Wolken*
Hendrix, Jimi: *Up from the Skies*
Moschner, Pinguin: *Gypsy Ears*
Hendrix, Jimi: *Voodoo Chile*
Moschner and Sachse: *Zombie Daddies*
Hendrix, Jimi: *Purple Haze*
Moschner and Sachse: *Red Mist*
Moschner and Sachse: *Candle Light in Disneyland*
Hendrix, Jimi: *Burning of the Midnight Lamp*
Sachse: *Lee Pizza, NE*
Hendrix, Jimi: *Spanish Castle Magic*
Hendrix, Jimi: *The Wind Cries Mary*
Moschner and Sachse: *Leave a Message after the Beep*
Moschner and Sachse: *If Sixty-nine Was Ninty-six*
Hendrix, Jimi: *If Six Was Nine*
Hendrix, Jimi: *Angel*
Roberts, William: *Hey Joe*
Hendrix, Jimi: *Little Wing*
Taylor: *Wild Thing*
Moschner and Sachse: *Mild Swing*
Moschner, Pinguin
Album Title: *Pinguin Moschner: A Tuba Love Story*
Personnel:
Label: Sound Aspects, LP: sas 005 digital
Moschner, Pinguin: *Love Story (und dann ging's heiss her)*
Moschner, Pinguin: *Majobiwomo*
Moschner, Pinguin: *Sax-Machine*
Moschner, Pinguin: *Bouillabaisse (Thanks, Maggie)*
Moschner, Pinguin: *Deep Throb*
Moschner, Pinguin: *Antartic Love Song*
Moschner, Pinguin: *Der Wurst lebt*
Moschner, Pinguin: *Waterloo*
Moschner, Pinquin; see European Tuba Quartet
Müller, Hartmut; see Melton Tuba-Quartett
Muros, Laszlo
Album Title: *The Magic Potion*
Personnel:
Label:
Hidas, Frigyes: *Tuba Concerto*
Murphy, Joe; see Modern Jazz Tuba Project
Murrow, Richard
Album Title: *Brazzology—Pick Yourself Up*
Personnel: Larry Spencer, trumpet; Steve Sonday, piano; Carl Hillman, bass; Dennis Durick, drums
Label: Brazzology Productions, 1997, CD: BPCD3101
Kern, Jerome/Spencer: *Pick Yourself Up*
Rodgers, Richard, and Lorenz Hart/Spencer: *My Funny Valentine*
Parker, Charlie/Spencer: *Little Suede Shoes*
Davis, Miles: *So What*
Spencer, Larry: *Ingrid*
Kern, Jerome/Spencer: *I Won't Dance*
Carmichael, Hoagy/Spencer: *Georgia on My Mind*
Parker, Charlie/Murrow and Spencer: *Au Privave*
Bach, Johann Sebastian/Murrow and Spencer: *Siciliano*
Murrow, R./Spencer: *Domi*
Satie, Erik: *Gymnopedie*
Lennon, John, and Paul McCartney/Stitzel: *Come Together*
Connelly, Reg/Murrow and Spencer: *Show Me the Way to Go Home*
Nahatzki, Richard
Album Title: *Lachenmann: Harmonica for Large Orchestra and Tuba*
Personnel: Saarbrucken Radio Symphony Orchestra; Hans Zender, conductor
Label: CPO Records, 1998, CD: CPO 999 484-2
Lachenmann, Helmut: *Harmonica for Large Orchestra and Tuba Solo*
Nahatzki, Richard
Album Title: *20th Century Wind Concertos*
Personnel: Berlin Symphony Orchestra; Hans E. Zimmer, conductor
Label: Capriccio, 1999, CD: #10522
Vaughan Williams, Ralph: *Concerto for Bass Tuba and Orchestra*
Neis, Leslie; see Tubalaté
Nelson, Mark
Album Title: *Aboriginal Voices*
Personnel: W. Ronald Yadeau, piano; Brian Justison, cymbals; Eric Hollenbeck, vibraphone
Label: Nelson, CD: 1
Ross, Walter: *Villanella*
Corwell, Neal: *Aboriginal Voices*
Grant, James: *Three Furies*
Read, Thomas: *Brillenbass*
Ayers, Jesse: *Dancing King*
Nielsen, Erik: *Spiritual Alloys*
Larsen, Libby: *Concertpiece for Tuba and Piano*
Nelson, Mark
Album Title: *New England Reveries*
Personnel: Sylvia Parker, piano
Label: Crystal, 1991, CD: CD 691; CS: C691
Cummings, Barton: *Fantasia Breve*
Persichetti, Vincent: *Parable for Solo Tuba, Op. 147*
Corwell, Neal: *New England Reveries*

Ross, Walter: *Escher's Sketches*
Calabro, Louis: *Sonata-Fantasia*
New Orleans Jazz Bands
Album Title: *Down Yonder*
Personnel: Olympia Jazz Band; Chosen Few; Rebirth Marching Jazz Band; Dirty Dozen
Brass Band
Label: Rounder Records, LP: 2062
New York Tuba Quartet
Album Title: *New York Tuba Quartet: Tubby's Revenge*
Personnel: Toby Hanks, Steven Johns, Sam Pilafian, Tony Price
Label: Crystal, 1976, LP: S221
Schuller, Gunther: *Five Moods for Tuba Quartet*
Heussenstamm, George: *Tubafour*
Purcell, Henry: *Allegro and Air*
Ross, Walter: *Fancy Dances for Three Bass Tubas*
Stevens, John: *Music 4 Tubas*
Parker, Charlie: *Au Privave*
Newberger, Eli
Album Title: *Don't Monkey with It*
Personnel: Black Eagle Jazz Band
Label: Stomp Off Records, 1987, LP: S. O. S. 1147, Volume 6
Monsborough, Abe: *Don't Monkey with It*
Oliver, Joe: *Chimes Blues*
Kassel and Stitzel: *Sobbin' Blues*
Armstrong, Louis, and F. "Jelly Roll" Morton: *Wild Man Blues*
Johnson, Bunk: *Moose Blues*
Brown, Sandy: *Tree Top Tall Papa*
Novick, Billy: *When She Cries*
Stitzel, Mel: *The Chant*
Newberger, Eli
Album Title: *The Men They Will Become*
Personnel: Jimmy Mazzy, banjo
Label: Stomp Off, 1998, CD: 1352
Blake and Sissle: *I'm Just Wild about Harry*
Grainger, Porter: *Put It Right Here*
Ager and Yellen: *Big Bad Bill*
Johnson and Mack: *Old Fashioned Love*
Hunter, Eugene: *Ain't Much Good in the Best of Men Now Days*
Price, Billy: *I Hate Myself for Loving You*
Williams and Palmer: *I Found a New Baby*
Sylva and Henderson: *Sonny Boy*
Morton, Jelly Roll: *I Hate a Man like You*
Overstreet and Higgins: *There'll Be Some Changes Made*
Overstreet and Higgins: *I Ain't Gonna Give Nobody None of My Jellyroll*
Dietz and Schwartz: *Sweet Music*
Porter, Cole: *Miss Otis Regrets*
Williams and Palmer: *Everybody Loves My Baby*
Handy and Brymn: *Aunt Hagar's Children*
Oliver and Melrose: *Doctor Jazz*
Newberger, Eli
Album Title: *Shake It Down*
Personnel: Jimmy Mazzy, banjo
Label: Stomp Off, 1985, LP: 1109
Williams and Urquhart: *Shake It Down*
Rainey and Arant: *Jelly Bean Blues*
Jones and Dickerson: *Tia Juanna Man*
Gershwin, George: *Prelude in C♯ minor*
Graham and Williams: *I Ain't Got Nobody*
Europe, Sissle, and Blake: *Goodnight, Angeline*
Smith, Jabbo: *Lina Blues*
MacDonald, Goodwin, and Hanley: *Breeze*
Lockhart and Seitz: *The World Is Waiting for the Sunrise*
Washington and Harline: *When You Wish upon a Star*
Morton, F. "Jelly Roll": *Chicago Breakdown*
Moret, Neil: *Song of the Wanderer*
Brown and Von Tilzer: *Dapper Dan*
Newberger, Eli
Album Title: *Skeletons in the Closet*
Personnel: Black Eagle Jazz Band
Label: Black Eagle, 1995, CD: BECD 2004
Newberger, Eli; see M'N'M Trio
Nickel, Hans
Album Title: *Cantuballade*
Personnel:
Label:
Vaughan Williams, Ralph: *Concerto for Bass Tuba and Orchestra*
Roost, Jan Van der: *Cantuballade*
Gregson, Edward: *Tuba Concerto*
Gregson, Edward: *Alarum for Solo Tuba*
Nickel, Hans
Album Title: *Tuba Obsessions*
Personnel: Gunther Herzfeld, piano; Henk Martens, Ad Tripels, percussions; Renato Meli, euphonium
Label:
Roost, Jan Van der: *Obsessions*
Newton, Rodney: *Capriccio*
Bedrich, Jan: *Dialogy*
Gregson, Edward: *Tuba Concerto (movement II)*
Schmidt, William: *Sonata for Tuba and Piano*
Hamers, Maurice: *Chameleon*
Forde, Jan Magne: *Folkevise*
Niquille, José; see Dites-Le-Moi Tuba
Nord, Lennart
Album Title: *Stockholm Symphonic Wind Orchestra*
Personnel: Stockholm Symphonic Wind Orchestra; Martin Turnovsky, conductor
Label: Caprice, 1992, LP: 214 14/1995; CD: CAP 21414
Gregson, Edward: *Tuba Concerto*
Norris, Tim
Album Title: *The Tuba Family Explored*
Personnel: Diana Owen, piano

Label: Winchester Music School CD/CS: WMS3
The Albert Hall Galop
Schumann, Robert: *Traumerei*
Kamen, Michael: *(Everything I Do) I Do It for You*
Pastoral Echoes
Habanera and Ragtime
Bizet, Georges: *Farandole from L'Arlesienne Suite No. 2*
Puccini, Giacomo: *"Nessun Dorma" from Turandot*
On Line
Rossini, Gioacchino: *Largo al factotum from "The Barber of Seville"*
Luther, Martin: *A Mighty Fortress Is Our God*
Little Fugue
Study in 8ths
Traditional: *Irish Washerwoman*
Still Swingin'
Romanze and Rondo
Traditional: *Tuba Smarties*
1st Movement—Tuba Concerto
Senaillé, Jean Baptiste/Catelinet: *Introduction and Allegro Spiritoso*

Norris, Tim
Album Title: *Tubby and Tim Take Off*
Personnel: Tim Norris and Friends
Label: Winchester Music School CD/CS: WMS2
Kleinsinger, George, and Paul Tripp: *Tubby the Tuba*
Arnold, Malcolm: *Fantasy for Solo Tuba*
Brand, Michael: *Tuba Tapestry for Tuba and Brass Band*
Gregson, Edward: *Tuba Concerto (first movement)*

Northcut, Timothy
Album Title: *Tennessee Tech Pride*
Personnel: Tennessee Tech University Symphony Band; Joseph Hermann, director
Label: Mark Custom Recording, 2003, CD: 4371-MCD
Danner, Greg: *Concerto for Tuba and Band*
Gliere, Reinhold: *Andante from Concerto for Coloratura*
Brusick, William: *Concerto for Tuba and Wind Orchestra*
Bartles, Alfred: *Tubossa—Concert Bossanova for Solo Tuba and Symphonic Band*
Puccini, Giacomo: *"Nessun Dorma" from Turandot*

Northern Tuba Lights
Album Title: *The Northern Tuba Lights*
Personnel: The Northern Tuba Lights
Label: The Northern Tuba Lights, 1991, CS:
Stevens, John: *Power*
Traditional/Minerd: *Sea Tubas*
Sousa, John Philip/Werden: *Stars and Stripes Forever*
Schooley, John: *Cherokee*
Niehaus, Lennie: *Brass Tacks*
Bach, Johann Sebastian/Sabourin: *Preludium*
Stevens, John: *Dances*
Sousa, John Philip/Werden: *Hands across the Sea*
Wolking, Henry: *Tuba Blues*
Mancini, Henry/Krush: *The Pink Panther*
Offenbach, Jacques/Fletcher: *Orpheus in the Underworld*

O'Bryant, Kelly
Album Title: *Carolina Morning*
Personnel: Dennis AsKew, tuba
Label: KoDa, CD: 1001
Traditional/Parker-Christianson: *Wonderous Love*
Copland, Aaron: *Three Old American Songs*
Carroll, Gregory: *Studies in American Folk Idiom*
Bernstein, Leonard: *Suite from "West Side Story"*
Green, Jonathan: *When We Were Giants*
Self, James: *Duh Suite*
Traditional: *Amazing Grace*

Palmer, Singleton
Album Title: *The Best Dixieland Band*
Personnel: Ben Thigpin, drums; Leon King, trombone; Bill Martin, trumpet; Norman Mason, clarinet; Gus Perryman, piano
Label: Norman Records, LP: NS 210
Blues in B♭
Big Butter and Egg Man
Shiek of Araby
Original Dixieland Jazz Band: *Fidgety Feet*
Hello, Dolly!
Rock of Ages
Alabama Jubilee
Cannon, Hughie: *Bill Bailey Won't You Please Come Home*

Palmer, Singleton
Album Title: *Dixie by Gaslight*
Personnel: Singleton Palmer and His Dixieland Band
Label: GNP Crescendo, LP: DJS 511
Melrose, Walter: *Tin Roof Blues*
Steele and Melrose: *High Society*
Koenig, Williams, and Handy: *Careless Love*
Bernie, Pinkard, and Casey: *Sweet Georgia Brown*
Maryland, My Maryland
Handy, W. C.: *St. Louis Blues*
Burris and Smith: *Ballin' the Jack*
Gilbert and Ory: *Muskrat Ramble*
Traditional: *When the Saints Go Marching In*

Palmer, Singleton
Album Title: *Sing Swings*
Personnel: Ben Thigpin, drums; Leon King, trombone; Bill Martin, trumpet; Norman Mason, clarinet; Gus Perryman, piano
Label: Opera House Records, LP: 1001
Sensation
Linger Awhile

Memphis Blues
When My Sugar Walks down the Street
Sousa, John Philip: *Stars and Stripes Forever*
Yellow Dog Blues
Fillmore, Henry: *Lassas Trombone*
South Rampart Street Parade
DeCosta and LaRocca: *Tiger Rag*

Palmer, Singleton
Album Title: *Singleton Palmer and His Dixieland Band at the Opera House*
Personnel: Lige Shaw, drums; Leon King, trombone; Bill Martin, trumpet; Norman Mason, clarinet; Gus Perryman, piano
Label: GNP Crescendo, 1974, LP: DJS 513
Morton, F. "Jelly Roll": *Wolverine Blues*
Petrie, H. W.: *Asleep in the Deep*
Gaskill and McHugh: *I Can't Believe That You're in Love with Me*
Handy, W. C.: *Beale Street Blues*
Allen, Sheale, and Robbins: *Washington and Lee Swing*
LaRocca, D.: *Original Dixieland One-Step*
Traditional: *Just a Closer Walk with Thee*
Williams, Clarence, and Spencer Williams: *Royal Garden Blues*
Meinken and Ringle: *Wabash Blues*
Fisher, F.: *Chicago*

Papaux, Nicolas; see Dites-Le-Moi Tuba

Patterson, Graham; see Stokes, David, and Graham Patterson; *Chalk Farm Band-Salvation Army*

Pearson, Norm
Album Title: *Edward Scissorhands [motion picture soundtrack]*
Personnel: Music by Danny Elfman; Norm Pearson, principal tuba; John Thomas (Tommy) Johnson, session tuba
Label: MCA Records, 1990, CD: MCAD-10133

Pearson, Norm; see Mighty Tubadours; see Self, James; *The Big Stretch*

Perantoni, Daniel
Album Title: *Chinary Ung*
Personnel: Judy May Sellheim, mezzo-soprano; Robert G. Hamilton, piano
Label: Composers Recordings, 1996, CD: #710
Ung, Chinary: *Spiral II,* for mezzo-soprano, piano, and tuba

Perantoni, Daniel
Album Title: *Curnow at Illinois*
Personnel: University of Illinois Band
Label: University of Illinois Band, 1983, LP: 108
Curnow, James: *Concertino for Tuba and Band*

Perantoni, Daniel
Album Title: *Daniel in the Lion's Den*
Personnel: Arizona State University Symphonic Band; Dr. Richard Strange, conductor; Eckart Selheim, piano; Saint Louis Brass Quintet
Label: Summit Records, 1994, CD: DCD-163
Arban, Jean Baptiste/Domek: *Carnival of Venice*
Mahler, Gustav/Perantoni: *Lieder eines Fahrenden Gesellen*
McBeth, Francis: *Daniel in the Lion's Den*
Penderecki, Krzysztof: *Capriccio for Solo Tuba*
Bernie, Pinkard, and Casey/Sellers: *Sweet Georgia Brown*
Plog, Anthony: *Three Miniatures*
Rachmaninoff, Sergei/Parentoni: *Vocalise, Op. 34, No. 14*

Perantoni, Daniel
Album Title: *In Concert with the University of Illinois Symphonic Band*
Personnel: University of Illinois Symphonic Band; Harry Begian, conductor
Label: University of Illinois Band, LP: 87
Jager, Robert: *Concerto for Bass Tuba and Band*

Perantoni, Daniel
Album Title: *In Concert with the University of Illinois Symphonic Band*
Personnel: University of Illinois Symphonic Band; Harry Begian, conductor
Label: College Presentation Series, LP: 106
Vaughan Williams, Ralph/Hare: *Concerto for Bass Tuba and Band*

Perantoni, Daniel
Album Title: *Morgan Powell: Music for Brass*
Personnel:
Label: University Brass Recording Series, 1975, LP: EN 203 Stereo
Powell, Morgan: *Midnight Realities*

Perantoni, Daniel
Album Title: *Paul Freeman Introduces . . . David N. Baker*
Personnel: Czech National Symphony Orchestra
Label: Albany Records, 2000, CD: #377
Baker, David N.: *Tuba Concerto*

Perantoni, Daniel
Album Title: *Perantoni Plays Perantoni*
Personnel: Eric Dalheim, piano; Caryl Conger, piano; Robert Hamilton, piano; Illinois Contemporary Chamber Players; Arthur Weisburg, conductor; University of Illinois Band; Harry Begian, conductor; Judy May Sellheim, Soprano; Matteson-Phillips TubaJazz Consort
Label: Mark, 1998, CD: 2433-MCD
George, Thom Ritter: *Sonata for Tuba and Piano*
Wyatt, Scott: *3 for 1 for Tuba and Tape*
Fredrickson, Thomas: *Tubalied*
Crozier, Daniel: *Fantasy for Tuba and Piano*
Jager, Robert: *Concerto for Bass Tuba and Band*

Ung, Chinary: *Spiral II*
Matteson, Rich: *Little Ole Softy* (TubaJazz Consort)

Perantoni, Daniel
Album Title: *Sterling Brass*
Personnel: David Hickman, Illinois Chamber Players, Paul Zonn, Edwin London
Label: Crystal, LP: S394
Hackbarth, Glenn: *Double Concerto*
Powell, Morgan: *Nocturnes*

Perantoni, Daniel
Album Title: *Symphonia #3—Symphonia Fantastique!*
Corwell, Neal: *The Wasteland*
[see full reference under Symphonia]

Perantoni, Daniel
Album Title: *Tuba in Recital*
Personnel: Eric Dalheim, piano
Label: University Brass Recording Series, LP: SN-101
Stevens, Halsey: *Sonatina for Tuba and Piano*
Hindemith, Paul: *Sonata for Bass Tuba and Piano*
Sibbing, Robert: *Sonata*
Zonn, Paul: *Divertimento No. 1* (Tuba, String Bass, Percussion)

Perantoni, Daniel
Album Title: *Symphonia Two—La Mort dell' Oom*
Jager, Robert: *Three Ludes for Tuba*
[see full reference under Symphonia]

Perantoni, Daniel
Album Title: *Tuba N' Spice*
Personnel: Eric Dalheim, piano; Illinois Contemporary Chamber Players; University of Illinois Symphonic Band
Label: Mark Educational Recordings, 1983, LP: MRS 37879
Fredrickson, Thomas: *Tubalied*
Jager, Robert: *Concerto for Bass Tuba and Band*
George, Thom Ritter: *Sonata for Tuba and Piano*
Wyatt, Scott: *Three for One*
(Note: On many copies of this record the labels are on the wrong sides)

Perantoni, Daniel; see Matteson-Phillips TubaJazz Consort; see Summit Tubas; *American Tribute-Summit Brass;* see Symphonia

Perrine, Matt
Album Title: *New Orleans Nightcrawlers*
Personnel: Kevin Clark, Barney Floyd, trumpets; Craig Klein, trombone; Eric Traub, tenor saxophone; Jason Mingledorff, clarinet; Ken Jacobs, baritone saxophone; Peter Kaplan, snare drum; Frank Oxley, bass drum
Label: Rounder Records, 1996, CD: 2147
Lastie, Mel: *Keep On Gwine*
Masakowski, Steve: *Sidewalk Strut*

Perrine, Matt
Album Title: *New Orleans Nightcrawlers—Funk City*
Personnel: Eric Traub, tenor saxophone; Rick Trolsen, trombone; Henry Butler, piano; Sista Teedy, vocals
Label: Rounder Records, 1997, CD: 2154
Bud's Delights
Pick up the Pieces
Royal Flush
Heavy Henry
Auz
Imperial March (of the Nightcrawlers)
Purple Gazelle
Crawlin'
Chicken
Reply
Funky Liza

Perrine, Matt
Album Title: *New Orleans Nightcrawlers—Live at the Old Point*
Personnel: Kevin Clark, Barney Floyd, trumpets; Craig Klein, Rick Trolsen, trombones; Jason Mingledorff, clarinet; Ken Jacobs, baritone saxophone; Kerry Hunter, snare drum; Tanio Hingle, bass drum
Label: Viper Records, 2000, CD: 6 04017-8888-2-0
Puente, Tito: *Oye Como Va*
McDermott, Tom: *Martin's Mambo*

Perry, Richard; see Modern Jazz Tuba Project

Phillips, Harvey
Album Title: *All-Star Concert Band*
Personnel: James Burke, conductor
Label: Golden Crest, LP: CRS 4025
Youmans, Vincent/ Norman: *Carioca*

Phillips, Harvey
Album Title: *The Burke-Phillips All Star Concert Band, Vol. II*
Personnel: James Burke, director
Label: Golden Crest, LP: CR 4040
Kling, Henri: *The Elephant and the Fly*

Phillips, Harvey
Album Title: *Cabin in the Sky—Curtis Fuller*
Personnel: Manny Albam, conductor
Label: Impulse Records

Phillips, Harvey
Album Title: *The Charleston City All-Stars Go Dixieland*
Personnel: Charleston City All-Stars
Label: Grand Award LP: G.A. 33-411
Burris and Smith: *Ballin' the Jack*

Phillips, Harvey
Album Title: *Cornell University Wind Ensemble*
Personnel: Cornell University Wind Ensemble; Maurice Stith, conductor
Label: LP: CUWE 17
Ross, Walter: *Tuba Concerto with Band*

Phillips, Harvey
Album Title: *David Baker's 21st Century Bebop Band*
Personnel: David Baker, cello; Hunt Butler, tenor sax; Jim Beard, piano; Kurt Bahn, bass; Keith Cronin, drums
Label: Laurel, 1983, LP: LR-503

Phillips, Harvey
Album Title: *Extended Voices*
Personnel: Brandeis University Chorus, Alvin Lucier, director
Label: Odyssey, LP: 32160156
Feldman, Morton: *Chorus and Instruments (II)*

Phillips, Harvey
Album Title: *Faculty Concert Band, Volume 1*
Personnel: Armed Forces School of Music Band
Label: Century, 1968, LP: FV 31721
Youmans, Vincent/Norman: *Carioca*

Phillips, Harvey
Album Title: *The Further Adventures of Tubby the Tuba*
Personnel:
Label: Golden Crest, 1960, LP: CR6000
Kleinsinger, George, and Paul Tripp: *The Further Adventures of Tubby the Tuba*

Phillips, Harvey
Album Title: *Harvey Phillips in Recital for Family and Friends*
Personnel: Arthur Harris, Bernie Leighton, piano; Andrew J. Lolya, flute; Bradley Spinney, percussion
Label: Golden Crest, LP: RE 7054
Hartley, Walter: *Suite for Flute and Tuba*
Bach, Johann Sebastian: *Invention No. 1* (flute and tuba)
Handel, George Friderik: *Selected Movements from Sonatas for Flute*
Wilder, Alec: *Suite No. 1 for Tuba and Piano (Effie the Elephant)*
Wilder, Alec: *Suite No. 2 (Jessie)*
Wilder, Alec: *Suite No. 3 (Little Harvey)*
Wilder, Alec: *Suite No. 4 (Thomas)*
Wilder, Alec: *Suite No. 5 (Ethan Ayer)*
Wilder, Alec: *Song for Carol*

Phillips, Harvey
Album Title: *Harvey Phillips in Recital, Vol. III*
Personnel: New York Horn Trio
Label: Golden Crest, LP: CRS 4122
Gould, Morton: *Tuba Suite for Tuba and Three Horns*
Baker, David N.: *Sonata for Tuba and String Quartet*

Phillips, Harvey
Album Title: *Harvey Phillips, Tuba*
Personnel: Milton Kaye, Bernie Leighton, piano
Label: Golden Crest, LP: RE 7006
Wilder, Alec: *Sonata*
Bach, Johann Sebastian/Bell: *Air and Bourree*
Handel, George Friderik: *Andante*
Corelli, Archangelo: *Gigue*
Mozart, Wolfgang Amadeus: *O Isis and Osiris*
Swann, Donald: *Two Moods for Tuba*

Phillips, Harvey
Album Title: *Harvey Phillips Tuba Company*
Personnel: Jim Williams, Norlan Bewley, Hitomi Yakata, Toby Oft, Todd Schendel, Eric Paull, euphoniums; Harvey Phillips, Gary Tirey, Brian Sands, Jerome Stover, Geoffrey Whitehead, Mitsunori Nikaido, tubas; Gary Potter, bass; Tom Harvey, drums
Label: HPF Recordings and Tapes, 1999, CD: HPF CD 002
Bewley, Norlan: *Octubafest Medley*
Bewley, Norlan: *Tubafiesta Medley*
Bewley, Norlan: *Tubarock Medley*
Bewley, Norlan: *Tubaswing Medley*

Phillips, Harvey
Album Title: *Interlochen Music Camp*
Personnel: Interlochen High School Camp Band
Label: Golden Crest, LP: S 403
Benson, Warren: *Helix for Solo Tuba and Concert Band*

Phillips, Harvey
Album Title: *Ithica High School Band*
Personnel: Frank Battisti, director
Label: Golden Crest, 1967, LP: CR 6001
Benson, Warren: *Helix for Solo Tuba and Concert Band*

Phillips, Harvey
Album Title: *John Downey Plays John Downey*
Personnel: John Downey, piano
Label: Gasparo, LP: GS-243; 1999, CD: GSS-2201
Downey, John: *Tabu for Tuba*

Phillips, Harvey
Album Title: *Lavalle in Hi-Fi*
Personnel: Paul Lavalle—His Woodwinds and His Band
Label: RCA Victor, 1958, LP: LSP-1516
Hupfeld, Herman: *When Yuba Plays the Rumba on the Tuba Down in Cuba* (with Joe Tarto)

Phillips, Harvey
Album Title: *Leasebreakers*
Personnel:
Label: United Artists, 1967, LP: LA 3423

Phillips, Harvey
Album Title: *Music for the Underdogs of the Orchestra*
Personnel: New England Conservatory Orchestra; Gunther Schuller, director
Label: GM Recordings, 1984, LP: GM 2004
Vaughan Williams, Ralph: *Concerto for Bass Tuba and Orchestra*
Schuller, Gunther: *Capriccio for Tuba and Orchestra*

Phillips, Harvey
Album Title: *Music for Tuba and French Horn*
Personnel: Bernie Leighton, Tait Sanford, piano; John Barrows, horn
Label: Golden Crest, 1963, LP: RE 7018
Persichetti, Vincent: *Serenade No. 12 for Solo Tuba*
Wilder, Alec: *Sonata for French Horn, Tuba, and Piano*

Phillips, Harvey
Album Title: *Texas Music Educators Association Presents Baylor University Wind Ensemble*
Personnel: Baylor University Wind Ensemble; Dick Floyd, conductor
Label: Crest Records (Silver Crest), 1978, LP: T-78-4
Vaughan Williams, Ralph/Hare: *Concerto for Bass Tuba and Band*

Phillips, Harvey
Album Title: *Tribute to a Friend*
Personnel: Milton Kaye, piano; John Barrows, horn; Valhalla Horn Choir
Label: Golden Crest, LP: CRS 4147
Heiden, Bernhard: *Variations for Tuba and Nine Horns*
Wilder, Alec: *Suite No. 2 for French Horn and Tuba*

Phillips, Harvey
Album Title: *20th Anniversary Mid-West Band and Orchestra Clinic*
Personnel: Clarence Central Senior High School Band; Norbert Buskey, director
Label: Century of Chicago, 1966, LP: 25834
Sauter, Eddie: *Conjectures for Tuba and Band*

Phillips, Harvey
Album Title: *Two Contemporary Composers: Alec Wilder and Don Hammond*
Personnel: New York Brass Quintet
Label: Golden Crest, LP: CR4017
Wilder, Alec: *Tuba Showpiece from Quintet for Brass*

Phillips, Harvey
Album Title: *Virtuosity—A Contemporary Look*
Personnel: Phil Smith, trumpet
Label: GM Recordings, CD: GM3017CD
Peasley, Richard: *The Devil's Herald*

Phillips, Harvey; see Bell, William; *The Directors Band;* see Matteson-Phillips TubaJazz Consort; see *Summit Tubas; American Tribute-Summit Brass*

Phillips, Harvey/TubaChristmas
Album Title: *Harvey Phillips and his Tuba-Santas and Merry TubaChristmas*
Personnel: Harvey Phillips' TubaSantas
Label: HPF Records and Tapes, 1991, CS: 1000-1
Bewley, Norlan: *Santa Wants a Tuba for Christmas* (vocal by Harvey Phillips)
Martin, Blaine/Bewley: *Have Yourself a Merry Little Christmas*
Tormé and Wells/Bewley: *The Christmas Song*
arr. Bewley: *TubaChristmas Suite*
arr. Bewley: *Fum, Fum, Fum*
arr. Bewley: *Good Christian Men Rejoice*
arr. Bewley: *Greensleeves*
arr. Bewley: *Bring a Torch, Jeanette, Isabella*
arr. Bewley: *Pat-a-Pan*
Leontovich and Wilhousky/Bewley: *Carol of the Bells*
Wilder, Alec: *Carols for a Merry TubaChristmas*

Phillips, Harvey/TubaChristmas
Album Title: *Merry TubaChristmas*
Personnel: TubaChristmas Choirs; Bloomington, Chicago, New York, Los Angeles, Dallas
Label: Harvey Phillips Foundation, 1980, LP: NR-1111-4; CS:
O Come All Ye Faithful
Deck the Halls
The First Noel
Go Tell It on the Mountain
O Little Town of Bethlehem
O Come, Oh Come Immanuel
We Three Kings
Handel, George Friderik: *Joy to the World*
Angels We Have Heard on High
Good King Wenceslas
It Came upon a Midnight Clear
God Rest Ye Merry, Gentlemen
Bach, Johann Sebastian: *Komm Süsser Tod*
Gruber, Franz: *Silent Night*

Piernik, Zdizislaw
Album Title: *Music from International Festival of Contemporary Music*
Personnel:
Label: SX 1847
Warsaw Autumn

Piernik, Zdizislaw
Album Title: *Plays Z. Piernik*
Personnel:
Label:
Penderecki, Krzysztof: *Capriccio for Solo Tuba*
Borkowski, Marian: *VOX per uno stromento ad ottone*
Kranowski, A.: *Sonata for Solo Tuba*
Dobrowski, A.: *Muzyka for Tuba Solo*
Szalonek, W.: *Piernikiana for Solo Tuba*

Piernik, Zdizislaw
Album Title: *Tuba Universale*
Personnel: Maciej Paderewski, piano
Label: Proviva/Deutsche Austrophon GMBH, 1980, LP: LC 6542
Piernik, Zdizislaw: *Dialogue für Tuba und Tonband*
Schäffer, Boguslaw: *Projekt für Tuba und Toneband*
Zajaczek, Roman: *Tema Cantabile con Piernicazioni per tuba universale e pianoforte*

Borkowski, Marian: *VOX per uno stromento ad ottone*
Sikora, Elzbieta: *Il Viaggio 1 per tuba solo con pianoforte*

Piernik, Zdizislaw
Album Title: *Virtuoso Tuba: Zdizislaw Piernik in Recital*
Personnel: Lech Lesniak, piano
Label: Stolat/Arista Records, 1981, LP: SZM 0115 (Reissue of Polskie Nagrania "MUZA" SX 1210)
Boccherini, Luigi: *Minuet*
Schubert, Franz Peter: *Serenade*
Dvorák, Antonin: *Humoresque*
Mussorgsky, Modest: *Bydlo from "Pictures at an Exhibition"*
Ecclés, Henry: *Sonata in G minor* (I. Prelude; II. Courant)
Mozart, Wolfgang Amadeus: *Rondo in E♭major, K. 371*
Paderewski, Ignacy Jan: *Minuet*
Saint-Saëns, Camille: *Morceau de Concerto* (III. Allegro non troppo)
Schumann, Robert: *Traumerai*
Saint-Saëns, Camille: *The Elephant and The Swan from "Carnival of the Animals"*

Pilafian, Sam
Album Title: *Alec Wilder: Music for Horn*
Personnel:
Label: Arabesque Recordings Z6665
Wilder, Alec: *Sonata No. 1 for Horn, Tuba and Piano*

Pilafian, Sam
Album Title: *Appel Direct* (Frank Vignola)
Personnel: Frank Vignola, guitars/banjo; John Goldsby, bass; Joseph Ascione, drums; Junior Mance, piano; Billy Mitchell, tenor saxophone
Label: Concord Records, CD: CCD-4576
Jimmy Smith
Ready 'n Able
Billy Mitchell
Whirly Twirly

Pilafian, Sam
Album Title: *Barbara Cook: It's Better with a Band*
Personnel: Barbara Cook, vocals; Wally Harper, piano; Jimmy Mitchell, banjo
Label: 1980, LP: CS: CD:
Pinkard, Casey, and Tauber: *Them There Eyes*

Pilafian, Sam
Album Title: *Boyadjian: Sonata, Epistles, Sareebar*
Personnel: John Ziarko, percussion
Label: Opus One, 1984, CD: 109
Boyadjian, Hayg: *Sareebar for Tuba and Percussion*

Pilafian, Sam
Album Title: *A Brassy Night at the Opera*
Personnel: Thomas Bacon, horn; David Hickman, trumpet; Arizona State University Chamber Orchestra; Timothy Russell, conductor
Label: Summit Records, 1997, CD: SMT 190
Mozart, Wolfgang Amadeus: *Queen of the Night Aria from "The Magic Flute"*
Verdi, Giuseppi: *Sempre libera from "La Traviata"*
Puccini, Giacomo: *Nessun dorma from "Turandot"*
Rossini, Gioacchino: *Largo al factotum from "The Barber of Seville"*
Rossini, Gioacchino: *All'idea di qual metallo from "The Barber of Seville"*
Mozart, Wolfgang Amadeus: *Champagne Aria from "Don Giovanni"*
Puccini, Giacomo: *Musetta's Waltz from "La Bohème"*

Pilafian, Sam
Album Title: *Christmas with Travelin' Light*
Personnel: Frank Vignola, guitar; Ken Peplowski, clarinet; Don Keiling, rhythm guitar; Joe Ascione, drums; Andy Kubiszewski, percussion
Label: Telarc Jazz, 1993, CD: CD-83330
Nelson and Rollins: *Frosty the Snowman*
Anderson, Leroy: *Sleigh Ride*
Pierpont, James: *Jingle Bells*
Livingston, J., and R. Evans: *Silver Bells*
Bernard and Smith: *Winter Wonderland*
Gillespie and Coots: *Santa Claus Is Coming to Town*
Conor, Thomas: *I Saw Mommy Kissing Santa Claus*
Marks, John: *Rudolph, the Red-Nosed Reindeer*
Tormé and Wells: *The Christmas Song*
Autry and Haldeman: *Here Comes Santa Claus*
Cahn and Styne: *Let It Snow*
Martin, Blaine: *Have Yourself a Merry Little Christmas*
Leontovich and Wilhousky: *Carol of the Bells*
The Twelve Days of Christmas
We Wish You a Merry Christmas
Gruber, Franz: *Silent Night*

Pilafian, Sam
Album Title: *Cookin' with Frank and Sam*
Personnel: Frank Vignola, guitar; Eric Bogart, guitar, drums, and washboard; Allen Farnham, piano
Label: Concord Records, 1995, CD: CCD-4647
Reinhardt, Django: *Manoir De mes Reves*
Monk, Thelonius: *Monk's Dream*
Salama and Grebenka: *Dark Eyes*
DeRose, Peter: *Deep Purple*
Jones, Sam: *Say It's So*
Brun and Gannon: *Under Paris Skies*
Davis, Miles: *Dig*
Ellington, Edward Kennedy "Duke": *Mood Indigo*
Ohmen, Kjell: *Alice's Fax*
Reinhardt, Django: *Nuages*

Rome, Harold J.: *FDR Jones*
Kern, Jerome: *Smoke Gets in Your Eyes*
Reinhardt, Django: *Song D'Automne*
Rodgers, Richard, and Lorenz Hart: *Lover*
Pilafian, Sam
Album Title: *Cool Brassy Night at the North Pole*
Personnel: David Hickman, trumpet; Thomas Bacon, French horn; Robert Spring, clarinet; Kate McLin, violin; Chuck Marohnic, piano; Warren L. Jones III, bass; Don Moio, drums/percussion
Label: Summit Records, CD: SMT-223
God Rest Ye Merry, Gentlemen
O Come, O Come, Emmanuel
Martin, Blaine: *Have Yourself a Merry Little Christmas*
Silent Night
The Christmas Song
Davis, Katherine: *Little Drummer Boy*
What Child Is This?
Gounod, Charles: *Ave Maria*
Let It Snow
Jesu, Joy of Man's Desiring
O Holy Night
Christmas Carnival
Pilafian, Sam
Album Title: *Dos Amigos with Tambores*
Personnel: Pat Sheridan, tuba
Label: Elf Records, 2002, CD: ELFCD 1013
Jobim, Antonio Carlos: *Agua de Beber*
Hernandez, Rafael: *El Cumbanchero*
Velasquez, Consuelo: *Besame Mucho*
Alberti, Luis: *Campadre Pedro Juan*
Grenet, Ernesto: *Drume Negrita*
Barroso, Ary: *Brazil*
Simons, Moises: *El Manisero*
Blades, Ruben: *Patria*
Prado, Damaso Perez: *Mambo #5*
Rodriquez, G./Green: *La Cumparsita*
Jobim, Antonio Carlos: *One Note Samba (But Which Note?)*
James, Pepper, and Russell/Rigsby: *Vaya Con Dios*
Pilafian, Sam
Album Title: *The 5 Sonatas for Brass and Piano/Paul Hindemith*
Personnel: David Korevaar, piano
Label: Kleos Classics, 2002, CD: KL 5118
Hindemith, Paul: *Sonata for Bass Tuba and Piano*
Pilafian, Sam
Album Title: *The Last Elephant: The Mandala Octet*
Personnel: John Medesk, piano; John Leaman, bass; Gene Caldarazzo, drums
Label: Accurate Recordings, 1993, CS: CD:
The Unknown Soldier
Pilafian, Sam
Album Title: *Makin' Whoopee*
Personnel: Frank Vignola, guitar; Ken Peplowski, clarinet; Don Keiling, rhythm guitar; Joe Ascione, drums; Andy Kubiszewski, percussion
Label: Telarc, 1993, CD: CD83324
Reinhardt, Django: *Micro*
Reinken, Fred: *Wabash Blues*
Winfree, Dick: *China Boy*
Davis, Jimmie: *You Are My Sunshine*
Cannon, Hughie: *Bill Bailey Won't You Please Come Home*
Weill, Kurt: *Mack the Knife*
Berlin, Irving: *Alexander's Ragtime Band*
Vignola, Frank: *Chasin' the Antelope*
Carmichael, Hoagy: *New Orleans*
Carmichael, Hoagy: *Up a Lazy River*
Parker, Charlie: *Little Suede Shoes*
Donalson, Walter, and Gus Kahn: *Makin' Whoopee*
Henley, James: *Indiana*
Williams, Hank: *Jumbalaya*
Carmichael, Hoagy: *Georgia on My Mind*
Youmans, Vincent: *Carioca*
Berlin, Irving: *What'll I Do?*
Pilafian, Samuel
Album Title: *Meltdown*
Personnel: The Pilafian Project: Scott Zimmer, saxophones; John O'Reilly, Jr., drums
Label: Summit Records, 1998, CD: SMT-227
Zimmer, Scott: *ACA Referendum*
Bartók, Béla: *Ruthenian Dance*
Ravel, Maurice: *Prelude*
Monk, Thelonius: *I Mean You*
Beefheart, Captain: *Dali's Car*
Bartók, Béla: *Sadness*
Bechet, Sidney: *Petit Fleur*
Pilafian, Sam: *Gesualdo Movement*
Coleman, Ornette: *Blues Connotation*
Pilafian, Sam: *Big Easy Groove*
Pilafian, Sam
Album Title: *Ready and Able: Frank Vignola*
Personnel: Frank Vignola, guitar; Billy Mitchell, tenor sax; Junior Mance, piano; John Golosky, bass
Label: Concord Jazz, 1993, CS: CD:
Whirly Twirly
Ready and Able
Pilafian, Sam
Album Title: *Silks and Rags*
Personnel: Ken Cooper, piano; Mark Gould, trumpet; Charles Nedich, clarinet
Label: Angel EMI, 1991, CS, CD: CDC 7541312
Joplin, Scott: *The Cascades*
Joplin, Scott: *Peacherine Rag*
Pilafian, Sam
Album Title: *Travelin' Light—Getting It Together for Beginning Jazz Improvisation*
Personnel: Frank Vignola, guitar
Label: Summit Records, 1995, CD: DCD 183
One- and two-chord play-along grooves

Pilafian, Sam
Album Title: *Travelin' Light*
Personnel: Frank Vignola, guitar; Jimmy George, guitar; Mark Shane, piano,
Label: Telarc, 1991, CD: CD80281
Bernie, Pinkard, and Casey: *Sweet Georgia Brown*
Ellington, Edward Kennedy "Duke": *Don't Get Around Much Anymore*
Arlen and Harburg: *If I Only Had a Brain*
Rose, Jolson, and DeSylva: *Avalon*
Kern, Jerome: *Ol' Man River*
Razof and Johnson: *Louisiana*
Palmer and Williams: *I Found a New Baby*
Fisher, Goodwin, and Shay: *When You're Smiling*
Williams, Spencer: *Basin Street Blues*
DeCosta and La Rocca: *Tiger Rag*
Waller, Thomas "Fats": *Black and Blue*
Reinhardt, Django: *Rhythm Futur*
Braham and Furber: *Limehouse Blues*
Gershwin, George: *Someone to Watch over Me*

Pilafian, Sam
Album Title: *Trumpets in Stride*
Personnel: Mark Gould, Marvin Stamm, Chris Gekker, David Bilger, Tom Bontrager, trumpets; Mark Shane, piano
Label: Summit Records, 1990, CD: DCD 113
Ellington, Edward Kennedy "Duke": *The Mooche*
Armstrong, Louis: *Cornet Chop Suey*
Carmichael, Hoagy: *New Orleans*
Morton, F. "Jelly Roll": *Grandpa's Spells*
Ellington, Edward Kennedy "Duke": *East St. Louis Toodle-Oo*
Morton, F. "Jelly Roll": *Black Bottom Stomp*
Creamer/Layton: *After You've Gone*
Morton, F. "Jelly Roll": *Buddy Bolden's Blues*

Pilafian, Samuel
Album Title: *Jazz!*
Personnel: Greg Hopkins, trumpet; Gary Carney, Russell Scarbrough, trombones; Scott Zimmer, alto sax; Bryon Ruth, tenor sax; Steven Van Wald, baritone sax; Chuck Marohnic, piano; Ed Frieland, bass; Dom Moio, drums
Label: Summit Records, 1999, CD: SMT-229
Henry, Cleo/Evans: *Boplicity*
Hopkins, Greg: *Hidden Agenda*
Hopkins, Greg: *Bas Relief*
Carisi, John: *Israel*
Tyner, McCoy: *Mode to John*
Marohnic, Chuck: *Just Blues*
Mercer, Johnny, and C. MacGregor/Evans: *Moondreams*
Hopkins, Greg: *Mystic Valley*

Pilafian, Samuel
Album Title: *Perception*
Personnel: Arizona State University Symphony Orchestra; Timothy Morrison, conductor
Label: D'Note Classics, 1998, CD: DND1027
Anderson, Eugene: *The Perception of War*
Anderson, Eugene: *Tuba Concerto No. 1 in B minor*
Anderson, Eugene: *Lyri-Tech for Solo Tuba*
Anderson, Eugene: *Baroque 'n Brass for Trumpet and Tuba*

Pilafian, Sam; see Gerhard Meinl's Tuba Sextet; *Tubas! A Six-Tuba Musical Romp;* see New York Tuba Quartet; *Tubby's Revenge;* see Sheridan, Patrick; *Bon Bons;* see Swoboda, Deanna; *Deanna's Wonderland;* see Symphonia

Pokorny, Gene
Album Title: *Big Boy*
Personnel: Jay Friedman, Michael Mulcahy, trombones; Bradley Haag, piano; Edward Ted Atkatz, percussion; Chris Willis, tapes
Label: Summit Records, 2001, CD: #283
Reynolds, Jeffrey: *Skirmish and Dance*
Prokofiev, Sergey: *Visions fugitives*
Penn, William: *Three Essays for Solo Tuba*
Satterwhite, Marc: *And What Rough Beast . . . ? for Tuba and Percussion*
McKimm, Barry: *Andante Tranquillo, for Solo Viola and Piano*
Penn, William: *Capriccio for Tuba and Marimba*

Pokorny, Gene
Album Title: *Hindemith, Paul: Complete Brass Works*
Personnel: Theodor Lichtmann, Piano
Label: Summit Records, 1991, 2CDs: DCD 115-2
Hindemith, Paul: *Sonata for Bass Tuba and Piano*

Pokorny, Gene
Album Title: *OrchestraPro Series: Orchestral Excerpts for Tuba*
Personnel:
Label: Summit Records, 1996, CD: DCD 142
Bartók, Béla: *Concerto for Orchestra (excerpt)*
Berlioz, Hector: *Damnation de Faust (excerpt)*
Berlioz, Hector: *Roméo et Juliette (excerpt)*
Berlioz, Hector: *Symphonie fantastique (excerpt)*
Bruckner, Anton: *Symphony No. 7 in E major ("Lyric") (excerpt)*
Gershwin, George: *An American in Paris (excerpt)*
Hindemith, Paul: *Symphonic Metamorphosis of Themes by Carl Maria von Weber (excerpt)*
Holst, Gustav: *The Planets (excerpt)*
Mahler, Gustav: *Symphony No. 1 in D major ("Titan") (excerpt)*
Mahler, Gustav: *Symphony No. 5 in C♯ minor (excerpt)*
Mahler, Gustav: *Symphony No. 6 in A minor ("Tragic") (excerpt)*

Mussorgsky, Modest: *Pictures at an Exhibition (excerpt)*
Prokofiev, Sergey: *Romeo and Juliet, Op. 64 (excerpt)*
Prokofiev, Sergey: *Symphony No. 5 in B♭ major, Op. 100 (excerpt)*
Respighi, Ottorino: *Fontane di Roma (excerpt)*
Strauss, Richard: *Also sprach Zarathustra (excerpt)*
Strauss, Richard: *Ein Heldenleben (excerpt)*
Strauss, Richard: *Till Eulenspiegels lustige Streiche (excerpt)*
Stravinsky, Igor: *Petroushka (excerpt)*
Wagner, Richard: *A Faust Overture (excerpt)*
Wagner, Richard: *Lohengrin (excerpt)*
Wagner, Richard: *Die Meistersinger von Nürnberg (excerpt)*
Wagner, Richard: *Ride of the Valkyries (excerpt)*

Pokorny, Gene
Album Title: *Star Wars Trilogy*
Personnel: Utah Symphony Orchestra; Varnjan Kojian, conductor
Label: Varese-Sarabande, 1983, CD: VCD47201
Williams, John: *Jabba the Hutt from "Return of the Jedi"*

Pokorny, Gene
Album Title: *Tuba Tracks*
Personnel: Roberta Garten, piano; Mary Mottl, piano; David "Red" Lehr and the Jazz Incredibles
Label: Summit Records, 1991, CD: DCD129; CS: DCD129
Handel, George Friderik: *Sonata in G Major*
Bach, Johann Sebastian: *Partita in A minor for Flute Alone*
Debussy, Claude/Schaefer: *General Levine—Eccentric*
Rachmaninoff, Sergei: *Three Songs*
Castérède, Jacques: *Serenade from Sonatine for Bass Saxhorn and Piano*
Ravel, Maurice: *Pavane pour une infante dufunte*
Debussy, Claude: *Prélude à "L'Après-midi d'un Faune"*
Vaughan Williams, Ralph: *Six Studies in English Folksong*
Pryor, Arthur: *Theme and Variation on the "Blue Bells of Scotland"*
Blake, Eubie: *Memories of You*

Pokorny, Gene; see Self, James; *The Big Stretch;* see Summit Tubas; *American Tribute—Summit Brass*

Poore, Melvyn
Album Title: *Electric Surrealistic Landscapes: The McClean Mix*
Personnel: Pricilla and Barton McClean
Label: Opus One, CD: 96
McLean, Pricilla: *Beneath the Horizon for Tuba and Taped Whale Songs*

Poore, Melvyn
Album Title: *Groundwork*
Personnel: Lawrence Casserley, live electronics
Label: Random Acoustics, 1994, CD: RA 005
Poore, Melvyn: *One, Two, Three*
Poore, Melvyn: *Stand Alone I*
Poore, Melvyn: *Stoneground*
Poore, Melvyn: *Playback I*
Poore, Melvyn: *Stand Alone II*
Poore, Melvyn: *Tubassoon*
Poore, Melvyn: *And Finally*
Poore, Melvyn: *Stand Alone III*
Poore, Melvyn: *Study in Moving Sounds*

Poore, Melvyn; see European Tuba Quartet

Popiel, Peter
Album Title: *Music for Young Bands, Vol. II*
Personnel: State University of New York—Fredonia Wind Ensemble
Label: Century Custom Recording Service, LP:
Dedrick, Art: *A Touch of Tuba*

Popiel, Peter
Album Title: *1974 Mid-West Band and Orchestra Clinic*
Personnel: Indian Trail Junior High School Concert Band
Label: Golden Crest, LP: MID-74-12
Frackenpohl, Arthur: *Variations for Tuba and Winds (Cobbler's Bench)*

Popiel, Peter
Album Title: *Peter Popiel: Recital Music for Tuba*
Personnel: Henry Fuchs, piano
Label: Mark Educational Recordings, LP: MRS 28437
Bach, Johann Sebastian/Bell: *Air and Bourree*
Handel, George Friderik/Ostrander: *Bourree from the Sixth Flute Sonata*
Mendelssohn, Felix: *It Is Enough from "Elijah"*
Semler-Collery, Jules: *Barcarolle et Chanson Bachique*
Hartley, Walter: *Sonatina*
Handel, George Friderik/Lafosse: *Concerto in G minor for Oboe and Orchestra*
Benson, Warren: *Arioso*
Hartley, Walter: *Suite for Unaccompanied Tuba*

Porter, David
Album Title: *44th Annual Mid-West International Band and Orchestra Clinic 1990*
Personnel: Roger Behrend, euphonium; Lake Braddock Secondary School Symphonic Band; Roy Holder and Jim Stegner, conductors
Label: Mark Recordings, 1990, CS: MW-90MC-19
Frackenpohl, Arthur: *Song and Dance for Euphonium, Tuba and Band*

Poulsen, Heick
Album Title: *Atlantis Transit*
Personnel:
Label: Olufsen Records, LP: DOC 5068
Powell, Jim; see Hoffnung, Gerard; *Hoffnung Music Festival Concert*
Price, Tony
Album Title: *Together Again—For the First Time: Mel Tormé and Buddy Rich*
Personnel: The Buddy Rich Band
Label: Jazz Heritage, 1978, CD: 512742L
Mercer, Johnny, and Harold Arlen: *Blues in the Night*
Price, Tony
Album Title: *Tree Music by Paul Chihara*
Personnel:
Label: Composer's Recordings, Inc., LP: CRI 269
Chihara, Paul: *Willow, Willow* (bass flute, tuba, percussion)
Price, Tony; see New York Tuba Quartet; *Tubby's Revenge*
Ramírez, Hernán
Album Title: *Tres Cánones y Tres Fanfarrias*
Personnel:
Label: Música Chilena de Siglo, 1998, CD: XX, Vol. II, SVR Producciones Limitada
Randolph, David
Album Title: *Contrasts in Contemporary Music*
Personnel: Peggy Randolph, piano; Richard Zimdars, piano
Label: ACA Digital Recording, 1992, CD: CM20018-18
George, Thom Ritter: *Sonata for Tuba and Piano*
Takács, Jenö: *Sonata Capricciosa, Op. 81*
Stevens, Halsey: *Sonatina for Tuba and Piano*
Baker, Claude: *Omaggi e Fantasie*
Randolph, David
Album Title: *Tuba Suites . . . And Other Sweets*
Personnel: Peggy Randolph, piano
Label: ACA Digital, 1995, CD: #20025
Defaye, Jean-Michel: *Suite Marine*
Lebedev, Alexei: *Concert Allegro*
Semler-Collery, Jules: *Barcarolle et Chanson Bachique*
Monti, Vittorio: *Csárdás*
Koetsier, Jan: *Sonatina for Trombone and Piano*
Jacob, Gordon: *Suite for Tuba and String Orchestra*
Mantia, Simone: *Believe Me If All Those Endearing Young Charms*
Swann, Donald: *Two Moods for Tuba*
Reilly, Timothy; see Mighty Tubadours; *Ve Iss Da Mighty Tubadours, Ya?*
Responsura, Judicanti; see Roper, William; *Juneteenth; Roper's Darn! Yarns*
Robinson, Jack
Album Title: *Windsongs*
Personnel: University of Northern Colorado Symphonic Band; David Wallace, conductor
Label: Soundmark, 1981, LP: R894 KM6748
Benson, Warren: *Helix for Solo Tuba and Concert Band*
Rojas, Marcus
Album Title: *Plunge—Falling with Grace*
Personnel: Mark McGrain, trombone and alphorn; Bob Moses, drums, percussion, and voice; Avishai Cohen, bass
Label: Accurate Records, 1995, CD:
McGrain, Mark: *Wagdanz*
McGrain, Mark, and Marcus Rojas: *394*
McGrain, Mark: *Beneath the Wheel*
McGrain, Mark: *Reveille*
McGrain, Mark: *Just like Alice*
McGrain, Mark: *Dog*
McGrain, Mark: *The Mist*
Moses, Bob: *Rafael's Drum/h.s.l.e.*
McGrain, Mark: *Mungo*
McGrain, Mark: *11:11*
McGrain, Mark: *Trick of the Light*
McGrain, Mark, and Bob Moses: *Running, Running*
Rojas, Marcus; see Johnson, Howard; *Howard Johnson & Gravity!!!*
Roper, William
Album Title: *Juneteenth*
Personnel: Judicanti Responsura, Zen Tsuba, tubas; Joseph Mitchell, percussion, vocals; Glenn Horichi, piano and shamisen; Lillian Nakano, shamisen; Francis Wong, flute; Tom Kurai, taiko
Label: Asian Improv, 2001, CD: AIR 0055
Roper, William: *Juneteenth*
Roper, William: *Pigs, Pigs, Oh! Those Tasty Pigs*
Vlatkovich: *The Perfect Construction of Decisive Moments*
Traditional: *Kagami Jishi*
Mitchell: *Dance of the Sophists*
Roper, William: *A Recondite State of Lorn*
Roper, William: *Lachrimae*
Roper, William
Album Title: *Roper's Darn! Yarns: Tales of Love and Woe*
Personnel: Judicanti Responsura, tuba; Francis Wong, woodwinds; Elliot Humberto, kavee-drums, cello; Joseph Mitchell, percussion, vocals; Glenn Horichi, piano and shamisen
Label: Asian Improv, 2002, CD: AIR 0058
Roper, William: *Em(M)*
Roper, William: *Golden Gate Park/You Don't Know What Love Is*
Horichi, Glenn: *Once upon a Time*
Rozen, Jay
Album Title: *Killer Tuba Songs*
Personnel: Vern Nelson, piano

Label: TTT Music, 1997
White, John: *Concert Duos*
Nelson, Vern: *Killer Tuba Songs*
White, John: *Three Movements from Basingstoke*
Rozen, Jay
Album Title: *Music of David Lang*
Personnel: Jay Rozen, electric tuba
Label: CRI, CD: 625
Rustic Bari-Tuba Ensemble
Album Title: *Rustic Bari-Tuba Ensemble*
Personnel: Fukuda Masanori, Makita Yoshiyuki, euphoniums; Muto Takayuki, Obana Jun, tubas
Label: Brain Music, 2001, CD: OSBR-17071
Bartles, Alfred: *When Tubas Waltz*
Debussy, Claude/Fukuda: *La Fille aux Cheveux de lin*
Schooley, John: *Cherokee*
Schooley, John: *Toccata*
Stevens, John: *Dances*
Frackenpohl, Arthur: *Pop Suite*
arr. Burrey: *Greensleeves*
Toda, Akira: *Euphonium Tuba Quartet*
Lacalle, J./Fukuda: *Amapola*
D'enza, Luigi/Fukuda: *Funiculi-Funicula Fantasy*
Meacham, Frank W./Konagaya: *American Tuba Patrol*
Sanden, Jan van de; see Dutch Tuba Quartet
Sass, Jonathon
Album Title: *Heavy Tuba and Jon Sass at the Montreaux Jazz Festival*
Personnel:
Label:
I Caught a Touch of Your Love
Concerto for Tuba
Didge I Do
Theme of Bolero
Para Ti
Toccata
Count Phenomium
Tadellos
Here Comes the Night
Sass, Jonathon
Album Title: *Symphonic Winds and Jon Sass*
Personnel: Symphonic Winds; Alexander Veit, conductor
Label: Amos, 1999, CD: 5901
Madden, Edward: *Elegy*
Youmans, Vincent: *Carioca*
Hausl, Johann: *Tubatubap*
Sass, Jonathon; see Gerhard Meinl's Tuba Sextet; *Tubas! A Six-Tuba Musical Romp;* see Heavy Tuba
Scandinavian Tuba Jazz
Album Title: *How Deep Is the Ocean*
Personnel: Michael Lind, Stein-Erik Tafjord, tubas; Torolf Mölgård, Frode Thingnäs, euphoniums; Göran Söderlund, piano; Sture Nordin, bass; Bjarne Rostvold, drums
Label: Four Leaf Records, 1986, LP: FLC 5093
Thingnäs, Frode: *Fink Finster*
McDermot, Ragni, and Rado/Bergman: *Dead End*
Hermann, Heinz: *Korn Blues*
Davis, Miles: *All Blues*
Berlin, Irving/Windfeld: *How Deep Is the Ocean?*
Hermann, Herman: *Y Luego*
Thingnäs, Frode: *Samba Loco*
Schiaffini, Giancarlo
Album Title: *Infernal Dream*
Personnel:
Label: Rofo Records, 1986, LP: CPR 17001
Schiaffini, Giancarlo: *Infernal Dream*
Schiaffini, Giancarlo
Album Title: *Space Blossoms—Dino Vander Noot*
Personnel:
Label: Innowo, 1989, CD: IN 813
Betti, Dino: *Space Blossoms*
Schiaffini, GianCarlo
Album Title: *Tuba Libre*
Personnel:
Label: Random Acoustics, 2000, CD: LC 04945
Schiaffini, GianCarlo: *Tuba Libre*
Schiaffini, GianCarlo: *Madrugada de laton*
Schiaffini, GianCarlo: *Scrap*
Schiaffini, GianCarlo: *Voz refracta*
Schiaffini, GianCarlo: *Sueno infernal*
Schiaffini, GianCarlo: *El carrousel de Juana la Loca*
Schiaffini, GianCarlo: *Mi mistico minimo Mi*
Schiaffini, GianCarlo: *Scratch*
Schiaffini, GianCarlo: *Cuba Mirum*
Schiaffini, GianCarlo: *El vuelo irresistibile del moscardon*
Schiaffini, GianCarlo: *Aqui el sol brilla mas*
Schmearer, William; see Stevens, John; *Power*
Schmid, Reinhold; see Heavy Tuba
Schmitz, Chester
Album Title: *The Boston Pops: Out of This World*
Personnel: The Boston Pops Orchestra; John Williams, conductor
Label: Philips, 1983, LP: 411 185-1
Williams, John: *Jabba the Hutt from "Return of the Jedi"*
Schmitz, Chester
Album Title: *Tubby the Tuba*
Personnel: Julia Childs, narrator; Boston Pops; Arthur Fiedler, conductor
Label: Polydor, 1970, LP: RD 5032
Kleinsinger, George, and Paul Tripp: *Tubby the Tuba*
Schneider, Christoph
Album Title: *Jean Francaix et . . .*
Personnel: Blaser Ensemble Amade: Philippe Boucly, Christiane Steffens, flutes; Stefan

Schilli, Dieter Salewski, oboes; Karl Heinz Steffens, Werner Mittelback, clarinets; Karl Ventulett, Matthias Roscher, bassoons; Johannes Ritzkowsky, Ursula Kepser, horns; Klaus Rainer Shoell, conductor
Label: ALCRA, ALC 5104-2
Francaix, Jean: *Petit valse europeenne pour tuba et double quintette a vents*

Schulz, Patrick: see Sotto Voce

Schumacker, Finn
Album Title: *Philip-Jones-Story*
Personnel: Südtiroler Bläserensemble
Label: Marcophon, CD: 952-2
Danielssohn, Christer: *Capriccio Da Camera for Solo Tuba and Brass Quintet*

Self, James
Album Title: *An American Tail II—Fieval Goes West [motion picture soundtrack]*
Personnel: Music by James Horner
Label: MCA, 1991, CD: MCAD-10416; CS: MCAC-10416

Self, James
Album Title: *Atlantis [motion picture soundtrack]*
Personnel: Score by James Newton Howard

Self, James
Album Title: *Basset Hound Blues*
Personnel: Pete Christlieb, tenor saxophone; Terry Trotter, piano; Tom Warrington, string bass; Steve Houghton, drums
Label: d'Note Records, 1997, CD: DND 1021
Self, James: *The Basset Hound Blues*
Brown, Tom: *One for Nick*
Loesser, Frank: *I've Never Been in Love Before*
Self, James: *Capriole*
Wright, Robert: *Baubles, Bangles and Beads*
Herman, Jerry: *Ribbons down My Back*
Morrey, Larry: *Some Day My Prince Will Come*
Sellers, Joey: *Terrible Twos*
Konitz, Lee: *No Splice*
Robin, Leo: *Easy Livin'*
Stanley the Bassett Hound: *Stanley's Last "Howl"*

Self, James
Album Title: *The Big Stretch*
Personnel: Tommy Johnson, Winston Morris, Norm Pearson, Gene Pokorny, Fred Greene, Doug Tornquist, tubas; Loren Marstellar, Ernie Carlson, euphoniums; John Magnussen, trombone; Malcolm McNab, Jon Lewis, trumpets; Dave Duke, horn; Wendy Prober, piano; Joann Turovsky, harp
Label: Basset Hound Records, 1999, CD: 106-2
Self, James: *Poker Chips*
Self, James: *Rondeau*
Self, James: *3 for 5*
Self, James: *Polka.com*
Newman, Maria: *9th Hour of Divine Office*
Grant, Jerome: *Time Cycles*
Scharnberg, Kim: *Waltz for Maya*
Tchaikovsky, Peter Ilyitch/Self: *Finale to Symphony #4*

Self, James
Album Title: *Bobby Jones, Stroke of Genius [motion picture soundtrack]*
Personnel: Score by James Horner

Self, James
Album Title: *Cat in the Hat [motion picture soundtrack]*
Personnel: Score by David Newman

Self, James
Album Title: *Changing Colors*
Personnel: Terry Trotter, piano; Doug Masek, alto saxophone; Burnette Dillon, Tony Ellis, trumpets; John Reynolds, horn; William Booth, trombone; Robert Sanders, bass trombone; Janet Lakatos, viola; David Speltz, cello; David Young, double bass; Gayle Levant, harp; Thomas Raney, percussion; David Rubenstein, synthesizer
Label: Summit Records, 1992, CD: DCD 132
Debussy, Claude: *Syrinx*
Stevens, Halsey: *Sonatina for Tuba and Piano*
Kochan, Gunter: *Sieben Miniaturen für Vier Tuben*
Self, James: *Courante*
Schumann, Robert/Self: *Scenes from Childhood, Op. 15*
Rubenstein, Arthur: *Bruegel—Dance Visions*
Capuzzi, Antonio/Self: *Rondo Allegro* (tuba with brass quintet)

Self, James
Album Title: *Close Encounters of the Third Kind [motion picture soundtrack]*
Personnel:
Label: Varese-Sarabande, 1977, CD: VSD 5275
Williams, John: *The Conversation*

Self, James
Album Title: *Don Ellis—Live at Montreaux*
Personnel: Don Ellis Band
Label: Atlantic

Self, James
Album Title: *Faces*
Personnel:
Label: Canary, 2001, CD:
Rodgers, Richard: *My Heart Stood Still*
Shorter, Wayne: *Adam's Apple*
Strayhorn, Billy: *Lush Life*
Parker, Dorothy: *I Wished on the Moon*

Self, James
Album Title: *Grinch Who Stole Christmas [motion picture soundtrack]*
Personnel: Score by James Horner

Self, James
Album Title: *Home Alone [motion picture soundtrack]*

Personnel: Music by John Williams
Label: CBS, 1990, CD: SK 46595; CS: ST 46595
Williams, John: *Home Alone*

Self, James
Album Title: *Home Alone II [motion picture soundtrack]*
Personnel: Music by John Williams
Label: Fox, 1992, CD: 07822-11000-2
Williams, John: *Home Alone II*

Self, James
Album Title: *Hook [motion picture soundtrack]*
Personnel: Music by John Williams
Label: Epic Soundtrax, 1991, CD: EK-4888; CS: ET-4888
Williams, John: *Hook*

Self, James
Album Title: *In Concert Tokyo*
Personnel: Mel Tormé and Marty Paitch
Label: Concord

Self, James
Album Title: *"InnerPlay"—Jim Self with Strings*
Personnel: Arranged by Brad Dechter. Featuring: Gary Foster, Pete Christlieb, Dan Higgins
Label: 2004, In preparation
Hancock, Herbie: *Speak like a Child*
Jones, Isham: *There Is No Greater Love*
Clare Fischer: *Pensativa*
Gershwin, George: *I Loves You Porgy/Bess You Is My Woman*
Huffsteter, Steve: *Cipriana*
Self, James: *That Morning in May*
Dechter, Brad: *The Underdog Has Arisen*
Jobim, Antonio Carlos: *No More Blues*
Silver, Horace: *Strollin'*
Alter, Louis: *Do You Know What It Means to Miss New Orleans?*

Self, James
Album Title: *Jim Morris—Brass Plus: Montage*
Personnel: Jim Morris, bass trombone; Bruce Fowler, trombone; Suzette Moriarty, horn; Steve Huffsteter, trumpet; Tom Adams, piano; Steve Moore, guitar; Jack Le Compte, drums; Jim Self, tuba and electric bass
Label: Mama Foundation, 1992, CD: MF 1005
Nelson, Oliver: *Blues and the Abstract Truth*
Adams, Tommy: *View from the Footplate*
Gale, Jack: *Picture of Dorian Blue*

Self, James
Album Title: *Jim Self and Friends "New Stuff"*
Personnel: James Self, tuba, bass trombone, electric bass, EVI (electronic valve instrument); Jon Kurnick, guitar; John Magnussen, percussion; Harvey Mason, drums;Ernie McDaniel, bass
Label: Trend Records, 1988, CD: TRCD-548
Harlos, Steve: *Breakthrough*
Brown, Tom: *New Stuff*
Morell, John: *Windsong*
Myers, Stanley: *Cavatina*
Brown, Tom: *Kilo*
Kurnick, Jon: *Bosque De Manaus*
Bach, Johann Sebastian/Self: *Sinfonia III*
Kalina, Ron: *Children at Play*
Waller, Thomas "Fats": *Jitterbug Waltz*
Eldsvoog, John: *Walt's Samba*
Rowles, Jimmy: *The Peacocks*
Mingus, Charlie: *Peggy's Blue Skylight*
McDaniel, Ernie: *Secrets*

Self, James
Album Title: *Jim Self Quintet—Children at Play*
Personnel: Ron Kalina, harmonica; Jon Kurnick, guitar; Ernie McDaniel, bass; Harold Mason, drums; Steve Forman, percussion
Label: Discovery, 1983, LP: DS-886
Kalina, Ron: *Children at Play*
Waller, Thomas "Fats": *Jitterbug Waltz*
Eldsvoog, John: *Walt's Samba*
Rowles, Jimmy: *The Peacocks*
Mingus, Charlie: *Peggy's Blue Skylight*
McDaniel, Ernie: *Secrets*

Self, James
Album Title: *Lemony Snicket [motion picture soundtrack]*
Personnel: Score by Tom Newman

Self, James
Album Title: *The Linguini Incident [motion picture soundtrack]*
Personnel: Music by Thomas Newman
Label: Varese-Sarabande, 1992, CD: VSD-5372; CS: VSC-5372
Newman, Thomas: *The Linguini Incident*

Self, James
Album Title: *Multiplicity [motion picture soundtrack]*
Personnel: Score by George Fenton

Self, James
Album Title: *My America*
Personnel: Burnette Dillon, trumpet; Bill Booth, trombone; Gary Foster, clarinet and saxes; Mike Lang, piano; Tim May, banjos and guitars; Dave Carpenter, basses; Bernie Dresel, drums; Joel Derouin, violin; Armen Ksadjikian, cello; Kim Scharnberg, synthesizer; Brian Kilgore, percussion; Chuck Niles, narration
Label: Basset Hound Records, 2002, CD BHR-107-2
Traditional: *I've Been Workin'*
DeSilva, Jolson, Meyer: *Yo, California*
King, Pee Wee, and Redd Stewart: *Tennessee Waltz*

Cannon, Hughie: *Bill Bailey, Please Call Your Service*
Foster, Stephen: *Old Homes*
Foster, Stephen: *Camptown Races*
Traditional: *Simple Gifts*
Traditional: *Turkey in the Straw (and Several Other Places)*
Traditional: *Shenandoah*
Gray, Jerry, and Carl Sigman: *Pennsylvania 6-5000 Polka*
Fisher, Fred: *My Flying Machine*
Foster, Stephen: *Beautiful Dreamer*
Lambert, Louis: *When Johnny Comes Marching Home*
Self, James: *Sousa, Phone Home!*
Scharnberg, Kim: *Juba Plays the FLUBA in Aruba*
Ward, Samuel A.: *America the Beautiful*
Gus and Buford: *Dog Tags*

Self, James
Album Title: *Music from Star Wars and Other Galaxies*
Personnel: Don Ellis Band
Label: Atlantic

Self, James
Album Title: *Mystic Solar Dance*
Personnel: Bingo Miki
Label: Kitty Jazz

Self, James
Album Title: *Reunion*
Personnel: Mel Tormé; Marty Paitch Decktette
Label: Concord

Self, James
Album Title: *Size Matters—The Bill Scarlett Quartet featuring Jim Self*
Personnel: Bill Scarlett, tenor saxophone; Bill Swann, piano; Taylor Coker, string bass; Daryll Johnson, drums
Label: Bassett Hound Records, 2003, CD: BHR 108-2
Rollins, Sonny: *Doxy*
Aldcroft, Randy: *Inner Self*
Wallington, George: *Godchild*
Meyer-Bretton, D., and S. Edwards: *For Heaven's Sake*
Brown, Tom: *Disgruntled Lullaby*
Self, James: *For Christina*
Ellington, Edward Kennedy "Duke": *In a Mellow Tone*
Wood, Guy, and Robert Mellin: *My One and Only Love*
Davis, Miles: *All Blues*

Self, James
Album Title: *Tricky Lix*
Personnel: Gary Foster, woodwinds; Warren Luening, trumpet; Bill Booth, trombone; Jon Kurnick, guitar; Joel Hamilton, bass; Alan Estes, drums
Label: Concord Records, 1990, CD: CCD-4430
Aldcroft, Randy: *Tricky Lix*
Berg, Curt: *Take the Stairs*
Monk, Williams, Hanighen: *'Round Midnight*
Brown, Tom: *Night Lights*
Broadbent, Alan: *Another Time*
Aldcroft, Randy: *Somebody's Samba*
Lerner, Alan Jay: *Heather on the Hill*
Porter, Cole: *I Love You*
Rodgers, Richard, and Lorenz Hart: *My Funny Valentine*
Berg, Curt: *The Farewell Burn*

Self, James
Album Title: *Troy [motion picture soundtrack]*
Personnel: Score by James Horner

Self, James; see Johnson, John Thomas (Tommy); *Beetlejuice; Capricorn One; Star Trek—The Motion Picture*

Seward, Steven
Album Title: *Classic Tuba*
Personnel:
Label: Walking Frog Records, CD: WFR504
CD format reissue of *The Virtuoso Tuba* and *The Virtuoso Tuba Vol. II*

Seward, Steven
Album Title: *Kansas City Dances*
Personnel: Vicki Berneking, piano; Patricia Higdon; David Diebold
Label: Walking Frog Records, CD: WFR444
Holsinger, David: *Kansas City Dances*
Sparke, Philip: *Fantasy for Euphonium and Brass Band*
Lax, Fred: *Fantasia of Popular Irish Airs*
Mendelssohn, Felix: *Concerto for Violin (third movement)*
Smith, Claude T.: *Ballade and Presto Dance*
Dukas, Paul: *Villanelle for Horn*
Telemann, Georg Philipp: *Sonata in E minor*
Mantia, Simone: *Believe Me If All Those Endearing Young Charms*

Seward, Steven
Album Title: *The Virtuoso Tuba*
Personnel: Vicki Berneking, piano; Eric Anderson, euphonium
Label: Golden Crest, 1979, LP: RE 7083, CD:
Bach, Johann Sebastian: *Suite in B♭ minor for Flute*
Handel, George Friderik/Fitzgerald: *Aria con Variazioni*
Bozza, Eugène: *Concertino for Tuba and Piano*
Telemann, Georg Philipp: *Sonata in F minor*
Vivaldi, Antonio: *Concerto in C major for Two Trumpets*

Seward, Steven
Album Title: *The Virtuoso Tuba, Vol. II*
Personnel: Vicki Berneking, piano
Label: Golden Crest, 1984, LP: RE-7096
Strauss, Richard: *Second Horn Concerto*
Pryor, Arthur: *The Blue Bells of Scotland*
Picchi, Ermanno/Mantia: *Fantasie Original*
Bach, Vincent: *Hungarian Melodies*

Sheridan, Patrick
Album Title: *Blazing Brass*
Personnel: Salvation Army New York Staff Band
Label: Summit Records, CD: SMT-1012
Doughty, G./Graham: *Variations on "Grandfather's Clock"*
Ellerby, Martin: *Tuba Concerto*
Norbury, Kevin: *Badinage*
Goedicke/Wm. Broughton: *Concert Etude*
Arban, Jean-Baptiste/Freeh: *Variations on a Tyrolean Song*

Sheridan, Patrick
Album Title: *Bon Bons*
Personnel: Rich Ridenour, Dave Ihlenfeld, piano; Dom Moio, bongos; Sam Pilafian, tuba
Label: Walking Frog Records, CD: WFR465
Dinicu, Grigoras: *Hora Staccato*
Ponce, Manuel: *Estrellita*
Chopin, Frédéric: *Minute Waltz*
Rachmaninoff, Sergei: *Vocalise Op. 34, No. 14*
Mendez, Rafael: *Mexican Hat Dance*
Fauré, Gabriel: *Après un Rêve*
Arban, Jean Baptiste: *Carnival of Venice*
Kreisler, Fritz: *Midnight Bells from the "Opera Ball"/Liebesfreud*
Bach, Johann Sebastian: *Ave Maria*
Davis: *Jenny Wren*
Foster, Stephen: *Jeannie with the Light Brown Hair*
Nero, Paul: *Hot Canary*
Ihlenfeld, Dave: *Clouds*
DeCosta and LaRocca: *Tiger Rag*
Loesser, Frank: *Fugue for Tinhorns from "Guys & Dolls"* (two tubas and bongos)

Sheridan, Patrick
Album Title: *Etudes with Style: Music for the Tuba*
Personnel:
Label: Tuba-Euphonium Press, 2004, book and CD: In preparation
Salotti, Harry: *Etudes with Style, Music for the Tuba*

Sheridan, Patrick
Album Title: *Lollipops*
Personnel: Rich Ridenour, piano
Label: Walking Frog Records, CD: WFR417
Monti, Vittorio: *Csárdás*
Kreisler, Fritz: *Liebesleid*
Kreisler, Fritz: *Schon Rosmarin*
Traditional: *Danny Boy (The Londonderry Air)*
Abreu, Zequinha: *Tico Tico*
Saint-Saëns, Camille: *The Swan from "Carnival of the Animals"*
Romberg, Sigmund: *Serenade from the "Student Prince"*
Drigo, Richard: *Valse Bluette*
Massenet, Jules: *Meditation from "Thais"*
Elgar, Edward: *La Capricieuse, Op. 17*
Elgar, Edward: *Salut D'Amour, Op. 12*
Gluck, Christopf: *Dance of the Blessed Spirits*
Rimmer, William: *Hailstorm*
Crockett, Edgar: *Mustique*
Rimsky-Korsakov, Nicholas: *Flight of the Bumblebee*
Kern, Jerome: *Ol' Man River*
Arndt, Felix: *Nola*
Chaplin, Charlie: *Smile*

Sheridan, Patrick
Album Title: *Storyteller*
Personnel: Johan Willem Friso Military Band; Gert D. Buitenhuis, conductor
Label: Elf Records, 2002, CD: 1014
Hummel, Johann Nepomuk: *Adagio, Theme and Variations, Op. 102*
Tchaikovsky, Peter Ilyitch: *Andante Cantabile*
Wilhelm, Rolf: *Concertino*
Barnes, James: *Yorkshire Ballad*
Barnes, James: *Concerto, Op. 96b*
Youmans, Vincent: *Carioca*

Sheridan, Patrick; see Pilafian; *Dos Amigos*

Sibley, Graham
Album Title:
Personnel: Hendon Band
Bratton, John W./Roberts: *Teddy Bear's Picnic*

Sinder, Philip
Album Title: *Aerodynamics*
Personnel: Deborah Moriarity, piano; Janine Gaboury-Sly, horn; Michigan State University Wind Symphony, John Whitwell, conductor
Label: Mark, CD: MCD-1701
Telemann, Georg Philipp: *Sonata in F*
Tcherepnin, Alexander: *Andante*
Broughton, Bruce: *Sonata [Concerto] for Tuba and Piano*
Gillingham, David: *Divertmento for Horn, Tuba, and Piano*
Ruggiero, Charles: *Fractured Mambos*
Benson, Warren: *Arioso*
Schmidt, William: *Tuba Mirum—Variations on a Gregorian Chant*

Skillen, Joseph
Album Title: *Blue Plate Special*
Personnel: Jan Grimes, piano
Label: Mark Custom Recording, 2000, CD3964-MCD
Plog, Anthony: *Three Miniatures for Tuba and Piano*
Schumann, Robert: *Adagio and Allegro in A♭, Op. 70*
Wilhelm, Rolf: *Concertino for Tuba and Piano*
Constantinides, Dinos: *Mutability Fantasy*
Hayden, Paul: *Chaconne*
Ewazen, Eric: *Concerto for Tuba*

Smith, Edgar; see New Orleans Jazz Bands; *Down Yonder*

Smith, J. R.
Album Title: *Chamber Music of Anthony Iannoccone*

Personnel: Carter Eggers, trumpet
Label: Coronet, LP: LPS 3038
Iannoccone, Anthony: *Sonatina for Trumpet and Tuba*

Sotto Voce
Album Title: *Consequences*
Personnel: Michael Forbes, Demondrae Thurman, euphoniums; Nat McIntosh, Patrick Schulz, tubas
Label: Summit Records, 2002, CD: SMT-322
Forbes, Mike: *Consequences,* for tuba quartet
Gasparini, Quirino: *Adoramus te Christe*
Bach, Johann Sebastian: *Contrapunctus 9 from Die Kunst der Fuge*
Kupferman, Meyer: *Kierkegaard, for Tuba Quartet*
Haydn, Franz Joseph: *Achieved Is the Glorious Work from "Die Schöpfung"*
Grovlez, Gabriel: *Petites Litanies de Jésus*
Schulz, Patrick: *Profiles,* for tuba quartet
Forbes, Mike: *Auburn Is the Colour*
Handel, George Friderik: *Suite for Keyboard (Suite de piece), Vol. 1, No. 5 in E major, HWV 430 (The Harmonious Blacksmith)*
Malotte, Albert Hay: *The Lord's Prayer*
Primrose, Joe: *St. James Infirmary*
Williams, Clarence, and Spencer Williams: *Royal Garden Blues*

Sotto Voce
Album Title: *Viva Voce: The Complete Quartets of John Stevens*
Personnel: Michael Forbes, Demondrae Thurman, euphoniums; Nat McIntosh, Patrick Schulz, tubas
Label: Summit Records, 2004, CD: 388
Stevens, John: *Power*
Stevens, John: *Music 4 Tubas*
Stevens, John: *Dances*
Stevens, John: *Manhattan Suite*
Stevens, John: *Diversions*
Stevens, John: *Moondance*
Stevens, John: *Fanfare for a Friend*
Stevens, John: *Viva Voce!*
Stevens, John: *Benediction*

Stachowiak, Bernard
Album Title: *Capriccio Vol. III—Beauty of Brass and Percussion*
Personnel:
Label: Sunrise Record 85403
Sheng-Tong, Tsai: *Capriccio for Tuba and Piano*

Steckar Elephant Tuba Horde
Album Title: *Steckar Elephant Tuba Horde*
Personnel: Jean-Jacques Justafre, tuben; Jean-Louis Damant, Christian Jous, Michel Nicolle, Marc Steckar, tenor tubas; Philippe Legris, Philippe Fritsch, Thierry Thibault, bass tubas; Bernard Lienard, Daniel Landréat, Didier Havet, contrabass tubas
Label: IDA Records, 1987, LP: IDA 011/ OMD 520
Steckar, Franck: *Rouleaux De Printemps*
Cugny, Laurent: *Molloy*
Michel, Marc: *Le Jour Oû Les Tubas*
Emler, Andy: *Gicael Mibbs*
Vigneron, Louis: *Sentier De Nuit*
Steckar, Franck: *Stabillo Steckardello*
Steckar, Marc: *Tubas au Fujiyama*
Goret, Didier: *Detournement Mineur*

Steckar Tubapack
Album Title: *In a Digital Mood*
Personnel: Marc Steckar, Christian Jous, euphoniums; Michel Godard, Daniel Landréat, tubas
Label: LP
Steckar, Franck: *Hurry Up*
Steckar, Marc: *Serie Noire*
Jenneau, Francois: *Paul et Mike*
Steckar, Franck: *In a Digital Mood*
Caratini, Patrice: *Demain il fera jour*
Steckar, Franck: *Tubapack Blues*
Fosset, Marc: *3a 5*
Quibel, Robert: *Danse Bizarre n o 3*
Arcadio, Bernard, and Marc Steckar: *Forêt Virge*
Steckar, Marc: *Dynozophorium*
Steckar, Marc: *Vendredi 13*

Steckar Tubapack
Album Title: *Kantation*
Personnel: Bernard Arcadio, piano, synthesizer, vocals
Label: JAM, 1981, LP:
Steckar, Marc: *Batuhop*
Arcadio, Bernard, and Andre Ceccarelli: *Leleo*
Steckar, Marc: *Megalo Fanfare*
Steckar, Franck: *Mon Cerveau a du Chagrin*
Arcadio, Bernard: *Splash*
Steckar, Marc: *Tuba Des Villes*
Arcadio, Bernard, and Marc Steckar: *Tubach*
Arcadio, Bernard, and Marc Steckar: *Kadanse et Kantation*
Arcadio, Bernard: *When the Bells Stopped Ringing*
Steckar, Marc: *Salammba*
Arcadio, Bernard, and Marc Steckar: *Konservatorium*
Arcadio, Bernard, and Andre Ceccarelli: *Amour Musique et Paix*
Steckar, Marc: *Tuba des Champs*

Steckar Tubapack
Album Title: *Suite a suivre*
Personnel: Marc Steckar, Christian Jous, euphoniums; Michel Godard, Daniel Landréat, tubas
Label: JAM DISC, 1982, LP: 0183/ MS 036
Steckar, Marc: *Suite a suivre*
Monk, Thelonius: *Blue Monk*
Godard/Steckar: *Et Le Kloxon Retentit Derchef Comme un Lezard Hongroise Eurhume*
Steckar, Marc: *Danse pour un Kangourou*

Bologneisi, J.: *Maria Alm*
Solal: *Tuba Only*
Steckar Tubapack
Album Title: *Tubakoustic*
Personnel: Marc Steckar, Christian Jous, euphoniums; Michel Godard, Daniel Landréat, tubas
Label: IDA Records, 1989, CD:
Steckar, Marc
Album Title: *Tuba International*
Personnel:
Label: Disc BIM, LP: O1TU
Galliano, R.: *French Tuba in Los Angeles*
Bologneisi, J.: *Quand le Tuba valse a Paris*
Steckar, Marc/Delaporte: *African Tuba Safari*
Galliano, R.: *Tubabando*
Steckar, Marc/Colombo: *Tuba Banjo Dixie*
Quibel, Robert: *Tuba Bouchka*
Janin, D.: *Swingin' Little Swiss Tuba . . . Cuckoo-clock*
Steckar, Marc/Galliano: *Tubacuba*
Steckar, Marc: *Tubas on Fujiyama*
Steckar, Marc/Galliano: *Bayerische Pop Tuba*
Steckar, Marc/Colombo: *Butacudatuba*
Coeuriot, M.: *Tuba Space*
Stern, Mary
Album Title: *Celebration*
Personnel: Staff Band of the Womens Royal Army Corp
Label: Band Leader, 1990, CD: BNA 5036
Clark, M.: *Tyrolean Tuba*
Stevens, John
Album Title: *Barnum!*
Personnel: Original Broadway Cast
Label: CBS Masterworks, 1980, LP: 36576; CS: 36576
Coleman, Cy, and Hershey Kay: *Come Follow the Band*
Stevens, John
Album Title: *A Horn of a Different Color*
Personnel: Jerry Peel, horn
Label: Friendly Bull Recordings, 1982, LP:
Stevens, John: *Thunder and Lightning*
Stevens, John
Album Title: *Power*
Personnel: James Jenkins, tuba; William Schmearer, tuba; Ray Stewart, tuba; Jerry Peel, horn; Joseph Stierli, trombone
Label: Mark Records, 1988, CD: MRS 20699
Stevens, John: *Suite No. 1 for Solo Tuba*
Stevens, John: *Triumph of the Demon Gods*
Stevens, John: *Splinters*
Stevens, John: *Suite for II*
Stevens, John: *Power*
Stevens, John; see Johnson, Howard; *Second Childhood;* see Symphonia
Stewart, Bob
Album Title: *Bluebells*
Personnel: Christoff Lauer, soprano and tenor saxophones; Wolfgang Puschnig, alto saxophone; Thomas Alkier, drums
Label: CMP Records, 1992, CD: EFA CD 03056/26
Lauer, Christoff: *Screwbirds*
Puschnig, Wolfgang: *Mixed Metaphors*
Stewart, Bob: *Tunk*
Lauer, Christoff: *Bluebells Nightmare*
Stewart, Bob: *Nonet*
Ann-Charlotte
Puschnig, Wolfgang: *Down Under*
Puschnig, Wolfgang: *Coming Home*
Stewart, Bob
Album Title: *Blythe Spirit*
Personnel: Arthur Blythe
Label: Columbia, 1981, LP: FC 37427
Stewart, Bob
Album Title: *Bush Baby*
Personnel: Arthur Blythe
Label: Adelphi, 1977, LP: 5008
Stewart, Bob
Album Title: *Charles Mingus Live at Avery Fischer Hall*
Personnel:
Label: Columbia, LP:
Let My Children Hear Music
Stewart, Bob
Album Title: *David Murray Big Band Live at Sweet Basil*
Personnel: David Murray Big Band
Label: Black Saint, 1984, BSR 0085
Stewart, Bob
Album Title: *European Tour 1977*
Personnel: Carla Bley Band
Label: Watt Works, 1977, LP: 8
Stewart, Bob
Album Title: *First Line*
Personnel: First Line Band
Label: JMT, 1987, LP: 834 414-1; CD: 834 414-2
Stewart, Bob: *First Line*
Stewart, Bob: *CJ*
Blythe, Arthur: *Metamorphosis*
Traditional: *Sometimes I Feel like a Motherless Child*
Stewart, Bob: *Nonet*
Traditional: *Hey Mama*
Blythe, Arthur: *Bush Baby*
Traditional: *Surinam*
Stewart, Bob: *Hambone*
Stewart, Bob
Album Title: *Goin' Home*
Personnel: First Line Band
Label: JMT, 1988, LP: 834 427-1; CD: 834 427-2; CS: 834 427-3
Bell, Kelvyn: *Suba La Nas Alturas*
Cherry, Don: *Art Deco*
Dara, Olu: *Bell and Ponce*
Stewart, Bob: *Tunk*
Stewart, Bob: *Sweet Georgia Brown Sweet*
Harper, Billy: *Priestess*
Stewart, Bob
Album Title: *The Grip*
Personnel: Arthur Blythe

Label: India Navigation, 1977, LP: 1029

Stewart, Bob
Album Title: *Heavy Life*
Personnel: Edward Vesala
Label: Leo Records, 1980, LP: 009

Stewart, Bob
Album Title: *Illusions*
Personnel: Arthur Blythe
Label: Columbia, 1980, LP: JC 36583

Stewart, Bob
Album Title: *Lenox Avenue Breakdown*
Personnel: Arthur Blythe
Label: Columbia, 1979, LP: JC 35638

Stewart, Bob
Album Title: *Light Blue*
Personnel: Arthur Blythe
Label: Columbia, 1983, 7464-38661-1

Stewart, Bob
Album Title: *Live in Germany*
Label: Circle Records, 1978 RK 101978/13

Stewart, Bob
Album Title: *Metamorphosis*
Personnel: Arthur Blythe
Label: Navigation, 1977, LP: 1038

Stewart, Bob
Album Title: *Musique Mecanique*
Personnel: Carla Bley Band
Label: Watt Works, 1978, LP: 9

Stewart, Bob
Album Title: *Rambler*
Personnel: Bill Frisell
Label: ECM, 1984, LP: 1287

Stewart, Bob
Album Title: *Then and Now*
Personnel: Dave Burell, piano; John Clark, French horn; Stanton Davis, trumpet; Fred Griffen, French horn; Jerome Harris, guitar; Graham Haynes, cornet/trumpet; Taj Mahal, guitar, vocals; Aaron Scott, drums; Marshall Sealy, French horn; Steve Turre, trombone; Carlos Ward, alto saxophone; Buddy Williams, drums; James Zolar, trumpet
Label: Postcards, 1996, CD: POST 1014
Stewart, Bob: *Hambone*
Mahal, Taj: *Big Kneed Gal*
Morton, F. "Jelly Roll": *King Porter Stomp*
Raye and DePaul: *You Don't Know What Love Is*
Stewart, Bob: *Rambler*
Mahal, Taj: *Fishin' Blues*
Ward, Carlos: *Nette*
Stewart, Bob: *Tunk*
Coleman, Ornette: *Law Years*
Ward, Carlos: *Nubian Stomp*

Stewart, Bob
Album Title: *13th House*
Personnel: McCoy Tyner
Label: Milestone, 1980, LP: M-9102
13th House
Song of the New World

Stewart, Ray; see Johnson, Howard; *Howard Johnson & Gravity!!!; Right Now!; Taj Mahal: The Real Thing;* see Stevens, John; *Power*

Stokes, David, and Graham Patterson
Album Title:
Personnel: Chalk Farm Band—Salvation Army
Label:
Condon, Leslie: *Radiant Pathway*

Strand, Donald
Album Title: *1979 Music Teachers National Association Collegiate Artists Winners*
Personnel: Peggy Randolph, piano
Label: Silver Crest, 1979, LP: MTNA-79-2B
Vaughan Williams, Ralph: *Concerto for Bass Tuba and Orchestra*

Stringer, Myron; see Tennessee Tech Tuba-Euphonium Quintet; *The Golden Sound of Euphoniums*

Summit Tubas
Album Title: *American Tribute-Summit Brass*
Personnel: Roger Bobo, Dan Perantoni, Harvey Phillips, Gene Pokorny
Label: Summit Records, 1991, CD: DCD 127
Stevens, John: *Moondance*

Swiss Tuba Quartet
Album Title: *Power*
Personnel: Michael Zoppas, Bernhard Wüthrich, tubas; Marcel Bossert, Rolf Aebersold, euphoniums
Label: Pro Music, 1996, CD: PM 736
Stevens, John: *Power*
Gourlay, James: *The Eagle Thunders*
Hazell, Chris: *Hallelujah Drive*
Rimsky-Korsakov, Nicholas/Wyss: *Flight of the Bumblebee*
Moren, Betrand: *Tubach*
Joplin, Scott/Picher: *Elite Syncopations*
Jewell, Fred/Smalley: *Battle Royal*
Handel, George Friderik/Michel: *Wassermusik*
Fritze, Gregory: *Prelude and Dance*
Cimarosa, D./Wuethrich: *The Impresario*
Schumann, Robert/Wyss: *Fughetta*
Rossini, Gioacchino/Cheseaux: *La Gazza Ladra*
Balet, William/Buttery: *Greensleeves*
Sousa, John Philip/Werden: *Stars and Stripes Forever*

Swoboda, Deanna
Album Title: *Deanna's Wonderland*
Personnel: Deanna Swoboda, tuba and vocals; Sam Pilafian, tuba; Gail Novak, piano; Dom Moio, drums and bongos; Steve McCallister, trombone; Clarke Rigsby, trumpet
Label: Summit Records, 2000, CD: DCD-245
Swoboda, Deanna: *Patricia Lee and Leah Marie*
Robinson, Keith: *Custard the Dragon*
Schultz, Mark: *T Rex*

Robinson, Keith: *Rainforest Etudes*
Wilder, Alec: *Suite No. 1 for Tuba and Piano (Effie the Elephant)*
Robinson, Keith, and Deanna Swoboda: *Wonderland Duets*
Wilder, Alec: *Elegy for the Whale*
Swoboda, Deanna: *Brass Rap!*

Sykes, Stephen
Album Title: *Firebird*
Personnel: Grimethorpe Colliery Band; Ray Farr, conductor
Label: Polyphonic, 1982, LP: PRL010; CS:
Golland, John: *Scherzo*

Sykes, Stephen
Album Title: *The Land of the Mountain and the Flood*
Personnel: C.W.S (Glasgow) Band; Geoffrey Brand, conductor
Label: Harlequin, 1993, CD: HAR 1123 CD
Ellerby, Martin: *Tuba Concerto*

Sykes, Stephen
Album Title: *Sovereign Soloists, Vol. I*
Personnel: Rochdale Band; Richard Evans, conductor
Label: Doyen, CD: DOY CD 003; CS: DOY MC 003
arr. Sykes: *Hefje Kati*
Newsome, Roy: *The Bass in the Ballroom*

Sykes, Steve
Album Title: *Sykology*
Personnel: Brenden Ashe, piano
Label: Martin-PM Sound, 1999, CD: PMSPCD M9927
Turrin, Joseph: *Escapade*
Schubert, Franz Peter/Sykes: *Ave Maria*
Sykes, Steve: *Carnival Cocktail*
Debussy, Claude: *Syrinx*
Kreisler, Fritz: *Liebesfreud*
Donizetti, Gaetano/Sykes: *Una Furtiva Lagrima*
Kneale, Peter: *Variations on a Welsh Theme*
Godard, Benjamin/Molenaar: *Berceuse De Jocelyn*
Jackman, Andrew: *Swing Rag*
Wood, Gareth: *Lullaby*
Monti, Vittorio/Sykes: *Csárdás*

Sykes, Steven
Album Title:
Personnel:
Label: KRO Records, KKCD 9204
Newton, Rodney: *Capriccio for E♭ Bass*
Mendez, Rafael: *Sambe Guitana*

Symphonia
Album Title: *Symphonia . . . A Super Sonic Ensemble in the Alternate Clef*
Personnel: Conductor: R. Winston Morris; Euphoniums: Thomas Ashworth, Brian Bowman, Larry Campbell, Neal Corwell, Paul Droste, Mark Fisher, Earle Louder, Denis Winter; Tubas: Marty Erickson, Hank Feldman, Jeff Funderburk, Fritz Kaenzig, Rex Martin, Daniel Perantoni, Sam Pilafian, John Stevens, Scott Watson, Jerry Young; Percussion: Mary Watson, Allison Shaw
Label: Mark, CD: 1982
Forte, Aldo Rafael: *Seguidillas/Adagio and Rondo*
Welcher, Dan: *Hauntings*
George, Thom Ritter: *Tubamobile*
Stevens, John: *Adagio*
Corwell, Neal: *The Furies*
Holst, Gustav: *Mars from "The Planets"*
Bach, Johann Sebastian: *Passacaglia and Fugue in C*
Pegram, Wayne: *Broadway Bash*
Krebs, Jesse: *Jesse's Jump*
Feldman, Hank: *Freedom*

Symphonia
Album Title: *Symphonia Two—La Mort dell' Oom*
Personnel: Conductor: R. Winston Morris; Euphoniums: Thomas Ashworth, Brian Bowman, Larry Campbell, Neal Corwell, Paul Droste, Mark Fisher, Earle Louder, Denis Winter; Tubas: Marty Erickson, Hank Feldman, Jeff Funderburk, Fritz Kaenzig, Rex Martin, Timothy Northcut, Daniel Perantoni, Sam Pilafian, John Stevens, Scott Watson, Jerry Young; Percussion: Mary Watson, Allison Shaw
Label: Mark, CD: 2808
Holst, Gustav: *March from Second Suite in F for Military Band*
Daugherty, Michael: *Timbuktuba*
Self, James: *La Morte dell'Oom (No Pah Intended)*
Stevens, John: *Talisman/Cookie's Revenge*
Barnes, James: *Yorkshire Ballad*
Duruflé, Maurice: *Ubi Caritas—Dance*
Shostakovich, Dmitri: *Festival Overture*
Puccini, Giacomo: *La Tregenda from "Le villi"*
Jager, Robert: *Three Ludes for Tuba* (Daniel Perantoni—Tuba solo)
Williams, John: *March from "1941"*
Sherwin, Manning: *A Nightingale Sang in Berkley Square*
Mingus, Charles: *Freedom*

Symphonia
Album Title: *Symphonia #3—Symphonia Fantastique!*
Personnel: Conductor: R. Winston Morris; Euphoniums: Thomas Ashworth, Brian Bowman, Larry Campbell, Neal Corwell, Paul Droste, Mark Fisher, Earle Louder, Denis Winter; Tubas: Marty Erickson, Hank Feldman, Jeff Funderburk, Fritz Kaenzig, Rex Martin, Timothy Northcut, Daniel Perantoni, Sam Pilafian, John Stevens, Scott Watson, Jerry Young; Percussion: Mary Watson, Allison Shaw
Label: Mark, CD: 3883

Rossini, Gioacchino: *Overture to William Tell*
Bach, Johann Sebastian: *Prelude and Fugue in D, BWV 554*
Berlioz, Hector: *Dream of a Witches Sabbath from "Symphonie Fantastique"*
Corwell, Neal: *The Wasteland* (Daniel Perantoni, soloist)
Barnes, James: *Tangents, Op. 109*
Barber, Samuel: *Adagio for Strings*
Verdi, Giuseppi: *Dies Irae from Requiem*
Raum, Elizabeth: *Jason and the Golden Fleece*
Mendez, Rafael: *La Virgin De La Macarena* (Brian Bowman, solo euphonium)
Bartles, Alfred: *The New When Tubas Waltz*
Kosma: *Autumn Leaves* (Thomas Ashworth, solo euphonium)

Szabo, Laszlo
Album Title: *Barcs 1986*
Personnel: Budapest Brass Quintet
Label: Hungaroton, 1987, LP: SLPX 12953
Farkas, Antal: *Tuba Variations*

Szentpáli, Roland
Album Title: *I Killed My Lips*
Personnel: Frigyes Sándor Chamber Orchestra; Roger Bobo, tuba
Label: Fenox, 1999, CD: 001
Bach, Johann Sebastian: *Es Ist Bollbracht*
Bach, Johann Sebastian: *Warum Willst du so Zornig Sein?*
Fauré, Gabriel: *Après un Rêve*
Gulya, R.: *Burlesk*
Handel, George Friderik: *Why Do the Nations?*
Kovács, Zoltán: *Golden Bells* (with Roger Bobo)
Paganini, Niccolò: *Moses-Fantasy*
Szentpáli, Roland: *Mi Amor*
Szentpáli, Roland: *Variations for a Children Song*
Szentpáli, Roland: *The Devil Never Sleeps*
Szentpáli, Roland: *Your Kisses like the Fire*

Tafjord, Stein-Erik; see Scandinavian Tuba Jazz
Takayuki, Muto; see Rustic Bari-Tuba Ensemble

Tarto, Joe
Album Title: *Sunday Band Concert*
Personnel: Cities Service Band of America; Paul Lavalle, conductor
Label: RCA Victor Records, LP: LPM 3120
Lavalle, Paul: *Big Joe, the Tuba*

Tarto, Joe
Album Title: *Titan of the Tuba*
Personnel: Red Nichols, Cliff Edwards, Joe Venuti, Carson Robison
Label: Broadway, LP: BR 108
Donaldson: *My Best Girl*
Bigelow-Bates: *Sob Sister Sadie*
Akst: *Steppin' in Society*
Bryan-Mayer: *Row, Row, Rosie*
Sherman-Bernie: *Marguriete*
Tarto, Joe: *Black Horse Stomp*
Napoleon and Signorelli: *Bass Ale Blues*
Nelson: *When You See that Aunt of Mine*
Gottler-Mitchell-Conrad: *Hittin' the Ceiling*
McHugh-Fields: *I Must Have That Man*
Robison: *Less Than That*
"The New Yorkers": *Onyx Club Revue*
Woods-Campbell-Connelly: *Just an Echo in the Valley*
Tarto, Joe, and Paul Lavelle: *Boy Scout—Be Prepared*
Tarto, Joe: *Medley—Salty Sailor Tunes*
Tarto, Joe, and Paul Lavelle: *The Trumpet Polka*

Tarto, Joe; see Phillips, Harvey; *Lavalle in Hi-Fi*
Taylor, Hal; see Tooba Blooze

Tennessee Tech Alumni Ensemble
Album Title: *For the Kings of Brass*
Personnel: R. Winston Morris, director
Label: Mark Records, 2001, CD: MCD 3713
Clinard, Fred Jr.: *Diversion for 7 Bass Clef Instruments*
Spears, Jared: *Divertimento for Tuba Ensemble*
Boone, Daniel: *Three Moods*
Krol, Bernhard: *Feiertagsmusik, Op. 107b*
Canter, James: *Siamang Suite*
Canter, James: *Appalachian Carol*
Holmes, Paul: *Quartet for Tubas*
Camphouse, Mark: *Ceremonial Sketch*
Wilson, Kenyon: *Dance #1*
Rogers, Thomas: *Air for Tuba Ensemble*
Brusick, William: *For the Kings of Brass*

Tennessee Tech Alumni Ensemble
Album Title: *Pierre Garbáge Festival*
Personnel: R. Winston Morris, director
Label: Mark Records, 2000, CD: MCD 3471
Garbáge, Pierre (a.k.a. Garrett, James): *Chaser #1*
Garbáge, Pierre (a.k.a. Garrett, James): *Bullfrog Rag*
Garbáge, Pierre (a.k.a. Garrett, James): *Pop-Rock Medley*
Garrett, James: *The Londonderry Air*
Garrett, James: *Mystical Music*
Garbáge, Pierre (a.k.a. Garrett, James): *Sousa Surrenders*
Garrett, James: *Wabash Canon Ball*
Garbáge, Pierre (a.k.a. Garrett, James): *Gay 50s Medley*
Garbáge, Pierre (a.k.a. Garrett, James): *Songs in the Fight against Rum*
Garbáge, Pierre (a.k.a. Garrett, James): *A Pierre Soliloquy—Ode to Pierre*

Tennessee Tech Alumni Ensemble
Album Title: *Tubalogy 601*
Personnel: R. Winston Morris, director; Darin Cochran, Kelly Thomas, Eric Paull, Lloyd Bone, euphoniums; Joe Murphy, Timothy Northcut, Richard Perry, Joe Skillen, Marcus Arnold, David Brown, tubas
Label: Mark Records, 1999, CD: 3051-MCD
Porter, Cole: *It's All Right with Me*
Moten, Bennie: *Moten Swing*

Loewe, Frederick: *Almost like Being in Love*
Mandel, Johnny: *A Time for Love*
Grolnick, Don: *Pools*
Arlen, Harold: *That Old Black Magic*
Silver, Horace: *Señor Blues*
Brown, Clifford: *Sandu*
Ellington, Edward Kennedy "Duke": *In a Mellow Tone*
Monk, Thelonius: *Round Midnight*
Gillespie, Dizzy: *Manteca*

Tennessee Tech Tuba-Euphonium Quintet
Album Title: *The Golden Sound of Euphoniums*
Personnel: R. Winston Morris, Bill Acuff, Myron Stringer, tubas; Bill Cherry, Alan Clark, euphoniums
Label: Mirafone flexible 33⅓ promotional
Bach, Johann Sebastian/Morris: *Contrapunctus I*
Joplin, Scott/Self: *The Entertainer*

Tennessee Technological University Tuba/Euphonium Ensemble
Album Title: *All That Jazz*
Personnel: R. Winston Morris, director
Label: Mark Records, 1985, CD: MES 20608
arr. Garrett: *Just a Closer Walk with Thee*
arr. Garrett: *Won't You Come Home Bill Bailey*
arr. Garrett: *Chimes Blues*
Ahbez, Eden/Cherry: *Nature Boy*
Harrison, Wayne: *Beneath the Surface*
Green, Freddie/Esleck: *Corner Pocket*
Morrison, Van/Kile: *Moondance*
Brown, Nacio Herb/Sample: *Two Tunes (You Stepped Out of a Dream; Temptation)*
Martin, Glenn: *Chops!*
Corea, Chick: *Spain*
Zawinul, Josef/Arnold: *Birdland*

Tennessee Technological University Tuba/Euphonium Ensemble
Album Title: *CARNEGIE VI*
Personnel: R. Winston Morris, director; Euphoniums: Cory Belvin, Anthony Brown, Seth Fletcher, Clint Isbill, Keith Kile, Aaron Marsee, Ben McMillan, Jacob Thorington; Tubas: Scott Beaver, Jesse Chavez, Chris Crunk, Brian DiDiego, James Gronewald, Joel Jones, Justin King, Angelo Kortyka, Richard Lawson, Jacqueline Newton, Josh Rose, Mark Smith, John Visel; Percussion: Paul Deatherage, Matt Sliger
Label: Mark Custom Recording Services, 2003, CD: 4769 MCB
Handel, George Friderik/Hauser: *Arrival of the Queen of Sheba*
Vivaldi, Antonio: *Winter from "The Seasons"* (Scott Beaver, solo tuba)
Fauré, Gabriel/K. Wilson: *Pavane, Op. 50*
Dvorák, Antonin/Butler: *Slavonic Dance, Op. 46, No. 1*
Prokofiev, Sergey/Butler: *Troika from "Lieutenant Kije"*
Danner, Greg/Vaden: *Scherzo*
Cosma, Vladimir/Fletcher: *Giocoso from "Euphonium Concerto"*
Mobberley, James C.: *On Thin Ice*
Osmon, Leroy: *Frescos De Bonampak*
Tull, Fisher: *Tubular Octad*

Tennessee Technological University Tuba/Euphonium Ensemble
Album Title: *Fifty-First Meeting Music Educators National Conference*
Personnel: R. Winston Morris, director
Label: Mark Custom Recording Service, 1988, CD: MENC88-1-4
Tchaikovsky, Peter Ilyitch/O'Conner: *Serenade for Tubas*
Camphouse, Mark: *Ceremonial Sketch*
Werle, Floyd: *Variations on an Old Hymn Tune*
O'Hara, Betty: *Euphonics*
Brubeck, Dave/Elseck and Murphy: *Blue Rondo alla Turk*
Hancock, Herbie/Perry: *Chameleon*

Tennessee Technological University Tuba/Euphonium Ensemble
Album Title: *Heavy Metal*
Personnel: R. Winston Morris, director
Label: Mark Custom Recording Services, 1987, LP: MES 20759
Pegram, Wayne: *Howdy!*
Gates, Crawford: *Tuba Quartet, Op. 59*
Lamb, Marvin: *Heavy Metal*
Shearing, George/Perry: *Lullaby of Birdland*
Wilson, Ted: *Wot Shigona Dew*
Garrett, James: *Miniature Jazz Suite*
Martin, Glenn: *Bluesin' Tubas*
Jarreau, Al/Murphy: *Boogie Down*

Tennessee Technological University Tuba/Euphonium Ensemble
Album Title: *Music of Jared Spears*
Personnel: R. Winston Morris, director
Label: KM Records, 1981, LP: KM 6549
Spears, Jared: *Divertimento for Tuba Ensemble*

Tennessee Technological University Tuba/Euphonium Ensemble
Album Title: *Play That Funky Tuba Right, Boy!*
Personnel: R. Winston Morris, director; Euphoniums: Cory Belvin, Anthony Brown, Seth Fletcher, Clint Isbill, Keith Kile, Aaron Marsee, Ben McMillan, Jacob Thorington; Tubas: Scott Beaver, Jesse Chavez, Chris Crunk, Brian DiDiego, James Gronewald, Angelo Kortyka, Richard Lawson, Jacqueline Newton, Josh Rose, Mark Smith, Josh Trent, John Visel; Mark Smith, bass; Paul Deatherage, drums; Matt Sliger, guitar
Label: Mark Custom Recording Service, Inc, 2003, CD: 757-MCD
Jarreau, Al/Murphy: *Boogie Down*

Parissi, Rob/Kortyka: *Play That Funky Tuba Right, Boy!*
Jackson, Michael/Rose: *Beat It*
King, Lapread, McClary, Orange, Richie, Williams/Murphy: *Brick House*
Corea, Chick/Arnold: *Spain*
Davis, Miles/Esleck: *Walkin'*
Morgan, Lee/Hauser: *Sidewinder*
Rodgers, Richard, and Oscar Hammerstein/Cherry: *My Favorite Things*
Cherry, Bill: *Musings*
Monk, Thelonius/Walker: *'Round Midnight*
Green, Freddie/Esleck: *Until I Met You (Corner Pocket)*
Silver, Horace/Hauser: *Sister Sadie*
Hayes, Isaac/Gottschalk: *Shaft*
Hancock, Herbie/Perry: *Chameleon*

Tennessee Technological University Tuba/Euphonium Ensemble
Album Title: *The Tennessee Tech Tuba Ensemble Live!*
Personnel: R. Winston Morris, director
Label: KM Educational Library, 1980, LP: KM 5661
Konagaya, Soichi: *Illusion*
Knox, Charles: *Scherzando for Tubular Octet*
Ruth, Matthew: *Exigencies*
DiGiovanni, Rocco: *Tuba Magic*
Gershwin, George/Sample: *Gershwin Medley*
arr. Arnold: *Corazon*

Tennessee Technological University Tuba/Euphonium Ensemble
Album Title: *Tennessee Tech Tuba Ensemble Presents Their Carnegie Recital Hall Program*
Personnel: R. Winston Morris, director
Label: Golden Crest, 1976, LP: CRS 4152
Beale, David: *Reflections on a Park Bench*
Bach, Johann Sebastian/Phillips: *"Air" from Suite No. 3 in D major for Orchestra, BWV 1068*
Stroud, Richard: *Treatments for Tuba*
Sample, Steve: *Nostalgia Medley*

Tennessee Technological University Tuba/Euphonium Ensemble
Album Title: *Tennessee Tech Tuba Ensemble, Vol. I*
Personnel: R. Winston Morris, director
Label: Golden Crest, 1975, LP: CRS 4139
Bartles, Alfred: *When Tubas Waltz*
Barroso, Ary/Morris: *Brazil*
Hutchison, Terry: *Tuba Juba Duba*
Lecuona, Ernesto/Morris: *Malagueña*
Ellington, Edward Kennedy "Duke"/Sample: *Tribute to Duke Ellington*
Bach, Johann Sebastian/Morris: *Toccata and Fugue in D minor*
Ross, Walter: *Concerto Basso*
Bach, Johann Sebastian/Sauter: *Komm Süsser Tod*

Tennessee Technological University Tuba/Euphonium Ensemble
Album Title: *The Tennessee Technological University Tuba Ensemble*
Personnel: R. Winston Morris, director
Label: KM Educational Library, 1980, LP: 4631
Cheetham, John: *Consortium*
George, Thom Ritter: *Tubasonatina*
Dodson, John: *Out of the Depths*
Porter, Cole/Sample: *Cole Porter Medley*
Bernie, Pinkard, and Casey/Garrett: *Sweet Georgia Brown*
Nyro, Laura/Cherry: *Eli's Coming*
Garrett, James: *A Tubalee Jubalee*
Rodgers, Richard, and Oscar Hammerstein/Cherry: *My Favorite Things*

Tennessee Technological University Tuba/Euphonium Ensemble
Album Title: *Unleash the Beast!!!*
Personnel: R. Winston Morris, director; Euphoniums: Lloyd Bone, Jon Oliver, Kelly Thomas, Ashley Sample, Ben Keen; Tubas: Jason Byrnes, Jim Vaden, Sean Mays, Anders Lund, Zack Buersmeyer, Scott Tignor, Michael Happenny, Justin Henderson, Andrew Lynn; Randy Gouge, guitar; Josh Wright, bass; Dolby Miller, drums; Devon Brewer, percussion
Label: Mark Records, 1995, CD: MCC 1800
Kamen, Michael/Oliver: *Robin Hood Fanfare*
Bach, Johann Sebastian/Beckman: *St. Anne's Fugue*
Wilson, Kenyon: *Tuba Quartet No. 1 in C, Op. 3*
Danner, Gregory: *Beast!*
Forte, Aldo Rafael: *Tubas Latinas*
Lockhart and Seitz/Butler: *The World Is Waiting for the Sunrise*
Johnston, Bruce/O'Connor: *Sunrise Lady*
Davis, Miles: *So What*
Davis, Miles/Esleck: *Walkin'*
James, Bob/O'Connor: *Courtship*
Foster, Frank/Perry: *Shiny Stockings*
Hancock, Herbie/Perry: *Chameleon*
Corea, Chick/Arnold: *La Fiesta*

Thibault, Thierry; see Steckar Elephant Tuba Horde

Thornton, Donald
Album Title: *Metropolis: The Klezmorin*
Personnel: The Klezmorin
Label: Flying Fish Records, LP:
Tuba Doina

Thornton, Michael
Album Title: *The Sound of a Tuba*
Personnel: Richard Jensen, percussion; Lisc Proto, piano; Barry Green, doublebass; Frank Proto, conductor
Label: QCA Red Mark/Liben Records, 1982, LP: RML 8202

Proto, Frank: *The Four Seasons for Tuba, Percussion, Strings and Stereo Tape*
Beethoven, Ludwig van/Proto: *Sonata in G major for Tuba and Piano* (Horn Sonata in F)
Elgar, Edward/Thornton: *Chanson de Matin, Op. 15, No. 2*

Thorton, Michael
Album Title: *Tubby the Tuba*
Personnel: Carol Channing, narrator
Label: Caedmon, LP: TC 1623
Kleinsinger, George, and Paul Tripp: *Tubby the Tuba*

Thuillier, Francois
Album Title: *Duo*
Personnel: Pierre Guignon, percussion
Label:
Steckar, Marc: *Tuba Boum*
Steckar, Marc: *Le Rêve d'lcare*
Thuillier, Francois: *Ballad for Inger*
Thuillier, Francois: *L'écureuil fou*
Guignon, Jean-Pierre: *Badintés*
Guignon, Jean-Pierre: *Tornade sur l'esplanade*
Guignon, Jean-Pierre: *La Ferte Alais*
Guignon, Jean-Pierre: *Des Athégiens au Sénégal*
Havet, Didier: *Le Jardin des Citrons*

Thuillier, Francois
Album Title: *Frantic Squirrel*
Personnel: Andy Emler, piano; Pierre Guignon, percussion; Jacelyn Loyer, piano; Serge Adam, trumpet; Daniel Casimir, trombone
Label: Zuk Records, 1998, CD: 309
Emler, Andy: *Tubastone No. 1, for Tuba and Piano*
Guignon, Jean-Pierre: *Tornade sur l'esplanade*
Caratini, P: *Miniatures for Tuba and Piano*
Thuillier, Francois: *Baguette Viennoise*
Havet, Didier: *Le Jardin des Citrons*
Steckar, Marc: *Duo Solo*
Thuillier, Francois: *L'écurreuil Fou*
Casimir, Daniel: *Sljivovica, for Tuba, Trumpet and Trombone*
Machado, Jean Marie: *La Peste*
Telemann, Georg Philipp: *Sonata for Oboe and Continuo*
Thuillier, Francois: *Equilibre Indifférent, for Tuba, Trumpet and Trombone*
Emler, Andy: *Improvisation for Tuba and Piano*
Casimir, Daniel: *Quand tu Veux, for Tuba, Trumpet and Trombone*

Thuillier, Francois
Album Title: *Hommage*
Personnel:
Label:
Thuillier, Francois: *80660*
Thuillier, Francois: *Hommage*
Thuillier, Francois: *Felka Miotta*
Thuillier, Francois: *L'insensible Gregiore*
Thuillier, Francois: *Faux-cils et vraies moustaches*
Thuillier, Francois: *Sale gosse*
Thuillier, Francois: *Vif, tendre et dangereux*
Thuillier, Francois: *A tot bien*
Adam: *Le cirque*
Casimir, Daniel: *Die Voralpen*
Casimir, Daniel: *Miss r and b*
Casimir, Daniel: *Les Satellites*
Bartók, Béla: *Hungarian Pictures*

Thuillier, Francois
Album Title: *Places des Vosges*
Personnel:
Label:
Machado, Jean Marie: *Tambours en colere*
Machado, Jean Marie: *Well, You Needn't*
Thuillier, Francois: *Places des Vosges*
Thuillier, Francois: *Timisoara*
Thuillier, Francois: *20h30*

Tietz, Henrik; see Melton Tuba-Quartett

Tooba Blooze
Album Title: *Tooba Blooze*
Personnel: Hal Taylor, tuba; Denny Wilson, acoustic and electric guitars; "Kaptain" Karl Streuber, harmonica, vocals; "Rotten" Rod Bradley, drums
Label: I WANNA Records, 1990, LP:
Wilson, Denny, and Hal Taylor: *7,000,000 Miles*
Wilson, Taylor, and Streuber: *Greedy Mr. Creed*
The Clash: *Brand New Cadillac*
Wilson, Denny, and Hal Taylor: *Stumble of the Fumble Bee*
Wilson, Denny, and Hal Taylor: *Livin' on the Wick*
Wilson, Taylor, and Streuber: *The Rainbow Song*

Torchinsky, Abe
Album Title: *Complete Brass Sonatas of Hindemith*
Personnel: Glenn Gould, piano
Label: Columbia Records, 1976, 2LPs: M2-33971 (rereleased on 2 CDs)
Hindemith, Paul: *Sonata for Bass Tuba and Piano*

Torchinsky, Abe
Album Title: *Glenn Gould Edition: Hindemith: Sonatas for Brass and Piano*
Personnel: Glenn Gould, piano
Label: Sony, 1992, CD: #52671
Hindemith, Paul: *Sonata for Bass Tuba and Piano*

Tornquist, Doug; see Self, James; *The Big Stretch*

Trice, Jerry
Album Title: *Opus One, Number Four*
Personnel: Robert Woodbury, tuba
Label: Opus One, LP: 4
Birchall, Steven: *Reciprocals II for Two Tubas*

Triebener, Heiko; see Hilgers, Walter; *Around the World 2; Bach 2000; On Tour;* see Melton Tuba-Quartett
Triendl, Oliver
Album Title: *Harald Genzmer: Musik für Blechbläser und Klavier*
Personnel:
Label: Thorofon, 2002, CD: #2427
Genzmer, Harald: *Sonata for Bass Tuba and Piano*
Tsuba, Zen; see Roper, William; *Juneteenth*
Tuba 4's
Album Title: *Tubas under the Boardwalk*
Personnel: Gail Robertson, Carmen Russo, euphoniums; Willie Clark, Patrick Glynn, tubas
Label: GAR Music, 1999, CD: TU4001
Mancini/Mercer/Robertson: *The Pink Panther*
Menken/Ashman/Robertson: *Friend like Me*
Young/Resnick/Robertson: *Under the Boardwalk*
Ellington/Mills/Bigard/Vaughan: *Mood Indigo*
Kaempfert/Gabler/Robertson: *L.O.V.E.*
Robinson/White/Robertson: *My Girl*
Gordon/Warren/Wolpe: *Chattanooga Choo Choo*
Rodgers, Richard, and Lorenz Hart/Robertson: *Blue Moon*
Menken/Schwartz/Robertson: *Colors of the Wind*
Cole/Mills/Robertson: *Straighten Up and Fly Right*
Collins/Robertson: *You'll Be in My Heart*
Brown/Homer/Green/Vaughan: *Sentimental Journey*
Ballard/Robertson: *Mister Sandman*
Barroso, Ary/Clark: *Barzil*
Wilder/Zippel/Robertson: *Reflection*
Ellington, Edward Kennedy "Duke"/Vaughan: *Satin Doll*
Newman/Robertson: *The Time of Your Life*
Zaret/North/Robertson: *Unchained Melody*
Alford, Kenneth/Robertson: *Colonel Bogey March*
Sherman/Sherman/Gaston: *I Wan'na Be like You*
Razaf/Goodman/Webb/Sampson/Mays: *Stompin' at the Savoy*
Martin/Blane/Wolpe: *The Trolley Song*
Mercer, Johnny/Vaughan: *Dream*
Traditional/Robertson: *Clarinet Polka*
Tubalaté
Album Title: *Earth and Moon*
Personnel: Ryan Breen, Leslie Neis, tubas; Paul Walton, John Powell, euphoniums
Label: Horizon, 2000, CD: TCD 4
McQueen, Ian: *The Heights of Halifax*
Roper, Antony: *A String of Tones*
Scott, Stuart: *Fellscape*
Seivewright, Andrew: *Gowbarrow Gavotte*
Bousted, Donald: *Tears*
Crump, Peter: *The March of the Hare*
Solomons, David: *Pieces of Eight*
Parfrey, Raymond: *Tributes to Tunesmiths*
Puw, Guto Pryderi: *Visages*
Regan, Michael J.: *Quartet*
Bayliss, Colin: *Tuba Quartet No. 2—Ale and Arty*
Parfrey, Raymond: *Male Voice for Brass*
Rice, Hugh Collins: *Earth and Moon*
Wood, Derek: *Tubafusion*
Tubalaté
Album Title: *Episodes*
Personnel: Ryan Breen, Leslie Neis, tubas; Paul Walton, John Powell, euphoniums
Label: ASC CS, 1999, CD: CD12
Hinchley, John: *Boogie Woogie Tuba Boy*
Bach, Johann Sebastian/Wood: *Air from Suite in D*
Mitchell-Davidson, Paul: *Tubafication*
Traditional/Forbes: *Scarborough Fair*
Kerwin, Simon: *Illustrations for Tubas*
Parker, Handel/Walton: *Deep Harmony*
Reeman, John: *Episodes*
Schifrin, Lalo/Smalley: *Mission Impossible*
Tubalaté
Album Title: *Light Metal*
Personnel: Ryan Breen, Leslie Neis, tubas; Paul Walton, John Powell, euphoniums
Label: TUBA CD, 1995, CD: 001
Sousa, John Philip: *The Thunderer*
Frackenpohl, Arthur: *Pop Suite*
Saint-Saëns, Camille/Minchin: *The Swan from "Carnival of the Animals"*
Saint-Saëns, Camille/Minchin: *The Elephant from "Carnival of the Animals"*
Traditional/Werden: *English Country Airs*
Handel, George Friderik/Minchin: *Air from Water Music*
Ivanovici, J./Konagaya: *Wave of the Danube*
Khatchaturian, Aram/Seitz: *Sabre Dance*
Proctor, S.: *Light Metal—I Talatasco*
Kreisler, Fritz/Woodcock: *Liebeslied*
Edgar, M./Powell: *Three Ha'Pence a Foot*
Moore, T.: *Three Piece Suite*
Lennon, John, and Paul McCartney/Miyagawa: *Yesterday*
Sousa, John Philip/Morris: *El Capitan*
Tchaikovsky, Peter Ilyitch/Butler: *Neopolitan Song*
Tubalaté
Album Title: *Move*
Personnel: Ryan Breen, Leslie Neis, tubas; Paul Walton, John Powell, euphoniums
Label: ASC CS, 2000, CD; CD 21
Kerwin, Simon: *March—FroT*
Skempton, Howard: *Rest and Recreation*
Traditional/Moore: *Three Negro Spirituals*
Naftel, Frederick: *Pascal's Victim*
Traditional/Plakidis: *Aija Zuzu*

Bach, Johann Sebastian/Smalley: *Fugue in G minor*
Primrose, Joe/Forbes: *St. James Infirmary*
Davidson, Matthew: *Move*
Gasparini, Quirino/Miller: *Adoramus te Christe*
Newsome, Roy: *The Basics*
Traditional/Forbes: *Just a Closer Walk*
Solomons, David: *Prayer before the Close of Day*

Turk, John
Album Title: *Low Blows*
Personnel: Dora Ohrenstein, soprano; Randall Fusco, piano; Lori Turk, piccolo; William Slocum, horn
Label: Dana Recording Project, 1991, CD: DRP-4
Hindemith, Paul: *Sonata for Bass Tuba and Piano*
Penn, William: *Three Essays for Solo Tuba*
Smith, Glenn: *Forowen 3* (tuba and piccolo)
Largent, Edward: *Four Shorts for Tuba and Piano*
Amato, Bruno: *Two Together* (tuba and soprano)
Rollin, Robert: *The Raven and the First Men* (tuba, horn, piano, electronics)

Turk, John
Album Title: *The Music of Warren Benson*
Personnel: Indiana University Symphonic Band; Fredrick Ebbs, director
Label: Coronet, 1966, LP: 2736
Benson, Warren: *Helix for Solo Tuba and Concert Band*

Turk, John
Album Title: *1974 Mid-West National Band and Orchestra Clinic*
Personnel: Cambridge High School Symphonic Band
Label: Silver Crest, 1974, LP: MID-74-9
Hartley, Walter: *Concertino for Tuba and Wind Ensemble*

United States Armed Forces Tuba-Euphonium Ensemble
Album Title: *Forty-Third Annual Mid-West International Band and Orchestra Clinic*
Personnel: R. Winston Morris, conductor
Label: Mark Custom Recording Services, 1989, CD: MW89MCD-8
Pegram, Wayne: *Howdy!*
Mozart, Wolfgang Amadeus/Gottschalk: *Overture from the "Marriage of Figaro"*
Rossini, Gioacchino/Kile: *Overture from the "Barber of Seville"*
Cheetham, John: *Consortium*
arr. Garrett: *The Londonderry Air*
Garret, James: *A Tubalee Jubalee*
Gershwin, George/Sample: *Gershwin Medley*
King, Karl L./Werden: *The Melody Shop*
King, Karl L./Morris: *Barnum and Bailey's Favorite*

United States Armed Forces Tuba-Euphonium Ensemble and Massed Ensemble
Album Title: *The United States Army Band Tuba-Euphonium Conference 1989*
Personnel: R. Winston Morris, conductor
Label: United States Army Band, 1989, CS: Public Service/Not for Sale
Also released by Mark Custom Recording Services, 1989, CD: MW89MCD-8
Bach, Johann Sebastian/Beckman: *St. Anne's Fugue*
Saint-Saëns, Camille/Cohen: *Marche Militaire Francaise*
Werle, Floyd: *Variations on an Old Hymn*
Camphouse, Mark: *Ceremonial Sketch*
Garbáge, Pierre (a.k.a. Garrett, James): *Sousa Surrenders*
Bach, Johann Sebastian: *Bist du bei mir, BWV 508*
Frank, Marcel G.: *Lyric Poem for Five Tubas*
Canter, James: *Appalachian Carol*
DiGiovanni, Rocco: *Tuba Magic*
Joplin, Scott/Self: *The Entertainer*
Huffine, G. H.: *Them Basses*
(Note: The Mark CD incorrectly lists Sousa: *Stars and Stripes Forever* as being on album)

United States Army Band "Pershing's Own"
Album Title: *United States Army Band Tuba-Euphonium Workshop Grand Concert*
Personnel: The United States Army Band "Pershing's Own," Colonel Eugene W. Allen,conductor
Label: United States Army Band, 1989, CS: Public Service/Not for Sale
Wilhelm, Rolf: *Concertino for Tuba and Wind Instruments* (Michael Bunn, soloist)
Smith, Claude T.: *Ballade and Presto Dance* (Robert Daniel, soloist)
Barat, Joseph Eduoard/Phillips: *Introduction and Dance* (Roger Bobo, soloist)
Dumitru, Ionel: *Romanian Dance No. 2* (Roger Bobo, soloist)
Arban, Jean-Baptiste/Berry: *Fantaisie and Variations on the "Carnival of Venice"* (Roger Bobo, soloist)

United States Coast Guard Tuba-Euphonium Quartet
Album Title: *The Musical Sounds of the Seasons: The United States Coast Guard Band*
Personnel: John Banker, Gary Buttery, tubas; Roger Behrend, David Werden, euphoniums
Label: U.S. Coast Guard, 1984, LP: Public Service/Not for Sale
Buttery, Gary: *An English Folk Christmas*

United States Coast Guard Tuba-Euphonium Quartet
Album Title: *The United States Coast Guard Band, Soloists and Chamber Players*

Personnel: Gary Buttery, David Chaput, tubas; David Werden, Dennis Winter, euphoniums
Label: U.S. Coast Guard, 1978, LP: USCG 122678-A; Public Service/Not for Sale
Persichetti, Vincent: *Serenade for Ten Wind Instruments*
Ramsöe, Emilio Wilhelm/Buttery: *Quartet for Brass*

United States Navy Band Tuba-Euphonium Quartet
Album Title: *The United States Navy Band Presents the Tuba Quartet*
Personnel: Roger Behrend, John Bowman, euphoniums; Keith Mehlan, Martin Erickson, tubas
Label: United States Navy Band, 1986, CS: Public Service/Not for Sale
Bulla, Stephen: *Quartet for Low Brass*
Ramsöe, Emilio Wilhelm/Buttery: *Quartet for Brass (third movement)*
Massenet, Jules/Margaret Erickson: *Argonaise from "Le Cid"*
Joplin, Scott/Werden: *Ragtime Dance*

University of Miami Tuba Ensemble
Album Title: *University of Miami Tuba Ensemble Greatest Hits*
Personnel: Constance Weldon, director
Label: Miami United Tuba Ensemble Society, LP: 14568
Payne, Frank Lynn: *Quartet for Tubas (The Condor)*
Frank, Marcel G.: *Lyric Poem for Five Tubas*
Hastings, Ross: *Little Madrigal for Big Horns*
Rogers, Thomas: *Music for Tuba Ensemble*
Boone, Daniel: *Three Moods*
Donaldson, W./Self: *Carolina in the Morning*
Gould, Morton/Woo: *Pavanne from the "Latin America Suite"*
Frackenpohl, Arthur: *Pop Suite for Barituba Ensemble*
Jones, Roger: *Duet No. 12 from "21 Distinctive Duets"*
Davis, Akst/Woo: *Baby Face*
Sousa, John Philip/Weldon: *Stars and Stripes Forever*

University of Michigan Tuba and Euphonium Ensemble
Album Title: *The Brass Menagerie*
Personnel: Abe Torchinsky, conductor
Label: School of Music LP Records, 1979, LP: SM0011
Byrd, William: *Agnus Dei*
Payne, Frank Lynn: *Quartet for Tubas (The Condor)*
Holmes, Paul: *Quartet for Tubas*
Stevens, John: *Manhattan Suite*
Mozart, Wolfgang Amadeus/Gottschalk: *Overture from the "Marriage of Figaro"*

University of Michigan Tuba Ensemble
Album Title: *University of Michigan Percussion and Tuba Ensembles*
Personnel: Abe Torchinsky, director; Uri Mayer, conductor
Label: Golden Crest, 1975, LP: CRS 4145
Iannaccone, Anthony: *Hades for Two Euphoniums and Two Tubas*
Presser, William: *Serenade for Four Tubas (third movement—Allegro)*
Iannaccone, Anthony: *Three Mythical Sketches for Four Tubas*
Gottschalk, Arthur: *Substructures for Ten Tubas*

Unkrodt, Dietrich
Album Title: *Dixieland Allstars Berlin—AMIGA*
Personnel:
Label: AMIGA Deutsche Schallplatten, LP: Stereo 855-350

Unkrodt, Dietrich
Album Title: *Musik für Blechbläser; Gruner Tubakonzert*
Personnel: Rundfunk-Sinfonie-Orchester Berlin; Joachim Willert; Berliner Blechbläserquintet
Label: NOVA Deutsche Schallplatten, 1982, LP: 885-208
Gruner, Joachim: *Konzert für Tuba und Orchester*

Unkrodt, Dietrich
Album Title: *Unkrodt/Zerbe*
Personnel: Hannes Zerbe, piano and synthesizer
Personnel: AMIGA, 1987, Stereo 856-336
Kanon
Die haltbare Graugans
Für H. S.
Spiralen
Calvados

Unternährer, Marc
Album Title: *Pilatus-Suite*
Personnel: Albins Alpin Quintett; Albin Brun, saxophones and schwyzerörgeli; Roland von Flüe, bass clarinet and tenor saxophone; Pascal Bruggisser, accordion and toy piano; Marco Käppeli, percussion and baby alphorn
Label: Altrisuoni, CD: LC 0504
Brun, Albin: *Widderfeld*
Brun, Albin: *Heitertannli*
Brun, Albin: *Holzwangflue*
Brun, Albin: *Laubrisleten*
Brun, Albin: *Goldwang*
Brun, Albin: *Chlingen*
Brun, Albin: *Ruessiflue*
Brun, Albin: *Intro Heuschlag*
Brun, Albin: *Heuschlag*
Brun, Albin: *Starrenwang*
Brun, Albin: *Lauelenegg*
Brun, Albin: *Schy*

Brun, Albin: *Galtigen*
Brun, Albin: *Intro Tomlishorn*
Brun, Albin: *Tomlishorn*
Brun, Albin: *Tumli*
Van Lier, Erik
Album Title: *First Brass*
Personnel: Allan Botschinsky, Derek Watkins, trumpet and flugelhorn; Bart Van Lier, trombone and euphonium
Label: M-A Music, 1986, LP:
Botschinsky, Allan: *Interlude No. 4*
Botschinsky, Allan: *October Sunshine*
Botschinsky, Allan: *Kubismus 502*
Brahms, Johannes: *Wiegenlied*
Botschinsky, Allan: *Don't Shoot the Banjo Player ('Cause We've Done It Already)*
Botschinsky, Allan: *Toot Your Roots*
Botschinsky, Allan: *The Lady in Blue*
Botschinsky, Allan: *Alster Promenade*
Botschinsky, Allan: *Chops a la Salsa*
Botschinsky, Allan: *Love Waltz*
Varner, Lesley
Album Title: *1977 Mid-West National Band and Orchestra Clinic*
Personnel: Victoria High School Band
Label: Crest Records, 1977, LP:
Grundman, Clare: *Tuba Rhapsody*
Veridaz, Benoit; see European Tuba Quartet; *Heavy Metal-Light Industry*
Vogt, Michael
Album Title: *Tuba Intim*
Personnel: Edwin Kaliga, percussion; Georg Shwark, tuba; Hans-Eckardt Wenzel, narrator; Michael Erxleben, violin; Christine Reumschussel, piano
Label: ReR, 1994, CD: Tuba1
Vogt, Michael: *Homo Ludens in Berlin*
Horwood, Michael S.: *Residue for Tuba and Vibraphone*
Zimmerlin, Alfred: *Toute l'etendur ne vaut pas un cri*
Stravinsky, Igor: *Elegie*
Luedeke, Raymond: *Wonderland Duets for Two Tubas and Narrator*
Schlunz, Annette: *ACH, ES . . . Music for Tuba Solo*
Feldman, Morton: *Durations 3 for Violin, Tuba and Piano*
Glandien, Lutz: *Aus Vertreutem ein Ganzes*
Wagner, Michael
Album Title: *Firestorm*
Personnel: U.S. Army Brass Band
Label: U.S. Army Brass Band/Public Service/ Not for Sale
Rimsky-Korsakov, Nicholas/Wyss: *Flight of the Bumblebee*
Wagner, Michael
Album Title: *The United States Army Ceremonial Brass and Percussion*
Personnel: The United States Army Ceremonial Brass and Percussion
Label: U.S. Army, 1986, LP: Public Service/ Not for Sale
Gregson, Edward: *Tuba Concerto*
Walsh, Thomas
Album Title: *Tuba Holiday*
Personnel: Philharmonic Chamber Orchestra of Munich; Michael Helmrath, conductor; Johannes Umbreit, piano; Beate Miller, soprano; Eomar Schloter, organ; Blechschaden; Bob Ross, conductor
Label: 1997, CD: 1/0267-210
Koetsier, Jan: *Concertino for Tuba and String Orchestra, Op. 77*
Etzel, Bernhard: *Fünf Miniaturen für Solotuba*
Koetsier, Jan: *Sonatine für Tuba unt Klavier, Op. 57*
Delanoff, Robert: *Wos hot er g'sogt?*
Rottler, Werner: *Sonatine für Tuba und Klavier, Op. 14*
Koetsier, Jan: *Choralfantasie ürber "Es ist ein Schnitter" für Tuba und Orgel, Op. 93*
Etzel, Bernhard: *Divertimento bassobavarese for Solo Tuba*
Carmichael, Hoagy/Iveson: *Stardust*
Washburn, Joe "Country"
Album Title:
Personnel: Spike Jones and His City Slickers
Label: RCA, LP: 10-2118
Hupfield, Herman: *When Yuba Plays the Rhumba on the Tuba Down in Cuba*
Watson, Scott
Album Title: *Rare Breeds and Dog-Eared Classics*
Personnel: Kansas Brass Quintet; Ellen R. Bottorff, piano
Label: University of Kansas, Lawrence, 2000, CD:
Bernstein, Leonard: *Waltz for Mippy III*
Watson, Scott; see Symphonia
Weaver, Mark
Album Title: *Protuberence—Treated and Released*
Personnel: Paul Pulaski, guitar; Dave Wayne, drums
Label: ZERX, 1999, CD: 019
Weaver, Mark: *Pocket*
Weaver, Mark: *Selvage*
Weaver, Mark: *Soon Enough*
Weaver, Mark: *Seven Enchiladas*
Weaver, Mark: *Pumpkin Pie*
Weaver, Mark: *Deflections*
Weaver, Mark: *Tee Vee/T. W.*
Weaver, Mark: *Movie*
Pulaski, Paul: *Wonamow*
Weaver, Mark: *Brown Blue*
Weaver, Mark: *Adhesive Colors*
Weaver, Mark: *Behind Your Face*
Weaver, Mark: *Land Shark*
Well, Christoph
Album Title: *Gruss Gott mein Bayernland*
Personnel:

Label: Mood Records, LP: 28631
Well, Christoph: *Wann der Dudelsack kraht u. a.*
Wendling, Philippe; see Miraphone Tuba Quartet
Whethem, Scott; see Albertasaurus Tuba Quartet
Wilhelm, Matthias
Album Title: *Amiri Baraka and Artra Live at the Amerikahaus Munich*
Personnel:
Label: Artra, 1981, LP: 1003
Wilhelm, Matthias
Album Title: *Artra-Artra*
Personnel: Loft
Label: Loft, 1980, LP: L1002
Wilhelm, Matthias
Album Title: *Band of Man-Carborundum*
Personnel:
Label: Artra, 1983, LP: 1001
Wilhelm, Matthias
Album Title: *Das Liedmobil*
Personnel:
Label: Deutsche Grammophon, 1981, LP: 254
Wilson, John L.; see Hoffnung, Gerard; *Hoffnung Music Festival Concert*
Winternheimer, Stefan
Album Title: *Tuba Stew, ein musikalischer Eintopf*
Personnel:
Label:
Wirth, Juergen; see Hilgers, Walter; *On Tour*
Wolff, Brian; see Drums and Tuba
Woodbury, Robert; see Trice, Jerry; *Opus One, Number One*
Woods, Gavin
Album Title: *Travelling by Tuba*
Personnel: Stewart Death, piano
Label: Tryfan, 1995, CD: TRF CD376
Corwell, Neal.: *New England Reveries*
Doughty, G.: *Variations on "Grandfather's Clock"*
Handel, George Friderik: *Oboe Concerto No. 3*
Hindemith, Paul: *Sonata for Bass Tuba and Piano*
Monti, Vittorio: *Csárdás*
Mozart, Wolfgang Amadeus: *Rondo*
Newsome, Roy: *The Bass in the Ballroom*
Rimsky-Korsakov, Nicholas: *Flight of the Bumblebee*
Sondheim, S.: *Send in the Clowns*
Waller, Thomas "Fats": *Ain't Misbehavin'*
Traditional: *Negro Spirituals*
Woods, Gavin
Album Title: *Travelling by Tuba 2*
Personnel: Stewart Death, piano; Simon Rebello, percussion; Jeffrey Box, bass
Label: Polyphonic, 1998, CD: QPRZ 022D
Brahms, Johannes: *Hungarian Dance*
Gluck, Christopf: *Dance of the Blessed Spirits*
Bach, Johann Sebastian: *Minuet and Badinerie from Suite #2*
Mozart, Wolfgang Amadeus: *Romanza and Rondo from Horn Concerto #4*
Clarke, Herbert L.: *Carnival of Venice*
Clarke, Herbert L.: *From the Shores of the Mighty Pacific*
Lebedev, Alexei: *Concerto for Tuba and Piano*
Kern, Jerome: *Ol' Man River*
Liszt, Franz: *Rhapsodic Fantasie*
Penderecki, Krzysztof: *Capriccio for Solo Tuba*
Gershwin, George: *The Man I Love*
Gershwin, George: *I Got Rhythm*
Castérède, Jacques: *Sonatine*
Ellington, Edward Kennedy "Duke": *It Don't Mean a Thing*
Wüthrich, Bernhard; see Swiss Tuba Quartet
Yasumoto, Hiroyuki
Album Title: *Solo Album for Wind Instruments: Tuba*
Personnel: Yuko Kusuyama, piano; Atsuhi Hairu, percussion
Label: Denon, 1990, CD: COCG-6536
Censhu, Jiro: *Verdurous Aubade for Tuba and Piano*
Konagaya, Soichi: *Fantasy for Tuba and Piano*
Toyama, Yuzo: *Trio Sonata for Tuba , Batteries [percussion], and Piano*
Kreisler, Fritz/Yasumoto: *Liebesfreud*
Martini, J. P. E./Yodo: *Piacer d'Amor*
Saint-Saëns, Camille/Yodo: *The Elephant from "Carnival of the Animals"*
Mori, Yoshiko: *Barcarolle for Tuba*
Traditional/Yamamoto: *Sakura Sakura*
Livingston, J., and R. Evans/Inomata: *To Each His Own*
Lennon, John, and Paul McCartney/Ito: *Yesterday*
McHugh, J., and D. Fields/Ito: *On the Sunny Side of the Street*
Young, Jerry; see Symphonia
Zerkel, David
Album Title: *American Music for Tuba: Something Old, Something New*
Personnel: Yuko Kusuyama, piano; Atsuhi Hairu, percussion
Label: Mark Recordings, CD: z5348-MCD
Cheetham, John: *Sonata for Tuba and Piano*
Persichetti, Vincent: *Serenade No. 12 for Solo Tuba*
Gillingham, David: *Diversive Elements for Euphonium, Tuba and Piano*
Hartley, Walter: *Sonata No. 1 for Tuba and Piano*
Woodward, James: *Tuba Concerto*
Zoppas, Michael; see Swiss Tuba Quartet

Tuba Recordings by Title

Note: Composers are underlined. Titles beginning with an English article are alphabetized according to the first substantive word.

A tot bien: Thuillier, Francois: Thuillier, Francois
Aboriginal Voices: Corwell, Neal: Brown, Velvet; Nelson, Mark
ACH, ES . . . . Music for Tuba Solo: Schlunz, Annette: Vogt, Michael
Achieved Is the Glorious Work from "Die Schöpfung": Haydn, Franz Joseph: Sotto Voce
Acousticon Theme: McIntosh, Nat
Adagio: Ecclés, Henry: Megules, Karl
Adagio: Shostakovich, Dmitri: Bobo, Roger
Adagio: Stevens, John: Symphonia
Adagio and Allegro in A♭ Op. 70: Schumann, Robert: Brewer, Robert; Cooley, Floyd; Dowling, Eugene; Funderburk, Jeff; Hanks, Toby; Skillen, Joseph
Adagio for Strings: Barber, Samuel: Symphonia
Adagio from Symphony No. 3: Saint-Saëns, Camille: British Tuba Quartet
Adagio from Toccata, Adagio and Fugue in C major: Bach, Johann Sebastian: Hilgers, Walter
Adagio, Theme and Variations, Op. 102: Hummel, Johann Nepomuk: Sheridan, Patrick
Adam's Apple: Shorter, Wayne: Self, James
Adhesive Colors: Weaver, Mark: Weaver, Mark
Adoramus te Christe: Gasparini, Quirino: Sotto Voce; Tubalaté
Adventures of Poo-Poo and Pee-Pee: Drums and Tuba: Drums and Tuba
African Tuba Safari: Steckar, Marc: Stecker, Marc
After You've Gone: Creamer: Pilafian, Sam
Agnus Dei: Byrd, William: University of Michigan Tuba and Euphonium Ensemble
Agua de Beber: Jobim, Antonio Carlos: Pilafian, Sam
Ah!, Vous Dirai-Je Maman, K. 265: Mozart, Wolfgang Amadeus: Alchemy
Aija Zuzu: Traditional: Tubalaté
Ain't Misbehavin': Waller, Thomas "Fats": Morgan, Kevin; Woods, Gavin
Ain't Much Good in the Best of Men Now Days: Hunter, Eugene: Newberger, Eli
Ain't My Fault: Johnson, Joseph: Dixie Power Trio
Air and Bourree: Bach, Johann Sebastian: Conner, Rex; Davis, Ronald; Phillips, Harvey; Popiel, Peter
Air and Bourree: Handel, George Friderik: Conner, Rex
Air con Variazioni from Suite No. 5 in E major: Handel, George Friderik: Dowling, Eugene
Air for the G String: Bach, Johann Sebastian: Bobo, Roger
Air for Tuba Ensemble: Rogers, Thomas: Tennessee Tech Alumni Ensemble
Air from Suite in D: Bach, Johann Sebastian: Tubalaté
Air from Suite No. 3: Bach, Johann Sebastian: British Tuba Quartet
"Air" from Suite No. 3 in D major for Orchestra, BWV 1068: Bach, Johann Sebastian: Atlantic Tuba Quartet; Tennessee Technological University Tuba/Euphonium Ensemble
Air from Water Music: Handel, George Friderik: Tubalaté
Alabama Jubilee: Palmer, Singleton
Alabamy Bound: Henderson, Ray: Lehr, David "Red"
Alarum for Solo Tuba: Gregson, Edward: Gourlay, James; Nickel, Hans
The Albert Hall Galop: Norris, Tim
Album, Album: Johnson, Howard: Johnson, Howard
Aldebaran, for Solo Tuba: Martin, Robert: Forman, Steven
Alexander's Ragtime Band: Berlin, Irving: Pilafian, Sam
Alice's Fax: Ohmen, Kjell: Pilafian, Sam
The Alisan Girl: Chinese traditional: Frey, Michael
All Alone Blues: Sheridan, John: Erickson, Martin
All Blues: Davis, Miles: Scandinavian Tuba Jazz; Self, James
Allegro and Air: Purcell, Henry: New York Tuba Quartet
Allegro et Finale: Bozza, Eugène: Georgie, Gerhard
Allegro from Sonata No. 3 in F major: Galliard, Johann Ernst: Arwood, Jeffrey
Allegro from Sonatina for Tuba: Thompson, Troy: Funderburk, Jeff
Allegro from Toccata in D minor for Klavier, BWV 913: Bach, Johann Sebastian: Atlantic Tuba Quartet
Allegro Molto from Quartet No. 4: Ramsöe, Emilio Wilhelm: Atlantic Tuba Quartet; Fletcher, John
Allegro Vivace: Hidas, Frigyes: Hötzel, Markus
All'idea di qual metallo from "The Barber of Seville": Rossini, Gioacchino: Pilafian, Sam
Almost like Being in Love: Loewe, Frederick: Tennessee Tech Alumni Ensemble
Also sprach Zarathustra (excerpt): Strauss, Richard: Pokorny, Gene
Alster Promenade: Botschinsky, Allan: Van Lier, Erik
Alte Kameraden: Teike, Carl: Miraphone Tuba Quartet
Always: Berlin, Irving: Erickson, Martin
Amapola: Lacalle, J.: Rustic Bari-Tuba Ensemble
Amazing Grace: Mancini, Henry: Johnson, John Thomas (Tommy)
Amazing Grace: Traditional: O'Bryant, Kelly
America: Carey, Henry: Daellenbach, Charles
America the Beautiful: Ward, Samuel A.: Self, James
An American in Paris (excerpt): Gershwin, George: Pokorny, Gene
An American Tail II—Fieval Goes West [motion picture soundtrack]: Horner, James: Self, James
American Tuba Patrol: Meacham, Frank W.: Rustic Bari-Tuba Ensemble
Amour Musique et Paix: Arcadio, Bernard, and Andre Ceccarelli: Steckar Tubapack

An die Musik, Op. 88, No. 4: Schubert, Franz Peter: Brewer, Robert; Daellenbach, Charles

And Finally: Poore, Melvyn: Poore, Melvyn

"and from the abyss" for tuba and tape: Felciano, Richard: Cooley, Floyd

And Leave Alone: McIntosh, Nat

And Then Again . . . : Blue, Kelly: Johnson, Howard

And What Rough Beast . . . ?, for Tuba and Percussion: Satterwhite, Marc: Pokorny, Gene

Andante: Handel, George Friderik: Phillips, Harvey

Andante: Tcherepnin, Alexander: Sinder, Philip

Andante and Rondo: Yoffe, Shlomo: Hershko, Shmuel "Adi"

Andante and Rondo from Concerto for Double Bass: Capuzzi, Antonio: Funderburk, Jeff; Jae Young, Heo

Andante Cantabile: Mozart, Wolfgang Amadeus: Albertasaurus Tuba Quartet

Andante Cantabile: Tchaikovsky, Peter Ilyitch: Sheridan, Patrick

Andante et Allegro: Lantier, Pierre: Michel, Guy

Andante for Tuba and Piano: Tscherepnin, Alexander: Hoppert, Manfred

Andante from Concerto for Coloratura: Gliere, Reinhold: Northcut, Timothy

Andante Quasi Allegretto: Ramsöe, Emilio Wilhelm: Melton Tuba-Quartett

Andante Tranquillo, for Solo Viola and Piano: McKimm, Barry: Pokorny, Gene

Angel: Hendrix, Jimi: Moschner, Pinguin

Angel Eyes: Dennis, Matt, and Earl Brent: Draper, Ray

Angels: Robinson, Perry: European Tuba Quartet

Angels We Have Heard on High: Phillips, Harvey/TubaChristmas

Anitra's Dance: Grieg, Edvard: Baadsvik, Øystein

Ann-Charlotte: Stewart, Bob

Another Blues: Callender, George Sylvester "Red"

Another Moment in the Past: Wittner, Gary: Johnson, Howard

Another Time: Broadbent, Alan: Self, James

Antartic Love Song: Moschner, Pinguin: Moschner, Pinguin

Appalachian Carol: Canter, James: Tennessee Tech Alumni Ensemble; United States Armed Forces Tuba-Euphonium Ensemble and Massed Ensemble

Appointment in Ghana: McLean, Jackie: Johnson, Howard

Après un Rêve: Fauré, Gabriel: Funderburk, Jeff; King, Ian; Sheridan, Patrick; Szentpáli, Roland

April Is in My Mistress' Face: Morley: British Tuba Quartet

Aqui el sol brilla mas: Schiaffini, GianCarlo: Schiaffini, GianCarlo

Argonaise from "Le Cid": Massenet, Jules: Monarch Tuba-Euphonium Quartet; United States Navy Band Tuba-Euphonium Quartet

Aria con Variazioni: Handel, George Friderik: Seward, Steven

Aria di coloratura: Lang, Istvan: Bazsinka, József

Arietta (Non posso disperar): Bononcini, Giovanni: Daellenbach, Charles

Arioso: Benson, Warren: Popiel, Peter; Sinder, Philip

Arpeggione Sonata: Schubert, Franz Peter: Jae Young, Heo

Arrival of the Queen of Sheba: Handel, George Friderik: Tennessee Technological University Tuba/Euphonium Ensemble

Art Deco: Cherry, Don: Stewart, Bob

"As When the Dove" from "Acis and Galatea": Handel, George Friderik: Brown, Velvet

Asleep in the Deep: Petrie, H. W.: Bell, William; Colonial Tuba Quartet; Mallon, Barney; Palmer, Singleton

At the Last Moment: Lindsay, Erica: Johnson, Howard

Athletic Conveyance: Taggart, Mark: Jarvis, Jeffrey

Atlantis [motion picture soundtrack]: Howard, James Newton: Self, James

Au Privave: Parker, Charlie: Mazura, János

Au Privave: Parker, Charlie: Murrow, Richard

Au Privave: Parker, Charlie: New York Tuba Quartet

Auburn Is the Colour: Forbes, Mike: Sotto Voce

Aunt Hagar's Children: Handy and Brymn: Newberger, Eli

aus "España," Op. 165: Albeniz, Isaac: Hilgers, Walter

Aus Allen Wolken: Moschner and Sachse: Moschner, Pinguin

aus Cantros de España, Op. 232, No. 2 "Chant d'Amour": Albeniz, Isaac: Hilgers, Walter

Aus Vertreutem ein Ganzes: Glandien, Lutz: Vogt, Michael

Autumn in New York: Callender, George Sylvester "Red"

Autumn Leaves: Kosma: Symphonia (Thomas Ashworth, solo euphonium)

Auz: Perrine, Matt

Avalanche: McIntosh, Nat

Avalon: Rose, Jolson, and DeSylva: Matteson, Rich; Pilafian, Sam

Ave Maria: Arcadelt, Jacob: Melton Tuba-Quartett

Ave Maria: Bach, Johann Sebastian: Sheridan, Patrick

Ave Maria: Gounod, Charles: Pilafian, Sam

Ave Maria: Schubert, Franz Peter: Sykes, Steve

Away in a Manger: Mueller: Mighty Tubadours

Baby Elephant Walk: Mancini, Henry: Melton Tuba-Quartett

Baby Face: Davis, Akst: University of Miami Tuba Ensemble

Baby Got Banjo: Smith, Zachary: Dixie Power Trio

Baby Let Me Hold Your Hand: Byrd, Roeland: Dixie Power Trio

Baby, You Keep Me up All Night: Smith, Zachary: Dixie Power Trio
Badinage: Norbury, Kevin: Sheridan, Patrick
Badintés: Guignon, Jean-Pierre: Thuillier, Francois
Baguette Viennoise: Thuillier, Francois: Thuillier, Francois
Ballad for Inger: Thuillier, Francois: Thuillier, Francois
Ballad for Tuba: Christensen, James: Cummings, Barton
Ballad of Enob Mort: Uber, David: Jae Young, Heo
Ballade: Hill, Helmar: Heavy Tuba
Ballade and Presto Dance: Smith, Claude T.: Daniel, Robert; Jae Young, Heo; Seward, Steven
Ballin' the Jack: Burris and Smith: Palmer, Singleton; Phillips, Harvey
Bandinerie: Bach, Johann Sebastian: Marshall, Oren; Melton Tuba-Quartett
Banjos and Tubas Forever: Cohan: Corella, Gil
Barcarolle et Chanson Bachique: Semler-Collery, Jules: Popiel, Peter; Randolph, David
Barcarolle for Tuba: Mori, Yoshiko: Yasumoto, Hiroyuki
The Bare Necessities: Gilkyson, Terry: Morgan, Kevin
Barnum and Bailey's Favorite: King, Karl L.: Mighty Tubadours; United States Armed Forces Tuba-Euphonium Ensemble
Baroque 'n Brass for Trumpet and Tuba: Anderson, Eugene: Pilafian, Sam
Bart's Piece for Tuba and Electronic Tape: Ott, Joseph: Cummings, Barton
Bas Relief: Hopkins, Greg: Pilafian, Sam
The Basics: Newsome, Roy: Tubalaté
Basin Street Blues: Williams, Spencer: Callender, George Sylvester "Red"; Lehr, David "Red"; Pilafian, Sam
Bass Ale Blues: Napoleon and Signorelli: Tarto, Joe
Bass Bees: Godard, Michel: Bargeron, Dave
The Bass in the Ballroom: Newsome, Roy: Sykes, Stephen; Woods, Gavin
Bass, for Solo Tuba and Percussion: Nilsson, Bo: Lind, Michael
Bassacat: Steckar, Marc: Miraphone Tuba Quartet
The Basset Hound Blues: Self, James: Self, James
Basso Continuo: Fritze, Gregory: Fritze, Gregory
Batida Diferente: Ferreira and Einhorn: Megules, Karl
Battle Hymn of the Republic: Howe, Julia Ward: Lehr, David "Red"
Battle Royal: Jewell, Fred: British Tuba Quartet; Swiss Tuba Quartet
Batubop: Steckar, Marc: Steckar Tubapack
Baubles, Bangles and Beads: Wright, Robert: Self, James
Bavarian Polka: Traditional: British Tuba Quartet
Bavarian Stew: Wilhelm, Rolf: Melton Tuba-Quartett
Bayerische Polka: Lohmann, Georg: Contraband (The); Gerhard Meinl's Tuba Sextet; Miraphone Tuba Quartet
Bayerische Pop Tuba: Steckar, Marc: Stecker, Marc
Bayerische Zell: Traditional: Gerhard Meinl's Tuba Sextet
Be No Evil: Johnson, Howard: Johnson, Howard
Beachcombers Dance: Uber, David: Hanks, Thompson (Toby)
Beale Street Blues: Handy, W. C.: Lehr, David "Red"; Palmer, Singleton
The Bear: Jacobs, Jacob: Corella, Gil
Bear Solo from "Petrouchka": Stravinsky, Igor: Jacobs, Arnold
Beast!: Danner, Gregory: Tennessee Technological University Tuba/Euphonium Ensemble
Beat It: Jackson, Michael: Tennessee Technological University Tuba/Euphonium Ensemble
Beautiful Dreamer: Foster, Stephen: Self, James
Beelzebub: Catozzi, A.: Jae Young, Heo
Beethoven's 5½: Beethoven, Ludwig van: Corella, Gil
Beetlejuice [motion picture soundtrack]: Elfman, Danny: Johnson, John Thomas (Tommy)
Behind Your Face: Weaver, Mark: Weaver, Mark
Believe Me If All Those Endearing Young Charms: Mantia, Simone: Griffiths, John; Randolph, David; Seward, Steven
Bell and Ponce: Dara, Olu: Stewart, Bob
Beneath the Horizon for Tuba and Taped Whale Songs: McLean, Pricilla: Poore, Melvyn
Beneath the Surface: Harrison, Wayne: Tennessee Technological University Tuba/Euphonium Ensemble
Beneath the Wheel: McGrain, Mark: Rojas, Marcus
Benediction : Stevens, John: Sotto Voce
Berceuse De Jocelyn: Godard, Benjamin: Sykes, Steve
Bertone: Drums and Tuba: Drums and Tuba
Besame Mucho: Velasquez, Consuelo: Pilafian, Sam
Betrayal for Tuba, Violin and Vibraphone, Op. 144: Christiansen, Henning: Andersen, Hans
Better Git It in Your Soul: Mingus, Charles: Frey, Michael
Bifurcation for Tuba and Piano: Baader-Nobs, Heidi: Bjørn-Larsen, Jens
Big Alice: Pullen, Don: Johnson, Howard
Big Bad Bill: Ager and Yellen: Newberger, Eli
Big Butter and Egg Man: Palmer, Singleton
Big Chief: Gaines and Quezerque: Dixie Power Trio
Big Easy Groove: Pilafian, Sam: Pilafian, Sam
Big Forehead: Wittner, Gary: Johnson, Howard
Big Joe, the Tuba: Lavalle, Paul: Tarto, Joe
Big Kneed Gal: Mahal, Taj: Stewart, Bob
Big Leg Woman: Lacen, Anthony "Tuba Fats"
Bill Bailey, Please Call Your Service: Cannon, Hughie: Self, James
Bill Bailey Won't You Please Come Home: Cannon, Hughie: Palmer, Singleton; Pilafian, Sam
Billie's Bounce: Parker, Charlie: Mazura, János
Bird: Hübsch, Carl Ludwig: European Tuba Quartet
Birdland: Zawinul, Josef: Tennessee Technological University Tuba/Euphonium Ensemble

Birks Werks: Gillespie, Dizzy: Feldman, Enrique "Hank" C.
Bist du bei mir, BWV 508: Bach, Johann Sebastian: Atlantic Tuba Quartet; Melton Tuba-Quartett; United States Armed Forces Tuba-Euphonium Ensemble and Massed Ensemble
Bivalve Suite for Euphonium and Tuba: Hartley, Walter: LeBlanc, Robert
Black and Blue: Waller, Thomas "Fats": Pilafian, Sam
Black Bottom Stomp: Morton, F. "Jelly Roll": Pilafian, Sam
Black Dog: Page/Plant: Carolino, Sérgio
Black Horse Stomp: Tarto, Joe: Tarto, Joe
Blackbird: Lennon, John, and Paul McCartney: Holmgaard, Lars
Blazevitch: Drums and Tuba: Drums and Tuba
Bloodshot: McIntosh, Nat
Blue in green: Davis, Miles: Frey, Michael
Blue Lights: Sass, Jonathon: Heavy Tuba
Blue Monk: Monk, Thelonius: Johnson, Howard; Steckar Tubapack
Blue Moon: Rodgers, Richard, and Lorenz Hart: Tuba 4's
Blue Rondo a la Turk: Brubeck, Dave: Modern Jazz Tuba Project; Tennessee Technological University Tuba/Euphonium Ensemble
Blue Wail: European Tuba Quartet
Bluebells Nightmare: Lauer, Christoff: Stewart, Bob
Blues and the Abstract Truth: Nelson, Oliver: Self, James
Blues Connotation: Coleman, Ornette: Pilafian, Sam
Blues for Bart: Williams, Danny: Cummings, Barton
Blues for E. L. C.: Smith, Warren: Johnson, Howard
Blues for Louie: Fritz, József Róbert: Mazura, János
Blues in B♭: Palmer, Singleton
Blues in the Night: Mercer, Johnny: Price, Tony
The Blues My Naughty Sweetie Gives to Me: Swanstone, McCarron, and Morgan: Dixie Power Trio; Lehr, David "Red"
Blues to Nasir: Felt, Brad: Felt, Brad
The Blues Walk: Brown: Gannett, Dave
Bluesin' Tubas: Martin, Glenn: Tennessee Technological University Tuba/Euphonium Ensemble
Bluzenfunky: Bulla, Stephen: Erickson, Martin
Boast: Colding-Jargensen, Henrik: Bazsinka, József
Bobby Jones, Stroke of Genius [motion picture soundtrack]: Horner, James: Self, James
Bocoxe: Aquino, Baden Powell de: Alchemy; Atlantic Tuba Quartet; British Tuba Quartet; Melton Tuba-Quartett
Bonampak: Gomez, Alice: Brown, Velvet
Boogie Down: Jarreau, Al: Tennessee Technological University Tuba/Euphonium Ensemble
Boogie Stop Shuffle: Mingus, Charles: Drums and Tuba
Boogie Woogie Tuba Boy: Hinchley, John: Tubalaté
Boplicity: Henry, Cleo: Barber, John William (Bill); Pilafian, Sam
Bosque De Manaus: Kurnick, Jon: Self, James
Boss-Swan-Nova: Tchaikovsky, Peter Ilyitch: Erickson, Martin
Bottoms Up Rag: Mehlan, Keith: Monarch Tuba-Euphonium Quartet
Bouillabaisse (Thanks, Maggie): Moschner, Pinguin: Moschner, Pinguin
Bourree from the Sixth Flute Sonata: Handel, George Friderik: Popiel, Peter
Bourree I and II from Suite for Solo Cello: Bach, Johann Sebastian: Bobo, Roger
Boy Scout—Be Prepared: Tarto, Joe, and Paul Lavelle: Tarto, Joe
Brand New Cadillac: Clash (The): Tooba Blooze
Brass Cuckoo: Hart, Bill: Alchemy
Brass Quintet No. 2: Wilder, Alec: Hanks, Thompson (Toby)
Brass Rap!: Swoboda, Deanna: Swoboda, Deanna
Brass Tacks: Niehaus, Lennie: Northern Tuba Lights
Brass Tax: European Tuba Quartet
Brazil: Barroso, Ary: Melton Tuba-Quartett; Pilafian, Sam; Tennessee Technological University Tuba/Euphonium Ensemble; Tuba 4's
Break Forth O Beauteous Light: Schop: Mighty Tubadours
Breakthrough: Harlos, Steve: Self, James
Breath and Sounds for Tuba and Tape: Witkin, Beatrice: Hanks, Thompson (Toby)
Breeze: MacDonald, Goodwin, and Hanley: Newberger, Eli
Brick House: King, Lapread, McClary, Orange, Richie, Williams: Tennessee Technological University Tuba/Euphonium Ensemble
Bride of the Waves: Clarke, Herbert L.: Frazier, Richard
Brief Case: Drums and Tuba: Drums and Tuba
Brillenbass: Read, Thomas: Nelson, Mark
Brilliant Corners: Monk, Thelonius: Carolino, Sérgio
Bring a Torch, Jeanette, Isabella: arr. Bewley: Phillips, Harvey/TubaChristmas
Broadway Bash: Pegram, Wayne: Symphonia
Brooklyn: McIntosh, Nat
Brown Blue: Weaver, Mark: Weaver, Mark
Bruckner Etude: Crespo, Enrique: Gerhard Meinl's Tuba Sextet
Bruegel—Dance Visions: Rubenstein, Arthur: Self, James
Bud's Delights: Perrine, Matt
Buddy Bolden's Blues: Morton, F. "Jelly Roll": Dixie Power Trio; Pilafian, Sam
Bullfrog Rag: Garbáge, Pierre (a.k.a. Garrett, James): Tennessee Tech Alumni Ensemble
Burlesk: Gulya, R.: Szentpáli, Roland
Burning of the Midnight Lamp: Hendrix, Jimi: Moschner, Pinguin
Bush Baby: Blythe, Arthur: Stewart, Bob
But Not for Me: Gershwin, George and Ira: Johnson, Howard
Butacudatuba: Steckar, Marc: Stecker, Marc
The Butcher: Drums and Tuba: Drums and Tuba

The Buzzard Song: Gershwin, George: Barber, John William (Bill)
Bydlo from "Pictures at an Exhibition": Mussorgsky, Modest: Piernik, Zdizislaw
Bye Bye Blackbird: Henderson, Ray: Mazura, János
Bye Bye Blues: Low/Gray/Bennett/Ha: Matteson-Phillips TubaJazz Consort
Cabaret: Kander, John Harold: Morgan, Kevin
Cadence VI for Tuba and Tape: Lazarof, Henri: Bobo, Roger
Cakewalk into Town: Mahal, Taj: Frey, Michael
Calvados: Unkrodt, Dietrich
Camouflage: McIntosh, Nat
Campadre Pedro Juan: Alberti, Luis: Pilafian, Sam
Camptown Races: Foster, Stephen: Self, James
Canadian Brass Blues: Boyd, Bill: Daellenbach, Charles
Candle Light in Disneyland: Moschner and Sachse: Moschner, Pinguin
Can't Let Go That Zydeco: Smith, Zachary: Dixie Power Trio
Canto VII for Solo Tuba: Adler, Samuel: Beauregard, Cherry
Cantuballade: Roost, Jan Van der: Nickel, Hans
Canzon per Sonare No. 2: Gabrieli, Giovanni: Jacobs, Arnold
Canzona, La Spiritata: Gabrieli, Giovanni: British Tuba Quartet
Canzona per Sonare No. 4: Gabrieli, Giovanni: Dutch Tuba Quartet; Gerhard Meinl's Tuba Sextet; Melton Tuba-Quartett
Capriccio Da Camera for Solo Tuba and Brass Quintet: Danielssohn, Christer: Hilgers, Walter; Jae Young, Heo; Lind, Michael; Schumacker, Finn
Capriccio for Solo Tuba: Penderecki, Krzysztof: Bazsinka, József; Bobo, Roger; Funderburk, Jeff; Jae Young, Heo; Labeyrie, Stéphane; Perantoni, Daniel; Piernik, Zdizislaw; Woods, Gavin
Capriccio for Tuba and Band: Presser, William: Astwood, Michael
Capriccio for Tuba and Marimba: Penn, William: Jarvis, Jeffrey; Pokorny, Gene
Capriccio for Tuba and Orchestra: Schuller, Gunther: Phillips, Harvey
Capriccio for Tuba and Piano: Sheng-Tong, Tsai: Stachowiak, Bernard
Capriccio in E♭ major: Newton, Rodney: Gourlay, James; Nickel, Hans; Sykes, Steven
Capricorn One [motion picture soundtrack]: Goldsmith, Jerry: Johnson, John Thomas (Tommy)
Capriole: Self, James: Self, James
Careless Love: Koenig, Williams, and Handy: Palmer, Singleton
Carioca: Youmans, Vincent: Arwood, Jeffrey; Phillips, Harvey; Pilafian, Sam; Sass, Jonathon; Sheridan, Patrick
Carlos the Cat: Drums and Tuba: Drums and Tuba
Carnival Cocktail: Sykes, Steve: Sykes, Steve
Carnival for Bass: Muscroft, Fred: Baker, Fred
Carnival of Venice: Arban, Jean Baptiste: Baadsvik, Øystein; Bell, William; Bobo, Roger; Lind, Michael; Jae Young, Heo; Perantoni, Daniel; Sheridan, Patrick
Carnival of Venice: Benedict, Julius: Daellenbach, Charles
Carnival of Venice: Clarke, Herbert L.: Jacobs, Arnold; Woods, Gavin
Carnival of Venice: Giampieri: Morgan, Kevin
Carnival of Venice: Howarth, Elgar: Fletcher, John
Carnival of Venice: LeClair, David: Contraband (The); Monarch Tuba-Euphonium Quartet
Carol of the Bells: Leontovich and Wilhousky: Phillips, Harvey/TubaChristmas; Pilafian, Sam
Carolina in the Morning: Donaldson, W.: University of Miami Tuba Ensemble
Carols for a Merry TubaChristmas: Wilder, Alec: Phillips, Harvey/TubaChristmas
Carol's Theme: Felt, Brad: Felt, Brad
Carrots: Drums and Tuba: Drums and Tuba
The Casbah of Tetouan: Miraphone Tuba Quartet
The Cascades: Joplin, Scott: British Tuba Quartet; Dites-Le-Moi Tuba; Johnson, John Thomas (Tommy); Pilafian, Sam
Castaldo Marsch: Novacek, Rudolf: Miraphone Tuba Quartet
Cat in the Hat [motion picture soundtrack]: Newman, David: Self, James
Cavatina: Myers, Stanley: Self, James
Celestial Morn: Condon, Leslie: Hornsberger, Albert
Celestial Suite: Bulla, Stephen: British Tuba Quartet
Cello Sonata No. 5 in E: Vivaldi, Antonio: King, Ian
Centerfold: Justman, S.: Dixie Power Trio
Ceremonial Sketch: Camphouse, Mark: Tennessee Tech Alumni Ensemble; Tennessee Technological University Tuba/Euphonium Ensemble; United States Armed Forces Tuba-Euphonium Ensemble and Massed Ensemble
Chaconne: Hayden, Paul: Skillen, Joseph
Chaconne: Sowerby, Leo: Davis, Ronald
Chamber Concerto for Tuba with 12 Winds and 12 Drums: Wuorinen, Charles: Braynard, David
Chameleon: Hamers, Maurice: Nickel, Hans
Chameleon: Hancock, Herbie: Tennessee Technological University Tuba/Euphonium Ensemble
Champagne Aria from "Don Giovanni": Mozart, Wolfgang Amadeus: Pilafian, Sam
Chanson de Matin, Op. 15, No. 2: Elgar, Edward: Fletcher, John; Thornton, Michael
The Chant: Stitzel, Mel: Dixie Power Trio; Matteson, Rich; Newberger, Eli
Chapeau Russia: Drums and Tuba: Drums and Tuba
Chaser #1: Garbáge, Pierre (a.k.a. Garrett, James): Tennessee Tech Alumni Ensemble
Chasin' the Antelope: Vignola, Frank: Pilafian, Sam
Chattanooga Choo Choo: Gordon/Warren/Wolpe: Tuba 4's
Cherokee: Noble, Ray: Erickson, Martin; Modern Jazz Tuba Project

Cherokee: Schooley, John: Melton Tuba-Quartett; Northern TubaLights; Rustic Bari-Tuba Ensemble
Chiacona: Bargeron, Dave
Chicago: Fisher, F.: Palmer, Singleton
Chicago Breakdown: Morton, F. "Jelly Roll": Newberger, Eli
Chicken: Perrine, Matt
A Child Is Born: Jones, Thad: Erickson, Martin
Children at Play: Kalina, Ron: Self, James
Chimes Blues: arr. Garrett: Tennessee Technological University Tuba/Euphonium Ensemble
Chimes Blues: Oliver, Joe: Newberger, Eli
Chin Up!: Kresin, Willibald: Contraband (The)
China Boy: Winfree, Dick: Pilafian, Sam
Chinatown: McIntosh, Nat
Chinatown, My Chinatown: Schwartz, Jean: Daellenbach, Charles
Chit Chat Polka: Strauss, Johann: British Tuba Quartet
Chlingen: Brun, Albin: Unternährer, Marc
Chompers: Wittner, Gary: Johnson, Howard
Chops!: Martin, Glenn: Tennessee Technological University Tuba/Euphonium Ensemble
Chops a la Salsa: Botschinsky, Allan: Van Lier, Erik
Chorale Prelude Op. 122, No. 8, "Es ist ein Ros' entsprungen": Brahms, Johannes: Jacobs, Arnold
Chorale Variations, "Jesu meine Fruede": Kreines: Jacobs, Arnold
Choralfantasie ürber "Es ist ein Schnitter" für Tuba und Orgel, Op. 93: Koetsier, Jan: Walsh, Thomas
Choro Loco: Bargeron, Dave
Chorus and Instruments (II): Feldman, Morton: Phillips, Harvey
Christmas Carnival: Pilafian, Sam
The Christmas Song: Tormé and Wells: Phillips, Harvey/TubaChristmas; Pilafian, Sam
The Chrysanthemum: Joplin, Scott: Johnson, John Thomas (Tommy)
Chummus, A Challa, and a Whole Lot of Chutzpah: Drums and Tuba: Drums and Tuba
Cipriana: Huffsteter, Steve: Self, James
Civilization and Its Discontents: Wilson, Richard Edward: Johns, Steven
CJ: Stewart, Bob: Stewart, Bob
Clara C: Bargeron, Dave
Clarinet Polka: Traditional: Davis, Ronald; Tuba 4's
Classical Jazz Suite: Copeland, Ray: Morris, Jim
Clearfield Driving: Bulla, Stephen: Erickson, Martin
Cleopha: Joplin, Scott: Johnson, John Thomas (Tommy)
Clifford's Kappa: Draper, Ray: Draper, Ray
Clones: Hamlin, Peter: Funderburk, Jeff
Close Case: Drums and Tuba: Drums and Tuba
Close Encounters of the Third Kind [motion picture soundtrack]: Williams, John: Self, James
Clouds: Ihlenfeld, Dave: Sheridan, Patrick
Cole Porter Medley: Porter, Cole: Tennessee Technological University Tuba/Euphonium Ensemble
Colline's Aria: Puccini, Giacomo: Daellenbach, Charles
Colonel Bogey March: Alford, Kenneth: Tuba 4's
Colonial Express: Stamp, Jack: Colonial Tuba Quartet
Colors of the Wind: Menken/Schwartz: Tuba 4's
Combination March: Joplin, Scott: Johnson, John Thomas (Tommy)
Come Back to Sorrento: Ernesto and Battista: Gannett, Dave
Come Dearest, the Daylight Is Gone: Anonymous: Mighty Tubadours
Come Follow the Band: Coleman, Cy, and Hershey Kay: Stevens, John
Come Together: Lennon, John, and Paul McCartney: Frey, Michael; Murrow, Richard
Come, Thou Fount of Every Blessing: American Folk Hymn: Daellenbach, Charles
Comedian's Galop: Kabalevski, Dmitri: Mighty Tubadours
Coming Home: Puschnig, Wolfgang: Stewart, Bob
Concert Allegro: Lebedev, Alexei: Funderburk, Jeff; Randolph, David
Concert Duos: White, John: Rozen, Jay
Concert Etude: Goedicke: Sheridan, Patrick
Concert Etudes for Solo Tuba: Osmon, Leroy: Kirk, David
Concert Music for Bass Tuba: Mueller, Florian: Conner, Rex
Concertante Suite for Tuba and Four Horns: Danielssohn, Christer: Hilgers, Walter; Hötzel, Markus; Lind, Michael
Concertino: Curnow, James: Cummings, Barton; McAdams, Charles; Perantoni, Daniel
Concertino: Wilhelm, Rolf: Sheridan, Patrick
Concertino for Three Brass and Band: Werle, Floyd: Angerstein, Fred
Concertino for Tuba and Band: Bencriscutto, Frank: Freese, Stanford
Concertino for Tuba and Concert Band: Wilhelm, Rolf: Bjørn-Larsen, Jens; Bunn, Michael
Concertino for Tuba and Piano: Bozza, Eugène: Bazsinka, József; Seward, Steven
Concertino for Tuba and Piano: Wilhelm, Rolf: Skillen, Joseph
Concertino for Tuba and String Orchestra, Op. 77: Koetsier, Jan: Brown, Velvet; Hoppert, Manfred; Walsh, Thomas
Concertino for Tuba and Strings: Frackenpohl, Arthur: Irmer, Benjamin
Concertino for Tuba and Wind Ensemble: Hartley, Walter: Turk, John
Concertino for Tuba, Percussion and Piano: Williams, Howard: Cummings, Barton
Concerto: Saglietti, Corrado Maria: Hötzel, Markus
Concerto Basso: Ross, Walter: Tennessee Technological University Tuba/Euphonium Ensemble

Concerto del Garda: Raum, Elizabeth: Griffiths, John
Concerto for Bass Tuba and Band: Jager, Robert: Morris, R. Winston; Perantoni, Daniel
Concerto for Bass Tuba and Band: Vaughan Williams, Ralph: Arwood, Jeffrey; Perantoni, Daniel; Phillips, Harvey
Concerto for Bass Tuba and Brass Band: Vaughan Williams, Ralph: Gourlay, James
Concerto for Bass Tuba and Orchestra: Vaughan Williams, Ralph: Catelinet, Philip; Cooley, Floyd; Dowling, Eugene; Fletcher, John; Harrild, Patrick; Hoppert, Manfred; Jacobs, Arnold; King, Ian; Lind, Michael; Morgan, Kevin; Nahatzki, Richard; Nickel, Hans; Phillips, Harvey; Strand, Donald
Concerto for Orchestra (excerpt): Bartók, Béla: Jacobs, Arnold; Pokorny, Gene
Concerto for Tuba: Sass, Jonathon
Concerto for Tuba: Bogar, Istvan: Bazsinka, József
Concerto for Tuba: Casas, Bartolomé Perez: Mas, Vicente Navarro
Concerto for Tuba: Ewazen, Eric: Skillen, Joseph
Concerto for Tuba: Williams, John: Brown, Velvet; Easener, Marc
Concerto for Tuba and Band: Danner, Greg: Northcut, Timothy
Concerto for Tuba and Brass Band: Horovitz, Joseph: Gourlay, James
Concerto for Tuba and Orchestra: Arutiunian, Alexander: Lidsle, Harri
Concerto for Tuba and Orchestra: Schmidt, Ole: Lind, Michael
Concerto for Tuba and Orchestra: Strukov, Valery: Bjørn-Larsen, Jens
Concerto for Tuba and Orchestra, Op. 52: Holmboe, Vagn: Bjørn-Larsen, Jens
Concerto for Tuba and Percussion Orchestra: Hartley, Walter: Jarvis, Jeffrey
Concerto for Tuba and Strings: Plau, Arild PLAU: Baadsvik, Øystein
Concerto for Tuba and Wind Orchestra: Brusick, William: Northcut, Timothy
Concerto for Tuba "Concerto Euphonique": Hopkinson: Michel, Guy
Concerto for Violin (third movement): Mendelssohn, Felix: Seward, Steven
Concerto Grosso for Tubas and Band: ANON
Concerto in C major for Two Trumpets: Vivaldi, Antonio: Seward, Steven
Concerto in G minor for Oboe and Orchestra: Handel, George Friderik: Popiel, Peter
Concerto in One Movement: Lebedev, Alexei: Arwood, Jeffrey; Funderburk, Jeff; Gourlay, James; Hoppert, Manfred; Woods, Gavin
Concerto No. 1 for Horn, Op. 11: Strauss, Richard: Cooley, Floyd; Jacobs, Arnold
Concerto No. 1 in G: Handel, George Friderik: Hilgers, Walter
Concerto, Op. 9, No. 2 in D: Albinoni, Tomaso: Hilgers, Walter
Concerto, Op. 96b: Barnes, James: Sheridan, Patrick
Concertpiece for Tuba and Piano: Larsen, Libby: Nelson, Mark
Concertpiece No. 1: Vaughan, Rodger: Conner, Rex; Davis, Ronald; Funderburk, Jeff
Conjectures for Tuba and Band: Sauter, Eddie: Phillips, Harvey
Consequences, for Tuba Quartet: Forbes, Mike: Sotto Voce
Consortium: Cheetham, John: British Tuba Quartet; Tennessee Technological University Tuba/Euphonium Ensemble; United States Armed Forces Tuba-Euphonium Ensemble
Contrapunctus I: Bach, Johann Sebastian: Tennessee Tech Tuba-Euphonium Quintet
Contrapunctus 9 from Die Kunst der Fuge: Bach, Johann Sebastian: Sotto Voce
The Conversation: Williams, John: Self, James
Cookin' at the Continental: Silver, Horace: Modern Jazz Tuba Project
A Cool Suite: Smalley, Peter: British Tuba Quartet
Corazon: arr. Arnold: Tennessee Technological University Tuba/Euphonium Ensemble
Corner Pocket: Green, Freddie: Tennessee Technological University Tuba/Euphonium Ensemble
Cornet Chop Suey: Armstrong, Louis: Pilafian, Sam
Count Phenomium: Sass, Jonathon
Courante: Self, James: Self, James
Courtship: James, Bob: Tennessee Technological University Tuba/Euphonium Ensemble
Cousins: Clarke, Herbert L.: Contraband (The)
Coventry Carol: arr. Vaughan: Mighty Tubadours
Crawlin': Perrine, Matt
Crespuscule with Nellie: Monk, Thelonius: Johnson, Howard
Crimson Tide [motion picture soundtrack]: Zimmer, Hans: Johnson, John Thomas (Tommy)
Cris: Callender, Red: Callender, George Sylvester "Red"
Criss-Cross: Monk, Thelonius: Johnson, Howard
The Cruel War Is Raging: American Folksong: Daellenbach, Charles
Csárdás: Monti, Vittorio: Baadsvik, Øystein; Contraband (The); Erickson, Martin; Hilgers, Walter; Jacobs, Arnold; Jae Young, Heo; King, Ian; Randolph, David; Sheridan, Patrick; Sykes, Steve; Woods, Gavin
C. T.'s Blues (Finger Filibuster): Terry, Clark: Matteson-Phillips TubaJazz Consort
Cuba Mirum: Schiaffini, GianCarlo: Schiaffini, GianCarlo
The Cuckoo, Lucerne Song: arr. Howarth: Fletcher, John
Culture:envy:war: McIntosh, Nat
Cumana: Lehr, David "Red"
Curtains: Drums and Tuba: Drums and Tuba
Custard the Dragon: Robinson, Keith: Swoboda, Deanna

D'un Souffle de Lumiere: Creuze, Roland: Lienard, Bernard
Da Bomba: McIntosh, Nat
Daahoud: Brown, Clifford: Dutch Tuba Quartet
Dali's Car: Beefheart, Captain: Pilafian, Sam
Damnation de Faust (excerpt): Berlioz, Hector: Pokorny, Gene
Dance No. 1: Wilson, Kenyon: Tennessee Tech Alumni Ensemble
Dance of Passion: Griffin, Johnny: Bargeron, Dave
Dance of the Big Fairries: Traditional: Flowers, Herbie
Dance of the Blessed Spirits: Gluck, Christopf: Sheridan, Patrick; Woods, Gavin
Dance of the Ocean Breeze: Kellaway, Roger: Bobo, Roger; Labeyrie, Stéphane
Dance of the Reedpipes: Tchaikovsky, Peter Ilyitch: Mighty Tubadours
Dance of the Sophists: Mitchell: Roper, William
Dance of the Sugar Plum Fairy: Tchaikovsky, Peter Ilyitch: British Tuba Quartet
Dance Suite for Tuba and Triangle: Beach, Bennie: Cummings, Barton
Dances: Pullig, Ken: Colonial Tuba Quartet
Dances: Stevens, John: Dutch Tuba Quartet; Hanks, Thompson (Toby); Melton Tuba-Quartett; Northern Tuba Lights; Rustic Bari-Tuba Ensemble; Sotto Voce
Dancing King: Ayers, Jesse: Nelson, Mark
Daniel in the Lion's Den: McBeth, Francis: Perantoni, Daniel
Danse Bizarre no 3: Quibel, Robert: Steckar Tubapack
Danse pour un Kangourou: Steckar, Marc: Steckar Tubapack
Danse Sacrée: Tomasi, Henri: Brown, Velvet
Danza Martelo from Bachianas Brasilieras No. 5: Villa-Lobos, Heitor: Alchemy
Dapper Dan: Brown and Von Tilzer: Newberger, Eli
Dark Eyes: Salama and Grebenka: M'N'M Trio; Pilafian, Sam
Darn That Dream: De-Lange: Callender, George Sylvester "Red"
Das Butterbrot: Mozart, Wolfgang Amadeus: Melton Tuba-Quartett
A Day at the Camptown Races: Uber, David: Hanks, Thompson (Toby)
Day Dream: Ellington, Edward Kennedy "Duke": Johnson, Howard
Dead End: McDermot, Ragni, and Rado: Scandinavian Tuba Jazz
Deck the Halls: Phillips, Harvey/TubaChristmas
Dedicated to the Blues: arr. Callender: Callender, George Sylvester "Red"
'Deed I Do: Hirsch/Rose: Gannett, Dave
Deep Harmony: Parker, Handel: Tubalaté
Deep Purple: DeRose, Peter: Pilafian, Sam
Deep River/Swing Low Sweet Chariot: Traditional: King, Ian
Deep Throb: Moschner, Pinguin: Moschner, Pinguin
Deflections: Weaver, Mark: Weaver, Mark
Demain il fera jour: Caratini, Patrice: Steckar Tubapack
Der Genesene an die Hoffnung: Wolf, Hugo: Hilgers, Walter
Der Khusid geyt Tantsn: Traditional: Dutch Tuba Quartet
Der Wurst lebt: Moschner, Pinguin: Moschner, Pinguin
Des Athégiens au Sénégal: Guignon, Jean-Pierre: Thuillier, Francois
Desert Song: Wauschke: European Tuba Quartet
Detournement Mineur: Goret, Didier: Steckar Elephant Tuba Horde
Deuxième sonate, Op. XIV: Boismortier, Joseph Bodin: Labeyrie, Stéphane
The Devil Never Sleeps: Szentpáli, Roland: Szentpáli, Roland
The Devil's Herald: Peasley, Richard: Phillips, Harvey
The Diagram: Drums and Tuba: Drums and Tuba
Dialogs: Jones, Robert: Funderburk, Jeff
Dialogue für Tuba und Tonband: Piernik, Zdzislaw: Piernik, Zdzislaw
Dialogy: Bedrich, Jan: Nickel, Hans
Diaspora: McIntosh, Nat
Didge I Do: Sass, Jonathon
Dido's Lament from "Dido and Aeneas": Purcell, Henry: British Tuba Quartet
Die Forelle (Trout) Theme and Variations 1–5: Schubert, Franz Peter: Contraband Tuba Quartet
Die haltbare Graugans: Unkrodt, Dietrich
Die Meistersinger von Nürnberg (excerpt): Wagner, Richard: Pokorny, Gene
Die Voralpen: Casimir, Daniel: Thuillier, Francois
Dies Irae for Tuba and Piano: Langgaard, Rued: Arnsted, Jørgen Voight
Dies Irae from Requiem: Verdi, Giuseppi: Symphonia
"Dies Irae" from "Symphonie Fantastique": Berlioz, Hector: Jacobs, Arnold; Pokorny, Gene
Dig: Davis, Miles: Pilafian, Sam
Disgruntled Lullaby: Brown, Tom: Self, James
Distressed Innocence Overture: Purcell, Henry: British Tuba Quartet
Diversion for 7 Bass Clef Instruments: Clinard, Fred Jr.: Tennessee Tech Alumni Ensemble
Diversions: Stevens, John: Sotto Voce
Diversita Continua: Choen, Michael: Hershko, Shmuel "Adi"
Diversive Elements for Euphonium, Tuba and Piano: Gillingham, David: Zerkel, David
Divertimento bassobavarese for Solo Tuba: Etzel, Bernhard: Walsh, Thomas
Divertimento for Tuba Ensemble: Spears, Jared: Tennessee Tech Alumni Ensemble; Tennessee Technological University Tuba/Euphonium Ensemble

Divertimento No. 1: Zonn, Paul: Perantoni, Daniel
Divertimento No. 2 in B♭: Mozart, Wolfgang Amadeus: Gerhard Meinl's Tuba Sextet
Divertissement for Tuba and Brass Quartet: Barboteu, Georges: Hilgers, Walter
Divertmento for Horn, Tuba and Piano: Gillingham, David: Sinder, Philip
Do Nothing 'Til You Hear from Me: Ellington, Edward Kennedy "Duke": Gannett, Dave
Do You Know What It Means to Miss New Orleans?: Alter, Louis: Self, James
Doctor Jazz: Oliver and Melrose: Newberger, Eli
Does It Suck to Be You: Drums and Tuba: Drums and Tuba
Dog: McGrain, Mark: Rojas, Marcus
Dog Tags: Gus and Buford: Self, James
Domi: Murrow, R.: Murrow, Richard
Dona Nobis Pacem: Ustvolskaya, Galina: LeClair, David
The Donkey and the Walrus: Drums and Tuba: Drums and Tuba
Donna Lee: Davis, Miles: Bargeron, Dave
Don't Forget to Mess Around: Barbarin and Armstrong: M'N'M Trio
Don't Get Around Much Anymore: Ellington, Edward Kennedy "Duke": Pilafian, Sam
Don't Hold On: Felt, Brad: Felt, Brad
Don't Let the Sun Catch You Cryin': Greene, Joe: Johnson, Howard
Don't Monkey with It: Monsborough, Abe: Newberger, Eli
Don't Shoot the Banjo Player ('Cause We've Done It Already): Botschinsky, Allan: Van Lier, Erik
Double Concerto: Hackbarth, Glenn: Perantoni, Daniel
Double Concerto for Saxophone, Tuba and Winds: Hartley, Walter: Erickson, Martin
Double Portraits for Trombone and Tuba: Uber, David: Lind, Michael
Down by the Old Mill Stream: Taylor, Tell: Mighty Tubadours
Down Under: Puschnig, Wolfgang: Stewart, Bob
Doxology: Bourgeois, Louis: Daellenbach, Charles
Doxy: Rollins, Sonny: Draper, Ray; Erickson, Martin; Mazura, János; Self, James
DPT Second Line: Smith, Zachary: Dixie Power Trio
Dream: Mercer, Johnny: Tuba 4's
Dream of a Witches Sabbath from "Symphonie Fantastique": Berlioz, Hector: Symphonia
Dreamer: Lindsay, Erica: Johnson, Howard
Drei Romanzen, Op. 94: Schumann, Robert: Cooley, Floyd
Drei Spielstucke: Katzenbeier, Hubert: Legris, Philippe; Bobo, Roger
Drinking Song from "Lucrezia Borgia": Donizetti, Gaetano: Daellenbach, Charles
Drume Negrita: Grenet, Ernesto: Pilafian, Sam
Dualismo for Tuba and Flute: Escovez, Fermin Ruiz: Mas, Vicente Navarro
Dudley Do-Right of the Mounties: Steiner: Gannett, Dave
Dudley Do-Wrong!: Steiner: Gannett, Dave
Duet for Tenor Tuba and Bass Tuba: Croft: Megules, Karl
Duet No. 12 from "21 Distinctive Duets": Jones, Roger: University of Miami Tuba Ensemble
Duett Duell: Moschner, Pinguin: European Tuba Quartet
Duh Suite: Self, James: O'Bryant, Kelly
Duo Solo: Steckar, Marc: Thuillier, Francois
Durations 3 for Violin, Tuba and Piano: Feldman, Morton: Butterfield, Don; Vogt, Michael
"Dutch" Suite (S. -16) for Bassoon and Tuba: Bach, P. D. Q. [Schikele, Peter]: Bishop, Ronald
Dynozophorium: Steckar, Marc: Steckar Tubapack
The Eagle Thunders: Gourlay, James: Swiss Tuba Quartet
The Eagle Thunders: Joule, James: Dutch Tuba Quartet
Earth and Moon: Rice, Hugh Collins: Tubalaté
East St. Louis Toodle-Oo: Ellington, Edward Kennedy "Duke": Pilafian, Sam
Easy Livin': Robin, Leo: Self, James
The Easy Winners: Joplin, Scott: Contraband (The); Dutch Tuba Quartet
Eclipse Finale? for Tuba and Brass Band: Meier, Jost: Baadsvik, Øystein
Edward Scissorhands [motion picture soundtrack]: Elfman, Danny: Johnson, John Thomas (Tommy); Pearson, Norm
1812 Overture (excerpt): Tchaikovsky, Peter Ilyitch: Jacobs, Arnold
Ein Heldenleben (excerpt): Strauss, Richard: Pokorny, Gene
Eine Kleine Nachtmusik: Mozart, Wolfgang Amadeus: Colonial Tuba Quartet; Fletcher, John; Melton Tuba-Quartett; Mighty Tubadours
Eine Kleine Schrecken Musik (A Little Fright Music): Mehlan, Keith: Monarch Tuba-Euphonium Quartet
Einzug Der Gladiatoren: Fucik, Julius: Miraphone Tuba Quartet
El Capitan: Sousa, John Philip: British Tuba Quartet; Monarch Tuba-Euphonium Quartet; Tubalaté
El carrousel de Juana la Loca: Schiaffini, GianCarlo: Schiaffini, GianCarlo
El Cumbanchero: Hernandez, Rafael: Pilafian, Sam
El Manisero: Simons, Moises: Pilafian, Sam
El vuelo irresistibile del moscardon: Schiaffini, Gian Carlo: Schiaffini, GianCarlo
Elegie: Stravinsky, Igor: Vogt, Michael
Elegy: Madden, Edward: Sass, Jonathon
Elegy: Zinos, Frederick: Cummings, Barton
Elegy for the Whale: Wilder, Alec: Hanks, Thompson (Toby); Swoboda, Deanna
The Elephant and the Fly: Kling, Henri: Erickson, Martin; Phillips, Harvey
The Elephant from "Carnival of the Animals": Saint-Saëns, Camille: Piernik, Zdzislaw; Tubalaté; Yasumoto, Hiroyuki
Elephant in the Livingroom: Pederson, Tommy: Mazura, János

Elephantine Polka: Laurendeau, L. P.: Erickson, Martin
The Elephant's Tango: Landes, B.: Bell, William
11:11: McGrain, Mark: Rojas, Marcus
Eli: Drums and Tuba: Drums and Tuba
Eli's Coming: Nyro, Laura: Tennessee Technological University Tuba/Euphonium Ensemble
Elite Syncopations: Joplin, Scott: British Tuba Quartet; Johnson, John Thomas (Tommy); Swiss Tuba Quartet
Ellen David: Haden, Charlie: Johnson, Howard
Em(M): Roper, William: Roper, William
Empty Streets: Draper, Ray: Draper, Ray
Encore Boz: Stevens, Thomas: Bobo, Roger
Encore: Cakewalk into Town: Mahal, Taj: Frey, Michael
Encore Piece (A Tubist's Showcase): Wilder, Alec: Bobo, Roger
Encounters II for Solo Tuba: Kraft, William: Baadsvik, Øystein; Bazsinka, József; Bobo, Roger; Jae Young, Heo
English Country Airs: Traditional: Tubalaté
An English Folk Christmas: Buttery, Gary: United States Coast Guard Tuba-Euphonium Quartet
The Entertainer: Joplin, Scott: Johnson, John Thomas (Tommy); Tennessee Tech Tuba-Euphonium Quintet; United States Armed Forces Tuba-Euphonium Ensemble and Massed Ensemble
Entrevue/Tribal: Miraphone Tuba Quartet
Episodes: Reeman, John: Tubalaté
Epistrophy: Monk, Thelonius: Frey, Michael
Epitaph V: Ellerby, Martin: Gourlay, James
Equilibre Indifférent, for Tuba, Trumpet and Trombone: Thuillier, Francois: Thuillier, Francois
Eria: Creuze, Roland: Legris, Philippe
Erich: Melillo, Stephen: Colonial Tuba Quartet
Erie Canal: American Folksong: Daellenbach, Charles
Es Ist Bollbracht: Bach, Johann Sebastian: Szentpáli, Roland
Escapade: Turrin, Joseph: Sykes, Steve
Escenas Latinas: Crespo, Enrique: Hilgers, Walter
Escher's Sketches: Ross, Walter: Nelson, Mark
Essii's Dance: Draper, Ray: Draper, Ray
Estampie: BL Lacerta: Gay, Les
Estrellita: Ponce, Manuel: Sheridan, Patrick
Et Le Kloxon Retentit Derchef Comme un Lezard Hongroise Eurhume: Godard: Steckar Tubapack
Être Ou Ne Pas Être! (monolog D'Hamlet) with three trombones: Tomasi, Henri: Bazsinka, József; Hanks, Thompson (Toby); Jacobs, Arnold *Etude No. 24:* Gugel/Pottag: Jacobs, Arnold
Etudes with Style, Music for the Tuba: Salotti, Harry: Sheridan, Patrick
Euphonic Sounds: Joplin, Scott: Atlantic Tuba Quartet; British Tuba Quartet
Euphonics: O'Hara, Betty: Tennessee Technological University Tuba/Euphonium Ensemble
Euphonium Tuba Quartet: Toda, Akira: Rustic Bari-Tuba Ensemble
Everybody Loves My Baby: Williams and Palmer: Newberger, Eli
(Everything I Do) I Do It for You: Kamen, Michael: Norris, Tim
Everything I Have Is Yours: Adamson: Barber, John William (Bill)
Exigencies: Ruth, Matthew: Tennessee Technological University Tuba/Euphonium Ensemble
Extrait des pêcheurs de perles: Bizet, Georges: Labeyrie, Stéphane
Facilita: Hartmann, John: Morgan, Kevin
"Fairest daughter of the graces" from Rigoletto: Verdi, Giuseppi: Morgan, Kevin
Fancy Dances for Three Bass Tubas: Ross, Walter: New York Tuba Quartet
Fanfare: Buxtehude, Dietrich: Jacobs, Arnold
Fanfare for a Friend : Stevens, John: Sotto Voce
Fanfare for the Millennium: Buttery, Gary: Alchemy
Fanfare No. 1: Taylor, Jeffrey: British Tuba Quartet; Monarch Tuba-Euphonium Quartet
Fanny Mae: Patorius, Jaco: Heavy Tuba
Fantaisie Brillante: Arban, Jean-Baptiste: Lienard, Bernard
Fantaisie Concertante: Castérède, Jacques: Lienard, Bernard
Fantasia Breve: Cummings, Barton: Jae Young, Heo; Nelson, Mark
Fantasia di Concerto: Boccalari, E.: Conner, Rex
Fantasia of Eastern European Village Dances: Buttery, Gary: Alchemy
Fantasia of Popular Irish Airs: Lax, Fred: Seward, Steven
Fantasia on China Song: Carpenter, Gary: Gourlay, James
Fantasie Original: Picchi, Ermanno: Colonial Tuba Quartet; Seward, Steven
Fantasiestücke, Op. 73: Schumann, Robert: Cooley, Floyd
Fantasy: Martino, Ralph: British Tuba Quartet; Miraphone Tuba Quartet; Monarch Tuba-Euphonium Quartet
Fantasy for Euphonium and Brass Band: Sparke, Philip: Seward, Steven
Fantasy for Solo Tuba: Arnold, Malcolm: Fletcher, John; Gourlay, James; Norris, Tim
Fantasy for Tuba and Piano: Crozier, Daniel: Perantoni, Daniel
Fantasy for Tuba and Piano: Konagaya, Soichi: Yasumoto, Hiroyuki
Fantasy in C minor: Telemann, Georg Philipp: Hanks, Thompson (Toby)
Fantezie Pentru Tuba si Pian: Dumitru, Ionel: Dumitru, Ionel
Farandole from L'Arlesienne Suite No. 2: Bizet, Georges: Norris, Tim
Farewell Blues: Schoebel, Maras, and Rapollo: Lehr, David "Red"
The Farewell Burn: Berg, Curt: Self, James
Fascinatin' Gershwin: Gershwin, George: British Tuba Quartet
Fat Cat: arr. Mitchell: Callender, George Sylvester "Red"

A Faust Overture (excerpt): Wagner, Richard: Pokorny, Gene
Faux-cils et vraies moustaches: Thuillier, Francois: Thuillier, Francois
The Favorite Rag: Joplin, Scott: British Tuba Quartet; Johnson, John Thomas (Tommy)
FDR Jones: Rome, Harold J.: Pilafian, Sam
Feiertagsmusik, Op. 107b: Krol, Bernhard: Tennessee Tech Alumni Ensemble
Felka Miotta: Thuillier, Francois: Thuillier, Francois
Fellscape: Scott, Stuart: Tubalaté
Festival Overture: Shostakovich, Dmitri: Symphonia
Fever: John, Little Willie: Johnson, Howard
Fidgety Feet: Original Dixieland Jazz Band: Dixie Power Trio; Palmer, Singleton
Figure of Speech: Eskelin, Ellery: Eskelin, Ellory
Filidia: Draper, Ray: Draper, Ray
Finale to Symphony No. 4: Tchaikovsky, Peter Ilyitch: Self, Jim
Fink Finster: Thingnäs, Frode: Scandinavian Tuba Jazz
Finlandia: Sibelius, Jean: Daellenbach, Charles
Fireworks: Frith, John: British Tuba Quartet
First Dream of Light: Subatnik, Morton: Bobo, Roger
First Line: Stewart, Bob: Stewart, Bob
First Movement: Lindsay, Erica: Johnson, Howard
First Noel: arr. Charlton: Mighty Tubadours
The First Noel: Phillips, Harvey/TubaChristmas
Fishin' Blues: Mahal, Taj: Stewart, Bob
Fishin' Blues: Thomas, Henry: Johnson, Howard
Fits of Spaghetti: Drums and Tuba: Drums and Tuba
Five Moods for Tuba Quartet: Schuller, Gunther: New York Tuba Quartet
Five Short Pieces: European Tuba Quartet
Five Studies for Tuba Alone: Reck, David: Hanks, Thompson (Toby)
5.24.94: Drums and Tuba: Drums and Tuba
Five-Four Blues: Callender, George Sylvester "Red"
Flander's Cauldron: Amos, Keith: British Tuba Quartet
Flickers: Waldron, Mal: Draper, Ray
Flight of the Bumblebee: Rimsky-Korsakov, Nicholas: Fletcher, John; Gourlay, James; Jae Young, Heo; Melton Tuba-Quartett; Morgan, Kevin; Sheridan, Patrick; Swiss Tuba Quartet; Wagner, Michael; Woods, Gavin
Floods of Spring: Rachmaninoff, Sergei: Feldman, Enrique "Hank" C.
Florentiner Marsch: Fucik, Julius: Miraphone Tuba Quartet
Flower Duet from "Lakmé": Delibes, Léo: British Tuba Quartet
Flutes and Tuba: BL Lacerta: Gay, Les
The Flying Ballerina: Drums and Tuba: Drums and Tuba
Fnugg: Baadsvik, Øystein: Baadsvik, Øystein
Foggy Day: Gershwin, George: Callender, George Sylvester "Red"
Folkevise: Forde, Jan Magne: Nickel, Hans
Fontane di Roma (excerpt): Respighi, Ottorino: Pokorny, Gene
For Christina: Self, James: Self, James
For Heaven's Sake: Meyer-Bretton, D., and S. Edwards: Self, James
For the Kings of Brass: Brusick, William: Tennessee Tech Alumni Ensemble
For Tuba .... with Strings Attached: Bazelon, Irwin: Baev, Bayo
Force of Destiny Overture: Verdi, Giuseppi: British Tuba Quartet
Forêt Virge: Arcadio, Bernard, and Marc Stecker: Steckar Tubapack
Forowen 3 (Tuba and Piccolo): Smith, Glenn: Turk, John
Forte/Formidable/Fortune/The Dragon's Dance: LeClair, David: Contraband (The)
42nd Street Selections: Dubin and Warren: British Tuba Quartet
Four: Davis, Miles: Johnson, Howard
Four Keen Guys: Gillis, Lew: Dutch Tuba Quartet
Four Miniatures: Fishkind, Larry: European Tuba Quartet
Four Pieces for Tuba: Ziffrin, Marilyn J.: Cummings, Barton
Four Pieces for Tuba Quartet: Jacob, Gordon: Dutch Tuba Quartet
The Four Seasons for Tuba, Percussion, Strings and Stereo Tape: Proto, Frank: Thornton, Michael
Four Shorts for Tuba and Piano: Largent, Edward: Turk, John
Four Tuba Blues: Roblee, Richard: Melton Tuba-Quartett
Fractured Mambos: Ruggiero, Charles: Sinder, Philip
Frame for the Blues: Hampton, Slide: Johnson, Howard
Freedom: Feldman, Hank: Symphonia
Freedom: Mingus, Charles: Symphonia
French Tuba in Los Angeles: Galliano, R.: Stecker, Marc
Frescos De Bonampak: Osmon, Leroy: Tennessee Technological University Tuba/Euphonium Ensemble
Freylekhs fun der Khupe: Traditional: Dutch Tuba Quartet
Friend like Me: Menken/Ashman: Tuba 4's
Fright of the Fumblebee: Rimsky-Korsakov, Nicholas: Corella, Gil
Frippery: Shaw, Lowell: Miraphone Tuba Quartet
From Now On: McIntosh, Nat
From the Shores of the Mighty Pacific: Clarke, Herbert L.: Hanks, Thompson (Toby); Woods, Gavin
Frosty the Snowman: Nelson and Rollins: Pilafian, Sam
Fughetta: Schumann, Robert: Swiss Tuba Quartet

Fugue for Tinhorns from "Guys and Dolls": Loesser, Frank: Sheridan, Patrick
Fugue from Fantasia and Fugue in G: Bach, Johann Sebastian: British Tuba Quartet
Fugue in G minor: Bach, Johann Sebastian: Anderson, Hans; British Tuba Quartet; Gerhard Meinl's Tuba Sextet; Mighty Tubadours; Tubalaté
Fum, Fum, Fum: arr. Bewley: Phillips, Harvey/TubaChristmas
Funeral March for a Marionette: Gounod, Charles: Mighty Tubadours
Fünf Miniaturen für Solotuba: Etzel, Bernhard: Walsh, Thomas
Funiculì Funiculà: Denza, Luigi: Morgan, Kevin
Funiculi-Funicula Fantasy: D'enza, Luigi: Rustic Bari-Tuba Ensemble
Funky Liza: Perrine, Matt
Für H. S.: Unkrodt, Dietrich
The Furies: Corwell, Neal: Brown, Velvet; Symphonia
The Further Adventures of Tubby the Tuba: Kleinsinger, George, and Paul Tripp: Johnson, John Thomas (Tommy); Phillips, Harvey
Galtigen: Brun, Albin: Unternährer, Marc
Gandolfo's Bounce: Draper, Ray
Gay 50s Medley: Garbáge, Pierre (a.k.a. Garrett, James): Tennessee Tech Alumni Ensemble
General Levine-Eccentric: Debussy, Claude: Pokorny, Gene
Gentle Old Sea: Wood, Philip D.: Draper, Ray
Georgia on My Mind: Carmichael, Hoagy: Contraband (The); Dites-Le-Moi Tuba; Matteson-Phillips TubaJazz Consort; Modern Jazz Tuba Project; Murrow, Richard; Pilafian, Sam
Gershwin Medley: Gershwin, George: Tennessee Technological University Tuba/Euphonium Ensemble; United States Armed Forces Tuba-Euphonium Ensemble
Gesualdo Movement: Pilafian, Sam: Pilafian, Sam
Get It On: Chase, Bill: Heavy Tuba
Get Me to the Church on Time: Lerner, Alan Jay: British Tuba Quartet
Giant Steps: Coltrane, John: Bargeron, Dave
Gicael Mibbs: Emler, Andy: Steckar Elephant Tuba Horde
Gigue: Corelli, Archangelo: Phillips, Harvey
Gimpel the Fool: Drums and Tuba: Drums and Tuba
Giocoso from "Euphonium Concerto": Cosma, Vladimir: Tennessee Technological University Tuba/Euphonium Ensemble
Give My Regards to Broadway: Cohan, George M.: Daellenbach, Charles
Gleichwie das Feuer: Schidlt, M.: Anderson, Hans
Glousteshire Wassail Song: arr. Harclerode: Mighty Tubadours
The Glyder Landscape: Smalley, Peter: British Tuba Quartet
Go Tell It on the Mountain: Phillips, Harvey/TubaChristmas
God Bows to Math: Minuteman (The): Drums and Tuba
God Rest Ye Merry, Gentlemen: arr. Vaughan: Mighty Tubadours
God Rest Ye Merry, Gentlemen: Phillips, Harvey/TubaChristmas; Pilafian, Sam
Godchild: Wallington, George: Barber, John William (Bill); Self, James
Going Up to the Country and Paint My Mailbox Blue: Mahal, Taj: Johnson, Howard
Going Uptown: Sass, Jonathon: Heavy Tuba
Golden Bells (with Roger Bobo): Kovács, Zoltán: Szentpáli, Roland
Golden Gate: European Tuba Quartet
Golden Gate Park/You Don't Know What Love Is: Roper, William: Roper, William
Goldwang: Brun, Albin: Unternährer, Marc
Golliwogg's Cakewalk: Debussy, Claude: Dutch Tuba Quartet
Gone with the Wind: Wrubel: Callender, George Sylvester "Red"
Good Christian Men Rejoice: arr. Bewley: Phillips, Harvey/TubaChristmas
Good King Wenceslas: Phillips, Harvey/Tuba Christmas
Good King Wenceslas; Il Est Ne: arr. Harclerode: Mighty Tubadours
Good Old New York: Morton, F. "Jelly Roll": M'N'M Trio
The Good, the Bad, and the Banjo: Smith, Zachary: Dixie Power Trio
Goodnight, Angeline: Europe, Sissle, and Blake: Newberger, Eli
Gospel Time: Agrell, Jeffrey: Miraphone Tuba Quartet
Gowbarrow Gavotte: Seivewright, Andrew: Tubalaté
Graf Zeppelin Marsch: Teike, Carl: Miraphone Tuba Quartet
Grand Slam: Niehaus, Lennie: British Tuba Quartet
Grandpa's Spells: Morton, F. "Jelly Roll": Pilafian, Sam
Gratitude: Lindsay, Erica: Johnson, Howard
Great Crush Collision: Joplin, Scott: Johnson, John Thomas (Tommy)
Great Gate of Kiev from "Pictures at an Exhibition": Mussorgsky, Modest: Jacobs, Arnold
Greedy Mr. Creed: Wilson, Taylor, and Streuber: Tooba Blooze
Greensleeves: Traditional: Atlantic Tuba Quartet; British Tuba Quartet; Melton Tuba-Quartett; Miraphone Tuba Quartet; Phillips, Harvey/TubaChristmas; Rustic Bari-Tuba Ensemble; Swiss Tuba Quartet
Gregory Is Here: Silver, Horace: Matteson-Phillips TubaJazz Consort; Modern Jazz Tuba Project
Grinch Who Stole Christmas [motion picture soundtrack]: Horner, James: Self, James
Grooveyard: Perkins: Erickson, Martin

Groteske Miniaturen: Poulheim, Bert: Legris, Philippe
Ground Zero: Heasley, Tom
Growing Up Together: LeClair, David: Contraband (The)
Gymnopedie: Satie, Erik: Murrow, Richard
Gypsy Ears: Moschner, Pinguin: Moschner, Pinguin
Habanera and Ragtime: Norris, Tim
Hades for Two Euphoniums and Two Tubas: Iannaccone, Anthony: University of Michigan Tuba Ensemble
Hail the Lord's Annointed: arr. Vaughan: Mighty Tubadours
Hailstorm: Rimmer, William: Sheridan, Patrick
Half-Way to Heaven: Dubin and Russell: M'N'M Trio
Hallelujah Drive: Hazell, Chris: Swiss Tuba Quartet
Haltungen (4) zu einem alten Thema, for Tuba: Hilprecht, Uwe: Bazsinka, József
Hambone: Stewart, Bob: Stewart, Bob
Handbags and Gladrags: Chase, Bill: Heavy Tuba
Hands across the Sea: Sousa, John Philip: Northern Tuba Lights
Happiness: Draper, Ray: Draper, Ray
Happy Soul: Wilkinson, Robert: Dutch Tuba Quartet
Harlem Rag: Turpin, Tom: Albertasaurus Tuba Quartet
Harmonica for Large Orchestra and Tuba Solo: Lachenmann, Helmut: Nahatzki, Richard
Harmony Club Waltz: Joplin, Scott: Johnson, John Thomas (Tommy)
Hauntings: Welcher, Dan: Symphonia
Havah Nagilah: Traditional: British Tuba Quartet
Have Yourself a Merry Little Christmas: Martin, Blaine: Phillips, Harvey/TubaChristmas; Pilafian, Sam
Heather on the Hill: Lerner, Alan Jay: Self, James
Heavy Henry: Perrine, Matt
Heavy Metal: Lamb, Marvin: Tennessee Technological University Tuba/Euphonium Ensemble
Hefje Kati: arr. Sykes: Sykes, Stephen
The Heights of Halifax: McQueen, Ian: Tubalaté
Heitertannli: Brun, Albin: Unternährer, Marc
Helix for Solo Tuba and Concert Band: Benson, Warren: Phillips, Harvey; Robinson, Jack; Turk, John
Hello, Dolly!: Palmer, Singleton
Hello Julius: Smith, Warren: Johnson, Howard
Helter Skelter: Lennon, John, and Paul McCartney: Heavy Tuba
Here Comes Santa Claus: Autry and Haldeman: Pilafian, Sam
Here Comes Sonny Man: Johnson, Howard: Johnson, Howard
Here Comes the Night: Sass, Jonathon
Here's That Rainy Day: Heusen, Van: British Tuba Quartet; Gannett, Dave
Heuschlag: Brun, Albin: Unternährer, Marc
Hey, Ho! Nobody Home: English Folksong: Daellenbach, Charles
Hey Joe: Roberts, William: Moschner, Pinguin
Hey Jude: Lennon, John, and Paul McCartney: Miraphone Tuba Quartet
Hey Mama: Traditional: Stewart, Bob
Hey Man!: Modern Jazz Tuba Project
Hidden Agenda: Hopkins, Greg: Pilafian, Sam
High Energy: BL Lacerta: Gay, Les
High Society: Steele and Melrose: Lehr, David "Red"; Palmer, Singleton
Highway Child: Hendrix, Jimi: Moschner, Pinguin
Hittin' the Ceiling: Gottler-Mitchell-Conrad: Tarto, Joe
Holzwangflue: Brun, Albin: Unternährer, Marc
Home: Wood, Philip D.: Draper, Ray
Home Alone [motion picture soundtrack]: Williams, John: Self, James
Home Alone II [motion picture soundtrack]: Williams, John: Self, James
Hommage: Thuillier, Francois: Thuillier, Francois
Homo Ludens in Berlin: Vogt, Michael: Vogt, Michael
Honeysuckle Rose: Waller, Thomas "Fats": Erickson, Martin
Hook [motion picture soundtrack]: Williams, John: Self, James
Hora Staccato: Dinicu, Grigoras: Sheridan, Patrick
Horn Concerto No. 4 in E♭ major, K. 495 Rondo: Mozart, Wolfgang Amadeus: Morgan, Kevin
Horn Sonata in F, Op. 17: Beethoven, Ludwig van: King, Ian
The Horse and the Tree: Drums and Tuba: Drums and Tuba
Hot Canary: Nero, Paul: Sheridan, Patrick
The House of Blue Lights: Raye and Slack: Dixie Power Trio
How Deep Is the Ocean?: Berlin, Irving: Scandinavian Tuba Jazz
How My Heart Sings: Zindars, Earl: Erickson, Martin
Howdy!: Pegram, Wayne: Tennessee Technological University Tuba/Euphonium Ensemble; United States Armed Forces Tuba-Euphonium Ensemble
Hugo Hugo: McPherson, John: Albertasaurus Tuba Quartet
80660: Thuillier, Francois: Thuillier, Francois
Human Nature: McIntosh, Nat
Human Nature Part 2: McIntosh, Nat
Humoresque: Dvorák, Antonin: Piernik, Zdizislaw
Hungarian Dance: Brahms, Johannes: Woods, Gavin
Hungarian March: Berlioz, Hector: Dutch Tuba Quartet
Hungarian Melodies: Bach, Vincent: Seward, Steven
Hungarian Pictures: Bartók, Béla: Thuillier, Francois
Hungarian Rhapsody No. 2: Liszt, Franz: Melton Tuba-Quartett

Hurry Up: Steckar, Franck: Steckar Tubapack
Hvezdonicka: Pecha, Antonin: Heavy Tuba
Hyldingsmarch: Grieg, Edvard: Anderson, Hans
The Hymn: Mall, Philippe: Frey, Michael
Hymne: Koetsier, Jan: Hötzel, Markus
I Ain't Gonna Give Nobody None of My Jellyroll: Overstreet and Higgins: Newberger, Eli
I Ain't Got Nobody: Graham and Williams: Newberger, Eli
I Can't Believe That You're in Love with Me: Gaskill and McHugh: Palmer, Singleton
I Can't Give You Anything but Love: Fields and McHugh: Lehr, David "Red"
I Caught a Touch of Your Love: Sass, Jonathon
I Could Have Danced All Night: Loewe, Frederick: Morgan, Kevin
I Found a New Baby: Palmer and Williams: Matteson, Rich; Newberger, Eli; Pilafian, Sam
I Got Rhythm: Gershwin, George: Woods, Gavin
I Hadn't Anyone Til You: Draper, Ray: Draper, Ray
I Hate a Man like You: Morton, F. "Jelly Roll": Newberger, Eli
I Hate Myself for Loving You: Price, Billy: Newberger, Eli
I Let the Song Go Out of My Heart: Ellington, Edward Kennedy "Duke": Erickson, Martin; Mazura, János
I Love You: Porter, Cole: Self, James
I Loves You Porgy/Bess You Is My Woman: Gershwin, George: Self, James
I Mean You: Monk, Thelonius: Pilafian, Sam
I Must Have That Man: McHugh-Fields: Tarto, Joe
I-95: Esleck, David L.: Modern Jazz Tuba Project
I Saw Her Standing There: Lennon, John, and Paul McCartney: Dixie Power Trio
I Saw Mommy Kissing Santa Claus: Conor, Thomas: Pilafian, Sam
I Talk to the Trees: Lerner, Alan Jay: Draper, Ray
I Wan'na Be like You: Sherman/Sherman/Gaston: Tuba 4's
I Want a Little Girl: arr. Mitchell: Callender, George Sylvester "Red"
I Wished on the Moon: Parker, Dorothy: Self, James
I Won't Dance: Kern, Jerome: Murrow, Richard
I'll Be Around: Callender, George Sylvester "Red"
I'll Never Forget Old What's Her Name: Wilson, Phil: Matteson, Rich
I'll Remember April: Raye, Don: Corella, Gil
I'm Getting Sentimental: Bassman, George: Corella, Gil
I'm Just Wild about Harry: Blake and Sissle: Newberger, Eli
I'm So Lonesome I Could Cry: Williams, Hank: Johnson, Howard
I've Been Workin': Traditional: Self, James
I've Never Been in Love Before: Loesser, Frank: Self, James
If I Only Had a Brain: Arlen and Harburg: Pilafian, Sam
If Six Was Nine: Hendrix, Jimi: Moschner, Pinguin
If Sixty-nine Was Ninty-six: Moschner and Sachse: Moschner, Pinguin
If You Ever Wanna: Trujillo, Tommy: Draper, Ray
Il Ritorno: Diero: British Tuba Quartet
Il Viaggio 1 per tuba solo con pianoforte: Sikora, Elzbieta: Piernik, Zdzislaw
Illusion: Konagaya, Soichi: Tennessee Technological University Tuba/Euphonium Ensemble
Illustrations for Tubas: Kerwin, Simon: Tubalaté
Images: Feldman, Hank C.: Feldman, Enrique "Hank" C.
Imperial March (of the Nightcrawlers): Perrine, Matt
Impre a tre: Funderburk, Jeff
The Impresario: Cimarosa, D.: Swiss Tuba Quartet
Impressions of a Parade: Baron, Samuel: Hanks, Thompson (Toby)
Impromptu for Tuba: Barry, Darrol: Ferguson, Kenneth
Impromptu in 2 Keys: Gershwin, George: Contraband Tuba Quartet
Improvisation for Tuba and Piano: Emler, Andy: Thuillier, Francois
In a Digital Mood: Steckar, Franck: Steckar Tubapack
In a Mellow Tone: Ellington, Edward Kennedy "Duke": Gannett, Dave; Matteson-Phillips Tuba-Jazz Consort; Self, James; Tennessee Tech Alumni Ensemble
In a Sentimental Mood: Ellington, Edward Kennedy "Duke": Callender, George Sylvester "Red"; Feldman, Enrique "Hank" C.
In a Shanty in Old Town: Young, Schuster, and Little: M'N'M Trio
In Case: Drums and Tuba: Drums and Tuba
In Darkness Dreaming: Cummings, Barton: Colonial Tuba Quartet
In Memoriam: Premru, Ray: British Tuba Quartet
In—Phase—Out: Tautenhahn, G.: Heavy Tuba
In the Gloryland: Lacen, Anthony "Tuba Fats"
In the Hall of the Mountain King: Grieg, Edvard: Bell, William
In the Sweet Bye and Bye: Lacen, Anthony "Tuba Fats"
Indian Summer: Herbert, Victor: Erickson, Martin
Indiana: Hanley and McDonald: Corella, Gil; Lehr, David "Red"; Pilafian, Sam
Inercia: Frazão, Alexandre: Carolino, Sérgio
Infant Holy: Kingsbury: Mighty Tubadours
Infernal Dream: Schiaffini, Giancarlo: Schiaffini, Giancarlo
Ingrid: Spencer, Larry: Murrow, Richard
Inner Self: Aldcroft, Randy: Self, James
The Inspector: Drums and Tuba: Drums and Tuba
The Inspector Returns: Drums and Tuba: Drums and Tuba
Interlude No. 4: Botschinsky, Allan: Van Lier, Erik
Intermezzo concertante for Tuba and Orchestra, Op. 171: Holmboe, Vagn: Bjørn-Larsen, Jens

Intro Heuschlag: Brun, Albin: Unternährer, Marc
Intro Tomlishorn: Brun, Albin: Unternährer, Marc
Introduction and Allegro Spiritoso: Senaillé, Jean Baptiste: Norris, Tim
Introduction and Dance: Barat, Joseph Eduoard: Bazsinka, József; Bobo, Roger; Jae Young, Heo
Introduction and Samba: Whitney: Erickson, Martin
Introduction to the Blues: Smith, Warren: Johnson, Howard
Invention No. 1: Bach, Johann Sebastian: Phillips, Harvey
Irish Black Bottom: Venable and Armstrong: M'N'M Trio
Irish Washerwoman: Traditional: Norris, Tim
Is an Elegy: McIntosh, Nat
Israel: Carisi, John: Pilafian, Sam
It Came upon a Midnight Clear: Willis: Mighty Tubadours; Phillips, Harvey/TubaChristmas
It Could Happen to You: Burke and Van Heusen: Felt, Brad
It Doesn't Wait: Eskelin, Ellery: Eskelin, Ellory
It Don't Mean a Thing: Ellington, Edward Kennedy "Duke": Woods, Gavin
It Is Enough from "Elijah": Mendelssohn, Felix: Popiel, Peter
It Might As Well Be Spring: Rodgers, Richard, and Oscar Hammerstein: Gannett, Dave
Italian Street Song: Herbert, Victor: Daellenbach, Charles
It's a Raggy Waltz: Brubeck, Dave: Erickson, Martin
It's All Over: McIntosh, Nat
It's All Right with Me: Porter, Cole: Tennessee Tech Alumni Ensemble
It's Getter Harder to Survive: Barron, Ronnie: Johnson, Howard
Jabba the Hutt from "Return of the Jedi": Williams, John: Pokorny, Gene; Schmitz, Chester
Jaroque Waltz/Mood: Morris, Jim: Morris, Jim
Jason and the Golden Fleece: Raum, Elizabeth: Symphonia
Jaws [motion picture soundtrack]: Williams, John: Johnson, John Thomas (Tommy)
Jazz Suite: *Gale, Jack:* Dites-Le-Moi Tuba
Jazzbo Jenkins: Brooks, Shelton: M'N'M Trio
Jeannie with the Light Brown Hair: Foster, Stephen: Sheridan, Patrick
Jelly Bean Blues: Rainey and Arant: Newberger, Eli
Jenny Jones, for Tuba Solo: Rimmer, William: Morgan, Kevin
Jenny Wren: Davis: Sheridan, Patrick
Jerkle Cirque: European Tuba Quartet
Jesse's Jump: Krebs, Jesse: Symphonia
Jesu, Joy of Man's Desiring: Bach, Johann Sebastian: British Tuba Quartet; Pilafian, Sam
The Jewish Life: Bloch, Ernst: Funderburk, Jeff
Jhon Come Kisse Me Now: Byrd, William: Atlantic Tuba Quartet; British Tuba Quartet
Jimmy Smith: Pilafian, Sam
Jingle Bell Waltz: Vaughan, Rodger: Mighty Tubadours
Jingle Bells: Pierpont, James: Pilafian, Sam
Jitterbug Waltz: Waller, Thomas "Fats": Self, James
Joanda: Bargeron, Dave: Bargeron, Dave
John, Ain't It Hard?: Mahal, Taj: Johnson, Howard
John Brown's Body: Traditional: Johnson, Howard
The Jolly Farmer Goes to Town: Schumann, Robert: Bell, William
Joy to the World: Handel, George Friderik: Phillips, Harvey/TubaChristmas
Juba Plays the FLUBA in Aruba: Scharnberg, Kim: Self, James
Jumbalaya: Williams, Hank: Pilafian, Sam
Jumbo's Holiday: Kalke, Ernst-Thilo: Melton Tuba-Quartett
Juneteenth: Roper, William: Roper, William
Just a Closer Walk with Thee: Traditional: Callender, George Sylvester "Red"; Daellenbach, Charles; Erickson, Martin; Lehr, David "Red"; Palmer, Singleton; Tennessee Technological University Tuba/Euphonium Ensemble; Tubalaté
Just an Echo in the Valley: Woods-Campbell-Connelly: Tarto, Joe
Just Blues: Marohnic, Chuck: Pilafian, Sam
Just like Alice: McGrain, Mark: Rojas, Marcus
Just Squeeze Me: Ellington, Edward Kennedy "Duke": Dixie Power Trio; Erickson, Martin
Kadanse et Kantation: Arcadio, Bernard, and Marc Steckar: Steckar Tubapack
Kagami Jishi: Traditional: Roper, William
Kanon: Unkrodt, Dietrich
Kansas City Dances: Holsinger, David: Mendoker, Scott; Seward, Steven
Keepin' Out of Mischief Now: Waller, Thomas "Fats": Gannett, Dave
Kelly Blue: Kelly, Wynton: Johnson, Howard
Kermit: Drums and Tuba: Drums and Tuba
Kermit the Frog Presents the Muppet Musicians of Bremen [TV soundtrack]: Elliott, Jack: Johnson, John Thomas (Tommy)
Kesh Jig: Traditional: Baadsvik, Øystein
Kierkegaard, for Tuba Quartet: Kupferman, Meyer: British Tuba Quartet; Sotto Voce
Killer Tuba Songs: Nelson, Vern: Rozen, Jay
Kilo: Brown, Tom: Self, James
King Porter Stomp: Morton, F. "Jelly Roll": Stewart, Bob
The King's Hunt: Bull, John: British Tuba Quartet
Kirkeby and Edvard Munch: Christiansen, Henning: Anderson, Hans
Kol Nidrei: Bruch, Max: Funderburk, Jeff
Komm Süsser Tod: Bach, Johann Sebastian: Megules, Karl; Phillips, Harvey/TubaChristmas; Tennessee Technological University Tuba/Euphonium Ensemble
Konservatorium: Arcadio, Bernard, and Marc Steckar: Steckar Tubapack

Konzert für Tuba und Orchester: Gruner, Joachim: Unkrodt, Dietrich
Kool Kube: Modern Jazz Tuba Project
Korn Blues: Hermann, Heinz: Scandinavian Tuba Jazz
Kubismus 502: Botschinsky, Allan: Van Lier, Erik
Kuc to Luc: Drums and Tuba: Drums and Tuba
La Capricieuse, Op. 17: Elgar, Edward: Sheridan, Patrick
La Cumparsita: Rodriquez, G.: Pilafian, Sam
La Danza: Miraphone Tuba Quartet
La Danza: Rossini, Gioacchino: British Tuba Quartet
La Ferte Alais: Guignon, Jean-Pierre: Thuillier, Francois
La Fiesta: Corea, Chick: Tennessee Technological University Tuba/Euphonium Ensemble
La Fille aux Cheveux de lin: Debussy, Claude: Rustic Bari-Tuba Ensemble
La Gazza Ladra: Rossini, Gioacchino: Swiss Tuba Quartet
La Morte dell'Oom (No Pah Intended): Self, James: Symphonia
La Peste: Machado, Jean Marie: Thuillier, Francois
La Tregenda from "Le villi": Puccini, Giacomo: Symphonia
La Virgin De La Macarena: Mendez, Rafael: Symphonia
Lachrimae: Roper, William: Roper, William
The Lady in Blue: Botschinsky, Allan: Van Lier, Erik
Lament: Smith, Warren: Johnson, Howard
Lamento: Beach, Bennie: Conner, Rex; LeBlanc, Robert
Land Shark: Weaver, Mark: Weaver, Mark
Landscape for Tuba and Strings: Lundquist, Torbjørn Iwan: Lind, Michael
Largo al factotum from "The Barber of Seville": Rossini, Gioacchino: Crowther, Shaun; Gourlay, James; Morgan, Kevin; Norris, Tim; Pilafian, Sam
Las Zorras Pocas: McDonald, Barry: Heavy Tuba
Lassas Trombone: Fillmore, Henry: Palmer, Singleton
Latin Fantasy: Taylor, Mark: Arwood, Jeffrey
Laubrisleten: Brun, Albin: Unternährer, Marc
Lauelenegg: Brun, Albin: Unternährer, Marc
Law Years: Coleman, Ornette: Stewart, Bob
Lazy Elephant Blues: Luis, Ingo: Melton Tuba-Quartett
Lazy Lullaby: Little, Donald: Davis, Ronald
Le cirque: Adam: Thuillier, Francois
Le Jardin des Citrons: Havet, Didier: Thuillier, Francois
Le Jour Oû Les Tubas: Michel, Marc: Steckar Elephant Tuba Horde
Le Rêve d'lcare: Steckar, Marc: Thuillier, Francois
Le Secret: Gautier, L.: Alchemy
Leave a Message after the Beep: Moschner and Sachse: Moschner, Pinguin
L'écureuil fou: Thuillier, Francois: Thuillier, Francois
Lee Pizza, NE: Sachse: Moschner, Pinguin
The Legend of Heimdall: Raum, Elizabeth: Griffiths, John
Leleo: Arcadio, Bernard, and Andre Ceccarelli: Steckar Tubapack
Lemony Snicket [motion picture soundtrack]: Newman, Thomas: Self, James
Lento: Handel, George Friderik: Daellenbach, Charles
Lento: Holmes, Paul: Conner, Rex; Davis, Ronald; LeBlanc, Robert
Les Baricades Misterieuses: Couperin, F.: Gerhard Meinl's Tuba Sextet
Les Satellites: Casimir, Daniel: Thuillier, Francois
Less Than That: Robison: Tarto, Joe
Let It Snow: Cahn and Styne: Pilafian, Sam
Let My Children Hear Music: Stewart, Bob
Let My People Go: Draper, Ray, and Richard Aplan: Draper, Ray
The Liberation of Sisyphus: Stevens, John: Bazsinka, József; Bobo, Roger
Liebesfreud: Kreisler, Fritz: Sykes, Steve; Yasumoto, Hiroyuki
Liebesleid: Kreisler, Fritz: Sheridan, Patrick; Tubalaté
Lieder eines Fahrenden Gesellen: Mahler, Gustav: Perantoni, Daniel
Lieder, Op. 135, D921: Schubert, Franz Peter: Labeyrie, Stéphane
Light Metal—I Talatasco: Proctor, S.: Tubalaté
Lilli's Funk (to Lillana)—Theme: Carolino, Sérgio: Carolino, Sérgio
Limehouse Blues: Furber and Braham: Dixie Power Trio; Matteson, Rich; Pilafian, Sam
Lina Blues: Smith, Jabbo: Newberger, Eli
Line for Lyons: Mulligan, Gerry: Johnson, Howard
Linger Awhile: Palmer, Singleton
Linguini Incident [motion picture soundtrack]: Newman, Thomas: Self, James
L'insensible Gregiore: Thuillier, Francois: Thuillier, Francois
L'Inverno (Winter) from The Four Seasons: Vivaldi, Antonio: Baadsvik, Øystein
Little Brown Jug: arr. Rosenthal: Hanks, Thompson (Toby)
Little Drummer Boy: Davis, Katherine: Pilafian, Sam
Little Fugue: Norris, Tim
Little Lullaby: Luis, Ingo: Melton Tuba-Quartett
Little Madrigal for Big Horns: Hastings, Ross: University of Miami Tuba Ensemble
Little Ole Softy: Matteson, Rich: Matteson-Phillips TubaJazz Consort; Perantoni, Daniel
Little Suede Shoes: Parker, Charlie: Erickson, Martin; Mazura, János; Murrow, Richard; Pilafian, Sam
Little Wing: Hendrix, Jimi: Moschner, Pinguin
Live and Let Live: Laumann, H.: Anderson, Hans
Livin in Heat: Chase, Bill: Heavy Tuba

Livin' on the Wick: Wilson, Denny, and Hal Taylor: Tooba Blooze
Loch Lomond: Scottish Folksong: Daellenbach, Charles
Locus Iste: Bruckner, Anton: Dutch Tuba Quartet
Lohengrin (excerpt): Wagner, Richard: Pokorny, Gene
Lohengrin (Introduction to Act III): Wagner, Richard: Jacobs, Arnold
The Londonderry Air (Danny Boy): Traditional: Melton Tuba-Quartett; Monarch Tuba-Euphonium Quartet; Sheridan, Patrick; Tennessee Tech Alumni Ensemble; United States Armed Forces Tuba-Euphonium Ensemble
Lonely Forest: Lully, Jean Baptiste: Daellenbach, Charles
The Lord's Prayer: Malotte, Albert Hay: Sotto Voce
Loteria: Drums and Tuba: Drums and Tuba
Lots of Luc: Drums and Tuba: Drums and Tuba
Louisiana: Razof and Johnson: Pilafian, Sam
L.O.V.E.: Kaempfert/Gabler: Tuba 4's
Love Song (Caro mio ben): Giordani, Giuseppi: Daellenbach, Charles
Love Story (und dann ging's heiss her): Moschner, Pinguin: Moschner, Pinguin
Love Waltz: Botschinsky, Allan: Van Lier, Erik
Lover: Rodgers, Richard, and Lorenz Hart: Pilafian, Sam
The Lowest: Callender, George Sylvester "Red"
Lucky Southern: Jarrett, Keith: Matteson-Phillips TubaJazz Consort
Lullaby: Wood, Gareth: Sykes, Steve
Lullaby of Birdland: Shearing, George: Albertasaurus Tuba Quartet; Tennessee Technological University Tuba/Euphonium Ensemble
Lush Life: arr. Callender: Callender, George Sylvester "Red"
Lush Life: Strayhorn, Billy: Self, James
Lute Dances: Anonymous: British Tuba Quartet
Lyri-Tech for Solo Tuba: Anderson, Eugene: Pilafian, Sam
Lyric Poem for Five Tubas: Frank, Marcel G.: United States Armed Forces Tuba-Euphonium Ensemble and Massed Ensemble; University of Miami Tuba Ensemble
Ma-Ma: Semanya, Caiphus: Johnson, Howard
Mack the Knife: Weill, Kurt: Pilafian, Sam
Mad about Him, Sad without Him, How Can I Be Glad without Him Blues: Charles, Dick: Mazura, János
Madrugada de laton: Schiaffini, GianCarlo: Schiaffini, GianCarlo
Magna: arr. Mitchell: Callender, George Sylvester "Red"
Majobiwomo: Moschner, Pinguin: Moschner, Pinguin
Makin' Whoopee: Donaldson, Walter, and Gus Kahn: Pilafian, Sam
Malagueña: Albeniz, Isaac: King, Ian
Malagueña: Lecuona, Ernesto: Tennessee Technological University Tuba/Euphonium Ensemble
Male Voice for Brass: Parfrey, Raymond: Tubalaté
Malta for Tuba and Tape: Hilles, Lejaren: Cummings, Barton
Mambo #5: Prado, Damaso Perez: Pilafian, Sam
The Man I Love: Gershwin, George: Woods, Gavin
Manhattan Suite: Stevens, John: Dutch Tuba Quartet; Miraphone Tuba Quartet; University of Michigan Tuba and Euphonium Ensemble; Sotto Voce
Manoir De mes Reves: Reinhardt, Django: Pilafian, Sam
Manteca: Gillespie, Dizzy: Tennessee Tech Alumni Ensemble
Maple Leaf Rag: Joplin, Scott: Johnson, John Thomas (Tommy)
March from "1941": Williams, John: Dutch Tuba Quartet; Symphonia
March from Second Suite in F for Military Band: Holst, Gustav: Symphonia
March—FroT: Kerwin, Simon: Tubalaté
The March of the Hare: Crump, Peter: Tubalaté
March of the Three Kings: arr. Harclerode: Mighty Tubadours
March of the Toy Soldiers: Herbert, Victor: Mighty Tubadours
March-Overture from "Nutcracker": Tchaikovsky, Peter Ilyitch: Mighty Tubadours
March to the Scaffold: Berlioz, Hector: British Tuba Quartet
Marche Militaire Francaise: Saint-Saëns, Camille: United States Armed Forces Tuba-Euphonium Ensemble and Massed Ensemble
Märchenbilder (Pictures of Fairyland), Op. 113: Schumann, Robert: Cooley, Floyd
Mardi Gras in New Orleans: Byrd, Roy: Dixie Power Trio
Mardi Gras Mambo: Welsch, Elliot, and Adams: Dixie Power Trio
Marguriete: Sherman-Bernie: Tarto, Joe
Maria Alm: Bologneisi, J.: Steckar Tubapack
Marine's Hymn: Offenbach, Jacques: Daellenbach, Charles
Mars from "The Planets": Holst, Gustav: Jacobs, Arnold; Symphonia
Martin's Mambo: McDermott, Tom: Perrine, Matt
Maruba: Wyre, John: Jarvis, Jeffrey
Maryland, My Maryland: Palmer, Singleton
Maskemåned for Trumpet and Tuba, Op. 148: Christiansen, Henning: Anderson, Hans
Material Girls: Hübsch, Carl Ludwig: European Tuba Quartet
Mazurcă: Wieniawski: Dumitru, Ionel
Mazurka No. 49: Chopin, Frédéric: Hoffnung, Gerard
Meat: Drums and Tuba: Drums and Tuba
Meditation from "Thais": Massenet, Jules: Sheridan, Patrick

Meditations on the Writings of Vasily Kandinsky: Bukvich, Daniel: Funderburk, Jeff
Mediterranean Rondo: Levy, Yeuda: Hershko, Shmuel "Adi"
Medley—Salty Sailor Tunes: Tarto, Joe: Tarto, Joe
Megalo Fanfare: Steckar, Marc: Steckar Tubapack
Mellon Dance: Gale, Jack: Dites-Le-Moi Tuba
The Melody Shop: King, Karl L.: Miraphone Tuba Quartet; United States Armed Forces Tuba-Euphonium Ensemble
Meltdown: Sass, Jonathon: Gerhard Meinl's Tuba Sextet; Heavy Tuba
Melton Marsch: Watz, Franz: Gerhard Meinl's Tuba Sextet; Melton Tuba-Quartett
Memoirs of the American Civil War: Vinson, Danny: Alchemy
Memories of You: Blake, Eubie: Pokorny, Gene
Memphis Blues: Palmer, Singleton
Mens Sana in Corpore Sano: Sprick, Geert: Miraphone Tuba Quartet
Merry Wives of Windsor Overture: Nicolai, Otto: British Tuba Quartet
Mess Around: Draper, Ray: Draper, Ray
Metamorphosis: Blythe, Arthur: Stewart, Bob
Meter Maid: Drums and Tuba: Drums and Tuba
Metropolitan 5tet: O'Reilly, John: Morris, Jim
Mevagissey Tales: Kalke, Ernst-Thilo: Hötzel, Markus
Mexican Hat Dance: Mendez, Rafael: Sheridan, Patrick
Mi Amor: Szentpáli, Roland: Szentpáli, Roland
Mi mistico minimo Mi: Schiaffini, GianCarlo: Schiaffini, GianCarlo
Micro: Reinhardt, Django: Pilafian, Sam
Midnight Bells from the "Opera Ball"/Liebesfreud: Kreisler, Fritz: Sheridan, Patrick
Midnight Realities: Powell, Morgan: Perantoni, Daniel
Midnight Variations for Tuba and Tape: Ross, Walter: Cummings, Barton
A Mighty Fortress Is Our God: Luther, Martin: Norris, Tim
Milano: Draper, Ray
Mild Swing: Moschner and Sachse: Moschner, Pinguin
Militärmarsch: Schubert, Franz Peter: Contraband (The)
Miniature Jazz Suite: Garrett, James: Tennessee Technological University Tuba/Euphonium Ensemble
Miniature Jazz Suite: Niehaus, Lennie: Melton Tuba-Quartett
Miniatures for Four Four-Valve Instruments: Hartley, Walter: Atlantic Tuba Quartet; British Tuba Quartet
Miniatures for Tuba and Piano: Caratini, P: Thuillier, Francois
Minina Moca (Young Lady): Antonio, Luis: Felt, Brad
Minor Dream: Draper, Ray: Draper, Ray
Minor Swing: Reinhardt, Django: Corella, Gil
Minuet: Beethoven, Ludwig van: Conner, Rex
Minuet: Boccherini, Luigi: Piernik, Zdizislaw
Minuet: Paderewski, Ignacy Jan: Piernik, Zdizislaw
Minuet and Badinerie from Suite No. 2: Bach, Johann Sebastian: Woods, Gavin
Minute Waltz: Chopin, Frédéric: Albertasaurus Tuba Quartet; British Tuba Quartet; Sheridan, Patrick
Miss Otis Regrets: Porter, Cole: Newberger, Eli
Miss R and B: Casimir, Daniel: Thuillier, Francois
Mission Impossible: Schifrin, Lalo: Tubalaté
Mississippi Mud: Barris and Cavanaugh: Matteson, Rich
The Mist: McGrain, Mark: Rojas, Marcus
Mister Sandman: Ballard: Tuba 4's
Misty: Garner, Erroll: Morgan, Kevin
Mixed Doubles for Trumpet, Tuba, Violin and Contrabass: Liptak, David: Kaenzig, Fritz
Mixed Metaphors: Puschnig, Wolfgang: Stewart, Bob
Miya Sama from "The Mikado": Sullivan, Arthur: Daellenbach, Charles
Mode to John: Tyner, McCoy: Pilafian, Sam
Molloy: Cugny, Laurent: Steckar Elephant Tuba Horde
The Moment: McIntosh, Nat
Mon Cerveau a du Chagrin: Steckar, Franck: Steckar Tubapack
Mon Coeur se Recommende a Vous: Di Lasso, Orlando: British Tuba Quartet
Mona Lisa: Evans, Ray: Corella, Gil
Monday Night: Pethel, Stan: Heavy Tuba
Monkey Chant: BL Lacerta: Gay, Les
Monk's Dream: Monk, Thelonius: Pilafian, Sam
Monodie III: Tisne, Antoine: Legris, Philippe
Monolog No. 9 for Unaccompanied Tuba: Koch, Erland von: Lind, Michael
Montagues and Capulets: Prokofiev, Sergey: British Tuba Quartet
Monterey Bay: Heasley, Tom
The Mooche: Ellington, Edward Kennedy "Duke": Pilafian, Sam
Mood Indigo: Ellington, Edward Kennedy "Duke": Gannett, Dave; Mighty Tubadours; Pilafian, Sam; Tuba 4's
Moon Mist Blues: Callender, Red: Callender, George Sylvester "Red"
Moondance: Morrison, Van: Tennessee Technological University Tuba/Euphonium Ensemble
Moondance: Stevens, John: Dutch Tuba Quartet; Melton Tuba-Quartett; Summit Tubas; Sotto Voce
Moondreams: Mercer, Johnny, and C. MacGregor: Pilafian, Sam
Moonlight Elephants: Moschner, Pinguin: European Tuba Quartet
Moose Blues: Johnson, Bunk: Newberger, Eli
Morceau de Concerto (III. Allegro non troppo): Saint-Saëns, Camille: Piernik, Zdizislaw
The Morning Song: Kellaway, Roger: Funderburk, Jeff

Norwegian Dance No. 1: Grieg, Edvard: Baadsvik, Øystein

Nostalgia Medley: Sample, Steve: Tennessee Technological University Tuba/Euphonium Ensemble

Notater for Three Trombones and Tuba: Holmboe, Vagn: Arnsted, Jørgen Voight

Notturno: Rimsky-Korsakov, Nicholas: British Tuba Quartet

Now Hear This: Dempsey, Raymond: British Tuba Quartet; Monarch Tuba-Euphonium Quartet

Nuages: Reinhardt, Django: Pilafian, Sam

Nubian Stomp: Ward, Carlos: Stewart, Bob

#107: Eskelin, Ellery: Eskelin, Ellory

"Nun komm'der Heiden Heiland, BWV 659: Bach, Johann Sebastian: Hilgers, Walter

O Come All Ye Faithful: Phillips, Harvey/TubaChristmas

O Come Little Children: Schulz: Mighty Tubadours

O Come, O Come, Emmanuel: Mighty Tubadours; Phillips, Harvey/TubaChristmas; Pilafian, Sam

O Du Mein Holder Abendstern from "Tannhauser": Wagner, Richard: Fletcher, John

O Holy Night: Adam: Pilafian, Sam

O Isis and Osiris: Mozart, Wolfgang Amadeus: Bell, William; Funderburk, Jeff; Phillips, Harvey

O Little Town of Bethlehem: Phillips, Harvey/TubaChristmas

"O Mensch bewein' dein SÜnde gross," BWV 622: Bach, Johann Sebastian: Hilgers, Walter

O Raggedy Man: Johnson, Howard: Johnson, Howard

O Sanctissumus: arr. Harclerode: Mighty Tubadours

O Tannenbaum: arr. Harclerode: Mighty Tubadours

O Vos Omnes: Victoria, Thomas Luis de: Melton Tuba-Quartett

Oboe Concerto No. 3: Handel, George Friderik: Woods, Gavin

Obsessions: Roost, Jan Van der: Nickel, Hans

October Sunshine: Botschinsky, Allan: Van Lier, Erik

Octubafest Medley: Bewley, Norlan: Phillips, Harvey

Ode to Joy: Beethoven, Ludwig van: Daellenbach, Charles

Ode to Low Brass: Butts, Carrol: Megules, Karl

Of Thee I Sing: Callender, George Sylvester "Red"

Oh, Daddy: Lehr, David "Red"

Oh How I Miss You Tonight: Lacen, Anthony "Tuba Fats"

Oh Little Town of Bethlehem: Redner: Mighty Tubadours

Oh, You Beautiful Doll: Brown and Ayer: Gannett, Dave

Ol' Man River: Kern, Jerome: Pilafian, Sam; Sheridan, Patrick; Woods, Gavin

Ol' Rockin' Chair's Got Me: Carmichael, Hoagy: Gannett, Dave

Ola, O che bon eccho: Di Lasso, Orlando: Gerhard Meinl's Tuba Sextet

Old Fashioned Love: Johnson and Mack: Newberger, Eli

Old Folks: Draper, Ray

Old Homes: Foster, Stephen: Self, James

The Old Rugged Cross: Brennard, George: Arwood, Jeffrey

The Old Rugged Cross: Dixie Power Trio

Old Star: Traditional: Melton Tuba-Quartett

Old Town: Bargeron, Dave

Oleo: Rollins, Sonny: Draper, Ray; Matteson-Phillips TubaJazz Consort; Modern Jazz Tuba Project

Omaggi e Fantasie: Baker, Claude: Randolph, David

On a Rocky Road: Templeton, Alec: Contraband Tuba Quartet

On a Slow Boat to China: Loesser, Frank: Gannett, Dave

On Chor: European Tuba Quartet

On Line: Norris, Tim

On My Own from "Les Miserables": Schoenberg, C. M.: British Tuba Quartet; Miraphone Tuba Quartet; Morgan, Kevin

On the Sunny Side of the Street: McHugh, J., and D. Fields: British Tuba Quartet; Gannett, Dave; Yasumoto, Hiroyuki

On Thin Ice: Mobberley, James C.: Tennessee Technological University Tuba/Euphonium Ensemble

Once in a Lifetime: Byrne, Eno: Dixie Power Trio

Once upon a Time: Horichi, Glenn: Roper, William

1 x 1 x 5: Foust, Alan: Morris, Jim

One for Nick: Brown, Tom: Self, James

One for the Whoofer: Taylor, Billy: Erickson, Martin

148 Street Blues: Sass, Jonathon: Heavy Tuba

One Note Samba (But Which Note?): Jobim, Antonio Carlos: Pilafian, Sam

One Room Country Shack: Traditional: Bargeron, Dave

One, Two, Three: Poore, Melvyn: Poore, Melvyn

Onyx Club Revue: New Yorkers (The): Tarto, Joe

Open Case: Drums and Tuba: Drums and Tuba

Original Dixieland One-Step: LaRocca, D.: Palmer, Singleton

Original Rags: Joplin, Scott: Johnson, John Thomas (Tommy); Lehr, David "Red"

Orpheus in the Underworld: Offenbach, Jacques: Northern Tuba Lights

Out of Case: Drums and Tuba: Drums and Tuba

Out of the Depths: Dodson, John: Tennessee Technological University Tuba/Euphonium Ensemble

Overture from the "Barber of Seville": Rossini, Gioacchino: United States Armed Forces Tuba-Euphonium Ensemble

Overture from the "Magic Flute": Mozart, Wolfgang Amadeus: Miraphone Tuba Quartet

Overture from the "Marriage of Figaro": Mozart, Wolfgang Amadeus: British Tuba Quartet; Monarch Tuba-Euphonium Quartet; United States Armed Forces Tuba-Euphonium Ensemble; University of Michigan Tuba and Euphonium Ensemble

Overture Miniature from "Nutcracker": Tchaikovsky, Peter Ilyitch: Fletcher, John

Overture to Russlan and Ludmila: Glinka, Michael: British Tuba Quartet; Miraphone Tuba Quartet
Oww: Bargeron, Dave
Oy Como Va: Puente, Tito: Perrine, Matt
Pale Young Curate: Sullivan, Arthur: Daellenbach, Charles
Para Ti: Sass, Jonathon
Parable for Solo Tuba, Op. 147: Persichetti, Vincent: Bazsinka, József; Nelson, Mark
Partita in A minor for Flute Alone: Bach, Johann Sebastian: Pokorny, Gene
Partita—Polacca: Rosler, J. J.: Gerhard Meinl's Tuba Sextet
Pascal's Victim: Naftel, Frederick: Tubalaté
Pascoal Joins the Dark Force: Delgado, Márlo: Carolino, Sérgio
Passacaglia and Fugue in C: Bach, Johann Sebastian: Symphonia
Passmezzo: Bargeron, Dave
Pastime Paradise: McIntosh, Nat
Pastoral Echoes: Norris, Tim
Pat-a-Pan: arr. Bewley: Phillips, Harvey/TubaChristmas
Patria: Blades, Ruben: Pilafian, Sam
Patricia Lee and Leah Marie: Swoboda, Deanna: Swoboda, Deanna
Paul et Mike: Jenneau, Francois: Steckar Tubapack
Paul's Pal: Draper, Ray: Draper, Ray
Pavane, Op. 50: Fauré, Gabriel: Hilgers, Walter; Tennessee Technological University Tuba/Euphonium Ensemble
Pavane pour une infante dufunte: Ravel, Maurice: Pokorny, Gene
Pavanne from the "Latin America Suite": Gould, Morton: University of Miami Tuba Ensemble
Peace: McIntosh, Nat
Peacherine Rag: Joplin, Scott: Pilafian, Sam
The Peacocks: Rowles, Jimmy: Self, James
Pearl Casters: Modern Jazz Tuba Project
Pearl Harbor [motion picture soundtrack]: Zimmer, Hans: Johnson, John Thomas (Tommy)
Peggy's Blue Skylight: Mingus, Charlie: Self, James
Pennies from Heaven: Burke and Johnston: Gannett, Dave
Pennsylvania 6-5000 Polka: Gray, Jerry, and Carl Sigman: Self, James
Pensativa: Clare Fischer: Self, James
The Perception of War: Anderson, Eugene: Pilafian, Sam
The Perfect Construction of Decisive Moments: Vlatkovich: Roper, William
Perpetual Motion: Cui, Cesar: Bobo, Roger
Perpetuum Mobile: Strauss, Johann: British Tuba Quartet
Pershing Concerto: Raum, Elizabeth: Griffiths, John
Petersburger Marsch: Volksweise: Miraphone Tuba Quartet
Pete's Dance: Drums and Tuba: Drums and Tuba
Petit Caprice in the Style of Offenbach: Rossini, Gioacchino: British Tuba Quartet; Monarch Tuba-Euphonium Quartet
Petit Fleur: Bechet, Sidney: Pilafian, Sam
Petit valse europeenne pour tuba et double quintette a vents: Francaix, Jean: Schneider, Christoph
Petites Litanies de Jésus: Grovlez, Gabriel: Sotto Voce
Petroushka (excerpt): Stravinsky, Igor: Pokorny, Gene
Piacer d'Amor: Martini, J. P. E.: Yasumoto, Hiroyuki
Piano Sonata No. 8 "Pathetique": Beethoven, Ludwig van: Albertasaurus Tuba Quartet
Pick Up the Pieces: Modern Jazz Tuba Project; Perrine, Matt
Pick Yourself Up: Kern, Jerome: Murrow, Richard
Pickin', Pluckin', Whistlin' and Walkin': Callender, George Sylvester "Red"
Pictural: Miraphone Tuba Quartet
A Picture of Dorian Blue: Gale, Jack: Morris, Jim; Self, James
Pictures at an Exhibition (excerpt): Mussorgsky, Modest: Pokorny, Gene
Pièce en form de Habanera: Ravel, Maurice: Dowling, Eugene; Hilgers, Walter
Pieces of Eight: Solomons, David: Tubalaté
Piernikiana for Solo Tuba: Szalonek, W.: Piernik, Zdzislaw
A Pierre Soliloquy—Ode to Pierre: Garbáge, Pierre (a.k.a. Garrett, James): Tennessee Tech Alumni Ensemble
Pies of Quincy: Draper, Ray
Pieta, Signora: Stradella, Alessandro: Megules, Karl
Pig Ears for Lily: Drums and Tuba: Drums and Tuba
Pigs: Ridout, Alan: British Tuba Quartet
Pigs, Pigs, Oh! Those Tasty Pigs: Roper, William: Roper, William
Piltdown Fragments: Ross, Walter: Cummings, Barton
The Pink Panther: Mancini, Henry: British Tuba Quartet; Dutch Tuba Quartet; Melton Tuba-Quartett; Northern Tuba Lights; Tuba 4's
Pipa Baquigrafo: Frazão, Alexandre: Carolino, Sérgio
"P.J. Lids": Felt, Brad: Felt, Brad
Places des Vosges: Thuillier, Francois: Thuillier, Francois
Planet of the Apes [motion picture soundtrack]: Elfman, Danny: Johnson, John Thomas (Tommy)
The Planets (excerpt): Holst, Gustav: Pokorny, Gene
Play That Country Tuba, Cowboy: Freese, Stanford: Freese, Stanford
Play That Funky Tuba Right, Boy!: Parissi, Rob: Tennessee Technological University Tuba/Euphonium Ensemble
Playback I: Poore, Melvyn: Poore, Melvyn
Pleasant Moments: Joplin, Scott: Dites-Le-Moi Tuba; Dutch Tuba Quartet
Pocket: Weaver, Mark: Weaver, Mark
Poeme: Camphouse, Mark: Arwood, Jeffrey
Poker Chips: Self, James: Self, Jim

Polka.com: Self, James: Self, Jim
Pompola: Martin, Carroll: Davis, Ronald
Poobah the Tuba: Wilder, Alec: Bell, William
Pools: Grolnick, Don: Tennessee Tech Alumni Ensemble
Poor Butterfly: Hubbel, Raymond: Mazura, János
Pop-Rock Medley: Garbáge, Pierre (a.k.a. Garrett, James): Tennessee Tech Alumni Ensemble
Pop Suite: Frackenpohl, Arthur: British Tuba Quartet; Dites-Le-Moi Tuba; Dutch Tuba Quartet; Megules, Karl; Rustic Bari-Tuba Ensemble; Tubalaté; University of Miami Tuba Ensemble
Popular Suite: Lebow, Leonard: Hanks, Thompson (Toby)
Pork Fat and Black-Eyed Peas: McDonald, Barry: Heavy Tuba
A Portrait: Gershwin, George: Dites-Le-Moi Tuba
Portrait of Teresa: Felt, Brad: Felt, Brad
Power: Stevens, John: Melton Tuba-Quartett; Miraphone Tuba Quartet; Northern Tuba Lights; Stevens, John; Sotto Voce
Powerful: BL Lacerta: Gay, Les
Praeludium: Hilgers, Walter: Gerhard Meinl's Tuba Sextet
Prayer before the Close of Day: Solomons, David: Tubalaté
Prayer for the Newborn: Luxion, Dennis: Johnson, Howard
Prayer (Il lascerato spirito): Verdi, Giuseppi: Daellenbach, Charles
Prelude: Heasley, Tom
Prelude: Bach, Johann Sebastian: Heavy Tuba; Legris, Philippe
Prélude: List, G.: Frey, Michael
Prelude: Ravel, Maurice: Pilafian, Sam
Prélude à "L'Après-midi d'un Faune": Debussy, Claude: Pokorny, Gene
Prélude and Allegro: Charpentier, Jacques: Bazsinka, József
Prelude and Dance: Fritze, Gregory: Colonial Tuba Quartet; Swiss Tuba Quartet
Prelude and Fugue in D BWV 554: Bach, Johann Sebastian: Symphonia
Prélude and Dance: Castérède, Jacques: Bazsinka, József
Prelude in C♯ minor: Gershwin, George: Newberger, Eli
Preludium: Bach, Johann Sebastian: Northern Tuba Lights
Preussens Gloria: Piefke, Gottfried: Miraphone Tuba Quartet
Priestess: Harper, Billy: Stewart, Bob
Primrose Lane: arr. Boyle: Callender, George Sylvester "Red"
Prince Meets the Phantom: Drums and Tuba: Drums and Tuba
The Prisoner's Song: Matteson, Rich
Profiles, for Tuba Quartet: Schulz, Patrick: Sotto Voce
Projekt für Tuba und Toneband: Schäffer, Boguslaw: Piernik, Zdizislaw
Promendade: Leopold, Louis J.: Jae Young, Heo
Puligny Montrachet: Godard, Michel: Bargeron, Dave
Pultany Bridge: Bargeron, Dave
Pumpkin Pie: Weaver, Mark: Weaver, Mark
Purple Gazelle: Perrine, Matt
Purple Haze: Hendrix, Jimi: Moschner, Pinguin
Put It Right Here: Grainger, Porter: Newberger, Eli
Puttin' on the Ritz: Berlin, Irving: British Tuba Quartet
Quand le Tuba valse a Paris: Bologneisi, J.: Stecker, Marc
Quand tu Veux, for Tuba, Trumpet and Trombone: Casimir, Daniel: Thuillier, Francois
Quartet: Regan, Michael J.: Tubalaté
Quartet for Brass: Ramsöe, Emilio Wilhelm: British Tuba Quartet; United States Coast Guard Tuba-Euphonium Quartet
Quartet for Low Brass: Bulla, Stephen: British Tuba Quartet; United States Navy Band Tuba-Euphonium Quartet
Quartet for Tubas: Holmes, Paul: British Tuba Quartet; Tennessee Tech Alumni Ensemble; University of Michigan Tuba and Euphonium Ensemble
Quartet for Tubas (The Condor): Payne, Frank Lynn: Dutch Tuba Quartet; Melton Tuba-Quartett; University of Miami Tuba Ensemble; University of Michigan Tuba and Euphonium Ensemble
Quatre Chansons: Dempsey, Raymond: Melton Tuba-Quartett; Monarch Tuba-Euphonium Quartet
Quatuor, Op. 109: Schmitt, Florent: Bazsinka, József
Queen of the Night Aria from "The Magic Flute": Mozart, Wolfgang Amadeus: Pilafian, Sam
A Question of Summer for Harp and Tuba: Childs, Barney: Hammond, Ivan
Quiet Nights of Quiet Stars: Jobim, Antonio Carlos: Gannett, Dave
Quintet for Tubas: Tarlow, Lawrence: Megules, Karl
Quittin' Time: Carlson, B.: Dixie Power Trio
Radetzky Marsch: Strauss, Johann: Miraphone Tuba Quartet
Radiant Pathway: Condon, Leslie: Stokes, David, and Graham Patterson
Rafael's Drum/h.s.l.e.: Moses, Bob: Rojas, Marcus
Ragtime: Frackenpohl, Arthur: Melton Tuba-Quartett
The Ragtime Dance: Joplin, Scott: Johnson, John Thomas (Tommy); United States Navy Band Tuba-Euphonium Quartet
Ragtime Rosie: Muir and Edgar: Lehr, David "Red"
The Rainbow Song: Wilson, Taylor, and Streuber: Tooba Blooze
Rainforest Etudes: Robinson, Keith: Swoboda, Deanna
Rakoczy (Hungarian) March from "Damnation of Faust" (excerpt): Berlioz, Hector: Jacobs, Arnold

Rambler: Stewart, Bob: Stewart, Bob
The Raven and the First Men (Tuba, Horn, Piano, Electronics): Rollin, Robert: Turk, John
Ready 'n Able: Pilafian, Sam
Reciprocals II for Two Tubas: Birchall, Steven: Trice, Jerry
A Recondite State of Lorn: Roper, William: Roper, William
Recordame: Henderson, Joe: Feldman, Enrique "Hank" C.
Red Mist: Moschner and Sachse: Moschner, Pinguin
Red Thread: Hübsch, Carl Ludwig: European Tuba Quartet
Reed Hornets: Fishkind, Larry: European Tuba Quartet
Reflection: Wilder/Zippel: Tuba 4's
Reflections on a Park Bench: Beale, David: Tennessee Technological University Tuba/Euphonium Ensemble
Refrain from "Pop Suite": Frackenpohl, Arthur: Miraphone Tuba Quartet
Regardez La Femme Charmante: Smith, Zachary: Dixie Power Trio
Release Me: Miller, Yount, Williams: Johnson, Howard
Rene's Song: Toledo, Rene Luis: Modern Jazz Tuba Project
Repentance (Chi sprezzando): Handel, George Friderik: Daellenbach, Charles
Reply: Perrine, Matt
Requiebros: Cassado: King, Ian
Requiem to a Dead Little Cat: Kalke, Ernst-Thilo: Melton Tuba-Quartett
Residue for Tuba and Vibraphone: Horwood, Michael S.: Vogt, Michael
Rest and Recreation: Skempton, Howard: Tubalaté
Reveille: McGrain, Mark: Rojas, Marcus
Rhapsodic Fantasie: Liszt, Franz: Woods, Gavin
Rhythm Futur: Reinhardt, Django: Pilafian, Sam
The Rhythm King: Hoover, J.: Dixie Power Trio
Rhythmic Contours (first movement): Uber, David: Cummings, Barton
Ribbons Down My Back: Herman, Jerry: Self, James
Ricercar: Gabrieli, Dominico: Davis, Ronald
Riddle Song: English Ballad: Daellenbach, Charles
Ride of the Valkyries (excerpt): Wagner, Richard: Pokorny, Gene
Riff Rock: Sarvello, Frank: Morris, Jim
Right Now: Tolliver, Charles: Johnson, Howard
Ripsey's Rumble: Sass, Jonathon: Heavy Tuba
Ritual: Corwell, Neal: Brown, Velvet
Riverboat Shuffle: Matteson, Rich
Roadway: Wittner, Gary: Johnson, Howard
Robin Hood Fanfare: Kamen, Michael: Tennessee Technological University Tuba/Euphonium Ensemble
Rock of Ages: Palmer, Singleton
Rocked in the Cradle of the Deep: Rollinson, T. H.: Lawhern, Tim
Romance: Elgar, Edward: Dowling, Eugene
Romance: Uber, David: Jae Young, Heo
Romanian Dance No. 2: Dumitru, Ionel: Bobo, Roger; United States Army Band "Pershing's Own"
Romanza and Rondo from Horn Concerto No. 4: Mozart, Wolfgang Amadeus: Woods, Gavin
Romanze and Rondo: Norris, Tim
Romeo and Juliet, Op. 64 (excerpt): Prokofiev, Sergey: Pokorny, Gene
Roméo et Juliette (excerpt): Berlioz, Hector: Jacobs, Arnold; Pokorny, Gene
Ronde and Saltarelle "Pour Quoy": Susato, Tielman: Atlantic Tuba Quartet
Rondeau: Self, James: Self, Jim
Rondo: Bach, Johann Sebastian: British Tuba Quartet
Rondo: Hook, J.: British Tuba Quartet
Rondo: Mouret, Jean Joseph: Mighty Tubadours
Rondo: Mozart, Wolfgang Amadeus: Woods, Gavin
Rondo alla Turca: Mozart, Wolfgang Amadeus: British Tuba Quartet
Rondo Allegro (Tuba with Brass Quintet): Capuzzi, Antonio: Self, James
Rondo in E♭ major, K371: Mozart, Wolfgang Amadeus: Piernik, Zdzislaw
Rondo Variato: Schlenker, Manfred: Hötzel, Markus
Rosetta: Wood and Hines: Gannett, Dave
Rouleaux De Printemps: Steckar, Franck: Steckar Elephant Tuba Horde
'Round Midnight: Monk, Thelonius, and Cootie Williams: Dites-Le-Moi Tuba; Johnson, Howard; Self, James; Tennessee Tech Alumni Ensemble; Tennessee Technological University Tuba/Euphonium Ensemble
Round One: McIntosh, Nat
Round the Block: Moschner, Pinguin: European Tuba Quartet
Roundarounds: Arbel, Chaya: Hershko, Shmuel "Adi"
Row, Row, Rosie: Bryan-Mayer: Tarto, Joe
Royal Flush: Perrine, Matt
Royal Garden Blues: Williams, Clarence, and Spencer Williams: Lehr, David "Red"; Palmer, Singleton; Sotto Voce
Royronus: Drums and Tuba: Drums and Tuba
Rudolph, the Red-Nosed Reindeer: Marks, John: Pilafian, Sam
Ruessiflue: Brun, Albin: Unternährer, Marc
Rumanian Dance No. 2: Dumitru, Ionel: Funderburk, Jeff
Rumpole of the Bailey: Horovitz, Joseph: British Tuba Quartet
Running Around: European Tuba Quartet
Running, Running: McGrain, Mark, and Bob Moses: Rojas, Marcus
Ruthenian Dance: Bartók, Béla: Pilafian, Sam
Sabre Dance: Khatchaturian, Aram: Melton Tuba-Quartett; Tubalaté
Sadiga: Draper, Ray
Sadness: Bartók, Béla: Pilafian, Sam

Sagenhaft: Cech, Christoph: Heavy Tuba
Sakura Sakura: Traditional: Yasumoto, Hiroyuki
Salammba: Steckar, Marc: Steckar Tubapack
Sale gosse: Thuillier, Francois: Thuillier, Francois
Salut D'Amour, Op.12: Elgar, Edward: Sheridan, Patrick
Salve Venere, Salve Marte: Stevens, John: Brown, Velvet
Samba Beach: Williams, Mason: Gannett, Dave
Samba de Orfeu: Bonfa, Luis: Corella, Gil
Samba Loco: Thingnäs, Frode: Scandinavian Tuba Jazz
Sambe Guitana: Mendez, Rafael: Sykes, Steven
Sandu: Brown, Clifford: Modern Jazz Tuba Project; Tennessee Tech Alumni Ensemble
Santa Claus Blues: Straight and Kahn: M'N'M Trio
Santa Claus Is Coming to Town: Gillespie: Mighty Tubadours; Pilafian, Sam
Santa Wants a Tuba for Christmas: Bewley, Norlan: Phillips, Harvey/TubaChristmas
Sarabande from English Suite No. 2 in A: Bach, Johann Sebastian: Hilgers, Walter
Sareebar for Tuba and Percussion: Boyadjian, Hayg: Pilafian, Sam
Satin Doll: Ellington, Edward Kennedy "Duke": Mazura, János; Mighty Tubadours; Tuba 4's
Saturnalis: Kupferman, Meyer: Bobo, Roger
The Satyr: Nielsen, Hans Peter: ANON
The Sauce Maker: Drums and Tuba: Drums and Tuba
Sax-Machine: Moschner, Pinguin: Moschner, Pinguin
Say It's So: Jones, Sam: Pilafian, Sam
Scarborough Fair: Traditional: Tubalaté
Scenes from Childhood, Op. 15: Schumann, Robert: Self, James
Scheherezade: Rimsky-Korsakov, Nicholas: Jacobs, Arnold
Scherzando for Tubular Octet: Knox, Charles: Tennessee Technological University Tuba/Euphonium Ensemble
Scherzo: Danner, Greg: Tennessee Technological University Tuba/Euphonium Ensemble
Scherzo: Golland, John: Sykes, Stephen
Schon Rosmarin: Kreisler, Fritz: King, Ian; Sheridan, Patrick
School Day: Berry, Chuck: Dixie Power Trio
Schy: Brun, Albin: Unternährer, Marc
Science Fiction: Gasner, Moshe: Hershko, Shmuel "Adi"
Scottie Pippen: Baron, Joey: Drums and Tuba
Scrap: Schiaffini, GianCarlo: Schiaffini, GianCarlo
Scrapple from an Apple: Parker, Charlie: Mazura, János
Scratch: Schiaffini, GianCarlo: Schiaffini, GianCarlo
Screwbirds: Lauer, Christoff: Stewart, Bob
Scyths: Mertens, Hardy: Dutch Tuba Quartet
Sea Tubas: Traditional: Northern Tuba Lights
Second Horn Concerto: Strauss, Richard: Seward, Steven
Second Line: Barbarin, P.: Dixe Power Trio
The Secret: Fauré, Gabriel: Daellenbach, Charles
Secrets: McDaniel, Ernie: Self, James
Seguidillas/Adagio and Rondo: Forte, Aldo Rafael: Symphonia
Selected Movements from Sonatas for Flute: Handel, George Friderik: Phillips, Harvey
Selvage: Weaver, Mark: Weaver, Mark
Semper Fidelis: Sousa, John Philip: British Tuba Quartet
Sempre libera from "La Traviata": Verdi, Giuseppi: Pilafian, Sam
Send in the Clowns: Sondheim, S.: Woods, Gavin
Send Me to the 'Lectric Chair: Brooks, George: M'N'M Trio
Señor Blues: Silver, Horace: Matteson-Phillips TubaJazz Consort; Tennessee Tech Alumni Ensemble
Sensation: Palmer, Singleton
Sentier De Nuit: Vigneron, Louis: Steckar Elephant Tuba Horde
Sentimental Journey: Brown/Homer/Green: Tuba 4's
Serenade: Schubert, Franz Peter: Bobo, Roger; Cummings, Barton; Piernik, Zdizislaw
Serenade for Four Tubas (third movement—Allegro): Presser, William: University of Michigan Tuba Ensemble
Serenade for Ten Wind Instruments: Persichetti, Vincent: United States Coast Guard Tuba-Euphonium Quartet
Serenade for Tuba and Piano: Schmidt, William: Conner, Rex; Johnson, John Thomas (Tommy)
Serenade for Tubas: Tchaikovsky, Peter Ilyitch: Tennessee Technological University Tuba/Euphonium Ensemble
Serenade from Sonatine for Bass Saxhorn and Piano: Castérède, Jacques: Pokorny, Gene
Serenade from the "Student Prince": Romberg, Sigmund: Sheridan, Patrick
Serenade No. 12 for Solo Tuba: Persichetti, Vincent: Legris, Philippe; Phillips, Harvey; Zerkel, David
Serie Noire: Steckar, Marc: Steckar Tubapack
Seven Enchiladas: Weaver, Mark: Weaver, Mark
7,000,000 Miles: Wilson, Denny, and Hal Taylor: Tooba Blooze
Shaft: Hayes, Isaac: Tennessee Technological University Tuba/Euphonium Ensemble
Shake It and Break It: Lacen, Anthony "Tuba Fats"
Shake It Down: Williams and Urquhart: Newberger, Eli
She Loves Me Anyway: Smith, Zachary: Dixie Power Trio
Shenandoah: Traditional: Self, James
Shepherd's Dance: Susato, Tielman: Alchemy
Shiek of Araby: Palmer, Singleton
Shiny Stockings: Foster, Frank: Tennessee Technological University Tuba/Euphonium Ensemble
Short Story: Eskelin, Ellery: Eskelin, Ellory
A Short Suspense Story: Rufeisen, Arie: Hershko, Shmuel "Adi"

Show Me the Way to Go Home: Connelly, Reg: Murrow, Richard
Shuckin' and Jivin': Matteson, Rich: Matteson-Phillips TubaJazz Consort
Siamang Suite: Canter, James: Tennessee Tech Alumni Ensemble
Siciliano: Bach, Johann Sebastian: Murrow, Richard
Sicilienne: Fauré, Gabriel: Funderburk, Jeff; King, Ian
Sidewinder: Morgan, Lee: Tennessee Technological University Tuba/Euphonium Ensemble
Sieben Durch Acht: Wefelmeyer, Bernd: Legris, Philippe
Sieben Miniaturen für Vier Tuben: Kochan, Gunter: Self, James
Siegfried (excerpts): Wagner, Richard: Cooley, Floyd
Signals for Trumpet, Tuba, and Brass Choir: Reynolds, Verne: Bobo, Roger
Silent Night: Gruber, Franz: Phillips, Harvey/TubaChristmas; Pilafian, Sam
Silver Bells: Livingston, J., and R. Evans: Pilafian, Sam
Silver Shadows: European Tuba Quartet
Simple Gifts: Traditional: Self, James
Simple Gifts/Yankee Doodle/When Jesus Wept/Chester/Edelweiss: Traditional: Colonial Tuba Quartet
Simplis Sonor: Rood, Hale: Morris, Jim
Since You've Asked: Collins, Judy: Atlantic Tuba Quartet; Dites-Le-Moi Tuba
Sine Nomine: Kilon, Moshe: Hershko, Shmuel "Adi"
Sinfonia III: Bach, Johann Sebastian: Self, James
Sing, Sing, Sing: Modern Jazz Tuba Project
Sister Sadie: Silver, Horace: Tennessee Technological University Tuba/Euphonium Ensemble
Six Studies in English Folksong: Vaughan Williams, Ralph: Dowling, Eugene; Pokorny, Gene
Skater's Waltz: Wauldteufel, Emil: Daellenbach, Charles
Sketches: McFarland, Michael: Kaenzig, Fritz
Skirmish and Dance: Reynolds, Jeffrey: Pokorny, Gene
Skylark: Carmichael, Hoagy: Gannett, Dave; Modern Jazz Tuba Project
Slavonic Dance, Op. 46, No. 1: Dvorák, Antonin: Tennessee Technological University Tuba/Euphonium Ensemble
Sleeping Giants: Niehaus, Lennie: Contraband (The)
Sleepytime Down South: Muse, C.: Dixie Power Trio
Sleigh Ride: Anderson, Leroy: Pilafian, Sam
Sljivovica, for Tuba, Trumpet and Trombone: Casimir, Daniel: Thuillier, Francois
Smile: Chaplin, Charlie: Erickson, Martin; Sheridan, Patrick
Smoke Gets in Your Eyes: Kern, Jerome: Pilafian, Sam
Só: Palma, J.: Carolino, Sérgio
So Little Time: De Rose and Hill: M'N'M Trio
So What: Davis, Miles: Murrow, Richard; Tennessee Technological University Tuba/Euphonium Ensemble
Sob Sister Sadie: Bigelow-Bates: Tarto, Joe
Sobbin' Blues: Kassel and Stitzel: Newberger, Eli
Social Studies: McIntyre, Earl
Softly, as a Morning Sunrise: Romberg, Sigmund, and O. Hammerstein: Feldman, Enrique "Hank" C.
Soji: Bargeron, Dave: Bargeron, Dave
Solace: Joplin, Scott: Daellenbach, Charles; Gannett, Dave
Solo No. 3 for Tuba: Dubrovay, Laszlo: Bazsinka, József
Solo Tuba Music: Lippe, Cort: Bazsinka, József
Solvejg's Lied: Grieg, Edvard: Jae Young, Heo
Some Day My Prince Will Come: Morrey, Larry: Self, James
Some Music: Fay, Tom: Hanks, Thompson (Toby)
Somebody's Samba: Aldcroft, Randy: Self, James
Someone to Watch over Me: Gershwin, George: Pilafian, Sam
Sometimes I Feel like a Motherless Child: Traditional: Stewart, Bob
Somewhere over the Rainbow: Arlen, Harold: Colonial Tuba Quartet
Sonata: Ewazen, Eric: Brown, Velvet; Funderburk, Jeff
Sonata: Pisciotta, Louis V: Hanks, Toby
Sonata: Reynolds, Verne: Brown, Velvet
Sonata: Sibbing, Robert: Perantoni, Daniel
Sonata: Wilder, Alec: Phillips, Harvey
Sonata Capricciosa, Op. 81: Takács, Jenö: Randolph, David
Sonata Concertante for Solo Tuba and Brass Quintet: Gaathaug, Morten: Baadsvik, Øystein
Sonata [Concerto] for Tuba and Piano: Broughton, Bruce: Brown, Velvet; Funderburk, Jeff; Sinder, Philip
Sonata-Fantasia: Calabro, Louis: Nelson, Mark
Sonata for Bass Tuba and Piano: Beversdorf, Thomas: Cummings, Barton; LeBlanc, Robert
Sonata for Bass Tuba and Piano: Genzmer, Harald: Triendl, Oliver
Sonata for Bass Tuba and Piano: Hindemith, Paul: Audenaert, Guy; Augustin, Rudiger; Baadsvik, Øystein; Barsotti, Mario; Bobo, Roger; Fletcher, John; Funderburk, Jeff; Georgie, Gerhard; Gourlay, James; Hilgers, Walter; Pokorny, Gene
Sonata for Bass Tuba and Piano: Uber, David: Jae Young, Heo
Sonata for French Horn, Tuba and Piano: Wilder, Alec: Phillips, Harvey; Pilafian, Sam
Sonata for Oboe and Continuo: Telemann, Georg Philipp: Thuillier, Francois
Sonata for Solo Tuba: Kranowski, A.: Piernik, Zdzislaw
Sonata for Tuba and Piano: Cheetham, John: Zerkel, David

Sonata for Tuba and Piano: George, Thom Ritter: Brewer, Robert; Perantoni, Daniel; Randolph, David
Sonata for Tuba and Piano: Madsen, Trygve: Baadsvik, Øystein; Bobo, Roger; Labeyrie, Stéphane
Sonata for Tuba and Piano: McIntyre, David: Griffiths, John
Sonata for Tuba and Piano: Schmidt, William: Hanks, Toby; Nickel, Hans
Sonata for Tuba and Piano: Sivelov, Niklas: Baadsvik, Øystein
Sonata for Tuba and Piano: White, Donald: Kaenzig, Fritz
Sonata in C major Op. 1, No. 7 for Tuba and Organ: Handel, George Friderik: Hilgers, Walter
Sonata in E minor: Telemann, Georg Philipp: Seward, Steven
Sonata in E♭ major: Bach, Johann Sebastian: Cooley, Floyd; Jae Young, Heo
Sonata in F: Telemann, Georg Philipp: Sinder, Philip
Sonata in F major for Tuba and Piano: Marcello, Benedetto: Lind, Michael
Sonata in F minor: Telemann, Georg Philipp: Seward, Steven
Sonata in F minor for Bassoon: Telemann, Georg Philipp: Jae Young, Heo
Sonata in G Dur: Bach, Johann Sebastian: Michel, Guy
Sonata in G Major: Handel, George Friderik: Pokorny, Gene
Sonata in G major for Tuba and Piano (Horn Sonata in F): Beethoven, Ludwig van: Thornton, Michael
Sonata in G minor (I. Prelude; II. Courant): Ecclés, Henry: Piernik, Zdizislaw
Sonata No. 1 for Tuba and Piano: Hartley, Walter: LeBlanc, Robert; Zerkel, David
Sonata No. 1 for Tuba and Piano: Wilder, Alec: Jae Young, Heo
Sonata No. 4 in C: Bach, Johann Sebastian: Dowling, Eugene
Sonata No. 5 in D minor: Galliard, Johann Ernst: Bobo, Roger
Sonata II for Tuba and Cembalo: Bach, Johann Sebastian: Hilgers, Walter
Sonate: Ecclés, Henry: Funderburk, Jeff; Lienard, Bernard
Sonatina: Hartley, Walter: Popiel, Peter
Sonatina: Sear, Walter: Davis, Ronald; Megules, Karl
Sonatina for Trombone and Piano: Koetsier, Jan: Randolph, David
Sonatina for Trumpet and Tuba: Iannoccone, Anthony: Smith, J. R.
Sonatina for Tuba and Piano: Stevens, Halsey: Brewer, Robert; Perantoni, Daniel; Randolph, David; Self, James
Sonatina for Tuba and Piano, Op. 57: Koetsier, Jan: Funderburk, Jeff; Hanks, Toby; Hoppert, Manfred; Walsh, Thomas
Sonatina for Tuba Quartet: Reeman, John: British Tuba Quartet
Sonatine: Bozza, Eugène: Jacobs, Arnold
Sonatine: Castérède, Jacques: Brown, Velvet; Funderburk, Jeff; Hanks, Toby; Woods, Gavin
Sonatine for Basstuba and Piano: Glass, Jennifer: Fletcher, John
Sonatine für Tuba und Klavier, Op. 14: Rottler, Werner: Walsh, Thomas
Song and Dance for Euphonium, Tuba and Band: Frackenpohl, Arthur: Porter, David
Song and Humoreske: Sinigaglia, Leone: Bobo, Roger
Song D'Automne: Reinhardt, Django: Pilafian, Sam
Song for Carol: Wilder, Alec: Phillips, Harvey
Song for Oliver: Laumann, H.: Anderson, Hans
Song of the Flea: Mussorgsky, Modest: Fletcher, John
Song of the New World: Stewart, Bob
Song of the Volga Boatman: Russian Folksong: Daellenbach, Charles
Song of the Wanderer: Moret, Neil: Newberger, Eli
Songs in the Fight against Rum: Garbáge, Pierre (a.k.a. Garrett, James): Tennessee Tech Alumni Ensemble
Sonny Boy: Brown, DeSylva, and Henderson: M'N'M Trio; Newberger, Eli
Sonoro for Horn, Bass Horn [Tuba], and Piano: Kellaway, Roger: Bobo, Roger; Labeyrie, Stéphane
Soon Enough: Weaver, Mark: Weaver, Mark
Sophisticated Lady: Ellington, Edward Kennedy "Duke": Callender, George Sylvester "Red"
Sortie in E♭: Lefebure-Wely: British Tuba Quartet
The Sound of the Wasp: Wilson, Phil: Matteson, Rich
Sousa, Phone Home!: Self, James: Self, James
Sousa Surrenders: Garbáge, Pierre (a.k.a. Garrett, James): Tennessee Tech Alumni Ensemble; United States Armed Forces Tuba-Euphonium Ensemble and Massed Ensemble
South: Charles, Moten, and Hayes: Matteson, Rich
South Rampart Street Parade: Palmer, Singleton
Space Blossoms: Betti, Dino: Schiaffini, Giancarlo
Spain: Corea, Chick: Tennessee Technological University Tuba/Euphonium Ensemble
Spanish Castle Magic: Hendrix, Jimi: Moschner, Pinguin
Spanish Dance, Op. 37, No. 2 and No. 5/Intermezzo from "Goyescas": Granados, Enrique: King, Ian
Speak like a Child: Hancock, Herbie: Self, James
Speak Low: Weill, Kurt: Callender, George Sylvester "Red"
Spiderman: Webster and Harris: Dixie Power Trio
Spiderman [motion picture soundtrack]: Elfman, Danny: Johnson, John Thomas (Tommy)
Spiderman 2 [motion picture soundtrack]: Elfman, Danny: Johnson, John Thomas (Tommy)
Spinning Wheel: Thomas, D. C.: Heavy Tuba
Spiral II, for Mezzo-Soprano, Piano and Tuba: Ung, Chinary: Perantoni, Daniel

Suite No. 2 (Jessie): Wilder, Alec: Phillips, Harvey
Suite No. 3 (Little Harvey): Wilder, Alec: Phillips, Harvey
Suite No. 4 (Thomas): Wilder, Alec: Phillips, Harvey
Suite No. 5 (Ethan Ayer): Wilder, Alec: Phillips, Harvey
Summer Knows: LeGrand, Michel: Modern Jazz Tuba Project
Summertime: Gershwin, George: Matteson-Phillips TubaJazz Consort
The Sun Has Got His Hat On: Butler: Crowther, Shaun
Sunday: Brahms, Johannes: Daellenbach, Charles
Sunrise Lady: Johnston, Bruce: Tennessee Technological University Tuba/Euphonium Ensemble
Surinam: Traditional: Stewart, Bob
Svengali's Summer/Waltz: Evans, Gil: Johnson, Howard
The Swan from "Carnival of the Animals": Saint-Saëns, Camille: Cummings, Barton; King, Ian; Morgan, Kevin; Piernik, Zdizislaw; Sheridan, Patrick; Tubalaté
Swannee River: Foster, Stephen: Matteson, Rich
Sweet Disposition: Snow, Phoebe: Johnson, Howard
Sweet Georgia Brown: Bernie, Pinkard, and Casey: Bargeron, Dave; Colonial Tuba Quartet; Matteson, Rich; Palmer, Singleton; Perantoni, Daniel; Pilafian, Sam; Tennessee Technological University Tuba/Euphonium Ensemble
Sweet Georgia Brown Sweet: Stewart, Bob: Stewart, Bob
Sweet Girl: M'N'M Trio
Sweet Lorraine: Burwell, C.: Dixie Power Trio
Sweet Mama Janisse: Mahal, Taj: Johnson, Howard
Sweet Music: Dietz and Schwartz: Newberger, Eli
Swing Castle: Ruga, Claudio: Dites-Le-Moi Tuba
Swing Low, Sweet Chariot: Spiritual: Contraband (The); Dutch Tuba Quartet
Swing Rag: Jackman, Andrew: Sykes, Steve
Swingin' Little Swiss Tuba . . . Cuckoo-clock: Janin, D.: Stecker, Marc
Swiss Air: Newsome, Roy: Crowther, Shaun
Symphonic Metamorphosis of Themes by Carl Maria von Weber (excerpt): Hindemith, Paul: Pokorny, Gene
Symphonie fantastique (excerpt): Berlioz, Hector: Pokorny, Gene
Symphony No. 1 in D major ("Titan") (excerpt): Mahler, Gustav: Pokorny, Gene
Symphony No. 2 (fifth movement excerpt): Mahler, Gustav: Jacobs, Arnold
Symphony No. 3 (first movement excerpts): Mahler, Gustav: Jacobs, Arnold
Symphony No. 4: Bruckner, Anton: Jacobs, Arnold
Symphony No. 4 excerpt: Neilsen, Carl: Jacobs, Arnold
Symphony No. 5 in B♭ major, Op. 100 (excerpt): Prokofiev, Sergey: Pokorny, Gene
Symphony No. 5 in C♯ minor (excerpt): Mahler, Gustav: Pokorny, Gene
Symphony No. 6 (fourth movement): Tchaikovsky, Peter Ilyitch: Jacobs, Arnold
Symphony No. 6 in A minor ("Tragic") (excerpt): Mahler, Gustav: Pokorny, Gene
Symphony No. 7 in E major: Bruckner, Anton: Pokorny, Gene
Symphony No. 8: Bruckner, Anton: Jacobs, Arnold
Syrinx: Debussy, Claude: Self, James; Sykes, Steve
"T" for Tuba: Raum, Elizabeth: Griffiths, John
T Rex: Schultz, Mark: Swoboda, Deanna
Tabu for Tuba: Downey, John: Phillips, Harvey
Tadellos: Sass, Jonathon
Tain't Nobody's Bizness If I Do: Grainger and Robbins: M'N'M Trio
Take Five: Desmond, Paul: Melton Tuba-Quartett
Take Me Out to the Ball Game: Tilzer, Albert von: Daellenbach, Charles
Take the Stairs: Berg, Curt: Self, James
Tales of the Cultural Revolution: Holmes, Brian: Fritze, Gregory
Talisman/Cookie's Revenge: Stevens, John: Symphonia
Tambours en colere: Machado, Jean Marie: Thuillier, Francois
Tangents, Op. 109: Barnes, James: Symphonia
Tangerine: Schertzinger, Victor, and Johnny Mercer: Corella, Gil; Gannett, Dave
Tannhauser Overture: Wagner, Richard: Jacobs, Arnold
Te Dago Mi: Brown, Velvet: Brown, Velvet
Tea for Two: Youmans/Ceasar: Callender, George Sylvester "Red"; Erickson, Martin
Tears: Bousted, Donald: Tubalaté
Teddy Bears' Picnic: Bratton, John: Morgan, Kevin; Sibley, Graham
Tee Vee/T. W.: Weaver, Mark: Weaver, Mark
Tell Me a Bedtime Story: Hancock, Herbie: Johnson, Howard
Tema Cantabile con Piernicazioni per tuba universale e pianoforte: Zajaczek, Roman: Piernik, Zdizislaw
The 10 Attacks of Dagger: Drums and Tuba: Drums and Tuba
Tennessee Waltz: King, Pee Wee, and Redd Stewart: Self, James
Terrible Twos: Sellers, Joey: Self, James
Territory: Drums and Tuba: Drums and Tuba
That Mellow Sousaphone: Montrell: Dixie Power Trio
That Morning in May: Self, James: Self, James
That Old Black Magic: Arlen, Harold: Tennessee Tech Alumni Ensemble
That's A-Plenty: Pollack, Lew: Lehr, David "Red"
That's What I Like about You: Skill: Dixie Power Trio
Thelonius: Monk, Thelonius: Johnson, Howard
Them Basses: Huffine, G. H.: United States Armed Forces Tuba-Euphonium Ensemble and Massed Ensemble
Them There Eyes: Pinkard, Casey, and Tauber: Pilafian, Sam

Theme and Variation on the "Blue Bells of Scotland": Pryor, Arthur: Pokorny, Gene; Seward, Steven
Theme and Variations: Paganini, Niccolò: Dumitru, Ionel
Theme for Malcolm: Modern Jazz Tuba Project
Theme of Bolero: Sass, Jonathon
There Is a Monster: Drums and Tuba: Drums and Tuba
There Is No Greater Love: Jones, Isham: Self, James
There'll Be Some Changes Made: Overstreet and Higgins: Newberger, Eli
They Can't Take That Away from Me: Gershwin, George: Callender, George Sylvester "Red"
They Didn't Believe Me: Kern, Jerome: British Tuba Quartet
Things Ain't What They Used to Be: Ellington, Edward Kennedy "Duke": Matteson-Phillips TubaJazz Consort
Third: BL Lacerta: Gay, Les
13th House: Stewart, Bob
This Is All I Ask: Jenkins: Gannett, Dave
This Masquerade: Modern Jazz Tuba Project
This Old Man: Nagel, Robert: Hanks, Thompson (Toby)
This Won't Hurt a Bit: Newman, Ron: Erickson, Martin
Three Easy Pieces: Hindemith, Paul: Hanks, Thompson (Toby)
Three Essays for Solo Tuba: Penn, William: Pokorny, Gene; Turk, John
Three Folksongs for Four Brass: Denson, Frank: Gerhard Meinl's Tuba Sextet
Three for One: Wyatt, Scott: Perantoni, Daniel
3 for 1 for Tuba and Tape: Wyatt, Scott: Perantoni, Daniel
3 for 5: Self, James: Self, Jim
3.4.7: Barretto, C.: Carolino, Sérgio
Three Furies for Solo Tuba: Grant, James: Nelson, Mark
Three Ha'Pence a foot: Edgar, M.: Tubalaté
Three Ludes for Tuba: Jager, Robert: Perantoni, Daniel
Three Milongas: Crespo, Enrique: Gerhard Meinl's Tuba Sextet
Three Miniatures for Tuba and Piano: Plog, Anthony: Bjørn-Larsen, Jens; Bobo, Roger; Perantoni, Daniel; Skillen, Joseph
Three Moods: Boone, Daniel: Tennessee Tech Alumni Ensemble; University of Miami Tuba Ensemble
Three Movements for Four Tubas: Beal, Keith: Dutch Tuba Quartet
Three Movements from Basingstoke: White, John: Rozen, Jay
Three Movements from "Quatre Chansons": arr. Dempsey: British Tuba Quartet
Three Mythical Sketches for Four Tubas: Iannaccone, Anthony: University of Michigan Tuba Ensemble
Three Negro Spirituals: Traditional: Tubalaté
394: McGrain, Mark, and Marcus Rojas: Rojas, Marcus
Three Old American Songs: Copland, Aaron: O'Bryant, Kelly
Three Piece Suite: Moore, T.: Tubalaté
Three Pieces: Ha, Jae Eu: Cummings, Barton
Three Portraits for Tuba and Chamber Orchestra: Sampson, David: Mendoker, Scott
Three Preludes: Gershwin, George: Contraband Tuba Quartet
Three Romanzes: Schumann, Robert: Cooley, Floyd
Three Salutations: End, Jack: Hanks, Thompson (Toby)
Three Songs: Rachmaninoff, Sergei: Pokorny, Gene
3a 5: Fosset, Marc: Steckar Tubapack
Thunder and Lightning: Stevens, John: Stevens, John
The Thunderer: Sousa, John Philip: British Tuba Quartet; Dutch Tuba Quartet; Tubalaté
Thursday: McIntosh, Nat
Tia Juanna Man: Jones and Dickerson: Newberger, Eli
Tico Tico: Abreu, Zequinha: Arwood, Jeffrey; Sheridan, Patrick
Tiger Rag: DeCosta and LaRocca: Corella, Gil; Dutch Tuba Quartet; Lehr, David "Red"; Palmer, Singleton; Pilafian, Sam; Sheridan, Patrick
The Tigger Movie [motion picture soundtrack]: Gregson-Williams, Harry: Johnson, John Thomas (Tommy)
Till Eulenspiegels lustige Streiche (excerpt): Strauss, Richard: Pokorny, Gene
Timbuktuba: Daugherty, Michael: Symphonia
Time after Time: Lauper and Hyman: Dixie Power Trio
Time Cycles: Grant, Jerome: Self, Jim
A Time for Love: Mandel, Johnny: Tennessee Tech Alumni Ensemble
The Time of Your Life: Newman: Tuba 4's
Time Out for Tuba (movement 1—Cycles): Ostrander, Linda: Cummings, Barton
Timisoara: Thuillier, Francois: Thuillier, Francois
Tin Roof Blues: Melrose, Walter: Palmer, Singleton
Ting a Ling: Lacen, Anthony "Tuba Fats"
To Be Tuba: Bargeron, Dave: Bargeron, Dave
To Come Together: McIntosh, Nat
To Each His Own: Livingston, J., and R. Evans: Yasumoto, Hiroyuki
Toby and Lynn: Hand, Frederic: Hanks, Thompson (Toby)
Toccata: Sass, Jonathon
Toccata: Schooley, John: Rustic Bari-Tuba Ensemble
Toccata and Fugue in D minor: Bach, Johann Sebastian: Tennessee Technological University Tuba/Euphonium Ensemble
Tom and Sally Drake: Mahal, Taj: Johnson, Howard
Tomlishorn: Brun, Albin: Unternährer, Marc
Too Fat Polka: Richardson, Arthur/McLean: Mighty Tubadours

Too Much Monkey Business: Berry, Chuck: Dixie Power Trio
Toot Your Roots: Botschinsky, Allan: Van Lier, Erik
Topolino: Drums and Tuba: Drums and Tuba
Torna a Surriento: Curtis, Eduardo de: Feldman, Enrique "Hank" C.
Tornade sur l'esplanade: Guignon, Jean-Pierre: Thuillier, Francois
A Touch of Tuba: Dedrick, Art: Popiel, Peter
Toute l'etendur ne vaut pas un cri: Zimmerlin, Alfred: Vogt, Michael
Transfigured Goat, for Solo Tuba: Wilson, Richard Edward: Johns, Steven
Trash Dance: Fishkind, Larry: European Tuba Quartet
Traumerei: Schumann, Robert: Melton Tuba-Quartett; Norris, Tim; Piernik, Zdizislaw
Treatments for Tuba: Stroud, Richard: Tennessee Technological University Tuba/Euphonium Ensemble
Tree Top Tall Papa: Brown, Sandy: Newberger, Eli
Trees: Rasbach, Oscar: Cummings, Barton
Trepek: Tchaikovsky, Peter Ilyitch: British Tuba Quartet
Tribute to Duke Ellington: Ellington, Edward Kennedy "Duke": Tennessee Technological University Tuba/Euphonium Ensemble
Tributes to Tunesmiths: Parfrey, Raymond: Tubalaté
Trick of the Light: McGrain, Mark: Rojas, Marcus
Tricky Lix: Aldcroft, Randy: Self, James
Trigon: Zindars, Earl: Cooley, Floyd
Trilogy: Wood, Philip D.: Draper, Ray
The Trilogy vs. Dr. Skooly: McIntosh, Nat
Trio for Xylophone, Soprano and Tuba: Ziffrin, Marilyn J.: Cummings, Barton
Trio Sonata for Tuba, Batteries [Percussion], and Piano: Toyama, Yuzo: Yasumoto, Hiroyuki
Triplet for 4 Tubas: Lundquist, Torbjørn Iwan: British Tuba Quartet
Triptych: Weeks, Clifford: Megules, Karl
Tritsch-Tratsch Polka: Strauss, Johann: Melton Tuba-Quartett
Triumph of the Demon Gods: Stevens, John: Stevens, John
Troika from "Lieutenant Kije": Prokofiev, Sergey: Tennessee Technological University Tuba/Euphonium Ensemble
The Trolley Song: Martin/Blane/Wolpe: Tuba 4's
Trombone Man Blues: Lehr, David "Red"
The Trouble with the Tuba Is: Relton, William: Crowther, Shaun
Troy [motion picture soundtrack]: Horner, James: Self, James
Truesome Whosome: Szalóky, Béla: Mazura, János
The Trumpet Polka: Tarto, Joe, and Paul Lavelle: Tarto, Joe
Tsiganochka: Traditional: Buttery, Gary
Tu bats le fer etc . . . : Steckar, Marc: Legris, Philippe
Tuba Ballet for Tuba and Woodwind Quintet: Jacobsen, Julius: Lind, Michael
Tuba Banjo Dixie: Steckar, Marc: Stecker, Marc
Tuba Blues: Wolking, Henry: British Tuba Quartet; Melton Tuba-Quartett; Northern Tuba Lights
Tuba Bouchka: Quibel, Robert: Stecker, Marc
Tuba Boum: Steckar, Marc: Thuillier, Francois
Tuba Buffo: Jacobsen, Julius: Lind, Michael
Tuba Concerto: Baker, David N.: Perantoni, Daniel
Tuba Concerto: Ellerby, Martin: Gourlay, James; Harrild, Patrick; Sheridan, Patrick; Sykes, Stephen
Tuba Concerto: Gregson, Edward: Cooley, Floyd; Fletcher, John; Gourlay, James; Jae Young, Heo; Lind, Michael; Maierhofer, Josef; Nickel, Hans; Nord, Lennart; Norris, Tim; Wagner, Michael
Tuba Concerto: Hidas, Frigyes: Griffiths, John; Muros, Laszlo
Tuba Concerto: Woodward, James: Zerkel, David
Tuba Concerto No. 1 in B minor: Anderson, Eugene: Pilafian, Sam
Tuba Concerto with Band: Ross, Walter: Phillips, Harvey
Tuba de Nod: Draper, Ray
Tuba des Champs: Steckar, Marc: Steckar Tubapack
Tuba Des Villes: Steckar, Marc: Steckar Tubapack
Tuba Doina: Thornton, Donald
Tuba Juba Duba: Hutchison, Terry: Melton Tuba-Quartett; Tennessee Technological University Tuba/Euphonium Ensemble
Tuba Libre: Schiaffini, GianCarlo: Schiaffini, GianCarlo
Tuba Magic: DiGiovanni, Rocco: Tennessee Technological University Tuba/Euphonium Ensemble; United States Armed Forces Tuba-Euphonium Ensemble and Massed Ensemble
Tuba Man: Carr, S.: Bell, William
Tuba Mirum—Variations on a Gregorian Chant: Schmidt, William: Sinder, Philip
Tuba Muckl: arr. Dankwart Schmidt: Contraband (The)
Tuba Only: Solal: Steckar Tubapack
Tuba Quartet No. 1 in C, Op. 3: Wilson, Kenyon: Tennessee Technological University Tuba/Euphonium Ensemble
Tuba Quartet No. 2—Ale and Arty: Bayliss, Colin: Tubalaté
Tuba Quartet, Op. 59: Gates, Crawford: Tennessee Technological University Tuba/Euphonium Ensemble
Tuba Quartett: Hidas, Frigyes: Melton Tuba-Quartett
Tuba Rhapsody: Grundman, Clare: Cummings, Barton; Varner, Lesley
Tuba Showpiece from Quintet for Brass: Wilder, Alec: Phillips, Harvey
Tuba Smarties: Traditional: Flowers, Herbie; Norris, Tim
Tuba Song: Drums and Tuba: Drums and Tuba
Tuba Space: Coeuriot, M.: Stecker, Marc
Tuba Suite: Jacob, Gordon: Dowling, Eugene
Tuba Suite for Tuba and Three Horns: Gould, Morton: Hötzel, Markus; Phillips, Harvey

Tuba Tapestry for Tuba and Brass Band: Brand, Michael: Anderson, Hans; Fletcher, John; Norris, Tim
Tuba Variations: Farkas, Antal: Szabo, Laszlo
Tuba Voluntary: Gibbons, Orlando: Alchemy
Tubabando: Galliano, R.: Stecker, Marc
Tubach: Arcadio, Bernard, and Marc Steckar: Steckar Tubapack
Tubach: Moren, Betrand: Swiss Tuba Quartet
TubaChristmas Suite: arr. Bewley: Phillips, Harvey/TubaChristmas
Tubacuba: Steckar, Marc: Stecker, Marc
Tubafication: Mitchell-Davidson, Paul: Tubalaté
Tubafiesta Medley: Bewley, Norlan: Phillips, Harvey
Tubafour: Heussenstamm, George: New York Tuba Quartet
Tubafusion: Wood, Derek: Tubalaté
Tubalation: Niehaus, Lennie: Dites-Le-Moi Tuba; Miraphone Tuba Quartet
A Tubalee Jubalee: Garrett, James: Tennessee Technological University Tuba/Euphonium Ensemble; United States Armed Forces Tuba-Euphonium Ensemble
Tubalied: Fredrickson, Thomas: Perantoni, Daniel
Tubamobile: George, Thom Ritter: Symphonia
"Tubaobab"—Concerto in Four Movements for Tuba and Big Wind Band: Steckar, Marc: Legris, Philippe
Tubapack Blues: Steckar, Franck: Steckar Tubapack
Tubarock Medley: Bewley, Norlan: Phillips, Harvey
Tubas au Fujiyama: Steckar, Marc: Steckar Elephant Tuba Horde
Tubas in the Moonlight: Anonymous: Gannett, Dave
Tubas Latinas: Forte, Aldo Rafael: Tennessee Technological University Tuba/Euphonium Ensemble
Tubas on Fujiyama: Steckar, Marc: Stecker, Marc
Tubasonatina: George, Thom Ritter: Tennessee Technological University Tuba/Euphonium Ensemble
Tubassoon: Poore, Melvyn: Poore, Melvyn
Tubastone No. 1, for Tuba and Piano: Emler, Andy: Bazsinka, József; Labeyrie, Stéphane; Thuillier, Francois
Tubaswing Medley: Bewley, Norlan: Phillips, Harvey
TubaTuba: Bargeron, Dave: Bargeron, Dave
Tubatubap: Hausl, Johann: Sass, Jonathon
Tubby the Tuba: Kleinsinger, George, and Paul Tripp: Bell, William; Bruno, Jerry; Jenkel, Herbert; Johnson, John Thomas (Tommy); Karella, Clarence; Norris, Tim; Schmitz, Chester; Thorton, Michael
Tubby the Tuba Joins the Circus: Kleinsinger, George, and Paul Tripp: Johnson, John Thomas (Tommy); Karella, Clarence
Tubby the Tuba Joins the Jazz Band: Kleinsinger, George, and Paul Tripp: Johnson, John Thomas (Tommy)
Tubossa—Concert Bossanova for Solo Tuba and Symphonic Band: Bartles, Alfred: Northcut, Timothy
Tubular Octad: Tull, Fisher: Tennessee Technological University Tuba/Euphonium Ensemble
Tumli: Brun, Albin: Unternährer, Marc
Tunk: Stewart, Bob: Stewart, Bob
Tuphonium: Hidas, Frigyes: Dutch Tuba Quartet
Turkey in the Straw (and Several Other Places): Traditional: Self, James
Turkish March: Mozart, Wolfgang Amadeus: Albertasaurus Tuba Quartet
Turkish Rondo: Mozart, Wolfgang Amadeus: Monarch Tuba-Euphonium Quartet
Tuxedo Junction: Hawkins, Erskin: Dutch Tuba Quartet; Melton Tuba-Quartett
The Twelve Days of Christmas: Pilafian, Sam
2 AM: Corwell, Neal: Brown, Velvet
Two Bourrees from Suite No. 3 for Solo Cello: Bach, Johann Sebastian: King, Ian
2 Fantasias: Banchieri, Adriano: Colonial Tuba Quartet
Two Menuets and Gigue from Suite No. 1 for Solo Cello: Bach, Johann Sebastian: King, Ian
Two Moods for Tuba: Swann, Donald: Phillips, Harvey; Randolph, David
Two Selections from "La Traviata": Verdi, Giuseppi: Albertasaurus Tuba Quartet
Two Songs: Spillman, Robert: Bobo, Roger
Two Sons: Draper, Ray: Draper, Ray
Two Together (Tuba and Soprano): Amato, Bruno: Turk, John
Two Tunes (You Stepped Out of a Dream; Temptation): Brown, Nacio Herb: Tennessee Technological University Tuba/Euphonium Ensemble
Tyrolean Tuba: Clark, M.: Stern, Mary
Ubi Caritas—Dance: Duruflé, Maurice: Symphonia
Un Poco Loco: Powell, B.: Carolino, Sérgio
Una Furtiva Lagrima: Donizetti, Gaetano: Sykes, Steve
Unchained Melody: Zaret/North: Tuba 4's
Undecided Now: Robin and Shavers: Lehr, David "Red"
Under Paris Skies: Brun and Gannon: Pilafian, Sam
Under Paris Skies: Draper, Ray: Draper, Ray
Under the Boardwalk: Young/Resnick: Tuba 4's
Under the Sea: Miraphone Tuba Quartet
Under Your Influence: McIntosh, Nat
The Underdog Has Arisen: Dechter, Brad: Self, James
Unit Seven: Jones, Sam: Frey, Michael
The Unknown Soldier: Pilafian, Sam
Unter Der Admiralsflagge: Fucik, Julius: Miraphone Tuba Quartet
Until I Met You (Corner Pocket): Green, Freddie: Tennessee Technological University Tuba/Euphonium Ensemble
Up a Lazy River: Carmichael, Hoagy: Pilafian, Sam
Up from the Skies: Hendrix, Jimi: Moschner, Pinguin
Valencia: Bargeron, Dave: Bargeron, Dave
Valkyrie (Magic Fire Music, Ride of the Valkyries): Wagner, Richard: Jacobs, Arnold
Valse Bluette: Drigo, Richard: Sheridan, Patrick

Valvin' on a Riff: Martin, Glenn: Modern Jazz Tuba Project
Variationen for Tuba and Nine Horns: Heiden, Bernhard: Hötzel, Markus; Phillips, Harvey
Variationen/Tempus Fugit/HoUsE miX: Beck, Jeremy: Funderburk, Jeff
Variations for a Children Song: Szentpáli, Roland: Szentpáli, Roland
Variations for Tuba and Winds (Cobbler's Bench): Frackenpohl, Arthur: Davis, Ronald; Popiel, Peter
Variations in Olden Style: Stevens, Thomas: Baadsvik, Øystein; Bobo, Roger
Variations on a Theme from "Judas Maccabeus": Beethoven, Ludwig van: Bell, William
Variations on a Tyrolean Song: Arban, Jean-Baptiste: Sheridan, Patrick
Variations on a Welsh Theme: Kneale, Peter: Sykes, Steve
Variations on an Old Hymn Tune: Werle, Floyd: Tennessee Technological University Tuba/Euphonium Ensemble; United States Armed Forces Tuba-Euphonium Ensemble and Massed Ensemble
Variations on "Grandfather's Clock": Doughty, G.: Sheridan, Patrick; Woods, Gavin
Variations on "Grandfather's Clock": Work, Henry Clay: Morgan, Kevin
Variations on the Scene: Draper, Ray
Vaya Con Dios: James, Pepper, and Russell: Pilafian, Sam
Vendredi 13: Steckar, Marc: Steckar Tubapack
Verdurous Aubade for Tuba and Piano: Censhu, Jiro: Yasumoto, Hiroyuki
Vier ernste Gesänge: Brahms, Johannes: Brewer, Robert; Cooley, Floyd
View from the Footplate: Adams, Tommy: Self, James
Vif, tendre et dangereux: Thuillier, Francois: Thuillier, Francois
Villanella: Ross, Walter: Nelson, Mark
Villanelle for Horn: Dukas, Paul: Seward, Steven
20h30: Thuillier, Francois: Thuillier, Francois
Viola da Gamba Sonata in G minor: Bach, Johann Sebastian: King, Ian
Viola da Gamba Sonata No. 1: Bach, Johann Sebastian: King, Ian
V. I. P.: McIntosh, Nat
Visages: Puw, Guto Pryderi: Tubalaté
Visions fugitives: Prokofiev, Sergey: Pokorny, Gene
Viva Voce!: Stevens, John: Sotto Voce
Vivace from Trio Sonata in C for Organ BWV 526: Bach, Johann Sebastian: Albertasaurus Tuba Quartet
Vocalise, Op. 34, No. 14: Rachmaninoff, Sergei: Feldman, Enrique "Hank" C.; Jae Young, Heo; LeBlanc, Robert; Perantoni, Daniel; Sheridan, Patrick
Volume, Too: Callender, George Sylvester "Red"
The Volunteer: Rogers, Walter: Arwood, Jeffrey
Von Himmel Hoch: Bach, Johann Sebastian: Mighty Tubadours
Voodoo Chile: Hendrix, Jimi: Heavy Tuba; Moschner, Pinguin
VOX per uno stromento ad ottone: Borkowski, Marian: Piernik, Zdzislaw
Voz refracta: Schiaffini, GianCarlo: Schiaffini, GianCarlo
Wabash Blues: Ringle and Meinken: Lehr, David "Red"; Palmer, Singleton; Pilafian, Sam
Wabash Cannonball: Traditional: British Tuba Quartet; Lehr, David "Red"
Wabash Canon Ball: Garrett, James: Tennessee Tech Alumni Ensemble
Wagdanz: McGrain, Mark: Rojas, Marcus
Walkin': Davis, Miles: Tennessee Technological University Tuba/Euphonium Ensemble
Walking Together: Lindsay, Erica: Johnson, Howard
Walt's Samba: Eldsvoog, John: Self, James
Waltz for Maya: Scharnberg, Kim: Self, Jim
Waltz for Mippy III: Bernstein, Leonard: Deck, Warren; Watson, Scott
Waltz from "Die Fledermaus": Strauss, Johann: Mighty Tubadours
Waltz from "Sleeping Beauty": Tchaikovsky, Peter Ilyitch: Fletcher, John
Waltzing Matilda: arr. Matteson: Matteson-Phillips TubaJazz Consort
Waltzing with Bears: Marxsen, Dale: Davis, Ronald
Wann der Dudelsack kraht u. a.: Well, Christoph: Well, Christoph
The Warrior Comes Out to Play: McIntosh, Nat
Warsaw Autumn: Piernik, Zdzislaw
Warum Willst du so Zornig Sein?: Bach, Johann Sebastian: Szentpáli, Roland
Washington and Lee Swing: Robbins, Allen, and Sheafe: Matteson, Rich; Palmer, Singleton
Washington Post March: Sousa, John Philip: British Tuba Quartet; Colonial Tuba Quartet; Contraband (The); Melton Tuba-Quartett; Miraphone Tuba Quartet
Wassermusik: Handel, George Friderik: Swiss Tuba Quartet
The Wasteland: Corwell, Neal: Perantoni, Daniel
Waterloo: Moschner, Pinguin: Moschner, Pinguin
Wave of the Danube: Ivanovici, J.: Tubalaté
Way 'Cross Georgia: Perkinson, Coleridge: Johnson, Howard
Wayfaring Stranger: American Folksong: Daellenbach, Charles
We Three Kings: Phillips, Harvey/TubaChristmas
We Three Kings: Hopkins: Mighty Tubadours
We Wish You a Merry Christmas: Pilafian, Sam
Well, You Needn't: Machado, Jean Marie: Thuillier, Francois
Western Sky: Heasley, Tom
Westminster Intrada: Forsyth, Kieran: British Tuba Quartet
The Westwood Song: Kellaway, Roger: Bobo, Roger
What Child Is This?: Pilafian, Sam
What I See in Your Eyes: Bargeron, Dave: Bargeron, Dave

What'll I Do?: Berlin, Irving: Pilafian, Sam
What's Her Name?: Wilson, Phil: Matteson, Rich
When Johnny Comes Marching Home: Lambert, Louis: Self, James
When My Sugar Walks down the Street: Palmer, Singleton
When She Cries: Novick, Billy: Newberger, Eli
When the Bells Stopped Ringing: Arcadio, Bernard: Steckar Tubapack
When the Saints Go Marching In: Traditional: Callender, George Sylvester "Red"; Palmer, Singleton
When Tubas Waltz: Bartles, Alfred: Contraband (The); Dites-Le-Moi Tuba; Mighty Tubadours; Rustic Bari-Tuba Ensemble; Tennessee Technological University Tuba/Euphonium Ensemble
When We Were Giants: Green, Jonathan: O'Bryant, Kelly
When You See That Aunt of Mine: Nelson: Tarto, Joe
When You Wish upon a Star: Washington and Harline: Newberger, Eli
When You're Smiling: Fisher, Goodwin, and Shay: Pilafian, Sam
When Yuba Plays the Rhumba on the Tuba Down in Cuba: Hupfeld, Herman: Bell, William; Phillips, Harvey; Washburn, Joe "Country"
Where e'er You Walk: Handel, George Friderik: Daellenbach, Charles
Where Flamingos Fly: Johnson, Howard
Where the Earth Meets the Sky: Heasley, Tom
While Soft Winds Shake the Barley: Traditional: Alchemy
Whirly Twirly: Billy Mitchell: Pilafian, Sam
Whisper Not: Golson, Benny: Felt, Brad
Whispered: Eskelin, Ellery: Eskelin, Ellory
White Christmas: Berlin, Irving: Mighty Tubadours
Who Is Sylvia?: Schubert, Franz Peter: Daellenbach, Charles
Whose Reality Is This Anyway?: Mall-Darby, Samira: Frey, Michael
Why Do the Nations?: Handel, George Friderik: Szentpáli, Roland
Wicked Jerk Chicken: Smith, Zachary: Dixie Power Trio
Widderfeld: Brun, Albin: Unternährer, Marc
Wiegenlied: Brahms, Johannes: Van Lier, Erik
Wild Man Blues: Armstrong, Louis, and F. "Jellyroll" Morton: Newberger, Eli
Wild Thing: Taylor: Moschner, Pinguin
Will There Be a Time?: Raum, Elizabeth: Griffiths, John
William Fell over the Chair: Rossini, Gioacchino: Corella, Gil
William Tell Overture: Rossini, Gioacchino: British Tuba Quartet; Symphonia
Willow Weep for Me: Ronell, Ann: Frey, Michael
Willow, Willow: Chihara, Paul: Price, Tony
The Wind Cries Mary: Hendrix, Jimi: Moschner, Pinguin
Windsong: Morell, John: Self, James
Winter from "The Four Seasons": Vivaldi, Antonio: Tennessee Technological University Tuba/Euphonium Ensemble (Scott Beaver, solo tuba)
Winter Wonderland: Bernard and Smith: Pilafian, Sam
Wolf the Cat: Schaars, Peter Kleine: Dutch Tuba Quartet
Wolkenschatten, Op. 136: Koetsier, Jan: Alchemy; Dutch Tuba Quartet
Wolverine Blues: Morton, F. "Jelly Roll": Lehr, David "Red"; Palmer, Singleton
The Woman Is Right: Smith, Zachary: Dixie Power Trio
Wonamow: Pulaski, Paul: Weaver, Mark
Wonderland Duets: Robinson, Keith, and Deanna Swoboda: Swoboda, Deanna
Wonderland Duets for Two Tubas and Narrator: Luedeke, Raymond: Vogt, Michael
Won't You Come Home Bill Bailey: arr. Garrett: Tennessee Technological University Tuba/Euphonium Ensemble
The World Is Waiting for the Sunrise: Lockhart and Seitz: Lehr, David "Red"; Newberger, Eli; Tennessee Technological University Tuba/Euphonium Ensemble
Wos hot er g'sogt?: Delanoff, Robert: Walsh, Thomas
Wot Shigona Dew: Wilson, Ted: Tennessee Technological University Tuba/Euphonium Ensemble
Xmas Tuba of the British Isles: Buttery, Gary: Alchemy
Y Luego: Hermann, Herman: Scandinavian Tuba Jazz
Ya'll Stay Up: McIntosh, Nat
Yakkety Tuba: Randolph, Boots: Gannett, Dave
Yankee Doodle: Traditional American: Daellenbach, Charles
Yardbird Suite: Parker, Charlie: Erickson, Martin
Yearning: Lacen, Anthony "Tuba Fats"
Year's End: Wittner, Gary: Johnson, Howard
The Yellow Bird: Tackett, Fred: Bobo, Roger
Yellow Dog Blues: Palmer, Singleton
Yesterday: Lennon, John, and Paul McCartney: Tubalaté; Yasumoto, Hiroyuki
Yesterdays: Kern, Jerome: Draper, Ray; Johnson, Howard
Yisrael V'oraita: Traditional: Feldman, Enrique "Hank" C.
Yo, California: DeSilva, Jolson, Meyer: Self, James
Yorkscher Marsch: Beethoven, Ludwig van: Miraphone Tuba Quartet
Yorkshire Ballad: Barnes, James: Sheridan, Patrick; Symphonia
You Ain't No Streetwalker, Mama Honey, But I Do Love the Way You Strutt Your Stuff: Mahal, Taj: Johnson, Howard
You Are My Sunshine: Davis, Jimmie: Pilafian, Sam
You Don't Know What Love Is: Raye and DePaul: Stewart, Bob
You Made Me Love You: McCarthy and Monaco: British Tuba Quartet; Gannett, Dave
You Rascal You: Theard, Sam: M'N'M Trio

You Took Advantage of Me: Rodgers, Richard, and Lorenz Hart: Erickson, Martin
You Wonderful You: Brooks and Chaplin: M'N'M Trio
You'd Be So Nice to Come Home to: Porter, Cole: Gannett, Dave
You'll Be in My Heart: Collins: Tuba 4's
You'll Long for Me: M'N'M Trio
You've Never Been There: Griffin, Johnny: Bargeron, Dave
Your Kisses like the Fire: Szentpáli, Roland: Szentpáli, Roland
Your Mama Ain't Got No Draws: Sheldon, Jack: Matteson-Phillips TubaJazz Consort
Zarathustra's Reincarnation: Strauss, Richard: Heavy Tuba
Zigzags: Silverman, Faye-Ellen: Brown, Velvet
Zing Went the Strings of My Heart: Hanley, James F.: Lehr, David "Red"
zoB erocnE: samohT,snevetS: Bobo, Roger
Zombie Daddies: Moschner and Sachse: Moschner, Pinguin
Zydeco Boogaloo: Dural, Stanley: Dixie Power Trio

Tuba Recordings by Composer

Abreu, Zequinha: *Tico Tico:* Arwood, Jeffrey; Sheridan, Patrick
Adam: *Le cirque:* Thuillier, Francois
Adam: *O Holy Night:* Pilafian, Sam
Adams, Tommy: *View from the Footplate:* Self, James
Adamson: *Everything I Have Is Yours:* Barber, John William (Bill)
Adler, Samuel: *Canto VII for Solo Tuba:* Beauregard, Cherry
Ager and Yellen: *Big Bad Bill:* Newberger, Eli
Agrell, Jeffrey: *Gospel Time:* Miraphone Tuba Quartet
Ahbez, Eden: *Nature Boy:* Tennessee Technological University Tuba/Euphonium Ensemble
Akst: *Steppin' in Society:* Tarto, Joe
Albam, Manny: *Morrisania Motion:* Morris, Jim
Albeniz, Isaac: *aus Cantros de España, Op. 232, No. 2 "Chant d'Amour":* Hilgers, Walter
Albeniz, Isaac: *aus "España," Op. 165:* Hilgers, Walter
Albeniz, Isaac: *Malagueña:* King, Ian
Alberti, Luis: *Campadre Pedro Juan:* Pilafian, Sam
Albinoni, Tomaso: *Concerto, Op. 9, No. 2 in D:* Hilgers, Walter
Aldcroft, Randy: *Inner Self:* Self, James
Aldcroft, Randy: *Somebody's Samba:* Self, James
Aldcroft, Randy: *Tricky Lix:* Self, James
Alford, Kenneth: *Colonel Bogey March:* Tuba 4's
Alter, Louis: *Do You Know What It Means to Miss New Orleans?:* Self, James
Amato, Bruno: *Two Together (Tuba and Soprano):* Turk, John
American Folk Hymn: *Come, Thou Fount of Every Blessing:* Daellenbach, Charles
American Folksong: *The Cruel War Is Raging:* Daellenbach, Charles
American Folksong: *Erie Canal:* Daellenbach, Charles
American Folksong: *Streets of Laredo:* Daellenbach, Charles
American Folksong: *Wayfaring Stranger:* Daellenbach, Charles
Amos, Keith: *Flander's Cauldron:* British Tuba Quartet
Anderson, Eugene: *Baroque 'n Brass for Trumpet and Tuba:* Pilafian, Sam
Anderson, Eugene: *Lyri-Tech for Solo Tuba:* Pilafian, Sam
Anderson, Eugene: *The Perception of War:* Pilafian, Sam
Anderson, Eugene: *Tuba Concerto No. 1 in B minor:* Pilafian, Sam
Anderson, Leroy: *Sleigh Ride:* Pilafian, Sam
Anonymous: *Come Dearest, the Daylight Is Gone:* Mighty Tubadours
Anonymous: *Lute Dances:* British Tuba Quartet
Anonymous: *Tubas in the Moonlight:* Gannett, Dave
Antonio, Luis: *Minina Moca (Young Lady):* Felt, Brad
Aquino, Baden Powell de: *Bocoxe:* Alchemy; Atlantic Tuba Quartet; British Tuba Quartet; Melton Tuba-Quartett
Arban, Jean Baptiste: *Carnival of Venice:* Baadsvik, Øystein; Bell, William; Bobo, Roger; Lind, Michael; Jae Young, Heo; Perantoni, Daniel; Sheridan, Patrick
Arban, Jean-Baptiste: *Fantaisie Brillante:* Lienard, Bernard
Arban, Jean-Baptiste: *Variations on a Tyrolean Song:* Sheridan, Patrick
Arbel, Chaya: *Roundarounds:* Hershko, Shmuel "Adi"
Arcadelt, Jacob: *Ave Maria:* Melton Tuba-Quartett
Arcadio, Bernard: *Splash:* Steckar Tubapack
Arcadio, Bernard: *When the Bells Stopped Ringing:* Steckar Tubapack
Arcadio, Bernard, and Andre Ceccarelli: *Amour Musique et Paix:* Steckar Tubapack
Arcadio, Bernard, and Andre Ceccarelli: *Leleo:* Steckar Tubapack
Arcadio, Bernard, and Marc Steckar: *Kadanse et Kantation:* Steckar Tubapack
Arcadio, Bernard, and Marc Steckar: *Konservatorium:* Steckar Tubapack
Arcadio, Bernard, and Marc Steckar: *Tubach:* Steckar Tubapack
Arcadio, Bernard, and Marc Stecker: *Forêt Virge:* Steckar Tubapack
Arlen and Harburg: *If I Only Had a Brain:* Pilafian, Sam
Arlen, Harold: *Somewhere over the Rainbow:* Colonial Tuba Quartet

Arlen, Harold: *That Old Black Magic:* Tennessee Tech Alumni Ensemble
Armstrong, Louis: *Cornet Chop Suey:* Pilafian, Sam
Armstrong, Louis, and F. "Jellyroll" Morton: *Wild Man Blues:* Newberger, Eli
Arndt, Felix: *Nola:* Sheridan, Patrick
Arnold, Malcolm: *Fantasy for Solo Tuba:* Fletcher, John; Gourlay, James; Norris, Tim
Arnold, arr.: *Corazon:* Tennessee Technological University Tuba/Euphonium Ensemble
Arutiunian, Alexander: *Concerto for Tuba and Orchestra:* Lidsle, Harri
Autry and Haldeman: *Here Comes Santa Claus:* Pilafian, Sam
Ayers, Jesse: *Dancing King:* Nelson, Mark
Baader-Nobs, Heidi: *Bifurcation for Tuba and Piano:* Bjørn-Larsen, Jens
Baadsvik, Øystein: *Fnugg:* Baadsvik, Øystein
Bach, Johann Sebastian: *Adagio from Toccata, Adagio and Fugue in C major:* Hilgers, Walter
Bach, Johann Sebastian: *Air and Bourree:* Conner, Rex; Davis, Ronald; Phillips, Harvey; Popiel, Peter
Bach, Johann Sebastian: *Air for the G String:* Bobo, Roger
Bach, Johann Sebastian: *Air from Suite in D:* Tubalaté
Bach, Johann Sebastian: *Air from Suite No. 3:* British Tuba Quartet
Bach, Johann Sebastian: *"Air" from Suite No. 3 in D major for Orchestra, BWV 1068:* Atlantic Tuba Quartet; Tennessee Technological University Tuba/Euphonium Ensemble
Bach, Johann Sebastian: *Allegro from Toccata in D minor for Klavier, BWV 913:* Atlantic Tuba Quartet
Bach, Johann Sebastian: *Ave Maria:* Sheridan, Patrick
Bach, Johann Sebastian: *Bandinerie:* Marshall, Oren; Melton Tuba-Quartett
Bach, Johann Sebastian: *Bist du bei mir, BWV 508:* Atlantic Tuba Quartet; Melton Tuba-Quartett; United States Armed Forces Tuba-Euphonium Ensemble and Massed Ensemble
Bach, Johann Sebastian: *Bourree I and II from Suite for Solo Cello:* Bobo, Roger
Bach, Johann Sebastian: *Contrapunctus I:* Tennessee Tech Tuba-Euphonium Quintet
Bach, Johann Sebastian: *Contrapunctus 9 from Die Kunst der Fuge:* Sotto Voce
Bach, Johann Sebastian: *Es Ist Bollbracht:* Szentpáli, Roland
Bach, Johann Sebastian: *Fugue from Fantasia and Fugue in G:* British Tuba Quartet
Bach, Johann Sebastian: *Fugue in G minor:* Anderson, Hans; British Tuba Quartet; Gerhard Meinl's Tuba Sextet; Mighty Tubadours; Tubalaté
Bach, Johann Sebastian: *Invention No. 1:* Phillips, Harvey
Bach, Johann Sebastian: *Jesu, Joy of Man's Desiring:* British Tuba Quartet; Pilafian, Sam
Bach, Johann Sebastian: *Komm Süsser Tod:* Megules, Karl; Phillips, Harvey/TubaChristmas; Tennessee Technological University Tuba/Euphonium Ensemble
Bach, Johann Sebastian: *Minuet and Badinerie from Suite No. 2:* Woods, Gavin
Bach, Johann Sebastian: *Nun komm'der Heiden Heiland, BWV 659:* Hilgers, Walter
Bach, Johann Sebastian: *"O Mensch bewein' dein Sünde gross," BWV 622:* Hilgers, Walter
Bach, Johann Sebastian: *Partita in A minor for Flute Alone:* Pokorny, Gene
Bach, Johann Sebastian: *Passacaglia and Fugue in C:* Symphonia
Bach, Johann Sebastian: *Prelude:* Heavy Tuba; Legris, Philippe
Bach, Johann Sebastian: *Prelude and Fugue in D, BWV 554:* Symphonia
Bach, Johann Sebastian: *Preludium:* Northern Tuba Lights
Bach, Johann Sebastian: *Rondo:* British Tuba Quartet
Bach, Johann Sebastian: *Sarabande from English Suite No. 2 in A:* Hilgers, Walter
Bach, Johann Sebastian: *Siciliano:* Murrow, Richard
Bach, Johann Sebastian: *Sinfonia III:* Self, James
Bach, Johann Sebastian: *Sonata in E♭ major:* Cooley, Floyd; Jae Young, Heo
Bach, Johann Sebastian: *Sonata in G Dur:* Michel, Guy
Bach, Johann Sebastian: *Sonata No. 4 in C:* Dowling, Eugene
Bach, Johann Sebastian: *Sonata II for Tuba and Cembalo:* Hilgers, Walter
Bach, Johann Sebastian: *St. Anne's Fugue:* Tennessee Technological University Tuba/Euphonium Ensemble; United States Armed Forces Tuba-Euphonium Ensemble and Massed Ensemble
Bach, Johann Sebastian: *Suite in B♭ minor for Flute:* Seward, Steven
Bach, Johann Sebastian: *Suite No. 1 in G major for Solo Cello (Minuet, Courante):* Fletcher, John
Bach, Johann Sebastian: *Toccata and Fugue in D minor:* Tennessee Technological University Tuba/Euphonium Ensemble
Bach, Johann Sebastian: *Two Bourrees from Suite No. 3 for Solo Cello:* King, Ian
Bach, Johann Sebastian: *Two Menuets and Gigue from Suite No. 1 for Solo Cello:* King, Ian
Bach, Johann Sebastian: *Viola da Gamba Sonata No. 1:* King, Ian
Bach, Johann Sebastian: *Viola da Gamba Sonata in G minor:* King, Ian
Bach, Johann Sebastian: *Vivace from Trio Sonata in C for Organ BWV 526:* Albertasaurus Tuba Quartet
Bach, Johann Sebastian: *Von Himmel Hoch:* Mighty Tubadours
Bach, Johann Sebastian: *Warum Willst du so Zornig Sein?:* Szentpáli, Roland

Bach, P. D. Q. [Schikele, Peter]: *"Dutch" Suite (S.-16) for Bassoon and Tuba:* Bishop, Ronald
Bach, Vincent: *Hungarian Melodies:* Seward, Steven
Baker, Claude: *Omaggi e Fantasie:* Randolph, David
Baker, David N.: *Tuba Concerto:* Perantoni, Daniel
Ballard: *Mister Sandman:* Tuba 4's
Banchieri, Adriano: *2 Fantasias:* Colonial Tuba Quartet
Barat, Joseph Eduoard: *Introduction and Dance:* Bazsinka, József; Bobo, Roger; Jae Young, Heo
Barbarin and Armstrong: *Don't Forget to Mess Around:* M'N'M Trio
Barbarin, P.: *Second Line:* Dixie Power Trio
Barber, Samuel: *Adagio for Strings:* Symphonia
Barboteu, Georges: *Divertissement for Tuba and Brass Quartet:* Hilgers, Walter
Bargeron, Dave: *Joanda:* Bargeron, Dave
Bargeron, Dave: *Soji:* Bargeron, Dave
Bargeron, Dave: *To Be Tuba:* Bargeron, Dave
Bargeron, Dave: *TubaTuba:* Bargeron, Dave
Bargeron, Dave: *Valencia:* Bargeron, Dave
Bargeron, Dave: *What I See in Your Eyes:* Bargeron, Dave
Barnes, James: *Concerto Op. 96b:* Sheridan, Patrick
Barnes, James: *Tangents Op. 109:* Symphonia
Barnes, James: *Yorkshire Ballad:* Sheridan, Patrick; Symphonia
Baron, Joey: *Scottie Pippen:* Drums and Tuba
Baron, Samuel: *Impressions of a Parade:* Hanks, Thompson (Toby)
Barretto, C.: *3.4.7:* Carolino, Sérgio
Barris and Cavanaugh: *Mississippi Mud:* Matteson, Rich
Barron, Ronnie: *It's Getter Harder to Survive:* Johnson, Howard
Barroso, Ary: *Brazil:* Melton Tuba-Quartett; Pilafian, Sam; Tennessee Technological University Tuba/Euphonium Ensemble; Tuba 4's
Barry, Darrol: *Impromptu for Tuba:* Ferguson, Kenneth
Bartles, Alfred: *The New When Tubas Waltz:* Symphonia
Bartles, Alfred: *Tubossa—Concert Bossanova for Solo Tuba and Symphonic Band:* Northcut, Timothy
Bartles, Alfred: *When Tubas Waltz:* Contraband (The); Dites-Le-Moi Tuba; Mighty Tubadours; Rustic Bari-Tuba Ensemble; Tennessee Technological University Tuba/Euphonium Ensemble
Bartók, Béla: *Concerto for Orchestra (excerpt):* Jacobs, Arnold; Pokorny, Gene
Bartók, Béla: *Hungarian Pictures:* Thuillier, Francois
Bartók, Béla: *Ruthenian Dance:* Pilafian, Sam
Bartók, Béla: *Sadness:* Pilafian, Sam
Bassman, George: *I'm Getting Sentimental:* Corella, Gil
Bayliss, Colin: *Tuba Quartet No. 2—Ale and Arty:* Tubalaté
Bazelon, Irwin: *For Tuba . . . with Strings Attached:* Baev, Bayo
Beach, Bennie: *Dance Suite for Tuba and Triangle:* Cummings, Barton
Beach, Bennie: *Lamento:* Conner, Rex; LeBlanc, Robert
Beal, Keith: *Three Movements for Four Tubas:* Dutch Tuba Quartet
Beale, David: *Reflections on a Park Bench:* Tennessee Technological University Tuba/Euphonium Ensemble
Bechet, Sidney: *Petit Fleur:* Pilafian, Sam
Beck, Jeremy: *Variationen/Tempus Fugit/HoUsE miX:* Funderburk, Jeff
Bedrich, Jan: *Dialogy:* Nickel, Hans
Beefheart, Captain: *Dali's Car:* Pilafian, Sam
Beethoven, Ludwig van: *Beethoven's 5½:* Corella, Gil
Beethoven, Ludwig van: *Horn Sonata in F, Op. 17:* King, Ian
Beethoven, Ludwig van: *Minuet:* Conner, Rex
Beethoven, Ludwig van: *Ode to Joy:* Daellenbach, Charles
Beethoven, Ludwig van: *Piano Sonata No. 8 "Pathetique":* Albertasaurus Tuba Quartet
Beethoven, Ludwig van: *Sonata in G major for Tuba and Piano (Horn Sonata in F):* Thornton, Michael
Beethoven, Ludwig van: *Variations on a Theme from "Judas Maccabeus":* Bell, William
Beethoven, Ludwig van: *Yorkscher Marsch:* Miraphone Tuba Quartet
Bell, Kelvyn: *Suba La Nas Alturas:* Stewart, Bob
Bencriscutto, Frank: *Concertino for Tuba and Band:* Freese, Stanford
Benedict, Julius: *Carnival of Venice:* Daellenbach, Charles
Benson, Warren: *Arioso:* Popiel, Peter; Sinder, Philip
Benson, Warren: *Helix for Solo Tuba and Concert Band:* Phillips, Harvey; Robinson, Jack; Turk, John
Berg, Curt: *The Farewell Burn:* Self, James
Berg, Curt: *Take the Stairs:* Self, James
Berlin, Irving: *Alexander's Ragtime Band:* Pilafian, Sam
Berlin, Irving: *Always:* Erickson, Martin
Berlin, Irving: *How Deep Is the Ocean?:* Scandinavian Tuba Jazz
Berlin, Irving: *Puttin' on the Ritz:* British Tuba Quartet
Berlin, Irving: *What'll I Do?:* Pilafian, Sam
Berlin, Irving: *White Christmas:* Mighty Tubadours
Berlioz, Hector: *Damnation de Faust (excerpt):* Pokorny, Gene
Berlioz, Hector: *"Dies Irae" from "Symphonie Fantastique":* Jacobs, Arnold; Pokorny, Gene
Berlioz, Hector: *Dream of a Witches Sabbath from "Symphonie Fantastique":* Symphonia
Berlioz, Hector: *Hungarian March:* Dutch Tuba Quartet

Berlioz, Hector: *March to the Scaffold:* British Tuba Quartet
Berlioz, Hector: *Rakoczy (Hungarian) March from "Damnation of Faust" (excerpt):* Jacobs, Arnold
Berlioz, Hector: *Roméo et Juliette (excerpt):* Jacobs, Arnold; Pokorny, Gene
Berlioz, Hector: *Symphonie fantastique (excerpt):* Pokorny, Gene
Bernard and Smith: *Winter Wonderland:* Pilafian, Sam
Bernie, Pinkard, and Casey: *Sweet Georgia Brown:* Bargeron, Dave; Colonial Tuba Quartet; Matteson, Rich; Palmer, Singleton; Perantoni, Daniel; Pilafian, Sam; Tennessee Technological University Tuba/Euphonium Ensemble
Bernstein, Leonard: *Suite from "West Side Story":* O'Bryant, Kelly
Bernstein, Leonard: *Waltz for Mippy III:* Deck, Warren; Watson, Scott
Berry, Chuck: *School Day:* Dixie Power Trio
Berry, Chuck: *Too Much Monkey Business:* Dixie Power Trio
Best, Denzil Decosta: *Move:* Atlantic Tuba Quartet; Barber, John William (Bill)
Betti, Dino: *Space Blossoms:* Schiaffini, Giancarlo
Beversdorf, Thomas: *Sonata for Bass Tuba and Piano:* Cummings, Barton; LeBlanc, Robert
Bewley, arr.: *Bring a Torch, Jeanette, Isabella:* Phillips, Harvey/TubaChristmas
Bewley, arr.: *Fum, Fum, Fum:* Phillips, Harvey/TubaChristmas
Bewley, arr.: *Good Christian Men Rejoice:* Phillips, Harvey/TubaChristmas
Bewley, arr.: *Pat-a-Pan:* Phillips, Harvey/TubaChristmas
Bewley, arr.: *TubaChristmas Suite:* Phillips, Harvey/TubaChristmas
Bewley, Norlan: *Octubafest Medley:* Phillips, Harvey
Bewley, Norlan: *Santa Wants a Tuba for Christmas:* Phillips, Harvey/TubaChristmas
Bewley, Norlan: *Tubafiesta Medley:* Phillips, Harvey
Bewley, Norlan: *Tubarock Medley:* Phillips, Harvey
Bewley, Norlan: *Tubaswing Medley:* Phillips, Harvey
Bigelow-Bates: *Sob Sister Sadie:* Tarto, Joe
Billy Mitchell: *Whirly Twirly:* Pilafian, Sam
Birchall, Steven: *Reciprocals II for Two Tubas:* Trice, Jerry
Bizet, Georges: *Extrait des pêcheurs de perles:* Labeyrie, Stéphane
Bizet, Georges: *Farandole from L'Arlesienne Suite No. 2:* Norris, Tim
BL Lacerta: *Estampie:* Gay, Les
BL Lacerta: *Flutes and Tuba:* Gay, Les
BL Lacerta: *High Energy:* Gay, Les
BL Lacerta: *Monkey Chant:* Gay, Les
BL Lacerta: *My Mother is Here:* Gay, Les
BL Lacerta: *Powerful:* Gay, Les
BL Lacerta: *Starts Same but Beautiful:* Gay, Les
BL Lacerta: *Stravinsky:* Gay, Les
BL Lacerta: *Third:* Gay, Les
Blades, Ruben: *Patria:* Pilafian, Sam
Blake and Sissle: *I'm Just Wild about Harry:* Newberger, Eli
Blake, Eubie: *Memories of You:* Pokorny, Gene
Bloch, Ernst: *The Jewish Life:* Funderburk, Jeff
Blue, Kelly: *And Then Again . . . :* Johnson, Howard
Blythe, Arthur: *Bush Baby:* Stewart, Bob
Blythe, Arthur: *Metamorphosis:* Stewart, Bob
Boccalari, E.: *Fantasia di Concerto:* Conner, Rex
Boccherini, Luigi: *Minuet:* Piernik, Zdizislaw
Bogar, Istvan: *Concerto for Tuba:* Bazsinka, József
Boismortier, Joseph Bodin: *Deuxième sonate, Op. XIV:* Labeyrie, Stéphane
Bologneisi, J.: *Maria Alm:* Steckar Tubapack
Bologneisi, J.: *Quand le Tuba valse a Paris:* Stecker, Marc
Bonfa, Luis: *Samba de Orfeu:* Corella, Gil
Bononcini, Giovanni: *Arietta (Non posso disperar):* Daellenbach, Charles
Boone, Daniel: *Three Moods:* Tennessee Tech Alumni Ensemble; University of Miami Tuba Ensemble
Borkowski, Marian: *VOX per uno stromento ad ottone:* Piernik, Zdizislaw
Botschinsky, Allan: *Alster Promenade:* Van Lier, Erik
Botschinsky, Allan: *Chops a la Salsa:* Van Lier, Erik
Botschinsky, Allan: *Don't Shoot the Banjo Player ('Cause We've Done It Already):* Van Lier, Erik
Botschinsky, Allan: *Interlude No. 4:* Van Lier, Erik
Botschinsky, Allan: *Kubismus 502:* Van Lier, Erik
Botschinsky, Allan: *The Lady in Blue:* Van Lier, Erik
Botschinsky, Allan: *Love Waltz:* Van Lier, Erik
Botschinsky, Allan: *October Sunshine:* Van Lier, Erik
Botschinsky, Allan: *Toot Your Roots:* Van Lier, Erik
Bourgeois, Louis: *Doxology:* Daellenbach, Charles
Bousted, Donald: *Tears:* Tubalaté
Boyadjian, Hayg: *Sareebar for Tuba and Percussion:* Pilafian, Sam
Boyd, Bill: *Canadian Brass Blues:* Daellenbach, Charles
Boyle, arr.: *Just a Closer Walk with Thee:* Callender, George Sylvester "Red"
Boyle, arr.: *Primrose Lane:* Callender, George Sylvester "Red"
Boyle, arr.: *When the Saints Go Marchin' In:* Callender, George Sylvester "Red"
Bozza, Eugène: *Allegro et Finale:* Georgie, Gerhard
Bozza, Eugène: *Concertino for Tuba and Piano:* Bazsinka, József; Seward, Steven
Bozza, Eugène: *New Orleans:* Bazsinka, József
Bozza, Eugène: *Sonatine:* Jacobs, Arnold
Braham and Furber: *Limehouse Blues:* (see Furber and Braham)
Braham-Furber: *Limehouse Blues:* (see Furber and Braham)
Brahms, Johannes: *Chorale Prelude, Op. 122, No. 8, "Es ist ein Ros' entsprungen":* Jacobs, Arnold

Brahms, Johannes: *Hungarian Dance:* Woods, Gavin
Brahms, Johannes: *Sunday:* Daellenbach, Charles
Brahms, Johannes: *Vier ernste Gesänge:* Brewer, Robert; Cooley, Floyd
Brahms, Johannes: *Wiegenlied:* Van Lier, Erik
Brand, Michael: *Tuba Tapestry for Tuba and Brass Band:* Anderson, Hans; Fletcher, John; Norris, Tim
Bratton, John: *Teddy Bears' Picnic:* Morgan, Kevin; Sibley, Graham
Brennard, George: *The Old Rugged Cross:* Arwood, Jeffrey
Broadbent, Alan: *Another Time:* Self, James
Brooks and Chaplin: *You Wonderful You:* M'N'M Trio
Brooks, George: *Send Me to the 'Lectric Chair:* M'N'M Trio
Brooks, Shelton: *Jazzbo Jenkins:* M'N'M Trio
Broughton, Bruce: *Sonata [Concerto] for Tuba and Piano:* Brown, Velvet; Funderburk, Jeff; Sinder, Philip
Brown: *The Blues Walk:* Gannett, Dave
Brown and Ayer: *Oh, You Beautiful Doll:* Gannett, Dave
Brown and Von Tilzer: *Dapper Dan:* Newberger, Eli
Brown, Clifford: *Daahoud:* Dutch Tuba Quartet
Brown, Clifford: *Sandu:* Modern Jazz Tuba Project; Tennessee Tech Alumni Ensemble
Brown, DeSylva, and Henderson: *Sonny Boy:* M'N'M Trio; Newberger, Eli
Brown, Nacio Herb: *Two Tunes (You Stepped Out of a Dream; Temptation):* Tennessee Technological University Tuba/Euphonium Ensemble
Brown, Sandy: *Tree Top Tall Papa:* Newberger, Eli
Brown, Tom: *Disgruntled Lullaby:* Self, James
Brown, Tom: *Kilo:* Self, James
Brown, Tom: *New Stuff:* Self, James
Brown, Tom: *Night Lights:* Self, James
Brown, Tom: *One for Nick:* Self, James
Brown, Velvet: *Negro Spirituals:* Brown, Velvet
Brown, Velvet: *Te Dago Mi:* Brown, Velvet
Brown/Homer/Green: *Sentimental Journey:* Tuba 4's
Brubeck, Dave: *Blue Rondo a la Turk:* Modern Jazz Tuba Project; Tennessee Technological University Tuba/Euphonium Ensemble
Brubeck, Dave: *It's a Raggy Waltz:* Erickson, Martin
Bruch, Max: *Kol Nidrei:* Funderburk, Jeff
Bruckner, Anton: *Locus Iste:* Dutch Tuba Quartet
Bruckner, Anton: *Symphony No. 4:* Jacobs, Arnold
Bruckner, Anton: *Symphony No. 7 in E major:* Pokorny, Gene
Bruckner, Anton: *Symphony No. 8:* Jacobs, Arnold
Brun and Gannon: *Under Paris Skies:* Pilafian, Sam
Brun, Albin: *Chlingen:* Unternährer, Marc
Brun, Albin: *Galtigen:* Unternährer, Marc
Brun, Albin: *Goldwang:* Unternährer, Marc
Brun, Albin: *Heitertannli:* Unternährer, Marc
Brun, Albin: *Heuschlag:* Unternährer, Marc
Brun, Albin: *Holzwangflue:* Unternährer, Marc
Brun, Albin: *Intro Heuschlag:* Unternährer, Marc
Brun, Albin: *Intro Tomlishorn:* Unternährer, Marc
Brun, Albin: *Laubrisleten:* Unternährer, Marc
Brun, Albin: *Lauelenegg:* Unternährer, Marc
Brun, Albin: *Ruessiflue:* Unternährer, Marc
Brun, Albin: *Schy:* Unternährer, Marc
Brun, Albin: *Starrenwang:* Unternährer, Marc
Brun, Albin: *Tomlishorn:* Unternährer, Marc
Brun, Albin: *Tumli:* Unternährer, Marc
Brun, Albin: *Widderfeld:* Unternährer, Marc
Brusick, William: *Concerto for Tuba and Wind Orchestra:* Northcut, Timothy
Brusick, William: *For the Kings of Brass:* Tennessee Tech Alumni Ensemble
Bryan-Mayer: *Row, Row, Rosie:* Tarto, Joe
Bukvich, Daniel: *Meditations on the Writings of Vasily Kandinsky:* Funderburk, Jeff
Bull, John: *The King's Hunt:* British Tuba Quartet
Bulla, Stephen: *Bluzenfunky:* Erickson, Martin
Bulla, Stephen: *Celestial Suite:* British Tuba Quartet
Bulla, Stephen: *Clearfield Driving:* Erickson, Martin
Bulla, Stephen: *Quartet for Low Brass:* British Tuba Quartet; United States Navy Band Tuba-Euphonium Quartet
Burke: *My Very Good Friend, the Milkman:* Erickson, Martin
Burke and Johnston: *Pennies from Heaven:* Gannett, Dave
Burke and Van Heusen: *Here's That Rainy Day:* Gannett, Dave
Burke and Van Heusen: *It Could Happen to You:* Felt, Brad
Burris and Smith: *Ballin' the Jack:* Palmer, Singleton; Phillips, Harvey
Burwell, C.: *Sweet Lorraine:* Dixie Power Trio
Butler: *The Sun Has Got His Hat On:* Crowther, Shaun
Buttery, Gary: *An English Folk Christmas:* United States Coast Guard Tuba-Euphonium Quartet
Buttery, Gary: *Fanfare for the Millennium:* Alchemy
Buttery, Gary: *Fantasia of Eastern European Village Dances:* Alchemy
Buttery, Gary: *Xmas Tuba of the British Isles:* Alchemy
Butts, Carrol: *Ode to Low Brass:* Megules, Karl
Butts, Carrol: *Suite for Tuba and Piano:* Cummings, Barton
Buxtehude, Dietrich: *Fanfare:* Jacobs, Arnold
Byrd, Roeland: *Baby Let Me Hold Your Hand:* Dixie Power Trio
Byrd, Roy: *Mardi Gras in New Orleans:* Dixie Power Trio
Byrd, William: *Agnus Dei:* University of Michigan Tuba and Euphonium Ensemble
Byrd, William: *Jhon Come Kisse Me Now:* Atlantic Tuba Quartet; British Tuba Quartet
Byrne, Eno: *Once in a Lifetime:* Dixie Power Trio

Christiansen, Henning: *MaskemÅned for Trumpet and Tuba, Op. 148:* Anderson, Hans
Cimarosa, D.: *The Impresario:* Swiss Tuba Quartet
Clare Fischer: *Pensativa:* Self, James
Clark, M.: *Tyrolean Tuba:* Stern, Mary
Clarke, Herbert L.: *Bride of the Waves:* Frazier, Richard
Clarke, Herbert L.: *Carnival of Venice:* Jacobs, Arnold; Woods, Gavin
Clarke, Herbert L.: *Cousins:* Contraband (The)
Clarke, Herbert L.: *From the Shores of the Mighty Pacific:* Hanks, Thompson (Toby); Woods, Gavin
Clarke, Herbert L.: *Stars in a Velvety Sky:* Brown, Velvet
Clash (The): *Brand New Cadillac:* Tooba Blooze
Clinard, Fred Jr.: *Diversion for 7 Bass Clef Instruments:* Tennessee Tech Alumni Ensemble
Coeuriot, M.: *Tuba Space:* Stecker, Marc
Cohan: *Banjos and Tubas Forever:* Corella, Gil
Cohan, George M.: *Give My Regards to Broadway:* Daellenbach, Charles
Colding-Jargensen, Henrik: *Boast:* Bazsinka, József
Cole/Mills: *Straighten Up and Fly Right:* Tuba 4's
Coleman, Cy, and Hershey Kay: *Come Follow the Band:* Stevens, John
Coleman, Ornette: *Blues Connotation:* Pilafian, Sam
Coleman, Ornette: *Law Years:* Stewart, Bob
Collette, Buddy: *Nice Day:* Callender, George Sylvester "Red"
Collins: *You'll Be in My Heart:* Tuba 4's
Collins, Judy: *Since You've Asked:* Atlantic Tuba Quartet; Dites-Le-Moi Tuba
Coltrane, John: *Giant Steps:* Bargeron, Dave
Condon, Leslie: *Celestial Morn:* Hornsberger, Albert
Condon, Leslie: *Radiant Pathway:* Stokes, David, and Graham Patterson
Connelly, Reg: *Show Me the Way to Go Home:* Murrow, Richard
Conor, Thomas: *I Saw Mommy Kissing Santa Claus:* Pilafian, Sam
Constantinides, Dinos: *Mutability Fantasy:* Skillen, Joseph
Copeland, Ray: *Classical Jazz Suite:* Morris, Jim
Copland, Aaron: *Three Old American Songs:* O'Bryant, Kelly
Corea, Chick: *La Fiesta:* Tennessee Technological University Tuba/Euphonium Ensemble
Corea, Chick: *Spain:* Tennessee Technological University Tuba/Euphonium Ensemble; Tennessee Technological University Tuba/Euphonium Ensemble
Corelli, Archangelo: *Gigue:* Phillips, Harvey
Corwell, Neal: *Aboriginal Voices:* Brown, Velvet; Nelson, Mark
Corwell, Neal: *The Furies:* Brown, Velvet; Symphonia
Corwell, Neal: *New England Reveries:* Nelson, Mark; Woods, Gavin
Corwell, Neal: *Ritual:* Brown, Velvet
Corwell, Neal: *2 AM:* Brown, Velvet
Corwell, Neal: *The Wasteland:* Perantoni, Daniel
Cosma, Vladimir: *Giocoso from "Euphonium Concerto":* Tennessee Technological University Tuba/Euphonium Ensemble
Couperin, F.: *Les Baricades Misteriueses:* Gerhard Meinl's Tuba Sextet
Creamer: *After You've Gone:* Pilafian, Sam
Crespo, Enrique: *Bruckner Etude:* Gerhard Meinl's Tuba Sextet
Crespo, Enrique: *Escenas Latinas:* Hilgers, Walter
Crespo, Enrique: *Three Milongas:* Gerhard Meinl's Tuba Sextet
Creuze, Roland: *D'un Souffle de Lumiere:* Lienard, Bernard
Creuze, Roland: *Eria:* Legris, Philippe
Crockett, Edgar: *Mustique:* Sheridan, Patrick
Croft: *Duet for Tenor Tuba and Bass Tuba:* Megules, Karl
Crozier, Daniel: *Fantasy for Tuba and Piano:* Perantoni, Daniel
Crump, Peter: *The March of the Hare:* Tubalaté
Cugny, Laurent: *Molloy:* Steckar Elephant Tuba Horde
Cui, Cesar: *Perpetual Motion:* Bobo, Roger
Cummings, Barton: *Fantasia Breve:* Jae Young, Heo; Nelson, Mark
Cummings, Barton: *In Darkness Dreaming:* Colonial Tuba Quartet
Curnow, James: *Concertino:* Cummings, Barton; McAdams, Charles; Perantoni, Daniel
Curtis, Eduardo de: *Torna a Surriento:* Feldman, Enrique "Hank" C.
Danielssohn, Christer: *Capriccio Da Camera for Solo Tuba and Brass Quintet:* Hilgers, Walter; Jae Young, Heo; Lind, Michael; Schumacker, Finn
Danielssohn, Christer: *Concertante Suite for Tuba and Four Horns:* Hilgers, Walter; Hötzel, Markus; Lind, Michael
Dankwart Schmidt, arr.: *Tuba Muckl:* Contraband (The)
Danner, Greg: *Concerto for Tuba and Band:* Northcut, Timothy
Danner, Greg: *Scherzo:* Tennessee Technological University Tuba/Euphonium Ensemble
Danner, Gregory: *Beast!:* Tennessee Technological University Tuba/Euphonium Ensemble
Danser, Jahn: *Suite:* Morris, Jim
Dara, Olu: *Bell and Ponce:* Stewart, Bob
Daugherty, Michael: *Timbuktuba:* Symphonia
Davidson, Matthew: *Move:* Tubalaté
Davis: *Jenny Wren:* Sheridan, Patrick
Davis, Akst: *Baby Face:* University of Miami Tuba Ensemble
Davis, Jimmie: *You Are My Sunshine:* Pilafian, Sam
Davis, Katherine: *Little Drummer Boy:* Pilafian, Sam
Davis, Miles: *All Blues:* Scandinavian Tuba Jazz; Self, James

Davis, Miles: *Blue in Green:* Frey, Michael
Davis, Miles: *Dig:* Pilafian, Sam
Davis, Miles: *Donna Lee:* Bargeron, Dave
Davis, Miles: *Four:* Johnson, Howard
Davis, Miles: *So What:* Murrow, Richard; Tennessee Technological University Tuba/Euphonium Ensemble
Davis, Miles: *Walkin':* Tennessee Technological University Tuba/Euphonium Ensemble
De Rose and Hill: *So Little Time:* M'N'M Trio
De-Lange: *Darn That Dream:* Callender, George Sylvester "Red"
Debussy, Claude: *General Levine—Eccentric:* Pokorny, Gene
Debussy, Claude: *Golliwogg's Cakewalk:* Dutch Tuba Quartet
Debussy, Claude: *La Fille aux Cheveux de lin:* Rustic Bari-Tuba Ensemble
Debussy, Claude: *Prélude à "L'Après-midi d'un Faune":* Pokorny, Gene
Debussy, Claude: *Syrinx:* Self, James; Sykes, Steve
Dechter, Brad: *The Underdog Has Arisen:* Self, James
DeCosta and LaRocca: *Tiger Rag:* Corella, Gil; Dutch Tuba Quartet; Lehr, David "Red"; Palmer, Singleton; Pilafian, Sam; Sheridan, Patrick
Dedrick, Art: *A Touch of Tuba:* Popiel, Peter
Defaye, Jean-Michel: *Suite Marine:* Randolph, David
Delanoff, Robert: *Wos hot er g'sogt?:* Walsh, Thomas
Delgado, Márlo: *Pascoal Joins the Dark Force:* Carolino, Sérgio
Delibes, Léo: *Flower Duet from "Lakmé":* British Tuba Quartet
Dempsey, arr.: *Quatro Chansons:* Monarch Tuba-Euphonium Quartet
Dempsey, arr.: *Three Movements from "Quatre Chansons":* British Tuba Quartet
Dempsey, Raymond: *Now Hear This:* British Tuba Quartet; Monarch Tuba-Euphonium Quartet
Dempsey, Raymond: *Quatre Chansons:* Melton Tuba-Quartett
Dennis, Matt, and Earl Brent: *Angel Eyes:* Draper, Ray
Denson, Frank: *Three Folksongs for Four Brass:* Gerhard Meinl's Tuba Sextet
Denza, Luigi: *Funiculì Funiculà:* Morgan, Kevin
D'enza, Luigi: *Funiculi-Funicula Fantasy:* Rustic Bari-Tuba Ensemble
DeRose, Peter: *Deep Purple:* Pilafian, Sam
Desenclos, Alfred: *Suite Brève:* Bazsinka, József
DeSilva, Jolson, Meyer: *Yo, California:* Self, James
Desmond, Paul: *Take Five:* Melton Tuba-Quartett
Di Lasso, Orlando: *Mon Coeur se Recommende a Vous:* British Tuba Quartet
Di Lasso, Orlando: *Ola, O che bon eccho:* Gerhard Meinl's Tuba Sextet
Diero: *Il Ritorno:* British Tuba Quartet
Dietz and Schwartz: *Sweet Music:* Newberger, Eli
DiGiovanni, Rocco: *Tuba Magic:* Tennessee Technological University Tuba/Euphonium Ensemble; United States Armed Forces Tuba-Euphonium Ensemble and Massed Ensemble
Dinicu, Grigoras: *Hora Staccato:* Sheridan, Patrick
Dobrowski, A.: *Muzyka for Tuba Solo:* Piernik, Zdizislaw
Dodson, John: *Out of the Depths:* Tennessee Technological University Tuba/Euphonium Ensemble
Donaldson: *My Best Girl:* Tarto, Joe
Donaldson, W.: *Carolina in the Morning:* University of Miami Tuba Ensemble
Donaldson, Walter, and Gus Kahn: *Makin' Whoopee:* Pilafian, Sam
Donizetti, Gaetano: *Drinking Song from "Lucrezia Borgia":* Daellenbach, Charles
Donizetti, Gaetano: *Una Furtiva Lagrima:* Sykes, Steve
Doughty, G.: *Variations on "Grandfather's Clock":* Sheridan, Patrick; Woods, Gavin
Downey, John: *Tabu for Tuba:* Phillips, Harvey
Draper, Ray: *Clifford's Kappa:* Draper, Ray
Draper, Ray: *Empty Streets:* Draper, Ray
Draper, Ray: *Essii's Dance:* Draper, Ray
Draper, Ray: *Filidia:* Draper, Ray
Draper, Ray: *Happiness:* Draper, Ray
Draper, Ray: *I Hadn't Anyone Til You:* Draper, Ray
Draper, Ray: *Mess Around:* Draper, Ray
Draper, Ray: *Minor Dream:* Draper, Ray
Draper, Ray: *Paul's Pal:* Draper, Ray
Draper, Ray: *Two Sons:* Draper, Ray
Draper, Ray: *Under Paris Skies:* Draper, Ray
Draper, Ray, and Richard Aplan: *Let My People Go:* Draper, Ray
Drigo, Richard: *Valse Bluette:* Sheridan, Patrick
Drums and Tuba: *Adventures of Poo-Poo and Pee-Pee:* Drums and Tuba
Drums and Tuba: *Bertone:* Drums and Tuba
Drums and Tuba: *Blazevitch:* Drums and Tuba
Drums and Tuba: *Brief Case:* Drums and Tuba
Drums and Tuba: *The Butcher:* Drums and Tuba
Drums and Tuba: *Carlos the Cat:* Drums and Tuba
Drums and Tuba: *Carrots:* Drums and Tuba
Drums and Tuba: *Chapeau Russia:* Drums and Tuba
Drums and Tuba: *Chummus, A Challa, and a Whole Lot of Chutzpah:* Drums and Tuba
Drums and Tuba: *Close Case:* Drums and Tuba
Drums and Tuba: *Curtains:* Drums and Tuba
Drums and Tuba: *The Diagram:* Drums and Tuba
Drums and Tuba: *Does It Suck to Be You:* Drums and Tuba
Drums and Tuba: *The Donkey and the Walrus:* Drums and Tuba
Drums and Tuba: *Eli:* Drums and Tuba
Drums and Tuba: *Fits of Spaghetti:* Drums and Tuba
Drums and Tuba: *5.24.94:* Drums and Tuba
Drums and Tuba: *The Flying Ballerina:* Drums and Tuba
Drums and Tuba: *Gimpel the Fool:* Drums and Tuba

Drums and Tuba: *The Horse and the Tree:* Drums and Tuba
Drums and Tuba: *In Case:* Drums and Tuba
Drums and Tuba: *The Inspector:* Drums and Tuba
Drums and Tuba: *The Inspector Returns:* Drums and Tuba
Drums and Tuba: *Kermit:* Drums and Tuba
Drums and Tuba: *Kuc to Luc:* Drums and Tuba
Drums and Tuba: *Loteria:* Drums and Tuba
Drums and Tuba: *Lots of Luc:* Drums and Tuba
Drums and Tuba: *Meat:* Drums and Tuba
Drums and Tuba: *Meter Maid:* Drums and Tuba
Drums and Tuba: *Neal Hamburger:* Drums and Tuba
Drums and Tuba: *No Accommodation for Buffalo:* Drums and Tuba
Drums and Tuba: *No Good with Words:* Drums and Tuba
Drums and Tuba: *Open Case:* Drums and Tuba
Drums and Tuba: *Out of Case:* Drums and Tuba
Drums and Tuba: *Pete's Dance:* Drums and Tuba
Drums and Tuba: *Pig Ears for Lily:* Drums and Tuba
Drums and Tuba: *Prince Meets the Phantom:* Drums and Tuba
Drums and Tuba: *Royronus:* Drums and Tuba
Drums and Tuba: *The Sauce Maker:* Drums and Tuba
Drums and Tuba: *The 10 Attacks of Dagger:* Drums and Tuba
Drums and Tuba: *Territory:* Drums and Tuba
Drums and Tuba: *There Is a Monster:* Drums and Tuba
Drums and Tuba: *Topolino:* Drums and Tuba
Drums and Tuba: *Tuba Song:* Drums and Tuba
Dubin and Russell: *Half-Way to Heaven:* M'N'M Trio
Dubin and Warren: *42nd Street Selections:* British Tuba Quartet
Dubrovay, Laszlo: *Solo No. 3 for Tuba:* Bazsinka, József
Dukas, Paul: *Villanelle for Horn:* Seward, Steven
Dumitru, Ionel: *Fantezie Pentru Tuba si Pian:* Dumitru, Ionel
Dumitru, Ionel: *Romanian Dance No. 2:* Bobo, Roger; Funderburk, Jeff; United States Army Band "Pershing's Own"
Dural, Stanley: *Zydeco Boogaloo:* Dixie Power Trio
Duruflé, Maurice: *Ubi Caritas—Dance:* Symphonia
Dvorák, Antonin: *Humoresque:* Piernik, Zdizislaw
Dvorák, Antonin: *Slavonic Dance, Op. 46, No. 1:* Tennessee Technological University Tuba/Euphonium Ensemble
Ecclés, Henry: *Adagio:* Megules, Karl
Ecclés, Henry: *Sonata in G minor (I. Prelude; II. Courant):* Piernik, Zdizislaw
Ecclés, Henry: *Sonate:* Funderburk, Jeff; Lienard, Bernard
Edgar, M.: *Three Ha'Pence a Foot:* Tubalaté
Edward, Gregson: *Tuba Concerto:* Fletcher, John
Eldsvoog, John: *Walt's Samba:* Self, James
Elfman, Danny: *Beetlejuice [motion picture soundtrack]:* Johnson, John Thomas (Tommy)
Elfman, Danny: *Edward Scissorhands[motion picture soundtrack]:* Johnson, John Thomas (Tommy); Pearson, Norm
Elfman, Danny: *Planet of the Apes[motion picture soundtrack]:* Johnson, John Thomas (Tommy)
Elfman, Danny: *Spiderman [motion picture soundtrack]:* Johnson, John Thomas (Tommy)
Elfman, Danny: *Spiderman 2 [motion picture soundtrack]:* Johnson, John Thomas (Tommy)
Elgar, Edward: *Chanson de Matin, Op. 15, No. 2:* Fletcher, John; Thornton, Michael
Elgar, Edward: *La Capricieuse, Op.17:* Sheridan, Patrick
Elgar, Edward: *Romance:* Dowling, Eugene
Elgar, Edward: *Salut D'Amour, Op.12:* Sheridan, Patrick
Ellerby, Martin: *Epitaph V:* Gourlay, James
Ellerby, Martin: *Tuba Concerto:* Gourlay, James; Harrild, Patrick; Sheridan, Patrick; Sykes, Stephen
Ellington, Edward Kennedy "Duke": *Day Dream:* Johnson, Howard
Ellington, Edward Kennedy "Duke": *Do Nothing 'Til You Hear from Me:* Gannett, Dave
Ellington, Edward Kennedy "Duke": *Don't Get Around Much Anymore:* Pilafian, Sam
Ellington, Edward Kennedy "Duke": *East St. Louis Toodle-Oo:* Pilafian, Sam
Ellington, Edward Kennedy "Duke": *I Let the Song Go Out of My Heart:* Erickson, Martin; Mazura, János
Ellington, Edward Kennedy "Duke": *In a Mellow Tone:* Gannett, Dave; Matteson-Phillips TubaJazz Consort; Self, James; Tennessee Tech Alumni Ensemble
Ellington, Edward Kennedy "Duke": *In a Sentimental Mood:* Callender, George Sylvester "Red"; Feldman, Enrique "Hank" C.
Ellington, Edward Kennedy "Duke": *It Don't Mean a Thing:* Woods, Gavin
Ellington, Edward Kennedy "Duke": *Just Squeeze Me:* Dixie Power Trio; Erickson, Martin
Ellington, Edward Kennedy "Duke": *The Mooche:* Pilafian, Sam
Ellington, Edward Kennedy "Duke": *Mood Indigo:* Gannett, Dave; Mighty Tubadours; Pilafian, Sam; Tuba 4's
Ellington, Edward Kennedy "Duke": *Satin Doll:* Mazura, János; Mighty Tubadours; Tuba 4's
Ellington, Edward Kennedy "Duke": *Sophisticated Lady:* Callender, George Sylvester "Red"
Ellington, Edward Kennedy "Duke": *Things Ain't What They Used to Be:* Matteson-Phillips Tuba-Jazz Consort
Ellington, Edward Kennedy "Duke": *Tribute to Duke Ellington:* Tennessee Technological University Tuba/Euphonium Ensemble
Elliott, Jack: *Kermit the Frog Presents the Muppet Musicians of Bremen [TV soundtrack]:* Johnson, John Thomas (Tommy)

Emler, Andy: *Gicael Mibbs:* Steckar Elephant Tuba Horde
Emler, Andy: *Improvisation for Tuba and Piano:* Thuillier, Francois
Emler, Andy: *Tubastone No. 1, for Tuba and Piano:* Bazsinka, József; Labeyrie, Stéphane; Thuillier, Francois
End, Jack: *Three Salutations:* Hanks, Thompson (Toby)
English Ballad: *Riddle Song:* Daellenbach, Charles
English Folksong: *Hey, Ho! Nobody Home:* Daellenbach, Charles
Ernesto and Battista: *Come Back to Sorrento:* Gannett, Dave
Escovez, Fermin Ruiz: *Dualismo for Tuba and Flute:* Mas, Vicente Navarro
Eskelin, Ellery: *Figure of Speech:* Eskelin, Ellory
Eskelin, Ellery: *It Doesn't Wait:* Eskelin, Ellory
Eskelin, Ellery: *#107:* Eskelin, Ellory
Eskelin, Ellery: *Short Story:* Eskelin, Ellory
Eskelin, Ellery: *Whispered:* Eskelin, Ellory
Esleck, David L.: *I-95:* Modern Jazz Tuba Project
Etzel, Bernhard: *Divertimento bassobavarese for Solo Tuba:* Walsh, Thomas
Etzel, Bernhard: *Fünf Miniaturen für Solotuba:* Walsh, Thomas
Europe, Sissle, and Blake: *Goodnight, Angeline:* Newberger, Eli
Evans, Gil: *Svengali's Summer/Waltz:* Johnson, Howard
Evans, Ray: *Mona Lisa:* Corella, Gil
Ewazen, Eric: *Concerto for Tuba:* Skillen, Joseph
Ewazen, Eric: *Sonata:* Brown, Velvet; Funderburk, Jeff
Farkas, Antal: *Tuba Variations:* Szabo, Laszlo
Fauré, Gabriel: *Après un Rêve:* Funderburk, Jeff; King, Ian; Sheridan, Patrick; Szentpáli, Roland
Fauré, Gabriel: *Pavane Op. 50:* Hilgers, Walter; Tennessee Technological University Tuba/ Euphonium Ensemble
Fauré, Gabriel: *The Secret:* Daellenbach, Charles
Fauré, Gabriel: *Sicilienne:* Funderburk, Jeff; King, Ian
Fay, Tom: *Some Music:* Hanks, Thompson (Toby)
Felciano, Richard: *"and from the abyss" for tuba and tape:* Cooley, Floyd
Feldman, Hank: *Freedom:* Symphonia
Feldman, Hank C.: *Images:* Feldman, Enrique "Hank" C.
Feldman, Hank C.: *Suenos Negros:* Feldman, Enrique "Hank" C.
Feldman, Morton: *Chorus and Instruments (II):* Phillips, Harvey
Feldman, Morton: *Durations 3 for Violin, Tuba and Piano:* Butterfield, Don; Vogt, Michael
Felt, Brad: *Blues to Nasir:* Felt, Brad
Felt, Brad: *Carol's Theme:* Felt, Brad
Felt, Brad: *Don't Hold On:* Felt, Brad
Felt, Brad: *"P.J. Lids":* Felt, Brad
Felt, Brad: *Portrait of Teresa:* Felt, Brad
Fenton, George: *Multiplicity [motion picture soundtrack]:* Self, James
Ferreira and Einhorn: *Batida Diferente:* Megules, Karl
Fields and McHugh: *I Can't Give You Anything but Love:* Lehr, David "Red"
Fields and McHugh: (see McHugh, J., and D. Fields)
Fillmore, Henry: *Lassas Trombone:* Palmer, Singleton
Fisher, F.: *Chicago:* Palmer, Singleton
Fisher, Fred: *My Flying Machine:* Self, James
Fisher, Goodwin, and Shay: *When You're Smiling:* Pilafian, Sam
Fishkind, Larry: *Four Miniatures:* European Tuba Quartet
Fishkind, Larry: *Reed Hornets:* European Tuba Quartet
Fishkind, Larry: *Trash Dance:* European Tuba Quartet
Foley, Red: *Just a Closer Walk with Thee:* Daellenbach, Charles
Forbes, Mike: *Auburn Is the Colour:* Sotto Voce
Forbes, Mike: *Consequences, for Tuba Quartet:* Sotto Voce
Forde, Jan Magne: *Folkevise:* Nickel, Hans
Forsyth, Kieran: *Westminster Intrada:* British Tuba Quartet
Forte, Aldo Rafael: *Seguidillas/Adagio and Rondo:* Symphonia
Forte, Aldo Rafael: *Tubas Latinas:* Tennessee Technological University Tuba/Euphonium Ensemble
Fosset, Marc: *3a 5:* Steckar Tubapack
Foster, Frank: *Shiny Stockings:* Tennessee Technological University Tuba/Euphonium Ensemble
Foster, Stephen: *Beautiful Dreamer:* Self, James
Foster, Stephen: *Camptown Races:* Self, James
Foster, Stephen: *Jeannie with the Light Brown Hair:* Sheridan, Patrick
Foster, Stephen: *Old Homes:* Self, James
Foster, Stephen: *Swannee River:* Matteson, Rich
Foust, Alan: *1 x 1 x 5:* Morris, Jim
Frackenpohl, Arthur: *Concertino for Tuba and Strings:* Irmer, Benjamin
Frackenpohl, Arthur: *Pop Suite:* British Tuba Quartet; Dites-Le-Moi Tuba; Dutch Tuba Quartet; Megules, Karl; Rustic Bari-Tuba Ensemble; Tubalaté; University of Miami Tuba Ensemble
Frackenpohl, Arthur: *Ragtime:* Melton Tuba-Quartett
Frackenpohl, Arthur: *Refrain from "Pop Suite":* Miraphone Tuba Quartet
Frackenpohl, Arthur: *Song and Dance for Euphonium, Tuba and Band:* Porter, David
Frackenpohl, Arthur: *Suite for Tuba Quartet:* Colonial Tuba Quartet
Frackenpohl, Arthur: *Variations for Tuba and Winds (Cobbler's Bench):* Davis, Ronald; Popiel, Peter
Francaix, Jean: *Petit valse europeenne pour tuba et double quintette a vents:* Schneider, Christoph

Frank, Marcel G.: *Lyric Poem for Five Tubas:* United States Armed Forces Tuba-Euphonium Ensemble and Massed Ensemble; University of Miami Tuba Ensemble
Frazão, Alexandre: *Inercia:* Carolino, Sérgio
Frazão, Alexandre: *Pipa Baquigrafo:* Carolino, Sérgio
Fredrickson, Thomas: *Tubalied:* Perantoni, Daniel
Freese, Stanford: *Play That Country Tuba, Cowboy:* Freese, Stanford
Frith, John: *Fireworks:* British Tuba Quartet
Fritz, József Róbert: *Blues for Louie:* Mazura, János
Fritze, Gregory: *Basso Continuo:* Fritze, Gregory
Fritze, Gregory: *Prelude and Dance:* Colonial Tuba Quartet; Swiss Tuba Quartet
Fucik, Julius: *Einzug Der Gladiatoren:* Miraphone Tuba Quartet
Fucik, Julius: *Florentiner Marsch:* Miraphone Tuba Quartet
Fucik, Julius: *Unter Der Admiralsflagge:* Miraphone Tuba Quartet
Furber and Braham: *Limehouse Blues:* Dixie Power Trio; Matteson, Rich; Pilafian, Sam
Gaathaug, Morten: *Sonata Concertante for Solo Tuba and Brass Quintet:* Baadsvik, Øystein
Gabrieli, Dominico: *Ricercar:* Davis, Ronald
Gabrieli, Giovanni: *Canzona, La Spiritata:* British Tuba Quartet
Gabrieli, Giovanni: *Canzon per Sonare No. 2:* Jacobs, Arnold
Gabrieli, Giovanni: *Canzona per Sonare No. 4:* Dutch Tuba Quartet; Gerhard Meinl's Tuba Sextet; Melton Tuba-Quartett
Gaines and Quezerque: *Big Chief:* Dixie Power Trio
Gale, Jack: *Jazz Suite:* Dites-Le-Moi Tuba
Gale, Jack: *Mellon Dance:* Dites-Le-Moi Tuba
Gale, Jack: *A Picture of Dorian Blue:* Morris, Jim; Self, James
Galliano, R.: *French Tuba in Los Angeles:* Stecker, Marc
Galliano, R.: *Tubabando:* Stecker, Marc
Galliard, Johann Ernst: *Allegro from Sonata No. 3 in F major:* Arwood, Jeffrey
Galliard, Johann Ernst: *Sonata No. 5 in D minor:* Bobo, Roger
Garbáge, Pierre (a.k.a. Garrett, James): *Bullfrog Rag:* Tennessee Tech Alumni Ensemble
Garbáge, Pierre (a.k.a. Garrett, James): *Chaser #1:* Tennessee Tech Alumni Ensemble
Garbáge, Pierre (a.k.a. Garrett, James): *Gay 50s Medley:* Tennessee Tech Alumni Ensemble
Garbáge, Pierre (a.k.a. Garrett, James): *A Pierre Soliloquy—Ode to Pierre:* Tennessee Tech Alumni Ensemble
Garbáge, Pierre (a.k.a. Garrett, James): *Pop-Rock Medley:* Tennessee Tech Alumni Ensemble
Garbáge, Pierre (a.k.a. Garrett, James): *Songs in the Fight Against Rum:* Tennessee Tech Alumni Ensemble
Garbáge, Pierre (a.k.a. Garrett, James): *Sousa Surrenders:* Tennessee Tech Alumni Ensemble; United States Armed Forces Tuba-Euphonium Ensemble and Massed Ensemble
Garner, Erroll: *Misty:* Morgan, Kevin
Garrett, arr.: *Chimes Blues:* Tennessee Technological University Tuba/Euphonium Ensemble
Garrett, arr.: *Just a Closer Walk with Thee:* Tennessee Technological University Tuba/Euphonium Ensemble
Garrett, arr.: *Won't You Come Home Bill Bailey:* Tennessee Technological University Tuba/Euphonium Ensemble
Garrett, James: *Miniature Jazz Suite:* Tennessee Technological University Tuba/Euphonium Ensemble
Garrett, James: *Mystical Music:* Tennessee Tech Alumni Ensemble
Garrett, James: *A Tubalee Jubalee:* Tennessee Technological University Tuba/Euphonium Ensemble; United States Armed Forces Tuba-Euphonium Ensemble
Garrett, James: *Wabash Canon Ball:* Tennessee Tech Alumni Ensemble
Gaskill and McHugh: *I Can't Believe That You're in Love with Me:* Palmer, Singleton
Gasner, Moshe: *Science Fiction:* Hershko, Shmuel "Adi"
Gasparini, Quirino: *Adoramus te Christe:* Sotto Voce; Tubalaté
Gates, Crawford: *Tuba Quartet, Op. 59:* Tennessee Technological University Tuba/Euphonium Ensemble
Gautier, L.: *Le Secret:* Alchemy
Genzmer, Harald: *Sonata for Bass Tuba and Piano:* Triendl, Oliver
George, Thom Ritter: *Sonata for Tuba and Piano:* Brewer, Robert; Perantoni, Daniel; Randolph, David
George, Thom Ritter: *Tubamobile:* Symphonia
George, Thom Ritter: *Tubasonatina:* Tennessee Technological University Tuba/Euphonium Ensemble
Gershwin, George: *An American in Paris (excerpt):* Pokorny, Gene
Gershwin, George: *The Buzzard Song:* Barber, John William (Bill)
Gershwin, George: *Fascinatin' Gershwin:* British Tuba Quartet
Gershwin, George: *Foggy Day:* Callender, George Sylvester "Red"
Gershwin, George: *Gershwin Medley:* Tennessee Technological University Tuba/Euphonium Ensemble; United States Armed Forces Tuba-Euphonium Ensemble
Gershwin, George: *I Got Rhythm:* Woods, Gavin
Gershwin, George: *I Loves You Porgy/Bess You Is My Woman:* Self, James
Gershwin, George: *Impromptu in 2 Keys:* Contraband Tuba Quartet
Gershwin, George: *The Man I Love:* Woods, Gavin
Gershwin, George: *A Portrait:* Dites-Le-Moi Tuba

Gershwin, George: *Prelude in C# minor:* Newberger, Eli
Gershwin, George: *Someone to Watch over Me:* Pilafian, Sam
Gershwin, George: *Summertime:* Matteson-Phillips TubaJazz Consort
Gershwin, George: *Three Preludes:* Contraband Tuba Quartet
Gershwin, George: *They Can't Take That Away from Me:* Callender, George Sylvester "Red"
Gershwin, George and Ira: *But Not for Me:* Johnson, Howard
Giampieri: *Carnival of Venice:* Morgan, Kevin
Gibbons, Orlando: *Tuba Voluntary:* Alchemy
Gilbert and Ory: *Muskrat Ramble:* Palmer, Singleton
Gilkyson, Terry: *The Bare Necessities:* Morgan, Kevin
Gillespie: *Santa Claus Is Coming to Town:* Mighty Tubadours; Pilafian, Sam
Gillespie, Dizzy: *Birks Werks:* Feldman, Enrique "Hank" C.
Gillespie, Dizzy: *Manteca:* Tennessee Tech Alumni Ensemble
Gillespie, Dizzy: *Night in Tunisia:* Feldman, Enrique "Hank" C.
Gillingham, David: *Diversive Elements for Euphonium, Tuba and Piano:* Zerkel, David
Gillingham, David: *Divertmento for Horn, Tuba and Piano:* Sinder, Philip
Gillis, Lew: *Four Keen Guys:* Dutch Tuba Quartet
Giordani, Giuseppi: *Love Song (Caro mio ben):* Daellenbach, Charles
Glandien, Lutz: *Aus Vertreutem ein Ganzes:* Vogt, Michael
Glass, Jennifer: *Sonatine for Basstuba and Piano:* Fletcher, John
Gliere, Reinhold: *Andante from Concerto for Coloratura:* Northcut, Timothy
Glinka, Michael: *Overture to Russlan and Ludmila:* British Tuba Quartet; Miraphone Tuba Quartet
Gluck, Christopf: *Dance of the Blessed Spirits:* Sheridan, Patrick; Woods, Gavin
Godard: *Et Le Kloxon Retentit Derchef Comme un Lezard Hongroise Eurhume:* Steckar Tubapack
Godard, Benjamin: *Berceuse De Jocelyn:* Sykes, Steve
Godard, Michel: *Bass Bees:* Bargeron, Dave
Godard, Michel: *The Night Is Still Young:* Bargeron, Dave
Godard, Michel: *Puligny Montrachet:* Bargeron, Dave
Goedicke: *Concert Etude:* Sheridan, Patrick
Goldsmith, Jerry: *Capricorn One [motion picture soundtrack]:* Johnson, John Thomas (Tommy)
Goldsmith, Jerry: *Star Trek—The Motion Picture [motion picture soundtrack]:* Johnson, John Thomas (Tommy)
Golland, John: *Scherzo:* Sykes, Stephen
Golson, Benny: *Whisper Not:* Felt, Brad
Gomez, Alice: *Bonampak:* Brown, Velvet
Gordon/Warren/Wolpe: *Chattanooga Choo Choo:* Tuba 4's
Goret, Didier: *Detournement Mineur:* Steckar Elephant Tuba Horde
Gottler-Mitchell-Conrad: *Hittin' the Ceiling:* Tarto, Joe
Gottschalk, Arthur: *Substructures for Ten Tubas:* University of Michigan Tuba Ensemble
Gould, Morton: *Pavanne from the "Latin America Suite":* University of Miami Tuba Ensemble
Gould, Morton: *Tuba Suite for Tuba and Three Horns:* Hötzel, Markus; Phillips, Harvey
Gounod, Charles: *Ave Maria:* Pilafian, Sam
Gounod, Charles: *Funeral March for a Marionette:* Mighty Tubadours
Gourlay, James: *The Eagle Thunders:* Swiss Tuba Quartet
Graham and Williams: *I Ain't Got Nobody:* Newberger, Eli
Grainger and Robbins: *Tain't Nobody's Bizness If I Do:* M'N'M Trio
Grainger, Porter: *Put It Right Here:* Newberger, Eli
Granados, Enrique: *Spanish Dance, Op. 37, No. 2 and No. 5/Intermezzo from "Goyescas":* King, Ian
Grant, James: *Three Furies for Solo Tuba:* Nelson, Mark
Grant, Jerome: *Time Cycles:* Self, Jim
Gray, Jerry, and Carl Sigman: *Pennsylvania 6-5000 Polka:* Self, James
Green, Freddie: *Corner Pocket:* Tennessee Technological University Tuba/Euphonium Ensemble
Green, Freddie: *Until I Met You (Corner Pocket):* Tennessee Technological University Tuba/Euphonium Ensemble
Green, Jonathan: *When We Were Giants:* O'Bryant, Kelly
Greene, Joe: *Don't Let the Sun Catch You Cryin':* Johnson, Howard
Gregson, Edward: *Alarum for Solo Tuba:* Gourlay, James; Nickel, Hans
Gregson, Edward: *Tuba Concerto:* Cooley, Floyd; Fletcher, John; Gourlay, James; Jae Young, Heo; Lind, Michael; Maierhofer, Josef; Nickel, Hans; Nord, Lennart; Norris, Tim; Wagner, Michael
Gregson-Williams, Harry: *The Tigger Movie [motion picture soundtrack]:* Johnson, John Thomas (Tommy)
Grenet, Ernesto: *Drume Negrita:* Pilafian, Sam
Grieg, Edvard: *Anitra's Dance:* Baadsvik, Øystein
Grieg, Edvard: *Hyldingsmarch:* Anderson, Hans
Grieg, Edvard: *In the Hall of the Mountain King:* Bell, William
Grieg, Edvard: *Norwegian Dance No. 1:* Baadsvik, Øystein
Grieg, Edvard: *Solvejg's Lied:* Jae Young, Heo
Griffin, Johnny: *Dance of Passion:* Bargeron, Dave
Griffin, Johnny: *You've Never Been There:* Bargeron, Dave
Grolnick, Don: *Pools:* Tennessee Tech Alumni Ensemble

Grovlez, Gabriel: *Petites Litanies de Jésus:* Sotto Voce

Gruber, Franz: *Silent Night:* Phillips, Harvey/TubaChristmas; Pilafian, Sam

Grundman, Clare: *Tuba Rhapsody:* Cummings, Barton; Varner, Lesley

Gruner, Joachim: *Konzert für Tuba und Orchester:* Unkrodt, Dietrich

Gugel/Pottag: *Etude No. 24:* Jacobs, Arnold

Guignon, Jean-Pierre: *Badintés:* Thuillier, Francois

Guignon, Jean-Pierre: *Des Athégiens au Sénégal:* Thuillier, Francois

Guignon, Jean-Pierre: *La Ferte Alais:* Thuillier, Francois

Guignon, Jean-Pierre: *Tornade sur l'esplanade:* Thuillier, Francois

Gulya, R.: *Burlesk:* Szentpáli, Roland

Gus and Buford: *Dog Tags:* Self, James

Ha, Jae Eu: *Three Pieces:* Cummings, Barton

Hackbarth, Glenn: *Double Concerto:* Perantoni, Daniel

Haddad, Don: *Suite for Tuba:* Conner, Rex; Davis, Ronald

Haden, Charlie: *Ellen David:* Johnson, Howard

Hamers, Maurice: *Chameleon:* Nickel, Hans

Hamlin, Peter: *Clones:* Funderburk, Jeff

Hampton, Slide: *Frame for the Blues:* Johnson, Howard

Hancock, Herbie: *Chameleon:* Tennessee Technological University Tuba/Euphonium Ensemble

Hancock, Herbie: *Speak like a Child:* Self, James

Hancock, Herbie: *Tell Me a Bedtime Story:* Johnson, Howard

Hand, Frederic: *Toby and Lynn:* Hanks, Thompson (Toby)

Handel, George Friderik: *Air and Bourree:* Conner, Rex

Handel, George Friderik: *Air con Variazioni from Suite No. 5 in E major:* Dowling, Eugene

Handel, George Friderik: *Air from Water Music:* Tubalaté

Handel, George Friderik: *Andante:* Phillips, Harvey

Handel, George Friderik: *Aria con Variazioni:* Seward, Steven

Handel, George Friderik: *Arrival of the Queen of Sheba:* Tennessee Technological University Tuba/Euphonium Ensemble

Handel, George Friderik: *"As When the Dove" from "Acis and Galatea":* Brown, Velvet

Handel, George Friderik: *Bourree from the Sixth Flute Sonata:* Popiel, Peter

Handel, George Friderik: *Concerto in G minor for Oboe and Orchestra:* Popiel, Peter

Handel, George Friderik: *Concerto No. 1 in G:* Hilgers, Walter

Handel, George Friderik: *Joy to the World:* Phillips, Harvey/TubaChristmas

Handel, George Friderik: *Lento:* Daellenbach, Charles

Handel, George Friderik: *Music for the Royal Fireworks:* Anderson, Hans

Handel, George Friderik: *Oboe Concerto No. 3:* Woods, Gavin

Handel, George Friderik: *Repentance (Chi sprezzando):* Daellenbach, Charles

Handel, George Friderik: *Selected Movements from Sonatas for Flute:* Phillips, Harvey

Handel, George Friderik: *Sonata in C major, Op. 1, No. 7 for Tuba and Organ:* Hilgers, Walter

Handel, George Friderik: *Sonata in G Major:* Pokorny, Gene

Handel, George Friderik: *Suite for Keyboard Vol. 1, No. 5 in E major, HWV 430 (The Harmonious Blacksmith):* Sotto Voce

Handel, George Friderik: *Wassermusik:* Swiss Tuba Quartet

Handel, George Friderik: *Where E'er You Walk:* Daellenbach, Charles

Handel, George Friderik: *Why Do the Nations?:* Szentpáli, Roland

Handy and Brymn: *Aunt Hagar's Children:* Newberger, Eli

Handy, W. C.: *Beale Street Blues:* Lehr, David "Red"; Palmer, Singleton

Handy, W. C.: *St. Louis Blues:* Dutch Tuba Quartet; Lehr, David "Red"; Melton Tuba-Quartett; Palmer, Singleton

Hanley and McDonald: *Indiana:* Corella, Gil; Lehr, David "Red"; Pilafian, Sam

Hanley, James F.: *Zing Went the Strings of My Heart:* Lehr, David "Red"

Harclerode, arr.: *Glousteshire Wassail Song:* Mighty Tubadours

Harclerode, arr.: *Good King Wenceslas; Il Est Ne:* Mighty Tubadours

Harclerode, arr.: *March of the Three Kings:* Mighty Tubadours

Harclerode, arr.: *O Sanctissumus:* Mighty Tubadours

Harclerode, arr.: *O Tannenbaum:* Mighty Tubadours

Harlos, Steve: *Breakthrough:* Self, James

Harper, Billy: *Priestess:* Stewart, Bob

Harrison, Wayne: *Beneath the Surface:* Tennessee Technological University Tuba/Euphonium Ensemble

Hart, Bill: *Brass Cuckoo:* Alchemy

Hartley, Walter: *Bivalve Suite for Euphonium and Tuba:* LeBlanc, Robert

Hartley, Walter: *Concertino for Tuba and Wind Ensemble:* Turk, John

Hartley, Walter: *Concerto for Tuba and Percussion Orchestra:* Jarvis, Jeffrey

Hartley, Walter: *Double Concerto for Saxophone, Tuba and Winds:* Erickson, Martin

Hartley, Walter: *Miniatures for Four Four-Valve Instruments:* Atlantic Tuba Quartet; British Tuba Quartet

Hartley, Walter: *Sonata No. 1 for Tuba and Piano:* LeBlanc, Robert; Zerkel, David

Hartley, Walter: *Sonatina:* Popiel, Peter
Hartley, Walter: *Suite for Flute and Tuba:* Phillips, Harvey
Hartley, Walter: *Suite for Unaccompanied Tuba:* Conner, Rex; Fletcher, John; Popiel, Peter
Hartmann, John: *Facilita:* Morgan, Kevin
Hastings, Ross: *Little Madrigal for Big Horns:* University of Miami Tuba Ensemble
Hausl, Johann: *Tubatubap:* Sass, Jonathon
Havet, Didier: *Le Jardin des Citrons:* Thuillier, Francois
Hawkins, Erskin: *Tuxedo Junction:* Dutch Tuba Quartet; Melton Tuba-Quartett
Hayden, Paul: *Chaconne:* Skillen, Joseph
Haydn, Franz Joseph: *Achieved Is the Glorious Work from "Die Schöpfung":* Sotto Voce
Hayes, Isaac: *Shaft:* Tennessee Technological University Tuba/Euphonium Ensemble
Hazell, Chris: *Hallelujah Drive:* Swiss Tuba Quartet
Heiden, Bernhard: *Variationen for Tuba and Nine Horns:* Hötzel, Markus; Phillips, Harvey
Henderson, Joe: *Recordame:* Feldman, Enrique "Hank" C.
Henderson, Ray: *Alabamy Bound:* Lehr, David "Red"
Henderson, Ray: *Bye Bye Blackbird:* Mazura, János
Hendrix, Jimi: *Angel:* Moschner, Pinguin
Hendrix, Jimi: *Burning of the Midnight Lamp:* Moschner, Pinguin
Hendrix, Jimi: *Highway Child:* Moschner, Pinguin
Hendrix, Jimi: *If Six Was Nine:* Moschner, Pinguin
Hendrix, Jimi: *Little Wing:* Moschner, Pinguin
Hendrix, Jimi: *Purple Haze:* Moschner, Pinguin
Hendrix, Jimi: *Spanish Castle Magic:* Moschner, Pinguin
Hendrix, Jimi: *Up from the Skies:* Moschner, Pinguin
Hendrix, Jimi: *Voodoo Chile:* Heavy Tuba; Moschner, Pinguin
Hendrix, Jimi: *The Wind Cries Mary:* Moschner, Pinguin
Henry, Cleo: *Boplicity:* Barber, John William (Bill); Pilafian, Sam
Herbert, Victor: *Indian Summer:* Erickson, Martin
Herbert, Victor: *Italian Street Song:* Daellenbach, Charles
Herbert, Victor: *March of the Toy Soldiers:* Mighty Tubadours
Herman, Jerry: *Ribbons down My Back:* Self, James
Hermann, Heinz: *Korn Blues:* Scandinavian Tuba Jazz
Hermann, Herman: *Y Luego:* Scandinavian Tuba Jazz
Hernandez, Rafael: *El Cumbanchero:* Pilafian, Sam
Heusen, Van: *Here's That Rainy Day:* British Tuba Quartet
Heussenstamm, George: *Tubafour:* New York Tuba Quartet
Hidas, Frigyes: *Allegro Vivace:* Hötzel, Markus
Hidas, Frigyes: *Tuba Concerto:* Griffiths, John; Muros, Laszlo
Hidas, Frigyes: *Tuba Quartett:* Melton Tuba-Quartett
Hidas, Frigyes: *Tuphonium:* Dutch Tuba Quartet
Hilgers, Walter: *Praeludium:* Gerhard Meinl's Tuba Sextet
Hill, Helmar: *Ballade:* Heavy Tuba
Hilles, Lejaren: *Malta for Tuba and Tape:* Cummings, Barton
Hilprecht, Uwe: *Haltungen (4) zu einem alten Thema, for tuba:* Bazsinka, József
Hinchley, John: *Boogie Woogie Tuba Boy:* Tubalaté
Hindemith, Paul: *Sonata for Bass Tuba and Piano:* Audenaert, Guy; Augustin, Rudiger; Baadsvik, Øystein; Barsotti, Mario; Bobo, Roger; Fletcher, John; Funderburk, Jeff; Georgie, Gerhard; Gourlay, James; Hilgers, Walter; Pokorny, Gene
Hindemith, Paul: *Symphonic Metamorphosis of Themes by Carl Maria von Weber (excerpt):* Pokorny, Gene
Hindemith, Paul: *Three Easy Pieces:* Hanks, Thompson (Toby)
Hirsch/Rose: *'Deed I Do:* Gannett, Dave
Hollomon, Samuel: *Music for Tuba:* Cummings, Barton
Holmboe, Vagn: *Concerto for Tuba and Orchestra, Op. 52:* Bjørn-Larsen, Jens
Holmboe, Vagn: *Intermezzo Concertante for Tuba and Orchestra, Op. 171:* Bjørn-Larsen, Jens
Holmboe, Vagn: *Notater for Three Trombones and Tuba:* Arnsted, Jørgen Voight
Holmes, Brian: *Tales of the Cultural Revolution:* Fritze, Gregory
Holmes, Paul: *Lento:* Conner, Rex; Davis, Ronald; LeBlanc, Robert
Holmes, Paul: *Quartet for Tubas:* British Tuba Quartet; Tennessee Tech Alumni Ensemble; University of Michigan Tuba and Euphonium Ensemble
Holsinger, David: *Kansas City Dances:* Mendoker, Scott; Seward, Steven
Holst, Gustav: *March from Second Suite in F for Military Band:* Symphonia
Holst, Gustav: *Mars from "The Planets":* Jacobs, Arnold; Symphonia
Holst, Gustav: *The Planets (excerpt):* Pokorny, Gene
Hook, J.: *Rondo:* British Tuba Quartet
Hoover, J.: *The Rhythm King:* Dixie Power Trio
Hopkins: *We Three Kings:* Mighty Tubadours
Hopkins, Greg: *Bas Relief:* Pilafian, Sam
Hopkins, Greg: *Hidden Agenda:* Pilafian, Sam
Hopkins, Greg: *Mystic Valley:* Pilafian, Sam
Hopkinson: *Concerto for Tuba "Concerto Euphonique":* Michel, Guy
Horichi, Glenn: *Once upon a Time:* Roper, William
Horner, James: *An American Tail II—Fieval Goes West [motion picture soundtrack]:* Self, James
Horner, James: *Bobby Jones, Stroke of Genius [motion picture soundtrack]:* Self, James

Horner, James: *Grinch Who Stole Christmas [motion picture soundtrack]:* Self, James
Horner, James: *Troy [motion picture soundtrack]:* Self, James
Horovitz, Joseph: *Concerto for Tuba and Brass Band:* Gourlay, James
Horovitz, Joseph: *Rumpole of the Bailey:* British Tuba Quartet
Horwood, Michael S.: *Residue for Tuba and Vibraphone:* Vogt, Michael
Howard, James Newton: *Atlantis [motion picture soundtrack]:* Self, James
Howarth, arr.: *The Cuckoo, Lucerne Song:* Fletcher, John
Howarth, Elgar: *Carnival of Venice:* Fletcher, John
Howe, Julia Ward: *Battle Hymn of the Republic:* Lehr, David "Red"
Hubbel, Raymond: *Poor Butterfly:* Mazura, János
Hübsch, Carl Ludwig: *Bird:* European Tuba Quartet
Hübsch, Carl Ludwig: *Material Girls:* European Tuba Quartet
Hübsch, Carl Ludwig: *Red Thread:* European Tuba Quartet
Huffine, G. H.: *Them Basses:* United States Armed Forces Tuba-Euphonium Ensemble and Massed Ensemble
Huffsteter, Steve: *Cipriana:* Self, James
Hummel, Johann Nepomuk: *Adagio, Theme and Variations, Op. 102:* Sheridan, Patrick
Hunter, Eugene: *Ain't Much Good in the Best of Men Now Days:* Newberger, Eli
Hupfeld, Herman: *When Yuba Plays the Rhumba on the Tuba Down in Cuba:* Bell, William; Phillips, Harvey; Washburn, Joe "Country"
Hutchison, Terry: *Tuba Juba Duba:* Melton Tuba-Quartett; Tennessee Technological University Tuba/Euphonium Ensemble
Iannaccone, Anthony: *Hades for Two Euphoniums and Two Tubas:* University of Michigan Tuba Ensemble
Iannaccone, Anthony: *Three Mythical Sketches for Four Tubas:* University of Michigan Tuba Ensemble
Iannoccone, Anthony: *Sonatina for Trumpet and Tuba:* Smith, J. R.
Ihlenfeld, Dave: *Clouds:* Sheridan, Patrick
Ivanovici, J.: *Wave of the Danube:* Tubalaté
Jackman, Andrew: *Swing Rag:* Sykes, Steve
Jackson, Michael: *Beat It:* Tennessee Technological University Tuba/Euphonium Ensemble
Jacob, Gordon: *Four Pieces for Tuba Quartet:* Dutch Tuba Quartet
Jacob, Gordon: *Suite for Tuba and String Orchestra:* Randolph, David
Jacob, Gordon: *Tuba Suite:* Dowling, Eugene
Jacobs, Jacob: *The Bear:* Corella, Gil
Jacobsen, Julius: *Tuba Ballet for Tuba and Woodwind Quintet:* Lind, Michael
Jacobsen, Julius: *Tuba Buffo:* Lind, Michael
Jager, Robert: *Concerto for Bass Tuba and Band:* Morris, R. Winston; Perantoni, Daniel
Jager, Robert: *Three Ludes for Tuba:* Perantoni, Daniel
James, Bob: *Courtship:* Tennessee Technological University Tuba/Euphonium Ensemble
James, Pepper, and Russell: *Vaya Con Dios:* Pilafian, Sam
Janin, D.: *Swingin' Little Swiss Tuba . . . Cuckoo-clock:* Stecker, Marc
Jarreau, Al: *Boogie Down:* Tennessee Technological University Tuba/Euphonium Ensemble
Jarrett, Keith: *Lucky Southern:* Matteson-Phillips TubaJazz Consort
Jenkins: *This Is All I Ask:* Gannett, Dave
Jenneau, Francois: *Paul et Mike:* Steckar Tubapack
Jewell, Fred: *Battle Royal:* British Tuba Quartet; Swiss Tuba Quartet
Jobim, Antonio Carlos: *Agua de Beber:* Pilafian, Sam
Jobim, Antonio Carlos: *No More Blues:* Self, James
Jobim, Antonio Carlos: *One Note Samba (But Which Note?):* Pilafian, Sam
Jobim, Antonio Carlos: *Quiet Nights of Quiet Stars:* Gannett, Dave
John, Little Willie: *Fever:* Johnson, Howard
Johnson and Mack: *Old Fashioned Love:* Newberger, Eli
Johnson, Bunk: *Moose Blues:* Newberger, Eli
Johnson, Howard: *Album, Album:* Johnson, Howard
Johnson, Howard: *Be No Evil:* Johnson, Howard
Johnson, Howard: *Here Comes Sonny Man:* Johnson, Howard
Johnson, Howard: *Music Written for Monterey:* Johnson, Howard
Johnson, Howard: *O Raggedy Man:* Johnson, Howard
Johnson, Joseph: *Ain't My Fault:* Dixie Power Trio
Johnston, Bruce: *Sunrise Lady:* Tennessee Technological University Tuba/Euphonium Ensemble
Jolson and Brown: *Sonny Boy:* (see Brown, DeSylva, and Henderson)
Jones and Dickerson: *Tia Juanna Man:* Newberger, Eli
Jones, Isham: *There Is No Greater Love:* Self, James
Jones, Robert: *Dialogs:* Funderburk, Jeff
Jones, Roger: *Duet No. 12 from "21 Distinctive Duets":* University of Miami Tuba Ensemble
Jones, Sam: *Say It's So:* Pilafian, Sam
Jones, Sam: *Unit Seven:* Frey, Michael
Jones, Thad: *A Child Is Born:* Erickson, Martin
Joplin, Scott: *The Cascades:* British Tuba Quartet; Dites-Le-Moi Tuba; Johnson, John Thomas (Tommy); Pilafian, Sam
Joplin, Scott: *The Chrysanthemum:* Johnson, John Thomas (Tommy)
Joplin, Scott: *Cleopha:* Johnson, John Thomas (Tommy)

Joplin, Scott: *Combination March:* Johnson, John Thomas (Tommy)
Joplin, Scott: *The Easy Winners:* Contraband (The); Dutch Tuba Quartet
Joplin, Scott: *Elite Syncopations:* British Tuba Quartet; Johnson, John Thomas (Tommy); Swiss Tuba Quartet
Joplin, Scott: *The Entertainer:* Johnson, John Thomas (Tommy); Tennessee Tech Tuba-Euphonium Quintet; United States Armed Forces Tuba-Euphonium Ensemble and Massed Ensemble
Joplin, Scott: *Euphonic Sounds:* Atlantic Tuba Quartet; British Tuba Quartet
Joplin, Scott: *The Favorite Rag:* British Tuba Quartet; Johnson, John Thomas (Tommy)
Joplin, Scott: *Great Crush Collision:* Johnson, John Thomas (Tommy)
Joplin, Scott: *Harmony Club Waltz:* Johnson, John Thomas (Tommy)
Joplin, Scott: *Maple Leaf Rag:* Johnson, John Thomas (Tommy)
Joplin, Scott: *Original Rags:* Johnson, John Thomas (Tommy); Lehr, David "Red"
Joplin, Scott: *Peacherine Rag:* Pilafian, Sam
Joplin, Scott: *Pleasant Moments:* Dites-Le-Moi Tuba; Dutch Tuba Quartet
Joplin, Scott: *The Ragtime Dance:* Johnson, John Thomas (Tommy); United States Navy Band Tuba-Euphonium Quartet
Joplin, Scott: *Solace:* Daellenbach, Charles; Gannett, Dave
Joplin, Scott: *The Strenuous Life:* Albertasaurus Tuba Quartet; Miraphone Tuba Quartet
Joule, James: *The Eagle Thunders:* Dutch Tuba Quartet
Justman, S.: *Centerfold:* Dixie Power Trio
Kabalevski, Dmitri: *Comedian's Galop:* Mighty Tubadours
Kaempfert/Gabler: *L.O.V.E.:* Tuba 4's
Kalina, Ron: *Children at Play:* Self, James
Kalke, Ernst-Thilo: *Jumbo's Holiday:* Melton Tuba-Quartett
Kalke, Ernst-Thilo: *Mevagissey Tales:* Hötzel, Markus
Kalke, Ernst-Thilo: *Requiem to a Dead Little Cat:* Melton Tuba-Quartett
Kamen, Michael: *(Everything I Do) I Do It for You:* Norris, Tim
Kamen, Michael: *Robin Hood Fanfare:* Tennessee Technological University Tuba/Euphonium Ensemble
Kander, John Harold: *Cabaret:* Morgan, Kevin
Kassel and Stitzel: *Sobbin' Blues:* Newberger, Eli
Katzenbeier, Hubert: *Drei Spielstucke:* Legris, Philippe; Bobo, Roger
Kellaway, Roger: *Dance of the Ocean Breeze:* Bobo, Roger; Labeyrie, Stéphane
Kellaway, Roger: *The Morning Song:* Funderburk, Jeff
Kellaway, Roger: *Sonoro for Horn, Bass Horn and Piano:* Bobo, Roger; Labeyrie, Stéphane
Kellaway, Roger: *The Westwood Song:* Bobo, Roger
Kelly, Wynton: *Kelly Blue:* Johnson, Howard
Kern, Jerome: *I Won't Dance:* Murrow, Richard
Kern, Jerome: *Ol' Man River:* Pilafian, Sam; Sheridan, Patrick; Woods, Gavin
Kern, Jerome: *Pick Yourself Up:* Murrow, Richard
Kern, Jerome: *Smoke Gets in Your Eyes:* Pilafian, Sam
Kern, Jerome: *They Didn't Believe Me:* British Tuba Quartet
Kern, Jerome: *Yesterdays:* Draper, Ray; Johnson, Howard
Kerwin, Simon: *Illustrations for Tubas:* Tubalaté
Kerwin, Simon: *March—FroT:* Tubalaté
Ketelby, Albert: *A Night in a Persian Caravan:* Albertasaurus Tuba Quartet
Khatchaturian, Aram: *Sabre Dance:* Melton Tuba-Quartett; Tubalaté
Kilon, Moshe: *Sine Nomine:* Hershko, Shmuel "Adi"
King, Karl L.: *Barnum and Bailey's Favorite:* Mighty Tubadours; United States Armed Forces Tuba-Euphonium Ensemble
King, Karl L.: *The Melody Shop:* Miraphone Tuba Quartet; United States Armed Forces Tuba-Euphonium Ensemble
King, Lapread, McClary, Orange, Richie, Williams: *Brick House:* Tennessee Technological University Tuba/Euphonium Ensemble
King, Pee Wee, and Redd Stewart: *Tennessee Waltz:* Self, James
Kingsbury: *Infant Holy:* Mighty Tubadours
Kleinsinger, George, and Paul Tripp: *The Further Adventures of Tubby the Tuba:* Johnson, John Thomas (Tommy); Phillips, Harvey
Kleinsinger, George, and Paul Tripp: *Tubby the Tuba:* Bell, William; Bruno, Jerry; Jenkel, Herbert; Johnson, John Thomas (Tommy); Karella, Clarence; Norris, Tim; Schmitz, Chester; Thorton, Michael
Kleinsinger, George, and Paul Tripp: *Tubby the Tuba Joins the Circus:* Johnson, John Thomas (Tommy); Karella, Clarence
Kleinsinger, George, and Paul Tripp: *Tubby the Tuba Joins the Jazz Band:* Johnson, John Thomas (Tommy)
Kling, Henri: *The Elephant and the Fly:* Erickson, Martin; Phillips, Harvey
Kneale, Peter: *Variations on a Welsh Theme:* Sykes, Steve
Knox, Charles: *Scherzando for Tubular Octet:* Tennessee Technological University Tuba/Euphonium Ensemble
Koch, Erland von: *Monolog No. 9 for Unaccompanied Tuba:* Lind, Michael
Kochan, Gunter: *Sieben Miniaturen für Vier Tuben:* Self, James
Koenig, Williams, and Handy: *Careless Love:* Palmer, Singleton
Koetsier, Jan: *Choralfantasie ürber "Es ist ein Schnitter" für Tuba und Orgel Op. 93:* Walsh, Thomas

Koetsier, Jan: *Concertino for Tuba and String Orchestra, Op. 77:* Brown, Velvet; Hoppert, Manfred; Walsh, Thomas
Koetsier, Jan: *Hymne:* Hötzel, Markus
Koetsier, Jan: *Sonatina for Trombone and Piano:* Randolph, David
Koetsier, Jan: *Sonatina for Tuba and Piano, Op. 57:* Funderburk, Jeff; Hanks, Toby; Hoppert, Manfred; Walsh, Thomas
Koetsier, Jan: *Wolkenschatten, Op. 136:* Alchemy; Dutch Tuba Quartet
Konagaya, Soichi: *Fantasy for Tuba and Piano:* Yasumoto, Hiroyuki
Konagaya, Soichi: *Illusion:* Tennessee Technological University Tuba/Euphonium Ensemble
Konitz, Lee: *No Splice:* Self, James
Kosma: *Autumn Leaves:* Symphonia
Kovács, Zoltán: *Golden Bells:* Szentpáli, Roland
Kraft, William: *Encounters II for Solo Tuba:* Baadsvik, Øystein; Bazsinka, József; Bobo, Roger; Jae Young, Heo
Kranowski, A.: *Sonata for Solo Tuba:* Piernik, Zdzislaw
Krebs, Jesse: *Jesse's Jump:* Symphonia
Kreines: *Chorale Variations, "Jesu meine Fruede":* Jacobs, Arnold
Kreisler, Fritz: *Liebesfreud:* Sykes, Steve; Yasumoto, Hiroyuki
Kreisler, Fritz: *Liebesleid:* Sheridan, Patrick; Tubalaté
Kreisler, Fritz: *Midnight Bells from the "Opera Ball"/Liebesfreud:* Sheridan, Patrick
Kreisler, Fritz: *Schon Rosmarin:* King, Ian; Sheridan, Patrick
Kresin, Willibald: *Chin Up!:* Contraband (The)
Kresin, Willibald: *Movin Groovin/Tuba Rodeo/Tango:* Contraband Tuba Quartet
Krol, Bernhard: *Feiertagsmusik, Op. 107b:* Tennessee Tech Alumni Ensemble
Kronk: *Mr. Bumble:* Morgan, Kevin
Kupferman, Meyer: *Kierkegaard, for Tuba Quartet:* British Tuba Quartet; Sotto Voce
Kupferman, Meyer: *Saturnalis:* Bobo, Roger
Kurnick, Jon: *Bosque De Manaus:* Self, James
Lacalle, J.: *Amapola:* Rustic Bari-Tuba Ensemble
Lachenmann, Helmut: *Harmonica for Large Orchestra and Tuba Solo:* Nahatzki, Richard
Lamb, Marvin: *Heavy Metal:* Tennessee Technological University Tuba/Euphonium Ensemble
Lambert, Louis: *When Johnny Comes Marching Home:* Self, James
Landes, B.: *The Elephant's Tango:* Bell, William
Lang, Istvan: *Aria di coloratura:* Bazsinka, József
Langgaard, Rued: *Dies Irae for Tuba and Piano:* Arnsted, Jørgen Voight
Lantier, Pierre: *Andante et Allegro:* Michel, Guy
Largent, Edward: *Four Shorts for Tuba and Piano:* Turk, John
LaRocca, D.: *Original Dixieland One-Step:* Palmer, Singleton
Larsen, Libby: *Concertpiece for Tuba and Piano:* Nelson, Mark
Lauer, Christoff: *Bluebells Nightmare:* Stewart, Bob
Lauer, Christoff: *Screwbirds:* Stewart, Bob
Laumann, H.: *Live and Let Live:* Anderson, Hans
Laumann, H.: *Song for Oliver:* Anderson, Hans
Lauper and Hyman: *Time after Time:* Dixie Power Trio
Laurendeau, L. P.: *Elephantine Polka:* Erickson, Martin
Lavalle, Paul: *Big Joe, the Tuba:* Tarto, Joe
Lax, Fred: *Fantasia of Popular Irish Airs:* Seward, Steven
Lazarof, Henri: *Cadence VI for Tuba and Tape:* Bobo, Roger
Lebedev, Alexei: *Concert Allegro:* Funderburk, Jeff; Randolph, David
Lebedev, Alexei: *Concerto in One Movement:* Arwood, Jeffrey; Funderburk, Jeff; Gourlay, James; Hoppert, Manfred; Woods, Gavin
Lebow, Leonard: *Popular Suite:* Hanks, Thompson (Toby)
LeClair, David: *Carnival of Venice:* Contraband (The); Monarch Tuba-Euphonium Quartet
LeClair, David: *Forte/Formidable/Fortune/The Dragon's Dance:* Contraband (The)
LeClair, David: *Growing Up Together:* Contraband (The)
Lecuona, Ernesto: *Malagueña:* Tennessee Technological University Tuba/Euphonium Ensemble
Lefebure-Wely: *Sortie in E♭:* British Tuba Quartet
LeGrand, Michel: *Summer Knows:* Modern Jazz Tuba Project
Lennon, John, and Paul McCartney: *Blackbird:* Holmgaard, Lars
Lennon, John, and Paul McCartney: *Come Together:* Frey, Michael; Murrow, Richard
Lennon, John, and Paul McCartney: *Helter Skelter:* Heavy Tuba
Lennon, John, and Paul McCartney: *Hey Jude:* Miraphone Tuba Quartet
Lennon, John, and Paul McCartney: *I Saw Her Standing There:* Dixie Power Trio
Lennon, John, and Paul McCartney: *Yesterday:* Tubalaté; Yasumoto, Hiroyuki
Leontovich and Wilhousky: *Carol of the Bells:* Phillips, Harvey/TubaChristmas; Pilafian, Sam
Leopold, Louis J.: *Promendade:* Jae Young, Heo
Lerner, Alan Jay: *Get Me to the Church on Time:* British Tuba Quartet
Lerner, Alan Jay: *Heather on the Hill:* Self, James
Lerner, Alan Jay: *I Talk to the Trees:* Draper, Ray
Levy, Yeuda: *Mediterranean Rondo:* Hershko, Shmuel "Adi"
Lindsay, Erica: *At the Last Moment:* Johnson, Howard
Lindsay, Erica: *Dreamer:* Johnson, Howard
Lindsay, Erica: *First Movement:* Johnson, Howard
Lindsay, Erica: *Gratitude:* Johnson, Howard
Lindsay, Erica: *Walking Together:* Johnson, Howard
Lippe, Cort: *Solo Tuba Music:* Bazsinka, József

Liptak, David: *Mixed Doubles for Trumpet, Tuba, Violin and Contrabass:* Kaenzig, Fritz
List, G.: *Prélude:* Frey, Michael
Liszt, Franz: *Hungarian Rhapsody No. 2:* Melton Tuba-Quartett
Liszt, Franz: *Rhapsodic Fantasie:* Woods, Gavin
Little, Donald: *Lazy Lullaby:* Davis, Ronald
Livingston, J., and R. Evans: *Silver Bells:* Pilafian, Sam
Livingston, J., and R. Evans: *To Each His Own:* Yasumoto, Hiroyuki
Lockhart and Seitz: *The World Is Waiting for the Sunrise:* Lehr, David "Red"; Newberger, Eli; Tennessee Technological University Tuba/Euphonium Ensemble
Loesser, Frank: *Fugue for Tinhorns from "Guys and Dolls":* Sheridan, Patrick
Loesser, Frank: *I've Never Been in Love Before:* Self, James
Loesser, Frank: *On a Slow Boat to China:* Gannett, Dave
Loewe, Frederick: *Almost like Being in Love:* Tennessee Tech Alumni Ensemble
Loewe, Frederick: *I Could Have Danced All Night:* Morgan, Kevin
Lohmann, Georg: *Bayerische Polka:* Contraband (The); Gerhard Meinl's Tuba Sextet; Miraphone Tuba Quartet
Low/Gray/Bennett/Ha: *Bye Bye Blues:* Matteson Phillips TubaJazz Consort
Luedeke, Raymond: *Wonderland Duets for Two Tubas and Narrator:* Vogt, Michael
Luis, Ingo: *Lazy Elephant Blues:* Melton Tuba-Quartett
Luis, Ingo: *Little Lullaby:* Melton Tuba-Quartett
Lully, Jean Baptiste: *Lonely Forest:* Daellenbach, Charles
Lundquist, Torbjørn Iwan: *Landscape for Tuba and Strings:* Lind, Michael
Lundquist, Torbjørn Iwan: *Triplet for 4 Tubas:* British Tuba Quartet
Luther, Martin: *A Mighty Fortress Is Our God:* Norris, Tim
Luxion, Dennis: *Prayer for the Newborn:* Johnson, Howard
Lyon, Max J.: *Suite for Four Bass Instruments:* Atlantic Tuba Quartet
MacDonald, Goodwin, and Hanley: *Breeze:* Newberger, Eli
Machado, Jean Marie: *La Peste:* Thuillier, Francois
Machado, Jean Marie: *Tambours en colere:* Thuillier, Francois
Machado, Jean Marie: *Well, You Needn't:* Thuillier, Francois
Madden, Edward: *Elegy:* Sass, Jonathon
Madsen, Trygve: *Sonata for Tuba and Piano:* Baadsvik, Øystein; Bobo, Roger; Labeyrie, Stéphane
Mahal, Taj: *Big Kneed Gal:* Stewart, Bob
Mahal, Taj: *Cakewalk into Town:* Frey, Michael
Mahal, Taj: *Encore—Cakewalk into Town:* Frey, Michael
Mahal, Taj: *Fishin' Blues:* Stewart, Bob
Mahal, Taj: *Going Up to the Country and Paint My Mailbox Blue:* Johnson, Howard
Mahal, Taj: *John, Ain't It Hard?:* Johnson, Howard
Mahal, Taj: *Sweet Mama Janisse:* Johnson, Howard
Mahal, Taj: *Tom and Sally Drake:* Johnson, Howard
Mahal, Taj: *You Ain't No Streetwalker, Mama Honey, But I Do Love the Way You Strutt Your Stuff:* Johnson, Howard
Mahler, Gustav: *Lieder eines Fahrenden Gesellen:* Perantoni, Daniel
Mahler, Gustav: *Symphony No. 1 in D major ("Titan") (excerpt):* Pokorny, Gene
Mahler, Gustav: *Symphony No. 2 (fifth movement excerpt):* Jacobs, Arnold
Mahler, Gustav: *Symphony No. 3 (first movement excerpts):* Jacobs, Arnold
Mahler, Gustav: *Symphony No. 5 in C♯ minor (excerpt):* Pokorny, Gene
Mahler, Gustav: *Symphony No. 6 in A minor ("Tragic") (excerpt):* Pokorny, Gene
Mall, Philippe: *The Hymn:* Frey, Michael
Mall-Darby, Samira: *Whose Reality Is This Anyway?:* Frey, Michael
Malotte, Albert Hay: *The Lord's Prayer:* Sotto Voce
Mancini, Henry: *Amazing Grace:* Johnson, John Thomas (Tommy)
Mancini, Henry: *Baby Elephant Walk:* Melton Tuba-Quartett
Mancini, Henry: *The Pink Panther:* British Tuba Quartet; Dutch Tuba Quartet; Melton Tuba-Quartett; Northern Tuba Lights; Tuba 4's
Mandel, Johnny: *A Time for Love:* Tennessee Tech Alumni Ensemble
Mantia, Simone: *Believe Me If All Those Endearing Young Charms:* Griffiths, John; Randolph, David; Seward, Steven
Marcello, Benedetto: *Sonata in F major for Tuba and Piano:* Lind, Michael
Marks, John: *Rudolph, the Red-Nosed Reindeer:* Pilafian, Sam
Marohnic, Chuck: *Just Blues:* Pilafian, Sam
Martin, Blaine: *Have Yourself a Merry Little Christmas:* Phillips, Harvey/TubaChristmas; Pilafian, Sam
Martin, Carroll: *Pompola:* Davis, Ronald
Martin, Glenn: *Bluesin' Tubas:* Tennessee Technological University Tuba/Euphonium Ensemble
Martin, Glenn: *Chops!:* Tennessee Technological University Tuba/Euphonium Ensemble
Martin, Glenn: *Valvin' on a Riff:* Modern Jazz Tuba Project
Martin, Robert: *Aldebaran, for Solo Tuba:* Forman, Steven
Martin/Blane/Wolpe: *The Trolley Song:* Tuba 4's
Martini, J. P. E.: *Piacer d'Amor:* Yasumoto, Hiroyuki
Martino, Ralph: *Fantasy:* British Tuba Quartet; Miraphone Tuba Quartet; Monarch Tuba-Euphonium Quartet

Marxsen, Dale: *Waltzing with Bears:* Davis, Ronald
Massenet, Jules: *Argonaise from "Le Cid":* Monarch Tuba-Euphonium Quartet; United States Navy Band Tuba-Euphonium Quartet
Massenet, Jules: *Meditation from "Thais":* Sheridan, Patrick
Matteson, arr.: *Waltzing Matilda:* Matteson-Phillips TubaJazz Consort
Matteson, Rich: *Little Ole Softy:* Matteson-Phillips TubaJazz Consort; Perantoni, Daniel
Matteson, Rich: *Shuckin' and Jivin':* Matteson-Phillips TubaJazz Consort
Matteson, Rich: *Spoofy:* Matteson-Phillips TubaJazz Consort
McBeth, Francis: *Daniel in the Lion's Den:* Perantoni, Daniel
McCarthy and Monaco: *You Made Me Love You:* Gannett, Dave
McDaniel, Ernie: *Secrets:* Self, James
McDermot, Ragni, and Rado: *Dead End:* Scandinavian Tuba Jazz
McDermott, Tom: *Martin's Mambo:* Perrine, Matt
McDonald, Barry: *Las Zorras Pocas:* Heavy Tuba
McDonald, Barry: *Pork Fat and Black-Eyed Peas:* Heavy Tuba
McFarland, Michael: *Sketches:* Kaenzig, Fritz
McGrain, Mark: *Beneath the Wheel:* Rojas, Marcus
McGrain, Mark: *Dog:* Rojas, Marcus
McGrain, Mark: *11:11:* Rojas, Marcus
McGrain, Mark: *Just like Alice:* Rojas, Marcus
McGrain, Mark: *The Mist:* Rojas, Marcus
McGrain, Mark: *Mungo:* Rojas, Marcus
McGrain, Mark: *Reveille:* Rojas, Marcus
McGrain, Mark: *Trick of the Light:* Rojas, Marcus
McGrain, Mark: *Wagdanz:* Rojas, Marcus
McGrain, Mark, and Bob Moses: *Running, Running:* Rojas, Marcus
McGrain, Mark, and Marcus Rojas: *394:* Rojas, Marcus
McHugh, J., and D. Fields: *On the Sunny Side of the Street:* British Tuba Quartet; Gannett, Dave; Yasumoto, Hiroyuki
McHugh-Fields: *I Must Have That Man:* Tarto, Joe
McIntyre, David: *Sonata for Tuba and Piano:* Griffiths, John
McKimm, Barry: *Andante Tranquillo, for Solo Viola and Piano:* Pokorny, Gene
McLean, Jackie: *Appointment in Ghana:* Johnson, Howard
McLean, Pricilla: *Beneath the Horizon for Tuba and Taped Whale Songs:* Poore, Melvyn
McPherson, John: *Hugo Hugo:* Albertasaurus Tuba Quartet
McQueen, Ian: *The Heights of Halifax:* Tubalaté
Meacham, Frank W.: *American Tuba Patrol:* Rustic Bari-Tuba Ensemble
Mehlan, Keith: *Bottoms Up Rag:* Monarch Tuba-Euphonium Quartet
Mehlan, Keith: *Eine Kleine Schrecken Musik (A Little Fright Music):* Monarch Tuba-Euphonium Quartet
Meier, Jost: *Eclipse Finale? For Tuba and Brass Band:* Baadsvik, Øystein
Meinken and Ringle: *Wabash Blues:* (see Ringle and Meinken)
Melillo, Stephen: *Erich:* Colonial Tuba Quartet
Melrose, Walter: *Tin Roof Blues:* Palmer, Singleton
Mendelssohn, Felix: *Concerto for Violin (third movement):* Seward, Steven
Mendelssohn, Felix: *It Is Enough from "Elijah":* Popiel, Peter
Mendez, Rafael: *La Virgin De La Macarena:* Symphonia
Mendez, Rafael: *Mexican Hat Dance:* Sheridan, Patrick
Mendez, Rafael: *Sambe Guitana:* Sykes, Steven
Menken/Ashman: *Friend like Me:* Tuba 4's
Menken/Schwartz: *Colors of the Wind:* Tuba 4's
Mercer, Johnny: *Blues in the Night:* Price, Tony
Mercer, Johnny: *Dream:* Tuba 4's
Mercer, Johnny: *Tangerine:* (see Schertzinger, Victor, and Johnny Mercer)
Mercer, Johnny, and C. MacGregor: *Moondreams:* Pilafian, Sam
Merle, John: *Mummers (Dance Grotesque):* Bell, William
Mertens, Hardy: *Scyths:* Dutch Tuba Quartet
Meyer-Bretton, D., and S. Edwards: *For Heaven's Sake:* Self, James
Michel, Marc: *Le Jour Oú Les Tubas:* Steckar Elephant Tuba Horde
Miller, Yount, Williams: *Release Me:* Johnson, Howard
Mingus, Charles: *Better Git It in Your Soul:* Frey, Michael
Mingus, Charles: *Boogie Stop Shuffle:* Drums and Tuba
Mingus, Charles: *Freedom:* Symphonia
Mingus, Charlie: *Peggy's Blue Skylight:* Self, James
Minuteman (The): *God Bows to Math:* Drums and Tuba
Mitchell: *Dance of the Sophists:* Roper, William
Mitchell, arr.: *Fat Cat:* Callender, George Sylvester "Red"
Mitchell, arr.: *I Want a Little Girl:* Callender, George Sylvester "Red"
Mitchell, arr.: *Magna:* Callender, George Sylvester "Red"
Mitchell-Davidson, Paul: *Tubafication:* Tubalaté
Mobberley, James C.: *On Thin Ice:* Tennessee Technological University Tuba/Euphonium Ensemble
Monaco: *You Made Me Love You:* (see McCarthy and Monaco)
Monk, Thelonius: *Blue Monk:* Johnson, Howard; Steckar Tubapack
Monk, Thelonius: *Brilliant Corners:* Carolino, Sérgio
Monk, Thelonius: *Crespuscule with Nellie:* Johnson, Howard
Monk, Thelonius: *Criss-Cross:* Johnson, Howard
Monk, Thelonius: *Epistrophy:* Frey, Michael

Mozart, Wolfgang Amadeus: *Romanza and Rondo from Horn Concerto No. 4:* Woods, Gavin
Mozart, Wolfgang Amadeus: *Rondo:* Woods, Gavin
Mozart, Wolfgang Amadeus: *Rondo alla Turca:* British Tuba Quartet
Mozart, Wolfgang Amadeus: *Rondo in E♭ major, K371:* Piernik, Zdzislaw
Mozart, Wolfgang Amadeus: *Turkish March:* Albertasaurus Tuba Quartet
Mozart, Wolfgang Amadeus: *Turkish Rondo:* Monarch Tuba-Euphonium Quartet
Mueller: *Away in a Manger:* Mighty Tubadours
Mueller, Florian: *Concert Music for Bass Tuba:* Conner, Rex
Muir and Edgar: *Ragtime Rosie:* Lehr, David "Red"
Mulligan, Gerry: *Line for Lyons:* Johnson, Howard
Murrow, R.: *Domi:* Murrow, Richard
Muscroft, Fred: *Carnival for Bass:* Baker, Fred
Muse, C.: *Sleepytime Down South:* Dixie Power Trio
Mussorgsky, Modest: *Bydlo from "Pictures at an Exhibition":* Piernik, Zdzislaw
Mussorgsky, Modest: *Great Gate of Kiev from "Pictures at an Exhibition":* Jacobs, Arnold
Mussorgsky, Modest: *Pictures at an Exhibition (excerpt):* Pokorny, Gene
Mussorgsky, Modest: *Song of the Flea:* Fletcher, John
Myers, Stanley: *Cavatina:* Self, James
Naftel, Frederick: *Pascal's Victim:* Tubalaté
Nagel, Robert: *This Old Man:* Hanks, Thompson (Toby)
Napoleon and Signorelli: *Bass Ale Blues:* Tarto, Joe
Neilsen, Carl: *Symphony No. 4 excerpt:* Jacobs, Arnold
Nelson: *When You See That Aunt of Mine:* Tarto, Joe
Nelson and Rollins: *Frosty the Snowman:* Pilafian, Sam
Nelson, Oliver: *Blues and the Abstract Truth:* Self, James
Nelson, Oliver: *Stolen Moments:* Johnson, Howard
Nelson, Vern: *Killer Tuba Songs:* Rozen, Jay
Nero, Paul: *Hot Canary:* Sheridan, Patrick
New Yorkers (The): *Onyx Club Revue:* Tarto, Joe
Newman: *The Time of Your Life:* Tuba 4's
Newman, David: *Cat in the Hat [motion picture soundtrack]:* Self, James
Newman, Maria: *9th Hour of Divine Office:* Self, Jim
Newman, Ron: *This Won't Hurt a Bit:* Erickson, Martin
Newman, Thomas: *Lemony Snicket [motion picture soundtrack]:* Self, James
Newman, Thomas: *Linguini Incident [motion picture soundtrack]:* Self, James
Newsome, Roy: *The Basics:* Tubalaté
Newsome, Roy: *The Bass in the Ballroom:* Sykes, Stephen; Woods, Gavin
Newsome, Roy: *Swiss Air:* Crowther, Shaun
Newton, Rodney: *Capriccio in E♭ major:* Gourlay, James; Nickel, Hans; Sykes, Steven
Nicolai, Otto: *Merry Wives of Windsor Overture:* British Tuba Quartet
Niehaus, arr.: *Spiritual Jazz Suite:* British Tuba Quartet
Niehaus, Lennie: *Brass Tacks:* Northern Tuba Lights
Niehaus, Lennie: *Grand Slam:* British Tuba Quartet
Niehaus, Lennie: *Miniature Jazz Suite:* Melton Tuba-Quartett
Niehaus, Lennie: *Sleeping Giants:* Contraband (The)
Niehaus, Lennie: *Spiritual Jazz Suite:* Dites-Le-Moi Tuba
Niehaus, Lennie: *Tubalation:* Dites-Le-Moi Tuba; Miraphone Tuba Quartet
Nielsen, Erik: *Spiritual Alloys:* Nelson, Mark
Nielsen, Hans Peter: *The Satyr:* ANON
Nilsson, Bo: *Bass, for Solo Tuba and Percussion:* Lind, Michael
Noble, Ray: *Cherokee:* Erickson, Martin; Modern Jazz Tuba Project
Norbury, Kevin: *Badinage:* Sheridan, Patrick
Nordhagen, Stig: *Nocturne:* Dutch Tuba Quartet
Novacek, Rudolf: *Castaldo Marsch:* Miraphone Tuba Quartet
Novick, Billy: *When She Cries:* Newberger, Eli
Nyro, Laura: *Eli's Coming:* Tennessee Technological University Tuba/Euphonium Ensemble
Offenbach, Jacques: *Marine's Hymn:* Daellenbach, Charles
Offenbach, Jacques: *Orpheus in the Underworld:* Northern Tuba Lights
O'Hara, Betty: *Euphonics:* Tennessee Technological University Tuba/Euphonium Ensemble
Ohmen, Kjell: *Alice's Fax:* Pilafian, Sam
Oliver and Melrose: *Doctor Jazz:* Newberger, Eli
Oliver, Joe: *Chimes Blues:* Newberger, Eli
O'Reilly, John: *Metropolitan 5tet:* Morris, Jim
Original Dixieland Jazz Band: *Fidgety Feet:* Dixie Power Trio; Palmer, Singleton
Osmon, Leroy: *Concert Etudes for Solo Tuba:* Kirk, David
Osmon, Leroy: *Frescos De Bonampak:* Tennessee Technological University Tuba/Euphonium Ensemble
Ostrander, Linda: *Time Out for Tuba (movement I—Cycles):* Cummings, Barton
Ott, Joseph: *Bart's Piece for Tuba and Electronic Tape:* Cummings, Barton
Overstreet and Higgins: *I Ain't Gonna Give Nobody None of My Jellyroll:* Newberger, Eli
Overstreet and Higgins: *There'll Be Some Changes Made:* Newberger, Eli
Paderewski, Ignacy Jan: *Minuet:* Piernik, Zdzislaw
Paganini, Niccolò: *Moses-Fantasy:* Szentpáli, Roland
Paganini, Niccolò: *Moto Perpetuo:* Bell, William
Paganini, Niccolò: *Theme and Variations:* Dumitru, Ionel
Page/Plant: *Black Dog:* Carolino, Sérgio

Palma, J.: *Só:* Carolino, Sérgio
Palmer and Williams: *I Found a New Baby:* Matteson, Rich; Newberger, Eli; Pilafian, Sam
Parfrey, Raymond: *Male Voice for Brass:* Tubalaté
Parfrey, Raymond: *Tributes to Tunesmiths:* Tubalaté
Parissi, Rob: *Play That Funky Tuba Right, Boy!:* Tennessee Technological University Tuba/Euphonium Ensemble
Parker, Charlie: *Au Privave:* Mazura, János; Murrow, Richard; New York Tuba Quartet
Parker, Charlie: *Billie's Bounce:* Mazura, János
Parker, Charlie: *Little Suede Shoes:* Erickson, Martin; Mazura, János; Murrow, Richard; Pilafian, Sam
Parker, Charlie: *Scrapple from an Apple:* Mazura, János
Parker, Charlie: *Yardbird Suite:* Erickson, Martin
Parker, Dorothy: *I Wished on the Moon:* Self, James
Parker, Handel: *Deep Harmony:* Tubalaté
Patorius, Jaco: *Fanny Mae:* Heavy Tuba
Payne, Frank Lynn: *Quartet for Tubas (The Condor):* Dutch Tuba Quartet; Melton Tuba-Quartett; University of Miami Tuba Ensemble; University of Michigan Tuba and Euphonium Ensemble
Peasley, Richard: *The Devil's Herald:* Phillips, Harvey
Pecha, Antonin: *Hvezdonicka:* Heavy Tuba
Pederson, Tommy: *Elephant in the Livingroom:* Mazura, János
Pegram, Wayne: *Broadway Bash:* Symphonia
Pegram, Wayne: *Howdy!:* Tennessee Technological University Tuba/Euphonium Ensemble; United States Armed Forces Tuba-Euphonium Ensemble
Penderecki, Krzysztof: *Capriccio for Solo Tuba:* Bazsinka, József; Bobo, Roger; Funderburk, Jeff; Jae Young, Heo; Labeyrie, Stéphane; Perantoni, Daniel; Piernik, Zdzislaw; Woods, Gavin
Penn, William: *Capriccio for Tuba and Marimba:* Jarvis, Jeffrey; Pokorny, Gene
Penn, William: *Three Essays for Solo Tuba:* Pokorny, Gene; Turk, John
Perkins: *Grooveyard:* Erickson, Martin
Perkinson, Coleridge: *Way 'Cross Georgia:* Johnson, Howard
Persichetti, Vincent: *Parable for Solo Tuba, Op. 147:* Bazsinka, József; Nelson, Mark
Persichetti, Vincent: *Serenade for Ten Wind Instruments:* United States Coast Guard Tuba-Euphonium Quartet
Persichetti, Vincent: *Serenade No. 12 for Solo Tuba:* Legris, Philippe; Phillips, Harvey; Zerkel, David
Peterson, Oscar: *Noreen's Nocturn:* Matteson-Phillips TubaJazz Consort
Pethel, Stan: *Monday Night:* Heavy Tuba
Petrie, H. W.: *Asleep in the Deep:* Bell, William; Colonial Tuba Quartet; Mallon, Barney; Palmer, Singleton
Picchi, Ermanno: *Fantasie Original:* Colonial Tuba Quartet; Seward, Steven
Piefke, Gottfried: *Preussens Gloria:* Miraphone Tuba Quartet
Piernik, Zdzislaw: *Dialogue für Tuba und Tonband:* Piernik, Zdzislaw
Pierpont, James: *Jingle Bells:* Pilafian, Sam
Pilafian, Sam: *Big Easy Groove:* Pilafian, Sam
Pilafian, Sam: *Gesualdo Movement:* Pilafian, Sam
Pinkard, Casey, and Tauber: *Them There Eyes:* Pilafian, Sam
Pinkard, Young, and Meyer: *Sugar:* Gannett, Dave
Pisciotta, Louis V: *Sonata:* Hanks, Toby
Plant and Page: *Stairway to Heaven:* Dixie Power Trio
Plau, Arild: *Concerto for Tuba and Strings:* Baadsvik, Øystein
Plog, Anthony: *Three Miniatures for Tuba and Piano:* Bjørn-Larsen, Jens; Bobo, Roger; Perantoni, Daniel; Skillen, Joseph
Pollack, Lew: *That's A-Plenty:* Lehr, David "Red"
Ponce, Manuel: *Estrellita:* Sheridan, Patrick
Poore, Melvyn: *And Finally:* Poore, Melvyn
Poore, Melvyn: *One, Two, Three:* Poore, Melvyn
Poore, Melvyn: *Playback I:* Poore, Melvyn
Poore, Melvyn: *Stand Alone I:* Poore, Melvyn
Poore, Melvyn: *Stand Alone II:* Poore, Melvyn
Poore, Melvyn: *Stand Alone III:* Poore, Melvyn
Poore, Melvyn: *Stoneground:* Poore, Melvyn
Poore, Melvyn: *Study in Moving Sounds:* Poore, Melvyn
Poore, Melvyn: *Tubassoon:* Poore, Melvyn
Porter, Cole: *Cole Porter Medley:* Tennessee Technological University Tuba/Euphonium Ensemble
Porter, Cole: *I Love You:* Self, James
Porter, Cole: *It's All Right with Me:* Tennessee Tech Alumni Ensemble
Porter, Cole: *Miss Otis Regrets:* Newberger, Eli
Porter, Cole: *You'd Be So Nice to Come Home to:* Gannett, Dave
Poulheim, Bert: *Groteske Miniaturen:* Legris, Philippe
Powell, B.: *Un Poco Loco:* Carolino, Sérgio
Powell, Morgan: *Midnight Realities:* Perantoni, Daniel
Powell, Morgan: *Nocturnes:* Perantoni, Daniel
Prado, Damaso Perez: *Mambo #5:* Pilafian, Sam
Premru, Ray: *In Memoriam:* British Tuba Quartet
Presser, William: *Capriccio for Tuba and Band:* Astwood, Michael
Presser, William: *Serenade for Four Tubas (third movement—Allegro):* University of Michigan Tuba Ensemble
Price, Billy: *I Hate Myself for Loving You:* Newberger, Eli
Primrose, Joe: *St. James Infirmary:* Dixie Power Trio; Sotto Voce; Tubalaté
Proctor, S.: *Light Metal—I Talatasco:* Tubalaté
Prokofiev, Sergey: *Montagues and Capulets:* British Tuba Quartet
Prokofiev, Sergey: *Romeo and Juliet, Op. 64 (excerpt):* Pokorny, Gene

Prokofiev, Sergey: *Symphony No. 5 in B♭ major, Op. 100 (excerpt):* Pokorny, Gene
Prokofiev, Sergey: *Troika from "Lieutenant Kije":* Tennessee Technological University Tuba/Euphonium Ensemble
Prokofiev, Sergey: *Visions fugitives:* Pokorny, Gene
Proto, Frank: *The Four Seasons for Tuba, Percussion, Strings and Stereo Tape:* Thornton, Michael
Pryor, Arthur: *Theme and Variation on the "Blue Bells of Scotland":* Pokorny, Gene; Seward, Steven
Puccini, Giacomo: *Colline's Aria:* Daellenbach, Charles
Puccini, Giacomo: *La Tregenda from "Le villi":* Symphonia
Puccini, Giacomo: *Musetta's Waltz from "La Bohème":* Pilafian, Sam
Puccini, Giacomo: *"Nessun Dorma" from Turandot:* Norris, Tim; Northcut, Timothy; Pilafian, Sam
Puente, Tito: *Oy Como Va:* Perrine, Matt
Pulaski, Paul: *Wonamow:* Weaver, Mark
Pullen, Don: *Big Alice:* Johnson, Howard
Pullig, Ken: *Dances:* Colonial Tuba Quartet
Purcell, Henry: *Allegro and Air:* New York Tuba Quartet
Purcell, Henry: *Dido's Lament from "Dido and Aeneas":* British Tuba Quartet
Purcell, Henry: *Distressed Innocence Overture:* British Tuba Quartet
Puschnig, Wolfgang: *Coming Home:* Stewart, Bob
Puschnig, Wolfgang: *Down Under:* Stewart, Bob
Puschnig, Wolfgang: *Mixed Metaphors:* Stewart, Bob
Puw, Guto Pryderi: *Visages:* Tubalaté
Quibel, Robert: *Danse Bizarre n o 3:* Steckar Tubapack
Quibel, Robert: *Tuba Bouchka:* Stecker, Marc
Rachmaninoff, Sergei: *Floods of Spring:* Feldman, Enrique "Hank" C.
Rachmaninoff, Sergei: *Three Songs:* Pokorny, Gene
Rachmaninoff, Sergei: *Vocalise, Op. 34, No. 14:* Feldman, Enrique "Hank" C.; Jae Young, Heo; LeBlanc, Robert; Perantoni, Daniel; Sheridan, Patrick
Rainey and Arant: *Jelly Bean Blues:* Newberger, Eli
Ramsöe, Emilio Wilhelm: *Allegro molto from Quartet No. 4:* Atlantic Tuba Quartet; Fletcher, John
Ramsöe, Emilio Wilhelm: *Andante Quasi Allegretto:* Melton Tuba-Quartett
Ramsöe, Emilio Wilhelm: *Quartet for Brass:* British Tuba Quartet; United States Coast Guard Tuba-Euphonium Quartet
Randolph, Boots: *Yakkety Tuba:* Gannett, Dave
Rasbach, Oscar: *Trees:* Cummings, Barton
Raum, Elizabeth: *Concerto del Garda:* Griffiths, John
Raum, Elizabeth: *Jason and the Golden Fleece:* Symphonia
Raum, Elizabeth: *The Legend of Heimdall:* Griffiths, John
Raum, Elizabeth: *Pershing Concerto:* Griffiths, John
Raum, Elizabeth: *"T" for Tuba:* Griffiths, John
Raum, Elizabeth: *Will There Be a Time?:* Griffiths, John
Ravel, Maurice: *Pavane pour une infante dufunte:* Pokorny, Gene
Ravel, Maurice: *Pièce en form de Habanera:* Dowling, Eugene; Hilgers, Walter
Ravel, Maurice: *Prelude:* Pilafian, Sam
Raye and DePaul: *You Don't Know What Love Is:* Stewart, Bob
Raye and Slack: *The House of Blue Lights:* Dixie Power Trio
Raye, Don: *I'll Remember April:* Corella, Gil
Razaf/Goodman/Webb/Sampson: *Stompin' at the Savoy:* Matteson-Phillips TubaJazz Consort; Tuba 4's
Razof and Johnson: *Louisiana:* Pilafian, Sam
Read, Thomas: *Brillenbass:* Nelson, Mark
Reck, David: *Five Studies for Tuba Alone:* Hanks, Thompson (Toby)
Redner: *Oh Little Town of Bethlehem:* Mighty Tubadours
Reeman, John: *Episodes:* Tubalaté
Reeman, John: *Sonatina for Tuba Quartet:* British Tuba Quartet
Regan, Michael J.: *Quartet:* Tubalaté
Reinhardt, Django: *Manoir De mes Reves:* Pilafian, Sam
Reinhardt, Django: *Micro:* Pilafian, Sam
Reinhardt, Django: *Minor Swing:* Corella, Gil
Reinhardt, Django: *Nuages:* Pilafian, Sam
Reinhardt, Django: *Rhythm Futur:* Pilafian, Sam
Reinhardt, Django: *Song D'Automne:* Pilafian, Sam
Reinken, Fred: *Wabash Blues:* (see Ringle and Meinken)
Relton, William: *The Trouble with the Tuba Is:* Crowther, Shaun
Respighi, Ottorino: *Fontane di Roma (excerpt):* Pokorny, Gene
Reynolds, Jeffrey: *Skirmish and Dance:* Pokorny, Gene
Reynolds, Verne: *Signals for Trumpet, Tuba, and Brass Choir:* Bobo, Roger
Reynolds, Verne: *Sonata:* Brown, Velvet
Rice, Hugh Collins: *Earth and Moon:* Tubalaté
Richardson, Arthur/McLean: *Too Fat Polka:* Mighty Tubadours
Ridout, Alan: *Pigs:* British Tuba Quartet
Rimmer, William: *Hailstorm:* Sheridan, Patrick
Rimmer, William: *Jenny Jones, for Tuba Solo:* Morgan, Kevin
Rimsky-Korsakov, Nicholas: *Flight of the Bumblebee:* Fletcher, John; Gourlay, James; Jae Young, Heo; Melton Tuba-Quartett; Morgan, Kevin; Sheridan, Patrick; Swiss Tuba Quartet; Wagner, Michael; Woods, Gavin
Rimsky-Korsakov, Nicholas: *Fright of the Fumblebee:* Corella, Gil

Rimsky-Korsakov, Nicholas: *Notturno:* British Tuba Quartet
Rimsky-Korsakov, Nicholas: *Scheherezade:* Jacobs, Arnold
Ringle and Meinken: *Wabash Blues:* Lehr, David "Red"; Palmer, Singleton; Pilafian, Sam
Robbins, Allen, and Sheafe: *Washington and Lee Swing:* Matteson, Rich
Roberts, William: *Hey Joe:* Moschner, Pinguin
Robin and Shavers: *Undecided Now:* Lehr, David "Red"
Robin, Leo: *Easy Livin':* Self, James
Robinson, Keith: *Custard the Dragon:* Swoboda, Deanna
Robinson, Keith: *Rainforest Etudes:* Swoboda, Deanna
Robinson, Keith, and Deanna Swoboda: *Wonderland Duets:* Swoboda, Deanna
Robinson, Perry: *Angels:* European Tuba Quartet
Robinson: *My Girl:* Tuba 4's
Robison: *Less Than That:* Tarto, Joe
Roblee, Richard: *Four Tuba Blues:* Melton Tuba-Quartett
Rodgers, Richard: *My Heart Stood Still:* Self, James
Rodgers, Richard, and Oscar Hammerstein: *It Might As Well Be Spring:* Gannett, Dave
Rodgers, Richard, and Oscar Hammerstein: *My Favorite Things:* Modern Jazz Tuba Project; Tennessee Technological University Tuba/Euphonium Ensemble
Rodgers, Richard, and Lorenz Hart: *Blue Moon:* Tuba 4's
Rodgers, Richard, and Lorenz Hart: *Lover:* Pilafian, Sam
Rodgers, Richard, and Lorenz Hart: *My Funny Valentine:* Murrow, Richard; Self, James
Rodgers, Richard, and Lorenz Hart: *You Took Advantage of Me:* Erickson, Martin
Rodriquez, G.: *La Cumparsita:* Pilafian, Sam
Rogers, Thomas: *Air for Tuba Ensemble:* Tennessee Tech Alumni Ensemble
Rogers, Thomas: *Music for Tuba Ensemble:* University of Miami Tuba Ensemble
Rogers, Walter: *The Volunteer:* Arwood, Jeffrey
Rollin, Robert: *The Raven and the First Men (Tuba, Horn, Piano, Electronics):* Turk, John
Rollins, Sonny: *Doxy:* Draper, Ray; Erickson, Martin; Mazura, János; Self, James
Rollins, Sonny: *Oleo:* Draper, Ray; Matteson-Phillips TubaJazz Consort; Modern Jazz Tuba Project
Rollinson, T. H.: *Rocked in the Cradle of the Deep:* Lawhern, Tim
Romberg, Sigmund: *Serenade from the "Student Prince":* Sheridan, Patrick
Romberg, Sigmund, and Hammerstein O.: *Softly, as a Morning Sunrise:* Feldman, Enrique "Hank" C.
Rome, Harold J.: *FDR Jones:* Pilafian, Sam
Ronell, Ann: *Willow Weep for Me:* Frey, Michael
Rood, Hale: *Simplis Sonor:* Morris, Jim
Roost, Jan Van der: *Cantuballade:* Nickel, Hans
Roost, Jan Van der: *Obsessions:* Nickel, Hans
Roper, Antony: *A String of Tones:* Tubalaté
Roper, William: *Em(M):* Roper, William
Roper, William: *Golden Gate Park/You Don't Know What Love Is:* Roper, William
Roper, William: *Juneteenth:* Roper, William
Roper, William: *Lachrimae:* Roper, William
Roper, William: *Pigs, Pigs, Oh! Those Tasty Pigs:* Roper, William
Roper, William: *A Recondite State of Lorn:* Roper, William
Rose and Richman: *Muddy Water:* M'N'M Trio
Rose, Jolson and DeSylva: *Avalon:* Matteson, Rich; Pilafian, Sam
Rosenthal, arr.: *Little Brown Jug:* Hanks, Thompson (Toby)
Rosler, J. J.: *Partita—Polacca:* Gerhard Meinl's Tuba Sextet
Ross, Walter: *Concerto Basso:* Tennessee Technological University Tuba/Euphonium Ensemble
Ross, Walter: *Escher's Sketches:* Nelson, Mark
Ross, Walter: *Fancy Dances for Three Bass Tubas:* New York Tuba Quartet
Ross, Walter: *Midnight Variations for Tuba and Tape:* Cummings, Barton
Ross, Walter: *Piltdown Fragments:* Cummings, Barton
Ross, Walter: *Tuba Concerto with Band:* Phillips, Harvey
Ross, Walter: *Villanella:* Nelson, Mark
Rossini, Gioacchino: *All'idea di qual metallo from "The Barber of Seville":* Pilafian, Sam
Rossini, Gioacchino: *La Danza:* British Tuba Quartet
Rossini, Gioacchino: *La Gazza Ladra:* Swiss Tuba Quartet
Rossini, Gioacchino: *Largo al factotum from "The Barber of Seville":* Crowther, Shaun; Gourlay, James; Morgan, Kevin; Norris, Tim; Pilafian, Sam
Rossini, Gioacchino: *Overture from the "Barber of Seville":* United States Armed Forces Tuba-Euphonium Ensemble
Rossini, Gioacchino: *Petit Caprice in the Style of Offenbach:* British Tuba Quartet; Monarch Tuba-Euphonium Quartet
Rossini, Gioacchino: *William Fell over the Chair:* Corella, Gil
Rossini, Gioacchino: *William Tell Overture:* British Tuba Quartet; Symphonia
Rottler, Werner: *Sonatine für Tuba und Klavier, Op. 14:* Walsh, Thomas
Rowles, Jimmy: *The Peacocks:* Self, James
Rubenstein, Arthur: *Bruegel–Dance Visions:* Self, James
Rufeisen, Arie: *A Short Suspense Story:* Hershko, Shmuel "Adi"
Ruga, Claudio: *Swing Castle:* Dites-Le-Moi Tuba
Ruggiero, Charles: *Fractured Mambos:* Sinder, Philip
Russell, Armand: *Suite Concertante:* Cooley, Floyd

Russian Folksong: *Song of the Volga Boatman:* Daellenbach, Charles
Ruth, Matthew: *Exigencies:* Tennessee Technological University Tuba/Euphonium Ensemble
Sachse: *Lee Pizza, NE:* Moschner, Pinguin
Saglietti, Corrado Maria: *Concerto:* Hötzel, Markus
Saint-Saëns, Camille: *Adagio from Symphony No. 3:* British Tuba Quartet
Saint-Saëns, Camille: *The Elephant from "Carnival of the Animals":* Piernik, Zdizislaw; Tubalaté; Yasumoto, Hiroyuki
Saint-Saëns, Camille: *Marche Militaire Francaise:* United States Armed Forces Tuba-Euphonium Ensemble and Massed Ensemble
Saint-Saëns, Camille: *Morceau de Concerto (III. Allegro non troppo):* Piernik, Zdizislaw
Saint-Saëns, Camille: *The Swan from "Carnival of the Animals":* Cummings, Barton; King, Ian; Morgan, Kevin; Piernik, Zdizislaw; Sheridan, Patrick; Tubalaté
Salama and Grebenka: *Dark Eyes:* M'N'M Trio; Pilafian, Sam
Salotti, Harry: *Etudes with Style, Music for the Tuba:* Sheridan, Patrick
samohT,snevetS: *zoB erocnE:* Bobo, Roger
Sample, Steve: *Nostalgia Medley:* Tennessee Technological University Tuba/Euphonium Ensemble
Sampson, David: *Three Portraits for Tuba and Chamber Orchestra:* Mendoker, Scott
Sarvello, Frank: *Riff Rock:* Morris, Jim
Sass, Jonathon: *Blue Lights:* Heavy Tuba
Sass, Jonathon: *Going Uptown:* Heavy Tuba
Sass, Jonathon: *Meltdown:* Gerhard Meinl's Tuba Sextet; Heavy Tuba
Sass, Jonathon: *148 Street Blues:* Heavy Tuba
Sass, Jonathon: *Ripsey's Rumble:* Heavy Tuba
Satie, Erik: *Gymnopedie:* Murrow, Richard
Satterwhite, Marc: *And What Rough Beast . . . ?, For Tuba and Percussion:* Pokorny, Gene
Sauter, Eddie: *Conjectures for Tuba and Band:* Phillips, Harvey
Schaars, Peter Kleine: *Wolf the Cat:* Dutch Tuba Quartet
Schäffer, Boguslaw: *Projekt für Tuba und Toneband:* Piernik, Zdizislaw
Scharnberg, Kim: *Juba Plays the FLUBA in Aruba:* Self, James
Scharnberg, Kim: *Waltz for Maya:* Self, Jim
Schertzinger, Victor, and Johnny Mercer: *Tangerine:* Corella, Gil; Gannett, Dave
Schiaffini, GianCarlo: *Aqui el sol brilla mas:* Schiaffini, GianCarlo
Schiaffini, GianCarlo: *Cuba Mirum:* Schiaffini, GianCarlo
Schiaffini, GianCarlo: *El carrousel de Juana la Loca:* Schiaffini, GianCarlo
Schiaffini, GianCarlo: *El vuelo irresistibile del moscardon:* Schiaffini, GianCarlo
Schiaffini, Giancarlo: *Infernal Dream:* Schiaffini, Giancarlo
Schiaffini, GianCarlo: *Madrugada de laton:* Schiaffini, GianCarlo
Schiaffini, GianCarlo: *Mi mistico minimo Mi:* Schiaffini, GianCarlo
Schiaffini, GianCarlo: *Scrap:* Schiaffini, GianCarlo
Schiaffini, GianCarlo: *Scratch:* Schiaffini, GianCarlo
Schiaffini, GianCarlo: *Sueno infernal:* Schiaffini, GianCarlo
Schiaffini, GianCarlo: *Tuba Libre:* Schiaffini, GianCarlo
Schiaffini, GianCarlo: *Voz refracta:* Schiaffini, GianCarlo
Schidlt, M.: *Gleichwie das Feuer:* Anderson, Hans
Schifrin, Lalo: *Mission Impossible:* Tubalaté
Schlenker, Manfred: *Rondo Variato:* Hötzel, Markus
Schlunz, Annette: *ACH, ES . . . Music for Tuba Solo:* Vogt, Michael
Schmidt, Ole: *Concerto for Tuba and Orchestra:* Lind, Michael
Schmidt, William: *Serenade for Tuba and Piano:* Conner, Rex; Johnson, John Thomas (Tommy)
Schmidt, William: *Sonata for Tuba and Piano:* Hanks, Toby; Nickel, Hans
Schmidt, William: *Tuba Mirum—Variations on a Gregorian Chant:* Sinder, Philip
Schmitt, Florent: *Quatuor, Op. 109:* Bazsinka, József
Schoebel, Maras, and Rapollo: *Farewell Blues:* Lehr, David "Red"
Schoenberg, C. M.: *On My Own from "Les Miserables":* British Tuba Quartet; Miraphone Tuba Quartet; Morgan, Kevin
Schooley, John: *Cherokee:* Melton Tuba-Quartett; Northern Tuba Lights; Rustic Bari-Tuba Ensemble
Schooley, John: *Toccata:* Rustic Bari-Tuba Ensemble
Schop: *Break Forth O Beauteous Light:* Mighty Tubadours
Schubert, Franz Peter: *An die Musik, Op. 88, No. 4:* Brewer, Robert; Daellenbach, Charles
Schubert, Franz Peter: *Arpeggione Sonata:* Jae Young, Heo
Schubert, Franz Peter: *Ave Maria:* Sykes, Steve
Schubert, Franz Peter: *Die Forelle (Trout) Theme and Variations 1–5:* Contraband Tuba Quartet
Schubert, Franz Peter: *Lieder, Op. 135, D921:* Labeyrie, Stéphane
Schubert, Franz Peter: *Militärmarsch:* Contraband (The)
Schubert, Franz Peter: *Serenade:* Bobo, Roger; Cummings, Barton; Piernik, Zdizislaw
Schubert, Franz Peter: *Ständchen:* Contraband (The)
Schubert, Franz Peter: *Who Is Sylvia?:* Daellenbach, Charles
Schuller, Gunther: *Capriccio for Tuba and Orchestra:* Phillips, Harvey

Schuller, Gunther: *Five Moods for Tuba Quartet:* New York Tuba Quartet
Schultz, Mark: *T Rex:* Swoboda, Deanna
Schulz: *O Come Little Children:* Mighty Tubadours
Schulz, Patrick: *Profiles, for Tuba Quartet:* Sotto Voce
Schumann, Robert: *Adagio and Allegro in A♭, Op. 70:* Brewer, Robert; Cooley, Floyd; Dowling, Eugene; Funderburk, Jeff; Hanks, Toby; Skillen, Joseph
Schumann, Robert: *Drei Romanzen, Op. 94:* Cooley, Floyd
Schumann, Robert: *Fantasiestücke, Op. 73:* Cooley, Floyd
Schumann, Robert: *Fughetta:* Swiss Tuba Quartet
Schumann, Robert: *The Jolly Farmer Goes to Town:* Bell, William
Schumann, Robert: *Märchenbilder (Pictures of Fairyland), Op. 113:* Cooley, Floyd
Schumann, Robert: *Scenes from Childhood, Op. 15:* Self, James
Schumann, Robert: *Traumerei:* Melton Tuba-Quartett; Norris, Tim; Piernik, Zdizislaw
Schwartz, Jean: *Chinatown, My Chinatown:* Daellenbach, Charles
Scott, Stuart: *Fellscape:* Tubalaté
Scottish Folksong: *Loch Lomond:* Daellenbach, Charles
Sear, Walter: *Sonatina:* Davis, Ronald; Megules, Karl
Seivewright, Andrew: *Gowbarrow Gavotte:* Tubalaté
Self, James: *The Basset Hound Blues:* Self, James
Self, James: *Capriole:* Self, James
Self, James: *Courante:* Self, James
Self, James: *Duh Suite:* O'Bryant, Kelly
Self, James: *For Christina:* Self, James
Self, James: *La Morte dell'Oom (No Pah Intended):* Symphonia
Self, James: *Poker Chips:* Self, Jim
Self, James: *Polka.com:* Self, Jim
Self, James: *Rondeau:* Self, Jim
Self, James: *Sousa, Phone Home!:* Self, James
Self, James: *That Morning in May:* Self, James
Self, James: *3 for 5:* Self, Jim
Sellers, Joey: *Terrible Twos:* Self, James
Semanya, Caiphus: *Ma-Ma:* Johnson, Howard
Semler-Collery, Jules: *Barcarolle et Chanson Bachique:* Popiel, Peter; Randolph, David
Senaillé, Jean Baptiste: *Introduction and Allegro Spiritoso:* Norris, Tim
Shaw, Lowell: *Frippery:* Miraphone Tuba Quartet
Shearing, George: *Lullaby of Birdland:* Albertasaurus Tuba Quartet; Tennessee Technological University Tuba/Euphonium Ensemble
Sheldon, Jack: *Your Mama Ain't Got No Draws:* Matteson-Phillips TubaJazz Consort
Sheng-Tong, Tsai: *Capriccio for Tuba and Piano:* Stachowiak, Bernard
Sheridan, John: *All Alone Blues:* Erickson, Martin
Sherman-Bernie: *Marguriete:* Tarto, Joe
Sherman/Sherman/Gaston: *I Wan'na Be Like You:* Tuba 4's
Sherwin, Manning: *A Nightingale Sang in Berkley Square:* British Tuba Quartet; Monarch Tuba-Euphonium Quartet; Symphonia
Shorter, Wayne: *Adam's Apple:* Self, James
Shostakovich, Dmitri: *Adagio:* Bobo, Roger
Shostakovich, Dmitri: *Festival Overture:* Symphonia
Sibbing, Robert: *Sonata:* Perantoni, Daniel
Sibelius, Jean: *Finlandia:* Daellenbach, Charles
Sikora, Elzbieta: *Il Viaggio 1 per tuba solo con pianoforte:* Piernik, Zdizislaw
Silver, Horace: *Cookin' at the Continental:* Modern Jazz Tuba Project
Silver, Horace: *Gregory Is Here:* Matteson-Phillips TubaJazz Consort; Modern Jazz Tuba Project
Silver, Horace: *Señor Blues:* Matteson-Phillips TubaJazz Consort; Tennessee Tech Alumni Ensemble
Silver, Horace: *Sister Sadie:* Tennessee Technological University Tuba/Euphonium Ensemble
Silver, Horace: *Strollin':* Self, James
Silverman, Faye-Ellen: *Zigzags:* Brown, Velvet
Simons, Moises: *El Manisero:* Pilafian, Sam
Sinigaglia, Leone: *Song and Humoreske:* Bobo, Roger
Sivelov, Niklas: *Sonata for Tuba and Piano:* Baadsvik, Øystein
Skeen, Lewis: *Suite for Brass:* Morris, Jim
Skempton, Howard: *Rest and Recreation:* Tubalaté
Skill: *That's What I Like about You:* Dixie Power Trio
Smalley, Peter: *A Cool Suite:* British Tuba Quartet
Smalley, Peter: *The Glyder Landscape:* British Tuba Quartet
Smith, Claude T.: *Ballade and Presto Dance:* Daniel, Robert; Jae Young, Heo; Seward, Steven
Smith, Glenn: *Forowen 3 (Tuba and Piccolo):* Turk, John
Smith, Jabbo: *Lina Blues:* Newberger, Eli
Smith, Warren: *Blues for E. L. C.:* Johnson, Howard
Smith, Warren: *Hello Julius:* Johnson, Howard
Smith, Warren: *Introduction to the Blues:* Johnson, Howard
Smith, Warren: *Lament:* Johnson, Howard
Smith, Zachary: *Baby Got Banjo:* Dixie Power Trio
Smith, Zachary: *Baby, You Keep Me Up All Night:* Dixie Power Trio
Smith, Zachary: *Can't Let Go That Zydeco:* Dixie Power Trio
Smith, Zachary: *DPT Second Line:* Dixie Power Trio
Smith, Zachary: *The Good, The Bad, and The Banjo:* Dixie Power Trio
Smith, Zachary: *Regardez La Femme Charmante:* Dixie Power Trio
Smith, Zachary: *She Loves Me Anyway:* Dixie Power Trio

Smith, Zachary: *Wicked Jerk Chicken:* Dixie Power Trio
Smith, Zachary: *The Woman Is Right:* Dixie Power Trio
Snow, Phoebe: *Sweet Disposition:* Johnson, Howard
Solal: *Tuba Only:* Steckar Tubapack
Solomons, David: *Pieces of Eight:* Tubalaté
Solomons, David: *Prayer before the Close of Day:* Tubalaté
Sondheim, S.: *Send in the Clowns:* Woods, Gavin
Sousa, John Philip: *El Capitan:* British Tuba Quartet; Monarch Tuba-Euphonium Quartet; Tubalaté
Sousa, John Philip: *Hands across the Sea:* Northern Tuba Lights
Sousa, John Philip: *Semper Fidelis:* British Tuba Quartet
Sousa, John Philip: *Stars and Stripes Forever:* Atlantic Tuba Quartet; Miraphone Tuba Quartet; Northern Tuba Lights; Palmer, Singleton; Swiss Tuba Quartet; University of Miami Tuba Ensemble
Sousa, John Philip: *The Thunderer:* British Tuba Quartet; Dutch Tuba Quartet; Tubalaté
Sousa, John Philip: *Washington Post March:* British Tuba Quartet; Colonial Tuba Quartet; Contraband (The); Melton Tuba-Quartett; Miraphone Tuba Quartet
Sowerby, Leo: *Chaconne:* Davis, Ronald
Sparke, Philip: *Fantasy for Euphonium and Brass Band:* Seward, Steven
Spears, Jared: *Divertimento for Tuba Ensemble:* Tennessee Tech Alumni Ensemble; Tennessee Technological University Tuba/Euphonium Ensemble
Spencer, Larry: *Ingrid:* Murrow, Richard
Spillman, Robert: *Two Songs:* Bobo, Roger
Spiritual: *Swing Low, Sweet Chariot:* Contraband (The); Dutch Tuba Quartet
Sprick, Geert: *Mens Sana in Corpore Sano:* Miraphone Tuba Quartet
Stamp, Jack: *Colonial Express:* Colonial Tuba Quartet
Stanley the Bassett Hound: *Stanley's Last "Howl":* Self, James
Steckar, Franck: *Hurry Up:* Steckar Tubapack
Steckar, Franck: *In a Digital Mood:* Steckar Tubapack
Steckar, Franck: *Mon Cerveau a du Chagrin:* Steckar Tubapack
Steckar, Franck: *Rouleaux De Printemps:* Steckar Elephant Tuba Horde
Steckar, Franck: *Stabillo Steckardello:* Steckar Elephant Tuba Horde
Steckar, Franck: *Tubapack Blues:* Steckar Tubapack
Steckar, Marc: *African Tuba Safari:* Stecker, Marc
Steckar, Marc: *Bassacat:* Miraphone Tuba Quartet
Steckar, Marc: *Batubop:* Steckar Tubapack
Steckar, Marc: *Bayerische Pop Tuba:* Stecker, Marc
Steckar, Marc: *Butacudatuba:* Stecker, Marc
Steckar, Marc: *Danse pour un Kangourou:* Steckar Tubapack
Steckar, Marc: *Duo Solo:* Thuillier, Francois
Steckar, Marc: *Dynozophorium:* Steckar Tubapack
Steckar, Marc: *Le Rêve d'lcare:* Thuillier, Francois
Steckar, Marc: *Megalo Fanfare:* Steckar Tubapack
Steckar, Marc: *Salammba:* Steckar Tubapack
Steckar, Marc: *Serie Noire:* Steckar Tubapack
Steckar, Marc: *Suite a suivre:* Steckar Tubapack
Steckar, Marc: *Tu bats le fer etc ...:* Legris, Philippe
Steckar, Marc: *Tuba Banjo Dixie:* Stecker, Marc
Steckar, Marc: *Tuba Boum:* Thuillier, Francois
Steckar, Marc: *Tuba des Champs:* Steckar Tubapack
Steckar, Marc: *Tuba Des Villes:* Steckar Tubapack
Steckar, Marc: *Tubacuba:* Stecker, Marc
Steckar, Marc: *"Tubaobab"–Concerto in Four Movements for Tuba and Big Wind Band:* Legris, Philippe
Steckar, Marc: *Tubas au Fujiyama:* Steckar Elephant Tuba Horde; Steckar, Marc
Steckar, Marc: *Vendredi 13:* Steckar Tubapack
Steele and Melrose: *High Society:* Lehr, David "Red"; Palmer, Singleton
Steiner: *Dudley Do-Right of the Mounties:* Gannett, Dave
Steiner: *Dudley Do-Wrong!:* Gannett, Dave
Stevens, Halsey: *Sonatina for Tuba and Piano:* Brewer, Robert; Perantoni, Daniel; Randolph, David; Self, James
Stevens, John: *Adagio:* Symphonia
Stevens, John: *Benediction:* Sotto Voce
Stevens, John: *Dances:* Dutch Tuba Quartet; Hanks, Thompson (Toby); Melton Tuba-Quartett; Northern Tuba Lights; Rustic Bari-Tuba Ensemble; Sotto Voce
Stevens, John: *Diversions:* Sotto Voce
Stevens, John: *Fanfare for a Friend:* Sotto Voce
Stevens, John: *The Liberation of Sisyphus:* Bazsinka, József; Bobo, Roger
Stevens, John: *Manhattan Suite:* Dutch Tuba Quartet; Miraphone Tuba Quartet; University of Michigan Tuba and Euphonium Ensemble; Sotto Voce
Stevens, John: *Moondance:* Dutch Tuba Quartet; Melton Tuba-Quartett; Summit Tubas; Sotto Voce
Stevens, John: *Music 4 Tubas:* New York Tuba Quartet; Sotto Voce
Stevens, John: *Power:* Melton Tuba-Quartett; Miraphone Tuba Quartet; Northern Tuba Lights; Stevens, John; Sotto Voce
Stevens, John: *Salve Venere, Salve Marte:* Brown, Velvet
Stevens, John: *Splinters:* Stevens, John
Stevens, John: *Suite for II:* Stevens, John
Stevens, John: *Suite No. 1 for Solo Tuba:* Stevens, John
Stevens, John: *Talisman/Cookie's Revenge:* Symphonia

Stevens, John: *Thunder and Lightning:* Stevens, John
Stevens, John: *Triumph of the Demon Gods:* Stevens, John
Stevens, John: *Viva Voce!:* Sotto Voce
Stevens, Thomas: *Encore Boz:* Bobo, Roger
Stevens, Thomas: *Variations in Olden Style:* Baadsvik, Øystein; Bobo, Roger
Stewart, Bob: *CJ:* Stewart, Bob
Stewart, Bob: *First Line:* Stewart, Bob
Stewart, Bob: *Hambone:* Stewart, Bob
Stewart, Bob: *Nonet:* Stewart, Bob
Stewart, Bob: *Rambler:* Stewart, Bob
Stewart, Bob: *Sweet Georgia Brown Sweet:* Stewart, Bob
Stewart, Bob: *Tunk:* Stewart, Bob
Stitzel, Mel: *The Chant:* Dixie Power Trio; Matteson, Rich; Newberger, Eli
Stradella, Alessandro: *Pieta, Signora:* Megules, Karl
Straight and Kahn: *Santa Claus Blues:* M'N'M Trio
Strauss, Johann: *Chit Chat Polka:* British Tuba Quartet
Strauss, Johann: *Perpetuum Mobile:* British Tuba Quartet
Strauss, Johann: *Radetzky Marsch:* Miraphone Tuba Quartet
Strauss, Johann: *Tritsch-Tratsch Polka:* Melton Tuba-Quartett
Strauss, Johann: *Waltz from "Die Fledermaus":* Mighty Tubadours
Strauss, Richard: *Also sprach Zarathustra (excerpt):* Pokorny, Gene
Strauss, Richard: *Concerto No. 1 for Horn, Op. 11:* Cooley, Floyd; Jacobs, Arnold
Strauss, Richard: *Ein Heldenleben (excerpt):* Pokorny, Gene
Strauss, Richard: *Second Horn Concerto:* Seward, Steven
Strauss, Richard: *Till Eulenspiegels lustige Streiche (excerpt):* Pokorny, Gene
Strauss, Richard: *Zarathustra's Reincarnation:* Heavy Tuba
Stravinsky, Igor: *Bear Solo from "Petrouchka":* Jacobs, Arnold
Stravinsky, Igor: *Elegie:* Vogt, Michael
Stravinsky, Igor: *Petroushka (excerpt):* Pokorny, Gene
Strayhorn, Billy: *Lush Life:* Self, James
Stroud, Richard: *Treatments for Tuba:* Tennessee Technological University Tuba/Euphonium Ensemble
Strukov, Valery: *Concerto for Tuba and Orchestra:* Bjørn-Larsen, Jens
Subatnik, Morton: *First Dream of Light:* Bobo, Roger
Sullivan, Arthur: *Miya Sama from "The Mikado":* Daellenbach, Charles
Sullivan, Arthur: *Pale Young Curate:* Daellenbach, Charles
Susato, Tielman: *Ronde and Saltarelle "Pour Quoy":* Atlantic Tuba Quartet
Susato, Tielman: *Shepherd's Dance:* Alchemy
Swann, Donald: *Two Moods for Tuba:* Phillips, Harvey; Randolph, David
Swanstone, McCarron, and Morgan: *The Blues My Naughty Sweetie Gives to Me:* Dixie Power Trio; Lehr, David "Red"
Swoboda, Deanna: *Brass Rap!:* Swoboda, Deanna
Swoboda, Deanna: *Patricia Lee and Leah Marie:* Swoboda, Deanna
Sykes, arr.: *Hefje Kati:* Sykes, Stephen
Sykes, Steve: *Carnival Cocktail:* Sykes, Steve
Sylva and Henderson: *Sonny Boy:* (see Brown, DeSylva, and Henderson)
Szalóky, Béla: *Truesome Whosome:* Mazura, János
Szalonek, W.: *Piernikiana for Solo Tuba:* Piernik, Zdizislaw
Szentpáli, Roland: *The Devil Never Sleeps:* Szentpáli, Roland
Szentpáli, Roland: *Mi Amor:* Szentpáli, Roland
Szentpáli, Roland: *Variations for a Children Song:* Szentpáli, Roland
Szentpáli, Roland: *Your Kisses like the Fire:* Szentpáli, Roland
Tackett, Fred: *The Yellow Bird:* Bobo, Roger
Taggart, Mark: *Athletic Conveyance:* Jarvis, Jeffrey
Takács, Jenö: *Sonata Capricciosa Op. 81:* Randolph, David
Tarlow, Lawrence: *Quintet for Tubas:* Megules, Karl
Tarto, Joe: *Black Horse Stomp:* Tarto, Joe
Tarto, Joe: *Medley——alty Sailor Tunes:* Tarto, Joe
Tarto, Joe, and Paul Lavelle: *Boy Scout—Be Prepared:* Tarto, Joe
Tarto, Joe, and Paul Lavelle: *The Trumpet Polka:* Tarto, Joe
Tautenhahn, G.: *In—Phase—Out:* Heavy Tuba
Taylor: *Wild Thing:* Moschner, Pinguin
Taylor, Billy: *One for the Whoofer:* Erickson, Martin
Taylor, Coleridge: *Substructure:* Johnson, Howard
Taylor, Jeffrey: *Fanfare No. 1:* British Tuba Quartet; Monarch Tuba-Euphonium Quartet
Taylor, Mark: *Latin Fantasy:* Arwood, Jeffrey
Taylor, Tell: *Down by the Old Mill Stream:* Mighty Tubadours
Tchaikovsky, Peter Ilyitch: *Andante Cantabile:* Sheridan, Patrick
Tchaikovsky, Peter Ilyitch: *Boss-Swan-Nova:* Erickson, Martin
Tchaikovsky, Peter Ilyitch: *Dance of the Reedpipes:* Mighty Tubadours
Tchaikovsky, Peter Ilyitch: *Dance of the Sugar Plum Fairy:* British Tuba Quartet
Tchaikovsky, Peter Ilyitch: *1812 Overture (excerpt):* Jacobs, Arnold
Tchaikovsky, Peter Ilyitch: *Finale to Symphony No. 4:* Self, Jim
Tchaikovsky, Peter Ilyitch: *March-Overture from "Nutcracker":* Mighty Tubadours

Tchaikovsky, Peter Ilyitch: *Neopolitan Song:* Tubalaté
Tchaikovsky, Peter Ilyitch: *Overture Miniature from "Nutcracker":* Fletcher, John
Tchaikovsky, Peter Ilyitch: *Serenade for Tubas:* Tennessee Technological University Tuba/Euphonium Ensemble
Tchaikovsky, Peter Ilyitch: *Symphony No. 6 (fourth movement):* Jacobs, Arnold
Tchaikovsky, Peter Ilyitch: *Trepek:* British Tuba Quartet
Tchaikovsky, Peter Ilyitch: *Waltz from "Sleeping Beauty":* Fletcher, John
Tcherepnin, Alexander: *Andante:* Sinder, Philip
Teike, Carl: *Alte Kameraden:* Miraphone Tuba Quartet
Teike, Carl: *Graf Zeppelin Marsch:* Miraphone Tuba Quartet
Telemann, Georg Philipp: *Fantasy in C minor:* Hanks, Thompson (Toby)
Telemann, Georg Philipp: *Sonata for Oboe and Continuo:* Thuillier, Francois
Telemann, Georg Philipp: *Sonata in E minor:* Seward, Steven
Telemann, Georg Philipp: *Sonata in F:* Sinder, Philip
Telemann, Georg Philipp: *Sonata in F minor:* Seward, Steven
Telemann, Georg Philipp: *Sonata in F minor for Bassoon:* Jae Young, Heo
Templeton, Alec: *Mr. Bach Goes to Town:* Contraband Tuba Quartet
Templeton, Alec: *On a Rocky Road:* Contraband Tuba Quartet
Terry, Clark: *C. T.'s Blues (Finger Filibuster):* Matteson-Phillips TubaJazz Consort
Theard, Sam: *You Rascal You:* M'N'M Trio
Thingnäs, Frode: *Fink Finster:* Scandinavian Tuba Jazz
Thingnäs, Frode: *Samba Loco:* Scandinavian Tuba Jazz
Thomas, D. C.: *Spinning Wheel:* Heavy Tuba
Thomas, Henry: *Fishin' Blues:* Johnson, Howard
Thompson, Troy: *Allegro from Sonatina for Tuba:* Funderburk, Jeff
Thuillier, Francois: *A tot bien:* Thuillier, Francois
Thuillier, Francois: *Baguette Viennoise:* Thuillier, Francois
Thuillier, Francois: *Ballad for Inger:* Thuillier, Francois
Thuillier, Francois: *Equilibre Indifférent, for Tuba, Trumpet and Trombone:* Thuillier, Francois
Thuillier, Francois: *Faux-cils et vraies moustaches:* Thuillier, Francois
Thuillier, Francois: *Felka Miotta:* Thuillier, Francois
Thuillier, Francois: *Hommage:* Thuillier, Francois
Thuillier, Francois: *80660:* Thuillier, Francois
Thuillier, Francois: *L'écureuil fou:* Thuillier, Francois
Thuillier, Francois: *L'insensible Gregiore:* Thuillier, Francois
Thuillier, Francois: *Places des Vosges:* Thuillier, Francois
Thuillier, Francois: *Sale gosse:* Thuillier, Francois
Thuillier, Francois: *Timisoara:* Thuillier, Francois
Thuillier, Francois: *Vif, tendre et dangereux:* Thuillier, Francois
Thuillier, Francois: *20h30:* Thuillier, Francois
Tilzer, Albert von: *Take Me Out to the Ball Game:* Daellenbach, Charles
Tisne, Antoine: *Monodie III:* Legris, Philippe
Toda, Akira: *Euphonium Tuba Quartet:* Rustic Bari-Tuba Ensemble
Toledo, Rene Luis: *Rene's Song:* Modern Jazz Tuba Project
Tolliver, Charles: *Right Now:* Johnson, Howard
Tomasi, Henri: *Danse Sacrée:* Brown, Velvet
Tomasi, Henri: *Être Ou Ne Pas Être! (monolog D'Hamlet) with three trombones:* Bazsinka, József; Hanks, Thompson (Toby); Jacobs, Arnold
Tormé and Wells: *The Christmas Song:* Phillips, Harvey/TubaChristmas; Pilafian, Sam
Toyama, Yuzo: *Trio Sonata for Tuba, Batteries [Percussion], and Piano:* Yasumoto, Hiroyuki
Traditional: *Aija Zuzu:* Tubalaté
Traditional: *Amazing Grace:* O'Bryant, Kelly
Traditional: *Bavarian Polka:* British Tuba Quartet
Traditional: *Bayerische Zell:* Gerhard Meinl's Tuba Sextet
Traditional: *Clarinet Polka:* Davis, Ronald; Tuba 4's
Traditional: *Dance of the Big Fairries:* Flowers, Herbie
Traditional: *Deep River/Swing Low Sweet Chariot:* King, Ian
Traditional: *Der Khusid geyt Tantsn:* Dutch Tuba Quartet
Traditional: *English Country Airs:* Tubalaté
Traditional: *Freylekhs fun der Khupe:* Dutch Tuba Quartet
Traditional: *Greensleeves:* Atlantic Tuba Quartet; British Tuba Quartet; Melton Tuba-Quartett; Miraphone Tuba Quartet; Phillips, Harvey/TubaChristmas; Rustic Bari-Tuba Ensemble; Swiss Tuba Quartet
Traditional: *Havah Nagilah:* British Tuba Quartet
Traditional: *Hey Mama:* Stewart, Bob
Traditional: *I've Been Workin':* Self, James
Traditional: *Irish Washerwoman:* Norris, Tim
Traditional: *John Brown's Body:* Johnson, Howard
Traditional: *Just a Closer Walk with Thee:* Callender, George Sylvester "Red"; Daellenbach, Charles; Erickson, Martin; Lehr, David "Red"; Palmer, Singleton; Tennessee Technological University Tuba/Euphonium Ensemble; Tubalaté
Traditional: *Kagami Jishi:* Roper, William
Traditional: *Kesh Jig:* Baadsvik, Øystein
Traditional: *The Londonderry Air (Danny Boy):* Melton Tuba-Quartett; Monarch Tuba-Euphonium Quartet; Sheridan, Patrick; Tennessee Tech Alumni Ensemble; United States Armed Forces Tuba-Euphonium Ensemble

Traditional: *Negro Spirituals:* Woods, Gavin
Traditional: *Old Star:* Melton Tuba-Quartett
Traditional: *One Room Country Shack:* Bargeron, Dave
Traditional: *Sakura Sakura:* Yasumoto, Hiroyuki
Traditional: *Scarborough Fair:* Tubalaté
Traditional: *Sea Tubas:* Northern Tuba Lights
Traditional: *Shenandoah:* Self, James
Traditional: *Simple Gifts:* Self, James
Traditional: *Simple Gifts/Yankee Doodle/When Jesus Wept/Chester/Edelweiss:* Colonial Tuba Quartet
Traditional: *Sometimes I Feel like a Motherless Child:* Stewart, Bob
Traditional: *Sponger Money:* Alchemy
Traditional: *Steal Away:* British Tuba Quartet
Traditional: *Surinam:* Stewart, Bob
Traditional: *Three Negro Spirituals:* Tubalaté
Traditional: *Tsiganochka:* Buttery, Gary
Traditional: *Tuba Smarties:* Flowers, Herbie; Norris, Tim
Traditional: *Turkey in the Straw (and Several Other Places):* Self, James
Traditional: *Wabash Cannonball:* British Tuba Quartet; Lehr, David "Red"
Traditional: *When the Saints Go Marching In:* Callender, George Sylvester "Red"; Palmer, Singleton
Traditional: *While Soft Winds Shake the Barley:* Alchemy
Traditional: *Yisrael V'oraita:* Feldman, Enrique "Hank" C.
Traditional American: *Yankee Doodle:* Daellenbach, Charles
Trujillo, Tommy: *If You Ever Wanna:* Draper, Ray
Tscherepnin, Alexander: *Andante for Tuba and Piano:* Hoppert, Manfred
Tull, Fisher: *Tubular Octad:* Tennessee Technological University Tuba/Euphonium Ensemble
Turpin, Tom: *Harlem Rag:* Albertasaurus Tuba Quartet
Turrin, Joseph: *Escapade:* Sykes, Steve
Tyner, McCoy: *Mode to John:* Pilafian, Sam
Uber, David: *Ballad of Enob Mort:* Jae Young, Heo
Uber, David: *Beachcombers Dance:* Hanks, Thompson (Toby)
Uber, David: *A Day at the Camptown Races:* Hanks, Thompson (Toby)
Uber, David: *Double Portraits for Trombone and Tuba:* Lind, Michael
Uber, David: *Music for the Stage:* Dutch Tuba Quartet
Uber, David: *Rhythmic Contours (first movement):* Cummings, Barton
Uber, David: *Romance:* Jae Young, Heo
Uber, David: *Sonata for Bass Tuba and Piano:* Jae Young, Heo
Ung, Chinary: *Spiral II, for Mezzo-soprano, Piano and Tuba:* Perantoni, Daniel
Urbaniak, Michael: *New York Polka:* Frey, Michael
Ustvolskaya, Galina: *Dona Nobis Pacem:* LeClair, David
Van Heusen, Jimmy, and Phil Silvers: *Nancy with the Laughing Face:* Arwood, Jeffrey
Vaughan, arr.: *Coventry Carol:* Mighty Tubadours
Vaughan, arr.: *God Rest Ye Merry, Gentlemen:* Mighty Tubadours
Vaughan, arr.: *Hail the Lord's Annointed:* Mighty Tubadours
Vaughan, arr.: *O Come, O Come Emmanuel:* Mighty Tubadours
Vaughan, Rodger: *Concertpiece No. 1:* Conner, Rex; Davis, Ronald; Funderburk, Jeff
Vaughan, Rodger: *Jingle Bell Waltz:* Mighty Tubadours
Vaughan Williams, Ralph: *Concerto for Bass Tuba and Band:* Arwood, Jeffrey; Perantoni, Daniel; Phillips, Harvey
Vaughan Williams, Ralph: *Concerto for Bass Tuba and Brass Band:* Gourlay, James
Vaughan Williams, Ralph: *Concerto for Bass Tuba and Orchestra:* Catelinet, Philip; Cooley, Floyd; Dowling, Eugene; Fletcher, John; Harrild, Patrick; Hoppert, Manfred; Jacobs, Arnold; King, Ian; Lind, Michael; Morgan, Kevin; Nahatzki, Richard; Nickel, Hans; Phillips, Harvey; Strand, Donald
Vaughan Williams, Ralph: *Six Studies in English Folksong:* Dowling, Eugene; Pokorny, Gene
Velasquez, Consuelo: *Besame Mucho:* Pilafian, Sam
Venable and Armstrong: *Irish Black Bottom:* M'N'M Trio
Verdi, Giuseppi: *Dies Irae from Requiem:* Symphonia
Verdi, Giuseppi: *"Fairest daughter of the graces" from Rigoletto:* Morgan, Kevin
Verdi, Giuseppi: *Force of Destiny Overture:* British Tuba Quartet
Verdi, Giuseppi: *Nabucco Overture (excerpt):* Jacobs, Arnold
Verdi, Giuseppi: *Prayer (Il lascerato spirito):* Daellenbach, Charles
Verdi, Giuseppi: *Sempre libera from "La Traviata":* Pilafian, Sam
Verdi, Giuseppi: *Two Selections from "La Traviata":* Albertasaurus Tuba Quartet
Victoria, Thomas Luis de: *O Vos Omnes:* Melton Tuba-Quartett
Vigneron, Louis: *Sentier De Nuit:* Steckar Elephant Tuba Horde
Vignola, Frank: *Chasin' the Antelope:* Pilafian, Sam
Villa-Lobos, Heitor: *Danza Martelo from Bachianas Brasilieras No. 5:* Alchemy
Vinson, Danny: *Memoirs of the American Civil War:* Alchemy
Vivaldi, Antonio: *Cello Sonata No. 5 in E:* King, Ian
Vivaldi, Antonio: *Concerto in C major for Two Trumpets:* Seward, Steven
Vivaldi, Antonio: *L'Inverno (Winter) from The Four Seasons:* Baadsvik, Øystein

Vivaldi, Antonio: *Winter from "The Four Seasons":* Tennessee Technological University Tuba/Euphonium Ensemble (Scott Beaver, solo tuba)
Vlatkovich: *The Perfect Construction of Decisive Moments:* Roper, William
Vogt, Michael: *Homo Ludens in Berlin:* Vogt, Michael
Volksweise: *Petersburger Marsch:* Miraphone Tuba Quartet
Wagner, Richard: *Die Meistersinger von Nürnberg (excerpt):* Pokorny, Gene
Wagner, Richard: *A Faust Overture (excerpt):* Pokorny, Gene
Wagner, Richard: *Lohengrin (excerpt):* Pokorny, Gene
Wagner, Richard: *Lohengrin (Introduction to Act III):* Jacobs, Arnold
Wagner, Richard: *O Du Mein Holder Abendstern from "Tannhauser":* Fletcher, John
Wagner, Richard: *Ride of the Valkyries (excerpt):* Pokorny, Gene
Wagner, Richard: *Siegfried (excerpts):* Cooley, Floyd
Wagner, Richard: *Tannhauser Overture:* Jacobs, Arnold
Wagner, Richard: *Valkyrie (Magic Fire Music, Ride of the Valkyries):* Jacobs, Arnold
Waldron, Mal: *Flickers:* Draper, Ray
Waller, Thomas "Fats": *Ain't Misbehavin':* Morgan, Kevin; Woods, Gavin
Waller, Thomas "Fats": *Black and Blue:* Pilafian, Sam
Waller, Thomas "Fats": *Honeysuckle Rose:* Erickson, Martin
Waller, Thomas "Fats": *Jitterbug Waltz:* Self, James
Waller, Thomas "Fats": *Keepin' Out of Mischief Now:* Gannett, Dave
Wallington, George: *Godchild:* Barber, John William (Bill); Self, James
Ward, Carlos: *Nette:* Stewart, Bob
Ward, Carlos: *Nubian Stomp:* Stewart, Bob
Ward, Samuel A.: *America the Beautiful:* Self, James
Washington and Harline: *When You Wish upon a Star:* Newberger, Eli
Watz, Franz: *Melton Marsch:* Gerhard Meinl's Tuba Sextet; Melton Tuba-Quartett
Wauldteufel, Emil: *Skater's Waltz:* Daellenbach, Charles
Wauschke: *Desert Song:* European Tuba Quartet
Weaver, Mark: *Adhesive Colors:* Weaver, Mark
Weaver, Mark: *Behind Your Face:* Weaver, Mark
Weaver, Mark: *Brown Blue:* Weaver, Mark
Weaver, Mark: *Deflections:* Weaver, Mark
Weaver, Mark: *Land Shark:* Weaver, Mark
Weaver, Mark: *Movie:* Weaver, Mark
Weaver, Mark: *Pocket:* Weaver, Mark
Weaver, Mark: *Pumpkin Pie:* Weaver, Mark
Weaver, Mark: *Selvage:* Weaver, Mark
Weaver, Mark: *Seven Enchiladas:* Weaver, Mark
Weaver, Mark: *Soon Enough:* Weaver, Mark
Weaver, Mark: *Tee Vee/T. W.:* Weaver, Mark
Webster and Harris: *Spiderman:* Dixie Power Trio
Weeks, Clifford: *Triptych:* Megules, Karl
Wefelmeyer, Bernd: *Sieben Durch Acht:* Legris, Philippe
Weill, Kurt: *Mack the Knife:* Pilafian, Sam
Weill, Kurt: *Speak Low:* Callender, George Sylvester "Red"
Welcher, Dan: *Hauntings:* Symphonia
Well, Christoph: *Wann der Dudelsack kraht u. a.:* Well, Christoph
Welsch, Elliot, and Adams: *Mardi Gras Mambo:* Dixie Power Trio
Werle, Floyd: *Concertino for Three Brass and Band:* Angerstein, Fred
Werle, Floyd: *Variations on an Old Hymn Tune:* Tennessee Technological University Tuba/Euphonium Ensemble; United States Armed Forces Tuba-Euphonium Ensemble and Massed Ensemble
White, Donald: *Sonata for Tuba and Piano:* Kaenzig, Fritz
White, John: *Concert Duos:* Rozen, Jay
White, John: *Three Movements from Basingstoke:* Rozen, Jay
Whitney: *Introduction and Samba:* Erickson, Martin
Wieniawski: *Mazurcâ:* Dumitru, Ionel
Wilder, Alec: *Brass Quintet No. 2:* Hanks, Thompson (Toby)
Wilder, Alec: *Carols for a Merry TubaChristmas:* Phillips, Harvey/TubaChristmas
Wilder, Alec: *Elegy for the Whale:* Hanks, Thompson (Toby); Swoboda, Deanna
Wilder, Alec: *Encore Piece (A Tubist's Showcase):* Bobo, Roger
Wilder, Alec: *Nonet:* Hötzel, Markus
Wilder, Alec: *Poobah the Tuba:* Bell, William
Wilder, Alec: *Sonata:* Phillips, Harvey
Wilder, Alec: *Sonata for French Horn, Tuba and Piano:* Phillips, Harvey; Pilafian, Sam
Wilder, Alec: *Sonata No. 1 for Tuba and Piano:* Jae Young, Heo
Wilder, Alec: *Song for Carol:* Phillips, Harvey
Wilder, Alec: *Suite No. 1 for Tuba and Brass Quintet (Effie the Elephant):* Hilgers, Walter
Wilder, Alec: *Suite No. 1 for Tuba and Piano (Effie the Elephant):* Bobo, Roger; Lind, Michael; Phillips, Harvey; Swoboda, Deanna
Wilder, Alec: *Suite No. 2 for French Horn and Tuba:* Phillips, Harvey
Wilder, Alec: *Suite No. 2 (Jessie):* Phillips, Harvey
Wilder, Alec: *Suite No. 3 (Little Harvey):* Phillips, Harvey
Wilder, Alec: *Suite No. 4 (Thomas):* Phillips, Harvey
Wilder, Alec: *Suite No. 5 (Ethan Ayer):* Phillips, Harvey
Wilder, Alec: *Tuba Showpiece from Quintet for Brass:* Phillips, Harvey

Zajaczek, Roman: *Tema Cantabile con Piernicazioni per tuba universale e pianoforte:* Piernik, Zdizislaw
Zaret/North: *Unchained Melody:* Tuba 4's
Zawinul, Josef: *Birdland:* Tennessee Technological University Tuba/Euphonium Ensemble
Ziffrin, Marilyn J.: *Four Pieces for Tuba:* Cummings, Barton
Ziffrin, Marilyn J.: *Trio for Xylophone, Soprano and Tuba:* Cummings, Barton
Zimmer, Hans: *Crimson Tide* [motion picture soundtrack]: Johnson, John Thomas (Tommy)
Zimmer, Hans: *Pearl Harbor* [motion picture soundtrack]: Johnson, John Thomas (Tommy)
Zimmerlin, Alfred: *Toute l'etendur ne vaut pas un cri:* Vogt, Michael
Zindars, Earl: *How My Heart Sings:* Erickson, Martin
Zindars, Earl: *Trigon:* Cooley, Floyd
Zinos, Frederick: *Elegy:* Cummings, Barton
Zonn, Paul: *Divertimento No. 1:* Perantoni, Daniel

Addresses of Recording Companies/ Distributors

A & R Records. Euphonium Concerts. 14274 Crystal Cove Drive South, Jacksonville, FL 32224
Abrasso
ACA Digital Recording. Department BR-T. P.O. Box 450727, Atlanta, GA 30345
Accura Recordings. P.O. Box 4260, Athens, OH 45701–4260
Accurate Records. 117 Columbia Street, Cambridge, MA 02139
ACUM
Adelphi Records. Box 7688, Silver Springs, MD 20907
Adi Hershko. 123 Stern Street, Kiron 55.000. Israel
AHO
Al Opland Recording Service. 1006 5th Ave S.W., Pipestone, MN 56164
Al Teare Digital Recordings. 9076 Willoughby Road, Pittsburgh, PA 15237. (412-367-1526)
Albany Records. 915 Broadway, Albany, NY 12207. USA. Tel: 518-436-8814. Email: infoalbany@aol.com. Web site: www.albanyrecords.com.
Alchemy. Web site: www.alchemyrecords.com
ALCRA.
Altrisuoni. Web site: www.altrisuoni.com
Amadeo. dist. PolyGram Group Distribution
AMIGA. Deutsche Schallplatten GmbH, Berlin, 1080, Reichstagsuger
Amos.
Angel. CEMA Distribution. 21700 Oxnard St. #700, Woodland Hills, CA 91367
Ann Arbor Jazz. 1700 McMullen-Booth Road, Suite C-3, Clearwater, FL 34619
Antilles. dist. PolyGram Group Distribution
AppleJazzRecords. 10825 Wheaton Court, Orlando, FL 32821. Tel: 888-241-2464 Email: info@applejazz.com. Web site: www.applejazz.com
AR University.
Arabesque Recordings. Arabesque Recordings, LLC. 420 Lexington Avenue Suite 340, New York, NY 10170. Tel: 800-966-1416. Email: info@arabesquerecords.com. Web site: www.arabesquerecordings.com
Arbor Jazz Records.
Argo. dist. PolyGram
Ariola. Division of BMG and Arista Records
Arista Records, Inc. 6 West 57th Street, New York, NY 10019
Arktos. 18432—55 Avenue, Edmonton, Alberta, Canada. T6M 1Y7. Tel: 780-469-2192. Fax: 780-469-2192. E-mail: arktos@arktosrecordings.com. Web site: www.arktosrecordings.com
Artlab.
Artra. Artist management for Pat Sheridan
Arts Music.
Aru Musici.
ASC CS.
ASI Records. 711 West Broadway, Minneapolis, MN 55411
ASV Living Era. Distributed by Bournemouth Classic Compact. Web site: http://www.bcc-classics.co.uk
Atlantic Jazz. dist. Warner-Electra-Atlantic Corp
ATS Records. Web site: http://members.aon.at/ats/
Audicom Corporation. 4950 Nome Street, Unit C, Denver, CO 80239
Audio Fidelity. dist. Leisure Audio
Audite. Koch International. 177 Cantiague Rock Road, Westbury, NY 11590
Avant. dist. Western International Music
Band Leader.
Barbirolli Society. 8 Tunnel Road, Retford Notts, DN22 7TA, England
Basset Hound Records. 2139 Kress Street, Los Angeles, CA 90046
Bayrischen Rundfunk. Qualition Imports. 24-02 40th Ave., Long Island City, NY 11101
Bear Productions.
Bernel Music Ltd. P.O. Box 2438, Cullowhee, NC 28723
BES.
BISRecords. Stationsvägen 20, SE-184 50 Åkersberga, Sweden. Tel.: +46-8-544 102-30. Fax: +46-8-544 102-40. Email: info@bis.se. Web site: www.bis.se
Black Eagle.
Black Saint. Sphere Marketing. P.O. Box 771. Manhassett, NY 11030
Blue Groove Records. Liebhartstal Strasse 15-5, A-1160 Vienna, Austria
BMG Entertainment. 1540 Broadway, New York, NY 10036
Borgen Records. Henning Christiansen. Bakkehojgaard. 4792 Askeby, Denmark

Brain Music.
Brazzology Productions. Jazz group with Richard Murrow
Broadway. P.O. Box 100, Brighton, Michigan 48116
BVHaast Records. BVHAAST, Prinseneiland 99, 1013 LN Amsterdam Holland. Tel: +31 20 6239799. Fax +31 20 6243534. Email bvhaast@xs4all.nl. Web site: www.xs4all.nl/~wbk/BVHAAST.html
C&CC.
Cadence. dist. North Country
Caedmon. Label recordings writers reading their works
Cala Records. Web site: www.calarecords.com
Campro Productions.
Candid. Website: Web site: www.candidrecords.com
Capital Records. 1750 N. Vine Street, Hollywood, CA 90028
Capra.
Capriccio. Web site: http://www.capricciousa.com/capriccio.html
Caprice, Svenska Rikskonserter. Box 1225, 111 27 Stockholm, Sweden
CBC. Web site: http://www.cbcrecords.ca/—Canadian classical label
CBS Inc. CBS Masterworks. 51 W. 52nd Street, New York, NY 10019
Century Custom Recording Service. dist. Century Records
Century of Chicago. dist. Century Records
Century Records. 303 North Pine Street. Prospect Heights, IL
Century Records. 303 North Pine Street, Prospect Heights, IL
Chandos Records, LTD. 41 Charing Cross Road, London WC2HOAR, England
Children's Records of America.
Circle Records. Collector's Record Club. GHB Jazz Foundation Building. 1206 Decatur St. New Orleans, LA 70116
Clean-feed Records. Web site: http://www.clean-feed-records.com/
CMP Records. Web site: http://www.artist-shop.com/cmp/
College Presentation Series. dist. University of Illinois Band
Colosseum Records. Qualition Imports. 24-02 40th Ave., Long Island City, NY 11101
Columbia Records. dist. CBS Inc.
Columbia. Columbia Legacy. dist. Sony Music Distribution
Composer's Recordings, Inc. 73 Spring Street, Room 506, New York, NY 10012
Concord Jazz.
Concord Records. P.O. Box 845, Concord, CA 94522
Cornell University Wind Ensemble. Band Office, Lincoln Hall, Cornell University, Ithaca, NY 14850
Coronet Recording Co. 4971 N. High Street, Columbus, OH 43214
CPO Records.
CR.
Crest Music. 33 Chambers Bridge Road. Lakewood, NJ 08901
Crest Records. dist. Golden Crest Records
Cricket Records.
Crown Records. Reissued on Red Records. P.O. Box 750. Reseda, CA 91335
Crystal Records. 28818 NE Hancock Road. Camas, WA 98607
D Flat Records
D'Note Classics. D'Note Records. Web site: http://www.dnote.com/mainframe.htm
Dana Recording Project. Dana School of Music. Youngstown State University. Youngstown, OH 44555
Dance Opus.
DaveGannett. 82452 US Hwy 231, Arab, AL 35016
Daybreak Express Records. P.O. Box 250, Van Brunt Station, Brooklyn, NY 11215
Decca. Decca Personality Series. dist. MCA Records
Denon. Web site: http://www.usa.denon.com/
Deutsche Grammophon. dist. PolyGram Group Distribution
Deutsche Schallplatten. DEUTSCHE SCHALLPLATTEN GMBH BERLIN Reichstagsufer 4–5 01080 Berlin. Tel.: (0049)(030) 2209-0. Fax: (0049)(030) 2209-218. Web site: http://www.discogs.com/label/Deutsche+Schallplatten
Diavolo Records. Schmid & Galke GbR. Kaiser Friedrich Strausse 4, Dusseldorf, Germany
Digitally Encoded Cassette Classics. dist. Mr. Cassette. 360 Supertest Road, Ontario, Canada M3J 2M2
Disc BIM. dist. North Country
Discophon. Calle Cardenal Tedeschini, 14-22, Esca: A—2o, 4a, Barcelona—27, Spain
Disneyland Records. Disneyland Productions. 350 S. Buena Vista, Burbank, CA 91521
Doyen Recordings, LTD. Doyen House. 17 Coupland Close, Moorside, Oldham, Lancs, England 0L4 2TQ
DPT.
East Coasting.
ECM. dist. PolyGram
Ed. RZ. Web site: http://www.justjazz.net.nz/index.html
Edipan. Web site: http://www.edipan.com/
Edition Wilhelm Hansen. Ole Schmidt. Brokbjergstrand 12, 4583 Sj. Odde, Denmark
Educational Brass Recordings. Web site: http://www.windsongpress.com
Electrecord. Allegro Imports. 3434 S.E. Milwaukie Ave., Portland, OR 97202
Elf Records. Web site: http://www.ludwigmusic.com
EMI. Angel EMI Records. Web site: http://www.emigroup.com/

ENJA. Web site: http://www.enjarecords.com/
Epic. Epic Soundtrax. dist. Sony Music Distribution
Equilibrium Records. Web site: http://www.equilibri.com/
Euphonia. Web site: http://www.euphonia.it/
Euphonium Concerts. 14274 Crystal Cove Drive South, Jacksonville, FL 32224
Excerpt Recording Company. P.O. Box 231, Kingsbridge Station, Bronx, NY 10463
Extraplatte. Web site: http://www.extraplatte.at/
Fanfare. Intersound International. P.O. Box 1724, Roswell, GA 30077
Fenox.
Flying Fish Records. 1304 W. Schubert, Chicago, IL 60614
Fonit-Cetra. Allegro Imports. 3434 S.E. Milwaukie Ave., Portland, OR 97202
Forces Command, Ft. McPherson. US Army Ground Forces Band, Fort McPherson, GA 30330-5000
Four Leaf Records. Box 1231, 172 24 Sundbyberg, Sweden
Fresh Sound Records, a product of Jazz Workshop S. L. Barcelona, Spain
Friendly Bull Recordings.
Furious Artisans. Web site: http://www.furiousartisans.com/
GAR Music. Web site: http://members.aol.com/ny91st/sound.html
Gasparo Records. P.O. Box 600, Jaffrey, NH 03452
Geffin Records. 9130 Sunset Blvd, Los Angeles, CA 90069-6197
German Brass Productions. Web site: http://www.german-brass.de/german_brass/contact/indexe.php
GHB Records. Web site: http://www.jazzology.com/ghb_records.php
GM Recordings. Gun Mar Music. 167 Dudley Road, Newton Centre, MA 02159
GNP Crescendo. 8400 Sunset Blvd, Los Angeles, CA 90069
Golden Crest Records, Inc. 220 Broadway, Huntington Station, NY 11746
Golden Records. 250 W. 57th Street, New York, NY 10019
Grammofonfirma BIS. Varingavagen 6. 182 63 Djursholm, Sweden
Grand Award. Web site: http://www.bsnpubs.com/abc/grandaward.html
Grasmere. Web site: http://www.crazyjazz.co.uk/labels/misc/miscgk.htm
Hal Leonard. 7777 West Bluemound Road. P.O. Box 13818, Milwaukee, WI 53213
Harlequin.info@harlequinrecords.com
Harvey Phillips Foundation. P.O. Box 933, Bloomington, IN 47402
Hat Art Records. Im Muhleboden 54, CH-4106 Therwil, Switzerland
Heartdance Music. Tel.: 1-(800)-884-8422. E-mail: hdance@mindspring.com
Heavyweight Records. P.O. Box 57, Kettering, Northants NN15 5PL, England
Hemisphere Records. P.O. Box 3578, New York, NY 10185
Hermitage. Web site: http://www.blueslandproductions.com/roadrecords/ngtb/
Himpsl Records. Zwergerstrasse 2c, D-85579 Neubiberg, Germany. Tel./Fax: (089) 637 27. E-mail: kontakt@unterbiberger.de
Horizon. Web site: http://www.horizonrecords.net
HPF Records and Tapes. P.O. Box 933, Bloomington, Indiana 47402
Hungaroton. Hungaroton Classics. Web site: http://www.hungaroton.hu
Hypnos Recordings. Web site: http://www.hypnos.com/
I WANNA Records. Web site: http://www.weewanna.com/main
IDA Records. dist. North Country. Web site: http://www.brittensmusic.co.uk/norway1.asp?label=IDA%20Records
Idielle Music.
Impulse. dist. MCA. Web site: http://www.vervemusicgroup.com
Impulse Records. dist. UNI. Web site: http://www.vervemusicgroup.com
India Navigation. 177 Franklin St., New York, NY 10013. dist. North Country
Innove Records. Web site: http://www.tomheasley.com/buycds.html
Innowo. Viale Verdi 1, 22037, Ponte Lambro, Italy
Invisible Music. Web site: http://www.invisiblemusicrecords.com/
IRIDA. Web site: http://www.deeplistening.org/dlc/95irida.html
JAM DISC. Web site: http://www.jamrecordings.com/catalog.php?alpha=vz
Jazz Heritage. 914 Lanyard Avenue, Kirkwood, MO 63122
JazzHausMusik. Web site: http://www.jazzhausmusik.de/
Jecklin Red Note. Web site: http://www.swiss-music-news.ch
JMT. dist. PolyGram Group Distribution. Web site: http://new.umusic.com
John Fletcher Trust Fund. 14 Hamilton Terrace, London NW8 UG
Kendor. P.O. Box 278, Delvan, NY 14042
Kitty Jazz. dist. Polydor Japan. Web site: http://www.polydor.co.uk
Kleos. Web site: http://www.heliconrecords.com
KM Educational Library. 2980 N. Ontario, Burbank, CA 91504
KM Records. dist. KM Educational Library
Koch Internationall. 177 Cantiague Rock Road, Westbury, NY 11590
KoDa contact: dwaskew@uncg.edu
Kompost Rekords. Beat Blaser. Steinenstrasse 28, CH-5406 Baden-Rutihof

Kosei Publishing Co. ELF Music. Ludwig Music Publishing Co., 557 East 140th Street, Cleveland, OH 44110, USA
KRO Records. Web site: http://allimportmusic.com/KRO-LAJ.html
Laurel. Web site: http://www.laurelrecord.com
Legacy. Sony Music Entertainment.
Legend Record Co. 12055 Burbank Blvd, N. Hollywood, CA 91607
Leisure Audio. P.O. Box 56757, New Orleans, LA 70156-6757. Tel.: (800) 321-1499
Leo Records. Box 193, 00101 Helsinki, Finland
Loft Records. Schlehecker Str. 114, 5064 Roesrath-Durbusch, Germany
London Records. dist. PolyGram Group Distribution
Lynx. Web site: http://www.lynxrecords.com
M-A Music. K-tel International, 15535 Medina Road, Plymouth, MN 55447
Mama Foundation. 555 E. Easy Street, Simi Valley, CA 93065
Marcophon. Im Schwantenmos 15, CH-8126 Zumikon, Switzerland
Mark College Jazz Series. dist. Mark Recordings
Mark Custom Recording Services. dist. Mark Recordings
Mark Educational Recordings. dist. Mark Recordings
Mark Nelson. Web site: http://members.aol.com/mnelson921/
Mark Recordings. 10815 Bodine Road, P.O. Box 406, Clarence, NY 14031-0406
Martin-PM Sound. Web site: http://www.cmc.ie/composers
MCA Records International. 70 Universal City Plaza, Universal City, CA 91608
MD&G Records. Web site: http://www.dvdpacific.com/audio
Mercury. dist. PolyGram Group Distribution
MGM. dist. PolyGram Group Distribution
MGM Children's Series. dist. PolyGram Group Distribution
Miami United Tuba Ensemble Society.
Milestone. Fantasy, Inc. 10th and Parker, Berkeley, CA 94710
MILS. E-mail: mils@netti.fi. Web site: http://www.tks.pp.fi/ecdlp.html
Mirafone. Web site: http://www.miraphone.de/
MMM. Web site: http://www.nuloop.com
Mole Records. dist. North Country. Web site: http://members.aol.com/molerecords206/mole. htm
Mood Records. DA Music, USA. 362 Pinehurst Lane, Marietta, GA 30068
Morehead State University Book Store. 4950 Nome Street, Unit C. Denver, CO 80239
Move Records. Web site: http://www.move.com.au/index.cfm
MPS Records. dist. PolyGram Group Distribution
mSi, Austria. Web site: http://www.rockdiscography.com
Music Minus One. Web site: http://www.musicminusone.com
Música Chilena de Siglo. Web site: http://www.latinoamerica-musica.net
Música de Arte. Web site: http://www.hellion.com.br
Musica Helvetica. Swiss Broadcasting Corporation. Swiss Radio International, 3000 Berne 15-Switzerland
Musical Heritage Society Orpheus. 1991 Broadway, New York, NY 10023
My Pal God. Web site: www.mypalgodrecords.com
Navigation. dist. India Navigation
New Age Sight and Sound. (404) 956-7956
New Columbian Brass Band.
Nicolai Music. P.O. Box 253, Clear Spring, MD 21722. Email: nicolaimusic@erols.com
Nippon Columbia Co. LTD. columbia.jp
Norman Records. Unit 1 Armley Park Court, Stanningley Road, Leeds, LS12 2AE, UK. Tel./Fax: +44 0113 2311114. E-mail: phil@normanrecords.com. Web site: www.normanrecords.com
North Country Cadence Building, Redwood, New York 13679, USA. Tel.: 315-287-2852. Fax: 315-287-2860. Email: cadence@cadencebuilding.com . Web site: www.cadencebuilding.com
Northern Tuba Lights. Harri Lidsle, Lautamiehenkatu 10B13, 15100 Lahti, Finland
NOVA. Deutsche Schallplatten GmbH, Berlin, 1080, Reichstagsuger
Nueve Composiciones de Camara.
Nurnichtnur. Dieter Schlensog GbR Gnadenthal 8, 47533 Kleve, Germany. Tel.: +49 2821 18666. Fax: +49 2821 24780. E-mail: info@nurnichtnur.com. Web site: www.nurnichtnur.com
NVA Production.
Odyssey. dist. Sony Music Distribution
Olufsen Records. Skt. Knudsvej 8. 1903 Frederiksberg C, Denmark
Opera House Records.
Opus One. 212 Lafayette Street, New York, NY 10012
Opus One. P.O. Box 604, Greenville, ME 04441
Ozone Music. Tel.: 212-247-1596. Web site: www.ozonemusic.com
Periferic. Web site: www.perifericrecords.com
Peter Pan Records. Peter Pan Industries, 88 St. Francis Street, Newark, NJ 07105
Philips. dist. PolyGram Group Distribution
Pierre Verany. www.arion-music.com
Plaene.
Plainsong.
Polydor. dist. PolyGram Group Distribution
PolyGram Group Distribution. Worldwide Plaza, 825 Eighth Avenue, New York, NY 10019
Polyphonic. 77–79 Dudden Hill Lane, London NW10 1BD, England
Postcards.

Prestige. Fantasy Records, Inc. 10th and Parker, Berkeley, CA 94710. Email: info@fantasyjazz.com. Web site: www.fantasyjazz.com

Pro Musica.

Proviva. Deutsche Austrophon. Deutsche Austrophon GMBH. D-2840 Diepholz, Bestell Nr.: ISPV 102

QCA Red Mark. Liben Records. Liben Music Publishers, 6265 Dawes Lane, Cincinnati, OH 45230

Random Acoustics. Haager Str. 5, D-81671 Munchen, Germany. Tel.: 49 89 45769190. Fax: 49 89 457691996. Web site: www.randomacoustics.de

RCA Red Seal. Bertelsman Music Group. 1133 Avenue of the Americas, New York, NY 10036

RCA Victor. Bertelsman Music Group. 1133 Avenue of the Americas, New York, NY 10036

RCA. RCA Red Seal. RCA Victor. dist. BMG Entertainment

Recorded Publications Company. 1100 State Street, Camden, NJ 08105

Red Lehr. Rural Route 1, Box 90, New Athens, IL 62264

Rene Gailly.

ReR. 79 Beulah Rd., Thornton Heath, Surrey CR7 8JG, UK. Tel.: 44 (0)20 8771 1063. Fax: 44 (0)20 8771 3138. Web site: www.rermegacorp.com

Ricordi. One World Records. 1250 W. Northwest Hwy, Suite 505, Palatine, IL 60067

Righteous Babe.

Rofo Records.

Rondo Grammofon & Danish Brass Publishing. Indepent Music OH, P.O. Box 49, 2680 Solrod Strand, Denmark

Rounder Records. 1 Camp Street, Cambridge, MA 02140. Tel.: 800-768-6337. E-mail: info@rounder.com. Web site: www.rounder.com

Saarländischer Rundfunk. Web site: www.sr-online.de

Saskatchewan Arts Board. 2135 Broad Street, Regina, Saskatchewan S4P 1Y6. Tel.: 306-787-4056. Fax: 306-787-4199. E-mail: sab@artsboard.sk.ca. Web site: www.artsboard.sk.ca

School of Music LP Records. University of Michigan, Ann Arbor, MI 48109

SEM Gramophone.

Serendipity.

Seven Seas Records.

Sica-Sound-Music. Steinamangererstrasse 187, A-7400 Oberwart, Austria

Silver Cornet Productions. P.O. Box 681992, Franklin, TN 37068-1992

Silver Crest. 408 Carew Tower, Cincinnati, OH 45202 (see Golden Crest)

SIMAX-PSC. ProMusica AS. Boks 4379, Torshov. N-0402 Oslo, Norway

Simon Says. Record Guild of America. 144 Milbar Blvd, Farmingdale, NY 11735

SoCal.

Sony Music Entertainment. 550 Madison Avenue, New York, NY 10022-3211. Web site: www.sonymusic.com

Soul Notes. Sphere Marketing. P.O. Box 771, Manhassett, NY 11030

Sound Aspects. Cai Sound Aspects. Pedro R. de Freitas. Im Bluetengarten 14, 7150 Backnang, Germany

Sound Mark. 4950-C Nome Street, Denver, CO 80239

SPLASC(H). Via Roma 11—P.O. Box 97, 21051 Arcisate, Italy

Stash Records. 140 W. 22nd St., New York, NY 10011. Tel.: 212-243-4321

Sterling Productions. 20 W. Verde Lane Tempe, Arizona 85284. Tel.: 480-838-8292. Fax: 480-413-0483. Web site: www.sterlingproductions.com

Stolat. Arista Records, Inc. 65 West 55th Street, New York, NY 19919

Stomp Off. Box 342, Dept. C., York, PA 17405. Web site: www.stompoffrecords.com

Strata-East Records. P.O. Box 36, G.C.S., New York, NY 10163. Web site: www.serecs.com

Studio fur Angewandte Musik. dist. Extraplatte

Summit Records. P.O. Box 26850, Tempe, AZ 85285. Tel.: 480-921-5212. Fax: 480-491-6433. Web site: www.summitrecords.com

Sunrise Records. 4069 Gordon Baker Rd., Toronto, Ontario M1W 2P3. Tel.: 416-498-6601. Fax: 416-494-8467. Web site: www.sunriserecords.com

Swedish Society Discofil. Allegro Imports. 3434 S.E. Milwaukie Ave., Portland, OR 97202

SWF.

T.A.P. Music Sales. 1992 Hunter Ave., Newton, Iowa 50208, USA. Tel.: 641-792-0352. E-mail: tapmusic@tapmusic.com. Web site: www.tapmusic.com

Telarc International Corporation. 23307 Commerce Park Road, Cleveland, OH 44122. Web site: www.telarc.com

Teldec. BMG Direct Marketing. 6550 East 30th Street, Indianapolis, IN 46219

The Army Ground Forces Band. 1777 Hardee Avenue SW, Ft. McPherson, GA 30330-1062. Tel.: 404-464-6381. E-mail: afcs-pa@forscom.army.mil. Web site: www.forscom.army.mil/band/

Thorofon.

Time Records. Time Jazz Series. 2 West 45th Street, New York, NY

TMK Köln. Website: www.tmk-gruppe.de

Tomato Records. CEMA Distribution. 21700 Oxnard St. #700, Woodland Hills, CA 91367. E-mail:info@tomatorecords.com. Website:www.tomatorecords.com

Tomorrow River Music. P.O. Box 165, Madison, WI 53701. Tel.: 608-423-3095

Tontraeger.

Tower. Tel.: 916-373-3050. Fax: 916-373-2930. Web site: www.towerrecords.com

Trend Records—Discovery Records. P.O. Box 48081, Los Angeles, CA 90048

Troy Records.

Tryfan.

TTT Music.

TUBA CD.

Tuba-Euphonium Press. 3811 Ridge Road, Annandale, VA 22003-1832. Fax: 703-916-0711. Web site: www.tubaeuphoniumpress.com

Twoten.

UMG Recordings. E-mail: communications@ umusic.com. Web site: www.umusic.com

UNI Distribution Corp, 10 Universal City Plaza, Universal City, CA 91608

Unit Records. Beat Blaser. Steinenstrasse 28, CH-5406 Baden-Rutihof, Switzerland

United Artists. Web site: www.unitedartists.com

United States Air Force Band. 201 McChord Street, Bolling AFB, DC 20032-0202. Web site: www.usafband.com

United States Air Force of Mid-America. 900 Chapman Dr., Scott Air Force Base, IL 62225-5115. Tel.: 618-229-8188. Fax: 681-229-0284. E-mail: amc-ba@scott.af.mil. Web site: public.amc.af.mil/band/

United States Army Band. 204 Lee Ave., Fort Myer, VA 22211-1199. Web site: www.army.mil/armyband/

United States Army Brass Band. 204 Lee Ave., Fort Myer, VA 22211-1199. Web site: www.army.mil/armyband/

United States Coast Guard. 15 Mohegan Ave., New London, CT 06320. E-mail: alyman@cga.uscg.mil. Web site: www.uscg.mil/band/

United States Navy Band. 617 Warrington Ave., S.E. Washington Navy Yard, DC 20374-5054. Tel.: 202-433-6090. E-mail: NavyBand.Public.Affairs@navy.mil. Web site: www.navyband.navy.mil

University Brass Recording Series. P.O. Box 2374, Station A., Champaign, IL 61820

University of Illinois Band. 140 Harding Band Building. 1103 S. 6th Street. Champaign, IL 61820; also: 2134 Music Building, 1114 W. Nevada Street, Urbana, Illinois 61801. Tel.: 217-333-2620. Web site: www.bands.uiuc.edu

University of Kansas, Lawrence. 1530 Naismith Drive, Lawrence, KS 66045-3102. Tel.: 785-864-3436. Fax: 785-864-5866. Web site: www.ku.edu

Varese-Sarabande. 13006 Saticoy Street, North Hollywood, CA 91605; also: 11846 Ventura Boulevard, Suite 130, Studio City, CA 91604. Tel: (800) 827-3734 or (818) 753-4143. Fax: (818) 753-7596. Web site: www.varesesarabande.com

VDE-Gallo. Qualition Imports. 24-02 40th Ave. Long Island City, NY 11101. In Switzerland (www.vdegallo.ch). The American distributor is Albany Music Distributors, Inc., 915 Boadway, Albany, NY 12207. Tel. : 518-436-8814. Fax: 518-436-0643. E-mail: LPAlbany@aol.com

Verve. dist. UMG Recordings

Viper Records. Viper Records 230 Mott St., New York, NY 10012. Tel: 212-873-4415. E-mail: info@viperrecords.com. Web site: www.viperrecords.com

Walking Frog Records. P.O. Box 680, Oskaloosa, IA 52577. Tel.: 641-673-8397. Fax: 888-673-4718. Web site: www.walkingfrog.com

Warner Brothers. 3300 Warner Blvd, Burbank, CA 91510. Tel: 818-846-9090. Web site: www.warnerbrosrecords.com/

Warner-Electra-Atlantic Corp. 111 N. Hollywood Way, Burbank, CA 91505. Web site: www.wea.com

Watt Works. dist. PolyGram Group Distribution

Weltmelodie. dist. Borgen Records

Western International Music. 3707 65th Avenue, Greeley, CO 80634-9626. Tel.: (970) 330-6901. Fax: (970) 330-7738. E-mail: wimbo@wiminc.com. Website: www.wiminc.com

Westmark Tapes. Opland Recordings. R.R. 10, Box 403, Sioux Falls, SD 57104

White Line.

Willson. DEG Music. N3475 Springfield Road, Lake Geneva, WI 53147. Tel.: 800-558-9416 or 262-248-8314. Web site: www.willsonbrass.com

Winchester Music School.

Wonderland. AA Wonderland Records. 12 Gelb Ave., Union, NJ 07083; also: 2 Moores Valley Road, Homedale P.O. Box 30-831, Wainuiomata, Wellington, New Zealand. Tel./fax: +64 4 939 7581

Woong-Jin Records. Web site: www.woongjinmedia.com. E-mail: webmaster@woongjinmedia.com

World Wind Music. Ariane 6 3824 MB Amersfoort, The Netherlands. Tel.: +31 (0)33 4555004. Fax: +31 (0)33 4552730. E-mail: wwm@mirasound.nl. Web site: www.mirasound.nl/wwm/

Young People's.

ZERX. 725 Van Buren Place, SE Albuquerque, NM 87108. Web site: www.zerxrecords.com/

Zuk Records. D-27568 Bremerhaven (Germany) Bürgermeister-Smidt-Straße 102. Tel.: +49 (0471) 49481. Fax: +49 (0471) 415378. E-mail: zuk-records@t-online.de. Web site: www.zuk-records.de/

APPENDIX: Addresses of Publishers and Composers

Compiled by Joseph Skillen

This list also appears in a constantly updated electronic format on the official website of the International Tuba and Euphonium Association (www.iteaonline.org <http://www.iteaonline.org>). Should there be further updates or additions to the list, please contact Joseph Skillen at Louisiana State University (jskille@lsu.edu).

A & L Musical Enterprises, Inc. 503 Tahoe Street, Natchitoches, LA 71457–5718, USA. Tel.: 318-357-0924. E-mail: ALMEI@aol.com. Web site: http://www.music-usa.org/conners

A.A. Kalmus Limited. 38 Eldon Way, Paddock Wood, Tonbridge, Kent, England

AAP. Edition AAP. Aas-Wangsvei 8, N-1613 Fredrikstad, Norway. Tel.: +47 69 31 09 64. E-mail: frank@nordensten.com

AB Carl Gehrmans Musikforlag. Box 6005, SE-102 31 Stockholm, Sweden. Tel.: +46 8 610 06 00. Fax: +46 8 610 06 25. E-mail: info@gehrmans.se. Web site: www.sk-gehrmans.se

Abingdon Press. 201 Eighth Avenue S, Box 801, Nashville, TN 37202-0801, USA. Tel.: 1-800-251-3320. Fax: 1-800-836-7802. E-mail: aadcock@abingdonpress.com. Web site: www.abingdonpress.com/abingdonpress/default.asp

Accentuate Music. 4524 14th Street, W. Bradenton, FL 34207–1428, USA

Accolade Press. 6303 Homestake Pl., Bowie, MD 20720, USA. Tel.: (301) 464–6969. E-mail: bbuck@ccconline.net

Accura Music. Box 4260, Athens, OH 45701–4260, USA

Adler Musikverlag. Postfach 9, A-8990 Bad Aussee, Germany. Tel.: +43(0)3622 / 54 588. Fax: +43(0)3622 / 55 266. E-mail: atp-records@aon.at. Web site: www.adler-musikverlag.com

Advance Music. Veronika Gruber GmbH, Maierackerstr, 18, D-72108 Rottenburg/N.Germany. Tel.: +49(0) 7472–1832. Fax: +49(0) 7472–24621 E-mail: mail@advancemusic.com. Web site: www.advancemusic.com

Åkerwall, Martin. Skt. Peders stræde 30 D. 1453 København, Denmark. Tel.: +45 33 16 33 40. E-mail: aakerwall@heaven.dk. Web site: www.aakerwall.com

Albam, Manny. 7 Glengary Road, Croton, NJ 10520, USA

Albert. See: J. Albert & Son Pty, Limited

Albian Publishing. 6971 Ridgeview Lane W298, Hartland, WI 53029, USA. Tel.: 262-538-1477. E-mail: albianjca@aol.com

Aldo Bruzzichelll Eds. U.S. Rep: Margun Music. Borgo S. Frediano 8, Florence 1-50124, Italy

Alessi Music Studio. 15 Anchorage Court, San Rafael, CA 94903, USA

Alfred Publishing Company Incorporated. 16380 Roscoe Blvd, Box 10003, Van Nuys, CA 91410, USA. Tel.: 818-891-5999. Fax: 818-891-2369. E-mail: customerservice@alfred.com. Web site: www.alfred.com

Allaire Music Publications. 212 2nd Ave., Bradley Beach, NJ 07720, USA. Tel.: 732-988-6188. E-mail: timbroege@aol.com. Out of business

Allans Publishing Limited. U.S. Rep: E. C. Schirmer. Level 1, Building 6, 64 Balmain Street, Richmond 3121, Victoria, Australia. Tel.: 61 3 8415 8000. Fax: 61 3 8415 8088. E-mail: sales@allanspublishing.com.au. Web site: www.allanspublishing.com.au/default.aspx

Allen Music Limited. 8168 Benton Way, Arvada, CO 80003-1810, USA

Almqvist & Wiksell Publishing Limited. P.O. Box 7634, S-103 94 Stockholm, Sweden. Tel.: +46 8 613 61 00. Fax: +46 8 24 25 43. E-mail: export@city.akademibokhandeln.se. Web site: www.akademibokhandeln.se/akb/awi.html

Alphonse Leduc Editions Paris. U.S.: see Robert King Music Sales. 175 Rue St. Honore, 75040, Paris Cedex 01, France. Tel.: +33 (0)1 42 96 89 11. Fax: +33 (0)1 42 86 02 83. Web site: www.alphonseleduc.com/english/

A.M. Percussion Publications. P.O. Box 436, Lancaster, NY 14086, USA. Tel. 1: 716 937–3705. Tel. 2: 1-800-317-2882. E-mail: AMPercPub@aol.com. Web site: www.ampercussion.com

Amadeus Verlag. Postfach 473, CH-8405 Winterthur, Switzerland. Tel.: +41(0) 52-233-2866. Fax: +41(0) 52-233-5401. E-mail: info@amadeusmusic.ch. Web site: www.amadeus-music.ch

Amazing Music World. See: SheetMusicNow.com

American Composers Alliance. American Composers Edition Incorporated. 73 Spring St. Rm. 505, New York, NY 10012, USA. Tel.: 212-362-8900.

Fax: 212-925-6798. E-mail: info@composers.com. Web site: www.composers.com

American Composers Edition, Incorporated. See: American Composers Alliance

American Music Center. 30 West 26th Street, Suite 1001, New York, NY 10010–2011, USA. Tel.: 212-366-5263. Fax: 212-366-5265. E-mail: www.amc.net/contact.html. Web site: www.amc.net

AMSI. 3706 East 34th Street, Minneapolis, MN 55406-2702. Fax: (612) 729–4487

Anderson, Mogens. Peter Rordamsvej 7, 2800 Lyngby, Denmark

Anderson's Arizona Originals. 524 E. 26th Avenue, Apache Jct., AZ 85219, USA. Tel.: 480-983-2350. Fax: 480-983-2602. E-mail: composer@andersons-originals.com. Web site: www.andersons-originals.com

Anglo-American Music Publishers (a.k.a. Worldwide Music Publishers). P.O. Box 161323, Altamonte Springs, FL 32716-1323, USA. Tel.: (407)464–9454. E-mail: wwm32716@yahoo.com. Web site: www.worldwidemusiconline.com

Animando Music Publishers. Tel. and Fax: +39 0342 211653. Web site: www.animando.com

Anton Boehm & Sohn. Postfach 110369—Lange Gasse 26, D—86028 Augsburg 11 Germany

Anton J. Benjamin. Werderstraße 44—Postfach 25 61, D—2000 Hamburg 13 Germany

A.R. Publishing Company. P.O. Box 292, Candlewood Isle, CT 06810, USA

Argee Music Press. 720 Terrace Lane, Greencastle, IN 46135, USA

Arizona University Music Press. School of Music, University of Arizona, 355 S. Euclid Ave. Suite 103, Tucson, AZ 85719. Tel.: 520-621-1441. Fax: 520-621-8899. Web site: www.uapress.arizona.edu/home.htm

Arpeges. 24 rue Etex, 75018 Paris, France. E-mail: accueil@arpeges.org. Web site: www.arpeges.org

Ars Nova. See: Theodore Presser Company

Ars Polona. Karkowskie Przedmiexcie #7, 00-068 Warszawa, Poland. Tel.: +48 (22) 826 12 01. Tel.: +48 (22) 826 47 58. Fax: +48 (22) 826 62 40. E-mail: arspolona@arspolona.com.pl. Web site: www.arspolona.com.pl/indexe.htm

Artia, Foreign Trade Corp. Ve Smeckkách 30, Praha 2, Czech Republic

Arts Lab. AR:Zak. 4 Gusta Green Aston, Birmingham B4 7ER, England

Ashley Dealers Incorporated. P.O. Box 337, Hasbrouck Heights, NJ 07604, USA

Assoc Board of the Royal School of Music. U.S. Rep: Theodore Presser Company. 24 Portland Place, London W1B 1LU, UK. Tel.: +44 (0)20 7636 5400. Fax: +44 (0)20 7637 0234. E-mail: abrsm@abrsm.ac.uk. Web site: www.abrsm.ac.uk

Associated Music Publishers. See: G. Schirmer, Inc.

Astoria Verlag. Hospitalstr. 19, D-40597, Düsseldorf, Germany. Tel.: (0211) 717996. Fax: (0211) 7184276. E-mail: astoriaverlag@t-online.de

Astute Music Ltd. P.O. Box 17, Winsford, Cheshire, UK. E-mail: info@astute-music.com. Web site: www.astute-music.com

Athens Music Publishing. 7230 Cloverhurst Court, Cumming, GA 30041. Fax: 770-754-7881. Web site: www.euphonium.com

Atlanta Brass Society Press. 953 Rosedale Road NE, Atlanta, GA 30306, USA. Tel.: 404-875-8822. E-mail: info@atlantabrass.com. Web site: userwww.service.emory.edu/~mmoor02/ABSPress.html

Atlantic Music Supply Corp. 6124 Selma Avenue, Hollywood, CA 90029, USA

Atlantis Publications. 406 E 31st Street, Baltimore, MD 21218, USA

Augsburg Fortress Publishers. P.O. Box 1209, Minneapolis, MN 55440, USA. Tel.: 612-330-3300. Fax: 612-330-3455. E-mail: www.augsburgfortress.org/company/contactus.asp. Web site: www.augsburgfortress.org

Augsburg Publishing Company. See: Augsburg Fortress Publishers

Aulos Music Publishers. P.O. Box 54, Montgomery, NY 12549, USA

Australian Music Centre. Level 4, The Arts Exchange, 18 Hickson Road, The Rocks, Sydney, NSW, Australia. Tel.: +61-2-9247 4677. Fax: +61-2-9241 2873. E-mail: info@amcoz.com.au. Web site: www.amcoz.com.au

Australian Trombone Education Magazine. Queensland Conservatorium of Music, P.O. Box 3428, South Brisbane Business Center, QLD 4101. Tel.: +07 3875 6360. Fax: 07 3875 6282

Avant Music. See: Western International Music

Avvakoumov, Valentin. Str. Schotman 9-1-232, St. Petersburg, 193232, Russia

Award Music Company, Oliveri Dist. Corp. P.O. Box 591, Oakdale, NY 11769, USA

Axelrod Music. 251 Weybosset Street, Providence, RI 02903, USA. Tel.: 401-421-4833. Fax: 401-621-3722

B. Schott's Sohne Mainz. U.S. Rep: European American Music. Weihergarten 5, D-55116 Mainz, Germany. Tel.: +49 6131 246-0. Fax: +49 6131 246–211. E-mail and Web site: www.schott-english.com/nocache/smi_en/#

Baadsvik Music Shop. Markaplassen 415, 7054 RANHEIM, Norway. Tel.: +47 73 57 43 45. Fax: +47 73 57 43 48. E-mail: oystein@baadsvik.com. Web site: www.baadsvik.com

Bales, Kenton. Department of Music, University of Nebraska at Omaha, Omaha, NE 68182–0245, USA. Tel. 1: 402 554-3359. Tel. 2: 402 213-4040. E-mail: kbales@mail.unomaha.edu. Web site: http://music.unomaha.edu/faculty_kbales.html

Baltimore Horn Club Publication. 7 Chapel Court, Lutherville, MD 21093, USA. Tel.: 410-561-9465

Banks Music Publications. The Old Forge, Sand Hutton, York YO41 1LB, England. Tel.:

(01904) 468472. Fax: (01904) 468679. E-mail: banksramsay@cwcom.net. Web site: www.banksmusicpublications.cwc.net/

Barenreiter Verlag. P.O. Box 10 03 29, D-34003 Kassel, Germany. Tel.: +49 561 3105-0. Fax: +49 561 3105-176. E-mail: info@barenreiter.com. Web site: www.barenreiter.com

Barnhouse. See: C. L. Barnhouse Company

Baron. See: M. Baron Company, Incorporated

Barry Ed. Com e Ind. Av. R. Saenz Pena 1185 80 „N.“ 1035 Buenos Aires, Argentine. Tel.: +54 1 382 3230. Fax: +54 1 383 3946. E-mail: barry@satlink.com

Bartles, Alfred. 3609A Wilbur Place, Nashville, TN 37204, USA. Tel.: 615-292-9157

Bartlesville Publishing Company. P.O. Box 265, Bartlesville, OK 74005, USA. Tel.: 918-333-1502

Basset Hound Music. 2139 Kress Street, Los Angeles, CA 90046, USA. Tel.: 213-656-6510. E-mail: jimself@BassetHoundMusic.com. Web site: www.jimself.com

Beasley, Rule. San Monica College, 1815 Pearl, Santa Monica, CA 90405, USA

Belaieff. See: M. P. Belaieff

Belden, George. 1211 LeLande, Anchorage, AK 99504, USA. Tel.: 907-786-1523. Fax: 907-786-1799. E-mail: beldenanchak@Web sitetv.net

Belmont Music Publishers. P.O. Box 231, Pacific Palisades, CA 90272, USA. Tel.: 310-454-1867. Fax: 310-573-1925. E-mail: belmontmusic90272 @yahoo.com. Web site: www.geocities.com/ belmontmusic

Belwin. See: CPP Belwin Incorporated

Benedetti, Donald. Trenton State College, Trenton, NJ 08625, USA

Benjamin. See: Anton J. Benjamin

Bennett, Malcolm. "Spennythorne" Cokes Lane, Little Chalfonts, Buckinghamshire HP8 4UD, United Kingdom

Berben Press. See: Edizioni Musical Berben

Berklee Press. See: Hal Leonard

Bernel Music LTD. P.O. Box 1118, Cartersville, GA 30120. Tel.: 678-721-1344. Fax: 501-694-6552. E-mail: sales@bernelmusic.com. Web site: www.bernelmusic.com

Bewley Music Incorporated. P.O. Box 9328, Dayton, OH 45409, USA. Tel./Fax: 937-253-5812. Web site: www.tubachristmas.com/bewley.html

Bizet (Editions) Belgium. 13 Rue de la Madeleine, Brussels 1, Belgium

BKJ Publications. P.O. Box 324, Astor Station, Boston, MA 02123, USA

Blasmusikverlag Fritz Schultz GmbH. Am Marzengraben 6, W-7800 Freiburg-Tiengen, Germany. Tel.: 07664/1431. Fax: 07664/5123

Blatter, Alfred. 3141 Chestnet Street, Rm#2018, MacAlister Hall, Philedelphia, PA 19104, USA. Tel.: 215-895-2451. E-mail: Alfred.blatter@ drexel.edu

Blis Music. 30 Grant Blvd, Brandon, Manitoba, Canada, R7B-2L5

Bliss, Marilyn. 34-40 79th Street, Apartment 5E, Jackson Heights, NY 11372, USA

BM. Bjørn Mellemberg. See: Norsk Musikforlag

Boccaccini & Spada Editori Rome. U.S. Rep: Theodore Presser Company. Via Arezzo, 17 00040 Pavona di Albano Laziale, Roma, Italy. Tel.: +39 (0) 6 9310217 or 9310561. Fax: +39 (0) 6 9311903. E-mail: info@boccacciniespada.com. Web site: www.boccacciniespada.com/

Boehm: See: Anton Boehm & Sohn

Bold Brass Studios. P.O. Box 77101, Vancouver, BC V5R 5T4, Canada

Bonesteel Music Company. P.O. Box 50862, Denton, TX 76206, USA

Booneslick Press. 3802 Frontenac Place, Columbia, MO 65203, USA. Tel.: 573-446-0450. E-mail: cheethamj@missouri.edu. Web site: www.booneslickpress.com

Boosey & Hawkes, Incorporated. 295 Regent Street, London W1B 2JH, United Kingdom. Tel.: +44 (0) 20 7291 7255. E-mail:www.boosey.com/pages/shop/help/Contact.asp. Web site: www.boosey.com

Borik Press

Bornemann (Editions) Paris. U.S. Rep: Theodore Presser Company. 15 Rue de Tournon, Paris F-75006, France

Boston Music Company. 215 Stuart Street, Boston, MA 02116, USA. Tel. 1: 800-863-5150. Tel. 2: 617-528-6100. Fax: 617-426-5100. E-mail: info@bostonmusiccompany.com. Web site: www.bostonmusiccompany.com

Boston Public Library. 700 Boylston St., Boston, MA 02117, USA. Tel.: 617-536-5400. E-mail: infor@bpl.org. Web site: www.bpl.org

Bosworth & Company, Limited, England. U.S. Rep: Brodt Music. 8/9 Frith Street, London W1V 5TZ, England. Tel.: +44 0171 7344961. Fax: +44 0171 7344961. E-mail: bosworthlon@ cityscape.co.uk

Bote and Bock K.G. Hardenbergstraße 9A. D—10623 Berlin, Germany. Tel.: +49 30 311003-0, Fax: +49 30 3124281

Bourne Company. 5 W. 37 Street, New York, NY 10018, USA. Tel.: 212-391-4300. Fax: 212-391-4306. E-mail: bournemusic@worldnet.att.net. Web site: www.bournemusic.com

Bowdoin College Music Press. Bowdoin College Library, 3000 College Station, Brunswick, ME 04011-8421. Tel.: 207-725-3288. E-mail: scaref@bowdoin.edu. Web site: library.bowdoin.edu/arch/archives/bcmpg.shtml

Brass Lion. P.O. Box 331, Southboro, MA 01772, USA

Brass Music Limited. See: Robert King

Brass Press, The. See: Robert King; also see: Editions BIM

Brass Wind Publications, 4 St Mary's Road, Manton, Oakham, Leics. LE15 8SU, England.

Tel.: 01572 737409 and 737210. Fax: 01572 737409. E-mail: brasswnd@glabalnet.co.uk

Brassquake Press. P.O. Box 86879, San Diego, CA 92138, USA. Tel.: 619-337-2848

Brassworks. 225 Regency Court, Wankesha, WI 53186, USA

Breakthrough Music. 5 Turnberry Drive, Wilmslow, Cheshire SK9 2QW, United Kingdom. E-mail: info@breakthroughmusic.co.uk. Web site: www.breakthroughmusic.co.uk

Breitkopf & HaerTel. Walkmühlstrasse 52, D-65195 Wiesbaden, Germany. Tel.: +49 611 45008 0. Fax: +49 611 45008 59-61. E-mail: info@breitkopf.com. Web site: www.breitkopf.com/

Brelmat Music. 241 Kohlers Hill Road, Kutztown, PA 19530-9181, USA. Tel.: 610-756-6324. E-mail: brelmat@gte.net. Web site: www.brelmat-music.com/

Bristol, Doug. 2106 Halcyon Blvd, Montgomery, AL 36117, USA. E-mail: doug@bristolnotes.com

Brixton Publications. 4311 Braemar Avenue, Lakeland, FL 33813, USA. Tel./Fax: 863-646-0961. E-mail: sales@BrixtonPublications.com. Web site: www.brixtonpublications.com

Broad River Press. P.O. Box 50329, Columbia, SC 29250, USA

Broadbent and Dunn Ltd. London. Tel.: +44 (0)1304 825604. Fax: +44 (0)870 135 3567. E-mail: music@broadbent-dunn.com. Web site: www.broadbent-dunn.com

Brodt Music Company. Box 9345, 1409 East Independence Blvd, Charlotte, NC 28299, USA. Tel. 1: 1-800-438-4129. Tel. 2: 704-332-2177. Fax: 800-446-0812. E-mail: orders@brodtmusic.com. Web site: www.brodtmusic.com

Broude Brothers Limited. 141 White Oaks Road, Williamstown, MA 01267-2257, USA. Tel.: 800 225-3197. Tel. 2: 413-458-8131. Fax: 413-458-5242. E-mail: broude@sover.net

Brusick, William R. 165 17th Avenue NE, St. Petersburg, FL 33704, USA. Tel.: 727-821-2494. Tel. 2: 727-527-1168. E-mail: sasha17@worldnet.att.net

BTQ Publications. Meadow View 10, Old Forge Road, Fenny Draton, Warwickshire CV13 6BD, England

Bugby, Colin. 32 Irchester Road, Rushden, Northamptonshire NN10 9XE, United Kingdom. Tel.: 01933 357838. E-mail: info@colinbugby.co.uk. Web site: http://www.colinbugby.co.uk

BVD Press. 79 Meetinghouse Lane, Ledyard, CT 06339, USA. Tel.: 860-536-2185. E-mail: bvdpress@snet.net. Web site: http://www.bvdpress.com

C & E Enterprises. 7341 Amberly Lane, Bldg. 33–410, Delray Beach, FL 33446, USA. Tel.: 561-495-0045

C & R Publishing Company, Incorporated. P.O. Box 53513, Fayetteville, NC 28305, USA

Camara Music Publishers. 23 LaFond Lane, Orinda, CA 94563, USA

Camden House. 668 Mount Hope Avenue, Rochester, NY 14620-2731, USA. Tel.: 585-275-0419. Fax: 585-271 8778. E-mail: boydell@boydellusa.net. Web site: www.camden-house.com

Camden Music. 19A North Villas, Camden Square, London NW1 9BJ, England

Camphouse, Mark D. P.O. Box 6968, East Main and Adams Streets, Radford, VA 24142, USA. Tel.: 540-831-5103. Fax: 540-831-6133. E-mail: mcamphou@radford.edu. Web site: www.radford.edu/~mcamphou/

Canadian Music Centre. 20 St. Joseph Street, Toronto, ON, Canada, M4Y 1J9. Tel.: 416-961-6601. Fax 416-961-7198. E-mail: info@musiccentre.ca. Web site: www.musiccentre.ca/

Canadian Musical Heritage Society. 120 Walnut Court, Unit 15, Ottawa, ON, Canada. K1R 7W2. Tel.: 613-230-3666. Fax: 613-230-6725. E-mail: enquiries@cliffordfordpublications. Web site: www.cmhs.carleton.ca/

Cantando. Cantando Forlag. P.O. Box 8019, N-4068 Stavanger, Norway. Tel.: +47 51 89 46 01. E-mail: order@cantando.com

Canzona Publications. P.O. Box 10123, Denver, CO 80210

Carl Fischer Incorporated. 65 Bleecker St., New York, NY 10012. Tel.: 212-777-0900. Fax: 212-477-6996. E-mail: cf-info@carlfischer.com. Web site: www.carlfischer.com

Carlin Music Publishing Company. P.O. Box 2289, Oakhurst, CA 93644, USA. Tel.: 209-683-7613. E-mail: www.carlinamerica.com/contact. Web site: www.carlinamerica.com

Carp Music, Incorporated. See: Theodore Presser Company

Carus-Verlag GmbH. U.S. Rep: Mark Foster. Sales Department, Sielminger Str. 51, D-70771 Lf.-Echterdingen. Tel.: +49/ (0) 711-797 330-0. Fax: +49/ (0) 711-797 330-29. E-mail: sales@carus-verlag.com. Web site: www.carus-verlag.com

Cautius Music. P.O. Box 32493, Kansas City, MO 64111

Cavata Music Publishers. See: Theodore Presser Company

Cazes Cuivres. Canada

Cellar Press. 322 Swain Avenue, Bloomington, IN 47401, USA

Celluloid Tubas. (see Fiegel, Todd)

Censhu, Jiro. 1-2-25-301 Terauchi, Toyonaka, Osaka 561-0872, Japan. Tel.: 06-6864-2834. Fax: 06-6864-2868. E-mail: jircen@u01.gate01.com

Ceskeho hudebniho fondu. 110 00 Praha 1, Parizska 3, Czechoslovakia

C. F. Peters Corporation. 70-30 80th Street, Glendale, NY 11385, USA. Tel.: 718-416-7800. Fax: 718-416-7805. E-mail: sales@cfpeters-ny.

com. Web site: www.edition-peters.com/home.html
Chamber Brass Library. See: Mentor Music
Chamber Music Library. 84 Jefferson St. #2-C, Hoboken, NJ 07030, USA
Chantry Music Press Incorporated. See: Augsberg Fortress Publishers
Chappell & Company, LTD. See: Hal Leonard Publications
Charles Colin. 315 West 53rd Street, New York, NY 10019, USA. Tel.: 212-581-1480. Fax: 212-489-5186. E-mail: info@charlescolin.com. Web site: www.charlescolin.com
Cherry Classics Music. E-mail: sales@cherry-classics.com. Web site: www.cherry-classics.com
Cherry Lane Music Company, Incorporated. 6 East 32nd Street, 11th Floor, New York, New York 10016, USA. Tel.: 212-561-3000. E-mail: publishing@cherrylane.com. Web site: www.cherrylane.com
Chester Music Limited. London. 8/9 Frith Street, GB-London W1V 5TZ, England, UK. Tel.: +47 0044 20 7434 0066. Fax: +47 0044 20 7287 6329. E-mail: music@musicsales.co.uk. Web site: www.musicsales.co.uk
Chicken Scratch Press. See: Windsong Press. Web site: www.windsongpress.com
Childs, Barney. School of Music, University of Redlands, Redlands, CA 92373, USA
Chiron Publications
Choristers Guild. 2834 W. Kingsley Road, Garland, TX 75041, USA. Tel.: 972-271-1521. Fax: 972-840-3113. E-mail: choristers@choristersguild.org. Web site: www.choristersguild.org
Cimarron Music and Productions. 722 Cimarron Trail, Irving, TX 75063. Tel.: 972-506-9033. Fax: 972-506-9043. E-mail: Cimarrontx@aol.com. Web site: www.cimarronmusic.com
Cirone Publications. See: CPP Belwin, Inc.
C. L. Barnhouse Company. Box 680, 205 Cowan Ave. West, Oskaloosa, IA 52577, USA. Tel.: 641-673-8397. Fax: 641-673-4718. E-mail: bbarnhouse@barnhouse.com. Web site: www.walkingfrog.com
Clark Baxley Publications. P.O. Box 417694, Sacramento, CA 95481, USA
Claude Benny Press. c/o Joseph Ott, Department of Music, Emporia State University, Emporia, KS 66801, USA
Coburn Press. See: Theodore Presser Company
Colding-Jorgensen, Henrik. Kildehuset 3, 3.tv. DK-2670 Greve, Denmark. Tel. +45 43 69 32 85. E-mail: mail@hc-j.dk. Web site: www.hc-j.dk/
Colin. See: Charles Colin
Collected Editions Limited. 750 Ralph McGill Blvd NE, Atlanta, GA 30312, USA. Fax: 404-525-4545
Columbia Pictures Publications. 15800 N.W. 48th Avenue, Miami, FL 33014, USA
Compello, Joseph. See: Joseph Compello Publications
Composers Library Editions. See: Theodore Presser Company
Composer's Manuscript Edition. 33 Springfield Gardens, London ORY NW9, England
Concordia Publishing House. 3558 South Jefferson Avenue, St. Louis, MO 63118, USA. Tel.: 314-268-1000. Fax: 314-268-1329. E-mail: order@cph.org. Web site: http://www.cph.org/
Conners Publications Inc. See: A & L Musical Enterprises, Inc.
Conservatory Publications. 18 Van Wyck, Croton-on-the-Hudson, NY 10520, USA
Consort Press. 1755 Monita Drive, Ventura, CA 93001, USA. Tel.: 800-995-7333. Fax: 805-643-9051. E-mail: office@consortpress.com. Web site: www.consortpress.com
Consortium Musical. See: Theodore Presser Company
Constantinides, Dinos. School of Music. Louisiana State University, Baton Rouge, LA 70803-2504, USA. Tel.: 225/578-4010. Fax: 225/578-2562. E-mail: cconsta@bellsouth.net. Web site: www.music.lsu.edu/facstaff_frameset.htm
Co-Op Press. Sy Brandon, P.O. Box 204, Wrightsville, PA 17368-0204, USA. Tel.: 717-252 3385. E-mail: cooppress@suscom.net. Web site: cooppress.hostrack.net/
Cor Publishing Company. 67 Bell Place, Massapequa, NY 11758, USA
CPP Belwin Incorporated. 15800 NW 48 Avenue, Miami, FL 33014, USA. Tel.: (305) 620-1500. Fax: (305) 625-3480
Creation Station. P.O. Box 301, Marlborough, NH 03455-0301, USA. Web site: http://regw9626.members.beeb.net/bpardus.htm
Criterion Music Corp. 6124 Selma Avenue, Hollywood, CA 90028, USA. Tel.: 323-469-2296. Fax: 323-962-5751
Crown Music Press. 612 Sedgwick Dr., Libertyville, IL 60048, USA. Tel.: 847-549-7124. Fax: 847-549-7136. E-mail: crownmusicpress@aol.com
Cumberland Press. 917 8th Avenue S., Nashville, TN 37203, USA
Czech Music Fund. 118 00 Praha 1, Besední 3, Czechoslovakia. Tel.: 257 320 008. Fax: 257 312 834. E-mail: nchf@gts.cz. Web site: www.nchf.cz
Da Capo Music. 26 Stanway Road, Whitefield, Manchester M45 8EG, United Kingdom. Tel.: 0044 161 766 5950. E-mail: colin@dacapomusic.freeserve.co.uk. Web site: www.dacapomusic.co.uk
DaCapo Press
Dako Publishers. 4225 Osage Avenue, Philadelphia, PA 19104, USA. Tel.: 215-386-7247
Danish Music Information Center. Gråbrødretorv 16, DK 1154 Copenhagen K, Denmark. Tel.: +45 33 11 20 66. Fax: +45 33 32 20 16. E-mail: mic@mic.dk. Web site: www.mic.dk
Dankwart, Schmidt. Seuerberger Str. 6, D-W-8196, Beuerberg/Achmule, Germany

Dantallan Incorporated. 11 Pembroke St., Newton, MA 02458-2122. Tel.: 617-244-7230. Fax: 617-244-7230. E-mail: dantinfo@dantalian.com. Web site: www.dantalian.com

David E. Smith Publications. 4826 Shabbona Road, Deckerville, MI 48427-9988, USA. Tel.: 810/376-9055. Fax: 810/376-8429. E-mail: despub@greatlakes.net. Web site: www.despub.com

Davis, D. Edward. E-mail: d_edwarddavis@yahoo.com. Web site: www.ickydog.com

DB Publishing Company. 64 Saint Philip Drive, Clifton, NJ 07013, USA

De haske muziekuitgave bv. Windas 2, 8441 RC, Heerenveen, Holland. 05139-493

DelDresser. Mark Dresser, Professor of Music, UCSD. E-mail: deldresser@aol.com. Web site: www.mark-dresser.com

Deutscher Verlag fur Musik. See: Breitkoph & HarTel

DID Publishing. 123 Steinmann Avenue, Middlebury, CT 06762, USA

DiGiovanni, Rocco. 10907 Camarillo Street, North Hollywood, CA 91602, USA

Dilia. Vysehradska 288, Nove Mesto, Pargue 2, Czechoslovakia. 2-966-515

Divertimento. Divertimento Music Edition. c/o Magne Murholt, P.O. Box 757, N-2604 Lillehammer, Norway

Dolmetsch Musical Instruments England. U.S. Rep: Theodore Presser Company

Domek, Richard. School of Music, University of Kentucky, Lexington, KY 40506 Tel.: 859-257-1966. E-mail: dicty@pop.uky.edu. Web site: www.uky.edu/FineArts/Music/faculty/richard_domek.htm

Doms. See: Johann Doms

Donemus Publishing House Amsterdam. U.S. Rep: Theodore Presser Company. Paulus Potterstraat 16, NL-1071 CZ Amsterdam, Netherlands. Tel.: +31 (0)20 3058900. Fax: +31 (0)20 673 35 88. E-mail: info@muziekgroep.nl. Web site: http://www.musiekgroep.nl

Dorn Publications, Incorporated. P.O. Box 206, Medfield, MA 02052, USA. Tel.: 508-359-1015. Fax: 508-359-7988. E-mail: dornpub@dornpub.com. Web site: www.dornpub.com

Dover Publications Incorporated. 31 E. Second Street, Mineola, NY 11501, USA. Tel.: 516-294-7000. Fax: 516-742-5049

Dramatic Publishing Company. P.O. Box 129, Woodstock, IL 60098-0129, USA. Tel.: 1-800-448-7469. Fax: 1-800-334-5302. E-mail: CustomerService@dpcplays.com. Web site: www.dramaticpublishing.com/welcome.html

Dunster Music. 22 Woodcote Avenue, Wallington, Surrey, England

Dunvagen Music Publishers Incorporated. 632 Broadway, 9th floor, New York, NY 10012, USA. Tel.: 212-979-2080. Fax: 212-473-2842. E-mail: info@dunvagen.com. Web site: www.dunvagen.com

Durand SA Editions Musicales France. U.S. Rep: Theodore Presser Company. 4–6, place de la Bourse, 75002 Paris, France

Dutton, Brent. San Diego State University, Music and Dance Room 236, 5500 Campanile Drive, San Diego, CA 92182, USA. Tel.: 619-594-4760. Fax: 619-594-1692. E-mail: dutton@mail.sdsu.edu. Web site: www.music.sdsu.edu

Earlham Press Limited. London. See: Theodore Presser Company

Easton, Ian. c/o Steve Rosse, P.O. Box R181, Royal Exchange, Sydney 1225, Australia. Tel.: 61 41 613 5854. E-mail: steve@tubamania.com.au

E. C. Schirmer Music Company, Incorporated. 138 Ipswich Street, Boston, MA 02215, USA. Tel.: 617-236-1935. Fax: 617-236-0261 E-mail: office@ecspub.com. Web site: www.ecspub.com

ECS Publishing. See: E. C. Schirmer Company

Ed. Feeling Musique. 15 Rue Guytoin de Moreveau, 75013, Paris, France

Editio Musica Budapest. Vörösmarty tér 1, H-1051 Budapest, Hungary. Tel.: +36-1-4833-100. E-mail: musicpubl@emb.hu. Web site: www.emb.hu

Editio Supraphon. Vodickova 27, 110 00, Praha 1, Czechoslovakia

Edition Andel Uitgave. Klaprozenlaan 28-30, B-8400 Oostende, Belgium. Tel.: +32 59 70 32 22. Fax: + 32 59 70 83 50. E-mail: andel@skynet.be. Web site: users.skynet.be/andel/

Edition Elvis. Runeberginkatu 15 A 11, 00100 Helsinki, Finland. Tel.: (09) 407 991. Fax: (09) 440 181. E-mail: elvis@elvissm.pp.fi. Web site: www.musicfinland.com/elvis/EE.html

Edition Eulenburg. See: European American Music

Edition Fazer. Warner/Chappell Music Finland OY. P.O. Box 169, FIN-02101 Espoo, Finland. Tel. +358-9-435 0141. Fax +358-9-455 2162

Edition Foetisch. 6, rue de Bourg, Lausanne, Switzerland. Fax: 41-21-311-50-11

Edition Hans Pizka. Pf.1136, D-85541 KIRCHHEIM, Germany. Tel.: +49 89 903-9548. Fax: +49 89 903-9414. E-mail: hans@pizka.de. Web site: www.pizka.de

Edition Helbling. AG. Pfaffikerstr. 6, CH-8604 Volketswil Zurich, Switzerland. Tel.: 01 908 1212. Fax: 01 945 6928

Edition Helios. Kirkeveg 26B, 5690 Tommerup, Denmark

Edition Ka We. Brederodestraat, 90. 1054 VE Amsterdam, Holland

Edition Marbot. Mühlenkamp 43, D-2000 Hamburg 60, Germany

Edition Wilhelm Hansen. U.S. Rep: G. Schirmer. Bornholmsgade 1, DK-1266 Copenhagen K, Denmark. Tel.: +45 33 11 78 88. Fax: +45 33 14 81 78. E-mail: ewh@ewh.dk. Web site: www.ewh.dk

Editions Aug. Zurfluh. 73 Boulevard Raspail, 75006 Paris, France. Tel.: 45.48.68.60. Fax: 42.22.

21.15. http://www.zurfluh.com. U.S. Agent: Presser

Editions Billaudot. 14 rue de l'Echiquier, 75010 Paris, France. Tel.: 00 33 1 47 70 14 46. Web site: www.billaudot.com

Editions Bim. P.O.Box 300, 1674 Vuarmarens, Switzerland. Tel.: ++41 (0)21 909 1000. Fax: +41 (0)21 909 1009. E-mail: order@editions-bim.com. Web site: www.editions-bim.com

Editions Choudens. 38, rue Jean-Mermoz, Paris 75008, France. Tel.: 01 42 66 62 97. E-mail: editions.choudens@wanadoo.fr

Editions de L'Oiseau Lyre. B.P. 515, MC-98015 Monaco Cedex. Tel.: +(377) 9330 0944. Fax: +(377) 9330 1915. E-mail: oiseaulyre@monaco-377.com. Web site: www.oiseaulyre.com/index.html

Editions du Petit Page. 57, rue Louis Blanc, 75010 Paris, France. Tel.: (+33)1-46-07-79-87. Fax: (+33)1-40-37-52-59. E-mail: commande@petitpage.biz. Web site: http://www.petitpage.biz

Editions Fertile Plaine. 11 rue de Rosny, 94120, Fontenay sous Bois, France. Tel.: (33) 1 48 77 38 12. Fax: (33) 1 48 77 39 85. E-mail: contact@fertileplaine.com. Web site: http://www.fertileplaine.com

Editions Francaises de Musique. 12, rue Magellan, 75008 Paris, France

Editions Henn. 8, rue de Hesse, CH—1204 Genève, Switzerland

Editions M. Combre. 14, BD Poissoniere, 75009 Paris, France. Tel.: 1 48 24 89 24. Fax: 1 42 46 98 82

Editions Marc Reift. Case postale 308, Route du Golf 122, CH-3963 Crans-Montana Switzerland. Tel.: +41 (0) 27 483 12 00. Fax: +41 (0) 27 483 42 43. E-mail: reift@tvs2net.ch. Web site: www.reift.ch

Editions Max Eschig. 4-6, Place de la Bourse, 75080 PARIS Cedex 2, France. Tel.: 33 1 44.88.73.73. Fax: 33 1 44.88.73.88. E-mail: gerald.hugon.durand-salabert-eschig@bmgintl.com

Editions Metropolis. Van Ertbornstr. 5. 2018, Antwerpen, Belgium. Tel.: 404.902.249

Editions Musicales Brogneaux. B-1000 Brussels, 73 Avenue Paul Janson, Belgium

Editions Musicales J. Maurer. Avenue du Verseau 7, B-1200, Brussels, Belgium. Tel.: 32 2 770 93 39. Fax: 32 2 770 93 39. E-mail: musicmaurer@hotmail.com

Editions Musicus. Box 1341, Stamford, CT 06904, USA

Editions Ricordi. See: Hal Leondard Publishing Corp.

Editions Rideau Rouge. 25 Bd Arago, 75013 Paris, France. Tel.: 01 55 43 08 45. Fax: 01 47 57 29 97

Editions Robert Martin. 106, Grande rue de la Coupée, F. 71850 Charnay Les Macon, France. Tel.: 03 85 34 46 81. Fax: 03 85 29 96 16. E-mail: www.edrmartin.com/contact/index.php?sessionID=420717639. Web site: www.edrmartin.com/index.php. (See also: Theodore Presser)

Editions Salabert. U.S. Rep: G. Schirmer & Hal Leonard

Editions Selmer. 18, rue la Fontaine au Roi, 75011 Paris, France

Editions 75. 75 rue de la Roquette, 75011 Paris, France. Tel.: 01 43 48 90 57. Web site: www.tom.johnson.org

Edizioni Curci. Galleria del Corso 4, 20122 Milan, Italy. Tel.: +39-02-760361. Fax:+39-02-7601.4504. E-mail: info@edizionicurci.it. Web site: www.edizionicurci.it

Edizioni Melodi. Via Quintiliano, 40 Milano, Italy

Edizioni Musical Berben. Via Redipuglia 65, i-60100 Ancona, Italy. Tel.: +39 (71) 20 44 28. Fax: +39 (71) 57 414

Edizioni Suvini Zerboni. Galleria del Corso, 4, 20122 Milano, Italy. Tel.: +39.02.770701. Fax: +39.02.77070261. E-mail: suvini.zerboni@sugarmusic.com. Web site: www.esz.it

Edward B. Marks Music Company. c/o Freddy Bienstock Enterprises, 126 East 38th Street, New York, NY 10016. Tel.: 212-779-7977. Fax: 212-779-7920. E-mail: bkalban@carlinamerica.com. Web site: www.ebmarks.com

Edwin Ashdown Limited. 19 Hanover Street, London W1, England

Edwin F. Kalmus & Company, Incorporated. See: CPP Belwin, Incorporated

EGI. Eivind Grovens Institutt. Ekebergvn. 59, N-1181 Oslo, Norway. Tel.: +47 22 67 91 23

Egtved ApS (Edition) Denmark. See: Wilhelm Hansen Musikverlag

Elite Music Company. 1314 W. Mountain Avenue, Fort Collins, CO 80521, USA

Elizabeth Thomi-Berg Verlag. Postfach 12 68, Bahnhofstr. 94 A, D-8032 Grafelfing bei Munchen, Germany. Tel.: 089/85 32 79. Fax: 89-854-1857

Elkan. See: Henri Elkan Music Publishing Company. Incorporated

Elkan-Vogel. See: Theodore Presser Company

Ellin, Ben. See: London Tuba Quartet. Web site: www.londontubaquartet.co.uk

Emberson, Steve. 1387 Ambridge Way, Ottawa, Ontario, K2C 3T3, Canada. Tel.: 613-727-3595

Emerson Edition Limited. Windmill Farm, High Street, Ampleforth, Yorkshire YO6 4HF, England. Tel.: 04393 324

EMI Music Publishing Limited. 138–149 Charing Cross Road, London WC2H 0LD, England

Encore Music Publishers. P.O. Box 786, Troy, MI 48099-0786,USA.Tel.:1-800-261-5676.Fax:1-800-261-5676. E-mail: encore@encoremupub.com. Web site: www.encoremupub.com

Engstrom & Sodring Musikforlag A/S. Borgergade 17 DK—1300, Copenhagen, Denmark

Ensemble Publications. P.O. Box 32, Ithaca, NY 14851-0032, USA. Tel.: 607-592-1778. Fax: 607-273-4655. E-mail: enspub@aol.com. Web site: members.aol.com/EnsPub

Euphonion Press Publications. P.O. Box 115, Ellerslie, MD 21529, USA. Tel.: 301-724-4286. E-mail: erkitchen@hereintown.net. Web site: euphonionpress.com

Euphplayer.com publications. T2F Kampung Warisan, Jalan Jelatek, Kuala Lumpur, 54200 Malaysia. E-mail: info@euphplayer.com. Web site: http://www.euphplayer.com

Euromusic GmbH. Neulerchenfelder Strasse 3–7, A-1160 Vienna, Austria

European American Music Distributors LLC. 15800 NW 48th Avenue, Miami, FL 33014, USA. Tel.: 305-521-1604. Fax: 305-521-1638. E-mail: eamdc@eamdc.com. Web site: www.eamdc.com

Ewoton Musikverlag. MitTelfeldstrasse, 4, D-66851 Queidersbach, Germany. Tel.: 06371/92300. Fax: 06371/17212. E-mail: vertrieb@ewoton.de. Web site: www.ewoton.de

Excelsior Music Publishing Company. See: Theodore Presser Company

Faber Music—Britain. 3 Queen Square, London WC1N 3AU, England. Tel.: +44 (0) 20 7833 7900. Fax: +44 (0) 20 7833 7939. E-mail: information@fabermusic.com. Web site: www.fabermusic.com

Faber Music Incorporated, Boston. 50 Cross Street, Winchester, MA 01890, USA. Fax: 617-729-2783

Facsimile Editions. See: Carl Fischer Incorporated

Faimo Edition. Abbotvägen 18, S-74695, Skokloster, Sweden. Tel.: +46 18 386268

Fazer Music Finland. P.O. Box 126, FIN-00521, Espoo, Finland. Tel.: +358 9 229 560. Fax: +358 0 455 2162. E-mail: ari.nieminen@warnerchappell.com

F.E.C. Leuckart Germany. See: Thomi-Berg, Rheingoldstraße 4, 80639 München, Germany. Tel.: 089-17 39 28. Fax: 089-17 60 54

Fema Music Publications. P.O. Box 395, Naperville, IL 60566

Fenette Music. 8 Horse and Dolphin Yard, London W1V 7LG, England

Fennica Gehrman. Lonnrotinkatu 20 B, PL 158, 00121 Helsinki, Finland. Tel.: (09) 7590 6311. Fax: (09) 7590 6312

Fentone Publications England. U.S. Rep: Theodore Presser Company. Fleming Road, Corby, Northants. NN17 4SN, England. Tel.: +44 1536 260981. Fax: +44 1536 401075. E-mail: music@fentone.com. Web site: www.fentone.com

Fest-Musik-Haus. P.O. Box 162, Medina, TX 78055, USA. Tel.: 830-589-2268. E-mail: herbert@festmusik.com. Web site: www.festmusik.com

Fetter, David. 3413 Oakenshaw Place, Baltimore, MD 21218, USA. Tel.: 410-659-8100. Fax: 410-783-8562. E-mail: davidf@peabody.jhu.edu. Web site: gigue.peabody.jhu.edu/~davidf/

Fidelio Music Publishing Company. 39 Danbury Avenue, Westport, CT 06880, USA. Tel.: 203-227-5709. Fax: 203-227-5715

Fiegel, E. Todd. 203 Artemos Drive, Missoula, MT 59803, USA. Tel.: 406-543-0841. E-mail: fiegel@celluloidtubas.com. Web site: www.celluloidtubas.com/html/comp.html

Finnish Music Information Centre. Lauttasaarentie 1, FI-00200 Helsinki, Finland. Tel.: +358 9 6810 1313. Fax: +358 9 682 0770. E-mail: info@fimic.fi. Web site: www.fimic.fi

Fischer, Carl. See: Carl Fischer, Incorporated

Fleischer Music Collection. Free Library of Philadelphia, Loga Square, Philadelphia, PA 19103, USA

F.M.I., Finnish Music Information. Lauttasaarentie 1, FIN-00200 Helsinki, Finland. Tel.: +358 9 6810 1313. Fax +358 9 682 0770. E-mail: info@mic.teosto.fi. Web site: www.fimic.fi/fimic/fimic.nsf?open

Folklore Productions Incorporated. 1671 Appian Way, Santa Monica, CA 90401, USA. Tel.: 213-451-0767. Fax: 213-458-6005

Foreign Music Distributors (Educational Music Service). 33 Elkay Drive, Chester, NY 10918, USA. Tel.: 845-469-5790. Fax: 845-469-5817. E-mail: sales@emsmusic.com. Web site: www.emsmusic.com

Forte, Aldo. 512 Waters Edge. Apt. E.. Newport News, VA 23606, USA. Tel.: 757-596-4444. E-mail: aldo@aldoforte.com. Web site: http://www.aldoforte.com

Frank E. Warren Music Service. 29 S. Main Street, Sharon, MA 02067, USA. Tel.: 781-784-0336. Fax: 781-784-0336. E-mail: fewpub@juno.com

The Franklin Edition. Five Fingers Music. 484 West 43 Street, Suite 21-L, New York, NY 10036, USA. E-mail: music@thefranklinedition.com. Web site: www.thefranklinedition.com/brass.htm

Frederick Music Publications. 120 N. Charles, McPherson, KS 67460, USA

Fredonia Press. 3947 Fredonia Drive, Hollywood, CA 90068, USA

Fredrickson, Thomas. School of Music, University of Illinois, 1111 W. Nevada, Urbana, IL 61801, USA

Friederich Hofmeister. Ubierstraße 20, 65719 Hofheim am Taunus, Germany. Fax: 06 192 21134

Friedrich Hofmeister Musikverlag. Büttnerstraße 10, D-04103 Leipzig, Germany. Tel.: +49-341/9 60 07 50. Fax: +49-341/9 60 30 55. Web site: www.friedrich-hofmeister.de

Friedrich, Kenneth. 1800 E. Stassney, 221, Austin, TX 78744, USA. E-mail: knuxie35@yahoo.com. Web site: www.kfsbrasschamber.homestead.com

Fritze, Gregory. 1140 Boylston Street, Boston, MA 02215-3695, USA. Tel.: 617-266-1400. E-mail: gfritze@berklee.edu. Web site: www.nii.net/~gfritze/questionaire.htm

Frog Peak Music. P.O. Box 1052, Lebanon, NH 03755. Tel./Fax: 603-643-9037. E-mail: fp@frogpeak.org. Web site: www.frogpeak.org

Frost. Frost Music A/S. P.O. Box 118 Skøyen, N-0212 Oslo, Norway. Tel.: +47 23 27 01 86. E-mail: philipkr@online.no

Frost Noter. A/S P.B. 79 Ankertorget 0133, Oslo, Norway

FTW Publishing. 415 Allyn St. #1, Akron, OH 44304, USA

G&M Brand Publications. P.O. Box 367, Aylesbury, Bucks. HP22 4LJ, UK. Tel.: 01296 682220. Fax: 01296 681989. E-mail: rsmithco@dircon.co.uk

G. Henie USA Incorporated, St. Louis. Box 1753, 2446 Centerline Ind'l Drive, Maryland Heights, MO 63043, USA. Fax: 304-991-3807

G. LeBlanc Company. 7001 Leblanc Blvd, Kenosha, WI 53141-1415, USA. Tel.: 262-658-1644. Fax: 262-658-2824. E-mail: gleblanc@gleblanc.com. Web site: www.gleblanc.com

G. Ricordi & Company. See: Hal Leonard

G. Ricordi & Company, Limited. London. See: Hal Leondard

G. Schirmer (Australia) Pty, Limited. See: Allans Publishing Pty Limited

G. Schirmer Incorporated. 257 Park Avenue S., New York, NY 10010, USA. Tel.: 212-254-2013. Fax: 212-254-2100. E-mail: schirmer@schirmer.com. Web site: www.schirmer.com

G. Zanibon. Liberia Musical Zanibon. Piazza Dei Signori 44, 35139 Padova, Italy. Tel.: 049 661033

Galaxy Music Corporation. See: E. C. Schirmer

Galliard Limited. Queen Anne's Road, Great Yarmouth, Norfolk, England

Garland Publishing. 29 W. 35th Street, New York, NY 10001-2299, USA. Tel.: 212-216-7800. Fax: 212-564-7854

Garrett, James. 5611 Forrester Ridge Road, Lyles, TN 37098, USA. (Deceased)

General Music Publishing Company. See: Boston Music Company

Georg Bauer Musikverlag. 47/49 Luisenstrasse, D-7500 Karlsruhe/Rhein, Germany

George, Thom Ritter. Department of Music, Idaho State University, PocaTelo, ID 83209, USA. Tel.: 208-282-2260. E-mail: georthom@isu.edu. Web site: www.isu.edu/~georthom/

Georges Delrieu & Cie. 45, Avenue Jean-Médecin F, 06000 Nice, France

Gérard Billaudot Éditeur. 14 rue de l'Echiquier, 75010 Paris, France. Tel.: +33 (0)1 47 70 14 46. Fax: +33 (0)1 45 23 22 54. Web site: www.billaudot.com

Gia Publications. 7404 South Mason Avenue, Chicago, IL 60638, USA. Tel.: 708-496-3800. Fax: 708 496-3828. E-mail: custserv@giamusic.com. Web site: www.giamusic.com

Gipps, Ruth. Allfarthings, Hermitage Road, Kenley, Surrey CR2 5EB, England

Glorious Sound bvba. De Hulsten 53, B2980 Zoersel, Belgium. Fax: +32 (0)3 605-04-42. E-mail: order@francoisglorieux.com

Glouchester Press. c/o Heilman Music, P.O. Box 1044, Fairmont, WV 26554, USA. Tel.: 304-367-4169. Fax: 304-367-4248. E-mail: tubajohn@mteer.com

Glover, Jim. 898 Promenade Lawnsberry Drive, Ottawa, Ontario K1E 1Y1, Canada. Tel.: 613-824-4294

GN. Gudbrandsdalsnoter. See: Frost Musi

Goddard, Mark. Spartan Press Music Publishers Ltd. Strathmashie House, Laggan Bridge, Scottish Highlands PH20 1BU, UK. Tel.: 01528 544770. Fax: 01528 544771. E-mail: Mail@SpartanPress.co.uk. Web site: www.SpartanPress.co.uk

Godiva Music. 18 Raleigh Road, Coventry, CV2 4AA, England. Tel.: 01203 459 409

Gorb, Adam. E-mail: Adam.gorb@rncm.ac.uk

Gordon Music Company. P.O. Box 2250, Canoga Park, CA 91307, USA. Tel.: (805) 647-4776

Gordon V. Thompson Limited. 85 Scarsdale Road, Don Mills, Ontario M3B 2R2, Canada

Gottschalk, Arthur. Shepard School of Music, 1606 Alice Pratt Brown Hall, Rice University, Houston, TX 77005-1892, USA. Tel.: 713-348-2567. E-mail: gottsch@rice.edu. Web site: www.ruf.rice.edu/~musi/facbios/gottschalk.htm

Gramercy Music. P.O. Box 41, Cheshire SK8 5HF, United Kingdom. Web site: www.gramercymusic.com

Grantwood Music Press. c/o James Grant, 7001 Charles Ridge Road, Baltimore, MD 21204, USA. Tel.: 410-825-1390. E-mail: jim@jamesgrantmusic.com. Web site: www.jamesgrantmusic.com

Great Works Publishing, Incorporated. See: Ludwig Music Publishing Company

Green Bay Music. 26 Dolbear Street, Green Bay, Auckkland 1007, New Zealand. Tel.: +64 9 817 3295. Fax: +64 9 849 4642. E-mail: 100243.2322@compuserve.com

Griffiths Edition. 21 Cefn. Coed, Bridgend, Mid Glamorgan CF31 4PH, Great Britain

Grosch-Musikverlag. Postfach 1268, Bahnhofstrabe 94A, D-8032 Grafelfing bei Munchen, Germany. Tel.: 089 85 32 79. Fax: 089 854 18 57

Grupo Real Musical. Carretera de Alcorcon a San Martin de Valdeiglesias, KM 9300, 28670 Villaviciosa de Odon, Madrid, Spain. Tel.: (34) 1 616 02 08. Fax: (34) 1 616 48 17. Web site: www.realmusical.com

GulfWind Music Press. P.O. Box 670545, Houston, TX 77267. Tel./Fax: 866-638-5879. Web site: http://home.earthlink.net/~gulfwindmusic. E-mail: gulfwindmusic@earthlink.net

GunMar Music, Incorporated. See: Margun/GunMar Music, Incorporated

Gustav Bosse Verlag. Von der Tann Straße 38, Postfach 417, D-8400 Regensburg 1, Germany
Haenssler Verlag. P.O. Box 50, Bismarckstrasse 4, 7303 Neuhausen, Stuttgart, Germany
Hal Leonard Publishing Corp. P.O. Box 13819, Milwaukee, WI 53213, USA. Tel.: 414-774-3630. Fax: 414-774-3259. E-mail: www.halleonard.com/contact.jsp. Web site: www.halleonard.com
Hallwag Verlag. Nordring 4, 3001 Bern, Switzerland. Fax: 41-31-41-41-33
Hamelle & Cie France. See: Theodore Presser Company
Hans Busch Musikforlag. Stubbstigen 3, Lidingo S-181 46, Sweden
Hans Schneider. Musikantiquariat U. Musikwiss. verlag. D 8132 Tutzing-Obb, Germany
Harald Lyche Musikforlag. Postboks 624, Strömsö, N-3003 Drammen, Norway. Tel.: +00 47 32 24 51 82. Fax: +00 47 32 24 51 89
Hargail Music Incorporated. See: CPP Belwin, Incorporated
Harmonia Uitgave. Nieuw-Loodsdrechtsedijk 105, Postbus 210, 1230 AE Loosdrecht, Nederland. Tel.: +31-35-5827595. Fax: +31-35-5827675
Harold Gore Publishing Company. 314 South Elm, Denton, TX 76201, USA. Tel.: 800-772-5918
Harvey Phillips Foundation. P.O. Box 933, Bloomington, IN 47402, USA. Tel.: 812-824-8833. Fax: 812-824-4462. E-mail: philliph@indiana.edu. Web site: www.tubachristmas.com
Heavy Metal Music. P.O. Box 954, Mundelein, IL 60060, USA
Heilman Music. P.O. Box 1044, Fairmont, WV 26554, USA. Tel.: 304-366-3758. Fax: 304-367-4248. E-mail: tubajohn@mteer.com
Heinick, David. Crane School of Music, 44 Pierrepont Avenue, Potsdam, NY 13676-2294, USA. Tel.: 315-267-2410. E-mail: heiniedg@potsdam.edu
Heinrichshofen Verlag. Liebigstraße 16, D-26389 Wilhelmshaven, Germany. Tel.: 0 44 21-92 67-0. Fax: 0 44 21-20 20 07. E-mail: info@heinrichshofen.de. Web site: www.heinrichshofen.de
Helicon Music Corporation. See: European American Music Distributors Corp.
Henie. See: G. Henie USA Incorporated
Henmar Press Incorporated. See: C. F. Peters
Henri Elkan Music Publishing Company, Incorporated. Box 965, Planetarium Station, New York, NY 10024, USA. Tel.: 212-877-8350. Fax: 212-877-8350. E-mail: helkan@aol.com
Henry Lemoine et Cie, France. See: Theodore Presser Company
Heritage Music Press. See: Lorenz Corporation
Hermann Moeck Verlag. See: European American Music Distributors Corp.
Heugel & Cie Paris. See: Theodore Presser
Heussenstamm, George. 5013 Lowell Avenue, La Crescenta, CA 91214, USA
Heuwekemeljer (Editions) Netherlands. See: Theodore Presser Company
Hewitt, Harry. 345 S. 19th Street, Apt. 3A, Philadelphia, PA 19103-6637, USA. Tel: 215-985-0963. Fax: 215-985-0736. E-mail: eh1958@tjburke.com
Hidalgo Music. P.O. Box 1928, Lyons, CO 80540, USA. Tel.:/Fax: 800 HID-ALGO. Tel./Fax: (303) 823-0152. E-mail: hidalgo@hidalgomusic.com. Web site: www.hidalgomusic.com
Hildegard Publishing Company. See: The Theodore Presser Company
Hinrichsen Edition, Limited. See: C. F. Peters Corporation
Hinshaw Music Incorporated. P.O. Box 470, Chapel Hill, NC 27514-0470, USA. Tel.: 919-933-1691. Fax: 919-967-3399. E-mail: krolleri@hinshawmusic.com. Web site: www.hinshawmusic.com
Hip-Bone Music. 119 W. 71st St. #8B, New York, NY 10023, USA. Tel.: 1-888-633-2663. E-mail: hip-bone@nyc.rr.com. Web site: www.hipbonemusic.com
HOA Music Publishers. 756 S. 3rd Street, DeKalb, IL 60115, USA. Tel.: 815-756-9730. E-mail: edgrieg@aol.com
Hofmeister. See: Friederich Hofmeister
HoneyRock. 396 Raystown Road, Everett, PA 15537, USA. Web site: http://www.honeyrock.net/ensm-3.htm
Hope Publishing Company. 380 S. Main Pl., Carol Stream, IL 60188, USA. Tel.: (630) 665-3200. Tel. 2: (800) 323-1049. Fax: (630) 665-2552. E-mail: hope@hopepublishing.com. Web site: www.hopepublishing.com
Horizon Press. P.O. Box 483, Newington, VA 22122, USA
Hornists' Nest, The. P.O. Box 253, Buffalo, NY 14226-0253, USA. Tel.: 716-626-9534. E-mail: Lowell.shaw@worldnet.att.net. Web site: home.att.net/~hornistsnest
Hornseth Music Company. 4318 Hamilton Street #10, Hyattsville, MD 20781, USA
Howe, Marvin C. 5105 Bush Road, Interlochen, MI 49643, USA
Hoyt Editions. 706 W. Halladey, Seattle, WA 98119, USA. E-mail: HoyEd@aol.com. Web site: www.hoyteditions.com
Hug & Company Musikverlage. Musik Hug AG. Stammhaus Limmatquai Postfach 28-30, CH-8022 Zürich, Switzerland. Tel.: 01/269 41 41. Fax: 01/269 41 01. E-mail: info.zuerich@musikhug.ch. Web site: http://www.musikhug.ch/
Huhn/Nobile Verlag. Aixhelmer Str. 25, 7000 Stuttgart 75, Germany
IACS. Postboks 157 Røa, N-0702 Oslo, Norway
Iceland Music Information Center. Sidumúli 34, 108 Reykjavík, Iceland. Tel.: +354 568 3122. Fax: +354 568 3124. E-mail: itm@mic.is. Web site: www.mic.is/english

Impero Verlag. See: Theodore Presser Company

Imudico Musikforlaget. Mårkærvej 13, DK2630 Tåstrup, Denmark. Tel.: 43 71 19 30. Fax: 43 71 19 45. E-mail: kleinert@kleinert.dk. Web site: www.kleinert.dk

Indiana Music Center. 322 Swain, Bloomington, IN 47401, USA

Instrumentalist, The. 200 Northfield Road, Northfield, IL 60093, USA. Tel.: 1-888-446-6888. Fax: 1-847-446-6263. E-mail: subscriptions@instrumentalistmagazine.com. Web site: www.instrumentalistmagazine.com

International Music Company. 5 West 37th Street, New York, NY 10018. Tel.: 212-391-4200. Fax: 212-391-4306. E-mail: salesmanager@internationalmusicco.com. Web site: www.internationalmusicco.com

International Trombone Association Press. 138 Fine Arts Center, University of Missouri–Columbia, Columbia, MO 65211, USA. Tel.: 573-882-0926. Fax: 573-884-7444

Intrada Music Group. 2220 Mountain Blvd, Suite 220, Oakland, CA 94611, USA. Tel.: 510-336-1612. Fax: 510-336-1615. E-mail: intrada@intrada.com. Web site: www.intrada.com

Ione Press. A division of ECS Publishing Boston Massachusetts

Iowa State University Press. 2121 State Ave., Ames, IA 50014-8300, USA. Tel.: 515-292-0140. Fax: 515-292-3348. E-mail: director@iowastatepress.com. Web site: www.iowastatepress.com

Israel Brass Woodwind Publications. P.O. Box 1126, Kfar Sava 44110, Israel. Tel.: +972-(0)9-767-9869. Fax: +972-(0)9-766-2855. E-mail: E-mail@ortav.com . Web site: www.ortav.com

Israel Music Institute. P.O. Box 8269, IL-61082 Tel Aviv, Israel. Tel.: (972)-03-6811010. Fax: (972)-03-6816070. E-mail: musicinst@bezeqint.net. Web site: www.aquanet.co.il/vip/imi/

Israeli Music Center. 73 Nordau Blvd, Tel Aviv, Israel

Israeli Music Publications Limited. U.S. Agent: Presser. 25 Keren Hayesod, Jerusalem, 94188, Israel

Italian Book Corporation. 1119 Shore Pkwy, Brooklyn, NY 11214, USA. Tel.: 718-236-5803. Fax: 718-236-5803. E-mail: italbook@worldnet.att.net

ITEA Journal. Jason Smith, 55 Sunnyside Drive, Athens, OH 45701, USA. Tel.: (740) 591-4075. E-mail: smithj10@ohio.edu. Web site: www.iteaonline.org

J. Albert & Son Pty, Limited. 9 Rangers Road, Neutral Bay, Sydney, NSW, Australia, 2089. Tel.: 61 2 9953 6038. Fax: 61 2 9953 1803. E-mail: contact@albertmusic.com. Web site: www.albertmusic.com

J. Maurer Editions Musicales. See: Editions Musicales J. Maurer

Jack Spratt Music Company. See: Plymouth Music Company, Incorporated

Jalni Publications. See: Boosey & Hawkes & Company

Jamey Aebersold. P.O. Box 1244, New Albany, IN 47151-1244, USA. Tel.: 1-812-945-4281. Fax: 1-812-949-2006. E-mail: staff@jazzbooks.com. Web site: www.jajazz.com

Japan Tuba Center. Chitate Kagawa. Shinoro 6-jo 5-chome 5-6, Kita-ku, Sapporo, Japan, 002-8026. Tel./Fax: (81) 11 771 0559. E-mail: order@japantubacenter.com. Web site: http://www.japantubacenter.com

Jasemusiikki. See: Edition Wilhelm Hansen

Jensen Publications. See: Hal Leonard Publications

JML Publications. John Luther, 4713 Contenta Ridge, Santa Fe, NM 87507, USA. Tel.: 505-424-1732. Fax: 505-424-1738. E-mail: jmlwords@msn.com

Johann Doms. Hubertusallee 24b, D-1000, Berlin 33, Germany

Jones, Roger. 303 Kenilworth Drive #29, Monroe, LA 71203, USA

Josef Weinberger. 12–14 Mortimer Street, London W1T 3JJ, UK. Tel.: 44 + (0)20 7580 2827. Fax: 44 + (0)20 7436 9616. E-mail: general.info@jwmail.co.uk. Web site: www.josef-weinberger.com/weinberger/index.html

Josef Weinberger (Germany). Oeder Weg 26, D-60318 Frankfurt am Main, Germany. Tel.: +49 69/955 288 30. Fax: +49 69/955 288 44. E-mail: mail@josefweinberger.de. Web site: www.josefweinberger.de

Josef Weinberger Wien GmbH. Music Publishing Group. Neulerchenfelderstraße 3–7, A-1160 Vienna; Austria. Tel.: +43 (0)1 403 59 91-0. Fax: +43 (0)1 403 59 91-13. E-mail: musik@weinberger.co.at. Web site: www.weinberger.co.at

Joseph Boonin. See: Jerona Music Corporation

Joseph Compello Publications. 11132 Old Carriage Road, Glen Arm, MD 21057, USA. Tel.: 668-1806

Joseph Wood Music Company. 148 East Main Street, Norton, MA 02766, USA

JTL Publications. See: E. C. Schirmer Co.

Jubilate Verlag. Friedhofgasse 8, D-85072 Eichstätt, Germany. Tel.: 08421-5332. Fax: 08421-4052. E-mail: info@Jubilate-Verlag.com. Web site: www.jubilate-verlag.com

Julio Tancredi. 78 Oakwood Avenue, Providence, RI 02909, USA. Tel.: 401-351-1128

Kaland. See: Norsk Musikksamling

Kallisti Music Press. 810 S. Saint Bernard Street, Philadelphia, PA 19143, USA. Tel.: 215-724-6511. E-mail: kallisti@ix.netcom.com. Web site: pw1.netcom.com/~kallisti/

Kalmus. See: A. A. Kalmus Limited

Karamar Publications. 255 Oser Avenue, Hauppauge, NY 11788, USA. Fax: 631-273-6349

Kelly Sebastian Music Publishers. PO Box 13, Hindmarsh, South Australia, 5007

Kendor Music Incorporated. 21 Grove Street, P.O. Box 278, Delevan, New York 14042-0278, USA. Tel.: 716-492-1254. Fax: 716-492-5124. E-mail: customerservice@kendormusic.com. Web site: www.kendormusic.com

Keyboard Percussion Publications. 392 Kirby Ave, Elberon, NJ 07740, USA. Tel.: 732-870-8600

Kibutz Movement League of Composers. 10 Dubnov Street, Tel-Aviv, Israel

Kirklee Music. 609 Bradford Road, Bailiff Bridge, Brighouse, West Yorkshire HD6 4DN, England. Tel.: +44 01484 722855. Fax: +44 01484 723591. E-mail: sales@kirkleesmusic.co.uk. Web site: www.kirkleesmusic.co.uk

Kistner & Siegel. Adrian-Kiels-Str. 2, 5000 Köln 90, Germany

KIWI Music Press. Box 1151, Groton, CT 06340, USA

Kjos. See: Neil A. Kjos Music Company

Kleooubger-Pfaff Music Company. c/o Dr. Paul Dorsam, Music Dept. Box 163, Wm Carey College, Hattiesburg, MS 39401, USA

Knox, Charles. (Lux Nova Press.) 2103 North Decatur Rd., #216, Decatur, GA 30033, USA. Tel. 1: 888-497-8956. Tel. 2: 404-218-2556. E-mail: luxnova@luxnova.com. Web site: www.luxnova.com/comp/cck/

Ko Ko Enterprises. 1515 Chickees Street, Johnson City, TN 37601, USA

Koff Music Company. P.O. Box 1442, Studio City, CA 91604, USA. Tel.: 323-656-2264

KSM Publishing Company. P.O. Box 3819, Dallas, TX 75208, USA

Kyodo Music. Web site: www.kyodo-music.com

Lackey, Jerry. 18050 Chipstead Drive, South Bend, IN 46637, USA. Tel.: 219-277-1938

Laissez-Faire Music. See: TUBA Press

Larrick, Geary. 2337 Jersey Street, Stevens Point, WI 54481, USA. Tel.: 715-341-4367

Larsen, Libby. 2205 Kenwood Avenue, Minneapolis, MN 55405, USA. E-mail: info@libbylarsen.com. Web site: www.libbylarsen.com

Lawson-Gould Music Publishers Incorporated. See: Warner/Chappell Music Inc.

Lea Pocket Scores. See: European American Music Distributors Corp.

LeBlanc. See: G. LeBlanc Company

L'Edition le Grand Orgue. Box 48, Syosset, NY 11791, USA

Leduc. See: Alphonse Leduc Editions Paris

Lema Musikforlag. Vetevagen 24, S 691 48, Karlskoga, Sweden. Tel.: 46 586 3 57 17. Fax: 46 586 3 99 20

Lemirre, Florent. 17 rue Roger Salengro, 59139 Wattignies, France. Tel.: 20.95.05.81

Lemoine. See: Henry Lemoine et Cie, France

Les Editions Ouvrieres. 12 Avenue Soeur-Roselie, Paris 13, France

Les Stallings Music Group. P.O. Box 1985, Brentwood, TN 37024-1985, USA

Leslie Music Supply Canada. 198 Speers Road, Unit 2, Oakville, Ontario, L6K 2E9, Canada. Tel.: 905 844-3109. Fax: 905 844-7637. E-mail: sales@lesliemusicsupply.com. Web site: www.lesliemusicsupply.com

Lewis Music Press. 124 Newmarket Stornoway, Isle of Lewis, Scotland HS2 0ED. Tel.: +44 (0) 1851 706549. E-mail: sales@lewismusicpress.com. Web site: www.lewismusicpress.com

Liben Music Publishers. 1191 Eversole Road, Cincinnati, OH 45230-3546, USA. Tel.: 513-232-6920. Fax: 1-513-232-1866. E-mail: info@liben.com. Web site: www.liben.com

Lillenas Publishing Company. 2923 Troost, Kansas City, MO 64109, USA. Tel.: 816-931-1900. Fax: 816-412-8390. E-mail and Web site: www.lillenas.com

Lindenfeld, Harris. See: Theodore Presser Co.

Lindsay Music England. 23 Hitchin Street, Biggleswade, Beds. SG18 8AX, England. Tel.: +44 (0)1767 316521. Fax: +44 (0)1767 317221. E-mail: sales@lindsaymusic.co.uk. Web site: www.lindsaymusic.co.uk

Lino Florenzo. 121 rue Barthelmy Delespaul, 59000 Lille, France

Lithuanian Music Information and Publishing Centre. Mickeviciaus 29, LT-600, Vilnius, Lithuania. Tel.: +370 2 726986. E-mail: center@mipc.vno.osf.lt. Web site: www.nkm.lt/mipc/index2.html

Litolff Verlag. See: C. F. Peters

London Pro Musica Edition. P.O. Box 1088, Bradford BD1 3XT, Great Britain. Tel.: +44 1274 728 884. Fax: +44 1274 728 882

London Tuba Quartet. Web site: www.londontubaquartet.co.uk

Long Island Brass Workshop. P.O. Box 85, Halesite, NY 11743, USA

Lorenz Corporation. Box 802. 501 E. Third Street, Dayton, OH 45401-0802, USA. Tel.: 1-800-444-1144. Fax: 937-223-2042. E-mail: info@lorenz.com. Web site: www.lorenz.com

Lorge, John. 4450 48th Street, San Diego, CA 92115, USA

Loux Music Publishing Company. 2 Hawley Ln, Hannacroix, NY 12087-0034, USA. Tel.: 518 756-2273. Fax: 518 756-2273. E-mail: recordershop@recordershop.com. Web site: www.recordershop.com

Luck's Music Library Incorporated. 32300 Edward, P.O. Box 71397, Madison Heights, MI 48071, USA. Tel.: 800-348-8749. Fax: 248-583-1114. E-mail: sales@lucksmusic.com. Web site: www.lucksmusic.com

Ludwig Doblinger K.G. Dorotheergasse 10, A-1010 Vienna, Austria. Tel.: 01/515 03-0. Fax: 01/515 03-51. E-mail: music@doblinger.at. Web site: www.doblinger.co.at

Ludwig Music Publishing Company. 1044 Vivian Drive, Grafton, OH 44044, USA. Tel.: 800-851-1150. E-mail: info@ludwigmusic.com. Web site: www.ludwigmusic.com

Lunde. Lunde & Co's Forlag. Sinsenvn. 25, N-0572 Oslo, Norway

Lusitanius Editions, Portugal. Web site: www.lusitanusensemble.net/editions

Lyceum Music Press. See: Ensemble Publications

Lyche. Edition Lyche. Nedre Eikervei 12, N-3045 Drammen, Norway. Tel.: +47 32 26 90 02. E-mail: order@lychemusikk.no

Lyra Music Company. 1841 Broadway Suite 1103, New York, NY 10023, USA. Tel.: 212-246-0724. Fax: 212-246-0781. E-mail: lyrahouse@aol.com. Web site: www.lyramusic.com

Lyric Brass Publishing. 380 North Colonial Avenue, Westminster, MD 21157, USA. Tel.: 410-751-2203. E-mail: publishing@lyricbrass.com. Web site: www.lyricbrass.com/publishing/

M. Baron Company, Incorporated. P.O. Box 149, South Road, Oyster Bay, NY 11771, USA. Tel.: 516-922-1657

M. P. Belaieff. See: C. F. Peters

Maecenas Music Limited. 5 Bushey Close, Old Barn Lane, Kenley, Surrey CR2 5AU, UK

Magnolia Music Press. 6319 Riverbend Blvd, Baton Rouge, LA 70800, USA

Magnolia Press Ltd. 344 Angela Court, Lexington, KY 40515, USA. Tel.: 606-272-9867

Malama Arts Incorporated. P.O. Box 1761, Honolulu, HI 96806, USA. Tel.: 1-808-329-5828. Fax: 1-808-329-5828. E-mail arts@ilhawaii.net

Malterer, Edward. Box 763, Morehead State University, Morehead, KY 40351, USA

Manas, Adriana I. Figueroa. Darwin 1281, Dorrego, Guaymallen, Mendoza 5519 Argentina. E-mail: adrifg@dynastar.com.ar

Manduca Music. 861 Washington Ave., Portland, ME 04103-2728, USA. Tel. 1: 207-773-7012. Tel. 2: 1-800-626-3822. Fax: 207-773-6597. E-mail: mark@manducamusic.com. Web site: www.manducamusic.com

Manhattan Beach Music. 1595 E. 46 Street, Brooklyn, NY 11234, USA. Tel.: 718-338-4137. E-mail: mbmband@aol.com. Web site: members.aol.com/mbmband/

Manncy Music. 7 Glengray Road, Crofton, NY 10520, USA

Manny Gold Music Publisher. 1060 East Ninth Street, Brooklyn, NY 11230, USA. Tel.: 718-258-0374. Fax: 718-258-0236

Manuscript Publications. Rt 2, Box 150A, Wrightville, PA 17368, USA

Mapa Mundl London. See: E. C. Schirmer

Mapleson Music Rental Library. 33 Elkay Drive, Chester, NY 10918, USA. Tel.: 845-469-5790. Fax: 845-469-5817. E-mail: rental@emsmusic.com. Web site: www.emsmusic.com

Margun Music, Incorporated. See: Shawnee Press

Margun/GunMar Music, Incorporated. 167 Dudley Road, Newton Center, MA 02159, USA. Tel.: 617-332-6398. Fax: 617-969-1079. E-mail: MargunMu@aol.com. Web site: members.aol.com/margunmus

Mark Foster Music Company. See: Shawnee Press

Mark Herman and Ronnie Apter. 5748 W. Brooks Road, Shepherd, MI 48883-9202, USA. Tel.: 517-774-3128. E-mail: ronnie.apter@cmich.edu

Mark Tezak. Postfach 101360, 5090 Leverkusen 1, Germany. Out of business. See: Georg Bauer Musikverlag

Marks Music. See: Edward B. Marks Music Company

Marseg Limited. 18 Farmstead Road, Willowdale, Ontario, ML 2G2, Canada

Mas, Vicente Navarro. Sergio Carolino. Bairro Da Ota, Do Cidral Lote 25, Vestiaria. 2460-743, Portugal. Tel.: 351-96-283-3260. E-mail: sergiofbc@hotmail.com

Masters Music. Tel.: 561-241-6169. Fax: 561-241-6347. E-mail: info@masters-music.com. Web site: www.masters-music.com

Max Hieber GmbH. P.O. Box 330429, 80064 Munich, Germany. Tel.: 089-29 00 80-0. Fax: 089-22 97 82. E-mail: info@musikhieber.de. Web site: www.musikhieber.de/index.htm

MCA Music Corp. See: Universal Music Publishing

McCoy Horn Library. P.O. Box 907, Houston, MN 55943, USA. Tel.: 507.896.4441. Fax: 507.896.4442. E-mail: info@mccoyshornlibrary.com. Web site: www.mccoyshornlibrary.com

McGinnis & Marx Music Publishers. 236 W. 26 Street No. 11-S, New York, NY 10001-6736, USA. Tel.: 212-243-5233. Fax: 212-675-1630

McKimm, Barry. See: Yarra Yarra Music

Media Press. P.O. Box 250, Elwyn, PA 19063 USA

Medici Music Press. 5017 Veach Road, Owensboro, KY 42303, USA. Tel.: 270-684-9233. E-mail: ronalddishinger@yahoo.com. Web site: www.medicimusic.com

Mel Bay Publications Inc. Box 66, #4 Industrial Drive, Pacific, MO 63069-0066, USA. Tel.: 800-863-5229. Fax: 636-257-5062. E-mail: E-mail@melbay.com. Web site: www.melbay.com

Menoche, Charles Paul. 237 Old Farm Drive, Newington, CT 06111, USA. Tel.: 860-667-9236. E-mail: menochec@ccsu.edu

Mentor Music Incorporated. 3301 Carlisle NE, Albuquerque, NM 87110, USA. Tel. 1: 1-800-545-6204. Tel. 2: 505-889-9777. Fax: 505-889-9070. E-mail: info@musicmart.com. Web site: www.musicmart.com

Metropolitan Museum c/o Henry Fischer. RR #1, Box 389, Sherman, CT 06784, USA

Mexicanas de Musica SA Ediciones Mexico. Avda Juarez 18 Despacho 206. Mexico. 06050. Mexico, D.F.

MGP. 10 Clifton Terrace, Winchester, Hants., England

Michigan State University Press. 1405 South Harrison Road, Suite 25 Manly Miles Building, East Lansing, MI 48823-5245, USA. Tel.: 517-355-9543. Fax: 517-432-2611. E-mail: msupress@msu.edu. Web site: msupress.msu.edu

MIC.NO(MS). Manuscript at Music Information Centre Norway. Tollbugt. 28, N-0157 Oslo, Norway. Tel.: +47 22 42 90 90. E-mail: info@mic.no

Middle Branch Music. P.O. Box 265, East Randolph, VT 05401, USA

Miserendino, Joe. Web site: www.joesmusicroom.com

M J Q Music Incorporated. 200 W.57th Street, New York, NY 10019, USA

MMB Music, Incorporated. Contemporary Arts Building, 3526 Washington Avenue, Saint Louis, MO 63103-1019, USA. Tel. 1: 314-531-9635. Tel. 2: 800-543-3771. Fax: 314-531-8384. E-mail: info@mmbmusic.com. Web site: www.mmbmusic.com

Modern Editions. P.O. Box 653, Taylor, TX 76574, USA

Modrana Music Publishers, Ltd. 41 Parklands Way, Poynton, Cheshire, England, SK121AL. Tel.: 01625 875389. Fax: 01625 875389. E-mail: info@modranamusicpromotions.com. Web site: www.modranamusicpromotions.com

Moore, David Arthur. 1746 South Canton Avenue, Tulsa, OK74112, USA. E-mail: davidcomposer@cox.net. Web site: http://members.cox.net/davidcomposer

Morning Star Music Publishers. 1727 Larkin Williams Rd, Fenton, MO 63026, USA. Tel.: 800-647-2117. Fax: 636-305-0121. E-mail: morningstar@morningstarmusic.com. Web site: www.morningstarmusic.com

Moseler Verlag. Hoffmann-v.-F.-Str. 8, 38304 Wolfenbüttel, Germany. Tel.: +49-5331-95970. Fax: +49-5331-959720. E-mail: info@moeseler-verlag.de. Web site: www.moeseler-verlag.de

Mother Lode Music. P.O. Box 110, Jamestown, CA 95327, USA. Tel.: 209-984-0681. Fax: 209-984-0681

MS Publications. 1045 Garfield, Oak Park, IL 60304, USA

Mueller, Frederick A. Music Department, Morehead State University, Morehead, KY 40351, USA

Mu-Hu. Musikk-Husets Forlag A/S. P.O. Box 822 Sentrum, N-0104 Oslo, Norway. Tel.: +47 22 82 59 00. E-mail: oslo@musikk-huset.no

Muradian, Vazgen. 269 W. 72nd. Street, Apt. 11A, New York, NY 10023-2713, USA. Tel.: 212-724-7452

Music Arts Company. P.O. Box 327, Ripon, WI 54971-0327, USA

Music Bona. Soukenicka 23. Box 45, 110 05 Praha 1, Czech Republic. Fax: +420 224 811 508. E-mail: contact@musicabona.com. Web site: www.musicabona.com

Music Box Dancer Publications Limited. Canada. See: Theodore Presser Company

Music Express. P.O. Box 331, Lambertville, NJ 08530, USA. Tel.: 800-841-1432. Fax: 609-882-3182

Music for Percussion. See: Plymouth Music Company, Incorporated

Music Graphics Press. 121 Washington Street, San Diego, CA 92103 USA. Tel.: 619-298-3629

Music in Action. See: Alfred Publishing Co.

Music Nove USA. 15 Falcon Road, Sharon, MA 02067, USA

Music Rara. Le Traversier, Chemin de la Buire, 84170 Monteux, France

Music Sales Corp. 257 Park Avenue S., New York, NY 10010, USA. Tel.: 212-254-2100. Fax: 212-254-2013. E-mail: info@musicsales.com. Web site: www.msc-catalog.com

Music 70 Music Publishers. See: Plymouth Music Company, Inc.

Music Theatre International. 421 West 54th Street, New York, NY 10019, USA. Tel.: 212-541-4684. Fax: 212-397-4684. E-mail: Licensing@MTIshows.com. Web site: www.mtishows.com

Music Treasure Publications. 620 Fort Washington Ave, No. 1-F, New York, NY 10040, USA

Musica Budapest (Edition) Hungary. See: Theodore Presser Company

Musica Islandica. Rejkjavik, Iceland

Musical Evergreen, The. See: Philharmusica Corporation

Musicc-Huset A/S. Postboks 1459 Vika, Oslo, Norway

Musicians Publications. 1076 River Road, Trenton, NJ 08628, USA. Tel.: 609-882-8139. Fax: 609-882-3182. E-mail: bhmuspub@aol.com

Musik Verlage Hans Sikorski. Johnsallee 23, D-20148 Hamburg, Germany. Tel.: +49 (0)40 41 41 00 0. Fax: +49 (0)40 41 41 00 41. E-mail: contact@sikorski.de. Web site: www.sikorski.de

Musikk-Huset Forlag. Postboks 822, Sentrum, N 0104, Oslo 1, Norway. Tel.: (+47) 22 82 59 00. Fax: (+47) 22 42 55 41. E-mail: oslo@musikk-huset.no. Web site: www.musikk-huset.no

Musikkverkstedet. Rolvseidet, N-1890 Rakkestad, Norway. Tel.: +47 69 32 29 50. E-mail: forlag@online.no. Web site: www.musikkverkstedet.no

Musikverlag Barbara Evans. Sybelstrasse 24, 1000 Berlin 12, Germany. Tel.: 030/323/55 98. Fax: 030/323/55 98

Musikverlag Bruno Uetz, Deutschland: See: Uetz Music Publishers

Musikverlag Johann Kliment KG. A-1090 Wien, Kolingasse 15, Austria. Tel.: 0043/1/317 51 47. Fax: 0043/1/310 08 27. E-mail: office@kliment.at. Web site: www.kliment.at

Musikverlag Martin Scherbacher. Blumenstetter Str. 6, 72379 Hechingen, Germany. Tel.: 0 74 71/4722. Fax: 0 74 71 / 1 26 65. E-mail: www.scherbacher.de/shop/enter.html. Web site: www.scherbacher.de

Musikverlag Robert Lienau. Strubbergstrasse 80, 60489 Frankfurt/Main, Germany. E-mail: info@lienau-frankfurt.de. Web site: www.zimmermann-frankfurt.de

Musikverlag Rundel GmbH. Untere Gewendhalde 27-29, 88430 Rot an der Rot, Germany. Tel.: ++49-8395-94260. Fax: ++49-8395-9426890. E-mail: info@rundel.de. Web site: www.rundel.de/englisch/a-frame.html

Musikverlag Stafan Reischl. A4181 Oberneukirchen 162, Germany

Musikverlag Wilhelm Halter. Gablonzerstr. 24, D-76185 Karlsruhe, Germany. Tel.: +49 (0) 721/567256. Fax +49 (0) 721/562674. E-mail: office@halter.de. Web site: www.halter.de

Muso's Media. P.O. Box 188, Kangaroo Flat, Australia, 3555. Tel.: +61 (0)3 5447-0873. Fax: +61 (0)3 5447-8178. Web site: www.musosmedia.com.au

Muziekuitgeverij Saul B. Groen. Ferdinand Bolstraat 6, Amsterdam, Holland

Nazarene Publishing House. See: Lillenas Publishing Company

Neil A. Kjos Music Company. P.O. Box 178270, San Diego, CA 92177-8270, USA. Tel.: 858-270-9800. Fax: 858-270-3507. E-mail: E-mail@kjos.com. Web site: www.kjos.com

Neilsen, Erik. See: Middle Branch Music

Neuschel Music. See: Studio Music

New Music West. See: Theodore Presser Co.

New Valley Music Press of Smith College. Smith College Music Dept, Sage Hall, Northampton, MA 01063, USA. Tel.: 413-585-3150. Fax: 413-585-3180

New World Enterprises of Montrose Incorporated. 2 Marisa Court, Montrose, NY 10548, USA. Tel.: 914-737-2232. Fax: 914-737-2232

New York Women Composers Incorporated. 114 Kelburne Avenue, North Tarrytown, NY 10591, USA. Tel.: 914-631-6444. E-mail: nywomencomposers@hotmail.com. Web site: www.ibiblio.org/nywc/

Nichols Music Company. See: Ensemble Publications

Nick Stamon Press. 4380 Middlesex Drive, San Diego, CA 92116, USA. Tel.: 619-283-1637

Nicolai Music. c/o Neal Corwell, P.O. Box 253, Clear Spring, MD 21722, USA. Tel.: 301-842-3307. E-mail: nicolaimusic@ erols.com

NKF. Norske Komponisters Forlag. c/o Norges Korforbund, Tollbugt. 28, N-0157 Oslo, Norway. Tel.: +4722 42 67 20. E-mail: korsenteret@korforbundet.no

NMO. Norsk Musikforlag AS. P.O. Box 1499 Vika, N-0116 Oslo, Norway. Tel.: +47 23 00 20 21. E-mail: order@musikforlaget.no

NMS(Ms). Manuscript with the National Library. Norsk Musikksamling. P.O. Box 2674, N-0203 Oslo, Norway. Tel.: +47 23 27 60 43. E-mail: musikk-nbo@nb.no. Website: www.nb.no/html/norsk_musikksamling.htm

Noga Music. See: Ensemble Publications. 00175 POB, 4025 Jerusalem, Israel. E-mail: eanogmus@netvision.net.il

Nordic Sounds Ltd. Postboks 726 4004, Stavanger, Norway. Tel.: +47 51 52 14 40. Fax: +47 5152 1406. E-mail: post@nordicsounds.com. Web site: www.nordicsounds.com

Nordiska Muslkforlaget Stockholm. See: G. Schirmer Incorporated

Norman Lee Publishing Company. See: C. L Barnhouse, Company

Norsk Musikforlag Oslo. See: MMB Music Incorporated. P.O. Box 1499 Vika, N-0116 Oslo, Norway. Tel.: +47 23 00 20 21. E-mail: order@musikforlaget.no

Norsk Notestik. See: Norsk Musikforlag

Northcut, Timothy. 5757 Stone Trace Drive, Mason, OH 45040, USA. Tel.: 513-336-0321. E-mail: Timothy.Northcut@uc.edu

Norwegian Music Center. Tollbugata 28, N-0157 Oslo, Norway. Tel.: +47 2242 9090. Fax: +47 2242 9091. E-mail: info@mic.no. Web site: www.mic.no/English

Noton. See: Norsk Musikforlag

Nova Music Limited, England. See: E. C. Schirmer

Novello & Company. See: Theodore Presser Company

O. Pagani & Brother Incorporated. c/o PD Mus. Headquarters, P.O. Box 252, Village Sta., New York, NY 10014, USA. Tel.: 212-242-5322

Obrasso Verlag AG. Baselstrasse 23c, CH-4537, Wiedlisbach, Switzerland. Tel.: +41 (0) 32-637-37-27. Fax: +41 (0) 32-636-26-44. E-mail: obrasso@bluewin.ch. Web site: www.obrasso.ch

OH Musik Aps. Jersie Strandvej 5, DK-2680 Sol rød Strand, Denmark. Tel.: (+45) 56 14 66 44. Fax: (+45) 56 14 66 67. E-mail: oh@ohmusik.dk. Web site: www.ohmusik.dk

Ohio University ITEA Chapter Composition Series. Jason Smith, 55 Sunnyside Drive, Athens, OH 45701, USA. Tel.: 740-591-4075. E-mail: smithj10@ohio.edu. Web site: oak.cats.ohiou.edu/~smithj10/

Ohio Valley Tuba Quartet Press. 1870 S. Springcrest Court, Beavercreek, OH 45432, USA

Ongaku No Tomo Sha Corp., Japan. See: Theodore Presser Company

ØNMF. Østnorsk Musikkforlag. c/o Hans-Olav Lien, Gullgata 15, N-3513 Hønefoss, Norway. Tel.: +47 32 12 63 96

Opus Music Publishers. 1315 Sherman Place, Evanston, IL 60201, USA. Tel.: 847-475-1544. Fax: 847-475-1544. Web site: www.opusmusic.net/opus.htm

Ott, Joseph. See: Claude Benny Press

Otto Heinrich Noetzel Verlag. Liebigstraße 16, D-26389 Wilhelmshaven, Germany. Tel: 0 44 21 92 67 0. Fax: 0 44 21 20 20 07. E-mail: info@heinrichshofen.de. Web site: www.heinrichshofen.de

Otto Wrede Regina Verlag. Schumannstrasse 35, Postfach 6148, D-65051 Wiesbaden 1, Germany. Tel.: (06 11) 52 31 18. Fax: (06 11) 52 07 73

Ovation. Markaplassen 415, 7054 Ranheim, Norway. Web site: www.baadsvik.com

Oxford University Press Incorporated. 189 Madison Avenue, New York, NY 10016, USA. Tel.: +1 212 726 6000. Fax: +1 212 726 6440. E-mail: custserv@oup-usa.org. Web site: www.oup-usa.org

Paganiniana Publications Incorporated. Box 427, 1 TFH Plaza, Third and Union, Neptune City, NJ 07753, USA. Tel.: 908-988-8400. Fax: 908-988-5466

Panton. See: Music Bona

Paolo Baratto. Rumelbachstr. 39, CH 8153 Rumlang, Switzerland

Parga Music. 113 Magnolia Lane, Princeton, NJ 08540, USA. Tel.: 609-921-6374

Parow'sche Musikalien. c/o Kagarice Brass Editions, P.O. Box 305302, Denton, TX 76203, USA. Web site: www.kagarice.com/contact

Pasquina Publishing Company. 5600 Snake Road, Oakland, CA 94611, USA

Paterson's Publications. See: Peters Edition

PatrickSheridan.com. #165. 610 N. Alma School Road, Suite #18, Chandler, AZ 85224-3687, USA. Tel.: 602-327-3765. E-mail: patsheridan@earthlink.net. Web site: www.patricksheridan.com

Paumanok Press. 974 Hardscrabble Road, Chappaqua, NY 10514, USA

Paxman Musical Instruments Ltd. Linton House, 164–80 Union Street, London SE1 0LH, UK. Tel.: (0)20 7620 2077. Fax: (0)20 7620 1688. E-mail: info@paxman.co.uk. Web site: www.paxman.co.uk

Payne, Frank Lynn. P.O. Box 60806, Oklahoma City, OK 73146, USA

Peer International Corporation. See: Theodore Presser Company

Peer Muslkverlag GmbH Hamburg. Postfach 602129, 22231 Hamburg, Germany Tel.: 040/278379-0. Fax: 040/278379-40. E-mail: classicaleur@peermusic.com

Peer-Southern Organization. See: Theodore Presser Company

Peermusic (UK) LTD. See: Theodore Presser Company

PEL Music Publications. W. 1761 River Oaks Drive, Marinette, WI 54143, USA. Tel.: 715-735-5273. Fax: 715-735-3613. E-mail: paul@pelmusic.com. Web site: www.pelmusic.com

Pelikan Musikverlag. Zurich, Switzerland

Peters. See: C. F. Peters Corp.

Peters Editions Limited. 10–12 Baches Street, London N1 6DN, England. Tel.: +44 (0)20 7553 4000. Fax: +44 (0)20 7490 4921. E-mail: sales@uk.edition-peters.com. Web site: www.edition-peters.com

PF Music Company. P.O. Box 8625, Woodcliff Lake, NJ 07675, USA

Philharmusica Corporation. 250 W. 57th Street, Suites 1527–195. New York, NY 10107, USA

Piccolo Press. Clifford Bevan c/o Piccolo Press, 10 Clifton Terrace, Winchester SO22 5BJ, England. E-mail: clifford.bevan@ntlworld.com. In the USA, c/o Piccolo Press, P.O. Box 50613, Columbia, SC 29250. E-mail: piccowinch@aol.com. Web site: www.berliozhistoricalbrass.org/piccolo.htm

Piedmont Music Company. See: Edward B. Marks Music Company

Pierre Noel, Editeur. 24, boulevard Poissoniere, 75009 Paris, France

Piston Reed Stick & Bow Publisher. P.O. Box 107, Convent Station, NJ 07961-0107, USA

Plymouth Music Company, Incorporated. 170 N.E. 33rd Street, Fort Lauderdale, FL 33334, USA. Tel.: 954-563-1844. Fax: 954-563-9006

Pocono Mountain Music Publishing. 208 Drexel Road, Tobyhanna, PA, USA. Tel.: 717-894-4177

Polskie Wydawnictwo Muzyczne. PWM-Edition. Al. Krasinskiego 11a, 31-111 Krakow, Poland. Tel.: 012 220174. Fax: 012 220174. E-mail: internet@pwm.com.pl. Web site: www.pwm.com.pl

PolyGram International Publishing Incorporated. 1416 N. La Brea Avenue, Los Angeles, CA 90028-7563, USA. Tel.: 818-843-4046. Fax: 818-840-0409

PP Music. See: Manduca Music

PRB Productions. 963 Peralta Avenue, Albany, CA 94706-2144, USA. Tel.: 510-526-0722. Fax: 510-527-4763. E-mail: PRBPrdns@aol.com. Web site: www.prbpro.com

Presser: See: Theodore Presser Company

Prima Musica. 1510 SW 155 Avenue, Weston, FL 33326, USA. Tel.: 877-877-5743. E-mail: info@primamusic.com. Web site: www.primamusic.com

Providence Music Press. See: Hope Publishing Company

Przedstawicielstwo Wydawnictw Polskich. Krakowskie Przedmiescie 7, Warszawa, Poland

Queen City Brass Publications. See: PP Music

Quiroga (Ediciones) Madrid. See: Theodore Presser Company

R. Smith and Company Limited. P.O. Box 367, Aylesbury, Bucks. HP22 4LW, England. Tel.: +44 (0) 1296 682 220. Fax: +44 (0) 1296 681 989. E-mail: sales@rsmith.co.uk. Web site: www.rsmith.co.uk

Raphael Valerio. P.O. Box 16045, Asheville, NC 28816, USA

Raum, Elizabeth. 88 Angus Crescent, Regina, Saskatchewan S4T 6N2, Canada. Tel.: 306-525-5585. E-mail: elizraum@sasktel.net. Web site: www.elizabethraum.com

RBC Music. P.O. Box 29128, San Antonio, TX 78229, USA. Tel.: 800-548-0917. Fax: 210-736-2919. E-mail: sales@rbcmusic.com. Web site: www.rbcmusic.com

RBC Publications. P.O. Box 29128, San Antonio, TX 78229, USA. Tel.: 800-548-0917. Fax:

210-736-2919. E-mail: sales@rbcmusic.com. Web site: www.rbcmusic.com

R.B.P. Music Publishers. 2615 Waugh Drive, PMB 198, Houston, TX 77006, USA. E-mail: rbpviola@aol.com. Web site: members.aol.com/rbpviola

Real Musical. See: Grupo Real Musical

Really Good Music, LLC. 121 E. Polk Ave, Eau Claire, WI 54701, USA. Tel.: 715-834-7530. Fax: 715-834-7530. E-mail: contact@reallygoodmusic.com. Web site: www.reallygoodmusic.com

Rebu Music Publications. Box 504, RD 1, Wallingford, VT 05773, USA. Tel.: 802-446-2630

Rebus Music. 10 E. 16th Street, No. 5., New York, NY 10003, USA

Red Frog Music. Boswinde 43, 1852 XG Heiloo, The Netherlands. Tel.: (072) 505 28 68. Fax: (072) 505 28 68. E-mail: info@redfrogmusic.nl. Web site: redfrogmusic.nl

Regina Verlag. See: Otto Wrede Regina Verlag

Regus Publisher. 10 Birchwood Lane, White Bear Lake, MN 55110, USA. Tel.: 612-426-4867

Reimers (Edition) Stockholm. U.S. Rep: Theodore Presser Company. Box 17051, S-161, 17 Bromma, Stockholm, Sweden. Tel.: (08) 704 02 80. Fax: (08) 80 42 28. E-mail: info@editionreimers.se. Web site: www.editionreimers.se

R.G.O., Orchestral Hire Library. Fuggerstr. 1, POB 27, W-8019 Glonn, Germany. Tel.: 8093-44-93. Fax: 8093-23-19

Richard Schauer Music Publishing London. See: Theodore Presser Company

Ricordi. See: G. Ricordi & Company

Rivera Editores, Valencia, Spain. Sergio Carolino, Bairro Da Ota, Do Cidral Lote 25, Vestiaria, 2460-743, Portugal. Tel.: 351-96-283-3260. E-mail: sergiofbc@hotmail.com

Robbins Music. c/o Columbia Pictures Publications

Robert Fairfax Birch Publications. See: Theodore Presser Company

Robert King Music Sales, Incorporated. 140 Main Street, North Easton, MA 02356-1499, USA. Fax: 508-238-2571. E-mail: commerce@rkingmusic.com. Web site: www.rkingmusic.com

Robert Martin Editions France. U.S. Rep: Theodore Presser Company. 106 Grande Rue de la Coupée, 71850 Charnay-lès-Macon, France. Tel.: 03 85 34 46 81. Fax: 03 85 29 96 16. Web site: www.edrmartin.com

Roberton Publications England. U.S. Rep: Theodore Presser Company. The Windmill Wendover, Aylesbury, Bucks. HP22 6JJ, England. Tel.: 01296 623107. Fax: 01296 696536

Roder Bernd. Presse ud Verlagsservice Baumweg 6, 5206 Neunkirchen-Seelscheid, Germany

Rodgers & Hammerstein Concert Library. 229 West 28th Street, 11th floor, New York, NY 10001, USA. Tel.: 212-268-9300. Fax: 212-268-1245. E-mail: editor@rnh.com. Web site: www.rnh.com

Roger Dean Publishing Company. See: Lorenz Corporation

Roger Rhodes Music Limited. 352 West 56th St #4-D, New York, NY 10019-4249, USA. Tel.: 212-245-5045. E-mail: roger@rogerrhodesmusic.net. Web site: www.rogerrhodesmusic.com

Rojker, Kjell. Kogevej 8 B, Frejerslev, 4690 Haslev, Denmark

Rondo-Independent Music Dist of Scandinavia. P.O. Box 49, Solod Strand, Denmark

Rosehill Music Publishing Company, Limited. See: Winwood Music

Rottler, Werner. Schmledberg 19, 8011 Buch am Buchsberg, Germany

Roundtree Music. P.O. Box 2254, Reston, VA 20195-2254, USA

Royal Danish Brass Pub. See: Oh Musik aps

Rozen, Jay. E-mail: jay_rozen@hotmail.com

Rubank, Incorporated. See: Hal Leonard

Rufer Verlag. Postfach 11 43, Hauptstrab e 23 u. 27, D-6946 Gorxheimertal, Germany. Tel.: 0 362 01 29 47-0. Fax: 0 62 01 29 47-20

Russell, Armand. University of Hawaii, Music. 2411 Dole Street, Honolulu, HI 96822, USA. E-mail: armrussell@earthlink.net

Ryker Associates, Inc. ryker@gol.com

Saga Music Press. 12550 9th Avenue NW, Seattle, WA 98177, USA

The Salvation Army USA Eastern Territory. 440 West Nyack Road, West Nyack, NY 10994-1739, USA. Web site: http://www.salvationarmy-usaeast.org/music/index.shtm

Salvationist Publishing & Supplies, Limited. 1 Tiverton Street, London SE1 6NT, England. Tel.: 020 7367 6580. E-mail: mail_order@sp-s.co.uk. Web site: archive.salvationarmy.org.uk/Shop/index.html

Sam Fox Music Sales. See: Plymoth Music Company, Inc.

Sam Fox Publishing Company. See: Theodore Presser Co.

Samfundet til udgivelse af Dansk Musik. Gråbrødrestræde 18.1, 1156 Copenhagen K, Denmark. Tel.: +45 33 13 54 45. Fax: +45 33 93 30 44. E-mail: sales@samfundet.dk. Web site: www.samfundet.dk

Sampson, David. 166 West Hanover Avenue, Morristown, NJ 07960, USA

Sanjo Music Company. P.O. Box 7000-104, Palos Verdes, CA 90274, USA. Tel.: 310-541-8213

Sarnia Music. 12 The Meadows, St Dennis, Cornwall P126 8DR, UK. Web site: www.sarnia-music.com

Sassetti, Bernardo. Sergio Carolino, Bairro Da Ota, Do Cidral Lote 25, Vestiaria, 2460-743, Portugal. Tel.: 351-96-283-3260. E-mail: sergiofbc@hotmail.com

Schaffner Publishing Company. 224 Penn Avenue, Westmont, NJ 08108-1839, USA. Tel.: 609-854-3760. Fax: 609-854-5584

Scherzando Editions Musicales. 14, rue Auguste Orts, Brussels, Belgium

Schirmer. See: E. C. Schirmer Music Company, Incorporated

Schirmer. See: G. Schirmer

Schmitt Publications. Schmitt Music Centers, 2400 Freeway Boulevard, Brooklyn Center, MN 55430-1799, USA. Tel.: 800-767-3434. Fax: 763-566-9932. E-mail: info@schmittmusic.com. Web site: www.schmittmusic.com

Schola Cantorum. 76, rue des Saints-Peres, 75007 Paris, France

Schott: See: B. Schott's Sohne Mainz

Schott & Company, Limited, London. U.S. Rep: European American Music. 48 Great Marlborough Street, London W1V 2BN, England. Tel.: (+44) 171 494 1487. Fax: (+44) 171 437 0263. E-mail: promotions@schott-music.com. Web site: www.schott-english.com

Schott Freres. 30, rue Saint Jean, Brussels, Belgium. Tel.: (02) 5123980. Fax: (02) 514845

Scottish Music Information Centre. 1 Bowmont Gardens, Glasgow G12 9LR, Scotland. Tel.: +44 (0) 141 334 6393. Fax: +44 (0) 141 337 1161. E-mail: info@smic.org.uk. Web site: www.smic.org.uk

Seesaw Music Corporation Publishers. 2067 Broadway, New York, NY 10023, USA. Tel.: 212-874-1200

Sekretariat for ny Kompositionsmusik. See: SNYK

Sengstack Group Limited. 180 Alexander Street, Princeton, NJ 08540, USA. Tel.: 609-497-3900. Fax: 609-924-1618

Serans, X. Carlos. Sergio Carolino, Bairro Da Ota, Do Cidral Lote 25, Vestiaria, 2460-743, Portugal. Tel.: 351-96-283-3260. E-mail: sergiofbc@hotmail.com

Shawnee Press Incorporated. Delaware Water Gap, PA 18327-1099, USA. Tel. 1: 800-962-8584. Tel. 2: 717-476-0550. Fax: 717-476-5247

Sheet Music Now A/S. Roarsvej 2, 1.t.v., 2000 Frederiksberg, Copenhagen, Denmark. Tel.: +45 3833 2823. Fax: +45 3833 2831. E-mail: info@sheetmusicnow.com. Web site: www.sheetmusicnow.com

SheetMusicNow.com. See: Sheet Music Now A/S

Sheridan, Patrick. See: PatrickSheridan.com

Simton Musikproduktion und Verlang. Berweg 2, 8170 Bad Tolz, Germany

Sloan, Gerald. 1735 E Overcrest St., Fayetteville, AR 72703, USA. Tel.: 479-443-4587

Sloway Music Editions. Web site: www.slowaymusic.com

Smith, Jason R. 2 Honeysuckle Way, Granite Falls, NC 28630, USA. Tel.: 513-784-9655

Smith Publications/Sonic Art Editions. 2617 Gwynndale Avenue, Baltimore, MD 21207, USA. Tel.: 410-298-6509. Fax: 410-944-5113. E-mail: sylvias@smith-publications.com. Web site: www.smith-publications.com

Snoek's Muziekhandel. Pannekoekstraat 62A, 3011 LJ Rotterdam, Holland. Tel: 010-4137874

Snow, David. 21 Bishop Street, New Haven, CT 06511, USA. E-mail: dsnow@erols.com

SNYK—Danish Secretariat for Contemporary Music. Gråbrødredtorv 16,2 tv., 1152 København K. Tel.: 33 93 00 24. E-mail: snyk@snyk.dk. Web site: www.snyk.dk

Societe d'Editions Musicales Internationales Paris. U.S. Rep: Peer-Southern Organization. 5 Rue Lincoln, Paris F-75008, France

Sohgaku-Sha. Tohky Bldg. 3F; Kami-Ochiai, Shinjuky-ku, Tokyo 161, Japan

Solid Brass Music Company. 71 Mt. Ranier Drive, San Rafael, CA 94903, USA. Tel. 1: 415-479-1337. Tel. 2: 800-873-9798. Fax: 415-472-0603. E-mail: dick@sldbrass.com. Web site: www.sldbrass.com

Sonante Publications. P.O. Box 74, Station F, Toronto, Ontario M4Y 2L4, Canada

Sonic Arts, Incorporated. Room 302, 3-3-14 Azabudai, Minato-ku pref 106, Japan

SOS Music Services. 1817 29th Avenue E., Tuscaloosa, AL 35405, USA

Sound Ideas Publications. P.O. Box 7612, Colorado Springs, CO 80933, USA

Soundspells Productions. 86 Livingston Street, Rhinebeck, NY 12572, USA. Tel.: 914-876-6295. Fax: 914-876-6295. Web site: www.jamesarts.com/soundspells.htm

Southern Music Company. P.O. Box 329, 1100 Broadway, San Antonio, TX 78292, USA. Tel. 1: 210-226-8167. Tel. 2: 800-284-5443. Fax: 210-223-4537. E-mail: info@southernmusic.com. Web site: www.southernmusic.com

Southern Music Publishing Company, Limited, London. U.S.: Peer-Southern Organization. 8 Denmark Street, London WC2 BLT, England

Southern Music Publishing Company (also see: Theodore Presser Company). 1740 Broadway, New York, NY 10019, USA

Spaeth/Schmid Blechbläsernoten. Lise-Meitner-Str.9, 72202 Nagold, Germany. Tel.: 0049/7452/818454. Fax: 0049/7452/818456. E-mail: info@spaeth-schmid.de

Spartan Press Music Publishers Ltd. Strathmashie House, Laggan Bridge, Scottish Highlands PH 20 1BU, UK. Tel.: 01528 544770. Fax: 01528 544771. E-mail: Mail@SpartanPress.co.uk. Web site: www.SpartanPress.co.uk

Spears, Jared. Box 2259, State University, AR 72467, USA

Spectrum Music Publishers. P.O. Box 5187, Greensboro, NC 27435, USA

Stadt- und Universitätsbibliothek. Bockenheimer Landstrasse 134–138, 60325 Frankfurt am Main 1, Germany. Tel.: (069) 21239-230. Fax: (069) 21 239-062. Web site: www.stub.uni-frankfurt.de

Stainer & Bell Limited, London. U.S. Agent: E. C. Schirmer Music Company. P.O. Box 110, Victoria House, 23 Gruneisen Road, London N3

1DZ, England. Tel.: +44 (0)20 8343 3303. Fax: +44 (0)20 8343 3024. E-mail: post@stainer.co.uk. Web site: www.stainer.co.uk

Stansfeld Music Company. 9709 Roosevelt Way NE, Seattle, WA 98115, USA

Stauffer Press. Box 101082, Birmingham, AL 35210, USA. Tel.: 205-951-3881

Stegmann, Richard. 87 Wurzburg, Waldkugelweg 5a, Germany

Step Two Musikverlag. Neulerchenfelder Strasse 3–7, A-1160 Vienna, Austria

Stephen Shoop Music Publications. 507 S.W. Main Street, Ennis, TX 75119, USA. Tel.: 972-875-9754. E-mail: tuba@hyperusa.com

Stevens, John D. 1606 Baker Avenue, Madison, WI 53705, USA. Tel.: 608-233-6199

STIM. See: Swedish Music Information Center

Stockhausen-Verlag. c/o Ione H. Stephens, 2832 Maple Lane, Fairfax, VA 22031, USA. Tel.: 703-560-3039

Stockhausen-Verlag. Kettenberg 15, 51515 Kürten, Germany. Web site: www.stockhausen.org/stockhausen_verlag.html

Stril. c/o Tom Brevik. Edvardsensgt. 19, N-5035 Bergen-Sandviken, Norway. Tel.: +47 55 32 42 54

Stroud, Richard. 131 Huntoon, Eureka, CA 95501, USA

Studio Music Company. 77–79 Dudden Hill Lane, London NW10 1BD, England. Tel.: 020-8830-0110. Fax: 020-8451-6470. Web site: www.studio-music.co.uk

Summy-Birchard Publishing Company. 15800 N.W. 48th Avenue, Miami, FL 33014, USA. Tel.: 305-620-1500. Fax: 305-621-1094

Svarda, William. 4532 Creek View Drive, Middletown, OH 45042, USA

Svensk Musik—Swedish Music Information Center. Box 27327, S-102 54 Stocholm, Sweden. Tel.: +46 08 783 88 00

Swand Publications. 120 North Longcross Road, Linthicum Heights, MD 21090, USA

Sweden Music AB. Mariehallsvagen 35, P.O. Box 20504, S -161 02 Bromma. Sweden. Tel.: 46 8 14 30 20. Fax: 46 8 21 53 33

Swedish Music Information Center—STIM. Sandhamnsgatan 79, Box 27327, S-102 54 Stockholm, Sweden. Tel.: +46 8 783 88 00. Fax: +46 8 783 95 10. E-mail: swedmic@stim.se. Web site: www.mic.stim.se

Swiss Music Edition. Tossertobelstrasse 12, CH-8400 Winterthur, Switzerland. Tel.: +41 52 213 55 27/29. Fax: +41 52 213 09 95. E-mail: info@edition-swiss-music.ch. Web site: www.edition-swiss-music.ch

Symphony Land. 24 Rue Utrillo, 93370 Montfermeil, France

SZK Music. 52 Briarwood St., Carindale, Q., Australia, 4152. E-mail: tuba@tubacentral.com. Web site: www.tubacentral.com

Szkutko, John. SZK Music. 52 Briarwood St, Carindale, Q., Australia, 4152. Web site: www.tubacentral.com/szkmusic

Taiga Press. P.O. Box 81382, Fairbanks, AK 99708, USA. Tel.: 907-455-6235. Fax: 907-455-4815. E-mail: jla@alaska.net

T.A.P. Music. See: TAP Music Sales

TAP Music Sales. 1992 Hunter Avenue, Newton, IA 50208, USA. Tel.: 641-792-0352. E-mail: tapmusic@tapmusic.com. Web site: www.tapmusic.com

Taunus Verlag Musikverlag H.-L. Grahl. Im Staffel 106, 60389 Frankfurt am Main, Germany. Tel.: 069-471588

Taurus Press. 17 The Common, Troston, Bury St. Edmunds, Suffolk, England

Tenuto Publications. See: Theodore Presser Company

Tezak. See: Mark Tezak

Themes & Variations. 39 Danbury Avenue, Westport, CT 06880, USA. Tel.: 203-227-5709. Fax: 203-227-5715. E-mail 1: jwwaxman@aol.com. E-mail 2: tnv@tnv.net. Web site: www.tnv.net

Theodore Presser Company. 588 North Gulph Road, King of Prussia, PA 19406, USA. Tel.: 610-525-3636. Fax: 610-527-7841. E-mail: presser@presser.com. Web site: www.presser.com

Thompson Edition. 231 Plantation Road, Rock Hill, SC 29732-9441, USA. Tel.: 803-366-4446. Fax: 360-234-5601. E-mail: sales@thompsonedition.com. Web site: www.thompsonedition.com

Thore Ehrling Musik AB. Box 21133, 10031 Stockholm, Sweden. Tel.: +46 8 30 50 25. Fax: +46 8 30 98 12

Thornes Music. 18 Sundorne Crescent, Sundorne, Shrewsbury, Shropshire SY1 4JE, England. Phone: 44 (0)1743 231150. E:mail: rogerthorne@thornesmusic.freeserve.co.uk

Tierolff Muziekcentrale. P.O. Box 18, Markt 90–92, 4700 AA Roosendaal, Holland. Tel.: +31 (0) 165 541255. Fax: +31 (0) 165 558339. E-mail: musicinfo@tierloff.nl. Web site: www.tierloff.nl

Tierra del Mar Music. 3348 S. Calle Del Albano, Green Valley, AZ 85614, USA. Tel.: 520-625-9005. E-mail: oboegreg@tierradelmar.org. Web site: tierradelmar.org

Tillander Enterprises. 260 West End Avenue, Suite 7A, New York, NY 10023, USA. Tel.: 212-874-4892

Tinoco, Luis. E-mail: sergiofbc@hotmail.com

T.I.S. Publications. P.O. Box 669, Bloomington, IN 47402, USA

Tokyo Bari Tuba Ensemble. c/o Toru Miura, 2-112, Shih Tamagawa Hgim, 1048-1 Nakanoshima, Kama-Ku, Kamasaki City, Kanagawa Prefecture, 214, Japan

Tonika. See: Norsk Musikforlag

Touch of Brass Music Corporation. c/o Ward Music Ltd. 412 W. Hastings Street, Vancouver, BC, V6B 1L3, Canada. Tel.: 604-682-5288

Toyama, Yuzo. c/o Kaijimoto Concert Management Company, Limited. attn: Junichi Isogai 8-6-25, Chuo-ku, Tokuo 104, Japan

Transatlantiques (Editions Musicales) Paris. U.S. Rep: Theodore Presser Company. 151 avenue Jean-Jaures, F-75019 Paris, France

Transcontinental Music Publications. 633 Third Avenue, 6th floor, New York, NY 10017-6778, USA. Tel. 1: 800-455-5223. Tel. 2: 212-650-4101. Fax: 212-650-4109. E-mail: tmp@uahc.org. Web site: www.etranscon.com

Trigram Music, Incorporated. See: Wimbledon Music Incorporated/Trigram Music Inc.

Triple Letter Brand. P.O. Box 396, Tenafly, NJ 07670, USA

Tritone Press. See: Theodore Presser Company

T.R.N. Music Publishers, Inc. P.O. Box 197-2700, Airport Road, Alto, NM 88312, USA. Tel. 1: 866-623-2472. Tel. 2: 505-336-2688. Fax: 505-336-2687. E-mail: sales@trnmusic.com. Web site: www.trnmusic.com

Tromba Publications. 2253 Bellaire Street, Denver, CO 80207, USA. Tel.: 303-322-8608. Fax: 303-322-8608. E-mail: gendsley@ecentral.com. Web site: www.dmamusic.org/tromba

Tuba Classics. P.O. Box 186, Kelly, WY 83011, USA. Tel.: 307-734-6868

Tuba Euphonium Press. 3811 Ridge Road, Annandale, VA 22003, USA. Fax: 703-916-0711. E-mail: dmiles@erols.com. Web site: www.tubaeuphoniumpress.com

Tuba/Euphonium Music Publications. Out of business

Tubalaté. Web site: www.dws.ndirect.co.uk/tubalate.htm

TubaMania International. P.O. Box R 181, Royal Exchange, Sydney, NSW 1225, Australia. Tel.: +61 41 613 5854. E-mail: Steve@tubamania.com.au

TubaMania Press. c/o Steve Rosse. E-mail: steve@tubamania.com.au

TUBA Journal. Jason Smith, 55 Sunnyside Drive, Athens, OH 45701, USA. Tel.: 740-591-4075. E-mail: smithj10@ohio.edu

TUBA Press. See: Tuba Euphonium Press

Uetz Music Publishers. Voigtei 39, D-38820 Halbertstadt, Germany. Tel.: +49-3941-570040. Fax: +49-3941-570041. Web site: www.uetz.de/music

Uitgave Molenaar. Postbus 19, N.V. Wormerveer, 1520AA, Holland

Unicorn Music Company. See: Boston Music Company

UNITUBA Press. Out of Business

Universal Edition. See: European American Music

Universal Songs BV. U.S. Rep: Theodore Presser Company. Oude Enghweg 24 Postbus 305, Hilversum, 1200 AH, Netherlands

Universe Publishers. See: Theodore Presser Company. P.O. Box 1900, Orem, UT 84059, USA

Universe Publishing. See: Universe Publishers

University Microfilm. 300 N. Zeeb Road, Ann Arbor, MI 48106-1346, USA. Tel. 1: 800-521-0600. Tel. 2: 734-761-4700. E-mail: info@il.proquest.com. Web site: www.umi.com

University of Massachusetts Press. Box 429, Amherst, MA 01004, USA. Tel. (Orders): 413-545-2219. Tel. (Editorial): 413-545-2217. Fax (Orders): 800-488-1144. Fax (Main): 413-545-1226. E-mail: info@umpress.umass.edu. Web site: www.umass.edu/umpress/

University of Miami Press. See: Sam Fox Music Sales

University of York Music Press. Department of Music, University of York, Heslington, York Y010 5DD, United Kingdom. Tel.: 01904 432434. E-mail: uymp@york.ac.uk. Web site: www.uymp.co.uk

Vanderbeek & Imrie Ltd, 15 Marvig, Lochs, Isle of Lewis, Scotland, PA86 9QP. Tel.: 01851 880216

Vaughan, Rodger D. 226 W. Borromeo, Placentia, CA 92670, USA

Veanova. Marcus Thranesgt. 18, 2821 Gjøvik, Norway. Tel.: +47 61 18 08 19. E-mail: ketilvea@lycos.com

Veb Friedrich Hofmeister—Leipzig. Karlstrasse 10, 0-7010 Leipzig, Germany. Tel.: 0341/20 99 08. Fax: 0341/29/51/14

Velvet Music Edition. Tel.: 814-867-3017. Fax: 814-867-3017. E-mail: velvet@lazerlink.com. Web site: www.velvetbrown.net

Verlag Merseburger. Postfach 10 38 80, 34038 Kassel, Berlin, Germany. Tel.: (0561) 78 98 09-0. Fax: (0561) 78 98 09-16. E-mail: info@merseburger.de. Web site: www.merseburger.de

Verlag Neue Musik. Grabbeallee 15, D-13156, Berlin, Germany. Tel.: +49-30-61 6981-0. Fax: +49-30-61 6981-21. E-mail: vnm@verlag-neue-musik.de. Web site: www.verlag-neue-musik.de

Verlag Von Paul Zschocher. Hamburg. Germany

Viola World Publications. 2 Inlander Road, Saratoga Springs, NY 12866, USA. Tel.: 518-583-7177. Fax: 518-583-7177. E-mail: violaworld@aol.com. Web site: www.viola.com/violaworld

Virgo Music Publishers. 9018 Walden Road, Silver Spring, MD 20901, USA. Tel.: 301-588-0836. Fax: 301-588-0836

Virgo Music Publishers. Virgo House. 47 Cole Bank Road, Hall Green, Birmingham B94 6DT, England. Tel.: +44 (0) 121-778-5569. Fax: +44 (0) 121-778-5569. E-mail: virog@printed-music.com

Visible Music. 276 Massachusetts Avenue No. 411, Arlington, MA 02174, USA. Tel.: 617-641-4741

Vivace Press. NW 310 Wawawai Road, Pullman, WA 99163-2959, USA. Tel.: 800-543-5429. Fax: 509-334-3551. E-mail: yordy@vivacepress.com. Web site: www.vivacepress.com

VNM. Vest-Norsk Musikkforlag. P.O. Box 59, N-5321 Kleppestø, Norway. Fax: +47 56 14 38 00

Vydavatelstvi Chf-Praha. 150 00 Praha 5-Smichov, Radlicka 99, Czechoslovakia. Tel.: 53 41 37-8. Fax: 54 86 27

W. W. Norton and Company, Incorporated. 500 Fifth Avenue, New York, NY 10110, USA. Tel. 1: 800-233-4830. Tel. 2: 212-354-5500. Fax 1: 800-458-6515. Fax 2: 212-869-0856

Walker, Gwyneth. Brainstorm Road. Braintree, VT 05060-9209, USA. Tel.: 212-656-1367. Fax: 212-656-1367. E-mail: walkermuse@aol.com. Web site: www.gwynethwalker.com

Wallan Music Company. 170 NE 33rd Street, Fort Lauderdale, FL 33334, USA

Wandle Music Limited. 26 Chiltern Street, London W1M 1PH, England

Warner Brothers Music. 265 Secaucus Road, Secaucus, NJ 07094-2037, USA

Warner/Chappell Music Incorporated. 9000 Sunset Boulevard, Penthouse, Los Angeles, CA 90069, USA. Tel.: 310-273-3323. Fax: 310-271-4843

Warner Chappel Music Scandinavia AB. Vendevagen 85B, S-182 15 Danderyd, Sweden. Tel.: 011-46-8-755-1210. Fax: 011-46-8-755-1596. Web site: www.warnerchappell.se/wcmse/home2.jsp

Warner Chappell Musikverlag GmbH. Diefenbachgasse 35, A-1150 Vienna, Austria. Tel.: 011-43-1-894-1920. Fax: 011-43-1-894-1615

Warren, Frank. See: Frank E. Warren Music Service

Warwick Music Limited. 1 Broomfield Road, Earlsdon, Coventry, England CV5 6JW. Tel.:+44 (0)24 7671 2081. Fax: +44 (0)24 7671 2550. E-mail: sales@warwickmusic.com. Web site: www.warwickmusic.com

Watts, Charles. 1503 Sherrill Boulevard, Murfreesboro, TN 37130, USA

Wehr's Music House. 3533 Baxter Drive, Winter Park, FL 32792, USA. Web site: www.wehrs-music-house.com

Weinberger. See: Josef Weinberger

Weintraub Music Company. See: G. Schirmer

Welcher, Dan. See: Theodore Presser Company

Wenström-Lekare, Lennart. Ynglävagen 20, 182 62 Djursholm, Sweden

Werle, Floyd. 5504 Aldrich Lane, Springfield, VA 22151, USA. Tel.: 703-941-5276

Wessner, John. 822 E. Joppa Road, Baltimore, MD 21204, USA

West Wind Music. 3072 S. Laredo Cir., Aurora, CO 80013-1806, USA

Western International Music. 3707 65th Avenue, Greeley, CO 80634-9626, USA. Tel.: 970-330-6901. Fax: 970-330-7738. E-mail: wimbo@wiminc.com. Web site: www.wiminc.com

Westleaf Editions. RD #2, Box 2770, Cox Brook Road, Northfield, VT 05663, USA. Tel.: 802-485-8019. Fax: 802-495-3972. E-mail: bathory@maltedmedia.com. Web site: members.aol.com/kalvos/westleaf.htm

Whaling Music Publishers. See: Cimarron Music & Productions

White, Ian. 13 Tugela Road, West Croydon, Surrey CR20 2HB, United Kingdom. E-mail: drianwhite@hotmail.com

White, Joseph Pollard. Department of Music, Christopher Newport University, Newport News, VA. Tel.: 757-594-8789. E-mail: joseph.white@cnu.edu

White, Winton. CNFJ N46, PSC 473 Box 12, EPO, AP 96349-0051. E-mail: Winton.C.White@biola.edu

Wilfredo Cardoso. Esmeraldo 1075, Buenos Aires 1007, Argentina

Wilhelm Hansen Musikforlag. Bornholmsgade 1, DK-1266 Copenhagen K, Denmark. Tel.: +45 33 11 78 88. Fax: +45 33 14 81 78. E-mail: ewh@ewh.dk. Web site: www.ewh.dk/index_en.asp

Wilhelm Zimmermann. Musikverlag Zimmermann. Strubbergstraße 80, 60489 Frankfurt am Main, Germany. Tel.: 069/97 82 86-72. Fax: 069/97 82 86-79. E-mail: info@zimmermann-frankfurt.de. Web site: www.zimmermann-frankfurt.de/v1.shtml

William A. Pfund. 35629 County Road #41, Eaton, CO 80615, USA. Tel.: 970-454-2642

William Elkin Music Services. Station Road Industrial Estate, Norwich, Norfolk NR13 6NS, England. Tel.: +44(0)1603 721302. Fax: +44(0)1603 721801. E-mail: info@elkinmusic.co.uk. Web site: www.elkinmusic.co.uk

William Grant Still Music. 1109 S. Univ. Plaza Way, Suite #109, Flagstaff, AZ 86001-6317, USA. Tel.: 928-526-9355. Fax: 928-526-0321. E mail: wgsmusic@bigplanet.com. Web site: www.williamgrantstill.com

Williams Music Publishing Company. 300 Fallen Leaf Lane, Roswell, GA 30075, USA. Tel.: 404-518-8861. E-mail: wmp@mindspring.com

Willis Music Company. 7380 Industrial Road, Florence, KY 41042, USA. Tel. 1: 800-354-9799. Tel. 2: 606-283-2050. Fax: 606-283-1784. E-mail: willis@willis-music.com. Web site: www.willismusic.com

Wilson, Curtis. Texas Christian University, School of Music, P.O. Box 297500, Ft. Worth, TX 76129, USA. Tel.: 817-257-6625. E-mail: c.wilson3@tcu.edu

Wilson, Kenyon. 1739 Bentridge Drive, Kennesaw, GA 30144, USA. Tel.: 404-694-1156. E-mail: kwilson@fulbrightweb.org

Wimbledon Music Incorporated/Trigram Music Inc. 1801 Century Park East (Suite 2400), Los Angeles, CA 90067-2326, USA. Tel.: 310-556-9683. Fax: 310-277-1278. E-mail: webmaster@wimbtri.com. Web site: www.wimbtri.com

Wind Music Incorporated. 153 Highland Parkway, Rochester, NY 14620, USA

WindSong Press. P.O. Box 146, Gurnee, IL 60031, USA. Tel.: 847 223-4586. Fax: 847 223-4580. E-mail: info@WindSongPress.com. Web site: www.windsongpress.com

Wingert-Jones Music, Incorporated. 11225 Colorado, Kansas City, MO 64137-2502, USA. Tel.: 1-800-625-3254. Fax: 1-816-765-3232. E-mail: wjmusic@wjmusic.com. Web site: www.wjmusic.com

Winteregg, Steven L. 419 Westview Place, Englewood, OH 45322, USA. Tel.: 936-836-8593. E-mail: Swint@erinet.com. Web site: ww.amc.net/member/Steven_Winteregg/home.html

Winwood Music Publishers. Unit 7, Fieldside Farm, Quainton, Bucks. HP22 4DQ, England. Tel.: 00 44 (0)1296 655777. Fax: 00 44 (0)1296 655778. E-mail: sales@winwoodmusic.com

Wiscasset Music Publishing Company. P.O. Box 380810, Cambridge, MA 02138-0810, USA. Tel.: 617-492-5720. Fax: 617-492-4031

Wolfgang G. Haas—Musikverlag Köln. 90 07 48, D-51117 Köln, Germany. Tel.: +49 (0)2203-98 88 3-0. Fax: 02203/98883-50. E-mail: info@hass-koeln.de. Web site: www.haas-koeln.de

Woodbrass Music SA. Rte de Fribourg 30, CH-1724 Praroman-Le Mouret, Switzerland. Tel.: +41 26 413 40 13. Fax: +41 26 413 45 55. E-mail: office@woodbrass-music.ch. Web site: www.woodbrass-music.ch

Woodsum Music, Limited. RFD 2 Box 244, Harrison, MA 04040, USA. Tel.: 207-583-4875

World Library Publications. 3815 N Willow Road, P.O. Box 2701, Schiller Park, IL 60176, USA. Tel.: 1-800-566-6150. Fax: 1-888-957-3291. International Tel.: 1-847-233-2752. International Fax: 1-847-671-5715. E-mail: wlpcs@jspaluch.com. Web site: www.wlpmusic.com

Wright & Round Limited. See: Solid Brass Music Company

Wspolczesna Muzyka Polska

Yamaha Kyohan Company Limited. Koshin Building 3F, 6-12-13 Ginza Chuo-ku, Tokyo pref. 104, Japan

Yamaha Music Foundation. 3-24-22, Shimo-Meguro, Meguro-ku, Tokyo 153-8666, Japan. Tel.: 03-5773-0808. Fax: 03-5773-0857. Web site: www.yamaha-mf.or.jp/conte.html

Yarra Yarra Music. P.O. Box 30, Warrandyte 3113 Victoria, Australia. Tel.: +61 3 9844 1194. E-mail: barrymckimm@hotmail.com

Ybarra Music. P.O. Box 665, Lemon Grove, CA 91946, USA. Tel.: 619 462-6538. Fax: 619 462-6565. E-mail: vbraun8368@aol.com

Zanibon. See: G. Zanibon

Zonn, Paul Martin. 122 Bay View Drive, Hendersonville, TN 37075, USA. Tel.: 615 264-6392. Fax: 615 264-6395. E-mail: wzonn@paulmartinzonn.com. Web site: www.paulmartinzonn.com

Zurfluh. See: Editions Aug. Zurfluh

EDITORS: Biographical Sketches

R. Winston Morris has been internationally recognized for the past four decades as one of the leaders in the advancement of the tuba. He is Professor of Music and Instructor of Tuba and Euphonium at Tennessee Technological University in Cookeville, Tennessee, where he has been on the faculty since 1967.

Daniel Perantoni is a legendary tuba artist, teacher, and pedagogue. He was given the Lifetime Achievement Award by the executive board of TUBA. He is currently Professor of Tuba at Indiana University.

Ronald Davis is currently Professor of Tuba and Euphonium at the University of South Carolina. He is currently preparing a history of the tuba and a profile of the major artists in the Los Angeles recording industry.

David D. Graves resides in Waco, Texas, where he serves as the Instructor of Euphonium and Tuba at Baylor University. Other duties at Baylor include performing in the Baylor Brass, coaching student chamber ensembles, and teaching low brass methods.

Timothy J. Northcut is presently Associate Professor of Music and Instructor of Tuba and Euphonium at the College-Conservatory of Music (CCM) of the University of Cincinnati in Cincinnati, Ohio. In addition, he serves as music director of the famed CCM Brass Choir and coordinator of the brass chamber music program.

Philip Sinder is Professor of Tuba and Euphonium, Chair of the Brass and Percussion Area, and a member of the faculty quintet "Beaumont Brass" at the Michigan State University School of Music. He is currently a member of the board of trustees for the Blue Lake Fine Arts Camp and the Leonard Falcone International Euphonium and Tuba Festival.

Joseph Skillen is on the faculty at Louisiana State University, where he teaches applied tuba and euphonium, coaches chamber music, performs with the faculty brass quintet, teaches graduate courses in literature and pedagogy, and guides research projects.

Kelly Thomas was appointed Tuba/Euphonium Instructor and Director of Pep Bands at the University of Arizona in 2001. A native of Flagstaff, Arizona, he began his studies with R. Winston Morris at Tennessee Technological University, where he earned a bachelor of music degree in music education. He holds a master of music degree in music education from Arizona State University, where he studied with Sam Pilafian. Kelly is currently completing a doctor of musical arts degree at Arizona State Univeristy.

Kenyon Wilson currently serves on the faculty at the University of Tennessee at Chattanooga and is principal tubist with the Augusta Symphony in Georgia and the Tuscaloosa Symphony in Alabama.

First Edition Editors

Jeffrey Funderburk is currently Professor of Tuba and Euphonium at the University of Northern Iowa, and since 1989 he has been principal tubist of the Cedar Rapids Symphony. From 1999 to 2002 he was also associated with the Staatliche Hochschule für Musik in Trossingen, Germany.

Skip Gray joined the faculty of the University of Kentucky School of Music in the fall of 1980 and was promoted to the rank of Professor of Music in 1991. He has appeared as a tuba soloist and clinician throughout North America, Europe, Japan, and Australia.

Charles A. McAdams is the Dean of the College of Arts and Sciences and Professor of Music at Northwest Missouri State University. He was elected College/University Vice President of the Missouri Music Educators Association and served as president of the Missouri Association of Schools and Departments of Music.

Mark A. Nelson is currently the Chair of Performing Arts at Pima Community College in Tucson, Arizona, and performs with Symphonia, the Southwest Brass Quintet, Big Band Express on bass trombone, the Southern Arizona Symphony, Arizona Symphonic Winds, and occasionally the Tucson Symphony Orchestra.

Jerry A. Young is Professor of Tuba and Euphonium and Coordinator of the Wind and Percussion Area at the University of Wisconsin–Eau Claire. Young has been a member of the music faculty at UW–Eau Claire since 1983, and he teaches tuba, euphonium, and courses in music education as well as in the university honors program.

INDEX